TYPES OF
DRAMA

TYPES OF
DRAMA
Plays and Contexts

EIGHTH EDITION

Sylvan Barnet

Tufts University

William Burto

University of Lowell

Lesley Ferris

The Ohio State University

Gerald Rabkin

Rutgers University

Longman

New York   San Francisco   Boston
London   Toronto   Sydney   Tokyo   Singapore   Madrid
Mexico City   Munich   Paris   Cape Town   Hong Kong   Montreal

Editor-in-Chief: Joseph Terry

Acquisitions Editor: Erika Berg

Associate Development Editor: Bennett Morrison

Marketing Manager: Melanie Goulet

Media Supplements Editor: Nancy Garcia

Associate Editor: Barbara Santoro

Production Manager: Joseph Vella

Project Coordination, Text Design, and Electronic Page Makeup: Nesbitt Graphics, Inc.

Cover Design Manager: John Callahan

Cover Designer: Maria Ilardi

Cover Photos: William Leach in *Death of a Salesman*, courtesy of the Utah Shakespearean Festival. Scenes from *Hamlet* and *In the Blood* courtesy of Michael Daniel/The Public Theatre, New York.

Photo Research: Photosearch, Inc.

Manufacturing Buyer: Roy Pickering

Printer and Binder: Courier-Stoughton

Cover Printer: The Lehigh Press

For permission to use copyrighted material, grateful acknowledgment is made to the copyright holders on pp. 1553–1560, which are hereby made part of this copyright page.

Library of Congress Cataloging-in-Publication Data

Types of drama : plays and contexts / Sylvan Barnet . . . [et al.].—8th ed.
    p. cm.
    Includes bibliographical references and index.
    ISBN 0-321-06506-9 (pbk.)
    1. Drama—Collections. 2. Drama—History and criticism. I. Barnet, Sylvan.

PN6112.T96 2000
808.82—dc21
                                00-048753

Please visit our website at http://www.ablongman.com/barnettod

ISBN 0-321-06506-9
  3 4 5 6 7 8 9 10—CRS—09 08 07 06 05 04

Contents

PART THREE   Writing About Drama

Preface

You need three things in the theater—the play, the actors, and the audience, and each must give something.

—Kenneth Haigh, actor

Kenneth Haigh's statement is true. Most obviously this book gives the play—actually 52 plays. Insofar as it is possible, it also gives something of the play on the stage, since it includes 18 interviews with playwrights and directors, 19 reviews of productions, and numerous stage histories, all of which will give the reader a sense of the play in production. As for the third ingredient, the audience, that is where you come in. The spectator or reader, as Haigh suggests, by responding emotionally and intellectually—by seeing the play "in the mind's eye," to use Hamlet's words—helps to bring the play to life and indeed gives meaning to the play. The apparatus in this book, for example the introductions to periods and the Topics for Critical Thinking, will help you to make your contribution to the life of the play.

Types of Drama, Eighth Edition is divided into three parts. **Part One: Getting Started,** a quick introduction to the language of the theater, moves from an examination of a play of only a few lines (the medieval *Whom Do You Seek?*) to brief discussions of basic matters such as audience awareness, plot, character, and theme. If we had to reduce all of this to a sentence, we might be tempted to quote one of Arthur Miller's remarks, "The structure of a play is always the story of how the birds come home to roost." (We include Miller's *Death of a Salesman,* so you can test his comment against his own play, if you wish. You may also want to test Miller's remark against a play with a very different structure, such as Caryl Churchill's *Top Girls.*) This brief introductory unit includes a photo essay, "The Language of Drama/ The Language of the Theater," where we illustrate points about theaters and performances with photographs, and we invite students to test our assertions against two short works, Susan Glaspell's *Trifles* and Rachel Rosenthal's *My Brazil.*

On the assumption that at this point most readers have read at least one short play and probably two and have thought about specific theatrical techniques, Part One then offers a review: "In Brief: How to Read a Play." Next it sketches the chief traditional dramatic forms, tragedy, comedy, and tragicomedy. Because drama is not merely art but is also life—plays are supported by the public, and sometimes productions are subsidized by the government—we conclude with some questions concerning "Drama and Society."

Part Two: A Collection of Plays is the heart of the book. The three short plays in Part One, with the editorial apparatus, were preliminary to the 49 plays of Part Two, ranging from plays of ancient Greece to the present; the most recent play is Suzan-Lori Parks's *In the Blood* written in 1999. Of these 49 plays, 20 are pretwentieth century (if we may count Chekhov's *The Cherry Orchard,* which in fact was produced in 1903). Here are the playwrights who for centuries have been accounted among the masters, for instance, Sophocles, Euripides, Shakespeare, Lope de Vega, Corneille, Molière, and Ibsen; among these classic writers, too, is Aphra Behn, immensely popular in her own day (the late seventeenth century) but later neglected and then rediscovered. We also include a *commedia dell'arte* scenario, never before published, and only recently translated from the Italian manuscript. Of the remaining 29 plays in this part, about one-third (for instance Odets's *Waiting for Lefty,* Brecht's *The Good Woman of Setzuan,* Miller's *Death of a Salesman,* and Arthur Laurents's *Gypsy*) are classics from the middle-third of the twentieth century; almost all of the remaining plays are from the last three decades of the twentieth century, with a strong representation of first-rate works by women and by minority authors (African American, Asian American, and Chicano).

Each play is preceded by a short biographical note and by an introductory commentary. The commentaries do not attempt to explicate the play, but they do contain, we think, useful and relevant points that will also be helpful with other plays. Thus, the introduction to *A Midsummer Night's Dream* includes a discussion of two traditions of comedy, "critical" (or "satiric") comedy and "romantic" comedy, material that is also relevant to other plays in the book, including Bernard Shaw's *Major Barbara* and Dario Fo's *We Won't Pay! We Won't Pay!* But even those commentaries that are sharply focused on a given play do not seek to utter the last word. On the contrary, they seek to provide material that will stimulate discussion in class or that may be the topic of a writing assignment. Following each play we give "Topics for Critical Thinking and Writing" (divided into "The Play on the Page" and "The Play on the Stage"); these are designed to assist readers to see the plays not only as literature but also as living theater—works written for the stage, or, if read, to be staged in the reader's mind.

To help readers envision the plays on the stage, we include stage histories for most plays, 19 reviews of productions, 10 discussions with directors—not only concerning productions of modern plays, such as the interviews with Jorge Huerta on Valdez's *Los Vendidos* and with the Nigerian director Ezekiel Kofoworola, who recently staged Wole Soyinka's *The Bacchae of Euripides: A Communion Right,* but also concerning productions of classical plays, such as interviews with directors who have staged Sophocles's *Oedipus* and Euripides's *Medea.* In Part Two we also include 8 discussions by playwrights, as well as 4 additional photo essays: Ancient Greek Drama Today, Staging Shakespeare, Then and Now, African Americans on the Stage, and Representations of Gender in the Theater. Further, Part Two includes introductions to historical periods, and additional short essays on such topics as The American Musical, Hispanic American Theater, Women's Theater, and Asian American Theater.

Part Three: Writing is devoted to writing essays about drama. We take seriously the view that college students should not only experience plays but should also be able to express their responses thoughtfully in coherent analytic essays. Indeed, we believe that the very process of writing an essay helps students to deepen their responses to the material. We therefore include substantial advice on such matters as finding a topic, converting it into a thesis, organizing a comparison, writing a review (we give two examples by students, which we annotate in an effort to help students to see the qualities that characterize an effective review), using the Internet as a research tool, and providing documentation.

A **Glossary, Bibliography,** and **List of Video Resources** conclude the book. The **glossary** contains more than two hundred terms, some defined briefly and some defined at length. Students and instructors have told us that the glossary can actually be read with interest, and that the definitions, far from perfunctory, are genuinely helpful.

The **Bibliography** begins with general works on theater, then gives works period by period and ends with works on each playwright represented in *Types of Drama,* Eighth Edition. This bibliography thus provides a starting point for students who wish to do further reading.

The **List of Video Resources** offers a range of general sources but, most important, for every play in the anthology we cite either a film/video version or background material on that playwright that is now available to instructors and students.

FEATURES OF THE EIGHTH EDITION

- **Expanded Coverage of Plays:** 52 plays are now included, 30 of which are new to this edition. Instructors in an introductory course in the history of theater will rightly expect a textbook to include such indispensable works as *Oedipus, Antigonê, Hamlet, Tartuffe, A Doll's House* and *Death of a Salesman*—these plays are indeed here, along with other classics—but instructors will also expect the anthology to go beyond the established canon, and to include (a) at least a few less familiar but nevertheless highly important older works (for instance a Noh play, *Dōjōji,* Elizabeth Robins's *Votes for Women,* and W. B. Yeats's *Purgatory*—a play influenced by the Noh tradition) and (b) a generous supply of contemporary plays. The canon today, in the early twenty-first century, is not what it was even in the late twentieth century, hence the extensive changes in the new edition of *Types of Drama.*

- **Expanded Coverage of Women and Contemporary Minority Authors:** Among the authors newly represented here are Elizabeth Robins, Sophie Treadwell, Gertrude Stein, Caryl Churchill, Maria Irene Fornes, Susan Yankowitz, Anna Deveare Smith, Suzan-Lori Parks, and the Caribbean playwright Derek Walcott

- **Expanded Coverage of the Play in Performance:** The Topics for Critical Thinking (notably, The Play on the Stage), the interviews with playwrights and directors, the numerous reviews of productions, and the rich photographic program make it clear to students that the plays are dynamic works that come to life on the stage and that plays change in response to the views of each generation of viewers.

- **Expanded Coverage of Writing about Drama:** Recognizing that instructors require students to write papers but do not have the time to offer instruction in writing, we have amplified this section. It now includes an extended discussion of writing about a filmed version of a play, which explains that the usual film does not simply record an actual stage production from a fixed camera position, but, rather, uses the camera creatively (for instance by close-up shots, or quick cuts), thereby commenting on the action. This quick course in film techniques, which includes a sample essay by a student on Kenneth Branagh's *Hamlet,* will assist students who are writing analyses of a filmed version of a play. We also include material concerning the use of the Internet: We provide a Checklist for Evaluating WWW Sites, a list of websites that will assist students who are doing research on theater topics, and material concerning documentation, both of print and electronic sources.

- **Companion Website and Instructor's Manual:** Types of Drama Online at **www.ablongman.com/barnettod**, provides a wealth of resources for students and instructors. Students will find links to different authors and theatrical periods, critical analysis exercises, and timelines to help them contextualize the plays studied in the text. In addition students can interact online with the use of chat and message board capabilities available on the site.

Types of Drama instructors will have access to the full text of the Instructor's Manual, which is conveniently offered on the companion website. This flexible resource replete witth discussion topics, lecture leads, and suggestions for in-class activities provides many useful ideas to enhance teaching. The heart of the manual is the "Teaching the Play" sections which offer classroom-tested tips and strategies on how to teach your students about each play through acting out scenes, collaborating in group exercises, and analyzing film productions and critical interpretations.

This manual is sure to be a valuable reference tool for the novice and experienced instructor alike. To access the Instructor's Manual, simply go to the Instructors Resources section of the website where you will have the opportunity to view and/or print the manual directly from the website.

ACKNOWLEDGMENTS

We have been fortunate in getting permission to reprint important plays and distinguished translations of older plays; we are grateful to the authors, translators, and publishers who have cooperated. They are all acknowledged starting on page 1553.

In preparing the eighth edition, we are grateful for the help we received from Barbara Bretcko, Raritan Valley Community College; Steve Budd, Bentley College; Barry Cavin, Biola University; Julie Empric, Eckerd College; Verna A. Foster, Loyola University; Leigh Harbin, Angelo State University; Christopher C. Hudgins, University of Las Vegas; Rob Jacklosky, College of Mount Saint Vincent; Albin W. Sandau, Black Hills State University; David K. Sauer, Spring Hill College; Janet M. Spencer, Wingate University; Salaam Yousif, California State University-San Bernardino; and Edward Zlotkowski, Bentley College; Mark Evans Bryan, Laura Farkas, Tonia Krueger, Karin Maresh, and Christy Stanlake (for the List of Video Resources), all at Ohio State University; and Esther Kim, University of Illinois–Champagne–Urbana. Ren Draya, Blackburn College, made valuable contributions to the preceding edition.

At Longman, we are indebted to Ben Morrison, whose contribution to this book cannot be overstated. His suggestions were invaluable, and (no less important) his patience was boundless. Lois Lombardo effectively presided over the process of converting an unwieldy manuscript into a book, and Marcy Lunetta equally effectively handled the difficult job of obtaining permission for copyrighted material. We wish every author such assistance.

We are also grateful to the many teachers who have given advice over the years: Jacob Adler, Purdue University; Joanne Altieri, University of Washington; Charles Bachman, Buffalo State College; Leonard Berkman, Smith College; David Boudreaux, Nicholls State University; Oscar Brockett, University of Texas at Austin; Terry Browne, State University of New York, Geneseo; Leslie Phillips Butterworth, Holyoke Community College; Michael Cadden, Princeton

University; Victor Cahn, Skidmore College; Kenneth Campbell, Virginia Commonwealth University; Lou F. Caton, University of Oregon; Cynthia Clegg, Pepperdine University; Douglas Cole, Northwestern University; Dorothy Crook, Central Connecticut State University; Joseph J. DaCrema, Villanova University; Charles L. Darn, University of Pittsburgh at Johnstown; E. T. A. Davidson, State University of New York/ Oneonta; Sherri R. Dienstfrey, Idaho State University; Cheryl Faraone, State University of New York, Geneseo; Jeanne Fosket, El Paso Community College; John C. Freeman, El Paso Community College; Catherine Gannon, California State University at San Bernardino; Russell Goldfarb, Western Michigan University; Anthony Graham-White, University of Illinois at Chicago; Charlotte Goodman, Skidmore College; John Gronbeck-Tedesco, University of Kansas; Virginia Hale, University of Hartford; Elsie Galbreath Haley, Metropolitan State College/Denver; Thomas Hatton, Southern Illinois University, Carbondale; JoAnn Holonbek, College of St. Catherine; Richard Homan, Rider College; Kathleen Klein, Southern Connecticut State University; Thomas Kranidas, State University of New York/Stony Brook; Jayne Lewis, University of California at Los Angeles; Helen Lojek, Boise State University; Mary J. McCue, College of San Mateo; Shannon M. McGuire, Louisiana State University; Grace McLaughlin, Portland Community College; Michael McVey, Miami University Middletown; Thomas J. Manning, University of Wisconsin-Oshkosh; Tim Martin, Rutgers University; Susan Vaneta Mason, California State University-Los Angeles; Don Moore, Louisiana State University; Lee Orchard, Northeast Missouri State University; John B. Pieters, University of Florida; Paige Price, University of Oregon; George Ray, Washington and Lee University; Bruce Robbins, Boise State University; Eric Rothstein, University of Wisconsin; Beverly Simpson, Ball State University; Gail Salo, George Mason University; David K. Sauer, Spring Hill College; Myron Simon, University of California at Irvine; Jyotsna Singh, Southern Methodist University; Keith Slocum, Montclair State College; Iris Smith, University of Kansas; Lucille Stelling, Normandale Community College; Edna M. Troiano, Charles County Community College; Robert L. Vales, Gannon University; Charles Watson, Jr., Syracuse University; Paul Wood, Villanova University; and Bruce E. Woodruff, Baker University.

We also gladly acknowledge our debts to Jeanne Newlin, formerly of the Harvard Theatre Collection; Arthur Friedman, University of Lowell; Lydia Forbes, Blackburn College; Roy Graham, Blackburn College; Dan McCandless; Laurence Senelick, Tufts University; and Marcia Stubbs, formerly of Wellesley College.

SYLVAN BARNET
WILLIAM BURTO
LESLEY FERRIS
GERALD RABKIN

TYPES OF
DRAMA

WHAT IS DRAMA?

Few books on drama fail to tell the reader that *drama* comes from a Greek word meaning "a deed," and that the Greek noun itself comes from a verb, *dran*, "to do." The idea is that a drama shows something in the doing, something being done. Drama is not simply the presentation of interesting characters (Macbeth and Lady Macbeth), or a matter of preaching interesting ideas (it doesn't pay to kill a king); rather, it is the presentation of human beings engaged in action.

How is this action presented? Although a play usually tells a story, "the medium of drama," as Ezra Pound observed, "is not words, but persons moving about on a stage using words." An equally brief statement about the essence of drama is Lope de Vega's assertion (made some four hundred years ago) that the essence of drama consists of three boards, two actors, and a passion—that is, a *place* (a playing-space, three boards), where *impersonators* (two actors) engage in a *conflict* (passion). The place may be a permanent theater-building, or it may be a street corner or a flat-top truck; the impersonators may be highly paid professionals, or they may be inexperienced amateurs; the conflict may be a trivial dispute over whose dog did what, and where, or it may be a matter of life and death. When thinking about even the most sophisticated plays, it's not a bad idea to recall from time to time the statements of Pound and Lope de Vega.

A play is written to be seen and to be heard, not just to be read. We go to *see* a play in a theater (*theater* is derived from a Greek word meaning "to watch"), but in the theater we also *hear* it, thus becoming an audience (*audience* is derived from a Latin word meaning "to hear"). Hamlet was speaking the ordinary language of his day when he said, "We'll hear a play tomorrow." When we read a play rather than see and hear it in a theater, we see it in the mind's eye (Hamlet's words), and we hear it in the mind's ear.

In reading a play it's not enough mentally to hear the lines. We must try to see the characters, costumed and moving with a specified setting; costumes, sets, and gestures are parts of the language of drama. When we are in the theater, our job is much easier, of course; we have only to pay attention to the performers. But when we are readers, we must do what we can to perform the play in the theater under our hat.

A MEDIEVAL EXAMPLE OF DRAMA

Let's look at a tiny example of early European drama—but first, a tiny bit of history. Although the ancient Greeks and Romans had developed drama to a high art, the early Christians opposed dramatic spectacles, partly because such spectacles included gladiatorial contests and naked dancing. After the Roman emperors made Christianity the official state religion, and after Rome was sacked by the Visigoths in 410 C.E. public acting was prohibited; and by the sixth century, drama had virtually disappeared from Europe, except for such rudimentary entertainments as puppet shows, minstrelsy, and acrobatics. Yet, amazingly, the drama was reborn within the church itself.

The New Testament reports that when women went to the tomb of the crucified Jesus in order to anoint the body, they found an angel, who told them that Jesus had risen from the tomb. Drawing on this narrative (chiefly Matthew 28.1–7 and Mark 16.1–8), the Church by the ninth century had developed an introductory text for the Mass on Easter Sunday morning, the anniversary of the Resurrection from the Dead of the Crucified Christ. The Latin words were chanted antiphonally, that is, with one voice or group of voices answering another. In translation the words go thus:

> FIRST VOICE. Whom do you seek in the tomb?
> SECOND VOICE. Jesus of Nazareth.
> FIRST VOICE. He is not here; he is risen as predicted when it was prophesied that he would rise from the dead.
> SECOND VOICE. Alleluia! The Lord is risen!
> ALL VOICES. Come and see the place.

Now suppose we take the lines of the First Voice, and we let them be sung by a priest who, dressed in white, represents an angel in the tomb—itself represented by the altar-table—and we take the lines of the Second Voice and we let them be sung by three priests who, dressed as women, represent the three Marys—the three women who, according to tradition, visited the tomb in order to anoint the corpse. Exactly such a development took place in the tenth century. In a document of about 970, Ethelwold, Bishop of Winchester, England, provides dialogue and stage directions for a miniature play to be performed by priests. What follows is a translation of Ethelwold's Latin account of the work known by its first words, *Quem Quaeritis* ("Whom do you seek?").

WHOM DO YOU SEEK?
(*QUEM QUAERITIS*)
Anonymous

While the third lesson is being chanted, let four brethren dress themselves. Let one of these, dressed in a white robe, enter as though to take part in the service, and let him go to the tomb without attracting attention and sit there quietly with a palm in his hand. While the third response is chanted, let the remaining three follow, and let them all, dressed in capes, bearing in their hand incense containers and stepping delicately as if seeking something, approach the tomb.

These things are done in imitation of the angel sitting on the tomb and the women with spices coming to anoint the body of Jesus. When, therefore, the seated one beholds the three approach him like wanderers who seek something, let him begin to sing in a sweet and moderate voice:

Whom do you seek in the tomb, O followers of Christ?

And when he has sung it to the end, let the three reply in unison:

Jesus of Nazareth who was crucified, O celestial one!

So he:

He is not here, He has risen as He foretold.
Go, announce that He is risen from the dead.

At the word of this bidding let those three turn to the choir and say:

Alleluia! The Lord is risen today,
The strong lion, Christ the Son of God! Unto God give thanks, eia!

This said, let the one, still sitting there and as if recalling them, say the anthem:

Come, and see the place where the Lord was laid,
Alleluia! Alleluia!

And saying this, let him rise, and lift the veil, and show them the place bare of the cross, but only the cloths laid there in which the cross was wrapped:

Go quickly, and tell the disciples that the Lord is risen.
Alleluia! Alleluia!

And when they have seen this, let them set down the incense containers which they bear in that same tomb, and take the cloth, and hold it up in the face of the clergy, and as if to demonstrate that the Lord has risen and is no longer wrapped therein, let them sing the anthem:

The Lord is risen from the tomb,
Who for us was hanged on the cross, alleluia!

and lay the cloth upon the altar. When the anthem is done, let the prior, sharing in their gladness at the triumph of Our King, in that, having vanquished death, He rose again, begin the hymn "We praise you, Lord." And this begun, all the bells chime out together.

All the elements of a play are here: an **imitation** by actors (here, priests) of an **action.** By "action" we do not mean the physical movements of the characters, but a story, a happening, in this case a story of characters moving from doubt to joyful certainty. Normally the action of a play includes a **conflict;** here we might say that the conflict is between the uncertainty and presumably the sorrow of the women, and the knowledge and joy of the angel. We can say, too, that the angel wins the women over to his side.

The dialogue of course is essential, but notice that the imitation is aided by **scenery** ("the place bare of the cross"), **hand properties** (incense vessels, representing the spices that the women brought to the tomb, and also the angel's palm branch), **costumes** (a white garment for the priest who plays the angel, and copes—capelike garments—for the priests who play the women), and **gestures** ("stepping delicately as if seeking something"). Even **sound effects** are used: "All the bells chime out together."[1]

---

[1]*Quem Quaeritis* is available on a videocassette, in *Early English Drama*, in the History of Drama series issued by Films for the Humanities and Sciences, Inc., Box 2053, Princeton, N.J. (telephone 1–800–257–5126)

MISTAKES, CONFLICTS, AND AUDIENCE-AWARENESS

MISTAKES AND CONFLICTS

If drama is the imitation of an action, an imitation of a happening, will any sort of happening do? Perhaps. Drama is so immensely varied that one is tempted to say there is no such thing as drama, only dramatists who produce dramas, plays of all sorts. Still, one notices a dominant pattern—or at least W. H. Auden, poet, librettist, and critic, noticed a pattern.

> Drama is based on the Mistake. I think someone is my friend when he really is my enemy, that I am free to marry a woman when in fact she is my mother, that this person is a chambermaid when it is a young nobleman in disguise, that this well-dressed young man is rich when he is really a penniless adventurer, or that if I do this such and such a result will follow when in fact it results in something very different. All good drama has two movements, first the making of the mistake, then the discovery that it was a mistake.
>
> "NOTES ON MUSIC AND OPERA" IN *THE DYER'S HAND* (1962)

If we think back to "Whom Do You Seek?" we see that the three "women with spices coming to anoint the body of Jesus" are making a mistake, and as the little play progresses they discover that mistake.

The conflict is scarcely visible, but it is nevertheless present. The women have come to the tomb to anoint the body of Jesus, but instead of finding the body they find an angel. The conflict, we can say, is between the mistaken quest of the women and the knowledge of the angel.

AUDIENCE-AWARENESS

The audience of "Whom Do You Seek?" of course knows how the story will turn out. There is nothing of the suspense that we find in a mystery novel, or in a soap opera. If there is any suspense, the audience wonders not what the outcome will be, but exactly what words will be uttered—exactly what the three women will say when they are given the good news.

Obviously if you are attending a classic play, perhaps *Romeo and Juliet*, you almost surely know what mistakes are made, what conflicts are set into motion, and how it all turns out. The audience knows—but Romeo does not—that Juliet is not dead but merely asleep; the audience knows—but Macbeth does not—that by murdering King Duncan he will lose rather than gain; the audience knows—but the young lovers in *A Midsummer Night's Dream* do not—that at the end of the play, all of the competing lovers will be properly paired. Much of our pleasure, in fact, results from our superior knowledge; we see characters engaging in certain actions that we know are mistaken, and a sort of conflict is set up between us and the characters, especially between the characters with whom we most sympathize, and to whom we feel like saying, "No, no, no, don't do that; can't you see that is exactly the wrong thing to do?"

But even if you do not already know the end of the play, you may find yourself engaged in this sort of sympathetic conflict with the characters. How can this be? Easy; most dramatists—putting aside those who write plays that are essentially detective stories—usually let the audience in on facts that some of the characters do not learn until later.

PLOT, CHARACTER, THEME

Although **plot** is sometimes equated with the gist of the narrative—the story—it is sometimes reserved to denote the writer's *arrangement* of the happenings in the story. Thus, all plays about the assassination of Julius Caesar have pretty much the same story, but by beginning with a scene of workmen enjoying a holiday (and thereby introducing the motif of the fickleness of the mob), Shakespeare's *Julius Caesar* has a plot different from a play that omits such a scene.

Handbooks on the drama often suggest that a plot (arrangement of happenings) should have a rising action, a climax, and a falling action. This sort of plot can be diagramed as a pyramid, the tension rising through complications, or crises, to a climax, at which point the fate of the protagonist (chief character) is firmly established; the climax is the apex, and the tension allegedly slackens as we witness the dénouement (unknotting). Shakespeare sometimes used a pyramidal structure, placing his climax neatly in the middle of what seems to us to be the third of five acts.[1] Roughly the first half of *Julius Caesar* shows Brutus rising, reaching his height in 3.1 with the death of Caesar; but later in this scene he gives Marc Antony permission to speak at Caesar's funeral and thus he sets in motion his own fall, which occupies the second half of

the play. In *Macbeth,* the protagonist attains his height in 3.1 ("Thou hast it now: King"), but he soon perceives that he is going downhill:

> I am in blood
> Stepped in so far, that, should I wade no more,
> Returning were as tedious as go o'er.

Of course, no law demands such a structure, and a hunt for the pyramid usually causes the hunter to overlook all the crises but the middle one. William Butler Yeats once suggestively diagrammed a good plot not as a pyramid but as a line moving diagonally upward, punctuated by several crises. Perhaps it is sufficient to say that a good plot has its moments of tension, but the location of these will vary with the play. They are the product of **conflict,** but not all conflict produces tension; there is conflict but little tension in a baseball game when the score is 10–0 in the ninth inning with two out and no one on base.

Regardless of how a plot is diagramed, the **exposition** is the part that tells the audience what it has to know about the past, the antecedent action. That is, the exposition tells the audience what the present situation is. When the three Marys say they are seeking Jesus "who was crucified," they are offering exposition, filling us in on what has already happened. In later plays, when two gossiping servants tell each other that after a year away in Paris the young master is coming home tomorrow with a new wife, they are giving the audience the exposition by introducing characters and defining relationships.

The Elizabethans and the Greeks sometimes tossed out all pretense at dialogue and began with a **prologue,** like the one spoken by the Chorus at the outset of *Romeo and Juliet:*

> Two households, both alike in dignity
>   In fair Verona, where we lay our scene.
> From ancient grudge break to new mutiny,
>   Where civil blood makes civil hands unclean.
> From forth the fatal loins of these two foes
>   A pair of star-crossed lovers take their life. . . .

And in Tennessee William's *The Glass Menagerie,* Tom's first speech is a sort of prologue. However, the exposition also may extend far into the play, so the audience keeps getting bits of information that clarify the present and build suspense about the future.

Character has two meanings: someone who appears in a play (for instance, Juliet), and second, the intel-

---

[1] An **act** is a main division in a drama or opera. Act divisions probably stem from Roman theory and derive ultimately from the Greek practice of separating episodes in a play by choral interludes, but Greek (and probably Roman) plays were performed without interruption, for the choral interludes were part of the plays themselves. Elizabethan plays, too, may have been performed without breaks; the division of Elizabethan plays into five acts is usually work of editors rather than of authors. Frequently an act division today (commonly indicated by lowering the curtain and turning up the houselights) denotes change in local and lapse of time. A **scene** is a smaller unit, either (1) a division with no change of locale or abrupt shift of time, or (2) a division consisting of an actor or group of actors on the stage; according to the second definition, the departure or entrance of an actor changes the composition of the group and thus introduces a new scene. (In an entirely different sense, the scene is the locale where a work is set.)

lectual, emotional, and moral qualities that add up to a personality (as when we say that Juliet's character is more complex than Romeo's).

When dramatic characters speak, they are doing at least two things: they are revealing themselves (if they are speaking deceitfully to their hearers, they are revealing themselves as deceivers to us), and they are also *doing things to other characters*, evoking from these characters agreement, anger, amusement, or whatever. **Dialogue,** then, is a form of action; when characters speak, they are bombarding other characters, who in turn reply and further advance the plot, perhaps by heightening the conflict.

One character may be in conflict either with another character or with a group of characters. In Susan Glaspell's *Trifles* (page 18), for instance, there is at first a subdued conflict between Mrs. Peters and Mrs. Hale (Mrs. Peters is stronger on the idea of dutifully following the law than Mrs. Hale is), but later the two women join forces in a conflict with the men. Each woman is a **foil** to the other, that is, a contrasting figure, one who helps to set off or define another figure.

Finally, one may ask, What does a play add up to? What is the underlying **theme,** or meaning, of a play?

Some critics, arguing that the concept of theme is meaningless, hold that any play gives us only an extremely detailed history of some imaginary people. But surely this view is desperate. Dramatists may begin by being fascinated by a particular character or by some particular happening (real or imagined), but as they work on their play they see to it that the characters and the plot add up to something. (A *plot* is what happens; a *theme* is what the happenings add up to.) *Quem Quaeritis,* for the believer, is about the conquest of death through the sacrifice of Jesus; *Trifles* is (at least in part) about a patriarchal society that foolishly underestimates the intelligence and resourcefulness of women. To the reply that the theme, when stated, is usually banal, we can counter that the plays present these ideas in such a way that they take on life and become a part of us. And surely we are in no danger of equating the play with the theme that we sense underlies it. We never believe that our rough statement of the theme is really the equivalent of the play itself. The play, we recognize, presents the theme with such detail that our statement of the theme is only a wedge that helps us to enter the play so we may more fully (in Henry James's words) "appropriate it."

PHOTO ESSAY:
The Language of Drama/
The Language of the Theater

■ DRAMA AND THEATER

We read plays and we see them performed. They exist in books, fixed with the immobility of the printed word. Drama represents, then, a major part of our literary tradition. The first great work of literary criticism, Aristotle's *Poetics*, is, after all, a work of dramatic criticism. But just as Aristotle theorized a century after the great outburst of Greek creativity, abstracting principles of tragic poetry from what had been the evolving practice of a living, changing drama, the literary history of dramatic expression is more often than not a rationalizing of stage popularity. Drama expresses itself through theater, a tyrannously contemporary art; in a play, the action is always expressed in the present tense. Works that are initially rejected or neglected may find their audiences later on, of course, but the fact of theater ties drama's survival much more stringently than poetry or fiction to immediate collective approval. So if drama is literature, it is also something more. With only a handful of exceptions, the history of drama is told through the history of those works that survive *on stage*.

Like music and dance, drama/theater is an art of performance necessarily dependent on other arts for completion. True, we can read a play as though it were intended for the printed page, but in so doing we must be aware that we are not accepting it fully on its own terms. What distinguishes "real" from "closet" drama is precisely its theatrical viability. Unlike poetry or fiction, drama interposes a series of interpretative artists—director, actor, scenic, sound, and costume designer, musician—between the writer and his or her audience. To "read" drama fully we must participate in a public event; we must be at a particular place at a particular time. And we must be attentive, because we cannot put it down and pick it up again. To read drama well we must try to transport ourselves into an imaginary audience. Music can serve as a model here: If indeed we possessed the skill to read a musical score, we surely would not confuse this experience with attending a concert.

Collaboration is a two-edged sword: The playwright's dramatic vision can be both enhanced and diminished by his or her interpreters. Theatrical experience is concrete and corporeal, literally embodying action in a continuous present. We watch *this* specific Hamlet at *this* specific time in *this* specific theater. The advantage of reading a play is that no possibly unwelcome physical presence is thrust before us downstage center. But remember the sword's other cutting edge: If theatrical mediocrity can degrade a great play, theatrical excellence can elevate an inferior one and even further enhance a great one. When interpretative artists succeed, they supplement the playwright's creative imagination with their own. The ideal conjunction of great performance and great play occurs infrequently, but when it does a summit of artistic achievement is reached. As Eric Bentley writes in *The Life of the Drama*,

> For anyone capable of relishing theatre—and that includes more people than know it—even though the written script has its own completeness, there is no pleasure to top that of seeing a dramatic masterpiece masterfully performed. What is added means so much in such an immediate, sensuous way. If plot, characterization and dialogue give body to the theme, and transform thought into wisdom, and a view into a vision, adequate performance helps them to do so in various ways but above all by adding that final and conclusive concretion, the living actor. (p. 149)

Like the legendary phoenix, theatrical tradition is replenished by the embers of past performances. As artifacts, the novel, the poem, the film remain fixed; the consciousness of their readers or viewers changes. But, paradoxically, the strength of drama lies in its very incompleteness, in the playwright's conscious acceptance of a loss of aesthetic control. We can only surmise what Shakespeare's fellow actor Richard Burbage brought personally to his characterization of Hamlet or Othello, the actor's art being necessarily ephemeral until the advent of the motion picture. But inasmuch as Shakespeare was first and foremost a man of the theatre—an actor and shareholder in the theatrical company's profits as well as a dramatist—his work assumes the necessity of this transient contribution. Shakespeare created not only great characters but great *roles*. His unbroken command of our literary tradition is paralleled by his unbroken command of the world stage. Even when translated, bowdlerized, or rewritten, his plays, in one tone or another, have spoken to all successive generations.

There can be, then, no definitive "edition" of a theatrical performance, no matter how impressive, for every age must create the play anew literally in its own image. After Laurence Olivier's magnificent film version of *Henry V*, it was asked how it would be possible to achieve a more perfect realization. But Olivier's heroic portrayal, the production of a nation at war, has given way to darker, less patriotic, even antiheroic characterizations by such as Ian Holm and Kenneth Branagh. Similarly, Peter Brook's great bleak Royal Shakespeare Company production of *King Lear* (1963) could have emerged only in an age that produced Samuel Beckett's *Endgame*, Peter Weiss's *Marat/Sade,* and Jan Kott's *Shakespeare Our Contemporary*. Indeed, even when it evokes the past, theater is always contemporary; its mediators live; its moment is *here, now*.

■ PLAYING-SPACES

Plays, we said earlier, are meant to be seen (*theater* is from a Greek word meaning "seeing-place") and heard (*audience* is from a Latin word connected with "to hear"). In all probability, however, if you are taking a course in drama, you will read more plays than you will see and hear. Still, when you read you will doubtless make an effort to experience the plays in the theater of your mind. This means that you will sometimes imagine the plays in the context of the distinctive theaters for which they were written. And you will (again, at least sometimes) keep in mind the dramatists' stage directions, which may describe the sets, costumes, gestures, and perhaps sound effects and lighting. Further,

you will try to imagine the gestures and movements that are called for by the dialogue even if they are not specified in stage directions.

Let's look at some pictures and try to see how they clarify our experience of drama. We will begin with some playing-spaces, since the space helps to shape the kind of play performed and also the spectator's response. The audience in an ancient **Greek theater** (pages 11 and 50, top), sitting on a hillside and looking down on the actors, had a somewhat godlike perspective: above were the heavens; behind the actors was a façade that resembled a temple or a palace; the plot concerned the actions of legendary figures (heroes, heroines), who played their parts in a world in which the gods intervened. And since the dramas were presented at fixed times at publicly supported dramatic festivals, the experience was communal; a relatively homogeneous audience (Athenian citizens— in fact, possibly only Athenian male citizens) heard again the great stories that were part of their heritage.

The Greek theater offered three levels for performers. On the ground level was the orchestra (literally, "dance place"), where the chorus—usually representing ordinary citizens—danced. At the rear of the orchestra, on a slightly elevated stage (there is some argument about the date when the stage was elevated above the orchestra), the actors performed with the *skene* or "scene-building" as a background. The third performing level was the roof of the *skene*; a human being might appear here, such as a watchman, but chiefly the roof was used to represent the realm of the gods.

Elizabethan theaters (pages 11 and 218), like Greek theaters, were open to the sky. More precisely, the so-called public theaters were essentially unroofed, but a canopy, called "the heaven," extended over part of the stage. (The canopy, whose underside was decorated with symbols of the zodiac, rested on two pillars that themselves rested on the stage.) Further, there were also smaller indoor theaters, customarily called "private" theaters, and plays were sometimes done at court in improvised theaters. For the most part, however, the plays of Shakespeare and his colleagues were written for theaters like the Globe—Shakespeare's theater—and the Swan, illustrated on page 218.

Although the Elizabethan theater, like the Greek theater, lacked a curtain at the front and therefore could not suddenly reveal elaborate settings, "discoveries" could be made by withdrawing a curtain from a doorway or perhaps from a small alcove at the back of the stage. And the architecture of the stage itself provided a degree of spectacle. Contemporary references indicate that the building itself was handsome, even splendid, and the performers thus moved against a fairly elaborate architectural background. When the Elizabethan *Hamlet* spoke of "this goodly frame, the earth," he moved against a sturdy and attractive background, and when (referring to the heavens) he spoke of "this majestical roof, fretted [i.e., adorned] with golden fire," he probably looked up and gestured toward the underside of the canopy. In many other scenes, spectacle was provided by colorful costumes and banners.

Further, the theater offered several levels for performers. The stage, jutting into the audience, served for most of the action, but windows above the stage could serve as Juliet's balcony in the famous scene with Romeo, or as the top of the city walls, from which residents might look down on a besieging army, or as the rigging of a ship, from which sailors would shout to those on deck below (i.e., on the main stage). In addition to the playing-spaces above the stage, there was a level below the stage called the cellarage or hell, reached by trapdoors. Probably when Hamlet leaped into the grave he leapt through a trapdoor, and quite possibly when a ghost or devil appeared on the main stage, it entered from a trap. The illustration from Marlowe's *Doctor Faustus* (page 12, top) cannot be regarded as an accurate picture of an Elizabethan stage, but it does give a good idea of how Faustus might have been costumed, and the emerging dragon-devil may well reflect theatrical practice.

▪ SETS

A proscenium theater (page 13, top), is a theater with a sort of picture frame separating the actors from the audience (in contrast to the theater with a thrust stage, such as the Elizabethan theater). It developed in Italy in the mid-sixteenth century and reached France and England in the next century. A proscenium stage can easily be equipped with a front curtain that can be raised to reveal actors in an elaborate setting. Further, these theaters used scenery painted on flats that ran in grooves across the breadth of the stage; the flats could be pulled off to the sides, thereby revealing another scene. Thus, the raising of the curtain revealed the performers in the first scene, who were backed by flats extending across the width of the stage; the withdrawal of the flats might reveal a second scene, and so on for a third or even a fourth scene. (For additional details, see pages 389–90.)

The proscenium theater lends itself to the box set, which is essentially a room constructed out of flats (often equipped with working doors and sometimes windows),

but with the front wall missing so the audience can see what goes on within the room. The box set, with its realistic furnishings, dominated later nineteenth-century European and American theater; it is the set in which, for instance, the plays of Ibsen and Chekhov were performed. **Realism** sought, obviously, to offer a close imitation of reality (page 13, middle, shows a 1976 version, of Ibsen's *A Doll's House*). But the theater—any theater—is essentially a place for symbolic action, and we can now see that even a realistic set of this sort can be symbolic. For instance, it may use overstuffed furniture, heavy drapes, and moralizing paintings on the walls to symbolize the crushing bourgeois life that the characters live.

Some sets use what has been called **selective realism.** A famous example is Jo Mielziner's set for the original production (1947) of *Death of a Salesman* (page 13, bottom). The bed, the refrigerator, the chairs—all of these are just what we might find in a house of the period—but the roof of the house is indicated by a skeletal-like structure. The set helps to convey both the commonplace yet oppressive world that the characters move in, and it is also suited, by its unreal aspects, to occasional scenes with flashbacks and fantasies.

The appearance of a set may have no connection, or almost no connection, with the way reality appears to our eye. Rather, it may represent a character's state of mind. For instance, Hamlet lives in a castle, but he finds not splendor but oppressiveness ("Denmark's a prison"). Hamlet's sense of reality, rather than optical reality, may be communicated by using a set that resembles a prison more than a palace, or by nothing much more than some clanking chains and clanging metal plates.

Similarly, although in Eugene O'Neill's *The Emperor Jones* the opening scene in the palace is usually represented realistically, with a throne, a red carpet, and so forth, the scenes in the jungle are represented symbolically, conveying Jones's sensations or experiences or ancient memories rather than what a dispassionate observer would actually see.

The **lighting** of course is part of the set. Here is part of the beginning stage direction in Arthur Miller's *Death of a Salesman:*

> Before us is the Salesman's house. We are aware of towering, angular shapes behind it, surrounding it on all sides. Only the blue light of the sky falls upon the house and forestage; the surrounding area shows an angry glow of orange.

Miller's lighting, especially the "angry glow of orange," is part of what we can call the language of the play.

Tennessee Williams uses lighting in a similar way in *The Glass Menagerie;* while two characters quarrel, the stage "is lit with turgid smoky red glow." These examples of symbolic lighting are obvious; less obvious are passages that at first glance seem merely naturalistic but, in fact, are also symbolic. In *A Doll's House,* as Nora's terror grows in the second act, Ibsen tells us in a brief but important stage direction, "It begins to grow dark."

Let's push the term *set* a bit far, so that we can include **sound effects.** After all, if a forest is part of the set, why not the sounds of the forest—whether the cheery twittering of birds or the menacing howl of the wind. In *Death of a Salesman,* before the curtain goes up, "A melody is heard, played upon a flute. It is small and fine, telling of grass and trees and the horizon." Then the curtain rises, revealing the Salesman's house, with "towering, angular shapes behind it, surrounding it on all sides." Obviously, the sound of the flute is meant to tell us about the world from which the Salesman is shut off. In *Quem Quaeritis* (page 2), the bells at the end help to communicate the joy and harmony of the action that the play sets forth.

A sound effect, however, need not be so evidently symbolic to be important. In Glaspell's *Trifles,* almost at the very end of the play we hear the "sound of a knob turning in the other room" (page 23). The sound has an electrifying effect on the audience, as it does on the two women on the stage, and it precedes a decisive action.

▪ PERFORMERS

In the Western theater, the performers now are almost always human beings, but puppet drama has been popular in much of the world and is still esteemed in some cultures, especially in Asia. In Japan, for instance, *bunraku* uses large puppets manipulated by a principal puppeteer and two hooded assistants, who are clothed in black and regarded as invisible (page 14, top). Outside of Asia, puppets or marionettes traditionally serve as entertainment for children.

But puppets and marionettes can still be used effectively, even in Western drama intended for adults. John Barton, in his 1974 production of Christopher Marlowe's *Doctor Faustus,* used two puppets—manipulated by Faustus—to represent the Good Angel and the Bad Angel (page 14, bottom). Doubtless, in Marlowe's day, two actors performed these roles, but since the characters represent (roughly speaking) Faustus's divided consciousness, it was effective to have Faustus manipulate the puppets that represented his conflicting thoughts.

Turning to human performers, we find that the use of females to play female roles is a relatively modern Western practice; in fact, it still is not the custom in Asia, where specially trained males perform the females roles in traditional drama—for instance in the Japanese Noh plays and Kabuki plays. Exactly *why* men have played women's roles is uncertain, but it may be related to the drama's roots in religious rituals. Although priestesses are important in many religions, some kinds of rites are off-limits to women, and it seems that males impersonated females in certain dealings with the gods. In any case, in Greece all of the performers were male, with masks making impersonation relatively easy. What is perhaps more surprising is that in medieval Christian drama—plays dramatizing biblical episodes—males took female roles, despite the injunction in the Hebrew Bible (Deuteronomy 22.5) against cross-dressing. (We have already seen, in *Quem Quaeritis* on page 2, that three priests impersonated the women who visited the tomb where they expected to find Jesus.) In the Elizabethan and Jacobean periods (the second half of the sixteenth century and the first half of the seventeen century) highly trained boys between the ages of approximately ten and thirteen played the females roles—for instance Juliet, Lady Macbeth, and Lear's three daughters. Although the English public of the period did occasionally see actresses in visiting French companies, the English stage did not routinely use actresses until 1660, when the theaters, which had been closed for almost two decades under Puritan rule, reopened.

We have almost no evidence about how early audiences reacted to boys or men playing the parts of women. The very few extant remarks from Shakespeare's day concerning boy actors uniformly praise the boys for their skill. *Possibly* there was some sniggering, some nudging with elbows, at the sight of a hero passionately addressing a boy dressed as a girl, but if we think that this *must* have been the reaction, we may simply be imposing our ideas on earlier centuries. Probably the convention of males playing female roles was so deeply entrenched that is was not thought about—just as we do not think about the music that accompanies the action in a movie. When you think about it, music accompanying lovers walking through a field, or soldiers dying in battle, is utterly unnatural, but no one bats an eyelash. On the other hand, we know for certain that in the past when a woman played a young romantic male role—what is called a breeches part—the audience was conscious of and titillated by the cross-dressing. In ages when women wore long dresses, male attire was a way for audiences to

see a female's legs. Today the chief breeches part is Peter Pan, though occasionally women play the male roles of Ariel (in Shakespeare's *The Tempest*), Puck (in *A Midsummer Night's Dream*), and the Fool in *King Lear*.

Having so completely accepted the idea that the actor's gender determines the available roles, we read with incredulity that Sarah Bernhardt in the late nineteenth century played Hamlet. It sounds eccentric, unnatural, a bad idea. The chief exceptions have been in farce, where it is considered hilarious for a man to disguise himself as a woman and to camp it up.

Today, however, chiefly under the stimulus of feminism and gay rights, gender-bending in serious drama is very much in style. A recent production of *Everyman*, for instance, cast women in the title role and in the role of Death (page 15, top left). The practice of casting against gender—having a woman play Everyman or Lear—is said to stimulate an inquiry into gender identity, making us see the plays and ourselves in a new light.

A related issue is casting against race. How do we feel about a black actor or an Asian actor playing Lear, with three white daughters? Does it bother some or all of us? If it bothers us, *why* does it bother us? Because of the lack of verisimilitude? Or because it touches some racist notion, a notion we do not wish to acknowledge? If it does bother some of us, is this perhaps a good thing, a means of jolting us out of our accustomed ways of thinking?

■ COSTUMES AND GESTURES

The performers, whether puppets or human, whether male or female, are costumed, and their costumes (like our own clothes) say something. When we wear jeans, a necktie, or running shoes, we are making statements about who we are—or who we want to be. Our clothes help us to create the role of student, professor, artist, police officer, chef, or lifeguard. Hamlet's "inky cloak" tells the viewers that he is in mourning, and—by its contrast with the colorful clothes that the other courtiers are wearing—it tells us that he remembers the death of his father in a way that no one else does. A change of costume is usually highly significant. In *Everyman* (page 184), near the beginning of the play we learn that the worldly Everyman is gaily dressed, a sign of his preoccupation with material things. Later in the play, when he has seen the folly of his ways, he puts off this worldly garment and dons "a garment of sorrow," perhaps a hair shirt. Neither garment is clearly described, but surely the change in garments symbolizes Everyman's spiritual development.

Or consider Nora Helmer's changes of costume in Ibsen's *A Doll's House*. In the first act, she wears ordinary clothing, presumably appropriate to a middle-class housewife, but in the middle of the second act, when she frantically rehearses her tarantella, a wild dance, she wears "a long, many-colored shawl." The shawl is appropriate to the Italian dance, but its multitude of colors also helps express Nora's conflicting emotions. Her extreme agitation is expressed, too, in the fact that "her hair comes loose and falls down over her shoulders," but "she doesn't notice." The shawl and her disheveled hair, then, *speak* to us as clearly as the dialogue does. In the middle of the third act, after the party and just before the showdown, Nora appears in her "Italian costume," and, her husband, Torvald, wears "evening dress" under an open black cloak. She is dressed for a masquerade (her whole life has been a masquerade, it turns out), and Torvald's formal suit and black cloak help express the stiffness and the blight that have forced her to present a false front throughout their years of marriage. (For an extremely expressive image of Torvald costumed as a Draculalike destructive being, see page 15, center.) A little later, Nora appears "in an everyday dress." The pretense is over. When she finally leaves the stage—leaves the house—she "wraps her shawl around her." This is not the "many-colored shawl" she used in rehearsing the dance, but the "big, black shawl" she wears when she returns from the dance. The blackness of this shawl helps express the death of the old way of life.

Gestures, too, are part of the language of life, as well as of drama. Every day, in the course of countless conversations, we shrug, lean forward or draw back, thrust our hands into our pockets, cross our legs, nod or shake our heads, and engage in hundred of little actions that reveal our states of mind. And so do characters in plays. Notice, as you study the photographs in this book, how much can be communicated by posture and gesture.

When we read a play can we fully envision it as though it is being performed on a stage? Of course not. But we must try, at least occasionally, to think about how we might perform a particular speech, or how we might stage a scene. In short, we must try to see and hear the play in what Shakespeare called "the mind's eye," and (to continue quoting Shakespeare) when we read what is nothing more than ink on paper, we must "give to airy nothings a local habitation."

This modern reconstruction of an ancient Greek theater in Athens gives a sense of the original circumstances: The audience sat on a hillside, looking down at a circular dancing place, behind which was an area where actors performed. A stone building behind the performers provided a background—its temple-like or palatial façade probably implied a world governed by divine law—and it also provided a means of entering and exiting the stage. See also page 50.

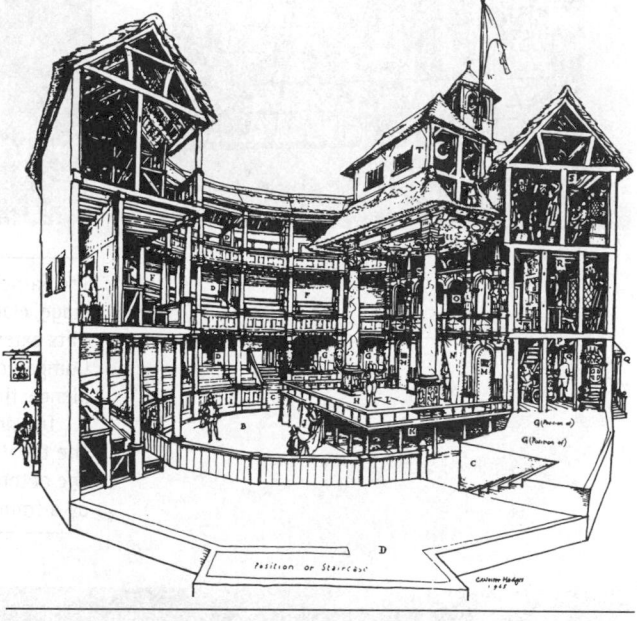

This modern sketch shows what an Elizabethan theater probably looked like. This stage is a "thrust stage," jutting out into the space where the audience stands (spectators who paid an extra fee sat in the galleries). Performers chiefly used the stage, but they might also appear at higher levels, and might use a trap door for a descent to the underworld. The contract for one theater of the period specifies that the stage is to be twenty-seven and one-half feet deep and forty-three feet wide.

For years we have had only drawings to indicate what an Elizabethan playhouse looked like. Now that has all changed with the reconstruction of Shakespeare's Globe Theatre on the South Bank of the River Thames in London. Located only 200 yards from the original 1599 site, the new Globe, which took 27 years of planning and fundraising, opened in 1996 and now provides playgoers and historians alike with a sense of what it must have been like to witness a play as Shakespeare and his fellow players intended. In this shot, you can see the interior with three levels of balcony-like seating that surrounds the thrust stage.

This title page from an early seventeenth-century edition of Marlowe's play *Doctor Faustus* shows us how the title character (here conjuring up a devil) may have been costumed. In the theater, the devil probably rose through a trapdoor.

The Farnese Theater, completed in 1618, uses a proscenium arch. With such a stage, elaborate sets could be revealed when a front curtain was raised, or when flats extending across the breadth of the stage were pulled to the right and left. Compared with the Elizabethan theater, which used a stage extending into the audience, this theater markedly separates the audience from the actors.

The proscenium stage is the stage that most of us are most familiar with. The theater consists of two boxes, one for the actors and one for the audience. The actors perform in their box, illuminated and separated from the audience by a frame, and the audience sits in a darkened box of their own.

In Pieter Brueghel the Younger's *Village Fair* (c. 1620) we see a temporary stage erected in a fairground. Such a stage, used by itinerant performers, consisted of a platform of boards elevated a few feet above the ground by trestles or barrels. At the rear of the platform a curtained booth served as a dressing room and a backdrop for the players. In Brueghel's painting we see the prompter peeking out from behind the curtain.

A proscenium theater is one in which an arch (the *proscenium arch,* or simply the *proscenium*) frames the stage, thus separating the performers from the audience. Such a building, though unknown to the Greeks, the Romans, and Shakespeare, today probably is the commonest type of theater. Although we often hear that a proscenium theater (in contrast to a thrust stage, where the performing area extends into the space of the audience) has the bad effect of distancing the spectators from the players, in fact spectators in proscenium theaters continue to be caught up in the action onstage. In this painting (c. 1860), Honoré Daumier catches both the broad style of acting that was required in large proscenium theaters where the spectators were far from the stage and also the rapt attention of the spectators. The play being acted here cannot be identified, but it may well be *Hamlet.*

A 1976 production of Ibsen's *A Doll's House* used a markedly realistic box set. But notice the doll: On a realistic level the doll is a child's toy, but in this context it is symbolic of Nora and perhaps of Torvald.

Jo Mielziner's set for Arthur Miller's *Death of a Salesman* combines realism (the beds) with abstraction or highly conventional scenery (the roof). It is admirably suited to a play that is chiefly realistic but also uses flashbacks and haunting memories.

The scene is from a famous *bunraku* (puppet) play, *The Double Suicide,* by Chikamatsu Monzaemon, one of Japan's greatest writers. The principal puppeteer (at the left) and his two hooded assistants are considered invisible. In Asia puppet drama is taken seriously by adults.

The street remains a significant site for performance as well as exciting design possibilities. Here the "Merry Monarch," a huge, inventive street puppet designed by Trinidad Carnival artist Peter Minshall, takes to the streets at the Caribana Festival in Toronto in 1987. Carnival, a festival that uses costumes, street performances, and music, takes place in cities around the world, for instance in Toronto, Brooklyn, London, and in Trinidad and Brazil, to name a few of the major sites. In New Orleans it is called Mardi Gras.

In John Barton's 1974 production of Marlowe's *Doctor Faustus,* the Good Angel and the Bad Angel, representing Faustus's conscience and his wicked impulses, were represented by hand puppets manipulated by Faustus.

In a 1996 production of *Everyman* at the Steppenwolf Theatre in Chicago, the roles of Death (left) and Everyman (center) were played by women, forcing the audience to rethink its attitudes about the issue of gender.

A 1972 production of Ibsen's *A Doll's House*—a notably "realistic" play—made Torvald Helmer's formal costume into a symbol of something threatening.

Body language—bodily gestures and facial expressions—is, of course, an important part of our daily behavior and also an actor's art. In this scene from Wole Soyinka's *The Bacchae of Euripides* (page 1064), members of the chorus watch in awe as Dionysus invokes the power of the gods as he points toward the sky. Dionysus, the god of wine and theater, is known for his physicality and chameleon-like ability to change shapes.

IN BRIEF: HOW TO READ A PLAY

If as a reader you develop the following principles into habits, you will get far more out of a play than if you read it as though it were a novel consisting only of dialogue.

1. **Pay attention to the list of characters, and carefully read whatever descriptions the playwright has provided.** Early dramatists, such as Shakespeare, did not provide much in the way of description ("Othello, the Moor" or "Iago, a villain" is about as much as we find in Elizabethan texts), but later playwrights are often very forthcoming. Here, for instance, is Tennessee Williams introducing us to Amanda Wingfield in *The Glass Menagerie*. (We give only the beginning of his longish description.)

> *Amanda Wingfield*; the mother. A little woman of great but confused vitality clinging frantically to another time and place.

And here is Susan Glaspell introducing us to all of the characters in her one-act play, *Trifles*:

> . . . the Sheriff comes in followed by the County Attorney and Hale. The Sheriff and Hale are men in middle life, the County Attorney is a young man; all are much bundled up and go at once to the stove. They are followed by the two women—the Sheriff's wife [Mrs. Peters] first; she is a slight wiry woman, a thin nervous face. Mrs. Hale is larger and would ordinarily be called more comfortable looking, but she is disturbed now and looks fearfully about as she enters. The women have come in slowly and stand close together near the door.

Glaspell's description of her character is not nearly so explicit as Tennessee Williams's, but Glaspell does tell a reader a good deal. What do we know about the men? They differ in age, they are bundled up, and they "go at once to the stove." What do we know about the women? Mrs. Peters is slight, and she has a "nervous face"; Mrs. Hale is "larger" but she too is "disturbed." The women enter "slowly," and they "stand close together near the door." In short, the men, who take over the warmest part of the room, are more confident than the women, who nervously huddle together near the door. It's a man's world.

2. **Pay attention to gestures and costumes that are specified in stage directions or are implied by the dialogue.** We have just seen how Glaspell distinguishes between the men and the women by what they do—the men take over the warm part of the room, the women stand insecurely near the door. Most dramatists from the late nineteenth century to the present have been fairly generous with their stage directions, but when we read the works of earlier dramatists we often have to deduce the gestures from the speeches. For instance, although Shakespeare has an occasional direction such as "She takes a sword and runs at him," for the most part he is very sparing. We must, then, infer the gestures from the dialogue. Consider this exchange between the Earl of Gloucester and King Lear. Early in the play Lear has acted despotically; then he suffers so greatly that his mind becomes unhinged. Gloucester, finding the mad king, says,

> O, let me kiss that hand.

Lear replies,

> Let me wipe it first; it smells of mortality.

Surely when Gloucester speaks his line he reaches for Lear's hand (and probably he also kneels), and Lear withdraws his hand and wipes it on his tattered clothing. Exactly *how* Lear withdraws his hand—suddenly, or with some dignity—is not specified in the words. Nor is it specified whether Lear smells his hand when he says, "It smells of mortality." All readers will have to decide such matters for themselves, but we can probably agree that although the words are immensely moving, the gestures that accompany them (Gloucester's gestures of humility and Lear's unwillingness to accept those gestures) are also part of the "language" of the play.

In addition to thinking about gestures, don't forget the costumes that the characters wear. Costumes, of course, identify the characters as soldiers or farmers or whatever, and changes of costume can be especially symbolic. When we first meet King Lear, for instance, he is dressed as a king. (The text doesn't specify this, but since he is engaged in officially giving away kingdoms, he presumably wears his crown and his robe of office.) Later, driven to madness, he tears off his clothing, thus showing his realization that he is powerless; and still later, after his madness has somewhat abated, he appears dressed in fresh clothing, a sign that at least to some degree he is restored to civilization. Or consider Ibsen's *A Doll's House*. In the first act Nora wears ordinary clothing, but in the middle of the second act she puts on "a long multi-colored shawl" when she frantically rehearses her Italian dance. The shawl not only is appropriate to the tarantella dance, but also in its multitude of colors it expresses Nora's emotional turmoil. In the middle of the third act, she is wearing her Italian costume, dressed for a masquerade—her life has been a masquerade—but later she returns in her "everyday dress." The pretense is over.

3. **Keep in mind the kind of theater for which the play was written.** The plays in this book were written for various kinds of theaters. Sophocles, author of *Antigone* and *King Oedipus,* wrote for the ancient Greek theater, essentially a space where performers acted in front of an audience seated on a hillside. (See the photo on page 50.) This theater was open to the heavens, with a structure representing a palace or temple behind the actors, in itself a kind of image of a society governed by the laws of the state and the laws of the gods. Moreover, the chorus enters the playing-space by marching down the side aisles, close to the audience, thus helping to unite the world of the audience with that of the players. On the other hand, the audience in most modern theaters sits in a darkened area, separated by a proscenium arch from the performers, and watches them move about in a boxlike setting. The box set of Ibsen's plays or of Glaspell's *Trifles*—a room with the front wall missing—is, it often seems, an appropriate image of the confined lives of the characters of the play.

4. **If the playwright describes the locale and the furnishings, try to envision the set clearly. Pay attention also to the lighting.** Glaspell, for instance, tells us a good deal about the set. We quote only the first part.

> The kitchen in the now abandoned farmhouse of John Wright, a gloomy kitchen, and left without having been put in order. . . .

These details about a gloomy and disordered kitchen may seem to be mere realism—after all, the play has to take place somewhere—but it turns out that the disorder and, for that matter, the gloominess are extremely important. You'll have to read the play to find out why.

Another example of a setting that provides important information is Arthur Miller's, in *Death of a Salesman*. Again we quote only the beginning of the description.

> Before us is the Salesman's house. We are aware of towering, angular shapes behind it, surrounding it on all sides. Only the blue light of the sky falls upon the house and forestage; the surrounding area shows an angry glow of orange.

Here the lighting, especially the "angry glow of orange," is also a part of the language of the dramatist. Tennessee Williams uses lighting in a similar way in *The Glass Menagerie;* while two characters quarrel, the stage "is lit with a turgid smoky red glow." These examples of symbolic lighting are obvious, but what at first seems to be merely realistic lighting may also be symbolic. In *A Doll's House,* as Nora's terror grows in the second act, Ibsen tells us in a stage direction, "It begins to grow dark."

If we read older drama, we find that playwrights do not give us much help, but by paying attention to the words we can at least to some degree visualize the locale. For instance, in *King Lear* Shakespeare establishes the setting by giving Gloucester this line:

> Alack, the night comes on, and the high winds
> Do sorely ruffle. For many miles about
> There's scarce a bush.

And, again, this locale says something about the impoverished people who move in it.

5. **Pay attention to whatever sound effects are specified in the play.** As we mentioned earlier, in *Death of a Salesman,* before the curtain goes up, "A melody is heard, played upon a flute. It is small and fine, telling of grass and trees and the horizon." Then the curtain rises, revealing the Salesman's house, with "towering, angular shapes behind it, surrounding it on all sides." The sound of the flute is meant to tell us of the world from which the Salesman is shut off. In *Quem Quaeritis,* the bells at the end help to communicate the joy and harmony of the action that the play sets forth.

6. **Pay attention, at least on second reading, to silences, including pauses within speeches or between speeches.** Late in *Trifles,* a stage direction tells us that "The women's eyes meet for an instant." We won't say what this exchange of looks indicates, but when you read the play you will see that the moment of silence is significant.

7. **Of course, dialogue is the most persistent sound in a play. Pay attention to what the characters say, but keep in mind that (like real people) dramatic characters are not always to be trusted.** An obvious case is Shakespeare's Edmund in *King Lear,* an utterly unscrupulous villain who knows that he is a liar, but a character may be self-deceived, or, to put it a bit differently, characters may say what they honestly think but may not know what they are talking about.

SUSAN Glaspell

Susan Glaspell (1882–1948) was born in Davenport, Iowa, and educated at Drake University in Des Moines. In 1903 she married George Cram Cook and, with Cook and other writers, actors, and artists, in 1915 founded the Provincetown Players. a group that remained vital until 1929. Glaspell wrote *Trifles* (1916) for the Provincetown Players, but she also wrote stories, novels, and a biography of her husband. In 1931 she won a Pulitzer Prize for *Alison's House,* a play about the family of a deceased poet who in some ways resembles Emily Dickinson.

■■■■■■■■■■■■■

TRIFLES
Susan Glaspell

SCENE

The kitchen in the now abandoned farmhouse of John Wright, a gloomy kitchen, and left without having been put in order—unwashed pans under the sink, a loaf of bread outside the breadbox, a dish towel on the table—other signs of incompleted work. At the rear the outer door opens, and the Sheriff comes in, followed by the County Attorney and Hale. The Sheriff and Hale are men in middle life, the County Attorney is a young man; all are much bundled up and go at once to the stove. They are followed by the two women—the Sheriff's Wife first; she is a slight wiry woman, a thin nervous face. Mrs. Hale is larger and would ordinarily be called more comfortable looking, but she is disturbed now and looks fearfully about as she enters. The women have come in slowly and stand close together near the door.

COUNTY ATTORNEY (*rubbing his hands*). This feels good. Come up to the fire, ladies.

MRS. PETERS (*after taking a step forward*). I'm not—cold.

SHERIFF (*unbottoning his overcoat and stepping away from the stove as if to the beginning of official business*). Now, Mr. Hale, before we move things about, you explain to Mr. Henderson just what you saw when you came here yesterday morning.

COUNTY ATTORNEY. By the way, has anything been moved? Are things just as you left them yesterday?

SHERIFF (*looking about*). It's just the same. When it dropped below zero last night, I thought I'd better send Frank out this morning to make a fire for us—no use getting pneumonia with a big case on; but I told him not to touch anything except the stove—and you know Frank.

COUNTY ATTORNEY. Somebody should have been left here yesterday.

SHERIFF. Oh—yesterday. When I had to send Frank to Morris Center for that man who went crazy—I want you to know I had my hands full yesterday. I knew you could get back from Omaha by today, and as long as I went over everything here myself—

COUNTY ATTORNEY. Well, Mr. Hale, tell just what happened when you came here yesterday morning.

HALE. Harry and I had started to town with a load of potatoes. We came along the road from my place; and as I got here, I said, "I'm going to see if I can't get John Wright to go in with me on a party telephone." I spoke to Wright about it once before, and he put me off, saying folks talked too much anyway, and all he asked was peace and quiet—I guess you know about how much he talked himself; but I thought maybe if I went to the house and talked about it before his wife, though I said to Harry that I didn't know as what his wife wanted made much difference to John—

COUNTY ATTORNEY. Let's talk about that later, Mr. Hale. I do want to talk about that, but tell now just what happened when you got to the house.

HALE. I didn't hear or see anything; I knocked at the door, and still it was all quiet inside. I knew they must be up, it was past eight o'clock. So I knocked again, and I thought I heard somebody say, "Come in." I wasn't sure, I'm not sure yet, but I opened the door—this door (*indicating the door by which the two women are still standing*), and there in that rocker—(*pointing to it*) sat Mrs. Wright. (*They all look at the rocker.*)

COUNTY ATTORNEY. What—was she doing?

HALE. She was rockin' back and forth. She had her apron in her hand and was kind of—pleating it.

COUNTY ATTORNEY. And how did she—look?

HALE. Well, she looked queer.

COUNTY ATTORNEY. How do you mean—queer?

HALE. Well, as if she didn't know what she was going to do next. And kind of done up.

COUNTY ATTORNEY. How did she seem to feel about your coming?

HALE. Why, I don't think she minded—one way or other. She didn't pay much attention. I said, "How do, Mrs. Wright, it's cold, ain't it?" And she said, "Is it?"—and went on kind of pleating at her apron. Well, I was surprised; she didn't ask me to come up to the stove, or to set down, but just sat there, not even looking at me, so I said, "I want to see John." And then she—laughed. I guess you would call it a laugh. I thought of Harry and the team outside, so I said a little sharp: "Can't I see John?" "No," she says, "he's home." "Then why can't I see him?" I asked her, out of patience. "'Cause he's dead," says she. *"Dead?"* says I. She just nodded her head, not getting a bit excited, but rockin' back and forth. "Why—where is he?" says I, not knowing what to say. She just pointed upstairs—like that (*himself pointing to the room above*). I got up, with the idea of going up there. I walked from there to here—then I says, "Why, what did he die of?" "He died of a rope around his neck," says she, and just went on pleatin' at her apron. Well, I went out and called Harry. I thought I might—need help. We went upstairs, and there he was lyin'—

COUNTY ATTORNEY. I think I'd rather have you go into that upstairs, where you can point it all out. Just go on now with the rest of the story.

HALE. Well, my first thought was to get that rope off. I looked . . . (*Stops, his face twitches.*) . . . but Harry, he went up to him, and he said, "No, he's dead all right, and we'd better not touch anything." So we went back downstairs. She was still sitting that same way. "Has anybody been notified?" I asked. "No," says she, unconcerned. "Who did this, Mrs. Wright?" said Harry. He said it businesslike—and she stopped pleatin' of her apron. "I don't know," she says. "You don't *know?*" says Harry. "No," says

she. "Weren't you sleepin' in the bed with him?" says Harry. "Yes," says she, "but I was on the inside." "Somebody slipped a rope round his neck and strangled him, and you didn't wake up?" says Harry. "I didn't wake up," she said after him. We must 'a looked as if we didn't see how that could be, for after a minute she said, "I sleep sound." Harry was going to ask her more questions, but I said maybe we ought to let her tell her story first to the coroner, or the sheriff, so Harry went fast as he could to Rivers' place, where there's a telephone.

COUNTY ATTORNEY. And what did Mrs. Wright do when she knew that you had gone for the coroner?

HALE. She moved from that chair to this over here . . . (*Pointing to a small chair in the corner.*) . . . and just sat there with her hands held together and looking down. I got feeling that I ought to make some conversation, so I said I had come in to see if John wanted to put in a telephone, and at that she started to laugh, and then she stopped and looked at me—scared. (*The County Attorney, who had his notebook out, makes a note.*) I dunno, maybe it wasn't scared. I wouldn't like to say it was. Soon Harry got back, and then Dr. Lloyd came, and you, Mr. Peters, and so I guess that's all I know that you don't.

COUNTY ATTORNEY (*looking around*). I guess we'll go upstairs first—and then out to the barn and around there. (*To the Sheriff.*) You're convinced that there was nothing important here—nothing that would point to the motive?

SHERIFF. Nothing here but kitchen things.

(*The County Attorney, after again looking around the kitchen, opens the door of a cupboard closet. He gets up on a chair and looks on a shelf. Pulls his hand away, sticky.*)

COUNTY ATTORNEY. Here's a nice mess.

(*The women draw nearer.*)

MRS. PETERS (*to the other woman*). Oh, her fruit; it did freeze. (*To the Lawyer.*) She worried about that when it turned so cold. She said the fir'd go out and her jars would break.

SHERIFF. Well, can you beat the women! Held for murder and worryin' about her preserves.

COUNTY ATTORNEY. I guess before we're through she may have something more serious than preserves to worry about.

HALE. Well, women are used to worrying over trifles.

(*The two women move a little closer together.*)

COUNTY ATTORNEY (*with the gallantry of a young politician*). And yet, for all their worries, what would we do without the ladies? (*The women do not unbend. He goes to the sink, takes a dipperful of water from the pail and, pouring it into a basin, washes his hands. Starts to wipe them on the roller towel, turns it for a cleaner place.*) Dirty towels! (*Kicks his foot against the pans under the sink.*) Not much of a housekeeper, would you say, ladies?

MRS. HALE (*stiffly*). There's a great deal of work to be done on a farm.

COUNTY ATTORNEY. To be sure. And yet . . . (*With a little bow to her.*) . . . I know there are some Dickson county farmhouses which do not have such roller towels. (*He gives it a pull to expose its full length again.*)

MRS. HALE. Those towels get dirty awful quick. Men's hands aren't always as clean as they might be.

COUNTY ATTORNEY. Ah, loyal to your sex, I see. But you and Mrs. Wright were neighbors. I suppose you were friends, too.

MRS. HALE (*shaking her head*). I've not seen much of her of late years. I've not been in this house—it's more than a year.

COUNTY ATTORNEY. And why was that? You didn't like her?

MRS. HALE. I liked her all well enough. Farmers' wives have their hands full, Mr. Henderson. And then—

COUNTY ATTORNEY. Yes—?

MRS. HALE (*looking about*). It never seemed a very cheerful place.

COUNTY ATTORNEY. No—it's not cheerful. I shouldn't say she had the homemaking instinct.

MRS. HALE. Well, I don't know as Wright had, either.

COUNTY ATTORNEY. You mean that they didn't get on very well?

MRS. HALE. No, I don't mean anything. But I don't think a place'd be any cheerfuler for John Wright's being in it.

COUNTY ATTORNEY. I'd like to talk more of that a little later. I want to get the lay of things upstairs now. (*He goes to the left, where three steps lead to a stair door.*)

SHERIFF. I suppose anything Mrs. Peters does'll be all right. She was to take in some clothes for her, you know, and a few little things. We left in such a hurry yesterday.

COUNTY ATTORNEY. Yes, but I would like to see what you take, Mrs. Peters, and keep an eye out for anything that might be of use to us.

MRS. PETERS. Yes, Mr. Henderson.

(*The women listen to the men's steps on the stairs, then look about the kitchen.*)

MRS. HALE. I'd hate to have men coming into my kitchen, snooping around and criticizing. (*She arranges the pans under sink which the Lawyer had shoved out of place.*)

MRS. PETERS. Of course it's no more than their duty.

MRS. HALE. Duty's all right, but I guess that deputy sheriff that came out to make the fire might have got a little of this on. (*Gives the roller towel a pull.*) Wish I'd thought of that sooner. Seems mean to talk about her for not having things slicked up when she had to come away in such a hurry.

MRS. PETERS (*who has gone to a small table in the left rear corner of the room, and lifted one end of a towel that covers a pan*). She had bread set. (*Stands still.*)

MRS. HALE (*eyes fixed on a loaf of bread beside the breadbox, which is on a low shelf at the other side of the room. Moves slowly toward it.*) She was going to put this in there. (*Picks up loaf, then abruptly drops it. In a manner of returning to familiar things.*) It's a shame about her fruit. I wonder if it's all gone. (*Gets up on the chair and looks.*) I think there's some here that's all right, Mrs. Peters. Yes—here; (*Holding it toward the window.*) this is cherries, too. (*Looking again.*) I declare I believe that's the only one. (*Gets down, bottle in her hand. Goes to the sink and wipes it off on the outside.*) She'll feel awful bad after all her hard work in the hot weather. I remember the afternoon I put up my cherries last summer. (*She puts the bottle on the big kitchen table, center of the room, front table. With a sigh, is about to sit down in the rocking chair. Before she is seated realizes what chair it is; with a slow look at it, steps back. The chair, which she has touched, rocks back and forth.*)

MRS. PETERS. Well, I must get those things from the front room closet. (*She goes to the door at the right, but after looking into the other room steps back.*) You coming with me, Mrs. Hale? You could help me carry them. (*They go into the other room; reappear, Mrs. Peters carrying a dress and skirt, Mrs. Hale following with a pair of shoes.*)

MRS. PETERS. My, it's cold in there. (*She puts the cloth on the big table, and hurries to the stove.*)

MRS. HALE (*examining the skirt*). Wright was close. I think maybe that's why she kept so much to herself. She didn't even belong to the Ladies' Aid. I suppose she felt she couldn't do her part, and then you don't enjoy things when you feel shabby. She used to wear pretty clothes and be lively, when she was Minnie Foster, one of the town girls singing in the choir. But that—oh, that was thirty years ago. This all you was to take in?

MRS. PETERS. She said she wanted an apron. Funny thing to want, for there isn't much to get you dirty in jail, goodness knows. But I suppose just to make her feel more natural. She said they was in the top drawer in this cupboard. Yes, here. And then her little shawl that always hung behind the door. (*Opens stair door and looks.*) Yes, here it is. (*Quickly shuts door leading upstairs.*)

MRS. HALE (*abruptly moving toward her.*) Mrs. Peters?

MRS. PETERS. Yes, Mrs. Hale?

MRS. HALE. Do you think she did it?

MRS. PETERS (*in a frightened voice*). Oh, I don't know.

MRS. HALE. Well, I don't think she did. Asking for an apron and her little shawl. Worrying about her fruit.

MRS. PETERS (*starts to speak, glances up, where footsteps are heard in the room above. In a low voice*). Mr. Peters says it looks bad for her. Mr. Henderson is awful sarcastic in speech, and he'll make fun of her sayin' she didn't wake up.

MRS. HALE. Well, I guess John Wright didn't wake when they were slipping that rope under his neck.

MRS. PETERS. No, it's strange. It must have been done awful crafty and still. They say it was such a—funny way to kill a man, rigging it up like that.

MRS. HALE. That's just what Mr. Hale said. There was a gun in the house. He says that's what he can't understand.

MRS. PETERS. Mr. Henderson said coming out that what was needed for the case was a motive; something to show anger, or—sudden feeling.

MRS. HALE (*who is standing by the table.*) Well, I don't see any signs of anger around here. (*She puts her hand on the dish towel which lies on the table, stands looking down at the table, one half of which is clean, the other half messy.*) It's wiped here. (*Makes a move as if to finish work, then turns and looks at loaf of bread outside the breadbox. Drops towel. In that voice of coming back to familiar things.*) Wonder how they are finding things upstairs? I hope she had it a little more red-up there. You know, it seems kind of *sneaking.* Locking her up in town and then coming out here and trying to get her own house to turn against her!

MRS. PETERS. But, Mrs. Hale, the law is the law.

MRS. HALE. I s'pose 'tis. (*Unbuttoning her coat.*) Better loosen up your things, Mrs. Peters. You won't feel them when you go out.

(*Mrs. Peters takes off her fur tippet, goes to hang it on hook at the back of room, stands looking at the under part of the small corner table.*)

MRS. PETERS. She was piecing a quilt. (*She brings the large basket, and they look at the bright pieces.*)

MRS. HALE. It's log cabin pattern. Pretty, isn't it? I wonder if she was goin' to quilt or just knot it?

(*Footsteps have been heard coming down the stairs. The Sheriff enters, followed by Hale and the County Attorney.*)

SHERIFF. They wonder if she was going to quilt it or just knot it. (*The men laugh, the women look abashed.*)

COUNTY ATTORNEY (*rubbing his hands over the stove*). Frank's fire didn't do much up there, did it? Well, let's go out to the barn and get that cleared up.

(*The men go outside.*)

MRS. HALE (*resentfully*). I don't know as there's anything so strange, our takin' up our time with little things while we're waiting for them to get the evidence. (*She sits down at the big table, smoothing out a block with decision.*) I don't see as it's anything to laugh about.

MRS. PETERS (*apologetically*). Of course they've got awful important things on their minds. (*Pulls up a chair and joins Mrs. Hale at the table.*)

MRS. HALE (*examining another block*). Mrs. Peters, look at this one. Here, this is the one she was working on, and look at the sewing! All the rest of it has been so nice and even. And look at this! It's all over the place! Why, it looks as if she didn't know what she was about! (*After she has said this, they look at each other, then started to glance back at the door. After an instant Mrs. Hale has pulled at a knot and ripped the sewing.*)

MRS. PETERS. Oh, what are you doing, Mrs. Hale?

MRS. HALE (*mildly*). Just pulling out a stitch or two that's not sewed very good. (*Threading a needle.*) Bad sewing always made me fidgety.

MRS. PETERS (*nervously*). I don't think we ought to touch things.

MRS. HALE. I'll just finish up this end. (*Suddenly stopping and leaning forward.*) Mrs. Peters?

MRS. PETERS. Yes, Mrs. Hale?

MRS. HALE. What do you suppose she was so nervous about?

MRS. PETERS. Oh—I don't know. I don't know as she was nervous. I sometimes sew awful queer when I'm just tried. (*Mrs. Hale starts to say something, looks at Mrs. Peters, then goes on sewing.*) Well, I must get these things wrapped up. They may be through sooner then we think. (*Putting apron and other things together.*) I wonder where I can find a piece of paper, and string.

MRS. HALE. In that cupboard, maybe.

MRS. PETERS (*looking in cupboard*). Why, here's a birdcage. (*Holds it up.*) Did she have a bird, Mrs. Hale?

MRS. HALE. Why, I don't know whether she did or not—I've not been here for so long. There was a man around last year selling canaries cheap, but I don't know as she took one; maybe she did. She used to sing real pretty herself.

MRS. PETERS (*glancing around*). Seems funny to think of a bird here. But she must have had one, or why should she have a cage? I wonder what happened to it?

MRS. HALE. I s'pose maybe the cat got it.

MRS. PETERS. No, she didn't have a cat. She's got that feeling some people have about cats—being afraid of them. My cat got in her room, and she was real upset and asked me to take it out.

MRS. HALE. My sister Bessie was like that. Queer, ain't it?

MRS. PETERS (*examining the cage*). Why, look at this door. It's broke. One hinge is pulled apart.

MRS. HALE (*looking, too*). Looks as if someone must have been rough with it.

MRS. PETERS. Why, yes. (*She brings the cage forward and puts it on the table.*)

MRS. HALE. I wish if they're going to find any evidence they'd be about it. I don't like this place.

MRS. PETERS. But I'm awful glad you came with me, Mrs. Hale. It would be lonesome for me sitting here alone.

MRS. HALE. It would, wouldn't it? (*Dropping her sewing.*) But I tell you what I do wish, Mrs. Peters. I wish I had come over sometimes when *she* was here. I—(*Looking around the room.*)—wish I had.

MRS. PETERS. But of course you were awful busy, Mrs. Hale— your house and your children.

MRS. HALE. I could've come. I stayed away because it weren't cheerful—and that's why I ought to have come. I—I've never liked this place. Maybe because it's down in a hollow, and you don't see the road. I dunno what it is, but it's a lonesome place and always was. I wish I had come over to see Minnie Foster sometimes. I can see now—(*Shakes her head.*)

MRS. PETERS. Well, you mustn't reproach yourself, Mrs. Hale. Somehow we just don't see how it is with other folks until—something comes up.

MRS. HALE. Not having children makes less work—but it makes a quiet house, and Wright out to work all day, and no company when he did come in. Did you know John Wright, Mrs. Peters?

MRS. PETERS. Not to know him; I've seen him in town. They say he was a good man.

MRS. HALE. Yes—good; he didn't drink, and kept his word as well as most, I guess, and paid his debts. But he was a hard man, Mrs. Peters. Just to pass the time of day with him. (*Shivers.*) Like a raw wind that gets to the bone. (*Pauses, her eye falling on the cage.*) I should think she would 'a wanted a bird. But what do you suppose went with it?

MRS. PETERS. I don't know, unless it got sick and died. (*She reaches over and swings her broken door, swings it again; both women watch it.*)

MRS. HALE. You weren't raised round here, were you? (*Mrs. Peters shakes her head.*) You didn't know—her?

MRS. PETERS. Not till they brought her yesterday.

MRS. HALE. She—come to think of it, she was kind of like a bird herself—real sweet and pretty, but kind of timid and—fluttery. How—she—did—change. (*Silence; then as if struck by a happy thought and relieved to get back to everyday things.*) Tell you what, Mrs. Peters, why don't you take the quilt in with you? It might take up her mind.

MRS. PETERS. Why, I think that's a real nice idea, Mrs. Hale. There couldn't possibly be any objection to it, could there? Now, just what would I take? I wonder if her patches are in here—and her things. (*They look in the sewing basket.*)

MRS. HALE. Here's some red. I expect this has got sewing things in it (*Brings out a fancy box.*) What a pretty box. Looks like something somebody would give you. Maybe her scissors are in here. (*Opens box. Suddenly puts her hand to her nose.*) Why—(*Mrs. Peters bends nearer, then turns her face away.*) There's something wrapped up in this piece of silk.

MRS. PETERS. Why, this isn't her scissors.

MRS. HALE (*lifting the silk*). Oh, Mrs. Peters—it's—(*Mrs. Peters bends closer.*)

MRS. PETERS. It's the bird.

MRS. HALE (*jumping up*). But, Mrs. Peters—look at it. Its neck! Look at its neck! It's all—other side *to*.

MRS. PETERS. Somebody—wrung—its neck.

(*Their eyes meet. A look of growing comprehension of horror. Steps are heard outside. Mrs. Hale slips box under quilt pieces, and sinks into her chair. Enter Sheriff and County Attorney. Mrs. Peters rises.*)

COUNTY ATTORNEY (*as one turning from serious things to little pleasantries*). Well, ladies, have you decided whether she was going to quilt it or knot it?

MRS. PETERS. We think she was going to—knot it.

COUNTRY ATTORNEY. Well, that's interesting, I'm sure. (*Seeing the birdcage.*) Has the bird flown?

MRS. HALE (*putting more quilt pieces over the box*). We think the—cat got it.

COUNTY ATTORNEY (*preoccupied*). Is there a cat?

(*Mrs. Hale glances in a quick covert way at Mrs. Peters.*)

MRS. PETERS. Well, not now. They're superstitious, you know. They leave.

COUNTY ATTORNEY (*to Sheriff Peters, continuing an interrupted conversation*). No sign at all of anyone having come from the outside. Their own rope. Now let's go up again and go over it piece by piece. (*They start upstairs.*) It would have to have been someone who knew just the—

(*Mrs. Peters sits down. The two women sit there not looking at one another, but as if peering into something and at the same time holding back. When they talk now, it is the manner of feeling their way over strange ground, as if afraid of what they are saying, but as if they cannot help saying it.*)

MRS. HALE. She liked the bird. She was going to bury it in that pretty box.

MRS. PETERS (*in a whisper*). When I was a girl—my kitten—there was a boy took a hatchet, and before my eyes—and before I could get there—(*Covers her face an instant.*) If they hadn't held me back, I would have—(*Catches herself, looks upstairs where steps are heard, falters weakly.*)—hurt him.

MRS. HALE (*with a slow look around her*). I wonder how it would seem never to have had any children around. (*Pause.*) No, Wright wouldn't like the bird—a thing that sang. She used to sing. He killed that, too.

MRS. PETERS (*moving uneasily*). We don't know who killed the bird.

MRS. HALE. I knew John Wright.

MRS. PETERS. It was an awful thing was done in this house that night, Mrs. Hale. Killing a man while he slept, slipping a rope around his neck that choked the life out of him.

MRS. HALE. His neck. Choked the life out of him.

(*Her hand goes out and rests on the birdcage.*)

MRS. PETERS (*with a rising voice*). We don't know who killed him. We don't *know*.

MRS. HALE (*her own feeling not interrupted*). If there'd been years and years of nothing, then a bird to sing to you, it would be awful—still, after the bird was still.

MRS. PETERS (*something within her speaking*). I know what stillness is. When we homesteaded in Dakota, and my first baby died—after he was two years old, and me with no other then—

MRS. HALE (*moving*). How soon do you suppose they'll be through, looking for evidence?

MRS. PETERS. I know what stillness is. (*Pulling herself back.*) The law has got to punish crime, Mrs. Hale.

MRS. HALE (*not as if answering that*). I wish you'd seen Minnie Foster when she wore a white dress with blue ribbons and stood up there in the choir and sang. (*A look around the room.*) Oh, I *wish* I'd come over here once in a while! That was a crime! That was a crime! Who's going to punish that?

MRS. PETERS (*looking upstairs*). We mustn't—take on.

MRS. HALE. I might have known she needed help! I know how things can be—for women. I tell you, it's queer, Mrs. Peters. We live close together and we live far apart. We all go through the same things—it's all just a different kind of the same thing. (*Brushes her eyes, noticing the bottle of fruit, reaches out for it.*) If I was you, I wouldn't tell her her fruit was gone. Tell her it *ain't*. Tell her it's all right. Take this in to prove it to her. She—she may never know whether it was broke or not.

MRS. PETERS (*takes the bottle, looks about for something to wrap it in; takes petticoat from the clothes brought from the other room, very nervously begins winding this around the bottle. In a false voice*). My, it's a good thing the men couldn't hear us. Wouldn't they just laugh! Getting all stirred up over a little thing like a—dead canary. As if that could have anything to do with—with—wouldn't they *laugh*!

(*The men are heard coming downstairs.*)

MRS. HALE (*under her breath*). Maybe they would—maybe they wouldn't.

COUNTY ATTORNEY. No, Peters, it's all perfectly clear except a reason for doing it. But you know juries when it comes to women. If there was some definite thing. Something to show—something to make a story about—a thing that would connect up with this strange way of doing it.

(*The women's eyes meet for an instant. Enter Hale from outer door.*)

HALE. Well, I've got the team around. Pretty cold out there.

COUNTY ATTORNEY. I'm going to stay here awhile by myself. (*To the Sheriff.*) You can send Frank out for me, can't you? I want to go over everything. I'm not satisfied that we can't do better.

SHERIFF. Do you want to see what Mrs. Peters is going to take in?

(*The Lawyer goes to the table, picks up the apron, laughs.*)

COUNTY ATTORNEY. Oh I guess they're not very dangerous things the ladies have picked up. (*Moves a few things about, disturbing the quilt pieces which cover the box. Steps back.*) No, Mrs. Peters doesn't need supervising. For that matter, a sheriff's wife is married to the law. Ever think of it that way, Mrs. Peters?

MRS. PETERS. Not—just that way.

SHERIFF (*chuckling*). Married to the law. (*Moves toward the other room.*) I just want you to come in here a minute, George. We ought to take a look at these windows.

COUNTY ATTORNEY (*scoffingly*). Oh, windows!

SHERIFF. We'll be right out, Mr. Hale.

(*Hale goes outside. The Sheriff follows the County Attorney into the other room. Then Mrs. Hale rises, hands tight together, looking intensely at Mrs. Peters, whose eyes take a slow turn, finally meeting, Mrs. Hale's. A moment Mrs. Hale holds her, then her own eyes point the way to where the box is concealed. Suddenly Mrs. Peters throws back quilt pieces and tries to put the box in the bag she is wearing. It is too big. She opens the box, starts to take the bird out, cannot touch it, goes to pieces, stands there helpless. Sound of a knob turning in the other room. Mrs. Hale snatches the box and puts it in the pocket of her big coat. Enter County Attorney and Sheriff.*)

COUNTY ATTORNEY (*facetiously*). Well, Henry, at least we found out that she was not going to quilt it. She was going to—what is it you call it, ladies?

MRS. HALE (*her hand against her pocket*). We call it—knot it, Mr. Henderson.

CURTAIN

TOPICS FOR CRITICAL THINKING AND WRITING

 ## The Play on the PAGE

1. How would you characterize Mr. Henderson, the county attorney?
2. In what ways or ways are Mrs. Peters and Mrs. Hale different from each other?

3. On page 22, when Mrs. Peters tells of the boys who killed her cat, she says, "If they hadn't held me back, I would have—(*catches herself, looks upstairs, where steps are heard, falters weakly.*)—hurt him."

What do you think she was about to say before she faltered? Why do you suppose Glaspell included the speech about Mrs. Peters's girlhood?

4. We never see Mrs. Wright on stage. Nevertheless, by the end of *Trifles* we know a great deal about her. Explain both what we know about her—physical characteristics, habits, interests, personality, life before her marriage and after—and *how* we know these things.

5. The title of the play is ironic—the "trifles" are important. What other ironies do you find in the play? (On *irony*, see Glossary.)

6. Do you think the play is immoral? Explain.

 The Play on the STAGE

7. Briefly describe the setting, indicating what it "says" and what atmosphere it evokes.

8. Several times the men "laugh" or "chuckle." In their contexts, what do these expressions of amusement convey?

9. On page 23, "*the women's eyes meet for an instant.*" What do you think this bit of action "says"? What do you understand by the exchange of glances?

A SECOND SHORT PLAY FOR STUDY: A PERFORMER-GENERATED SCRIPT

In our discussion of "Mistakes, Conflict, and Audience-Awareness" (page 3) we quoted W. H. Auden to the effect that mistakes are at the heart of drama. We mentioned, too, that dramatists often take the audience into their confidence, giving the audience information that the characters do not have. In *Trifles*, for example, Susan Glaspell gives the audience important facts that she denies to the sheriff and the county attorney. The audience therefore sees (and enjoys, with an ironic detachment) the mistakes made by the overly confident men. In reading or seeing *Trifles*, much of our pleasure resides in the fact that we know more than the men do.

The following script provides us with a very different way of approaching Auden's notion of mistakes as an impetus for the dramatic and the issue of audience-awareness. The conventional way of writing a play has been the playwright working in isolation to produce a script to be performed by actors in a theater. Although this is still a standard, viable, and often-practiced format, significant changes in the theatrical process and practice took place in the late twentieth century. One of the changes is that in the past several decades there has been a gradual but increasing emphasis on **performer-generated scripts.** This kind of work arises when the actor on stage is also the creator of the material performed. In many of the examples of this kind of work, the material performed is autobiographical.

In the following script the notion of conflict is still present. Here, however, the conflict takes place inside of one character: Rachel Rosenthal. *My Brazil* recalls Rosenthal's family's escape to Brazil when she was thirteen, and her performance chronicles the vivid feelings of death and rebirth that she experienced there. She juxtaposes romantic memories of lush tropical landscapes and carnival exuberance of this South American country with the dramatic, terrifying realities of the Nazi takeover of her home. She draws a parallel between her younger self and her adult self as she addresses the issue of change and awakening. Rosenthal states,

> I take aspects of my life that I feel were useless and worthless, and through performance redeem them. It's a means of understanding and re-creation. Putting them in an art form has a mythmaking quality. It is also an order making. . . . What a lot of people don't realize about . . . performance is that it is happening right there before their eyes. No matter how much you work on the text, how much you prepare beforehand, the actual transformation is happening right there in front of the audience.

MARIA ROTH, ED. *RACHEL ROSENTHAL*. BALTIMORE: JOHN HOPKINS UP, 1997.

RACHEL Rosenthal

Rachel Rosenthal, born in Paris in 1926, was the daughter of Russian Jewish émigrés who were patrons of the arts. As a child she lived a privileged life of servants, private schooling, ballet lessons, and concerts in her house by the leading musicians of the day. At the age of thirteen her idyllic life was shattered when her family hurriedly fled France in the wake of the Nazi invasion. They were able to take a boat to Brazil where they lived for seven months before settling in New York City. After the war, Rosenthal returned to Paris for a time where she discovered experimental theater and the writing of Antonin Artaud. His celebrated book *The Theater and Its Double,* both a theoretical statement about the power of performance and a vision of the theater artist as someone who intervenes and jolts the public, became Rosenthal's "theater Bible" (Roth 6). During her time in Paris she also studied theater with the actor-director Jean-Louis Barrault. Around 1949 she became involved with avant-garde artists in New York City, befriending the choreographer Merce Cunningham and composer John Cage. In 1954 she lived in the same building as the artist Jasper Johns and exhibited some sculpture in a group show with him. In 1956 she founded an improvisational theater company called Instant Theater in Los Angeles. When the company disbanded in 1966, she returned to painting and sculpting. In 1971 she attended a conference on women artists and was introduced to feminism for the first time. Her exposure to this work radically altered her concept of herself as a working artist, and she began to rethink and reconsider her career. In 1975 she created *Replays,* a solo performance piece that began her prolific career of autobiographical performance work. In addition to *My Brazil* (1979), she has written and performed *Leave Her in Naxos* (1981), *Gaia, Mon Amour* (1983), *The Others* (1985), *L.O.W. in Gaia* (1986), and *Rachel's Brain* (1987). Much of Rosenthal's more recent work, which she continues to tour, connects social issues such as animal rights and environmental concerns to personal experience. She states,

> My concern about broader issues, the state of the world, starts, of course, from my very personal self. Who are you and what you make cannot be separated. There is a continuum between life and art. We make up artificial borderlines trying to imprison phenomena into certain categories.

> ELKE LAMPE. "RACHEL ROSENTHAL CREATING HER SELVES." *TDR* 117 (SPRING 1988): 170–90.

MY BRAZIL
A RECITAL
Rachel Rosenthal

A 4' × 8' platform against the wall. Sheets of Mylar hang from ceiling to floor and line the sides of the platform. There is a stool stage left on the platform and a microphone on a stand stage right. Two sparklers and a lighter are placed on the platform, upstage.

The lighting is in pink, lavender, green, blue-green and blue tones.

A PA system with two large speakers. An audiotape runs through the speakers.

Before the performance, an assistant distributes both sparklers and matchbooks to the audience. The matchbooks are silver, with "My Brazil" by Rachel Rosenthal etched in green on the covers. The assistant tells the audience to light up when Rosenthal does.

Blackout. A male voice on tape.

The New York Times, July 16, 1940. "Readers of this newspaper have been able to learn from Mr. Russel B. Porter's

Rachel Rosenthal performs her autobiographical piece *My Brazil* in 1979 at the Institute for Dance and Experimental Arts in Santa Monica, California. Anthony Canty accompanies her on the drums. Note the mylar back drop that reflects the audience's own images in a fractured and distorted manner.

informative dispatches in recent weeks what the Nazi menace is like in Brazil. In Mr. Porter's opinion it already amounts to an *undeclared war.* The Nazi efforts are deliberate and unmistakable. Spying, terrorism, economic pressure, physical violence, the boycott, misuse of the schools, the radio, newspapers, the motion pictures—all have been used and each is used as circumstances permit. The tricks are precisely those employed by the Nazis in the Balkans, in Scandinavia, in Holland, Belgium, Spain and France. If Hitler has not yet laid claim to the million Germans of Southern Brazil there is every sign that he will do so whenever he feels strong enough. The 'Dry War' has, in short, been brought to this hemisphere by the Nazis."

Segue into "O Que Que A Bahiana Tem," a vintage record by Carmen Miranda, sung in Portuguese. Record ends.

Lights. Rosenthal enters, accompanied by the Drummer. She is wearing a Grecian-type turquoise gown, high heels, and a white orchid in her hair. The Drummer is black, stripped to the waist, wearing white pants and Yoruba beads. He carries a large conga drum and is barefoot. They step up onto the platform.

Rosenthal and the Drummer bow to the audience and to each other. He sits on the stool and she picks up the mike from the stand. She sings a cappella:

JARDINHEIRA
Jardinheira porque está tão triste?
O que foi que aconteceu?
Foi a camélia que caiu do galho,
deu dois suspiros e depois morreu.

Oh Jardinheira, O meu amor!
Não ficas triste nesse mundo,
é tudo seu e tu es muito
mais bonita que a camélia que morreu.

Rosenthal then steps downstage and the Drummer taps a simple beat. She talks and swings her hips.

Sometimes I prune a Creeping Charlie. I cut off the small piece and place it in a glass decanter with water. I pinch it first. It reacts as if goosed. Some weeks later, the decanter water turns a greenish hue. Vague clouds of green meander about aimlessly, gathering momentum. The Charlie forages with a newly harbored white Chinaman's whisker, says good-bye, and emigrates to dirt. The green scum sloshes angrily awhile and then subsides. I lose interest and pay attention elsewhere. It's all assumed to be as it is, as it was, as it always will be. Appalling, isn't it? I grow complacent. Will I die not having known the rapture of the deep? I can't swim too well in all this algae.

On muggy days I look up and see a timber wolf sitting quietly on my doorstep, watching me discreetly. When Mother was about to die, she saw the Wilis, in white tutu, like in *Giselle.* She was afraid of spooks. I'm not afraid of wolves. The decanter sits on the sill, filling with slugs and water moccasins. I dreamt it was a Trojan Fish, filled with piranhas. One day, I pick up my objects and find them all brittle and light. Desiccated and eviscerated. All empty pods. Whatever happened? Time sends me messages in envelopes but forgot to insert the note. Something is going to brush me gently with its wings, I'm sure. Never say die! I anoint myself, just in case. Don't laugh. When I stop suiciding, I'm a robust Queen of the Jungle. And I rarely need a straitjacket nowadays, which was difficult to tie anyway since I insisted on doing it all myself. But I suffer from Life's Cramp. I am dying.

The Drummer stops. Rosenthal sings:

AURORA
Si você fosse sincera
ô-ô-ô-ô Aurora
veja só que bom que era
ô-ô-ô-ô Aurora!
Um belo apartamento com porteiro e elevador
e ar refrigerado para os dias de calor
"Madame" antes do nome você teria agora
ô-ô-ô-ô Aurora!

The Drummer resumes, with a slightly more complex beat. Rosenthal speaks, and her dancing becomes more accentuated.

When I lived in Tarzana, just before the events that led to my leaving home, I was swimming in our pool one day, when I happened to look up at the sky. Way up there, very high and very small, was what I later recognized to be a white sheet of paper, waltzing and zigzagging in air currents, ascending, descending, dancing its gradual approach to earth. For some reason, I couldn't take my eyes off it, and it became a kite, with my gaze the string it was attached to. And I reeled it in, slowly but surely, until that piece of paper fluttered down into the pool beside me, within two feet of where I was standing! I felt singled out somehow, and vaguely heard a call, but didn't recognize the voice.

A long time ago, a similar event took place.

I was with my parents, high above Rio de Janeiro, at the base of the forty-foot Christ on top of Corcovado mountain. It was in 1940. Some new friends took us sightseeing in their car. It was just before the rainy season and the sky was stridently clear. As I was walking around the big statue, I was eyeing uneasily a huge, jet black butterfly flapping about in the hot, still air. I had a butterfly phobia. Suddenly, a gust of wind swept him away in the direction of the sea. I looked out at the string of sparkling bays in the white-hot sun under the cycloramic blue sky. And then I saw a black cloud, like a tiny spot on the horizon. The air around us began to churn. The black butterfly was whirled back as I watched that speck of black cloud racing toward us at vertiginous speed, progressively blotting out the blue of sky, until it was all around us, and wind howling, huge raindrops pelting us as we ran for the car and as the black butterfly fought for balance trying to reach the shelter of the jungle growth. We raced down the mountain road, but by the time we reached bottom there was an ocher-colored flood in the streets and our car fairly floated.

I know today but didn't know it then, that I had died as I am dying now. I was born then, in Brazil, in 1940.

This corpse was born in Rio, age thirteen, the product of a cosmic upheaval and a very private alchemy.

The Drummer stops. Rosenthal sings:

HELENA
Eu ontem cheguei em casa, Helena,
teo procurei mais não encontrei.
Fiquei tristonho a chorar . . .
Passei o resto da noite a chamar.
Helena, Helena, vem me consolar!
Depois de cansado
teu nome eu chamava baixinho.
Helena dos meus encantos
Vem me fazer um carinho.
Eu fiquei desesperado,
cadê Helena meu bem?
O dia ja vem raiando e
minha Helena ão vem.
Porquê será?

The beat is now lilting. Rosenthal is dancing the samba during the next text.

There is an awesome theory of quantum physics called the Many Worlds Theory. It states that all possibilities in the wave function of an observed system actualize, but in different worlds that coexist with ours. Who is in these worlds? We are. In other words, the choices between various possibilities are illusion. With each and every choice we make, the world splits into separate and mutually inaccessible branches, each of which contains different editions of the same actors performing different acts at the same time, on different stages that are somehow located in the same place.

In 1940, there is a Rachel who sailed across the Atlantic. There is another Rachel who remained in France. The Rachel who stayed splits into a heroine who fought the Germans in the Resistance, and another who hid like a coward in some remote countryside with secret cellars filled with hams and sausages hanging from the rafters. Either Rachel or both split again, into one who survives and one who is caught by the Nazis and tortured. That one divides into she who tells all, causing the deaths of many, and she who dies in a concentration camp, having allowed the abject desecration of her body in order to save her soul. The Rachels who survive become, one, a "grande bougeoise" married to a snob, two, an artist, whose modernist tastes are shaken in 1948 with the arrival in Paris of John Cage and Merce Cunningham, whom she meets, befriends, and follows to New York. But wait a minute. . . . That wave function must have joined with another and merged, for I was there, in Paris, in 1948, and I met Merce and John . . .

Anyway, the other wave function that brought me to that point crossed the equator on the Atlantic in September 1940. The others, all the others, in their equal and separate universes, are somehow and inexplicably a part of me as well, as I am of each and every one of them. I am the hatred of the Germans, the fear of the knock in the night, the coward, the horder, I am the hero parachuted behind enemy lines, the horror and nausea of torture, the panic of incarceration, the guilty survival and the battered death.

The Drummer stops. Rosenthal sings:

A LA-LA-O
  Alá-la-ô ô-ô-ô ô-ô-ô
  Mais que calor ô-ô-ô ô-ô-ô!
  Viemos do Egito
  e muitas vezes nós tivemos que rezar:
  Alá! Alá! Alá, meu bom Alá!
  Mande agua pra loyõ!
  Mande agua par layá!
  Alá, meu bom Alá!

A strong, rolling beat.

Before I was thirteen, I dreamt recurringly of being swallowed by a tidal wave, relaxing into it, and experiencing bliss. The wave appeared over the horizon like those gigantic Picasso "Women at the Beach" of his surrealist period. In Rio, 1940–41, I played in the Copacabana surf. The waves were often twenty feet high and higher. My girlfriend Janine and I would let ourselves be sucked into the huge wave's undertow, maneuvering and calculating so that, at the exact moment when the wave was about to break into bone-crushing white water, we would propel ourselves with superhuman effort out of the accelerating suction and dive into the glaucous green underbelly, emerging on the other side, battered and breathless, ready to face the gathering of power of another colossal wave. It was fantastic! I didn't fight the waves. I tuned my body to resonate with equal power. I heard the mighty rhythms and obeyed them. To fight would have broken the flow, and the wave would have shattered me to pieces on the sand.

    In the sea, I was a hero. Out of the water, I was a tadpole: large head, my body trailing behind me like a snail-trail of mucus. I had abandoned in the Northern Hemisphere the blood clots of first menstruation and the muddy bogs of pubescent feelings. I was in love with my brother Pierre. In Brazil, I spent hours on my bed, eyes closed, drowning in nostalgia and making Proustian efforts to recapture the feel, the smell, the exact taste of love and lust lost. At night, macumba drums wafted from the many jungle-covered little sugarloaf hills of the city, I slept in a hammock, a lion of lights glided across Botafogo Bay advertising Lyons Tea. "When the war is over, Pierrot!" I would whisper like Scarlett O'Hara to Ashley. Pierre was killed in North Africa, a great hero and posthumous Croix de Guerre and Legion d'Honneur, in the Sahara Campaign of 1943.

    I am experiencing death in a very real way. In my body. There is an entropic tendency below the skin. I dream of devilish geometries in an attempt to organize this sloppy information. I dream that Satan slices a man in four with his eyes, each quarter neatly encased in skin, like grapefruit segments. They fall to the floor, shaped like swastika. I also dream of letting my animals die, untended, in some forgotten room.

    In Rio, a business acquaintance of my father's, a man called Pereira, sought to ingratiate himself to us by bringing me baby animals that his men caught in the jungle. The first was a baby anteater. I called him Tatú for that was his name in Portuguese. The Tatú slept in my bed, I didn't know how to feed it or what to do. I was always afraid he'd escape and fall down the elevator shaft. Later on, Pereira brought me a baby alligator. We put it in the bathtub. He created even greater problems. We were invited to the *fazenda* of Monsieur and Madame Hammond, for Christmas. The Hammonds owned a small zoo and we decided to bring them the animals. We placed them in boxes, with breathing holes. The *fazenda* was in Terezopolis, in the mountains above Rio de Janeiro. We took a little wooden train that cranked us up the steep mountainside, surrounded on both sides with virgin forest. The jungle was impenetrable, emerald green, overgrown with pink and white orchids, and teeming with brilliantly colored birds. All the way up, the little train stopped in villages where the cars were besieged by dozens of vendors, women in multicolored skirts and turbans carrying piles of fruit on their heads, little boys with baskets of *guaraná* (the Brazilian Coke), men with trays of pastries covered with flies, everyone laughing, shouting, singing. . . . For the duration of the trip, the Tatú panicked. He kept pushing his little snout desperately through the breathing hole and struggling. I could see his little eyes filling with pus. When we got to the *fazenda*, he was ice-cold. He died within a few days. The last time I saw the alligator, he was in a bathtub, again, only this time with a frog that somehow had parked there. The two were eyeing each other mournfully.

The drumming stops. Rosenthal sings:

EU NESSE PASSO VOU ATE HONOLULU
  Eu nesse passo vou até Honolul, ô-ô-ô,
  ô-ô-ô-ô, devagar!
  Lá no meu clube só se dança o kanguru ô-ô-ô
  das dêz as três sem parar.
  Parece valsa, fox-trot, tango, rumba,
  hula-hula e macumba,
  até maracatu, uh!
  Pois lá no clube toda gente cai na dança
  leva no colo criança
  pensa até que é kanguru!

A fast, samba beat.

I feel I am in the process of being sucked into a black hole. At what stage does one stop fighting it? There must be a point in time and space when all is in balance, poised, where all stands still, and then there is a tremendous, cosmic sigh, and one gives in, and all becomes easy, the pull of the hole accelerating toward the singularity, where being and annihilation coincide, where you are squeezed for an infinitesimally tiny moment into the singular essence of what you are, and then you emerge on the other side, unrecognizable even to yourself, but with the roaring pulse of matter burst forth from the womb! I can't wait . . . . Not because I'm in such a hurry for all this, but because the oscillating tension between being a hero or an asshole is killing me!

The drumming stops. Rosenthal sings:

O-O-O OPA! QUE DANCA SOPA!
O-ô-ô Opá! Que Dança sopa!
que os Indios sem roupa
me ensinaram a dançar.
Todo mundo diz que vai, mas não vai
e fica pulando no mesmo lugar . . .
O-ô-ô Opá! Que Dança sopa . . .

A very sensual rhythm. Rosenthal has been dancing more strenuously to the various rhythms as she speaks. The movement is dissociated from the words and spoken rhythms.

Brazil! Site of the second chakra! Sexual susurration of the language—a Portuguese caressed and tongued into insinuation and quasi-obscene nakedness. The colors of sex: red, orange, gold, green, purple. . . . The dance. The dance everywhere. The imperative of the dance. Its demands, its orders. The abandon of all non-Dionysiac modes. The singleness of purpose of the life-force, buttressed by anxiety, lonesomeness, fear. The billows of love. I am tunneled with love as by maggots. I am rotting with love. Nowhere to cast it but back on myself and my father and mother. Watertight. Self-enthralled. I am an infant again, cradled and rocked, but this time in my mother's arms. I am the center of the world. I am enervated. I have leapt feet first into dependence. I wear a dogtag. I am a slave of love. My thirteen-year-old infant flesh imbibes it. My head inflates with fear. I am encephalitic for a week. My head is so swollen and painful that I can't move it from side to side on the pillow without screaming. The doctors can't diagnose.

And how could they? Other refugees complain of sores between their fingers, of toenails turning soft and falling off. Tropical diseases, we say. The truth is that our bodies are liquefying under the impact of a world where fortunes are squandered in three bacchanalian days, where gorgeous black bodies always ripple to audible or silent beats, where forests are studded with myriad orchids like millefleur tapestries gone wild, where giant cockroaches fly, and where there are two dozen different kinds of bananas. Brazil is there for the taking. My father is poised, with grandiose plans. We are ready, Daddy Vampire, Mommy Vampire and Baby Vampire, to bite into the succulent land. But we didn't. Jews are jailed right and left. Some even disappear. One day, the American consul calls, "off the record," and tells Mr. Rosenthal

to heed his brotherly advice and be on the next boat to the U.S. within four days.

And we were. Abandoning the diamond mines and real-estate bonanzas to the Fifth Column. We had lived in Brazil seven months. During that time I died, I was born, I was weaned, reimprinted and bonded for good. I may even have been dwarfed and bonsaied too. I don't know if I ever grew up. Worse yet, I don't know if I'm a giant compared to the Rachel who stayed.

The drumming stops. Rosenthal sings:

E NO BOLIMBOLAIXO
É no bolimbolaixo
que eu quero ver você!
É no bolimbolaixo
que eu quero ver você!
Bolimbolaixo
bola em cima
bola em baixo!

A slow beat.

I am falling. My arms and legs, flailing the ether, become swastika-shaped. I spin faster and faster. This stigma at my core must melt. When I learned of Pierre's death, my face screwed up into a grin. Negation. Refusal. Amputation and death. I cannot love, except the beasts. I atone for the Tatú. Pierre had the sharp muzzle and luminous eyes of a wolf. I spin and spin and the branches of the swastika melt away, flowing in an unbroken circle. I must liquefy this accursed sign that saws me into a duality no longer liveable and that robs me of the last, the only wave.

Vision: a Nazi rally. Huge stadium. Floodlights. People in thirties clothes. A hundred thousand heiling soldiers. I swoop down on them, tear their backs open with knives, hoist them up with meat hooks, decapitate them with swords. Then I am with Pierre, at the Borj des Monopoles, in Tunisia, where he is alone, having ordered his men to fall back, manning a machine gun, facing the advancing Germans. We are together, machine-gunning hundreds, in intoxicating syncopation. He is hit in the chest and the head. All around us, in the Borj and along the flanks of the adjoining cliffs, are bodies of German soldiers, bleeding. Countless rivulets of blood trickle down to form a lake of blood. From the depth of the lake, black dinosaurs surface. They are like huge bubbles and they float up into the air. Pierre grows. He grows taller than the hills. Taller than the clouds. Then he flays himself and his skin falls off like a banana peel. His form remains like a pillar of light. He picks me up in his arms and together we fly over the Earth. The beautiful, the dazzling Earth. We glide over meadows covered with flowers. Over oceans and mountains. Over Grand Canyon. We then leave the Earth and fly to the Moon. And from the Moon to each planet of the system in turn, including Jupiter and its moons, Saturn and its rings. We leave the system and fly to the stars, the nebulae, the distant galaxies. Pierre becomes a cosmic cloud and tells me: "I am everything. I will teach you from all there is." I leave him and return to Earth.

The drumming stops. Rosenthal sings:

"COWBOY" DO AMOR
Quando monto o meu cavalo e jogo laço
prendo logo, prendo logo um coração.
Sou Cowboy mas gosto muito de um abraço:
"Mãos ao alto! e não vai dizer que não!"
Sou vaqueiro capataz de uma fazenda.
Nas horas vagas também toco o violão.
O meu cavalo
está ensinado a
tomar bilhete para a filha do patrão!

A very strong, rolling beat. Vigorous dancing.

Yes, I am searching for the perfect wave, knowing full well where it's been all this time. When I was little, I had trouble skipping rope because I couldn't jump into the circling rhythm. One day, I will close my eyes and take a flying leap. Then, I and the flow will stand still, in perfect unison, watching the river banks speed by. I will cuddle up inside the wave's curl forever, the roar of the water in my ears, silence in my heart. Then slowly, but with progressively lovelier configurations, I will break into splashes of drops like fireworks, waterworks, sparks. I will shatter and re-form in an infinite variety of ways on my feet, my fins, my claws, my beaks, my trunks, my antennae. . . . I will fly with the fish and dive with the birds. I will be a geyser and a waterfall. I will be a black water spout and a white tornado. I will erupt from Krakatoa and evaporate in Mono Lake. I will perspire from your pores and drink myself from a straw. I will have fulfilled all the promises and be none the wiser. I will become what I have always been and go back to where I never left. So if one day you cannot find me, just remember: I will be Missing In Action!

TOPICS FOR CRITICAL THINKING AND WRITING

The Play on the PAGE

1. References to death and dying appear throughout Rosenthal's script. Select three moments when this is discussed and explain why she is preoccupied with death.
2. Rosenthal's text recalls a range of adolescent anxieties that are made larger by the context of her family's escape from the Nazis. How does the script work to create a sense of dramatic conflict through these anxieties?
3. Despite the overriding sense of despair in this script, several critics of Rosenthal's work describe how she ends with a sense of hope. Do you agree with this assessment? If so, why? If not, why not?

The Play on the STAGE

4. In autobiographical performance there is no attempt to hide the actor beneath the fictional character. With Rosenthal's performance the character (which is Rosenthal herself) and the actor cannot be separated. How will this kind of theater affect an audience differently than the standard approach found in the previous play by Susan Glaspell?
5. The stage directions describe a simple set hung from ceiling to floor with sheets of Mylar (a thin plastic material that has a shiny and mirrorlike surface). One of the reviews of Rosenthal's performance described the Mylar as providing a viewing screen with the images of the drummer and Rosenthal refracted in the shiny surface. At the end of the performance the lights black out and Rosenthal lights two sparklers (and the audience is invited to join in with sparklers they were given at the beginning of the performance). What effect will the sparklers make on this set? Discuss possible meanings the set and sparklers give to Rosenthal's performance.
6. At regular intervals throughout her performance, Rosenthal interrupts her monologue and sings various songs a cappella in Portuguese. What is the significance of the songs and the drumming in this script?

SOME KINDS OF DRAMA

TRAGEDY AND COMEDY

Whimsical assertions that all of us are Platonists or Aristotelians, or liberals or conservatives ("Nature wisely does contrive / That every boy and every gal / That's born into the world alive / Is either a little Liberal / Or else a little Conservative"), reveal a tendency to divide things into two. Two is about right: peace and war, man and woman, day and night, life and death. There may be middle cases; Edmund Burke suggested that no one can point to the precise moment that divides day from night—but Burke also suggested that everyone can make the useful distinction between day and night. The distinction between comedy and tragedy may not always be easy to make, but until the twentieth century it was usually clear enough. *Hamlet*, which in Horatio's words is concerned with "woe or wonder," is a tragedy; *A Midsummer Night's Dream*, which in Puck's words is concerned with things that pleasingly "befall preposterously," is a comedy. The best plays of our century, however, are another thing, and discussions of these plays—somewhat desperately called tragicomedy—will be postponed until later in this chapter.

What befalls—preposterous or not—is the action of the play. The gestures on the stage are, of course, "actions," but they are not the action of the play in the sense of Aristotle's use of **praxis,** or "action" in *The Poetics*, a fragmentary treatise of the fourth century B.C.E. that remains the starting point for most discussions of drama.

Imitation of an Action

For Aristotle, drama is the imitation (i.e., representation, re-presentation, re-creation) by impersonators, of an action. In tragedy the action is serious and important, something that matters, done by people who count (e.g., King Oedipus's discovery that he has killed his father and married his mother); in comedy (for Aristotle), the action is done by unimportant, laughable people who make mistakes that do not cause us pain. Commonly the tragic action is a man's percep-

tion of a great mistake he has made; he suffers intensely and perhaps dies, having exhausted all the possibilities of his life. (Female tragic heroes are rare.) The comic action often is the exposure of folly and the renewal rather than the exhaustion of human nature. Crabby parents, for example, find that they cannot keep young lovers apart, and so they join in the marriage festivities. Byron jocosely put the matter thus:

> All tragedies are finished by a death,
> All comedies are ended by a marriage.

All tragedies and all comedies do not in fact end this way, but the idea is right; tragedy has the solemnity, seriousness, and finality we often associate with death,[1] and comedy has the joy and fertility and suggestion of a new life we often associate with marriage.

This concept of *an action* (i.e., an underlying motif, not merely gestures) in tragedy and in comedy makes clear that comedy is not a mere matter of jokes or funny bits of business. It also makes clear what the Greek comic playwright Menander meant when he told a friend that he had composed a play, and now had only to write the dialogue: He had worked out the happenings that would embody the action, and there remained only the slighter task of providing the spirited words. The same idea is implicit in Ibsen's comment that the drafts of his plays differed "very much from each other in characterization, not in action." The action or happening dramatized in a tragedy or a comedy may be conceived of as a single course or train of events manifested on the stage by a diversity of activities. Think of such expressions as "the closing of the frontier," or "the revival of learning"; each might be said to denote an action, although such action is seen only in its innumerable manifestations.

---

[1]Shakespeare's tragedies all end with the death of the tragic hero, but a good many Greek tragedies do not. In *Oedipus the King* the hero remains alive, but he is blind and banished and seems to have exhausted the possibilities of his life. Some other Greek tragedies have what can reasonably be called a happy ending; that is, some sort of joyful reconciliation. For example, in Sophocles's *Philoctetes,* the weapon which has been taken from the sick Philoctetes is returned to him, and Heracles, a messenger from Zeus, announces that Philoctetes will be healed. But these tragedies with happy endings, like those with unhappy endings, deal with "important" people, and they are about "serious" things. If there is finally joy, it is a solemn joy.

Happenings and Happenings

Tragic playwrights take some happening, from history (for example, the assassination of Julius Caesar) or from fiction (Shakespeare derived Othello from an Italian short story), or from their own imagination, and they make or shape or arrange episodes that clarify the action. They make (in common terminology) a *plot* that embodies the action or spiritual content. Even when playwrights draw on history, they make their own plot because they select and rearrange the available historical facts. A reenactment of everything that Julius Caesar did during his last days or hours would not be a play with an action, for drama is not so much concerned with what in fact *happened* as with some sort of typical and coherent or unified thing that *happens*, a significant action. Sometimes, of course, history provides substantial material for drama, but even Shakespeare's *Julius Caesar* takes frequent liberties with the facts as Shakespeare knew them, and Shakespeare's source, the biographer Plutarch, doubtless had already assimilated the facts to a literary form. At most we can say that history provided Shakespeare with a man whose life lent itself well to an established literary form. Not every life does lend itself thus.

Unity

We are told that Aeschylus, the earliest tragic playwright who has left us many complete plays, was killed when an eagle mistook his bald head for a rock and dropped a turtle on it to break the shell. Aeschylus's death was a great loss, but it did not have the unified significant action required of tragedy. By chance an eagle that had captured a turtle was near to Aeschylus, and Aeschylus by chance (or rather by his chemistry) was bald. There is no relation between these two circumstances; Aeschylus's death (allegedly) happened this way, and we can account for it, but the event has no intelligible unity. (A sentence from Vladimir Nabokov's *Pale Fire* comes to mind: If one is contemplating suicide, "jumping from a high bridge is not recommended even if you cannot swim, for wind and water abound in weird contingencies, and tragedy ought not to culminate in a record dive or a policeman's promotion.")

In tragedy things cohere. The hero normally does some deed and suffers as a consequence. Actions have consequences in the moral world no less than in the materialistic world of the laboratory. The tragic playwright's solemn presentation of "the remorseless working of things," Alfred North Whitehead pointed out

(in his *Science and the Modern World*, 1925), is "the vision possessed by science," and it cannot be accidental that the two great periods of tragic drama, fifth-century B.C.E. Athens and England around 1600, were periods of scientific inquiry.

The Tragic Hero

This emphasis on causality means that the episodes are related, connected, and not merely contiguous. Generally the formula is to show the tragic hero moving toward committing some deed that will cause great unintended suffering, committing it, and then, by seeing the consequences, learning the true nature of his deed. The plot, that is, involves a credible character whose doings are related to his nature.

Hamartia

For Aristotle, in the best sort of tragedy the tragic hero is an important person, almost preeminently virtuous, who makes some sort of great mistake that entails great suffering. Calamity does not descend upon him from above, does not happen *to* him, nor does he consciously will a destructive act; he merely makes a great mistake. The mistake is Aristotle's **hamartia,** sometimes translated as "error," sometimes as "flaw." Probably Aristotle did not mean by *hamartia* a trait, such as rashness or ambition, which the translation "flaw" implies, but simply meant an action based on a mental error, a sort of false step. Oedipus, erroneously thinking that Polybus and Meropê are his parents, flees from them when he hears that he will kill his father and sleep with his mother. His action is commendable, but it happens to be a great mistake because it brings him to his real parents. Nevertheless, despite the scholarly elucidations of Aristotle, we can sometimes feel that the erring action proceeds from a particular kind of character, that a person with different traits would not have acted in the same way. The Oedipus that we see in the play, for example, is a self-assured quick-tempered man—almost a rash man, we might say—who might well have neglected to check the facts before he fled from Corinth. There are at least times, even when reading *Oedipus the King*, when one feels with George Meredith (1828–1909) that

in tragic life, God wot,
No villain need be! Passions spin the plot:
We are betrayed by what is false within.

Hybris

From this it is only a short step to identifying *hamartia* with a flaw, and the flaw most often attributed to the tragic hero is **hybris,** a word that for the Greeks meant something like "bullying," "abuse of power," but in dramatic criticism usually is translated as "overweening pride." The tragic hero forgets that (in Montaigne's words) "on the loftiest throne in the world we are still sitting only on our own rear," and he believes his actions are infallible. King Lear, for example, banishes his daughter Cordelia with "Better thou / Hadst not been born than not t' have pleased me better." Macbeth, told that he will be king of Scotland, chooses to make the prophecy come true by murdering his guest, King Duncan; Brutus decides that Rome can be saved from tyranny only by killing Caesar, and he deludes himself into thinking he is not murdering Caesar but sacrificing Caesar for the welfare of Rome.

Peripeteia

We have talked of *hamartia* and *hybris* in tragedy; two more Greek words, **peripeteia** and **anagnorisis,** also common in discussions of tragedy, ought to be mentioned. A peripeteia (sometimes anglicized to *peripety* or translated as "reversal") occurs when the action takes a course not intended by the doer. Aristotle gives two examples: (1) the Messenger comes to cheer up Oedipus by freeing him from fears but the message heightens Oedipus's fears; (2) Danaus (in a lost play) prosecutes a man but is himself killed.

A few other examples of reversals may be useful; Oedipus flees from Corinth to avoid contact with his parents, but his flight brings him to them; Macbeth kills Duncan to gain the crown but his deed brings him fearful nights instead of joyful days; Lear, seeking a peaceful old age, puts himself in the hands of two daughters who maltreat him, and banishes the one daughter who later will comfort him. The Bible—especially the Hebrew Bible—is filled with such peripeties or ironic actions. For example, the Philistines brought Samson before them to entertain them, and he performed his most spectacular feat by destroying his audience. But the archetypal tragic story is that of Adam and Eve: Aiming to be like gods, they lost their immortality and the earthly paradise, and brought death to themselves.

Anagnorisis

The other Greek word, **anagnorisis,** translated as "recognition" or "discovery" or "disclosure," seems to have meant for Aristotle a clearing up of some misunderstanding, such as the proper identification of someone or the revelation of some previously unknown fact. But later critics have given it a richer meaning and used it to describe the hero's perception of his or her true nature or true plight. In the narrow sense, it is an *anagnorisis,* or "recognition" when King Lear learns that Regan and Goneril are ungrateful and cruel. In the wider sense, the *anagnorisis* is in his speech in 3.4, when he confesses his former ignorance and his neglect of his realm:

> Poor naked wretches, wheresoe'er you are,
> That bide the pelting of this pitiless storm,
> How shall your houseless heads and unfed sides,
> Your looped and windowed raggedness, defend you
> From seasons such as these? O, I have ta'en
> Too little care of this! Take physic, pomp;
> Expose thyself to feel what wretches feel,
> That thou mayst shake the superflux to them,
> And show the heavens more just.

Similarly, Hamlet's "There is special providence in the fall of a sparrow," and Othello's "one that loved not wisely, but too well," may be called recognition scenes. Here is Macbeth's recognition that his purpose has been frustrated, that his deed has been ironic:

> My way of life
> Is fall'n into the sear, the yellow leaf
> And that which should accompany old age,
> As honor, love, obedience, troops of friends,
> I must not look to have.

The Social World of Comedy

"Troops of friends" abound in comedy. Where tragedy is primarily the dramatization of the single life that ripens and then can only rot, that reaches its fullest and then is destroyed, comedy is primarily the dramatization of the renewing of the self and of social relationships. Tragic heroes are isolated from society, partly by their different natures, and partly by their tragic acts; comedy suggests that selfhood is found not in assertion of individuality, but in joining in the fun, in becoming part of the flow of common humanity.

Where tragedy suggests an incompatibility between the energy or surge of the individual life and the laws of life or the norms of society, comedy suggests that norms are valid and necessary.

Tragic Isolation

Tragic heroes do what they feel compelled to do; they assert themselves, and are intensely aware that they are special persons and not members of the crowd. But that their mistake always reveals that they are hybristic is not at all certain. The Greek tragic hero is commonly set against a chorus of ordinary mortals who caution him, wring their hands, and lament the hero's boldness, but these ordinary mortals are always aware that if they are law-abiding people, they are also less fully human beings than the hero. That they obey society's laws is not due to superior virtue, to the triumph of reason over will, to self-discipline; rather, their obedience is due to a lower vision, or to timidity, and indeed sometimes to a fear of what resides in their own breasts.

Tragic Virtue

Tragic heroes are, of course, in one way inferior to those about them; their actions cost them great suffering, and they are thus immobilized as the others are not. But their greatness remains indisputable; the anguish that at times paralyzes Hamlet also makes him greater than, say, Horatio and Laertes. In fact, tragic heroes are circumscribed, certainly after the deed, when they are necessarily subject to the consequences (Brutus kills Caesar and finds that he brings to Rome a turmoil that makes him flee from Rome and ultimately makes him take his own life); even before doing the tragic deed, the heroes are circumscribed because their action proceeds from something, either from their personality or from their circumstances. Still, their action seems to them to be freely theirs, and indeed we feel it is an action that lesser persons could not perform. This perception is almost a way of arguing that a tragic hero may err not so much from weakness as from strength. Why can Iago so easily deceive Othello? Not because Othello is an unthinking savage, or an unsophisticated foreigner, but because (as Iago admits) Othello is of a "loving noble nature," and, again,

The Moor is of *a free and open nature*
That thinks men honest that but seem to be so;
And will as tenderly be led by th' nose
As asses are.

Why can Claudius see to it that Laertes murders Hamlet during a fencing match? Not because Hamlet is a poor fencer, or a coward, but because Hamlet

Most generous, and free from all contriving,
Will not peruse the foils.

Tragic Joy

This is not to say that tragic heroes are faultless, or that they are quite happy with themselves and with their action; but they do experience a kind of exultation even in their perception that disaster is upon them. If they grieve over their deeds, we sense a glory in their grief, for they find, like Captain Ahab, that in their topmost grief lies their topmost greatness. At last they see everything and know that nothing more can be experienced. They have lived their lives to the limits. Othello put it thus:

Here is my journey's end, here is my butt,
And very seamark of my utmost sail.

(In a comedy Shakespeare tells us that "journeys end in lovers meeting," that is, the end is a new beginning.)

In "Under Ben Bulben" William Butler Yeats (1865–1939) suggests the sense of completeness that the tragic hero experiences when, under the influence of a great passion, he exhausts his nature and seems to be not a man among men but a partner (rather than a subject) of fate:

Know that when all words are said
And a man is fighting mad,
Something drops from eyes long blind,
He completes his partial mind,
For an instant stands at ease,
Laughs aloud, his heart at peace.
Even the wisest man grows tense
With some sort of violence
Before he can accomplish fate,
Know his work or choose his mate.

Elsewhere Yeats put his distinction between the tragic hero and the world the hero is up against thus: "Some

Frenchman[2] has said that farce is the struggle against a ridiculous object, comedy against a movable object, tragedy against an immovable object; and because the will, or energy, is greatest in tragedy, tragedy is the more noble; but I add that 'will or energy is eternal delight,' and when its limit is reached it may become a pure, aimless joy, though the man, the shade, still mourns his lost object."

Comic Assertion

What of the contexts and times when we find passionate self-assertion funny? Much depends on what is being asserted, and on what or who the antagonist is. King Lear against his tigerish daughters is a tragic figure, but a pedant against a dull schoolboy may be a comic one. The lament of the tragic hero is proportionate to the event, but the effort extended by the comic figure is absurdly disproportionate. Furthermore, as Henri Bergson (1859–1941) pointed out, the comic figure usually is a sort of mechanism, repeating his actions and catch phrases with clocklike regularity in contexts where they are inappropriate. He quotes Latin on every occasion, or he never travels without his pills, or she always wants to know how much something costs, or he is forever spying on his wife. Bergson, who suggested that the comic is "the mechanical encrusted on the living," illustrated his point by telling of the customs officers who bravely rescue the crew of a sinking vessel, and then ask, the moment the shore is reached, "Have you anything to declare?" The mechanical question, inappropriate in the situation, reveals that the officers value trivial regulations as much as they do life itself. In *The Circus* Charlie Chaplin is dusting things off; he comes upon the magician's bowl of goldfish, takes the fish out and wipes them, and then returns them to the bowl.

Comic Joy

The comic world seems to be presided over by a genial, tolerant deity who enjoys the variety that crosses the stage. The sketchbooks of the Japanese artist Hokusai (1760–1849) wonderfully reveal this comic delight in humantiy. There are pages of fat men, pages of thin men (no less engagingly drawn), pages of men making

---

[2]Yeats is rather freely summarizing Ferdinand Brunetière's *La Loi du théâtre*. A translation of Brunetière's treatise is available in *European Theories of the Drama*, ed. Barrett H. Clark.

---

funny faces, and there is a delightful drawing of a man holding a magnifying glass in front of his face so that his nose seems enormous. Comic playwrights give us something of this range of types and grotesques, and they give us also variety in language (e.g., puns, inverted clichés, malapropisms) and variety in episodes (much hiding behind screens, dressing in disguise).

Comic Isolation

The characters, then, who insist on being themselves, who mechanically hold to a formula of language or of behavior, are laughably out of place in the world of varied people who live and let live. What comedy does not tolerate is intolerance; it regularly suggests that the intolerant—for example, the pedant and the ascetic—are fools and probably hypocrites. Here is the self-righteous Alceste, in Molière's *The Misanthrope*:

> Some men I hate for being rogues: the others,
> I hate because they treat the rogues like brothers,
> And, lacking a virtuous scorn for what is vile,
> Receive the villain with a complaisant smile.
> Notice how tolerant people choose to be
> Toward that bold rascal who's at law with me.

Philinte genially replies,

> Let's have an end of rantings and of railings,
> And show some leniency toward human failings.
> This world requires a pliant rectitude;
> Too stern a virtue makes one stiff and rude.

Here is the puritanical Malvolio in *Twelfth Night*, trying to quiet down some tipsy but genial revelers:

> My masters, are you mad? Or what are you? Have you no wit, manners nor honesty, but to gabble like tinkers at this time of night? Do ye make an alehouse of my lady's house? . . . Is there not respect of place, persons, nor time in you?

He is aptly answered:

> Art any more than a steward? Dost thou think, because thou art virtuous, there shall be no more cakes and ale?

This suspicion of a "virtue" that is opposed to cakes and ale runs through the history of comedy.

In Shakespeare's *Love's Labor Lost*, the young noblemen who vow to devote themselves to study, and to forgo the company of women, are laughed at until they accept their bodies and admit interest in those of the ladies. The celebration of the human body, or at least the good-natured acceptance of it that is present in comedy, is well put by the General in Anouilh's *The Waltz of the Toreadors*:

> You're in the ocean, splashing about, doing your damndest not to drown, in spite of whirlpools and cross currents. The main thing is to do the regulation breaststroke and if you're not a clod, never to let the life-buoy ["the ideal"] out of sight. No one expects any more than that out of you. Now if you relieve yourself in the water now and then, that's your affair. The sea is big, and if the top half of your body still looks as though it's doing the breaststroke, nobody will say a word.

Detachment and Engagement

One way of distinguishing between comedy and tragedy is summarized in Horace Walpole's aphorism "This world is a comedy to those that think, a tragedy to those that feel." Life seen thoughtfully, with considerable detachment, viewed from above, as it were, is an amusing pageant, and the comic writer gives us something of this view. With Puck we look at the antics in the forest, smile tolerantly, and say with a godlike perspective, "Lord, what fools these mortals be!" But in tragedy we are to a greater degree engaged; the tragic dramatist manages to make us in large measure identify ourselves with the hero, feel his plight as if it were our own, and value his feelings as he values them.[3] Yeats noticed this when he said that "character is continuously present in comedy alone," and that "tragedy must always be a drowning and breaking of the dykes that separate man from man. . . . It is upon these dykes comedy keeps house." And Yeats again: "Nor when the tragic reverie is at its height do we say, 'How well that man is realised, I should know him were I to meet him in the street,' for it is always ourselves that we see upon the [tragic] stage."

Tragic Fate and Comic Fortune in Plots

One consequence of this distinction between tragedy and comedy, between looking-at and feeling-with, is that the comic plot is usually more intricate than the tragic plot, and less plausible. The comic plot continues

---

[3]Bergson's theory that a human being—an organism—is comical when it behaves mechanically requires, as Bergson said, a modification: Feelings must be suppressed. A crippled man is not comic despite his mechanical limp, because we feel for him. Comedy requires, Bergson said, an "anesthesia of the heart."

to trip up its characters, bringing them into numerous situations that allow them to display their folly over and over again. The complex comic plot is often arbitrary, full of the workings of Fortune or Chance, and we delight at each new unexpected or unlikely happening. In tragedy, Fate (sometimes in the form that "character is destiny") or Necessity rules, there is the consistency and inevitability, the "remorseless working of things," that has already been mentioned. If Macbeth were struck dead by a falling roof tile while he dozed in the palace after a good meal, instead of dying on Macduff's sword, or if Brutus were to die by slipping in his bath, instead of dying on the very sword with which he killed Caesar, we would have arbitrary happenings that violate the spirit of everything that precedes. But the unexpected letters and the long-lost relatives that often turn up at the close of a comedy are thoroughly in the spirit of the comic vision, which devalues not only rigidly consistent character but rigidity of every sort, even of plot. Tragedy usually follows a straight course, comedy a delightfully twisted one.

Comic Beginnings and Endings

The rigid behavior of some of comedy's laughably serious characters (e.g., misers, jealous husbands, stern fathers) is paralleled in the rigid circumstances that often are sketched at the beginning of a comedy. In *A Midsummer Night's Dream* the Athenian law requires that a young woman marry the man of her father's choice, or be put to death, or live chastely in a nunnery. Gilbert and Sullivan, to draw on familiar material, afford plenty of examples of comedy's fondness for a cantankerous beginning: *The Mikado* opens with a chorus of Japanese noblemen whose code of etiquette makes them appear to be "worked by strings"; they live in a town where a law ordered that "all who flirted, leered or winked / Should forthwith be beheaded." (Comedy often begins with a society dominated by some harsh law.) Although this law has been suspended, another harsh decree is in effect: The pretty Yum-Yum is betrothed to her old guardian, Ko-Ko. We learn, too, that her appropriate wooer, Nanki-Poo, is a prince who has had to disguise himself as a humble wandering minstrel to escape his father's decree that he marry Katisha, an old and ugly lady of the court.

After various doings in a comedy, a new—presumably natural, prosperous, fertile, and free—society is formed, usually centered on young lovers who are going to be married. Yum-Yum and Nanki-Poo finally contrive to get married, evading Katisha and Ko-Ko, who make the best of things by marrying each other. The whole business is satisfactorily explained to the Mikado, who affably accepts, and ruffled tempers are soothed:

> The threatened cloud has passed away,
> And brightly shines the dawning day;
> What though the night may come too soon,
> We've years and years of afternoon!

> Then let the throng
> Our joy advance,
> With laughing song
>   And merry dance,
> With joyous shout and ringing cheer,
> Inaugurate our new career!

The first four lines are sung by the young lovers, the remaining six are sung by "All," the new, or renewed, society, free from unnatural law. *H.M.S. Pinafore* begins with lovers who cannot marry because of disparity in rank, but ends with appropriate shifts in rank so that there can be "three loving pairs on the same day united."

Self-Knowledge

In comedy there is often not only an improbable turn in events but an improbable (but agreeable) change in character—or at least in rank; troublesome persons become enlightened, find their own better nature, and join in the fun, commonly a marriage feast. Finding one's own nature is common in tragedy, too, but there self-knowledge is coterminous with death or some deathlike condition, such as blindness. *Oedipus the King* ends with a note of finality, even though Oedipus is alive at the end; the fact that twenty-five years later Sophocles decided to write a play showing Oedipus's apotheosis does not allow us to see the earlier play as less than complete. The chorus in *Oedipus the King* has the last word:

> This man was Oedipus.
> That mighty King, who knew the riddle's mystery,
> Whom all the city envied, Fortune's favorite.
> Behold, in the event, the storm of his calamities,
> And, being mortal, think on that last day of death,
> Which all must see, and speak of no man's happiness
> Till, without sorrow, he hath passed the goal of life.

Or consider the irreparable loss at the end of Shakespeare's tragedies: "This was the noblest Roman of them all"; "We that are young / Shall never see so much, nor live so long"; "The rest is silence." But comedy ends with a new beginning, a newly formed society, usually a wedding party; the tragic figure commonly awakens to the fact that he has made a big mistake and his life is over, but the comic figure commonly awakens to his better nature. He usually sheds his aberration and is restored to himself and to a renewed society. Alceste's refusal to change, at the end of *The Misanthrope*, helps to push that comedy toward the borderline between comedy and tragedy. Oedipus learns that his parents were not those whom he had supposed, and he learns that even the mighty Oedipus can be humbled. Othello comes to see himself as a man "that loved not wisely but too well," and, having reached his journey's end, he executes justice upon himself by killing himself. That is, at the end of the play he finds himself, but this finding of the self separates him forever from those around him, whereas the comic figure who finds himself usually does so by putting aside in some measure his individuality and by submitting himself to a partner or to the group.

Comedy and tragedy offer different visions and represent different psychological states. And they are equally useful. The tragic vision may have more prestige, but it is no small thing to make people laugh, to call attention amusingly to the follies and joys of life, and to help develop the sense of humor—and humility—that may be indispensable to survival in a world continually threatened by aggressive ideals that demand uncritical acceptance. Infants smile easily, and children laugh often, but growing up is often attended by a frightening seriousness. True, hostile laughter, the scarcely veiled aggressiveness that manifests itself in derision, remains an adult possession, but the laughter evoked by the best comedy is good-natured while it is critical, and it is in part directed at ourselves. We look at bumbling humanity and we recall Puck's words, "Lord, what fools these mortals be." This is not to say that the comic vision is cynical; rather, it attributes to folly what less generous visions attribute to ill will or to hopeless corruption, and when it laughs it forgives. Analyses of laughter are sometimes funny but more often they are tedious; still, they at least pay the comic spirit the compliment of recognizing it as worthy of our best efforts.

TRAGICOMEDY

Tragicomedy Before 1900

The word *tragicomedy* is several hundred years newer than the words *tragedy* and *comedy*; it first appeared about 186 B.C.E. when Plautus spoke of *tragicocomoedia* in his *Amphitryon*, a Roman comedy in which gods assume mortal shapes in order to dupe a husband and seduce his wife. Mercury, in a joking prologue to the play, explains the author's dilemma:

> I'll make it a mixture, a tragicomedy. It wouldn't be right for me to make it all a comedy since kings and gods appear. Well, then, since there's a slave part too, I'll do as I said and make it a tragicomedy.

But the play is a traditional comedy, unalloyed with the solemnity, terror, and pity of tragedy. It shows laughable activities that finally turn out all right. It should be mentioned again, however, that although tragedy and comedy were clearly separated in the ancient world, not all ancient tragedies ended with death, or even ended unhappily. Aeschylus's trilogy, *The Oresteia*, ends with reconciliation and solemn joy (but it has been bought at the price of great suffering), and Sophocles's *Philoctetes* and Euripides's *Iphigeneia at Taurus* end with catastrophes averted. They were tragic for the Greeks because momentous issues were treated seriously, though we might say that the plots have a comic structure because they end happily.

In the Renaissance there was much fussing over the meanings of tragedy, comedy, and tragicomedy, but most theoreticians inclined to the view that tragedy dealt with noble figures engaged in serious actions, was written in a lofty style, and ended unhappily; comedy dealt with humbler figures engaged in trivial actions, was written in relatively common diction, and ended happily. Tragicomedy, whether defined as some mixture (e.g., high people in trivial actions) or as a play in which, to quote Sir Philip Sidney, the writer "thrust in the clown by head and shoulders to play a part in majestical matters," was for the most part scorned by academic critics as a mongrel. It was merely additive, bits of comedy added to a tragedy. At best the advocates for tragicomedy could argue that a play without the terror of tragedy and the absurdity of comedy can cover a good deal of life and can please a good many tastes. But this sort of play, unlike modern tragicomedy, is not so much a union of tragedy and comedy as an exclusion of both, lacking, for example, the awe we associate with tragedy and the fun we associate with comedy.

In the twentieth century the word and the form have become thoroughly respectable; indeed, it is now evident that many of the best plays of our century are best described not as tragedies or as comedies but as tragicomedies—distinctive fusions (not mere aggregations) of tragedy and comedy. For a start we can take William Hazlitt's statement that "man is the only animal that laughs and weeps; for he is the only animal that is struck with the difference between what things are, and what they ought to be." Another way of putting it is to say that human beings have an ideal of conduct, but circumstances and human limitations prevent them from fulfilling this ideal. This pursuit of the ideal thus can seem noble, or foolish, or a mixture of the two.

Detachment and Engagement Again

Many of the best playwrights of the twentieth century have adopted the more complicated mixed view. Comedy had customarily invoked a considerable degree of detachment; in Bergson's formula (1900), already quoted, comedy requires an anesthesia of the spectators' hearts as they watch folly on the stage. Tragedy, on the other hand, has customarily invoked a considerable degree of involvement or sympathy; in Walpole's formula, also already quoted, "The world is a comedy to those that think, a tragedy to those that feel." But tragicomedy shows us comic characters for whom we feel deep sympathy. Pirandello, in his essay *Umorismo* (1908), gives an interesting example of the phenomenon. Suppose, he says, we see an elderly woman with dyed hair and much too much makeup. We find her funny; but if we realize that she is trying to hold the attention of her husband, our sympathy is aroused. Our sense of her absurdity is not totally dissipated, but we feel for her and so our laughter is combined with pity.

Theater of the Absurd

In the third quarter of the twentieth century the theater that was most vital was not the Broadway musical, the earnest problem-play, or the well-made drawing-room comedy (although these continued to be written) but a fairly unified body of drama called the absurd, whose major writers are Beckett, Genet, Ionesco, Pinter, and

Albee. Their theme is human anguish, but their techniques are those of comedy: improbable situations and unheroic characters who say funny things. These writers differ, of course, and differ from play to play, but they are all preoccupied with the loneliness of people in a world without the certainties afforded by God or by optimistic rationalism. This loneliness is heightened by a sense of impotence derived partly from an awareness of our inability to communicate in a society that has made language meaningless, and partly from an awareness of the precariousness of our existence in an atomic age.

Behind this vision are some two hundred years of thinking that have conspired to make it difficult to think of any person as a hero who confronts a mysterious cosmic order. Man, Ionesco says in *Notes and Counter Notes*, is "cut off from his religious and metaphysical roots." One of the milestones in the journey toward contemporary nihilism is the bourgeois drama of the middle of the eighteenth century, which sought to show the dignity of the common people but which, negatively put, undermined the concept of a tragic hero. Instead of showing a heroic yet universal figure, it showed ordinary people in relation to their society, thus paving the way for Arthur Miller's Willy Loman, who apparently would have been okay, as we all would be, if our economic system allowed for early retirement. Miller's play makes no claim for Willy's grandeur or for the glory of life; it claims only that he is an ordinary man at the end of his rope in a deficient society and that he is entitled to a fair deal.

Diminution of Human Beings

Other landmarks on the road to our awareness of our littleness are, like bourgeois drama, developments in thinking that were believed by their builders to be landmarks on the road to our progressive conquest of fear. Among these we can name Darwin's *The Origin of Species* (1859), which, in the popular phrase, seemed to record progress "up from apes," but which, more closely read, reduced human beings to the product of "accidental variations" and left God out of the picture, substituting for a cosmic order a barbaric struggle for existence. (In the second edition, 1860, Darwin spoke of life as "breathed by the creator," but the creator was not Darwin's concern and he later abandoned all religious beliefs. Probably he retained his belief that the process of "natural selection works solely by and for the good of each being," but by 1889 his disciple T. H. Huxley saw it differently. Huxley said he knew of no

study "so unutterably saddening as that of the evolution of humanity.") Karl Marx, studying the evolution of societies at about the same time, was attributing our sense of alienation to economic forces, thereby implying that we have no identity we can properly call our own. Moreover, Marxist thinking, like Darwinian thinking, suggested that human beings could not do anything of really great importance, nor could they be blamed for their misfortunes. At the end of the nineteenth century, and in the early twentieth century, Freud, also seeking to free us from tyranny, turned to the forces within our mind. Ironically, the effort to chart our unconscious drives and anarchic impulses in order to help us to know ourselves induced a profound distrust of the self: We can scarcely be confident of our behavior, for we know that apparently heroic behavior has unconscious unheroic motives rooted in the experiences of infancy. Tragic heroes are people with complexes, and religious codes are only wishful thinking.

Dissolution of Character and Plot

The result of such developments in thought seems to be that a "tragic sense" in the twentieth century commonly means a despairing or deeply uncertain view, something very different from what it meant in Greece and in Elizabethan England. This uncertainty is not merely about the cosmos but even about character or identity. In 1888, in the Preface to *Miss Julie*, August Strindberg called attention to the new sense of the instability of character:

> I have made the people in my play fairly "characterless." The middle-class conception of a fixed character was transferred to the stage, where the middle class has always ruled. A character there came to mean an actor who was always one and the same, always drunk, always comic or always melancholy, and who needed to be characterized only by some physical defect such as a club foot, a wooden leg, or a red nose, or by the repetition of some such phrase such as, "That's capital," or "Barkis is willin'." . . . Since the persons in my play are modern characters, living in a transitional era more hurried and hysterical than the previous one at least, I have depicted them as more unstable, as torn and divided, a mixture of the old and the new.

In 1902, in his preface to *A Dream Play*, he is more explicit: "Anything may happen, anything seems possible and probable. . . . The characters split, double, multiply, vanish, solidify, blur, clarify." Strindberg's view of the fluidity of character—the characterless of character, one might say—has continued and is apparent in almost all of Pirandello's work, in the underground film, and in much of the theater of the absurd. Ionesco, in *Fragments of a Journal,* says, "I often find it quite impossible to hold an opinion about a fact, a thing or a person. Since it's all a matter of interpretation, one has to choose a particular interpretation." In *Notes and Counter Notes* Ionesco said, "chance formed us," and that we would be different if we had different experiences; characteristically, a few years later he said he was no longer sure that he believed in chance.

Along with the sense of characterlessness, or at least of the mystery of character, there developed in the drama (and in the underground film and the novel) a sense of plotlessness, or fundamental untruthfulness of the traditional plot that moved by cause and effect "Plots," Ionesco has said in *Conversations,* "are never interesting," and again he has said that a play should be able to stop at any point; it ends only because "the audience has to go home to bed. . . . It's true for real life. Why should it be different for art?" Ionesco has treated his own plots very casually, allowing directors to make "all the cuts needed" and suggesting that endings other than those he wrote are possibilities. After all, in a meaningless world one can hardly take a dramatic plot seriously. In Ionesco's *Victims of Duty* a character defends a new kind of irrational, anti-Aristotelian drama: "The theater of my dreams would be irrationalist. . . . The contemporary theater doesn't reflect the cultural tone of our period, it's not in harmony with the general drift of the other manifestations of the modern spirit. . . . We'll get rid of the principle of identity and unity of character. . . . Personality doesn't exist." A policeman-psychologist (a materialist who demands law and order) offers an old-fashioned view: "I don't believe in the absurd, everything hangs together, everything can be comprehended . . . thanks to the achievements of human thought and science," but he is murdered by the anti-Aristotelian.

Thus, Becket's *Waiting for Godot* ends—as the first act ended—without anything ending:

VLADIMIR. Well? Shall we go?
ESTRAGON. Yes, let's go.

They do not move.

CURTAIN

To bring an action to a completion, as drama traditionally did, is to imply an orderly world of cause and effect, of beginnings and endings, but for the dramatists of the absurd, there is no such pattern. At best it is *Hamlet* as Tom Stoppard's Rosencrantz and Guildenstern see it: They are supposed to do a job they don't understand, and instead of a pattern or "order" they encounter only "Incidents! Incidents! Dear God, is it too much to expect a little sustained action?" Well, yes; it is too much to expect.

The Tragedy of Comedy

There can be no tragedy, because, as Ionesco explains in *Notes,* tragedy admits the existence of fate or destiny, which is to say it admits the existence of objective (however incomprehensible) laws ruling the universe, whereas the new comic perception of incongruity is that existence itself is absurd because there is no objective law. The new comic vision is far darker than the old tragic vision; it has nothing in it of what Yeats called "tragic joy." But what is our reaction to this joyless comedy? Let Ionesco, whose plays sometimes include meaningless babble, have the last word:

> The fact of being astonishes us, in a world that now seems all illusion and pretense, in which all human behavior tells of absurdity and all history of absolute futility; all reality and all language appear to lose their articulation, to disintegrate and collapse, so what possible reaction is there left, when everything has ceased to matter, but laugh at it all.[4]

DRAMA AND SOCIETY: SIX QUESTIONS

Our government supports the arts, including the theater, by giving grants to numerous institutions. But the amount that the government contributes (for example, through the National Endowment for the Arts and the National Endowment for the Humanities) is extremely small when compared to the amounts given to the arts by most European governments. It is estimated that federal subsidies amount to about 5 percent of the funding of established arts institutions, whereas in Europe they amount to something over 60 percent. The government of Germany, for instance, gives more to its theaters than our government gives to *all* of the arts combined.

Of course one might reply that our government offers relatively little support because private philan-

[4]*Notes and Counter Notes: Writings on the Theatre* (New York: Grove Press, 1964), p. 163.

thropies offer so much—and one can add that that is the way it ought to be. Why, after all, should the government support the arts? Why should taxpayers who have little or no interest in the arts be forced to subsidize them? Doesn't this use of tax dollars involve a sort of reverse Robin Hoodism, taking money from the poor and giving it to the rich, who go to the theaters and the museums?

Let's begin, then, by formulating a few questions:

1. Should taxpayers' dollars be used to support the arts, in particular the theater in America? Why, or why not? Is it relevant to say that even if, on principle, the arts deserve to be supported, we cannot afford to give them money when we are confronted with such problems as homelessness, AIDS, and inadequate health care?

2. What possible public benefit(s) can come from supporting the arts? Can one argue that, in effect, we should support the arts for the same reasons that we support the public schools; that is, in order to have a civilized citizenry?

3. If dollars should be given to the arts, should the political content of the works be taken into account, or only the aesthetic merit? Can we always, or sometimes, or never, separate political content from aesthetic content?

4. Is it censorship not to award public funds to artists or groups whose work is not approved of, or is it simply a matter of refusing to reward them with taxpayers' dollars?

5. Should decisions about grants be made chiefly by federal officials or chiefly by experts in the field? Why?

6. If the arts are funded, should the funds go only to bring the classics to the public—in our case, to subsidize productions of plays that have withstood the test of time, therefore becoming a part of our cultural heritage—or should funds also be used to support new playwrights?

We hope that you will occasionally think about these questions when you read the plays—and when you go to the theater.

Classical Greek Theater

With a Note on Roman Drama

We begin this anthology with examples of classical Greek drama that have continued to be performed into modern times. Pictured here is a scene from *Oedipus Rex* starring Christopher Plummer as he appeared in the 1952 television program "Omnibus."

THE PLAYING SPACE IN GREEK THEATER

The great age of the Greek drama was the fifth century B.C.E. All the the Greek plays in this book are from that period, and all were presented in the Theater of Dionysus at Athens. The audience sat on wooden benches or stone tiers of seats on a hillside (see photos, pages 11 and 50), looking down at a flat circular dancing place (the *orchestra*), about sixty-five feet in diameter, in the middle of which was an altar to Dionysus. Behind the dancing place was a stage or playing area, which logic (but almost no concrete evidence) suggests may have been slightly elevated. Visible behind the playing area was the *skene,* a wooden "scene-building" introduced about 458 B.C.E. that served as a background (as in our word "scenery"), as a place for actors to make entrances from and exits to (through a door or doors in the front), and as a dressing room where actors could change masks and costumes.

To speak of these elements in a little more detail: The seating area, which held some fourteen thousand people, was the *theatron* ("seeing-place"); fan-shaped or horseshoe-shaped, it swept around the orchestra in a segment greater than a semicircle. The chorus of singers and dancers, entering by an aisle (*parodos*) at each side of the *theatron,* danced in the orchestra. The *skene* or scene-building (or stage-building) was about twelve feet deep, and consisted of two stories. A god might appear on the roof, or (as in *Antigonê*) even a watchman. Since most of the spectators were looking down from the hillside, a performer on the roof would be easily visible. The front (i.e., the façade) of the *skene* (or perhaps a temporary screen) and sometimes the playing area in front of it seem to have been called the *proskenion.* Though the *skene's* façade perhaps suggested the front of a temple or a palace, there were further efforts at indicating locale: Sophocles is said to have invented scene painting (a painted cloth or screen in front of the *skene?*), and there are allusions to *periaktoi,* upright prisms bearing a different decoration on each side. Apparently when a new locality in the same town was to be indicated, the *periaktos* at the right was turned; when an entirely new locality was to be indicated, both *periaktoi* were turned. Other machines were the *eccyclema,* a platform that was rolled out of the *skene* to indicate a scene indoors, and the *mechane,* a crane from which a god could descend or by means of which a character could soar through the air. (See, in the Glossary, *deus ex machina.*)

The playing area or stage in front of the *skene* was probably about twenty-five feet wide, eight or nine feet deep, and if it was elevated it was connected to the orchestra by a few steps. On the whole the actors confined themselves to the stage, backed by the *skene,* and the chorus confined itself to the *orchestra,* but there are a few instances of intermingling. For example, in *Medea,* at one point the chorus ventures onto the stage and hammers at the door of the *skene.*

Stage Symbolism

Speaking a bit broadly, we can say that the Greek theater, open to the heavens, with its orchestra representing a city square and the *skene* representing a temple or palace, is itself a symbol of the ancient Athenian worldview of a society that operates under divine and human law. Further, the diminutive size of the actors in the vast theater, and the background of trees and mountains, must also have conveyed a sense of the sublime natural world surrounding human passions.

Plays were put on chiefly during two holidays, the **Lenaea** (Feast of the Wine Press) in January, and the **Great** (or **City**) **Dionysia** in March or April. The Lenaea was chiefly associated with comedy, the Great Dionysia with tragedy. At the latter, on each of three mornings, a tragic dramatist presented three tragedies and one **satyr-play.** The expense was borne by a *choregos,* a rich citizen ordered by the state to assume the financial burden.

THE ORIGINS OF GREEK DRAMA AND THE STRUCTURE OF GREEK TRAGEDY

The Theory of an Origin in Dionysian Rituals

Although the ancient Greeks were fairly confident that they knew the origin and history of drama, modern scholars are less certain. The Greeks—notably Aristotle (384–322 B.C.E.)—said that both tragedy and comedy originated in improvisations; tragedy, according to Aristotle, originated in improvisations in choral poems honoring Dionysus (the god of fertility and wine), and comedy originated in improvisations in phallic songs. Around the middle of the sixth century B.C.E. a man named Thespis stepped out of the chorus and, singing in a different meter, became an impersonator who sang not *about* a god but *in the role of* a god. Thespis thus was the first actor, and by taking on an identity apart from the chorus, he and his successors made possible dialogue between a charater and the chorus. (The chorus numbered twelve or fifteen performers.) Later the playwright Aeschylus (525–456 B.C.E.) added a second actor, thus increasing the dramatic (as opposed to the lyric and narrative) element, and still later Sophocles (c. 496–406 B.C.E.) added the third. The number of actors became fixed at three, so in ancient Greek drama there are never more than three speaking parts onstage at one time. However, since the actors could double in roles, there may be eight or even ten speaking parts in a play.

Unfortunately, there is little evidence to support the assertion that Greek tragedy originated in festivals honoring Dionysus. The chief evidence for the theory, aside from Aristotle's assertion (made some three centuries after the supposed fact), is that tragic plays from 534 B.C.E. were indeed performed at a festival called the Dionysia, honoring Dionysus. But, surprisingly, Dionysus figures importantly in only one Greek tragedy, which is puzzling if Greek tragedy really did originate in songs honoring him. The old view dies hard, however, and one still usually reads that tragedy originated in choral songs sung at fertility festivals honoring Dionysus, and that at some decisive moment Thespis impersonated him or some other god, and tragic drama was born.

A sort of corollary goes this way: Since Dionysus was god of the vine, the original songs were performed during revels in honor of the rebirth of the vine, which was seen as the rebirth of the year, the renewal of life after the death of the year in winter. The celebration of the renewal of the "year spirit" involved dramatizing the death of this divine power, and that's what Greek tragedy supposedly shows, though the "divine power" or "year spirit" came to be put into the forms of Greek heroes rather than of the god Dionysus. This is all pretty imaginative; skeptics have asked not only why Dionysus virtually disappears from the plays but also why these plays, supposedly rooted in festivals honoring the renewal of the year, end with death and lamentation rather than with renewal and joy. To the second objection, the answer is sometimes made that the plays do indeed include a suggestion of renewal; the hero comes to perceive his or her fate, and in recognizing it, and in magnificently singing about it, shows a sort of spiritual rebirth. Confronted with this answer, skeptics remain (justifiably) skeptical.

The Use of Masks

One other alleged connection with ritual should be mentioned. We know that Greek actors wore masks when they performed. Advocates of the ritual origin of Greek drama argue that the masks derived from masks that priests wore for two reasons: to impersonate the gods, and to disguise themselves lest the gods be displeased with them. Skeptics reply that the masks, with their bold, stylized features, were necessary in order to identify the characters to the audience in the vast theaters, since a Greek theater held some 15,000 people. That is, even a spectator at a great distance from the stage would immediately be able to know, upon seeing a character enter with a stereotyped mask, that this was a tragic king, or a young woman, or a messenger. It is also argued that the mouths of the masks were designed to serve as megaphones, though in fact the acoustics in Greek theaters are so remarkably good that megaphones seem unnecessary.

The Structure of Greek Tragedy

A tragedy commonly begins with a *prologue*, during which the exposition is given. Next comes the chorus's *ode* of entrance, sung while the chorus marches into the theater, through the side aisles and onto the orchestra. The ensuing *scene* is followed by a choral song or *stasimon*. Usually there are four or five scenes, alternating with odes. Each of these choral odes has a *strophe* (lines presumably sung while the chorus dances in one direction) and an *antistrophe* (lines presumably sung while the chorus retraces its steps). Sometimes a third part, an *epode*, concludes an ode. (In addition to odes that are *stasima*—the plural of stasimon— there can be odes within episodes; the fourth episode of *Antigonê* contains an ode complete with *epode*.) After the last part of the last ode comes the *epilogue*, or final scene.

The actors (all male) seem to have chanted much of the play. Perhaps the total result of combining speech with music and dancing was a sort of music-drama roughly akin to opera with some spoken dialogue, such as Mozart's *Magic Flute*.

For a brief additional remark about Dionysus, see the entry on him in the Glossary.

■■■■■■■■■■■■■■■ A NOTE ON ROMAN DRAMA

The ancient Romans claimed that their drama was rooted in native material, and at least for comedy there is some evidence of skits belonging to a genre called "Atellan farce," named for the city of Attelae in southern Italy, near Naples. Atellan farce was built on stock characters (the oaf, the crabby old man, the clever slave, etc.), but it was not written down, and so we know little more than can be garnered from references to the titles of the skits. In any case, the Roman plays that exist—tragedies as well as comedies—are clearly derived from Greek plays. Greece early exerted an influence on southern Italy (the region south of Naples was called Greater Greece), and the influence spread to Rome. Around the middle of the third century B.C.E. Latin adaptations of Greek plays—tragedies and comedies—were performed in Rome, and these were followed by new plays, in Latin, on themes derived from ancient Greek plays.

In the first century B.C.E., Roman poets seem to have written tragedies not as productions for the stage but as literary exercises—works that might be read to a select group. It is customarily said that one reason serious writers now shunned the stage was that the stage was occupied by pantomime, a form in which a masked dancer (the *pantomimus*) performed all the roles while a chorus sang the story. The dancer might use more than one mask, and on occasion two or even three dancers performed.

But Romans *did* write plays that are comedies and tragedies, and we will now glance at these. The two chief writers of comedy are Plautus (c. 254–184 B.C.E.) and Terence (c. 190–159 B.C.E.), and though their names are forever linked, they actually were very different sorts of people—like, say, Laurel and Hardy. But they did share certain qualities. They adapted their plays from Greek New Comedy, which, we will see (page 138), is essentially a comedy of intrigue: It usually shows a young man achieving his goal— for instance outwitting an old man and getting the girl he wants. It thus combines an element of satire (ridicule for those who get in the way of the resourceful youths) and a story of intrigue (getting the girl). In Roman comedy, the names of the characters are

Greek, and the settings are said to be Greek. Although the plots of Plautus and Terence resemble each other, there is a great difference in tone. A traditional comparison holds that Plautus is a blacksmith, Terence a watchmaker. That is, the twenty-one extant plays of Plautus emphasize boisterous fun, whereas the six extant plays of Terence emphasize elegant language and human tolerance.

Titus Macius Plautus ("Titus, the Flatfooted Clown") does not hesitate to allow his characters to step out of character if a laugh can be had. The plays are relatively short by today's standard—they run for about an hour—and they are built chiefly on what today is called situation comedy, with a good deal of physical humor. One situation that the Romans invented is the confusion caused by identical twins; Plautus uses this device in *Menaechmi (The Menaechmus Brothers)*, which is the major source for Shakespeare's *The Comedy of Errors*—and also for a Rodgers and Hart musical, *The Boys from Syracuse* (1938).

Terence—more properly, Publius Terentius Afer—is said to have been a freed slave from Carthage. Six plays are attributed to him, and compared with the plays of Plautus these works are models of subtlety and restraint, with elegant language and with relatively little physical humor. Further, the follies of Terence's characters are not boisterously exposed and subjected to guffaws, but are treated genially and sympathetically. His tolerance is evident in what is his most famous line: "I am a man; nothing human is alien to me" *(Homo sum; humani nil a me alienum puto)*. Consider, too, some of his other famous lines: "Moderation in all things"; "Lovers' quarrels are the renewal of love"; "Time removes distress"; "Extreme law is often extreme injustice"; "Nothing is said that has not been said before." It is easy to see why schoolteachers have liked Terence. One unexpected product of Terence's influence is the work of Hrotsvitha of Gandersheim (c. 935–73), a German noblewoman who lived within a religious order, though she was not a nun. Hrotsvitha wrote six prose plays in Latin about martyrs and the triumph of virginity, as examples of what a Christian Terence might write. Virtually all scholars agree that she did not intend her plays for performance.

In Roman tragedy, Seneca (c. 4 B.C.E.–65 C.E.) is the chief name. Ten plays are ascribed to him, including a *Medea* (derived from Euripides) and an *Oedipus* (derived from Sophocles). Although the plays are derived from Greek themes, they are distinctive, partly because of a greater emphasis on the supernatural (ghosts and dreams) and especially on madness. Curiously, the mad speeches are combined with clever epigrams and with elaborate rhetorical effects. In the view of many readers—the plays are rarely staged—these tragedies dwell too lovingly on the morbid, and for all of their passionate assertion they are lacking in drama. On the other hand, Seneca has appealed to serious students who emphasize the drama's roots in ancient ritual and who believe that drama should shock an audience into primal feelings rather than merely entertain an audience. Although the issue has not been settled, it is generally believed that Seneca's plays were intended for recitation to a small private audience rather than for stage production. In any case, because in the sixteenth and seventeenth century Seneca was much read in the schools, these works had an enormous influence on the drama, evident not only in a minor work such as Shakespeare's *Titus Andronicus* but also in *Hamlet*.

A few words should be said about the Roman stage. There is evidence that in the third century B.C.E. the Romans sometimes erected temporary wood stages, but a permanent theater was not built until very late, 55 B.C.E., when Pompey the Great ordered that a stone theater be built. It no longer stands, but evidence indicates that it was semicircular, following the tradition of the Greek theater. In the next few decades several other theaters were built, including the Theater of Marcellus (13 B.C.E.), which seated twenty thousand spectators, and whose walls still stand in

Rome. Theaters in the Roman Empire were Greek in inspiration, but instead of being built into a hillside they were built upward, on flat terrain. Thus, the *scaena* (based on the Greek *skene* or scene-building, which provided a background for the action) and the *cavea* (the auditorium) were fully surrounded. The area in front of the *scaena* was known as the *proscaena*, which gives us our word *proscenium*. The chorus was used only rarely, and so there was no need for the *orchestra* (dancing place) of the Greek theater. Perhaps spectators in the enclosed Roman theater had a heightened feeling of being in a world apart from the real world. The opening shows at Pompey's theater consisted not of plays but of the slaughter of exotic animals. Later entertainments in Roman theaters included throwing Christian martyrs to wild beasts. Not surprisingly, when Christianity triumphed in Rome, the theater was seen as an enemy, and the theaters fell into disuse.

Ancient Greek Drama Today

The ancient plays are alive and well. In Greece they are regularly performed at festivals in the surviving ancient theaters, notably at Epidaurus and Herodes. Of course, they are also performed in modern Greek theaters as well as elsewhere in Europe, and in fact throughout the world.

Speaking broadly, when the plays are staged in ancient theaters in Greece, an effort is made to produce the plays in a manner that at least somewhat resembles the manner in which they were originally done—or were thought to have been done, since we really know very little about the original productions. This means that the costuming is classical, masks may be used, the chorus is large, and there is music and dancing. But outside of Greece, where directors do not feel obligated to present the national heritage, they are less likely to aim at what has been called "museum drama."

At least five chief decisions (beyond the choice of a play and of a translation) must be made.

1. Will masks be used? If so, full masks (which most actors find very uncomfortable), or half-masks (but what is the point of a half-mask)?
2. How will the play be costumed? Here the choices usually come to these: (a) in costumes that more or less evoke ancient Greece; (b) in contemporary dress; (c) in a period other than ancient and other than contemporary, for instance the Victorian period; (d) in some sort of unidentifiable but perhaps evocative and seemingly archetypal dress, that is, outfits that no one ever wore, but that seem expressive of tragedy.
3. What sort of set will be used? Obviously this decision is closely connected with the decision about costuming. If one costumes the play in ancient Greek garments, probably one will want a set that evokes the ancient world, perhaps the façade of a palace or a temple. But there are other possibilities, for instance a nonrepresentational background.
4. How many people will make up the chorus? It is thought that Sophocles and Euripides used choruses of fifteen, but most modern productions reduce the chorus to a handful, often three. A large chorus makes sense in an enormous theater, but in a theater that seats only a few hundred spectators the stage is not likely to be large enough to accommodate a chorus of fifteen. On the other hand, when the number is diminished the grandeur of the play lessens. Whatever the number, should the chorus speak in unison or should the lines be distributed among the performers? In the interest of intelligibility, most modern productions distribute the lines rather than have them spoken in unison.
5. Will the chorus sing and dance, and, if so, what kinds of music and what kinds of dances will be used? Almost nothing is known about ancient music, though it seems a flute was certainly used in dramatic performances, and probably percussion instruments were also used. Even less is known for sure about ancient dance. Some modern productions use certain performers to speak the lines of the chorus, and use others—trained dancers—to dance. The dances are likely to be either something that can pass for ancient dance, or, on the other hand, they may be obviously contemporary. What is sometimes thought to be a middle position is to use Greek folk dances.

The theater at Epidaurus is the best preserved ancient Greek theater, though the *skene* ("scene-building" or stage house) at the left is in ruins. Although the evidence is scant, it seems to indicate that the fifth-century *skene* had two stories, was about twelve feet deep, and had a double door in the center. A few comedies call for more than one point of entrance, so there probably were additional (less prominent) doors near each end of the *skene*. Whether there was an elevated stage in the fifth century has been much disputed, but the one surviving contemporary picture (about 420 B.C.E.) of actors and an audience shows a low stage, connected to the orchestra by four steps. The actors perform on the stage, and the chorus sings and dances in the orchestra. It is thought that during the strophe the chorus danced around the orchestra to the right, during the antistrophe it danced to the left, and during the epode it stood still. A reference to "the double dance" is taken to mean that two half-choruses faced each other.

Two photographs of the production of *Oedipus* directed by Tyrone Guthrie at Stratford, Canada, in 1954. As Guthrie says in the essay that we reprint on pages 83–84, Oedipus's mask was gold (the sun), Jocasta's was silver (the moon), and Creon's was bronze. The chorus wore earth-colored clothes of varying hues of grayish greens and grayish browns.

Two pictures of Laurence Olivier as Oedipus, in the Old Vic production of 1945. The columns of course echo Greek architecture, and the costuming is vaguely "classical," though in its colorfulness it departs from the popular idea of classical garb.

A German production of *Oedipus*, directed by G. R. Sellner, in Darmstadt, 1952. Here no attempt is made to evoke the Greek world; the scenery is abstract, and although masks are used, they are clearly not used in the ancient Greek manner. Costumes and sets that more accurately represented the ancient world would (in the director's view) serve only to limit the audience's response; they might be archaeologically acceptable but they would fail to connect with some sort of universal dream-world archetype.

Jane Lapotaire as Antigonê, in a production directed by John Burgess and Peter Gill in London in 1984. The floor was bare, and the back wall was unadorned but vaguely suggested a stone building. Modern dress was used, but of the 1930s, thus distancing the play a bit from the contemporary world. The chorus (for the most part seated on kitchen chairs) wore gray suits and felt hats with black bands, and they held walking sticks; the guards wore berets and khaki uniforms, and Ismene and Antigonê wore frocks and toques (red for Antigonê, blue for Ismene). For a review of this production, see pages 107–108.

During World War II Jean Anouilh wrote a version of Antigonê, which was staged in Paris under the German occupation. Members of the French Resistance are said to have seen themselves as Antigonê, but apparently the Germans did not mind being thought of as Creon, since Creon is presented quite sympathetically in this version. In 1946 the play was performed in New York, with Katherine Cornell in the role of Antigonê. As in Paris, the actors wore contemporary formal clothing. In this photograph, the figure at the left is the Narrator, Anouilh's substitution for the Greek chorus. Antigonê is seated in the center; Haemon and Ismene stand at the right.

Diana Rigg, in a blood-red dress, as Medea, in a production of 1992–94. The set (discussed on pages 131 and 134), consisting of massive rusting squares that clanged when struck, was abstract but nevertheless suggested a prison. In the photo below Medea talks with Aegeus; in the background is the chorus of three women. In the picture at the left Medea is about to enter the palace, shortly before the end of the play.

Judith Anderson, widely regarded as the greatest tragic actress of the American stage, played Medea in 1947. In this picture she is seated on the palace steps. The set is both realistic and abstract—it is recognizably a palace but instead of being an archaeologically accurate reproduction it seeks to evoke a world of primitive forces.

Sophocles

Sophocles (c. 496–406 B.C.E.), the son of a wealthy Athenian, is one of the three Greek tragic writers whose work survives. (The other two are Aeschylus and Euripides.) Of Sophocles's more than one hundred twenty plays, we have seven. The exact dates of most of Sophocles's plays are unknown. *Antigonê* probably was written about 441 B.C.E.; *Oedipus the King,* which deals with earlier material concerning the House of Oedipus, was written later, about 430 B.C.E. Some twenty-five years later, when he was almost ninety, Sophocles wrote *Oedipus at Colonus,* dramatizing Oedipus's last deeds.

■■■■■■■■■■■■■■■

COMMENTARY ON *OEDIPUS REX*

Classroom discussions of *Oedipus Rex,* like discussions in books, are usually devoted to the problem of fate versus free will. Students (who ought to be filled with youthful confidence in the freedom of the will) generally argue that Oedipus is fated; instructors (who ought to be old enough to know that the inexplicable and unwilled often comes about) generally argue that Oedipus is free and performs of his own accord the actions that fulfill the prophecy. Prophecy or prediction or foreknowledge, instructors patiently explain, is not the same as foreordination. The physician who says that the newborn babe will never develop mentally beyond the age of six is predicting, not ordaining or willing. So, the argument usually runs, the oracle who predicted that Oedipus would kill his father and marry his mother was not *causing* Oedipus to do these things but was simply, in his deep knowledge, announcing what a man like Oedipus would do. But that may be too sophisticated a reading, and a reading that derives from the much later European view of human beings as creatures who can shape their destiny. It is hard for us—especially if the tragedy we know best is Shakespeare's—to recognize the possibility of another sort of tragic drama that does not relate the individual's suffering to his or her own actions but that postulates some sort of necessity that works within an individual.

Whatever the merits of these views, the spectators or readers undeniably already know, when they set out to see or read the play, that Oedipus must end wretchedly. The story is known to all, fixed in Sophocles's text, and Oedipus cannot extricate himself from it. Something along these lines was suggested in the middle of the fourth century B.C.E. when a Greek comic dramatist complained that the comic writer's task was harder than the tragic writer's: "Tragedy has the best of it since the stories are known beforehand to the spectators even before anyone speaks; so the poet only has to remind them. For if I merely say the name Oedipus, they all know the rest—his father Laius, mother Iocasta, daughters, who his sons are, what will happen to him, what he did."

Nonetheless, the tragic writer's task was not quite so easy. First of all, we have Aristotle's statement that "even the known legends are known to only a few," and, second, we have evidence that the tragic writer could vary the details. In Homer's *Iliad* we read that Oedipus continued to rule even after his dreadful history was known, but Sophocles exiles him. And a fragment of Euripides indicates that his Oedipus was blinded by Laius's followers, whereas Sophocles's Oedipus blinds himself. These are details, but they are rather important ones. Probably the ancient Greeks knew the legends in a rough sort of way, as most of us know the Bible or some nuggets of Roman history. Robert Frost and Archibald MacLeish have both drawn from the Book of Job, but their works are enormously different. Writers today who use Job can scarcely omit Job's great suffering, and they can assume that their audience will know that Job had a wife and some comforters, but they are free to go on from there.

Still, the main outline of Oedipus's life must have been fixed, and for us even the details are forever fixed in Sophocles's version. (We know that the Greeks wrote a dozen plays about Oedipus's discovery of his terrible actions, but only Sophocles's survives.) This means that as we read or watch it, each speech has for us a meaning somewhat different from the meaning it has for the speaker and the audience on the stage. Oedipus says he will hunt out the polluted man; we know, as he and the Thebans do not, that *he* is the hunted as well as the hunter. Oedipus says the killer of King Laius may well try to strike at him; we know that Oedipus will find himself out and will strike out his own eyes. A messenger from Corinth tries to allay Oedipus's fears, but instead increases them.

What we are talking about, of course, is tragic irony, or Sophoclean irony, in which words and deeds have a larger meaning for the spectator and the reader than for the dramatis personae. Because Sophocles so persistently uses this device of giving speeches a second, awesome significance, we feel the plot is a masterpiece of construction in which Oedipus is caught. If ever a man has confidence in his will, it is Oedipus, but if ever a man moves toward a predicted point, it is Oedipus. He solved the riddle of the sphinx (by himself, without the aid of birds, he somewhat hybristically boasts), but he does not yet know himself. That knowledge comes later, when he commendably pursued the quest for Laius's slayer and inevitably found himself. The thing is as inevitable as the history described in the sphinx's riddle, which in J. T. Sheppard's version goes like this:

A thing there is whose voice is one;
Whose feet are four and two and three.

So mutable a thing is none
That moves in earth or sky or sea.
When on most feet this thing doth go,
Its strength is weakest and its pace most slow.

This is the history of humanity. In Sophocles's time people grew from crawling infancy, through erect adulthood, to bent old age supported by a stick, and so they do in our time, as the child's rhyme still claims:

Walks on four feet,
On two feet, on three,
The more feet it walks on,
The weaker it be.

There was scarcely an infant weaker than the maimed Oedipus; there was scarcely a man stronger than King Oedipus at his height; and there was scarcely a man more in need of a staff than the blind exile. However free each of his actions—and we can only feel that the figure we see on the stage is acting freely when he abuses Teiresias and Creon—Oedipus was by fate a human being, and thus the largest pattern of his life could be predicted easily enough.

OEDIPUS REX
Sophocles

An English Version by Dudley Fitts and Robert Fitzgerald

LIST OF CHARACTERS

OEDIPUS

A PRIEST

CREON

TEIRESIAS

IOCASTÊ

MESSENGER

SHEPHERD OF LAÏOS

SECOND MESSENGER

CHORUS OF THEBAN ELDERS

SCENE

Before the palace of Oedipus, King of Thebes. A central door and two lateral doors open onto a platform which runs the length of the façade. On the platform, right and left, are altars; and three steps lead down into the "orchestra," or chorus-ground. At the beginning of the action these steps are crowded by Suppliants who have brought branches and chaplets of olive leaves and who lie in various attitudes of despair. Oedipus enters.

PROLOGUE

OEDIPUS.

    My children, generations of the living

    In the line of Kadmos,° nursed at his ancient hearth;

    Why have you strewn yourselves before these altars

    In supplication, with your boughs and garlands?

5   The breath of incense rises from the city

    With a sound of prayer and lamentation.

                          Children,

    I would not have you speak through messengers,

    And therefore I have come myself to hear you—

    I, Oedipus, who bear the famous name.

10   (*To a Priest.*) You, there, since you are eldest in the company,

    Speak for them all, tell me what preys upon you,

    Whether you come in dread, or crave some blessing:

    Tell me, and never doubt that I will help you

    In every way I can; I should be heartless

15   Were I not moved to find you suppliant here.

PRIEST.

    Great Oedipus, O powerful King of Thebes!

    You see how all the ages of our people

    Cling to your altar steps: here are boys

    Who can barely stand alone, and here are priests

20   By weight of age, as I am a priest of God,

    And young men chosen from those yet unmarried;

    As for the others, all that multitude,

    They wait with olive chaplets in the squares,

    At the two shrines of Pallas,° and where Apollo°

    Speaks in the glowing embers.

                        Your own eyes   25

    Must tell you: Thebes is in her extremity

    And cannot lift her head from the surge of death.

    A rust consumes the buds and fruits of the earth;

    The herds are sick; children die unborn,

    And labor is vain. The god of plague and pyre   30

    Raids like detestable lightning through the city,

    And all the house of Kadmos is laid waste,

    All emptied, and all darkened: Death alone

    Battens upon the misery of Thebes.

    You are not one of the immortal gods, we know;   35

    Yet we have come to you to make our prayer

    As to the man of all men best in adversity

    And wisest in the ways of God. You saved us

    From the Sphinx,° that flinty singer, and the tribute

    We paid to her so long; yet you were never   40

    Better informed than we, nor could we teach you:

    It was some god breathed in you to set us free.

---

2 Kadmos mythical founder of Thebes

24 Pallas Athena, goddess of wisdom, protectress of Athens **Apollo** god of light and healing   **39 Sphinx** a monster (body of a lion, wings of a bird, face of a woman) who asked the riddle, "What goes on four legs in the morning, two at noon, and three in the evening?" and who killed those who could not answer. When Oedipus responded correctly that man crawls on all fours in infancy, walks upright in maturity, and uses a staff in old age, the Sphinx destroyed herself.

45 Therefore, O mighty King, we turn to you:
Find us our safety, find us a remedy,
Whether by counsel of the gods or the men.
A king of wisdom tested in the past
Can act in a time of troubles, and act well.
Noblest of men, restore
Life to your city! Think how all men call you
50 Liberator for your triumph long ago;
Ah, when your years of kingship are remembered,
Let them not say *We rose, but later fell*—
Keep the State from going down in the storm!
Once, years ago, with happy augury,
55 You brought us fortune; be the same again!
No man questions your power to rule the land:
But rule over men, not over a dead city!
Ships are only hulls, citadels are nothing,
When no life moves in the empty passageways.

OEDIPUS.
60 Poor children! You may be sure I know
All that you longed for in your coming here.
I know that you are deathly sick; and yet,
Sick as you are, not one is as sick as I.
Each of you suffers in himself alone
65 His anguish, not another's; but my spirit
Groans for the city, for myself, for you.

I was not sleeping, you are not waking me.
No, I have been in tears for a long while
And in my restless thought walked many ways.
70 In all my search, I found one helpful course,
And that I have taken: I have sent Creon,
Son of Menoikeus, brother of the Queen,
To Delphi, Apollo's place of revelation,
To learn there, if he can,
75 What act or pledge of mine may save the city.
I have counted the days, and now, this very day,
I am troubled, for he has overstayed his time.
What is he doing? He has been gone too long.
Yet whenever he comes back, I should do ill
80 To scant whatever hint the god may give.

PRIEST.
It is a timely promise. At this instant
They tell me Creon is here.

OEDIPUS.   O Lord Apollo!
May his news be fair as his face is radiant!

PRIEST.
It could not be otherwise: he is crowned with bay,
The chaplet is thick with berries.

85 OEDIPUS.   We shall soon know;
He is near enough to hear us now.

Enter Creon.

                              O Prince:
Brother: son of Menoikeus:
What answer do you bring us from the god?

CREON.
It is favorable. I can tell you, great afflictions
Will turn out well, if they are taken well.   90

OEDIPUS.
What was the oracle? These vague words
Leave me still hanging between hope and fear.

CREON.
Is it your pleasure to hear me with all these
Gathered around us? I am prepared to speak,
But should we not go in?

OEDIPUS.   Let them all hear it.   95
It is for them I suffer, more than myself.

CREON.
Then I will tell you what I heard at Delphi.

In plain words
The god commands us to expel from the land of Thebes
An old defilement that it seems we shelter.   100
It is a deathly thing, beyond expiation.
We must not let it feed upon us longer.

OEDIPUS.
What defilement? How shall we rid ourselves of it?

CREON.
By exile or death, blood for blood. It was
Murder that brought the plague-wind on the city.   105

OEDIPUS.
Murder of whom? Surely the god has named him?

CREON.
My lord: long ago Laïos was our king,
Before you came to govern us.

OEDIPUS.   I know;
I learned of him from others; I never saw him.

CREON.
He was murdered; and Apollo commands us now   110
To take revenge upon whoever killed him.

OEDIPUS.
Upon whom? Where are they? Where shall we find a clue
To solve that crime, after so many years?

CREON.
Here in this land, he said.

                              If we make enquiry,
We may touch things that otherwise escape us.   115

OEDIPUS.
Tell me: Was Laïos murdered in his house,
Or in the fields, or in some foreign country?

CREON.
He said he planned to make a pilgrimage.
He did not come home again.

OEDIPUS.   And was there no one,
No witness, no companion, to tell what happened?   120

CREON.
They were all killed but one, and he got away
So frightened that he could remember one thing only.

OEDIPUS.
What was that one thing? One may be the key

To everything, if we resolve to use it.

CREON.

125   He said that a band of highwaymen attacked them,
      Outnumbered them, and overwhelmed the King.

OEDIPUS.

      Strange, that a highwayman should be so daring—
      Unless some faction here bribed him to do it.

CREON.

      We thought of that. But after Laïos' death
130   New troubles arose and we had no avenger.

OEDIPUS.

      What troubles could prevent your hunting down the
            killers?

CREON.

      The riddling Sphinx's song
      Made us deaf to all mysteries but her own

OEDIPUS.

      Then once more I must bring what is dark to light.
135   It is most fitting that Apollo shows,
      As you do, this compunction for the dead.
      You shall see how I stand by you, as I should,
      To avenge the city and the city's god,
      And not as though it were for some distant friend,
140   But for my own sake, to be rid of evil.
      Whoever killed King Laïos might—who knows?—
      Decide at any moment to kill me as well.
      By avenging the murdered king I protect myself.
      Come, then, my children: leave the altar steps,
      Lift up your olive boughs!
145   One of you go
      And summon the people of Kadmos to gather here.
      I will do all that I can; you may tell them that.

                                        (*Exit a Page.*)

      So, with the help of God,
      We shall be saved—or else indeed we are lost.

PRIEST.

150   Let us rise, children. It was for this we came,
      And now the King has promised it himself.
      Phoibos° has sent us an oracle; may he descend
      Himself to save us and drive out the plague.

      Exeunt Oedipus and Creon into the palace by the central
      door. The Priest and the Suppliants disperse right and left.
      After a short pause the Chorus enters the orchestra.

PÁRODOS

Strophe 1

CHORUS.

      What is God singing in his profound
      Delphi of gold and shadow?

152 Phoibos Phoebus Apollo, the sun god

What oracle for Thebes, the sunwhipped city?
Fear unjoints me, the roots of my heart tremble.
Now I remember, O Healer, your power, and wonder;   5
Will you send doom like a sudden cloud, or weave it
Like nightfall of the past?
Speak, speak to us, issue of holy sound:
Dearest to our expectancy: be tender!

Antistrophe 1

Let me pray to Athenê, the immortal daughter of Zeus,   10
And to Artemis her sister
Who keeps her famous throne in the market ring,
And to Apollo, bowman at the far butts of heaven—

O gods, descend! Like three streams leap against
The fires of our grief, the fires of darkness;   15
Be swift to bring us rest!
As in the old time from the brilliant house
Of air you stepped to save us, come again!

Strophe 2

Now our afflictions have no end,
Now all our stricken host lies down   20
And no man fights off death with his mind;

The noble plowland bears no grain,
And groaning mothers cannot bear—
See, how our lives like birds take wing,
Like sparks that fly when a fire soars,   25
To the shore of the god of evening.

Antistrophe 2

The plague burns on, it is pitiless
Though pallid children laden with death
Lie unwept in the stony ways,
And old gray women by every path   30
Flock to the strand about the altars

There to strike their breasts and cry
Worship of Phoibos in wailing prayers:
Be kind, God's golden child!

Strophe 3

There are no swords in this attack by fire,   35
No shields, but we are ringed with cries.
Send the besieger plunging from our homes
Into the vast sea-room of the Atlantic
Or into the waves that foam eastward of Thrace—
For the day ravages what the night spares—   40

Destroy our enemy, lord of the thunder!
Let him be riven by lightning from heaven!

Antistrophe 3

Phoibos Apollo, stretch the sun's bowstring,
That golden cord, until it sing for us,
Flashing arrows in heaven!
45   Artemis, Huntress,
Race with flaring lights upon our mountains!
O scarlet god, O golden-banded brow,
O Theban Bacchos° in a storm of Maenads,°

Enter Oedipus, center.

Whirl upon Death, that all the Undying hate!
50   Come with blinding cressets, come in joy!

SCENE 1

OEDIPUS.
Is this your prayer? It may be answered. Come,
Listen to me, act as the crisis demands,
And you shall have relief from all these evils.

Until now I was a stranger to this tale,
5   As I had been a stranger to the crime.
Could I track down the murderer without a clue?
But now, friends,
As one who became a citizen after the murder,
I make this proclamation to all Thebans:
10   If any man knows by whose hand Laïos, son of Labdakos,
Met his death, I direct that man to tell me everything,
No matter what he fears for having so long withheld it.
Let it stand as promised that no further trouble
Will come to him, but he may leave the land in safety.

15   Moreover: If anyone knows the murderer to be foreign,
Let him not keep silent: he shall have his reward from me.
However, if he does conceal it, if any man
Fearing for his friend or for himself disobeys this edict,
Hear what I propose to do:

20   I solemnly forbid the people of this country,
Where power and throne are mine, ever to receive that
        man
Or speak to him, no matter who he is, or let him
Join in sacrifice, lustration, or in prayer.
I decree that he be driven from every house,

25   Being, as he is, corruption itself to us: the Delphic
Voice of Zeus has pronounced this revelation.
Thus I associate myself with the oracle

And take the side of the murdered king.
As for the criminal, I pray to God—
Whether it be a lurking thief, or one of a number—   30
I pray that that man's life be consumed in evil and
        wretchedness.
And as for me, this curse applies no less
If it should turn out that the culprit is my guest here,
Sharing my hearth.
                         You have heard the penalty.   35
I lay it on you now to attend to this
For my sake, for Apollo's, for the sick
Sterile city that heaven has abandoned.
Suppose the oracle had given you no command:
Should this defilement go uncleansed for ever?
You should have found the murderer: your king,   40
A noble king, had been destroyed!
                              Now I,
Having the power that he held before me,
Having his bed, begetting children there
Upon his wife, as he would have, had he lived—
Their son would have been my children's brother,   45
If Laïos had had luck in fatherhood!
(But surely ill luck rushed upon his reign)—
I say I take the son's part, just as though
I were his son, to press the fight for him
And see it won! I'll find the hand that brought   50
Death to Labdakos' and Polydoros' child,
Heir of Kadmos' and Agenor's line.
And as for those who fail me,
May the gods deny them the fruit of the earth,
Fruit of the womb, and may they rot utterly!   55
Let them be wretched as we are wretched, and worse!

For you, for loyal Thebans, and for all
Who find my actions right, I pray the favor
Of justice, and of all the immortal gods.
CHORAGOS.°
Since I am under oath, my lord, I swear   60
I did not do the murder, I cannot name
The murderer. Might not the oracle
That has ordained the search tell where to find him?
OEDIPUS.
An honest question. But no man in the world
Can make the gods do more than the gods will.   65
CHORAGOS.
There is one last expedient—
OEDIPUS.   Tell me what it is.
Though it seem slight, you must not hold it back.
CHORAGOS.
A lord clairvoyant to the lord Apollo,
As we all know, is the skilled Teiresias.
One might learn much about this from him, Oedipus.   70

---

48 Bacchos Dionysos, god of wine, thus scarlet-faced   **48 Mae-nads** Dionysos's female attendants

60 Choragos leader of the Chorus

OEDIPUS.
    I am not wasting time:
    Creon spoke of this, and I have sent for him—
    Twice, in fact; it is strange that he is not here.
CHORAGOS.
    The other matter—that old report—seems useless.
OEDIPUS.
75   Tell me. I am interested in all reports.
CHORAGOS.
    The King was said to have been killed by highwaymen.
OEDIPUS.
    I know. But we have no witnesses to that.
CHORAGOS.
    If the killer can feel a particle of dread,
    Your curse will bring him out of hiding!
OEDIPUS.   No.
80   The man who dared that act will fear no curse.

Enter the blind seer Teiresias led by a Page.

CHORAGOS.
    But there is one man who may detect the criminal.
    This is Teiresias, this is the holy prophet
    In whom, alone of all men, truth was born.
OEDIPUS.
85   Teiresias: seer: student of mysteries,
    Of all that's taught and all that no man tells,
    Secrets of Heaven and secrets of the earth:
    Blind though you are, you know the city lies
    Sick with plague; and from this plague, my lord,
    We find that you alone can guard or save us.

90   Possibly you did not hear the messengers?
    Apollo, when we sent to him,
    Sent us back word that this great pestilence
    Would lift, but only if we established clearly
    The identity of those who murdered Laïos.
    They must be killed or exiled.
95   Can you use
    Birdflight or any art of divination
    To purify yourself, and Thebes, and me
    From this contagion? We are in your hands.
    There is no fairer duty
100   Than that of helping others in distress.
TEIRESIAS.
    How dreadful knowledge of the truth can be
    When there's no help in truth! I knew this well,
    But did not act on it: else I should not have come.
OEDIPUS.
    What is troubling you? Why are your eyes so cold?
TEIRESIAS.
105   Let me go home. Bear your own fate, and I'll
    Bear mine. It is better so: trust what I say.
OEDIPUS.
    What you say is ungracious and unhelpful
    To your native country. Do not refuse to speak.

TEIRESIAS.
    When it comes to speech, your own is neither temperate
    Nor opportune. I wish to be more prudent.   110
OEDIPUS.
    In God's name, we all beg you—
TEIRESIAS.   You are all ignorant.
    No; I will never tell you what I know.
    Now it is my misery; then, it would be yours.
OEDIPUS.
    What! You do know something, and will not tell us?
    You would betray us all and wreck the State?   115
TEIRESIAS.
    I do not intend to torture myself, or you.
    Why persist in asking? You will not persuade me.
OEDIPUS.
    What a wicked man you are! You'd try a stone's
    Patience! Out with it! Have you no feeling at all?
TEIRESIAS.
    You call me unfeeling. If you could only see   120
    The nature of your feelings . . .
OEDIPUS.   Why,
    Who would not feel as I do? Who could endure
    Your arrogance toward the city?
TEIRESIAS.   What does it matter!
    Whether I speak or not, it is bound to come.
OEDIPUS.
    Then, if "it" is bound to come, you are bound to tell me.   125
TEIRESIAS.
    No, I will not go on. Rage as you please.
OEDIPUS.
    Rage? Why not!
                            And I'll tell you what I think:
    You planned it, you had it done, you all but
    Killed him with your own hands: if you had eyes,
    I'd say the crime was yours, and yours alone.   130
TEIRESIAS.
    So? I charge you, then,
    Abide by the proclamation you have made.
    From this day forth
    Never speak again to these men or to me;
    You yourself are the pollution of this country.   135
OEDIPUS.
    You dare say that! Can you possibly think you have
    Some way of going free, after such insolence?
TEIRESIAS.
    I have gone free. It is the truth sustains me.
OEDIPUS.
    Who taught you shamelessness? It was not your craft.
TEIRESIAS.
    You did. You made me speak. I did not want to.   140
OEDIPUS.
    Speak what? Let me hear it again more clearly.
TEIRESIAS.
    Was it not clear before? Are you tempting me?

OEDIPUS.
　　I did not understand it. Say it again.
TEIRESIAS.
　　I say that you are the murderer whom you seek.
OEDIPUS.
145　　Now twice you have spat out infamy. You'll pay for it!
TEIRESIAS.
　　Would you care for more? Do you wish to be really
　　　　angry?
OEDIPUS.
　　Say what you will. Whatever you say is worthless.
TEIRESIAS.
　　I say you live in hideous shame with those
　　Most dear to you. You cannot see the evil.
OEDIPUS.
150　　It seems you can go on mouthing like this for ever.
TEIRESIAS.
　　I can, if there is power in truth.
OEDIPUS.   There is:
　　But not for you, not for you,
　　You sightless, witless, senseless, mad old man!
TEIRESIAS.
　　You are the madman. There is no one here
155　　Who will not curse you soon, as you curse me.
OEDIPUS.
　　You child of endless night! You cannot hurt me
　　Or any other man who sees the sun.
TEIRESIAS.
　　True: it is not from me your fate will come.
　　That lies within Apollo's competence,
　　As it is his concern.
160 OEDIPUS.   Tell me:
　　Are you speaking for Creon, or for yourself?
TEIRESIAS.
　　Creon is no threat. You weave your own doom.
OEDIPUS.
　　Wealth, power, craft of statesmanship!
　　Kingly position, everywhere admired!
165　　What savage envy is stored up against these,
　　If Creon, whom I trusted, Creon my friend,
　　For this great office which the city once
　　Put in my hands unsought—if for this power
　　Creon desires in secret to destroy me!

170　　He has brought this decrepit fortune-teller, this
　　Collector of dirty pennies, this prophet fraud—
　　Why, he is no more clairvoyant than I am!
　　　　　　　　　　　　　　　　　　　　Tell us:
　　Has your mystic mummery ever approached the
　　　　truth?
　　When that hellcat the Sphinx was performing here,
175　　What help were you to these people?
　　Her magic was not for the first man who came along:
　　It demanded a real exorcist. Your birds—

What good were they? or the gods, for the matter of that?
But I came by,
Oedipus, the simple man, who knows nothing—   180
I thought it out for myself, no birds helped me!
And this is the man you think you can destroy,
That you may be close to Creon when he's king!
Well, you and your friend Creon, it seems to me,
Will suffer most. If you were not an old man,   185
You would have paid already for your plot.
CHORAGOS.
　　We cannot see that his words or yours
　　Have spoken except in anger, Oedipus,
　　And of anger we have no need. How can God's will
　　Be accomplished best? That is what most concerns us.   190
TEIRESIAS.
　　You are a king. But where argument's concerned
　　I am your man, as much a king as you.
　　I am not your servant, but Apollo's.
　　I have no need of Creon to speak for me.

　　Listen to me. You mock my blindness, do you?   195
　　But I say that you, with both your eyes, are blind:
　　You cannot see the wretchedness of your life,
　　Not in whose house you live, no, nor with whom.
　　Who are your father and mother? Can you tell me?
　　You do not even know the blind wrongs   200
　　That you have done them, on earth and in the world
　　　　below.
　　But the double lash of your parents' curse will whip you
　　Out of this land some day, with only night
　　Upon your precious eyes.
　　Your cries then—where will they not be heard?   205
　　What fastness of Kithairon° will not echo them?
　　And that bridal-descant of yours—you'll know it then,
　　The song they sang when you came here to Thebes
　　And found your misguided berthing.
　　All this, and more, that you cannot guess at now,   210
　　Will bring you to yourself among your children.
　　Be angry, then. Curse Creon. Curse my words.
　　I tell you, no man that walks upon the earth
　　Shall be rooted out more horribly than you.
OEDIPUS.
　　Am I to bear this from him?—Damnation   215
　　Take you! Out of this place! Out of my sight!
TEIRESIAS.
　　I would not have come at all if you had not
　　　　asked me.
OEDIPUS.
　　Could I have told that you'd talk nonsense, that
　　You'd come here to make a fool of yourself, and
　　　　of me?

206 fastness of Kithairon stronghold in a mountain near Thebes

TEIRESIAS.
220   A fool? Your parents thought me sane enough.
OEDIPUS.
    My parents again!—Wait: who were my parents?
TEIRESIAS.
    This day will give you a father, and break your
        heart.
OEDIPUS.
    Your infantile riddles! Your damned abracadabra!
TEIRESIAS.
    You were a great man once at solving riddles.
OEDIPUS.
225   Mock me with that if you like; you will find it true.
TEIRESIAS.
    It was true enough. It brought about your ruin.
OEDIPUS.
    But if it saved this town.
TEIRESIAS (to the Page).   Boy, give me your hand.
OEDIPUS.
    Yes, boy; lead him away.
                        —While you are here
    We can do nothing. Go; leave us in peace.
TEIRESIAS.
230   I will go when I have said what I have to say.
    How can you hurt me? And I tell you again:
    The man you have been looking for all this time,
    The damned man, the murderer of Laïos,
    That man is in Thebes. To your mind he is foreign-
        born,
235   But it will soon be shown that he is a Theban,
    A revelation that will fail to please
                            A blind man
    Who has his eyes now; a penniless man, who is
        rich now;
    And he will go tapping the strange earth with his
        staff;
    To the children with whom he lives now he will be
240   Brother and father—the very same; to her
    Who bore him, son and husband—the very same
    Who came to his father's bed, wet with his father's
        blood.
    Enough. Go think that over.
    If later you find error in what I have said,
245   You may say that I have no skill in prophecy.

    *Exit Teiresias, led by his Page. Oedipus goes into the
    palace.*

ODE 1

Strophe 1

CHORUS.
    The Delphic stone of prophecies
    Remembers ancient regicide

And a still bloody hand.
That killer's hour of flight has come.
He must be stronger than riderless   5
Coursers of untiring wind,
For the son of Zeus° armed with his father's thunder
Leaps in lightning after him;
And the Furies° follow him, the sad Furies.

Antistrophe 1

Holy Parnossos' peak of snow   10
Flashes and blinds that secret man,
That all shall hunt him down:
Though he may roam the forest shade
Like a bull gone wild from pasture
To rage through glooms of stone.   15
Doom comes down on him; flight will not avail him;
For the world's heart calls him desolate,
And the immortal Furies follow, for ever follow.

Strophe 2

But now a wilder thing is heard
From the old man skilled at hearing Fate in   20
    the wingbeat of a bird.
Bewildered as a blown bird, my soul hovers and cannot
    find
Foothold in this debate, or any reason or rest of mind.
But no man ever brought—none can bring
Proof of strife between Thebes' royal house,
Labdakos' line,° and the son of Polybos;°   25
And never until now has any man brought word
Of Laïos dark death staining Oedipus the King.

Antistrophe 2

Divine Zeus and Apollo hold
Perfect intelligence alone of all tales ever told;
And well though this diviner works, he works in his own   30
    night;
No man can judge that rough unknown or trust in
    second sight,
For wisdom changes hands among the wise.
Shall I believe my great lord criminal.
At a raging word that a blind old man let fall?
I saw him, when the carrion woman faced him of old,   35
Prove his heroic mind! These evil words are lies.

---

7 son of Zeus Apollo   9 Furies avenging deities   25 Labdakos'
line family of Laïos   son of Polybos Oedipus (so the Chorus
believes)

SCENE II

CREON.

Men of Thebes:
I am told that heavy accusations
Have been brought against me by King Oedipus.
I am not the kind of man to bear this tamely.

5   If in these present difficulties
He holds me accountable for any harm to him
Through anything I have said or done—why, then,
I do not value life in this dishonor.
It is not as though this rumor touched upon

10   Some private indiscretion. The matter is grave.
The fact is that I am being called disloyal
To the State, to my fellow citizens, to my friends.

CHORAGOS.

He may have spoken in anger, not from his mind.

CREON.

But did you hear him say I was the one

15   Who seduced the old prophet into lying?

CHORAGOS.

The thing was said; I do not know how seriously.

CREON.

But you were watching him! Were his eyes steady?
Did he look like a man in his right mind?

CHORAGOS.   I do not know.
I cannot judge the behavior of great men.
But here is the King himself.

Enter Oedipus.

20

OEDIPUS.   So you dared come back.
Why? How brazen of you to come to my house,
You murderer!
                    Do you think I do not know
That you plotted to kill me, plotted to steal my throne?

25   Tell me, in God's name: am I coward, a fool,
That you should dream you could accomplish this?
A fool who could not see your slippery game?
A coward, not to fight back when I saw it?
You are the fool, Creon, are you not? hoping

30   Without support or friends to get a throne?
Thrones may be won or bought: you could do neither.

CREON.

Now listen to me. You have talked; let me talk, too.
You cannot judge unless you know the facts.

OEDIPUS.

You speak well: there is one fact; but I find it hard
To learn from the deadliest enemy I have.

35 CREON.

That above all I must dispute with you.

OEDIPUS.

That above all I will not hear you deny.

CREON.

If you think there is anything good in being stubborn

Against all reason, then I say you are wrong.

OEDIPUS.

If you think a man can sin against his own kind
And not be punished for it, I say you are mad.   40

CREON.

I agree. But tell me: what have I done to you?

OEDIPUS.

You advised me to send for that wizard, did you not?

CREON.

I did. I should do it again.

OEDIPUS.   Very well. Now tell me:
How long has it been since Laïos—

CREON.   What of Laïos?

OEDIPUS.

Since he vanished in that onset by the road?   45

CREON.

It was long ago, a long time.

OEDIPUS.   And this prophet,
Was he practicing here then?

CREON.   He was; and with honor, as now.

OEDIPUS.

Did he speak of me at that time?

CREON.   He never did;
At least, not when I was present.

OEDIPUS.   But . . . the enquiry?
I suppose you held one?

CREON.   We did, but we learned nothing.   50

OEDIPUS.

Why did the prophet not speak against me then?

CREON.

I do not know; and I am the kind of man
Who holds his tongue when he has no facts to go
    on.

OEDIPUS.

There's one fact that you know, and you could tell it.

CREON.

What fact is that? If I know it, you shall have it.   55

OEDIPUS.

If he were not involved with you, he could not say
That it was I who murdered Laïos.

CREON.

If he says that, you are the one that knows it!—
But now it is my turn to question you.

OEDIPUS.

Put your questions. I am no murderer.   60

CREON.

First, then: You married my sister?

OEDIPUS.   I married your sister.

CREON.

And you rule the kingdom equally with her?

OEDIPUS.

Everything that she wants she has from me.

CREON.

And I am the third, equal to both of you?

OEDIPUS.

That is why I call you a bad friend.   65

CREON.

    No. Reason it out, as I have done.
    Think of this first. Would any sane man prefer
    Power, with all a king's anxieties,
    To that same power and the grace of sleep?

70   Certainly not I.
    I have never longed for the king's power—only his rights.
    Would any wise man differ from me in this?
    As matters stand, I have my way in everything
    With your consent, and no responsibilities.

75   If I were king, I should be a slave to policy.
    How could I desire a scepter more
    Than what is now mine—untroubled influence?
    No, I have not gone mad; I need no honors,
    Except those with the perquisites I have now.

80   I am welcome everywhere; every man salutes me,
    And those who want your favor seek my ear,
    Since I know how to manage what they ask.
    Should I exchange this ease for that anxiety?
    Besides, no sober mind is treasonable.

85   I hate anarchy
    And never would deal with any man who likes it.

    Test what I have said. Go to the priestess
    At Delphi, ask if I quoted her correctly.
    And as for this other thing: if I am found

90   Guilty of treason with Teiresias,
    Then sentence me to death! You have my word
    It is a sentence I should cast my vote for—
    But not without evidence!
                   You do wrong
    When you take good men for bad, bad men for good.

95   A true friend thrown aside—why, life itself
    Is not more precious!
                  In time you will know this well:
    For time, and time alone, will show the just man,
    Though scoundrels are discovered in a day.

CHORAGOS.

    This is well said, and a prudent man would ponder it.

100   Judgments too quickly formed are dangerous.

OEDIPUS.

    But is he not quick in his duplicity?
    And shall I not be quick to parry him?
    Would you have me stand still, hold my peace, and let
    This man win everything, through my inaction?

CREON.

105   And you want—what is it, then? To banish me?

OEDIPUS.

    No, not exile. It is your death I want,
    So that all the world may see what treason means.

CREON.

    You will persist, then? You will not believe me?

OEDIPUS.

    How can I believe you?

CREON.   Then you are a fool.

OEDIPUS.

    To save myself?

CREON.   In justice, think of me.   110

OEDIPUS.

    You are evil incarnate.

CREON.   But suppose that you are wrong?

OEDIPUS.

    Still I must rule.

CREON.   But not if you rule badly.

OEDIPUS.

    O city, city!

CREON.   It is my city, too!

CHORAGOS.

    Now, my lords, be still. I see the Queen,
    Iocastê, coming from her palace chambers;   115
    And it is time she came, for the sake of you both.
    This dreadful quarrel can be resolved through her.

Enter Iocastê.

IOCASTÊ.

    Poor foolish men, what wicked din is this?
    With Thebes sick to death, is it not shameful
    That you should rake some private quarrel up?   120
    (*To Oedipus.*) Come into the house.
                     —And you, Creon,
      go now: Let us have no more of this tumult over nothing.

CREON.

    Nothing? No, sister: what your husband plans for me
    Is one of two great evils: exile or death.

OEDIPUS.

    He is right.
               Why, woman, I have caught him squarely   125
    Plotting against my life.

CREON.   No! Let me die
    Accurst if ever I have wished you harm!

IOCASTÊ.

    Ah, believe it, Oedipus!
    In the name of the gods, respect this oath of his
    For my sake, for the sake of these people here!   130

Strophe 1

CHORAGOS.

    Open your mind to her, my lord. Be ruled
      by her, I beg you!

OEDIPUS.

    What would you have me do?

CHORAGOS.

    Respect Creon's word. He has never spoken like a fool,
    And now he has sworn an oath.

OEDIPUS.
    You know what you ask?
CHORAGOS.   I do.
135 OEPIDUS.   Speak on, then.
CHORAGOS.
    A friend so sworn should not be baited so,
    In blind malice, and without final proof.
OEDIPUS.
    You are aware, I hope, that what you say
    Means death for me, or exile at the least.

Strophe 2

CHORAGOS.
140 No, I swear by Helios,° first in Heaven!
    May I die friendless and accurst,
    The worst of deaths, if ever I meant that!
        It is the withering fields
            That hurt my sick heart:
145   Must we bear all these ills,
            And now your bad blood as well?
OEDIPUS.
    Then let him go. And let me die, if I must,
    Or be driven by him in shame from the land of Thebes.
    It is your unhappiness, and not his talk,
    That touches me.
150   As for him—
    Wherever he is, I will hate him as long as I live.
CREON.
    Ugly in yielding, as you were ugly in rage!
    Natures like yours chiefly torment themselves.
OEDIPUS.
    Can you not go? Can you not leave me?
CREON.   I can.
155 You do not know me; but the city knows me,
    And in its eyes I am just, if not in yours.

                                                (*Exit Creon.*)

Antistrophe 1

CHORAGOS.
    Lady Iocastê, did you not ask the King
        to go to his chambers?
IOCASTÊ.
    First tell me what has happened.
CHORAGOS.
    There was suspicion without evidence; yet it rankled
    As even false charges will.
IOCASTÊ.   On both sides?

140 Helios sun god

CHORAGOS.   On both.
IOCASTÊ.   But   160
    what was said?
CHORAGOS.
    Oh let it rest, let it be done with!
    Have we not suffered enough?
OEDIPUS.
    You see to what your decency has brought you:
    You have made difficulties where my heart saw none.

Antistrophe 2

CHORAGOS.
    Oedipus, it is not once only I have told you—   165
    You must know I should count myself unwise
    To the point of madness, should I now forsake you—
        You, under whose hand,
            In the storm of another time,
        Our dear land sailed out free,   170
            But now stand fast at the helm!
IOCASTÊ.
    In God's name, Oedipus, inform your wife as well:
    Why are you so set in this hard anger?
OEDIPUS.
    I will tell you, for none of these men deserves
    My confidence as you do. It is Creon's work,   175
    His treachery, his plotting against me.
IOCASTÊ.
    Go on, if you can make this clear to me.
OEDIPUS.
    He charges me with the murder of Laïos.
IOCASTÊ.
    Has he some knowledge? Or does he speak from hearsay?
OEDIPUS.
    He would not commit himself to such a charge,   180
    But he has brought in that damnable soothsayer
    To tell his story.
IOCASTÊ.   Set your mind at rest.
    If it is a question of soothsayers, I tell you
    That you will find no man whose craft gives knowledge
    Of the unknowable.
                                  Here is my proof.   185
    An oracle was reported to Laïos once
    (I will not say from Phoibos himself, but from
    His appointed ministers, at any rate)
    That his doom would be death at the hands of his own
        son—
    His son, born of his flesh and of mine!   190

    Now, you remember the story: Laïos was killed
    By marauding strangers where three highways meet;
    But his child had not been three days in this world
    Before the King had pierced the baby's ankles
    And left him to die on a lonely mountainside.   195

Thus, Apollo never caused that child
To kill his father, and it was not Laïos fate
To die at the hands of his son, as he had feared.
This is what prophets and prophecies are worth!
Have no dread of them.
200   It is God himself
Who can show us what he wills, in his own way.

OEDIPUS.
How strange a shadowy memory crossed my mind,
Just now while you were speaking; it chilled my heart.

IOCASTÊ.
What do you mean? What memory do you speak of?

OEDIPUS.
205   If I understand you, Laïos was killed
At a place where three roads meet.

IOCASTÊ.   So it was said;
We have no later story.

OEDIPUS.   Where did it happen?

IOCASTÊ.
Phokis, it is called: at a place where the Theban Way
Divides into the roads towards Delphi and Daulia.

OEDIPUS.
When?

210   IOCASTÊ. We had the news not long before you came
And proved the right to your succession here.

OEDIPUS.
Ah, what net has God been weaving for me?

IOCASTÊ.
Oedipus! Why does this trouble you?

OEDIPUS.   Do not ask me yet.
First, tell me how Laïos looked, and tell me
How old he was.

215   IOCASTÊ.   He was tall, his hair just touched
With white; his form was not unlike your own.

OEDIPUS.
I think that I myself may be accurst
By my own ignorant edict.

IOCASTÊ.   You speak strangely.
It makes me tremble to look at you, my King.

OEDIPUS.
220   I am not sure that the blind man cannot see.
But I should know better if you were to tell me—

IOCASTÊ.
Anything—though I dread to hear you ask it.

OEDIPUS.
Was the King lightly escorted, or did he ride
With a large company, as a ruler should?

IOCASTÊ.
225   There were five men with him in all: one was a herald;
And a single chariot, which he was driving.

OEDIPUS.
Alas, that makes it plain enough!
                          But who—
Who told you how it happened?

IOCASTÊ.   A household servant,
The only one to escape.

OEDIPUS.   And is he still
A servant of ours?

IOCASTÊ.   No; for when he came back at last   230
And found you enthroned in the place of the dead king,
He came to me, touched my hand with his, and begged
That I would send him away to the frontier district
Where only the shepherds go—
As far away from the city as I could send him.   235
I granted his prayer; for although the man was a slave,
He had earned more than this favor at my hands.

OEDIPUS.
Can he be called back quickly?

IOCASTÊ.   Easily.
But why?

OEDIPUS.   I have taken too much upon myself
Without enquiry; therefore I wish to consult him.   240

IOCASTÊ.
Then he shall come.
                     But am I not one also
To whom you might confide these fears of yours!

OEDIPUS.
That is your right; it will not be denied you,
Now least of all; for I have reached a pitch
Of wild foreboding. Is there anyone   245
To whom I should sooner speak?
Polybos of Corinth is my father.
My mother is a Dorian: Meropê.
I grew up chief among the men of Corinth
Until a strange thing happened—   250
Not worth my passion, it may be, but strange.

At a feast, a drunken man maundering in his cups
Cries out that I am not my father's son!

I contained myself that night, though I felt anger
And a sinking heart. The next day I visited   255
My father and mother, and questioned them. They
     stormed,
Calling it all the slanderous rant of a fool;
And this relieved me. Yet the suspicion
Remained always aching in my mind;
I knew there was talk; I could not rest;   260
And finally, saying nothing to my parents,
I went to the shrine at Delphi.
The god dismissed my question without reply;
He spoke of other things.
                     Some were clear,
Full of wretchedness, dreadful, unbearable: 265
As, that I should lie with my own mother, breed
Children from whom all men would turn their eyes;
And that I should be my father's murderer.

I heard all this, and fled. And from that day
Corinth to me was only in the stars   270

Descending in that quarter of the sky,
As I wandered farther and farther on my way
To a land where I should never see the evil
Sung by the oracle. And I came to this country
275   Where, so you say, King Laïos was killed.
I will tell you all that happened there, my lady.

There were three highways
Coming together at a place I passed;
And there a herald came towards me, and a chariot
280   Drawn by horses, with a man such as you describe
Seated in it. The groom leading the horses
Forced me off the road at his lord's command;
But as this charioteer lurched over toward me
I struck him in my rage. The old man saw me
285   And brought his double goad down upon my head
As I came abreast.
                        He was paid back, and more!
Swinging my club in this right hand I knocked him
Out of his car, and he rolled on the ground.
                                        I killed him.
I killed them all.
290   Now if that stranger and Laïos were—kin,
Where is a man more miserable than I?
More hated by the gods? Citizen and alien alike
Must never shelter me or speak to me—
I must be shunned by all.
                              And I myself
295   Pronounced this malediction upon myself!

Think of it: I have touched you with these hands,
These hands that killed your husband. What defilement!

Am I all evil, then? It must be so,
Since I must flee from Thebes, yet never again
300   See my own countrymen, my own country,
For fear of joining my mother in marriage
And killing Polybos, my father.
                                    Ah,
If I was created so, born to this fate,
Who could deny the savagery of God?

305   O holy majesty of heavenly powers!
May I never see that day! Never!
Rather let me vanish from the race of men
Than know the abomination destined me!

CHORAGOS.
We too, my lord, have felt dismay at this.
310   But there is hope: you have yet to hear the shepherd.

OEDIPUS.
Indeed, I fear no other hope is left me.

IOCASTÊ.
What do you hope from him when he comes?

OEDIPUS.   This much:
If his account of the murder tallies with yours,
Then I am cleared.

IOCASTÊ.   What was it that I said
Of such importance?

OEDIPUS.   Why, "marauders," you said,   315
Killed the King, according to this man's story.
If he maintains that still, if there were several,
Clearly the guilt is not mine: I was alone.
But if he says one man, singlehanded, did it,
Then the evidence all points to me.   320

IOCASTÊ.
You may be sure that he said there were several;
And can he call back that story now? He cannot.
The whole city heard it as plainly as I.
But suppose he alters some detail of it:
He cannot ever show that Laïos' death   325
Fulfilled the oracle: for Apollo said
My child was doomed to kill him; and my child—
Poor baby!—it was my child that died first.

No. From now on, where oracles are concerned,
I would not waste a second thought on any.   330

OEDIPUS.
You may be right.
                        But come: let someone go
For the shepherd at once. This matter must be settled.

IOCASTÊ.
I will send for him.
I would not wish to cross you in anything,
And surely not in this.—Let us go in.   335

                                    (*Exeunt into the palace.*)

ODE II

Strophe 1

CHORUS.
Let me be reverent in the ways of right,
Lowly the paths I journey on;
Let all my words and actions keep
The laws of the pure universe
From highest Heaven handed down.   5
For Heaven is their bright nurse,
Those generations of the realms of light;
Ah, never of mortal kind were they begot,
Nor are they slaves of memory, lost in sleep:
Their Father is greater than Time, and ages not.   10

Antistrophe 1

The tyrant is a child of Pride
Who drinks from his great sickening cup
Recklessness and vanity,
Until from his high crest headlong
He plummets to the dust of hope.   15
That strong man is not strong.

But let no fair ambition be denied;
May God protect the wrestler for the State
In government, in comely policy,
20 Who will fear God, and on His ordinance wait.

Strophe 2

Haughtiness and the high hand of disdain
Tempt and outrage God's holy law;
And any mortal who dares hold
No immortal Power in awe
25 Will be caught up in a net of pain:
The price for which his levity is sold.
Let each man take due earnings, then,
And keep his hands from holy things,
And from blasphemy stand apart—
30 Else the crackling blast of heaven
Blows on his head, and on his desperate heart;
Though fools will honor impious men,
In their cities no tragic poet sings.

Antistrophe 2

Shall we lose faith in Delphi's obscurities,
35 We who have heard the world's core
Discredited, and the sacred wood
Of Zeus at Elis praised no more?
The deeds and the strange prophecies
Must make a pattern yet to be understood.
40 Zeus, if indeed you are lord of all,
Throned in light over night and day,
Mirror this in your endless mind:
Our masters call the oracle
Words on the wind, and the Delphic vision blind!
45 Their hearts no longer know Apollo,
And reverence for the gods has died away.

SCENE III

Enter Iocastê.

IOCASTÊ.
Princes of Thebes, it has occurred to me
To visit the altars of the gods, bearing
These branches as a suppliant, and this incense.
Our King is not himself: his noble soul
5 Is overwrought with fantasies of dread,
Else he would consider
The new prophecies in the light of the old.
He will listen to any voice that speaks disaster,
And my advice goes for nothing.

She approaches the altar, right.

To you, then, Apollo,
Lycean lord, since you are nearest, I turn in prayer.   10
Receive these offerings, and grant us deliverance
From defilement. Our hearts are heavy with fear
When we see our leader distracted, as helpless sailors
Are terrified by the confusion of their helmsman.

Enter messenger.

MESSENGER.
Friends, no doubt you can direct me: 15
Where shall I find the house of Oedipus,
Or, better still, where is the King himself?
CHORAGOS.
It is this very place, stranger; he is inside.
This is his wife and mother of his children.
MESSENGER.
I wish her happiness in a happy house,   20
Blest in all the fulfillment of her marriage.
IOCASTÊ.
I wish as much for you: your courtesy
Deserves a like good fortune. But now, tell me:
Why have you come? What have you to say to us?
MESSENGER.
Good news, my lady, for your house and your husband.   25
IOCASTÊ.
What news? Who sent you here?
MESSENGER.   I am from Corinth.
The news I bring ought to mean joy for you,
Though it may be you will find some grief in it.
IOCASTÊ.
What is it? How can it touch us in both ways?
MESSENGER.
The people of Corinth, they say,   30
Intend to call Oedipus to be their king.
IOCASTÊ.
But old Polybos—is he not reigning still?
MESSENGER.
No. Death holds him in his sepulchre.
IOCASTÊ.
What are you saying? Polybos is dead?
MESSENGER.
If I am not telling the truth, may I die myself.   35
IOCASTÊ (*to a maidservant*).
Go in, go quickly; tell this to your master.

O riddlers of God's will, where are you now!
This was the man whom Oedipus, long ago,
Feared so, fled so, in dread of destroying him—
But it was another fate by which he died.   40

Enter Oedipus, center.

OEDIPUS.
Dearest Iocastê, why have you sent for me?
IOCASTÊ.
Listen to what this man says, and then tell me

What has become of the solemn prophecies.
OEDIPUS.
   Who is this man? What is his news for me?
IOCASTÊ.
45   He has come from Corinth to announce your father's
     death!
OEDIPUS.
   Is it true, stranger? Tell me in your own words.
MESSENGER.
   I cannot say it more clearly: the King is dead.
OEDIPUS.
   Was it by treason? Or by an attack of illness?
MESSENGER.
   A little thing brings old men to their rest.
OEDIPUS.
   It was sickness, then?
50 MESSENGER.   Yes, and his many years.
OEDIPUS.
   Ah!
   Why should a man respect the Pythian hearth,° or
   Give heed to the birds that jangle above his head?
   They prophesied that I should kill Polybos,
55   Kill my own father; but he is dead and buried,
   And I am here—I never touched him, never,
   Unless he died in grief for my departure,
   And thus, in a sense, through me. No Polybos
   Has packed the oracles off with him underground.
   They are empty words.
60 IOCASTÊ.   Had I not told you so?
OEDIPUS.
   You had; it was my faint heart that betrayed me.
IOCASTÊ.
   From now on never think of those things again.
OEDIPUS.
   And yet—must I not fear my mother's bed?
IOCASTÊ.
   Why should anyone in this world be afraid,
65   Since Fate rules us and nothing can be foreseen?
   A man should live only for the present day.
   Have no more fear of sleeping with your mother
   How many men, in dreams, have lain with their mothers!
   No reasonable man is troubled by such things.
OEDIPUS.
70   That is true; only—
   If only my mother were not still alive!
   But she is alive. I cannot help my dread.
IOCASTÊ.
   Yet this news of your father's death is wonderful.

OEDIPUS.
   Wonderful. But I fear the living woman.
MESSENGER.
   Tell me, who is this woman that you fear?   75
OEDIPUS.
   It is Meropê, man; the wife of King Polybos.
MESSENGER.
   Meropê? Why should you be afraid of her?
OEDIPUS.
   An oracle of the gods, a dreadful saying.
MESSENGER.
   Can you tell me about it or are you sworn to silence?
OEDIPUS.
   I can tell you, and I will.   80
   Apollo said through his prophet that I was the man
   Who should marry his own mother, shed his father's blood
   With his own hands. And so, for all these years
   I have kept clear of Corinth, and no harm has come—
   Though it would have been sweet to see my parents   85
     again.
MESSENGER.
   And is this the fear that drove you out of Corinth?
OEDIPUS.
   Would you have me kill my father?
MESSENGER.   As for that
   You must be reassured by the news I gave you.
OEDIPUS.
   If you could reassure me, I would reward you.
MESSENGER.
   I had that in mind, I will confess: I thought   90
   I could count on you when you returned to Corinth.
OEDIPUS.
   No: I will never go near my parents again.
MESSENGER.
   Ah, son, you still do not know what you are doing—
OEDIPUS.
   What do you mean? In the name of God tell me!
MESSENGER.
   —If these are your reasons for not going home—   95
OEDIPUS.
   I tell you, I fear the oracle may come true.
MESSENGER.
   And guilt may come upon you through your parents?
OEDIPUS.
   That is the dread that is always in my heart.
MESSENGER.
   Can you not see that all your fears are groundless?
OEDIPUS.
   How can you say that? They are my parents, surely?   100
MESSENGER.
   Polybos was not your father.
OEDIPUS.   Not my father?
MESSENGER.
   No more your father than the man speaking to you.

---

52 Pythian hearth Delphi (also called Pytho because a great snake
had lived there), where Apollo spoke through a priestess

OEDIPUS.
But you are nothing to me!

MESSENGER.   Neither was he.

OEDIPUS.
Then why did he call me son?

MESSENGER.   I will tell you:
105 Long ago he had you from my hands, as a gift.

OEDIPUS.
Then how could he love me so, if I was not his?

MESSENGER.
He had no children, and his heart turned to you.

OEDIPUS.
What of you? Did you buy me? Did you find me by
       chance?

MESSENGER.
I came upon you in the crooked pass of Kithairon.

OEDIPUS.
And what were you doing there?

110 MESSENGER.   Tending my flocks.

OEDIPUS.
A wandering shepherd?

MESSENGER.   But your savior, son, that day.

OEDIPUS.
From what did you save me?

MESSENGER.   Your ankles should tell you
       that.

OEDIPUS.
Ah, stranger, why do you speak of that childhood pain?

MESSENGER.
I cut the bonds that tied your ankles together.

115 OEDIPUS.
I have had the mark as long as I can remember.

MESSENGER.
That was why you were given the name you bear.°

OEDIPUS.
God! Was it my father or my mother who did it?
Tell me!

MESSENGER.
I do not know. The man who gave you to me
120 Can tell you better than I.

OEDIPUS.
It was not you that found me, but another?

MESSENGER.
It was another shepherd gave you to me.

OEDIPUS.
Who was he? Can you tell me who he was?

MESSENGER.
I think he was said to be one of Laïos' people.

OEDIPUS.
125 You mean the Laïos who was king here years ago?

116 **name you bear** *Oedipus* means "swollen-foot"

MESSENGER.
Yes; King Laïos; and the man was one of his herdsmen.

OEDIPUS.
Is he still alive? Can I see him?

MESSENGER.   These men here
Know best about such things.

OEDIPUS.   Does anyone here
Know this shepherd that he is talking about?
Have you seen him in the fields, or in the town?   130
If you have, tell me. It is time things were made plain.

CHORAGOS.
I think the man he means is that same shepherd
You have already asked to see. Iocastê perhaps
Could tell you something.

OEDIPUS.   Do you know anything
About him, Lady? Is he the man we have summoned?   135
Is that the man this shepherd means?

IOCASTÊ.   Why think of him?
Forget this herdsman. Forget it all.
This talk is a waste of time.

OEDIPUS.   How can you say that,
When the clues to my true birth are in my hands?

IOCASTÊ.
For God's love, let us have no more questioning!   140
Is your life nothing to you?
My own is pain enough for me to bear.

OEDIPUS.
You need not worry. Suppose my mother a slave,
And born of slaves: no baseness can touch you.

IOCASTÊ.
Listen to me, I beg you: do not do this thing!   145

OEDIPUS.
I will not listen; the truth must be made known.

IOCASTÊ.
Everything that I say is for your own good!

OEDIPUS.   My own good
Snaps my patience, then: I want none of it.

IOCASTÊ.
You are fatally wrong! May you never learn who you are!

OEDIPUS.
Go, one of you, and bring the shepherd here.   150
Let us leave this woman to brag of her royal name.

IOCASTÊ.
Ah, miserable!
That is the only word I have for you now.
That is the only word I can ever have.

                                    (*Exit into the palace.*)

CHORAGOS.
Why has she left us, Oedipus? Why has she gone   155
In such a passion of sorrow? I fear this silence:
Something dreadful may come of it.

OEDIPUS.   Let it come!
However base my birth, I must know about it.

160 The Queen, like a woman, is perhaps ashamed
To think of my low origin. But I
Am a child of luck; I cannot be dishonored.
Luck is my mother; the passing months, my brothers,
Have seen me rich and poor. If this is so,
165 How could I wish that I were someone else?
How could I not be glad to know my birth?

ODE III

Strophe

CHORUS.

If ever the coming time were known
To my heart's pondering,
Kithairon, now by Heaven I see the torches
At the festival of the next full moon,
5 And see the dance, and hear the choir sing
A grace to your gentle shade:
Mountain where Oedipus was found,
O mountain guard of a noble race!
May the god who heals us lend his aid,
10 And let that glory come to pass
For our king's cradling-ground.

Antistrophe

Of the nymphs that flower beyond the years.
Who bore you, royal child,
To Pan of the hills or the timberline Apollo,
15 Cold in delight where the upland clears.
Or Hermês for whom Kyllenê's° heights are piled?
Or flushed as evening cloud,
Great Dionysos, roamer of mountains,
He—was it he who found you there,
20 And caught you up in his own proud
Arms from the sweet god-ravisher°
Who laughed by the Muses' fountains?

SCENE IV

OEDIPUS.

Sirs: though I do not know the man,
I think I see him coming, this shepherd we want:
He is old, like our friend here, and the men
Bringing him seem to be servants of my house.
5 But you can tell, if you have ever seen him.

Enter shepherd escorted by servants.

16 **Hermês . . . Kyllenê's** Hermês, messenger of the gods, was said
to have been born on Mt. Kyllenê   21 **the sweet god-ravisher** the
presumed mother, the nymph whom the god found irresistible

CHORAGOS.

I know him, he was Laïos' man. You can trust him.

OEDIPUS.

Tell me first, you from Corinth: is this the shepherd
We were discussing?

MESSENGER.   This is the very man.

OEDIPUS (*to shepherd*).

Come here. No, look at me. You must answer
Everything I ask.—You belonged to Laïos?   10

SHEPHERD.

Yes: born his slave, brought up in his house.

OEDIPUS.

Tell me: what kind of work did you do for him?

SHEPHERD.

I was a shepherd of his, most of my life.

OEDIPUS.

Where mainly did you go for pasturage?

SHEPHERD.

Sometimes Kithairon, sometimes the hills near-by.   15

OEDIPUS.

Do you remember ever seeing this man out there?

SHEPHERD.

What would he be doing there? This man?

OEDIPUS.

This man standing here. Have you ever seen him before?

SHEPHERD.

No. At least, not to my recollection.

MESSENGER.

And that is not strange, my lord. But I'll refresh   20
His memory: he must remember when we two
Spent three whole seasons together, March to September,
On Kithairon or thereabouts. He had two flocks;
I had one. Each autumn I'd drive mine home
And he would go back with his to Laïos' sheepfold.—   25
Is this not true, just as I have described it?

SHEPHERD.

True, yes; but it was all so long ago.

MESSENGER.

Well, then: do you remember, back in those days
That you gave me a baby boy to bring up as my own?

SHEPHERD.

What if I did? What are you trying to say?   30

MESSENGER.

King Oedipus was once that little child.

SHEPHERD.

Damn you, hold your tongue!

OEDIPUS.   No more of that!
It is your tongue needs watching, not this man's.

SHEPHERD.

My King, my Master, what is it I have done wrong?

OEDIPUS.

You have not answered his question about the boy.   35

SHEPHERD.

He does not know . . . He is only making trouble . . .

OEDIPUS.
   Come, speak plainly, or it will go hard with you.
SHEPHERD.
   In God's name, do not torture an old man!
OEDIPUS.
   Come here, one of you; bind his arms behind him.
SHEPHERD.
40   Unhappy king! What more do you wish to learn?
OEDIPUS.
   Did you give this man the child he speaks of?
SHEPHERD.   I did.
   And I would to God I had died that very day.
OEDIPUS.
   You will die now unless you speak the truth.
SHEPHERD.
   Yet if I speak the truth, I am worse than dead.
OEDIPUS.
45   Very well; since you insist upon delaying—
SHEPHERD.
   No! I have told you already that I gave him the boy.
OEDIPUS.
   Where did you get him? From your house?
   From somewhere else?
SHEPHERD.
   Not from mine, no. A man gave him to me.
OEDIPUS.
   Is that man here? Do you know whose slave he was?
SHEPHERD.
50   For God's love, my King, do not ask me any more!
OEDIPUS.
   You are a dead man if I have to ask you again.
SHEPHERD.
   Then . . . Then the child was from the palace of Laïos.
OEDIPUS.
   A slave child? or a child of his own line?
SHEPHERD.
   Ah, I am on the brink of dreadful speech!
OEDIPUS.
55   And I of dreadful hearing. Yet I must hear.
SHEPHERD.
   If you must be told, then . . .
                              They said it was Laïos' child,
   But it is your wife who can tell you about that.
OEDIPUS.
   My wife!—Did she give it to you?
SHEPHERD.   My lord, she did.
OEDIPUS.
   Do you know why?
SHEPHERD.   I was told to get rid of it.
OEDIPUS.
   An unspeakable mother!
60 SHEPHERD.   There had been prophecies . . .
OEDIPUS.
   Tell me.

SHEPHERD. It was said that the boy would kill his own father.
OEDIPUS.
   Then why did you give him over to this old man?
SHEPHERD.
   I pitied the baby, my King,
   And I thought that this man would take him far away
   To his own country.
                        He saved him—but for what a fate!   65
   For if you are what this man says you are,
   No man living is more wretched than Oedipus.
OEDIPUS.
   Ah God!
            It was true!
                        All the prophecies!
                                            —Now,
   O Light, may I look on you for the last time!   70
   I, Oedipus,
   Oedipus, damned in his birth, in his marriage damned,
   Damned in the blood he shed with his own hand!

He rushes into the palace.

ODE IV

Strophe 1

CHORUS.
   Alas for the seed of men.
   What measure shall I give these generations
   That breathe on the void and are void
   And exist and do not exist?

   Who bears more weight of joy   5
   Than mass of sunlight shifting in images,
   Or who shall make his thought stay on
   That down time drifts away?

   Your splendor is all fallen.

   O naked brow of wrath and tears,   10
   O change of Oedipus!
   I who saw your days call no man blest—
   Your great days like ghósts góne.

Antistrophe 1

   That mind was a strong bow.
   Deep, how deep you drew it then, hard archer,   15
   At a dim fearful range,
   And brought dear glory down!

   You overcame the stranger—
   The virgin with her hooking lion claws—
   And though death sang, stood like a tower   20
   To make pale Thebes take heart.

   Fortress against our sorrow!

Divine king, giver of laws,
Majestic Oedipus!
25   No prince in Thebes had ever such renown,
No prince won such grace of power.

Strophe 2

And now of all men ever known
Most pitiful is this man's story:
His fortunes are most changed, his state
30   Fallen to a low slave's
Ground under bitter fate.

O Oedipus, most royal one!
The great door that expelled you to the light
Gave it night—ah, gave night to your glory:
35   As to the father, to the fathering son.

All understood too late.

How could that queen whom Laïos won,
The garden that he harrowed at his height,
Be silent when that act was done?

Antistrophe 2

40   But all eyes fail before time's eye,
All actions come to justice there.
Though never willed, though far down the deep past,
Your bed, your dread sirings,
Are brought to book at last.
45   Child by Laïos doomed to die,
Then doomed to lose that fortunate little death,
Would God you never took breath in this air
That with my wailing lips I take to cry:

For I weep the world's outcast.

50   I was blind, and now I can tell why:
Asleep, for you had given ease of breath
To Thebes, while the false years went by.

EXODOS

Enter, from the palace, second messenger.

SECOND MESSENGER.
Elders of Thebes, most honored in this land,
What horrors are yours to see and hear, what weight
Of sorrow to be endured, if, true to your birth,
You venerate the line of Labdakos!
5   I think neither Istros nor Phasis, those great rivers,
Could purify this place of the corruption
It shelters now, or soon must bring to light—
Evil not done unconsciously, but willed.

The greatest griefs are those we cause ourselves.
CHORAGOS.
Surely, friend, we have grief enough already;   10
What new sorrow do you mean?
SECOND MESSENGER.   The Queen is dead.
CHORAGOS.
Iocastê? Dead? But at whose hand?
SECOND MESSENGER.   Her own.
The full horror of what happened you cannot know,
For you did not see it; but I, who did, will tell you
As clearly as I can how she met her death.   15

When she had left us,
In passionate silence, passing through the court,
She ran to her apartment in the house,
Her hair clutched by the fingers of both hands.
She closed the doors behind her; then, by that bed   20
Where long ago the fatal son was conceived—
That son who should bring about his father's death—
We heard her call upon Laïos, dead so many years,
And heard her wail for the double fruit of her marriage,
A husband by her husband, children by her child.   25

Exactly how she died I do not know:
For Oedipus burst in moaning and would not let us
Keep vigil to the end: it was by him
As he stormed about the room that our eyes were caught.
From one to another of us he went, begging a sword,   30
Cursing the wife who was not his wife, the mother
Whose womb had carried his own children and himself.
I do not know: it was none of us aided him,
But surely one of the gods was in control!
For with a dreadful cry   35
He hurled his weight, as though wrenched out of himself,
At the twin doors: the bolts gave, and he rushed in.
And there we saw her hanging, her body swaying
From the cruel cord she had noosed about her neck.
A great sob broke from him heartbreaking to hear,   40
As he loosed the rope and lowered her to the ground.

I would blot out from my mind what happened next!
For the King ripped from her gown the golden brooches
That were her ornament, and raised them, and plunged
     them down
Straight into his own eyeballs, crying, "No more,   45
No more shall you look on the misery about me,
The horrors of my own doing! Too long you have known
The faces of those whom I should never have seen,
Too long been blind to those for whom I was searching!
From this hour, go in darkness!" And as he spoke,   50
He struck at his eyes—not once, but many times;
And the blood spattered his beard,
Bursting from his ruined sockets like red hail.

So from the unhappiness of two this evil has sprung,
A curse on the man and woman alike. The old   55

Happiness of the house of Labdakos
Was happiness enough: where is it today?
It is all wailing and ruin, disgrace, death—all
The misery of mankind that has a name—
60   And it is wholly and for ever theirs.
CHORAGOS.
     Is he in agony still? Is there no rest for him?
SECOND MESSENGER.
     He is calling for someone to lead him to the gates
     So that all the children of Kadmos may look upon
     His father's murderer, his mother's—no,
     I cannot say it!
65   And then he will leave Thebes,
     Self-exiled, in order that the curse
     Which he himself pronounced may depart from the house.
     He is weak, and there is none to lead him,
     So terrible is his suffering.
70   But you will see:
     Look, the doors are opening; in a moment
     You will see a thing that would crush a heart of stone.

     The central door is opened; Oedipus, blinded, is led in.

CHORAGOS.
     Dreadful indeed for men to see.
     Never have my own eyes
     Looked on a sight so full of fear.

75   Oedipus!
     What madness came upon you, what daemon°
     Leaped on your life with heavier
     Punishment than a mortal man can bear?
     No: I cannot even
80   Look at you, poor ruined one.
     And I would speak, question, ponder,
     If I were able. No.
     You make me shudder.
OEDIPUS.
     God. God.
85   Is there a sorrow greater?
     Where shall I find harbor in this world?
     My voice is hurled far on a dark wind.
     What has God done to me?
CHORAGOS.
     Too terrible to think of, or to see.

Strophe 1

OEDIPUS.
90   O cloud of night,
     Never to be turned away: night coming on,
     I cannot tell how: night like a shroud!

76 daemon a spirit, not necessarily evil

My fair winds brought me here.
                    Oh God. Again
The pain of the spikes where I had sight,
The flooding pain   95
Of memory, never to be gouged out.
CHORAGOS.
     This is not strange.
     You suffer it all twice over, remorse in pain,
     Pain in remorse.

Antistrophe 1

OEDIPUS.
     Ah dear friend   100
     Are you faithful even yet, you alone?
     Are you still standing near me, will you stay here,
     Patient, to care for the blind?
                              The blind man!
     Yet even blind I know who it is attends me,
     By the voice's tone—   105
     Though my new darkness hide the comforter.
CHORAGOS.
     Oh fearful act!
     What god was it drove you to rake black
     Night across your eyes?

Strophe 2

OEDIPUS.
     Apollo. Apollo. Dear   110
     Children, the god was Apollo.
     He brought my sick, sick fate upon me.
     But the blinding hand was my own!
     How could I bear to see
     When all my sight was horror everywhere?   115
CHORAGOS.
     Everywhere; that is true.
OEDIPUS.
     And now what is left?
     Images? Love? A greeting even,
     Sweet to the senses? Is there anything?
     Ah, no, friends: lead me away.   120
     Lead me away from Thebes.
                              Lead the great wreck
     And hell of Oedipus, whom the gods hate.
CHORAGOS.
     Your fate is clear, you are not blind to that.
     Would God you had never found it out!

Antistrophe 2

OEDIPUS.
     Death take the man who unbound   125
     My feet on that hillside

And delivered me from death to life! What life?
If only I had died,
This weight of monstrous doom
130 Could not have dragged me and my darlings down.
CHORAGOS.
    I would have wished the same.
OEDIPUS.
    Oh never to have come here
With my father's blood upon me! Never
To have been the man they call his mother's husband!
135 Oh accurst! O child of evil,
To have entered that wretched bed—
                                    the selfsame one!
More primal than sin itself, this fell to me.
CHORAGOS.
    I do not know how I can answer you.
    You were better dead than alive and blind.
OEDIPUS.
140 Do not counsel me any more. This punishment
That I have laid upon myself is just.
If I had eyes,
I do not know how I could bear the sight
Of my father, when I came to the house of Death,
145 Or my mother: for I have sinned against them both
So vilely that I could not make my peace
By strangling my own life.
                            Or do you think my children,
Born as they were born, would be sweet to my eyes?
Ah never, never! Nor this town with its high walls,
Nor the holy images of the gods.
150   For I,
Thrice miserable—Oedipus, noblest of all the line
Of Kadmos, have condemned myself to enjoy
These things no more, by my own malediction
Expelling that man whom the gods declared
155 To be a defilement in the house of Laïos.
After exposing the rankness of my own guilt,
How could I look men frankly in the eyes?
No, I swear it,
If I could have stifled my hearing at its source,
160 I would have done it and made all this body
A tight cell of misery, blank to light and sound:
So I should have been safe in a dark agony
Beyond all recollection.
                        Ah Kithairon!
Why did you shelter me? When I was cast upon you,
165 Why did I not die? Then I should never
Have shown the world my execrable birth.

Ah Polybos! Corinth, city that I believed
The ancient seat of my ancestors: how fair
I seemed, your child! And all the while this evil
Was cancerous within me!
170   For I am sick
In my daily life, sick in my origin.

O three roads, dark ravine, woodland and way
Where three roads met: you, drinking my father's blood,
My own blood, spilled by my own hand: can you remember
The unspeakable things I did there, and the things   175
I went on from there to do?
                            O marriage, marriage!
The act that engendered me, and again the act
Performed by the son in the same bed—
                                    Ah, the net
Of incest, mingling fathers, brothers, sons,
With brides, wives, mothers: the last evil   180
That can be known by men: no tongue can say
How evil!
            No. For the love of God, conceal me
Somewhere far from Thebes; or kill me; or hurl me
Into the sea, away from men's eyes for ever.
Come, lead me. You need not fear to touch me.   185
Of all men, I alone can bear this guilt.

Enter Creon.

CHORAGOS.
    We are not the ones to decide; but Creon here
    May fitly judge of what you ask. He only
    Is left to protect the city in your place.
OEDIPUS.
    Alas, how can I speak to him? What right have I   190
    To beg his courtesy whom I have deeply wronged?
CREON.
    I have not come to mock you, Oedipus,
    Or to reproach you, either.
    (*To attendants.*)   —You, standing there:
    If you have lost all respect for man's dignity,
    At least respect the flame of Lord Helios: 195
    Do not allow this pollution to show itself
    Openly here, an affront to the earth
    And Heaven's rain and the light of day. No, take him
    Into the house as quickly as you can.
    For it is proper   200
    That only the close kindred see his grief.
OEDIPUS.
    I pray you in God's name, since your courtesy
    Ignores my dark expectation, visiting
    With mercy this man of all men most execrable:
    Give me what I ask—for your good, not for mine.   205
CREON.
    And what is it that you would have me do?
OEDIPUS.
    Drive me out of this country as quickly as may be
    To a place where no human voice can ever greet me.
CREON.
    I should have done that before now—only,
    God's will had not been wholly revealed to me.   210

OEDIPUS.
    But his command is plain: the parricide
    Must be destroyed. I am that evil man.
CREON.
    That is the sense of it, yes; but as things are,
    We had best discover clearly what is to be done.
OEDIPUS.
215   You would learn more about a man like me?
CREON.
    You are ready now to listen to the god.
OEDIPUS.
    I will listen. But it is to you.
    That I must turn for help. I beg you, hear me.

    The woman in there—
220   Give her whatever funeral you think proper:
    She is your sister.
             —But let me go, Creon!
    Let me purge my father's Thebes of the pollution
    Of my living here, and go out to the wild hills,
    To Kithairon, that has won such fame with me,
225   The tomb my mother and father appointed for me,
    And let me die there, as they willed I should.
    And yet I know
    Death will not ever come to me through sickness
    Or in any natural way: I have been preserved
230   For some unthinkable fate. But let that be.
    As for my sons, you need not care for them.
    They are men, they will find some way to live.
    But my poor daughters, who have shared my table,
    Who never before have been parted from their father—
235   Take care of them, Creon; do this for me.
    And will you let me touch them with my hands
    A last time, and let us weep together?
    Be kind, my lord,
    Great prince, be kind!
               Could I but touch them,
240   They would be mine again, as when I had my eyes.

Enter Antigonê and Ismenê, attended.

    Ah, God!
    Is it my dearest children I hear weeping?
    Has Creon pitied me and sent my daughters?
CREON.
    Yes, Oedipus: I knew that they were dear to you
245   In the old days, and know you must love them still.
OEDIPUS.
    May God bless you for this—and be a friendlier
    Guardian to you than he has been to me!
    Children, where are you?
    Come quickly to my hands: they are your brother's—
250   Hands that have brought your father's once clear eyes
    To this way of seeing—
             Ah dearest ones,
    I had neither sight nor knowledge then, your father

    By the woman who was the source of his life!
    And I weep for you—having no strength to see you—,
    I weep for you when I think of the bitterness   255
    That men will visit upon you all your lives.
    What homes, what festivals can you attend
    Without being forced to depart again in tears?
    And when you come to marriageable age,
    Where is the man, my daughters, who would dare   260
    Risk the bane that lies on all my children?
    Is there any evil wanting? Your father killed
    His father; sowed the womb of her who bore him;
    Engendered you at the fount of his own existence!
    That is what they will say of you.
                          Then, whom   265
    Can you ever marry? There are no bridegrooms for you,
    And your lives must wither away in sterile dreaming.
    O Creon, son of Menoikeus!
    You are the only father my daughters have,
    Since we, their parents, are both of us gone forever.   270
    They are your own blood: you will not let them
    Fall into beggary and loneliness;
    You will keep them from the miseries that are mine!
    Take pity on them; see, they are only children,
    Friendless except for you. Promise me this,   275
    Great Prince, and give me your hand in token of it.

Creon clasps his right hand.

    Children:
    I could say much, if you could understand me,
    But as it is, I have only this prayer for you:
    Live where you can, be as happy as you can—
    Happier, please God, than God has made your father!
CREON.
    Enough. You have wept enough. Now go within.
OEDIPUS.
    I must; but it is hard.
CREON.   Time eases all things.
OEDIPUS.
    But you must promise—
CREON.   Say what you desire.
OEDIPUS.
    Send me from Thebes!
CREON.   God grant that I may!   285
OEDIPUS.
    But since God hates me . . .
CREON.   No, he will grant your wish.
OEDIPUS.
    You promise?
CREON.   I cannot speak beyond my knowledge.
OEDIPUS.
    Then lead me in.
CREON.   Come now, and leave your children.
OEDIPUS.
    No! Do not take them from me!

CREON.   Think no longer
290   That you are in command here, but rather think
       How, when you were, you served your own destruction.

           (*Exeunt into the house all but the Chorus; the Choragos
                            chants directly to the audience.*)

CHORAGOS.
       Men of Thebes: look upon Oedipus.

This is the king who solved the famous riddle
And towered up, most powerful of men.
No mortal eyes but looked on him with envy,   295

Yet in the end ruin swept over him.
Let every man in mankind's frailty
Consider his last day; and let none
Presume on his good fortune until he find
Life, at his death, a memory without pain.   300

TOPICS FOR CRITICAL THINKING AND WRITING

The Play on the PAGE

1. On the basis on lines 1–149, characterize Oedipus. Does he seem an effective leader? What additional traits are revealed in lines 205–491?

2. In your opinion, how fair is it to say that Oedipus is morally guilty? Does he argue that he is morally innocent because he did not intend to do immoral deeds? Can it be said that he is guilty of *hybris* but that *hybris* (see page 34) has nothing to do with his fall?

3. Oedipus says that he blinds himself in order not to look upon people he should not. What further reasons can be given? Why does he not (like Iocastê) commit suicide?

4. Does the play show the futility of human efforts to act intelligently?

5. In *Oedipus* do you find the gods evil?

6. Are the choral odes lyrical interludes that serve to separate the scenes, or do they advance the dramatic action?

7. Matthew Arnold said that Sophocles saw life steadily and saw it whole. But in this play is Sophocles facing the facts of life? Or, on the contrary, is he avoiding what we think of as normal life, and presenting a series of unnatural and outrageous coincidences? In either case, do you think the play is relevant today?

8. Can you describe your emotions at the end of the play? Do they include pity for Oedipus? Pity for all human beings, including yourself? Fear that you might be punished for some unintended transgression? Awe, engendered by a perception of the interrelatedness of things? Relief that the story is only a story? Exhilaration? Explain your reaction.

9. Examine Aristotle's comments on tragedy (p. 78), and evaluate three of his points with relevance to *Oedipus*.

The Play on the STAGE

10. During your first consideration of the play, start with a reading of lines 1–149. Choose someone from the group to stand on a chair (Oedipus), two other readers to stand nearby (the Priest and Creon), and several others to kneel or lie on the floor (Theban citizens). After this rough enactment, ask the readers how they felt about their roles. Then discuss the ways a modern staging could create a powerful opening for the play. Some questions to consider: Do the Thebans ever touch Oedipus? Should the actor playing Oedipus make eye contact with anyone on the stage?

11. Originally the Greek chorus chanted and danced. What are your recommendations for a director today? Choose a particular passage from the play to illustrate your ideas.

12. Imagine that you are directing a production of *Oedipus*. Propose a cast for the principal roles, using well-known actors or people from your own circle. Explain the reasons for your choices.

13. What might be gained or lost by performing the play in modern dress? Or is there some period other than ancient Greece—let's say the Victorian period—in which you think the play might be effectively set?

14. Alan MacVey, in his comment on a production (page 84), wishes the royalty had been clothed in "power suits." What is your response to this idea?

A Context for *OEDIPUS REX*

ARISTOTLE
The Poetics
Translated by L. J. Potts

It is no exaggeration to say that the history of tragic criticism is a series of footnotes to Aristotle. In a fragmentary treatise usually called the *Poetics*, Aristotle (384–322 B.C.E.) raises almost all the points that have subsequently been argued, such as the nature of the hero, the emotional effect on the spectator, the coherence of the plot. Whether or not he gave the right answers, it has seemed for more than two thousand years that he asked the right questions.

[Art Is Imitation]

Let us talk of the art of poetry as a whole, and its different species with the particular force of each of them; how the fables must be put together if the poetry is to be well formed; also what are its elements and their different qualities; and all other matters pertaining to the subject.

To begin in the proper order, at the beginning. The making of epics and tragedies, and also comedy, and the art of the dithyramb, and most flute and lyre art, all have this in common, that they are imitations. But they differ from one another in three respects: the different kinds of medium in which they imitate, the different objects they imitate, and the different manner in which they imitate (when it does differ). . . . When the imitators imitate the doings of people, the people in the imitation must be either high or low; the characters almost always follow this line exclusively, for all men differ in character according to their degree of goodness or badness. They must therefore be either above our norm, or below it, or normal; as, in painting, Polygnōtus depicted superior, Pauson inferior, and Dionysius normal, types. It is clear that each variant of imitation that I have mentioned will have these differences, and as the object imitated varies in this way so the works will differ. Even in the ballet, and in flute and lyre music, these dissimilarities can occur; and in the art that uses prose, or verse without music. . . . This is the difference that marks tragedy out from comedy; comedy is inclined to imitate persons below the level of our world, tragedy persons above it.

[Origins of Poetry]

There seem to be two causes that gave rise to poetry in general, and they are natural. The impulse to imitate is inherent in man from his childhood; he is distinguished among the animals by being the most imitative of them, and he takes the first steps of his education by imitating. Everyone's enjoyment of imitation is also inborn. What happens with works of art demonstrates this: though a thing itself is disagreeable to look at, we enjoy contemplating the most accurate representations of it—for instance, figures of the most despicable animals, or of human corpses. The reason for this lies in another fact: learning is a great pleasure, not only to philosophers but likewise to everyone else, however limited his gift for it may be. He enjoys looking at these representations, because in the act of studying them he is learning—identifying the object by an inference (for instance, recognizing who is the original of a portrait); since, if he happens not to have already seen the object depicted, it will not be the imitation as such that is giving him pleasure, but the finish of the workmanship, or the colouring, or some such other cause.

And just as imitation is natural to us, so also are music and rhythm (metres, clearly, are constituent parts of rhythms). Thus, from spontaneous beginnings, mankind developed poetry by a series of mostly minute changes out of these improvisations.

[The Elements of Tragedy]

Let us now discuss tragedy, having first picked up from what has been said the definition of its essence that has so far emerged. Tragedy, then, is an imitation of an action of high importance, complete and of some amplitude; in language enhanced by distinct and varying beauties; acted not narrated; by means of pity and fear effecting its purgation of these emotions. By the beauties enhancing the language I mean rhythm and melody; by "distinct and varying" I mean that some are produced by metre alone, and others at another time by melody.

Now since the imitating is done by actors, it would follow of necessity that one element in a tragedy must be the *Mise en scène* [i.e. setting]. Others are Melody and Language, for these are the media in which the imitating is done. By Language, I mean the component parts of the verse, whereas Melody has an entirely sensuous effect. Again, since the object imitated is an action, and doings are done by persons, whose individuality will be determined by their Character and their Thought (for these are the factors we have in mind when we define the quality of their doings), it follows that there are two natural causes of these doings, Thought and Character; and these causes determine the good or ill fortune of everyone. But the Fable is the imitation of the action; and by the Fable I mean the whole structure of the incidents. By Character I mean the factor that enables us to define the particular quality of the people involved in the doings; and Thought is shown in everything they say when they are demonstrating a fact or disclosing an opinion. There are therefore necessarily six elements in every tragedy, which give it its quality; and they are the Fable, Character, Language, Thought, the *Mise en scène*, and Melody. Two of these are the media in which the imitating is done, one is the manner of imitation, and three are its objects; there is no other element besides these. Numerous poets have turned these essential components to account; all of them are always present—the *Mise en scène*, Character, the Fable, Language, Melody, and Thought.

The chief of these is the plotting of the incidents; for tragedy is an imitation not of men but of doings, life, happiness; unhappiness is located in doings, and our end is a certain kind of doing, not a personal quality; it is their characters that give men their quality, but their doings that make them happy or the opposite. So it is not the purpose of the actors to imitate character, but they include character as a factor in the doings. Thus it is the incidents (that is to say the Fable) that are the end for which tragedy exists; and the end is more important than anything else. Also, without an action there could not be a tragedy, but without Character there could. (In fact, the tragedies of most of the moderns are non-moral, and there are many non-moral poets of all periods; this also applies to the paintings of Zeuxis, if he is compared with

Polygnōtus, for whereas Polygnōtus is a good portrayer of character the painting of Zeuxis leaves it out.) Again, if any one strings together moral speeches with the language and thought well worked out, he will be doing what is the business of tragedy; but it will be done much better by a tragedy that handles these elements more weakly, but has a fable with the incidents connected by a plot. Further, the chief means by which tragedy moves us, Irony of events and Disclosure, are elements in the Fable. A pointer in the same direction is that beginners in the art of poetry are able to get the language and characterization right before they can plot their incidents, and so were almost all the earliest poets.

So the source and as it were soul of tragedy is the Fable; and Character comes next. For, to instance a parallel from the art of painting, the most beautiful colours splashed on anyhow would not be as pleasing as a recognizable picture in black and white. Tragedy is an imitation of an action, and it is chiefly for this reason that it imitates the persons involved.

Third comes Thought: that is, the ability to say what circumstances allow and what is appropriate to them. It is the part played by social morality and rhetoric in making the dialogue: the old poets made their characters talk like men of the world, whereas our contemporaries make them talk like public speakers. Character is what shows a man's disposition—the kind of things he chooses or rejects when his choice is not obvious. Accordingly those speeches where the speaker shows no preferences or aversions whatever are non-moral. Thought, on the other hand, is shown in demonstrating a matter of fact or disclosing a significant opinion.

Fourth comes the Language. By Language I mean, as has already been said, words used semantically. It has the same force in verse as in prose.

Of the remaining elements, Melody is the chief of the enhancing beauties. The *Mise en scène* can excite emotion, but it is the crudest element and least akin to the art of poetry; for the force of tragedy exists even without stage and actors; besides, the fitting out of a *Mise en scène* belongs more to the wardrobe-master's art than to the poet's.

[The Tragic Fable]

So much for analysis. Now let us discuss in what sort of way the incidents should be plotted, since that is the first and chief consideration in tragedy. Our data are that tragedy is an imitation of a whole and complete action of some amplitude (a thing can be whole and yet quite lacking in amplitude). Now a whole is that which has a beginning, a middle, and an end. A beginning is that which does not itself necessarily follow anything else, but which leads naturally to another event or development; an end is the opposite, that which itself naturally (either of necessity or most commonly) follows something else, but nothing else comes after it; and a middle is that which itself follows something else and is followed by another thing. So, well-plotted fables must not begin or end casually, but must follow the pattern here described.

But, besides this, a picture, or any other composite object, if it is to be beautiful, must not only have its parts properly arranged, but be of an appropriate size; for beauty depends on size and structure. Accordingly, a minute picture cannot be beautiful (for when our vision has almost lost its sense of time it becomes confused); nor can an immense one (for we cannot take it all in together, and so our vision loses its unity and wholeness)—imagine a picture a thousand miles long! So, just as there is a proper size for bodies and pictures (a size that can be well surveyed), there is also a proper amplitude for fables (what can be kept well in one's mind). The length of the performance on the stage has nothing to do with art; if a hundred tragedies had to be produced, the length of the production would be settled by the clock, as the story goes that another kind of performance once was. But as to amplitude, the invariable rule dictated by the nature of the action is the fuller the more beautiful so long as the outline remains clear; and for a simple rule of size, the number of happenings that will make a chain of probability (or necessity) to change a given situation from misfortune to good fortune or from good fortune to misfortune is the minimum.

[Unity]

Unity in a fable does not mean, as some think, that it has one man for its subject. To any one man many things happen—an infinite number—and some of them do not make any sort of unity; and in the same way one man has many doings which cannot be made into a unit of action. . . . Accordingly, just as in the other imitative arts the object of each imitation is a unit, so, since the fable is an imitation of an action, that action must be a complete unit, and the events of which it is made up must be so plotted that if any of these elements is moved or removed the whole is altered and upset. For when a thing can be included or not included without making any noticeable difference, that thing is no part of the whole.

[Probability]

From what has been said it is also clear that it is not the poet's business to tell what has happened, but the kind of things that would happen—what is possible according to probability or necessity. The difference between the historian and the poet is not the difference between writing in verse or prose; the work of Herodotus could be put into verse, and it would be just as much a history in verse as it is in prose. The difference is that the one tells what has happened, and the other the kind of things that would happen. It follows therefore that poetry is more philosophical and of higher value than history; for poetry unifies more, whereas history aggregates. To unify is to make a man of a certain description say or do the things that suit him, probably or necessarily, in the circumstances (this is the point of the descriptive proper names in poetry); what Alcibiades did or what happened to him is an aggregation. In comedy this has now become clear. They first plot the fable on a base of probabilities, and then find imaginary names for the people—unlike the lampooners, whose work was an aggregation of personalities. But in tragedy they keep to the names of real people. This is because possibility depends on conviction; if a thing has not happened we are not yet convinced that it is possible, but if it has happened it is clearly possible, for it would not have happened if it were impossible. Even tragedies, however, sometimes have all their persons fictitious except for one or two known names; and sometimes they have not a single known name, as in the *Anthos* of Agathon, in which both the events and the names are equally fictitious, without in the least reducing the delight it gives. It is not, therefore, requisite at all costs to keep to the traditional fables from which our tragedies draw their subject-matter. It would be absurd to insist on that, since even the known legends are known only to a few, and yet the delight is shared by everyone. . . .

[Simple and Complex Fables]

The action imitated must contain incidents that evoke fear and pity, besides being a complete action; but this effect is accentuated when these incidents occur logically as well as unexpectedly, which will be more sensational than if they happen arbitrarily, by chance. Even when events are accidental the sensation is greater if they appear to have a purpose, as when the statue of Mitys at Argos killed the man who had caused his death, by falling on him at a public entertainment. Such things appear not to have happened blindly. Inevitably, therefore, plots of this sort are finer.

Some fables are simple, others complex: for the obvious reason that the original actions imitated by the fables are the one or the other. By a simple action I mean one that leads to the catastrophe in the way we have laid down, directly and singly, without Irony of events or Disclosure.

An action is complex when the catastrophe involves Disclosure, or Irony, or both. But these complications should develop out of the very structure of the fable, so that they fit what has gone before, either necessarily or probably. To happen after something is by no means the same as to happen because of it.

[Irony]

Irony is a reversal in the course of events, of the kind specified, and, as I say, in accordance with probability or necessity. Thus in the *Oedipus* the arrival of the messenger, which was expected to cheer Oedipus up by releasing him from his fear about his mother, did the opposite by showing him who he was; and in the *Lynceus* [Abas], who was awaiting sentence of death, was acquitted, whereas his prosecutor Dănaüs was killed, and all this arose out of what had happened previously.

A Disclosure, as the term indicates, is a change from ignorance to knowledge; if the people are marked out for good fortune it leads to affection, if for misfortune, to enmity. Disclosure produces its finest effect when it is connected with Irony, as the disclosure in the *Oedipus* is. There are indeed other sorts of Disclosure: the process I have described can even apply to inanimate objects of no significance, and mistakes about what a man has done or not done can be cleared up. But the sort I have specified is more a part of the fable and of the action than any other sort; for this

coupling of Irony and Disclosure will carry with it pity or fear, which we have assumed to be the nature of the doings tragedy imitates; and further, such doings will constitute good or ill fortune. Assuming then that it is a disclosure of the identity of persons, it may be of one person only, to the other, when the former knows who the latter is; or sometimes both have to be disclosed—for instance, the sending of the letter led Orestes to the discovery of Iphigeneia, and there had to be another disclosure to make him known to her.

This then is the subject-matter of two elements in the Fable, Irony and Disclosure. A third element is the Crisis of feeling. Irony and Disclosure have been defined; the Crisis of feeling is a harmful or painful experience, such as deaths in public, violent pain, physical injuries, and everything of that sort.

[The Tragic Pattern]

Following the proper order, the next subject to discuss after this would be: What one should aim at and beware of in plotting fables; that is to say, What will produce the tragic effect. Since, then, tragedy, to be at its finest, requires a complex, not a simple, structure, and its structure should also imitate fearful and pitiful events (for that is the peculiarity of this sort of imitation), it is clear: first, that decent people must not be shown passing from good fortune to misfortune (for that is not fearful or pitiful but disgusting); again, vicious people must not be shown passing from misfortune to good fortune (for that is the most untragic situation possible—it has none of the requisites, it is neither humane, nor pitiful, nor fearful); nor again should an utterly evil man fall from good fortune into misfortune (for though a plot of that kind would be humane, it would not induce pity or fear—pity is induced by undeserved misfortune, and fear by the misfortunes of normal people, so that this situation will be neither pitiful nor fearful). So we are left with the man between these extremes: that is to say, the kind of man who neither is distinguished for excellence and virtue, nor comes to grief on account of baseness and vice, but on account of some error; a man of great reputation and prosperity, like Oedipus and Thyestes and conspicuous people of such families as theirs. So, to be well informed, a fable must be single rather than (as some say) double—there must be no change from misfortune to good fortune, but only the opposite, from good fortune to misfortune; the cause must not be vice, but a great error; and the man must be either of the type specified or better, rather than worse. This is borne out by the practice of poets; at first they picked a fable at random and made an inventory of its contents, but now the finest tragedies are plotted, and concern a few families—for example, the tragedies about Alcmeon, Oedipus, Orestes, Mĕlĕāger, Thyestes, Tēlĕphus, and any others whose lives were attended by terrible experiences or doings.

This is the plot that will produce the technically finest tragedy. Those critics are therefore wrong who censure Euripides on this very ground—because he does this in his tragedies, and many of them end in misfortune; for it is, as I have said, the right thing to do. This is clearly demonstrated on the stage in the competitions, where such plays, if they succeed, are the most tragic, and Euripides, even if he is inefficient in every other respect, still shows himself the most tragic of our poets. The next best plot, which is said by some people to be the best, is the tragedy with a double plot, like the *Odyssey*, ending in one way for the better people and in the opposite way for the worse. But it is the weakness of theatrical performances that gives priority to this kind; when poets write what the audience would like to happen, they are in leading strings. This is not the pleasure proper to tragedy, but rather to comedy, where the greatest enemies in the fable, say Orestes and Aegisthus, make friends and go off at the end, and nobody is killed by anybody.

[The Tragic Emotions]

The pity and fear can be brought about by the *Mise en scène;* but they can also come from the mere plotting of the incidents, which is preferable, and better poetry. For, without seeing anything, the fable ought to have been so plotted that if one heard the bare facts, the chain of circumstances would make one shudder and pity. That would happen to anyone who heard the fable of the *Oedipus.* To produce this effect by the *Mise en scène* is less artistic and puts one at the mercy of the technician; and those who use it not to frighten but merely to startle have lost touch with tragedy altogether. We should not try to get all sorts of pleasure from tragedy, but the particular tragic pleasure. And clearly, since this pleasure coming from pity and fear has to be produced by imitation, it is by his handling of the incidents that the poet must create it.

Let us, then, take next the kind of circumstances that seem terrible or lamentable. Now, doings of that kind must be between friends, or enemies, or neither. If any enemy injures an enemy, there is no pity either beforehand or at the time, except on account of the bare fact; nor is there if they are neutral; but when sufferings are engendered among the affections—for example, if murder is done or planned, or some similar outrage is committed, by brother on brother, or son on father, or mother on son, or son on mother—that is the thing to aim at.

Though it is not permissible to ruin the traditional fables—I mean, such as the killing of Clytemnestra by Orestes, or Erĭphȳle by Alcmeon—the poet should use his own invention to refine on what has been handed down to him. Let me explain more clearly what I mean by "refine." The action may take place, as the old poets used to make it, with the knowledge and understanding of the participants; this was how Euripides made Medea kill her children. Or they may do it, but in ignorance of the horror of the deed, and then afterwards discover the tie of affection, like the Oedipus of Sophocles; his act was outside the play, but there are examples where it is inside the tragedy itself—Alcmeon in the play by Astydămas, or Tēlĕgōnus in *The Wounded Odysseus.* Besides these, there is a third possibility: when a man is about to do some fatal act in ignorance, but is enlightened before he does it. These are the only possible alternatives. One must either act or not act, and either know or not know. Of these alternatives, to know, and to be about to act, and then not to act, is thoroughly bad—it is disgusting without being tragic, for there is no emotional crisis; accordingly poets only rarely create such situations, as in the *Antigone,* when Haemon fails to kill Creon. Next in order is to act; and if the deed is done in ignorance and its nature is disclosed afterwards, so much the better—there is no bad taste in it, and the revelation is overpowering. But the last is best; I mean, like Mĕrŏpe in the *Cresphontes,* intending to kill her son, but recognizing him and not killing him; and the brother and sister in the *Iphigeneia;* and in the *Helle,* the son recognizing his mother just as he was going to betray her.—This is the reason for what was mentioned earlier: that the subject-matter of our tragedies is drawn from a few families. In their search for matter they discovered this recipe in the fables, not by cunning but by luck. So they are driven to have recourse to those families where such emotional crises have occurred. . . .

[Character]

And in the characterization, as in the plotting of the incidents, the aim should always be either necessity or probability: so that they say or do such things as it is necessary or probable that they would, being what they are; and that for this to follow that is either necessary or probable. . . . As for extravagant incidents, there should be none in the story, or if there are they should be kept outside the tragedy, as is the one in the *Oedipus* of Sophocles.

Since tragedy is an imitation of people above the normal, we must be like good portrait-painters, who follow the original model closely, but refine on it; in the same way the poet, in imitating people whose character is choleric or phlegmatic, and so forth, must keep them as they are and at the same time make them

attractive. So Homer made Achilles noble, as well as a pattern of obstinacy. . . .

[Chorus]

Treat the chorus as though it were one of the actors; it should be an organic part of the play and reinforce it, not as it is in Euripides, but as in Sophocles. In their successors the songs belong no more to the fable than to that of any other tragedy. This has led to the insertion of borrowed lyrics, an innovation for which Agathon was responsible.

The Play in PERFORMANCE

Because the story of Oedipus was ancient even in Sophocles's day, one cannot attribute all later versions of the story to the influence of Sophocles, but the version by the Roman dramatist Seneca (4 B.C.E.–65 C.E.) so closely resembles Sophocles's *Oedipus the King* that the influence is evident. Other famous versions of *Oedipus* are by the French writer Corneille (1659); the English writers John Dryden and Nathaniel Lee (1679; this version is noted for its combination of melodrama and low comedy); and Voltaire (1718; this version clearly puts the blame on cruel gods). In the twentieth century, Jean Cocteau's *The Infernal Machine* (1934)—the universe is conceived as a destructive and therefore infernal machine—is a four-act play

about Oedipus, but only the fourth act is essentially Sophocles's play.

Sophocles's *Oedipus* has been esteemed for centuries, but Freud's comments on the Oedipus complex have given the play a special prominence in the twentieth century. *Oedipus* is often produced, not only in colleges and universities but occasionally in the professional theater. Among the most distinguished productions in the twentieth century were those by Laurence Olivier (1945) and by Tyrone Guthrie (1954). We reprint, immediately following, an essay in which Guthrie discusses some of the issues confronting a director, and an interview with Alan MacVey, who directed a more recent production.

TYRONE GUTHRIE
King Oedipus *in Canada*

Tyrone Guthrie (1900–71), for whom the Guthrie Theatre in Minneapolis is named, achieved fame as a director in Britain, Canada, and the United States. In the following essay he discusses his 1954 production of *Oedipus the King*.

To maintain that this or that way of doing something is the Right Way is not a wise idea. Even so simple an action as hammering a nail may be done in many different ways, none of them perfectly right, but many of

them defensibly reasonable, defensibly even the best possible way in given circumstances. So, in the very much more complex matter of presenting a Greek tragedy, no way can possibly be right; many ways can be reasonably defended.

Our Canadian *King Oedipus* was produced with a high degree of stylization. The great personages of the play—Oedipus, Jokasta and Creon—wore masks, one and a half times life size; and "cothurni" which made them taller than their own height by about the length of a hand. The masks designed by Tanya Moiseiwitsch, were boldly stylized and painted to represent metal—Oedipus in gold, a sun image; Jokasta, silver, like the moon; Creon, of darker baser metal than the others, in bronze. The mask of Tiresias, the Seer, resembled a great, sightless bird. The chorus masks and dresses suggested that they were very near to the earth; the head appeared to be carved out of wood, and their heavy robes were colored like lichen, brown and gray and saffron.

The verse—we used the free translation of the great Irish poet, W.B. Yeats—was declaimed in a bold, operatic fashion with few concessions to naturalism; the choruses were elaborate set-pieces of chanting and mime. Our attempt was to raise the performance to a level of religious ritual, both movement and speech being as "abstract" as we dared to make them. The reason for all this was to remove the characters and the story from the realm of the particular into something more nearly related to the universal. Oedipus, for instance, was not to be A King and A Man, but the embodiment of kingship and manhood. The great golden mask was not, of course, susceptible to fine shades of subtle expression; but it did make it possible for the actor to suggest superhuman majesty, and an extraordinarily powerful, if abstract, expression of suffering.

Deliberately, we risked a production that was extreme, and might have seemed extremely pretentious. To some it may indeed have been so, but the general reaction of press and audience was markedly good.

This was four years ago. Looking back, I now wish that I had had the courage to be even more pretentious, more stylized and more extreme. These dramas are, in my opinion, only reduced by concessions to the prevalent naturalistic mode in the theatre; the emotion of the audience is diminished from tragedy to pathos.

If it ever falls to my lot again to direct a Greek tragedy, I hope to be able to stage it in so bold a manner that the personages bear no more realistic resemblance to human individuals than do the people in Rouault's paintings or the sculpture of Henry Moore; and that their utterance has little in common with the bourgeois verisimilitude of the naturalistic theatre; but relates rather to the crash of waves, the sighing of the wind, or the roars of enraged or wounded beasts. The result may be absurd; but that risk must, in the theatre, always apply to any departure from current fashion.

ALAN MACVEY
Directing Oedipus

Professor Alan MacVey, who teaches at the University of Iowa, in 1982 directed a production of *Oedipus* at Princeton. The play was performed by the Acting Ensemble; all principal roles were played by professional actors but the chorus consisted chiefly of students. The play was done in a small space, about sixty by forty feet, with the audience seated in two rows all around, to give the largest possible playing area. In a recent interview MacVey discussed the production.

Can you tell me something about the scenic design for your Oedipus?

I liked the scenic design of the production very much. We grappled with ways to suggest a marble landscape and the scene designer [Karen Schultz] arrived at a brilliant solution. She spread white butcher paper over the entire playing area. It was hard, cold, white, like marble, but wasn't trying to disguise itself as anything else. Each night we replaced the paper after it was scarred by blood and dirt. In the middle of the area we built an open pit out of real rocks and dirt.

Above this dried, baked area hung a large bronze pan, suspended by chains from the high ceiling. It contained fire. The play began with an offering placed in it. Later Tiresius walked across the holy area, as if in defiance of its power. The remaining element of the set was composed of two white walls kitty-corner from each other. Both were as tall as we could make them in a relatively small space. They had doorways and most entrances were made from one or the other. They were functional, but weren't massive enough really to do the trick.

What about the costumes? Did you try to evoke the classical world?

After going round and round we decided to stay with a Greek design. The principal characters wore colored "togas" (for lack of a better word) that were simple and elegant and looked very beautiful. Strong, bold colors—purple, blue . . . I can't remember what else. The chorus wore similar clothes, off-white in color, much rattier, torn with dried mud at the bottom. They wore a kind of headdress too.

At one point we debated putting the royalty in contemporary "power suits" and using a large, black round table—like a huge conference table—as the set. In hindsight I wish that we had gone this direction. Though the royal togas looked good, I wish we had been bolder. I think the suits would have looked great against the white and would have startled everyone. Given our realistic production the suits would have said power with a capital P. But we didn't do this, in part because we kept seeing togas in our minds' eyes. Since that time, in most of my Shakespeare productions, I've experimented with a kind of "modern-myth" approach to costuming that begins in the modern era and sprawls as is appropriate through other periods. I learned to do that by *not* doing it in *Oedipus*. Nonetheless, all in all the production was handsome and successful in visual terms.

Did you use masks? I suppose that everyone knows that the Greeks used masks—but modern actors aren't used to masks. What did you do?

We didn't use masks because we were exploring a more psychological approach. I think the intimate approach worked extremely well until Oedipus came out blind. Then it didn't work. Something about that scene cried out for a more distanced approach, and a mask would have been better. But we couldn't use a mask at that point in the evening. Instead we used a bloody blindfold, but it wasn't effective enough.

What about the chorus? One person or many? And did the chorus sing or speak to music?

The chorus was composed of about fifteen people, male and female, mostly students. Most of their words were sung. We hired a fine composer from Princeton to set the words to music and arrange accompaniment, et cetera. He did a fine job. The music was very powerful. It was more liturgical than I had in mind, and in some ways not as strange as it should have been. But it was complex and musically demanding, and gave a strong identity to the whole evening. Accompaniment, as I recall now, was limited. I think much of the music was sung without instrumental accompaniment—but there were surely drums on occasion.

Everyone says that Greek choruses danced, but no one knows much about ancient Greek dance. Did your chorus dance?

One of the most important things I've ever learned as a director came from dealing with the chorus and its movement. We hired a movement-choreographer to help with the chorus. She did a good job, adding movement to the singing. We tried to keep the movement fairly simple and there wasn't too much dance—mostly a kind of gesture that seemed appropriate.

Can you say a little more about the movement and its relation to the words?

At the first dress rehearsal I felt something was very wrong. It took me a while to realize what it was. It was the chorus, and specifically the movement. We were doing too much. It was a kind of meaningless layer. It made sense conceptually and looked as if it ought to be there—this was a Greek play, after all—but it was detracting from the impulse behind the words. As I thought further I realized that I hadn't really done the most important thing, which was to make sure that the chorus's words were coming from their mouths in the immediate present moment of the play for a reason that related to their experience of the events. Instead, I think we all took the chorus's words to be vaguely "choral"—that is, the words of the author, or some kind of comment on the action, or a musical interlude—something other than the direct human experience of those people in the play. After that rehearsal we simplified the movements to practically nothing. We focused the purpose of each ode directly on the immediate present, and sang directly, very intimately and personally, of fear, happiness, or whatever formed the heart of the ode. This improved the production enormously. I learned always to be sure that the words in a play come from the mouths of the characters, really from them, not from the playwright or from some "idea" of the way something was supposed to be.

It sounds as though you regard the production as quite successful.

I think the production worked very well until the closing scenes. From the blinding until the end of the play it didn't work. Perhaps the problem came from me and the actor playing Oedipus—perhaps we just weren't up to the demands of the play—but no matter what we tried, everything felt inadequate. We were stuck in a psychological approach to the material. We couldn't rise to the level of myth. The result was certainly interesting, and at times it was quite theatrical, but I felt the production failed the play at the end. Until then our approach was successful.

Did you make any cuts, or did you add anything?

We made few cuts and no additions. This was partly because we were using Bob Fagles' new translation, but also because I found the play swift and clear. The odes were not realistic, we discovered. But they too had immediacy and energy.

Did the actor playing Oedipus have to face any special difficulties?

One of the hardest things he faced was how "not to know" what the character found out until he found it out. The process of discovery is central to the play. John Doolittle (the actor) had to work hard to forget all the little details that Oedipus didn't know until he discovered them.

I imagine that the role of Tiresius is especially difficult. Did the actor seem satisfactory to you?

Yes. Paul Zimet played Tiresius brilliantly. He came up with the idea to have a woman's breasts but be dressed basically as a man. He used his amazing vocal range to move up and down the scales without ever making us feel it was technical. He barked and cried out and whispered. It was a brilliant performance because it was so bold and because it stemmed from a concept of Tiresius as man-woman.

If you were to do the play again, do you think you would pretty much repeat what you had done?

No. If I were to do the play again I'd probably try it in exactly the opposite way—nonrealistic, nonliturgical. I'm not certain any of these Greek plays can work fully for us. Who knows whether they even worked fully for the Greeks. Much of the language is mysterious for us, many of the references have little or no resonance. Even the great myths themselves, fleshed out in stories that are no longer immediate for us, are difficult to animate. The style is a mystery. Imagine doing *Oklahoma* two thousand years from now. Already that great musical is out of date, we have to find new ways to animate it. The Greeks are a giant problem. And yet I think the energy in the plays is very real and the possibility of power is there. I believe now that we need to seek the strangeness, the foreign-ness of the texts. Rather than bringing them as close to us as possible—as I tried with this production—we might look for their alien-ness. Perhaps in exploring this we'll find our way to the heart of these very strange plays.

Sophocles

Sophocles (c. 496–406 B.C.E.), the son of a wealthy Athenian, is one of the three Greek tragic writers whose work survives. (The other two are Aeschylus and Euripides.) Of Sophocles's more than one hundred twenty plays, we have seven. The exact dates of most of his plays are unknown. *Antigonê* was written about 441 B.C.E.; *Oedipus the King*, which deals with earlier material concerning the house of Oedipus, was written later, probably about 430 B.C.E.

■■■■■■■■■■■■■■

COMMENTARY ON *ANTIGONÊ*

The German philosopher George Wilhelm Friedrich Hegel, in the early nineteenth century, offered a view that makes a good starting point for considering *Antigonê*, although few have accepted it without qualification. For Hegel, the play is not a conflict of right against wrong; rather, it shows "a collision between the two highest moral powers," the rightful demands of the family versus those of the state. "The public law of the state and the instinctive family-love and duty towards a brother are here set in conflict." And elsewhere in Hegel: "Each of these two sides realizes only one of the moral powers . . . , and the meaning of eternal justice is shown in this, that both end in injustice because they are one-sided." Moreover, this conflict between ties of kinship and the claims of society reflects a conflict of divine law (the duty of the ruler to govern so as to preserve order, and of the citizen to obey). For Hegel, then, Sophocles' *Antigonê* denies neither the claim of the family nor the claim of the state; what it denies is the absoluteness of either claim.

Few modern readers have agreed with Hegel that Creon and Antigonê are equally right and equally wrong. Most readers find Antigonê much more sympathetic than Creon. Suppose, then, we briefly make a case for Antigonê. We can say, first of all, that she is right and Creon is wrong. (Even Creon's strongest defenders finally cannot say that Creon is right and Antigonê is wrong.) She acts bravely, persisting in a course that she knows will bring her to suffering. And she does this not out of any hope of private gain. Moreover, she persists even though she sees that her course of action isolates her from everyone else—from her sister Ismene, and from the chorus of men (Creon's counselors).

What can be said against Antigonê? Some readers have found her to be a bit too eager for martyrdom, a bit too headstrong, a bit too aware of her superiority to Ismene. There is, perhaps, also some validity to Hegel's comment that "the gods she reveres are the Gods of the Underworld, the instinctive powers of feeling, love, and blood, not the daylight gods of a free, self-conscious life of nation and people."

And what of Creon? The play itself, of course, refutes his early view that he is right in denying burial to Polyneices. And he is in many ways, even from the start, unattractive. One can note, for instance, his touchy male chauvinism, in such a passage as this:

Who is the man here,
She or I, if this crime goes unpunished?

(PAGE 95)

He soon comes to feel that the city is his personal property, so that his word is law—whether just or not. Can anything be said on his behalf? Perhaps at least this: First, he is new on the throne, and his inexperience apparently makes him suspicious, uneasy, and quick to act. Second, as ruler, he does indeed have the responsibility of maintaining order in a city that has recently undergone a civil war. Third, his refusal to allow Polyneices to be buried is not based on personal hatred of Polyneices; he believes (wrongly, it turns out, but perhaps understandably) that the gods cannot sympathize with a man who has come to burn their shrines. Fourth, perhaps it can be said in his behalf that the last third of the play arouses some sympathy (or at least pity) for him; although he repents, he is nevertheless terribly punished by the deaths of his son and his wife, and he must live with the knowledge that these deaths, as well as Antigonê's, are his responsibility.

Much more, of course, can be said—must be said—about both Antigonê and Creon; a reader of the play may well feel that not only can more be said but that less can be said, since several of the assertions just made about the two chief figures may strike some readers as scarcely relevant. For instance, one might say, "Yes, Creon is new on the throne, and, yes, he is ruling during a state of emergency, but that's of no importance since he is so clearly in the wrong." One might tentatively test this assertion by looking to see what the chorus has to say. To what degree does it support Creon, and to what degree does it support Antigonê? But of course there is a problem here: the chorus is a character in the play, not simply Sophocles's spokesperson. Indeed, it is quite interesting to study this chorus of rather conventional male advisers to Creon. They give Antigonê a little sympathy when she is led off to her death, but not until after they hear Teiresias (the seer) do they advise Creon to reverse his order. And, to take only one passage, we can notice that at the end of the first choral ode, celebrating civilization and the city, the chorus utters cautious words to the effect that the laws must be observed, and the "anarchic" person must be shunned. These words seem aimed at the rebel who has defied Creon, but at the end of the play the audience may well apply them not to Antigonê but to Creon.

The more one reads the play and thinks about it, the more subtle it becomes. This is not to suggest that one cannot come out and say "Antigonê is the tragic hero, and Creon is clearly wrong"; but it is to suggest that as soon as one has come out and said such a thing, one realizes that there is more to be said. For instance, to continue with the position just taken, one wants to see and to say exactly why and how Creon is "wrong," and even while listing his faults one finds that he holds one's attention. He acts—he believes—in the best interests of Thebes. And of course even those few who find Antigonê a headstrong girl (readers familiar with *Oedipus the King* may think she has inherited her father's irritability), a bit too intent on martyrdom, must, on reading the play, admit that she compels our admiration. Scholarly books on ancient Greece rightly tell us that women played a severely limited role in Athenian society. Pericles, the Athenian statesman and general, probably summed up the average man's view when he said, "A woman's glory is not to show more weakness than is natural to her sex, and not to be talked about, for good or for evil, among men." The scholarly books on ancient

Athens are probably right, in the main. Luckily, Sophocles didn't read them.

In 1849 Matthew Arnold published a splendid poem in which he said that Sophocles "saw life steadily, and saw it whole." But Arnold, no indiscriminate admirer of Sophocles's work, a few years later granted that the interests of the ancient writers were sometimes so remote from ours that "we can no longer sympathize. An action like the action of the *Antigonê* of Sophocles, which turns upon the conflict between the heroine's duty to her brother's corpse and that to the laws of her country, is no longer one in which it is possible that we should feel a deep interest."

One might indeed think that a play which makes a fuss about ancient Greek burial rites could be of only remote interest to later readers, and yet Sophocles's *Antigonê* has seemed highly relevant to later ages. Modern writers have sometimes shown this interest by rewriting the play, finding in the old story a new meaning. For instance, during World War II, when France was occupied by the Nazis, Jean Anouilh produced his own version of *Antigonê* in which it was evident that Antigonê stood for the French resistance and that Creon, efficient and ruthless, stood for the Nazis. But Sophocles's play itself—not merely the gist of his plot as reinterpreted by later playwrights—continues to hold our interest, too.

Behind the story of Antigonê is the story of her father, Oedipus (as told in Sophocles's *Oedipus the King*; see pp. 56–77), who unknowingly killed his own father and slept with his own mother. The curse on the house of Oedipus outlived him and descended to his children: His sons Polyneices and Eteocles quarreled and killed each other, and his daughter Antigonê was put to death when she sought to confer on Polyneices the burial rites she felt were his due.

More precisely, after the fall of Oedipus his two sons inherited the rule of Thebes. They were to rule jointly, but they quarreled and Eteocles banished his brother Polyneices. Polyneices returned to Thebes, armed with allies, and in the ensuing conflict both brothers were killed. Creon, their maternal uncle (and Antigonê's), thereupon set about ruling the city. One of his first acts was to order that Eteocles be given a state funeral but that Polyneices, who had come in arms against his own city and had thereby (in Creon's opinion) assaulted the gods of the city, be denied burial. For the Greeks, the denial of funeral rites—a fate reserved for the worst criminals—meant that the soul of the corpse could not enter the next world and be honored.

Antigonê defied her uncle's edict, gave the corpse a symbolic burial, was caught, and was sent to death. Creon ultimately relented, but his change of mind came too late: Antigonê was dead, and so were Creon's wife and son.

Matthew Arnold notwithstanding, even a single reading of the play will let a reader see that it is not simply about ancient rites. Nor is it about the workings of fate, for although the household curse is several times mentioned in the play, the tragic outcome does not seem to be arbitrarily imposed on the characters. But what, then, is the play about?

ANTIGONÊ
Sophocles

An English Version by Dudley Fitts and Robert Fitzgerald

LIST OF CHARACTERS

ANTIGONÊ
ISMENÊ
EURYDICÊ
CREON
HAIMON
TEIRESIAS
A SENTRY
A MESSENGER
CHORUS

SCENE

Before the palace of Creon, King of Thebes. A central double door, and two lateral doors. A platform extends the length of the façade, and from this platform three steps lead down into the "orchestra," or chorus-ground.

TIME

Dawn of the day after the repulse of the Argive army from the assault on Thebes.

PROLOGUE

Antigonê and Ismenê enter from the central door of the palace.

ANTIGONÊ.
  Ismenê, dear sister,
  You would think that we had already suffered enough
  For the curse on Oedipus.°
  I cannot imagine any grief
5 That you and I have not gone through. And now—
  Have they told you of the new decree of our King
     Creon?

ISMENÊ.
  I have heard nothing: I know
  That two sisters lost two brothers, a double death
  In a single hour; and I know that the Argive army
10 Fled in the night; but beyond this, nothing.

ANTIGONÊ.
  I thought so. And this is why I wanted you
  To come out here with me. There is something we must
    do.

ISMENÊ.
  Why do you speak so strangely?

---

3 Oedipus, once King of Thebes, was the father of Antigonê and Ismenê, and of their brothers Polyneicês and Eteoclês. Oedipus unwittingly killed his father, Laïos, and married his own mother Iocastê. When he learned what he had done, he blinded himself and left Thebes. Eteoclês and Polyneicês quarreled; Polyneicês was driven out but returned to assault Thebes. In the battle each brother killed the other; Creon became king and ordered that Polyneicês be left to rot unburied on the battlefield as a traitor.

ANTIGONÊ.
  Listen, Ismenê:
  Creon buried our brother Eteoclês   15
  With military honors, gave him a soldier's funeral,
  And it was right that he should; but Polyneicês,
  Who fought as bravely and died as miserably,—
  They say that Creon has sworn
  No one shall bury him, no one mourn for him,   20
  But his body must lie in the fields, a sweet treasure
  For carrion birds to find as they search for food.
  That is what they say, and our good Creon is coming here
  To announce it publicly; and the penalty—
  Stoning to death in the public square!
                  There it is,   25
  And now you can prove what you are:
  A true sister, or a traitor to your family.

ISMENÊ.
  Antigonê, you are mad! What could I possibly do?

ANTIGONÊ.
  You must decide whether you will help me or not.

ISMENÊ.
  I do not understand you. Help you in what?   30

ANTIGONÊ.
  Ismenê. I am going to bury him. Will you come?

ISMENÊ.
  Bury him! You have just said the new law forbids it.

ANTIGONÊ.
  He is my brother. And he is your brother, too.

ISMENÊ.
  But think of the danger! Think what Creon will do!

ANTIGONÊ.
  Creon is not strong enough to stand in my way.   35

ISMENÊ.
　　Ah sister!
　　Oedipus died, everyone hating him
　　For what his own search brought to light, his eyes
　　Ripped out by his own hand; and Iocastê died,
40　　His mother and wife at once: she twisted the cords
　　That strangled her life; and our two brothers died,
　　Each killed by the other's sword. And we are left:
　　But oh, Antigonê,
　　Think how much more terrible than these
45　　Our own death would be if we should go against Creon
　　And do what he has forbidden! We are only women,
　　We cannot fight with men, Antigonê!
　　The law is strong, we must give in to the law
　　In this thing, and in worse. I beg the Dead
50　　To forgive me, but I am helpless: I must yield
　　To those in authority. And I think it is dangerous
　　　　business
　　To be always meddling.
ANTIGONÊ.　　　　　　　　　　　　If that is what you think,
　　I should not want you, even if you asked to come.
　　You have made your choice, you can be what you want
　　　　to be.
55　　But I will bury him; and if I must die,
　　I say that this crime is holy: I shall lie down
　　With him in death, and I shall be as dear
　　To him as he to me.
　　　　　　　　　　　　It is the dead,
　　Not the living, who make the longest demands:
　　We die for ever. . . .
60　　　　　　　　　　　　You may do as you like.
　　Since apparently the laws of the gods mean nothing to
　　　　you.
ISMENÊ.
　　They mean a great deal to me; but I have no strength
　　To break laws that were made for the public good.
ANTIGONÊ.
　　That must be your excuse, I suppose. But as for me,
　　I will bury the brother I love.
65　ISMENÊ.　　　　　　　　　　　　Antigonê,
　　I am so afraid for you!
ANTIGONÊ.　　　　　　　　You need not be:
　　You have yourself to consider, after all.
ISMENÊ.
　　But no one must hear of this, you must tell no one!
　　I will keep it a secret, I promise!
ANTIGONÊ.　　　　　　　　　　　O tell it! Tell everyone!
70　　Think how they'll hate you when it all comes out
　　If they learn that you knew about it all the time!
ISMENÊ.
　　So fiery! You should be cold with fear.
ANTIGONÊ.
　　Perhaps. But I am doing only what I must.
ISMENÊ.
　　But can you do it? I say that you cannot.

ANTIGONÊ.
　　Very well: when my strength gives out,
　　I shall do no more.   75
ISMENÊ.
　　Impossible things should not be tried at all.
ANTIGONÊ.
　　Go away, Ismenê:
　　I shall be hating you soon, and the dead will too,
　　For your words are hateful. Leave me my foolish plan:
　　I am not afraid of the danger; if it means death,   80
　　It will not be the worst of deaths—death without honor.
ISMENÊ.
　　Go then, if you feel that you must.
　　You are unwise,
　　But a loyal friend indeed to those who love you.

Exit into the palace. Antigonê goes off, left. Enter the
Chorus.

PÁRODOS

Strophe 1

CHORUS.
　　Now the long blade of the sun, lying
　　Level east to west, touches with glory
　　Thebes of the Seven Gates. Open, unlidded
　　Eye of golden day! O marching light
　　Across the eddy and rush of Dircê's stream,°   5
　　Striking the white shields of the enemy
　　Thrown headlong backward from the blaze of morning!
CHORAGOS.°
　　Polyneicês their commander
　　Roused them with windy phrases,
　　He the wild eagle screaming   10
　　Insults above our land,
　　His wings their shields of snow,
　　His crest their marshalled helms.

Antistrophe 1

CHORUS.
　　Against our seven gates in a yawning ring
　　The famished spears came onward in the night: 15
　　But before his jaws were sated with our blood,
　　Or pinefire took the garland of our towers,
　　He was thrown back; and as he turned, great Thebes—

5 Dircê's stream a stream west of Thebes　**8 Choragos** leader of
the Chorus

No tender victim for his noisy power—
20   Rose like a dragon behind him, shouting war.
CHORAGOS.
For God hates utterly
The bray of bragging tongues;
And when he beheld their smiling,
Their swagger of golden helms,
25   The frown of his thunder blasted
Their first man from our walls.

Strophe 2

CHORUS.
We heard his shout of triumph high in the air
Turn to a scream; far out in a flaming arc
He fell with his windy torch, and the earth struck him.
30   And others storming in fury no less than his
Found shock of death in the dusty joy of battle.
CHORAGOS.
Seven captains at seven gates
Yielded their clanging arms to the god
That bends the battle-line and breaks it.
35   These two only, brothers in blood,
Face to face in matchless rage.
Mirroring each the other's death,
Clashed in long combat.

Antistrophe 2

CHORUS.
But now in the beautiful morning of victory
40   Let Thebes of the many chariots sing for joy!
With hearts for dancing we'll take leave of war:
Our temples shall be sweet with hymns of praise,
And the long nights shall echo with our chorus.

SCENE 1

CHORAGOS.
But now at last our new King is coming:
Creon of Thebes, Menoikeus' son.
In this auspicious dawn of his reign
What are the new complexities
5   That shifting Fate has woven for him?
What is his counsel? Why has he summoned
The old men to hear him?

*Enter Creon from the palace, center. He addresses the
Chorus from the top step.*

CREON. Gentlemen: I have the honor to inform you that our
Ship of State, which recent storms have threatened to
10   destroy, has come safely to harbor at last, guided by the
merciful wisdom of Heaven. I have summoned you here
this morning because I know that I can depend upon you:
your devotion to King Laïos was absolute; you never hesitated in your duty to our late ruler Oedipus; and when
Oedipus died, your loyalty was transferred to his children.   15
Unfortunately, as you know, his two sons, the princes
Eteoclês and Polyneicês, have killed each other in battle;
and I, as the next in blood, have succeeded to the full
power of the throne.
I am aware, of course, that no Ruler can expect com-   20
plete loyalty from his subjects until he has been tested in
office. Nevertheless, I say to you at the very outset that I
have nothing but contempt for the kind of Governor
who is afraid, for whatever reason, to follow the course
that he knows is best for the State; and as for the man   25
who sets private friendship above the public welfare,—I
have no use for him, either. I call God to witness that if I
saw my country headed for ruin, I should not be afraid to
speak out plainly; and I need hardly remind you that I
would never have any dealings with an enemy of the peo-   30
ple. No one values friendship more highly than I: but we
must remember that friends made at the risk of wrecking
our Ship are not real friends at all.
These are my principles, at any rate, and that is why I
have made the following decision concerning the sons of   35
Oedipus: Eteoclês, who died as a man should die, fighting
for his country, is to be buried with full military honors,
with all the ceremony that is usual when the greatest heroes die; but his brother Polyneicês, who broke his exile
to come back with fire and sword against his native city   40
and the shrines of his fathers' gods, whose one idea was to
spill the blood of his blood and sell his own people into
slavery—Polyneicês, I say, is to have no burial: no man is
to touch him or say the least prayer for him; he shall lie
on the plain, unburied; and the birds and the scavenging   45
dogs can do with him whatever they like.
This is my command, and you can see the wisdom behind it. As long as I am King, no traitor is going to be
honored with the loyal man. But whoever shows by word
and deed that he is on the side of the State—he shall   50
have my respect while he is living and my reverence
when he is dead.
CHORAGOS.
If that is your will, Creon son of Menoikeus,
You have the right to enforce it: we are yours.
CREON.
That is my will. Take care that you do your part.   55
CHORAGOS.
We are old men: let the younger ones carry it out.
CREON.
I do not mean that: the sentries have been appointed.
CHORAGOS.
Then what is it that you would have us do?
CREON.
You will give no support to whoever breaks this law.
CHORAGOS.
Only a crazy man is in love with death!   60

CREON.
　　And death it is; yet money talks, and the wisest
　　Have sometimes been known to count a few coins too
　　　　many.

Enter Sentry from left.

SENTRY. I'll not say that I'm out of breath from running,
　　King, because every time I stopped to think about what I
65　　have to tell you, I felt like going back. And all the time a
　　voice kept saying, "You fool, don't you know you're walk-
　　ing straight into trouble?"; and then another voice: "Yes,
　　but if you let somebody else get the news to Creon first, it
　　will be even worse than that for you!" But good sense
70　　won out, at least I hope it was good sense, and here I am
　　with a story that makes no sense at all; but I'll tell it any-
　　how, because, as they say, what's going to happen's going
　　to happen and—
CREON.
　　Come to the point. What have you to say?
75　SENTRY. I did not do it. I did not see who did it. You must not
　　punish me for what someone else has done.
CREON.
　　A comprehensive defense! More effective, perhaps, if I
　　　　knew its purpose. Come: what is it?
SENTRY.
　　A dreadful thing . . . I don't know how to put it—
CREON.
　　Out with it!
80　SENTRY.　　　　　Well, then;
　　The dead man—
　　　　　　　Polyneicês—

*Pause. The sentry is overcome, fumbles for words. Creon
waits impassively.*

　　　　　　　　　out there—
　　　　　　　　　　　　someone,—
　　New dust on the slimy flesh!

Pause. No sign from Creon.

　　Someone has given it burial that way, and
　　Gone . . . .

Long pause. Creon finally speaks with deadly control.

CREON.
　　And the man who dared do this?
85　SENTRY.　　　　　　　　I swear I
　　Do not know! You must believe me!
　　　　　　　　Listen:
　　The ground was dry, not a sign of digging, no,
　　Not a wheeltrack in the dust, no trace of anyone.
　　It was when they relieved us this morning: and one of
　　　　them,
　　The corporal, pointed to it.
90　　　　　　　There it was,

The strangest—
　　　　Look:
The body, just mounded over with light dust: you see?
Not buried really, but as if they'd covered it
Just enough for the ghost's peace. And no sign
Of dogs or any wild animal that had been there.　　　　95

And then what a scene there was! Every man of us
Accusing the other: we all proved the other man did it,
We all had proof that we could not have done it.
We were ready to take hot iron in our hands,
Walk through fire, swear by all the gods,　　　　　100
It was not I!
I do not know who it was, but it was not I!

*Creon's rage has been mounting steadily, but the Sentry is
too intent upon his story to notice it.*

And then, when this came to nothing, someone said
A thing that silenced us and made us stare
Down at the ground: you had to be told the news,　　105
And one of us had to do it! We threw the dice,
And the bad luck fell to me. So here I am,
No happier to be here than you are to have me:
Nobody likes the man who brings bad news.
CHORAGOS.
　　I have been wondering, King: can it be that the gods　110
　　　　have done this?
CREON (*furiously*).
　　Stop!
　　Must you doddering wrecks
　　Go out of your heads entirely? "The gods"!
　　Intolerable!　　　　　　　　　　　　115
　　The gods favor this corpse? Why? How had he served
　　　　them?
　　Tried to loot their temples, burn their images,
　　Yes, and the whole State, and its laws with it!
　　Is it your senile opinion that the gods love to honor bad
　　　　men?
　　A pious thought!—
　　　　　　　　No, from the very beginning　　120
　　There have been those who have whispered together,
　　Stiff-necked anarchists, putting their heads together,
　　Scheming against me in alleys. These are the men,
　　And they have bribed my own guard to do this thing.
　　(*Sententiously.*) Money!　　　　　　　125
　　There's nothing in the world so demoralizing as money.
　　Down go your cities,
　　Homes gone, men gone, honest hearts corrupted.
　　Crookedness of all kinds, and all for money!
　　(*To Sentry.*)　　　　　　　But you—!
　　I swear by God and by the throne of God,　　　130
　　The man who has done this thing shall pay for it!
　　Find that man, bring him here to me, or your death
　　Will be the least of your problems: I'll string you up
　　Alive, and there will be certain ways to make you

135   Discover your employer before you die;
       And the process may teach you a lesson you seem to
           have missed:
       The dearest profit is sometimes all too dear:
       That depends on the source. Do you understand me?
       A fortune won is often misfortune.
       SENTRY.
           King, may I speak?
140   CREON.   Your very voice distresses me.
       SENTRY.
           Are you sure that it is my voice, and not your conscience?
       CREON.
           By God, he wants to analyze me now!
       SENTRY.
           It is not what I say, but what has been done, that hurts
               you.
       CREON.
           You talk too much.
       SENTRY.   Maybe; but I've done nothing.
       CREON.
145   Sold your soul for some silver: that's all you've done.
       SENTRY.
           How dreadful it is when the right judge judges wrong!
       CREON.
           Your figures of speech
           May entertain you now; but unless you bring me the man,
           You will get little profit from them in the end.

       Exit Creon into the palace.

       SENTRY.
150   "Bring me the man"—!
       I'd like nothing better than bringing him the man!
       But bring him or not, you have seen the last of me here.
       At any rate, I am safe!

                                               (*Exit Sentry.*)

ODE 1

Strophe 1

       CHORUS.
           Numberless are the world's wonders, but not
           More wonderful than man; the stormgray sea
           Yields to his prows, the huge crests bear him high;
           Earth, holy and inexhaustible, is graven
   5   With shining furrows where his plows have gone
           Year after year, the timeless labor of stallions.

Antistrophe 1

           The lightboned birds and beasts that cling to cover,
           The lithe fish lighting their reaches of dim water,
           All are taken, tamed in the net of his mind;
  10   The lion on the hill, the wild horse windy-maned,

       Resign to him; and his blunt yoke has broken
       The sultry shoulders of the mountain bull.

Strophe 2

       Words also, and thought as rapid as air,
       He fashions to his good use; statecraft is his,
       And his the skill that deflects the arrows of snow,   15
       The spears of winter rain: from every wind
       He has made himself secure—from all but one:
       In the late wind of death he cannot stand.

Antistrophe 2

       O clear intelligence, force beyond all measure!
       O fate of man, working both good and evil!   20
       When the laws are kept, how proudly his city stands!
       When the laws are broken, what of his city then?
       Never may the anarchic man find rest at my hearth,
       Never be it said that my thoughts are his thoughts.

SCENE II

Reenter Sentry leading Antigonê.

       CHORAGOS.
           What does this mean? Surely this captive woman
           Is the Princess, Antigonê. Why should she be taken?
       SENTRY.
           Here is the one who did it! We caught her
           In the very act of burying him.—Where is Creon?
       CHORAGOS.
           Just coming from the house.

       Enter Creon, center.

       CREON.   What has happened?   5
           Why have you come back so soon?
       SENTRY (*expansively*).   O King,
           A man should never be too sure of anything:
           I would have sworn
           That you'd not see me here again: your anger
           Frightened me so, and the things you threatened me   10
               with;
           But how could I tell then
           That I'd be able to solve the case so soon?
           No dice-throwing this time: I was only too glad to come!
           Here is this woman. She is the guilty one:
           We found her trying to bury him.   15
           Take her, then; question her; judge her as you will.
           I am through with the whole thing now, and glad of it.
       CREON.
           But this is Antigonê! Why have you brought her here?
       SENTRY.
           She was burying him, I tell you!
       CREON (*severely*).   Is this the truth?

SENTRY.
20   I saw her with my own eyes. Can I say more?
CREON.
      The details: come, tell me quickly!
SENTRY.   It was like this:
      After those terrible threats of yours, King,
      We went back and brushed the dust away from the body.
      The flesh was soft by now, and stinking,
25   So we sat on a hill to windward and kept guard.
      No napping this time! We kept each other awake.
      But nothing happened until the white round sun
      Whirled in the center of the round sky over us:
      Then, suddenly,
30   A storm of dust roared up from the earth, and the sky
      Went out, the plain vanished with all its trees
      In the stinging dark. We closed our eyes and endured it.
      The whirlwind lasted a long time, but it passed;
      And then we looked, and there was Antigonê!
35   I have seen
      A mother bird come back to a stripped nest, heard
      Her crying bitterly a broken note or two
      For the young ones stolen. Just so, when this girl
      Found the bare corpse, and all her love's work wasted,
40   She wept, and cried on heaven to damn the hands
      That had done this thing.
                               And then she brought more dust
      And sprinkled wine three times for her brother's ghost.

      We ran and took her at once. She was not afraid,
      Not even when we charged her with what she had done.
      She denied nothing.
45   And this was a comfort to me,
      And some uneasiness: for it is a good thing
      To escape from death, but it is no great pleasure
      To bring death to a friend.
                                  Yet I always say
      There is nothing so comfortable as your own safe skin!
CREON (*slowly, dangerously*).
50   And you, Antigonê,
      You with your head hanging,—do you confess this thing?
ANTIGONÊ.
      I do. I deny nothing.
CREON (*to Sentry*).
                          You may go.
                                      (*Exit Sentry.*)

      (*To Antigonê.*) Tell me, tell me briefly:
      Had you heard my proclamation touching this matter?
ANTIGONÊ.
55   It was public. Could I help hearing it?
CREON.
      And yet you dared defy the law.
ANTIGONÊ.   I dared.
      It was not God's proclamation. That final Justice
      That rules the world below makes no such laws.

Your edict, King, was strong.
But all your strength is weakness itself against   60
The immortal unrecorded laws of God.
They are not merely now: they were, and shall be,
Operative for ever, beyond man utterly.
I knew I must die, even without your decree:
I am only mortal. And if I must die   65
Now, before it is my time to die,
Surely this is no hardship: can anyone
Living, as I live, with evil all about me,
Think Death less than a friend? This death of mine
Is of no importance; but if I had left my brother   70
Lying in death unburied, I should have suffered.
Now I do not.
              You smile at me. Ah Creon,
Think me a fool, if you like; but it may well be
That a fool convicts me of folly.
CHORAGOS.
Like father, like daughter: both headstrong, deaf to   75
   reason!
She has never learned to yield.
CREON.   She has much to learn.
The inflexible heart breaks first, the toughest iron
Cracks first, and the wildest horses bend their necks
At the pull of the smallest curb.
                                  Pride? In a slave?
This girl is guilty of a double insolence,   80
Breaking the given laws and boasting of it.
Who is the man here,
She or I, if this crime goes unpunished?
Sister's child, or more than sister's child,
Or closer yet in blood—she and her sister   85
Win bitter death for this!
(*To servants.*)   Go, some of you,
Arrest Ismenê. I accuse her equally.
Bring her: you will find her sniffling in the house there.

Her mind's a traitor: crimes kept in the dark
Cry for light, and the guardian brain shudders;   90
But how much worse than this
Is brazen boasting of barefaced anarchy!
ANTIGONÊ.
Creon, what more do you want than my death?
CREON.   Nothing.
That gives me everything.
ANTIGONÊ.   Then I beg you: kill me.
This talking is a great weariness: your words   95
Are distasteful to me, and I am sure that mine
Seem so to you. And yet they should not seem so:
I should have praise and honor for what I have done.
All these men here would praise me
Were their lips not frozen shut with fear of you.   100
(*Bitterly.*) Ah the good fortune of kings,
Licensed to say and do whatever they please!

CREON.
    You are alone here in that opinion.
ANTIGONÊ.
    No, they are with me. But they keep their tongues in
        leash.
CREON.
105   Maybe. But you are guilty, and they are not.
ANTIGONÊ.
    There is no guilt in reverence for the dead.
CREON.
    But Eteoclês—was he not your brother too?
ANTIGONÊ.
    My brother too.
CREON.   And you insult his memory?
ANTIGONÊ (softly).
    The dead man would not say that I insult it.
CREON.
110   He would: for you honor a traitor as much as him.
ANTIGONÊ.
    His own brother, traitor or not, and equal in blood.
CREON.
    He made war on his country. Eteoclês defended it.
ANTIGONÊ.
    Nevertheless, there are honors due all the dead.
CREON.
    But not the same for the wicked as for the just.
ANTIGONÊ.
115   Ah Creon, Creon,
    Which of us can say what the gods hold wicked?
CREON.
    An enemy is an enemy, even dead.
ANTIGONÊ.
    It is my nature to join in love, not hate.
CREON (finally losing patience).
    Go join them then; if you must have your love,
120   Find it in hell!
CHORAGOS.
    But see, Ismenê comes:

    Enter Ismenê, guarded.

    Those tears are sisterly, the cloud
    That shadows her eyes rains down gentle sorrow.
CREON.
    You too, Ismenê,
125   Snake in my ordered house, sucking my blood
    Stealthily—and all the time I never knew
    That these two sisters were aiming at my throne!
                                        Ismenê,
    Do you confess your share in this crime, or deny it?
    Answer me.
ISMENÊ.
130   Yes, if she will let me say so. I am guilty.
ANTIGONÊ (coldly).
    No, Ismenê. You have no right to say so.

You would not help me, and I will not have you help me.
ISMENÊ.
    But now I know what you meant; and I am here
    To join you, to take my share of punishment.
ANTIGONÊ.
    The dead man and the gods who rule the dead   135
    Know whose act this was. Words are not friends.
ISMENÊ.
    Do you refuse me, Antigonê? I want to die with you:
    I too have a duty that I must discharge to the dead.
ANTIGONÊ.
    You shall not lessen my death by sharing it.
ISMENÊ.
    What do I care for life when you are dead?   140
ANTIGONÊ.
    Ask Creon. You're always hanging on his opinions.
ISMENÊ.
    You are laughing at me. Why, Antigonê?
ANTIGONÊ.
    It's a joyless laughter, Ismenê.
ISMENÊ.   But can I do nothing?
ANTIGONÊ.
    Yes. Save yourself. I shall not envy you.
    There are those who will praise you; I shall have honor,   145
        too.
ISMENÊ.
    But we are equally guilty!
ANTIGONÊ.   No more, Ismenê.
    You are alive, but I belong to Death.
CREON (to the chorus).
    Gentlemen, I beg you to observe these girls:
    One has just now lost her mind; the other,
    It seems, has never had a mind at all.   150
ISMENÊ.
    Grief teaches the steadiest minds to waver, King.
CREON.
    Yours certainly did, when you assumed guilt with the
        guilty!
ISMENÊ.
    But how could I go on living without her?
CREON.   You are.
    She is already dead.
ISMENÊ.   But your own son's bride!
CREON.
    There are places enough for him to push his plow.   155
    I want no wicked women for my sons!
ISMENÊ.
    O dearest Haimon, how your father wrongs you!
CREON.
    I've had enough of your childish talk of marriage!
CHORAGOS.
    Do you really intend to steal this girl from your son?
CREON.
    No; Death will do that for me.

160 CHORAGOS.   Then she must die?
CREON (*ironically*).
     You dazzle me.
                    —But enough of this talk!
     (*To guards.*) You, there, take them away and guard them
          well:
     For they are but women, and even brave men run
     When they see Death coming.

                                (*Exeunt Ismenê, Antigonê, and guards.*)

ODE II

Strophe 1

CHORUS.
     Fortunate is the man who has never tasted God's
          vengeance!
     Where once the anger of heaven has struck, that house
          is shaken
     For ever: damnation rises behind each child
     Like a wave cresting out of the black northeast,
5   When the long darkness under sea roars up
     And bursts drumming death upon the windwhipped sand.

Antistrophe 1

     I have seen this gathering sorrow from time long past
     Loom upon Oedipus' children: generation from generation
     Takes the compulsive rage of the enemy god.
10   So lately this last flower of Oedipus' line
     Drank the sunlight! but now a passionate word
     And a handful of dust have closed up all its beauty.

Strophe 2

     What mortal arrogance
     Transcends the wrath of Zeus?
15   Sleep cannot lull him nor the effortless long months
     Of the timeless gods: but he is young for ever,
     And his house is the shining day of high Olympos.
     All that is and shall be,
     And all the past, is his.
20   No pride on earth is free of the curse of heaven.

Antistrophe 2

     The straying dreams of men
     May bring them ghosts of joy:
     But as they drowse, the waking embers burn them;
     Or they walk with fixed eyes, as blind men walk.
25   But the ancient wisdom speaks for our own time:

     Fate works most for woe
       With Folly's fairest show.
     Man's little pleasure is the spring of sorrow.

SCENE III

CHORAGOS.
     But here is Haimon, King, the last of all your sons.
     Is it grief for Antigonê that brings him here,
     And bitterness at being robbed of his bride?

     Enter Haimon.

CREON.
     We shall soon see, and no need of diviners.
                                        —Son,
     You have heard my final judgment on that girl: 5
     Have you come here hating me, or have you come
     With deference and with love, whatever I do?
HAIMON.
     I am your son, father. You are my guide.
     You make things clear for me, and I obey you.
     No marriage means more to me than your continuing   10
          wisdom.
CREON.
     Good. That is the way to behave: subordinate
     Everything else, my son, to your father's will.
     This is what a man prays for, that he may get
     Sons attentive and dutiful in his house,
     Each one hating his father's enemies,   15
     Honoring his father's friends. But if his sons
     Fail him, if they turn out unprofitably,
     What has he fathered but trouble for himself
     And amusement for the malicious?
                                So you are right
     Not to lose your head over this woman.   20
     Your pleasure with her would soon grow cold, Haimon,
     And then you'd have a hellcat in bed and elsewhere.
     Let her find her husband in Hell!
     Of all the people in this city, only she
     Has had contempt for my law and broken it.   25

     Do you want me to show myself weak before the people?
     Or to break my sworn word? No, and I will not.
     The woman dies.
     I suppose she'll plead "family ties." Well, let her.
     If I permit my own family to rebel,   30
     How shall I earn the world's obedience?
     Show me the man who keeps his house in hand,
     He's fit for public authority.
                                I'll have no dealings
     With lawbreakers, critics of the government:
     Whoever is chosen to govern should be obeyed—   35
     Must be obeyed, in all things, great and small,
     Just and unjust! O Haimon,

The man who knows how to obey, and that man only,
Knows how to give commands when the time comes.
40 You can depend on him, no matter how fast
The spears come: he's a good soldier, he'll stick it out.

Anarchy, anarchy! Show me a greater evil!
This is why cities tumble and the great houses rain down,
This is what scatters armies!

45 No, no: good lives are made so by discipline.
We keep the laws then, and the lawmakers,
And no woman shall seduce us. If we must lose,
Let's lose to a man, at least! Is a woman stronger than we?

CHORAGOS.
Unless time has rusted my wits,
50 What you say, King, is said with point and dignity.

HAIMON (*boyishly earnest*).
Father:
Reason is God's crowning gift to man, and you are right
To warn me against losing mine. I cannot say—
I hope that I shall never want to say!—that you
55 Have reasoned badly. Yet there are other men
Who can reason, too; and their opinions might be helpful.
You are not in a position to know everything
That people say or do, or what they feel:
Your temper terrifies—everyone
60 Will tell you only what you like to hear.
But I, at any rate, can listen; and I have heard them
Muttering and whispering in the dark about this girl.
They say no woman has ever, so unreasonably,
Died so shameful a death for a generous act:
65 "She covered her brother's body. Is this indecent?
She kept him from dogs and vultures. Is this a crime?
Death?—She should have all the honor that we can give
    her!"

This is the way they talk out there in the city.

You must believe me:
70 Nothing is closer to me than your happiness.
What could be closer? Must not any son
Value his father's fortune as his father does his?
I beg you, do not be unchangeable:
Do not believe that you alone can be right.
75 The man who thinks that,
The man who maintains that only he has the power
To reason correctly, the gift to speak, the soul—
A man like that, when you know him, turns out empty.

It is not reason never to yield to reason!

80 In flood time you can see how some trees bend,
And because they bend, even their twigs are safe,
While stubborn trees are torn up, roots and all.
And the same thing happens in sailing:
Make your sheet fast, never slacken,—and over you go,
85 Head over heels and under: and there's your voyage.
Forget you are angry! Let yourself be moved!

I know I am young; but please let me say this:
The ideal condition
Would be, I admit, that men should be right by instinct;
But since we are all too likely to go astray,   90
The reasonable thing is to learn from those who can
    teach.
CHORAGOS.
You will do well to listen to him, King,
If what he says is sensible. And you, Haimon,
Must listen to your father.—Both speak well.
CREON.
You consider it right for a man of my years and   95
    experience
To go to school to a boy?
HAIMON.   It is not right
If I am wrong. But if I am young, and right,
What does my age matter?
CREON.
You think it right to stand up for an anarchist?
HAIMON.
Not at all. I pay no respect to criminals.   100
CREON.
Then she is not a criminal?
HAIMON.
The City would deny it, to a man.
CREON.
And the City proposes to teach me how to rule?
HAIMON.
Ah. Who is it that's talking like a boy now?
CREON.
My voice is the one voice giving orders in this City!   105
HAIMON.
It is no City if it takes orders from one voice.
CREON.
The State is the King!
HAIMON.   Yes, if the State is a desert.

Pause.

CREON.
This boy, it seems, has sold out to a woman.
HAIMON.
If you are a woman: my concern is only for you.
CREON.
So? Your "concern"! In a public brawl with your father!   110
HAIMON.
How about you, in a public brawl with justice?
CREON.
With justice, when all that I do is within my rights?
HAIMON.
You have no right to trample on God's right.
CREON (*completely out of control*).
Fool, adolescent fool! Taken in by a woman!
HAIMON.
You'll never see me taken in by anything vile.   115

CREON.
    Every word you say is for her!
HAIMON (*quietly, darkly*).   And for you.
    And for me. And for the gods under the earth.
CREON.
    You'll never marry her while she lives.
HAIMON.
    Then she must die.—But her death will cause another.
CREON.
120   Another?
    Have you lost your senses? Is this an open threat?
HAIMON.
    There is no threat in speaking to emptiness.
CREON.
    I swear you'll regret this superior tone of yours!
    You are the empty one!
HAIMON.   If you were not my father,
125   I'd say you were perverse.
CREON.
    You girlstruck fool, don't play at words with me!
HAIMON.
    I am sorry. You prefer silence.
CREON.   Now, by God—
    I swear, by all the gods in heaven above us,
    You'll watch it, I swear you shall!
    (*To the servants.*)   Bring her out!
130   Bring the woman out! Let her die before his eyes!
    Here, this instant, with her bridegroom beside her!
HAIMON.
    Not here, no; she will not die here, King.
    And you will never see my face again.
    Go on raving as long as you've a friend to endure
      you.

                       (*Exit Haimon.*)

CHORAGOS.
135   Gone, gone.
    Creon, a young man in a rage is dangerous!
CREON.
    Let him do, or dream to do, more than a man can.
    He shall not save these girls from death.
CHORAGOS.   These girls?
    You have sentenced them both?
CREON.   No, you are right.
140   I will not kill the one whose hands are clean.
CHORAGOS.
    But Antigonê?
CREON (*somberly*). I will carry her far away
    Out there in the wilderness, and lock her
    Living in a vault of stone. She shall have food,
    As the custom is, to absolve the State of her death.
145   And there let her pray to the gods of hell:
    They are her only gods:
    Perhaps they will show her an escape from death,

Or she may learn,
            though late,
That piety shown the dead is piety in vain.

                       (*Exit Creon.*)

ODE III

Strophe

CHORUS.
    Love, unconquerable
    Waster of rich men, keeper
    Of warm lights and all-night vigil
    In the soft face of a girl:
    Sea-wanderer, forest-visitor!   5
    Even the pure Immortals cannot escape you,
    And the mortal man, in his one day's dusk,
    Trembles before your glory.

Antistrophe

    Surely you swerve upon ruin
    The just man's consenting heart,   10
    As here you have made bright anger
    Strike between father and son—
    And none has conquered by Love!
    A girl's glánce wórking the will of heaven:
    Pleasure to her alone who mocks us,   15
    Merciless Aphroditê.°

SCENE IV

CHORAGOS (*as Antigonê enters guarded*).
    But I can no longer stand in awe of this,
    Nor, seeing what I see, keep back my tears.
    Here is Antigonê, passing to that chamber
    Where all find sleep at last.

Strophe 1

ANTIGONÊ.
    Look upon me, friends, and pity me   5
    Turning back at the night's edge to say
    Good-by to the sun that shines for me no longer;
    Now sleepy Death
    Summons me down to Acheron,° that cold shore:
    There is no bridesong there, nor any music.   10
CHORUS.
    Yet not unpraised, not without a kind of honor,

---

16 Aphroditê goddess of love   **9 Acheron** a river of the underworld, which was ruled by Hades

You walk at last into the underworld;
Untouched by sickness, broken by no sword.
What woman has ever found your way to death?

Antistrophe 1

ANTIGONÊ.

15   How often I have heard the story
              of Niobê,°
        Tantalos' wretched daughter, how the stone
        Clung fast about her, ivy-close: and they say
        The rain falls endlessly
        And sifting soft snow; her tears are never done.
20   I feel the loneliness of her death in mine.

CHORUS.

        But she was born of heaven, and you
        Are woman, woman-born. If her death is yours,
        A mortal woman's, is this not for you
        Glory in our world and in the world beyond?

Strophe 2

ANTIGONÊ.

25   You laugh at me. Ah, friends, friends
        Can you not wait until I am dead? O Thebes,
        O men many-charioted, in love with Fortune,
        Dear springs of Dircê, sacred Theban grove,
        Be witnesses for me, denied all pity,
30   Unjustly judged! and think a word of love
        For her whose path turns
        Under dark earth, where there are no more tears.

CHORUS.

        You have passed beyond human daring and come at last
        Into a place of stone where Justice sits.
35   I cannot tell
        What shape of your father's guilt appears in this.

Antistrophe 2

ANTIGONÊ.

        You have touched it at last:
        That bridal bed
        Unspeakable, horror of son and mother mingling:
40   Their crime, infection of all our family!
        O Oedipus, father and brother!

15 Niobê Niobê boasted of her numerous children, provoking Leto, the mother of Apollo, to destroy them. Niobê wept profusely, and finally was turned to stone on Mount Sipylus, whose streams are her tears.

Your marriage strikes from the grave to murder mine.
I have been a stranger here in my own land:
All my life
The blasphemy of my birth has followed me.   45

CHORUS.

        Reverence is a virtue, but strength
        Lives in established law: that must prevail.
        You have made your choice,
        Your death is the doing of your conscious hand.

Epode

ANTIGONÊ.

        Then let me go, since all your words are bitter,   50
        And the very light of the sun is cold to me.
        Lead me to my vigil, where I must have
        Neither love nor lamentation; no song, but silence.

Creon interrupts impatiently.

CREON.

        If dirges and planned lamentations could put off death,
        Men would be singing for ever.
        (*To the servants.*)   Take her, go!   55
        You know your orders: take her to the vault
        And leave her alone there. And if she lives or dies,
        That's her affair, not ours: our hands are clean.

ANTIGONÊ.

        O tomb, vaulted bride-bed in eternal rock,
        Soon I shall be with my own again   60
        Where Persephonê° welcomes the thin ghosts under-
              ground:
        And I shall see my father again, and you, mother,
        And dearest Polyneicês—
                              dearest indeed
        To me, since it was my hand
        That washed him clean and poured the ritual wine: 65
        And my reward is death before my time!

        And yet, as men's hearts know, I have done no wrong,
        I have not sinned before God. Or if I have,
        I shall know the truth in death. But if the guilt
        Lies upon Creon who judged me, then, I pray,   70
        May his punishment equal my own.

CHORAGOS.   O passionate heart,
        Unyielding, tormented still by the same winds!

CREON.

        Her guards shall have good cause to regret their delaying.

ANTIGONÊ.

        Ah! That voice is like the voice of death!

CREON.

        I can give you no reason to think you are mistaken.   75

61 Persephonê queen of the underworld

ANTIGONÊ.

Thebes, and you my fathers' gods,
And rulers of Thebes, you see me now, the last
Unhappy daughter of a line of kings,
Your kings, led away to death. You will remember
80   What things I suffer, and at what men's hands,
Because I would not transgress the laws of heaven.
(*To the guards, simply.*) Come: let us wait no longer.

(*Exit Antigonê, left, guarded.*)

ODE IV

Strophe 1

CHORUS.

All Danaê's beauty was locked away
In a brazen cell where the sunlight could not come:
A small room still as any grave, enclosed her.
Yet she was a princess too,
5   And Zeus in a rain of gold poured love upon her.
O child, child,
No power in wealth or war
Or tough sea-blackened ships
Can prevail against untiring Destiny!

Antistrophe 1

And Dryas' son° also, that furious king,
Bore the god's prisoning anger for his pride:
Sealed up by Dionysos in deaf stone,
His madness died among echoes.
So at the last he learned what dreadful power
15   His tongue had mocked:
For he had profaned the revels,
And fired the wrath of the nine
Implacable Sisters° that love the sound of the flute.

Strophe 2

And old men tell a half-remembered tale
20   Of horror where a dark ledge splits the sea
And a double surf beats on the gráy shóres:
How a king's new woman,° sick

10 Dryas' son Lycurgus, King of Thrace   **18 Sisters** the Muses
22 king's new woman Eidothea, second wife of King Phineus,
blinded her stepsons. Their mother, Cleopatra, had been imprisoned in a cave. Phineus was the son of a king, and Cleopatra, his
first wife, was the daughter of Boreas, the North wind, but this
illustrious ancestry could not protect his sons from violence and
darkness.

With hatred for the queen he had imprisoned,
Ripped out his two sons' eyes with her bloody hands
While grinning Arês° watched the shuttle plunge   25
Four times: four blind wounds crying for revenge,

Antistrophe 2

Crying, tears and blood mingled.—
      Piteously born,
Those sons whose mother was of heavenly birth!
Her father was the god of the North Wind
And she was cradled by gales,   30
She raced with young colts on the glittering hills
And walked untrammeled in the open light:
But in her marriage deathless Fate found means
To build a tomb like yours for all her joy.

SCENE V

*Enter blind Teiresias, led by a boy. The opening speeches
of Teiresias should be in singsong contrast to the realistic
lines of Creon.*

TEIRESIAS.

This is the way the blind man comes, Princes, Princes,
Lock-step, two heads lit by the eyes of one.

CREON.

What new thing have you to tell us, old Teiresias?

TEIRESIAS.

I have much to tell you: listen to the prophet, Creon.

CREON.

I am not aware that I have ever failed to listen.   5

TEIRESIAS.

Then you have done wisely, King, and ruled well.

CREON.

I admit my debt to you. But what have you to say?

TEIRESIAS.

This, Creon: you stand once more on the edge of fate.

CREON.

What do you mean? Your words are a kind of dread.

TEIRESIAS.

Listen, Creon: 10
I was sitting in my chair of augury, at the place
Where the birds gather about me. They were all a-chatter,
As is their habit, when suddenly I heard
A strange note in their jangling, a scream, a
Whirring fury; I knew that they were fighting,   15
Tearing each other, dying
In a whirlwind of wings clashing. And I was afraid.
I began the rites of burnt-offering at the altar,

25 Arês god of war

But Hephaistos° failed me: instead of bright flame,
20   There was only the sputtering slime of the fat thigh-flesh
Melting: the entrails dissolved in gray smoke,
The bare bone burst from the welter. And no blaze!

This was a sign from heaven. My boy described it,
Seeing for me as I see for others.

25   I tell you, Creon, you yourself have brought
This new calamity upon us. Our hearths and altars
Are stained with the corruption of dogs and carrion birds
That glut themselves on the corpse of Oedipus' son.
The gods are deaf when we pray to them, their fire
30   Recoils from our offering, their birds of omen
Have no cry of comfort, for they are gorged
With the thick blood of the dead.
                                        O my son,
These are no trifles! Think: all men make mistakes,
But a good man yields when he knows his course is
        wrong,
35   And repairs the evil. The only crime is pride.

Give in to the dead man, then: do not fight with a
        corpse—
What glory is it to kill a man who is dead?
Think, I beg you:
It is for your own good that I speak as I do.
40   You should be able to yield for your own good.

CREON.
    It seems that prophets have made me their especial
        province.
    All my life long
    I have been a kind of butt for the dull arrows
    Of doddering fortune-tellers!
                                No, Teiresias:
45   If your birds—if the great eagles of God himself
    Should carry him stinking bit by bit to heaven,
    I would not yield. I am not afraid of pollution:
    No man can defile the gods.
                                Do what you will,
    Go into business, make money, speculate
50   In India gold or that synthetic gold from Sardis,
    Get rich otherwise than by my consent to bury him.
    Teiresias, it is a sorry thing when a wise man
    Sells his wisdom, lets out his words for hire!

TEIRESIAS.
    Ah Creon! Is there no man left in the world—

CREON.
55   To do what?—Come, let's have the aphorism!

TEIRESIAS.
    No man who knows that wisdom outweighs any
        wealth?

CREON.
    As surely as bribes are baser than any baseness.

TEIRESIAS.
    You are sick, Creon! You are deathly sick!

19 **Hephaistos** god of fire

CREON.
    As you say: it is not my place to challenge a prophet.

TEIRESIAS.
    Yet you have said my prophecy is for sale.   60

CREON.
    The generation of prophets has always loved gold.

TEIRESIAS.
    The generation of kings has always loved brass.

CREON.
    You forget yourself! You are speaking to your King.

TEIRESIAS.
    I know it. You are a king because of me.

CREON.
    You have a certain skill; but you have sold out.   65

TEIRESIAS.
    King, you will drive me to words that—

CREON.
                                Say them, say
        them!
    Only remember: I will not pay you for them.

TEIRESIAS.
    No, you will find them too costly.

CREON.
                                No doubt. Speak:
    Whatever you say, you will not change my will.

TEIRESIAS.
    Then take this, and take it to heart!   70
    The time is not far off when you shall pay back
    Corpse for corpse, flesh of your own flesh.
    You have thrust the child of this world into living night,
    You have kept from the gods below the child that is theirs:
    The one in a grave before her death, the other,   75
    Dead, denied the grave. This is your crime:
    And the Furies and the dark gods of Hell
    Are swift with terrible punishment for you.

    Do you want to buy me now, Creon?
                                Not many days,
    And your house will be full of men and women weeping,   80
    And curses will be hurled at you from far
    Cities grieving for sons unburied, left to rot
    Before the walls of Thebes.

    These are my arrows, Creon: they are all for you.

    (*To boy.*) But come, child: lead me home.   85
    Let him waste his fine anger upon younger men.
    Maybe he will learn at last
    To control a wiser tongue in a better head.

                                (*Exit Teiresias.*)

CHORAGOS.
    The old man has gone, King, but his words
    Remain to plague us. I am old, too,   90
    But I cannot remember that he was ever false.

CREON.
    That is true. . . . It troubles me.
    Oh it is hard to give in! but it is worse
    To risk everything for stubborn pride.

CHORAGOS.
  Creon: take my advice.
95 CREON.   What shall I do?
CHORAGOS.
  Go quickly: free Antigonê from her vault
  And build a tomb for the body of Polyneicês.
CREON.
  You would have me do this!
CHORAGOS.   Creon, yes!
  And it must be done at once: God moves
100 Swiftly to cancel the folly of stubborn men.
CREON.
  It is hard to deny the heart! But I
  Will do it: I will not fight with destiny.
CHORAGOS.
  You must go yourself, you cannot leave it to others.
CREON.
  I will go.
      —Bring axes, servants:
105 Come with me to the tomb. I buried her, I
  Will set her free.
          Oh quickly!
  My mind misgives—
  The laws of the gods are mighty, and a man must serve
    them
  To the last day of his life!

                              (*Exit Creon.*)

PAEAN°

Strophe 1

CHORAGOS.
  God of many names
CHORUS.   O Iacchos
              son
  of Kadmeian Sémelê
            O born of the Thunder!
  Guardian of the West
            Regent
  of Eleusis' plain
            O Prince of maenad Thebes
5 and the Dragon Field by rippling Ismenós:°

Antistrophe 1

CHORAGOS.
  God of many names

CHORUS.   the flame of torches
  flares on our hills
            the nymphs of Iacchos
  dance at the spring of Castalia:°
  from the vine-close mountain
                come ah come in ivy:
  Evohé evohé! sings through the streets of Thebes   10

Strophe 2

CHORAGOS.
  God of many names
CHORUS.   Iacchos of Thebes
  heavenly Child
          of Sémelê bride of the Thunderer!
  The shadow of plague is upon us:
                  come
  with clement feet
            oh come from Parnassos
  down the long slopes
            across the lamenting water   15

Antistrophe 2

CHORAGOS.
  Iô Fire! Chorister of the throbbing stars!
  O purest among the voices of the night!
  Thou son of God, blaze for us!
CHORUS.
  Come with choric rapture of circling Maenads
  Who cry *Iô Iacche!*
          God of many names!   20

EXODOS

Enter Messenger from left.

MESSENGER.
  Men of the line of Kadmos,° you who live
  Near Amphion's citadel,°
              I cannot say
  Of any condition of human life "This is fixed,
  This is clearly good, or bad." Fate raises up,
  And Fate casts down the happy and unhappy alike: 5
  No man can foretell his Fate.
              Take the case of Creon:
  Creon was happy once, as I count happiness:
  Victorious in battle, sole governor of the land,
  Fortunate father of children nobly born.

Paean a hymn (here dedicated to Iacchos, also called Dionysos. His father was Zeus, his mother was Sémelê, daughter of Kadmos. Iacchos's worshipers were the Maenads, whose cry was "Evohé evohé") **5 Ismenós** a river east of Thebes (from a dragon's teeth, sown near the river, there sprang men who became the ancestors of the Theban nobility)

8 Castalia a spring on Mount Parnassos   **1 Kadmos,** who sowed the dragon's teeth, was founder of Thebes   **2 Amphion's citadel** Amphion played so sweetly on his lyre that he charmed stones to form a wall around Thebes

10 And now it has all gone from him! Who can say
That a man is still alive when his life's joy fails?
He is a walking dead man. Grant him rich,
Let him live like a king in his great house:
If his pleasure is gone, I would not give
15 So much as the shadow of smoke for all he owns.

CHORAGOS.
Your words hint at sorrow: what is your news for us?

MESSENGER.
They are dead. The living are guilty of their death.

CHORAGOS.
Who is guilty? Who is dead? Speak!

MESSENGER.   Haimon.
Haimon is dead; and the hand that killed him
Is his own hand.

CHORAGOS.
20 His father's? or his own?

MESSENGER.
His own, driven mad by the murder his father had done.

CHORAGOS.
Teiresias, Teiresias, how clearly you saw it all!

MESSENGER.
This is my news: you must draw what conclusions you
    can from it.

CHORAGOS.
But look: Eurydicê, our Queen:
25 Has she overheard us?

Enter Eurydicê from the palace, center.

EURYDICÊ.
I have heard something, friends:
As I was unlocking the gate of Pallas'° shrine,
For I needed her help today, I heard a voice
Telling of some new sorrow. And I fainted
30 There at the temple with all my maidens about me.
But speak again: whatever it is, I can bear it:
Grief and I are no strangers.

MESSENGER.   Dearest Lady,
I will tell you plainly all that I have seen.
I shall not try to comfort you: what is the use,
35 Since comfort could lie only in what is not true?
The truth is always best.

                          I went with Creon
To the outer plain where Polyneicês was lying,
No friend to pity him, his body shredded by dogs.
We made our prayers in the place to Hecatê
40 And Pluto,° that they would be merciful. And we
    bathed
The corpse with holy water, and we brought

Fresh-broken branches to burn what was left of it,
And upon the urn we heaped up a towering barrow
Of the earth of his own land.

                          When we were done, we ran
To the vault where Antigonê lay on her couch of stone.   45
One of the servants had gone ahead,
And while he was yet far off he heard a voice
Grieving within the chamber, and he came back
And told Creon. And as the King went closer,
The air was full of wailing, the words lost,   50
And he begged us to make all haste. "Am I a prophet?"
He said, weeping, "And must I walk this road,
The saddest of all that I have gone before?
My son's voice calls me on. Oh quickly, quickly!
Look through the crevice there, and tell me   55
If it is Haimon, or some deception of the gods!"

We obeyed; and in the cavern's farthest corner
We saw her lying:
She had made a noose of her fine linen veil
And hanged herself. Haimon lay beside her,   60
His arms about her waist, lamenting her,
His love lost under ground, crying out
That his father had stolen her away from him.

When Creon saw him the tears rushed to his eyes
And he called to him: "What have you done, child?
    Speak to me.   65
What are you thinking that makes your eyes so strange?
O my son, my son, I come to you on my knees!"
But Haimon spat in his face. He said not a word,
Staring—
              And suddenly drew his sword
And lunged. Creon shrank back, the blade missed; and   70
    the boy,
Desperate against himself, drove it half its length
Into his own side, and fell. And as he died
He gathered Antigonê close in his arms again,
Choking, his blood bright red on her white cheek.
And now he lies dead with the dead, and she is his   75
At last, his bride in the house of the dead.

                          (*Exit Eurydicê into the palace.*)

CHORAGOS.
She has left us without a word. What can this mean?

MESSENGER.
It troubles me, too; yet she knows what is best,
Her grief is too great for public lamentation,
And doubtless she has gone to her chamber to weep   80
For her dead son, leading her maidens in his dirge.

Pause.

CHORAGOS.
It may be so: but I fear this deep silence.

MESSENGER.
I will see what she is doing. I will go in.

---

27 **Pallas** Pallas Athene, goddess of wisdom   40 **Hecatê / And
Pluto** Hecatê and Pluto (also known as Hades) were deities of the
underworld

(Exit messenger into the palace.)

Enter Creon with attendants, bearing Haimon's body.

CHORAGOS.
    But here is the king himself: on look at him,
85 Bearing his own damnation in his arms.
CREON.
    Nothing you say can touch me any more.
    My own blind heart has brought me
    From darkness to final darkness. Here you see
    The father murdering, the murdered son—
90 And all my civic wisdom!

    Haimon my son, so young, so young to die,
    I was the fool, not you; and you died for me.
CHORAGOS.
    That is the truth; but you were late in learning it.
CREON.
    This truth is hard to bear. Surely a god
95 Has crushed me beneath the hugest weight of heaven,
    And driven me headlong a barbaric way
    To trample out the thing I held most dear.

    The pains that men will take to come to pain!

Enter Messenger from the palace.

MESSENGER.
    The burden you carry in your hands is heavy,
100 But it is not all: you will find more in your house.
CREON.
    What burden worse than this shall I find there?
MESSENGER.
    The Queen is dead.
CREON.
    O port of death, deaf world,
    Is there no pity for me? And you, Angel of evil,
105 I was dead, and your words are death again.
    Is it true, boy? Can it be true?
    Is my wife dead? Has death bred death?
MESSENGER.
    You can see for yourself.

The doors are opened and the body of Eurydicê is disclosed within.

CREON.
    Oh pity!
110 All true, all true, and more than I can bear!
    O my wife, my son!
MESSENGER.
    She stood before the altar, and her heart

Welcomed the knife her own hand guided,
And a great cry burst from her lips for Megareus° dead,
And for Haimon dead, her sons; and her last breath   115
Was a curse for their father, the murderer of her sons.
And she fell, and the dark flowed in through her closing
    eyes.
CREON.
    O God, I am sick with fear.
    Are there no swords here? Has no one a blow for me?
MESSENGER.
    Her curse is upon you for the deaths of both.   120
CREON.
    It is right that it should be. I alone am guilty.
    I know it, and I say it. Lead me in,
    Quickly, friends.
    I have neither life nor substance. Lead me in.
CHORAGOS.
    You are right, if there can be right in so much wrong.   125
    The briefest way is best in a world of sorrow.
CREON.
    Let it come,
    Let death come quickly, and be kind to me.
    I would not ever see the sun again.
CHORAGOS.
    All that will come when it will; but we, meanwhile,   130
    Have much to do. Leave the future to itself.
CREON.
    All my heart was in that prayer!
CHORAGOS.
    Then do not pray any more: the sky is deaf.
CREON.
    Lead me away. I have been rash and foolish.
    I have killed my son and my wife.   135
    I look for comfort; my comfort lies here dead.
    Whatever my hands have touched has come to nothing.
    Fate has brought all my pride to a thought of dust.

As Creon is being led into the house, the Choragos advances and speaks directly to the audience.

CHORAGOS.
    There is no happiness where there is no wisdom;
    No wisdom but in submission to the gods.   140
    Big words are always punished,
    And proud men in old age learn to be wise.

---

114 Megareus Megareus, brother of Haimon, had died in the assault on Thebes

TOPICS FOR CRITICAL THINKING AND WRITING

The Play on the PAGE

1. If you have read *Oedipus*, compare and contrast the Creon of *Antigonê* with the Creon of *Oedipus*.
2. Although Sophocles called his play *Antigonê*, many critics say that Creon is the real tragic hero, pointing out that Antigonê is absent from the last third of the play. Evaluate this view.
3. In some Greek tragedies, fate plays a great role in bringing about the downfall of the tragic hero. Though there are references to the curse on the House of Oedipus in *Antigonê*, do we feel that Antigonê goes to her death as a result of the workings of fate? Do we feel that fate is responsible for Creon's fall? Are both Antigonê and Creon the creators of their own tragedy?
4. Are the words *hamartia* and *hybris* (pages 33–34) relevant to Antigonê? To Creon?

5. Why does Creon, contrary to the Chorus's advice (Scene 5, lines 96–97), bury the body of Polyneicês before he releases Antigonê? Does his action show a zeal for piety as short-sighted as his earlier zeal for law? Is his action plausible, in view of the facts that Teiresias has dwelt on the wrong done to Polyneicês and that Antigonê has ritual food to sustain her? Or are we not to worry about Creon's motive?
6. A *foil* is a character who, by contrast, sets off or helps define another character. To what extent is Ismene a foil to Antigonê? Is she entirely without courage?
7. What function does Eurydicê serve? How deeply do we feel about her fate?

The Play on the STAGE

8. Would you use masks for some (or all) of the characters? If so, would they be masks that fully cover the face, Greek-style, or some sort of half-masks? (A full mask enlarges the face, and conceivably the mouthpiece can amplify the voice, but only an exceptionally large theater might require such help. Perhaps half-masks are enough if the aim is chiefly to distance the actors from the audience and from daily reality, and to force the actors to develop resources other than facial gestures. One director, arguing in favor of half-masks, has said that actors who wear even a half-mask learn to act not with the eyes but with the neck.)
9. How would you costume the players? Would you dress them as the Greeks might have? Why? One

argument sometimes used by those who hold that modern productions of Greek drama should use classical costumes is that Greek drama *ought* to be remote and ritualistic. Evaluate this view. What sort of modern dress might be effective?
10. If you were directing a college production of *Antigonê*, how large a chorus would you use? (Sophocles is said to have used a chorus of fifteen.) Would you have the chorus recite (or chant) the odes in unison, or would you assign lines to single speakers? In Sophocles's day, the chorus danced. Would you use dance movements? If not, in what sorts of movements might they engage?

The Play in PERFORMANCE

Sophocles's *Antigonê* has had a great influence, especially in the twentieth century, but its influence may first have manifested itself in a version of the play by his younger contemporary, Euripides. Euripides's text is known only from a few fragments, however, so a detailed comparison cannot be made. In any case, we know that Sophocles's *Antigonê* was highly esteemed in the century after it was written, and that it influenced a Roman version of the play. After the collapse of the Roman Empire, however, Greek drama was absent from the public stage until the nineteenth century. When *Antigonê* was produced in Greece in 1861, it had the distinction of being the first ancient Greek play to be performed for the general public in modern times. (Earlier in the century Greek drama survived on the stage only in occasional performances by and for university students.)

In the twentieth century *Antigonê* has been much in view, for instance in a pacifist version by Walter Hasenclever (1919), in a version by Jean Cocteau (1922), and especially in a version by Jean Anouilh (written in 1942 and produced in occupied France in 1944). Anouilh's version resembles Sophocles's, but it includes modern references, for instance to cigarettes, and it was done in modern dress (evening gowns and tuxedos). This version is often said to have been staged as a protest against the Nazi occupation of Paris, and apparently those who resisted the German occupation took it that way. In fact, however, Creon is presented very sympathetically, and because the play emphasizes fulfilling the roles that fate assigns to us, it suited the Nazis quite as much as it suited the French Resistance. The version by Bertolt Brecht (1948), however, is unambiguously hostile to Creon, who is presented as a materialistic brute. Similarly, Creon is clearly presented as a villain in Athol Fugard's *The Island* (1973), a play in which black political prisoners in a South African jail stage an abbreviated version of *Antigonê*. Fugard's point obviously is that the prisoners, like Antigonê, have transgressed the law of an oppressive society.

For a discussion of what *Antigonê* has meant to successive generations, see George Steiner, *Antigones* (1984).

MICHAEL BILLINGTON
Antigonê *in Modern Dress*

The following review of a production in England by the National Theatre Company, directed by John Burgess and Peter Gill in 1984, originally appeared in *The Guardian*, May 18, 1984. For a photo, see page 52.

How does one play Greek tragedy? In ancient or modern dress? In masks or with bared faces? In dense-packed or limpid verse? Peter Hall's *Oresteia* favoured the former approach: John Burgess and Peter Gill's production of *Antigonê* at the Cottesloe goes for the latter. And, while acknowledging the vast difference between the two plays and venues, I lean heavily towards the updated approach on the grounds of sheer theatrical immediacy.

What Burgess and Gill have done, with some skill, is to tread a fine line between modernity and stylisation. Taking a leaf from Peter Stein's Schaubühne *Oresteia*, they turn the Chorus into old men in grey suits and felt hats (modern directors clearly like being Svengalis to their actors' trilbies). Antigonê and Ismenê sport red and blue Forties frocks and matching toques. The Guards wear berets and khaki uniforms. At the same time, the two sisters move with exaggeratedly long strides. The Chorus rise from their front-bench chairs to become part of the action. Staccato drumbeats punctuate the drama. The production thus manages to acquire a contemporary feel without lapsing into simple naturalism.

But the real test of any version of Sophocles's *Antigonê* is whether it manages to achieve a precise balance between the two antagonists rather than becoming a crude melodrama about a brute tyrant who refuses the heroine burial rites for her brother. Maurice Bowra once suggested that the Sophoclean irony is that we start by thinking Creon must be right and then switch our sympathies to Antigonê. In performance, I find the exact reverse happens. Creon at first seems a narrow paternalist and Antigonê the upholder of moral law. But by the end Creon seems the one who suffers more in losing both son and wife precisely because he has broken the family bonds that underpin any society.

It is a deeply complex play that asks a lot of still-pertinent questions (does one break a law if one's conscience tells one it is bad?). But Greek tragedy is also nothing without passion and this production is unafraid of gut emotion. Jane Lapotaire's Antigonê is a tense, desperate woman who senses death is the penalty but who is still dragged kicking and screaming to her entombment and who instantly buckles at the knees when reminded of her father's sins: she moves one because she is specific rather than general. And

Peter Sproule's bullet-headed, blue-suited Creon likewise is no vague despot but an increasingly panic-stricken figure beseechingly asking the Chorus, after prophecies of disaster, "What must I do?" Both principals, in fact, follow a basic acting-rule of playing the characters from their own point of view.

Even this production, gripping and urgent as it is, can't solve every problem. I like the way the Chorus become constantly reacting figures, emitting an audible sign at Antigonê's defiance and visibly cringing at

Creon's blasphemy, but their speaking of C. A. Trypanis's translation is sometimes a little furry and their canes occasionally suggest an impending soft-shoe shuffle. But it is a well-acted evening (Ron Pember and Vincenzo Nicoli as the Guards report news of fresh disasters as if they meant it), the narrative is clear and strong, and the gesture towards the present-day brings the drama home and removes the chill aura of a pious cultural event.

Euripides

Euripides's approximate dates (484–406 B.C.E.) mark him as a younger contemporary of Sophocles. Thus, while Sophocles was already old when the disastrous struggle between Greek city-states, the Peloponnesian War, began in 431 B.C.E., Euripides was in his maturity. In fact, 431 was the year in which he wrote *Medea*.

More open to current intellectual trends than Sophocles, Euripides reflects a doubting, skeptical mood. Further, his extant dramas are of more varied kinds than those of Sophocles, for in addition to writing tragedies he wrote tragicomedies and melodramas. Relatively unpopular in his day (he won only five prizes, although he wrote ninety-two plays) and often maligned, he was of a retiring and bookish nature. In his last months he voluntarily left Athens and settled in Macedonia, where he may have enjoyed the excellent company of other great self-exiled Athenians, including the painter Zeuxis and the historian Thucydides.

■■■■■■■■■■■■■■■

COMMENTARY ON *MEDEA*

In our introductory remarks to *Oedipus* we mention that although the Greek tragic playwrights used traditional legends, within broad limits they were free to make significant changes. In fact, the inherited legends often included contradictory details, so the dramatists had to select as well as to amplify. In the story of Medea, for instance, all of the legends indicate that her children died at Corinth, but the cause of their death was variously explained. In one version the children are killed by the Corinthians, in revenge for Medea's murder of their king and his daughter, but in Euripides's version she herself murders them. In any case, allowing for variations, we can say that the gist of the story that Euripides dramatized in *Medea* went along the following lines.

Jason was the rightful heir to the kingdom of Iolcus in western Turkey, but his uncle, Pelias, usurped the throne. When Jason tried to claim the throne, Pelias tricked him into setting out on what seemed an impossible quest—obtaining the Golden Fleece, a fleece that hung in a sacred grove at Colchis, guarded by a dragon that never slept. (Colchis was south of the Caucasus Mountains, on the Black Sea, in what is now Georgia.) Jason set out in a boat called the *Argo*, whose crew of fifty-six (the Argonauts, i.e., "those who sailed in the *Argo*") consisted of fifty-four paired heroes who served as rowers, a helmsman, and the poet Orpheus, who calmed the seas by singing to them and who called out the rhythm to the rowers. Eventually Jason reached Colchis, ruled by King Aeetes. Aeetes,

who was a sorcerer and the son of Helios the sun god, sought to kill Jason by requiring him to perform impossibly dangerous tasks. For instance, he had to harness fire-breathing bulls and plow a field with them, and he had to sow the teeth of a dragon, each of which turned into an armed soldier who strove to kill Jason.

Medea, King Aeetes's daughter and herself a sorceress, fell in love with Jason, and in exchange for his promise to marry her she enabled him to accomplish the impossible. For instance, she gave Jason a balm that made him fireproof; he anointed his body and thus was able to harness the fire-breathing bulls. But Medea did more than disobey her father in the course of helping Jason: When her father pursued her, she dismembered her brother and scattered the pieces, thereby delaying her father, who paused to gather the pieces of his murdered son.

Fleeing Colchis, Jason and Medea took refuge in Corinth, where Jason found that he could improve his lot by putting Medea aside—despite the oaths he had vowed—and by marrying the daughter of Creon, King of Corinth. Euripides's play begins at this point. Although the story of Jason and the Golden Fleece is one of the great romantic tales of the world, we will find no romance in the sequel in Corinth. True, even in Colchis the heroic Jason required Medea's aid, but the Jason we see in the play is not in any way heroic; rather, he is a petty self-server. Figures like Euripides's Jason allowed the next generation of Greeks to say that Sophocles showed men as they should be, Euripides as they are. But if the earlier legends do not prepare us for Euripides's Jason, neither do they—with their cunning sorceress—prepare us for Euripides's compelling Medea.

After the Nurse's prologue, Medea, speaking to the Chorus of Women of Corinth, utters one of the great feminist speeches (241–60) in literature. In part it runs thus:

> Men say we live a lazy life at home,
> while they must go to war—what fools they are!
> I'd rather face the enemy three times
> than undergo the pains of labor once.
>
> (257–60)

Later, in one of the great lyrics of the play, the Chorus will celebrate women:

> Let the rivers flow back to their holy sources,
> Justice and all things reverse direction!
> It is men whose plans are full of deceit,
> and no one can trust in the gods. But now
> the story is being transformed: we women
> demand the respect we deserve. Our life
> is just as worthy of note. We refuse
> to stay imprisoned in stereotypes.
>
> The doddering bards will stop writing their ditties
> about how *mobile la donna* is.
> *We* were not granted access to song,
> were discouraged from writing what we believe.
> Otherwise we would have answered back
> the race of males with a tale of our own.
> The past holds many things it could say
> about what men *and* women have done.
>
> (415–30)

What the Chorus is saying, in part, is of course obviously true: Men have done most of the writing, and therefore they have glorified themselves and paid little attention to the accomplishments of women. We need not say that Jason is a typical man, but if we want to know what attitudes Athenian men had toward women, probably Jason's words to Medea give us a fairly good idea. Consider, for instance, his remark that

> women have gotten to such a point that you
> think if your sex life's good, then everything
> is perfect; but a problem in that area
> makes you turn the best things people have
> into a battleground.
>
> (581–85)

We can pause here, briefly, to say a few things about the status of women in ancient Greece. According to

Thucydides, Euripides's contemporary, the great statesman Pericles said that "a woman's glory is not to be mentioned, whether for good or ill." Women were married at about the age of fifteen—in arranged marriages, of course—to men of thirty or so. Women were brought up apart from males, and, as wives, they lived in separate quarters within the household. Aristocratic women did not eat with their husbands and his male friends, and they did not go out of the house except to attend religious festivals or dramatic performances, and they were always accompanied by an attendant. Their job was to supervise the household slaves, and to produce children to inherit the land. A husband could divorce his wife merely by announcing his plan in the presence of witnesses, but a wife could divorce a husband only after a judicial proceeding and for a serious cause. Incidentally, because women rarely appeared in public, dramatists sometimes had to invent explanations to account for the presence of a woman in an outdoor scene. An example is Medea's speech in lines 226–28. Another way of surmounting the difficulty of representing an aristocratic woman was to use a go-between, such as the nurse in Medea, who would report the words and actions of her mistress.

With Euripides, we get (as we do not get from the other tragic dramatists) serious discussions of the roles of women. This is not to say, however, that the other dramatists neglected women. Quite the contrary. Although, as we have briefly seen, ancient Greece was a man's world, almost half of the extant Greek tragedies are either named for individual women (e.g., *Antigonê, Medea*) or for groups of women (e.g., *The Suppliant Women, The Trojan Women*), and in most of the plays which are chiefly about women the Chorus consists of women (though not in *Antigonê*, where Sophocles emphasizes Antigonê's isolation by setting her against a chorus of old men). But in most of these plays by Euripides's predecessors, the women are presented—with a few notable exceptions, such as Sophocles's *Antigonê*—as relatively conventional figures, and they are usually presented as pathetic creatures who undergo suffering but who scarcely initiate action.

Obviously Medea is of a different sort, strong-willed and imaginative. We can only wonder what the Greek audience—chiefly male—thought when it heard Medea denounce the traditional heroic ideas that men are important because they fight battles, and that women are unimportant because they deal with routine domestic matters. Possibly they dismissed Euripides as a gadfly, or possibly they thought that Medea's ideas were self-evidently nonsense, exactly the kind of raving that a barbarian woman was capable of—so un-Greek, so irrational. Or possibly they recognized that Euripides was a dramatist of a different sort from Sophocles, someone more like (say) Henrik Ibsen or George Bernard Shaw, dramatists who saw themselves as concerned with the problems of their day.

Certainly, if the audience was paying attention, it must have realized that although Medea is (in Greek eyes) from a primitive part of the world, Jason's arguments defending his abandonment of Medea are shallow, even despicable. He has deserted her, despite his earlier vows, in order to better his social position in Corinth. And he will learn that Medea—stimulated by his ignominious behavior—has a strength of purpose that will destroy his life, not by killing him but by killing his new wife and his children, that is, by killing everything that he wants to live for. We should remember, too, when we read or hear Medea's prediction of Jason's empty future, that in ancient Greece, where there were no pensions or insurance plans, aged people depended on their grown children for support. Notice, further, that Medea predicts an *un*heroic death for Jason. Instead of dying gloriously, he will be struck down by a timber from the rotting *Argo*, the very ship that brought him to Medea.

MEDEA
Euripides

Translated by Mary-Kay Gamel

CHARACTERS IN ORDER OF APPEARANCE

Medea's childhood NURSE
TUTOR *of Medea's children*
CHILDREN *of Jason and Medea*
MEDEA, *formerly princess of Colchis, wife of Jason*
CREON, *King of Corinth*

JASON, *formerly prince of Iolchos, Medea's husband*
AEGEUS, *King of Athens*
MESSENGER, *slave in Creon's palace*
CHORUS *of women of Corinth*

All the action takes place in front of Medea's house in Corinth.

NURSE.
    Oh how I wish that boat the Argo had never
    flown through the dark clashing rocks to Colchis' shore!
    I wish the pine that made it had never been felled
    in the groves of Thessaly! Wish the heroes sent
5   for the Golden Fleece by Pelias never had rowed it!
    My lady Medea, battered by love for Jason,
    would never have sailed off with him to his home, Iolchos.
    She wouldn't have killed the king, by tricking his daughters
    to do it; she wouldn't be in exile now in this land,
10   Corinth, along with her husband and children. Here
    she's tried to please the residents of her new city,
    and gone along with Jason in everything.
    (That's stability—a wife never taking a stand
    against her husband!) That was then. But now
15   all is hatred; what's dearest to me is dying.
    Jason's betrayed his own sons, and my lady,
    by wallowing in a royal marriage bed
    with King Creon's daughter. Medea, dishonored,
    wounded, calls out "promises!" remembers how
20   he pledged his faith by clasping her hand, and asks
    the gods to see how Jason swindles her.
    She doesn't eat. Her body aches. She spends
    every moment weeping, ever since
    she found out she had been betrayed. She stares
25   at the ground, never lifts her eyes. She's like a rock,
    or the crashing surf. She can't hear the words
    of those who love her giving her advice.
    Sometimes she shakes her head, talks to herself,
    whispers her father's name, her own land,
30   home—all the things she gave up for Jason.
    He gives *her* up now. In this disaster
    she's found out, poor woman, what it means
    to have no country. She hates her children, gets
    no pleasure from seeing them. She scares me.

    I'm afraid she's planning something awful,   35
    awful as she can be. Someone who dares
    to take her on won't leave the field alive.
    But here are the children coming from their games,
    completely unaware of their mother's pain.
    Of course—young folks don't know what suffering is.   40

[*Enter Tutor.*]

TUTOR.
    Old fixture of my lady's household, why
    are you standing out here in front alone, fretting
    to yourself about things? How is it Medea
    is willing for you to leave her alone in the house?
NURSE.
    Old servant of Jason's children, to a good slave,   45
    troubles which fall on the master hit her too
    and bruise her heart. I'm so far gone with sadness
    I couldn't resist coming out here to tell
    all earth and heaven of my mistress' grief.
TUTOR.
    Hasn't she stopped suffering yet, poor thing?   50
NURSE.
    Far from it—the pain has only just begun.
TUTOR.
    She's a fool, then—though she is my lady.
    She doesn't know the latest awful news.
NURSE.
    What is it, old man? Don't refuse to speak!
TUTOR.
    No! Nothing! Sorry I said anything.   55
NURSE.
    I beg you, don't hold back from your fellow slave.
    I can keep my mouth shut if need be.
TUTOR.
    Down by Pirene fountain, where the old men
    play checkers in the sun, I heard someone

60 (he didn't notice me) say that King Creon
    means to send these children out of Corinth,
    their mother too. Of course, I don't know if
    the story's true. I hope it isn't. But—

NURSE.
    Will Jason stand for this—his children exiled—
65 even if he is at odds with their mother?

TUTOR.
    Old ties give way when new ones come along.
    That man's no friend to this family any more.

NURSE.
    We're done for, then! A new disaster, before
    we've bailed out the earlier ones! We're swamped!

TUTOR.
70 Listen, you: it's no time for the mistress
    to learn this. Just keep quiet! Not a word!

NURSE.
    Children, hear what kind of father you have?
    Damn him! No—he is my master. But
    he's guilty of ignoring those he ought to love.

TUTOR.
75 So who isn't? Are you learning this just now,
    that no one loves his neighbor as himself?
    Jason's remarried. Of course he doesn't love them.

NURSE.
    Children, go inside the house, that'll be better.
    You—keep them by themselves as much as you can;
80 don't let them near their mother in her fury.
    I've already seen her staring at them like a bull,
    about to do something. She won't give up her rage,
    I know, until she rushes someone. Please,
    make it an enemy, not someone she loves.

MEDEA [within].
    I'm so unhappy!
    I can't stand it!
    I want to die!

NURSE.
    That's it, boys!
    Mother's going
90 into a rage.
    Hurry up, get in
    the house! Keep out
    of sight, don't come
    near her! Watch out
95 for her temper—savage,
    stiff with hate.
    Go! She's a storm cloud
    gathering force,
    wounded, hurting,
100 pregnant with power,
    soon to fork lightning
    hard to put out.
    What is she going to do?

MEDEA.
    Oh God! I've suffered

such awful things.   105
I've got a right
to scream! Children
of a hated mother,
die! You're doomed!
Your father too!   110
All of us must die!

NURSE.
Lord, oh Lord!
Why mix up the boys
in their father's crime?
Why hate them?   115
Children, I'm terrified
you'll be destroyed.
Powerful people
aren't like us:
they get what they want,   120
don't know how to give way;
their moods are unstable.
It's better to know
how to live together,
all equal: let me   125
get old in security
rather than wealth.
(People always
assert that, but
working at it is best.)   130
To try for too much
brings no good to folks.
When the gods get enraged
they've got more to wreck.

[*Exeunt Children and Tutor into the house.*]

[*Enter Chorus.*]

CHORUS.
Standing at my door   135
I heard a voice,
that piercing cry
the outsider let out.
She hasn't calmed down.
Old lady, speak: 140
your family troubles
make me so sad.
I come as a friend.

NURSE.
Family? What family?
That's all over with.   145
The husband in bed
with the princess, the wife
in her room, weeping,
wears herself out.
Friendly words   150
are not what she needs.

MEDEA [*within*].
　　O God! Earth! Sun!
　　Send a lightning flash
　　through my brain! Why, why
155　　must I stay alive?
　　I want to leave
　　this life I hate,
　　and find escape in death.

CHORUS.[1]
　　Did you hear? She called out "God! Earth! Sun!"
160　　What a dreadful cry from the wretched wife!
　　The husband she's eager for now is Death.
　　But Death is already hurrying here—
　　don't goad him on! If your husband prefers
　　to sleep in a new bed, that's up to him.
165　　Don't take it so hard—let God be his judge.
　　You're wasting away bewailing your man.

MEDEA.
　　O great Justice!
　　Mighty Artemis!
　　Don't you see
170　　what I'm going through?
　　I bound my husband
　　with powerful oaths,
　　but he broke them all!
　　For him I abandoned
175　　my father, butchered
　　my brother!
　　I want to see him,
　　and his bride,
　　and all they love,
180　　lie peeled and bleeding.

NURSE.
　　Hear how she calls
　　on Justice, Zeus
　　who guards all contracts?
　　This anger will end
185　　in nothing small.

CHORUS.
　　Then how can she see me? Hear my words?
　　But if she can let her anger go
　　and alter her mood, I'm going to be
　　a trustworthy friend. Won't you please go in
190　　and bring her out here? You can say I've come,
　　and I'm anxious to help. Please hurry, before
　　something terrible happens inside.
　　Something awful is starting to stir.

NURSE.
　　I'll go, but I

[1]At this point the chorus break into an "ode," a formal song accompanied by the flute; in the original production the chorus would have danced while singing. Medea and the Nurse continue in the movement meter, indicating that Medea is in the process of coming out. (Translator's note)

don't know if she   195
will listen. When
someone comes near
to speak to her
she glares like a lioness
newly cubbed,   200
butting away
all words. Some call
those songs men sing
at banquets "life's
sweet sounds"—how stupid!   205
No one has ever
soothed away hatred
with rippling chords,
stopped death and disaster
with rhyme. Of course,   210
if poetry could
put an end to pain,
what a gift it would be.
But when there's food
on the table, who needs   215
empty words? The food
is good enough by itself.

　　　　　　　　　　　　　　　　　　[*Exit Nurse.*]

CHORUS.
　　Shrill with pain
　　she curses the liar,
　　the double-crosser.   220
　　Sailing by night
　　through the dangerous straits,
　　she made it to Greece,
　　and gets paid back like this.
　　God, is that justice?   225

[*Enter Medea.*]

MEDEA.
　　Women of Corinth, I don't want you to blame me.
　　So I've come out. Many people are too proud,
　　in public or private. Those who keep to themselves
　　acquire a bad reputation for being aloof.
　　It's unfair, though, when people make snap judgments, 230
　　and decide to dislike someone who's done no harm
　　before they even know her. A foreigner
　　has to work very hard not to seem odd,
　　but locals too become disliked if they're
　　stuck up and don't know how to act.

　　　　　　　　　　　　　　　　　As for me,   235
　　this thing has fallen on me so suddenly
　　it's wrecked me. Giving up all joy in life,
　　I'm done for friends; I only want to die.
　　My husband, the man who could have made me know
　　a happy life, has proved the worst of men.   240
　　As women we are more abused than anything
　　that lives and has a mind. With a rich dowry

we first must buy a husband. Then we have
to give our bodies up to a master's control.
245 That's still more painful, but here's the worst:
he might be sweet, or abusive—we can't know.
There's no way out—we can't stay single, and
divorce makes the woman involved look bad.
So—you move into a stranger's house,
250 where things are done his way. (You can't learn that
at home—you have to read his mind.) If you
work hard, and your husband's ball and chain doesn't
chafe,
you're lucky. But if not, you're better off dead.
Whenever a man gets bored with life at home,
255 he can go out to amuse himself with friends,
while we must set our sights on only one.
Men say we live a lazy life at home,
while they must go to war—what fools they are!
I'd rather face the enemy three times
260 than undergo the pains of labor once.

Yet your situation is very different from mine.
This is your land, your family home is here,
you get some pleasure from life, being with friends.
I am an exile, homeless, carried off
265 like a trophy from an exotic land, the victim
of my husband. Mother, brother, no one near
can harbor me in time of trouble. So
I ask you, friends, for this one favor: if
I find a way to make my husband pay
270 for what he's done, keep quiet. Other times
a woman's scared to pick up naked steel;
but when her home is threatened, then her will
grows firm and dyes itself with criminal blood.

CHORUS.
I promise to say nothing. I agree:
275 you have a right to rage, and you are right
to seek revenge. Look! I see Creon, ruler
of this land, bringing some new decision.

[Enter Creon.]

CREON.
Hey you! Yes, you, the frowning one, the one
who hates her husband, Medea: I've decreed
280 that you must leave this place, and take your children.
No delays. I came to tell you this,
and I'm not going home until I see
you've gone beyond the limit of this land.

MEDEA.
Oh, no! Please no! I'm ruined! With full sail
285 my enemies pursue me, and there's no
safe place to land. Miserable as I am,
I have to ask: why are you doing this?

CREON.
You terrify me. No need to mince my words.
You might do something awful to my daughter,

something I couldn't stop. I have good reason: 290
your nature's cunning, you have evil skills,
you're angry at being divested of your husband.
They say you threaten to harm the father-in-law
and the bridegroom and the bride herself.
That's what I'm taking precautions against. I'd rather   295
have you hate me now than soften up
and then be sorry later.

MEDEA.   Oh, my God!
This is my reputation damaging me—
not the first time it has happened. Creon,
someone who's smart should never give his children   300
too much education. First, they'll be
"overqualified" for menial jobs.
Then, your neighbors think they look down on them
and start to resent them. What a double bind:
dimwits call an unconventional thinker   305
"impractical!" "too smart for his own good!"
while those who like to think they know it all
resent someone who's smarter than they are.
This is my problem: some are jealous of me,
others find me formidable. But I   310
am not so wise. You're afraid of me?
Think I can make you suffer? I am hardly
in any position to hurt a man like you.
You needn't fear me. You've done nothing to me.
You gave your daughter to a man you liked.   315
It's my husband I hate. As for you, I think
you've acted quite correctly, and I hope
all your affairs go well. More marriages!
Many happy returns! But let me stay
here in this land. Though I'm badly treated,   320
I'll keep quiet, giving way to those in control.

CREON.
Very soft-spoken! But I shudder to think
what evil thing you're planning; your mild words
make me trust you even less than I did before.
A woman who shows her anger is easier   325
to guard against than one who holds her tongue.
No more speeches! Get out, immediately!
That's how things stand. Since you're my enemy
none of your skill can keep you here with us.

MEDEA.
No, Creon! I beg you, in your daughter's name!   330

CREON.
You're wasting your breath. You'll never change my mind.

MEDEA.
You're forcing me out? You won't hear my appeal?

CREON.
You matter less to me than my family does.

MEDEA.
The memory of my homeland comes back to me now.

CREON.
Homeland's important—but children count the most.   335

MEDEA.
Every kind of love can make you suffer.

CREON.
Of course, it all depends on the circumstances.
MEDEA.
God! Don't forget who's responsible for all this!
CREON.
You're crazy! Get moving! Give my mind a rest!
MEDEA.
340   A rest? It's you who are arresting me!
CREON.
Move, or my men will move you out by force.
MEDEA.
No—not that! Creon, I beg of you—

[Sinks to her knees.]

CREON.
As usual, Medea, you're drawing a crowd.
MEDEA.
I promise to leave. That's not what I'm asking.
CREON.
345   Why are you grovelling, then? Get up off the ground!
MEDEA.
Just let me stay for one more day, so I
can figure out where we can go, and get
a new start for my children, since their father
doesn't see the need to provide for them.
350   They're the ones who need your sympathy.
You are a father—how can you be so hard?
Moving on won't bother me: it's them
I'm sorry for, involved in my bad luck.
CREON.
My nature is hardly authoritarian. I
355   have often gotten in trouble by being too nice.
I know I'm probably making a big mistake
but—all right, you can stay. I warn you, though:
you and your sons must go by dawn tomorrow.
If you're still on my land after that,
360   you die. That's a promise. One day is all
you get. I'm still afraid you might do something
terrible . . . but you won't.

[Exit Creon.]

CHORUS.
Poor thing! No end
to your problems. Where
365   will you go? Who
will take you in?
Where will you
find shelter from your pain?
In a sea of troubles
370   God has set you adrift.
MEDEA.
Yes, all is over: who could deny it? Right?
[Fiercely.] Don't you believe it! It's not over yet.
The newlyweds still have some hurdles before them;
the in-laws will have a few little problems too.

Do you think I would ever have grovelled at that man's   375
feet
if I didn't have something to gain, some plan in mind?
I wouldn't have spoken one word, much less touched him.
He's such a fool! By throwing me out, he could
have blocked my entire scheme—but no, he gives me
this whole day, which is all I need. Today   380
I will make the three of them into corpses:
the father, the daughter, and the loving husband.
So many ways I can make them die! I can't
decide which one to try out first, my friends.
A little *plastique* in the bridal suite?° Or shall   385
I sneak into the house, find them in bed,
and shove a knife through both their guts? One thing
bothers me, though: if I get caught, and put
to death, that'll give them a good laugh. No—
better to use the direct method, the one   390
we women know best: poison. So—now they're dead.
Where can I go? Who will give me asylum?
Someone who doesn't know me to save my skin.
If during the short time I have left I find
someone to watch over me I'll use deceit   395
and get my revenge by secret machinations.
But if there's no way out, I'll have to run
the greater risk. Even if I must die,
I'll take up the knife and kill them with my own hands.
I swear by Hekate,° the leader whom I reverence   400
more than all others, who has been my ally,
who lives in the darkest corners of my house,
not one of them will laugh after hurting me.
I'll make this wedding taste bitter; they will weep
for making this alliance, banishing me.   405
Proceed, Medea! Leave out nothing of what
you have in mind, plotting and scheming! Go
to the awful thing! Your courage is on trial.
You know what they've done to you, and you
know how to pay them back. Will the Sisyphus family   410
laugh at Helios' grand-daughter because her man
has married their daughter? Never! Women, we
are helpless when virtue is demanded, but
incomparable architects of crime.
CHORUS.
Let the rivers flow back to their holy sources,   415
Justice and all things reverse direction!
It is men whose plans are full of deceit,
and no one can trust in the gods. But now
the story is being transformed: we women
demand the respect we deserve. Our life   420
is just as worthy of note. We refuse
to stay imprisoned in stereotypes.

The doddering bards will stop writing their ditties

385 *plastique* bomb   400 Hekate (also Hecate) goddess of the
underworld and of magic

about how *mobile la donna* is.°
425 *We* were not granted access to song,
were discouraged from writing what we believe.
Otherwise we would have answered back
the race of males with a tale of our own.
The past holds many things it could say
430 about what men *and* women have done.

Medea, crazy with love, you sailed
away from your father's land, dividing
the Rocks which clash on passing ships.
Now you live in a foreign land;
435 your husband has left, your bed is abandoned,
you're driven out of your rightful place,
discarded, deprived of your legal rights.
At one time a person's word meant something;
promises were made to be kept.
440 Trustworthiness now is a thing of the past;
look for respect in this land no more.
No father's house will harbor you now
in your trouble. A woman who's stronger than you
moves into your bed and takes over your life.

[*Enter Jason.*]

JASON.
445 This isn't the first time. I have often seen
how difficult to deal with stubbornness is.
If you'd only taken it easy, you could have stayed
right here and kept the house. But no, not you—
your crazy words have gotten you thrown out.
450 And I don't give a damn: please, keep right on
calling Jason the worst man in the world.
But as for what you've said about our leaders—
be grateful all they're doing is throwing you out.
I kept trying to smoothe the royal anger,
455 kept asking them to let you stay. But you
refused to shut up, kept those stupid accusations
against them coming, and now you're exiled. Well,
I came to help you, not to write you off,
so that you and the children won't be sent off
460 without sufficient funds for your daily needs.
(I know first-hand how difficult exile is).
Even if you hate me, I'll never be
anything but quite concerned about you.

MEDEA.
Jason, I have this to say to you,
465 the worst thing one could say to a *real* man:
you have no balls! You're just a spineless coward!
You've come to see me, have you, after what you did?
To look someone in the eye who used to be dear,
someone you've hurt terribly, that isn't courage!
470 That isn't bravery! It's smug arrogance,
a cancer that poisons human relations. Still,

424 how *mobile la donna* is how fickle a woman is

you did the right thing by coming. I will feel
much better after telling you how I despise you
and after hearing it you'll feel much worse.
I'll start from the very beginning.   475
As all the Greeks know, those who sailed in the ship
with you, I saved your life. Those terrible tasks
they gave you! Yoking the bulls breathing fire,
sowing the seed from which armed men sprang up,
and that great serpent coiled around the prize,   480
the Golden Fleece, never sleeping, always on guard,
was killed—by me. *I* delivered you from evil.
I was too eager to be prudent; I betrayed
my father, my family, and came away with you
to Iolchos. There I murdered your uncle Pelias,   485
who sent you on that trip to get you killed,
and then stole your inheritance. He died
the worst of deaths: by his own children's hands.
So I ruined the entire family. And after
I did all this for you, you bastard, you   490
betrayed me, procuring a new bride for yourself,
despite the fact that I bore you two sons.
If you were still childless, I could understand
your wanting this marriage. But as things are, where
are all those promises you proffered? Gone!   495
I can't figure it out: do you think the gods
of former times no longer rule? or that
a new code of ethics has been established?
You must, since you know you've broken your promise to
     me.
Look at my right hand—remember how often   500
you grasped it? And how you'd go right down on your
     knees?
You made me hope for things that would never happen!
Enough. I'll share with you, as if with a friend
—but why? what do I expect to gain?—
anyway, you'll look worse when I question you.   505
Where am I to turn? To my father's house,
my country, which I betrayed for you? Back
to your cousins, perhaps? No doubt they'd be delighted
to welcome their father's murderer into their home.
This is how things stand: a state of war   510
exists between the ones I loved at home,
people I never should have hurt, and me—
all because of favors I did for you.
In return, I'm blessed among Greek women:
I have you, a marvelous husband, so   515
kind and so trustworthy—the more fool I!
If we are driven out of here in exile
the children and I, completely alone, no one
whom we can turn to, what a juicy scandal—
the bridegroom's children begging on the street,   520
along with the woman who saved him. Oh, God! Why
are there simple tests that tell us whether gold
has been adulterated, yet no stamp
upon the skin to tell good men from bad?

CHORUS.
525   When love turns into war between two lovers,
       that's a terrible passion which has no cure.
JASON.
       I see. I have to be a rhetorician,
       an expert yachtsman, furl my sails, ride out
       the storm of your tongue-lashing, woman. You
530   enumerate those favors you did for me,
       but I say the only one of gods and men
       responsible for my salvation was—Love.°
       (You do have a clever mind). It would be crude
       to spell out in detail how lust took over
535   and drove you to save my body—I won't put
       too fine a point on it. What service you did do
       was not without its value. But you got
       better than you gave from saving me.
       Look at it this way. First, you now live in Greece
540   instead of that backward land. Moreover, here
       you can experience justice, the rule of law
       instead of brute force. Here might does not make right.
       And now the Greeks all know how skilled you are.
       You have a reputation! If you were still
545   out at the ends of the earth, no one would ever
       have heard of you. As far as I'm concerned,
       being rich, or able to strum a better tune
       than Orpheus himself means less to me
       than being well-known: a star, a celebrity.
550   That's what I have to say about my exploits.
       (You're the one who started the debate).
       As for your whining about my royal marriage,
       I'll prove to you how sensible I was,
       how smart . . . in fact, this marriage shows
555   how much I love you and my kids. Shut up!
       When I came here from Iolchos, dragging a load
       of disasters behind me, what greater streak of luck
       could I have found than marrying Creon's daughter?
       Me, an outcast! You think I got tired
560   of screwing you, and fell madly in love
       with someone new: that's what burns you up.
       But it's not true. I have no interest, either,
       in seeing how many children I can father.
       Ours are sufficient. I have no complaints.
565   The reason I married her was the most basic
       motive anyone could have—so we
       could be well off, live comfortably, and not
       have any needs go unfulfilled. I know
       "a friend in need is a friend indeed" but when
570   you're poor friends fade away fast. I married her
       so I could raise my children in a style
       appropriate to my family background, make
       new brothers for them, treat them just the same

532 Love literally, "Aphrodite," the goddess who inspired sexual
desire. (Translator's note)

as those I have with you: and thanks to me
we'll be one big happy family!   575
Why do you need children? But I gain
if I can benefit the ones now living
by means of children who are still to come.
My plans weren't so bad, were they, wouldn't you say?
You would if you weren't sexually jealous. But   580
women have gotten to such a point that you
think if your sex life's good, then everything
is perfect; but a problem in that area
makes you turn the best things people have
into a battleground. There should have been   585
some other way for children to be born,
so there would be no women. In that case
men would be a carefree, happy race.
CHORUS.
Jason, your presentation was elegant.
But even though I'm contradicting you   590
I think your betrayal of your wife was wrong.
MEDEA.
I'm quite different from most people. I
think someone who does wrong, but who is slick
at speaking, gets the greatest blame. Someone
who boasts that he can always cover up   595
criminal actions with convincing words
is capable of anything. And yet
he's not so smart. Don't you come to me
with your nice getup, your deceptive speech.
A single word from me will lay you flat.   600
If you're not a coward, why marry in secret?
Why not tell the ones you love so much?
JASON.
Oh, sure! If I *had* told you of my plans,
why, you'd have jumped right on the bandwagon!
You, who can't let go of your rage even now!   605
MEDEA.
That wasn't what held you back. You're getting old.
Your unconventional marriage was starting to look
bizarre in the public eye: not good for a star.
JASON.
Just get this: it wasn't for a woman
that I made this royal marriage alliance.   610
I'm trying to help you, as I said before,
and father children, offspring to my own,
noble offspring to keep my line secure.
MEDEA.
Security like that I do not want.
That kind of money has too high a price!   615
JASON.
You know how you can change, and have more sense?
Stop looking at good luck as if it were bad;
stop agonizing when you should be glad.
MEDEA.
Go ahead, gloat: you've got your security.
I'm homeless now. I have to leave this place.   620

JASON.
    The choice was yours. You can't blame anyone else.
MEDEA.
    Of course! I married and abandoned *you*.
JASON.
    You made terrible threats against the king.
MEDEA.
    Soon I'm going to be a threat to you.
JASON.
625   I'm not going to discuss these things any more.
    But if you want a little financial support
    for the children and yourself, just say the word.
    I'm ready to give it with an open hand.
    I have friends who can help you; I'll write them.
630   You're crazy if you don't accept. Give up
    your anger. You have everything to gain.
MEDEA.
    I'll take nothing from your friends! Nothing
    from you! Don't you offer me a cent!
    I won't let a criminal buy me off!
JASON.
635   Well, I tried to help you and the kids,
    God knows. But being nice to you's no good.
    You stubbornly push away people on your side
    and only make things worse for yourself.

                         [*Exit Jason.*]
MEDEA.   Go on!
    Seized by lust, no doubt, you suddenly think
640   how long you're dawdling far from your new bride.
    Happy honeymoon! But perhaps—as God's
    my witness—you'll wish you'd never married!
CHORUS.
    When love comes on too strong, too much,
    it brings no honor, makes no one
645   look good. But nothing is so sweet
    when it goes right. Goddess of love,
    don't wound me with your golden bow
    and arrows dripping with desire.[2]

    What I want is sensible love,
650   the best the gods can give. No lust
    which drives me into a stranger's bed,
    brings arguments which never end.
    Look carefully at marriages;

[2]This choral song reflects the ancient attitude towards erotic love, which was seen as a kind of frenzy sent by a god on an individual rather than as an expression of the individual self. This passion was depicted as dangerous, upsetting, undesirable rather than pleasurable and fulfilling. This song can be understood as referring both to Medea's passion for Jason and to Jason's involvement with the princess, suggesting that it was desire for her that drove him from Medea. Jason says, however (609–13) that his motive was security, not passion. (Translator's note)

    leave the peaceful ones alone.

    My home, my country! May I never be   655
    a refugee, whose life drags on,
    dependent on others, miserable,
    pitied by all—intolerable!
    I'd rather die, and end such a life!   660
    No fate is worse than losing your home.
    I don't say this from hearsay; I
    have seen it. Medea, you've endured
    the worst of trials, yet no one
    consoles you. I will never respect   665
    a man who closes his heart to a friend.
    Let him die alone, unloved, unmourned!

[*Enter Aegeus.*]

AEGEUS.
    Medea! God be with you! There is no
    more gratifying greeting between old friends.
MEDEA.
    God be with you, Aegeus, Pandion's son!
    Where do you come from, visiting this place?   670
AEGEUS.
    I come from Apollo's ancient oracle.
MEDEA.
    Why did you go to consecrated Delphi?
AEGEUS.
    To find out how I can become a father.
MEDEA.
    Good Lord! You have no children, at your age?
AEGEUS.
    No children. That's the will of God, it seems.   675
MEDEA.
    But you are married, right?
AEGEUS.   I have a wife.
MEDEA.
    What did Apollo say to you about children?
AEGEUS.
    Something too hard for a man to figure out.
MEDEA.
    Would it be all right for me to hear what it was?
AEGEUS.
    Of course—intelligence is just what's needed.   680
MEDEA.
    Well, what did he say? Tell me!
AEGEUS.   Not
    to uncork the wine in my big bottle.
MEDEA.   Till
    you did something, or reached some place?
AEGEUS.   Not till
    I came to my own home again.
MEDEA.   Then why
    are you coming this way? It's not on your route.   685
AEGEUS.
    You've heard of Pittheus, King of Troezen?

MEDEA.

Yes—Pelops' son. They say he's very pious.

AEGEUS.

I want to ask his advice about these words.

MEDEA.

He's a wise man, knows all about such things.

AEGEUS.

690   And he's the closest of my foreign friends.

MEDEA.

Well, good luck. I hope you get what you want.

AEGEUS.

Wait—why are you weeping? And so pale?

MEDEA.

Aegeus, my husband's the cruellest of all to me!

AEGEUS.

What's this? You're unhappy? Tell me all about it.

MEDEA.

695   I've done nothing to him, but he betrays me.

AEGEUS.

By doing what? Be more specific, please.

MEDEA.

He's made another woman mistress of his house.

AEGEUS.

Surely he didn't do such an awful thing!

MEDEA.

He did. He cares nothing for his former wife.

AEGEUS.

700   Did he fall in love, or just get tired of you?

MEDEA.

A powerful love made him turn out false to us.

AEGEUS.

Well, if he's as bad as you say, forget him.

MEDEA.

It's power he's in love with, a royal marriage.

AEGEUS.

He married a king's daughter? Tell me more.

MEDEA.

705   His father-in-law is Creon, King of Corinth.

AEGEUS.

Then I can see why you're so unhappy, Medea.

MEDEA.

I'm done for! I'm even banished from this land!

AEGEUS.

Another blow! Who's sending you away?

MEDEA.

Creon wants to drive me out of Corinth.

AEGEUS.

710   And Jason lets this happen? It's an outrage!

MEDEA.

He *says* he doesn't agree, but forces himself
to bear it like a man. At your feet
I ask, I beg you, plead with you, oh please
take pity on me in my suffering!

715   Don't let me perish as a refugee!
Take me in—to your country, to your home!

If you do this, I pray the gods may grant
your wish to father children and die happy.
You don't know what luck you've found today.
I'll make you fertile! I'm the one will end   720
your childlessness! I know certain ways . . .[3]

AEGEUS.

I have good reason to help you, Medea. First,
God blesses those who aid the needy. Next,
you bring good news about my future sons.
(Regarding that I'm utterly good for nothing.)   725
Here's what I'll do. If you come to my land
it's only right I should help you out, and I will.
But this much I must also tell you: I
will not help you get out of here. If you
come to my house, you'll stay there unmolested.   730
I won't hand you over to anyone.
Just get out of this place by yourself.
In a foreign land I don't want to offend.

MEDEA.

Fine. Now if you give me your word on this
you'll have given me everything I want.   735

AEGEUS.

What's the problem? You mean you don't trust me?

MEDEA.

I trust *you*. But Creon, and Pelias' family
are my enemies. When they come after me,
and send you threats, if you haven't sworn by the gods
you might make friends with them. But if you're held 740
by firm agreements, you won't let me go.
I'm weak, and all alone, while they control
vast wealth, and power, and a royal house.

AEGEUS.

What thorough advance planning you display!
Well, if you want me to, I won't refuse.   745
In fact, it's safer for me if I have
some kind of excuse to show your enemies,
safer for you too. By what shall I swear?

MEDEA.

Swear by Earth, and Sun my father's father;
add the whole huge race of gods as well.   750

AEGEUS.

To do or not do what? Speak.

MEDEA.   Never
cast me out yourself from your land; never,
if one of my enemies tries to drag me off,
let me go voluntarily, so long as you live.

AEGEUS.

By Earth, by Sun's holy light, by all the gods,   755
I swear I will comply with what you say.

---

[3]The obvious reference is to Medea's knowledge of magic, but
she is also suggesting her own proven fertility. According to
other sources Medea did marry Aegeus after arriving in Athens,
but rather than help him in his quest for progeny she attempted
to murder his son Theseus. (Translator's note)

MEDEA.

Good. And if you break this oath, what then?

AEGEUS.

I suffer the fate of a man who defies the gods.

MEDEA.

Be happy, proceed on your journey. All is well.

760   I'll come to you as quickly as I can,
when I've done what I intend and got what I want.

[*Exit Aegeus.*]

CHORUS.

May Hermes conduct
you safe to your home,
and may you achieve
765   what you're hoping for,
since to me you seem
a noble man.

MEDEA.

O God! Divine Justice! Glorious Sun!
Now I will triumph over my enemies.
770   I've taken the first step upon the road.
Now I know I'll pay my enemies back,
since this man, just when all was lost, appeared
like a safe harbor protecting all my schemes.
As soon as I get to Athens' citadel
775   I'll moor myself to him and hold him fast.
Now I can tell you everything I'll do.
Listen to me. I don't think you will laugh.
    I'll send one of my servants to Jason, ask him
nicely, please won't he come here and see me.
780   He'll come. I'll wheedle him with tender words,
agree with him completely: he was right
to make his royal marriage, abandon me.
It was a wonderful plan, so well thought out.
I'll ask that my children stay. Oh, I don't intend
785   to leave them in a hostile land, so my foes
can have their way with them. No. This
is my way to kill another child: the king's.
I'll send them holding presents in their hands,
gifts for the bride—a delicate dress, a crown
790   of finely beaten gold. If she just touches
this loveliness, lays it on her skin,
she will die the most appalling death,
and so will anyone who touches her—
so deadly the poison in which I dip my gifts.
795   Now I have to break off my strategy . . .
oh God! What a thing I have to do after this!
I'm going to kill my children! There's no one
who can take them away from me—save them from me.
Then, after I destroy Jason's whole world,
800   I'll leave this place, escaping from my sweetest
babies' murder—an awful, God-cursed act!
I won't stand for my enemies mocking me!
    Wait. What good is there for me in life?
I have no place to go, no family,

no refuge from my pain. When I left home,   805
that's when I made my big mistake, seduced
by a Greek man's words. But with God's help he'll pay!
He'll never see again, alive, the sons
he had with me. And he won't spawn new ones
from his new bride: she has to die, badly,   810
as she deserves, poisoned by my drugs.
No one should think I'm unimportant, weak
or lazy. Quite the opposite—kind
to my friends, implacable to my enemies.[4]
To such a character comes greatest fame.   815

CHORUS.

You have shared your thoughts with me, and I
want to help you, but still obey the law.
I'm telling you: you must not do these things!

MEDEA.

There's no other way. Of course you can't approve.
But you're not going through this pain: I am.   820

CHORUS.

Woman, will you have the heart to kill your children?

MEDEA.

To cause my husband the greatest possible pain.

CHORUS.

But *you* will be the most unhappy woman!

MEDEA.

Enough of these words! They stand between me and my
    plan.
[*To the Nurse.*] Go on, bring Jason here. I trust you com-   825
    pletely.
Say nothing of what I have in mind, if you
are loyal to your mistress—and a woman.

[*Exit Nurse.*]

CHORUS.

Of old the Athenians prosper; the happy
descendants of blessed gods, they inhabit
a land which has never been pillaged. They feed   830
on glorious Wisdom; lightly they step
through the radiant air. It is there, people say,
the Muses conceived golden Harmony.

Beside the beautiful river of Cephisus,
Aphrodite breathes sweet gentle breezes   835
over the fertile savannahs. Wreathing
a garland of roses in fragrant hair,
she sends Love to be a companion to Wisdom;
together they give all the blessings of life.

How can a sacred city, which gives   840
sanctuary to friends, take you,

---

[4]This creed, quite different from the Golden Rule, was the accepted standard of Greek male behavior; Medea is here explicitly adopting a masculine code of honor. (Translator's note)

killer of children? You will infect
every thing that you touch. Just think
what a murder you'll carry out—
845   to gash and hack your children! No!
On my knees, I beg you, please,
somehow, anyhow, don't kill your sons!

Where will you get the courage, when
you come close to that awful deed?
850   Won't your heart and hand flinch back?
Looking them in the face, will you
carry out your role and strike,
shedding no tears? When they plead for their lives,
will you bathe your hands in innocent blood?
855   No! You won't be able to do it!

[*Enter Jason.*]

JASON.
You sent for me. I came. Though you are angry
at me, I'll always grant you this: I'll listen.
What new thing do you want from me now, woman?
MEDEA.
Jason, I beg you to forgive me for
860   the things I said. It's only right for you
to put up with my temper—I've helped you out.
Why, I've even taken myself to task
and said "You fool! Why are you crazy? Mad
at those who only wish you well! You've made
865   the ruler of this land your enemy—
your husband too, who's doing his best by us
by marrying the princess, making sons,
brothers to ours. Won't you give up your rage?
Why do you take it so hard? The gods direct
870   all well. Don't you have children? Don't you know
we're going into exile, and are short
of friends?" Thinking like this, I realized
how totally unreasonable I had been,
how useless all my furious anger was.
875   Now I agree with you. I think you're right
to make this merger for us. I was wrong
I should have shared in all your strategies,
shared in your marriage, standing by the bed,
taking pleasure in your bride with you.
880   However, we women are as we are: I
won't say we're bad. But you men should not share
our mistakes, answer our foolishness
with more stupidity. I've let that go.
I admit I was wrong before, but now
885   I've done so much more careful reasoning.[5]

---

[5]Many of Medea's comments here are not lies, but true in a different sense from the way she knows Jason will understand her. Here her "careful reasoning" has made her realize that she was wrong to reveal her anger previously. (Translator's note)

Children! Come here! Leave the house.

[*Enter children with Tutor.*]

Now kiss
your father, speak to him with me. Think
of him as a friend, not an enemy,
together with your mother. We've made peace.
The anger's all gone. Take his right hand. [*Screams.*]   890
    Ohhh!
[*Recovers.*] I'm thinking awful things could always happen.
Children, all your lives long, will you stretch
your sweet hands out to me like this? Poor me—
the tears just come. I'm superstitious.
Giving up my anger towards your father   895
after such a long time makes me cry.
CHORUS.
My eyes too are filled with tears. May no
worse thing take place than what is happening now.
JASON.
Good for you, woman. I have no complaints.
It's natural for a woman to get annoyed   900
when her man smuggles in another wife.
But your heart's changed for the better—though
it did take time to see my plan was right.
Now you're acting like a sensible woman.
Children, your father has carefully provided   905
security for you—with the gods' help, of course.
I foresee in time to come you'll be
the leading men of Corinth—along with your brothers.
Just grow up. Your father will take care
of all the rest—with the gods' help, of course.   910
I want to see you coming to adolescence
strong, to triumph over my enemies.
[*To Medea.*] You there—why do you have tears in your
    eyes?
Why do you turn away your pallid face?
Aren't you pleased with what I said just now?   915
MEDEA.
It's nothing. I was just thinking about these boys.
JASON.
Oh, cheer up! I will take good care of them.
MEDEA.
I'll do that. I've no doubt of what you say.
Women are nurturers, always ready to weep.
JASON.
Why do you make such a fuss about these kids?   920
MEDEA.
I gave birth to them. When you prayed just now
that they might live, tenderness rushed on me,
uncertainty if that will ever be.
    But the reason I asked you to come,
what I wanted to say, I've covered some;   925
now I'll continue. Since the king sees fit
to send us away—I too think this is best,
I know it very clearly—not stay on,

an obstacle to you and the royal ones.
930 I seem to be quite dangerous to them.
So I will sail off into exile, but
you should bring the children up yourself.
Ask Creon not to send them away from here.

JASON.
I don't know if I'll succeed; I'll try.

MEDEA.
935 Then order your wife to ask her father too
not to send the children away from here.

JASON.
All right—I'm pretty sure I can persuade her.

MEDEA.
You will, if she's a woman like the rest.
I'll also take a part in this attempt:
940 I'll send her gifts—the most perfect things that earth
possesses. The children will take a delicate dress,
a crown of finely beaten gold. At once!
Let one of the servants bring the treasure here.
She'll have so many reasons to rejoice—
945 you, the best of men, to sleep with her,
and now the ornaments my father's father
Helios gave to his own progeny.
Pick up these presents, children, in your hands,
and give them to the happy royal bride.
950 She won't be able to find fault with them.

JASON.
What? You're crazy to let these out of your hands!
You think the royal house is deficient in dresses?
Or golden jewelry? Keep them, don't give them away.
If my new wife thinks I'm worth anything,
955 she'll put my wishes ahead of material wealth.

MEDEA.
Don't tell me no. They say gifts can persuade
the gods themselves. To human beings they
have much more power than a thousand words.
Her star is rising, God is on her side,
960 she's young and in control. I wouldn't trade
just gold, but life, to keep my children out
of exile. Children! Carry these rich presents
to the new wife of your father—she's
my mistress too. Hurry! Ask her not
965 to send you away from here. Put the gifts
into her own hands. It's very important—
make sure she herself receives them. Go,
as fast as you can. I pray you may fare well
and come back bringing news I long to hear.

[Exeunt children, Jason, Tutor.]

CHORUS.
970 Now there is no longer hope for the children—
none! They are already walking towards death.
The new bride—unlucky!—will pick up disaster,
a curse from the golden tiara. Accepting
that loveliness, she will position Death

with her own hands on her shining blond hair.   975

That heavenly beauty, the glittering charm
of the golden dress will seduce her to try
the crown, so carefully worked, as she decks
herself as a bride—for a wedding in Hell.
What a trap she is falling into, accursed,   980
devoted to death. There is no way out.

God help you, Jason! You have made
a terrible royal marriage alliance.
You don't know it, but you've brought
an awful death on your wife and sons,   985
not even knowing what's going on!
But most of all I share your pain,
unhappy mother of the children—
the ones whom you will slaughter, since
your husband left you, wrongly. Now   990
he sleeps in another woman's bed.

[Enter Tutor and children.]

TUTOR.
Mistress! The children are set free from exile!
The princess was delighted with the gifts:
a reconciliation on their part
                              What's this?
Why are you just standing there amazed?   995

MEDEA.
Oh no!

TUTOR.
That cry is out of tune with my good news.

MEDEA.
No! No!!

TUTOR.
Maybe I don't
quite understand some part of the news? Have I   1000
made some mistake? It seemed like wonderful news.

MEDEA.
You've made your announcement. Fault's not yours.

TUTOR.
Why are you staring at the ground, in tears?

MEDEA.
Old man, I have my reasons. Gods have made
their evil machinations. So have I.   1005

TUTOR.
Cheer up! Because of your children, you'll come home.

MEDEA.
I'll send them home before me—damned as I am!

TUTOR.
You're not the only one to lose your kids.
You're human. Have to take disasters lightly.

MEDEA.
Yes. I will. Now go into the house.   1010
Get ready what they need on any day.

[Exit Tutor.]

Children, children! You have a place to go,
a house, a city. Leaving me behind,
without your mother you will live there always.
1015   I am going to another land,
exiled, before I can enjoy you, watch
you grow, adorn your brides, prepare for you
the bridal bed and lift the wedding torch . . .
it was not for this I raised you, children!
1020   not for this I struggled and took the pain,
twisting under the cruel spasms of birth.
I had such plans for you once—I thought that you
would take good care of me when I got old,
and when I died would lay me out properly—
1025   what every person hopes will happen. Now
that pleasant expectation is all gone.
Parted from you, I'll live an awful life,
filled with bitter memories. And you
won't see your mother any more; you'll go
1030   to quite another kind of life. Oh God!
Children, why are you looking at me like that?
Why are you smiling at me with your last smile?
What shall I do? My heart is giving way
as I look into my children's shining eyes.
1035   I could never do it! Goodbye, plans!
I'll take the children with me out of this land!
To make their father suffer, why should I
butcher my babies? I'll suffer twice as much!
Goodbye, my plans!
                            What's happening to me?
1040   Let my enemies get away scot-free
and earn their laughter? Is that what I want?
I have to do it. What a fool I was
putting a poultice of soft words on my heart!
Go into the house, children. If anyone here
1045   thinks it not right to attend my sacrifice,
that is your business. My hand will not fail.
        No! You cannot do this thing! You can't
Let them go, woman! Spare your children!
They can live on with you and make you happy.
1050   In the name of those punishers who dwell below
in Hell, I swear that this will never happen:
I will not deliver up my children,
victims to my enemies' abuse.
The deed is done. There's no way out.
1055   Right now the bride is putting on her crown
and melting in her dress: I see her, now.
I'm walking down the hardest road of all;
the road I send them on is harder still.
I want to speak to them. Children, give,
1060   give me your hands for Mother to hold. Oh
darling hands, and mouths I love so much,
straight bodies, and aristocratic faces!
I pray you both fare well—but not here. Here
is where your father threw it all away.
1065   How sweet you are to touch! Such tender skin,

such gentle babies' breath! Go, go away!
I can't keep looking at you any more.
The pain is stronger than I am. Now I know
what an awful thing it is I'm going to do.
But rage is stronger than this understanding—   1070
rage, the greatest cause of human pain.

CHORUS.
        I've spent time in careful thinking,
arguments too, trying to know
more than is right for a woman's mind.
We too have gifts which live with us   1075
and make us wise. Not all, perhaps
but some of us do seek the truth.
Women are not fools.
And to this verdict I have come:
those who have borne no children, who   1080
know nothing at all of parenting
are much better off than those who do.
Are children a curse or a blessing?
The childless never debate the question.
Their lack of experience saves them pain.   1085
But I see those with children at home,
those sweet offshoots, worn out with care.
They must figure out how to raise them right,
how to get them enough to live on. Next,
they can't know whether they're good or bad,   1090
the ones they're spending that effort on.
But worst of all the problems is this:
suppose we secure a decent living,
the children are healthy, they grow in strength,
they turn out to have good character, too.   1095
But if a god decides it, they're gone!
Death carries off their bodies to Hell.
For the gods to add this worst pain of all
to all the others we humans have—
what good does it do? Why bear a child?   1100

MEDEA.
        Friends, I've been standing here for a long time, waiting
to learn how events would turn out at the palace.
Now I see one of Jason's men coming here.
How hard he pants! Must have some awful news.

[Enter Messenger.]

MESSENGER.
        Medea! You've done the most awful deed, illegal,   1105
unholy! Go! Flee! You have to consider
how to make your escape, by land or sea!
MEDEA.
        What has happened that I should take to flight?
MESSENGER.
        She's dead—the princess! Just this minute. Creon
too, her father. Your magic poisons did it.   1110
MEDEA.
        Wonderful words! From now on I'll count you

among my friends, who do good things for me.
MESSENGER.
    What are you saying? Are you sane, or mad?
    You've attacked the royal family,
1115 yet hearing this you're pleased and not afraid?
MEDEA.
    I have plenty to say in response to you.
    But please, first tell me all, my friend. Don't hurry.
    How did they die? You'll give me twice the pleasure
    if their deaths were utterly horrible.
MESSENGER.
1120 When your two children arrived along with their father
    and entered the rooms of the newly married pair,
    we were all pleased, we servants who were pained
    by your unhappiness. Immediately
    the story went buzzing through our ears that you
1125 and Jason had settled your previous bitter feud.
    Someone kissed the hand of one of the children,
    another stroked a blond head. I myself
    followed the children to the women's quarters,
    I was so delighted. Till she saw
1130 your boys, the mistress—the one we look to now
    instead of you—was casting eager eyes
    on Jason. Then she went pale, and shut her eyes,
    and turned her head away; she was offended,
    seeing them. Your husband tried to calm
1135 her feelings, soothe the young girl's anger, saying:
    "You mustn't resent the ones I care about.
    Leave off this pouting. Turn your head around.
    You must love the ones your husband loves.
    Won't you accept these gifts, and ask your father
1140 to cancel his order banishing these boys?
    You'll do it, won't you, as a favor to me?"
    She said she would—as soon as she saw the gifts.
    She exclaimed to him about their beauty, and
    before her father and the children left
1145 the rooms, she took the delicate dress and wrapped
    herself up in it. Placing the golden garland
    on her curls, she arranged her hair. The mirror
    showed her own dead image laughing at her.
    Got up then, and walked across the room,
1150 prancing lightly on her little white feet,
    so pleased with her presents, glancing back
    to see just how the dress hung down behind.
    But then there was a terrible sight to see.
    Her color went; she staggered; body all
1155 convulsed, almost fell down, collapsed in her chair.
    An old maidservant, thinking one of the gods
    had sent a frenzy on her, called "God bless!"
    But when she saw the white foam on her lips,
    saw her eyes twisted back into her skull,
1160 saw her bloodless face, another cry
    came out—a scream of terror and despair.
    Off to the father's rooms ran one, another
    to the new husband, telling the bride's collapse.

Whole house was thundering with running feet.
It all happened fast: a runner would have turned   1165
and been close to the finish line, when the poor girl
    stirred,
opening her clenchedshut eyes, and moaned.
Two kinds of pain were making war on her:
the golden crown was sending out a stream
of eerie hungry fire around her head.   1170
The delicate dress—the gift your children brought—
was lapping up her delicate flesh. She jumps
up from her chair and bursts into flame; she tries
to run away, tossing her head, her hair,
pulling, tearing the garland off—but it   1175
was a manacle of gold, it held on tight,
and when she shook her head, the fire roared up
more brightly than before. She crashes down;
the enemy wins; she's hard to recognize—
only a father would know that she was his.   1180
You couldn't see her eyes, melted into her face;
her pretty face itself was gone; her scalp
was oozing blood like lava seething flame.
The way a pine exudes its viscous tears,
the flesh was dripping off her bones: the poison   1185
had its teeth deep into her. We all
were terrified to touch the corpse: we took
a lesson from what had happened to her.
                 And then
her father, unaware of this disaster,
comes in suddenly, sees the corpse, kneels down   1190
sobbing and gathers it into his arms, kissing,
talking to it: "My poor baby, what
demon has done this to you? Who's made me
into an orphan, an empty tomb, without you?
Oh God, I want to die with you, my child!"   1195
But then he quit his moaning and lamenting,
and tried to straighten up his body, but
the delicate dress was clutching him, like shoots
of ivy crawling over laurel. Then
there was an awful wrestling-match: he tried   1200
to rise, she grappled, pulled him down. He struggled
hard; she peeled the flesh from his old bones.
After a while, he had no more strength; he gasped
his last, extinguished by the power. Now
daughter and aged father lie together: 1205
this is an event which longs for tears.
    I'll say nothing about your situation.
You yourself will know how to find a way out.
This is not the first time I've understood
that everything people do is just a dream.   1210
I'd even say that those who seem to know
the most, who handle words so well, it's those
who get the greatest blame. Real happiness
belongs to no man. Sure, you slather on
a coating of good luck, and someone's life   1215
seems so much better than another's. But

who gets secure good fortune. No one can.

CHORUS.
It seems a god has taken Jason's measure,
fitting him with disaster—as he deserves.
1220 It's you we're sorry for, miserable princess,
heading down to Hades for marrying him.

MEDEA.
It's all decided, friends. As soon as I
can kill my children, I will leave this land.
I won't waste time and hand them over to
1225 some other, more sadistic murderer.
They have to die. And since they must,
it's I who'll kill them, I who gave them life.
Medea, put your armor on. What
are you waiting for? The thing that you must do
1230 is awful, but you have no choice. Come on!
Here's your heroic, wretched hand. Pick up
the sword. Pick it up. You're walking towards the end,
but it's the starting-point of a painful life.
Don't be a coward. Don't think about the children,
1235 how sweet they are, how you gave birth to them—
Forget about them for just a few minutes now;
later you can weep for them. Although
you're going to kill them, they were sweet, were yours—
I am a woman whom the gods have cursed!

[Exit Medea.]

CHORUS.
1240 O Mother Earth! O glittering rays
of the sun, look down and examine a woman
who is destroyed, and destroying, before
she can lift up her hand to slaughter her children.
To do it is just like killing herself.
1245 They are young shoots from your own famous line;
it is fearful for offspring of gods to be slain!
O heavenly light, prevent her! Expel
from the house this unhappy, murderous Fury
whose longing for vengeance comes straight out of Hell!

1250 All that labor of raising the children
all wasted, all worthless! You gave birth in vain,
you loved them for nothing! Then was it for this
you sailed here, defeating the sea's clashing rocks?
Unhappy Medea, why let this resentment
1255 take over your spirit? Is murder the answer?
To pour out the blood of your blood on the earth
leaves a poisonous stain which can never be clean,
and into the life of a butcher the gods
will orchestrate an echoing pain.

[Children scream within.]

CHORUS.
1260 A scream! Do you hear?
The children! A scream!

CHILDREN.
She wants to kill us![6]
What can we do?

CHILDREN.
I don't know, brother!
There's no way out!   1265

CHORUS.
Let's go in and stop
her killing the children!
Now! Come on![7]

CHILDREN.
Help us, for God's sake!

CHILDREN.
The knife's at my throat!   1270

CHORUS.
Only one woman has done such a thing,
killing her own dear children, and she
was insane: when the wife of Zeus drove her out
of her house and into the wilderness, Ino
went raving out to the shoreline, and stepped   1275
over a cliff to split on the rocks.
In her arms she carried her own two babes
She murdered them, but she died with them.
Can something more awful than that take place?
Marriage is so full of pain for a woman   1280
its evils reach out to touch others too.

[Enter Jason.]

JASON.
Women! You there, standing near the house,
is Medea, that criminal, still inside? or has
she already taken to flight? She'll have to hide
beneath the earth, or lift her body on wings   1285
and fly into the sky, to get away
from paying the penalty to the royal house.
Does she think she can kill the leaders of our land
and just sail out of here, safe and secure?

---

[6]Children appear and even speak onstage in Euripides' plays—Alcestis' son, for example, delivers a lament over his mother's body. Given the limited number of actors used in Greek drama, most scholars assume that child actors did play the roles but did not speak, that adult actors spoke their parts. Although Medea's children are certainly old enough to speak, they have no lines until these desperate cries, which were probably spoken by an actor within the stage-building (presumably the actor playing Medea). (Translator's note)

[7]In the non-illusionistic Greek theater, the chorus almost never intervenes in the action, even at moments like this, when not to do so seems absurd. (Translator's note)

1290 Yet it's not her I'm concerned about, but my children.
     Those that she attacked will pay her back,
     but I came here to save my children's lives.
     The king's family might take out on them
     the revenge their mother's ungodly crime deserves.
     CHORUS.
1295 Jason, poor man, you don't even know how far
     you've marched into misery. You wouldn't have said
        what you did.
     JASON.
     What's that? You mean she wants to kill me too?
     CHORUS.
     Your children are murdered. Their own mother did it.
     JASON.
     Oh, no! What are you saying? Your words destroy me.
     CHORUS.
1300 You must believe it: your children are dead and gone.
     JASON.
     Where did she kill them? Out here, or in the house?
     CHORUS.
     If you open the doors, you'll see your children's bodies.
     JASON.
     Hurry up, slaves! Open up the locks! Shatter
     the bolts! I want to see both parts of this crime:
1305 my children, dead, and her—I'll get revenge!

     [*Medea appears above the palace in the Chariot of the Sun.*]

     MEDEA.
     Why are you rushing around and storming the doors?
     Looking for your dead children and the one who killed
        them?
     Give yourself a rest. If you have something
     you need to say to me, just say it. But
1310 you will not lay a hand on me. The Sun,
     my father's father, gave me this chariot.
     It protects me from my enemies.
     JASON.
     You're disgusting! hated by the gods,
     by me, by every human being, you
1315 dared to use a sword on your own sons.
     How can you stay alive, see the sun and earth,
     after you've done the most ungodly acts?
     God damn you! Now I know you, but I didn't
     back when I took you out of that backward land
1320 and brought you home to Greece, an evil thing,
     a traitor to her father and fatherland.
     The gods have set on me the punishment
     which you deserved for killing your own brother
     and then embarking on our beautiful ship.
1325 And that was only the beginning. Next,
     after marrying me and bearing my children,
     you murdered them, and why? Because of sex.
     No Greek woman would dare to do such a thing,

and yet instead I chose to marry you.
I made a contract with an enemy,   1330
not a woman—a vicious lioness
more savage than the monster Scylla, who
devours ships in the Tyrrhenian Sea.
Enough! No use to gnaw at you with insults—
you have no sense of shame that can be touched. 1335
You criminal, child-killer, go to hell!
I have to weep for my own fate. I won't
ever get any profit from my bride.
I've lost my children, the ones I bore and raised.
I'll never be able to see them alive again.   1340
MEDEA.
I could provide a very long rebuttal
to what you've said, but there's no reason.
God the Father knows what I have done.
He also knows what you have done. There was
no way you were going to lead a happy life   1345
after disregarding our marriage and mocking me.
Not the princess either, or the father-in-law,
were about to get rid of me without paying a price.
Go right ahead and call me a lioness,
the monster Scylla in the Tyrrhenian Sea.   1350
I sank my claws in your heart—as you deserved.
JASON.
You feel it too; you share the pain.
MEDEA.   You're right.
But it's worth the pain for you not to laugh at me.
JASON.
Poor children! What a bad mother you got for yourselves!
MEDEA.
Poor children! Your father infected you with death. 1355
JASON.
You can't say it was my hand that killed them.
MEDEA.
No—your arrogance, and your new marriage.
JASON.
Because of my *marriage* you decided to kill them?
MEDEA.
Do you think that's such a small thing to a woman?
JASON.
To a sane one, yes. But you turn everything bad.   1360
MEDEA.
This will torment you: your sons are dead and gone.
JASON.
They're not! They'll come to take revenge on you.
MEDEA.
No—the gods know who started all this pain.
JASON.
What they know is how revolting you are.
MEDEA.
Go on, hate me: I despise your pretty attacks.   1365
JASON.
As I do yours. But it's easy to stop all this.

MEDEA.
Oh, really? Wonderful. What should I do?

JASON.
Give me the children's bodies to mourn and bury.

MEDEA.
Never! I'm going to bury them myself,
1370 far off, in the shrine of Hera on the cape,
so that no enemy can dig up the grave
and violate their bodies. In this land
I'll establish sacred rites to last forever,
recompense for their unholy death.
1375 I myself am off to Athens; there
I'll live with Aegeus, son of Pandion.
You will die badly, just as you deserve,
hit on the head by a piece of your ship the Argo.
You've seen the bitter result of your marriage to me.

JASON.
1380 May the children's Furies
get the justice
their blood demands,
destroying you!

MEDEA.
What god listens
1385 to one who lies
and breaks his word?

JASON.
You're a disgusting
killer of children!

MEDEA.
Go to the house
1390 and bury your wife.

JASON.
I'll go, deprived
of my two sons.

MEDEA.
You don't feel it yet.
Wait till you're old.

JASON.
1395 My dearest children!

MEDEA.
Dear to their mother,
not to you.

JASON.
So why did you kill them?

MEDEA.
To make you suffer.

JASON.
I want to kiss   1400
my babies' lips.

MEDEA.
Now you talk to them.
Now you love them.
Then you ignored them.

JASON.
Please, in the gods' names,   1405
just let me touch
my children's skin.

MEDEA.
No. Your words are worthless.

[Exit Medea.]

JASON.
God! Do you hear
how I'm pushed aside?   1410
What this loathsome monster,
this killer of children,
is doing to me?
I'll do what I can
to mourn my children,   1415
asking the gods
to see how you killed them,
then stopped me from touching,
from burying them.
Now that I see them murdered by you,   1420
I wish they had never even been born!

CHORUS.
Zeus in Olympus
has much in store.
Gods do their work
unpredictably.   1425
What we don't expect,
the gods bring about,
and what seems sure,
doesn't happen after all.
And that is how this story turned out.   1430

TOPICS FOR CRITICAL THINKING AND WRITING

The Play on the PAGE

1. The classical scholar Gilbert Murray once summed up Medea and Jason thus: "Love to her is the whole world, to him it is a stale memory." How adequate is this summary? Explain.

2. Another classical scholar, Denys L. Page, in the preface to his edition of the Greek text of the play (1938), says,

> Here, indeed, for the first time in the Greek theatre, the power of the drama lies rather in the characters than in their actions. Medea's emotions are far more moving than her revenge; Jason's state of mind is more interesting than his calamity. The murder of children, caused by jealousy and anger against their father, is mere brutality: if it moves us at all, it does so towards incredulity and horror. . . . But the emotions of the woman whose love turned to hatred, and equally those of the man who loves no longer, represent something eternal and unchangeable in human nature; here we find, what in great drama we must always seek, the universal in this particular.   (xiv–xv)

   To what extent do you agree or disagree? Explain.

3. Denys L. Page, again in the preface to his edition, says (p. xiv):

> The heart of the play is the quarrel between Medea and Jason, the deserted wife and the deserting husband. It must be clearly understood that the poet does not attempt to solve the problem which they propound. The fantastic conclusion of his play—child-murder, dragon-chariot—is an end and not an answer. This is no longer a part of life, but of myth and magic; no longer about a woman, but about a barbarian sorceress.

   Your view of Page's comments?

4. In popular legend and in a later play by Seneca, Medea is a cold-blooded murderer. Do you think Euripides's Medea is sufficiently human, or is she a monstrous freak? Explain. (One way to think about the issue is to ask yourself if there is any way to make sense of her murder of the children.)

5. Jason offers several arguments defending his conduct. For instance, he suggests that he has Medea's welfare in mind, in addition to his own. Do you think he is hypocritical? Or sincere but stupid? Or what? Do you find any of his arguments convincing? If so, which ones?

6. Aristotle found the scene with Aegeus irrelevant. Do you agree, or do you think it serves some useful function(s)? Explain.

7. Do you think Euripides in effect is saying, "Life is sometimes like this?" or is he implying that something should be done to improve the status of women in Greek society?

The Play on the STAGE

8. Here are three translations of the opening lines of the play, spoken by the Nurse. (The first, by Mary-Kay Gamel, is the version that we print in this book.) Do the different versions require different styles of acting? If you were an actor, which version would you use? Why? (*Note:* The second and third versions, more literal than the first, mention by name the *Symplegades* ["clashing ones"], two dark blue rocks or islands near the entrance of the Black Sea. These rocks supposedly closed and crushed ships that tried to pass between them.)

Oh how I wish that boat the Argo had never
flown through the dark clashing rocks to Colchis'
   shore!
I wish the pine that made it had never been felled
in the groves of Thessaly! Wish the heroes sent
for the Golden Fleece by Pelias never had rowed it!
(TRANS. MARY-KAY GAMEL)

If only the Argo, skimming its way among
The blue Symplegades, had never reached
The land of Colchis, nor the ax-hewn pine

Been felled in Pelion's glen to furnish oars
To put into the hands of warrior princes
Whom Pelias urged to seek the Golden Fleece!

(TRANS. SIMON GOLDFIELD)

How I wish the Argo never had reached the land
Of Colchis, skimming through the blue Symple-
    gades,
Nor ever had fallen in the glades of Pelion
The smitten fir-tree to furnish oars for the hands
Of heroes who in Pelias's name attempted
The Golden Fleece!

(TRANS. REX WARNER)

9. Here are three versions (lines 257–60) of part of
Medea's speech comparing the sufferings of women
with those of men. As with the preceding question,
consider whether the translations require different
styles of acting, and consider, too, which translation you would prefer to speak.

Men say we live a lazy life at home
while they must go to war—what fools they are!
I'd rather face the enemy three times
than undergo the pains of labor once.

(TRANS. MARY-KAY GAMEL)

They say we lead a life devoid of danger
At home while they do battle with the spear,
But they are wrong. I'd three times rather stand
And face a line of shields than once give birth.

(TRANS. SIMON GOLDFIELD)

What they say of us is that we have a peaceful time
Living at home, while they do the fighting in war.

How wrong they are! I would very much rather
    stand
Three times in the front of battle than bear one
    child.

(TRANS. REX WARNER)

10. Choose one key scene that includes Medea and
propose two opposed ways of staging it. (Consider
blocking—the director's organization of movement
on the stage—lighting, gestures, and, of course,
emphases.)

11. What are some difficulties (or challenges) for an
actor who plays Jason? Support your answer with
references to specific scenes.

12. Start by listing Medea's major one-on-one scenes
(with the Nurse, with Creon, etc.). Take two of
these, and indicate how the actress playing Medea
should do each scene. What specific instructions
would you give the actress?

13. How would you clothe, block, and choreograph
the Chorus?

14. Suppose that you are the set designer for a production of Medea. The theater seats three hundred
(not twelve thousand), and it is not open to the
heavens; the stage is a traditional proscenium
arrangement, and your budget is modest. Prepare
an annotated sketch of a usable one-set design.
(Consider the possibility of several acting levels,
and the suggestions of walls and windows, and the
need for one dominant entrance.) Or consider an
open-air site on your campus—for instance, in
front of a particular building—where the play
might be staged during good weather. Why did you
choose this site?

The Play in PERFORMANCE

We know that when Medea was first performed at the
festival in Athens it won third prize, but we know
nothing in particular about how the play was staged.
Still, we can say a few things. Almost surely Medea's
costume (including the headdress on her mask)
marked her as a foreigner; paintings of Medea on
vases, though admittedly of a slightly later date than
Euripides's play, regularly show her wearing distinctive—"foreign"—clothing.

In some Greek plays it is not always clear when a
character enters or exits, but there are no such problems in Medea, though it is not clear at what point
Medea prepares the deadly gifts. Possibly she goes inside and poisons the gifts during the choral song that
begins at line 828. Or perhaps the magic poison works
only on her enemies, so she and her children can handle the gifts even though they are deadly. In any case,
the robe was part of the traditional story, and it there-

fore caused no surprise. But an audience probably was surprised to learn that Medea herself kills the children. The Chorus seems to assume that the children will be killed by the Corinthians, in retaliation for bringing destruction to the princess and to Creon. And surely there is a surprise near the end of the play, when Medea appears above the palace, in a chariot of the sun. We have heard the children scream, and we have heard the Chorus talk of murder. Jason pounds at the doors, and presumably the audience expects the doors to open and the *eccyclema* (a wheeled platform) to roll out, revealing a tableau of dead bodies, perhaps presided over by Medea. Instead, Euripides uses the Greek theater's other theatrical machine, the *mechane,* or crane. Medea in the chariot, hoisted from behind the scene-building, comes into view on the roof of the scene-building, and we get, in effect, a *dea ex machina,* a "goddess out of a machine." From this elevated position Medea confronts Jason for the last time, and we see—quite literally—the great gap between the two. With her last words, presumably the crane reverses its action, lowers her out of sight, and the Chorus exits.

Medea was enormously influential on later Western literature; it was widely quoted, and several important playwrights were moved to write their own plays on the subject, notably Seneca in Rome, Corneille in France, and Grillparzer in Germany. A film (1970) by Pier Passolini, with Maria Callas as Medea, was inspired by Euripides's play, and quoted a few lines, but it cannot by any means be considered a filmed version of the play. An experimental production of *Medea* in New York in 1972 by Andrei Serban radically interpolated some of Seneca into Euripides, with the conflated texts performed in the original Greek and Latin. Influenced by Peter Brook's search for a transcendent theater language, Serban (with the aid of Elizabeth Swados's percussive score for archaic instruments) aimed to connect with tragedy's ritualistic core.

In the United States, the poet Robinson Jeffers did a very free translation that was performed with much acclaim in 1947, with Judith Anderson—a leading classical actress—in the title role. Anderson gave a performance in a somewhat old-fashioned, highly theatrical or melodramatic style, which she managed to bring off, in part because of her reputation and in part because it seemed appropriate to an ancient Greek tragedy. John Gielgud played Jason, in a colorless manner that suited the role and allowed Anderson to dominate the play. In 1982 the role was played by Zoe Caldwell—with Judith Anderson, age eighty-four, playing the Nurse. Caldwell emphasized Medea's sexuality, with a good deal of orgiastic writhing. Reviewers who remembered Anderson in the role tended to find Caldwell lacking in power.

In 1992 a London company, with Diana Rigg as Medea, achieved acclaim and came to New York in 1994, where it received enthusiastic reviews. Rigg, her hair pulled back into a single braid, wore a blood red dress—symbolism obvious enough—but she emphasized not the sexuality of the role but the intellectuality. It was evident that Medea was the smartest person on the stage, and the ingenuity that she had used to help Jason win the Golden Fleece now was turned into an effort to destroy him, not by killing him but by killing his new wife and his children, so that he had nothing left to live for. Rigg was highly praised, but the set aroused almost as much praise. Two bronze façades, made of rusting squares, stood three stories tall, looking like the massive walls of a prison cell in a courtyard. Medea was sometimes seen in a window in a wall, a friendless foreigner, virtually in prison. And the corroded metal also suggested her tormented, burning mind. These qualities—imprisonment and mental chaos—were symbolized, too, by the clangings and groanings given out when the metal walls were struck. Two quotations from reviews may help to suggest something of the production, and something of the enthusiasm that it evoked. In the *Wall Street Journal,* April 13, 1994, Edwin Wilson commented on two aspects of staging:

> In the scene where Medea is agonizing over whether or not to carry through her infanticide, a harsh, triangular beam of light slashes across the stage, pinning her in a corner. At the climax of the play, after Medea has murdered her sons inside her palace, three enormous metal panels break loose, falling with a clangor that lifts spectators from their seats.

William A. Henry, writing in *Time,* April 25, 1994, described the ending in more detail:

> A wall topples to reveal Diana Rigg apparently already at sea. Hunched during her period of rage and oppression, she stands proud as a ship's figurehead, clouds streaming past, golden light burnishing her. Then she turns and looks back, toward the scene of her unrepented misdeeds and, surely, toward an audience agape at the beauty and power of this finale.

L. L. WEST
Directing Medea

Director L. L. West produced *Medea* in the fall of 1994. The production was sponsored by the Utah Classical Greek Festival and toured throughout Utah, Colorado, New Mexico, and California. Venues for the production were split between indoor "traditional" proscenium stages and outdoor "classical" stages. Since the performance space changed radically with each performance, audience size varied from three hundred to fifteen hundred.

What made you decide to do a Greek play and why Medea?

Well, first off you need to know that the decision to produce a Greek play happened long before I became involved. The Utah Classical Greek Festival has produced at least one Greek play for the past twenty-four years. There is a huge classical tradition in Utah. Yes . . . Utah of all places. To my knowledge, it is the oldest festival of its kind in the country. So, as a freelance director, I was honored to be invited to direct the 1994 production. Since I had directed for the festival before—*Iphigenia at Aulis* in 1985 and *Helen* in 1988—I had some voice in the actual play selection. My first thought was to do Euripides's *Medea* . . . a brutal, raw, passionate, and loving *Medea*.

What is it about Medea?

Understand that it's more than *Medea*. It's Euripides's *Medea*. As far as Greek plays and playwrights, my taste seems to run full speed to Euripides. There is a frightening God-in-Man/Man-in-God conflict that I find very twentieth-century American. There is something brutal and passionate about Euripides's characters, especially his women. When I direct, I want to spend my time and energy with plays that touch my soul. I want to wrap myself around characters that are still a bit of an enigma. I figure if I know a character's motives and needs at the beginning of the process then what's the purpose—or the fun—of the journey? So as I looked at Euripides's *Medea*, I thought, "This play has all the stuff of a very scary ride and I'm not quite sure where it's going."

So, you decided on Euripides's Medea. *Then what?*

Finding a translation. Finding the right translation for this production.

How did you go about finding the "right" translation?

Shortly after we decided to do *Medea*, I happened to take an inhumanely long bus ride from Utah to Kansas. It was January at its bleakest. I knew the winter landscape through Wyoming and Nebraska would be flat and depressing . . . so I armed myself with at least ten translations of *Medea*. With most of the translations, I would read for a while then doze then read again. With Mary-Kay Gamel's translation, it was as if I was reading *Medea* for the first time. I started reading just outside Cheyenne and finished as we pulled into Ogalalla. Professor Gamel had managed to fill the characters—especially Medea and Jason—with a blood and a passion. There was a sense of ritual with the language that I found wonderfully dark and compelling. But the thing that impressed me most was that the story was told with painstaking clarity.

As a director, one of your biggest decisions is how to visually present the play. What did you want your audience to see?

In terms of the setting, I wanted the feel to be extremely theatrical. I felt that it was important to present an environment for the action that was unique to every theatre where we performed. We created a skeleton proscenium—very Greek-like in shape—that allowed the audience to see the surrounding space. When we performed outside, the audience saw rocks and trees; when we performed on traditional indoor stages, our audiences saw the backstage of that particular theatre.

What about costumes?

In the beginning, I knew what I didn't want. I'd seen far too many classical white chiton productions. They all seem so pristine and bloodless. Nor did I want a twentieth-century French production with tuxedos and evening dresses . . . I wanted costumes that would capture the passion and power of the Euripides/Gamel *Medea*. Our goal with the costume design was to create an archetypal world where magic and ritual exist. It was never our desire to place our characters in a specific time frame. Consequently we borrowed from many different sources: superhero comics, ritual voodoo garb, and *Mad Max* movies.

What about masks? I imagine that everyone who goes to see a Greek play knows that originally masks were used—chiefly, it is thought, because theaters were so huge. But since the theaters where you performed were much smaller, did you feel the need to use masks?

For *Medea* I felt that some type of masking was important to set a sense of other-world-ness and ritual. Ritual played a large part in this production. We decided to avoid the traditional masks and chose instead to find other ways to hide the face. For the Chorus, each costume was designed with a cowl at the neck that could be pulled up to mask the face. In addition, each chorus member wore a headband that covered most of his or her forehead. So with the cowl up and the headband, there was a only a slit for the eyes . . . it was very much a mask. I chose not to mask the individual characters. I wanted our audiences to identify with the characters and I felt that masking would distance them.

You mentioned the Chorus. How did you use them? How many?

I used five chorus members. There was rarely a time when they were not on stage. They provided counterpoint for the action with Medea and Jason, they played music, they became Medea's friends and critics, Creon's guards, and Jason's cohorts. With the exception of Medea and Jason, all of the characters in the play—Creon, the Messenger, the Nurse, the Tutor—were pulled from the Chorus.

In all your talking about the characters, you have not mentioned the Children.

I didn't cast children. I felt that there was a more effective, more theatrical way to present the children than to have actual actors. Each time the children appeared I had the chorus leader "become" the children. She had a stylized mask on each hand that represented each boy. Her movements—again, very stylized and ritualistic—created the two children.

Of course we know virtually nothing about Greek dances and about Greek music, but it seems pretty

certain that the chorus sang and—perhaps at the same time—sometimes danced. Did your chorus do any dancing? Any singing?

They probably sang more than they danced, although movement was extremely important to the overall mood and feel of the production. There was music written for all the choral odes and it was sung by the chorus. Describing the music as primitive and ritualistic is an understatement. The feel of the music was more like a voodoo incantation than a Greek ode. I would say that the music was more strident than melodic, more percussive than rhythmic. The mood that was created was dark and frightening.

The question about dance reminds me that I should have asked about musical instruments. I think scholars agree that the ancient Greeks used a flute, but there is not much more agreement than that. Sometimes in scholarly books on Greek drama one comes across statements such as "probably in addition to flute, percussion instruments were used." What musical instruments did you use?

Well, I'm sorry to disappoint the scholars . . . but we didn't use a single flute. We did, however, begin the play and end it with a saxophone solo. It had a strange and wonderful quality that we liked . . . it also kept the play in "the now." All the music within the play was vocal with a strong drum accompaniment.

One final question. At the end of the play Medea is flown away in a golden chariot. How did you accomplish that bit of Deus ex Machina—*or, I guess in this case,* Dea ex Machina?

Very simply and theatrically. I am a great believer in my audience's imagination. I placed Medea on one side of the stage with a chair; her focus was out and down as if she were flying. On the opposite side of the stage I grouped the Chorus and Jason; their focus was out and up as if they were looking to her rising higher and higher. The dialogue and the actors created flying chariot and the audience believed.

DAVID RICHARDS
Medea *with Diana Rigg*

The following review of a New York production with Diana Rigg appeared in the *New York Times*, April 8, 1994. For two photographs of the production, see page 51.

Mountain climbers have Everest. Swimmers have the English Channel. Actresses have *Medea*.

The title character of Euripides' tragedy is one of the huge, ravenous roles of dramatic literature. It will take everything a performer can give, then ask for more. Sheer talent is not enough. Courage and a certain recklessness are required to conquer it. A wild and exotic creature who knows potions that cure and poisons that kill, Medea is also a forsaken wife and tortured mother. She is one of us and not like us at all.

In the London-born production that began a limited engagement last night at the Longacre Theater, Diana Rigg brings a blazing intelligence and an elegant ferocity to the part. In the course of the 90-minute production, she grovels ignominiously at the feet of men. But by the end, she stands over them like the mighty figurehead of a ship about to sail for distant lands. For the actress, who has always managed to suggest impeccable breeding even when she is behaving abominably, the evening is a triumph.

It can also be counted a considerable success for the director, Jonathan Kent, who has set the play in an abstract box that could be the courtyard of a grim prison. The three-story walls are made of rusting metal panels. Whenever someone pounds on them, they produce thunderous echoes. The doors shut with a clang. Peter J. Davison's austere design does more than convey a sense of Medea's exile in a foreign land—an incarceration, really—it is a potent image for an inhospitable universe, conceived by the gods for man's misery and pain.

Working closely, Mr. Kent and Mr. Davison have engineered a spectacular climax for a tragedy that consists primarily of a series of increasingly horrible revelations. Abandoned by Jason for a younger woman, Medea won't rest until she has poisoned her rival and her rival's father, Creon. If she spares her errant husband, it is only so she can drive him into deepest despair by slaughtering their two young sons. Atrocity follows atrocity. Then, vengeance taken, she locks herself behind the rusted walls.

The biggest jolt is still to come, however. "Unbar the doors," howls a grief-stricken Jason (Tim Oliver Woodward), desperate to see the corpses of his sons but unable to find a way in. Suddenly, as if shaken by an earthquake, the metal wall before him collapses, the panels crashing to the ground with a colossal din. There, high above, stands Medea in a blood-soaked gown: victorious, remorseless, inhuman. Jason's pleading exasperates her. The last word out of her mouth before the lights fade is "rubbish." She virtually spits it down at him.

The women of Corinth (Judith Paris, Jane Loretta Lowe, Nuala Willis), who make up the chorus, are the sorts of Greek peasants who hover like crows on the fringes of "Zorba." Their clothes are black and their faces are lined. Sometimes they sing their choral passages (Jonathan Dove has written the haunting musical line). Sometimes they speak them. But for all their grand and woeful thoughts, they mostly communicate a fearful helplessness, before taking to wooden chairs on the side lines. The play is Medea's. So is the agony.

Unlike Zoe Caldwell, who emphasized the sexuality of the character (and won a Tony Award in 1982 for her efforts), Ms. Rigg sees Medea as a woman of restless intellect. An orgiastic fervor informed Ms. Caldwell's performance; she had a savage growl in her voice. A passionate sense of injustice propels Ms. Rigg, whose voice never entirely loses its intrinsic musicality. Her hair is swept back into a tight braid, a style that sets off her grave and handsome features. Initially, only the aggressive jut of her chin and the smolder in her eyes give her away.

While some of Paul Brown's modernistic costumes—in particular, a greatcoat for the king that seems to be growing hair—are a bit wacky, the lighting by Wayne Dowdeswell and Rui Rita is almost brutal in its directness. At one point, a merciless shaft of light actually forces Medea into a corner, even as she is wrestling with her conscience and trying to steel herself to the awful deeds ahead. In what may be the best messenger role ever written, Dan Mullane, motionless in a fierce spotlight, describes ghastly offstage events with frozen horror. He could be responding to a police grilling.

The male characters in *Medea* don't come off well. But then they never have, and Alistair Elliot's stripped-for-action translation of the play further emphasizes Euripides' feminist sympathies. Either the men are smug and patronizing (like John Turner's Creon) or else they're smug and self-serving (like Mr. Woodward's Jason). Although Aegeus (Donald Douglas) shows some understanding of Medea's plight and promises her asylum in Athens, he's got a prudent streak running down his back and makes it clear that she'll have to get there by herself.

None of them can hold their own against her on moral or dramatic grounds. And when Ms. Rigg allows herself to indulge in some traditional feminine wiles, their defenses prove pathetically weak. "I am clever," she admits boldly to Creon, before realizing her error

and backing down. The voice softens, and she adds, "but I am not *that* clever." The qualification is shrewd, self-protective. She's not ready for the kill yet.

Let men boast that they take all of life's risks while women sit safely at home. "I'd rather stand three times in battle by my shield," she responds, "than once give birth." Ms. Rigg, who has always had a wry wit, does not forgo it here. In addition to the knife in the folds of her robe, irony is one of her weapons. Medea, a victim, is also a victimizer.

The contradictions are tantalizing.

Aristophanes

Nothing of much interest is known about Aristophanes (c. 450–c. 385 B.C.E.). An Athenian, he competed for about forty years in the annual festivals of comic drama to which three playwrights each contributed one play. His first play was produced in 427 B.C.E., his last extant play in 388 B.C.E., but he is known to have written two comedies after this date. Of the forty or so plays he wrote, eleven survive. *Lysistrata* was produced in 411 B.C.E.

■■■■■■■■■■■■■■

COMMENTARY ON *LYSISTRATA*

Of the hundreds of ancient Greek comedies that were written, only eleven by Aristophanes and four by Menander (c. 342–299 B.C.E.) are extant, and three of Menander's four survive only in long fragments. Aristophanes seems to have written about forty plays, Menander more than twice as many. Hundreds of other men wrote comedies in ancient Greece, but they are mere names, or names attached to brief fragments. This means that when we talk about Greek comedy we are really talking about a fraction of Aristophanes's work, and an even smaller fraction of Menander's.

Greek comedy is customarily divided into three kinds: Old Comedy (486 B.C.E., when comedy was first given official recognition at the festival called the City Dionysia, to 404 B.C.E., the end of the Peloponnesian War, when Athens was humbled and freedom of speech was curtailed); Middle Comedy (404 B.C.E.–336 B.C.E., the accession of Alexander, when Athens was no longer free); and New Comedy (336 B.C.E.–c. 250 B.C.E., the approximate date of the last fragments). Of Old Comedy, there are Aristophanes's plays; of Middle Comedy, there is *Plutus*, one of Aristophanes's last plays; of New Comedy, there are Menander's fragments and his recently discovered *Dyskolos* (*The Disagreeable Man*).

Old Comedy—*Lysistrata* is an example—is a curious combination of obscenity, farce, political allegory, satire, and lyricism. Puns, literary allusions, phallic jokes, and political jibes periodically give way to joyful song; Aristophanes seems to have been something of a combination of Joyce, Swift, and Shelley. Other comparisons may be helpful. Perhaps we can say that in their loosely connected episodes and their rapid shifts from lyricism and fantasy to mockery the plays are

something like a Marx Brothers movie (Harpo's musical episodes juxtaposed with Groucho's irreverent wisecracks and outrageous ogling), though the plays are more explicitly political; and they are something like the rock musical *Hair*, which combined lyricism and politics with sex. The players of male roles wore large phalluses, and all the players wore masks, usually with grotesque expressions.

Aristophanes's plays usually have the following structure:

1. *Prologos:* prologue or exposition. Someone has a bright idea and sets it forth either in monologue or dialogue. In *Lysistrata*, the prologue consists of lines 1–212, in which Lysistrata persuades the women to refrain from sex with their husbands and thus compel their husbands to give up the war.
2. *Parados:* entrance of the chorus. The twenty-four or so members of the chorus express their opinion of the idea. (The *koryphaios*, or leader of the chorus, perhaps sings some lines by himself.) *Lysistrata* is somewhat unusual in having two half-choruses (*hemichori*), one of Old Men and another of Old Women, each with its own leader. Probably each half-chorus had twelve members.
3. *Epeisodion:* episode or scene. In the first scene of *Lysistrata* the women defeat the Commissioner. (A scene in this position, that is, before the *parabasis*, is sometimes called the *agon*, or debate.)
4. *Parabasis:* usually an elaborate composition in which the leader of the chorus ordinarily sheds his dramatic character and addresses the audience on the poet's behalf, the other actors having briefly retired. The *parabasis* in *Lysistrata* is unusual: It is much shorter than those in Aristophanes's earlier

plays, and the chorus does not speak directly for the playwright.

5. *Epeisodia*: episodes or scenes, sometimes briefly separated by choral songs. These episodes have to do with the working out of the original bright idea. In *Lysistrata* the first scene of this group (labeled Scene II because we have already had one scene before the *parabasis*) shows the women seeking to desert the cause, the second shows Myrrhine—loyal to the idea—tormenting her husband Kinesias, the third shows the Spartan herald discomfited by an erection, and the fourth shows the Spartan ambassadors similarly discomfited.

6. *Exodos*: final scene, customarily of reconciliation and rejoicing. There is often talk of a wedding and a feast. In this play a Spartan sings in praise not only of Sparta but also of Athens, and the chorus praises the deities worshiped in both states.

Perhaps all Old Comedy was rather like this, but it should be remembered that even Aristophanes's eleven plays do not all follow the pattern exactly. *Lysistrata*, for example, is unusual in having two hemichori and in having the chorus retain its identity during the *parabasis*. But *Lysistrata* (the accent is on the second syllable, and the name in effect means "Disbander-of-the-Army") is typical in its political concern, in its fantasy, in its bawdiness, and in its revelry. It touches on serious, destructive themes, but it is joyous and extravagant, ending with a newly unified society. These points require some explanation.

First, Aristophanes's political concern. *Lysistrata* is the last of Aristophanes's three plays opposing the Peloponnesian War (the earlier two are *Acharnians* and *Peace*). This drawn-out war (431–404 B.C.E.), named for a peninsula forming the southern part of Greece, was fought between Athens (with some allies) and a confederacy headed by Sparta. Though enemies when the play was performed in 411 B.C.E., Athens and Sparta and other communities had been allies in 478 B.C.E. in order to defeat a common enemy, the Persians, but once the Persian threat was destroyed, Athens deprived most of its allies of their autonomy and, in effect, Athens ruled an empire.

Moreover, Athens tried to extend its empire. The war ultimately cost Athens its overseas empire and its leadership on the mainland. In 413 B.C.E. Athens had suffered an especially disastrous naval defeat; it had made something of a recovery by the time of *Lysistrata*, but the cost in manpower and money was enormous.

Yet Athens persisted in its dream of conquest and of colonizing.

To counter this fantastic idea Aristophanes holds up another fantastic idea: The women will end the war by a sex strike. Actually, this is not one fantastic idea but two, for the idea of a sex strike is no more fantastic (for Athenians of the fifth century B.C.) than the idea of women playing a role—not to speak of a decisive role—in national affairs. Lysistrata, reporting her husband's view, is reporting the view of every Athenian: "War's a man's affair." (He was quoting from Homer's *Iliad*, so the point was beyond dispute.) And so there is something wild in her suggestion that the women can save the Greek cities (her hope goes beyond Athens, to Sparta and the other combatants), and in her comparison of the state to a ball of tangled yarn:

COMMISSIONER.
  All this is beside the point.
                                 Will you be so kind
  as to tell me how you mean to save Greece?
LYSISTRATA.   Of course.
  Nothing could be simpler.
COMMISSIONER.   I assure you, I'm all ears.
LYSISTRATA.
  Do you know anything about weaving?
  Say the yarn gets tangled: we thread it
  this way and that through the skein, up and down,
  until it's free. And it's like that with war.
  We'll send our envoys
  up and down, this way and that, all over Greece,
  until it's finished.
COMMISSIONER.
  Yarn? Thread? Skein?
  Are you out of your mind? I tell you,
  war is a serious business.
LYSISTRATA.   So serious
  that I'd like to go on talking about weaving.
COMMISSIONER.
  All right. Go ahead.
LYSISTRATA.   The first thing we have to do
  is to wash our yarn, get the dirt out of it.
  You see? Isn't there too much dirt here in Athens?
  You must wash those men away.
                      Then our spoiled
  wool—that's like your job-hunters, out for a life
  of no work and big pay. Back to the basket,
  citizens or not, allies or not,
  or friendly immigrants.
                And your colonies?
  Hanks of wool lost in various places. Pull them
  together, weave them into one great whole,
  and our voters are clothed for ever.

To the Commissioner, this is utterly fantastic:

> COMMISSIONER.   It would take a
> woman to reduce state questions to a matter of card-
> ing and weaving.

Such is the male view, and so these fantastic women, in order to exert influence, must resort to another fantastic idea, the sex strike, and here we encounter Aristophanes's famous ribaldry. In fact the play's reputation for bawdry is grossly exaggerated. Until recently, when pornography was hard to get, *Lysistrata*—because it was literature—provided one of the few available texts that talked of erections and of female delight in sex, and Aubrey Beardsley's illustrations (1896) doubtless helped to establish the book's reputation as a sexual stimulus. But it is really pretty tame stuff compared to what is now readily available, and the play, for all its sexual jokes, is not really about sex but about peace, harmony, and union—union between husbands and wives, between all in Athens, and between Athens and the other Greek-speaking communities.

One final point: The whole play, of course, not only is utterly improbable but also is utterly impossible. The women complain that they are sex-starved because the men are away at the war, but we soon find that the women will remedy this situation by withholding sex from the men—who, we thought, were away at war.

How can one withhold sex from men who are supposedly not present? But Old Comedy never worried about such consistency.

A few words should be said about Middle Comedy and New Comedy. Middle Comedy is a convenient label to apply to the lost plays that must have marked the transition from Old Comedy to New Comedy— that is, to the surviving work of Menander. In New Comedy, written when Athens's political greatness was gone, and when political invective was impossible, the chorus has dwindled to musicians and dancers who perform intermittently, characters tend to be types (the young lover, the crabby old father, etc.), and the plot is regularly a young man's wooing of a maid. Fortune seems unfair and unpredictable, but in the end the virtuous are rewarded. The personal satire and obscenity of Old Comedy are gone, and in their place is a respectably conducted tale showing how, after humorous difficulties, the young man achieves his goal. The plot steadily moves toward the happy ending, which is far more integral than the more or less elusive allegoric (or metaphoric) union at the end of *Lysistrata*. It was New Comedy that influenced Rome (which could scarcely have imitated the political satire of Old Comedy), and through Rome modern Europe. Shakespeare, for example, whose comedies have been described as obstacle races to the altar, was a descendant of Menander though he knew nothing of Menander's work firsthand.

LYSISTRATA
Aristophanes

English version by Dudley Fitts

LIST OF CHARACTERS

LYSISTRATA [*pronounced* Ly SIS tra ta]
KALONIKE [*pronounced* Ka lo NI ke]
MYRRHINE [*pronounced* MYR rhi nee]
LAMPITO [*pronounced* LAM pee toe]
CHORUS
COMMISSIONER
KINESIAS [*pronounced* ki NEE see as]
SPARTAN HERALD
SPARTAN AMBASSADOR
A SENTRY

Until the exodos, the Chorus is divided into two hemi-chori: the first, of Old Men; the second, of Old Women. Each of these has its Koryphaios (i.e., leader). In the ex-odos, the hemichori return as Athenians and Spartans.

The supernumeraries include the baby son of Kinesias; Stratyllis, a member of the hemichorus of Old Women; various individual speakers, both Spartan and Athenian.

SCENE

Athens. First, a public square; later, beneath the walls of the Akropolis; later, a courtyard within the Akropolis.

PROLOGUE

(Athens; a public square; early morning; Lysistrata alone.)

LYSISTRATA.

If someone had invited them to a festival—
of Bacchos, say; or to Pan's shrine, or to Aphrodite's°
over at Kolias—, you couldn't get through the streets,
what with the drums and the dancing. But now,
not a woman in sight!

5   Except—oh, yes!

Enter Kalonike.

Here's one of my neighbors, at last. Good
morning, Kalonike.

KALONIKE.   Good morning, Lysistrata. Darling,
don't frown so! You'll ruin your face!

LYSISTRATA.   Never mind my face.
Kalonike,
10 the way we women behave! Really, I don't blame the
      men
for what they say about us.

KALONIKE.   No; I imagine they're right.

LYSISTRATA.

For example: I call a meeting

2 Bacchos, Pan, Aphrodite the first two are gods associated with wine; Aphrodite is the goddess of love

to think out a most important matter—and what
      happens?
The women all stay in bed!

KALONIKE.   Oh, they'll be along.
It's hard to get away, you know: a husband, a cook,   15
a child . . . Home life can be *so* demanding!

LYSISTRATA.

What I have in mind is even more demanding.

KALONIKE.

Tell me: what is it?

LYSISTRATA.   It's big.

KALONIKE.   Goodness! *How* big?

LYSISTRATA.

Big enough for all of us.

KALONIKE.   But we're not all here!

LYSISTRATA.

We would be, if *that's* what was up!
                                          No, Kalonike,   20
this is something I've been turning over for nights,
long sleepless nights.

KALONIKE.   It must be getting worn down, then,
if you've spent so much time on it.

LYSISTRATA.   Worn down or not,
it comes to this: Only we women can save Greece!

KALONIKE.

Only we women? Poor Greece!

LYSISTRATA.   Just the same,   25
it's up to us. First, we must liquidate
the Peloponnesians—

KALONIKE.   Fun, fun!

LYSISTRATA.   —and then the Boiotians.°
KALONIKE.
Oh! But not those heavenly eels!
LYSISTRATA.   You needn't worry.
I'm not talking about eels.—But here's the point:
30 If we can get the women from those places—
all those Boiotians and Peloponnesians—
to join us women here, why, we can save
all Greece!
KALONIKE.   But dearest Lysistrata!
How can women do a thing so austere, so
35 political? We belong at home. Our only armor's
our perfumes, our saffron dresses and
our pretty little shoes!
LYSISTRATA.   Exactly. Those
transparent dresses, the saffron, the
perfume, those pretty shoes—
KALONIKE.   Oh?
LYSISTRATA.   Not a single man
would lift his spear—
40 KALONIKE.   I'll send my dress to the dyer's tomorrow!
LYSISTRATA.
—or grab a shield—
KALONIKE.   The sweetest little negligée—
LYSISTRATA.
—or haul out his sword.
KALONIKE.   I know where I can buy
the dreamiest sandals!
LYSISTRATA.   Well, so you see. Now shouldn't
the women have come?
KALONIKE.   Come? They should have *flown!*
LYSISTRATA.
Athenians are always late.
                               But imagine!
45 There's no one here from the South Shore, or from
    Salamis.
KALONIKE.
Things are hard over in Salamis, I swear.
They have to get going at dawn.
LYSISTRATA.   And nobody from
Acharnai. I thought they'd be here hours ago.
KALONIKE.   Well, you'll get
50 that awful Theagenes woman: she'll be
a sheet or so in the wind.
                             But look!
Someone at last! Can you see who they are?

Enter Myrrhine and other women.

LYSISTRATA.
They're from Anagyros.
KALONIKE.   They certainly are.
You'd know them anywhere, by the scent.

27 **Boiotia** a country north of Attika, noted for the crudity of its inhabitants and the excellence of its seafood

MYRRHINE.
Sorry to be late, Lysistrata.
                                Oh come,   55
don't scowl so. Say something!
LYSISTRATA.   My dear Myrrhine,
what is there to say? After all,
you've been pretty casual about the whole thing.
MYRRHINE.   Couldn't
find my girdle in the dark, that's all.
                              But what *is*
"the whole thing"?
KALONIKE.   No, we've got to wait   60
for those Boiotians and Peloponnesians.
LYSISTRATA.
That's more like it.—But, look!
Here's Lampito!

Enter Lampito with women from Sparta.

LYSISTRATA.   Darling Lampito,
how pretty you are today! What a nice color!
Goodness, you look as though you could strangle a bull!   65
LAMPITO.
Ah think Ah could! It's the work-out
In the gym every day; and, of co'se that dance of ahs
where y' kick yo' own tail.
KALONIKE.   What an adorable figure!
LAMPITO.
Lawdy, when y' touch me lahk that,
Ah feel lahk a heifer at the altar!
LYSISTRATA.   And this young lady?   70
Where is she from?
LAMPITO.   Boiotia. Social-Register type.
LYSISTRATA.
Ah. "Boiotia of the fertile plain."
KALONIKE.   And if you look,
you'll find the fertile plain has just been mowed.
LYSISTRATA.
And this lady?
LAMPITO.   Hagh, wahd, handsome. She comes from
Korinth.
KALONIKE.
High and wide's the word for it.
LAMPITO.   Which one of you   75
called this heah meeting, and why?
LYSISTRATA.   I did.
LAMPITO.   Well, then, tell
us: What's up?
MYRRHINE.   Yes, darling, what *is* on your mind, after all?
LYSISTRATA.
I'll tell you.—But first, one little question.
MYRRHINE.   Well?
LYSISTRATA.
It's your husbands. Fathers of your children. Doesn't it
bother you
that they're always off with the Army? I'll stake my life,   80

not one of you has a man in the house this minute!
KALONIKE.
    Mine's been in Thrace the last five months, keeping an
      eye on that General.
MYRRHINE.   Mine's been in Pylos for seven.
LAMPITO.   And
    mahn, whenever he gets a *discharge*, he goes raht back
85   with that li'l ole shield of his, and enlists again!
LYSISTRATA.
    And not the ghost of a lover to be found!
    From the very day the war began—
                       those Milesians!
    I could skin them alive!
                —I've not seen so much, even,
    as one of those leather consolation prizes.—
90   But there! What's important is: If I've found a way
    to end the war, are you with me?
MYRRHINE.   I should *say* so!
    Even if I have to pawn my best dress and
    drink up the proceeds.
KALONIKE.   Me, too! Even if they split me
    right up the middle, like a flounder.
LAMPITO.   Ah'm shorely with you.
95   Ah'd crawl up Taygetos° on mah knees
    if that'd bring peace.
LYSISTRATA.   All right, then; here it is:
    Women! Sisters!
    If we really want our men to make peace,
    we must be ready to give up—
MYRRHINE.   Give up what?
    Quick, tell us!
LYSISTRATA.
    But *will* you?
100 MYRRHINE.   We will, even if it kills us.
LYSISTRATA.
    Then we must give up going to bed with our men.

    (*Long silence.*)

    Oh? So now you're sorry? Won't look at me?
    Doubtful? Pale? All teary-eyed?
                But come: be frank with me.
    Will you do it, or not? Well? Will you do it?
MYRRHINE.   I couldn't. No.
    Let the war go on.
105 KALONIKE.   Nor I. Let the war go on.
LYSISTRATA.
    You, you little flounder,
    ready to be split up the middle?
KALONIKE.   Lysistrata, no!
    I'd walk through the fire for you—you *know* I would! but
      don't
    ask us to give up *that!* Why, there's nothing like it!

95 Taygetos a mountain range

LYSISTRATA.
    And you?
BOIOTIAN.   No. I must say *I'd* rather walk through fire.   110
LYSISTRATA.
    What an utterly perverted sex we women are!
    No wonder poets write tragedies about us.
    There's only one thing we can think of.
                        But you from Sparta:
    If you stand by me, we may win yet! Will you?
    It means so much!
LAMPITO.   Ah sweah, it means *too* much!   115
    By the Two Goddesses, it does! Asking a girl
    to sleep—Heaven knows how long!—in a great big bed
    with nobody there but herself! But Ah'll stay with you!
    Peace comes first!
LYSISTRATA.   Spoken like a true Spartan!
KALONIKE.
    But if—
        oh dear!
                  —if we give up what you tell us to,   120
    will there *be* any peace?
LYSISTRATA.   Why, mercy, of course there will!
    We'll just sit snug in our very thinnest gowns,
    perfumed and powdered from top to bottom, and those
      men
    simply won't stand still! And when we say No,
    they'll go out of their minds! And there's your peace.   125
    You can take my word for it.
LAMPITO.   Ah seem to remember
    that Colonel Menelaos threw his sword away
    when he saw Helen's breast all bare.
KALONIKE.   But, goodness me!
    What if they just get up and leave us?
LYSISTRATA.   In that case
    we'll have to fall back on ourselves, I suppose.   130
    But they won't.
KALONIKE.   I must say that's not much help. But
    what if they drag us into the bedroom?
LYSISTRATA.   Hang on to the door.
KALONIKE.
    What if they slap us?
LYSISTRATA.   If they do, you'd better give in.
    But be sulky about it. Do I have to teach you how?
    You know there's no fun for men when they have to   135
      force you.
    There are millions of ways of getting them to see reason.
    Don't you worry: a man
    doesn't like it unless the girl co-operates.
KALONIKE.
    I suppose so. Oh, all right. We'll go along.
LAMPITO.
    Ah imagine us Spahtans can arrange a peace. But you   140
    Athenians! Why, you're just war-mongerers!
LYSISTRATA.   Leave that to
    me. I know how to make them listen.

LAMPITO.   Ah don't see how.
After all, they've got their boats; and there's lots of money
piled up in the Akropolis.°
LYSISTRATA.   The Akropolis? Darling,
145   we're taking over the Akropolis today!
That's the older women's job. All the rest of us
are going to the Citadel to sacrifice—you understand me?
And once there, we're in for good!
LAMPITO.   Whee! Up the rebels!
Ah can see you're a good strat*eg*ist.
LYSISTRATA.   Well, then, Lampito,
150   what we have to do now is take a solemn oath.
LAMPITO.
Say it. We'll sweah.
LYSISTRATA.   This is it.
—But where's our Inner Guard?
                          —Look, Guard: you see this shield?
Put it down here. Now bring me the victim's entrails.
KALONIKE.
But the oath?
LYSISTRATA.
You remember how in Aischylos' *Seven*
155   they killed a sheep and swore on a shield? Well, then?
KALONIKE.
But I don't see how you can swear for peace on a shield.
LYSISTRATA.
What else do you suggest?
KALONIKE.   Why not a white horse?
We could swear by that.
LYSISTRATA.   And where will you get a white horse?
KALONIKE.
I never thought of that. *What* can we do?
LYSISTRATA.   I have it!
160   Let's set this big black wine-bowl on the ground
and pour in a gallon or so of Thasian, and swear
not to add one drop of water.
LAMPITO.   Ah lahk *that* oath!
LYSISTRATA.
Bring the bowl and the wine-jug.
KALONIKE.   Oh, what a simply *huge* one!
LYSISTRATA.
Set it down. Girls, place your hands on the gift-offering.
165   O Goddess of Persuasion! And thou, O Loving-cup:
Look upon this our sacrifice, and
be gracious!
KALONIKE.
See the blood spill out. How red and pretty it is!
LAMPITO.
And Ah must say it smells good.
MYRRHINE.   Let me swear first!
KALONIKE.
170   No, by Aphrodite, we'll match for it!

144 Akropolis at the beginning of the war, Perikles stored emergency funds in the Akropolis, the citadel sacred to Athene

LYSISTRATA.
Lampito: all of you women: come, touch the bowl,
and repeat after me—remember, this is an oath—:
I WILL HAVE NOTHING TO DO WITH MY
    HUSBAND OR MY LOVER
KALONIKE.
I will have nothing to do with my husband or my lover
LYSISTRATA.
THOUGH HE COME TO ME IN PITIABLE   175
    CONDITION
KALONIKE.
Though he come to me in pitiable condition
(Oh Lysistrata! This is killing me!)
LYSISTRATA.
IN MY HOUSE I WILL BE UNTOUCHABLE
KALONIKE.
In my house I will be untouchable
LYSISTRATA.
IN MY THINNEST SAFFRON SILK   180
KALONIKE.
In my thinnest saffron silk
LYSISTRATA.
AND MAKE HIM LONG FOR ME.
KALONIKE.
And make him long for me.
LYSISTRATA.
I WILL NOT GIVE MYSELF
KALONIKE.
I will not give myself   185
LYSISTRATA.
AND IF HE CONSTRAINS ME
KALONIKE.
And if he constrains me
LYSISTRATA.
I WILL BE COLD AS ICE AND NEVER MOVE
KALONIKE.
I will be cold as ice and never move
LYSISTRATA.
I WILL NOT LIFT MY SLIPPERS TOWARD THE   190
    CEILING
KALONIKE.
I will not lift my slippers toward the ceiling
LYSISTRATA.
OR CROUCH ON ALL FOURS LIKE THE LIONESS
    IN THE CARVING
KALONIKE.
Or crouch on all fours like the lioness in the carving
LYSISTRATA.
AND IF I KEEP THIS OATH LET ME DRINK FROM
    THIS BOWL
KALONIKE.
And if I keep this oath let me drink from this bowl   195
LYSISTRATA.
IF NOT, LET MY OWN BOWL BE FILLED WITH
    WATER.

KALONIKE.
If not, let my own bowl be filled with water.
LYSISTRATA.
You have all sworn?
MYRRHINE.   We have.
LYSISTRATA.   Then thus
I sacrifice the victim.

(*Drinks largely.*)

KALONIKE.   Save some for us!
200 Here's to you, darling, and to you, and to you!

(*Loud cries off-stage.*)

LAMPITO.
What's all *that* whoozy-goozy?
LYSISTRATA.   Just what I told you.
The older women have taken the Akropolis.
Now you, Lampito,
rush back to Sparta. We'll take care of things here. Leave
these girls here for hostages.
205   The rest of you,
up to the Citadel: and mind you push in the bolts.
KALONIKE.
But the men? Won't they be after us?
LYSISTRATA.   Just you leave
the men to me. There's not fire enough in the world,
or threats either, to make me open these doors
except on my own terms.
210 KALONIKE.   I hope not, by Aphrodite!
After all, we've got a reputation for bitchiness to live up
to.

(*Exeunt.*)

PARADOS

CHORAL EPISODE

(*The hillside just under the Akropolis. Enter Chorus of
Old Men with burning torches and braziers; much puffing
and coughing.*)

KORYPHAIOS(MAN).
Forward march, Drakes, old friend: never mind
That damn big log banging hell down on your back.

Strophe 1

CHORUS(MEN).
There's this to be said for longevity:
You see things you thought that you'd never see.
5   Look, Strymodoros, who would have thought it?
   We've caught it—
            the New Femininity!
The wives of our bosom, our board, our bed—

Now, by the gods, they've gone ahead
And taken the Citadel (Heaven knows why!),
Porfanéd the sacred statuar-y,   10
            And barred the doors,
            The subversive whores!
KORYPHAIOS(M).
Shake a leg there, Philurgos, man: the Akropolis or bust!
Put the kindling around here. We'll build one almighty
   big
bonfire for the whole bunch of bitches, every last one;   15
and the first we fry will be old Lykon's woman.

Antistrophe 1

CHORUS(M).
They're not going to give me the old horselaugh!
No, by Demeter, they won't pull this off!
   Think of Kleomenes: even he
   Didn't go free
            till he brought me his stuff.   20
A good man he was, all stinking and shaggy,
Bare as an eel except for the bag he
Covered his rear with. God, what a mess!
Never a bath in six years, I'd guess.
            Pure Sparta, man!   25
            He also ran.
KORYPHAIOS(M).
That was a siege, friends! Seventeen ranks strong
we slept at the Gate. And shall we not do as much
against these women, whom God and Euripides hate?
If we don't, I'll turn in my medals from Marathon.   30

Strophe 2

CHORUS(M).
Onward and upward! A little push,
   And we're there.
Ouch, my shoulders! I could wish
   For a pair
Of good strong oxen. Keep your eye   35
   On the fire there, it mustn't die.
            Akh! Akh!
The smoke would make a cadaver cough!

Antistrophe 2

Holy Herakles, a hot spark
   Bit my eye!   40
Damn this hellfire, damn this work!
   So say I.
Onward and upward just the same.
(Laches, remember the Goddess: for shame!)
            Akh! Akh!   45
The smoke would make a cadaver cough!

KORYPHAIOS(M).

At last (and let us give suitable thanks to God
for his infinite mercies) I have managed to bring
my personal flame to the common goal. It breathes, it
    lives.

50   Now, gentlemen, let us consider. Shall we insert
the torch, say, into the brazier, and thus extract
a kindling brand? And shall we then, do you think
push on to the gate like valiant sheep? On the whole, yes.
But I would have you consider this, too: if they—

55   I refer to the women—should refuse to open,
what then? Do we set the doors afire
and smoke them out? At ease, men. Mediate.
Akh, the smoke! Woof! What we really need
is the loan of a general or two from the Samos
    Command.

60   At least we've got this lumber off our backs.
That's something. And now let's look to our fire.
O Pot, brave Brazier, touch my torch with flame!
Victory, Goddess, I invoke thy name!
Strike down these paradigms of female pride,

65   And we shall hang our trophies up inside.

Enter Chorus of Old Women on the walls of the Akropolis, carrying jars of water.

KORYPHAIOS(WOMAN).

Smoke, girls, smoke! There's smoke all over the place!
Probably fire, too. Hurry, girls! Fire! Fire!

Strophe 1

CHORUS(WOMEN).

Nikodike, run!
Or Kalyke's done

70   To a turn, and poor Kritylla's
Smoked like a ham.
                        Damn
These old men! Are we too late?
I nearly died down at the place
Where we fill our jars:

75   Slaves pushing and jostling—
    Such a hustling
I never saw in all my days.

Antistrophe 1

But here's water at last.
Haste, sisters, haste!

80   Slosh it on them, slosh it down,
The silly old wrecks!
                        Sex
Almighty! What they want's
A hot bath? Good. Send one down.
Athena of Athens town,

Trito-born!° Helm of Gold!   85
    Cripple the old
Firemen! Help us help them drown!

(The Old Men capture a woman, Stratyllis.)

STRATYLLIS.

Let me go! Let me go!

KORYPHAIOS(W).   You walking corpses,
have you no shame?

KORYPHAIOS(M).   I wouldn't have believed it!
An army of women in the Akropolis!   90

KORYPHAIOS(W).

So we scare you, do we? Grandpa, you've seen
only our pickets yet!

KORYPHAIOS(M).   Hey, Phaidrias!
Help me with the necks of these jabbering hens!

KORYPHAIOS(W).

Down with your pots, girls! We'll need both hands
if these antiques attack us.

KORYPHAIOS(M).   Want your face kicked in?   95

KORYPHAIOS(W).

Want your balls chewed off?

KORYPHAIOS(M).   Look out! I've got a stick!

KORYPHAIOS(W).

You lay a half-inch of your stick on Stratyllis,
and you'll never stick again!

KORYPHAIOS(M).

Fall apart!

KORYPHAIOS(W).

I'll spit up your guts!

KORYPHAIOS(M).   Euripides!° Master!
How well you knew women!

KORYPHAIOS(W).   Listen to him, Rhodippe,   100
up with the pots!

KORYPHAIOS(M).   Demolition of God,
what good are your pots?

KORYPHAIOS(W).   You refugee from the tomb,
what good is your fire?

KORYPHAIOS(M).   Good enough to make a pyre
to barbecue you!

KORYPHAIOS(W).   We'll squizzle your kindling!

KORYPHAIOS(M).

You think so?

KORYPHAIOS(W). Yah! Just hang around a while!   105

KORYPHAIOS(M).

Want a touch of my torch?

KORYPHAIOS(W).   It needs a good soaping.

KORYPHAIOS(M).

How about you?

KORYPHAIOS(W). Soap for a senile bridegroom!

---

85 Trito-born Athene, said to be born near Lake Tritonis, in Libya
99 Euripides a tragic dramatist

KORYPHAIOS(M).
    Senile? Hold your trap!
KORYPHAIOS(W).   Just *you* try to hold it!
KORYPHAIOS(M).
    The yammer of women!
KORYPHAIOS(W).   Oh is that so?
110   You're not in the jury room now, you know.
KORYPHAIOS(M).
    Gentlemen, I beg you, burn off that woman's hair!
KORYPHAIOS(W).
    Let it come down!

(They empty their pots on the men.)

KORYPHAIOS(M).
    What a way to drown!
KORYPHAIOS(W).   Hot, hey?
KORYPHAIOS(M).   Say,
    enough!
KORYPHAIOS(W). Dandruff
115   needs watering. I'll make you
    nice and fresh.
KORYPHAIOS(M). For God's sake, you,
    hold off!

SCENE 1

Enter a Commissioner accompanied by four constables.

COMMISSIONER.
    These degenerate women! What a racket of little drums,
    what a yapping for Adonis on every house-top!
    It's like the time in the Assembly when I was listening
    to a speech—out of order, as usual—by that fool
5   Demostratos,° all about troops for Sicily,°
    that kind of nonsense—
                        and there was his wife
    trotting around in circles howling
    Alas for Adonis!°—
                        and Demostratos insisting
    we must draft every last Zakynthian that can walk—
10   and his wife up there on the roof,
    drunk as an owl, yowling
    Oh weep for Adonis!—
                        and that damned ox Demostratos
    mooing away through the rumpus. That's what we get
    for putting up with this wretched woman-business!
KORYPHAIOS(M).
15   Sir, you haven't heard the half of it. They laughed at us!
    Insulted us! They took pitchers of water

---

5 Demostratos Athenian orator and jingoist politician **Sicily** a
reference to the Sicilian Expedition (416 B.C.E.), in which Athens
was decisively defeated   **8 Adonis** fertility god

and nearly drowned us! We're still wringing out our
    clothes,
for all the world like unhousebroken brats.
COMMISSIONER.
    Serves you right, by Poseidon!
    Whose fault is it if these women-folk of ours   20
    get out of hand? We coddle them,
    we teach them to be wasteful and loose. You'll see a
        husband
    go into a jeweler's. "Look," he'll say,
    "jeweler," he'll say, "you remember that gold choker
    you made for my wife? Well, she went to a dance last   25
        night
    and broke the clasp. Now, I've got to go to Salamis,
    and can't be bothered. Run over to my house tonight,
    will you, and see if you can put it together for her."
    Or another one goes to a cobbler—a good strong
        workman, too,
    with an awl that was never meant for child's play.   30
        "Here,"
    he'll tell him, "one of my wife's shoes is pinching
    her little toe. Could you come up about noon
    and stretch it out for her?"
                        Well, what do you expect?
    Look at me, for example, I'm a Public Officer,
    and it's one of my duties to pay off the sailors.   35
    And where's the money? Up there in the Akropolis!
    And those blasted women slam the door in my face!
    But what are we waiting for?
                        —Look here, constable,
    stop sniffing around for a tavern, and get us
    some crowbars. We'll force their gates! As a matter of   40
        fact,
    I'll do a little forcing myself.

*Enter Lysistrata, above, with Myrrhine, Kalonike, and the
Boiotian.*

LYSISTRATA.   No need of forcing.
    Here I am, of my own accord. And all this talk
    about locked doors—! We don't need locked doors,
    but just the least bit of common sense.
COMMISSIONER.
    Is that so, ma'am!
                        —Where's my constable?
                                —Constable,   45
    arrest that woman, and tie her hands behind her.
LYSISTRATA.
    If he touches me, I swear by Artemis
    there'll be one scamp dropped from the public payroll to-
        morrow!
COMMISSIONER.
    Well constable? You're not afraid, I suppose? Grab her,
    two of you, around the middle!
KALONIKE.   No, by Pandrosos!   50

Lay a hand on her, and I'll jump on you so hard
your guts will come out the back door!

COMMISSIONER.   That's what *you* think!
Where's the sergeant?—Here, you: tie up that trollop
     first,
the one with the pretty talk!

MYRRHINE.   By the Moon-Goddess,
55   just try! They'll have to scoop you up with a spoon!

COMMISSIONER.
Another one!
                    Officer, seize that woman!
                                        I swear
I'll put an end to this riot!

BOIOTIAN.   By the Taurian,
one inch closer, you'll be one screaming baldhead!

COMMISSIONER.
Lord, what a mess! And my constables seem ineffective.
60   But—women get the best of us? By God, no!
                                        —Skythians!
Close ranks and forward march!

LYSISTRATA.   "Forward," indeed!
By the Two Goddesses, what's the sense in *that*?
They're up against four companies of women
armed from top to bottom.

COMMISSIONER.   Forward, my Skythians!

LYSISTRATA.
65   Forward, yourselves, dear comrades!
You grainlettucebeanseedmarket girls!
You garlicandonionbreadbakery girls!
Give it to 'em! Knock 'em down! Scratch 'em!
Tell 'em what you think of 'em!

(*General mêlée; the Skythians yield.*)

                                        —Ah, that's enough!
70   Sound a retreat: good soldiers don't rob the dead.

COMMISSIONER.
A nice day *this* has been for the police!

LYSISTRATA.
Well, there you are.—Did you really think we women
would be driven like slaves? Maybe now you'll admit
that a woman knows something about spirit.

COMMISSIONER.   Spirit enough,
75   especially spirits in bottles! Dear Lord Apollo!

KORYPHAIOS(M).
Your Honor, there's no use talking to them. Words
mean nothing whatever to wild animals like these.
Think of the sousing they gave us! and the water
was not, I believe, of the purest.

KORYPHAIOS(W).
80   You shouldn't have come after us. And if you try it again,
you'll be one eye short!—Although, as a matter of fact,
what I like best is just to stay at home and read,
like a sweet little bride: never hurting a soul, no,

never going out. But if you *must* shake hornets' nests,
look out for the hornets.   85

Strophe

CHORUS(M).
Of all the beasts that God hath wrought
     What monster's worse than woman?
Who shall encompass with his thought
     Their guile unending? No man.

They've seized the Heights, the Rock, the Shrine—   90
     But to what end? I wot not.
Sure there's some clue to their design!
     Have you the key? I thought not.

KORYPHAIOS(M).
We might question them, I suppose. But I warn you sir,
don't believe anything you hear! It would be un-   95
     Athenian
not to get to the bottom of this plot.

COMMISSIONER.   Very well.
My first question is this: Why, so help you God,
did you bar the gates of the Akropolis?

LYSISTRATA.   Why?
To keep the money, of course. No money, no war.

COMMISSIONER.
You think that money's the cause of war?

LYSISTRATA.   I do.   100
Money brought about that Peisandros° business
and all the other attacks on the State. Well and good!
They'll not get another cent here!

COMMISSIONER.   And what will you do?

LYSISTRATA.
What a question! From now on, we intend
to control the Treasury.

COMMISSIONER.   Control the Treasury!   105

LYSISTRATA.
Why not? Does that seem strange? After all,
we control our household budgets.

COMMISSIONER.   But that's different!

LYSISTRATA.
"Different"? What do you mean?

COMMISSIONER.   I mean simply this:
it's the Treasury that pays for National Defense.

LYSISTRATA.
Unnecessary. We propose to abolish war.   110

COMMISSIONER.
Good God.—And National Security?

LYSISTRATA.   Leave that to us.

COMMISSIONER.
You?

LYSISTRATA.
Us.

101 Peisandros a plotter against the Athenian democracy

COMMISSIONER.
            We're done for, then!
LYSISTRATA.   Never mind.
    We women will save you in spite of yourselves.
COMMISSIONER.   What nonsense!
LYSISTRATA.
    If you like. But you must accept it, like it or not.
COMMISSIONER.
    Why, this is downright subversion!
115 LYSISTRATA.   Maybe it is.
    But we're going to save you, Judge.
COMMISSIONER.   I don't *want* to be saved.
LYSISTRATA.
    Tut. The death-wish. All the more reason.
COMMISSIONER.   But the idea
    of women bothering themselves about peace and war!
LYSISTRATA.
    Will you listen to me?
COMMISSIONER.   Yes. But be brief, or I'll—
LYSISTRATA.
    This is no time for stupid threats.
120 COMMISSIONER.   By the gods,
    I can't stand any more!
AN OLD WOMAN.   Can't stand? Well, well.
COMMISSIONER.
    That's enough out of you, you old buzzard!
    Now, Lysistrata: tell me what you're thinking.
LYSISTRATA.
    Glad to.
            Ever since this war began
125 We women have been watching you men, agreeing with
            you,
    keeping our thoughts to ourselves. That doesn't mean
    we were happy: we weren't, for we saw how things were
            going;
    but we'd listen to you at dinner
    arguing this way and that.
                        —Oh you, and your big
    Top Secrets!—
130   And then we'd grin like little patriots
    (though goodness knows we didn't feel like grinning)
            and ask you:
    "Dear, did the Armistice come up in Assembly today?"
    And you'd say, "None of your business! Pipe down!,"
            you'd say.
    And so we would.
AN OLD WOMAN.   *I* wouldn't have, by God!
COMMISSIONER.
    You'd have taken a beating, then!
135   —Go on.
LYSISTRATA.
    Well, we'd be quiet. But then, you know, all at once
    you men would think up something worse than ever.
    Even *I* could see it was fatal. And, "Darling," I'd say,

"have you gone completely mad?" And my husband
            would look at me
and say, "Wife, you've got your weaving to attend to.   140
Mind your tongue, if you don't want a slap. 'War's a
    man's affair!'"°
COMMISSIONER.
    Good words, and well pronounced.
LYSISTRATA.
    You're a fool if you think so.
                            It was hard enough
to put up with all this banquet-hall strategy.
But then we'd hear you out in the public square: 145
"Nobody left for the draft-quota here in Athens?"
you'd say; and, "No," someone else would say, "not a
    man!"
And so we women decided to rescue Greece.
You might as well listen, to us now: you'll have to, later.
COMMISSIONER.
    You rescue Greece? Absurd.
LYSISTRATA.   You're the absurd one.   150
COMMISSIONER.
    You expect me to take orders from a woman?
                                        I'd die first!
LYSISTRATA.
    Heavens, if that's what's bothering you, take my veil,
    here, and wrap it around your poor head.
KALONIKE.   Yes,
    and you can have my market-basket, too.
    Go home, tighten your girdle, do the washing, mind   155
    your beans! "War's
    a woman's affair!"
KORYPHAIOS(W).   Ground pitchers! Close ranks!

Antistrophe

CHORUS(W).
        This is a dance that I know well,
            My knees shall never yield.
        Wobble and creak I may, but still   160
            I'll keep the well-fought field.
        Valor and grace march on before,
            Love prods us from behind.
        Our slogan is EXCELSIOR,
            Our watchword SAVE MANKIND.   165
KORYPHAIOS(W).
    Women, remember your grandmothers! Remember
    that little old mother of yours, what a stinger she was!
    On, on, never slacken. There's a strong wind astern!
LYSISTRATA.
    O Eros of delight! O Aphrodite! Kyprian!

141 War's a man's affair quoted from Homer's *Iliad*, VI, 492, Hector to his wife Andromache

170 If ever desire has drenched our breasts or dreamed
in our thighs, let it work so now on the men of Hellas
that they shall tail us through the land, slaves, slaves
to Woman, Breaker of Armies!

COMMISSIONER.   And if we do?

LYSISTRATA.

175 Well, for one thing, we shan't have to watch you
going to market, a spear in one hand, and heaven knows
what in the other.

KALONIKE.   Nicely said, by Aphrodite!

LYSISTRATA.

As things stand now, you're neither men nor women.
Armor clanking with kitchen pans and pots—
you sound like a pack of Korybantes!

COMMISSIONER.

A man must do what a man must do.

180 LYSISTRATA.   So I'm told.
But to see a General, complete with Gorgon-shield,
jingling along the dock to buy a couple of herrings!

KALONIKE.

I saw a Captain the other day—lovely fellow he was,
nice curly hair—sitting on his horse; and—can you believe it?—

185 he'd just bought some soup, and was pouring it into his
helmet!
And there was a soldier from Thrace
swishing his lance like something out of Euripides,
and the poor fruit-store woman got so scared
that she ran away and let him have his figs free!

COMMISSIONER.

All this is beside the point

190   Will you be so kind
as to tell me how you mean to save Greece?

LYSISTRATA.   Of course.
Nothing could be simpler.

COMMISSIONER.   I assure you, I'm all ears.

LYSISTRATA.

Do you know anything about weaving?
Say the yarn gets tangled: we thread it

195 this way and that through the skein, up and down,
until it's free. And it's like that with war.
We'll send our envoys
up and down, this way and that, all over Greece,
until it's finished.

COMMISSIONER.   Yarn? Thread? Skein?

200 Are you out of your mind? I tell you,
war is a serious business.

LYSISTRATA.   So serious
that I'd like to go on talking about weaving.

COMMISSIONER.

All right. Go ahead.

LYSISTRATA.   The first thing we have to do
is to wash our yarn, get the dirt out of it.

205 You see? Isn't there too much dirt here in Athens?
You must wash those men away.

Then our spoiled wool—
that's like your job-hunters, out for a life
of no work and big pay. Back to the basket,
citizens or not, allies or not,
or friendly immigrants.

                     And your colonies?   210
Hanks of wool lost in various places. Pull them
together, weave them into one great whole,
and our voters are clothed for ever.

COMMISSIONER.   It would take a woman
to reduce state questions to a matter of carding and
weaving.

LYSISTRATA.

You fool! Who were the mothers whose sons sailed off   215
to fight for Athens in Sicily?

COMMISSIONER.   Enough!
I beg you, do not call back those memories.

LYSISTRATA.   And then,
instead of the love that every woman needs,
we have only our single beds, where we can dream
of our husbands off with the Army.

                                Bad enough for wives!   220
But what about our girls, getting older every day,
and older, and no kisses?

COMMISSIONER.   Men get older, too.

LYSISTRATA.

Not in the same sense.
                         A soldier's discharged,
and he may be bald and toothless, yet he'll find
a pretty young thing to go to bed with.

                                    But a woman!   225
Her beauty is gone with the first gray hair.
She can spend her time
consulting the oracles and the fortune-tellers,
but they'll never send her a husband.

COMMISSIONER.

Still, if a man can rise to the occasion—   230

LYSISTRATA.

Rise? Rise, yourself!

(*Furiously.*)

Go invest in a coffin!
                    You've money enough.
                                    I'll bake you
a cake for the Underworld.
                            And here's your funeral
wreath!

(*She pours water upon him.*)

MYRRHINE.

And here's another!

(*More water.*)

KALONIKE.   And here's
my contribution!

(*More water.*)

235 LYSISTRATA.   What are you waiting for?
All aboard Styx Ferry!
                        Charon's° calling for you!
It's sailing-time: don't disrupt the schedule!

COMMISSIONER.
The insolence of women! And to me!
No, by God, I'll go back to town and show
240 the rest of the Commission what might happen to them.

                                (*Exit Commissioner.*)

LYSISTRATA.
Really, I suppose we should have laid out his corpse
on the doorstep, in the usual way.
                                But never mind.
We'll give him the rites of the dead tomorrow morning.

            (*Exit Lysistrata with Myrrhine and Kalonike.*)

PARABASIS

CHORAL EPISODE

Ode 1

KORYPHAIOS(M).
Sons of Liberty, awake! The day of glory is at hand.
CHORUS(M).
I smell tyranny afoot, I smell it rising from the land.
I scent a trace of Hippias,° I sniff upon the breeze
A dismal Spartan hogo that suggests King Kleisthenes.°
5   Strip, strip for action, brothers!
    Our wives, aunts, sisters, mothers
Have sold us out: the streets are full of godless female
    rages.
Shall we stand by and let our women confiscate our
    wages?

Epirrhema 1°

KORYPHAIOS(M).
Gentlemen, it's a disgrace to Athens, a disgrace
10   to all that Athens stands for, if we allow these grandmas
to jabber about spears and shields and making friends
with the Spartans. What's a Spartan? Give me a wild wolf
any day. No. They want the Tyranny back, I suppose.
Are we going to take that? No. Let us look like
15   the innocent serpent, but be the flower under it,
as the poet sings. And just to begin with,

236 **Charon** god who ferried the souls of the newly dead across
the Styx to Hades   3 **Hippias** an Athenian tyrant (d. 490 B.C.E.)
4 **Kleisthenes** an ambisexual Athenian   8 **Epirrhema** a satiric
speech spoken by the leader of half of the chorus. The **antode** (line
18) and the **Antepirrhema,** sung by the leader of the other half of
the chorus, balance the **Ode** (line 1) and the Epirrhema.

I propose to poke a number of teeth
down the gullet of that harridan over there.

Antode 1

KORYPHAIOS(W).
Oh, is that so? When you get home, your own mammá
    won't know you!
CHORUS(W).
Who do you think we are, you senile bravos? Well, I'll   20
    show you.
I bore the sacred vessels in my eighth year, and at ten
I was pounding out the barley for Athena Goddess; then
    They made me Little Bear
    At the Braunonian Fair;
I'd held the Holy Basket by the time I was of age,   25
The Blessed Dry figs had adorned my plump décolletage.

Antepirrhema 1

KORYPHAIOS(W).
A "disgrace to Athens," am I, just at the moment
I'm giving Athens the best advice she ever had?
Don't I pay taxes to the State? Yes, I pay them
in baby boys. And what do you contribute,   30
you impotent horrors? Nothing but waste: all
our Treasury,° dating back to the Persian Wars,
gone! rifled! And not a penny out of your pockets!
Well, then? Can you cough up an answer to that?
Look out for your own gullet, or you'll get a crack   35
from this old brogan that'll make your teeth see stars!

Ode 2

CHORUS(M).
        Oh insolence!
        Am I unmanned?
        Incontinence!
        Shall my scarred hand   40
        Strike never a blow
        To curb this flow-
        ing female curse?
        Leipsydrion!°
        Shall I betray   45
        The laurels won
        On that great day?

32 **Treasury** money originally contributed by Athens and her allies, intended to finance an extension of the sea war against Persia.
Since the failure of the Sicilian Expedition, the contributions of
the allies had fallen off; and the fund itself was now being raided by
Athenian politicians   44 **leipsydrion** a place where patriots had
gallantly fought

Come, shake a leg,
Shed old age, beg
50   The years reverse!

Epirrhema 2

KORYPHAIOS(M).
Give them an inch, and we're done for! We'll have them
launching boats next and planning naval strategy,
sailing down on us like so many Artemisias.
Or maybe they have ideas about the cavalry.
55   That's fair enough, women are certainly good
in the saddle. Just look at Mikon's paintings,
All those Amazons wrestling with all those men!
On the whole, a straitjacket's their best uniform.

Antode 2

CHORUS(W).
Tangle with me,
60   And you'll get cramps.
Ferocity
's no use now, Gramps!
By the Two,
I'll get through
65   To you wrecks yet!

I'll scramble your eggs,
I'll burn your beans,
With my two legs.
You'll see such scenes
70   As never yet
Your two eyes met.
A curse? You bet!

Antepirrhema 2

KORYPHAIOS(W).
If Lampito stands by me, and that delicious Theban girl,
Ismenia—what good are *you*? You and your seven
75   Resolutions! Resolutions? Rationing Boiotian eels
and making our girls go with them at Hekate's Feast!
That was statesmanship! And we'll have to put up with it
and all the rest of your decrepit legislation
until some patriot—God give him strength!—
80   grabs you by the neck and kicks you off the Rock.

SCENE 11

Re-enter Lysistrata and her lieutenants.

KORYPHAIOS(W) (*Tragic tone*).
Great Queen, fair Architect of our emprise,
Why lookst thou on us with foreboding eyes?
LYSISTRATA.
The behavior of these idiotic women!

There's something about the female temperament
that I can't bear!
KORYPHAIOS(W).   What in the world do you mean?   5
LYSISTRATA.
Exactly what I say.
KORYPHAIOS(W).   What dreadful thing has happened?
Come, tell us: we're all your friends.
LYSISTRATA.   It isn't easy
to say it; yet, God knows, we can't hush it up.
KORYPHAIOS(W).
Well, then? Out with it!
LYSISTRATA.   To put it bluntly,
we're dying to get laid.
KORYPHAIOS(W).   Almighty God!   10
LYSISTRATA.
Why bring God into it?—No, it's just as I say.
I can't manage them any longer: they've gone man-crazy,
they're all trying to get out.
                              Why, look:
one of them was sneaking out the back door
over there by Pan's cave; another   15
was sliding down the walls with rope and tackle;
another was climbing aboard a sparrow, ready to take off
for the nearest brothel—I dragged *her* back by the hair!
They're all finding some reason to leave.
                              Look there!
There goes another one.
                    —Just a minute, you!   20
Where are you off to so fast?
FIRST WOMAN.   I've got to get home.
I've a lot of Milesian wool, and the worms are spoiling it.
LYSISTRATA.
Oh bother you and your worms! Get back inside!
FIRST WOMAN.
I'll be back right away, I swear I will.
I just want to get it stretched out on my bed.   25
LYSISTRATA.
You'll do no such thing. You'll stay right here.
FIRST WOMAN.   And my wool?
You want it ruined?
LYSISTRATA.   Yes, for all I care.
SECOND WOMAN.
Oh dear! My lovely new flax from Amorgos—
I left it at home, all uncarded!
LYSISTRATA.   Another one!
And all she wants is someone to card her flax.   30
Get back in there!
SECOND WOMAN.   But I swear by the Moon-Goddess,
the minute I get it done, I'll be back!
LYSISTRATA.   I say No.
If you, why not all the other women as well?
THIRD WOMAN.
O Lady Eileithyia!° Radiant goddess! Thou

34 Eileithyia goddess of childbirth

35   intercessor for women in childbirth! Stay, I pray thee,
oh stay this parturition. Shall I pollute
a sacred spot?
LYSISTRATA.   And what's the matter with *you*?
THIRD WOMAN.
I'm having a baby—any minute now.
LYSISTRATA.
But you weren't pregnant yesterday.
THIRD WOMAN.   Well, I am today.
40   Let me go home for a midwife, Lysistrata:
there's not much time.
LYSISTRATA.   I never heard such nonsense.
What's that bulging under your cloak?
THIRD WOMAN.   A little baby boy.
LYSISTRATA.
It certainly isn't. But it's something hollow,
like a basin or—Why, it's the helmet of Athena!
And you said you were having a baby.
45   THIRD WOMAN.   Well, I am! So there!
LYSISTRATA.
Then why the helmet?
THIRD WOMAN.   I was afraid that my pains
might begin here in the Akropolis; and I wanted
to drop my chick into it, just as the dear doves do.
LYSISTRATA.
Lies! Evasions!—But at least one thing's clear:
50   you can't leave the place before your purification.
THIRD WOMAN.
But I can't stay here in the Akropolis! Last night I
dreamed of the Snake.
FIRST WOMAN.   And those horrible owls, the
noise they make!
I can't get a bit of sleep; I'm just about dead.
LYSISTRATA.
You useless girls, that's enough: Let's have no more lying.
55   Of course you want your men. But don't you imagine
that they want you just as much? I'll give you my word,
their nights must be pretty hard.
Just stick it out!
A little patience, that's all, and our battle's won.
I have heard an Oracle. Should you like to hear it?
FIRST WOMAN.
An Oracle? Yes, tell us!
60   LYSISTRATA.   Here is what it says:
WHEN SWALLOWS SHALL THE HOOPOE SHUN
AND SPURN HIS HOT DESIRE,
ZEUS WILL PERFECT WHAT THEY'VE BEGUN
AND SET THE LOWER HIGHER.
FIRST WOMAN.
65   Does that mean we'll be on top?
LYSISTRATA.
BUT IF THE SWALLOWS SHALL FALL OUT
AND TAKE THE HOOPOE'S BAIT,
A CURSE MUST MARK THEIR HOUR OF DOUBT,
INFAMY SEAL THEIR FATE.

THIRD WOMAN.
I swear, *that* Oracle's all too clear.
FIRST WOMAN.   Oh the dear gods!   70
LYSISTRATA.
Let's not be downhearted, girls. Back to our places!
The god has spoken. How can we possibly fail him?

(*Exit Lysistrata with the dissident women.*)

CHORAL EPISODE

Strophe

CHORUS(M).
I know a little story that I learned way back in school.
Goes like this:
Once upon a time there was a young man—and no   75
fool—
Named Melanion; and his
One aversion was marriage. He loathed the very
thought.
So he ran off to the hills, and in a special grot
Raised a dog, and spent his days
Hunting rabbits. And it says   80
That he never never never did come home.
It might be called a refuge *from* the womb.
All right,
all right,
all right!
We're as bright as young Melanion, and we hate the very
sight
Of you women!   85
A MAN.
How about a kiss, old lady?
A WOMAN.
Here's an onion for your eye!
A MAN.
A kick in the guts, then?
A WOMAN.
Try, old bristle-tail, just try!
A MAN.
Yet they say Myronides   90
On hands and knees
Looked just as shaggy fore and aft as I!

Antistrophe

CHORUS(W).
Well, *I* know a little story, and it's just as good as yours.
Goes like this:
Once there was a man named Timon—a rough diamond,   95
of course,
And that whiskery face of his
Looked like murder in the shrubbery. By God, he was a
son

Of the Furies, let me tell you! And what did he do but run
From the world and all its ways,
100   Cursing mankind! And it says
That his choicest execrations as of then
Were leveled almost wholly at *old* men.
All right,
          all right,
                    all right,
But there's one thing about Timon: he could always
          stand the sight
105   Of us women.
A WOMAN.
How about a crack in the jaw, Pop?
A MAN.
I can take it, Ma—no fear!
A WOMAN.
How about a kick in the face?
A MAN.
You'd reveal your old caboose?
A WOMAN.
110   What I'd show,
I'll have you know,
Is an instrument you're too far gone to use.

SCENE III

Re-enter Lysistrata.

LYSISTRATA.
Oh, quick, girls, quick! Come here!
A WOMAN.   What is it?
LYSISTRATA.   A man.
A man simply bulging with love.
                              O Kyprian Queen,°
O Paphian, O Kythereian! Hear us and aid us!
A WOMAN.
Where is this enemy?
LYSISTRATA.   Over there, by Demeter's shrine.
A WOMAN.
Damned if he isn't. But who *is* he?
5   MYRRHINE.   My husband.
Kinesias.
LYSISTRATA.
          Oh, then, get busy! Tease him! Undermine him!
Wreck him! Give him everything—kissing, tickling,
          nudging,
whatever you generally torture him with—: give him
          everything
except what we swore on the wine we would not give.
MYRRHINE.
Trust me.
10   LYSISTRATA. I do. But I'll help you get him started.
The rest of you women, stay back.

2 Kyprian Queen Aphrodite, goddess of love

Enter Kinesias.

KINESIAS.   Oh God! Oh my God!
I'm stiff from lack of exercise. All I can do to stand up.
LYSISTRATA.
Halt! Who are you, approaching our lines?
KINESIAS.   Me? I.
LYSISTRATA.
A man?
KINESIAS. You have eyes, haven't you?
LYSISTRATA.   Go away.
KINESIAS.
Who says so?
LYSISTRATA.   Officer of the Day.
KINESIAS.   Officer, I beg you,   15
by all the gods at once, bring Myrrhine out.
LYSISTRATA.
Myrrhine? And who, my good sir, are you?
KINESIAS.
Kinesias. Last name's Pennison. Her husband.
LYSISTRATA.
Oh, of course. I beg your pardon. We're glad to see you.
We've heard so much about you. Dearest Myrrhine   20
is always talking about Kinesias—never nibbles an egg
or an apple without saying
"Here's to Kinesias!"
KINESIAS.   Do you really mean it?
LYSISTRATA.   I do.
When we're discussing men, she always says
"Well, after all, there's nobody like Kinesias!"   25
KINESIAS.
Good God.—Well, then, please send her down here.
LYSISTRATA.
And what do *I* get out of it?
KINESIAS.   A standing promise.
LYSISTRATA.
I'll take it up with her.

                              (Exit Lysistrata.)

KINESIAS.   But be quick about it!
Lord, what's life without a wife? Can't eat. Can't sleep.
Every time I go home, the place is so empty, so   30
insufferably sad. Love's killing me, Oh,
hurry!

*Enter Manes, a slave, with Kinesias' baby; the voice of
Myrrhine is heard off-stage.*

MYRRHINE.   But of course I love him! Adore him—
                                        But no,
he hates love. No. I won't go down.

Enter Myrrhine, above.

KINESIAS.   Myrrhine!
Darlingest Myrrhinette! Come down quick!
MYRRHINE.
Certainly not.

KINESIAS.

35   Not? But why, Myrrhine?

MYRRHINE.

Why? You don't need me.

KINESIAS.   Need you? My God, *look* at me!

MYRRHINE.

So long!

(Turns to go.)

KINESIAS.   Myrrhine, Myrrhine, Myrrhine!
If not for my sake, for our child!

(Pinches Baby.)

                       —All right, you: pipe up!

BABY.

Mummie! Mummie! Mummie!

KINESIAS.   You hear that?

40   Pitiful, I call it. Six days now
with never a bath; no food; enough to break your heart!

MYRRHINE.

My darlingest child! What a father *you* acquired!

KINESIAS.

At least come down for his sake.

MYRRHINE.   I suppose I must.
Oh, this mother business!

                     (Exit.)

KINESIAS.   How pretty she is! And younger!
The harder she treats me, the more bothered I get.

(Myrrhine enters, below.)

45   MYRRHINE.   Dearest child,
you're as sweet as your father's horrid. Give me a kiss.

KINESIAS.

Now don't you see how wrong it was to get involved
in this scheming League of women? It's bad
for us both.

MYRRHINE.   Keep both hands to yourself!

KINESIAS.   But our house
going to rack and ruin?

MYRRHINE.   *I* don't care.

50   KINESIAS.   And your knitting
all torn to pieces by the chickens? Don't you care?

MYRRHINE.

Not at all.

KINESIAS.   And our debt to Aphrodite?
Oh, *won't* you come back?

MYRRHINE.   No.—At least, not until you men
make a treaty and stop this war.

KINESIAS.   Why, I suppose
that might be arranged.

55   MYRRHINE.   Oh? Well, I suppose
I might come down then. But meanwhile,
I've sworn not to.

KINESIAS.   Don't worry.—Now let's have fun.

MYRRHINE.

No! Stop it! I said no!

           —Although, of course,
I *do* love you.

KINESIAS.   I know you do. Darling Myrrhine:
come, shall we?

MYRRHINE.

          Are you out of your mind? In front of the child?   60

KINESIAS.

Take him home, Manes.

                (Exit Manes with Baby.)

               There. He's gone.

                  Come on!
There's nothing to stop us now.

MYRRHINE.   You devil! But where?

KINESIAS.

In Pan's cave. What could be snugger than that?

MYRRHINE.

But my purification before I go back to the Citadel?

KINESIAS.

Wash in the Klepsydra.°

MYRRHINE.   And my oath?

KINESIAS.

               Leave the oath to me.   65
After all, I'm the man.

MYRRHINE.   Well . . . if you say so.

                 I'll go find a bed.

KINESIAS.

Oh, bother a bed! The ground's good enough for me.

MYRRHINE.

No. You're a bad man, but you deserve something better
than dirt.

                (Exit Myrrhine.)

KINESIAS.

What a love she is! And how thoughtful!

Re-enter Myrrhine.

MYRRHINE.   Here's your bed.
Now let me get my clothes off.

         But good horrors!   70
We haven't a mattress.

KINESIAS.   Oh, forget the mattress!

MYRRHINE.   No.
Just lying on blankets? Too sordid.

KINESIAS.   Give me a kiss.

MYRRHINE.

Just a second.

                (Exit Myrrhine.)

KINESIAS.   I swear, I'll explode!

65 Klepsydra a sacred spring beneath the walls of the Akropolis.
Kinesias's suggestion has overtones of blasphemy.

Re-enter Myrrhine.

MYRRHINE.   Here's your mattress.
I'll just take my dress off.
                    But look—
where's our pillow?
KINESIAS.   I don't *need* a pillow!
MYRRHINE.

75   Well, *I* do.

                    (*Exit Myrrhine.*)

KINESIAS.
I don't suppose even Herakles
would stand for this!

Re-enter Myrrhine.

MYRRHINE.   There we are. Ups-a-daisy!
KINESIAS.
So we are. Well, come to bed.
MYRRHINE.   But I wonder:
is everything ready now?
KINESIAS.   I can swear to that. Come, darling!
MYRRHINE.
Just getting out of my girdle.
80   But remember, now
what you promised about the treaty.
KINESIAS.   Yes, yes, yes!
MYRRHINE.
But no coverlet!
KINESIAS.   Damn it, I'll be
your coverlet!
MYRRHINE.
Be right back.

                    (*Exit Myrrhine*)

KINESIAS.   This girl and her coverlets
will be the death of me.

Re-enter Myrrhine.

MYRRHINE.   Here we are. Up you go!
KINESIAS.
Up? I've been up for ages.
85 MYRRHINE.   Some perfume?
KINESIAS.
No, by Apollo!
MYRRHINE.   Yes, by Aphrodite!
I don't care whether you want it or not.

                    (*Exit Myrrhine.*)

KINESIAS.
For love's sake, hurry!

Re-enter Myrrhine.

MYRRHINE.
Here, in your hand. Rub it right in.

KINESIAS.   Never cared for perfume.
And this is particularly strong. Still, here goes.   90
MYRRHINE.
What a nitwit I am! I brought the Rhodian bottle.
KINESIAS.
Forget it.
MYRRHINE.   No trouble at all. You just wait here.

                    (*Exit Myrrhine.*)

KINESIAS.
God damn the man who invented perfume!

Re-enter Myrrhine.

MYRRHINE.
At last! The right bottle!
KINESIAS.   I've got the rightest
bottle of all, and it's right here waiting for you.   95
Darling, forget everything else. Do come to bed.
MYRRHINE.
Just let me get my shoes off.
                    —And, by the way,
you'll vote for the treaty?
KINESIAS.   I'll think about it.

                    (*Myrrhine runs away.*)

There! That's done it! The damned woman,
she gets me all bothered, she half kills me,
and off she runs! What'll I do? Where   100
can I get laid?
                    —And you, little prodding pal,
who's going to take care of *you?* No, you and I
had better get down to old Foxdog's Nursing Clinic.
CHORUS(M).
    Alas for the woes of man, alas   105
        Specifically for you.
    She's brought you to a pretty pass:
        What are you going to do?
    Split, heart! Sag, flesh! Proud spirit, crack!
    Myrrhine's got you on your back.   110
KINESIAS.
The agony, the protraction!
KORYPHAIOS(M).   Friend,
    What woman's worth a damn?
They bitch us all, world without end.
KINESIAS.
Yet they're so damned sweet, man!
KORYPHAIOS(M).
Calamitous, that's what I say.   115
You should have learned that much today.
CHORUS(M).
O blessed Zeus, roll womankind.
    Up into one great ball;
Blast them aloft on a high wind,
    And once there, let them fall.   120
Down, down they'll come, the pretty dears,

And split themselves on our thick spears.

                                        (*Exit Kinesias.*)

SCENE IV

Enter a Spartan Herald.

HERALD.
  Gentlemen, Ah beg you will be so kind
  as to direct me to the Central Committee.
  Ah have a communication.

  Re-enter Commissioner.

COMMISSIONER.   Are you a man,
  or a fertility symbol?
HERALD.   Ah refuse to answer that question!
5 Ah'm a certified herald from Spahta, and Ah've come
  to talk about an ahmistice.
COMMISSIONER.   Then why
  that spear under your cloak?
HERALD.   Ah have no speah!
COMMISSIONER.
  You don't walk naturally, with your tunic
  poked out so. You have a tumor, maybe,
  or a hernia?
HERALD.   You lost yo' mahnd, man?
10 COMMISSIONER.   Well,
  something's up, I can see that. And I don't like it.
HERALD.
  Colonel, Ah resent this.
COMMISSIONER.   So I see. But what *is* it?
HERALD.   A staff
  with a message from Spahta.
COMMISSIONER.   Oh. I know about those
  staffs.
  Well, then, man, speak out: How are things in Sparta?
HERALD.
15 Hahd, Colonel, hahd! We're at a standstill.
  Cain't seem to think of anything but women.
COMMISSIONER.
  How curious! Tell me, do you Spartans think
  that maybe Pan's to blame?
HERALD.
  Pan? No. Lampito and her little naked friends.
20 They won't let a man come nigh them.
COMMISSIONER.
  How are you handling it?
HERALD.   Losing our mahnds,
  if y' want to know, and walking around hunched over
  lahk men carrying candles in a gale.
  The women have swohn they'll have nothing to do with
    us
  until we get a treaty.
25 COMMISSIONER.   Yes. I know.
  It's a general uprising, sir, in all parts of Greece.

But as for the answer—
                          Sir: go back to Sparta
and have them send us your Armistice Commission.
I'll arrange things in Athens.
                              And I may say
that my standing is good enough to make them listen. 30
HERALD.
  A man after mah own haht! Seh, Ah thank you.

                                        (*Exit Herald.*)

CHORAL EPISODE

Strophe

CHORUS(M).
  Oh these women! Where will you find
  A slavering beast that's more unkind? Where a hotter fire?
  Give me a panther, any day.
  He's not so merciless as they,   35
    And panthers don't conspire.

Antistrophe

CHORUS(W).
    We may be hard, you silly old ass,
      But who brought you to this stupid pass?
        You're the ones to blame.
    Fighting with us, your oldest friends,   40
    Simply to serve your selfish ends—
        Really, you have no shame!
KORYPHAIOS(M).
  No, I'm through with women forever.
KORYPHAIOS(W).   If you say so.
  Still, you might put some clothes on. You look too ab-
    surd
  standing around naked. Come, get into this cloak.   45
KORYPHAIOS(M).
  Thank you; you're right. I merely took it off
  because I was in such a temper.
KORYPHAIOS(W).   That's much better
  Now you resemble a man again.
                              Why have you been so horrid?
  And look: there's some sort of insect in your eye.
  Shall I take it out?
KORYPHAIOS(M).   An insect, is it? So that's   50
  what's been bothering me. Lord, yes: take it out!
KORYPHAIOS(W).
  You might be more polite.
                          —But, heavens!
  What an enormous mosquito!
KORYPHAIOS(M).   You've saved my life.
  That mosquito was drilling an artesian well
  in my left eye.
KORYPHAIOS (W). Let me wipe   55
  those tears away.—And now: one little kiss?

KORYPHAIOS(M).
  No, no kisses.
KORYPHAIOS(W).   You're so difficult.
KORYPHAIOS(M).
  You impossible women! How you do get around us!
  The poet was right: Can't live with you, or without you.
60 But let's be friends.
  And to celebrate, you might join us in an Ode.

Strophe 1

CHORUS(M AND W).
      Let it never be said
      That my tongue is malicious:
      Both by word and by deed
65 I would set an example that's noble and gracious.
      We've had sorrow and care
      Till we're sick of the tune.
      Is there anyone here
      Who would like a small loan?
70   My purse is crammed,
        As you'll soon find;
  And you needn't pay me back if the Peace gets
  signed.

Strophe 2

      I've invited to lunch
      Some Karystian° rips—
75   An esurient bunch,
  But I've ordered a menu to water their lips.
      I can still make soup
      And slaughter a pig.
      You're all coming, I hope?
80   But a bath first, I beg!
        Walk right up
        As though you owned the place,
  And you'll get the front door slammed to in your
  face.

SCENE V

Enter Spartan Ambassador, with entourage.

KORYPHAIOS(M).
  The Commission has arrived from Sparta.
                              How oddly
  they're walking!
                  Gentlemen, welcome to Athens!
  How is life in Lakonia?
AMBASSADOR.   Need we discuss that?
  Simply use your eyes.
CHORUS(M).   The poor man's right:
                    What a sight!
AMBASSADOR.   Words fail me.

74 Karystians were known for their crudity

But come, gentlemen, call in your Commissioners,   5
  and let's get down to a Peace.
CHORAGOS(M).   The state we're in! Can't bear
  a stitch below the waist. It's a kind of pelvic
  paralysis.
COMMISSIONER.
  Won't somebody call Lysistrata?—Gentlemen,
  we're no better off than you.
AMBASSADOR.   So I see.   10
A SPARTAN.
  Seh, do y'all feel a certain strain
  early in the morning?
AN ATHENIAN.   I do, sir. It's worse than a strain.
  A few more days, and there's nothing for us but
      Kleisthenes,
  that broken blossom.
CHORAGOS(M).   But you'd better get dressed again.
  You know these people going around Athens with
      chisels,   15
  looking for statues of Hermes.°
ATHENIAN.   Sir, you are right.
SPARTAN.
  He certainly is! Ah'll put mah own clothes back on.

Enter Athenian Commissioners.

COMMISSIONER.
  Gentlemen from Sparta, welcome. This is a sorry
      business.
SPARTAN (*To one of his own group*).
  Colonel, we got dressed just in time. Ah sweah,
  if they'd seen us the way we were, there'd have been a
      new wah   20
  between the states.
COMMISSIONER.
  Shall we call the meeting to order?
                          Now, Lakonians,
  what's your proposal?
AMBASSADOR.   We propose to consider peace.
COMMISSIONER.
  Good. That's on our minds, too.
                          —Summon Lysistrata.
  We'll never get anywhere without her.
AMBASSADOR.   Lysistrata?   25
  Summon Lysis-*anybody*! Only, summon!
KORYPHAIOS(M).   No need to summon:
  here she is, herself.

Enter Lysistrata.

16 statues of Hermes The statues were the Hermai, stone posts set
up in various parts of Athens. Just before the sailing of the Sicilian
Expedition, a group of anonymous vandals mutilated these statues
with chisels. This was considered an unhappy augury.

COMMISSIONER.   Lysistrata! Lion of women!
  This is your hour to be
  hard and yielding, outspoken and shy, austere and
30 gentle. You see here
  the best brains of Hellas (confused, I admit,
  by your devious charming) met as one man
  to turn the future over to you.
LYSISTRATA.   That's fair enough,
  unless you men take it into your heads
35 to turn to each other instead of us. But I'd know
  soon enough if you did.
                              —Where is Reconciliation?
  Go, some of you: bring her here.

                              (*Exeunt two women.*)

                              And now, women,
  lead the Spartan delegates to me: not roughly
  or insultingly, as our men handle them, but gently,
40 politely, as ladies should. Take them by the hand,
  or by anything else if they won't give you their hands.

(*The Spartans are escorted over.*)

There.—The Athenians next, by any convenient
  handle.

(*The Athenians are escorted.*)

Stand there, please.—Now, all of you, listen to me.

(*During the following speech the two women reenter, carrying an enormous statue of a naked girl; this is Reconciliation.*)

I'm only a woman, I know; but I've a mind,
45 and, I think, not a bad one: I owe it to my father
  and to listening to the local politicians.
  So much for that.
                      Now, gentlemen,
  since I have you here, I intend to give you a scolding.
  We are all Greeks.
50 Must I remind you of Thermopylai,° of Olympia,
  of Delphoi? names deep in all our hearts?
  Are they not a common heritage?
                              Yet you men
  go raiding through the country from both sides,
  Greek killing Greek, storming down Greek cities—
55 and all the time the Barbarian across the sea
  is waiting for his chance!
                              —That's my first point.
AN ATHENIAN.
  Lord! I can hardly contain myself.
LYSISTRATA.   As for you Spartans:

Was it so long ago that Perikleides°
came here to beg our help? I can see him still,
his gray face, his sombre gown. And what did he want?   60
An army from Athens. All Messene
was hot at your heels, and the sea-god splitting your land.
Well, Kimon and his men,
four thousand strong, marched out and saved all Sparta.
And what thanks do we get? You come back to murder   65
  us.
AN ATHENIAN.
  They're aggressors, Lysistrata!
A SPARTAN.   Ah admit it.
  When Ah look at those laigs, Ah sweah Ah'll aggress
    mahself!
LYSISTRATA.
  And you, Athenians: do you think you're blameless?
  Remember that bad time when we were helpless,
  and an army came from Sparta,   70
  and that was the end of the Thessalian menace,
  the end of Hippias and his allies.
                              And that was Sparta,
  and only Sparta; but for Sparta, we'd be
  cringing slaves today, not free Athenians.

(*From this point, the male responses are less to Lysistrata than to the statue.*)

A SPARTAN.
  A well-shaped speech.
AN ATHENIAN.   Certainly it has its points.   75
LYSISTRATA.
  Why are we fighting each other? With all this history
  of favors given and taken, what stands in the way
  of making peace?
AMBASSADOR.   Spahta is ready, ma'am,
  so long as we get that place back.
LYSISTRATA.   What place, man?
AMBASSADOR.
  Ah refer to Pylos.
COMMISSIONER.   Not a chance, by God!   80
LYSISTRATA.
  Give it to them, friend.
COMMISSIONER.   But—what shall we have to bar-
  gain with?
LYSISTRATA.
  Demand something in exchange.
COMMISSIONER.   Good idea.—Well, then:
  Cockeville first, and the Happy Hills, and the country
  between the Legs of Megara.
AMBASSADOR.   Mah government objects.
LYSISTRATA.
  Over-ruled. Why fuss about a pair of legs?   85

50 **Thermopylai** a narrow pass where, in 480 B.C.E, an army of 300 Spartans held out for three days against a vastly superior Persian force

58 **Perikleides** a Spartan ambassador to Athens who successfully urged Athenians to aid Sparta in putting down a rebellion

(General assent. The statue is removed.)

AN ATHENIAN.
    I want to get out of these clothes and start my plowing.
A SPARTAN.
    Ah'll fertilize mahn first, by the Heavenly Twins!
LYSISTRATA.
    And so you shall,
    once you've made peace. If you are serious,
90   go, both of you, and talk with your allies.
COMMISSIONER.
    Too much talk already. No, we'll stand together.
    We've only one end in view. All that we want
    is our women; and I speak for our allies.
AMBASSADOR.
    Mah government concurs.
AN ATHENIAN.   So does Karystos.
LYSISTRATA.
95   Good.—But before you come inside
    to join your wives at supper, you must perform
    the usual lustration. Then we'll open
    our baskets for you, and all that we have is yours.
    But you must promise upright good behavior
100   from this day on. Then each man home with his woman!
AN ATHENIAN.
    Let's get it over with.
A SPARTAN.   Lead on. Ah follow.
AN ATHENIAN.
    Quick as a cat can wink!

(Exeunt all but the Choruses.)

Antistrophe 1

CHORUS(W).
    Embroideries and
    Twinkling ornaments and
105   Pretty dresses—I hand
    Them all over to you, and with never a qualm.
    They'll be nice for your daughters
    On festival days.
    When the girls bring the Goddess
110   The ritual prize.
    Come in, one and all:
    Take what you will.
    I've nothing here so tightly corked that you can't make
    it spill.

Antistrophe 2

    You may search my house
115   But you'll not find
    The least thing of use,

    Unless your two eyes are keener than mine.
    Your numberless brats
    Are half starved? and your slaves?
    Courage, grandpa! I've lots   120
    Of grain left, and big loaves.
    I'll fill your guts,
    I'll go the whole hog;
    But if you come too close to me, remember: 'ware the
    dog!

(Exeunt Choruses.)

EXODOS

A Drunken Citizen enters, approaches the gate, and is halted by a sentry.

CITIZEN.
    Open. The. Door.
SENTRY.   Now, friend, just shove along!
    —So you want to sit down. If it weren't such an old joke,
    I'd tickle your tail with this torch. Just the sort of gag
    this audience appreciates.
CITIZEN.   I. Stay. Right. Here.
SENTRY.
    Get away from there, or I'll scalp you! The gentlemen
        from Sparta   5
    are just coming back from dinner.

(Exit Citizen; the general company reenters; the two Choruses now represent Spartans and Athenians.)

A SPARTAN.   Ah must say,
    Ah never tasted better grub.
AN ATHENIAN.   And those Lakonians!
    They're gentlemen, by the Lord! Just goes to show,
    a drink to the wise is sufficient.
COMMISSIONER.   And why not?
    A sober man's an ass.   10
    Men of Athens, mark my words: the only efficient
    Ambassador's a drunk Ambassador. Is that clear?
    Look: we go to Sparta,
    and when we get there we're dead sober. The result?
    Everyone cackling at everyone else. They make speeches;   15
    and even if we understand, we get it all wrong
    when we file our reports in Athens. But today—!
    Everybody's happy. Couldn't tell the difference
    between *Drink to Me Only* and
    The Star-Spangled Athens.
                          What's a few lies,   20
    washed down in good strong drink?

Re-enter the Drunken Citizen.

SENTRY.   God almighty,
  he's back again!
CITIZEN.   I. Resume. My. Place.
A SPARTAN (*To an Athenian*).
  Ah beg yo', seh,
  take yo' instrument in yo' hand and play for us.
25 Ah'm told
  yo' understand the in*tr*icacies of the floot?
  Ah'd lahk to execute a song and dance
  in honor of Athens,
               and, of cohse, of Spahta.
CITIZEN.
  Toot. On. Your. Flute.

(The following song is a solo—an aria—accompanied by
the flute. The Chorus of Spartans begins a slow dance.)

A SPARTAN.
30   O Memory,
     Let the Muse speak once more
     In my young voice. Sing glory.
     Sing Artemision's shore,
     Where Athens fluttered the Persians. *Alalai,*
35   Sing glory, that great
     Victory! Sing also
     Our Leonidas and his men,
     Those wild boars, sweat and blood
     Down in a red drench. Then, then
40   The barbarians broke, though they had stood
     Numberless as the sands before!

     O Artemis,°
     Virgin Goddess, whose darts
     Flash in our forests: approve
45   This pact of peace and join our hearts,
     From this day on, in love.
     Huntress, descend!
LYSISTRATA.
  All that will come in time.
             But now, Lakonians,
  take home your wives. Athenians, take yours.
50 Each man be kind to his woman; and you, women,
  be equally kind. Never again, pray God,
  shall we lose our way in such madness.
KORYPHAIOS (*Athenian*). And now
  let's dance our joy.

(From this point the dance becomes general.)

CHORUS(Athenian).
  Dance, you Graces
           Artemis, dance

42 Artemis goddess of virginity, of the hunt, and of childbirth

  Dance, Phoibos,° Lord of dancing
                 Dance,   55
  In a scurry of Maenads, Lord Dionysos°
             Dance, Zeus Thunderer
        Dance, Lady Hera°
  Queen of the sky.
             Dance, dance, all you gods
  Dance witness everlasting of our pact
  Evohí Evohé   60
  Dance for the dearest
             the Bringer of Peace
  Deathless Aphrodite!
COMMISSIONER.
  Now let us have another song from Sparta.
CHORUS(SPARTAN).
     From Taygetos, from Taygetos,
      Lakonian Muse, come down.   65
     Sing to the Lord Apollo
      Who rules Amyklai Town.

     Sing Athena of the House of Brass!°
     Sing Leda's Twins,° that chivalry
     Resplendent on the shore   70
     Of our Eurotas; sing the girls
      That dance along before:
     Sparkling in dust their gleaming feet,
      Their hair a Bacchant fire,
     And Leda's daughter, thyrsos° raised,   75
      Leads their triumphant choir.
CHORUSES(S AND A).
    Evohé!
      Evohaí!
        Evohé!
          We pass
     Dancing
        dancing
           to greet
  Athena of the House of Brass.

55 Phoibos god of the sun **56 Maenads, Lord Dionysos** The maenads were ecstatic women in the train of Dionysos, god of wine **57 Hera** wife of Zeus **68 Athena of the House of Brass** a temple standing on the Akropolis of Sparta **69 Leda's Twins** Leda, raped by Zeus, bore quadruplets: two daughters, Helen and Klytaimnestra, and two sons, Kastor and Polydeukes **75 thyrsos** a staff twined with ivy, carried by Dionysus and his followers

TOPICS FOR CRITICAL THINKING AND WRITING

The Play on the PAGE

1. According to *Lysistrata*, what are the causes of war? What do you think are the causes of war?
2. What connection, if any, is there between the sex strike and the seizure of the Akropolis?

3. An antiwar play might be expected to call attention to cruelty, innocent suffering, and death. How much of this do you find in *Lysistrata*?

The Play on the STAGE

4. How would you costume the play?
5. Take a passage of some fifty lines and specify the gestures and blocking that you would use if you were directing the play.
6. There is much about sex here. How much is there about love?

7. Evaluate the view that the real heroine of the play is not Lysistrata but the nude female statue, Reconciliation.

The Play in PERFORMANCE

Lysistrata requires at least four actors, in addition to the chorus and to a few mute figures.

Most ancient Greek plays require only one doorway through which actors enter and exit, but *Lysistrata* (as well as a few other comedies) seems to require two or even three doors. The *skene,* or "scene-building" apparently had one permanent central entrance with double doors, but additional entrances could be created at each side. Thus, in *Lysistrata* at the end of the prologue the central door is identified as the gateway to the Acropolis. Perhaps at the start of the play Lysistrata enters from a side door, or from the *parodos,* stands in front of the central door, and then is greeted by her neighbor Kalonike, who enters from the other side door.

The play requires that actors appear not only on ground level but also at an elevation. We know that performers—usually in the role of gods—sometimes appeared on the roof of the *skene;* in *Lysistrata* the heroine appears on the roof, and so do some of the other women.

The costumes of the actors presumably resembled the costumes of the audience, that is, of contemporary society, though some of the male characters are equipped with erect phalluses. About the only other

costume that requires mention is that of Reconciliation, a female figure who is said to be nude. Since all of the roles were played by males, female nakedness presumably was represented by males in bodysuits adorned with female breasts and genitalia.

Probably the most important decision a director must make is whether to use actresses or (following ancient Greek practice) to use an all-male cast. It is important to realize that the parts of the women must be convincingly played; if men play the parts in drag, and camp it up, most of the joke is lost, since the male characters must be understood to be sexually aroused by the sight of the women. Or, let's say, a campy drag version becomes something very different from Aristophanes's play.

In modern times the play has occasionally been done by pacifists and also by feminists—always with women in the female roles. There are records of such productions as early as 1912. The Moscow Art Theater did a version, and brought it to the United States in 1925. In 1930 a rather free version of *Lysistrata* had a brief but successful professional run in Philadelphia and in New York, but chiefly the play is produced in college and university theaters.

Medieval Theater
England and Japan

Like classical Greek drama, medieval morality plays are often updated and staged in contemporary settings. In this 1995 adaptation of *Everyman*, Sarah Hasky (standing) plays Everyman in a contemporary Appalachian setting. Joel Saunders plays Goods.

ENGLAND

The word *medieval* comes from two Latin words: *medius*, meaning "middle," and *aevum*, meaning "age." In this view, Western European history was divided into three periods: The first was a period of classical (Greek and Roman) civilization, ending with the disintegration of the Roman empire in the fourth and fifth centuries C.E. The second was the middle period, the Middle Ages, though of course no one in this period knew that he or she was living in the middle period; the third was the Renaissance (a French word for "rebirth"), when classical ideas, and indeed the arts themselves, were supposedly reborn after the centuries of darkness. (The Middle Ages have also been called the *Dark Ages*, although the term is no longer used.) The Middle Ages are usually said to end in Italy in the fourteenth century but in England they continued throughout the fifteenth and even into the sixteenth. Of course no precise dates can be given for these periods, any more than one can give a precise moment when day turns into night. It is fair to say that certain kinds of English medieval plays that were popular in the fourteenth century were still popular in the late sixteenth, but by the end of the sixteenth century kinds of drama had emerged that were notably different from those in the Middle Ages. To take a single fact: Throughout the Middle Ages, though plays were staged outdoors and indoors (for instance in churches, and sometimes in the residences of nobles), there was no building in all of England that was designed specifically for the staging of plays. In 1576, however, a building was constructed outside of London for the sole purpose of staging plays. It was a new age.

Christian Opposition to Drama

In 410 C.E. Alaric, King of the Visigoths, crossed the Alps and sacked Rome. In the next five centuries probably no plays were written in Europe and no theaters were built there. But the drama had encountered an enemy even before Alaric entered Rome: The Christian church had long opposed theatrical entertainments, partly because they included spectacles of nudity, fights with wild beasts, and the like; partly because Christians were fed to lions or were tarred and set afire in entertainments offered to the pagan Romans; and partly because the church's hatred of "falsehood" included among the untruths—the fictions—of literature the art of acting, which involves the impersonation of one man by another, and—even worse—of a woman by a man by means of transvestism. Here is the biblical text that is usually cited: "The woman shall not wear that which pertaineth unto a man, neither shall a man put on a woman's garment; for all that do so are abomination unto the Lord God" (Deuteronomy 22.5).

The Rise of Liturgical Drama, and "The Play of Corpus Christi"

In the fifth century, after a monk attempted to interfere in a gladiatorial combat and was stoned to death, the Roman emperors (who in 378 had adopted Christianity as the official state religion) prohibited public spectacles. For all practical purposes, the theater in Europe and Britain ceased to exist, except for quasi-dramatic events such as tournaments and ritual practices in pagan festivals and such meager performances as were put on by itinerant minstrels, owners of performing animals, mimes, jugglers, and puppeteers.

And yet, despite the opposition of Christianity, which held that drama is immoral because it presents false appearances, the drama was reborn within the church in what is known as liturgical drama. A liturgy is a prescribed form of worship, including the singing of the Mass, in which bread and wine are consecrated as the body and blood of Christ. Some liturgical texts were arranged in dialogue form, with choric chants divided antiphonally, that is with one voice (or set of voices) responding to another. For instance, one of the introductory antiphons for the Easter Mass consists of an exchange in song between a voice or set of voices speaking for an angel and another set of voices speaking for the women who visited Christ's tomb in order to anoint the corpse. The angel asks whom they seek, they reply that they seek Jesus, and the angel explains that Jesus has risen from the tomb. Such a service, with chanting priests and a choir—a voice or voices answering a voice or voices—resembles a dramatic exchange, but it is not quite drama, since there is little or no emphasis on impersonation. Still, before the end of the tenth century it was clear that drama was reborn in the church.

Earlier in this book (pages 2–3), in our essay in which we consider the essence of drama, we discuss the liturgical drama called *Quem Quaeritis* ("Whom do you seek?"), described by Bishop Ethelwold. We need not repeat that discussion here. Suffice it to say that adaptations soon followed; for instance, similar dramatic renditions celebrated the birth of Jesus and the journey of the Magi. These compositions probably were not initially conceived of as educational; in time they must have been recognized as a means by which an illiterate congregation could better grasp the miraculous realities. In 1264, some three hundred years after Bishop Ethelwold set down his instructions, Pope Urban IV promulgated a new Feast Day, Corpus Christi (medieval Latin, "body of Christ"), which was finally instituted by Pope Clement V in 1311. Celebrated on the Thursday following Trinity Sunday, and commemorating Christ's sacrifice of his life for the salvation of humankind, Corpus Christi Day occurred nine weeks after Easter Sunday. Although in the modern calendar it falls in late May or in June, in the Middle Ages, because the calendar was inaccurate, Corpus Christi Day fell at a time equivalent to our June or early July. It became a joyful midsummer festival, marked by a procession in which the communion chalice, escorted by local dignitaries, was carried through the streets.

Plays soon became part of the Feast of Corpus Christi, and so, for example, in Italy in the early fourteenth century Corpus Christi Day was celebrated by an almost cosmic cycle of plays on sacred history, in Latin, ranging from the Fall of Lucifer, the Crucifixion of Christ, the Harrowing of Hell, Christ's Ascension, and on up to the Day of Judgment. By the end of the fourteenth century the celebration of Corpus Christi included plays performed not in Latin but in the vernacular, on Old Testament and New Testament subjects, sponsored not only by the Church but by civic organizations. Guilds sponsored plays deemed appropriate; thus, the shipwrights were responsible for the play about Noah's Ark, the bakers for The Last Supper, and so on. The plays as a groups were called "the play of Corpus Christi," and each episode was a pageant, but scholars usually call the individual episodes **miracle plays**—a term sometimes used in the Middle Ages—or **mystery plays** because they were sponsored by various trades or "mysteries," a word derived, like the French *métier*, from the Latin *minister*, "attendant," "servant."

How does one account for this widespread and vast medieval cyclical drama? Did it "develop" from *Quem Quaeritis*, or was it engendered afresh? In the late nineteenth and early twentieth centuries, scholars customarily held a sort of Darwinian view, suggesting that the late medieval cycles "evolved" out of *Quem Quaeritis*. In this view, the drama gradually but naturally grew, adding one story to another, expanding the length of the stories, inevitably shifting from Latin into the vernacular, and equally inevitably moving out of the Church and into the marketplace. The current prevailing scholarly view, however, tends to deemphasize a "natural" evolution and to hold that the plays are the result of self-conscious efforts to set forth scriptural history—a history of the wonders of God—in dramatic form. That is, the plays are now seen as an effort to provide visible evidence explaining the significance of the Feast of Corpus Christi.

The Staging of Miracle Plays

In England four great cycles of miracle plays are extant: forty-eight plays were done at York, thirty-two at Wakefield, twenty-four at Chester, and forty-three at an unidentified town (formerly thought to be Coventry). Moreover, this sort of medieval drama, enormously popular in the late fourteenth century and in the fifteenth, survived until well into the Renaissance, that is, for several decades after Henry VIII split with the Church of Rome and established the Church of England. The cycles were given at Chester until 1574 and at Coventry (only fourteen miles from Shakespeare's Stratford) until 1581, when Shakespeare was seventeen. They apparently were abandoned not because the people lost interest in religious drama but for two other reasons: (1) Protestantism was hostile to a drama that had developed under Roman Catholic auspices, and (2) better dramatic entertainment was becoming available. The late sixteenth century saw the rise of small companies of professional strolling players, who could put on a better show than could the local amateurs. In 1576, the last year that the plays were staged at Wakefield, James Burbage erected England's first permanent theater, in London. In York the plays were revived in 1951 to celebrate "The Festival of Britain." Much to the producers' and community's surprise, audiences found the old scripts exciting drama. Today, all around Britain the medieval plays are staged often—in medieval and in modern dress—and audiences respond to both the spiritual and theatrical elements.

Something (but not a great deal) is known about the staging of medieval plays. There is evidence of performances on temporary stages made of planks resting on trestles or barrels; there is also evidence of performances in the round (i.e., with the audience on all sides), and of performances on wagons or floats called **pageants.** In some towns pageants were drawn to several announced localities where separate audiences waited. In this method of staging, each audience stayed in one place, seeing a succession of scenes, and the wagons traveled on to other audiences waiting at other locations. But it may also be the case, for some vast cycles, that although the wagons were first drawn through the town, they were then assembled in a circle in one place, for instance in a public square, where the plays were performed one by one with the audience in the center of the ring of wagons.

A stage, or a pageant, might simultaneously display several sets (called *sedes,* literally "seats," or *mansions*) to indicate different locales; a structure representing Hell (the head of a monster, from whose gaping mouth smoke poured forth) might be at one side, and a structure representing Heaven might be at the other. In between were structures representing various places, such as the manger where Jesus was born, the hill where he was crucified, and so forth. There is also evidence that the performers sometimes left their stages and entered the open space (the *platea*) where the audience stood. In short, the productions were closer to today's "street theater" than to what goes on in our modern playhouses.

Martial Rose, in *The Wakefield Mystery Plays* (a book with a long introduction to a modernized text of the plays), offers some conjectures about how the town of Wakefield in the mid-fifteenth century may have staged its cycle of thirty-two plays, ranging from the creation of the world through the fall of humankind, the redemption, and the judgment. (It must be remembered that the evidence is very fragmentary, and Rose's account therefore is highly conjectural, but it is as reasonable as any other that has been offered.) Perhaps, Rose says, soon after dawn on Corpus Christi Day, twenty or thirty pageants set out on the Corpus Christi procession. Sponsored by the trade guilds—each guild was associated with a particular pageant—the procession of wagons, guilds—men, minstrels, and clergy went to the parish church. Here, at the service, the Host of the Lord was raised, carried out of the church, and carried (with the procession following) to various stations in the town. At each station the pageants would produce, in pantomime, the climax of the play that they would perform in full in the following three days. During the next three days, the plays were performed at only one location (perhaps the marketplace, the common, or the land adjoining the church), where an audience assembled in a circle around an open space to watch as each pageant entered through an aisle and its actors performed. Rose conjectures that perhaps Heaven and Hell were brought in first and remained in view throughout, while the other wagons came and went. Or possibly the audience assembled in the center, and all of the wagons were assembled around the perimeter of the circle.

The wagon for *The Second Shepherd's Play* might have used two mansions, one for Mak's house and one for Mary and Jesus. The space between and in front of the two mansions (the *platea*) could have served for the fields, though some scholars conjecture a third mansion, a fence, to represent the sheepfold.

For a further discussion of the staging of *The Second Shepherd's Play*, see the introduction (page 166) to the play.

JAPAN

Many historians of Japan use the term *the Middle Ages* to refer to the period of, roughly, the tenth century, when a new system of land allotment was introduced, to the middle of the sixteenth century, when the warrior class wrested power from the emperor. The real power was with the shogun, a warrior, and the emperor became a figurehead.

We do not wish to suggest, even remotely, that there was any contact between medieval England and medieval Japan, but there are some similarities. To begin with, the Noh drama, the form we are concerned with here, is essentially a fourteenth-century development, which is to say it was contemporary with the English miracle or mystery plays. Second, and more important, in medieval Japan, as in medieval England, religion was a powerful force. Most Noh plays are deeply Buddhist. Briefly, Buddhism preaches the need to free oneself form "attachment" to things of this world—not only things like money and power, but also attachment to sexual objects, and even nonsexual attachment to friends and family. When one is free from desire of every sort, one has reached *nirvana*, and is no longer subject to the cycle of reincarnation. If this idea of the need to renounce nonsexual passion or attachment even to members of one's family seems utterly foreign to you, recall that it is not absent from Christian thinking. For instance, in Matthew 10.37 Jesus says, "He that loveth father or mother more than me is not worthy of me; and he that loveth son or daughter more than me is not worthy of me"; and in Matthew 19.29 Jesus says, "And everyone that hath forsaken houses, or brethren, or sisters, or father, or mother, or wife, or children, or lands, for my name's sake, shall receive an hundredfold, and shall inherit everlasting life."

Japan of course has developed forms of drama other than the Noh. The most famous are *bunraku* (plays using large puppets or dolls) and *kabuki* (a form derived from Noh, but far more secular). Both of these forms, however, belong not to the Middle Ages but to what historians of Japan customarily call the Early Modern Period.

The Wakefield Master

The anonymous author of five plays in The Wakefield Cycle (which has a total of thirty-two plays) is called The Wakefield Master. He is thought to have been a clergyman active in the first half of the fifteenth century, but nothing is known for certain about him. (The cycle is also known as the Towneley Cycle, from the name of a family that owned the manuscript, but Wakefield is a better designation for two reasons: The manuscript specifically mentions Wakefield, a town in Yorkshire, England, and it is known that a cycle of plays was in fact performed there.)

The Wakefield Cycle probably originated in the late fourteenth century, but it was revised and amplified. The five plays attributed to the Wakefield Master are characterized by the liveliness of the roles and by a distinctive nine-line stanza. The first four lines of each stanza use identical end-rhymes and also internal rhymes. In the last five lines, lines 5 and 9 rhyme, and lines 6, 7, and 8 rhyme. The first four lines each have four stresses, line 5 has only one stress, lines 6, 7, and 8 have three stresses each, and line 9 has two stresses. This stanza is used only in the five plays attributed to the Wakefield Master and in a few passages in another play that he apparently revised.

■■■■■■■■■■■■■

COMMENTARY ON *THE SECOND SHEPHERDS' PLAY*

The play that we print is called *The Second Shepherds' Play* because in the Wakefield cycle it is the second of two plays about the shepherds who received the news of the birth of Jesus, as told in the second chapter of the Gospel according to Saint Luke. Here is the biblical material, in the King James Version (1611)—a translation that appeared almost two hundred years later than the play. After reporting that Mary gave birth to Jesus in a stable, Luke says,

8 And there were in the same country shepherds abiding in the fields, keeping watch over their flock by night.

9 And, lo, the angel of the Lord came upon them, and the glory of the Lord shone round about them: and they were sore afraid.

10 And the angel said unto them, "Fear not: for behold, I bring you good tidings of great joy, which shall be to all people.

11 For unto you is born this day in the city of David a Savior, which is Christ the Lord.

12 And this shall be a sign unto you; Ye shall find the babe wrapped in swaddling clothes, lying in a manger."

13 And suddenly there was with the angel a multitude of the heavenly host praising God, and saying,

14 "Glory to God in the highest, and on earth peace, good will toward men."

15 And it came to pass, as the angels were gone away from them into heaven, the shepherds said one to another, "Let us now go even unto Bethlehem, and see this thing which is come to pass, which the Lord hath made known unto us."

16 And they came with haste, and found Mary, and Joseph, and the babe lying in a manger.

17 And when they had seen it, they made known abroad the saying which was told them concerning the child.

The life of Jesus, from his birth through his crucifixion and resurrection, underlies the numerous episodes of the cycle of plays that was known as *The Play of Corpus Christi*. The cycle begins with the Creation of the World, moves through various episodes in the Hebrew Bible, including such momentous episodes as the Fall of Adam and Eve, Abraham and Isaac, and Noah's Flood, and then gives us the turning point of history, the birth of Jesus, which, through the Crucifixion, leads to the salvation of humankind. In short, the pageants in *The Play of Corpus Christi* dramatize episodes of the Old Testament in order to show how they are fulfilled in the New Testament. But the plays often go beyond the sources, elaborating the biblical stories with invented details. Thus, Luke's ten verses concerning the shepherds are expanded in *The Second Shepherds' Play* into a drama of 794 lines—and what is more amazing, the first 637 lines of the play, concerning a stolen sheep that is disguised as an infant, are sheer invention, having nothing explicitly to do with the news of the birth of Jesus. But of course there are dramatic connections—most obviously in the contrast between the pseudo-birth scene in Mak's cottage (with the swaddled stolen sheep, horned like the devil) and the nativity of the Christ Child, announced in the last part of the play. Similarly, the initial complaints of the laboring men in an unjust world are connected, by way of contrast, with the joy in a spiritually renewed world at the end of the play.

The Second Shepherds' Play is comic in two senses. First, it is amusing, with its grumbling figures and the sheep-stealer who adopts a dialect in order to impersonate a man of rank and who tries to pass off a stolen sheep as his newborn infant. Second, it is comic in its overall action, that is, in its movement from bad fortune to good fortune (the recovery of the stolen sheep), from sorrow to joy (the news of the birth of Jesus), from the cruelty of nature and of humankind to generosity (the giving of gifts), from winter to an anticipation of spring (in the presentation of the bunch of cherries) and renewed life.

A Note on the Translation

Something should be said about the language of the original play and about our translation. The anonymous author, writing in the middle of the fifteenth century, used an English that often is close to modern English, and often it is not. Thus, the first line of the original,

> Lord, what these weders are cold! And I am ill
> happyd,

may be translated fairly literally as

> Lord, how this weather is cold! And I am poorly
> clothed.

We translate it as:

> Lord, but this weather is cold! And I am ill
> wrapped.

By substituting "wrapped" for the obscure "happyd," we can spare the reader from consulting a gloss and yet we can also preserve the rhyme of *happyd* / *nappyd* / *chappyd* of the original. Or consider the very last lines of the play:

> To sing ar we bun—
> Let take on loft!

Literally this means, "To sing are we bound, / Begin [the song] loudly." We render the last line as "Ring it aloft," which avoids the need to gloss "Let take" as "begin," and which yet preserves the rhyme with "Full oft," as in the original.

THE SECOND SHEPHERDS' PLAY
The Wakefield Master

Modernized Version by the Editors

LIST OF CHARACTERS

FIRST SHEPHERD [*Coll*]
SECOND SHEPHERD [*Gib*]
THIRD SHEPHERD [*Daw*]
MAK [*a sheep-stealer*]
HIS WIFE [*Gill*]

ANGEL
MARY
CHRIST-CHILD

A field.

FIRST SHEPHERD.
    Lord, but these weathers are cold! And I am ill wrapped
    I am near-hand dold,° so long have I napped;
    My legs they fold, my fingers are chapped.
    It is not as I would, for I am all lapped
5   In sorrow.
    In storms and tempest,
    Now in the east, now in the west,
    Woe is him has never rest
    Midday nor morrow!

10   But we simple husbands° that walk on the moor,
    In faith we are near-hands out of the door.
    No wonder, as it stands, if we be poor,
    For the tilth of our lands lies fallow as the floor,
    As ye ken.°
15   We are so lamed,
    O'ertaxed and maimed,
    We are made hand-tamed
    By these gentlery men.

    Thus they rob us our rest, our Lady them harry!
20   These men that are lord-fast, they make the plough tarry.
    What men say is for the best, we find it contrary.
    Thus are husbands oppressed, about to miscarry
    In life.
    Thus hold they us under,
25   Thus they bring us in blunder;
    It were great wonder
    If ever should we thrive.

    There shall come a swain as proud as a po;°
    He must borrow my wain, my plough also;
30   Then I am full fain° to grant ere he go.
    Thus live we in pain, anger, and woe,

    By night, and day.
    He must have it for sure,
    Though I remain poor;
    I'll be pushed out of door   35
    If I once say nay.

    If he has braid on his sleeve or a badge nowadays,
    Woe to him that him grieve or ever gainsays!
    No complaint he'll receive, whatever his ways.
    And yet may none believe one word that he says,   40
    No letter.
    He can make his demands
    With boasts and commands,
    And all because he stands
    For men who are greater.   45

    It does me good, as I walk thus by mine own,
    Of this world for to talk in manner of moan.
    To my sheep will I stalk, and hearken anon,°
    And there will I halt and sit on a stone
    Full soon.   50
    For I trust, pardie,°
    True men if there be,
    We get more company
    Ere it be noon.

[*Enter the Second Shepherd, who does not see the First Shepherd.*]

SECOND SHEPHERD.
    Blessings upon us, what may this bemean?   55
    Why fares this world thus? Such we seldom have seen.
    Lord, these weathers are spiteous, and the winds full keen,
    And the frosts so hideous they water mine eyne,°
    No lie!

---

2 dold nearly numb   **10 husbands** husbandmen, that is, shepherds
14 ken know   **28 po** peacock   **30 fain** pleased

48 anon soon   **51 pardie** by God   **58 eyne** eyes

60   Now in dry, now in wet,
      Now in snow, now in sleet,
      When my shoes freeze to my feet
      It is not all easy.

      But as far as I've been, or yet as I know,
65   We poor wedded-men suffer great woe;
      We sorrow now and again; it falls oft so.
      Silly Caple, our hen, both to and fro
      She cackles;
      But begins she to croak,
70   To groan or to cluck,
      Woe is him, our cock,
      For he is in her shackles.

      These men that are wed have not all their will;
      When they're full hard bestead,° they sigh full still.
75   God knows they are led full hard and full ill;
      In bower nor in bed they say nought theretil.°
      This tide°
      My part have I found,
      I know my ground!
80   Woe is him that is bound,
      For he must abide.

      But now late in our lives—a marvel to me,
      That I think my heart rives such wonders to see;
      Whate'er destiny drives, it must so be—
85   Some men will have two wives, and some men three
      In store;
      Some are grieved that have any.
      But so far ken I—
      Woe is him that has many,
90   For he feels sore.

      [*Addresses the audience.*]

      But, young men, of wooing, for God who you bought,°
      Be well ware of wedding, and think in your thought,
      "Had I known" is a thing that serves us of nought.
      Much constant mourning has wedding home brought,
95   And griefs,
      With many a sharp shower;
      For thou may catch in an hour
      What shall savor full sour
      As long as thou lives.

100 For, as e'er read I epistle, I have one for my dear
      As sharp as thistle, as rough as a brier;
      She is browed like a bristle, with a sour-looking cheer;°
      Had she once wet her whistle, she could sing full clear
      Her Paternoster.
105 She is as great as a whale,
      She has a gallon of gall;

      By Him that died for us all,
      I would I had run till I had lost her!

      [*The First Shepherd interrupts him.*]

FIRST SHEPHERD.
      The like I never saw! Full deafly ye stand.
SECOND SHEPHERD.
      Be the devil in thy maw, so tariand!°   110
      Saw thou ought of Daw?
FIRST SHEPHERD.
      Yea, on pasture-land
      Heard I him blaw.° He comes here at hand,
      Not far.
      Standstill.
SECOND SHEPHERD.
      Why?
FIRST SHEPHERD.
      For he comes here, think I.   115
SECOND SHEPHERD.
      He will tell us both a lie
      Unless we beware.

      [*Enter the Third Shepherd, a boy, who does not see the
      others.*]

THIRD SHEPHERD.
      Christ's cross, my creed, and Saint Nicholas!
      Thereof had I need; it is worse than it was.
      Whoso could take heed and let the world pass,   120
      It is ever in dread and brittle as glass
      And slides.
      This world fared never sure,
      With marvels more and more—
      Now with rich, now with poor,   125
      Nothing abides.

      Never since Noah's flood were such floods seen,
      Winds and rains so rude, and storms so keen—
      Some stammered, some stood in fear, as I ween,°
      Now God turn all to good! I say as I mean,   130
      For, ponder:
      These floods so they drown,
      Both in fields and in town,
      And bear all down;
      And that is a wonder.   135

      [*He sees the others.*]

      We that walk in the nights, our cattle to keep,
      We see sudden sights when other men sleep.
      Yet methinks my heart lights; I see rogues peep.
      Ye are two tall wights°—I will give my sheep
      A turn.   140

---

74 bestead oppressed   **76 theretil** thereto   **77 tide** time   **91 bought** redeemed   **102 cheer** face

110 tariand for tarrying   **112 blaw** blow on his shepherd's pipe
129 ween fear   **139 wights** men

But much ill have I meant;
As I walk on this bent,°
I may lightly repent,
My toes if I spurn.°

[*The other two advance.*]

145 Ah, sir, God you save, and master mine!
A drink fain would I have, and somewhat to dine.
FIRST SHEPHERD.
Christ's curse, my knave, thou art lazy, I find!
SECOND SHEPHERD.
How the boy will rave! Wait for a time;
You have fed.
150 Bad luck on your brow;
The rogue came just now,
Yet would he, I vow,
Sit down to his bread.
THIRD SHEPHERD.
Such servants as I, that sweats and swinks,°
155 Eats our bread full dry, a sorrow methinks.
We are oft wet and weary when master-men winks;°
Yet comes full tardy both dinners and drinks.
But truly.
Both our dame and our sire,
160 When we have run in the mire,
They can nip at our hire,°
And pay us full slowly.

But hear my mind, master: for the bread that I break,
I shall toil thereafter—work as I take.
165 I shall do but little, sir, and always hold back,
For yet lay my supper never on my stomach
In fields.
Why should I complain?
With my staff I can run;
170 And men say, "A bargain
Little profit yields."
FIRST SHEPHERD.
You'd be a poor lad to go a-walking
With a man that had but little for spending.
SECOND SHEPHERD.
Peace, boy, I said. No more jangling,
175 Or I shall make thee afraid, by the heaven's king!
Thy joke—
Where are our sheep, boy?—we scorn.
THIRD SHEPHERD.
Sir, this same day at morn
I them left in the corn,°
180 When the dawn broke.

They have pasture good, they can not go wrong.

FIRST SHEPHERD.
That is right. By the rood,° these nights are long!
Ere we went, how I would, that one gave us a song.
SECOND SHEPHERD.
So I thought as I stood, to mirth us among.
THIRD SHEPHERD.
I grant.
FIRST SHEPHERD.
Let me sing the tenory. 185
SECOND SHEPHERD.
And I the treble so high.
THIRD SHEPHERD.
Then the mean falls to me.
Let see how ye chant.

[*They sing.*]
Then Mak enters with a cloak drawn over his tunic.

MAK.
Now, Lord, for Thy names seven, that made both beast
    and bird,
Well more than I can mention, Thy will leaves me 190
    unstirred.
I am all uneven; that upsets my brains.
Now would God I were in heaven, for there weep no
    bairns°
So still.°
FIRST SHEPHERD.
Who is that pipes so poor?
MAK.
Would God ye knew how I were! 195
Lo, a man that walks on the moor,
And has not all his will.
SECOND SHEPHERD.
Mak, where hast thou gone?
Tell us tiding.
THIRD SHEPHERD.
Is he come? Then each one take heed to his thing. 200

He takes the cloak from Mak.

MAK.
What! Ich° be a yeoman, I tell you, of the king,
The self and the same, agent of a lording,
And sich.
Fie on you! Go hence
Out of my presence! 205
I must have reverence.
Why, who be Ich?
FIRST SHEPHERD.
Why make ye it so quaint? Mak, ye do wrong.

---

142 **bent** heath   144 **spurn** perhaps: If I trip, I can easily expiate
my evil thoughts   154 **swinks** works   156 **winks** sleeps
161 **nip . . . hire** reduce our wages   179 **corn** wheat

182 **rood** cross   192 **bairns** children   193 **still** continuously
201 **Ich** Mak here adopts a southern dialect, but slips back into the
northern dialect at times.

SECOND SHEPHERD.
Mak, play ye the saint? I think not for long.
THIRD SHEPHERD.
210 I think the rogue can feign, may the devil him hang!
MAK.
I shall make complaint, and make you all to thwang°
At a word,
And tell even how ye doth.
FIRST SHEPHERD.
But, Mak, is that truth?
215 Now take out that Southern tooth,
And put in a turd!
SECOND SHEPHERD.
Mak, the devil in your eye! A stroke would I beat you.
THIRD SHEPHERD.
Mak, know ye not me? By God, I could grieve you.
MAK.
God save you all three! Me thought I had seen you.
Ye are a fair company.
FIRST SHEPHERD.
220 What is it that mean you?
SECOND SHEPHERD.
Shrew,° peep!
Thus late as thou goes,
What will men suppose?
Thou hast a good nose
225 For stealing a sheep.
MAK.
And I am true as steel, all men state;
But a sickness I feel that will not abate:
My belly fares not well; it is out of estate.
THIRD SHEPHERD.
Seldom lies the devil dead by the gate.
MAK.
230 Therefore,
Full sore am I and sick;
May I stand like a stick
If I've had a bit
For a month and more.
FIRST SHEPHERD.
235 How fares thy wife? By the hood, what say you?
MAK.
Lies wallowing—by the rood—by the fire, lo!
And a house full of brood. She drinks well, too;
There's no other good that she will do!
But she
240 Eats as fast as may be,
And every year that we see
She brings forth a baby—
And, some years, two.

Were I even more prosperous and richer by some,

I were eaten out of house and even of home. 245
Yet is she a foul souse, if ye come near;
There is none that goes or anywhere roams
Worse than she.
Now will ye see what I proffer?
To give all in my coffer, 250
Tomorrow early to offer
Her head-masspenny.°
SECOND SHEPHERD.
I know so forwaked° is none in this shire;
I would sleep, if I taked less for my hire.°
THIRD SHEPHERD.
I am cold and naked, and would have a fire. 255
FIRST SHEPHERD.
I am weary, all ached, and run in the mire—
Watch, thou.

[Lies down.]

SECOND SHEPHERD.
Nay, I will lie near by,
For I must sleep, truly.

[Lies down beside him.]

THIRD SHEPHERD.
As good a man's son was I 260
As any of you.

[Lies down.]

But, Mak, come thou here. Between us you'll stay.
MAK.
Then could I stop you if evil you'd say,
No dread.
From my top to my toe, 265
Manus tuas commendo,
Poncio Pilato;°
May Christ's cross me clear.

Then he gets up, the shepherds still sleeping, and says:

Now's the time for a man that lacks what he would
To stalk privily then into a fold, 270
And nimbly to work then, and be not too bold,
For he might pay for the bargain, if it were told
At the end.
Only time now will tell;
But he needs good counsel 275
Who fain would fare well,
And has little to spend.

[Mak casts a spell over them.]

252 **head-masspenny** payment for funeral mass   253 **forwaked** worn out with watching   254 **taked less . . . hire** even though I accepted less wages   266-7 *Manus . . . Pilato* "Into thy hands I commend, Pontius Pilate."

211 **thwang** be flogged   221 **shrew** rogue

Here about you a circle, as round as a moon,
Till I have done what I will, till that it be noon,
280   May ye lie stone-still till that I have done;
And I shall say theretil a few good words soon:
A height,
Over your heads, my hand I lift.
Out go your eyes! Black out your sight!
285   But yet I must make better shift
If it go right.

[*The shepherds begin to snore.*]

Lord, how they sleep hard. That may ye all hear.
I was never a shepherd, but now will I lere.°
Though the flock be scared, yet shall I draw near.
290   How! Draw hitherward! Now mends our cheer
From sorrow;
A fat sheep, I dare say,
A good fleece, dare I lay.
Pay back when I may,
295   But this will I borrow.

[*He takes the sheep home.*]

How, Gill, art thou in? Get us some light.
WIFE.
Who makes such din this time of the night?
I am set for to spin; I don't think there might
Be a penny to win; I curse them, all right!
300   So fares
The housewife that has been
Called from her work by a din.
Thus I earn not a pin
For such small chores.
MAK.
305   Good wife, open the hatch! See'st thou not what I bring?
WIFE.
I will let you draw the latch. Ah, come in, my sweeting.
MAK.
Thou care not a scratch of my long standing.
WIFE.
By thy naked neck art thou like for to hang.
MAK.
Away!
310   I am worthy my meat,
For in a pinch can I get
More than they that swink and sweat
All the long day. [*Shows her the sheep.*]
Thus it fell to my lot, Gill; I had such grace.
WIFE.
315   It were a foul blot to be hanged for the case.
MAK.
I have 'scaped, Jelott, oft as hard a place.
WIFE.
"But so long goes the pot to the water," men says,

288 **lere** learn

"At last
Comes it home broken."
MAK.
Well know I the token,   320
But let it never be spoken.
But come and help fast.

I would it were slain; I would well eat.
This twelvemonth was I not so fain of one sheep-meat.
WIFE.
Come they ere it be slain, and hear the sheep bleat—   325
MAK.
Then might I be ta'en. That were a cold sweat!
Go bar
The gate-door.
WIFE.   Yes, Mak,
And if they're close at thy back—
MAK.
Then might I get, from all the pack,   330
The devil and more.
WIFE.
A good trick have I spied, since thou know none:
Here shall we him hide, till they be gone—
In my cradle abide. Let me alone,
And I shall lie beside in childbed, and groan.   335
MAK.
Good head!
And I shall say thou was light°
Of a boy-child this night.
WIFE.
For sure was the day bright
On which I was bred!   340
This is a good guise and a fair cast;
A woman's advice helps at the last.
I fear someone spies; again go thou fast.
MAK.
If I'm gone when they rise, they'll blow a cold blast.
I will go sleep. [*Returns to the shepherds.*]   345
Still they sleep, these three men,
And I shall softly creep in,
As though I had not been
He who stole their sheep.

[*He resumes his place.*]

[*The First and Second Shepherds awake.*]

FIRST SHEPHERD.
Resurrex a mortruus!° Give me a hand.   350
Judas carnas dominus!° I can not well stand;
My foot sleeps, by Jesus, and I totter on land.
I thought that we laid us full near England.

337 **light** delivered   350 ***Resurrex a mortruus*** garbled Latin:
"Resurrection from the dead"   351 ***Judas carnas dominus*** "Judas,
lord of the flesh"

SECOND SHEPHERD.
 Ah, yea?
355 Lord, but I have slept well!
 As fresh as an eel,
 As light I me feel
 As leaf on a tree.

[*The Third Shepherd awakes.*]

THIRD SHEPHERD.
 Blessing be herein! My heart so quakes,
360 My heart is out of skin, hear how it shakes.
 Who makes all this din? How my brow aches!
 To the door will I spin. Hark, fellows, wake!
 Four we were—
 See ye ought of Mak now?
FIRST SHEPHERD.
365 We were up ere thou.
SECOND SHEPHERD.
 Man, I give God a vow,
 That he did not stir.
THIRD SHEPHERD.
 Methought he was lapped in a wolf-skin.
FIRST SHEPHERD.
 So are many wrapped now, namely within.
THIRD SHEPHERD.
370 When we had long napped, methought with a gin°
 A fat sheep he trapped; but he made no din.
SECOND SHEPHERD.
 Be still!
 Thy dream makes thee wood;°
 It is but phantom, by the rood.
FIRST SHEPHERD.
375 Now God turn all to good,
 If it be his will.

[*They awaken Mak.*]

SECOND SHEPHERD.
 Rise, Mak, for shame! Thou liest right long.
MAK.
 Now Christ's holy name be us among.
 What is this? For Saint Jame, I may not go strong.
380 I trust I be the same. Ah, my neck has lain wrong
 Enough.

[*The others help him to his feet.*]

 Many thanks! Since yester-even,
 Now by Saint Steven,
 I was scared by a dream—
385 That makes me full gruff.

 I thought Gill began to croak and travail full sad,
 Well-nigh at the first cock, of a young lad

To add to our flock. Then be I never glad;
I have more of my stock, more than ever I had.
Ah, my head! 390
A house full of young dolts,
The devil cut up their throats!
Woe is him has many colts,
And only little bread.

I must go home, by your leave, to Gill, as I thought. 395
I pray look up my sleeve, that I steal nought:
I am loath you to grieve, or from you take ought.

[*Leaves.*]

THIRD SHEPHERD.
 Go forth, ill may'st thou 'chieve!
 Now would I we sought,
 This morn, 400
 That we had all our store.
FIRST SHEPHERD.
 But I will go before;
 Let us meet.
SECOND SHEPHERD.
 Where?
THIRD SHEPHERD.
 At the crooked thorn. [*They go out.*] 405

[*Mak outside his own door.*]

MAK.
 Undo this door! Who is here? How long shall I stand?
WIFE.
 Who is it that's near? Go walk in the quicksand!
MAK.
 Ah, Gill, what cheer? It is I, Mak, your husband.
WIFE.
 Then may we see here the devil in a band,°
 Sir Guile. 410
 Lo, he comes with a roar,
 As he were chased by a boar!
 I may not work at my chore
 A little while.
MAK.
 Will ye hear what fuss she makes to get her a glose?° 415
 And does naught but shirks, and claws her toes.
WIFE.
 Why, who wanders, who wakes? Who comes, who goes?
 Who brews, who bakes? Who makes us our hose?
 And then
 It is sad to behold— 420
 Now in hot, now in cold,
 Full woeful is the household
 What lacks a woman.

 What end has thou made with the shepherds, Mak?

370 gin trap **373 wood** crazy **409 band** that is, bound up **415 glose** explanation

MAK.

425   The last word that they said when I turned my back
    They would look that they had their sheep, all the pack.
    I think they will not be allayed when they their sheep
        lack,
    Pardie!
    But howso the ball fly,
430   To me they will hie,
    And make a foul cry
    And shout out upon me.
    But thou must do it aright.

WIFE.   I accord me theretil;
    I shall swaddle him right in my cradle.

[Gill puts the sheep in the cradle.]

435   If it were a greater sleight, yet could I help still,
    I will lie down straight. Come wrap me.

MAK.   I will.

[Covers her.]

WIFE.

    Behind!
    Come Coll and his mate,
    They will nip us full straight.

MAK.

440   But I may cry out, "Wait!"
    The sheep if they find.

WIFE.

    Harken well when they call; they will come anon.
    Come and make ready all, and sing all alone;
    Sing "Lullay" thou shall, for I must groan,
445   And cry out by the wall on Mary and John,
    In pain
    Sing "Lullay" so fast
    When thou hearest at last;
    And if I play a false cast,
450   Don't trust me again.

[The shepherds meet at the thorn tree.]

THIRD SHEPHERD.

    Ah, Coll, good morn. Why sleepest thou not?

FIRST SHEPHERD.

    Alas, that ever was I born. We have a foul blot—
    Of a sheep we have been shorn.

THIRD SHEPHERD.   The devil! Say what!

SECOND SHEPHERD.

    Who should do us that scorn?
455   That is a foul plot.

FIRST SHEPHERD.

    Some shrew.
    I have sought with my dogs

    All Horbury bogs,
    And of fifteen hogs°
    Found all but one ewe.   460

THIRD SHEPHERD.

    Now trust me, if ye will—by Saint Thomas of Kent,
    Either Mak or Gill was at that assent.

FIRST SHEPHERD.

    Peace, man, be still. I saw when he went.
    Thou slanderest him ill; thou ought to repent
    With speed.   465

SECOND SHEPHERD.

    Now as ever might thrive I,
    Though I should even here die,
    It were he, I'd reply,
    That did that same deed.

THIRD SHEPHERD.

    Go we thither, let's tread, and run on our feet.   470
    I shall never eat bread, till the truth is complete.

FIRST SHEPHERD.

    No drink in my head, till him I can meet.

SECOND SHEPHERD.

    I will rest in no stead till that I him greet.
    My brother,
    One pledge I will plight: 475
    Till I see him in sight,
    Shall I never sleep one night
    Where I do another.

*[As the shepherds approach Mak's cottage, Mak's Wife be-
gins to groan, and Mak sings a tuneless lullaby.]*

THIRD SHEPHERD.

    Will ye hear how they hack?°
    Our sire can croon.   480

FIRST SHEPHERD.

    Heard I never none crack so clear out of tune.
    Call to him.

SECOND SHEPHERD.

    Mak, undo your door soon!

MAK.

    Who is that spake, as it were noon
    Aloft?   485
    Who is that, I say?

THIRD SHEPHERD.

    Good fellows, were it day!

MAK.

    As much as ye can, *[Opens the door.]*
    Sirs, speak soft,

    Over a sick woman's head that is at malaise;   490
    I had rather be dead than she had any disease.

WIFE.

    Go elsewhere instead. I may not well wheeze;
    Each foot that ye tread makes my nose sneeze.

459 hogs young sheep   **479 hack** split a note

Ah, me!

FIRST SHEPHERD.
495   Tell us, Mak, if ye may,
    How fare ye, I say?

MAK.
    But are ye in this town today?
    Now how fare ye?

    Ye have run in the mire, and are wet yet;
500   I shall make you a fire, if ye will sit.
    A nurse would I hire. Think ye on it?
    Well paid is my hire—my dream, this is it—
    In season. [*Points to the cradle.*]
    I have sons, if ye knew,
505   Well more than a few;
    But we must drink as we brew,
    And that is but reason.

    Ere ye go take some food. Me think that ye sweat.

SECOND SHEPHERD.
    Nay, neither mends our mood, drink nor meat.

MAK.
510   Why, sir, is something not good?

THIRD SHEPHERD.
    Yea, our sheep that we get
    Were stolen as they stood. Our loss is great.

MAK.
    Sirs, drink!
    Had I been there,
515   Some should have felt it full dear.

FIRST SHEPHERD.
    Marry, some men hold that ye were,
    And that's what I think.

SECOND SHEPHERD.
    Mak, some men propose that it were ye.

THIRD SHEPHERD.
    Either ye or your spouse, so say
520   We.

MAK.
    Now, if ye suppose it of Gill or of me—
    Come and search our house, and then may ye see
    Who had it.
    If I any sheep got
525   Either cow or stot°—
    And Gill, my wife, rose not
    And here she lies yet—
    As I am true in zeal, to God here I pray
    That this be the first meal that I shall eat this day.

    [*Points to the cradle.*]

FIRST SHEPHERD.
530   Mak, as have I weal, be careful, I say:
    "He learned early to steal who could not say nay."

[*The shepherds begin to search.*]

WIFE.
    I shake!
    Out, thieves, from our home.
    Ye come to rob us of our own.

MAK.
    Hear ye not how she groans?   535
    Your hearts should break.

[*The shepherds approach the cradle.*]

WIFE.
    Off, thieves, from my son. Nigh him not there.

MAK.
    Know ye how she had done, your hearts would have care.
    Ye do wrong, I you warn, that thus come before
    To a woman that has born—but I say no more.   540

WIFE.
    Ah, my middle!
    I pray to God so mild,
    If ever I you beguiled,
    May I eat this child
    That lies in this cradle.   545

MAK.
    Peace, woman, for God's pain, and cry not so.
    You injure your brain, and make me great woe.

SECOND SHEPHERD.
    I think our sheep be slain. What find ye two?

THIRD SHEPHERD.
    Our work is in vain; we may as well go.
    But hatters!°   550
    I can find no meat,
    Salt nor sweet,
    Nothing to eat—
    But two bare platters.
    Livestock like this, tame or wild, [*Points to cradle.*] 555
    None, as have I bliss, has smelled so vile.

WIFE.
    No, so God me bliss, and give me joy of my child.

FIRST SHEPHERD.
    We have gone amiss; I hold us beguiled.

SECOND SHEPHERD.
    We're done.
    Sir—our Lady him save—   560
    Is your child a knave?°

MAK.
    Any lord might him have,
    This child, as his son.

    When he wakens he grips, such joy it's to see.

THIRD SHEPHERD.
    May heirs spring from his hips, happy he be.   565
    But who were his gossips° so soon ready?

525 stot heifer   **550 hatters** confound it   **561 knave** boy   **566 gossips** godparents

MAK.

Blessings on their lips.

FIRST SHEPHERD.

[*Aside.*] Hark now, a lie!

MAK.

So God them thanks,

570   Parkin, and Gibbon Waller, I say,

And gentle John Horne, in good play—

He made us all gay—

With his great shanks.

SECOND SHEPHERD.

Mak, friends will we be, for we are all one.

MAK.

575   We? No, I'm out for me, for help get I none.

Farewell all three. [*Aside.*] I wish they were gone.

THIRD SHEPHERD.

Fair words may there be, but love is there none

This year.

[*The shepherds leave the cottage.*]

FIRST SHEPHERD.

Gave ye the child anything?

SECOND SHEPHERD.

580   I swear not one farthing.

THIRD SHEPHERD.

Quickly back will I fling;

Abide ye me here. [*He runs back.*]

Mak, take it to no grief if I come to thy son.

MAK.

Nay, thou dost me great mischief, and foul hast thou done.

THIRD SHEPHERD.

585   The child will it not grieve, that daystar one?

Mak, with your leave, let me give your son

But sixpence.

MAK.

Nay, go way! He sleeps.

THIRD SHEPHERD.

Methinks he peeps.

MAK.

590   When he wakens he weeps.

I pray you, go hence!

[*The others return.*]

THIRD SHEPHERD.

Give me leave him to kiss, and lift up the clout.° [*He lifts up the cover.*]

What the devil is this? He has a long snout!

FIRST SHEPHERD.

He is shapèd amiss. Let's not wait about.

SECOND SHEPHERD.

"Ill-spun weft," iwis, "aye comes foul out."°   595

A son! [*Recognizes the sheep.*]

He is like to our sheep!

THIRD SHEPHERD.

How, Gib, may I peep?

FIRST SHEPHERD.

"How nature will creep

Where it cannot run!"   600

SECOND SHEPHERD.

This was a quaint gaud and a far cast;°

It was a high fraud.

THIRD SHEPHERD.

Yea, sirs, was't.

Let's burn this bawd and bind her fast.

A false scold hangs at the last;   605

So shalt thou.

Will ye see how they swaddle

His four feet in the middle?

Saw I never in a cradle

A horned lad ere now.   610

MAK.

Peace, bid I. What! Leave off your care!

I am he that begat, and yond woman him bare.

FIRST SHEPHERD.

How named is your brat? "Mak?" Lo, God, Mak's heir.

SECOND SHEPHERD.

Let be all that. Now God curse his fare,

This boy.   615

WIFE.

A pretty child is he

As sits on a woman's knee;

A dillydown, pardie,

To give a man joy.

THIRD SHEPHERD.

I know him by the ear-mark; that is a good token.   620

MAK.

I tell you, sirs, hark!—his nose was broken.

I was told by a clerk a spell had been spoken.

FIRST SHEPHERD.

This is a false work; my vengeance is woken.

Get weapon!

WIFE.

He was taken by an elf,   625

I saw it myself;

When the clock struck twelve

Was he misshapen.

SECOND SHEPHERD.

Ye two are most deft, but we're not misled.

FIRST SHEPHERD.

Since they stand by their theft, let's see them both dead.   630

---

592 clout cloth

595 "Ill-spun . . . out" "An ill-spun weft," indeed, "comes ever out foul," that is, the deformity of the parents appears in the offspring.

601 quaint . . . cast a clever prank and a sly trick

MAK.
　If I trespass eft,° strike off my head.
　With you will I be left.
THIRD SHEPHERD.　　　　Sirs, let them dread:
　For this trespass
　We will neither curse nor fight,
635　Strike nor smite;
　But hold him tight,
　And cast him in canvas.

[*They toss Mak in a sheet, and return to the field.*]

FIRST SHEPHERD.
　Lord, how I am sore, and ready to burst.
　Faith, I can do no more; therefore will I rest.
SECOND SHEPHERD.
640　As a sheep of seven score Mak weighed in my fist.
　For to sleep anywhere me think that I must.
THIRD SHEPHERD.
　Now I pray you
　Lie on grass yonder.
FIRST SHEPHERD.
　On these thieves I still ponder.
THIRD SHEPHERD.
645　Wherefore should ye wonder?
　Do as I say.

[*They lie down and fall asleep.*]

An Angel sings "Gloria in excelsis," and then says:

ANGEL.
　Rise, herdsmen kind, for now is he born
　Who shall take from the fiend what from Adam was
　　　drawn;
　That warlock° to rend, this night is he born.
650　God is made your friend now at this morn.
　He requests
　To Bethlehem haste
　Where lies that Grace
　In a crib low placed,
655　Betwixt two beasts.

[*The Angel withdraws.*]

FIRST SHEPHERD.
　This was the finest voice that ever yet I heard.
　It is a marvel to rejoice, thus to be stirred.
SECOND SHEPHERD.
　Of God's son so bright he spoke the word.
　All the wood in a light methought that he made
660　Appear.

THIRD SHEPHERD.
　He spoke of a bairn
　In Bethlehem born.
FIRST SHEPHERD.
　That betokens yon starn; [*Points to the star.*]
　Let us seek him there.
SECOND SHEPHERD.
　Say, what was his song? Heard ye not how he cracked° it,　665
　Three breves to a long?
THIRD SHEPHERD.
　Yea, marry, he hacked it:
　Was no crotchet wrong, nor nothing that lacked it.
FIRST SHEPHERD.
　For to sing us among, right as he knacked it,
　I can.　　　　　　　　　　　　　　　　　　　670
SECOND SHEPHERD.
　Let see how ye croon!
　Can ye bark at the moon?
THIRD SHEPHERD.
　Hold your tongues! Have done!
FIRST SHEPHERD.
　Hark after, then.

[*He sings.*]

SECOND SHEPHERD.
　To Bethl'em he bade that we be gone;　　　　　675
　I am afraid that we tarry too long.
THIRD SHEPHERD.
　Be merry and not sad—of mirth is our song.
　Now may we be glad and hasten in throng;
　Say not nay.
FIRST SHEPHERD.
　Go we thither quickly,　　　　　　　　　680
　Though we be wet and weary,
　To that child and that lady;
　We must never delay.

[*He begins to sing again.*]

SECOND SHEPHERD.
　The olden prophets bid—let be your din—
　Isaiah and David and more than I min°—　　　685
　With great learning they said that in a virgin
　Should he light and lie, to atone for our sin,
　And slake it,
　Our kindred, from woe;

---

665 In the next few lines the shepherds use technical musical terms in describing the Angel's singing: **cracked,** split a note; **Three breves to a long,** three short notes to one long one; **hacked,** split a note; **crotchet,** a quarter note; **knacked,** trilled.　**685 min** remember

631 eft again　**649 warlock** devil

690   Isaiah said so:
        Ecce virgo
        Concipiet° a child that is naked.
        THIRD SHEPHERD.
        Full glad may we be, and abide that day
        That Glory to see, whom all things obey.
695   Lord, well were me, for once and for aye,
        Might I kneel on my knee, some word for to say
        To that child.
        But the angel said
        In a crib was he laid;
700   He was poorly arrayed,
        So meek and so mild.
        FIRST SHEPHERD.
        Patriarchs that have been, and prophets beforn,
        They desired to have seen this child that is born.
        They are gone full clean—they were forlorn.
705   We shall see him, I ween,° ere it be morn,
        As token.
        When I see him and feel,
        Then know I full well
        It is true as steel
710   That prophets have spoken:
        To so poor as we are that he would appear,
        Find us, and declare by his messenger.
        SECOND SHEPHERD.
        Go we now, let us fare; the place is us near.
        THIRD SHEPHERD.
        I am ready, I swear; go we with cheer
715   To that joy.
        Lord, if thy will be—
        We are simple all three—
        Now grant us that we
        May comfort thy boy.

        [*They enter the stable. The First Shepherd kneels.*]

        FIRST SHEPHERD.
720   Hail, comely and clean! Hail, young child!
        Hail maker, as I mean, of a maiden so mild!
        Thou hast beaten, I ween, the warlock so wild:
        The beguiler of men, now goes he beguiled.
        Lo, he merries!
725   Lo, he laughs, my sweeting!
        A welcome meeting.
        I here give my greeting:
        Have a bob° of cherries.

        [*The Second Shepherd kneels.*]

        SECOND SHEPHERD.
        Hail, sovereign savior, for thou hast us sought!

        Hail, noble child, the flower, who all thing has wrought!   730
        Hail, full of favor, that made all of nought!
        Hail! I kneel and I cower. A bird have I brought
        To my bairn.
        Hail, little tiny mop!°
        Of our creed thou art crop;°   735
        I would drink of thy cup,
        Little day-starn.

        [*The Third Shepherd kneels.*]

        THIRD SHEPHERD.
        Hail, darling dear, full of Godhead!
        I pray thee be near when that I have need!
        Hail, sweet is thy cheer! My heart would bleed   740
        To see thee sit here in so poor weed,°
        With no pennies.
        Hail! Put forth thy hand small.
        I bring thee but a ball:
        Have it and play withal,   745
        And go to the tennis.
        MARY.
        The father of heaven, God omnipotent,
        That made all in seven, his son has he sent.
        My name did he mention; I conceived ere he went.
        I fulfilled God's intention through his might, as he   750
            meant;
        And now is he born.
        He keep you from woe!
        I shall pray him so.
        Tell forth as ye go,
        And mind you this morn.   755
        FIRST SHEPHERD.
        Farewell, lady, so fair to behold,
        With thy child on thy knee.
        SECOND SHEPHERD.
        But he lies full cold.
        Lord, well is me. Now we go, thou behold.
        THIRD SHEPHERD.
        Forsooth, already it seems to be told   760
        Full oft.
        FIRST SHEPHERD.
        What grace we have found.
        SECOND SHEPHERD.
        Come forth; now are we sound.
        THIRD SHEPHERD.
        To sing are we bound—
        Ring it aloft.   [*They go out singing.*] 765

692–3 Ecce . . . concipiet "Behold, a virgin shall conceive." (Isaiah 7.14)   **705 ween** know   **728 bob** bunch   **734 mop** moppet, babe   **735 crop** head   **741 weed** clothing

TOPICS FOR CRITICAL THINKING AND WRITING

The Play on the PAGE

1. The play presents two scenes of nativity. What details bind the two scenes together? Does the first nativity strike you as blasphemous? Does the second nativity seem to you to be tacked on? The view in the nineteenth century, and until fairly recently in the twentieth, was that in *The Second Shepherds' Play* we have an example of a virtually independent comic secular play (the business of the sheep-stealing), which is made acceptable by attaching it to a brief dramatization of Christ's nativity. The commonest scholarly view today, however, is that the comedy is subservient to the sacred theme. (For instance, some critics insist that the anachronisms—such as calling on Jesus even before the birth of Jesus has been announced—serve, during the comic scenes, to focus the audience's attention on the profound religious meaning.) Do you find either of these views convincing? To what degree? What other view can you offer?

2. Exactly why do the shepherds return to Mak's house? Taking into account their motive for returning and the outcome of their return visit, at the risk of being a little heavy-handed, what might one say the moral is for this part of the play? How does such a moral fit with the rest of the play?

3. The medieval punishment for stealing sheep was death, but the shepherds punish Mak only by tossing him in a blanket. Why does the play depart from reality in this respect?

The Play on the STAGE

4. Examine the references to music, chiefly song, with an eye toward seeing how music functions in the play. What sort of music would you use if you were directing the play?

5. After Mak is tossed in a blanket, we hear nothing more about him. If you were directing the play, would you have him go off to his house and watch the rest of the play? Or might you have him sleep on the ground, as the other shepherds do, but remain sleeping, unaware of the good tidings that are granted to the other shepherds? Or should he wake with the others and join them on the journey to Bethlehem? Or can you think of some other staging? Explain your preference.

The Play in PERFORMANCE

In our section introduction to the Medieval Theater we offered a few remarks about the staging of medieval drama, but here we must add some details. First, it should be noted that although scholars have made thorough searches of medieval records and have found many documents of great interest, there is still relatively little firm information about the staging of the plays. For instance, although we know that in some locales—but probably not in all—*pageants* (wheeled playing areas, in today's terminology, *floats*) were used, because we have no contemporary picture of an English pageant, we cannot be sure of what they looked like. We do have early seventeenth-century pictures of Flemish pageants, and they deserve to be considered seriously, but we cannot be confident that the English wagons of two centuries earlier were identical to them. We do not even have any detailed contemporary verbal descriptions of the pageants. The only substantial descriptions of the English pageants are relatively late (late sixteenth century, and later), and they are not very specific. Here is one such description, from 1565: "A pageant, that is to say, a house of wainscot painted and builded on a car with four wheels. A square top to set over the said house." Here is a second description, this one from 1609: "This pageant or carriage was a high place made like a house with two rooms, being open on the top; in the lower room they apparelled themselves, and in the higher room they played; and they stood upon six wheels." These descriptions are something—but not very much, and if (drawing on the Flemish pictures) we start to talk about the elaborate decoration of pageants, the flexibility of multiple heights for playing, and so forth, we are going beyond the hard evidence, at least so far as medieval drama goes.

Similarly, some of the English plays include very interesting stage directions, but there is much uncertainty about how typical they are. Consider, for instance, a stage direction in a medieval play on the Slaughter of the Innocents. According to the gospels of Matthew and Luke, King Herod ordered a massacre of infants in Bethlehem. The stage direction in the play says, "Here Herod rages in the pageant and in the street also." Doubtless the raging actor who played Herod leaped off the pageant, and stormed about among the spectators in the *platea* (the Latin word, translated as *place*, common in stage directions), and then climbed back onto the pageant. But we do not know how typical such an effect was. Some scholars, eager to emphasize the flexibility of the medieval stage and the intimate connection between actors and audience, assume—on very little more evidence than this stage direction—that actors often entered into the audience. So we read, in some discussions of *The Second Shepherds' Play* that when Mak steals the sheep, in order to indicate his journey from the fields to his house he climbs down from one end of the wagon, moves through the *platea*, and then climbs up the other end of the wagon, where he shows the sheep to Gill. Later we perhaps get another journey through the *platea*, when the shepherds go from Mak's house to what used to be the sheepfold but which now represents the manger where Jesus is born. Perhaps—but the text of the play does not specify even one journey through the audience.

In fact, the text does not specify that one end of the wagon represents one locale, the other end another locale. True, it is reasonable to think that the wagon is divided by two sets or *mansions*, one mansion (perhaps indicated by a fence) representing a sheepfold, the other mansion (perhaps indicated by a chair and a cradle) representing Mak's and Gill's house, but we cannot be confident about any of this.

In short, the original text of *The Second Shepherds' Play* does not include any instructions concerning properties or scenery, or any instructions concerning methods of performing. The favored view, but it is only a conjecture, is that a few props (a cradle, chair, and perhaps a table) at one end of the wagon indicated Mak's and Gill's house, and a cradle and chair at the other end indicated the manger where Jesus was born. The space between them and in front of them—the *platea*—would serve for the fields, and for the area covered by Mak's journey.

One further detail about staging should be mentioned: In today's performances, the angel who announces the birth of Jesus usually appears in an elevated place, on the assumption that in medieval times he appeared at the top of a structure on the wagon.

The Shepherds' Play in Spanish, in the New World

The medieval English cycles of miracle plays were part of a European phenomenon; that is, plays on biblical subjects were performed not only in England but in Europe. A Spanish play about the shepherds (*Los Pastores*) who were called to Bethlehem was brought by Spanish Franciscan friars to Mexico, and was performed for Spanish soldiers in what is now Mexico City at a Christmas entertainment, on January 9, 1526. Further, records indicate that in 1538 a Franciscan friar arranged for dramatic performances on the Feast of Corpus Christi, as well as on other feast days. Performed in the Nahuatl language, the plays were part of a far-reaching program to convert the native peoples to Christianity.

Although these dramatic programs were organized by churchmen, they met with opposition from other churchmen. In 1544 or 1545 a bishop denounced and banned dramatic events:

> Y cosas de gran desacato y desvergüenza parece que ante el Santisimo Sacramento vayan los hombres con máscaras y en hábitos de mujeres, danzando y saltando con meneos deshonestos y lascivos, haciendo estruendo, estorbando los cantos de Iglesia, representando profanos triunfos, como el del Dios del Amor . . . .

> [It is a matter of great disrespect and shame that before the Holy Sacrament men should go about with masks and in women's attire, dancing and jumping

about with immodest and lascivious motions, making a racket, disrupting Church singing, performing profane celebrations, like those of the God of Love. . . .]

This translation—like all of the rest of the information contained in this note—comes from Robert Potter's fascinating article, "The Illegal Immigration of Medieval Drama to California," in *Comparative Drama* 27:1 (Spring 1993): 141–58. Potter traces the transplantation, survival (despite opposition from the bishops), and development of *Los Pastores* from Spain to Mexico and then to southern California. Thus, Potter points out that in 1585 we again encounter a prohibition against religious plays, with Nativity plays specifically mentioned—a sure sign that despite earlier bans the plays were being performed. And, as with the English *Second Shepherds' Play*, the Spanish *Los Pastores* included much humorous material that to pious eyes seemed irrelevant and even impious. In fact, the *Pastorela*—a Christmas entertainment developed around a nucleus of the story of the annunciation—

spread into southern California at least as early as the late eighteenth century. One might reasonably think that this Spanish (or, better, Mexican) dramatic form would have died outside of Mexico after the Mexican-American War of 1846–48, when Mexico was forced to give up its claims to vast areas that are now part of the United States, but in fact it survived, especially in isolated villages in New Mexico and southern California. In the first half of the twentieth century anthropologists duly recorded it, with the sense that they were taking note of a dying phenomenon. In fact, however, with the recent increase of immigration from Mexico the *Pastorela* in the United States has gained new life. For instance, in 1975 it was revived by Luis Valdez and El Teatro Campesino (on Valdez, see page 937), first as a puppet show and then as an entertainment with live performers, and it has continued to thrive in California. Valdez has also made a film version. For details, see Robert Potter's article, mentioned earlier in this paragraph.

Anonymous

Everyman was published at least four times between 1508 and 1537. It closely resembles a Dutch play, *Elckerlijc* (i.e., Everyman), first printed in 1495, and although there used to be a good deal of argument as to which play was the original and which was the translation, virtually all scholars now believe that the Dutch play is the original.

■■■■■■■■■■■■■■

COMMENTARY ON *EVERYMAN*

The Middle Ages produced not only the numerous pageants or miracle plays such as *The Second Shepherds' Play* (page 168) that dramatized the spiritual history of the world, from the Creation to Doomsday, but also other forms of drama, notably the **morality play,** of which *Everyman* is the most impressive example in English. The morality play, a drama of ideas, uses allegorical representations—a system of equivalents—to set forth a religious or moral lesson. Thus, in a play called *The Pride of Life* (c. 1400–25), a character called the King of Life is supported by such characters as Strength, Mirth, and Health. His queen, Wisdom, warns him to live virtuously so that he can die well, that is, so that when he dies his soul will be saved. The foolish king, however, sends Mirth to proclaim that he can conquer anyone, even Death. At this point the manuscript breaks off, but we know how the play ended because a prologue tells us that Death kills the king, the king's soul is grasped by fiends, but Our Lady prays to her son for the soul's release.

Because morality plays use abstractions in order to speak about the lives of contemporary individuals, it is easy to think of them as utterly different from miracle plays, which dramatize the lives of specific biblical characters. But both forms, however different they may seem, emerge from the idea that human beings are fallen creatures who can be saved only through God's intervention in human history. Both forms—the one using specific, historical figures, the other using abstractions—seek to convey the essential truth of existence.

A morality play, through its use of abstractions such as Everyman, Goods, and Good Deeds, is about *us*; it seeks to teach us how to live. Here are the first words of the beginning of *Everyman:*

> I pray you all give your audience,
> And hear this matter with reverence,
> By figure a moral play.
> The *Summoning of Everyman* called it is,
> That of our lives and ending shows   5
> How transitory we be all day.
> This matter is wondrous precious,
> But the intent of it is more gracious,
> And sweet to bear away.

The *figure* (line 3) is the particular literary form, in this case "a moral play." The *matter* (7) is the story (Everyman's encounter with Death, and his responses) and the moral doctrine (we are saved by repentance and by God's grace); the *intent* (8) is the purport, the dramatist's hope that we will heed the lesson and live virtuously so that (like Everyman at the end of the play) we may "be crowned" (917) in heaven.

About sixty English morality plays survived, from the late fourteenth century to about 1570. They are not concerned with representing in realistic detail the complexities of human character; rather, they are concerned with representing, through allegory, what life is really about, that is, with representing the spiritual conditions of life. The largest group of moralities dramatizes the conflict between the vices and the virtues for the possession of the human soul, but some illustrate moral texts (for instance, *All for Money*, which is about avarice) or even religious or political controversy, and some, like *Everyman*, are about the coming of death.

Today we are apt to think of allegory as mechanical and lifeless—unless we remember George Orwell's *Animal Farm*, a twentieth-century classic. But to see how dramatically effective allegory can be, let's briefly look at Everyman's first encounter with Death, beginning with line 87. When Death, accosting Everyman, asks if he has forgotten God, Everyman does not offer a direct answer but cagily asks, "Why askest thou?" Death says that God has sent him to Everyman, and—since few of us in the prime of life can believe that our time has come—Everyman responds incredulously, "What! Sent to me?" When Death again says that God has sent him, Everyman asks Death, "What desireth God of me?" Death explains that God wants to clear the account, now, and Everyman very humanly asks for more time: "To give a reckoning longer leisure I crave" (101). When Death presses him, Everyman blusteringly takes another tack: "I know thee not. What messenger art thou?" Death continues to press, Everyman is reduced to asking for pity, and when this fails he tries to bribe Death:

> Yet of my good will I give thee, if thou will be kind;
> Yea, a thousand pound shalt thou have. . . .
>
> (121–22)

We need not continue this examination; our point is the obvious but important one that the characters, though abstractions, are uncannily human. Just as Everyman's first responses to Death move through a believable sequence from denial to the plea for more time and to the attempt to bribe, similarly his spiritual progress, whereby he comes to an acceptance of death, is convincingly charted. He learns that externals (Fellowship, Kindred, Cousin, and Goods) are of no avail, and when he turns to himself, he finds that certain qualities, such as strength and Beauty, also in the end are of no avail. Even Knowledge—spiritual awareness, we might say—leaves him at the grave; only Good Deeds accompanies him on the final steps of his journey to heaven.

Morality plays exerted a profound influence on Renaissance tragic drama. This may at first sound paradoxical, since morality plays are, by virtue of their happy endings—sinners are saved—comic rather than tragic. But in their depiction of vices and virtues in conflict (let's say, material Goods versus Good Deeds)

and in their dramatization of the coming of death they provided traditions that shaped Elizabethan tragedy. For instance, in Christopher Marlowe's *Doctor Faustus* (page 223) two characters called Good Angel and Bad Angel seek to guide the hero. The morality tradition is only a little less obvious in *Macbeth*, where Macbeth is flanked by a virtue and by vice, the saintly King Duncan on one side, and the vicious Lady Macbeth and the witches on the other. Like Faustus (and unlike Everyman), Macbeth makes the wrong choice. In *Othello*, "the divine Desdemona" stands at one side of the hero, and the villainous Iago at the other. King Lear, similarly flanked, yields to his two wicked daughters and rejects the virtuous words of Kent and Cordelia.

Admittedly, the morality play puts little emphasis on the protagonist's earlier folly, but his recognition and remorse and his consequent suffering do reflect the sequence we find in tragedy. After all, the basic plot of *Everyman* concerns Everyman's recognition that he has lived the wrong sort of life. In tragedy, the hero or heroine customarily comes to a recognition of an error. In his discussion of tragedy Aristotle uses the word *anagnorisis* for what in English is commonly called *recognition* or *disclosure*. (See pages 34 and 81.) The tragic figure finds that the customary values by which he or she has lived do not suffice. The familiar world seems to drop away, the supports all collapse, and the central figure is isolated. "My dismal scene I needs must act alone," says Juliet, speaking, we might say, for Oedipus, Antigone, Hamlet, Lear, and a host of other tragic figures. In *Everyman* the sense of isolation is not given the emphasis that it is given in Greek or Elizabethan tragedies, but it is there, notably when Everyman experiences a series of desertions by aspects of the world that he had mistakenly trusted. But, again, *Everyman* has a happy ending; the desertions are subordinated to the loyalty of a few allies in a play that celebrates the salvation of the hero.

EVERYMAN
Anonymous

CHARACTERS

GOD
MESSENGER
DEATH
EVERYMAN
FELLOWSHIP
KINDRED
COUSIN
GOODS
GOOD DEEDS
KNOWLEDGE
CONFESSION

BEAUTY
STRENGTH
DISCRETION
FIVE WITS
ANGEL
DOCTOR

Here Beginneth a Treatise how the High Father of Heaven Sendeth Death to Summon Every Creature to Come and Give Account of their Lives in this World, and is in Manner of a Moral Play.

[*Enter Messenger as a Prologue.*]

MESSENGER.
I pray you all give your audience,
And hear this matter with reverence,
By figure° a moral play.
The *Summoning of Everyman* called it is,
5   That of our lives and ending shows
How transitory we be all day.
This matter is wondrous precious,
But the intent° of it is more gracious,
And sweet to bear away.
10   The story saith: Man, in the beginning
Look well, and take good heed to the ending,
Be you never so gay!
Ye think sin in the beginning full sweet,
Which in the end causeth the soul to weep,
15   When the body lieth in clay.
Here shall you see how Fellowship and Jollity,
Both Strength, Pleasure, and Beauty,
Will fade from thee as flower in May;
For ye shall hear how our Heaven King
20   Calleth Everyman to a general reckoning.
Give audience, and hear what he doth say.   [*Exit.*]

God speaketh.

GOD.
I perceive, here in my majesty,
How that all creatures be to me unkind,°
Living without dread in worldly prosperity.
Of ghostly sight° the people be so blind,   25
Drowned in sin, they know me not for their God.
In worldly riches is all their mind;
They fear not my rightwiseness,° the sharp rod.
My law that I showed, when I for them died,
They forget clean, and shedding of my blood red;   30
I hanged between two, it cannot be denied;
To get them life I suffered° to be dead;
I healed their feet, with thorns hurt was my head.
I could do no more than I did, truly;
And now I see the people do clean forsake me.   35
They use the seven deadly sins° damnable,
As pride, covetise, wrath, and lechery
Now in the world be made commendable;
And thus they leave of angels, the heavenly company.
Every man liveth so after his own pleasure,   40
And yet of their life they be nothing sure.
I see the more that I them forbear
The worse they be from year to year.
All that liveth appaireth° fast;

2–3 matter . . . figure the *matter* is the story and the moral doctrine; the *figure* is the literary form, in this case a play   **8 intent** meaning

22 unkind (1) unnatural (2) ungrateful   **25 ghostly sight** spiritual insight   **28 rightwiseness** righteousness   **32 suffered** allowed **36 seven deadly sins** four are named in the next line; the other three are envy, gluttony, and sloth   **44 appaireth** becomes worse

Cjere begynneth a treatyse how y hye
fader of heuen sendeth dethe to so-
mon euery creature to come and
gyue a counte of theyr lyues in
this worlde/and is in maner
of a morall playe.
✠

This woodcut of Everyman and Death is from the first printed
edition (circa 1530) of the play. Although it does not illustrate an
actual performance of the play—for instance, Death here holds
the lid of a coffin, something not mentioned anywhere in the
text—it may suggest fairly accurately the costume that Everyman
wears before he changes into "a garment of sorrow." For a photograph of a recent production of *Everyman,* see page 15.

45   Therefore I will, in all the haste,
      Have a reckoning of every man's person;
      For, and° I leave the people thus alone
      In their life and wicked tempests,
      Verily they will become much worse than beasts;
50   For now one would by envy another up eat;
      Charity° they do all clean forget.
      I hoped well that every man
      In my glory should make his mansion,
      And thereto I had them all elect.
      But now I see, like traitors deject,   55
      They thank me not for the pleasure that I to them
          meant,
      Nor yet for their being that I them have lent.
      I proffered the people great multitude of mercy,
      And few there be that asketh it heartily.
      They be so cumbered with worldly riches   60
      That needs on them I must do justice,
      On every man living, without fear.
      Where art thou, Death, thou mighty messenger?

      [*Enter Death.*]

DEATH.
      Almighty God, I am here at your will,
      Your commandment to fulfill.   65
GOD.
      Go thou to Everyman,
      And show him, in my name,
      A pilgrimage he must on him take,
      Which he in no wise may escape;
      And that he bring with him a sure reckoning   70
      Without delay or any tarrying.   [*Exit God*]
DEATH.
      Lord, I will in the world go run overall,°
      And cruelly outsearch both great and small.
      Every man will I beset that liveth beastly
      Out of God's laws, and dreadeth not folly.   75
      He that loveth riches I will strike with my dart,
      His sight to blind, and from heaven to depart°—
      Except that alms be his good friend—
      In hell for to dwell, world without end.
      Lo, yonder I see Everyman walking.   80
      Full little he thinketh on my coming;
      His mind is on fleshly lusts and his treasure,
      And great pain it shall cause him to endure
      Before the Lord, Heaven King.

      [*Enter Everyman.*]

      Everyman, stand still! Whither art thou going   85
      Thus gaily? Hast thou thy Maker forget?
EVERYMAN.
      Why askest thou?
      Wouldest thou wit?°
DEATH.
      Yea, sir; I will show you:
      In great haste I am sent to thee   90
      From God out of his majesty.
EVERYMAN.
      What, sent to me?

---

47 and if **51 Charity** love (of God and of one's fellows)   **72 overall** everywhere **77 depart** sunder **88 wit** know

DEATH.

    Yea, certainly.

    Though thou have forget him here,

95   He thinketh on thee in the heavenly sphere,

    As, ere we depart, thou shalt know.

EVERYMAN.

    What desireth God of me?

DEATH.

    That shall I show thee:

    A reckoning he will needs have

100   Without any longer respite.

EVERYMAN.

    To give a reckoning longer leisure I crave;

    This blind° matter troubleth my wit.

DEATH.

    On thee thou must take a long journey;

    Therefore thy book of count° with thee thou bring,

105   For turn again° thou cannot by no way.

    And look thou be sure of thy reckoning,

    For before God thou shalt answer, and show

    Thy many bad deeds, and good but a few;

    How thou hast spent thy life, and in what wise,

110   Before the chief Lord of paradise.

    Have ado that we were in that way,°

    For, wit thou well, thou shalt make none attorney.°

EVERYMAN.

    Full unready I am such reckoning to give.

    I know thee not. What messenger art thou?

DEATH.

115   I am Death, that no man dreadeth,°

    For every man I rest,° and no man spareth;

    For it is God's commandment

    That all to me shall be obedient.

EVERYMAN.

    O Death, thou comest when I had thee least in mind!

120   In thy power it lieth me to save;

    Yet of my good° will I give thee, if thou will be kind;

    Yea, a thousand pound shalt thou have,

    And defer this matter till another day.

DEATH.

    Everyman, it may not be, by no way.

125   I set not by gold, silver, nor riches,

    Ne° by pope, emperor, king, duke, ne princes;

    For, and I would receive gifts great,

    All the world I might get;

    But my custom is clean contrary.

130   I give thee no respite. Come hence, and not tarry.

EVERYMAN.

    Alas, shall I have no longer respite?

    I may say Death giveth no warning!

    To think on thee, it maketh my heart sick,

    For all unready is my book of reckoning.

135   But twelve year and I might have abiding,

    My counting-book I would make so clear

    That my reckoning I should not need to fear.

    Wherefore, Death, I pray thee, for God's mercy,

    Spare me till I be provided of remedy.

DEATH.

140   Thee availeth not to cry, weep, and pray;

    But haste thee lightly° that thou were gone that journey,

    And prove thy friends, if thou can;

    For, wit thou well, the tide° abideth no man,

    And in the world each living creature

145   For Adam's sin must die of nature.°

EVERYMAN.

    Death, if I should this pilgrimage take,

    And my reckoning surely make,

    Show me, for° Saint Charity,

    Should I not come again shortly?

DEATH.

150   No, Everyman; and thou be once there,

    Thou mayst never more come here,

    Trust me verily.

EVERYMAN.

    O gracious God in the high seat celestial,

    Have mercy on me in this most need!

155   Shall I have no company from this vale terrestrial

    Of mine acquaintance, that way me to lead?

DEATH.

    Yea, if any be so hardy

    That would go with thee and bear thee company.

    Hie° thee that thou were gone to God's magnificence,

160   Thy reckoning to give before his presence.

    What, weenest° thou thy life is given thee,

    And thy worldly goods also?

EVERYMAN.

    I had wend° so, verily.

DEATH.

    Nay, nay; it was but lent thee;

165   For as soon as thou art go,

    Another a while shall have it, and then go therefro,°

    Even as thou hast done.

    Everyman, thou art mad! Thou hast thy wits five,

    And here on earth will not amend thy life;

170   For suddenly I do come.

---

102 **blind** obscure   104 **book of count** account book   105 **turn
again** return   111 **Have . . . way** Get ready that we may be on
that road   112 **make none attorney** have no attorney   115 **no
man dreadeth** dreads no man   116 **rest** arrest   121 **good** wealth
126 **Ne** Nor

141 **lightly** quickly   143 **tide** time   145 **of nature** as a natural
thing   148 **for** in the name of   159 **Hie** Hurry   161 **weenest**
think   163 **wend** thought   166 **therefro** from it

EVERYMAN.
> O wretched caitiff,° whither shall I flee,
> That I might scape this endless sorrow?
> Now, gentle Death, spare me till tomorrow,
> That I may amend me
175 > With good advisement.°

DEATH.
> Nay, thereto I will not consent,
> Nor no man will I respite;
> But to the heart suddenly I shall smite
> Without any advisement.
180 > And now out of thy sight I will me hie.
> See thou make thee ready shortly,
> For thou mayst say this is the day
> That no man living may scape away.   [*Exit Death.*]

EVERYMAN.
> Alas, I may well weep with sighs deep!
185 > Now have I no manner of company
> To help me in my journey, and me to keep;
> And also my writing is full unready.
> How shall I do now for to excuse me?
> I would to God I had never be get!°
190 > To my soul a full great profit it had be;
> For now I fear pains huge and great.
> The time passeth. Lord, help, that all wrought!
> For though I mourn it availeth nought.
> The day passeth, and is almost ago.°
195 > I wot° not well what for to do.
> To whom were I best my complaint to make?
> What and I to Fellowship thereof spake,
> And showed him of this sudden chance?
> For in him is all mine affiance;°
200 > We have in the world so many a day
> Be good friends in sport and play.
> I see him yonder certainly.
> I trust that he will bear me company;
> Therefore to him will I speak to ease my sorrow.
205 > Well met, good Fellowship, and good morrow!

Fellowship speaketh.

FELLOWSHIP.
> Everyman, good morrow, by this day!
> Sir, why lookest thou so piteously?
> If any thing be amiss, I pray thee me say,
> That I may help to remedy.

EVERYMAN.
210 > Yea, good Fellowship, yea;
> I am in great jeopardy.

FELLOWSHIP.
> My true friend, show to me your mind;
> I will not forsake thee to my life's end
> In the way of good company.

EVERYMAN.
215 > That was well spoken, and lovingly.

FELLOWSHIP.
> Sir, I must needs know your heaviness;°
> I have pity to see you in any distress.
> If any have you wronged, ye shall revenged be,
> Though I on the ground be slain for thee,
220 > Though that I know before that I should die.

EVERYMAN.
> Verily, Fellowship, gramercy.°

FELLOWSHIP.
> Tush! by thy thanks I set not a straw.
> Show me your grief, and say no more.

EVERYMAN.
> If I my heart should to you break,°
225 > And then you to turn your mind from me,
> And would not me comfort when ye hear me speak,
> Then should I ten times sorrier be.

FELLOWSHIP.
> Sir, I say as I will do, indeed.

EVERYMAN.
> Then be you a good friend at need!
230 > I have found you true here before.

FELLOWSHIP.
> And so ye shall evermore;
> For, in faith, and thou go to hell,
> I will not forsake thee by the way.

EVERYMAN.
> Ye speak like a good friend; I believe you well.
235 > I shall deserve it, and I may.

FELLOWSHIP.
> I speak of no deserving, by this day!
> For he that will say, and nothing do,
> Is not worthy with good company to go;
> Therefore show me the grief of your mind,
240 > As to your friend most loving and kind.

EVERYMAN.
> I shall show you how it is:
> Commanded I am to go a journey—
> A long way, hard and dangerous—
> And give a strait count, without delay,
245 > Before the high Judge, Adonai.°
> Wherefore, I pray you, bear me company,
> As ye have promised, in this journey.

---

171 **wretched caitiff** captive wretch   175 **good advisement** proper reflection   189 **be get** been born   194 **ago** gone by   195 **wot** know   199 **affiance** trust

216 **heaviness** sorrow   221 **gramercy** thanks   224 **break** open   245 **Adonai** a Hebrew name for God; in Christian liturgy, Christ

FELLOWSHIP.
    That is matter indeed. Promise is duty;
    But, and I should take such a voyage on me,
250   I know it well, it should be to my pain.
    Also it maketh me afeard, certain.
    But let us take counsel here as well as we can,
    For your words would fear° a strong man.

EVERYMAN.
    Why, ye said if I had need
255   Ye would me never forsake, quick° ne dead,
    Though it were to hell, truly.

FELLOWSHIP.
    So I said, certainly,
    But such pleasures be set aside, the sooth° to say.
    And also, if we took such a journey,
260   When should we come again?

EVERYMAN.
    Nay, never again, till the day of doom.

FELLOWSHIP.
    In faith, then will not I come there!
    Who hath you these tidings brought?

EVERYMAN.
    Indeed, Death was with me here.

FELLOWSHIP.
265   Now, by God that all hath bought,°
    If Death were the messenger,
    For no man that is living today
    I will not go that loath journey—
    Not for the father that begat me!

EVERYMAN.
270   Ye promised otherwise, pardie.°

FELLOWSHIP.
    I wot well I said so, truly.
    And yet if thou wilt eat, and drink, and make good cheer,
    Or haunt to women the lusty company,°
    I would not forsake you while the day is clear,
275   Trust me verily.

EVERYMAN.
    Yea, thereto ye would be ready!
    To go to mirth, solace, and play,
    Your mind will sooner apply,
    Than to bear me company in my long journey.

FELLOWSHIP.
280   Now, in good faith, I will not that way.
    But and thou will murder, or any man kill,
    In that I will help thee with a good will.

EVERYMAN.
    O, that is a simple advice, indeed.

    Gentle fellow, help me in my necessity!
    We have loved long, and now I need;   285
    And now, gentle Fellowship, remember me.

FELLOWSHIP.
    Whether ye have loved me or no,
    By Saint John, I will not with thee go.

EVERYMAN.
    Yet, I pray thee, take the labor, and do so much for me
    To bring me forward,° for Saint Charity,   290
    And comfort me till I come without the town.

FELLOWSHIP.
    Nay, and thou would give me a new gown,
    I will not a foot with thee go;
    But, and thou had tarried, I would not have left thee so.
    And as now God speed thee in thy journey,   295
    For from thee I will depart as fast as I may.

EVERYMAN.
    Whither away, Fellowship? Will you forsake me?

FELLOWSHIP.
    Yea, by my fay!° To God I betake° thee.

EVERYMAN.
    Farewell, good Fellowship; for thee my heart is sore.
    Adieu for ever! I shall see thee no more.   300

FELLOWSHIP.
    In faith, Everyman, farewell now at the end,
    For you I will remember that parting is mourning.

                                 [Exit Fellowship.]

EVERYMAN.
    Alack! shall we thus depart° indeed—
    Ah, Lady, help!—without any more comfort?
    Lo, Fellowship forsaketh me in my most need.   305
    For help in this world whither shall I resort?
    Fellowship here before with me would merry make,
    And now little sorrow for me doth he take.
    It is said, "In prosperity men friends may find,
    Which in adversity be full unkind."   310
    Now whither for succor shall I flee,
    Sith that° Fellowship hath forsaken me?
    To my kinsmen I will, truly,
    Praying them to help me in my necessity.
    I believe that they will do so,   315
    For "kind° will creep where it may not go."
    I will go say,° for yonder I see them go.
    Where be ye now, my friends and kinsmen?

    [Enter Kindred and Cousin.]

KINDRED.
    Here be we now at your commandment.

---

253 **fear** frighten   255 **quick** alive   258 **sooth** truth   265
bought redeemed   270 **pardie** by God   273 **haunt . . . company**
frequent the delightful company of women

290 **bring me forward** accompany me   298 **fay** faith   303 **depart**
separate   312 **Sith that** Since   316 **kind** kinship, family (the idea
is that blood ties will find a way)   317 **say** try, essay

320   Cousin, I pray you show us your intent
      In any wise, and do not spare.°
COUSIN.
      Yea, Everyman, and to us declare
      If ye be disposed to go any whither;
      For, wit you well, we will live and die together.
KINDRED.
325   In wealth and woe we will with you hold,
      For over his kin a man may be bold.°
EVERYMAN.
      Gramercy, my friends and kinsmen kind.
      Now shall I show you the grief of my mind:
      I was commanded by a messenger,
330   That is a high king's chief officer;
      He bade me go a pilgrimage, to my pain,
      And I know well I shall never come again;
      Also I must give a reckoning strait,
      For I have a great enemy° that hath me in wait,
335   Which intendeth me for to hinder.
KINDRED.
      What account is that which ye must render?
      That would I know.
EVERYMAN.
      Of all my works I must show
      How I have lived and my days spent;
340   Also of ill deeds that I have used°
      In my time sith life was me lent;
      And of all virtues that I have refused.
      Therefore, I pray you, go thither with me
      To help to make mine account, for Saint Charity.
COUSIN.
345   What, to go thither? Is that the matter?
      Nay, Everyman, I had leifer fast° bread and water
      All this five year and more.
EVERYMAN.
      Alas, that ever I was bore!°
      For now shall I never be merry,
350   If that you forsake me.
KINDRED.
      Ah, sir, what, ye be a merry man!
      Take good heart to you, and make no moan.
      But one thing I warn you, by Saint Anne—
      As for me, ye shall go alone.
EVERYMAN.
355   My Cousin, will you not with me go?
COUSIN.
      No, by Our Lady! I have the cramp in my toe.
      Trust not to me, for, so God me speed,°
      I will deceive you in your most need.

KINDRED.
      It availeth not us to tice.°
      Ye shall have my maid with all my heart;   360
      She loveth to go to feasts, there to be nice,°
      And to dance, and abroad to start.°
      I will give her leave to help you in that journey,
      If that you and she may agree.
EVERYMAN.
      Now show me the very effect of your mind: 365
      Will you go with me, or abide behind?
KINDRED.
      Abide behind? Yea, that will I, and I may!
      Therefore farewell till another day.   [*Exit Kindred.*]
EVERYMAN.
      How should I be merry or glad?
      For fair promises men to me make,   370
      But when I have most need they me forsake.
      I am deceived; that maketh me sad.
COUSIN.
      Cousin Everyman, farewell now,
      For verily I will not go with you.
      Also of mine own an unready reckoning   375
      I have to account; therefore I make tarrying.
      Now God keep thee, for now I go.   [*Exit Cousin.*]
EVERYMAN.
      Ah, Jesus, is all come hereto?°
      Lo, fair words maketh fools fain;°
      They promise, and nothing will do certain.   380
      My kinsmen promised me faithfully
      For to abide with me steadfastly;
      And now fast away do they flee.
      Even so Fellowship promised me.
      What friend were best me of to provide?°   385
      I lose my time here longer to abide.
      Yet in my mind a thing there is;
      All my life I have loved riches;
      If that my Good° now help me might,
      He would make my heart full light.   390
      I will speak to him in this distress.
      Where art thou, my Goods and riches?
GOODS.
      [*Within.*] Who calleth me? Everyman? What! hast thou
            haste?
      I lie here in corners, trussed and piled so high,
      And in chests I am locked so fast,   395
      Also sacked in bags. Thou mayst see with thine eye
      I cannot stir; in packs low I lie.
      What would ye have? Lightly me say.

---

321 spare hold back   **326 over his kin . . . hold** a man may command his kinsmen   **334 enemy** that is, the Devil   **340 used** practiced   **344 leifer fast** would rather have nothing but   **348 bore** born   **357 so God me speed** so may God cause me to prosper

359 tice entice   **361 nice** wanton   **362 abroad to start** go gadding about   **378 hereto** to this   **379 fain** glad   **385 of me to provide** to provide me with   **389 Good** wealth

EVERYMAN.
　　Come hither, Good, in all the haste thou may,
400　For of counsel I must desire thee.

　　[Enter Goods.]

GOODS.
　　Sir, and ye in the world have sorrow or adversity,
　　That can I help you to remedy shortly.
EVERYMAN.
　　It is another disease that grieveth me;
　　In this world it is not, I tell thee so.
405　I am sent for another way to go,
　　To give a strait count general
　　Before the highest Jupiter of all;
　　And all my life I have had joy and pleasure in thee,
　　Therefore, I pray thee, go with me;
410　For, peradventure, thou mayst before God Almighty
　　My reckoning help to clean and purify;
　　For it is said ever among°
　　That "money maketh all right that is wrong."
GOODS.
　　Nay, Everyman, I sing another song.
415　I follow no man in such voyages;
　　For, and I went with thee,
　　Thou shouldst fare much the worse for me;
　　For because on me thou did set thy mind,
　　Thy reckoning I have made blotted and blind,
420　That thine account thou cannot make truly—
　　And that hast thou for the love of me.
EVERYMAN.
　　That would grieve me full sore,
　　When I should come to that fearful answer.
　　Up, let us go thither together.
GOODS.
425　Nay, not so! I am too brittle, I may not endure.
　　I will follow no man one foot, be ye sure.
EVERYMAN.
　　Alas, I have thee loved, and had great pleasure
　　All my life-days on good and treasure.
GOODS.
　　That is to thy damnation, without lesing,°
430　For my love is contrary to the love everlasting.
　　But if thou had me loved moderately during,
　　As to the poor to give part of me,
　　Then shouldst thou not in this dolor be,
　　Nor in this great sorrow and care.
EVERYMAN.
435　Lo, now was I deceived ere I was ware,
　　And all I may wite° misspending of time.

GOODS.
　　What, weenest thou that I am thine?
EVERYMAN.
　　I had wend so.
GOODS.
　　Nay, Everyman, I say no.
　　As for a while I was lent thee;　　　　　　　　　440
　　A season thou hast had me in prosperity.
　　My condition is man's soul to kill;
　　If I save one, a thousand I do spill.°
　　Weenest thou that I will follow thee?
　　Nay, not from this world, verily.　　　　　　　445
EVERYMAN.
　　I had wend otherwise.
GOODS.
　　Therefore to thy soul Good is a thief;
　　For when thou art dead, this is my guise°—
　　Another to deceive in this same wise
　　As I have done thee, and all to his soul's reprief.°　450
EVERYMAN.
　　O false Good, cursed may thou be,
　　Thou traitor to God, that hast deceived me
　　And caught me in thy snare!
GOODS.
　　Mary!° thou brought thyself in care,
　　Whereof I am right glad;　　　　　　　　　　455
　　I must needs laugh, I cannot be sad.
EVERYMAN.
　　Ah, Good, thou hast had long my heartly° love;
　　I gave thee that which should be the Lord's above.
　　But wilt thou not go with me indeed?
　　I pray thee truth to say.　　　　　　　　　　460
GOODS.
　　No, so God me speed!
　　Therefore farewell, and have good day.　　[Exit Goods.]
EVERYMAN.
　　O, to whom shall I make my moan
　　For to go with me in that heavy journey?
　　First Fellowship said he would with me gone—　465
　　His words were very pleasant and gay,
　　But afterward he left me alone.
　　Then spake I to my kinsmen, all in despair,
　　And also they gave me words fair—
　　They lacked no fair speaking,　　　　　　　　470
　　But all forsook me in the ending.
　　Then went I to my Goods, that I loved best,
　　In hope to have comfort, but there had I least;
　　For my Goods sharply did me tell
　　That he bringeth many into hell.　　　　　　　475

---

412 **ever among** every now and then　429 **lesing** lying　436 **wite** blame on

443 **spill** destroy　448 **guise** custom, practice　450 **reprief** reproof　454 **Mary** By Mary (an expletive)　457 **heartly** hearty

Then of myself I was ashamed,
And so I am worthy to be blamed.
Thus may I well myself hate.
Of whom shall I now counsel take?
480   I think that I shall never speed
Till that I go to my Good Deed.
But, alas, she is so weak
That she can neither go° nor speak.
Yet will I venture on her now.
485   My Good Deeds, where be you?

[*Good Deeds speaks from the ground.*]

GOOD DEEDS.
Here I lie, cold in the ground.
Thy sins hath me sore bound,
That I cannot stir.
EVERYMAN.
O Good Deeds, I stand in fear!
490   I must you pray of counsel,
For help now should come right well.
GOOD DEEDS.
Everyman, I have understanding
That ye be summoned account to make
Before Messias, of Jerusalem King;
495   And you do by me,° that journey with you will I take.
EVERYMAN.
Therefore I come to you, my moan to make.
I pray you that ye will go with me.
GOOD DEEDS.
I would full fain, but I cannot stand, verily.
EVERYMAN.
Why, is there anything on you fall?
GOOD DEEDS.
500   Yea, sir, I may thank you of° all;
If ye had perfectly cheered me,
Your book of count full ready had be.
Look, the books of your works and deeds eke!°
Behold how they lie under the feet
505   To your soul's heaviness.
EVERYMAN.
Our Lord Jesus help me!
For one letter here I cannot see.
GOOD DEEDS.
There is a blind reckoning in time of distress.
EVERYMAN.
Good Deeds, I pray you help me in this need,
510   Or else I am for ever damned indeed;
Therefore help me to make reckoning
Before the Redeemer of all thing,
That King is, and was, and ever shall.

483 go walk   **495 And you do by me** If you do as I advise   **500
of** for   **503 eke** also

GOOD DEEDS.
Everyman, I am sorry of your fall,
And fain would I help you, and I were able.   515
EVERYMAN.
Good Deeds, your counsel I pray you give me.
GOOD DEEDS.
That shall I do verily;
Though that on my feet I may not go,
I have a sister that shall with you also,
Called Knowledge,° which shall with you abide,   520
To help you to make that dreadful reckoning.

[*Enter Knowledge.*]

KNOWLEDGE.
Everyman, I will go with thee, and be thy guide,
In thy most need to go by thy side.
EVERYMAN.
In good condition I am now in every thing,
And am wholly content with this good thing,   525
Thanked be God my creator.
GOOD DEEDS.
And when she hath brought you there
Where thou shalt heal thee of thy smart,°
Then go you with your reckoning and your Good Deeds
together,
For to make you joyful at heart   530
Before the Blessed Trinity.
EVERYMAN.
My Good Deeds, gramercy!
I am well content, certainly,
With your words sweet.
KNOWLEDGE.
Now go we together lovingly   535
To Confession, that cleansing river.
EVERYMAN.
For joy I weep; I would we were there!
But, I pray you give me cognition
Where dwelleth that holy man, Confession?
KNOWLEDGE.
In the House of Salvation: 540
We shall find him in that place,
That shall us comfort, by God's grace.

[*Knowledge leads Everyman to Confession.*]

Lo, this is Confession. Kneel down and ask mercy,
For he is in good conceit° with God Almighty.

520 Knowledge acknowledgement of sin, the first step to contrition (*Knowledge* is not scientific knowledge, but is knowledge of Christianity—the knowledge that tells us we are dependent on God's grace)   **528 smart** pain   **544 good conceit** high esteem

EVERYMAN.

545   O glorious fountain, that all uncleanness doth clarify,
    Wash from me the spots of vice unclean,
    That on me no sin may be seen.
    I come with Knowledge for my redemption,
    Redempt with heart and full contrition;
550   For I am commanded a pilgrimage to take,
    And great accounts before God to make.
    Now I pray you, Shrift,° mother of Salvation,
    Help my Good Deeds for my piteous exclamation.

CONFESSION.

    I know your sorrow well, Everyman.
555   Because with Knowledge ye come to me,
    I will you comfort as well as I can,
    And a precious jewel I will give thee,
    Called penance, voider of adversity;
    Therewith shall your body chastised be,
560   With abstinence and perseverance in God's service.
    Here shall you receive that scourge of me,
    Which is penance strong that ye must endure,
    To remember thy Savior was scourged for thee
    With sharp scourges, and suffered it patiently;
565   So must thou, ere thou scape that painful pilgrimage.
    Knowledge, keep him in this voyage,
    And by that time Good Deeds will be with thee.
    But in any wise be siker° of mercy,
    For your time draweth fast; and° ye will saved be,
570   Ask God mercy, and he will grant truly.
    When with the scourge of penance man doth him° bind,
    The oil of forgiveness then shall he find.

EVERYMAN.

    Thanked be God for his gracious work!
    For now I will my penance begin;
575   This hath rejoiced and lighted my heart,
    Though the knots be painful and hard within.

KNOWLEDGE.

    Everyman, look your penance that ye fulfill,
    What pain that ever it to you be;
    And Knowledge shall give you counsel at will
580   How your account ye shall make clearly.

EVERYMAN.

    O eternal God, O heavenly figure,
    O way of rightwiseness, O goodly vision,
    Which descended down in a virgin pure
    Because he would every man redeem,
585   Which Adam forfeited by his disobedience,
    O blessed Godhead, elect and high divine,
    Forgive my grievous offense;
    Here I cry thee mercy in this presence.
    O ghostly treasure, O ransomer and redeemer,

    Of all the world hope and conductor,°   590
    Mirror of joy, and founder of mercy,
    Which enlumineth heaven and earth thereby,
    Hear my clamorous complaint, though it late be;
    Receive my prayers, unworthy of thy benignity.
    Though I be a sinner most abominable,   595
    Yet let my name be written in Moses' table.
    O Mary, pray to the Maker of all thing,
    Me for to help at my ending,
    And save me from the power of my enemy,
    For Death assaileth me strongly.   600
    And, Lady, that I may by mean of thy prayer
    Of your Son's glory to be partner,
    By the means of his passion, I it crave.
    I beseech you help my soul to save.
    Knowledge, give me the scourge of penance;   605
    My flesh therewith shall give acquittance.°
    I will now begin, if God give me grace.

KNOWLEDGE.

    Everyman, God give you time and space!
    Thus I bequeath you in the hands of our Savior.
    Now may you make your reckoning sure.   610

EVERYMAN.

    In the name of the Holy Trinity,
    My body sore punished shall be.
    Take this, body, for the sin of the flesh! [*Scourges himself.*]
    Also thou delightest to go gay and fresh,
    And in the way of damnation thou did me bring;   615
    Therefore suffer now strokes of punishing.
    Now of penance I will wade the water clear,
    To save me from purgatory, that sharp fire.

[*Good Deeds rises from the floor.*]

GOOD DEEDS.

    I thank God, now I can walk and go,
    And am delivered of my sickness and woe.   620
    Therefore with Everyman I will go, and not spare;
    His good works I will help him to declare.

KNOWLEDGE.

    Now, Everyman, be merry and glad!
    Your Good Deeds cometh now; ye may not be sad.
    Now is your Good Deeds whole and sound,   625
    Going upright upon the ground.

EVERYMAN.

    My heart is light, and shall be evermore;
    Now will I smite faster than I did before.

GOOD DEEDS.

    Everyman, pilgrim, my special friend,
    Blessed be thou without end;   630
    For thee is preparate° the eternal glory.

---

552 Shrift Confession   **568 siker** certain   **569 and** if   **571 him** himself   **590 conductor** guide   **606 acquittance** atonement   **631 preparate** prepared

Ye have me made whole and sound,
Therefore I will bide by thee in every stound.°
EVERYMAN.
    Welcome, my Good Deeds! Now I hear thy voice,
635   I weep for very sweetness of love.
KNOWLEDGE.
    Be no more sad, but ever rejoice;
    God seeth thy living in his throne above.
    Put on this garment to thy behove,°
    Which is wet with your tears,
640   Or else before God you may it miss,
    When ye to your journey's end come shall.
EVERYMAN.
    Gentle Knowledge, what do ye it call?
KNOWLEDGE.
    It is a garment of sorrow;
    From pain it will you borrow;°
645   Contrition it is,
    That getteth forgiveness;
    It pleaseth God passing well.
GOOD DEEDS.
    Everyman, will you wear it for your heal?
EVERYMAN.
    Now blessed be Jesu, Mary's Son,
650   For now have I on true contrition.
    And let us go now without tarrying.
    Good Deeds, have we clear our reckoning?
GOOD DEEDS.
    Yea, indeed, I have here.
EVERYMAN.
    Then I trust we need not fear.
655   Now, friends, let us not part in twain.
KNOWLEDGE.
    Nay, Everyman, that will we not, certain.
GOOD DEEDS.
    Yet must thou lead with thee
    Three persons of great might.
EVERYMAN.
    Who should they be?
GOOD DEEDS.
660   Discretion and Strength they hight,°
    And thy Beauty may not abide behind.
KNOWLEDGE.
    Also ye must call to mind
    Your Five Wits° as for your counselors.
GOOD DEEDS.
    You must have them ready at all hours.

EVERYMAN.
    How shall I get them hither?   665
KNOWLEDGE.
    You must call them all together,
    And they will hear you incontinent.°
EVERYMAN.
    My friends, come hither and be present,
    Discretion, Strength, my Five Wits, and Beauty.

[*Enter Beauty, Strength, Discretion, and Five Wits.*]

BEAUTY.
    Here at your will we be all ready.   670
    What will ye that we should do?
GOOD DEEDS.
    That ye would with Everyman go,
    And help him in his pilgrimage.
    Advise you, will ye with him or not in that voyage?
STRENGTH.
    We will bring him all thither,   675
    To his help and comfort, ye may believe me.
DISCRETION.
    So will we go with him all together.
EVERYMAN.
    Almighty God, loved may thou be!
    I give thee laud that I have hither brought
    Strength, Discretion, Beauty, and Five Wits. Lack I   680
        nought.
    And my Good Deeds, with Knowledge clear,
    All be in my company at my will here.
    I desire no more to° my business.
STRENGTH.
    And I, Strength, will by you stand in distress,
    Though thou would in battle fight on the ground.   685
FIVE WITS.
    And though it were through the world round,
    We will not depart for sweet ne sour.
BEAUTY.
    No more will I unto death's hour,
    Whatsoever thereof befall.
DISCRETION.
    Everyman, advise you° first of all;   690
    Go with a good advisement and deliberation.
    We all give you virtuous monition°
    That all shall be well.
EVERYMAN.
    My friends, harken what I will tell:
    I pray God reward you in his heavenly sphere.   695
    Now harken, all that be here,
    For I will make my testament
    Here before you all present:

---

633 stound moment (i.e., in every fierce attack) **638 behove** benefit **644 borrow** redeem **660 hight** are called **663 Five Wits** five physical senses (they are Everyman's "counselors" because they provide him with sensory data on which Discretion, that is, reason, operates)

667 incontinent immediately **683 to** for **690 advise you** consider the matter **692 monition** admonition

In alms half my good I will give with my hands twain
700 In the way of charity with good intent,
And the other half still shall remain
In queth,° to be returned there° it ought to be.
This I do in despite of the fiend of hell,
705 To go quite out of his peril
Ever after and this day.

KNOWLEDGE.

Everyman, harken what I say:
Go to Priesthood, I you advise,
And receive of him in any wise
The holy sacrament and ointment together.
710 Then shortly see ye turn again hither;
We will all abide you here.

FIVE WITS.

Yea, Everyman, hie you that ye ready were.
There is no emperor, king, duke, ne baron,
That of God hath commission
715 As hath the least priest in the world being;°
For of the blessed sacraments pure and benign
He bareth the keys, and thereof hath the cure°
For man's redemption—it is ever sure—
Which God for our soul's medicine
720 Gave us out of his heart with great pain
Here in this transitory life, for thee and me.
The blessed sacraments seven there be:
Baptism, confirmation, with priesthood good,
And the sacrament of God's precious flesh and blood,
725 Marriage, the holy extreme unction, and penance.
These seven be good to have in remembrance,
Gracious sacraments of high divinity.

EVERYMAN.

Fain would I receive that holy body,
And meekly to my ghostly° father I will go.

FIVE WITS.

730 Everyman, that is the best that ye can do.
God will you to salvation bring,
For priesthood exceedeth all other thing:
To us Holy Scripture they do teach,
And converteth man from sin heaven to reach;
735 God hath to them more power given
Than to any angel that is in heaven.
With five words° he may consecrate,
God's body in flesh and blood to make,
And handleth his Maker between his hands.
740 The priest bindeth and unbindeth all bands,
Both in earth and in heaven.

Thou ministers° all the sacraments seven;
Though we kissed thy feet, thou were worthy;
Thou art surgeon that cureth sin deadly;
No remedy we find under God   745
But all only° priesthood.
Everyman, God gave priests that dignity,
And setteth them in his stead among us to be.
Thus be they above angels in degree.

[*Exit Everyman to receive the last sacraments
from the priest.*]

KNOWLEDGE.

If priests be good, it is so,° surely.   750
But when Jesus hanged on the cross with great smart,
There he gave out of his blessed heart
The same sacrament in great torment.
He sold them not to us, that Lord omnipotent.
Therefore Saint Peter the apostle doth say   755
That Jesu's curse hath all they
Which God their Savior do buy or sell,
Or they for any money do take or tell.°
Sinful priests giveth the sinners example bad;
Their children sitteth by other men's fires, I have heard;   760
And some haunteth women's company
With unclean life, as lusts of lechery:
These be with sin made blind.

FIVE WITS.

I trust to God no such may we find.
Therefore let us priesthood honor,   765
And follow their doctrine for our souls' succor.
We be their sheep, and they shepherds be,
By whom we all be kept in surety.
Peace, for yonder I see Everyman come,
Which hath made true satisfaction.   770

GOOD DEEDS.

Methink it is he indeed.

[*Re-enter Everyman.*]

EVERYMAN.

Now Jesu be your alder speed!°
I have received the sacrament for my redemption,
And then mine extreme unction.
Blessed be all they that counseled me to take it!   775
And now, friends, let us go without longer respite;
I thank God that ye have tarried so long.
Now set each of you on this rod° your hand,
And shortly follow me.
I go before there° I would be; God be our guide!   780

702 queth bequest   there where   715 being living   717 cure
charge, spiritual responsibility (with a pun on medical healing, indicated in 719)   729 ghostly spiritual   737 five words Hoc est
enim corpus meum (For this is my body), from the sacrament of the
Eucharist

742 ministers administers   746 only except   750 it is so that
is, "above angels in degree"   758 tell count   772 Now Jesu . . .
speed Now may Jesus let you all prosper   778 rod cross   780
there where

STRENGTH.
Everyman, we will not from you go
Till ye have done this voyage long.

DISCRETION.
I, Discretion, will bide by you also.

KNOWLEDGE.
And though this pilgrimage be never so strong,°
785 I will never part you fro.

STRENGTH.
Everyman, I will be as sure by thee
As ever I did by Judas Maccabee.°

[They go together to the grave.]

EVERYMAN.
Alas, I am so faint I may not stand;
My limbs under me doth fold.
790 Friends, let us not turn again to this land,
Not for all the world's gold;
For into this cave must I creep
And turn to earth, and there to sleep.

BEAUTY.
What, into this grave? Alas!

EVERYMAN.
795 Yea, there shall ye consume, more and less.°

BEAUTY.
And what, should I smother here?

EVERYMAN.
Yea, by my faith, and never more appear.
In this world live no more we shall,
But in heaven before the highest Lord of all.

BEAUTY.
800 I cross out all this! Adieu, by Saint John!
I take my cap in my lap, and am gone.

EVERYMAN.
What, Beauty, whither will ye?

BEAUTY.
Peace, I am deaf; I look not behind me,
Not and thou wouldest give me all the gold in thy chest.

[Exit Beauty.]

EVERYMAN.
805 Alas, whereto may I trust?
Beauty goeth fast away from me;
She promised with me to live and die.

STRENGTH.
Everyman, I will thee also forsake and deny;
Thy game liketh° me not at all.

EVERYMAN.
810 Why, then, ye will forsake me all?
Sweet Strength, tarry a little space.

STRENGTH.
Nay, sir, by the rood of grace!
I will hie me from thee fast,
Though thou weep till they heart to-brast.°

EVERYMAN.
Ye would ever bide by me, ye said. 815

STRENGTH.
Yea, I have you far enough conveyed.
Ye be old enough, I understand,
Your pilgrimage to take on hand;
I repent me that I hither came.

EVERYMAN.
Strength, you to displease I am to blame; 820
Yet promise is debt, this ye well wot.

STRENGTH.
In faith, I care not.
Thou are but a fool to complain;
You spend your speech and waste your brain.
Go, thrust thee into the ground!   [Exit Strength.] 825

EVERYMAN.
I had wend surer I should you have found.
He that trusteth in his Strength
She him deceiveth at the length.
Both Strength and Beauty forsaketh me;
Yet they promised me fair and lovingly. 830

DISCRETION.
Everyman, I will after Strength be gone;
As for me, I will leave you alone.

EVERYMAN.
Why, Discretion, will ye forsake me?

DISCRETION.
Yea, in faith, I will go from thee,
For when Strength goeth before 835
I follow after evermore.

EVERYMAN.
Yet, I pray thee, for the love of the Trinity,
Look in my grave once piteously.

DISCRETION.
Nay, so nigh will I not come;
Farewell, everyone!   [Exit Discretion.] 840

EVERYMAN.
O, all thing faileth, save God alone—
Beauty, Strength, and Discretion;
For when Death bloweth his blast,
They all run from me full fast.

FIVE WITS.
Everyman, my leave now of thee I take; 845
I will follow the other, for here I thee forsake.

EVERYMAN.
Alas, then may I wail and weep,
For I took you for my best friend.

784 strong hard   **787 Judas Maccabee** Judas Maccabeus, ancient
Jewish leader noted for his military exploits   **795 more and less**
high and low, that is, people of all ranks   **809 liketh** pleases

814 to-brast burst to pieces

FIVE WITS.
I will no longer thee keep;
850   Now farewell, and there an end.   [*Exit Five Wits.*]
EVERYMAN.
O Jesu, help! All hath forsaken me.
GOOD DEEDS.
Nay, Everyman; I will bide with thee.
I will not forsake thee indeed;
Thou shalt find me a good friend at need.
EVERYMAN.
855   Gramercy, Good Deeds! Now may I true friends see.
They have forsaken me, every one;
I loved them better than my Good Deeds alone.
Knowledge, will ye forsake me also?
KNOWLEDGE.
Yea, Everyman, when ye to Death shall go;
860   But not yet, for no manner of danger.
EVERYMAN.
Gramercy, Knowledge, with all my heart.
KNOWLEDGE.
Nay, yet I will not from hence depart
Till I see where ye shall be come.
EVERYMAN.
Methink, alas, that I must be gone
865   To make my reckoning and my debts pay,
For I see my time is nigh spent away.
Take example, all ye that this do hear or see,
How they that I loved best do forsake me,
Except my Good Deeds that bideth truly.
GOOD DEEDS.
870   All earthly things is but vanity:
Beauty, Strength, and Discretion do man forsake,
Foolish friends, and kinsmen, that fair spake—
All fleeth save Good Deeds, and that am I.
EVERYMAN.
Have mercy on me, God most mighty;
875   And stand by me, thou mother and maid, Holy Mary.
GOOD DEEDS.
Fear not; I will speak for thee.
EVERYMAN.
Here I cry God mercy.
GOOD DEEDS.
Short° our end, and minish° our pain;
Let us go and never come again.
EVERYMAN.
880   Into thy hands, Lord, my soul I commend;
Receive it, Lord, that it be not lost.
As thou me boughtest, so me defend,
And save me from the fiend's boast,
That I may appear with that blessed host
885   That shall be saved at the day of doom.

878 Short Shorten   minish diminish

In manus tuas, of might's most
For ever, *commendo spiritum meum.*°

    [*Everyman and Good Deeds descend into the grave.*]

KNOWLEDGE.
Now hath he suffered that we all shall endure;
The Good Deeds shall make all sure.
Now hath he made ending.   890
Methinketh that I hear angels sing,
And make great joy and melody
Where Everyman's soul received shall be.

[*Enter Angel.*]

ANGEL.
Come, excellent elect spouse, to Jesu!
Here above thou shalt go   895
Because of thy singular virtue.
Now the soul is taken the body fro,
Thy reckoning is crystal clear.
Now shalt thou in to the heavenly sphere,
Unto the which all ye shall come   900
That liveth well before the day of doom.

    [*Exit Knowledge.*]

Enter Doctor [*of Theology*]

DOCTOR.
This moral men may have in mind.
Ye hearers, take it of worth,° old and young,
And forsake Pride, for he deceiveth you in the end;
And remember Beauty, Five Wits, Strength, and Discre-   905
    tion,
They all at the last do every man forsake,
Save° his Good Deeds there doth he take.
But beware, and they be small
Before God, he hath no help at all;
None excuse may be there for every man.   910
Alas, how shall he do then?
For after death amends may no man make,
For then mercy and pity doth him forsake.
If his reckoning be not clear when he doth come,
God will say: "*Ite, maledicti, in ignem eternum.*"°   915
And he that hath his account whole and sound,
High in heaven he shall be crowned;
Unto which place God bring us all thither,
That we may live body and soul together.
Thereto help the Trinity!   920
Amen, say ye, for Saint Charity.   [*Exit Doctor.*]

THUS ENDETH THIS MORAL PLAY OF *Everyman.*

886–87 In manus . . . meum "Into thy hands I commit my spirit";
Christ's last words, according to Luke 23.46   903 take it of worth
value it   907 Save Only   915 Ite . . . eternum "Depart from me,
ye cursed, into everlasting fire" (Christ's words in Matthew 25.41)

TOPICS FOR CRITICAL THINKING AND WRITING

The Play on the PAGE

1. The Messenger's speech at the beginning of *Everyman* announces the theme and suggests the gist of the plot. Do you think that by giving this information the speech diminishes the possibility of suspense, and thereby weakens the play? Explain.

2. In the play, Death is an abstraction, of course, but what characteristics does the author give him?

The Play on the STAGE

3. If you were producing *Everyman*, how would you costume Death? As a skeleton, wearing a cloak? As a businessperson in a three-piece suit? Or what? Do you think a woman can perform the role effectively? Explain.

4. Take one of the abstractions other than Death and Everyman and examine the degree to which it is made concrete and interesting. Suggest appropriate stage business for several speeches of this character. And how would you costume him or her? Do you assume that certain roles should necessarily be played by a male (e.g., Strength) and certain roles by a woman (e.g., Beauty)? (Note that in line 828 strength is spoken of as "she.") Or can we disregard the sex of the actor? Explain.

5. If you were staging the play would you use the same actor for the Messenger (who opens the play) and the Doctor (who closes it), in the same costume? Why, or why not?

6. Lines 707–49, on the powers of the priesthood, are sometimes deleted from modern productions. What arguments can you offer, pro or con?

The Play in PERFORMANCE

Because *Everyman* was printed four times early in the sixteenth century, we can infer that it probably was performed as well as read, but we do not have a single reference to a performance before William Poel's revival in 1901, which we will discuss later. We do not know, therefore, if it was performed outdoors, perhaps on some sort of booth-and-trestle stage, or indoors, in a castle, court, or school. Probably it was performed under a variety of circumstances, sometimes perhaps by students, sometimes by amateurs or semiprofessional actors—let's say a group of talented part-time actors who took their local productions to neighboring towns—but all of this is only conjecture. What we do know is that the required stage properties are few (perhaps a cross, and a chair or two), that with some doubling of roles it can be done by a cast of seven, and that from about 1400 there were indeed small touring companies of actors. The trouble is, we do not know which plays these companies performed; the records that prove their existence are for the most part records of payments for "a play" or payments to "players of interludes."

In *Everyman*, we have no hard evidence concerning the methods of production; in fact, we have only four stage directions in the entire play: "God speketh," after line 21; "Dethe" (i.e., "enter Death"), after line 63; "Euery Man" (i.e., "enter Everyman"), after 86 (but we place it a bit earlier), and "Felawshyp speketh," after 205. We must examine the text, then, with an eye toward what *might* have been done, but with the understanding that we cannot speak with certainty.

Costumes

The first character to speak is a Messenger. Perhaps he wore some sort of garb that identified him as such, but nothing is specified. The next character to speak is God. We know, from a few medieval records of performances, that in miracle plays God was distinctively costumed. One document speaks of "five sheep-skins for God's coat," and another, concerning a late (1565) production of *Creation of Eve and Expulsion from Eden,* calls for "A face [i.e., a mask] and hair [a wig] for the Father." Perhaps, then, in *Everyman* God wore a mask and a wig. In any case, because in his very first line God refers to his "majesty," probably he is dressed as a king or emperor. If today we wish to stage *Everyman* in a way that might resemble its original staging, we can easily find pictures of monarchs. On the other hand, although in the Middle Ages troupes did not hesitate to use actors to impersonate God, some modern directors prefer to keep God offstage, and to represent him only by his voice. Similarly, although we are told nothing about the appearance of the angel who speaks in line 894, he probably was represented much as angels appear in medieval paintings—winged, white-robed, with gold hair. And, again, some modern directors prefer to have the angel heard but not seen.

God calls on Death. What does Death look like? In the Middle Ages Death was often depicted as a skeleton, sometimes holding a scythe (the Grim Reaper), or holding an hourglass (to symbolize the passage of time), or holding a dart (to strike down his prey), or holding a coffin-lid. It happens that in his first speech in *Everyman,* Death actually mentions his dart (line 76), and in line 178 he says he will "smite" Everyman to the heart, but the dart is never again mentioned, so Death probably did not carry a dart in sixteenth-century productions. The illustration in one of the earliest editions of the play shows Death carrying a board for a coffin (see page 185), but the play makes no reference to such a prop, so again we can assume it probably was not used. In fact, since Everyman does not at first recognize Death, perhaps Death is *not* immediately identifiable by his costume or by a hand prop; perhaps he is identifiable only when, saying "I am Death that no man dredeth" (i.e., "I am Death, who dreads no man"), he removes a hood or cloak and reveals a skull or skeleton. In short, we can offer ideas, but we cannot say with any certainty what Death looked like in *Everyman.*

Similarly, we cannot say for sure what the various personified abstractions, such as Kindred and Good Deeds, looked like, though we can guess that Goods held a money bag or a money box, and Beauty doubtless was beautiful. Finally, the Doctor at the end of the play presumably wore an academic robe, indicating that he was a learned man.

Looking further at the text, still with an eye toward the costumes, we find that Death asks Everyman, "Whither are thou going / Thus gaily?" (85–86). From this line we may infer that Everyman is dressed in some sort of colorful, fashionably tailored apparel. In line 638, when Everyman is in "the House of Salvation," Knowledge says to him, "Put on this garment," and a few lines later Knowledge explains that it is "a garment of sorrow." Here, most likely, Everyman changes from his worldly garments to some sort of austere garment, thus *visibly* communicating the change in his spiritual condition.

Scenery and Locales

But what is this "House of Salvation" (540) where Confession dwells? It stands for the Church, but how was it represented on the stage? We do not know. Possibly a cross, or a cross and a chair would be enough, but possibly there was some further indication of a house, for instance a framework covered with canvas. We know that in other plays painted or constructed scenery was used to represent such things as "the city of Jerusalem, with towers and pinnacles," "a prison," and "a fiery cloud." Perhaps to help represent the House of Salvation, God stood there, or even sat atop it.

If the staging of the House of Salvation is uncertain, so too is the staging of other locales. It seems reasonable to assume that, at the beginning of the play, God appears on some sort of elevated structure, indicating heaven, and that most of the action takes place beneath him. God's "I perceive" and his repeated "I see" add to the likelihood that he is aloft, looking down on his creation. Possibly from a lofty position he watches the entire action; possibly, however, he joins Everyman in the House of Salvation; or possibly we see God only at the start of the play. It is even possible, as we have already said, that we do not see him but only hear his voice. Let's assume, however, that at least at the start God stands or sits above the other players: The audience sees two realms, the spiritual and the earthly. When Everyman dies, does he descend into a lower realm? Consider these lines:

> For into this cave must I creep / And turn to earth (792–93)

> What, into this grave? (794)

> Look in my grave once piteously (838)

Good Deeds says he will go with Everyman, and the editors of this text have added a stage direction, "Everyman and Good Deeds descend into the grave." We have added this direction (887) because the text strongly suggests that they descend through a trapdoor, but possibly they simply walk offstage, that is, disappear behind a curtain or screen.

Before looking briefly at the play's stage history, we want to mention one other conjectural bit of staging, and our comments may strike readers as extremely eccentric. Many medieval illustrations show, just above a dying man's head, Mary holding—receiving—a small, naked figure. This figure represents the soul of the dying man, which has escaped from the gesticulating devils at the bottom of the illustration. Now, such pictures illustrate what all morality plays are essentially about, the salvation of the repentant soul. And the happy ending, in art, is almost always shown by a depiction of the soul, symbolized by an infant, in the arms of Mary, or in heaven. And so, when at the end of the play Knowledge says that he hears angels sing (891), and the angel says, "Come, excellent spouse, to Jesu" (894), it is possible or (we think) even probable that the audience heard music and actually saw a representation of Everyman's soul rise out of the grave and go to the angel, presumably in an elevated place.

Stage History

Solid information about *Everyman* on the stage begins in 1901, with a production by William Poel, an Englishman who founded the Elizabethan Stage Society. Poel tried to stage early plays in the way that (he thought) they were originally staged. He therefore rejected the elaborate sets, with realistic scenery, common in the Victorian period. The late nineteenth-century use of illusionistic sets—trees that looked like trees, rooms with substantial walls, and so forth—had two consequences: (1) Intermissions were introduced, so that the sets could be changed, and (2) the original sequence of scenes was altered, in an effort to reduce the number of changes. For instance, two forest scenes that had been separated by, say, a scene in court were run together. Poel assumed that early plays should be performed without cuts, without transpositions of scenes, and without interruptions. The stage thus was kept relatively bare, with a few props brought on as needed.

On July 13, 1901, Poel produced *Everyman*. He wanted to stage it in the cloisters of Westminster Abbey, but he had been turned down, and turned down again when he had asked for permission to use Canterbury Cathedral. He then settled for the Master's Court (an old gray quadrangle) of the Charterhouse, a former monastery but in Poel's day a home for the aged. Poel played God (Adonai), and a famous actress, Edith Wynne Mathison, played Everyman, the idea being that a woman's voice would make an effective contrast against the male voices of God and Death. Death, a skeleton, carried a drum. Otherwise the costumes were derived chiefly from Flemish tapestries of the fifteenth century, and from the two woodcuts that appear in some copies of the earliest editions of *Everyman* (see illustration page 185).

Poel's staging involved two levels, an upper level (a battlement) for God, and a main level, for the rest of the action. His production was very popular, and Poel staged it elsewhere in England and also in Scotland and Ireland. His company also played in America, where it opened in New York on October 13, 1902. It toured the United States, and in fact the British company returned again and again, with changes in the cast, of course, until the 1930s.

Poel's *Everyman* engendered a more famous version, *Jedermann* (Everyman), a German version produced by Max Reinhardt. Reinhardt saw Poel's production, and commissioned the German writer Hugo von Hofmannsthal to write a version of the play. Hofmannsthal complied, and his *Jedermann* achieved fame, especially in its annual productions at the Salzburg Festival (1920 to the present, except for 1937–45), where it was staged in front of the cathedral.

Everyman is occasionally performed by students and by religious groups. It requires only a fairly small company (the actors who play Fellowship, Kindred, Cousin, and Goods usually double as Discretion, Strength, Five Wits, and Beauty), and only a few props, for instance a scourge, and perhaps some money bags or a money box for Goods. Most productions today are performed either within a church or against the façade of a church, thereby borrowing a religious background, though for outdoor staging almost any stone building seems to provide an adequate background. When the play is staged, directors often use artificial light to reveal the characters to whom Everyman appeals for help, and then cause them to disappear with a blackout. Costumes tend to be either medieval or contemporary. Sometimes masks are used for the various abstractions (e.g., Goods, Beauty, Strength) to whom Everyman turns for help, but the mouth-openings have to be almost grotesquely large to make sure that the speeches can be heard, and, in any case, amateurs usually find masks uncomfortable.

JOHN ASTINGTON
Everyman *in Toronto*

In 1979 John Astington staged *Everyman* in Toronto. Music was incorporated at two points in the play—at Everyman's entrance (treated as a kind of dance, accompanied by a dance-song played on a recorder by a seated actor) and, second, during Knowledge's final speech (the Antiphon from the Office of the Dead, sung by the Angel).

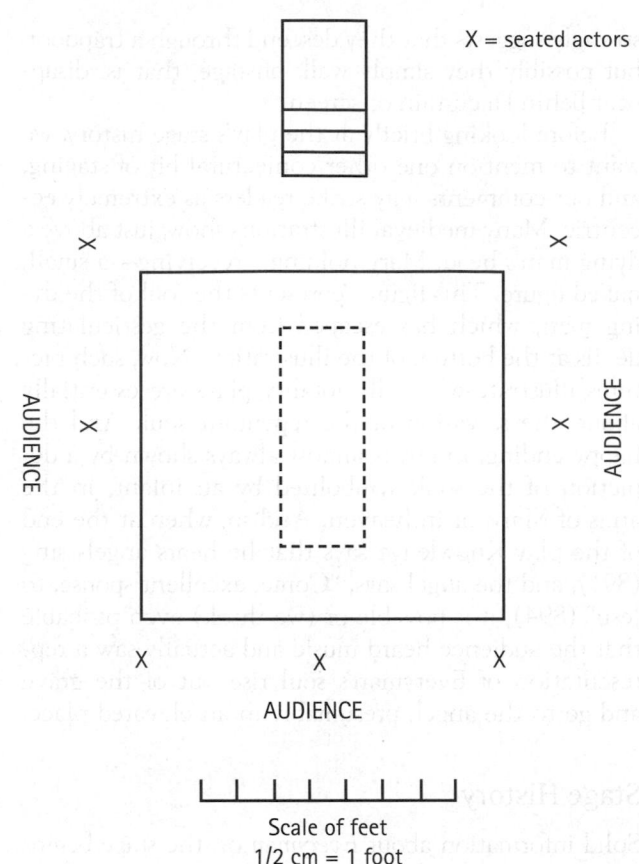

A plain modern style was chosen for this production. The play was acted in three-quarter round, on and around a simple wooden platform ten feet square and eighteen inches high. The stage had a central hinged trap, with crawl spaces to gain access to it from below. A small square platform three feet in height, with steps down to floor level, represented both heaven and the house of salvation. General area lighting illuminated the audience and acting area, with the stage slightly brighter, lit by spotlights.

The generally austere, spare style of the production was intended to place stress on the action and words of the play. The doubling of parts, and the presence of the actors before and after they appeared on the stage as specific characters were intended to stimulate the imaginative involvement of the audience with the play, by limiting the fiction that the actors "were" the characters they played.

The actors were dressed alike in plain modern clothes in dark colours, predominantly black: cloth shoes, trousers, and leotard tops or T-shirts. The actresses playing Good Deeds and Knowledge wore long skirts. The only other items of costume were the robe of contrition, a simple, full-length, sleeveless gown, and two long, coloured sashes, one red and one gold, which were used at Everyman's entrance to symbolise his rich clothing. Death carried a staff, one end of which was sharpened and the other surmounted by a hooded skull.

The actors entered together before the start of the play and sat in a ring on the floor, facing inward towards the stage, where they remained throughout the play when they were not on stage. Entrances were made from these positions, and exits simply required the actor to move to his or her place and sit. Staging of particular passages conformed to the general style dictated by this approach. God was not revealed, but the actor simply rose and took a standing position on the platform as the Messenger ended his speech, extending his arms as he began to speak. After the command to Death, the actor unobtrusively dropped his pose and returned to his place. The entry of Everyman was made into a tableau: to a dance tune Everyman was teasingly pulled around the edge of the stage by two companions, who wrapped and entangled him in long, coloured sashes. At Death's summons this dance abruptly stopped, the companions fled, and the cloth sashes dropped to the ground around Everyman's feet. The trap was not used for the entry of Death, but was opened by Everyman himself as he searched for Goods, and thereafter remained open. Goods was played primarily by one actress, who crawled into the trap from below, but the opening lines were split up among four other actors, who crept and rolled into positions roughly at the four corners of the stage. Goods thus became multiple, as his name suggests: he spoke from many places and with different voices, and the laughter at the end of the scene could build and echo as the actors rolled and staggered back to their positions. During the activity of the opening of this scene the actress playing Good Deeds could slip under the edge of the stage unnoticed, to be ready for her entrance. There was a deliberate visual contrast between the two entrances from the trap.

The play was managed with seven actors rather than eight by having the actor playing Discretion, who had already played Confession, simply leave the group around Everyman after l. 705 and mount the higher platform to become Priesthood. The extreme unction was played with Everyman kneeling on the steps; once Everyman returned to the central platform, about l. 775, Priesthood moved down to resume his role as Discretion. Beauty was played by a man; it is Everyman's beauty, after all, and though the character is referred to as 'she,' so is Strength (l. 828). The line that does indicate a female dress and occupation, 'I take my cap in my lap and am gone,' is fairly obscure to a modern audience.

The journey of the soul to heaven (l. 894 ff) was not staged; the Angel spoke towards the grave into which Everyman had sunk. The Angel remained in position, and Knowledge remained kneeling at the head of the grave as the Doctor delivered the final speech.

A deliberate effect of the visual austerity of the production was that properties had a strong visual emphasis. The book particularly was made into a central property. The Messenger carried it as he came on to the stage, and left it lying there, whence it was picked up by Death, and subsequently delivered to Everyman. Everyman tried to rid himself of it by throwing it at Death's feet on l. 113; it was roughly thrust back at him on l. 130. Thereafter it always lay in view on the stage, liable to catch Everyman's eye as he looked about him, and was picked up to be shown to Kindred, and then to Good Deeds, who took it from him and carried it until he required it to recite his testament. He then laid it at the foot of the grave, where it remained until the entrance of the Doctor, who picked it up and carried it during his final speech.

Noh stage

1. *butai* (main stage)
2. *wakiza* (side stage)
3. *atoza* (rear stage)
4. *hashigakari* (bridge)
5. *kagami no ma* ("mirror" room)
6. strip of pebbles
7. first pine
8. second pine
9. third pine
10. two pine trees upstage of bridge
11. *kagamiita* ("mirror" board, acoustic)
12. *kirido* (sliding door)
13. *kizahashi* (three steps)
14. *kyōgen-bashira* (comedian's pillar)
15. *shité-bashira* (principal actor's pillar)
16. *metsuke-bashira* ("eye-fixing" pillar)
17. *waki-bashira* (subordinate actor's pillar)
18. *fue-bashira* ("flute" pillar)
19. curtain

A few of the terms need explanation:

5 *kagami no ma* ("mirror" room): The dressing room is connected to the main stage by a bridge; major characters enter the stage from the mirror room, whereas subordinate characters, musicians, and stage attendants enter the stage from the door marked **12**, upstage left.

14 *kyōgen-bashira* (comedian's pillar): If a comic actor appears in the interlude of a serious play, he sits at this pillar, upstage where the bridge and the rear stage join.

15, 16 *shité-bashira* (principal actor's pillar) and *metsuki bashira* ("eye-fixing" pillar): After entering the stage from the bridge, the principal actor (*shité*) stops at the principal actor's pillar (**15**), upstage right, and announces his name and from where he comes. Because his mask impedes his vision, he gets his bearings by facing the "eye-fixing pillar" (**16**), downstage right.

17 *waki-bashira* (subordinate actor's pillar): The *waki* (subordinate actor) sits at this pillar, downstage left, during much of the play.

18 *fue-bashira* ("flute" pillar): The pillar (upstage left) where the flute player sits.

Anonymous

Who wrote *Dōjōji*—and when? Early scholarship attributed the play to Kannami (1333–1384), the father of Noh. But later scholars have attributed the play to Kanze Kojiro Nobumitsu (1457–1518), the last important Noh dramatist. Still other scholars believe that in its present form *Dōjōji* cannot predate the sixteenth century. As Japanese scholar Donald Keene writes in his introduction to *20 Plays of the Nô Theatre*, "The difficulties confronting the would-be critic of Nô are enormous. Not a single play is dated, . . . some plays can be dated only by century, and others seem to have been rewritten so often that the establishment of a single date of composition would be impossible" (p. 3). And questions of authorship are just as perplexing: Early scholars attributed more than half of the current Noh repertoire to Zeami (1363–1443), the son of Kannami. But recent scholarship has reduced considerably the number of plays Zeami probably wrote. Undoubtedly, Zeami adapted works by his father and other early playwrights to fit his theater's needs. We can assume, however, that the main outlines of a piece—indeed much of its poetry—stayed the same. This was most probably true of *Dōjōji*, whoever wrote it.

■■■■■■■■■■■■■■

COMMENTARY ON *DOJOJI*

Noh and Ritual

Of all existing theater traditions, the 600-year-old Japanese classical theater called *Noh* (literally, skill, craft, talent) is perhaps the most remote to a Western audience. In almost every respect it confounds our popular notions of what theater should be. Austere, static, and slow, it is an art of exquisite subtlety foreign to our impulses toward action and realism. It demolishes the boundaries between drama, dance, and music—between text and performance. Its actors move ethereally through a fixed theatrical universe intoning strange strangulated cries interspersed with sporadic percussive thumpings by onstage musicians. It is like witnessing an unfamiliar religious ritual whose exoticism is mystifying but riveting.

Noh's uncompromising purity, its closeness to ritual, its non-naturalistic aesthetic have bred a fascination among twentieth-century Western artists (from W.B. Yeats and Gordon Craig to Robert Wilson and Peter Brook) dissatisfied with the constraints of realism and the marketplace. There is a yearning to connect with the metaphysical values Noh embodies: the power of spirituality, the acceptance of life's impermanence and fragility. And to learn from Noh's aesthetic means: the disregard of ordinary concepts of space and time, the distancing of character through performance style and conventions (like masks), and the inseparability of language and gesture.

Noh seems to offer a mythic key because of the unbroken continuity of its dramatic and theatrical tradi-

tion. What wouldn't we give to *really* know how Greek and Elizabethan plays were specifically staged in their original theater spaces? Most of Western performance tradition has been lost by historical disruption. But geographically isolated Japan has been able to sustain a continuous theater tradition for over a millennium despite bloody political upheavals because of deeply ingrained values of order and hierarchy and the capacity to assimilate rather than be engulfed by outside cultures. Noh theater represents, then, a window to the past the likes of which we do not possess—a continuous, centuries-old heritage that is still very much alive.

This is not to claim that contemporary Noh performances (which, of course, we rarely see) exactly recreate the conventions of the fourteenth century—no such total historical resuscitation is possible. Like all art, Noh evolved from what preceded it, and continued to shape itself in the act of self-definition. Noh evolved out of popular ceremonial dance forms and temple entertainments, particularly *Dengaku*, a dance form rooted in harvest rituals, and *Sarugaku*, a form of mime with origins in earthy interludes designed to break the solemnity of Shinto-inspired dance.

Zeami's Contribution

By 1374—a time (see the introduction to this section, page 165) when the feudal barons (the *daimyos*) had ascended to power—the time was ripe for the emergence of a form of greater complexity than simple entertainments and ceremonies. The powerful Ashikaga shogun Yoshimitsu was so impressed by one skillful *Sarugaku* performer, Kannami, that he invited him and his twelve-year-old son, Zeami, to become part of the Shogun's household. In this new courtly atmosphere, Kannami innovatively embued elements of *Sarugaku* and other theater dance forms with Buddhist ideals to develop an elevated form suited to the Shogun and his retainers. Building on his father's innovations, Zeami deepened and refined the art to its classic maturity. He is simultaneously its greatest dramatist (of the approximately 240 plays in the current Noh repertoire Zeami wrote more than any other playwright) and its great theorist, writing treatises which define Noh's aesthetic goals, treatises that were lost until the beginning of the twentieth century.

It is striking to note that, although he was a playwright, in these treatises Zeami directs his focus primarily toward performance—the actor and the audience—rather than toward dramatic text. In contrast, we may note Aristotle's denigration of "spectacle" as the least important characteristic of tragedy. Although the ritualized Greek theater must have had great affinities to Noh, Aristotle's total lack of interest in "stage machinery" has left us in the dark about Greek theatrical means. The contrasting theories of Aristotle and Zeami encapsulate the essential difference between Western and Asian visions of theater: In the West, for all our performance tradition, the play's the thing; in the East, language is always complementary to mime, gesture, music, and dance. Here is a Balinese saying: "Dancing is not there to be looked at nor music to be listened to; both are only to be seen and heard like trees in a wood."

Zeami stressed that Noh should balance *monomane* (which we could translate as "imitation") with *yugen* (spirit, soul, grace). Some scholars contend that the delicate balance Zeami placed at the heart of Noh was lost when it became an exclusively aristocratic entertainment from which commoners were legally prohibited. At the beginning of the seventeenth century, the Tokagawa shogunate enshrined (and petrified) Noh as court ceremony, *the* official national performing art. The pursuite of *yugen* at the expense of *monomane* banished the often emotional audience reactions of Zeami's time, and performances were attenuated to twice their previous length.

Nonetheless, Noh's essential spirit still derives from the fourteenth and fifteenth centuries. The core dramatic repertoire remains, and we have a direct line back to Zeami's time in the art's unbroken performance tradition, passed on from father to son. Four of the five current schools of Noh leading actors trace their ori-

gins to the period of Noh's emergence. Indeed, nearly half of the 1,500 or so present-day Noh performers belong to the school directly descended from the troupe led by Kannami and Zeami, hence their conflated name, the *Kanze* school. Although Noh lost its official patronage in the Meiji period (1868–1912) when Japan westernized, the performers regrouped, found private sponsors, taught the art to amateurs, and rewon recognition as bearers of a great national tradition.

Noh Today

Noh theater schools, however, are *not* organized on our prized ideal of the ensemble. Noh's impressive artistic synthesis is created paradoxically through solitary specialization; the individual artist trains in one of four schools defined by the categories of roles in Noh performance—including the *shité* (pronounced "sh'tay"—the principal character, or "doer," who may wear the mask of warrior, lady, ghost, or demon), the *waki* (the "side-person" or "the witness," the unmasked player of secondary roles, often priests), the *kyogen* (comic servant) role, and the *hayashikata* (musicians). The haunting, percussive music of Noh—provided by two or three drummers and a flutist—is as crucial as other performance elements, never mere accompaniment. A few days before a performance all artists meet to discuss possible variations within the highly codified form. But they never rehearse collectively, and their coming together on stage for the first time is a highly charged, spontaneous event.

Noh actors are magnificently appareled in richly embroidered silk costumes and masks of painted wood that are themselves art objects, many going back centuries. It is unfortunate that only once (to my knowledge) has the traditional Noh playhouse been reconstructed on a major American tour (in 1987 in the East Wing of the National Gallery of Art in Washington, D.C., as part of a wide-ranging exhibition entitled "Japan: The Shaping of Daimyo Culture 1185–1868.") For the traditional Noh theater, to a Western observer, resembles an Elizabethan playhouse with Japanese temple variations. It has a thrust stage, replete with "heavens." This is an austere but intimate space befitting an austere but intimate art, *not* the huge concert halls Noh troupes are invariably booked into on international concert tours.

All of the performers are men, for Noh preserves what was also true about Greek and Elizabethan theater practice—the prohibition of female performance. The frequent representations of women (usually by the *shité*), however, never attempt female impersonation through falsetto or feminine gait, as was to be the case in *Kabuki,* another (later) form of Japanese theater. The objective is not to play femininity but to express the woman's heart and mind. But as befits their inferior status, the principal women characters in Noh plays are usually loyally subservient or, as in *Dōjōji,* rebelliously demonic. In this play—one of the greatest and most difficult plays in the Noh repertoire—a beautiful dancer, who has wheedled her way onto the forbidden grounds of Dōjōji (i.e., Dōjō temple) the day a new bell is to be dedicated, transforms herself into a vengeful serpentine demon. The demon represents the spirit of a woman carnally spurned by a priest whom she pursued to this temple and incinerated in a bell in which he had hidden himself. The priests of Dōjōji confront the demon, who reemerges from the new bell, and, through prayers and struggle, drive it off.

This cautionary Buddhist legend may indeed be grist for feminist analysis, but the still-powerful play represents the quintessence of Noh performance artistry. So dangerous are its demands that even the greatest *shités* may play it only once or twice in their careers. The bell that is the play's central prop duplicates traditional artistic renderings of the legend; it must be large enough to safely fall over the actor who must then transform himself onstage from dancer to demon. The bell used by the Kanze troupe weighs more than 800 pounds. The moment of its crash and envelopment of the *shité* demands the ultimate in timing, technique, and concentration. I can attest from having witnessed the performance at the National Gallery that it is a thrilling *coup de théâtre* second to none.

Noh arose in a turbulent, violent era that took solace from a disciplined, distilled form suffused with Buddhist spiritual concerns about the deceptions of the flesh, the sin of killing, the troubled spirits of the dead, the transcience of life. That it thrived in more peaceful times and survived Japan's rage to modernize in the nineteenth century reveals the timelessness of its vision. For us in the West, its unbroken traditions embody what we have lost: an authentic stylistic encounter with past ritual and myth, a world in which ghosts, gods, and demons are as palpable as the performers before us.

DOJOJI
Anonymous

Translated by Donald Keene

LIST OF CHARACTERS

THE ABBOTT OF DOJOJI (*waki* ["side-person," i.e., subordinate actor])
TWO PRIESTS OF THE TEMPLE (*wakizure* [companions of the *waki*])
TWO TEMPLE SERVANTS (*kyōgen* [menials])
A DANCER (*mae-jite* ["before-shité," i.e., the shité or "doer" in the first part of a two-part play])
THE SERPENT DEMON (*nochi-jite* ["after-shité," i.e., the transformed shité or "doer" in the second part])

PLACE

Dōjōji, a temple in Kii Province

TIME

The third month

(*As the opening flute is played the Abbot, the Two Priests, and the First Servant enter. The Priests and the Servant kneel on the bridgeway, but the Abbot continues on to the stage.*)

ABBOT. I am the abbot of Dōjōji, a temple in the Province of Kii. For many years no bell has hung in the belfry tower of the temple, and for a good reason. I have decided lately to restore the ancient custom and at my order a new bell has been cast. In the calendar today is a day of good omen. I have ordered that the bell be raised into the tower and that there be a service of dedication.

(*He calls towards the bridgeway.*)

Servant!

FIRST SERVANT. Here I am, sir.

ABBOT. Today is marked in the calendar as a lucky day, and I want you to hoist the bell into the belfry.

FIRST SERVANT. Yes, certainly, sir.

(*As the Servant stands the two Priests enter the stage from the bridgeway and sit at the waki-position[1] behind the waki. The Servant leaves the bridgeway but returns shortly with another Servant. They carry between them on bamboo poles the prop, a huge bell. Two stage assistants help them.*)

FIRST SERVANT. *Ei tō, ei tō.*
SECOND SERVANT. *Ei ya, ei ya.*
FIRST SERVANT. *Ei tō, ei tō.*
SECOND SERVANT. *Ei ya, ei ya.*

(*Groaning under the strain, they lower the bell halfway down the bridgeway.*)

[1]**the waki position** the *waki*, or "side-person" (subordinate actor), customarily sits near a pillar at front stage left when he is not part of the action. See position 17 in the picture on page 202.

FIRST SERVANT. Let's rest a while.
SECOND SERVANT. A good idea.
FIRST SERVANT. It's certainly a heavy bell.
SECOND SERVANT. Amazingly heavy.
FIRST SERVANT. Well, shall we lift it again?
SECOND SERVANT. All right.

(*They lift the bell again.*)

FIRST SERVANT. *Ei tō, ei tō.*
SECOND SERVANT. *Ei ya, ei ya.*
FIRST SERVANT. *Ei tō, ei tō.*
SECOND SERVANT. *Ei ya, ei ya.*

(*They reach the middle of the stage.*)

FIRST SERVANT. Let's put it down right here.
SECOND SERVANT. Right you are.
FIRST SERVANT. Everything under control?
SECOND SERVANT. Everything's going fine.

(*With appropriate cries they set the bell down.*)

FIRST SERVANT. Now for hoisting it into the belfry.
SECOND SERVANT. Right you are.

(*The two Servants, helped by the stage assistants, use poles to thread the rope of the prop through the ring set in the ceiling. Then, with rhythmic shouts they hoist the prop to the appropriate height.*)

FIRST SERVANT. It looks more impressive than ever, now that we've hoisted it up there.
SECOND SERVANT. That's right. It's certainly an impressive sight.

The standing figure at the right is a temple servant. He is warning the principal actor (*the shité*) who wears the mask of a woman in her twenties, not to enter the temple grounds. In the Noh drama, all of the performers are male.

FIRST SERVANT. Let's waste no time in telling the Abbot about this.

(*The First Servant goes before the gazing-pillar and addresses the Abbot.*)

FIRST SERVANT. Excuse me, sir. We've raised the bell into the belfry.

ABBOT. You've raised it, you say?

FIRST SERVANT. Yes, that's just what I said, sir.

ABBOT. Then we will hold the dedication service today. For certain reasons best known to me, women are not to be admitted to the couryard where the ceremonies are held. Make sure that everyone understands this.

FIRST SERVANT. Your orders shall be obeyed.

(*He goes to the naming-place where he addresses people off-stage.*)

Listen, you people! The new bell of the Dōjōji is to be dedicated today. All who wish to attend the ceremony are welcome. However, for reasons known only to himself, the Abbot has ordered that women are not to be allowed inside the courtyard where the service will take place. Take care you all obey his orders!

(*He goes to kneel before the flute player. The Dancer enters. She wears the* fukai *mask,[2] a long wig, a brocade outer robe, an inner kimono with a fish-scale pattern, and* a crested garment tied around her waist. She stands at the shité-position[3] and faces the area before the musicians.)

DANCER. My sin, my guilt, will melt away,
My sin, my guilt, will melt away,
I will go to the service for the bell.

(*She faces forward*).

I am a dancer who lives in a remote village of this Province of Kii. I have heard that a bell is to be dedicated at the Dōjōji, and so I am hurrying there now, in the hopes of improving my chances of salvation.
The moon will soon be sinking;
As I pass the groves of little pines
The rising tide weaves veils of mist around them.
But look—can it be my heart's impatience?—

(*She takes a few steps to the right, then returns to her original position. This indicates she has reached the temple.*)

Dusk has not yet fallen, the sun's still high,
But I have already arrived:
I am here at the Temple of Dōjōji.

(*She faces forward.*)

My journey has been swift, and no I have reached the temple. I shall go at once to watch the ceremony.

(*She moves toward the center of the stage. The First Servant rises.*)

---

[2]**fukai mask** the mask of a middle-aged woman: thin eyebrows, hair parted in center, heavy eyelids to indicate unhappiness, unsmiling mouth

[3]**shité position** the position where the *shité*, or "doer" (chief role) stands, at a pillar near the rear, stage right. See position 15, page 202.

FIRST SERVANT. Stop! You can't go into the courtyard. Women aren't allowed.

DANCER But I'm not like other women. I'm only a dancer. I live nearby and I am to perform a dance at the dedication of the bell. Please let me see the ceremony.

FIRST SERVANT (*to himself*). A dancer? That's right, I suppose she doesn't count as an ordinary woman. (*to Dancer*) Very well, I'll let you into the courtyard on my own, but in return you must dance for me. (*He goes before flute player, picks up a tall court cap lying on the stage, and brings it to the Dancer.*) Here, take this hat.[4] It just happened to be around. Put it on and let's see you dance.

DANCER. With pleasure. I'll dance for you as best I can.

(*She retires to stage assistant's position to alter her costume. The Servant returns to his original place and sits. The Dancer puts on the hat and goes to the first pine on the bridgeway. She looks beyond the pillar at the bell, then glides onto the stage to the suddenly stepped-up tempo of large drum. She stops just past the* shité-*pillar.*)

DANCER. How happy you have made me! I will dance for you. (*She describes her actions.*) Borrowing for a moment a courtier's hat, she puts it on her head.
Her feet already stamp the rhythm.
Apart from cherry blossoms,
There are only the pines,
Apart from cherry blossoms,
There are only the pines.
When the darkness starts to fall
The temple bell will resound.

(*She lifts the hem of her robe a little with her left hand, and dances the following passage as if she were climbing step by step up to the bell. This is the famous* rambyōshi[5] *dance, accompanied by the weird cries and pounding of the* kotsuzumi *drum.*)

Prince Michinari, at the imperial command,
First raised these sacred walls.
And because the temple was his work,
Tachibana no Michinari,
They called it Dōjōji.[6]

(*The rhythm of the dance grows more rapid and intense.*)

CHORUS (*for the Dancer*).
   To a temple in the mountains
   Now, on this evening in spring,

[4]**hat** Professional dancers wore a tall hat when they danced.
[5]**rambyoshi dance** The drummer utters a call, the dancer bends at the waist, lifts and turns a leg, and stamps at a drum beat. The dancer moves on the stage in triangular patterns, matching the triangles on the costume, which represent a serpent's scales.
[6]**Dōjōji** The name *Michinari* is pronounced in Sino-Japanese reading as Dojo. *Dōjōji* would therefore mean the "temple of Michinari" (translator's note).

I have come, I have seen

CHORUS.
   The blossoms scattered with the evening bell,
   The blossoms scatter, the blossoms fall.

DANCER.
   And all the while,
   And all the while,
   At temples everywhere across the land
   The sinking moon strikes the bell.
   The birds sing, and frost and snow fills the sky;
   Soon the swelling tide will recede.
   The peaceful fishers will show their lights
   In villages along the river banks—
   And if the watchers sleep when danger threatens
   I'll not let my chances pass me by!

(*The Servants have become hypnotized by the rhythm of the dance. The Dancer looks at the Abbot and the Priests. The Chrous describes her actions.*)

CHORUS.
   Up the bell she stealthily creeps
   Pretending to go on with her dance.

(*She holds her fan and looks at the bell.*)

She starts to strike it!

(*She swings the fan back and forth like a bell-hammer.*)

This loathsome bell, now I remember it!

(*She unfastens the cord of her hat, then strikes the hat from her hand with a blow of her fan. She stands under the bell.*)

Placing her hand on the dragon-head boss,[7]
She seems to fly upward into the bell.
She wraps the bell around her,
She has disappeared.

(*At the words, "Placing her hand," the Dancer rests her hand on the edge of the bell, then leaps up into it. At the same moment the stage assistant loosens the rope and drops the bell over her. The Servants, who have been drowsing, hypnotized by the dance, wake up, startled by the noise of the bell falling. The First Servant tumbles in confusion on the stage; the Second Servant falls on the bridgeway.*)

BOTH SERVANTS (*variously*). Ho! Hi! What was that frightful noise? That awful crashing racket? I'm so frightened I don't know what I'm doing!

FIRST SERVANT. That certainly was a terrible crash. I wonder where the other fellow went. (*He sees the Second Servant.*) Hey there, are you all right?

[7]**dragon-head boss** ornamental dragon-head on the bell

SECOND SERVANT. How about you?

FIRST SERVANT. I still don't know yet.

SECOND SERVANT. No wonder. We got so carried away by her dance we dozed off. Then came that awful bang. What do you think that was?

FIRST SERVANT. Do you suppose it was thunder? If it was thunder, there should have been some sort of warning—a little clap or two before the big one. Strange, very strange.

SECOND SERVANT. Yes, you're right. Whatever it was, the earth shook something terrible.

FIRST SERVANT. I don't think it was an earthquake. Look— come over here. (*He discovers the bell and claps his hands in recognition.*) Here's what made the noise.

SECOND SERVANT. You're right!

FIRST SERVANT. I hung it up very carefully, but the loop must've snapped. How else could it fall?

SECOND SERVANT. No. Look. The loop's all right. Nothing's broken. It's certainly a mystery. (*He touches the bell.*) Oww! This bell is scorching hot!

FIRST SERVANT. Why should falling make it hot? (*He too touches the bell.*) Oww! Boiling hot!

SECOND SERVANT. It's a problem, all right. What do you suppose it can mean? It's beyond me. Well, we'd better report what's happened. We can't leave things this way.

FIRST SERVANT. That's a good idea. Too bad if the Abbot heard about it from anyone but us! We've got to do something. But I don't think I should be the one to tell. You tell him.

SECOND SERVANT. Telling him is no problem, but it would look peculiar if I went. You tell him—you were left in charge.

FIRST SERVANT. That's what makes it so hard! You tell him, please.

(*He pushes the Second Servant forward.*)

SECOND SERVANT. No, it's not my business to tell him. *You* tell him. Hurry! (*He pushes the First Servant.*)

FIRST SERVANT. Please, I beg of you, as a favor. You tell him.

SECOND SERVANT. Why should I? You tell him. I don't know anything about it. (*The Second Servant leaves. The First Servant watches him go.*)

FIRST SERVANT. He's gone! Now I have no choice. I'll have to tell the Abbot, and it's going to get me into trouble. Well, I'll get it over with. (*He goes up to the Abbot.*) It fell down.

ABBOT. What fell down?

FIRST SERVANT. The bell. It fell from the belfry.

ABBOT. What? Our bell? From the belfry?

FIRST SERVANT. Yes, Master.

ABBOT. What caused it?

FIRST SERVANT. I fastened it very carefully, but all the same it fell down. Ah! That reminds me. There was a dancer here a little while ago. She said she lives nearby and asked me to let her into the courtyard to see the dedication of the bell. Of course I told her that it wasn't allowed, but she said she wasn't an ordinary woman, and

that she was going to offer a dance. So I let her in. I wonder if she had something to do with this?

ABBOT. You idiot! What a stupid thing to do! I knew this would happen. That's why I forbade you strictly to allow any women in here! You blundering fool!

FIRST SERVANT. Ahhhh. (*He bows to the ground.*)

ABBOT. I suppose I must go now and take a look.

FIRST SERVANT. Yes, Master. Please hurry. Help! Help! (*He exits, still crying for help.*)

ABBOT (*to the Priests*). Priests, come with me. (*They stand and go to the bell.*) Do you know why I gave the order that no woman was to be permitted to enter the temple during the dedication of the bell?

PRIEST. No, Master. We have no idea.

ABBOT. Then I will tell you.

PRIESTS. Yes, please tell us the whole story.

ABBOT. Many years ago there lived in this region a man who was the steward of the manor of Manago, and he had an only daughter. In those days too there was a certain *yamabushi*[8] priest who came here every year from the northern provinces on his way to worship at the shrine of Kumano, and he would always stay with this same steward. The priest never forgot to bring charming little presents for the steward's daughter, and the steward, who doted on the girl, as a joke once told her, "Some day that priest will be your husband, and you will be his wife!" In her childish innocence the girl thought he was speaking the truth, and for months and years she waited.

Time passed and once again the priest came to the landlord's house. Late one night, after everyone else was asleep, the girl went to his bedroom and chided him: "Do you intend to leave me here forever? Claim me soon as your wife."

Amazed to hear these words, the priest turned the girl away with a joking answer. That night he crept out into the darkness and came to this temple, imploring us to hide him. But having nowhere else we could hide him, we lowered the bell and hid him inside. Soon the girl followed, swearing she would never let him go. At that time the River Hitaka was swollen to a furious flood and the girl could not cross over. She ran up and down the bank, wild with rage, until at last her jealous fury turned her into a venomous snake, and she easily swam across the river.

The serpent glided here, to the Temple of Dōjōji, and searched here and there until her suspicions were aroused by the lowered bell. Taking the metal loop between her teeth, she coiled herself around the bell in seven coils. Then, breathing smoke and flames, she lashed the bell

[8]*yamabushi* literally, "one who lies in the mountains," a name given to ascetics who practiced austerities in the mountains in order to gain holy powers

with her tail. At once the bronze grew hot, boiling hot, and the monk, hidden inside, was roasted alive. (*to the Priests*) Isn't that a horrible story?

PRIEST. Unspeakable! The worst I have ever heard!

ABBOT. I have felt her jealous ghost about here, and I feared she might bring some harm to our new bell. All of our austerities and penances have been for strength in this moment. Pray with all your hearts. Let us try to raise the bell again.

PRIESTS. We will, Master. (*The Abbot and the Priests stand on either side of the bell, facing it.*)

ABBOT. Though the waters of Hitaka River seethe and dry up,
Though the sands of its shores run out,
Can the sacred strength of our holy order fail?

(*They pray, their rosaries clasped in their hands.*)

PRIESTS (*describing their actions*). All raise their voices together

ABBOT. To the East,[9] the Guardian King, Conqueror of the Three Realms;

PRIESTS. To the South, the Guardian King, Conqueror of the Demons;

ABBOT. To the West, the Guardian King, Conqueror of Evil Serpents and Dragons;

PRIESTS. To the North, the Guardian King, Conqueror of Frightful Monsters;

ABBOT. And you in the Center, Messenger of the Sun, All Holy Immovable One,

TOGETHER.
Will you make the bell move?
Show us the power of your avenging noose!
Namaku Samanda Basarada
Senda Makaroshana Sowataya
Un Tarata Kamman
"I dedicate[10] myself to the universal diamond,"
May this raging fury be destroyed!"
"He who hearkens to My Law shall gain enlightenment,
He who knows My Heart will be a Buddha in this flesh."
Now that we have prayed
For the serpent's salvation,
What rancor could it bear us?
As the moon at daybreak

ABBOT. Strikes the hanging bell—

CHORUS.
Look! Look! It moves!
Pray with all your hearts!
Pray to raise the bell!

(*They rub their rosaries frantically. The stage assistant lifts the bell a little and the Demon shakes it from within.*)

Here the Priests, joining hands,

---

[9]**To the East** What follows is a *yamabushi* prayer invoking wrathful (but beneficient) deities who oppose evil.

[10]**I dedicate** What follows is a mantra of Fudo the Immovable, a chief wrathful deity.

Invoke the sacred spell of the Thousand-Handed-One,
The Song of Salvation of the Guardian King,
The Immovable One, the Flaming One.
Black smoke rises from their frantic prayers.
And as they pray,
And as they pray,
Though no one strikes the bell, it sounds!

(*The Demon inside the bell strikes cymbals.*)

Though no one tugs the rope, the bell begins to dance!

(*The stage assistant pulls the bell up farther, and the Demon shakes it.*)

Soon it rises to the belfry tower,
Look! A serpent form emerges!

(*The stage assistant lifts the bell completely. The Dancer, now transformed into a Demon, wears the hannya mask. She has removed her outer brocade robe. When she is clear of the bell she takes up her mallet, then picks up her outer robe in both hands and wraps it around her waist. She stands and tries to drive the Abbot away. The Abbot and Priests pray, trying to subdue her. The Demon is driven onto the bridgeway where she drops her outer robe. Then she is forced back as far as the curtain, only to turn on the Abbot again, this time compelling him to withdraw. She stands with her back to the shité-pillar, throws one arm around it, pauses, and then invades the stage again. She tries to pull the bell down, but the Abbot forces her to the ground with the power of his rosary. The Demon rises again, and during the following passage sung by the Chorus, she and the Abbot struggle.*)

CHORUS.
Humbly we ask the help of the Green-bodied,
The Green Dragon of the East;
Humbly we ask the help of the White-bodied,
The White Dragon of the West;
Humbly we ask the help of the Yellow-bodied,
The Yellow Dragon of the Center,
All ye countless Dragon Kings of the three thousand worlds:
Have mercy, hear our prayers!
If now you show your mercy, your benevolence,
What refuge can the serpent find?
And as we pray,
Defeated by our prayers,
Behold the serpent fall!

(*She staggers back under the pressure of the Abbot's prayers and drops to the ground.*)

Again she springs to her feet,
The breath she vomits at the bell

Has turned to raging flames.

(*She rises and rushes to the bridgeway.*)

Her body burns in her own fire.
She leaps into the river pool,

(*She rushes through the curtain.*)

Into the waves of the River Hitaka,
And there she vanishes.
The Priests, their prayers granted,
Return to the temple,
Return to the temple.

(*The Abbot gives a final stamp of the foot near the shité-pillar.*)

TOPICS FOR CRITICAL THINKING AND WRITING

The Play on the PAGE

1. Compare this play with a medieval mystery play like *The Second Shepherds' Play* or a morality play like *Everyman.* What religious and philosophical values do each display? Are there beliefs in common? How do the values of Christianity and Buddhism as revealed in the plays differ?
2. Comment on the combination of reverence and comedy in these plays.

3. By the measure of Greek tragedy this play is very short textually, although its musical and dance elements would make it play longer. Does it, then, in your view, succeed or not in conveying dramatic intensity through the act of reading?
4. How much do ceremonial elements contribute to the meaning of the play?
5. Is the play essentially sexist?

The Play on the STAGE

6. To a Western audience what is the effect of having some performers masked and others unmasked?
7. Contemporary attempts to add to the traditional Noh repertoire have not been very successful (the last play that entered the current repertoire was written in 1928). Can a theater form have vitality if it almost always presents "classics"? What about grand opera in this regard?
8. Think about the intersection between text and performance by comparing the relationship between choreographer and dancer in ballet or modern dance and composer and performer—often the same—in jazz.

A Context for *DOJOJI*

LEONARD PRONKO
*Nô Theatre and Samuel Beckett**

The avant-garde, [Eugene] Ionesco has said, is not only seeking new forms of theater, it is also attempting to return to primitive but not elementary) the-

*From Leonard Pronko, *Theatre East & West* (Berkeley: University of California Press, 1967), pp. 106–10.

ater as well. Beckett's work, in the context of the Nô, is a good example of such a return. The fact that Beckett is today recognized as one of the most significant dramatists of our era seems to indicate that even so exotic a form as the Nô may not be so inaccessible as it at first seems. Perhaps it is *not*, as Gabriel Marcel [French playwright and philosopher] claimed, really from another planet! The most striking resemblance between Beckett's drama and the Nô lies in the sense of compression and concentration which one experiences, for example, in *Hagoromo*, or *Sotoba Komachi*, *Endgame* or *Krapp's Last Tape*. One has the impression that these plays have been reduced to their essence, pared down to almost skeletal proportions, with muscle and sinew, but surely no excess fat. What Ionesco (judging form his latest play *Thirst and Hunger*) has not learned from reading Zeami's writings, Beckett has learned without reading them.

The action of a Nô play is always reduced, so much so that [Paul] Claudel [French poet and playwright] contrasted Nô with Western drama by saying that in drama *something* comes about, while in the Nô someone comes about ("quelque chose arrive / quelqu'un arrive"). Perhaps it is pushing things too far to say that in Beckett's theater "someone comes about." Even in so "static" a play as *Endgame*, however, we note a structure remarkably similar to that of the Nô. *Endgame* is not, of course, an imitation of a Nô play, and is somewhat more complex structurally, but the major outline is surprisingly similar. . . .

Ruby Cohn [in *Samuel Beckett: The Comic Gamut*] has described *Endgame* as the presentation of the "death of the stock props of Western civilization—family cohesion, filial devotion, parental and connubial love, faith in God, empirical knowledge, and artistic creation." If her analysis is correct, then there comes a moment when Hamm is reduced to nothing other than himself, divorced totally from any meaningful relationship with people or even with objects—a terrifying revelation. Clov has left him, or so he believes, and in the finale of the play Hamm performs what might well be called his farewell dance, once more going through the trivial motions that were his life, but now only for himself, and in anything but rapid tempo. Unlike the Nô plays, *Endgame* carries no suggestion of release or of any kind of happiness, attained or attainable.

If Beckett's characters—in *Endgame* more than in *Waiting for Godot* and in the later plays more than in *Endgame*—are turned toward the past, constantly reenacting the events of a life already lived, it is because they, like the Buddhist ghosts of the Nô, are tied to the wheel of life, unable to escape the effects of their past, unable to free themselves from a cycle that has become meaninglessly repetitious. Only the kind of faith possessed by the priests and ghosts of old Japan, but so tragically lacking in Beckett's world, could bring some cessation to the suffering of his pathetic protagonists. . . . Arthur Waley speaks of the Nô story as creeping "at its subject warily." Since the action is [often] presented as a memory evoked by a dead man "we get . . . a vision of life indeed, but painted with the colours of memory, longing or regret" [*The Nô Plays of Japan*]. Such a description applies to *Krapp's Last Tape* and *Embers*, in which the protagonists are ghosts and the action is evoked, for it took place long ago. . . .

Since Beckett works outside an established theatrical tradition, he cannot depend upon an accepted symbolic vocabulary, as could Zeami. And yet, with incredible skill and imagination, the Western playwright has managed to fill his scripts with objects and movements as meaningful to the modern man as was the fan or the twig of the Nô character to the Japanese. What Beckett cannot do is to give his actors a highly stylized mode of moving and speaking. Our theater has moved so far from the concept of the dramatist who is also actor and director that the actor now almost resents any interference from the dramatist. Beckett, we are told, is keenly interested in the *mise en scene* of his plays, and takes great pains, if he attends rehearsals, to indicate precisely what he wishes. Indeed, his scripts are quite exemplary in this regard, and become more so as his dramaturgy develops. Scenic indications in *Godot*, while plentiful, cannot compare with those in Beckett's later drama, *Play*. Divorced from a tradition that would allow the actor to know precisely how to intone the text or how to move, Beckett has clearly attempted to compensate for this loss by detailed stage directions.

There is quite clearly a kinship between Beckett's plays and the Nô drama, but there is just as clearly no true influence. If I have made this excursion it is not in an attempt to show influence where there is none, but to suggest that Beckett's drama, like that of some of his fellow writers, has made us sensitive to forms of theater that fifteen or twenty years ago might have struck us as slow, insignificant, and dull. *Waiting for Godot* seemed static in 1953 partly because the action it embodies is unlike any action we had witnessed on the stage before. In the years since that most important premiere, we have learned to look for other things in our theater; we have broadened our dramatic horizons, sharpened our perceptivity, and deepened our understanding. Beckett has shown us that a drama may at first strike us as strange, exotic, difficult, even undramatic, and upon closer acquaintance, prove to be a meaningful addition to our aesthetic and human experience.

The Play in PERFORMANCE

The following combines program notes offered at a performance of the play in the National Gallery, Washington, D.C. on October 27, 1988, with this editor's personal notes from that performance.

(1) First a group of musicians, then a group of chorus members, then a group of stagehands—all dressed in formal kimono—slowly enter in silence and take their places on the Nô stage. Then several kyogen players enter bearing an imposingly large, heavy temple bell. As they carefully proceed to install the bell, they are tense with excitement.

(2) A special flute prelude summons to the scene the head priest, the abbot, of Dōjōji and his priests. The abbot assembles the temple servants and gives them strict orders that no women are to be allowed to enter the temple grounds.

(3) When the priests withdraw, a beautiful dancer (the *shité*) makes "her" entrance to the accompaniment of flute and drums. She chants her opening lines three times, a chant echoed in a low tone by the chorus. This, I was informed, is one of the special effects of the "Akagashira variation" of the play being performed.

(4) Entranced by the beauty of the dancer, the temple servants disregard the head priest's warning and permit her to enter the temple grounds to perform a dance in celebration of the installation of the new bell.

(5) The dancer withdraws to don a formal lacquered hat and prepares to perform her dance. But her graceful movements are arrested for a dramatic moment when she casts a malevolent look at the temple bell.

(6) Her first dance is an exciting interaction of rising intensity between the solo dancer and a single percussionist, whose reverberating drumbeats are interspersed with the musicians' piercing cries. In the Akagashira variation, a special effect is created by reversing the direction of the dance pattern: Instead of circling to the left to trace a triangular movement symbolizing the scales of the snake, the dancer circles to the right. The dance is shorter but all the more intense. The dancer first advances to the forestage to perform the *cha no dan*. Then, in the next section, called the *ranbyôshi*, a two-line chant is inserted, followed by the moves to the right in the special Akagashira tradition. When the dancer returns to the forestage, two more separate lines are chanted. When

the chorus chants the first line of the poetic motif, "*Yamadera no ya . . .*" ("To a temple in the mountains . . . "), the tempo suddenly increases, and the dancer begins a new dance, the *kyûnomai*.

(7) The other musicians join the performance of the *kyûnomai*, which expresses the intense turmoil compelling the dancer finally to approach the bell in a furious rush. She sweeps off her hat, gives a last, violent stamp, and leaps up into the bell, which falls over with a terrifying, reverberating crash.

(8) The role of the senior stagehand is critical at this moment. He must literally be breathing in unison with the dancer in order to know the exact second at which to drop the bell. This is a serious business: The dancer's life is at stake.

(9) The temple servants come running at the sound of the crash only to recoil as they approach the bell, which they indicate radiates a scorching heat. A comic squabble ensues (which relieves the tension of the moment): Who's going to tell the abbot what's happened? One goes to get him and a report is made; then the servants are told the reason for the prohibition against admitting women to the temple grounds.

(10) Meanwhile, the *shité* is performing another virtuoso feat sight unseen: changing costumes, masks, and wigs inside the bell. In a standard performance, he would have only to remove one outer robe, rearrange the wig slightly, change masks, and take up a prop (the demon's hammer); in the challenging "Akagashira" version, however, the costume change is more complex, involving several layers of garments.

(11) The final struggle begins: Prayers are said by all the priests as the bell is raised to reveal a demonic, serpentine figure. An epic struggle begins, the priest vigorously rubbing his sacred accoutrements, the demon attacks and retreats in stylized movements. Finally, the serpent's skin symbolically bursts and is shed, entwining itself around a pillar.

(12) In the finale, the performer (in Washington, Shigeyoshi Mori, who has been accorded the highest traditional cultural honor of designation as a "Living National Treasure") draws upon centuries of tradition as well as his individual imagination to create an unforgettable effect: a choreographic coda as the demon serpent leaps off the stage (according to legend into the waters of the Hitaka River) and disappears from sight.

English Renaissance Theater

Movement and dance played a significant role in the Peter Brook 1971 Royal Shakespeare Company production of *A Midsummer Night's Dream*, pictured here.

No one, of course, knew that he or she was living in the Middle Ages. Historians define the Middle Ages as the period between, on the one hand, the classical civilization of Greece from the sixth century B.C.E. through the disintegration of the Roman Empire in the fifth century C.E., and, on the other hand, the revival of an interest in the classical world, beginning in Italy in the fourteenth century, reaching England around 1500, and at its height in England during Shakespeare's lifetime (1564–1616). But if people in the Middle Ages could not know that later ages would look back and see them as in the middle of something, many people in the *Renaissance*—a French word that means "rebirth"—were aware that something was reborn.

The Italian artist and biographer Giorgio Vasari, author of the *Lives of the Most Excellent Painters, Sculptors, and Architects* (1550, enlarged in 1568), as early as 1550 used the world *rináscita* ("new birth"), to convey his idea that after a centuries-long absence, the creative spirit of the classical world was now reborn. In Italy the Renaissance is usually said to have begun with the poet Petrarch (1304–74), and to have reached its height in the first half of the sixteenth century, with Leonardo (1452–1519) and with Michelangelo (1475–1564). For Vasari, as for many of his contemporaries and his immediate predecessors, art had achieved a high level of perfection in classical antiquity, but had then declined and was reborn with Petrarch's earlier contemporary, the painter Giotto (1267–1337).

But we must modify these remarks. In the first place, of course periods are not sharply defined. If we are talking about the Renaissance in England, as a sort of shorthand we can speak of the Elizabethan period, but we should remember that Elizabeth I (1558–1603) died before Shakespeare wrote such works as *King Lear, Macbeth,* and *The Tempest.* Second, many scholars would argue that the idea of a rebirth is misleading: There were changes, of course (we look at some of them in a moment), but—some scholars say—the idea that Italy in the fifteenth and sixteenth centuries, or England in the late sixteenth century and the early seventeenth century, saw a "rebirth" of classical culture is nonsense. To believe this, they say, is to buy Vasari's propaganda, and not to realize he was defending a particular sort of painting that he himself practiced. For various reasons, then, some scholars today do not use the word "Renaissance," and instead speak of "Early Modern Italy" or "Early Modern England." Our own view is that "Renaissance" is a convenient word, and that although it can be misleading if one takes it too seriously, it does catch some of the newness of the period; no one can doubt that in these years men and women were aware that the world had changed rapidly.

What were some of the enormous changes? A few can be easily dated, and we begin with these. First, Johann Gutenberg (1397?–1478) invented movable type about 1436 or 1437. The effect was that books, which previously had been written by hand, became relatively cheap, and literacy greatly increased within a century. Second, in 1453 Constantinople fell to the Turks, with the result that scholars familiar with Greek texts were forced to move to Western Europe, where they soon communicated their learning to an eager audience. (Some medieval Western Europeans had known Greek authors, notably Aristotle, but chiefly in Latin versions.) The stimulus given to classical studies, along with the increase in literacy, resulted in translations of such authors as Virgil, Ovid, Horace, and Plutarch (Shakespeare drew on a 1579 translation of Plutarch's *The Lives of the Noble Grecians and Romans* for his *Julius Caesar, Antony and Cleopatra, Coriolanus,* and *Timon of Athens*). Third, in 1492 Columbus discovered America, initiating exploration on an unprecedented scale. Fourth, Nicholas Copernicus (1473–1543) established that the earth rotates around the sun, in contrast to the Ptolemaic view that held the reverse. (Copernicus published his treatise when he was on his deathbed, but he had developed the ideas by 1530.) Fifth, in England, in 1534 parliament passed the Act of Supremacy, which made the English monarch (Henry VIII) the head of an English church, whereas until then the church in England had been part of a vast unified body, the Roman Catholic church, headed by the pope. Between 1536 and 1542 the extensive properties of the monasteries in England were distributed to persons whose allegiance was to the king, not the pope.

Other happenings cannot be so easily dated, but they include a shift from an essentially Christian view of the world to a relatively secular view—in the formula of the famous Swiss historian Jacob Burckhardt, the Renaissance marked humans' discovery of themselves and of the world around them. One evident sign of this shift is the devaluation of the medieval view that the contemplative life is superior to the active life, and the highest goal of contemplation is knowledge of divine things; in the Renaissance the active life is elevated, and the highest wisdom is that of the statesman who advises his prince or king. (We get a glimpse of the vision of an ideal Renaissance man when Ophelia characterizes Hamlet as a courtier, soldier, and scholar, all in one.) Secularization was aided by the Reformation; from the reformer's point of view the Reformation marked a return to a purer form of Christianity, but from the historian's point of view it shattered the unity of medieval Christianity, thereby weakening the hold of the Church and thus contributing to the secularization of society. Further, the rise of the middle class marked a new social system, for it did not fit into the medieval view that society consisted of three groups: the clergy, who ministered to spiritual needs; the nobility, who protected others; and the peasants, whose labor supported the first two groups. Indeed, the emergence of professional actors and playwrights such as Shakespeare—persons who, if successful, were members of the middle class—is a sign that we are no longer in the Middle Ages, a period where there are no professional writers other than scribes and no professional actors other than minstrels and clowns.

Our concern, however, is with the theater of Renaissance England, so we can say the most obvious thing that was new was the presence of a permanent theater, a building designed specifically for the staging of plays, a kind of building unknown in the Middle Ages. Closely connected with this development, indeed a necessary prelude to it, was the development of professional companies of actors, and it is to these matters that we now turn.

■■■■■■■■■■■■■■ THE ELIZABETHAN PLAYHOUSE

The first permanent structure built in England for plays was The Theater, built outside the city limits of London in 1576 by James Burbage. It soon had several competitors, but little is known about any of these playhouses. The contract for one, The Fortune (built in 1600) survives; it tells us that the three-storied building was square, eight feet on the outside, fifty-five feet on the inside. The stage was forty-three feet broad and twenty-seven-and-a-half feet deep. It had been calculated that about 800 people (the *groundlings*) could stand around the three sides of the stage on the ground that was called the *yard*, and another 1500 could be seated in the three galleries. The other chief pieces of evidence concerning the physical nature of the theater are (1) the "de Witt drawing," which is really a copy of a sketch made by a visitor (c. 1596) to The Swan (see illustration, page 218); (2) the discovery in 1989 of the foundations of the Rose Theater; and (3) bits of evidence that can be gleaned from the plays themselves, such as "Enter a Fairy at one door, and Robin Goodfellow at another." Conclusions vary and scholarly tempers run high; the following statements are not indisputable.

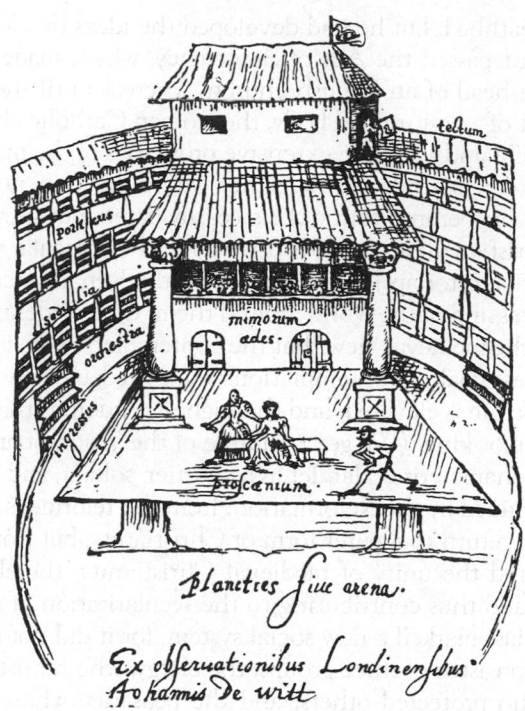

Planeties ſiue arena.

Ex obſeruationibus Londinenſibus
Johannis de witt

Arend Van Buchel's copy of a drawing of the Swan Theater, made by Johannes de Witt about 1596. The absence of spectators is puzzling; perhaps Van Buchel attended a rehearsal, or perhaps he didn't bother to attempt to draw a crowd. For a modern drawing based chiefly on de Witt's drawing, see page 11.

Most theaters were polygonal or round structures (Shakespeare calls the theater a "wooden O") with three galleries; the yard was open to the sky. From one side a raised stage (or open *platform*) jutted in the middle. A sort of wooden canopy (the *heavens*, or the *shadow*) projected over the stage and in some theaters rested on two pillars; these pillars could conveniently serve as a hiding place for an actor supposed to be unseen by the other characters. At the rear of the stage there sometimes was a curtained alcove or booth, which when uncurtained might represent a room or a cave. The curtain is often called an *arras*, and it was probably behind this curtain that Polonius hid, only to be stabbed. At the rear of the stage (flanking the curtained space?) there were perhaps also two or three doors, through which entrances and exits were made. Probably the *tiring house* ("attiring house," i.e., dressing room) was behind the stage. Above the alcove or booth was an area that could be used for an *upper stage* (for example, in scenes of people standing on a city's walls); flanking the upper stage were windows, one of which may have served Juliet for her misnamed balcony scene. Some scholars argue that in a yet higher place were musicians, and at the very top—called the *top*—was an opening from which an actor could look; in *Henry VI, Part I*, Joan of Arc appears "on the top, thrusting out a torch burning."

Most of the acting was done on the main stage (the platform), but the "inner stage," "upper stage," "windows," and "top" must have been useful occasionally (if they existed). The *cellar* (beneath the stage) was used, for example, for the voice of the ghost in *Hamlet* and for Ophelia's grave. Though some scenery was used, the absence of a front curtain precluded many elaborate scenic effects (much, however, could be done by carrying banners) and encouraged continuous action. The stage that was a battlefield could become in an instant, by the introduction of a throne, a room in a palace. Two readable books are A. M. Nagler, *Shakespeare's Stage*, and C. Walter Hodges, *The Globe Restored*. Nagler (Ch. 12) also gives information about a second kind of Elizabethan theater—basically a platform at one end of a hall—that catered to a courtly group. For a more detailed study, see Andrew Gurr, *The Shakespearean Stage, 1542–1642,* third edition, and Christine Eccles, *The Rose Theatre.*

▪▪▪▪▪▪▪▪▪▪▪▪▪▪ THE THEATRICAL COMPANIES

In England the profession of player developed during the sixteenth century. In the Middle Ages there were of course amateur actors in the mystery plays, but the closest to professional actors were the minstrels and clowns who may have performed semi-dramatic bits. At the very end of the fifteenth century we hear of short secular plays being done as entertainments in great houses, and in the sixteenth century we hear of traveling troupes, usually consisting of four men and a boy—the boy would play female roles. These traveling players, in order to avoid being classified as "rogues and vagabonds," usually had the protection of a noble, whose "servants" they nominally were. Their duties were to entertain his household on holidays, and at weddings or other special occasions, but the rest of the time they were free to travel, setting up a temporary stage in an inn yard or in the hall of someone who paid for a performance.

By the later sixteenth century, a company consisted of (1) eight or ten adult males who were senior actors and who shared in the profits; (2) two boys apprenticed at the age of ten or so to senior actors (until they were about twenty years of age they would play females roles); and (3) hirelings, who for a small fee would play minor roles and serve as stagehands. By our standards an Elizabethan company was small, but actors doubled in several parts. We know, for instance, that fifteen players performed *Julius Caesar,* a play that has thirty-five named parts.

Until fairly recently scholars were content to mention that boys played the female parts; these scholars also mentioned that this convention continued the medieval practice of using males in female roles, and that other theaters, notably in ancient Greece and in China and Japan, also used males in female roles. (In classical Noh drama in Japan, males still play the female roles.) Prudery may have been at the root of the academic failure to talk much about the use of boy actors, or maybe there really is not much more to say than that it was a convention of a male-centered culture (Stephen Greenblatt's view, in *Shakespearan Negotiations* [1988]). Further, the very nature of a convention is that it is not thought about: Hamlet is a Dane and Julius Caesar is a Roman, but in Shakespeare's plays they speak English, and we in the audience never give this odd fact a thought. Similarly, a character may speak in the presence of others and we understand, again without thinking about it, that he or she is not heard by the figures on the stage (the aside); a character alone on the stage may speak (the soliloquy), and we do not take the character to be unhinged; in a realistic (box) set, the fourth wall, which allows us to see what is going on, is miraculously missing. The no-nonsense view, then, is that the boy actor was an accepted convention, accepted unthinkingly—just as today we know that Kenneth Branagh is not Hamlet, Al Pacino is not Richard III, and Denzel Washington is not the Prince of Aragon. In this view, the audience takes the performer for the role, and that is that; such is the argument we now make for color-blind casting, in which African Americans and Asians can play roles of persons who lived in medieval Denmark and ancient Rome. But gender perhaps is different, at least today. It is a matter of abundant academic study: The Elizabethan theater is now sometimes called a transvestite theater, and we hear much about cross-dressing.

Shakespeare himself in a very few passages calls attention to the use of boys in female roles. At the end of *As You Like It* the boy who played Rosalind addresses the audience, and says, "O men, . . . if I were a woman, I would kiss as many of you as had beards that pleased me." But this is in the Epilogue; the plot is over, and the actor is stepping out of the play and into the audience's everyday world. A second reference to the practice of boys playing female roles occurs in *Antony and Cleopatra*, when Cleopatra imagines that she and Antony will be the subject of crude plays, her role being performed by a boy:

> The quick comedians
> Extemporally will stage us, and present
> Our Alexandrian revels; Antony
> Shall be brought drunken forth, and I shall see
> Some squeaking Cleopatra boy my greatness.
> (5.2.216–20)

In Hamlet, when the players arrive in 2.2, Hamlet jokes with the boy who plays a female role. The boy has grown since Hamlet last saw him: "By'r Lady, your ladyship is nearer to heaven than when I saw you last by the altitude of a chopine" (a lady's thick-soled shoe). He goes on: "Pray God your voice . . . be not cracked" (434–38).

Exactly how sexual, how erotic, this material was and is, is now much disputed. Again, the use of boys may have been unnoticed, or, rather, not thought about—an unexamined convention—by most or all spectators most of the time, perhaps *all* of the time, except when Shakespeare calls the convention to the attention of the audience, as in the passages just quoted. Still, an occasional bit seems to invite erotic thoughts. The clearest example is the name that Rosalind takes in *As You Like It*, Ganymede—the beautiful youth whom Zeus abducted. Did boys dressed to play female roles carry homoerotic appeal for straight men (Lisa Jardine's view, in *Still Harping on Daughters* [1983]), or for gay men, or for some or all women in the audience? Further, when the boy actor played a woman who (for the purposes of the plot) disguised herself as a male, as Rosalind, Viola, and Portia do—so we get a boy playing a woman playing a man—what sort of appeal was generated, and for what sort of spectator?

Some scholars have argued that the convention empowered women by letting female characters display a freedom unavailable in Renaissance patriarchal society; the convention, it is said, undermined rigid gender distinctions. In this view, the convention (along with plots in which female characters for a while disguised themselves as young men) allowed Shakespeare to say what some modern gender critics say: Gender is a constructed role rather than a biological given, something we make, rather than a fixed binary opposition of male and female (see Juliet Dusinberre, in *Shakespeare and the Nature of Women* [1975]). On the other hand, some scholars have maintained that the male disguise assumed by some female characters serves only to reaffirm traditional social distinctions, since female characters who don male garb (notably Portia in *The Merchant of Venice* and Rosalind in *As You Like It*) return to their female garb and at least implicitly (these critics say) reaffirm the status quo. (For this last view, see Clara Claiborne Park, in an essay in *The Woman's Part*, ed. Carolyn Ruth Swift Lenz et al. [1980].) Perhaps no one answer is right for all plays; in *As You Like It* cross-dressing empowers Rosalind, but in *Twelfth Night* cross-dressing comically traps Viola.

CHRISTOPHER Marlowe

Christopher Marlowe (1564–1593) was born in Canterbury, England, in the year of Shakespeare's birth. Like Shakespeare, he was of a prosperous middle-class family (his father was a shoemaker), but unlike Shakespeare he went to a university, Corpus Christi College, Cambridge, where he received his B.A. degree in 1584 and his M.A. in 1587. The terms of his scholarship implied that he was preparing for the clergy, but he did not become a clergyman. Shortly before he received his M.A., the university seems to have wished to withhold it, apparently suspecting him of conversion to Roman Catholicism, but the queen's Privy Council intervened on his behalf, stating that he "had done her majesty good service" and had been employed "in matters touching the benefit of his country." His precise service is unknown. Marlowe's first play, *Tamburlaine the Great* (c. 1587), in blank verse (unrhymed iambic pentameter) inaugurated the great age of Elizabethan drama with its "mighty" line. While continuing his career as dramatist, he apparently lived a turbulent life in London: In 1589, involved in a brawl in which a man was killed, Marlowe was jailed (though later released); in 1593 he was again arrested, this time accused of atheism. He was not imprisoned, but before his case could be decided, he was dead, only six years after having left Cambridge, stabbed in a tavern fight. Marlowe wrote seven plays—the dates are uncertain—the most important of which, besides *Doctor Faustus* (c. 1593), were *The Jew of Malta* (c. 1588) and *Edward II* (c. 1591). He did a verse translation of Ovid's *Amores* and left unfinished at the time of his death the long poem *Hero and Leander*.

COMMENTARY ON *DOCTOR FAUSTUS*

The exact date of *Doctor Faustus* is unknown, but the play was probably written not long before Marlowe was stabbed to death in 1593. It is universally acknowledged as the first great English tragedy (Shakespeare was barely starting at the time), but behind *Doctor Faustus* stands the tradition of the morality play, a form that had originated in the late fourteenth century and survived until the latter part of the sixteenth. As readers of *Everyman* (page 184) know, the morality play uses allegorical figures to dramatize a representative person's struggle in a world of deceitful appearances. Thus, *Everyman* (late fifteenth century) shows a figure called Everyman who has put his trust in Goods, Kindred, Fellowship, and so forth, but who learns—when faced with Death—that these are false friends who will abandon him; he rightly turns to Good Deeds, who assists him to achieve eternal felicity after death. Despite its happy ending, then, the morality play dramatizes guilt, suffering, and sometimes even death, and thus it approaches tragedy.

In a morality play, good and evil are sharply delineated and the spectator never doubts which is which. Wicked deeds are repaid with suffering, virtuous deeds with eternal happiness. Performers portraying good and bad angels sometimes engage in lively struggles—visible demonstrations of the conscience being tempted by the agents of Satan. In tragedy, however, the issues may be more complicated; the suffering hero may say, with King Lear, "I am a man more sinned against than sinning," and the audience may feel the truth of his assertion. Or the tragic hero may act in defiance of the conventional good, and the audience may not find it in their hearts to condemn the action, partly because the conventional good may seem severely limited, and the defiant act may seem, at least in some degree, noble. We leave it to you to think about whether Faustus's acts are noble, ignoble, or a mixture.

Textual Note

The earliest edition of *Doctor Faustus* was published in 1604, eleven years after Marlowe's death. Scholars call it the A-text, or A1. The text was reprinted in 1609 (A2) and again in 1611 (A3); A2 and A3 differ from A only by virtue of small errors that they introduce. In 1616, however, a very different version of *Doctor Faustus* was published, conventionally called the B-text. Whereas the A-text contains 1,517 lines, the B-text contains 2,121 lines. The B-text has:

some passages that are very close to A;

some episodes that are broadly parallel to A, but with little verbal similarity;

some deletions of material found in A, especially material that might be thought blasphemous;

approximately 600 more lines than A, chiefly devoted to comic scenes; the last act is notably fuller in B, which has a final visit of the angels, and the discovery of Faustus's mangled body. But although longer than A, B lacks some material found in A.

Because it is known that in 1602 a theatrical entrepreneur named Philip Henslowe paid William Bird and Samuel Rowley "for their adicyones in doctor fostes," it was believed until fairly recently that all or nearly all of the new material in B consisted of un-Marlovian additions, and that A, the shorter text, therefore was closer to Marlowe's own play. But today most scholars believe that B is closer to Marlowe's play. Instead of seeing B as containing un-Marlovian additions to an authentic text represented by A, scholars now see A as being an abridged version of Marlowe's play. That is, some or much of the material found only in B is now thought to be Marlowe's.

But even if it is agreed that A is abridged, and that B is closer to Marlowe's final manuscript, it is evident that some passages in B are not by Marlowe. For example, B prints "O mercy heauen," which almost surely is a censored version of A's "My God, my God." The text that follows is essentially the B text, but the "blasphemy" of A has been restored, and in a few other places, where A makes better sense than B, we print the A version.

For convenience in reference, we add act and scene divisions in square brackets [ ], though no edition of the play was so divided until relatively recent times.

DOCTOR FAUSTUS
Christopher Marlowe

Edited by Sylvan Barnet

SPEAKING CHARACTERS

CHORUS
DOCTOR FAUSTUS
WAGNER, *his student and servant*
GOOD ANGEL
BAD ANGEL
VALDES ⎱ *magicians*
CORNELIUS ⎰
Three SCHOLARS
LUCIFER, *prince of devils*
MEPHOSTOPHILIS, *a devil*
ROBIN, *a clown*
BELZEBUB, *a devil*
DICK, *a clown*
POPE ADRIAN
PRIDE
COVETOUSNESS
ENVY
WRATH ⎱ *the Seven Deadly Sins*
GLUTTONY
SLOTH
LECHERY
RAYMOND, King of Hungary
BRUNO, *rival Pope appointed by the Emperor*
Two CARDINALS
ARCHBISHOP OF RHEIMS
FRIARS
VINTNER
The German Emperor, CHARLES THE FIFTH

MARTINO
FREDERICK ⎱ *gentlemen at the Emperor's court*
BENVOLIO
DUKE OF SAXONY
Two SOLDIERS
HORSE-COURSER, *a clown*

MUTE CHARACTERS

DARIUS OF PERSIA
ALEXANDER THE GREAT
ALEXANDER'S PARAMOUR
HELEN OF TROY
DEVILS
PIPER
CARDINALS
CARTER, *a clown*
HOSTESS *of a Tavern*
DUKE OF VANHOLT
DUCHESS OF VANHOLT
SERVANT
OLD MAN

MONKS
FRIARS
ATTENDANTS
SOLDIERS
SERVANTS
Two CUPIDS

[PROLOGUE]

(*Enter Chorus.*°)

Not marching in the fields of Trasimene°
Where Mars did mate° the warlike Carthagens,

Chorus a single actor (here, perhaps, Wagner, Faustus's servant-student)   **1 Trasimene** Lake Trasimene, site of one of Hannibal's victories over the Romans, 217 B.C.E. (Marlowe is not known to have written on this subject, though lines 3–4 may refer to his *Edward II*, and line 5 to his *Tamburlaine*)   **2 Mars did mate** that is, the Roman army encountered

Nor sporting in the dalliance of love
In courts of kings where state° is overturned,
Nor in the pomp of proud audacious deeds   5
Intends our muse° to vaunt° his heavenly verse.
Only this, gentles—We must now perform
The form of Faustus' fortunes, good or bad:
And now to patient judgments we appeal
And speak for Faustus in his infancy.   10
Now is he born of parents base of stock
In Germany within a town called Rhode;°

4 state government   **6 muse** poet   **vaunt** proudly display   **12 Rhode** Roda

The photograph illustrates Clifford Williams's Royal Shakespeare Company production (1968–1969) of *Doctor Faustus*, with Eric Porter (extreme right) in the title role. Faustus is watching the antics of the Seven Deadly Sins (2.2). This production did not seek to recreate an Elizabethan performance, but purists who object to introducing highly spectacular elements in modern production of Elizabethan plays should remember that the Elizabethan theater did as much as possible to introduce striking visual effects. Marlowe's text, for instance, calls for splendidly costumed figures (e.g., the pope), and it includes scenes with fireworks. For another picture of a production of *Doctor Faustus,* see page 14.

At riper years to Wittenberg he went
Whereas° his kinsmen chiefly brought him up.
15 So much he profits in divinity
That shortly he was graced° with doctor's name,
Excelling all, and sweetly can dispute
In th' heavenly matters of theology;
Till swoll'n with cunning, of a self-conceit,°
20 His waxen wings° did mount above his reach
And melting, heavens conspired his overthrow!
For falling to a devilish exercise
And glutted now with learning's golden gifts
He surfeits upon cursèd necromancy:°
25 Nothing so sweet as magic is to him
Which he prefers before his chiefest bliss°—
And this the man that in his study sits.

(*Exit.*)

[1.1] (*Faustus in his study.*°)

FAUSTUS.
Settle thy studies Faustus, and begin

To sound the depth of that thou wilt profess.°
Having commenced,° be a divine in show—
Yet level° at the end of every art
And live and die in Aristotle's works.   5
Sweet *Analytics,*° 'tis thou hast ravished me.
Bene disserere est finis logices.°
Is to dispute well logic's chiefest end?
Affords this art no greater miracle?
Then read no more, thou hast attained that end.   10
A greater subject fitteth Faustus' wit:°
Bid *on kai me on*° farewell, and Galen° come:
Be a physician Faustus, heap up gold,
And be eternized for some wondrous cure.
Summum bonum medicinae sanitas,°   15
The end of physic° is our body's health.
Why Faustus hast thou not attained that end?
Are not thy bills° hung up as monuments
Whereby whole cities have escaped the plague
And thousand desperate maladies been cured?   20
Yet art thou still but Faustus and a man.
Could'st thou make men to live eternally
Or being dead raise them to life again,
Then this profession were to be esteemed.

14 Whereas where   16 graced (alluding to the official "grace" permitting the student to take his degree)   19 cunning, of a self-conceit ingenuity born of arrogance   20 waxen wings (alluding to Icarus, who flew by means of wings made of feathers waxed to a framework; despite the warning of his father, Icarus soared too near the sun, the wax melted, and he plunged to his death)   24 necromancy (literally divination by means of the spirits of the dead, but here probably equivalent to black magic)   26 prefers before his chiefest bliss sets above his hope of salvation   1.1.s.d. Faustus in his study (probably at his last line the Chorus drew back a curtain at the rear of the stage, disclosing Faustus)

2 profess study and teach   3 commenced taken a degree   4 level aim   6 Analytics title of two treatises by Aristotle on logic   7 Bene . . . logices the end (i.e., purpose) of logic is to argue well (Latin)   11 wit intelligence   12 on kai me on being and not being (Greek)   Galen Greek authority on medicine, second century C.E.   15 Summum . . . sanitas health is the greatest good of medicine (Latin, translated from Aristotle's *Nichomachean Ethics*)   16 physic medicine   18 bills prescriptions

25   Physic farewell! Where is Justinian?°
      Si una eademque res legatur duobus, alter rem, alter valorem
          rei, et cetera.°
      A petty case of paltry legacies.
      Exhereditare filium non potest pater, nisi°—
30   Such is the subject of the *Institute*
      And universal body of the law!
      This study fits a mercenary drudge
      Who aims at nothing but external trash,
      Too servile and illiberal for me.
35   When all is done, divinity is best.
      Jerome's Bible,° Faustus, view it well.
      Stipendium peccati mors est.° Ha! *Stipendium et cetera.* The
          reward of sin is death? That's hard: *Si peccasse nega-*
          mus, fallimur, et nulla est in nobis veritas.° If we say
40   that we have no sin, we deceive ourselves, and there
          is no truth in us. Why, then belike, we must sin, and
          so consequently die.
      Ay, we must die an everlasting death.
      What doctrine call you this? *Che serà, serà:*°
45   What will be, shall be! Divinity, adieu!
      These metaphysics° of magicians
      And negromantic° books are heavenly;
      Lines, circles, letters, characters—
      Ay, these are those that Faustus most desires.
50   O, what a world of profit and delight,
      Of power, of honor, and omnipotence
      Is promised to the studious artisan!°
      All things that move between the quiet° poles
      Shall be at my command: emperors and kings
55   Are but obeyed in their several provinces
      But his dominion that exceeds in this°
      Stretcheth as far as doth the mind of man:
      A sound magician is a demi-god!

Here tire my brains to get° a deity!

(*Enter Wagner.*)

Wagner, commend me to my dearest friends,   60
The German Valdes and Cornelius.
Request them earnestly to visit me.
WAGNER. I will, sir. (*Exit.*)
FAUSTUS.
      Their conference° will be a greater help to me
      Than all my labors, plod I ne'er so fast.   65

(*Enter the [Good] Angel and the [Evil] Spirit.*°)

GOOD ANGEL.
      O Faustus, lay that damnèd book aside
      And gaze not on it lest it tempt thy soul
      And heap God's heavy wrath upon thy head!
      Read, read the Scriptures—that° is blasphemy!
BAD ANGEL.
      Go forward Faustus, in that famous art   70
      Wherein all nature's treasure is contained.
      Be thou on earth as Jove is in the sky,
      Lord and commander of these elements!

                                            (*Exeunt Angels.*)
FAUSTUS.
      How am I glutted with conceit of this!°
      Shall I make spirits fetch me what I please?   75
      Resolve me of° all ambiguities?
      Perform what desperate enterprise I will?
      I'll have them fly to India° for gold,
      Ransack the ocean for orient° pearl,
      And search all corners of the new-found world   80
      For pleasant fruits and princely delicates;
      I'll have them read me strange philosophy
      And tell the secrets of all foreign kings;
      I'll have them wall all Germany with brass
      And make swift Rhine circle fair Wittenberg;   85
      I'll have them fill the public schools° with silk
      Wherewith the students shall be bravely° clad.
      I'll levy soldiers with the coin they bring
      And chase the Prince of Parma° from our land
      And reign sole king of all the provinces!   90
      Yea, stranger engines for the brunt° of war

---

25 Justinian Roman emperor and authority on law (483–565) who ordered the compilation of the *Institutes* (see line 30)   **26–27 Si . . . et cetera** if one thing is willed to two persons, one of them shall have the thing itself, the other the value of the thing, and so forth (Latin)   **29 Exhereditare . . . nisi** a father cannot disinherit his son unless (Latin)   **36 Jerome's Bible** the Latin translation made by St. Jerome (c. 340–420)   **37 Stipendium . . . est** the wages of sin is death (Romans 6.23; if Faustus had gone on to read the rest of the verse, he would have found that "the gift of God is eternal life through Jesus Christ our Lord")   **38–39 Si . . . veritas** from I John 1.8, translated in the next two lines; Faustus neglects the following verse: "If we confess our sins, He is faithful and just to forgive us our sins, and to cleanse us from all unrighteousness"   **44 Che serà, serà** (Italian; translated in the first half of the next line)   **46 metaphysics** subjects lying beyond (or studied after) physics   **47 negromantic** black magical (though probably here also associated with "necromantic," that is, concerned with raising the spirits of the dead)   **52 artisan** that is, expert   **53 quiet** motionless   **56 this** that is, magic

59 get beget   **64 conference** conversation   **65 s.d. Spirit** Bad Angel, devil (the two angels probably enter the stage from separate doors)   **69 that** that is, the book of magic   **74 conceit of this** that is, the conception of being a magician   **76 Resolve me of** explain to me   **78 India** either the West Indies (America) or the East Indies   **79 orient** lustrous and precious   **86 public schools** universities   **87 bravely** splendidly   **89 Prince of Parma** Spanish governor-general of the Low Countries during 1579–92   **91 brunt** assault

Than was the fiery keel° at Antwerp bridge
I'll make my servile spirits to invent.

(*Enter Valdes and Cornelius.*)

Come German Valdes and Cornelius
95   And make me blest with your sage conference.
Valdes, sweet Valdes, and Cornelius,
Know that your words have won me at the last
To practice magic and concealèd arts.
Philosophy is odious and obscure,
100   Both law and physic are for petty wits,
Divinity is basest of the three—
Unpleasant, harsh, contemptible, and vile.
'Tis magic, magic, that hath ravished me!
Then, gentle friends, aid me in this attempt
105   And I, that have with subtle syllogisms
Graveled° the pastors of the German church
And made the flow'ring pride of Wittenberg
Swarm to my problems° as th' infernal spirits
On sweet Musaeus° when he came to hell,
110   Will be as cunning as Agrippa° was,
Whose shadows made all Europe honor him.

VALDES.
Faustus, these books, thy wit, and our experience
Shall make all nations to canonize us.
As Indian Moors° obey their Spanish lords,
115   So shall the spirits of every element
Be always serviceable to us three:
Like lions shall they guard us when we please,
Like Almain rutters° with their horsemen's staves
Or Lapland giants trotting by our sides;
120   Sometimes like women or unwedded maids
Shadowing° more beauty in their airy brows
Than has the white breasts of the queen of love;
From Venice shall they drag huge argosies
And from America the golden fleece
125   That yearly stuffs old Philip's° treasury,
If learnèd Faustus will be resolute.

FAUSTUS.
Valdes, as resolute am I in this
As thou to live; therefore object it not.

CORNELIUS.
The miracles that magic will perform

Will make thee vow to study nothing else.   130
He that is grounded in astrology,
Enriched with tongues, well seen° in minerals,
Hath all the principles magic doth require.
Then doubt not Faustus but to be renowned
And more frequented for this mystery°   135
Than heretofore the Delphian oracle.°
The spirits tell me they can dry the sea
And fetch the treasure of all foreign wracks,
Yea, all the wealth that our forefathers hid
Within the massy° entrails of the earth.   140
Then tell me Faustus, what shall we three want?°

FAUSTUS.
Nothing, Cornelius. O, this cheers my soul!
Come, show me some demonstrations magical
That I may conjure° in some bushy grove
And have these joys in full possession.   145

VALDES.
Then haste thee to some solitary grove,
And bear wise Bacon's° and Albanus'° works,
The Hebrew Psalter, and New Testament;
And whatsoever else is requisite
We will inform thee ere our conference cease.   150

CORNELIUS.
Valdes, first let him know the words of art,
And then, all other ceremonies learned,
Faustus may try his cunning by himself.

VALDES.
First I'll instruct thee in the rudiments,
And then wilt thou be perfecter than I.   155

FAUSTUS.
Then come and dine with me, and after meat
We'll canvass every quiddity° thereof,
For ere I sleep I'll try what I can do:
This night I'll conjure though I die therefor!

(*Exeunt omnes.°*)

[1.2] (*Enter two Scholars.*)

I SCHOLAR. I wonder what's become of Faustus that was wont
to make our schools ring with *sic probo*.°

(*Enter Wagner.*)

II SCHOLAR. That shall we presently° know. Here comes his
boy.°

---

92 **fiery keel** burning ship sent by the Netherlanders in 1585
against a bridge erected by Parma to blockade Antwerp (Antwerp
here is an adjective, not genitive) 106 **Graveled** confounded
108 **problems** questions proposed for disputation 109 **Musaeus**
legendary Greek poet 110 **Agrippa** Cornelius Agrippa of
Nettesheim (1486–1535), German author of *De occulta philosophia*,
a survey of Renaissance magic; Agrippa was believed to have raised
spirits ("shadows") from the dead 114 **Indian Moors** American
Indians 118 **Almain rutters** German cavalrymen 121 **Shadow-
ing** sheltering 125 **Philip** King Philip II of Spain (1527–98)

132 **well seen** skilled 135 **frequented for this mystery** resorted
to for this art 136 **Delphian oracle** oracle of Apollo at Delphi
140 **massy** massive 141 **want** lack 144 **conjure** raise spirits
147 **Bacon** Roger Bacon, medieval friar and scientist **Albanus**
perhaps Pietro d'Abano, medieval writer on medicine and philosophy 157 **canvass every quiddity** discuss every essential detail
159 **s.d. omnes** all (Latin) 1.2.2 **sic probo** thus I prove it (Latin)
3 **presently** at once 4 **boy** servant (an impoverished student)

5 I SCHOLAR. How now sirrah,° where's thy master?
   WAGNER. God in heaven knows.
   I SCHOLAR. Why, dost not thou know then?
   WAGNER. Yes, I know, but that follows not.
   I SCHOLAR. Go to° sirrah, leave your jesting and tell us where
10   he is.
   WAGNER. That follows not by force of argument, which you,
      being licentiates,° should stand upon;° therefore ac-
      knowledge your error and be attentive.
   II SCHOLAR. Then you will not tell us?
15 WAGNER. You are deceived, for I will tell you. Yet if you were
      not dunces,° you would never ask me such a question. For
      is he not *corpus naturale?* And is not that *mobile?*° Then
      wherefore should you ask me such a question? But that I
      am by nature phlegmatic,° slow to wrath, and prone to
20   lechery—to love, I would say—it were not for you to
      come within forty foot of the place of execution°—al-
      though I do not doubt but to see you both hanged the
      next sessions.° Thus, having triumphed over you, I will
      set my countenance like a precisian° and begin to speak
25   thus: Truly, my dear brethren, my master is within at din-
      ner, with Valdes and Cornelius, as this wine, if it could
      speak, would inform your worships; and so, the Lord bless
      you, preserve you, and keep you, my dear brethren. (*Exit.*)
   I SCHOLAR.
      O Faustus, then I fear that which I have long suspected,
30   That thou art fall'n into that damnèd art
      For which they two are infamous through the world.
   II SCHOLAR.
      Were he a stranger, not allied to me,
      The danger of his soul would make me mourn.
      But come, let us go and inform the rector.°
35   It may be his grave counsel may reclaim him.
   I SCHOLAR.
      I fear me nothing will reclaim him now.
   II SCHOLAR.
      Yet let us see what we can do.   (*Exeunt.*)

   [1.3] (*Thunder. Enter Lucifer and four Devils.*° *Faustus
   to them with this speech.*)

   FAUSTUS.
      Now that the gloomy shadow of the night,

Longing to view Orion's° drizzling look,
Leaps from th' antarctic world unto the sky
And dims the welkin° with her pitchy breath,
Faustus, begin thine incantations   5
And try if devils will obey thy hest,
Seeing thou hast prayed and sacrificed to them.
Within this circle° is Jehovah's name
Forward and backward anagrammatized,
Th' abbreviated names of holy saints,   10
Figures of every adjunct to° the heavens,
And characters of signs and erring stars,°
By which the spirits are enforced to rise:
Then fear not, Faustus, to be resolute
And try the utmost magic can perform.   15

                                              (*Thunder.*)

*Sint mihi dei Acherontis propitii! Valeat numen triplex Iehovae!
Ignei, aerii, aquatici, spiritus, salvete! Orientis princeps, Belzebub inferni ardentis monarcha, et Demogorgon, propitiamus vos
ut appareat et surgat Mephostophilis! Quid tu moraris? Per Ieho-*
vam, Gehennam, et consecratam aquam quam nunc spargo,   20
*signumque crucis quod nunc facio, et per vota nostra, ipse nunc
surgat nobis dicatus Mephostophilis!*°

(*Enter a Devil.*°)

I charge thee to return and change thy shape,
Thou art too ugly to attend on me.
Go, and return an old Franciscan friar: 25
That holy shape becomes a devil best.

                                              (*Exit Devil.*)

I see there's virtue in my heavenly words.
Who would not be proficient in this art?
How pliant is this Mephostophilis,
Full of obedience and humility,   30
Such is the force of magic and my spells.

---

5 sirrah (term of address used to an inferior) **9 Go to** (exclamation of impatience) **12 licentiates** possessors of a degree preceding the master's degree **stand upon** make much of **16 dunces** (1) fools (2) hairsplitters **17 *corpus naturale . . . mobile*** natural matter . . . movable (Latin, scholastic definition of the subject-matter of physics) **19 phlegmatic** sluggish **21 the place of execution** the place of action, that is, the dining room (with quibble on gallows) **23 sessions** sittings of a court **24 precisian** Puritan (Wagner goes on to parody the style of the Puritans) **34 rector** head of the university **1.3.s.d. Enter . . . Devils** (they are invisible to Faustus; perhaps they enter through a trapdoor and climb to the upper playing area, as implied in V.ii.s.d.)

2 Orion constellation appearing at the beginning of winter, associated with rain **4 welkin** sky **8 circle** circle the conjuror draws around him on the ground, to call the spirits and to protect himself from them **11 adjunct to** heavenly body fixed to **12 signs and erring stars** signs of the Zodiac and planets **16–22 *Sint . . .* *Mephostophilis*** may the gods of the lower region be favorable to me. Away with the trinity of Jehovah. Hail, spirits of fire, air, water. Prince of the east, Belzebub monarch of burning hell, and Demogorgon, we pray to you that Mephostophilis may appear and rise. Why do you delay? By Jehovah, Gehenna, and the holy water which now I sprinkle, and the sign of the cross which now I make, and by our vows, may Mephostophilis himself now rise to serve us (Latin) **22 s.d. Devil** (the word "dragon" oddly appears, after "surgat Mephostophilis," in the preceding conjuration. It makes no sense in the sentence, and it has therefore been omitted from the present text, but perhaps it indicates that a dragon briefly appears at that point, or perhaps the devil referred to in the present stage direction is disguised as a dragon)

(*Enter Mephostophilis.*)

MEPHOSTOPHILIS.
    Now Faustus, what wouldst thou have me do?
FAUSTUS.
    I charge thee wait upon me whilst I live
    To do whatever Faustus shall command,
35 Be it to make the moon drop from her sphere
    Or the ocean to overwhelm the world.
MEPHOSTOPHILIS.
    I am a servant to great Lucifer
    And may not follow thee without his leave.
    No more than he commands must we perform.
FAUSTUS.
40 Did not he charge thee to appear to me?
MEPHOSTOPHILIS.
    No, I came now hither of mine own accord.
FAUSTUS.
    Did not my conjuring raise thee? Speak.
MEPHOSTOPHILIS.
    That was the cause, but yet *per accidens:*°
    For when we hear one rack° the name of God,
45 Abjure the Scriptures and his savior Christ,
    We fly in hope to get his glorious° soul.
    Nor will we come unless he use such means
    Whereby he is in danger to be damned.
    Therefore the shortest cut for conjuring
50 Is stoutly to abjure the Trinity
    And pray devoutly to the prince of hell.
FAUSTUS.
    So Faustus hath already done, and holds this principle,
    There is no chief but only Belzebub:
    To whom Faustus doth dedicate himself.
55 This word "damnation" terrifies not me
    For I confound hell in Elysium:°
    My ghost° be with the old° philosophers!
    But leaving these vain trifles of men's souls,
    Tell me, what is that Lucifer thy lord?
MEPHOSTOPHILIS.
60 Arch-regent and commander of all spirits.°
FAUSTUS.
    Was not that Lucifer an angel once?
MEPHOSTOPHILIS.
    Yes Faustus, and most dearly loved of God.
FAUSTUS.
    How comes it then that he is prince of devils?
MEPHOSTOPHILIS.
    O, by aspiring pride and insolence,
65 For which God threw him from the face of heaven.

FAUSTUS.
    And what are you that live with Lucifer?
MEPHOSTOPHILIS.
    Unhappy spirits that fell with Lucifer,
    Conspired against our God with Lucifer,
    And are forever damned with Lucifer.
FAUSTUS.
70 Where are you damned?
MEPHOSTOPHILIS.
    In hell.
FAUSTUS.
    How comes it then that thou art out of hell?
MEPHOSTOPHILIS.
    Why this is hell, nor am I out of it.
    Think'st thou that I who saw the face of God
75 And tasted the eternal joys of heaven
    Am not tormented with ten thousand hells
    In being deprived of everlasting bliss?
    O Faustus, leave these frivolous demands
    Which strikes° a terror to my fainting soul!
FAUSTUS.
80 What, is great Mephostophilis so passionate°
    For being deprivèd of the joys of heaven?
    Learn thou of Faustus manly fortitude
    And scorn those joys thou never shalt possess.
    Go bear these tidings to great Lucifer:
85 Seeing Faustus hath incurred eternal death
    By desperate thoughts against Jove's deity,
    Say he surrenders up to him his soul
    So he will spare him four and twenty years,
    Letting him live in all voluptuousness,
90 Having thee ever to attend on me,
    To give me whatsoever I shall ask,
    To tell me whatsoever I demand,
    To slay mine enemies and to aid my friends
    And always be obedient to my will.
95 Go and return to mighty Lucifer
    And meet me in my study at midnight,
    And then resolve° me of thy master's mind.
MEPHOSTOPHILIS.
    I will, Faustus.
FAUSTUS.
    Had I as many souls as there be stars
100 I'd give them all for Mephostophilis.
    By him I'll be great emperor of the world,
    And make a bridge through° the moving air
    To pass the ocean with a band of men;
    I'll join the hills that bind the Afric shore

43 *per accidens* the immediate (but not ultimate) cause (Latin)
44 **rack** torture 46 **glorious** (1) splendid (2) presumptuous
56 **confound hell in Elysium** do not distinguish between hell and
Elysium 57 **ghost** spirit **old** pre-Christian 60 **spirits** devils

79 **strikes** (it is not unusual to have a plural subject—especially
when it has a collective force—take a verb ending in -s) 80 **passionate** emotional 97 **resolve** inform 102 **through** (pronounced "thorough")

105   And make that country continent to° Spain,
      And both contributary to my crown;
      The Emperor shall not live but by my leave,
      Nor any potentate of Germany.
      Now that I have obtained what I desired
110   I'll live in speculation° of this art
      Till Mephostophilis return again.   (*Exit.*)

                                    [*Exeunt Lucifer and Devils.*]

[1.4] (*Enter Wagner and [Robin] the Clown.°*)

WAGNER. Come hither, sirrah boy.
ROBIN. Boy! O, disgrace to my person! Zounds,° boy in your
      face! You have seen many boys with such pickadevants,°
      I am sure.
5   WAGNER. Sirrah, hast thou no comings in?°
ROBIN. Yes, and goings out too, you may see sir.
WAGNER. Alas, poor slave! See how poverty jests in his
      nakedness. I know the villain's out of service, and so hun-
      gry that I know he would give his soul to the devil for a
10   shoulder of mutton, though it were blood-raw.
ROBIN. Not so, neither! I had need to have it well roasted,
      and good sauce to it, if I pay so dear, I can tell you.
WAGNER. Sirrah, wilt thou be my man and wait on me? And
      I will make thee go like *Qui mihi discipulus.°*
15   ROBIN. What, in verse?
WAGNER. No, slave, in beaten° silk and stavesacre.°
ROBIN. Stavesacre? That's good to kill vermin! Then, belike,
      if I serve you I shall be lousy.
WAGNER. Why, so thou shalt be, whether thou dost it or no;
20   for sirrah, if thou dost not presently bind thyself to me for
      seven years, I'll turn all the lice about thee into familiars°
      and make them tear thee in pieces.
ROBIN. Nay sir, you may save yourself a labor, for they are as
      familiar with me as if they paid for their meat and drink, I
25   can tell you.
WAGNER. Well sirrah, leave your jesting and take these
      guilders.°
ROBIN. Yes marry° sir, and I thank you too.
WAGNER. So, now thou art to be at an hour's warning when-
30   soever and wheresoever the devil shall fetch thee.

ROBIN. Here, take your guilders, I'll none of 'em!
WAGNER. Not I, thou art pressed.° Prepare thyself, for I will
      presently raise up two devils to carry thee away. Banio!
      Belcher!
ROBIN. Belcher! And° Belcher come here I'll belch him. I   35
      am not afraid of a devil!

                                    (*Enter two Devils.*)

WAGNER. How now sir, will you serve me now?
ROBIN. Ay, good Wagner, take away the devil then.
WAGNER. Spirits, away! [*Exeunt Devils.*] Now sirrah, follow
      me.   40
ROBIN. I will sir! But hark you master, will you teach me this
      conjuring occupation?
WAGNER. Ay sirrah, I'll teach thee to turn thyself to a dog or
      a cat or a mouse or a rat or anything.
ROBIN. A dog or a cat or a mouse or a rat? O brave° Wagner!   45
WAGNER. Villain, call me Master Wagner. And see that you
      walk attentively, and let your right eye be always diame-
      trally° fixed upon my left heel, that thou mayst *quasi ves-
      tigiis nostris insistere.°*
ROBIN. Well sir, I warrant you.   (*Exeunt.*)   50

[2.1] (*Enter Faustus in his study.*)

FAUSTUS.
      Now, Faustus, must thou needs be damned;
      Canst thou not be saved!
      What boots° it then to think on God or heaven?
      Away with such vain fancies, and despair—
      Despair in God and trust in Belzebub!   5
      Now go not backward. Faustus, be resolute!
      Why waver'st thou? O something soundeth in mine ear,
      "Abjure this magic, turn to God again."
      Ay, and Faustus will turn to God again.
      To God? He loves thee not;   10
      The god thou serv'st is thine own appetite
      Wherein is fixed the love of Belzebub!
      To him I'll build an altar and a church
      And offer lukewarm blood of newborn babes!

                                    (*Enter the two Angels.*)

BAD ANGEL.
      Go forward, Faustus, in that famous art.   15
GOOD ANGEL.
      Sweet Faustus, leave that execrable art.
FAUSTUS.
      Contrition, prayer, repentance, what of these?
GOOD ANGEL.
      O, they are means to bring thee unto heaven.

---

105 continent to continuous with   **110 speculation** contemplation   **1.4.s.d. Clown** buffoon   **2 Zounds** by God's wounds   **3
pickadevants** pointed beards   **5 comings in** income (the Clown
then quibbles on "goings out," i.e., expenses and also holes in his
clothes through which his body pokes)   **14 *Qui mihi discipulus***
one who is my disciple, that is, like the servant of a learned man
(the Latin is the beginning of a poem, familiar to Renaissance
schoolboys, on proper behavior)   **16 beaten** embroidered (leading
to the quibble on the sense "hit")   **stavesacre** preparation from
seeds of delphinium, used to kill vermin   **21 familiars** attendant
demons   **27 guilders** Dutch coins   **28 marry** indeed (a mild oath,
from "by the Virgin Mary")

32 pressed enlisted into service   **35 And** if   **45 brave** splendid
47–48 diametrally directly   **48–49 *quasi vestigiis nostris insis-
tere*** as if to step in our footsteps   **2.1.3 boots** avails

BAD ANGEL.
    Rather illusions, fruits of lunacy,
20   That make men foolish that do use them most.
GOOD ANGEL.
    Sweet Faustus, think of heaven and heavenly things.
BAD ANGEL.
    No Faustus, think of honor and of wealth.

                                  (Exeunt Angels.)

FAUSTUS.
    Wealth!
    Why, the signory of Emden° shall be mine!
25   When Mephostophilis shall stand by me
    What power can hurt me? Faustus, thou art safe.
    Cast no more doubts! Mephostophilis, come,
    And bring glad tidings from great Lucifer.
    Is't not midnight? Come Mephostophilis,
30   *Veni, veni, Mephostophile!*°

    (Enter Mephostophilis.)

    Now tell me, what saith Lucifer thy lord?
MEPHOSTOPHILIS.
    That I shall wait on Faustus whilst he lives,
    So he will buy my service with his soul.
FAUSTUS.
    Already Faustus hath hazarded that for thee.
MEPHOSTOPHILIS.
35   But now thou must bequeath it solemnly
    And write a deed of gift with thine own blood,
    For that security craves Lucifer.
    If thou deny it I must back to hell.
FAUSTUS.
    Stay Mephostophilis and tell me
40   What good will my soul do thy lord?
MEPHOSTOPHILIS.
    Enlarge his kingdom.
FAUSTUS.
    Is that the reason why he tempts us thus?
MEPHOSTOPHILIS.
    Solamen miseris socios habuisse doloris.°
FAUSTUS.
    Why, have you any pain that torture other?°
MEPHOSTOPHILIS.
45   As great as have the human souls of men.
    But tell me, Faustus, shall I have thy soul—
    And I will be thy slave and wait on thee
    And give thee more than thou hast wit to ask?
FAUSTUS.
    Ay Mephostophilis, I'll give it him.°

MEPHOSTOPHILIS.
    Then, Faustus, stab thy arm courageously   50
    And bind thy soul that at some certain day
    Great Lucifer may claim it as his own.
    And then be thou as great as Lucifer!
FAUSTUS.
    Lo, Mephostophilis, for love of thee
    Faustus hath cut his arm and with his proper° blood   55
    Assures° his soul to be great Lucifer's,
    Chief lord and regent of perpetual night.
    View here this blood that trickles from mine arm
    And let it be propitious for my wish.
MEPHOSTOPHILIS.
    But Faustus,   60
    Write it in manner of a deed of gift.
FAUSTUS.
    Ay so I do—But Mephostophilis,
    My blood congeals and I can write no more.
MEPHOSTOPHILIS.
    I'll fetch thee fire to dissolve it straight.

                                    (Exit.)

FAUSTUS.
    What might the staying of my blood portend?   65
    Is it unwilling I should write this bill?°
    Why streams it not that I may write afresh:
    "Faustus gives to thee his soul"? O there it stayed.
    Why shouldst thou not? Is not thy soul thine own?
    Then write again: "Faustus gives to thee his soul."   70

    (Enter Mephostophilis with the chafer° of fire.)

MEPHOSTOPHILIS.
    See Faustus, here is fire. Set it° on.
FAUSTUS.
    So, now the blood begins to clear again.
    Now will I make an end immediately.
MEPHOSTOPHILIS [*aside*].
    What will not I do to obtain his soul!
FAUSTUS.
    Consummatum est!° This bill is ended: 75
    And Faustus hath bequeathed his soul to Lucifer.
    —But what is this inscription on mine arm?
    Homo fuge!° Whither should I fly?
    If unto God, He'll throw me down to hell.
    My senses are deceived, here's nothing writ.   80
    O yes, I see it plain! Even here is writ
    Homo fuge! Yet shall not Faustus fly!

---

24 **signory of Emden** lordship of the rich German port at the mouth of the Ems 30 *Veni, veni, Mephostophile* come, come, Mephostophilis (Latin) 43 *Solamen . . . doloris* misery loves company (Latin) **44 other** others **49 him** that is, to Lucifer

55 **proper** own **56 Assures** conveys by contract **66 bill** contract **70 s.d. chafer** portable grate **71 it** that is, the receptacle containing the congealed blood **75 *Consummatum est*** it is finished (Latin; a blasphemous repetition of Christ's words on the Cross; see John 19.30) **78 *Homo fuge*** fly, man (Latin)

MEPHOSTOPHILIS [*aside*].
  I'll fetch him somewhat to delight his mind.

                                              (*Exit.*)

(*Enter Devils giving crowns and rich apparel to Faustus.
They dance and then depart.*)

(*Enter Mephostophilis.*)

FAUSTUS.
  What means this show? Speak, Mephostophilis.
MEPHOSTOPHILIS.
85   Nothing Faustus, but to delight thy mind
     And let thee see what magic can perform.
FAUSTUS.
     But may I raise such spirits when I please?
MEPHOSTOPHILIS.
     Ay Faustus, and do greater things than these.
FAUSTUS.
     Then, Mephostophilis, receive this scroll,
90   A deed of gift of body and of soul:
     But yet conditionally that thou perform
     All covenants and articles between us both.
MEPHOSTOPHILIS.
     Faustus, I swear by hell and Lucifer
     To effect all promises between us both.
FAUSTUS.
95   Then hear me read it, Mephostophilis:
     "On these conditions following:
     First, that Faustus may be a spirit° in form and sub-
        stance.
     Secondly, that Mephostophilis shall be his servant and
100   be by him commanded.
     Thirdly, that Mephostophilis shall do for him and bring
        him whatsoever.
     Fourthly, that he shall be in his chamber or house invisi-
        ble.
105 Lastly, that he shall appear to the said John Faustus at all
        times in what form or shape soever he please:
     I, John Faustus of Wittenberg, Doctor, by these presents,
        do give both body and soul to Lucifer, prince of the
        east, and his minister Mephostophilis, and further-
110   more grant unto them that, four and twenty years be-
        ing expired, and these articles above written being
        inviolate,° full power to fetch or carry the said John
        Faustus, body and soul, flesh, blood, or goods, into
        their habitation wheresoever.
115   By me John Faustus.
MEPHOSTOPHILIS. Speak Faustus, do you deliver this as your
        deed?

FAUSTUS. Ay, take it, and the devil give thee good of it!
MEPHOSTOPHILIS. So now Faustus, ask me what thou wilt.
FAUSTUS. First will I question with thee about hell. Tell me,   120
     where is the place that men call hell?
MEPHOSTOPHILIS. Under the heavens.
FAUSTUS.
     Ay, so are all things else, but whereabouts?
MEPHOSTOPHILIS.
     Within the bowels of these elements
     Where we are tortured and remain forever.   125
     Hell hath no limits nor is circumscribed
     In one self place, but where we are is hell,
     And where hell is there must we ever be.
     And to be short, when all the world dissolves
     And every creature shall be purified   130
     All places shall be hell that is not heaven!
FAUSTUS.
     I think hell's a fable.
MEPHOSTOPHILIS.
     Ay, think so still—till experience change thy mind!
FAUSTUS.
     Why, dost thou think that Faustus shall be damned?
MEPHOSTOPHILIS.
     Ay, of necessity, for here's the scroll   135
     In which thou hast given thy soul to Lucifer.
FAUSTUS.
     Ay, and body too; but what of that?
     Think'st thou that Faustus is so fond° to imagine
     That after this life there is any pain?
     No, these are trifles and mere old wives' tales.   140
MEPHOSTOPHILIS.
     But I am an instance to prove the contrary,
     For I tell thee I am damned and now in hell!
FAUSTUS.
     Nay, and this be hell, I'll willingly be damned—
     What, sleeping, eating, walking, and disputing?
     But leaving this, let me have a wife, the fairest maid in 145
        Germany, for I am wanton and lascivious and cannot
        live without a wife.
MEPHOSTOPHILIS.
     Well Faustus, thou shalt have a wife.

(*He fetches in a woman Devil* [*with fireworks*].)

FAUSTUS.
     What sight is this?
MEPHOSTOPHILIS.
     Now Faustus, wilt thou have a wife?   150
FAUSTUS.
     Here's a hot whore indeed! No, I'll no wife.
MEPHOSTOPHILIS.
     Marriage is but a ceremonial toy,°

                                          [*Exit She-Devil.*]

---

97 spirit evil spirit, devil (but to see Faustus as transformed now
into a devil deprived of freedom to repent is to deprive the remainder of the play of much of its meaning)   **112 inviolate** unviolated

138 fond foolish   **152 toy** trifle

And if thou lovest me, think no more of it.
I'll cull thee out° the fairest courtesans
155 And bring them every morning to thy bed.
She whom thine eye shall like thy heart shall have,
Were she as chaste as was Penelope,°
As wise as Saba,° or as beautiful
As was bright Lucifer before his fall.
160 Here, take this book and peruse it well.
The iterating° of these lines brings gold;
The framing° of this circle on the ground
Brings thunder, whirlwinds, storm, and lightning;
Pronounce this thrice devoutly to thyself,
165 And men in harness° shall appear to thee,
Ready to execute what thou command'st.

FAUSTUS.
Thanks Mephostophilis for this sweet book.
This will I keep as chary as my life.

(*Exeunt.°*)

[2.2] (*Enter Faustus in his study and Mephostophilis.*)

FAUSTUS.
When I behold the heavens, then I repent
And curse thee, wicked Mephostophilis,
Because thou has deprived me of those joys.
MEPHOSTOPHILIS.
'Twas thine own seeking Faustus, thank thyself.
5 But think'st thou heaven is such a glorious thing?
I tell thee, Faustus, it is not half so fair
As thou or any man that breathe on earth.
FAUSTUS.
How prov'st thou that?
MEPHOSTOPHILIS.
'Twas made for man; then he's more excellent.
FAUSTUS.
10 If heaven was made for man, 'twas made for me!
I will renounce this magic and repent.

(*Enter the two Angels.*)

GOOD ANGEL.
Faustus, repent: yet° God will pity thee!
BAD ANGEL.
Thou art a spirit: God cannot pity thee!
FAUSTUS.
Who buzzeth in mine ears I am a spirit?

Be I a devil, yet God may pity me—   15
Yea, God will pity me if I repent.
BAD ANGEL.
Ay, but Faustus never shall repent.

(*Exit Angels.*)

FAUSTUS.
My heart is hardened, I cannot repent.
Scarce can I name salvation, faith, or heaven,
Swords, poison, halters, and envenomed steel   20
Are laid before me to dispatch myself.
And long ere this I should have done the deed
Had not sweet pleasure conquered deep despair.
Have not I made blind Homer sing to me
Of Alexander's love and Oenon's° death?   25
And hath not he° that built the walls of Thebes
With ravishing sound of his melodious harp
Made music with my Mephostophilis?
Why should I die then or basely despair?
I am resolved, Faustus shall not repent!   30
Come Mephostophilis, let us dispute again
And reason of divine astrology.
Speak, are there many spheres above the moon?
Are all celestial bodies but one globe
As is the substance of this centric° earth?   35
MEPHOSTOPHILIS.
As are the elements, such° are the heavens,
Even from the moon unto the empyreal orb
Mutually folded in each others' spheres,
And jointly move upon one axle-tree,
Whose terminè° is termed the world's wide pole.   40
Nor are the names of Saturn, Mars, or Jupiter
Feigned but are erring stars.°
FAUSTUS.
But have they all one motion,
Both *situ et tempore?*°
MEPHOSTOPHILIS. All move from east to west in four and   45
twenty hours upon the poles of the world but differ in
their motions upon the poles of the zodiac.
FAUSTUS.
These slender questions Wagner can decide.
Hath Mephostophilis no greater skill?
Who knows not the double motion of the planets?   50
That the first is finished in a natural day.°

154 cull thee out select for you   157 Penelope wife of Ulysses,
famed for her fidelity   158 Saba the Queen of Sheba   161 iterat-
ing repetition   162 framing drawing   165 harness armor   168
s.d. Exeunt (a scene following this stage direction has probably
been lost. Earlier Wagner hired the Clown; later the Clown is an
ostler possessed of one of Faustus's conjuring books. Possibly, then,
the lost scene was a comic one, showing the Clown stealing a book
and departing)   2.2.12 yet still, even now

25 Alexander . . . Oenone Paris, also called Alexander, was Oenone's
lover, but he later deserted her for Helen of Troy, causing the Trojan
War, the subject of Homer's *Iliad*   26 he Amphion, whose music
charmed stones to form the walls of Thebes   35 centric central   36
such that is, separate but combined; the idea is that the heavenly bodies are separate but their spheres are concentric ("folded"), and all—
from the nearest (the moon) to the farthest ("the empyreal orb" or
empyrean)—move on one axletree   40 terminè end, extremity   42
erring stars planets   44 *situ et tempore* in place and in time   51
natural day twenty-four hours

The second thus: Saturn in thirty years;
Jupiter in twelve; Mars in four; the sun, Venus, and Mer-
cury in a year; the moon in twenty-eight days. These
55   are freshmen's suppositions.° But tell me, hath every
sphere a dominion or *intelligentia*?°
MEPHOSTOPHILIS. Ay.
FAUSTUS. How many heavens or spheres are there?
MEPHOSTOPHILIS. Nine: the seven planets, the firmament,
60   and the empyreal heaven.
FAUSTUS. But is there not *coelum igneum et crystallinum*?°
MEPHOSTOPHILIS. No Faustus, they be but fables.
FAUSTUS. Resolve me then in this one question. Why are not
conjunctions, oppositions, aspects, eclipses all at one
65   time,° but in some years we have more, in some less?
MEPHOSTOPHILIS. *Per inaqualem motum respectu totius*.°
FAUSTUS. Well, I am answered. Now tell me, who made the
world?
MEPHOSTOPHILIS. I will not.
70   FAUSTUS. Sweet Mephostophilis, tell me.
MEPHOSTOPHILIS. Move° me not, Faustus!
FAUSTUS. Villain, have not I bound thee to tell me anything?
MEPHOSTOPHILIS. Ay, that is not against our kingdom.
75   This is. Thou are damned. Think thou of hell!
FAUSTUS.
   Think, Faustus, upon God, that made the world.
MEPHOSTOPHILIS.
   Remember this!   (*Exit.*)
FAUSTUS.
   Ay, go accursèd spirit to ugly hell!
   'Tis thou hast damned distressèd Faustus' soul.—
80   Is't not too late?

(*Enter the two Angels.*)

BAD ANGEL.
   Too late.
GOOD ANGEL.
   Never too late, if Faustus will repent.
BAD ANGEL.
   If thou repent, devils will tear thee in pieces.
GOOD ANGEL.
   Repent, and they shall never raze° thy skin.

(*Exeunt Angels.*)

FAUSTUS.
85   O Christ, my savior, my savior!
   Help to save distressèd Faustus' soul.

(*Enter Lucifer, Belzebub, and Mephostophilis.*)

LUCIFER.
   Christ cannot save thy soul, for He is just.
   There's none but I have interest in° the same.
FAUSTUS.
   O, what art thou that look'st so terribly?
LUCIFER.
   I am Lucifer   90
   And this is my companion prince in hell.
FAUSTUS.
   O Faustus, they are come to fetch thy soul!
BELZEBUB.
   We are come to tell thee thou dost injure us.
LUCIFER.
   Thou call'st on Christ contrary to thy promise.
BELZEBUB.
   Thou should'st not think on God.   95
LUCIFER.   Think on the Devil.
BELZEBUB.
   And his dam° too.
FAUSTUS.
   Nor will Faustus henceforth. Pardon him for this,
   And Faustus vows never to look to heaven!
   Never to name God or to pray to Him,   100
   To burn His Scriptures, slay His ministers,
   And make my spirits pull His churches down.
LUCIFER.
   So shalt thou show thyself an obedient servant,
   And we will highly gratify thee for it.
BELZEBUB. Faustus, we are come from hell in person to show   105
   thee some pastime. Sit down and thou shalt behold the
   Seven Deadly Sins° appear to thee in their own proper
   shapes and likeness.
FAUSTUS. That sight will be as pleasant to me as Paradise was
   to Adam the first day of his creation.   110
LUCIFER. Talk not of Paradise or creation but mark the show.
   Go Mephostophilis, fetch them in.

(*Enter the Seven Deadly Sins [led by a Piper].*)

BELZEBUB. Now Faustus, question them of their names and
   dispositions.
FAUSTUS. That shall I soon. What art thou, the first?   115
PRIDE. I am Pride. I disdain to have any parents. I am like to
   Ovid's flea,° I can creep into every corner of a wench:
   sometimes, like a periwig I sit upon her brow; next, like a
   necklace I hang about her neck; then, like a fan of feathers I kiss her; and then, turning myself to a wrought   120
   smock,° do what I list—But fie, what a smell is here! I'll

---

55 suppositions premises   **56 dominion or *intelligentia*** governing angel or intelligence (believed to impart motion to the sphere) **61 *coelum igneum et crystallinum*** a heaven of fire and a crystalline sphere (Latin)   **64–65 at one time** that is, at regular intervals   **66 Per . . . totius** because of unequal speed within the system (Latin)   **71 Move** anger   **84 raze** scratch

88 interest in legal claim on   **97 dam** mother   **107 Seven Deadly Sins** (so called because they cause spiritual death; they are Pride, Covetousness, Envy, Wrath, Gluttony, Sloth, Lechery) **117 Ovid's flea** flea in *Carmen de pulce*, a lewd poem mistakenly attributed to Ovid   **120–121 wrought smock** decorated petticoat

not speak a word more for a king's ransom unless the ground be perfumed and covered with cloth of arras.°

FAUSTUS. Thou art a proud knave indeed.

125 What art thou, the second?

COVETOUSNESS. I am Covetousness, begotten of an old churl in a leather bag;° and might I now obtain my wish, this house, you and all, should turn to gold that I might lock you safe into my chest. O my sweet gold!

130 FAUSTUS. And what art thou, the third?

ENVY. I am Envy, begotten of a chimney-sweeper and an oyster-wife.° I cannot read and therefore wish all books burned. I am lean with seeing others eat. O, that there would come a famine over all the world that all might die

135 and I live alone! Then thou shouldst see how fat I'd be. But must thou sit and I stand? Come down, with a vengeance!

FAUSTUS. Out, envious wretch! But what art thou, the fourth?

140 WRATH. I am Wrath. I had neither father nor mother. I leapt out of a lion's mouth when I was scarce an hour old and ever since have run up and down the world with these case° of rapiers, wounding myself when I could get none to fight withal. I was born in hell! And look to it, for

145 some of you shall be my father.

FAUSTUS. And what art thou, the fifth?

GLUTTONY. I am Gluttony. My parents are all dead, and the devil a penny they have left me, but a small pension: and that buys me thirty meals a day and ten bevers,° a small

150 trifle to suffice nature. I come of a royal pedigree. My father was a gammon° of bacon, and my mother was a hogshead of claret wine. My godfathers were these: Peter Pickled-herring and Martin Martlemas-beef.° But my godmother, O, she was an ancient gentlewoman: her

155 name was Margery March-beer.° Now Faustus, thou hast heard all my progeny,° wilt thou bid me to supper?

FAUSTUS. Not I.

GLUTTONY. Then the devil choke thee!

FAUSTUS. Choke thyself, glutton! What art thou, the sixth?

160 SLOTH. Heigh-ho!° I am Sloth. I was begotten on a sunny bank. Heigh-ho, I'll not speak a word more for a king's ransom.

FAUSTUS. And what are you, Mistress Minx, the seventh and last?

LECHERY. Who, I, I sir? I am one that loves an inch of raw   165
mutton° better than an ell of fried stockfish,° and the first letter of my name begins with Lechery.

LUCIFER. Away to hell, away! On, piper!

(*Exeunt the Seven Sins.*)

FAUSTUS.
O, how this sight doth delight my soul!

LUCIFER.
But Faustus, in hell is all manner of delight.   170

FAUSTUS.
O, might I see hell and return again safe, how happy were I then!

LUCIFER.
Faustus, thou shalt. At midnight I will send for thee. Meanwhile peruse this book and view it thoroughly, And thou shalt turn thyself into what shape thou wilt.   175

FAUSTUS.
Thanks mighty Lucifer.
This will I keep as chary° as my life.

LUCIFER.
Now Faustus, farewell.

FAUSTUS.
Farewell great Lucifer. Come Mephostophilis.

(*Exeunt omnes several° ways.*)

[2.3] (*Enter [Robin] the Clown.*)

ROBIN. What, Dick, look to the horses there till I come again! I have gotten one of Doctor Faustus' conjuring books, and now we'll have such knavery as't passes.

(*Enter Dick.*)

DICK. What, Robin, you must come away and walk the horses.

ROBIN. I walk the horses? I scorn't, 'faith. I have other mat-   5
ters in hand. Let the horses walk themselves an° they will. [*Reading*] A per se°—a; t, h, e—the; o per se—o; deny orgon—gorgon.° Keep further from me, O thou illiterate and unlearned hostler!

DICK. 'Snails,° what hast thou got there, a book? Why, thou   10
canst not tell ne'er a word on't.

ROBIN. That thou shalt see presently. Keep out of the circle, I say, lest I send you into the hostry° with a vengeance.

---

123 **cloth of arras** Flemish cloth used for tapestries   127 **leather bag** moneybag (?)   131–132 **chimney-sweeper ... oyster-wife** that is, dirty and smelly   142–143 **these case** this pair   149 **bevers** snacks (literally drinks)   151 **gammon** haunch   153 **Martlemas-beef** cattle slaughtered at Martinmas (11 November) and salted for winter consumption   155 **March-beer** strong beer brewed in March   156 **progeny** ancestry   160 **Heigh-ho** (a yawn or tired greeting)

165–166 **inch of raw mutton** that is, penis ("mutton" in a bawdy sense commonly alludes to a prostitute, but since here the speaker is a woman, the allusion must be to a male)   166 **an ell of ... stockfish** forty-five inches of dried cod   177 **chary** carefully   179 **s.d. several** various   2.3.6 **an** if   7 **per se** by itself (Latin; the idea is, "A by itself spells A")   7–8 **deny orgon—gorgon** (Robin is trying to read the name "Demogorgon")   10 **'Snails** by God's nails   13 **hostry** hostelry, inn

DICK. That's like, 'faith! You had best leave your foolery, for
15 an my master come, he'll conjure you, 'faith.
ROBIN. My master conjure me? I'll tell thee what. An my
master come here, I'll clap as fair a pair of horns° on's
head as e'er thou sawest in thy life.
DICK. Thou need'st not do that, for my mistress hath done it.
20 ROBIN. Ay, there be of us here that have waded as deep into
matters as other men—if they were disposed to talk.
DICK. A plague take you! I thought you did not sneak up and
down after her for nothing. But I prithee tell me in good
sadness° Robin, is that a conjuring book?
25 ROBIN. Do but speak what thou't have me to do, and I'll do't.
If thou't dance naked, put off thy clothes, and I'll conjure
thee about presently. Or if thou't go but to the tavern
with me, I'll give thee white wine, red wine, claret wine,
sack,° muscadine, malmsey, and whippincrust°—hold-
30 belly-hold. And we'll not pay one penny for it.
DICK. O brave! Prithee let's to it presently, for I am as dry as a
dog.
ROBIN. Come then, let's away.   (*Exeunt.*)

[3] (*Enter the Chorus.*)

Learnèd Faustus,
To find the secrets of astronomy
Graven in the book of Jove's high firmament,
Did mount him up to scale Olympus' top:
5 Where, sitting in a chariot burning bright
Drawn by the strength of yokèd dragons' necks,
He views the clouds, the planets, and the stars,
The tropics, zones,° and quarters of the sky,
From the bright circle° of the hornèd moon
10 Even to the height of *primum mobile:*°
And whirling round with this circumference
Within the concave compass of the pole,
From east to west his dragons swiftly glide
And in eight days did bring him home again.
15 Not long he stayed within his quiet house
To rest his bones after his weary toil
But new exploits do hale him out again.
And mounted then upon a dragon's back,
That with his wings did part the subtle air,
20 He now is gone to prove cosmography,°
That measures coasts and kingdoms of the earth,
And as I guess will first arrive at Rome
To see the Pope and manner of his court

And take some part of holy Peter's feast,
The which this day is highly solemnized.   25

(*Exit.*)

[3.1] (*Enter Faustus and Mephostophilis.*)

FAUSTUS.
Having now, my good Mephostophilis,
Passed with delight the stately town of Trier,°
Environed round with airy mountain tops,
With walls of flint, and deep-entrenchèd lakes,°
Not to be won by any conquering prince: 5
From Paris next, coasting the realm of France,
We saw the river Main fall into Rhine,
Whose banks are set with groves of fruitful vines:
Then up to Naples, rich Campania,
Whose buildings fair and gorgeous to the eye,   10
The streets straight forth and paved with finest brick,
Quarters the town in four equivalents.
There saw we learnèd Maro's° golden tomb,
The way he cut an English mile in length
Through° a rock of stone in one night's space.   15
From thence to Venice, Padua, and the rest,
In one of which a sumptuous temple stands
That threats the stars with her aspiring top,
Whose frame is paved with sundry colored stones
And roofed aloft with curious work in gold.   20
Thus hitherto hath Faustus spent his time.
But tell me now, what resting-place is this?
Hast thou, as erst I did command,
Conducted me within the walls of Rome?
MEPHOSTOPHILIS.
I have, my Faustus, and for proof thereof   25
This is the goodly palace of the Pope,
And 'cause we are no common guests
I choose his privy chamber for our use.
FAUSTUS.
I hope his Holiness will bid us welcome.
MEPHOSTOPHILIS.
All's one, for we'll be bold with his venison.   30
But now my Faustus, that thou may'st perceive
What Rome contains for to delight thine eyes,
Know that this city stands upon seven hills
That underprop the groundwork of the same:
Just through the midst runs flowing Tiber's stream   35
With winding banks that cut it in two parts,
Over the which four stately bridges lean°
That make safe passage to each part of Rome.

17 horns (as the next speech indicates, horns were said to adorn
the head of a man whose wife was unfaithful)   **23–24 in good sadness** seriously   **29 sack** sherry   **whippincrust** illiterate pronunciation of "hippocras," a spiced wine   **3 Chorus 8 zones** segments of
the sky   **9 circle** orbit   **10 *primum mobile*** the outermost sphere,
the empyrean   **20 prove cosmography** test maps, that is, explore
the universe

3.1.2 Trier German city on the Moselle, also known as Trèves   **4
deep-entrenchèd lakes** moats   **13 Maro** Vergil (Publius Vergilius
Maro, 70–19 B.C.E.)   **15 Through** (pronounced "thorough")   **37
lean** bend

Upon the bridge called Ponte Angelo
40 Erected is a castle passing strong
Where thou shalt see such store of ordinance
As that the double cannons forged of brass
Do match the number of the days contained
Within the compass of one complete year,
45 Beside the gates and high pyramides°
That Julius Caesar brought from Africa.

FAUSTUS.
Now, by the kingdoms of infernal rule,
Of Styx, of Acheron, and the fiery lake
Of ever-burning Phlegethon,° I swear
50 That I do long to see the monuments
And situation of bright-splendent Rome.
Come therefore, let's away.

MEPHOSTOPHILIS.
Nay stay my Faustus. I know you'd see the Pope
And take some part of holy Peter's feast,
55 The which this day with high solemnity,
This day, is held through Rome and Italy
In honor of the Pope's triumphant victory.

FAUSTUS.
Sweet Mephostophilis, thou pleasest me.
Whilst I am here on earth let me be cloyed
60 With all things that delight the heart of man.
My four and twenty years of liberty
I'll spend in pleasure and in dalliance,
That Faustus' name, whilst this bright frame doth stand,
May be admirèd through the furthest land.

MEPHOSTOPHILIS.
65 'Tis well said, Faustus, come then, stand by me
And thou shalt see them come immediately.

FAUSTUS.
Nay stay my Faustus. I know you'd see the Pope
And grant me my request, and then I go.
Thou know'st, within the compass of eight days
70 We viewed the face of heaven, of earth, and hell.
So high our dragons soared into the air
That looking down the earth appeared to me
No bigger than my hand in quantity—
There did we view the kingdoms of the world,
75 And what might please mine eye I there beheld.
Then in this show let me an actor be
That this proud Pope may Faustus' cunning see!

MEPHOSTOPHILIS.
Let it be so, my Faustus, but first stay
And view their triumphs° as they pass this way.
80 And then devise what best contents thy mind
By cunning in thine art to cross the Pope
Or dash the pride of this solemnity—

To make his monks and abbots stand like apes
And point like antics° at his triple crown,
To beat the beads about the friars' pates,   85
Or clap huge horns upon the cardinals' heads,
Or any villainy thou canst devise—
And I'll perform it, Faustus. Hark, they come!
This day shall make thee be admired° in Rome!

(*Enter the Cardinals and Bishops, some bearing crosiers,
some the pillars; Monks and Friars singing their procession; then the Pope and Raymond King of Hungary, with
Bruno° led in chains.*)

POPE.
Cast down our footstool.   90

RAYMOND.   Saxon Bruno, stoop,
Whilst on thy back his Holiness ascends
Saint Peter's chair and state° pontifical.

BRUNO.
Proud Lucifer, that state belongs to me—
But thus I fall to Peter, not to thee.   95

POPE.
To me and Peter shalt thou grov'lling lie
And crouch before the papal dignity!
Sound trumpets then, for thus Saint Peter's heir
From Bruno's back ascends Saint Peter's chair!

(*A flourish° while he ascends.*)

Thus as the gods creep on with feet of wool   100
Long ere with iron hands they punish men,
So shall our sleeping vengeance now arise
And smite with death thy hated enterprise.
Lord Cardinals of France and Padua,
Go forthwith to our holy consistory°   105
And read amongst the statutes decretal°
What by the holy council held at Trent°
The sacred synod° hath decreed for him
That doth assume the papal government
Without election and a true consent.   110
Away, and bring us word with speed!

I CARDINAL.
We go my lord.   (*Exeunt [two] Cardinals.*)

POPE.
Lord Raymond—   [*Talks to him apart.*]

FAUSTUS.
Go haste thee, gentle Mephostophilis,
Follow the cardinals to the consistory   115

---

84 antics grotesque figures, buffoons **89 admired** wondered at **s.d. Raymond King of Hungary . . . Bruno** (unhistorical figures; Bruno is the emperor's nominee for the papal throne) **93 state** throne **99 s.d. flourish** trumpet fanfare **105 consistory** that is, meeting-place of the papal consistory or senate **106 statutes decretal** that is, ecclesiastical laws **107 council held at Trent** (intermittently from 1545 to 1563) **108 synod** council

45 pyramides obelisk (pronounced py-ràm-i-des) **48–49 Styx, Acheron, Phlegethon** rivers of the underworld **79 triumphs** spectacular displays

And as they turn their superstitious books
Strike them with sloth and drowsy idleness
And make them sleep so sound that in their shapes
Thyself and I may parley with this Pope,
120 This proud confronter of the Emperor!
—And in despite of all his holiness
Restore this Bruno to his liberty
And bear him to the states of Germany!

MEPHOSTOPHILIS.
Faustus, I go.

FAUSTUS.
125 Dispatch it soon.
The Pope shall curse that Faustus came to Rome.

(*Exit Faustus and Mephostophilis.*)

BRUNO.
Pope Adrian, let me have some right of law:
I was elected by the Emperor.

POPE.
We will depose the Emperor for that deed
130 And curse the people that submit to him.
Both he and thou shalt stand excommunicate
And interdict from church's privilege
And all society of holy men.
He grows too proud in his authority,
135 Lifting his lofty head above the clouds,
And like a steeple overpeers the church.
But we'll pull down his haughty insolence.
And as Pope Alexander,° our progenitor,°
Trod on the neck of German Frederick,
140 Adding this golden sentence to our praise:
"That Peter's heirs should tread on emperors
And walk upon the dreadful adder's back,
Treading the lion and the dragon down,
And fearless spurn the killing basilisk"°—
145 So will we quell that haughty schismatic
And by authority apostolical
Depose him from his regal government.

BRUNO.
Pope Julius swore to princely Sigismond,
For him and the succeeding Popes of Rome,
150 To hold the emperors their lawful lords.

POPE.
Pope Julius did abuse the church's rites
And therefore none of his decrees can stand.
Is not all power on earth bestowed on us?
And therefore though we would, we cannot err.
155 Behold this silver belt whereto is fixed
Seven golden keys fast sealed with seven seals
In token of our sevenfold power from heaven

To bind or loose, lock fast, condemn, or judge,
Resign° or seal, or whatso pleaseth us.
Then he and thou and all the world shall stoop—   160
Or be assured of our dreadful curse
To light as heavy as the pains of hell.

(*Enter Faustus and Mephostophilis like the cardinals.*)

MEPHOSTOPHILIS [*aside*].
Now tell me Faustus, are we not fitted well?

FAUSTUS [*aside*].
Yes Mephostophilis, and two such cardinals
Ne'er served a holy Pope as we shall do.   165
But whilst they sleep within the consistory
Let us salute his reverend Fatherhood.

RAYMOND.
Behold my lord, the cardinals are returned.

POPE.
Welcome grave fathers, answer presently,°
What have our holy council there decreed   170
Concerning Bruno and the Emperor
In quittance of° their late conspiracy
Against our state and papal dignity?

FAUSTUS.
Most sacred patron of the church of Rome,
By full consent of all the synod   175
Of priests and prelates it is thus decreed:
That Bruno and the German Emperor
Be held as lollards° and bold schismatics
And proud disturbers of the church's peace.
And if that Bruno by his own assent,   180
Without enforcement of the German peers,
Did seek to wear the triple diadem
And by your death to climb Saint Peter's chair,
The statutes decretal have thus decreed:
He shall be straight condemned of heresy   185
And on a pile of fagots burnt to death.

POPE.
It is enough. Here, take him to your charge
And bear him straight to Ponte Angelo
And in the strongest tower enclose him fast.
Tomorrow, sitting in our consistory   190
With all our college of grave cardinals
We will determine of his life or death.
Here, take his triple crown along with you
And leave it in the church's treasury.
Make haste again,° my good lord cardinals,   195
And take our blessing apostolical.

MEPHOSTOPHILIS [*aside*].
So, so! Was never devil thus blessed before.

---

138 Pope Alexander Pope Alexander III (d. 1181) compelled the
emperor Frederick Barbarossa to kneel before him   **progenitor** predecessor   **144 basilisk** fabulous monster said to kill with a glance

159 Resign unseal   **169 presently** immediately   **172 quittance
of** requital for   **178 lollards** heretics   **195 again** that is, to return

FAUSTUS [*aside*].
    Away sweet Mephostophilis, be gone!
    The cardinals will be plagued for this anon.

        (*Exeunt Faustus and Mephostophilis [with Bruno].*)

POPE.
200   Go presently and bring a banquet forth,
    That we may solemnize Saint Peter's feast
    And with Lord Raymond, King of Hungary,
    Drink to our late and happy victory.

                (*Exeunt.*)

[3.2] (*A sennet° while the banquet is brought in, and then
enter Faustus and Mephostophilis in their own shapes.*)

MEPHOSTOPHILIS.
    Now Faustus, come prepare thyself for mirth.
    The sleepy cardinals are hard at hand
    To censure Bruno, that is posted hence,
    And on a proud-paced steed as swift as thought
5   Flies o'er the Alps to fruitful Germany,
    There to salute the woeful Emperor.
FAUSTUS.
    The Pope will curse them for their sloth today
    That slept both Bruno and his crown away.
    But now, that Faustus may delight his mind
10   And by their folly make some merriment,
    Sweet Mephostophilis, so charm me here
    That I may walk invisible to all
    And do whate'er I please unseen of any.
MEPHOSTOPHILIS.
    Faustus, thou shalt. Then kneel down presently,
15   Whilst on thy head I lay my hand
    And charm thee with this magic wand.
    First wear this girdle, then appear
    Invisible to all are here:
    The planets seven, the gloomy air,
20   Hell, and the Furies' forkèd hair,°.
    Pluto's blue fire, and Hecat's°. tree
    With magic spells so compass thee
    That no eye may thy body see.

    So Faustus, now for all their holiness,
25   Do what thou wilt, thou shalt not be discerned.

3.2.s.d. **sennet** set of notes played on a trumpet signaling an approach or a departure   **20 Furies' forkèd hair** (the hair of the Furies consisted of snakes, whose forked tongues may be implied here) **21 Hecat** Hecate, goddess of magic (possibly her "tree" is the gallows-tree, but possibly "tree" is a slip for "three," Hecate being the triple goddess of heaven, earth, and hell)

FAUSTUS.
    Thanks Mephostophilis. Now friars, take heed
    Lest Faustus make your shaven crowns to bleed.
MEPHOSTOPHILIS.
    Faustus, no more. See where the cardinals come.

    (*Enter Pope [and Friars] and all the Lords [with King Raymond and the Archbishop of Rheims]. Enter the [two] Cardinals with a book.*)

POPE.
    Welcome lord cardinals. Come, sit down.
    Lord Raymond, take your seat. Friars, attend,   30
    And see that all things be in readiness
    As best beseems this solemn festival.
I CARDINAL.
    First may it please your sacred Holiness
    To view the sentence of the reverend synod
    Concerning Bruno and the Emperor.   35
POPE.
    What needs this question? Did I not tell you
    Tomorrow we would sit i' th' consistory
    And there determine of his punishment?
    You brought us word, even now, it was decreed
    That Bruno and the cursèd Emperor   40
    Were by the holy council both condemned
    For loathèd lollards and base schismatics.
    Then wherefore would you have me view that book?
I CARDINAL.
    Your Grace mistakes. You gave us no such charge.
RAYMOND.
    Deny it not; we all are witnesses   45
    That Bruno here was late delivered you
    With his rich triple crown to be reserved
    And put into the church's treasury.
BOTH CARDINALS.
    By holy Paul we saw them not.
POPE.
    By Peter you shall die   50
    Unless you bring them forth immediately.
    Hale them to prison, lade their limbs with gyves.°
    False prelates, for this hateful treachery
    Cursed be your souls to hellish misery.

        [*Exeunt Attendants with two Cardinals.*]

FAUSTUS.
    So, they are safe. Now Faustus, to the feast.   55
    The Pope had never such a frolic guest.
POPE.
    Lord Archbishop of Rheims, sit down with us.
ARCHBISHOP.
    I thank your Holiness.

---

52 gyves fetters

FAUSTUS.
     Fall to,° the devil choke you an you spare!
POPE.
60   Who's that spoke? Friars, look about.
     Lord Raymond, pray fall to. I am beholding
     To the Bishop of Milan for this so rare a present.
FAUSTUS [*aside*].
     I thank you, sir!   [*Snatches the dish.*]
POPE.
     How now! Who snatched the meat from me?
65   Villains, why speak you not?
     My good Lord Archbishop, here's a most dainty dish
     Was sent me from a cardinal in France.
FAUSTUS [*aside*].
     I'll have that too!   [*Snatches the dish.*]
POPE.
     What lollards do attend our Holiness
70   That we receive such great indignity!
     Fetch me some wine.
FAUSTUS [*aside*].
     Ay, pray do, for Faustus is adry.
POPE.
     Lord Raymond, I drink unto your Grace.
FAUSTUS [*aside*].
     I pledge your Grace.   [*Snatches the goblet.*]
POPE.
75   My wine gone too? Ye lubbers, look about
     And find the man that doth this villainy,
     Or by our sanctitude you all shall die.
     I pray, my lords, have patience at this troublesome ban-
        quet.
ARCHBISHOP.
     Please it your Holiness, I think it be some ghost crept
80   out of purgatory, and now is come unto your Holiness
        for his pardon.
POPE.
     It may be so:
     Go then, command our priests to sing a dirge
     To lay the fury of this same troublesome ghost.

                                              [*Exit Attendant.*]

[*The Pope crosses himself before eating.*]

FAUSTUS.
85   How now! Must every bit be spiced with a cross?
     Nay then, take that! [*Strikes the Pope.*]
POPE.
     O, I am slain! Help me my lords!
     O come and help to bear my body hence.
     Damned be this soul forever for this deed.

                                    (*Exeunt the Pope and his train.*)

59 Fall to set to work (here, as commonly, "start eating")

MEPHOSTOPHILIS.
     Now Faustus, what will you do now?   90
     For I can tell you, you'll be cursed with bell, book, and
        candle.°
FAUSTUS.
     Bell, book, and candle. Candle, book, and bell.
     Forward and backward, to curse Faustus to hell!

(*Enter the Friars, with bell, book, and candle for the
dirge.*)

I FRIAR.
     Come brethren, let's about our business with good devo-
        tion.
     Cursèd be he that stole his Holiness' meat from the
        table.   95
     Maledicat Dominus!°
     Cursèd be he that struck his Holiness a blow on the face.
     Maledicat Dominus!

                                              [*Faustus strikes a Friar.*]

     Cursèd be he that took Friar Sandelo a blow on the pate.
     Maledicat Dominus!   100
     Cursèd be he that disturbeth our holy dirge.
     Maledicat Dominus!
     Cursèd be he that took away his Holiness' wine.
     Maledicat Dominus!

([*Faustus and Mephostophilis*] *beat the Friars, fling fireworks
                                    among them and exeunt.*)

[3.3] (*Enter [Robin the] Clown and Dick with a cup.*)

DICK. Sirrah Robin, we were best look that your devil can
     answer the stealing of this same cup, for the vintner's boy
     follows us at the hard heels.°
ROBIN. 'Tis no matter, let him come! An he follow us I'll so
     conjure him as he was never conjured in his life, I war-   5
     rant him. Let me see the cup.

(*Enter Vintner.*)

DICK. Here 'tis. Yonder he comes. Now Robin, now or never
     show thy cunning.
VINTNER. O, are you here? I am glad I have found you. You
     are a couple of fine companions!° Pray, where's the cup   10
     you stole from the tavern?
ROBIN. How, how! We steal a cup? Take heed what you say.
     We look not like cup-stealers, I can tell you.

91 bell, book, and candle implements used in excommunicating
(the bell was tolled, the book closed, the candle extinguished)
96 Maledicat Dominus may the Lord curse him (Latin)   **3.3.3 at
the hard heels** hard at heel, closely   **10 companions** fellows (contemptuous)

VINTNER. Never deny't, for I know you have it, and I'll
15   search you.
ROBIN. Search me? Ay, and spare not! [*Aside.*] Hold the cup,
Dick.—Come, come. Search me, search me.

[*Vintner searches him.*]

VINTNER. Come on sirrah, let me search you now.
DICK. Ay ay, do do. [*Aside.*] Hold the cup, Robin.—I fear not
20   your searching. We scorn to steal your cups, I can tell
you.

[*Vintner searches him.*]

VINTNER. Never outface me for the matter, for sure the cup is
between you two.
ROBIN. Nay, there you lie! 'Tis beyond us both.°
25   VINTNER. A plague take you. I thought 'twas your knavery to
take it away. Come, give it me again.
ROBIN. Ay, much! When, can you tell?° [*Aside.*] Dick, make
me a circle and stand close at my back and stir not for thy
life. Vintner, you shall have your cup anon. [*Aside.*] Say
30   nothing, Dick! O *per se*, o; Demogorgon, Belcher, and
Mephostophilis!

(*Enter Mephostophilis.* [*Exit Vintner.*])

MEPHOSTOPHILIS.
You princely legions of infernal rule,
How am I vexèd by these villains' charms!
From Constantinople have they brought me now
35   Only for pleasure of these damnèd slaves.
ROBIN. By lady sir, you have had a shrewd° journey of it. Will
it please you to take a shoulder of mutton to supper and a
tester° in your purse and go back again?
DICK. Ay, I pray you heartily, sir. For we called you but in
40   jest, I promise you.
MEPHOSTOPHILIS.
To purge the rashness of this cursèd deed,
First be thou turnèd to this ugly shape,
For apish° deeds transformèd to an ape.
ROBIN. O brave! An ape! I pray sir, let me have the carrying
45   of him about to show some tricks.
MEPHOSTOPHILIS. And so thou shalt. Be thou transformed to
a dog and carry him upon thy back. Away, be gone!
ROBIN. A dog! That's excellent. Let the maids look well to
their porridge-pots, for I'll into the kitchen presently.
50   Come Dick, come.

(*Exeunt the two Clowns.*)

MEPHOSTOPHILIS.
Now with the flames of ever-burning fire

---

24 **beyond us both** (apparently Robin has managed to place the
cup at some distance from where he now stands)   27 **When, can
you tell** (a scornful reply)   36 **shrewd** bad   38 **tester** sixpence
43 **apish** (1) foolish (2) imitative

I'll wing myself and forthwith fly amain
Unto my Faustus, to the Great Turk's court.

(*Exit.*)

[4] (*Enter Chorus.*)

When Faustus had with pleasure ta'en the view
Of rarest things and royal courts of kings,
He stayed his course and so returnèd home,
Where such as bare his absence but with grief,
I mean his friends and nearest companions,   5
Did gratulate° his safety with kind words.
And in their conference° of what befell
Touching his journey through the world and air
They put forth questions of astrology
Which Faustus answered with such learnèd skill   10
As they admired and wondered at his wit.
Now is his fame spread forth in every land.
Amongst the rest the Emperor is one,
Carolus the Fifth,° at whose palace now
Faustus is feasted 'mongst his noblemen.   15
What there he did in trial of his art
I leave untold, your eyes shall see performed.

(*Exit.*)

[4.1] (*Enter Martino and Frederick at several° doors.*)

MARTINO.
What ho, officers, gentlemen!
Hie to the presence°to attend the Emperor.
Good Frederick, see the rooms be voided straight,°
His Majesty is coming to the hall.
Go back and see the state° in readiness.   5
FREDERICK.
But where is Bruno, our elected Pope,
That on a fury's back came post from Rome?
Will not his Grace consort° the Emperor?
MARTINO.
O yes, and with him comes the German conjurer,
The learnèd Faustus, fame of Wittenberg,   10
The wonder of the world for magic art:
And he intends to show great Carolus
The race of all his stout progenitors
And bring in presence of his Majesty
The royal shapes and warlike semblances   15
Of Alexander and his beauteous paramour.°
FREDERICK.
Where is Benvolio?

---

4 **Chorus** 6 **gratulate** express joy in   **7 conference** discussion   **14
Carolus the Fifth** Charles V (1500–58), Holy Roman Emperor
4.1.s.d. several separate   **2 presence** presence-chamber   **3 voided
straight** emptied immediately   **5 state** chair of state, throne   **8
consort** attend   **16 Alexander and his beauteous paramour**
Alexander the Great and his mistress Thaïs

MARTINO.   Fast asleep, I warrant you.
  He took his rouse with stoups° of Rhenish wine
  So kindly yesternight to Bruno's health
20 That all this day the sluggard keeps his bed.
FREDERICK.
  See, see, his window's ope. We'll call to him.
MARTINO.
  What ho, Benvolio!

  (*Enter Benvolio above at a window, in his nightcap,*
  buttoning.)

BENVOLIO.
  What a devil ail you two?
MARTINO.
  Speak softly sir, lest the devil hear you,
25 For Faustus at the court is late arrived
  And at his heels a thousand furies wait
  To accomplish whatsoever the doctor please.
BENVOLIO.
  What of this?
MARTINO.
  Come, leave thy chamber first, and thou shalt see
30 This conjurer perform such rare exploits
  Before the Pope° and royal Emperor
  As never yet was seen in Germany.
BENVOLIO.
  Has not the Pope enough of conjuring yet?
  He was upon the devil's back late enough!
35 And if he be so far in love with him
  I would he would post with him to Rome again.
FREDERICK.
  Speak, wilt thou come and see this sport?
BENVOLIO.   Not I.
MARTINO.
  Wilt thou stand in thy window and see it then?
BENVOLIO.
  Ay, and I fall not asleep i' th' meantime.
MARTINO.
40 The Emperor is at hand, who comes to see
  What wonders by black spells may compassed be.
BENVOLIO. Well, go you attend the Emperor. I am content for
  this once to thrust my head out at a window, for they say
  if a man be drunk overnight the devil cannot hurt him in
45 the morning. If that be true, I have a charm in my head
  shall control him as well as the conjurer, I warrant you.

  (*Exit* [*Martino with Frederick. Benvolio remains at*
  window].°)

18 took his rouse with stoups had drinking bouts with full goblets
31 the Pope that is, Bruno **46 s.d. Benvolio remains at window**
(because Benvolio does not leave the stage, this scene cannot properly be said to be ended. But the present edition, following its predecessors for convenience of reference, begins a new scene)

[4.2] (*A sennet.° Charles the German Emperor, Bruno,*
[*Duke of*] *Saxony, Faustus, Mephostophilis, Frederick,*
Martino, and Attendants.)

EMPEROR.
  Wonder of men, renowned magician,
  Thrice-learnèd Faustus, welcome to our court.
  This deed of thine in setting Bruno free
  From his and our professèd enemy,
  Shall add more excellence unto thine art   5
  Than if by powerful necromantic spells
  Thou could'st command the world's obedience.
  For ever be beloved of Carolus!
  And if this Bruno thou hast late redeemed°
  In peace possess the triple diadem   10
  And sit in Peter's chair despite of chance,
  Thou shalt be famous through all Italy
  And honored of the German Emperor.
FAUSTUS.
  These gracious words, most royal Carolus,
  Shall make poor Faustus to his utmost power   15
  Both love and serve the German Emperor
  And lay his life at holy Bruno's feet.
  For proof whereof, if so your Grace be pleased,
  The doctor stands prepared by power of art
  To cast his magic charms that shall pierce through   20
  The ebon gates of ever-burning hell,
  And hale the stubborn furies from their caves
  To compass whatsoe'er your Grace commands.
BENVOLIO. Blood! He speaks terribly. But for all that I do not
  greatly believe him. He looks as like a conjurer as the   25
  Pope to a costermonger.°
EMPEROR.
  Then Faustus, as thou late didst promise us,
  We would behold that famous conqueror
  Great Alexander and his paramour
  In their true shapes and state majestical,   30
  That we may wonder at their excellence.
FAUSTUS.
  Your Majesty shall see them presently.—
  Mephostophilis away,
  And with a solemn noise of trumpets' sound
  Present before this royal Emperor   35
  Great Alexander and his beauteous paramour.
MEPHOSTOPHILIS.
  Faustus, I will.   [*Exit.*]
BENVOLIO. Well master doctor, an your devils come not away
  quickly, you shall have me asleep presently. Zounds,° I

4.2.s.d. sennet trumpet fanfare (the absence of a verb in the rest of
the stage direction perhaps indicates that the Emperor and his party
do not enter but rather are "discovered," as Faustus may have been
discovered at the beginning of I.i, if the Chorus drew back a curtain) **9 redeemed** freed **26 costermonger** fruit-seller **39
Zounds** by God's wounds

40   could eat myself for anger to think I have been such an
      ass all this while to stand gaping after the devils' gover-
      nor and can see nothing.

FAUSTUS.
      I'll make you feel something anon if my art fail me not!
      My lord, I must forewarn your Majesty
45   That when my spirits present the royal shapes
      Of Alexander and his paramour,
      Your Grace demand no questions of the King
      But in dumb silence let them come and go.

EMPEROR.
      Be it as Faustus please; we are content.
50 BENVOLIO. Ay, ay, and I am content too. And thou bring
      Alexander and his paramour before the Emperor, I'll be
      Actaeon° and turn myself to a stag.

FAUSTUS [*aside*]. And I'll play Diana and send you the horns
      presently.

      (*Sennet. Enter at one [door] the Emperor Alexander, at
      the other Darius.° They meet. Darius is thrown down.
      Alexander kills him, takes off his crown, and offering to go
      out, his Paramour meets him. He embraceth her and sets
      Darius' crown upon her head, and coming back both
      salute the Emperor; who leaving his state offers to embrace
      them, which Faustus seeing suddenly stays him. Then
      trumpets cease and music sounds.*)

55   My gracious lord, you do forget yourself.
      These are but shadows, not substantial.

EMPEROR.
      O pardon me, my thoughts are so ravished
      With sight of this renownèd Emperor,
      That in mine arms I would have compassed° him.
60   But Faustus, since I may not speak to them,
      To satisfy my longing thoughts at full,
      Let me this tell thee: I have heard it said
      That this fair lady whilst she lived on earth,
      Had on her neck a little wart or mole.
65   How may I prove that saying to be true?

FAUSTUS.
      Your Majesty may boldly go and see.

EMPEROR.
      Faustus, I see it plain!
      And in this sight thou better pleasest me
      Than if I gained another monarchy.

FAUSTUS.
70   Away, be gone!   (*Exit show.*)
      See, see, my gracious lord, what strange beast is yon that
         thrusts his head out at the window!

EMPEROR.
      O wondrous sight! See, Duke of Saxony,
      Two spreading horns most strangely fastened
      Upon the head of young Benvolio.   75

SAXONY.
      What, is he asleep or dead?

FAUSTUS.
      He sleeps my lord, but dreams not of his horns.

EMPEROR.
      This sport is excellent. We'll call and wake him.
      What ho, Benvolio!

BENVOLIO. A plague upon you! Let me sleep awhile.   80

EMPEROR. I blame thee not to sleep much, having such a
      head of thine own.

SAXONY. Look up Benvolio! 'Tis the Emperor calls.

BENVOLIO. The Emperor! Where? O zounds, my head!

EMPEROR. Nay, and thy horns hold, 'tis no matter for thy   85
      head, for that's armed sufficiently.

FAUSTUS. Why, how now Sir Knight? What, hanged by the
      horns?° This is most horrible! Fie fie, pull in your head
      for shame! Let not all the world wonder at you.

BENVOLIO. Zounds doctor, is this your villainy?   90

FAUSTUS.
      Oh, say not so sir: The doctor has no skill,
      No art, no cunning to present these lords
      Or bring before this royal Emperor
      The mighty monarch, warlike Alexander.
      If Faustus do it, you are straight resolved   95
      In bold Actaeon's shape to turn a stag.
      And therefore my lord, so please your Majesty,
      I'll raise a kennel of hounds shall hunt him so
      As all his footmanship shall scarce prevail
      To keep his carcass from their bloody fangs.   100
      Ho, Belimote, Argiron, Asterote!

BENVOLIO. Hold, hold! Zounds, he'll raise up a kennel of
      devils I think, anon. Good my lord, entreat for me.
      'Sblood,° I am never able to endure these torments.

EMPEROR.
      Then good master doctor,   105
      Let me entreat you to remove his horns.
      He has done penance now sufficiently.

FAUSTUS. My gracious lord, not so much for injury done to
      me, as to delight your Majesty with some mirth, hath
      Faustus justly requited this injurious° knight; which be- 110
      ing all I desire, I am content to remove his horns.
      Mephostophilis, transform him. And hereafter sir, look
      you speak well of scholars.

BENVOLIO [*aside*]. Speak well of ye! 'Sblood, and scholars be
      such cuckold-makers to clap horns of honest men's heads 115

---

52 Actaeon legendary hunter who saw the naked goddess Diana
bathing. She transformed him into a stag, and he was torn to
pieces by his own hounds   **54 s.d. Darius** King of Persia, defeated by Alexander in 334 B.C.E.   **59 compassed** encompassed,
embraced

87–88 hanged by the horns (the spreading horns prevent Benvolio
from pulling his head inside the window)   **104 'Sblood** by God's
blood   **110 injurious** insulting

o' this order, I'll ne'er trust smooth faces and small ruffs°.
more. But an I be not revenged for this, would I might be
turned to a gaping oyster and drink nothing but salt wa-
ter.   [*Exit.*]

EMPEROR.
120   Come Faustus, while the Emperor lives,
      In recompense of this thy high desert,
      Thou shalt command the state of Germany
      And live beloved of mighty Carolus.

                                                          (*Exeunt omnes.*)

[4.3] (*Enter Benvolio, Martino, Frederick, and Soldiers.*)

MARTINO.
      Nay, sweet Benvolio, let us sway thy thoughts
      From this attempt against the conjurer.
BENVOLIO.
      Away! You love me not to urge me thus.
      Shall I let slip° so great an injury
5   When every servile groom jests at my wrongs
      And in their rustic gambols proudly say,
      "Benvolio's head was graced with horns today"?
      O, may these eyelids never close again
      Till with my sword I have that conjurer slain!
10   If you will aid me in this enterprise,
      Then draw your weapons and be resolute;
      If not, depart. Here will Benvolio die
      But° Faustus' death shall quit° my infamy.
FREDERICK.
      Nay, we will stay with thee, betide what may,
15   And kill that doctor if he come this way.
BENVOLIO.
      Then, gentle Frederick, hie thee to the grove
      And place our servants and our followers
      Close in an ambush there behind the trees.
      By this, I know, the conjurer is near.
20   I saw him kneel and kiss the Emperor's hand
      And take his leave laden with rich rewards.
      Then soldiers, boldly fight. If Faustus die,
      Take you the wealth, leave us the victory.
FREDERICK.
      Come soldiers, follow me unto the grove.
25   Who kills him shall have gold and endless love.

                                      (*Exit Frederick with the Soldiers.*)

BENVOLIO.
      My head is lighter than it was by th' horns—
      But yet my heart more ponderous than my head,
      And pants until I see that conjurer dead.

MARTINO.
      Where shall we place ourselves, Benvolio?
BENVOLIO.
      Here will we stay to bide the first assault.   30
      O, were that damnèd hell-hound but in place
      Thou soon should'st see me quit my foul disgrace.

(*Enter Frederick.*)

FREDERICK.
      Close, close! The conjurer is at hand
      And all alone comes walking in his gown.
      Be ready then and strike the peasant° down!   35
BENVOLIO.
      Mine be that honor then! Now sword, strike home!
      For horns he gave I'll have his head anon.

(*Enter Faustus with the false head.*)

MARTINO.
      See see, he comes.
BENVOLIO.   No words. This blow ends all!

                                                          [*Strikes Faustus.*]

      Hell take his soul, his body thus must fall.
FAUSTUS.
      O!   40
FREDERICK.
      Groan you, master doctor?
BENVOLIO.
      Break may his heart with groans! Dear Frederick, see,
      Thus will I end his griefs immediately.

[*Cuts off Faustus's false head.*]

MARTINO.
      Strike with a willing hand! His head is off.
BENVOLIO.
      The devil's dead, the furies now may laugh.   45
FREDERICK.
      Was this that stern aspect, that awful frown,
      Made the grim monarch of infernal spirits
      Tremble and quake at his commanding charms?
MARTINO.
      Was this that damnèd head whose heart conspired
      Benvolio's shame before the Emperor?   50
BENVOLIO.
      Ay, that's the head, and here the body lies
      Justly rewarded for his villainies.
FREDERICK.
      Come let's devise how we may add more shame
      To the black scandal of his hated name.
BENVOLIO.
      First, on his head in quittance of my wrongs   55

116 small ruffs (worn by scholars, in contrast to the large ruffs
worn by courtiers) **4.3.4 let slip** ignore **13 But** unless **quit**
avenge

35 peasant low fellow

I'll nail huge forkèd horns and let them hang
Within the window where he yoked me first
That all the world may see my just revenge.
MARTINO.
   What use shall we put his beard to?
60 BENVOLIO. We'll sell it to a chimney-sweeper. It will wear out
   ten birchen brooms, I warrant you.
FREDERICK. What shall eyes do?
BENVOLIO. We'll put out his eyes, and they shall serve for
   buttons to his lips to keep his tongue from catching cold.
65 MARTINO. An excellent policy! And now sirs, having di-
   vided him, what shall the body do?

                                              [*Faustus rises.*]

BENVOLIO. Zounds, the devil's alive again!
FREDERICK. Give him his head for God's sake!
FAUSTUS.
   Nay keep it. Faustus will have heads and hands,
70   Ay, all your hearts, to recompense this deed.
   Knew you not, traitors, I was limited
   For four and twenty years to breathe on earth?
   And had you cut my body with your swords
   Or hewed this flesh and bones as small as sand,
75   Yet in a minute had my spirit returned
   And I had breathed a man made free from harm.
   But wherefore do I dally my revenge?
   Asteroth, Belimoth, Mephostophilis!

   (*Enter Mephostophilis and other Devils.*)

   Go horse these traitors on your fiery backs
80   And mount aloft with them as high as heaven,
   Thence pitch them headlong to the lowest hell.
   Yet stay, the world shall see their misery,
   And hell shall after plague their treachery.
   Go Belimoth, and take this caitiff° hence
85   And hurl him in some lake of mud and dirt:
   Take thou this other, drag him through the woods
   Amongst the pricking thorns and sharpest briars:
   Whilst with my gentle Mephostophilis
   This traitor flies unto some steepy rock
90   That rolling down may break the villain's bones
   As he intended to dismember me.
   Fly hence, dispatch my charge immediately!
FREDERICK.
   Pity us, gentle Faustus, save our lives!
FAUSTUS.
   Away!
FREDERICK.
95   He must needs go that the devil drives.

                   (*Exeunt Spirits with the Knights.*)

84 caitiff wretch

(*Enter the ambushed Soldiers.*)

I SOLDIER.
   Come sirs, prepare yourselves in readiness.
   Make haste to help these noble gentlemen.
   I heard them parley with the conjurer.
II SOLDIER.
   See where he comes, dispatch, and kill the slave!
FAUSTUS.
   What's here, an ambush to betray my life?   100
   Then Faustus, try thy skill. Base peasants, stand!
   For lo, these trees remove° at my command
   And stand as bulwarks 'twixt yourselves and me
   To shield me from your hated treachery!
   Yet to encounter this your weak attempt   105
   Behold an army comes incontinent.°

(*Faustus strikes the door, and enter a Devil playing on a
drum, after him another bearing an ensign, and divers with
weapons: Mephostophilis with fireworks: they set upon the
Soldiers and drive them out.*)

                                              [*Exeunt all.*]

[4.4] (*Enter at several doors Benvolio, Frederick, and
Martino, their heads and faces bloody and besmeared with
mud and dirt, all having horns on their heads.*)

MARTINO.
   What ho, Benvolio!
BENVOLIO.   Here! What, Frederick, ho!
FREDERICK.
   O, help me gentle friend. Where is Martino?
MARTINO.
   Dear Frederick, here,
   Half smothered in a lake of mud and dirt,
   Through which the furies dragged me by the heels.   5
FREDERICK.
   Martino, see, Benvolio's horns again.
MARTINO.
   O misery! How now Benvolio?
BENVOLIO.
   Defend me, heaven! Small I be haunted° still?
MARTINO.
   Nay fear not man, we have no power to kill.
BENVOLIO.
   My friends transformèd thus! O hellish spite,   10
   Your heads are all set with horns.
FREDERICK.
                              You hit it right:
   It is your own you mean. Feel on your head.

102 remove move **106 incontinent** immediately **4.4.8
haunted** (the following line suggests that there is a quibble on
"hunted," Benvolio now resembling a stag)

BENVOLIO.
    Zounds, horns again!
MARTINO.
                        Nay chafe° not man, we all are sped.°
BENVOLIO.
    What devil attends this damned magician,
15   That spite of spite our wrongs are doubled?
FREDERICK.
    What may we do that we may hide our shames?
BENVOLIO.
    If we should follow him to work revenge
    He'd join long asses' ears to these huge horns
    And make us laughing-stocks to all the world.
MARTINO.
20   What shall we then do, dear Benvolio?
BENVOLIO.
    I have a castle joining near these woods,
    And thither we'll repair and live obscure
    Till time shall alter this our brutish shapes.
    Sith° black disgrace hath thus eclipsed our fame,
25   We'll rather die with grief than live with shame.

                            (*Exeunt omnes.*)

[4.5] (*Enter Faustus and the Horse-Courser.*°)

HORSE-COURSER. I beseech your worship, accept of these
    forty dollars.°
FAUSTUS. Friend, thou canst not buy so good a horse for so
    small a price. I have no great need to sell him, but if thou
5   likest him for ten dollars more, take him, because I see
    thou hast a good mind to him.
HORSE-COURSER. I beseech you sir, accept of this. I am a very
    poor man and have lost very much of late by horse-flesh,°
    and this bargain will set me up again.
10 FAUSTUS. Well, I will not stand° with thee. Give me the
    money. Now sirrah, I must tell you that you may ride him
    o'er hedge and ditch and spare him not. But, do you hear,
    in any case ride him not into the water.
HORSE-COURSER. How sir, not into the water! Why, will he
15   not drink of all waters?°
FAUSTUS. Yes, he will drink of all waters, but ride him not
    into the water: o'er hedge and ditch or where thou wilt,
    but not into the water. Go bid the hostler deliver him
    unto you, and remember what I say.
20 HORSE-COURSER. I warrant you sir. O joyful day! Now am I a
    made man forever.   (*Exit.*)

---

13 **chafe** fret   **sped** done for, ruined (because of the horns)
24 **Sith** since   **4.5.s.d. Horse-Courser** horse trader   **2 dollars**
German coins   **8 horse-flesh** (the possibility of a quibble on
"whores' flesh" is increased by "set me up" and "stand" in the ensuing dialogue)   **10 stand** haggle   **15 drink of all waters** that is, go
anywhere

FAUSTUS.
    What art thou, Faustus, but a man condemned to die?
    Thy fatal time° draws to a final end;
    Despair doth drive distrust into my thoughts.
    Confound these passions with a quiet sleep.   25
    Tush, Christ did call the thief upon the cross!°
    Then rest thee Faustus, quiet in conceit.°

                                        (*He sits to sleep.*)

(*Enter the Horse-Courser wet.*)

HORSE-COURSER. O what a cozening° doctor was this! I rid-
    ing my horse into the water, thinking some hidden mys-
    tery had been in the horse, I had nothing under me but a   30
    little straw and had much ado to escape drowning. Well,
    I'll go rouse him and make him give me my forty dollars
    again. Ho, sirrah doctor, you cozening scab! Master doc-
    tor, awake and rise, and give me my money again, for
    your horse is turned to a bottle° of hay. Master doctor!   35

                                        (*He pulls off his leg.*)

    Alas, I am undone! What shall I do? I have pulled off his
    leg.
FAUSTUS. O help, help! The villain hath murdered me!
HORSE-COURSER. Murder or not murder, now he has but one
    leg I'll outrun him, and cast this leg into some ditch or   40
    other.   [*Exit.*]
FAUSTUS. Stop him, stop him, stop him!—Ha, ha, ha! Faus-
    tus hath his leg again, and the horse-courser a bundle of
    hay for his forty dollars.

(*Enter Wagner.*)

    How now, Wagner? What news with thee?   45
WAGNER. If it please you, the Duke of Vanholt doth earnestly
    entreat your company, and hath sent some of his men to
    attend you with provision fit for your journey.
FAUSTUS. The Duke of Vanholt's an honorable gentleman,
    and one to whom I must be no niggard of my cunning.   50
    Come, away!

                                            (*Exeunt.*)

[4.6] (*Enter [Robin the] Clown, Dick, Horse-courser,
and a Carter.*)

CARTER. Come my masters, I'll bring you to the best beer in
    Europe. What ho, hostess! Where be these whores?

(*Enter Hostess.*)

---

23 **fatal time** life span   **26 Christ . . . cross** (in Luke 23.39–43
Christ promised one of the thieves that he would be with Christ in
paradise)   **27 quiet in conceit** with a quiet mind   **28 cozening**
deceiving   **35 bottle** bundle

HOSTESS. How now? What lack you? What, my old guests, welcome.

5 ROBIN [*aside*]. Sirrah Dick, dost thou know why I stand so mute?

DICK [*aside*]. No Robin, why is't?

ROBIN [*aside*]. I am eighteen pence on the score.° But say nothing. See if she have forgotten me.

10 HOSTESS. Who's this that stands so solemnly by himself? What, my old guest!

ROBIN. O, hostess, how do you? I hope my score stands still.

HOSTESS. Ay, there's no doubt of that, for methinks you make no haste to wipe it out.

15 DICK. Why hostess, I say, fetch us some beer!

HOSTESS. You shall, presently.—Look up into th' hall there, ho!   (*Exit.*)

DICK. Come sirs, what shall we do now till mine hostess comes?

20 CARTER. Marry sir, I'll tell you the bravest tale how a conjurer served me. You know Doctor Fauster?

HORSE-COURSER. Ay, a plague take him! Here's some on's have cause to know him. Did he conjure thee too?

CARTER. I'll tell you how he served me. As I was going to

25 Wittenberg t'other day with a load of hay, he met me and asked me what he should give me for as much hay as he could eat. Now sir, I thinking that a little would serve his turn, bad him take as much as he would for three farthings. So he presently gave me my money and fell to

30 eating; and as I am a cursen° man, he never left eating till he had eat up all my load of hay.

ALL. O monstrous, eat a whole load of hay!

ROBIN. Yes yes, that may be, for I have heard of one that has eat a load of logs.°

35 HORSE-COURSER. Now sirs, you shall hear how villainously he served me. I went to him yesterday to buy a horse of him, and he would by no means sell him under forty dollars. So sir, because I knew him to be such a horse as would run over hedge and ditch and never tire, I gave

40 him his money. So, when I had my horse, Doctor Fauster bade me ride him night and day and spare him no time. "But," quoth he, "in any case ride him not into the water." Now sir, I thinking the horse had had some quality that he would not have me know of, what did I but rid

45 him into a great river—and when I came just in the midst, my horse vanished away and I sate straddling upon a bottle of hay.

ALL. O brave doctor!

HORSE-COURSER. But you shall hear how bravely I served

50 him for it. I went me home to his house, and there I found him asleep. I kept ahallowing and whooping in his ears, but all could not wake him. I seeing that, took him by the leg and never rested pulling till I had pulled me his leg quite off, and now 'tis at home in mine hostry.°

DICK. And has the doctor but one leg then? That's excellent, 55 for one of his devils turned me into the likeness of an ape's face.

CARTER. Some more drink, hostess!

ROBIN. Hark you, we'll into another room and drink awhile, and then we'll go seek out the doctor.   (*Exeunt omnes.*) 60

[4.7] (*Enter the Duke of Vanholt, his [Servants,] Duchess, Faustus, and Mephostophilis.*)

DUKE. Thanks master doctor, for these pleasant sights. Nor know I how sufficiently to recompense your great deserts in erecting that enchanted castle in the air, the sight whereof so delighted me,

As nothing in the world could please me more. 5

FAUSTUS. I do think myself, my good lord, highly recompensed in that it pleaseth your Grace to think but well of that which Faustus hath performed.—But gracious lady, it may be that you have taken no pleasure in those sights. Therefore I pray you tell me what is the thing you most 10 desire to have: be it in the world it shall be yours. I have heard that great-bellied° women do long for things are rare and dainty.

DUCHESS. True master doctor, and since I find you so kind, I will make known unto you what my heart desires to have: 15 and were it now summer, as it is January, a dead time of the winter, I would request no better meat° than a dish of ripe grapes.

FAUSTUS.

This is but a small matter. Go Mephostophilis, away!

           (*Exit Mephostophilis.*)

Madam, I will do more than this for your content. 20

(*Enter Mephostophilis again with the grapes.*)

Here, now taste ye these. They should be good, For they come from a far country, I can tell you.

DUKE. This makes me wonder more than all the rest, that at this time of the year when every tree is barren of his fruit, from whence you had these ripe grapes. 25

FAUSTUS. Please it your Grace, the year is divided into two circles° over the whole world, so that when it is winter with us, in the contrary circle it is likewise summer with them, as in India, Saba,° and such countries that lie far east, where they have fruit twice a year. From whence, by 30 means of a swift spirit that I have, I had these grapes brought as you see.

DUCHESS. And trust me, they are the sweetest grapes that e'er I tasted.

(*The Clowns [Robin, Dick, Carter, and Horse-Courser] bounce° at the gate within.*)

4.6.8 on the score in debt   **30 cursen** that is, Christian (dialect form)   **34 eat a load of logs** been drunk   **54 hostry** inn

4.7.12 great-bellied that is, pregnant   **17 meat** food   **27 two circles** that is, the northern and the southern hemispheres (though later in the speech he talks of east and west rather than of north and south)   **29 Saba** Sheba   **34 s.d. bounce** knock

DUKE.

35   What rude disturbers have we at the gate?
     Go pacify their fury, set it ope,
     And then demand of them what they would have.

     (*They knock again and call out to talk with Faustus.*)

SERVANT.

     Why, how now masters, what a coil° is there!
     What is the reason° you disturb the Duke?

40 DICK. We have no reason for it, therefore a fig for him!

SERVANT.

     Why saucy varlets, dare you be so bold!

HORSE-COURSER. I hope sir, we have wit enough to be more
     bold than welcome.

SERVANT.

     It appears so. Pray be bold elsewhere

45   And trouble not the Duke.

DUKE. What would they have?

SERVANT.

     They all cry out to speak with Doctor Faustus.

CARTER. Ay, and we will speak with him.

DUKE. Will you sir? Commit° the rascals.

50 DICK. Commit with us! He were as good commit with his fa-
     ther as commit with us!

FAUSTUS.

     I do beseech your Grace, let them come in.
     They are good subject for a merriment.

DUKE.

     Do as thou wilt, Faustus, I give thee leave.

FAUSTUS.

55   I thank your Grace.

     (*Enter [Robin] the Clown, Dick, Carter, and Horse-
     courser.*)

                         Why, how now my good friends?
     'Faith, you are too outrageous; but come near,
     I have procured your pardons. Welcome all.

ROBIN. Nay sir, we will be welcome for our money, and we
     will pay for what we take. What ho, give's half a dozen of

60   beer here, and be hanged!

FAUSTUS.

     Nay, hark you, can you tell me where you are?

CARTER. Ay, marry can I, we are under heaven.

SERVANT.

     Ay, but Sir Sauce-box, know you in what place?

HORSE-COURSER. Ay ay, the house is good enough to drink

65   in. Zounds, fill us some beer, or we'll break all the barrels

in the house and dash out all your brains with your bottles.

FAUSTUS.

     Be not so furious. Come, you shall have beer.
     My lord, beseech you give me leave awhile;
     I'll gage° my credit 'twill content your Grace.   70

DUKE.

     With all my heart, kind doctor, please thyself.
     Our servants and our court's at thy command.

FAUSTUS.

     I humbly thank your Grace.—Then fetch some beer.

HORSE-COURSER. Ay marry, there spake a doctor indeed!
     And 'faith, I'll drink a health to thy wooden leg for that   75
     word.

FAUSTUS.

     My wooden leg? What dost thou mean by that?

CARTER. Ha, ha, ha, dost hear him Dick? He has forgot his
     leg.

HORSE-COURSER. Ay ay, he does not stand much upon° that.   80

FAUSTUS.

     No, 'faith, not much upon a wooden leg.

CARTER. Good lord, that flesh and blood should be so frail
     with your worship! Do not you remember a horse-courser
     you sold a horse to?

FAUSTUS. Yes, I remember I sold one a horse.   85

CARTER. And do you remember you bid he should not ride
     into the water?

FAUSTUS. Yes, I do very well remember that.

CARTER. And do you remember nothing of your leg?

FAUSTUS. No, in good sooth.   90

CARTER. Then I pray remember your curtsy.°

FAUSTUS. I thank you sir.

CARTER. 'Tis not so much worth. I pray you tell me one
     thing.

FAUSTUS. What's that?   95

CARTER. Be both your legs bedfellows every night together?

FAUSTUS. Would'st thou make a colossus° of me that thou
     askest me such questions?

CARTER. No, truly sir, I would make nothing of you, but I
     would fain know that.   100

     (*Enter Hostess with drink.*)

FAUSTUS. Then I assure thee certainly they are.

CARTER. I thank you, I am fully satisfied.

FAUSTUS. But wherefore dost thou ask?

CARTER. For nothing, sir, but methinks you should have a
     wooden bedfellow of one of 'em.   105

---

38 coil turmoil   **39 reason** (pronounced like "raisin," leading to
the quibble on "fig"; a "fig" here is an obscene contemptuous gesture in which the hand is clenched and the thumb is thrust between the first and second fingers, making the thumb resemble the
stem of a fig, or a penis)   **49 Commit** imprison (Dick proceeds to
quibble on the idea of committing adultery)

70 gage pledge   **80 stand much upon** (quibble on "attach much
importance to")   **91 curtsy** (also called "a leg," hence there is a
quibble on the Carter's previous speech)   **97 colossus** huge statue
in the harbor at Rhodes, between whose legs ships were said to have
sailed

HORSE-COURSER. Why, do you hear sir, did not I pull off one
of your legs when you were asleep?

FAUSTUS. But I have it again now I am awake. Look you here
sir.

110 ALL. O horrible! Had the doctor three legs?

CARTER. Do you remember sir, how you cozened me and eat
up my load of—

(*Faustus charms him dumb.*)

DICK. Do you remember how you made me wear an ape's—
[*Faustus charms him.*]

HORSE-COURSER. You whoreson conjuring scab! Do you re-
115 member how you cozened me with a ho—

[*Faustus charms him.*]

ROBIN. Ha' you forgotten me? You think to carry it away with
your "hey-pass" and "re-pass"?° Do you remember the
dog's fa—

([*Faustus charms him.*] *Exeunt Clowns.*)

HOSTESS. Who pays for the ale? Hear you master doctor, now
120 you have sent away my guests, I pray who shall pay me for
my a—

([*Faustus charms her.*] *Exit Hostess.*)

DUCHESS.
My lord,
We are much beholding to this learnèd man.

DUKE.
So are we madam, which we will recompense
125 With all the love and kindness that we may:
His artful sport drives all sad thoughts away.

(*Exeunt.*)

[5.1] (*Thunder and lightning. Enter Devils with covered
dishes: Mephostophilis leads them into Faustus's study.
Then enter Wagner.*)

WAGNER. I think my master means to die shortly. He has
made his will and given me his wealth: his house, his
goods, and store of golden plate—besides two thousand
ducats ready coined. I wonder what he means. If death
5 were nigh, he would not frolic thus. He's now at supper
with the scholars, where there's such belly-cheer as Wagner in his life ne'er saw the like! And see where they
come. Belike° the feast is done.°   (*Exit.*)

(*Enter Faustus, Mephostophilis, and two or three Scholars.*)

I SCHOLAR. Master Doctor Faustus, since our conference
about fair ladies, which was the beautifulest in all the   10
world, we have determined with ourselves that Helen of
Greece was the admirablest lady that ever lived. Therefore master doctor, if you will do us so much favor as to
let us see that peerless dame of Greece, whom all the
world admires for majesty, we should think ourselves   15
much beholding unto you.

FAUSTUS.
Gentlemen,
For that I know your friendship is unfeigned,
It is not Faustus' custom to deny
The just request of those that wish him well: 20
You shall behold that peerless dame of Greece
No otherwise for pomp or majesty
Than when Sir Paris crossed the seas with her
And brought the spoils° to rich Dardania.°
Be silent then, for danger is in words.   25

(*Music sounds. Mephostophilis brings in Helen: she passeth over the stage.*)

II SCHOLAR.
Was this fair Helen, whose admired worth
Made Greece with ten years' wars afflict poor Troy?

III SCHOLAR.
Too simple is my wit to tell her worth,
Whom all the world admires for majesty.

SCHOLAR.
Now we have seen the pride of nature's work,   30
We'll take our leaves, and for this blessèd sight
Happy and blest be Faustus evermore.

FAUSTUS.
Gentlemen, farewell, the same wish I to you.

(*Exeunt Scholars.*)

(*Enter an Old Man.*)

OLD MAN.
O gentle Faustus, leave this damnèd art,
This magic that will charm thy soul to hell   35
And quite bereave° thee of salvation.
Though thou hast now offended like a man,
Do not persever° in it like a devil.
Yet, yet, thou hast an amiable soul°
If sin by custom grow not into nature.   40
Then, Faustus, will repentance come too late!
Then, thou art banished from the sight of heaven!
No mortal can express the pains of hell!
It may be this my exhortation
Seems harsh and all unpleasant. Let it not.   45

117 hey-pass, re-pass conjuring expressions   5.1.8 Belike most
likely   1–8 I think . . . done (though printed as prose in the
quarto, as here, perhaps this speech should be verse, the lines ending *shortly, wealth, plate, coined, nigh, supper, belly-cheer, like, done*)

24 spoils booty (including Helen)   Dardania Troy   36 bereave
deprive   38 persever (accent on second syllable)   39 an amiable
soul a soul worthy of love

For gentle son, I speak it not in wrath
Or envy of thee but in tender love
And pity of thy future misery:
And so have hope that this my kind rebuke,
50   Checking° thy body, may amend thy soul.
FAUSTUS.
Where art thou, Faustus? Wretch, what hast thou done!

(*Mephostophilis gives him a dagger.*)

Hell claims his right and with a roaring voice
Says "Faustus, come, thine hour is almost come!"
And Faustus now will come to do thee right!
OLD MAN.
55   O stay, good Faustus, stay thy desperate steps!
I see an angel hover o'er thy head,
And with a vial full of precious grace
Offers to pour the same into thy soul:
Then call for mercy and avoid despair.
FAUSTUS.
60   O friend,
I feel thy words to comfort my distressèd soul:
Leave me awhile to ponder on my sins.
OLD MAN.
Faustus, I leave thee, but with grief of heart,
Fearing the enemy of thy hapless soul.

(*Exit.*)

FAUSTUS.
65   Accursèd Faustus! Wretch, what hast thou done!
I do repent, and yet I do despair:
Hell strives with grace for conquest in my breast!
What shall I do to shun the snares of death?
MEPHOSTOPHILIS.
Thou traitor Faustus, I arrest thy soul
70   For disobedience to my sovereign lord.
Revolt,° or I'll in piecemeal tear thy flesh.
FAUSTUS.
I do repent I e'er offended him.
Sweet Mephostophilis, entreat thy lord
To pardon my unjust presumption,
75   And with my blood again I will confirm
The former vow I made to Lucifer.
MEPHOSTOPHILIS.
Do it then, Faustus, with unfeignèd heart
Lest greater dangers do attend thy drift.
FAUSTUS.
Torment, sweet friend, that base and agèd man
80   That durst dissuade me from thy Lucifer,
With greatest torment that our hell affords.
MEPHOSTOPHILIS.
His faith is great. I cannot touch his soul.
But what I may afflict his body with
I will attempt, which is but little worth.

50 **Checking** rebuking   71 **Revolt** return (to your allegiance)

FAUSTUS.
One thing, good servant, let me crave of thee   85
To glut the longing of my heart's desire:
That I may have unto my paramour
That heavenly Helen which I saw of late,
Whose sweet embraces may extinguish clear
Those thoughts that do dissuade me from my vow,   90
And keep mine oath I made to Lucifer.
MEPHOSTOPHILIS.
This or what else my Faustus shall desire
Shall be performed in twinkling of an eye.

(*Enter Helen again, passing over between two Cupids.*)

FAUSTUS.
Was this the face that launched a thousand ships
And burnt the topless° towers of Ilium?°   95
Sweet Helen, make me immortal with a kiss.
Her lips suck forth my soul. See where it flies!
Come Helen, come, give me my soul again.
Here will I dwell, for heaven is in these lips
And all is dross that is not Helena.   100
I will be Paris, and for love of thee
Instead of Troy shall Wittenberg be sacked;
And I will combat with weak Menelaus°
And wear thy colors on my plumèd crest.
Yea, I will wound Achilles° in the heel   105
And then return to Helen for a kiss.
O, thou art fairer than the evening's air
Clad in the beauty of a thousand stars,
Brighter art thou than flaming Jupiter
When he appeared to hapless Semele,°   110
More lovely than the monarch of the sky
In wanton Arethusa's° azure arms,
And none but thou shalt be my paramour.

(*Exeunt.*)

[5.2] [*Thunder,   Enter   Lucifer,   Belzebub,   and
Mephostophilis.°*]

LUCIFER.
Thus from infernal Dis° do we ascend
To view the subjects of our monarchy,
Those souls which sin seals the black sons of hell.

95 **topless** that is, so tall their tops are beyond sight   **Ilium** Troy
103 **Menelaus** Greek king, deserted by Helen for Paris
105 **Achilles** greatest of the Greek warriors   110 **Semele** beloved
by Jupiter, who promised to do whatever she wished; she asked to
see him in his full splendor, and the sight incinerated her
112 **Arethusa** a nymph, here apparently loved by Jupiter, "the
monarch of the sky"   **5.2.s.d. Enter Lucifer, Belzebub, and
Mephostophilis** (probably they rise out of a trapdoor and ascend to
the upper stage, Mephostophilis descending to the main stage at
line 108)   **1 infernal Dis** the underworld (named for its ruler)

’Mong which as chief, Faustus, we come to thee,
5   Bringing with us lasting damnation
To wait upon thy soul. The time is come
Which makes it forfeit.
MEPHOSTOPHILIS.   And this gloomy night
Here in this room will wretched Faustus be.
BELZEBUB.
And here we’ll stay
10   To mark him how he doth demean himself.
MEPHOSTOPHILIS.
How should he but in desperate lunacy?
Fond° worldling, now his heart blood dries with grief,
His conscience kills it, and his laboring brain
Begets a world of idle fantasies
15   To overreach the devil; but all in vain:
His store of pleasures must be sauced with pain!
He and his servant Wagner are at hand.
Both come from drawing Faustus’ latest will.
See where they come.

(*Enter Faustus and Wagner.*)

FAUSTUS.
20   Say Wagner, thou hast perused my will;
How dost thou like it?
WAGNER.   Sir, so wondrous well
As in all humble duty I do yield
My life and lasting service for your love.

(*Enter the Scholars.*)

FAUSTUS.
Gramercies,° Wagner.—Welcome gentlemen.

[*Exit Wagner.*]

25 I SCHOLAR. Now worthy Faustus, methinks your looks are
changed.
FAUSTUS.
O gentlemen!
II SCHOLAR.
What ails Faustus?
FAUSTUS. Ah my sweet chamber-fellow, had I lived with
30   thee, then had I lived still!—But now must die eternally.
Look sirs, comes he not, comes he not?
I SCHOLAR. O my dear Faustus, what imports this fear?
II SCHOLAR. Is all our pleasure turned to melancholy?
III SCHOLAR. He is not well with being oversolitary.
35 II SCHOLAR. If it be so, we’ll have physicians and Faustus
shall be cured.
III SCHOLAR. ’Tis but a surfeit° sir, fear nothing.

12 Fond foolish   **24 Gramercies** thank you   **37 a surfeit** indigestion

FAUSTUS. A surfeit of deadly sin that hath damned both
body and soul!
II SCHOLAR. Yet Faustus, look up to heaven and remember   40
mercy is infinite.
FAUSTUS. But Faustus’ offense can ne’er be pardoned. The
serpent that tempted Eve may be saved, but not Faustus!
O gentlemen, hear with patience and tremble not at my
speeches. Though my heart pant and quiver to remember   45
that I have been a student here these thirty years, O,
would I had never seen Wittenberg, never read book.—
And what wonders I have done all Germany can witness,
yea all the world, for which Faustus hath lost both Germany and the world, yea heaven itself—heaven, the seat   50
of God, the throne of the blessèd, the kingdom of joy—
and must remain in hell forever! hell, O hell forever!
Sweet friends, what shall become of Faustus being in hell
forever?
II SCHOLAR. Yet Faustus, call on God.   55
FAUSTUS. On God, whom Faustus hath abjured? On God,
whom Faustus hath blasphemed? O my God, I would
weep, but the devil draws in my tears! Gush forth blood
instead of tears, yea life and soul! O, he stays my tongue!
I would lift up my hands, but see, they hold ’em, they   60
hold ’em!
ALL. Who, Faustus?
FAUSTUS. Why, Lucifer and Mephostophilis. O gentlemen, I
gave them my soul for my cunning.
ALL. O, God forbid!   65
FAUSTUS. God forbade it indeed, but Faustus hath done it.
For the vain pleasure of four and twenty years hath Faustus lost eternal joy and felicity. I writ them a bill with
mine own blood. The date is expired. This is the time.
And he will fetch me.   70
I SCHOLAR. Why did not Faustus tell us of this before, that
divines might have prayed for thee?
FAUSTUS. Oft have I thought to have done so, but the devil
threatened to tear me in pieces if I named God—to fetch
me body and soul if I once gave ear to divinity; and now   75
’tis too late! Gentlemen, away, lest you perish with me.
II SCHOLAR. O, what may we do to save Faustus?
FAUSTUS. Talk not of me but save yourselves and depart.
III SCHOLAR. God will strengthen me. I will stay with Faustus.
I SCHOLAR. Tempt not God, sweet friend, but let us into the   80
next room and pray for him.
FAUSTUS. Ay, pray for me, pray for me. And what noise soever
you hear, come not unto me, for nothing can rescue me.
II SCHOLAR. Pray thou, and we will pray that God may have
mercy upon thee.   85
FAUSTUS. Gentlemen, farewell! If I live till morning, I’ll visit
you. If not, Faustus is gone to hell.
ALL. Faustus, farewell.   (*Exeunt Scholars.*)
MEPHOSTOPHILIS.
Ay, Faustus, now thou hast no hope of heaven.

90 Therefore, despair! Think only upon hell,
For that must be thy mansion, there to dwell.
FAUSTUS.
O thou bewitching fiend, 'twas thy temptation
Hath robbed me of eternal happiness.
MEPHOSTOPHILIS.
I do confess it Faustus, and rejoice.
95 'Twas I, that when thou wert i' the way to heaven
Dammed up thy passage. When thou took'st the book
To view the Scriptures, then I turned the leaves
And led thine eye.
What, weep'st thou! 'Tis too late, despair, farewell!
100 Fools that will laugh on earth, most weep in hell.

(*Exit.*)

(*Enter the Good Angel and the Bad Angel at several doors.*)

GOOD ANGEL.
O Faustus, if thou hadst given ear to me
Innumerable joys had followèd thee.
But thou did'st love the world.
BAD ANGEL.
Gave ear to me,
And now must taste hell's pains perpetually.
GOOD ANGEL.
105 O, what will all thy riches, pleasures, pomps
Avail thee now?
BAD ANGEL.
Nothing but vex thee more,
To want in hell, that had on earth such store.

(*Music while the throne° descends.*)

GOOD ANGEL.
O, thou hast lost celestial happiness,
Pleasures unspeakable, bliss without end.
110 Had'st thou affected° sweet divinity,
Hell or the devil had had no power on thee.
Had'st thou kept on that way, Faustus behold
In what resplendent glory thou had'st sat
In yonder throne, like those bright shining saints,
115 And triumphed over hell! That hast thou lost.

[*Throne ascends.*]

And now, poor soul, must thy good angel leave thee,
The jaws of hell are open to receive thee.

(*Exit.*)

(*Hell is discovered.*)

107 s.d. **throne** (symbolic of heaven) 110 **affected** preferred

BAD ANGEL.
Now Faustus, let thine eyes with horror stare
Into that vast perpetual torture-house.
120 There are the furies, tossing damnèd souls
On burning forks. Their bodies boil in lead.
There are live quarters° broiling on the coals,
That ne'er can die: this ever-burning chair
Is for o'er-tortured souls to rest them in.
125 These that are fed with sops of flaming fire
Were gluttons and loved only delicates
And laughed to see the poor starve at their gates.
But yet all these are nothing. Thou shalt see
Ten thousand tortures that more horrid be.
FAUSTUS.
130 O, I have seen enough to torture me.
BAD ANGEL.
Nay, thou must feel them, taste the smart of all:
He that loves pleasure must for pleasure fall.
And so I leave thee Faustus, till anon:
Then wilt thou tumble in confusion.° (*Exit.*)

(*The clock strikes eleven.*)

FAUSTUS.
135 O Faustus!
Now hast thou but one bare hour to live
And then thou must be damned perpetually.
Stand still, you ever-moving spheres of Heaven
That time may cease and midnight never come:
140 Fair nature's eye, rise, rise again and make
Perpetual day, or let this hour be but a year,
A month, a week, a natural day—
That Faustus may repent and save his soul.
O lente lente currite noctis equi!°
145 The stars move still, time runs, the clock will strike:
The devil will come, and Faustus must be damned!
O, I'll leap up to my God! Who pulls me down?
See, see where Christ's blood streams in the firmament!
One drop of blood will save me. O my Christ!—
150 Rend not my heart for naming of my Christ!
Yet will I call on Him! O spare me, Lucifer!—
Where is it now? 'Tis gone: and see where God
Stretcheth out His arm and bends His ireful brows!
Mountains and hills, come, come and fall on me
155 And hide me from the heavy wrath of God!
No?
Then will I headlong run into the earth.
Gape earth! O no, it will not harbor me.
You stars that reigned at my nativity,

122 **quarters** bodies 134 **confusion** destruction 144 **O . . .**
equi slowly, slowly run, O horses of the night (Latin, adapted from
Ovid's *Amores*, I.xiii.40, where a lover regretfully thinks of the
coming of the dawn)

160 Whose influence hath allotted death and hell,
Now draw up Faustus like a foggy mist
Into the entrails of yon laboring cloud
That when you vomit forth into the air,
My limbs may issue from your smoky mouths—
165 But let my soul mount and ascend to heaven!

(*The watch strikes.*)

O half the hour is passed! 'Twill all be passed anon!
O God,
If thou wilt not have mercy on my soul,
Yet for Christ's sake, whose blood hath ransomed me,
170 Impose some end to my incessant pain!
Let Faustus live in hell a thousand years,
A hundred thousand, and at last be saved!
No end is limited to° damnèd souls!
Why wert thou not a creature wanting soul?
175 Or why is this immortal that thou hast?
O, Pythagoras' metempsychosis,° were that true
This soul should fly from me and I be changed
Into some brutish beast.
All beasts are happy, for when they die
180 Their souls are soon dissolved in elements.
But mine must live still° to be plagued in hell!
Cursed be the parents that engendered me!
No Faustus, curse thyself, curse Lucifer
That hath deprived thee of the joys of heaven.

(*The clock strikes twelve.*)

185 It strikes, it strikes! Now body, turn to air,
Or Lucifer will bear thee quick° to hell!
O soul, be changed into small water-drops
And fall into the ocean, ne'er be found.

(*Thunder, and enter the Devils.*)

My God, my God! Look not so fierce on me!
190 Adders and serpents, let me breathe awhile!
Ugly Hell, gape not! Come not Lucifer!
I'll burn my books!—O Mephostophilis!

(*Exeunt [Devils with Faustus.]°*)

[5.3] (*Enter the Scholars.*)

I SCHOLAR.
Come gentlemen, let us go visit Faustus,
For such a dreadful night was never seen
Since first the world's creation did begin!
Such fearful shrieks and cries were never heard!
Pray heaven, the doctor have escaped the danger.   5

II SCHOLAR.
O, help us heaven, see, here are Faustus' limbs
All torn asunder by the hand of death!

III SCHOLAR.
The devils whom Faustus served have torn him thus:
For 'twixt the hours of twelve and one, methought
I heard him shriek and call aloud for help,   10
At which self° time the house seemed all on fire
With dreadful horror of these damnèd fiends.

II SCHOLAR.
Well gentlemen, though Faustus' end be such
As every Christian heart laments to think on,
Yet for he was a scholar once admired   15
For wondrous knowledge in our German schools,
We'll give his mangled limbs due burial;
And all the students, clothed in mourning black,
Shall wait upon° his heavy° funeral.

(*Exeunt.*)

(*Enter Chorus.*)

Cut is the branch that might have grown full straight   20
And burnèd is Apollo's laurel bough°
That sometime grew within this learnèd man.
Faustus is gone: regard his hellish fall,
Whose fiendful fortune may exhort the wise
Only to wonder at° unlawful things,   25
Whose deepness doth entice such forward wits
To practice more than heavenly power permits.

[*Exit.*]

Terminat hora diem; terminat Author opus.°

FINIS

---

173 **limited to** set for 176 **metempsychosis** transmigration of souls (a doctrine held by Pythagoras, philosopher of the sixth century B.C.E.) 181 **still** always 186 **quick** alive 192 **s.d. Exeunt [Devils with Faustus]** (possibly the devils drag Faustus into the "hell" that was "discovered" at 5.2.117, and then toss his limbs onto the stage, or possibly the limbs are revealed in 5.3.6 by withdrawing a curtain at the rear of the stage)

5.3.11 **self** same 19 **wait upon** attend **heavy** sad 21 **laurel bough** symbol of wisdom, here associated with Apollo, god of divination 25 **Only to wonder at** that is, merely to observe at a distance, with awe 28 **Terminat . . . opus** the hour ends the day; the author ends his work (this Latin tag probably is not Marlowe's but the printer's, though it is engaging to believe Marlowe wrote it, ending his play at midnight, the hour of Faustus's death)

TOPICS FOR CRITICAL THINKING AND WRITING

The Play on the PAGE

1. Characterize Faustus, calling attention to his virtues (if any) and to his weaknesses. In 1.1.74–93, for instance, how mixed are his motives? Elsewhere in the play do you find evidence of *hybris* (see Glossary)? In Faustus's last scene (5.2) do you find indications that he has grown morally? Explain.

2. What evidence can you offer to support the idea that Faustus is a victim, trapped by diabolic forces?

3. What evidence can you offer to support the idea that Faustus freely chooses damnation?

4. In 1.3.23–24 Faustus says to a devil, "I charge thee to return and change thy shape, / Thou art too ugly to attend on me." What does this statement tell us about Faustus?

5. Take at least two comic scenes and examine them with the idea that perhaps these scenes can be justified in one way or another as related to the story of Faustus. Or are the scenes irrelevant material added to fill out the play?

6. Faustus often engages in low fooling, rather than in heroic errors. Can we satisfactorily explain this comic stuff? How?

7. Do you find the final scene integral to the dramatic wholeness of the play? Provide specific arguments.

The Play on the STAGE

8. If you were directing the play, exactly what blocking and what gestures would you prescribe for the Chorus at the beginning of the play and for Faustus in his first speech?

9. Do you think the devils can be played in such a way that at least in some scenes they are genuinely terrifying, or do you think that a modern audience can see them only as absurd? Explain.

10. Much of the fooling, especially with the Horse-courser and with the Pope, is deleted in most modern productions, on the grounds that it is unfunny and that it trivializes the tragic hero. Are there certain comic scenes that you would cut, and others that you would retain? Why?

11. If you were staging the play would you try to suggest that Faustus is basically a heroic figure who finds himself in conflict with an oppressive morality, or would you try to suggest that Faustus is essentially a talented but shallow person, overly fond of coarse fun? Or a neurotic? Or would you try to develop some other view? (One way to think about the problem is this: Does Faustus *enjoy* the jokes—in which case he is shallow and vulgar—or does Marlowe somehow distance Faustus from the comedy, perhaps even suggesting that Faustus's clowning represents his unsatisfactory attempt to alleviate his painful awareness of the limitations imposed upon humanity.)

12. Clifford Williams, in his 1968 production (discussed in Gareth Lloyd Evans's essay, which follows), used a nude Helen. If you were directing the play, and if you thought that the law would allow you to present Helen nude, would you do so? Why, or why not?

13. In some modern productions, the role of Helen has been played by a man, thus making clear that the devils have duped Faustus. What do you think of this idea?

14. In John Barton's 1974 production, a devil—rather than the Chorus—spoke the final lines of the play. How do you feel about this?

The Play in PERFORMANCE

The date of the composition of *Doctor Faustus* is uncertain, but it probably was first performed during the winter of 1592–93, and it was certainly performed in September 1594, with Edward Alleyn—the leading tragic actor of the period—in the title role. We know that it was popular for the next few years, and we know that in 1602 Philip Henslowe, a theater owner and manager, paid William Bird and William Rowley for "additions" to the play. Subsequent performances, therefore—including those of today—surely include some material that Marlowe did not write. Unfortunately, it is not certain which scenes or lines are the "additions."

The play was popular until the theaters were closed in 1642, at the outbreak of the English Civil War. We can get some idea of what these early performances were like from Sir John Melton, who in a work published in 1620 says that at a production of *Doctor Faustus*

> a man may behold shagge-hayr'd Deuills runne roaring ouer the Stage with Squibs [i.e., firecrackers] in their mouthes, while Drummers make thunder in the Tyring-house [i.e., the area at the back of the projecting stage], and the twelue-penny Hirelings [i.e., stagehands] make artificiall Lightning in their heauens.

The text of the play supports Melton's comment. For instance, 1.3 begins with "thunder"; in 2.1 when Faustus calls for a wife, Mephostophilis provides a female devil with fireworks; 3.2 tells us that Faustus and Mephostophilis "fling fireworks" at the friars. We know for certain that the stage effects were not only frightening but also were comic, since (for instance) when Faustus gives up his desire for a wife, he jokes that the fireworks-throwing female devil is "a hot whore indeed." (With the word "hot," he is punning on her lasciviousness and also suggesting that she is burning with venereal disease.) It may be hard for some of us to take seriously the spectacular events and the talk of the supernatural, but apparently the Elizabethans were impressed. For instance, stories circulated that during a performance the actors suddenly found one devil more on the stage than there should have been. According to one report, when the actors perceived that the devil himself was among them, they were so unnerved that they terminated the performance. Edward Alleyn's retirement was traditionally attributed to the appearance of a devil during the play.

Beyond the fact that drums provided the thunder, and firecrackers and lightning were used, what do we know about the earliest productions of the play? Not a great deal for sure, but we probably can make some safe guesses. The Chorus, who opens the play, probably wore a black cloak—traditional for such a role—and possibly he wore a crown of bays, emblematic of the poet. When he ends his first speech with "And this the man that in his study sits," he probably pulls back a curtain at the rear of the stage, revealing Faustus in his study.

From here, however, we enter upon less firm ground. Probably the study was equipped with some books and with some magic symbols, for instance a magic circle on the floor, as is seen on the title page of an edition of the play. (This picture shows a dragon emerging from the floor; possibly in the play a devil appeared in the form of a dragon. See page 12.) Faustus probably wore a scholar's robe—maybe the fur-trimmed gown of a Doctor of Divinity—and he may have held a magician's wand, again as in the woodcut on the title page. Probably when Faustus dismissed each field of learning in his first speech (philosophy, medicine, law, theology) he read from a different book, and then cast it aside. With the entrance of Wagner in the first scene, Faustus probably came forth from the alcove at the rear and moved forward, onto the platform stage, in a sense bringing his locale with him. The audience would then understand that (so long as Faustus was on the stage) the scene was still within his study, even though whatever scenery there was—for instance an astrological chart—probably was confined to the alcove at the rear of the platform.

The Good Angel and the Bad Angel entered and exited through different doors (the text says they enter "at several doors"); possibly some or all devils showed their underworld nature by entering onto the stage through a trapdoor. Perhaps during his last speech, when he says he will burn his books, Faustus rushed into his study, an alcove at the rear of the stage, and perhaps devils then pulled him down into an opened trap. In keeping with the other medieval aspects of the play, this trap may have been covered by a conventional medieval hellmouth, a gaping mouth of a monster or a devil, from which infernal smoke issued. The curtain could then have been pulled closed, the hellmouth removed, and when the curtain was drawn back the limbs of Faustus would be discovered.

We know, of course, that the Elizabethan stage not only made use of traps, but it also made use of playing spaces *above* the stage. When Lucifer begins 5.2 by saying, "Thus from infernal Dis [the underworld] do we ascend," he and his cohorts may have climbed out of a trapdoor and then continued climbing onto an elevated position above the stage, where for a while they looked down on their victim. An area above the platform stage is also indicated by a stage direction in 5.2, which tells us that "the throne descends," that is, a symbol from heaven manifests itself on the stage.

From 1642 to 1660, during the Civil War between the Parliamentarians and the Royalists (1642–52) and during the Commonwealth Period (1649–60) when Oliver Cromwell and his son were dictators, the theaters were closed, but in 1662, during the Restoration, *Doctor Faustus* was revived. The play was performed again in 1675, and then it disappeared from the stage for more than two hundred years, until July 1896, when William Poel, founder of the Elizabethan Stage Society, revived it on a stage that approximated an Elizabethan stage. (Poel's revival of *Everyman* in 1901 is discussed on page 199.)

Perhaps a director's first act of interpretation is the decision about which text to use—the 1604 text, or the longer (chiefly because of comic scenes) 1616 text. The choice makes a big difference not only in the playing time but also in the interpretation of the central figure, because the abundant comic scenes of 1616 tend to trivialize Faustus. Directors who wish to suggest that Faustus is a grand Renaissance hero whose fault—let's say an overly aspiring mind—is tragic, usually choose the shorter text.

For the 1896 production (and again for a revival in 1906), William Poel relied chiefly on the shorter text, partly because he believed that the longer text included additions not by Marlowe, and partly because he saw Faustus as a heroic figure, driven by a quest for knowledge. In keeping with the ideals of the Elizabethan Stage Society—the idea was to produce the plays as they might have been done in the sixteenth century, with relatively little scenery and therefore with no intervals between changes of scene—Poel dispensed with the usual Victorian scenery that clearly established the particular setting as a room or a forest or whatever. The players merely entered the stage through curtains, in effect establishing the particular locale by their dialogue and their costumes (for instance, the costumes of cardinals or of a pope indicated that the scene was Rome). A reviewer of Poel's production tells us that for some scenes, however, a curtain at the rear was drawn back to reveal "a great dragon's mouth wide open, representing the mouth of hell. Out of this mouth came Mephostophilis, and un-

der his escort the Seven Deadly Sins, Alexander and his paramour, and Helen."

Three other points about Poel's production should be mentioned. (1) The Chorus was a woman (odd, since the Elizabethan Stage Society sought to imitate Elizabethan practice, and the Elizabethan stage did not use actresses). (2) Faustus's encounter with Helen was very chaste (Helen kissed his forehead, and he kissed her hand), though in the 1906 revival, Poel—or Faustus—was a little bolder, since Faustus brushed Helen's cheek with his lips. (3) The devil-wife of 2.1, seen from the front, seemed a beautiful woman, but when she turned around the audience perceived a skeleton—an interesting idea that to the best of our knowledge has not been used in later productions.

We cannot discuss all of the subsequent productions, but a few deserve special mention. In 1937 Orson Welles—not yet twenty-two and therefore still regarded as a boy genius—produced the play under the auspices of the Federal Theatre Project (part of Franklin Delano Roosevelt's Works Project Administration, a plan to find work for the unemployed during the Depression). John Houseman (later known to a vast public as the law professor in the television series, *Paper Chase*) was the director of the unit in which Welles worked, and the two staged an impressive version. In fact, Welles was a devoted amateur magician, and—given his high estimate of himself and his fondness for breaking rules—he must have identified strongly with the role of Faustus. He cut much of the comedy and stressed the heroic aspects of Faustus, but he did retain some of the comedy where he could indulge in conjuring. Thus, the cardinals' hats flew through the air, the pope's miter arose, splendidly dressed papal servants carrying dishes of food were astonished to find the food—a side of beef, a pudding, roasted chickens—fly through the air and disappear. Welles's set appeared to be not much more than a background of black velvet, but this set was the key to the magic. Houseman, in *Run-Through*, an autobiography, explains a system that professional magicians call "black magic."

Used for vanishing acts and miraculous appearances, it exploits the absorbent properties of black velvet so that, under certain lighting conditions, not only do black surfaces become totally invisible against each other, but all normal sense of space, depth and perspective becomes lost and confused in the eye of the spectator. . . . By using almost no front light and crisscrossing the stage with parallel light curtains and clusters of units carefully focused from the sides and overhead, [Welles] was able to achieve mystifications that would have impressed the great Thurston. . . .

This mystification was accomplished with the aid of eight dancers, dressed from head to foot in black velvet, moving alongside the procession [of servants carrying food], just far enough upstage to be out of the blaze of the light curtain and thus completely invisible to the audience against the darkness of black velvet. In their black-gloved hands, they held . . . thin, black, flexible steel rods whose ends were affixed to the meats, the pudding and the episcopal headgear that were marked for flight. On cue the boys in black swung those loaded rods up over their heads and brought them down behind them where their own black costumes formed a screen for them till they were able to leave the stage unobserved in the confusion of the dissolving parade.

(233–34)

Although most of the comedy was cut, those clown scenes that were staged were played strictly for comedy—Faustus was just fooling around—and they did not seem to interfere with Welles's heroic interpretation of the role. The Seven Deadly Sins were puppets that appeared onstage by wriggling up through openings in the floor; as we will see in a moment, later productions follow Welles in tending to use puppets rather than human actors for the Seven Deadly Sins.

One other point should be made about this production. Welles used an African American actor, Jack Carter, in the role of Mephostophilis. The employment of a single black actor in the role of a devil today scarcely seems to be daring, but it was an innovation in the 1930s, when casts were almost never integrated.

In 1968 Clifford Williams directed the Royal Shakespeare Company's production of *Doctor Faustus*, with Eric Porter in the title role. Because this production is discussed in Gareth Lloyd Evans's essay, which follows, we need not comment at length here, but we do want briefly to describe the staging of Faustus's last exit. Faustus grovelled in terror as he made his final speech, but when the clock finished striking twelve and nothing happened, he raised his head, looked at the emptiness around, and then laughed. At this point, sections of the back wall fell away, revealing a red glow, through which were seen steel spikes, the teeth of a hellmouth. Devils slowly came forward, surrounded Faustus, and then carried him screaming back into the hellmouth, which then closed.

The 1974 production by John Barton, first in Edinburgh and then in London, starred Ian McKellen as Faustus. Barton cut almost all of the comedy, replacing some of it with passages from the source of the play, a prose account of Faustus. All of the action took place within Faustus's study, and Barton gave the final lines of the play, in the original spoken by the Chorus, to a devil. Despite the deletion of the comic material, which might indicate that the director was aiming at an heroic Faustus, Barton's Faustus was not a grand figure but rather struck most viewers as a neurotic pedant. He peered through spectacles, twitched, grimaced, and hugged himself with glee. All of the magical figures—the Seven Deadly Sins, Helen, and so forth—were puppets or dummies of one sort or another. The Good Angel and Bad Angel, for instance, were hand puppets manipulated by Faustus, who spoke their lines. Helen of Troy was merely a blonde wig, a mask, and a bit of cloth, which Faustus caressed and took to bed. The effect was to diminish Faustus. After all, what sort of a man would be delighted with these toys? Reviews tended to be unfavorable, with much severe talk about the director who dared to cut the text and to impose his views on what was left of it, but, as we have seen, no one really knows what Marlowe's original text was like.

For further discussion of these and of other productions, see Michael Hattaway, *Elizabethan Popular Theatre* (1982, chiefly on the earliest productions), and William Tydeman, *Doctor Faustus: Text and Performance* (1984, on productions in the later twentieth century).

GARETH LLOYD EVANS
The Royal Shakespeare Company Production of Doctor Faustus

Gareth Lloyd Evans, a distinguished specialist in Elizabethan drama, here reviews a 1968 production at Stratford-upon-Avon.

Stratford made its most explicit committal to the era of permissiveness when it announced that Helen in *Doctor Faustus* was to appear naked. The result of this decision and of the attention it incited was a mere confirmation that she did, in fact, appear naked—and that is all. It is a respectable and traditional view that a sweet disorder in dress kindles wantonness, and that total exposure has an anesthetic effect. Helen's appearance proved this. At one stroke the expectations of the lascivious were dampened and the wanton and desperate passion of Faustus's speech to Helen reduced to superfluous triviality. The best answer to any theory the director may have had that a naked Helen was essential to his interpretation is the fact that the understudy appeared fully clothed and Eric Porter's speech gained immensely in evocative power.

This production is, indeed, noteworthy for other qualities. Visually it was the most inventive of the whole season, and often successfully. The claustrophobic and dark recesses of Faustus's study were exactly and economically achieved—the designer had resisted the usual temptation of depicting 'Elizabethanism' by a vast clutter of dusty books, skulls, astrolabes and olde mappes. Hell enclosed about Faustus in a sensational explosion of colour, noise and shape—a medieval conception boosted by twentieth-century technical aids. The Seven Deadly Sins, out of Bosch by Gerald Scarfe, cavorted and shrieked. They were startlingly ugly and malformed and had a great theatrical impact. At the same time they raised the question, 'Would Faustus or anyone be tempted by such grotesque ugliness?' In a way Faustus is a demonstration of Wilde's dictum that the only way to resist temptation is to yield to it. These Sins made a mockery of any urge to yield. Perhaps the director had concluded that their appearance is calculated less to allure Faustus than to convince him of Lucifer's theatrical inventiveness; if this is so, it begs many questions about the relationship of Faustus to the Devil and, more pertinently, of the meaning of the bond.

Eric Porter, in the name part, created, with thoughtful precision, the various stages of Faustus's spiritual and physical journey—the curiosity, the doubt, the urge for more and yet more sensation, the regret, the terror. Technically and intellectually, his reading of the text was excellent. What was lacking (and this where it was most needed—in the final monologue) was passion. At any point in this performance one could sense a strong intellectual engagement with the character, but missed the sense of a heart and soul moving in parallel with the mind's experience. The pathos of this play comes from our observation of a man wasting great gifts and entering into a trap. It was Terrence Hardiman's Mephistopheles, rather than Faustus, who induced the pity of it in a performance characterized by quiet grief, mordant humour, and resigned dignity. His performance was the more touching since the overall interpretation stressed wryness and grim humour—this was increased by the brilliantly controlled and realized comic scenes. These did not attempt comic relief (for which Marlowe's text is not conspicuously well equipped) but underlined the dangerous absurdity of playing with the devil's fire.

PHOTO ESSAY:
Staging Shakespeare, Then and Now

Although many details remain unclear, we have a pretty good idea of how Shakespeare's plays were originally staged. We know that although there were properties (chairs, tables, torches, and so on) there was no bulky scenery. This is not to say, however, that the stage seemed barren. The architecture of the playing area itself was attractive, and costumes and banners would add color. We know, too, that the action could take place on several levels, and we know that the actors—all were male, boys taking the female parts—for the most part wore Elizabethan clothing. If they were performing a play set in ancient times, the chief actors wore something that passed for a toga, but much of the clothing nevertheless was Elizabethan.

Consider the costuming and the staging of the Ghost's appearance in *Hamlet*. The dialogue tells us that at his first appearance (1.1) the Ghost appears "In the same figure like the King that's dead," in the "fair and warlike form / In which the majesty of buried Denmark / did sometime march." That is, the Ghost is wearing the armor that the King of Denmark wore ("warlike form"). At its last appearance, in 3.4, the Ghost is dressed differently, at least according to the First Quarto, which specifies, "Enter the ghost in his night gowne," that is, in what we would call a dressing gown, a garment worn while relaxing at home. In all of its appearances, however, it appears as a human being in human apparel. Nothing in the text suggests that it is accompanied by unearthly sounds or by strange lighting. Of course, since Shakespeare's plays were written to be performed by daylight in an unroofed theater, little could be done with special lighting effects, though we do know that for some plays stage lighting was produced by blowing powdered resin through a tube into the flame of a candle.

We know that the Elizabethan stage made use of a trapdoor, and it may be tempting to think the Ghost appeared and disappeared through a trap, but the language of the text suggests that at least in its first appearance it appears and disappears through a doorway that leads to the platform stage. When it first appears Bernardo says, "Look where it comes again," *not* "Look where it rises," or even "Look where it appears." Appearance through a door rather than a trap is not necessarily without drama. Let's look at the lines that lead up to the ghost's first appearance. Bernardo says,

Last night of all,
When yond same star that's westward from the pole
Had made his course t'illume that part of Heaven
Where now it burns, Marcellus and myself
The bell then beating one—

Enter Ghost (1.1.39–43)

If Bernardo is downstage and points heavenward when he speaks of "yond same star," his gesture catches the audience's attention and allows the Ghost to appear in the doorway now or in the next line, unnoticed by the audience (or by most of it) until Marcellus says, "Peace, break thee off! Look where it comes again!" In any case, the text suggests that the Ghost makes the first disappearance by walking off rather than by descending through a trap, since just before it disappears Bernardo says, "See, it stalks away," words hardly compatible with a supernatural mode of disappearance. A modern student of the Elizabethan stage, C. Walter Hodges, conjectures (see his drawings, page 259) that the Ghost enters from one door, crosses the stage, and exits through the other. Hodges's view is entirely reasonable. The dialogue that accompanies the Ghost's second disappearance (still in the first scene), however, suggests some sort of special effect.

BERNARDO. 'Tis here.
HORATIO. 'Tis here.
MARCELLUS. 'Tis gone.

Conceivably it vanishes through a trap, or perhaps it vanishes through one door, immediately reappears (actually a double for the actor) at the other door, and then again vanishes. But this is mere conjecture. When it appears in 1.5, it again probably enters through a door, as earlier, but when it disappears in 1.5.92 it may well go through a trapdoor, as Hodges assumes, since later in this scene the Ghost's voice is heard beneath the stage, that it, the Ghost is supposed to be speaking from within the earth. (An original stage direction [Q2] specifically says, "Ghost cries under the Stage.") Modern directors, of course, do not assume that they are bound to stage the scene as the Elizabethans may have staged it, and fairly often they prefer to represent the Ghost only by a great shadow, or by other lighting effects and an offstage voice.

Hamlet, 1.4 and 1.5. Entrances and departures of the Ghost.

The Oregon Shakespeare Festival Theater, in Ashland, Oregon, opened in 1935. Scholarly efforts to stage plays in the Elizabethan manner inevitably produced some new theaters that were based at least in part on Elizabethan theaters. The Oregon theater more or less imitates the façade and the thrust stage of what we think an Elizabethan theater was like. Doors right and left, pillars, windows, and a musicians' gallery on the third level all can be justified on the basis of Elizabethan evidence, but the "inner stage" and the "upper stage" are less certain. The building itself is the chief element in the set of any play staged here; obviously one would not use a highly elaborate set that took time to assemble on stage. Equally obviously, this stage is better suited to performances in which the performers wear Elizabethan costume than to performances in modern dress.

Charles Witham's watercolor of the churchyard scene for *Hamlet* at Booth's Theatre, 1970.

Contemporary clothing was used throughout the seventeenth century and well into the eighteenth, but at the end of the eighteenth century and through much of the nineteenth the emphasis shifted to historical accuracy, both in costumes and in stage sets. (A problem, of course, is this: What *is* the dress and architecture of Hamlet's Denmark? Or, for that matter, what is the architecture in the Athens of *A Midsummer Night's Dream,* and what is the bower of a fairy queen?)

The productions of the American actor and manager Edwin Booth (1833–93; brother of John Wilkes Booth), like their Victorian counterparts, were noted for their spectacular effects and their attempts at historical accuracy. His *Hamlet* (1870) wa accompanied by a brochure, telling the reader that the play was staged with Norman architecture, and the performers (equipped with blond wigs) wore not the usual colorful silk apparel associated with the Renaissance but rather heavy woolen Saxon garments appropriate to tenth-century Denmark. The scenery (eleven elaborate sets) by Charles Witham was highly praised by reviewers, who commented on its solidity. Here we reproduce Witham's watercolor for the graveyard scene in the fifth act. Watercolor is a light medium, especially suited for airy effects, but even in this watercolor you can get an idea of the massiveness of the sets. Foliage frames the stage, and tombs, trees, and a chapel leave little empty space. Lighting indicated that the time was night (moonlight pierced the branches), although nothing in the text suggests the funeral takes place at night.

The use of elaborate sets, which of course could not quickly be dismantled and then set up again for a later scene, meant that in productions of this sort some scenes were deleted, and the surviving scenes might be rearranged; scenes with the same set, though separated in the original play, were run together in order to avoid time-consuming shifts of scenery. A further disadvantage of a highly realistic (i.e., illusionistic) set, offered in the name of historical accuracy, is that its very detail may obscure what we may call the universal qualities of the play.

early in the twentieth century both sorts of antiquarianism seemed inadequate, and directors turned toward more imaginative kinds of staging—sometimes using symbolic decor and sometimes using modern dress.

Barry Jackson (1879–1961) founded the Birmingham Repertory Company in England in 1911, and served as its artistic director. Believing that traditional productions and highly "poetic" acting alienated audiences from the plays themselves, Jackson decided to set the plays in the present and to act them as though they were modern plays. His *Cymbeline* (1923) was the first important production in modern dress, but his *Hamlet* (1925) arrested even more attention. It was thought by some reviewers to be a spoof, but it was seriously intended and for the most part it was well received. The photograph shows the duel between Hamlet and Laertes in 5.2, with Hamlet toward the left in knickers, and Laertes toward the right. Osric, in the dress of a naval officer, is behind Laertes. Because the play is set in the court, it allows—even when modern dress is used—for fancy costumes, notably formal attire and military garb. Thus, in some scenes the ambassadors and Polonius wore tailcoats and white ties, and Hamlet wore a tuxedo. In other scenes, however, Ophelia wore a short skirt characteristic of the 1920s, the young men wore tweeds, and Hamlet wore loose knickers known as plus fours. Many later productions, for instance Kenneth Branagh's film version, have found that military costumes, whether contemporary or of the nineteenth century, provide an eye-catching spectacle that most modern dress does not afford, and yet these costumes allow the production to avoid what is thought of as the fusty antiquarianism of Elizabethan dress.

The most obvious sort of antiquarianism is the desire to use historically accurate costumes and architecture for the play (medieval Denmark for *Hamlet,* Renaissance Italy for *Romeo and Juliet*), but another sort of antiquarianism is the desire to stage the plays as the Elizabethans staged them, on a relatively bare stage and in Elizabethan costume. (We have already briefly discussed Elizabethan revivalism in our comments on William Poel's productions of *Everyman* [page 199] and *Doctor Faustus* [page 255].) But fairly

Tourists who visit Stratford-upon-Avon to see the Royal Shakespeare Company do a play presumably expect a good show for their money, and the RSC has tended to comply, with lavish productions. But Stratford also has a smaller theater nearby, "The Other Place," a corrugated-iron shed, used for offbeat productions. It was here that Buzz Goodbody (the first woman to direct for the RSC) in 1974 directed *Hamlet* on a tiny budget. The idea was to do a "Village Hall" production, the play as it might be staged by locals with a very small budget. At one end of the room was a door through which actors and audience entered; at the other end was a stage about ten feet deep with sliding paper screens at the rear. Costumes were contemporary, with Claudius in an expensively tailored striped suit (very much an Establishment figure in this radical production), Fortinbras in combat gear, Horatio in corduroys, and Hamlet first in black but later in a brown suit and a baggy overcoat. For the play-within-the play, the performers wore simple masks and were accompanied by Charles Dance on the guitar.

The word "expressionism" seems to have been coined in 1901, to indicate a kind of painting in which the artist seeks to express his or her emotional experience rather than convey an optically accurate illusion of external reality. If you are familiar with such pictures as van Gogh's *Starry Night* or Edward Munch's *The Scream,* you are familiar with expressionistic works. In the theater, expressionist productions use *non*illusionistic scenery and lighting to convey emotions rather than to imitate daylight, candlelight, and so on.

In Ron Daniels's production (Royal Shakespeare Company, at Stratford-upon-Avon, 1989), walls sloped steeply, lighting changed disconcertingly to reflect moods rather than times of day, the ghost was accompanied by creepy music and a red glow, and costumes were a mixed lot, with Claudius in a plum-colored suit and Hamlet sometimes in striped pajamas. Hamlet (Mark Rylance) spoke the opening lines of his first soliloquy with his back to the audience, indicating his alienation. Not surprisingly, some reviewers said that the production was more concerned with shocking viewers than with presenting Shakespeare effectively.

Sir Herbert Beerbohm Tree's production (1900) of *A Midsummer Night's Dream* used elaborate sets, seeking to evoke a forest that looked as real as possible. Such sets could be impressive in themselves, but in order to eliminate intervals during which sets were erected, taken down, and again erected, directors rearranged the sequence of scenes, or simply deleted some scenes.

Harley Granville Barker's production (1914) of *A Midsummer Night's Dream* marked a striking departure from the traditional staging. For the palace of Theseus, in Athens, Granville Barker used a relatively realistic, solidly built structure in black and silver, but for the forest he used stylized scenery. In the center of the stage was a green velvet mound—clearly artificial and therefore quite different from the grasslike textures and real plants commonly used in Victorian productions (e.g., Beerbohm Tree's)—and at the rear was a spangled backcloth, green at the bottom and bluish-purple toward the top. Trees were suggested by bands of green, blue, and violet hanging cloth. Suspended above the green velvet mound was a wreath of flowers, ten feet in diameter, from which hung a gauze curtain that constituted Titania's bower. In order to further emphasize the contrast between the two worlds—the world of the mortals (represented by Theseus's palace) and the world of the fairies (represented by Titania's bower)—Granville Barker dressed the fairies in bronze-colored tights and he gilded their faces and hands. Further, instead of moving with the childlike skipping steps of the cute fairies of Victorian productions, his fairies moved in a jerky fashion—causing some uneasiness even among his admirers. On the whole, Granville Barker was the chief force in moving early twentieth-century Shakespearean production away from realism and toward stylization.

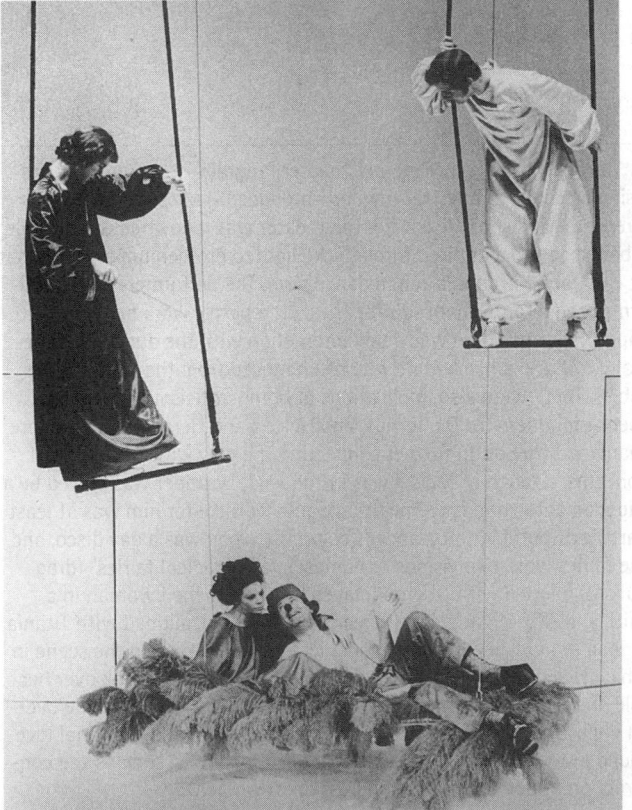

Peter Brook's production (1970) at Stratford-upon-Avon was for the second half of the twentieth century what Granville Barker's production (see photo above) was for the first half. Brook has said that after failing to find a symbol for the fairy world, he "turned to the arts of the circus, the tumblers, the acrobats, the jugglers and the slapstick comedy of the clowns. I wanted to make it a joyful production and I felt a display of sheer physical virtuosity would achieve this." The setting consisted of simple white flats surrounded by a catwalk, with trapezes. In one scene Oberon and Puck were on trapezes, and the magic flower that Oberon gave to Puck was a disk spinning on a wand, passed from Oberon's wand to Puck's. The fairies—chiefly males wearing pajamalike garb or track suits—sometimes seemed to be doing gymnastics, and at other times acted as stagehands or circus roustabouts, for instance sweeping up confetti. (For additional comments about this production, see page 299.)

Especially in the United States and in England, there has been a tendency in recent years to locate Shakespeare's plays in an environment other than the one indicated in the play. In this 1987 New York Shakespeare Festival production, the action was moved to the Caribbean. Doubtless part of the reason for this particular setting is that New York now has a substantial Caribbean population, but the setting can also be justified by the (now traditional) argument that a fresh setting helps us to see the plays freshly and prevents them from becoming static museum pieces.

In 1991 the Asian/Experimental Theater Program—a group that uses Asian methods of physical training—produced *A Midsummer Night's Dream* in Madison, Wisconsin. The theater was renovated to resemble a bar; spectators entered through the lighted proscenium and then sat at café tables around a raised dance floor. The performers wore modern clothing (an Armani suit for Theseus, a purple lycra mini-dress for Hippolyta), and there was much interaction with the audience, especially by Puck, a black male who often moved from the stage to the tables. There were also implications of homoeroticism: Egeus had a special fondness for Demetrius, and Helena and Hermia seemed more than good friends. In further connecting the play with today's chief concerns, a touch of racism was introduced; Lysander was played by a Nigerian actor, and it seemed that Egeus's dislike for him was at least partly attributable to Lysander's color. The wood was a gay disco, and the fairies were two visions of homosexuals—"radical fairies" (drag queens) aligned with Oberon (played by a mustached woman in a suit), and ACT-UP activists (in jeans and T-shirts), aligned with Titania (a man in high-heeled shoes and a leather mini-skirt). In the scene in which Helena invites Demetrius to beat her, the fairies took over her role and Demetrius's, wearing masks to indicate the switch. The overall implication was that the play revealed not only the irrational love found in the real world but also other irrationalities, such as the construction of gender and the oppression of women.

WILLIAM Shakespeare

William Shakespeare (1564–1616) was born in Stratford, England, of middle-class parents. Nothing of interest is known about his early years, but by 1590 he was acting and writing plays in London. He worked early in all three Elizabethan dramatic genres—tragedy, comedy, and history. *Romeo and Juliet*, for example, was written about 1595, the year of *Richard II*, and in the following year he wrote *A Midsummer Night's Dream*. Other major comedies are *The Merchant of Venice* (1596–97), *As You Like It* (1599–1600), and *Twelfth Night* (1599–1600). His last major works, *The Winter's Tale* (1610–11) and *The Tempest* (1611), are usually called "romances"; these plays have happy endings but they seem more meditative and less joyful than the earlier comedies.

COMMENTARY ON *A MIDSUMMER NIGHT'S DREAM*

Speaking broadly, there are in the Renaissance two comic traditions, which may be called "critical comedy" (or "bitter comedy") and "romantic comedy" (or "sweet comedy"). The former claims, in Hamlet's words, that the "purpose of playing . . . is to hold, as 'twere, the mirror up to nature; to show virtue her own feature, scorn her own image, and the very age and body of the time his form and pressure." Because it aims to hold a mirror up to the audience, its dramatis personae are usually urban citizens—jealous husbands, foolish merchants, and the like. These are ultimately punished, at times merely by exposure, at times by imprisonment or fines or some such thing. The second kind of comedy, romantic comedy, seeks less to correct than to delight with scenes of pleasant behavior. It does not hold a mirror to the audience: Rather, it leads the audience into an elegant dream world where charming gentlefolk live in a timeless world. Thomas Heywood, a playwright contemporary with Shakespeare, briefly set forth the characteristics of both traditions in *An Apology for Actors* (1612). A comedy, he said,

is pleasantly contrived with merry accidents, and intermixed with apt and witty jests. . . . and what then is the subject of this harmless mirth? Either in the shape of a clown to show others their slovenly behavior, that they may reform that simplicity in themselves, which others make their sport, . . . or to refresh such weary spirits as are tired with labors or study, to moderate the cares and heaviness of the mind, that they may return to their trades and faculties with more zeal and earnestness, after some small soft and pleasant retirement.

When we think of *A Midsummer Night's Dream*, we think not of critical comedy that seeks to reform "slovenly behavior" but of romantic comedy that offers "harmless mirth" and the refreshing of "such weary spirits as are tired with labors or study." Yet even *A Midsummer Night's Dream* has its touches of critical comedy, its elements that, in Heywood's words, "may reform" by holding up a mirror to unsocial behavior. There is some satire—a little satire of the crabby father, Egeus, and rather more of the young lovers and of the well-meaning rustics who bumblingly stage a play in an effort to please their duke (and to win pensions), but mostly the play is pervaded by genial spirits and a humane vision that make it moral without moralizing. The first book on Shakespeare's morality, Elizabeth Griffith's *The Morality of Shakespeare's Dramas* (1775), rather impatiently dismissed *A Midsummer Night's Dream*: "I shall not trouble my readers with the Fable of this piece, as I can see no general moral that can be deducted from the Argument."

For one thing, all of the people—including the fairies—in *A Midsummer Night's Dream* are basically decent creatures. Egeus is at first irascible, but at the end of the play we hear no more of his insistence that his daughter marry the young man of his choice; Theseus had engaged in youthful indiscretions, but that was long ago and in another country, and now he is the very model of a benevolent ruler; the fairy king and queen bicker, but at the end they are reconciled and they bless the bridal beds of the newlyweds. The rustics, though inept actors and sometimes too impressed by their own theatrical abilities, are men of good intentions. And if in the last act the young aristocratic lovers are a little too confident of their superiority to the rustic actors, we nevertheless feel that they are fundamentally decent; after all, their comments on the performance are more or less in tune with our own.

If *A Midsummer Night's Dream*, then, employs satire only sparingly, what does it do, and what is it about? Perhaps we can get somewhere near to an answer by briefly looking at some of the interrelationships of the stories that make up the intricate plot. There is the story of Theseus and Hippolyta, who will be married in four days; the story of the four young lovers; the story of Bottom and his fellow craftsmen, who are rehearsing a play; and the story of the quarreling fairies. All these stories are related, and eventually come together: The lovers marry on the same day as Theseus and Hippolyta; the craftsmen perform their play at the wedding; the fairies come to witness the wedding and bless it.

One of the play's themes, of course, is love, as shown in the contrasts between the stately love of Theseus and Hippolyta, the changeable romantic love of the four young Athenians, the love of Pyramus and Thisby in the play that the craftsmen are rehearsing, the quarrel between the fairy king and queen, and even Titania's infatuation with Bottom. All these stories play against one another, sometimes very subtly, and sometimes explicitly, as when Lysander, having shifted his affection from Hermia to Helena, says, "Reason says you are the worthier maid" (2.2.122), and Bottom in

the next scene accepts Titania's love, saying, "Reason and love keep little company together nowadays" (3.1.143–44). The nature of reason is also implicitly discussed in the play, in the numerous references to "fantasy" and "fancy," or imagination. There is scarcely a scene that does not touch on the matter of the power of the imagination. In the opening scene, for example, Egeus says that Lysander has corrupted Hermia's fantasy (1.1.32), and Duke Theseus tells Hermia that she must perceive her suitors as her father perceives them. The most famous of these references is Theseus's speech on "the lunatic, the lover, and the poet" (5.1.7). In addition to setting the time and place, the images help to define the nature of fantasy: There is an emphasis on night and moonlight during the period of confusion, and then references to the "morning lark," "day," and so on, when Theseus (the spokesman for reason) enters the woods and the lovers are properly paired (4.1.102 ff.). The last scene reintroduces night, and the lovers have moved from the dark wood back to the civilized world of Athens, and the night will bring them to bed. The plot of *A Midsummer Night's Dream*, then, juxtaposes speech against speech, image against image, and scene against scene, telling not simply a story but a story that "grows to something of great constancy, . . . strange and admirable."[1]

[1]The last two paragraphs of commentary are from *The Complete Signet Classic Shakespeare*, edited by Sylvan Barnet. Copyright © 1972 by Harcourt Brace Jovanovich. Reprinted by permission.

A MIDSUMMER NIGHT'S DREAM*
William Shakespeare

Edited by David Bevington

DRAMATIS PERSONAE

THESEUS, *Duke of Athens*
HIPPOLYTA, *Queen of the Amazons, betrothed to Theseus*
PHILOSTRATE, *Master of the Revelsy*
EGEUS, *father of Hermia*

HERMIA, *daughter of Egeus, in love with Lysander*
LYSANDER, *in love with Hermia*
DEMETRIUS, *in love with Hermia and favored by Egeus*
HELENA, *in love with Demetrius*

OBERON, *King of the Fairies*
TITANIA, *Queen of the Fairies*
PUCK, *or* ROBIN GOODFELLOW

PEASEBLOSSOM,
COBWEB,
MOTE, } *fairies attending Titania*
MUSTARDSEED,
Other FAIRIES *attending*

PETER QUINCE, *a carpenter,*   PROLOGUE
NICK BOTTOM, *a weaver,*   PYRAMUS
FRANCIS FLUTE, *a bellows mender,*   THISBE
TOM SNOUT, *a tinker,* } *representing*   WALL
SNUG, *a joiner,*   LION
ROBIN STARVELING, *a tailor,*   MOONSHINE
Lords and Attendants on Theseus and Hippolyta

SCENE

Athens, and a wood near it

[1.1] *Enter Theseus, Hippolyta, [and Philostrate,] with others.*

THESEUS.
  Now, fair Hippolyta, our nuptial hour
  Draws on apace. Four happy days bring in
  Another moon; but, O, methinks, how slow
  This old moon wanes! She lingers° my desires,
5 Like to a stepdame° or a dowager°
  Long withering out° a young man's revenue.
HIPPOLYTA.
  Four days will quickly steep themselves in night,

Four nights will quickly dream away the time;
And then the moon, like to a silver bow
New bent in heaven, shall behold the night   10
Of our solemnities.
THESEUS.   Go, Philostrate,
  Stir up the Athenian youth to merriments,
  Awake the pert and nimble spirit of mirth,
  Turn melancholy forth to funerals;
  The pale companion° is not for our pomp.°   15
                        [*Exit Philostrate.*]
  Hippolyta, I wooed thee with my sword°
  And won thy love doing thee injuries;
  But I will wed thee in another key,
  With pomp, with triumph,° and with reveling.

Enter Egeus and his daughter Hermia, and Lysander, and Demetrius.

EGEUS.
  Happy be Theseus, our renowned duke!   20
THESEUS.
  Thanks, good Egeus. What's the news with thee?

A Midsummer Night's Dream was first published in 1600 in a small book of a type called a quarto. A second quarto edition, printed in 1616 but based on the 1600 text, introduces a few corrections, but it also introduces many errors. The 1619 text in turn was the basis for the text in the first collected edition of Shakespeare's plays, the First Folio (1623). Bevington's edition is of course based on the text of 1600, but it includes a few corrections, and it modifies the punctuation in accordance with modern usage. Material added by the editor, such as amplifications in the *dramatis personae*, is enclosed within square brackets [ ]. **1.1 Location: Athens, Theseus' court**
4 lingers postpones, delays the fulfillment of   **5 stepdame** stepmother   **dowager** i.e., a widow (whose right of inheritance from her dead husband is eating into her son's estate)   **6 withering out** causing to dwindle

15 companion fellow   **pomp** ceremonial magnificence   **16 with my sword** i.e., in a military engagement against the Amazons, when Hippolyta was taken captive   **19 triumph** public festivity

Shakespeare's *A Midsummer Night's Dream* is a common offering in outdoor summer dramatic festivals. Among the most successful versions was this elegant modern-dress production at the Colorado Shakespeare Festival in 1988, directed by Robert Cohen, with scenery by Douglas-Scott Goheen. The circular stage and a large white marble disk (with a door in it) kept the moon themes in view. For the forest, the disk slid to stage right, revealing an opening in which hung ropes suggestive of vines and foliage.

EGEUS.
    Full of vexation come I, with complaint
    Against my child, my daughter Hermia.
    Stand forth, Demetrius. My noble lord,
25   This man hath my consent to marry her.
    Stand forth, Lysander. And, my gracious Duke,
    This man hath bewitched the bosom of my child.
    Thou, thou, Lysander, thou hast given her rhymes
    And interchanged love tokens with my child.
30   Thou hast by moonlight at her window sung
    With feigning voice verses of feigning° love,
    And stol'n the impression of her fantasy°
    With bracelets of thy hair, rings, gauds,° conceits,°
    Knacks,° trifles, nosegays, sweetmeats—messengers
35   Of strong prevailment in° unhardened youth.
    With cunning hast thou filched my daughter's heart,
    Turned her obedience, which is due to me,
    To stubborn harshness. And, my gracious Duke,
    Be it so° she will not here before Your Grace
40   Consent to marry with Demetrius,
    I beg the ancient privilege of Athens:
    As she is mine, I may dispose of her,

Which shall be either to this gentleman
Or to her death, according to our law
Immediately° provided in that case.   45
THESEUS.
    What say you, Hermia? Be advised, fair maid.
    To you your father should be as a god—
    One that composed your beauties, yea, and one
    To whom you are but as a form in wax
    By him imprinted, and within his power   50
    To leave° the figure or disfigure° it.
    Demetrius is a worthy gentleman.
HERMIA.
    So is Lysander.
THESEUS.   In himself he is;
    But in this kind,° wanting° your father's voice,°
    The other must be held the worthier.   55
HERMIA.
    I would my father looked but with my eyes.
THESEUS.
    Rather your eyes must with his judgment look.
HERMIA.
    I do entreat Your Grace to pardon me.
    I know not by what power I am made bold,
    Nor how it may concern° my modesty   60

---

31 feigning (1) counterfeiting (2) faining, desirous **32 And . . . fantasy** and made her fall in love with you (imprinting your image on her imagination) by stealthy and dishonest means **33 gauds** playthings **conceits** fanciful trifles **34 Knacks** knickknacks **35 prevailment in** influence on **39 Be it so** if

45 Immediately directly, with nothing intervening **51 leave** i.e., leave unaltered **disfigure** obliterate **54 kind** respect **wanting** lacking **voice** approval **60 concern** befit

In such a presence here to plead my thoughts;
But I beseech Your Grace that I may know
The worst that may befall me in this case
If I refuse to wed Demetrius.

THESEUS.

65 Either to die the death or to abjure
Forever the society of men.
Therefore, fair Hermia, question your desires,
Know of your youth, examine well your blood,°
Whether, if you yield not to your father's choice,

70 You can endure the livery° of a nun,
For aye° to be in shady cloister mewed,°
To live a barren sister all your life,
Chanting faint hymns to the cold fruitless moon.
Thrice blessèd they that master so their blood

75 To undergo such maiden pilgrimage;
But earthlier happy° is the rose distilled
Than that which, withering on the virgin thorn,
Grows, lives, and dies in single blessedness.

HERMIA.

So will I grow, so live, so die, my lord,

80 Ere I will yield my virgin patent° up
Unto his lordship, whose unwishèd yoke
My soul consents not to give sovereignty.

THESEUS.

Take time to pause, and by the next new moon—
The sealing day betwixt my love and me

85 For everlasting bond of fellowship—
Upon that day either prepare to die
For disobedience to your father's will,
Or° else to wed Demetrius, as he would,
Or on Diana's altar to protest°

90 For aye austerity and single life.

DEMETRIUS.

Relent, sweet Hermia, and, Lysander, yield
Thy crazèd° title to my certain right.

LYSANDER.

You have her father's love, Demetrius;
Let me have Hermia's. Do you marry him.

EGEUS.

95 Scornful Lysander! True, he hath my love,
And what is mine my love shall render him.
And she is mine, and all my right of her
I do estate unto° Demetrius.

LYSANDER.

I am, my lord, as well derived° as he,

100 As well possessed;° my love is more than his;

My fortunes every way as fairly° ranked,
If not with vantage,° as Demetrius';
And, which is more than all these boasts can be,
I am beloved of beauteous Hermia.
Why should not I then prosecute my right?   105
Demetrius, I'll avouch it to his head,°
Made love to Nedar's daughter, Helena
And won her soul; and she, sweet lady, dotes,
Devoutly dotes, dotes in idolatry,
Upon this spotted° and inconstant man.   110

THESEUS.

I must confess that I have heard so much,
And with Demetrius thought to have spoke thereof;
But, being overfull of self-affairs,°
My mind did lose it. But, Demetrius, come,
And come, Egeus, you shall go with me;   115
I have some private schooling° for you both.
For you, fair Hermia, look you arm° yourself
To fit your fancies° to your father's will;
Or else the law of Athens yields you up—
Which by no means we may extenuate°—   120
To death or to a vow of single life.
Come, my Hippolyta. What cheer, my love?
Demetrius and Egeus, go° along.
I must employ you in some business
Against° our nuptial and confer with you   125
Of something nearly that° concerns yourselves.

EGEUS.

With duty and desire we follow you.

Exeunt [all but Lysander and Hermia].

LYSANDER.

How now, my love, why is your cheek so pale?
How chance the roses there do fade so fast?

HERMIA.

Belike° for want of rain, which I could well   130
Beteem° them from the tempest of my eyes.

LYSANDER.

Ay me! For aught that I could ever read,
Could ever hear by tale or history,
The course of true love never did run smooth
But either it was different in blood°—   135

HERMIA.

O cross!° Too high to be enthralled to low.

---

68 **blood** passions 70 **livery** habit 71 **aye** ever. **mewed** shut in. (Said of a hawk, poultry, etc.) 76 **earthlier happy** happier as respects this world 80 **patent** privilege 88 **Or** either 89 **protest** vow 92 **crazèd** cracked, unsound 98 **estate unto** settle or bestow upon 99 **derived** descended, i.e., as well born 100 **possessed** endowed with wealth

101 **fairly** handsomely 102 **vantage** superiority 106 **head** i.e., face 110 **spotted** i.e., morally stained 113 **self-affairs** my own concerns 116 **schooling** admonition 117 **look you arm** take care you prepare 118 **fancies** likings, thoughts of love 120 **extenuate** mitigate 123 **go** i.e., come 125 **Against** in preparation for 126 **nearly that** that closely 130 **Belike** very likely 131 **Beteem** grant, afford 135 **blood** hereditary station 136 **cross** vexation

LYSANDER.
    Or else misgrafted° in respect of years—
HERMIA.
    O spite! Too old to be engaged to young.
LYSANDER.
    Or else it stood upon the choice of friends°—
HERMIA.
140   O hell, to choose love by another's eyes!
LYSANDER.
    Or if there were a sympathy° in choice,
    War, death, or sickness did lay siege to it,
    Making it momentany° as a sound,
    Swift as a shadow, short as any dream,
145   Brief as the lightning in the collied° night,
    That in a spleen° unfolds° both heaven and earth,
    And ere a man hath power to say "Behold!"
    The jaws of darkness do devour it up.
    So quick° bright things come to confusion.°
HERMIA.
150   If then true lovers have been ever crossed,°
    It stands as an edict in destiny.
    Then let us teach our trial patience,°
    Because it is a customary cross,
    As due to love as thoughts and dreams and sighs,
155   Wishes and tears, poor fancy's° followers.
LYSANDER.
    A good persuasion.° Therefore, hear me, Hermia:
    I have a widow aunt, a dowager
    Of great revenue, and she hath no child.
    From Athens is her house remote seven leagues;
160   And she respects° me as her only son.
    There, gentle Hermia, may I marry thee,
    And to that place the sharp Athenian law
    Cannot pursue us. If thou lovest me, then,
    Steal forth thy father's house tomorrow night;
165   And in the wood, a league without the town,
    Where I did meet thee once with Helena
    To do observance to a morn of May,°
    There will I stay for thee.
HERMIA.   My good Lysander!
    I swear to thee by Cupid's strongest bow,
170   By his best arrow° with the golden head,

By the simplicity° of Venus' doves,°
By that which knitteth souls and prospers loves,
And by that fire which burned the Carthage queen°
When the false Trojan° under sail was seen,
By all the vows that ever men have broke,   175
In number more than ever women spoke,
In that same place thou hast appointed me
Tomorrow truly will I meet with thee.
LYSANDER.
    Keep promise, love. Look, here comes Helena.

    Enter Helena.

HERMIA.
    God speed, fair° Helena! Whither away?   180
HELENA.
    Call you me fair? That "fair" again unsay.
    Demetrius loves your fair.° O happy fair!°
    Your eyes are lodestars,° and your tongue's sweet air°
    More tunable° than lark to shepherd's ear
    When wheat is green, when hawthorn buds appear.   185
    Sickness is catching. O, were favor° so!
    Yours would I catch, fair Hermia, ere I go;
    My ear should catch your voice, my eye your eye,
    My tongue should catch your tongue's sweet melody.
    Were the world mine, Demetrius being bated,°   190
    The rest I'd give to be to you translated.°
    O, teach me how you look and with what art
    You sway the motion° of Demetrius' heart.
HERMIA.
    I frown upon him, yet he loves me still.
HELENA.
    O, that your frowns would teach my smiles such skill!   195
HERMIA.
    I give him curses, yet he gives me love.
HELENA.
    O, that my prayers could such affection° move!°
HERMIA.
    The more I hate, the more he follows me.
HELENA.
    The more I love, the more he hateth me.
HERMIA.
    His folly, Helena, is no fault of mine.   200

---

137 **misgrafted** ill grafted, badly matched   139 **friends** relatives
141 **sympathy** agreement   143 **momentany** lasting but a moment
145 **collied** blackened (as with coal dust), darkened   146 **in a
spleen** in a swift impulse, in a violent flash   **unfolds** discloses
149 **quick** quickly; or, perhaps, living, alive   **confusion** ruin   150
ever crossed always thwarted   152 **teach . . . patience** i.e., teach
ourselves patience in this trial   155 **fancy's** amorous passion's
156 **persuasion** conviction   160 **respects** regards
167 **do . . . May** perform the ceremonies of May Day   170 **best arrow** (Cupid's best gold-pointed arrows were supposed to induce
love; his blunt leaden arrows, aversion.)

171 **simplicity** innocence   **doves** i.e., those that drew Venus' chariot   173, 174 **Carthage queen, false Trojan** (Dido, Queen of
Carthage, immolated herself on a funeral pyre after having been deserted by the Trojan hero Aeneas.)   180 **fair** fair-complexioned
(generally regarded by the Elizabethans as more beautiful than dark
complexioned)   182 **your fair** your beauty (even though Hermia
is dark-complexioned)   **happy fair** lucky fair one   183 **lodestars**
guiding stars   **air** music   184 **tunable** tuneful, melodious   186
favor appearance, looks   190 **bated** excepted   191 **translated**
transformed   193 **motion** impulse   197 **affection** passion.
move arouse

HELENA.

None but your beauty. Would that fault were mine!

HERMIA.

Take comfort. He no more shall see my face.

Lysander and myself will fly this place.

Before the time I did Lysander see

205　Seemed Athens as a paradise to me.

O, then, what graces in my love do dwell

That he hath turned a heaven unto a hell!

LYSANDER.

Helen, to you our minds we will unfold.

Tomorrow night, when Phoebe° doth behold

210　Her silver visage in the watery glass,°

Decking with liquid pearl the bladed grass,

A time that lovers' flights doth still° conceal,

Through Athens' gates have we devised to steal.

HERMIA.

And in the wood, where often you and I

215　Upon faint° primrose beds were wont to lie,

Emptying our bosoms of their counsel° sweet,

There my Lysander and myself shall meet;

And thence from Athens turn away our eyes,

To seek new friends and stranger companies.

220　Farewell, sweet playfellow. Pray thou for us,

And good luck grant thee thy Demetrius!

Keep word, Lysander. We must starve our sight

From lovers' food till morrow deep midnight.

LYSANDER.

I will, my Hermia. *Exit Hermia.*

Helena, adieu.

225　As you on him, Demetrius dote on you!　　*Exit Lysander.*

HELENA.

How happy some o'er other some can be!°

Through Athens I am thought as fair as she.

But what of that? Demetrius thinks not so;

He will not know what all but he do know.

230　And as he errs, doting on Hermia's eyes,

So I, admiring of° his qualities.

Things base and vile, holding no quantity,°

Love can transpose to form and dignity.

Love looks not with the eyes, but with the mind,

235　And therefore is winged Cupid painted blind.

Nor hath Love's mind of any judgment taste;°

Wings, and no eyes, figure° unheedy haste.

And therefore is Love said to be a child,

Because in choice he is so oft beguiled.

As waggish° boys in game° themselves forswear,　　240

So the boy Love is perjured everywhere.

For ere Demetrius looked on Hermia's eyne,°

He hailed down oaths that he was only mine;

And when this hail some heat from Hermia felt,

So he dissolved, and showers of oaths did melt.　　245

I will go tell him of fair Hermia's flight.

Then to the wood will he tomorrow night

Pursue her; and for this intelligence°

If I have thanks, it is a dear expense.°

But herein mean I to enrich my pain,　　250

To have his sight thither and back again.

Exit.

*[1.2] Enter Quince the carpenter, and Snug the joiner,
and Bottom the weaver, and Flute the bellows mender,
and Snout the tinker, and Starveling the tailor.*

QUINCE. Is all our company here?

BOTTOM. You were best to call them generally,° man by man,
　according to the scrip.°

QUINCE. Here is the scroll of every man's name which is
　thought fit, through all Athens, to play in our interlude　　5
　before the Duke and the Duchess on his wedding day at
　night.

BOTTOM. First, good Peter Quince, say what the play treats
　on, then read the names of the actors, and so grow to° a
　point.　　10

QUINCE. Marry,° our play is "The most lamentable comedy
　and most cruel death of Pyramus and Thisbe."

BOTTOM. A very good piece of work, I assure you, and a
　merry. Now, good Peter Quince, call forth your actors by
　the scroll. Masters, spread yourselves.　　15

QUINCE. Answer as I call you. Nick Bottom,° the weaver.

BOTTOM. Ready. Name what part I am for, and proceed.

QUINCE. You, Nick Bottom, are set down for Pyramus.

BOTTOM. What is Pyramus? A lover or a tyrant?

QUINCE. A lover, that kills himself most gallant for love.　　20

BOTTOM. That will ask some tears in the true performing of
　it. If I do it, let the audience look to their eyes. I will
　move storms; I will condole° in some measure. To the

209 Phoebe Diana, the moon　**210 glass** mirror　**212 still** always
215 faint pale　**216 counsel** secret thought　**226 o'er . . . can** be
can be in comparison to some others　**231 admiring of** wondering
at　**232 holding no quantity** i.e., unsubstantial, unshapely　**236
Nor . . . taste** i.e., nor has Love, which dwells in the fancy or imagination, any *taste* or least bit of judgment or reason　**237 figure** are
a symbol of

240 waggish playful, mischievous　**game** sport, jest　**242 eyne**
eyes (Old form of plural.)　**248 intelligence** information　**249 a
dear expense** i.e., a trouble worth taking (**dear** costly)　**1.2 Location: Athens**　**2 generally** (Bottom's blunder for *individually*.)　**3
scrip** scrap (Bottom's error for *script*.)　**9 grow to** come to　**11
Marry** (A mild oath; originally the name of the Virgin Mary.)　**16
Bottom** (As a weaver's term, a *bottom* was an object around which
thread was wound.)　**23 condole** lament, arouse pity

rest—yet my chief humor° is for a tyrant. I could play
25   Ercles° rarely, or a part to tear a cat° in, to make all split.°

"The raging rocks
And shivering shocks
Shall break the locks
    Of prison gates:
30   And Phibbus' car°
Shall shine from far
And make and mar
    The foolish Fates."

This was lofty! Now name the rest of the players. This is
35   Ercles' vein, a tyrant's vein. A lover is more condoling.
QUINCE. Francis Flute, the bellows mender.
FLUTE. Here, Peter Quince.
QUINCE. Flute, you must take Thisbe on you.
FLUTE. What is Thisbe? A wandering knight?
40   QUINCE. It is the lady that Pyramus must love.
FLUTE. Nay, faith, let not me play a woman. I have a beard
    coming.
QUINCE. That's all one.° You shall play it in a mask, and you
    may speak as small° as you will.
45   BOTTOM. An° I may hide my face, let me play Thisbe too.
    I'll speak in a monstrous little voice, "Thisne, Thisne!"
    "Ah Pyramus, my lover dear! Thy Thisbe dear, and lady
    dear!"
QUINCE. No, no, you must play Pyramus, and, Flute, you
50   Thisbe.
BOTTOM. Well, proceed.
QUINCE. Robin Starveling, the tailor.
STARVELING. Here, Peter Quince.
QUINCE. Robin Starveling, you must play Thisbe's mother.
55   Tom Snout, the tinker.
SNOUT. Here, Peter Quince.
QUINCE. You, Pyramus' father; myself, Thisbe's father; Snug,
    the joiner, you, the lion's part, and I hope here is a play
    fitted.
60   SNUG. Have you the lion's part written? Pray you, if it be,
    give it me, for I am slow of study.
QUINCE. You may do it extempore, for it is nothing but roar-
    ing.
BOTTOM. Let me play the lion too. I will roar that I will do
65   any man's heart good to hear me. I will roar that I will
    make the Duke say, "Let him roar again, let him roar
    again."
QUINCE. An you should do it too terribly, you would fright
    the Duchess and the ladies, that they would shriek; and
70   that were enough to hang us all.

ALL. That would hang us, every mother's son.
BOTTOM. I grant you, friends, if you should fright the ladies
    out of their wits, they would have no more discretion but
    to hang us; but I will aggravate° my voice so that I will
    roar you° as gently as any sucking dove;° I will roar you   75
    an 'twere any nightingale.
QUINCE. You can play no part but Pyramus; for Pyramus is a
    sweet-faced man, a proper° man as one shall see in a sum-
    mer's day, a most lovely gentlemanlike man. Therefore
    you must needs play Pyramus.   80
BOTTOM. Well, I will undertake it. What beard were I best to
    play it in?
QUINCE. Why, what you will.
BOTTOM. I will discharge° it in either your° straw-color
    beard, your orange-tawny beard, your purple-in-grain°   85
    beard, or your French-crown-color° beard, your perfect
    yellow.
QUINCE. Some of your French crowns° have no hair at all,
    and then you will play barefaced. But, masters, here are
    your parts. [He distributes parts.] And I am to entreat you,   90
    request you, and desire you to con° them by tomorrow
    night; and meet me in the palace wood, a mile without
    the town, by moonlight. There will we rehearse; for if we
    meet in the city, we shall be dogged with company, and
    our devices° known. In the meantime I will draw a bill°   95
    of properties, such as our play wants. I pray you, fail me
    not.
BOTTOM. We will meet, and there we may rehearse most ob-
    scenely° and courageously. Take pains, be perfect;°
    adieu.   100
QUINCE. At the Duke's oak we meet.
BOTTOM. Enough. Hold, or cut bowstrings.°   Exeunt.

[2.1] Enter a Fairy at one door, and Robin Goodfellow
[Puck] at another.

PUCK.
    How now, spirit, whither wander you?
FAIRY.
        Over hill, over dale,
            Thorough° bush, thorough brier,

---

24 humor inclination, whim   25 Ercles Hercules (The tradition
of ranting came from Seneca's Hercules Furens.)   tear a cat i.e.,
rant   make all split i.e., cause a stir, bring the house down   30
Phibbus' car Phoebus', the sun-god's, chariot   43 That's all one it
makes no difference   44 small high-pitched   45 An if (also at
l. 68)

74 aggravate (Bottom's blunder for moderate.)   75 roar you i.e.,
roar for you   sucking dove (Bottom conflates sitting dove and sucking lamb, two proverbial images of innocence.)   78 proper handsome   84 discharge perform   your i.e., you know the kind I mean
85 purple-in-grain dyed a very deep red (From grain, the name
applied to the dried insect used to make the dye.)
86 French-crown-color i.e., color of a French crown, a gold coin
88 crowns heads bald from syphilis, the "French disease"   91 con
learn by heart   95 devices plans   bill list   98–99 obscenely (An
unintentionally funny blunder, whatever Bottom meant to say.)
perfect i.e., letter-perfect in memorizing your parts   102 Hold . . .
bowstrings (An archers' expression not definitely explained, but
probably meaning here "keep your promises, or give up the play.")
2.1 Location: A wood near Athens   3 Thorough through

Over park, over pale,°
5   Thorough flood, thorough fire,
I do wander everywhere,
Swifter than the moon's sphere;°
And I serve the Fairy Queen,
To dew her orbs° upon the green.
10   The cowslips tall her pensioners° be.
In their gold coats spots you see:
Those be rubies, fairy favors;°
In those freckles live their savors.°

I must go seek some dewdrops here
15   And hang a pearl in every cowslip's ear.
Farewell, thou lob° of spirits: I'll be gone.
Our Queen and all her elves come here anon.°

PUCK.
The King doth keep his revels here tonight.
Take heed the Queen come not within his sight.
20   For Oberon is passing fell° and wrath,°
Because that she as her attendant hath
A lovely boy, stolen from an Indian king;
She never had so sweet a changeling.°
And jealous Oberon would have the child
25   Knight of his train, to trace° the forests wild.
But she perforce° withholds the lovèd boy,
Crowns him with flowers, and makes him all her joy.
And now they never meet in grove or green,
By fountain° clear, or spangled starlight sheen,°
30   But they do square,° that all their elves for fear
Creep into acorn cups and hide them there.

FAIRY.
Either I mistake your shape and making quite,
Or else you are that shrewd° and knavish sprite°
Called Robin Goodfellow. Are not you he
35   That frights the maidens of the villagery,°
Skim milk, and sometimes labor in the quern,°
And bootless° make the breathless huswife° churn,
And sometimes make the drink to bear no barm,°
Mislead night wanderers, laughing at their harm?
40   Those that "Hobgoblin" call you, and "Sweet Puck,"
You do their work, and they shall have good luck.
Are you not he?

PUCK.   Thou speakest aright;

I am that merry wanderer of the night.
I jest to Oberon and make him smile
When I a fat and bean-fed horse beguile,   45
Neighing in likeness of a filly foal;
And sometimes lurk I in a gossip's° bowl,
In very likeness of a roasted crab,°
And when she drinks, against her lips I bob
And on her withered dewlap° pour the ale.   50
The wisest aunt,° telling the saddest° tale,
Sometimes for three-foot stool mistaketh me;
Then slip I from her bum, down topples she,
And "Tailor"° cries, and falls into a cough;
And then the whole choir° hold their hips and laugh,   55
And waxen° in their mirth, and neeze,° and swear
A merrier hour was never wasted there.
But, room,° fairy! Here comes Oberon.

FAIRY.
And here my mistress. Would that he were gone!

Enter [Oberon] the King of Fairies at one door, with his
train; and [Titania] the Queen at another, with hers.

OBERON.
Ill met by moonlight, proud Titania.   60
TITANIA.
What, jealous Oberon? Fairies, skip hence.
I have forsworn his bed and company.
OBERON.
Tarry, rash wanton.° Am not I thy lord?
TITANIA.
Then I must be thy lady; but I know
When thou hast stolen away from Fairyland   65
And in the shape of Corin° sat all day,
Playing on pipes of corn° and versing love
To amorous Phillida.° Why art thou here
Come from the farthest step° of India
But that, forsooth, the bouncing Amazon,   70
Your buskined° mistress and your warrior love,
To Theseus must be wedded, and you come
To give their bed joy and prosperity.
OBERON.
How canst thou thus for shame, Titania,
Glance at my credit with Hippolyta,°   75

---

4 pale enclosure   **7 sphere** orbit   **9 orbs** circles, i.e., fairy rings
(circular bands of grass, darker than the surrounding area, caused by
fungi enriching the soil)   **10 pensioners** retainers, members of the
royal bodyguard   **12 favors** love tokens   **13 savors** sweet smells
16 lob country bumpkin   **17 anon** at once   **20 passing fell** exceedingly angry   **wrath** wrathful   **23 changeling** child exchanged
for another by the fairies   **25 trace** range through   **26 perforce**
forcibly   **29 fountain** spring   **starlight sheen** shining starlight
30 square quarrel   **33 shrewd** mischievous   **sprite** spirit   **35**
villagery village population   **36 quern** handmill   **37 bootless** in
vain   **huswife** housewife   **38 barm** yeast, head on the ale

47 gossip's old woman's   **48 crab** crab apple   **50 dewlap** loose
skin on neck   **51 aunt** old woman   **saddest** most serious   **54 Tai-**
lor (possibly because she ends up sitting cross-legged on the floor,
looking like a tailor.)   **55 choir** company   **56 waxen** increase.
neeze sneeze   **58 room** stand aside, make room   **63 wanton** headstrong creature   **66, 68 Corin, Phillida** (Conventional names of
pastoral lovers.)   **67 corn** (Here, oat stalks.)   **69 step** farthest
limit of travel, or, perhaps, *steep*, mountain range   **71 buskined**
wearing half-boots called buskins   **75 Glance . . . Hippolyta** make
insinuations about my favored relationship with Hippolyta

Knowing I know thy love to Theseus?
Didst not thou lead him through the glimmering night
From Perigenia,° whom he ravishèd?
And make him with fair Aegles° break his faith,
80   With Ariadne° and Antiopa?°

TITANIA.
These are the forgeries of jealousy;
And never, since the middle summer's spring,°
Met we on hill, in dale, forest, or mead,
By pavèd° fountain or by rushy° brook,
85   Or in° the beachèd margent° of the sea,
To dance our ringlets° to the whistling wind,
But with thy brawls thou hast disturbed our sport.
Therefore the winds, piping to us in vain,
As in revenge, have sucked up from the sea
90   Contagious° fogs; which, falling in the land,
Hath every pelting° river made so proud
That they have overborne their continents.°
The ox hath therefore stretched his yoke in vain,
The plowman lost his sweat, and the green corn°
95   Hath rotted ere his youth attained a beard;
The fold° stands empty in the drownèd field,
And crows are fatted with the murrain° flock;
The nine-men's-morris° is filled up with mud,
And the quaint mazes° in the wanton° green
100   For lack of tread are undistinguishable.
The human mortals want° their winter° here;
No night is now with hymn or carol blessed.
Therefore° the moon, the governess of floods,
Pale in her anger, washes all the air,
105   That rheumatic diseases° do abound.
And thorough this distemperature° we see

The seasons alter: hoary-headed frosts
Fall in the fresh lap of the crimson rose,
And on old Hiems'° thin and icy crown
An odorous chaplet of sweet summer buds   110
Is, as in mockery, set. The spring, the summer,
The childing° autumn, angry winter, change
Their wonted liveries,° and the mazèd° world
By their increase° now knows not which is which.
And this same progeny of evils comes   115
From our debate,° from our dissension;
We are their parents and original.°

OBERON.
Do you amend it, then; it lies in you.
Why should Titania cross her Oberon?
I do but beg a little changeling boy   120
To be my henchman.°

TITANIA.   Set your heart at rest.
The fairy land buys not the child of me.
His mother was a vot'ress of my order,
And in the spicèd Indian air by night
Full often hath she gossiped by my side   125
And sat with me on Neptune's yellow sands,
Marking th' embarkèd traders° on the flood,°
When we have laughed to see the sails conceive
And grow big-bellied with the wanton° wind;
Which she, with pretty and with swimming° gait, 130
Following—her womb then rich with my young squire—
Would imitate, and sail upon the land
To fetch me trifles, and return again
As from a voyage, rich with merchandise.
But she, being mortal, of that boy did die;   135
And for her sake do I rear up her boy,
And for her sake I will not part with him.

OBERON.
How long within this wood intend you stay?

TITANIA.
Perchance till after Theseus' wedding day.
If you will patiently dance in our round°   140
And see our moonlight revels, go with us;
If not, shun me, and I will spare° your haunts.

OBERON.
Give me that boy and I will go with thee.

TITANIA.
Not for thy fairy kingdom. Fairies, away!
We shall chide downright if I longer stay.   145

Exeunt [*Titania with her train*].

---

78 Perigenia i.e., Perigouna, one of Theseus' conquests (This and the following women are named in Thomas North's translation of Plutarch's "Life of Theseus.")   **79 Aegles** i.e., Aegle, for whom Theseus deserted Ariadne according to some accounts   **80 Ariadne** the daughter of Minos, King of Crete, who helped Theseus to escape the labyrinth after killing the Minotaur; later she was abandoned by Theseus.   **Antiopa** Queen of the Amazons and wife of Theseus; elsewhere identified with Hippolyta, but here thought of as a separate woman   **82 middle summer's spring** beginning of midsummer   **84 pavèd** with pebbled bottom   **rushy** bordered with rushes   **85 in** on   **margent** edge, border   **86 ringlets** dances in a ring (See *orbs* in line 9.)   **90 Contagious** noxious   **91 pelting** paltry   **92 continents** banks that contain them   **94 corn** grain of any kind   **96 fold** pen for sheep or cattle   **97 murrain** having died of the plague   **98 nine-men's-morris** i.e., portion of the village green marked out in a square for a game played with nine pebbles or pegs   **99 quaint mazes** i.e., intricate paths marked out on the village green to be followed rapidly on foot as a kind of contest   **wanton** luxuriant   **101 want** lack   **winter** i.e., regular winter season; or, proper observances of winter, such as the *hymn or carol* in the next line (?)   **103 Therefore** i.e., as a result of our quarrel   **105 rheumatic diseases** colds, flu, and other respiratory infections   **106 distemperature** disturbance in nature

109 Hiems' the winter god's   **112 childing** fruitful, pregnant   **113 wonted liveries** usual apparel   **mazèd** bewildered   **114 their increase** their yield, what they produce   **116 debate** quarrel   **117 original** origin   **121 henchman** attendant, page   **127 traders** trading vessels   **flood** flood tide   **129 wanton** sportive   **130 swimming** smooth, gliding   **140 round** circular dance   **142 spare** shun

OBERON.
　　Well, go thy way. Thou shalt not from° this grove
　　Till I torment thee for this injury.
　　My gentle Puck, come hither. Thou rememb'rest
　　Since° once I sat upon a promontory,
150　And heard a mermaid on a dolphin's back
　　Uttering such dulcet and harmonious breath°
　　That the rude° sea grew civil at her song,
　　And certain stars shot madly from their spheres
　　To hear the sea-maid's music?
PUCK.　　　　　　　　　　　　I remember.
OBERON.
155　That very time I saw, but thou couldst not,
　　Flying between the cold moon and the earth,
　　Cupid all° armed. A certain aim he took
　　At a fair vestal° thronèd by the west,
　　And loosed° his love shaft smartly from his bow
160　As° it should pierce a hundred thousand hearts;
　　But I might° see young Cupid's fiery shaft
　　Quenched in the chaste beams of the watery moon,
　　And the imperial vot'ress passèd on
　　In maiden meditation, fancy-free.°
165　Yet marked I where the bolt° of Cupid fell:
　　It fell upon a little western flower,
　　Before milk-white, now purple with love's wound,
　　And maidens call it "love-in-idleness."°
　　Fetch me that flower; the herb I showed thee once.
170　The juice of it on sleeping eyelids laid
　　Will make or man or° woman madly dote
　　Upon the next live creature that it sees.
　　Fetch me this herb, and be thou here again
　　Ere the leviathan° can swim a league.
PUCK.
175　I'll put a girdle round about the earth
　　In forty° minutes.　　　　　　　　　[*Exit.*]
OBERON.　　　　　　　Having once this juice,
　　I'll watch Titania when she is asleep
　　And drop the liquor of it in her eyes.
　　The next thing then she waking looks upon,
180　Be it on lion, bear, or wolf, or bull,
　　On meddling monkey, or on busy ape,
　　She shall pursue it with the soul of love.
　　And ere I take this charm from off her sight,
　　As I can take it with another herb,
185　I'll make her render up her page to me.

But who comes here? I am invisible,
And I will overhear their conference.

Enter Demetrius, Helena following him.

DEMETRIUS.
　　I love thee not; therefore pursue me not.
　　Where is Lysander and fair Hermia?
　　The one I'll slay; the other slayeth me.　　　190
　　Thou toldst me they were stol'n unto this wood;
　　And here am I, and wode° within this wood,
　　Because I cannot meet my Hermia.
　　Hence, get thee gone, and follow me no more.
HELENA.
　　You draw me, you hardhearted adamant!°　　195
　　But yet you draw not iron, for my heart
　　Is true as steel. Leave° you your power to draw,
　　And I shall have no power to follow you.
DEMETRIUS.
　　Do I entice you? Do I speak you fair?°
　　Or rather do I not in plainest truth　　　200
　　Tell you I do not nor I cannot love you?
HELENA.
　　And even for that do I love you the more.
　　I am your spaniel; and, Demetrius,
　　The more you beat me, I will fawn on you.
　　Use me but as your spaniel, spurn me, strike me,　205
　　Neglect me, lose me; only give me leave,
　　Unworthy as I am, to follow you.
　　What worser place can I beg in your love—
　　And yet a place of high respect with me—
　　Than to be usèd as you use your dog?　　　210
DEMETRIUS.
　　Tempt not too much the hatred of my spirit,
　　For I am sick when I do look on thee.
HELENA.
　　And I am sick when I look not on you.
DEMETRIUS.
　　You do impeach° your modesty too much
　　To leave the city and commit yourself　　　215
　　Into the hands of one that loves you not,
　　To trust the opportunity of night
　　And the ill counsel of a desert° place
　　With the rich worth of your virginity.
HELENA.
　　Your virtue° is my privilege°. For that°　　220
　　It is not night when I do see your face,

---

146 from go from　**149 Since** when　**151 breath** voice, song
152 rude rough　**157 all** fully　**158 vestal** vestal virgin (Contains
a complimentary allusion to Queen Elizabeth as a votaress of Diana
and probably refers to an actual entertainment in her honor at El-
vetham in 1591.)　**159 loosed** released　**160 As** as if　**161 might**
could　**164 fancy-free** free of love's spell　**165 bolt** arrow　**168
love-in-idleness** pansy, heartsease　**171 or . . . or** either . . . or
174 leviathan sea monster, whale　**176 forty** (Used indefinitely.)

192 wode mad (Pronounced "wood" and often spelled so.)　**195
adamant** lodestone, magnet (with pun on *hardhearted*, since
adamant was also thought to be the hardest of all stones and was
confused with the diamond)　**197 Leave** give up　**199 fair** courteously　**214 impeach** call into question　**218 desert** deserted
220 virtue goodness or power to attract　**privilege** safeguard; warrant　**For that** because

Therefore I think I am not in the night;
Nor doth this wood lack worlds of company,
For you, in my respect,° are all the world.
225   Then how can it be said I am alone
When all the world is here to look on me?

DEMETRIUS.
I'll run from thee and hide me in the brakes,°
And leave thee to the mercy of wild beasts.

HELENA.
The wildest hath not such a heart as you.
230   Run when you will, the story shall be changed:
Apollo flies and Daphne holds the chase,°
The dove pursues the griffin,° the mild hind°
Makes speed to catch the tiger—bootless° speed,
When cowardice pursues and valor flies!

DEMETRIUS.
235   I will not stay° thy questions.° Let me go!
Or if thou follow me, do not believe
But I shall do thee mischief in the wood.

HELENA.
Ay, in the temple, in the town, the field,
You do me mischief. Fie, Demetrius!
240   Your wrongs do set a scandal on my sex.°
We cannot fight for love, as men may do;
We should be wooed and were not made to woo.

[Exit Demetrius.]

I'll follow thee and make a heaven of hell,
To die upon° the hand I love so well.   [Exit.]

OBERON.
245   Fare thee well, nymph. Ere he do leave this grove,
Thou shalt fly him and he shall seek thy love.

Enter Puck.

Hast thou the flower there? Welcome, wanderer.

PUCK.
Ay, there it is.   [He offers the flower.]

OBERON.   I pray thee, give it me.
I know a bank where the wild thyme blows,°
250   Where oxlips° and the nodding violet grows,
Quite overcanopied with luscious woodbine,°

With sweet muskroses° and with eglantine.°
There sleeps Titania sometimes of the night,
Lulled in these flowers with dances and delight;
And there the snake throws° her enameled skin,   255
Weed° wide enough to wrap a fairy in.
And with the juice of this I'll streak° her eyes
And make her full of hateful fantasies.
Take thou some of it, and seek through this grove.

[He gives some love juice.]

A sweet Athenian lady is in love   260
With a disdainful youth. Anoint his eyes,
But do it when the next thing he espies
May be the lady. Thou shalt know the man
By the Athenian garments he hath on.
Effect it with some care, that he may prove   265
More fond on° her than she upon her love;
And look thou meet me ere the first cock crow.

PUCK.
Fear not, my lord, your servant shall do so.

Exeunt.

[2.2] Enter Titania, Queen of Fairies, with her train.

TITANIA.
Come, now a roundel° and a fairy song;
Then, for the third part of a minute, hence—
Some to kill cankers° in the muskrose buds,
Some war with reremice° for their leathern wings
To make my small elves coats, and some keep back
The clamorous owl, that nightly hoots and wonders   5
At our quaint° spirits. Sing me now asleep.
Then to your offices, and let me rest.

Fairies sing.

FIRST FAIRY.
You spotted snakes with double° tongue,
Thorny hedgehogs, be not seen;
Newts° and blindworms, do no wrong,   10
Come not near our Fairy Queen.

CHORUS.
Philomel,° with melody

---

224 in my respect as far as I am concerned   227 brakes thickets
231 Apollo . . . chase (In the ancient myth, Daphne fled from
Apollo and was saved from rape by being transformed into a laurel
tree; here it is the female *who holds the chase*, or pursues, instead of
the male.)   232 griffin a fabulous monster with the head of an eagle and the body of a lion   hind female deer   233 bootless fruitless   235 stay wait for   questions talk or argument   240 Your
. . . sex i.e., the wrongs that you do me cause me to act in a manner
that disgraces my sex   244 upon by   249 blows blooms   250
oxlips flowers resembling cowslip and primrose   251 woodbine
honeysuckle

252 muskroses a kind of large, sweet-scented rose   eglantine
sweetbrier, another kind of rose   255 throws sloughs off, sheds
256 Weed garment   257 streak anoint, touch gently   266 fond
on doting on   2.2 Location: The wood   1 roundel dance in a
ring   3 cankers cankerworms (i.e., caterpillars or grubs)   4
reremice bats   7 quaint dainty   9 double forked   11 Newts water lizards (considered poisonous, as were *blindworms*—small snakes
with tiny eyes—and spiders)   13 Philomel the nightingale
(Philomela, daughter of King Pandion, was transformed into a
nightingale, according to Ovid's *Metamorphoses* 6, after she had
been raped by her sister Procne's husband, Tereus.)

Sing in our sweet lullaby;
15 Lulla, lulla, lullaby, lulla, lulla, lullaby.
        Never harm
        Nor spell nor charm
        Come our lovely lady nigh.
        So good night, with lullaby.
    FIRST FAIRY.
20   Weaving spiders, come not here;
            Hence, you long-legged spinners, hence!
        Beetles black, approach not near;
            Worm nor snail, do no offense.
    CHORUS.
        Philomel, with melody
25   Sing in our sweet lullaby;
        Lulla, lulla, lullaby, lulla, lulla, lullaby.
        Never harm
        Nor spell nor charm
        Come our lovely lady nigh.
30   So good night, with lullaby.

                                    [*Titania sleeps.*]

    SECOND FAIRY.
        Hence, away! Now all is well.
        One aloof stand sentinel.   [*Exeunt Fairies.*]

    *Enter Oberon [and squeezes the flower on Titania's eye-
    lids].*

    OBERON.
        What thou seest when thou dost wake,
        Do it for thy true love take;
35   Love and languish for his sake.
        Be it ounce,° or cat, or bear,
        Pard,° or boar with bristled hair,
        In thy eye that shall appear
        When thou wak'st, it is thy dear.
40   Wake when some vile thing is near.   [*Exit.*]

    Enter Lysander and Hermia.

    LYSANDER.
        Fair love, you faint with wandering in the wood;
            And to speak truth, I have forgot our way.
        We'll rest us, Hermia, if you think it good,
            And tarry for the comfort of the day.
    HERMIA.
45   Be it so, Lysander. Find you out a bed,
        For I upon this bank will rest my head.
    LYSANDER.
        One turf shall serve as pillow for us both;
        One heart, one bed, two bosoms, and one troth.°
    HERMIA.
        Nay, good Lysander, for my sake, my dear,

Lie further off yet; do not lie so near.   50
LYSANDER.
    O, take the sense, sweet, of my innocence!°
    Love takes the meaning in love's conference.°
    I mean that my heart unto yours is knit
    So that but one heart we can make of it;
    Two bosoms interchainéd with an oath—   55
    So then two bosoms and a single troth.
    Then by your side no bed-room me deny,
    For lying so, Hermia, I do not lie.°
HERMIA.
    Lysander riddles very prettily.
    Now much beshrew° my manners and my pride   60
    If Hermia meant to say Lysander lied.
    But, gentle friend, for love and courtesy
    Lie further off, in human° modesty;
    Such separation as may well be said
    Becomes a virtuous bachelor and a maid,   65
    So far be distant; and good night, sweet friend.
    Thy love ne'er alter till thy sweet life end!
LYSANDER.
    Amen, amen, to that fair prayer, say I,
    And then end life when I end loyalty!
    Here is my bed. Sleep give thee all his rest! 70
HERMIA.
    With half that wish the wisher's eyes be pressed!°

                    [*They sleep, separated by a short distance.*]

    Enter Puck.

PUCK.
    Through the forest have I gone,
    But Athenian found I none
    On whose eyes I might approve°
    This flower's force in stirring love.   75
    Night and silence.—Who is here?
    Weeds of Athens he doth wear.
    This is he, my master said,
    Despisèd the Athenian maid;
    And here the maiden, sleeping sound,   80
    On the dank and dirty ground.
    Pretty soul, she durst not lie
    Near this lack-love, this kill-courtesy.
    Churl, upon thy eyes I throw
    All the power this charm doth owe.°   85

---

51 take . . . innocence i.e., interpret my intention as innocent   **52
Love . . . conference** i.e., when lovers confer, love teaches each
lover to interpret the other's meaning lovingly   **58 lie** tell a falsehood (with a riddling pun on *lie*, recline)   **60 beshrew** curse. (But
mildly meant.)   **63 human** courteous   **71 With . . . pressed** i.e.,
may we share your wish, so that your eyes too are *pressed*, closed, in
sleep   **74 approve** test   **85 owe** own

36 ounce lynx   **37 Pard** leopard   **48 troth** faith, trothplight

[He applies the love juice.]

When thou wak'st, let love forbid
Sleep his seat on thy eyelid.
So awake when I am gone,
For I must now to Oberon.   *Exit.*

Enter Demetrius and Helena, running.

HELENA.
90   Stay, though thou kill me, sweet Demetrius!
DEMETRIUS.
      I charge thee, hence, and do not haunt me thus.
HELENA.
      O, wilt thou darkling° leave me? Do not so.
DEMETRIUS.
      Stay, on thy peril!° I alone will go.   *[Exit.]*
HELENA.
      O, I am out of breath in this fond° chase!
95   The more my prayer, the lesser is my grace.°
      Happy is Hermia, wheresoe'er she lies,
      For she hath blessèd and attractive eyes.
      How came her eyes so bright? Not with salt tears;
      If so, my eyes are oftener washed than hers.
100   No, no, I am as ugly as a bear;
      For beasts that meet me run away for fear.
      Therefore no marvel though Demetrius
      Do, as a monster, fly my presence thus.°
      What wicked and dissembling glass of mine
105   Made me compare° with Hermia's sphery eyne?°
      But who is here? Lysander, on the ground?
      Dead, or asleep? I see no blood, no wound.
      Lysander, if you live, good sir, awake.
LYSANDER *[Awaking]*.
      And run through fire I will for thy sweet sake.
110   Transparent° Helena! Nature shows art,
      That through thy bosom makes me see thy heart.
      Where is Demetrius? O, how fit a word
      Is that vile name to perish on my sword!
HELENA.
      Do not say so, Lysander, say not so.
115   What though he love your Hermia? Lord, what though?
      Yet Hermia still loves you. Then be content.
LYSANDER.
      Content with Hermia? No! I do repent
      The tedious minutes I with her have spent.
      Not Hermia but Helena I love.
120   Who will not change a raven for a dove?
      The will of man is by his reason swayed,

And reason says you are the worthier maid.
Things growing are not ripe until their season;
So I, being young, till now ripe not° to reason.
And touching° now the point° of human skill,°   125
Reason becomes the marshal to my will
And leads me to your eyes, where I o'erlook°
Love's stories written in love's richest book.
HELENA.
      Wherefore° was I to this keen mockery born?
      When at your hands did I deserve this scorn?   130
      Is 't not enough, is 't not enough, young man,
      That I did never, no, nor never can,
      Deserve a sweet look from Demetrius' eye,
      But you must flout my insufficiency?
      Good troth,° you do me wrong, good sooth,° you do, 135
      In such disdainful manner me to woo.
      But fare you well. Perforce I must confess
      I thought you lord of° more true gentleness.°
      O, that a lady, of° one man refused,
      Should of another therefore be abused!°   *Exit.* 140
LYSANDER.
      She sees not Hermia. Hermia, sleep thou there,
      And never mayst thou come Lysander near!
      For as a surfeit of the sweetest things
      The deepest loathing to the stomach brings,
      Or as the heresies that men do leave   145
      Are hated most of those they did deceive,°
      So thou, my surfeit and my heresy,
      Of all be hated, but the most of me!
      And, all my powers, address° your love and might
      To honor Helen and to be her knight!   *Exit.* 150
HERMIA *[Awaking]*.
      Help me, Lysander, help me! Do thy best
      To pluck this crawling serpent from my breast!
      Ay me, for pity! What a dream was here!
      Lysander, look how I do quake with fear.
      Methought a serpent ate my heart away,   155
      And you sat smiling at his cruel prey.°
      Lysander! What, removed? Lysander! Lord!
      What, out of hearing? Gone? No sound, no word?
      Alack, where are you? Speak, an if° you hear;
      Speak, of all loves!° I swoon almost with fear.   160
      No? Then I well perceive you are not nigh.
      Either death, or you, I'll find immediately.

                          Exit. [The sleeping Titania remains.]

92 **darkling** in the dark   93 **on thy peril** i.e., on pain of danger to you if you don't obey me and stay   94 **fond** doting   95 **my grace** the favor I obtain   102–103 **no marvel . . . thus** i.e., no wonder that Demetrius flies from me as from a monster   105 **compare** vie. **sphery eyne** eyes as bright as stars in their spheres   110 **Transparent** (1) radiant (2) able to be seen through

124 **ripe not** (am) not ripened   125 **touching** reaching.   **point** summit.   **skill** judgment   127 **o'erlook** read   129 **Wherefore** why   135 **Good troth,   good sooth** i.e., indeed, truly   138 **lord of** i.e., possessor of   **gentleness** courtesy   139 **of** by   140 **abused** ill treated   145–146 **as . . . deceive** as renounced heresies are hated most by those persons who formerly were deceived by them   149 **address** direct, apply   156 **prey** act of preying   159 **an if** if   160 **of all loves** for all love's sake

[3.1] *Enter the clowns* [*Quince, Snug, Bottom, Flute, Snout, and Starveling*].

BOTTOM. Are we all met?

QUINCE. Pat, pat;° and here's a marvelous convenient place for our rehearsal. This green plot shall be our stage, this hawthorn brake° our tiring-house,° and we will do it in
5   action as we will do it before the Duke.

BOTTOM. Peter Quince?

QUINCE. What sayest thou, bully° Bottom?

BOTTOM. There are things in this comedy of Pyramus and Thisbe that will never please. First, Pyramus must draw a
10   sword to kill himself, which the ladies cannot abide. How answer you that?

SNOUT. By 'r lakin,° a parlous° fear.

STARVELING. I believe we must leave the killing out, when all is done.°

15   BOTTOM. Not a whit. I have a device to make all well. Write me° a prologue, and let the prologue seem to say we will do no harm with our swords, and that Pyramus is not killed indeed; and for the more better assurance, tell them that I, Pyramus, am not Pyramus but Bottom the
20   weaver. This will put them out of fear.

QUINCE. Well, we will have such a prologue, and it shall be written in eight and six.°

BOTTOM. No, make it two more; let it be written in eight and eight.

25   SNOUT. Will not the ladies be afeard of the lion?

STARVELING. I fear it, I promise you.

BOTTOM. Masters, you ought to consider with yourselves, to bring in—God shield us!—a lion among ladies° is a most dreadful thing. For there is not a more fearful° wildfowl
30   than your lion living; and we ought to look to 't.

SNOUT. Therefore another prologue must tell he is not a lion.

BOTTOM. Nay, you must name his name, and half his face must be seen through the lion's neck, and he himself
35   must speak through, saying thus, or to the same defect:° "Ladies"—or "Fair ladies—I would wish you"—or "I would request you"—or "I would entreat you—not to fear, not to tremble; my life for yours.° If you think I

come hither as a lion, it were pity of my life.° No, I am no such thing: I am a man as other men are." And there in-   40
deed let him name his name and tell them plainly he is Snug the joiner.

QUINCE. Well, it shall be so. But there is two hard things: that is, to bring the moonlight into a chamber; for, you know, Pyramus and Thisbe meet by moonlight.   45

SNOUT. Doth the moon shine that night we play our play?

BOTTOM. A calendar, a calendar! Look in the almanac. Find out moonshine, find out moonshine.

[*They consult an almanac.*]

QUINCE. Yes, it doth shine that night.

BOTTOM. Why, then, may you leave a casement of the great   50
chamber window, where we play, open, and the moon may shine in at the casement.

QUINCE. Ay; or else one must come in with a bush of thorns° and a lantern and say he comes to disfigure,° or to pre-sent,° the person of Moonshine. Then there is another   55
thing: we must have a wall in the great chamber; for Pyramus and Thisbe, says the story, did talk through the chink of a wall.

SNOUT. You can never bring in a wall. What say you, Bot-tom?   60

BOTTOM. Some man or other must present Wall. And let him have some plaster, or some loam, or some roughcast° about him, to signify wall; or let him hold his fingers thus, and through that cranny shall Pyramus and Thisbe whisper.   65

QUINCE. If that may be, then all is well. Come, sit down, every mother's son, and rehearse your parts. Pyramus, you begin. When you have spoken your speech, enter into that brake, and so everyone according to his cue.

Enter Robin [*Puck*].

PUCK.
What hempen homespuns° have we swaggering here   70
So near the cradle° of the Fairy Queen?
What, a play toward?° I'll be an auditor;
An actor too perhaps, if I see cause.

QUINCE. Speak, Pyramus. Thisbe, stand forth.

BOTTOM [*As Pyramus*]. "Thisbe, the flowers of odious savors   75
sweet—"

QUINCE. Odors, odors.

BOTTOM.
"—Odors savors sweet;

3.1. Location: The action is continuous. 2 Pat on the dot, punctually **4 brake** thicket **tiring-house** attiring area, hence backstage **7 bully** i.e., worthy, jolly, fine fellow **12 By 'r lakin** by our ladykin, i.e., the Virgin Mary **parlous** alarming **13–14 when all is done** i.e., when all is said and done **15–16 Write me** i.e., write at my suggestion. (*Me* is used colloquially.) **22 eight and six** alternate lines of eight and six syllables, a common ballad measure **28 lion among ladies** (A contemporary pamphlet tells how at the christening in 1594 of Prince Henry, eldest son of King James VI of Scotland, later James I of England, a "black-amoor" instead of a lion drew the triumphal chariot, since the lion's presence might have "brought some fear to the nearest.") **29 fearful** fear inspiring **35 defect** (Bottom's blunder for *effect*.) **38 my life for yours** i.e., I pledge my life to make your lives safe

39 it were . . . life my life would be endangered **53 bush of thorns** bundle of thornbush faggots (part of the accoutrements of the man in the moon, according to the popular notions of the time, along with his lantern and his dog) **54 disfigure** (Quince's blunder for *figure*.) **54–55 present** represent **62 roughcast** a mixture of lime and gravel used to plaster the outside of buildings **70 hempen homespuns** i.e., rustics dressed in clothes woven of coarse, homespun fabric made from hemp **71 cradle** i.e., Titania's bower **72 toward** about to take place

So hath thy breath, my dearest Thisbe dear.
But hark, a voice! Stay thou but here awhile,
80   And by and by I will to thee appear."   *Exit.*
PUCK. A stranger Pyramus than e'er played here.°   [*Exit.*]
FLUTE. Must I speak now?
QUINCE. Ay, marry, must you; for you must understand he
    goes but to see a noise that he heard, and is to come
85   again.
FLUTE [*As Thisbe*].
    "Most radiant Pyramus, most lily-white of hue,
        Of color like the red rose on triumphant° brier,
    Most brisky juvenal° and eke° most lovely Jew,°
    As true as truest horse, that yet would never tire.
90   I'll meet thee, Pyramus, at Ninny's tomb."
QUINCE. "Ninus'° tomb," man. Why, you must not speak that
    yet. That you answer to Pyramus. You speak all your part°
    at once, cues and all. Pyramus, enter. Your cue is past; it is
    "never tire."
FLUTE.
95   O—"As true as truest horse, that yet would never tire."

    [*Enter Puck, and Bottom as Pyramus with the ass head.°*]

BOTTOM. "If I were fair,° Thisbe, I were° only thine."
QUINCE. O, monstrous! O, strange! We are haunted. Pray,
    masters! Fly, masters! Help!

            [*Exeunt Quince, Snug, Flute, Snout, and Starveling.*]

PUCK.
    I'll follow you, I'll lead you about a round,°
100   Through bog, through bush, through brake, through
        brier.
    Sometimes a horse I'll be, sometimes a hound,
        A hog, a headless bear, sometimes a fire;°
    And neigh, and bark, and grunt, and roar, and burn,
    Like horse, hound, hog, bear, fire, at every turn.   *Exit.*
105 BOTTOM. Why do they run away? This is a knavery of them
    to make me afeard.

    Enter Snout.

SNOUT. O Bottom, thou art changed! What do I see on thee?

BOTTOM. What do you see? You see an ass head of your own,
    do you?

                        [*Exit Snout.*]

    Enter Quince.

QUINCE. Bless thee, Bottom, bless thee! Thou art translated.°   110
                                                        Exit.
BOTTOM. I see their knavery. This is to make an ass of me, to
    fright me, if they could. But I will not stir from this place,
    do what they can. I will walk up and down here, and will
    sing, that they shall hear I am not afraid.   [*Sings.*]

    The ouzel cock° so black of hue,   115
        With orange-tawny bill,
    The throstle° with his note so true,
        The wren with little quill°—

TITANIA [*Awaking*].
    What angel wakes me from my flowery bed?
BOTTOM [*Sings*].

    The finch, the sparrow, and the lark,   120
        The plainsong° cuckoo gray,
    Whose note full many a man doth mark,
        And dares not answer nay°—
    For, indeed, who would set his wit to so foolish a bird?
        Who would give a bird the lie,° though he cry   125
        "cuckoo" never so?°
TITANIA.
    I pray thee, gentle mortal, sing again.
    Mine ear is much enamored of thy note;
    So is mine eye enthrallèd to thy shape;
    And thy fair virtue's force° perforce doth move me   130
    On the first view to say, to swear, I love thee.
BOTTOM. Methinks, mistress, you should have little reason
    for that. And yet, to say the truth, reason and love keep
    little company together nowadays. The more the pity
    that some honest neighbors will not make them friends.   135
    Nay, I can gleek° upon occasion.
TITANIA.
    Thou art as wise as thou art beautiful.
BOTTOM. Not so, neither. But if I had wit enough to get out
    of this wood, I have enough to serve mine own turn.°
TITANIA.
    Out of this wood do not desire to go.   140
    Thou shalt remain here, whether thou wilt or no.
    I am a spirit of no common rate.°

---

81 A stranger . . . here (Puck indicates that he has conceived of
his plan to present a "stranger" Pyramus than ever seen before, and
so Puck exits to put his plan into effect.)   **87 triumphant** magnificent   **88 brisky juvenal** lively youth   **eke** also   **Jew** (Probably
an absurd repetition of the first syllable of *juvenal*, or Flute's error
for *jewel*.)   **91 Ninus** mythical founder of Nineveh (whose wife,
Semiramis, was supposed to have built the walls of Babylon where
the story of Pyramus and Thisbe takes place)   **92 part** (An actor's
part was a script consisting only of his speeches and their cues.)
95 s.d. with the ass head (This stage direction, taken from the Folio, presumably refers to a standard stage property.)   **96 fair** handsome   **were** would be   **99 about a round** roundabout   **102 fire**
will-o'-the-wisp

110 translated transformed   **115 ouzel cock** male blackbird   **117
throstle** song thrush   **118 quill** (Literally, a reed pipe; hence, the
bird's piping song.)   **121 plainsong** singing a melody without variations   **123 dares . . . nay** i.e., cannot deny that he is a cuckold
125 give . . . lie call the bird a liar   **126 never so** ever so much
130 thy . . . force the power of your beauty   **136 gleek** scoff, jest
139 serve . . . turn answer my purpose   **142 rate** rank, value

The summer still° doth tend upon my state,°
And I do love thee. Therefore go with me.
145 I'll give thee fairies to attend on thee
And they shall fetch thee jewels from the deep,
And sing while thou on pressèd flowers dost sleep.
And I will purge thy mortal grossness° so
That thou shalt like an airy spirit go.
150 Peaseblossom, Cobweb, Mote,° and Mustardseed!

*Enter four Fairies [Peaseblossom, Cobweb, Mote, and
Mustardseed].*

PEASEBLOSSOM.
   Ready.
COBWEB.
   And I.
MOTE.   And I.
MUSTARDSEED.   And I.
ALL.   Where shall we go?
TITANIA.
   Be kind and courteous to this gentleman.
   Hop in his walks and gambol in his eyes;°
155 Feed him with apricots and dewberries,°
   With purple grapes, green figs, and mulberries;
   The honey bags steal from the humble-bees,
   And for night tapers crop their waxen thighs
   And light them at the fiery glowworms' eyes,
160 To have my love to bed and to arise;
   And pluck the wings from painted butterflies
   To fan the moonbeams from his sleeping eyes.
   Nod to him, elves, and do him courtesies.
PEASEBLOSSOM.
   Hail, mortal!
COBWEB.
165 Hail!
MOTE.
   Hail!
MUSTARDSEED.
   Hail!
BOTTOM. I cry your worships mercy, heartily. I beseech your
   worship's name.
COBWEB.
170 Cobweb.
BOTTOM. I shall desire you of more acquaintance, good Mas-
   ter Cobweb. If I cut my finger, I shall make bold with
   you.°—Your name, honest gentleman?
PEASEBLOSSOM.
   Peaseblossom.

BOTTOM. I pray you, commend me to Mistress Squash,° your   175
   mother, and to Master Peascod,° your father. Good Master Peaseblossom, I shall desire you of more acquaintance
   too.—Your name, I beseech you, sir?
MUSTARDSEED.
   Mustardseed.
BOTTOM. Good Master Mustardseed I know your patience°   180
   well. That same cowardly giantlike ox-beef hath devoured many a gentleman of your house. I promise you,
   your kindred hath made my eyes water° ere now. I desire
   you of more acquaintance, good Master Mustardseed.
TITANIA.
   Come, wait upon him; lead him to my bower.   185
      The moon methinks looks with a watery eye;
   And when she weeps,° weeps every little flower,
      Lamenting some enforcèd° chastity.
   Tie up my lover's tongue,° bring him silently.

                         [Exeunt.]

[3.2] *Enter [Oberon,] King of Fairies.*

OBERON.
   I wonder if Titania be awaked;
   Then what it was that next came in her eye,
   Which she must dote on in extremity.

[Enter] Robin Goodfellow [Puck].

   Here comes my messenger. How now, mad spirit?
   What night-rule° now about this haunted°   5
      grove?
PUCK.
   My mistress with a monster is in love.
   Near to her close° and consecrated bower,
   While she was in her dull° and sleeping hour,
   A crew of patches,° rude mechanicals,°
   That work for bread upon Athenian stalls,°   10
   Were met together to rehearse a play
   Intended for great Theseus' nuptial day.
   The shallowest thick-skin of that barren sort,°
   Who Pyramus presented° in their sport,
   Forsook his scene° and entered in a brake.   15
   When I did him at this advantage take,

---

143 **still** ever, always   **doth . . . state** waits upon me as a part of my royal retinue   148 **mortal grossness** materiality (i.e., the corporal nature of a mortal being)   150 **Mote** i.e., speck (The two words *moth* and *mote* were pronounced alike, and both meanings may be present.)   154 **in his eyes** in his sight (i.e., before him)   155 **dewberries** blackberries   172–173 **If . . . you** (Cobwebs were used to stanch bleeding.)

175 **Squash** unripe pea pod   176 **Peascod** ripe pea pod   180 **your patience** what you have endured   183 **water** (1) weep for sympathy (2) smart, sting   187 **she weeps** i.e., she causes dew   188 **enforcèd** forced, violated; or, possibly, constrained (since Titania at this moment is hardly concerned about chastity)   189 **Tie . . . tongue** (Presumably Bottom is braying like an ass.)   **3.2. Location: The wood**   5 **night-rule** diversion for the night.   **haunted** much frequented   7 **close** secret, private   8 **dull** drowsy   9 **patches** clowns, fools   **rude mechanicals** ignorant artisans   10 **stalls** market booths   13 **barren sort** stupid company or crew   14 **presented** acted   15 **scene** playing area

An ass's noll° I fixèd on his head.
Anon his Thisbe must be answered,
And forth my mimic° comes. When they him spy,
20 As wild geese that the creeping fowler° eye,
Or russet-pated choughs,° many in sort,°
Rising and cawing at the gun's report,
Sever° themselves and madly sweep the sky,
So, at his sight, away his fellows fly;
25 And, at our stamp, here o'er and o'er one falls;
He "Murder!" cries and help from Athens calls.
Their sense thus weak, lost with their fears thus strong,
Made senseless things begin to do them wrong,
For briers and thorns at their apparel snatch;
30 Some, sleeves—some, hats; from yielders all things
     catch.°
I led them on in this distracted fear
And left sweet Pyramus translated there,
When in that moment, so it came to pass,
Titania waked and straightway loved an ass.

OBERON.
35 This falls out better than I could devise.
But hast thou yet latched° the Athenian's eyes
With the love juice, as I did bid thee do?

PUCK.
I took him sleeping—that is finished too—
And the Athenian woman by his side,
40 That, when he waked, of force° she must be eyed.

Enter Demetrius and Hermia.

OBERON.
Stand close. This is the same Athenian.

PUCK.
This is the woman, but not this the man.

                                      [*They stand aside.*]

DEMETRIUS.
O, why rebuke you him that loves you so?
Lay breath so bitter on your bitter foe.

HERMIA.
45 Now I but chide; but I should use thee worse,
For thou, I fear, hast given me cause to curse.
If thou hast slain Lysander in his sleep,
Being o'er shoes° in blood, plunge in the deep,
And kill me too.
50 The sun was not so true unto the day
As he to me. Would he have stolen away
From sleeping Hermia? I'll believe as soon
This whole° earth may be bored, and that the moon

May through the center creep, and so displease
Her brother's° noontide with th' Antipodes.°   55
It cannot be but thou hast murdered him;
So should a murderer look, so dead,° so grim.

DEMETRIUS.
So should the murdered look, and so should I
Pierced through the heart with your stern cruelty.
Yet you, the murderer, look as bright, as clear,   60
As yonder Venus in her glimmering sphere.

HERMIA.
What's this to° my Lysander? Where is he?
Ah, good Demetrius, wilt thou give him me?

DEMETRIUS.
I had rather give his carcass to my hounds.

HERMIA.
Out, dog! Out, cur! Thou driv'st me past the bounds 65
Of maiden's patience. Hast thou slain him, then?
Henceforth be never numbered among men.
O, once tell true, tell true, even for my sake:
Durst thou have looked upon him being awake?
And hast thou killed him sleeping? O brave touch!°   70
Could not a worm,° an adder, do so much?
An adder did it; for with doubler tongue
Than thine, thou serpent, never adder stung.

DEMETRIUS.
You spend your passion° on a misprised mood.°
I am not guilty of Lysander's blood,   75
Nor is he dead, for aught that I can tell.

HERMIA.
I pray thee, tell me then that he is well.

DEMETRIUS.
An if I could, what should I get therefor?

HERMIA.
A privilege never to see me more.
And from thy hated presence part I so.   80
See me no more, whether he be dead or no.   *Exit.*

DEMETRIUS.
There is no following her in this fierce vein.
Here therefore for a while I will remain.
So sorrow's heaviness doth heavier° grow
For debt that bankrupt° sleep doth sorrow owe;   85
Which now in some slight measure it will pay,
If for his tender here I make some stay.°

                              Lie[s] down [and sleeps].

17 **noll** noddle, head 19 **mimic** burlesque actor 20 **fowler** hunter of game birds 21 **russet-pated choughs** reddish brown or gray-headed jackdaws **in sort** in a flock 23 **Sever** i.e., scatter 30–31 **from . . . catch** i.e., everything preys on those who yield to fear 36 **latched** fastened, snared 40 **of force** perforce 48 **o'er shoes** i.e., so far gone 53 **whole** solid

55 **Her brother's** i.e., the sun's **th' Antipodes** the people on the opposite side of the earth (where the moon is imagined bringing night to noontime) 57 **dead** deadly, or deathly pale 62 **to** to do with 70 **brave touch** noble exploit (Said ironically.) 71 **worm** serpent 74 **passion** violent feelings **misprised mood** anger based on misconception 84 **heavier** (1) harder to bear (2) more drowsy 85 **bankrupt** (Demetrius is saying that his sleepiness adds to the weariness caused by sorrow.) 86–87 **Which . . . stay** i.e., to a small extent I will be able to "pay back" and hence find some relief from sorrow, if I pause here awhile (*make some stay*) while sleep "tenders" or offers itself by way of paying the debt owed to sorrow

OBERON.
What hast thou done? Thou hast mistaken quite
And laid the love juice on some true love's sight.
90   Of thy misprision° must perforce ensue
Some true love turned, and not a false turned true.
PUCK.
Then fate o'errules, that, one man holding troth,°
A million fail, confounding oath on oath.°
OBERON.
About the wood go swifter than the wind,
95   And Helena of Athens look° thou find.
All fancy-sick° she is and pale of cheer°
With sighs of love, that cost the fresh blood° dear.
By some illusion see thou bring her here.
I'll charm his eyes against she do appear.°
PUCK.
100   I go. I go, look how I go,
Swifter than arrow from the Tartar's bow.°   [*Exit*].
OBERON [*Applying love juice to Demetrius' eyes*].
Flower of this purple dye,
Hit with Cupid's archery,
Sink in apple of his eye.
105   When his love he doth espy,

Let her shine as gloriously
As the Venus of the sky.
When thou wak'st, if she be by,
Beg of her for remedy.

Enter Puck.

PUCK.
110   Captain of our fairy band,
Helena is here at hand,
And the youth, mistook by me,
Pleading for a lover's fee.°
Shall we their fond pageant° see?
115   Lord, what fools these mortals be!
OBERON.
Stand aside. The noise they make
Will cause Demetrius to awake.
PUCK.
Then will two at once woo one;
That must needs be sport alone.°
120   And those things do best please me
That befall preposterously.°

[They stand aside.]

Enter Lysander and Helena.

LYSANDER.
Why should you think that I should woo in scorn?
Scorn and derision never come in tears.
Look when° I vow, I weep; and vows so born,
In their nativity all truth appears.°   125
How can these things in me seem scorn to you,
Bearing the badge° of faith to prove them true?
HELENA.
You do advance° your cunning more and more.
When truth kills truth,° O, devilish-holy fray!
These vows are Hermia's. Will you give her o'er?   130
Weigh oath with oath, and you will nothing weigh.
Your vows to her and me, put in two scales,
Will even weigh, and both as light as tales.°
LYSANDER.
I had no judgment when to her I swore.
HELENA.
Nor none, in my mind, now you give her o'er.   135
LYSANDER.
Demetrius loves her, and he loves not you.
DEMETRIUS [*Awaking*].
O Helen, goddess, nymph, perfect, divine!
To what, my love, shall I compare thine eyne?
Crystal is muddy. O, how ripe in show°
Thy lips, those kissing cherries, tempting grow!   140
That pure congealèd white, high Taurus'° snow,
Fanned with the eastern wind, turns to a crow°
When thou hold'st up thy hand. O, let me kiss
This princess of pure white, this seal° of bliss!
HELENA.
O spite! O hell! I see you all are bent   145
To set against° me for your merriment.
If you were civil and knew courtesy,
You would not do me thus much injury.
Can you not hate me, as I know you do,
But you must join in souls to mock me too?   150
If you were men, as men you are in show,
You would not use a gentle lady so—
To vow, and swear, and superpraise° my parts,°
When I am sure you hate me with your hearts.
You both are rivals, and love Hermia;   155
And now both rivals, to mock Helena.
A trim° exploit, a manly enterprise,

---

90 **misprision** mistake   92 **troth** faith   93 **confounding . . . oath** i.e., invalidating one oath with another   95 **look** i.e., be sure   96 **fancy-sick** lovesick   **cheer** face   97 **sighs . . . blood** (An allusion to the physiological theory that each sigh costs the heart a drop of blood.)   99 **against . . . appear** in anticipation of her coming   101 **Tartar's bow** (Tartars were famed for their skill with the bow.)   113 **fee** privilege, reward   114 **fond pageant** foolish exhibition   119 **alone** unequaled   121 **preposterously** out of the natural order

124 **Look when** whenever   124–125 **vows . . . appears** i.e., vows made by one who is weeping give evidence thereby of their sincerity   127 **badge** identifying device such as that worn on servants' livery (here, his tears)   128 **advance** carry forward, display   129 **truth kills truth** i.e., one of Lysander's vows must invalidate the other   133 **tales** lies   139 **show** appearance   141 **Taurus** a lofty mountain range in Asia Minor   142 **turns to a crow** i.e., seems black by contrast   144 **seal** pledge   146 **set against** attack   153 **superpraise** overpraise   **parts** qualities   157 **trim** pretty, fine (Said ironically.)

To conjure tears up in a poor maid's eyes
With your derision! None of noble sort°
160   Would so offend a virgin and extort°
A poor soul's patience, all to make you sport.

LYSANDER.
You are unkind, Demetrius. Be not so;
For you love Hermia; this you know I know.
And here, with all good will, with all my heart,
165   In Hermia's love I yield you up my part;
And yours of Helena to me bequeath,
Whom I do love and will do till my death.

HELENA.
Never did mockers waste more idle breath.

DEMETRIUS.
Lysander, keep thy Hermia; I will none.°
170   If e'er I loved her, all that love is gone.
My heart to her but as guest-wise sojourned,°
And now to Helen is it home returned,
There to remain.

LYSANDER.   Helen, it is not so.

DEMETRIUS.
Disparage not the faith thou dost not know,
175   Lest, to thy peril, thou aby° it dear.
Look where thy love comes; yonder is thy dear.

Enter Hermia.

HERMIA.
Dark night, that from the eye his° function takes,
The ear more quick of apprehension makes;
Wherein it doth impair the seeing sense
180   It pays the hearing double recompense.
Thou art not by mine eye, Lysander, found;
Mine ear, I thank it, brought me to thy sound.
But why unkindly didst thou leave me so?

LYSANDER.
Why should he stay whom love doth press to go?

HERMIA.
185   What love could press Lysander from my side?

LYSANDER.
Lysander's love, that would not let him bide—
Fair Helena, who more engilds° the night
Than all yon fiery oes° and eyes of light.
Why seek'st thou me? Could not this make thee know,
190   The hate I bear thee made me leave thee so?

HERMIA.
You speak not as you think. It cannot be.

HELENA.
Lo, she is one of this confederacy!
Now I perceive they have conjoined all three

To fashion this false sport in spite of me.°
Injurious Hermia, most ungrateful maid!   195
Have you conspired, have you with these contrived°
To bait° me with this foul derision?
Is all the counsel° that we two have shared,
The sisters' vows, the hours that we have spent,
When we have chid the hasty-footed time   200
For parting us—O, is all forgot?
All schooldays' friendship, childhood innocence?
We, Hermia, like two artificial° gods,
Have with our needles created both one flower,
Both on one sampler, sitting on one cushion,   205
Both warbling of one song, both in one key,
As if our hands, our sides, voices, and minds
Had been incorporate.° So we grew together
Like to a double cherry, seeming parted
But yet an union in partition,   210
Two lovely° berries molded on one stem;
So with two seeming bodies but one heart,
Two of the first, like coats in heraldry,
Due but to one and crownèd with one crest.°
And will you rend our ancient love asunder   215
To join with men in scorning your poor friend?
It is not friendly, 'tis not maidenly.
Our sex, as well as I, may chide you for it,
Though I alone do feel the injury.

HERMIA.
I am amazèd at your passionate words.   220
I scorn you not. It seems that you scorn me.

HELENA.
Have you not set Lysander, as in scorn,
To follow me and praise my eyes and face?
And made your other love, Demetrius,
Who even but now did spurn me with his foot,   225
To call me goddess, nymph, divine and rare,
Precious, celestial? Wherefore speaks he this
To her he hates? And wherefore doth Lysander
Deny your love, so rich within his soul,
And tender° me, forsooth, affection,   230
But by your setting on, by your consent?
What though I be not so in grace° as you,
So hung upon with love, so fortunate,
But miserable most, to love unloved?
This you should pity rather than despise.   235

HERMIA.
I understand not what you mean by this.

---

159 **sort** character, quality   160 **extort** twist, torture   169 **will none** i.e., want no part of her   171 **to . . . sojourned** only visited with her   175 **aby** pay for   177 **his** its   187 **engilds** brightens with a golden light   188 **oes** spangles (here, stars)

194 **in spite of me** to vex me   196 **contrived** plotted   197 **bait** torment, as one sets on dogs to bait a bear   198 **counsel** confidential talk   203 **artificial** skilled in art or creation   208 **incorporate** of one body   211 **lovely** loving   213–214 **Two . . . crest** i.e., we have two separate bodies, just as a coat of arms in heraldry can be represented twice on a shield but surmounted by a single crest   230 **tender** offer   232 **grace** favor

HELENA.
　Ay, do! Persever, counterfeit sad° looks,
　Make mouths° upon° me when I turn my back.
　Wink each at other, hold the sweet jest up.°
240　This sport, well carried,° shall be chronicled.
　If you have any pity, grace, or manners,
　You would not make me such an argument.°
　But fare ye well. 'Tis partly my own fault,
　Which death, or absence, soon shall remedy.
LYSANDER.
245　Stay, gentle Helena; hear my excuse,
　My love, my life, my soul, fair Helena!
HELENA.
　O excellent!
HERMIA [*To Lysander*].
　Sweet, do not scorn her so.
DEMETRIUS.
　If she cannot entreat,° I can compel.
LYSANDER.
250　Thou canst compel no more than she entreat.
　Thy threats have no more strength than her weak
　　prayers.
　Helen, I love thee, by my life I do!
　I swear by that which I will lose for thee,
　To prove him false that says I love thee not.
DEMETRIUS.
255　I say I love thee more than he can do.
LYSANDER.
　If thou say so, withdraw, and prove it too.
DEMETRIUS.
　Quick, come!
HERMIA.　　　　Lysander, whereto tends all this?
LYSANDER.
　Away, you Ethiop!°

　　　[*He tries to break away from Hermia.*]

DEMETRIUS.
　　　　No, no; he'll
　Seem to break loose; take on as° you would follow,
260　But yet come not. You are a tame man, go!
LYSANDER.
　Hang off,° thou cat, thou burr! Vile thing, let loose,
　Or I will shake thee from me like a serpent!
HERMIA.
　Why are you grown so rude? What change is this,
　Sweet love?

LYSANDER.　　Thy love? Out, tawny Tartar, out!
　Out, loathèd med'cine!° O hated potion, hence!　265
HERMIA.
　Do you not jest?
HELENA.
　　　　Yes, sooth,° and so do you.
LYSANDER.
　Demetrius, I will keep my word with thee.
DEMETRIUS.
　I would I had your bond, for I perceive
　A weak bond° holds you. I'll not trust your word.
LYSANDER.
　What, should I hurt her, strike her, kill her dead?　270
　Although I hate her, I'll not harm her so.
HERMIA.
　What, can you do me greater harm than hate?
　Hate me? Wherefore? O me, what news,° my love?
　Am not I Hermia? Are not you Lysander?
　I am as fair now as I was erewhile.°　　　　　275
　Since night you loved me; yet since night you left me.
　Why, then you left me—O, the gods forbid!—
　In earnest, shall I say?
LYSANDER.　　　　　Ay, by my life!
　And never did desire to see thee more.
　Therefore be out of hope, of question, of doubt;　280
　Be certain, nothing truer. 'Tis no jest
　That I do hate thee and love Helena.
HERMIA [*to Helena*].
　O me! You juggler! You cankerblossom!°
　You thief of love! What, have you come by night
　And stol'n my love's heart from him?
HELENA.　　　　　　　　Fine, i' faith!　285
　Have you no modesty, no maiden shame,
　No touch of bashfulness? What, will you tear
　Impatient answers from my gentle tongue?
　Fie, fie! You counterfeit, you puppet,° you!
HERMIA.
　"Puppet"? Why, so!° Ay, that way goes the game.　290
　Now I perceive that she hath made compare
　Between our statures: she hath urged her height,
　And with her personage, her tall personage,
　Her height, forsooth, she hath prevailed with him.
　And are you grown so high in his esteem　　　295
　Because I am so dwarfish and so low?
　How low am I, thou painted maypole? Speak!
　How low am I? I am not yet so low
　But that my nails can reach unto thine eyes.

---

237 **sad** grave, serious　238 **mouths** i.e., mows, faces, grimaces.
upon at　239 **hold . . . up** keep up the joke　240 **carried** managed　242 **argument** subject for a jest　249 **entreat** i.e., succeed by entreaty　258 **Ethiop** (Referring to Hermia's relatively dark hair and complexion; see also *tawny Tartar* six lines later.)　259 **take on as** act as if　261 **Hang off** let go

265 **med'cine** i.e., poison　266 **sooth** truly　269 **weak bond** i.e., Hermia's arm (with a pun on *bond*, oath, in the previous line)　273 **what news** what is the matter　275 **erewhile** just now　283 **cankerblossom** worm that destroys the flower bud (?)　289 **puppet** (1) counterfeit (2) dwarfish woman (in reference to Hermia's smaller stature)　290 **Why, so** i.e., Oh, so that's how it is

[She flails at Helena but is restrained.]

HELENA.

300   I pray you, though you mock me, gentlemen,
        Let her not hurt me. I was never curst;°
        I have no gift at all in shrewishness;
        I am a right° maid for my cowardice.
        Let her not strike me. You perhaps may think,
305   Because she is something° lower than myself,
        That I can match her.

HERMIA.   Lower? Hark, again!

HELENA.

        Good Hermia, do not be so bitter with me.
        I evermore did love you, Hermia,
        Did ever keep your counsels, never wronged you;
310   Save that, in love unto Demetrius,
        I told him of your stealth° unto this wood.
        He followed you; for love I followed him.
        But he hath chid me hence° and threatened me
        To strike me, spurn me, nay, to kill me too.
315   And now, so° you will let me quiet go,
        To Athens will I bear my folly back
        And follow you no further. Let me go.
        You see how simple and how fond° I am.

HERMIA.

        Why, get you gone. Who is 't that hinders you?

HELENA.

320   A foolish heart, that I leave here behind.

HERMIA.

        What, with Lysander?

HELENA.   With Demetrius.

LYSANDER.

        Be not afraid; she shall not harm thee, Helena.

DEMETRIUS.

        No, sir, she shall not, though you take her part.

HELENA.

        O, when she is angry, she is keen° and shrewd.°
325   She was a vixen when she went to school,
        And though she be but little, she is fierce.

HERMIA.

        "Little" again? Nothing but "low" and "little"?
        Why will you suffer her to flout me thus?
        Let me come to her.

LYSANDER.   Get you gone, you dwarf!
330   You minimus,° of hindering knotgrass° made!
        You bead, you acorn!

DEMETRIUS.   You are too officious

In her behalf that scorns your services.
Let her alone. Speak not of Helena;
Take not her part. For, if thou dost intend°
Never so little show of love to her,   335
Thou shalt aby° it.

LYSANDER.   Now she holds me not;
Now follow, if thou dar'st, to try whose right,
Of thine or mine, is most in Helena.   *[Exit.]*

DEMETRIUS.

Follow? Nay, I'll go with thee, cheek by jowl.°

                        [Exit, following Lysander.]

HERMIA.

You, mistress, all this coil° is 'long of° you.   340
Nay, go not back.°

HELENA.   I will not trust you, I,
Nor longer stay in your curst company.
Your hands than mine are quicker for a fray;
My legs are longer, though, to run away.   *[Exit.]*

HERMIA.

I am amazed and know not what to say.   *Exit.*   345

[Oberon and Puck come forward.]

OBERON.

This is thy negligence. Still thou mistak'st,
Or else committ'st thy knaveries willfully.

PUCK.

Believe me, king of shadows, I mistook.
Did not you tell me I should know the man
By the Athenian garments he had on?   350
And so far blameless proves my enterprise
That I have 'nointed an Athenian's eyes;
And so far am I glad it so did sort,°
As° this their jangling I esteem a sport.

OBERON.

Thou seest these lovers seek a place to fight.   355
Hie° therefore, Robin, overcast the night;
The starry welkin° cover thou anon
With drooping fog as black as Acheron,°
And lead these testy rivals so astray
As one come not within another's way.   360
Like to Lysander sometimes frame thy tongue,
Then stir Demetrius up with bitter wrong;°
And sometimes rail thou like Demetrius.
And from each other look thou lead them thus,
Till o'er their brows death-counterfeiting sleep   365
With leaden legs and batty° wings doth creep.

---

301 curst shrewish   **303 right** true   **305 something** somewhat
311 stealth stealing away   **313 chid me hence** driven me away
with his scolding   **315 so** if only   **318 fond** foolish   **324 keen**
fierce, cruel   **shrewd** shrewish   **330 minimus** diminutive creature.   **knotgrass** a weed, an infusion of which was thought to stunt
the growth

334 intend give sign of   **336 aby** pay for   **339 cheek by jowl** i.e.,
side by side   **340 coil** turmoil, dissension   **'long of** on account of
341 go not back i.e., don't retreat (Hermia is again proposing a
fight.)   **353 sort** turn out   **354 As** that (also at l. 360)   **356 Hie**
hasten   **357 welkin** sky   **358 Acheron** river of Hades (here representing Hades itself)   **362 wrong** insults   **366 batty** batlike

Then crush this herb° into Lysander's eye,   [*Giving herb*]
Whose liquor hath this virtuous° property,
To take from thence all error with his° might
370 And make his eyeballs roll with wonted° sight.
When they next wake, all this derision°
Shall seem a dream and fruitless vision,
And back to Athens shall the lovers wend
With league whose date° till death shall never end.
375 Whiles I in this affair do thee employ,
I'll to my queen and beg her Indian boy;
And then I will her charmèd eye release
From monster's view, and all things shall be peace.
PUCK.
My fairy lord, this must be done with haste,
380 For night's swift dragons° cut the clouds full fast,
And yonder shines Aurora's harbinger,°
At whose approach, ghosts, wand'ring here and there,
Troop home to churchyards. Damnèd spirits all,
That in crossways and floods have burial,°
385 Already to their wormy beds are gone.
For fear lest day should look their shames upon,
They willfully themselves exile from light
And must for aye° consort with black-browed night.
OBERON.
But we are spirits of another sort.
390 I with the Morning's love° have oft made sport,
And, like a forester,° the groves may tread
Even till the eastern gate, all fiery red,
Opening on Neptune with fair blessèd beams,
Turns into yellow gold his salt green streams.
395 But notwithstanding, haste, make no delay.
We may effect this business yet ere day.   [*Exit.*]
PUCK.
Up and down, up and down,
I will lead them up and down.
I am feared in field and town.
400 Goblin, lead them up and down.
Here comes one.

Enter Lysander.

LYSANDER.
Where art thou, proud Demetrius? Speak thou now.

PUCK [*Mimicking Demetrius*].
Here, villain, drawn° and ready. Where art thou?
LYSANDER.
I will be with thee straight.°
PUCK.   Follow me, then,
To plainer° ground.

          [*Lysander wanders about,° following the voice.*]

Enter Demetrius.

DEMETRIUS.   Lysander! Speak again!   405
Thou runaway, thou coward, art thou fled?
Speak! In some bush? Where dost thou hide thy head?
PUCK [*Mimicking Lysander*].
Thou coward, art thou bragging to the stars,
Telling the bushes that thou look'st for wars,
And wilt not come? Come, recreant;° come, thou child,   410
I'll whip thee with a rod. He is defiled
That draws a sword on thee.
DEMETRIUS.   Yea, art thou there?
PUCK.
Follow my voice. We'll try° no manhood here.

                                        Exeunt.

[*Lysander returns.*]

LYSANDER.
He goes before me and still dares me on.
When I come where he calls, then he is gone.   415
The villain is much lighter-heeled than I.
I followed fast, but faster he did fly,
That fallen am I in dark uneven way,
And here will rest me. [*He lies down.*] Come, thou gentle
     day!
For if but once thou show me thy gray light,   420
I'll find Demetrius and revenge this spite. [*He sleeps.*]

[*Enter*] Robin [*Puck*] *and Demetrius.*

PUCK.
Ho, ho, ho! Coward, why com'st thou not?
DEMETRIUS.
Abide° me, if thou dar'st; for well I wot°
Thou runn'st before me, shifting every place,
And dar'st not stand nor look me in the face.   425
Where art thou now?
PUCK.   Come hither. I am here.
DEMETRIUS.
Nay, then, thou mock'st me. Thou shalt buy° this dear,°
If ever I thy face by daylight see.

---

367 **this herb** i.e., the antidote (mentioned in 2.1.184) to love-in-idleness   368 **virtuous** efficacious   369 **his** its   370 **wonted** accustomed   371 **derision** laughable business   374 **date** term of existence   380 **dragons** (Supposed by Shakespeare to be yoked to the car of the goddess of night.)   381 **Aurora's harbinger** the morning star, precursor of dawn   384 **crossways . . . burial** (Those who had committed suicide were buried at crossways, with a stake driven through them; those drowned, i.e., buried in floods or great waters, would be condemned to wander disconsolate for want of burial rites.)   388 **for aye** forever   390 **Morning's love** Cephalus, a beautiful youth beloved by Aurora; or perhaps the goddess of the dawn herself   391 **forester** keeper of a royal forest

403 **drawn** with drawn sword   404 **straight** immediately   405 **plainer** more open   **s.d. Lysander wanders about** (It is not clearly necessary that Lysander exit at this point; neither exit nor reentrance is indicated in the early texts.)   410 **recreant** cowardly wretch   413 **try** test   423 **Abide** confront, face   **wot** know   427 **buy** aby, pay for   **dear** dearly

430 Now, go thy way. Faintness constraineth me
To measure out my length on this cold bed.
By day's approach look to be visited.

> [*He lies down and sleeps.*]

Enter Helena.

HELENA.
O weary night, O long and tedious night,
Abate° thy hours! Shine comforts from the east,
That I may back to Athens by daylight,
435   From these that my poor company detest;
And sleep, that sometimes shuts up sorrow's eye,
Steal me awhile from mine own company.

> [*She lies down and*] *sleep*[*s*].

PUCK.
Yet but three? Come one more;
Two of both kinds makes up four.
440   Here she comes, curst° and sad.
Cupid is a knavish lad,
Thus to make poor females mad.

[*Enter Hermia.*]

HERMIA.
Never so weary, never so in woe,
Bedabbled with the dew and torn with briers
445   I can no further crawl, no further go;
My legs can keep no pace with my desires.
Here will I rest me till the break of day.
Heavens shield Lysander, if they mean a fray!

PUCK.   [*She lies down and sleeps.*]
On the ground
450   Sleep sound.
I'll apply
To your eye,
Gentle lover, remedy.

> [*Squeezing the juice on Lysander's eyes.*]

When thou wak'st,
455   Thou tak'st
True delight
In the sight
Of thy former lady's eye;
And the country proverb known,
460   That every man should take his own,
In your waking shall be shown:
Jack shall have Jill;°
Naught shall go ill;

The man shall have his mare again, and all shall be well.

> [*Exit. The four sleeping lovers remain.*]

[**4.1**] *Enter* [*Titania*] *Queen of Fairies, and* [*Bottom the*] *clown, and Fairies; and* [*Oberon,*] *the King, behind them.*

TITANIA.
Come, sit thee down upon this flowery bed,
While I thy amiable° cheeks do coy,°
And stick muskroses in thy sleek smooth head,
And kiss thy fair large ears, my gentle joy.

> [*They recline.*]

BOTTOM. Where's Peaseblossom?   5
PEASEBLOSSOM.
Ready.
BOTTOM. Scratch my head, Peaseblossom. Where's Monsieur Cobweb?
COBWEB.
Ready.
BOTTOM. Monsieur Cobweb, good monsieur, get you your   10
weapons in your hand, and kill me a red-hipped humble-
bee on the top of a thistle; and, good monsieur, bring me
the honey bag. Do not fret yourself too much in the ac-
tion, monsieur, and, good monsieur, have a care the
honey bag break not; I would be loath to have you over-   15
flown with a honey bag, signor. [*Exit Cobweb.*] Where's
Monsieur Mustardseed?
MUSTARDSEED.
Ready.
BOTTOM. Give me your neaf,° Monsieur Mustardseed. Pray
you, leave your courtesy,° good monsieur.   20
MUSTARDSEED.
What's your will?
BOTTOM. Nothing, good monsieur, but to help Cavalery° Cob-
web° to scratch. I must to the barber's, monsieur, for me-
thinks I am marvelous hairy about the face; and I am such
a tender ass, if my hair do but tickle me, I must scratch.   25
TITANIA.
What, wilt thou hear some music, my sweet love?
BOTTOM. I have a reasonable good ear in music. Let's have
the tongs and the bones.°

> [*Music: tongs, rural music.*°]

**4.1 Location: The action is continuous. The four lovers are still
asleep onstage. 2 amiable** lovely.   **coy** caress   **19 neaf** fist   **20
leave your courtesy** i.e., stop bowing, or put on your hat   **22 Cav-
alery** cavalier. (Form of address for a gentleman.)   **23 Cobweb**
(Seemingly an error, since Cobweb has been sent to bring honey
while Peaseblossom has been asked to scratch.)   **28 tongs . . .
bones** instruments for rustic music. (The tongs were played like a
triangle, whereas the bones were held between the fingers and used
as clappers.)   **s.d. Music . . . music** (This stage direction is added
from the Folio.)

---

433 Abate lessen, shorten   **440 curst** ill-tempered   **462 Jack
shall have Jill** (Proverbial for "boy gets girl.")

TITANIA.
   Or say, sweet love, what thou desirest to eat.

30 BOTTOM. Truly, a peck of provender.° I could munch your
   good dry oats. Methinks I have a great desire to a bottle°
   of hay. Good hay, sweet hay, hath no fellow.°

TITANIA.
   I have a venturous fairy that shall seek
   The squirrel's hoard, and fetch thee new nuts.

35 BOTTOM. I had rather have a handful or two of dried peas.
   But, I pray you, let none of your people stir° me. I have
   an exposition° of sleep come upon me.

TITANIA.
   Sleep thou, and I will wind thee in my arms.
   Fairies, begone, and be all ways° away.

                                          [Exeunt Fairies.]

40 So doth the woodbine the sweet honeysuckle
    Gently entwist; the female ivy so
    Enrings the barky fingers of the elm.
    O, how I love thee! How I dote on thee!

                                              [They sleep.]

    Enter Robin Goodfellow [Puck].

OBERON [Coming forward].
   Welcome, good Robin. Seest thou this sweet sight?
45 Her dotage now I do begin to pity.
   For, meeting her of late behind the wood,
   Seeking sweet favors° for this hateful fool,
   I did upbraid her and fall out with her.
   For she his hairy temples then had rounded
50 With coronet of fresh and fragrant flowers;
   And that same dew, which sometime° on the buds
   Was wont to swell like round and orient pearls,°
   Stood now within the pretty flowerets' eyes
   Like tears that did their own disgrace bewail.
55 When I had at my pleasure taunted her,
   And she in mild terms begged my patience,
   I then did ask of her her changeling child,
   Which straight she gave me, and her fairy sent
   To bear him to my bower in Fairyland.
60 And, now I have the boy, I will undo
   This hateful imperfection of her eyes.
   And, gentle Puck, take this transformèd scalp
   From off the head of this Athenian swain,
   That he, awaking when the other° do,
65 May all to Athens back again repair,°

And think no more of this night's accidents
But as the fierce vexation of a dream.
But first I will release the Fairy Queen.

                              [He squeezes a herb on her eyes.]

   Be as thou wast wont to be;
   See as thou wast wont to see.   70
   Dian's bud° o'er Cupid's flower
   Hath such force and blessèd power.

Now, my Titania, wake you, my sweet queen.
TITANIA [Waking].
   My Oberon! What visions have I seen!
   Methought I was enamored of an ass.   75
OBERON.
   There lies your love.
TITANIA.   How came these things to pass?
   O, how mine eyes do loathe his visage now!
OBERON.
   Silence awhile. Robin, take off this head.
   Titania, music call, and strike more dead
   Than common sleep of all these five° the sense.   80
TITANIA.
   Music, ho! Music, such as charmeth° sleep!

                                                   [Music.]

PUCK [Removing the ass head].
   Now, when thou wak'st, with thine own fool's eyes peep.
OBERON.
   Sound, music! Come, my queen, take hands with me,
   And rock the ground whereon these sleepers be.
                                              [They dance.]
   Now thou and I are new in amity,   85
   And will tomorrow midnight solemnly°
   Dance in Duke Theseus' house triumphantly,
   And bless it to all fair prosperity.
   There shall the pairs of faithful lovers be
   Wedded, with Theseus, all in jollity.   90
PUCK.
   Fairy King, attend, and mark:
   I do hear the morning lark.
OBERON.
   Then, my queen, in silence sad,°
   Trip we after night's shade.
   We the globe can compass soon,   95
   Swifter than the wandering moon.
TITANIA.
   Come, my lord, and in our flight

---

30 **peck of provender** one-quarter bushel of grain   31 **bottle** bundle   32 **fellow** equal   36 **stir** disturb   37 **exposition** (Bottom's
word for *disposition*.)   39 **all ways** in all directions   47 **favors** i.e.,
gifts of flowers   51 **sometime** formerly   52 **orient pearls** i.e., the
most beautiful of all pearls, those coming from the Orient   64
other others   65 **repair** return

71 **Dian's bud** (Perhaps the flower of the *agnus castus* or chaste-
tree, supposed to preserve chastity; or perhaps referring simply to
Oberon's herb by which he can undo the effects of "Cupid's flower,"
the love-in-idleness of 2.1.166–168.)   80 **these five** i.e., the four
lovers and Bottom   81 **charmeth** brings about, as though by a
charm   86 **solemnly** ceremoniously   93 **sad** sober

Tell me how it came this night
That I sleeping here was found
100   With these mortals on the ground.   *Exeunt.*

                            Wind horn [within].

Enter Theseus and all his train; [Hippolyta, Egeus].

THESEUS.
    Go, one of you, find out the forester,
    For now our observation° is performed;
    And since we have the vaward° of the day,
    My love shall hear the music of my hounds.
105   Uncouple° in the western valley, let them go.
    Dispatch, I say, and find the forester.   *[Exit an Attendant.]*
    We will, fair queen, up to the mountain's top
    And mark the musical confusion
    Of hounds and echo in conjunction.
HIPPOLYTA.
110   I was with Hercules and Cadmus° once,
    When in a wood of Crete they bayed° the bear
    With hounds of Sparta.° Never did I hear
    Such gallant chiding;° for, besides the groves,
    The skies, the fountains, every region near
115   Seemed all one mutual cry. I never heard
    So musical a discord, such sweet thunder.
THESEUS.
    My hounds are bred out of the Spartan kind,°
    So flewed,° so sanded;° and their heads are hung
    With ears that sweep away the morning dew;
120   Crook-kneed, and dewlapped° like Thessalian bulls;
    Slow in pursuit, but matched in mouth like bells,
    Each under each.° A cry° more tunable°
    Was never holloed to, nor cheered° with horn,
    In Crete, in Sparta, nor in Thessaly.
125   Judge when you hear. [*He sees the sleepers.*] But, soft!
      What nymphs are these?
EGEUS.
    My lord, this is my daughter here asleep,
    And this Lysander; this Demetrius is,
    This Helena, old Nedar's Helena.
    I wonder of° their being here together.
THESEUS.
130   No doubt they rose up early to observe

The rite of May, and hearing our intent,
Came here in grace of our solemnity.°
But speak, Egeus. Is not this the day
That Hermia should give answer of her choice?
EGEUS.
    It is, my lord.   135
THESEUS.
    Go, bid the huntsmen wake them with their horns.

                            [Exit an Attendant.]

Shout within. Wind horns. They all start up.

Good morrow, friends. Saint Valentine° is past.
Begin these woodbirds but to couple now?
LYSANDER.
    Pardon, my lord.   *[They kneel.]*
THESEUS.   I pray you all, stand up.
    I know you two are rival enemies;   140
    How comes this gentle concord in the world,
    That hatred is so far from jealousy°
    To sleep by hate and fear no enmity?
LYSANDER.
    My lord, I shall reply amazedly,
    Half sleep, half waking; but as yet, I swear,   145
    I cannot truly say how I came here.
    But, as I think—for truly would I speak,
    And now I do bethink me, so it is—
    I came with Hermia hither. Our intent
    Was to be gone from Athens, where° we might,   150
    Without° the peril of the Athenian law—
EGEUS.
    Enough, enough, my lord; you have enough.
    I beg the law, the law, upon his head.
    They would have stol'n away; they would, Demetrius,
    Thereby to have defeated° you and me,   155
    You of your wife and me of my consent,
    Of my consent that she should be your wife.
DEMETRIUS.
    My lord, fair Helen told me of their stealth,
    Of this their purpose hither° to this wood,
    And I in fury hither followed them,   160
    Fair Helena in fancy following me.
    But, my good lord, I wot not by what power—
    But by some power it is—my love to Hermia,
    Melted as the snow, seems to me now
    As the remembrance of an idle gaud°   165
    Which in my childhood I did dote upon;

---

102 observation i.e., observance to a morn of May (1.1.167)
103 vaward vanguard, i.e., earliest part   **105 Uncouple** set free for
the hunt   **110 Cadmus** mythical founder of Thebes. (This story
about him is unknown.)   **111 bayed** brought to bay   **112 hounds
of Sparta** (A breed famous in antiquity for their hunting skill.)
113 chiding i.e., yelping   **117 kind** strain, breed   **118 So flewed**
similarly having large hanging chaps or fleshly covering of the jaw.
sanded of sandy color   **120 dewlapped** having pendulous folds of
skin under the neck   **121–122 matched . . . each** i.e., harmo-
niously matched in their various cries like a set of bells, from treble
down to bass   **122 cry** pack of hounds   **tunable** well tuned, melodious   **123 cheered** encouraged   **129 wonder of** wonder at

132 in . . . solemnity in honor of our wedding   **137 Saint Valentine** (Birds were supposed to choose their mates on Saint Valentine's Day.)   **142 jealousy** suspicion   **150 where** wherever; or, to
where   **151 Without** outside of, beyond   **155 defeated** defrauded
159 hither in coming hither   **165 idle gaud** worthless trinket

And all the faith, the virtue of my heart,
The object and the pleasure of mine eye,
Is only Helena. To her, my lord,
170 Was I betrothed ere I saw Hermia,
But like a sickness did I loathe this food;
But, as in health, come to my natural taste,
Now I do wish it, love it, long for it,
And will for evermore be true to it.

THESEUS.
175 Fair lovers, you are fortunately met.
Of this discourse we more will hear anon.
Egeus, I will overbear your will;
For in the temple, by and by, with us
These couples shall eternally be knit.
180 And, for° the morning now is something° worn,
Our purposed hunting shall be set aside.
Away with us to Athens. Three and three,
We'll hold a feast in great solemnity.
Come, Hippolyta.

        [Exeunt Theseus, Hippolyta, Egeus, and train.]

DEMETRIUS.
185 These things seem small and undistinguishable,
Like far-off mountains turnèd into clouds.

HERMIA.
Methinks I see these things with parted° eye,
When everything seems double.

HELENA.   So methinks;
And I have found Demetrius like a jewel,
Mine own, and not mine own.°

190 DEMETRIUS.   Are you sure
That we are awake? It seems to me
That yet we sleep, we dream. Do not you think
The Duke was here, and bid us follow him?

HERMIA.
Yea, and my father.

HELENA.   And Hippolyta.

LYSANDER.
195 And he did bid us follow to the temple.

DEMETRIUS.
Why, then, we are awake. Let's follow him,
And by the way let us recount our dreams.   *[Exeunt.]*

BOTTOM *[Awaking]*. When my cue comes, call me, and I will
answer. My next is, "Most fair Pyramus." Heigh—ho! Pe-
200 ter Quince! Flute, the bellows mender! Snout, the tinker! Starveling! God's° my life, stolen hence and left me
asleep! I have had a most rare vision. I have had a dream,
past the wit of man to say what dream it was. Man is but
an ass if he go about° to expound this dream. Methought

I was—there is no man can tell what. Methought I was— 205
and methought I had—but man is but a patched° fool if
he will offer° to say what methought I had. The eye of
man hath not heard, the ear of man hath not seen, man's
hand is not able to taste, his tongue to conceive, nor his
heart to report,° what my dream was. I will get Peter 210
Quince to write a ballad of this dream. It shall be called
"Bottom's Dream," because it hath no bottom; and I will
sing it in the latter end of a play, before the Duke. Peradventure, to make it the more gracious, I shall sing it at
her° death.   *[Exit.]* 215

[4.2] *Enter Quince, Flute, [Snout, and Starveling].*

QUINCE. Have you sent to Bottom's house? Is he come home
yet?

STARVELING. He cannot be heard of. Out of doubt he is
transported.°

FLUTE. If he come not, then the play is marred. It goes not 5
forward, doth it?

QUINCE. It is not possible. You have not a man in all Athens
able to discharge° Pyramus but he.

FLUTE. No, he hath simply the best wit° of any handicraft
man in Athens. 10

QUINCE. Yea, and the best person° too, and he is a very paramour for a sweet voice.

FLUTE. You must say "paragon." A paramour is, God bless us,
a thing of naught.°

Enter Snug the joiner.

SNUG. Masters, the Duke is coming from the temple and 15
there is two or three lords and ladies more married. If our
sport had gone forward, we had all been made men.°

FLUTE. O sweet bully Bottom! Thus hath he lost sixpence a
day during his life; he could not have scaped sixpence a
day. An the Duke had not given him sixpence a day° for 20
playing Pyramus, I'll be hanged. He would have deserved
it. Sixpence a day in Pyramus, or nothing.

Enter Bottom.

BOTTOM. Where are these lads? Where are these hearts?°

QUINCE. Bottom! O most courageous day! O most happy
hour! 25

BOTTOM. Masters, I am to discourse wonders.° But ask me
not what; for if I tell you, I am no true Athenian. I will
tell you everything, right as it fell out.

---

206 patched wearing motley, i.e., a dress of various colors.
207 offer venture   **207–210 The eye . . . report** (Bottom garbles
the terms of 1 Corinthians 2:9)   **215 her** Thisbe's (?)   **4.2 Location: Athens   4 transported** carried off by fairies; or, possibly,
transformed   **8 discharge** perform   **9 wit** intellect   **11 person**
appearance   **14 a . . . naught** a shameful thing   **17 we . . . men**
i.e., we would have had our fortunes made   **20 sixpence a day** i.e.,
as a royal pension   **23 hearts** good fellows   **26 am . . . wonders**
have wonders to relate

180 for since   **something** somewhat   **187 parted** improperly focused   **189–190 like . . . mine own** i.e., like a jewel that one finds
by chance and therefore possesses but cannot certainly consider
one's own property   **201 God's** may God save   **204 go about** attempt

QUINCE. Let us hear, sweet Bottom.

30 BOTTOM. Not a word of° me. All that I will tell you is—that the Duke hath dined. Get your apparel together, good strings° to your beards, new ribbons to your pumps;° meet presently° at the palace; every man look o'er his part; for the short and the long is, our play is preferred.° In any

35 case, let Thisbe have clean linen; and let not him that plays the lion pare his nails, for they shall hang out for the lion's claws. And, most dear actors, eat no onions nor garlic, for we are to utter sweet breath; and I do not doubt but to hear them say it is a sweet comedy. No more

40 words. Away! Go, away!

[*Exeunt.*]

[**5.1**] *Enter Theseus, Hippolyta, and Philostrate, [lords, and attendants].*

HIPPOLYTA.
'Tis strange, my Theseus, that° these lovers
   speak of.
THESEUS.
More strange than true. I never may° believe
These antique° fables nor these fairy toys.°
Lovers and madmen have such seething brains,
Such shaping fantasies,° that apprehend°
5 More than cool reason ever comprehends.°
The lunatic, the lover, and the poet
Are of imagination all compact.°
One sees more devils than vast hell can hold;
10 That is the madman. The lover, all as frantic,
Sees Helen's° beauty in a brow of Egypt.°
The poet's eye, in a fine frenzy rolling,
Doth glance from heaven to earth, from earth to heaven;
And as imagination bodies forth
15 The forms of things unknown, the poet's pen
Turns them to shapes and gives to airy nothing
A local habitation and a name.
Such tricks hath strong imagination
That, if it would but apprehend some joy,
20 It comprehends some bringer° of that joy;
Or in the night, imagining some fear,°
How easy is a bush supposed a bear!
HIPPOLYTA.
But all the story of the night told over,
And all their minds transfigured so together,

More witnesseth than fancy's images° 25
And grows to something of great constancy;°
But, howsoever,° strange and admirable.°

Enter lovers: Lysander, Demetrius, Hermia, and Helena.

THESEUS.
Here come the lovers, full of joy and mirth.
Joy, gentle friends! Joy and fresh days of love
Accompany your hearts!
LYSANDER.   More than to us   30
Wait in your royal walks, your board, your bed!
THESEUS.
Come now, what masques,° what dances shall we have
To wear away this long age of three hours
Between our after-supper and bedtime?
Where is our usual manager of mirth?   35
What revels are in hand? Is there no play
To ease the anguish of a torturing hour?
Call Philostrate.
PHILOSTRATE.   Here, mighty Theseus.
THESEUS.
Say what abridgment° have you for this evening?
What masque? What music? How shall we beguile   40
The lazy time, if not with some delight?
PHILOSTRATE [*Giving him a paper*].
There is a brief° how many sports are ripe.
Make choice of which Your Highness will see first.
THESEUS [*Reads*].
"The battle with the Centaurs,° to be sung
By an Athenian eunuch to the harp"?   45
We'll none of that. That have I told my love,
In glory of my kinsman° Hercules.
[*Reads.*] "The riot of the tipsy Bacchanals,
Tearing the Thracian singer in their rage"?°
That is an old device;° and it was played   50
When I from Thebes came last a conqueror.
[*Reads.*] "The thrice three Muses mourning for the death
Of Learning, late deceased in beggary"?°

---

30 **of** out of 32 **strings** (to attach the beards) **pumps** light shoes or slippers. 33 **presently** immediately 34 **preferred** selected for consideration **5.1 Location: Athens. The palace of Theseus.** 1 **that** that which 2 **may** can 3 **antique** old-fashioned (punning too on *antic*, strange, grotesque). **fairy toys** trifling stories about fairies 5 **fantasies** imaginations. **apprehend** conceive, imagine 6 **comprehends** understands 8 **compact** formed, composed 11 **Helen's** i.e., of Helen of Troy, pattern of beauty. **brow of Egypt** i.e., face of a gypsy 20 **bringer** i.e., source 21 **fear** object of fear

25 **More . . . images** testifies to something more substantial than mere imaginings 26 **constancy** certainty 27 **howsoever** in any case **admirable** a source of wonder 32 **masques** courtly entertainments 39 **abridgment** pastime (to abridge or shorten the evening) 42 **brief** short written statement, summary 44 **battle . . . Centaurs** (Probably refers to the battle of the Centaurs and the Lapithae, when the Centaurs attempted to carry off Hippodamia, bride of Theseus' friend Pirothous.) 47 **kinsman** (Plutarch's "Life of Theseus" states that Hercules and Theseus were near kinsmen. Theseus is referring to a version of the battle of the Centaurs in which Hercules was said to be present.) 48–49 **The riot . . . rage** (This was the story of the death of Orpheus, as told in *Metamorphoses* 9.) 50 **device** show, performance 52–53 **The thrice . . . beggary** (Possibly an allusion to Spenser's *Tears of the Muses*, 1591, though "satires" deploring the neglect of learning and the creative arts were commonplace.)

That is some satire, keen and critical,
55   Not sorting with° a nuptial ceremony.
     [*Reads*.] "A tedious brief scene of young Pyramus
     And his love Thisbe; very tragical mirth"?
     Merry and tragical? Tedious and brief?
     That is hot ice and wondrous strange° snow.
60   How shall we find the concord of this discord?

PHILOSTRATE.
     A play there is, my lord, some ten words long,
     Which is as brief as I have known a play;
     But by ten words, my lord, it is too long,
     Which makes it tedious. For in all the play
65   There is not one word apt, one player fitted.
     And tragical, my noble lord, it is,
     For Pyramus therein doth kill himself.
     Which, when I saw rehearsed, I must confess,
     Made mine eyes water; but more merry tears
70   The passion of loud laughter never shed.

THESEUS.
     What are they that do play it?

PHILOSTRATE.
     Hard-handed men that work in Athens here,
     Which never labored in their minds till now,
     And now have toiled° their unbreathed° memories
75   With this same play, against° your nuptial.

THESEUS.
     And we will hear it.

PHILOSTRATE.   No, my noble lord,
     It is not for you. I have heard it over,
     And it is nothing, nothing in the world;
     Unless you can find sport in their intents,
80   Extremely stretched° and conned° with cruel pain
     To do you service.

THESEUS.   I will hear that play;
     For never anything can be amiss
     When simpleness° and duty tender it.
     Go bring them in; and take your places, ladies.

                [*Philostrate goes to summon the players*.]

HIPPOLYTA.
85   I love not to see wretchedness o'ercharged,°
     And duty in his service° perishing.

THESEUS.
     Why, gentle sweet, you shall see no such thing.

HIPPOLYTA.
     He says they can do nothing in this kind.°

THESEUS.
     The kinder we, to give them thanks for nothing.
     Our sport shall be to take what they mistake;   90
     And what poor duty cannot do, noble respect°
     Takes it in might, not merit.°
     Where I have come, great clerks° have purposèd
     To greet me with premeditated welcomes;
     Where I have seen them shiver and look pale,   95
     Make periods in the midst of sentences,
     Throttle their practiced accent° in their fears,
     And in conclusion dumbly have broke off,
     Not paying me a welcome. Trust me, sweet,
     Out of this silence yet I picked a welcome;   100
     And in the modesty of fearful duty
     I read as much as from the rattling tongue
     Of saucy and audacious eloquence.
     Love, therefore, and tongue-tied simplicity
     In least° speak most, to my capacity.°   105

[*Philostrate returns*.]

PHILOSTRATE. So please Your Grace, the Prologue° is ad-
     dressed.°
THESEUS. Let him approach.   [*A flourish of trumpets*.]

Enter the Prologue [*Quince*].

PROLOGUE.
     If we offend, it is with our good will.
     That you should think, we come not to offend,   110
     But with good will. To show our simple skill,
     That is the true beginning of our end.
     Consider then, we come but in despite.
     We do not come, as minding° to content you,
     Our true intent is. All for your delight.   115
     We are not here. That you should here repent you,
     The actors are at hand, and, by their show,
     You shall know all that you are like to know.
THESEUS. This fellow doth not stand upon points.°
LYSANDER. He hath rid° his prologue like a rough° colt; he   120
     knows not the stop.° A good moral, my lord: it is not
     enough to speak, but to speak true.
HIPPOLYTA. Indeed he hath played on his prologue like a
     child on a recorder°; a sound, but not in government.°

91 respect evaluation, consideration   **92 Takes . . . merit** values
it for the effort made rather than for the excellence achieved   **93
clerks** learned men   **97 practiced accent** i.e., rehearsed speech; or,
usual way of speaking   **105 least** i.e., saying least.   **to my capacity**
in my judgment and understanding   **106 Prologue** speaker of the
prologue.   **107 addressed** ready   **114 minding** intending   **119
stand upon points** (1) heed niceties or small points (2) pay attention to punctuation in his reading (The humor of Quince's speech
is in the blunders of its punctuation.)   **120 rid** ridden.   **rough** unbroken   **121 stop** (1) the stopping of a colt by reining it in (2)
punctuation mark   **124 recorder** a wind instrument like a flute or
flageolet   **government** control

55 sorting with befitting   **59 strange** (Sometimes emended to an
adjective that would contrast with *snow*, just as *hot* contrasts with
ice.)   **74 toiled** taxed   **unbreathed** unexercised   **75 against** in
preparation for   **80 stretched** strained   **conned** memorized   **83
simpleness** simplicity   **85 wretchedness** **o'ercharged** incompe-
tence overburdened   **86 his service** its attempt to serve   **88 kind**
kind of thing

125 THESEUS. His speech was like a tangled chain: nothing° impaired, but all disordered. Who is next?

Enter Pyramus [Bottom] and Thisbe [Flute], and Wall [Snout], and Moonshine [Starveling], and Lion [Snug].

PROLOGUE.
Gentles, perchance you wonder at this show,
    But wonder on, till truth makes all things plain.
This man is Pyramus, if you would know;
130   This beauteous lady Thisbe is certain.
This man with lime and roughcast doth present
    Wall, that vile Wall which did these lovers sunder;
And through Wall's chink, poor souls, they are content
    To whisper. At the which let no man wonder.
135 This man, with lantern, dog, and bush of thorn,
    Presenteth Moonshine; for, if you will know,
By moonshine did these lovers think no scorn°
    To meet at Ninus' tomb, there, there to woo.
This grisly beast, which Lion hight° by name,
140 The trusty Thisbe coming first by night
Did scare away, or rather did affright;
And as she fled, her mantle she did fall,°
    Which Lion vile with bloody mouth did stain.
Anon comes Pyramus, sweet youth and tall,°
145   And finds his trusty Thisbe's mantle slain;
Whereat, with blade, with bloody blameful blade,
    He bravely broached° his boiling bloody breast.
And Thisbe, tarrying in mulberry shade,
    His dagger drew, and died. For all the rest,
150 Let Lion, Moonshine, Wall, and lovers twain
At large° discourse while here they do remain.

Exeunt Lion, Thisbe, and Moonshine.

THESEUS. I wonder if the lion be to speak.
DEMETRIUS. No wonder, my lord. One lion may, when many asses do.
WALL.
155 In this same interlude° it doth befall
That I, one Snout by name, present a wall;
And such a wall as I would have you think
That had in it a crannied hole or chink,
Through which the lovers, Pyramus and Thisbe,
160 Did whisper often, very secretly.
This loam, this roughcast, and this stone doth show
That I am that same wall; the truth is so.
And this the cranny is, right and sinister,°

Through which the fearful lovers are to whisper.
THESEUS. Would you desire lime and hair to speak better?   165
DEMETRIUS. It is the wittiest partition° that ever I heard discourse, my lord.

[Pyramus comes forward.]

THESEUS. Pyramus draws near the wall. Silence!
PYRAMUS.
O grim-looked° night! O night with hue so black!
    O night, which ever art when day is not!   170
O night, O night! Alack, alack, alack,
    I fear my Thisbe's promise is forgot.
And thou, O wall, O sweet, O lovely wall,
    That stand'st between her father's ground and mine,
Thou wall, O wall, O sweet and lovely wall,   175
    Show me thy chink to blink through with mine eyne!

[Wall makes a chink with his fingers.]

Thanks, courteous wall. Jove shield thee well for this.
    But what see I? No Thisbe do I see.
O wicked wall, through whom I see no bliss!
    Cursed by they stones for thus deceiving me!   180
THESEUS. The wall, methinks, being sensible,° should curse again.
PYRAMUS. No, in truth, sir, he should not. "Deceiving me" is Thisbe's cue: she is to enter now, and I am to spy her through the wall. You shall see, it will fall pat° as I told   185
you. Yonder she comes.

Enter Thisbe.

THISBE.
O wall, full often hast thou heard my moans,
    For parting my fair Pyramus and me.
My cherry lips have often kissed thy stones,
    Thy stones with lime and hair knit up in thee.   190
PYRAMUS.
I see a voice. Now will I to the chink,
    To spy an° I can hear my Thisbe's face.
Thisbe!
THISBE.
My love! Thou art my love, I think.
PYRAMUS.
Think what thou wilt, I am thy lover's grace,°   195
And like Limander° am I trusty still.
THISBE.
And I like Helen,° till the Fates me kill.

125 **nothing** not at all   137 **think no scorn** think it no disgraceful matter   139 **hight** is called   142 **fall** let fall   144 **tall** courageous   147 **broached** stabbed   151 **At large** in full, at length   155 **interlude** play   163 **right and sinister** i.e., the right side of it and the left; or, running from right to left, horizontally

166 **partition** (1) wall (2) section of a learned treatise or oration   169 **grim-looked** grim-looking   181 **sensible** capable of feeling   185 **pat** exactly   192 **an** if   195 **lover's grace** i.e., gracious lover   196, 197 **Limander, Helen** (Blunders for *Leander* and *Hero*.)

PYRAMUS.

    Not Shafalus to Procrus° was so true.

THISBE.

    As Shafalus to Procrus, I to you.

PYRAMUS.

200   O, kiss me through the hole of this vile wall!

THISBE.

    I kiss the wall's hole, not your lips at all.

PYRAMUS.

    Wilt thou at Ninny's tomb meet me straightway?

THISBE.

    'Tide° life, 'tide death, I come without delay.

[Exeunt Pyramus and Thisbe.]

WALL.

    Thus have I, Wall, my part dischargèd so;

205   And, being done, thus Wall away doth go.   *[Exit.]*

THESEUS. Now is the mural down between the two neighbors.

DEMETRIUS. No remedy, my lord, when walls are so willful° to hear without warning.°

210 HIPPOLYTA. This is the silliest stuff that ever I heard.

THESEUS. The best in this kind° are but shadows;° and the worst are no worse, if imagination amend them.

HIPPOLYTA. It must be your imagination then, and not theirs.

215 THESEUS. If we imagine no worse of them than they of themselves, they may pass for excellent men. Here come two noble beasts in, a man and a lion.

Enter Lion and Moonshine.

LION.

    You, ladies, you whose gentle hearts do fear

      The smallest monstrous mouse that creeps on floor,

220   May now perchance both quake and tremble here,

      When lion rough in wildest rage doth roar.

    Then know that I, as Snug the joiner, am

    A lion fell,° nor else no lion's dam;

    For, if I should as lion come in strife

225   Into this place, 'twere pity on my life.

THESEUS. A very gentle beast, and of a good conscience.

DEMETRIUS. The very best at a beast, my lord, that e'er I saw.

LYSANDER. This lion is a very fox for his valor.°

THESEUS. True; and a goose for his discretion.°

DEMETRIUS. Not so, my lord; for his valor cannot carry his 230 discretion; and the fox carries the goose.

THESEUS. His discretion, I am sure, cannot carry his valor; for the goose carries not the fox. It is well. Leave it to his discretion, and let us listen to the moon.

MOON.

    This lanthorn° doth the hornèd moon present— 235

DEMETRIUS. He should have worn the horns on his head.°

THESEUS. He is no crescent, and his horns are invisible within the circumference.

MOON.

    This lanthorn doth the hornèd moon present;

    Myself the man i' the moon do seem to be. 240

THESEUS. This is the greatest error of all the rest. The man should be put into the lanthorn. How is it else the man i' the moon?

DEMETRIUS. He dares not come there for the° candle, for you see, it is already in snuff.° 245

HIPPOLYTA. I am aweary of this moon. Would he would change!

THESEUS. It appears, by his small light of discretion, that he is in the wane; but yet, in courtesy, in all reason, we must stay the time. 250

LYSANDER. Proceed, Moon.

MOON. All that I have to say is to tell you that the lanthorn is the moon, the man i' the moon, this thornbush my thornbush, and this dog my dog.

DEMETRIUS. Why, all these should be in the lanthorn, for all 255 these are in the moon. But silence! Here comes Thisbe.

Enter Thisbe.

THISBE.

    This is old Ninny's tomb. Where is my love?

LION *[Roaring]*.

    O!

DEMETRIUS. Well roared, Lion.

[Thisbe runs off, dropping her mantle.]

THESEUS. Well run, Thisbe. 260

HIPPOLYTA. Well shone, Moon. Truly, the moon shines with a good grace.

[The Lion worries Thisbe's mantle.]

THESEUS. Well moused,° Lion.

---

198 Shafalus, Procrus (Blunders for *Cephalus* and *Procris,* also famous lovers.) **203 'Tide** betide, come **208 willful** willing **209 without warning** i.e., without warning the parents (Demetrius makes a joke on the proverb "Walls have ears.") **211 in this kind** of this sort **shadows** likenesses, representations **223 lion fell** fierce lion (with a play on the idea of "lion skin") **228 is . . . valor** i.e., his valor consists of craftiness and discretion **229 goose . . . discretion** i.e., as discreet as a goose, that is, more foolish than discreet

235 lanthorn (This original spelling, *lanthorn,* may suggest a play on the *horn* of which lanterns were made, and also on a cuckold's horns; but the spelling *lanthorn* is not used consistently for comic effect in this play or elsewhere. At 5.1.135, for example, the word is *lantern* in the original.) **236 on his head** (as a sign of cuckoldry) **244 for the** because of the **245 in snuff** (1) offended (2) in need of snuffing or trimming **263 moused** shaken, torn, bitten

Enter Pyramus.   [*Exit Lion.*]

DEMETRIUS. And then came Pyramus.

265 LYSANDER. And so the lion vanished.

PYRAMUS.

    Sweet Moon, I thank thee for thy sunny beams;
       I thank thee, Moon, for shining now so bright;
    For, by thy gracious, golden, glittering gleams,
       I trust to take of truest Thisbe sight.

270   But stay, O spite!
        But mark, poor knight,
    What dreadful dole° is here?
        Eyes, do you see?
        How can it be?

275   O dainty duck! O dear!
        Thy mantle good,
        What, stained with blood!
    Approach, ye Furies° fell!°
        O Fates,° come, come,

280   Cut thread and thrum;°
    Quail,° crush, conclude, and quell!°

THESEUS. This passion, and the death of a dear friend, would
    go near to make a man look sad.°

HIPPOLYTA. Beshrew my heart, but I pity the man.

PYRAMUS.

285   O, wherefore, Nature, didst thou lions frame?
    Since lion vile hath here deflowered my dear,
    Which is—no, no, which was—the fairest dame
    That lived, that loved, that liked, that looked with
       cheer.°

        Come, tears, confound,
290   Out, sword, and wound
    The pap° of Pyramus;
        Ay, that left pap,
        Where heart doth hop.   [*He stabs himself.*]
    Thus die I, thus, thus, thus.
295   Now am I dead,
        Now am I fled;
    My soul is in the sky.
        Tongue, lose thy light;
        Moon, take thy flight.   [*Exit Moonshine.*]
300   Now die, die, die, die, die.   [*Pyramus dies.*]

DEMETRIUS. No die, but an ace,° for him; for he is but one.°

LYSANDER. Less than an ace, man; for he is dead, he is noth-
    ing.

THESEUS. With the help of a surgeon he might yet recover,
    and yet prove an ass.°   305

HIPPOLYTA. How chance Moonshine is gone before Thisbe
    comes back and finds her lover?

THESEUS. She will find him by starlight.

[*Enter Thisbe.*]

    Here she comes, and her passion ends the play.

HYPPOLYTA. Methinks she should not use a long one for such   310
    a Pyramus. I hope she will be brief.

DEMETRIUS. A mote° will turn the balance, which Pyramus,
    which° Thisbe, is the better: he for a man, God warrant
    us; she for a woman, God bless us.

LYSANDER. She hath spied him already with those sweet eyes.   315

DEMETRIUS. And thus she means,° videlicet:°

THISBE.

        Asleep, my love?
        What, dead, my dove?
    O Pyramus, arise!
        Speak, speak. Quite dumb?   320
        Dead, dead? A tomb
    Must cover thy sweet eyes.
        These lily lips,
        This cherry nose,
    These yellow cowslip cheeks,   325
        Are gone, are gone!
        Lovers, make moan.
    His eyes were green as leeks.
        O Sisters Three,°
        Come, come to me,   330
    With hands as pale as milk;
        Lay them in gore,
        Since you have shore°
    With shears his thread of silk.
        Tongue, not a word.   335
        Come, trusty sword,
    Come, blade, my breast imbrue!°   [*Stabs herself.*]
        And farewell, friends.
        Thus Thisbe ends.
    Adieu, adieu, adieu.   [*She dies.*]   340

THESEUS. Moonshine and Lion are left to bury the dead.

---

272 **dole** grievous event   278 **Furies** avenging goddesses of Greek myth   **fell** fierce   279 **Fates** the three goddesses (Clotho, Lachesis, Atropos) of Greek myth who drew and cut the thread of human life   280 **thread and thrum** the warp in weaving and the loose end of the warp   281 **Quail** overpower   **quell** kill, destroy   282–283 **This . . . sad** i.e., if one had other reason to grieve, one might be sad, but not from this absurd portrayal of passion   289 **cheer** countenance   291 **pap** breast

301 **ace** the side of the die featuring the single pip, or spot (The pun is on *die* as a singular of *dice*; Bottom's performance is not worth a whole *die* but rather one single face of it, one small portion.)   **one** (1) an individual person (2) unique   305 **ass** (with a pun on *ace*)   312 **mote** small particle   **which . . . which** whether . . . or   316 **means** moans, laments   **videlicet** to wit   329 **Sisters Three** the Fates   333 **shore** shorn   337 **imbrue** stain with blood

DEMETRIUS. Ay, and Wall too.

BOTTOM [*Starting up, as Flute does also*]. No, I assure you, the
wall is down that parted their fathers. Will it please you

345 to see the epilogue, or to hear a Bergomask dance° between two of our company?

[*The other players enter.*]

THESEUS. No epilogue, I pray you; for your play needs no excuse. Never excuse; for when the players are all dead,
there need none to be blamed. Marry, if he that writ it

350 had played Pyramus and hanged himself in Thisbe's
garter, it would have been a fine tragedy; and so it is,
truly, and very notably discharged. But, come, your
Bergomask. Let your epilogue alone.   [*A dance.*]
The iron tongue° of midnight hath told° twelve.

355 Lovers, to bed, 'tis almost fairy time.
I fear we shall outsleep the coming morn
As much as we this night have overwatched.°
This palpable-gross° play hath well beguiled
The heavy° gait of night. Sweet friends, to bed.

360 A fortnight hold we this solemnity,
In nightly revels and new jollity.   *Exeunt.*

Enter Puck [carrying a broom].

PUCK.
　　Now the hungry lion roars,
　　　And the wolf behowls the moon;
　　Whilst the heavy° plowman snores,
365 　　All with weary task fordone.°
　　Now the wasted brands° do glow,
　　　Whilst the screech owl, screeching loud
　　Puts the wretch that lies in woe
　　　In remembrance of a shroud.
370 　　Now it is the time of night
　　　That the graves, all gaping wide,
　　Every one lets forth his sprite,°
　　　In the church-way paths to glide.
　　And we fairies, that do run
375 　　By the triple Hecate's° team
　　From the presence of the sun,
　　　Following darkness like a dream,
　　Now are frolic.° Not a mouse
　　　Shall disturb this hallowed house.

I am sent with broom before,   380
To sweep the dust behind° the door.

*Enter [Oberon and Titania,] King and Queen of Fairies,
with all their train.*

OBERON.
　　Through the house give glimmering light,
　　　By the dead and drowsy fire;
　　Every elf and fairy sprite
　　　Hop as light as bird from brier;   385
　　And this ditty, after me,
　　Sing, and dance it trippingly.

TITANIA.
　　First, rehearse your song by rote,
　　To each word a warbling note.
　　Hand in hand, with fairy grace,   390
　　Will we sing, and bless this place.

[*Song and dance.*]

OBERON.
　　Now, until the break of day,
　　Through this house each fairy stray.
　　To the best bride-bed will we,
　　Which by us shall blessèd be;   395
　　And the issue there create°
　　Ever shall be fortunate.
　　So shall all the couples three
　　Ever true in loving be;
　　And the blots of Nature's hand   400
　　Shall not in their issue stand;
　　Never mole, harelip, nor scar,
　　Nor mark prodigious,° such as are
　　Despisèd in nativity,
　　Shall upon their children be.   405
　　With this field dew consecrate°
　　Every fairy take his gait,°
　　And each several° chamber bless,
　　Through this palace, with sweet peace;
　　And the owner of it blest   410
　　Ever shall in safety rest.
　　Trip away; make no stay;
　　Meet me all by break of day.

Exeunt [Oberon, Titania, and train].

PUCK [*To the audience*].
　　If we shadows have offended,
　　Think but this, and all is mended,   415

---

345 **Bergomask dance** a rustic dance named from Bergamo, a
province in the state of Venice   354 **iron tongue** i.e., of a bell.
told counted, struck ("tolled")   357 **overwatched** stayed up too
late   358 **palpable-gross** gross, obviously crude   359 **heavy**
drowsy, dull   364 **heavy** tired   365 **fordone** exhausted   366
wasted brands burned-out logs   372 **Every . . . sprite** every grave
lets forth its ghost   375 **triple Hecate's** (Hecate ruled in three capacities: as Luna or Cynthia in heaven, as Diana on earth, and as
Proserpina in hell.)   378 **frolic** merry

381 **behind** from behind. (Robin Goodfellow was a household
spirit who helped good housemaids and punished lazy ones.)   396
create created   403 **prodigious** monstrous, unnatural   406 **consecrate** consecrated   407 **take his gait** go his way   408 **several**
separate

That you have but slumbered here°
While these visions did appear.
And this weak and idle theme,
No more yielding but° a dream,
420   Gentles, do not reprehend.
If you pardon, we will mend.°
And, as I am an honest Puck,

If we have unearnèd luck
Now to scape the serpent's tongue,°
We will make amends ere long;   425
Else the Puck a liar call.
So, good night unto you all.
Give me your hands,° if we be friends,
And Robin shall restore amends.°   [*Exit.*]

416 **That . . . here** i.e., that it is a "midsummer night's dream"
419 **No . . . but** yielding no more than   421 **mend** improve

424 **serpent's tongue** i.e., hissing   428 **Give . . . hands** applaud
429 **restore amends** give satisfaction in return

TOPICS FOR CRITICAL THINKING AND WRITING

The Play on the PAGE

1. What impression do you get of Theseus in the first scene?
2. Characterize Bottom in the second scene.
3. The love story is really complete by the end of the fourth act. What does the fifth act contribute to the play?

4. What ironies (see the Glossary) do you find in the play?
5. What do you find funny about *A Midsummer Night's Dream?*

The Play on the STAGE

6. Take one scene and compose detailed stage directions for it, indicating exactly how you would stage the scene.
7. What challenges do the roles of Lysander, Demetrius, Hermia, and Helena offer the actors? Take either the pair of men or the pair of women and set forth the suggestions you would give to the performers if you were directing a production.
8. If a small company were producing the play, which roles might be double- (or triple-) cast?
9. If you were directing and had decided on modern dress, what costumes and stage actions might be

suitable for Theseus and Hippolyta in the first scene? For the Rude Mechanicals when they stage *Pyramus and Thisby?*
10. Propose three very different stage or film actors or actresses who might play Puck, and explain the strengths each would bring to the role.
11. When the St. Louis Shakespeare Company staged the play, they cast a young child to play the changeling over whom Oberon and Titania quarrel. He appeared on stage in all the relevant scenes. What do you think of this decision? Why?

The Play in PERFORMANCE

In the last few decades, the productions of *A Midsummer Night's Dream* that have aroused the most interest are the ones that have emphasized the dark aspects of the comedy. This concern with "the fierce vexation of a dream" (Oberon's words, in 4.1.68) makes a marked contrast with the sweet, opulent productions that from the middle of the nineteenth century until the second decade of the twentieth century prettified the play with butterfly-winged child fairies, gauzy sets, and Mendelssohn's music. When Theseus smoothly says to Hippolyta, "I wooed thee with my sword," directors and spectators—heirs to Brecht, and to Artaud's Theater of Cruelty—can easily perceive the violence of rape. And so a play that a century ago was thought to be an airy trifle, full of high jinks and lovely sentiments about love, is now seen largely as an image of brutality. Thus, in John Hancock's production (San Francisco, 1965, New York, 1967), Hippolyta in leopard skins was brought onstage as a captive, Hermia was a transvestite, Demetrius wore an electrified codpiece; the emphasis was on the malevolence of the fairies, and the cruelty and lust of the humans. Mendelssohn's music was used—but ironically, since it blared from a jukebox.

It is not puzzling that our time should emphasize the eroticism and the violence of the play, just as it is not puzzling that the second half of the nineteenth century emphasized the lyricism; what is puzzling is that *A Midsummer Night's Dream*—Shakespeare's play as opposed to operatic versions of it—was in effect banished from the theater from the second half of the seventeenth century until 1840, when Madame Vestris staged a fairly full text at Covent Garden in London. Her version served as the basis for all productions of the play until Harley Granville Barker staged an uncut version in 1914. Rejecting the realistic scenery that had characterized productions of the late nineteenth and early twentieth centuries, Barker used what he called "decorative" settings. (See page 263 for an illustration, and for a brief additional account of his production.)

For the next fifty years most productions seemed either to echo Granville Barker or to react against him. One production, however, neither echoed nor answered him: This was Louis Armstrong's and Benny Goodman's *Swingin' the Dream*, done in 1939 with a predominantly black cast that included Armstrong as Bottom, Butterfly McQueen as Puck, Maxine Sullivan as Titania, and the Dandridge Sisters as three fairies. The book was by Gilbert Seldes and Erik Charell, the locale was New Orleans in the late nineteenth century, and the scenery was indebted to Walt Disney. Despite all of this talent, it was unsuccessful, running for only thirteen performances.

Of all the productions of Shakespeare's play since Barker's the most widely discussed was Peter Brook's Stratford version, given in 1970. Brook has said that he was influenced by Jan Kott's *Shakespeare Our Contemporary*, which emphasizes the night world of sex and violence. In the spirit of Kott, Brook said that Oberon furnishes Titania with "the crudest sex machine he can find"—though one might pedantically point out that Oberon doesn't choose Bottom, or anyone, for it is only by chance that Bottom enters Titania's line of sight. Curiously, given the stimulus of Kott, the production was in many ways attractive and elegant, with a brightly lit box set consisting of three white walls surrounded by a catwalk. Brook has said that he was influenced by the circus, and the circus element was evident from the start, when the entire company entered to a roll of drums, removed their white capes and revealed their costumes. (For an illustration and a further comment on this production, see page 263.)

Most productions of *A Midsummer Night's Dream* are somewhat more traditional than Brook's, but the emphasis on anti-illusionism and on aggressive sexuality continue, and since 1964, when Kott's book was published in English, most productions have been influenced by Kott's vision of the play as a work concerned with violence and power. For instance, Liviu Ciulei at the Guthrie Theater in Minneapolis in 1985, and in Purchase, New York, in 1986, used a blood-red vinyl set in order, he said, to represent passion in a play about a society in which males dominate. His Hippolyta, a black woman, in an opening dumb show at first appeared in dark battle fatigues. Female attendants removed her clothes, tossed them onto a glowing brazier, and then wrapped her in white clothes taken from mannequins. (Thus Ciulei gave the play racial overtones too.) Theseus then entered and offered casual approval of the transformation of a passionate black into a tamed pseudo-white. Violence of a less subtle sort was provided by the switchblades of the lovers, which are more threatening to a twentieth-century audience than swords would have been.

ALAN MacVEY
Directing A Midsummer Night's Dream

Alan MacVey teaches at the University of Iowa. In the following interview he discusses a production he directed in 1980 at the Bread Loaf School of English. The cast included Equity actors, faculty, and students from the school.

It's my impression that A Midsummer Night's Dream *is a special favorite in our time. Do you agree?*

Yes. One of the reasons this play has been so popular on the contemporary stage is that it gives directors great opportunities to play. It can work as a romantic comedy, as an investigation of unconscious desires, as an explosion of sexual energy (violent or not), as an exploration of gender roles, or as a dark rumination on power. I've done the play three times in three different ways. In each case the production was very much about the power of sex to change individuals and determine relationships, but the style and feel of each production was quite different.

What was the conception behind the productions?

In each of the productions I began with the same image: a rock in the forest. The top of the rock is rubbed clean. It's nearly white. Lift the rock up, however, and you find insects, mold, and all kinds of things you wouldn't have imagined.

Which of the three productions pleased you most?

I was happy with all three productions, but I'll discuss the middle one, done at Bread Loaf in 1980. I set the play in the modern world. Costumes were white with bits of color here and there; they included a few Elizabethan touches (in design) and a hint of Greek (in color), but were basically modern. Much of the first part of the play was done in front of a white wall. Later, when the characters entered the forest, the wall spun away and revealed a deep, dark setting inhabited by strange beings. Arriving back in the palace at the end of the play we repeated the wall, now divided into smaller sections that gave both space and organization.

In addition to visual effects, you must have been concerned with aural effects, for instance with music.

Yes. Music is important in *Midsummer*. It can arise from almost any period and can be romantic, mysterious, strange, even violent. Perhaps it's best if it touches all these bases. Our production used a mixture of classical music (for the court scenes) and electronic/computer music for the forest scenes. The forest music was based on recordings of spoken poetry. It was extraordinarily beautiful but also very strange, and drew us into a subconscious world where words and the meaning of words were turned into pure sound—yet where something remained of the words themselves. The fairies added to the strangeness with their own "natural sounds," twisted and turned by the human voice. The final scene of the play, in which Oberon and Titania blessed the house, was graced by simple, beautiful music whose rhythm matched that of the verse.

Did some central idea dominate your presentation?

The central conflict in the play—between Titania and Oberon—requires the director to decide what's really going on here. Does Oberon have any right to the changeling child, or is he just muscling in on Titania? If we say that he has no right to the child except that he's king and he wants it, then the play spins out as the victory of male over female, king over queen, sexual dominance over another kind of love. This journey will strongly influence all the other scenes in the forest and the end of the play; in our day, it can't help but have dark overtones. On the other hand, if Oberon has some right to the child—if, for example, he's the father—then the play can become a journey in which the male feels what it's like to be abandoned (Oberon can feel jealousy, envy, even sorrow as he watches Titania with Bottom), and the female can feel what it's like to be irrationally and powerfully attracted to someone she shouldn't like. In this reading, each learns something about the other's experience of life.

Did you use a particular kind of acting style?

We played most of the lovers' exchanges (as well as those of Titania and Oberon) very physically. We kept the comedy, permitted violent colors to arise as they do in the text, and allowed the play to move very quickly from physical comedy to threatening situation. We didn't cross the boundary to violence, though we suggested it was possible at any moment.

In almost every production I've seen the mechanicals are very funny. Audiences don't have to pretend to find them funny. Did your mechanicals succeed in this way?

They did, and they did so by playing their parts very straight. They never "hammed it up." The characters weren't very bright and were very inexperienced on the stage, but the actors never pushed for laughs. They were very real and while we laughed at them we didn't make fun of them because they, too, changed over the course of the evening. They arrived in the first act on a truck with a keg of beer; five acts later, transformed into a little troupe of fledgling artists, they left the stage proud of their work and aware, for the first time, of how little they knew. Their artistry, in the end, came from their simplicity. Though Thisby's death is funny, for example, we found it also to be very moving. Here was a person—Thisby—ready to die for love. And when she died she did it simply, gently, next to Bottom. The stage audience was touched, though they didn't know what to do with those feelings.

But earlier, during the play-within-a-play, what did you do with the stage audience?

That's a very good question. It opens up a series of complex possibilities. Neither Hermia nor Helena says a word, and that's a clue. The men work very hard to be clever. Their jokes aren't too successful and I believe that's what Shakespeare intended. Hippolyta seems to make a transition from sarcasm to appreciation, and I believe she leads the others to experience the play in a surprising way. The "audience" should not be central to our experience of the scene—the mechanicals are the most important element—but their interruptions should not be cut because they suggest how difficult it is for art (yes, even Pyramus and Thisby is art) to get through to people. In our production the "art" did finally have its effect and the "audience" was moved by the simple presentation of a love story not very different from their own.

How did you play the final scene?

We did the final scene—as many productions do—as a blessing. A senior colleague at Bread Loaf had drowned that summer and the community was very shaken. So in the last scene Oberon and Titania blessed the audience and the community. They did it with great simplicity. Reeds were dipped into a bowl of field dew and waved gently above the audience, with beautiful music beneath. I believe Shakespeare intended us to travel a great distance in this play and experience all the anticipation, fear, excitement, and danger of a first sexual encounter (perhaps on a wedding night). At the end of the journey we bless the moment, in hope, simplicity, and love. We acknowledge all the dark places of the spirit, and, in the finest moment of any comedy ever written, unite with the generative forces of the universe in an act that is both physical and spiritual.

WILLIAM Shakespeare

William Shakespeare (1564–1616) was born in Stratford, England, of middle-class parents. Nothing of interest is known about his early years, but by 1590 he was acting and writing plays in London. He early worked in all three Elizabethan dramatic genres—tragedy, comedy, and history. *Romeo and Juliet,* for example, was written about 1595, the year of *Richard II,* and the following year he wrote *A Midsummer Night's Dream. Hamlet* (1600–01) was probably written fairly soon after two of the great comedies, *As You Like It* and *Twelfth Night.* Among the plays that followed *Hamlet* are *Othello* (1603–04), *King Lear* (1605–06), *Macbeth* (1605–06), and several "romances," for example, *The Tempest* (1611)—plays that have happy endings but seem more meditative and closer to tragedy than the comedies already mentioned.

■■■■■■■■■■■■■■■■

COMMENTARY ON *HAMLET, PRINCE OF DENMARK*

"Something is rotten in the state of Denmark" (1.4.90) is one of more than two hundred lines from *Hamlet* given in *Bartlett's Familiar Questions.* What, we may ask, is rotten in the state of Denmark?

Readers or viewers of the play soon learn from the Ghost, in 1.5.10–92, exactly what is rotten. Claudius poisoned the king, Hamlet's father, but the Danes (including Hamlet's mother, who is now married to the murderer) mistakenly believe that the king died from the bite of a serpent. Hamlet will share the truth with Horatio, and late in the play with Gertrude, but for the most part he must keep the Ghost's revelation to himself. The result is that, in the eyes of some of the other characters in the play, Hamlet is the rotten apple. Yes, it is appropriate for him to grieve for his father, but why (they may well ask) does he continue whining, does he behave rudely, does he fail to recognize that (as Claudius patiently explains to Hamlet in 1.2) the "death of fathers" is perfectly natural? The terrible knowledge that he carries—the knowledge that his father has been murdered and his mother is married to the murderer—almost unhinges him (here we are touching on the famous question, "Is Hamlet mad, or only pretending to be?"), and infects his dealings with his fellows. He speaks rudely and bitterly to Ophelia and to her father Polonius, and he taunts his former schoolmates Rosencrantz and Guildenstern. He is indirectly responsible for the death of Ophelia, and directly responsible for the deaths of Polonius, Rosencrantz, and Guildenstern. We should remember that Polonius, however fatuous, does not know that

Claudius is a murderer. Polonius, as a courtier, merely does what courtiers are supposed to do: He flatters, he eavesdrops, and he gives advice to his monarch. Similarly, Rosencrantz and Guildenstern, however vacuous, are (again, from the point of view of the characters within the play, i.e., characters who do not know that Claudius is a murderer) guilty of nothing more than keeping watch over a friend who, from everyone's point of view, has been acting very strangely, and reported his doings to the monarch.

Curiously, Bernard Shaw—a dramatist who knows about the way drama works—does not talk about Hamlet from the point of a member of the audience (*we* know that Claudius is a murderer). Rather, Shaw judges Hamlet almost from the point of view of a character within the play, a character who is unaware of what in fact the audience knows about Claudius. In the preface to his one-act play about Shakespeare, *The Dark Lady of the Sonnets,* Shaw says, "Hamlet, who does not dream of apologizing for the three murders he commits, is always apologizing because he has not yet committed a fourth. . . ."

Hamlet begins with a question "Who's there?" and questions continue into the last scene, "What is it you would see?" (this last question might be rephrased, "What have we seen?") The Ghost comes in a "questionable shape" (Hamlet's words, in 1.4.43), but even here we get into uncertainties and ambiguities, since "questionable" means "able to respond to questions" and also "dubious." No wonder that almost everyone who sits down to write something about Hamlet is, like Hamlet, assailed by doubts, and uneasily recalls Hamlet's sharp words to Rosencrantz and Guildenstern. "You would pluck out the heart of my mystery, you would sound me from my lowest note to the top of my compass" ("compass" here means "range," specifically the range of his voice). Still, we can try to say a few helpful things about the play, or we can at least try to touch on some topics that will set the reader thinking.

WHY DOES HAMLET DELAY?

Let's begin by looking at a few sentences from the earliest extended comment on *Hamlet,* an anonymous essay, "Some Remarks on the Tragedy of *Hamlet Prince of Denmark*" (1736), perhaps written by one George Stubbes. (Earlier comments on the play are not much more than phrases, or at most a sentence or two, usually praising an actor in the role.) Stubbes (if indeed he wrote the essay) raises an issue that has plagued criticism ever since: Why does Hamlet delay? (Some critics reply that Hamlet does not delay. We will consider their view in a moment.) Here is the crucial passage, in which Stubbes raises the issue of delay and explains it by the no-nonsense view that Hamlet *has to* delay because if he doesn't, the play will be over almost as soon as it begins.

> To speak truth, our poet, by keeping too close to the ground-work of his plot, has fallen into an absurdity; for there appears no reason at all in nature, why the young prince does not put the usurper to death as soon as possible, especially as Hamlet is represented as a youth so brave, and so careless of his own life.
>
> The case indeed is this: Had Hamlet gone naturally to work, as we could suppose such a prince to do in parallel circumstances, there would have been an end of our play. The poet therefore was obliged to delay his hero's revenge, but then he should have contrived some good reason for it.

Stubbes offers this comment in connection with Hamlet's soliloquy at the end of 2.2. Hamlet, having heard the Player deliver the speech about Pyrrhus slaughtering Priam, in a soliloquy rebukes himself for not having killed Claudius:

> o'er ere this
> I should ha' fatted all the region kites
> With this slave's offal. . . .
> This is most brave,
> That I, the son of a dear father murdered,
> Prompted to my revenge by heaven and hell,
> Must like a whore unpack my heart with words. . . .

Elsewhere, too, Hamlet rebukes himself, notably in a soliloquy 4.4, after seeing Fortinbras and his army cross the stage, en route to fight with Poland over a worth-

less bit of land. Stubbes suggests that part of the reason Shakespeare created this scene was to provide Hamlet with some "reflections" which "tend to give some reason for his deferring the punishment of the usurper." In fact, in this speech Hamlet does not give any explicit reasons for not having acted; on the contrary, he says that everything around him (e.g., Fortinbras's willingness to engage in a battle with the Poles) seems to denounce his own *in*action:

> I do not know
> Why yet I live to say "This thing's to do."
> Sith I have cause, and will, and strength, and means
> To do.

Certainly he does have "cause," but does he have the "will" and does he have the "means"? Let's put aside what may be the chief issue, Hamlet's "will," and talk for a moment about "means." One can argue that when we are in the theater, watching the play, it probably never occurs to us that Hamlet has the means to kill Claudius, except in 3.3, when the King is on his knees, praying, and Hamlet says, "Now might I do it pat." And indeed at this moment he might, the King is absorbed in thought, presumably unarmed (if he usually wears a sword, he has removed it), unaware of Hamlet, who is probably behind him. But surely almost no one wants Hamlet to kill the King in this circumstance. Later in the play, in 4.7.127, Laertes tells Claudius that his hatred for Hamlet is so great—Hamlet has killed Laertes's father, Polonius—that he would "cut his throat i' the church," and the murderer Claudius unctuously approves: "No place, indeed, should murder sanctuarize." But Laertes's passionate avowal of action scarcely provides the viewer or the reader with an ideal of behavior against which we judge Hamlet. If anything, Laertes's line reveals his own limitations, limitations emphasized a moment later when with Claudius he plots to use a poisoned foil in the fencing match with Hamlet. Laertes, apparently the man of action, clearly is by no means a figure we can regard as superior to Hamlet.

THE GHOSTS

We will return to the issue of delay, but first let's consider two important aspects in the play, the Ghost and the issue of revenge. The basic narrative of *Hamlet* is ultimately derived from a history of Denmark, written in Latin around 1220, by a monk known as Saxo Grammaticus. This work was first printed in 1514, and then adapted into French by Belleforest, in his *His-*

toires Tragiques (1576). But what has this to do with the Ghost in *Hamlet?* Nothing—and that is the point. In the Latin and French versions of the story, there is no Ghost. The murder of the king was done openly, so the plot does not require a ghost to inform the prince that his uncle is the murderer. In these early versions, Hamlet (his name is Amleth in Saxo) pretends to be a harmless idiot so his uncle will mistakenly think no harm can come from this gibbering fool. But in a lost English play, known to have been staged in the late 1580s, and presumably drawn from Belleforest, we know there was a ghost that called upon Hamlet for revenge. This lost play, conventionally called by scholars the *Ur-Hamlet* (i.e., the *Original Hamlet*), is known because of several surviving contemporary references to it. The earliest reference is by Thomas Nashe, a university graduate, who in 1589 complained that some uneducated men who have taken up the craft of playwriting in effect plagiarize by borrowing from translations of the Roman tragic writer Seneca:

> English Seneca . . . yields many good sentences, as "Blood is a beggar" and so forth, and if you entreat him fair in a frosty morning, he will afford you whole *Hamlets,* I should say handfuls of tragical speeches . . .

In 1596, and here we get closer to our main point, the writer Thomas Lodge speaks of the "ghost who cried so miserably at the Theatre, like an oyster-wife, 'Hamlet, revenge.'" In short, when Shakespeare wrote his own *Hamlet,* around 1600–01, the ghost was an important part of the story, at least insofar as the story had been shown on the English stage.

What are we to make of Shakespeare's Ghost? What is its nature? First, does it exist? Gertrude does not see it in 3.4 when Hamlet sees it, but we can eliminate the view that the Ghost is a figment of Hamlet's imagination, since Bernardo, Marcellus, and Horatio see it. We can also eliminate the idea that the Ghost comes, like Seneca's ghosts, from a pagan underworld, since it explicitly refers to Christian rituals and the play includes numerous other references to a Christian world. The Ghost, then, is either what it says it is, or it is a demon who has taken the form of Hamlet's father in order to do mischief on earth—for instance to destroy Hamlet by enticing him to wickedness. In Hamlet's words, the Ghost is either a "spirit of health" or a "goblin damned." This second view has occasionally been argued. The gist is this: The Ghost says it is in purgatory ("doomed for a certain term to walk the night, / and for the day confirmed to fast in fires, / Till

the foul crimes [i.e., sins] done in my days of nature / Are burnt and purged away" (1.5.10–13), but a ghost released from Purgatory, presumably for some heavenly purpose, would not seek revenge. The Ghost (in this view) therefore must be a demon. Its suspicious actions—for instance its disappearance when Horatio invokes heaven in 1.1.49—are used to support this view.

What can be said against the view that the Ghost is a demon disguised as Hamlet's father, seeking to tempt Hamlet? Only this (and we think it is decisive): Nothing in the play confirms this view. When the Ghost first appears to Horatio, and then to Hamlet, they do not raise the possibility that it is a demon, so the audience—after all, we are talking about a play—would not consider this possibility. Later, they do consider the possibility (Horatio as early as 1.4.69–74), but nothing later confirms it. Even when the "Ghost cries under the stage" (1.5.148, stage direction), no one suggests it is a demon. Further, the Ghost instructs Hamlet, "Taint not thy mind, nor let thy soul contrive / Against thy mother aught" (5.85–86). Admittedly, this wholesome advice might be part of the clever demon's strategy to make his deception plausible, but could an audience possibly understand that this figure is not what it says it is?

Can the case be definitively proved to everyone's satisfaction? Apparently not, but doesn't it make sense to see *Hamlet* as a play about a man who learns, from his father's spirit, that a terrible crime has been committed, and who feels obliged to set it right? In the course of facing this great task Hamlet surprisingly has doubts including doubts about the Ghost and about his own worthiness, but the play itself provides no substantial evidence to indicate that when Hamlet overcomes his doubts about the Ghost he is making a disastrous error. Still, one may conceivably be uneasy with the Ghost's demand for revenge, and this brings us to the next issue.

REVENGE

"Revenge his foul and most unnatural murder" (1.5.25): Revenge, beyond all doubt, is widely condemned in Elizabethan writing, but if we look at some of Shakespeare's uses of the word *revenge* we will find that our responses (and surely the responses of the original audiences) must vary, depending on the context. In *Macbeth*, Malcomb, counseling the grief-stricken Macduff (Macbeth has murdered Macduff's wife and children) says, "Let's make us med'cines of our great revenge / To cure the deadly grief" (4.3.214–15), and we clearly regard the goal—killing Macbeth—as proper. Elsewhere in *Macbeth*, when Banquo is slain, he calls out to his son, Fleance, "O treachery! Fly, good Fleance, fly, fly, fly! Thou mayst revenge." Elizabethan authorities were fond of telling their subjects that vengeance belonged to the Lord or to his representative on earth, the monarch (they cited Paul, Epistle to the Romans, 12.19: "Vengeance is mine; I will repay, saith the Lord"), but in fact the Elizabethan tolerated revenge in various circumstances. For instance, the "Homily against Disobedience and Wilful Rebellion" prohibited rebellion against lawful princes but not against usurpers, and the Bond of Association, signed by thousands in 1584, specified that subjects are obliged "to take the uttermost revenge" on anyone who harms the rightful monarch. Hamlet comes to know that Claudius has murdered the legitimate monarch, so we might conclude that Hamlet as dutiful son and as loyal subject has an obligation to kill the man who killed his father.

In fact, putting aside Claudius's hypocritical pious comment about the justice of Laertes killing Hamlet even in a church, the question of the morality of revenge comes up only once in the play, and then almost casually. Just after the passage in which he says he has sent Rosencrantz and Guildenstern to their deaths but their deaths "are not near [his] conscience," Hamlet lists Claudius's offenses, as he sees them: Claudius has murdered Hamlet's father, married Hamlet's mother, taken over the throne that in Hamlet's view should have gone to Hamlet himself, and made an attempt on Hamlet's life. It is perfectly in keeping with the dictates of conscience, Hamlet says, to "quit" (requite, pay back) Claudius, that is, to kill Claudius, by Hamlet's own hand.

> Does it not, think thee, stand me now upon—
> He that hath killed my king and whored my mother,
> Popped in between th'election and my hopes,
> Thrown out his angle for my proper life,
> And with such cozenage—is't not perfect conscience
> To quit him with this arm? And is't not to be
>   damned
> To let this canker of our nature come
> In further evil.
>
> (5.2.63–70)

There is a slight problem here; the last three lines appear only in the Folio (1623), not the Second Quarto

(1604). (On the complicated business of the three versions of *Hamlet*, see page 380.) Perhaps the compositor accidentally omitted them in the 1604 text, or perhaps Shakespeare added them to the text that was ultimately printed in 1623, but in any case it is clear that Hamlet does not doubt the appropriateness of taking revenge, nor does anyone else.

While we are talking about revenge, it is worth mentioning that in most tragedies, for instance *King Lear* and *Macbeth*, the tragic hero sets into motion the chain of events that destroys him. Most tragedies begin with the hero in a situation of power, we might say in a prosperous condition. The play then shows the hero making what Aristotle calls a tragic error, and we watch the hero fall into misery. But in revenge tragedy the hero does not initiate the action, does *not* begin in a situation of power. On the contrary, in revenge tragedy the hero is caught up in a situation not at all of his making. In *Hamlet*, the prince's father has been murdered, and his mother has married the murderer. The avenger, especially in plays that owe some debt to the Roman tragedy, begins at a disadvantage and therefore is forced to engage in intrigue. Caught up in a situation not of his own making, and confronted with a powerful and unscrupulous foe, the avenger—we are of course talking partly about Hamlet—is forced to perform deeds that may be as monstrous as those that goad him into action.

We do not know much about the *Ur-Hamlet*, the lost *Hamlet* that preceded Shakespeare's play, but we do know that other avengers in Elizabethan drama, forced by circumstances to exceed in guile the villains who have injured them, become deeply tainted. If we absolve them, it is on the grounds that, like the tragic heroes in Seneca's plays, the injuries they suffered drove them to insanity. Quite possibly when Hamlet warns his friends that he may in the future behave fantastically, or, in his own words, he may "put an antic disposition on" (1.5.181), he foresees that he may be unable to behave rationally, given the terrible revelations of the Ghost. In any case, in the absence of the *Ur-Hamlet* we cannot speak with confidence, but it probably was Shakespeare's distinctive idea to present a new sort of avenger, a man who has been horribly wronged and who succeeds in avenging the wrong without himself becoming deeply corrupted.

If we wish to see an avenger who, unlike Hamlet, does become deeply corrupted, we need look no further than Laertes, who treacherously applies poison to a foil used in what is supposed to be a mere fencing match. Laertes huffily talks about his honor

(5.2.233–42), but even while speaking thus, he holds the poisoned foil. A few moments later, dying from the poison he had prepared for Hamlet, he confesses "the foul practice [i.e., deception]" (311). He regains a bit of lost honor by revealing that the King has planned the affair, and by forgiving Hamlet for the death of Polonius.

> It is a poison tempered by himself.
> Exchange forgiveness with me, noble Hamlet
> Mine and my father's death come not upon thee. . . .
>   (321–23)

DELAY REVISITED

Having touched on what are almost the last lines of the play, we can now go back to a question we raised earlier. Why does Hamlet delay? As we mentioned, George Stubbes in 1736 suggested that Shakespeare ought to have motivated the delay, or the apparent delay. Some have argued that although Hamlet does rebuke himself for delay, in fact he does not delay, and a spectator sees only one missed opportunity, in the scene when Claudius is praying.

Some critics, denying that Hamlet delays, have argued that he has no opportunity to kill the King because the King is always closely guarded, but in 4.5 Laertes breaks in upon the King, and, further, nothing in the dialogue suggests that guards insulate Claudius from Hamlet. Other critics, granting that Hamlet does delay, assume the delay is due to some fault in his character. Laurence Olivier's film begins with a notorious interpretation, "This is the tragedy of a man who could not make up his mind." The implication is that Hamlet had the bad luck to be a certain sort of person, someone who procrastinates because he can't come to a decision. Others have held that Hamlet ordinarily is a well-balanced man, indeed a man of action, but the death of his father and the prompt marriage of this mother to the murderer have shattered his world, and have induced in him a deep melancholy that for the most part inhibits action—though he acts effectively when he kills Polonius, and when he boards the pirate ship. The Ghost orders him to avenge the murder, but (it has been asked) how will killing Claudius bring back the dead father, and how will the death of Claudius erase from Hamlet's mind the image of his mother's desertion of her first husband? It is sometimes said that this delay in killing Claudius is due to an entirely reasonable (though unspoken) awareness that action against Claudius cannot bring back his father or restore honor to his mother.

Perhaps the most famous explanation for Hamlet's delay (if he does delay) is the explanation offered by Ernest Jones, who developed an idea that Freud in 1900 offered in a footnote in *The Interpretation of Dreams:* Hamlet cannot take vengeance on the man who killed his father and slept with his mother because these actions are fulfillments of Hamlet's own repressed Oedipal wishes. Jones amplified this point in an article in the *American Journal of Psychology,* January 1910, and at greater length in a small book, *Hamlet and Oedipus* (1949). Essentially Jones argues that Hamlet delays because if he killed Claudius he would be killing the man who fulfilled his own desires; to kill Claudius would be to kill part of himself.

A SATISFYING ENDING

Whether or not Hamlet delays, the question we must ask is this: How is Hamlet to fulfill the Ghost's demands *in a way that will be satisfying to us?* Suppose we briefly compare him to two other young men who have lost their fathers, Laertes and Fortinbras. Laertes is certainly a man of action: He bursts in upon the King, and he vows he would cut Hamlet's throat in the church, but we soon see that this passionate young man who is so concerned with honor is in fact dishonorable and easily manipulated by Claudius. Surely we do not want a Hamlet who has the passion and the easily adjusted sense of honor that Laertes has. What of Fortinbras? In 4.4 a Captain in Fortinbras's army tells Hamlet that a battle will be fought over a worthless piece of land. Stirred by this report of an action soon to be begun, Hamlet in a soliloquy rebukes himself for not having acted, and he praises Fortinbras as a man of action: Fortinbras, a man "whose spirit, with divine ambition puffed," will act "even for an eggshell," and will "find quarrel in a straw / When honor's at the stake." Meditation on Fortinbras's imminent battle stirs Hamlet to thoughts of honor, and he resolves, "O, from this time forth, / My thoughts be bloody, or be nothing worth." But surely the words Hamlet uses *undercut* this sort of honor, which is "puffed," and which is connected with an "eggshell" and "straw." Fortinbras's battle doubtless will produce much blood, but why? And do we want Hamlet's thoughts to be "bloody"? Probably not. After all, one of the commands that the Ghost gave Hamlet in 1.5 was "Taint not thy mind." What *do* we want?

We want Hamlet to avenge his father in a way that we find satisfying. And Shakespeare satisfies our desire primarily in three ways—by changing Hamlet's mood, by establishing a ritual setting for the act of revenge (really an act of justice), and by having Hamlet act spontaneously—without plotting—in circumstances that his enemy has established (Claudius, so to speak, kills himself).

We will begin with Hamlet's mood. There is not space here to go through the play speech by speech, but most readers agree that when Hamlet returns from the sea journey he seems poised, almost serene at times. There will still be outbursts, notably in the struggle with Laertes in the grave (5.1), but a change seems to have come over him after he had some sort of premonition, stole Claudius's letter that Rosencrantz and Guildenstern were taking to the King of England, forged a new letter, and boarded the pirate ship. Now in Denmark again, he tells Horatio that on the ship he acted "rashly,"

> And praised be rashness for it—let us know
> Our indiscretion sometimes serves us well
> When our deep plots do pall, and that should learn
>   us
> There's a divinity that shapes our ends,
> Rough-hew them how we will.
>
> (5.2.7–11)

When he is asked how he managed to forge the letter, which would require the royal seal, he replies, "Even in that was heaven ordinant." Later in the scene, shortly before the duel with Laertes, he says, "There is special providence in the fall of a sparrow," a line that surely evokes (in the minds of those who know the New Testament) Matthew 10.29, in which Jesus says, "Not a sparrow shall fall on the ground without your father's knowledge." A moment later he says, "The readiness is all." For some readers and members of the audience, Hamlet has reached a new low; he has (in this view) fallen into a weary fatalism, and has rejected all sense of responsibility. For others (including the writer of this page) Hamlet has achieved a new state of mind, a state that marks a welcome development in his character. His task is not to contrive but to be ready, to act when the moment presents itself.

Claudius himself presents Hamlet with the right moment. It is, after all, Claudius who contrives the deadly fencing match and who prepares the poisoned cup. True, Laertes adds the envenomed foil, but the plan as a whole is Claudius's. When Claudius and Laertes die from the poison, they die by Hamlet's hand, but we are in the mysteriously yet justly governed world of the Hebrew Bible, "Whoso shall diggeth a pit, shall fall therein, and he that rolleth a stone, it will return" (Proverbs 26.27).

The ceremoniousness of the fencing match, ironically provided not by a contriving Hamlet but by the criminal himself, adds a ritual dignity to the execution of justice. A long stage direction tells us that a table is prepared, "trumpets" and "drums" sound, and wine is brought in. Then we get further ceremonial actions, notably Hamlet's apology to Laertes, the sound of trumpets when the King drinks, and the fencing match itself. When Laertes is wounded by his own poisoned foil, he accepts his guilt ("I am justly killed with mine own treachery"), and he confesses the plot, publicly exposing Claudius's role:

> The foul practice
> Hath turned itself on me. Lo, here I lie,
> Never to rise again. Thy mother's poisoned.
> I can no more. The King, the King's to blame.

Hamlet, now publicly vindicated, and using the weapons at hand—provided by the villain and the villain's cat's-paw—stabs the King with the poisoned foil and forces him to drink from the poisoned cup. Laertes voices what must be the audience's thoughts concerning Claudius, "He is justly served," and then Laertes and Hamlet exchange forgiveness. It is hard to imagine how Hamlet could more fittingly—more satisfyingly in a reader's or a viewer's eyes—have avenged the death of his father, and, for that matter, the death that we have just seen Claudius inflict upon Hamlet.

Earlier in the play Hamlet has committed acts that are almost unspeakable—but the Ghost delivered to him the otherwise unspeakable news about the murder of his father. Hamlet is not untainted; his ill treatment of Ophelia and the murder of Polonius are understandable, but his behavior distresses us. In some of his lines we can hear something of the unattractive avenger-become-villain, as when he seems to gloat about the fate to which he delivered Rosencrantz and Guildenstern:

> They must sweep my way
> And marshal me to knavery. Let it work.
> For 'tis the sport to have the enginer
> Hoist with his own petard, and 't shall go hard
> But I will delve one yard below their mines
> And blow them at the moon. O, 'tis most sweet
> When in one line two crafts directly meet.
>
> (3.4.211–17)

Now, the end of the play, we are grateful that Hamlet hoists Claudius with Claudius's "own petard," but we are grateful too that no "knavery" and no "craft" on Hamlet's part were brought into play. Claudius is dead, at Hamlet's hand, but by Claudius's own contriving. Fortinbras, the successful warrior, soon enters. Is it going too far to say that Hamlet has been a warrior too, and has won his battle, though at the cost of his own life? Fortinbras, expressing recognition of Hamlet as a fellow-soldier, speaks the last lines and he orders the firing of cannon in salute ("the soldiers' music"). This is the third time we have heard cannon. The first was when the usurper, Claudius, drank (1.4.6 stage direction); the second was when, earlier in the final act, Hamlet scored a hit in the fencing match and Claudius, claiming to drink to Hamlet's success, in reality drinks to Hamlet's death; and now, for a third time, the cannon are fired, this time in tribute to a man who has succeeded in performing an almost unbelievably difficult and horrible duty.

HAMLET, PRINCE OF DENMARK
William Shakespeare

[DRAMATIS PERSONAE

GHOST *of Hamlet, the former King of Denmark*
CLAUDIUS, *King of Denmark, the former King's brother*
GERTRUDE, *Queen of Denmark, widow of the former King and now wife of Claudius*
HAMLET, *Prince of Denmark, son of the late King and of Gertrude*
POLONIUS, *councillor to the King*
LAERTES, *his son*
OPHELIA, *his daughter*
REYNALDO, *his servant*
HORATIO, *Hamlet's friend and fellow student*

VOLTIMAND,
CORNELIUS,
ROSENCRANTZ,
GUILDENSTERN, } *members of the Danish court*
OSRIC,
A GENTLEMAN,
A LORD,

BERNARDO,
FRANCISCO, } *officers and soldiers on watch*
MARCELLUS,

FORTINBRAS, *Prince of Norway*
CAPTAIN *in his army*
Three or four PLAYERS, *taking the roles of* PROLOGUE, PLAYER KING, PLAYER QUEEN, *and* LUCIANUS
Two MESSENGERS
FIRST SAILOR
Two CLOWNS, *a gravedigger and his companion*
PRIEST
FIRST AMBASSADOR *from England*
Lords, Soldiers, Attendants, Guards, other Players, Followers of Laertes, other Sailors, another Ambassador or Ambassadors from England

SCENE

Denmark]

1.1 *Enter Bernardo and Francisco, two sentinels, [meeting].*

BERNARDO.
Who's there?
FRANCISCO.
Nay, answer me.° Stand and unfold yourself.°
BERNARDO.
Long live the King!
FRANCISCO.
Bernardo?
BERNARDO.
He.
FRANCISCO.
You come most carefully upon your hour.
BERNARDO.
'Tis now struck twelve. Get thee to bed, Francisco.

FRANCISCO.
For this relief much thanks. 'Tis bitter cold,
And I am sick at heart.
BERNARDO.
Have you had quiet guard?   10
FRANCISCO.
Not a mouse stirring.
BERNARDO.
Well, good night.
If you do meet Horatio and Marcellus,
The rivals° of my watch, bid them make haste.

Enter Horatio and Marcellus.

FRANCISCO.
I think I hear them.—Stand, ho! Who is there?   15
HORATIO.
Friends to this ground.°
MARCELLUS.
And liegemen to the Dane.°

1.1 Location: Elsinore castle. A guard platform. **2 me** (Francisco emphasizes that *he* is the sentry currently on watch.) **unfold yourself** reveal your identity

14 rivals partners **16 ground** country, land **17 liegemen to the Dane** men sworn to serve the Danish king

FRANCISCO.
Give° you good night.

MARCELLUS.
O, farewell, honest soldier. Who hath relieved you?

FRANCISCO.
20   Bernardo hath my place. Give you good night.

Exit Francisco.

MARCELLUS.
Holla! Bernardo!

BERNARDO.
Say, what, is Horatio there?

HORATIO.
A piece of him.

BERNARDO.
Welcome, Horatio. Welcome, good Marcellus.

HORATIO.
25   What, has this thing appeared again tonight?

BERNARDO.
I have seen nothing.

MARCELLUS.
Horatio says 'tis but our fantasy,°
And will not let belief take hold of him
Touching this dreaded sight twice seen of us.
30   Therefore I have entreated him along°
With us to watch° the minutes of this night,
That if again this apparition come
He may approve° our eyes and speak to it.

HORATIO.
Tush, tush, 'twill not appear.

BERNARDO.   Sit down awhile,
35   And let us once again assail your ears,
That are so fortified against our story,
What° we have two nights seen.

HORATIO.   Well, sit we down,
And let us hear Bernardo speak of this.

BERNARDO.
Last night of all,°
40   When yond same star that's westward from the pole°
Had made his° course t' illume° that part of heaven
Where now it burns, Marcellus and myself,
The bell then beating one—

Enter Ghost.

MARCELLUS.
Peace, break thee off! Look where it comes again!

BERNARDO.
45   In the same figure like the King that's dead.

MARCELLUS.
Thou art a scholar.° Speak to it, Horatio.

BERNARDO.
Looks 'a° not like the King? Mark it, Horatio.

HORATIO.
Most like. It harrows me with fear and wonder.

BERNARDO.
It would be spoke to.°

MARCELLUS.   Speak to it, Horatio.

HORATIO.
What art thou that usurp'st° this time of night,   50
Together with that fair and warlike form
In which the majesty of buried Denmark°
Did sometime° march? By heaven, I charge thee, speak!

MARCELLUS.
It is offended.

BERNARDO.   See, it stalks away.

HORATIO.
Stay! Speak, speak! I charge thee, speak!   55

Exit Ghost.

MARCELLUS.
'Tis gone and will not answer.

BERNARDO.
How now, Horatio? You tremble and look pale.
Is not this something more than fantasy?
What think you on 't?°

HORATIO.
Before my God, I might not this believe   60
Without the sensible° and true avouch°
Of mine own eyes.

MARCELLUS.   Is it not like the King?

HORATIO.
As thou art to thyself.
Such was the very armor he had on
When he the ambitious Norway° combated.   65
So frowned he once when, in an angry parle,°
He smote the sledded° Polacks° on the ice.
'Tis strange.

MARCELLUS.
Thus twice before, and jump° at this dead hour,
With martial stalk° hath he gone by our watch.   70

HORATIO.
In what particular thought to work° I know not,

---

18 **Give** i.e., may God give   27 **fantasy** imagination   30 **along** to
come along   31 **watch** keep watch during   33 **approve** corrobo-
rate   37 **What** with what   39 **Last . . . all** i.e., this *very* last night.
(Emphatic.)   40 **pole** polestar, north star   41 **his** its **illume** illuminate

46 **scholar** one learned enough to know how to question a ghost
properly   47 **'a** he   49 **It . . . to** (It was commonly believed that a
ghost could not speak until spoken to.)   50 **usurp'st** wrongfully
takes over   52 **buried Denmark** the buried King of Denmark   53
sometime formerly   59 **on 't** of it   61 **sensible** confirmed by the
senses **avouch** warrant, evidence   65 **Norway** King of Norway
66 **parle** parley   67 **sledded** traveling on sleds **Polacks** Poles
69 **jump** exactly   70 **stalk** stride   71 **to work** i.e., to collect my
thoughts and try to understand this

But in the gross and scope° of mine opinion
This bodes some strange eruption to our state.

MARCELLUS.

75   Good now,° sit down, and tell me, he that knows,
Why this same strict and most observant watch
So nightly toils° the subject° of the land,
And why such daily cast° of brazen cannon
And foreign mart° for implements of war,
80   Why such impress° of shipwrights, whose sore task
Does not divide the Sunday from the week.
What might be toward,° that this sweaty haste
Doth make the night joint-laborer with the day?
Who is 't that can inform me?

HORATIO.   That can I;

85   At least, the whisper goes so. Our last king,
Whose image even but now appeared to us,
Was, as you know, by Fortinbras of Norway,
Thereto pricked on° by a most emulate° pride,°
Dared to the combat; in which our valiant Hamlet—
For so this side of our known world° esteemed him—
90   Did slay this Fortinbras; who by a sealed° compact
Well ratified by law and heraldry
Did forfeit, with his life, all those his lands
Which he stood seized° of, to the conqueror;
Against the° which a moiety competent°
95   Was gagèd° by our king, which had returned°
To the inheritance° of Fortinbras
Had he been vanquisher, as, by the same cov'nant°
And carriage of the article designed,°
His fell to Hamlet. Now, sir, young Fortinbras,
100   Of unimprovèd mettle° hot and full,
Hath in the skirts° of Norway here and there
Sharked up° a list° of lawless resolutes°
For food and diet° to some enterprise
That hath a stomach° in 't, which is no other—
105   As it doth well appear unto our state—

But to recover of us, by strong hand
And terms compulsatory, those foresaid lands
So by his father lost. And this, I take it,
Is the main motive of our preparations,
110   The source of this our watch, and the chief head°
Of this posthaste and rummage° in the land.

BERNARDO.

I think it be no other but e'en so.
Well may it sort° that this portentous figure
Comes armèd through our watch so like the King
115   That was and is the question° of these wars.

HORATIO.

A mote° it is to trouble the mind's eye.
In the most high and palmy° state of Rome,
A little ere the mightiest Julius fell,
The graves stood tenantless, and the sheeted° dead
120   Did squeak and gibber in the Roman streets;
As° stars with trains° of fire and dews of blood,
Disasters° in the sun; and the moist star°
Upon whose influence Neptune's° empire stands°
Was sick almost to doomsday° with eclipse.
125   And even the like precurse° of feared events,
As harbingers° preceding still° the fates
And prologue to the omen° coming on,
Have heaven and earth together demonstrated
Unto our climatures° and countrymen.

Enter Ghost.

But soft,° behold! Lo, where it comes again!
130   I'll cross° it, though it blast° me. [*It spreads his° arms.*]
Stay, *illusion!*
If thou hast any sound or use of voice,
Speak to me!
If there be any good thing to be done
135   That may to thee do ease and grace to me,
Speak to me!
If thou art privy to° thy country's fate,
Which, happily,° foreknowing may avoid,
O, speak!
140   Or if thou hast uphoarded in thy life
Extorted treasure in the womb of earth,

---

72 gross and scope general drift   **74 Good now** (An expression denoting entreaty or expostulation.)   **76 toils** causes to toil   **subject** subjects   **77 cast** casting   **78 mart** buying and selling   **79 impress** impressment, conscription   **81 toward** in preparation   **87 pricked on** incited.   **emulate** emulous, ambitious   **Thereto . . . pride** (Refers to old Fortinbras, not the Danish King.)   **89 this . . . world** i.e., all Europe, the Western world   **90 sealed** certified, confirmed   **93 seized** possessed   **94 Against the** in return for   **moiety competent** corresponding portion   **95 gagèd** engaged, pledged   **had returned** would have passed   **96 inheritance** possession   **97 cov'nant** i.e., the *sealed compact* of line 90   **98 carriage . . . designed** carrying out of the article or clause drawn up to cover the point   **100 unimprovèd mettle** untried, undisciplined spirits   **101 skirts** outlying regions, outskirts   **102 Sharked up** gathered up, as a shark takes fish   **list** i.e., troop   **resolutes** desperadoes   **103 For food and diet** i.e., they are to serve as *food,* or "means," *to some enterprise*; also they serve in return for the rations they get   **104 stomach** (1) a spirit of daring (2) an appetite that is fed by the *lawless resolutes*

110 head source   **111 rummage** bustle, commotion   **113 sort** suit   **115 question** focus of contention   **116 mote** speck of dust   **117 palmy** flourishing   **119 sheeted** shrouded   **121 As** (This abrupt transition suggests that matter is possibly omitted between lines 120 and 121.)   **trains** trails   **122 Disasters** unfavorable signs or aspects   **moist star** i.e., moon, governing tides   **123 Neptune** god of the sea   **stands** depends   **124 sick . . . doomsday** (See Matthew 24.29 and Revelation 6.12.)   **125 precurse** heralding, foreshadowing   **126 harbingers** forerunners   **still** continually   **127 omen** calamitous event   **129 climatures** regions   **130 soft** i.e., enough, break off   **131 cross** stand in its path, confront   **blast** wither, strike with a curse   **s.d. his** its   **137 privy to** in on the secret of   **138 happily** haply, perchance

For which, they say, you spirits oft walk in death,
Speak of it! [*The cock crows.*] Stay and speak!—Stop it,
  Marcellus.

MARCELLUS.
  Shall I strike at it with my partisan?°

HORATIO.
145 Do, if it will not stand.   [*They strike at it.*]

BERNARDO.
  'Tis here!

HORATIO.
  'Tis here!

[*Exit Ghost.*]

MARCELLUS.
  'Tis gone.
  We do it wrong, being so majestical,
150 To offer it the show of violence,
  For it is as the air invulnerable,
  And our vain blows malicious mockery.

BERNARDO.
  It was about to speak when the cock crew.

HORATIO.
  And then it started like a guilty thing
155 Upon a fearful summons. I have heard
  The cock, that is the trumpet° to the morn,
  Doth with his lofty and shrill-sounding throat
  Awake the god of day, and at his warning,
  Whether in sea or fire, in earth or air,
160 Th' extravagant and erring° spirit hies°
  To his confine; and of the truth herein
  This present object made probation.°

MARCELLUS.
  It faded on the crowing of the cock.
  Some say that ever 'gainst° that season comes
165 Wherein our Savior's birth is celebrated,
  This bird of dawning singeth all night long,
  And then, they say, no spirit dare stir abroad;
  The nights are wholesome, then no planets strike,°
  No fairy takes,° nor witch hath power to charm,
170 So hallowed and so gracious° is that time.

HORATIO.
  So have I heard and do in part believe it.
  But, look, the morn in russet mantle clad
  Walks o'er the dew of yon high eastward hill.
  Break we our watch up, and by my advice
175 Let us impart what we have seen tonight
  Unto young Hamlet; for upon my life,
  This spirit, dumb to us, will speak to him.

Do you consent we shall acquaint him with it,
As needful in our loves, fitting our duty?

MARCELLUS.
  Let's do 't, I pray, and I this morning know   180
  Where we shall find him most conveniently.

Exeunt.

1.2 *Flourish. Enter Claudius, King of Denmark,
Gertrude the Queen, [the] Council, as° Polonius and his
son Laertes, Hamlet, cum aliis° [including Voltimand and
Cornelius].*

KING.
  Though yet of Hamlet our° dear brother's death
  The memory be green, and that it us befitted
  To bear our hearts in grief and our whole kingdom
  To be contracted in one brow of woe,
  Yet so far hath discretion fought with nature   5
  That we with wisest sorrow think on him
  Together with remembrance of ourselves.
  Therefore our sometime° sister, now our queen,
  Th' imperial jointress° to this warlike state,
  Have we, as 'twere with a defeated joy—   10
  With an auspicious and a dropping eye,°
  With mirth in funeral and with dirge in marriage,
  In equal scale weighing delight and dole°—
  Taken to wife. Nor have we herein barred
  Your better wisdoms, which have freely gone   15
  With this affair along. For all, our thanks.
  Now follows that you know° young Fortinbras,
  Holding a weak supposal° of our worth,
  Or thinking by our late dear brother's death
  Our state to be disjoint and out of frame,   20
  Co-leaguèd with° this dream of his advantage,°
  He hath not failed to pester us with message
  Importing° the surrender of those lands
  Lost by his father, with all bonds° of law,
  To our most valiant brother. So much for him.   25
  Now for ourself and for this time of meeting.
  Thus much the business is: we have here writ
  To Norway, uncle of young Fortinbras—
  Who, impotent° and bed-rid, scarcely hears
  Of this his nephew's purpose—to suppress   30

---

144 partisan long-handled spear **156 trumpet** trumpeter **160
extravagant and erring** wandering beyond bounds (The words have
similar meaning.) **hies** hastens **162 probation** proof **164
'gainst** just before **168 strike** destroy by evil influence **169
takes** bewitches **170 gracious** full of grace

1.2 Location: The castle. **s.d. as** i.e., such as, including **cum
aliis** with others **1 our** my (The royal "we"; also in the following
lines.) **8 sometime** former **9 jointress** woman possessing property with her husband **11 With . . . eye** with one eye smiling and
the other weeping **13 dole** grief **17 that you know** what you
know already, that; or, that you be informed as follows **18 weak
supposal** low estimate **21 Co-leaguèd** with joined to, allied with
dream . . . advantage illusory hope of having the advantage. (His
only ally is this hope.) **23 Importing** pertaining to **24 bonds**
contracts **29 impotent** helpless

His° further gait° herein, in that the levies,
The lists, and full proportions are all made
Out of his subject;° and we here dispatch
You, good Cornelius, and you, Voltimand,
35   For bearers of this greeting to old Norway,
Giving to you no further personal power
To business with the King more than the scope
Of these dilated° articles allow.   [*He gives a paper.*]
Farewell, and let your haste commend your duty.°

CORNELIUS, VOLTIMAND.
40   In that, and all things, will we show our duty.

KING.
We doubt it nothing.° Heartily farewell.

[*Exeunt Voltimand and Cornelius.*]

And now, Laertes, what's the news with you?
You told us of some suit; what is 't, Laertes?
You cannot speak of reason to the Dane°
45   And lose your voice.° What wouldst thou beg, Laertes,
That shall not be my offer, not thy asking?
The head is not more native° to the heart,
The hand more instrumental° to the mouth,
Than is the throne of Denmark to thy father.
What wouldst thou have, Laertes?

50   LAERTES.   My dread lord,
Your leave and favor° to return to France,
From whence though willingly I came to Denmark
To show my duty in your coronation,
Yet now I must confess, that duty done,
55   My thoughts and wishes bend again toward France
And bow them to your gracious leave and pardon.°

KING.
Have you your father's leave? What says Polonius?

POLONIUS.
H'ath,° my lord, wrung from me my slow leave
By laborsome petition, and at last
60   Upon his will I sealed° my hard° consent.
I do beseech you, give him leave to go.

KING.
Take thy fair hour,° Laertes. Time be thine,
And thy best graces spend it at thy will!°

But now, my cousin° Hamlet, and my son—

HAMLET.
A little more than kin, and less than kind.°   65

KING.
How is it that the clouds still hang on you?

HAMLET.
Not so, my lord. I am too much in the sun.°

QUEEN.
Good Hamlet, cast thy nighted color° off,
And let thine eye look like a friend on Denmark.°
Do not forever with thy vailèd lids°   70
Seek for thy noble father in the dust.
Thou know'st 'tis common,° all that lives must die,
Passing through nature to eternity.

HAMLET.
Ay, madam, it is common.

QUEEN.   If it be,
Why seems it so particular° with thee?   75

HAMLET.
Seems, madam? Nay, it is. I know not "seems."
'Tis not alone my inky cloak, good Mother,
Nor customary° suits of solemn black,
Nor windy suspiration° of forced breath,
No, nor the fruitful° river in the eye,   80
Nor the dejected havior° of the visage,
Together with all forms, moods,° shapes of grief,
That can denote me truly. These indeed seem,
For they are actions that a man might play.
But I have that within which passes show;   85
These but the trappings and the suits of woe.

KING.
'Tis sweet and commendable in your nature, Hamlet,
To give these mourning duties to your father.
But you must know your father lost a father,
That father lost, lost his, and the survivor bound   90
In filial obligation for some term
To do obsequious° sorrow. But to persever°
In obstinate condolement° is a course
Of impious stubbornness. 'Tis unmanly grief.

---

31 His i.e., Fortinbras's **gait** proceeding **31–33 in that . . . subject** since the levying of troops and supplies is drawn entirely from the King of Norway's own subjects **38 dilated** set out at length **39 let . . . duty** let your swift obeying of orders, rather than mere words, express your dutifulness **41 nothing** not at all **44 the Dane** the Danish king **45 lose your voice** waste your speech **47 native** closely connected, related **48 instrumental** serviceable **51 leave and favor** kind permission **56 bow . . . pardon** entreatingly make a deep bow, asking your permission to depart **58 H'ath** he has **60 sealed** (as if sealing a legal document) **hard** reluctant **62 Take thy fair hour** enjoy your time of youth **63 And . . . will** and may your finest qualities guide the way you choose to spend your time

64 cousin any kin not of the immediate family **65 A little . . . kind** i.e., closer than an ordinary nephew (since I am stepson), and yet more separated in natural feeling (with pun on *kind* meaning "affectionate" and "natural," "lawful." This line is often read as an aside, but it need not be. The King chooses perhaps not to respond to Hamlet's cryptic and bitter remark.) **67 the sun** i.e., the sunshine of the King's royal favor (with pun on *son*) **68 nighted color** (1) mourning garments of black (2) dark melancholy **69 Denmark** the King of Denmark **70 vailèd lids** lowered eyes **72 common** of universal occurrence (But Hamlet plays on the sense of "vulgar" in line 74.) **75 particular** personal **78 customary** (1) socially conventional (2) habitual with me **79 suspiration** sighing **80 fruitful** abundant **81 havior** expression **82 moods** outward expression of feeling **92 obsequious** suited to obsequies or funerals **persever** persevere **93 condolement** sorrowing

95 It shows a will most incorrect to heaven,
A heart unfortified,° a mind impatient,
An understanding simple° and unschooled.
For what we know must be and is as common
As any the most vulgar thing to sense,°
100 Why should we in our peevish opposition
Take it to heart? Fie, 'tis a fault to heaven,
A fault against the dead, a fault to nature,
To reason most absurd, whose common theme
Is death of fathers, and who still° hath cried,
105 From the first corpse° till he that died today,
"This must be so." We pray you, throw to earth
This unprevailing° woe and think of us
As of a father; for let the world take note,
You are the most immediate° to our throne,
110 And with no less nobility of love
Than that which dearest father bears his son
Do I impart toward° you. For° your intent
In going back to school° in Wittenberg,°
It is most retrograde° to our desire,
115 And we beseech you bend you° to remain
Here in the cheer and comfort of our eye,
Our chiefest courtier, cousin, and our son.

QUEEN.
Let not thy mother lose her prayers, Hamlet.
I pray thee, stay with us, go not to Wittenberg.

HAMLET.
120 I shall in all my best° obey you, madam.

KING.
Why, 'tis a loving and a fair reply.
Be as ourself in Denmark. Madam, come.
This gentle and unforced accord of Hamlet
Sits smiling to° my heart, in grace° whereof
125 No jocund° health that Denmark drinks today
But the great cannon to the clouds shall tell,
And the King's rouse° the heaven shall bruit again,°
Respeaking earthly thunder.° Come away.

Flourish. Exeunt all but Hamlet.

HAMLET.
O, that this too too sullied° flesh would melt,
130 Thaw, and resolve itself into a dew!

Or that the Everlasting had not fixed
His canon° 'gainst self-slaughter! O God, God,
How weary, stale, flat, and unprofitable
Seem to me all the uses° of this world!
Fie on 't, ah fie! 'Tis an unweeded garden 135
That grows to seed. Things rank and gross in nature
Possess it merely.° That it should come to this!
But two months dead—nay, not so much, not two.
So excellent a king, that was to° this
Hyperion° to a satyr,° so loving to my mother 140
That he might not beteem° the winds of heaven
Visit her face too roughly. Heaven and earth,
Must I remember? Why, she would hang on him
As if increase of appetite had grown
By what it fed on, and yet within a month— 145
Let me not think on 't; frailty, thy name is woman!—
A little month, or ere° those shoes were old
With which she followed my poor father's body,
Like Niobe,° all tears, why she, even she—
O God, a beast, that wants discourse of reason,° 150
Would have mourned longer—married with my uncle,
My father's brother, but no more like my father
Than I to Hercules. Within a month,
Ere yet the salt of most unrighteous tears
Had left the flushing in her gallèd° eyes, 155
She married. O, most wicked speed, to post°
With such dexterity to incestuous° sheets!
It is not, nor it cannot come to good.
But break, my heart, for I must hold my tongue.

Enter Horatio, Marcellus, and Bernardo.

HORATIO.
Hail to your lordship!

HAMLET.   I am glad to see you well. 160
Horatio!—or I do forget myself.

HORATIO.
The same, my lord, and your poor servant ever.

HAMLET.
Sir, my good friend; I'll change that name° with you.

---

96 **unfortified** i.e., against adversity   97 **simple** ignorant   99 **As . . . sense** as the most ordinary experience   104 **still** always   105 **the first corpse** (Abel's)   107 **unprevailing** unavailing, useless   109 **most immediate** next in succession   112 **impart toward** i.e., bestow my affection on   **For** as for   113 **to school** i.e., to your studies   **Wittenberg** famous German university founded in 1502   114 **retrograde** contrary   115 **bend you** incline yourself   120 **in all my best** to the best of my ability   124 **to** i.e., at   **grace** thanksgiving   125 **jocund** merry   127 **rouse** drinking of a draft of liquor   **bruit again** loudly echo   128 **thunder** i.e., of trumpet and kettledrum, sounded when the King drinks; see 1.4.8–12   129 **sullied** defiled (The early quartos read *sallied*; the Folio, *solid*.)

132 **canon** law   134 **all the uses** the whole routine   137 **merely** completely   139 **to** in comparison to   140 **Hyperion** Titan sungod, father of Helios   **satyr** a lecherous creature of classical mythology, half-human but with a goat's legs, tail, ears, and horns   141 **beteem** allow   147 **or ere** even before   149 **Niobe** Tantalus' daughter, Queen of Thebes, who boasted that she had more sons and daughters than Leto; for this, Apollo and Artemis, children of Leto, slew her fourteen children. She was turned by Zeus into a stone that continually dropped tears.   150 **wants . . . reason** lacks the faculty of reason   155 **gallèd** irritated, inflamed   156 **post** hasten   157 **incestuous** (In Shakespeare's day, the marriage of a man like Claudius to his deceased brother's wife was considered incestuous.)   163 **change that name** i.e., give and receive reciprocally the name of "friend" (rather than talk of "servant")

And what make you from° Wittenberg, Horatio?
165 Marcellus.

MARCELLUS.
My good lord.

HAMLET.
I am very glad to see you. [*To Bernardo.*] Good even,
    sir.—
But what in faith make you from Wittenberg?

HORATIO.
A truant disposition, good my lord.

HAMLET.
170 I would not hear your enemy say so,
Nor shall you do my ear that violence
To make it truster of your own report
Against yourself. I know you are no truant.
But what is your affair in Elsinore?
175 We'll teach you to drink deep ere you depart.

HORATIO.
My lord, I came to see your father's funeral.

HAMLET.
I prithee, do not mock me, fellow student;
I think it was to see my mother's wedding.

HORATIO.
Indeed, my lord, it followed hard° upon.

HAMLET.
180 Thrift, thrift, Horatio! The funeral baked meats°
Did coldly° furnish forth the marriage tables.
Would I had met my dearest° foe in heaven
Or ever° I had seen that day, Horatio!
My father!—Methinks I see my father.

HORATIO.
Where, my lord?

185 HAMLET.   In my mind's eye, Horatio.

HORATIO.
I saw him once. 'A° was a goodly king.

HAMLET.
'A was a man. Take him for all in all,
I shall not look upon his like again.

HORATIO.
My lord, I think I saw him yesternight.

HAMLET.
190 Saw? Who?

HORATIO.
My lord, the King your father.

HAMLET.
The King my father?

HORATIO.
Season your admiration° for a while
With an attent° ear till I may deliver,

Upon the witness of these gentlemen,   195
This marvel to you.

HAMLET.   For God's love, let me hear!

HORATIO.
Two nights together had these gentlemen,
Marcellus and Bernardo, on their watch,
In the dead waste° and middle of the night,
Been thus encountered. A figure like your father,   200
Armèd at point° exactly, cap-à-pie,°
Appears before them, and with solemn march
Goes slow and stately by them. Thrice he walked
By their oppressed and fear-surprisèd eyes
Within his truncheon's° length, whilst they, distilled° 205
Almost to jelly with the act° of fear,
Stand dumb and speak not to him. This to me
In dreadful° secrecy impart they did,
And I with them the third night kept the watch,
Where, as they had delivered, both in time,   210
Form of the thing, each word made true and good,
The apparition comes. I knew your father;
These hands are not more like.

HAMLET.   But where was this?

MARCELLUS.
My lord, upon the platform where we watch.

HAMLET.
Did you not speak to it?

HORATIO.   My lord, I did,   215
But answer made it none. Yet once methought
It lifted up its head and did address
Itself to motion, like as it would speak;°
But even then° the morning cock crew loud,
And at the sound it shrunk in haste away   220
And vanished from our sight.

HAMLET.   'Tis very strange.

HORATIO.
As I do live, my honored lord, 'tis true,
And we did think it writ down in our duty
To let you know of it.

HAMLET.
Indeed, indeed, sirs. But this troubles me.   225
Hold you the watch tonight?

ALL.   We do, my lord.

HAMLET.
Armed, say you?

ALL.
Armed, my lord.

HAMLET.
From top to toe?

---

164 **make you from** are you doing away from 179 **hard** close
180 **baked meats** meat pies 181 **coldly** i.e., as cold leftovers
182 **dearest** closest (and therefore deadliest) 183 **Or ever** before
186 **'A** he 193 **Season your admiration** restrain your astonishment 194 **attent** attentive

199 **dead waste** desolate stillness 201 **at point** correctly in every
detail **cap-à-pie** from head to foot 205 **truncheon** officer's staff
distilled dissolved 206 **act** action, operation 208 **dreadful** full
of dread 217–218 **did . . . speak** began to move as though it were
about to speak 219 **even then** at that very instant

ALL.
230   My lord, from head to foot.
HAMLET.
    Then saw you not his face?
HORATIO.
    O, yes, my lord, he wore his beaver° up.
HAMLET.
    What° looked he, frowningly?
HORATIO.
    A countenance more in sorrow than in anger.
HAMLET.
235   Pale or red?
HORATIO.
    Nay, very pale.
HAMLET.
    And fixed his eyes upon you?
HORATIO.
    Most constantly.
HAMLET.
    I would I had been there.
HORATIO.
240   It would have much amazed you.
HAMLET.
    Very like, very like. Stayed it long?
HORATIO.
    While one with moderate haste might tell° a hundred.
MARCELLUS, BERNARDO.
    Longer, longer.
HORATIO.
    Not when I saw 't.
HAMLET.
245   His beard was grizzled°—no?
HORATIO.
    It was, as I have seen it in his life,
    A sable silvered.°
HAMLET.   I will watch tonight.
    Perchance 'twill walk again.
HORATIO.   I warrant° it will.
HAMLET.
    If it assume my noble father's person,
250   I'll speak to it though hell itself should gape
    And bid me hold my peace. I pray you all,
    If you have hitherto concealed this sight,
    Let it be tenable° in your silence still,
    And whatsoever else shall hap tonight,
255   Give it an understanding but no tongue.
    I will requite your loves. So, fare you well.
    Upon the platform twixt eleven and twelve
    I'll visit you.
ALL.   Our duty to your honor.

232 beaver visor on the helmet   233 What how   242 tell count
245 grizzled gray   247 sable silvered black mixed with white
248 warrant assure you   253 tenable held

HAMLET.
    Your loves, as mine to you. Farewell.

                              Exeunt [all but Hamlet].

    My father's spirit in arms! All is not well.   260
    I doubt° some foul play. Would the night were come!
    Till then sit still, my soul. Foul deeds will rise,
    Though all the earth o'erwhelm them, to men's eyes.

                                                      Exit.

1.3 *Enter Laertes and Ophelia, his sister.*

LAERTES.
    My necessaries are embarked. Farewell.
    And, sister, as the winds give benefit
    And convoy is assistant,° do not sleep
    But let me hear from you.
OPHELIA.   Do you doubt that?
LAERTES.
    For Hamlet, and the trifling of his favor,   5
    Hold it a fashion and a toy in blood,°
    A violet in the youth of primy° nature,
    Forward,° not permanent, sweet, not lasting,
    The perfume and suppliance° of a minute—
    No more.
OPHELIA.   No more but so?
LAERTES.   Think it no more.   10
    For nature crescent° does not grow alone
    In thews° and bulk, but as this temple° waxes
    The inward service of the mind and soul
    Grows wide withal.° Perhaps he loves you now,
    And now no soil° nor cautel° doth besmirch   15
    The virtue of his will;° but you must fear,
    His greatness weighed,° his will is not his own.
    For he himself is subject to his birth.
    He may not, as unvalued persons do,
    Carve° for himself, for on his choice depends   20
    The safety and health of this whole state,
    And therefore must his choice be circumscribed
    Unto the voice and yielding° of that body
    Whereof he is the head. Then if he says he loves you,
    It fits your wisdom so far to believe it   25
    As he in his particular act and place°
    May give his saying deed, which is no further

261 doubt suspect   1.3 Location: Polonius's chambers.   3 con-
voy is assistant means of conveyance are available   6 toy in blood
passing amorous fancy   7 primy in its prime, springtime   8 Forward precocious   9 suppliance supply, filler   11 crescent growing, waxing   12 thews bodily strength   temple i.e., body   14
Grows wide withal grows along with it   15 soil blemish   cautel
deceit   16 will desire   17 His greatness weighed if you take into
account his high position   20 Carve i.e., choose   23 voice and
yielding assent, approval   26 in . . . place in his particular restricted circumstances

Than the main voice° of Denmark goes withal.°
Then weigh what loss your honor may sustain
30 If with too credent° ear you list° his songs,
Or lose your heart, or your chaste treasure open
To his unmastered importunity.
Fear it, Ophelia, fear it, my dear sister,
And keep you in the rear of your affection,°
35 Out of the shot and danger of desire.
The chariest° maid is prodigal enough
If she unmask° her beauty to the moon.°
Virtue itself scapes not calumnious strokes.
The canker galls° the infants of the spring
40 Too oft before their buttons° be disclosed,°
And in the morn and liquid dew° of youth
Contagious blastments° are most imminent.
Be wary then; best safety lies in fear.
Youth to itself rebels,° though none else near.
OPHELIA.
45 I shall the effect of this good lesson keep
As watchman to my heart. But, good my brother,
Do not, as some ungracious° pastors do,
Show me the steep and thorny way to heaven,
Whiles like a puffed° and reckless libertine
50 Himself the primrose path of dalliance treads,
And recks° not his own rede.°

Enter Polonius.

LAERTES.   O, fear me not.°
I stay too long. But here my father comes.
A double° blessing is a double grace;
Occasion smiles upon a second leave.°
POLONIUS.
55 Yet here, Laertes? Aboard, aboard, for shame!
The wind sits in the shoulder of your sail,
And you are stayed for. There—my blessing with thee!
And these few precepts in thy memory
Look° thou character.° Give thy thoughts no tongue,
60 Nor any unproportioned° thought his° act.
Be thou familiar,° but by no means vulgar.°

Those friends thou hast, and their adoption tried,°
Grapple them unto thy soul with hoops of steel,
But do not dull thy palm° with entertainment
Of each new-hatched, unfledged courage.° Beware   65
Of entrance to a quarrel, but being in,
Bear 't that° th' opposèd may beware of thee.
Give every man thy ear, but few thy voice;
Take each man's censure,° but reserve thy judgment.
Costly thy habit° as thy purse can buy,   70
But not expressed in fancy;° rich, not gaudy,
For the apparel oft proclaims the man,
And they in France of the best rank and station
Are of a most select and generous chief in that.°
Neither a borrower nor a lender be,   75
For loan oft loses both itself and friend,
And borrowing dulleth edge of husbandry.°
This above all: to thine own self be true,
And it must follow, as the night the day,
Thou canst not then be false to any man.   80
Farewell. My blessing season° this in thee!
LAERTES.
Most humbly do I take my leave, my lord.
POLONIUS.
The time invests° you. Go, your servants tend.°
LAERTES.
Farewell, Ophelia, and remember well
What I have said to you.   85
OPHELIA.
'Tis in my memory locked,
And you yourself shall keep the key of it.
LAERTES.
Farewell.

Exit Laertes.

POLONIUS.
What is 't, Ophelia, he hath said to you?
OPHELIA.
So please you, something touching the Lord Hamlet.   90
POLONIUS.
Marry,° well bethought.
'Tis told me he hath very oft of late
Given private time to you, and you yourself
Have of your audience been most free and bounteous.
If it be so—as so 'tis put on° me,   95

28 main voice general assent   **withal** along with   **30 credent**
credulous   **list** listen to   **34 keep . . . affection** don't advance as
far as your affection might lead you (A military metaphor.)   **36
chariest** most scrupulously modest   **37 If she unmask** if she does
no more than show her beauty   **moon** (Symbol of chastity.)   **39
canker galls** cankerworm destroys   **40 buttons** buds   **disclosed**
opened   **41 liquid dew** i.e., time when dew is fresh and bright
42 blastments blights   **44 Youth . . . rebels** youth is inherently rebellious   **47 ungracious** ungodly   **49 puffed** bloated, or swollen
with pride   **51 recks** heeds   **rede** counsel   **fear me not** don't
worry on my account   **53 double** (Laertes has already bid his father good-bye.)   **54 Occasion . . . leave** happy is the circumstance
that provides a second leave-taking. (The goddess Occasion, or Opportunity, smiles.)   **59 Look** be sure that   **character** inscribe   **60
unproportioned** badly calculated, intemperate   **his** its   **61 familiar** sociable   **vulgar** common

62 and their adoption tried and also their suitability for adoption
as friends having been tested   **64 dull thy palm** i.e., shake hands
so often as to make the gesture meaningless   **65 courage** young
man of spirit   **67 Bear 't that** manage it so that   **69 censure**
opinion, judgment   **70 habit** clothing   **71 fancy** excessive ornament, decadent fashion   **74 Are . . . that** are of a most refined and
well-bred preeminence in choosing what to wear   **77 husbandry**
thrift   **81 season** mature   **83 invests** besieges, presses upon
tend attend, wait   **91 Marry** i.e., by the Virgin Mary. (A mild
oath.)   **95 put on** impressed on, told to

And that in way of caution—I must tell you
You do not understand yourself so clearly
As it behooves° my daughter and your honor.
What is between you? Give me up the truth.

OPHELIA.

100   He hath, my lord, of late made many tenders°
Of his affection to me.

POLONIUS.

Affection? Pooh! You speak like a green girl,
Unsifted° in such perilous circumstance.
Do you believe his tenders, as you call them?

OPHELIA.

105   I do not know, my lord, what I should think.

POLONIUS.

Marry, I will teach you. Think yourself a baby
That you have ta'en these tenders for true pay
Which are not sterling.° Tender° yourself more dearly,
Or—not to crack the wind° of the poor phrase,
110   Running it thus—you'll tender me a fool.°

OPHELIA.

My lord, he hath importuned me with love
In honorable fashion.

POLONIUS.

Ay, fashion° you may call it. Go to,° go to.

OPHELIA.

And hath given countenance° to his speech, my lord,
115   With almost all the holy vows of heaven.

POLONIUS.

Ay, springes° to catch woodcocks.° I do know,
When the blood burns, how prodigal° the soul
Lends the tongue vows. These blazes, daughter,
Giving more light than heat, extinct in both
120   Even in their promise as it° is a-making,
You must not take for fire. From this time
Be something° scanter of your maiden presence.
Set your entreatments° at a higher rate
Than a command to parle.° For Lord Hamlet,
125   Believe so much in him° that he is young,
And with a larger tether may he walk
Than may be given you. In few,° Ophelia,

Do not believe his vows, for they are brokers,°
Not of that dye° which their investments° show,
But mere implorators° of unholy suits,   130
Breathing° like sanctified and pious bawds,
The better to beguile. This is for all:°
I would not, in plain terms, from this time forth
Have you so slander° any moment° leisure
As to give words or talk with the Lord Hamlet.   135
Look to 't, I charge you. Come your ways.°

OPHELIA.

I shall obey, my lord.

                                                      Exeunt.

1.4 *Enter Hamlet, Horatio, and Marcellus.*

HAMLET.

The air bites shrewdly;° it is very cold.

HORATIO.

It is a nipping and an eager° air.

HAMLET.

What hour now?

HORATIO.   I think it lacks of° twelve.

MARCELLUS.

No, it is struck.

HORATIO.   Indeed? I heard it not.
It then draws near the season°   5
Wherein the spirit held his wont° to walk.

A flourish of trumpets, and two pieces° go off [within].

What does this mean, my lord?

HAMLET.

The King doth wake° tonight and takes his rouse,°
Keeps wassail,° and the swaggering upspring° reels;°
And as he drains his drafts of Rhenish° down,   10
The kettledrum and trumpet thus bray out
The triumph of his pledge.°

HORATIO.   It is a custom?

HAMLET.

Ay, marry, is 't,
But to my mind, though I am native here
And to the manner° born, it is a custom   15

---

98 behooves befits   **100 tenders** offers   **103 Unsifted** i.e., un-tried   **108 sterling** legal currency   **Tender** hold, look after, offer   **109 crack the wind** i.e., run it until it is broken-winded   **110 tender me a fool** (1) show yourself to me as a fool (2) show me up as a fool (3) present me with a grandchild. (*Fool* was a term of endearment for a child.)   **113 fashion** mere form, pretense   **Go to** (An expression of impatience.)   **114 countenance** credit, confirmation   **116 springes** snares   **woodcocks** birds easily caught; here used to connote gullibility   **117 prodigal** prodigally   **120 it** i.e., the promise   **122 something** somewhat   **123 entreatments** negotiations for surrender. (A military term.)   **124 parle** discuss terms with the enemy. (Polonius urges his daughter, in the metaphor of military language, not to meet with Hamlet and consider giving in to him merely because he requests an interview.)   **125 so ... him** this much concerning him   **127 In few** briefly

128 brokers go-betweens, procurers   **129 dye** color or sort   **investments** clothes. (The vows are not what they seem.)   **130 mere implorators** out and out solicitors   **131 Breathing** speaking   **132 for all** once for all, in sum   **134 slander** abuse, misuse   **moment** moment's   **136 Come your ways** come along   **1.4 Location: The guard platform.   1 shrewdly** keenly, sharply   **2 eager** biting   **3 lacks of** is just short of   **5 season** time   **6 held his wont** was accustomed.   **s.d. pieces** i.e., of ordnance, cannon   **8 wake** stay awake and hold revel.   **takes his rouse** carouses   **9 wassail** carousal   **upspring** wild German dance   **reels** dances   **10 Rhenish** Rhine wine   **12 The triumph ... pledge** i.e., his feat in draining the wine in a single draft   **15 manner** custom (of drinking)

More honored in the breach than the observance.°
This heavy-headed revel east and west°
Makes us traduced and taxed of° other nations.
They clepe° us drunkards, and with swinish phrase°
20 Soil our addition;° and indeed it takes
From our achievements, though performed at height,°
The pith and marrow of our attribute.°
So, oft it chances in particular men,
That for° some vicious mole of nature° in them,
25 As in their birth—wherein they are not guilty,
Since nature cannot choose his° origin—
By their o'ergrowth of some complexion,°
Oft breaking down the pales° and forts of reason,
Or by some habit that too much o'erleavens°
30 The form of plausive° manners, that these men,
Carrying, I say, the stamp of one defect,
Being nature's livery° or fortune's star,°
His virtues else,° be they as pure as grace,
As infinite as man may undergo,°
35 Shall in the general censure° take corruption
From that particular fault. The dram of evil
Doth all the noble substance often dout
To his own scandal.°

Enter Ghost.

HORATIO.   Look, my lord, it comes!
HAMLET.
Angels and ministers° of grace defend us!
40 Be thou° a spirit of health° or goblin damned,
Bring° with thee airs from heaven or blasts from hell,
Be thy intents° wicked or charitable,
Thou com'st in such a questionable° shape
That I will speak to thee. I'll call thee Hamlet,
45 King, father, royal Dane. O, answer me!

Let me not burst in ignorance, but tell
Why thy canonized° bones, hearsèd° in death,
Have burst their cerements;° why the sepulcher
Wherein we saw thee quietly inurned°
50 Hath oped his ponderous and marble jaws
To cast thee up again. What may this mean,
That thou, dead corpse, again in complete steel,°
Revisits thus the glimpses of the moon,°
Making night hideous, and we fools of nature°
55 So horridly to shake our disposition°
With thoughts beyond the reaches of our souls?
Say, why is this? Wherefore? What should we do?

[*The Ghost*] *beckons* [*Hamlet*].

HORATIO.
It beckons you to go away with it,
As if it some impartment° did desire
To you alone.
MARCELLUS.   Look with what courteous action   60
It wafts you to a more removèd ground.
But do not go with it.
HORATIO.   No, by no means.
HAMLET.
It will not speak. Then I will follow it.
HORATIO.
Do not, my lord!
HAMLET.   Why, what should be the fear?
I do not set my life at a pin's fee,°   65
And for my soul, what can it do to that,
Being a thing immortal as itself?
It waves me forth again. I'll follow it.
HORATIO.
What if it tempt you toward the flood,° my lord,
Or to the dreadful summit of the cliff   70
That beetles o'er° his° base into the sea,
And there assume some other horrible form
Which might deprive your sovereignty of reason°
And draw you into madness? Think of it.
The very place puts toys of desperation,°   75
Without more motive, into every brain
That looks so many fathoms to the sea
And hears it roar beneath.

16 **More . . . observance** better neglected than followed   17 **east and west** i.e., everywhere   18 **taxed of** censured by   19 **clepe** call   **with swinish phrase** i.e., by calling us swine   20 **addition** reputation   21 **at height** outstandingly   22 **The pith . . . attribute** the essence of the reputation that others attribute to us   24 **for** on account of   **mole of nature** natural blemish in one's constitution   26 **his** its   27 **their o'ergrowth . . . complexion** the excessive growth in individuals of some natural trait   28 **pales** palings, fences (as of a fortification)   29 **o'erleavens** induces a change throughout (as yeast works in dough)   30 **plausive** pleasing   32 **nature's livery** sign of one's servitude to nature.   **fortune's star** the destiny that chance brings   33 **His virtues else** i.e., the other qualities of *these men* (line 30)   34 **may undergo** can sustain   35 **general censure** general opinion that people have of him   36–38 **The dram . . . scandal** i.e., the small drop of evil blots out or works against the noble substance of the whole and brings it into disrepute. To *dout* is to blot out. (A famous crux.)   39 **ministers of grace** messengers of God   40 **Be thou** whether you are   **spirit of health** good angel   41 **Bring** whether you bring   42 **Be thy intents** whether your intentions are   43 **questionable** inviting question

47 **canonized** buried according to the canons of the church   **hearsèd** coffined   48 **cerements** grave clothes   49 **inurned** entombed   52 **complete steel** full armor   53 **glimpses of the moon** pale and uncertain moonlight   54 **fools of nature** mere men, limited to natural knowledge and subject to nature   55 **So . . . disposition** to distress our mental composure so violently   59 **impartment** communication   65 **fee** value   69 **flood** sea   71 **beetles o'er** overhangs threateningly (like bushy eyebrows)   **his** its   73 **deprive . . . reason** take away the rule of reason over your mind   75 **toys of desperation** fancies of desperate acts, i.e., suicide

HAMLET.
　　It wafts me still.—Go on, I'll follow thee.
MARCELLUS.
　　You shall not go, my lord.　　　　　[*They try to stop him.*]
80　HAMLET.　　　　　　　　　Hold off your hands!
HORATIO.
　　Be ruled. You shall not go.
HAMLET.　　　　　　　　　My fate cries out,°
　　And makes each petty° artery° in this body
　　As hardy as the Nemean lion's° nerve.°
　　Still am I called. Unhand me, gentlemen.
85　By heaven, I'll make a ghost of him that lets° me!
　　I say, away!—Go on, I'll follow thee.

Exeunt Ghost and Hamlet.

HORATIO.
　　He waxes desperate with imagination.
MARCELLUS.
　　Let's follow. 'Tis not fit thus to obey him.
HORATIO.
　　Have after.° To what issue° will this come?
MARCELLUS.
90　Something is rotten in the state of Denmark.
HORATIO.
　　Heaven will direct it.°
MARCELLUS.　　　　　　　Nay, let's follow him.

Exeunt.

1.5 *Enter Ghost and Hamlet.*

HAMLET.
　　Whither wilt thou lead me? Speak. I'll go no further.
GHOST.
　　Mark me.
HAMLET.　　I will.
GHOST.　　　　　　My hour is almost come,
　　When I to sulfurous and tormenting flames
　　Must render up myself.
HAMLET.　　　　　　　Alas, poor ghost!
GHOST.
5　Pity me not, but lend thy serious hearing
　　To what I shall unfold.
HAMLET.
　　Speak. I am bound° to hear.

GHOST.
　　So art thou to revenge, when thou shalt hear.
HAMLET.
　　What?
GHOST.
　　I am thy father's spirit,　　　　　　　　　　　　10
　　Doomed for a certain term to walk the night,
　　And for the day confined to fast° in fires,
　　Till the foul crimes° done in my days of nature°
　　Are burnt and purged away. But that° I am forbid
　　To tell the secrets of my prison house,　　　　　15
　　I could a tale unfold whose lightest word
　　Would harrow up° thy soul, freeze thy young blood,
　　Make thy two eyes like stars start from their spheres,°
　　Thy knotted and combinèd locks° to part,
　　And each particular hair to stand on end　　　　20
　　Like quills upon the fretful porcupine.
　　But this eternal blazon° must not be
　　To ears of flesh and blood. List, list, O, list!
　　If thou didst ever thy dear father love—
HAMLET.
　　O God!　　　　　　　　　　　　　　　　　　25
GHOST.
　　Revenge his foul and most unnatural murder.
HAMLET.
　　Murder?
GHOST.
　　Murder most foul, as in the best° it is,
　　But this most foul, strange, and unnatural.
HAMLET.
　　Haste me to know 't, that I, with wings as swift　　30
　　As meditation or the thoughts of love,
　　May sweep to my revenge.
GHOST.　　　　　　　　　I find thee apt;
　　And duller shouldst thou be° than the fat° weed
　　That roots itself in ease on Lethe° wharf,
　　Wouldst thou not stir in this. Now, Hamlet, hear.　　35
　　'Tis given out that, sleeping in my orchard,°
　　A serpent stung me. So the whole ear of Denmark
　　Is by a forgèd process° of my death
　　Rankly abused.° But know, thou noble youth,
　　The serpent that did sting thy father's life　　　　40
　　Now wears his crown.

81 My fate cries out my destiny summons me　**82 petty** weak. **artery** (through which the vital spirits were thought to have been conveyed)　**83 Nemean lion** one of the monsters slain by Hercules in his twelve labors　**nerve** sinew　**85 lets** hinders　**89 Have after** let's go after him　**issue** outcome　**91 it** i.e., the outcome　**1.5 Location: The battlements of the castle.**　**7 bound** (1) ready (2) obligated by duty and fate. (The Ghost, in line 8, answers in the second sense.)

12 fast do penance by fasting　**13 crimes** sins　**of nature** as a mortal　**14 But that** were it not that　**17 harrow up** lacerate, tear　**18 spheres** i.e., eye-sockets, here compared to the orbits or transparent revolving spheres in which, according to Ptolemaic astronomy, the heavenly bodies were fixed　**19 knotted . . . locks** hair neatly arranged and confined　**22 eternal blazon** revelation of the secrets of eternity　**28 in the best** even at best　**33 shouldst thou be** you would have to be　**fat** torpid, lethargic　**34 Lethe** the river of forgetfulness in Hades　**36 orchard** garden　**38 forgèd process** falsified account　**39 abused** deceived

HAMLET.
O, my prophetic soul! My uncle!

GHOST.
Ay, that incestuous, that adulterate° beast,
With witchcraft of his wit, with traitorous gifts°—
45 O wicked wit and gifts, that have the power
So to seduce!—won to his shameful lust
The will of my most seeming-virtuous queen.
O Hamlet, what a falling off was there!
From me, whose love was of that dignity
50 That it went hand in hand even with the vow°
I made to her in marriage, and to decline
Upon a wretch whose natural gifts were poor
To° those of mine!
But virtue,° as it° never will be moved,
55 Though lewdness court it in a shape of heaven,°
So lust, though to a radiant angel linked,
Will sate itself in a celestial bed°
And prey on garbage.
But soft, methinks I scent the morning air.
60 Brief let me be. Sleeping within my orchard,
My custom always of the afternoon,
Upon my secure° hour thy uncle stole,
With juice of cursèd hebona° in a vial,
And in the porches of my ears° did pour
65 The leprous distillment,° whose effect
Holds such an enmity with blood of man
That swift as quicksilver it courses through
The natural gates and alleys of the body,
And with a sudden vigor it doth posset°
70 And curd, like eager° droppings into milk,
The thin and wholesome blood. So did it mine,
And a most instant tetter° barked° about,
Most lazar-like,° with vile and loathsome crust,
All my smooth body.
75 Thus was I, sleeping, by a brother's hand
Of life, of crown, of queen at once dispatched,°
Cut off even in the blossoms of my sin,
Unhouseled,° disappointed,° unaneled,°

No reckoning° made, but sent to my account
With all my imperfections on my head. 80
O, horrible! O, horrible, most horrible!
If thou hast nature° in thee, bear it not.
Let not the royal bed of Denmark be
A couch for luxury° and damnèd incest.
But, howsoever thou pursues this act, 85
Taint not thy mind nor let thy soul contrive
Against thy mother aught. Leave her to heaven
And to those thorns that in her bosom lodge,
To prick and sting her. Fare thee well at once.
The glowworm shows the matin° to be near, 90
And 'gins to pale his° uneffectual fire.
Adieu, adieu, adieu! Remember me.

[*Exit.*]

HAMLET.
O all you host of heaven! O earth! What else?
And shall I couple° hell? O, fie! Hold,° hold, my heart,
And you, my sinews, grow not instant° old, 95
But bear me stiffly up. Remember thee?
Ay, thou poor ghost, whiles memory holds a seat
In this distracted globe.° Remember thee?
Yea, from the table° of my memory
I'll wipe away all trivial fond° records, 100
All saws° of books, all forms,° all pressures° past
That youth and observation copied there,
And thy commandment all alone shall live
Within the book and volume of my brain,
Unmixed with baser matter. Yes, by heaven! 105
O most pernicious woman!
O villain, villain, smiling, damnèd villain!
My tables°—meet it is° I set it down
That one may smile, and smile, and be a villain.
At least I am sure it may be so in Denmark. 110

[*Writing.*]

So uncle, there you are.° Now to my word:
It is "Adieu, adieu! Remember me."
I have sworn't.

Enter Horatio and Marcellus.

HORATIO.
My lord, my lord!

MARCELLUS.
Lord Hamlet! 115

43 **adulterate** adulterous   44 **gifts** (1) talents (2) presents   **50 even with the vow** with the very vow   **53 To** compared to   **54 virtue, as it** as virtue   **55 shape of heaven** heavenly form   **57 sate . . . bed** cease to find sexual pleasure in a virtuously lawful marriage   **62 secure** confident, unsuspicious   **63 hebona** a poison (The word seems to be a form of *ebony*, though it is thought perhaps to be related to *henbane*, a poison, or to *ebenus*, "yew.")   **64 porches of my ears** ears as a porch or entrance of the body   **65 leprous distillment** distillation causing leprosylike disfigurement   **69 posset** coagulate, curdle   **70 eager** sour, acid   **72 tetter** eruption of scabs   **barked** recovered with a rough covering, like bark on a tree   **73 lazar-like** leperlike   **76 dispatched** suddenly deprived   **78 Unhouseled** without having received the Sacrament   **disappointment** unready (spiritually) for the last journey   **unaneled** without having received extreme unction

79 **reckoning** settling of accounts   **82 nature** i.e., the promptings of a son   **84 luxury** lechery   **90 matin** morning   **91 his** its   **94 couple** add   **Hold** hold together   **95 instant** instantly   **98 globe** (1) head (2) world   **99 table** tablet, slate   **100 fond** foolish   **101 saws** wise sayings   **forms** shapes or images copied onto the slate; general ideas   **pressures** impressions stamped   **108 tables** writing tablets   **meet it is** it is fitting   **111 there you are** i.e., there, I've written that down against you

HORATIO.
Heavens secure him!°

HAMLET.
So be it.

MARCELLUS.
Hilo, ho, ho, my lord!

HAMLET.
Hillo, ho, ho, boy! Come, bird, come.°

MARCELLUS.
120   How is 't, my noble lord?

HORATIO.
What news, my lord?

HAMLET.
O, wonderful!

HORATIO.
Good my lord, tell it.

HAMLET.
No, you will reveal it.

HORATIO.
125   Not I, my lord, by heaven.

MARCELLUS.
Nor I, my lord.

HAMLET.
How say you, then, would heart of man once° think it?
But you'll be secret?

HORATIO, MARCELLUS.   Ay, by heaven, my lord.

HAMLET.
There's never a villain dwelling in all Denmark
130   But he's an arrant° knave.

HORATIO.
There needs no ghost, my lord, come from the grave
To tell us this.

HAMLET.   Why, right, you are in the right.
And so, without more circumstance° at all,
I hold it fit that we shake hands and part,
135   You as your business and desire shall point you—
For every man hath business and desire,
Such as it is—and for my own poor part,
Look you, I'll go pray.

HORATIO.
These are but wild and whirling words, my lord.

HAMLET.
140   I am sorry they offend you, heartily;
Yes, faith, heartily.

HORATIO.   There's no offense, my lord.

HAMLET.
Yes, but Saint Patrick,° but there is, Horatio,

And much offense° too. Touching this vision here,
It is an honest ghost,° that let me tell you.
For your desire to know what is between us,   145
O'ermaster 't as you may. And now, good friends,
As you are friends, scholars, and soldiers,
Give me one poor request.

HORATIO.
What is 't, my lord? We will.

HAMLET.
Never make known what you have seen tonight.   150

HORATIO, MARCELLUS.
My lord, we will not.

HAMLET.
Nay, but swear 't.

HORATIO.
In faith, my lord, not I.°

MARCELLUS.
Nor I, my lord, in faith.

HAMLET.
Upon my sword.°   [He holds out his sword.]   155

MARCELLUS.
We have sworn, my lord, already.°

HAMLET.
Indeed, upon my sword, indeed.

GHOST [cries under the stage]. Swear.

HAMLET.
Ha, ha, boy, sayst thou so? Art thou there, truepenny?°
Come on, you hear this fellow in the cellarage.   160
Consent to swear.

HORATIO.   Propose the oath, my lord.

HAMLET.
Never to speak of this that you have seen,
Swear by my sword.

GHOST [beneath].
Swear.   [They swear.°]

HAMLET.
Hic et ubique?° Then we'll shift our ground.   165

                                        [He moves to another spot.]

Come hither, gentlemen,
And lay your hands again upon my sword.

116 secure him keep him safe   119 Hilo . . . come (A falconer's call to a hawk in air. Hamlet mocks the hallooing as though it were a part of hawking.)   127 once ever   130 arrant thoroughgoing   133 circumstance ceremony, elaboration   142 Saint Patrick (The keeper of Purgatory and patron saint of all blunders and confusion.)

143 offense (Hamlet deliberately changes Horatio's "no offense taken" to "an offense against all decency.")   144 an honest ghost i.e., a real ghost and not an evil spirit   153 In faith . . . I i.e., I swear not to tell what I have seen. (Horatio is not refusing to swear.)   155 sword i.e., the hilt in the form of a cross   156 We . . . already i.e., we swore in *faith*   159 truepenny honest old fellow   164 s.d. They swear (Seemingly they swear here, and at lines 170 and 190, as they lay their hands on Hamlet's sword. Triple oaths would have particular force; these three oaths deal with what they have seen, what they have heard, and what they promise about Hamlet's *antic disposition*.)   165 Hic et ubique here and everywhere. (Latin.)

Swear by my sword
Never to speak of this that you have heard.
GHOST [*beneath*].
170   Swear by his sword.   [*They swear.*]
HAMLET.
Well said, old mole. Canst work i' th' earth so fast?
A worthy pioneer!°—Once more removed, good friends.

                              [*He moves again.*]

HORATIO.
O day and night, but this is wondrous strange!
HAMLET.
And therefore as a stranger° give it welcome.
175   There are more things in heaven and earth, Horatio,
Than are dreamt of in your philosophy.°
But come;
Here, as before, never, so help you mercy,°
How strange or odd soe'er I bear myself—
180   As I perchance hereafter shall think meet
To put an antic° disposition on—
That you, at such times seeing me, never shall,
With arms encumbered° thus, or this headshake,
Or by pronouncing of some doubtful phrase
185   As "Well, we know," or "We could, an if° we would,"
Or "If we list° to speak," or "There be, an if they
      might,"°
Or such ambiguous giving out,° to note°
That you know aught° of me—this do swear,
So grace and mercy at your most need help you.
GHOST [*beneath*].
190   Swear.   [*They swear.*]
HAMLET.
Rest, rest, perturbèd spirit! So, gentlemen,
With all my love I do commend me to you;°
And what so poor a man as Hamlet is
May do t' express his love and friending° to you,
195   God willing, shall not lack.° Let us go in together,
And still° your fingers on your lips, I pray.
The time° is out of joint. O cursèd spite°
That ever I was born to set it right!

                [*They wait for him to leave first.*]

---

172 **pioneer** foot soldier assigned to dig tunnels and excavations
174 **as a stranger** i.e., needing your hospitality   176 **your philosophy** this subject called "natural philosophy" or "science" that people talk about   178 **so help you mercy** as you hope for God's mercy when you are judged   181 **antic** fantastic   183 **encumbered** folded   185 **an if** if   186 **list** wished.   **There . . . might** i.e., there are people here (we, in fact) who could tell news if we were at liberty to do so   187 **giving out** intimation.   **note** draw attention to the fact   188 **aught** i.e., something secret   192 **do . . . you** entrust myself to you   194 **friending** friendliness   195 **lack** be lacking   196 **still** always   197 **The time** the state of affairs   **spite** i.e., the spite of Fortune

Nay, come, let's go together.°

                                Exeunt.

2.1 *Enter old Polonius with his man [Reynaldo].*

POLONIUS.
Give him this money and these notes, Reynaldo.

                    [*He gives money and papers.*]

REYNALDO.
I will, my lord.
POLONIUS.
You shall do marvelous° wisely, good Reynaldo,
Before you visit him, to make inquire°
Of his behavior.
REYNALDO.   My lord, I did intend it.   5
POLONIUS.
Marry, well said, very well said. Look you, sir,
Inquire me first what Danskers° are in Paris,
And how, and who, what means,° and where they keep,°
What company, at what expense; and finding
By this encompassment° and drift° of question   10
That they do know my son, come you more nearer
Than your particular demands will touch it.°
Take you,° as 'twere, some distant knowledge of him,
As thus, "I know his father and his friends,
And in part him." Do you mark this, Reynaldo?   15
REYNALDO.
Ay, very well, my lord.
POLONIUS.
"And in part him, but," you may say, "not well.
But if 't be he I mean, he's very wild,
Addicted so and so," and there put on° him
What forgeries° you please—marry, none so rank°   20
As may dishonor him, take heed of that,
But, sir, such wanton,° wild, and usual slips
As are companions noted and most known
To youth and liberty.
REYNALDO.
As gaming, my lord.   25
POLONIUS.
Ay, or drinking, fencing, swearing,

---

199 **let's go together** (Probably they wait for him to leave first, but he refuses this ceremoniousness.)   **2.1 Location:** Polonius's chambers.   3 **marvelous** marvelously   4 **inquire** inquiry   7 **Danskers** Danes   8 **what means** what wealth (they have)   **keep** dwell   10 **encompassment** roundabout talking   **drift** gradual approach or course   11–12 **come . . . it** you will find out more this way than by asking pointed questions (*particular demands*)   13 **Take you** assume, pretend   19 **put on** impute to   20 **forgeries** invented tales   **rank** gross   22 **wanton** sportive, unrestrained

Quarreling, drabbing°—you may go so far.

REYNALDO.
My lord, that would dishonor him.

POLONIUS.
Faith, no, as you may season° it in the charge.
30 You must not put another scandal on him
That he is open to incontinency;°
That's not my meaning. But breathe his faults so
    quaintly°
That they may seem the taints of liberty,°
The flash and outbreak of a fiery mind,
35 A savageness in unreclaimèd blood,
Of general assault.°

REYNALDO.
But, my good lord—

POLONIUS.
Wherefore should you do this?

REYNALDO.
Ay, my lord, I would know that.

POLONIUS.
40 Marry, sir, here's my drift,
And I believe it is a fetch of warrant.°
You laying these slight sullies on my son,
As 'twere a thing a little soiled wi' the working,°
Mark you,
45 Your party in converse,° him you would sound,°
Having ever° seen in the prenominate crimes°
The youth you breathe° of guilty, be assured
He closes with you in this consequence:°
"Good sir," or so, or "friend," or "gentleman,"
50 According to the phrase or the addition°
Of man and country.

REYNALDO.   Very good, my lord.

POLONIUS. And then, sir, does 'a this—'a does—what was I
about to say? By the Mass, I was about to say something.
Where did I leave?

REYNALDO.
55 At "closes in the consequence."

POLONIUS.
At "closes in the consequence," ay, marry.
He closes thus: "I know the gentleman,
I saw him yesterday," or "th' other day,"
Or then, or then, with such or such, "and as you say,

There was 'a gaming," "there o'ertook in 's rouse,"°   60
"There falling out° at tennis," or perchance
"I saw him enter such a house of sale,"
Videlicet° a brothel, or so forth. See you now,
Your bait of falsehood takes this carp° of truth;
And thus do we of wisdom and of reach,°   65
With windlasses° and with assays of bias,°
By indirections find directions° out.
So by my former lecture and advice
Shall you my son. You have° me, have you not?

REYNALDO.
My lord, I have.

POLONIUS.   God b'wi'° ye; fare ye well.   70

REYNALDO.
Good my lord.

POLONIUS.
Observe his inclination in yourself.°

REYNALDO.
I shall, my lord.

POLONIUS.
And let him ply his music.

REYNALDO.
Well, my lord.   75

POLONIUS.
Farewell.

Exit Reynaldo.

Enter Ophelia.

            How now, Ophelia, what's the matter?

OPHELIA.
O my lord, my lord, I have been so affrighted!

POLONIUS.
With what, i' the name of God?

OPHELIA.
My lord, as I was sewing in my closet,°
Lord Hamlet, with his doublet° all unbraced,°   80
No hat upon his head, his stockings fouled,
Ungartered, and down-gyvèd° to his ankle,
Pale as his shirt, his knees knocking each other,
And with a look so piteous in purport°
As if he had been loosèd out of hell   85
To speak of horrors—he comes before me.

27 **drabbing** whoring 29 **season** temper, soften 31 **incontinency** habitual sexual excess 32 **quaintly** artfully, subtly 33 **taints of liberty** faults resulting from free living 35–36 **A savageness . . . assault** a wildness in untamed youth that assails all indiscriminately 41 **fetch of warrant** legitimate trick 43 **soiled wi' the working** soiled by handling while it is being made, i.e., by involvement in the ways of the world 45 **converse** conversation **sound** i.e., sound out 46 **Having ever** if he has ever **prenominate crimes** before-mentioned offenses 47 **breathe** speak 48 **closes . . . consequence** takes you into his confidence in some fashion, as follows 50 **addition** title

60 **o'ertook in 's rouse** overcome by drink 61 **falling out** quarreling 63 **Videlicet** namely 64 **carp** a fish 65 **reach** capacity, ability 66 **windlasses** i.e., circuitous paths (Literally, circuits made to head off the game in hunting.) **assays of bias** attempts through indirection (like the curving path of the bowling ball, which is biased or weighted to one side) 67 **directions** i.e., the way things really are 69 **have** understand 70 **b'wi'** be with 72 **in yourself** in your own person (as well as by asking questions) 79 **closet** private chamber 80 **doublet** close-fitting jacket. **unbraced** unfastened 82 **down-gyvèd** fallen to the ankles (like gyves or fetters) 84 **in purport** in what it expressed

POLONIUS.
Mad for thy love?
OPHELIA.   My lord, I do not know,
But truly I do fear it.
POLONIUS.   What said he?
OPHELIA.
He took me by the wrist and held me hard.
90   Then goes he to the length of all his arm,
And, with his other hand thus o'er his brow
He falls to such perusal of my face
As° 'a would draw it. Long stayed he so.
At last, a little shaking of mine arm
95   And thrice his head thus waving up and down,
He raised a sigh so piteous and profound
As it did seem to shatter all his bulk°
And end his being. That done, he lets me go,
And with his head over his shoulder turned
100   He seemed to find his way without his eyes,
For out o' doors he went without their helps,
And to the last bended their light on me.
POLONIUS.
Come, go with me. I will go seek the King.
This is the very ecstasy° of love,
105   Whose violent property° fordoes° itself
And leads the will to desperate undertakings
As oft as any passion under heaven
That does afflict our natures. I am sorry.
What, have you given him any hard words of late?
OPHELIA.
110   No, my good lord, but as you did command
I did repel his letters and denied
His access to me.
POLONIUS.   That hath made him mad.
I am sorry that with better heed and judgment
I had not quoted° him. I feared he did but trifle
115   And meant to wrack° thee. But beshrew my jealousy!°
By heaven, it is as proper to our age°
To cast beyond° ourselves in our opinions
As it is common for the younger sort
To lack discretion. Come, go we to the King.
This must be known,° which, being kept close,° might
120   move
More grief to hide than hate to utter love.°
Come.

Exeunt.

93 **As** as if (also in line 97)   97 **bulk** body   104 **ecstasy** madness
105 **property** nature   **fordoes** destroys   114 **quoted** observed
115 **wrack** ruin, seduce   **beshrew my jealousy** a plague upon my
suspicious nature   116 **proper . . . age** characteristic of us (old)
men   117 **cast beyond** overshoot, miscalculate (A metaphor from
hunting.)   120 **known** made known (to the King)   **close** secret
120–121 **might . . . love** i.e., might cause more grief (because of
what Hamlet might do) by hiding the knowledge of Hamlet's
strange behavior to Ophelia than unpleasantness by telling it

2.2 *Flourish. Enter King and Queen, Rosencrantz, and
Guildenstern [with others].*

KING.
Welcome, dear Rosencrantz and Guildenstern.
Moreover that° we much did long to see you,
The need we have to use you did provoke
Our hasty sending. Something have you heard
Of Hamlet's transformation—so call it,   5
Sith nor° th' exterior nor the inward man
Resembles that° it was. What it should be,
More than his father's death, that thus hath put him
So much from th' understanding of himself,
I cannot dream of. I entreat you both   10
That, being of so young days° brought up with him,
And sith so neighbored to° his youth and havior,°
That you vouchsafe your rest° here in our court
Some little time, so by your companies
To draw him on to pleasures, and to gather   15
So much as from occasion° you may glean,
Whether aught to us unknown afflicts him thus
That, opened,° lies within our remedy.
QUEEN.
Good gentlemen, he hath much talked of you,
And sure I am two men there is not living   20
To whom he more adheres. If it will please you
To show us so much gentry° and good will
As to expend your time with us awhile
For the supply and profit of our hope,°
Your visitation shall receive such thanks   25
As fits a king's remembrance.°
ROSENCRANTZ.   Both Your Majesties
Might, by the sovereign power you have of° us,
Put your dread° pleasures more into command
Than to entreaty.
GUILDENSTERN.   But we both obey,
And here give up ourselves in the full bent°   30
To lay our service freely at your feet,
To be commanded.
KING.
Thanks, Rosencrantz and gentle Guildenstern.
QUEEN.
Thanks, Guildenstern and gentle Rosencrantz.

2.2 Location: The castle. **2 Moreover that** besides the fact that
6 Sith nor since neither   **7 that** what   **11 of . . . days** from such
early youth   **12 And sith so neighbored to** and since you are (or,
and since that time you are) intimately acquainted with   **havior**
demeanor   **13 vouchsafe your rest** please to stay   **16 occasion**
opportunity   **18 opened** being revealed   **22 gentry** courtesy   **24
supply . . . hope** aid and furtherance of what we hope for   **26 As
fits . . . remembrance** as would be a fitting gift of a king who rewards true service   **27 of** over   **28 dread** inspiring awe   **30 in
. . . bent** to the utmost degree of our capacity (An archery
metaphor.)

35   And I beseech you instantly to visit
       My too much changèd son. Go, some of you,
       And bring these gentlemen where Hamlet is.
GUILDENSTERN.
       Heavens make our presence and our practices°
       Pleasant and helpful to him!
QUEEN.   Ay, amen!

       Exeunt Rosencrantz and Guildenstern [with some attendants].

       Enter Polonius.

POLONIUS.
40   Th' ambassadors from Norway, my good lord,
       Are joyfully returned.
KING.
       Thou still° hast been the father of good news.
POLONIUS.
       Have I, my lord? I assure my good liege
       I hold° my duty, as° I hold my soul,
45   Both to my God and to my gracious king;
       And I do think, or else this brain of mine
       Hunts not the trail of policy° so sure
       As it hath used to do, that I have found
       The very cause of Hamlet's lunacy.
KING.
50   O, speak of that! That do I long to hear.
POLONIUS.
       Give first admittance to th' ambassadors.
       My news shall be the fruit° to that great feast.
KING.
       Thyself do grace° to them and bring them in.

                                        [Exit Polonius.]

       He tells me, my dear Gertrude, he hath found
55   The head and source of all your son's distemper.
QUEEN.
       I doubt° it is no other but the main,°
       His father's death and our o'erhasty marriage.

       *Enter Ambassadors [Voltimand and Cornelius, with Polo-
       nius].*

KING.
       Well, we shall sift him.°—Welcome, my good friends!
       Say, Voltimand, what from our brother° Norway?
VOLTIMAND.
60   Most fair return of greetings and desires.°

       Upon our first,° he sent out to suppress
       His nephew's levies, which to him appeared
       To be a preparation 'gainst the Polack,
       But, better looked into, he truly found
       It was against Your Highness. Whereat grieved   65
       That so his sickness, age, and impotence°
       Was falsely borne in hand,° sends out arrests°
       On Fortinbras, which he, in brief, obeys,
       Receives rebuke from Norway, and in fine°
       Makes vow before his uncle never more   70
       To give th' assay° of arms against Your Majesty.
       Whereon old Norway, overcome with joy,
       Gives him three thousand crowns in annual fee
       And his commission to employ those soldiers,
       So levied as before, against the Polack,   75
       With an entreaty, herein further shown,   *[giving a paper]*
       That it might please you to give quiet pass
       Through your dominions for this enterprise
       On such regards of safety and allowance°
       As therein are set down.
KING.   It likes° us well,   80
       And at our more considered° time we'll read,
       Answer, and think upon this business.
       Meantime we thank you for your well-took labor.
       Go to your rest; at night we'll feast together.
       Most welcome home!

                                        Exeunt Ambassadors.

POLONIUS.   This business is well ended.   85
       My liege, and madam, to expostulate°
       What majesty should be, what duty is,
       Why day is day, night night, and time is time,
       Were nothing but to waste night, day, and time.
       Therefore, since brevity is the soul of wit,°   90
       And tediousness the limbs and outward flourishes,
       I will be brief. Your noble son is mad.
       Mad call I it, for, to define true madness,
       What is 't but to be nothing else but mad?
       But let that go.
QUEEN.   More matter, with less art.   95
POLONIUS.
       Madam, I swear I use no art at all.
       That he's mad, 'tis true; 'tis true 'tis pity,
       And pity 'tis 'tis true—a foolish figure,°
       But farewell it, for I will use no art.
       Mad let us grant him, then, and now remains   100

38 **practices** doings   42 **still** always   44 **hold** maintain   **as** as
firmly as   47 **policy** sagacity   52 **fruit** dessert   53 **grace** honor
(punning on *grace* said before a *feast*, line 52)   56 **doubt** fear, suspect   **main** chief point, principal concern   58 **sift him** question
Polonius closely   59 **brother** fellow king   60 **desires** good wishes

61 **Upon our first** at our first words on the business   66 **impotence** helplessness   67 **borne in hand** deluded, taken advantage of
arrests orders to desist   69 **in fine** in conclusion   71 **give th' assay** make trial of strength, challenge   79 **On . . . allowance** i.e.,
with such considerations for the safety of Denmark and permission
for Fortinbras   80 **likes** pleases   81 **considered** suitable for deliberation   86 **expostulate** expound, inquire into   90 **wit** sense or
judgment   98 **figure** figure of speech

That we find out the cause of this effect,
Or rather say, the cause of this defect,
For this effect defective comes by cause.°
Thus it remains, and the remainder thus.
105   Perpend.°
I have a daughter—have while she is mine—
Who, in her duty and obedience, mark,
Hath given me this. Now gather and surmise.°
[*He reads the letter.*] "To the celestial and my soul's idol,
110   the most beautified Ophelia"—
That's an ill phrase, a vile phrase; "beautified" is a vile
      phrase. But you shall hear. Thus: [*He reads.*]
"In her excellent white bosom,° these,° etc."
   QUEEN.
     Came this from Hamlet to her?
115 POLONIUS. Good madam, stay° awhile, I will be faithful.°
                                [*He reads.*]
      "Doubt thou the stars are fire,
        Doubt that the sun doth move,
      Doubt° truth to be a liar,
        But never doubt I love.
120   O dear Ophelia, I am ill at these numbers.° I have
     not art to reckon° my groans. But that I love thee
     best, O most best, believe it. Adieu.
         Thine evermore, most dear lady, whilst this
                  machine is to him, Hamlet."
125   This in obedience hath my daughter shown me,
And, more above,° hath his solicitings,
As they fell out° by° time, by means, and place,
All given to mine ear.°
   KING.   But how hath she
     Received his love?
   POLONIUS.   What do you think of me?
   KING.
130   As of a man faithful and honorable.
   POLONIUS.
     I would fain° prove so. But what might you think,
When I had seen this hot love on the wing—
As I perceived it, I must tell you that,
Before my daughter told me—what might you,
135   Or my dear Majesty your queen here, think,
If I had played the desk or table book,°

Or given my heart a winking,° mute and dumb,
Or looked upon this love with idle sight?°
What might you think? No, I went round° to work,
And my young mistress thus I did bespeak:°   140
"Lord Hamlet is a prince out of thy star;°
This must not be." And then I prescripts° gave her,
That she should lock herself from his resort,°
Admit no messengers, receive no tokens.
Which done, she took the fruits of my advice;   145
And he, repellèd—a short tale to make—
Fell into a sadness, then into a fast,
Thence to a watch,° thence into a weakness,
Thence to a lightness,° and by this declension°
Into the madness wherein now he raves,   150
And all we° mourn for.
KING [*to the Queen*].   Do you think 'tis this?
QUEEN.
     It may be, very like.
POLONIUS.
     Hath there been such a time—I would fain know that—
That I have positively said "'Tis so,"
When it proved otherwise?
KING.   Not that I know.   155
POLONIUS.
     Take this from this,° if this be otherwise.
If circumstances lead me, I will find
Where truth is hid, though it were hid indeed
Within the center.°
KING.   How may we try° it further?
POLONIUS.
     You know sometimes he walks four hours together   160
     Here in the lobby.
QUEEN.   So he does indeed.
POLONIUS.
     At such a time I'll loose° my daughter to him.
Be you and I behind an arras° then.
Mark the encounter. If he love her not
And be not from his reason fall'n thereon,°   165
Let me be no assistant for a state,
But keep a farm and carters.°

---

103 **For . . . cause** i.e., for this defective behavior, this madness, has a cause 105 **Perpend** consider 108 **gather and surmise** draw your own conclusions 113 **In . . . bosom** (The letter is poetically addressed to her heart.) **these** i.e., the letter 115 **stay** wait **faithful** i.e., in reading the letter accurately 118 **Doubt** suspect 120 **ill . . . numbers** unskilled at writing verses 121 **reckon** (1) count (2) number metrically, scan 123 **machine** i.e., body 126 **more above** moreover 127 **fell out** occurred. **by** according to 128 **given . . . ear** i.e., told me about 131 **fain** gladly 136 **played . . . table book** i.e., remained shut up, concealing the information

137 **given . . . winking** closed the eyes of my heart to this 138 **with idle sight** complacently or incomprehendingly 139 **round** roundly, plainly 140 **bespeak** address 141 **out of thy star** above your sphere, position 142 **prescripts** orders 143 **his resort** his visits 148 **watch** state of sleeplessness 149 **lightness** lightheadedness **declension** decline, deterioration (with a pun on the grammatical sense) 151 **all we** all of us, or, into everything that we 156 **Take this from this** (The actor probably gestures, indicating that he means his head from his shoulders, or his staff of office or chain from his hands or neck, or something similar.) 159 **center** middle point of the earth (which is also the center of the Ptolemaic universe) **try** test, judge 162 **loose** (as one might release an animal that is being mated) 163 **arras** hanging, tapestry 165 **thereon** on that account 167 **carters** wagon drivers

KING.   We will try it.

Enter Hamlet [reading on a book].

QUEEN.
But look where sadly° the poor wretch comes reading.
POLONIUS.
Away, I do beseech you both, away.
170   I'll board° him presently.° O, give me leave.°

Exeunt King and Queen [with attendants].

How does my good Lord Hamlet?
HAMLET.
Well, God-a-mercy.°
POLONIUS.
Do you know me, my lord?
HAMLET.
Excellent well. You are a fishmonger.°
POLONIUS.
175   Not I, my lord.
HAMLET.
Then I would you were so honest a man.
POLONIUS.
Honest, my lord?
HAMLET. Ay, sir. To be honest, as this world goes, is to be one
man picked out of ten thousand.
180   POLONIUS. That's very true, my lord.
HAMLET. For if the sun breed maggots in a dead dog, being a
good kissing carrion°—Have you a daughter?
POLONIUS. I have, my lord.
HAMLET. Let her not walk i' the sun.° Conception° is a bless-
185   ing, but as your daughter may conceive, friend, look to 't.
POLONIUS [aside]. How say you by that? Still harping on my
daughter. Yet he knew me not at first; 'a° said I was a fishmonger. 'A is far gone. And truly in my youth I suffered
much extremity for love, very near this. I'll speak to him
190   again.—What do you read, my lord?
HAMLET. Words, words, words.
POLONIUS. What is the matter,° my lord?
HAMLET. Between who?
POLONIUS. I mean, the matter that you read, my lord.
195   HAMLET. Slanders, sir; for the satirical rogue says here that
old men have gray beards, that their faces are wrinkled,
their eyes purging° thick amber° and plum-tree gum, and

that they have a plentiful lack of wit,° together with
most weak hams. All which, sir, though I most powerfully
and potently believe, yet I hold it not honesty° to have it   200
thus set down, for yourself, sir, shall grow old° as I am, if
like a crab you could go backward.
POLONIUS [aside]. Though this be madness, yet there is
method in 't.—Will you walk out of the air,° my lord?
HAMLET. Into my grave.   205
POLONIUS. Indeed, that's out of the air. [Aside.] How preg-
nant° sometimes his replies are! A happiness° that often
madness hits on, which reason and sanity could not so
prosperously° be delivered of. I will leave him and sud-
denly° contrive the means of meeting between him and   210
my daughter.—My honorable lord, I will most humbly
take my leave of you.
HAMLET. You cannot, sir, take from me anything that I will
more willingly part withal°—except my life, except my
life, except my life.   215

Enter Guildenstern and Rosencrantz.

POLONIUS. Fare you well, my lord.
HAMLET. These tedious old fools!°
POLONIUS. You go to seek the Lord Hamlet. There he is.
ROSENCRANTZ [to Polonius]. God save you, sir!

[Exit Polonius.]

GUILDENSTERN. My honored lord!   220
ROSENCRANTZ. My most dear lord!
HAMLET. My excellent good friends! How dost thou,
Guildenstern? Ah, Rosencrantz! Good lads, how do you
both?
ROSENCRANTZ. As the indifferent° children of the earth.   225
GUILDENSTERN. Happy in that we are not overhappy.
On Fortune's cap we are not the very button.
HAMLET. Nor the soles of her shoe?
ROSENCRANTZ. Neither, my lord.
HAMLET. Then you live about her waist, or in the middle of   230
her favors?°
GUILDENSTERN. Faith, her privates we.°
HAMLET. In the secret parts of Fortune? O, most true, she is a
strumpet.° What news?
ROSENCRANTZ. None, my lord, but the world's grown honest.   235

---

168 sadly seriously **170 board** accost **presently** at once **give
me leave** i.e., excuse me, leave me alone (Said to those he hurries
offstage, including the King and Queen.) **172 God-a-mercy** God
have mercy, i.e., thank you **174 fishmonger** fish merchant
181–182 a good kissing carrion i.e., a good piece of flesh for kissing, or for the sun to kiss **184 i' the sun** in public (with additional implication of the sunshine of princely favors) **Conception**
(1) understanding (2) pregnancy **187 'a** he **192 matter** substance. (But Hamlet plays on the sense of "basis for a dispute.")
197 purging discharging **amber** i.e., resin, like the resinous *plum-
tree gum*

198 wit understanding **200 honesty** decency, decorum **201 old**
as old **204 out of the air** (The open air was considered dangerous
for sick people.) **207 pregnant** quick-witted, full of meaning
happiness felicity of expression **209 prosperously** successfully
210 suddenly immediately **214 withal** with **217 old fools** i.e.,
old men like Polonius **225 indifferent** ordinary, at neither extreme of fortune or misfortune **231 favors** i.e., sexual favors
232 her privates we i.e., (1) we are sexually intimate with Fortune,
the fickle goddess who bestows her favors indiscriminately (2) we
are her private citizens **234 strumpet** prostitute (A common epi-
thet for indiscriminate Fortune; see line 452.)

HAMLET. Then is doomsday near. But your news is not true. Let me question more in particular. What have you, my good friends, deserved at the hands of Fortune that she sends you to prison hither?

240 GUILDENSTERN. Prison, my lord?

HAMLET. Denmark's a prison.

ROSENCRANTZ. Then is the world one.

HAMLET. A goodly one, in which there are many confines,° wards,° and dungeons, Denmark being one o' the worst.

245 ROSENCRANTZ. We think not so, my lord.

HAMLET. Why then 'tis none to you, for there is nothing either good or bad but thinking makes it so. To me it is a prison.

ROSENCRANTZ. Why then, your ambition makes it one. 'Tis too narrow for your mind.

250 HAMLET. O God, I could be bounded in a nutshell and count myself a king of infinite space, were it not that I have bad dreams.

GUILDENSTERN. Which dreams indeed are ambition, for the very substance of the ambitious° is merely the shadow of
255 a dream.

HAMLET. A dream itself is but a shadow.

ROSENCRANTZ. Truly, and I hold ambition of so airy and light a quality that it is but a shadow's shadow.

HAMLET. Then are our beggars bodies,° and our monarchs
260 and outstretched° heroes the beggars' shadows. Shall we to the court? For, by my fay,° I cannot reason.

ROSENCRANTZ, GUILDENSTERN. We'll wait upon° you.

HAMLET. No such matter. I will not sort° you with the rest of my servants, for, to speak to you like an honest man, I am
265 most dreadfully attended.° But, in the beaten way° of friendship, what make° you at Elsinore?

ROSENCRANTZ. To visit you, my lord, no other occasion.

HAMLET. Beggar that I am, I am even poor in thanks; but I thank you, and sure, dear friends, my thanks are too dear
270 a halfpenny.° Were you not sent for? Is it your own inclining? Is it a free° visitation? Come, come, deal justly with me. Come, come. Nay, speak.

GUILDENSTERN. What should we say, my lord?

HAMLET. Anything but to the purpose.° You were sent for,
275 and there is a kind of confession in your looks which your modesties° have not craft enough to color.° I know the good King and Queen have sent for you.

ROSENCRANTZ. To what end, my lord?

HAMLET. That you must teach me. But let me conjure° you, by the rights of our fellowship, by the consonancy of our 280 youth,° by the obligation of our ever-preserved love, and by what more dear a better° proposer could charge° you withal, be even° and direct with me whether you were sent for or no.

ROSENCRANTZ [aside to Guildenstern]. What say you? 285

HAMLET [aside]. Nay, then, I have an eye of° you.—If you love me, hold not off.°

GUILDENSTERN. My lord, we were sent for.

HAMLET. I will tell you why; so shall my anticipation prevent your discovery,° and your secrecy to the King and Queen 290 molt no feather.° I have of late—but wherefore I know not—lost all my mirth, forgone all custom of exercises; and indeed it goes so heavily with my disposition that this goodly frame, the earth, seems to me a sterile promontory; this most excellent canopy, the air, look 295 you, this brave° o'erhanging firmament, this majestical roof fretted° with golden fire, why, it appeareth nothing to me but a foul and pestilent congregation° of vapors. What a piece of work° is a man! How noble in reason, how infinite in faculties, in form and moving how ex- 300 press° and admirable, in action how like an angel, in apprehension° how like a god! The beauty of the world, the paragon of animals! And yet, to me, what is this quintessence° of dust? Man delights not me—no, nor woman neither, though by your smiling you seem to say so. 305

ROSENCRANTZ. My lord, there was no such stuff in my thoughts.

HAMLET. Why did you laugh, then, when I said man delights not me?

ROSENCRANTZ. To think, my lord, if you delight not in man, 310 what Lenten entertainment° the players shall receive from you. We coted° them on the way, and hither are they coming to offer you service.

HAMLET. He that plays the king shall be welcome; His Majesty shall have tribute° of° me. The adventurous 315 knight shall use his foil and target,° the lover shall not

243 **confines** places of confinement   244 **wards** cells   253–254 **the very . . . ambitious** that seemingly very substantial thing that the ambitious pursue   259 **bodies** i.e., solid substances rather than shadows (since beggars are not ambitious)   260 **outstretched** (1) far-reaching in their ambition (2) elongated as shadows   261 **fay** faith   262 **wait upon** accompany, attend. (But Hamlet uses the phrase in the sense of providing menial service.)   263 **sort** class, categorize   265 **dreadfully attended** waited upon in slovenly fashion   **beaten way** familiar path, tried-and-true course   266 **make** do   269–270 **too dear a halfpenny** (1) too expensive at even a halfpenny, i.e., of little worth (2) too expensive by a halfpenny in return for worthless kindness   271 **free** voluntary   274 **Anything but to the purpose** anything except a straightforward answer. (Said ironically.)   276 **modesties** sense of shame   **color** disguise

279 **conjure** adjure, entreat   281 **the consonancy of our youth** our closeness in our younger days   282 **better** more skillful   **charge** urge.   283 **even** straight, honest   286 **of** on   287 **hold not off** don't hold back   289–290 **so . . . discovery** in that way my saying it first will spare you from revealing the truth   291 **molt no feather** i.e., not diminish in the least   296 **brave** splendid   297 **fretted** adorned (with fretwork, as in a vaulted ceiling)   298 **congregation** mass.   299 **piece of work** masterpiece   300–301 **express** well-framed, exact, expressive   302–303 **apprehension** power of comprehending   303–304 **quintessence** the fifth essence of ancient philosophy, beyond earth, water, air, and fire, supposed to be the substance of the heavenly bodies and to be latent in all things   311 **Lenten entertainment** meager reception (appropriate to Lent)   312 **coted** overtook and passed by   315 **tribute** (1) applause (2) homage paid in money   **of** from   316 **foil and target** sword and shield

sigh gratis,° the humorous man° shall end his part in peace,° the clown shall make those laugh whose lungs are tickle o' the sear,° and the lady shall say her mind freely, or the blank verse shall halt° for 't. What players are they?

320

ROSENCRANTZ. Even those you were wont to take such delight in, the tragedians° of the city.

HAMLET. How chances it they travel? Their residence,° both in reputation and profit, was better both ways.

325

ROSENCRANTZ. I think their inhibition° comes by the means of the late° innovation.°

HAMLET. Do they hold the same estimation they did when I was in the city? Are they so followed?

ROSENCRANTZ. No, indeed are they not.

330

HAMLET. How comes it? Do they grow rusty?

ROSENCRANTZ. Nay, their endeavor keeps° in the wonted° pace. But there is, sir, an aerie° of children, little eyases,° that cry out on the top of question° and are most tyrannically° clapped for 't. These are now the fashion, and so

335

berattle° the common stages°—so they call them—that many wearing rapiers° are afraid of goose quills° and dare scarce come thither.

HAMLET. What, are they children? Who maintains 'em? How are they escoted?° Will they pursue the quality° no longer

340

than they can sing?° Will they not say afterwards, if they should grow themselves to common° players—as it is most like,° if their means are no better°—their writers do them wrong to make them exclaim against their own succession?°

345

ROSENCRANTZ. Faith, there has been much to-do° on both sides, and the nation holds it no sin to tar° them to con-

troversy. There was for a while no money bid for argument unless the poet and the player went to cuffs in the question.°

HAMLET. Is 't possible?

350

GUILDENSTERN. O, there has been much throwing about of brains.

HAMLET. Do the boys carry it away?°

ROSENCRANTZ. Ay, that they do, my lord—Hercules and his load° too.°

355

HAMLET. It is not very strange; for my uncle is King of Denmark, and those that would make mouths° at him while my father lived give twenty, forty, fifty, a hundred ducats° apiece for his picture in little.° 'Sblood,° there is something in this more than natural, if philosophy° could find

360

it out.

A flourish [of trumpets within].

GUILDENSTERN. There are the players.

HAMLET. Gentlemen, you are welcome to Elsinore. Your hands, come then. Th' appurtenance° of welcome is fashion and ceremony. Let me comply° with you in this

365

garb,° lest my extent° to the players, which, I tell you, must show fairly outwards,° should more appear like entertainment° than yours. You are welcome. But my uncle-father and aunt-mother are deceived.

GUILDENSTERN. In what, my dear lord?

370

HAMLET. I am but mad north-north-west.° When the wind is southerly I know a hawk from a handsaw.°

Enter Polonius.

POLONIUS. Well be with you, gentlemen!

HAMLET. Hark you, Guildenstern, and you too; at each ear a hearer. That great baby you see there is not yet out of his

375

swaddling clouts.°

---

317 gratis for nothing **humorous man** eccentric character, dominated by one trait or "humor" **318 in peace** i.e., with full license **319 tickle o' the sear** easy on the trigger, ready to laugh easily (A *sear* is part of a gunlock.) **320 halt** limp **322 tragedians** actors **323 residence** remaining in their usual place, i.e., in the city **325 inhibition** formal prohibition (from acting plays in the city) **326 late** recent **innovation** i.e., the new fashion in satirical plays performed by boy actors in the "private" theaters; or possibly a political uprising; or the strict limitations set on the theaters in London in 1600 **331 keeps** continues **wonted** usual **332 aerie** nest **eyases** young hawks **333 cry ... question** speak shrilly, dominating the controversy (in decrying the public theaters) **333–334 tyrannically** outrageously **335 berattle** berate, clamor against **common stages** public theaters **336 many wearing rapiers** i.e., many men of fashion, afraid to patronize the common players for fear of being satirized by the poets writing for the boy actors **goose quills** i.e., pens of satirists **339 escoted** maintained **quality** (acting) profession **339–340 no longer ... sing** i.e., only until their voices change **341 common** regular, adult **342 like** likely **if ... better** if they find no better way to support themselves **343–344 succession** i.e., future careers **345 to-do** ado **346 tar** set on (as dogs)

347–349 There ... question i.e., for a while, no money was offered by the acting companies to playwrights for the plot to a play unless the satirical poets who wrote for the boys and the adult actors came to blows in the play itself **353 carry it away** i.e., win the day **354–355 Hercules ... load** (Thought to be an allusion to the sign of the Globe Theatre, which was Hercules bearing the world on his shoulders.) **330–355 How ... load too** (The passage, omitted from the early quartos, alludes to the so-called War of the Theaters, 1599–1602, the rivalry between the children's companies and the adult actors.) **357 mouths** faces **358 ducats** gold coins **359 in little** in miniature **'Sblood** by God's (Christ's) blood **360 philosophy** i.e., scientific inquiry **364 appurtenance** proper accompaniment **365 comply** observe the formalities of courtesy **366 garb** i.e., manner. **my extent** that which I extend, i.e., my polite behavior **367 show fairly outwards** show every evidence of cordiality **367–368 entertainment** a (warm) reception **371 north-north-west** just off true north, only partly **372 hawk, handsaw** two very different things, though also perhaps meaning a mattock (or *hack*) and a carpenter's cutting tool, respectively; also birds, with a play on *hernshaw*, or heron **376 swaddling clouts** cloths in which to wrap a newborn baby

ROSENCRANTZ. Haply° he is the second time come to them,
  for they say an old man is twice a child.

HAMLET. I will prophesy he comes to tell me of the players.
380 Mark it.—You say right, sir, o' Monday morning, 'twas
  then indeed.

POLONIUS. My lord, I have news to tell you.

HAMLET. My lord, I have news to tell you. When Roscius°
  was an actor in Rome—

385 POLONIUS. The actors are come hither, my lord.

HAMLET. Buzz,° buzz!

POLONIUS. Upon my honor—

HAMLET. Then came each actor on his ass.

POLONIUS. The best actors in the world, either for tragedy,
390 comedy, history, pastoral, pastoral-comical, historical-
  pastoral, tragical-historical, tragical-comical-historical-
  pastoral, scene individable,° or poem unlimited.°
  Seneca° cannot be too heavy, nor Plautus° too light. For
  the law of writ and the liberty,° these° are the only men.

395 HAMLET. O Jephthah, judge of Israel,° what a treasure hadst
  thou!

POLONIUS. What a treasure had he, my lord?

HAMLET.
  Why,
    "One fair daughter, and no more,
400   The which he lovèd passing° well."

POLONIUS [aside]. Still on my daughter.

HAMLET. Am I not i' the right, old Jephthah?

POLONIUS. If you call me Jephthah, my lord, I have a daughter that I love passing well.

405 HAMLET. Nay, that follows not.

POLONIUS. What follows then, my lord?

HAMLET. Why,
    "As by lot,° God wot,"°
  and then, you know,
410   "It came to pass, as most like° it was"—
  the first row° of the pious chanson° will show you more,
  for look where my abridgement° comes.

Enter the Players.

You are welcome, masters; welcome, all. I am glad to see
thee well. Welcome, good friends. O, old friend! Why,
thy face is valanced° since I saw thee last. Com'st thou   415
to beard° me in Denmark? What, my young lady° and
mistress! By 'r Lady,° your ladyship is nearer to heaven
than when I saw you last, by the altitude of a chopine.°
Pray God your voice, like a piece of uncurrent° gold, be
not cracked within the ring.° Masters, you are all wel-   420
come. We'll e'en to 't° like French falconers, fly at anything we see. We'll have a speech straight.° Come, give
us a taste of your quality.° Come, a passionate speech.

FIRST PLAYER. What speech, my good lord?

HAMLET. I heard thee speak me a speech once, but it was   425
never acted, or if it was, not above once, for the play, I remember, pleased not the million; 'twas caviar to the general.° But it was—as I received it, and others, whose
judgments in such matters cried in the top of° mine—an
excellent play, well digested° in the scenes, set down   430
with as much modesty° as cunning.° I remember one said
there were no sallets° in the lines to make the matter savory, nor no matter in the phrase that might indict° the
author of affectation, but called it an honest method, as
wholesome as sweet, and by very much more handsome°   435
than fine.° One speech in 't I chiefly loved: 'twas Aeneas'
tale to Dido, and thereabout of it especially when he
speaks of Priam's slaughter.° If it live in your memory, begin at this line: let me see, let me see—
  "The rugged Pyrrhus,° like th' Hyrcanian° beast"—   440
'Tis not so. It begins with Pyrrhus:
  "The rugged° Pyrrhus, he whose sable° arms,
  Black as his purpose, did the night resemble

---

415 valanced fringed (with a beard) **416 beard** confront, challenge (with obvious pun) **young lady** i.e., boy playing women's
parts **417 By 'r Lady** by Our Lady **418 chopine** thick-soled
shoe of Italian fashion **419 uncurrent** not passable as lawful
coinage **420 cracked . . . ring** i.e., changed from adolescent to
male voice, no longer suitable for women's roles. (Coins featured
rings enclosing the sovereign's head; if the coin was cracked within
this ring, it was unfit for currency.) **421 e'en to 't** go at it **422
straight** at once **423 quality** professional skill **427–428 caviar
to the general** caviar to the multitude, i.e., a choice dish too elegant for coarse tastes **429 cried in the top of** i.e., spoke with
greater authority than **430 digested** arranged, ordered **431
modesty** moderation, restraint **cunning** skill **432 sallets** i.e.,
something savory, spicy improprieties **433 indict** convict **435
handsome** well-proportioned. **436 fine** elaborately ornamented,
showy **438 Priam's slaughter** the slaying of the ruler of Troy,
when the Greeks finally took the city **440 Pyrrhus** a Greek hero
in the Trojan War, also known as Neoptolemus, son of Achilles—
another avenging son **Hyrcanian beast** i.e., tiger. (On the death
of Priam, see Virgil, *Aeneid,* 2.506 ff.; compare the whole speech
with Marlowe's *Dido Queen of Carthage,* 2.1.214 ff. On the *Hyrcanian* tiger, see *Aeneid,* 4.366–367. Hyrcania is on the Caspian Sea.)
442 rugged shaggy, savage **sable** black (for reasons of camouflage
during the episode of the Trojan horse)

---

377 Haply perhaps **383 Roscius** a famous Roman actor who died
in 62 B.C. **386 Buzz** (An interjection used to denote stale news.)
392 scene individable a play observing the unity of place; or perhaps one that is unclassifiable, or performed without intermission
poem unlimited a play disregarding the unities of time and place;
one that is all-inclusive **393 Seneca** writer of Latin tragedies
Plautus writer of Latin comedy **394 law . . . liberty** dramatic
composition both according to the rules and disregarding the rules
these i.e., the actors **395 Jephthah . . . Israel** (Jephthah had to
sacrifice his daughter; see Judges 11. Hamlet goes on to quote from
a ballad on the theme.) **400 passing** surpassingly **408 lot**
chance **wot** knows **410 like** likely, probable **411 row** stanza.
chanson ballad, song **412 my abridgement** something that cuts
short my conversation; also, a diversion

When he lay couchèd° in the ominous horse,°
445   Hath now this dread and black complexion smeared
With heraldry more dismal.° Head to foot
Now is he total gules,° horridly tricked°
With blood of fathers, mothers, daughters, sons,
Baked and impasted° with the parching streets,°
450   That lend a tyrannous° and a damnèd light
To their lord's° murder. Roasted in wrath and fire,
And thus o'ersizèd° with coagulate gore,
With eyes like carbuncles,° the hellish Pyrrhus
Old grandsire Priam seeks."

455 So proceed you.

POLONIUS.
  'Fore God, my lord, well spoken, with good accent and
  good discretion.

FIRST PLAYER.   "Anon he finds him
Striking too short at Greeks. His antique° sword,
460   Rebellious to his arm, lies where it falls,
Repugnant° to command. Unequal matched,
Pyrrhus at Priam drives, in rage strikes wide,
But with the whiff and wind of his fell° sword
Th' unnervèd° father falls. Then senseless Ilium,°
465   Seeming to feel this blow, with flaming top
Stoops to his° base, and with a hideous crash
Takes prisoner Pyrrhus' ear. For, lo! His sword,
Which was declining° on the milky° head
Of reverend Priam, seemed i' th' air to stick.
470   So as a painted° tyrant Pyrrhus stood,
And, like a neutral to his will and matter,°
Did nothing.
But as we often see against° some storm
A silence in the heavens, the rack° stand still,
475   The bold winds speechless, and the orb° below
As hush as death, anon the dreadful thunder
Doth rend the region,° so, after Pyrrhus' pause,
A rousèd vengeance sets him new a-work
And never did the Cyclops'° hammers fall

On Mars's armor forged for proof eterne°   480
With less remorse° than Pyrrhus' bleeding sword
Now falls on Priam.
Out, out, thou strumpet Fortune! All you gods
In general synod° take away her power!
Break all the spokes and fellies° from her wheel,   485
And bowl the round nave° down the hill of heaven°
As low as to the fiends!"

POLONIUS. This is too long.

HAMLET. It shall to the barber's with your beard.—Prithee,
say on. He's for a jig° or a tale of bawdry, or he sleeps. Say   490
on; come to Hecuba.°

FIRST PLAYER.
  "But who, ah woe! had° seen the moblèd° queen"—

HAMLET. "The moblèd queen?"

POLONIUS. That's good. "Moblèd queen" is good.

FIRST PLAYER.
  "Run barefoot up and down, threat'ning the flames°   495
With bisson rheum,° a clout° upon that head
Where late° the diadem stood, and, for a robe,
About her lank and all o'erteemèd° loins
A blanket, in the alarm of fear caught up—
Who this had seen, with tongue in venom steeped,   500
'Gainst Fortune's state° would treason have pro-
  nounced.°
But if the gods themselves did see her then
When she saw Pyrrhus make malicious sport
In mincing with his sword her husband's limbs,
The instant burst of clamor that she made,   505
Unless things mortal move them not at all,
Would have made milch° the burning eyes of heaven,°
And passion° in the gods."

POLONIUS. Look whe'er° he has not turned his color and has
tears in 's eyes. Prithee, no more.   510

HAMLET. 'Tis well; I'll have thee speak out the rest of this
soon.—Good my lord, will you see the players well bestowed?° Do you hear, let them be well used, for they are
the abstract° and brief chronicles of the time. After your
death you were better have a bad epitaph than their ill   515
report while you live.

POLONIUS. My lord, I will use them according to their desert.

---

444 couchèd concealed   **ominous horse** fateful Trojan horse, by
which the Greeks gained access to Troy   **446 dismal** ill-omened
447 total gules entirely red. (A heraldic term.)   **tricked** spotted
and smeared. (Heraldic.)   **449 impasted** crusted, like a thick paste
with . . . streets by the parching heat of the streets (because of the
fires everywhere)   **450 tyrannous** cruel   **451 their lord's** i.e.,
Priam's   **452 o'ersizèd** covered as with size or glue   **453 carbun-**
cles large fiery-red precious stones thought to emit their own light
459 antique ancient, long-used   **461 Repugnant** disobedient, resistant   **463 fell** cruel   **464 unnervèd** strengthless   **senseless Il-**
ium inanimate citadel of Troy   **466 his** its   **468 declining** descending   **milky** white-haired   **470 painted** i.e., painted in a
picture   **471 like . . . matter** i.e., as though suspended between his
intention and its fulfillment   **473 against** just before   **474 rack**
mass of clouds   **475 orb** globe, earth   **477 region** sky   **479 Cy-**
clops giant armor makers in the smithy of Vulcan

480 proof eterne eternal resistance to assault   **481 remorse** pity
484 synod assembly   **485 fellies** pieces of wood forming the rim of
a wheel   **486 nave** hub   **hill of heaven** Mount Olympus   **490 jig**
comic song and dance often given at the end of a play   **491**
Hecuba wife of Priam   **492 who . . . had** anyone who had (also in
line 500)   **moblèd** muffled   **495 threat'ning the flames** i.e.,
weeping hard enough to dampen the flames   **496 bisson rheum**
blinding tears   **clout** cloth   **497 late** lately   **498 all o'erteemèd**
utterly worn out with bearing children   **501 state** rule, managing
pronounced proclaimed   **507 milch** milky, moist with tears
burning eyes of heaven i.e., heavenly bodies   **508 passion** overpowering emotion   **509 whe'er** whether   **513 bestowed** lodged
514 abstract summary account

HAMLET. God's bodikin,° man, much better. Use every man
after his desert, and who shall scape whipping? Use them
520 after° your own honor and dignity. The less they deserve,
the more merit is in your bounty. Take them in.

POLONIUS. Come, sirs.

[*Exit.*]

HAMLET. Follow him, friends. We'll hear a play tomorrow.
[*As they start to leave, Hamlet detains the First Player.*] Dost
525 thou hear me, old friend? Can you play *The Murder of
Gonzago?*

FIRST PLAYER. Ay, my lord.

HAMLET. We'll ha 't° tomorrow night. You could, for a need,
study° a speech of some dozen or sixteen lines which I
530 would set down and insert in 't, could you not?

FIRST PLAYER. Ay, my lord.

HAMLET. Very well. Follow that lord, and look you mock him
not. (*Exeunt Players.*) My good friends, I'll leave you till
night. You are welcome to Elsinore.

535 ROSENCRANTZ. Good my lord!

Exeunt [*Rosencrantz and Guildenstern*].

HAMLET.
Ay, so, goodbye to you.—Now I am alone.
O, what a rogue and peasant slave am I!
Is it not monstrous that this player here,
But° in a fiction, in a dream of passion,
540 Could force his soul so to his own conceit°
That from her working° all his visage wanned,°
Tears in his eyes, distraction in his aspect,°
A broken voice, and his whole function suiting
With forms to his conceit?° And all for nothing!
545 For Hecuba!
What's Hecuba to him, or he to Hecuba,
That he should weep for her? What would he do
Had he the motive and the cue for passion
That I have? He would drown the stage with tears
550 And cleave the general ear° with horrid° speech,
Make mad the guilty and appall° the free,°
Confound the ignorant,° and amaze° indeed
The very faculties of eyes and ears. Yet I,
A dull and muddy-mettled° rascal, peak°

Like John-a-dreams,° unpregnant of° my cause,   555
And can say nothing—no, not for a king
Upon whose property° and most dear life
A damned defeat° was made. Am I a coward?
Who calls me villain? Breaks my pate° across?
Plucks off my beard and blows it in my face?   560
Tweaks me by the nose? Gives me the lie i' the throat°
As deep as to the lungs? Who does me this?
Ha, 'swounds,° I should take it; for it cannot be
But I am pigeon-livered° and lack gall
To make oppression bitter,° or ere this   565
I should ha' fatted all the region kites°
With this slave's offal.° Bloody, bawdy villain!
Remorseless,° treacherous, lecherous, kindless° villain!
O, vengeance!
Why, what an ass am I! This is most brave,°   570
That I, the son of a dear father murdered,
Prompted to my revenge by heaven and hell,
Must like a whore unpack my heart with words
And fall a-cursing, like a very drab,°
A scullion!° Fie upon 't, foh! About,° my brains!   575
Hum, I have heard
That guilty creatures sitting at a play
Have by the very cunning° of the scene°
Been struck so to the soul that presently°
They have proclaimed their malefactions;   580
For murder, though it have no tongue, will speak
With most miraculous organ. I'll have these players
Play something like the murder of my father
Before mine uncle. I'll observe his looks;
I'll tent° him to the quick.° If 'a do blench,°   585
I know my course. The spirit that I have seen
May be the devil, and the devil hath power
T' assume a pleasing shape; yea, and perhaps,
Out of my weakness and my melancholy,
As he is very potent with such spirits,°   590
Abuses° me to damn me. I'll have grounds
More relative° than this. The play's the thing

518 God's bodikin by God's (Christ's) little body, *bodykin* (Not to
be confused with *bodkin*, "dagger.")   **520 after** according to   **528
ha 't** have it   **529 study** memorize   **539 But** merely   **540 force
. . . conceit** bring his innermost being so entirely into accord with
his conception (of the role)   **541 from her working** as a result of,
or in response to, his soul's activity   **wanned** grew pale   **542 aspect** look, glance   **543–544 his whole . . . conceit** all his bodily
powers responding with actions to suit his thought   **550 the general ear** everyone's ear   **horrid** horrible   **551 appall** (Literally,
make pale.)   **free** innocent   **552 Confound the ignorant** i.e.,
dumbfound those who know nothing of the crime that has been committed   **amaze** stun   **554 muddy-mettled** dull-spirited   **peak**
mope, pine

555 John-a-dreams a sleepy, dreaming idler   **unpregnant of** not
quickened by   **557 property** i.e., the crown; also character, quality
558 damned defeat damnable act of destruction   **559 pate** head
561 Gives . . . throat calls me an out-and-out liar   **563 'swounds**
by his (Christ's) wounds   **564 pigeon-livered** (The pigeon or dove
was popularly supposed to be mild because it secreted no gall.)   **565
bitter** i.e., bitter to me   **566 region kites** kites (birds of prey) of the
air   **567 offal** entrails   **568 Remorseless** pitiless   **kindless** unnatural   **570 brave** fine, admirable (Said ironically.)   **574 drab** whore
575 scullion menial kitchen servant (apt to be foulmouthed)
About about it, to work   **578 cunning** art, skill   **scene** dramatic
presentation   **579 presently** at once   **585 tent** probe   **the quick**
the tender part of a wound, the core   **blench** quail, flinch   **590
spirits** humors (of melancholy)   **591 Abuses** deludes   **592 relative**
cogent, pertinent

Wherein I'll catch the conscience of the King.

Exit.

3.1 *Enter King, Queen, Polonius, Ophelia, Rosencrantz,*
Guildenstern, lords.

KING.

And can you by no drift of conference°
Get from him why he puts on this confusion,
Grating so harshly all his days of quiet
With turbulent and dangerous lunacy?

ROSENCRANTZ.

5   He does confess he feels himself distracted,
But from what cause 'a will by no means speak.

GUILDENSTERN.

Nor do we find him forward° to be sounded,°
But with a crafty madness keeps aloof
When we would bring him on to some confession
Of his true state.

10   QUEEN.   Did he receive you well?

ROSENCRANTZ.

Most like a gentleman.

GUILDENSTERN.

But with much forcing of his disposition.°

ROSENCRANTZ.

Niggard° of question,° but of our demands
Most free in his reply.

QUEEN.   Did you assay° him

15   To any pastime?

ROSENCRANTZ.

Madam, it so fell out that certain players
We o'erraught° on the way. Of these we told him,
And there did seem in him a kind of joy
To hear of it. They are here about the court,
20   And, as I think, they have already order
This night to play before him.

POLONIUS.   'Tis most true,
And he beseeched me to entreat Your Majesties
To hear and see the matter.

KING.

With all my heart, and it doth much content me
25   To hear him so inclined.
Good gentlemen, give him a further edge°
And drive his purpose into these delights.

ROSENCRANTZ.

We shall, my lord.

Exeunt Rosencrantz and Guildenstern.

KING.   Sweet Gertrude, leave us too,
For we have closely° sent for Hamlet hither,
That he, as 'twere by accident, may here   30
Affront° Ophelia.
Her father and myself, lawful espials,°
Will so bestow ourselves that seeing, unseen,
We may of their encounter frankly judge,
And gather by him, as he is behaved,   35
If 't be th' affliction of his love or no
That thus he suffers for.

QUEEN.   I shall obey you.
And for your part, Ophelia, I do wish
That your good beauties be the happy cause
Of Hamlet's wildness. So shall I hope your virtues 40
Will bring him to his wonted° way again,
To both your honors.

OPHELIA.   Madam, I wish it may.

[Exit Queen.]

POLONIUS.

Ophelia, walk you here.—Gracious,° so please you,
We will bestow° ourselves. [*To Ophelia.*] Read on this
    book,

[giving her a book]

That show of such an exercise° may color°   45
Your loneliness.° We are oft to blame in this—
'Tis too much proved°—that with devotion's visage
And pious action we do sugar o'er
The devil himself.

KING [*aside*].

O, 'tis too true!   50
How smart a lash that speech doth give my conscience!
The harlot's cheek, beautied with plastering art,
Is not more ugly to° the thing° that helps it
Than is my deed to my most painted word.
O heavy burden!   55

POLONIUS.

I hear him coming. Let's withdraw, my lord.

[The King and Polonius withdraw.°]

Enter Hamlet. [Ophelia pretends to read a book.]

---

29 closely privately   **31 Affront** confront, meet   **32 espials** spies
41 wonted accustomed   **43 Gracious** Your Grace (i.e., the King)
44 bestow conceal   **45 exercise** religious exercise. (The book she
reads is one of devotion.)   **color** give a plausible appearance to
46 loneliness being alone   **47 too much proved** too often shown
to be true, too often practiced   **53 to** compared to   **the thing** i.e.,
the cosmetic   **56 s.d. withdraw** (The King and Polonius may retire behind an arras. The stage directions specify that they "enter"
again near the end of the scene.)

3.1 Location: The castle. **1 drift of conference** directing of conversation   **7 forward** willing   **sounded** questioned   **12 disposition** inclination   **13 Niggard** stingy   **question** conversation   **14
assay** try to win   **17 o'erraught** overtook   **26 edge** incitement

HAMLET.
To be, or not to be, that is the question:
Whether 'tis nobler in the mind to suffer
The slings° and arrows of outrageous fortune,
60   Or to take arms against a sea of troubles
And by opposing end them. To die, to sleep—
No more—and by a sleep to say we end
The heartache and the thousand natural shocks
That flesh is heir to. 'Tis a consummation
65   Devoutly to be wished. To die, to sleep;
To sleep, perchance to dream. Ay, there's the rub,°
For in that sleep of death what dreams may come,
When we have shuffled° off this mortal coil,°
Must give us pause. There's the respect°
70   That makes calamity of so long life.°
For who would bear the whips and scorns of time,
Th' oppressor's wrong, the proud man's contumely,°
The pangs of disprized° love, the law's delay,
The insolence of office,° and the spurns°
75   That patient merit of th' unworthy takes,°
When he himself might his quietus° make
With a bare bodkin?° Who would fardels° bear,
To grunt and sweat under a weary life,
But that the dread of something after death,
80   The undiscovered country from whose bourn°
No traveler returns, puzzles the will,
And makes us rather bear those ills we have
Than fly to others that we know not of?
Thus conscience does make cowards of us all;
85   And thus the native hue° of resolution
Is sicklied o'er with the pale cast° of thought,
And enterprises of great pitch° and moment°
With this regard° their currents° turn awry
And lose the name of action.—Soft you° now,
90   The fair Ophelia. Nymph, in thy orisons°
Be all my sins remembered.
OPHELIA.   Good my lord,
How does your honor for this many a day?
HAMLET.
I humbly thank you; well, well, well.

OPHELIA.
My lord, I have remembrances of yours,
That I have longèd long to redeliver.   95
I pray you, now receive them.   [*She offers tokens.*]
HAMLET.
No, not I, I never gave you aught.
OPHELIA.
My honored lord, you know right well you did,
And with them words of so sweet breath composed
As made the things more rich. Their perfume lost,   100
Take these again, for to the noble mind
Rich gifts wax poor when givers prove unkind.
There, my lord.   [*She gives tokens.*]
HAMLET. Ha, ha! Are you honest?°
OPHELIA. My lord?   105
HAMLET. Are you fair?°
OPHELIA. What means your lordship?
HAMLET. That if you be honest and fair, your honesty° should
admit no discourse° to your beauty.
OPHELIA. Could beauty, my lord, have better commerce°   110
than with honesty?
HAMLET. Ay, truly, for the power of beauty will sooner trans-
form honesty from what it is to a bawd than the force of
honesty can translate beauty into his° likeness. This was
sometime° a paradox,° but now the time° gives it proof. I   115
did love you once.
OPHELIA. Indeed, my lord, you made me believe so.
HAMLET. You should not have believed me, for virtue cannot
so inoculate° our old stock but we shall relish of it.° I
loved you not.   120
OPHELIA. I was the more deceived.
HAMLET. Get thee to a nunnery.° Why wouldst thou be a
breeder of sinners? I am myself indifferent honest,° but
yet I could accuse me of such things that it were better
my mother had not borne me: I am very proud, revenge- 125
ful, ambitious, with more offenses at my beck° than I
have thoughts to put them in, imagination to give them
shape, or time to act them in. What should such fellows
as I do crawling between earth and heaven? We are arrant knaves all; believe none of us. Go thy ways to a nun- 130
nery. Where's your father?
OPHELIA. At home, my lord.

---

59 slings missiles   **66 rub** (Literally, an obstacle in the game of
bowls.)   **68 shuffled** sloughed, cast   **coil** turmoil   **69 respect**
consideration   **70 of . . . life** so long-lived, something we willingly
endure for so long (also suggesting that long life is itself a calamity)
72 contumely insolent abuse   **73 disprized** unvalued   **74 office**
officialdom   **spurns** insults   **75 of . . . takes** receives from unworthy persons   **76 quietus** acquittance; here, death   **77 a bare bodkin** a mere dagger, unsheathed   **fardels** burdens   **80 bourn** frontier, boundary   **85 native hue** natural color, complexion   **86 cast**
tinge, shade of color   **87 pitch** height (as of a falcon's flight)   **moment** importance   **88 regard** respect, consideration   **currents**
courses   **89 Soft you** i.e., wait a minute, gently   **90 orisons**
prayers

104 honest (1) truthful (2) chaste   **106 fair** (1) beautiful (2) just,
honorable   **108 your honesty** your chastity   **109 discourse** to familiar dealings with   **110 commerce** dealings, intercourse   **114
his** its   **115 sometime** formerly   **a paradox** a view opposite to
commonly held opinion   **the time** the present age   **119 inocu-
late** graft, be engrafted to   **but . . . it** that we do not still have
about us a taste of the old stock, i.e., retain our sinfulness   **122
nunnery** convent (with possibly an awareness that the word was
also used derisively to denote a brothel)   **123 indifferent honest**
reasonably virtuous   **126 beck** command

HAMLET. Let the doors be shut upon him, that he may play
the fool nowhere but in 's own house. Farewell.

135 OPHELIA. O, help him, you sweet heavens!

HAMLET. If thou dost marry, I'll give thee this plague for thy
dowry: be thou as chaste as ice, as pure as snow, thou
shalt not escape calumny. Get thee to a nunnery,
farewell. Or, if thou wilt needs marry, marry a fool, for

140 wise men know well enough what monsters° you° make
of them. To a nunnery, go, and quickly too. Farewell.

OPHELIA. Heavenly powers, restore him!

HAMLET. I have heard of your paintings too, well enough.
God hath given you one face, and you make yourselves

145 another. You jig,° you amble,° and you lisp, you nickname God's creatures,° and make your wantonness your
ignorance.° Go to, I'll no more on 't;° it hath made me
mad. I say we will have no more marriage. Those that are
married already—all but one—shall live. The rest shall

150 keep as they are. To a nunnery, go.

Exit.

OPHELIA.
O, what a noble mind is here o'erthrown!
The courtier's, soldier's, scholar's, eye, tongue, sword,
Th' expectancy° and rose° of the fair state,
The glass of fashion and the mold of form,°

155 Th' observed of all observers,° quite, quite down!
And I, of ladies most deject and wretched,
That sucked the honey of his music° vows,
Now see that noble and most sovereign reason
Like sweet bells jangled out of tune and harsh,

160 That unmatched form and feature of blown° youth
Blasted° with ecstasy.° O, woe is me,
T' have seen what I have seen, see what I see!

Enter King and Polonius.

KING.
Love? His affections° do not that way tend;

165 Nor what he spake, though it lacked form a little,
Was not like madness. There's something in his soul
O'er which his melancholy sits on brood,°
And I do doubt° the hatch and the disclose°

Will be some danger; which for to prevent,
I have in quick determination
Thus set it down:° he shall with speed to England   170
For the demand of° our neglected tribute.
Haply the seas and countries different
With variable objects° shall expel
This something-settled matter in his heart,°
Whereon his brains still° beating puts him thus   175
From fashion of himself.° What think you on 't?

POLONIUS.
It shall do well. But yet do I believe
The origin and commencement of his grief
Sprung from neglected love.—How now, Ophelia?
You need not tell us what Lord Hamlet said;   180
We heard it all.—My lord, do as you please,
But, if you hold it fit, after the play
Let his queen-mother° all alone entreat him
To show his grief. Let her be round° with him;
And I'll be placed, so please you, in the ear   185
Of all their conference. If she find him not,°
To England send him, or confine him where
Your wisdom best shall think.

KING.   It shall be so.
Madness in great ones must not unwatched go.

Exeunt.

3.2 *Enter Hamlet and three of the Players.*

HAMLET. Speak the speech, I pray you, as I pronounced it to
you, trippingly on the tongue. But if you mouth it, as
many of our players° do, I had as lief° the town crier
spoke my lines. Nor do not saw the air too much with
your hand, thus, but use all gently; for in the very torrent,   5
tempest, and, as I may say, whirlwind of your passion, you
must acquire and beget a temperance that may give it
smoothness. O, it offends me to the soul to hear a robus-
tious° periwig-pated° fellow tear a passion to tatters, to
very rags, to split the ears of the groundlings,° who for   10
the most part are capable of° nothing but inexplicable
dumb shows° and noise. I would have such a fellow

---

140 **monsters** (An illusion to the horns of a cuckold.)   **you** i.e.,
you women   145 **jig** dance   **amble** move coyly   145–146 **you
nickname . . . creatures** i.e., you give trendy names to things in
place of their God-given names   146–147 **make . . . ignorance**
i.e., excuse your affectation on the grounds of pretended ignorance
147 **on 't** of it   153 **expectancy** hope   **rose** ornament   154 **The
glass . . . form** the mirror of true fashioning and the pattern of
courtly behavior   155 **Th' observed . . . observers** i.e., the center
of attention and honor in the court   157 **music** musical, sweetly
uttered   160 **blown** blooming   161 **Blasted** withered   **ecstasy**
madness   163 **affections** emotions, feelings   166 **sits on brood**
sits like a bird on a nest, about to *hatch* mischief (line 162)   167
doubt fear   **disclose** disclosure, hatching

170 **set it down** resolved   171 **For . . . of** to demand   173 **variable objects** various sights and surroundings to divert him   174
This something . . . heart the strange matter settled in his heart
175 **still** continually   176 **From . . . himself** out of his natural
manner   183 **queen-mother** queen and mother   184 **round**
blunt   186 **find him not** fails to discover what is troubling him
3.2 Location: The castle. 3 our players players nowadays   **I had
as lief** I would just as soon   8–9 **robustious** violent, boisterous
periwig-pated wearing a wig   10 **groundlings** spectators who paid
least and stood in the yard of the theater   11 **capable of** able to
understand   12 **dumb shows** mimed performances, often used before Shakespeare's time to precede a play or each act

whipped for o'erdoing Termagant.° It out-Herods
Herod.° Pray you, avoid it.

15 FIRST PLAYER. I warrant your honor.

HAMLET. Be not too tame neither, but let your own discretion be your tutor. Suit the action to the word, the word
to the action, with this special observance, that you o'er-
step not the modesty° of nature. For anything so o'erdone
20 is from° the purpose of playing, whose end, both at the
first and now, was and is to hold as 't were the mirror up
to nature, to show virtue her feature, scorn° her own image, and the very age and body of the time° his° form and
pressure.° Now this overdone or come tardy off,° though
25 it makes the unskillful° laugh, cannot but make the judicious grieve, the censure of the which one° must in your
allowance° o'erweigh a whole theater of others. O, there
be players that I have seen play, and heard others praise,
and that highly, not to speak it profanely,° that, neither
30 having th' accent of Christians° nor the gait of Christian,
pagan, nor man,° have so strutted and bellowed that I
have thought some of nature's journeymen° had made
men and not made them well, they imitated humanity so
abominably.°

35 FIRST PLAYER. I hope we have reformed that indifferently°
with us, sir.

HAMLET. O, reform it altogether. And let those that play
your clowns speak no more than is set down for them; for
there be of them° that will themselves laugh, to set on
40 some quantity of barren° spectators to laugh too, though
in the meantime some necessary question of the play be
then to be considered. That's villainous, and shows a
most pitiful ambition in the fool that uses it. Go make
you ready.

                                                        [*Exeunt Players.*]

Enter Polonius, Guildenstern, and Rosencrantz.

How now, my lord, will the King hear this piece of work?   45
POLONIUS.
And the Queen too, and that presently.°
HAMLET.
Bid the players make haste.

                                                        [*Exit Polonius.*]

Will you two help to hasten them?
ROSENCRANTZ.
Ay, my lord.

                                                        Exeunt they two.

HAMLET.   What ho, Horatio!

Enter Horatio.

HORATIO.
Here, sweet lord, at your service.   50
HAMLET.
Horatio, thou art e'en as just a man
As e'er my conversation coped withal.°
HORATIO.
O, my dear lord—
HAMLET.   Nay, do not think I flatter,
For what advancement may I hope from thee
That no revenue hast but thy good spirits   55
To feed and clothe thee? Why should the poor be flat-
    tered?
No, let the candied° tongue lick absurd pomp,
And crook the pregnant° hinges of the knee
Where thrift° may follow fawning. Dost thou hear?
Since my dear soul was mistress of her choice   60
And could of men distinguish her election,°
Sh' hath sealed thee° for herself, for thou hast been
As one, in suffering all, that suffers nothing,
A man that Fortune's buffets and rewards
Hast ta'en with equal thanks; and blest are those   65
Whose blood° and judgment are so well commeddled°
That they are not a pipe for Fortune's finger
To sound what stop° she please. Give me that man
That is not passion's slave, and I will wear him
In my heart's core, ay, in my heart of heart,   70
As I do thee.—Something too much of this.—
There is a play tonight before the King.
One scene of it comes near the circumstance
Which I have told thee of my father's death.
I prithee, when thou seest that act afoot,   75

---

13 Termagant a supposed deity of the Mohammedans, not found in
any English medieval play but elsewhere portrayed as violent and
blustering **14 Herod** Herod of Jewry. (A character in *The Slaughter of the Innocents* and other cycle plays. The part was played with
great noise and fury.) **19 modesty** restraint, moderation **20
from** contrary to **22 scorn** i.e., something foolish and deserving
of scorn **23 the very . . . time** i.e., the present state of affairs **his**
its **24 pressure** stamp, impressed character **come tardy off** inadequately done **25 the unskillful** those lacking in judgment **26
the censure . . . one** the judgment of even one of whom **27 your
allowance** your scale of values **29 not . . . profanely** (Hamlet an-
ticipates his idea in lines 27–29 that some men were not made by
God at all.) **30 Christians** i.e., ordinary decent folk **31 nor
man** i.e., nor any human being at all **32 journeymen** laborers
who are not yet masters in their trade **34 abominably** (Shakespeare's usual spelling, *abhominably*, suggests a literal though etymo-
logically incorrect meaning, "removed from human nature.") **35
indifferently** tolerably **39 of them** some among them **40 barren** i.e., of wit

46 presently at once **52 my . . . withal** my dealings encountered
57 candied sugared, flattering **58 pregnant** compliant **59 thrift**
profit **61 could . . . election** could make distinguishing choices
among persons **62 sealed thee** (Literally, as one would seal a legal
document to mark possession.) **66 blood** passion **commeddled**
commingled **68 stop** hole in a wind instrument for controlling
the sound

Even with the very comment of thy soul°
Observe my uncle. If his occulted° guilt
Do not itself unkennel° in one speech,
It is a damnèd° ghost that we have seen,
80   And my imaginations are as foul
As Vulcan's stithy.° Give him heedful note,
For I mine eyes will rivet to his face,
And after we will both our judgments join
In censure of his seeming.°

HORATIO.   Well, my lord.
85   If 'a steal aught° the whilst this play is playing
And scape detecting, I will pay the theft.

[*Flourish.*] *Enter trumpets and kettledrums, King, Queen,*
Polonius, Ophelia, [Rosencrantz, Guildenstern, and other
lords, with guards carrying torches].

HAMLET.
They are coming to the play. I must be idle.°
Get you a place.   [*The King, Queen, and courtiers sit.*]
KING. How fares our cousin° Hamlet?
90   HAMLET. Excellent, i' faith, of the chameleon's dish:° I eat
the air, promise-crammed. You cannot feed capons° so.
KING. I have nothing with° this answer, Hamlet. These
words are not mine.°
HAMLET. No, nor mine now.° [*To Polonius.*] My lord, you
95   played once i' th' university, you say?
POLONIUS. That did I, my lord, and was accounted a good ac-
tor.
HAMLET. What did you enact?
POLONIUS. I did enact Julius Caesar. I was killed i' the Capi-
100   tol; Brutus killed me.
HAMLET. It was a brute° part° of him to kill so capital a calf°
there.—Be the players ready?
ROSENCRANTZ. Ay, my lord. They stay upon° your patience.
QUEEN. Come hither, my dear Hamlet, sit by me.
105   HAMLET. No, good Mother, here's metal° more attractive.

POLONIUS [*to the King*]. O, ho, do you mark that?
HAMLET. Lady, shall I lie in your lap?

[*Lying down at Ophelia's feet.*]

OPHELIA. No, my lord.
HAMLET. I mean, my head upon your lap?
OPHELIA. Ay, my lord.   110
HAMLET. Do you think I meant country matters?°
OPHELIA. I think nothing, my lord.
HAMLET. That's a fair thought to lie between maids' legs.
OPHELIA. What is, my lord?
HAMLET. Nothing.°   115
OPHELIA. You are merry, my lord.
HAMLET. Who, I?
OPHELIA. Ay, my lord.
HAMLET. O God, your only jig maker.° What should a man
do but be merry? For look you how cheerfully my mother   120
looks, and my father died within 's° two hours.
OPHELIA. Nay, 'tis twice two months, my lord.
HAMLET. So long? Nay then, let the devil wear black, for I'll
have a suit of sables.° O heavens! Die two months ago,
and not forgotten yet? Then there's hope a great man's   125
memory may outlive his life half a year. But, by 'r Lady, 'a
must build churches, then, or else shall 'a suffer not
thinking on,° with the hobbyhorse, whose epitaph is "For
O, for O, the hobbyhorse is forgot."°

The trumpets sound. Dumb show follows.

Enter a King and a Queen [very lovingly]; the Queen em-
bracing him, and he her. [She kneels, and makes show of
protestation unto him.] He takes her up, and declines his
head upon her neck. He lies him down upon a bank of
flowers. She, seeing him asleep, leaves him. Anon comes
in another man, takes off his crown, kisses it, pours poison
in the sleeper's ears, and leaves him. The Queen returns,
finds the King dead, makes passionate action. The Poi-
soner with some three or four come in again, seem to con-

76 very . . . soul your most penetrating observation and consideration   **77 occulted** hidden   **78 unkennel** (As one would say of a
fox driven from its lair.)   **79 damnèd** in league with Satan   **81
stithy** smithy, place of stiths (anvils)   **84 censure of his seeming**
judgment of his appearance or behavior   **85 If 'a steal aught** if he
gets away with anything   **87 idle** (1) unoccupied (2) mad   **89
cousin** i.e., close relative   **90 chameleon's dish** (Chameleons were
supposed to feed on air. Hamlet deliberately misinterprets the
King's *fares* as "feeds." By his phrase *eat the air* he also plays on the
idea of feeding himself with the promise of succession, of being the
heir.)   **91 capons** roosters castrated and crammed with feed to
make them succulent   **92 have . . . with** make nothing of, or gain
nothing from   **93 are not mine** do not respond to what I asked
94 nor mine now (Once spoken, words are proverbially no longer
the speaker's own—and hence should be uttered warily.)   **101
brute** (The Latin meaning of *brutus*, "stupid," was often used pun-
ningly with the name Brutus.)   **part** (1) deed (2) role   **calf** fool
103 stay upon await   **105 metal** substance that is *attractive*, i.e.,
magnetic, but with suggestion also of *mettle*, "disposition"

111 country matters sexual intercourse (making a bawdy pun on
the first syllable of *country*)   **115 Nothing** the figure zero or
naught, suggesting the female sexual anatomy. (*Thing* not infrequently has a bawdy connotation of male or female anatomy, and
the reference here could be male.)   **119 only jig maker** very best
composer of jigs, i.e., pointless merriment. (Hamlet replies sardonically to Ophelia's observation that he is merry by saying, "If you're
looking for someone who is really merry, you've come to the right
person.")   **121 within** 's within this (i.e., these)   **124 suit of
sables** garments trimmed with the fur of the sable and hence suited
for a wealthy person, not a mourner (but with a pun on *sable*,
"black," ironically suggesting mourning once again)   **127–128
suffer . . . on** undergo oblivion   **128–129 For . . . forgot** (Verse of
a song occurring also in *Love's Labor's Lost*, 3.1.27–28. The hobbyhorse was a character made up to resemble a horse and rider, appearing in the morris dance and such May-game sports. This song
laments the disappearance of such customs under pressure from the
Puritans.)

dole with her. The dead body is carried away. The Poisoner woos the Queen with gifts; she seems harsh awhile, but in the end accepts love.

[Exeunt players.]

130 OPHELIA. What means this, my lord?

HAMLET. Marry, this' miching mallico;° it means mischief.

OPHELIA. Belike° this show imports the argument° of the play.

Enter Prologue.

HAMLET. We shall know by this fellow. The players cannot
135   keep counsel;° they'll tell all.

OPHELIA. Will 'a tell us what this show meant?

HAMLET. Ay, or any show that you will show him. Be not you° ashamed to show, he'll not shame to tell you what it means.

OPHELIA.
140   You are naught,° you are naught. I'll mark the play.

PROLOGUE.
    For us, and for our tragedy,
    Here stooping° to your clemency,
    We beg your hearing patiently.

[Exit.]

HAMLET.
    Is this a prologue, or the posy of a ring?°

OPHELIA.
145   'Tis brief, my lord.

HAMLET.
    As woman's love.

Enter [two Players as] King and Queen.

PLAYER KING.
    Full thirty times hath Phoebus' cart° gone round
    Neptune's salt wash° and Tellus'° orbèd ground,
    And thirty dozen moons with borrowed° sheen
150   About the world have times twelve thirties been,
    Since love our hearts and Hymen° did our hands
    Unite commutual° in most sacred bands.°

PLAYER QUEEN.
    So many journeys may the sun and moon
    Make us again count o'er ere love be done!
155   But, woe is me, you are so sick of late,

So far from cheer and from your former state,
That I distrust° you. Yet, though I distrust,
Discomfort° you, my lord, it nothing° must.
For women's fear and love hold quantity;°
In neither aught, or in extremity.°   160
Now, what my love is, proof° hath made you know,
And as my love is sized,° my fear is so.
Where love is great, the littlest doubts are fear;
Where little fears grow great, great love grows there.

PLAYER KING.
    Faith, I must leave thee, love, and shortly too;   165
    My operant powers° their functions leave to do.°
    And thou shalt live in this fair world behind,°
    Honored, beloved; and haply one as kind
    For husband shalt thou—

PLAYER QUEEN.   O, confound the rest!
    Such love must needs be treason in my breast.   170
    In second husband let me be accurst!
    None° wed the second but who° killed the first.

HAMLET.
    Wormwood,° wormwood.

PLAYER QUEEN.
    The instances° that second marriage move°
    Are base respects of thrift,° but none of love.   175
    A second time I kill my husband dead
    When second husband kisses me in bed.

PLAYER KING.
    I do believe you think what now you speak,
    But what we do determine oft we break.
    Purpose is but the slave to memory,°   180
    Of violent birth, but poor validity,°
    Which° now, like fruit unripe, sticks on the tree,
    But fall unshaken when they mellow be.
    Most necessary 'tis that we forget
    To pay ourselves what to ourselves is debt.°   185
    What to ourselves in passion we propose,
    The passion ending, doth the purpose lose.
    The violence of either grief or joy
    Their own enactures° with themselves destroy.
    Where joy most revels, grief doth most lament;   190

131 **this' miching mallico** this is sneaking mischief   132 **Belike** probably   **argument** plot   135 **counsel** secret   137–138 **Be not you** provided you are not   140 **naught** indecent (Ophelia is reacting to Hamlet's pointed remarks about not being ashamed to show all.)   142 **stooping** bowing   144 **posy . . . ring** brief motto in verse inscribed in a ring   147 **Phoebus' cart** the sun-god's chariot, making its yearly cycle   148 **salt wash** the sea   **Tellus** goddess of the earth, of the *orbèd ground*   149 **borrowed** i.e., reflected   151 **Hymen** god of matrimony   152 **commutual** mutually   **bands** bonds

157 **distrust** am anxious about   158 **Discomfort** distress   **nothing** not at all   159 **hold quantity** keep proportion with one another   160 **In . . . extremity** i.e., women fear and love either too little or too much, but the two, fear and love, are equal in either case   161 **proof** experience   162 **sized** in size   166 **operant powers** vital functions   **leave to do** cease to perform   167 **behind** after I have gone   172 **None** i.e., let no woman   **but who** except the one who   173 **Wormwood** i.e., how bitter. (Literally, a bitter-tasting plant.)   174 **instances** motives   **move** motivate   175 **base . . . thrift** ignoble considerations of material prosperity   180 **Purpose . . . memory** our good intentions are subject to forgetfulness   181 **validity** strength, durability   182 **Which** i.e., purpose   184–185 **Most . . . debt** it's inevitable that in time we forget the obligations we have imposed on ourselves   189 **enactures** fulfillments

Grief joys, joy grieves, on slender accident.°
This world is not for aye,° nor 'tis not strange
That even our loves should with our fortunes change;
For 'tis a question left us yet to prove,
195   Whether love lead fortune, or else fortune love.
The great man down,° you mark his favorite flies;
The poor advanced makes friends of enemies.°
And hitherto° doth love on fortune tend;°
For who not needs° shall never lack a friend,
200   And who in want° a hollow friend doth try°
Directly seasons him° his enemy.
But, orderly to end where I begun,
Our wills and fates do so contrary run°
That our devices still° are overthrown;
205   Our thoughts are ours, their ends° none of our own.
So think thou wilt no second husband wed,
But die thy thoughts when thy first lord is dead.

PLAYER QUEEN.
Nor° earth to me give food, nor heaven light,
Sport and repose lock from me day and night,°
210   To desperation turn my trust and hope,
An anchor's cheer° in prison be my scope!°
Each opposite that blanks° the face of joy
Meet what I would have well and it destroy!°
Both here and hence° pursue me lasting strife
215   If, once a widow, ever I be wife!

HAMLET.
If she should break it now!

PLAYER KING.
'Tis deeply sworn. Sweet, leave me here awhile;
My spirits° grow dull, and fain I would beguile
The tedious day with sleep.

PLAYER QUEEN.   Sleep rock thy brain,
220   And never come mischance between us twain!

                              [He sleeps.] Exit [Player Queen].

HAMLET. Madam, how like you this play?
QUEEN. The lady doth protest too much,° methinks.
HAMLET. O, but she'll keep her word.
KING. Have you heard the argument?° Is there no offense in 't?
HAMLET. No, no, they do but jest,° poison in jest. No of-   225
    fense° i' the world.
KING. What do you call the play?
HAMLET. The Mousetrap. Marry, how? Tropically.° This play
    is the image of a murder done in Vienna. Gonzago is the
    Duke's° name, his wife, Baptista. You shall see anon. 'Tis   230
    a knavish piece of work, but what of that? Your Majesty,
    and we that have free° souls, it touches us not. Let the
    galled jade° wince, our withers° are unwrung.°

Enter Lucianus.

This is one Lucianus, nephew to the King.
OPHELIA. You are as good as a chorus,° my lord.   235
HAMLET. I could interpret° between you and your love, if I
    could see the puppets dallying.°
OPHELIA. You are keen,° my lord, you are keen.
HAMLET. It would cost you a groaning to take off mine edge.
OPHELIA. Still better, and worse.°   240
HAMLET. So° you mis-take° your husbands. Begin, murder;
    leave thy damnable faces and begin. Come, the croaking
    raven doth bellow for revenge.
LUCIANUS.
Thoughts black, hands apt, drugs fit, and time agreeing,
Confederate season,° else° no creature seeing,°   245
Thou mixture rank, of midnight weeds collected,

190–191 Where ... accident the capacity for extreme joy and
grief go together, and often one extreme is instantly changed into
its opposite on the slightest provocation   192 aye ever   196
down fallen in fortune   197 The poor ... enemies when one of
humble station is promoted, you see his enemies suddenly becoming his friends   198 hitherto up to this point in the argument, or,
to this extent   tend attend   199 who not needs he who is not in
need (of wealth)   200 who in want he who, being in need   try
test (his generosity)   201 seasons him ripens him into   203 Our
... run what we want and what we get go so contrarily   204 devices still intentions continually   205 ends results   208 Nor let
neither   209 Sport ... night may day deny me its pastimes and
night its repose   211 anchor's cheer anchorite's or hermit's fare
my scope the extent of my happiness   212 blanks causes to
blanch or grow pale   212–213 Each ... destroy may every ad-
verse thing that causes the face of joy to turn pale meet and destroy
everything that I desire to see prosper   214 hence in the life hereafter   218 spirits vital spirits

222 doth ... much makes too many promises and protestations
224 argument plot   225 jest make believe   224–226 offense
... offense cause for objection ... actual injury, crime   228 Tropically figuratively (The First Quarto reading, trapically, suggests a
pun on trap in Mousetrap.)   230 Duke's i.e., King's (A slip that
may be due to Shakespeare's possible source, the alleged murder of
the Duke of Urbino by Luigi Gonzaga in 1538.)   232 free guiltless
233 galled jade horse whose hide is rubbed by saddle or harness
withers the part between the horse's shoulder blades   unwrung
not rubbed sore   235 chorus (In many Elizabethan plays, the
forthcoming action was explained by an actor known as the "chorus"; at a puppet show, the actor who spoke the dialogue was known
as an "interpreter," as indicated by the lines following.)   236 interpret (1) ventriloquize the dialogue, as in puppet show (2) act as
pander   237 puppets dallying (With suggestion of sexual play,
continued in keen, "sexually aroused," groaning, "moaning in pregnancy," and edge, "sexual desire" or "impetuosity.")   238 keen
sharp, bitter   240 Still ... worse more keen, always bettering what
other people say with witty wordplay, but at the same time more offensive   241 So even thus (in marriage)   mis-take take false-
heartedly and cheat on (The marriage vows say "for better, for
worse.")   245 Confederate season the time and occasion conspir-
ing (to assist the murderer)   else otherwise   seeing seeing me

With Hecate's ban° thrice blasted, thrice infected,
Thy natural magic and dire property°
On wholesome life usurp immediately.

[*He pours the poison into the sleeper's ear.*]

250   HAMLET. 'A poisons him i' the garden for his estate.° His°
name's Gonzago. The story is extant, and written in very
choice Italian. You shall see anon how the murderer gets
the love of Gonzago's wife.

[*Claudius rises.*]

OPHELIA.
The King rises.
HAMLET.
255   What, frighted with false fire?°
QUEEN.
How fares my lord?
POLONIUS.
Give o'er the play.
KING.
Give me some light. Away!
POLONIUS.
Lights, lights, lights!

Exeunt all but Hamlet and Horatio.

HAMLET.
260   "Why, let the strucken deer go weep,
The hart ungallèd° play.
For some must watch,° while some must sleep;
Thus runs the world away."°
Would not this,° sir, and a forest of feathers°—if the rest
265   of my fortunes turn Turk with° me—with two Provincial
roses° on my razed° shoes, get me a fellowship in a cry°
of players?°
HORATIO. Half a share.
HAMLET. A whole one, I.
270   "For thou dost know, O Damon° dear,
This realm dismantled° was

Of Jove himself, and now reigns here
A very, very—pajock."°
HORATIO. You might have rhymed.
HAMLET. O good Horatio, I'll take the ghost's word for a   275
thousand pound. Didst perceive?
HORATIO. Very well, my lord.
HAMLET. Upon the talk of the poisoning?
HORATIO. I did very well note him.

Enter Rosencrantz and Guildenstern.

HAMLET.
Aha! Come, some music! Come, the recorders.°   280
"For if the King like not the comedy,
Why then, belike, he likes it not, perdy."°
Come, some music.
GUILDENSTERN. Good my lord, vouchsafe me a word with
you.   285
HAMLET. Sir, a whole history.
GUILDENSTERN. The King, sir—
HAMLET. Ay, sir, what of him?
GUILDENSTERN. Is in his retirement° marvelous distem-
pered.°   290
HAMLET. With drink, sir?
GUILDENSTERN. No, my lord, with choler.°
HAMLET. Your wisdom should show itself more richer to sig-
nify this to the doctor, for for me to put him to his purga-
tion° would perhaps plunge him into more choler.   295
GUILDENSTERN. Good my lord, put your discourse into some
frame° and start° not so wildly from my affair.
HAMLET. I am tame, sir. Pronounce.
GUILDENSTERN. The Queen, your mother, in most great affliction of spirit, hath sent me to you.   300
HAMLET. You are welcome.
GUILDENSTERN. Nay, good my lord, this courtesy is not of the
right breed.° If it shall please you to make me a wholesome answer, I will do your mother's commandment; if
not, your pardon° and my return shall be the end of my   305
business.

---

247 Hecate's ban the curse of Hecate, the goddess of witchcraft
248 dire property baleful quality   **250 estate** i.e., the kingship
His i.e., the King's   **255 false fire** the blank discharge of a gun
loaded with powder but no shot   **260–263 Why . . . away** (Probably from an old ballad, with allusion to the popular belief that a
wounded deer retires to weep and die; compare with *As You Like It,*
2.1.33–66.)   **261 ungallèd** unafflicted   **262 watch** remain awake
263 Thus . . . away thus the world goes   **264 this** i.e., the play
feathers (Allusion to the plumes that Elizabethan actors were fond
of wearing.)   **265 turn Turk with** turn renegade against, go back
on   **266 Provincial roses** rosettes of ribbon, named for roses
grown in a part of France   **razed** with ornamental slashing   **267
cry** pack (of hounds)   **fellowship . . . players** partnership in a theatrical company   **270 Damon** the friend of Pythias, as Horatio is
friend of Hamlet; or, a traditional pastoral name   **271 dismantled**
stripped, divested

271–273 This realm . . . pajock i.e., Jove, representing divine authority and justice, has abandoned this realm to its own devices,
leaving in his stead only a peacock or vain pretender to virtue
(though the rhyme-word expected in place of *pajock* or "peacock"
suggests that the realm is now ruled over by an "ass")   **280
recorders** wind instruments of the flute kind   **282 perdy** (A corruption of the French *par dieu,* "by God.")   **289 retirement** withdrawal to his chambers   **289–290 distempered** out of humor (But
Hamlet deliberately plays on the wider application to any illness of
mind or body, as in line 324–25, especially to drunkenness.)   **292
choler** anger (But Hamlet takes the word in its more basic humoral
sense of "bilious disorder.")   **294–295 purgation** (Hamlet hints at
something going beyond medical treatment to bloodletting and the
extraction of confession.)   **297 frame** order   **start** shy or jump
away (like a horse; the opposite of *tame* in line 298)   **303 breed**
(1) kind (2) breeding, manners   **305 pardon** permission to depart

HAMLET. Sir, I cannot.

ROSENCRANTZ. What, my lord?

HAMLET. Make you a wholesome answer; my wit's diseased.
310   But, sir, such answer as I can make, you shall command,
      or rather, as you say, my mother. Therefore no more, but
      to the matter. My mother, you say—

ROSENCRANTZ. Then thus she says: your behavior hath
      struck her into amazement and admiration.°

315   HAMLET. O wonderful son, that can so stonish a mother! But
      is there no sequel at the heels of this mother's admira-
      tion? Impart.

ROSENCRANTZ. She desires to speak with you in her closet°
      ere you go to bed.

320   HAMLET. We shall obey, were she ten times our mother. Have
      you any further trade with us?

ROSENCRANTZ. My lord, you once did love me.

HAMLET. And do still, by these pickers and stealers.°

ROSENCRANTZ. Good my lord, what is your cause of distem-
325   per? You do surely bar the door upon your own liberty° if
      you deny° your griefs to your friend.

HAMLET. Sir, I lack advancement.

ROSENCRANTZ. How can that be, when you have the voice of
      the King himself for your succession in Denmark?

330   HAMLET. Ay, sir, but "While the grass grows"°—the proverb
      is something° musty.

Enter the Players° with recorders.

      O, the recorders. Let me see one.   [*He takes a recorder.*]
      To withdraw° with you: why do you go about to recover
      the wind° of me, as if you would drive me into a toil?°

335   GUILDENSTERN. O, my lord, if my duty be too bold, my love is
      too unmannerly.°

HAMLET. I do not well understand that.° Will you play upon
      this pipe?

GUILDENSTERN. My lord, I cannot.

340   HAMLET. I pray you.

GUILDENSTERN. Believe me, I cannot.

HAMLET. I do beseech you.

GUILDENSTERN. I know no touch of it, my lord.

HAMLET. It is as easy as lying. Govern these ventages° with

---

314 **admiration** bewilderment   318 **closet** private chamber   323
pickers and stealers i.e., hands (So called from the catechism, "to
keep my hands from picking and stealing.")   325 **liberty** i.e., being
freed from *distemper,* line 324–25; but perhaps with a veiled threat
as well   326 **deny** refuse to share   330 **While . . . grows** (The
rest of the proverb is "the silly horse starves"; Hamlet may not live
long enough to succeed to the kingdom.)   331 **something** somewhat   **s.d. Players** actors   333 **withdraw** speak privately
333–334 **recover the wind** get to the windward side (thus driving
the game into the *toil,* or "net")   334 **toil** snare   335–336 **if . . .
unmannerly** if I am using an unmannerly boldness, it is my love
that occasion it   337 **I . . . that** i.e., I don't understand how genuine love can be unmannerly   344 **ventages** finger-holes or *stops*
(line 328) of the recorder

---

your fingers and thumb, give it breath with your mouth,   345
and it will discourse most eloquent music. Look you,
these are the stops.

GUILDENSTERN. But these cannot I command to any utterance of harmony. I have not the skill.

HAMLET. Why, look you now, how unworthy a thing you   350
make of me! You would play upon me, you would seem to
know my stops, you would pluck out the heart of my mystery, you would sound° me from my lowest note to the
top of my compass,° and there is much music, excellent
voice, in this little organ,° yet cannot you make it speak.   355
'Sblood, do you think I am easier to be played on than a
pipe? Call me what instrument you will, though you can
fret° me, you cannot play upon me.

Enter Polonius.

God bless you, sir!

POLONIUS. My lord, the Queen would speak with you, and   360
presently.°

HAMLET. Do you see yonder cloud that's almost in shape of a
camel?

POLONIUS. By the Mass and 'tis, like a camel indeed.

HAMLET. Methinks it is like a weasel.   365

POLONIUS. It is backed like a weasel.

HAMLET. Or like a whale.

POLONIUS. Very like a whale.

HAMLET. Then I will come to my mother by and by.° [*Aside.*]
They fool me° to the top of my bent.°—I will come by   370
and by.

POLONIUS. I will say so.

[*Exit.*]

HAMLET. "By and by" is easily said. Leave me, friends.

[*Exeunt all but Hamlet.*]

'Tis now the very witching time° of night,
When churchyards yawn and hell itself breathes out   375
Contagion to this world. Now could I drink hot blood
And do such bitter business as the day
Would quake to look on. Soft, now to my mother.
O heart, lose not thy nature!° Let not ever
The soul of Nero° enter this firm bosom.   380
Let me be cruel, not unnatural;

---

353 **sound** (1) fathom (2) produce sound in   354 **compass** range
(of voice)   355 **organ** musical instrument   358 **fret** irritate (with
a quibble on *fret,* meaning the piece of wood, gut, or metal that reg-
ulates the fingering on an instrument)   361 **presently** at once
369 **by and by** quite soon   370 **fool me** trifle with me, humor my
fooling   **top of my bent** limit of my ability or endurance. (Literally, the extent to which a bow may be bent.)   374 **witching time**
time when spells are cast and evil is abroad   379 **nature** natural
feeling   380 **Nero** murderer of his mother, Agrippina

I will speak daggers to her, but use none.
My tongue and soul in this be hypocrites:
How in my words soever° she be shent,°
To give them seals° never my soul consent!

                                        Exit.

385 (line marker)

3.3 *Enter King, Rosencrantz, and Guildenstern.*

KING.
  I like him° not, nor stands it safe with us
  To let his madness range. Therefore prepare you.
  I your commission will forthwith dispatch,°
  And he to England shall along with you.
5 The terms of our estate° may not endure
  Hazard so near 's as doth hourly grow
  Out of his brows.°
GUILDENSTERN.   We will ourselves provide.
  Most holy and religious fear° it is
  To keep those many many bodies safe
10 That live and feed upon Your Majesty.
ROSENCRANTZ.
  The single and peculiar° life is bound
  With all the strength and armor of the mind
  To keep itself from noyance,° but much more
  That spirit upon whose weal depends and rests
15 The lives of many. The cess° of majesty
  Dies not alone, but like a gulf° doth draw
  What's near it with it; or it is a massy° wheel
  Fixed on the summit of the highest mount,
  To whose huge spokes ten thousand lesser things
20 Are mortised° and adjoined, which, when it falls,°
  Each small annexment, petty consequence,°
  Attends° the boisterous ruin. Never alone
  Did the King sigh, but with a general groan.
KING.
  Arm° you, I pray you, to this speedy voyage,
25 For we will fetters put about this fear,
  Which now goes too free-footed.
ROSENCRANTZ.   We will haste us.

     Exeunt gentlemen [Rosencrantz and Guildenstern].

Enter Polonius.

POLONIUS.
  My lord, he's going to his mother's closet.
  Behind the arras° I'll convey myself
  To hear the process.° I'll warrant she'll tax him home,°
  And, as you said—and wisely was it said—   30
  'Tis meet° that some more audience than a mother,
  Since nature makes them partial, should o'erhear
  The speech, of vantage.° Fare you well, my liege.
  I'll call upon you ere you go to bed
  And tell you what I know.
KING.   Thanks, dear my lord.   35

                            Exit [Polonius].

  O, my offense is rank! It smells to heaven.
  It hath the primal eldest curse° upon 't,
  A brother's murder. Pray can I not,
  Though inclination be as sharp as will;°
  My stronger guilt defeats my strong intent,   40
  And like a man to double business bound°
  I stand in pause where I shall first begin,
  And both neglect. What if this cursèd hand
  Were thicker than itself with brother's blood,
  Is there not rain enough in the sweet heavens   45
  To wash it white as snow? Whereto serves mercy
  But to confront the visage of offense?°
  And what's in prayer but this twofold force,
  To be forestallèd° ere we come to fall,
  Or pardoned being down? Then I'll look up.   50
  My fault is past. But O, what form of prayer
  Can serve my turn? "Forgive me my foul murder"?
  That cannot be, since I am still possessed
  Of those effects for which I did the murder:
  My crown, mine own ambition, and my Queen.   55
  May one be pardoned and retain th' offense?°
  In the corrupted currents° of this world
  Offense's gilded hand° may shove by° justice,
  And oft 'tis seen the wicked prize° itself

---

384 How . . . soever however much by my words **shent** rebuked
385 give them seals i.e., confirm them with deeds **3.3 Location:**
The castle. **1 him** i.e., his behavior **3 dispatch** prepare, cause to
be drawn up **5 terms of our estate** circumstances of my royal position **7 Out of** his brows i.e., from his brain, in the form of plots
and threats **8 religious fear** sacred concern **11 single and peculiar** individual and private **13 noyance** harm **15 cess** decease,
cessation **16 gulf** whirlpool **17 massy** massive **20 mortised**
fastened (as with a fitted joint) **when it falls** i.e., when it descends, like the wheel of Fortune, bringing a king down with it **21
Each . . . consequence** i.e., every hanger-on and unimportant person or thing connected with the King **22 Attends** participates in
24 Arm prepare

28 arras screen of tapestry placed around the walls of household
apartments. (On the Elizabethan stage, the arras was presumably
over a door or discovery space in the tiring-house facade.) **29
process** proceedings **tax him home** reprove him severely **31
meet** fitting **33 of vantage** from an advantageous place, or, in addition **37 the primal eldest curse** the curse of Cain, the first murderer; he killed his brother Abel **39 Though . . . will** though my
desire is as strong as my determination **41 bound** (1) destined (2)
obliged. (The King wants to repent and still enjoy what he has
gained.) **46–47 Whereto . . . offense** what function does mercy
serve other than to meet sin face to face? **49 forestallèd** prevented (from sinning) **56 th' offense** the thing for which one offended **57 currents** courses **58 gilded hand** hand offering gold
as a bribe **shove by** thrust aside **59 wicked prize** prize won by
wickedness

60 Buys out the law. But 'tis not so above.
    There° is no shuffling,° there the action lies°
    In his° true nature, and we ourselves compelled,
    Even to the teeth and forehead° of our faults,
    To give in° evidence. What then? What rests?°
65 Try what repentance can. What can it not?
    Yet what can it, when one cannot repent?
    O wretched state, O bosom black as death,
    O limèd° soul that, struggling to be free,
    Art more engaged!° Help, angels! Make assay.°
70 Bow, stubborn knees, and heart with strings of steel,
    Be soft as sinews of the newborn babe!
    All may be well.   [He kneels.]

    Enter Hamlet.

HAMLET.
    Now might I do it pat,° now 'a is a-praying;
    And now I'll do 't. [He draws his sword.] And so 'a goes
        to heaven,
75 And so am I revenged. That would be scanned:°
    A villain kills my father, and for that,
    I, his sole son, do this same villain send
    To heaven.
    Why, this is hire and salary, not revenge.
80 'A took my father grossly, full of bread,°
    With all his crimes broad blown,° as flush° as May;
    And how his audit° stands who knows save° heaven?
    But in our circumstance and course of thought°
    'Tis heavy with him. And am I then revenged,
85 To take him in the purging of his soul,
    When he is fit and seasoned° for his passage?
    No!
    Up, sword, and know thou a more horrid hent.°

                                    [He puts up his sword.]

    When he is drunk asleep, or in his rage,°
90 Or in th' incestuous pleasure of his bed,
    At game,° a-swearing, or about some act
    That has no relish° of salvation in 't—

---

61 There i.e., in heaven   **shuffling** escape by trickery   **the action
lies** the accusation is made manifest (A legal metaphor.)   **62 his**
its   **63 to the teeth and forehead** face to face, concealing nothing
64 give in provide.   **rests** remains   **68 limèd** caught as with
birdlime, a sticky substance used to ensnare birds   **69 engaged** entangled   **assay** trial. (Said to himself.)   **73 pat** opportunely   **75
would be scanned** needs to be looked into, or, would be interpreted
as follows   **80 grossly, full of bread** i.e., enjoying his worldly pleasures rather than fasting (See Ezekiel 16:49.)   **81 crimes broad
blown** sins in full bloom   **flush** vigorous   **82 audit** account   **save**
except for   **83 in . . . thought** as we see it from our mortal perspective   **86 seasoned** matured, readied   **88 know . . . hent** await to
be grasped by me on a more horrid occasion   **hent** act of seizing
89 drunk . . . rage dead drunk, or in a fit of sexual passion   **91
game** gambling   **92 relish** trace, savor

    Then trip him, that his heels may kick at heaven,
    And that his soul may be as damned and black
    As hell, whereto it goes. My mother stays.°   95
    This physic° but prolongs thy sickly days.

                                    Exit.

KING.
    My words fly up, my thoughts remain below.
    Words without thoughts never to heaven go.

                                    Exit.

3.4 Enter [Queen] Gertrude and Polonius.

POLONIUS.
    'A will come straight. Look you lay home° to him.
    Tell him his pranks have been too broad° to bear with,
    And that Your Grace hath screened and stood between
    Much heat° and him. I'll shroud° me even here.
    Pray you, be round° with him.   5
HAMLET [within].
    Mother, Mother, Mother!
QUEEN.
    I'll warrant you, fear me not.
    Withdraw, I hear him coming.

                        [Polonius hides behind the arras.]

    Enter Hamlet.

HAMLET.
    Now, Mother, what's the matter?
QUEEN.
    Hamlet, thou hast thy father° much offended.   10
HAMLET.
    Mother, you have my father much offended.
QUEEN.
    Come, come, you answer with an idle° tongue.
HAMLET.
    Go, go, you question with a wicked tongue.
QUEEN.
    Why, how now, Hamlet?
HAMLET.   What's the matter now?
QUEEN.
    Have you forgot me?°
HAMLET.   No, by the rood,° not so: 15

---

95 stays awaits (me)   **96 physic** purging (by prayer), or, Hamlet's
postponement of the killing   **3.4 Location: The Queen's private
chamber.**   **1 lay home** thrust to the heart, reprove him soundly   **2
broad** unrestrained   **4 Much heat** i.e., the King's anger   **shroud
conceal** (with ironic fitness to Polonius' imminent death. The word
is only in the First Quarto: the Second Quarto and the Folio read
"silence.")   **5 round** blunt   **10 thy father** i.e., your stepfather,
Claudius   **12 idle** foolish   **15 forgot me** i.e., forgotten that I am
your mother   **rood** cross of Christ

You are the Queen your husband's brother's wife,
And—would it were not so!—you are my mother.

QUEEN.

Nay, then, I'll set those to you that can speak.°

HAMLET.

Come, come, and sit you down; you shall not budge.
20   You go not till I set you up a glass
Where you may see the inmost part of you.

QUEEN.

What wilt thou do? Thou wilt not murder me?
Help, ho!

POLONIUS [behind the arras].

What ho! Help!

HAMLET [drawing].

25   How now? A rat? Dead for a ducat,° dead!

        [He thrusts his rapier through the arras.]

POLONIUS [behind the arras].

O, I am slain!   [He falls and dies.]

QUEEN.   O me, what hast thou done?

HAMLET.

Nay, I know not. Is it the King?

QUEEN.

O, what a rash and bloody deed is this!

HAMLET.

A bloody deed—almost as bad, good Mother,
30   As kill a King, and marry with his brother.

QUEEN.

As kill a King!

HAMLET.   Ay, lady, it was my word.

        [He parts the arras and discovers Polonius.]

Thou wretched, rash, intruding fool, farewell!
I took thee for thy better. Take thy fortune.
Thou find'st to be too busy° is some danger.—
35   Leave wringing of your hands. Peace, sit you down,
And let me wring your heart, for so I shall,
If it be made of penetrable stuff,
If damnèd custom° have not brazed° it so
That it be proof° and bulwark against sense.°

QUEEN.

40   What have I done, that thou dar'st wag thy tongue
In noise so rude against me?

HAMLET.   Such an act
That blurs the grace and blush of modesty,
Calls virtue hypocrite, takes off the rose
From the fair forehead of an innocent love
45   And sets a blister° there, makes marriage vows

As false as dicers' oaths. O, such a deed
As from the body of contraction° plucks
The very soul, and sweet religion makes°
A rhapsody° of words. Heaven's face does glow
O'er this solidity and compound mass   50
With tristful visage, as against the doom,
Is thought-sick at the act.°

QUEEN.   Ay me, what act,
That roars so loud and thunders in the index?°

HAMLET [showing her two likenesses].

Look here upon this picture, and on this,
The counterfeit presentment° of two brothers.   55
See what a grace was seated on this brow:
Hyperion's° curls, the front° of Jove himself,
An eye like Mars° to threaten and command,
A station° like the herald Mercury°
New-lighted° on a heaven-kissing hill—   60
A combination and a form indeed
Where every god did seem to set his seal°
To give the world assurance of a man.
This was your husband. Look you now what follows:
Here is your husband, like a mildewed ear,°   65
Blasting° his wholesome brother. Have you eyes?
Could you on this fair mountain leave° to feed
And batten° on this moor?° Ha, have you eyes?
You cannot call it love, for at your age
The heyday° in the blood° is tame, it's humble,   70
And waits upon the judgment, and what judgment
Would step from this to this? Sense,° sure, you have,
Else could you not have motion, but sure that sense
Is apoplexed,° for madness would not err,°
Nor sense to ecstasy was ne'er so thralled,   75
But° it reserved some quantity of choice

---

18 **speak** i.e., to someone so rude   25 **Dead for a ducat** i.e., I bet a ducat he's dead; or, a ducat is his life's fee   34 **busy** nosey   38 **damnèd custom** habitual wickedness   **brazed** brazened, hardened   39 **proof** armor   **sense** feeling   45 **sets a blister** i.e., brands as a harlot

47 **contraction** the marriage contract   48 **sweet religion makes** i.e., makes marriage vows   49 **rhapsody** senseless string   49–52 **Heaven's . . . act** heaven's face blushes at this solid world compounded of the various elements, with sorrowful face as though the day of doom were near, and is sick with horror at the deed (i.e., Gertrude's marriage)   53 **index** table of contents, prelude or preface   55 **counterfeit presentment** portrayed representation   57 **Hyperion's** the sun-god's   **front** brow   58 **Mars** god of war   59 **station** manner of standing   **Mercury** winged messenger of the gods   60 **New-lighted** newly alighted   62 **set his seal** i.e., affix his approval   65 **ear** i.e., of grain   66 **Blasting** blighting   67 **leave** cease   68 **batten** gorge   **moor** barren or marshy ground (suggesting also "dark-skinned")   70 **heyday** state of excitement   **blood** passion   72 **Sense** perception through the five senses (the functions of the middle or sensible soul)   74 **apoplexed** paralyzed (Hamlet goes on to explain that, without such a paralysis of will, mere madness would not so err, nor would the five senses so enthrall themselves to *ecstasy* or lunacy; even such deranged states of mind would be able to make the obvious choice between Hamlet Senior and Claudius.)   **err** so err   76 **But** but that

To serve in such a difference.° What devil was 't
That thus hath cozened° you at hoodman-blind?°
Eyes without feeling, feeling without sight,
80 Ears without hands or eyes, smelling sans° all,
Or but a sickly part of one true sense
Could not so mope.° O shame, where is thy blush?
Rebellious hell,
If thou canst mutine° in a matron's bones,
85 To flaming youth let virtue be as wax
And melt in her own fire.° Proclaim no shame
When the compulsive ardor gives the charge,
Since frost itself as actively doth burn,
And reason panders will.°

QUEEN.
90 O Hamlet, speak no more!
Thou turn'st mine eyes into my very soul,
And there I see such black and grainèd° spots
As will not leave their tinct.°

HAMLET.   Nay, but to live
In the rank sweat of an enseamèd° bed,
95 Stewed° in corruption, honeying and making love
Over the nasty sty!

QUEEN.
O, speak to me no more!
These words like daggers enter in my ears.
No more, sweet Hamlet!

HAMLET.   A murderer and a villain,
100 A slave that is not twentieth part the tithe°
Of your precedent lord,° a vice° of kings,
A cutpurse of the empire and the rule,
That from a shelf the precious diadem stole
And put it in his pocket!

QUEEN.
105 No more!

Enter Ghost [in his nightgown].

HAMLET.
A king of shreds and patches°—

Save me, and hover o'er me with your wings,
You heavenly guards! What would your gracious figure?

QUEEN.
Alas, he's mad!

HAMLET.
Do you not come your tardy son to chide, 110
That, lapsed° in time and passion, lets go by
Th' important° acting of your dread command?
O, say!

GHOST.
Do not forget. This visitation
Is but to whet thy almost blunted purpose. 115
But look, amazement° on thy mother sits.
O, step between her and her fighting soul!
Conceit° in weakest bodies strongest works.
Speak to her, Hamlet.

HAMLET.   How is it with you, lady?

QUEEN.
Alas, how is 't with you, 120
That you do bend your eye on vacancy,
And with th' incorporal° air do hold discourse?
Forth at your eyes your spirits wildly peep,
And, as the sleeping soldiers in th' alarm,°
Your bedded° hair, like life in excrements,° 125
Start up and stand on end. O gentle son,
Upon the heat and flame of thy distemper°
Sprinkle cool patience. Whereon do you look?

HAMLET.
On him, on him! Look you how pale he glares!
His form and cause conjoined,° preaching to stones, 130
Would make them capable.°—Do not look upon me,
Lest with this piteous action you convert
My stern effects.° Then what I have to do
Will want true color—tears perchance for blood.°

QUEEN.
To whom do you speak this? 135

HAMLET.
Do you see nothing there?

QUEEN.
Nothing at all, yet all that is I see.

HAMLET.
Nor did you nothing hear?

77 To . . . difference to help in making a choice between two such
men **78 cozened** cheated **hoodman-blind** blindman's buff (In
this game, says Hamlet, the devil must have pushed Claudius toward Gertrude while she was blindfolded.) **80 sans** without **82
mope** be dazed, act aimlessly **84 mutine** incite mutiny **85–86
be as wax . . . fire** melt like a candle or stick of sealing wax held
over the candle flame **86–89 Proclaim . . . will** call it no shameful business when the compelling ardor of youth delivers the attack,
i.e., commits lechery, since the *frost* of advanced age burns with as
active a fire of lust and reason perverts itself by fomenting lust
rather than restraining it **92 grainèd** dyed in grain, indelible **93
leave their tinct** surrender their color **94 enseamèd** saturated in
the grease and filth of passionate lovemaking **95 Stewed** soaked,
bathed (with a suggestion of "stew," brothel) **100 tithe** tenth part
101 precedent lord former husband **vice** buffoon (A reference to
the Vice of the morality plays.) **106 shreds and patches** i.e., motley, the traditional costume of the clown or fool

111 lapsed delaying **112 important** importunate, urgent **116
amazement** distraction **118 Conceit** imagination **122 incorpo-
ral** immaterial **124 as . . . alarm** like soldiers called out of sleep by
an alarum **125 bedded** laid flat **like life in excrements** i.e., as
though hair, an outgrowth of the body, had a life of its own (Hair
was thought to be lifeless because it lacks sensation, and so its
standing on end would be unnatural and ominous.) **127 distemper** disorder **130 His . . . conjoined** his appearance joined to his
cause for speaking **131 capable** receptive **132–133 convert . . .
effects** divert me from my stern duty **134 want . . . blood** lack
plausibility so that (with a play on the normal sense of *color*) I shall
shed colorless tears instead of blood

QUEEN.
No, nothing but ourselves.

HAMLET.
140　Why, look you there, look how it steals away!
My father, in his habit° as° he lived!
Look where he goes even now out at the portal!

Exit Ghost.

QUEEN.
This is the very° coinage of your brain.
This bodiless creation ecstasy
145　Is very cunning in.°

HAMLET.
Ecstasy?
My pulse as yours doth temperately keep time,
And makes as healthful music. It is not madness
That I have uttered. Bring me to the test,
150　And I the matter will reword,° which madness
Would gambol° from. Mother, for love of grace,
Lay not that flattering unction° to your soul
That not your trespass but my madness speaks.
It will but skin° and film the ulcerous place,
155　Whiles rank corruption, mining° all within,
Infects unseen. Confess yourself to heaven,
Repent what's past, avoid what is to come,
And do not spread the compost° on the weeds
To make them ranker. Forgive me this my virtue;°
160　For in the fatness° of these pursy° times
Virtue itself of vice must pardon beg,
Yea, curb° and woo for leave° to do him good.

QUEEN.
O Hamlet, thou hast cleft my heart in twain.

HAMLET.
O, throw away the worser part of it,
165　And live the purer with the other half.
Good night. But go not to my uncle's bed;
Assume a virtue, if you have it not.
That monster, custom, who all sense doth eat,°
Of habits devil,° is angel yet in this,
170　That to the use of actions fair and good
He likewise gives a frock or livery°

That aptly° is put on. Refrain tonight,
And that shall lend a kind of easiness
To the next abstinence; the next more easy;
For use° almost can change the stamp of nature,°   175
And either° . . . the devil, or throw him out
With wondrous potency. Once more, good night;
And when you are desirous to be blest,
I'll blessing beg of you.° For this same lord,

[*pointing to Polonius.*]

I do repent; but heaven hath pleased it so   180
To punish me with this, and this with me,
That I must be their scourge and minister.°
I will bestow° him, and will answer° well
The death I gave him. So, again, good night.
I must be cruel only to be kind.   185
This° bad begins, and worse remains behind.°
One word more, good lady.

QUEEN.   What shall I do?

HAMLET.
Not this by no means that I bid you do:
Let the bloat° King tempt you again to bed,
Pinch wanton° on your cheek, call you his mouse,   190
And let him, for a pair of reechy° kisses,
Or paddling° in your neck with his damned fingers,
Make you to ravel all this matter out°
That I essentially am not in madness,
But mad in craft.° 'Twere good° you let him know,   195
For who that's but a Queen, fair, sober, wise,
Would from a paddock,° from a bat, a gib,°
Such dear concernings° hide? Who would do so?
No, in despite of sense and secrecy,°
Unpeg the basket° on the house's top,   200
Let the birds fly, and like the famous ape,°

---

141 **habit** clothes　**as** as when　143 **very** mere　144–145 **This . . . in** madness is skillful in creating this kind of hallucination　150 **reword** repeat word for word　151 **gambol** skip away　152 **unction** ointment　154 **skin** grow a skin for　155 **mining** working under the surface　158 **compost** manure　159 **this my virtue** my virtuous talk in reproving you　160 **fatness** grossness　**pursy** flabby, out of shape　162 **curb** bow, bend the knee　**leave** permission　168 **who . . . eat** which consumes all proper or natural feeling, all sensibility　169 **Of habits devil** devil-like in prompting evil habits　171 **livery** an outer appearance, a customary garb (and hence a predisposition easily assumed in time of stress)

172 **aptly** readily　175 **use** habit.　**the stamp of nature** our inborn traits　176 **And either** (A defective line, usually emended by inserting the word *master* after *either,* following the Fourth Quarto and early editors.)　178–179 **when . . . you** i.e., when you are ready to be penitent and seek God's blessing, I will ask your blessing as a dutiful son should　182 **their scourge and minister** i.e., agent of heavenly retribution (By *scourge,* Hamlet also suggests that he himself will eventually suffer punishment in the process of fulfilling heaven's will.)　183 **bestow** stow, dispose of　**answer** account or pay for　186 **This** i.e., the killing of Polonius　**behind** to come　189 **bloat** bloated　190 **Pinch wanton** i.e., leave his love pinches on your cheeks, branding you as wanton　191 **reechy** dirty, filthy　192 **paddling** fingering amorously　193 **ravel . . . out** unravel, disclose　195 **in craft** by cunning　**good** (Said sarcastically; also the following eight lines.)　197 **paddock** toad　**gib** tomcat　198 **dear concernings** important affairs　199 **sense and secrecy** secrecy that common sense requires　200 **Unpeg the basket** open the cage, i.e., let out the secret　201 **famous ape** (In a story now lost.)

To try conclusions,° in the basket creep
And break your own neck down.°

QUEEN.
Be thou assured, if words be made of breath,
205   And breath of life, I have no life to breathe
What thou hast said to me.

HAMLET.
I must to England. You know that?

QUEEN.   Alack,
I had forgot. 'Tis so concluded on.

HAMLET.
There's letters sealed, and my two schoolfellows,
210   Whom I will trust as I will adders fanged,
They bear the mandate; they must sweep my way
And marshal me to knavery.° Let it work.°
For 'tis the sport to have the enginer°
Hoist with° his own petard,° and 't shall go hard
215   But I will° delve one yard below their mines°
And blow them at the moon. O, 'tis most sweet
When in one line° two crafts° directly meet.
This man shall set me packing.°
I'll lug the guts into the neighbor room.
220   Mother, good night indeed. This counselor
Is now most still, most secret, and most grave,
Who was in life a foolish prating knave.—
Come, sir, to draw toward an end° with you.—
Good night, Mother.

Exeunt [separately, Hamlet dragging in Polonius].

4.1 *Enter King and Queen,° with Rosencrantz and Guildenstern.*

KING.
There's matter° in these sighs, these profound heaves.°

You must translate; 'tis fit we understand them.
Where is your son?

QUEEN.
Bestow this place on us a little while.

[Exeunt Rosencrantz and Guildenstern.]

Ah, mine own lord, what have I seen tonight!   5

KING.
What, Gertrude? How does Hamlet?

QUEEN.
Mad as the sea and wind when both contend
Which is the mightier. In his lawless fit,
Behind the arras hearing something stir,
Whips out his rapier, cries, "A rat, a rat!"   10
And in this brainish apprehension° kills
The unseen good old man.

KING.   O heavy° deed!
It had been so with us,° had we been there.
His liberty is full of threats to all—
To you yourself, to us, to everyone.
Alas, how shall this bloody deed be answered?°   15
It will be laid to us, whose providence°
Should have kept short,° restrained, and out of haunt°
This mad young man. But so much was our love,
We would not understand what was most fit,   20
But, like the owner of a foul disease,
To keep it from divulging,° let it feed
Even on the pith of life. Where is he gone?

QUEEN.
To draw apart the body he hath killed,
O'er whom his very madness, like some ore°   25
Among a mineral° of metals base,
Shows itself pure: 'a weeps for what is done.

KING.
O Gertrude, come away!
The sun no sooner shall the mountains touch
But we will ship him hence, and this vile deed   30
We must with all our majesty and skill
Both countenance° and excuse.—Ho, Guildenstern!

Enter Rosencrantz and Guildenstern.

Friends both, go join you with some further aid.
Hamlet in madness hath Polonius slain,
And from his mother's closet hath he dragged him.   35
Go seek him out, speak fair, and bring the body
Into the chapel. I pray you, haste in this.

[Exeunt Rosencrantz and Guildenstern.]

202 try conclusions test the outcome (in which the ape apparently enters a cage from which birds have been released and then tries to fly out of the cage as they have done, falling to its death) **203 down** in the fall; utterly **211–212 sweep ... knavery** sweep a path before me and conduct me to some *knavery* or treachery prepared for me **212 work** proceed **213 enginer** maker of military contrivances **214 Hoist with** blown up by. **petard** an explosive used to blow in a door or make a breach **214–215 't shall ... will** unless luck is against me, I will **215 mines** tunnels used in warfare to undermine the enemy's emplacements; Hamlet will countermine by going under their mines **217 in one line** i.e., mines and countermines on a collision course, or the countermines directly below the mines **crafts** acts of guile, plots **218 set me packing** set me to making schemes, and set me to lugging (him), and, also, send me off in a hurry **223 draw ... end** finish up (with a pun on *draw*, "pull") **4.1 Location: The castle. s.d. Enter ... Queen** (Some editors argue that Gertrude never exits in 3.4 and that the scene is continuous here, as suggested in the Folio, but the Second Quarto marks an entrance for her and at line 35 Claudius speaks of Gertrude's *closet* as though it were elsewhere. A short time has elapsed, during which the King has become aware of her highly wrought emotional state.) **1 matter** significance **heaves** heavy sighs

11 brainish apprehension headstrong conception **12 heavy** grievous **13 us** i.e., me (The royal "we"; also in line 15.) **16 answered** explained **17 providence** foresight **18 short** i.e., on a short tether. **out of haunt** secluded **22 divulging** becoming evident **25 ore** vein of gold **26 mineral** mine **32 countenance** put the best face on

Come, Gertrude, we'll call up our wisest friends
And let them know both what we mean to do
40   And what's untimely done°. . . . .
Whose whisper o'er the world's diameter,°
As level° as the cannon to his blank,°
Transports his poisoned shot, may miss our name
And hit the woundless° air. O, come away!
45   My soul is full of discord and dismay.

Exeunt.

4.2 *Enter Hamlet.*

HAMLET.
Safely stowed.
ROSENCRANTZ, GUILDENSTERN [*within*].
Hamlet! Lord Hamlet!
HAMLET.
But soft, what noise? Who calls on Hamlet? O, here they
come.

Enter Rosencrantz and Guildenstern.

ROSENCRANTZ.
5   What have you done, my lord, with the dead body?
HAMLET. Compounded it with dust, whereto 'tis kin.
ROSENCRANTZ.
Tell us where 'tis, that we may take it thence
And bear it to the chapel.
HAMLET.
Do not believe it.
ROSENCRANTZ.
10   Believe what?
HAMLET. That I can keep your counsel and not mine own.°
Besides, to be demanded of° a sponge, what replication°
should be made by the son of a king?
ROSENCRANTZ. Take you me for a sponge, my lord?
15 HAMLET. Ay, sir, that soaks up the King's countenance,° his
rewards, his authorities.° But such officers do the King
best service in the end. He keeps them, like an ape, an
apple, in the corner of his jaw, first mouthed to be last
swallowed. When he needs what you have gleaned, it is
20   but squeezing you, and, sponge, you shall be dry again.
ROSENCRANTZ. I understand you not, my lord.
HAMLET. I am glad of it. A knavish speech sleeps in° a foolish
ear.

ROSENCRANTZ. My lord, you must tell us where the body is
and go with us to the King.   25
HAMLET. The body is with the King, but the King is not with
the body.° The King is a thing—
GUILDENSTERN. A thing, my lord?
HAMLET. Of nothing.° Bring me to him. Hide fox, and all after!°   30

Exeunt [*running*].

4.3 *Enter King, and two or three.*

KING.
I have sent to seek him, and to find the body.
How dangerous is it that this man goes loose!
Yet must not we put the strong law on him.
He's loved of° the distracted° multitude,
Who like not in their judgment, but their eyes,°   5
And where 'tis so, th' offender's scourge° is weighed,°
But never the offense. To bear all smooth and even,°
This sudden sending him away must seem
Deliberate pause.° Diseases desperate grown
By desperate appliance° are relieved,   10
Or not at all.

Enter Rosencrantz, [*Guildenstern,*] *and all the rest.*

How now, what hath befall'n?
ROSENCRANTZ.
Where the dead body is bestowed, my lord,
We cannot get from him.
KING.   But where is he?
ROSENCRANTZ. Without, my lord; guarded, to know your
pleasure.   15
KING. Bring him before us.
ROSENCRANTZ.   Ho! Bring in the lord.

They enter [*with Hamlet*].

KING. Now, Hamlet, where's Polonius?
HAMLET. At supper.
KING. At supper? Where?
HAMLET. Not where he eats, but where 'a is eaten. A certain   20

---

40 And . . . done (A defective line; conjectures as to the missing
words include So, *haply, slander* [Capell and others]; For, *haply, slander* [Theobald and others]; and *So envious slander* [Jenkins].) **41
diameter** extent from side to side **42 As level** with as direct aim
his blank its target at point-blank range **44 woundless** invulnerable **4.2 Location: The castle. 11 That . . . own** i.e., that I can
follow your advice (by telling where the body is) and still keep my
own secret **12 demanded of** questioned by **replication** reply
15 countenance favor **16 authorities** delegated power, influence
22 sleeps in has no meaning to

26–27 The . . . body (Perhaps alludes to the legal commonplace of
"the king's two bodies," which drew a distinction between the sacred
office of kingship and the particular mortal who possessed it at any
given time. Hence, although Claudius's body is necessarily a part of
him, true kingship is not contained in it. Similarly, Claudius will
have Polonius's body when it is found, but there is no kingship in this
business either.) **29–30 Of nothing** (1) of no account (2) lacking
the essence of kingship, as in lines 24–25 and note **Hide . . . after**
(An old signal cry in the game of hide-and-seek, suggesting that
Hamlet now runs away from them.) **4.3 Location: The castle.   4
of** by. **distracted** fickle, unstable **5 Who . . . eyes** who choose not
by judgment but by appearance **6 scourge** punishment (Literally,
blow with a whip.) **weighed** sympathetically considered **7 To . . .
even** to manage the business in an unprovocative way **9 Deliberate
pause** carefully considered action **10 appliance** remedies

convocation of politic worms° are e'en° at him. Your
worm° is your only emperor for diet.° We fat all creatures
else to fat us, and we fat ourselves for maggots. Your fat
king and your lean beggar is but variable service°—two
25 dishes, but to one table. That's the end.

KING. Alas, alas!

HAMLET. A man may fish with the worm that hath eat° of a
king, and eat of the fish that hath fed of that worm.

KING. What dost thou mean by this?

30 HAMLET. Nothing but to show you how a king may go a
progress° through the guts of a beggar.

KING. Where is Polonius?

HAMLET. In heaven. Send thither to see. If your messenger
find him not there, seek him i' th' other place yourself.
35 But if indeed you find him not within this month, you
shall nose him as you go up the stairs into the lobby.

KING [to some attendants]. Go seek him there.

HAMLET. 'A will stay till you come.

[Exeunt attendants.]

KING.
Hamlet, this deed, for thine especial safety—
40 Which we do tender,° as we dearly° grieve
For that which thou hast done—must send thee hence
With fiery quickness. Therefore prepare thyself.
The bark° is ready, and the wind at help,
Th' associates tend,° and everything is bent°
45 For England.

HAMLET. For England!

KING. Ay, Hamlet.

HAMLET. Good.

KING. So is it, if thou knew'st our purposes.

50 HAMLET. I see a cherub° that sees them. But come, for England! Farewell, dear mother.

KING. Thy loving father, Hamlet.

HAMLET. My mother. Father and mother is man and wife,
man and wife is one flesh, and so, my mother. Come, for
55 England!

Exit.

KING.
Follow him at foot;° tempt him with speed aboard.

Delay it not. I'll have him hence tonight.
Away! For everything is sealed and done
That else leans on° th' affair. Pray you, make haste.

[Exeunt all but the King.]

And, England,° if my love thou hold'st at aught°—   60
As my great power thereof may give thee sense,°
Since yet thy cicatrice° looks raw and red
After the Danish sword, and thy free awe°
Pays homage to us—thou mayst not coldly set°
Our sovereign process,° which imports at full,°   65
By letters congruing° to that effect,
The present° death of Hamlet. Do it, England,
For like the hectic° in my blood he rages,
And thou must cure me. Till I know 'tis done,
Howe'er my haps,° my joys were ne'er begun.   70

Exit.

4.4 *Enter Fortinbras with his army over the stage.*

FORTINBRAS.
Go, Captain, from me greet the Danish king.
Tell him that by his license° Fortinbras
Craves the conveyance of° a promised march
Over his kingdom. You know the rendezvous.
If that His Majesty would aught with us,   5
We shall express our duty° in his eye;°
And let him know so.

CAPTAIN.
I will do 't, my lord.

FORTINBRAS.
Go softly° on.

[Exeunt all but the Captain.]

Enter Hamlet, Rosencrantz, [Guildenstern,] etc.

HAMLET.
Good sir, whose powers° are these?   10

CAPTAIN.
They are of Norway, sir.

HAMLET.
How purposed, sir, I pray you?

---

21 politic worms crafty worms (suited to a master spy like Polonius).   **e'en** even now   **21–22 Your worm** your average worm
(Compare *your fat king and your lean beggar* in line 24.)   **22 diet**
food, eating (with a punning reference to the Diet of Worms, a famous *convocation* held in 1521)   **24 variable service** different
courses of a single meal   **27 eat** eaten (Pronounced *et*.)   **31
progress** royal journey of state   **40 tender** regard, hold dear
dearly intensely   **43 bark** sailing vessel   **44 tend** wait   **bent** in
readiness   **50 cherub** (Cherubim are angels of knowledge. Hamlet
hints that both he and heaven are onto Claudius's tricks.)   **56 at
foot** close behind, at heel

59 leans on bears upon, is related to   **60 England** i.e., King of
England   **at aught** at any value   **61 As . . . sense** for so my great
power may give you a just appreciation of the importance of valuing
my love   **62 cicatrice** scar   **63 free awe** voluntary show of respect
64 coldly set regard with indifference   **65 process** command.
imports at full conveys specific directions for   **66 congruing**
agreeing   **67 present** immediate   **68 hectic** persistent fever   **70
haps** fortunes   **4.4 Location: The coast of Denmark.**   **2 license**
permission   **3 the conveyance** of escort during   **6 duty** respect
eye presence   **9 softly** slowly, circumspectly   **10 powers** forces

CAPTAIN.
   Against some part of Poland.
HAMLET.
   Who commands them, sir?
CAPTAIN.
15   The nephew to old Norway, Fortinbras.
HAMLET.
   Goes it against the main° of Poland, sir,
   Or for some frontier?
CAPTAIN.
   Truly to speak, and with no addition,°
   We go to gain a little patch of ground
20   That hath in it no profit but the name.
   To pay° five ducats, five, I would not farm it;°
   Nor will it yield to Norway or the Pole
   A ranker° rate, should it be sold in fee.°
HAMLET.
   Why, then the Polack never will defend it.
CAPTAIN.
25   Yes, it is already garrisoned.
HAMLET.
   Two thousand souls and twenty thousand ducats
   Will not debate the question of this straw.°
   This is th' impostume° of much wealth and peace,
   That inward breaks, and shows no cause without
30   Why the man dies. I humbly thank you, sir.
CAPTAIN.
   God b'wi' you, sir.

                                          [Exit.]

ROSENCRANTZ.   Will 't please you go, my lord?
HAMLET.
   I'll be with you straight. Go a little before.

                          [Exeunt all except Hamlet.]

   How all occasions do inform against° me
   And spur my dull revenge! What is a man,
35   If his chief good and market of° his time
   Be but to sleep and feed? A beast, no more.
   Sure he that made us with such large discourse,°
   Looking before and after,° gave us not
   That capability and godlike reason
40   To fust° in us unused. Now, whether it be
   Bestial oblivion,° or some craven° scruple

Of thinking too precisely° on th' event°—
A thought which, quartered, hath but one part wisdom
And ever three parts coward—I do not know
Why yet I live to say "This thing's to do,"   45
Sith° I have cause, and will, and strength, and means
To do 't. Examples gross° as earth exhort me:
Witness this army of such mass and charge,°
Led by a delicate and tender° prince,
Whose spirit with divine ambition puffed   50
Makes mouths° at the invisible event,°
Exposing what is mortal and unsure
To all that fortune, death, and danger dare,°
Even for an eggshell. Rightly to be great
Is not to stir without great argument,   55
But greatly to find quarrel in a straw
When honor's at the stake.° How stand I, then,
That have a father killed, a mother stained,
Excitements of° my reason and my blood,
And let all sleep, while to my shame I see   60
The imminent death of twenty thousand men
That for a fantasy° and trick° of fame
Go to their graves like beds, fight for a plot°
Whereon the numbers cannot try the cause,°
Which is not tomb enough and continent°   65
To hide the slain? O, from this time forth
My thoughts be bloody or be nothing worth!

                                          Exit.

4.5 *Enter Horatio, [Queen] Gertrude, and a Gentleman.*

QUEEN.
   I will not speak with her.
GENTLEMAN.   She is importunate,
   Indeed distract.° Her mood will needs be pitied.
QUEEN.
   What would she have?
GENTLEMAN.
   She speaks much of her father, says she hears
   There's tricks° i' the world, and hems,° and beats her
      heart,°   5

16 **main** main part   18 **addition** exaggeration   21 **To pay** i.e., for
a yearly rental of.   **farm it** take a lease of it   23 **ranker** higher   **in
fee** fee simple, outright   27 **debate . . . straw** settle this trifling
matter   28 **impostume** abscess   33 **inform against** denounce, betray; take shape against   35 **market of** profit of, compensation for
37 **discourse** power of reasoning   38 **Looking before and after**
able to review past events and anticipate the future   40 **fust** grow
moldy   41 **oblivion** forgetfulness   **craven** cowardly

42 **precisely** scrupulously   **event** outcome   46 **Sith** since   47
gross obvious   48 **charge** expense   49 **delicate and tender** of fine
and youthful qualities   51 **Makes mouths** makes scornful faces.
invisible event unforeseeable outcome   53 **dare** could do (to him)
54–57 **Rightly . . . stake** true greatness does not normally consist of
rushing into action over some trivial provocation; however, when
one's honor is involved, even a trifling insult requires that one respond greatly(?)   **at the stake** (A metaphor from gambling or bear-
baiting.)   59 **Excitements of** promptings by   62 **fantasy** fanciful
caprice, illusion   **trick** trifle, deceit   63 **plot** plot of ground   64
Whereon . . . cause on which there is insufficient room for the soldiers needed to engage in a military contest   65 **continent** receptacle; container   **4.5 Location: The castle.**   2 **distract** distracted   5
tricks deceptions   **hems** makes "hmm" sounds   **heart** i.e., breast

Spurns enviously at straws,° speaks things in doubt°
That carry but half sense. Her speech is nothing,
Yet the unshapèd use° of it doth move
The hearers to collection;° they yawn° at it,
10   And botch° the words up fit to their own thoughts,
Which,° as her winks and nods and gestures yield° them,
Indeed would make one think there might be thought,°
Though nothing sure, yet much unhappily.°

HORATIO.
'Twere good she were spoken with, for she may strew
15   Dangerous conjectures in ill-breeding° minds.

QUEEN.
Let her come in.   [Exit Gentleman.]
[Aside.] To my sick soul, as sin's true nature is,
Each toy° seems prologue to some great amiss.°
So full of artless jealousy is guilt,
20   It spills itself in fearing to be spilt.°

Enter Ophelia° [distracted].

OPHELIA.
Where is the beauteous majesty of Denmark?

QUEEN.
How now, Ophelia?

OPHELIA [she sings].
"How should I your true love know
From another one?
25   By his cockle hat° and staff,
And his sandal shoon."°

QUEEN.
Alas, sweet lady, what imports this song?

OPHELIA.
Say you? Nay, pray you, mark.
"He is dead and gone, lady,
30   He is dead and gone;   [Song.]
At his head a grass-green turf,
At his heels a stone."
O, ho!

QUEEN.
Nay, but Ophelia—

OPHELIA.
Pray you, mark.   [Sings.]   35
"White his shroud as the mountain snow"—

Enter King.

QUEEN.
Alas, look here, my lord.

OPHELIA.
"Larded° with sweet flowers;   [Song.]
Which bewept to the ground did not go
With true-love showers."°   40

KING. How do you, pretty lady?

OPHELIA. Well, God 'ild° you! They say the owl° was a
baker's daughter. Lord, we know what we are, but know
not what we may be. God be at your table!

KING. Conceit° upon her father.   45

OPHELIA. Pray let's have no words of this; but when they ask
you what it means, say you this:
"Tomorrow is Saint Valentine's day,   [Song.]
All in the morning betime,°
And I a maid at your window,   50
To be your Valentine.
Then up he rose, and donned his clothes,
And dupped° the chamber door,
Let in the maid, that out a maid
Never departed more."   55

KING. Pretty Ophelia—

OPHELIA. Indeed, la, without an oath, I'll make an end on 't:
[Sings.]
"By Gis° and by Saint Charity,
Alack, and fie for shame!
Young men will do 't, if they come to 't;   60
By Cock,° they are to blame.
Quoth she, 'Before you tumbled me,
You promised me to wed.' "
He answers:
" 'So would I ha' done, by yonder sun,   65
An° thou hadst not come to my bed.' "

KING. How long hath she been thus?

OPHELIA. I hope all will be well. We must be patient, but I
cannot choose but weep to think they would lay him i'
the cold ground. My brother shall know of it. And so I   70
thank you for your good counsel. Come, my coach! Good
night, ladies, good night, sweet ladies, good night, good
night.

6 Spurns . . . straws kicks spitefully, takes offense at trifles   in
doubt obscurely   8 unshapèd use incoherent manner   9 collection inference, a guess at some sort of meaning   yawn gape, wonder; grasp. (The Folio reading, aim, is possible.)   10 botch patch
11 Which which words   yield deliver, represent   12 thought intended   13 unhappily unpleasantly near the truth, shrewdly   15
ill-breeding prone to suspect the worst and to make mischief   18
toy trifle   amiss calamity   19–20 So . . . split guilt is so full of
suspicion that it unskillfully betrays itself in fearing betrayal   20
s.d. Enter Ophelia (In the First Quarto, Ophelia enters, "playing
on a lute, and her hair down, singing.")   25 cockle hat hat with
cockle-shell stuck in it as a sign that the wearer had been a pilgrim
to the shrine of Saint James of Compostela in Spain   26 shoon
shoes

38 Larded decorated   40 showers i.e., tears   42 God 'ild God
yield or reward   owl (Refers to a legend about a baker's daughter
who was turned into an owl for being ungenerous when Jesus
begged a loaf of bread.)   45 Conceit brooding   49 betime early
53 dupped did up, opened   58 Gis Jesus   61 Cock (A perversion
of "God" in oaths; here also with a quibble on the slang word for
penis.)   66 An if

[*Exit.*]

KING [*to Horatio*].
   Follow her close. Give her good watch, I pray you.

[*Exit Horatio.*]

75   O, this is the poison of deep grief; it springs
     All from her father's death—and now behold!
     O Gertrude, Gertrude,
     When sorrows come, they come not single spies,°
     But in battalions. First, her father slain;
80   Next, your son gone, and he most violent author
     Of his own just remove;° the people muddied,°
     Thick and unwholesome in their thoughts and whispers
     For good Polonius' death—and we have done but
        greenly,°
     In hugger-mugger° to inter him; poor Ophelia
85   Divided from herself and her fair judgment,
     Without the which we are pictures or mere beasts;
     Last, and as much containing° as all these,
     Her brother is in secret come from France,
     Feeds on this wonder, keeps himself in clouds,°
90   And wants° not buzzers° to infect his ear
     With pestilent speeches of his father's death,
     Wherein necessity,° of matter beggared,°
     Will nothing stick our person to arraign
     In ear and ear.° O my dear Gertrude, this,
95   Like to a murdering piece,° in many places
     Gives me superfluous death.°   *A noise within.*
QUEEN.
     Alack, what noise is this?
KING.
     Attend!°
     Where is my Switzers?° Let them guard the door.

Enter a Messenger.

     What is the matter?
100 MESSENGER.   Save yourself, my lord!
     The ocean, overpeering of his list,°

Eats not the flats° with more impetuous° haste
Than young Laertes, in a riotous head,°
O'erbears your officers. The rabble call him lord,
And, as° the world were now but to begin,   105
Antiquity forgot, custom not known,
The ratifiers and props of every word,°
They cry, "Choose we! Laertes shall be king!"
Caps,° hands, and tongues applaud it to the clouds,
"Laertes shall be king, Laertes king!"   110
QUEEN.
How cheerfully on the false trail they cry!

                                    A noise within.

O, this is counter,° you false Danish dogs!

Enter Laertes with others.

KING. The doors are broke.
LAERTES. Where is this King?—Sirs, stand you all without.
ALL. No, let's come in.   115
LAERTES. I pray you, give me leave.
ALL. We will, we will.
LAERTES. I thank you. Keep the door. [*Exeunt followers.*] O
     thou vile king,
     Give me my father!
QUEEN [*RESTRAINING HIM*]. Calmly, good Laertes.
LAERTES.
     That drop of blood that's calm proclaims me bastard, 120
     Cries cuckold to my father, brands the harlot
     Even here, between° the chaste unsmirchèd brow
     Of my true mother.
KING.   What is the cause, Laertes,
     That thy rebellion looks so giantlike?
     Let him go, Gertrude. Do not fear our° person.   125
     There's such divinity doth hedge° a king
     That treason can but peep to what it would,°
     Acts little of his will.° Tell me, Laertes,
     Why thou art thus incensed. Let him go, Gertrude.
     Speak, man.
LAERTES.   Where is my father?
KING.   Dead.   130
QUEEN.
     But not by him.

---

78 spies scouts sent in advance of the main force   **81 remove** removal   **muddied** stirred up, confused   **83 greenly** in an inexperienced way, foolishly   **84 hugger-mugger** secret haste   **87 as much containing** as full of serious matter   **89 Feeds . . . clouds** feeds his resentment or shocked grievance, holds himself inscrutable and aloof amid all this rumor   **90 wants** lacks   **buzzers** gossipers, informers   **92 necessity** i.e., the need to invent some plausible explanation   **of matter beggared** unprovided with facts   **93–94 Will . . . ear** will not hesitate to accuse my (royal) person in everybody's ears   **95 murdering piece** cannon loaded so as to scatter its shot   **96 Gives . . . death** kills me over and over   **98 Attend** i.e., guard me   **99 Switzers** Swiss guards, mercenaries   **101 overpeering of his list** overflowing its shore, boundary

102 flats i.e., flatlands near shore   **impetuous** violent (perhaps also with the meaning of *impiteous* [*impitious*, Q2], "pitiless")   **103 head** insurrection   **105 as** as if   **107 The ratifiers . . . word** i.e., *antiquity* (or tradition) and *custom* ought to confirm (*ratify*) and underprop our every word or promise.   **109 Caps** (The caps are thrown in the air.)   **112 counter** (A hunting term, meaning to follow the trail in a direction opposite to that which the game has taken.)   **122 between** in the middle of   **125 fear our** fear for my   **126 hedge** protect, as with a surrounding barrier   **127 can . . . would** can only peep furtively, as through a barrier, at what it would intend   **128 Acts . . . will** (but) performs little of what it intends

KING.   Let him demand his fill.

LAERTES.

How came he dead? I'll not be juggled with.°
To hell, allegiance! Vows, to the blackest devil!
Conscience and grace, to the profoundest pit!
135 I dare damnation. To this point I stand,°
That both the worlds I give to negligence,°
Let come what comes, only I'll be revenged
Most throughly° for my father.

KING.

Who shall stay you?

LAERTES.

140 My will, not all the world's.°
And for° my means, I'll husband them so well
They shall go far with little.

KING.   Good Laertes,
If you desire to know the certainty
Of your dear father, is 't writ in your revenge
145 That, swoopstake,° you will draw both friend and foe,
Winner and loser?

LAERTES.

None but his enemies.

KING.

Will you know them, then?

LAERTES.

To his good friends thus wide I'll ope my arms,
150 And like the kind life-rendering pelican°
Repast° them with my blood.

KING.   Why, now you speak
Like a good child and a true gentleman.
That I am guiltless of your father's death,
And am most sensibly° in grief for it,
155 It shall as level° to your judgment 'pear
As day does to your eye.   *A noise within.*

LAERTES.

How now, what noise is that?

Enter Ophelia.

KING.   Let her come in.

LAERTES.

O heat, dry up my brains! Tears seven times salt
Burn out the sense and virtue° of mine eye!

By heaven, thy madness shall be paid with weight°   160
Till our scale turn the beam.° O rose of May!
Dear maid, kind sister, sweet Ophelia!
O heavens, is 't possible a young maid's wits
Should be as mortal as an old man's life?
Nature is fine in° love, and where 'tis fine   165
It sends some precious instance° of itself
After the thing it loves.°

OPHELIA.

"They bore him barefaced on the bier,   (*Song.*)
    Hey non nonny, nonny, hey nonny,
    And in his grave rained many a tear—"   170
Fare you well, my dove!

LAERTES. Hadst thou thy wits and didst persuade° revenge,
It could not move thus.

OPHELIA. You must sing "A-down a-down," and you "call
him a-down-a."° O, how the wheel° becomes it! It is the   175
false steward° that stole his master's daughter.

LAERTES. This nothing's more than matter.°

OPHELIA. There's rosemary,° that's for remembrance; pray
you, love, remember. And there is pansies;° that's for
thoughts.   180

LAERTES. A document° in madness, thoughts and remembrance fitted.

OPHELIA. There's fennel° for you, and columbines.° There's
rue° for you, and here's some for me; we may call it herb
of grace o' Sundays. You must wear your rue with a differ-   185
ence.° There's a daisy.° I would give you some violets,°
but they withered all when my father died. They say 'a
made a good end—
[*Sings.*] "For bonny sweet Robin is all my joy."

LAERTES.

Thought° and affliction, passion,° hell itself,   190

---

132 **juggled with** cheated, deceived   135 **To . . . stand** I am resolved in this   136 **both . . . negligence** i.e., both this world and
the next are of no consequence to me   138 **throughly** thoroughly
140 **My will . . . world's** I'll stop (*stay*) when my will is accomplished, not for anyone else's   141 **for** as for   145 **swoopstake**
i.e., indiscriminately (Literally, taking all stakes on the gambling
table at once. *Draw* is also a gambling term, meaning "take from.")
150 **pelican** (Refers to the belief that the female pelican fed its
young with its own blood.)   151 **Repast** feed   154 **sensibly** feelingly   155 **level** plain   159 **virtue** faculty, power

160 **paid with weight** repaid, avenged equally or more   161 **beam**
crossbar of a balance   165 **fine in** refined by   166 **instance** token
167 **After . . . loves** i.e., into the grave, along with Polonius   172
persuade argue cogently for   174–175 **You . . . a-down-a** (Ophelia assigns the singing of refrains, like her own "Hey non nonny," to
others present.)   175 **wheel** spinning wheel as accompaniment to
the song, or refrain   176 **false steward** (The story is unknown.)
177 **This . . . matter** this seeming nonsense is more eloquent than
sane utterance   178 **rosemary** (Used as a symbol of remembrance
both at weddings and at funerals.)   179 **pansies** (Emblems of love
and courtship; perhaps from French *pensées*, "thoughts.")   181
document instruction, lesson   183 **fennel** (Emblem of flattery.)
columbines (Emblems of unchastity or ingratitude.)   184 **rue**
(Emblem of repentance—a signification that is evident in its popular name, *herb of grace.*)   185–186 **with a difference** (A device
used in heraldry to distinguish one family from another on the coat
of arms, here suggesting that Ophelia and the others have different
causes of sorrow and repentance; perhaps with a play on *rue* in the
sense of "ruth," "pity.")   186 **daisy** (Emblem of dissembling, faith-
lessness.)   **violets** (Emblems of faithfulness.)   190 **Thought**
melancholy   **passion** suffering

She turns to favor° and to prettiness.

OPHELIA.

> "And will 'a not come again?   [*Song.*]
> And will 'a not come again?
>   No, no, he is dead.
>   Go to thy deathbed,
> 195   He never will come again.

> "His beard was as white as snow,
> All flaxen was his poll.°
>   He is gone, he is gone,
> 200   And we cast away moan.
> God ha' mercy on his soul!"

And of all Christian souls, I pray God. God b' wi' you.

[*Exit, followed by Gertrude.*]

LAERTES.
    Do you see this, O God?

KING.
    Laertes, I must commune with your grief,
205   Or you deny me right. Go but apart,
    Make choice of whom° your wisest friends you will,
    And they shall hear and judge twixt you and me.
    If by direct or by collateral hand°
    They find us touched,° we will our kingdom give,
210   Our crown, our life, and all that we call ours
    To you in satisfaction; but if not,
    Be you content to lend your patience to us,
    And we shall jointly labor with your soul
    To give it due content.

LAERTES.   Let this be so.
215   His means of death, his obscure funeral—
    No trophy,° sword, nor hatchment° o'er his bones,
    No noble rite, nor formal ostentation°—
    Cry to be heard, as 'twere from heaven to earth,
    That° I must call 't in question.°

KING.   So you shall,
220   And where th' offense is, let the great ax fall.
    I pray you, go with me.

Exeunt.

4.6 *Enter Horatio and others.*

HORATIO.
    What are they that would speak with me?

GENTLEMAN.
    Seafaring men, sir. They say they have letters for you.

HORATIO.
    Let them come in.

[*Exit Gentleman.*]

I do not know from what part of the world
I should be greeted, if not from Lord Hamlet.   5

Enter Sailors.

FIRST SAILOR. God bless you, sir.

HORATIO. Let him bless thee too.

FIRST SAILOR. 'A shall, sir, an 't° please him. There's a letter
    for you, sir—it came from th' ambassador° that was
    bound for England—if your name be Horatio, as I am let   10
    to know it is.   [*He gives a letter.*]

HORATIO [*reads*]. "Horatio, when thou shalt have over-
    looked° this, give these fellows some means° to the King;
    they have letters for him. Ere we were two days old at sea,
    a pirate of very warlike appointment° gave us chase.   15
    Finding ourselves too slow of sail, we put on a compelled
    valor, and in the grapple I boarded them. On the instant
    they got clear of our ship, so I alone became their pris-
    oner. They have dealt with me like thieves of mercy,° but
    they knew what they did: I am to do a good turn for   20
    them. Let the King have the letters I have sent, and re-
    pair° thou to me with as much speed as thou wouldest fly
    death. I have words to speak in thine ear will make thee
    dumb, yet are they much too light for the bore° of the
    matter. These good fellows will bring thee where I am.   25
    Rosencrantz and Guildenstern hold their course for Eng-
    land. Of them I have much to tell thee. Farewell.

                         He that thou knowest thine, Hamlet."
Come, I will give you way° for these your letters,
And do 't the speedier that you may direct me   30
To him from whom you brought them.

Exeunt.

4.7 *Enter King and Laertes.*

KING.
    Now must your conscience my acquittance seal,°
    And you must put me in your heart for friend,
    Sith° you have heard, and with a knowing ear,
    That he which hath your noble father slain
    Pursued my life.

LAERTES.   It well appears. But tell me   5
    Why you proceeded not against these feats°

---

191 favor grace, beauty   **198 poll** head   **206 whom** whichever of
208 collateral hand indirect agency   **209 us touched** me implicated   **216 trophy** memorial   **hatchment** tablet displaying the ar-
morial bearings of a deceased person   **217 ostentation** ceremony
219 That so that   **call 't in question** demand an explanation
4.6 Location: The castle.

8 an 't if it   **9 th' ambassador** (Evidently Hamlet. The sailor is being circumspect.)   **12–13 overlooked** looked over   **13 means**
means of access   **15 appointment** equipage   **19 thieves of mercy**
merciful thieves   **21–22 repair** come   **24 bore** caliber, i.e., importance   **29 way** means of access   **4.7 Location: The castle.**   **1
my acquittance seal** confirm or acknowledge my innocence   **3
Sith** since   **6 feats** acts

So crimeful and so capital° in nature,
As by your safety, greatness, wisdom, all things else,
You mainly° were stirred up.

KING.
10   O, for two special reasons,
Which may to you perhaps seem much unsinewed,°
But yet to me they're strong. The Queen his mother
Lives almost by his looks, and for myself—
My virtue or my plague, be it either which—
15   She is so conjunctive° to my life and soul
That, as the star moves not but in his° sphere,°
I could not but by her. The other motive
Why to a public count° I might not go
Is the great love the general gender° bear him,
20   Who, dipping all his faults in their affection,
Work° like the spring° that turneth wood to stone,
Convert his gyves° to graces, so that my arrows,
Too slightly timbered° for so loud° a wind,
Would have reverted° to my bow again
25   But not where I had aimed them.

LAERTES.
And so have I a noble father lost,
A sister driven into desperate terms,°
Whose worth, if praises may go back° again,
Stood challenger on mount° of all the age
30   For her perfections. But my revenge will come.

KING.
Break not your sleeps for that. You must not think
That we are made of stuff so flat and dull
That we can let our beard be shook with danger
And think it pastime. You shortly shall hear more.
35   I loved your father, and we love ourself;
And that, I hope, will teach you to imagine—

Enter a Messenger with letters.

How now? What news?

MESSENGER.
Letters, my lord, from Hamlet:
This to Your Majesty, this to the Queen.

[*He gives letters.*]

KING.
From Hamlet? Who brought them?   40

MESSENGER.
Sailors, my lord, they say. I saw them not.
They were given me by Claudio. He received them
Of him that brought them.

KING.   Laertes, you shall hear them.—
Leave us.

[*Exit Messenger.*]

[*He reads.*] "High and mighty, you shall know I am set   45
naked° on your kingdom. Tomorrow shall I beg leave
to see your kingly eyes, when I shall, first asking your
pardon,° thereunto recount the occasion of my sudden and more strange return.
                                        Hamlet."
What should this mean? Are all the rest come back?
Or is it some abuse,° and no such thing?°   50

LAERTES.
Know you the hand?

KING.   'Tis Hamlet's character.° "Naked!"
And in a postscript here he says "alone."
Can you devise° me?

LAERTES.
I am lost in it, my lord. But let him come.
It warms the very sickness in my heart   55
That I shall live and tell him to his teeth,
"Thus didst thou."°

KING.   If it be so, Laertes—
As how should it be so? How otherwise?°—
Will you be ruled by me?

LAERTES.   Ay, my lord,
So° you will not o'errule me to a peace.   60

KING.
To thine own peace. If he be now returned,
As checking at° his voyage, and that° he means
No more to undertake it, I will work him
To an exploit, now ripe in my device,°
Under the which he shall not choose but fall;   65
And for his death no wind of blame shall breathe,
But even his mother shall uncharge the practice°
And call it accident.

---

7 capital punishable by death   **9 mainly** greatly   **11 unsinewed**
weak   **15 conjunctive** closely united (An astronomical
metaphor.)   **16 his** its   **sphere** one of the hollow spheres in
which, according to Ptolemaic astronomy, the planets were supposed to move   **18 count** account, reckoning, indictment   **19**
general gender common people   **21 Work** operate, act   **spring**
i.e., a spring with such a concentration of lime that it coats a piece
of wood with limestone, in effect gilding and petrifying it   **22**
gyves fetters (which, gilded by the people's praise, would look like
badges of honor)   **23 slightly timbered** light.   **loud** (suggesting
public outcry on Hamlet's behalf)   **24 reverted** returned   **27**
terms state, condition   **28 go back** i.e., recall what she was   **29**
on mount set up on high

46 naked destitute, unarmed, without following   **48 pardon** permission   **50 abuse** deceit   **no such thing** not what it appears   **51**
character handwriting   **53 devise** explain to   **57 Thus didst**
thou i.e., here's for what you did to my father   **58 As ... other-**
wise how can this (Hamlet's return) be true? Yet how otherwise
than true (since we have the evidence of his letter)?   **60 So** provided that   **62 checking at** i.e., turning aside from (like a falcon
leaving the quarry to fly at a chance bird)   **that** if   **64 device** devising, invention   **67 uncharge the practice** acquit the stratagem
of being a plot

LAERTES.   My lord, I will be ruled,
 The rather if you could devise it so
 That I might be the organ.°
70 KING.   It falls right.
 You have been talked of since your travel much,
 And that in Hamlet's hearing, for a quality
 Wherein they say you shine. Your sum of parts°
 Did not together pluck such envy from him
75 As did that one, and that, in my regard,
 Of the unworthiest siege.°
 LAERTES.
 What part is that, my lord?
 KING.
 A very ribbon in the cap of youth,
 Yet needful too, for youth no less becomes°
80 The light and careless livery that it wears
 Than settled age his sables° and his weeds°
 Importing health and graveness.° Two months since
 Here was a gentleman of Normandy.
 I have seen myself, and served against, the French,
85 And they can well° on horseback, but this gallant
 Had witchcraft in 't; he grew unto his seat,
 And to such wondrous doing brought his horse
 As had he been incorpsed and demi-natured°
 With the brave beast. So far he topped° my thought
90 That I in forgery° of shapes and tricks
 Come short of what he did.
 LAERTES.   A Norman was 't?
 KING.
 A Norman.
 LAERTES.
 Upon my life, Lamord.
 KING.   The very same.
 LAERTES.
 I know him well. He is the brooch° indeed
95 And gem of all the nation.
 KING.
 He made confession° of you,
 And gave you such a masterly report
 For art and exercise in your defense,°
 And for your rapier most especial,
100 That he cried out 'twould be a sight indeed
 If one could match you. Th' escrimers° of their nation,

He swore, had neither motion, guard, nor eye
If you opposed them. Sir, this report of his
Did Hamlet so envenom with his envy
That he could nothing do but wish and beg   105
Your sudden° coming o'er, to play° with you.
Now, out of this—
LAERTES.   What out of this, my lord?
KING.
Laertes, was your father dear to you?
Or are you like the painting of a sorrow,
A face without a heart?
LAERTES.   Why ask you this?   110
KING.
Not that I think you did not love your father,
But that I know love is begun by time,°
And that I see, in passages of proof,°
Time qualifies° the spark and fire of it.
There lives within the very flame of love   115
A kind of wick or snuff° that will abate it,
And nothing is at a like goodness still,°
For goodness, growing to a pleurisy,°
Dies in his own too much.° That° we would do,
We should do when we would; for this "would" changes   120
And hath abatements° and delays as many
As there are tongues, are hands, are accidents,°
And then this "should" is like a spendthrift sigh,°
That hurts by easing.° But, to the quick o' th' ulcer:°
Hamlet comes back. What would you undertake   125
To show yourself in deed your father's son
More than in words?
LAERTES.   To cut his throat i' the church.
KING.
No place, indeed, should murder sanctuarize;°
Revenge should have no bounds. But good Laertes,
Will you do this,° keep close within your chamber.   130
Hamlet returned shall know you are come home.
We'll put on those shall° praise your excellence

---

70 organ agent, instrument   **73 Your ... parts** i.e., all your other virtues   **76 unworthiest siege** least important rank   **79 no less becomes** is no less suited by   **81 his sables** its rich robes furred with sable.   **weeds** garments   **82 Importing ... graveness** signifying a concern for health and dignified prosperity; also, giving an impression of comfortable prosperity   **85 can well** are skilled   **88 As ... demi-natured** as if he had been of one body and nearly of one nature (like the centaur)   **89 topped** surpassed   **90 forgery** imagining   **94 brooch** ornament   **96 confession** testimonial, admission of superiority   **98 For ... defense** with respect to your skill and practice with your weapon   **101 escrimers** fencers

106 sudden immediate   **play** fence   **112 begun by time** i.e., created by the right circumstance and hence subject to change   **113 passages of proof** actual instances that prove it   **114 qualifies** weakens, moderates   **116 snuff** the charred part of a candlewick   **117 nothing ... still** nothing remains at a constant level of perfection   **118 pleurisy** excess, plethora (Literally, a chest inflammation.)   **119 in ... much** of its own excess   **That** that which   **121 abatements** diminutions   **122 As ... accidents** as there are tongues to dissuade, hands to prevent, and chance events to intervene   **123 spendthrift sigh** (An allusion to the belief that sighs draw blood from the heart.)   **124 hurts by easing** i.e., costs the heart blood and wastes precious opportunity even while it affords emotional relief   **quick o' th' ulcer** i.e., heart of the matter   **128 sanctuarize** protect from punishment (Alludes to the right of sanctuary with which certain religious places were invested.)   **130 Will you do this** if you wish to do this   **132 put on those shall** arrange for some to

And set a double varnish on the fame
The Frenchman gave you, bring you in fine° together,
135   And wager on your heads. He, being remiss,°
Most generous,° and free from all contriving,
Will not peruse the foils, so that with ease,
Or with a little shuffling, you may choose
A sword unbated,° and in a pass of practice°
Requite him for your father.

140   LAERTES.   I will do 't,
And for that purpose I'll anoint my sword.
I bought an unction° of a mountebank°
So mortal that, but dip a knife in it,
Where it draws blood no cataplasm° so rare,
145   Collected from all simples° that have virtue°
Under the moon,° can save the thing from death
That is but scratched withal. I'll touch my point
With this contagion, that if I gall° him slightly,
It may be death.

      KING.   Let's further think of this,
150   Weigh what convenience both of time and means
May fit us to our shape.° If this should fail,
And that our drift look through our bad performance,°
'Twere better not assayed. Therefore this project
Should have a back or second, that might hold
155   If this did blast in proof.° Soft, let me see.
We'll make a solemn wager on your cunnings°—
I ha 't!
When in your motion you are hot and dry—
As° make your bouts more violent to that end—
160   And that he calls for drink, I'll have prepared him
A chalice for the nonce,° whereon but sipping,
If he by chance escape your venomed stuck,°
Our purpose may hold there. [A cry within.] But stay,
      what noise?

      Enter Queen.

QUEEN.
One woe doth tread upon another's heel,

So fast they follow. Your sister's drowned, Laertes.   165
LAERTES.
Drowned! O, where?
QUEEN.
There is a willow grows askant° the brook,
That shows his hoar leaves° in the glassy stream;
Therewith fantastic garlands did she make
Of crowflowers, nettles, daisies, and long purples,°   170
That liberal° shepherds give a grosser name,°
But our cold° maids do dead men's fingers call them.
There on the pendent° boughs her crownet° weeds
Clamb'ring to hang, an envious sliver° broke,
When down her weedy° trophies and herself   175
Fell in the weeping brook. Her clothes spread wide,
And mermaidlike awhile they bore her up,
Which time she chanted snatches of old lauds,°
As one incapable of° her own distress,
Or like a creature native and endued°   180
Unto that element. But long it could not be
Till that her garments, heavy with their drink,
Pulled the poor wretch from her melodious lay
To muddy death.
LAERTES.   Alas, then she is drowned?
QUEEN.
Drowned, drowned.   185
LAERTES.
Too much of water hast thou, poor Ophelia,
And therefore I forbid my tears. But yet
It is our trick;° nature her custom holds,
Let shame say what it will. [He weeps.] When these are
      gone,   190
The woman will be out.° Adieu, my lord.
I have a speech of fire that fain would blaze,
But that this folly douts° it.   Exit.
KING.   Let's follow, Gertrude.
How much I had to do to calm his rage!
Now fear I this will give it start again;   195
Therefore let's follow.

                                        Exeunt.

---

134 in fine finally   135 remiss negligently unsuspicious   136 generous noble-minded   139 unbated not blunted, having no button   pass of practice treacherous thrust   142 unction ointment   mountebank quack doctor   144 cataplasm plaster or poultice   145 simples herbs   virtue potency   146 Under the moon i.e., anywhere (with reference perhaps to the belief that herbs gathered at night had a special power)   148 gall graze, wound   151 shape part we propose to act   152 drift . . . performance intention should be made visible by our bungling   155 blast in proof burst in the test (like a cannon)   156 cunnings respective skills   159 As i.e., and you should   161 nonce occasion   162 stuck thrust (From stoccado, a fencing term.)

167 askant aslant   168 hoar leaves white or gray undersides of the leaves   170 long purples early purple orchids   171 liberal free-spoken   a grosser name (The testicle-resembling tubers of the orchid, which also in some cases resemble dead men's fingers, have earned various slang names like "dogstones" and "cullions.")   172 cold chaste   173 pendent overhanging   crownet made into a chaplet or coronet   174 envious sliver malicious branch   175 weedy i.e., of plants   178 lauds hymns   179 incapable of lacking capacity to apprehend   180 endued adapted by nature   188 It is our trick i.e., weeping is our natural way (when sad)   189–190 When . . . out when my tears are all shed, the woman in me will be expended, satisfied   192 douts extinguishes (The Second Quarto reads "drowns.")

5.1 *Enter two Clowns*° [*with spades and mattocks*].

FIRST CLOWN. Is she to be buried in Christian burial, when
  she willfully seeks her own salvation?°

SECOND CLOWN. I tell thee she is; therefore make her grave
  straight.° The crowner° hath sat on her,° and finds it°
5 Christian burial.

FIRST CLOWN. How can that be, unless she drowned herself
  in her own defense?

SECOND CLOWN. Why, 'tis found so.°

FIRST CLOWN. It must be *se offendendo*,° it cannot be else. For
10 here lies the point: if I drown myself wittingly, it argues
  an act, and an act hath three branches—it is to act, to
  do, and to perform. Argal,° she drowned herself wittingly.

SECOND CLOWN. Nay, but hear you, goodman° delver—

FIRST CLOWN. Give me leave. Here lies the water; good. Here
15 stands the man; good. If the man go to this water and
  drown himself, it is, will he, nill he,° he goes, mark you
  that. But if the water come to him and drown him, he
  drowns not himself. Argal, he that is not guilty of his
  own death shortens not his own life.

20 SECOND CLOWN. But is this law?

FIRST CLOWN. Ay, marry, is 't—crowner's quest° law.

SECOND CLOWN. Will you ha' the truth on 't? If this had not
  been a gentlewoman, she should have been buried out o'
  Christian burial.

25 FIRST CLOWN. Why, there thou sayst.° And the more pity
  that great folk should have countenance° in this world to
  drown or hang themselves, more than their even-Christian.° Come, my spade. There is no ancient° gentlemen
  but gardeners, ditchers, and grave makers. They hold up°
30 Adam's profession.

SECOND CLOWN. Was he a gentleman?

FIRST CLOWN. 'A was the first that ever bore arms.°

SECOND CLOWN. Why, he had none.

FIRST CLOWN. What, art a heathen? How dost thou understand the Scripture? The Scripture says Adam digged.   35
  Could he dig without arms?° I'll put another question to
  thee. If thou answerest me not to the purpose, confess
  thyself°—

SECOND CLOWN. Go to.

FIRST CLOWN. What is he that builds stronger than either the   40
  mason, the shipwright, or the carpenter?

SECOND CLOWN. The gallows maker, for that frame° outlives
  a thousand tenants.

FIRST CLOWN. I like thy wit well, in good faith. The gallows
  does well.° But how does it well? It does well to those   45
  that do ill. Now thou dost ill to say the gallows is built
  stronger than the church. Argal, the gallows may do well
  to thee. To 't again, come.

SECOND CLOWN. "Who builds stronger than a mason, a shipwright, or a carpenter?"   50

FIRST CLOWN. Ay, tell me that, and unyoke.°

SECOND CLOWN. Marry, now I can tell.

FIRST CLOWN. To 't.

SECOND CLOWN. Mass,° I cannot tell.

Enter Hamlet and Horatio [*at a distance*].

FIRST CLOWN. Cudgel thy brains no more about it, for your   55
  dull ass will not mend his pace with beating; and when
  you are asked this question next, say "a grave maker."
  The houses he makes lasts till doomsday. Go get thee in
  and fetch me a stoup° of liquor.

[*Exit Second Clown. First Clown digs.*]

Song.

"In youth, when I did love, did love,°   60
  Methought it was very sweet,
  To contract—O—the time for—a—my behove,°
  O, methought there—a—was nothing—a—meet."°

HAMLET. Has this fellow no feeling of his business, 'a° sings
  in grave-making?   65

HORATIO. Custom hath made it in him a property of easiness.°

5.1 Location: A churchyard.   **s.d. Clowns** rustics   **2 salvation**
(A blunder for "damnation," or perhaps a suggestion that Ophelia
was taking her own shortcut to heaven.)   **4 straight** straightway,
immediately. (But with a pun on *strait*, "narrow.")   **crowner** coroner.   **sat on her** conducted an inquest on her case   **finds it** gives
his official verdict that her means of death was consistent with   **8
found so** determined so in the coroner's verdict   **9 *se offendendo***
(A comic mistake for *se defendendo*, a term used in verdicts of justifiable homicide.)   **12 Argal** (Corruption of *ergo*, "therefore.")
13 goodman (An honorific title often used with the name of a profession or craft.)   **16 will he, nill he** whether he will or no, willy-
nilly   **21 quest** inquest   **25 there thou sayst** i.e., that's right   **26
countenance** privilege   **27–28 even-Christian** fellow Christians
28 ancient going back to ancient times   **29 hold up** maintain
32 bore arms (To be entitled to bear a coat of arms would make
Adam a gentleman, but as one who bore a spade, our common ancestor was an ordinary delver in the earth.)

36 arms i.e., the arms of the body   **37–38 confess thyself** (The
saying continues, "and be hanged.")   **42 frame** (1) gallows (2)
structure   **45 does well** (1) is an apt answer (2) does a good turn
51 unyoke i.e., after this great effort, you may unharness the team
of your wits   **54 Mass** by the Mass   **59 stoup** two-quart measure
60 In . . . love (This and the two following stanzas, with nonsensical variations, are from a poem attributed to Lord Vaux and printed
in *Tottel's Miscellany*, 1557. The O and *a* [for "ah"] seemingly are
the grunts of the digger.)   **62 To contract . . . behove** i.e., to
shorten the time for my own advantage (Perhaps he means to *prolong* it.)   **63 meet** suitable, i.e., more suitable   **64 'a** that he   **66
property of easiness** something he can do easily and indifferently

HAMLET. 'Tis e'en so. The hand of little employment hath the daintier sense.°

FIRST CLOWN.   *Song.*

"But age with his stealing steps
70   Hath clawed me in his clutch,
        And hath shipped me into the land,°
        As if I had never been such."

[He throws up a skull.]

HAMLET. That skull had a tongue in it and could sing once.
How the knave jowls° it to the ground, as if 'twere Cain's
75   jawbone, that did the first murder! This might be the
        pate of a politician,° which this ass now o'erreaches,° one
        that would circumvent God, might it not?

HORATIO. It might, my lord.

HAMLET. Or of a courtier, which could say, "Good morrow,
80   sweet lord! How dost thou, sweet lord?" This might be
        my Lord Such-a-one, that praised my Lord Such-a-one's
        horse when 'a meant to beg it, might it not?

HORATIO. Ay, my lord.

HAMLET. Why, e'en so, and now my Lady Worm's, chapless,°
85   and knocked about the mazard° with a sexton's spade.
        Here's fine revolution,° an° we had the trick to see° 't.
        Did these bones cost no more the breeding but° to play at
        loggets° with them? Mine ache to think on 't.

FIRST CLOWN.   *Song.*

"A pickax and a spade, a spade,
90   For and° a shrouding sheet;
        O, a pit of clay for to be made
        For such a guest is meet."

[He throws up another skull.]

HAMLET. There's another. Why may not that be the skull of a
        lawyer? Where be his quiddities° now, his quillities,° his
95   cases, his tenures,° and his tricks? Why does he suffer this
        mad knave now to knock him about the sconce° with a

dirty shovel, and will not tell him of his action of battery?° Hum, this fellow might be in 's time a great buyer
of land, with his statutes, his recognizances,° his fines, his
double° vouchers,° his recoveries.° Is this the fine of his   100
fines and the recovery of his recoveries, to have his fine
pate full of fine dirt?° Will his vouchers vouch him no
more of his purchases, and double ones too, than the
length and breadth of a pair of indentures?° The very
conveyances° of his lands will scarcely lie in this box,°   105
and must th' inheritor° himself have no more, ha?

HORATIO. Not a jot more, my lord.

HAMLET. Is not parchment made of sheepskins?

HORATIO. Ay, my lord, and of calves' skins too.

HAMLET. They are sheep and calves which seek out assurance   110
in that.° I will speak to this fellow.—Whose grave's this,
sirrah?°

FIRST CLOWN. Mine, sir.   *[Sings.]*
"O, pit of clay for to be made
        For such a guest is meet."   115

HAMLET. I think it be thine, indeed, for thou liest in 't.

FIRST CLOWN. You lie out on 't, sir, and therefore 'tis not
yours. For my part, I do not lie in 't, yet it is mine.

HAMLET. Thou dost lie in 't, to be in 't and say it is thine. 'Tis
for the dead, not for the quick;° therefore thou liest.   120

FIRST CLOWN. 'Tis a quick lie, sir; 'twill away again from me
to you.

HAMLET. What man dost thou dig it for?

FIRST CLOWN. For no man, sir.

HAMLET. What woman, then?   125

FIRST CLOWN. For none, neither.

HAMLET. Who is to be buried in 't?

FIRST CLOWN. One that was a woman, sir, but, rest her soul,
she's dead.

HAMLET. How absolute° the knave is! We must speak by the   130
card,° or equivocation° will undo us. By the Lord, Horatio, this three years I have took° note of it: the age is

---

68 daintier sense more delicate sense of feeling   **71 into the land**
i.e., toward my grave(?) (But note the lack of rhyme in *steps, land.*)
74 jowls dashes (with a pun on *jowl,* "jawbone")   **76 politician**
schemer, plotter   **o'erreaches** circumvents, gets the better of (with
a quibble on the literal sense)   **84 chapless** having no lower jaw
85 mazard i.e., head. (Literally, a drinking vessel.)   **86 revolution**
turn of Fortune's wheel, change   **an** if   **trick to see** knack of seeing   **87 cost . . . but** involve so little expense and care in upbringing that we may   **88 loggets** a game in which pieces of hard wood
shaped like Indian clubs or bowling pins are thrown to lie as near as
possible to a stake   **90 For and** and moreover   **94 quiddities** subtleties, quibbles. (From Latin *quid,* "a thing.")   **quillities** verbal
niceties, subtle distinctions. (Variation of *quiddities.*)   **95 tenures**
the holding of a piece of property or office, or the conditions or period of such holding   **96 sconce** head

97–98 action of battery lawsuit about physical assault   **99
statutes, recognizances** legal documents guaranteeing a debt by attaching land and property   **99–100 fines, recoveries** ways of converting entailed estates into "fee simple" or freehold   **100 double**
signed by two signatories   **vouchers** guarantees of the legality of a
title to real estate   **100–103 fine of his fines . . . fine pate . . .
fine dirt** end of his legal maneuvers . . . elegant head . . . minutely
sifted dirt   **104 pair of indentures** legal document drawn up in duplicate on a single sheet and then cut apart on a zigzag line so that
each pair was uniquely matched. (Hamlet may refer to two rows of
teeth or dentures.)   **105 conveyances** deeds   **box** (1) deed box
(2) coffin. ("Skull" has been suggested.)   **106 inheritor** possessor,
owner   **110–111 assurance in that** safety in legal parchments
112 sirrah (A term of address to inferiors.)   **120 quick** living
130 absolute strict, precise   **130–131 by the card** i.e., with precision (Literally, by the mariner's compass-card, on which the points
of the compass were marked.)   **131 equivocation** ambiguity in the
use of terms   **132 took** taken

grown so picked° that the toe of the peasant comes so near the heel of the courtier, he galls his kibe.°—How long hast thou been grave maker?

135

FIRST CLOWN. Of all the days i' the year, I came to 't that day that our last king Hamlet overcame Fortinbras.

HAMLET. How long is that since?

FIRST CLOWN. Cannot you tell that? Every fool can tell that. It was that very day that young Hamlet was born—he that is mad and sent into England.

140

HAMLET. Ay, marry, why was he sent into England?

FIRST CLOWN. Why, because 'a was mad. 'A shall recover his wits there, or if 'a do not, 'tis no great matter there.

145

HAMLET. Why?

FIRST CLOWN. 'Twill not be seen in him there. There the men are as mad as he.

HAMLET. How came he mad?

FIRST CLOWN. Very strangely, they say.

150

HAMLET. How strangely?

FIRST CLOWN. Faith, e'en with losing his wits.

HAMLET. Upon what ground?°

FIRST CLOWN. Why, here in Denmark. I have been sexton here, man and boy, thirty years.

155

HAMLET. How long will a man lie i' th' earth ere he rot?

FIRST CLOWN. Faith, if 'a be not rotten before 'a die—as we have many pocky° corpses nowadays, that will scarce hold the laying in°—'a will last you° some eight year or nine year. A tanner will last you nine year.

160

HAMLET. Why he more than another?

FIRST CLOWN. Why, sir, his hide is so tanned with his trade that 'a will keep out water a great while, and your water is a sore° decayer of your whoreson° dead body. [*He picks up a skull.*] Here's a skull now hath lien you° i' th' earth three-and-twenty years.

165

HAMLET. Whose was it?

FIRST CLOWN. A whoreson mad fellow's it was. Whose do you think it was?

HAMLET. Nay, I know not.

170

FIRST CLOWN. A pestilence on him for a mad rogue! 'A poured a flagon of Rhenish° on my head once. This same skull, sir, was, sir, Yorick's skull, the King's jester.

HAMLET. This?

FIRST CLOWN. E'en that.

175

HAMLET. Let me see. [*He takes the skull.*] Alas, poor Yorick! I knew him, Horatio, a fellow of infinite jest, of most ex-

cellent fancy. He hath bore° me on his back a thousand times, and now how abhorred in my imagination it is! My gorge rises° at it. Here hung those lips that I have kissed I know not how oft. Where be your gibes now? Your gambols, your songs, your flashes of merriment that were wont° to set the table on a roar? Not one now, to mock your own grinning?° Quite chopfallen?° Now get you to my lady's chamber and tell her, let her paint an inch thick, to this favor° she must come. Make her laugh at that. Prithee, Horatio, tell me one thing.

180

185

HORATIO. What's that, my lord?

HAMLET. Dost thou think Alexander looked o' this fashion i' th' earth?

HORATIO. E'en so.

190

HAMLET. And smelt so? Pah! [*He throws down the skull.*]

HORATIO. E'en so, my lord.

HAMLET. To what base uses we may return, Horatio! Why may not imagination trace the noble dust of Alexander till 'a find it stopping a bunghole?°

195

HORATIO. 'Twere to consider too curiously° to consider so.

HAMLET. No, faith, not a jot, but to follow him thither with modesty° enough, and likelihood to lead it. As thus: Alexander died, Alexander was buried, Alexander returneth to dust, the dust is earth, of earth we make loam,° and why of that loam whereto he was converted might they not stop a beer barrel?

200

Imperious° Caesar, dead and turned to clay,
Might stop a hole to keep the wind away.
O, that that earth which kept the world in awe
Should patch a wall t' expel the winter's flaw!°

205

Enter King, Queen, Laertes, and the corpse [of Ophelia, in procession, with Priest, lords, etc.].

But soft,° but soft awhile! Here comes the King,
The Queen, the courtiers. Who is this they follow?
And with such maimèd° rites? This doth betoken
The corpse they follow did with desperate hand
Fordo° its own life. 'Twas of some estate.°
Couch we° awhile and mark.

210

[He and Horatio conceal themselves. Ophelia's body is taken to the grave.]

---

133 **picked** refined, fastidious 134 **galls his kibe** chafes the courtier's chilblain 152 **ground** cause (But, in the next line, the grave-digger takes the word in the sense of "land," "country.") 157 **pocky** rotten, diseased (Literally, with the pox, or syphilis.) 158 **hold the laying in** hold together long enough to be interred **last you** last. (*You* is used colloquially here and in the following lines.) 163 **sore** i.e., terrible, great **whoreson** i.e., vile, scurvy 164 **lien you** lain. (See the note at line 158.) 172 **Rhenish** Rhine wine

177 **bore** borne 178–179 **My gorge rises** i.e., I feel nauseated 181–182 **were wont** used 182–183 **mock your own grinning** mock at the way your skull seems to be grinning (just as you used to mock at yourself and those who grinned at you) 183 **chopfallen** (1) lacking the lower jaw (2) dejected 185 **favor** aspect, appearance 195 **bunghole** hole for filling or emptying a cask 196 **curiously** minutely 198 **modesty** plausible moderation 200 **loam** mortar consisting chiefly of moistened clay and straw 203 **Imperious** imperial 206 **flaw** gust of wind 207 **soft** i.e., wait, be careful 209 **maimèd** mutilated, incomplete 211 **Fordo** destroy. **estate** rank 212 **Couch we** let's hide, lie low

LAERTES.
    What ceremony else?
HAMLET [to Horatio].
    That is Laertes, a very noble youth. Mark.
LAERTES.
215   What ceremony else?
PRIEST.
    Her obsequies have been as far enlarged
    As we have warranty.° Her death was doubtful,
    And but that great command o'ersways the order°
    She should in ground unsanctified been lodged°
220   Till the last trumpet. For° charitable prayers,
    Shards,° flints, and pebbles should be thrown on her.
    Yet here she is allowed her virgin crants,°
    Her maiden strewments,° and the bringing home
    Of bell and burial.°
LAERTES.
    Must there no more be done?
225 PRIEST.   No more be done.
    We should profane the service of the dead
    To sing a requiem and such rest° to her
    As to peace-parted souls.°
LAERTES.   Lay her i' th' earth,
    And from her fair and unpolluted flesh
230   May violets° spring! I tell thee, churlish priest,
    A ministering angel shall my sister be
    When thou liest howling.°
HAMLET [to Horatio].   What, the fair Ophelia!
QUEEN [scattering flowers].
    Sweets to the sweet! Farewell.
    I hoped thou shouldst have been my Hamlet's wife.
235   I thought thy bride-bed to have decked, sweet maid,
    And not t' have strewed thy grave.
LAERTES.   O, treble woe
    Fall ten times treble on that cursèd head
    Whose wicked deed thy most ingenious sense°
    Deprived thee of! Hold off the earth awhile,
240   Till I have caught her once more in mine arms.

    [He leaps into the grave and embraces Ophelia.]

    Now pile your dust upon the quick and dead,
    Till of this flat a mountain you have made

    T' o'ertop old Pelion or the skyish head
    Of blue Olympus.°
HAMLET [coming forward].
    What is he whose grief   245
    Bears such an emphasis,° whose phrase of sorrow
    Conjures the wandering stars° and makes them stand
    Like wonder-wounded° hearers? This is I,
    Hamlet the Dane.°
LAERTES [grappling with him°].
    The devil take thy soul!   250
HAMLET.
    Thou pray'st not well.
    I prithee, take thy fingers from my throat,
    For though I am not splenitive° and rash,
    Yet have I in me something dangerous,
    Which let thy wisdom fear. Hold off thy hand.   255
KING.
    Pluck them asunder.
QUEEN.
    Hamlet, Hamlet!
ALL.
    Gentlemen!
HORATIO.
    Good my lord, be quiet.

    [Hamlet and Laertes are parted.]

HAMLET.
    Why, I will fight with him upon this theme   260
    Until my eyelids will no longer wag.°
QUEEN.
    O my son, what theme?
HAMLET.
    I loved Ophelia. Forty thousand brothers
    Could not with all their quantity of love
    Make up my sum. What wilt thou do for her?   265
KING.
    O, he is mad, Laertes.
QUEEN.
    For love of God, forbear him.°

243–244 Pelion, Olympus sacred mountains in the north of Thessaly; see also Ossa, at line 277   246 emphasis i.e., rhetorical and florid emphasis. (Phrase has a similar rhetorical connotation.) 247 wandering stars planets   248 wonder-wounded struck with amazement   249 the Dane (This title normally signifies the King; see 1.1.17 and note.)   s.d. grappling with him The testimony of the First Quarto that "Hamlet leaps in after Laertes" and the "Elegy on Burbage" ("Oft have I seen him leap into the grave") seem to indicate one way in which this fight was staged; however, the difficulty of fitting two contenders and Ophelia's body into a confined space (probably the trapdoor) suggests to many editors the alternative, that Laertes jumps out of the grave to attack Hamlet.)   253 splenitive quick-tempered   261 wag move. (A fluttering eyelid is a conventional sign that life has not yet gone.)   267 forbear him leave him alone

217 warranty i.e., ecclesiastical authority   218 great ... order orders from on high overrule the prescribed procedures   219 She should ... lodged she should have been buried in unsanctified ground   220 For in place of   221 Shards broken bits of pottery 222 crants garlands betokening maidenhood   223 strewments flowers strewn on a coffin   223–224 bringing ... burial laying the body to rest, to the sound of the bell   227 such rest i.e., to pray for such rest   228 peace-parted souls those who have died at peace with God   230 violets (See 4.5.183 and note)   232 howling i.e., in hell   238 ingenious sense a mind that is quick, alert, of fine qualities

HAMLET.
    'Swounds,° show me what thou'lt do.
    Woo't° weep? Woo't fight? Woo't fast? Woo't tear thy-
       self?
270   Woo't drink up° eisel?° Eat a crocodile?°
    I'll do 't. Dost come here to whine?
    To outface me with leaping in her grave?
    Be buried quick° with her, and so will I.
    And if thou prate of mountains, let them throw
275   Millions of acres on us, till our ground,
    Singeing his pate° against the burning zone,°
    Make Ossa° like a wart! Nay, an° thou'lt mouth,°
    I'll rant as well as thou.
QUEEN.   This is mere° madness,
    And thus awhile the fit will work on him;
280   Anon, as patient as the female dove
    When that her golden couplets° are disclosed,°
    His silence will sit drooping.
HAMLET.   Hear you, sir,
    What is the reason that you use me thus?
    I loved you ever. But it is no matter.
285   Let Hercules himself do what he may,
    The cat will mew, and dog will have his day.°

                             Exit Hamlet.

KING.
    I pray thee, good Horatio, wait upon him.

                          [Exit] Horatio.

    [To Laertes.] Strengthen your patience in° our last night's
       speech;
    We'll put the matter to the present push.°—
290   Good Gertrude, set some watch over your son.—
    This grave shall have a living° monument.
    An hour of quiet° shortly shall we see;

268 'Swounds by His (Christ's) wounds **Woo't** wilt thou **270
drink up** drink deeply **eisel** vinegar **crocodile** (Crocodiles were
tough and dangerous, and were supposed to shed hypocritical
tears.) **273 quick** alive **276 his pate** its head, i.e., top **burning
zone** zone in the celestial sphere containing the sun's orbit, between the tropics of Cancer and Capricorn **277 Ossa** another
mountain in Thessaly (In their war against the Olympian gods, the
giants attempted to heap Ossa on Pelion to scale Olympus.) **an if
mouth** i.e., rant **278 mere** utter **281 golden couplets** two baby
pigeons, covered with yellow down **disclosed** hatched **285–286
Let . . . day** i.e., (1) even Hercules couldn't stop Laertes's theatrical
rant (2) I, too, will have my turn; i.e., despite any blustering attempts at interference, every person will sooner or later do what he
or she must do **288 in** i.e., by recalling **289 present push** immediate test **291 living** lasting. (For Laertes's private understanding, Claudius also hints that Hamlet's death will serve as such a
monument.) **292 hour of quiet** time free of conflict

Till then, in patience our proceeding be.

                             Exeunt.

5.2 *Enter Hamlet and Horatio.*

HAMLET.
    So much for this, sir; now shall you see the other.°
    You do remember all the circumstance?
HORATIO.
    Remember it, my lord!
HAMLET.
    Sir, in my heart there was a kind of fighting
    That would not let me sleep. Methought I lay   5
    Worse than the mutines° in the bilboes.° Rashly,°
    And praised be rashness for it—let us know°
    Our indiscretion° sometimes serves us well
    When our deep plots do pall,° and that should learn° us
    There's a divinity that shapes our ends,   10
    Rough-hew° them how we will—
HORATIO.   That is most certain.
HAMLET.
    Up from my cabin,
    My sea-gown° scarfed° about me, in the dark
    Groped I to find out them,° had my desire,
    Fingered° their packet, and in fine° withdrew   15
    To mine own room again, making so bold,
    My fears forgetting manners, to unseal
    Their grand commission; where I found, Horatio—
    Ah, royal knavery!—an exact command,
    Larded° with many several° sorts of reasons   20
    Importing° Denmark's health and England's too,
    With, ho! such bugs° and goblins in my life,°
    That on the supervise,° no leisure bated,°
    No, not to stay° the grinding of the ax,
    My head should be struck off.   25
HORATIO.   Is 't possible?
HAMLET *[giving a document]*.
    Here's the commission. Read it at more leisure.
    But wilt thou hear now how I did proceed?

5.2 Location: The castle. 1 see the other hear the other news
6 mutines mutineers **bilboes** shackles **Rashly** on impulse (This
adverb goes with lines 12ff.) **7 know** acknowledge **8 indiscretion** lack of foresight and judgment (not an indiscreet act) **9 pall**
fail, falter, go stale **learn** teach **11 Rough-hew** shape roughly
13 sea-gown seaman's coat **scarfed** loosely wrapped **14 them**
i.e., Rosencrantz and Guildenstern **15 Fingered** pilfered, pinched
in fine finally, in conclusion **20 Larded** garnished **several** different **21 Importing** relating to **22 bugs** bugbears, hobgoblins
in my life i.e., to be feared if I were allowed to live **23 supervise**
reading **leisure bated** delay allowed **24 stay** await

HORATIO.
    I beseech you.
HAMLET.
    Being thus benetted round with villainies—
30   Ere I could make a prologue to my brains,
    They had begun the play°—I sat me down,
    Devised a new commission, wrote it fair.°
    I once did hold it, as our statists° do,
    A baseness° to write fair, and labored much
35   How to forget that learning, but, sir, now
    It did me yeoman's° service. Wilt thou know
    Th' effect° of what I wrote?
HORATIO.   Ay, good my lord.
HAMLET.
    An earnest conjuration° from the King,
    As England was his faithful tributary,
40   As love between them like the palm° might flourish,
    As peace should still° her wheaten garland° wear
    And stand a comma° 'tween their amities,
    And many suchlike "as" es° of great charge,°
    That on the view and knowing of these contents,
45   Without debatement further more or less,
    He should those bearers put to sudden death,
    Not shriving time° allowed.
HORATIO.   How was this sealed?
HAMLET.
    Why, even in that was heaven ordinant.°
    I had my father's signet° in my purse,
50   Which was the model° of that Danish seal;
    Folded the writ° up in the form of th' other,
    Subscribed° it, gave 't th' impression,° placed it safely,
    The changeling° never known. Now, the next day
    Was our sea fight, and what to this was sequent°
55   Thou knowest already.
HORATIO.
    So Guildenstern and Rosencrantz go to 't.
HAMLET.
    Why, man, they did make love to this employment.
    They are not near my conscience. Their defeat°

Does by their own insinuation° grow.
'Tis dangerous when the baser° nature comes   60
Between the pass° and fell° incensèd points
Of mighty opposites.°
HORATIO.   Why, what a king is this!
HAMLET.
    Does it not, think thee, stand me now upon°—
    He that hath killed my king and whored my mother,
    Popped in between th' election° and my hopes,   65
    Thrown out his angle° for my proper° life,
    And with such cozenage°—is 't not perfect conscience
    To quit° him with this arm? And is 't not to be damned
    To let this canker° of our nature come
    In° further evil?   70
HORATIO.
    It must be shortly known to him from England
    What is the issue of the business there.
HAMLET.
    It will be short. The interim is mine,
    And a man's life's no more than to say "one."°
    But I am very sorry, good Horatio,   75
    That to Laertes I forgot myself,
    For by the image of my cause I see
    The portraiture of his. I'll court his favors.
    But, sure, the bravery° of his grief did put me
    Into a tow'ring passion.
HORATIO.   Peace, who comes here?   80

Enter a Courtier [Osric].

OSRIC. Your lordship is right welcome back to Denmark.
HAMLET. I humbly thank you, sir. [*To Horatio.*] Dost know
    this water fly?
HORATIO. No, my good lord.
HAMLET. Thy state is the more gracious, for 'tis a vice to   85
    know him. He hath much land, and fertile. Let a beast be
    lord of beasts, and his crib° shall stand at the King's
    mess.° 'Tis a chuff,° but, as I say, spacious in the posses-
    sion of dirt.
OSRIC. Sweet lord, if your lordship were at leisure, I should   90
    impart a thing to you from His Majesty.

30–31 **Ere . . . play** before I could consciously turn my brain to the
matter, it had started working on a plan   **32 fair** in a clear hand
33 statists statesmen   **34 baseness** i.e., lower-class trait   **36 yeoman's** i.e., substantial, faithful, loyal   **37 effect** purport   **38 conjuration** entreaty   **40 palm** (An image of health; see Psalm 92:12)
41 still always.   **wheaten garland** (Symbolic of fruitful agriculture,
of peace and plenty.)   **42 comma** (Indicating continuity, link.)
43 "as"es (1) the "whereases" of a formal document (2) asses.
charge (1) import (2) burden (appropriate to asses)   **47 shriving
time** time for confession and absolution   **48 ordinant** directing
49 signet small seal   **50 model** replica   **51 writ** writing   **52
Subscribed** signed (with forged signature).   **impression** i.e., with a
wax seal   **53 changeling** i.e., substituted letter (Literally, a fairy
child substituted for a human one)   **54 was sequent** followed   **58
defeat** destruction

59 insinuation intrusive intervention, sticking their noses in my
business   **60 baser** of lower social station   **61 pass** thrust. **fell**
fierce   **62 opposites** antagonists   **63 stand me now upon** become
incumbent on me now   **65 election** (The Danish monarch was
"elected" by a small number of high-ranking electors.)   **66 angle**
fishhook. **proper** very   **67 cozenage** trickery   **68 quit** requite,
pay back   **69 canker** ulcer   **69–70 come In** grow into   **74 a
man's . . . "one"** one's whole life occupies such a short time, only
as long as it takes to count to 1   **79 bravery** bravado   **87 crib**
manger   **86–87 Let . . . mess** i.e., if a man, no matter how beast-
like, is as rich in livestock and possessions as Osric, he may eat at
the King's table   **87 chuff** boor, churl (The Second Quarto
spelling, *chough,* is a variant spelling that also suggests the meaning
here of "chattering jackdaw.")

HAMLET.
　I will receive it, sir, with all diligence of spirit.
　Put your bonnet° to his° right use; 'tis for the head.

OSRIC. I thank your lordship, it is very hot.

95　HAMLET. No, believe me, 'tis very cold. The wind is
　northerly.

OSRIC. It is indifferent° cold, my lord, indeed.

HAMLET. But yet methinks it is very sultry and hot for my
　complexion.°

100　OSRIC. Exceedingly, my lord. It is very sultry, as 'twere—I
　cannot tell how. My lord, His Majesty bade me signify to
　you that 'a has laid a great wager on your head. Sir, this is
　the matter—

HAMLET. I beseech you, remember.

　[Hamlet moves him to put on his hat.]

105　OSRIC. Nay, good my lord; for my ease,° in good faith. Sir,
　here is newly come to court Laertes—believe me, an ab-
　solute° gentleman, full of most excellent differences,° of
　very soft society° and great showing.° Indeed, to speak
　feelingly° of him, he is the card° or calendar° of gentry,°
110　for you shall find in him the continent of what part a
　gentleman would see.°

HAMLET. Sir, his definement° suffers no perdition° in you,°
　though I know to divide him inventorially° would dozy°
　th' arithmetic of memory, and yet but yaw° neither° in
115　respect of° his quick sail. But, in the verity of extolment,°
　I take him to be a soul of great article,° and his infusion°
　of such dearth and rareness° as, to make true diction° of
　him, his semblable° is his mirror and who else would
　trace° him his umbrage,° nothing more.

120　OSRIC. Your lordship speaks most infallibly of him.

HAMLET. The concernancy,° sir? Why do we wrap the gentle-
　man in our more rawer breath?°

OSRIC. Sir?

HORATIO. Is 't not possible to understand in another
　tongue?° You will do 't,° sir, really.　125

HAMLET. What imports the nomination° of this gentleman?

OSRIC. Of Laertes?

HORATIO [*to Hamlet*]. His purse is empty already; all 's golden
　words are spent.

HAMLET. Of him, sir.　130

OSRIC. I know you are not ignorant—

HAMLET. I would you did, sir. Yet in faith if you did, it would
　not much approve° me. Well, sir?

OSRIC. You are not ignorant of what excellence Laertes is—

HAMLET. I dare not confess that, lest I should compare with　135
　him in excellence. But to know a man well were to know
　himself.°

OSRIC. I mean, sir, for° his weapon; but in the imputation
　laid on him by them,° in his meed° he's unfellowed.°

HAMLET. What's his weapon?　140

OSRIC. Rapier and dagger.

HAMLET. That's two of his weapons—but well.°

OSRIC. The King, sir, hath wagered with him six Barbary
　horses, against the which he° has impawned,° as I take it,
　six French rapiers and poniards,° with their assigns,° as　145
　girdle, hangers,° and so.° Three of the carriages,° in faith,
　are very dear to fancy,° very responsive° to the hilts, most
　delicate° carriages, and of very liberal conceit.°

HAMLET. What call you the carriages?

HORATIO [*to Hamlet*]. I knew you must be edified by the mar-　150
　gent° ere you had done.

OSRIC. The carriages, sir, are the hangers.

HAMLET. The phrase would be more germane to the matter if
　we could carry a cannon by our sides; I would it might be
　hangers till then. But, on: six Barbary horses against six　155
　French swords, their assigns, and three liberal-conceited

---

93 **bonnet** any kind of cap or hat　**his** its　97 **indifferent** somewhat　99 **complexion** temperament　105 **for my ease** (A conventional reply declining the invitation to put his hat back on.)
106–107 **absolute** perfect　107–108 **differences** special qualities
108 **soft society** agreeable manners　**great showing** distinguished
appearance　109 **feelingly** with just perception　**card** chart, map
calendar guide　**gentry** good breeding　110–111 **the continent
. . . see** one who contains in him all the qualities a gentleman
would like to see (A *continent* is that which contains.)　112 **de-
finement** definition (Hamlet proceeds to mock Osric by throwing
his lofty diction back at him.)　**perdition** loss, diminution　**you**
your description　113 **divide him inventorially** enumerate his
graces　**dozy** dizzy　114 **yaw** swing unsteadily off course (Said of a
ship.)　**neither** for all that　114–115 **in respect of** in comparison
with　115 **in . . . extolment** in true praise (of him)　116 **of great
article** one with many articles in his inventory　**infusion** essence,
character infused into him by nature　117 **dearth and rareness**
rarity　**make true diction** speak truly　118 **semblable** only true
likeness　118–119 **who . . . trace** any other person who would
wish to follow　119 **umbrage** shadow　121 **concernancy** import,
relevance　122 **rawer breath** unrefined speech that can only come
short in praising him

124–125 **to understand . . . tongue** i.e., for you, Osric, to understand when someone else speaks your language (Horatio twits Osric
for not being able to understand the kind of flowery speech he himself uses, when Hamlet speaks in such a vein. Alternatively, all this
could be said to Hamlet.)　125 **You will do 't** i.e., you can if you
try, or, you may well have to try (to speak plainly)　126 **nomination** naming　133 **approve** commend　135–137 **I dare . . . himself** I dare not boast of knowing Laertes's excellence lest I seem to
imply a comparable excellence in myself. Certainly, to know another person well, one must know oneself.　138 **for** i.e., with
138–139 **imputation . . . them** reputation given him by others
139 **meed** merit.　**unfellowed** unmatched　142 **but well** but
never mind　144 **he** i.e., Laertes.　**impawned** staked, wagered
145 **poniards** daggers.　**assigns** appurtenances　146 **hangers**
straps on the sword belt (*girdle*), from which the sword hung　**and
so** and so on　**carriages** (An affected way of saying *hangers;* literally, gun carriages.)　147 **dear to fancy** delightful to the fancy.
responsive corresponding closely, matching or well adjusted　148
delicate (i.e., in workmanship)　**liberal conceit** elaborate design
150–151 **margent** margin of a book, place for explanatory notes

carriages; that's the French bet against the Danish. Why is this impawned, as you call it?

OSRIC. The King, sir, hath laid,° sir, that in a dozen passes°
160 between yourself and him, he shall not exceed you three hits. He hath laid on twelve for nine, and it would come to immediate trial, if your lordship would vouchsafe the answer.°

HAMLET. How if I answer no?

165 OSRIC. I mean, my lord, the opposition of your person in trial.

HAMLET. Sir, I will walk here in the hall. If it please His Majesty, it is the breathing time° of day with me. Let° the foils be brought, the gentleman willing, and the King
170 hold his purpose, I will win for him an I can; if not, I will gain nothing but my shame and the odd hits.

OSRIC. Shall I deliver you° so?

HAMLET. To this effect, sir—after what flourish your nature will.

175 OSRIC. I commend° my duty to your lordship.

HAMLET. Yours, yours. [Exit Osric.] 'A does well to commend it himself; there are no tongues else for 's turn.°

HORATIO. This lapwing° runs away with the shell on his head.

180 HAMLET. 'A did comply with his dug° before 'a sucked it. Thus has he—and many more of the same breed that I know the drossy° age dotes on—only got the tune° of the time and, out of an habit of encounter,° a kind of yeasty° collection,° which carries them through and through the
185 most fanned and winnowed opinions;° and do° but blow them to their trial, the bubbles are out.°

Enter a Lord.

LORD. My lord, His Majesty commended him to you by young Osric, who brings back to him that you attend him in the hall. He sends to know if your pleasure hold to play with Laertes, or that° you will take longer time. 190

HAMLET. I am constant to my purposes; they follow the King's pleasure. If his fitness speaks, mine is ready;° now or whensoever, provided I be so able as now.

LORD. The King and Queen and all are coming down.

HAMLET. In happy time.° 195

LORD. The Queen desires you to use some gentle entertainment° to Laertes before you fall to play.

HAMLET. She well instructs me.   [Exit Lord.]

HORATIO. You will lose, my lord.

HAMLET. I do not think so. Since he went into France, I have 200 been in continual practice; I shall win at the odds. But thou wouldst not think how ill all's here about my heart; but it is no matter.

HORATIO. Nay, good my lord—

HAMLET. It is but foolery, but it is such a kind of gaingiving° 205 as would perhaps trouble a woman.

HORATIO. If your mind dislike anything, obey it. I will forestall their repair° hither and say you are not fit.

HAMLET. Not a whit, we defy augury. There is special providence in the fall of a sparrow. If it be now, 'tis not to come; 210 if it be not to come, it will be now; if it be not now, yet it will come. The readiness is all. Since no man of aught he leaves knows, what is 't to leave betimes? Let be.°

A table prepared. [Enter] trumpets, drums, and officers with cushions; King, Queen, [Osric,] and all the state; foils, daggers, [and wine borne in;] and Laertes.

KING.
Come, Hamlet, come and take this hand from me.

[The King puts Laertes' hand into Hamlet's.]

HAMLET [to Laertes].
Give me your pardon, sir. I have done you wrong, 215
But pardon 't as you are a gentleman.
This presence° knows,
And you must needs have heard, how I am punished°

---

159 **laid** wagered   **passes** bouts (The odds of the betting are hard to explain. Possibly the King bets that Hamlet will win at least five out of twelve, at which point Laertes raises the odds against himself by betting he will win nine.)   **162–163 vouchsafe the answer** be so good as to accept the challenge (Hamlet deliberately takes the phrase in its literal sense of replying.)   **168 breathing time** exercise period.   **Let** i.e., if   **172 deliver you** report what you say   **175 commend** commit to your favor (A conventional salutation, but Hamlet wryly uses a more literal meaning, "recommend," "praise," in line 163.)   **177 for 's turn** for his purposes, i.e., to do it for him   **178 lapwing** (A proverbial type of youthful forwardness. Also, a bird that draws intruders away from its nest and was thought to run about with its head in the shell when newly hatched; a seeming reference to Osric's hat.)   **180 comply . . . dug** observe ceremonious formality toward his nurse's or mother's teat   **182 drossy** laden with scum and impurities, frivolous   **tune** temper, mood, manner of speech   **183 an habit of encounter** a demeanor in conversing (with courtiers of his own kind)   **yeasty** frothy   **184 collection** i.e., of current phrases   **184–185 carries . . . opinions** sustains them right through the scrutiny of persons whose opinions are select and refined (Literally, like grain separated from its chaff. Osric is both the chaff and the bubbly froth on the surface of the liquor that is soon blown away.)   **185 and do** yet do   **185–186 blow . . . out** test them by merely blowing on them, and their bubbles burst

190 that if   **192 If . . . ready** if he declares his readiness, my convenience waits on his   **195 In happy time** (A phrase of courtesy indicating that the time is convenient.)   **196–197 entertainment** greeting   **205 gaingiving** misgiving   **208 repair** coming   **212–213 Since . . . Let be** since no one has knowledge of what he is leaving behind, what does an early death matter after all? Enough; don't struggle against it.   **217 presence** royal assembly   **218 punished** afflicted

With a sore distraction. What I have done
220　That might your nature, honor, and exception°
Roughly awake, I here proclaim was madness.
Was 't Hamlet wronged Laertes? Never Hamlet.
If Hamlet from himself be ta'en away,
And when he's not himself does wrong Laertes,
225　Then Hamlet does it not, Hamlet denies it.
Who does it, then? His madness. If 't be so,
Hamlet is of the faction° that is wronged;
His madness is poor Hamlet's enemy.
Sir, in this audience
230　Let my disclaiming from a purposed evil
Free me so far in your most generous thoughts
That I have° shot my arrow o'er the house
And hurt my brother.

LAERTES.　　　　　　　I am satisfied in nature,°
Whose motive° in this case should stir me most
235　To my revenge. But in my terms of honor
I stand aloof, and will no reconcilement
Till by some elder masters of known honor
I have a voice° and precedent of peace°
To keep my name ungored.° But till that time
240　I do receive your offered love like love,
And will not wrong it.

HAMLET.　　　　　　　I embrace it freely,
And will this brothers' wager frankly° play.—
Give us the foils. Come on.

LAERTES.　　　　　　　Come, one for me.

HAMLET.
I'll be your foil,° Laertes. In mine ignorance
245　Your skill shall, like a star i' the darkest night,
Stick fiery off° indeed.

LAERTES.　　　　　　　You mock me, sir.

HAMLET.
No, by this hand.

KING.
Give them the foils, young Osric. Cousin Hamlet,
You know the wager?

HAMLET.　　　　　　　Very well, my lord.
250　Your Grace has laid the odds o'° the weaker side.

KING.
I do not fear it; I have seen you both.
But since he is bettered,° we have therefore odds.

LAERTES.
This is too heavy. Let me see another.

　　　　　　　　　[*He exchanges his foil for another.*]

HAMLET.
This likes me° well. These foils have all a length?

　　　　　　　　　[*They prepare to play.*]

OSRIC.
Ay, my good lord.　　　　　　　　　　　　　255

KING.
Set me the stoups of wine upon that table.
If Hamlet give the first or second hit,
Or quit in answer of the third exchange,°
Let all the battlements their ordnance fire.
The King shall drink to Hamlet's better breath,°　260
And in the cup an union° shall he throw
Richer than that which four successive kings
In Denmark's crown have worn. Give me the cups,
And let the kettle° to the trumpet speak,
The trumpet to the cannoneer without,　　　　265
The cannons to the heavens, the heaven to earth,
"Now the King drinks to Hamlet." Come, begin.

　　　　　　　　　　　　Trumpets the while.

And you, the judges, bear a wary eye.

HAMLET.
Come on, sir.

LAERTES.
Come, my lord.　　　　[*They play. Hamlet scores a hit.*]　270

HAMLET.
One.

LAERTES.
No.

HAMLET.
Judgment.

OSRIC.　　　　A hit, a very palpable hit.

　　　Drum, trumpets, and shot. Flourish. A piece goes off.

LAERTES.
Well, again.

KING.
Stay, give me drink. Hamlet, this pearl is thine.　275

　　　[*He drinks, and throws a pearl in Hamlet's cup.*]

Here's to thy health. Give him the cup.

---

220 exception disapproval　**227 faction** party　**232 That I have** as if I had　**233 in nature** i.e., as to my personal feelings　**234 motive** prompting　**238 voice** authoritative pronouncement　**of peace** for reconciliation　**239 name ungored** reputation unwounded　**242 frankly** without ill feeling or the burden of rancor　**244 foil** thin metal background which sets a jewel off (with pun on the blunted rapier for fencing)　**246 Stick fiery off** stand out brilliantly　**250 laid the odds o'** bet on, backed　**252 is bettered** has improved; is the odds-on favorite (Laertes's handicap is the "three hits" specified in line 159.)

254 likes me pleases me　**258 Or . . . exchange** i.e., or requites Laertes in the third bout for having won the first two　**260 better breath** improved vigor　**261 union** pearl (So called, according to Pliny's *Natural History*, 9, because pearls are *unique*, never identical.)　**264 kettle** kettledrum

HAMLET.
I'll play this bout first. Set it by awhile.
Come. [*They play.*] Another hit; what say you?
LAERTES.
A touch, a touch, I do confess 't.
KING.
Our son shall win.
280   QUEEN.   He's fat° and scant of breath.
Here, Hamlet, take my napkin,° rub thy brows.
The Queen carouses° to thy fortune, Hamlet.
HAMLET.
Good, madam!
KING.
Gertrude, do not drink.
QUEEN.
285   I will, my lord, I pray you pardon me.   [*She drinks.*]
KING [*aside*].
It is the poisoned cup. It is too late.
HAMLET.
I dare not drink yet, madam; by and by.
QUEEN.
Come, let me wipe thy face.
LAERTES [*to King*].
My lord, I'll hit him now.
KING.   I do not think 't.
LAERTES [*aside*].
290   And yet it is almost against my conscience.
HAMLET.
Come, for the third, Laertes. You do but dally.
I pray you, pass° with your best violence;
I am afeard you make a wanton of me.°
LAERTES.
Say you so? Come on.   [*They play.*]
OSRIC.
295   Nothing neither way.
LAERTES.
Have at you now!

[*Laertes wounds Hamlet; then, in scuffling, they change
rapiers,° and Hamlet wounds Laertes.*]

KING.   Part them! They are incensed.
HAMLET.
Nay, come, again.   [*The Queen falls.*]
OSRIC.   Look to the Queen there, ho!

HORATIO.
They bleed on both sides. How is it, my lord?
OSRIC.
How is 't, Laertes?
LAERTES.
Why, as a woodcock° to mine own springe,° Osric;   300
I am justly killed with mine own treachery.
HAMLET.
How does the Queen?
KING.   She swoons to see them bleed.
QUEEN.
No, no, the drink, the drink—O my dear Hamlet—
The drink, the drink! I am poisoned.   [*She dies.*]
HAMLET.
O villainy! Ho, let the door be locked!   305
Treachery! Seek it out.

                              [*Laertes falls. Exit Osric.*]

LAERTES.
It is here, Hamlet. Hamlet, thou art slain.
No med'cine in the world can do thee good;
In thee there is not half an hour's life.
The treacherous instrument is in thy hand,   310
Unbated° and envenomed. The foul practice°
Hath turned itself on me. Lo, here I lie,
Never to rise again. Thy mother's poisoned.
I can no more. The King, the King's to blame.
HAMLET.
The point envenomed too? Then, venom, to thy work.   315
                              [*He stabs the King.*]
ALL.
Treason! Treason!
KING.
O, yet defend me, friends! I am but hurt.
HAMLET [*forcing the King to drink*].
Here, thou incestuous, murderous, damnèd Dane,
Drink off this potion. Is thy union° here?
Follow my mother.   [*The King dies.*]
LAERTES.   He is justly served.   320
It is a poison tempered° by himself.
Exchange forgiveness with me, noble Hamlet.
Mine and my father's death come not upon thee,
Nor thine on me!   [*He dies.*]
HAMLET.
Heaven make thee free of it! I follow thee.   325
I am dead, Horatio. Wretched Queen, adieu!
You that look pale and tremble at this chance,°

---

280 **fat** not physically fit, out of training   281 **napkin** handkerchief   283 **carouses** drinks a toast   292 **pass** thrust   293 **make . . . me** i.e., treat me like a spoiled child, trifle with me   296 **s.d. in scuffling, they change rapiers** (This stage direction occurs in the Folio. According to a widespread stage tradition, Hamlet receives a scratch, realizes that Laertes's sword is unbated, and accordingly forces an exchange.)

300 **woodcock** a bird, a type of stupidity or as a decoy   **springe** trap, snare   311 **Unbated** not blunted with a button   **practice** plot   319 **union** pearl (See line 245; with grim puns on the word's other meanings: marriage, shared death.)   321 **tempered** mixed   327 **chance** mischance

That are but mutes° or audience to this act,
Had I but time—as this fell° sergeant,° Death,
330   Is strict° in his arrest°—O, I could tell you—
But let it be. Horatio, I am dead;
Thou livest. Report me and my cause aright
To the unsatisfied.
HORATIO.   Never believe it.
I am more an antique Roman° than a Dane.
Here's yet some liquor left.

[*He attempts to drink from the poisoned cup.
Hamlet prevents him.*]

335   HAMLET.   As thou'rt a man,
Give me the cup! Let go! By heaven, I'll ha 't.
O God, Horatio, what a wounded name,
Things standing thus unknown, shall I leave behind me!
If thou didst ever hold me in thy heart,
340   Absent thee from felicity awhile,
And in this harsh world draw thy breath in pain
To tell my story. *A march afar off* [*and a volley within*].
What warlike noise is this?

Enter Osric.

OSRIC.
Young Fortinbras, with conquest come from Poland,
345   To th' ambassadors of England gives
This warlike volley.
HAMLET.   O, I die, Horatio!
The potent poison quite o'ercrows° my spirit.
I cannot live to hear the news from England,
But I do prophesy th' election lights
350   On Fortinbras. He has my dying voice.°
So tell him, with th' occurents° more and less
Which have solicited°—the rest is silence.   [*He dies.*]
HORATIO.
Now cracks a noble heart. Good night, sweet prince,
And flights of angels sing thee to thy rest!

[*March within.*]

355   Why does the drum come hither?

Enter Fortinbras, with the [*English*] *Ambassadors* [*with
drum, colors, and attendants*].

FORTINBRAS.
Where is this sight?
HORATIO.   What is it you would see?
If aught of woe or wonder, cease your search.
FORTINBRAS.
This quarry° cries on havoc.° O proud Death,
What feast° is toward° in thine eternal cell,
That thou so many princes at a shot   360
So bloodily hast struck?
FIRST AMBASSADOR.   The sight is dismal,
And our affairs from England come too late.
The ears are senseless that should give us hearing,
To tell him his commandment is fulfilled,
That Rosencrantz and Guildenstern are dead.   365
Where should we have our thanks?
HORATIO.   Not from his° mouth,
Had it th' ability of life to thank you.
He never gave commandment for their death.
But since, so jump° upon this bloody question,°
You from the Polack wars, and you from England,   370
And here arrived, give order that these bodies
High on a stage° be placèd to the view,
And let me speak to th' yet unknowing world
How these things came about. So shall you hear
Of carnal, bloody, and unnatural acts,   375
Of accidental judgments,° casual° slaughters,
Of deaths put on° by cunning and forcèd cause,°
And, in this upshot, purposes mistook
Fall'n on th' inventors' heads. All this can I
Truly deliver.
FORTINBRAS.   Let us haste to hear it,   380
And call the noblest to the audience.
For me, with sorrow I embrace my fortune.
I have some rights of memory° in this kingdom,
Which now to claim my vantage° doth invite me.
HORATIO.
Of that I shall have also cause to speak,   385
And from his mouth whose voice will draw on more.°
But let this same be presently° performed,
Even while men's minds are wild, lest more mischance

---

328 mutes silent observers (Literally, actors with nonspeaking parts.) **329 fell** cruel. **sergeant** sheriff's officer **330 strict** (1) severely just (2) unavoidable. **arrest** (1) taking into custody (2) stopping my speech **334 Roman** (Suicide was an honorable choice for many Romans as an alternative to a dishonorable life.) **347 o'ercrows** triumphs over (like the winner in a cockfight) **350 voice** vote **351 occurents** events, incidents **352 solicited** moved, urged (Hamlet doesn't finish saying what the events have prompted—presumably, his acts of vengeance, or his reporting of those events to Fortinbras.)

358 quarry heap of dead. **cries on havoc** proclaims a general slaughter **359 feast** i.e., Death feasting on those who have fallen **toward** in preparation **366 his** i.e., Claudius's **369 jump** precisely, immediately **question** dispute, affair **372 stage** platform **376 judgments** retributions **casual** occurring by chance **377 put on** instigated **forced cause** contrivance **383 of memory** traditional, remembered, unforgotten **384 vantage** favorable opportunity **386 voice ... more** vote will influence still others **387 presently** immediately

On° plots and errors happen.

FORTINBRAS.   Let four captains
390   Bear Hamlet, like a soldier, to the stage,
       For he was likely, had he been put on,°
       To have proved most royal; and for his passage,°
       The soldiers' music and the rite of war

Speak° loudly for him.
Take up the bodies. Such a sight as this   395
Becomes the field,° but here shows much amiss.
Go bid the soldiers shoot.

*Exeunt [marching, bearing off the dead bodies; a peal of
ordnance is shot off].*

389 **On** on the basis of; on top of   391 **put on** i.e., invested in royal office and so put to the test   392 **passage** i.e., from life to death

394 **Speak** (let them) speak   396 **Becomes the field** suits the field of battle.

TOPICS FOR CRITICAL THINKING AND WRITING

The Play on the PAGE

ACT 1

1. The first scene (like many other scenes in this play) is full of expressions of uncertainty. What are some of these uncertainties?

2. Does the King's opening speech in 1.2 reveal him to be an accomplished public speaker—or are lines 10–14 offensive? In his second speech (lines 41–49), what is the effect of naming Laertes four times? Claudius sometimes uses the royal pronouns ("we," "our"), sometimes the more intimate "I" and "my." Study his use of these in lines 1–4 and in 106–117. What do you think he is getting at?

3. Hamlet's first soliloquy (1.2.129–59) reveals that more than just his father's death distresses him. Be as specific as possible about the causes of Hamlet's anguish here. What traits does Hamlet reveal in his conversation with Horatio (1.2.160–258)?

4. What do you make of Polonius's advice to Laertes (1.3.55–81)? Is it sound? Sound advice, but here uttered by a fool? Ignoble advice? How would one follow the advice of line 78: "to thine own self be true"? In his words to Ophelia in 1.3.102–36, what does he reveal about himself?

5. Can 1.4.17–38 reasonably be taken as a speech on the "tragic flaw"? (On this idea, see page 33.) Or is the passage a much more limited discussion, a comment simply on Danish drinking habits?

ACT 2

6. Characterize Polonius on the basis of 2.1.1–76.

7. In light of what we have seen of Hamlet, is Ophelia's report of his strange behavior when he visits her understandable?

8. Is "the hellish Pyrrhus" (2.2.453) Hamlet's version of Claudius? Or is he Hamlet, who soon will be responsible for the deaths of Polonius, Rosencrantz and Guildenstern, Claudius, Gertrude, Ophelia, and Laertes? Explain.

9. In 2.2.536–75 Hamlet rebukes himself for not acting. Why has he not acted? Because he is a coward (line 538)? Because he has a conscience? Because no action can restore his father and his mother's purity? Because he doubts the Ghost? What reason(s) can you offer?

ACT 3

10. What do you make out of Hamlet's assertion to Ophelia: "I loved you not" (3.1.119–20)? Of his characterization of himself as full of "offenses" (3.1.123–30)? Why is Hamlet so harsh to Ophelia?

11. In 3.3.36–72 Claudius's conscience afflicts him. But is he repentant? What makes you say so?

12. The Ghost speaks of Hamlet's "almost blunted purpose" (3.4.115). Is the accusation fair? Explain.

ACT 4

13. Is Gertrude protecting Hamlet when she says he is mad (4.1.7), or does she believe that he is mad? If she believes he is mad, does it follow that she no longer feels ashamed and guilty? Explain.

14. Why should Hamlet hide Polonius's body (in 4.2)? Is he feigning madness? Is he on the edge of madness? Explain.

15. Judging from 4.5, what has driven Ophelia mad? Is Laertes heroic, or somewhat foolish? Consider also the way Claudius treats him in 4.7.

ACT 5

16. Would anything be lost if the gravediggers in 5.1 were omitted?

17. To what extent do we judge Hamlet severely for sending Rosencrantz and Guildenstern to their deaths, as he reports in 5.2? On the whole, do we think of Hamlet as an intriguer? What other intrigues has he engendered? How successful were they?

18. Does 5.2.209–13 show a paralysis of the will, or a wise recognition that more is needed than mere human scheming? Explain.

19. Does 5.2.295 suggest that Laertes takes advantage of a momentary pause and unfairly stabs Hamlet? Is the exchange of weapons accidental, or does Hamlet (as in Olivier's film version), realizing that he has been betrayed, deliberately get possession of Laertes's deadly weapon?

The Play on the STAGE

20. The Ghost first appears at 1.1.43. Does his appearance surprise us, or have we been prepared for it? Or is there both preparation and surprise?

21. Is the First Player's speech (2.2.440 ff.) a huffing speech? If so, why? To distinguish it from the poetry of the play itself? To characterize deeds that Hamlet cannot descend to?

22. In 3.3.74–97, is Hamlet abhorrent? Do we want him to kill Claudius at this moment, when Claudius (presumably with his back to Hamlet) is praying? Do you suppose that when we *see* the episode on the stage, as opposed to when we *read* it, our response differs? Why?

23. Fortinbras is often cut from the play. How much is lost by the cut?

24. If you were directing the play, would you want the audience to believe in some episodes Hamlet is mad or very nearly so, or would you want the audience to believe the madness is always feigned? Discuss two scenes in particular.

25. When Hamlet tells his mother, "Look here upon this picture, and on this" (3.4), the two pictures are miniatures, one of Hamlet Senior worn on a chain around Hamlet's neck, the other of Claudius, worn by Gertrude. Showing the pictures of course brings Hamlet and his mother into close physical contact, perhaps with a sexual undertone. But the pictures can also be portraits hanging on a wall or framed on a desk. How would you stage the scene? Why?

26. The play has been variously costumed—notably in what passes for medieval Danish clothing, Elizabethan clothing, contemporary clothing, and (as in Kenneth Branagh's film) late nineteenth-century dress with the men in fancy military dress and the women in ball gowns. What can be said for and against each of these approaches?

The Play in PERFORMANCE

Hamlet to 1800

Hamlet advises the players, in 3.2.1–4, to "Speak the speech ... trippingly on the tongue"—but exactly what are the speeches that add up to *Hamlet*? *Hamlet* exists in three versions: Q1 (published in 1603), 2,154 lines; Q2 (1604), 3,723 lines; and F (1623), 3,604 lines. (Much depends on how one counts the lines, but that's not important now.) Most scholars agree that F (that is, the version printed in the Folio of 1623) is an *acting* version, that is, a text somewhat abridged for the stage. They also agree that Q1 is a much more drastic abridgement, apparently prepared from memory by an actor or actors without access to a copy of the manuscript. The text of Q1 is often very poor (sometimes it is gibberish), but occasionally it gives insights into the performance of the play—our topic here—that are not found in either of the fuller and more coherent versions. For instance, only Q1 gives us a stage direction telling us that in 5.1.242 Hamlet leaps into Ophelia's grave.

When people speak of an "uncut *Hamlet*," or of a "full text *Hamlet*," they are speaking of a version that probably never was performed in Shakespeare's time, a version that begins with Q2 (the longest of the three texts) and adds to it the passages in F that are not found in Q2. This composite text, running to about 3,900 lines, takes four or even four and a quarter hours to perform. Most performances of an abridged text run to about three hours, which usually means that about a fourth of the text is cut. There are, roughly speaking, two ways of cutting: one is to leave out some characters (for example, Fortinbras and everything connected with him, including the talk in 1.1 about the quarrel between Hamlet Senior and Fortinbras's father); the other is to keep a little of everything, trimming down longer speeches, especially reflective or descriptive ones. Laertes's advice to Ophelia, Polonius's advice to Laertes, Hamlet's disquisition on drunkenness, his musings on Alexander, and his advice to the players may be reduced to tokens. If one follows the first method, omitting, say, material concerning Fortinbras, one eliminates four speaking characters (Fortinbras, Cornelius, Voltemand, the Captain), and one thus focuses more sharply on Hamlet's problem in a corrupt court. The play becomes more domestic, more personal, and in some ways more manageable, but it necessarily loses its political dimension, for instance in the contrast between the thinking man (Hamlet) and the active man (Fortinbras). It also loses, of course, Shakespeare's ending, which shows order being restored after violence. If one follows the second method of cutting, thinning down the speeches, no single theme may be utterly neglected, but the play loses so much of its complexity or texture or depth that it may seem to be not much more than a melodrama.

The role of Hamlet is long and complex, and *Hamlet* is the most frequently staged of Shakespeare's plays; this short essay can look at only a very few productions, and can comment on only some of their most distinctive features. We must begin by mentioning Richard Burbage (c. 1567–1619), a member of Shakespeare's theatrical company, who is known to have played the role—but nothing is really known about how he played it. The next actor of note who performed the role was Thomas Betterton (c. 1635–1710), who played his first

Hamlet in 1661, when he was about twenty-six, and played his last Hamlet in 1709, when he was in his seventies. Betterton's text was a relatively slight abridgment of the folio text—it deletes about 816 lines, but, as we have seen, the Elizabethans themselves probably abridged the play. Among the cuts are the roles of Voltemand and Cornelius, all of the Fortinbras material except the entry of Fortinbras at the end of the play, Polonius's advice to Laertes, Polonius's scene with Reynaldo, Hamlet's advice to the Players, and Hamlet's soliloquy beginning "How all occasions do inform against me." Among the speeches that are thinned out rather than entirely cut are Horatio's explanation of the preparation for war, the king's reproof of Hamlet's excessive grief, Laertes's advice to Ophelia, the Mouse Trap, and the closet scene with Gertrude. Minor changes include some elevation of the diction, in accordance with new ideas of decorum. Thus, instead of "The kettledrum and trumpet thus *bray out* / The triumph of his pledge" (1.4.11–12), we get "The kettledrum and trumpet thus *proclaim* / The triumph of his health."

People who saw Betterton spoke of his "vivacity" and "enterprize," and they described his performance as "manly." Putting together such scraps of evidence as we have, we can say that Betterton's Hamlet (played in the dress of a courtier of Charles II, and later with a cocked hat and powdered wig) was not a neurotic or a weakling but "the glass of fashion," and a vigorous young man—even when Betterton was seventy.

In the middle of the eighteenth century, viewers used pretty much the same words that had described Betterton to describe the performance of David Garrick (1717–79), who first played the role in 1742. In the next thirty years, like his predecessors and his successors, Garrick used a somewhat abridged text, from time to time slightly altering it both by additions and deletions, but in 1772 he made a drastic revision. Although he restored 629 lines that had not been heard for a century (these included such passages as the king at prayer, and the soliloquy beginning "How all occasions do inform against me"), Garrick also in effect rewrote the fifth act, more or less in line with neoclassical ideals of decorum. (As early as 1661 John Evelyn wrote, "I saw *Hamlet, Prince of Denmark* played, but now the old plays begin to disgust this refined age.") Garrick's aim, he said, was to rescue "that whole play from all the rubbish of the fifth act." The rubbish included the gravediggers and (as it must have seemed to eighteenth-century taste) the boorish struggle between Hamlet and Laertes at Ophelia's grave. Clowns did not, in the strict neoclassical view, belong in tragedies, and courtly gentlemen did not engage in fisticuffs at a funeral. Briefly, in Garrick's revision of the fifth act, the king commands Hamlet to go to England, and Hamlet replies by stabbing him. Laertes, seeking vengeance for the deaths of Polonius and Ophelia, mortally wounds Hamlet. Horatio is about to kill Laertes when Hamlet commands him to desist, saying that Laertes has been guided by heaven to give Hamlet the "precious balm" for all his wounds. Hamlet, before he dies, lectures his mother, and commands Laertes and Horatio "to calm the troubled land." But what is most relevant to our purpose here is this: Garrick's Hamlet, though perhaps touched with melancholy, was a man of action. For the rest of the century, Garrick's interpretation remained the touchstone by which other performances of the role were judged.

Hamlet in the Nineteenth Century

After Garrick, so many notable actors played Hamlet that this essay can do little more than make what must seem to be arbitrary choices. Our first choice is Henry Irving (1838–1905). Irving, who played Hamlet from 1864 to 1885, somewhat varied his conception over the years, but essentially his Hamlet was a man overpowered by his love of Ophelia. (For a thorough discussion of Irving's interpretations of Hamlet, see Alan Hughes, *Henry Irving*.) In his first version, Irving followed tradition in cutting all references to Fortinbras, but he also cut everything that seemed to him to diminish Hamlet, for instance Hamlet's bawdy remarks (and of course Ophelia's bawdy songs, too), Hamlet's callous description of the deaths of Rosencrantz and Guildenstern, his soliloquy about murdering Claudius under particularly reprehensible conditions (3.3.72–97), and his claim in his apology to Laertes that he was mad (Irving at first believed that Hamlet's madness always was feigned). Irving later restored the soliloquy, and he also (by 1884) allowed that Hamlet was hysterical in four scenes—after the visitation by the Ghost, with Ophelia in the nunnery scene, in the queen's closet, and at Ophelia's grave. And of course he altered some of his stage business over the years. In the nunnery scene, for instance, in 1885 he added Edmund Kean's business of returning to Ophelia, after "To a nunnery, go," and kissing her hand. One of Irving's invented pieces of business was severely criticized. In the closet scene, when Hamlet tells his mother to "Look here upon this pic-

ture, and on this" (3.4.54), the usual business was for Hamlet to call attention to miniature portraits: Hamlet wore a miniature of his father, Gertrude a miniature of Claudius. (An alternate tradition used two framed portraits in the queen's room.) Irving, however, used no real pictures. He gesticulated his hand downstage, as though the portraits hung on the missing fourth wall between the audience and the actors—or existed in Hamlet's mind.

One other point should be made about Irving's *Hamlet*. Staging in the nineteenth century was noted for its spectacle and its illusionism, and Irving's productions were especially known for these qualities. Thus, reviewers comment admiringly on a scene in which the Ghost stands among huge rocks in moonlight, as dawn steals across a great expanse of water. Another especially memorable scene was the procession to Ophelia's grave: All available members of the cast served as priests, monks, and miscellaneous mourners, while a bell tolled and a hymn was played on a harmonium. All of this, of course, took time, which means that the text had to be fairly heavily cut.

Reacting against such productions, in 1881 William Poel, amateur actor and Elizabethan enthusiast, staged *Hamlet* in Elizabethan costumes on a stage with only a few chairs and a platform for the play-within-the play. This was, he believed, the Elizabethan manner. Moreover, the text he chose for his production was Q1, the so-called "Bad Quarto" of 1603, "bad" because it represents an actor's corrupt abridgment of a performance of *Hamlet*. (See pages 380–82.) But the fact that Q1 is based on a performance made it especially attractive to Poel. He recognized that some passages of Q1 were so corrupt that they were gibberish, but, as he explained in a letter, he also believed that this text "represents more truly [Shakespeare's] dramatic conception than either Quarto 2 or our stage version."

Poel's production, which took only two hours, was reviewed most unfavorably, partly because it offended contemporary taste, and partly because it was indeed a thoroughly amateur affair. (Poel himself played Hamlet; unfortunately, his skill as an actor did not equal his enthusiasm for Elizabethan drama.) In this production, he was more concerned with the text than with the staging—that is, more concerned with showing that Q1 is good theater than with showing how an Elizabethan play ought to be staged—but critics seized on inconsistencies in his method of production. Why not, they asked, use boys to play Ophelia and Gertrude? (Poel had in fact used a boy for the Player Queen.)

Why not do the play by daylight? Why not do it in contemporary—i.e., late nineteenth century—garb, since in Shakespeare's time the actors wore the clothing of their own age? The production indeed was inconsistent, and weak, and it added little to the interpretation of Hamlet—though Poel did insist that Hamlet is not a sentimental moper but an Elizabethan gallant; but the production nevertheless marked a milestone in the recovery of Shakespeare's stage, a neutral space that allows one scene to follow another rapidly.

Hamlet in Modern Dress

When reviewers teased Poel by asking why he didn't stage the play in modern dress, they touched on an important issue. In a sense, up to the late eighteenth century, Hamlet had regularly been done in modern dress. That is, the early performers, such as Burbage, Betterton, Garrick, and Kemble wore the clothes of their own period—Kemble, for example, at first played in modern court dress and powdered hair. But in the late eighteenth century, Kemble began to wear what has been called a Vandyck costume, with a lace collar open at the neck, thus invoking a somewhat romantic past. Edmund Kean, perhaps from the late 1820s, wore a sort of stage Elizabethan costume, thus again evoking a romantic past, and actors later in the century experimented with what were thought to be historically accurate medieval Danish costumes, though Elizabethan costume remained popular.

In short, if one goes back to the seventeenth and eighteenth centuries, one finds plenty of productions of Hamlet in the "modern dress," though apparently after the late eighteenth century there were none until 1925, when Barry Jackson's Birmingham Repertory opened a production in London, directed by H. K. Ayliff, with Colin Keith-Johnston as Hamlet. Reviewers recognized that Jackson was not offering merely a gimmick; rather, he was trying to see the play freshly, to think about it not as a period piece to be declaimed but as something to be spoken naturally. Hamlet was not only dressed as a modern play, but was also acted as a modern play. (The negative side is that this conception encouraged an antipoetic reading of the lines.) Modern dress did not (for the most part) seem incongruous, partly because much of the play is set at court, allowing or even requiring formal dress and military costumes—themselves kinds of theatrical costumes. Thus, in the court scenes, the ambassadors and Polo-

nius wore tailcoats and white ties, and Hamlet wore a tuxedo. In other scenes, however, Ophelia wore a short skirt characteristic of the twenties, the young men wore tweeds, and, in the graveyard scene, Hamlet wore loose sports knickers known as plus fours.

Modern-dress productions today are so commonplace that it is hard to realize how novel Jackson's production was. Since 1925 there has been a fashion for setting Hamlet in some sort of post-Elizabethan period. For instance, in 1948 Michael Benthall direct Paul Scofield in a Victorian Hamlet at Stratford-upon-Avon. Benthall, having already done an Elizabethan Hamlet in doublet and hose, concluded that the Elizabethan costume robbed the play of its "essential modern realism." Why Victorian? Because, Benthall said, the Victorian period was

> near enough to our own to heighten the play's realism, and yet far enough distant to give scope for that picturesque romanticism modern life has largely betrayed. . . . And I set the play in a mid-European court where the juxtaposition of crinolines, uniforms, and evening and levee clothes would create the atmosphere of color and romance associated with royalty of the period. I hoped in this way to retain the grandeur of the tragedy without destroying the play's vital contemporary relevance.

For Richard Burton's Hamlet, directed by John Gielgud in 1964, we have a highly detailed record. Richard L. Sterne's John Gielgud Directs Richard Burton in Hamlet: A Journal of Rehearsals. This remarkable book summarizes and sometimes quotes at length from tape recordings made during rehearsals. It also includes the prompt-script of the production, an interview with Gielgud, and an interview with Burton. (Also useful is a book by the actor who played Guildenstern, William Redfield's Letters from an Actor.) The idea behind the production was unusual: Struck by the observation that actors sometimes perform better in a rehearsal run-through, with improvised props and without fancy costumes and sets, than in a public performance, Gielgud conceived of this production as a rehearsal of Hamlet. Thus, the play began with some actors (who later played courtiers) bringing a few chairs onto the stage (one of the chairs, an upholstered armchair, served for Claudius's throne); the set was the brick rear wall of the theater (not a real brick wall, but a set looking like a brick wall). The actors wore ordinary clothes—but in fact the clothes were faintly symbolic; Burton wore a black sweater or turtleneck, Hume

Cronyn (Polonius) wore a business suit, and Alfred Drake (Claudius) wore a shirt and tie, and a sport jacket. As the play progressed, and pressures on Claudius increased, he loosened his necktie. The lighting, too, pretended to be rehearsal lighting. There were, for instance, no sudden blackouts, but the lights faded or gradually rose where dramatically appropriate. Stern's transcription of the tapes indicates that much of Gielgud's effort was directed toward restraining Burton's abundant energy—Burton tended to shout—but, even so, the performance was intense rather than sensitive. The production was extremely successful financially, but this success may have been due partly to the publicity attending Burton's recent marriage to Elizabeth Taylor (they had married during the tryouts in Toronto); reviews were mixed.

Film Versions

Laurence Olivier's film, made in 1948, has been much written about. (The basic sources are Alan Dent, ed., *Hamlet: The Film and the Play*, and Brenda Cross, ed., *The Film Hamlet*.) Olivier had played Hamlet at Elsinore in 1937, but when he first thought of directing a film of the play he did not intend to take the title role. "I feel that my style of acting," he said, "is more suited to stronger character roles, such as Hotspur and Henry V, rather than to the lyrical, poetical role of Hamlet." (This quotation tells us a good deal about Olivier's conception of the role of Hamlet. It is hard to imagine Burbage, Betterton, or Garrick talking about Hamlet this way.) At the beginning of the film, we are told: "This is the tragedy of a man who could not make up his mind," a simplistic view that, fortunately, does not come anywhere near to summarizing the interpretation offered in the film. In fact, the underlying theme really seems to be the Freudian interpretation that Hamlet cannot easily avenge his father's death because he (like everyone) has an Oedipus complex, that is, he wishes (or wished) to kill his father and to sleep with his mother. Hamlet thus cannot bring himself to act against the man who has done what he himself wanted to do. (Although Freud initiated this explanation of Hamlet's alleged irresolution at least as early as 1900, he did not discuss the play at length. The classic psychoanalytic discussion of the play is by Ernest Jones, in *Hamlet and Oedipus*.) When Tyrone Guthrie directed Olivier in the 1937 *Hamlet* at Elsinore, he drew on Freud's remarks, and Olivier even discussed the idea with Jones. Not surprisingly, then, Olivier returned to

this interpreation when he made his film. The most obvious signs of Freud are in the passionate kisses (some of the scenes between Hamlet and Gertrude are virtually love scenes) and in the emphasis on the queen's bedroom, indeed on the bed itself. The text of the play tells us that Hamlet encounters Gertrude in "his mother's closet" (3.3.27), that is, in a private room. There is no need to think of this as a bedroom— it might well be furnished only with a small writing desk and a couple of chairs—but a bed now seems to have become indispensable. The sexual focus in Olivier's film is sharpened by Olivier's deletion of the entire Fortinbras story; that is, Olivier reduces the political elements in order to concentrate on Hamlet's relationship with his family.

The emphasis on Hamlet's psyche is partly conveyed by the set. Responding to Olivier's desire for a dreamlike cavernous area, the designer provided a castle with vast columns, long (often empty) corridors, and winding staircases, presumably symbolizing the puzzled mind. Exteriors tend to be misty. The camera does lots of panning and tracking, slowing down the action by dwelling on the set. Olivier seems to be trying to make scenes last as long as possible, ending them with dreamlike dissolves—a notable contrast, by the way, to the straight cuts used in the 1964 Russian film version by Grigori Kozintsev. Olivier exploits the camera as fully as possible. For example, the camera moves down from a great height, approaching the seated Hamlet, who then delivers his first soliloquy. Similarly, when the Ghost leaves at 1.5.91, the camera soars into the air (as though with the Ghost), moving above Hamlet, and showing him fainting on the battlement. Olivier also uses the cinematic device of voice-over for parts of some of the soliloquies; that is, we hear Hamlet's thoughts, but his lips do not move. Olivier took advantage also, perhaps needlessly, of the camera's ability to show us scenes that could not be staged, for instance Ophelia's drowning and Hamlet's encounter with the pirates. Olivier's *Hamlet*, in short, is a film, not a filmed version of a stage presentation.

A word about the end of Olivier's film: Laertes unfairly thrusts at Hamlet and wounds him, drawing blood. Having perceived that Laertes's foil is unbated, in the next round Hamlet knocks Laertes's foil out of his hand, retrieves it for his own use, and gives Laertes the bated foil. After wounding Laertes, Hamlet assumes the throne (the courtiers kneel before him), asks Horatio to tell his story, and dies. The film ends with a procession, cannon are fired, the camera goes through the castle, passing the now-empty throne and Gertrude's bedroom, and up to a tower, where Hamlet's bearers are silhouetted against the sky.

Kenneth Branagh's film version (1996, with Branagh as Hamlet, Derek Jacobi as Claudius, Julie Christie as Gertrude, and Kate Winslet as Ophelia) gives us as much text as possible—the longest version (Q2) with the addition of the lines found only in the Folio version. It runs three hours and fifty-eight minutes, not including an intermission, whereas Olivier's version runs only 152 minutes. The intermission (after two hours and thirty-five minutes) comes at the end of 4.4, after Hamlet's last soliloquy ("How all occasions do inform against me"), which means that before the intermission we get the whole story up to the time of Hamlet's departure for England. This is a long haul, and after about two hours some spectators find themselves wondering if at *this* screening there will be no intermission.

Branagh's Hamlet—he had already played the role twice on the stage, in 1988, directed by Derek Jacobi, and in 1993, directed by Adrian Noble—is a robust (even a swashbuckling) prince, not a disaffected student. The film is set in a late nineteenth-century kingdom, where the men wear handsome military uniforms (Hamlet in black, Claudius in red, Laertes in white) and the women wear ball gowns. Serving as the exterior of the castle at Elsinore is one of England's baroque masterpieces, the palace at Blenheim Park (1724), and the interior shots show ornate rooms, often with mirrored doors. The visual splendor, doubtless partly an attempt to hold the viewer's interest through a very long film, works well, though occasionally one feels that the eye is given too much. There is overkill in, for instance, Hamlet's scene with the ghost in 1.5, where the earth heaves, and smoke and fire issue forth. (The music is also a good deal too loud here.)

Doubtless also in an effort to hold the viewer's attention, during long narrative speeches Branagh sometimes shows actors silently performing what the character is reporting. Thus, when the ghost tells Hamlet how he was poisoned, we see the episode enacted, including the writhings of Hamlet Senior as the poison takes its effect. Although viewers who know the play well may wish that Branagh had been content here to let the words do the work, current dogma insists that film is a visual medium, and that talking heads are anathema. There is something to the idea that by showing what a character is describing at length, a long narrative

speech is not only enlivened but is also clarified. Still, the visual imagery during the ghost's narrative may have the wrong effect; it convinces the viewer that the episode did indeed happen—we see the episode with our own eyes, and we therefore conclude that the ghost is indeed an honest ghost—whereas at this point, although we should be fully taken by the horror of the ghost's narrative, we should not yet be entirely certain of its truth. At least we (with Hamlet) should later be able entertain the possibility that the ghost was fabricating.

A second and much more offensive added flashback shows Hamlet and Ophelia nude, copulating. This addition is merely an attempt to make Shakespeare sexy. Nothing in the text suggests that they have been to bed, and it is difficult to imagine the dutiful Ophelia would have slept with a man. It is even difficult for most readers to imagine that Hamlet would have seduced her, since he is presented as an ideal gentleman. (Although audiences today may find the idea risible, Shakespeare valued virginity; in *Macbeth* [4.3.125–26]. Malcolm—soon to be crowned monarch of Scotland—in assuring Macduff of his fitness to rule says, "I am yet / Unknown to woman.")

Other visual additions in Branagh's *Hamlet*, however, are of considerable interest, especially the pantomime of the fall of Troy, narrated by the Player in 2.2.440–508. Branagh has said that he wished to pay tribute to John Gielgud (Priam) and Judi Dench (Hecuba), and we are glad to see them here, even if they don't speak and the visual addition is not really needed. Several other famous performers, notably Billy Crystal, Gérard Depardieu, Rosemary Harris, Charlton Heston, and Robin Williams play small parts, doubtless in order to attract large audiences.

Branagh's treatment of Fortinbras is both good and bad; good in that Fortinbras has not been omitted (most productions do without him), bad in that he is overemphasized, first near the beginning, when descriptions of him are accompanied by visual images, and near the end, when we see his army invading the palace. The duel between Hamlet and Laertes is intercut with shots of Fortinbras's soldiers advancing on the castle, possessing the courtyard, entering the corridors, and then bursting through the mirrored doors of the great hall. All of this greatly diminishes an immensely important scene, the fatal duel and the deaths of Claudius and Gertrude. And at the very end, when Hamlet's body is carried out, we see Fortinbras's soldiers hacking at the great statue of Hamlet's father, which finally topples, probably reminding viewers of television footage of statues of Lenin and Stalin being pulled down when the Soviet Union dissolved. Strange, that a director who is so eager to give us all of the words of the play should undercut them with irrelevant visuals. After all, who cares about Fortinbras's triumph? (Probably the answer to the question is that Branagh thought that the general public share the current academic interest in a politicized Shakespeare.) What we care about is Hamlet's trial, and his tragic (woeful and wonderful) success. Still, Branagh's film offers so much that is good, that we must be grateful to Branagh, even as we wish he had left well enough alone.

There are dozens—even hundreds—of other productions that one could talk about, but beyond the few that we have discussed, the rest (for our purposes) is silence.

Bibliographic Note: In addition to the sources already cited here, the following are of special interest. On the 1985 staging of Q1 (the First Quarto) by Orange Tree, see Bryan Loughrey in *The Hamlet First Published*, ed. Thomas Clayton (1992), and Nicholas Shrimpton in *Shakespeare Survey* 39 (1986): 191–206. On the 1992 production of Q1 by the Medieval Players, see Peter Holland in *Shakespeare Survey* 46 (1994): 156–62. For traditional stage business in productions up to the beginning of the twentieth century, see Arthur Colby Sprague, *Shakespeare and the Actors: The Stage Business in His Plays 1660–1905* (1944). Robert Hapgood's edition (1999) of *Hamlet*, in series called Shakespeare in Production, has a 96-page introduction on the history of productions and then gives the text of the play with annotations reporting stage business over the centuries.

See also Marvin Rosenberg, *The Masks of Hamlet* (1992, an exhaustive study of the ways in which scenes have been done); Ralph Berry, *Changing Styles in Shakespeare* (1981, on productions from 1948 to the 1970s); Ralph Berry, *Shakespeare in Performance* (1993, a chapter on productions in the 1970s and 1980s, and another chapter on the doubling of roles in the play); on modern productions, see Peter Thomson's chapter in Jonathan Bate and Russell Jackson, *Shakespeare: An Illustrated Stage History* (1996); and also Peter Davison, *"Hamlet": Text and Performance* (1983). For general histories, see John A. Mills, *"Hamlet" on Stage: The Great Tradition* (1985), and Raymond Mander and Joe Mitchenson, *"Hamlet" Though the Ages: A Pictorial Record from 1709* (1952).

For film and television versions, see Bernice Kilman, *Hamlet: Film, Television, and Audio Performance* (1988); H. R. Coursen, *Shakespearean Performance as an Interpretation* (1992); and H. R. Coursen, *Watching Shakespeare on Television* (1993). The Olivier and Branagh film versions have been published.

WHAT IS THE TEXT OF A PLAY BY SHAKESPEARE?

THE PLAY TEXT AS A COLLABORATION

Shakespeare's fellow dramatist Ben Jonson reported that the actors said of Shakespeare, "In his writing, whatsoever he penned, he never blotted out line," i.e., never crossed out material and revised his work while composing. None of Shakespeare's plays survives in manuscript (with the possible exception of a scene in *Sir Thomas More*), so we cannot fully evaluate the comment, but in a few instances the published work clearly shows that he revised his manuscript. Consider the following passage (shown here in facsimile) from the best early text of *Romeo and Juliet*, the Second Quarto (1599):

> *Ro.* Would I were sleepe and peace so sweet to rest
> The grey eyde morne smiles on the frowning night,
> Checkring the Easterne Clouds with streaks of light,
> And darknesse fleckted like a drunkard reeles,
> From forth daies pathway, made by *Tytans* wheeles.
> Hence will I to my ghostly Friers close cell,
> His helpe to craue, and my deare hap to tell.
>
> *Exit.*
>
> *Enter Frier alone with a basket.* (night,
> *Fri.* The grey-eyed morne smiles on the frowning
> Checking the Easterne clowdes with streaks of light:
> And fleckeld darknesse like a drunkard reeles,
> From forth daies path, and *Titans* burning wheeles:
> Now ere the sun aduance his burning eie,

Romeo rather elaborately tells us that the sun at dawn is dispelling the night (morning is smiling, the eastern clouds are checked with light, and the sun's chariot—Titan's wheels—advances), and he will seek out his spiritual father, the friar. He exits and, oddly, the Friar enters and says pretty much the same thing about the sun. Both speakers say that "the gray-eyed morn smiles on the frowning night," but there are small differences, perhaps having more to do with the business of printing the book than with the author's composition: For Romeo's "checkring," "fleckted," and "pathway," we get the Friar's "checking," "fleckeld," and "path." (Notice, by the way, the inconsistency in Elizabethan spelling: Romeo's "clouds" become the Friar's "clowdes.")

Both versions must have been in the printer's copy, and it seems safe to assume that both were in Shakespeare's manuscript. He must have written one version—let's say he first wrote Romeo's closing lines for the scene—and then he decided, no, it's better to give this lyrical passage to the Friar, as the opening of a new scene, but he neglected to delete the first version. Editors must make a choice, and they may feel that the reasonable thing to do is to print the text as Shakespeare intended it. But how can we know what he intended? Almost all modern editors delete the lines from Romeo's speech, and retain the Friar's lines. They don't do this because they know Shakespeare's intention, however. They give the lines to the Friar because the first published version (1597) of *Romeo and Juliet* gives only the Friar's version, and this text (though in many ways inferior to the 1599 text) is thought to derive from the memory of some actors, that is, it is thought to represent a performance, not just a script. Maybe during the course of rehearsals Shakespeare—an actor as well as an author—unilaterally decided that the Friar should speak the lines; if so (remember that we don't know this to be a fact) his final intention was to give the speech to the Friar. Maybe, however, the actors talked it over and settled on the Friar, with or without Shakespeare's approval. On the other hand, despite the 1597 version, one might argue (if only weakly) on behalf of giving the lines to Romeo rather than to the Friar, thus: (1) Romeo's comment on the coming of the daylight emphasizes his separation from Juliet, and (2) the figurative language seems more appropriate to Romeo than to the Friar.

A playwright sold a script to a theatrical company. The script thus belonged to the company, not the author, and author and company alike must have regarded this script not as a literary work but as the basis for a play that the actors would create on the stage. We speak of Shakespeare as the author of the plays, but readers should bear in mind that the texts they read, even when derived from a single text, such as the First Folio (1623), is inevitably the collaborative work not simply of Shakespeare with his company—doubtless during rehearsals the actors would suggest alterations—but also with other forces of the age. One force was governmental censorship. In 1606 parliament passed "an Act to restrain abuses of players," prohibiting the utterance of oaths and the name of God. So where the earliest text of *Othello* gives us "By heaven" (3.3.106), the first Folio gives "Alas," presumably reflecting the compliance of stage practice with the law. Similarly, the 1623 version of *King Lear* omits the oath "Fut" (probably from "By God's foot") at 1.2.142, again presumably reflecting the line as it was spoken on the stage. Editors who seek to give the reader the play that Shakespeare initially conceived— the "authentic" play conceived by the solitary Shakespeare—probably will restore the missing oaths and references to God. Other editors, who see the play as a collaborative work, a construction made not only by Shakespeare but also by actors and compositors and even government censors, may claim that what counts is the play as it was actually performed. Such editors regard the censored text as legitimate, since it is the play that was (presumably) finally put on. A performed text, they argue, has more historical reality than a text produced by an editor who has sought to get at what Shakespeare initially wrote. In this view, the text of a play is rather like the script of a film; the script is not the film, and the play text is not the performed play. Even if we want to talk about the play that Shakespeare "intended", we will find ourselves talking about a script that he handed over to a company with the intention that it be implemented by actors. The "intended" play is the one that the actors—we might almost say "society"—would help to construct.

Further, it is now widely held that a play is also the work of readers and spectators, who do not simply receive meaning, but who create it when they respond to the play. This idea is fully in accord with contemporary post-structuralist critical thinking, notably Roland Barthes's "The Death of the Author," in *Image-Music-Text* (1977) and Michel Foucault's "What Is an Author?", in *The Foucault Reader* (1984). The gist of the idea is that an author is not an isolated genius; rather, authors are subject to the politics and other social structures of their age. A dramatist especially is a worker in a collaborative project, working most obviously with actors—parts may be written for particular actors—but working also with the audience. Consider the words of Samuel Johnson, written to be spoken by the actor David Garrick at the opening of a theater in 1747:

> The stage but echoes back the public voice;
> The drama's laws, the drama's patrons give,
> For we that live to please, must please to live.

EDITING TEXTS

Though eighteen of his plays were published during his lifetime, Shakespeare seems never to have supervised their publication. There is nothing unusual here; when a playwright sold a play to a theatrical company he surrendered his ownership to it. Normally a company would not publish the play, because to publish it meant to allow competitors to acquire the piece. Some plays did get published: Apparently hard up actors sometimes pieced together a play for a publisher; sometimes a company in need of money sold a play; and sometimes a company allowed publication of a play that no longer drew audiences. That Shakespeare did not concern himself with publication is not remarkable; of his contemporaries, only Ben Jonson carefully supervised the publication of his own plays.

In 1623, seven years after Shakespeare's death, John Heminges and Henry Condell (two senior members of Shakespeare's company, who had worked with him for about twenty years) collected his plays—published and unpublished—into a large volume, of a kind called a folio. (A folio is a volume consisting of large sheets that have been folded once, each sheet thus making two leaves, or four pages. The size of the page of course depends on the size of the sheet—a folio can range in height from twelve to sixteen inches, and in width from eight to eleven; the pages in the 1623 edition of Shakespeare, commonly called the First Folio, are approximately thirteen inches tall and eight inches wide.) The eighteen plays published during Shakespeare's lifetime had been issued one play per volume in small formats called quartos. (Each sheet in a quarto has been folded twice, making four leaves, or eight pages, each page being about nine inches tall and seven inches wide, roughly the size of a large paperback.)

Heminges and Condell suggest in an address "To the great variety of readers" that the republished plays are presented in better form than in the quartos:

> Before you were abused with diverse stolen and surreptitious copies, maimed and deformed by the frauds and stealths of injurious imposters that exposed them; even those, are now offered to your view cured and perfect of their limbs, and all the rest absolute in their numbers, as he [i.e. Shakespeare] conceived them.

There is a good deal of truth to this statement, but some of the quarto versions are better than others; some are in fact preferable to the Folio text.

Modern editors of Shakespeare must first select their copy; no problem if the play exists only in the Folio, but a considerable problem if the relationship between a Quarto and the Folio is unclear. As we will see in a moment, the relationships among texts of *Hamlet* are highly uncertain.

THE TEXTS OF *HAMLET*

Probably the most famous line in Western literature is "To be or not to be, that is the question," from Hamlet's soliloquy in 3.1.57–91. But in fact this soliloquy exists in three forms—in a text published in 1603, a text published in 1604–1605, and a text published in 1623. First, let's look at the beginning of the 1603 version. This book is a quarto (we have already mentioned that a quarto is a fairly small book whose pages were made by folding a sheet of paper twice, producing four leaves, or eight pages); this edition is called Q1 because it is the first quarto version of *Hamlet*. If you are at all familiar with the speech, the Q1 version may strike you as comic, almost a parody. (Spelling and punctuation are modernized in the three versions given here.)

> To be or not to be, aye, there's the point
> To die, to sleep; is that all? Aye, all.
> No, to sleep, to dream, aye, marry, there it goes,
> For in that dream of death, when we awake,
> And borne before an everlasting judge,
> From whence no passenger ever returned,
> The undiscovered country, at whose sight
> The happy smile, and the accursed damned.
> But for this, the joyful hope of this.
> Who'd bear the scorns and flattery of the world,
> Scorned by the right rich, the rich cursed of the
>   poor?
> The widow being oppressed, the orphan wronged,
> The taste of hunger, or a tyrant's reign. . . .

No, we did not mistakenly omit "That is the question." And even if this version were quoted in full, you would not find such familiar phrases as "the slings and arrows of outrageous fortune," or "take arms against a sea of troubles." (See facsimile, page 381.)

Before we comment on Q1, let's look at the beginning of the next version, from Q2 (i.e., the second quarto version), published in 1604–1605. This version, will strike you as familiar. Line numbers keyed to the present text are added.

> To be or not to be: that is the question:
> Whether 'tis nobler in the mind to suffer
> The slings and arrows of outrageous fortune,
> Or to take arms against a sea of troubles,   60
> And by opposing end them. To die, to sleep—
> No more—and by a sleep to say we end
> The heartache, and the thousand natural shocks
> That flesh is heir to! 'Tis a consummation
> Devoutly to be wished. To die, to sleep—   65
> To sleep—perchance to dream: ay, there's the rub,
> For in that sleep of death what dreams may come
> When we have shuffled off this mortal coil,
> Must give us pause. There's the respect
> That makes calamity of so long life: 70
> For who would bear the whips and scorns of time,
> Th' oppressor's wrong, the proud man's contumely,
> The pangs of despised love, the law's delay. . . .
>
> (3.1.57–73)

The third version, almost the same as the second, appears in the collection of Shakespeare's plays called the First Folio, printed in 1623. (A folio, you recall, consists of pages made by folding a large sheet only once rather than twice, thereby producing two leaves or four pages, instead of a quarto's four leaves and eight pages.) In the original printings, the second and third versions (Q2 and F) often differ in spelling and punctuation—for instance, in the first line of the Folio version, the word "question" is capitalized and it is followed by a colon, whereas in Q2 "question" is not capitalized and it is followed by a comma—but despite such differences the two versions of the speech are very close to each other. Putting aside spelling and punctuation, the two chief differences in the quoted passage are "proud" (Q2) versus "poor" (F) in line 72, and "despised" (Q1) versus "disprized," i.e. "undervalued" (F) in line 73.

Let's now look at the three texts in some detail.

The First Quarto (Q1, 1603)

Only two copies of Q1 are extant. This version has 2,154 lines which is to say that it is much shorter than Q2 (about 3,764 lines), and than F (about 3,535 lines). (Methods of counting lines differ, so you may find slightly different figures in some other source.) In this version, for example, Laertes's speech to Ophelia in 1.3, warning her against Hamlet (5–44), is less than half the length it is in Q2 and F. The Player's speech about Pyrrhus at 2.2.440–508 is twenty lines shorter, and Hamlet's praise of Horatio at 3.2.60–86 is a dozen lines shorter. In the nineteenth century Q1 was commonly regarded either as a stage version of the pre-Shakespearean *Hamlet* or as the early play with some revisions by Shakespeare, i.e., as a sort of first version of Shakespeare's *Hamlet*. Today almost everyone agrees that, partly because many speeches are much shorter than in Q2 and F, and partly because a fair amount of the text is banal and some passages are close to nonsense, whereas some other passages show Shakespeare at the top of his form, it is not a pre-Shakespearean play and it is not an early version by Shakespeare; rather, it is an actor's garbled memory of what Shakespeare wrote. A still-unexplained feature of this version, however, is the fact that Polonius is called Corambis—something that cannot be attributed to a faulty memory.

Probably an actor who had performed in an abridged version of the play—maybe a version created for a company that toured the provinces—provided the printer with the copy. Such a text is characterized as a "reported text" or a "post-performance" text or a "memorial reconstruction"—something based on the memory of an actor or actors.

In this instance, it is all but certain that the actor who gave the copy to the printer had played Marcellus. Why Marcellus? Because his lines in Q1 correspond very closely with the two other texts, and indeed the lines of characters who are on stage at the same time as Marcellus correspond pretty well, whereas many other passages depart widely and wildly—presumably because the actor was offstage and he was more or less forced to invent speeches he only vaguely recalled. On the other hand, because Lucianus's six-line speech in 3.2.244–49 is perfect—and because Voltemand's long speech in 2.2.60–79 corresponds closely with the other texts, it is likely that the actor who played Marcellus doubled in these other roles.

What value can such a text have? Only a little, but especially in recent years, when there has been an emphasis on the play as a *performance* rather than as a text, claims have been made that whereas the two other versions are "literary," the Q1 version gives us the play as it was actually produced on the stage. It is thus supposedly closer to the real *Hamlet*, the *Hamlet* that the Elizabethans saw, than are the other texts, which are said in any case to be impossibly long. Thus, Graham Holderness and Bryan Loughrey say in their introduction to a reprint (1992) of Q1, "What we can assume with reasonable confidence is that this text

The Tragedy of Hamlet

And so by continuance, and weakenesse of the braine
Iuto this frensie, which now posseffeth him:
And if this be not true, take this from this.

   King Thinke you t'is so?

   Cor. How? so my Lord, I would very faine knovv
That thing that I haue saide t'is so, positiuely,
And it hath fallen out otherwise.
Nay, if circumstances leade me on,
Ile finde it out, if it were hid
As deepe as the centre of the earth.

   King. how should wee trie this same?

   Cor. Mary my good lord thus,
The Princes walke is here in the galery,
There let *Ofelia*, walke vntill hee comes:
Your selfe and I will stand close in the study,
There shall you heare the effect of all his hart,
And if it proue any otherwise then loue,
Then let my censure faile an other time.

   King. see where hee comes poring vppon a booke.

       Enter Hamlet.

   Cor. Madame, will it please your grace
To leaue vs here?

   Que. With all my hart.   *exit.*

   Cor. And here *Ofelia*, reade you on this booke,
And walke aloofe, the King shal be vnseene.

   Ham. To be, or not to be, I there's the point,
To Die, to sleepe, is that all? I all:
No, to sleepe, to dreame, I mary there it goes,
For in that dreame of death, when wee awake,
And borne before an euerlasting Iudge,
From whence no passenger euer returnd,
The vndiscouered country, at whose sight
The happy smile, and the accursed damn'd.
But for this, the ioyfull hope of this,
Whol'd beare the scornes and flattery of the world,
Scorned by the right rich, the rich curssed of the poore?

                                     Th

The beginning of "To be or not to be," as given in the First Quarto (Q1, 1603).

comes closer than the other texts to actual Jacobean stage practice" (page 14). But we *cannot* say that this text gives us the play as it was performed. The title page says that the play "hath beene diuerse times acted by his Highnesse seruants in the Cittie of London: as also in the two Vniuersities of Cambridge and Oxford, and else-where," but this is a statement about the play, not about this particular text; and in any case it is an advertisement, not a document whose truth is beyond question. At best Q1 gives us the play as one actor or perhaps a few actors *remembered* it. Further, we don't have direct access to their memories, but only to the compositor's version, filled with printer's errors. For instance, old Norway in Q1 is said to be "impudent" ("impudent / And bed-rid"), but in Q2 (1.2.29) he is "impotent" ("impotent and bedred"). The context (whether "bed-rid" or "bedred") clearly calls for Q2's "impotent," not Q1's "impudent." Whether the actor's memory failed or the compositor misread the handwriting or the compositor's mind wandered we cannot know, but one hardly wants to say that because Q1 has "impudent," this is the word that was spoken in production, much less that it therefore is quite as legitimate as whatever Shakespeare wrote in his lost manuscript.

On the other hand, we can value Q1 because it includes some stage directions not found in the other texts that do indeed seem to give us a sense of how the play was staged. For instance, Q1 has a stage direction, *"Enter Ofelia playing on a Lute, and her haire downe singing"* (4.5.20 s.d.) where Q2 has merely *"Enter Ophelia"* and the Folio text (1623) has merely *"Enter Ophelia distracted."* A second example of an interesting stage direction in Q1: only Q1 tells us that Hamlet leaps into Ophelia's grave in 5.1.250: *"Hamlet leapes in after Leartes"* (sic). (This stage direction, by the way, causes uneasiness among some editors because it makes Hamlet the aggressor.) Again, this is not to say that these stage directions are Shakespeare's; the most that we can say is that they help to give us a glimpse of what an Elizabethan audience may have seen.

The Second Quarto (Q2, 1604–1605)

Q2, the second published version, printed in 1604 and 1605, contains about 3,764 lines. It is the longest of Shakespeare's texts (it is almost twice as long as *Macbeth*), and it claims to be "Newly imprinted and enlarged to almost as much againe as it was, according to the true and perfect Coppie." Despite it's length, how-

ever, it omits some material that is found in the third text, for Folio, which we will look at later.

There is much dispute about exactly what "the true and perfect Coppie" was, but it may well have been Shakespeare's manuscript—sheets that scholars customarily call "foul papers," as opposed, for instance, to a neat scribal copy (a "fair copy"), or a scribal copy with later annotations that would serve as a prompt copy for actors. A brief reminder is called for at this point: When we speak of Shakespeare's "completed manuscript" or his "final version" we may be talking about something that never existed. No Shakespeare play survives in manuscript; we do not know how he worked, and we do not know if he thought of the play as finished when he turned over a manuscript, or—a very different thing—when the play was in some degree reworked during rehearsal. And we do not know if, after the early productions, he revised the play for later productions. Fifty years ago almost no one talked of the possibility that Shakespeare revised plays after they have been staged, but today some scholars argue that the texts of *Hamlet, The Second Part of Henry IV, Troilus and Cressida, Othello,* and *King Lear* all show evidence of revision, i e. there are (some people say) two authentic versions for each play.

Now to return to Q2 as "foul papers." At the beginning of 2.1 we get a stage direction: *"Enter old Polonius, with his man or two."* Such a direction suggests foul papers rather than a prompt copy; Shakespeare, in the process of beginning the scene, was not yet entirely sure about how the scene would go—maybe he would need two servants, and maybe he wouldn't. As it turns out, only one servant, Reynaldo, is needed. Presumably in a copy prepared for a stage production (a promptbook), such a direction would be corrected to something like, *"Enter Polonius and Reynaldo,"* and (if we may briefly get ahead of our story) that is exactly what we do find in the next version we will look at, the Folio version, which surely is a text based on a manuscript that reflects a production.

Of course, *"with his man or two"* might survive from Shakespeare's manuscript into a clean copy that a scribe prepared for the theatrical company, but additional evidence that the source of Q2 was Shakespeare's manuscript is the fact that Q2 prints many words that are obvious misreadings of handwriting, or guesses as to what the writer intended. Thus, in 3.2.350 it gives *"the vmber"* where the sense requires *"thumb"* (Hamlet is talking about fingering a musical instrument), and in 4.7.62 it gives *"the King"* where the sense requires *"checking."*

In addition to working from some sort of manuscript, the compositors of Q2 made occasional use of a printed text, Q1; especially in the first five scenes there are otherwise inexplicable similarities in typography and layout. Apparently the compositors of Q2 consulted Q1 when they were puzzled by something in their manuscript.

The Folio (1623)

The third early printed version (3,535 lines), in the posthumous First Folio, entitled *Mr. William Shakespeares Comedies, Histories, & Tragedies*, is a little shorter than Q2. The title page says the plays are "Published according to the True Originall Copies," but exactly what the printer's copy was for *Hamlet* is uncertain. Most students of the problem believe the compositor worked from a heavily annotated copy of Q2—the text in F contains some of Q2's errors as well as some new errors, and it also contains some of Q2's unusual spellings—but G. R. Hibbard in his Oxford edition of *Hamlet* (1987) offers strong arguments against this view. Still, even if the compositors of F did not use Q2 (or the 1611 reprint of it, Q3) as printer's copy, they may have consulted it on occasion, when their manuscript was unclear.

In any case, although F is slightly shorter than Q2, it is not simply a shortened version; it contains about eighty lines *not* found in Q2. Consider this small example. In the scene with the grave diggers, in Q2 the grave digger (in the speech prefixes he is called a clown) identifies the skull of Yorick, and we then (5.1.174–77) get this dialogue:

> HAM. This?
> CLOW. Een that.
> HAM. Alas poore *Yoricke*, I knew him *Horatio*.
>   . . .

But in the Folio text, Hamlet's second speech is different:

> HAM. Let me see. Alas poore *Yorick*, I knew him
>   *Horatio*. . . .

The Folio's addition of "Let me see" is very interesting. Probably the words were not in Shakespeare's foul papers (Q2); we can strongly suspect that "Let me see"—words indicating that Hamlet takes the skull from the grave digger—was a bit of dialogue added during the course of producing the play.

True, some of the lines that appear only in F may have been in the manuscript for Q2 and were acciden-

tally omitted when Q2 was printed, but some of the F-only material must be additions. Additions by whom? Are they revisions that actors made as they worked and reworked the play? Or are they revisions that Shakespeare himself made, perhaps after he saw early productions of the play? Here are some examples of small additions which to most editors sound like the sorts of things that actors might add. In 2.2.213, where in Q2 Hamlet says, "You cannot take from me . . . ," in F he says, "You cannot, sir, take from me . . ." In Hamlet's second soliloquy, "O, what a rogue and peasant slave am I," in an extended passage of blank verse (unrhymed lines of ten syllables) we get a line that consists only of, "O vengeance" (593). A third example, and the most interesting, concerns Hamlet's last words in 5.2.352. In both Q2 and F they are, "the rest is silence," but F goes on to add, as his utterance, "O, o, o, o." This string of *o*'s probably is meant to represent a sigh, and it may well be something that an actor added to Shakespeare's text.

Consider a slightly longer but still a brief example of an addition in F. In Q2, after Rosencrantz and Guildenstern tell Hamlet he must go with them and inform the kind where Polonius's body is, Hamlet says, "Bring me to him." But in F, Hamlet adds to these words, "Hide fox, and all after" (4.2.30–31)—presumably the cry from a game like hide-and-seek—and he probably runs off. Is this an authorial revision, adding liveliness to the scene and also perhaps suggesting (at least to Rosencrantz and Guildenstern) that Hamlet is a bit mad? Or is it, on the other hand, despite its theatrical effectiveness, a showy bit added by actors, and in fact *less* effective as an exit line than the simple "Bring me to him"? Or is it a revision—maybe for the worse—by Shakespeare himself?

Even if we grant that many of the small additions found in F probably are the work of actors, we should remember that Shakespeare was an actor, a member of the company that bought his plays, and we should not be too quick to dismiss the changes as unauthorized additions by meddlesome actors.

What of the longer passages found only in F, notably the thirty-odd lines in 2.2 concerning what is conventionally called The War of the Theaters, lines about the competition that companies of children were offering to the adult companies? No one doubts that the passage is authentic Shakespeare, but is it evidence that Shakespeare revised the play after it had already been on the stage? That is, was this passage absent from the manuscript behind Q2 and added in the

The Tragedie of Hamlet. 265

With turbulent and dangerous Lunacy.

Rosin. He does confesse he feeles himselfe distracted,
But from what cause he will by no meanes speake.

Guil. Nor do we finde him forward to be sounded,
But with a crafty Madnesse keepes aloose:
When we would bring him on to some Confession
Of his true state.

Qu. Did he receiue you well?

Rosin. Most like a Gentleman.

Guild. But with much forcing of his disposition.

Rosin. Niggard of question, but of our demands
Most free in his reply.

Qu. Did you assay him to any pastime?

Rosin. Madam, it so fell out, that certaine Players
We ore-wrought on the way: of these we told him,
And there did seeme in him a kinde of ioy
To heare of it: They are about the Court,
And (as I thinke) they haue already order
This night to play before him.

Pol. 'Tis most true:
And he beseech'd me to intreate your Maiesties
To heare, and see the matter.

King. With all my heart, and it doth much content me
To heare him so inclin'd. Good Gentlemen,
Giue him a further edge, and driue his purpose on
To these delights.

Rosin. We shall my Lord.   *Exeunt.*

King. Sweet *Gertrude* leaue vs too,
For we haue closely sent for *Hamlet* hither,
That he, as 'twere by accident, may there
Affront *Ophelia.* Her Father, and my selfe (lawful espials)
Will so bestow our selues, that seeing vnseene
We may of their encounter frankely iudge,
And gather by him, as he is behaued,
If t be th'affliction of his loue, or no,
That thus he suffers for.

Qu. I shall obey you,
And for your part *Ophelia,* I do wish
That your good Beauties be the happy cause
Of *Hamlets* wildenesse: so shall I hope your Vertues
Will bring him to his wonted way againe,
To both your Honors.

Ophe. Madam, I wish it may.

Pol. *Ophelia,* walke you heere. Gracious so please ye
We will bestow our selues: Reade on this booke,
That shew of such an exercise may colour
Your lonelinesse. We are oft too blame in this,
'Tis too much prou'd, that with Deuotions visage,
And pious Action, we do surge o're
The diuell himselfe.

King. Oh 'tis true:
How smart a lash that speech doth giue my Conscience?
The Harlots Cheeke beautied with plaist'ring Art
Is not more vgly to the thing that helpes it,
Then is my deede, to my most painted word.
Oh heauie burthen!

Pol. I heare him comming, let's withdraw my Lord.
          Exeunt.

Enter Hamlet.

Ham. To be, or not to be, that is the Question:
Whether 'tis Nobler in the minde to suffer
The Slings and Arrowes of outragious Fortune,
Or to take Armes against a Sea of troubles,
And by opposing end them: to dye, to sleepe
No more; and by a sleepe, to say we end
The Heart-ake, and the thousand Naturall shockes

That Flesh is heyre too? 'Tis a consummation
Deuoutly to be wish'd. To dye to sleepe,
To sleepe, perchance to Dreame; I, there's the rub,
For in that sleepe of death, what dreames may come,
When we haue shuffel'd off this mortall coile,
Must giue vs pawse. There's the respect
That makes Calamity of so long life:
For who would beare the Whips and Scornes of time,
The Oppressors wrong, the poore mans Contumely,
The pangs of dispriz'd Loue, the Lawes delay,
The insolence of Office, and the Spurnes
That patient merit of the vnworthy takes,
When he himselfe might his *Quietus* make
With a bare Bodkin? Who would these Fardles beare
To grunt and sweat vnder a weary life,
But that the dread of something after death,
The vndiscouered Countrey, from whose Borne
No Traueller returnes, Puzels the will,
And makes vs rather beare those illes we haue,
Then flye to others that we know not of.
Thus Conscience does make Cowards of vs all,
And thus the Natiue hew of Resolution
Is sicklied o're, with the pale cast of Thought,
And enterprizes of great pith and moment,
With this regard their Currants turne away,
And loose the name of Action. Soft you now,
The faire *Ophelia*? Nimph, in thy Orizons
Be all my sinnes remembred.

Ophe. Good my Lord,
How does your Honor for this many a day?

Ham. I humbly thanke you: well, well, well.

Ophe. My Lord, I haue Remembrances of yours,
That I haue longed long to re-deliuer.
I pray you now, receiue them.

Ham. No, no, I neuer gaue you ought.

Ophe. My honor'd Lord, I know right well you did,
And with them words of so sweet breath compos'd,
As made the things more rich, then perfume left:
Take these againe, for to the Noble minde
Rich gifts wax poore, when giuers proue vnkinde.
There my Lord.

Ham. Ha, ha: Are you honest?

Ophe. My Lord.

Ham. Are you faire?

Ophe. What meanes your Lordship?

Ham. That if you be honest and faire, your Honesty
should admit no discourse to your Beautie.

Ophe. Could Beautie my Lord, haue better Comerce
then your Honestie?

Ham. I trulie: for the power of Beautie, will sooner
transforme Honestie from what it is, to a Bawd, then the
force of Honestie can translate Beautie into his likenesse.
This was sometime a Paradox, but now the time giues it
proofe. I did loue you once.

Ophe. Indeed my Lord, you made me beleeue so.

Ham. You should not haue beleeued me. For vertue
cannot so innocculate our old stocke, but we shall rellish
of it. I loued you not.

Ophe. I was the more deceiued.

Ham. Get thee to a Nunnerie. Why would'st thou
be a breeder of Sinners? I am my selfe indifferent honest,
but yet I could accuse me of such things, that it were better my Mother had not borne me. I am very prowd, re-
uengefull, Ambitious, with more offences at my becke,
then I haue thoughts to put them in imagination, to giue
them shape, or time to acte them in. What should such
Fel-

"To be or not to be" (the speech begins near the bottom of the left-hand column) as given in the First Folio (F1, 1623).

manuscript behind F, or was it present in the Q2 ms but omitted from the printed version (perhaps because it seemed to be an undramatic digression), in which case it was not so much *added* to F as it was *restored* by F? The short answer is that inconclusive arguments have been offered on both sides. Similarly, take the passage in 5.2.57—which is found only in F—where Hamlet, talking to Horatio, says of Rosencrantz and Guildenstern,

Why, man, they did make love to this employment.

Did Q2 accidentally omit this line, or did Shakespeare add it, in the course of revising the play, in order to further reveal Hamlet's character, specifically to show him justifying the action by which he sends these two men to their deaths?

The 220-odd lines *not* in F also raise questions. For instance, the soliloquy beginning "How all occasions do inform against me" (4.4.33), present in Q2, is not in F. Does its omission let us glimpse Shakespeare revising the play? Did Shakespeare come to think (as some readers and viewers think) that the speech is redundant? Or did he decide to alter the character of Hamlet, in this case by revealing less of his thoughts? Or is the omission due merely to the company's attempt to shorten the performance time of the play? The same questions can be asked of another passage not in F, Hamlet's comment to his mother about Rosencrantz and Guildenstern:

There's letters sealed, and my two schoolfellows,
Whom I will trust as I will adders fanged,
They bear the mandate; they must sweep my way
And marshal me to knavery. Let it work;
For 'tis sport to have the enginer
Hoist with his own petar, and 't shall go hard
But I will delve one yard below their mines
And blow them to the moon. O, 'tis most sweet
When in one line two crafts directly meet.

(3.4.203–11)

Did Shakespeare have second thoughts, some time after the play had been on the stage, and decide to delete this passage, perhaps because it showed an unattractive cast to Hamlet's thinking? Or perhaps because it is inconsistent with Hamlet's later speech, when he tells Horatio that during the voyage to England he was suddenly inspired in a moment of "rashness" to forge the papers that send Rosencrantz and Guildenstern to their deaths? If so, in the course of removing the passage he deleted what was to become one of his most famous phrases, "Hoist with his own petar."

In short, in F, some omissions of material that is present in Q2 are very brief, and may be accidental; other omissions are longer, and must be deliberate cuts but we do not know if the cuts were made by Shakespeare or by someone or some group of actors charged with preparing a text for production. (It is uncertain how a manuscript became a promptbook.) Conceivably, some omissions are due to Shakespeare, some to the company, and some to carelessness.

There are also several hundred small differences—variants—between Q2 and F, such as the famous "too too solid flesh" of F, versus the "sallied" (i.e. sullied) flesh of Q2. Similarly, in 1.4.49, speaking to the ghost, Hamlet says in Q2 that its bones were "quietly interr'd," but in F he says they were "quietly enurn'd." Did Shakespeare in the course of revising think that "interred" was a bit bland, and therefore substitute "inurned"? Or did an actor make the change—or did a compositor misread the manuscript? Whether such differences are due to Shakespeare revising, actors altering the text, or compositors blundering (perhaps the word was the same in both manuscripts, but one compositor got it right and one got it wrong), cannot be established. Possibly some are authorial revisions, some are alterations made by actors, and some are errors made by compositors; everyone agrees, however, that in *some* instances (as when Q2 gives the nonsensical "*the vmber*" and F gives the meaningful "*thumb*"), Q2 is mistaken and F is correct.

It should also be mentioned that F includes some stage directions, such as "On scuffling they change Rapiers," that suggest it is based on a text prepared for performance—but it also omits many necessary exits and entrances. Perhaps the most we can say about the copy for F is that whoever made it began with Shakespeare's foul papers and added some stage directions and some material—whether by Shakespeare or by the actors is uncertain—that has come to be part of the play.

The Present Text

We use the text prepared by David Bevington, of the University of Chicago. Bevington relies chiefly on Q2, but he also draws on F and (rarely) on Q1.

Seventeenth-Century Drama: England and the Continent

The plays in this volume have been performed by professional theater companies and students alike. Pictured here is a 1993 production of Lope de Vega's *Fuente Ovejuna* by the Yale School of Drama.

THE END OF THE RENAISSANCE, THE PURITAN INTERREGNUM, THE RESTORATION, AND THE INTRODUCTION OF ACTRESSES

In England, radical and sudden changes to the theater establishment occurred during the middle of the seventeenth century. After an incredibly rich, creative period of theatrical activity—with Marlowe, Shakespeare, and the establishment of theater as a profession in the late sixteenth century—in 1642 the Puritans, who had come to power, succeeded in closing the theaters until 1660.

What happened was this: Even in the later sixteenth century, when theatrical activity was vigorous, Puritans and many other respectable folk disapproved of the theater and sought to regulate it as closely as they could. To escape such interference, James Burbage built The Theater, the first permanent structure built in England for plays, outside of the city limits of London in 1576. He soon had competition; other theaters were built—also outside of London—on the south bank of the River Thames and in the northern suburbs. In the earlier part of the seventeenth century, theatrical activity continued to flourish, but always with Puritan opposition. Puritan power increased during the reign of King Charles I (1629–49). From 1629 to 1642 Charles ruled without Parliament, but when financial difficulty forced him to call a session, the members of Parliament refused to raise taxes for him, insisting that limits be set on his power. Charles refused, civil war broke out between his supporters (the Royalists) and his Puritan opponents, and in 1642 the Puritans were sufficiently powerful to shut down virtually all theatrical activity. "Virtually all," rather than all, because there is indeed evidence of occasional surreptitious performances, but for all practical purposes the theater came to a halt. In 1649 Charles was beheaded, and England was ruled by a military dictatorship headed by Oliver Cromwell. Thus ended one of the most brilliant periods in theater history.

Cromwell died in 1658, and his son Richard attempted to succeed him, but the Puritan government fell apart, thus ending the Interregnum—the period between two monarchs. In 1660 the son of the late Charles I (the prince was living in exile in France) was invited to return to England, and was restored to the English throne, as Charles II, thus introducing the period called the Restoration, which runs to about 1700. In France Charles had witnessed numerous theater performances, both in the French court and in the public theaters in Paris. In France women had been performing the female roles for some time, unlike the practice in his homeland where boys played female parts. Upon his return Charles II instituted a radical reform for the theater profession in Britain: Women must play their own roles. When the theaters opened again, a new profession was available to women. The introduction of women on the English public stages was a significant change on many levels. Imagine what it must have been like as a playwright to write a role for a woman and to know that a woman would actually perform the role. The significance of this was not lost on Aphra Behn, the first professional woman playwright, whose scripts often made connections between herself as a writer for the stage and those women who played the roles she wrote.

A very practical aspect of women performing was the creation of "breeches roles," parts in which women cross-dress as men. Numerous plays from prerevolutionary England used cross-dressing, often for comic purposes. For instance, in Shakespeare's *Twelfth Night* and *As You Like It,* Viola and Rosalind dress as youths and are not recognized even by the young men who love them. These female characters, however, disguise themselves as men as part of the plot; that is, the role is female, though in some scenes the performer wears male attire. Such roles became very popular, leading to the creation of male roles played by a female performer. That is, where on Shakespeare's stage, boy performers played female roles and sometimes disguised themselves as men, now, in the Restoration theater, women played certain male roles. The convention became pervasive; it has been estimated that between 1660 and 1700 nearly one-third of all new plays contained breeches parts. Their popularity presumably had at least two sources: (1) Women spectators were delighted to see women on the stage dressed as men, that is, women assuming a sense of authority denied them off stage; (2) male spectators were happy to see women display their legs in public. And of course cross-dressing allowed both sexes to enjoy sexual innuendoes.

THE DEVELOPMENT OF THE SEVENTEENTH-CENTURY PROSCENIUM THEATER

In our discussion of the Greek theater (page 50) we mentioned that the actors performed in front of the *skene*, literally a hut or tent, but in this case a "scene-building," a structure that served two purposes: It served as a place from which the actors entered onto the performing areas and into which they exited, and it also served as a background for the actors (*skene* gives us our word *scene*).

The word *proscenium*, a Latinized form of a Greek word, is made up of *pro* = in front of, *skene* = hut, and *-ion*, a diminutive suffix, rather like the *-ette* in kitchenette. The *proscenium*, then, is a little something in front of the *skene*. In the Hellenistic world (Greece after the death of Alexander, in 323 B.C.E.), the word could refer to decorated panels set against the *skene*, or it could refer to the raised stage in front of the *skene*. For the ancient Romans, it almost always meant the raised stage, but in Italy in the sixteenth century it began to take on another meaning, *something in front of the scenery*—in particular, an arch that acted somewhat like a frame around a picture, in this case the picture being the set on the stage.

Such an arch has come to separate the actors from the audience, but in the early proscenium theaters the division was not sharp. True, the stage was no longer the *thrust stage* (or *platform stage*) of the Elizabethan theater (see pages 11 and 259), but it did extend beyond the proscenium, allowing actors to perform in what can be thought of as the audience's space. (This protruding segment of the stage is called the *apron*, and today's proscenium theaters retain a trace of the apron, thought it is scarcely deep enough to allow for much action. It is now chiefly used when actors take curtain calls at the end of a performance.)

Theaters of course varied from decade to decade, and from country to country—an Italian theater of 1550 can scarcely be expected to be identical with a French theater of 1600 or with an English theater of 1670—but we can say that the development of the proscenium theater allowed for increasingly pictorial effects, and it also reduced the intimacy between performers and audiences. In the English theaters of the late seventeenth century—the theaters of Aphra Behn, one of whose plays we include in this book, two doors were built into each side of the proscenium, and above the doors were windows or balconies. Because actors entered and exited through the doors, they were indeed in front of the proscenium, but much of the action nevertheless took place behind the proscenium. These theaters were equipped with **wings** and with **shutter settings.** Wings—rectangular painted canvases in wooden frames, often set into grooves—were used at the sides to help decorate the stage setting. Shutters were similar contrivances, usually in pairs, extending from one side of the stage to the other. Thus, when a pair of shutters was pulled back, another scene could be revealed. The depth of the space between one pair of shutters and the pair behind it varied, but the space could be considerable. The withdrawing of the front pair could reveal, for instance, a fairly large group of actors, thus changing the scene from, say, a street in front of a house to a banquet hall within the house. The use of rather elaborate painted scenery means that actors did not have to announce—as they did in the Elizabethan theater—what the scene was. In *King Lear,* for instance, we get such helpful dialogue as this (2.4.304–06), and we know what time of day it is and what the setting is:

> Alack, the night comes on, and the high winds
> Do sorely ruffle. For many miles about
> There's scarce a bush.

With painted scenery—although the characters will still have to tell us what time of day it is—we know where we are, without dialogue. Further, a theater that uses painted scenery is likely to use it a good deal. The stage directions in Behn's *The Rover* indicate that the scene often changes. For instance, 3.2 is set in "Lucetta's house," but Lucetta soon exits, and after a few lines spoken by two other characters we are told that the scene changes. That is, 3.3 begins thus:

> The scene changes to a chamber with an alcove bed in it, a table, etc. Lucetta in bed. Enter Sancho and Blunt, who takes the candle of Sancho at the door.

The change was accomplished by drawing back the shutters, thereby revealing Lucetta's bedchamber. Perhaps the alcove specified in the stage direction was simply painted on a shutter at the rear. The bedroom scene then yields to a scene (3.4) that begins with Blunt pulling himself up out of a sewer (a "common-shore"):

> The scene changes, and discovers Blunt, creeping out of a common-shore, his face, etc. all dirty.

The sharp changes of locale are immediately evident, even without dialogue. Sometimes even the change from one street to another is marked by a change of scenery, whereas in the Elizabethan theater the audience would have been given nothing more than the entrance of new characters, and perhaps a few words indicating where they are. In *The Rover,* however, 4.3, which is set in "A street," is followed by a scene which is set in "Another street." Presumably at the end of 4.3 shutters were withdrawn to mark the change.

For additional details about the English theater in the late seventeenth century, see Jocelyn Powell, *Restoration Theater Production* (1984); John Loftis et al., *The Revels History of Drama in English,* vol. 5 (1976); J. L. Styan, *Restoration Comedy in Performance* (1986).

Lope de Vega

Lope Félix de Vega Carpio, known as Lope de Vega (1562–1635), was born in Madrid and studied as a child with the Jesuits. Legend claims that by the time he was five he was composing verses and reading both Latin and Spanish. He entered the University of Alcalá, now known as the University of Madrid, and by 1585 he had established himself not only as a celebrated poet, but also as a man who lived an adventurous, often scandalous life. Married twice while having numerous affairs with actresses, he became a priest after the death of his second wife in 1614. As a young man he seems to have sailed with the ill-fated Spanish Armada and later wrote an epic poem that attacked the English victor of the battle, Sir Francis Drake. He served as secretary consecutively to two royal dukes, while managing to write plays, novels, and poetry. He probably did not write the 1500 plays attributed to him, but contemporary scholars have identified at least 314 as genuine. His reputation for excellence caused other lesser writers to attribute their works to him. Lope's theater work was so pervasive and popular that the term *es de Lope* entered the language as an expression meaning "it's of real quality!" Although he did not invent a new form of theater, Lope de Vega developed and established the three-act verse play known as a *comedia*, which was to become the major theatrical form of Spanish theater. As part of his innovation, he developed the subplot to complement the main story, and in his poetry he used varied rhythms with many shifts in rhymes to characterize differences in the plot. Between 1604 and 1635 Lope published more than twenty volumes of work. In 1609, in a poem entitled *New Rules for Writing Plays Today*, he defended his writing against the attacks of the classicists who demanded that plays must be written according to certain rules. The chief rule, he argued, is that the audience must enjoy the play. On his death in 1635 the Duke of Sessa, for whom he worked as secretary, acknowledged his reputation by paying for an elaborate funeral in Madrid that lasted nine days.

COMMENTARY ON *FUENTE OVEJUNA*

The sixteenth and seventeenth centuries in Spain produced so rich an array of literature (including drama) and art that this period is now referred to as the Golden Age. By the time Lope de Vega died in 1635, professional theaters created within courtyards, or *corrales*, were active in nearly all Spanish towns and cities. These productions added to the rich eclectic mix of theater activity: religious drama dominated by the Jesuits, private performances produced in palaces, and street theater from Italy, the ever popular commedia dell'arte. Similar to England, the plays were written in verse and playwrights were called *poetas*. Another similarity to English theater was the lack of strict separation between comedy and tragedy. Like Shakespeare, Lope included humorous scenes or characters in a serious play when it seemed appropriate.

Unlike England, however, the commercial theater in Spain was a mixture of private enterprise and municipal planning. City governments granted the right to build and administer a theater to local charities. The charities acted as business managers to the theater companies, returning profit from the enterprise back to the hospitals and poorhouses administered by the charities. Although Spanish theater was not immune to antitheatrical attacks, this financial arrangement gave the companies a respectability unavailable to theater artists in England. The charitable institutions relied heavily on this source of revenue, so much that closures of the theaters were kept at an absolute minimum, even during periods of royal mourning.

These public theaters, or *corrales*, were rectangular-shaped yards enclosed by blocks of houses. The stage was a raised platform, or apron, at one end of the yard, which had its own roof. Most of the spectators stood on the ground exposed to the sky, like the groundlings in Shakespeare's theater, but wealthy patrons were seated at the windows of the houses looking out into the yard, which were transformed into expensive boxes.

The subject matter for the plays was wide-ranging, coming from Spanish history, legends, Italian stories, lives of the saints, and biblical stories. Another distinction between English and Spanish theater is that the English tended to focus on a theater of character, whereas the Spanish focused on a theater of theme. While Shakespeare created believable characters in relatively realistic situations, Spanish theater subordinated characterization and action to the main theme. Spectators enjoyed watching the theme work itself out in front of them. Spanish theater is essentially a theater of ideas, and during the Golden Age the great themes of the drama were honor, love, and religion.

Fuente Ovejuna is based on a real incident that took place in 1476 in a Spanish village of this name (literally "sheep's well") in the southern province of Cór-

doba. In the play, the peasants of the village rebel against a rapacious military tyrant, Commander Fernanado Goméz de Guzmán. The central theme is the concept of honor, and Lope de Vega asks us to consider why the common people, the peasants, cannot be allowed their share of honor. In Lope's day the standard, accepted idea of honor was that it was accorded only to those of privileged birth or rank. In a remarkably powerful examination of this idea—radical for its day—*Fuente Ovejuna* asks us to question the notion that honor, reputation, and public respect depend only on class.

FUENTE OVEJUNA
Lope de Vega

Adapted by Adrian Mitchell

CHARACTERS

COMMANDER FERNANDO GÓMEZ DE GUZMÁN
CAPTAIN FLORES
SERGEANT ORTUÑO
GRAND MASTER RODRIGO TÉLLEZ GIRÓN
LAURENCIA
PASCUALA
JACINTA
FRONDOSO
MENGO
BARRILDO
JUAN ROJO
ESTEBAN

ALONSO
LEONELO
CIMBRANOS
QUEEN ISABELLA OF CASTILLE
KING FERDINAND OF ARAGON
DON MANRIQUE
FIRST ALDERMAN
SECOND ALDERMAN
THE FARMER
SOLDIERS
A BOY
WOMEN

ACT 1
SCENE 1

[*An ante-chamber in the house of the Master of the Order of Calatrava—a powerful organization which takes as its insignia a red cross*]

[*Enter Commander Fernando Goméz de Guzmán of the Order. He is dynamic, in his early forties, a successful and ruthless soldier*]

[*With him are his permanent aides—the young Captain Flores and the veteran Sergeant Ortuño. They have been travelling. Soldiers stand on guard*]

COMMANDER.
Does the Grand Master know I'm here?
FLORES.
He knows.
ORTUÑO.
He's seventeen sir.
It's an arrogant age.
COMMANDER.
Does he know Fernando Gómez is waiting?
FLORES.
He doesn't know much. He's only a lad.
COMMANDER.
He's old enough to respect my rank.

ORTUÑO.
He's one boy surrounded by a hundred advisers.
They're telling him:
Don't play favourites, take your time,
Keep your distance and keep them waiting.
COMMANDER.
They ought to teach him a few old proverbs:
"Punctuality is the politeness of kings."
FLORES.
Be rude to an equal—that's stupidity.
Be rude to a lesser man—that's tyrany.
COMMANDER.
Lesser man? Am I less a man
Than this pubescent?
ORTUÑO.
He's new to all this, sir. He'll learn.
COMMANDER.
He'd better learn fast.
Power brings obligations.
When he was eight years old they presented him
With the great sword of Calatrava
And the Red Cross of our Order
Was pinned, in burning rubies, on his breast.
That day alone should have taught our Master
Something about courtesy.
ORTUÑO.
If you feel insulted, we'd better leave.
COMMANDER.
I want to see what the boy's made of.

In Lope de Vega's *Fuente Ovejuna*—the name of a village, "Sheep Well"—the female peasants stir the cowardly men into rebelling against official injustice. This photograph is from a production at the Court Theatre in Chicago.

[*Enter the Grand Master of Calatrava and his following, which includes Guards and Advisers*]

MASTER.
Commander, I'm sorry, you must forgive me—
Fernando Goméz.

[*Master embraces Commander*]

I've only just been told of your arrival.
For me to keep you waiting—
you must be furious.

COMMANDER.
Well, I'm used to respect, I value respect
And you, Grand Master, owe me some respect
For my loyalty and my battle-scars.

MASTER.
I owe you more than I can ever repay.
I honour you and, once again, embrace you.
Brave Fernando.

[*Master embraces Commander again*]

COMMANDER.
Well, I have risked my neck for you
And once, that time when the Pope was angry,
I intervened for you.

MASTER.
It's true, I remember
And, by the holy crosses on both our breasts,
I honour you as I honour my father.

COMMANDER.
I'm pleased with you, Rodrigo.

Yes, you seem more mature—

MASTER.
—But this is not a social visit . . .
I think your message said—military matters?

COMMANDER.
Listen to me. I'll explain
What your next move has to be.

MASTER.
I'm listening, Commander.

COMMANDER.
Grand Master, you were raised
To your high office by the worth
Of your illustrious father.
He named you his successor
As the Grand Master of our Order.
As such it is your duty to support
King Alonso of Portugal
In his rightful claim to all Castile.

MASTER.
King Ferdinand and Queen Isabella
Claim the same lands, of course.

COMMANDER.
But their claim's muddy. It's fraudulent.
Besides, you're related to King Alonso.
So I'll presume to offer some advice.
Assemble all the Knights of Calatrava.
Lay siege to the city of Cuidad Real
And capture it, then you'll control
The vital pass which is the gateway
From Andalusia into Castile.

You won't need many men.
You'll only be opposed
By shopkeepers, beggars
And a fistful of minor aristocrats
Pledged by Ferdinand and Isabella.

Don Rodrigo, they say you're just a boy.
They say the red cross is too heavy
For adolescent shoulders.
They are liars. Of course. But you have to prove it.
Remember your great ancestors—
The lords of Urueña and Villena.
Draw your great sword and let it slice
Into the red flesh of our enemies.
When that white sword is running with blood
The whole world will salute you.

MASTER.
Fernando Goméz, rest assured—
I will support my kinsman.
Your summary, I think, is a little biased
And yet justice is on your side.

Since Cuidad Real must be captured
I'll take that city like a thunderbolt.

They say I am young.
Yes I am young.
But my eyes are clear
And my heart is strong.
With the cross on my breast
Into battle I'll ride
And the white of my sword
Shall be reddened by blood.

Commander, do you have many soldiers?

COMMANDER.
Not many, but they're all hand-picked.
They can fight. I call them my lion-pack.
The men and women of Fuente Ovejuna
Are peasants. They're not trained at all—
Except in the use of sickles, forks and spades.

MASTER.
Fuente Ovejuna? Is that your headquarters?

COMMANDER.
Just a shabby old town up in the hills.
My country house is there. It's my fortress too.

MASTER.
Summon my soldiers.

COMMANDER.
Cuidad Real will collapse.

MASTER.
That's right, Commander. Let's consult the maps.

SCENE 2

[*The Town Square of Fuente Ovejuna. One public building with pillars. A couple of trees. Benches in the shade.*

*Old houses. A spring which pours into a large drinking
trough on wheels*]

[*Enter Laurencia and Pascuala, two young peasant
women, fetching water from the spring*]

LAURENCIA.
I hope we've seen the last of that Commander.

PASCUALA.
Now there's a funny thing.
I had the feeling
That you were slightly put about
When he rode off.

LAURENCIA.
Put about? I hope to God
We're rid of him for good.

PASCUALA.
Laurencia, I've seen plenty of women
As proud as you and harder to please,
But their little hearts betrayed them—
Slippery as candle-grease.

LAURENCIA.
My heart's as dry as an old oak tree
And that's how it's going to stay.

PASCUALA.
Come on, it's daft even to think:
There is some water I'd never drink.

LAURENCIA.
I swear by the sun that I never will,
Though Fuente Ovejuna drinks its fill.
Pascuala, what'd be the point
In going to bed with Commander Goméz?
Is he likely to marry me?

PASCUALA.
Not in this world.

LAURENCIA.
How many of the local girls
Have listened to the Commander's promises,
Taken a walk in the woods and tottered back
All tears and belly?

PASCUALA.
I've lost count.
But it'll be a miracle
If you escape that cunning bastard.

LAURENCIA.
Don't bet on that!
The Commander's chased me for more than a month
And all he's got to show for it is blisters.
His two friends, that Captain Flores
And crafty old Sergeant Ortuño,
Offered me a pair of yellow shoes
And a silver necklace with doves in flight
And a sort of spiderweb silky dress.
They went on and on and on and on
About their wonderful Commander,
On and on till I was scared, Pascuala.

But they can't do anything to break me down.

PASCUALA.

Where did this happen?

LAURENCIA.

Down by the river where we wash the clothes.
Down by the river six days ago.

PASCUALA.

Laurencia, I wouldn't die of horror
If one day you surrendered.

LAURENCIA.

You think I'm a spring chicken?
No. I'm a tough little hen.
And I'll chase Commander Goméz out of my backyard.
He can crow somewhere else.

[*Sings.*] I'd rather
Get up at daybreak
And light up the fireplace
Stack plenty of dry wood beside it.
And then
Make a tortilla
The size of a cartwheel
With cupfuls of basil inside it.

I'd rather
Set the pot frothing
With rabbit and cabbage
United with garlic and spices.
And then
Fix up a marriage
Between some good bacon
And hundreds of aubergine slices.

I'd rather
Walk in the sunset
And pick me a necklace
Of grapes on the vine
Green and glowing.
And then
Heat up a pork chop
With olives and peppers
And anything else that is going.

I'd rather
Go to bed weary
With belly contented
And heart free of all obligation.
And then
Fall asleep praying
For more food the next day:
Deliver us, Lord, from temptation.

Pascuala—
You know these villains
They wheedle and woo us

And promise their love's to be trusted
And then
Call round at nightfall
Play with us till cockcrow
Then leave us and say they're disgusted.

PASCUALA.

You're right Laurencia.
When men cease to love you
They become unpleasant
As the ungrateful sparrow
To the generous peasant.

LAURENCIA.

So sing me the story, Pascuala.

PASCUALA.

[*Sings*]

In winter, when the fields are ice
The sparrow longs to eat.
He flies down from the roof and lands
Beside the peasant's feet.
He opens up his trembling beak
And calls the peasant "sweet".
Sweet! Sweet!
He calls the peasant sweet.

That's how the sparrow earns his crumbs
Amid the snow and sleet,
But when the springtime swings around
And all the world's on heat,
The sparrow dances on the roof
And calls the peasant "Cheat".
Cheat! Cheat!
He calls the peasant cheat.

And men are sparrow when they long
To lay us on a sheet.
We are their life, their everything,
Their soul and their heartbeat.
But when they're cooler, they begin
To call the woman "cheat".
Cheat! Cheat!
And things I'll not repeat.

LAURENCIA.

I remember a line from some ancient poem:
Don't trust men farther than you can throw 'em.

[*Enter three young peasant men from the town—Frondoso, who is in love with Laurencia, Barrildo and Mengo, who is somewhat stout. Mengo takes a bottle of wine which he has previously left to cool in the drinking trough, uncorks it, swigs and passes it round among his friends*]

FRONDOSO.

Give up, Barrildo, he'll never give in.

BARRILDO.
Well, here's a pair of qualified judges.
They're always ready to say what's right,
Or, more likely, what's wrong.
MENGO.
Before you ask them, let's make a deal.
If they decide I'm right,
you both have to give me some sort of prize
For winning the debate.
BARRILDO.
Done. But, Mengo, suppose you lose.
What've you got to give to us?
MENGO.
My little pipe. [*Produces penny whistle*]
It's worth more than a full granary—
It gives me more pleasure, anyway.
BARRILDO.
I'll shake on that.

[*Barrildo and Mengo shake hands*]

FRONDOSO.
Beautiful morning, lovely ladies!
LAURENCIA.
Frondoso, are you calling us ladies?
FRONDOSO.
It's just the modern manner of speech—
All students today are called "intellectuals."
Misers are "economical"
And the deaf are "hard of hearing."
If you're loudmouthed, they say you're "powerful,"
The busybody "cares about people,"
A bully is "strong-willed"
And a raving maniac is "so original."
So if you catch the pox, call it a "cold sore."
If you're a hunchback, call yourself "round-shouldered."
That's the fashion and I'm in the fashion
Up to my neck when I call the pair of you
"Ladies." Ladies, shall I go on.
LAURENCIA.
I suppose, Frondoso, that in the city
People would frame that speech and hang it on their
   walls.
Well, I'm just a peasant and I wouldn't feed it to the
   pigs.
FRONDOSO.
Explain to me where I'm wrong, learned Laurencia.
LAURENCIA.
You're looking at it the wrong way up.
Let me tell you how people are judged.

A serious person is called "boring."
Those who seek justice are "heretics."
You keep your promise—you're "old-fashioned."
Be polite—"what an awful crawler!"

You give to a beggar—"hypocrite."
You're generous to everyone—"Ostentatious!"
If a woman tells the truth
She's called a bitch
But if she won't go to be with you—
Call her a snobbish whore.
And a wife who's faithful—but that'll do.
Frondoso—have I silenced you?
MENGO.
The devil's got into her tongue.
BARRILDO.
She's as tough as leather
And cold as scandal.
MENGO.
Send for a priest
With a bell, book and candle.
LAURENCIA.
What was your famous debate about?
FRONDOSO.
I'll tell you, but can you listen?
LAURENCIA.
There's no wax in my ears.
FRONDOSO.
But seriously—we must settle a bet.
LAURENCIA.
What's the wager?
FRONDOSO.
Barrildo and I say Mengo's wrong.
LAURENCIA.
And what does Mengo say?
BARRILDO.
Mengo denies the existence of something
Which is obviously indispensable.
MENGO.
No. I simply say that it doesn't exist
Because I know it doesn't exist.
LAURENCIA.
Please—somebody translate from Mengoese.
BARRILDO.
He says there's no such thing as love.
LAURENCIA.
Most people find they can't manage without it.
BARRILDO.
Love is a madness, but I agree.
Without love, the world would shut up shop.
MENGO.
In the old days, they used to imagine
That before the world came, there was Chaos.
Now Chaos was made up of whizzing atoms
And all the atoms were fighting each other.
But one day Love crept in the back door
And Love linked all the atoms together
And that was the end of Chaos.
Do you follow me?

BARRILDO.

And so everything in this world
Harmonised with everything else.
Which proves my point, for harmony
Is only another word for love.

MENGO.

One moment, Barrildo. Listen to this.
First let me say I don't deny
The existence and importance of *self-love*.
Self-love rules the universe,
Self-love maintains the balance of nature.
No, I've never denied, not for one minute
That we all have a kind of love we're born with
Which helps us to survive.
If you try to thump me on the nose
My hand flies up automatically,
My eyelashes slam their shutters
To protect my eyes
And my feet start sprinting away
To save my invaluable hooter.
But all this is *self-love*, not love itself.

PASCUALA.

Where does that leave the argument?

LAURENCIA.

Up a fig tree.

MENGO.

No, my point is, there's no greater love
Than that of a man for his own self.

PASCUALA.

Sorry, Mengo, but you're wrong.
The passion with which a man loves a woman
Or a lion loves a lioness
Or a buck rabbit loves a doe—
That passion's real, you can't deny it.

MENGO.

But that's not love at all.
That's what I call self-love.
Tell me, Laurencia, what is love?

LAURENCIA.

To love is to desire

MENGO.

Good. To love is to desire what?

LAURENCIA.

To desire beauty.

MENGO.

Beauty—yes—but why should love want beauty?

LAURENCIA.

To enjoy it.

MENGO.

Precisely. And this enjoyment the lover hopes to
    have—
Is it not for himself?

LAURENCIA.

It is.

MENGO.

Therefore, because he loves himself
He pursues beauty, hoping to catch it,
So it will make him happy?

LAURENCIA.

That is true.

MENGO.

Since this is so,
The love we're talking about
Is the love I pursue
For my own pleasure.
It's all for me, myself. Self-love. You see?

BARRILDO.

The other day Father Oliver preached
About another thinker like you called Plato.
Now Plato had a great deal to say
On the subject of love and what to do about it.
Plato saved all of his love for the soul
And the virtue of the person he loved.

PASCUALA.

Yes, there are colleges in the cities
Overflowing with similar old men
Who spend all day and half the night
Discussing love. They're called philosophers
And they get paid for it.

LAURENCIA.

I will pronounce my verdict.
Barrildo's right about Barrildo
And Mengo's right about himself.
Mengo, thank your lucky stars
That you don't know what love is.

MENGO.

Laurencia, do you love anybody?

LAURENCIA.

Oh I love my virtue. I'm just like Plato.

FRONDOSO.

May God punish you for that remark
By striking you with jealousy.

BARRILDO.

Who won the debate?

MENGO.

Who won the bet?

PASCUALA.

Take your problem to Father Oliver,
I think he knows something about love,
But if he can't oblige, write a nice letter
To Don Plato at the university.
Laurencia's never been in love
And I've only a passing acquaintance with it—
So how can we be judges?

FRONDOSO.

By making fun of us poor men.
Oh it's a wicked business when
The sheet of paper mocks the pen.

[*Enter Captain Flores*]

FLORES.
    Beautiful morning, ladies and gentlemen.
PASCUALA.
    Here comes the Commander's ploughboy.
    Master comes later to sow the seed.
LAURENCIA.
    Sir, you're a polite sort of vulture today—
    Where have you flown in from?
FLORES.
    From the battle, sweetheart, isn't that obvious?
LAURENCIA.
    Will Comander Goméz be coming back?
FLORES.
    He's well. The fighting's finished with now.
    But it cost up plenty in blood and friends.
FRONDOSO.
    What happened, Captain?
FLORES.
    I saw it. I was there.
    Our mission was to capture Cuidad Real.
    The Grand Master assembled his forces:
    Two thousand vassals as soldiers on foot.
    Three hundred Brothers of the Order
    Riding on horseback, red crosses blazing.

    Our brave young Master rode out that day
    In a green cloak embroidered with gold
    Fastened with silken cords over his bright armour.
    A magnificent horse, well-fleshed and firm,
    A dappled silver-grey like a gale-born cloud,
    A steed raised on the clear water of the Betis river
    And the deep rich grasses of its meadowbanks,
    Its tail was covered by plaited strips
    Of cunningly-worked leather, and its mane
    Tied in tight curls with whitest ribbons
    Which matched the snow-flake marks
    Flecking his pale grey flanks.

    At his right hand rode Commander Goméz,
    Your overlord, upon a sturdy
    Stallion the colour of crystallised honey,
    With a jet-black mane and tail, but a white underlip.
    The Commander wore a cloak
    Of flowing, orange-coloured silk
    With golden tracery and milky pearls.
    His white-plumed helmet seemed to be
    Bursting with orange blossom, and he bore
    That famout pine-tree of a lance
    Before which proud Granada trembles.

    We advanced, through the dust, towards Cuidad Real.
    The city fathers were stubborn.
    They took up arms
    Shouting "For Ferdinand and Isabella!"

They fought hard, but we beat them down.
Our young Master gave his orders.
Rebel leaders were beheaded.
Their followers were gagged and flogged through the
    streets.
Now the city fears him, the city admires him,
For a youth so suddenly turned conqueror
Will surely grow into a giant
Who will become the scourge of Africa
And overcome a million crescent moons
With his triumphant cross of blood.

He has been generous, too,
Heaping rare gifts upon us,
And he let us plunder the city as freely
As if it were his private property.

But here comes our Commander. Greet him joyfully.
Your smiles and cheers must crown his victory.

[*Enter the Commander with Sergeant Ortuño, Soldiers,
Musicians, local councillors including Juan Rojo, and the
joint Mayors of Fuente Ovejuna, Alonso and Esteban. Esteban is also Chief Magistrate and is the father of Laurencia*]

PEOPLE OF FUENTE OVEJUNA.
    [*Sing*]
        Welcome the Commander
        Who killed our enemies
        Welcome the Commander
        For he beat them to their knees

        Long live Commander Goméz
        Who is terrible in war
        But in peacetime he is peaceful
        May he live for evermore

        Long live Commander Goméz
        Our mighty overlord
        For he cut up the rebels
        With his celebrated sword

        Now he comes back to Fuente
        For this is where his home is
        We hope he stays for ever
        Long live Commander Goméz!

COMMANDER.
    People of Fuente Ovejuna
    I thank you with all my heart
    For the affection you have shown today.
ALONSO.
    Commander, our town has only shown
    A little part of its true feelings.
JUAN ROJO.
    Commander, Senor Esteban,
    Who is our Chief Magistrate
    And joint Mayor with Alonso here

Would like to make a presentation.

COMMANDER.
I am obliged to him. Proceed.

MENGO.
[*To Esteban*]
Here's the speech I wrote for you.

[*Esteban clears his throat and reads from the piece of paper, gesturing towards a cart loaded with presents*]

ESTEBAN.
I speak for Fuente Ovejuna, I start
By begging, from the bottom of my heart,
You to accept the presents in this cart.

Baskets shallow and baskets deep,
Blankets bright enough to make you weep,
A set of dinner plates painted with sheep.

Your courage the whole town celebrates
With strings of onions, boxes of dates
And oranges burning in their crates.

Preserved in brine you'll find delicate young
Piglets and calves—kidneys, brains, heart, lung
And there's our specialty—jellied tongue.

Sheepskins black and sheepskins white
And Mengo made this lamp—it shines as bright
As any angel. And it lasts all night.

We can't offer gold watches or works of art
Only the contents of this cart
And the golden love of the people's heart

And that's fine gold, and to show you how fine
Here are three hundred gallons of wine
To renew your courage whenever you dine.

Your popularity is proved by these
Heart-felt tokens. Accept them, please.
And, may I recommend the local cheese?

[*Applause*]

COMMANDER.
I'd like to thank you and the town council.
[*To Soldiers*] Take the cart to my country house.

ALONSO.
Sir, you deserve a holiday.
You are welcome back to Fuente Ovejuna.
May the nearest tree to your house be struck by moonlight
And bear diamonds big as oranges.

COMMANDER.
Let's hope it does. I'll see you soon.

[*Exit Commander into the door of the public building. Musicians strike up and the People of Fuente Ovejuna,*

apart from Laurencia and Pascuala, march away with them]

PEOPLE OF FUENTE OVEJUNA
[*Sing*]
    Now he comes back to Fuente
    For this is where his home is
    We hope he stays for ever
    Long life Commander Goméz!

[*Commander looks out of the window of the public building*]

COMMANDER.
You two. Stay here.

LAURENCIA.
What can we do for you, sir?

COMMANDER.
The other day you were rude to me
Just before I had to go
And risk my life on the battlefield.

LAURENCIA.
Pascuala, were you rude to him?

PASCUALA.
I'm never rude to men, poor things.

COMMANDER.
You both insulted me.
Listen. Who rules this district?

LAURENCIA.
The power's in your hands, Commander.

COMMANDER.
And therefore you are in my power. Correct?

PASCUALA.
Certainly, sir, politically speaking,
But not in any other sense.

COMMANDER.
I'd like a word with you both in here.
Plenty of people around, don't worry.

LAURENCIA.
My father the Mayor will be back soon.
When he goes into the Council Offices
I will go in as well . . .

COMMANDER.
Captain Flores!

FLORES.
[*Appearing in the Square*] Sir!

COMMANDER.
What's wrong with these women?
Why won't they do what they're told?

FLORES.
Come on, ladies, in we go.

[*Laurencia and Pascuala fight off Flores during the following exchanges.*]

LAURENCIA.
Keep your monkey claws off me.

FLORES.
Come on, ladies, let's be sensible.

PASCUALA.
    Not a chance.
    You'd barricade us in with the Commander.
FLORES.
    He only wants you to take a look
    At what he's brought back from the wars.
COMMANDER.

    [*Appearing at window*]

    When they come in, lock the doors behind 'em.

    [*Commander disappears*]

LAURENCIA.
    Out of our way, Captain.

    [*Enter Ortuño. He joins in the struggle*]

ORTUÑO.
    Weren't you two presented to us
    Along with all the other rubbish on the cart?
PASCUALA.
    I'll bite your bloody nose off.
FLORES.
    Let 'em go. They're hopeless.
LAURENCIA.
    Isn't your Commander satisfied
    With all that wine and meat?
ORTUÑO.
    It's your meat he's after.
LAURENCIA.
    He'd choke on it.

    [*Exit Laurencia and Pascuala*]

FLORES.
    How can we face him empty-handed?
    He'll curse us purple.
ORTUÑO.
    Part of the job, sir, if you can't take
    An officer's abuse
    Better quit the army and live as a beggar
    On fishbones and lemon juice.

                              [*Exit Flores and Ortuño*]

SCENE 3

[*The Palace of King Ferdinand and Queen Isabella. King,
Queen, Don Manrique their minister, and their following
enter*]

QUEEN.
    My lord, we must move straight away.
    The King of Portugal's troops are poised to strike.
    At any moment they may cut off your army.
    Cuidad Real must be recaptured.
KING.
    We can rely on Navarre and Aragon?

QUEEN.
    Of course.
KING.
    I've been reorganising
    My Castillian battalions.
    We'll need them too.
    Be patient, Isabella. We must think ahead.
QUEEN.
    Your majesty's convinced
    That we have time for thinking?
MANRIQUE.
    Your majesties, two aldermen
    Escaped from the massacre at Cuidad Real.
    They're here, begging to see you.
KING.
    We'll see them now.
MANRIQUE.
    You may come in.

    [*Enter, travel-weary, two Aldermen*]

QUEEN.
    Let's hear your news.
FIRST ALDERMAN.
    King Ferdinand, Queen Isabella,
    Whom Heaven sent to help us.
    We are humbly here from Cuidad Real
    To plead for your protection.
    Once we were proud and lucky men
    Because we were your subjects.
    But now we've lost that honour.

    The Grand Master of Calatrava
    Is greedy for more lands.
    He is a lion of courage
    Though a mere cub in years.
    He laid siege to our city—
    A most bitter siege.
    All of us fought back so angrily
    That every white-washed street
    Was smeared with the blood of the dead.
    In the end he conquered us
    But he never could have done it
    Without Commander Goméz
    Who gave support, advice and soldiers.
    Now the Grand Master rules Cuidad Real
    And we're his sullen slaves.
KING.
    Where are your fighting men?
SECOND ALDERMAN.
    Some, sir, are prisoners.
    And some are maimed and some are dead.
    We have no other fighting men.
QUEEN.
    We must strike now.
    We must, or the Portuguese
    Will swarm all over our territories.

KING.
    Don Manrique, march on Cuidad Real.
    Take two companies with you.
    Show no mercy to our enemies.
MANRIQUE.
    I'll put an end to this boy's adventures
    Or die in the attempt.
QUEEN.
    You will not die. I have no doubts at all.
KING.
    Where is Commander Goméz now?
FIRST ALDERMAN.
    In Fuente Ovejuna, sire.
    That's where he has his house
    And what he calls his seat of justice.
    And there he grabs, with his bony hand,
    Their goods, their women and their land.

                                        [*Exeunt All*]

SCENE 4

[*A wood near Fuente Ovejuna. Enter Laurencia and Frondoso*]

LAURENCIA.
    Frondoso, you've made me climb all this way,
    Leaving my washing half wrung out
    Down by the stream. Sweet Jesus, what a climb,
    And all so we can talk together
    Without the town exploding with gossip.
    You're such a trouble to me, Frondoso.
    The town's talking anyway:
    "He fancies her, you know," "She after him."
    Just because you're quick on your feet
    And, some of my friends say, quite good-looking,
    Well, not deformed, and just because
    You're generally slightly better dressed
    Than most of the shepherds on the hill
    And just because you've not been elected
    To be this year's village idiot—
    There's not a boy or a girl in the whole of Fuente Ove-
        juna
    Who's not certain as sin that we're lovers already
    And they're simply counting the days until
    Father Oliver stops playing his old bassoon
    And mutters warnings to us from the pulpit.
    They've decided how many children we'll have—
    The whole business is out of control.
FRONDOSO.
    What do you feel about marrying me?
LAURENCIA.
    I don't feel much, one way or the other.
FRONDOSO.
    Please, Laurencia,
    I'm in such a state,

I risk my life
Whenever I dare
Look into your eyes
Or listen to your voice.
You know I want to marry you
So why to you laugh at me?
LAURENCIA.
    I'm sorry, but little things make me laugh.
FRONDOSO.
    Aren't you upset that I'm so upset?
    When I close my eyes, I see your face
    I can't sleep or eat or even drink.
    How can an angel be so cruel?
    God's honour, but you're driving me mad.
LAURENCIA.
    So go see a doctor, Frondoso.
FRONDOSO.
    You're the only doctor who can cure me

    Laurencia
    We'll be like two doves
    Gliding side by side
    Over the mountains

    Laurencia
    We'll be like two doves
    Perching on a branch
    And cooing harmonies.
LAURENCIA.
    Have a quiet word with my uncle and my father.
    It's not that I'm lovesick, but I'm beginning
    To feel some of the symptoms.
FRONDOSO.
    Christ! It's the Commander.
LAURENCIA.
    He's out hunting deer.
FRONDOSO.
    Hide here.
LAURENCIA.
    There's no room. I'll hide over here.

[*Laurencia and Frondoso hide separately. Enter the Commander carrying a crossbow. He spots Laurencia and grabs her wrist, dragging her into the open*]

COMMANDER.
    Looks like my day.
    I go out deer hunting
    And catch a little doe.
LAURENCIA.
    I've just had a rest
    After doing my washing.
    I'll be off back down to the stream.
    So good morning to you, Commander.
COMMANDER.
    Shame that your manners aren't

As pretty as your face.
You're a peculiar creature, aren't you?
You've given me the slip
Several times in the town
But way out here—
In this lonely, secret wood,
Why, you're at bay, Laurencia,
You're trapped, Laurencia.
The only woman in Fuente Ovejuna
Too high and mighty to look in the eyes
Of her lord and master.
The other women like me, Laurencia,
Respectable married ladies and all.
You know Sebastiana?
Pedro Redondo's wife?
We did it together, Laurencia.
And Martin del Pozo's bride,
What was her name?
Just two days after she married him
We did it together, Laurencia.

LAURENCIA.
Yes, I do know those women, Commander.
They've always been most generous
To men of every kind.
You know, if you weren't wearing that cross
I'd take you for the devil himself.
Go chase your deer and God be with you.

[*Commander puts down his crossbow*]

COMMANDER.
I'm going to teach you a lesson, Laurencia,
With my arms and with my hands
And with my naked body.

LAURENCIA.
You'd rape me? You're crazy!

[*Frondoso creeps out of hiding and takes the crossbow*]

COMMANDER.
It's no use. I've got you. Here. Come on.

LAURENCIA.
Get off me, you bastard!

COMMANDER.
Come on. You want it, don't you?
Come on. There's nobody here.

[*Frondoso pokes Commander in the back with the crossbow*]

FRONDOSO.
Let her go, Commander.
Let her go or I'll be forced to
Aim at the red cross on your chest
And shoot your heart out.

COMMANDER.
Get out, you scruffy dog.

FRONDOSO.
There's no dog here.

Laurencia, run for it.

LAURENCIA.
Be careful, Frondoso.

FRONDOSO.
Run to your father's house.

[*Exit Laurencia*]

COMMANDER.
I put the crossbow down, you know.
I didn't threaten her with it.

FRONDOSO.
All I have to do
Is press my finger—here—
And you're dead Commander

COMMANDER.
She's got away. You know this is treason?
Lay down that crossbow, you bastard.

FRONDOSO.
And let you shoot me?
I'm warning you—I love Laurencia—
And I'm as angry as a scorpion.

COMMANDER.
Oh I see, so a gentleman
Is expected to walk away
Offering his back as a target
To a mad young peasant?
All right, you son of a rat,
Shoot me—and then watch out for yourself.

FRONDOSO.
Oh no, Commander, I don't shoot my betters.
I have this strange ambition
To become an old peasant one day.
So I think I'll take your crossbow away.

[*Exit Frondoso*]

COMMANDER.
To be insulted by a slave
And fall for a surprise attack!
I swear to God I'll pay him back
And I'll teach that little bitch how to behave
By screwing her on her sweetheart's grave.

[END OF ACT ONE]

ACT 2

SCENE 1

[*The Town Square, Esteban and Alonso sitting on bench*]

ESTEBAN.
We've got to think of the public good.
We mustn't draw on our reserve stocks of grain.
It looks like a bad year. Time to hang on
Whatever the rest of the council say.

ALONSO.
>I'm with you. Caution's always been my policy.
>That's why this town's such a peaceful place.

ESTEBAN.
>We'll appeal to Commander Gomez about it.
>We mustn't be fooled by these astrologers
>Who know less than lizards about the weather
>But try to convince us, with their turgid language,
>They know secrets hidden from God himself.
>They talk like bishops with hangovers. You've heard 'em:
>"The past and the future form one great mystic circle."
>All very fine, but if you ask
>About something that matters here and now
>Like where to lay drains or a sick donkey
>They're about as much use as a woollen bucket.
>Do you think, in their studies, there are stars and planets
>And miniature galaxies whizzing around?
>How else can they know what's happening in the skies
>So they can peddle us their cheapjack prophecies?
>While we're out sowing the fields,
>They're indoors, doing their calculations:
>Let's order a crop of so much wheat, barley, cereals,
>So many tons of mustard, so many cucumbers—
>Look, I've grown pumpkins with better brains on 'em.
>The prophets announce: "A brown horse shall expire"—
>And behold, it comes to pass—in Transylvania.
>Or they tell us: "Lo, there shall be much beer
>In Germany and verily behold
>There will be cheese in Holland and rain in Scotland"
>I'm not clairvoyant, but this I will say:
>After April next year, with some luck, we'll have May.

[Enter Leonelo, a student newly returned from the University of Salamanca, talking with Barrildo]

LEONELO.
>Enough, Barrildo, that's more than enough.
>I can't keep up with all the local gossip.

BARRILDO.
>What's it like in Salamanca?
>How do they treat you at the University?

LEONELO.
>That's a long story.

BARRILDO.
>You'll be very learned now?

LEONELO.
>I know a lot less than Pedro the barber
>And that's true of most of the other students.

BARRILDO.
>Go on. They must have taught you a lot.

LEONELO.
>I'm beginning to learn what really matters.

BARRILDO.
>Now they've started printing all these books

The whole country's suddenly full of great thinkers.

LEONELO.
>So many books—and so much confusion!
>All around us an ocean of print
>And most of it covered in froth.

BARRILDO.
>But books are good. Everyone knows, Leonelo.

LEONELO.
>You know that printing was invented
>In Germany by Gutenberg?
>So far so good. What happened then?
>All the most famous men in Europe
>Rushed into print, but once they were published
>Their ignorance was obvious to all.
>Next there arrived, like a swarm of fleas,
>The bawdy scribblers and the gallows hacks
>Writing any old cabbage for the sake of cash.

BARRILDO.
>Leonelo, printing's essential.

LEONELO.
>We managed without it for thousands of years.
>In this great age of printing we haven't seen
>Any new author reach the heights
>Of Homer or Saint Augustine.

BARRILDO.
>Leave it at that. Sit down. You're just being awkward.
>A holiday from thinking
>Is what you badly need.
>Whatever you say against printing
>I wish I was able to read.

[Enter Juan Rojo and another middle-aged Farmer]

JUAN ROJO.
>If you sold four farms and their stock
>You couldn't raise a dowry for your daughter,
>Not after the taxmen take their whack.
>You want to know why? The men who rule us
>Don't know there's any difference between
>Trying to grow corn out of dusty rock
>And selling necklaces in Madrid.

FARMER.
>What's the latest on the Commander?

JUAN ROJO.
>Pesters the life out of my niece, Laurencia.

FARMER.
>What a shit! I'd like to see
>Him swinging from an olive tree.

[Enter the Commander, Flores and Ortuño]

COMMANDER.
>Another lovely evening, gentlemen?

ALONSO.
>Sir.

COMMANDER.
  Please—sit yourselves down.
ESTEBAN.
  Commander—be seated wherever you like.
  We would prefer to stand.
COMMANDER.
  But I'd prefer you to be seated.
ESTEBAN.
  And I prefer to choose
  The company I keep.
COMMANDER.
  Sit down, Chief Magistrate,
  I want a word with you.

[*Esteban sits*]

ESTEBAN.
  Did you see my greyhound racing yesterday?
COMMANDER.
  No, but the Captain tells me
  It has an astonishing turn of speed.
ESTEBAN.
  Yes, an incredible animal.
  You know, I think it can move as fast
  As a wanted criminal on the run
  Or the tongue of a coward under torture.
COMMANDER.
  I'd like to take that greyhound of yours
  And set it on the trail of a hare
  Which keeps eluding me.
ESTEBAN.
  Of course. And where's this hare?
COMMANDER.
  In your daughter's shoes.
ESTEBAN.
  My daughter?
COMMANDER.
  Yes.
ESTEBAN.
  The daughter of a small-town Mayor . . .
  Surely she's not good enough
  For a Commander?
COMMANDER.
  You'd better teach her the way of the world.
ESTEBAN.
  What do you mean?
COMMANDER.
  She's been upsetting me.
  You see that woman—over there—
  Looks cold and snobbish, doesn't she?
  I scribbled her a little note.
  She was warming up my bed
  Before the ink was dry.
ESTEBAN.
  If she did, she shouldn't have,

And neither should you boast about it.
COMMANDER.
  A preaching peasant! Captain Flores,
  Please order for Senor Esteban
  A copy of Aristotle on Politics. He needs it.
ESTEBAN.
  Sir, here in Fuente Ovejuna
  We like the quiet life.
  We're good citizens, we pay our taxes
  And you should treat us with respect.
LEONELO.
  It's outrageous.
COMMANDER.
  Oh dear, have I said something
  That's upset you, boy?
LEONELO.
  You mustn't talk to us like that.
  It's not right for you to insult
  The honour of our town.
COMMANDER.
  Oh, you have honour, do you?
  Are you my brothers in arms
  In the great Order of Calatrava?
LEONELO.
  Some wearers of the Cross of Calatrava
  May be less honourable than cattle.
COMMANDER.
  And am I dirtying the muck of your cowshed
  By walking through it, boy?
LEONELO.
  You're not making it any cleaner.

[*Commander strikes Leonelo. Ortuño restrains Leonelo*]

COMMANDER.
  Is that so? Well, I'm honouring your cows by serving
    them.
  Now get your slimy face out of my town.
  If you ever come back I promise you
  an interesting death.
LEONELO.
  You'll—
COMMANDER.
  Out of my town!

[*Ortuño forces Leonelo out of the Square and off*]

ESTEBAN.
  Commander, you dishonour yourself.
COMMANDER.
  These yokels are pathetic.
  Life in the cities is so much freer—
  No-one stops a man having his fun
  So long as he's a gentleman.
  City husbands are perfectly happy
  For their wives to entertain me.

ESTEBAN.

No they're not. You want us to ignore
What's going on under our noses.
There is still such a thing as love in this town.
There is still such a thing as jealousy.
There is still such a thing as brutal lust.
There is still such a thing as sudden revenge.

COMMANDER.

[To Soldiers] Clear the Square!
[To Townspeople] Get out of here!

ESTEBAN.

You mean just us two,
Or the entire population of the town?

COMMANDER.

Out of this square!
Everybody out of this square!

ESTEBAN.

Don't worry, we're going.

COMMANDER.

Not in a mob like that! Disperse them!

FLORES.

Easy does it, sir.

COMMANDER.

These peasants imagine
They can gang up on me
As soon as my back's turned.

ORTUÑO.

[Returning]
I think it's best if we all keep calm.

COMMANDER.

I'm absolutely calm.
Back to your nasty little homes!

[Exeunt all the Townspeople]

COMMANDER.

Back to their holes, like mice.

ORTUÑO.

Don't hide your feelings do you sir?

COMMANDER.

What d'you mean, Sergeant!

ORTUÑO.

You don't like 'em not liking you.

COMMANDER.

I don't give a damn—
But they fancy they're as good as me.

FLORES.

Not really, sir.

COMMANDER.

What about that damn peasant?
Are you going to let him keep my crossbow?

FLORES.

Last night we had him cornered
Outside Laurencia's door.

ORTUÑO.

I tripped him up,

Gave him a good kicking.

FLORES.

I started to whip him, then I saw
It wasn't the right peasant.

ORTUÑO.

Had the same build.

FLORES.

All look alike.

ORTUÑO.

Must've taught him something.

COMMANDER.

Where's this damned Frondoso?

FLORES.

The word is that he's still around.

COMMANDER.

Tries to kill me—and he's still around?

ORTUÑO.

Fish are attracted magically
Towards the wriggling bait.
All an angler has to do
Is hold his rod and wait.

COMMANDER.

A shepherd threatens a Commander!
Flores, what's the world coming to?

FLORES.

Love causes all the trouble.

ORTUÑO.

And the lover's still alive.

COMMANDER.

I'm a very patient man, Sergeant,
Otherwise I'd have taken my sword
And carved Laurencia's name
All over his stupid body.
But I've been trained to hold myself back
Till the best moment for an attack.

[Consults a list]

Well, I'll take Pascuala.

FLORES.

Pascuala's very sorry—
Says she's getting married.

COMMANDER.

I've no objection to that.

FLORES.

To tell you the truth, I think she's dead scared—
But we'll talk her round to it eventually.

COMMANDER.

What about Olalla?

ORTUÑO.

That one likes a laugh.

COMMANDER.

Yes, she's a lively little creature.
What does Olalla say?

ORTUÑO.

Her brand-new husband hides her away

Like wheat inside a bin
But she says as soon as she can get out
You shall be first man in.

COMMANDER.

Well done, Ortuño!
But her husband's watching her.

ORTUÑO.

And he's got a temper
Like a rhinoceros with gout.

COMMANDER.

And Ines?

FLORES.

Which Ines?

COMMANDER.

Ines with the—you know—Anton's wife.

FLORES.

Pop round any day
Between nine and four
Please bring a bottle
Use the back door.

COMMANDER.

She's not much better
Than a marketday whore.
If only women
Esteemed themselves more.

FLORES.

There's nothing sweeter than the pain
Of delayed satisfaction.
If they give in too easily you miss
Drinking the wine of anticipation
Which make us stagger with love.

COMMANDER.

When I get all worked up
It's great if they give in.
But how can you value a woman much
If she opens up at the very first touch?

[*Enter Cimbranos, a messenger*]

CIMBRANOS.

Where's the Commander?

ORTUÑO.

Use your eyes.

CIMBRANOS.

O brave Commander Goméz,
Put on your white-plumed helmet and bright armour.
Cuidad Real, won with so much blood and pain,
Is in the greatest danger.
All round its walls they're closing in
Lit by a thousand smoky torches,
The Master of Calatrava is at bay.
Mount your horse now, sir, for the sight of you
Will rout our enemies and save our Master.

COMMANDER.

Enough. Ortuño, have the bugle sounded.
How many horsemen do I have?

ORTUÑO.

Fifty-four, sir.

COMMANDER.

Tell them to mount and join me.

CIMBRANOS.

They must be quick or Cuidad Real will fall
To Ferdinand and Isabella.

COMMANDER.

Have no fear of that.

[*Exeunt*]

[*Enter Laurencia, Mengo and Pascuala, running*]

PASCUALA.

Stay with us, Mengo.
The Commander's out to get us.

MENGO.

What can I do?

LAURENCIA.

The more we stay together
The harder things are for the Commander.

MENGO.

He's a devil.

LAURENCIA.

He's a curse on the town.

MENGO.

God send a thunderbolt
And split him down the middle.

LAURENCIA.

He's worse than arsenic and the Black Death
Rolled into one.

MENGO.

Is it true that Frondoso, out in the woods,
Pointed a crossbow at his chest
So you could run away?

LAURENCIA.

I used to hate all men,
But that moment changed my mind.
I'm scared they'll kill him for it.

MENGO.

Well he'd better get out of Fuente Ovejuna.

LAURENCIA.

I tell him that, although I love him.
But it makes him angry. He insists on staying
And the Commander has sworn
To string him up by one foot
And then skin him alive.

PASCUALA.

That Commander needs strangling.

MENGO.

Stoning would be better.
I use a sling to guard my sheep.
You can bet your boots
That, if I let fly at him with a stone,
The leather thong would no sooner creak

Than his forehead would burst open like an egg.

[*Enter Jacinta, running*]

JACINTA.
Jesus Christ, help me!
LAURENCIA.
Jacinta! What's the matter?
JACINTA.
Some of the Commander's men
Broke down our front door with clubs.
They said the Commander wanted me.
They're after me now.
LAURENCIA.
We'd all better hide. God help you Jacinta.

[*Exit Laurencia*]

PASCUALA.
He's after both of us as well.

[*Exit Pascuala*]

MENGO.
Men are supposed to fight, I suppose
We'll, I've got a man's name and a man's body.
Jacinta, stand behing me.
JACINTA.
If only we had a gun.
MENGO.
We'll have to use stones.

[*Mengo produces his sling. Enter Flores and Ortuño*]

FLORES.
I see—you thought you'd run away?
JACINTA.
Mengo—it's them.
MENGO.
Excuse me, sir.
These poor country girls . . .
ORTUÑO.
What's this then?
Are you standing up for her?
MENGO.
Well, I'll stand up with words.
Sir, I'm Jacinta's cousin, so I must
Protect her if I can.
FLORES.
Get him, Sergeant.
MENGO.
Listen, if I lose my temper
And let fly with my slingshot
You'll bleed enough to fill a horse trough.

[*Enter Commander and Cimbranos*]

COMMANDER.
Must I dismount to deal with brawlers?
FLORES.
One of the peasants from this filthy town
Which you should have burned down long ago
In my humble opinion, sir.
He was obstructing us, disobeying orders
And finally threatening us.
MENGO.
Commander, sir, if you care about justice,
You ought to punish these soldiers of yours.
They've tried to carry off a country girl
From her own parents' home.
Please let me take her back to them.
COMMANDER.
I'll let my men
Take their revenge on you.
Drop that sling.
MENGO.
[*Doing so*] Sir!
COMMANDER.
Flores. Ortuño. Cimbranos.
Use it to tie his hands together.
MENGO.
Is this the way you defend the peace?
COMMANDER.
Tell me, lad,
What do the peasants of Fuente Ovejuna say about me?
MENGO.
Sir, how have I offended you.
How has Fuente Ovejuna offended you?
FLORES.
Shall we kill him, sir?
COMMANDER.
Don't waste your bullets.
You'll need them at Cuidad Real.
ORTUÑO.
What shall we do with him?
COMMANDER.
Tie him to that oak tree.
Strip him naked.
Use your horse's reins
And whip him—
MENGO.
Mercy!
COMMANDER.
Whip him until his back
Is one dripping pattern of bright red and dark red.
MENGO.
God!

[*Exit Flores, Ortuño and Cimbranos with Mengo*]

COMMANDER.
Jacinta, why were you running away?

JACINTA.
  Give me back to my father and mother!
COMMANDER.
  You're safe with me, Jacinta.
  I belong to an order of chivalry.
JACINTA.
  My father is an honest man.
  You're far more rich and powerful
  And your parents may be aristocrats,
  But my father is much better than you—
  He always acts in an honourable way.
COMMANDER.
  Jacinta, you're being insolent.
  That's not the way to pacify
  A soldier when he's angry.
  Over there with you.
  I'll give it to you here and now.

[*Sounds of whipping and Mengo's cries offstage*]

JACINTA.
  Watch what you're doing.

[*Jacinta fights off the Commander, scratching his face*]

COMMANDER.
  All right, Jacinta, I understand.
  You'll be pleased to know I don't want you now.
  I'll hand you over to my troops—
  They'll queue up and screw you one by one.
JACINTA.
  I'll kill myself.
COMMANDER.
  You'll love it, peasant.
JACINTA.
  Please, Commander, show some mercy.
COMMANDER.
  I don't have any of that stuff.
JACINTA.
  God will take his revenge on you.
COMMANDER.
  That's up to him.

[*Exit Commander forcing Jacinta before him, her arm twisted
                                                    behind her*]

[*Enter Laurencia and Frondoso*]

LAURENCIA.
  My love, please, it's too dangerous.
FRONDOSO.
  I love you completely.
  I had to tell you.
  I saw you in the square
  And I wasn't scared any more.

LAURENCIA.
  The Commander—
FRONDOSO.
  Let's hope the people of Cuidad Real
  Finish off that bastard.
LAURENCIA.
  Don't say that.
  They say when you wish a man should die
  He usually lives to be
  A great-great grandfather.
FRONDOSO.
  Then I hope he lives a thousand painful years—
  And that takes care of him.
  Laurencia—I have to know—
  How do you feel about me and my love?
  You know how the town talks about us?
  They always couple our names together—
  Frondoso-Laurencia, Laurencia-Frondoso—
  And they wonder why we aren't coupling too.
  Darling is it yes or no?
LAURENCIA.
  I think there's only one of us.
FRONDOSO.
  Kiss me Laurencia.
  [*They kiss.*]
  I feel as if I've just been born.
LAURENCIA.
  No time for speeches.
  Go talk with my father,
  That's the important thing.
  There he is, strolling with my uncle.
  Don't worry, they'll be for the marriage.
FRONDOSO.
  God help me, I hope so.

[*Laurencia moves out of sight, but within hearing. Enter
Esteban with Alonso*]

ESTEBAN.
  The way he behaved . . .
  There was nearly a riot.
  He's just a bully. Everyone was shocked.
  And as for poor Jacinta . . .
ALONSO.
  A terrible thing.
  Such a gentle girl.
ESTEBAN.
  And poor old Mengo beaten.
ALONSO.
  They whipped him raw. Disgraceful.
ESTEBAN.
  And we're the Council.
  But what's the point of having a Council
  When he kicks us all around like this?
  I heard that just the other day

He caught Pedro Redondo's wife
Down by the waterside
And when he'd finished with her
He gave her to his Captain
Who took his turn, then passed her to the Sergeant,

ALONSO.
Just a moment. Who's that?

FRONDOSO.
Only me. Can I have a word?

ALONSO.
Of course, Frondoso,
You're my favourite nephew.

FRONDOSO.
Well, I want to ask you a favour, sir.

ESTEBAN.
Has that Commander Goméz
Given you trouble?

FRONDOSO.
All kinds of trouble.

ESTEBAN.
I thought as much.

FRONDOSO.
The love you show me gives me the courage
To tell you this: I love Laurencia.
I want to marry her.
I'm sorry if you think this is too abrupt,
Blurting it out like this—

ESTEBAN.
Not at all, Frondoso, your timing is perfect.
There's been a splinter of dread in my heart
But you've removed it and saved my life.
I'm grateful to God for your love for Laurencia.
I have always been a lucky man.

ALONSO.
Shouldn't you ask Laurencia first?

ESTEBAN.
Don't worry your head about that, Alonso.
Laurencia must have said yes
Or he wouldn't have dared to ask me.
Let's settle the question of the dowry.
Gold coins, I thought.

FRONDOSO.
I don't need any dowry.

ALONSO.
You're a lucky man, Esteban,
He'll take her as nature made her.

ESTEBAN.
I'll see what she has to say about dowries.

ALONSO.
That'd be just as well.

FRONDOSO.
Certainly. I don't want
To trample on anyone's feelings,
Particularly hers.

ESTEBAN.
Daughter! Laurencia!

[Enter Laurencia]

ESTEBAN.
What an obedient daughter!
I call and she appears.

LAURENCIA.
I was shopping at the fruit-stall.

ESTEBAN.
Laurencia,
I have been asked for your opinion.
Come over here please.
D'you think it's a good idea
For Frondoso here to get married
To your curly-haired friend Gila?
He is the most intelligent young man
In Fuente Ovejuna—

LAURENCIA.
Gila's getting married?
To Frondoso?

ESTEBAN.
D'you think she's good enough for him?

LAURENCIA.
Too good if anything.

ESTEBAN.
Very generous. But I don't agree.
Frondoso could do better for himself.
He might, for instance, marry you.

LAURENCIA.
You will have your awful little joke, won't you?
Even at your age.

ESTEBAN.
Do you want this boy?

LAURENCIA.
I've always like him.
He's always like me.
I was biding my time.
But now, because of you know who—

ESTEBAN.
Shall I say yes?

LAURENCIA.
You say it for me, sir.

ESTEBAN.
Consider it said.

ALONSO.
Come, let's go look
For Frondoso's father.

ESTEBAN.
My son, about the dowry.
It'll be in gold.

FRONDOSO.
I'd rather not, sir,
I'd be insulted.

ESTEBAN.

Swallow that insult, or you'll find instead
You're swallowing crusts of mouldy bread.

[*Exit Esteban and Alonso*]

LAURENCIA.

Tell me, Frondoso, are you happy?

FRONDOSO.

I'm too happy to say anything at all.

[*Exit Laurencia and Frondoso*]

SCENE 2

[*Outside the city of Cuidad Real. A battle raging off-stage*]

[*Enter the Master of Calatrava, Commander Goméz, Flores and Ortuño*]

COMMANDER.

Only one thing to do now, sir—take flight.

MASTER.

The city walls were flimsy.
Our enemies are mighty.

COMMANDER.

It's cost them more men than they can count.

MASTER.

But they will never boast of winning
The standard of Calatrava.

COMMANDER.

All your ambitions, Master,
Trampled in the mud.

MASTER.

What could I do? Fortune decides.
One day she lifts you to the throne;
Next day, down to the dungeons.

VOICES.

[*Off*] Ferdinand and Isabella!
Victory! Victory!
Ferdinand and Isabella!

MASTER.

They're lighting beacons on the battlements.
Down from the windows of high towers
Their banners unroll like the tongues of dragons.

COMMANDER.

An expensive celebration—paid for in blood.

MASTER.

Fernando Goméz,
I shall return to Calatrava.

COMMANDER.

And I'll go back to Fuente Ovejuna.
You must make up your own mind
Whether to fight on in this cause

Or bow your kneee to Ferdinand and Isabella.

MASTER.

I'll write to you about these matters.

COMMANDER.

Time will advise you.

MASTER.

I am still young. I can't tell what will be.
But time's already tricked me cruelly.

[*Exeunt*]

SCENE 3

[*The Town Square in Fuente Ovejuna. The square is decorated for the celebration of a wedding. Music. Enter the wedding party for Laurencia and Frondoso. Musicians, Mengo, Frondoso, Laurencia, Pascuala, Barrildo, Esteban, Juan Rojo, Alonso, the priest Father Oliver etc. Villagers launch into a mocking song in which individuals improvise alternate lines to answer chorus lines*]

ALL.

[*Sing*]

Viva! Viva! The newly-weds!
May they never sleep in different beds.
Viva! Viva! The happy pair!
Twenty-one children may they bear.
Viv! Viva! The happy bride!
She's not the one who is terrified!
Viva! Viva! The happy groom!
May his little pistol go boom boom boom.
Viva Laurencia!
Viva Frondoso!
Viva Laurencia!
Viva Frondoso!

[*All dance*]

MENGO.

What a lot of dog-eared doggerel.

BARRILDO.

I'd like to see you make up a better song.

FRONDOSO.

Mengo knows more about whips than he does about
song-making.

MENGO.

Just to wipe that grin off your face Frondoso,
Let me tell you this.
I know a man lives down the valley—
The Commander took him—

BARRILDO.

—Shut up, Mengo.
Just hearing the name of that butcher
Puts a blight on the day.

MENGO.

>One hundred strokes they gave me
>For lawful possession of a slingshot.
>But this man down the valley—
>The Commander had him given
>An enema of purple dye and pebbles.
>I won't say the man's name
>But he's highly respected by everyone.
>How can we live with that sort of thing?

BARRILDO.

>It's the Commander's idea of a joke.

MENGO.

>Enemas are no laughing matter.

FRONDOSO.

>Come on, Mengo, give us the song
>You made up for our wedding.

MENGO.

[*Sings*]

>I wish the bride and bridegroom
>May live a cheerful life
>And never hit each other
>With frying pan or knife
>
>May they have many children
>And lots of meat and wine
>And may they live forever
>Or till they're ninety-nine
>
>This is the song of Mengo
>For two of his best friends
>I do hope they'll be happy
>And so my ditty ends.

[*Laurencia kisses Mengo*]

FRONDOSO.

>If you're a poet, I'm the Pope.

BARRILDO.

>And he made it up as he went along!

MENGO.

>I'm so glad you like it. I'll do you another.
>A song about cooking fritters.

[*Sings*]

>Have you seen a fritter fryer
>When he's frying fritters?
>The fat in the frying pan,
>The pan upon the fire.
>The fritter fryer takes some batter
>When the fat is fizzing,
>He flings it in the frying pan
>And blows the fire higher.
>
>When the fritter fryer takes the
>Fritters from the fryer,
>They're different shapes and sizes—
>Like a squid or like a ball.

>There's pretty ones and ugly ones and
>Some are quite disgusting
>They're frizzled to a frazzle
>Or they're hardly fried at all.
>
>That's how I think of poets
>Making up their verses.
>Their batter is their matter
>And the paper is their pan.
>There's pretty ones and ugly ones and
>Some are quite revolting,
>And nobody can swallow them
>Unless the poet can!

BARRILDO.

>That's enough clowning.
>Silence for the bride!

LAURENCIA.

>I'm going to kiss you all.

[*Applause*]

ESTEBAN.

>Please God
>Give my daughter and her husband
>A life as beautiful
>As a deep lake in autumn time
>Reflecting the golden trees.

FRONDOSO.

>To us and all of you as well.

[*Applause*]

FATHER OLIVER.

>Now they are man and wife—
>Give us more music!

BARRILDO.

[*Sings*]

>There was a maiden from the hill
>Went walking by the stream
>There came a knight from far away
>He followed in a dream
>
>She hid herself among the leaves
>For she was young and shy
>He sought her down the waterside
>And he began to cry:
>
>"Why do you hide yourself from me
>O fairest of them all?
>My love is long, my love is strong
>And it breaks down every wall."
>
>His sword it cut through bush and briar
>Towards her hiding place.
>She drew a branch in front of her
>To hide her lily face.
>
>But when he pulled that branch away

A bright snake did appear.
The snake did bite that lusty knight
And whispered in his ear:

"Why do you hid yourself from me,
O fairest of them all?
My love is long, my love is strong
And it breaks down every wall."

[*Enter Commander, Flores, Ortuño and Soldiers*]

COMMANDER.
Please don't stop the celebrations—
Not on my account.

JUAN ROJO.
We are happy to obey you, sir, in this.
Perhaps you'd care to join our party?
How did your battle go?
Did you win? But what a question!

FRONDOSO.
I'm as good as dead.

LAURENCIA.
Frondoso—run!

COMMANDER.
Oh no. Arrest him. Tie his hands.

JUAN ROJO.
Give yourself up, lad.

FRONDOSO.
You want to see me killed?

JUAN ROJO.
What do you mean?

[*Soldiers seize and bind Frondoso*]

COMMANDER.
I'm not the kind of soldier
Who shoots down unarmed peasants.
If I was these men of mine
Would've skewered this hooligan by now.
He goes to jail—and his father-in-law
Can sit in judgement on him.
Take him away.

[*Soldiers drag off Frondoso*]

PASCUALA.
But Commander, what's he done?

COMMANDER.
He stole my crossbow.
Tried to murder me.

PASCUALA.
Sir, he's just getting married.

COMMANDER.
Fancy that, he's just getting married.
There are plenty of other louts in the town
The bride can marry instead.

PASCUALA.
Please be generous, Commander.

Let him off this time.

COMMANDER.
Pascuala, it's not up to me.
His offence was against the Order which I serve
And against the Grand Master, God protect him.
This many must be punished as an example
Or Fuente Ovejuna will breed more rebels.
He pointed a crossbow at my chest.

ESTEBAN.
I'm his father-in-law.
Let me try to excuse him.
It's not amazing that a man who's a lover
Should occasionally forget himself.
You tried to take his wife away.
Wasn't it natural to defend her?

COMMANDER.
Esteban—you're an idiot.

ESTEBAN.
For your reputation's sake—

COMMANDER.
—I never tried to take his wife.
The boy wasn't even married.

ESTEBAN.
Yes, you did. Don't argue with me.
In Castile now a King and Queen
Are bringing peace to all the people
And stamping out petty tyrants.
When they have won the last of their battles
They will do well to cut down any man
Who preys upon the helpless.
Let King Ferdinand wear the red cross
For that insignia was made
Only for noble breasts.

COMMANDER.
Remove his chain of office.

ESTEBAN.

[*Handing it over*]

Take it, sir, you're welcome.

COMMANDER.

[*To Flores and Ortuño*]

Use this chain. Beat the magistrate.
The way I do when I break a horse.

ESTEBAN.
You are our overlord. Do what you like.

PASCUALA.
You'd beat an old man?

LAURENCIA.
You only beat him because he's my father.
Why him? Why not me?

COMMANDER.
Later perhaps. Take them both away.
I want a guard of ten soldiers on them.

[*Exit Commander and Soldiers with Esteban and Laurencia
under arrest*]

PASCUALA.

The wedding's turned into a funeral.

[Exit Pascuala]

BARRILDO.

Is nobody man enough to stand up to him?

MENGO.

I've had one whipping already.

My bruises are still ripe.

BARRILDO.

Let's all speak out together.

MENGO.

Let's all keep quiet. They have the weapons.

I can still hear that leather crack

And I look like raw steak from the back.

[END OF ACT 2]

ACT 3

SCENE 1

[A modest meeting room. A hot day. Enter Esteban,
Alonso and Barrildo]

ESTEBAN.

Just look who's turned up for the meeting!

BARRILDO.

Nobody.

ESTEBAN.

Pathetic.

BARRILDO.

Everybody in town was told.

ESTEBAN.

Frondoso chained up in the jail.

Leonelo thrown out of town.

Laurencia taken God knows where.

Great God Almighty!

BARRILDO.

And they beat you too.

[Enter Juan Rojo and a Farmer]

JUAN ROJO.

Keep your voices down.

It's meant to be a secret meeting.

ESTEBAN.

It's a wonder we're not screaming.

[Enter Mengo]

MENGO.

Is this the secret meeting?

ESTEBAN.

Sit down, Mengo.

Fellow citizens,

I speak as an old man

So pardon an old man's tears.

We ought to be in mourning

For the honour of our beloved town.

Which has been nailed into its coffin

And stuck in the cold depths of the earth.

How can we go on living, when all of us

Have been insulted by this thug?

Tell me, is there one man here

Whose life he hasn't wrecked?

You see, it's a disaster.

JUAN ROJO.

Worse than an earthquake.

ESTEBAN.

But who can help us?

JUAN ROJO.

King Ferdinand and Queen Isabella

Have turned Córdoba into a peaceful place.

Let's send two council members

To ask them to save us.

BARRILDO.

King Ferdinand's too busy fighting battles

To worry about Fuente Ovejuna.

FARMER.

If anyone wants to know what I think,

I think we should abandon the town,

That's what I think.

ALONSO.

They steal our wives and daughters.

They treat us like slaves.

JUAN ROJO.

So what can the town do?

ALONSO.

Kill these soldiers before they kill us.

There's plenty of us—not many of them.

MENGO.

They can always get more.

We can't.

BARRILDO.

Let's share out the few weapons we have—and fight!

ESTEBAN.

God and the King and Queen—they're our only rulers—

Not these strutting military men.

What have we got to lose?

MENGO.

Now just a moment, sir, hang on.

Let's show a little caution, shall we?

I represent the ordinary shepherd

And he's always the one who comes off worst

When important people fight it out.

I would suggest that we wait and see—

Speaking on behalf of the ordinary shepherd, that is.

[Enter Laurencia, dishevelled]

LAURENCIA.

Out of my way and let me in

To this all-wise, all-male Council meeting.

You may not allow a woman to vote
But you can't stop her yelling.
Don't you know me, for God's sake?
ESTEBAN.
　Yes, you're my daughter.
JUAN ROJO.
　Laurencia!
LAURENCIA.
　Hard to recognise me, isn't it,
　The state I'm in?
ESTEBAN.
　My daughter!
LAURENCIA.
　Don't call me that.
ESTEBAN.
　Why not?
LAURENCIA.
　For lots of good reasons—
　The chief ones are these:
　Because you let those soldiers take me
　Without lifting a finger.
　Because you left it to Frondoso
　To protect me when that's a father's job
　Till after the wedding night.
　For, even if you buy a diamond ring
　It isn't yours till it's on your finger.
　So why did Frondoso have to run
　The gauntlet of those vicious troops?
ESTEBAN.
　They beat me too, you know, when I protested.
LAURENCIA.
　They did, yes, I'm sorry, yes they did, but these others—
　When the Commander took me off
　You stood and goggled like cowardly shepherds
　While the wolf ran off with your lamb.
　Oh, did they hold you back with swords?
　Well, they held me down with violent abuse,
　With violent threats, with violent hands,
　With every kind of violence
　So he could violate me.

　Doesn't my hair tell it's own story?
　Can you see the blood on my skirt?
　Can you see the bruises
　Where they clutched me?
　Where they hit me?
　Can you see anything at all?

　Call yourselves respected councillors?
　Call yourselves my kinsmen?
　Your guts should burst out of your bellies
　To see Laurencia like this.

　Fuente Ovejuna—the spring for sheep.
　Sheep, that's all you are, a flock of sheep.

Sheepspring's the right name for this town.
Give me your weapons
You're a heap of stones,
A shelf of plaster idols,
A knot of cold-hearted snakes—
No, that's not fair on snakes—
A snake at least
Follows the hunters who steal its eggs
And lashes out, biting into their legs,
Injecting venom before they can reach
The safety of their saddles.

You gang of rabbits—stay down your holes!
Ancient cockerels, loafing around the dunghill
While other men screw your wives.
Give me your swords.
Take my sewing needles.

My God, do we women have to show you
How to smash those bastards
And wash yourself clean in a trough of their blood?

Stones! Rabbits! Sheep! Eunuchs!

Tomorrow we women will dress you up
In our best skirts and blouses.
We'll paint and powder you prettily
And lead you round the houses.

Listen, the Commander has made up his mind
To murder Frondoso at his headquarters.
There'll be no trial. There'll be no verdict.
And maybe his body will be found in the river.
And maybe his body will never be found.

And when the Commander takes the rest of you,
One by one, week by week, and strings you up
While your fellow-councillors hold secret meetings—
I'll be laughing my head off—little boys!
O when he's killed all the men of this town
Then the age of Amazons will return
And women will show the world what courage means.
ESTEBAN.
　Laurencia, I won't swallow those insults.
　I'll go out alone to fight, even though
　An army of devils marches against me.
JUAN ROJO.
　I'm scared, it't true.
　But I'll come too.
ALONSO.
　Let's risk everything and die together.
BARRILDO.
　Tie a rag to the top of a stick,
　Hold it high in the wind.
　We'll kill those monsters.

JUAN ROJO.
> What sort of order shall we march in?

MENGO.
> Just kill 'em, don't worry about what order.
> Stamp along in a thumping great mob,
> All of the townspeople, all together.

ESTEBAN.
> Take crossbows, lances,
> Kitchen knives, hammers—

MENGO.
> Slingshots?

ESTEBAN.
> Anything that can cut or batter.

MENGO.
> Long live our lords
> The King and Queen,
> Ferdinand and Isabella!

ALL.
> Long live the King and Queen!

MENGO.
> Death to all traitors!
> Death to all tyrants!

ALL.
> Death to all traitors!
> Death to all tyrants!

[*Exit all but Laurencia. She goes to the window*]

LAURENCIA.
> When sheep march out to the attack
> It's terrible news for the wolf-pack.

[*Shouts*]

> Women of Fuente Ovejuna!
> Come and win your good names back!
> Women of Fuente Ovejuna!
> Everyone of you is needed!

[*Enter Pascuala, Jacinta and other Women*]

PASCUALA.
> What's up? What are you shouting about?

LAURENCIA.
> Don't you see the men are marching out
> To assassinate Commander Goméz?
> Men, young lads and little boys,
> All rushing out to finish him off.
> D'you think it's right for the men of the town
> To tackle this alone?
> They've suffered less
> Than any of us women.

JACINTA.
> What can we do?

LAURENCIA.
> Form up in ranks and take part in an action
> Which will shake the world.

> Jacinta, because of what they did to you,
> You shall march at the head of our column.

JACINTA.
> They hurt you as much as me.

LAURENCIA.
> Pascuala, you be standard bearer.

PASCUALA.
> Just give me a moment to hoist
> The flag up on a pole
> I'll bear it proudly, just watch me.

LAURENCIA.
> No time for embroidering banners.
> Hold up your shawls, let them flow in the wind.

PASCUALA.
> We ought to elect a captain.

LAURENCIA.
> No.

PASCUALA.
> Why not?

LAURENCIA.
> Because we can fight bravely enough
> Without a leader telling us how to die.

LAURENCIA AND THE WOMEN.

[*March and sing*]

> The hands of ladies and gentlemen
> Are soft as Chinese silk.
> The hands of ladies and gentlemen
> Are white as purest milk.
> But we're not ladies or gentlemen
> And we're not soft or white,
> For we are women with peasants' hands
> And our hands can caress or fight.

> For our hands fight the tough old soil
> With hoe and spade and plough.
> They light the first and pour the oil
> And they milk the goat and cow.

> And our hands help old lives to end
> And they help new lives to start.
> And they show affection to our friends
> And put courage in our lover's heart,
> And put courage in our lover's heart.

> The hands of ladies and gentlemen
> Are soft as Chinese silk.
> The hands of ladies and gentlemen
> Are white as purest milk.
> But we're not ladies or gentlemen
> And we're not soft or white,
> For we are women with peasants' hands
> And our hands can caress or fight.

> And our hands plant the corn you eat
> And weave the clothes you wear,

And scrub the floors and cook the meat
And they comb the children's hair.

But if a wolf attacks our flocks
Our hands will take its life
With crossbows and with well-aimed rocks,
With a sickle and a carving knife,
With a sickle and a carving knife.

Oh the hands of ladies and gentlemen . . .

[*Laurencia and the Women march out of sight*]

SCENE 2

[*Inside the Commander's country house. Enter Frondoso, his hands bound, led by Flores and Ortuño followed by the Commander*]

COMMANDER.
String him up on the beam
And then we'll have some fun with him.
FLORES.
Right you are, Commander.
FRONDOSO.
They all call you Commander.
I know a better name for you.

[*Commander hits Frondoso*]

COMMANDER.
Rope over the beam,
Haul him up backwards by the arms.
Drop him a few times.
And then we can begin.
FRONDOSO.
I could've killed you that day.

[*Sounds of off-stage singing and marching*]

FLORES.
What's happening out there?
ORTUÑO.
We're going to be interrupted.

[*Looks out of the window*]

They're breaking down the gates, sir.
LAURENCIA.

[*Off*]

Break it down!
Tear it down!
Burn it down!
ORTUÑO.
It's a mutiny, sir.
The whole damn town.

COMMANDER.
Rebelling against me?
FLORES.
They're armed. They're out for blood.
The gates are down, sir.
COMMANDER.
Untie the lad.
Frondoso, you've got to go
And calm them down.

[*Flores unties Frondoso*]

FRONDOSO.
I'll do what I can.
COMMANDER.
What's the problem?
What's got into them?
FRONDOSO.
Love.

[*Exit Frondoso*]

MENGO.

[*Off*]

Long live Ferdinand and Isabella!
Death to all traitors!
FLORES.
For Christ's sake, sir,
Don't let them corner you.
COMMANDER.
There's guards outside.
They'll never get in.
FLORES.
When people are pushed so far
That they take up arms
They don't give them up till they've tasted blood.
COMMANDER.
We'll shoot them down.
ORTUÑO.
Too many of them, sir.
FRONDOSO.

[*Off*]

Long live Fuente Ovejuna!
COMMANDER.
They're mad. But I can cure them.
FLORES.
We're mad if we stay here.

[*Enter Townspeople including Esteban, Juan Rojo, Pascuala, Laurencia, Jacinta, Mengo, Frondoso, Barrildo etc, all armed with weapons and farming implements*]

ESTEBAN.
The tyrant and his apes!

Long live Fuente Ovejuna!
Death to all traitors!
COMMANDER.
Now just a minute . . .
LAURENCIA.
We've no time to waste.
We're here to put things right.
COMMANDER.
Just tell me your complaints.
If I've made some mistakes, I'll do my utmost
To make up for them—I just want to say—
TOWNSPEOPLE.
Fuente Ovenjuna! Fuente Ovejuna!
Death to rapists! Death to traitors!
COMMANDER.
Listen to me! I'm talking to you.
I'm the Commander of this district.
LAURENCIA.
Our only commanders are the King and Queen.
COMMANDER.
Wait. Let me—
TOWNSPEOPLE.
Fuente Ovejuna! Fuente Ovejuna!
Death to the Commander!
COMMANDER.
I must appeal to the women of the town—
LAURENCIA.
We're not women—we're soldiers now.
PASCUALA.
Come on, let's drink his blood.
JACINTA.
Cut him up for mincemeat!
PASCUALA.
Blood and mincemeat!

[*Townspeople have closed in on the Commander, Flores and Ortuño*]

ESTEBAN.
Try this, Commander!
COMMANDER.
You're killing me.
Have pity, Esteban. Mercy!
BARRILDO.
Here's Captain Flores.
MENGO.
Let him have it.
He gave me two thousand lashes.
FRONDOSO.
I won't be happy until he's dead.
LAURENCIA.
Let me at him.
PASCUALA.
Easy now. Make sure they don't escape.

BARRILDO.
Don't give me prayers!
Don't give me I'm so sorry!
You're a toy soldier!
LAURENCIA.
Pascuala, I'm going in for the kill.
My knife's so thirsty that it's shaking.
BARRILDO.
I've found that Sergeant.
FRONDOSO.
Carve him up.

[*Flores breaks out of the mob, Mengo after him*]

FLORES.
Mengo, have mercy.
I was under orders.
MENGO.
It wasn't just my flogging.
You pimped for the Commander.
PASCUALA.
Let him go, Mengo.
The women want him.
MENGO.
Take him, you're welcome.
PASCUALA.
I'll pay him for your whipping.
MENGO.
Carry on.
JACINTA.
Kill the bastard!
FLORES.
Torn to pieces by women!
PASCUALA.
Thought you liked women!
JACINTA.
Cut his throat.
FLORES.
Ladies! Mercy!

[*Ortuño breaks out of the mob, chased by Laurencia*]

ORTUÑO.
It wasn't me. It wasn't me!
LAURENCIA.
I know who you are.
Down on your knees.
Women, here's one more.
PASCUALA.
I'll kill him if it kills me.
TOWNSPEOPLE.
Long live Fuente Ovejuna!

[*Townspeople kill Ortuño, Flores, badly wounded, manages to escape as Townspeople crowd round Commander's corpse*]

SCENE 3

[*The Palace of Ferdinand and Isabella. Enter King Ferdinand, Queen Isabella and Don Manrique*]

MANRIQUE.
We moved at the right time, your majesties.
We won the day with little opposition.
Now our forces occupy Cuidad Real
In case the enemy attacks again.

KING.
Well done. We shall send reinforcements.
That city commands the pass to Portugal.
We intend to hold it forever—
A bastion against the Portuguese.

[*Flores is helped on, wounded*]

FLORES.
Your majesties. Bad news.
The worse atrocity.

QUEEN.
Tell us.

FLORES.
Your majesty, my wounds.
I can't hold out much longer.
They brought me here from Fuente Ovejuna.
The people of that town, the men and the women,
Murdered Commander Goméz.
They worked themselves up
Over nothing at all—
Tore him to shreds, sir.
The whole damned town,
Fuente Ovejuna,
Shouting: Down with the tyrant!
Got so excited by their own shouting
They broke down the doors of his house
And in they burst
And they took no notice when he swore on his honour
To repay anything he owed them,
They took no notice and they struck him down,
Stabbing right through the red cross on his breast
With a thousand vicious gashes,
And they picked him up and sent him flying down
From a high window
And a mob of howling women underneath
Caught his body on the points of pitchforks,
Tossed him, caught him,
Tossed him, dropped him,
Dragged him into a barn.
They fought each other to pull out his hair,
Scratched his face to pieces with their nails.
It was hysteria, your majesties,
So bad that when they'd finished hacking him
The biggest pieces left were his two ears.

They burned his coat of arms.
They sacked his house and looted it.

I was mobbed too,
But managed to find a hiding place.
From there I watched and saw all this.
Later I escaped, was found by your soldiers
And brought here.

Your majesties, punish these barbarians.
The Commander's blood cries out for justice.

KING.
Catpain Flores, you may rest assured
They will not go unpunished.
Don Manrique, I appoint you Judge.
Go find out all the facts of the case
And punish the offenders.

QUEEN.
Send a strong troop of soldiers with the Judge.
He'll need protection in such a place.

KING.
Bind up this soldier's wounds and give
Him all your care—

FLORES.
—I do not want to live.

[*Exeunt*]

SCENE 4

[*The Town Square at Fuente Ovejuna. Enter Townspeople and Musicians celebrating, with the Commander's head stuck on a pole*]

TOWNSPEOPLE.

[*Sing*]

Have you seen our Commander
With his boots and medals on?
Have you seen our Commander?
No I think our Commander's gone.

BARRILDO.
Frondoso—sing your verse.

FRONDOSO.
Here goes—and if you don't like it,
You make up a better one.

[*Sings*]

The first time I saw the Commander
He was strutting down the street.
The last time I saw the Commander
He looked like sausage-meat.

TOWNSPEOPLE.
Have you seen our Commander

With his boots and medals on?
Have you seen our Commander?
No I think our Commander's gone.

LAURENCIA.
Your turn, Barrildo.

BARRILDO.
Listen carefully.
Took a long time to compose this.

PASCUALA.
Well, sing it slowly then.

BARRILDO.

[Sings]

The first time I saw the Commander
He was courting someone's wife
The last time I saw our Commander
He was pleading for his life.

TOWNSPEOPLE.
Have you seen our Commander
With his boots and medals on?
Have you seen our Commander?
No I think our Commander's gone.

LAURENCIA.
Mengo's turn.

FRONDOSO.
Come on, Mengo.

MENGO.
My verse is very tasty.

PASCUALA.
Like tripe.

MENGO.
The first time I saw the Commander
He was whipping me half-dead.
The last time I saw the Commander
The Commander lost his head.

TOWNSPEOPLE.
Have you seen our Commander
With his boots and medals on?
Have you seen our Commander?
No I think our Commander's gone.

ESTEBAN.
Take his head away and give it decent burial.

MENGO.
Yes, he's a miserable looking sod.

[Alonso brings out two glorious coats of arms]

PASCUALA.
What are those for?

ALONSO.
They are the coats of arms of our true lords—
King Ferdinand and Queen Isabella.

ESTEBAN.
Hang them here, each side of the Town Hall door.

[Juan Rojo brings out a simple plaque painted with a sheep rampant and a fountain]

JUAN ROJO.
And here's Fuente Ovejuna's coat of arms.

FRONDOSO.
It's a fine piece of work. Who painted it?

[Mengo tries to look modest]

LAURENCIA.
Hang it between the other two.
A new day is dawning for Fuente Ovejuna.

ESTEBAN.
But it won't be long before the dark arrives.

MENGO.
What do you mean?

ESTEBAN.
The King and Queen are sending a Judge.
He and his investigators
Will do anything to find out
Who killed the Commander.
We must all agree
On what we're going to tell them.

FRONDOSO.
What can we say?

ESTEBAN.
If they ask you who killed him
And they put you to the torture
Die saying "Fuente Ovejuna"
Nobody budge from that.

FRONDOSO.
And it's the truth—
Fuente Ovenjuna did kill the Commander.

ESTEBAN.
What will you say?

ALL.
[Raggedly]
Fuente Ovejuna.

ESTEBAN.
I'd better show you what I mean.
Let's rehearse it. I'll be the torturer.
Now who can be the one who's being questioned?
Ah yes . . . Mengo!

MENGO.
Couldn't you find someone feebler than me?

ESTEBAN.
Impossible. Come on, man.
We'll only pretend to torture you.

MENGO.
All right. Do your worst. Pretending.

ESTEBAN.
Mengo, who killed the Commander?

MENGO.
Fuente Ovejuna did it.

ESTEBAN.
  What if I torture you? Will you change your story?
MENGO.
  Not even if you kill me dead. It was Fuente Ovejuna.
ESTEBAN.
  Confess, you scum.
MENGO.
  All right, I'll confess.
ESTEBAN.
  Who did it then?
MENGO.
  Fuente Ovejuna.
ESTEBAN.
  Tear out his nails.
MENGO.
  That's nothing. Fuente Ovejuna!

[Enter Alonso, agitated]

ALONSO.
  The Judge has arrived. With a troop of soldiers.
ESTEBAN.
  Everyone, go to your homes.
ALONSO.
  They're rounding up everyone.
ESTEBAN.
  Don't be afraid.
  You all know what you have to say?
ALL.
  Yes!
ALONSO.
  What's that?
ESTEBAN.
  When we're asked who killed the Commander
  We say—Mengo, who killed the Commander?
MENGO.
  Fuente Ovejuna!

[Enter Manrique with Soldiers]

MANRIQUE.
  Ladies and gentlemen,
  Judgement has come to Fuente Ovejuna.
  I represent the King and Queen today
  And I am here to investigate the death
  of Commander Goméz de Guzmán.
  I will conduct my interviews in the Town Hall
  And I want to talk with every one of you.

                                        [Exeunt]

SCENE 5

[The Master of Calatrava's tent. The Master seated, a
Soldier standing]

MASTER.
  That was a terrible way to die.
  You, I shall have you killed
  For bringing me such news.
SOLDIER.
  I'm only the messenger, sir,
  I meant no harm.
MASTER.
  A town of savages!
  They dared do such a thing?
  Well, I shall take five hundred men
  And Fuente Ovejuna shall be burned.
  That town will be a black patch on the ground.
  I'll burn their bones and their children's bones.
SOLDIER.
  Control your anger, sir.
  The people of Fuente Ovejuna have declared their loy-
      alty
  To Ferdinand and Isabella.
  You're on the wrong side of the King already.
MASTER.
  How can they declare for the King and Queen
  When the Order of Calatrava owns their town?
SOLDIER.
  You'll have to settle that with King Ferdinand.
  I suppose you could bring a law-suit against him.
MASTER.
  Idiot! How could I ever win?
  No, I'll bank down my anger
  And seek an audience with the King and Queen.
  I have been a rebel, but I may be pardoned
  By such a gracious Queen and King.
  Youth's an excuse for anything.

                                        [Exeunt]

SCENE 6

[The Town Square. Frondoso and Laurencia stand and
listen to the interrogations taking place off stage]

LAURENCIA.
  My love, I'm terrified they'll kill you.
  For God's sake, get out of this town.
FRONDOSO.
  I'm not going to abandon my friends
  Just to save my own skin.

[Screams from the hall]

LAURENCIA.
  Listen. What's happening.
MANRIQUE.

  [Off]

Come on, grandad, I want the truth.

FRONDOSO.

They're torturing an old man.

LAURENCIA.

Bastards.

ESTEBAN.

[*Off*]

Give me a minute's peace!

MANRIQUE.

[*Off*]

Slacken off a bit.
Tell me, who killed Commander Goméz?

ESTEBAN.

[*Off*]

Fuente Ovejuna did it.

LAURENCIA.

God bless you, father.

FRONDOSO.

He's a brave man.

MANRIQUE.

[*Off*]

Take that boy.
That's right.
I know you know who did it, you little pig.
You won't talk?
Tighten it!
Who killed him?

BOY.

[*Off*]

Fuente Ovejuna, sir.

MANRIQUE.

[*Off*]

Peasants!
I'll hang the lot of you with my own two hands.
Who killed the Commander?

FRONDOSO.

He's only a boy.

BOY.

[*Off*]

Fuente Ovejuna!

LAURENCIA.

It's a brave town.

FRONDOSO.

Brave and strong.

MANRIQUE.

[*Off*]

Now that woman.
Hold her down.
Begin!

LAURENCIA.

He's going mad.

MANRIQUE.

[*Off*]

I'll skin you all alive.
I'm warning you.
Come on, who killed the Commander?

PASCUALA.

[*Off*]

Fuente Ovenjuna.

MANRIQUE.

[*Off*]

Now! Show her what pain is!

FRONDOSO.

Pascuala! She'll never hold out.

LAURENCIA.

Pascuala won't break.

MANRIQUE.

[*Off*]

I think they're enjoying it.
Don't play games with me, girl.
Let her have it.

PASCUALA.

[*Off*]

Jesus Christ!

MANRIQUE.

[*Off*]

I said let her have it!
Are you deaf?

PASCUALA.

[*Off*]

Fuente Ovejuna did it.

MANRIQUE.

[*Off*]

I'll take the fat one next.

LAURENCIA.

Poor old Mengo! That must be him.

FRONDOSO.

Mengo! He's bound to crack.

MENGO.

[*Off*]

Oh! Oh!

MANRIQUE.

[Off]

Turn it again.

MENGO.

[Off]

Oh!

MANRIQUE.

[Off]

Tighter. Do I have to help you?

MENGO.

[Off]

Oh! Oh!

MANRIQUE.

[Off]

Who killed the Commander?

MENGO.

[Off]

Stop! I'll tell you, sir.

MANRIQUE.

[Off]

Slacken it off a little.

FRONDOSO.

He's going to talk.

MANRIQUE.

[Off]

Ready to start again?

MENGO.

[Off]

I know who killed him!

MANRIQUE.

[Off]

Who?

MENGO.

[Off]

Fuente Ovejuna.

MANRIQUE.

[Off]

A townful of idiots!
They're laughing at the pain.
I was sure I'd break that fat one down.
Oh, let them go for the moment.

[Enter Mengo, Esteban, Pascuala and Boy, with other Townspeople]

FRONDOSO.

Mengo! You're a hero.

ESTEBAN.

That's what I say too.

MENGO.

Oh God!

ESTEBAN.

[Producing a flask] Have a drink, Mengo.

MENGO.

[Drinking and spluttering]

What is that stuff?

ESTEBAN.

Home-brewed brandy. Don't you like it?

MENGO.

Oh God. Give me another go at it.

FRONDOSO.

Must be good.

ESTEBAN.

Have another.

MENGO.

Yes please.

FRONDOSO.

You deserve it.

LAURENCIA.

Put a blanket round him, he's shivering.

ESTEBAN.

Want some more?

MENGO.

Well, just a few more.

PASCUALA.

Pass it round, we all need a drink.
[Drinks] Oh good Lord above.

LAURENCIA.

What's the matter?

PASCUALA.

It's a bit rough. [Takes another swig]

FRONDOSO.

[Producing another flask] Here, try mine.
Mengo, who killed the Commander?

MENGO.

Fuente Ovejuna did it.

[Exit all but Laurencia and Frondoso]

FRONDOSO.

Tell me, my love, now we're all alone . . .
Who did kill the Commander?

LAURENCIA.

Fuente Ovejuna, my darling.

FRONDOSO.

Who killed him?

LAURENCIA.
  Frondoso, I'm scared.
  Well, it was Fuente Ovejuna.
FRONDOSO.
  And me, what do I kill you with?
LAURENCIA.
  What with? With loving you so much.

[Exit Laurencia and Frondoso]

SCENE 7

[The Palace of King Ferdinand and Queen Isabella. Enter
King and Queen, meeting]

QUEEN.
  How lucky I am, my lord,
  To welcome you home again
  To your palace and my arms.
KING.
  My eyes are stinging with the dust
  Which rises from the yellow roads—
  I look at you—my eyes feel young again.
  But tell me, what is happening in Castile?
QUEEN.
  Castile is peaceful once again,
  Orderly, in control.
KING.
  Hardly surprising, under your rule, my lady.

[Enter Cimbranos]

CIMBRANOS.
  The Master of Calatrava
  Implores you to grant him an audience.
QUEEN.
  I've heard so much talk about the boy
  That I'm fascinated to see what he's like.
KING.
  He's a very young man—
  They're all much the same.
CIMBRANOS.
  He has fought bravely in two battles
  And he has aged considerably.

[Exit Cimbranos. Enter the Master of Calatrava. He kneels]

MASTER.
  The Master of Calatrava
  Most humbly begs your royal forgiveness.

  I was wrong, I was deceived.
  I struggled against you and I stole from you—
  And all because I am so young.
  The bad advice of Commander Goméz
  And my own vanity and self-interest

Sent me galloping headlong down a wicked road—
So I beg for your forgiveness.

And if you can forget my sins
I will engage from this day on
To serve you most wholeheartedly,
For I would ride along with you
To that great battleground to which you go
And there, in bright Granada, there I'll prove my
    courage.

My sword, the moment it's unsheathed
Will spread terror amongst your foes
And you shall see red crosses spring
From all Granada's battlements.
And furthermore, I'll bring with me
Five hundred soldiers and a vow
That I will serve you all my life.
KING.
  Rise, Master, from your knees.
  You came to us bravely of your own accord,
  So you are very welcome.
MASTER.
  You are the healer of the sick.
QUEEN.
  Your prowess in battle, I am told,
  Even excels your skill with words.
MASTER.
  You are as beautiful as Esther was
  And you, sir, merciful as Xerxes.

[Enter Cimbranos]

CIMBRANOS.
  Your majesties, your Judge
  Is back from Fuente Ovejuna.
KING.
  [To Queen] You shall pass judgement on these rioters.
MASTER.
  It is, of course, your Majesty, your concern,
  But were it mine, I would teach them a lesson
  For killing their Commander.
KING.
  It is no longer your concern.

[Enter Manrique]

MANRIQUE.
  Your majesties, I travelled to Fuente Ovejuna
  And, as you requested,
  Conducted my inquiry
  With care and diligence.
  However, in all the evidence I found
  We do not have one single page,
  No, not a single sentence written down
  Which names the perpetrator of this crime.

The people of the town were stubborn.
Whenever I asked the name of the murderer
All they would say was: "Fuente Ovejuna".

I interrogated three hundred of them.
All the approved tortures, rigorously applied.
Old men, women, ten year old boys,
But I could get nothing out of them
Except the cry of "Fuente Ovejuna."

QUEEN.
But if it's impossible
To find out who it was
We'll either have to pardon them
Or execute them all.

MANRIQUE.
They are all here.

KING.
Let them be brought before us.

[*Enter the Townspeople of* Fuente Ovejuna, *guarded*]

LAURENCIA.
Is that the King and Queen?

FRONDOSO.
The rulers of Castile and Aragon.

LAURENCIA.
Oh, they are so beautiful.
St. Anthony's blessings fall upon them!

QUEEN.
Are these the barbarians, the murderers?

ESTEBAN.
Your majesties,
The town of Fuente Ovejuna stands before you.
A town which is loyal and longs to serve you.
The cruelty of the late Commander
Was the root of all our troubles.
He stole our farms. He raped our women.
He had no pity for anyone.

FRONDOSO.
That's right.
This is the young woman
God sent me for a bride.
I was the luckiest man alive—

LAURENCIA.
—But on our wedding night
The Commander and his men carried me off—

FRONDOSO.
And she resisted and they hurt her—

MENGO.
Permission, sir, to say a few words?
Permission, madam? Prepare yourselves
To be dumbfounded by my account
Of the behaviour of Fernando Goméz.

Because I tried to protect a young woman
From being abducted by his bullies,
That little Nero had me flogged
Till my back looked like a side of smoked salmon.
Three burly soldiers beat my drum
With such rhythmic energy
That I've had to spend my life savings on
Linament and myrtle powder.
I can prove all this, your majesties.
Would you care to inspect my scars?

KING.
Later, perhaps.

ESTEBAN.
Sir, we wish to live under your rule.
You are our rightful overlord.
My lady, we ask for your leniency.
Hoping you'll understand
The innocence and courage of our town.

QUEEN.
No written evidence exists
Naming the person who
Committed this most vicious crime—
So we must pardon you.

[*Cheers*]

KING.
Fuente Ovejuna, you turned to us for help,
Therefore your town shall be
Ruled by ourselves from this day on—
And we'll watch you carefully,
Till we can find a new Commander
Who's fit to govern such a town
As Fuente Ovejuna.

LAURENCIA.
Your gracious majesties, we must
Thank you for being both kind and just
And it's on this happy note, good friends,
That the story of Fuente Ovejuna ends.

[THE END]

TOPICS FOR CRITICAL THINKING AND WRITING

The Play on the PAGE

1. In what ways does Lope de Vega let us know that Commander Fernando Goméz de Guzmán is the villain in the play? What characteristics does the Commander possess and what acts does he do to make him villainous?
2. After the theme of honor, Lope de Vega utilizes the secondary theme of the relationship between love and harmony. In what ways does he do this and how does love and harmony connect to the concept of honor?
3. One critic describes the play "as the most democratic in all of Spanish drama" (Ingber, 236). What evidence in the play allows us to call it "democratic"?
4. In 3.1 Laurencia confronts her father and the other men assembled at a secret meeting, admonishing them for allowing the Commander to steal her away on her wedding day. To what does she liken the men for their lack of action? Why is she particularly upset with her father for not fending off the Commander? What does this tell us about seventeenth-century Spain?

The Play on the STAGE

5. The play has eight different settings, ranging from a palace to a wooded area outside of the village, that quickly shift from one location to another. How might the stage be designed in order to encompass all of these settings?
6. In reviews of the Royal National Theater production directed by Declan Donnellan, critics praised his ability to stage the large group scenes leading up to the climactic peasant insurrection. Select three moments in the play where the roles of peasants need to demonstrate a clear sense of collective action and suggest ways for staging these scenes.
7. What kind of costumes would the characters wear? How would the costumes help tell the story?

The Play in PERFORMANCE

Fuente Ovejuna was written in 1612–14 and first published in 1619, but the original performance date is unknown. In the Spanish-speaking world, it is one of Lope de Vega's most produced plays. Peasant insurrection has been a recurrent theme in twentieth-century Spain, and in 1932 an almost exact replica of the events in the play took place in the village of Castilblanco. The Spanish playwright Federico García Lorca directed a modern dress production of the play in the following year that toured to villages in southern Spain. Produced just prior to the Spanish Civil War, this production had special relevance as García Lorca used it to comment on the deteriorating political situation in his country. In the year that he died—he was murdered by right-wing extremists at the outbreak of the war in 1936—the first English-language production was staged by the Experimental Theater of Vassar College in Poughkeepsie, New York. More recently the Royal National Theater of Great Britain commissioned a new translation of the play by the London-born poet and dramatist Adrian Mitchell. This lively translation, which is reprinted here, was directed by Declan Donnellan in 1989 in a brilliant production that included live Spanish music on the guitar and spirited dancing.

PIERRE Corneille

Pierre Corneille (1606–84), the first major French playwright, was born in the city of Rouen, where he received his early education in a Jesuit school. Later, following the family tradition, he studied law, a career in which—due to a speech defect—it is not surprising he did not prosper. Having been a fascinated spectator of the various troupes of strolling players who regularly played Rouen, Corneille decided to try his hand at writing a play, *Mélite,* a comedy of intrigue (1629). The play impressed one of the leading actor-managers of the time, Mont-dory (the future Rodrigue in *Le Cid*), who took it—and its author—to Paris. Most of the novice dramatist's first seven plays were comedies, and though they enjoyed considerable contemporary success, only one of them—*L'Illusion comique*—has had much stage afterlife. His first venture into tragedy was based on *Medea* (*Médée,* 1635), which was followed by the play upon which his reputation rests: the spectacularly successful but controversial *Le Cid* (1636). The tremendous popularity of the play—with its classical irregularities—inevitably inspired the envy of several fellow authors as well as the displeasure of Cardinal Richelieu (for a complex of reasons) and led to the famous *"querelle* [quarrel] *du Cid"* (see later), which was referred to the newly formed Académie Française for resolution. The 192-page "mixed review" the august body finally issued obviously left its mark on Corneille, for the plays that followed—*Horace* (1640), *Cinna* (1640–41), and *Polyeucte* (1641–42)—made a deliberate attempt to more strictly observe classical rules. Corneille's later plays—among them *Nicoméde* (1651) and *Œdipe* (1652)—are generally considered inferior to his major work, and he himself recognized that his star was being eclipsed by his younger contemporary Jean Racine.

■ ■ ■ ■ ■ ■ ■ ■ ■ ■ ■ ■ ■ ■ ■ ■

COMMENTARY ON *THE CID*

The Cid arrived at a moment when France and its art began to establish a national identity. Because of the intense religious conflict between Catholic and Protestant in the late sixteenth century, France was unable to achieve the political stability which, in England and Spain, had permitted the flourishing of art, particularly the public art of theater. Finally, a modus vivendi was achieved by the Edict of Nantes (1598), and with the ascension to the throne of Louis XIII with his adviser Cardinal Richelieu, a national unity was imposed that now unleashed artistic energies. When Louis XIV succeeded his father (1643), the groundwork for a new "Golden Age"—a definitively French Golden Age—had been laid. Unlike England, France now admitted a new specialist into the brotherhood of artists—the critic, whose job was to direct the energies of art through the establishment of rules, which, significantly, he had the power to enforce. A critic wrote, "The generation of Descartes, of Corneille, of Chapelain, of Guez de Balzac, organized Parnassus as thoroughly as Richelieu had organized the kingdom." Note the names: one philosopher, one playwright, and *two* critics.

Richelieu was to institutionalize this new self-consciousness by establishing an academy dedicated to maintaining artistic order: the French Academy, or Académie Française (1635). The Academy still exists, and French culture remains defined by the symbiosis of art and criticism to this day.

Richelieu's actions were driven by his veneration of the Italians' rediscovery of the classics; on attaining power he was determined to impose the order of the Italian Renaissance on the medieval disorder he felt still reigned in French art. And nowhere was this disorder more evident than in the public theater that had risen at the end of the sixteenth century. Unlike the Italians who had rediscovered Aristotle, France's first professional playwright, the prolific Alexandre Hardy (1572–1632), paid little or no attention to the classical unities and showed violent action on stage. Moreover, the dominant style of staging utilized what was called *décor simultanée* (simultaneous setting) in which, in medieval style, different locales were represented on stage at the same time by different *compartements,* or set pieces. The place from which the actor entered defined the entire stage. When too many characters entered in near proximity it could get very confusing.

In his first play, *Mélite*, Corneille could not change the *décor*, but he could, as he pointed out, change the play by reducing the number of locales and eliminating extraneous subplots. So it is ironic that Corneille would soon find himself in trouble with those newly authorized to defend values he himself believed in. Part of the problem was the very unclassical nature of the source of the play with which he was to achieve his greatest success; and part of the problem was that one can only look so far ahead. Like Marlowe's *Doctor Faustus*, *The Cid*—unclassically labeled at first a *tragi-comédie*—is a transitional work with roots in conventions it very much wanted to reform. Although it was staged originally with *décor simultanée*, Corneille tried to mitigate the confusion by radically restricting the number of locales where scenes took place. (In later revivals, Italianate neoclassical theatrical principles were applied.)

Corneille's masterwork is based on a contemporary play by the Spanish playwright Guillén de Castro, *Las Mocedades del Cid* (*The Exploits of the Cid*; 1621), which is itself based on the exploits of the national hero who inspired the classic Spanish epic poem. Corneille was clearly taken by Castro's flamboyance and energy, which he very much wanted to retain, but he realized that the play's rambling lyrical style, its mixture of tragedy and comedy, its subplots, its many characters, and its long passages of time might please the Spanish public but would never please the French. And so, adhering to the letter of Aristotle's suggestion in the *Poetics* that "tragedy endeavors, as far as possible, to confine itself to a single revolution of the sun," Corneille radically simplified the plot and condensed the action into a single day. He reduced the number of characters, eliminated the subplots, and toned down or eliminated anything that he thought might offend the French taste for decorum and verisimilitude. But, by far, his greatest innovation was to radically reduce the scope of action by focusing the play on one essential theme: the conflict between the contrary obligations necessarily accepted by the hero and his beloved. The quarrel between the fathers of the star-crossed lovers Rodrigue and Chimène leads to an insult that the young man is duty bound to avenge; his killing of Chimène's father in the attendant duel creates for her an impossible dilemma: the obligation to honor her father by seeking justice against the man she is in love with. Only after Rodrigue has repulsed the Moors and been victor in a royally sanctioned trial of combat, does a *rap-prochement* between the lovers—the "happy ending" of marriage—become possible as Chimène seemingly bows to the King's will.

Corneille obviously struck just the right balance between Spanish ardor and French restraint, between the old dramaturgy and the new. The play was a fantastic success; all Paris, said the critic Boileau, had for Rodrigue the eyes of Chimène. But success invariably exacts a price: The jealousy of less successful rivals soon surfaced and initiated a public quarrel on the virtues and vices of the play, the famous *Querelle du Cid*. First to attack was the anonymous author of a pamphlet called *Observations sur le Cid*, who tried to prove that the play's "subject is worthless, that it defies the major rules of a Dramatic Poem, that its development is lacking judgment . . ." Corneille was attacked for crowding events implausibly into one day, and, most importantly, for immorally consenting to the marriage of a daughter with her father's murderer. Corneille responded with a scathing *Lettre apologique*, but he disdained to answer the attack point by point. Others, however, sprang to his defense. In a pamphlet called *La deffense* [sic] *du Cid*, an anonymous supporter wrote, "I have never read Aristotle, and I know nothing of the rules of the theater, but I judge plays according to the pleasure they give me." Throughout early 1637 the debate raged in a fury of pamphlets. Finally, the author of the *Observations* identified himself as the author Georges de Scudéry, who then petitioned the newly formed French Academy to investigate his charges, a request to which Corneille assented.

Eagerly awaited, a long, thorough opinion—*Sentimens* [sic] *de l'Académie française sur la tragi-comédie du Cid* (largely written by the critic Jean Chapelain)—appeared the following year. It considered each of Scudéry's arguments in detail, in effect providing a scene-by-scene analysis of the play. On many points it found fault with the criticism of Corneille's language and the believability of his characters. Scudéry, it was observed, was insufficiently Aristotelian in his analysis. But the Academy found that much of the criticism of the play *was* warranted. They found that Corneille had indeed violated the rules of verisimilitude (*vraisemblance*) by crowding so much action into a single day. And, most significantly, they agreed with the major charge that Corneille was morally irresponsible in permitting a "girl introduced as virtuous" to consent, even after due hesitation, to marry her father's slayer. They asserted the duty of the critical elite to protect the general populace from that which is morally dangerous. That what is depicted may actually have happened is no defense. "There are monstrous truths that must be repressed for the good of society."

Corneille was bloody but unbowed. He rose to his own defense against objections raised in the "querelle" many times in his future writing. But, as a practicing playwright, he also much more carefully observed the new rules as the Academy laid them down. He never returned to Spanish subjects nor again achieved the dramatic vitality of *The Cid*. He later changed the designation of the play, claiming that tragedy did not demand death, only high seriousness. But, however labeled and whatever its inconsistencies, *The Cid*, by initiating a new form, style, and tone, in effect inaugurated serious French drama.

THE CID
A TRAGEDY
Pierre Corneille

English Version by James Schevill in collaboration with Robert and Angela Goldsby

This translation is dedicated to the memory of Rudolph Schevill, whose devotion and scholarly insight into French and Spanish literature influenced many generations of American students in the classroom, and whose books and articles will continue to influence many new generations of students.

CHARACTERS

THE KING, *Ferdinand the First of Castile [died 1065]*

THE INFANTA, *his daughter*

COUNT DE GORMAS, *father of Chimena and the King's foremost warrior*

CHIMENA,* *daughter of the Count de Gormas, in love with Rodrigo*

DON DIEGO, *father of Rodrigo, an old man who was once the King's foremost warrior*

RODRIGO, *Don Diego's son, who becomes The Cid* [a title deriving from the Arabic* El Seid, *the Lord]*

DON ARIAS } *two Castilian noblemen*
DON ALONSO }

DON SANCHO, *a young Castilian nobleman who is a suitor of Chimena*

LEONORA, *a lady in waiting to the Infanta*

ELVIRA, *a lady in waiting to Chimena*

A PAGE

The scene of the play is laid in Seville.

ACT 1

SCENE 1

[*Chimena's house*]
[*Enter Chimena, Elvira*]

CHIMENA.
Elvira, you hold back the truth, I swear.
What did my father say you will not share?

ELVIRA.
His words have all my senses quite enthralled.
He favors Rodrigo whom your heart has called,
5   And if I were to guess, I should believe
His final choice will not cause you to grieve.

CHIMENA.
I beg you, tell me more, I will rejoice.
Why are you certain he'll approve my choice?
Give me again that hope I long to cherish
10   For those sweet words you speak should never perish.

* A somewhat Anglicized pronunciation is recommended: *Shimayna; The Sid* (not *Seed*).

Oh, why withhold your precious tale? I pray
Love's flame will soar to light the dark with day.
Did father heed Don Sancho with good grace,
Or did he favor my Rodrigo's place?
You took great care, I hope, not to make clear   15
That I am only glad when one is near.

ELVIRA.
I painted you indifferent, but tense,
Granting some hope, yet also cruel suspense.
And neither stern nor sweet as you await
Your father's choice of men to be your mate.   20
How much this touched him was an easy measure
In the proud look he gave me, filled with pleasure.
Since you must linger on his every word
I shall repeat the phrases which I heard: 25
"She does well. Either man is worthy of her.
Both come of noble stock with loyal valor;
Young men in whose bold eyes one looks to see
The prideful spirit of their ancestry.
In Rodrigo's eyes, it's not so hard to trace   30
The courageous image of a hero's face,
Born to a family whose victorious name
Shines on the pages of our country's fame.

The star-crossed lovers Chimena (Sarah Karbasnikoff) and Rodrigo (William Nadylam) struggle between the demands of love and honor in Declan Donnelan's anti-heroic, Avignon-festival version of Pierre Corneille's *The Cid*.

On his father's brow is etched the story
35   Of the might that was our Spanish glory.
If the son commands an echo of the sire,
Chimena's love for him is my desire."
That moment the King's Council was to meet
And he did leave, his thought cut incomplete.
40   But his few words on your bold, wooing gallants
Gave your loved one the favorable balance.
The King must choose a tutor for his son
And this post, by your father will be won.
His choice is certain, and his noble spirit
45   Can have no fear of any rival merit.
Since his exploits have been so far outstanding
The King can find no other claim demanding.
Rodrigo, it seems, has gained his father's aid
To ask your hand after the choice is made.
50   You must agree that all things seem to bring
The joy which promises love's wedding ring.

CHIMENA.
    For some dim reason, my distrusting heart
    Accepts no happiness and beats apart
    In fear. Time, suddenly, today, tomorrow,
55   Can change the greatest joy to darkest sorrow.

ELVIRA.
    Soon your silly, childish fears will mend.

CHIMENA.
    Well, come what may, let us await the end.

[Exeunt]

SCENE 2

[*The Infanta's house*]
[*Enter The Infanta, Leonora, a Page*]

THE INFANTA, *to the Page.*
    Go, tell Chimena, I dislike delay.
    She waits too long in seeing me today.
    Let her know she hurts me, acting this part.

Exit the Page.

LEONORA.
    Daily, this strange desire moves in your heart,
    Madam; you call her here with the demand   5
    To question her about Rodrigo's hand.

THE INFANTA.
    I have my valid reasons. It is my fault
    Chimena's spirit flew into this vault
    Of love for Rodrigo. I gave him to her.
    It was my will that furnished them the spur,   10
    And now my conscience thinks: Who locks love's chains
    Must spare no effort to release love's pains.

LEONORA.
    But, Madam, as they seek love's richest treasure,
    You watch them meet with sorrow and displeasure.
    Why should their love, which fills them with such gladness,   15
    Cause in your noble heart this clinging sadness?
    Why should the happiness with which they meet

Bring grief that twists their love into deceit?
But I am indiscreet and should not ask.

THE INFANTA.

20 My sorry would rage higher behind the mask
Of secrecy. If I tell of my soul,
You'll see how love plays a cruel tyrant's role.
This youth, this lover whom I gave away,
Is still my love.

LEONORA.

                    For love you still pray?

THE INFANTA.

25 If you placed your soft hand upon my heart,
It would confess by its impulsive start
How much I love him.

LEONORA.

                    Madam, please excuse me
If I think this is madness that I see.
Can a great lady so forget her place

30 And love a cavalier to her disgrace?
What would the King proclaim? Or proud Castile?
You have not thought how your father would feel?

THE INFANTA.

I know too well, that if my rank were stained
By love, it would be just if death had reigned;

35 For noble love commands the bloodless fact
Of title joining title as love's act.
But if my passion only sought a ruse,
A thousand legends would serve for excuse.
Yet honor has the strength still to suppress

40 My strong desire, however hard the stress.
I must recall I am a proud King's daughter
And history must say that great kings sought her.
When I did find my heart had no defense,
I cast off love so warm and so intense.

45 Instead, I placed Chimena in this net
Of love for Rodrigo, to ease my debt.
Can you still wonder why I must await
Impatiently, their marriage as my fate?
You see the way to death my peace has led;

50 Love lives by hope and dies when hope is dead.
Its fire fades from lack of nourishment;
Despite all of the pain I have been sent,
Although this marriage will bring bitter bane
To hope, it set my spirit free again.

55 Till then my anguish has no boundary;
In dream, Rodrigo hovers close to me.
My will commands I lose, but how to lose?
That's my secret torment: I cannot choose.
With shame I feel my love invite his kiss

60 And know that all his love can bring no bliss.
My soul must writhe, divided, torn apart,
Into a broken will and a lost heart.
This marriage is death to me! I must fear it,
Yet desire it, though this goal can only split

65 My life apart; whichever hope may win—

Love or honor—the end is death or sin.

LEONORA.

Madam, what can I say to answer you?
I cannot help, although I would be true.
You've won my pity for your sorry plight.

70 Since with deep grief your spirit must in flight
Depart from love, you will conquer desire
And find in time the peace which calms love's fire.
Have faith in God; His justice is too great
To make you suffer always from this fate.

THE INFANTA.

75 My only hope lies in the loss of hope.

The Page returns.

PAGE.

Chimena's here . . .

THE INFANTA.

                    Ask her to wait. For peace I grope.

Exit the Page.

LEONORA.

Madam, why brood alone in fantasy?

THE INFANTA.

Go, give me a time of rest to steady
Myself. I'll come as soon as I am ready.

                                        [*Exit Leonora*]

SCENE 3

[*The same*]

THE INFANTA, *alone.*

Oh God, to whom we kneel in prayer and
    sing
With love, spare me from this endless suffering.
Grant honor to me and restore my peace
That giving bliss, my pain may find release.

5 For this wedding now, three hearts are praying.
Bring it to pass and keep my heart from straying!
Marriage, that will make these lovers one
Will break my chains, however much it stun.
I wait too long; Chimena I must see

10 And ease my pain by their new love's decree.

                                        [*Exit*]

SCENE 4

[*In front of the Palace.*]
[*Enter The Count, Don Diego*]

THE COUNT.

You've won what I desired. The King's great hand
Has conferred on you the honor of the land.

You are to teach the young Prince of Castile.
DON DIEGO.
    This adds a luster to my family seal;
5   It proves to all the justice of our King
    And the reward old services can bring.
THE COUNT.
    However great our kings may be, their flaws
    Are like our own and errors mark their laws.
    This choice proves to each member of the court
10   That present services gain ill report.
DON DIEGO.
    Let us say nothing more to vex your mind
    About his choice. Because he is so kind
    He may have chosen me, not just for merit.
    But still we owe too much respect to sit
15   In judgment on the King who is supreme;
    So, please I pray you add another theme:
    You have a daughter, I an only son.
    Give your permission now to make them one
    In marriage, and, suddenly, there'll be no flaw
20   To friendship. My son will be your son-in-law.
THE COUNT.
    Your son should dream of a loftier aim,
    And this new honor given to your claim
    Should build his hopes and cause his heart to swell.
    Perform your duties, Sir. Instruct the Prince well.
25   Teach him how a province should be ruled,
    How fear is law before his word has cooled;
    To leave bad men afraid; gain love from good.
    Then add a captain's god-like virtues, whose flood
    Of heavy duties must endure all hardships:
30   Fight to triumph; face pain with smiling lips;
    Pass lengthy days and nights on horseback; rattle
    Fully armed in sleep; scale walls in battle
    That victory is his and his alone!
    Teach him by acts, and make his pride like stone.
DON DIEGO.
35   Despite your jealousy, I shall not need
    To teach him what I've learned, and let him read
    The history of my old life. There, long
    Succession of heroic deeds are strong,
    Bright proofs of how to build an army's fame,
40   Attack a fortress, win a lasting name.
THE COUNT.
    Living examples furnish better guides.
    From musty books, princes learn false prides,
    And, to be blunt, what has your ancient praise
    To equal one of my heroic days?
45   I hold the power, for your strength is poor,
    And my strong arm keeps this kingdom secure
    My sword subdues Granada; Aragon quails,
    My fame is in Castile's proudest tales.
    Without me you would soon obey the cause
50   Of foreign kings who would create your laws.
    Each moment of each day adds to my glory,

Praise leads to praise and further victory.
If the good Prince rode with me into battle,
Protected by my arm, he'd prove his mettle,
And learn to conquer from my own example.   55
Soon, his nature's grace would find an ample
Realm . . .
DON DIEGO.
    I know. I saw you fight under me.
    You've served the King well—thus far I'll agree.
    Now that old age fills up my veins with ice
    The King favors your courage and advice.   60
    Enough said. It is not difficult to see
    That you're today what I was formerly.
    However, this honor shows one strong change;
    The King seeks to reward my life's rich range.
THE COUNT.
    You have stolen the honor I deserved!   65
DON DIEGO.
    The King's true faith in me has never swerved.
THE COUNT.
    My loyal deeds have also won his grace.
DON DIEGO.
    Denial is not grace in your vain case.
THE COUNT.
    Your old, sly courtier's tricks won you the post!
DON DIEGO.
    You lie! My reputation counted most.   70
THE COUNT.
    You mean the King showed his respect for age.
DON DIEGO.
    My courage was the King's primary gauge.
THE COUNT.
    Then he should have favored me with his grace.
DON DIEGO.
    Who cannot win, does not deserve the place.
THE COUNT.
    I not deserve it?   75
DON DIEGO.
            No!
THE COUNT.
            Your impudence,
    You rash old man, deserves just recompense!

He slaps Don Diego across the face.

DON DIEGO, *drawing his sword.*
    Draw and kill me after this cold shame,
    The first disgrace that ever marked my name.
THE COUNT.
    Weak as you are, can you fight with a boast?

He disarms Don Diego.

DON DIEGO.
    Oh God! My strength's gone when I need it most.   80

THE COUNT.

    Your sword is mine, but you might be too vain
    If I kept it; false pride whirls in your brain.

He throws the sword contemptuously at the feet of Don Diego.

    Good-by. Have the Prince read your true story
    For his instruction. Though he cheer your glory,
85   This punishment of aged insolence
    Should ornament your words with glittering sense.

                             [*Exit*]

SCENE 5

[*The same*]

DON DIEGO, *alone*.

    What senseless fury and impotent rage
    One feels at the hard weakness of old age!
    Have I lived but to suffer this disgrace?
    What does it mean, my courtier's rich lace,
5   All the laurels of war, when in one day
    Reputation fades and withers away?
    Look at my arm, once the wonder of Spain,
    Which saved the throne from all the world's disdain;
    More than the throne, my country did redeem.
10   Why must my strength fail and a vision seem?
    This is a cruel reminder of my deeds.
    The flower of my name withers to weeds;
    And the King's award, fatal to happiness
    Because I lost honor in time of stress.
15   Must I watch the Count triumph again
    And die without revenge, with this dark stain?
    No, Count, you be the tutor of my Prince;
    Not one who was humiliated since
    He won the place. No shame has this office known,
20   And I stand here unworthy and alone.

He picks up his sword.

    This sword, that bravely hewed out all my fame,
    Is now in my old age a useless claim,
    A sword that can my weakness never cure,
    Lost symbol of a time when strength was pure.
25   My son is coming. Revenge demands
    That I give you into his youthful hands.

SCENE 6

[*The same*]
[*Enter Don Rodrigo*]

DON DIEGO

    My son, have you courage?

RODRIGO.

                    No man should doubt it.

    My father's call will not find me without it.

DON DIEGO.

    I like your answer and the flame of truth
    Which echoes the lost spirit of my youth.
    It quickens me and gives me cause to hope   5
    You shall avenge honor for which I grope.
    You must avenge me.

RODRIGO.

                 For what shame?

DON DIEGO.

                        For cruelty
    To an old man's reputation. He slapped me;
    A slap! I tell you that I wished to kill
    Him, but my weak arm betrayed my will.   10
    This sword, which I can never use again,
    I give to you to still my vengeful brain.
    Against his arrogance, your courage prove.
    For only blood can this dark act remove.
    Kill him or go and die yourself. I know   15
    He is an enemy whose mind will glow
    With shrewdness. I've seen him covered with dust
    And blood, holding an army at sword's thrust,
    And break a hundred squadrons in attack.
    No. Courage is a trait he'll never lack.   20
    You must be careful. More than his bravery,
    He is . . .

RODRIGO.

          Why are you silent? Who is he?

DON DIEGO.

    Chimena's father.

RODRIGO.

               Her father!

DON DIEGO.

                    Can your youthful song
    Of love be greater to you than a wrong?
    Love the offender, the offense is worse.   25
    You've heard my wrong. Its cure is now your curse.
    Enough of this. Avenge yourself and me;
    Remember your father was and is the key
    To this dark paradox that guides your fate.
    I go. Make sure your vengeance is not late.   30

                             [*Exit*]

SCENE 7

[*The same*]

RODRIGO, *alone*.

                  Into my heart
    Cuts the cold steel of a dagger's thrust;
    I must avenge a cause that is so just.
    A net of fate twists me away from love;
    I stand, my heart confused and torn,   5

My soul on fire.
So near at last to find love's healing sense;
              Oh God, to learn
My father was insulted, and the offense
Done by her father . . . Where shall I turn?

              In this storm,
My love is mocked whichever way I move.
10 If I avenge my father, I kill my love;
Honor compels me, yet love holds my arm.
If I marry her, all men will scorn me
              For this love.
There's evil in each choice that must be made.
              Oh God, unjust!
How can I leave an insult unrepaid?
15 How kill Chimena's father? Yet I must.

              Father, mistress,
My pleasures dead or glory in the tomb,
Soft arms of love or duty that is doom;
One leaves me wretched and the other worthless.

He stares at his sword.

And you, my sword, you would betray my heart
20   With your sharp point;
Bright foe of all my dreams of ecstasy,
              Cause of my pain!
Were you meant to avenge my ancestry,
Or given me my only love to stain?

25   To drink death's chalice?
I owe mistress and father equal debt;
Without revenge with scorn I am beset,
While this dark deed of duty wins her malice.
Oh my sweet love, I must your name deface,
30   Or honor lose.
My anguish grows. My search must end in failure,
              Rising grief.
My soul accepts my death as the one cure,
For death will bring Chimena's pain relief.

              Yet die without revenge,
35 To turn a family's fame to infamy,
Leaving all Spain to mock my memory
As if I were a coward who must cringe;
All this to gain a love I know so well
              Forever doomed.
Listen no more to this cruel devil's thought
              Of love star-crossed.
40 Come, sword, the goal of honor must be sought;
Whatever comes, Chimena's love is lost.

              Love blinded me.
My father's cause is just, a loyal claim.
Although by sword or grief I die, the same
Blood which he gave, I'll give in purity.
45 How could a longing dream of love's lost grave

              Prevent my fate?
Dispel these hopeless, lovesick dreams of pity,
              That honor stain;
This foul slap revealed no charity,
And love is lost in one short night of pain.

              [*Exit*]

ACT II

SCENE 1

[*A room in the Palace.*]
[*Enter Don Arias, the Count*]

THE COUNT.
    Agreed. This quarrel rose with too great heat,
    Sparked by a word which made us indiscreet.
    But the deed is done. There is no remedy.
DON ARIAS.
    Your pride must yield to your great King's decree.
    For he is deeply moved, and in this cause   5
    Will use against you his vast power of laws.
    You have no just defense with which to plead.
    The gross act and the victim's age, all lead
    To your indebtedness, to your submission
    Greater than a payment of contrition.   10
THE COUNT.
    The King may turn my life as he pleases.
DON ARIAS.
    After this deed, your sinful pride increases.
    The King still loves you. Appease his rage today.
    When he says, *My desire,* you disobey?
THE COUNT.
    To keep all that I value in this time,   15
    A disobedience can't be a crime;
    Yet, were it such, my deeds would overwhelm
    A minor act of shame unto the realm.
DON ARIAS.
    However great the glory of one's acts,
    The King is not indebted to such facts.   20
    You flatter pride you've gained from war's rich booty,
    But service to the King is your one duty.
    You'll ruin yourself with this stubbornness.
THE COUNT.
    Not yet are you a prophet of success.   25
DON ARIAS.
    You should consent, and fear the King's stern
        power.
THE COUNT.
    I shall outlive the displeasure of the hour.
    Let the whole state be armed when judgment calls.
    If I should perish, then the kingdom falls.
DON ARIAS.
    Do you then fear so little the King's might?

THE COUNT.
30 Without me his scepter will fall from light.
 He knows how his fortune would fade, sink down;
 My head in falling would strike off his crown.
DON ARIAS.
 I beg you by your reason be guided.
 Take counsel.
THE COUNT.
    It is no use. I have decided.
DON ARIAS.
35 What shall I tell the King? I must report.
THE COUNT.
 Say I'll not plead dishonor to the court.
DON ARIAS.
 A King's great will is always absolute.
THE COUNT.
 I cannot change. I, too, am resolute.
DON ARIAS.
 Farewell, then. I came to you in vain. Your path,
40 Though laurel-strewn, awaits the lightning's wrath.
THE COUNT.
 I shall not fear.
DON ARIAS.
    The end will be the same.
THE COUNT.
 Then it shall win Don Diego's acclaim.

       [*Exit Don Arias*]

He is now alone.

 He who fears not death can fear no threats.
 My heart can bear the worst that life begets.
45 Without the King, I'll live in misery,
 But life without honor is death to me.

SCENE 2

[*The same*]
[*Enter Rodrigo*]

RODRIGO.
 Count, a word.
THE COUNT.
    Speak!
RODRIGO.
      First, resolve my doubt.
 You know Don Diego?
THE COUNT.
    Yes.
RODRIGO.
      Do not speak out
 So proudly. Listen to me. Is it true
 That virtue did this old man's life imbue?

THE COUNT.
 Perhaps.   5
RODRIGO.
    In my presence, can you foresee
 My father's vengeance?
THE COUNT.
      Why say this to me?
RODRIGO.
 My challenge to a duel should make it plain.
THE COUNT.
 What young presumption!
RODRIGO.
      You speak with the disdain
 Of pride; I am young, but more than my few years
 I have the courage of a race of peers.   10
THE COUNT.
 You dare to challenge me? Your words are grand,
 But have you held a sword within your hand?
RODRIGO.
 Some men don't require reputation's yoke.
 Their first sword's thrust can be the final stroke.
THE COUNT.
 Do you know who I am?   15
RODRIGO.
      I do not shun
 Your skill; I know your reputation.
 The honors you've received for victories
 Would seem to spell my death in their decrees,
 But I'll attack the symbol of your arm
 With courage; faith may save me from great harm. 20
 A father's honor should be a strong shield.
 Unconquered still, you can be made to yield.
THE COUNT.
 Your fearless heart rings through these words you say.
 My eyes have watched you grow from day to day.
 I've seen the future hero of Castile.   25
 I thought Chimena's marriage soon would seal
 This hope. I know your love, and I admire
 The honor which you've shown as your desire.
 Love hasn't weakened you with hesitation
 And you are richer in my estimation.   30
 I wished a soldier for my son-in-law;
 It pleases me my choice now shows no flaw.
 But you arouse my love for open truth.
 While I admire courage, I pity youth.
 Don't let your first duel become your last. 35
 Release me from this most unequal test.
 Though I should win, no honor would then follow.
 To conquer without peril is most hollow.
 That I did kill with ease, men would believe,
 And there would only be your death to grieve. 40
RODRIGO.
 Your arrogance must lead to further strife.

You take my honor and yet fear my life?
THE COUNT.
    Leave this room.
RODRIGO.
                When you will leave with me.
THE COUNT.
    Are you so tired of life?
RODRIGO.
                        Or you to die?
45 THE COUNT.
    Come, then. You do your duty. A son is base
    Who views in silence his proud sire's disgrace.

                                        [*Exeunt*]

SCENE 3

[*The Infanta's room.*]
[*Enter the Infanta, Chimena, Leonora*]

THE INFANTA.
    Chimena, do not grieve so much. Borrow
    Strength to bear the burden of your sorrow.
    After this transient storm a calm will come.
    Only a small cloud makes your bliss seem numb
5   And you shall lose nothing though hope's deferred.
CHIMENA.
    I dare not hope. My heart with pain is stirred.
    Upon a placid sea, a smiling face,
    This storm brings shipwreck with too swift a pace.
    Before I set my sales, my journey's done.
10 I loved, was loved, our fathers thought as one,
    And then, as I told you these joyful tidings,
    Disaster sprang from their accursed chidings,
    And changed my hope of love that seemed so near
    To dreams of woe which I must always fear.
15 Insane folly, wretched, vain ambition,
    Tyrants that bring the noblest to perdition,
    When pride must cause desire to be lost
    How many sighs and tears shall mark the cost.
THE INFANTA.
    You are too sure this quarrel merits fear.
20 Born quickly, it will quickly disappear.
    Too many talk of it; it must be mended.
    The King has ordered that it be so ended,
    And you know my affection for your right
    Will do all that it can to ease your plight.
CHIMENA.
25 Too late for reconciliation now.
    Insults defeat what reason should avow.
    The King's authority will be in vain;
    Though wounds are healed, the anguish shall remain.
    This hate that's locked by force within the heart
30 Burns secretly with a cold, searing art.

THE INFANTA.
    When you are married to Rodrigo, then must
    Your father's hatred wither into dust;
    And we shall see love silence all discord
    When happiness of marriage is your lord.
CHIMENA.
    I cannot hope although that's my desire.   35
    Don Diego is too proud; I know my sire.
    I try to staunch my tears, but I must weep.
    The past is torment; the future brings no sleep.
THE INFANTA.
    What do you fear? An old man's feeble arm?
CHIMENA.
    Rodrigo's courage.   40
THE INFANTA.
    He is too young to harm.
CHIMENA.
    Brave men can be heroes in their first duel.
THE INFANTA.
    You have no cause to think he'd be so cruel.
    He is too much in love to do this deed.
    A word from you to halt is all you need.
CHIMENA.
    If he did not obey, what fatal whim!   45
    Yet if he yields, what would men think of him?
    Born great, he cannot suffer such outrage.
    If he does yield to love, or to old age,
    I'll be ashamed by his so weak compliance
    Or crushed by love refusing our alliance.   50
THE INFANTA.
    Chimena, in your soul, whatever cost,
    The lasting truth of love cannot be lost.
    What if I stay your fears of this sad feud,
    Command him into prison to ease your mood,
    And thus deny all action to his threat?   55
    Would your proud, loving heart be in my debt?
CHIMENA.
    Oh, Madam, then I would be free from fear.

SCENE 4

[*The same*]
[*Enter the Page*]

THE INFANTA.
    Page, summon Rodrigo. Go, bring him here.
PAGE.
    He and the Count . . .
CHIMENA.
                        Oh, God, I am bereft!
THE INFANTA, *to the Page*.
    What did you see?
PAGE.
                    I saw them as they left.

CHIMENA.
  Alone?
PAGE.
        Alone, and deep in argument.
CHIMENA.
5   They fight! All words are now a sad lament.
  Madam, forgive my haste, but I must go.

                    [*Exeunt Page and Chimena*]

SCENE 5

[*The same*]
[*Enter The Infanta, Leonora*]

THE INFANTA.
  Alas! My spirit bends like a taut bow.
  I mourn her loss, but love enraptures me.
  Desire tears me; gone is tranquility.
  The fate that is to part them now, again
5   Renews my desperate longing and my pain.
  Their separation causes me to mourn,
  But in my heart an ecstasy is born.
LEONORA.
  How can the noble virtue of your soul
  So swiftly founder on this darkened shoal?
THE INFANTA.
10   Not dark, but bright, the song my heart must sing;
  It makes the laws to which I turn and cling.
  Respect it, as it is a love I cherish.
  Though honor fights, I cannot see it perish,
  And caught in hope that is but vain and senseless,
15   My heart in search of his love is defenseless.
LEONORA.
  Is your great courage lost that grew the stronger?
  Does reason guide and rule your mind no longer?
THE INFANTA.
  How reason's formal voice does fade, grow faint,
  When heart's inflamed with this sweet poison's taint;
20   The patient loves the painful malady
  And lives without a hope for remedy.
LEONORA.
  Your illness lures you with romantic dreams.
  Rodrigo's lost in such proud, lovesick schemes.
THE INFANTA.
  Too well I know this, but if pride should yield,
25   See how love soothes the heart it seeks to shield.
  If now Rodrigo wins this duel of fate—
  If he defeats a fame so great—
  I shall feel free to love him without shame.
  Think of him with this conquest to his name!
30   I dare imagine he will then be free
  To conquer kingdoms, rule them by decree.
  My love tells me I shall see him with time
  The King of all Granada in his prime.

  The vanquished Moors will bow to him in terror,
  Proud Aragon welcome its conqueror,   35
  And Portugal will fall; across the sea
  His deeds will bear him to his destiny:
  The blood of Africans will mark his laurels;
  Since famous captains make their code of morals,
  He'll rank with heroes of most famous story   40
  And in his love I'll find my lasting glory.
LEONORA.
  Madam, your dream of conquests to be won
  Depends upon a duel that's not begun.
THE INFANTA.
  Rodrigo's with the Count, his father's foe.
  They left together. Is there more to know?   45
LEONORA.
  If you insist, I'll grant that they will fight.
  But is his love the same that blinds your sight?
THE INFANTA.
  Bear with me. I am mad; my dream's a snare.
  What evil does my love for him prepare?
  Come to my chamber; console me with kindness.   50
  Do not forsake me in my secret blindness.

                              [*Exeunt*]

SCENE 6

[*The Court*]
[*Enter The King, Don Arias, Don Sancho*]

THE KING.
  Is this Count in his pride bereft of sense?
  Does he expect pardon for his offense?
DON ARIAS.
  I talked to him at length, Sire. He is blind.
  Nothing I said could change his stubborn mind.
THE KING.
  Just Heaven, is this respect for my decrees?   5
  Does he then take so little care to please?
  By this insult what does he think to gain?
  In my own court, he seeks to mock my reign.
  No matter how brave, or how great his role,
  I have the means to tame his haughty soul.   10
  Were he the God of Battle here today
  He should learn what it means to disobey.
  He seeks the insolence he has displayed.
  I thought I might by leniency be swayed,
  But since he casts off mercy, from this hour   15
  I order him imprisoned by my power.
DON SANCHO.
  A little time might soothe his raging spurt
  Of temper. He is still seething from his hurt.
  You know, Sire, such a spirit cannot yield
  And wears its first fierce anger like a shield.   20
  He knows his wrong, but caught in this vault

Of rage, his soul cannot confess his fault.

THE KING.

    Hold your peace, Don Sancho, for you should know
    That he who shields the guilty is my foe.

DON SANCHO.

25   I will obey. But, in your gracious way
    Permit me just one word . . .

THE KING.

                     What is there to say?

DON SANCHO.

    Who is accustomed to the noblest deeds
    Cannot abase himself before your needs.
    Apologies to him are only masks of shame,
30   And this prevents him from accepting blame.
    As your subject, he's troubled by his part,
    But would obey if he had weaker heart.
    Command his strength, as proved in valiant action,
    To heal this deed; he'll give full satisfaction.
35   Before then, who dares challenge him to fight,
    I'll answer till the Count speaks for his right.

THE KING.

    You lack respect to me; but you are young
    And I forgive your youthful, zealous tongue.
    To rule his subjects with consummate care
40   A King must never let his temper flare.
    I must respect their lives, conserving them
    As hand is servant of the body's stem.
    My reason's not the same to which you cling.
    You speak as soldier, but I act as King.
45   Whatever you may dare think of his plea,
    He loses nothing in obeying me.
    My crown is tarnished by the act he's done.
    He scorned my choice for tutor of my son.
    To strike Don Diego has slandered me,
50   Challenged both my command and dignity.
    No more of this . . . Ten vessels have been seen,
    Flying the flag of our enemy's spleen.
    They've sailed up where the river starts to swell.

DON ARIAS.

    By force the Moors have learned to know you well.
55   You've conquered them so often, they fear the wing
    Of hope; they dare not fight so great a King.

THE KING.

    They'll never see without a jealous frown
    Bright Andalusia ruled by my crown.
    This lovely land, which, once, they did possess.
60   They hope again, from envy, to caress.
    That is the reason why I did decide
    My throne should rise here in Seville's rich pride:
    To watch the Moors closely, and thus to break
    Whatever follies they might undertake.

DON ARIAS.

65   At cost of the most valiant soldiers' lives,
    your presence takes the honey from their hives.

    You've nothing to fear.

THE KING.

                  Only some negligence.
    Disaster's bred when courage conquers sense.
    You know how easily, since they are near,
    The Moors, with changing tide, could sail here.   70
    Yet I'd be guilty of a fatal error
    If I aroused my people with this terror.
    The fear that would be caused by such alarm
    At night would pierce the city with great harm.
    Double the guards upon the walls instead.   75
    Enough for now.

                  [Exit Don Arias, Enter Don Alonso]

SCENE 7

[The same]

DON ALONSO.

                Sire, the Count is dead.
    Rodrigo has revenged his father's wrong.

THE KING.

    I feared his hope for vengeance would be strong
    After this deed, and hoped for God's relief.

DON ALONSO.

    Chimena's coming, seized with bitter grief.   5
    Through tears, for justice she will seek to plead.

THE KING.

    Although I pity her cause in this deed,
    The Count's rash act appears to have deserved
    The punishment with which he has been served.
    And yet, however just his sudden fate,   10
    I must regret his loss, who was so great.
    After such lengthy service to my crown,
    His blood for me a thousand times poured down,
    Although his arrogance was plain to see,
    His sudden death causes me injury.   15

SCENE 8

[The same]
[Enter Don Diego, Don Arias, Chimena]

CHIMENA.

    Sire, I plead for justice!

DON DIEGO.

                  No, hear my pleas!

CHIMENA.

    I kneel at your feet.

DON DIEGO.

                I clasp your knees!

CHIMENA.

    I beg for justice.

DON DIEGO.

              Please hear my defense.

CHIMENA.

    Punish the crime of this youth's insolence.

5   He struck down the support of your proud throne;

    He killed my father.

DON DIEGO.

              He avenged his own.

CHIMENA.

    Justice is owed to us when we appeal.

DON DIEGO.

    A just revenge is what she does conceal.

THE KING.

    Rise, both of you; and speak to me with calm.

10   Chimena, I share your sorrow. With qualm

    No less than yours, my heart must now decree.

To Don Diego.

    You shall speak later. Do not halt her plea.

CHIMENA.

    My father, Sire, is dead. No one can hide

    The stream of blood that gushed from his torn side;

15   That blood which has so often saved your walls;

    That blood which fought for you at battle's calls;

    That blood which smoked with anger as it flowed

    Because on someone else than you bestowed;

    That blood which many dangers could not thwart,

20   Rodrigo spilled within your sacred court.

    Trembling and pale I ran to that grim place.

    I found him dead. Avenge, Sire, this disgrace.

    I cannot speak of it, but only wail.

    My tears can better tell this bitter tale.

THE KING.

25   Have courage, child, for since your father's dead,

    Your King will serve as father in his stead.

CHIMENA.

    Such honor cannot cure my misery.

    My father's killed and by his enemy.

    His wound lay open and to it I'm bound;

30   His blood wrote out my duty on the ground;

    All of his greatness fallen in the dust

    Called for revenge through that wound's fatal crust,

    And to be heard by you, most just of kings,

    My voice through that sad, twisted mouth now rings.

35   Sire, do not let the glory of your reign

    Be tarnished with the license of this stain,

    Exposing your best warriors' defense

    To thrusts of every young man's insolence.

    Let not this youth defame their glory's plea,

40   Bathe in their blood, and mock their memory.

    If this brave warrior gains no reward,

    Then he who serves you will lay down his sword.

    Since my father is dead, I demand vengeance

    For your sake, Sire, not for my allegiance.

    Your loss is great when such a man is killed.   45

    You must rule that Rodrigo's death is willed:

    A sacrifice, not mine, Your Majesty,

    But yours, that all your subjects justice see;

    A sacrifice to honor all your realm,

    To show that madness does not guide our helm.   50

THE KING.

    Don Diego, answer her.

DON DIEGO.

              How free from strife,

    When strength is gone, is he who loses life!

    Old age prepares a trap of pain and hate

    For noble-minded men who live too late.

    I, whose long labors have won me acclaim,   55

    Whom victory has followed with some fame,

    Must see myself now doomed by sagging age,

    Insulted, vanquished by my body's cage.

    What neither combat, lengthy siege, ambush,

    Nor jealous rivals, what no foe could crush,   60

    Not even Aragon, this Count has done,

    Done in your court; before your throne he's won

    Against your choice, with pride in his rash scorn,

    Thus leaving me in feeble age forlorn.

    Sire, beneath my helmet my hair's turned white;   65

    This blood, so often shed to serve your light—

    This arm, which once your enemies did fear—

    Would have fallen, been lost, dishonored here

    To die, had I not had a son to cling

    To honor for his country and his King!   70

    He lent his youth to me; killed for my name,

    My dignity, to wash away my shame.

    To show such courage as in him was pent,

    If to avenge a slap brings punishment,

    On me alone should fall the storm of law.   75

    Punish the head whose arm commits some flaw.

    Whether or not his action has done harm,

    I am the head, Sire; he is but the arm.

    Chimena cries that her father is dead.

    Had I the strength, for vengeance I'd have bled   80

    To sacrifice my life which age has bowed,

    And spare my son for service to you vowed.

    Let my blood flow to satisfy her pain.

    I won't resist; I will accept its stain,

    And far from arguing this stern decree,   85

    I'll die possessing honor, silently.

THE KING.

    This matter needs a long deliberation

    In full council with due consideration.

    Don Sancho, guide Chimena home to rest.

    Don Diego, here will be my guest.   90

    While we decide. Go, fetch his son.

To Chimena.

                  Justice I'll give.

CHIMENA.

    His death is just, or justice cannot live.

THE KING.

    Go, rest, my child, to calm your bitter grief.

CHIMENA.

    Rest brings a greater anguish, not relief.

                                             [Exeunt]

ACT III

SCENE 1

[Chimena's house]
[Enter Rodrigo, Elvira]

ELVIRA.

    Rodrigo, why are you here? What have you done?

RODRIGO.

    I follow my fate as a cursèd son.

ELVIRA.

    What vanity is yours, this prideful scorning
    Of a stricken house you've filled with mourning.
5   Will you challenge the Count's white, ghostly face?
    Did you not kill him?

RODRIGO.

                  His life was my disgrace.
    My honor forced my hand to do this deed.

ELVIRA.

    But safety in your victim's house to plead.
    What murderer could find asylum there?

RODRIGO.

10   I give myself into my judge's care.
    Do not look at me in astonishment.
    I search for death, and death for me has sent.
    My judge is my Chimena, my belovèd.
    My death shall free her since we cannot wed,
15   And I have come to beg one last request:
    Death from her lips and hand will bring me rest.

ELVIRA.

    No! Flee her sight, flee from her violent hand.
    Spare her the anguish of your cruel demand.
    Do not add to her present suffering
20   With all this further grief you seem to bring.

RODRIGO.

    My dearest love whom I have deeply wronged
    Must seek to punish me if life's prolonged.
    I shall exchange a hundred deaths for peace,
    If she can speed my search for death's release.

ELVIRA.

25   Crushed with her grief, Chimena's gone to plead
    Her cause. She is not unaccompanied.
    Rodrigo, you must flee and spare my fear.
    What would men think if they should find you here?

You'd seek the cry of some false slanderer
That she did hide her father's murderer?   30
Soon she'll return. You must protect her pride.
I see her! She is coming. You must hide.

[Rodrigo hides]

SCENE 2

[The same]
[Enter Don Sancho, Chimena]

DON SANCHO.

    Yes, Madam, blood is sacrificed for blood;
    Your anger and distress a daughter's flood.
    I shall not seek by cunning words or art
    To soothe your anger and console your heart;
    But if I can serve what you must now decree,   5
    Command my sword to punish him who's free.
    Command my love with vengeance to be troubled;
    In this command my arm's strength will be doubled.

CHIMENA.

    How miserable I am!

DON SANCHO.

                  Accept my sword.

CHIMENA.

    I'd wrong the King who promised just reward.   10

DON SANCHO.

    You know how justice moves so tediously
    That it gives the criminal a chance to flee.
    Its course is often lost in time.
    Permit my sword to save you from this crime.
    That way is certain, justice to assure.   15

CHIMENA.

    This is the last resort. If you must cure
    My woe; if that time comes, and you still pity,
    You may defend my cause before this city.

DON SANCHO.

    For that one happiness, my soul was sent,
    And with the hope of it I go, content.   20

                                        [Exit]

SCENE 3

[The same]

CHIMENA.

    At last I'm free to show without restraint,
    The burning coldness of my grief's complaint.
    To you I need not mask my piercing sadness,
    My emptiness of heart, the end of gladness.
    My father's dead; it was Rodrigo's sword   5

That cut away his life from which blood poured.
Weep, weep my eyes! My tears to blind and smother!
Half of my youthful life has killed the other,
And for that stroke of death, I'm forced to cry.
10   Vengeance against the love for which I sigh.

ELVIRA.
You must be calm and rest, Madam.

CHIMENA.
                                        What use
Is it to talk of rest in pain's abuse?
How shall my sorrow ever be appeased
If I can't hate the hand that did the deed?
15   What can I hope but torment of the damned
If I avenge, yet love the guilty hand?

ELVIRA.
He killed your father and you love him still?

CHIMENA.
I do. I worship him with all my will.
My passion fights against what I've been taught;
20   My lover in my enemy is caught.
Another duel clashes in my soul;
Rodrigo fights my father for love's goal,
Attacks him, drives him back, defends and yields,
Now weak, now strong, his sword in triumph wields;
25   In this awful war of love and wrath
He wins my heart, but cannot change my path.
Whatever hold my love has over me,
I'll search wherever light of duty be.
Without false step, I'll walk where honor waits.
30   Rodrigo is my love. I mourn the fates.
My heart will not forsake the hope to wed,
But then I see my father lying dead.

ELVIRA.
And you will seek revenge?

CHIMENA.
                                    Oh cruel chase!
Love torn with duty's hate is always base.
35   I pray his death, yet hope my prayer is weak.
My death shall follow his, yet his I seek.

ELVIRA.
Madam, you must renounce so cruel a task.
Your love is warped by this avenging mask.

CHIMENA.
When, almost in my arms, my father dies,
40   Shall I not hear how blood for vengeance cries?
My heart, deceived by love's call which it hears,
Should give my father only useless tears?
Shall I through love my duty betray
And stifle in such shame, honor's proud way?

ELVIRA.
45   Believe me, Madam, none would expect of you
Revenge against a lover who is true,
One whom you love. You've done all that you should.
You know the King must wear the judge's hood.
Be not so adamant in your strange mood.

CHIMENA.
Honor demands that vengeance be pursued.   50
However love may blind us with desire,
Excuse is shameful to a soul of fire.

ELVIRA.
But you love him. You cannot wish him harm.

CHIMENA.
That's true.

ELVIRA.
                    Then why create this great alarm?

CHIMENA.
To save my honor from God's savage whim,   55
I'll hunt him to his death, die after him!

SCENE 4

[*The same*]
[*Enter Rodrigo*]

RODRIGO.
Take my life now, and grant to us death's grace,
To save you from the anguish of this chase.

CHIMENA.
Elvira, where are we? Betrayed by spies?
Rodrigo in my house, burning my eyes!

RODRIGO.
Do not spare me. I won't resist. Enjoy   5
The sweetness of my death, revenge's toy.

CHIMENA.
Alas.

RODRIGO.
        Listen to me.

CHIMENA.
                        No.

RODRIGO.
                            Please . . .

CHIMENA.
                                        Let me die.

RODRIGO.
Grant me a word. You know I shall not lie.

She turns away.

Then speak to me with my despairing sword.

He draws his sword and she recoils from it.

CHIMENA.
My father's blood like some dumb beast you've gored!   10

RODRIGO.
Chimena.

CHIMENA.
            Take that devil's blade away,
Flashing your bloody crime in sunlit day.

RODRIGO.
No, look at it and kill me with your hate.
Let it increase your wrath and be your fate.

CHIMENA.
15   It's stained with my father's blood.
RODRIGO.

                                        Plunge it in mine
      And see how it will lose its red design.
CHIMENA.
      How cruel is God, in one short day we die:
      My father with a sword, his daughter by
      It's sight. Take it away. I cannot stare;
20   You wish to speak and kill me with its glare.
RODRIGO, *sheathing the sword.*
      I will do as you wish, but I still hope
      For mercy. My lost life can only grope
      Through darkness. And yet you must never think
      Because I love you that I hate this link
25   With honor. An impossible, gross act
      Dishonored my father and left me racked
      With shame. You know what such a brutal slap
      Does to an old man's pride. This sprung the trap
      Of fate in which we're caught. How could I rest
30   When part of that insult struck at my breast?
      I sought your father then. I could not deny
      My duty to avenge my father's cry.
      Through time of torture, I argued the love due
      My father against all of my love for you.
35   Judge love's great power to endure outrage,
      For I still hoped to flee revenge's cage.
      My choice was cold disgrace or loss of love,
      I thought of you as gentle as a dove.
      I told myself I had too hot a temper
40   And your great beauty almost made the slur
      Against me fade away, but then I thought:
      Without honor, how could your love be sought?
      Even though I have a place in your heart,
      Disloyalty would tear our love apart.
45   To listen to love's lure and heed its voice
      Would separate us and condemn your choice.
      I told you this, which I must now repeat,
      Although it tears my heart out with defeat.
      I wronged you greatly, but was forced to act
50   To earn respect. This is the shameful fact.
      To this strange goal of honor I've been true
      And now I've come to pay my debt to you.
      I paid one debt and for that duty's blame,
      I offer you my life as duty's claim;
55   Your father's death reveals a world of vice.
      I cannot save you from a sacrifice.
      With courage you must renounce the man
      Whose pride caused blood to run against love's ban.
CHIMENA.
      Oh Rodrigo, how can I ever blame
60   You as a foe for refusing shame?
      Whichever way my loving grief must flow,
      I hate the evil I have learned to know.
      With this insult to your proud ancestry,

      The call to honor was a simple plea,
      And you have done your duty as you saw,   65
      But doing it, have shown me honor's claw.
      Your desperate courage marks the way for me.
      You avenged your father to pay honor's fee,
      And caught in this trap, I'll do the same—
      Avenge my father and preserve my name.   70
      Still I have found a reason to despair.
      If someone else had robbed me of my care,
      My soul would find its joy in seeing you
      And you would give the comfort I pursue.
      Deep in my grief, I would have found it sweet   75
      For you to kiss my tears and, kissing, meet;
      But I must lose you after losing him.
      Honor's revealed its dark and bloody whim,
      And this duty, which seeks to conquer me,
      Bids me kill you to end the mystery.   80
      Despite my love, do not expect my grace,
      The force of duty now must line my face.
      Though still our love does plead its youthful cause,
      My strength, like yours, must follow deadly laws.
      By wronging you, you proved to me love's birth,   85
      And, by your death, I must prove my true worth.
RODRIGO.
      You must not bend to my love any longer.
      Honor demands my death. Its law is stronger
      And seeks the sacrifice of love, of pity.
      My death is welcome. I cannot flee this city   90
      To wait in vain for justice that denies
      Your honor, turns our love to mocking lies.
      I shall die happy, dying by your hand.
CHIMENA.
      Please go, I can accuse you where you stand,
      Not in an executioner's black shroud.   95
      "She killed her love!" then men would whisper loud.
      I must attack, you must defend what's true,
      And I must prosecute, not murder you.
RODRIGO.
      Our love must not destroy your strength to kill
      And turn you from fate's deadly, chosen will.   100
      Believe me, dear Chimena, another day
      Of vengeance for your father's not my way.
      My hand alone avenged my father's shame,
      Your hand ought to avenge your father's name.
CHIMENA.
      Why do you cling so cruelly to your point?   105
      Is honor but a balm you can anoint?
      Do not seek to aid me. I am too proud
      To wish praise from the righteous, common crowd.
      I will not sacrifice my father's care
      To your love's urging or your lost despair.   110
RODRIGO.
      It is you who cling to your stubborn course.
      Whatever happens, show me your remorse.
      Kill me for love, if not your father's face,

For pity, if not vengeance, or disgrace.
115   Killed by your love I would be happier dead
       Than with your bitter hate to live instead.
CHIMENA.
       No, please, I do not hate you.
RODRIGO.
                                        But you should.
CHIMENA.
       I cannot.
RODRIGO.
                      You'll hear dark rumors like a hood
       Cover the truth. When men learn of your deed,
120   Their bitter tongues will spread an evil seed,
       But if you kill me, you'll enforce their silence,
       And prove by duty's sense their lies of violence.
CHIMENA.
       The truth shines brighter still if you're not dead;
       Then slander will have no false tongue to spread
125   Its lies to Heaven, but only mourn my woe
       Knowing I seek your death, yet love you so.
       Leave me alone in my greatest sorrow
       And say no more what I must lose tomorrow.
       Hide your departure in shadows of night
130   Or else my honor will not see the light.
       Your presence here would only be a reason
       For idle tongues to gossip in their season.
       Give no one evil cause to blame my virtue.
RODRIGO.
       Oh, let me die!
CHIMENA.
                              Please, go!
RODRIGO.
                                                What will you do?
CHIMENA.
135   Although my love for you forbids my hate
       I must avenge my father's violent fate,
       But I confess that deep within my soul,
       I hope and pray I shall not gain my goal.
RODRIGO.
       Your love is a miracle.
CHIMENA.
                                        Death is near.
RODRIGO.
140   Our fathers caused this curse of pain and fear.
CHIMENA.
       Rodrigo, who could have thought . . . ?
RODRIGO.
                                                        Who could have known?
CHIMENA.
       That happiness so close would turn to stone.
RODRIGO.
       So close; and yet a sudden storm could move
       With fury unforeseen and shatter love.
CHIMENA.
145   Men make their grief.

RODRIGO.
                              Remorse burns like a sore.
CHIMENA.
       Leave now, I cannot listen any more.
RODRIGO.
       Farewell, until your search frees me from dread
       By killing me, living I'll live as dead.
CHIMENA.
       If I should win, I promise you my breath
       Shall cease the first moment after your death.   150
       Farewell, my love. You must not be seen.

                                        Exit Rodrigo.

ELVIRA, coming forward.
       Madam, whatever evil God may mean . . .
CHIMENA.
       Leave me! Do not vex me when my pain is deep.
       I need the silence of the night to weep.

                                        [Exeunt]

SCENE 5

[A public square]
[Enter Don Diego]

DON DIEGO, alone.
       Never can we taste a perfect happiness.
       Our happiest success mingles with sadness.
       Our dream of contentment is always troubled
       By care, like winter fields in shadows stubbled.
       Against my happiness, this shadow nears   5
       To darken joy and threaten me with fears.
       My enemy is dead who outraged me,
       But my son is lost who has avenged me.
       In vain I seek for him to meet this pity
       For an old, broken man who scours the city.   10
       What little strength age leaves me to besmirch,
       I pour out fruitlessly within my search.
       Each hour, each moment caught in this black night,
       I think I shall embrace his shadow's flight;
       My love for him deceived by this false vision   15
       Forms new shadows of fear and cold suspicion.
       I cannot find where my dear son has fled.
       I fear the Count's friends since they know he's dead;
       Their strength and power suddenly has risen.
       Rodrigo may be dead or held in prison.   20

He sees a figure approaching.

       Oh God, does my desire still come to mock,
       Or have You given me this hopeful shock?
       If this is Rodrigo, my prayer's transcended,
       My fear dispelled, and my great sorrow ended.

SCENE 6

[*The same*]
[*Enter Rodrigo*]

DON DIEGO.
God has sent you as an answer to my cry.

RODRIGO.
Alas.

DON DIEGO.
Do not confound my joy with a sigh,
But let me catch my breath that I may praise;
I cannot disavow you in these days.
5 You have inherited courage; your daring
Makes our ancestors live through your bold faring.
From them you come; from me springs your design;
Your sword's first thrust has equaled all of mine,
And with a noble ardor, your bold youth
10 Has claimed renown in this trial of truth.
You are my blessing, the prop of my old age,
Which you have given back to honor's page.
Come, kiss this cheek, and recognize the place
Where fell the slap whose stain you did efface.

RODRIGO.
15 The honor's yours. I could not seek for less
Since I was reared by the conduct you bless.
It was a gift of God, that I defile
My love, and not my father with denial.
But, in your pleasure, please do not be grieved,
20 If by your joy I cannot be decieved.
Let my despair burst form my aching heart
Where this deed's kept it hidden from the start.
I don't repent my service as your son,
But give me back the happiness I won.
25 I armed myself against my love for you
And with one stroke I cut my heart in two.
Speak no consolation. I have lost all.
I repaid my debt, although I fall.

DON DIEGO.
The fruit of victory is your reward.
30 I gave you life, my honor you restored.
And though honor is dearer to me than life,
I owe you more to justify your strife.
But drive this weakness from your mind apart.
Many women will live to soothe your heart.
35 Love is but passing pleasure; honor is grace.

RODRIGO.
What are you saying?

DONDON DIEGO.
Only what you should face.

RODRIGO.
Our sullied honor is avenged by me
And you ask shame of infidelity!
The coward-soldier and the faithless lover
40 Both find an equal shame on them must hover.
Do not insult my strong will to be loyal.

Let me be noble without thoughts that soil.
My love's too strong by you to be undone;
My love still binds though she cannot be won,
And while Chimena I must leave again,   45
The death I seek will soon bring end to pain.

DON DIEGO.
The time has not yet come to walk death's path,
For now your King and country need your wrath.
The fleet we feared has entered this great river
To sack the startled city with death's shiver.   50
The Moors are coming and the tide and night
Will bring them silently within our sight.
The court's confused and people shout alarms;
Their cries are everywhere instead of arms.
In this chaos, it was my fortune going   55
To my house to find some friends, who, knowing
Of my shame, driven on by loyalty,
Had all come there with offers to avenge me.
This you have done, but their swift anger's flood
Will seem nobler stained with Moorish blood.   60
Go march at their head at honor's demand.
They wish you to lead them and to command.
Force this attack of enemies to cease,
And then, if you wish death, find noble peace.
Take up this battle fate weaves on its loom   65
And make the King owe safety to your doom;
Or, for my sake, return with flag on high,
Be not content to serve revenge's eye.
When you subdue the Moor's invading violence,
That act will force Chimena then to silence.   70
If you love her, the way to her again
Is to return as conqueror, with train.
But time's too precious now for us to waste;
My words delay when we require haste.
You'll fight to show the King that though he lost   75
When Count de Gormas died, you're worth the cost!

ACT IV

SCENE 1

[*Chimena's house*]
[*Enter Chimena, Elvira*]

CHIMENA.
Elvira, is this true, the news you bring?

ELVIRA.
It is beyond belief how some men sing
The praise of glorious deeds by this young knight,
And raise them in glad song to Heaven's sight.
The Moors who fought him won a savage death.   5
Swift in attack, their retreat drew swifter breath.
Three hours of battle brought him his reward
And made two kings surrender to his sword.
His courage overcame all obstacles.

CHIMENA.

10   Rodrigo's courage did these miracles?

ELVIRA.

He conquered them; his leadership was wise,
The capture of two kings his greatest prize.

CHIMENA.

Who came and told you these amazing things?

ELVIRA.

Everyone! There is not one who brings

15   A word but praise of him who's made us free,
The guardian angel of our destiny.

CHIMENA.

The King, what does he think of these great deeds?

ELVIRA.

Rodrigo has not seen the King. He pleads
For time, but Don Diego has presented

20   The captive kings in honor of the Cid,
And begged the King to grant his conquering son
A royal pardon for this deed he's done.

CHIMENA.

Was he wounded?

ELVIRA.

I do not know.
Be calm, I fear the paleness that you show.

CHIMENA.

25   It is my wrath that has been made to falter;
Through love for him, my duty seems to alter.
In his glory, his praise, my heart is pent,
My duty hesitates, my pride is rent.
Oh love, be gone, let anger grow in peace.

30   He conquers kings, our love can never cease.
My black raiment of woe is loathsome fee
Caused by his sword's first fatal victory.
Whatever else of him that may be said,
I know that by his hand my father's dead.

35   You who can fill me full with bitterness—
In this veil and crepe, grief's nightly dress
Which he gave to me when he killed my sire—
Uphold my pride against my heart's desire;
And when my love becomes too strong in me,

40   Speak to my soul of my sad destiny;
To seek love's death and die in maiden's weeds.

ELVIRA.

Be calm. The princess comes to aid your needs.

SCENE 2

[*The same*]
[*Enter The Infanta, Leonora*]

THE INFANTA.

I come not to bring your sadness quick relief,
But to join my sighs with your tears of grief.

CHIMENA.

You should join in the people's revelment,
Madam, and share their joy which God has sent.

I am the only one who has to sigh.   5
Rodrigo banished peril. Your hopes are high,
And there is safety in his arm's brave shield.
Today, the only tears are ones I yield.
He has served his King well, as all know;   10
To me alone his valiant arm brings woe.

THE INFANTA.

In truth it is a miracle he's wrought.

CHIMENA.

This news leaves me in greater heartbreak caught,
For I shall hear his name by all extolled
As my lost lover who's now the warrior bold.

THE INFANTA.

Where do you find such pain in all of this?   15
This son of Mars once brought a lover's bliss.
He ruled your heart, as you ruled his days.
Your choice is honored by each word of praise.

CHIMENA.

Whoever lauds him, grants him what he's due,
But with this praise does torture me anew.   20
My pain is heightened as they raise him higher.
All that he is, is all that I desire.
Of, this is cruel to a woman's heart:
To make our love stronger when we must part.
Yet honor shines above love's waiting beauty;   25
To seek his death can be my only duty.

THE INFANTA.

That sense of duty won you yesterday
Approval, for you seemed with love to sway
The sympathy of the entire court,
And all did seek to lend your cause support.   30
As friend, I have advice for you to heed.

CHIMENA.

Not to obey you would be base indeed.

THE INFANTA.

Today the justice of your cause is bated
But joyous peace which Rodrigo has created.
He is our greatest hope, by all adored   35
As Castile's guardian, by the Moors abhorred.
The King himself gives sanction to this truth,
And says your father lives within this youth.
In short, you must listen to words of reason;
To kill this man would be an act of treason.   40
To revenge a father, can it be lawful
To condemn your country? This is more awful,
In that we're punished as though participants
In a crime of which we are the innocents.
You need not seek, since your great heart refuses, 45
A marriage which your father's death accuses.
I plead with you to quench this useless strife;
Deprive him of your love, but leave his life.

CHIMENA.

Too late; how can I grant him mercy now?
I cannot shame a daughter's sacred vow,   50
Although my heart cries out in his behalf.

Of King and country he may be the staff,
Surrounded by his Army, but I must blot
His laurels, surround him with a cypress plot.

THE INFANTA.

55 Duty is noble even though it leads
Against the dictates of your heart's deep needs.
But it would be nobler if you withstood
Your pride and sacrificed for public good.
The cruelest punishment you can bestow
60 Would be denying him your love. I know
Your country calls on you to guard its fame.
You will not act against the King's great name?

CHIMENA.

He may refuse, but I cannot keep still.

THE INFANTA

Think well before you seek the death you will.
65 Farewell, and think of all there is to lose.

CHIMENA.

Since father's death, one way is left to choose.

SCENE 3

[*The King's Palace*]
[*Enter The King, Don Diego, Rodrigo, Don Arias, Don Sancho*]

THE KING, *to Rodrigo*.

Brave son of an illustrious house, whose zeal
Has always been the glory of Castile,
Your victory has soared over the train
Of deeds your ancestors have done for Spain.
5 I have no power to grant a just reward.
Your virtue to my might is overlord.
Our land's deliverance from savage foes,
The glory which on my scepter glows,
The Moor's defeat, before in night's alarm
10 I could give orders to repulse their harm,
Are exploits that I cannot recompense;
But here the captive kings can grant their sense,
For in my presence they have called you Cid.
This means to them as Lord and King you're bid.
15 No one can grudge you such a glorious name.
Be henceforth called The Cid, the word a flame
To Granada and Toledo. It shall prove
To all beneath my rule of law, my love
For you, and this proud title then will show
20 How great you are, how much to you I owe.

RODRIGO.

Your Majesty places too high a praise
Upon an act that followed duty's ways.
I blush to hear before my gracious King
The honors that my victory does bring.
25 I know that to the welfare of your land,
I owe my life whenever you command,
And had I lost it in this sacred cause,
I would have only followed duty's laws.

THE KING.

None of my officers, engaged by scores,
30 Has shown duty and courage such as yours.
When valor goes not to the point of stress,
It cannot bring such rare and great success.
Permit us then to praise you, and tell me
The circumstances of your victory.

RODRIGO.

35 Sire, you know that when the Moorish stranger
Throughout the city sent his chill of danger,
Some friends assembled at my father's home
Compelled my mind which still in love did roam . . .
But, Sire, please pardon my temerity
40 For I acted without authority.
As danger threatened, I thought of all the dead,
And how at court I would have risked my head,
For if I had to lose it, I would rather
Fight now for you as I fought for my father.

THE KING.

45 I do forgive your vengeance that was just
As you have saved the state from evil's thurst.
When Chimena comes to ask for my decision,
We'll grant her but the grace of pity's vision.
Continue, please.

RODRIGO.

                          Forward I led our flanks
50 As a new confidence grew in our ranks.
We were five hundred, but our cause did throng,
And at the port we were three thousand strong.
Even the timid at this final stage,
Drew courage from our Army's massive rage.
55 Most of my men I then concealed, for shock,
In holds of our vessels lying at the dock.
The rest, whose numbers grew with every hour,
Impatiently grouped near my central power,
Lay noiselessly upon the ground, out of sight,
60 And so we passed a large part of the night.
The harbor guard, by order, followed suit
To help my stratagem, thus hidden, mute.
Boldly, I pretended that my new orders
Came from my King since Moors had crossed our bor-
     ders.
65 At least with darkling light of stars for guide,
We saw their sails floating on the full tide.
The heavy swell bore them up to the land
Where our men lay awaiting my command.
None stayed the Moors; all seemed at peace; no calls
70 Of guards upon the wharfs or on the walls.
Deceived by silence, they could never doubt
That their surprise attack prepared a rout.
They neared and cast their anchors quickly down,
Rushed forward fearlessly to sack the town.
75 Our men rose up and a tremendous roar
Exploded to Heaven with the sound of war.
Those in our ships echoed that battle shriek;

They plunged forth armed; the Moors, confused, were
      weak
   With terror, for but half their men had landed.
80 Before the fight began their cause was stranded.
   Bent on swift pillage, they met red slaughter.
   We pressed them hard upon the land and water.
   Their blood, in rivers, flowed upon the banks
   Before they could resist and form in ranks.
85 But then, despite us, their princes rallied them;
   Their courage flamed, and fear they did condemn.
   The shame of death without attempt to fight,
   Stopped their disorder and restored their might.
   Against us, standing firm, their scimitars
90 Drew blood, that flowed into their bloody scars.
   Earth, river, harbor, were all battlegrounds
   With death's triumphant screams the only sounds.
   How many deeds passed by without the mark
   Of glory since they went unseen in dark
95 Where each man struck along his blows of hate
   And could not see the hidden shoals of fate.
   I encouraged our men on every side,
   Made some regroup and some advance in pride,
   Sent forth the new arrivals to the fray
100 And could not know the outcome until day.
   At last the dawn showed coming victory,
   And, suddenly, the Moors began to flee.
   When sounds of our fresh troops drummed quickly near,
   The Moorish lust to conquer turned to fear.
105 They reached their ships and cut their anchor ropes,
   Screaming in fear, retreating from their hopes;
   In such confusion fled that no one saw
   Their two great kings unable to withdraw.
   Their panic drove their loyalty astray
110 And the receding tide swept them away.
   Caught in our midst, their kings, with some few men,
   Fought fiercely to break from our trap again.
   Pierced by our thrusts, they sold their lives too dearly.
   "Surrender!" I cried, but they refused to hear me,
115 And, with their scimitars, they struck instead.
   Then, seeing all their soldiers cut down, dead,
   And that, alone, they did defend their tender
   Lives, they called for me and gave surrender.
   I sent them both to you in morning light,
120 The battle won after that bloody night.
   It was in this way, Sire, for your service . . .

SCENE 4

[*The same*]
[*Enter Don Alonso*]

DON ALONSO.
   Sire, Chimena comes in search of justice.
THE KING.
   A troubled duty to which I must be true.

To Rodrigo.

Go, I shall not force her yet to see you.
I must send you away from Spain's sweet earth.
Let me embrace you and applaud your worth.   5

He embraces him. Exit Rodrigo.

DON DIEGO.
   Chimena loves, but vengeance does deter.
THE KING.
   That shoe loves him, we'll prove by testing her.
   Put on a mask of sadness.

SCENE 5

[*The same*]
[*Enter Chimena, Elvira*]

THE KING.
                        At last be content,
   Chimena, for success to you has bent.
   Rodrigo did defeat the Moor's uprise,
   But died from savage wounds before our eyes.
   Give thanks to God, who has avenged you now.   5

To Don Diego.

See how her color drains away her vow!
DON DIEGO.
   Look, Sire, she swoons and in that swoon supplies
   A proof of love beyond all fatal cries.
   Her grief betrays her vengeance lives apart;
   You can no longer doubt her loving heart.   10
CHIMENA.
   It's true he's dead?
THE KING.
                        No, no, he is alive,
   And still for you in lasting love would strive.
   Cast off the grief that seized you for his sake.
CHIMENA.
   Sire, joy does also faintness make.
   Too much of pleasure turns us soft and weak,   15
   And must obscure that honor which we seek.
THE KING.
   You ask us in this falsehood to abstain?
   Chimena, your true grief was all too plain.
CHIMENA.
   Sire, add this then to my misery,
   And call my swoon the act of grief's decree.   20
   Misfortune did conspire to make me mute
   For death would save his head from my pursuit.
   If death for his great country him had greeted,
   My vengeance would be lost, my aims defeated.
   An end so fair would bring no satisfaction.   25
   I ask his death, but not in glorious action;
   Not one so brilliant that it honors him,
   No hero's death, but on the scaffold grim;

Death for my father, not for this land of Spain,
30 A death that will his name forever stain.
To die a hero's death can bring no shame,
But only wins much praise, immortal fame.
I love his victory; this love's no crime;
The State is safe, my victim grows sublime,
35 Famous, a hero welcomed at gay balls,
And crowned with honors in your palace halls.
It seems his life is worthy then to take
In royal justice for my father's sake . . .
Alas! What dream is this I hope to see?
40 Rodrigo has nothing to fear from me.
What good are tears which all of you despise?
Your empire gives him freedom for his prize.
Wherever you rule, you heed his plea;
As with the Moors, he triumphs over me.
45 Justice, whose voice is stifled in war's pain,
Serves as a trophy for this conqueror's gain.
With kings his prisoners and your applause,
He drives his chariot over the laws.

THE KING.
Too violently, Chimena, your words call.
50 A King dispensing justice must weigh all.
A plea for vengeance you've come to uphold,
But justice, without mercy, must grow cold.
Before berating me for clemency,
Consult your heart; let love bend your proud knee.
55 Then, secretly, your joy shall thank your King,
Whose favor such a love to you can bring.

CHIMENA.
To me? My enemy whom I must hate,
Who wrote in blood my lord and father's fate?
My father's death is looked upon so lightly
60 That it's a favor now to listen rightly!
Since you refuse, Sire, justice to my cause,
Permit me, then, the sword of ancient laws.
He injured me through peril of his sword
And, by a duel, I deserve reward.
65 From all your cavaliers, I ask his head;
To him who brings this prize, I shall be wed.
Let them fight, Sire, and when blood runs again,
I'll marry the victor if Rodrigo's slain.
Let this be published with your authority.

THE KING.
70 This custom was established anciently.
To punish in a duel, deprives the State
Of all the warriors who've made us great.
Often the sad outcome of this abuse
Serves to ambition as a subtle ruse.
75 I do exempt Rodrigo from such need;
He is too precious for this fatal creed.
Whatever sins sprang from his sword's bright hilt,
The fleeing Moors have carried off his guilt.

DON DIEGO.
What, Sire, you change custom for him alone,

A law which gives your Court its ancient tone?   80
What will your subjects think? Whom will they shun,
If he find shelter in this hope you've spun?
If he does make a pretext not to go
Where men of honor seek death's final glow?
Such favor would deny his present glory   85
And shame his deeds, his legendary story.
He slew the Count who had insulted me.
He was a brave man then, and still must be.

THE KING.
Since you desire it, I shall let him fight.
But challenges I'll limit to his might;   90
To win Chimena's hand in marriage pleas
Would make all cavaliers his enemies.
For him to face them all would be too cruel.
Once only, then, shall he be forced to duel.
Choose whom you wish, Chimena, for this score,   95
But after this combat ask nothing more.

DON DIEGO.
Do not excuse those who his sword do fear,
But leave the combat open; none will come near.
After the deeds he has to this day willed,
Who has the senseless courage to be killed?   100
Who would dare to fight with such a foe,
In this foolhardness would only show.

DON SANCHO.
Open the lists. My challenge you shall hear.
Though it may seem in vain, I shall not fear.

To Chimena.

Permit this favor as my heart's last fee,   105
Madam. You know what you have promised me.

THE KING, *to Chimena.*
Did you accept his offer in your sorrow?

CHIMENA.
Sire, I promised.

THE KING.
                          Be ready then tomorrow.

DON DIEGO.
No, Sire, there is no reason for delay.
One who is brave and just can fight today.   110

THE KING.
How can he fight fresh from this battle's feud?

DON DIEGO.
In telling you his tale, his life renewed.

THE KING.
Still, he should have a longer time of rest.
To show this duel cannot by me be blessed,
For fear it might become a precedent   115
To which I've wrongly given my consent,
I shall not witness it, nor shall my Court.

To Don Arias.

To you as only judge I will resort.
Assure this combat honorably is fought

120 And that they both acquit them as they ought.
    Whoever wins, the prize shall be the same.
    With my own hand, I'll pledge Chimena's name,
    And his reward shall be her marriage vow.
    CHIMENA.
    How can you, Sire, so cruelly make me bow?
    THE KING.
125 You complain, but if your love should win,
    You shall accept him as love conquers sin.
    Cease murmuring against this mild decree,
    For he who triumphs shall your husband be.

                                            [*Exeunt*]

ACT V

SCENE 1

[*Chimena's house*]
[*Enter Rodrigo, Chimena*]

CHIMENA.
    Rodrigo, here by day! How dare you show
    This boldness against my honor? Go, please go!
RODRIGO.
    Madam, I go to die, and came to tell
    You of my love before my last farewell,
5   The sacred love which binds me to your need
    And takes my life in homage to your creed.
CHIMENA.
    You go to die?
RODRIGO.
                    I hasten toward the end
    Where my blood with your father's then shall blend.
CHIMENA.
    You go to die! Don Sancho is a foe
10 Who strikes into your heart this coward's woe?
    Who has made you so weak or him so strong?
    Rodrigo goes to fight and thinks his wrong
    Already needs his death! You scorned the Moor
    And killed my sire, yet tremble as if poor
15 Of heart at Sancho! Your courage is spent.
RODRIGO.
    I seek no combat, but my punishment.
    When you ask for my death in this strife,
    I am unwilling to defend my life.
    My courage is the same, but not my arm
20 Which yearns to hold you as a shield from harm.
    Last night I would have sought death to atone
    Had I been fighting for my cause alone.
    But to betray by death country and King,
    I could not, and so to life I had to cling.
25 In my spirit I could not find good reason
    To lose my life by a base act of treason.
    Now that I fight for nothing but my name,
    You claim my death, and I accept your claim.
    You've chosen Sancho's yoke, his hot demand

30 To fight me. I did not deserve your hand
    To cause my death. I shall not strike a blow.
    Respect to him who fights to you I owe.
    I shall rejoice knowing his trust is yours,
    Since for your gracious honor his blade soars.
35 I'll meet his challenge with unguarded breast,
    For in his hand, your hand will bring me rest.
CHIMENA.
    If justice and the violence of my task
    Force me to wear a prosecutor's mask,
    Inflict so harsh a law upon your love
40 That helpless to this duel you must move,
    Remember in your blindness that your fame
    Departs with life; and that Rodrigo's name
    When dead will bear the stain of a defeat.
    Honor is more to you than love's deceit,
45 For in my father's blood your hands were stained;
    The bonds of honor our pure love restrained;
    Yet now you think this is so little true
    You care not who it is that conquers you.
    How inconsistent with yourself you are;
50 You debase honor, yet place it on a star.
    Are you so noble in humility?
    Are you so cruel to my sire, then flee
    That having conquered him you will submit
    To any hand? Forsake this devil's wit.
55 Though I attack you till your final breath,
    Defend your honor though you seek your death.
RODRIGO.
    The Count is dead. Our enemy, the Moor, bleeds
    In defeat. Must I perform yet other deeds?
    Chimena, my honor needs no defense.
60 Men know my courage swept beyond all sense
    Of expectation; if honor should die
    The world would waste beneath a sunless sky.
    No, if I should lose this final duel,
    If can but aid your justice of pursual.
65 No one will dare to think my courage failed,
    Or claim my conqueror with joy be hailed;
    For men shall only say, "Love was his fate.
    He could not live and still endure her hate.
    He yielded willingly to fate's dark flood
70 Which forced his own dear love to seek his blood.
    She had to seek his head, and his denial
    Would have placed the gift of love on trial.
    For honor's sake, in combat he was hurled;
    For his sweet mistress, he renounced this world
75 And died, preferring dreams of her as wife,
    His honor to Chimena, her love to life."
    Thus you shall see my death in this fight
    Will spread the sun of honor in my night,
    And by my death proclaim your honor's glory,
80 That no one's life but mine could end this story.
CHIMENA.
    Since life and honor have so little power

To keep you from this entrance to death's tower,
Rodrigo, if you love me, fight your foe,
Defend yourself to save me from this woe;
85 Release me from this compact so forlorn,
And fight to save me from a man I scorn.
What shall I add? Please think of your defense
To force my hand to silent innocence;
And if your love has not hardened to ice,
90 Defeat him when Chimena is the price.
Farewell! This last word makes me blush with shame.

[Exit Chimena.]

RODRIGO, *alone.*

Is there any enemy I fear in name?
Castilians, Moors, whoever dares to take
The field against us, now one Army make:
95 Let all the valiant men whom Spain has nourished
Join together, and their greatness, flourished,
Will shatter against the sweetness of her light;
To gain her love with whom dare I not fight?

SCENE 2

[The Infanta's house]

THE INFANTA, *alone.*

Shall I consider still my birth and rank
    Which make my love a crime?
Or shall I listen, love, to you whose claim
Makes me rebel against my royal time?
5   Unhappy Princess, choose,
        For either choice must lose
The hope of happiness. My royal grace
Would mock me as I kissed Rodrigo's face.

Pitiless fate that sternly separates
10   My glory from desire;
Why must the choice of courage that is rare
Bring to my heart this hot, despairing fire?
        Oh God, how many years
        My heart must blend with fears
15 Until this long torment can end forever
And either quell my love, or my love sever.

Too long have I been scrupulous.
    Why must I condemn my choice?
Although my birth gives me to kings alone,
20 To claim Rodrigo's name I can rejoice.
        Striking two kings down,
        He will achieve a crown.
His wondrous name of Cid—does this not prove
That he should rule a princess and her love?

25 Yet worthy of my birth, he is Chimena's.
    I gave him to her at love's decree.
Not even her father's death could make them hate,
Though from her duty now she cannot flee.

I dare not hope for bliss tomorrow
    From his crime or from my sorrow,   30
Since ruthless fate, to punish me, foresees
That they shall keep their love, though enemies.

SCENE 3

[The same]
[Enter Leonora]

THE INFANTA.
Why are you here, Leonora?
LEONORA.
                            Madam, my heart glows
With joy to know that you have found repose.
THE INFANTA.
How can a heart so filled with grief find rest?
LEONORA.
If love requires hope, with hope is blessed,
Rodrigo can no longer claim your heart.   5
You know the duel in which he plays his part.
Since he must die or else Chimena wed,
Your soul is cured for then your hope is dead.
THE INFANTA.
Ah, if that were true!
LEONORA.
                        What do you mean?
THE INFANTA.
How kill the hope that in my mind you've seen?   10
If under these conditions Rodrigo duels,
Have I not power to silence tongues of fools?
Sweet love, who causes cruel suffering,
Teaches too easily how lovers cling.
LEONORA.
How can you breed a discontent between them?   15
Her father's death could not their great love stem;
And by her conduct Chimena clearly shows
That her pursuit from hatred never flows.
She asks a trial by combat, and reveres
As champion the first who volunteers;
She does not choose an expert for this task;   20
A man famous for valor she doesn't ask;
Instead, Don Sancho satisfied her turn,
Who never yet in war did merit earn.
She loves in him his inexperienced hand;
Thus, her anxiety fears no demand,   25
And she fulfills her duty in her aim
To then permit at last Rodrigo's claim.
THE INFANTA.
Well do I know this guile, and yet my heart,
Competing with Chimena, is torn apart.
Unfortunate love; what shall I best decide?   30
LEONORA.
Remember that your lineage you can't hide.

You love a subject, while God grants you a King.
THE INFANTA.
   My love has changed. No longer does my hope sing
   Of Rodrigo as a simple cavalier.
35   No, my love now thinks of him as peer.
   If I love, it is the Cid whose name atones
   For lack of rank, since he has conquered thrones.
   Yet I shall give up love, not from a share
   Of blame, but for the sacred love they bear.
40   If he did gain a crown to seal our rift,
   I still could not accept his lover's gift.
   Since in this duel, he is sure to win,
   I'll give him to Chimena to heal my sin;
   And you who know the anguish I have won,
45   Come, see me finish what I have begun.

                           [*Exeunt*]

SCENE 4

[*Chimena's house*]
[*Enter Chimena, Elvira*]

CHIMENA.
   Elvira, how I should be pitied! I hope
   And yet there's only fear in which to grope.
   I dare not give consent to my desires.
   A swift repentance follows their bright fires.
5   I made two rivals take up arms for me;
   The happiest result of fate's decree
   Will see my lover slain within this net,
   Or else my father still demands my debt.
ELVIRA.
   You shall be recompensed on either side.
10   You'll have Rodrigo, or revenge's pride.
   Whatever fate ordains this day for you,
   It saves your honor, grants a husband true.
CHIMENA.
   Which husband? He whose love has been my prayer,
   Or Sancho whom I hate, Rodrigo's slayer?
15   In either case I earn a husband stained
   With blood of him who in my mind is grained.
   My heart rebels whatever the decision.
   I fear this quarrel's end more than death's vision.
   Go, vengeance, love, you that possess my soul.
20   You cannot aid me now to reach your goal;
   And you, creator of my violent fate,
   Decide this combat equally, without hate;
   That neither be the victor nor the vanquished.
ELVIRA.
   Such a cruel end should not by you be wished.
25   This duel is fresh punishment for you
   If it demands again that you must sue
   For justice, always in resentment live,
   Pursue to death the man you would love give.
   Madam, it were better if this violence

Makes him victor and commands your silence,   30
And that the King who has become your Sire
Should force you to comply with your desire.
CHIMENA.
   If he is conqueror, how can I yield?
   My duty is too strong, too great a shield;
   And to command me, even combat's laws   35
   Are not enough; nor even the King's proud cause.
   Yet, though Rodrigo break Don Sancho's guard,
   Chimena's honor will remain unscarred.
   However the King rewards the victor's pleas,
   I shall fight him with a thousand enemies.   40
ELVIRA.
   Take care lest Heaven punish your strange pride,
   And grant you vengeance that you cannot hide.
   Will you reject this final happiness
   Which your true silence could with honor bless?
   What would you then pretend? What could you hope?   45
   You would find one more death with which to cope?
   Is one misfortune not enough? Would you heap
   Loss upon loss, and greater sorrow reap?
   In your pride, you do not deserve in this
   The lover who is destined for your kiss,   50
   And Heaven whose anger you wish to provoke,
   Instead will bind you to Don Sancho's yoke.
CHIMENA.
   Elvira, the torment which I seek to flee
   Is only swollen by your prophecy.
   I would, if possible, avoid them both.   55
   If not, Rodrigo's love was my sworn oath.
   No dream of peace inclines my heart to him,
   But if he fails I must please Sancho's whim.
   This apprehension causes all my hate.

Enter Don Sancho.

   Look, Elvira! Oh God! It is too late.   60

SCENE 5

[*The same*]

DON SANCHO.
   Madam, I must present this sword to you.
CHIMENA.
   See! Rodrigo's blood! Can this be true?
   Traitor, how can you shamefully come here
   When you have killed my love and caused my fear?
   Cry out, my love, the anguish that I feel.   5
   My father is avenged; love can't conceal
   This sword that frees my love to every stare,
   Assures my honor, but creates despair.
DON SANCHO.
   Hear me with calmer . . .
CHIMENA.
                     How dare you speak   10
   When this proud hero's death you wished to seek?

Your triumph was through treachery! Please, go!
Rodrigo never could have felt your blow.
Hope for nothing from me in this cruel strife;
Searching for vengeance, you have taken my life.

DON SANCHO.

15   You are wrong, Madam. Yet further hear me.

CHIMENA.

How shall I hear your fatal boast or see
The prideful insolence with which you mime
Your courage, his misfortune, and my crime?

[Exeunt]

SCENE 6

[*The Palace*]
[*Enter The King, Don Diego, Don Arias, Don Sancho,
Don Alonso, Chimena, Elvira*]

CHIMENA.

Sire, there is no longer need to hide
The truth which could not be concealed by pride.
For my father, I sought to rise above
My hope, and to condemn the man I love.
5   Your Majesty has seen with sorrow how
I made my love yield to my duty's vow.
But the shadow of death has come to hover
Over me, change me to a bitter lover.
The vengeance that I to my father owed
10   How now upon my lover been bestowed.
By his defense, Sancho has cut love's ties,
Yet for his doing so I'm made his prize.
Sire, if your pity moves you, please withdraw
The cruelty of this barbaric law,
15   All that I have is his, but to atone
For killing love, let him leave me alone.
Send me to a cloister where I'll mourn
The two from whose great love I have been torn.

DON DIEGO.

At last she loves, Sire, and shall no longer claim
20   It is a crime to speak love's blessèd name.

THE KING.

Chimena, you are wrong and speak in error.
Don Sancho has deceived you in your terror.

DON SANCHO.

Sire, this is unjust. She speaks from passion's sway.
I came here straight to tell her of the way
25   In which Rodrigo did my sword disarm.
This noble swordsman, with her heart in charm,
Told me to fear nothing. "I mean to leave
This victory uncertain lest she grieve,"
He said. "But since my duty must attend
30   The King, to her I will his sword now send
Through you as messenger of your defeat."
With these instructions, I came here to greet

Her, but she thought that I had conquered him;
And then her anger turned into this whim
Of grief that did so rob her reason's sense   35
I could not win a moment's audience.
For my part, though I suffer in defeat,
And though, in love, we shall never meet,
I must bow to the cause of my distress
Which brings a greater love this bright success.   40

THE KING.

You must not be ashamed of such a love,
My daughter, or seek means to disapprove.
Your honor is fulfilled and free from shame;
Your duty paid unto your family's name.
Your father's satisfied, he rests in peace,   45
While Rodrigo's dangers cannot yet cease.
You see how Heaven has decreed this end:
Since you are free, I have seen fit to send
For Rodrigo; in respect to my command,
Accept your husband with a loving hand.   50

SCENE 7

[*The same*]
[*Enter The Infanta, Leonora, Rodrigo*]

THE INFANTA.

Chimena, dry your tears; from your Princess
Take this hero whom with love you bless.

RODRIGO, *kneeling before Chimena.*

Be not offended, Sire, if I fail to greet
Your regal presence and kneel here at her feet.

To Chimena.

I came not to demand you for my wife,   5
But once again to offer you my life.
The law of combat I shall never plead,
Nor ask the King to recognize my deed.
If all that's done cannot appease death's cry,
Tell me what means is left to satisfy.   10
Must I still fight a thousand enemies,
Extend my deeds across the distant seas,
Defeat an Army, attack a camp alone,
Surpass the greatest heroes, to atone?
If guilt does pass, and we are not deceived,   15
I dare to hope that this can be achieved;
But if proud honor in its forceful course
Cannot be silent without death's remorse,
No longer seek through others your demands.
My life is yours. Take it with your own hands.   20
Your hands alone can conquer the unconquered;
For you alone by vengeance can be stirred;
But let my death suffice to punish me
And do not cut me from your memory.
Then righteous death shall keep your honor bright,   25
And you will hold your dream of love's delight
In lamentation for your hope to wed,

Crying, "He loved and, therefore, he is dead."

CHIMENA.

Arise, Rodrigo. I have said too much,
30 Sire, to deny the truth. My love is such
As I have said, and him I cannot hate.
At your command I must obey my fate;
Your Majesty condemns me to this marriage,
But, Sire, how shall you see the wedding carriage?
35 And when before the priest we kneel to pray,
Will all your great justice rule there that day?
Rodrigo has become a hero now;
Must I with marriage his reward avow,
And yield myself to an eternal flood
40 Of guilt, my hands stained with my father's blood?

THE KING.

The laws of reason change in course of time
And show the truth of what may seem a crime.
Rodrigo has won you; you must be wise;
But though you are today his valor's prize,
45 It would insult your honor to decree,
So soon, a wedding for his victory.
Delaying this marriage no law can break;

No date was set when you his hand must take.
You have a year then, if you wish, to mourn.
Meanwhile, Rodrigo still the Moors must scorn,   50
And having conquered them upon our shores,
Repulsed them and destroyed their Army's stores,
Must take the war into their bloodstained land
And ravage it beneath his sword's command.
They'll tremble when the name of Cid shall ring!   55
They'll call you Lord, and soon will make you King;
But do from faithful love this mighty deed;
If possible, return with love to plead,
And let your acts create in her such pride
That she shall then no honor lose as bride.   60

RODRIGO.

For my Chimena, Sire, and for your throne,
You need but ask and I'll seek to atone.
Though I shall suffer distant from her face,
Yet I can hope, for in that hope is grace.

THE KING.

Rely upon your valor and my word,   65
And since the pledge of love from her you've heard,
Let time, your courage, and your King remove
The point of honor that obstructs your love.

TOPICS FOR CRITICAL THINKING AND WRITING

The Play on the PAGE

1. The French Academy found the scenes with the Infanta beautiful, but useless to the action of the play. What do you think?
2. In what way is Rodrigue's idea of honor similar to that of his father? In what way is it different?
3. Describe the character of the King. Is he an entirely sympathetic figure?

4. What do you think about the controversial bone of contention: Under *any* circumstances, can you marry your parent's killer?
5. What would Falstaff have thought about the lovers' dilemmas?

The Play on the STAGE

6. If you were directing this play, how would you make the theme of honor believable to the audience?
7. Would you set the play in Spain or in France? Or elsewhere?
8. Would you modernize it?
9. Declan Donnellan staged the play essentially on a bare stage. Why do you think he did it this way?
10. How would *you* stage it? In what style?
11. Assume for the moment that you are translating into English a French play about Spaniards. The

French play uses the French version of Spanish names, (e.g. *Rodrigue* for the Spanish *Rodrigo*, *Diegue* for the Spanish *Diego*). Presumably three possibilities confront the translator: (1) retain the French names; (2) translate the names into Spanish (3) translate the names into English (in this last instance, the French *Diegue* and the Spanish *Diego* will become "James"). Which course will you choose, and why?

The Play in Performance

Like certain rare wines, French neoclassical tragedy has not traveled well, especially to Anglo-Saxon countries. Even during the Restoration, with a British aristocracy newly returned from exile in France with acquired French tastes, it is significant that there are few productions of serious French drama, and these invariably are adaptations such as Thomas Otway's *Titus and Berenice* (1667) and John Crown's *Andromache* (1674). Although a few of Corneille's plays (*Le Cid, Pompée, Horace*) are translated into English (*Le Cid* almost immediately) there are no records of productions of any of them. The British will make their own attempt to write heroic tragedy in such plays as John Dryden's *All for Love* and William Davenant's *Siege of Rhodes*. As the brief reign of English neoclassicism wanes, as Marlowe's mighty blank verse reconquers the heroic couplet, there is even less reason to put on stage the plays of France's classic playwrights. So Irish director Declan Donnellan may well be right when he claims that his revelatory 1986 version of *The Cid* by his innovative theater group Cheek By Jowl at the Almeida theater in London was the first professional British production of the play—an extraordinarily late debut for the ex-lawyer from Rouen.

In France, of course, the reverse is true. The plays of Corneille in general, and *Le Cid* in particular, hold not only the classroom, but the French stage as well. Indeed, between 1680 and 1966 (the last date for which we could find statistics), the most often revived noncomedy in the repertoire of the Comédie Française is *Le Cid*, with 1480 performances to Racine's *Phèdre's* 1350. (*Tartuffe* is the box-office champ with 2761 performances.) Ever since Montdory's original triumph as Rodrigue, the role has become for French actors the same kind of summit that Hamlet represents for the British. In our era the most acclaimed performance of the role occurred mid-twentieth century at the then young Avignon Festival, founded in 1947 by Jean Vilar. In 1951 Vilar directed an intelligent, disturbing production of the play starring the then popular film actor Gérard Philipe in the leading role. Ironically, so definitive seemed Philipe's performance that few later actors have been willing to compete with its memory. When Declan Donnellan was asked to direct a play at Avignon in the 1990s, he remembered his past success in London and suggested a new production of *Le Cid* in French. Initially appalled by the idea, the directors of the festival came to realize that if ever the play was to be renovated and escape the aura of Philipe (who died young and was buried in Rodrigue's third-act costume), it would have to be by a foreigner without the anxiety of influence.

This production was an unqualified success (see following review) not only at Avignon and around France but in its ventures abroad, including the Brooklyn Academy of Music in 1999. Donnellan had stringently modernized its interpretation: First of all, he cast the play multiracially, with black actors playing both Rodrigue and the King. The Andalusian court evoked both Franco Spain and an African military dictatorship. The soldiers wore khaki uniforms; the women, severe two-piece suits. The play unfolded on a bare stage devoid of any scenic elements save three Cordovan leather chairs. All this, at first glance, seems familiarly "trendy." But what impressed viewers (including this one) most strongly was that Donnellan did not, as so many superficial experimental versions of classics do, impose an anachronistic modernity on the play. He did not bend the text to ironically contradict it. No, he showed that the play was more complex than it first seems. He found beneath the surface rhetoric about *gloire, devoir, honneur,* a countertension that subtextually challenged the assumptions of the ruling abstractions *for the characters themselves.* He showed that the play itself is rich enough to sustain an interpretation of Rodrigue as a tormented and reluctant hero, a Hamlet more than a Henry V.

We must also cite here a production of the play a few years earlier (1994) at the Royal National Theatre, London. In the theater's experimental space, the Cottesloe, Jonathan Kent directed a less revelatory but still admirable version that seized the play's vitality and proved it dramatically engrossing. Together with several recent exciting reinterpretations of the plays of Racine (*Brittanicus* as well as *Phèdre*), the British theater and its innovative young directors are discovering in French tragedy dramatic values hitherto unnoticed. Who would have thought the old man had so much blood left in him?

The French Academy on "The Cid"

Excerpts from Sentimens de l'Académie française sur la tragi-comédie du Cid, *1638**

Some, too much inclined, it seems, toward pleasure, hold that delight is the true purpose of dramatic poetry. Others . . . holding [time] too dear to be given over to amusements which yield only pleasure and no profit, maintain that its real end is to instruct. Though each expresses himself in such different terms, it will on closer examination be seen that both are in agreement. . . . Those who claim pleasure as the sole end are too reasonable to exclude anything that is not conformable to reason. We must believe—if we would do them justice—that by pleasure they mean the pleasure which is not the enemy but the instrument of virtue, and which purges men, insensibly and without disgust, of their vicious practices, and which is useful because it is good, and which can never leave regret in the mind for having surprised it, nor in the soul for having corrupted it. . . .

Hence, they are at one, and we agree with them both, and we can all of us together say that a play is good when it produces a feeling of reasonable content. But, as in music and painting, we should not consider every concert and every picture good if it please the people but fail in the observance of the rules of their respective arts, and if the experts, who are the sole judges, did not by their approval confirm that of the multitude. Hence, we must *not* say with the crowd that a poem is good merely because it pleases, unless the learned and the expert are also pleased. . . . Nor have we to do with pleasing those who are ignorant and untutored, who would be no more moved at seeing the sufferings of Penelope than of Clytemnestra. Evil examples are contagious, even in the theater, the representations even of feigned acts produce only too many real crimes; and there is great danger in diverting the people with pleasures which may someday result in public catastrophes. . . . It is impossible to please anyone with disorder and confusion, and if it happens that irregular plays sometimes please, it is only by reason of

what is regular in them, because of certain unquestioned and extraordinary beauties which transport the soul so far that for a long time after it is incapable of detecting the deformities which accompany them, and which serve imperceptibly to bring out the faults, while the understanding is yet dazzled by the brilliancy of the good. And, on the other hand, if certain regularly constructed plays give little pleasure, it must not be thought that this is the fault of the rules, but of the author, whose sterile wit was unable to exercise his art upon sufficiently rich material. . . .

Now, the Natural, rather than the True is, according to Aristotle, the province of epic and dramatic poetry, which, having for its purpose pleasure and profit of the auditor or the spectator, the epic or dramatic poet can the more surely encompass by making use of the natural, or verisimilar, rather than what is simply true or matter of fact, because it convinces men the more easily as it finds no resistance in them, which it would if the poet adhered to mere facts, and which might well be so strange and incredible that they would think them false and refuse to be persuaded of them. But since several things are required to make a story natural—that is, observation of time, of place, of the condition, age, manners and customs, and passions—the principal point of all is that each personage must behave according to his character as set forth early in the poem. For instance, an evil man must not do good deeds. And the reason why this exact observation is required is that there is no other way of producing the Marvelous, which delights the mind with astonishment and pleasure, and is the perfect means adopted by poetry to arrive at the end of profit. It is indeed a great undertaking to try to create the rare effect of the Marvelous from so common a thing as the Natural. And so, we believe with the Masters that herein lies the greatest merit for him who knows well how to do it; and as the difficulty is great, there are few who can succeed. And that is why so many, despairing of success, resort to that false Marvelous which results in the unnatural, what is not true to lfe, and which may be called the Monstrous, and try to pass off on the crowd as the true Marvelous that which deserves only the name of Miraculous.

*Barrett H. Clark, *European Theories of the Drama*. Newly revised by Henry Popkin (New York: Crown, 1965), pp. 89–91.

The Playwright Replies to His Critics

From Corneille's Examen (or self-examination) of The Cid that appeared in the 1682 edition of the play.*

Due to this poetic play's advantages in its choice of subject matter and in the continual ingenuity of its ideas, most audiences have permitted themselves to be carried away by the pleasures of its performance, and have had no desire to search for defects in its structure. Although it is—of all my plays—the one in which I have permitted myself much license, it remains judged the best by those who do not attach too much importance to the strictness of rules; for fifty years† it has held the stage, and neither history nor critical effort has dimmed its lustre. It also has met the two great conditions that Aristotle demands of perfect tragedies, conditions rarely found simultaneously in classic works *or* contemporary. Indeed, it combines its virtues more strongly and nobly than the examples offered by that philosopher: A woman in love whom duty forces to pursue the death of her lover—a result she dreads—displays passions more intense and enflamed than those which may pass between husband and wife, between mother and son, between brother and sister. It proves that the high virtue of a nature susceptible to these passions must triumph over these passions gloriously without weakening them. . . .

The great outburst of love she [Chimène] releases when she believes . . . [Rodrigue] dead is followed by her vigorous opposition to the fulfilling of the pledge giving her to his vanquisher, and she ceases to protest only after the king postpones judgment and allows her to hope that time will reveal some new obstacle. I know well that silence normally passes for consent, for when kings speak a contradiction appears: one never fails to applaud when one agrees with them; if one does not, the only way to express this contradiction is through silence, to preserve the hope that something unforeseen may alter circumstances.

It is true that in this plot all that is necessary is to remove Rodrigue from danger, without pushing to the point of consummating his marriage with Chimène. This is historical and pleased everyone in its time; but it would surely *not* please everyone today, and I remain surprised that Chimène consents to it in the Spanish play, even if the Spanish author allows his play to span more than three years. Not to contradict history, I could not altogether jettison this action, but I consciously left the outcome in doubt in order to reconcile stage decorum with factual circumstances.

The two visits Rodrigue makes to his mistress shocks decor in that she permits them: strict duty demands that she shut herself in her chambers and refuse to speak or listen to him. But permit me to say with one of the leading minds of our century, that "their conversation is full of such elevated sentiments that this lapse in propriety remains unnoticed or ignored." If I may go further: almost everyone *wanted* these intimate exchanges to take place; I noticed in the first performances that when the unhappy Rodrigue presented himself before his beloved that a perceptible shudder could be discerned in the audience expressing a marvelous curiosity and a redoubling of attentiveness to hear what the lovers had to say to one another in such pitiable circumstances.

Aristotle says that there are absurdities that should be left in a work when it can be expected that they will be well received; and it is the duty of the poet, in this case, to cover them with brilliance so they dazzle. I leave to the judgment of my audiences if I have so succeeded in justifying these two intimate scenes. The lovers's thoughts in the first of the two are too spiritually elevated to be uttered by deeply afflicted characters; but apart from the fact of having paraphrased the Spanish original, if we artists were not allowed to poeticize the banal language of passion, in the mouths of actors great sorrows would be reduced to "Woe!" and "Alas!" I must admit that the scenes in which Rodrigue offers his sword to Chimène and offers to let Don Sanche kill him do not please me today. These actions were appropriate in their time but are no longer. The first comes from the Spanish original, and the second is based on that model of stage action. Both have won me favor, but I shall take scrupulous care not to spread similar actions in the future on our stage.

---

*Translated by Gerald Rabkin.
†Actually 46 years.

JEAN-LOUIS PERRIER
The "Cid" Superb and Anti-Heroic*
Declan Donnellan plays cat and mouse with Cornielle

Avignon Summer Festival

Avignon has a pleasant surprise: forty years after the seminal version with Gérard Phillipe, The *Cid* has been stood on its head, tidied up, and transposed to the twentieth century by the Irish director Declan Donnellan in an anti-heroic version so full of inventiveness that the audience at the Theatre Municipal were brought to their feet.

In 1951, The *Cid* so glorified Avignon that it could afford to stay away for two generations. Now it returns in the spirit of our times. The foreign director Donnellan, has boldly uprooted Rodrigue from his age and transported him to ours: khaki uniforms haunt the Castilian Court. The impetuous ardor and heroism of Phillipe have been thrown fearlessly away. Here we have . . . an agitated boy more a kid than a Cid, but a boy with a unique conscience who unhappily lives in a society confined by ossified rules.

Donnellan does not deconstruct the *Cid;* on the contrary, he follows the text with complete fidelity. What he does is to upset the delicate Corneillian balance, something no one has dared to do until now. He adds dissonance to the characters, puts them in danger even as they strive to recover their lost bearings. In this reading of the play, the familiar lines etched in our memories still go straight to the heart, but the *alexandrines* sing differently. Transcending rhetoric, they now become a feared and delicious trap where passion, con-

*Le Monde 14 July 1998. Translated by Gerald Rabkin.

tempt, and weakness are exhibited. After this production, it would be laughable to try to resurrect an antiquated *Cid*.

The director plays a game of cat and mouse with Corneille. Whereas Rodrigue traditionally affects his modesty in order to achieve his goals, Donnellan here renders him truly modest precisely in order to escape them. At the onset, William Nadylarn (a young black actor) stands in front of his father and his King, his heels firmly planted impeccably, possessed by fear, a fear tinged with disgust at the idea of fighting. He realizes he embodies to a nauseating degree an anachronistic code of honor. He is trapped in the contradiction between his appetite for life and his necessary submission to pompous, mortifying speeches. And finally, he is a devout Catholic, who prays fervently over the body of the Count that he has just murdered. And when he returns, a hero in spite of himself, from the battle against the Moors, his story is sober, painful, and ridden with the heavy burden of death. His victory he sees as a defeat, an indelible stain on his conscience. Rodrigue is crowned the "Cid" by default, against his will.

Donnellan varies his angles of attack. His heroine is presented as a flashy blond in a suit: this Chimène (Sarah Karbasnikoff) . . . occupies the center of the stage: a fired-up flirt, no-shrinking violet . . . for whom the word *"gloire"* really means something. In contrast with her lover's delaying tactics, she is life itself, embodied in a performance that will not rest; one full of ideas which dynamically raise the dead. In an effort to give prestige to his play four years after its composition, Corneille renounced the title of "tragicomedy" to call it a "tragedy." Whatever its designation, *Le Cid* is explored by Donnellan with full justice and wit.

Anonymous

Although some other scripts in this volume have no named author—such as *Everyman* and *The Second Shepherds' Play*—these works probably were written by a single person. The composition of *The Insane Asylum*, however, more fully reflects the collaborative nature of theater as an art form. Here the author is unknown, but it is likely that the "author" is the collective voice of the actors who originally performed this work. Every *commedia dell'arte* troupe possessed a store of scenarios that were used over and over again, and, with each performance, were embellished and refined. Scenarios were written down only to serve as a goad to the actors' memory, to remind them of the plot and key elements of comic business. Publication was never intended, but in 1611 Flaminio Scala, an actor with the famous I Gelosi *commedia* troupe, published fifty of the company's most popular scenarios. Although *commedia* companies traveled widely throughout Italy and Europe, they had geographical allegiances, I Gelosi's home base was in northern Italy and their scenarios were published in Venice.

The scenario published here appears in English translation for the first time. This work, from the Casamarciano manuscript in the National Library in Naples, attests to the vibrant tradition of *commedia dell'arte* in and around Naples from 1650 to 1700. The manuscript, written in a mixture of Italian and Neopolitan (the native dialect of Naples), contains 181 scenarios, 176 of which can still be deciphered. It took Italian scholar Francesco Cotticelli ten years to transcribe the original manuscripts into readable Italian and a translation team of Cotticelli, Thomas Heck, and Ann Goodrich Heck a year to translate the scenarios into English.

■■■■■■■■■■■■■■■

COMMENTARY ON *THE INSANE ASYLUM*

No one knows exactly how or when *commedia dell'arte* began, but by 1550 it was an established form of Italian public theater. *Commedia dell'arte* translates as "professional comedy," "comedy of artists," or even "comedy of the profession." This term distinguishes it from other forms of theater in Italy that retained an amateur status, such as performances at religious festivals or in the Italian courts or educational academies. These latter productions catered exclusively for coterie, aristocratic audiences. It was also known by other names that reveal certain of its characteristics: *commedia improviso* (improvised comedy) and *commedia alla maschera* (masked comedy).

This form of popular comedy developed under circumstances very different from those of the institutionally sanctioned cycle plays of medieval Europe. Particularly in its early period, *commedia* was a grassroots form of entertainment. Most of the companies were family-based structures where husband and wife teams led the players. It was customary for the parents to hand down their roles to sons or daughters, and evidence exists of such "inheritances" lasting three or four generations. Women played the female roles in *commedia*, providing the first significant record of professional actresses over a century before women were permitted to act in England. The family structure of the companies, linked with the precarious and unpredictable earnings of itinerant actors, made it an economical necessity for the women to act and to take part in running the company.

The origins of the *commedia* are uncertain. One theory links the comic figures of the medieval cycle plays to the comic types found in *commedia*. In particular *The Second Shepherds' Play*, which we studied earlier in this volume, with its comic characters and knock-about farce, has been cited as a possible candidate. Another theory persuasively suggests that *commedia*'s origins are found even further back in history with a raucous comic form from ancient Rome called Atellan farce, which utilized masks. One character from *commedia*, Pulcinella, seems to be a descendant from the Roman comic figure known as Maccus. They both have a slight humpback, a swollen potbelly, large hooked nose, and a white loose-fitting tunic. Another connection is to the comedies of the Roman playwright Plautus, whose popular plays often featured a clever comic servant outwitting his master, similar to stories used again and again in *commedia* performances.

Although the origins of *commedia* still remain essentially a mystery, the influence of this popular form of theater was widespread. Some *commedia* companies began to be invited to perform at court or indoor in conventional theaters. The most famous *commedia* troupes were active between 1570 and 1650. The history of the companies is often difficult to trace, since they traveled widely and did not keep records. The Ganassa company spent ten years in Spain and is credited with influencing Spanish theater. Lope de Vega, whose work appears in this section, developed a comic servant role that is clearly a cousin of the *commedia* servants, known as *zanni*. (*Zanni*, incidently, gives us the English word *zany*). In France, *commedia* was so popular that the king invited one company to have a permanent residency under royal protection in Paris. Known as the Comédie-Italienne, after a period of time they abandoned improvisation and began to perform scripted plays in French. Molière, in his early ca-

reer the head of an itinerant group of French actors himself, greatly admired the Italian performers, and much of the comic wit of his early works was inspired by *commedia* performance. More recently, Dario Fo, whose comedy appears later in this volume, sees himself as a descendant of the Italian comic tradition of itinerant players. In this country San Francisco Mime Company, founded in 1959, continues to create theater pieces based on the physicalized comedy of *commedia dell'arte*.

The Insane Asylum has the standard set of characters: two old men, Magnifico and the Dottore; two clown servants, Pulcinella and Coviello; two sets of young lovers, Silvio and Flaminia and Lavinia and Orazio. The story begins with Silvio proclaiming his love for Flaminia and the two lecherous old men agreeing to marry each other's daughter.

THE INSANE ASYLUM
A COMMEDIA DELL'ARTE SCENARIO

Translated by Francesco Cotticelli, Anne Goodrich Heck, and Thomas F. Heck

DRAMATIS PERSONAE

MAGNIFICO, *father of*
LAVINIA *and*
SILVIO, *his children*
PULCINELLA, *their servant*
DOTTORE, *father of*
FLAMINIA
ROSETTA, *their servant*
ORAZIO (*no relation*)
COVIELLO (*no relation*)
AN ASYLUM WARDEN
SOME MADMEN (*inmates*)

PROPERTIES

*A basket containing some stories
and a costume for a storyteller
A courier's attire
for Coviello, with a letter
Clothes for the madmen
Two sticks and several wineskins
A bed sheet
An enema syringe
Some prison cells onstage*

CITY

Milan

ACT 1

SCENE 1

Flaminia and Rosetta
After talking about their lovers, Silvio and Pulcinella, who are in Padua for [Silvio's] studies, Flaminia sends Rosetta to the post office to get Silvio's letters. [Silvio writes to her] under the name of Medoro Gentile. Rosetta exits. Flaminia goes inside.

SCENE 2

Orazio and Coviello
[They come on stage] from opposite sides. Orazio [speaks of] his love for Flaminia. Coviello [speaks of] his love for Rosetta. Then they meet and, after their scene, share their stories, reckoning their love [pursuits to be] hopeless. At that,

SCENE 3

Rosetta and the above
She arrives, saying that there were no letters [at the post office]. Coviello tries to flirt with her. She refuses him. Orazio begs her [to intercede for him] with Flaminia. Rosetta [says that] it is impossible. Finally, after this scene, she tells him that he can speak to her [himself], when she informs [Flaminia] that there was no mail. She knocks [at Dottore's].

SCENE 4

Flaminia and the above
[After Flaminia] hears Rosetta's message, Orazio comes forward and woos her. Flaminia rejects him and goes inside with Rosetta. [Orazio and Coviello] stay behind, in despair. Then Coviello devises a plan; he will play a courier, with a letter stating that Silvio and Pulcinella have gotten married. They leave.

SCENE 5

Magnifico and Dottore
They promise their daughters to each other in marriage. Then Magnifico knocks [at his own house].

SCENE 6

Lavinia and the above
She learns that her father has promised her to Dottore, refuses, and goes inside. After the [old men do] their scene, Dottore knocks [at his own house].

SCENE 7

Flaminia and the above
She learns that her father has promised her to Magnifico, refuses, and goes inside. Scorned, the old men do their scene, then leave to draw up the marriage contracts.

SCENE 8

Flaminia and Rosetta, then Coviello
While they are discussing what happened, Coviello comes out, dressed as a courier. After some *lazzi* [bits of comic business], he hands a letter to Flaminia. It states that Silvio and Pulcinella got married in Padua. With the lazzo [business] of

A contemporary rendering of a commedia mask from an artisan in Venice. The mask is one of the many zanni masks; one of the servant clown roles. The device of the half mask makes it possible for the actor to have full use of the mouth for both speaking and facial expression.

the passport, the women beat the courier, who runs off. In despair, they swear they will take their revenge. At that,

SCENE 9

Magnifico, Dottore, Flaminia, and Rosetta
Out of spite, Flaminia, pretending to obey her father, takes Magnifico's hand as a sign of marriage. Happy, Magnifico calls [his daughter].

SCENE 10

Lavinia and the above
Lavinia, following Flaminia's example (although against her will), accepts Dottore. At that,

SCENE 11

Coviello and the above
Coviello asks for Rosetta's hand. Out of spite, Rosetta agrees. The old men give their consent. Magnifico, Flaminia, Coviello, and Rosetta go into Magnifico's house. Dottore brings Lavinia to his home.

SCENE 12

Silvio and Pulcinella
[They say] they are returning from studies in Padua. After their scene, they knock at [Magnifico's].

SCENE 13

Magnifico and the above
After a scene of greetings, [Magnifico] tells them about his marriage (not saying with whom). Silvio asks to see the bride. Magnifico knocks [at his own house].

SCENE 14

Flaminia and the above
On seeing her, Silvio faints flat on his face. The others carry him inside, as if he were dead. Pulcinella is stunned. At that,

SCENE 15

Coviello and Pulcinella
[Coviello] is happy at Pulcinella's arrival, then tells him about his marriage (not saying with whom). Pulcinella asks to see the bride. Coviello knocks [at Magnifico's].

SCENE 16

Rosetta and the above
On seeing her, Pulcinella faints flat on his face. With lazzi Coviello carries him inside as if he were dead. So ends the first act.

ACT II

SCENE 1

Magnifico and Pulcinella
Desperate, [believing], that Silvio has gone out of his mind, Magnifico leaves to search for a doctor; Pulcinella remains. At that,

SCENE 2

Silvio, Coviello, and Pulcinella
Dressed as a madman, Silvio does a scene, speaking nonsense and beating [the others] with wineskins. Then Coviello calls [for help].

SCENE 3

The asylum warden, some inmates, and the above
They lead Silvio by force to the asylum. Coviello leaves to find Magnifico; Pulcinella remains. At that,

SCENE 4

Flaminia and Pulcinella
[She speaks] of Silvio, and talks to Pulcinella, who gently sets her straight. In the end, after she begs him, he calls [the warden].

The *commedia dell'arte* used a dozen or so stock figures, three of whom are shown here. Harlequin, a servant, wears a costume of patches, which later became stylized diamond-shapes. Zany Cornetto, a clown, gives us the English word *zany* (from the Italian *Zanni,* a dialectical form of *Gianni,* an affectionate form of *Giovanni* or John). The third character here, Pantalone, is the old, lustful, miserly Venetian merchant. He wears narrow trousers that were called pantaloons (hence his name) and slippers. The basic plot of most of the plays is the farcical outwitting of old characters such as Pantalone.

SCENE 5

The asylum warden and the above
Flaminia tells [the warden] that she is Silvio's sister and wants to speak to him. Pulcinella exits. The warden orders that the gates be opened, and leaves. Flaminia stays behind. At that,

SCENE 6

Silvio and Flaminia
Behind the bars, [Silvio] does his scene with Flaminia, and withdraws. Flaminia remains, and decides she will pretend to be mad too. She departs.

SCENE 7

Orazio, alone
Orazio, having overheard what Flaminia said last, that she will pretend to be mad, decides he will pretend to be mad too, and exits.

SCENE 8

Magnifico and Coviello
[Magnifico speaks] of Silvio. Coviello advises him to send [Silvio] away again to study. They call [the warden].

SCENE 9

The asylum warden and the above
The warden [says] that Silvio is doing better. They ask that he be brought out. The warden goes inside; they remain.

SCENE 10

Silvio, Magnifico, and Coviello
Silvio comes out half-dressed. Magnifico sends Coviello inside to fetch some clothes. Coviello goes inside, then comes out with some clothes. They do a scene of lucid intervals.* Magnifico sends [Silvio] off with Coviello, telling him to escort Silvio beyond the city gates, [so he can be] on his way to Padua. Silvio [does] his lazzi of going into [his] house, and after this scene (since Magnifico doesn't want to let him in), he leaves with Coviello. Magnifico [also] exits.

SCENE 11

Dottore and Pulcinella
[They arrive] from different directions. Dottore sympathizes with Magnifico, having learned that Silvio has gone out of

*A "scena di luce d'intervallo" is ambiguous in Italian, and could also be translated "a scene of alternating light [and darkness]." We opted for something that makes sense in English.

his mind. Pulcinella complains that he is dying of hunger, because the house is topsy-turvy. At that,

SCENE 12

Flaminia and the above
[Flaminia,] pretending to be mad, does her scene with them. They call [the warden].

SCENE 13

The asylum warden, some inmates and the above
They take [Flaminia] to the asylum. Dottore exits. Pulcinella remains. At that,

SCENE 14

Coviello and Pulcinella
Coviello [appears,] saying that Silvio has fled. Then he meets Pulcinella, who says that Rosetta belongs to him. They hurl insults at each other. After their lazzi they challenge each other to a duel. Pulcinella turns to go inside, to fetch his weapons. At that,

SCENE 15

Orazio and the above
Dressed as a madman, Orazio does his nonsense scene with them. Coviello summons [the warden]. Pulcinella exits.

SCENE 16

The asylum warden, some inmates, Orazio, and Coviello
They take Orazio to the asylum and all exit.

SCENE 17

Pulcinella, alone
With an enema syringe, [he intends] to play a prank on Coviello. At that,

SCENE 18

Silvio [and Pulcinella]
Silvio, as a madman, does the scene of the enema, and then departs. Pulcinella stays behind, laughing, and goes on playing the fool. At that,

SCENE 19

Coviello, then the asylum warden, some inmates, and Pulcinella
Having observed Pulcinella's foolish behavior, Coviello calls the warden, who comes out with some inmates. They all jump on Pulcinella, and with this uproar the second act ends.

ACT III

SCENE 1

Pulcinella, alone
To reproach Rosetta for her unfaithfulness, he knocks [at Dottore's].

SCENE 2

Rosetta [and Pulcinella]
Pulcinella scolds her. After their scene, they clear everything up, and arm in arm go inside to take their pleasure.

SCENE 3

Coviello, alone
[He talks] about the prank he played on Pulcinella, then about having fled, and then [goes on] about the inmates. Finally, he [says] he wants to go home and recuperate, and goes inside.

SCENE 4

Orazio and Flaminia
[Orazio emerges] from the asylum, pursuing Flaminia. She flees, rejecting him, and enters [Dottore's] house. Orazio stays behind. At that,

SCENE 5

Lavinia and Orazio
[Lavinia emerges] from the asylum, begging Orazio [to love her]. He flees, rejecting her, and departs. Lavinia enters [Magnifico's] house.

SCENE 6

Dottore and Magnifico
[They talk about] what happened with all these crazy people. At that,

SCENE 7

Coviello, Pulcinella, Rosetta, and the above
Coviello is pursuing Pulcinella and Rosetta, who appear on stage, both wrapped in a sheet. After this scene, Rosetta tells the old men she is in love with Pulcinella, [saying] that she has not yet consummated the marriage with Coviello. The old men grant her this point, and Rosetta marries Pulcinella. Still wrapped in the sheet (which they have worn for the whole scene), they go inside to [resume] their pleasure. The old men exit, but Coviello remains. At that,

SCENE 8

Silvio and Coviello

Silvio [comes out] dressed as a storyteller, selling his stories. Coviello asks what stories he is selling. Silvio replies, "Coviello's story." After lazzi, [Coviello] says he wants to hear it. Silvio reads "The Story of Coviello," speaking ill of him. Coviello tears the story up, and leaves. Silvio remains. At that,

SCENE 9

Magnifico and Silvio

They do the same scene as before, reading "Magnifico's story," [Silvio] speaking ill of him. Magnifico tears the story up, and leaves. Silvio remains. At that,

SCENE 10

Dottore and Silvio

They do the same scene, and [Silvio] speaks ill of Dottore, who tears the story up, and exits. Silvio stays behind. At that,

SCENE 11

Pulcinella and Silvio

They do the same scene, and [Silvio] speaks ill of Pulcinella, who tears the story up, and exits. Silvio stands behind. At that,

SCENE 12

Flaminia and Silvio

They do the same scene. Silvio reads her story to her, saying that she betrayed her lover, Silvio. She says that it's not true, and shows him the letter that the courier brought her. Silvio reveals his true identity, saying that he didn't write that letter either. It was a betrayal, and he swears he will have his revenge. At that,

LAST SCENE

Everyone

They make their marriage matches (since none of the earlier marriages was consummated): Silvio and Flaminia, Orazio and Lavinia, Pulcinella and Rosetta. And after they all make peace, the comedy ends with rejoicing.

THE END

TOPICS FOR CRITICAL THINKING AND WRITING

The Play on the PAGE

1. Is it possible to get a sense of the story and knockabout comedy from reading a scenario as opposed to a full-blown script with dialogue?

2. In the mid–1700s Italian playwright Carlo Goldoni began scripting dialogue based on old *commedia* scenarios. One of his most well-known plays is *Harlequin, Servant of Two Masters.* Goldoni was committed to reforming Italian comedy and ridding it of its sometimes raunchy humor and improvisational excesses. Some critics have praised Goldoni for "cleaning up" *commedia;* others have criticized him for contributing to *commedia's* demise, for once the scripted plays became in vogue, the improvisational aspect to the performance disappeared. Discuss why or why not improvisation was possible with scripted plays.

The Play on the STAGE

3. Comic business—or *lazzi*—appears throughout the scenario executed by the two clowns Pulcinella and Coviello. Can you describe one of these moments?

4. Many critics have commented that *commedia* performance must have been like watching a Marx Brothers film, or a film by Mel Brooks. What do these films have in common with *commedia* performance?

5. The numerous sets of lovers and would-be lovers could add endless confusion to the story. How do you think the performers were able to keep the story line clear to the audience?

The Play in PERFORMANCE

Unlike the other plays in this volume, *The Insane Asylum* is not a traditional script but a scenario. A scenario is a plot outline detailing the main course of action for individual scenes and specifying which characters are needed for each scene. It contains no dialogue. The actors followed the plot and improvised their words and actions as they performed. *Commedia* companies had a variety of plots and characters at their disposal that they developed or copied from other performers. When they got ready to perform, a scenario was selected, posted for all the actors to see behind the playing area before the performance began, and referred to during the course of the performance. *Commedia* companies were tight-knit groups who played together so much that they developed a strong sense of ensemble.

Traveling from town to town the players used the street as their theater performing at busy street corners, town squares, and special festivals or fairs. The actors traveled with a kind of portable stage, a simple platform that could be easily set up on a cart or on sawhorses. Known as a platform or trestle stage, this type of staging placed the actors at a higher level than the audience, making them visible to the many spectators who gathered around them. (For an illustration of a platform stage, see page 12.) The better visibility the spectators had, the more they would be willing to pay for the performance. The stages often included a simple back curtain that could be easily erected at the rear of the platform. *Commedia* performance required great physical dexterity on the part of the actors. Dancing, tumbling, acrobatics, mime, and comic timing were attributes of every good *commedia* performer.

The stories performed by *commedia* companies were farcical comedy centered on conventional themes of greed, love, and social status. Each performer in the company always played the same character no matter what scenario was performed, and the roles performed usually consisted of the following types: two aging men of high social status one of whom is demanding, greedy, and sometimes lustful, the other a pompous fool; two male clown figures, known as *zanni*, (from *Gianni*, i.e., John), servants to the two older men; at least one pair of innocent young lovers, called *innamoretta*. These kinds of roles are known as *stock characters*. Easily identifiable—both through their costumes and their attributes—*commedia* characters became well-established types. The audience's enjoyment is based partly on its familiarity with the types, and partly on its curiosity about how a particular actor would play the part.

A defining aspect of this theater was that most of the characters wore masks, or more precisely, half-masks, that covered the upper half of the face and left the mouth and jaw free. They were made of thin leather lined with linen and through frequent wear would often shape themselves, without losing particular physical attributes, comfortably to the actor's face. The major exceptions to the use of masks were female roles and the young lovers. The most popular characters were the clowns; Arlecchino [Harlequin], the simpleton intermittently given to flashes of keen wit always trying to confound his master, and Pulcinella, the slyly intelligent country bumpkin. Arlecchino's costume was a colorful array of patches (often stylized into diamond shapes), and he also sported a stick or sword that he wore tucked into his belt. This stick consisted of two thin pieces of wood tied together at the handle. As part of his comic stage business, Arlecchino would often smack someone with his bat, producing a loud cracking or slapping sound. This instrument, known as a "slapstick," has given its name to a boisterous, raucous form of physical comedy marked by wild chases and practical jokes.

A standard feature of every *commedia* performance was the comic stage business, or routines, known in Italian as *lazzi*. *Lazzi* could be performed again and again without regard to the plot, and many farcical moments became the trademarks of certain performers. In the scenario the phrase "Pulcinella does his *lazzo*" occurs several times (*lazzo* is the singular of *lazzi* in Italian). This meant that the actor had a series of signature gestures (compare Groucho Marx wagging his cigar, or Harpo Marx tooting a horn when he sees a girl), verbal repartees, or routines that he would use, often interrupting the story line, to create a humorous moment or a hilarious conclusion to an act.

Molière

Jean Baptiste Poquelin (1622–73), who took the name Molière, was born into a prosperous middle-class family. For a while he studied law and philosophy, but by 1643 he was acting. He became the head of a theatrical company that had initial difficulties but later, thanks largely to Molière's comedies, had great successes. In 1662, he married Armande Béjart. The marriage apparently was unhappy, but the capricious and flirtatious Armande proved to be an accomplished actress. Molière continued to act, with great success in comedy until his death. In one of those improbable things that happen in real life but that are too strange for art, Molière died of a hemorrhage that he suffered while playing the title role in his comedy *The Hypochondriac*. The early plays are highly farcical; among the later and greater plays are *The Highbrow Ladies* (1659), *Tartuffe* (1664), *Don Juan* (1665), *The Misanthrope* (1666), and *The Miser* (1668).

■■■■■■■■■■■■■■■■

COMMENTARY ON *TARTUFFE*

The introduction to this book makes the rather obvious point that in both tragedy and comedy we have characters who are motivated by some ideal, and that (for example) the tragic hero who hunts out the polluted man in Thebes, or who in Denmark avenges his father by killing his father's murderer, is neither more nor less impassioned than the comic lover who ardently vows eternal love to his newest mistress. Whether the passion is noble or comic depends not on its depth, or its persistence, but on its context, and especially on its object. In *Tartuffe*, Orgon's obsession with Tartuffe, in its crazy way, is as consuming as Oedipus's quest for the polluted man or Hamlet's desire to avenge his father. But it is comic, or laughable, because we see how misplaced it is, how unworthy Tartuffe is. Orgon's intensity is, so to speak, wasted.

But why is a person who is obsessed with an unworthy object funny? Here we can get some help from the philosopher Henri Bergson, who in *Laughter* (1900), a small book on comedy, offers an explanation, with examples sometimes drawn from Molière. According to Bergson, the actions of the human being, an organic creature, ought to be free, spontaneous, varied, appropriately responsive to the particular situation, but in comic figures we see a sort of mechanical behavior. The jealous husband is jealous no matter who speaks with his wife, the miser is afraid that whoever rings the doorbell will steal his money, the pedant gives absurdly inappropriate lectures, even to his dog. According to Bergson, in comic behavior we see "the machine inside

the living" (*du mècanique dans le vivant*), or, translated somewhat more freely, the mechanical encrusted on the living. A famous instance (cited by Bergson) occurs in *Tartuffe*, 1.4, when Orgon is told that his wife has been ill. Orgon's response: "Ah. And Tartuffe?" He is then told that Tartuffe is "Bursting with health, and excellently fed," to which he responds, "Poor fellow." Told yet again that his wife suffers severe head pains, he says, "Ah. And Tartuffe?" Told that Tartuffe "ate his meal with relish," Orgon again responds, "Poor fellow!"

What is the point of writing a play about someone blinded by or possessed of an absurd passion, a passion that reduces him or her to a machine? The classical view, going back to a remark attributed to Cicero (106–43 B.C.E.), holds that "Comedy is the imitation of life, the mirror of custom, the image of truth." (If this sounds familiar, it may be because you recall one of Hamlet's comments, in 3.2, to the traveling actors who come to Elsinore: "The purpose of playing," Hamlet explains, "both at the first and now, was and is to hold as 'twere the mirror up to nature, to show virtue her feature, scorn her own image, and the very age and body of the time his form and pressure.") The absurd figures on the comic stage, that is, are a mirror in which we can see our own absurd behavior. We laugh at these figures and (the theory goes), seeing that they are laughable, we resolve not to behave as they do. In the words of the Latin poet Horace (65–68 B.C.E.), who echoed Cicero, comedy "*castigat ridendo mores*," that is, comedy chastises behavior by laughing at it.

Molière draws on this tradition in a petition (1664) he wrote to King Louis XIV, defending *Tartuffe*:

As the duty of comedy is to correct men by amusing them, I believed that in my occupation I could do nothing better than attack the vices of my age by making them ridiculous; and as hypocrisy is undoubtedly one of the most common, most improper, and most dangerous, I thought, Sire, that I would perform a service for all good men of your kingdom if I wrote a comedy which denounced hypocrites and placed in proper view all of the contrived poses of these incredibly virtuous men, all of the concealed villainies of these counterfeit believers who would trap others with a fraudulent piety and a pretended virtue.

Five years later he again drew on this tradition, in his Preface (1669) to *Tartuffe*, when he says, "The function of comedy is to correct men's vices." In the Preface he goes on to explain why satiric comedy is able to correct: Although people are quite willing to behave badly, and can easily ignore moral lectures, they cannot stand being made fun of:

The most forceful lines of a serious moral statement are usually less powerful than those of satire; and nothing will reform most men better than the depiction of their faults. It is a vigorous blow to vices to expose them to public laughter. Criticism is taken lightly, but men will not tolerate satire. They are quite willing to be mean, but they never like to be ridiculed.

We cannot doubt, then, that Molière was familiar with the classical defense of comedy, but we can doubt that the defense is sound, and we can even doubt that Molière believed it and was guided by it. To take the first point: Do we see our own vices (or even our foibles) on the stage, or do we somehow see in the comic figures only the vices and foibles of our neighbors? As for the second point, whether Molière believed the theory, we cannot help but notice that he uses this venerable idea in documents in which he is justifying his play against censorship; beleaguered by courtiers and clergymen who found his play objectionable, he doubtless was pleased to be able to use a venerable argument as justification for his satirical comedy. But in an earlier work, *The Critique of the School of Wives*, through the mouth of his spokesman, Dorante, he says something that strikes us as truer than the classical formula:

It's a strange undertaking, that, of making decent people laugh (*c'est une étrange enterprise que celle de faire rire les honnêtes gens*).

Here Molière recognizes, first, that writing comedies is not something that can be reduced to a formula, and, second, that the usual audience consists of *honnêtes gens* who come for a laugh, not vicious people who come so they can reform their behavior.

This is not to say that Molière thought people were chiefly rational, and irrational behavior was unusual. In *Tartuffe*, Cléante, whom we may well take as Molière's spokesman or *raisonneur* (literally a person who reasons, but in dramatic terminology a character who expresses the author's standpoint), suggests we are all a bit odd, and we too easily behave irrationally:

Ah, brother, man's a strangely fashioned creature
Who seldom is content to follow Nature,
But recklessly pursues his inclination
Beyond the narrow bounds of moderation
And often, by transgressing Reason's laws,
Perverts a lofty aim or noble cause.

(1.5.81–86)

Cléante recognizes that most of us have irrational tendencies, but he assumes we can listen to reason when our fellows point out our odd bits of behavior. At the very end of the play, when Tartuffe is arrested, Orgon quite naturally is again impassioned, this time with anger directed against Tartuffe: "Well, traitor, now you see. . . ." Cléante again urges Orgon to try to act with moderation, and Cléante even goes so far as to suggest that Orgon should wish for Tartuffe's reformation. Here are the last three speeches of the play:

ORGON (*to Tartuffe*).
Well, traitor, now you see . . .
CLÉANTE.
                                     Ah, Brother, please,
Let's not descend to such indignities.
Leave the poor wretch to his unhappy fate,
And don't say anything to aggravate
His present woes; but rather hope that he
Will soon embrace an honest piety,
And mend his ways, and by a true repentance
Move our just King to moderate his sentence.
Meanwhile, go kneel before your sovereign's throne
And thank him for the mercies he has shown.
ORGON.
Well said: let's go at once and, gladly kneeling,
Express the gratitude which all are feeling.
Then, when that first great duty has been done,
We'll turn with pleasure to a second one,

And give Valère whose love has proven so true,
The wedded happiness which is his due.

Cléante's advice is good, and doubtless we are all glad to hear Orgon at last talk sense and look forward to the wedding of the young people, but whether *Tartuffe* can indeed prevent viewers from acting badly by showing them images of bad behavior (Tartuffe's hypocrisy and lust, Orgon's credulity) is doubtful. What is undoubted, however, is that the play has entertained viewers and readers for more than three hundred years, and this may be enough for any play to do.

TARTUFFE
Molière

Translated by Richard Wilbur

CHARACTERS

MME PERNELLE, *Orgon's mother*
ORGON, *Elmire's husband*
ELMIRE, *Orgon's wife*
DAMIS, *Orgon's son, Elmire's stepson*
MARIANE, *Orgon's daughter, Elmire's stepdaughter, in love with Valère*
VALÈRE, *in love with Mariane*
CLÉANTE, *Orgon's brother-in-law*

TARTUFFE, *a hypocrite*
DORINE, *Mariane's lady's maid*
M. LOYAL, *a bailiff*
A POLICE OFFICER
FLIPOTE, *Mme Pernelle's maid*

THE SCENE THROUGHOUT

Orgon's house in Paris

ACT 1

SCENE 1

MADAME PERNELLE and FLIPOTE, her maid
ELMIRE   DORINE   CLÉANTE   MARIANE   DAMIS

MADAME PERNELLE.
    Come, come, Flipote; it's time I left this place.
ELMIRE.
    I can't keep up, you walk at such a pace.
MADAM PERNELLE.
    Don't trouble, child; no need to show me out.
    It's not your manners I'm concerned about.
ELMIRE.
5   We merely pay you the respect we owe.
    But, Mother, why this hurry? Must you go?
MADAME PERNELLE.
    I must. This house appalls me. No one in it
    Will pay attention for a single minute.
    Children, I take my leave much vexed in spirit.
10   I offer good advice, but you won't hear it.
    You all break in and chatter on and on.
    It's like a madhouse with the keeper gone.
DORINE.
    If . . .
MADAME PERNELLE.
        Girl, you talk too much, and I'm afraid
    You're far too saucy for a lady's-maid.
15   You push in everywhere and have your say.
DAMIS.
    But . . .

MADAME PERNELLE.
    You, boy, grow more foolish every day.
    To think my grandson should be such a dunce!
    I've said a hundred times, if I've said it once,
    That if you keep the course on which you've started,
    You'll leave your worthy father broken-hearted.   20
MARIANE.
    I think . . .
MADAME PERNELLE.
        And you, his sister, seems so pure,
    So shy, so innocent, and so demure.
    But you know what they say about still waters.
    I pity parents with secretive daughters.
ELMIRE.
    Now, Mother . . .
MADAME PERNELLE.   And as for you, child, let me add   25
    That your behavior is extremely bad,
    And a poor example for these children, too.
    Their dear, dead mother did far better than you.
    You're much too free with money, and I'm distressed
    To see you so elaborately dressed.   30
    When it's one's husband that one aims to please,
    One has no need of costly fripperies.
CLÉANTE.
    Oh, Madam, really . . .
MADAME PERNELLE.   You are her brother, Sir,
    And I respect and love you; yet if I were
    My son, this lady's good and pious spouse,   35
    I wouldn't make you welcome in my house.
    You're full of worldly counsels which, I fear,
    Aren't suitable for decent folk to hear.
    I've spoken bluntly, Sir; but it behooves us

Tartuffe can be staged very effectively in modern dress, as was done
in this 1996 adaptation set in Baton
Rouge, Louisiana and presented by
Circle in the Square. John Glover
(left) played Tartuffe and Haviland
Morris (right) played Elmire.

40   Not to mince words when righteous fervor moves us.
       DAMIS.
          Your man Tartuffe is full of holy speeches . . .
       MADAME PERNELLE.
          And practises precisely what he preaches.
          He's a fine man, and should be listened to.
          I will not hear him mocked by fools like you.
       DAMIS.
45   Good God! Do you expect me to submit
          To the tyranny of that carping hypocrite?
          Must we forgo all joys and satisfactions
          Because that bigot censures all our actions?
       DORINE.
          To hear him talk—and he talks all the time—
50   There's nothing one can do that's not a crime.
          He rails at everything, your dear Tartuffe.
       MADAME PERNELLE.
          Whatever he reproves deserves reproof.
          He's out to save your souls, and all of you
          Must love him, as my son would have you do.
       DAMIS.
55   Ah no, Grandmother, I could never take
          To such a rascal, even for my father's sake.
          That's how I feel, and I shall not dissemble
          His every action makes me seethe and tremble
          With helpless anger, and I have no doubt
60   That he and I will shortly have it out.

       DORINE.
          Surely it is a shame and a disgrace
          To see his man usurp the master's place—
          To see this beggar who, when he first came,
          Had not a shoe or shoestring to his name
          So far forget himself that he behaves   65
          As if the house were his, and we his slaves.
       MADAME PERNELLE.
          Well, mark my words, your souls would fare far better
          If you obeyed his precepts to the letter
       DORINE.
          You see him as a saint. I'm far less awed;
          In fact, I see right through him. He's a fraud.   70
       MADAME PERNELLE.
          Nonsense!
       DORINE.   His man Laurent's the same, or worse;
          I'd not trust either with a penny purse.
       MADAME PERNELLE.
          I can't say what his servant's morals may be;
          His own great goodness I can guarantee.
          You all regard him with distaste and fear   75
          Because he tells you what you're loath to hear,
          Condemns your sins, points out your moral flaws,
          And humbly strives to further Heaven's cause.
       DORINE.
          If sin is all that bothers him, why is it
          He's so upset when folk drop in to visit?   80

Is Heaven so outraged by a social call
That he must prophesy against us all?
I'll tell you what I think; if you ask me,
He's jealous of my mistress' company.

MADAME PERNELLE.

85   Rubbish! (*To Elmire.*) He's not alone, child, in com-
            plaining
Of all your promiscuous entertaining.
Why, the whole neighborhood's upset, I know,
By all these carriages that come and go,
With crowds of guests parading in and out
90   And noisy servants loitering about.
In all of this, I'm sure there's nothing vicious;
But why give people cause to be suspicious?

CLÉANTE.

They need no cause; they'll talk in any case.
Madam, this world would be a joyless place
95   If, fearing what malicious tongues might say,
We locked our doors and turned our friends away.
And even if one did so dreary a thing,
D'you think those tongues would cease their chattering?
One can't fight slander; it's a losing battle;
100   Let us instead ignore their tittle-tattle.
Let's strive to live by conscience' clear decrees,
And let the gossips gossip as they please.

DORINE.

If there is talk against us, I know the source:
It's Daphne and her little husband, of course.
105   Those who have greatest cause for guilt and shame
Are quickest to besmirch a neighbor's name.
When there's a chance for libel, they never miss it;
When something can be made to seem illicit
They're off at once to spread the joyous news,
110   Adding to fact what fantasies they choose.
By talking up their neighbor's indiscretions
They seek to camouflage their own transgressions,
Hoping that others' innocent affairs
Will lend a hue of innocence to theirs,
115   Or that their own black guilt will come to seem
Part of a general shady color-scheme.

MADAME PERNELLE.

All that is quite irrelevant. I doubt
That anyone's more virtuous and devout
Than dear Orante; and I'm informed that she
120   Condemns your mode of life most vehemently.

DORINE.

Oh, yes, she's strict, devout, and has no taint
Of worldliness; in short, she seems a saint.
But it was time which taught her that disguise;
She's thus because she can't be otherwise.
125   So long as her attractions could enthrall,
She flounced and flirted and enjoyed it all,
But now that they're no longer what they were
She quits the world which fast is quitting her,

And wears a veil of virtue to conceal
Her bankrupt beauty and her lost appeal.   130
That's what becomes of old coquettes today;
Distressed when all their lovers fall away,
They see no recourse but to play the prude,
And so confer a style on solitude.
Thereafter, they're severe with everyone,   135
Condemning all our actions, pardoning none,
And claiming to be pure, austere, and zealous
When, if the truth were known, they're merely jealous,
And cannot bear to see another know
The pleasures time has forced them to forgo.   140

MADAME PERNELLE (*initially to Elmire*).

That sort of talk is what you like to hear;
Therefore you'd have us all keep still, my dear,
While Madam rattles on the livelong day.
Nevertheless, I mean to have my say.
I tell you that you're blest to have Tartuffe   145
Dwelling, as my son's guest, beneath this roof;
That Heaven has sent him to forestall its wrath
By leading you, once more, to the true path;
That all he reprehends its reprehensible,
And that you'd better heed him, and be sensible.   150
These visits, balls, and parties in which you revel
Are nothing but inventions of the Devil.
One never hears a word that's edifying:
Nothing but chaff and foolishness and lying,
As well as vicious gossip in which one's neighbor   155
Is cut to bits with epee, foil, and saber.
People of sense are driven half-insane
At such affairs, where noise and folly reign
And reputations perish thick and fast.
As a wise preacher said on Sunday last,   160
Parties are Towers of Babylon, because
The guests all babble on with never a pause;
And then he told a story which, I think . . .
(*To Cléante.*) I heard that laugh, Sir, and I saw that wink!
Go find your silly friends and laugh some more!   165
Enough; I'm going; don't show me to the door.
I leave this household much dismayed and vexed;
I cannot say when I shall see you next.
(*Slapping Flipote.*) Wake up, don't stand there gaping
            into space!
I'll slap some sense into that stupid face.   170
Move, move, you slut.

SCENE 2

CLÉANTE   DORINE

CLÉANTE. I think I'll stay behind;
I want no further pieces of her mind.
How that old lady . . .

DORINE.   Oh, what wouldn't she say

If she could hear you speak of her that way!
5   She'd thank you for the *lady*, but I'm sure
She'd find the *old* a little premature.

CLÉANTE.
My, what a scene she made, and what a din!
And how this man Tartuffe has taken her in!

DORINE.
Yes, but her son is even worse deceived;
10   His folly must be seen to be believed.
In the late troubles, he played an able part
And served his king with wise and loyal heart,
But he's quite lost his senses since he fell
Beneath Tartuffe's infatuating spell.
15   He calls him brother, and loves him as his life,
Preferring him to mother, child, or wife.
In him and him alone will he confide;
He's made him his confessor and his guide;
He pets and pampers him with love more tender
20   Than any pretty mistress could engender,
Gives him the place of honor when they dine,
Delights to see him gorging like a swine,
Stuffs him with dainties till his guts distend,
And when he belches, cries, "God bless you, friend!"
25   In short, he's mad; he worships him; he dotes;
His needs he marvels at, his words he quotes,
Thinking each act a miracle, each word
Oracular as those that Moses heard.
Tartuffe, much pleased to find so easy a victim,
30   Has in a hundred ways beguiled and tricked him.
Milked him of money, and with his permission
Established here a sort of Inquisition.
Even Laurent, his lackey, dares to give
Us arrogant advice on how to live;
35   He sermonizes us in thundering tones
And confiscates our ribbons and colognes.
Last week he tore a kerchief into pieces
Because he found it pressed in a *Life of Jesus:*
He said it was a sin to juxtapose
40   Unholy vanities and holy prose.

SCENE 3

ELMIRE   DAMIS   DORINE   MARIANE   CLÉANTE

ELMIRE (*to Cléante*).
You did well not to follow, she stood in the door
And said *verbatim* all she'd said before.
I saw my husband coming. I think I'd best
Go upstairs now, and take a little rest.

CLÉANTE.
5   I'll wait and greet him here; then I must go.
I've really only time to say hello.

DAMIS.
Sound him about my sister's wedding, please.

I think Tartuffe's against it, and that he's
Been urging Father to withdraw his blessing.
As you well know, I'd find that most distressing.   10
Unless my sister and Valère can marry,
My hopes to wed his sister will miscarry,
And I'm determined . . .

DORINE.   He's coming.

SCENE 4

ORGON   CLÉANTE   DORINE

ORGON.   Ah, Brother, good-day.

CLÉANTE.
Well, welcome back. I'm sorry I can't stay.
How was the country? Blooming, I trust, and green?

ORGON.
Excuse me, Brother, just one moment.
(*To Dorine.*)   Dorine . . .
(*To Cléante.*) To put my mind at rest, I always learn   5
The household news the moment I return.
(*To Dorine.*) Has all been well, these two days I've been
   gone?
How are the family? What's been going on?

DORINE.
Your wife, two days ago, had a very bad fever,
And a fierce headache which refused to leave her.   10

ORGON.
Ah. And Tartuffe?

DORINE.   Tartuffe? Why, he's round and red,
Bursting with health, and excellently fed.

ORGON.
Poor fellow!

DORINE.   That night, the mistress was unable
To take a single bite at the dinner-table.
Her headache-pains, she said, were simply hellish.   15

ORGON.
Ah. And Tartuffe?

DORINE.   He ate his meal with relish,
And zealously devoured in her presence
A leg of mutton and a brace of pheasants.

ORGON.
Poor fellow!

DORINE.   Well, the pains continued strong,
And so she tossed and tossed the whole night long,   20
Now icy-cold, now burning like a flame.
We sat beside her bed till morning came.

ORGON.
Ah. And Tartuffe?

DORINE.   Why, having eaten, he rose
And sought his room, already in a doze,
Got into his warm bed, and snored away   25
In perfect peace until the break of day.

ORGON.
Poor fellow!

DORINE.   After much ado, we talked her
Into dispatching someone for the doctor.
He bled her, and the fever quickly fell.

ORGON.
Ah. And Tartuffe?

30 DORINE.   He bore it very well.
To keep his cheerfulness at any cost,
And make up for the blood *Madame* had lost,
He drank, at lunch, four beakers full of port.

ORGON.
Poor fellow!

DORINE.   Both are doing well, in short.
35 I'll go and tell *Madame* that you've expressed
Keen sympathy and anxious interest.

SCENE 5

ORGON   CLÉANTE

CLÉANTE.
That girl was laughing in your face, and though
I've no wish to offend you, even so
I'm bound to say that she had some excuse.
How can you possibly be such a goose?
5 Are you dazed by this man's hocus-pocus
That all the world, save him, is out of focus?
You've given him clothing, shelter, food, and care;
Why must you also . . .

ORGON.   Brother, stop right there.
You do not know the man of whom you speak.

CLÉANTE.
10 I grant you that. But my judgment's not so weak
That I can't tell, by his effect on others . . .

ORGON.
Ah, when you meet him, you two will be like brothers!
There's been no loftier soul since time began.
He is a man who . . . a man who . . . an excellent man.
15 To keep his precepts is to be reborn,
And view this dunghill of a world with scorn.
Yes, thanks to him I'm a changed man indeed.
Under his tutelage my soul's been freed
From earthly loves, and every human tie:
20 My mother, children, brother, and wife could die,
And I'd not feel a single moment's pain.

CLÉANTE.
That's a fine sentiment, Brother; most humane.

ORGON.
Oh, had you seen Tartuffe as I first knew him.
Your heart, like mine, would have surrendered to him.
25 He used to come into our church each day
And humbly kneel nearby, and start to pray.
He'd draw the eyes of everybody there

By the deep fervor of his heartfelt prayer;
He'd sigh and weep, and sometimes with a sound
Of rapture he would bend and kiss the ground; 30
And when I rose to go, he'd run before
To offer me holy-water at the door.
His serving-man, no less devout than he,
Informed me of his master's poverty;
I gave him gifts, but in his humbleness 35
He'd beg me every time to give him less.
"Oh, that's too much," he'd cry, "too much by twice!
I don't deserve it. The half, Sir, would suffice."
And when I wouldn't take it back, he'd share
Half of it with the poor, right then and there. 40
At length, Heaven prompted me to take him in
To dwell with us, and free our souls from sin.
He guides our lives, and to protect my honor
Stays by my wife, and keeps an eye on her;
He tells me whom she sees, and all she does, 45
And seems more jealous than I ever was!
And how austere he is! Why, he can detect
A mortal sin where you would least suspect;
In smallest trifles, he's extremely strict.
Last week, his conscience was severely pricked 50
Because, while praying, he had caught a flea
And killed it, so he felt, too wrathfully.

CLÉANTE.
Good God, man! Have you lost your common sense—
Or is this all some joke at my expense?
How can you stand there and in all sobriety . . . 55

ORGON.
Brother, your language savors of impiety.
Too much free-thinking's made your faith unsteady,
And as I've warned you many times already,
'Twill get you into trouble before you're through.

CLÉANTE.
So I've been told before by dupes like you: 60
Being blind, you'd have all others blind as well;
The clear-eyed man you call an infidel,
And he who sees through humbug and pretense
Is charged, by you, with want of reverence.
Spare me your warnings, Brother; I have no fear 65
Of speaking out, for you and Heaven to hear,
Against affected zeal and pious knavery
There's true and false in piety, as in bravery,
And just as those whose courage shines the most
In battle, are the least inclined to boast, 70
So those whose hearts are truly pure and lowly
Don't make a flashy show of being holy.
There's a vast difference, so it seems to me.
Between true piety and hypocrisy:
How do you fail to see it, may I ask? 75
Is not a face quite different from a mask?
Cannot sincerity and cunning art,
Reality and semblance, be told apart?

Are scarecrows just like men, and do you hold
80 That a false coin is just as good as gold?
Ah, Brother, man's a strangely fashioned creature
Who seldom is content to follow Nature,
But recklessly pursues his inclination
Beyond the narrow bounds of moderation,
85 And often, by transgressing Reason's laws,
Perverts a lofty aim or noble cause.
A passing observation, but it applies.

ORGON.
I see, dear Brother, that you're profoundly wise;
You harbor all the insight of the age.
90 You are our one clear mind, our only sage,
The era's oracle, its Cato too
And all mankind are fools compared to you.

CLÉANTE.
Brother, I don't pretend to be a sage,
Nor have I all the wisdom of the age.
95 There's just one insight I would dare to claim:
I know that true and false are not the same;
And just as there is nothing I more revere
Than a soul whose faith is steadfast and sincere,
Nothing that I more cherish and admire
100 Than honest zeal and true religious fire,
So there is nothing that I find more base
Than specious piety's dishonest face—
Than these bold mountebanks, these histrios
Whose impious mummeries are hollow shows
105 Exploit our love of Heaven, and make a jest
Of all that men think holiest and best;
These calculating souls who offer prayers
Not to their Maker, but as public wares,
And seek to buy respect and reputation
110 With lifted eyes and sighs of exultation;
These charlatans, I say, whose pilgrim souls
Proceed, by way of Heaven, toward earthly goals,
Who weep and pray and swindle and extort,
Who preach the monkish life, but haunt the court,
115 Who make their zeal the partner of their vice—
Such men are vengeful, sly, and cold as ice,
And when there is an enemy to defame
They cloak their spite in fair religion's name,
Their private spleen and malice being made
120 To seem a high and virtuous crusade,
Until, to mankind's reverent applause,
They crucify their foe in Heaven's cause.
Such knaves are all too common; yet, for the wise,
True piety isn't hard to recognize,
125 And, happily, these present times provide us
With bright examples to instruct and guide us.
Consider Ariston and Périandre;
Look at Oronte, Alcidamas, Clitandre;
Their virtue is acknowledged; who could doubt it?
130 But you won't hear them beat the drum about it.

They're never ostentatious, never vain,
And their religion's moderate and humane;
It's not their way to criticize and chide:
They think censoriousness a mark of pride,
And therefore, letting others preach and rave,   135
They show, by deeds, how Christians should behave.
They think no evil of their fellow man,
But judge of him as kindly as they can.
They don't intrigue and wangle and conspire;
To lead a good life in their one desire;   140
The sinner wakes no rancorous hate in them;
It is the sin alone which they condemn;
Nor do they try to show a fiercer zeal
For Heaven's cause than Heaven itself could feel.
These men I honor, these men I advocate   145
As models for us all to emulate.
Your man is not their sort at all. I fear:
And, while your praise of him is quite sincere,
I think that you've been dreadfully deluded.

ORGON.
Now then, dear Brother, is your speech concluded?   150

CLÉANTE.
Why, yes.

ORGON.   Your servant, Sir. (*He turns to go.*)

CLÉANTE.   No, Brother; wait.
There's one more matter. You agreed of late
That young Valère might have your daughter's hand.

ORGON.
I did.

CLÉANTE. And set the date, I understand.

ORGON.
Quite so.

CLÉANTE.   You've now postponed it; is that true? 155

ORGON.
No doubt.

CLÉANTE.
The match no longer pleases you?

ORGON.
Who knows?

CLÉANTE.   D'you mean to go back on your word?

ORGON.
I won't say that.

CLÉANTE.   Has anything occurred
Which might entitle you to break your pledge?

ORGON.
Perhaps.

CLÉANTE. Why must you hem, and haw, and hedge?   160
The boy asked me to sound you in this affair . . .

ORGON.
It's been a pleasure.

CLÉANTE.
But what shall I tell Valère?

ORGON.
Whatever you like.

CLÉANTE.   But what have you decided?
    What are your plans?
ORGON.   I plan, Sir, to be guided
    By Heaven's will.
CLÉANTE.   Come, Brother, don't talk rot.
165   You've given Valère your word; will you keep it, or not?
ORGON.
    Good day.
CLÉANTE.   This looks like poor Valère's undoing;
    I'll go and warn him that there's trouble brewing.

ACT II

SCENE 1

ORGON   MARIANE

ORGON.
    Mariane.
MARIANE.   Yes, Father?
ORGON.   A word with you; come here.
MARIANE.
    What are you looking for?
ORGON (*peering into a small closet*).
    Eavesdroppers, dear.
    I'm making sure we shan't be overheard.
    Someone in there could catch our every word.
5   Ah, good, we're safe. Now, Mariane, my child,
    You're a sweet girl who's tractable and mild,
    Whom I hold dear, and think most highly of.
MARIANE.
    I'm deeply grateful, Father, for your love.
ORGON.
    That's well said, Daughter; and you can repay me
10   If, in all things, you'll cheerfully obey me.
MARIANE.
    To please you, Sir, is what delights me best
ORGON.
    Good, good, Now, what d'you think of Tartuffe, our guest?
MARIANE.
    I, Sir?
ORGON. Yes. Weigh your answer; think it through.
MARIANE.
    Oh, dear. I'll say whatever you wish me to.
ORGON.
15   That's wisely said, my Daughter. Say of him, then,
    That he's the very worthiest of men,
    And that you're fond of him and would rejoice
    In being his wife, if that should be my choice.
    Well?
MARIANE.
    What?
ORGON.   What's that?

MARIANE.   I . . .
ORGON.   Well?
MARIANE.   Forgive me, pray.
ORGON.
    Did you not hear me?
MARIANE.   Of *whom*, sir, must I say   20
    That I am fond of him, and would rejoice
    In being his wife, if that should be your choice?
ORGON.
    Why, of Tartuffe.
MARAINE.   But, Father, that's false, you know.
    Why would you have me say what isn't so?
ORGON.
    Because I am resolved it shall be true.   25
    That it's my wish should be enough for you.
MARIANE.
    You can't mean, Father . . .
ORGON.   Yes, Tartuffe shall be
    Allied by marriage to this family,
    And he's to be your husband, is that clear?   30
    It's a father's privilege . . .

SCENE 2

DORINE   ORGON   MARIANE

ORGON (*to Dorine*).   What are you doing in here?
    Is curiosity so fierce a passion
    With you, that you must eavesdrop in this fashion?
DORINE.
    There's lately been a rumor going about—
    Based on some hunch or chance remark, no doubt—
    That you mean Mariane to wed Tartuffe.   5
    I've laughed it off, of course, as just a spoof.
ORGON.
    You find it so incredible?
DORINE.   Yes, I do.
    I won't accept that story, even from you.
ORGON.
    Well, you'll believe it when the thing is done.   10
DORINE.
    Yes, yes, of course. Go on and have your fun.
ORGON.
    I've never been more serious in my life.
DORINE.
    Ha!
ORGON.   Daughter, I mean it; you're to be his wife.
DORINE.
    No, don't believe your father; it's all a hoax.
ORGON.
    See here, young woman . . .
DORINE.   Come, Sir, no more jokes;   15
    You can't fool us.

ORGON.   How dare you talk that way?
DORINE.
    All right, then: we believe you, sad to say.
    But how a man like you, who looks so wise
    And wears a moustache of such splendid size,
    Can be so foolish as to . . .
20 ORGON.   Silence please!
    My girl, you take too many liberties.
    I'm master here, as you must not forget.
DORINE.
    Do let's discuss this calmly; don't be upset.
    You can't be serious, Sir, about this plan.
    What should that bigot want with Mariane?
25   Praying and fasting ought to keep him busy.
    And then, in terms of wealth and rank, what is he?
    Why should a man of property like you
    Pick out a beggar son-in-law?
ORGON.   That will do.
30   Speak of his poverty with reverence.
    His is a pure and saintly indigence
    Which far transcends all worldly pride and pelf.
    He lost his fortune, as he says himself,
    Because he cared for Heaven alone, and so
35   Was careless of his interests here below.
    I mean to get him out of his present straits
    And help him to recover his estates—
    Which, in his part of the world, have no small fame.
    Poor though he is, he's a gentleman just the same.
DORINE.
40   Yes, so he tells us; and Sir, it seems to me
    Such pride goes very ill with piety.
    A man whose spirit spurns this dungy earth
    Ought not to brag of lands and noble birth;
    Such worldly arrogance will hardly square
45   With meek devotion and the life of prayer.
    . . . But this approach, I see, has drawn a blank;
    Let's speak, then, of his person, not his rank.
    Doesn't is seem to you a trifle grim
    To give a girl like her to a man like him?
50   When two are so ill-suited, can't you see
    What the sad consequence is bound to be?
    A young girl's virtue is imperilled, Sir,
    When such a marriage is imposed on her;
    For if one's bridegroom isn't to one's taste,
55   It's hardly an inducement to be chaste,
    And many a man with horns upon his brow
    Has made his wife the thing that she is now.
    It's hard to be a faithful wife, in short,
    To certain husbands of a certain sort,
60   And he who gives his daughter to a man she hates
    Must answer for her sins at Heaven's gates.
    Think, Sir, before you play so risky a role.
ORGON.
    This servant-girl presumes to save my soul!

DORINE.
    You would do well to ponder what I've said.
ORGON.
    Daughter, we'll disregard this dunderhead.   65
    Just trust your father's judgement. Oh, I'm aware
    That once I promised you to young Valère;
    But now I hear he gambles, which greatly shocks me;
    What's more, I've doubts about his orthodoxy.
    His visits to church, I note, are very few.   70
DORINE.
    Would you have him go at the same hours as you,
    And kneel nearby, to be sure of being seen?
ORGON.
    I can dispense with such remarks, Dorine.
    (*To Mariane.*) Tartuffe, however, is sure of Heaven's
      blessing,
    And that's the only treasure worth possessing.   75
    This match will bring you joys beyond all measure;
    Your cup will overflow with every pleasure;
    You two will interchange your faithful loves
    Like two sweet cherubs, or two turtle-doves.
    No harsh word shall be heard, no frown be seen,   80
    And he shall make you happy as a queen.
DORINE.
    And she'll make him a cuckold, just wait and see.
ORGON.
    What language!
DORINE.   Oh, he's a man of destiny;
    He's *made* for horns, and what the stars demand
    Your daughter's virtue surely can't withstand.   85
ORGON.
    Don't interrupt me further. Why can't you learn
    That certain things are none of your concern?
DORINE.
    It's for your own sake that I interfere.

(*She repeatedly interrupts Orgon just as he is turning to
speak to his daughter:*)

ORGON.
    Most kind of you. Now, hold your tongue, d'you hear?
DORINE.
    If I didn't love you . . .
ORGON.   Spare me your affection.   90
DORINE.
    I love you, Sir, in spite of your objection.
ORGON.
    Blast!
DORINE. I can't bear, Sir, for your honor's sake,
    To let you make this ludicrous mistake.
ORGON.
    You mean to go on talking?
DORINE.   If I didn't protest
    This sinful marriage, my conscience couldn't rest.   95

ORGON.
    If you don't hold you tongue, you little shrew . . .
DORINE.
    What, lost your temper? A pious man like you?
ORGON.
    Yes! Yes! You talk and talk. I'm maddened by it.
    Once and for all, I tell you to be quiet.
DORINE.
100   Well, I'll be quiet. But I'll be thinking hard.
ORGON.
    Think all you like, but you had better guard
    That saucy tongue of yours, or I'll . . .
    (*Turning back to Mariane.*)   Now, child,
    I've weighed this matter fully.
DORINE (*aside*).   It drives me wild
    That I can't speak.

    (*Orgon turns his head, and she is silent.*)

ORGON.   Tartuffe is no young dandy,
    But, still, his person . . .
105 DORINE (*aside*).   Is as sweet as candy,
ORGON.
    Is such that, even if you shouldn't care
    For his other merits . . .

    (*He turns and stands facing Dorine, arms crossed.*)

DORINE (*aside*).   They'll make a lovely pair.
    If I were she, no man would marry me
    Against my inclination, and go scot-free.
110   He'd learn, before the wedding-day was over.
    How readily a wife can find a lover.
ORGON (*to Dorine*).
    It seems you treat my orders as a joke.
DORINE.
    Why, what's the matter? 'Twas not to you I spoke.
ORGON.
    What *were* you doing?
DORINE.   Talking to myself, that's all.
ORGON.
115   Ah! (*aside*.) One more bit of impudence and gall,
    And I shall give her a good slap in the face.

    (*He puts himself in position to slap her; Dorine, whenever
    he glances at her, stands immobile and silent:*)

    Daughter, you shall accept, and with good grace,
    The husband I've selected . . . Your wedding-day . . .
    (*To Dorine.*) Why don't you talk to yourself?
DORINE.   I've nothing to say.
ORGON.
    Come, just one word.
120 DORINE.   No thank you, Sir. I pass.
ORGON.
    Come, speak; I'm waiting.
DORINE.   I'd not be such an ass.

ORGON (*turning to Mariane*).
    In short, dear Daughter, I mean to be obeyed,
    And you must bow to the sound choice I've made.
DORINE (*moving away*).
    I'd not wed such a monster, even in jest.

    (*Orgon attempts to slap her, but misses.*)

ORGON.
    Daughter, that maid of yours is a thorough pest;   125
    She makes me sinfully annoyed and nettled.
    I can't speak further; my nerves are too unsettled.
    She's so upset me by her insolent talk,
    I'll calm myself by going for a walk.

SCENE 3

DORINE   MARIANE

DORINE (*returning*).
    Well, have you lost your tongue, girl? Must I play
    Your part, and say the lines you ought to say?
    Faced with a fate so hideous and absurd,
    Can you not utter one dissenting word?
MARIANE.
    What good would it do? A father's power is great.   5
DORINE.
    Resist him now, or it will be too late.
MARIANE.
    But . . .
DORINE.   Tell him one cannot love at a father's whim;
    That you shall marry for yourself, not him;
    That since it's you who are to be the bride,
    It's you, not he, who must be satisfied;   10
    And that if his Tartuffe is so sublime,
    He's free to marry him at any time.
MARIANE.
    I've bowed so long to Father's strict control,
    I couldn't oppose him now, to save my soul.
DORINE.
    Come, come, Mariane. Do listen to reason, won't you?   15
    Valère has asked your hand. Do you love him, or don't
        you?
MARIANE.
    Oh, how unjust of you! What can you mean
    By asking such a question, dear Dorine?
    You know the depth of my affection for him;
    I've told you a hundred times how I adore him.   20
DORINE.
    I don't believe in everything I hear;
    Who knows if your professions were sincere?
MARIANE.
    They were, Dorine, and you do me wrong to doubt it;
    Heaven knows that I've been all too frank about it.
DORINE.
    You love him, then?

25 MARIANE.   Oh, more than I can express.
   DORINE.
      And he, I take it, cares for you no less?
   MARIANE.
      I think so.
   DORINE.   And you both, with equal fire,
      Burn to be married?
   MARIANE.   That is our one desire.
   DORINE.
      What of Tartuffe, then? What of your father's plan?
   MARIANE.
30   I'll kill myself, if I'm forced to wed that man.
   DORINE.
      I hadn't thought of that recourse. How splendid!
      Just die, and all your troubles will be ended!
      A fine solution. Oh, it maddens me
      To hear you talk in that self-pitying key.
   MARIANE.
35   Dorine, how harsh you are! It's most unfair.
      You have no sympathy for my despair.
   DORINE.
      I've none at all for people who talk drivel
      And, faced with difficulties, whine and snivel.
   MARIANE.
      No doubt I'm timid, but it would be wrong . . .
   DORINE.
40   True love requires a heart that's firm and strong.
   MARIANE.
      I'm strong in my affection for Valère,
      But coping with my father is his affair.
   DORINE.
      But if your father's brain has grown so cracked
      Over his dear Tartuffe that he can retract
45   His blessing, though your wedding-day was named,
      It's surely not Valère who's to be blamed.
   MARIANE.
      If I defied my father, as you suggest,
      Would it not seem unmaidenly, at best?
      Shall I defend my love at the expense
50   Of brazenness and disobedience?
      Shall I parade my heart's desires, and flaunt . . .
   DORINE.
      No, I ask nothing of you. Clearly you want
      To be Madame Tartuffe, and I feel bound
      Not to oppose a wish so very sound.
55   What right have I to criticize the match?
      Indeed, my dear, the man's a brilliant catch.
      Monsieur Tartuffe! Now, there's a man of weight!
      Yes, yes, Monsieur Tartuffe, I'm bound to state,
      Is quite a person; that's not to be denied;
60   'Twill be no little thing to be his bride.
      The world already rings with his renown;
      He's a great noble—in his native town;
      His ears are red, he has a pink complexion,

      And all in all, he'll suit you to perfection.
   MARIANE.
      Dear God!
   DORINE.   Oh, how triumphant you will feel   65
      At having caught a husband so ideal!
   MARIANE.
      Oh, do stop teasing, and use your cleverness
      To get me out of this appalling mess.
      Advise me, and I'll do whatever you say.
   DORINE.
      Ah no, a dutiful daughter must obey   70
      Her father, even if he weds her to an ape.
      You've a bright future, why struggle to escape?
      Tartuffe will take you back where his family lives,
      To a small town aswarm with relatives—
      Uncles and cousins whom you'll be charmed to meet. 75
      You'll be received at once by the elite,
      Calling upon the bailiff's wife, no less—
      Even, perhaps, upon the mayoress,
      Who'll sit you down in the *best* kitchen chair.
      Then, once a year, you'll dance at the village fair 80
      To the drone of bagpipes—two of them, in fact—
      And see a puppet-show, or an animal act.
      Your husband . . .
   MARIANE.   Oh, you turn my blood to ice!
      Stop torturing me, and give me your advice.
   DORINE (*threatening to go*).
      Your servant, Madam.
   MARIANE.   Dorine, I beg of you . . .   85
   DORINE.
      No, you deserve it; this marriage must go through.
   MARIANE.
      Dorine!
   DORINE.   No.
   MARIANE.   Not Tartuffe! You know I think him . . .
   DORINE.
      Tartuffe's your cup of tea, and you shall drink him.
   MARIANE.
      I've always told you everything, and relied . . .
   DORINE.
      No, you deserve to be tartuffified.   90
   MARIANE.
      Well, since you mock me and refuse to care,
      I'll henceforth seek my solace in despair;
      Despair shall be my counsellor and friend,
      And help me bring my sorrows to an end.

      (*She starts to leave.*)

   DORINE.
      There now, come back; my anger has subsided.   95
      You do deserve some pity, I've decided.
   MARIANE.
      Dorine, if Father makes me undergo
      This dreadful martyrdom, I'll die, I know.

DORINE.
> Don't fret; it won't be difficult to discover
100 > Some plan of action . . . But here's Valère, your lover.

SCENE 4

VALÈRE   MARIANE   DORINE

VALÈRE.
> Madam, I've just received some wondrous news
> Regarding which I'd like to hear your views.

MARIANE.
> What news?

VALÈRE.   You're marrying Tartuffe.

MARIANE.   I find
> That Father does have such a match in mind.

VALÈRE.
> Your father, Madam . . .

5 MARIANE.   . . . has just this minute said
> That it's Tartuffe he wishes me to wed.

VALÈRE.
> Can he be serious?

MARIANE.   Oh, indeed he can;
> He's clearly set his heart upon the plan.

VALÈRE.
> And what position do you propose to take, Madam?

MARIANE.
> Why—I don't know.

10 VALÈRE.   For heaven's sake—
> You don't know?

MARIANE.   No.

VALÈRE.   Well, well!

MARIANE.   Advise me, do.

VALÈRE.
> Marry the man. That's my advice to you.

MARIANE.
> That's your advice?

VALÈRE.   Yes.

MARIANE.   Truly?

VALÈRE.   Oh, absolutely.
> You couldn't choose more wisely, more astutely.

MARIANE.
15 > Thanks for this counsel; I'll follow it, of course.

VALÈRE.
> Do, do; I'm sure 'twill cost you no remorse.

MARIANE.
> To give it didn't cause your heart to break.

VALÈRE.
> I gave it, Madam, only for your sake.

MARIANE.
> And it's for your sake, that I take it, Sir.

DORINE (*withdrawing to the rear of the stage*).
> Let's see which fool will prove the stubborner.   20

VALÈRE.
> So! I am nothing to you, and it was flat
> Deception when you . . .

MARIANE.   Please, enough of that.
> You've told me plainly that I should agree
> To wed the man my father's chosen for me,
> And since you've designed to counsel me so wisely,   25
> I promise, Sir, to do as you advise me.

VALÈRE.
> Ah, no, 'twas not by me that you were swayed.
> No, your decision was already made;
> Though now, to save appearances, you protest
> That you're betraying me at my behest.   30

MARIANE.
> Just as you say.

VALÈRE.   Quite so. And I now see
> That you were never truly in love with me.

MARIANE.
> Alas, you're free to think so if you choose.

VALÈRE.
> I choose to think so, and here's a bit of news:
> You've spurned my hand, but I know where to turn   35
> For kinder treatment, as you shall quickly learn.

MARIANE.
> I'm sure you do. Your noble qualities
> Inspire affection . . .

VALÈRE.   Forget my qualities, please.
> They don't inspire you overmuch, I find.
> But there's anther lady I have in mind   40
> Whose sweet and generous nature will not scorn
> To compensate me for the loss I've borne.

MARIANE.
> I'm no great loss, and I'm sure that you'll transfer
> Your heart quite painlessly from me to her.

VALÈRE.
> I'll do my best to take it in my stride.   45
> The pain I feel at being cast aside
> Time and forgetfulness may put an end to.
> Or if I can't forget, I shall pretend to.
> No self-respecting person is expected
> To go on loving once he's been rejected.   50

MARIANE.
> Now, that's a fine, high-minded sentiment.

VALÈRE.
> One to which any sane man would assent.
> Would you prefer it if I pined away
> In hopeless passion till my dying day?
> Am I to yield you to a rival's arms   55
> And not console myself with other charms?

MARIANE.
> Go then: console yourself; don't hesitate
> I wish you to; indeed, I cannot wait.

VALÈRE.
You wish me to?
MARIANE.   Yes.
VALÈRE.   That's the final straw.
60   Madame, farewell. Your wish shall be my law.

(*He starts to leave, and then returns: this repeatedly.*)

MARIANE.
Splendid.
VALÈRE (*coming back again*).
            This breach, remember, is of your making;
It's you who've driven me to the step I'm taking.
MARIANE.
Of course.
VALÈRE (*coming back again*).
                Remember, too, that I am merely
Following your example.
MARIANE.   I see that clearly.
VALÈRE.
65   Enough. I'll go and do your bidding, then.
MARIANE.
Good.
VALÈRE (*coming back again*).
            You shall never see my face again.
MARIANE.
Excellent.
VALÈRE (*walking to the door, then turning about*).
                Yes?
MARIANE.   What?
VALÈRE.   What's that? What did you say?
MARIANE.
Nothing. You're dreaming.
VALÈRE.   Ah. Well, I'm on my way.
Farewell, Madame.

(*He moves slowly away.*)

MARIANE.   Farewell.
70 DORINE (*to Mariane*).   If you ask me,
Both of you are as mad as mad can be.
Do stop this nonsense, now. I've only let you
Squabble so long to see where it would get you.
Whoa there, Monsiere Valère!

(*She goes and seizes Valère by the arm; he makes a great
show of resistance.*)

VALÈRE.   What's this, Dorine?
DORINE.
Come here.
VALÈRE.   No, no, my heart's too full of spleen.
75   Don't hold me back, her wish must be obeyed.
DORINE.
Stop!
VALÈRE. It's too late now; my decision's made.

DORINE.
Oh, pooh!
MARIANE (*aside*).
He hates the sight of me, that's plain.
I'll go, and so deliver him from pain.
DORINE (*leaving Valère, running after Mariane*).
And now *you* run away! Come back!
MARIANE.   No, no.
Nothing you say will keep me here. Let go!   80
VALÈRE (*aside*).
She cannot bear my presence, I perceive.
To spare her further torment, I shall leave.
DORINE (*leaving Mariane, running after Valère*).
Again! You'll not escape, Sir; don't you try it.
Come here, you two. Stop fussing, and be quiet.

(*She takes Valère by the hand, then Mariane, and draws
them together.*)

VALÈRE (*to Dorine*).
What do you want of me?
MARIANE (*to Dorine*).   What is the point of this?   85
DORINE.
We are going to have a little armistice.
(*To Valère.*) Now weren't you silly to get so overheated?
VALÈRE.
Didn't you see how badly I was treated?
DORINE (*to Mariane*).
Aren't you a simpleton, to have lost your head?
MARIANE.
Didn't you hear the hateful things he said?   90
DORINE (*to Valère*).
You're both great fools. Her sole desire, Valère,
Is to be yours in marriage. To that I'll swear.
(*To Mariane.*) He loves you only, and he wants no wife
But you, Mariane. On that I'll stake my life.
MARIANE (*to Valère*).
Then why you advised me so, I cannot see.   95
VALÈRE (*to Mariane*).
On such a question, why ask advice of *me*?
DORINE.
Oh, you're impossible. Give me your hands, you two.
(*To Valère.*) Yours first.
VALÈRE (*giving Dorine his hand*).
But why?
DORINE (*to Mariane*).
                And now a hand from you.
MARIANE (*also giving Dorine her hand*).
What are you doing?
DORINE.   There: a perfect fit.
You suit each other better than you'll admit.   100

(*Valère and Mariane hold hands for some time without
looking at each other.*)

VALÈRE (*turning toward Mariane*).
    Ah, come, don't be so haughty. Give a man
    A look of kindness, won't you, Mariane?

    (*Mariane turns towards Valère and smiles.*)

DORINE.
    I tell you, lovers are completely mad!
VALÈRE (*to Mariane*).
    Now come, confess that you were very bad
105   To hurt my feelings as you did just now.
    I have a just complaint, you must allow.
MARIANE.
    You must allow that you were most unpleasant . . .
DORINE.
    Let's table that discussion for the present;
    Your father has a plan which must be stopped.
MARIANE.
110   Advise us, then; what means must we adopt?
DORINE.
    We'll use all manner of means, and all at once.
    (*To Mariane.*) Your father's addled; he's acting like a
        dunce.
    Therefore you'd better humor the old fossil.
    Pretend to yield to him, be sweet and docile,
115   And then postpone, as often as necessary,
    The day on which you have agreed to marry.
    You'll thus gain time, and time will turn the trick.
    Sometimes, for instance, you'll be taken sick.
    And that will seem good reason for delay;
120   Or some bad omen will make you change the day—
    You'll dream of muddy water, or you'll pass
    A dead man's hearse, or break a looking glass.
    If all else fails, no man can marry you
    Unless you take his ring and say "I do."
125   But now, let's separate. If they should find
    Us talking here, our plot might be divined.
    (*To Valère.*) Go to your friends, and tell them what's oc-
        curred,
    And have them urge her father to keep his word.
    Meanwhile, we'll stir her brother into action.
130   And get Elmire, as well, to join our faction.
    Good-bye.
VALÈRE (*to Mariane*).
    Though each of us will do his best
    It's your true heart on which my hopes shall rest.
MARIANE (*to Valère*).
    Regardless of what Father may decide,
    None but Valère shall claim me as his bride.
VALÈRE.
135   Oh, how those words content me! Come what will . . .
DORINE.
    Oh, lovers, lovers! Their tongues are never still.
    Be off, now.

VALÈRE (*turning to go, then turning back*).
        One last word . . .
DORINE.
                No time to chat:
    You leave by this door; and you leave by that.

    (*Dorine pushes them, by the shoulders, toward opposing
    doors.*)

ACT III

SCENE 1

DAMIS   DORINE

DAMIS.
    May lightening strike me even as I speak,
    May all men call me cowardly and weak,
    If any fear or scruple holds me back
    From settling things, at once, with that great quack!
DORINE.
    Now, don't give way to violent emotion.   5
    Your father's merely talked about this notion,
    And words and deeds are far from being one.
    Much that is talked about is left undone.
DAMIS.
    No, I must stop that scoundrel's machinations;
    I'll go and tell him off; I'm out of patience.   10
DORINE.
    Do calm down and be practical. I had rather
    My mistress dealt with him—and with your father.
    She has some influence with Tartuffe, I've noted.
    He hangs upon her words, seems most devoted,
    And may, indeed, be smitten by her charm.   15
    Pray Heaven it's true! 'Twould do our cause no harm.
    She sent for him, just now, to sound him out
    On this affair you're so incensed about;
    She'll find out where he stands, and tell him, too,
    What dreadful strife and trouble will ensue   20
    If he lends countenance to your father's plan.
    I couldn't get in to see him, but his man
    Says that he's almost finished with his prayers.
    Go, now. I'll catch him when he comes downstairs.
DAMIS.
    I want to hear this conference, and I will.   25
DORINE.
    No, they must be alone.
DAMIS.
                Oh, I'll keep still.
DORINE.
    Not you. I know your temper. You'd start a brawl,
    And shout and stamp your foot and spoil it all.
    Go on.
DAMIS.
    I won't; I have a perfect right . . .

DORINE.
30   Lord, you're a nuisance! He's coming; get out of sight.

(Damis conceals himself in a closet at the rear of the stage.)

SCENE 2

TARTUFFE   DORINE

TARTUFFE *(observing Dorine. and calling to his manservant off-stage).*
    Hang up my hair-shirt, put my scourge in place,
    And pray, Laurent, for Heaven's perpetual grace.
    I'm going to the prison now, to share
    My last few coins with the poor wretches there.
DORINE *(aside).*
5   Dear God, what affectation! What a fake!
TARTUFFE.
    You wished to see me?
DORINE.   Yes . . .
TARTUFFE *(taking a handkerchief from his pocket).*
                               For mercy's sake,
    Please take this handkerchief, before you speak.
DORINE.
    What?
TARTUFFE. Cover that bosom, girl. The flesh is weak,
    And unclean thoughts are difficult to control.
    Such sights as that can undermine the soul.
DORINE.
10   Your soul, it seems has very poor defenses,
    And flesh makes quite an impact on your senses.
    It's strange that you're so easily excited;
    My own desires are not so soon ignited,
    And if I saw you naked as a beast,
    Not all your hide would tempt me in the least.
15 TARTUFFE.
    Girl, speak more modestly; unless you do,
    I shall be forced to take my leave of you.
DORINE.
    Oh, no, it's I who must be on my way;
    I've just one little message to convey.
    Madame is coming down, and begs you, Sir,
20   To wait and have a word or two with her.
TARTUFFE.
    Gladly.
DORINE *(aside).*
    That had a softening effect!
    I think my guess about him was correct.
TARTUFFE.
    Will she be long?

DORINE.   No: that's her step I hear.   25
    Ah, here she is , and I shall disappear.

SCENE 3

ELMIRE   TARTUFFE

TARTUFFE.
    May Heaven, whose infinite goodness we adore.
    Preserve your body and soul forevermore.
    And bless your days, and answer thus the plea
    Of one who is its humblest votary.
ELMIRE.
    I thank you for that pious wish. But please,   5
    Do take a chair and let's be more at ease.

(They sit down.)

TARTUFFE.
    I trust that you are once more well and strong?
ELMIRE.
    Oh, yes: the fever didn't last for long.
TARTUFFE.
    My prayers are too unworthy, I am sure
    To have gained from Heaven this most gracious cure;   10
    But lately, Madam, my every supplication
    Has had for object your recuperation.
ELMIRE.
    You shouldn't have troubled so. I don't deserve it.
TARTUFFE.
    Your health is priceless, Madam, and to preserve it
    I'd gladly give my own, in all sincerity.   15
ELMIRE.
    Sir, you outdo us all in Christian charity.
    You've been most kind. I count myself your debtor.
TARTUFFE.
    'Twas nothing, Madam. I long to serve you better.
ELMIRE.
    There's a private matter I'm anxious to discuss.
    I'm glad there's no one here to hinder us.   20
TARTUFFE.
    I too am glad; it floods my heart with bliss
    To find myself alone with you like this.
    For just this chance I've prayed with all my power—
    But prayed in vain, until this happy hour.
ELMIRE.
    This won't take long, Sir, and I hope you'll be   25
    Entirely frank and unconstrained with me.
TARTUFFE.
    Indeed, there's nothing I had rather do
    Than bare my inmost heart and soul to you.
    First, let me say that what remarks I've made
    About the constant visits you are paid
    Were prompted not by any mean emotion,   30

But rather by a pure and deep devotion,
A fervent zeal . . .

ELMIRE.   No need for explanation.
Your sole concern, I'm sure, was my salvation.

TARTUFFE (*taking Elmire's hand and pressing her fingertips*).
Quite so; and such great fervor do I feel . . .

ELMIRE.
35   Ooh! Please! You're pinching!

TARTUFFE.   'Twas from excess of zeal.
I never meant to cause you pain, I swear.
I'd rather . . .

(*He places his hand on Elmire's knee.*)

ELMIRE.
What can your hand be doing there?

TARTUFFE.
40   Feeling your gown; what soft, fine-woven stuff!

ELMIRE.
Please, I'm extremely ticklish. That's enough.

(*She draws her chair away, Tartuffe pulls his after her.*)

TARTUFFE (*fondling the lace collar of her gown*).
My, my, what lovely lacework on your dress!
The workmanship's miraculous, no less.
I've not seen anything to equal it.

ELMIRE.
45   Yes, quite. But let's talk business for a bit.
They say my husband means to break his word
And give his daughter to you, Sir. Had you heard?

TARTUFFE.
He did once mention it. But I confess
I dream of quite a different happiness.
50   It's elsewhere, Madam, that my eyes discern
The promise of that bliss for which I yearn.

ELMIRE.
I see: you care for nothing here below.

TARTUFFE.
Ah, well—my heart's not made of stone, you know.

ELMIRE.
All your desires mount heavenward, I'm sure,
55   In scorn of all that's earthly and impure.

TARTUFFE.
A love of heavenly beauty does not preclude
A proper love for earthly pulchritude;
Our senses are quite rightly captivated
By perfect works our Maker has created.
60   Some glory clings to all that Heaven has made;
In you, all Heaven's marvels are displayed.
On that fair face, such beauties have been lavished,
The eyes are dazzled and the heart is ravished;
How could I look on you, O flawless creature,
65   And not adore the Author of all Nature,
Feeling a love both passionate and pure

For you, his triumph of self-portraiture?
At first, I trembled lest that love should be
A subtle snare that Hell had laid for me;
I vowed to flee the sight of you, eschewing   70
A rapture that might prove my soul's undoing;
But soon, fair being, I became aware
That my deep passion could be made to square
With rectitude, and with my bounden duty.
I thereupon surrendered to your beauty.
It is, I know, presumptuous on my part   75
To bring you this poor offering of my heart,
And it is not my merit, Heaven knows,
But your compassion on which my hopes repose.
You are my peace, my solace, my salvation;
On you depends my bliss—or desolation;   80
I bide your judgment and, as you think best,
I shall be either miserable or blest.

ELMIRE.
Your declaration is most gallant, Sir,
But don't you think it's out of character?
You'd have done better to restrain your passion   85
And think before you spoke in such a fashion.
It ill becomes a pious man like you . . .

TARTUFFE.
I may be pious, but I'm human too:
With your celestial charms before his eyes,
A man has not the power to be wise.   90
I know such words sound strangely, coming from me,
But I'm no angel, nor was meant to be,
And if you blame my passion, you must needs
Reproach as well the charms on which it feeds.
Your loveliness I had no sooner seen   95
Than you became my soul's unrivalled queen;
Before your seraph glance, divinely sweet,
My heart's defenses crumbled in defeat,
And nothing fasting, prayer, or tears might do
Could stay my spirit from adoring you.   100
My eyes, my sighs have told you in the past
What now my lips make bold to say at last,
And if, in your great goodness, you will deign
To look upon your slave, and ease his pain—
If, in compassion for my soul's distress,   105
You'll stoop to comfort my unworthiness,
I'll raise to you, in thanks for that sweet manna,
And endless hymn, an infinite hosanna.
With me, of course, there need be no anxiety,
No fear of scandal or of notoriety.   110
These young court gallants, whom all the ladies fancy,
Are vain in speech, in action rash and chancy;
When they succeed in love, the world soon knows it;
No favor's granted them but they disclose it
And by the looseness of their tongues profane   115
The very altar where their hearts have lain.
Men of my sort, however, love discreetly,

And one may trust our reticence completely.
My keen concern for my good name insures
120 The absolute security of yours;
In short, I offer you, my dear Elmire,
Love without scandal, pleasure without fear.

ELMIRE.
I've heard your well-turned speeches to the end,
And what you urge I clearly apprehend.
125 Aren't you afraid that I may take a notion
To tell my husband of your warm devotion,
And that, supposing he were duly told,
His feelings toward you might grow rather cold?

TARTUFFE.
I know, dear lady, that your exceeding charity
130 Will lead your heart to pardon my temerity;
That you'll excuse my violent affection
As human weakness, human imperfection;
And that—O fairest—you will bear in mind
That I'm but flesh and blood, and am not blind.

ELMIRE.
135 Some women might do otherwise, perhaps,
But I shall be discreet about your lapse;
I'll tell my husband nothing of what's occurred
If, in return, you'll give your solemn word
To advocate as forcefully as you can
140 The marriage of Valère and Mariane,
Renouncing all desire to dispossess
Another of his rightful happiness,
And . . .

SCENE 4

DAMIS ELMIRE TARTUFFE

DAMIS (*emerging from the closet where he has been hiding*).
         No! we'll not hush up about this vile affair;
I heard it all inside that closet there,
Where Heaven, in order to confound the pride
Of this great rascal, prompted me to hide.
5 Ah, now I have my long-awaited chance
To punish his deceit and arrogance.
And give my father clear and shocking proof
Of the black character of his dear Tartuffe.

ELMIRE.
Ah, no, Damis; I'll be content if he
10 Will study to deserve my leniency.
I've promised silence—don't make me break my word;
To make a scandal would be too absurd.
Good wives laugh off such trifles, and forget them;
Why should they tell their husbands, and upset them?

DAMIS.
15 You have your reasons for taking such a course,

And I have reasons, too, of equal force.
To spare him now would be insanely wrong.
I've swallowed my just wrath for far too long
And watched this insolent bigot bringing strife
And bitterness into our family life. 20
Too long he's meddled in my father's affairs,
Thwarting my marriage-hopes, and poor Valère's.
It's high time that my father was undeceived,
And now I've proof that can't be disbelieved—
Proof that was furnished me by Heaven above. 25
It's too good not to take advantage of.
This is my chance, and I deserve to lose it
If, for one moment, I hesitate to use it.

ELMIRE.
Damis . . .

DAMIS.   No, I must do what I think right.
Madam, my heart is bursting with delight, 30
And, say whatever you will, I'll not consent
To lose the sweet revenge on which I'm bent.
I'll settle matters without much ado;
And here, most opportunely, is my cue.

SCENE 5

ORGON TARTUFFE DAMIS ELMIRE

DAMIS.
Father, I'm glad you've joined us. Let us advise you
Of some fresh news which doubtless will surprise you.
You've just now been repaid with interest
For all your loving-kindness to our guest.
He's proved his warm and grateful feelings towards you; 5
It's with a pair of horns he would reward you.
Yes, I surprised him with your wife, and heard
His whole adulterous offer, every word.
She, with her all too gentle disposition,
Would not have told you of his proposition; 10
But I shall not make terms with brazen lechery,
And feel that not to tell you would be treachery.

ELMIRE.
And I hold that one's husband's peace of mind
Should not be spoilt by tattle of this kind.
One's honor doesn't require it: to be proficient 15
In keeping men at bay is quite sufficient.
These are my sentiments, and I wish, Damis,
That you had heeded me and held your peace.

SCENE 6

ORGON DAMIS TARTUFFE

ORGON.
Can it be true, this dreadful thing I hear?

TARTUFFE.
  Yes, Brother, I'm a wicked man, I fear:
  A wretched sinner, all depraved and twisted,
  The greatest villain that has ever existed.
5 My life's one heap of crimes, which grows each minute;
  There's naught but foulness and corruption in it;
  And I perceive that Heaven, outraged by me,
  Has chosen this occasion to mortify me.
  Charge me with any deed you wish to name;
10 I'll not defend myself, but take the blame.
  Believe what you are told, and drive Tartuffe
  Like some base criminal from beneath your roof;
  Yes, drive me hence, and with a parting curse:
  I shan't protest, for I deserve far worse.
ORGON (to Damis).
15 Ah, you deceitful boy, how dare you try
  To stain his purity with so foul a lie?
DAMIS.
  What! Are you taken in by such a bluff?
  Did you not hear . . . ?
ORGON.   Enough, you rogue, enough!
TARTUFFE.
  Ah, Brother, let him speak: you're being unjust.
20 Believe his story; the boy deserves your trust.
  Why, after all, should you have faith in me?
  How can you know what I might do, or be?
  Is it on my good actions that you base
  Your favor? Do you trust my pious face?
25 Ah, no, don't be deceived by hollow shows;
  I'm far, alas, from being what men suppose;
  Though the world takes me for a man of worth,
  I'm truly the most worthless man on earth.
  (To Damis.) Yes, my dear son, speak out now; call me the
    chief
30 Of sinners, a wretch, a murderer, a thief;
  Load me with all the names men most abhor;
  I'll not complain; I've earned them all, and more;
  I'll kneel here while you pour them on my head
  As a just punishment for the life I've led.
ORGON (to Tartuffe).
  This is too much, dear Brother.
35 (To Damis.)   Have you no heart?
DAMIS.
  Are you so hoodwinked by this rascal's art . . . ?
ORGON.
  Be still, you monster.
  (To Tartuffe.)   Brother, I pray you, rise.
  (To Damis) Villain!
DAMIS.   But . . .
ORGON.   Silence!
DAMIS.   Can't you realize . . . ?
ORGON.
  Just one word more, and I'll tear you limb from limb.
TARTUFFE.
40 In God's name, Brother, don't be harsh with him.

  I'd rather far be tortured at the stake
  Than see him bear one scratch for my poor sake.
ORGON (to Damis).
  Ingrate!
TARTUFFE. If I must beg you, on bended knee,
  To pardon him . . .
ORGON (falling to his knees, addressing Tartuffe).
  Such goodness cannot be!
  (To Damis.)   Now, there's true charity!
DAMIS.   What, you . . . ?
ORGON.   Villain, be still! 45
  I know your motives; I know you wish him ill:
  Yes, all of you—wife, children, servants, all—
  Conspire against him and desire his fall,
  Employing every shameful trick you can
  To alienate me from this saintly man. 50
  Ah, but the more you seek to drive him away,
  The more I'll do to keep him. Without delay,
  I'll spite this household and confound its pride
  By giving him my daughter as his bride.
DAMIS.
  You're going to force her to accept his hand? 55
ORGON.
  Yes, and this very night, d'you understand?
  I shall defy you all, and make it clear
  That I'm the one who gives the orders here.
  Come, wretch, kneel down and clasp his blessed feet,
  And ask his pardon for your black deceit. 60
DAMIS.
  I ask that swindler's pardon? Why I'd rather . . .
ORGON.
  So! You insult him, and defy your father!
  A stick! A stick! (To Tartuffe.) No, no—release me, do.
  (To Damis.) Out of my house this minute! Be off with you,
  And never dare set foot in it again. 65
DAMIS.
  Well, I shall go, but . . .
ORGON.   Well, go quickly, then.
  I disinherit you; an empty purse
  Is all you'll get from me—except my curse!

SCENE 7

ORGON   TARTUFFE

ORGON.
  How he blasphemed your goodness! What a son!
TARTUFFE.
  Forgive him, Lord, as I've already done.
  (To Orgon.)   You can't know how it hurts when some-
    one tries
  To blacken me in my dear Brother's eyes.

ORGON.

    Ahh!

TARTUFFE.

5   The mere thought of such ingratitude

    Plunges my soul into so dark a mood . . .

    Such horror grips my heart . . . I gasp for breath,

    And cannot speak, and feel myself near death.

ORGON (*He runs, in tears, to the door through which he has just
driven his son.*)

    You blackguard! Why did I spare you? Why did I not

10   Break you in little pieces on the spot?

    Compose yourself, and don't be hurt, dear friend.

TARTUFFE.

    These scenes, these dreadful quarrels, have got to end.

    I've much upset your household, and I perceive

    That the best thing will be for me to leave.

ORGON.

    What are you saying!

15 TARTUFFE.   They're all against me here;

    They'd have you think me false and insincere.

ORGON.

    Ah, what of that? Have I ceased believing in you?

TARTUFFE.

    Their adverse talk will certainly continue,

    And charges which you now repudiate

20   You may find credible at a later date.

ORGON.

    No, Brother, never.

TARTUFFE.   Brother, a wife can sway

    Her husband's mind in many a subtle way.

ORGON.

    No, no.

TARTUFFE. To leave at once is the solution;

    Thus only can I end their persecution.

ORGON.

25   No, no, I'll not allow it; you shall remain.

TARTUFFE.

    Ah, well; 'twill mean much martyrdom and pain,

    But if you wish it . . .

ORGON.   Ah!

TARTUFFE.   Enough, so be it.

    But one thing must be settled, as I see it.

    For your dear honor, and for our friendship's sake,

30   There's one precaution I feel bound to take.

    I shall avoid your wife, and keep away . . .

ORGON.

    No, you shall not, whatever they may say.

    It pleases me to vex them, and for spite

    I'd have them see you with her day and night.

35   What's more, I'm going to drive them to despair

    By making you my only son and heir;

    This very day, I'll give to you alone

    Clear deed and title to everything I own.

    A dear, good friend and son-in-law-to-be

40   Is more than wife, or child, or kin to me.

    Will you accept my offer, dearest son?

TARTUFFE.

    In all things, let the will of Heaven be done.

ORGON.

    Poor fellow! Come, we'll go draw up the deed.

    Then let them burst with disappointed greed!

ACT IV

SCENE 1

CLÉANTE   TARTUFFE

CLÉANTE.

    Yes, all the town's discussing it, and truly,

    Their comments do not flatter you unduly.

    I'm glad we've met, Sir, and I'll give my view

    Of this sad matter in a word or two.

    As for who's guilty, that I shan't discuss;   5

    Let's say it was Damis who caused the fuss;

    Assuming then, that you have been ill-used

    By young Damis, and groundlessly accused,

    Ought not a Christian to forgive, and ought

    He not to stifle every vengeful thought?   10

    Should you stand by and watch a father make

    His only son an exile for your sake?

    Again I tell you frankly, be advised:

    The whole town, high and low, is scandalized;

    This quarrel must be mended, and my advice is   15

    Not to push matters to a further crisis.

    No, sacrifice your wrath to God above,

    And help Damis regain his father's love.

TARTUFFE.

    Alas, for my part I should take great joy

    In doing so, I've nothing against the boy.   20

    I pardon all, I harbor no resentment;

    To serve him would afford me much contentment.

    But Heaven's interest will not have it so:

    If he comes back, then I shall have to go.

    After his conduct—so extreme, so vicious—   25

    Our further intercourse would look suspicious.

    God knows what people would think! Why, they'd

        describe

    My goodness to him as a sort of bribe;

    They'd say that out of guilt I made pretense

    Of loving-kindness and benevolence—   30

    That, fearing my accuser's tongue, I strove

    To buy his silence with a show of love.

CLÉANTE.

    Your reasoning is badly warped and stretched,

    And these excuses, Sir, are most far-fetched.

    Why put yourself in charge of Heaven's cause?   35

    Does Heaven need our help to enforce its laws?

    Leave vengeance to the Lord, Sir; while we live,

Our duty's not to punish, but forgive;
And what the Lord commands, we should obey
40 Without regard to what the world may say.
What! Shall the fear of being misunderstood
Prevent our doing what is right and good?
No, no; let's simply do what Heaven ordains,
And let no other thoughts perplex our brains.

TARTUFFE.

45 Again, Sir, let me say that I've forgiven
Damis, and thus obeyed the laws of Heaven;
But I am not commanded by the Bible
To live with one who smears my name with libel.

CLÉANTE.

Were you commanded, Sir, to indulge the whim
50 Of poor Orgon, and so encourage him
In suddenly transferring to your name
A large estate to which you have no claim?

TARTUFFE.

'Twould never occur to those who know me best
To think I acted from self-interest.
55 The treasures of this world I quite despise;
Their specious glitter does not charm my eyes;
And if I have resigned myself to taking
The gift which my dear Brother insists on making,
I do so only, as he well understands,
60 Lest so much wealth fall into wicked hands,
Lest those to whom it might descend in time
Turn it to purposes of sin and crime,
And not, as I shall do, make use of it
For Heaven's glory and mankind's benefit.

CLÉANTE.

65 Forget these trumped-up fears. Your argument
Is one the rightful heir might well resent;
It *is* a moral burden to inherit
Such wealth, but give Damis a chance to bear it.
And would it not be worse to be accused
70 Of swindling, than to see that wealth misused?
I'm shocked that you allowed Orgon to broach
This matter, and that you feel no self-reproach;
Does true religion teach that lawful heirs
May freely be deprived of what is theirs?
75 And if the Lord has told you in your heart
That you and young Damis must dwell apart,
Would it not be the decent thing to beat
A generous and honorable retreat,
Rather than let the son of the house be sent,
80 For your convenience, into banishment?
Sir, if you wish to prove the honesty
Of your intentions . . .

TARTUFFE.   Sir, it is half-past three.
I've certain pious duties to attend to,
And hope my prompt departure won't offend you.

CLÉANTE (*alone*).
Damn.

SCENE 2

ELMIRE   CLÉANTE   MARIANE   DORINE

DORINE. Stay, Sir, and help Mariane, for Heaven's sake!
She's suffering so, I fear her heart will break.
Her father's plan to marry her off tonight
Has put the poor child in a desperate plight.
I hear him coming. Let's stand together, now,   5
And see if we can't change his mind, somehow,
About this match we all deplore and fear.

SCENE 3

ORGON   MARIANE   DORINE   ELMIRE   CLÉANTE

ORGON.
Hah! Glad to find you all assembled here.
(*To Mariane.*)   This contract, child, contains your happiness,
And what it says I think your heart can guess.

MARIANE (*falling to her knees*).
Sir, by that Heaven which sees me here distressed,
And by whatever else can move your breast,   5
Do not employ a father's power, I pray you,
To crush my heart and force it to obey you,
Nor by your harsh commands oppress me so
That I'll begrudge the duty which I owe—
And do not so embitter and enslave me   10
That I shall hate the very life you gave me.
If my sweet hopes must perish, if you refuse
To give me to the one I've dared to choose,
Spare me at least—I beg you—I implore—
The pain of wedding one whom I abhor;   15
And do not, by a heartless use of force,
Drive me to contemplate some desperate course.

ORGON (*feeling himself touched by her*).
Be firm, my soul. No human weakness, now.

MARIANE.
I don't resent your love for him. Allow
Your heart free rein, Sir; give him your property,   20
And if that's not enough, take mine from me;
He's welcome to my money; take it, do,
But don't, I pray, include my person too.
Spare me, I beg you; and let me end the tale
Of my sad days behind a convent veil.   25

ORGON.
A convent! Hah! When crossed in their amours,
All lovesick girls have the same thought as yours.
Get up! The more you loathe the man, and dread him,
The more ennobling it will be to wed him.
Marry Tartuffe, and mortify your flesh!   30
Enough; don't start that whimpering afresh.

DORINE.
But why . . .
ORGON.   Be still, there. Speak when you're spoken to.
Not one more bit of impudence out of you.
CLÉANTE.
If I may offer a word of counsel here . . .
ORGON.
35   Brother, in counseling you have no peer;
All your advice is forceful, sound, and clever;
I don't propose to follow it, however.
ELMIRE (*to Orgon*).
I am amazed, and don't know what to say;
Your blindness simply takes my breath away.
40   You are indeed bewitched, to take no warning
From our account of what occurred this morning.
ORGON.
Madam, I know a few plain facts, and one
Is that you're partial to my rascal son;
Hence, when he sought to make Tartuffe the victim
45   Of a base lie, you dared not contradict him.
Ah, but you underplayed your part, my pet;
You should have looked more angry, more upset.
ELMIRE.
When men make overtures, must we reply
With righteous anger and a battle-cry?
50   Must we turn back their amorous advances
With sharp reproaches and with fiery glances?
Myself, I find such offers merely amusing,
And make no scenes and fusses in refusing;
My taste is for good-natured rectitude,
55   And I dislike the savage sort of prude
Who guards her virtue with her teeth and claws,
And tear's men's eyes out for the slightest cause:
The Lord preserve me from such honor as that,
Which bites and scratches like an alley-cat!
60   I've found that a polite and cool rebuff
Discourages a lover quite enough.
ORGON.
I know the facts, and I shall not be shaken.
ELMIRE.
I marvel at your power to be mistaken.
Would it, I wonder, carry weight with you
65   If I could *show* you that our tale was true?
ORGON.
Show me?
ELMIRE.   Yes.
ORGON.   Rot.
ELMIRE.   Come, what if I found a way
To make you see the facts as plain as day?
ORGON.
Nonsense.
ELMIRE.   Do answer me; don't be absurd.
I'm not now asking you to trust our word.
70   Suppose that from some hiding-place in here

You learned the whole sad truth by eye and ear—
What would you say of your good friend, after that?
ORGON.
Why, I'd say . . . nothing, by Jehoshaphat!
It can't be true.
ELMIRE.   You've been too long deceived,
And I'm quite tired of being disbelieved.   75
Come now: let's put my statements to the test,
And you shall see the truth made manifest.
ORGON.
I'll take that challenge. Now do your uttermost.
We'll see how you make good your empty boast.
ELMIRE (*to Dorine*).
Send him to me.
DORINE.   He's crafty; it may be hard
To catch the cunning scoundrel off his guard.   80
ELMIRE.
No, amorous men are gullible. Their conceit
So blinds them that they're never hard to cheat.
Have him come down (*To Cléante and Mariane*.) Please
leave us, for a bit.

SCENE 4

ELMIRE   ORGON

ELMIRE.
Pull up this table, and get under it.
ORGON.
What?
ELMIRE.   It's essential that you be well-hidden.
ORGON.
Why there?
ELMIRE.   Oh, Heavens! Just do as you are bidden.
I have my plans; we'll soon see how they fare.
Under the table, now; and once you're there,   5
Take care that you are neither seen nor heard.
ORGON.
Well, I'll indulge you, since I gave my word
To see you through this infantile charade.
ELMIRE.
Once it is over, you'll be glad we played.
(*To her husband, who is now under the table*.) I'm going to   10
act quite strangely, now, and you
Must not be shocked at anything I do.
Whatever I may say, you must excuse
As part of that deceit I'm forced to use.
I shall employ sweet speeches in the task
Of making that imposter drop his mask;   15
I'll give encouragement to his bold desires,
And furnish fuel to his amorous fires.
Since it's for your sake, and for his destruction,
That I shall seem to yield to his seduction,

20   I'll gladly stop whenever you decide
       That all your doubts are fully satisfied.
       I'll count on you, as soon as you have seen
       What sort of man he is, to intervene,
       And not expose me to his odious lust
25   One moment longer than you feel you must.
       Remember: you're to save me from my plight
       Whenever . . . He's coming! Hush! Keep out of sight!

SCENE 5

TARTUFFE   ELMIRE   ORGON

TARTUFFE.
       You wish to have a word with me, I'm told.
ELMIRE.
       Yes. I've a little secret to unfold.
       Before I speak, however, it would be wise
       To close that door, and look about for spies.

5   (*Tartuffe goes to the door, closes it, and returns.*)

       The very last thing that must happen now
       Is a repetition of this morning's row.
       I've never been so badly caught off guard.
       Oh, how I feared for you! You saw how hard
10   I tried to make that troublesome Damis
       Control his dreadful temper, and hold his peace.
       In my confusion, I didn't have the sense
       Simply to contradict his evidence;
       But as it happened, that was for the best,
15   And all has worked out in our interest.
       This storm has only bettered your position;
       My husband doesn't have the least suspicion,
       And now, in mockery of those who do,
       He bids me be continually with you.
       And that is why, quite fearless of reproof,
20   I now can be alone with my Tartuffe,
       And why my heart—perhaps too quick to yield—
       Feels free to let its passion be revealed.
TARTUFFE.
       Madam, your words confuse me. Not long ago,
       You spoke in quite a different style, you know.
ELMIRE.
25   Ah, Sir, if that refusal made you smart,
       It's little that you know of woman's heart,
       Or what that heart is trying to convey
       When it resists in such a feeble way!
       Always, at first, our modesty prevents
30   The frank avowal of tender sentiments;
       However high the passion which inflames us,
       Still, to confess its power somehow shames us.
       Thus we reluct, at first, yet in a tone
       Which tells you that our heart is overthrown,

That what our lips deny, our pulse confesses,   35
And that, in time, all noes will turn to yesses.
I fear my words are all too frank and free,
And a poor proof of woman's modesty;
But since I'm started, tell me if you will—
Would I have tried to make Damis be still,   40
Would I have listened, calm and unoffended,
Until your lengthy offer of love was ended,
And been so very mild in my reaction,
Had your sweet words not given me satisfaction?
And when I tried to force you to undo   45
The marriage-plans my husband had in view,
What did my urgent pleading signify
If not that I admired you, and that I
Deplored the thought that someone else might own
Part of a heart I wished for mine alone?   50
TARTUFFE.
Madam, no happiness is so complete
As when, from lips we love, come words so sweet;
Their nectar floods my every sense, and drains
In honeyed rivulets through all my veins.
To please you is my joy, my only goal;   55
Your love is the restorer of my soul;
And yet I must beg leave, now, to confess
Some lingering doubts as to my happiness.
Might this not be a trick? Might not the catch
Be that you wish me to break off the match   60
With Mariane, and so have feigned to love me?
I shan't quite trust your fond opinion of me
Until the feelings you've expressed so sweetly
Are demonstrated somewhat more concretely,
And you have shown, by certain kind concessions,   65
That I may put my faith in your professions.
ELMIRE. (*She coughs, to warn her husband*).
Why be in such a hurry? Must my heart
Exhaust it's bounty at the very start?
To make that sweet admission cost me dear,
But you'll not be content, it would appear,   70
Unless my store of favors is disbursed
To the last farthing, and at the very first.
TARTUFFE.
The less we merit, the less we dare to hope,
And with our doubts, mere words can never cope.
We trust no promised bliss till we receive it;
Not till a joy is ours can we believe it.   75
I, who so little merit your esteem,
Can't credit this fulfillment of my dream,
And shan't believe it, Madam, until I savor
Some palpable assurance of your favor.   80
ELMIRE.
My, how tyrannical your love can be,
And how it flusters and perplexes me!
How furiously you take one's heart in hand,
And make your every wish a fierce command!

85   Come, must you hound and harry me to death?
     Will you not give me time to catch my breath?
     Can it be right to press me with such force,
     Give me no quarter, show me no remorse,
     And take advantage, by your stern insistence,
90   Of the fond feelings which weaken my resistance?
TARTUFFE.
     Well, if you look with favor upon my love,
     Why, then, begrudge me some clear proof thereof?
ELMIRE.
     But how can I consent without offense
     To Heaven, toward which you feel such reverence?
TARTUFFE.
95   If Heaven is all that holds you back, don't worry.
     I can remove that hindrance in a hurry.
     Nothing of that sort need obstruct our path.
ELMIRE.
     Must one not be afraid of Heaven's wrath?
TARTUFFE.
     Madam, forget such fears, and be my pupil,
100 And I shall teach you how to conquer scruple.
     Some joys, it's true, are wrong in Heaven's eyes;
     Yet Heaven is not averse to compromise;
     There is a science, lately formulated,
     Whereby one's conscience may be liberated,
105 Any any wrongful act you care to mention
     May be redeemed by purity of intention.
     I'll teach you, Madam, the secrets of that science;
     Meanwhile, just place on me your full reliance.
     Assuage my keen desires, and feel no dread:
110 The sin, if any shall be on my head.

     (*Elmire coughs, this time more loudly.*)

     You've a bad cough.
ELMIRE.   Yes, yes, it's bad indeed.
TARTUFFE (*producing a little paper bag*).
     A bit of licorice may be what you need.
ELMIRE.
     No, I've a stubborn cold, it seems. I'm sure it
     Will take much more than licorice to cure it.
TARTUFFE.
     How aggravating.
115 ELMIRE.   Oh, more than I can say.
TARTUFFE.
     If you're still troubled, think of things this way:
     No one shall know our joys, save us alone,
     And there's no evil till the act is known;
     It's scandal, Madam, which makes it an offense,
120 And it's no sin to sin in confidence.
ELMIRE (*having coughed once more*).
     Well, clearly I must do as you require,
     And yield to your importunate desire.
     It is apparent, now, that nothing less

     Will satisfy you, and so I acquiesce.
     To go so far is much against my will;   125
     I'm vexed that it should come to this; but still,
     Since you are determined on it, since you
     Will not allow mere language to convince you,
     And since you ask for concrete evidence, I
     See nothing for it, now, but to comply.   130
     If this is sinful, if I'm wrong to do it.
     So much the worse for him who drove me to it.
     The fault can surely not be charged to me.
TARTUFFE.
     Madam, the fault is mine, if fault there be,
     And . . .
ELMIRE.
     Open the door a little, and peek out;   135
     I wouldn't want my husband poking about.
TARTUFFE.
     Why worry about the man? Each day he grows
     More gullible; one can lead him by the nose.
     To find us here would fill him with delight,
     And if he saw the worst, he'd doubt his sight.   140
ELMIRE.
     Nevertheless, do step out for a minute
     Into the hall, and see that no one's in it.

SCENE 6

ORGON   ELMIRE

ORGON (*coming out from under the table*).
     That man's a perfect monster, I must admit!
     I'm simply stunned. I can't get over it.
ELMIRE.
     What, coming out so soon? How premature!
     Get back in hiding, and wait until you're sure.   5
     Stay till the end, and be convinced completely;
     We mustn't stop till things are proved concretely.
ORGON.
     Hell never harbored anything so vicious!
ELMIRE.
     Tut, don't be hasty. Try to be judicious.
     Wait, and be certain that there's no mistake.
     No jumping to conclusions, for Heaven's sake!   10

     (*She places Orgon behind her, as Tartuffe re-enters.*)

SCENE 7

TARTUFFE   ELMIRE   ORGON

TARTUFFE (*not seeing Orgon*).
     Madam, all things have worked out to perfection;

I've given the neighboring rooms a full inspection;
No one's about; and now I may at last . . .
ORGON (*intercepting him*).
    Hold on, my passionate fellow, not so fast!
5   I should advise a little more restraint.
    Well, so you thought you'd fool me, my dear saint!
    How soon you wearied of the saintly life—
    Wedding my daughter, and coveting my wife!
    I've long suspected you, and had a feeling
10 That soon I'd catch you at your double-dealing.
    Just now, you've given me evidence galore;
    It's quite enough; I have no wish for more.
ELMIRE (*to Tartuffe*).
    I'm sorry to have treated you so slyly,
    But circumstances forced me to be wily.
TARTUFFE.
    Brother, you can't think . . .
15 ORGON.   No more talk from you;
    Just leave this household, without more ado.
TARTUFFE.
    What I intended . . .
ORGON.   That seems fairly clear.
    Spare me your falsehoods and get out of here.
TARTUFFE.
    No, I'm the master, and you're the one to go!
20 This house belongs to me, I'll have you know,
    And I shall show you that you can't hurt *me*
    By this contemptible conspiracy.
    That those who cross me know not what they do,
    And that I've means to expose and punish you,
25 Avenge offended Heaven, and make you grieve
    That ever you dared order me to leave.

SCENE 8

ELMIRE   ORGON

ELMIRE.
    What was the point of all that angry chatter?
ORGON.
    Dear God, I'm worried. This is no laughing matter.
ELMIRE.
    How so?
ORGON.   I fear I understood his drift.
    I'm much disturbed about that deed of gift.
ELMIRE.
    You gave him . . . ?
5   ORGON.   Yes, it's all been drawn and signed.
    But one thing more is weighing on my mind.
ELMIRE.
    What's that?
ORGON.   I'll tell you; but first let's see if there's
    A certain strong-box in his room upstairs.

ACT V

SCENE 1

ORGON   CLÉANTE

CLÉANTE.
    Where are you going so fast?
ORGON.   God knows!
CLÉANTE.   Then wait;
    Let's have a conference, and deliberate
    On how this situation's to be met.
ORGON.
    That strong-box has me utterly upset;
    This is the worst of many, many shocks.   5
CLÉANTE.
    Is there some fearful mystery in that box?
ORGON.
    My poor friend Argas brought that box to me
    With his own hands, in utmost secrecy;
    'Twas on the very morning of his flight.
    It's full of papers, which, if they came to light,   10
    Would ruin him—or such is my impression.
CLÉANTE.
    Then why did you let it out of your possession?
ORGON.
    Those papers vexed my conscience, and it seemed best
    To ask the counsel of my pious guest.
    The cunning scoundrel got me to agree   15
    To leave the strong-box in his custody.
    So that, in case of an investigation,
    I could employ a slight equivocation
    And swear I didn't have it, and thereby,
    At no expense to conscience, tell a lie.   20
CLÉANTE.
    It looks to me as if you're out on a limb.
    Trusting him with that box, and offering him
    That deed of gift, were actions of a kind
    Which scarcely indicate a prudent mind.
    With two such weapons, he has the upper hand,   25
    And since you're vulnerable, as matters stand,
    You erred once more in bringing him to bay.
    You should have acted in some subtler way.
ORGON.
    Just think of it: behind that fervent face,
    A heart so wicked, and a soul so base!   30
    I took him in, a hungry beggar, and then . . .
    Enough, by God! I'm through with pious men:
    Henceforth I'll hate the whole false brotherhood,
    And persecute them worse than Satan could.
CLÉANTE.
    Ah, there you go—extravagant as ever!   35
    Why can you not be rational? You never
    Manage to take the middle course, it seems,

But jump, instead between absurd extremes.
You've recognized your recent grave mistake
40 In falling victim to a pious fake;
Now, to correct that error, must you embrace
An even greater error in its place,
And judge our worthy neighbors as a whole
By what you've learned of one corrupted soul?
45 Come, just because one rascal made you swallow
A show of zeal which turned out to be hollow,
Shall you conclude that all men are deceivers,
And that, today, there are no true believers?
Let atheists make that foolish inference,
50 Learn to distinguish virtue from pretense,
Be cautious in bestowing admiration,
And cultivate a sober moderation.
Don't humor fraud, but also don't asperse
True piety; the latter fault is worse,
55 And it is best to err, if err one must.
As you have done, upon the side of trust.

SCENE 2

DAMIS   ORGON   CLÉANTE

DAMIS.
    Father, I hear that scoundrel's uttered threats
    Against you; that he pridefully forgets
    How, in his need, he was befriended by you,
    And means to use your gifts to crucify you.
ORGON.
5   It's true, my boy. I'm too distressed for tears.
DAMIS.
    Leave it to me, Sir; let me trim his ears.
    Faced with such insolence, we must not waver.
    I shall rejoice in doing you the favor
    Of cutting short his life, and your distress.
CLÉANTE.
10   What a display of young hotheadedness!
    Do learn to moderate your fits of rage.
    In this just kingdom, this enlightened age,
    One does not settle things by violence.

SCENE 3

MADAME PERNELLE   DORINE   ORGON
MARIANE   DAMIS   CLÉANTE   ELMIRE

MADAME PERNELLE.
    I hear strange tales of very strange events.
ORGON.
    Yes, strange events which these two eyes beheld.

The man's ingratitude is unparalleled.
I save a wretched pauper from starvation,
House him, and treat him like a blood relation,   5
Shower him every day with my largesse,
Give him my daughter, and all that I possess;
And meanwhile the unconscionable knave
Tries to induce my wife to misbehave;
And not content with such extreme rascality,   10
Now threatens me with my own liberality,
And aims, by taking base advantage of
The gifts I gave him out of Christian love,
To drive me from my house, a ruined man,
And make me end a pauper, as he began.   15
DORINE.
    Poor fellow!
MADAME PERNELLE.
                    No, my son. I'll never bring
    Myself to think him guilty of such a thing.
ORGON.
    How's that?
MADAME PERNELLE.
                The righteous always were maligned.
ORGON.
    Speak clearly, Mother. Say what's on your mind.
MADAME PERNELLE.
    I mean that I can smell a rat, my dear.   20
    You know how everybody hates him, here.
ORGON.
    That has no bearing on the case at all.
MADAME PERNELLE.
    I told you a hundred times, when you were small,
    That virtue in this world is hated ever;
    Malicious men may die, but malice never.   25
ORGON.
    No doubt that's true, but how does it apply?
MADAME PERNELLE.
    They've turned you against him by a clever lie.
ORGON.
    I've told you, I was there and saw it done.
MADAME PERNELLE.
    Ah, slanderers will stop at nothing, Son.
ORGON.
    Mother, I'll lose my temper . . . For the last time,   30
    I tell you I was witness to the crime.
MADAME PERNELLE.
    The tongues of spite are busy night and noon,
    And to their venom no man is immune.
ORGON.
    You're talking nonsense. Can't you realize
    I saw it; saw it; saw it with my eyes?   35
    Saw, do you understand me? Must I shout it
    Into your ears before you'll cease to doubt it?
MADAME PERNELLE.
    Appearances can deceive, my son. Dear me,

We cannot always judge by what we see.
ORGON.
      Drat! Drat!
MADAME PERNELLE.
40   One often interprets things awry;
      Good can seem evil to a suspicious eye.
ORGON.
      Was I to see his pawing at Elmire
      As an act of charity?
MADAME PERNELLE.   Till his guilt is clear,
      A man deserves the benefit of the doubt
      You should have waited, to see how things turned out.
45 ORGON.
      Great God in Heaven, what more proof did I need?
      Was I to sit there, watching, until he'd . . .
      You drive me to the brink of impropriety.
MADAME PERNELLE.
      No, no, man of such surpassing piety
      Could not do such a thing. You cannot shake me.
50   I don't believe it, and you shall not make me.
ORGON.
      You vex me so that, if you weren't my mother,
      I'd say to you . . . some dreadful thing or other.
DORINE.
      It's your turn now, Sir, not to be listened to;
      You'd not trust us, and now she won't trust you.
55 CLÉANTE.
      My friends, we're wasting time which should be spent
      In facing up to our predicament.
      I fear that scoundrel's threats weren't made in sport.
DAMIS.
      Do you think he'd have the nerve to go to court?
ELMIRE.
60   I'm sure he won't: they'd find it all too crude
      A case of swindling and ingratitude.
CLÉANTE.
      Don't be too sure. He won't be at a loss
      To give his claims a high and righteous gloss;
      And clever rogues with far less valid cause
65   Have trapped their victims in a web of laws.
      I say again that to antagonize
      A man so strongly armed was most unwise.
ORGON.
      I know it; but the man's appalling cheek
      Outraged me so, I couldn't control my pique.
CLÉANTE.
70   I wish to Heaven that we could devise
      Some truce between you, or some compromise.
ELMIRE.
      If I had known what cards he held, I'd not
      Have roused his anger by my little plot.
ORGON (*to Dorine as M. Loyal enters*).
      What is that fellow looking for? Who is he?
75   Go talk to him—and tell him that I'm busy.

SCENE 4

MONSIEUR LOYAL   DAMIS   ELMIRE
MADAME PERNELLE   MARIANE   CLÉANTE
ORGON   DORINE

MONSIEUR LOYAL.
      Good day, dear sister. Kindly let me see
      Your master.
DORINE.   He's involved with company.
      And cannot be disturbed just now, I fear.
MONSIEUR LOYAL.
      I hate to intrude; but what has brought me here
      Will not disturb your master, in any event.   5
      Indeed, my news will make him most content.
DORINE.
      Your name?
MONSIEUR LOYAL. Just say that I bring greetings from
      Monsieur Tartuffe, on whose behalf I've come.
DORINE (*to Orgon*).
      Sir, he's a very gracious man, and bears
      A message from Tartuffe, which, he declares   10
      Will make you most content.
CLÉANTE.   Upon my word,
      I think this man had best be seen, and heard.
ORGON.
      Perhaps he has some settlement to suggest.
      How shall I treat him? What manner would be best?
CLÉANTE.
      Control your anger, and if he should mention,   15
      Some fair adjustment, give him your full attention.
MONSIEUR LOYAL.
      Good health to you, good Sir. May Heaven confound
      Your enemies, and may your joys abound.
ORGON (*aside to Cléante*).
      A gentle salutation: it confirms
      My guess that he is here to offer terms.   20
MONSIEUR LOYAL.
      I've always held your family most dear;
      I served your father, Sir, for many a year.
ORGON.
      Sir, I must ask your pardon; to my shame,
      I cannot now recall your face or name.
MONSIEUR LOYAL.
      Loyal's my name, I come from Normandy,   25
      And I'm a bailiff, in all modesty.
      For forty years, praise God, it's been my boast
      To serve with honor in that vital post,
      And I am here, Sir, if you will permit
      The liberty, to serve you with this writ . . .   30
ORGON.
      To—*what?*
MONSIEUR LOYAL.
      Now, please, Sir, let us have no friction:

It's nothing but an order of eviction.
You are to move your goods and family out
And make way for new occupants, without
35   Deferment or delay, and give me the keys . . .
ORGON.
I? Leave this house?
MONSIEUR LOYAL.   Why yes, Sir, if you please.
This house, Sir, from the cellar to the roof,
Belongs now to the good Monsieur Tartuffe,
And he is lord and master of your estate
40   By virtue of a deed of present date,
Drawn in due form, with clearest legal phrasing . . .
DAMIS.
Your insolence is utterly amazing!
MONSIEUR LOYAL.
Young man, my business here is not with you,
But with your rise and temperate father, who,
45   Like every worthy citizen, stands in awe
Of justice, and would never obstruct the law.
ORGON.
But . . .
MONSIEUR LOYAL.
Not for a million, Sir, would you rebel
Against authority; I know that well.
You'll not make trouble, Sir, or interfere
50   With the execution of my duties here.
DAMIS.
Someone may execute a smart tattoo
On that black jacket of yours, before you're through.
MONSIEUR LOYAL.
Sir, bid your son be silent. I'd much regret
Having to mention such a nasty threat
55   Of violence, in writing my report.
DORINE (*aside*).
This man Loyal's a most disloyal sort!
MONSIEUR LOYAL.
I love all men of upright character,
And when I agreed to serve these papers, Sir,
It was your feelings that I had in mind.
60   I couldn't bear to see the case assigned
To someone else, who might esteem you less
And so subject you to unpleasantness.
ORGON.
What's more unpleasant than telling a man to leave
His house and home?
MONSIEUR LOYAL.   You'd like a short reprieve?
65   If you desire it, Sir, I shall not press you,
But wait until tomorrow to dispossess you.
Splendid. I'll come and spend the night here, then,
Most quietly, with half a score of men.
For forms sake, you might bring me, just before
70   You go to bed, the keys to the front door.
My men, I promise, will be on their best
Behavior, and will not disturb your rest.

But bright and early, Sir, you must be quick
And move out all your furniture, every stick:
The men I've chosen are both young and strong,   75
And with their help it shouldn't take you long.
In short, I'll make things pleasant and convenient,
And since I'm being so extremely lenient,
Please show me, Sir, a like consideration,
And give me your entire cooperation.   80
ORGON (*aside*).
I may be all but bankrupt, but I vow
I'd give a hundred louis, here and now,
Just for the pleasure of landing one good clout
Right on the end of that complacent snout.
CLÉANTE.
Careful; don't make things worse.
DAMIS.   My bootsole itches   85
To give that beggar a good kick in the breeches.
DORINE.
Monsieur Loyal, I'd love to hear the whack
Of a stout stick across your fine broad back.
MONSIEUR LOYAL.
Take care: a woman too may go to jail if
She uses threatening language to a bailiff.   90
CLÉANTE.
Enough, enough, Sir. This must not go on.
Give me that paper, please, and then begone.
MONSIEUR LOYAL.
Well, *au revoir*, God give you all good cheer!
ORGON.
May God confound you, and him who sent you here!

SCENE 5

ORGON   ELMIRE   DORINE
CLÉANTE   MADAME PERNELLE   DAMIS   MARIANE

ORGON.
Now, Mother, was I right or not? This writ
Should change your notion of Tartuffe a bit.
Do you perceive his villainy at last?
MADAME PERNELLE.
I'm thunderstuck. I'm utterly aghast.
DORINE.
Oh, come be fair. You mustn't take offense   5
At this new proof of his benevolence.
He's acting out of selfless love, I know.
Material things enslave the soul, and so
He kindly has arranged your liberation
From all that might endanger your salvation.   10
ORGON.
Will you not ever hold your tongue, you dunce?
CLÉANTE.
Come, you must take some action, and at once.

ELMIRE.

    Go tell the world of the low trick he's tried.
    The deed of a gift is surely nullified
15   By such behavior, and public rage will not
    Permit the wretch to carry out his plot.

SCENE 6

VALÈRE   ELMIRE   DAMIS
ORGON   MARIANE   DORINE
CLÉANTE   MADAME PERNELLE

VALÈRE.

    Sir, though I hate to bring you more bad news,
    Such is the danger that I cannot choose.
    A friend who is extremely close to me
    And knows my interest in your family
5   Has, for my sake, presumed to violate
    The secrecy that's due to things of state,
    And sends me word that you are in a plight
    From which your one salvation lies in flight.
    That scoundrel who's imposed upon you so
10   Denounced you to the King an hour ago
    And, as supporting evidence, displayed
    The strong-box of a certain renegade
    Whose secret papers, so he testified,
    You had disloyally agreed to hide.
15   I don't know just what charges may be pressed,
    But there's a warrant out for your arrest;
    Tartuffe has been instructed, furthermore,
    To guide the arresting officer to your door.

CLÉANTE.

    He's clearly done this to facilitate
20   His seizure of your house and your estate.

ORGON.

    That man, I must say, is a vicious beast!

VALÈRE.

    Quick, Sir; you mustn't tarry in the least.
    My carriage is outside, to take you hence;
    This thousand louis should cover all expense.
25   Let's lose no time, or you shall be undone;
    The sole defense, in this case, is to run.
    I shall go with you all the way, and place you
    In a safe refuge to which they'll never trace you.

ORGON.

    Alas, dear boy, I wish that I could show you
30   My gratitude for everything I owe you.
    But now is not the time; I pray the Lord
    That I may live to give you your reward.
    Farewell, my dears; be careful . . .

CLÉANTE.   Brother, hurry.
    We shall take care of things; you needn't worry.

SCENE 7

THE OFFICER   ELMIRE   DORINE
TARTUFFE   MARIANE   CLÉANTE
VALÈRE   MADAME PERNELLE   DAMIS   ORGON

TARTUFFE.

    Gently, Sir, gently; stay right where you are.
    No need for haste; your lodging isn't far.
    You're off to prison, by order of the Prince.

ORGON.

    This is the crowning blow, you wretch; and since
    It means my total ruin and defeat,   5
    Your villainy is now at last complete.

TARTUFFE.

    You needn't try to provoke me; it's no use.
    Those who serve Heaven must expect abuse.

CLÉANTE.

    You are indeed most patient, sweet and blameless.

DORINE.

    How he exploits the name of Heaven! It's shameless.   10

TARTUFFE.

    Your taunts and mockeries are all for naught;
    To do my duty is my only thought.

MARIANE.

    Your love of duty is most meritorious,
    And what you've done is little short of glorious.

TARTUFFE.

    All deeds are glorious, Madam, which obey   15
    The sovereign prince who sent me here today.

ORGON.

    I rescued you when you were destitute;
    Have you forgotten that, you thankless brute?

TARTUFFE.

    No, no, I well remember everything;
    But my first duty is to serve my King.   20
    That obligation is so paramount
    That other claims, beside it, do not count;
    And for it I would sacrifice my wife,
    My family, my friend, or my own life.

ELMIRE.

    Hypocrite!

DORINE.   All that we most revere, he uses   25
    To cloak his plots and camouflage his ruses.

CLÉANTE.

    If it is true that you are animated
    By pure and loyal zeal, as you have stated,
    Why was this zeal not roused until you'd sought
    To make Orgon a cuckhold, and been caught?   30
    Why weren't you moved to give your evidence
    Until your outraged host had driven you hence?
    I shan't say that the gift of all his treasure
    Ought to have damped your zeal in any measure;
    But if he is a traitor, as you declare,   35

How could you condescend to be his heir?
TARTUFFE (*to the Officer*).
   Sir, spare me all this clamor; it's growing shrill.
   Please carry out your orders, if you will.
   OFFICER.
   Yes, I've delayed too long, Sir. Thank you kindly.
40   You're just the proper person to remind me.
   Come, you are off to join the other boarders
   In the King's prison, according to his orders.
   TARTUFFE.
   Who? I, Sir?
   OFFICER.   Yes.
   TARTUFFE.   To prison? This can't be true!
   OFFICER.
   I owe an explanation, but not to you.
45   (*To Orgon*.) Sir, all is well; rest easy, and be grateful.
   We serve a Prince to whom all sham is hateful,
   A Prince who sees into our inmost hearts,
   And can't be fooled by any trickster's arts.
   His royal soul, though generous and human,
50   Views all things with discernment and acumen;
   His sovereign reason is not lightly swayed,
   And all his judgements are discreetly weighed.
   He honors righteous men of every kind,
   And yet his zeal for virtue is not blind,
55   Nor does his love of piety numb his wits
   And make him tolerant of hypocrites.
   'Twas hardly likely that this man could cozen
   A King who's foiled such liars by the dozen.
   With one keen glance, the King perceived the whole
60   Perverseness and corruption of his soul,
   And thus high Heaven's justice was displayed:
   Betraying you, the rogue stood self-betrayed.
   The King soon recognized Tartuffe as one
   Notorious by another name, who'd done
65   So many vicious crimes that one could fill
   Ten volumes with them, and be writing still.
   But to be brief: our sovereign was appalled
   By this man's treachery toward you, which he called
   The last, worst villainy of a vile career,

   And bade me follow the imposter here   70
   To see how gross his impudence could be,
   And force him to restore your property.
   Your private papers, by the King's command,
   I hereby seize and give into your hand.
   The King, by royal order, invalidates   75
   The deed which gave this rascal your estates,
   And pardons, furthermore, your grave offense
   In harboring an exile's documents.
   By these decrees, your Prince rewards you for
   Your loyal deeds in the late civil war,   80
   And shows how heartfelt in his satisfaction
   In recompensing any worthy action,
   How much he prizes merit, and how he makes
   More of men's virtues than of their mistakes.
   DORINE.
   Heaven be praised!
   MADAME PERNELLE.   I breathe again, at last.   85
   ELMIRE.
   We're safe.
   MARIANE.   I can't believe the danger's past.
   ORGON (*to Tartuffe*).
   Well, traitor, now you see . . .
   CLÉANTE.   Ah, brother please,
   Let's not descend to such indignities.
   Leave the poor wretch to his unhappy fate,
   And don't say anything to aggravate   90
   His present woes; but rather hope that he
   Will soon embrace an honest piety,
   And mend his ways, and by a true repentance
   Move our just King to moderate his sentence.
   Meanwhile, go kneel before your sovereign's throne   95
   And thank him for the mercies he has shown.
   ORGON.
   Well said: let's go at once and, gladly kneeling,
   Express the gratitude which all are feeling.
   Then, when the first great duty has been done,
   We'll turn with pleasure to the second one,   100
   And give Valère, whose love has proven so true,
   The wedded happiness which is his due.

TOPICS FOR CRITICAL THINKING AND WRITING

The Play on the PAGE

1. Satiric comedy is usually justified on the grounds that the spectators not only laugh at the folly or vice depicted on the stage, but, seeing the absurdity of folly and vice, they also reform their own characters. What is your view?
2. Is Orgon a comic (laughable) figure? Would he be more comic or less comic if Tartuffe was genuinely pious? Does Orgon deserve the treatment he gets from Tartuffe?
3. Is Tartuffe a comic (laughable) figure? Why, or why not?
4. What is our attitude toward Tartuffe? Is it possible to admire him as well as find him loathsome?
5. Is there a fundamental inconsistency in the play: Tartuffe is a clever schemer, and yet his scheme is evident to everyone except Orgon? Some productions suggest that Orgon is erotically attracted to Tartuffe. Is this an adequate explanation? Is it a helpful explanation?
6. The play ends with a messenger from the king, a *deus ex machina* (if the term is unfamiliar, consult the glossary in this book). Is the ending unsatisfactory? Or is it acceptable on the grounds that in fact the king in the seventeenth century was regarded as semidivine, able to see and to punish injustice almost miraculously?
7. It is commonplace to say that the play criticizes hypocrisy, not religion. Do you agree or disagree? Why?
8. Molière was certainly influenced by the *commedia dell'arte*. If you are familiar with the *commedia dell'arte* (see pages 459–60), what evidence of its influence do you see in this play?

The Play on the STAGE

9. How would you costume the play? It is set in bourgeois Paris in the seventeenth century—a period of colorful costumes—but might there be reasons to change the period? Is the Victorian period a candidate? Explain.
10. As the brief note on "The Play in Performance" indicates, Tartuffe has sometimes been costumed in near-clerical garb, sometimes in secular garb. How would you costume him? Why?
11. Dorine is often cast as a pretty, saucy young girl, though occasionally she is presented as an older woman, a servant who has been with the family for decades. How would you cast Dorine? Why?
12. Take one scene that you especially like, and explain how you would stage it. Consider placement of the characters on the stage, their gestures, and their tones of voice.
13. Several directors of recent productions have treated ironically the speech of the police officer in the final scene, usually by having it delivered swiftly, mechanically, unfeelingly, or even unintelligibly. What are your thoughts about this way of delivering a speech?
14. If a spectator does not know the play, do you suppose he or she fears that evil may triumph?

The Play in PERFORMANCE

Molière had trouble getting the play onto the stage. In 1664 a three-act version was performed at Versailles; King Louis XIV was amused, but the archbishop of Paris and some other members of the clergy protested, as did some powerful courtiers, and the play was banned. Because this three-act version was not published, its nature is unknown. Conjectures are idle, but that has not stopped scholars from conjecturing (e.g., that it consisted of acts 1, 3 and 4 of the five-act version we now have). Also uncertain, but less so, is

Tartuffe's costume; substantial evidence indicates that he wore a cassock or some sort of modified clerical garb suggestive of Jesuit attire, and this costume partly accounted for the hostility of the Church.

In 1664–65 a five-act version was privately performed, and it was given one public performance in Paris in 1667. The play was now titled *L'Imposteur*, Tartuffe was renamed Panulphe, and his appearance was not that of a cleric but of a man of fashion (long hair, lace, and a sword). Despite the attempt to emphasize the protagonist's secular status, this version too was suppressed by the clergy after the single public performance in 1667. We know some details about this version because they are specified in a work discussing it, *Lettre sur la Comédie de l'Imposteur*, perhaps partly written by Molière.

In 1669 the ban was lifted, and the play—in five acts—was performed and published. Some evidence (though it is not decisive) indicates that Tartuffe (the original name was restored) wore black, and he has often worn black in later productions. The play has had such a rich stage history that here we can indicate only a handful of some of the most interesting productions of the twentieth century. In 1968 it was produced in the United States by the Theater of the City of Villeurbanne, directed by Roger Planchon, with a set by René Allis. This play began with an elaborately furnished room, but at the end of each act properties and parts of the set vanished into the flies, so that by the end of the play, when the actors were performing against a wooden frame with paper wall, the implication was that the bare truth had been revealed. In this production Tartuffe was played with dignity, but in many other productions (e.g. Ingmar Bergman's German production in Munich in 1979) Tartuffe has been played as something of a madman, or at least as a crazed schemer. Bergman's production was very highly

theatrical; changes of scenery were visible, made by costumed stagehands. The play's end was treated ironically: The King's Officer rushed through his proclamation in French (German had been the language onstage up to this point), speaking it so mechanically that is was self-evidently absurd. Cléante, who in this scene was in a wheelchair (at the beginning of the play he used a cane, later crutches), leaped as though cured by the manifestation of justice, but the effect was intentionally absurd. A 1980 production at the Comédie Française was odd in a different way: It used a modern setting, and at the end Tartuffe was shot by the police.

Finally, it should be mentioned that in the last thirty or so years, there have been several homoerotic productions, such as one by Roger Planchon in 1977, where Orgon's interest in Tartuffe was at least partly sexual. Bergman's 1979 version, too, approached this theme: Orgon clearly was someone seeking to be loved, and Tartuffe exploited this need. In 1981–82, Brian Bedford's British production, staged at the Kennedy Center, in Washington, D.C., followed this line: Orgon clearly had a crush on Tartuffe, and on one occasion, when his arm was at first around Tartuffe's shoulder he allowed his arm to lower and his hand slip to Tartuffe's buttocks. In the scene when Orgon, under a table, spies on Tartuffe attempting to seduce Orgon's wife Elmire, Orgon in this production seemed wounded not because Tartuffe was lustful but by the fact that Tartuffe's attention was not directed to him. One might consider whether the play is strengthened by attempts to—in effect—make Orgon's behavior plausible, that is, to provide Orgon with convincing motivation. Against such attempts it can perhaps be argued that making comic behavior plausible is likely to make it less comic, less amusing.

APHRA Behn

Very little is known for certain about Aphra Behn. We are not sure of the year or the place of her birth in England, her maiden name, the date of her marriage or the nationality and the profession of her husband, or even of the exact number of plays that she wrote. Some biographers, however, have been quick to report as fact what is really conjecture. She is usually said to have been born about 1640, probably into a family named Johnson. It is commonly asserted that her father was appointed Lieutenant General of Surinam, then a British colony and now Dutch Guiana, but that he died on the voyage to Surinam, and that Aphra lived only briefly there and then returned to England. In fact, the chief authority for her visit to Surinam is a passage in her novel, *Oroonoko* (1688), which was then reported as a biographical fact in the first (anonymous) biography of Behn issued after her death. There is no compelling reason, however, to assume that *Oroonoko* is in any way autobiographical—such details as it does include about Surinam could well have been derived from other books—and there is no compelling reason to believe that the anonymous biography is authoritative, though some scholars believe it is by Behn herself. The biography may or may not be by Behn, and if it is by Behn it may or may not be truthful.

Still, there are some facts. In 1666 Aphra Behn served in Antwerp as a spy for England, but her services were deemed of no value and she was not paid. In 1667 she returned to England, impoverished, and in 1668 she was imprisoned for debt. She began her career as a playwright in 1670, with a tragicomedy called *The Forced Marriage*. It ran for six performances, which means that it was a success, although today a play must run far longer if it is to earn any money for the author. At least fifteen more of her plays were produced during her lifetime, including *The Rover* (1677), *The Second Part of the Rover* (1681), and *The Emperor of the Moon* (1687). It is not known how she became associated with the theater, but perhaps it was through Thomas Killigrew, a playwright and later a theatrical entrepreneur, with whom Behn had corresponded when she was in Antwerp. (*The Rover* is partly based on a play by Killigrew, *Thomaso*.) Behn also wrote an important antislavery novel, *Oronooko* (1688), which was dramatized by Thomas Southerne in 1695 and was popular throughout the eighteenth century.

Behn was not the first woman in England to write plays, but she was the first to make a living as a playwright. (Two women who were her contemporaries must be mentioned: The Marchioness of Newcastle published two collections of plays, in 1662 and 1668, but they were never performed; Catherine Phillips [or Katherine Philips] did have a play performed, *Pompey*, but she was not a professional playwright.) Behn died in 1689, and is buried in Westminster Abbey.

■■■■■■■■■■■■

COMMENTARY ON *THE ROVER*

Let's begin with words by Aphra Behn herself, though not words from *The Rover*. In the preface to another of her plays, *The Lucky Chance* (1686), she complained that her plays were given low marks simply because it was known that they were by a woman, and the age believed that it took a man to write a good play:

> Had the Plays I have writ come forth under any Mans Name, and never known to have been mine, I appeal to all unbyast Judges of Sense, if they had not said that Person had made as many good Comedies, as any one Man that has writ in our Age; but a Devil on't the

> Woman damns the Poet. . . . All I ask, is the Priviledge for my Masculine Part the Poet in me.

Behn is asking that she be judged on her work, not on her gender. When she writes, she is (she says) doing what is usually done only by men. She is using what the age would think of as her "Masculine Part"—for instance the power to imagine characters, or the power to organize episodes into a coherent plot. But if some readers of Behn's day were skeptical that a woman could write a play, some readers of our day are skeptical that a woman can write the same sort of play that a man can write. The idea is this: Given the fact that the experience of being a woman is different from the experience of being a man, men and women must in some degree see things differently.

Take, for instance, the common use of women as commodities in marriage. An impoverished male aristocrat might marry a rich middle-class woman in order to improve his finances, and a shopkeeper might marry in order to have a cheap housekeeper. A woman usually married in order to have economic security. All of this may have seemed perfectly natural to the men and the women involved, but clearly marriage had one meaning for men and another for women. A related point: Prostitution is accepted by many men because it is an institution that affords them pleasure, but for women prostitution is a means of livelihood. In Behn's day, women had few choices: marriage (arranged by men, for business reasons), the cloister (again arranged by men), domestic service, and prostitution.

Speaking of prostitution, we should mention that when the theaters in England reopened in 1660, after the period of Puritan rule, actresses appeared on the English stage in place of young boys who had taken the female roles in earlier years. These actresses were widely regarded—with some justification—as prostitutes; some of them were the mistresses of courtiers, and Nell Gwynne, perhaps the most famous actress of her day, for a while was the mistress of King Charles II. It is not entirely surprising, then, that prostitution becomes a topic for discussion in the plays, as we will see in a moment.

Although some men have profited financially from prostitution, it is largely a woman's business. Partly for this reason, as well as for moral reasons, prostitution has been scorned by men and has been regarded as the antithesis of marriage, which was regarded as an institution that offered a respectable career for women. But some women have been quick to point out a connection between the business of marriage and the business of prostitution. For instance, Polly Adler, a brothel-keeper, in a book called *A House Is Not a Home* (1953), wrote:

> The women who take husbands not out of love but out of greed, to get their bills paid, to get a fine house and clothes and jewels; the women who marry to get out of a tiresome job, or to get away from disagreeable relatives, or to avoid being called an old maid—these are whores in everything but in name.

In several passages in *The Rover* Aphra Behn raises a similar point. For instance, when Willmore, in 2.2, rebukes Angellica for demanding money for her services, Angellica replies by commenting on the financial aspects of respectable marriage:

> Pray tell me, sir, are not you guilty of the same mercenary crime? When a lady is proposed to you for a wife, you never ask how fair, discreet, or virtuous she is, but what's her fortune—which if but small, you cry, "She will not do my business" and basely leave her, though she languish for you. . . .

Because we know that *The Rover* was written by a woman, it is hard not to hear a distinctive female sensibility in such a passage, and indeed it would be hard to find comparable lines in the work of a male dramatist of the period. On the other hand, we should make two points about dramatic traditions that Behn is working in. First, there is the tradition of "the love-game comedy," in which a witty young man and a witty young woman engage in verbal combat. A famous example is Shakespeare's *Much Ado About Nothing,* in which Beatrice and Benedict enjoy themselves and give enjoyment to audiences by putting each other down, and then at last find what everyone has long known—that they love each other and will make an excellent couple. In Behn's play, Willmore and Angellica do *not* marry, and the business aspect of what passes as respectable marriage is subjected to an irony not found in Shakespeare's comedies, but Behn was by no means the first dramatist to present a clever woman who speaks hard truths.

Second, the skeptical view of marriage that Behn offers is found in many other comic writers of the time. Consider, for instance, this song from a comedy by John Dryden, *Marriage a-la-Mode,* written in 1671:

> Why should a foolish marriage vow,
>   Which long ago was made,
> Oblige us to each other now
>   When passion is decayed?
> We loved, and we loved, as long as we could,
>   Till our love was loved out in us both:
> But our marriage is dead, when the pleasure is fled:
>   'Twas pleasure first made it an oath.

If we go back a century from Dryden and Behn to Shakespeare's songs about marriage—delightful lyrics about true love and undying passion—in the last decade of the sixteenth century and the first decade or so of the seventeenth, we realize how greatly the English theater had changed.

Even in Shakespeare's day, the English theater can be said to have been divided between two theatrical publics. There was the broad, general public that paid a penny to enter a large theater which was open to the elements, and there was a smaller, richer public that paid sixpence to enter an indoor theater, a so-called private theater. The difference can be exaggerated—certain authors wrote for both theaters, and the richer members of the theater-going public could go to both theaters—but, still, the price of admission meant that there was a difference. For one thing, English history plays were more popular with the general Elizabethan public than with the smaller, richer public.

What we are saying about the effect of an audience's taste on those who make a living by satisfying that taste is nothing new. Dr. Samuel Johnson in 1747 made the point memorably, in a verse prologue he wrote in honor of his former pupil David Garrick—the greatest actor of the day—who had just became joint owner of a theater. After sketching the history of English drama, Johnson says that the playwrights and actors respond to the public—"The stage but echoes back the public voice." Then he goes on to offer this memorable formula:

The drama's laws the drama's patrons give,
For we that live to please, must please to live.

But who were "the drama's patrons" when Aphra Behn was writing, in the 1670s and 1680s? A bit of historical background must be offered. King Charles I (reigned 1625–49) sought to limit the powers of Parliament and in particular to suppress the Puritans, but in 1642 Parliament passed legislation limiting the power of the throne. One of Parliament's actions was to close the London theaters, and though there were some surreptitious performances, for all practical purposes theatrical activity ceased in England. The civil war which in 1642 broke out between the Parliamentary and the Royalist forces more or less ended with the capture of Charles in 1646, and it decisively ended in 1649, when Charles was executed. His wife and children (including the future Charles II) escaped to France, where they were joined by some loyal followers, called the cavaliers. (*The Rover* is about such followers, though it is set in Naples rather than in France.) The management of what had been the kingdom but now was called the Commonwealth fell chiefly into the hands of Oliver Cromwell, a Puritan who held the title of Lord Protector of the Realm.

Cromwell died in 1658, and in 1660, when the monarchy was restored, Charles II returned from the Continent. Even in exile he had lived a life of ease and pleasure, and when he was restored to the throne one of the first actions of "The Merry Monarch" was to give patents or licenses to William Davenant and Thomas Killigrew, each of whom was permitted to operate a theater—the so-called theaters-royal. Each of the two theater buildings held fewer spectators than an Elizabethan theater had held, but even so, the new theaters did not prosper, and from 1682 until 1695 the two companies survived only by uniting into a single company. This means that a relatively small group of performers did all of the acting, and a relatively small audience witnessed the plays. The composition of the audience cannot be determined exactly, but we know that the king himself attended the first recorded performance of *The Rover,* and where the king is, courtiers are not far behind. And we can notice in the plays a mild contempt for bourgeois values—for the values of "the cits," as they are called. We are told that Angellica Bianca, a courtesan, is "the only adored beauty of all the youth in Naples," something that perhaps gives us pause if we think of the beautiful, chaste women in Shakespeare's comedies. In *The Rover,* all of the men except Belvile attempt to rape women, but no one seems to think this activity is especially reprehensible; alcohol and youth are considered sufficient excuses for such assaults. Willmore, the hero, is lust incarnate, and he therefore finds it difficult to believe that any woman can be virtuous:

A virtuous mistress? Death, what a thing thou has found out for me! Why, what the devil should I do with a virtuous woman, a sort of ill-natured creature that take a pride to torment a lover. Virtue is but an infirmity in woman, a disease that renders even the handsome ungrateful; whilst the ill-favored, for want of solicitations and address, only fancy themselves so. I have lain with a woman of quality who has all the while been railing at whores. (4.2)

Presumably the audience that enjoyed this speech regarded itself as highly sophisticated—witty, skeptical, enlightened, adventurous—especially sexually adventurous, which gets us back to the passage by Dryden, asking why "a foolish marriage vow" should oblige a couple to stay together, and the passage by Behn, asking if prostitution is much different from marriage.

What are we to make of this world of rovers, of men and women who condone adultery, and who, speaking broadly, live in a world in which the values seem utterly remote from traditional values—or at least from the values expressed earlier on the English stage, say in *A Midsummer Night's Dream? (A Midsummer Night's*

Dream ends with fairies blessing the marriage bed; *The Rover* ends with Willmore talking of "the storms o' th' marriage bed.") In 1822, in a famous essay called "On the Artificial Comedy of the Last Century," Charles Lamb offered one way of thinking about this. Lamb's word "artificial" is the key. According to Lamb, the comic world that we see on the Restoration stage has no connection with our world, the real world. Rather, the characters belong to a fairy-tale world of utterly unreal—but thoroughly entertaining—people. These characters do not offend our moral sense because they are not moving in a moral world:

> They seem engaged in their proper element. They break through no laws or conscientious restraints. They know of none. They have got out of Christendom into the land—what shall I call it?—of cuckoldry—the Utopia of gallantry, where pleasure is duty, and the manners perfect freedom. It is altogether a speculative scene of things, which has no reference whatever to the world that is. No good person can be justly offended as a spectator, because no good person suffers on the stage. Judged morally, every character in these plays—the few exceptions only are *mistakes*—is alike essentially vain and worthless. . . . The whole is a passing pageant, where we should sit as unconcerned at the issues, for life or death, as at the battle of the frogs and mice.

Whereas the moralist might say that plays are morally damaging to spectators if (as in *The Rover*) characters who think that rape is fun go unpunished, Lamb says that these plays—far from damaging us—have a beneficial effect, at least on him, since they entertain him and therefore allow him to return to his job refreshed. "I come back to my cage and my restraint the fresher and more healthy for it. I wear my shackles more contentedly for having respired the breath of an imaginary freedom."

Today, most scholars of Restoration drama believe that Lamb was mistaken when he said that the plays had no connection with real life. On the other hand, even if he was mistaken on this point, we probably cannot simply dismiss his view that a certain amount of imaginative liberty—let's say fantasizing—is actually healthful. Lamb's assertion that after witnessing a Restoration comedy we return, refreshed, to the "cage" of the real world, can be tested against your own response to, say, a Marx Brothers movie, where mayhem rules, or even your response to a Chaplin movie, since in the films Chaplin engages in all sorts of deceits that in the real world would be reprehensible. Lamb's theory can also be related to Aristotle's theory of catharsis, which holds that we somehow are made better by seeing on the stage actions—let's say an action such as the suffering of Oedipus—that in real life would pain us.

If we accept Lamb's view that the world in a Restoration comedy is unrelated to our world, we undermine the view that the comedy probes our social institutions and sets out to make us think. In particular, Lamb's view would diminish the idea that because Behn was a woman—an outsider, so to speak, in the man's world of playwriting—she was in a particularly good position to examine male values, and to stimulate skeptical thought in her audience. Perhaps the twentieth century offers a synthesis: We can hold both views, sometimes with Lamb seeing *The Rover* as a play that offers a never-never land in which fantasy reigns, and sometimes with today's critics seeing *The Rover* as a searching criticism of patriarchy.

THE ROVER; OR, THE BANISHED CAVALIERS*
Aphra Behn

PROLOGUE

Wits, like physicians, never can agree,
When of a different society.
And Rabel's drops[1] were never more cried down
By all the learned doctors of the town,
Than a new play whose author is unknown.
Nor can those doctors with more malice sue
(And powerful purses) the dissenting few,
Than those, with an insulting pride, do rail
At all who are not of their own cabal.[2]
  If a young poet hit your humor[3] right,
You judge him then out of revenge and spite.
So amongst men there are ridiculous elves,
Who monkeys hate for being too like themselves.
So that the reason of the grand debate
Why wit so oft is damned when good plays take,
Is that you censure as you love, or hate.
  Thus like a learned conclave poets sit,
Catholic judges[4] both of sense and wit,
And damn or save as they themselves think fit.
Yet those who to others' faults are so severe,
Are not so perfect but themselves may err.
Some write correct, indeed, but then the whole
(Bating[5] their own dull stuff i'th' play) is stole:
As bees do suck from flowers their honeydew,
So they rob others striving to please you.
  Some write their characters genteel and fine,
But then they do so toil for every line,
That what to you does easy seem, and plain,
Is the hard issue of their laboring brain.
And some th' effects of all their pains, we see,
Is but to mimic good extempore.[6]
Others, by long converse about the town,
Have wit enough to write a lewd lampoon,
But their chief skill lies in a bawdy song.
In short, the only wit that's now in fashion,
Is but the gleanings of good conversation.
As for the author of this coming play,

I asked him[7] what he thought fit I should say
In thanks for your good company today:
He called me fool, and said it was well known
You came not here for our sakes, but your own.
New plays are stuffed with wits, and with deboches,[8]
That crowd and sweat like cits[9] in May-Day coaches.[10]

WRITTEN BY A PERSON OF QUALITY

THE ACTORS' NAMES

[Men]
DON ANTONIO, *the Viceroy's son*
DON PEDRO, *a noble Spaniard, his friend*
BELVILE, *an English colonel in love with Florinda*
WILLMORE, *the Rover*[11]
FREDERICK, *an English gentleman, and friend to Belvile and Blunt*
BLUNT, *an English country gentleman*
STEPHANO, *servant to Don Pedro*
PHILIPPO, *Lucetta's gallant*
SANCHO, *pimp to Lucetta*
BISKEY *and* SEBASTIAN, *two Bravos*[12] *to Angellica*
OFFICER *and* SOLDIERS
[DIEGO,] *Page to Don Antonio*

[Women]
FLORINDA, *sister to Don Pedro*
HELLENA, *a gay young woman designed for a nun, and sister to Florinda*
VALERIA, *a kinswoman to Florinda*
ANGELLICA BIANCA, *a famous courtesan*
MORETTA, *her woman*
CALLIS, *governess to Florinda and Hellena*
LUCETTA, *a jilting wench*
SERVANTS, *other* MASQUERADERS, MEN *and* WOMEN

THE SCENE

Naples, in carnival time.

---

*Cavaliers supporters of the English monarchy during the English civil war. After the execution of Charles I in 1649, many cavaliers left England.   [1]Rabel's drops a patent medicine   [2]cabal secret group   [3]hit your humor accurately portray your characteristics   [4]Catholic judges broadminded judges   [5]Bating excepting   [6]extempore that is, a performance given without adequate preparation

[7]him the play was published anonymously, and the writer of the prologue speaks of the author as a male   [8]deboches dissipations   [9]Cits tradesman and their families (a mildly contemptuous term)   [10]May-Day coaches on May 1, pretentious "cits" customarily took a carriage ride through Hyde Park   [11]Rover wanderer (also *pirate*)   [12]Bravos hired ruffians

Setting her play during Carnival in Naples, Aphra Behn took full advantage of the comic device of mistaken identity through the use of carnival masks. Here Florinda, with her governess Callis, stops her lover Belvile (who she does not recognize) from dueling with Don Pedro, her brother, in Act 4, Scene 2 of *The Rover*.

ACT 1

SCENE 1

(*A Chamber. Enter Florinda and Hellena.*)

FLORINDA. What an impertinent thing is a young girl bred in a nunnery! How full of questions! Prithee no more, Hellena; I have told thee more than thou understand'st already.

HELLENA. The more's my grief. I would fain[13] know as much as you, which makes me so inquisitive; nor is't enough I know you're a lover, unless you tell me too who 'tis you sigh for.

FLORINDA. When you're a lover I'll think you fit for a secret of that nature.

HELLENA. 'Tis true, I never was a lover yet, but I begin to have a shrewd guess what 'tis to be so, and fancy it very pretty to sigh, and sing, and blush, and wish, and dream and wish, and long and wish to see the man, and when I do, look pale and tremble, just as you did when my brother brought home the fine English colonel to see you. What do you call him? Don Belvile?

FLORINDA. Fie, Hellena.

HELLENA. That blush betrays you. I am sure 'tis so. Or is it Don Antonio the Viceroy's son? Or perhaps the rich old Don Vincentio, whom my father designs you for a husband? Why do you blush again?

FLORINDA. With indignation; and how near soever my father thinks I am to marrying that hated object, I shall let him see I understand better what's due to my beauty, birth, and fortune, and more to my soul, than to obey those unjust commands.

HELLENA. Now hang me, if I don't love thee for that dear disobedience. I love mischief strangely, as most of our sex do who are come to love nothing else. But tell me, dear Florinda, don't you love that fine *Anglese*?[14] For I vow, next to loving him myself, 'twill please me most that you do so, for he is so gay and so handsome.

FLORINDA. Hellena, a maid designed for a nun ought not to be so curious in a discourse of love.

HELLENA. And dost thou think that ever I'll be a nun? Or at least till I'm so old I'm fit for nothing else? Faith no, sister; and that which makes me long to know whether you love Belvile, is because I hope he has some mad companion or other that will spoil my devotion. Nay, I'm resolved to provide myself this Carnival, if there be e'er a handsome proper fellow of my humor[15] above ground, though I ask first.

FLORINDA. Prithee be not so wild.

HELLENA. Now you have provided yourself of a man you take no care of poor me. Prithee tell me, what dost thou see about me that is unfit for love? Have I not a world of youth? A humor gay? A beauty passable? A vigor desirable? Well shaped? Clean limbed? Sweet breathed? And sense enough to know how all these ought to be employed to the best advantage? Yes, I do and will; therefore lay aside your hopes of my fortune by my being a devote,[16] and tell me how you came acquainted with this

---

[13]**fain** gladly

[14]***Anglese*** Englishman, that is, Belvile   [15]**Humor** mood   [16]**devote** nun

Belvile. For I perceive you knew him before he came to Naples.

FLORINDA. Yes, I knew him at the siege of Pamplona;[17] he was then a colonel of French horse,[18] who when the town was ransacked, nobly treated my brother and myself, preserving us from all insolences. And I must own, besides great obligations, I have I know not what that pleads kindly for him about my heart, and will suffer no other to enter. But see, my brother.

(*Enter Don Pedro, Stephano with a masking habit,[19] and Callis.*)

PEDRO. Good morrow, sister. Pray when saw you your lover Don Vincentio?

FLORINDA. I know not, sir. Callis, when was he here? For I consider it so little I know not when it was.

PEDRO. I have a command from my father here to tell you you ought not to despise him, a man of so vast a fortune, and such a passion for you.—Stephano, my things.

(*Puts on his masking habit.*)

FLORINDA. A passion for me? 'Tis more than e'er I saw, or he had a desire should be known. I hate Vincentio, sir, and I would not have a man so dear to me as my brother follow the ill customs of our country and make a slave of his sister. And, sir, my father's will I'm sure you may divert.

PEDRO. I know not how dear I am to you, but I wish only to be ranked in your esteem equal with the English colonel Belvile. Why do you frown and blush? Is there any guilt belongs to the name of that cavalier?

FLORINDA. I'll not deny I value Belvile. When I was exposed to such dangers as the licensed lust of common soldiers threatened when rage and conquest flew through the city, then Belvile, this criminal for my sake, threw himself into all dangers to save my honor. And will you not allow him my esteem?

PEDRO. Yes, pay him what you will in honor, but you must consider Don Vincentio's fortune, and the jointure[20] he'll make you.

FLORINDA. Let him consider my youth, beauty, and fortune, which ought not to be thrown away on his age and jointure.

PEDRO. 'Tis true, he's not so young and fine a gentleman as that Belvile. But what jewels will that cavalier present you with? Those of his eyes and heart?

HELLENA. And are not those better than any Don Vincentio has brought from the Indies?

PEDRO. Why, how now! Has your nunnery breeding taught you to understand the value of hearts and eyes?

HELLENA. Better than to believe Vincentio's deserve value from any woman. He may perhaps increase her bags, but not her family.[21]

PEDRO. This is fine! Go! Up to your devotion! You are not designed for the conversation of lovers.

HELLENA (*aside*). Nor saints yet a while, I hope.—Is't not enough you make a nun of me, but you must cast my sister away too, exposing her to a worse confinement than a religious life?

PEDRO. The girl's mad! It is a confinement to be carried into the country to an ancient villa belonging to the family of the Vincentios these five hundred years, and have no other prospect than that pleasing one of seeing all her own that meets her eyes: a fine air, large fields, and gardens where she may walk and gather flowers?

HELLENA. When, by moonlight? For I am sure she dares not encounter with the heat of the sun; that were a task only for Don Vincentio and his Indian breeding, who loves it in the dog days.[22] And if these be her daily divertissements,[23] what are those of the night? To lie in a wide moth-eaten bedchamber with furniture in fashion in the reign of King Sancho the First; the bed, that which his forefathers lived and died in.

PEDRO. Very well.

HELLENA. This apartment, new furbrushed[24] and fitted out for the young wife, he out of freedom makes his dressing room; and being a frugal and a jealous coxcomb,[25] instead of a valet to uncase[26] his feeble carcass, he desires you to do that office. Signs of favor, I'll assure you, and such as you must not hope for unless your woman be out of the way.

PEDRO. Have you done yet?

HELLENA. That honor being past, the giant stretches itself, yawns and sighs a belch or two loud as a musket, throws himself into bed, and expects you in his foul sheets; and ere you can get yourself undressed, calls you with a snore or two. And are not these fine blessings to a young lady?

PEDRO. Have you done yet?

HELLENA. And this man you must kiss, nay you must kiss none but him too, and nuzzle through his beard to find his lips. And this you must submit to for threescore years, and all for a jointure.

PEDRO. For all your character of Don Vincentio, she is as like to marry him as she was before.

HELLENA. Marry Don Vincentio! Hang me, such a wedlock would be worse than adultery with another man. I had

---

[17]**Pamplona** town in northern Spain   [18]**of French horse** in the French cavalry   [19]**masking habit** masquerade costume for the Carnival   [20]**jointure** a marriage settlement providing for the wife's support after her husband's death

[21]**increase . . . family** that is he may make her rich but he is too old to make her pregnant   [22]**dog days** hot summer days   [23]**divertissements** diversions   [24]**new furbrushed** refurbished   [25]**coxcomb** conceited fop   [26]**uncase** undress

rather see her in the *Hostel de Dieu*,[27] to waste her youth there in vows, and be a handmaid to lazars[28] and cripples, than to lose it in such a marriage.

PEDRO. You have considered, sister, that Belvile has no fortune to bring you to; banished his country, despised at home, and pitied abroad.

HELLENA. What then? The Viceroy's son is better than that old Sir Fifty. Don Vincentio! Don Indian! He thinks he's trading to Gambo[29] still, and would barter himself—that bell and bauble—for your youth and fortune.

PEDRO. Callis, take her hence and lock her up all this Carnival, and at Lent she shall begin her everlasting penance in a monastery.

HELLENA. I care not; I had rather be a nun than be obliged to marry as you would have me if I were designed for't.

PEDRO. Do not fear the blessing of that choice. You shall be a nun.

HELLENA (*aside*). Shall I so? You may chance to be mistaken in my way of devotion. A nun! Yes, I am like to make a fine nun! I have an excellent humor for a grate![30] No, I'll have a saint of my own to pray to shortly, if I like any that dares venture on me.

PEDRO. Callis, make it your business to watch this wildcat.— As for you, Florinda, I've only tried you all this while and urged my father's will; but mine is that you would love Antonio: He is brave and young, and all that can complete the happiness of a gallant maid. This absence of my father will give us opportunity to free you from Vincentio by marrying here, which you must do tomorrow.

FLORINDA. Tomorrow!

PEDRO. Tomorrow, or 'twill be too late. 'Tis not my friendship to Antonio which makes me urge this, but love to thee and hatred to Vincentio; therefore resolve upon tomorrow.

FLORINDA. Sir, I shall strive to do as shall become your sister.

PEDRO. I'll both believe and trust you. Adieu.

(*Exeunt*[31] *Pedro and Stephano.*)

HELLENA. As becomes his sister! That is to be as resolved your way as he is his.

(*Hellena goes to Callis.*)

FLORINDA.
I ne'er till now perceived my ruin near.
I've no defense against Antonio's love,
For he has all the advantages of nature,
The moving arguments of youth and fortune.

HELLENA. But hark you, Callis, you will not be so cruel to lock me up indeed, will you?

CALLIS. I must obey the commands I have. Besides, do you consider what a life you are going to lead?

HELLENA. Yes, Callis, that of a nun; and till then I'll be indebted a world of prayers to you if you'll let me now see what I never did, the divertissements of a Carnival.

CALLIS. What, go in masquerade? 'Twill be a fine farewell to the world, I take it. Pray what would you do there?

HELLENA. That which all the world does, as I am told: Be as mad as the rest and take all innocent freedoms. Sister, you'll go too, will you not? Come, prithee be not sad. We'll outwit twenty brothers if you'll be ruled by me. Come, put off this dull humor with your clothes, and assume one as gay and as fantastic as the dress my cousin Valeria and I have provided, and let's ramble.

FLORINDA. Callis, will you give us leave to go?

CALLIS (*aside*). I have a youthful itch of going myself.— Madam, if I thought your brother might not know it, and I might wait on you; for by my troth I'll not trust young girls alone.

FLORINDA. Thou seest my brother's gone already, and thou shalt attend and watch us.

(*Enter Stephano.*)

STEPHANO. Madam, the habits[32] are come, and your cousin Valeria is dressed and stays for you.

FLORINDA (*aside*). 'Tis well. I'll write a note, and if I chance to see Belvile and want an opportunity to speak to him, that shall let him know what I've resolved in favor of him.

HELLENA. Come, let's in and dress us.

(*Exeunt.*)

SCENE 2

(*A long street. Enter Belvile, melancholy; Blunt and Frederick.*)

FREDERICK. Why, what the devil ails the colonel, in a time when all the world is gay to look like mere Lent thus? Hadst thou been long enough in Naples to have been in love, I should have sworn some such judgment had befallen thee.

BELVILE. No, I have made no new amours since I came to Naples.

FREDERICK. You have left none behind you in Paris?

BELVILE. Neither.

FREDERICK. I cannot divine the cause then, unless the old cause, the want of money.

BLUNT. And another old cause, the want of a wench. Would not that revive you?

BELVILE. You are mistaken, Ned.

---

[27]**Hostel de Dieu** hospital run by nuns   [28]**lazars** lepers   [29]**Gambo** Gambia, in West Africa   [30]**grate** a grille covering a convent window (i.e., the convent)   [31]**Exeunt** they go out (Latin)

[32]**habits** costumes (of a religious order)

BLUNT. Nay, 'adsheartlikins,[33] then thou'rt past cure.

FREDERICK. I have found it out: Thou hast renewed thy acquaintance with the lady that cost thee so many sighs at the siege of Pamplona—pox on't, what d'ye call her—her brother's a noble Spaniard, nephew to the dead general. Florinda. Ay, Florinda. And will nothing serve thy turn but that damned virtuous woman, whom on my conscience thou lov'st in spite too, because thou seest little or no possibility of gaining her.

BELVILE. Thou art mistaken; I have int'rest enough in that lovely virgin's heart to make me proud and vain, were it not abated by the severity of a brother, who, perceiving my happiness—

FREDERICK. Has civilly forbid thee the house?

BELVILE. 'Tis so, to make way for a powerful rival, the Viceroy's son, who has the advantage of me in being a man of fortune, a Spaniard, and her brother's friend; which gives him liberty to make his court, whilst I have recourse only to letters and distant looks from her window, which are as soft and kind as those which heaven sends down on penitents.

BLUNT. Heyday! 'Adsheartlikins, simile! By this light the man is quite spoiled. Fred, what the devil are we made of that we cannot be thus concerned for a wench? 'Adsheartlikins, our Cupids are like the cooks of the camp: They can roast or boil a woman, but they have none of the fine tricks to set 'em off; no hogoes[34] to make the sauce pleasant and the stomach sharp.

FREDERICK. I dare swear I have had a hundred as young, kind, and handsome as this Florinda; and dogs eat me if they were not as troublesome to me i'th' morning as they were welcome o'er night.

BLUNT. And yet I warrant he would not touch another woman if he might have her for nothing.

BELVILE. That's thy joy, a cheap whore.

BLUNT. Why, 'adsheartlikins, I love a frank soul. When did you ever hear of an honest woman that took a man's money? I warrant 'em good ones. But gentlemen, you may be free; you have been kept so poor with parliaments and protectors[35] that the little stock you have is not worth preserving. But I thank my stars I had more grace than to forfeit my estate by cavaliering.

BELVILE. Me thinks only following the court should be sufficient to entitle 'em to that.

BLUNT. 'Adsheartlikins, they know I follow it to do it no good, unless they pick a hole in my coat for lending you money now and then, which is a greater crime to my conscience, gentlemen, than to the Commonwealth.[36]

(*Enter Willmore.*)

WILLMORE. Ha! Dear Belvile! Noble colonel!

BELVILE. Willmore! Welcome ashore, my dear rover! What happy wind blew us this good fortune?

WILLMORE. Let me salute my dear Fred, and then command me.—How is't, honest lad?

FREDERICK. Fair, sir, the old compliment, infinitely the better to see my dear mad Willmore again. Prithee, why camest thou ashore? And where's the Prince?[37]

WILLMORE. He's well, and reigns still lord of the wat'ry element. I must aboard again within a day or two, and my business ashore was only to enjoy myself a little this Carnival.

BELVILE. Pray know our new friend, sir; he's but bashful, a raw traveler, but honest, stout, and one of us. (*Embraces Blunt.*)

WILLMORE. That you esteem him gives him an int'rest[38] here.

BLUNT. Your servant, sir.

WILLMORE. But well, faith, I'm glad to meet you again in a warm climate, where the kind sun has its godlike power still over the wine and women. Love and mirth are my business in Naples, and if I mistake not the place, here's an excellent market for chapmen[39] of my humor.

BELVILE. See, here be those kind merchants of love you look for.

(*Enter several men in masking habits, some playing on music, others dancing after; women dressed like courtesans, with papers pinned on their breasts, and baskets of flowers in their hands.*)

BLUNT. 'Adsheartlikins, what have we here?

FREDERICK. Now the game begins.

WILLMORE. Fine pretty creatures! May a stranger have leave to look and love? What's here? "Roses for every month"?
                                          (*Reads the papers.*)

BLUNT. Roses for every month? What means that?

BELVILE. They are, or would have you think they're courtesans, who here in Naples are to be hired by the month.

WILLMORE. Kind and obliging to inform us, pray where do these roses grow? I would fain plant some of 'em in a bed of mine.

WOMAN. Beware such roses, sir.

WILLMORE. A pox of fear:[40] I'll be baked with thee between a pair of sheets, and that's thy proper still;[41] so I might but strew such roses over me and under me. Fair one, would you would give me leave to gather at your bush this idle month; I would go near to make somebody smell of it all the year after.

---

[33]**'adsheartlikins** God's little heart (a mild oath)   [34]**hogoes** relishes
[35]**protectors** Oliver Cromwell used this title   [36]**Commonwealth** the republican government of England, 1649–53, replaced by the Proctorate

[37]**Prince** Charles II, who was in exile on the Continent during Cromwell's reign in England   [38]**int'rest** recommendation   [39]**chapmen** merchants (of love)   [40]**pox of fear** a curse on fear   [41]**baked … still** a bawdy joke comparing women to roses, which are distilled to make rose water; the bawdiness continues in *bush*, that is, pubic hair

BELVILE. And thou hast need of such a remedy, for thou stink'st of tar and ropes' ends like a dock or pesthouse.

(*The Woman puts herself into the hands of a man and exeunt.*)

WILLMORE. Nay, nay, you shall not leave me so.

BELVILE. By all means use no violence here.

WILLMORE. Death! Just as I was going to be damnably in love, to have her led off! I could pluck that rose out of his hand, and even kiss the bed the bush grew in.

FREDERICK. No friend to love like a long voyage at sea.

BLUNT. Except a nunnery, Fred.

WILLMORE. Death! But will they not be kind? Quickly be kind? Thou know'st I'm no tame sigher, but a rampant lion of the forest.

(*Advances from the farther end of the scenes two men dressed all over with horns[42] of several sorts, making grimaces at one another, with papers pinned on their backs.*)

BELVILE. Oh the fantastical rogues, how they're dressed! 'Tis a satire against the whole sex.

WILLMORE. Is this a fruit that grows in this warm country?

BELVILE. Yes, 'tis pretty to see these Italians start, swell, and stab at the word cuckold, and yet stumble at horns on every threshold.

WILLMORE. See what's on their back. (*Reads.*) "Flowers of every night." Ah, rogue! And more sweet than roses of every month! This is a gardener of Adam's own breeding.

(*They dance.*)

BELVILE. What think you of these grave people? Is a wake[43] in Essex half so mad or extravagant?

WILLMORE. I like their sober grave way; 'tis a kind of legal authorized fornication, where the men are not chid[44] for't, nor the women despised, as amongst our dull English. Even the monsieurs[45] want[46] that part of good manners.

BELVILE. But here in Italy, a monsieur is the humblest best-bred gentleman: Duels are so baffled by bravos that an age shows not one but between a French man and a hangman, who is as much too hard for him on the Piazza as they are for a Dutchman on the New Bridge.[47] But see, another crew.

(*Enter Florinda, Hellena, and Valeria, dressed like gypsies; Callis and Stephano, Lucetta, Philippo, and Sancho in masquerade.*)

HELLENA. Sister, there's your Englishman, and with him a handsome proper fellow. I'll to him, and instead of telling him his fortune, try my own.

WILLMORE. Gypsies, on my life. Sure these will prattle if a man cross their hands.[48] (*Goes to Hellena.*)—Dear, pretty, and, I hope, young devil, will you tell an amorous stranger what luck he's like to have?

HELLENA. Have a care how you venture with me, sir, lest I pick your pocket, which will more vex your English humor than an Italian fortune will please you.

WILLMORE. How the devil cam'st thou to know my country and humor?

HELLENA. The first I guess by a certain forward impudence, which does not displease me at this time; and the loss of your money will vex you because I hope you have but very little to lose.

WILLMORE. Egad, child, thou'rt i'th' right; it is so little I dare not offer it thee for a kindness. But cannot you divine what other things of more value I have about me that I would more willingly part with?

HELLENA. Indeed no, that's the business of a witch, and I am but a gypsy yet. Yet without looking in your hand, I have a parlous guess[49] 'tis some foolish heart you mean, an inconstant English heart, as little worth stealing as your purse.

WILLMORE. Nay, then thou dost deal with the devil, that's certain. Thou hast guessed as right as if thou hadst been one of that number it has languished for. I find you'll be better acquainted with it, nor can you take it in a better time; for I am come from sea, child, and Venus not being propitious to me in her own element,[50] I have a world of love in store. Would you would be good-natured and take some on't[51] off my hands.

HELLENA. Why, I could be inclined that way, but for a foolish vow I am going to make to die a maid.

WILLMORE. Then thou art damned without redemption, and as I am a good Christian, I ought in charity to divert so wicked a design. Therefore prithee, dear creature, let me know quickly when and where I shall begin to set a helping hand to so good a work.

HELLENA. If you should prevail with my tender heart, as I begin to fear you will, for you have horrible loving eyes, there will be difficulty in't that you'll hardly undergo for my sake.

WILLMORE. Faith, child, I have been bred in dangers, and wear a sword that has been employed in a worse cause than for a handsome kind woman. Name the danger; let it be anything but a long siege, and I'll undertake it.

HELLENA. Can you storm?[52]

[42]**horns** allusion to the old belief that a cuckolded husband sprouted horns on his forehead that could be seen by everyone but himself [43]**wake** vigil over a corpse   [44]**chid** chided   [45]**monsieurs** Frenchmen   [46]**want** lack   [47]**Dutchman . . . Bridge** a reference to recent French military successes in Flanders

[48]**prattle . . . hands** tell his fortune if he gives them silver   [49]**a parlous guess** a hunch   [50]**Venus . . . element** Venus, the goddess of love, was born from sea foam   [51]**on't** of it   [52]**storm** attack

WILLMORE. Oh, most furiously.

HELLENA. What think you of a nunnery wall? For he that wins me must gain that first.

WILLMORE. A nun! Oh, now I love thee for't! There's no sinner like a young saint. Nay, now there's no denying me; the old law had no curse to a woman like dying a maid: Witness Jeptha's daughter.[53]

HELLENA. A very good text this, if well handled; and I perceive, Father Captain, you would impose no severe penance on her who were inclined to console herself before she took orders.[54]

WILLMORE. If she be young and handsome.

HELLENA. Ay, there's it. But if she be not—

WILLMORE. By this hand, child, I have an implicit faith, and dare venture on thee with all faults. Besides, 'tis more meritorious to leave the world when thou hast tasted and proved the pleasure on't. Then 'twill be a virtue in thee, which now will be pure ignorance.

HELLENA. I perceive, good Father Captain, you design only to make me fit for heaven. But if, on the contrary, you should quite divert me from it, and bring me back to the world again, I should have a new man to seek, I find. And what a grief that will be; for when I begin, I fancy I shall love like anything; I never tried yet.

WILLMORE. Egad, and that's kind! Prithee, dear creature, give me credit for a heart, for faith, I'm a very honest fellow. Oh, I long to come first to the banquet of love! And such a swinging appetite I bring. Oh, I'm impatient. Thy lodging, sweetheart, thy lodging, or I'm a dead man!

HELLENA. Why must we be either guilty of fornication or murder if we converse with you men? And is there no difference between leave to love me, and leave to lie with me?

WILLMORE. Faith, child, they were made to go together.

LUCETTA (pointing to Blunt). Are you sure this is the man?

SANCHO. When did I mistake your game?

LUCETTA. This is a stranger, I know by his gazing; if he be brisk he'll venture to follow me, and then, if I understand my trade, he's mine. He's English, too, and they say that's a sort of good-natured loving people, and have generally so kind an opinion of themselves that a woman with any wit may flatter 'em into any sort of fool she pleases.

(She often passes by Blunt and gazes on him; he struts and cocks, and walks and gazes on her.)

BLUNT. 'Tis so, she is taken; I have beauties which my false glass[55] at home did not discover.[56]

FLORINDA (aside). This woman watches me so, I shall get no opportunity to discover myself to him, and so miss the in-

tent of my coming.—[To Belvile.] But as I was saying, sir, by this line you should be a lover.

(Looking in his hand.)

BELVILE. I thought how right you guessed: All men are in love, or pretend to be so. Come, let me go; I'm weary of this fooling.   (Walks away.)

FLORINDA. I will not, sir, till you have confessed whether the passion that you have vowed Florinda be true or false.

(She holds him; he strives to get from her.)

BELVILE. Florinda!   (Turns quick toward her.)

FLORINDA. Softly.

BELVILE. Thou hast nam'd one will fix me here forever.

FLORINDA. She'll be disappointed then, who expects you this night at the garden gate. And if you fail not, as—(Looks on Callis, who observes 'em.) Let me see the other hand— you will go near to do, she vows to die or make you happy.

BELVILE. What canst thou mean?

FLORINDA. That which I say. Farewell.

(Offers to go.)

BELVILE. O charming sibyl,[57] stay; complete that joy which as it is will turn into distraction! Where must I be? At the garden gate? I know it. At night, you say? I'll sooner forfeit heaven than disobey.

(Enter Don Pedro and other maskers, and pass over the stage.)

CALLIS. Madam, your brother's here.

FLORINDA. Take this to instruct you farther.

(Gives him a letter, and goes off.)

FREDERICK. Have a care, sir, what you promise; this may be a trap laid by her brother to ruin you.

BELVILE. Do not disturb my happiness with doubts.

(Opens the letter.)

WILLMORE. My dear pretty creature, a thousand blessings on thee! Still in this habit, you say? And after dinner at this place?

HELLENA. Yes, if you will swear to keep your heart and not bestow it between this and that.

WILLMORE. By all the little gods of love, I swear; I'll leave it with you, and if you run away with it, those deities of justice[58] will revenge me.

(Exeunt all the women [except Lucetta].)

FREDERICK. Do you know the hand?

BELVILE. 'Tis Florinda's.

All blessings fall upon the virtuous maid.

[53]**Jeptha's daughter** the virgin daughter of a Hebrew judge who rashly sacrificed her. See Judges 11:39–40.   [54]**took orders** entered a convent   [55]**false glass** lying mirror   [56]**discover** reveal

[57]**sybil** prophetess, here a fortuneteller   [58]**deities of justice** in Greek mythology, the Erynys, avenging spirits

FREDERICK. Nay, no idolatry; a sober sacrifice I'll allow you.

BELVILE. Oh friends, the welcom'st news! The softest letter! Nay, you shall all see it. And could you now be serious, I might be made the happiest man the sun shines on!

WILLMORE. The reason of this mighty joy?

BELVILE. See how kindly she invites me to deliver her from the threatened violence of her brother. Will you not assist me?

WILLMORE. I know not what thou mean'st, but I'll make one at any mischief where a woman's concerned. But she'll be grateful to us for the favor, will she not?

BELVILE. How mean you?

WILLMORE. How should I mean? Thou know'st there's but one way for a woman to oblige me.

BELVILE. Do not profane; the maid is nicely virtuous.

WILLMORE. Who, pox,[59] then she's fit for nothing but a husband. Let her e'en go, colonel.

FREDERICK. Peace, she's the colonel's mistress, sir.

WILLMORE. Let her be the devil; if she be thy mistress, I'll serve her. Name the way.

BELVILE. Read here this postscript.

(Gives him a letter.)

WILLMORE (*reads*). "At ten at night, at the garden gate, of which, if I cannot get the key, I will contrive a way over the wall. Come attended with a friend or two."—Kind heart, if we three cannot weave a string to let her down a garden wall, 'twere pity but the hangman wove one for us all.

FREDERICK. Let her alone for that; your woman's wit, your fair kind woman, will outtrick a broker or a Jew, and contrive like a Jesuit[60] in chains. But see, Ned Blunt is stolen out after the lure of a damsel.

(Exeunt Blunt and Lucetta.)

BELVILE. So, he'll scarce find his way home again unless we get him cried by the bellman[61] in the market place. And 'twould sound prettily: "A lost English boy of thirty."

FREDERICK. I hope 'tis some common crafty sinner, one that will fit him. It may be she'll sell him for Peru:[62] The rogue's sturdy, and would work well in a mine. At least I hope she'll dress him for our mirth, cheat him of all, then have him well-favoredly banged, and turned out at midnight.

WILLMORE. Prithee what humor is he of, that you wish him so well?

BELVILE. Why, of an English elder brother's humor: educated in a nursery, with a maid to tend him till fifteen, and lies with his grandmother till he's of age; one that knows no pleasure beyond riding to the next fair, or going up to London with his right worshipful father in parliament time, wearing gay clothes, or making honorable love to his lady mother's laundry maid; gets drunk at a hunting match, and ten to one then gives some proofs of his prowess. A pox upon him, he's our banker, and has all our cash about him; and if he fail, we are all broke.

FREDERICK. Oh, let him alone for that matter; he's of a damned stingy quality that will secure our stock. I know not in what danger it were indeed if the jilt[63] should pretend she's in love with him, for 'tis a kind believing coxcomb; otherwise, if he part with more than a piece of eight,[64] geld him—for which offer he may chance to be beaten if she be a whore of the first rank.

BELVILE. Nay, the rogue will not be easily beaten; he's stout enough. Perhaps if they talk beyond his capacity he may chance to exercise his courage upon some of them, else I'm sure they'll find it as difficult to beat as to please him.

WILLMORE. 'Tis a lucky devil to light upon so kind a wench!

FREDERICK. Thou hadst a great deal of talk with thy little gypsy; couldst thou do no good upon her? For mine was hardhearted.

WILLMORE. Hang her, she was some damned honest person of quality, I'm sure, she was so very free and witty. If her face be but answerable to her wit and humor, I would be bound to constancy this month to gain her. In the meantime, have you made no kind acquaintance since you came to town? You do not use to be honest[65] so long, gentlemen.

FREDERICK. Faith, love has kept us honest: We have been all fir'd with a beauty newly come to town, the famous Paduana[66] Angellica Bianca.

WILLMORE. What, the mistress of the dead Spanish general?

BELVILE. Yes, she's now the only ador'd beauty of all the youth in Naples, who put on all their charms to appear lovely in her sight: Their coaches, liveries, and themselves all gay as on a monarch's birthday to attract the eyes of this fair charmer, while she has the pleasure to behold all languish for her that see her.

FREDERICK. 'Tis pretty to see with how much love the men regard her, and how much envy the women.

WILLMORE. What gallant has she?

BELVILE. None; she's exposed to sale, and four days in the week she's yours, for so much a month.

WILLMORE. The very thought of it quenches all manner of fire in me. Yet prithee, let's see her.

BELVILE. Let's first to dinner, and after that we'll pass the day as you please. But at night ye must all be at my devotion.

WILLMORE. I will not fail you.

[Exeunt.]

---

[59]**pox** damn   [60]**Jew ... Jesuit** Jews and Jesuits were widely distrusted and feared in this period   [61]**the bellman** town crier   [62]**sell ... Peru** sell him as a slave to Peru

[63]**jilt** whore   [64]**piece of eight** obsolete Spanish coin   [65]**honest** chaste   [66]**Paduana** Angellica comes from Padua

ACT 2

SCENE 1

(*The long street. Enter Belvile and Frederick in masking habits, and Willmore in his own clothes, with a vizard[67] in his hand.*)

WILLMORE. But why thus disguised and muzzled?

BELVILE. Because whatever extravagances we commit in these faces, our own may not be obliged to answer 'em.

WILLMORE. I should have changed my eternal buff,[68] too; but no matter, my little gypsy would not have found me out then. For if she should change hers, it is impossible I should know her unless I should hear her prattle. A pox on't, I cannot get her out of my head. Pray heaven, if ever I do see her again, she prove damnably ugly, that I may fortify myself against her tongue.

BELVILE. Have a care of love, for o' my conscience she was not of a quality to give thee any hopes.

WILLMORE. Pox on 'em, why do they draw a man in then? She has played with my heart so, that 'twill never lie still till I have met with some kind wench that will play the game out with me. Oh, for my arms full of soft, white, kind woman—such as I fancy Angellica.

BELVILE. This is her house, if you were but in stock to get admittance. They have not dined yet; I perceive the picture is not out.[69]

(*Enter Blunt.*)

WILLMORE. I long to see the shadow of the fair substance; a man may gaze on that for nothing.

BLUNT. Colonel, thy hand. And thine, Fred. I have been an ass, a deluded fool, a very coxcomb from my birth till this hour, and heartily repent my little faith.

BELVILE. What the devil's the matter with thee, Ned?

BLUNT. Oh, such a mistress, Fred! Such a girl!

WILLMORE. Ha! Where?

FREDERICK. Ay, where?

BLUNT. So fond, so amorous, so toying, and so fine! And all for sheer love, ye rogue! Oh, how she looked and kissed! And soothed my heart from my bosom! I cannot think I was awake, and yet methinks I see and feel her charms still. Fred, try if she have not left the taste of her balmy kisses upon my lips.   (*Kisses him.*)

BELVILE. Ha! Ha! Ha!

WILLMORE. Death, man, where is she?

BLUNT. What a dog was I to stay in dull England so long! How have I laughed at the colonel when he sighed for love! But now the little archer[70] has revenged him! And by this one dart I can guess at all his joys, which then I took for fancies, mere dreams and fables. Well, I'm resolved to sell all in Essex and plant here forever.

BELVILE. What a blessing 'tis, thou hast a mistress thou dar'st boast of; for I know thy humor is rather to have a proclaimed clap[71] than a secret amour.

WILLMORE. Dost know her name?

BLUNT. Her name? No, 'adsheartlikins. What care I for names? She's fair, young, brisk and kind, even to ravishment! And what a pox care I for knowing her by any other title?

WILLMORE. Didst give her anything?

BLUNT. Give her? Ha! Ha! Ha! Why, she's a person of quality. That's a good one! Give her? 'Adsheartlikins, dost think such creatures are to be bought? Or are we provided for such a purchase? Give her, quoth ye? Why, she presented me with this bracelet for the toy of a diamond I used to wear. No, gentlemen, Ned Blunt is not everybody. She expects me again tonight.

WILLMORE. Egad, that's well; we'll all go.

BLUNT. Not a soul! No, gentlemen, you are wits; I am a dull country rogue, I.

FREDERICK. Well, sir, for all your person of quality, I shall be very glad to understand your purse be secure; 'tis our whole estate at present, which we are loath to hazard in one bottom.[72] Come sir, unlade.

BLUNT. Take the necessary trifle useless now to me, that am beloved by such a gentlewoman. 'Adsheartlikins, money! Here, take mine too.

FREDERICK. No, keep that to be cozened,[73] that we may laugh.

WILLMORE. Cozened? Death! Would I could meet with one that would cozen me of all the love I could spare tonight.

FREDERICK. Pox, 'tis some common whore, upon my life.

BLUNT. A whore? Yes, with such clothes, such jewels, such a house, such furniture, and so attended! A whore!

BELVILE. Why yes, sir, they are whores, though they'll neither entertain you with drinking, swearing, or bawdry; are whores in all those gay clothes and right[74] jewels; are whores with those great houses richly furnished with velvet beds, store of plate,[75] handsome attendance, and fine coaches; are whores, and errant[76] ones.

WILLMORE. Pox on't, where do these fine whores live?

BELVILE. Where no rogues in office, ycleped[77] constables, dare give 'em laws, nor the wine-inspired bullies of the town break their windows; yet they are whores though this Essex calf[78] believe 'em persons of quality.

---

[67]**vizard** mask   [68]**buff** leather military coat   [69]**the picture ... out** when Angellica's picture is hung, she is open for business; see stage direction line later in the scene, referring to a great picture of Angellica

[70]**the little archer** Cupid   [71]**proclaimed clap** sexual disease that everyone knows of   [72]**loath ... bottom** reluctant to risk cargo in one ship   [73]**cozened** cheated   [74]**right** real   [75]**plate** silverware   [76]**errant** arrant, unmitigated   [77]**ycleped** called   [78]**Essex calf** fool from Essex (Blunt's county in England)

BLUNT. 'Adsheartlikins, y'are all fools. There are things about this Essex calf that shall take with the ladies, beyond all your wit and parts. This shape and size, gentlemen, are not to be despised; my waist, too, tolerably long, with other inviting signs that shall be nameless.

WILLMORE. Egad, I believe he may have met with some person of quality that may be kind to him.

BELVILE. Dost thou perceive any such tempting things about him that should make a fine woman, and of quality, pick him out from all mankind to throw away her youth and beauty upon; nay, and her dear heart, too? No, no, Angellica has raised the price too high.

WILLMORE. May she languish for mankind till she die, and be damned for that one sin alone.

(*Enter two Bravos and hang up a great picture of Angellica's against the balcony, and two little ones at each side of the door.*)

BELVILE. See there the fair sign to the inn where a man may lodge that's fool enough to give her price.

(*Willmore gazes on the picture.*)

BLUNT. 'Adsheartlikins, gentlemen, what's this?

BELVILE. A famous courtesan, that's to be sold.

BLUNT. How? To be sold? Nay, then I have nothing to say to her. Sold? What impudence is practiced in this country; with what order and decency whoring's established here by virtue of the Inquisition![79] Come, let's be gone; I'm sure we're no chapmen[80] for this commodity.

FREDERICK. Thou art none, I'm sure, unless thou couldst have her in thy bed at a price of a coach in the street.

WILLMORE. How wondrous fair she is! A thousand crowns a month? By heaven, as many kingdoms were too little! A plague of this poverty, of which I ne'er complain but when it hinders my approach to beauty which virtue ne'er could purchase.

(*Turns from the picture.*)

BLUNT. What's this? (*Reads.*) "A thousand crowns a month"! 'Adsheartlikins, here's a sum! Sure 'tis a mistake.—[*To one of the Bravos.*] Hark you, friend, does she take or give so much by the month?

FREDERICK. A thousand crowns! Why, 'tis a portion for the Infanta![81]

BLUNT. Hark ye, friends, won't she trust?[82]

BRAVO. This is a trade, sir, that cannot live by credit.

(*Enter Don Pedro in masquerade, followed by Stephano.*)

BELVILE. See, here's more company; let's walk off a while.

(*Exeunt English;[83] Pedro reads.*)

PEDRO. Fetch me a thousand crowns; I never wished to buy this beauty at an easier rate.   (*Passes off.*)

(*Enter Angellica and Moretta in the balcony, and draw a silk curtain.*)

ANGELLICA. Prithee, what said those fellows to thee?

BRAVO. Madam, the first were admirers of beauty only, but no purchasers; they were merry with your price and picture, laughed at the sum, and so passed off.

ANGELLICA. No matter, I'm not displeased with their rallying; their wonder feeds my vanity, and he that wishes but to buy gives me more pride than he that gives my price can make my pleasure.

BRAVO. Madam, the last I knew through all his disguises to be Don Pedro, nephew to the general, and who was with him in Pamplona.

ANGELLICA. Don Pedro? My old gallant's nephew? When his uncle died he left him a vast sum of money; it is he who was so in love with me at Padua, and who used to make the general so jealous.

MORETTA. Is this he that used to prance before our window, and take such care to show himself an amorous ass? If I am not mistaken, he is the likeliest man to give your price.

ANGELLICA. The man is brave and generous, but of a humor so uneasy and inconstant that the victory over his heart is as soon lost as won; a slave that can add little to the triumph of the conqueror. But inconstancy's the sin of all mankind, therefore I'm resolved that nothing but gold shall charm my heart.

MORETTA. I'm glad on't; 'tis only interest that women of our profession ought to consider, though I wonder what has kept you from that general disease of our sex so long; I mean, that of being in love.

ANGELLICA. A kind but sullen star under which I had the happiness to be born. Yet I have had no time for love; the bravest and noblest of mankind have purchased my favors at so dear a rate, as if no coin but gold were current with our trade. But here's Don Pedro again; fetch me my lute, for 'tis for him or Don Antonio the Viceroy's son that I have spread my nets.

(*Enter at one door Don Pedro, Stephano; Don Antonio and Diego [his page] at the other door, with people following him in masquerade, antically attired, some with music. They both go up to the picture.*)

ANTONIO. A thousand crowns! Had not the painter flattered her, I should not think it dear.[84]

PEDRO. Flattered her? By heaven, he cannot. I have seen the original, nor is there one charm here more than adorns

[79]**Inquisition** prostitutes forced out of Spain by the Spanish Inquisition came to Italy   [80]**chapmen** merchants   [81]**portion . . . Infanta** dowry for the Spanish princess   [82]**trust** extend credit

[83]**English** all the Englishmen   [84]**dear** expensive

her face and eyes; all this soft and sweet, with a certain languishing air that no artist can represent.

ANTONIO. What I heard of her beauty before had fired my soul, but this confirmation of it has blown it to a flame.

PEDRO. Ha!

PAGE. Sir, I have known you throw away a thousand crowns on a worse face, and though y'are near your marriage, you may venture a little love here; Florinda will not miss it.

PEDRO (aside). Ha! Florinda! Sure 'tis Antonio.

ANTONIO. Florinda! Name not those distant joys; there's not one thought of her will check my passion here.

PEDRO [aside]. Florinda scorned! (A noise of a lute above.) And all my hopes defeated of the possession of Angellica! (Antonio gazes up.) Her injuries, by heaven, he shall not boast of!

(Song to a lute above.)

SONG

[I]
When Damon first began to love
He languished in a soft desire,
And knew not how the gods to move,
To lessen or increase his fire.
For Caelia in her charming eyes
Wore all love's sweets, and all his cruelties.

II

But as beneath a shade he lay,
Weaving of flowers for Caelia's hair,
She chanced to lead her flock that way,
And saw the am'rous shepherd there.
She gazed around upon the place,
And saw the grove, resembling night,
To all the joys of love invite,
Whilst guilty smiles and blushes dressed her face.
At this the bashful youth all transport grew,
And with kind force he taught the virgin how
To yield what all his sighs could never do.

(Angellica throws open the curtains and bows to Antonio, who pulls off his vizard and bows and blows up kisses. Pedro, unseen, looks in's face. [The curtains close.])

ANTONIO. By heaven, she's charming fair!

PEDRO (aside). 'Tis he, the false Antonio!

ANTONIO (to the Bravo[85]).
Friend, where must I pay my off'ring of love?
My thousand crowns I mean.

PEDRO.
That off'ring I have designed to make,
And yours will come too late.

ANTONIO.
Prithee begone; I shall grow angry else,
And then thou art not safe.

PEDRO.
My anger may be fatal, sir, as yours,
And he that enters here may prove this truth.

ANTONIO. I know not who thou art, but I am sure thou'rt worth my killing, for aiming at Angellica.

(They draw and fight.)

(Enter Willmore and Blunt, who draw and part 'em.)

BLUNT. 'Adsheartlikins, here's fine doings.

WILLMORE. Tilting[86] for the wench, I'm sure. Nay, gad, if that would win her I have as good a sword as the best of ye. Put up, put up, and take another time and place, for this is designed for lovers only.   (They all put up.)

PEDRO.
We are prevented; dare you meet me tomorrow on the Molo?[87]
For I've a title to a better quarrel,
That of Florinda, in whose credulous heart
Thou'st made an int'rest, and destroyed my hopes.

ANTONIO. Dare!
I'll meet thee there as early as the day.

PEDRO. We will come thus disguised, that whosoever chance to get the better, he may escape unknown.

ANTONIO. It shall be so.

(Exeunt Pedro and Stephano.)

—Who should this rival be? Unless the English colonel, of whom I've often heard Don Pedro speak. It must be he, and time he were removed who lays a claim to all my happiness.

(Willmore, having gazed all this while on the picture[s], pulls down a little one.)

WILLMORE.
This posture's loose and negligent;
The sight on't would beget a warm desire
In souls whom impotence and age had chilled.
This must along with me.

BRAVO. What means this rudeness, sir? Restore the picture.

ANTONIO. Ha! Rudeness committed to the fair Angellica!— Restore the picture, sir.

WILLMORE. Indeed I will not, sir.

ANTONIO. By heaven, but you shall.

WILLMORE. Nay, do not show your sword; if you do, by this dear beauty, I will show mine too.

ANTONIO. What right can you pretend to't?

WILLMORE. That of possession, which I will maintain. You, perhaps, have a thousand crowns to give for the original.

ANTONIO. No matter, sir, you shall restore the picture.

([The curtains open.] Angellica and Moretta above.)

ANGELLICA. Oh, Moretta, what's the matter?

---

[85]**Bravo** ruffian
[86]**Tilting** fighting (normally charging on horseback, with a lance)
[87]**Molo** stone pier

ANTONIO. Or leave your life behind.

WILLMORE. Death! You lie; I will do neither.

(*[Willmore and Antonio] fight. The Spaniards join with Antonio, Blunt [joins with Willmore,] laying on like mad.*)

ANGELLICA. Hold, I command you, if for me you fight.

(*They leave off and bow.*)

WILLMORE [*aside*]. How heavenly fair she is! Ah, plague of her price!

ANGELLICA. You sir, in buff, you that appear a soldier, that first began this insolence—

WILLMORE. 'Tis true, I did so, if you call it insolence for a man to preserve himself. I saw your charming picture and was wounded; quite through my soul each pointed beauty ran; and wanting a thousand crowns to procure my remedy, I laid this little picture to my bosom, which, if you cannot allow me, I'll resign.

ANGELLICA. No, you may keep the trifle.

ANTONIO. You shall first ask me leave, and this.

(*Fight again as before.*)

(*Enter Belvile and Frederick, who join with the English.*)

ANGELLICA. Hold! Will you ruin me?—Biskey! Sebastian! Part 'em!

(*The Spaniards are beaten off.*)

MORETTA. Oh, madam, we're undone. A pox upon that rude fellow; he's set on to ruin us. We shall never see good days again till all these fighting poor rogues are sent to the galleys.

(*Enter Belvile, Blunt, Frederick, and Willmore with's shirt bloody.*)

BLUNT. 'Adsheartlikins, beat me at this sport and I'll ne'er wear sword more.

BELVILE (*to Willmore*). The devil's in thee for a mad fellow; thou art always one at an unlucky adventure. Come, let's be gone whilst we're safe, and remember these are Spaniards, a sort of people that know how to revenge an affront.

FREDERICK. You bleed! I hope you are not wounded.

WILLMORE. Not much. A plague on your dons; if they fight no better they'll ne'er recover Flanders.[88] What the devil was't to them that I took down the picture?

BLUNT. Took it! 'Adsheartlikins, we'll have the great one too; 'tis ours by conquest. Prithee help me up and I'll pull it down.

ANGELLICA [*to Willmore*]. Stay, sir, and ere you affront me farther let me know how you durst commit this outrage. To you I speak, sir, for you appear a gentleman.

WILLMORE. To me, madam?—Gentlemen, your servant.

(*Belvile stays him.*)

BELVILE. Is the devil in thee? Dost know the danger of ent'ring the house of an incensed courtesan?

WILLMORE. I thank you for your care, but there are other matters in hand, there are, though we have no great temptation. Death! Let me go!

FREDERICK. Yes, to your lodging if you will, but not in here. Damn these gay harlots; by this hand I'll have as sound and handsome a whore for a patacoon.[89] Death, man, she'll murder thee!

WILLMORE. Oh, fear me not. Shall I not venture where a beauty calls? A lovely charming beauty! For fear of danger? When, by heaven, there's none so great as to long for her whilst I want money to purchase her.

FREDERICK. Therefore 'tis loss of time unless you had the thousand crowns to pay.

WILLMORE. It may be she may give a favor; at least I shall have the pleasure of saluting her when I enter and when I depart.

BELVILE. Pox, she'll as soon lie with thee as kiss thee, and sooner stab than do either. You shall not go.

ANGELLICA. Fear not, sir, all I have to wound with is my eyes.

BLUNT. Let him go. 'Adsheartlikins, I believe the gentlewoman means well.

BELVILE. Well, take thy fortune; we'll expect you in the next street. Farewell, fool, farewell.

WILLMORE. 'Bye, colonel.   (*Goes in.*)

FREDERICK. The rogue's stark mad for a wench.

(*Exeunt.*)

SCENE 2

(*A fine chamber. Enter Willmore, Angellica, and Moretta.*)

ANGELLICA. Insolent sir, how durst you pull down my picture?

WILLMORE. Rather, how durst you set it up to tempt poor am'rous mortals with so much excellence, which I find you have but too well consulted by the unmerciful price you set upon't. Is all this heaven of beauty shown to move despair in those that cannot buy? And can you think th'effects of that despair should be less extravagant than I have shown?

ANGELLICA. I sent for you to ask my pardon, sir, not to aggravate your crime. I thought I should have seen you at my feet imploring it.

WILLMORE. You are deceived. I came to rail at you, and rail such truths too, as shall let you see the vanity of that pride which taught you how to set such price on sin. For such it is whilst that which is love's due

[88]**Flanders** in 1659 Spain ceded the Netherlands to France

[89]**patacoon** Spanish coin

Is meanly bartered for.

ANGELLICA. Ha! Ha! Ha! Alas, good captain, what pity 'tis your edifying doctrine will do no good upon me. Moretta, fetch the gentleman a glass,[90] and let him survey himself to see what charms he has.—(*Aside, in a soft tone.*) And guess my business.

MORETTA. He knows himself of old: I believe those breeches and he have been acquainted ever since he was beaten at Worcester.[91]

ANGELLICA. Nay, do not abuse the poor creature.

MORETTA. Good weather-beaten corporal, will you march off? We have no need of your doctrine, though you have of our charity. But at present we have no scraps; we can afford no kindness for God's sake. In fine, sirrah, the price is too high i'th' mouth[92] for you, therefore troop, I say.

WILLMORE. Here, good forewoman of the shop, serve me and I'll be gone.

MORETTA. Keep it to pay your laundress; your linen stinks of the gun room. For here's no selling by retail.

WILLMORE. Thou hast sold plenty of thy stale ware at a cheap rate.

MORETTA. Ay, the more silly kind heart I, but this is an age wherein beauty is at higher rates. In fine, you know the price of this.

WILLMORE. I grant you 'tis here set down, a thousand crowns a month. Pray, how much may come to my share for a pistole? Bawd, take your black lead[93] and sum it up, that I may have a pistole's worth[94] of this vain gay thing, and I'll trouble you no more.

MORETTA. Pox on him, he'll fret me to death! Abominable fellow, I tell thee we only sell by the whole piece.

WILLMORE. 'Tis very hard, the whole cargo or nothing. Faith, madam, my stock will not reach it; I cannot be your chapman. Yet I have countrymen in town, merchants of love like me; I'll see if they'll put in for a share. We cannot lose much by it, and what we have no use for, we'll sell upon the Friday's mart at "Who gives more?"—I am studying, madam, how to purchase you, though at present I am unprovided of money.

ANGELLICA (*aside*). Sure this from any other man would anger me; nor shall he know the conquest he has made.—Poor angry man, how I despise this railing.

WILLMORE.
Yes, I am poor. But I'm a gentleman,
And one that scorns this baseness which you practice.
Poor as I am I would not sell myself,
No, not to gain your charming high-prized person.
Though I admire you strangely for your beauty,
Yet I contemn your mind.

---

[90]**glass** mirror   [91]**Worcester** Cromwell defeated Charles II at Worcester and forced him into exile   [92]**high i'th' mouth** expensive   [93]**black lead** pencil   [94]**a pistole's worth** as much as a Spanish gold coin will buy

And yet I would at any rate enjoy you;
At your own rate; but cannot. See here
The only sum I can command on earth:
I know not where to eat when this is gone.
Yet such a slave I am to love and beauty
This last reserve I'll sacrifice to enjoy you.
Nay, do not frown, I know you're to be bought,
And would be bought by me. By me,
For a meaning trifling sum, if I could pay it down.
Which happy knowledge I will still repeat,
And lay it to my heart: It has a virtue in't,
And soon will cure those wounds your eyes have made.
And yet, there's something so divinely powerful there—
Nay, I will gaze, to let you see my strength.

(*Holds her, looks on her, and pauses and sighs.*)

By heav'n, bright creature, I would not for the world
Thy fame were half so fair as is thy face.

(*Turns her away from him.*)

ANGELLICA (*aside*).
His words go through me to the very soul.—
If you have nothing else to say to me—

WILLMORE.
Yes, you shall hear how infamous you are—
For which I do not hate thee—
But that secures my heart, and all the flames it feels
Are but so many lusts:
I know it by their sudden bold intrusion.
The fire's impatient and betrays; 'tis false.
For had it been the purer flame of love,
I should have pined and languished at your feet,
Ere found the impudence to have discovered it.
I now dare stand your scorn and your denial.

MORETTA. Sure she's bewitched, that she can stand thus tamely and hear his saucy railing.—Sirrah, will you be gone?

ANGELLICA (*to Moretta*). How dare you take this liberty! Withdraw!—Pray tell me, sir, are not you guilty of the same mercenary crime? When a lady is proposed to you for a wife, you never ask how fair, discreet, or virtuous she is, but what's her fortune; which, if but small, you cry "She will not do my business," and basely leave her, though she languish for you. Say, is not this as poor?

WILLMORE. It is a barbarous custom, which I will scorn to defend in our sex, and do despise in yours.

ANGELLICA.
Thou'rt a brave fellow! Put up thy gold, and know,
That were thy fortune as large as is thy soul,
Thou shouldst not buy my love
Couldst thou forget those mean effects of vanity
Which set me out to sale,
And as a lover prize my yielding joys.
Canst thou believe they'll be entirely thine,
Without considering they were mercenary?

WILLMORE.
I cannot tell, I must bethink me first.
(*Aside*.) Ha! Death, I'm going to believe her.
ANGELLICA.
Prithee confirm that faith, or if thou canst not,
Flatter me a little: 'Twill please me from thy mouth.
WILLMORE (*aside*).
Curse on thy charming tongue! Dost thou return
My feigned contempt with so much subtlety?—
Thou'st found the easiest way into my heart,
Though I yet know that all thou say'st is false.

(*Turning from her in rage*.)

ANGELLICA.
By all that's good, 'tis real;
I never loved before, though oft a mistress.
Shall my first vows be slighted?
WILLMORE (*aside*).
What can she mean?
ANGELLICA (*in an angry tone*).
I find you cannot credit me.
WILLMORE.
I know you take me for an errant ass,
An ass that may be soothed into belief,
And then be used at pleasure;
But, madam, I have been so often cheated
By perjured, soft, deluding hypocrites,
That I've no faith left for the cozening sex,
Especially for women of your trade.
ANGELLICA.
The low esteem you have of me perhaps
May bring my heart again:
For I have pride that yet surmounts my love.

(*She turns with pride; he holds her*.)

WILLMORE.
Throw off this pride, this enemy to bliss,
And show the power of love: 'Tis with those arms
I can be only vanquished, made a slave.
ANGELLICA.
Is all my mighty expectation vanished?
No, I will not hear thee talk; thou hast a charm
In every word that draws my heart away,
And all the thousand trophies I designed
Thou hast undone. Why art thou soft?
Thy looks are bravely rough, and meant for war.
Couldst thou not storm on still?
I then perhaps had been as free as thou.
WILLMORE (*aside*).
Death, how she throws her fire about my soul!—
Take heed, fair creature, how you raise my hopes,
Which once assumed pretends to all dominion:
There's not a joy thou hast in store
I shall not then command.
For which I'll pay you back my soul, my life!

Come, let's begin th'account this happy minute!
ANGELLICA.
And will you pay me then the price I ask?
WILLMORE.
Oh, why dost thou draw me from an awful worship,
By showing thou art no divinity.
Conceal the fiend, and show me all the angel!
Keep me but ignorant, and I'll be devout
And pay my vows forever at this shrine.

(*Kneels and kisses her hand*.)

ANGELLICA.
The pay I mean is but thy love for mine.
Can you give that?
WILLMORE. Entirely. Come, let's withdraw where I'll renew
my vows, and breathe 'em with such ardor thou shalt not
doubt my zeal.
ANGELLICA. Thou hast a power too strong to be resisted.

(*Exeunt Willmore and Angellica*.)

MORETTA. Now my curse go with you! Is all our project fallen
to this? To love the only enemy to our trade? Nay, to love
such a shameroon;[95] a very beggar; nay, a pirate beggar,
whose business is to rifle and be gone; a no-purchase, no-
pay tatterdemalion, and English picaroon;[96] a rogue that
fights for daily drink, and takes a pride in being loyally
lousy? Oh, I could curse now, if I durst. This is the fate of
most whores.

Trophies, which from believing fops we win,
Are spoils to those who cozen us again.

[*Exit*.]

ACT 3

SCENE 1

(*A street. Enter Florinda, Valeria, Hellena, in antic[97] different dresses from what they were in before; Callis attending*.)

FLORINDA. I wonder what should make my brother in so ill a
humor? I hope he has not found out our ramble this
morning.
HELLENA. No, if he had, we should have heard on't at both
ears, and have been mew'd up[98] this afternoon, which I
would not for the world should have happened. Hey ho,
I'm as sad as a lover's lute.
VALERIA. Well, methinks we have learnt this trade of gypsies
as readily as if we had been bred upon the road to
Loretto, and yet I did so fumble when I told the stranger
his fortune that I was afraid I should have told my own

---

[95]**shameroon** deceiver [96]**picaroon** rogue [97]**antic** grotesque
[98]**mew'd up** confined

and yours by mistake. But methinks Hellena has been very serious ever since.

FLORINDA. I would give my garters she were in love, to be revenged upon her for abusing me. How is't, Hellena?

HELLENA. Ah, would I had never seen my mad monsieur. And yet, for all your laughing, I am not in love. And yet this small acquaintance, o' my conscience, will never out of my head.

VALERIA. Ha! Ha! Ha! I laugh to think how thou art fitted with a lover, a fellow that I warrant loves every new face he sees.

HELLENA. Hum, he has not kept his word with me here, and may be taken up. That thought is not very pleasant to me. What the deuce should this be now that I feel?

VALERIA. What is't like?

HELLENA. Nay, the Lord knows, but if I should be hanged I cannot choose but be angry and afraid when I think that mad fellow should be in love with anybody but me. What to think of myself I know not: Would I could meet with some true damned gypsy, that I might know my fortune.

VALERIA. Know it! Why there's nothing so easy: Thou wilt love this wand'ring inconstant till thou find'st thyself hanged about his neck, and then be as mad to get free again.

FLORINDA. Yes, Valeria, we shall see her bestride his baggage horse and follow him to the campaign.

HELLENA. So, so, now you are provided for there's no care taken of poor me. But since you have set my heart a-wishing, I am resolved to know for what; I will not die of the pip,[99] so I will not.

FLORINDA. Art thou mad to talk so? Who will like thee well enough to have thee, that hears what a mad wench thou art?

HELLENA. Like me? I don't intend every he that likes me shall have me, but he that I like. I should have stayed in the nunnery still if I had liked my lady abbess as well as she liked me. No, I came thence not, as my wise brother imagines, to take an eternal farewell of the world, but to love and to be beloved; and I will be beloved, or I'll get one of your men, so I will.

VALERIA. Am I put into[100] the number of lovers?

HELLENA. You? Why, coz, I know thou'rt too good-natured to leave us in any design; thou wouldst venture a cast[101] though thou comest off a loser, especially with such a gamester. I observed your man, and your willing ear incline that way; and if you are not a lover, 'tis an art soon learnt—that I find.   (Sighs.)

FLORINDA. I wonder how you learnt to love so easily. I had a thousand charms to meet my eyes and ears ere I could yield, and 'twas the knowledge of Belvile's merit, not the surprising person, took my soul. Thou art too rash, to give a heart at first sight.

HELLENA. Hang your considering lover! I never thought beyond the fancy that 'twas a very pretty, idle, silly kind of pleasure to pass one's time with: to write little soft nonsensical billets,[102] and with great difficulty and danger receive answers in which I shall have my beauty praised, my wit admired, though little or none, and have the vanity and power to know I am desirable. Then I have the more inclination that way because I am to be a nun, and so shall not be suspected to have any such earthly thoughts about me; but when I walk thus—and sigh thus—they'll think my mind's upon my monastery, and cry, "How happy 'tis she's so resolved." But not a word of man.

FLORINDA. What a mad creature's this!

HELLENA. I'll warrant, if my brother hears either of you sigh, he cries gravely, "I fear you have the indiscretion to be in love, but take heed of the honor of our house, and your own unspotted fame"; and so he conjures on till he has laid the soft winged god in your hearts, or broke the bird's nest.[103] But see, here comes your lover, but where's my inconstant? Let's step aside, and we may learn something.

(Go aside.)

(Enter Belvile, Frederick, and Blunt.)

BELVILE. What means this! The picture's taken in.

BLUNT. It may be the wench is good-natured, and will be kind gratis.[104] Your friend's a proper handsome fellow.

BELVILE. I rather think she has cut his throat and is fled; I am mad he should throw himself into dangers. Pox on't, I shall want him, too, at night. Let's knock and ask for him.

HELLENA. My heart goes a-pit, a-pat, for fear 'tis my man they talk of.

(Knock; Moretta above.)

MORETTA. What would you have?

BELVILE. Tell the stranger that entered here about two hours ago that his friends stay here for him.

MORETTA. A curse upon him for Moretta: Would he were at the devil! But he's coming to you.

(Enter Willmore.)

HELLENA. Ay, ay 'tis he. Oh, how this vexes me!

BELVILE. And how and how, dear lad, has fortune smiled? Are we to break her windows, or raise up altars to her, hah?

WILLMORE. Does not my fortune sit triumphant on my brow? Dost not see the little wanton god there all gay and smiling? Have I not an air about my face and eyes that distinguish me from the crowd of common lovers? By heaven, Cupid's quiver has not half so many darts as her eyes! Oh,

---

[99]**die of the pip** die of some minor ailment   [100]**into** among   [101]**venture a cast** throw dice

[102]**billets** love notes   [103]**laid . . . bird's nest** stimulated your love, or destroyed the place where love dwells (*bird* = Cupid)   [104]**gratis** freely

such a *bona roba!*[105] To sleep in her arms is lying *in fresco,*[106] all perfumed air about me.

HELLENA (*aside*). Here's fine encouragement for me to fool on!

WILLMORE. Hark'ee, where didst thou purchase that rich Canary[107] we drank today? Tell me, that I may adore the spigot and sacrifice to the butt.[108] The juice was divine; into which I must dip my rosary, and then bless all things that I would have bold or fortunate.

BELVILE. Well, sir, let's go take a bottle and hear the story of your success.

FREDERICK. Would not French wine do better?

WILLMORE. Damn the hungry balderdash![109] Cheerful sack[110] has a generous virtue in't inspiring a successful confidence, gives eloquence to the tongue and vigor to the soul, and has in a few hours completed all my hopes and wishes! There's nothing left to raise a new desire in me. Come, let's be gay and wanton. And, gentlemen, study; study what you want, for here are friends that will supply gentlemen. [*Jingles gold coins.*] Hark what a charming sound they make! 'Tis he and she gold whilst here, and shall beget new pleasures every moment.

BLUNT. But hark'ee, sir, you are not married, are you?

WILLMORE. All the honey of matrimony but none of the sting, friend.

BLUNT. 'Adsheartlikins, thou'rt a fortunate rogue!

WILLMORE. I am so, sir: let these inform you! Ha, how sweetly they chime! Pox of poverty: It makes a man a slave, makes wit and honor sneak. My soul grew lean and rusty for want of credit.

BLUNT. 'Adsheartlikins, this I like well; it looks like my lucky bargain! Oh, how I long for the approach of my squire, that is to conduct me to her house again. Why, here's two provided for!

FREDERICK. By this light, y'are happy men.

BLUNT. Fortune is pleased to smile on us, gentlemen, to smile on us.

(*Enter Sancho and pulls down Blunt by the sleeve; they go aside.*)

SANCHO. Sir, my lady expects you. She has removed all that might oppose your will and pleasure, and is impatient till you come.

BLUNT. Sir, I'll attend you.—Oh the happiest rogue! I'll take no leave, lest they either dog me or stay me.

(*Exit with Sancho.*)

BELVILE. But then the little gypsy is forgot?

WILLMORE. A mischief on thee for putting her into my thoughts! I had quite forgot her else, and this night's debauch had drunk her quite down.

HELLENA. Had it so, good captain!

(*Claps him on the back.*)

WILLMORE (*aside*). Ha! I hope she did not hear me!

HELLENA. What, afraid of such a champion?

WILLMORE. Oh, you're a fine lady of your word, are you not? To make a man languish a whole day—

HELLENA. In tedious search of me.

WILLMORE. Egad, child, thou'rt in the right. Hadst thou seen what a melancholy dog I have been ever since I was a lover, how I have walked the streets like a Capuchin,[111] with my hands in my sleeves—faith, sweetheart, thou wouldst pity me.

HELLENA [*aside*]. Now if I should be hanged I can't be angry with him, he dissembles so heartily.—Alas, good captain, what pains you have taken; now were I ungrateful not to reward so true a servant.

WILLMORE. Poor soul, that's kindly said; I see thou barest a conscience. Come then, for a beginning show me thy dear face.

HELLENA. I'm afraid, my small acquaintance, you have been staying that swinging stomach you boasted of this morning. I then remember my little collation[112] would have gone down with you without the sauce of a handsome face. Is your stomach so queasy now?

WILLMORE. Faith, long fasting, child, spoils a man's appetite. Yet if you durst treat, I could so lay about me still—

HELLENA. And would you fall to before a priest says grace?

WILLMORE. O fie, fie, what an old out-of-fashioned thing hast thou named? Thou couldst not dash me more out of countenance shouldst thou show me an ugly face.

(*Whilst he is seemingly courting Hellena, enter Angellica, Moretta, Biskey, and Sebastian, all in masquerade. Angellica sees Willmore and stares.*)

ANGELLICA. Heavens, 'tis he! And passionately fond to see another woman!

MORETTA. What could you less expect from such a swaggerer?

ANGELLICA.
Expect? As much as I paid him: a heart entire,
Which I had pride enough to think when'er I gave,
It would have raised the man above the vulgar,
Made him all soul, and that all soft and constant.

HELLENA. You see, captain, how willing I am to be friends with you, till time and ill luck make us lovers; and ask you the question first rather than put your modesty to the blush by asking me. For alas, I know you captains are such strict men, and such severe observers of your vows

---

[105]**bona roba** courtesan [106]**in fresco** outdoors [107]**Canary** sweet wine, from the Canary Islands [108]**butt** large cask [109]**hungry balderdash** cheap mixture of liquor [110]**sack** dry wine from Spain

[111]**Capuchin** monk [112]**collation** light meal

to chastity, that 'twill be hard to prevail with your tender conscience to marry a young willing maid.

WILLMORE. Do not abuse me, for fear I should take thee at thy word and marry thee indeed, which I'm sure will be revenge sufficient.

HELLENA. O' my conscience, that will be our destiny, because we are both of one humor: I am as inconstant as you, for I have considered, captain, that a handsome woman has a great deal to do whilst her face is good. For then is our harvest-time to gather friends, and should I in these days of my youth catch a fit of foolish constancy, I were undone: 'tis loitering by daylight in our great journey. Therefore, I declare I'll allow but one year for love, one year for indifference, and one year for hate; and then go hang yourself, for I profess myself the gay, the kind, and the inconstant. The devil's in't if this won't please you!

WILLMORE. Oh, most damnably. I have a heart with a hole quite through it too; no prison mine, to keep a mistress in.

ANGELLICA (aside). Perjured man! How I believe thee now!

HELLENA. Well, I see our business as well as humors are alike: yours to cozen as many maids as will trust you, and I as many men as have faith. See if I have not as desperate a lying look as you can have for the heart of you. (Pulls off her vizard; he starts.) How do you like it, captain?

WILLMORE. Like it! By heaven, I never saw so much beauty! Oh, the charms of those sprightly black eyes! That strangely fair face, full of smiles and dimples! Those soft round melting cherry lips and small even white teeth! Not to be expressed, but silently adored! [She replaces her mask.] Oh, one look more, and strike me dumb, or I shall repeat nothing else till I'm mad.

(He seems to court her to pull off her vizard; she refuses.)

ANGELLICA. I can endure no more. Nor is it fit to interrupt him, for if I do, my jealousy has so destroyed my reason I shall undo him. Therefore I'll retire, and you, Sebastian (to one of her Bravos), follow that woman and learn who 'tis; while you (to the other Bravo) tell the fugitive I would speak to him instantly.   (Exit.)

(This while Florinda is talking to Belvile, who stands sullenly; Frederick courting Valeria.)

VALERIA [to Belvile]. Prithee, dear stranger, be not so sullen, for though you have lost your love you see my friend frankly offers you hers to play with in the meantime.

BELVILE. Faith, madam, I am sorry I can't play at her game.

FREDERICK [to Valeria]. Pray leave your intercession and mind your own affair. They'll better agree apart: He's a modest sigher in company, but alone no woman 'scapes him.

FLORINDA [aside]. Sure he does but rally. Yet, if it should be true? I'll tempt him farther.—Believe me, noble stranger, I'm no common mistress. And for a little proof on't, wear this jewel. Nay, take it, sir, 'tis right, and bills of exchange may sometimes miscarry.

BELVILE. Madam, why am I chose out of all mankind to be the object of your bounty?

VALERIA. There's another civil question asked.

FREDERICK [aside]. Pox of's modesty; it spoils his own markets and hinders mine.

FLORINDA. Sir, from my window I have often seen you, and women of my quality have so few opportunities for love that we ought to lose none.

FREDERICK [to Valeria]. Ay, this is something! Here's a woman! When shall I be blest with so much kindness from your fair mouth?—(Aside to Belvile.) Take the jewel, fool!

BELVILE. You tempt me strangely, madam, every way—

FLORINDA (aside). So, if I find him false, my whole repose is gone.

BELVILE. And but for a vow I've made to a very fair lady, this goodness had subdued me.

FREDERICK [aside to Belvile]. Pox on't, be kind, in pity to me be kind. For I am to thrive here but as you treat her friend.

HELLENA. Tell me what you did in yonder house, and I'll unmask.

WILLMORE. Yonder house? Oh, I went to a—to—why, there's a friend of mine lives there.

HELLENA. What, a she or a he friend?

WILLMORE. A man, upon honor, a man. A she friend? No, no, madam, you have done my business, I thank you.

HELLENA. And was't your man friend that had more darts in's eyes than Cupid carries in's whole budget[113] of arrows?

WILLMORE. So—

HELLENA. "Ah, such a bona roba! To be in her arms is lying in fresco, all perfumed air about me." Was this your man friend too?

WILLMORE. So—

HELLENA. That gave you the he and the she gold, that begets young pleasures?

WILLMORE. Well, well, madam, then you can see there are ladies in the world that will not be cruel. There are, madam, there are.

HELLENA. And there be men, too, as fine, wild, inconstant fellows as yourself. There be, captain, there be, if you go to that now. Therefore, I'm resolved—

WILLMORE. Oh!

HELLENA. To see your face no more—

WILLMORE. Oh!

HELLENA. Till tomorrow.

WILLMORE. Egad, you frighted me.

HELLENA. Nor then neither, unless you'll swear never to see that lady more.

WILLMORE. See her! Why, never to think of womankind again.

HELLENA. Kneel and swear.

(Kneels; she gives him her hand.)

---

[113]**budget** bag, quiver

WILLMORE. I do, never to think, to see, to love, nor lie, with any but thyself.

HELLENA. Kiss the book.

WILLMORE. Oh, most religiously.   (*Kisses her hand.*)

HELLENA. Now what a wicked creature am I, to damn a proper fellow.

CALLIS (*to Florinda*). Madam, I'll stay no longer: 'tis e'en dark.

FLORINDA [*to Belvile*]. However, sir, I'll leave this with you, that when I'm gone you may repent the opportunity you have lost by your modesty.

(*Gives him the jewel, which is her picture, and exits. He gazes after her.*)

WILLMORE [*to Hellena*]. 'Twill be an age till tomorrow, and till then I will most impatiently expect you. Adieu, my dear pretty angel.

(*Exeunt all the women.*)

BELVILE. Ha! Florinda's picture! 'Twas she herself. What a dull dog was I! I would have given the world for one minute's discourse with her.

FREDERICK. This comes of your modesty. Ah, pox o' your vow; 'twas ten to one but we had lost the jewel by't.

BELVILE. Willmore, the blessed'st opportunity lost! Florinda, friends, Florinda!

WILLMORE. Ah, rogue! Such black eyes! Such a face! Such a mouth! Such teeth! And so much wit!

BELVILE. All, all, and a thousand charms besides.

WILLMORE. Why, dost thou know her?

BELVILE. Know her! Ay, ay, and a pox take me with all my heart for being so modest.

WILLMORE. But hark'ee, friend of mine, are you my rival? And have I been only beating the bush all this while?

BELVILE. I understand thee not. I'm mad! See here—

(*Shows the picture.*)

WILLMORE. Ha! Whose picture's this? 'Tis a fine wench!

FREDERICK. The colonel's mistress, sir.

WILLMORE. Oh, oh, here. (*Gives the picture back.*) I thought't had been another prize. Come, come, a bottle will set thee right again.

BELVILE. I am content to try, and by that time 'twill be late enough for our design.

WILLMORE. Agreed.

> Love does all day the soul's great empire keep,
> But wine at night lulls the soft god asleep.

(*Exeunt.*)

SCENE 2

(*Lucetta's house. Enter Blunt and Lucetta with a light.*)

LUCETTA. Now we are safe and free: no fears of the coming home of my old jealous husband, which made me a little thoughtful when you came in first. But now love is all the business of my soul.

BLUNT. I am transported!—(*Aside.*) Pox on't, that I had but some fine things to say to her, such as lovers use. I was a fool not to learn of Fred a little by heart before I came. Something I must say.—'Adsheartlikins, sweet soul, I am not used to compliment, but I'm an honest gentleman, and thy humble servant.

LUCETTA. I have nothing to pay for so great a favor, but such a love as cannot but be great, since at first sight of that sweet face and shape it made me your absolute captive.

BLUNT (*aside*). Kind heart, how prettily she talks! Egad, I'll show her husband a Spanish trick: Send him out of the world and marry her; she's damnably in love with me, and will ne'er mind settlements,[114] and so there's that saved.

LUCETTA. Well, sir, I'll go and undress me, and be with you instantly.

BLUNT. Make haste then, for 'adsheartlikins, dear soul, thou canst not guess at the pain of a longing lover when his joys are drawn within the compass of a few minutes.

LUCETTA. You speak my sense, and I'll make haste to prove it.   (*Exit.*)

BLUNT. 'Tis a rare girl, and this one night's enjoyment with her will be worth all the days I ever passed in Essex. Would she would go with me into England, though to say truth, there's plenty of whores already. Put a pox on 'em, they are such mercenary prodigal whores that they want such a one as this, that's free and generous, to give 'em good examples. Why, what a house she has, how rich and fine!

(*Enter Sancho.*)

SANCHO. Sir, my lady has sent me to conduct you to her chamber.

BLUNT. Sir, I shall be proud to follow.—(*Aside.*) Here's one of her servants too; 'adsheartlikins, by this garb and gravity he might be a justice of peace in Essex, and is but a pimp here.

(*Exeunt.*)

SCENE 3

(*The scene changes to a chamber with an alcove bed in't, a table, etc.; Lucetta in bed. Enter Sancho and Blunt, who takes the candle of Sancho at the door.*)

SANCHO. Sir, my commission reaches no farther.

BLUNT. Sir, I'll excuse your compliment.

[*Exit Sancho.*]

—What, in bed, my sweet mistress?

LUCETTA. You see, I still outdo you in kindness.

[114]**settlements** prenuptial agreement settling property on a wife

BLUNT. And thou shalt see what haste I'll make to quit scores. Oh, the luckiest rogue!

(*He undresses himself.*)

LUCETTA. Should you be false or cruel now—

BLUNT. False! 'Adsheartlikins, what dost thou take me for, a Jew? An insensible heathen? A pox of thy old jealous husband: An[115] he were dead, egad,[116] sweet soul, it should be none of my fault if I did not marry thee.

LUCETTA. It never should be mine.

BLUNT. Good soul! I'm the fortunatest dog!

LUCETTA. Are you not undressed yet?

BLUNT. As much as my impatience will permit.

(*Goes toward the bed in his shirt, drawers, etc.*)

LUCETTA. Hold, sir, put out the light; it may betray us else.

BLUNT. Anything; I need no other light but that of thine eyes.—(*Aside.*) 'Adsheartlikins, there I think I had it.

(*Puts out the candle; the bed descends; he gropes about to find it.*)

Why, why, where am I got? What, not yet? Where are you, sweetest?—Ah, the rogue's silent now. A pretty love-trick this; how she'll laugh at me anon!—You need not, my dear rogue, you need not! I'm all on fire already; come, come, now call me, in pity.—Sure I'm enchanted! I have been round the chamber, and can find neither woman nor bed. I locked the door; I'm sure she cannot go that way, or if she could, the bed could not.—Enough, enough, my pretty wanton; do not carry the jest too far! (*Lights on a trap, and is let down.*)—Ha! Betrayed! Dogs! Rogues! Pimps! Help! Help!

(*Enter Lucetta, Philippo, and Sancho with a light.*)

PHILIPPO. Ha! Ha! Ha! He's dispatched finely.

LUCETTA. Now, sir, had I been coy, we had missed of this booty.

PHILIPPO. Nay, when I saw 'twas a substantial fool, I was mollified. But when you dote upon a serenading coxcomb, upon a face, fine clothes, and a lute, it makes me rage.

LUCETTA. You know I was never guilty of that folly, my dear Philippo, but with yourself. But come, let's see what we have got by this.

PHILIPPO. A rich coat; sword and hat; these breeches, too, are well lined! See here, a gold watch! A purse—Ha! Gold! At least two hundred pistoles! A bunch of diamond rings, and one with the family arms! A gold box, with a medal of his king, and his lady mother's picture! These were sacred relics, believe me. See, the waistband of his breeches have a mine of gold—old queen Bess's![117] We have a

quarrel to her ever since eighty-eight,[118] and may therefore justify the theft: The Inquisition might have committed it.

LUCETTA. See, a bracelet of bowed[119] gold! These his sisters tied about his arm at parting. But well, for all this, I fear his being a stranger may make a noise and hinder our trade with them hereafter.

PHILIPPO. That's our security: He is not only a stranger to us, but to the country too. The common shore[120] into which he is descended, thou know'st, conducts him into another street, which this light will hinder him from ever finding again. He knows neither your name, nor that of the street where your house is; nay, nor the way to his own lodgings.

LUCETTA. And art thou not an unmerciful rogue, not to afford him one night for all this? I should not have been such a Jew.

PHILIPPO. Blame me not, Lucetta, to keep as much of thee as I can to myself. Come, that thought makes me wanton; let's to bed.—Sancho, lock up these.

This is the fleece which fools do bear,
Designed for witty men to shear.

(*Exeunt.*)

SCENE 4

(*The scene changes, and discovers Blunt creeping out of a common shore; his face, etc., all dirty.*)

BLUNT (*climbing up*). Oh, Lord, I am got out at last, and, which is a miracle, without a clue. And now to damning and cursing! But if that would ease me, where shall I begin? With my fortune, myself, or the quean[121] that cozened me? What a dog was I to believe in woman! Oh, coxcomb! Ignorant conceited coxcomb! To fancy she could be enamored with my person! At first sight enamored! Oh, I'm a cursed puppy! 'Tis plain, fool was writ upon my forehead! She perceived it; saw the Essex calf there. For what allurements could there be in this countenance, which I can endure because I'm acquainted with it. Oh dull, silly dog, to be thus soothed into a cozening! Had I been drunk, I might fondly have credited the young quean; but as I was in my right wits to be thus cheated, confirms it: I am a dull believing English country fop. But my comrades! Death and the devil, there's the worst of all! Then a ballad will be sung tomorrow on the Prado,[122] to a lousy tune of the enchanted squire and the annihilated damsel. But Fred—that rogue—and the colonel will abuse me beyond all Christian patience. Had

---

[115]**An** if   [116]**egad** a mild oath   [117]**old queen Bess** Queen Elizabeth I (reigned 1558–1603)   [118]**eighty-eight** 1588, the year the English defeated the Spanish Armada   [119]**bowed** curved(?) braided(?)   [120]**common shore** sewer   [121]**quean** harlot   [122]**Prado** promenade

she left me my clothes, I have a bill of exchange at home would have saved my credit. But now all hope is taken from me. Well, I'll home, if I can find the way, with this consolation: that I am not the first kind believing coxcomb; but there are, gallants, many such good natures amongst ye.

> And though you've better arts to hide your follies,
>   'Adsheartlikins, y'are all as errant cullies.[123]

(*Exit.*)

SCENE 5

(*Scene: the garden in the night. Enter Florinda in an undress,[124] with a key and a little box.*)

FLORINDA. Well, thus far I'm in my way to happiness. I have got myself free from Callis; my brother too, I find by yonder light, is got into his cabinet,[125] and thinks not of me; I have by good fortune got the key of the garden back door. I'll open it to prevent Belvile's knocking: A little noise will now alarm my brother. Now am I as fearful as a young thief. (*Unlocks the door.*) Hark! What noise is that? Oh, 'twas the wind that played amongst the boughs. Belvile stays long, methinks; it's time. Stay, for fear of a surprise, I'll hide these jewels in yonder jasmine.

(*She goes to lay down the box.*)

(*Enter Willmore, drunk.*)

WILLMORE. What the devil is become of these fellows Belvile and Frederick? They promised to stay at the next corner for me, but who the devil knows the corner of a full moon? Now, whereabouts am I? Ha, what have we here? A garden! A very convenient place to sleep in. Ha! What has God sent us here? A female! By this light, a woman! I'm a dog if it be not a very wench!

FLORINDA. He's come! Ha! Who's there?

WILLMORE. Sweet soul, let me salute thy shoestring.

FLORINDA [*aside*]. 'Tis not my Belvile. Good heavens, I know him not!—Who are you, and from whence come you?

WILLMORE. Prithee, prithee, child, not so many hard questions! Let is suffice I am here, child. Come, come kiss me.

FLORINDA. Good gods! What luck is mine?

WILLMORE. Only good luck, child, parlous[126] good luck. Come hither.—'Tis a delicate shining wench. By this hand, she's perfumed, and smells like any nosegay.— Prithee, dear soul, let's not play the fool and lose time— precious time. For as Gad shall save me, I'm as honest a fellow as breathes, though I'm a little disguised[127] at present. Come, I say. Why, thou mayst be free with me: I'll

be very secret. I'll not boast who 'twas obliged me, not I; for hang me if I know thy name.

FLORINDA. Heavens! What a filthy beast is this!

WILLMORE. I am so, and thou ought'st the sooner to lie with me for that reason. For look you, child, there will be no sin in't, because 'twas neither designed nor premeditated: 'Tis pure accident on both sides. That's a certain thing now. Indeed, should I make love to you, and you vow fidelity, and swear and lie till you believed and yielded— that were to make it willful fornication, the crying sin of the nation. Thou art, therefore, as thou art a good Christian, obliged in conscience to deny me nothing. Now, come be kind without any more idle prating.

FLORINDA. Oh, I am ruined! Wicked man, unhand me!

WILLMORE. Wicked? Egad, child, a judge, were he young and vigorous, and saw those eyes of thine, would know 'twas they gave the first blow, the first provocation. Come, prithee let's lose no time, I say. This is a fine convenient place.

FLORINDA. Sir, let me go, I conjure[128] you, or I'll call out.

WILLMORE. Ay, ay, you were best to call witness to see how finely you treat me. Do!

FLORINDA. I'll cry murder, rape, or anything, if you do not instantly let me go!

WILLMORE. A rape? Come, come, you lie, you baggage, you lie. What! I'll warrant you would fain have the world believe now that you are not so forward as I. No, not you. Why at this time of night was your cobweb door set open, dear spider, but to catch flies? Ha! Come, or I shall be damnably angry. Why, what a coil[129] is here!

FLORINDA. Sir, can you think—

WILLMORE. That you would do't for nothing? Oh, oh, I find what you would be at. Look here, here's a pistole[130] for you. Here's a work indeed! Here, take it, I say!

FLORINDA. For heaven's sake, sir, as you're a gentleman—

WILLMORE. So now, now, she would be wheedling me for more! What, you will not take it then? You are resolved you will not? Come, come, take it or I'll put it up again, for look ye, I never give more. Why, how now, mistress, are you so high i'th' mouth[131] a pistole won't down with you? Ha! Why, what a work's here! In good time! Come, no struggling to be gone. But an y'are good at a dumb wrestle, I'm for ye. Look ye, I'm for ye.

(*She struggles with him.*)

(*Enter Belvile and Frederick.*)

BELVILE. The door is open. A pox of this mad fellow! I'm angry that we've lost him; I durst have sworn he had followed us.

FREDERICK. But you were so hasty, colonel, to be gone.

[123]**errant cullies** arrant fools [124]**undress** informal clothing [125]**cabinet** private room [126]**parlous** excessively, with pun on perilous [127]**disguised** drunk

[128]**conjure** implore [129]**coil** disturbance [130]**pistole** gold coin [131]**high i'th' mouth** stuck up

FLORINDA. Help! Help! Murder! Help! Oh, I am ruined!

BELVILE. Ha! Sure that's Florinda's voice (*Comes up to them.*) A man!—Villain, let go that lady!

(*A noise; Willmore turns and draws; Frederick interposes.*)

FLORINDA. Belvile! Heavens! My brother too is coming, and 'twill be impossible to escape. Belvile, I conjure you to walk under my chamber window, from whence I'll give you some instructions what to do. This rude man has undone us.   (*Exit.*)

WILLMORE. Belvile!

(*Enter Pedro, Stephano, and other servants, with lights.*)

PEDRO. I'm betrayed! Run, Stephano, and see if Florinda be safe.

(*Exit Stephano.*)

(*They fight, and Pedro's party beats 'em out.*)

—So, whoe'er they be, all is not well. I'll to Florinda's chamber.   (*Going out, meets Stephano.*)

STEPHANO. You need not, sir: The poor lady's fast asleep, and thinks no harm. I would not awake her, sir, for fear of frighting her with your danger.

PEDRO. I'm glad she's there.—Rascals, how came the garden door open?

STEPHANO. That question comes too late, sir. Some of my fellow servants masquerading, I'll warrant.

PEDRO. Masquerading! A lewd custom to debauch our youth! There's something more in this than I imagine.

(*Exeunt.*)

SCENE 6

(*Scene changes to the street. Enter Belvile in rage, Frederick holding him, Willmore melancholy.*)

WILLMORE. Why, how the devil should I know Florinda?

BELVILE. Ah, plague of your ignorance! If it had not been Florinda, must you be a beast? A brute? A senseless swine?

WILLMORE. Well, sir, you see I am endued[132] with patience: I can bear. Though egad, y'are very free with me, methinks. I was in good hopes the quarrel would have been on my side, for so uncivilly interrupting me.

BELVILE. Peace, brute, whilst thou'rt safe. Oh, I'm distracted!

WILLMORE. Nay, nay, I'm an unlucky dog, that's certain.

BELVILE. Ah, curse upon the star that ruled my birth, or whatsoever other influence that makes me still so wretched.

WILLMORE. Thou break'st my heart with these complaints. There is no star in fault, no influence but sack, the cursed sack I drunk.

FREDERICK. Why, how the devil came you so drunk?

WILLMORE. Why, how the devil came you so sober?

BELVILE. A curse upon his thin skull, he was always beforehand that way.

FREDERICK. Prithee, dear colonel, forgive him; he's sorry for his fault.

BELVILE. He's always so after he has done a mischief. A plague on all such brutes!

WILLMORE. By this light, I took her for an errant harlot.

BELVILE. Damn your debauched opinion! Tell me, sot, hadst thou so much sense and light about thee to distinguish her woman, and couldst not see something about her face and person to strike an awful reverence into thy soul?

WILLMORE. Faith no, I considered her as mere a woman as I could wish.

BELVILE. 'Sdeath, I have no patience. Draw, or I'll kill you!

WILLMORE. Let that alone till tomorrow, and if I set not all right again, use your pleasure.

BELVILE.
Tomorrow! Damn it,
The spiteful light will lead me to no happiness.
Tomorrow is Antonio's, and perhaps
Guides him to my undoing. Oh, that I could meet
This rival, this powerful fortunate!

WILLMORE. What then?

BELVILE. Let thy own reason, or my rage, instruct thee.

WILLMORE. I shall be finely informed then, no doubt. Hear me, colonel, hear me; show me the man and I'll do his business.

BELVILE. I know him no more than thou, or if I did I should not need thy aid.

WILLMORE. This you say is Angellica's house; I promised the kind baggage to lie with her tonight.

(*Offers to go in.*)

(*Enter Antonio and his Page. Antonio knocks on the hilt of his sword.*)

ANTONIO. You paid the thousand crowns I directed?

PAGE. To the lady's old woman, sir, I did.

WILLMORE. Who the devil have we here?

BELVILE. I'll now plant myself under Florinda's window, and if I find no comfort there, I'll die.

(*Exeunt Belvile and Frederick.*)

(*Enter Moretta.*)

MORETTA. Page?

PAGE. Here's my lord.

WILLMORE. How is this? A picaroon[133] going to board my frigate?—Here's one chase gun for you!

(*Drawing his sword, justles Antonio, who turns and draws. They fight; Antonio falls.*)

MORETTA. Oh, bless us! We're all undone!

---

[132]**endued** endowed

[133]**picaroon** pirate

(*Runs in and shuts the door.*)

PAGE. Help! Murder!

(*Belvile returns at the noise of fighting.*)

BELVILE. Ha! The mad rogue's engaged in some unlucky adventure again.

(*Enter two or three Masqueraders.*)

MASQUERADER. Ha! A man killed!

WILLMORE. How, a man killed? Then I'll go home to sleep.

(*Puts up and reels out. Exeunt Masqueraders another way.*)

BELVILE. Who should it be? Pray heaven the rogue is safe, for all my quarrel to him.

(*As Belvile is groping about, enter an Officer and six Soldiers.*)

SOLDIER. Who's there?

OFFICER. So, here's one dispatched. Secure the murderer.

BELVILE. Do not mistake my charity for murder! I came to his assistance!

(*Soldiers seize on Belvile.*)

OFFICER. That shall be tried, sir. St. Jago! Swords drawn in the Carnival time!   (*Goes to Antonio.*)

ANTONIO. Thy hand, prithee.

OFFICER. Ha! Don Antonio! Look well to the villain there.—How is it, sir?

ANTONIO. I'm hurt.

BELVILE. Has my humanity made me a criminal?

OFFICER. Away with him!

BELVILE. What a curst chance is this!

(*Exeunt soldiers with Belvile.*)

ANTONIO [*aside*]. This is the man that has set upon me twice.—(*To the officer.*) Carry him to my apartment till you have further orders from me.

(*Exit Antonio, led.*)

ACT 4

SCENE 1

(*A fine room. Discovers Belvile as by dark alone.*)

BELVILE. When shall I be weary of railing on fortune, who is resolved never to turn with smiles upon me? Two such defeats in one night none but the devil and that mad rogue could have contrived to have plagued me with. I am here a prisoner. But where, heaven knows. And if there be murder done, I can soon decide the fate of a stranger in a nation without mercy. Yet this is nothing to the torture my soul bows with when I think of losing my fair, my dear Florinda. Hark, my door opens. A light! A man, and seems of quality. Armed, too! Now shall I die like a dog, without defense.

(*Enter Antonio in a nightgown, with a light; his arm in a scarf, and a sword under his arm. He sets the candle on the table.*)

ANTONIO. Sir, I come to know what injuries I have done you, that could provoke you to so mean an action as to attack me basely without allowing time for my defense?

BELVILE. Sir, for a man in my circumstances to plead innocence would look like fear. But view me well, and you will find no marks of coward on me, nor anything that betrays that brutality you accuse me with.

ANTONIO. In vain, sir, you impose upon my sense. You are not only he who drew on me last night, but yesterday before the same house, that of Angellica. Yet there is something in your face and mien[134] that makes me wish I were mistaken.

BELVILE. I own I fought today in the defense of a friend of mine with whom you, if you're the same, and your party were first engaged. Perhaps you think this crime enough to kill me; but if you do, I cannot fear you'll do it basely.

ANTONIO. No sir, I'll make you fit for a defense with this. (*Gives him the sword.*)

BELVILE. This gallantry surprises me, nor know I how to use this present, sir, against a man so brave.

ANTONIO. You shall not need. For know, I come to snatch you from a danger that is decreed against you: perhaps your life, or long imprisonment. And 'twas with so much courage you offended, I cannot see you punished.

BELVILE. How shall I pay this generosity?

ANTONIO. It had been safer to have killed another than have attempted me. To show your danger, sir, I'll let you know my quality:[135] And 'tis the Viceroy's son whom you have wounded.

BELVILE. The Viceroy's son!—(*Aside.*) Death and confusion! Was this plague reserved to complete all the rest? Obliged by[136] him, the man of all the world I would destroy!

ANTONIO. You seem disordered, sir.

BELVILE. Yes, trust me, I am, and 'tis with pain that man receives such bounties who wants the power to pay 'em back again.

ANTONIO. To gallant spirits 'tis indeed uneasy, but you may quickly overpay me, sir.

BELVILE (*aside*). Then I am well. Kind heaven, but set us even, that I may fight with him and keep my honor safe.—Oh, I'm impatient, sir, to be discounting the mighty debt I owe you. Command me quickly.

ANTONIO. I have a quarrel with a rival, sir, about the maid we love.

---

[134]**mien** manner   [135]**quality** rank   [136]**Obliged by** favored by

BELVILE (*aside*). Death, 'tis Florinda he means! That thought destroys my reason, and I shall kill him.

ANTONIO. My rival, sir, is one has all the virtues man can boast of—

BELVILE (*aside*). Death, who should this be?

ANTONIO. He challenged me to meet him on the Molo[137] as soon as day appeared, but last night's quarrel has made my arm unfit to guide a sword.

BELVILE. I apprehend you, sir. You'd have me kill the man that lays a claim to the maid you speak of. I'll do't. I'll fly to do't!

ANTONIO. Sir, do you know her?

BELVILE. No, sir, but 'tis enough she is admired by you.

ANTONIO. Sir, I shall rob you of the glory on't, for you must fight under my name and dress.

BELVILE. That opinion must be strangely obliging that makes you think I can personate the brave Antonio, whom I can but strive to imitate.

ANTONIO. You say too much to my advantage. Come, sir, the day appears that calls you forth. Within, sir, is the habit.[138]   (*Exit Antonio.*)

BELVILE.
Fantastic fortune, thou deceitful light,
That cheats the wearied traveler by night,
Though on a precipice each step you tread,
I am resolved to follow where you lead.

(*Exit.*)

SCENE 2

(*The Molo. Enter Florinda and Callis in masks, with Stephano.*)

FLORINDA (*aside*). I'm dying with my fears: Belvile's not coming as I expected under my window makes me believe that all those fears are true.—Canst thou not tell with whom my brother fights?

STEPHANO. No, madam, they were both in masquerade. I was by when they challenged one another, and they had decided the quarrel then, but were prevented by some cavaliers; which made 'em put it off till now. But I am sure 'tis about you they fight.

FLORINDA (*aside*). Nay, then, 'tis with Belvile, for what other lover have I that dares fight for me except Antonio, and he is too much in favor with my brother. If it be he, for whom shall I direct my prayers to heaven?

STEPHANO. Madam, I must leave you, for if my master see me, I shall be hanged for being your conductor. I escaped narrowly for the excuse I made for you last night i'th' garden.

FLORINDA. I'll reward thee for't. Prithee, no more.

(*Exit Stephano.*)

(*Enter Don Pedro in his masking habit.*)

PEDRO. Antonio's late today; the place will fill, and we may be prevented.[139]

(*Walks about.*)

FLORINDA (*aside*). Antonio? Sure I heard amiss.

PEDRO.
But who will not excuse a happy lover
When soft fair arms confine the yielding neck,
And the kind whisper languishingly breathes
"Must you be gone so soon?"
Sure I had dwelt forever on her bosom—
But stay, he's here.

(*Enter Belvile dressed in Antonio's clothes.*)

FLORINDA [*aside*]. 'Tis not Belvile; half my fears are vanished.

PEDRO. Antonio!

BELVILE (*aside*). This must be he.—You're early, sir; I do not use to be outdone this way.

PEDRO.
The wretched, sir, are watchful, and 'tis enough
You've the advantage of me in Angellica.

BELVILE (*aside*).
Angellica! Or[140] I've mistook my man, or else Antonio!
Can he forget his interest in Florinda
And fight for common prize?

PEDRO.
Come, sir, you know our terms.

BELVILE (*aside*).
By heaven, not I.
No talking; I am ready, sir.

(*Offers to fight; Florinda runs in.*)

FLORINDA (*to Belvile*).
Oh, hold! Whoe'er you be, I do conjure you hold!
If you strike here, I die!

PEDRO. Florinda!

BELVILE. Florinda imploring for my rival!

PEDRO.
Away; this kindness is unseasonable.

(*Puts her by; they fight; she runs in just as Belvile disarms Pedro.*)

FLORINDA.
Who are you, sir, that dares deny my prayers?

BELVILE.
Thy prayers destroy him; if thou wouldst preserve him,
Do that thou'rt unacquainted with, and curse him.

(*She holds him.*)

FLORINDA.
By all you hold most dear, by her you love,
I do conjure you, touch him not.

BELVILE.
By her I love?

See, I obey, and at your feet resign
The useless trophy of my victory.

                (*Lays his sword at her feet.*)

PEDRO. Antonio, you've done enough to prove you love
     Florinda.

BELVILE. Love Florinda! Does heaven love adoration, prayer,
     or penitence? Love her? Here, sir, your sword again.

(*Snatches up the sword and gives it to him.*)

Upon this truth I'll fight my life away.

PEDRO. No, you've redeemed my sister, and my friendship.

(*He gives him Florinda, and pulls off his vizard to show his
face, and puts it on again.*)

BELVILE. Don Pedro!

PEDRO.
     Can you resign your claims to other women,
     And give your heart entirely to Florinda?

BELVILE.
     Entire, as dying saints' confessions are!
     I can delay my happiness no longer:
     This minute let me make Florinda mine.

PEDRO.
     This minute let it be. No time so proper:
     This night my father will arrive from Rome,
     And possibly may hinder what we purpose.

FLORINDA. O, heavens! This minute?

(*Enter Masqueraders and pass over.*)

BELVILE. Oh, do not ruin me!

PEDRO. The place begins to fill, and that we may not be ob-
     served, do you walk off to St. Peter's church, where I will
     meet you and conclude your happiness.

BELVILE. I'll meet you there.—(*Aside.*) If there be no more
     saints' churches in Naples.

FLORINDA.
     Oh, stay, sir, and recall your hasty doom!
     Alas, I have not yet prepared my heart
     To entertain so strange a guest.

PEDRO.
     Away; this silly modesty is assumed too late.

BELVILE.
     Heaven, madam, what do you do?

FLORINDA.
     Do? Despise the man that lays a tyrant's claim
     To what he ought to conquer by submission.

BELVILE.
     You do not know me. Move a little this way.

                (*Draws her aside.*)

FLORINDA.
     Yes, you may force me even to the altar,
     But not the holy man that offers there
     Shall force me to be thine.

                (*Pedro talks to Callis this while.*)

BELVILE.
     Oh, do not lose so blest an opportunity!

                (*Pulls off his vizard.*)

     See, 'tis your Belvile, not Antonio,
     Whom your mistaken scorn and anger ruins.

FLORINDA. Belvile!
     Where was my soul it could not meet thy voice,
     And take this knowledge in.

(*As they are talking, enter Willmore, finely dressed, and
Frederick.*)

WILLMORE. No intelligence? No news of Belvile yet? Well, I
     am the most unlucky rascal in nature. Ha! Am I de-
     ceived, or is it he? Look, Fred! 'Tis he, my dear Belvile!

(*Runs and embraces him; Belvile's vizard falls out on's
hand.*)

BELVILE. Hell and confusion seize thee!

PEDRO. Ha! Belvile! I beg your pardon, sir.

                (*Takes Florinda from him.*)

BELVILE.
     Nay, touch her not. She's mine by conquest, sir;
     I won her by my sword.

WILLMORE.
     Didst thou so? And egad, child, we'll keep her by the
     sword.

                (*Draws on Pedro; Belvile goes between.*)

BELVILE.
     Stand off!
     Thou'rt so profanely lewd, so curst by heaven,
     All quarrels thou espousest must be fatal.

WILLMORE.
     Nay, an you be so hot, my valor's coy,
     And shall be courted when you want it next.

                (*Puts up his sword.*)

BELVILE (*to Pedro*).
     You know I ought to claim a victor's right,
     But you're the brother to divine Florinda,
     To whom I'm such a slave. To purchase her
     I durst not hurt the man she holds so dear.

PEDRO.
     'Twas by Antonio's, not by Belvile's sword
     This question should have been decided, sir.
     I must confess much to your bravery's due,
     Both now and when I met you last in arms;
     But I am nicely punctual in my word,
     As men of honor ought, and beg your pardon:
     For this mistake another time shall clear.

(*Aside to Florinda as they are going out.*)

—This was some plot between you and Belvile,
But I'll prevent you.

[*Exeunt Pedro and Florinda.*]

(*Belvile looks after her and begins to walk up and down in rage.*)

WILLMORE. Do not be modest now and lose the woman. But if we shall fetch her back so—

BELVILE. Do not speak to me!

WILLMORE. Not speak to you? Egad, I'll speak to you, and will be answered, too.

BELVILE. Will you, sir?

WILLMORE. I know I've done some mischief, but I'm so dull a puppy that I'm the son of a whore if I know how or where. Prithee inform my understanding.

BELVILE. Leave me, I say, and leave me instantly!

WILLMORE. I will not leave you in this humor, nor till I know my crime.

BELVILE. Death, I'll tell you, sir—

(*Draws and runs at Willmore; he runs out, Belvile after him; Frederick interposes.*)

(*Enter Angellica, Moretta, and Sebastian.*)

ANGELLICA. Ha! Sebastian, is that not Willmore? Haste! haste and bring him back.

[*Exit Sebastian.*]

FREDERICK [*aside*]. The colonel's mad: I never saw him thus before. I'll after 'em lest he do some mischief, for I am sure Willmore will not draw on him.   (*Exit.*)

ANGELLICA.
I am all rage! My first desires defeated!
For one for aught he knows that has no
Other merit than her quality,
Her being Don Pedro's sister. He loves her!
I know 'tis so. Dull, dull, insensible,
He will not see me now, though oft invited,
And broke his word last night. False perjured man!
He that but yesterday fought for my favors,
And would have made his life a sacrifice
To've gained one night with me,
Must now be hired and courted to my arms.

MORETTA. I told you what would come on't, but Moretta's an old doting fool. Why did you give him five hundred crowns, but to set himself out for other lovers? You should have kept him poor if you had meant to have had any good from him.

ANGELLICA.
Oh, name not such mean trifles! Had I given
Him all my youth has earned from sin,
I had not lost a thought nor sigh upon't.
But I have given him my eternal rest,
My whole repose, my future joys, my heart!
My virgin heart, Moretta! Oh, 'tis gone!

MORETTA. Curse on him, here he comes. How fine she has made him, too.

(*Enter Willmore and Sebastian; Angellica turns and walks away.*)

WILLMORE.
How now, turned shadow?
Fly when I pursue, and follow when I fly?   (*Sings.*)

Stay, gentle shadow of my dove,
    And tell me ere I go,
Whether the substance may not prove
    A fleeting thing like you.

(*As she turns she looks on him.*)

There's a soft kind look remaining yet.

ANGELLICA. Well, sir, you may be gay: All happiness, all joys pursue you still. Fortune's your slave, and gives you every hour choice of new hearts and beauties, till you are cloyed[141] with the repeated bliss which others vainly languish for. But know, false man, that I shall be revenged.

(*Turns away in rage.*)

WILLMORE. So, gad, there are of those faint-hearted lovers, whom such a sharp lesson next their hearts would make as impotent as fourscore.[142] Pox o' this whining; my business is to laugh and love. A pox on't, I hate your sullen lover: A man shall lose as much time to put you in humor now as would serve to gain a new woman.

ANGELLICA.
I scorn to cool that fire I cannot raise,
Or do the drudgery of your virtuous mistress.

WILLMORE. A virtuous mistress? Death, what a thing thou hast found out for me! Why, what the devil should I do with a virtuous woman, a sort of ill-natured creatures that take a pride to torment a lover. Virtue is but an infirmity in woman, a disease that renders even the handsome ungrateful; whilst the ill-favored, for want of solicitations and address, only fancy themselves so. I have lain with a woman of quality who has all the while been railing at whores.

ANGELLICA.
I will not answer for your mistress's virtue,
Though she be young enough to know no guilt;
And I could wish you would persuade my heart
'Twas the two hundred thousand crowns you courted.

WILLMORE. Two hundred thousand crowns! What story's this? What trick? What woman, ha?

ANGELLICA. How strange you make it. Have you forgot the creature you entertained on the Piazzo last night?

WILLMORE (*aside*). Ha! My gypsy worth two hundred thousand crowns! Oh, how I long to be with her! Pox, I knew she was of quality.

---

[141]**cloyed** sickened   [142]**as fourscore** as an eighty-year old

ANGELLICA.
    False man! I see my ruin in thy face.
    How many vows you breathed upon my bosom
    Never to be unjust. Have you forgot so soon?

WILLMORE. Faith, no; I was just coming to repeat 'em. But here's a humor indeed would make a man a saint.—(*Aside.*) Would she would be angry enough to leave me, and command me not to wait on her.

(*Enter Hellena dressed in man's clothes.*)

HELLENA. This must be Angellica: I know it by her mumping[143] matron here. Ay, ay, 'tis she. My mad captain's with her, too, for all his swearing. How this unconstant humor makes me love him!—Pray, good grave gentlewoman, is not this Angellica?

MORETTA. My too young sir, it is.—[*Aside.*] I hope 'tis one from Don Antonio.   (*Goes to Angellica.*)

HELLENA (*aside*). Well, something I'll do to vex him for this.

ANGELLICA. I will not speak with him. Am I in humor to receive a lover?

WILLMORE. Not speak with him? Why, I'll be gone, and wait your idler minutes. Can I show less obedience to the thing I love so fondly?

(*Offers to go.*)

ANGELLICA. A fine excuse this! Stay—

WILLMORE. And hinder your advantage? Should I repay your bounties so ungratefully?

ANGELLICA [*to Hellena*].
    Come hither, boy.—[*To Willmore.*] That I may let you see
    How much above the advantages you name
    I prize one minute's joy with you.

WILLMORE (*impatient to be gone*). Oh, you destroy me with this endearment.—[*Aside.*] Death, how shall I get away?—Madam, 'twill not be fit I should be seen with you. Besides, it will not be convenient. And I've a friend—that's dangerously sick.

ANGELLICA. I see you're impatient. Yet you shall stay.

WILLMORE (*aside*). And miss my assignation with my gypsy.

(*Walks about impatiently; Moretta brings Hellena, who addresses herself to Angellica.*)

HELLENA.
    Madam,
    You'll hardly pardon my instrusion
    When you shall know my business,
    And I'm too young to tell my tale with art;
    But there must be a wondrous store of goodness
    Where so much beauty dwells.

ANGELLICA.
    A pretty advocate, whoever sent thee.

Prithee proceed. (*To Willmore, who is stealing off.*)—Nay, sir, you shall not go.

WILLMORE (*aside*). Then I shall lose my dear gypsy forever. Pox on't, she stays me out of spite.

HELLENA.
    I am related to a lady, madam,
    Young, rich, and nobly born, but has the fate
    To be in love with a young English gentleman.
    Strangely she loves him, at first sight she loved him,
    But did adore him when she heard him speak;
    For he, she said, had charms in every word
    That failed not to surprise, to wound and conquer.

WILLMORE (*aside*). Ha! Egad, I hope this concerns me.

ANGELLICA (*aside*).
    'Tis my false man he means. Would he were gone:
    This praise will raise his pride, and ruin me. (*To Willmore.*)—Well,
    Since you are so impatient to be gone,
    I will release you, sir.

WILLMORE (*aside*). Nay, then I'm sure 'twas me he spoke of: This cannot be the effects of kindness in her.—No, Madam, I've considered better on't, and will not give you cause of jealousy.

ANGELLICA. But sir, I've business that—

WILLMORE. This shall not do; I know 'tis but to try me.

ANGELLICA. Well, to your story, boy.—(*Aside*). Though 'twill undo me.

HELLENA.
    With this addition to his other beauties,
    He won her unresisting tender heart.
    He vowed, and sighed, and swore he loved her dearly;
    And she believed the cunning flatterer,
    And thought herself the happiest maid alive.
    Today was the appointed time by both
    To consummate their bliss:
    The virgin, altar, and the priest were dressed;
    And whilst she languished for th'expected bridegroom,
    She heard he paid his broken vows to you.

WILLMORE (*aside*). So, this is some dear rogue that's in love with me, and this way lets me know it. Or, if it be not me, he means someone whose place I may supply.

ANGELLICA. Now I perceive
    The cause of thy impatience to be gone,
    And all the business of this glorious dress.

WILLMORE. Damn the young prater; I know not what he means.

HELLENA. Madam,
    In your fair eyes I read too much concern
    To tell my further business.

ANGELLICA.
    Prithee, sweet youth, talk on: Thou mayst perhaps
    Raise here a storm that may undo my passion,
    And then I'll grant thee anything.

HELLENA.
    Madam, 'tis to entreat you (oh unreasonable)
    You would not see this stranger.

---

[143]**mumping** moping

For if you do, she vows you are undone;
Though nature never made a man so excellent,
And sure he 'ad been a god, but for inconstancy.

WILLMORE (*aside*). Ah, rogue, how finely he's instructed! 'Tis plain, some woman that has seen me *en passant*.[144]

ANGELLICA. Oh, I shall burst with jealousy! Do you know the man you speak of?

HELLENA. Yes, madam, he used to be in buff and scarlet.

ANGELLICA (*to Willmore*). Thou false as hell, what canst thou say to this?

WILLMORE. By heaven—

ANGELLICA. Hold, do not damn thyself—

HELLENA. Nor hope to be believed.

(*He walks about; they follow.*)

ANGELLICA. Oh perjured man!
Is't thus you pay my generous passion back?

HELLENA. Why would you, sir, abuse my lady's faith?

ANGELLICA. And use me so unhumanely.

HELLENA. A maid so young, so innocent—

WILLMORE. Ah, young devil!

ANGELLICA. Dost thou not know thy life is in my power?

HELLENA. Or think my lady cannot be revenged?

WILLMORE (*aside*). So, so, the storm comes finely on.

ANGELLICA.
Now thou art silent: Guilt has struck thee dumb.
Oh, hadst thou still been so, I'd lived in safety.

(*She turns away and weeps.*)

WILLMORE (*aside to Hellena*). Sweetheart, the lady's name and house—quickly! I'm impatient to be with her.

(*Looks toward Angellica to watch her turning, and as she comes towards them he meets her.*)

HELLENA (*aside*). So, now is he for another woman.

WILLMORE.
The impudent'st young thing in nature:
I cannot persuade him out of his error, madam.

ANGELLICA.
I know he's in the right; yet thou'st a tongue
That would persuade him to deny his faith.

(*In rage walks away.*)

WILLMORE (*said softly to Hellena*). Her name, her name, dear boy!

HELLENA. Have you forgot it, sir?

WILLMORE (*aside*). Oh, I perceive he's not to know I am a stranger to his lady.—Yes, yes, I do know, but I have forgot the—

(*Angellica turns.*)

By heaven, such early confidence I never saw.

ANGELLICA.
Did I not charge you with this mistress, sir?

Which you denied, though I beheld your perjury.
This little generosity of thine has rendered back my
   heart.   (*Walks away.*)

WILLMORE (*to Hellena*). So, you have made sweet work here, my little mischief. Look your lady be kind and good-natured now, or I shall have but a cursed bargain on't.

(*Angellica turns toward them.*)

—The rogue's bred up to mischief;
Art thou so great a fool to credit him?

ANGELLICA.
Yes, I do, and you in vain impose upon me.
Come hither, boy. Is not this he you spake of?

HELLENA. I think it is. I cannot swear, but I vow he has just such another lying lover's look.

(*Hellena looks in his face; he gazes on her.*)

WILLMORE (*aside*).
Ha! Do I not know that face?
By heaven, my little gypsy! What a dull dog was I:
Had I but looked that way I'd known her.
Are all my hopes of a new woman banished?—
Egad, if I do not fit thee for this, hang me.—
[*To Angellica.*] Madam, I have found out the plot.

HELLENA [*aside*]. Oh lord, what does he say? Am I discovered now?

WILLMORE. Do you see this young spark here?

HELLENA [*aside*]. He'll tell her who I am.

WILLMORE. Who do you think this is?

HELLENA [*aside*]. Ay, ay, he does know me.—
Nay, dear captain, I am undone if you discover me.

WILLMORE. Nay, nay, no cogging;[145] she shall know what a precious mistress I have.

HELLENA. Will you be such a devil?

WILLMORE. Nay, nay, I'll teach you to spoil sport you will not make.—This small ambassador comes not from a person of quality, as you imagine and he says, but from a very errant gypsy: the talking'st, prating'st, canting'st little animal thou ever saw'st.

ANGELLICA. What news you tell me, that's the thing I mean.

HELLENA (*aside*). Would I were well off the place! If ever I go a-captain-hunting again—

WILLMORE. Mean that thing? That gypsy thing? Thou mayst as well be jealous of thy monkey or parrot as of her. A German motion[146] were worth a dozen of her, and a dream were a better enjoyment—a creature of a constitution fitter for heaven than man.

HELLENA (*aside*). Though I'm sure he lies, yet this vexes me.

ANGELLICA. You are mistaken: she's a Spanish woman made up of no such dull materials.

WILLMORE. Materials? Egad, and she be made of any that will either dispense or admit of love, I'll be bound to continence.

HELLENA (*aside to him*). Unreasonable man, do you think so?

144**en passant** in passing   145**cogging** fawning   146**motion** puppet show

WILLMORE. You may return, my little brazen head, and tell your lady, that till she be handsome enough to be beloved, or I dull enough to be religious, there will be small hopes of me.

ANGELLICA. Did you not promise, then, to marry her?

WILLMORE. Not I, by heaven.

ANGELLICA. You cannot undeceive my fears and torments, till you have vowed you will not marry her.

HELLENA (*aside*). If he swears that, he'll be revenged on me indeed for all my rogueries.

ANGELLICA. I know what arguments you'll bring against me: fortune and honor.

WILLMORE. Honor! I tell you, I hate it in your sex; and those that fancy themselves possessed of that foppery are the most impertinently troublesome of all womankind, and will transgress nine commandments to keep one. And to satisfy your jealousy, I swear—

HELLENA (*aside to him*). Oh, no swearing, dear captain.

WILLMORE. If it were possible I should ever be inclined to marry, it should be some kind young sinner: one that has generosity enough to give a favor handsomely to one that can ask it discreetly, one that has wit enough to manage an intrigue of love. Oh, how civil such a wench is to a man that does her the honor to marry her.

ANGELLICA. By heaven, there's no faith in anything he says.

(*Enter Sebastian.*)

SEBASTIAN. Madam, Don Antonio—

ANGELLICA. Come hither.

HELLENA [*aside*]. Ha! Antonio! He may be coming hither, and he'll certainly discover me. I'll therefore retire without a ceremony.   (*Exit Hellena.*)

ANGELLICA. I'll see him. Get my coach ready.

SEBASTIAN. It waits you, madam.

WILLMORE [*aside*]. This is lucky.—What, madam, now I may be gone and leave you to the enjoyment of my rival?

ANGELLICA.
Dull man, that canst not see how ill, how poor,
That false dissimulation looks. Be gone,
And never let me see thy cozening face again,
Lest I relapse and kill thee.

WILLMORE. Yes, you can spare me now. Farewell, till you're in better humor.—[*Aside.*] I'm glad of this release.
Now for my gypsy:
For though to worse we change, yet still we find
New joys, new charms, in a new miss that's kind.

(*Exit Willmore.*)

ANGELLICA.
He's gone, and in this ague[147] of my soul
The shivering fit returns.
Oh, with what willing haste he took his leave,
As if the longed-for minute were arrived

Of some blest assignation.
In vain I have consulted all my charms,
In vain this beauty prized, in vain believed
My eyes could kindle any lasting fires;
I had forgot my name, my infamy,
And the reproach that honor lays on those
That dare pretend a sober passion here.
Nice[148] reputation, though it leave behind
More virtues than inhabit where that dwells,
Yet that once gone, those virtues shine no more.
Then since I am not fit to be beloved,
I am resolved to think on a revenge
On him that soothed[149] me thus to my undoing.

(*Exeunt.*)

SCENE 3

(*A street. Enter Florinda and Valeria in habits different from what they have been seen in.*)

FLORINDA. We're happily escaped, and yet I tremble still.

VALERIA. A lover, and fear? Why, I am but half an one, and yet I have courage for any attempt. Would Hellena were here: I would fain have had her as deep in this mischief as we; she'll fare but ill else, I doubt.

FLORINDA. She pretended a visit to the Augustine nuns; but I believe some other design carried her out; pray heaven we light on her. Prithee, what didst do with Callis?

VALERIA. When I saw no reason would do good on her, I followed her into the wardrobe, and as she was looking for something in a great chest, I toppled her in by the heels, snatched the key of the apartment where you were confined, locked her in, and left her bawling for help.

FLORINDA. 'Tis well you resolve to follow my fortunes, for thou darest never appear at home again after such an action.

VALERIA. That's according as the young stranger and I shall agree. But to our business. I delivered your note to Belvile when I got out under pretense of going to mass. I found him at his lodging, and believe me it came seasonably, for never was man in so desperate a condition. I told him of your resolution of making your escape today if your brother would be absent long enough to permit you; if not, to die rather than be Antonio's.

FLORINDA. Thou should'st have told him I was confined to my chamber upon my brother's suspicion that the business on the Molo was a plot laid between him and I.

VALERIA. I said all this, and told him your brother was now gone to his devotion; and he resolves to visit every church till he find him, and not only undeceive him in that, but caress him so as shall delay his return home.

FLORINDA. Oh heavens! He's here, and Belvile with him, too.

(*They put on their vizards.*)

(*Enter Don Pedro, Belvile, Willmore; Belvile and Don Pedro seeming in serious discourse.*)

VALERIA. Walk boldly by them, and I'll come at a distance, lest he suspect us.

(*She walks by them and looks back on them.*)

WILLMORE. Ha! A woman, and of excellent mien!

PEDRO. She throws a kind look back on you.

WILLMORE. Death, 'tis a likely wench, and that kind look shall not be cast away. I'll follow her.

BELVILE. Prithee do not.

WILLMORE. Do not? By heavens, to the antipodies,[150] with such an invitation.

(*She goes out, and Willmore follows her.*)

BELVILE. 'Tis a mad fellow for a wench.

(*Enter Frederick.*)

FREDERICK. Oh, colonel, such news!

BELVILE. Prithee what?

FREDERICK. News that will make you laugh in spite of fortune.

BELVILE. What, Blunt has had some damned trick put upon him? Cheated, banged, or clapped?[151]

FREDERICK. Cheated, sir, rarely cheated of all but his shirt and drawers; the unconscionable whore too turned him out before consummation, so that, traversing the streets at midnight, the watch found him in this *fresco* and conducted him home. By heaven, 'tis such a sight, and yet I durst as well been hanged as laughed at him or pity him: He beats all that do but ask him a question, and is in such an humor.

PEDRO. Who is't has met with this ill usage, sir?

BELVILE. A friend of ours whom you must see for mirth's sake.—(*Aside.*) I'll employ him to give Florinda time for an escape.

PEDRO. What is he?

BELVILE. A young countryman of ours, one that has been educated at so plentiful a rate he yet ne'er knew the want of money; and 'twill be a great jest to see how simply he'll look without it. For my part, I'll lend him none: And the rogue know not how to put on a borrowing face and ask first, I'll let him see how good 'tis to play our parts whilst I play his. Prithee, Fred, do you go home and keep him in that posture till we come.   (*Exeunt.*)

(*Enter Florinda from the farther end of the scene, looking behind her.*)

FLORINDA. I am followed still. Ha! My brother too advancing this way! Good heavens defend me from being seen by him! (*She goes off.*)

(*Enter Willmore, and after him Valeria, at a little distance.*)

WILLMORE. Ah, there she sails! She looks back as she were willing to be boarded; I'll warrant her prize.[152]

(*He goes out, Valeria following.*)

(*Enter Hellena, just as he goes out, with a page.*)

HELLENA. Ha, is not that my captain that has a woman in chase? 'Tis not Angellica.—Boy, follow those people at a distance, and bring me an account where they go in. (*Exit Page.*)—I'll find his haunts, and plague him everywhere. Ha! My brother!

(*Belvile, Willmore, Pedro cross the stage; Hellena runs off.*)

SCENE 4

(*Scene changes to another street. Enter Florinda.*)

FLORINDA.
What shall I do? My brother now pursues me.
Will no kind power protect me from his tyranny?
Ha! Here's a door open; I'll venture in, since nothing can be worse than to fall into his hands. My life and honor are at stake, and my necessity has no choice.

(*She goes in.*)

(*Enter Valeria, Hellena's Page peeping after Florinda.*)

PAGE. Here she went in; I shall remember this house.

(*Exit Boy.*)

VALERIA. This is Belvile's lodging; she's gone in as readily as if she knew it. Ha! Here's that mad fellow again; I dare not venture in. I'll watch my opportunity. (*Goes aside.*)

(*Enter Willmore, gazing about him.*)

WILLMORE. I have lost her hereabouts. Pox on't, she must not 'scape me so.   (*Goes out.*)

SCENE 5

(*Scene changes to Blunt's chamber, discovers him sitting on a couch in his shirt and drawers, reading.*)

BLUNT. So, now my mind's a little at peace, since I have resolved revenge. A pox on this tailor, though, for not bringing home the clothes I bespoke. And a pox of all poor cavaliers: A man can never keep a spare suit for 'em, and I shall have these rogues come in and find me naked,

---

[150]**antipodies** Antipodes, on the opposite side of the earth
[151]**clapped** (1) beaten; or (2) infected with a venereal disease

[152]**warrant her prize** consider her worthy of pursuing

and then I'm undone. But I'm resolved to arm myself: The rascals shall not insult over me too much. (*Puts on an old rusty sword and buff belt.*) Now, how like a morris dancer[153] I am equipped! A fine ladylike whore to cheat me thus without affording me a kindness for my money! A pox light on her, I shall never be reconciled to the sex more; she has made me as faithless as a physician, as uncharitable as a churchman, and as ill-natured as a poet. Oh, how I'll use all womankind hereafter! What would I give to have one of 'em within my reach now! Any mortal thing in petticoats, kind fortune, send me, and I'll forgive thy last night's malice.—Here's a cursed book, too— a warning to all young travelers—that can instruct me how to prevent such mischiefs now 'tis too late. Well, 'tis a rare convenient thing to read a little now and then, as well as hawk and hunt.

(*Sits down again and reads.*)

(*Enter to him Florinda.*)

FLORINDA. This house is haunted, sure: 'Tis well furnished, and no living thing inhabits it. Ha! A man! Heavens, how he's attired! Sure 'tis some rope dancer, or fencing master. I tremble now for fear, and yet I must venture now to speak to him.—Sir, if I may not interrupt your meditations—

(*He starts up and gazes.*)

BLUNT. Ha, what's here? Are my wishes granted? And is not that a she creature? 'Adsheartlikins, 'tis.—What wretched thing art thou, ha?

FLORINDA. Charitable sir, you've told yourself already what I am: a very wretched maid, forced by a strange unlucky accident to seek a safety here, and must be ruined if you do not grant it.

BLUNT. Ruined! Is there any ruin so inevitable as that which now threatens thee? Dost thou know, miserable woman, into what den of mischiefs thou art fallen; what abyss of confusion, ha? Dost not see something in my looks that frights thy guilty soul, and makes thee wish to change that shape of woman for any humble animal, or devil? For those were safer for thee, and less mischievous.

FLORINDA. Alas, what mean you, sir? I must confess, your looks have something in 'em makes me fear, but I beseech you, as you seem a gentleman, pity a harmless virgin that takes your house for sanctuary.

BLUNT. Talk on, talk on; and weep, too, till my faith return. Do, flatter me out of my senses again. A harmless virgin with a pox; as much one as t'other, 'adsheartlikins. Why, what the devil, can I not be safe in my house for you, not in my chamber? Nay, not even being naked too cannot secure me? This is an impudence greater than has invaded me yet. Come, no resistance.   (*Pulls her rudely.*)

FLORINDA. Dare you be so cruel?

BLUNT. Cruel? 'Adsheartlikins, as a galley slave, or a Spanish whore. Cruel? Yes, I will kiss and beat thee all over, kiss and see thee all over; thou shalt lie with me too, not that I care for the enjoyment, but to let thee see I have ta'en deliberated malice to thee, and will be revenged on one whore for the sins of another. I will smile and deceive thee; flatter thee, and beat thee; embrace thee and rob thee, as she did me; fawn on thee, and strip thee stark naked; then hang thee out at my window by the heels, with a paper of scurvy verses fastened to thy breast in praise of damnable women. Come, come, along.

FLORINDA. Alas, sir, must I be sacrificed for the crimes of the most infamous of my sex? I never understood the sins you name.

BLUNT. Do, persuade the fool you love him, or that one of you can be just or honest; tell me I was not an easy coxcomb, or any strange impossible tale: It will be believed sooner than thy false showers or protestations. A generation of damned hypocrites! To flatter my very clothes from my back! Dissembling witches! Are these the returns you make an honest gentleman that trusts, believes, and loves you? But if I be not even with you—Come along, or I shall—   (*Pulls her again.*)

(*Enter Frederick.*)

FREDERICK. Ha, what's here to do?

BLUNT. 'Adsheartlikins, Fred, I am glad thou art come, to be a witness of my dire revenge.

FREDERICK. What's this, a person of quality too, who is upon the ramble[154] to supply the defects of some grave impotent husband?

BLUNT. No, this has another pretense: Some very unfortunate accident brought her hither, to save a life pursued by I know not who or why, and forced to take sanctuary here at fool's haven. 'Adsheartlikins, to me of all mankind for protection? Is the ass to be cajoled again, think ye? No, young one, no prayers or tears shall mitigate my rage; therefore prepare for both my pleasures of enjoyment and revenge. For I am resolved to make up my loss here on thy body: I'll take it out in kindness and in beating.

FREDERICK. Now, mistress of mine, what do you think of this?

FLORINDA. I think he will not, dares not be so barbarous.

FREDERICK. Have a care, Blunt, she fetched a deep sigh; she is enamored with thy shirt and drawers. She'll strip thee even of that; there are of her calling such unconscionable baggages and such dexterous thieves, they'll flea[155] a man and he shall ne'er miss his skin till he feels the cold. There was a countryman of ours robbed of a row of teeth whilst he was a-sleeping, which the jilt made him buy again when he waked. You see, lady, how little reason we have to trust you.

---

[153]**morris dancer** fantastically attired dancer

[154]**upon the ramble** wandering   [155]**flea** flay

BLUNT. 'Adsheartlikins, why this is most abominable!

FLORINDA. Some such devils there may be, but by all that's holy, I am none such. I entered here to save a life in danger.

BLUNT. For no goodness, I'll warrant her.

FREDERICK. Faith, damsel, you had e'en confessed the plain truth, for we are fellows not to be caught twice in the same trap. Look on that wreck: a tight vessel when he set out of haven, well trimmed and laden. And see how a female picaroon of this island of rogues has shattered him, and canst thou hope for any mercy?

BLUNT. No, no, gentlewoman, come along; 'adsheartlikins, we must be better acquainted.—We'll both lie with her, and then let me along to bang her.

FREDERICK. I'm ready to serve you in matters of revenge that has a double pleasure in't.

BLUNT. Well said.—You hear, little one, how you are condemned by public vote to the bed within; there's no resisting your destiny, sweetheart.

(*Pulls her.*)

FLORINDA. Stay, sir. I have seen you with Belvile, an English cavalier. For his sake, use me kindly. You know him, sir.

BLUNT. Belvile? Why yes, sweeting, we do know Belvile, and wish he were with us now. He's a cormorant at whore and bacon:[156] He'd have a limb or two of thee, my virgin pullet. But 'tis no matter; we'll leave him the bones to pick.

FLORINDA. Sir, if you have any esteem for that Belvile, I conjure you to treat me with more gentleness; he'll thank you for the justice.

FREDERICK. Hark'ee, Blunt, I doubt we are mistaken in this matter.

FLORINDA. Sir, if you find me not worth Belvile's care, use me as you please. And that you may think I merit better treatment than you threaten, pray take this present.

(*Gives him a ring; he looks on it.*)

BLUNT. Hum, a diamond! Why, 'tis a wonderful virtue now that lies in this ring, a mollifying virtue. 'Adsheartlikins, there's more persuasive rhetoric in't than all her sex can utter.

FREDERICK. I begin to suspect something, and 'twould anger us vilely to be trussed up for a rape upon a maid of quality, when we only believe we ruffle a harlot.

BLUNT. Thou art a credulous fellow, but 'adsheartlikins, I have no faith yet. Why, my saint prattled as parlously as this does; she gave me a bracelet, too, a devil on her! But I sent my man to sell it today for necessaries, and it proved as counterfeit as her vows of love.

FREDERICK. However, let it reprieve her till we see Belvile.

BLUNT. That's hard, yet I will grant it.

(*Enter a Servant.*)

[156]**cormorant . . . bacon** glutton for sex

SERVANT. Oh, sir, the colonel is just come in with his new friend and a Spaniard of quality, and talks of having you to dinner with 'em.

BLUNT. 'Adsheartlikins, I'm undone! I would not see 'em for the world. Hark'ee, Fred, lock up the wench in your chamber.

FREDERICK. Fear nothing, madam: Whate'er he threatens, you are safe whilst in my hands.

(*Exeunt Frederick and Florinda.*)

BLUNT. And sirrah, upon your life, say I am not at home, or that I'm asleep, or—or—anything. Away; I'll prevent their coming this way.

(*Locks the door, and exeunt.*)

ACT 5

(*Blunt's chamber. After a great knocking as at his chamber door, enter Blunt softly crossing the stage, in his shirt and drawers as before.*)

[voices] (*call within*). Ned! Ned Blunt! Ned Blunt!

BLUNT. The rogues are up in arms. 'Adsheartlikins, this villainous Frederick has betrayed me: They have heard of my blessed fortune.

[voices] (*and knocking within*). Ned Blunt! Ned! Ned!

BELVILE [*within*]. Why, he's dead, sir, without dispute dead; he has not been seen today. Let's break open the door. Here, boy—

BLUNT. Ha, break open the door? 'Adsheartlikins, that mad fellow will be as good as his word.

BELVILE [*within*]. Boy, bring something to force the door.

(*A great noise within, at the door again.*)

BLUNT. So, now must I speak in my own defense; I'll try what rhetoric will do.—Hold, hold! What do you mean, gentlemen, what do you mean?

BELVILE (*within*). Oh, rogue, art alive? Prithee open the door and convince us.

BLUNT. Yes, I am alive, gentlemen, but at present a little busy.

BELVILE (*within*). How, Blunt grown a man of business? Come, come, open and let's see this miracle.

BLUNT. No, no, no, no, gentlemen, 'tis no great business. But—I am—at—my devotion. 'Adsheartlikins, will you not allow a man time to pray?

BELVILE (*within*). Turned religious? A greater wonder than the first! Therefore open quickly, or we shall unhinge, we shall.

BLUNT [*aside*]. This won't do.—Why hark'ee, colonel, to tell you the truth, I am about a necessary affair of life: I have a wench with me. You apprehend me?—The devil's in't if they be so uncivil as to disturb me now.

WILLMORE [*within*]. How, a wench? Nay then, we must enter and partake. No resistance. Unless it be your lady of quality, and then we'll keep our distance.

BLUNT. So, the business is out.

WILLMORE [*within*]. Come, come, lend's more hands to the door. Now heave, all together. (*Breaks open the door.*) So, well done, my boys.

(*Enter Belvile [and his Page], Willmore, Frederick, and Pedro. Blunt looks simply,[157] they all laugh at him; he lays his hand on his sword, and comes up to Willmore.*)

BLUNT. Hark'ee, sir, laugh out your laugh quickly, d'ye hear, and be gone. I shall spoil your sport else, 'adsheartlikins, sir. I shall. The jest has been carried on too long.— (*Aside.*) A plague upon my tailor!

WILLMORE. 'Sdeath, how the whore has dressed him! Faith, sir, I'm sorry.

BLUNT. Are you so, sir? Keep't to yourself then, sir, I advise you, d'ye hear, for I can as little endure your pity as his mirth.

(*Lays his hand on's sword.*)

BELVILE. Indeed, Willmore, thou wert a little too rough with Ned Blunt's mistress. Call a person of quality whore, and one so young, so handsome, and so eloquent? Ha, ha, he.

BLUNT. Hark'ee, sir, you know me, and know I can be angry. Have a care, for 'adsheartlikins, I can fight, too, I can, sir. Do you mark me? No more.

BELVILE. Why so peevish, good Ned? Some disappointments, I'll warrant. What, did the jealous count, her husband, return just in the nick?

BLUNT. Or the devil, sir. (*They laugh.*) D'ye laugh? Look ye settle me a good sober countenance, and that quickly, too, or you shall know Ned Blunt is not—

BELVILE. Not everybody, we know that.

BLUNT. Not an ass to be laughed at, sir.

WILLMORE. Unconscionable sinner! To bring a lover so near his happiness—a vigorous passionate lover—and then not only cheat him of his movables, but his very desires, too.

BELVILE. Ah, sir, a mistress is a trifle with Blunt; he'll have a dozen the next time he looks abroad. His eyes have charms not to be resisted; there needs no more than to expose that taking person to the view of the fair, and he leads 'em all in triumph.

PEDRO. Sir, though I'm a stranger to you, I am ashamed at the rudeness of my nation; and could you learn who did it, would assist you to make an example of 'em.

BLUNT. Why ay, there's one speaks sense now, and handsomely. And let me tell you, gentlemen, I should not have showed myself like a jack pudding[158] thus to have made you mirth, but that I have revenge within my power. For know, I have got into my possession a female, who had better have fallen under any curse than the ruin I design her. 'Adsheartlikins, she assaulted me here in my own lodgings, and had doubtless committed a rape upon me, had not this sword defended me.

FREDERICK. I know not that, but o' my conscience thou had ravished her, had she not redeemed herself with a ring. Let's see't, Blunt.

(*Blunt shows the ring.*)

BELVILE [*aside*]. Ha! The ring I gave Florinda when we exchanged our vows!—Hark'ee, Blunt—

(*Goes to whisper to him.*)

WILLMORE. No whispering, good colonel, there's a woman in the case. No whispering.

BELVILE [*aside to Blunt*]. Hark'ee, fool, be advised, and conceal both the ring and the story for your reputation's sake. Do not let people know what despised cullies[159] we English are; to be cheated and abused by one whore, and another rather bribe thee than be kind to thee, is an infamy to our nation.

WILLMORE. Come, come, where's the wench? We'll see her; let her be what she will, we'll see her.

PEDRO. Ay, ay, let us see her. I can soon discover whether she be of quality, or for your diversion.

BLUNT. She's in Fred's custody.

WILLMORE. Come, come, the key—

(*To Frederick, who gives him the key; they are going.*)

BELVILE [*aside*]. Death, what shall I do?—Stay, gentlemen.— [*Aside.*] Yet if I hinder 'em, I shall discover all.—Hold, let's go one at once.[160] Give me the key.

WILLMORE. Nay, hold there, colonel, I'll go first.

FREDERICK. Nay, no dispute, Ned and I have the propriety of her.

WILLMORE. Damn propriety! Then we'll draw cuts. (*Belvile goes to whisper [to] Willmore.*) Nay, no corruption, good colonel. Come, the longest sword carries her.

(*They all draw, forgetting Don Pedro, being a Spaniard, had the longest.*)

BLUNT. I yield up my interest to you, gentlemen, and that will be revenge sufficient.

WILLMORE (*to Pedro*). The wench is yours.—[*Aside.*] Pox of his Toledo,[161] I had forgot that.

FREDERICK. Come, sir, I'll conduct you to the lady.

(*Exeunt Frederick and Pedro.*)

BELVILE (*aside*). To hinder him will certainly discover her.— Dost know, dull beast, what mischief thou hast done?

(*Willmore walking up and down, out of humor.*)

---

[157]**simply** foolishly   [158]**jack pudding** clown   [159]**cullies** dupes   [160]**one at once** one after the other   [161]**Toledo** sword made in Toledo

WILLMORE. Ay, ay, to trust our fortune to lots! A devil on't, 'twas madness, that's the truth on't.

BELVILE. Oh, intolerable sot—

(*Enter Florinda running, masked, Pedro after her; Willmore gazing round her.*)

FLORINDA (*aside*). Good heaven defend me from discovery!

PEDRO. 'Tis but in vain to fly me; you're fallen to my lot.

BELVILE [*aside*]. Sure she's undiscovered yet, but now I fear there is no way to bring her off.

WILLMORE [*aside*]. Why, what a pox, is not this my woman, the same I followed but now?

(*Pedro talking to Florinda, who walks up and down.*)

PEDRO. As if I did not know ye, and your business here.

FLORINDA (*aside*). Good heaven, I fear he does indeed!

PEDRO. Come, pray be kind; I know you meant to be so when you entered here, for these are proper gentlemen.

WILLMORE. But sir, perhaps the lady will not be imposed upon: She'll choose her man.

PEDRO. I am better bred than not to leave her choice free.

(*Enter Valeria, and is surprised at sight of Don Pedro.*)

VALERIA (*aside*). Don Pedro here! There's no avoiding him.

FLORINDA (*aside*). Valeria! Then I'm undone.

VALERIA (*to Pedro, running to him*). Oh, I have found you, sir! The strangest accident—if I had breath—to tell it.

PEDRO. Speak! Is Florinda safe? Hellena well?

VALERIA. Ay, ay, sir. Florinda is safe.—[*Aside.*] From any fears of you.

PEDRO. Why, where's Florinda? Speak!

VALERIA. Ay, where indeed, sir; I wish I could inform you. But to hold you no longer in doubt—

FLORINDA (*aside*). Oh, what will she say?

VALERIA. She's fled away in the habit—of one of her pages, sir. But Callis thinks you may retrieve her yet, if you make haste away. She'll tell you, sir, the rest.—(*Aside.*) If you can find her out.

PEDRO. Dishonorable girl, she has undone my aim.—[*To Belvile.*] Sir, you see my necessity of leaving you, and I hope you'll pardon it. My sister, I know, will make her flight to you; and if she do, I shall expect she should be rendered back.

BELVILE. I shall consult my love and honor, sir.

(*Exit Pedro.*)

FLORINDA (*to Valeria*). My dear preserver, let me embrace thee.

WILLMORE. What the devil's all this?

BLUNT. Mystery, by this light.

VALERIA. Come, come, make haste and get yourselves married quickly, for your brother will return again.

BELVILE. I'm so surprised with fears and joys, so amazed to find you here in safety, I can scarce persuade my heart into a faith of what I see.

WILLMORE. Hark'ee, colonel, is this that mistress who has cost you so many sighs, and me so many quarrels with you?

BELVILE. It is.—[*To Florinda.*] Pray give him the honor of your hand.

WILLMORE. Thus it must be received, then. (*Kneels and kisses her hand.*) And with it give your pardon, too.

FLORINDA. The friend to Belvile may command me anything.

WILLMORE (*aside*). Death, would I might; 'tis a surprising beauty.

BELVILE. Boy, run and fetch a father[162] instantly.

(*Exit Boy.*)

FREDERICK. So, now do I stand like a dog, and have not a syllable to plead my own cause with. By this hand, madam, I was never thoroughly confounded before, nor shall I ever more dare look up with confidence, till you are pleased to pardon me.

FLORINDA. Sir, I'll be reconciled to you on one condition: that you'll follow the example of your friend in marrying a maid that does not hate you, and whose fortune, I believe, will not be unwelcome to you.

FREDERICK. Madam, had I no inclinations that way, I should obey your kind commands.

BELVILE. Who, Fred marry? He has so few inclinations for womankind that had he been possessed of paradise he might have continued there to this day, if no crime but love could have disinherited him.

FREDERICK. Oh, I do not use to boast of my intrigues.

BELVILE. Boast! Why, thou dost nothing but boast. And I dare swear, wert thou as innocent from the sin of the grape as thou art from the apple, thou might'st yet claim that right in Eden which our first parents lost by too much loving.

FREDERICK. I wish this lady would think me so modest a man.

VALERIA. She would be sorry then, and not like you half so well. And I should be loath to break my word with you, which was, that if your friend and mine agreed, it should be a match between you and I.   (*She gives him her hand.*)

FREDERICK. Bear witness, colonel, 'tis a bargain.

(*Kisses her hand.*)

BLUNT (*to Florinda*). I have a pardon to beg, too; but 'ads-heartlikins, I am so out of countenance that I'm a dog if I can say anything to purpose.

FLORINDA. Sir, I heartily forgive you all.

BLUNT. That's nobly said, sweet lady.—Belvile, prithee present her her ring again, for I find I have not courage to approach her myself.

(*Gives him the ring; he gives it to Florinda.*)

(*Enter Boy.*)

---

[162]**father** priest

BOY. Sir, I have brought the father that you sent for.

[Exit Boy.]

BELVILE. 'Tis well. And now, my dear Florinda, let's fly to complete that mighty joy we have so long wished and signed for.—Come, Fred, you'll follow?

FREDERICK. Your example, sir, 'twas ever my ambition in war, and must be so in love.

WILLMORE. And must not I see this juggling[163] knot tied?

BELVILE. No, thou shalt do us better service and be our guard, lest Don Pedro's sudden return interrupt the ceremony.

WILLMORE. Content; I'll secure this pass.

(Exeunt Belvile, Florinda, Frederick, and Valeria.)

(Enter Boy.)

BOY *(to Willmore)*. Sir, there's a lady without would speak to you.

WILLMORE. Conduct her in; I dare not quit my post.

BOY *[to Blunt]*. And sir, your tailor waits you in your chamber.

BLUNT. Some comfort yet: I shall not dance naked at the wedding.

(Exeunt Blunt and Boy.)

(Enter again the Boy, conducting in Angellica in a masking habit and a vizard. Willmore runs to her.)

WILLMORE *[aside]*. This can be none but my pretty gypsy.— Oh, I see you can follow as well as fly. Come, confess thyself the most malicious devil in nature; you think you have done my business with Angellica—

ANGELLICA. Stand off, base villain!

(She draws a pistol and holds it to his breast.)

WILLMORE. Ha, 'tis not she! Who art thou, and what's thy business?

ANGELLICA. One thou hast injured, and who comes to kill thee for't.

WILLMORE. What the devil canst thou mean?

ANGELLICA. By all my hopes to kill thee—

(Holds still the pistol to his breast; he going back, she following still.)

WILLMORE. Prithee, on what acquaintance? For I know thee not.

ANGELLICA.
Behold this face so lost to thy remembrance,

(Pulls off her vizard.)

And then call all thy sins about thy soul,
And let 'em die with thee.

WILLMORE. Angellica!

ANGELLICA.
Yes, traitor!
Does not thy guilty blood run shivering through thy
    veins?
Hast thou no horror at this sight, that tells thee
Thou hast not long to boast thy shameful conquest?

WILLMORE. Faith, no, child. My blood keeps its old ebbs and flows still, and that usual heat too, that could oblige thee with a kindness, had I but opportunity.

ANGELLICA. Devil! Dost wanton with my pain? Have at thy heart!

WILLMORE. Hold, dear virago![164] Hold thy hand a little; I am not now at leisure to be killed. Hold and hear me.— *(Aside.)* Death, I think she's in earnest.

ANGELLICA *(aside, turning from him)*.
Oh, if I take not heed,
My coward heart will leave me to his mercy.—
What have you, sir, to say?—But should I hear thee,
Thoud'st talk away all that is brave about me,
And I have vowed thy death by all that's sacred.

(Follows him with the pistol to his breast.)

WILLMORE.
Why then, there's an end of a proper handsome fellow,
That might 'a lived to have done good service yet.
That's all I can say to't.

ANGELLICA *(pausingly)*.
Yet—I would give thee time for—penitence.

WILLMORE.
Faith, child, I thank God I have ever took
Care to lead a good, sober, hopeful life, and am of a religion
That teaches me to believe I shall depart in peace.

ANGELLICA.
So will the devil! Tell me,
How many poor believing fools thou hast undone?
How many hearts thou hast betrayed to ruin?
Yet these are little mischiefs to the ills
Thou'st taught mine to commit: Thou'st taught it love.

WILLMORE.
Egad, 'twas shrewdly hurt the while.

ANGELLICA.
Love, that has robbed it of its unconcern,
Of all that pride that taught me how to value it.
And in its room
A mean submissive passion was conveyed,
That made me humbly bow, which I ne'er did
To anything but heaven.
Thou, perjured man, didst this; and with thy oaths,
Which on thy knees thou didst devoutly make,
Softened my yielding heart, and then I was a slave.
Yet still had been content to've worn my chains,
Worn 'em with vanity and joy forever,
Hadst thou not broke those vows that put them on.

---

[163]**juggling** deceptive

[164]**virago** dominating woman

'Twas then I was undone.

(*All this while follows him with the pistol to his breast.*)

WILLMORE. Broke my vows? Why, where hast thou lived? Amongst the gods? For I never heard of mortal man that has not broke a thousand vows.

ANGELLICA. Oh, impudence!

WILLMORE. Angellica, that beauty has been too long tempting, not to have made a thousand lovers languish; who, in the amorous fever, no doubt have sworn like me. Did they all die in that faith, still adoring? I do not think they did.

ANGELLICA. No, faithless man; had I repaid their vows, as I did thine, I would have killed the ingrateful that had abandoned me.

WILLMORE. This old general has quite spoiled thee: Nothing makes a woman so vain as being flattered. Your old lover ever supplies the defects of age with intolerable dotage, vast charge, and that which you call constancy; and attributing all this to your own merits, you domineer, and throw your favors in's teeth, upbraiding him still with the defects of age, and cuckold him as often as he deceives your expectations. But the gay, young, brisk lover, that brings his equal fires, and can give you dart for dart, you'll find will be as nice as you sometimes.

ANGELLICA.
All this thou'st made me know, for which I hate thee.
Had I remained in innocent security,
I should have thought all men were born my slaves,
And worn my power like lightning in my eyes,
To have destroyed at pleasure when offended.
But when love held the mirror, the undeceiving glass
Reflected all the weakness of my soul, and made me know
My richest treasure being lost, my honor,
All the remaining spoil could not be worth
The conqueror's care or value.
Oh, how I feel, like a long-worshiped idol,
Discovering all the cheat.
Would not the incense and rich sacrifice
Which blind devotion offered at my altars
Have fallen to thee?
Why wouldst thou then destroy my fancied power?

WILLMORE.
By heaven, thou'rt brave, and I admire thee strangely.
I wish I were that dull, that constant thing
Which thou wouldst have, and nature never meant me.
I must, like cheerful birds, sing in all groves,
And perch on every bough,
Billing the next kind she that flies to meet me;
Yet, after all, could build my nest with thee,
Thither repairing when I'd loved my round,
And still reserve a tributary flame.
To gain your credit, I'll pay you back your charity,
And be obliged for nothing but for love.

(*Offers her a purse of gold.*)

ANGELLICA.
Oh, that thou wert in earnest!
So mean a thought of me
Would turn my rage to scorn, and I should pity thee,
And give thee leave to live;
Which for the public safety of our sex,
And my own private injuries, I dare not do.
Prepare—(*Follows still, as before.*)
I will no more be tempted with replies.

WILLMORE. Sure—

ANGELLICA. Another word will damn thee! I've heard thee talk too long.

(*She follows him with the pistol ready to shoot; he retires, still amazed. Enter Don Antonio, his arm in a scarf, and lays hold on the pistol.*)

ANTONIO. Ha! Angellica!

ANGELLICA. Antonio! What devil brought thee hither?

ANTONIO.
Love and curiosity, seeing your coach at door.
Let me disarm you of this unbecoming instrument of death.

(*Takes away the pistol.*)

Amongst the number of your slaves was there not one worthy the honor to have fought your quarrel?—
[*To Willmore.*] Who are you, sir, that are so very wretched
To merit death from her?

WILLMORE. One, sir, that could have made a better end of an amorous quarrel without you, than with you.

ANTONIO. Sure 'tis some rival. Ha! The very man took down her picture yesterday; the very same that set on me last night! Blessed opportunity—

(*Offers to shoot him.*)

ANGELLICA. Hold, you're mistaken, sir.

ANTONIO. By heaven, the very same!—Sir, what pretensions have you to this lady?

WILLMORE. Sir, I do not use to be examined, and am ill at all disputes but this—

(*Draws; Antonio offers to shoot.*)

ANGELLICA (*to Willmore*).
Oh, hold! You see he's armed with certain death.
—And you, Antonio, I command you hold,
By all the passion you've so lately vowed me.

(*Enter Don Pedro, sees Antonio, and stays.*)

PEDRO (*aside*). Ha! Antonio! And Angellica!

ANTONIO.
When I refuse obedience to your will,
May you destroy me with your mortal hate.

By all that's holy, I adore you so,
That even my rival, who has charms enough
To make him fall a victim to my jealousy,
Shall live; nay, and have leave to love on still.

PEDRO (*aside*). What's this I hear?

ANGELLICA (*pointing to Willmore*).
Ah thus, 'twas thus he talked, and I believed.
Antonio, yesterday
I'd not have sold my interest in his heart
For all the sword has won and lost in battle.
—But now, to show my utmost of contempt,
I give thee life; which, if thou wouldst preserve,
Live where my eyes may never see thee more.
Live to undo someone whose soul may prove
So bravely constant to revenge my love.

(*Goes out. Antonio follows, but Pedro pulls him back.*)

PEDRO. Antonio, stay.

ANTONIO. Don Pedro!

PEDRO.
What coward fear was that prevented thee
From meeting me this morning on the Molo?

ANTONIO. Meet thee?

PEDRO. Yes, me; I was the man that dared thee to't.

ANTONIO.
Hast thou so often seen me fight in war,
To find no better cause to excuse my absence?
I sent my sword and one to do thee right,
Finding myself uncapable to use a sword.

PEDRO.
But 'twas Florinda's quarrel that we fought,
And you, to show how little you esteemed her,
Sent me your rival, giving him your interest.
But I have found the cause of this affront,
And when I meet you fit for the dispute,
I'll tell you my resentment.

ANTONIO.
I shall be ready, sir, ere long, to do you reason.

(*Exit Antonio.*)

PEDRO. If I could find Florinda, now whilst my anger's high, I think I should be kind, and give her to Belvile in revenge.

WILLMORE. Faith, sir, I know not what you would do, but I believe the priest within has been so kind.

PEDRO. How? My sister married?

WILLMORE. I hope by this time he is, and bedded too, or he has not my longings about him.

PEDRO. Dares he do this? Does he not fear my power?

WILLMORE. Faith, not at all; if you will go in and thank him for the favor he has done your sister, so; if not, sir, my power's greater in this house than yours: I have a damned surly crew here that will keep you till the next tide, and then clap you on board for prize. My ship lies but a league

off the Molo, and we shall show your donship a damned Tramontana[165] rover's trick.

(*Enter Belvile.*)

BELVILE. This rogue's in some new mischief. Ha! Pedro returned!

PEDRO. Colonel Belvile, I hear you have married my sister.

BELVILE. You have heard truth then, sir.

PEDRO. Have I so? Then, sir, I wish you joy.

BELVILE. How?

PEDRO. By this embrace I do, and I am glad on't.

BELVILE. Are you in earnest?

PEDRO.
By our long friendship and my obligations to thee, I am;
The sudden change I'll give you reasons for anon.
Come, lead me to my sister,
That she may know I now approve her choice.

(*Exit Belvile with Pedro.*)

(*Willmore goes to follow them. Enter Hellena, as before in boy's clothes, and pulls him back.*)

WILLMORE. Ha! My gypsy! Now a thousand blessings on thee for this kindness. Egad, child, I was e'en in despair of ever seeing thee again; my friends are all provided for within, each man his kind woman.

HELLENA. Ha! I thought they had served me some such trick!

WILLMORE. And I was e'en resolved to go aboard, and condemn myself to my lone cabin, and the thoughts of thee.

HELLENA. And could you have left me behind? Would you have been so ill natured?

WILLMORE. Why, 'twould have broke my heart, child. But since we are met again, I defy foul weather to part us.

HELLENA. And would you be a faithful friend now, if a maid should trust you?

WILLMORE. For a friend I cannot promise: Thou art of a form so excellent, a face and humor too good for cold dull friendship. I am parlously afraid of being in love, child; and you have not forgotten how severely you have used me?

HELLENA. That's all one; such usage you must still look for: to find out all your haunts, to rail at you to all that love you, till I have made you love only me in your own defense, because nobody else will love you.

WILLMORE. But hast thou no better quality to recommend thyself by?

HELLENA. Faith, none, captain. Why, 'twill be the greater charity to take me for thy mistress. I am a lone child, a kind of orphan lover; and why I should die a maid, and in a captain's hands too, I do not understand.

WILLMORE. Egad, I was never clawed away with broadsides from any female before. Thou hast one virtue I adore—good nature. I hate a coy demure mistress, she's as trou-

---

[165]**Tramontana** in Northern Italy (literally: beyond the mountains)

blesome as a colt; I'll break none. No, give me a mad mistress when mewed, and in flying, one I dare trust upon the wing, that whilst she's kind will come to the lure.[166]

HELLENA. Nay, as kind as you will, good captain, whilst it lasts. But let's lose no time.

WILLMORE. My time's as precious to me as thine can be. Therefore, dear creature, since we are so well agreed, let's retire to my chamber; and if ever thou wert treated with such savory love! Come, my bed's prepared for such a guest all clean and sweet as thy fair self. I love to steal a dish and a bottle with a friend, and hate long graces. Come, let's retire and fall to.

HELLENA. 'Tis but getting my consent, and the business is soon done. Let but old gaffer Hymen[167] and his priest say amen to't, and I dare lay my mother's daughter by as proper a fellow as your father's son, without fear or blushing.

WILLMORE. Hold, hold, no bug words,[168] child. Priest and Hymen? Prithee add a hangman to 'em to make up the consort. No, no, we'll have no vows but love, child, nor witness but the lover: The kind deity enjoins naught but love and enjoy. Hymen and priest wait still upon portion and jointure; love and beauty have their own ceremonies. Marriage is as certain a bane to love as lending money is to friendship. I'll neither ask nor give a vow, though I could be content to turn gypsy and become a left-handed bridegroom to have the pleasure of working that great miracle of making a maid a mother, if you durst venture. 'Tis upse gypsy[169] that, and if I miss I'll lose my labor.

HELLENA. And if you do not lose, what shall I get? A cradle full of noise and mischief, with a pack of repentance at my back? Can you teach me to weave incle[170] to pass my time with? 'Tis upse gypsy that, too.

WILLMORE. I can teach thee to weave a true love's knot better.

HELLENA. So can my dog.

WILLMORE. Well, I see we are both upon our guards, and I see there's no way to conquer good nature but by yielding. Here, give me thy hand: One kiss, and I am thine.

HELLENA. One kiss! How like my page he speaks! I am resolved you shall have none, for asking such a sneaking sum. He that will be satisfied with one kiss will never die of that longing. Good friend single-kiss, is all your talking come to this? A kiss, a caudle![171] Farewell, captain single-kiss.

(Going out; he stays her.)

WILLMORE. Nay, if we part so, let me die like a bird upon a bough, at the sheriff's charge. By heaven, both the Indies shall not buy thee from me. I adore thy humor and will marry thee, and we are so of one humor it must be a bargain. Give me thy hand. (Kisses her hand.) And now let the blind ones, love and fortune, do their worst.

HELLENA. Why, god-a-mercy, captain!

WILLMORE. But hark'ee: the bargain is now made, but is it not fit we should know each other's names, that when we have reason to curse one another hereafter, and people ask me who 'tis I give to the devil, I may at least be able to tell what family you came of?

HELLENA. Good reason, captain; and where I have cause, as I doubt not but I shall have plentiful, that I may know at whom to throw my—blessings, I beseech ye your name.

WILLMORE. I am called Robert the Constant.

HELLENA. A very fine name! Pray was it your faulkner[172] or butler that christened you? Do they not use to whistle when they call you?

WILLMORE. I hope you have a better, that a man may name without crossing himself—you are so merry with mine.

HELLENA. I am called Hellena the Inconstant.

(Enter Pedro, Belvile, Florinda, Frederick, Valeria.)

PEDRO. Ha! Hellena!

FLORINDA. Hellena!

HELLENA. The very same. Ha! My brother! Now, captain, show your love and courage; stand to your arms and defend me bravely, or I am lost forever.

PEDRO. What's this I hear? False girl, how came you hither, and what's your business? Speak!

(Goes roughly to her.)

WILLMORE. Hold off, sir; you have leave to parley[173] only.

(Puts himself between.)

HELLENA. I had e'en as good tell it, as you guess it. Faith, brother, my business is the same with all living creatures of my age: to love and be beloved—and here's the man.

PEDRO. Perfidious maid, hast thou deceived me too; deceived thyself and heaven?

HELLENA.
'Tis time enough to make my peace with that;
Be you but kind, let me alone with heaven.

PEDRO. Belvile, I did not expect this false play from you. Was't not enough you'd gain Florinda, which I pardoned, but your lewd friends too must be enriched with the spoils of a noble family?

BELVILE. Faith, sir, I am as much surprised at this as you can be. Yet, sir, my friends are gentlemen, and ought to be esteemed for their misfortunes, since they have the glory to

---

[166]**whilst . . . lure** will follow her nature and will do what she should(?); while she is happy with him she will be faithful(?) [167]**gaffer Hymen** old Hymen, God of Marriage   [168]**bug words** frightening words, threats   [169]**upse gypsy** like a gypsy   [170]**incle** linen tape   [171]**caudle** warm drink given to the sick

[172]**faulkner** falconer, a trainer of falcons   [173]**parley** speak

suffer with the best of men and kings. 'Tis true, he's a rover of fortune, yet a prince aboard his little wooden world.

PEDRO. What's this to the maintenance of a woman of her birth and quality?

WILLMORE. Faith, sir, I can boast of nothing but a sword which does me right where'er I come, and has defended a worse cause than a woman's; and since I loved her before I either knew her birth or name, I must pursue my resolution and marry her.

PEDRO. And is all your holy intent of becoming a nun debauched into a desire of man?

HELLENA. Why, I have considered the matter, brother, and find the three hundred thousand crowns my uncle left me, and you cannot keep from me, will be better laid out in love than in religion, and turn to as good an account. Let most voices carry it: for heaven or the captain?

ALL CRY. A captain! A captain!

HELLENA. Look ye, sir, 'tis a clear case.

PEDRO. Oh, I am mad!—(*Aside.*) If I refuse, my life's in danger.—Come, there's one motive induces me. Take her; I shall now be free from fears of her honor. Guard it you now, if you can; I have been a slave to't long enough.

(*Gives her to him.*)

WILLMORE. Faith, sir, I am of a nation that are of opinion a woman's honor is not worth guarding when she has a mind to part with it.

HELLENA. Well said, captain.

PEDRO (*to Valeria*). This was your plot, mistress, but I hope you have married one that will revenge my quarrel to you.

VALERIA. There's no altering destiny, sir.

PEDRO. Sooner than a woman's will; therefore I forgive you all, and wish you may get my father's pardon as easily, which I fear.

(*Enter Blunt dressed in a Spanish habit, looking very ridiculous; his Man adjusting his band.[174]*)

MAN. 'Tis very well, sir.

BLUNT. Well, sir! 'Adsheartlikins, I tell you 'tis damnable ill, sir. A Spanish habit! Good Lord! Could the devil and my tailor devise no other punishment for me but the mode of a nation I abominate?

BELVILE. What's the matter, Ned?

BLUNT. Pray view me round, and judge.

(*Turns round.*)

BELVILE. I must confess thou art a kind of an odd figure.

BLUNT. In a Spanish habit with a vengeance! I had rather be in the Inquisition for Judaism[175] than in this doublet and breeches; a pillory were an easy collar to this, three handfuls high; and these shoes, too, are worse than the stocks,

with the sole an inch shorter than my foot. In fine, gentlemen, methinks I look like a bag of bays[176] stuffed full of fool's flesh.

BELVILE. Methinks 'tis well, and makes thee look e'en cavalier. Come, sir, settle your face and salute our friends. Lady—

BLUNT (*to Hellena*). Ha! Sayst thou so, my little rover? Lady, if you be one, give me leave to kiss your hand, and tell you, 'adsheartlikins, for all I look so, I am your humble servant. A pox of my Spanish habit!

(*Music is heard to play.*)

WILLMORE. Hark! What's this?

(*Enter Boy.*)

BOY. Sir, as the custom is, the gay people in masquerade, who make every man's house their own, are coming up.

(*Enter several men and women in masking habits, with music; they put themselves in order and dance.*)

BLUNT. 'Adsheartlikins, would 'twere lawful to pull off their false faces, that I might see if my doxy[177] were not amongst 'em.

BELVILE (*to the maskers*). Ladies and gentlemen, since you are come so *a propos*,[178] you must take a small collation with us.

WILLMORE (*to Hellena*). Whilst we'll to the good man within, who stays to give us a cast of his office.[179] Have you no trembling at the near approach?

HELLENA. No more than you have in an engagement or a tempest.

WILLMORE. Egad, thou'rt a brave girl, and I admire thy love and courage.

Lead on; no other dangers they can dread,
Who venture in the storms o'th' marriage bed.

(*Exeunt.*)

EPILOGUE

The banished cavaliers! A roving blade!
A popish carnival! A masquerade!
The devil's in't if this will please the nation
In these our blessed times of reformation,
When conventickling[180] is so much in fashion.
And yet—
That mutinous tribe[181] less factions do beget,
Than your continual differing in wit.
Your judgment's, as your passion's, a disease:

---

[174]**band** neckband   [175]**Inquisition for Judaism** the Spanish Inquisition persecuted Jews as well as heretics

[176]**bag of bays** bag of spices used in cooking   [177]**doxy** prostitute [178]***a propos*** opportunely   [179]**cast of office** sample of his work (in marrying people)   [180]**conventickling** attending conventicles, that is, participating in secret meetings of religious dissenters (with a pun on *tickling*)   [181]**mutinous tribe** dissenters

Nor muse nor miss your appetite can please;
You're grown as nice as queasy consciences,
Whose each convulsion, when the spirit moves,
Damns everything that maggot[182] disapproves.
    With canting[183] rule you would the stage refine,
And to dull method all our sense confine.
With th'insolence of commonwealths you rule,
Where each gay fop and politic grave fool
On monarch wit impose, without control.
As for the last, who seldom sees a play,
Unless it be the old Blackfriars[184] way;
Shaking his empty noddle[185] o'er bamboo,[186]
He cries, "Good faith, these plays will never do!
Ah, sir, in my young days, what lofty wit,
What high-strained scenes of fighting there were writ.
These are slight airy toys. But tell me, pray,
What has the House of Commons done today?"
Then shows his politics, to let you see
Of state affairs he'll judge as notably
As he can do of wit and poetry.
The younger sparks, who hither do resort,
Cry,
"Pox o' your genteel things! Give us more sport!
Damn me, I'm sure 'twill never please the court."
    Such fops are never pleased, unless the play
Be stuffed with fools as brisk and dull as they.
Such might the half-crown[187] spare, and in a glass
At home behold a more accomplished ass.
Where they may set their cravats, wigs, and faces,
And practice all their buffoonry grimaces:
See how this huff becomes, this damny,[188] stare,
Which they at home may act because they dare,
But must with prudent caution do elsewhere.

---

[182]**maggot** the inner light (the *spirit* of the preceding line) that guides dissenters   [183]**canting** hypocritical   [184]**Blackfriars** a London theater, closed in 1642   [185]**noddle** head   [186]**bamboo** a cane, that is, an infirm man is shaking his head   [187]**half-crown** coin   [188]**damny** damn me

Oh that our Nokes, or Tony Lee,[189] could show
A fop but half so much to th' life as you.

POSTSCRIPT

This play had been sooner in print, but for a report about the town (made by some either very malicious or very ignorant) that 'twas *Thomaso*[190] altered; which made the booksellers fear some trouble from the proprietor of that admirable play, which indeed has wit enough to stock a poet, and is not to be pieced or mended by any but the excellent author himself. That I have stolen some hints from it, may be a proof that I valued it more than to pretend to alter it, had I the dexterity of some poets, who are not more expert in stealing than in the art of concealing, and who even that way outdo the Spartan boys.[191] I might have appropriated all to myself; but I, vainly proud of my judgment, hang out the sign of Angellica (the only stolen object) to give notice where a great part of the wit dwelt; though if the *Play of the Novella*[192] were as well worth remembering as *Thomaso*, they might (bating[193] the name) have as well said I took it from thence. I will only say the plot and business (not to boast on't) is my own; as for the words and characters, I leave the reader to judge and compare 'em with *Thomaso*, to whom I recommend the great entertainment of reading it. Though had this succeeded ill, I should have had no need of imploring that justice from the critics, who are naturally so kind to any that pretend to usurp their dominion, especially of our sex: They would doubtless have given me the whole honor on't. Therefore I will only say in English what the famous Vergil does in Latin: I make verses, and others have the fame.

---

[189]**Nokes . . . Lee** James Nokes and Anthony Leigh, two comedians of the period   [191]***Thomaso*** play by Thomas Killigrew, *Thomaso; or, The Wanderer* (1654)   [191]**Spartan boys** soldiers who hid in the Trojan horse   [192]***Play of the Novella*** Richard Brome's *The Novella* (1632)   [193]**bating** excepting

TOPICS FOR CRITICAL THINKING AND WRITING

The Play on the PAGE

1. What (if anything) makes Blunt's pursuit of Lucetta different from Willmore's pursuit of Angellica?
2. Angellica falls in love with Willmore. Do you think he is convincing enough for her to love him as the play indicates?
3. How disturbed are we by Willmore's rejection of Angellica's love? Is his rejection of Angellica so

disturbing that the play *as a comedy* suffers? Explain.
4. Angellica and Hellena both comment on Willmore's eloquence. How eloquent do you find him? Is it important that we find him eloquent, or is it enough for the characters to say that *they* find him eloquent? (Cite several speeches to support your point.)

5. Angellica's future is left unresolved at the end of the play. Some critics take this to mean that Aphra Behn is suggesting that in the real world there is no place for women like Angellica. Do you agree with this interpretation? Explain. Two related questions: (a) Is Angellica too rounded a figure—too convincing a figure—for a comedy? (b) Do you think Behn is signaling readers that Angellica Bianca is her spokesperson by using a character whose initials—A. B.—correspond with her own?

The Play on the STAGE

6. Two questions about Blunt: (a) We laugh at him, but do we also sometimes feel that he is badly treated? Support your answer by pointing to specific episodes; (b) since Blunt is companion of Belvile and Willmore, does the role need to portray him as something more than a buffoon?

7. It is customary to stage Restoration comedies (English comedies of the late seventeenth century) in the costume of the period—women draped under yards of heavy material, men in clothing adorned with gold braid and lace, and men and women with towering wigs. In short, the usual costuming emphasizes the artifice of the behavior. What might be gained or lost by staging the play in another period, for instance in the 1920s?

8. Suggest a casting for *The Rover*, choosing from today's film or stage performers, or from your own circle of friends. Explain your reasons.

The Play in PERFORMANCE

The Rover was first performed at the Dorset Garden Theatre in 1677, with King Charles II present. We cannot be certain of every performance, but we know that it was revived in 1680, 1685, and in 1696, and throughout the first half of the eighteenth century it was a regular part of the repertory, with several performances in almost every year. After 1761, however, it disappeared, until it was brought back in 1790 in a shortened and somewhat moralized form (*Love in Many Masks*) by John Philip Kemble. In Kemble's version, Willmore is less often in pursuit of women, and the final lines of the play suggest that the marriage may turn out well. *Love in Many Masks*, however, did not see many productions, and the original went unproduced for well over a century. A new interest in Behn, begun by feminist literary historians in the 1970s, brought *The Rover* (with some cuts) back to the stage. It is now again fairly popular, especially on college campuses but also occasionally in the professional theater. In 1986 John Barton, directing the Royal Shakespeare Company, with Jeremy Irons as Willmore, did a heavily revised version at Stratford-upon-Avon. Barton cut about five hundred fifty lines and added about three hundred fifty lines, some of them from Behn's chief source, Thomas Killigrew's *Thomaso*. In Barton's version, Belvile is a black soldier of fortune, and the setting is an unspecified Spanish colony in the Caribbean, rather than Naples. Because the production met with considerable popular success at Stratford-upon-Avon, it was produced in London in the following year, but on a different kind of stage. In the Stratford production Barton used a bare thrust stage—such a stage would have seemed terribly old-fashioned to Behn and her audience, who valued the relatively new invention of painted scenery—thereby bringing the actors into close contact with the audience. In fact, the actors sometimes addressed the audience, as when Florinda appealed to the audience to stop the fight between Pedro and Belvile.

In 1987 the Williamstown Theater in Massachusetts staged a more conventional production, with Christopher Reeve as Willmore and Kate Burton (Richard Burton's daughter) as Florinda. Finally, it should be mentioned that although most productions emphasize the high spirits and energy of the play, in 1991 the New Cross Theatre in London emphasized the darker aspects of the play; the desperation of the characters seemed not so much funny as disturbing.

CAROL ELLIOTT MACVEY
Directing The Rover

Carol Elliott MacVey, a member of the Department of Theatre at the University of Iowa, directed *The Rover* at Princeton University in 1985. In this interview, she discusses the production.

Why did you choose to stage The Rover?

I found it satisfied my needs for an undergraduate production—many young roles for college-aged actors, lots of comic shenanigans, sword fights, and women who prevailed. I recognized an innate sense of theatricality in Behn's script and prayed I could find enough actors who loved long sentences and had breath enough to speak them.

What did you cut, and what did you add?

I did a lot of cutting—of speeches, of scenes, whole pages. I also interpolated events in the carnival scenes. As it turned out, the carnival scenes played a major role in my production, providing a mother lode of theatrical energy which both dazzled and entertained. Every time the setting shifted to the carnival, two events happened. First, there was an explosion of Dionysian activity with carnival acts being performed everywhere: dancing, juggling, fire-swallowing, singing, acrobatics, whatever. This was followed, center stage, by an episode of an ongoing commedia dumb-show entitled *Marriage a-la-Mode* (or as one of the actors renamed it, *Marriage with Ice Cream*). These episodes depicted a series of arranged marriages in one woman's lifetime.

Episode 1: youth—she is physically dragged by her father to the altar to marry a very senile, very old man.

Episode 2: woman—she is carrying ten bambinos and is forced to marry a very ugly old man with ten bambinos of his own. He has two bags of gold.

Episode 3: midlife—she is carrying thirty bambinos and is forced to marry a very old, very mean man with multo bambinos of his own. He has many bags of gold.

Episode 4: old age—she is carrying several bags of gold, has no bambinos, no teeth, no hair, sans everything, and a very handsome young man is being physically dragged to the altar to marry her.

Willmore's initial entrance into the carnival conveyed much about what one might expect from his character. One of the many carnival figures was a giantess, a hoop-skirted woman on stilts. She was huge and grotesque. Suddenly she screamed, no one knowing if the scream was a result of surprise or of pleasure. All activity stopped and everyone focused on her. Then, out from under her skirts, smug and satisfied, strutted Willmore. She picked him up, smothered him in her oversized balloon breasts and hurled him to the ground, much to everyone's delight. Let's ramble!

Are you familiar with Peter Hall's adaptation of The Rover?

Yes. I regret to say that it is the version that is popularly done. Behn's original script opens with two sisters discussing how to solve their respective problems. Florinda is in love but is being forced to marry a septuagenarian while Hellena is being forced to go to a convent. Hall's script, on the other hand, opens with a band of Cavaliers entering Naples trying to figure out how, while they are ashore, they will woo and win women in order to satisfy their long-delayed sexual yearnings. What Behn gives us in the original version is unusual and ought to be fiercely protected—a play that opens with women's energies generating the machinations of the plot and creating a landscape into which the men will enter. What Hall gives us is the usual "good ole boy" formula: Let the men create and organize the world and then let women enter into it as devices for their pleasure. Even though much of the rest of Hall's script reflects Behn's original version, the damage has been done: He has sabotaged and violated and subverted all the primal female energy with which Behn obviously intended the play to begin.

Do you think the original version ends satisfactorily?

I'm interested in the unresolved tensions at the end of a play. I find Angellica's problem to be a curious one. The courtesan, for the first time, falls in love. She loves Willmore with a passion she has never experienced with any other man and yet she, unlike the other lovers in the play, ends up rejected, alone. The final image in my production was of Angellica on a balcony, alone, watching the paired lovers exit as the festive carnival music brought the play to an end.

What design decisions did you make about The Rover?

The action took place on a three-quarter-round stage, with the audience quite close to the actors; there was a balcony upstage. The only set pieces were huge pillows which were used in various ways throughout, allowing the playing to be extremely physical, even for the women. At the opening of the first scene, the pillows were piled center stage and we heard raucous screaming offstage. Then, Florinda ran in, wildly pursued by Hellena, who eventually tackled her sister, threw her onto the piles of pillows, straddled her, and pinned her down. Florinda, struggling to be free, exclaims, "What an impertinent thing is a young girl bred in a nunnery! Prithee, no more Hellena! I have told you more than thou understand'st already." From the outset, Hellena is someone to reckon with, not only verbally, but physically.

The costume design was modified Restoration, which meant that one could easily identify the period but there was enough flexibility and physical freedom for the women to cavort when needed. Although the women do prevail primarily by their wits I also wanted to provide them with other options.

Classic Modern Drama

Jean (played by Peter Stormare) suggests "a way out of this" to Julie (Lena Olin) in this touring production of August Strindberg's *Miss Julie* at the Brooklyn Academy of Music. This production was originally directed by Ingmar Bergman at the Royal National Theater in Stockholm.

In the mid-1870s, Émile Zola, French novelist, playwright, man of letters, wrote dramatic criticism for several Parisian newspapers. In one piece he gloomily contemplated what fare yet another theater season would bring: sentimental melodramas, overplotted "well-made" plays, lifeless imitations of classical tragedy, empty spectacles, extravagant overacting, exotic displays of "knights and ladies, manufactured strange sets with castles pinnacled over sheer gorges, . . . dungeons dripping with moisture, forests pocked with moonlight." His depressed mood, however, was softened by a hope: that maybe *this* season a "dramatist of genius" will emerge to "bring about a rebirth in an art degraded by its practitioners to the simple-minded requirements of the crowd." But it would be no simple task to put on stage "the real human drama in place of the ridiculous untruths that are on display today." So engrained are these untruths that nothing less than a radical demolition is called for if we want to admit "a shiver of life to the painted trees, letting in through the backcloth the great, free air of reality."

This was not a vain hope because change *was* in the artistic air. It was already evident in fiction, in the novels of Honoré de Balzac and Gustave Flaubert. A new adjective was being used to describe them. By the 1850s, the term "realism" had arisen to describe writing that tried to record the world truthfully and objectively, with the author minimizing his or her intervention. This artistic approach was an inevitable response to the enormous political, social, and scientific changes that were occurring in the nineteenth century. The French Revolution at the end of the eighteenth century had broken up the old order, and the "modern" world, as we know it, began to be formed. The most radical change came from the Industrial Revolution, which had irrevocably transformed ordinary life by replacing the old craft system with the factory system, a change that forced people into cities to become a "working class." The technological advances that created the Industrial Revolution were made possible by an explosion of scientific knowledge that inevitably redefined the way the world was looked at philosophically. What we call the social sciences—anthropology, sociology, psychology—broke off from history and theology to define themselves as independent disciplines. Even the traditional sciences such as medicine succumbed to materialist theories of physical development (Claude Bernard, *Introduction to Experimental Medicine,* 1865). Karl Marx, of course, radically shaped this new materialism into a politically revolutionary doctrine.

Zola asks, How can it be that theater art is so oblivious to all this change? "It seems impossible that the movement of inquiry and analysis, which is precisely the movement of the nineteenth century, can have revolutionized all the sciences and arts and left dramatic art to one side, as if isolated." And so he offers his own doctrine, which incorporates and intensifies the principles of realism: He calls his theory "naturalism," and he raises it as a banner around which he urges all theater innovators to congregate. With new experimental science as his model, Zola proposes a naturalist theater that would not only *reproduce* human life accurately, it would *explain* how heredity and environment and history crucially shape—indeed *determine*—that life, not only for kings and princes but for all humanity. Instead of stereotypic and conventionalized characters with names like Pinchwife and Cléante, let us have characters with full names who have unique personal histories and who live in a socially defined world. (See *naturalism* in the glossary for further discussion.) The job of the artist, then, is to abandon artificial conventions in favor of all the realities that govern the human condition: "There must be no more schools, no more formulas, . . . there is just life itself, an immense field where everybody can explore and create at his heart's content." Look at the world truthfully, Zola pleads: "Take our present environment and try to make men live in it; you will write great works. . . . It will be proved that there is more poetry in the little apartment of a bourgeois than in all the empty, worm-eaten palaces of history."

Stirring words, but theories do not create art; artists do. Zola had indeed tried to write naturalistic plays (*Thérèse Raquin*, 1873—a dramatic adaptation of his own novel—is the best known), but as is always the case, it is easier to predict or promote genius than to achieve it; Zola himself recognized that his plays did not really do the naturalist job (he was later to do so in fiction in his major novels *L'Assommoir*, 1877, and *Germinal*, 1885), and in 1875 asked, "When will our Corneilles, Molières and Racines appear to establish our new theater? We must hope and wait." The waiting was not very long.

In December 1879 an expatriate Norwegian published in Copenhagen a play—*A Doll's House*—that immediately became notorious and hence successful. Henrik Ibsen was not then a young man, having been born in 1828, and he had written plays for the Norwegian theater before retiring to Italy to write poetic plays more highly regarded now than then—*Brand* and *Peer Gynt* (1866, 1867). In his middle years he began writing "social" plays in a new realistic mode: *The League of Youth* and *Pillars of Society*. *A Doll's House*, their successor, with its heroine who abandons her husband and family *without the author's condemnation*, in the words of a contemporary, "pronounced a death sentence on accepted social ethics." But if its impact as a book was immediate, as a theater piece it had to wait at least two years before it was widely produced; indeed, it was ten years or more before France, England, and America saw on stage a recognizably faithful version of the play (although corrupt adaptations made brief and unsuccessful appearances). The tempest became international, and the dour middle-aged Norwegian became the archetype of subversion.

The reason for the productional delay is obvious: In response to a startling urban population spurt, the major theaters of Europe had grown into huge, oversized barns seating thousands, hardly appropriate venues for plays demanding the truthfulness of small gestures and nondeclamation. As our man Zola had indeed recognized earlier, "Everything is interdependent in the theater. Lifelike costumes look wrong if the sets, the diction, the plays themselves are not lifelike. They must all march in step along the naturalistic road." As a new drama emerged—a drama that rejected empty spectacle and rhetoric, easy sentimentality, melodramatic contrivance, moral obtuseness, conventional morality—it was clear a new *theater* had to emerge. Zola's dream was realized because a realistic theater art was an idea whose time had come. Indeed, without his personal participation, Zola was at the heart of the theatrical revolution that was about to start. A young clerk at the Paris Gas Company, André Antoine, decided to start a theater group dedicated to new works. He chose as his debut piece a dramatization of a story by Zola, *Jacques D'Amour*, set in quarters behind a butcher shop. Antoine obtained the use of a room above a café, carted his mother's furniture across Paris to use as the set, and, *voilà!*, the Théâtre libre (Free Theater) was born. March 30, 1887, the opening performance of the Théâtre libre, may well mark the beginning of the modern theater. It established a way of making theater that had never existed before and which remains with us as a model of youthful independent production.

The immediate success of the Théâtre libre initiated a little theater movement that rapidly spread across Europe: Two years later, led by a man named Otto Brahm, a group was established in Berlin called the Freie Bühne (Free Stage) dedicated to "Truth on every path of life." Significantly, its first production was *Ghosts*, the equally controversial play followed *A Doll's House*, a play that had the temerity to treat the subject of venereal disease. After all, truth demanded that no subject was taboo, no matter how grim. Indeed, truth more often that not *was* grim and adversarial. The Freie Bühne discovered a native naturalist in Gerhart Hauptmann who, in *The Weavers*, examined the social cost the new capitalist society was exacting. In England, Ibsen had become a rallying cry, with William Archer rushing to translate the plays as soon as they were published. His Irish friend, George Bernard Shaw, was so energized by the Norwegian that he abandoned a mediocre start as a novelist to embark on his own dramatic career. Shaw also became Ibsen's champion in *The Quintessence of Ibsenism* (1981). But it took a young Dutchman, J.T. Grein, to actually put Ibsen on stage in England by establishing in London the Independent Theater (1891), and again with *Ghosts*, a production with the distinction of receiving some of the vilest reviews ever written ("an open drain, a loathsome sore unbandaged, a dirty act done publicly.")

By far the best known of the European independent theaters was the last established: In Moscow in 1897, Konstantin Alexeyev (soon to change his name to Stanislavski), an industrialist's son who led a local amateur literary society, and Vladimir Nemirovich-Danchenko, a jounalist and teacher of acting, met in a café for a legendary meeting after which they decided to form an art theater. After indifferent response to their first three productions of Russian and international classics, the Moscow Art Theater found its way by remounting *The Sea Gull*, a failed play by a contemporary writer, Anton Chekhov, thus beginning one of the greatest, if all too brief, collaborations between dramatist and theater artists in history. With the riches of Chekhov's (and others') plays to work with, Stanislavski was able to turn Zola's ideal of truthful acting into practical methodology.

Yes, build it and they will come: With intimate theaters now proliferating, dramatists emerged across the landscape (though it really is a chicken and the egg problem; Zola or Ibsen might well have said: write it and it will be staged)—the aforementioned Hauptmann and Shaw in Germany and England, Maxim Gorki following Chekhov in Russia, and preeminently, that other towering Scandinavian, the prolific, mercurial, crazy, provocative genius, August Strindberg. The truth of Realism—the truth of verisimilitude—was soon to be followed by other "truths"—the truth of Ibsen's later symbolism, the truth of Shaw's new thematic wine in old dramatic bottles; above all, the influential truths of Strindberg's proto-expressionistic and surrealistic forays into the states of dreams and nightmares. The modern drama, in all its infinite variety, had begun.

HENRIK Ibsen

Henrik Ibsen (1828–1906) was born in Skien, Norway, of wealthy parents who soon after his birth lost their money. Ibsen worked as a pharmacist's apprentice, but at the age of twenty-two he had written his first play, a promising melodrama entitled *Cataline.* He engaged in theater work first in Norway and then in Denmark and Germany. By 1865 his plays had won him a state pension that enabled him to settle in Rome. After writing romantic, historic, and poetic plays, he turned to realistic drama with *The League of Youth* (1869). Among the major realistic "problem plays" are *A Doll's House* (1879), *Ghosts* (1881), and *An Enemy of the People* (1882). In *The Wild Duck* (1884) he moved toward a more symbolic tragic comedy, and his last plays, written in the nineties, are highly symbolic.

■■■■■■■■■■■■■

COMMENTARY ON *A DOLL'S HOUSE*

Before he was forty Ibsen had written two masterpieces of poetic drama, *Brand* (1866) and *Peer Gynt* (1867). But a few years later he came to feel, along with many others, that the future of dramatic literature was not in poetic language, but in language that closely resembled ordinary speech. He devoted his subsequent efforts to prose drama, and we find him, in his letters, occasionally prophesying that poetic drama has no future and warning his translators to avoid all expressions that depart from "everyday speech." In the 1870s and 1880s he wrote the so-called problem plays (including *A Doll's House, Ghosts,* and *An Enemy of the People*) that for the next seventy-five years made his name familiar to the English-speaking world. A problem play, or "play of ideas," or *pièce à thèse,* is concerned with a serious political or social issue, its author hoping to arouse the audience to do something about the problem (for example, to modify the divorce laws, to extend the ballot, to alter the tax structure). The more successful the play, the more it ensures its own demise, for when the social institutions have been altered and the problem has been solved, the play has no relevance to experience; it is merely a thing of historical importance, a museum curio. The violent reviews that *A Doll's House, Ghosts,* and some of Ibsen's other plays engendered are evidence that more was at stake than aesthetic matters; discussions of the plays inevitably became discussions of divorce, venereal disease, incest, and so forth. A century later, we see readers have found that Ibsen has something more to offer than thoughts on how to improve society.

First of all, we have come to see that Ibsen's prose dramas, which he said were written in "the straightforward plain language spoken in daily life," are more than realistic copies of aspects of behavior. With Ibsen, realism often becomes a form of symbolism. Let's begin with the stage and its setting. When the curtain goes up on a performance of *A Doll's House,* the audience sees "a comfortably and tastefully but not expensively furnished room." Additional details, such as "engravings on the walls," and "a small bookcase with leather-bound books," tell us much about the kind of people who live here. We shall learn more about these people when we see the clothes that they wear and hear the words that they speak, but even now—from seeing their living room—we know that they are people who hold the conventional middle-class values. The leather-bound books in the bookcase, for example, are more for show than for reading.

In some plays there are several sets—sometimes in sharp contrast—but in *A Doll's House* there is only one set, and perhaps we come to feel that this omnipresent room is a sort of prison that stifles its inhabitants or, as the title of the play implies, that this room keeps its inhabitants at a distance from the realities of life. At the end of the play, Nora escapes from this box and enters the real world. We might look, too, at the ways in which some of the furniture and the properties work in the play. Very early, when Torvald begins to lecture Nora about incurring debts, she "goes over towards the stove." It is scarcely too subtle to conclude that she is seeking a place of warmth or security when confronted by Torvald's chilling words. We may not *consciously* come to this conclusion, but that doesn't matter. Indeed, later in this act, Torvald, sitting near the stove, says quite naturally, "Ah, how cozy and peaceful it is here."

Or consider the use Ibsen makes of the Christmas tree. In the first act, when Nora's world is still relatively undisturbed, the tree, adorned with candles and flowers, is in the center of the stage. By the end of this act Nora is terrified, and when the curtain goes up for the second act, we see the tree thrust into a corner, "stripped and disheveled," with burnt-down candles. Again, we may not consciously conclude that Ibsen, through the tree, is telling us something about Nora, but surely the tree—at first gay, then forlorn—somehow has an impact on us.

It would be easy to go on at length, discussing the ways in which Ibsen as a dramatist produces meanings, but we now should step back and ask a large question: What does the play add up to? Before we try to answer such a question, it may be useful to mention that Ibsen actually knew a woman who had forged a check to pay for a trip that her husband's health required. When the husband learned the truth, he turned on her and had her committed to an asylum, though later, for the sake of their children, he allowed her to return to their home. This episode apparently set Ibsen thinking, and when he set to work on A Doll's House he jotted down some "Notes for a Modern Tragedy":

> There are two kinds of moral law, two kinds of conscience, one in man and a completely different one in woman. They do not understand each other; but in matters of practical living the woman is judged by man's law, as if she were not a woman but a man.
>
> The wife in the play ends up quite bewildered and not knowing right from wrong; her natural instincts on the one side and her faith in authority on the other leave her completely confused.

Of course, Ibsen probably began by thinking about the real woman who forged a check to pay for the trip to save her sick husband, but the passage just quoted is the earliest writing relevant to the play. As Ibsen worked on the play, he (not surprisingly) produced characters and a plot that have a life of their own; but even if they depart from his preliminary note, these characters and this plot add up to something. (A *plot* is what happens; a *theme* is what the happenings add up to.) Some readers see in A Doll's House a play about a woman's place in a man's world, or a play about women's rights, but Ibsen himself (years after writing the play) said he had a larger theme: "I am not even sure what women's rights really are. To me it has been a question of human rights." Certainly the play deals, as Ibsen implies, with the enslavement of one person by another. At last Torvald dimly seems to recognize that Nora is a human being, not a doll; and Nora perceives that such a recognition could lead to "a true marriage."

A DOLL'S HOUSE
Henrik Ibsen

Translated by James McFarlane

CHARACTERS

TORVALD HELMER, *a lawyer*
NORA, *his wife*
DR. RANK
MRS. KRISTINE LINDE
NILS KROGSTAD

ANNE MARIE, *the nursemaid*
HELENE, *the maid*
THE HELMERS' THREE CHILDREN
A PORTER

The action takes place in the Helmers' flat.

ACT 1

A pleasant room, tastefully but not expensively furnished. On the back wall, one door on the right leads to the entrance hall, a second door on the left leads to Helmer's study. Between these two doors, a piano. In the middle of the left wall, a door; and downstage from it, a window. Near the window a round table with armchairs and a small sofa. In the right wall, upstage, a door; and on the same wall downstage, a porcelain stove with a couple of armchairs and a rocking chair. Between the stove and the door a small table. Etchings on the walls. A whatnot with china and other small objets d'art; a small bookcase with books in handsome bindings. Carpet on the floor; a fire burns in the stove. A winter's day.

The front door-bell rings in the hall; a moment later, there is the sound of the front door being opened. Nora comes into the room, happily humming to herself. She is dressed in her outdoor things, and is carrying lots of parcels which she then puts down on the table, right. She leaves the door into the hall standing open; a Porter can be seen outside holding a Christmas tree and a basket; he hands them to the Maid who has opened the door for them.

NORA. Hide the Christmas tree away carefully, Helene. The children mustn't see it till this evening when it's decorated. [*To the Porter, taking out her purse.*] How much?
PORTER. Fifty öre.
NORA. There's a crown. Keep the change.

[*The Porter thanks her and goes. Nora shuts the door. She continues to laugh quietly and happily to herself as she takes off her things. She takes a bag of macaroons out of her pocket and eats one or two; then she walks stealthily across and listens at her husband's door.*]

NORA. Yes, he's in.

[*She begins humming again as she walks over to the table, right.*]

HELMER [*in his study*]. Is that my little sky-lark chirruping out there?
NORA [*busy opening some of the parcels*]. Yes, it is.
HELMER. Is that my little squirrel frisking about?
NORA. Yes!
HELMER. When did my little squirrel get home?
NORA. Just this minute. [*She stuffs the bag of macaroons in her pocket and wipes her mouth.*] Come on out, Torvald, and see what I've bought.
HELMER. I don't want to be disturbed! [*A moment later, he opens the door and looks out, his pen in his hand.*] 'Bought', did you say? All that? Has my little spendthrift been out squandering money again?
NORA. But, Torvald, surely this year we can spread ourselves just a little. This is the first Christmas we haven't had to go carefully.
HELMER. Ah, but that doesn't mean we can afford to be extravagant, you know.
NORA. Oh yes, Torvald, surely we can afford to be just a little bit extravagant now, can't we? Just a teeny-weeny bit. You are getting quite a good salary now, and you are going to earn lots and lots of money.
HELMER. Yes, after the New Year. But it's going to be three whole months before the first pay cheque comes in.
NORA. Pooh! We can always borrow in the meantime.
HELMER. Nora! [*Crosses to her and takes her playfully by the ear.*] Here we go again, you and your frivolous ideas! Suppose I went and borrowed a thousand crowns today, and you went and spent it all over Christmas, then on New Year's Eve a slate fell and hit me on the head and there I was. . . .

Ingmar Bergman's 1989 production of *A Doll's House* at the Royal Dramatic Theatre in Stockholm kept all of the characters on stage throughout the play, or, more precisely, those characters who were not speaking were seated, in view of the audience, at the side of the stage. In the illustrated scene we see Nora taking leave of her husband, Torvald. Bergman emphasized Torvald's vulnerability by having him in bed, nude. For additional photographs of productions of *A Doll's House*, see pages 13 and 15.

NORA [*putting her hand over his mouth*]. Sh! Don't say such horrid things.

HELMER. Yes, but supposing something like that did happen . . . what then?

NORA. If anything as awful as that did happen, I wouldn't care if I owed anybody anything or not.

HELMER. Yes, but what about the people I'd borrowed from?

NORA. Them? Who cares about them! They are only strangers!

HELMER. Nora, Nora! Just like a woman! Seriously though, Nora, you know what I think about these things. No debts! Never borrow! There's always something inhibited, something unpleasant, about a home built on credit and borrowed money. We two have managed to stick it out so far, and that's the way we'll go on for the little time that remains.

NORA [*walks over to the stove*]. Very well, just as you say, Torvald.

HELMER [*following her*]. There, there! My little singing bird mustn't go drooping her wings, eh? Has it got the sulks, that little squirrel of mine? [*Takes out his wallet.*] Nora, what do you think I've got here?

NORA [*quickly turning round*]. Money!

HELMER. There! [*He hands her some notes*]. Good heavens, I know only too well how Christmas runs away with the housekeeping.

NORA [*counts*]. Ten, twenty, thirty, forty. Oh, thank you, thank you, Torvald! This will see me quite a long way.

HELMER. Yes, it'll have to.

NORA. Yes, yes, I'll see that it does. But come over here, I want to show you all the things I've bought. And so

cheap! Look, some new clothes for Ivar . . . and a little sword. There's a horse and a trumpet for Bob. And a doll and a doll's cot for Emmy. They are not very grand but she'll have them all broken before long anyway. And I've got some dress material and some handkerchiefs for the maids. Though, really, dear old Anne Marie should have had something better.

HELMER. And what's in this parcel here?

NORA [*shrieking*]. No, Torvald! You mustn't see that till tonight!

HELMER. All right. But tell me now, what did my little spendthrift fancy for herself?

NORA. For me? Puh, I don't really want anything.

HELMER. Of course you do. Anything reasonable that you think you might like, just tell me.

NORA. Well, I don't really know. As a matter of fact, though, Torvald . . .

HELMER. Well?

NORA [*toying with his coat buttons, and without looking at him*]. If you did want to give me something, you could . . . you could always . . .

HELMER. Well, well, out with it!

NORA [*quickly*]. You could always give me money, Torvald. Only what you think you could spare. And then I could buy myself something with it later on.

HELMER. But Nora. . . .

NORA. Oh, please, Torvald dear! Please! I beg you. Then I'd wrap the money up in some pretty gilt paper and hang it on the Christmas tree. Wouldn't that be fun?

HELMER. What do we call my pretty little pet when it runs away with all the money?

NORA. I know, I know, we call it a spendthrift. But please let's do what I said, Torvald. Then I'll have a bit of time to think about what I need most. Isn't that awfully sensible, now, eh?

HELMER [*smiling*]. Yes, it is indeed—that is, if only you really could hold on to the money I gave you, and really did buy something for yourself with it. But it just gets mixed up with the housekeeping and frittered away on all sorts of useless things, and then I have to dig into my pocket all over again.

NORA. Oh but, Torvald. . . .

HELMER. You can't deny it, Nora dear. [*Puts his arm round her waist.*] My pretty little pet is very sweet, but it runs away with an awful lot of money. It's incredible how expensive it is for a man to keep such a pet.

NORA. For shame! How can you say such a thing? As a matter of fact I save everything I can.

HELMER [*laughs*]. Yes, you are right there. Everything you *can*. But you simply can't.

NORA [*hums and smiles quietly and happily*]. Ah, if you only knew how many expenses the likes of us sky-larks and squirrels have, Torvald!

HELMER. What a funny little one you are! Just like your father. Always on the look-out for money, wherever you can lay your hands on it; but as soon as you've got it, it just seems to slip through your fingers. You never seem to know what you've done with it. Well, one must accept you as you are. It's in the blood. Oh yes, it is, Nora. That sort of thing is hereditary.

NORA. Oh, I only wish I'd inherited a few more of Daddy's qualities.

HELMER. And I wouldn't want my pretty little song-bird to be the least bit different from what she is now. But come to think of it, you look rather . . . rather . . . how shall I put it? . . . rather guilty today. . . .

NORA. Do I?

HELMER. Yes, you do indeed. Look me straight in the eye.

NORA [*looks at him*]. Well?

HELMER [*wagging his finger at her*]. My little sweet-tooth surely didn't forget herself in town today?

NORA. No, whatever makes you think that?

HELMER. She didn't just pop into the confectioner's for a moment?

NORA. No, I assure you, Torvald . . . !

HELMER. Didn't try sampling the preserves?

NORA. No, really I didn't.

HELMER. Didn't go nibbling a macaroon or two?

NORA. No, Torvald, honestly, you must believe me . . . !

HELMER. All right then! It's really just my little joke. . . .

NORA [*crosses to the table*]. I would never dream of doing anything you didn't want me to.

HELMER. Of course not, I know that. And then you've given me your word. . . . [*Crosses to her.*] Well then, Nora dearest, you shall keep your little Christmas secrets. They'll all come out tonight, I dare say, when we light the tree.

NORA. Did you remember to invite Dr. Rank?

HELMER. No. But there's really no need. Of course he'll come and have dinner with us. Anyway, I can ask him when he looks in this morning. I've ordered some good wine. Nora, you can't imagine how I am looking forward to this evening.

NORA. So am I. And won't the children enjoy it, Torvald!

HELMER. Oh, what a glorious feeling it is, knowing you've got a nice, safe job, and a good fat income. Don't you agree? Isn't it wonderful, just thinking about it?

NORA. Oh, it's marvellous!

HELMER. Do you remember last Christmas? Three whole weeks beforehand you shut yourself up every evening till after midnight making flowers for the Christmas tree and all the other splendid things you wanted to surprise us with. Ugh, I never felt so bored in all my life.

NORA. I wasn't the least bit bored.

HELMER [*smiling*]. But it turned out a bit of an anticlimax, Nora.

NORA. Oh, you are not going to tease me about that again! How was I to know the cat would get in and pull everything to bits?

HELMER. No, of course you weren't. Poor little Nora! All you wanted was for us to have a nice time—and it's the thought behind it that counts, after all. All the same, it's a good thing we've seen the back of those lean times.

NORA. Yes, really it's marvellous.

HELMER. Now there's no need for me to sit here all on my own, bored to tears. And you don't have to strain your dear little eyes, and work those dainty little fingers to the bone. . . .

NORA [*clapping her hands*]. No, Torvald, I don't, do I? Not any more. Oh, how marvellous it is to hear that! [*Takes his arm.*] Now I want to tell you how I've been thinking we might arrange things, Torvald. As soon as Christmas is over. . . . [*The door-bell rings in the hall.*] Oh, there's the bell. [*Tidies one or two things in the room.*] It's probably a visitor. What a nuisance!

HELMER. Remember I'm not at home to callers.

MAID [*in the doorway*]. There's a lady to see you, ma'am.

NORA. Show her in, please.

MAID [*to Helmer*]. And the doctor's just arrived, too, sir.

HELMER. Did he go straight into my room?

MAID. Yes, he did, sir.

[*Helmer goes into his study. The Maid shows in Mrs. Linde, who is in travelling clothes, and closes the door after her.*]

MRS. LINDE [*subdued and rather hesitantly*]. How do you do, Nora?

NORA [*uncertainly*]. How do you do?

MRS. LINDE. I'm afraid you don't recognize me.

NORA. No, I don't think I . . . And yet I seem to. . . . [*Bursts out suddenly.*] Why! Kristine! Is it really you?

MRS. LINDE. Yes, it's me.

NORA. Kristine! Fancy not recognizing you again! But how was I to, when . . . [*Gently.*] How you've changed, Kristine!

MRS. LINDE. I dare say I have. In nine . . . ten years. . . .

NORA. Is it so long since we last saw each other? Yes, it must be. Oh, believe me these last eight years have been such a happy time. And now you've come up to town, too? All that long journey in wintertime. That took courage.

MRS. LINDE. I just arrived this morning on the steamer.

NORA. To enjoy yourself over Christmas, of course. How lovely! Oh, we'll have such fun, you'll see. Do take off your things. You are not cold, are you? [*Helps her.*] There now! Now let's sit down here in comfort beside the stove. No, here, you take the armchair, I'll sit here on the rocking chair. [*Takes her hands.*] Ah, now you look a bit more like your old self again. It was just that when I first saw you. . . . But you are a little paler, Kristine . . . and perhaps even a bit thinner!

MRS. LINDE. And much, much older, Nora.

NORA. Yes, perhaps a little older . . . very, very little, not really very much. [*Stops suddenly and looks serious.*] Oh, what a thoughtless creature I am, sitting here chattering on like this! Dear, sweet Kristine, can you forgive me?

MRS. LINDE. What do you mean, Nora?

NORA [*gently*]. Poor Kristine, of course you're a widow now.

MRS. LINDE. Yes, my husband died three years ago.

NORA. Oh, I remember now. I read about it in the papers. Oh, Kristine, believe me I often thought at the time of writing to you. But I kept putting it off, something always seemed to crop up.

MRS. LINDE. My dear Nora, I understand so well.

NORA. No, it wasn't very nice of me, Kristine. Oh, you poor thing, what you must have gone through. And didn't he leave you anything?

MRS. LINDE. No.

NORA. And no children?

MRS. LINDE. No.

NORA. Absolutely nothing?

MRS. LINDE. Nothing at all . . . not even a broken heart to grieve over.

NORA [*looks at her incredulously*]. But, Kristine, is that possible?

MRS. LINDE [*smiles sadly and strokes Nora's hair*]. Oh, it sometimes happens, Nora.

NORA. So utterly alone. How terribly sad that must be for you. I have three lovely children. You can't see them for the moment, because they're out with their nanny. But now you must tell me all about yourself. . . .

MRS. LINDE. No, no, I want to hear about you.

NORA. No, you start. I won't be selfish today. I must think only about your affairs today. But there's just one thing I really must tell you. Have you heard about the great stroke of luck we've had in the last few days?

MRS. LINDE. No. What is it?

NORA. What do you think? My husband has just been made Bank Manager!

MRS. LINDE. Your husband? How splendid!

NORA. Isn't it tremendous! It's not a very steady way of making a living, you know, being a lawyer, especially if he refuses to take on anything that's the least bit shady—which of course is what Torvald does, and I think he's quite right. You can imagine how pleased we are! He starts at the Bank straight after New Year, and he's getting a big salary and lots of commission. From now on we'll be able to live quite differently . . . we'll do just what we want. Oh, Kristine, I'm so happy and relieved. I must say it's lovely to have plenty of money and not have to worry. Isn't it?

MRS. LINDE. Yes. It must be nice to have enough, at any rate.

NORA. No, not just enough, but pots and pots of money.

MRS. LINDE [*smiles*]. Nora, Nora, haven't you learned any sense yet? At school you used to be an awful spendthrift.

NORA. Yes, Torvald still says I am. [*Wags her finger.*] But little Nora isn't as stupid as everybody thinks. Oh, we haven't really been in a position where I could afford to spend a lot of money. We've both had to work.

MRS. LINDE. You too?

NORA. Yes, odd jobs—sewing, crochet-work, embroidery and things like that. [*Casually.*] And one or two other things, besides. I suppose you know that Torvald left the Ministry when we got married. There weren't any prospects of promotion in his department, and of course he needed to earn more money than he had before. But the first year he wore himself out completely. He had to take on all kinds of extra jobs, you know, and he found himself working all hours of the day and night. But he couldn't go on like that; and he became seriously ill. The doctors said it was essential for him to go South.

MRS. LINDE. Yes, I believe you spent a whole year in Italy, didn't you?

NORA. That's right. It wasn't easy to get away, I can tell you. It was just after I'd had Ivar. But of course we had to go. Oh, it was an absolutely marvellous trip. And it saved Torvald's life. But it cost an awful lot of money, Kristine.

MRS. LINDE. That I can well imagine.

NORA. Twelve hundred dollars. Four thousand eight hundred crowns. That's a lot of money, Kristine.

MRS. LINDE. Yes, but in such circumstances, one is very lucky if one has it.

NORA. Well, we got it from Daddy, you see.

MRS. LINDE. Ah, that was it. It was just about then your father died, I believe, wasn't it?

NORA. Yes, Kristine, just about then. And do you know, I couldn't even go and look after him. Here was I expecting Ivar any day. And I also had poor Torvald, gravely ill, on my hands. Dear, kind Daddy! I never saw him again, Kristine. Oh, that's the saddest thing that has happened to me in all my married life.

MRS. LINDE. I know you were very fond of him. But after that you left for Italy?

NORA. Yes, we had the money then, and the doctors said it was urgent. We left a month later.

MRS. LINDE. And your husband came back completely cured?

NORA. Fit as a fiddle!

MRS. LINDE. But . . . what about the doctor?

NORA. How do you mean?

MRS. LINDE. I thought the maid said something about the gentleman who came at the same time as me being a doctor.

NORA. Yes, that was Dr. Rank. But this isn't a professional visit. He's our best friend and he always looks in at least once a day. No, Torvald has never had a day's illness since. And the children are fit and healthy, and so am I. [*Jumps up and claps her hands.*] Oh God, oh God, isn't it marvellous to be alive, and to be happy, Kristine! . . . Oh, but I ought to be ashamed of myself . . . Here I go on talking about nothing but myself. [*She sits on a low stool near Mrs. Linde and lays her arms on her lap.*] Oh, please, you mustn't be angry with me! Tell me, is it really true that you didn't love your husband? What made you marry him, then?

MRS. LINDE. My mother was still alive; she was bedridden and helpless. And then I had my two young brothers to look after as well. I didn't think I would be justified in refusing him.

NORA. No, I dare say you are right. I suppose he was fairly wealthy then?

MRS. LINDE. He was quite well off, I believe. But the business was shaky. When he died, it went all to pieces, and there just wasn't anything left.

NORA. What then?

MRS. LINDE. Well, I had to fend for myself, opening a little shop, running a little school, anything I could turn my hand to. These last three years have been one long relentless drudge. But now it's finished, Nora. My poor dear mother doesn't need me any more, she's passed away. Nor the boys either; they're at work now, they can look after themselves.

NORA. What a relief you must find it. . . .

MRS. LINDE. No, Nora! Just unutterably empty. Nobody to live for any more. [*Stands up restless.*] That's why I couldn't stand it any longer being cut off up there. Surely it must be a bit easier here to find something to occupy your mind. If only I could manage to find a steady job of some kind, in an office perhaps. . . .

NORA. But, Kristine, that's terribly exhausting; and you look so worn out even before you start. The best thing for you would be a little holiday at some quiet little resort.

MRS. LINDE [*crosses to the window*]. I haven't any father I can fall back on for the money, Nora.

NORA [*rises*]. Oh, please, you mustn't be angry with me!

MRS. LINDE [*goes to her*]. My dear Nora, you mustn't be angry with me either. That's the worst thing about people in my position, they become so bitter. One has nobody to work for, yet one has to be on the look-out all the time. Life has to go on, and one starts thinking only of oneself. Believe it or not, when you told me the good news about

your step up, I was pleased not so much for your sake as for mine.

NORA. How do you mean? Ah, I see. You think Torvald might be able to do something for you.

MRS. LINDE. Yes, that's exactly what I thought.

NORA. And so he shall, Kristine. Just leave things to me. I'll bring it up so cleverly . . . I'll think up something to put him in a good mood. Oh, I do so much want to help you.

MRS. LINDE. It is awfully kind of you, Nora, offering to do all this for me, particularly in your case, where you haven't known much trouble or hardship in your own life.

NORA. When I . . . ? I haven't known much . . . ?

MRS. LINDE [*smiling*]. Well, good heavens, a little bit of sewing to do and a few things like that. What a child you are, Nora!

NORA [*tosses her head and walks across the room*]. I wouldn't be too sure of that, if I were you.

MRS. LINDE. Oh?

NORA. You're just like the rest of them. You all think I'm useless when it comes to anything really serious. . . .

MRS. LINDE. Come, come. . . .

NORA. You think I've never had anything much to contend with in this hard world.

MRS. LINDE. Nora dear, you've only just been telling me all the things you've had to put up with.

NORA. Pooh! They were just trivialities! [*Softly.*] I haven't told you about the really big thing.

MRS. LINDE. What big thing? What do you mean?

NORA. I know you rather tend to look down on me, Kristine. But you shouldn't, you know. You are proud of having worked so hard and so long for your mother.

MRS. LINDE. I'm sure I don't look down on anybody. But it's true what you say: I am both proud and happy when I think of how I was able to make Mother's life a little easier towards the end.

NORA. And you are proud when you think of what you have done for your brothers, too.

MRS. LINDE. I think I have every right to be.

NORA. I think so too. But now I'm going to tell you something, Kristine. I too have something to be proud and happy about.

MRS. LINDE. I don't doubt that. But what is it you mean?

NORA. Not so loud. Imagine if Torvald were to hear! He must never on any account . . . nobody must know about it, Kristine, nobody but you.

MRS. LINDE. But what is it?

NORA. Come over here. [*She pulls her down on the sofa beside her.*] Yes, Kristine, I too have something to be proud and happy about. I was the one who saved Torvald's life.

MRS. LINDE. Saved . . . ? How . . . ?

NORA. I told you about our trip to Italy. Torvald would never have recovered but for that. . . .

MRS. LINDE. Well? Your father gave you what money was necessary. . . .

NORA [*smiles*]. That's what Torvald thinks, and everybody else. But . . .

MRS. LINDE. But . . . !

NORA. Daddy never gave us a penny. I was the one who raised the money.

MRS. LINDE. You? All that money?

NORA. Twelve hundred dollars. Four thousand eight hundred crowns. What do you say to that!

MRS. LINDE. But, Nora, how was it possible? Had you won a sweepstake or something?

NORA [*contemptuously*]. A sweepstake? Pooh! There would have been nothing to it then.

MRS. LINDE. Where did you get it from, then?

NORA [*hums and smiles secretively*]. H'm, tra-la-la!

MRS. LINDE. Because what you couldn't do was borrow it.

NORA. Oh? Why not?

MRS. LINDE. Well, a wife can't borrow without her husband's consent.

NORA [*tossing her head*]. Ah, but when it happens to be a wife with a bit of a sense for business . . . a wife who knows her way about things, then. . . .

MRS. LINDE. But, Nora, I just don't understand. . . .

NORA. You don't have to. I haven't said I did borrow the money. I might have got it some other way. [*Throws herself back on the sofa.*] I might even have got it from some admirer. Anyone as reasonably attractive as I am. . . .

MRS. LINDE. Don't be so silly!

NORA. Now you must be dying of curiosity, Kristine.

MRS. LINDE. Listen to me now, Nora dear—you haven't done anything rash, have you?

NORA [*sitting up again*]. Is it rash to save your husband's life?

MRS. LINDE. I think it was rash to do anything without telling him. . . .

NORA. But the whole point was that he mustn't know anything. Good heavens, can't you see! He wasn't even supposed to know how desperately ill he was. It was me the doctors came and told his life was in danger, that the only way to save him was to go South for a while. Do you think I didn't try talking him into it first? I began dropping hints about how nice it would be if I could be taken on a little trip abroad, like other young wives. I wept, I pleaded. I told him he ought to show some consideration for my condition, and let me have a bit of my own way. And then I suggested he might take out a loan. But at that he nearly lost his temper, Kristine. He said I was being frivolous, that it was his duty as a husband not to give in to all these whims and fancies of mine—as I do believe he called them. All right, I thought, somehow you've got to be saved. And it was then I found a way. . . .

MRS. LINDE. Did your husband never find out from your father that the money hadn't come from him?

NORA. No, never. It was just about the time Daddy died. I'd intended letting him into the secret and asking him not to give me away. But when he was so ill . . . I'm sorry to say it never became necessary.

MRS. LINDE. And you never confided in your husband?

NORA. Good heavens, how could you ever imagine such a thing! When he's so strict about such matters! Besides, Torvald is a man with a good deal of pride—it would be terribly embarrassing and humiliating for him if he thought he owed anything to me. It would spoil everything between us; this happy home of ours would never be the same again.

MRS. LINDE. Are you never going to tell him?

NORA [*reflectively, half-smiling*]. Oh yes, some day perhaps . . . in many years time, when I'm no longer as pretty as I am now. You mustn't laugh! What I mean of course is when Torvald isn't quite so much in love with me as he is now, when he's lost interest in watching me dance, or get dressed up, or recite. Then it might be a good thing to have something in reserve. . . . [*Breaks off.*] What nonsense! That day will never come. Well, what have you got to say to my big secret, Kristine? Still think I'm not much good for anything? One thing, though, it's meant a lot of worry for me, I can tell you. It hasn't always been easy to meet my obligations when the time came. You know in business there is something called quarterly interest, and other things called instalments, and these are always terribly difficult things to cope with. So what I've had to do is save a little here and there, you see, wherever I could. I couldn't really save anything out of the housekeeping, because Torvald has to live in decent style. I couldn't let the children go about badly dressed either—I felt any money I got for them had to go on them alone. Such sweet little things!

MRS. LINDE. Poor Nora! So it had to come out of your own allowance?

NORA. Of course. After all, I was the one it concerned most. Whenever Torvald gave me money for new clothes and such-like, I never spent more than half. And always I bought the simplest and cheapest things. It's a blessing most things look well on me, so Torvald never noticed anything. But sometimes I did feel it was a bit hard, Kristine, because it is nice to be well dressed, isn't it?

MRS. LINDE. Yes, I suppose it is.

NORA. I have had some other sources of income, of course. Last winter I was lucky enough to get quite a bit of copying to do. So I shut myself up every night and sat and wrote through to the small hours of the morning. Oh, sometimes I was so tired, so tired. But it was tremendous fun all the same, sitting there working and earning money like that. It was almost like being a man.

MRS. LINDE. And how much have you been able to pay off like this?

NORA. Well, I can't tell exactly. It's not easy to know where you are with transactions of this kind, you understand. All I know is I've paid off just as much as I could scrape together. Many's the time I was at my wit's end. [*Smiles.*] Then I used to sit here and pretend that some rich old gentleman had fallen in love with me. . . .

MRS. LINDE. What! What gentleman?

NORA. Oh, rubbish! . . . and that now he had died, and when they opened his will, there in big letters were the words: 'My entire fortune is to be paid over, immediately and in cash, to charming Mrs. Nora Helmer.'

MRS. LINDE. But my dear Nora—who is this man?

NORA. Good heavens, don't you understand? There never was any old gentleman; it was just something I used to sit here pretending, time and time again, when I didn't know where to turn next for money. But it doesn't make very much difference; as far as I'm concerned, the old boy can do what he likes, I'm tired of him; I can't be bothered any more with him or his will. Because now all my worries are over. [*Jumping up.*] Oh God, what a glorious thought, Kristine! No more worries! Just think of being without a care in the world . . . being able to romp with the children, and making the house nice and attractive, and having things just as Torvald likes to have them! And then spring will soon be here, and blue skies. And maybe we can go away somewhere. I might even see something of the sea again. Oh yes! When you're happy, life is a wonderful thing!

[*The door-bell is heard in the hall.*]

MRS. LINDE [*gets up*]. There's the bell. Perhaps I'd better go.

NORA. No, do stay, please. I don't suppose it's for me; it's probably somebody for Torvald . . .

MAID [*in the doorway*]. Excuse me, ma'am, but there's a gentleman here wants to see Mr. Helmer, and I didn't quite know . . . because the Doctor is in there. . . .

NORA. Who is the gentleman?

KROGSTAD [*in the doorway*]. It's me, Mrs. Helmer.

[*Mrs. Linde starts, then turns away to the window.*]

NORA [*tense, takes a step towards him and speaks in a low voice*]. You? What is it? What do you want to talk to my husband about?

KROGSTAD. Bank matters . . . in a manner of speaking. I work at the bank, and I hear your husband is to be the new manager. . . .

NORA. So it's . . .

KROGSTAD. Just routine business matters, Mrs. Helmer. Absolutely nothing else.

NORA. Well then, please go into his study.

[*She nods impassively and shuts the hall door behind him; then she walks across and sees to the stove.*]

MRS. LINDE. Nora . . . who was that man?

NORA. His name is Krogstad.

MRS. LINDE. So it really was him.

NORA. Do you know the man?

MRS. LINDE. I used to know him . . . a good many years ago. He was a solicitor's clerk in our district for a while.

NORA. Yes, so he was.

MRS. LINDE. How he's changed!

NORA. His marriage wasn't a very happy one, I believe.

MRS. LINDE. He's a widower now, isn't he?

NORA. With a lot of children. There, it'll burn better now.

[*She closes the stove door and moves the rocking chair a little to one side.*]

MRS. LINDE. He does a certain amount of business on the side, they say?

NORA. Oh? Yes, it's always possible. I just don't know. . . . But let's not think about business . . . it's all so dull.

[*Dr. Rank comes in from Helmer's study.*]

DR. RANK [*still in the doorway*]. No, no, Torvald, I won't intrude. I'll just look in on your wife for a moment. [*Shuts the door and notices Mrs. Linde.*] Oh, I beg your pardon. I'm afraid I'm intruding here as well.

NORA. No, not at all! [*Introduces them.*] Dr. Rank . . . Mrs. Linde.

RANK. Ah! A name I've often heard mentioned in this house. I believe I came past you on the stairs as I came in.

MRS. LINDE. I have to take things slowly going upstairs. I find it rather a trial.

RANK. Ah, some little disability somewhere, eh?

MRS. LINDE. Just a bit run down, I think, actually.

RANK. Is that all? Then I suppose you've come to town for a good rest—doing the rounds of the parties?

MRS. LINDE. I have come to look for work.

RANK. Is that supposed to be some kind of sovereign remedy for being run down?

MRS. LINDE. One must live, Doctor.

RANK. Yes, it's generally thought to be necessary.

NORA. Come, come, Dr. Rank. You are quite as keen to live as anybody.

RANK. Quite keen, yes. Miserable as I am, I'm quite ready to let things drag on as long as possible. All my patients are the same. Even those with a moral affliction are no different. As a matter of fact, there's a bad case of that kind in talking with Helmer at this very moment . . .

MRS. LINDE [*softly*]. Ah!

NORA. Whom do you mean?

RANK. A person called Krogstad—nobody you would know. He's rotten to the core. But even he began talking about having to *live*, as though it were something terribly important.

NORA. Oh? And what did he want to talk to Torvald about?

RANK. I honestly don't know. All I heard was something about the Bank.

NORA. I didn't know that Krog . . . that this Mr. Krogstad had anything to do with the Bank.

RANK. Oh yes, he's got some kind of job down there. [*To Mrs. Linde.*] I wonder if you've got people in your part of the country too who go rushing round sniffing out cases of moral corruption, and then installing the individuals concerned in nice, well-paid jobs where they can keep them under observation. Sound, decent people have to be content to stay out in the cold.

MRS. LINDE. Yet surely it's the sick who most need to be brought in.

RANK [*shrugs his shoulders*]. Well, there we have it. It's that attitude that's turning society into a clinic.

[*Nora, lost in her own thoughts, breaks into smothered laughter and claps her hands.*]

RANK. Why are you laughing at that? Do you know in fact what society is?

NORA. What do I care about your silly old society? I was laughing about something quite different . . . something frightfully funny. Tell me, Dr. Rank, are all the people who work at the Bank dependent on Torvald now?

RANK. Is that what you find so frightfully funny?

NORA [*smiles and hums*]. Never you mind! Never you mind! [*Walks about the room.*] Yes, it really is terribly amusing to think that we . . . that Torvald now has power over so many people. [*She takes the bag out of her pocket.*] Dr. Rank, what about a little macaroon?

RANK. Look at this, eh? Macaroons. I thought they were forbidden here.

NORA. Yes, but these are some Kristine gave me.

MRS. LINDE. What? I . . . ?

NORA. Now, now, you needn't be alarmed. You weren't to know that Torvald had forbidden them. He's worried in case they ruin my teeth, you know. Still . . . what's it matter once in a while! Don't you think so, Dr. Rank? Here! [*She pops a macaroon into his mouth.*] And you too, Kristine. And I shall have one as well; just a little one . . . or two at the most. [*She walks about the room again.*] Really I am so happy. There's just one little thing I'd love to do now.

RANK. What's that?

NORA. Something I'd love to say in front of Torvald.

RANK. Then why can't you?

NORA. No, I daren't. It's not very nice.

MRS. LINDE. Not very nice?

RANK. Well, in that case it might not be wise. But to us, I don't see why. . . . What is this you would love to say in front of Helmer?

NORA. I would simply love to say: 'Damn.'

RANK. Are you mad!

MRS. LINDE. Good gracious, Nora . . . !

RANK. Say it! Here he is!

NORA [*hiding the bag of macaroons*]. Sh! Sh!

[*Helmer comes out of his room, his overcoat over his arm and his hat in his hand.*]

NORA [*going over to him*]. Well, Torvald dear, did you get rid of him?

HELMER. Yes, he's just gone.

NORA. Let me introduce you. This is Kristine, who has just arrived in town. . . .

HELMER. Kristine . . . ? You must forgive me, but I don't think I know . . .

NORA. Mrs. Linde, Torvald dear. Kristine Linde.

HELMER. Ah, indeed. A school-friend of my wife's, presumably.

MRS. LINDE. Yes, we were girls together.

NORA. Fancy, Torvald, she's come all this long way just to have a word with you.

HELMER. How is that?

MRS. LINDE. Well, it wasn't really . . .

NORA. The thing is, Kristine is terribly clever at office work, and she's frightfully keen on finding a job with some efficient man, so that she can learn even more. . . .

HELMER. Very sensible, Mrs. Linde.

NORA. And then when she heard you'd been made Bank Manager—there was a bit in the paper about it—she set off at once. Torvald please! You *will* try and do something for Kristine, won't you? For my sake?

HELMER. Well, that's not altogether impossible. You are a widow, I presume?

MRS. LINDE. Yes.

HELMER. And you've had some experience in business?

MRS. LINDE. A fair amount.

HELMER. Well, it's quite probable I can find you a job, I think. . . .

NORA [*clapping her hands*]. There, you see!

HELMER. You have come at a fortunate moment, Mrs. Linde. . . .

MRS. LINDE. Oh, how can I ever thank you . . . ?

HELMER. Not a bit. [*He puts on his overcoat.*] But for the present I must ask you to excuse me. . . .

RANK. Wait. I'm coming with you.

[*He fetches his fur coat from the hall and warms it at the stove.*]

NORA. Don't be long, Torvald dear.

HELMER. Not more than an hour, that's all.

NORA. Are you leaving too, Kristine?

MRS. LINDE [*putting on her things*]. Yes, I must go and see if I can't find myself a room.

HELMER. Perhaps we can all walk down the road together.

NORA [*helping her*]. What a nuisance we are so limited for space here. I'm afraid it just isn't possible. . . .

MRS. LINDE. Oh, you mustn't dream of it! Goodbye, Nora dear, and thanks for everything.

NORA. Goodbye for the present. But . . . you'll be coming back this evening, of course. And you too, Dr. Rank? What's that? If you are up to it? Of course you'll be up to it. Just wrap yourself up well.

[*They go out, talking, into the hall; children's voices can be heard on the stairs.*]

NORA. Here they are! Here they are! [*She runs to the front door and opens it. Anne Marie, the nursemaid, enters with* the children.] Come in! Come in! [*She bends down and kisses them.*] Ah! my sweet little darlings. . . . You see them, Kristine? Aren't they lovely!

RANK. Don't stand here chattering in this draught!

HELMER. Come along, Mrs. Linde. The place now becomes unbearable for anybody except mothers.

[*Dr. Rank, Helmer and Mrs. Linde go down the stairs: the Nursemaid comes into the room with the children, then Nora, shutting the door behind her.*]

NORA. How fresh and bright you look! My, what red cheeks you've got! Like apples and roses. [*During the following, the children keep chattering away to her.*] Have you had a nice time? That's splendid. And you gave Emmy and Bob a ride on your sledge? Did you now! Both together! Fancy that! There's a clever boy, Ivar. Oh, let me take her a little while, Anne Marie. There's my sweet little baby-doll! [*She takes the youngest of the children from the nursemaid and dances with her.*] All right, Mummy will dance with Bobby too. What? You've been throwing snowballs? Oh, I wish I'd been there. No, don't bother, Anne Marie, I'll help them off with their things. No, please, let me—I like doing it. You go on in, you look frozen. You'll find some hot coffee on the stove. [*The nursemaid goes into the room, left. Nora takes off the children's coats and hats and throws them down anywhere, while the children all talk at once.*] Really! A great big dog came running after you? But he didn't bite. No, the doggies wouldn't bite my pretty little dollies. You mustn't touch the parcels, Ivar! What are they? Wouldn't you like to know! No, no, that's nasty. Now? Shall we play something? What shall we play? Hide and seek? Yes, let's play hide and seek. Bob can hide first. Me first? All right, let me hide first.

[*She and the children play, laughing and shrieking, in this room and in the adjacent room on the right. Finally Nora hides under the table; the children come rushing in to look for her but cannot find her; they hear her stifled laughter, rush to the table, lift up the tablecloth and find her. Tremendous shouts of delight. She creeps out and pretends to frighten them. More shouts. Meanwhile there has been a knock at the front door, which nobody has heard. The door half opens, and Krogstad can be seen. He waits a little; the game continues.*]

KROGSTAD. I beg your pardon, Mrs. Helmer. . . .

NORA [*turns with a stifled cry and half jumps up*]. Ah! What do you want?

KROGSTAD. Excuse me. The front door was standing open. Somebody must have forgotten to shut it. . . .

NORA [*standing up*]. My husband isn't at home, Mr. Krogstad.

KROGSTAD. I know.

NORA. Well . . . what are you doing here?

KROGSTAD. I want a word with you.

NORA. With . . . ? [*Quietly, to the children.*] Go to Anne Marie. What? No, the strange man won't do anything to Mummy. When he's gone we'll have another game. [*She leads the children into the room, left, and shuts the door after them; tense and uneasy.*] You want to speak to me?

KROGSTAD. Yes, I do.

NORA. Today? But it isn't the first of the month yet. . . .

KROGSTAD. No, it's Christmas Eve. It depends entirely on you what sort of Christmas you have.

NORA. What do you want? Today I can't possibly . . .

KROGSTAD. Let's not talk about that for the moment. It's something else. You've got a moment to spare?

NORA. Yes, I suppose so, though . . .

KROGSTAD. Good. I was sitting in Olsen's café, and I saw your husband go down the road . . .

NORA. Did you?

KROGSTAD. . . . with a lady.

NORA. Well?

KROGSTAD. May I be so bold as to ask whether that lady was a Mrs. Linde?

NORA. Yes.

KROGSTAD. Just arrived in town?

NORA. Yes, today.

KROGSTAD. And she's a good friend of yours?

NORA. Yes, she is. But I can't see . . .

KROGSTAD. I also knew her once.

NORA. I know.

KROGSTAD. Oh? So you know all about it. I thought as much. Well, I want to ask you straight: is Mrs. Linde getting a job in the Bank?

NORA. How dare you cross-examine me like this, Mr. Krogstad? You, one of my husband's subordinates? But since you've asked me, I'll tell you. Yes, Mrs. Linde *has* got a job. And I'm the one who got it for her, Mr. Krogstad. Now you know.

KROGSTAD. So my guess was right.

NORA [*walking up and down*]. Oh, I think I can say that some of us have a little influence now and again. Just because one happens to be a woman, that doesn't mean. . . . People in subordinate positions, ought to take care they don't offend anybody . . . who . . . hm . . .

KROGSTAD. . . . has influence?

NORA. Exactly.

KROGSTAD [*changing his tone*]. Mrs. Helmer, will you have the goodness to use your influence on my behalf?

NORA. What? What do you mean?

KROGSTAD. Will you be so good as to see that I keep my modest little job at the Bank?

NORA. What do you mean? Who wants to take it away from you?

KROGSTAD. Oh, you needn't try and pretend to me you don't know. I can quite see that this friend of yours isn't particularly anxious to bump up against me. And I can also see now whom I can thank for being given the sack.

NORA. But I assure you. . . .

KROGSTAD. All right, all right. But to come to the point: there's still time. And I advise you to use your influence to stop it.

NORA. But, Mr. Krogstad, I *have* no influence.

KROGSTAD. Haven't you? I thought just now you said yourself . . .

NORA. I didn't mean it that way, of course. Me? What makes you think I've got any influence of that kind over my husband?

KROGSTAD. I know your husband from our student days. I don't suppose he is any more steadfast than other married men.

NORA. You speak disrespectfully of my husband like that and I'll show you the door.

KROGSTAD. So the lady's got courage.

NORA. I'm not frightened of you any more. After New Year's I'll soon be finished with the whole business.

KROGSTAD [controlling himself]. Listen to me, Mrs. Helmer. If necessary I shall fight for my little job in the Bank as if I were fighting for my life.

NORA. So it seems.

KROGSTAD. It's not just for the money, that's the last thing I care about. There's something else . . . well, I might as well out with it. You see it's like this. You know as well as anybody that some years ago I got myself mixed up in a bit of trouble.

NORA. I believe I've heard something of the sort.

KROGSTAD. It never got as far as the courts; but immediately it was as if all paths were barred to me. So I started going in for the sort of business you know about. I had to do something, and I think I can say I haven't been one of the worst. But now I have to get out of it. My sons are growing up; for their sake I must try and win back what respectability I can. That job in the Bank was like the first step on the ladder for me. And now your husband wants to kick me off the ladder again, back into the mud.

NORA. But in God's name, Mr. Krogstad, it's quite beyond my power to help you.

KROGSTAD. That's because you haven't the will to help me. But I have ways of making you.

NORA. You wouldn't go and tell my husband I owe you money?

KROGSTAD. Suppose I did tell him?

NORA. It would be a rotten shame. [Half choking with tears.] That secret is all my pride and joy—why should he have to hear about it in this nasty, horrid way . . . hear about it from *you*. You would make things horribly unpleasant for me. . . .

KROGSTAD. Merely unpleasant?

NORA [vehemently]. Go on, do it then! It'll be all the worse for you. Because then my husband will see for himself what a bad man you are, and then you certainly won't be able to keep your job.

KROGSTAD. I asked whether it was only a bit of domestic unpleasantness you were afraid of?

NORA. If my husband gets to know about it, he'll pay off what's owing at once. And then we'd have nothing more to do with you.

KROGSTAD [taking a pace towards her]. Listen, Mrs. Helmer, either you haven't a very good memory, or else you don't understand much about business. I'd better make the position a little bit clearer for you.

NORA. How do you mean?

KROGSTAD. When your husband was ill, you came to me for the loan of twelve hundred dollars.

NORA. I didn't know of anybody else.

KROGSTAD. I promised to find you the money. . . .

NORA. And you did find it.

KROGSTAD. I promised to find you the money on certain conditions. At the time you were so concerned about your husband's illness, and so anxious to get the money for going away with, that I don't think you paid very much attention to all the incidentals. So there is perhaps some point in reminding you of them. Well, I promised to find you the money against an IOU which I drew up for you.

NORA. Yes, and which I signed.

KROGSTAD. Very good. But below that I added a few lines, by which your father was to stand security. This your father was to sign.

NORA. Was to . . . ? He did sign it.

KROGSTAD. I had left the date blank. The idea was that your father was to add the date himself when he signed it. Remember?

NORA. Yes, I think. . . .

KROGSTAD. I then gave you the IOU to post to your father. Wasn't that so?

NORA. Yes.

KROGSTAD. Which of course you did at once. Because only about five or six days later you brought it back to me with your father's signature. I then paid out the money.

NORA. Well? Haven't I paid the instalments regularly?

KROGSTAD. Yes, fairly. But . . . coming back to what we were talking about . . . that was a pretty bad period you were going through then, Mrs. Helmer.

NORA. Yes, it was.

KROGSTAD. Your father was seriously ill, I believe.

NORA. He was very near the end.

KROGSTAD. And died shortly afterwards?

NORA. Yes.

KROGSTAD. Tell me, Mrs. Helmer, do you happen to remember which day your father died? The exact date, I mean.

NORA. Daddy died on 29 September.

KROGSTAD. Quite correct. I made some inquiries. Which brings up a rather curious point [takes out a paper] which I simply cannot explain.

NORA. Curious . . . ? I don't know . . .

KROGSTAD. The curious thing is, Mrs. Helmer, that your father signed this document three days after his death.

NORA. What? I don't understand. . . .

KROGSTAD. Your father died on 29 September. But look here. Your father has dated his signature 2 October. Isn't that rather curious, Mrs. Helmer? [*Nora remains silent.*] It's also remarkable that the words '2 October' and the year are not in your father's handwriting, but in a handwriting I rather think I recognize. Well, perhaps that could be explained. Your father might have forgotten to date his signature, and then somebody else might have made a guess at the date later, before the fact of your father's death was known. There is nothing wrong in that. What really matters is the signature. And *that* is of course genuine, Mrs. Helmer? It really was your father who wrote his name here?

NORA [*after a moment's silence, throws her head back and looks at him defiantly*]. No, it wasn't. It was me who signed father's name.

KROGSTAD. Listen to me. I suppose you realize that that is a very dangerous confession?

NORA. Why? You'll soon have all your money back.

KROGSTAD. Let me ask you a question: why didn't you send that document to your father?

NORA. It was impossible. Daddy was ill. If I'd asked him for his signature, I'd have to tell him what the money was for. Don't you see, when he was as ill as that I couldn't go and tell him that my husband's life was in danger. It was simply impossible.

KROGSTAD. It would have been better for you if you had abandoned the whole trip.

NORA. No, that was impossible. This was the thing that was to save my husband's life. I couldn't give it up.

KROGSTAD. But did it never strike you that this was fraudulent . . . ?

NORA. That wouldn't have meant anything to me. Why should I worry about you? I couldn't stand you, not when you insisted on going through with all those cold-blooded formalities, knowing all the time what a critical state my husband was in.

KROGSTAD. Mrs. Helmer, it's quite clear you still haven't the faintest idea what it is you've committed. But let me tell you, my own offence was no more and no worse than that, and it ruined my entire reputation.

NORA. You? Are you trying to tell me that you once risked everything to save your wife's life?

KROGSTAD. The law takes no account of motives.

NORA. Then they must be very bad laws.

KROGSTAD. Bad or not, if I produce this document in court, you'll be condemned according to them.

NORA. I don't believe it. Isn't a daughter entitled to try and save her father from worry and anxiety on his deathbed? Isn't a wife entitled to save her husband's life? I might not know very much about the law, but I feel sure of one thing: it must say somewhere that things like this are allowed. You mean to say you don't know that—you, when it's your job? You must be a rotten lawyer, Mr. Krogstad.

KROGSTAD. That may be. But when it comes to business transactions—like the sort between us two—perhaps you'll admit I know something about *them*? Good. Now you must please yourself. But I tell you this: if I'm pitched out a second time, you are going to keep me company.

[*He bows and goes out through the hall.*]

NORA [*stands thoughtfully for a moment, then tosses her head*]. Rubbish! He's just trying to scare me. I'm not such a fool as all that. [*Begins gathering up the children's clothes; after a moment she stops.*] Yet . . . ? No, it's impossible! I did it for love, didn't I?

THE CHILDREN [*in the doorway, left*]. Mummy, the gentleman's just gone out of the gate.

NORA. Yes, I know. But you mustn't say anything to anybody about that gentleman. You hear? Not even to Daddy!

THE CHILDREN. All right, Mummy. Are you going to play again?

NORA. No, not just now.

THE CHILDREN. But Mummy, you promised!

NORA. Yes, but I can't just now. Off you go now, I have a lot to do. Off you go, my darlings. [*She herds them carefully into the other room and shuts the door behind them. She sits down on the sofa, picks up her embroidery and works a few stitches, but soon stops.*] No! [*She flings her work down, stands up, goes to the hall door and calls out.*] Helene! Fetch the tree in for me, please. [*She walks across to the table, left, and opens the drawer; again pauses.*] No, really, it's quite impossible!

MAID [*with the Christmas tree*]. Where shall I put it, ma'am?

NORA. On the floor there, in the middle.

MAID. Anything else you want me to bring?

NORA. No, thank you. I've got what I want.

[*The maid has put the tree down and goes out.*]

NORA [*busy decorating the tree*]. Candles here . . . and flowers here—Revolting man! It's all nonsense! There's nothing to worry about. We'll have a lovely Christmas tree. And I'll do anything you want me to, Torvald; I'll sing for you, dance for you. . . .

[*Helmer, with a bundle of documents under his arm, comes in by the hall door.*]

NORA. Ah, back again already?

HELMER. Yes. Anybody been?

NORA. Here? No.

HELMER. That's funny. I just saw Krogstad leave the house.

NORA. Oh? O yes, that's right. Krogstad was here a minute.

HELMER. Nora, I can tell by your face he's been asking you to put a good word in for him.

NORA. Yes.

HELMER. And you were to pretend it was your own idea? You were to keep quiet about his having been here. He asked you to do that as well, didn't he?

NORA. Yes, Torvald. But . . .

HELMER. Nora, Nora, what possessed you to do a thing like that? Talking to a person like him, making him promises? And then on top of everything, to tell me a lie!

NORA. A lie . . . ?

HELMER. Didn't you say that nobody had been here? [*Wagging his finger at her.*] Never again must my little song-bird do a thing like that! Little song-birds must keep their pretty little beaks out of mischief; no chirruping out of tune! [*Puts his arm round her waist.*] Isn't that the way we want things to be? Yes, of course it is. [*Lets her go.*] So let's say no more about it. [*Sits down by the stove.*] Ah, nice and cosy here!

[*He glances through his papers.*]

NORA [*busy with the Christmas tree, after a short pause*]. Torvald!

HELMER. Yes.

NORA. I'm so looking forward to the fancy dress ball at the Stenborgs on Boxing Day.

HELMER. And I'm terribly curious to see what sort of surprise you've got for me.

NORA. Oh, it's too silly.

HELMER. Oh?

NORA. I just can't think of anything suitable. Everything seems so absurd, so pointless.

HELMER. Has my little Nora come to *that* conclusion?

NORA [*behind his chair, her arms on the chairback*]. Are you very busy, Torvald?

HELMER. Oh. . . .

NORA. What are all those papers?

HELMER. Bank matters.

NORA. Already?

HELMER. I have persuaded the retiring manager to give me authority to make any changes in organisation or personnel I think necessary. I have to work on it over the Christmas week. I want everything straight by the New Year.

NORA. So that was why that poor Krogstad. . . .

HELMER. Hm!

NORA [*still leaning against the back of the chair, running her fingers through his hair*]. If you hadn't been so busy, Torvald, I'd have asked you to do me an awfully big favour.

HELMER. Let me hear it. What's it to be?

NORA. Nobody's got such good taste as you. And the thing is I do so want to look my best at the fancy dress ball. Torvald, couldn't you give me some advice and tell me what you think I ought to go as, and how I should arrange my costume?

HELMER. Aha! So my impulsive little woman is asking for somebody to come to her rescue, eh?

NORA. Please, Torvald, I never get anywhere without your help.

HELMER. Very well, I'll think about it. We'll find something.

NORA. That's sweet of you. [*She goes across to the tree again; pause.*] How pretty these red flowers look.—Tell me, was it really something terribly wrong this man Krogstad did?

HELMER. Forgery. Have you any idea what that means?

NORA. Perhaps circumstances left him no choice?

HELMER. Maybe. Or perhaps, like so many others, he just didn't think. I am not so heartless that I would necessarily want to condemn a man for a single mistake like that.

NORA. Oh no, Torvald, of course not!

HELMER. Many a man might be able to redeem himself, if he honestly confessed his guilt and took his punishment.

NORA. Punishment?

HELMER. But that wasn't the way Krogstad chose. He dodged what was due to him by a cunning trick. And that's what has been the cause of his corruption.

NORA. Do you think it would . . . ?

HELMER. Just think how a man with a thing like that on his conscience will always be having to lie and cheat and dissemble; he can never drop the mask, not even with his own wife and children. And the children—*that's* the most terrible part of it, Nora.

NORA. Why?

HELMER. A fog of lies like that in a household, and it spreads disease and infection to every part of it. Every breath the children take in that kind of house is reeking with evil germs.

NORA [*closer behind him*]. Are you sure of that?

HELMER. My dear Nora, as a lawyer I know what I'm talking about. Practically all juvenile delinquents come from homes where the mother is dishonest.

NORA. Why mothers particularly?

HELMER. It's generally traceable to the mothers, but of course fathers can have the same influence. Every lawyer knows that only too well. And yet there's Krogstad been poisoning his own children for years with lies and deceit. That's the reason I call him morally depraved. [*Holds out his hands to her.*] That's why my sweet little Nora must promise me not to try putting in any more good words for him. Shake hands on it. Well? What's this? Give me your hand. There now! That's settled. I assure you I would have found it impossible to work with him. I quite literally feel physically sick in the presence of such people.

NORA [*draws her hand away and walks over to the other side of the Christmas tree*]. How hot it is in here! And I still have such a lot to do.

HELMER [*stands up and collects his papers together*]. Yes, I'd better think of getting some of this read before dinner. I must also think about your costume. And I might even be able to lay my hands on something to wrap in gold paper and hang on the Christmas tree. [*He lays his hand on her head.*] My precious little singing bird.

[*He goes into his study and shuts the door behind him.*]

NORA [*quietly, after a pause*]. Nonsense! It can't be. It's impossible. It *must* be impossible.

MAID [*in the doorway, left*]. The children keep asking so nicely if they can come in and see Mummy.

NORA. No, no, don't let them in! You stay with them, Anne
     Marie.

MAID. Very well, ma'am.

[*She shuts the door.*]

NORA [*pale with terror*]. Corrupt my children . . . ! Poison my
     home? [*Short pause; she throws back her head.*] It's not true!
     It could never, never be true!

ACT II

*The same room. In the corner beside the piano stands the
Christmas tree, stripped, bedraggled and with its candles
burnt out. Nora's outdoor things lie on the sofa. Nora,
alone there, walks about restlessly; at last she stops by the
sofa and picks up her coat.*

NORA [*putting her coat down again*]. Somebody's coming!
     [*Crosses to the door, listens.*] No, it's nobody. Nobody will
     come today, of course, Christmas Day—nor tomorrow, ei-
     ther. But perhaps. . . . [*She opens the door and looks out.*]
     No, nothing in the letter box; quite empty. [*Comes for-
     ward.*] Oh, nonsense! He didn't mean it seriously. Things
     like that *can't* happen. It's impossible. Why, I have three
     small children.

[*The Nursemaid comes from the room, left, carrying a big
cardboard box.*]

NURSEMAID. I finally found it, the box with the fancy dress
     costumes.

NORA. Thank you. Put it on the table, please.

NURSEMAID [*does this*]. But I'm afraid they are in an awful
     mess.

NORA. Oh, if only I could rip them up into a thousand pieces!

NURSEMAID. Good heavens, they can be mended all right,
     with a bit of patience.

NORA. Yes, I'll go over and get Mrs. Linde to help me.

NURSEMAID. Out again? In this terrible weather? You'll catch
     your death of cold, Ma'am.

NORA. Oh, worse things might happen.—How are the chil-
     dren?

NURSEMAID. Playing with their Christmas presents, poor lit-
     tle things, but . . .

NORA. Do they keep asking for me?

NURSEMAID. They are so used to being with their Mummy.

NORA. Yes, Anne Marie, from now on I can't be with them
     as often as I was before.

NURSEMAID. Ah well, children get used to anything in time.

NORA. Do you think so? Do you think they would forget
     their Mummy if she went away for good?

NURSEMAID. Good gracious—for good?

NORA. Tell me, Anne Marie—I've often wondered—how on
     earth could you bear to hand your child over to strangers?

NURSEMAID. Well, there was nothing else for it when I had
     to come and nurse my little Nora.

NORA. Yes but . . . how could you *bring* yourself to do it?

NURSEMAID. When I had the chance of such a good place?
     When a poor girl's been in trouble she must make the
     best of things. Because *he* didn't help, the rotter.

NORA. But your daughter will have forgotten you.

NURSEMAID. Oh no, she hasn't. She wrote to me when she
     got confirmed, and again when she got married.

NORA [*putting her arms round her neck*]. Dear old Anne Marie,
     you were a good mother to me when I was little.

NURSEMAID. My poor little Nora never had any other
     mother but me.

NORA. And if my little ones only had you, I know you
     would. . . . Oh, what am I talking about! [*She opens the
     box.*] Go in to them. I must . . . Tomorrow I'll let you see
     how pretty I am going to look.

NURSEMAID. Ah, there'll be nobody at the ball as pretty as
     my Nora.

[*She goes into the room, left.*]

NORA [*begins unpacking the box, but soon throws it down*]. Oh,
     if only I dare go out. If only I could be sure nobody would
     come. And that nothing would happen in the mean-
     time here at home. Rubbish—nobody's going to come. I
     mustn't think about it. Brush this muff. Pretty gloves,
     pretty gloves! I'll put it right out of my mind. One, two,
     three, four, five, six. . . . [*Screams.*] Ah, they are coming.
     . . . [*She starts towards the door, but stops irresolute. Mrs.
     Linde comes from the hall, where she has taken off her things.*]
     Oh, it's you, Kristine. There's nobody else out there, is
     there? I'm so glad you've come.

MRS. LINDE. I heard you'd been over looking for me.

NORA. Yes, I was just passing. There's something you must
     help me with. Come and sit beside me on the sofa here.
     You see, the Stenborgs are having a fancy dress party up-
     stairs tomorrow evening, and now Torvald wants me to
     go as a Neapolitan fisher lass and dance the tarantella. I
     learned it in Capri, you know.

MRS. LINDE. Well, well! So you are going to do a party piece?

NORA. Torvald says I should. Look, here's the costume, Tor-
     vald had it made for me down there. But it's got all torn
     and I simply don't know. . . .

MRS. LINDE. We'll soon have that put right. It's only the
     trimming come away here and there. Got a needle and
     thread? Ah, here's what we are after.

NORA. It's awfully kind of you.

MRS. LINDE. So you are going to be all dressed up tomorrow,
     Nora? Tell you what—I'll pop over for a minute to see
     you in all your finery. But I'm quite forgetting to thank
     you for the pleasant time we had last night.

NORA [*gets up and walks across the room*]. Somehow I didn't
     think yesterday was as nice as things generally are.—You
     should have come to town a little earlier, Kristine.—Yes,
     Torvald certainly knows how to make things pleasant
     about the place.

MRS. LINDE. You too, I should say. You are not your father's daughter for nothing. But tell me, is Dr. Rank always as depressed as he was last night?

NORA. No, last night it was rather obvious. He's got something seriously wrong with him, you know. Tuberculosis of the spine, poor fellow. His father was a horrible man, who used to have mistresses and things like that. That's why the son was always ailing, right from being a child.

MRS. LINDE [*lowering her sewing*]. But my dear Nora, how do you come to know about things like that?

NORA [*walking about the room*]. Huh! When you've got three children, you get these visits from . . . women who have had a certain amount of medical training. And you hear all sorts of things from them.

MRS. LINDE [*begins sewing again; short silence*]. Does Dr. Rank call in every day?

NORA. Every single day. He was Torvald's best friend as a boy, and he's a good friend of *mine*, too. Dr. Rank is almost like one of the family.

MRS. LINDE. But tell me—is he really genuine? What I mean is: doesn't he sometimes rather turn on the charm?

NORA. No, on the contrary. What makes you think that?

MRS. LINDE. When you introduced me yesterday, he claimed he'd often heard my name in this house. But afterwards I noticed your husband hadn't the faintest idea who I was. Then how is it that Dr. Rank should. . . .

NORA. Oh yes, it was quite right what he said, Kristine. You see Torvald is so terribly in love with me that he says he wants me all to himself. When we were first married, it even used to make him sort of jealous if I only as much as mentioned any of my old friends from back home. So of course I stopped doing it. But I often talk to Dr. Rank about such things. He likes hearing about them.

MRS. LINDE. Listen, Nora! In lots of ways you are still a child. Now, I'm a good deal older than you, and a bit more experienced. I'll tell you something: I think you ought to give up all this business with Dr. Rank.

NORA. Give up what business?

MRS. LINDE. The whole thing, I should say. Weren't you saying yesterday something about a rich admirer who was to provide you with money. . . .

NORA. One who's never existed, I regret to say. But what of it?

MRS. LINDE. Has Dr. Rank money?

NORA. Yes, he has.

MRS. LINDE. And no dependents?

NORA. No, nobody. But . . . ?

MRS. LINDE. And he comes to the house every day?

NORA. Yes, I told you.

MRS. LINDE. But how can a man of his position want to pester you like this?

NORA. I simply don't understand.

MRS. LINDE. Don't pretend, Nora. Do you think I don't see now who you borrowed the twelve hundred from?

NORA. Are you out of your mind? Do you really think that? A friend of ours who comes here every day? The whole situation would have been absolutely intolerable.

MRS. LINDE. It *really* isn't him?

NORA. No, I give you my word. It would never have occurred to me for one moment. . . . Anyway, he didn't have the money to lend then. He didn't inherit it till later.

MRS. LINDE. Just as well for you, I'd say, my dear Nora.

NORA. No, it would never have occurred to me to ask Dr. Rank. . . . All the same I'm pretty certain if I were to ask him . . .

MRS. LINDE. But of course you won't.

NORA. No, of course not. I can't ever imagine it being necessary. But I'm quite certain if ever I were to mention it to Dr. Rank. . . .

MRS. LINDE. Behind your husband's back?

NORA. I have to get myself out of that other business. That's also behind his back. I *must* get myself out of that.

MRS. LINDE. Yes, that's what I said yesterday. But . . .

NORA [*walking up and down*]. A man's better at coping with these things than a woman. . . .

MRS. LINDE. Your own husband, yes.

NORA. Nonsense! [*Stops.*] When you've paid everything you owe, you do get your IOU back again, don't you?

MRS. LINDE. Of course.

NORA. And you can tear it up into a thousand pieces and burn it—the nasty, filthy thing!

MRS. LINDE [*looking fixedly at her, puts down her sewing and slowly rises*]. Nora, you are hiding something from me.

NORA. Is it so obvious?

MRS. LINDE. Something has happened to you since yesterday morning. Nora, what is it?

NORA [*going towards her*]. Kristine! [*Listens.*] Hush! There's Torvald back. Look, you go and sit in there beside the children for the time being. Torvald can't stand the sight of mending lying about. Get Anne Marie to help you.

MRS. LINDE [*gathering a lot of the things together*]. All right, but I'm not leaving until we have thrashed this thing out.

[*She goes into the room, left; at the same time Helmer comes in from the hall.*]

NORA [*goes to meet him*]. I've been longing for you to be back, Torvald, dear.

HELMER. Was that the dressmaker . . . ?

NORA. No, it was Kristine; she's helping me with my costume. I think it's going to look very nice . . .

HELMER. Wasn't that a good idea of mine, now?

NORA. Wonderful! But wasn't it also nice of me to let you have your way?

HELMER [*taking her under the chin*]. Nice of you—because you let your husband have his way? All right, you little rogue, I know you didn't mean it that way. But I don't want to disturb you. You'll be wanting to try the costume on, I suppose.

NORA. And I dare say you've got work to do?

HELMER. Yes. [*Shows her a bundle of papers.*] Look at this. I've been down at the Bank. . . .

[*He turns to go into his study.*]

NORA. Torvald!

HELMER [*stopping*]. Yes.

NORA. If a little squirrel were to ask ever so nicely . . . ?

HELMER. Well?

NORA. Would you do something for it?

HELMER. Naturally I would first have to know what it is.

NORA. Please, if only you would let it have its way, and do what it wants, it'd scamper about and do all sorts of marvellous tricks.

HELMER. What is it?

NORA. And the pretty little sky-lark would sing all day long. . . .

HELMER. Huh! It does that anyway.

NORA. I'd pretend I was an elfin child and dance a moonlight dance for you, Torvald.

HELMER. Nora—I hope it's not that business you started on this morning?

NORA [*coming closer*]. Yes, it is, Torvald. I implore you!

HELMER. You have the nerve to bring that up again?

NORA. Yes, yes, you *must* listen to me. You must let Krogstad keep his job at the Bank.

HELMER. My dear Nora, I'm giving his job to Mrs. Linde.

NORA. Yes, it's awfully sweet of you. But couldn't you get rid of somebody else in the office instead of Krogstad?

HELMER. This really is the most incredible obstinacy! Just because you go and make some thoughtless promise to put in a good word for him, you expect me . . .

NORA. It's not that, Torvald. It's for your own sake. That man writes in all the nastiest papers, you told me that yourself. He can do you no end of harm. He terrifies me to death. . . .

HELMER. Aha, now I see. It's your memories of what happened before that are frightening you.

NORA. What do you mean?

HELMER. It's your father you are thinking of.

NORA. Yes . . . yes, that's right. You remember all the nasty insinuations those wicked people put in the papers about Daddy? I honestly think they would have had him dismissed if the Ministry hadn't sent you down to investigate, and you hadn't been so kind and helpful.

HELMER. My dear little Nora, there is a considerable difference between your father and me. Your father's professional conduct was not entirely above suspicion. Mine is. And I hope it's going to stay that way as long as I hold this position.

NORA. But nobody knows what some of these evil people are capable of. Things could be so nice and pleasant for us here, in the peace and quiet of our home—you and me and the children, Torvald! That's why I implore you. . . .

HELMER. The more you plead for him, the more impossible you make it for me to keep him on. It's already known down at the Bank that I am going to give Krogstad his notice. If it ever got around that the new manager had been talked over by his wife. . . .

NORA. What of it?

HELMER. Oh, nothing! As long as the little woman gets her own stubborn way . . . ! Do you want me to make myself a laughing stock in the office? . . . Give people the idea that I am susceptible to any kind of outside pressure? You can imagine how soon I'd feel the consequences of that! Anyway, there's one other consideration that makes it impossible to have Krogstad in the Bank as long as I am manager.

NORA. What's that?

HELMER. At a pinch I might have overlooked his past lapses. . . .

NORA. Of course you could, Torvald!

HELMER. And I'm told he's not bad at his job, either. But we knew each other rather well when we were younger. It was one of those rather rash friendships that prove embarrassing in later life. There's no reason why you shouldn't know we were once on terms of some familiarity. And he, in his tactless way, makes no attempt to hide the fact, particularly when other people are present. On the contrary, he thinks he has every right to treat me as an equal, with his 'Torvald this' and 'Torvald that' every time he opens his mouth. I find it extremely irritating, I can tell you. He would make my position at the Bank absolutely intolerable.

NORA. Torvald, surely you aren't serious?

HELMER. Oh? Why not?

NORA. Well, it's all so petty.

HELMER. What's that you say? Petty? Do you think I'm petty?

NORA. No, not at all, Torvald dear! And that's why . . .

HELMER. Doesn't make any difference! . . . You call my motives petty; so I must be petty too. Petty! Indeed! Well, we'll put a stop to that, once and for all. [*He opens the hall door and calls.*] Helene!

NORA. What are you going to do?

HELMER [*searching among his papers*]. Settle things. [*The Maid comes in.*] See this letter? I want you to take it down at once. Get hold of a messenger and get him to deliver it. Quickly. The address is on the outside. There's the money.

MAID. Very good, sir.

[*She goes with the letter.*]

HELMER [*putting his papers together*]. There now, my stubborn little miss.

NORA [*breathless*]. Torvald . . . what was that letter?

HELMER. Krogstad's notice.

NORA. Get it back, Torvald! There's still time! Oh, Torvald, get it back! Please for my sake, for your sake, for the sake of the children! Listen, Torvald, please! You don't realize what it can do to us.

HELMER. Too late.

NORA. Yes, too late.

HELMER. My dear Nora, I forgive you this anxiety of yours, although it is actually a bit of an insult. Oh, but it is, I tell you! It's hardly flattering to suppose that anything this miserable pen-pusher wrote could frighten *me*! But I forgive you all the same, because it is rather a sweet way of showing how much you love me. [*He takes her in his arms.*] This is how things must be, my own darling Nora. When it comes to the point, I've enough strength and enough courage, believe me, for whatever happens. You'll find I'm man enough to take everything on myself.

NORA [*terrified*]. What do you mean?

HELMER. Everything, I said. . . .

NORA [*in command of herself*]. That is something you shall never, never do.

HELMER. All right, then we'll share it, Nora—as man and wife. That's what we'll do. [*Caressing her.*] Does that make you happy now? There, there, don't look at me with those eyes, like a little frightened dove. The whole thing is sheer imagination.—Why don't you run through the tarantella and try out the tambourine? I'll go into my study and shut both the doors, then I won't hear anything. You can make all the noise you want. [*Turns in the doorway.*] And when Rank comes, tell him where he can find me.

[*He nods to her, goes with his papers into his room, and shuts the door behind him.*]

NORA [*wild-eyed with terror, stands as though transfixed*]. He's quite capable of doing it! He would do it! No matter what, he'd do it.—No, never in this world! Anything but that! Help? Some way out . . . ? [*The door-bell rings in the hall.*] Dr. Rank . . . ! Anything but that, *anything*! [*She brushes her hands over her face, pulls herself together and opens the door into the hall. Dr. Rank is standing outside hanging up his fur coat. During what follows it begins to grow dark.*] Hello, Dr. Rank. I recognized your ring. Do you mind not going in to Torvald just yet, I think he's busy.

RANK. And you?

[*Dr. Rank comes into the room and she closes the door behind him.*]

NORA. Oh, you know very well I've always got time for you.

RANK. Thank you. A privilege I shall take advantage of as long as I am able.

NORA. What do you mean—as long as you are able?

RANK. Does that frighten you?

NORA. Well, it's just that it sounds so strange. Is anything likely to happen?

RANK. Only what I have long expected. But I didn't think it would come quite so soon.

NORA [*catching at his arm*]. What have you found out? Dr. Rank, you must tell me!

RANK. I'm slowly sinking. There's nothing to be done about it.

NORA [*with a sigh of relief*]. Oh, it's *you* you're . . . ?

RANK. Who else? No point in deceiving oneself. I am the most wretched of all my patients, Mrs. Helmer. These last few days I've made a careful analysis of my internal economy. Bankrupt! Within a month I shall probably be lying rotting up there in the churchyard.

NORA. Come now, what a ghastly thing to say!

RANK. The whole damned thing is ghastly. But the worst thing is all the ghastliness that has to be gone through first. I only have one more test to make; and when that's done I'll know pretty well when the final disintegration will start. There's something I want to ask you. Helmer is a sensitive soul; he loathes anything that's ugly. I don't want him visiting me. . . .

NORA. But Dr. Rank. . . .

RANK. On no account must he. I won't have it. I'll lock the door on him.—As soon as I'm absolutely certain of the worst, I'll send you my visiting card with a black cross on it. You'll know then the final horrible disintegration has begun.

NORA. Really, you are being quite absurd today. And here was I hoping you would be in a thoroughly good mood.

RANK. With death staring me in the face? Why should I suffer for another man's sins? What justice is there in that? Somewhere, somehow, every single family must be suffering some such cruel retribution. . . .

NORA [*stopping up her ears*]. Rubbish! Do cheer up!

RANK. Yes, really the whole thing's nothing but a huge joke. My poor innocent spine must do penance for my father's gay subaltern life.

NORA [*by the table, left*]. Wasn't he rather partial to asparagus and *pâté de foie gras*?

RANK. Yes, he was. And truffles.

NORA. Truffles, yes. And oysters, too, I believe?

RANK. Yes, oysters, oysters, of course.

NORA. And all the port and champagne that goes with them. It does seem a pity all these delicious things should attack the spine.

RANK. Especially when they attack a poor spine that never had any fun out of them.

NORA. Yes, that is an awful pity.

RANK [*looks at her sharply*]. Hm. . . .

NORA [*after a pause*]. Why did you smile?

RANK. No, it was you who laughed.

NORA. No, it was you who smiled, Dr. Rank!

RANK [*getting up*]. You are a bigger rascal than I thought you were.

NORA. I feel full of mischief today.

RANK. So it seems.

NORA [*putting her hands on his shoulders*]. Dear, dear Dr. Rank, you mustn't go and die on Torvald and me.

RANK. You wouldn't miss me for long. When you are gone, you are soon forgotten.

NORA [*looking at him anxiously*]. Do you think so?

RANK. People make new contacts, then . . .

NORA. Who make new contacts?

RANK. Both you and Helmer will, when I'm gone. You yourself are already well on the way, it seems to me. What was this Mrs. Linde doing here last night?

NORA. Surely you aren't jealous of poor Kristine?

RANK. Yes, I am. She'll be my successor in this house. When I'm done for, I can see this woman. . . .

NORA. Hush! Don't talk so loud, she's in there.

RANK. Today as well? There you are, you see!

NORA. Just to do some sewing on my dress. Good Lord, how absurd you are! [*She sits down on the sofa.*] Now Dr. Rank, cheer up. You'll see tomorrow how nicely I can dance. And you can pretend I'm doing it just for you—and for Torvald as well, of course. [*She takes various things out of the box.*] Come here, Dr. Rank. I want to show you something.

RANK [*sits*]. What is it?

NORA. Look!

RANK. Silk stockings.

NORA. Flesh-coloured! Aren't they lovely! Of course, it's dark here now, but tomorrow. . . . No, no, no, you can only look at the feet. Oh well, you might as well see a bit higher up, too.

RANK. Hm. . . .

NORA. Why are you looking so critical? Don't you think they'll fit?

RANK. I couldn't possibly offer any informed opinion about that.

NORA [*looks at him for a moment*]. Shame on you. [*Hits him lightly across the ear with the stockings.*] Take that! [*Folds them up again.*]

RANK. And what other delights am I to be allowed to see?

NORA. Not another thing. You are too naughty. [*She hums a little and searches among her things.*]

RANK [*after a short pause*]. Sitting here so intimately like this with you, I can't imagine . . . I simply cannot conceive what would have become of me if I had never come to this house.

NORA [*smiles*]. Yes, I rather think you do enjoy coming here.

RANK [*in a low voice, looking fixedly ahead*]. And the thought of having to leave it all . . .

NORA. Nonsense. You aren't leaving.

RANK [*in the same tone*]. . . . without being able to leave behind even the slightest token of gratitude, hardly a fleeting regret even . . . nothing but an empty place to be filled by the first person that comes along.

NORA. Supposing I were to ask you to . . . ? No . . .

RANK. What?

NORA. . . . to show me the extent of your friendship . . .

RANK. Yes?

NORA. I mean . . . to do me a tremendous favour. . . .

RANK. Would you really, for once, give me that pleasure?

NORA. You have no idea what it is.

RANK. All right, tell me.

NORA. No, really I can't, Dr. Rank. It's altogether too much to ask . . . because I need your advice and help as well. . . .

RANK. The more the better. I cannot imagine what you have in mind. But tell me anyway. You do trust me, don't you?

NORA. Yes, I trust you more than anybody I know. You are my best and my most faithful friend. I know that. So I will tell you. Well then, Dr. Rank, there is something you must help me to prevent. You know how deeply, how passionately Torvald is in love with me. He would never hesitate for a moment to sacrifice his life for my sake.

RANK [*bending towards her*]. Nora . . . do you think he's the only one who . . . ?

NORA [*stiffening slightly*]. Who . . . ?

RANK. Who wouldn't gladly give his life for your sake.

NORA [*sadly*]. Oh!

RANK. I swore to myself you would know before I went. I'll never have a better opportunity. Well, Nora! Now you know. And now you know too that you can confide in me as in nobody else.

NORA [*rises and speaks evenly and calmly*]. Let me past.

RANK [*makes way for her, but remains seated*]. Nora. . . .

NORA [*in the hall doorway*]. Helene, bring the lamp in, please. [*Walks over to the stove.*] Oh, my dear Dr. Rank, that really was rather horrid of you.

RANK [*getting up*]. That I have loved you every bit as much as anybody? Is *that* horrid?

NORA. No, but that you had to go and tell me. When it was all so unnecessary. . . .

RANK. What do you mean? Did you know . . . ?

[*The Maid comes in with the lamp, puts it on the table, and goes out again.*]

RANK. Nora . . . Mrs. Helmer . . . I'm asking you if you knew?

NORA. How can I tell whether I did or didn't. I simply can't tell you. . . . Oh, how could you be so clumsy, Dr. Rank! When everything was so nice.

RANK. Anyway, you know now that I'm at your service, body and soul. So you can speak out.

NORA [*looking at him*]. After this?

RANK. I beg you to tell me what it is.

NORA. I can tell you nothing now.

RANK. You must. You can't torment me like this. Give me a chance—I'll do anything that's humanly possible.

NORA. You can do nothing for me now. Actually, I don't really need any help. It's all just my imagination, really it is. Of course! [*She sits down in the rocking chair, looks at him and smiles.*] I must say, you are a nice one, Dr. Rank!

Don't you feel ashamed of yourself, now the lamp's been brought in?

RANK. No, not exactly. But perhaps I ought to go—for good?

NORA. No, you mustn't do that. You must keep coming just as you've always done. You know very well Torvald would miss you terribly.

RANK. And *you*?

NORA. I always think it's tremendous fun having you.

RANK. That's exactly what gave me wrong ideas. I just can't puzzle you out. I often used to feel you'd just as soon be with me as with Helmer.

NORA. Well, you see, there are those people you love and those people you'd almost rather *be* with.

RANK. Yes, there's something in that.

NORA. When I was a girl at home, I loved Daddy best, of course. But I also thought it great fun if I could slip into the maids' room. For one thing they never preached at me. And they always talked about such exciting things.

RANK. Aha! So it's their role I've taken over!

NORA [*jumps up and crosses to him*]. Oh, my dear, kind Dr. Rank, I didn't mean that at all. But you can see how it's a bit with Torvald as it was with Daddy. . . .

[*The Maid comes in from the hall.*]

MAID. Please, ma'am . . . !

[*She whispers and hands her a card.*]

NORA [*glances at the card*]. Ah!

[*She puts it in her pocket.*]

RANK. Anything wrong?

NORA. No, no, not at all. It's just . . . it's my new costume. . . .

RANK. How is that? There's your costume in there.

NORA. That one, yes. But this is another one. I've ordered it. Torvald mustn't hear about it. . . .

RANK. Ah, so that's the big secret, is it!

NORA. Yes, that's right. Just go in and see him, will you? He's in the study. Keep him occupied for the time being. . . .

RANK. Don't worry. He shan't escape me.

[*He goes into Helmer's study.*]

NORA [*to the maid*]. Is he waiting in the kitchen?

MAID. Yes, he came up the back stairs. . . .

NORA. But didn't you tell him somebody was here?

MAID. Yes, but it was no good.

NORA. Won't he go?

MAID. No, he won't till he's seen you.

NORA. Let him in, then. But quietly. Helene, you mustn't tell anybody about this. It's a surprise for my husband.

MAID. I understand, ma'am. . . .

[*She goes out.*]

NORA. Here it comes! What I've been dreading! No, no, it can't happen, it *can't* happen.

[*She walks over and bolts Helmer's door. The maid opens the hall door for Krogstad and shuts it again behind him. He is wearing a fur coat, over-shoes, and a fur cap.*]

NORA [*goes towards him*]. Keep your voice down, my husband is at home.

KROGSTAD. What if he is?

NORA. What do you want with me?

KROGSTAD. To find out something.

NORA. Hurry, then. What is it?

KROGSTAD. You know I've been given notice.

NORA. I couldn't prevent it, Mr. Krogstad, I did my utmost for you, but it was no use.

KROGSTAD. Has your husband so little affection for you? He knows what I can do to you, yet he dares. . . .

NORA. You don't imagine he knows about it!

KROGSTAD. No, I didn't imagine he did. It didn't seem a bit like my good friend Torvald Helmer to show that much courage. . . .

NORA. Mr. Krogstad, I must ask you to show some respect for my husband.

KROGSTAD. Oh, sure! All due respect! But since you are so anxious to keep this business quiet, Mrs. Helmer, I take it you now have a rather clearer idea of just what it is you've done, than you had yesterday.

NORA. Clearer than *you* could ever have given me.

KROGSTAD. Yes, being as I am such a rotten lawyer. . . .

NORA. What do you want with me?

KROGSTAD. I just wanted to see how things stood, Mrs. Helmer. I've been thinking about you all day. Even a mere money-lender, a hack journalist, a—well, even somebody like me has a bit of what you might call feeling.

NORA. Show it then. Think of my little children.

KROGSTAD. Did you or your husband think of mine? But what does it matter now? There was just one thing I wanted to say: you needn't take this business too seriously. I shan't start any proceedings, for the present.

NORA. Ah, I knew you wouldn't.

KROGSTAD. The whole thing can be arranged quite amicably. Nobody need know. Just the three of us.

NORA. My husband must never know.

KROGSTAD. How can you prevent it? Can you pay off the balance?

NORA. No, not immediately.

KROGSTAD. Perhaps you've some way of getting hold of the money in the next few days.

NORA. None I want to make use of.

KROGSTAD. Well, it wouldn't have been very much help to you if you had. Even if you stood there with the cash in your hand and to spare, you still wouldn't get your IOU back from me now.

NORA. What are you going to do with it?

KROGSTAD. Just keep it—have it in my possession. Nobody who isn't implicated need know about it. So if you are thinking of trying any desperate remedies . . .

NORA. Which I am. . . .

KROGSTAD. . . . if you happen to be thinking of running away . . .

NORA. Which I am!

KROGSTAD. . . . or anything worse . . .

NORA. How did you know?

KROGSTAD. . . . forget it!

NORA. How did you know I was thinking of *that*?

KROGSTAD. Most of us think of *that*, to begin with. I did, too; but I didn't have the courage. . . .

NORA. [*tonelessly*]. I haven't either.

KROGSTAD. [*relieved*]. So you haven't the courage either, eh?

NORA. No, I haven't! I haven't!

KROGSTAD. It would also be very stupid. There'd only be the first domestic storm to get over. . . . I've got a letter to your husband in my pocket here. . . .

NORA. And it's all in there?

KROGSTAD. In as tactful a way as possible.

NORA. [*quickly*]. He must never read that letter. Tear it up. I'll find the money somehow.

KROGSTAD. Excuse me, Mrs. Helmer, but I've just told you. . . .

NORA. I'm not talking about the money I owe you. I want to know how much you are demanding from my husband, and I'll get the money.

KROGSTAD. I want no money from your husband.

NORA. What do you want?

KROGSTAD. I'll tell you. I want to get on my feet again, Mrs. Helmer; I want to get to the top. And your husband is going to help me. For the last eighteen months I've gone straight; all that time it's been hard going; I was content to work my way up, step by step. Now I'm being kicked out, and I won't stand for being taken back again as an act of charity. I'm going to get to the top, I tell you. I'm going back into that Bank—with a better job. Your husband is going to create a new vacancy, just for me. . . .

NORA. He'll never do that!

KROGSTAD. He will do it. I know him. He'll do it without so much as a whimper. And once I'm in there with him, you'll see what's what. In less than a year I'll be his right-hand man. It'll be Nils Krogstad, not Torvald Helmer, who'll be running that Bank.

NORA. You'll never live to see that day!

KROGSTAD. You mean you . . . ?

NORA. Now I have the courage.

KROGSTAD. You can't frighten me! A precious pampered little thing like you. . . .

NORA. I'll show you! I'll show you!

KROGSTAD. Under the ice, maybe? Down in the cold, black water? Then being washed up in the spring, bloated, hairless, unrecognizable. . . .

NORA. You can't frighten me.

KROGSTAD. You can't frighten me, either. People don't do that sort of thing, Mrs. Helmer. There wouldn't be any point to it, anyway, I'd still have him right in my pocket.

NORA. Afterwards? When I'm no longer . . .

KROGSTAD. Aren't you forgetting that your reputation would then be entirely in my hands? [*Nora stands looking at him, speechless.*] Well, I've warned you. Don't do anything silly. When Helmer gets my letter, I expect to hear from him. And don't forget: it's him who is forcing me off the straight and narrow again, your own husband! That's something I'll never forgive him for. Goodbye, Mrs. Helmer.

[*He goes out through the hall.* NORA *crosses to the door, opens it slightly, and listens.*]

NORA. He's going. He hasn't left the letter. No, no, that would be impossible! [*Opens the door further and further.*] What's he doing? He's stopped outside. He's not going down the stairs. Has he changed his mind? Is he . . . ? [*A letter falls into the letter-box. Then Krogstad's footsteps are heard receding as he walks downstairs. Nora gives a stifled cry, runs across the room to the sofa table; pause.*] In the letter-box! [*She creeps stealthily across to the hall door.*] There it is! Torvald, Torvald! It's hopeless now!

MRS. LINDE [*comes into the room, left, carrying the costume*]. There, I think that's everything. Shall we try it on?

NORA. [*in a low, hoarse voice*]. Kristine, come here.

MRS. LINDE [*throws the dress down on the sofa*]. What's wrong with you? You look upset.

NORA. Come here. Do you see that letter? *There*, look! Through the glass in the letter-box.

MRS. LINDE. Yes, yes, I can see it.

NORA. It's a letter from Krogstad.

MRS. LINDE. Nora! It was Krogstad who lent you the money!

NORA. Yes. And now Torvald will get to know everything.

MRS. LINDE. Believe me, Nora, it's best for you both.

NORA. But there's more to it than that. I forged a signature. . . .

MRS. LINDE. Heavens above!

NORA. Listen, I want to tell you something, Kristine, so you can be my witness.

MRS. LINDE. What do you mean 'witness'? What do you want me to . . . ?

NORA. If I should go mad . . . which might easily happen . . .

MRS. LINDE. Nora!

NORA. Or if anything happened to me . . . which meant I couldn't be here. . . .

MRS. LINDE. Nora, Nora! Are you out of your mind?

NORA. And if somebody else wanted to take it all upon himself, the whole blame, you understand. . . .

MRS. LINDE. Yes, yes. But what makes you think . . . ?

NORA. Then you must testify that it isn't true, Kristine. I'm not out of my mind; I'm quite sane now. And I tell you this: nobody else knew anything, I alone was responsible for the whole thing. Remember that!

MRS. LINDE. I will. But I don't understand a word of it.

NORA. Why should you? You see something miraculous is going to happen.

MRS. LINDE. Something miraculous?

NORA. Yes, a miracle. But something so terrible as well, Kristine—oh, it must *never* happen, not for anything.

MRS. LINDE. I'm going straight over to talk to Krogstad.

NORA. Don't go. He'll only do you harm.

MRS. LINDE. There was a time when he would have done anything for me.

NORA. Him!

MRS. LINDE. Where does he live?

NORA. How do I know . . . ? Wait a minute. [*She feels in her pocket.*] Here's his card. But the letter, the letter . . . !

HELMER [*from his study, knocking on the door*]. Nora!

NORA [*cries out in terror*]. What's that? What do you want?

HELMER. Don't be frightened. We're not coming in. You've locked the door. Are you trying on?

NORA. Yes, yes, I'm trying on. It looks so nice on me, Torvald.

MRS. LINDE [*who has read the card*]. He lives just round the corner.

NORA. It's no use. It's hopeless. The letter is there in the box.

MRS. LINDE. Your husband keeps the key?

NORA. Always.

MRS. LINDE. Krogstad must ask for his letter back unread, he must find some sort of excuse. . . .

NORA. But this is just the time that Torvald generally . . .

MRS. LINDE. Put him off! Go in and keep him busy. I'll be back as soon as I can.

[*She goes out hastily by the hall door. Nora walks over to Helmer's door, opens it and peeps in.*]

NORA. Torvald!

HELMER [*in the study*]. Well, can a man get into his own living-room again now? Come along, Rank, now we'll see . . . [*In the doorway.*] But what's this?

NORA. What, Torvald dear?

HELMER. Rank led me to expect some kind of marvellous transformation.

RANK [*in the doorway*]. That's what I thought too, but I must have been mistaken.

NORA. I'm not showing myself off to anybody before tomorrow.

HELMER. Nora dear, you look tired. You haven't been practising too hard?

NORA. No, I haven't practised at all yet.

HELMER. You'll have to, though.

NORA. Yes, I certainly must, Torvald. But I just can't get anywhere without your help: I've completely forgotten it.

HELMER. We'll soon polish it up.

NORA. Yes, do help me, Torvald. Promise? I'm so nervous. All those people. . . . You must devote yourself exclusively to me this evening. Pens away! Forget all about the office! Promise me, Torvald dear!

HELMER. I promise. This evening I am wholly and entirely at your service . . . helpless little thing that you are. Oh, but while I remember, I'll just look first . . .

[*He goes towards the hall door.*]

NORA. What do you want out there?

HELMER. Just want to see if there are any letters.

NORA. No, don't, Torvald!

HELMER. Why not?

NORA. Torvald, *please!* There aren't any.

HELMER. Just let me see.

[*He starts to go. Nora, at the piano, plays the opening bars of the tarantella.*]

HELMER [*at the door, stops*]. Aha!

NORA. I shan't be able to dance tomorrow if I don't rehearse it with you.

HELMER. [*walks to her*]. Are you really so nervous, Nora dear?

NORA. Terribly nervous. Let me run through it now. There's still time before supper. Come and sit here and play for me, Torvald dear. Tell me what to do, keep me right—as you always do.

HELMER. Certainly, with pleasure, if that's what you want.

[*He sits at the piano. Nora snatches the tambourine out of the box, and also a long gaily-coloured shawl which she drapes round herself, then with a bound she leaps forward.*]

NORA. [*shouts*]. Now play for me! Now I'll dance!

[*Helmer plays and Nora dances; Dr. Rank stands at the piano behind Helmer and looks on.*]

HELMER [*playing*]. Not so fast! Not so fast!

NORA. I can't help it.

HELMER. Not so wild, Nora!

NORA. This is how it has to be.

HELMER [*stops*]. No, no, that won't do at all.

NORA [*laughs and swings the tambourine*]. Didn't I tell you?

RANK. Let me play for her.

HELMER [*gets up*]. Yes, do. Then I'll be better able to tell her what to do.

[*Rank sits down at the piano and plays. Nora dances more and more wildly. Helmer stands by the stove giving her repeated directions as she dances; she does not seem to hear them. Her hair comes undone and falls about her shoulders; she pays no attention and goes on dancing. Mrs. Linde enters.*]

MRS. LINDE [*standing as though spellbound in the doorway*]. Ah . . . !

NORA [*dancing*]. See what fun we are having, Kristine.

HELMER. But my dear darling Nora, you are dancing as though your life depended on it.

NORA. It does.

HELMER. Stop, Rank! This is sheer madness. Stop, I say.

[*Rank stops playing and Nora comes to a sudden halt.*]

HELMER [*crosses to her*]. I would never have believed it. You have forgotten everything I ever taught you.

NORA [*throwing away the tambourine*]. There you are, you see.

HELMER. Well, some more instruction is certainly needed there.

NORA. Yes, you see how necessary it is. You must go on coaching me right up to the last minute. Promise me, Torvald?

HELMER. You can rely on me.

NORA. You mustn't think about anything else but me until after tomorrow . . . mustn't open any letters . . . mustn't touch the letter-box.

HELMER. Ah, you are still frightened of what that man might . . .

NORA. Yes, yes, I am.

HELMER. I can see from your face there's already a letter there from him.

NORA. I don't know. I think so. But you mustn't read anything like that now. We don't want anything horrid coming between us until all this is over.

RANK [*softly to Helmer*]. I shouldn't cross her.

HELMER [*puts his arm round her*]. The child must have her way. But tomorrow night, when your dance is done. . . .

NORA. Then you are free.

MAID [*in the doorway, right*]. Dinner is served, madam.

NORA. We'll have champagne, Helene.

MAID. Very good, madam.

[*She goes.*]

HELMER. Aha! It's to be quite a banquet, eh?

NORA. With champagne flowing until dawn. [*Shouts.*] And some macaroons, Helene . . . lots of them, for once in a while.

HELMER [*seizing her hands*]. Now, now, not so wild and excitable! Let me see you being my own little singing bird again.

NORA. Oh yes, I will. And if you'll just go in . . . you, too, Dr. Rank. Kristine, you must help me to do my hair.

RANK [*softly, as they leave*]. There isn't anything . . . anything as it were, impending, is there?

HELMER. No, not at all, my dear fellow. It's nothing but these childish fears I was telling you about.

[*They go out to the right.*]

NORA. Well?

MRS. LINDE. He's left town.

NORA. I saw it in your face.

MRS. LINDE. He's coming back tomorrow evening. I left a note for him.

NORA. You shouldn't have done that. You must let things take their course. Because really it's a case for rejoicing, waiting like this for the miracle.

MRS. LINDE. What is it you are waiting for?

NORA. Oh, you wouldn't understand. Go and join the other two. I'll be there in a minute.

[*Mrs. Linde goes into the dining-room. Nora stands for a moment as though to collect herself, then looks at her watch.*]

NORA. Five. Seven hours to midnight. Then twenty-four hours till the next midnight. Then the tarantella will be over. Twenty-four and seven? Thirty-one hours to live.

HELMER [*in the doorway, right*]. What's happened to our little sky-lark?

NORA [*running towards him with open arms*]. Here she is!

ACT III

The same room. The round table has been moved to the centre of the room, and the chairs placed round it. A lamp is burning on the table. The door to the hall stands open. Dance music can be heard coming from the floor above. Mrs. Linde is sitting by the table, idly turning over the pages of a book; she tries to read, but does not seem able to concentrate. Once or twice she listens, tensely, for a sound at the front door.

MRS. LINDE [*looking at her watch*]. Still not here. There isn't much time left. I only hope he hasn't . . . [*She listens again.*] Ah, there he is. [*She goes out into the hall, and cautiously opens the front door. Soft footsteps can be heard on the stairs. She whispers.*] Come in. There's nobody here.

KROGSTAD [*in the doorway*]. I found a note from you at home. What does it all mean?

MRS. LINDE. I *had* to talk to you.

KROGSTAD. Oh? And did it have to be here, in this house?

MRS. LINDE. It wasn't possible over at my place, it hasn't a separate entrance. Come in. We are quite alone. The maid's asleep and the Helmers are at a party upstairs.

KROGSTAD [*comes into the room*]. Well, well! So the Helmers are out dancing tonight! Really?

MRS. LINDE. Yes, why not?

KROGSTAD. Why not indeed!

MRS. LINDE. Well then, Nils. Let's talk.

KROGSTAD. Have we two anything more to talk about?

MRS. LINDE. We have a great deal to talk about.

KROGSTAD. I shouldn't have thought so.

MRS. LINDE. That's because you never really understood me.

KROGSTAD. What else was there to understand, apart from the old, old story? A heartless woman throws a man over the moment something more profitable offers itself.

MRS. LINDE. Do you really think I'm so heartless? Do you think I found it easy to break it off?

KROGSTAD. Didn't you?

MRS. LINDE. You didn't really believe that?

KROGSTAD. If that wasn't the case, why did you write to me as you did?

MRS. LINDE. There was nothing else I could do. If I had to make the break, I felt in duty bound to destroy any feeling that you had for me.

KROGSTAD [clenching his hands]. So that's how it was. And all that . . . was for money!

MRS. LINDE. You mustn't forget I had a helpless mother and two young brothers. We couldn't wait for you, Nils. At that time you hadn't much immediate prospect of anything.

KROGSTAD. That may be. But you had no right to throw me over for somebody else.

MRS. LINDE. Well, I don't know. Many's the time I've asked myself whether I was justified.

KROGSTAD [more quietly]. When I lost you, it was just as if the ground had slipped away from under my feet. Look at me now: a broken man clinging to the wreck of his life.

MRS. LINDE. Help might be near.

KROGSTAD. It was near. Then you came along and got in the way.

MRS. LINDE. Quite without knowing, Nils. I only heard today it's you I'm supposed to be replacing at the Bank.

KROGSTAD. If you say so, I believe you. But now you do know, aren't you going to withdraw?

MRS. LINDE. No, that wouldn't benefit you in the slightest.

KROGSTAD. Benefit, benefit . . . ! I would do it just the same.

MRS. LINDE. I have learned to go carefully. Life and hard, bitter necessity have taught me that.

KROGSTAD. And life has taught me not to believe in pretty speeches.

MRS. LINDE. Then life has taught you a very sensible thing. But deeds are something you surely must believe in?

KROGSTAD. How do you mean?

MRS. LINDE. You said you were like a broken man clinging to the wreck of his life.

KROGSTAD. And I said it with good reason.

MRS. LINDE. And I am like a broken woman clinging to the wreck of her life. Nobody to care about, and nobody to care for.

KROGSTAD. It was your own choice.

MRS. LINDE. At the time there was no other choice.

KROGSTAD. Well, what of it?

MRS. LINDE. Nils, what about us two castaways joining forces.

KROGSTAD. What's that you say?

MRS. LINDE. Two of us on one wreck surely stand a better chance than each on his own.

KROGSTAD. Kristine!

MRS. LINDE. Why do you suppose I came to town?

KROGSTAD. You mean, you thought of me?

MRS. LINDE. Without work I couldn't live. All my life I have worked, for as long as I can remember; that has always been my one great joy. But now I'm completely alone in the world, and feeling horribly empty and forlorn. There's no pleasure in working only for yourself. Nils, give me somebody and something to work for.

KROGSTAD. I don't believe all this. It's only a woman's hysteria, wanting to be all magnanimous and self-sacrificing.

MRS. LINDE. Have you ever known me hysterical before?

KROGSTAD. Would you really do this? Tell me—do you know all about my past?

MRS. LINDE. Yes.

KROGSTAD. And you know what people think about me?

MRS. LINDE. Just now you hinted you thought you might have been a different person with me.

KROGSTAD. I'm convinced I would.

MRS. LINDE. Couldn't it still happen?

KROGSTAD. Kristine! You know what you are saying, don't you? Yes, you do. I can see you do. Have you really the courage . . . ?

MRS. LINDE. I need someone to mother, and your children need a mother. We two need each other. Nils, I have faith in what, deep down, you are. With you I can face anything.

KROGSTAD [seizing her hands]. Thank you, thank you, Kristine. And I'll soon have everybody looking up to me, or I'll know the reason why. Ah, but I was forgetting. . . .

MRS. LINDE. Hush! The tarantella! You must go!

KROGSTAD. Why? What is it?

MRS. LINDE. You hear that dance upstairs? When it's finished they'll be coming.

KROGSTAD. Yes, I'll go. It's too late to do anything. Of course, you know nothing about what steps I've taken against the Helmers.

MRS. LINDE. Yes, Nils, I do know.

KROGSTAD. Yet you still want to go on. . . .

MRS. LINDE. I know how far a man like you can be driven by despair.

KROGSTAD. Oh, if only I could undo what I've done!

MRS. LINDE. You still can. Your letter is still there in the box.

KROGSTAD. Are you sure?

MRS. LINDE. Quite sure. But . . .

KROGSTAD [regards her searchingly]. Is that how things are? You want to save your friend at any price? Tell me straight. Is that it?

MRS. LINDE. When you've sold yourself *once* for other people's sake, you don't do it again.

KROGSTAD. I shall demand my letter back.

MRS. LINDE. No, no.

KROGSTAD. Of course I will, I'll wait here till Helmer comes. I'll tell him he has to give me my letter back . . . that it's only about my notice . . . that he mustn't read it. . . .

MRS. LINDE. No, Nils, don't ask for it back.

KROGSTAD. But wasn't that the very reason you got me here?

MRS. LINDE. Yes, that was my first terrified reaction. But that was yesterday, and it's quite incredible the things I've witnessed in this house in the last twenty-four hours. Helmer must know everything. This unhappy secret must come out. Those two must have the whole thing out between them. All this secrecy and deception, it just can't go on.

KROGSTAD. Well, if you want to risk it. . . . But one thing I can do, and I'll do it at once. . . .

MRS. LINDE [*listening*]. Hurry! Go, go! The dance has stopped. We aren't safe a moment longer.

KROGSTAD. I'll wait for you downstairs.

MRS. LINDE. Yes, do. You must see me home.

KROGSTAD. I've never been so incredibly happy before.

[*He goes out by the front door. The door out into the hall remains standing open.*]

MRS. LINDE [*tidies the room a little and gets her hat and coat ready*]. How things change! How things change! Somebody to work for . . . to live for. A home to bring happiness into. Just let me get down to it. . . . I wish they'd come. . . . [*Listens.*] Ah, there they are. . . . Get my things.

[*She takes her coat and hat. The voices of Helmer and Nora are heard outside. A key is turned and Helmer pushes Nora almost forcibly into the hall. She is dressed in the Italian costume, with a big black shawl over it. He is in evening dress, and over it a black cloak, open.*]

NORA [*still in the doorway, reluctantly*]. No, no, not in here! I want to go back up again. I don't want to leave so early.

HELMER. But my dearest Nora . . .

NORA. Oh, please, Torvald, I beg you. . . . *Please*, just for another hour.

HELMER. Not another minute, Nora my sweet. You remember what we agreed. There now, come along in. You'll catch cold standing there.

[*He leads her, in spite of her resistance, gently but firmly into the room.*]

MRS. LINDE. Good evening.

NORA. Kristine!

HELMER. Why, Mrs. Linde. You here so late?

MRS. LINDE. Yes. You must forgive me but I did so want to see Nora all dressed up.

NORA. Have you been sitting here waiting for me?

MRS. LINDE. Yes, I'm afraid I wasn't in time to catch you before you went upstairs. And I felt I couldn't leave again without seeing you.

HELMER [*removing Nora's shawl*]. Well take a good look at her. I think I can say she's worth looking at. Isn't she lovely, Mrs. Linde?

MRS. LINDE. Yes, I must say. . . .

HELMER. Isn't she quite extraordinarily lovely? That's what everybody at the party thought, too. But she's dreadfully stubborn . . . the sweet little thing! And what shall we do about that? Would you believe it, I nearly had to use force to get her away.

NORA. Oh Torvald, you'll be sorry you didn't let me stay, even for half an hour.

HELMER. You hear that, Mrs. Linde? She dances her tarantella, there's wild applause—which was well deserved, although the performance was perhaps rather realistic . . . I mean, rather more so than was strictly necessary from the artistic point of view. But anyway! The main thing is she was a success, a tremendous success. Was I supposed to let her stay after that? Spoil the effect? No thank you! I took my lovely little Capri girl—my capricious little Capri girl, I might say—by the arm, whisked her once round the room, a curtsey all round, and then—as they say in novels—the beautiful vision vanished. An exit should always be effective, Mrs. Linde. But I just can't get Nora to see that. Phew! It's warm in here. [*He throws his cloak over a chair and opens the door to his study.*] What? It's dark. Oh yes, of course. Excuse me. . . .

[*He goes in and lights a few candles.*]

NORA [*quickly, in a breathless whisper*]. Well?

MRS. LINDE [*softly*]. I've spoken to him.

NORA. And . . . ?

MRS. LINDE. Nora . . . you must tell your husband everything.

NORA [*tonelessly*]. I knew it.

MRS. LINDE. You've got nothing to fear from Krogstad. But you must speak.

NORA. I won't.

MRS. LINDE. Then the letter will.

NORA. Thank you, Kristine. Now I know what's to be done. Hush . . . !

HELMER [*comes in again*]. Well, Mrs. Linde, have you finished admiring her?

MRS. LINDE. Yes. And now I must say good night.

HELMER. Oh, already? Is this yours, this knitting?

MRS. LINDE [*takes it*]. Yes, thank you. I nearly forgot it.

HELMER. So you knit, eh?

MRS. LINDE. Yes.

HELMER. You should embroider instead, you know.

MRS. LINDE. Oh? Why?

HELMER. So much prettier. Watch! You hold the embroidery like this in the left hand, and then you take the needle in the right hand, like this, and you describe a long, graceful curve. Isn't that right?

MRS. LINDE. Yes, I suppose so. . . .

HELMER. Whereas knitting on the other hand just can't help being ugly. Look! Arms pressed into the sides, the knitting needles going up and down—there's something Chinese about it. . . . Ah, that was marvellous champagne they served tonight.

MRS. LINDE. Well, good night, Nora! And stop being so stubborn.

HELMER. Well said, Mrs. Linde!

MRS. LINDE. Good night, Mr. Helmer.

HELMER [accompanying her to the door]. Good night, good night! You'll get home all right, I hope? I'd be only too pleased to. . . . But you haven't far to walk. Good night, good night! [She goes; he shuts the door behind her and comes in again.] There we are, got rid of her at last. She's a frightful bore, that woman.

NORA. Aren't you very tired, Torvald?

HELMER. Not in the least.

NORA. Not sleepy?

HELMER. Not at all. On the contrary, I feel extremely lively. What about you? Yes, you look quite tired and sleepy.

NORA. Yes, I'm very tired. I just want to fall straight off to sleep.

HELMER. There you are, you see! Wasn't I right in thinking we shouldn't stay any longer.

NORA. Oh, everything you do is right.

HELMER [kissing her forehead]. There's my little sky-lark talking common sense. Did you notice how gay Rank was this evening?

NORA. Oh, was he? I didn't get a chance to talk to him.

HELMER. I hardly did either. But it's a long time since I saw him in such a good mood. [Looks at Nora for a moment or two, then comes nearer her.] Ah, it's wonderful to be back in our own home again, and quite alone with you. How irresistibly lovely you are, Nora!

NORA. Don't look at me like that, Torvald!

HELMER. Can't I look at my most treasured possession? At all this loveliness that's mine and mine alone, completely and utterly mine.

NORA. [walks round to the other side of the table]. You mustn't talk to me like that tonight.

HELMER [following her]. You still have the tarantella in your blood, I see. And that makes you even more desirable. Listen! The guests are beginning to leave now. [Softly.] Nora . . . soon the whole house will be silent.

NORA. I should hope so.

HELMER. Of course you do, don't you, Nora my darling? You know, whenever I'm out at a party with you . . . do you know why I never talk to you very much, why I always stand away from you and only steal a quick glance at you now and then . . . do you know why I do that? It's because I'm pretending we are secretly in love, secretly engaged and nobody suspects there is anything between us.

NORA. Yes, yes. I know your thoughts are always with me, of course.

HELMER. And when it's time to go, and I lay your shawl round those shapely, young shoulders, round the exquisite curve of your neck . . . I pretend that you are my young bride, that we are just leaving our wedding, that I am taking you to our new home for the first time . . . to be alone with you for the first time . . . quite alone with your young and trembling loveliness! All evening I've been longing for you, and nothing else. And as I watched you darting and swaying in the tarantella, my blood was on fire . . . I couldn't bear it any longer . . . and that's why I brought you down here with me so early. . . .

NORA. Go away, Torvald! Please leave me alone. I won't have it.

HELMER. What's this? It's just your little game isn't it, my little Nora. Won't! Won't! Am I not your husband . . . ?

[There is a knock on the front door.]

NORA [startled]. Listen . . . !

HELMER [going towards the hall]. Who's there?

RANK [outside]. It's me. Can I come in for a minute?

HELMER [in a low voice, annoyed]. Oh, what does he want now? [Aloud] Wait a moment. [He walks across and opens the door.] How nice of you to look in on your way out.

RANK. I fancied I heard your voice and I thought I would just look in. [He takes a quick glance round.] Ah yes, this dear, familiar old place! How cosy and comfortable you've got things here, you two.

HELMER. You seemed to be having a pretty good time upstairs yourself.

RANK. Capital! Why shouldn't I? Why not make the most of things in this world? At least as much as one can, and for as long as one can. The wine was excellent. . . .

HELMER. Especially the champagne.

RANK. You noticed that too, did you? It's incredible the amount I was able to put away.

NORA. Torvald also drank a lot of champagne this evening.

RANK. Oh?

NORA. Yes, and that always makes him quite merry.

RANK. Well, why shouldn't a man allow himself a jolly evening after a day well spent?

HELMER. Well spent? I'm afraid I can't exactly claim that.

RANK [clapping him on the shoulder]. But I can, you see!

NORA. Dr. Rank, am I right in thinking you carried out a certain laboratory test today?

RANK. Exactly.

HELMER. Look at our little Nora talking about laboratory tests!

NORA. And may I congratulate you on the result?

RANK. You may indeed.

NORA. So it was good?

RANK. The best possible, for both doctor and patient—certainty!

NORA [*quickly and searchingly*]. Certainty?

RANK. Absolute certainty. So why shouldn't I allow myself a jolly evening after that?

NORA. Quite right, Dr. Rank.

HELMER. I quite agree. As long as you don't suffer for it in the morning.

RANK. Well, you never get anything for nothing in this life.

NORA. Dr. Rank . . . you are very fond of masquerades, aren't you?

RANK. Yes, when there are plenty of amusing disguises. . . .

NORA. Tell me, what shall we two go as next time?

HELMER. There's frivolity for you . . . thinking about the next time already!

RANK. We two? I'll tell you. You must go as Lady Luck. . . .

HELMER. Yes, but how do you find a costume to suggest *that*?

RANK. Your wife could simply go in her everyday clothes. . . .

HELMER. That was nicely said. But don't you know what you would be?

RANK. Yes, my dear friend, I know exactly what I shall be.

HELMER. Well?

RANK. At the next masquerade, I shall be invisible.

HELMER. That's a funny idea!

RANK. There's a big black cloak . . . haven't you heard of the cloak of invisibility? That comes right down over you, and then nobody can see you.

HELMER [*suppressing a smile*]. Of course, that's right.

RANK. But I'm clean forgetting what I came for. Helmer, give me a cigar, one of the dark Havanas.

HELMER. With the greatest of pleasure.

[*He offers his case.*]

RANK [*takes one and cuts the end off*]. Thanks.

NORA [*strikes a match*]. Let me give you a light.

RANK. Thank you. [*She holds out the match and he lights his cigar.*] And now, goodbye!

HELMER. Goodbye, goodbye, my dear fellow!

NORA. Sleep well, Dr. Rank.

RANK. Thank you for that wish.

NORA. Wish me the same.

RANK. You? All right, if you want me to. . . . Sleep well. And thanks for the light.

[*He nods to them both, and goes.*]

HELMER [*subdued*]. He's had a lot to drink.

NORA [*absently*]. Very likely.

[*Helmer takes a bunch of keys out of his pocket and goes out into the hall.*]

NORA. Torvald . . . what do you want there?

HELMER. I must empty the letter-box, it's quite full. There'll be no room for the papers in the morning. . . .

NORA. Are you going to work tonight?

HELMER. You know very well I'm not. Hello, what's this? Somebody's been at the lock.

NORA. At the lock?

HELMER. Yes, I'm sure of it. Why should that be? I'd hardly have thought the maids . . . ? Here's a broken hair-pin. Nora, it's one of yours. . . .

NORA [*quickly*]. It must have been the children. . . .

HELMER. Then you'd better tell them not to. Ah . . . there . . . I've managed to get it open. [*He takes the things out and shouts into the kitchen.*] Helene! . . . Helene, put the light out in the hall. [*He comes into the room again with the letters in his hand and shuts the hall door.*] Look how it all mounts up. [*Runs through them.*] What's this?

NORA. The letter! Oh no, Torvald, no!

HELMER. Two visiting cards . . . from Dr. Rank.

NORA. From Dr. Rank?

HELMER [*looking at them*]. Dr. Rank, Medical Practitioner. They were on top. He must have put them in as he left.

NORA. Is there anything on them?

HELMER. There's a black cross above his name. Look. What an uncanny idea. It's just as if he were announcing his own death.

NORA. He is.

HELMER. What? What do you know about it? Has he said anything to you?

NORA. Yes. He said when these cards came, he would have taken his last leave of us. He was going to shut himself up and die.

HELMER. Poor fellow! Of course I knew we couldn't keep him with us very long. But so soon. . . . And hiding himself away like a wounded animal.

NORA. When it has to happen, it's best that it should happen without words. Don't you think so, Torvald?

HELMER [*walking up and down*]. He had grown so close to us. I don't think I can imagine him gone. His suffering and his loneliness seemed almost to provide a background of dark cloud to the sunshine of our lives. Well, perhaps it's all for the best. For him at any rate. [*Pauses.*] And maybe for us as well, Nora. Now there's just the two of us. [*Puts his arms round her.*] Oh, my darling wife, I can't hold you close enough. You know, Nora . . . many's the time I wish you were threatened by some terrible danger so I could risk everything, body and soul, for your sake.

NORA [*tears herself free and says firmly and decisively*]. Now you must read your letters, Torvald.

HELMER. No, no, not tonight. I want to be with you, my darling wife.

NORA. Knowing all the time your friend is dying . . . ?

HELMER. You are right. It's been a shock to both of us. This ugly thing has come between us . . . thoughts of death and decay. We must try to free ourselves from it. Until then . . . we shall go our separate ways.

NORA [*her arms round his neck*]. Torvald . . . good night! Good night!

HELMER [*kisses her forehead*]. Goodnight, my little singing bird. Sleep well, Nora, I'll just read through my letters.

[*He takes the letters into his room and shuts the door behind him.*]

NORA [*gropes around her, wild-eyed, seizes Helmer's cloak, wraps it round herself, and whispers quickly, hoarsely, spasmodically*]. Never see him again. Never, never, never. [*Throws her shawl over her head.*] And never see the children again either. Never, never. Oh, that black icy water. Oh, that bottomless . . . ! If only it were all over! He's got it now. Now he's reading it. Oh no, no! Not yet! Torvald, goodbye . . . and my children. . . .

[*She rushes out in the direction of the hall; at the same moment Helmer flings open his door and stands there with an open letter in his hand.*]

HELMER. Nora!

NORA [*shrieks*]. Ah!

HELMER. What is this? Do you know what is in this letter?

NORA. Yes, I know. Let me go! Let me out!

HELMER [*holds her back*]. Where are you going?

NORA [*trying to tear herself free*]. You mustn't try to save me, Torvald!

HELMER [*reels back*]. True! Is it true what he writes? How dreadful! No, no, it can't possibly be true.

NORA. It *is* true. I loved you more than anything else in the world.

HELMER. Don't come to me with a lot of paltry excuses!

NORA [*taking a step towards him*]. Torvald . . . !

HELMER. Miserable woman . . . what is this you have done?

NORA. Let me go. I won't have you taking the blame for me. You mustn't take it on yourself.

HELMER. Stop play-acting! [*Locks the front door.*] You are staying here to give an account of yourself. Do you understand what you have done? Answer me! Do you understand?

NORA [*looking fixedly at him, her face hardening*]. Yes, now I'm really beginning to understand.

HELMER [*walking up and down*]. Oh, what a terrible awakening this is. All these eight years . . . this woman who was my pride and joy . . . a hypocrite, a liar, worse than that, a criminal! Oh, how utterly squalid it all is! Ugh! Ugh! [*Nora remains silent and looks fixedly at him.*] I should have realized something like this would happen. I should have seen it coming. All your father's irresponsible ways. . . . Quiet! All your father's irresponsible ways are coming out in you. No religion, no morals, no sense of duty. . . . Oh, this is my punishment for turning a blind eye to him. It was for your sake I did it, and this is what I get for it.

NORA. Yes, this.

HELMER. Now you have ruined my entire happiness, jeopardized my whole future. It's terrible to think of. Here I am, at the mercy of a thoroughly unscrupulous person; he can do whatever he likes with me, demand anything he wants, order me about just as he chooses . . . and I daren't even whimper. I'm done for, a miserable failure, and it's all the fault of a feather-brained woman!

NORA. When I've left this world behind, you will be free.

HELMER. Oh, stop pretending! Your father was just the same, always ready with fine phrases. What good would it do me if you left this world behind, as you put it? Not the slightest bit of good. He can still let it all come out, if he likes; and if he does, people might even suspect me of being an accomplice in these criminal acts of yours. They might even think I was the one behind it all, that it was I who pushed you into it! And it's you I have to thank for this . . . and when I've taken such good care of you, all our married life. Now do you understand what you have done to me?

NORA [*coldly and calmly*]. Yes.

HELMER. I just can't understand it, it's so incredible. But we must see about putting things right. Take that shawl off. Take it off, I tell you! I must see if I can't find some way or other of appeasing him. The thing must be hushed up at all costs. And as far as you and I are concerned, things must appear to go on exactly as before. But only in the eyes of the world, of course. In other words you'll go on living here; that's understood. But you will not be allowed to bring up the children, I can't trust you with them. . . . Oh, that I should have to say this to the woman I loved so dearly, the woman I still. . . . Well, that must be all over and done with. From now on, there can be no question of happiness. All we can do is save the bits and pieces from the wreck, preserve appearances. . . . [*The front door-bell rings. Helmer gives a start.*] What's that? So late? How terrible, supposing. . . . If he should . . . ? Hide, Nora! Say you are not well.

[*Nora stands motionless. Helmer walks across and opens the door into the hall.*]

MAID [*half dressed, in the hall*]. It's a note for Mrs. Helmer.

HELMER. Give it to me. [*He snatches the note and shuts the door.*] Yes, it's from him. You can't have it. I want to read it myself.

NORA. You read it then.

HELMER [*by the lamp*]. I hardly dare. Perhaps this is the end, for both of us. Well, I must know. [*He opens the note hurriedly, reads a few lines, looks at another enclosed sheet, and gives a cry of joy.*] Nora! [*Nora looks at him inquiringly.*] Nora! I must read it again. Yes, yes, it's true! I am saved! Nora, I am saved!

NORA. And me?

HELMER. You too, of course, we are both saved, you as well as me. Look, he's sent your IOU back. He sends his regrets and apologies for what he has done. . . . His luck has changed. . . . Oh, what does it matter what he says. We are saved, Nora! Nobody can do anything to you now. Oh, Nora, Nora . . . but let's get rid of this disgusting thing first. Let me see. . . . [*He glances at the IOU.*] No, I don't want to see it. I don't want it to be anything but a dream. [*He tears up the IOU and both letters, throws all the pieces into the stove and watches them burn.*] Well, that's the end of that. He said in his note you'd known since Christmas Eve. . . . You must have had three terrible days of it, Nora.

NORA. These three days haven't been easy.

HELMER. The agonies you must have gone through! When the only way out seemed to be. . . . No, let's forget the whole ghastly thing. We can rejoice and say: It's all over! It's all over! Listen to me, Nora! You don't seem to understand: it's all over! Why this grim look on your face? Oh, poor little Nora, of course I understand. You can't bring yourself to believe I've forgiven you. But I have, Nora, I swear it. I forgive you everything. I know you did what you did because you loved me.

NORA. That's true.

HELMER. You loved me as a wife should love her husband. It was simply that you didn't have the experience to judge what was the best way of going about things. But do you think I love you any the less for that; just because you don't know how to act on your own responsibility? No, no, you just lean on me, I shall give you all the advice and guidance you need. I wouldn't be a proper man if I didn't find a woman doubly attractive for being so obviously helpless. You mustn't dwell on the harsh things I said in that first moment of horror, when I thought everything was going to come crashing down about my ears. I have forgiven you, Nora, I swear it! I have forgiven you!

NORA. Thank you for your forgiveness.

[*She goes out through the door, right.*]

HELMER. No, don't go! [*He looks through the doorway.*] What are you doing in the spare room?

NORA. Taking off this fancy dress.

HELMER [*standing at the open door*]. Yes, do. You try and get some rest, and set your mind at peace again, my frightened little song-bird. Have a good long sleep; you know you are safe and sound under my wing. [*Walks up and down near the door.*] What a nice, cosy little home we have here, Nora! Here you can find refuge. Here I shall hold you like a hunted dove I have rescued unscathed from the cruel talons of the hawk, and calm your poor beating heart. And that will come, gradually, Nora, believe me. Tomorrow you'll see everything quite differently. Soon everything will be just as it was before. You won't need me to keep on telling you I've forgiven you; you'll feel convinced of it in your own heart. You don't really imagine me ever thinking of turning you out, or even of reproaching you? Oh, a real man isn't made that way, you know, Nora. For a man, there's something indescribably moving and very satisfying in knowing that he has forgiven his wife—forgiven her, completely and gen-

uinely, from the depths of his heart. It's as though it made her his property in a double sense: he has, as it were, given her a new life, and she becomes in a way both his wife and at the same time his child. That is how you will seem to me after today, helpless, perplexed little thing that you are. Don't you worry your pretty little head about anything, Nora. Just you be frank with me, and I'll take all the decisions for you. . . . What's this? Not in bed? You've changed your things?

NORA [*in her everyday dress*]. Yes, Torvald, I've changed.

HELMER. What for? It's late.

NORA. I shan't sleep tonight.

HELMER. But my dear Nora. . . .

NORA [*looks at her watch*]. It's not so terribly late. Sit down, Torvald. We two have a lot to talk about.

[*She sits down at one side of the table.*]

HELMER. Nora, what is all this? Why so grim?

NORA. Sit down. It'll take some time. I have a lot to say to you.

HELMER [*sits down at the table opposite her*]. You frighten me, Nora. I don't understand you.

NORA. Exactly. You don't understand me. And I have never understood you, either—until tonight. No, don't interrupt. I just want you to listen to what I have to say. We are going to have things out, Torvald.

HELMER. What do you mean?

NORA. Isn't there anything that strikes you about the way we two are sitting here?

HELMER. What's that?

NORA. We have now been married eight years. Hasn't it struck you this is the first time you and I, man and wife, have had a serious talk together?

HELMER. Depends what you mean by 'serious.'

NORA. Eight whole years—no, more, ever since we first knew each other—and never have we exchanged one serious word about serious things.

HELMER. What did you want me to do? Get you involved in worries that you couldn't possibly help me to bear?

NORA. I'm not talking about worries. I say we've never once sat down together and seriously tried to get to the bottom of anything.

HELMER. But, my dear Nora, would that have been a thing for you?

NORA. That's just it. You have never understood me . . . I've been greatly wronged, Torvald. First by my father, and then by you.

HELMER. What! Us two! The two people who loved you more than anybody?

NORA [*shakes her head*]. You two never loved me. You only thought how nice it was to be in love with me.

HELMER. But, Nora, what's this you are saying?

NORA. It's right, you know, Torvald. At home, Daddy used to tell me what he thought, then I thought the same. And if

I thought differently, I kept quiet about it, because he wouldn't have liked it. He used to call me his baby doll, and he played with me as I used to play with my dolls. Then I came to live in your house. . . .

HELMER. What way is that to talk about our marriage?

NORA [*imperturbably*]. What I mean is: I passed out of Daddy's hands into yours. You arranged everything to your tastes, and I acquired the same tastes. Or I pretended to . . . I don't really know . . . I think it was a bit of both, sometimes one thing and sometimes the other. When I look back, it seems to me I have been living here like a beggar, from hand to mouth. I lived by doing tricks for you, Torvald. But that's the way you wanted it. You and Daddy did me a great wrong. It's your fault that I've never made anything of my life.

HELMER. Nora, how unreasonable . . . how ungrateful you are! Haven't you been happy here?

NORA. No, never. I thought I was, but I wasn't really.

HELMER. Not . . . not happy!

NORA. No, just gay. And you've always been so kind to me. But our house has never been anything but a play-room. I have been your doll wife, just as at home I was Daddy's doll child. And the children in turn have been my dolls. I thought it was fun when you came and played with me, just as they thought it was fun when I went and played with them. That's been our marriage, Torvald.

HELMER. There is some truth in what you say, exaggerated and hysterical though it is. But from now on it will be different. Play-time is over; now comes the time for lessons.

NORA. Whose lessons? Mine or the children's?

HELMER. Both yours and the children's, my dear Nora.

NORA. Ah, Torvald, you are not the man to teach me to be a good wife for you.

HELMER. How can you say that?

NORA. And what sort of qualifications have I to teach the children?

HELMER. Nora!

NORA. Didn't you say yourself, a minute or two ago, that you couldn't trust me with that job.

HELMER. In the heat of the moment! You shouldn't pay any attention to that.

NORA. On the contrary, you were quite right. I'm not up to it. There's another problem needs solving first. I must take steps to educate myself. You are not the man to help me there. That's something I must do on my own. That's why I'm leaving you.

HELMER [*jumps up*]. What did you say?

NORA. If I'm ever to reach any understanding of myself and the things around me, I must learn to stand alone. That's why I can't stay here with you any longer.

HELMER. Nora! Nora!

NORA. I'm leaving here at once. I dare say Kristine will put me up for tonight. . . .

HELMER. You are out of your mind! I won't let you! I forbid you!

NORA. It's no use forbidding me anything now. I'm taking with me my own personal belongings. I don't want anything of yours, either now or later.

HELMER. This is madness!

NORA. Tomorrow I'm going home—to what used to be my home, I mean. It will be easier for me to find something to do there.

HELMER. Oh, you blind, inexperienced . . .

NORA. I must set about *getting* experience, Torvald.

HELMER. And leave your home, your husband and your children? Don't you care what people will say?

NORA. That's no concern of mine. All I know is that this is necessary for me.

HELMER. This is outrageous! You are betraying your most sacred duty.

NORA. And what do you consider to be my most sacred duty?

HELMER. Does it take me to tell you that? Isn't it your duty to your husband and your children?

NORA. I have another duty equally sacred.

HELMER. You have not. What duty might *that* be?

NORA. My duty to myself.

HELMER. First and foremost, you are a wife and mother.

NORA. That I don't believe any more. I believe that first and foremost I am an individual, just as much as you are—or at least I'm going to try to be. I know most people agree with you, Torvald, and that's also what it says in books. But I'm not content any more with what most people say, or with what it says in books. I have to think things out for myself, and get things clear.

HELMER. Surely you are clear about your position in your own home? Haven't you an infallible guide in questions like these? Haven't you your religion?

NORA. Oh, Torvald, I don't really know what religion is.

HELMER. What do you say!

NORA. All I know is what Pastor Hansen said when I was confirmed. He said religion was this, that and the other. When I'm away from all this and on my own, I'll go into that, too. I want to find out whether what Pastor Hansen told me was right—or at least whether it's right for *me*.

HELMER. This is incredible talk from a young woman! But if religion cannot keep you on the right path, let me at least stir your conscience. I suppose you do have some moral sense? Or tell me—perhaps you don't?

NORA. Well, Torvald, that's not easy to say. I simply don't know. I'm really very confused about such things. All I know is my ideas about such things are very different from yours. I've also learnt that the law is different from what I thought; but I simply can't get it into my head that that particular law is right. Apparently a woman has no right to spare her old father on his deathbed, or to save her husband's life, even. I just don't believe it.

HELMER. You are talking like a child. You understand nothing about the society you live in.

NORA. No, I don't. But I shall go into that too. I must try to discover who is right, society or me.

HELMER. You are ill, Nora. You are delirious. I'm half inclined to think you are out of your mind.

NORA. Never have I felt so calm and collected as I do tonight.

HELMER. Calm and collected enough to leave your husband and children?

NORA. Yes.

HELMER. Then only one explanation is possible.

NORA. And that is?

HELMER. You don't love me any more.

NORA. Exactly.

HELMER. Nora! Can you say that!

NORA. I'm desperately sorry, Torvald. Because you have always been so kind to me. But I can't help it. I don't love you any more.

HELMER [*struggling to keep his composure*]. Is that also a 'calm and collected' decision you've made?

NORA. Yes, absolutely calm and collected. That's why I don't want to stay here.

HELMER. And can you also account for how I forfeited your love?

NORA. Yes, very easily. It was tonight, when the miracle didn't happen. It was then I realized you weren't the man I thought you were.

HELMER. Explain yourself more clearly. I don't understand.

NORA. For eight years I have been patiently waiting. Because, heavens, I knew miracles didn't happen every day. Then this devastating business started, and I became absolutely convinced the miracle *would* happen. All the time Krogstad's letter lay there, it never so much as crossed my mind that you would ever submit to that man's conditions. I was absolutely convinced you would say to him: Tell the whole wide world if you like. And when that was done . . .

HELMER. Yes, then what? After I had exposed my own wife to dishonour and shame . . . !

NORA. When that was done, I was absolutely convinced you would come forward and take everything on yourself, and say: I am the guilty one.

HELMER. Nora!

NORA. You mean I'd never let you make such a sacrifice for my sake? Of course not. But what would my story have counted for against yours?—That was the miracle I went in hope and dread of. It was to prevent it that I was ready to end my life.

HELMER. I would gladly toil day and night for you, Nora, enduring all manner of sorrow and distress. But nobody sacrifices his *honour* for the one he loves.

NORA. Hundreds and thousands of women have.

HELMER. Oh, you think and talk like a stupid child.

NORA. All right. But you neither think nor talk like the man I would want to share my life with. When you had got over your fright—and you weren't concerned about me but only about what might happen to you—and when all danger was past, you acted as though nothing had happened. I was your little sky-lark again, your little doll, exactly as before; except you would have to protect it twice as carefully as before, now that it had shown itself to be so weak and fragile. [*Rises.*] Torvald, that was the moment I realised that for eight years I'd been living with a stranger, and had borne him three children. . . . Oh, I can't bear to think about it! I could tear myself to shreds.

HELMER. [*sadly*]. I see. I see. There is a tremendous gulf dividing us. But, Nora, is there no way we might bridge it?

NORA. As I am now, I am no wife for you.

HELMER. I still have it in me to change.

NORA. Perhaps . . . if you have your doll taken away.

HELMER. And be separated from you! No, no, Nora, the very thought of it is inconceivable.

NORA [*goes into the room, right*]. All the more reason why it must be done.

[*She comes back with her outdoor things and a small travelling bag which she puts on the chair beside the table.*]

HELMER. Nora, Nora, not now! Wait till the morning.

NORA [*putting on her coat*]. I can't spend the night in a strange man's room.

HELMER. Couldn't we go on living here like brother and sister . . . ?

NORA. [*tying on her hat*]. You know very well that wouldn't last. [*She draws the shawl round her.*] Goodbye, Torvald. I don't want to see the children. I know they are in better hands than mine. As I am now, I can never be anything to them.

HELMER. But some day, Nora, some day . . . ?

NORA. How should I know? I've no idea what I might turn out to be.

HELMER. But you are my wife, whatever you are.

NORA. Listen, Torvald, from what I've heard, when a wife leaves her husband's house as I am doing now, he is absolved by law of all responsibility for her. I can at any rate free you from all responsibility. You must not feel in any way bound, any more than I shall. There must be full freedom on both sides. Look, here's your ring back. Give me mine.

HELMER. That too?

NORA. That too.

HELMER. There it is.

NORA. Well, that's the end of that. I'll put the keys down here. The maids know where everything is in the house—better than I do, in fact. Kristine will come in the morning after I've left to pack up the few things I brought with me from home. I want them sent on.

HELMER. The end! Nora, will you never think of me?

NORA. I dare say I'll often think about you and the children and this house.

HELMER. May I write to you, Nora?

NORA. No, never. I won't let you.

HELMER. But surely I can send you . . .

NORA. Nothing, nothing.

HELMER. Can't I help you if ever you need it?

NORA. I said 'no.' I don't accept things from strangers.

HELMER. Nora, can I never be anything more to you than a stranger?

NORA [*takes her bag*]. Ah, Torvald, only by a miracle of miracles . . .

HELMER. Name it, this miracle of miracles!

NORA. Both you and I would have to change to the point where. . . . Oh, Torvald, I don't believe in miracles any more.

HELMER. But I *will* believe. Name it! Change to the point where . . . ?

NORA. Where we could make a real marriage of our lives together. Goodbye!

[*She goes out through the hall door.*]

HELMER [*sinks down on a chair near the door, and covers his face with his hands*]. Nora! Nora! [*He rises and looks round.*] Empty! She's gone! [*With sudden hope.*] The miracle of miracles . . . ?

[*The heavy sound of a door being slammed is heard from below.*]

TOPICS FOR CRITICAL THINKING AND WRITING

The Play on the PAGE

1. Near the beginning of the play, how does Mrs. Linde's presence help to define Nora's character? How does Nora's response to Krogstad's entrance tell us something about Nora?

2. What does Dr. Rank contribute to the play? If he were eliminated, what would be lost?

3. In view of the fact that the last act several times seems to be moving toward a "happy ending" (e.g., Krogstad promises to recall his letter), what is wrong with the alternate ending (see page 584) that Ibsen reluctantly provided for a German production?

4. Can it be argued that although at the end Nora goes out to achieve self-realization, her abandonment of her children—especially to Torvald's loathsome conventional morality—is a crime? (By the way, exactly why does Nora leave the children? She seems to imply, in some passages, that because she forged a signature she is unfit to bring them up. But do you agree with her?)

5. Michael Meyer, in his splendid biography *Henrik Ibsen*, says that the play is not so much about women's rights as about "the need of every individual to find out the kind of person he or she really is, and to strive to become that person." What evidence can you offer to support or refute this interpretation?

6. In *The Quintessence of Ibsenism* Bernard Shaw says that Ibsen, reacting against a common theatrical preference for strange situations, "saw that . . . the more familiar the situation, the more interesting the play. Shakespeare had put ourselves on the stage but not our situations. Our uncles seldom murder our fathers and . . . marry our mothers. . . . Ibsen . . . gives us not only ourselves, but ourselves in our own situations. The things that happen to his stage figures are things that happen to us. One consequence is that his plays are much more important to us than Shakespeare's. Another is that they are capable both of hurting us cruelly and of filling us with excited hopes of escape from idealistic tyrannies, and with visions of intenser life in the future." How much of this do you believe?

The Play on the STAGE

7. In some interpretations, Nora is at the start a ninny, who matures during the play. In other interpretations, she is cunning at the start. If you were directing the play, would you lean toward one or the other of these interpretations, and if so, how would you direct the actress playing Nora? What specific bits of business might you give her?

8. Does it matter if Helmer is especially handsome or not? And whatever his physical appearance, should he display any signs of weakness? Actors of-

ten emphasize one trait, for instance his silliness, or his brutality, or his affection. Do you think one trait is dominant, and should be evident to the audience?

9. As costume designer for a staging of *A Doll's House*, what colors and fabrics would you use for Torvald, Nora, Mrs. Linde, Krogstad, and Dr. Rank?

10. If you were directing a production, what gestures and movements would you give to Nora and Krogstad when they first meet in the play?

11. Nora's tarantella is usually performed as an attempt to distract Helmer from the letterbox. In Bergman's production (see page 585), the dance—performed on top of the dining room table—expressed Nora's anger, and it ended with Nora dropping her tambourine, indicating that the masquerade was over. How would you stage the dance?

12. Working from the last three pages of the script, do you suggest any physical contact between Nora and her husband? If so, point to the specific passages and describe the contact. If you think there should be no physical contact, explain why.

13. Keeping in mind Ibsen's wintry setting—specifically, Christmastime—what kinds of sound effects might be effective in a production?

14. The play is occasionally updated, for instance to an Indiana farm in the 1950s, or to suburban San Diego in the 1990s. What might be gained by some such updating? Do you think that more would be lost than gained? Explain.

Contexts for *A DOLL'S HOUSE*

HENRIK IBSEN
Notes for the Tragedy of Modern Times

[The University Library, Oslo, has the following preliminary notes for *A Doll's House:*]

Rome 19.10.78

There are two kinds of moral law, two kinds of conscience, one in man and a completely different one in woman. They do not understand each other; but in matters of practical living the woman is judged by man's law, as if she were not a woman but a man.

The wife in the play ends up quite bewildered and not knowing right from wrong; her natural instincts on the one side and her faith in authority on the other leave her completely confused.

A woman cannot be herself in contemporary society, it is an exclusively male society with laws drafted by men, and with counsel and judges who judge feminine conduct from the male point of view.

She has committed a crime, and she is proud of it; because she did it for love of her husband and to save his life. But the husband, with his conventional views of honor, stands on the side of the law and looks at the affair with male eyes.

Mental conflict. Depressed and confused by her faith in authority, she loses faith in her moral right and ability to bring up her children. Bitterness. A mother in contemporary society, just as certain insects go away and die when she has done her duty in the propagation of the race [sic]. Love of life, of home and husband and children and family. Now and then, woman-like, she shrugs off her thoughts. Sudden return of dread and terror. Everything must be borne alone. The catastrophe approaches, ineluctably, inevitably. Despair, resistance, defeat.

[*The following note was later added in the margin:*]

Krogstad has done some dishonest business, and thus made a bit of money; but his prosperity does not help him, he cannot recover his honor.

HENRIK IBSEN
Adaptation of A Doll's House *for a German Production*

[Because Norwegian works were not copyrighted in Germany, German theaters could stage and freely adapt Ibsen's works without his consent. When he heard that a German director was going to change the ending to a happy one, Ibsen decided that he had better do the adaptation himself, though he characterized it as "a barbaric outrage" against the play.]

NORA. . . . Where we could make a real marriage out of our lives together. Goodbye. (*Begins to go.*)

HELMER. Go then! (*Seizes her arm.*) But first you shall see your children for the last time!

NORA. Let me go! I will not see them! I cannot!

HELMER (*draws her over to the door, left*). You shall see them. (*Opens the door and says softly.*) Look, there they are asleep, peaceful and carefree. Tomorrow, when they wake up and call for their mother, they will be—motherless.

NORA (*trembling*). Motherless . . . !

HELMER. As you once were.

NORA. Motherless! (*Struggles with herself, lets her travelling bag fall, and says.*) Oh, this is a sin against myself, but I cannot leave them. (*Half sinks down by the door.*)

HELMER (*joyfully, but softly*). Nora!

(THE CURTAIN FALLS.)

HENRIK IBSEN
Speech at the Banquet of the Norwegian League for Women's Rights

[A month after the official birthday celebrations for Ibsen's seventieth birthday were over, Ibsen and his wife were invited to a banquet in his honor given by the leading Norwegian feminist society.]

Christiania, May 26, 1898

I am not a member of the Women's Rights League. Whatever I have written has been without any conscious thought of making propaganda. I have been more the poet and less the social philosopher than people generally seem inclined to believe. I thank you for the toast, but must disclaim the honor of having consciously worked for the women's rights movement. I am not even quite clear as to just what this women's rights movement really is. To me it has seemed a problem of mankind in general. And if you read my books carefully you will understand this. True enough, it is desirable to solve the woman problem, along with all the others; but that has not been the whole purpose. My task has been the *description of humanity*. To be sure, whenever such a description is felt to be reasonably true, the reader will read his own feelings and sentiments into the work of the poet. These are then attributed to the poet; but incorrectly so. Every reader remolds the work beautifully and neatly, each according to his own personality. Not only those who write but also those who read are poets. They are collaborators. They are often more poetical than the poet himself.

The Play in PERFORMANCE

A *Doll's House* is probably Ibsen's most frequently staged play, which means that it is probably the most frequently staged modern drama, and probably only the major plays of Shakespeare are more frequently performed.

A *Doll's House* had its première in Copenhagen, in 1879; as early as 1882 it was produced in English (under the title of *The Child Wife*) in Milwaukee, but with a revised ending in which Nora remained with her family. In the first London production (an amateur production, in 1884), too, Nora did not leave home, and for a German production of 1880 Ibsen himself reluctantly wrote a happy ending, rather than allow someone else to write it (see above, on this page).

It is inconceivable today that the ending would be revised thus, and indeed most productions probably can be characterized as traditional. That is to say, the play is regarded as a classic of realistic drama, and it is staged appropriately, with characters in the dress of the period, and with the appropriate setting. But there have been some notable departures. In Stockholm in 1967 Peter Zadek used a bare room (in contrast to the usual room full of overstuffed furniture), and he rearranged the text into a series of scenes each of which ended with a blackout. In a 1972 production in Stockholm, transferred to Frankfurt in 1973, Hans Neunfels directed a production with surrealistic qualities. The set was an immense room, which of course diminished the characters. At the rear were tall glass doors topped by a kitten (at the left) and a lioness (at the right), symbolizing Nora's dual nature. (For a photograph from this production, see page 15.)

In 1981 the Swedish director Ingmar Bergman offered a severely cut version in Munich, entitled *Nora*, which with some changes was repeated (again called *Nora*) in 1989 in Stockholm. In his first version Bergman omitted the children in order to concentrate on the adult couple, but he later regretted this decision and in the Stockholm version he used one child. Bergman's Helmer was the traditional stuffy figure, but his Nora was from the start an angry woman, and his Dr. Rank was a warmer man than the usual Rank. In the stocking scene, each of these characters brought to the other a warmth that was nowhere else to be found in the play.

Bergman's staging was highly unusual. He used three sets: a living room, with a massive dark sofa, a chair, and in the background a Christmas tree with two dolls, a doll's bed, and other presents; a dining room, with a large round table and four chairs; and a bedroom, with a brass bed that resembled a miniature doll's bed that was among the toys in the first scene. But the use of several rooms instead of only one, far from making the Helmer household seem relatively open, made it more oppressive than the usual living room set does, since none of the rooms had windows or door, except in the final scene when a door appeared in the background. Each set appeared on a platform,

and the platform itself was surrounded by high walls with small barred windows at the top. The platform thus was a sort of inner stage, and each room was itself imprisoned within the tall outer walls. The actors were always in view of the audience; in the first (Munich) version, when called upon to perform, they stepped onto the platform from the background (in effect, they entered the inner stage), performed their parts, and then returned to the background. In the Stockholm version, they sat in simple chairs at the sides, and, when called upon to perform in the action, they stepped up onto the platform, played their parts, and then returned to their chairs, where they watched the others perform. Thus the actors were spectators as well as actors, with the implication that life is a matter of role playing.

Most astounding was Bergman's ending. He did not, of course, use the happy ending that in earlier days some directors had foisted on the play, but he did something almost as daring—he staged the end of the scene in the Helmer bedroom. Helmer was asleep (presumably he had gone to bed thinking that he and Nora were reconciled), when Nora entered, carrying a small suitcase. Helmer awakened, flooded with light (Nora was in the dark), sat up, and the audience realized that he was naked. (See the photo on page 554.) Moving in and out of the light Nora spoke to Helmer, who—for reasons of modesty dared not get out of bed, despite years of marriage. Nora exited and was replaced by her daughter, who carried the doll—a Christmas present—that the audience had seen at the start. Nora reentered, and then made a final exit from the platform, walking past Mrs. Linde and Krogstad, who were sitting offstage, and she then walked through the auditorium.

For an extended discussion of productions of the play, see Egil Tornqvist, *Ibsen: A Doll's House* (1995). For a briefer discussion, see Frederick J. Marker and Lise-Lone Marker, *Ibsen's Lively Art* (1989). On Bergman's *Nora*, see Ingmar Bergman, *A Project for the Theatre*, ed. Frederick J. Marker and Lise-Lone Marker (1983).

CAROL ELLIOT MACVEY
Directing A Doll's House

Carol Elliot MacVey, a member of the theater department at the University of Iowa, directed *A Doll's House* at Princeton in 1991.

Did you make any cuts? If so, why?

When asked about cutting an Ibsen text the question ought to be, almost *has* to be, "If you made any cuts, *how* did you manage to do so?" My own rule: if you're going to cut, *cut big*. Ibsen's dialogue is so finely crafted that it is often virtually impossible to excise a sentence without confusing what directly follows. There is a verbal dependency between speaker's sentences. Many responses repeat a word mentioned in the previous sentence, frustrating the possibility of doing much interdialogue cutting. This pattern is consistent throughout the text. This careful forging of each link to form a whole is quintessentially Ibsen, his characteristic rhythm. It isn't surprising to read that once on meeting an architect Ibsen commented, "Yes; it is, as you know, my own trade."

And wouldn't you agree that some very brief passages of dialogue are highly important to the plot and to connections between characters?

There is a weighty history to the personal and relational events of the play. Ibsen might well have entitled this play *Ghosts* too, since each of the characters in this play is haunted by sins of the past. The actors, directors, and designers must be vigilant in detecting clues to what these sins of the past might be and how they relate to the other characters. What appears to be a casual or cryptic comment by one character can actually turn out to be significant in decoding that character's past.

What might be an example?

When Krogstad confronts Nora with having forged her father's signature, Krogstad says,

> "But business, the kind of business we two have been transacting—I think you'll admit I understand something about that?"

Precisely what does he mean by "the kind of business"? With some research and poetic license I deduced from that comment something along these lines: When, years earlier, Torvald and Krogstad, both government legal inspectors, investigated Nora's father's firm, they found the old gentleman guilty of improprieties. But because Torvald was then engaged to Nora he didn't want to bring charges against her father so he "turned a blind eye"; Krogstad, out of friendship to Torvald, submitted a false report and altered one or more bank documents that might have incriminated Nora's father. I assume that Krogstad falsified these documents by forging the old man's signature. Meanwhile, Torvald resigned his government job, married Nora, and within months Nora's father died. Later there was some questioning about one of the aforementioned bank documents and Krogstad was accused of forgery and subsequently fired. Therefore, when Krogstad says to Nora that he knows about "the kind of business," he is alluding to his own experience with forgery, ironically linking him and Nora in a similar crime motivated by the same reason: Torvald's salvation. So aside from violating the exact verbal architecture of the play, it is also difficult to cut text without excising some of the irony, morality, history, and complexity of the characters.

What are some other ways in which you see connections between characters?

There is a kind of incestuousness with these characters' lives, each one having been connected with another at some time in his or her past. With Ibsen's own words those relationships may also be projected into the future as well. Consider the relationship between Nora and Mrs. Linde. As a character construct, Christine is somewhat of a döppelganger for Nora: When they first meet in Act I, Christine is needy, Nora has everything; at the end Christine is poised for security, Nora is practically destitute. Imagine that some time has passed since Nora's departure at the end of the play and the two friends meet. The exchange from their first meeting in Act I, as scripted by Ibsen, could be recycled almost word for word except that the speakers would be switched and the resonances of their pasts altered. It would read as follows:

NORA (*shyly and a little hesitantly*). Good evening, Christine.
MRS. LINDE (*uncertainly*). Good evening—
NORA. I don't suppose you recognize me.
MRS. LINDE. No, I'm afraid I—Yes, wait a minute—surely—(*Exclaims.*) Why, Nora! Is it really you?
NORA. Yes, it's me.
MRS. LINDE. And I didn't recognize you! But how could I—? (*More quietly.*) How you've changed, Nora!

NORA. Yes, I know. It's been nine years—nearly ten—

MRS. LINDE. Is it so long? Yes, it must be. Oh, these last eight years have been such a happy time for me! So you've come to town? All that way in winter! How brave of you!

NORA. I arrived by the steamer this morning.

MRS. LINDE. Yes, of course—to enjoy yourself over Christmas. Oh, how splendid! We'll have to celebrate! But take off your coat. You're not cold, are you? (*Helps her off with it.*) There! Now let's sit down here by the stove and be comfortable. No, you take the armchair. I'll sit here in the rocking-chair. (*Clasps Nora's hands.*) Yes, now you look like your old self. It was just at first that—you've got a little paler, though, Nora. And perhaps a bit thinner.

NORA. And older, Christine. Much, much older.

This is one of several examples I could point out. We actually used these character/line reversals in rehearsal as improvisations to discover character relationships. I contend that the incestuousness of the characters' past lives also extends to their very words. Again, any cutting would have to be judicious.

But you did make a big cut late in the play, didn't you?

Yes. Once Nora stood up and said, "Torvald, in that moment I realized that for eight years I had been living here with a complete stranger and had borne him three children! Oh, I can't bear to think of it. I could tear myself to pieces!" the actors spoke no more lines from the text. Originally the actors had memorized and spoken all of the text and we had rehearsed it intact. But one day, as a rehearsal technique—a favorite of mine—we played the scene (from the time Nora stands to the end of play) as a silent movie, without any words. It turned out that everything essential was conveyed in movement and sound and that in the process we had gained tremendous emotional resonances. As a result of bypassing the literal word, we discovered firsthand what Peter Brook says about a word being "a small visible portion of a gigantic unseen formation." We drew from a primordial stratum of human sounds that we associate with a life and death situation, which is what the ending is for Nora and Torvald, and it yielded a powerful spectacle.

Did you do anything special with Nora's departure at the end? Everyone expects the door to slam.

Oh yes, the door did slam in our production, the climax of a litany of orchestrated sounds—not arbitrary sounds but ones suggested by the text. One such sequence played especially well. At the very end of the play when Nora walked to the door to exit she found that the door was locked. Torvald had locked it earlier (via Ibsen's stage directions), but he had not yet unlocked it (Ibsen never indicated that he should have) and he still had the key. Nora desperately tried to pull and kick the door open. That didn't work. Torvald refused to give her the key. And in one of the more powerful images of the production she tried climbing out up over the walls of the room but was not successful. Finally, in desperation, she had to assault Torvald physically in order to extricate the key from him. Throughout all of this, there were no words, but there was language and sound: Nora's footsteps, the grappling with the doorknob, her kicking the door, her heaving and panting, her fingernails and feet scratching the walls, her pummelling Torvald, their cries as they struggled. It was a brutal fight, but she prevailed and got the key. Some evenings the audience actually applauded and cheered at this point. When, at last, we finally heard the sound of the key in the door and saw the door open wide and heard her hard footsteps go into the hall and heard the final slam of the outside door we knew it was not only an act of will but also a result of great courage and we felt that she could and would survive. I hoped as much.

Purists are shocked that I cut those final last exchanges about "the miracle of miracles" but I felt we lost nothing essential and gained a visual and visceral power that the words never unpacked. To this day, when asked what I feel most successful about as a director I always reply, "The last act of *A Doll's House*."

What design decisions did you make about A Doll's House? *How did you costume it?*

One particular costume was the lynchpin for our thinking about the rest of the costume design: Nora's Neapolitan dress. What a theatrical genius Ibsen is! He built into this play a truly stunning stage image executed by a costume; unfortunately, it's easy to miss since it's buried in a stage direction: *Nora removes the dress from a box.* We wanted to underscore the drama and import of that event so we consciously chose to color-starve our audience up until that moment of unpacking the dress. Our palette for the set and costumes was combinations of mauves, tans, and endless shades of off-white. When Nora took her tarantella dress out of its box and all that brilliant redness ignited the stage, it was a thrilling event. Each night, when that dress appeared, there were audible gasps from the audience. I wish I could take sole credit for the idea, but I can't; it's right there in Ibsen's text.

What was the set like?

We started our set design discussions with a principle, a fact, and a question—principle: Space is destiny; fact: The only object Ibsen insisted be present on the set of A Doll's House was a painting of the Madonna and Child; question: What, if anything, should be visible outside the room's windows? We ended up fusing those three elements. The walls of the room, which were papered in a delicate Victorian design, were rounded and very, very high. There were three doors, which were also wallpapered like the walls, an idea inspired by Strindberg's design for The Father. When these doors were closed they created one continuous seamless wall and the sense of confinement was total: Nora's space was the physical correlative of Nora's character. The only other objects in the room were three chairs, a small table, and a stove. But the most visually exciting and dominating aspect of the design was Ibsen's called-for portrait of the Virgin and Infant. In the center of the room was a very large window—maybe eight feet high—outside of which was hung a bigger than life-size painting of the Madonna and Child. We believed that if there was a single image of what that society held up as the model for motherhood, femininity, and womanhood it was the image of the Madonna. We intended that the image be pervasive. It was. For the last act the painting of the Madonna was covered in black velvet, giving the effect of an ominous bleakness and void "out there" to which Nora would exit. There were no models of womanhood or femininity or motherhood for Nora at the end of the play.

Do you think that the play may come across as a melodrama?

In the reading of it, yes. I had always been daunted by Ibsen. In part I feared the inherent melodrama—you know, those coincidences that make one want to snicker aloud and roll one's eyes in disbelief as one reads the stage directions announcing a knock at the door and—gasp!—the entrance of the very person just whispered about and least expected. But much to my surprise, what was melodramatic on the page most often became simply dramatic on the stage. And the truth is that each of our lives, when reduced to a plot summary, sounds very melodramatic, doesn't it? Often in recounting important moments in our lives, don't we tell about unbelievable coincidences? So I embraced the artifice of those selected coincidences and constructed events and constricted time and concentrated on making the characters real people, which is where the actual power of the performance lies. Plays are artifices; people aren't.

Two questions: Is this a feminist piece? And, is it dated?

As a director, I have always been interested in the unresolved tensions at the end of a play: What remains in that final moment? Of equal theatrical importance are the two final events of the play: Nora's leaving and Torvald's remaining. Consider the final image in our production: Nora has exited and the door has slammed. But that's not the end of the play, not in my imagination, not in Ibsen's text. The final image belongs to Torvald. He is alone on stage as the sound of Nora's door slamming reverberates (and in our production he was on the floor in a totally empty room, weeping, distraught, bewildered, rocking himself in a prenatal position). It is the single most powerful image I know of in dramatic literature which suggests both the 1880s as well as the 1990s response of the majority of men vis-à-vis the feminist movement: silence and perhaps an unspoken "How could this have happened?" What was and remains both feminist and timely then is Nora's struggle to achieve the miracle of miracles, which has yet to be achieved in any culture, and Torvald's reaction to his wife's departure which has not yet, sad to say, been fully processed and understood by many men and even by many women.

AUGUST Strindberg

August Strindberg (1849–1912) was born in Sweden two months after the marriage of his parents (who already had three children). After a desperately unhappy childhood and youth, he turned to playwriting; King Charles XV of Sweden was impressed by one drama and granted Strindberg a small scholarship to the university. The king, however, soon died, and Strindberg found employment in the Royal Library, where he studied Chinese. In 1877 he married a divorced baroness, but the marriage was extremely stormy and they separated in 1891. During the period when he was married, however, he wrote his great naturalistic plays, all of which deal with sexual conflict: *The Father* (1887), *Miss Julie* (1888), and *The Creditors* (1889). (*Miss Julie* includes autobiographical elements—Strindberg's mother was a servant, yet he married a baroness.) In 1893 he married an Austrian woman and again separated, and lastly, after a period in a sanatorium, he married and separated for a third time. During and between marriages he worked fiercely at Chinese, dramaturgy, and, for a while, chemistry.

His early plays are mostly either historical (on Swedish history from the thirteenth to the eighteenth century) or realistic; his later ones, notably *The Dance of Death* (1901), wherein he tries to dramatize the conflict of the soul, are symbolic and expressionistic; that is, they present not life as we all see it but life as the artist passionately feels it to be. In all, he wrote some seventy plays, as well as several autobiographical novels.

■■■■■■■■■■■■■

COMMENTARY ON *MISS JULIE*

Realism, as practiced by Ibsen, insists that the drama ought to be a close copy of life. People on the stage should sound pretty much like people off the stage, the scenery and the properties should look like the real thing—if the set is a kitchen, the pots and pans should not be obviously painted on the wall but should be real pots and pans—and the story dramatized should be one in which we ourselves might participate. But realism is not allied to any particular philosophy, and in this it is unlike naturalism.

Naturalism is an artistic movement characterized not merely by an attempt to imitate life and life's dialogue, but also by a basic assumption about the nature of existence. Heavily influenced by scientific—especially biological—research, the naturalists believed that human actions are less free than had generally been supposed, and are in fact the results of influences exerted by heredity and environment. In this view, genetics (our biological inheritance) and history (the shape of our society, and our assigned role in it) largely determine what we are and what we do. As early as the second quarter of the nineteenth century, for example, Balzac in his novels had examined human beings partly by examining their environment, working on the biological assumption that the creature's nature is partly determined by its surroundings. But, as Strind-

berg points out in his preface to *Miss Julie*, though naturalism has, by appealing to factors outside of humans' control, abolished guilt, the consequences of human actions nevertheless remain.

Naturalism, then, aims not merely at presenting a "slice of life," but, assuming that we are motivated by our biological inheritance and our milieu, it has a definite attitude as to what life is like. It thus dethrones reason, and for free will it substitutes biological drives (notably hunger and sex) and sometimes economic pressures. In 1881 Zola published a collection of essays, *Naturalism in the Theater*, demanding that the drama not only set aside old theatrical conventions such as unconvincing scenery but that it also take account of scientific research—meaning the influence of heredity and environment—and in 1887 André Antoine, founder of the Théâtre libre, a dramatic group dedicated to realism—illusionism in costume and setting—and to serious drama rather than to farce and melodrama, staged a dramatization of one of Zola's naturalistic stories. Because it emphasizes environment, naturalism tends to concentrate on what used to be called the lower classes, whose basic drives and economic pressures are most obviously manifested in actions. (Strindberg closely followed newspapers reports of Antoine's activities.) Zola, in his novel, *L'Assommoir* (The Tavern), for example, using the appropriate slang, describes the influence of a lazy drunkard (who ultimately dies in an asylum) on his mistress (who ultimately dies of starvation). But Zola, despite the protests he evoked, was basically moral; although he depicted the influence of environment, he nevertheless held his characters morally responsible for their actions. In early twentieth-century America, Theodore Dreiser's characters range, in a series of novels, from frightened young men to ruthless financiers, but Dreiser excuses their crimes and lies by assuming that, given their "chemistry" and their situation, they could do nothing else.

Because naturalism generally explores an environment, and in addition often traces actions back to one's ancestors, the novel, by virtue of its breadth, is more suited to its needs than is the drama. Strindberg, however, found its philosophy congenial to his own obviously irrational nature and sought to write plays for the naturalistic theater. He succeeded admirably, and Eugene O'Neill called him "the greatest interpreter in the theater of the characteristic spiritual conflicts which constitute the drama—the blood—of our lives today." *Miss Julie* (1888), written as Strindberg's contribution to the new drama promoted by Antoine, characterized by Strindberg in a letter to his publisher as "the Swedish drama's first naturalistic tragedy," is among the most important products of naturalism. It has had much success on the stage, and a Swedish motion picture version brought *Miss Julie* to an even wider public than before. The germ of the play, Strindberg claimed, was a real story of which he had heard, though he admitted altering the ending. (Incidentally, if his account is accurate, by reworking the facts he violated one of the tenets of naturalism.)

Technically, the play (which lasts about an hour and a half) has no intermission; Strindberg, in his concern with realism, did not want to destroy the dramatic illusion by a break, which would allow the spectators to be reminded that they are watching a play, not life itself. But we move from realism to naturalism in the tragic outcome of the conflict of wills, where Strindberg gives us a conflict equivalent to the Darwinian struggle for existence. The actions, Strindberg insists in his preface (see pages 606–08), are not the outcome of this or that obvious motive but are the products of a number of forces, some almost invisible, uniting with a particular circumstance to produce deeds not rationally willed. Julie's motives, he says, are deliberately complex, for whereas (he claims) older drama falsely suggests that a character is motivated by one trait, such as pride, or love, or hate, Strindberg's figures have all the complexity of life itself. Jean, the count's valet, on Midsummer Eve (a night, when the sun does not set, devoted to festive dancing and celebration) seduces Julie, his master's daughter, and then drives her to suicide. Why does Julie yield? As a matter of fact, a reading of the play will show that this summary is misleading, for Jean is seduced by Julie as much as she is by him. Strindberg states that she is undone by many causes: her father's faulty care of her; his absence; the aphrodisiacal influence of flowers; the excitement of the dance; and chance, which happens to bring her into proximity with an excited, aggressive man.

Coupled with this picture of human beings as victims of heredity, environment, and chance is Strindberg's assumption that, in addition to the conflict between individuals and more especially between the male and the female, there is a larger battle, the class struggle. Thus, Julie and Jean represent not only the struggle between the sexes but also the clash between a decaying aristocracy and a rising working class. Strindberg himself reports in one of his autobiographies how delighted he was by the thought that he, the son of poor parents, had married—conquered—a daughter of the aristocracy, Baron Wrangel's wife. But whether the conflict is sexual or economic, behind the struggle of the individual looms Fate, now composed of heredity and environment, absolving human beings from moral responsibility. Furthermore, Strindberg assumes that the conflicts are irreconcilable; no compromise can be worked out in these struggles, which must be to the death. Drawing on his own unhappy marital experiences, he assumed that each individual is propelled by a desire to dominate, and though life is ghastly, we irrationally desire to prolong it. Why, then, does Julie commit suicide? Because, Strindberg explained in a letter to a friend, she is ashamed, depressed, under the influence of a will stronger than her own, and near a razor. Her tragedy, Strindberg implies, is pathetic as she struggles against a destiny that cannot be averted, and at last yields, semivoluntarily.

MISS JULIE
August Strindberg

Translated by Harry G. Carlson

CHARACTERS

MISS JULIE, *25 years old*
JEAN, *her father's valet, 30 years old*
KRISTINE, *her father's cook, 35 years old*

(*The action takes place in the Count's kitchen on midsummer eve.*)

SETTING

(*A large kitchen, the ceiling and side walls of which are hidden by draperies. The rear wall runs diagonally from down left to up right. On the wall down left are two shelves with copper, iron, and pewter utensils; the shelves are lined with scalloped paper. Visible to the right is most of a set of large, arched glass doors, through which can be seen a fountain with a statue of Cupid, lilac bushes in bloom, and the tops of some Lombardy poplars. At down left is the corner of a large tiled stove; a portion of its hood is showing. At right, one end of the servants' white pine dining table juts out; several chairs stand around it. The stove is decorated with birch branches; juniper twigs are strewn on the floor. On the end of the table stands a large Japanese spice jar, filled with lilac blossoms. An ice box, a sink, and a washstand. Above the door is an old-fashioned bell on a spring; to the left of the door, the mouthpiece of a speaking tube is visible.*)

(*Kristine is frying something on the stove. She is wearing a light-colored cotton dress and an apron. Jean enters. He is wearing livery and carries a pair of high riding boots with spurs, which he puts down on the floor where they can be seen by the audience.*)

JEAN. Miss Julie's crazy again tonight; absolutely crazy!

KRISTINE. So you finally came back?

JEAN. I took the Count to the station and when I returned past the barn I stopped in for a dance. Who do I see but Miss Julie leading off the dance with the gamekeeper! But as soon as she saw me she rushed over to ask me for the next waltz. And she's been waltzing ever since—I've never seen anything like it. She's crazy!

KRISTINE. She always has been, but never as bad as the last two weeks since her engagement was broken off.

JEAN. Yes, I wonder what the real story was there. He was a gentleman, even if he wasn't rich. Ah! These people have such romantic ideas. (*Sits at the end of the table.*) Still, it's strange, isn't it? I mean that she'd rather stay home with the servants on midsummer eve instead of going with her father to visit relatives?

KRISTINE. She's probably embarrassed after that row with her fiancé.

JEAN. Probably! He gave a good account of himself, though. Do you know how it happened, Kristine? I saw it, you know, though I didn't let on I had.

KRISTINE. No! You saw it?

JEAN. Yes, I did.——That evening they were out near the stable, and she was "training" him—as she called it. Do you know what she did? She made him jump over her riding crop, the way you'd teach a dog to jump. He jumped twice and she hit him each time. But the third time he grabbed the crop out of her hand, hit her with it across the cheek, and broke it in pieces. Then he left.

KRISTINE. So, that's what happened! I can't believe it!

JEAN. Yes, that's the way it went!——What have you got for me that's tasty, Kristine?

KRISTINE (*serving him from the pan*). Oh, it's only a piece of kidney I cut from the veal roast.

JEAN (*smelling the food*). Beautiful! That's my favorite *délice*.[1] (*Feeling the plate.*) But you could have warmed the plate!

KRISTINE. You're fussier than the Count himself, once you start! (*She pulls his hair affectionately.*)

JEAN (*angry*). Stop it, leave my hair alone! You know I'm touchy about that.

KRISTINE. Now, now, it's only love, you know that. (*Jean eats. Kristine opens a bottle of beer.*)

JEAN. Beer? On midsummer eve? No thank you! I can do better than that. (*Opens a drawer in the table and takes out a bottle of red wine with yellow sealing wax.*) See that? Yellow seal! Give me a glass! A wine glass! I'm drinking this *pur*.[2]

---

[1] **délice** delight [2] **pur** pure; without water

Jean (played by Peter Francis James) seduces—or is seduced by—Miss Julie (Kim
Catrall), in a production at the McCarter Theatre, in Princeton, New Jersey. Like most productions of Miss Julie, this one used sets and
costumes that evoked the period in which the
play was written and set.

KRISTINE (*returns to the stove and puts on a small saucepan*).
God help the woman who gets you for a husband! What
a fussbudget.

JEAN. Nonsense! You'd be damned lucky to get a man like
me. It certainly hasn't done you any harm to have people
call me your sweetheart. (*Tastes the wine.*) Good! Very
good! Just needs a little warming. (*Warms the glass between his hands.*) We bought this in Dijon. Four francs a
liter, not counting the cost of the bottle, or the customs
duty.——What are you cooking now? It stinks like hell!

KRISTINE. Oh, some slop Miss Julie wants to give Diana.

JEAN. Watch your language, Kristine. But why should you
have to cook for that damn mutt on midsummer eve? Is
she sick?

KRISTINE. Yes, she's sick! She sneaked out with the gatekeeper's dog—and now there's hell to pay. Miss Julie
won't have it!

JEAN. Miss Julie has too much pride about some things and
not enough about others, just like her mother was. The
Countess was most at home in the kitchen and the cow-
sheds, but a *one*-horse carriage wasn't elegant enough for
her. The cuffs of her blouse were dirty, but she had to
have her coat of arms on her cufflinks.——And Miss
Julie won't take proper care of herself either. If you ask
me, she just isn't refined. Just now, when she was dancing
in the barn, she pulled the gamekeeper away from Anna
and made him dance with her. *We* wouldn't behave like
that, but that's what happens when aristocrats pretend
they're common people—they get *common!*——But she
is quite a woman! Magnificent! What shoulders, and
what—et cetera!

KRISTINE. Oh, don't overdo it! I've heard what Clara says,
and she dresses her.

JEAN. Ha, Clara! You're all jealous of each other! I've been
out riding with her. . . . And the way she dances!

KRISTINE. Listen, Jean! You're going to dance with me, when
I'm finished here, aren't you?

JEAN. Of course I will.

KRISTINE. Promise?

JEAN. Promise? When I say I'll do something, I do it! By the
way, the kidney was very good. (*Corks the bottle.*)

JULIE (*in the doorway to someone outside*). I'll be right back!
You go ahead for now! (*Jean sneaks the bottle back into the
table drawer and gets up respectfully. Miss Julie enters and
crosses to Kristine by the stove.*) Well? Is it ready? (*Kristine
indicates that Jean is present.*)

JEAN (*gallantly*). Are you ladies up to something secret?

JULIE (*flicking her handkerchief in his face*). None of your business!

JEAN. Hmm! I like the smell of violets!

JULIE (*coquettishly*). Shame on you! So you know about perfumes, too? You certainly know how to dance. Ah, ah!
No peeking! Go away.

JEAN (*boldly but respectfully*). Are you brewing up a magic potion for midsummer eve? Something to prophesy by under a lucky star, so you'll catch a glimpse of your future
husband!

JULIE (*caustically*). You'd need sharp eyes to see him! (*To
Kristine.*) Pour out half a bottle and cork it well.——
Come and dance a schottische[3] with me, Jean . . .

³**schottische** a Scottish round dance

JEAN (*hesitating*). I don't want to be impolite to anyone, and I've already promised this dance to Kristine . . .

JULIE. Oh, she can have another one—can't you, Kristine? Won't you lend me Jean?

KRISTINE. It's not up to me, ma'am. (*To Jean.*) If the mistress is so generous, it wouldn't do for you to say no. Go on, Jean, and thank her for the honor.

JEAN. To be honest, and no offense intended, I wonder whether it's wise for you to dance twice running with the same partner, especially since these people are quick to jump to conclusions . . .

JULIE (*flaring up*). What's that? What sort of conclusions? What do you mean?

JEAN (*submissively*). If you don't understand, ma'am, I must speak more plainly. It doesn't look good to play favorites with your servants. . . .

JULIE. Play favorites! What an idea! I'm astonished! As mistress of the house, I honor your dance with my presence. And when I dance, I want to dance with someone who can lead, so I won't look ridiculous.

JEAN. As you order, ma'am! I'm at your service!

JULIE (*gently*). Don't take it as an order! On a night like this we're all just ordinary people having fun, so we'll forget about rank. Now, take my arm!——Don't worry, Kristine! I won't steal your sweetheart! (*Jean offers his arm and leads Miss Julie out.*)

MIME

(*The following should be played as if the actress playing Kristine were really alone. When she has to, she turns her back to the audience. She does not look toward them, nor does she hurry as if she were afraid they would grow impatient. Schottische music played on a fiddle sounds in the distance. Kristine hums along with the music. She clears the table, washes the dishes, dries them, and puts them away. She takes off her apron. From a table drawer she removes a small mirror and leans it against the bowl of lilacs on the table. She lights a candle, heats a hairpin over the flame, and uses it to set a curl on her forehead. She crosses to the door and listens, then returns to the table. She finds the handkerchief Miss Julie left behind, picks it up, and smells it. Then, preoccupied, she spreads it out, stretches it, smoothes out the wrinkles, and folds it into quarters, and so forth.*)

JEAN (*enters alone*). God, she really *is* crazy! What a way to dance! Everybody's laughing at her behind her back. What do you make of it, Kristine?

KRISTINE. Ah! It's that time of the month for her, and she always gets peculiar like that. Are you going to dance with me now?

JEAN. You're not mad at me, are you, for leaving . . . ?

KRISTINE. Of course not!——Why should I be, for a little thing like that? Besides, I know my place . . .

JEAN (*puts his arm around her waist*). You're a sensible girl, Kristine, and you'd make a good wife . . .

JULIE (*entering; uncomfortably surprised; with forced good humor*). What a charming escort—running away from his partner.

JEAN. On the contrary, Miss Julie. Don't you see how I rushed back to the partner I abandoned!

JULIE (*changing her tone*). You know, you're a superb dancer!——But why are you wearing livery on a holiday? Take it off at once!

JEAN. Then I must ask you to go outside for a moment. You see, my black coat is hanging over here . . . (*Gestures and crosses right.*)

JULIE. Are you embarrassed about changing your coat in front of me? Well, go in your room then. Either that or stay and I'll turn my back.

JEAN. With your permission, ma'am! (*He crosses right. His arm is visible as he changes his jacket.*)

JULIE (*to Kristine*). Tell me, Kristine—you two are so close—. Is Jean your fiancé?

KRISTINE. Fiancé? Yes, if you wish. We can call him that.

JULIE. What do you mean?

KRISTINE. You had a fiancé yourself, didn't you? So . . .

JULIE. Well, we were properly engaged . . .

KRISTINE. But nothing came of it, did it? (*Jean returns dressed in a frock coat and bowler hat.*)

JULIE. *Très gentil, monsieur Jean! Très gentil!*

JEAN. *Vous voulez plaisanter, madame!*

JULIE. *Et vous voulez parler français!*[4] Where did you learn that?

JEAN. In Switzerland, when I was wine steward in one of the biggest hotels in Lucerne!

JULIE. You look like a real gentleman in that coat! *Charmant!*[5] (*Sits at the table.*)

JEAN. Oh, you're flattering me!

JULIE (*offended*). Flattering you?

JEAN. My natural modesty forbids me to believe that you would really compliment someone like me, and so I took the liberty of assuming that you were exaggerating, which polite people call flattering.

JULIE. Where did you learn to talk like that? You must have been to the theater often.

JEAN. Of course. And I've done a lot of traveling.

JULIE. But you come from here, don't you?

JEAN. My father was a farmhand on the district attorney's estate nearby. I used to see you when you were little, but you never noticed me.

JULIE. No! Really?

JEAN. Sure. I remember one time especially . . . but I can't talk about that.

---

[4]**Très gentil . . . français!** Very nice, Mr. Jean. You are joking, madam! And you want to speak French!   [5]**Charmant** charming

JULIE. Oh, come now! Why not? Just this once!

JEAN. No, I really couldn't, not now. Some other time, perhaps.

JULIE. Why some other time? What's so dangerous about now?

JEAN. It's not dangerous, but there are obstacles.——Her, for example. (*Indicating Kristine, who has fallen asleep in a chair by the stove.*)

JULIE. What a pleasant wife she'll make! She probably snores, too.

JEAN. No, she doesn't, but she talks in her sleep.

JULIE (*cynically*). How do *you* know?

JEAN (*audaciously*). I've heard her! (*Pause, during which they stare at each other.*)

JULIE. Why don't you sit down?

JEAN. I couldn't do that in your presence.

JULIE. But if I order you to?

JEAN. Then I'd obey.

JULIE. Sit down, then.——No, wait. Can you get me something to drink first?

JEAN. I don't know what we have in the ice box. I think there's only beer.

JULIE. Why do you say "only"? My tastes are so simple I prefer beer to wine. (*Jean takes a bottle of beer from the ice box and opens it. He looks for a glass and a plate in the cupboard and serves her.*)

JEAN. Here you are, ma'am.

JULIE. Thank you. Won't you have something yourself?

JEAN. I'm not partial to beer, but if it's an order . . .

JULIE. An order?——Surely a gentleman can keep his lady company.

JEAN. You're right, of course. (*Opens a bottle and gets a glass.*)

JULIE. Now, drink to my health! (*He hesitates.*) What? A man of the world—and shy?

JEAN (*in mock romantic fashion, he kneels and raises his glass*). Skål to my mistress!

JULIE. Bravo!——Now kiss my shoe, to finish it properly. (*Jean hesitates, then boldly seizes her foot and kisses it lightly.*) Perfect! You should have been an actor.

JEAN (*rising*). That's enough now, Miss Julie! Someone might come in and see us.

JULIE. What of it?

JEAN. People talk, that's what! If you knew how their tongues were wagging just now at the dance, you'd . . .

JULIE. What were they saying? Tell me!——Sit down!

JEAN (*sits*). I don't want to hurt you, but they were saying things——suggestive things, that, that . . . well, you can figure it out for yourself! You're not a child. If a woman is seen drinking alone with a man—let alone a servant—at night—then . . .

JULIE. Then what? Besides, we're not alone. Kristine is here.

JEAN. Asleep!

JULIE. Then I'll wake her up. (*Rising.*) Kristine! Are you asleep? (*Kristine mumbles in her sleep.*)

JULIE. Kristine!——She certainly can sleep!

KRISTINE (*in her sleep*). The Count's boots are brushed—put the coffee on—right away, right away—uh, huh—oh!

JULIE (*grabbing Kristine's nose*). Will you wake up!

JEAN (*severely*). Leave her alone—let her sleep!

JULIE (*sharply*). What?

JEAN. Someone who's been standing over a stove all day has a right to be tired by now. Sleep should be respected . . .

JULIE (*changing her tone*). What a considerate thought—it does you credit—thank you! (*Offering her hand.*) Come outside and pick some lilacs for me! (*During the following, Kristine awakens and shambles sleepily off right to bed.*)

JEAN. Go with you?

JULIE. With me!

JEAN. We couldn't do that! Absolutely not!

JULIE. I don't understand. Surely you don't imagine . . .

JEAN. No, I don't, but the others might.

JULIE. What? That I've fallen in love with a servant?

JEAN. I'm not a conceited man, but such things happen—and for these people, nothing is sacred.

JULIE. I do believe you're an aristocrat!

JEAN. Yes, I am.

JULIE. And I'm stepping down . . .

JEAN. Don't step down, Miss Julie, take my advice. No one'll believe you stepped down voluntarily. People will always say you fell.

JULIE. I have a higher opinion of people than you. Come and see!——Come! (*She stares at him broodingly.*)

JEAN. You're very strange, do you know that?

JULIE. Perhaps! But so are you!——For that matter, everything is strange. Life, people, everything. Like floating scum, drifting on and on across the water, until it sinks down and down! That reminds me of a dream I have now and then. I've climbed up on top of a pillar. I sit there and see no way of getting down. I get dizzy when I look down, and I must get down, but I don't have the courage to jump. I can't hold on firmly, and I long to be able to fall, but I don't fall. And yet I'll have no peace until I get down, no rest unless I get down, down on the ground! And if I did get down to the ground, I'd want to be under the earth . . . Have you ever felt anything like that?

JEAN. No. I dream that I'm lying under a high tree in a dark forest. I want to get up, up on top, and look out over the bright landscape, where the sun is shining, and plunder the bird's nest up there, where the golden eggs lie. And I climb and climb, but the trunk's so thick and smooth, and it's so far to the first branch. But I know if I just reached that first branch, I'd go right to the top, like up a ladder. I haven't reached it yet, but I will, even if it's only in a dream!

JULIE. Here I am chattering with you about dreams. Come, let's go out! Just into the park! (*She offers him her arm, and they start to leave.*)

JEAN. We'll have to sleep on nine midsummer flowers, Miss Julie, to make our dreams come true! (*They turn at the door. Jean puts his hand to his eye.*)

JULIE. Did you get something in your eye?

JEAN. It's nothing—just a speck—it'll be gone in a minute.

JULIE. My sleeve must have brushed against you. Sit down and let me help you. (*She takes him by the arm and seats him. She tilts his head back and with the tip of a handkerchief tries to remove the speck.*) Sit still, absolutely still! (*She slaps his hand.*) Didn't you hear me?——Why, you're trembling; the big, strong man is trembling! (*Feels his biceps.*) What muscles you have!

JEAN (*warning*). Miss Julie!

JULIE. Yes, *monsieur* Jean.

JEAN. *Attention! Je ne suis qu'un homme*[6]

JULIE. Will you sit still!——There! Now it's gone! Kiss my hand and thank me.

JEAN (*rising*). Miss Julie, listen to me!——Kristine has gone to bed!——Will you listen to me!

JULIE. Kiss my hand first!

JEAN. Listen to me!

JULIE. Kiss my hand first!

JEAN. All right, but you've only yourself to blame!

JULIE. For what?

JEAN. For what? Are you still a child at twenty-five? Don't you know that it's dangerous to play with fire?

JULIE. Not for me. I'm insured.

JEAN (*boldly*). No, you're not! But even if you were, there's combustible material close by.

JULIE. Meaning you?

JEAN. Yes! Not because it's me, but because I'm young——

JULIE. And handsome—what incredible conceit! A Don Juan perhaps! Or a Joseph![7] Yes, that's it, I do believe you're a Joseph!

JEAN. Do you?

JULIE. I'm almost afraid so. (*Jean boldly tries to put his arm around her waist and kiss her. She slaps his face.*) How dare you?

JEAN. Are you serious or joking?

JULIE. Serious.

JEAN. Then so was what just happened. You play games too seriously, and that's dangerous. Well, I'm tired of games. You'll excuse me if I get back to work. I haven't done the Count's boots yet and it's long past midnight.

JULIE. Put the boots down!

JEAN. No! It's the work I have to do. I never agreed to be your playmate, and never will. It's beneath me.

JULIE. You're proud.

JEAN. In certain ways, but not in others.

JULIE. Have you ever been in love?

JEAN. We don't use that word, but I've been fond of many girls, and once I was sick because I couldn't have the one I wanted. That's right, sick, like those princes in the Arabian Nights—who couldn't eat or drink because of love.

JULIE. Who was she? (*Jean is silent.*) Who was she?

JEAN. You can't force me to tell you that.

JULIE. But if I ask you as an equal, as a—friend! Who was she?

JEAN. You!

JULIE (*sits*). How amusing . . .

JEAN. Yes, if you like! It was ridiculous!——You see, that was the story I didn't want to tell you earlier. Maybe I will now. Do you know how the world looks from down below?——Of course you don't. Neither do hawks and falcons, whose backs we can't see because they're usually soaring up there above us. I grew up in a shack with seven brothers and sisters and a pig, in the middle of a wasteland, where there wasn't a single tree. But from our window I could see the tops of apple trees above the wall of your father's garden. That was the Garden of Eden, guarded by angry angels with flaming swords. All the same, the other boys and I managed to find our way to the Tree of Life.——Now you think I'm contemptible, I suppose.

JULIE. Oh, all boys steal apples.

JEAN. You say that, but you think I'm contemptible anyway. Oh well! One day I went into the Garden of Eden with my mother, to weed the onion beds. Near the vegetable garden was a small Turkish pavilion in the shadow of jasmine bushes and overgrown with honeysuckle. I had no idea what it was used for, but I'd never seen such a beautiful building. People went in and came out again, and one day the door was left open. I sneaked close and saw walls covered with pictures of kings and emperors, and red curtains with fringes at the windows—now you know the place I mean. I——(*Breaks off a sprig of lilac and holds it in front of Miss Julie's nose.*)——I'd never been inside the manor house, never seen anything except the church—but this was more beautiful. From then on, no matter where my thoughts wandered, they returned—there. And gradually I got a longing to experience, just once, the full pleasure of—*enfin*,[8] I sneaked in, saw, and marveled! But then I heard someone coming! There was only one exit for ladies and gentlemen, but for me there was another, and I had no choice but to take it! (*Miss Julie, who has taken the lilac sprig, lets it fall on the table.*) Afterwards, I started running. I crashed through a raspberry bush, flew over a strawberry patch, and came up onto the rose terrace. There I caught sight of a pink dress and a pair of white stockings—it was you. I crawled under a pile of weeds, and I mean under—under thistles that pricked me and wet dirt that stank. And I looked at you as you walked among the roses, and I thought: If it's true that a thief can enter heaven and be with the angels, then why can't a farmhand's son here on God's earth enter the manor house garden and play with the Count's daughter?

[6]**Attention! . . . homme!** Watch out! I am only a man! [7]**Don Juan . . . Joseph:** Don Juan is a seducer of women; in the Hebrew Bible (Genesis 39.6–20) Joseph resists the advances of Potiphar's wife

[8]**enfin** finally

JULIE (*romantically*). Do you think all poor children would have thought the way you did?

JEAN (*at first hesitant, then with conviction*). If *all* poor—yes—of course. Of course!

JULIE. It must be terrible to be poor!

JEAN (*with exaggerated suffering*). Oh, Miss Julie!Oh!——A dog can lie on the Countess's sofa, a horse can have his nose patted by a young lady's hand, but a servant—— (*Changing his tone.*)——oh, I know—now and then you find one with enough stuff in him to get ahead in the world, but how often?—Anyhow, do you know what I did then?—I jumped in the millstream with my clothes on, was pulled out, and got a beating. But the following Sunday, when my father and all the others went to my grandmother's, I arranged to stay home. I scrubbed myself with soap and water, put on my best clothes, and went to church so that I could see you! I saw you and returned home, determined to die. But I wanted to die beautifully and pleasantly, without pain. And then I remembered that it was dangerous to sleep under an elder bush. We had a big one, and it was in full flower. I plundered its treasures and bedded down under them in the oat bin. Have you ever noticed how smooth oats are?—and soft to the touch, like human skin . . . ! Well, I shut the lid and closed my eyes. I fell asleep and woke up feeling very sick. But I didn't die, as you can see. What was I after?——I don't know. There was no hope of winning you, of course.——You were a symbol of the hopelessness of ever rising out of the class in which I was born.

JULIE. You're a charming storyteller. Did you ever go to school?

JEAN. A bit, but I've read lots of novels and been to the theater often. And then I've listened to people like you talk—that's where I learned most.

JULIE. Do you listen to what we say?

JEAN. Naturally! And I've heard plenty, too, driving the carriage or rowing the boat. Once I heard you and a friend . . .

JULIE. Oh?——What did you hear?

JEAN. I'd better not say. But I was surprised a little. I couldn't imagine where you learned such words. Maybe at bottom there isn't such a great difference between people as we think.

JULIE. Shame on you! We don't act like you when we're engaged.

JEAN (*staring at her*). Is that true?——You don't have to play innocent with me, Miss . . .

JULIE. The man I gave my love to was a swine.

JEAN. That's what you all say—afterwards.

JULIE. All?

JEAN. I think so. I know I've heard that phrase before, on similar occasions.

JULIE. What occasions?

JEAN. Like the one I'm talking about. The last time . . .

JULIE (*rising*). Quiet! I don't want to hear any more!

JEAN. That's interesting—that's what *she* said, too.

Well, if you'll excuse me, I'm going to bed.

JULIE (*gently*). To bed? On midsummer eve?

JEAN. Yes! Dancing with the rabble out there doesn't amuse me much.

JULIE. Get the key to the boat and row me out on the lake. I want to see the sun come up.

JEAN. Is that wise?

JULIE. Are you worried about your reputation?

JEAN. Why not? Why should I risk looking ridiculous and getting fired without a reference, just when I'm trying to establish myself. Besides, I think I owe something to Kristine.

JULIE. So, now it's Kristine . . .

JEAN. Yes, but you, too.——Take my advice, go up and go to bed!

JULIE. Am I to obey you?

JEAN. Just this once—for your own good! Please! It's very late. Drowsiness makes people giddy and liable to lose their heads! Go to bed! Besides—unless I'm mistaken—I hear the others coming to look for me. And if they find us together, you'll be lost!

(*The Chorus approaches, singing.*)

> The swineherd found his true love
> a pretty girl so fair,
> The swineherd found his true love
> but let the girl beware.
>
> For then he saw the princess
> the princess on the golden hill,
> but then saw the princess,
> so much fairer still.
>
> So the swineherd and the princess
> they danced the whole night through,
> and he forgot his first love,
> to her he was untrue.
>
> And when the long night ended,
> and in the light of day, of day,
> the dancing too was ended,
> and the princess could not stay.
>
> Then the swineherd lost his true love,
> and the princess grieves him still,
> and never more she'll wander
> from atop the golden hill.

JULIE. I know all these people and I love them, just as they love me. Let them come in and you'll see.

JULIE (*listening*).What are they singing?

JEAN. It's a dirty song! About you and me!

JULIE. Disgusting! Oh! How deceitful!——

JEAN. The rabble is always cowardly! And in a battle like this, you don't fight; you can only run away!

JULIE. Run away? But where? We can't go out—or into Kristine's room.

JEAN. True. But there's my room. Necessity knows no rules. Besides, you can trust me. I'm your friend and I respect you.

JULIE. But suppose—suppose they look for you in there?

JEAN. I'll bolt the door, and if anyone tries to break in, I'll shoot!——Come! (*On his knees.*) Come!

JULIE (*urgently*). Promise me . . . ?

JEAN. I swear! (*Miss Julie runs off right. Jean hastens after her.*)

BALLET

(*Led by a fiddler, the servants and farm people enter, dressed festively, with flowers in their hats. On the table they place a small barrel of beer and a keg of schnapps, both garlanded. Glasses are brought out, and the drinking starts. A dance circle is formed and "The Swineherd and the Princess" is sung. When the dance is finished, everyone leaves, singing.*)

(*Miss Julie enters alone. She notices the mess in the kitchen, wrings her hands, then takes out her powder puff and powders her nose.*)

JEAN (*enters, agitated*). There, you see? And you heard them. We can't possibly stay here now, you know that.

JULIE. Yes, I know. But what can we do?

JEAN. Leave, travel, far away from here.

JULIE. Travel? Yes, but where?

JEAN. To Switzerland, to the Italian lakes. Have you ever been there?

JULIE. No. Is it beautiful?

JEAN. Oh, an eternal summer—oranges growing everywhere, laurel trees, always green . . .

JULIE. But what'll we do there?

JEAN. I'll open a hotel—with first-class service for first-class people.

JULIE. Hotel?

JEAN. That's the life, you know. Always new faces, new languages. No time to worry or be nervous. No hunting for something to do—there's always work to be done: bells ringing night and day, train whistles blowing, carriages coming and going, and all the while gold rolling into the till! That's the life!

JULIE. Yes, it sounds wonderful. But what'll I do?

JEAN. You'll be mistress of the house: the jewel in our crown! With your looks . . . and your manner—oh—success is guaranteed! It'll be wonderful! You'll sit in your office like a queen and push an electric button to set your slaves in motion. The guests will file past your throne and timidly lay their treasures before you.——You have no idea how people tremble when they get their bill.——I'll salt the bills and you'll sweeten them with your prettiest smile.——Let's get away from here——(*Takes a timetable out of his pocket.*)——Right away, on the next train!—— We'll be in Malmö six-thirty tomorrow morning, Hamburg at eight-forty; from Frankfort to Basel will take a day, then on to Como by way of the St. Gotthard Tunnel, in, let's see, three days. Three days!

JULIE. That's all very well! But Jean—you must give me courage!——Tell me you love me! Put your arms around me!

JEAN (*hesitating*). I want to—but I don't dare. Not in this house, not again. I love you—never doubt that—you don't doubt it, do you, Miss Julie?

JULIE (*shy; very feminine*). "Miss!"——Call me Julie! There are no barriers between us anymore. Call me Julie!

JEAN (*tormented*). I can't! There'll always be barriers between us as long as we stay in this house.——There's the past and there's the Count. I've never met anyone I had such respect for.——When I see his gloves lying on a chair, I feel small.——When I hear that bell up there ring, I jump like a skittish horse.——And when I look at his boots standing there so stiff and proud, I feel like bowing! (*Kicking the boots.*) Superstitions and prejudices we learned as children—but they can easily be forgotten. If I can just get to another country, a republic, people will bow and scrape when they see my livery—*they'll* bow and scrape, you hear, not me! I wasn't born to cringe. I've got stuff in me, I've got character, and if I can only grab onto that first branch, you watch me climb! I'm a servant today, but next year I'll own my own hotel. In ten years I'll have enough to retire. Then I'll go to Rumania and be decorated. I could—mind you I said *could*—end up a count!

JULIE. Wonderful, wonderful!

JEAN. Ah, in Rumania you just buy your title, and so you'll be a countess after all. My countess!

JULIE. But I don't care about that—that's what I'm putting behind me! Show me you love me, otherwise—otherwise, what am I?

JEAN. I'll show you a thousand times—afterwards! Not here! And whatever you do, no emotional outbursts, or we'll both be lost! We must think this through coolly, like sensible people. (*He takes out a cigar, snips the end, and lights it.*) You sit there, and I'll sit here. We'll talk as if nothing happened.

JULIE (*desperately*). Oh, my God! Have you no feelings?

JEAN. Me? No one has more feelings than I do, but I know how to control them.

JULIE. A little while ago you could kiss my shoe—and now!

JEAN (*harshly*). Yes, but that was before. Now we have other things to think about.

JULIE. Don't speak harshly to me!

JEAN. I'm not—just sensibly! We've already done one foolish thing, let's not have any more. The Count could return any minute, and by then we've got to decide what to do with our lives. What do you think of my plans for the future? Do you approve?

JULIE. They sound reasonable enough. I have only one question: For such a big undertaking you need capital—do you have it?

JEAN (*chewing on the cigar*). Me? Certainly! I have my professional expertise, my wide experience, and my knowledge of languages. That's capital enough, I should think!

JULIE. But all that won't even buy a train ticket.

JEAN. That's true. That's why I'm looking for a partner to advance me the money.

JULIE. Where will you find one quickly enough?

JEAN. That's up to you, if you want to come with me.

JULIE. But I can't; I have no money of my own. (*Pause.*)

JEAN. Then it's all off . . .

JULIE. And . . .

JEAN. Things stay as they are.

JULIE. Do you think I'm going to stay in this house as your lover? With all the servants pointing their fingers at me? Do you imagine I can face my father after this? No! Take me away from here, away from shame and dishonor——Oh, what have I done! My God, my God! (*She cries.*)

JEAN. Now, don't start that old song!——What have you done? The same as many others before you.

JULIE (*screaming convulsively*). And now you think I'm contemptible!——I'm falling, I'm falling!

JEAN. Fall down to my level and I'll lift you up again.

JULIE. What terrible power drew me to you? The attraction of the weak to the strong? The falling to the rising? Or was it love? Was this love? Do you know what love is?

JEAN. Me? What do you take me for? You don't think this was my first time, do you?

JULIE. The things you say, the thoughts you think!

JEAN. That's the way I was taught, and that's the way I am! Now don't get excited and don't play the grand lady, because we're in the same boat now!——Come on, Julie, I'll pour you a glass of something special! (*He opens a drawer in the table, takes out a wine bottle, and fills two glasses already used.*)

JULIE. Where did you get that wine?

JEAN. From the cellar.

JULIE. My father's burgundy!

JEAN. That'll do for his son-in-law, won't it?

JULIE. And I drink beer! Beer!

JEAN. That only shows I have better taste.

JULIE. Thief!

JEAN. Planning to tell?

JULIE. Oh, oh! Accomplice of a common thief! Was I drunk? Have I been walking in a dream the whole evening? Midsummer eve! A time of innocent fun!

JEAN. Innocent, eh?

JULIE (*pacing back and forth*). Is there anyone on earth more miserable than I am at this moment?

JEAN. Why should you be? After such a conquest? Think of Kristine in there. Don't you think she has feelings, too?

JULIE. I thought so awhile ago, but not any more. No, a servant is a servant . . .

JEAN. And a whore is a whore!

JULIE (*on her knees, her hands clasped*). Oh, God in heaven, end my wretched life! Take me away from the filth I'm sinking into! Save me! Save me!

JEAN. I can't deny I feel sorry for you. When I lay in that onion bed and saw you in the rose garden, well . . . I'll be frank . . . I had the same dirty thoughts all boys have.

JULIE. And you wanted to die for me!

JEAN. In the oat bin? That was just talk.

JULIE. A lie, in other words!

JEAN (*beginning to feel sleepy*). More or less! I got the idea from a newspaper story about a chimney sweep who curled up in a firewood bin full of lilacs because he got a summons for not supporting his illegitimate child . . .

JULIE. So, that's what you're like . . .

JEAN. I had to think of something. And that's the kind of story women always go for.

JULIE. Swine!

JEAN. *Merde!*

JULIE. And now you've seen the hawk's back . . .

JEAN. Not exactly its *back* . . .

JULIE. And I was to be the first branch . . .

JEAN. But the branch was rotten . . .

JULIE. I was to be the sign on the hotel . . .

JEAN. And I the hotel . . .

JULIE. Sit at your desk, entice your customers, pad their bills . . .

JEAN. That I'd do myself . . .

JULIE. How can anyone be so thoroughly filthy?

JEAN. Better clean up then!

JULIE. You lackey, you menial, stand up, when I speak to you!

JEAN. Menial's strumpet, lackey's whore, shut up and get out of here! Who are you to lecture me on coarseness? None of my kind is ever as coarse as you were tonight. Do you think one of your maids would throw herself at a man the way you did? Have you ever seen any girl of my class offer herself like that? I've only seen it among animals and streetwalkers.

JULIE (*crushed*). You're right. Hit me, trample on me. I don't deserve any better. I'm worthless. But help me! If you see any way out of this, help me, Jean, please!

JEAN (*more gently*). I'd be lying if I didn't admit to a sense of triumph in all this, but do you think that a person like me would have dared even to look at someone like you if you hadn't invited it? I'm still amazed . . .

JULIE. And proud . . .

JEAN. Why not? Though I must say it was too easy to be really exciting.

JULIE. Go on, hit me, hit me harder!

JEAN (*rising*). No! Forgive me for what I've said! I don't hit a man when he's down, let alone a woman. I can't deny though, that I'm pleased to find out that what looked so dazzling to us from below was only tinsel, that the hawk's back was only gray, after all, that the lovely complexion was only powder, that those polished fingernails had black edges, and that a dirty handkerchief is still dirty, even if it smells of perfume . . . ! On the other hand, it hurts me to find out that what I was striving for wasn't finer, more substantial. It hurts me to see you sunk so low that you're inferior to your own cook. It hurts like watching flowers beaten down by autumn rains and turned into mud.

JULIE. You talk as if you were already above me.

JEAN. I am. You see, I could make you a countess, but you could never make me a count.

JULIE. But I'm the child of a count—something you could never be!

JEAN. That's true. But I could be the father of counts—if . . .

JULIE. But you're a thief. I'm not.

JEAN. There are worse things than being a thief! Besides, when I'm working in a house, I consider myself sort of a member of the family, like one of the children. And you don't call it stealing when a child snatches a berry off a full bush. (*His passion is aroused again.*) Miss Julie, you're a glorious woman, much too good for someone like me! You were drinking and you lost your head. Now you want to cover up your mistake by telling yourself that you love me! You don't. Maybe there was a physical attraction—but then your love is no better than mine.——I could never be satisfied to be no more than an animal to you, and I could never arouse real love in you.

JULIE. Are you sure of that?

JEAN. You're suggesting it's possible——Oh, I could fall in love with you, no doubt about it. You're beautiful, you're refined——(*approaching and taking her hand*)——cultured, lovable when you want to be, and once you start a fire in a man, it never goes out. (*Putting his arm around her waist.*) You're like hot, spicy wine, and one kiss from you . . . (*He tries to lead her out, but she slowly frees herself.*)

JULIE. Let me go!?——You'll never win me like that.

JEAN. *How* then?——Not like that? Not with caresses and pretty speeches. Not with plans about the future or rescue from disgrace! *How* then?

JULIE. How? How? I don't know!——I have no idea!——I detest you as I detest rats, but I can't escape from you.

JEAN. Escape with me!

JULIE (*pulling herself together*). Escape? Yes, we must escape!——But I'm so tired. Give me a glass of wine? (*Jean pours the wine. She looks at her watch.*) But we must talk first. We still have a little time. (*She drains the glass, then holds it out for more.*)

JEAN. Don't drink so fast. It'll go to your head.

JULIE. What does it matter?

JEAN. What does it matter? It's vulgar to get drunk! What did you want to tell me?

JULIE. We must escape! But first we must talk, I mean I must talk. You've done all the talking up to now. You told

about your life, now I want to tell about mine, so we'll know all about each other before we go off together.

JEAN. Just a minute! Forgive me! If you don't want to regret it afterwards, you'd better think twice before revealing any secrets about yourself.

JULIE. Aren't you my friend?

JEAN. Yes, sometimes! But don't rely on me.

JULIE. You're only saying that.——Besides, everyone already knows my secrets.——You see, my mother was a commoner—very humble background. She was brought up believing in social equality, women's rights, and all that. The idea of marriage repelled her. So, when my father proposed, she replied that she would never become his wife, but he could be her lover. He insisted that he didn't want the woman he loved to be less respected than he. But his passion ruled him, and when she explained that the world's respect meant nothing to her, he accepted her conditions. But now his friends avoided him and his life was restricted to taking care of the estate, which couldn't satisfy him. I came into the world—against my mother's wishes, as far as I can understand. She wanted to bring me up as a child of nature, and, what's more, to learn everything a boy had to learn, so that I might be an example of how a woman can be as good as a man. I had to wear boy's clothes and learn to take care of horses, but I was never allowed in the cowshed. I had to groom and harness the horses and go hunting—and even had to watch them slaughter animals—that was disgusting! On the estate men were put on women's jobs and women on men's jobs—with the result that the property became run down and we became the laughingstock of the district. Finally, my father must have awakened from his trance because he rebelled and changed everything his way. My parents were then married quietly. Mother became ill—I don't know what illness it was—but she often had convulsions, hid in the attic and in the garden, and sometimes stayed out all night. Then came the great fire, which you've heard about. The house, the stables, and the cowshed all burned down, under very curious circumstances, suggesting arson, because the accident happened the day after the insurance had expired. The quarterly premium my father sent in was delayed because of a messenger's carelessness and didn't arrive in time. (*She fills her glass and drinks.*)

JEAN. Don't drink any more!

JULIE. Oh, what does it matter.——We were left penniless and had to sleep in the carriages. My father had no idea where to find money to rebuild the house because he had so slighted his old friends that they had forgotten him. Then my mother suggested that he borrow from a childhood friend of hers, a brick manufacturer who lived nearby. Father got the loan without having to pay interest, which surprised him. And that's how the estate was rebuilt.——(*Drinks again.*) Do you know who started the fire?

JEAN. The Countess, your mother.

JULIE. Do you know who the brick manufacturer was?

JEAN. Your mother's lover?

JULIE. Do you know whose money it was?

JEAN. Wait a moment—no, I don't.

JULIE. It was my mother's.

JEAN. You mean the Count's, unless they didn't sign an agreement when they were married.

JULIE. They didn't.——My mother had a small inheritance which she didn't want under my father's control, so she entrusted it to her—friend.

JEAN. Who stole it!

JULIE. Exactly! He kept it.——All this my father found out, but he couldn't bring it to court, couldn't repay his wife's lover, couldn't prove it was his wife's money! It was my mother's revenge for being forced into marriage against her will. It nearly drove him to suicide—there was a rumor that he tried with a pistol, but failed. So, he managed to live through it and my mother had to suffer for what she'd done. You can imagine that those were a terrible five years for me. I loved my father, but I sided with my mother because I didn't know the circumstances. I learned from her to hate men—you've heard how she hated the whole male sex—and I swore to her I'd never be a slave to any man.

JEAN. But you got engaged to that lawyer.

JULIE. In order to make him my slave.

JEAN. And he wasn't willing?

JULIE. He was willing, all right, but I wouldn't let him. I got tired of him.

JEAN. I saw it—out near the stable.

JULIE. What did you see?

JEAN. I saw—how he broke off the engagement.

JULIE. That's a lie! I was the one who broke it off. Has he said that he did? That swine . . .

JEAN. He was no swine, I'm sure. So, you hate men, Miss Julie?

JULIE. Yes!——Most of the time! But sometimes—when the weakness comes, when passion burns! Oh, God, will the fire never die out?

JEAN. Do you hate me, too?

JULIE. Immeasurably! I'd like to have you put to death, like an animal . . .

JEAN. I see—the penalty for bestiality—the woman gets two years at hard labor and the animal is put to death. Right?

JULIE. Exactly!

JEAN. But there's no prosecutor here—and no animal. So, what'll we do?

JULIE. Go away!

JEAN. To torment each other to death?

JULIE. No! To be happy for—two days, a week, as long as we can be happy, and then—die . . .

JEAN. Die? That's stupid! It's better to open a hotel!

JULIE (without listening). ——on the shore of Lake Como, where the sun always shines, where the laurels are green at Christmas and the oranges glow.

JEAN. Lake Como is a rainy hole, and I never saw any oranges outside the stores. But tourists are attracted there because there are plenty of villas to be rented out to lovers, and that's a profitable business.——Do you know why? Because they sign a lease for six months—and then leave after three weeks!

JULIE (naively). Why after three weeks?

JEAN. They quarrel, of course! But they still have to pay the rent in full! And so you rent the villas out again. And that's the way it goes, time after time. There's never a shortage of love—even if it doesn't last long!

JULIE. You don't want to die with me?

JEAN. I don't want to die at all! For one thing, I like living, and for another, I think suicide is a crime against the Providence which gave us life.

JULIE. You believe in God? You?

JEAN. Of course I do. And I go to church every other Sunday.——To be honest, I'm tired of all this, and I'm going to bed.

JULIE. Are you? And do you think I can let it go at that? A man owes something to the woman he's shamed.

JEAN (taking out his purse and throwing a silver coin on the table). Here! I don't like owing anything to anybody.

JULIE (pretending not to notice the insult). Do you know what the law states . . .

JEAN. Unfortunately the law doesn't state any punishment for the woman who seduces a man!

JULIE (as before). Do you see any way out but to leave, get married, and then separate?

JEAN. Suppose I refuse such a mésalliance?[9]

JULIE. Mésalliance . . .

JEAN. Yes, for me! You see, I come from better stock than you. There's no arsonist in my family.

JULIE. How do you know?

JEAN. You can't prove otherwise. We don't keep charts on our ancestors—there's just the police records! But I've read about your family. Do you know who the founder was? He was a miller who let the king sleep with his wife one night during the Danish War. I don't have any noble ancestors like that. I don't have any noble ancestors at all, but I could become one myself.

JULIE. This is what I get for opening my heart to someone unworthy, for giving my family's honor . . .

JEAN. Dishonor!——Well, I told you so: When people drink, they talk, and talk is dangerous!

JULIE. Oh, how I regret it!——How I regret it!——If you at least loved me.

JEAN. For the last time—what do you want? Shall I cry; shall I jump over your riding crop? Shall I kiss you and lure you off to Lake Como for three weeks, and then God knows what . . . ? What shall I do? What do you want? This is getting painfully embarrassing! But that's what happens

---

[9]**mésalliance** mismatch

when you stick your nose in women's business. Miss Julie! I see that you're unhappy. I know you're suffering, but I can't understand you. We don't have such romantic ideas; there's not this kind of hate between us. Love is a game we play when we get time off from work, but we don't have all day and night, like you. I think you're sick, really sick. Your mother was crazy, and her ideas have poisoned your life.

JULIE. Be kind to me. At least now you're talking like a human being.

JEAN. Be human yourself, then. You spit on me, and you won't let me wipe myself off——

JULIE. Help me! Help me! Just tell me what to do, where to go!

JEAN. In God's name, if I only knew myself!

JULIE. I've been crazy, out of my mind, but isn't there any way out?

JEAN. Stay here and keep calm! No one knows anything!

JULIE. Impossible! The others know and Kristine knows.

JEAN. No they don't, and they'd never believe a thing like that!

JULIE (*hesitantly*). But—it could happen again!

JEAN. That's true!

JULIE. And then?

JEAN (*frightened*). Then?——Why didn't I think about that? Yes, there is only one thing to do—get away from here! Right away! I can't come with you, then we'd be finished, so you'll have to go alone—away—anywhere!

JULIE. Alone?——Where?——I can't do that!

JEAN. You must! And before the Count gets back! If you stay, you know what'll happen. Once you make a mistake like this, you want to continue because the damage has already been done. . . . Then you get bolder and bolder—until finally you're caught! So leave! Later you can write to the Count and confess everything—except that it was me! He'll never guess who it was, and he's not going to be eager to find out, anyway.

JULIE. I'll go if you come with me.

JEAN. Are you out of your head? Miss Julie runs away with her servant! In two days it would be in the newspapers, and that's something your father would never live through.

JULIE. I can't go and I can't stay! Help me! I'm so tired, so terribly tired.——Order me! Set me in motion—I can't think or act on my own . . .

JEAN. What miserable creatures you people are! You strut around with your noses in the air as if you were the lords of creation! All right, I'll order you. Go upstairs and get dressed! Get some money for the trip, and then come back down!

JULIE (*in a half-whisper*). Come up with me!

JEAN. To your room?——Now you're crazy again! (*Hesitates for a moment.*) No! Go, at once! (*Takes her hand to lead her out.*)

JULIE (*as she leaves*). Speak kindly to me, Jean!

JEAN. An order always sounds unkind—now you know how it feels. (*Jean, alone, sighs with relief. He sits at the table, takes out a notebook and pencil, and begins adding up figures, counting aloud as he works. He continues in dumb show until Kristine enters, dressed for church. She is carrying a white tie and shirt front.*)

KRISTINE. Lord Jesus, what a mess! What have you been up to?

JEAN. Oh, Miss Julie dragged everybody in here. You mean you didn't hear anything? You must have been sleeping soundly.

KRISTINE. Like a log.

JEAN. And dressed for church already?

KRISTINE. Of course! You remember you promised to come with me to communion today!

JEAN. Oh, yes, that's right.——And you brought my things. Come on, then! (*He sits down. Kristine starts to put on his shirt front and tie. Pause. Jean begins sleepily.*) What's the gospel text for today?

KRISTINE. On St. John's Day?—the beheading of John the Baptist, I should think!

JEAN. Ah, that'll be a long one, for sure.——Hey, you're choking me!——Oh, I'm sleepy, so sleepy!

KRISTINE. Yes, what have you been doing, up all night? Your face is absolutely green.

JEAN. I've been sitting here gabbing with Miss Julie.

KRISTINE. She has no idea what's proper, that one! (*Pause.*)

JEAN. You know, Kristine . . .

KRISTINE. What?

JEAN. It's really strange when you think about it.——Her!

KRISTINE. What's so strange?

JEAN. Everything! (*Pause.*)

KRISTINE (*looking at the half-empty glasses standing on the table*). Have you been drinking together, too?

JEAN. Yes.

KRISTINE. Shame on you!——Look me in the eye!

JEAN. Well?

KRISTINE. Is it possible? Is it possible?

JEAN (*thinking it over for a moment*). Yes, it is.

KRISTINE. Ugh! I never would have believed it! No, shame on you, shame!

JEAN. You're not jealous of her, are you?

KRISTINE. No, not of her! If it had been Clara or Sofie I'd have scratched your eyes out!——I don't know why, but that's the way I feel.——Oh, it's disgusting!

JEAN. Are you angry at her, then?

KRISTINE. No, at you! That was an awful thing to do, awful! Poor girl!——No, I don't care who knows it—I won't stay in a house where we can't respect the people we work for.

JEAN. Why should we respect them?

KRISTINE. You're so clever, you tell me! Do you want to wait on people who can't behave decently? Do you? You disgrace yourself that way, if you ask me.

JEAN. But it's a comfort to know they aren't any better than us.

KRISTINE. Not for me. If they're no better, what do we have to strive for to better ourselves.——And think of the Count! Think of him! As if he hasn't had enough misery in his life! Lord Jesus! No, I won't stay in this house any longer!——And it had to be with someone like you! If it had been that lawyer, if it had been a real gentleman . . .

JEAN. What do you mean?

KRISTINE. Oh, you're all right for what you are, but there are men and gentlemen, after all!——No, this business with Miss Julie I can never forget. She was so proud, so arrogant with men, you wouldn't have believed she could just go and give herself—and to someone like you! And she was going to have poor Diana shot for running after the gatekeepers' mutt!——Yes, I'm giving my notice, I mean it—I won't stay here any longer. On the twenty-fourth of October, I leave!

JEAN. And then?

KRISTINE. Well, since the subject has come up, it's about time you looked around for something since we're going to get married, in any case.

JEAN. Where am I going to look? I couldn't find a job like this if I was married.

KRISTINE. No, that's true. But you can find work as a porter or as a caretaker in some government office. The state doesn't pay much, I know, but it's secure, and there's a pension for the wife and children . . .

JEAN (grimacing). That's all very well, but it's a bit early for me to think about dying for a wife and children. My ambitions are a little higher than that.

KRISTINE. Your ambitions, yes! Well, you have obligations, too! Think about them!

JEAN. Don't start nagging me about obligations. I know what I have to do! (Listening for something outside.) Besides, this is something we have plenty of time to think over. Go and get ready for church.

KRISTINE. Who's that walking around up there?

JEAN. I don't know, unless it's Clara.

KRISTINE (going). You don't suppose it's the Count, who came home without us hearing him?

JEAN (frightened). The Count? No, I don't think so. He'd have rung.

KRISTINE (going). Well, God help us! I've never seen anything like this before. (The sun has risen and shines through the treetops in the park. The light shifts gradually until it slants in through the windows. Jean goes to the door and signals. Miss Julie enters, dressed in travel clothes and carrying a small bird cage, covered with a cloth, which she places on a chair.)

JULIE. I'm ready now.

JEAN. Shh! Kristine is awake.

JULIE (very nervous during the following). Does she suspect something?

JEAN. She doesn't know anything. But my God, you look awful!

JULIE. Why? How do I look?

JEAN. You're pale as a ghost and—excuse me, but your face is dirty.

JULIE. Let me wash up then.——(She goes to the basin and washes her hands and face.) Give me a towel!——Oh—the sun's coming up.

JEAN. Then the goblins will disappear.

JULIE. Yes, there must have been goblins out last night!——Jean, listen, come with me! I have some money now.

JEAN (hesitantly). Enough?

JULIE. Enough to start with. Come with me! I just can't travel alone on a day like this—midsummer day on a stuffy train—jammed in among crowds of people staring at me. Eternal delays at every station, while I'd wish I had wings. No, I can't, I can't! And then there'll be memories, memories of midsummer days when I was little. The church—decorated with birch leaves and lilacs; dinner at the big table with relatives and friends; the afternoons in the park, dancing, music, flowers, and games. Oh, no matter how far we travel, the memories will follow in the baggage car, with remorse and guilt!

JEAN. I'll go with you—but right away, before it's too late. Right this minute!

JULIE. Get dressed, then! (Picking up the bird cage.)

JEAN. But no baggage! It would give us away!

JULIE. No, nothing! Only what we can have in the compartment with us.

JEAN (has taken his hat). What've you got there? What is it?

JULIE. It's only my greenfinch. I couldn't leave her behind.

JEAN. What? Bring a bird cage with us? You're out of your head! Put it down!

JULIE. It's the only thing I'm taking from my home—the only living being that loves me, since Diana was unfaithful. Don't be cruel! Let me take her!

JEAN. Put the cage down, I said!——And don't talk so loudly—Kristine will hear us!

JULIE. No, I won't leave her in the hands of strangers! I'd rather you killed her.

JEAN. Bring the thing here, then, I'll cut its head off!

JULIE. Oh! But don't hurt her! Don't . . . no, I can't.

JEAN. Bring it here! I can!

JULIE (taking the bird out of the cage and kissing it). Oh, my little Serena, must you die and leave your mistress?

JEAN. Please don't make a scene! Your whole future is at stake! Hurry up! (He snatches the bird from her, carries it over to the chopping block, and picks up a meat cleaver. Miss Julie turns away.) You should have learned how to slaughter chickens instead of how to fire pistols. (He chops off the bird's head.) Then you wouldn't feel faint at the sight of blood.

JULIE (screaming). Kill me, too! Kill me! You, who can slaughter an innocent animal without blinking an eye! Oh, how I hate, how I detest you! There's blood between us now! I curse the moment I set eyes on you! I curse the moment I was conceived in my mother's womb!

JEAN. What good does cursing do? Let's go!

JULIE (*approaching the chopping block, as if drawn against her will*). No, I don't want to go yet. I can't . . . until I see . . . Shh! I hear a carriage——(*She listens, but her eyes never leave the cleaver and the chopping block.*) Do you think I can't stand the sight of blood? You think I'm so weak . . . Oh—I'd like to see your blood and your brains on a chopping block!——I'd like to see your whole sex swimming in a sea of blood, like my little bird . . . I think I could drink from your skull! I'd like to bathe my feet in your open chest and eat your heart roasted whole!——You think I'm weak. You think I love you because my womb craved your seed. You think I want to carry your spawn under my heart and nourish it with my blood—bear your child and take your name! By the way, what is your family name? I've never heard it.——Do you have one? I was to be Mrs. Bootblack—or Madame Pigsty.——You dog, who wears my collar, you lackey, who bears my coat of arms on your buttons—do I have to share you with my cook, compete with my own servant? Oh! Oh! Oh!——You think I'm a coward who wants to run away! No, now I'm staying—and let the storm break! My father will come home . . . to find his desk broken open . . . and his money gone! Then he'll ring—that bell . . . twice for his valet—and then he'll send for the police . . . and then I'll tell everything! Everything! Oh, what a relief it'll be to have it all end—if only it will end!——And then he'll have a stroke and die . . . That'll be the end of all of us—and there'll be peace . . . quiet . . . eternal rest!—And then our coat of arms will be broken against his coffin—the family title extinct—but the valet's line will go on in an orphanage . . . win laurels in the gutter, and end in jail!

JEAN. There's the blue blood talking! Very good, Miss Julie! Just don't let that miller out of the closet! (*Kristine enters, dressed for church, with a psalmbook in her hand.*)

JULIE (*rushing to Kristine and falling into her arms, as if seeking protection*). Help me, Kristine! Help me against this man!

KRISTINE (*unmoved and cold*). What a fine way to behave on a Sunday morning! (*Sees the chopping block.*) And look at this mess!——What does all this mean? Why all this screaming and carrying on?

JULIE. Kristine! You're a woman and my friend! Beware of this swine!

JEAN (*uncomfortable*). While you ladies discuss this, I'll go in and shave. (*Slips off right.*)

JULIE. You must listen to me so you'll understand!

KRISTINE. No, I could never understand such disgusting behavior! Where are you off to in your traveling clothes?——And he had his hat on.——Well?——Well?——

JULIE. Listen to me, Kristine! Listen, and I'll tell you everything——

KRISTINE. I don't want to hear it . . .

JULIE. But you must listen to me . . .

KRISTINE. What about? If it's about this silliness with Jean, I'm not interested, because it's none of my business. But if you're thinking of tricking him into running out, we'll soon put a stop to that!

JULIE (*extremely nervous*). Try to be calm now, Kristine, and listen to me! I can't stay here, and neither can Jean—so we must go away . . .

KRISTINE. Hm, hm!

JULIE (*brightening*). You see, I just had an idea——What if all three of us go—abroad—to Switzerland and start a hotel together?——I have money, you see–and Jean and I could run it—and I thought you, you could take care of the kitchen . . . Wouldn't that be wonderful?——Say yes! And come with us, and then everything will be settled!——Oh, do say yes! (*Embracing Kristine and patting her warmly.*)

KRISTINE (*coolly, thoughtfully*). Hm, hm!

JULIE (*presto tempo*)[10]. You've never traveled, Kristine.——You must get out and see the world. You can't imagine how much fun it is to travel by train—always new faces—new countries.——And when we get to Hamburg, we'll stop off at the zoo—you'll like that.——and then we'll go to the theater and the opera–and when we get to Munich, dear, there we have museums, with Rubens and Raphael, the great painters, as you know.——You've heard of Munich, where King Ludwig lived—the king who went mad.——And then we'll see his castles—they're still there and they're like castles in fairy tales.——And from there it isn't far to Switzerland—and the Alps.——Imagine—the Alps have snow on them even in the middle of summer!——And oranges grow there and laurel trees that are green all year round——(*Jean can be seen in the wings right, sharpening his razor on a strop which he holds with his teeth and his left hand. He listens to the conversation with satisfaction, nodding now and then in approval. Miss Julie continues tempo prestissimo.*)[11] And then we'll start a hotel—and I'll be at the desk, while Jean greets the guests . . . does the shopping . . . writes letters.——You have no idea what a life it'll be—the train whistles blowing and the carriages arriving and the bells ringing in the rooms and down in the restaurant.——And I'll make out the bills—and I know how to salt them! . . . You'll never believe how timid travelers are when they have to pay their bills!——And you—you'll be in charge of the kitchen.——Naturally, you won't have to stand over the stove yourself.——And since you're going to be seen by people, you'll have to wear beautiful clothes.——And you, with your looks—no, I'm not flattering you—one fine day you'll grab yourself a husband!——You'll see!——A rich Englishman—they're so easy to——(*Slowing down.*)——catch—and then we'll get rich—and build ourselves a villa on Lake

---

[10]**presto tempo** quickly   [11]**tempo prestissimo** very quickly

Como.——It's true it rains there a little now and then, but——(*Dully.*)——the sun has to shine sometimes—although it looks dark—and then . . . of course we could always come back home again——(*Pause.*)——here—or somewhere else——

KRISTINE. Listen, Miss Julie, do you believe all this?

JULIE (*crushed*). Do I believe it?

KRISTINE. Yes!

JULIE (*wearily*). I don't know. I don't believe in anything anymore. (*She sinks down on the bench and cradles her head in her arms on the table.*) Nothing! Nothing at all!

KRISTINE (*turning right to where Jean is standing*). So, you thought you'd run out!

JEAN (*embarrassed; puts the razor on the table*). Run out? That's no way to put it. You hear Miss Julie's plan, and even if she is tired after being up all night, it's still a practical plan.

KRISTINE. Now you listen to me! Did you think I'd work as a cook for that . . .

JEAN (*sharply*). You watch what you say in front of your mistress! Do you understand?

KRISTINE. Mistress!

JEAN. Yes!

KRISTINE. Listen to him! Listen to him!

JEAN. Yes, you listen! It'd do you good to listen more and talk less! Miss Julie is your mistress. If you despise her, you have to despise yourself for the same reason!

KRISTINE. I've always had enough self-respect——

JEAN. ——to be able to despise other people!

KRISTINE. ——to stop me from doing anything that's beneath me. You can't say that the Count's cook has been up to something with the groom or the swineherd! Can you?

JEAN. No, you were lucky enough to get hold of a gentleman!

KRISTINE. Yes, a gentleman who sells the Count's oats from the stable.

JEAN. You should talk—taking a commission from the grocer and bribes from the butcher.

KRISTINE. What?

JEAN. And you say you can't respect your employers any longer. You, you, you!

KRISTINE. Are you coming to church with me, now? You could use a good sermon after your fine deed!

JEAN. No, I'm not going to church today. You'll have to go alone and confess what you've been up to.

KRISTINE. Yes, I'll do that, and I'll bring back enough forgiveness for you, too. The Savior suffered and died on the Cross for all our sins, and if we go to Him with faith and a penitent heart, He takes all our sins on Himself.

JEAN. Even grocery sins?

JULIE. And do you believe that, Kristine?

KRISTINE. It's my living faith, as sure as I stand here. It's the faith I learned as a child, Miss Julie, and kept ever since. "Where sin abounded, grace did much more abound!"

JULIE. Oh, if I only had your faith. If only . . .

KRISTINE. Well, you see, we can't have it without God's special grace, and that isn't given to everyone——

JULIE. Who is it given to then?

KRISTINE. That's the great secret of the workings of grace, Miss Julie, and God is no respecter of persons, for the last shall be the first . . .

JULIE. Then He does respect the last.

KRISTINE (*continuing*). . . . and it is easier for a camel to go through the eye of a needle, than for a rich man to enter the Kingdom of God. That's how it is, Miss Julie! Anyhow, I'm going now—alone, and on the way I'm going to tell the groom not to let any horses out, in case anyone wants to leave before the Count gets back!——Goodbye! (*Leaves.*)

JEAN. What a witch!——And all this because of a greenfinch!——

JULIE (*dully*). Never mind the greenfinch!——Can you see any way out of this? Any end to it?

JEAN (*thinking*). No!

JULIE. What would you do in my place?

JEAN. In your place? Let's see—as a person of position, as a woman who had—fallen. I don't know—wait, now I know.

JULIE (*taking the razor and making a gesture*). You mean like this?

JEAN. Yes! But—understand—*I* wouldn't do it! That's the difference between us!

JULIE. Because you're a man and I'm a woman? What sort of difference is that?

JEAN. The usual difference—between a man and a woman.

JULIE (*with the razor in her hand*). I want to, but I can't!——My father couldn't either, the time he should have done it.

JEAN. No, he shouldn't have! He had to revenge himself first.

JULIE. And now my mother is revenged again, through me.

JEAN. Didn't you ever love your father, Miss Julie?

JULIE. Oh yes, deeply, but I've hated him, too. I must have done so without realizing it! It was he who brought me up to despise my own sex, making me half woman, half man. Whose fault is what's happened? My father's, my mother's, my own? My own? I don't have anything that's my own. I don't have a single thought that I didn't get from my father, not an emotion that I didn't get from my mother, and this last idea—that all people are equal—I got that from my fiancé.——That's why I called him a swine! How can it be my fault? Shall I let Jesus take on the blame, the way Kristine does?——No, I'm too proud to do that and too sensible—thanks to my father's teachings.——And as for someone rich not going to heaven, that's a lie. But Kristine won't get in—how will she explain the money she has in the savings bank? Whose fault is it?——What does it matter whose fault it is? I'm still the one who has to bear the blame, face the consequences . . .

JEAN. Yes, but . . . (*The bell rings sharply twice. Miss Julie jumps up. Jean changes his coat.*) The Count is back! Do you suppose Kristine— (*He goes to the speaking tube, taps the lid, and listens.*)

JULIE. He's been to his desk!

JEAN. It's Jean, sir! (*Listening, the audience cannot hear the Count's voice.*) Yes, sir! (*Listening.*) Yes, sir! Right away! (*Listening.*) At once, sir! (*Listening.*) I see, in half an hour!

JULIE (*desperately frightened*). What did he say? Dear Lord, what did he say?

JEAN. He wants his boots and his coffee in half an hour.

JULIE. So, in half an hour! Oh, I'm so tired. I'm not able to do anything. I can't repent, can't run away, can't stay, can't live—can't die! Help me now! Order me, and I'll obey like a dog! Do me this last service, save my honor, save his name! You know what I *should* do, but don't have the will to . . . You will it, you order me to do it!

JEAN. I don't know why——but now I can't either——I don't understand.——It's as if this coat made it impossible for me to order you to do anything.——And now, since the Count spoke to me—I—I can't really explain it—but—ah, it's the damn lackey in me!——I think if the Count came down here now—and ordered me to cut my throat, I'd do it on the spot.

JULIE. Then pretend you're he, and I'm you!——You gave such a good performance before when you knelt at my feet.——You were a real nobleman.——Or—have you ever seen a hypnotist in the theater? (*Jean nods.*) He says to his subject: "Take the broom," and he takes it. He says: "Sweep," and he sweeps——

JEAN. But the subject has to be asleep.

JULIE (*ecstatically*). I'm already asleep.——The whole room is like smoke around me . . . and you look like an iron stove . . . shaped like a man in black, with a tall hat—and your eyes glow like coals when the fire is dying—and your face is a white patch, like ashes——(*The sunlight has reached the floor and now shines on Jean.*)——it's so warm and good——(*She rubs her hands as if warming them before a fire.*)——and bright—and so peaceful!

JEAN (*taking the razor and putting it in her hand*). Here's the broom! Go now while it's bright—out to the barn—and . . . (*Whispers in her ear.*)

JULIE (*awake*). Thank you. I'm going now to rest! But just tell me—that those who are first can also receive the gift of grace. Say it, even if you don't believe it.

JEAN. The first? No, I can't——But wait—Miss Julie—now I know! You're no longer among the first—you're now among—the last!

JULIE. That's true.——I'm among the last. I'm the last one of all! Oh!——But now I can't go!——Tell me once more to go!

JEAN. No, now I can't either! I can't!

JULIE. And the first shall be the last!

JEAN. Don't think, don't think! You're taking all my strength from me, making me a coward.——What was that? I thought the bell moved!——No! Shall we stuff paper in it?——To be so afraid of a bell!——But it isn't just a bell.——There's someone behind it—a hand sets it in motion—and something else sets the hand in motion.——Maybe if you cover your ears—cover your ears! But then it rings even louder! rings until someone answers.——And then it's too late! And then the police come—and—then——(*The bell rings twice loudly. Jean flinches, then straightens up.*) It's horrible! But there's no other way!——Go! (*Miss Julie walks firmly out through the door.*)

TOPICS FOR CRITICAL THINKING AND WRITING

 ### The Play on the PAGE

1. In his preface, Strindberg emphasizes that the play is realistic, but many readers and viewers have found it highly symbolic. What symbolic elements, if any, do you find? Do you consider, for instance, the "statue of Cupid" (specified in the opening stage direction) to be symbolic?

2. Do you think the ending of *Miss Julie* is plausible? (Some contemporary critics found Julie's suicide improbable because she cannot know if she is pregnant. Strindberg argued that she would have killed herself because of her sense of honor.) Support your response with reasons.

3. Do you think the play is a tragedy? Explain.

The Play on the STAGE

4. Reread Strindberg's opening stage direction, and make a rough sketch of the set. Notice that "the rear wall runs diagonally from down left to up right." Usually the rear wall of a box set runs parallel to the rear wall of the theater. What effect do you think this diagonal has on the spectators?

5. Usually directors ignore Strindberg's wishes and place an intermission after the interlude of the dancing peasants. If you were staging the play would you include an intermission? Explain.

6. In a 1985 production in South Africa, Jean was played by a black, Julie by a white. What is your response to this decision? Explain.

A Context for *MISS JULIE*

Selections from Strindberg's Preface

In the following play, instead of trying to do anything new—which is impossible—I have simply modernized the form in accordance with demands I think contemporary audiences make upon this art. Toward this end, I have chosen, or let myself be moved by, a theme that can be said to lie outside partisan politics since the problem of social climbing or falling, of higher or lower, better or worse, man or woman, are, have been, and will be of lasting interest. When I took this theme from a true story I heard told some years ago, which made a strong impression on me, I found it appropriate for tragedy, for it still seems tragic to see someone favored by fortune go under, much more to see a family die out. Perhaps the time will come when we will be so advanced, so enlightened, that we can witness with indifference what now seem the coarse, cynical, heartless dramas life has to offer, when we have closed down those lower, unreliable mechanisms of thought called feelings, because better developed organs of judgment will have found them superfluous and harmful. The fact that the heroine arouses compassion is because we are too weak to resist the fear that the same fate could overtake us. A hypersensitive spectator may not be satisfied with compassion alone, while a man with faith in the future may demand some positive proposals to remedy the evil, in other words, a program of some kind. But for one thing there is no absolute evil. The fall of one family can mean a chance for another family to rise, and the alternation of rising and falling fortunes is one of life's greatest delights since happiness lies only in comparison. And to the man who wants a program to remedy the unpleasant fact that the bird of prey eats the dove and the louse eats the bird of prey I ask: why should it be remedied? Life is not so idiotically mathematical that only the great eat the small; it is just as common for a bee to kill a lion or at least drive it mad.

If my tragedy depresses many people, it is their own fault. When we become as strong as the first French revolutionaries, it will afford nothing but pleasure and relief to witness the thinning out in royal parks of overage, decaying trees that have long stood in the way of others equally entitled to their time in the sun, the kind of relief we feel when we see someone incurably ill die!

. . .

I have motivated Miss Julie's tragic fate by a great number of circumstances: her mother's primary instincts, her father raising her incorrectly, her own nature, and the influence of her fiancé on her weak and degenerate brain. Also, more particularly: the festive atmosphere of midsummer night, her father's absence, her monthly indisposition, her preoccupation with animals, the provocative effect of the dancing, the magical midsummer twilight, the powerfully aphrodisiac influence of flowers, and, finally, the chance that drives the couple together into a room alone—plus the boldness of the aroused man.

My treatment of the subject has thus been neither one-sidedly physiological nor exclusively psychological. I have not put the entire blame on what she inherited from her mother, nor on her monthly indisposition, nor on immorality. I have not even preached morality—this I left to the cook in the absence of a minister.

. . .

Miss Julie is a modern character. Not that the man-hating half-woman has not existed in all ages but because now that she has been discovered, she has come out in the open to make herself heard. The half-woman is a type who pushes her way ahead, selling herself nowadays for power, decorations, honors, and diplomas, as formerly she used to do for money. The type implies a retrogressive step in evolution, an inferior species who cannot endure. Unfortunately, they are able to pass on their wretchedness; degenerate men seem unconsciously to choose their mates from among them. And so they breed, producing an indeterminate sex for whom life is a torture. Fortunately, the offspring go under either because they are out of harmony with reality or because their repressed instincts break out uncontrollably or because their hopes of achieving equality with men are crushed. The type is tragic, revealing the drama of a desperate struggle against Nature, tragic as the romantic heritage now being dissipated by naturalism, which has a contrary aim: happiness, and happiness belongs only to the strong and skillful species.

But Miss Julie is also: a relic of the old warrior nobility now giving way to a new nobility of nerve and intellect, a victim of her own flawed constitution, a victim of the discord caused in a family by a mother's "crime," a victim of the delusions and conditions of her age—and together these are the equivalent of the concept of Destiny, or Universal Law, of antiquity. Guilt has been abolished by the naturalist, along with God, but the consequences of an action—punishment, imprisonment or the fear of it—that he cannot erase, for the simple reason that they remain, whether he pronounces acquittal or not. Those who have been injured are not as kind and understanding as an unscathed outsider can afford to be. Even if her father felt constrained not to seek revenge, his daughter would wreak vengeance upon herself, as she does here, out of an innate or acquired sense of honor, which the upper classes inherit—from where? From barbarism, from the ancient Aryan home of the race, from medieval chivalry. It is a beautiful thing, but nowadays a hindrance to the survival of the race. It is the nobleman's harikari, which compels him to slit open his own stomach when someone insults him and which survives in a modified form in the duel, that privilege of the nobility. That is why Jean, the servant, lives, while Miss Julie cannot live without honor. The slave's advantage over the nobleman is that he lacks this fatal preoccupation with honor. But in all of us Aryans there is something of the nobleman, or a Don Quixote. And so we sympathize with the suicide, whose act means a loss of honor. We are noblemen enough to be pained when we see the mighty fallen and as superfluous as a corpse, yes, even if the fallen should rise again and make amends through an honorable act. The servant Jean is a race-founder, someone in whom the process of differentiation can be detected. Born the son of a tenant farmer, he has educated himself in the things a gentleman should know. He has been quick to learn, has finely developed senses (smell, taste, sight) and a feeling for what is beautiful. He is already moving up in the world and is not embarrassed about using other people's help. He is alienated from his fellow servants, despising them as parts of a past he has already put behind him. He fears and flees them because they know his secrets, pry into his intentions, envy his rise, and look forward eagerly to his fall. Hence his dual, indecisive nature, vacillating between sympathy for people in high social positions and hatred for those who currently occupy those positions. He is an aristocrat, as he himself says, has learned the secrets of good society, is polished on the surface but coarse beneath, wears a frock coat tastefully but without any guarantee that his body is clean.

He has respect for Miss Julie, but is afraid of Kristine because she knows his dangerous secrets. He is sufficiently callous not to let the night's events disturb his plans for the future. With both a slave's brutality and a master's lack of squeamishness, he can see blood without fainting and shake off misfortune easily. Consequently, he comes through the struggle unscathed and will probably end up an innkeeper. And even if *he* does not become a Romanian count, his son will become a university student and possibly a county police commissioner.

. . .

Apart from the fact that Jean is rising in the world, he is superior to Miss Julie because he is a man. Sexually, he is an aristocrat because of his masculine strength, his more keenly developed senses, and his capacity for taking the initiative. His sense of inferiority is mostly due to the social circumstances in which he happens to be living, and he can probably shed it along with his valet's jacket.

His slave mentality expresses itself in the fearful respect he has for the Count (the boots) and his religious superstition; but he respects the Count mainly as the occupant of the kind of high position to which he himself aspires; and the respect remains even after he has conquered the daughter of the house and seen how empty the lovely shell was. I do not believe that love in any "higher" sense can exist between two people of such different natures, and so I have Miss Julie's love as something she fabricates in order to protect and excuse herself; and I have Jean suppose himself capable of loving her under other social circumstances. I think it is the same with love as with the hyacinth, which must take root in darkness *before* it can produce a sturdy flower. Here a flower shoots up, blooms, and goes to seed all at once, and that is why it dies so quickly.

Kristine, finally, is a female slave. Years standing over the stove have made her conventional and lethargic; instinctively hypocritical, she uses morality and religion as cloaks and scapegoats. A strong person would not need these because he can either bear his guilt or reason it away. Kristine goes to church as a quick and easy way to unload her household thefts on Jesus and to take on a new charge of innocence.

The Play in PERFORMANCE

Miss Julie—Strindberg's most popular play—exists in at least twenty English translations, and it has been made into a film, an opera, and a ballet. It has been staged countless times throughout the world—chiefly in Europe and the United States, of course, but also in Latin America, Asia, and Africa.

Miss Julie had its world premiere in Copenhagen in 1889, performed by the Scandinavian Experimental Theater, a small group that Strindberg had organized under the influence of André Antoine's Théâtre libre. Because the Danish censor had banned the play, it was performed privately for an invited audience rather than publicly staged. Four years later, in 1893, Antoine staged *Miss Julie* in his theater in Paris, where it received mixed reviews, because some critics considered that naturalistic drama was already old-fashioned. The early productions of course used realistic settings and a style of acting that was thought to be realistic, in accordance with Strindberg's wishes, and indeed most productions continue to be realistic, but in recent decades productions have departed very far from Strindberg's vision. For instance, in a German production of 1974 five old women in black moved about on the stage, a sort of silent chorus. Further, all three of Strindberg's characters were visible throughout the play; when a character was not onstage, he or she sat on a chair at the side and watched the performance. In the following year, another German production offered a different variant: The scene in which Julie says she would like to see Jean's blood and his brains on the chopping block was played as an affectionate love scene between bantering lovers. In 1979 a production in London set the play in South Africa, using a black Jean and a white Julie—an idea repeated by a company in South Africa, where for the first time in South African history a black man was seen to kiss a white woman on the stage. In this production, it was clear that all talk about class was really talk about race. A 1982 production in Gothenburg (Sweden) took a strong feminist line: Jean was made up to look like Strindberg, Julie was quite pleasant, and in the final scene a woman came onstage and silently watched the ending, implicitly condemning the misogynistic author.

A highly praised English production in 1983 was much more traditional. It opened in the tiny (one hundred and twenty seats) Lyric Theatre, Hammersmith, but after a few weeks it was transferred to a theater whose capacity was five times greater. Strindberg would have been delighted with the highly realistic set, which included a dripping faucet that unnerved the spectators. The director had wanted to set the play in nineteenth-century Ireland—the servants were to have Irish accents, Julie an English accent—but the actress playing Kristine could not produce an acceptable accent, and so this interpretation was not put onto the stage until that play had changed theaters and the actress in question had been replaced.

The next major production was in Tokyo in 1984, where Strindberg's demand that the set be naturalistic was ignored. The set was not the usual room without a fourth wall but was a birdcage without a fourth wall, and the characters perched on pedestals. The play began with a flirtation between Jean and Kristine, with Jean holding a boot between his legs as a phallus. A 1986 Swedish production was even less faithful to the letter of the play, which was updated to the 1920s and presented with a highly symbolic set—a glowing stove, a table that was a block for slaughtering an animal, and huge meat hooks. Even more obvious was the symbolism used when Julie and Jean left the stage for Jean's room—a peasant came by and placed a midsummer wreath over the tip of a maypole.

The Swedish director Ingmar Bergman staged the play, under the title *Julie*, in Stockholm in 1981, as part of a program that included *Nora*—Bergman's version of Ibsen's *A Doll's House*. Bergman's interpretation of the play was heavily based on a detail that Strindberg deleted from his manuscript. In the manuscript version of the speech in which Kristine tells Jean that Julie made her lover jump over her whip, there is a sentence—never published—to the effect that the lover jumped twice, but on the third command he "grabbed the whip from her and slashed her face with it, leaving a long scratch on her left cheek." In Bergman's produc-

tion, it was evident that Julie was heavily made up, but after the sexual encounter with Jean the makeup has come off, and a bleeding scar was evident on her cheek. As Bergman explains in his account of the production, *A Project for the Theatre*, he wanted to show that Julie had already been wounded. "Then, you see, when Jean gives her this second 'wound'—her second physical humiliation at the hands of a man—it destroys her" (15).

For brief discussions of numerous productions, see Egil Tornqvist and Barry Jacobs, *Strindberg's "Miss Julie": A Play and Its Transpositions* (1988). For an interview with Ingmar Bergman concerning his production, as well as a discussion of his *Julie*, see Bergman's *A Project for the Theatre*, ed. Frederick J. Marker and Lise-Lone Marker (1993).

OSCAR Wilde

Oscar Wilde (1854–1900) was born in Dublin. He distinguished himself as a student at Trinity College, Dublin, and at Oxford and then turned to a career of writing, lecturing, and in other ways making himself a public figure in England: His posture as an aesthete (he was alleged to have walked down Piccadilly with a flower in his hand) was caricatured by Gilbert and Sullivan in *Patience*. But it became no laughing matter when in 1895 he was arrested and convicted of homosexuality. After serving two years at hard labor, he was released from jail. He then went to France, where he lived under an assumed name until he died. His Irish birth did not ally him to the Irish Renaissance at the end of the nineteenth century; when W. B. Yeats was writing plays on Irish legends, Wilde was writing drawing-room comedies.

■■■■■■■■■■■■■■

COMMENTARY ON *THE IMPORTANCE OF BEING EARNEST*

The gist of the plot of *The Importance of Being Earnest* is the gist of the plot of many comedies: A young man and a young woman wish to marry, but an apparently insurmountable obstacle interposes. The obstacle, however, is surmounted, and so at the end we get a happy, united society. Wilde doubles the lovers, giving us two young men and two young women, but this is scarcely an innovation, for we get two pairs of lovers in several of Shakespeare's comedies, including *A Midsummer Night's Dream*, which, after what has been called an obstacle race to the altar, similarly concludes with all of the lovers happily paired.

Our entry on *farce* in the Glossary suggests that farce is "a sort of comedy based not on clever language or subtleties of character, but on broadly humorous situations," such as a man mistakenly entering the ladies' locker room. Generally the emphasis in farce is on surprise and on swift physical action, with much frantic hiding under beds, desperate putting on of absurd disguises, and so forth. But it is widely (though not universally) agreed that *The Importance of Being Earnest* is a farce, an utterly improbable play with virtually no connection with life as we know or feel it. Those who hold this view, however, see this play as unique, the one farce that depends on language rather than physical action. Writing in 1902, of a revival staged seven years after the original production of *The Importance of Being Earnest*, Max Beerbohm said,

> In scheme, of course, it is a hackneyed farce—the story of a young man coming up to London "on the spree," and of another young man going down conversely to the country, and of the complications that ensue. . . . [But] the fun depends mainly on what the characters say, rather than on what they do. They speak a kind of beautiful nonsense—the language of high comedy, twisted into fantasy. Throughout the dialogue is the horseplay of a distinguished intellect and a distinguished imagination—a horse-play among words and ideas, conducted with poetic dignity.

A few critics, however, have insisted that under the glittering but apparently trivial surface (Wilde said this play was "written by a butterfly for butterflies") there are serious topics, and that Wilde is indeed saying serious things—disguised as nonsense—about society. He is, in this view, joking in earnest; that is, he is writing satirically and only pretending to be playful. (On *satire*, see the Glossary entry.) Among the topics that critics have singled out are marriage, money, education, sincerity (the importance—or unimportance—of being earnest), class relationships, and death. In effect, the question comes down to this: When we hear, for instance, Lady Bracknell commenting on the absurd circumstances of Jack's infancy, do our minds turn to a criticism of the snobbish speaker, or do they (delighting in the absurd speech) relish the lines themselves and take pleasure in the speaker? Here is the passage in question:

> To be born, or at any rate, bred in a handbag, whether it had handles or not, seems to me to display a contempt for the ordinary decencies of family life that reminds one of the worst excesses of the French Revolution. And I presume you know what that unfortunate movement led to?

Readers are invited to try thinking about the play both ways—as a work of art divorced from reality, and as a work of art that repeatedly if indirectly comments on life—and to come to their own conclusions about the truth of the two views we have set forth. Possibly they will conclude, with Algernon, that "The truth is rarely pure, and never simple."

THE IMPORTANCE OF BEING EARNEST
A TRIVIAL COMEDY FOR SERIOUS PEOPLE
Oscar Wilde

CHARACTERS

JOHN WORTHING, J.P.
ALGERNON MONCRIEFF
REV. CANON CHASUBLE, D.D.
MERRIMAN (*butler*)
LANE (*manservant*)
LADY BRACKNELL
HON. GWENDOLEN FAIRFAX
CECILY CARDEW
MISS PRISM (*governess*)

THE SCENES OF THE PLAY

ACT I, *Algernon Moncrieff's flat in Half-Moon Street, W.*
ACT II, *The garden at the Manor House, Woolton*
ACT III, *Drawing-room of the Manor House, Woolton*

TIME

The Present

PLACE

London

ACT 1

SCENE: *Morning-room in Algernon's flat in Half-Moon Street. The room is luxuriously and artistically furnished. The sound of a piano is heard in the adjoining room.*

(*Lane is arranging afternoon tea on the table, and after the music has ceased, Algernon enters.*)

ALGERNON. Did you hear what I was playing, Lane?

LANE. I didn't think it polite to listen, sir.

ALGERNON. I'm sorry for that, for your sake. I don't play accurately—anyone can play accurately—but I play with wonderful expression. As far as the piano is concerned, sentiment is my forte. I keep science for Life.

LANE. Yes, sir.

ALGERNON. And, speaking of the science of Life, have you got the cucumber sandwiches cut for Lady Bracknell?

LANE. Yes, sir. (*Hands them on a salver.*)

ALGERNON (*inspects them, takes two, and sits down on the sofa*). Oh! . . . by the way, Lane, I see from your book that on Thursday night, when Lord Shoreman and Mr. Worthing were dining with me, eight bottles of champagne are entered as having been consumed.

LANE. Yes, sir; eight bottles and a pint.

ALGERNON. Why is it that at a bachelor's establishment the servants invariably drink the champagne? I ask merely for information.

LANE. I attribute it to the superior quality of the wine, sir. I have often observed that in married households the champagne is rarely of a first-rate brand.

ALGERNON. Good Heavens! Is marriage so demoralizing as that?

LANE. I believe it *is* a very pleasant state, sir. I have had very little experience of it myself up to the present. I have only been married once. That was in consequence of a misunderstanding between myself and a young woman.

ALGERNON (*languidly*). I don't know that I am much interested in your family life, Lane.

LANE. No, sir; it is not a very interesting subject. I never think of it myself.

ALGERNON. Very natural, I am sure. That will do, Lane, thank you.

LANE. Thank you, sir. (*Lane goes out.*)

ALGERNON. Lane's views on marriage seem somewhat lax. Really, if the lower orders don't set us a good example, what on earth is the use of them? They seem, as a class, to have absolutely no sense of moral responsibility.

(*Enter Lane.*)

LANE. Mr. Ernest Worthing.

(*Enter Jack. Lane goes out.*)

ALGERNON. How are you, my dear Ernest? What brings you up to town?

JACK. Oh, pleasure, pleasure! What else should bring one anywhere? Eating as usual, I see, Algy!

ALGERNON (*stiffly*). I believe it is customary in good society to take some slight refreshment at five o'clock. Where have you been since last Thursday?

JACK (*sitting down on the sofa*). In the country.

ALGERNON. What on earth do you do there?

JACK (*pulling off his gloves*). When one is in town one amuses oneself. When one is in the country one amuses other people. It is excessively boring.

ALGERNON. And who are the people you amuse?

JACK (*airily*). Oh, neighbours, neighbours.

ALGERNON. Got nice neighbours in your part of Shropshire?

JACK. Perfectly horrid! Never speak to one of them.

ALGERNON. How immensely you must amuse them! (*Goes over and takes sandwich.*) By the way, Shropshire is your county, is it not?

JACK. Eh? Shropshire? Yes, of course. Hallo! Why all these cups? Why cucumber sandwiches? Why such reckless extravagance in one so young? Who is coming to tea?

ALGERNON. Oh! merely Aunt Augusta and Gwendolen.

JACK. How perfectly delightful!

ALGERNON. Yes, that is all very well; but I am afraid Aunt Augusta won't quite approve of your being here.

JACK. May I ask why?

ALGERNON. My dear fellow, the way you flirt with Gwendolen is perfectly disgraceful. It is almost as bad as the way Gwendolen flirts with you.

JACK. I am in love with Gwendolen. I have come up to town expressly to propose to her.

ALGERNON. I thought you had come up for pleasure? . . . I call that business.

JACK. How utterly unromantic you are!

ALGERNON. I really don't see anything romantic in proposing. It is very romantic to be in love. But there is nothing romantic about a definite proposal. Why, one may be accepted. One usually is, I believe. Then the excitement is all over. The very essence of romance is uncertainty. If ever I get married, I'll certainly try to forget the fact.

JACK. I have no doubt about that, dear Algy. The Divorce Court was specially invented for people whose memories are so curiously constituted.

ALGERNON. Oh! there is no use speculating on that subject. Divorces are made in Heaven–(*Jack puts out his hand to take a sandwich. Algernon at once interferes.*) Please don't touch the cucumber sandwiches. They are ordered specially for Aunt Augusta. (*Takes one and eats it.*)

JACK. Well, you have been eating them all the time.

ALGERNON. That is quite a different matter. She is my aunt. (*Takes plate from below.*) Have some bread and butter. The bread and butter is for Gwendolen. Gwendolen is devoted to bread and butter.

JACK (*advancing to table and helping himself*). And very good bread and butter it is, too.

ALGERNON. Well, my dear fellow, you need not eat as if you were going to eat it all. You behave as if you were married to her already. You are not married to her already, and I don't think you ever will be.

JACK. Why on earth do you say that?

ALGERNON. Well, in the first place girls never marry the men they flirt with. Girls don't think it right.

JACK. Oh, that is nonsense!

ALGERNON. It isn't. It is a great truth. It accounts for the extraordinary number of bachelors that one sees all over the place. In the second place, I don't give my consent.

JACK. Your consent!

ALGERNON. My dear fellow, Gwendolen is my first cousin. And before I allow you to marry her, you will have to clear up the whole question of Cecily. (*Rings bell.*)

JACK. Cecily! What on earth do you mean? What do you mean, Algy, by Cecily? I don't know anyone of the name of Cecily.

(*Enter Lane.*)

ALGERNON. Bring me that cigarette case Mr. Worthing left in the smoking-room the last time he dined here.

LANE. Yes, sir. (*Lane goes out.*)

JACK. Do you mean to say you have had my cigarette case all this time? I wish to goodness you had let me know. I have been writing frantic letters to Scotland Yard about it. I was very nearly offering a large reward.

ALGERNON. Well, I wish you would offer one. I happen to be more than usually hard up.

JACK. There is no good offering a large reward now that the thing is found.

(*Enter Lane with the cigarette case on a salver. Algernon takes it at once. Lane goes out.*)

ALGERNON. I think that is rather mean of you, Ernest, I must say. (*Opens case and examines it.*) However, it makes no matter, for, now that I look at the inscription, I find that the thing isn't yours after all.

JACK. Of course it's mine. (*Moving to him.*) You have seen me with it a hundred times, and you have no right whatsoever to read what is written inside. It is a very ungentlemanly thing to read a private cigarette case.

ALGERNON. Oh! it is absurd to have a hard-and-fast rule about what one should read and what one shouldn't. More than half of modern culture depends on what one shouldn't read.

JACK. I am quite aware of the fact, and I don't propose to discuss modern culture. It isn't the sort of thing one should talk of in private. I simply want my cigarette case back.

ALGERNON. Yes; but this isn't your cigarette case. This cigarette case is a present from someone of the name of Cecily, and you said you didn't know anyone of that name.

JACK. Well, if you want to know, Cecily happens to be my aunt.

ALGERNON. Your aunt!

JACK. Yes. Charming old lady she is, too. Lives at Tunbridge Wells. Just give it back to me, Algy.

ALGERNON (*retreating to back of sofa*). But why does she call herself little Cecily if she is your aunt and lives at Tunbridge Wells? (*Reading.*) "From little Cecily with her fondest love."

JACK (*moving to sofa and kneeling upon it*). My dear fellow, what on earth is there in that? Some aunts are tall, some aunts are not tall. That is a matter that surely an aunt may be allowed to decide for herself. You seem to think that every aunt should be exactly like your aunt! That is absurd! For Heaven's sake give me back my cigarette case. (*Follows Algernon round the room.*)

ALGERNON. Yes. But why does your aunt call you her uncle? "From little Cecily, with her fondest love to her dear Uncle Jack." There is no objection, I admit, to an aunt being a small aunt, but why an aunt, no matter what her size may be, should call her own nephew her uncle, I can't quite make out. Besides, your name isn't Jack at all; it is Ernest.

JACK. It isn't Ernest; it's Jack.

ALGERNON. You have always told me it was Ernest. I have introduced you to everyone as Ernest. You answer to the name of Ernest. You look as if your name was Ernest. You are the most ernest looking person I ever saw in my life. It is perfectly absurd your saying that your name isn't Ernest. It's on your cards. Here is one of them. (*Taking it from case.*) "Mr. Ernest Worthing, B 4, The Albany." I'll keep this as a proof your name is Ernest if ever you attempt to deny it to me, or to Gwendolen, or to anyone else. (*Puts the card in his pocket.*)

JACK. Well, my name is Ernest in town and Jack in the country, and the cigarette case was given to me in the country.

ALGERNON. Yes, but that does not account for the fact that your small Aunt Cecily, who lives at Tunbridge Wells, calls you her dear uncle. Come, old boy, you had much better have the thing out at once.

JACK. My dear Algy, you talk exactly as if you were a dentist. It is very vulgar to talk like a dentist when one isn't a dentist. It produces a false impression.

ALGERNON. Well, that is exactly what dentists always do. Now, go on! Tell me the whole thing. I may mention that I have always suspected you of being a confirmed and secret Bunburyist; and I am quite sure of it now.

JACK. Bunburyist? What on earth do you mean by a Bunburyist?

ALGERNON. I'll reveal to you the meaning of that incomparable expression as soon as you are kind enough to inform me why you are Ernest in town and Jack in the country.

JACK. Well, produce my cigarette case first.

ALGERNON. Here it is. (*Hands cigarette case.*) Now produce your explanation, and pray make it improbable. (*Sits on sofa.*)

JACK. My dear fellow, there is nothing improbable about my explanation at all. In fact it's perfectly ordinary. Old Mr. Thomas Cardew, who adopted me when I was a little boy, made me in his will guardian to his granddaughter, Miss Cecily Cardew. Cecily, who addresses me as her uncle from motives of respect that you could not possibly appreciate, lives at my place in the country under the charge of her admirable governess, Miss Prism.

ALGERNON. Where is that place in the country, by the way?

JACK. That is nothing to you, dear boy. You are not going to be invited. . . . I may tell you candidly that the place is not in Shropshire.

ALGERNON. I suspected that, my dear fellow! I have Bunburyed all over Shropshire on two separate occasions. Now, go on. Why are you Ernest in town and Jack in the country?

JACK. My dear Algy, I don't know whether you will be able to understand my real motives. You are hardly serious enough. When one is placed in the position of guardian, one has to adopt a very high moral tone on all subjects. It's one's duty to do so. And as a high moral tone can hardly be said to conduce very much to either one's health or one's happiness, in order to get up to town I have always pretended to have a younger brother of the name of Ernest, who lives in the Albany, and gets into the most dreadful scrapes. That, my dear Algy, is the whole truth pure and simple.

ALGERNON. The truth is rarely pure and never simple. Modern life would be very tedious if it were either, and modern literature a complete impossibility!

JACK. That wouldn't be at all a bad thing.

ALGERNON. Literary criticism is not your forte, my dear fellow. Don't try it. You should leave that to people who haven't been at a University. They do it so well in the daily papers. What you really are is a Bunburyist. I was quite right in saying you were a Bunburyist. You are one of the most advanced Bunburyists I know.

JACK. What on earth do you mean?

ALGERNON. You have invented a very useful younger brother called Ernest, in order that you may be able to come up to town as often as you like. I have invented an invaluable permanent invalid called Bunbury, in order that I may be able to go down into the country whenever I choose. Bunbury is perfectly invaluable. If it wasn't for Bunbury's extraordinary bad health, for instance, I wouldn't be able to dine with you at Willis's to-night, for I have been really engaged to Aunt Augusta for more than a week.

JACK. I haven't asked you to dine with me anywhere tonight.

ALGERNON. I know. You are absolutely careless about sending out invitations. It is very foolish of you. Nothing annoys people so much as not receiving invitations.

JACK. You had much better dine with your Aunt Augusta.

ALGERNON. I haven't the smallest intention of doing anything of the kind. To begin with, I dined there on Monday, and once a week is quite enough to dine with one's own relatives. In the second place, whenever I do dine there I am always treated as a member of the family, and sent down with either no woman at all, or two. In the third place, I know perfectly well whom she will place me next to, tonight. She will place me next Mary Farquhar, who always flirts with her own husband across the dinner-table. That is not very pleasant. Indeed, it is not even decent . . . and that sort of thing is enormously on the increase. The amount of women in London who flirt with their own husbands is perfectly scandalous. It looks so bad. It is simply washing one's clean linen in public. Besides, now that I know you to be a confirmed Bunburyist I naturally want to talk to you about Bunburying. I want to tell you the rules.

JACK. I'm not a Bunburyist at all. If Gwendolen accepts me, I am going to kill my brother, indeed I think I'll kill him in any case. Cecily is a little too much interested in him. It is rather a bore. So I am going to get rid of Ernest. And I strongly advise you to do the same with Mr. . . . with your invalid friend who has the absurd name.

ALGERNON. Nothing will induce me to part with Bunbury, and if you ever get married, which seems to me extremely problematic, you will be very glad to know Bunbury. A man who marries without knowing Bunbury has a very tedious time of it.

JACK. That is nonsense. If I marry a charming girl like Gwendolen, and she is the only girl I ever saw in my life that I would marry, I certainly won't want to know Bunbury.

ALGERNON. Then your wife will. You don't seem to realize, that in married life three is company and two is none.

JACK (*sententiously*). That, my dear young friend, is the theory that the corrupt French Drama has been propounding for the last fifty years.

ALGERNON. Yes; and that the happy English home has proved in half the time.

JACK. For heaven's sake, don't try to be cynical. It's perfectly easy to be cynical.

ALGERNON. My dear fellow, it isn't easy to be anything now-a-days. There's such a lot of beastly competition about. (*The sound of an electric bell is heard.*) Ah! that must be Aunt Augusta. Only relatives, or creditors, ever ring in that Wagnerian manner. Now, if I get her out of the way for ten minutes, so that you can have an opportunity for proposing to Gwendolen, may I dine with you to-night at Willis's?

JACK. I suppose so if you want to.

ALGERNON. Yes, but you must be serious about it. I hate people who are not serious about meals. It is so shallow of them.

(*Enter Lane.*)

LANE. Lady Bracknell and Miss Fairfax. (*Algernon goes forward to meet them. Enter Lady Bracknell and Gwendolen.*)

LADY BRACKNELL. Good afternoon, dear Algernon, I hope you are behaving very well.

ALGERNON. I'm feeling very well, Aunt Augusta.

LADY BRACKNELL. That's not quite the same thing. In fact the two things rarely go together. (*Sees Jack and bows to him with icy coldness.*)

ALGERNON (*to Gwendolen*). Dear me, you are smart!

GWENDOLEN. I am always smart! Aren't I, Mr. Worthing?

JACK. You're quite perfect, Miss Fairfax.

GWENDOLEN. Oh! I hope I am not that. It would leave no room for developments, and I intend to develop in *many directions*. (*Gwendolen and Jack sit down together in the corner.*)

LADY BRACKNELL. I'm sorry if we are a little late, Algernon, but I was obliged to call on dear Lady Harbury. I hadn't been there since her poor husband's death. I never saw a woman so altered; she looks quite twenty years younger. And now I'll have a cup of tea, and one of those nice cucumber sandwiches you promised me.

ALGERNON. Certainly, Aunt Augusta. (*Goes over to tea-table.*)

LADY BRACKNELL. Won't you come and sit here, Gwendolen?

GWENDOLEN. Thanks, mamma, I'm quite comfortable where I am.

ALGERNON (*picking up empty plate in horror*). Good heavens! Lane! Why are there no cucumber sandwiches? I ordered them specially.

LANE (*gravely*). There were no cucumbers in the market this morning, sir. I went down twice.

ALGERNON. No cucumbers!

LANE. No, sir. Not even for ready money.

ALGERNON. That will do, Lane, thank you.

LANE. Thank you sir. (*Goes out.*)

ALGERNON. I am greatly distressed, Aunt Augusta, about there being no cucumbers, not even for ready money.

LADY BRACKNELL. It really makes no matter, Algernon. I had some crumpets with Lady Harbury, who seems to me to be living entirely for pleasure now.

ALGERNON. I hear her hair has turned quite gold from grief.

LADY BRACKNELL. It certainly has changed its colour. From what cause I, of course, cannot say. (*Algernon crosses and hands tea.*) Thank you. I've quite a treat for you to-night, Algernon. I am going to send you down with Mary Farquhar. She is such a nice woman, and so attentive to her husband. It's delightful to watch them.

ALGERNON. I am afraid, Aunt Augusta, I shall have to give up the pleasure of dining with you to-night after all.

LADY BRACKNELL (*frowning*). I hope not, Algernon. It would put my table completely out. Your uncle would have to dine upstairs. Fortunately he is accustomed to that.

ALGERNON. It is a great bore, and, I need hardly say, a terrible disappointment to me, but the fact is I have just had a telegram to say that my poor friend Bunbury is very ill again. (*Exchanges glances with Jack.*) They seem to think I should be with him.

LADY BRACKNELL. It is very strange. This Mr. Bunbury seems to suffer from curiously bad health.

ALGERNON. Yes; poor Bunbury is a dreadful invalid.

LADY BRACKNELL. Well, I must say, Algernon, that I think it is high time that Mr. Bunbury made up his mind whether he was going to live or to die. This shilly-shallying with the question is absurd. Nor do I in any way approve of the modern sympathy with invalids. I consider it morbid. Illness of any kind is hardly a thing to be encouraged in others. Health is the primary duty of life. I am always telling that to your poor uncle, but he never seems to take much notice . . . as far as any improvement in his ailments goes. I should be much obliged if you would ask Mr. Bunbury, from me, to be kind enough not to have a relapse on Saturday, for I rely on you to arrange my music for me. It is my last reception and one wants something that will encourage conversation, particularly at the end of the season when everyone has practically said whatever they had to say, which, in most cases, was probably not much.

ALGERNON. I'll speak to Bunbury, Aunt Augusta, if he is still conscious, and I think I can promise you he'll be all right by Saturday. You see, if one plays good music, people don't listen, and if one plays bad music people don't talk. But I'll run over the programme I've drawn out, if you will kindly come into the next room for a moment.

LADY BRACKNELL. Thank you, Algernon. It is very thoughtful of you. (*Rising, and following Algernon.*) I'm sure the programme will be delightful, after a few expurgations. French songs I cannot possibly allow. People always seem to think that they are improper, and either look shocked, which is vulgar, or laugh, which is worse. But German sounds a thoroughly respectable language, and indeed, I believe is so. Gwendolen, you will accompany me.

GWENDOLEN. Certainly, mamma. (*Lady Bracknell and Algernon go into the music-room, Gwendolen remains behind.*)

JACK. Charming day it has been, Miss Fairfax.

GWENDOLEN. Pray don't talk to me about the weather, Mr. Worthing. Whenever people talk to me about the weather, I always feel quite certain that they mean something else. And that makes me so nervous.

JACK. I do mean something else.

GWENDOLEN. I thought so. In fact, I am never wrong.

JACK. And I would like to be allowed to take advantage of Lady Bracknell's temporary absence . . .

GWENDOLEN. I would certainly advise you to do so. Mamma has a way of coming back suddenly into a room that I have often had to speak to her about.

JACK (*nervously*). Miss Fairfax, ever since I met you I have admired you more than any girl . . . I have ever met since . . . I met you.

GWENDOLEN. Yes, I am quite aware of the fact. And I often wish that in public, at any rate, you had been more demonstrative. For me you have always had an irresistible fascination. Even before I met you I was far from indifferent to you. (*Jack looks at her in amazement.*) We live, as I hope you know, Mr. Worthing, in an age of ideals. The fact is constantly mentioned in the more expensive monthly magazines, and has reached the provincial pulpits I am told: and my ideal has always been to love some one of the name of Ernest. There is something in that name that inspires absolute confidence. The moment Algernon first mentioned to me that he had a friend called Ernest, I knew I was destined to love you.

JACK. You really love me, Gwendolen?

GWENDOLEN. Passionately!

JACK. Darling! You don't know how happy you've made me.

GWENDOLEN. My own Ernest!

JACK. But you don't really mean to say that you couldn't love me if my name wasn't Ernest?

GWENDOLEN. But your name is Ernest.

JACK. Yes, I know it is. But supposing it was something else? Do you mean to say you couldn't love me then?

GWENDOLEN (*glibly*). Ah! that is clearly a metaphysical speculation, and like most metaphysical speculations has very little reference at all to the actual facts of real life, as we know them.

JACK. Personally, darling, to speak quite candidly, I don't much care about the name of Ernest . . . I don't think that name suits me at all.

GWENDOLEN. It suits you perfectly. It is a divine name. It has a music of its own. It produces vibrations.

JACK. Well, really, Gwendolen, I must say that I think there are lots of other much nicer names. I think, Jack, for instance, a charming name.

GWENDOLEN. Jack? . . . No, there is very little music in the name Jack, if any at all, indeed. It does not thrill. It produces absolutely no vibration. . . . I have known several Jacks, and they all, without exception, were more than usually plain. Besides, Jack is a notorious domesticity for John! And I pity any woman who is married to a man called John. She would probably never be allowed to know the entrancing pleasure of a single moment's solitude. The only really safe name is Ernest.

JACK. Gwendolen, I must get christened at once—I mean we must get married at once. There is no time to be lost.

GWENDOLEN. Married, Mr. Worthing?

JACK (*astounded*). Well . . . surely. You know that I love you, and you led me to believe, Miss Fairfax, that you were not absolutely indifferent to me.

GWENDOLEN. I adore you. But you haven't proposed to me yet. Nothing has been said at all about marriage. The subject has not even been touched on.

JACK. Well . . . may I propose to you now?

GWENDOLEN. I think it would be an admirable opportunity. And to spare you any possible disappointment, Mr. Worthing, I think it only fair to tell you quite frankly beforehand that I am fully determined to accept you.

JACK. Gwendolen!

GWENDOLEN. Yes, Mr. Worthing, what have you got to say to me?

JACK. You know what I have got to say to you.

GWENDOLEN. Yes, but you don't say it.

JACK. Gwendolen, will you marry me? (*Goes on his knees.*)

GWENDOLEN. Of course I will, darling. How long you have been about it! I am afraid you have had very little experience in how to propose.

JACK. My own one, I have never loved anyone in the world but you.

GWENDOLEN. Yes, but men often propose for practice. I know my brother Gerald does. All my girl-friends tell me so. What wonderfully blue eyes you have, Ernest! They are quite, quite blue. I hope you will always look at me just like that, especially when there are other people present.

(*Enter Lady Bracknell.*)

LADY BRACKNELL. Mr. Worthing! Rise, sir, from this semi-recumbent posture. It is most indecorous.

GWENDOLEN. Mamma! (*He tried to rise; she restrains him.*) I must beg you to retire. This is no place for you. Besides, Mr. Worthing has not quite finished yet.

LADY BRACKNELL. Finished what, may I ask?

GWENDOLEN. I am engaged to Mr. Worthing, mamma. (*They rise together.*)

LADY BRACKNELL. Pardon me, you are not engaged to anyone. When you do become engaged to some one, I, or your father, should his health permit him, will inform you of the fact. An engagement should come on a young girl as a surprise, pleasant or unpleasant, as the case may be. It is hardly a matter that she could be allowed to arrange for herself. . . . And now I have a few questions to put to you, Mr. Worthing. While I am making these inquiries, you, Gwendolen, will wait for me below in the carriage.

GWENDOLEN (*reproachfully*). Mamma!

LADY BRACKNELL. In the carriage, Gwendolen! (*Gwendolen goes to the door. She and Jack blow kisses to each other behind Lady Bracknell's back. Lady Bracknell looks vaguely about as if she could not understand what the noise was. Finally turns round.*) Gwendolen, the carriage!

GWENDOLEN. Yes, mamma. (*Goes out, looking back at Jack.*)

LADY BRACKNELL (*sitting down*). You can take a seat, Mr. Worthing. (*Looks in her pocket for note-book and pencil.*)

JACK. Thank you, Lady Bracknell, I prefer standing.

LADY BRACKNELL (*pencil and notebook in hand*). I feel bound to tell you that you are not down on my list of eligible young men, although I have the same list as the dear Duchess of Bolton has. We work together, in fact. However, I am quite ready to enter your name, should your answers be what a really affectionate mother requires. Do you smoke?

JACK. Well, yes, I must admit I smoke.

LADY BRACKNELL. I am glad to hear it. A man should always have an occupation of some kind. There are far too many idle men in London as it is. How old are you?

JACK. Twenty-nine.

LADY BRACKNELL. A very good age to be married at. I have always been of opinion that a man who desires to get married should know either everything or nothing. Which do you know?

JACK (*after some hesitation*). I know nothing, Lady Bracknell.

LADY BRACKNELL. I am pleased to hear it. I do not approve of anything that tampers with natural ignorance. Ignorance is like a delicate exotic fruit; touch it and the bloom is gone. The whole theory of modern education is radically unsound. Fortunately in England, at any rate, education produces no effect whatsoever. If it did, it would prove a serious danger to the upper classes, and probably lead to acts of violence in Grosvenor Square. What is your income?

JACK. Between seven and eight thousand a year.

LADY BRACKNELL (*makes a note in her book*). In land, or in investments?

JACK. In investments, chiefly.

LADY BRACKNELL. That is satisfactory. What between the duties expected of one during one's life-time, and the duties exacted from one after one's death, land has ceased to be either a profit or a pleasure. It gives one position, and prevents one from keeping it up. That's all that can be said about land.

JACK. I have a country house with some land, of course, attached to it, about fifteen hundred acres, I believe; but I don't depend on that for my real income. In fact, as far as I can make out, the poachers are the only people who make anything out of it.

LADY BRACKNELL. A country house! How many bedrooms? Well, that point can be cleared up afterwards. You have a town house, I hope? A girl with a simple, unspoiled nature, like Gwendolen, could hardly be expected to reside in the country.

JACK. Well, I own a house in Belgrave Square, but it is let by the year to Lady Bloxham. Of course, I can get it back whenever I like, at six months' notice.

LACY BRACKNELL. Lady Bloxham? I don't know her.

JACK. Oh, she goes about very little. She is a lady considerably advanced in years.

LADY BRACKNELL. Ah, now-a-days that is no guarantee of respectability of character. What number in Belgrave Square?

JACK. 149.

LADY BRACKNELL (*shaking her head*). The unfashionable side. I thought there was something. However, that could easily be altered.

JACK. Do you mean the fashion, or the side?

LADY BRACKNELL (*sternly*). Both, if necessary, I presume. What are your politics?

JACK. Well, I am afraid I really have none. I am a Liberal Unionist.

LADY BRACKNELL. Oh, they count as Tories. They dine with us. Or come in the evening, at any rate. Now to minor matters. Are your parents living?

JACK. I have lost both my parents.

LADY BRACKNELL. Both? . . . That seems like carelessness. Who was your father? He was evidently a man of some wealth. Was he born in what the Radical papers call the purple of commerce, or did he rise from the ranks of the aristocracy?

JACK. I am afraid I really don't know. The fact is, Lady Bracknell, I said I had lost my parents. It would be nearer the truth to say that my parents seem to have lost me . . . I don't actually know who I am by birth. I was . . . well, I was found.

LADY BRACKNELL. Found!

JACK. The late Mr. Thomas Cardew, an old gentleman of a very charitable and kindly disposition, found me, and gave me the name of Worthing, because he happened to have a first-class ticket for Worthing in his pocket at the time. Worthing is a place in Sussex. It is a seaside resort.

LADY BRACKNELL. Where did the charitable gentleman who had a first-class ticket for this seaside resort find you?

JACK (gravely). In a hand-bag.

LADY BRACKNELL. A hand-bag?

JACK (very seriously). Yes, Lady Bracknell. I was in a hand-bag—a somewhat large, black leather hand-bag, with handles to it—an ordinary hand-bag in fact.

LADY BRACKNELL. In what locality did Mr. James, or Thomas, Cardew come across this ordinary hand-bag?

JACK. In the cloak-room at Victoria Station. It was given to him in mistake for his own.

LADY BRACKNELL. The cloak-room at Victoria Station?

JACK. Yes. The Brighton line.

LADY BRACKNELL. The line is immaterial. Mr. Worthing, I confess I feel somewhat bewildered by what you have just told me. To be born, or at any rate bred, in a hand-bag, whether it had handles or not, seems to me to display a contempt for the ordinary decencies of family life that remind one of the worst excesses of the French Revolution. And I presume you know what that unfortunate movement led to? As for the particular locality in which the hand-bag was found, a cloak-room at a railway station might serve to conceal a social indiscretion—has probably, indeed, been used for the purpose before now—but it could hardly be regarded as an assured basis for a recognized position in good society.

JACK. May I ask you then what you would advise me to do? I need hardly say I would do anything in the world to ensure Gwendolen's happiness.

LADY BRACKNELL. I would strongly advise you, Mr. Worthing, to try and acquire some relations as soon as possible, and to make a definite effort to produce at any rate one parent, of either sex, before the season is quite over.

JACK. Well, I don't see how I could possibly manage to do that. I can produce the hand-bag at any moment. It is in my dressing-room at home. I really think that should satisfy you, Lady Bracknell.

LADY BRACKNELL. Me, sir! What has it to do with me? You can hardly imagine that I and Lord Bracknell would dream of allowing our only daughter—a girl brought up with the utmost care—to marry into a cloak-room, and form an alliance with a parcel? Good morning, Mr. Worthing! (Lady Bracknell sweeps out in majestic indignation.)

JACK. Good morning! (Algernon, from the other room, strikes up the Wedding March. Jack looks perfectly furious, and goes to the door.) For goodness' sake don't play that ghastly tune, Algy! How idiotic you are! (The music stops, and Algernon enters cheerily.)

ALGERNON. Didn't it go off all right, old boy? You don't mean to say Gwendolen refused you? I know it is a way she has. She is always refusing people. I think it is most ill-natured of her.

JACK. Oh, Gwendolen is as right as a trivet. As far as she is concerned, we are engaged. Her mother is perfectly unbearable. Never met such a Gorgon . . . I don't really know what a Gorgon is like, but I am quite sure that Lady Bracknell is one. In any case, she is a monster, without being a myth, which is rather unfair. . . . I beg your pardon, Algy, I suppose I shouldn't talk about your own aunt in that way before you.

ALGERNON. My dear boy, I love hearing my relations abused. It is the only thing that makes me put up with them at all. Relations are simply a tedious pack of people, who haven't got the remotest knowledge of how to live, nor the smallest instinct about when to die.

JACK. Oh, that is nonsense!

ALGERNON. It isn't!

JACK. Well, I won't argue about the matter. You always want to argue about things.

ALGERNON. That is exactly what things were originally made for.

JACK. Upon my word, if I thought that, I'd shoot myself . . . (A pause.) You don't think there is any chance of Gwendolen becoming like her mother in about a hundred and fifty years, do you, Algy?

ALGERNON. All women become like their mothers. That is their tragedy. No man does. That's his.

JACK. Is that clever?

ALGERNON. It is perfectly phrased! and quite as true as any observation in civilized life should be.

JACK. I am sick to death of cleverness. Everybody is clever now-a-days. You can't go anywhere without meeting clever people. The thing has become an absolute public nuisance. I wish to goodness we had a few fools left.

ALGERNON. We have.

JACK. I should extremely like to meet them. What do they talk about?

ALGERNON. The fools? Oh! about the clever people, of course.

JACK. What fools!

ALGERNON. By the way, did you tell Gwendolen the truth about your being Ernest in town, and Jack in the country?

JACK (*in a very patronising manner*). My dear fellow, the truth isn't quite the sort of thing one tells to a nice, sweet, refined girl. What extraordinary ideas you have about the way to behave to a woman!

ALGERNON. The only way to behave to a woman is to make love to her, if she is pretty, and to someone else if she is plain.

JACK. Oh, that is nonsense.

ALGERNON. What about your brother? What about the profligate Ernest?

JACK. Oh, before the end of the week I shall have got rid of him. I'll say he died in Paris of apoplexy. Lots of people die of apoplexy, quite suddenly, don't they?

ALGERNON. Yes, but it's hereditary, my dear fellow. It's a sort of thing that runs in families. You had much better say a severe chill.

JACK. You are sure a severe chill isn't hereditary, or anything of that kind?

ALGERNON. Of course it isn't!

JACK. Very well, then. My poor brother Ernest is carried off suddenly in Paris, by a severe chill. That gets rid of him.

ALGERNON. But I thought you said that . . . Miss Cardew was a little too much interested in your poor brother Ernest? Won't she feel his loss a good deal?

JACK. Oh, that is all right. Cecily is not a silly, romantic girl, I am glad to say. She has got a capital appetite, goes for long walks, and pays no attention at all to her lessons.

ALGERNON. I would rather like to see Cecily.

JACK. I will take very good care you never do. She is excessively pretty, and she is only just eighteen.

ALGERNON. Have you told Gwendolen yet that you have an excessively pretty ward who is only just eighteen?

JACK. Oh! one doesn't blurt these things out to people. Cecily and Gwendolen are perfectly certain to be extremely great friends. I'll bet you anything you like that half an hour after they have met, they will be calling each other sister.

ALGERNON. Women only do that when they have called each other a lot of other things first. Now, my dear boy, if we want to get a good table at Willis's, we really must go and dress. Do you know it is nearly seven?

JACK (*irritably*). Oh! it always is nearly seven.

ALGERNON. Well, I'm hungry.

JACK. I never knew you when you weren't. . . .

ALGERNON. What shall we do after dinner? Go to a theatre?

JACK. Oh, no! I loathe listening.

ALGERNON. Well, let us go to the Club?

JACK. Oh, no! I hate talking.

ALGERNON. Well, we might trot round to the Empire at ten?

JACK. Oh, no! can't bear looking at things. It is so silly.

ALGERNON. Well, what shall we do?

JACK. Nothing!

ALGERNON. It is awfully hard work doing nothing. However, I don't mind hard work where there is no definite object of any kind.

(*Enter Lane.*)

LANE. Miss Fairfax.

(*Enter Gwendolen. Lane goes out.*)

ALGERNON. Gwendolen, upon my word!

GWENDOLEN. Algy, kindly turn your back. I have something very particular to say to Mr. Worthing.

ALGERNON. Really, Gwendolen, I don't think I can allow this at all.

GWENDOLEN. Algy, you always adopt a strictly immoral attitude towards life. You are not quite old enough to do that. (*Algernon retires to the fireplace.*)

JACK. My own darling!

GWENDOLEN. Ernest, we may never be married. From the expression on mamma's face I fear we never shall. Few parents now-a-days pay any regard to what their children say to them. The old-fashioned respect for the young is fast dying out. Whatever influence I ever had over mamma, I lost at the age of three. But although she may prevent us from becoming man and wife, and I may marry someone else, and marry often, nothing that she can possibly do can alter my eternal devotion to you.

JACK. Dear Gwendolen.

GWENDOLEN. The story of your romantic origin, as related to me by mamma, with unpleasing comments, has naturally stirred the deeper fibers of my nature. Your Christian name has an irresistible fascination. The simplicity of your character makes you exquisitely incomprehensible to me. Your town address at the Albany I have. What is your address in the country?

JACK. The Manor House, Woolton, Hertfordshire. (*Algernon, who has been carefully listening, smiles to himself, and writes the address on his shirt-cuff. Then picks up the Railway Guide.*)

GWENDOLEN. There is a good postal service, I suppose? It may be necessary to do something desperate. That, of course, will require serious consideration. I will communicate with you daily.

JACK. My own one!

GWENDOLEN. How long do you remain in town?

JACK. Till Monday.

GWENDOLEN. Good! Algy, you may turn round now.

ALGERNON. Thanks, I've turned round already.

GWENDOLEN. You may also ring the bell.

JACK. You will let me see you to your carriage, my own darling?

GWENDOLEN. Certainly.

JACK (*to Lane, who now enters*). I will see Miss Fairfax out.

LANE. Yes, sir. (*Jack and Gwendolen go off. Lane presents several letters on a salver to Algernon. It is to be surmised that they are bills, as Algernon, after looking at the envelopes, tears them up.*)

ALGERNON. A glass of sherry, Lane.

LANE. Yes, sir.

ALGERNON. To-morrow, Lane, I'm going Bunburying.

LANE. Yes, sir.

ALGERNON. I shall probably not be back till Monday. You can put up my dress clothes, my smoking jacket, and all the Bunbury suits . . .

LANE. Yes, sir. (*Handing sherry.*)

ALGERNON. I hope to-morrow will be a fine day, Lane.

LANE. It never is, sir.

ALGERNON. Lane, you're a perfect pessimist.

LANE. I do my best to give satisfaction, sir.

(*Enter Jack. Lane goes off.*)

JACK. There's a sensible, intellectual girl! the only girl I ever cared for in my life. (*Algernon is laughing immoderately.*) What on earth are you so amused at?

ALGERNON. Oh, I'm a little anxious about poor Bunbury, that's all.

JACK. If you don't take care, your friend Bunbury will get you into a serious scrape some day.

ALGERNON. I love scrapes. They are the only things that are never serious.

JACK. Oh, that's nonsense, Algy. You never talk anything but nonsense.

ALGERNON. Nobody ever does. (*Jack looks indignantly at him, and leaves the room. Algernon lights a cigarette, reads his shirt-cuff and smiles.*)

ACT 2

SCENE: *Garden at the Manor House. A flight of gray stone steps leads up to the house. The garden, an old-fashioned one, full of roses. Time of year, July. Basket chairs, and a table covered with books, are set under a large yew tree.*

(*Miss Prism discovered seated at the table. Cecily is at the back watering flowers.*)

MISS PRISM (*calling*). Cecily, Cecily! Surely such a utilitarian occupation as the watering of flowers is rather Moulton's duty than yours? Especially at a moment when intellectual pleasures await you. Your German grammar is on the table. Pray open it at page fifteen. We will repeat yesterday's lesson.

CECILY (*coming over very slowly*). But I don't like German. It isn't at all a becoming language. I know perfectly well that I look quite plain after my German lesson.

MISS PRISM. Child, you know how anxious your guardian is that you should improve yourself in every way. He laid particular stress on your German, as he was leaving for town yesterday. Indeed, he always lays stress on your German when he is leaving for town.

CECILY. Dear Uncle Jack is so very serious! Sometimes he is so serious that I think he cannot be quite well.

MISS PRISM (*drawing herself up*). Your guardian enjoys the best of health, and his gravity of demeanour is especially to be commended in one so comparatively young as he is. I know no one who has a higher sense of duty and responsibility.

CECILY. I suppose that is why he often looks a little bored when we three are together.

MISS PRISM. Cecily! I am surprised at you. Mr. Worthing has many troubles in his life. Idle merriment and triviality would be out of place in his conversation. You must remember his constant anxiety about that unfortunate young man, his brother.

CECILY. I wish Uncle Jack would allow the unfortunate young man, his brother, to come down here sometimes. We might have a good influence over him, Miss Prism. I am sure you certainly would. You know German, and geology, and things of that kind influence a man very much. (*Cecily begins to write in her diary.*)

MISS PRISM (*shaking her head*). I do not think that even I could produce any effect on a character that, according to his own brother's admission, is irretrievably weak and vacillating. Indeed, I am not sure that I would desire to reclaim him. I am not in favour of this modern mania for turning bad people into good people at a moment's notice. As a man sows so let him reap. You must put away your diary, Cecily. I really don't see why you should keep a diary at all.

CECILY. I keep a diary in order to enter the wonderful secrets of my life. If I didn't write them down I should probably forget all about them.

MISS PRISM. Memory, my dear Cecily, is the diary that we all carry about with us.

CECILY. Yes, but it usually chronicles the things that have never happened, and couldn't possibly have happened. I believe that Memory is responsible for nearly all the three-volume novels that Mudie sends us.

MISS PRISM. Do not speak slightingly of the three-volume novel, Cecily. I wrote one myself in earlier days.

CECILY. Did you really, Miss Prism? How wonderfully clever you are! I hope it did not end happily? I don't like novels that end happily. They depress me so much.

MISS PRISM. The good ended happily, and the bad unhappily. That is what Fiction means.

CECILY. I suppose so. But it seems very unfair. And was your novel ever published?

MISS PRISM. Alas! no. The manuscript unfortunately was abandoned. I use the word in the sense of lost or mislaid. To your work, child, these speculations are profitless.

CECILY (*smiling*). But I see dear Dr. Chasuble coming up through the garden.

MISS PRISM (*rising and advancing*). Dr. Chasuble! This is indeed a pleasure.

(*Enter Canon Chasuble.*)

CHASUBLE. And how are we this morning? Miss Prism, you are, I trust, well?

CECILY. Miss Prism has just been complaining of a slight headache. I think it would do her so much good to have a short stroll with you in the park, Dr. Chasuble.

MISS PRISM. Cecily, I have not mentioned anything about a headache.

CECILY. No, dear Miss Prism, I know that, but I felt instinctively that you had a headache. Indeed I was thinking about that, and not about my German lesson, when the Rector came in.

CHASUBLE. I hope, Cecily, you are not inattentive.

CECILY. Oh, I am afraid I am.

CHASUBLE. That is strange. Were I fortunate enough to be Miss Prism's pupil, I would hang upon her lips. (*Miss Prism glares.*) I spoke metaphorically.—My metaphor was drawn from bees. Ahem! Mr. Worthing, I suppose, has not returned from town yet?

MISS PRISM. We do not expect him till Monday afternoon.

CHASUBLE. Ah, yes, he usually likes to spend his Sunday in London. He is not one of those whose sole aim is enjoyment, as by all accounts, that unfortunate young man, his brother, seems to be. But I must not disturb Egeria and her pupil any longer.

MISS PRISM. Egeria? My name is Lætitia, Doctor.

CHASUBLE (*bowing*). A classical allusion merely, drawn from the Pagan authors. I shall see you both no doubt at Evensong.

MISS PRISM. I think, dear Doctor, I will have a stroll with you. I find I have a headache after all, and a walk might do it good.

CHASUBLE. With pleasure, Miss Prism, with pleasure. We might go as far as the schools and back.

MISS PRISM. That would be delightful. Cecily, you will read your Political Economy in my absence. The chapter on the Fall of the Rupee you may omit. It is somewhat too sensational. Even these metallic problems have their melodramatic side.

(*Goes down the garden with Dr. Chasuble.*)

CECILY (*picks up books and throws them back on table*). Horrid Political Economy! Horrid Geography! Horrid, horrid German!

(*Enter Merriman with a card on a salver.*)

MERRIMAN. Mr. Ernest Worthing has just driven over from the station. He has brought his luggage with him.

CECILY (*takes the card and reads it*). "Mr. Ernest Worthing, B 4 The Albany, W." Uncle Jack's brother! Did you tell him Mr. Worthing was in town?

MERRIMAN. Yes, Miss. He seemed very much disappointed. I mentioned that you and Miss Prism were in the garden. He said he was anxious to speak to you privately for a moment.

CECILY. Ask Mr. Ernest Worthing to come here. I suppose you had better talk to the housekeeper about a room for him.

MERRIMAN. Yes, Miss.   (*Merriman goes off.*)

CECILY. I have never met any really wicked person before. I feel rather frightened. I am so afraid he will look just like everyone else.

(*Enter Algernon, very gay and debonair.*)

He does!

ALGERNON (*raising his hat*). You are my little cousin Cecily, I'm sure.

CECILY. You are under some strange mistake. I am not little. In fact, I am more than usually tall for my age. (*Algernon is rather taken aback.*) But I am your cousin Cecily. You, I see from your card, are Uncle Jack's brother, my cousin Ernest, my wicked cousin Ernest.

ALGERNON. Oh! I am not really wicked at all, cousin Cecily. You mustn't think that I am wicked.

CECILY. If you are not, then you have certainly been deceiving us all in a very inexcusable manner. I hope you have not been leading a double life, pretending to be wicked and being really good all the time. That would be hypocrisy.

ALGERNON (*looks at her in amazement*). Oh! of course I have been rather reckless.

CECILY. I am glad to hear it.

ALGERNON. In fact, now you mention the subject, I have been very bad in my own small way.

CECILY. I don't think you should be so proud of that, though I am sure it must have been very pleasant.

ALGERNON. It is much pleasanter being here with you.

CECILY. I can't understand how you are here at all. Uncle Jack won't be back till Monday afternoon.

ALGERNON. That is a great disappointment. I am obliged to go up by the first train on Monday morning. I have a business appointment that I am anxious . . . to miss.

CECILY. Couldn't you miss it anywhere but in London?

ALGERNON. No; the appointment is in London.

CECILY. Well, I know, of course, how important it is not to keep a business engagement, if one wants to retain any sense of the beauty of life, but still I think you had better wait till Uncle Jack arrives. I know he wants to speak to you about your emigrating.

ALGERNON. About my what?

CECILY. Your emigrating. He has gone up to buy your outfit.

ALGERNON. I certainly wouldn't let Jack buy my outfit. He has no taste in neckties at all.

CECILY. I don't think you will require neckties. Uncle Jack is sending you to Australia.

ALGERNON. Australia! I'd sooner die.

CECILY. Well, he said at dinner on Wednesday night, that you would have to choose between this world, the next world, and Australia.

ALGERNON. Oh, well! The accounts I have received of Australia and the next world, are not particularly encouraging. This world is good enough for me, cousin Cecily.

CECILY. Yes, but are you good enough for it?

ALGERNON. I'm afraid I'm not that. That is why I want you to reform me. You might make that your mission, if you don't mind, cousin Cecily.

CECILY. I'm afraid I've not time, this afternoon.

ALGERNON. Well, would you mind my reforming myself this afternoon?

CECILY. That is rather Quixotic of you. But I think you should try.

ALGERNON. I will. I feel better already.

CECILY. You are looking a little worse.

ALGERNON. That is because I am hungry.

CECILY. How thoughtless of me. I should have remembered that when one is going to lead an entirely new life, one requires regular and wholesome meals. Won't you come in?

ALGERNON. Thank you. Might I have a button-hole first? I never have any appetite unless I have a button-hole first.

CECILY. A Maréchal Niel? (*Picks up scissors.*)

ALGERNON. No, I'd sooner have a pink rose.

CECILY. Why? (*Cuts a flower.*)

ALGERNON. Because you are like a pink rose, cousin Cecily.

CECILY. I don't think it can be right for you to talk to me like that. Miss Prism never says such things to me.

ALGERNON. Then Miss Prism is a short-sighted old lady. (*Cecily puts the rose in his button-hole.*) You are the prettiest girl I ever saw.

CECILY. Miss Prism says that all good looks are a snare.

ALGERNON. They are a snare that every sensible man would like to be caught in.

CECILY. Oh! I don't think I would care to catch a sensible man. I shouldn't know what to talk to him about. (*They pass into the house. Miss Prism and Dr. Chasuble return.*)

MISS PRISM. You are too much alone, dear Dr. Chasuble. You should get married. A misanthrope I can understand—a womanthrope, never!

CHASUBLE (*with a scholar's shudder*). Believe me, I do not deserve so neologistic a phrase. The precept as well as the practice of the Primitive Church was distinctly against matrimony.

MISS PRISM (*sententiously*). That is obviously the reason why the Primitive Church has not lasted up to the present day. And you do not seem to realize, dear Doctor, that by persistently remaining single, a man converts himself into a permanent public temptation. Men should be careful; this very celibacy leads weaker vessels astray.

CHASUBLE. But is a man not equally attractive when married?

MISS PRISM. No married man is ever attractive except to his wife.

CHASUBLE. And often, I've been told, not even to her.

MISS PRISM. That depends on the intellectual sympathies of the woman. Maturity can always be depended on. Ripeness can be trusted. Young women are green. (*Dr. Chasuble starts.*) I spoke horticulturally. My metaphor was drawn from fruits. But where is Cecily?

CHASUBLE. Perhaps she followed us to the schools.

(*Enter Jack slowly from the back of the garden. He is dressed in the deepest mourning, with crepe hatband and black gloves.*)

MISS PRISM. Mr. Worthing!

CHASUBLE. Mr. Worthing?

MISS PRISM. This is indeed a surprise. We did not look for you till Monday afternoon.

JACK (*shakes Miss Prism's hand in a tragic manner*). I have returned sooner than I expected. Dr. Chasuble, I hope you are well?

CHASUBLE. Dear Mr. Worthing, I trust this garb of woe does not betoken some terrible calamity?

JACK. My brother.

MISS PRISM. More shameful debts and extravagance?

CHASUBLE. Still leading his life of pleasure?

JACK (*shaking his head*). Dead!

CHASUBLE. Your brother Ernest dead?

JACK. Quite dead.

MISS PRISM. What a lesson for him! I trust he will profit by it.

CHASUBLE. Mr. Worthing, I offer you my sincere condolence. You have at least the consolation of knowing that you were always the most generous and forgiving of brothers.

JACK. Poor Ernest! He had many faults, but it is a sad, sad blow.

CHASUBLE. Very sad indeed. Were you with him at the end?

JACK. No. He died abroad; in Paris, in fact. I had a telegram last night from the manager of the Grand Hotel.

CHASUUBLE. Was the cause of death mentioned?

JACK. A severe chill, it seems.

MISS PRISM. As a man sows, so shall he reap.

CHASUBLE (*raising his hand*). Charity, dear Miss Prism, charity! None of us are perfect. I myself am peculiarly susceptible to draughts. Will the interment take place here?

JACK. No. He seems to have expressed a desire to be buried in Paris.

CHASUBLE. In Paris! (*Shakes his head.*) I fear that hardly points to any very serious state of mind at the last. You would no doubt wish me to make some slight allusion to this tragic domestic affliction next Sunday. (*Jack presses his hand convulsively.*) My sermon on the meaning of the manna in the wilderness can be adapted to almost any occasion, joyful, or, as in the present case, distressing. (*All sigh.*) I have preached it at harvest celebrations, christenings, confirmations, on days of humiliation and festal days. The last time I delivered it was in the Cathedral, as a charity sermon on behalf of the Society for the Prevention of Discontentment among the Upper Orders. The Bishop, who was present, was much struck by some of the analogies I drew.

JACK. Ah, that reminds me, you mentioned christenings I think, Dr. Chasuble? I suppose you know how to christen all right? (*Dr. Chasuble looks astounded.*) I mean, of course, you are continually christening, aren't you?

MISS PRISM. It is, I regret to say, one of the Rector's most constant duties in this parish. I have often spoken to the poorer classes on the subject. But they don't seem to know what thrift is.

CHASUBLE. But is there any particular infant in whom you are interested, Mr. Worthing? Your brother was, I believe, unmarried, was he not?

JACK. Oh, yes.

MISS PRISM (*bitterly*). People who live entirely for pleasure usually are.

JACK. But it is not for any child, dear Doctor. I am very fond of children. No! the fact is, I would like to be christened myself, this afternoon, if you have nothing better to do.

CHASUBLE. But surely, Mr. Worthing, you have been christened already?

JACK. I don't remember anything about it.

CHASUBLE. But have you any grave doubts on the subject?

JACK. I certainly intend to have. Of course, I don't know if the thing would bother you in any way, or if you think I am a little too old now.

CHASUBLE. Not at all. The sprinkling, and, indeed, the immersion of adults is a perfectly canonical practice.

JACK. Immersion!

CHASUBLE. You need have no apprehensions. Sprinkling is all that is necessary, or indeed I think advisable. Our weather is so changeable. At what hour would you wish the ceremony performed?

JACK. Oh, I might trot around about five if that would suit you.

CHASUBLE. Perfectly, perfectly! In fact I have two similar ceremonies to perform at that time. A case of twins that occurred recently in one of the outlying cottages on your own estate. Poor Jenkins the carter, a most hard-working man.

JACK. Oh! I don't see much fun in being christened along with other babies. It would be childish. Would half-past five do?

CHASUBLE. Admirably! Admirably! (*Takes out watch.*) And now, dear Mr. Worthing, I will not intrude any longer into a house of sorrow. I would merely beg you not to be too much bowed down by grief. What seem to us bitter trials at the moment are often blessings in disguise.

MISS PRISM. This seems to me a blessing of an extremely obvious kind.

(*Enter Cecily from the house.*)

CECILY. Uncle Jack! Oh, I am pleased to see you back. But what horrid clothes you have on! Do go and change them.

MISS PRISM. Cecily!

CHASUBLE. My child! my child! (*Cecily goes towards Jack; he kisses her brow in a melancholy manner.*)

CECILY. What is the matter, Uncle Jack? Do look happy! You look as if you had a toothache and I have such a surprise for you. Who do you think is in the dining-room? Your brother!

JACK. Who?

CECILY. Your brother Ernest. He arrived about half an hour ago.

JACK. What nonsense! I haven't got a brother.

CECILY. Oh, don't say that. However badly he may have behaved to you in the past he is still your brother. You couldn't be so heartless as to disown him. I'll tell him to come out. And you will shake hands with him, won't you, Uncle Jack? (*Runs back into the house.*)

CHASUBLE. There are very joyful tidings.

MISS PRISM. After we had all been resigned to his loss, his sudden return seems to me peculiarly distressing.

JACK. My brother is in the dining-room? I don't know what it all means. I think it is perfectly absurd.

(*Enter Algernon and Cecily hand in hand. They come slowly up to Jack.*)

JACK. Good heavens! (*Motions Algernon away.*)

ALGERNON. Brother John, I have come down from town to tell you that I am very sorry for all the trouble I have given you, and that I intend to lead a better life in the future. (*Jack glares at him and does not take his hand.*)

CECILY. Uncle Jack, you are not going to refuse your own brother's hand.

JACK. Nothing will induce me to take his hand. I think his coming down here disgraceful. He knows perfectly well why.

CECILY. Uncle Jack, do be nice. There is good in everyone. Ernest has just been telling me about his poor invalid friend, Mr. Bunbury, whom he goes to visit so often. And surely there must be much good in one who is kind to an invalid, and leaves the pleasures of London to sit by a bed of pain.

JACK. Oh, he has been talking about Bunbury, has he?

CECILY. Yes, he has told me all about poor Mr. Bunbury, and his terrible state of health.

JACK. Bunbury! Well, I won't have him talk to you about Bunbury or about anything else. It is enough to drive one perfectly frantic.

ALGERNON. Of course I admit that the faults were all on my side. But I must say that I think that Brother John's coldness to me is peculiarly painful. I expected a more enthusiastic welcome, especially considering it is the first time I have come here.

CECILY. Uncle Jack, if you don't shake hands with Ernest I will never forgive you.

JACK. Never forgive me?

CECILY. Never, never, never!

JACK. Well, this is the last time I shall ever do it. (*Shakes hands with Algernon and glares.*)

CHASUBLE. It's pleasant, is it not, to see so perfect a reconciliation? I think we might leave the two brothers together.

MISS PRISM. Cecily, you will come with us.

CECILY. Certainly, Miss Prism. My little task of reconciliation is over.

CHASUBLE. You have done a beautiful action to-day, dear child.

MISS PRISM. We must not be premature in our judgments.

CECILY. I feel very happy. (*They all go off.*)

JACK. You young scoundrel, Algy, you must get out of this place as soon as possible. I don't allow any Bunburying here.

(*Enter Merriman.*)

MERRIMAN. I have put Mr. Ernest's things in the room next to yours, sir. I suppose that is all right?

JACK. What?

MERRIMAN. Mr. Ernest's luggage, sir. I have unpacked it and put it in the room next to your own.

JACK. His luggage?

MERRIMAN. Yes, sir. Three portmanteaus, a dressing-case, two hat-boxes, and a large luncheon-basket.

ALGERNON. I am afraid I can't stay more than a week this time.

JACK. Merriman, order the dog-cart at once. Mr. Ernest has been suddenly called back to town.

MERRIMAN. Yes, sir. (*Goes back into the house.*)

ALGERNON. What a fearful liar you are, Jack. I have not been called back to town at all.

JACK. Yes, you have.

ALGERNON. I haven't heard anyone call me.

JACK. Your duty as a gentleman calls you back.

ALGERNON. My duty as a gentleman has never interfered with my pleasures in the smallest degree.

JACK. I can quite understand that.

ALGERNON. Well, Cecily is a darling.

JACK. You are not to talk of Miss Cardew like that. I don't like it.

ALGERNON. Well, I don't like your clothes. You look perfectly ridiculous in them. Why on earth don't you go up and change? It is perfectly childish to be in deep mourning for a man who is actually staying for a whole week with you in your house as a guest. I call it grotesque.

JACK. You are certainly not staying with me for a whole week as a guest or anything else. You have got to leave . . . by the four-five train.

ALGERNON. I certainly won't leave you so long as you are in mourning. It would be most unfriendly. If I were in mourning you would stay with me, I suppose. I should think it very unkind if you didn't.

JACK. Well, will you go if I change my clothes?

ALGERNON. Yes, if you are not too long. I never saw anybody take so long to dress, and with such little result.

JACK. Well, at any rate, that is better than being always overdressed as you are.

ALGERNON. If I am occasionally a little over-dressed, I make up for it by being always immensely over-educated.

JACK. Your vanity is ridiculous, your conduct an outrage, and your presence in my garden utterly absurd. However, you have got to catch the four-five, and I hope you will have a pleasant journey back to town. This Bunburying, as you call it, has not been a great success for you. (*Goes into the house.*)

ALGERNON. I think it has been a great success. I'm in love with Cecily, and that is everything. (*Enter Cecily at the back of the garden. She picks up the can and begins to water the flowers.*) But I must see her before I go, and make arrangements for another Bunbury. Ah, there she is.

CECILY. Oh, I merely came back to water the roses. I thought you were with Uncle Jack.

ALGERNON. He's gone to order the dog-cart for me.

CECILY. Oh, is he going to take you for a nice drive?

ALGERNON. He's going to send me away.

CECILY. Then have we got to part?

ALGERNON. I am afraid so. It's a very painful parting.

CECILY. It is always painful to part from people whom one has known for a very brief space of time. The absence of old friends one can endure with equanimity. But even a momentary separation from anyone to whom one has just been introduced is almost unbearable.

ALGERNON. Thank you.

(*Enter Merriman.*)

MERRIMAN. The dog-cart is at the door, sir. (*Algernon looking appealingly at Cecily.*)

CECILY. It can wait, Merriman . . . for . . . five minutes.

MERRIMAN. Yes, miss. (*Exit Merriman.*)

ALGERNON. I hope, Cecily, I shall not offend you if I state quite frankly and openly that you seem to me to be in every way the visible personification of absolute perfection.

CECILY. I think your frankness does you great credit, Ernest. If you will allow me I will copy your remarks into my diary. (*Goes over to table and begins writing in diary.*)

ALGERNON. Do you really keep a diary? I'd give any thing to look at it. May I?

CECILY. Oh, no. (*Puts her hand over it.*) You see, it is simply a very young girl's record of her own thoughts and impressions, and consequently meant for publication. When it appears in volume form I hope you will order a copy. But pray, Ernest, don't stop. I delight in taking down from dictation. I have reached "absolute perfection." You can go on. I am quite ready for more.

ALGERNON (*somewhat taken aback*). Ahem! Ahem!

CECILY. Oh, don't cough, Ernest. When one is dictating one should speak fluently and not cough. Besides I don't know how to spell a cough. (*Writes as Algernon speaks.*)

ALGERNON (*speaking very rapidly*). Cecily, ever since I first looked upon your wonderful and incomparable beauty, I have dared to love you wildly, passionately, devotedly, hopelessly.

CECILY. I don't think that you should tell me that you love me wildly, passionately, devotedly, hopelessly. Hopelessly doesn't seem to make much sense, does it?

ALGERNON. Cecily!

(*Enter Merriman.*)

MERRIMAN. The dog-cart is waiting, sir.

ALGERNON. Tell it to come round next week, at the same hour.

MERRIMAN (*looks at Cecily, who makes no sign*). Yes, sir.

(*Merriman retires.*)

CECILY. Uncle Jack would be very much annoyed if he knew you were staying on till next week, at the same hour.

ALGERNON. Oh, I don't care about Jack. I don't care for anybody in the whole world but you. I love you, Cecily. You will marry me, won't you?

CECILY. You silly you! Of course. Why, we have been engaged for the last three months.

ALGERNON. For the last three months?

CECILY. Yes, it will be exactly three months on Thursday.

ALGERNON. But how did we become engaged?

CECILY. Well, ever since dear Uncle Jack first confessed to us that he had a younger brother who was very wicked and bad, you of course have formed the chief topic of conversation between myself and Miss Prism. And of course a man who is much talked about is always very attractive. One feels there must be something in him after all. I daresay it was foolish of me, but I fell in love with you, Ernest.

ALGERNON. Darling! And when was the engagement actually settled?

CECILY. On the 14th of February last. Worn out by your entire ignorance of my existence, I determined to end the matter one way or the other, and after a long struggle with myself I accepted you under this dear old tree here. The next day I bought this little ring in your name, and this is the little bangle with the true lovers' knot I promised you always to wear.

ALGERNON. Did I give you this? It's very pretty, isn't it?

CECILY. Yes, you've wonderfully good taste, Ernest. It's the excuse I've always given for your leading such a bad life. And this is the box in which I keep all your dear letters. (*Kneels at table, opens box, and produces letters tied up with blue ribbon.*)

ALGERNON. My letters! But my own sweet Cecily, I have never written you any letters.

CECILY. You need hardly remind me of that, Ernest. I remember only too well that I was forced to write your letters for you. I wrote always three times a week, and sometimes oftener.

ALGERNON. Oh, do let me read them, Cecily?

CECILY. Oh, I couldn't possibly. They would make you far too conceited. (*Replaces box.*) The three you wrote me after I had broken off the engagement are so beautiful, and so badly spelled, that even now I can hardly read them without crying a little.

ALGERNON. But was our engagement ever broken off?

CECILY. Of course it was. On the 22nd of last March. You can see the entry if you like. (*Shows diary.*) "Today I broke off my engagement with Ernest. I feel it is better to do so. The weather still continues charming."

ALGERNON. But why on earth did you break it off? What had I done? I had done nothing at all, Cecily. I am very much hurt indeed to hear you broke it off. Particularly when the weather was so charming.

CECILY. It would hardly have been a really serious engagement if it hadn't been broken off at least once. But I forgave you before the week was out.

ALGERNON (*crossing to her, and kneeling*). What a perfect angel you are, Cecily.

CECILY. You dear romantic boy. (*He kisses her, she puts her fingers through his hair.*) I hope your hair curls naturally, does it?

ALGERNON. Yes, darling, with a little help from others.

CECILY. I am so glad.

ALGERNON. You'll never break off our engagement again, Cecily?

CECILY. I don't think I could break it off now that I have actually met you. Besides, of course, that is the question of your name.

ALGERNON. Yes, of course. (*Nervously.*)

CECILY. You must not laugh at me, darling, but it had always been a girlish dream of mine to love some one whose name was Ernest. (*Algernon rises, Cecily also.*) There is something in that name that seems to inspire absolute confidence. I pity any poor married woman whose husband is not called Ernest.

ALGERNON. But, my dear child, do you mean to say you could not love me if I had some other name?

CECILY. But what name?

ALGERNON. Oh, any name you like—Algernon, for instance. . . .

CECILY. But I don't like the name of Algernon.

ALGERNON. Well, my own dear, sweet, loving little darling, I really can't see why you should object to the name of Algernon. It is not at all a bad name. In fact, it is rather an aristocratic name. Half of the chaps who get into the Bankruptcy Court are called Algernon. But seriously, Cecily . . . (*Moving to her*) . . . if my name was Algy, couldn't you love me?

CECILY (*rising*). I might respect you, Ernest, I might admire your character, but I fear that I should not be able to give you my undivided attention.

ALGERNON. Ahem! Cecily! (*Picking up hat.*) Your Rector here is, I suppose, thoroughly experienced in the practice of all the rites and ceremonials of the church?

CECILY. Oh, yes. Dr. Chasuble is a most learned man. He has never written a single book, so you can imagine how much he knows.

ALGERNON. I must see him at once on a most important christening—I mean on most important business.

CECILY. Oh!

ALGERNON. I sha'n't be away more than half an hour.

CECILY. Considering that we have been engaged since February the 14th, and that I only met you to-day for the first time, I think it is rather hard that you should leave me for so long a period as half an hour. Couldn't you make it twenty minutes?

ALGERNON. I'll be back in no time. (*Kisses her and rushes down the garden.*)

CECILY. What an impetuous boy he is. I like his hair so much. I must enter his proposal in my diary.

(*Enter Merriman.*)

MERRIMAN. A Miss Fairfax has just called to see Mr. Worthing. On very important business, Miss Fairfax states.

CECILY. Isn't Mr. Worthing in his library?

MERRIMAN. Mr. Worthing went over in the direction of the Rectory some time ago.

CECILY. Pray ask the lady to come out here; Mr. Worthing is sure to be back soon. And you can bring tea.

MERRIMAN. Yes, miss.   (*Goes out.*)

CECILY. Miss Fairfax! I suppose one of the many good elderly women who are associated with Uncle Jack in some of his philanthropic work in London. I don't quite like women who are interested in philanthropic work. I think it is so forward of them.

(*Enter Merriman.*)

MERRIMAN. Miss Fairfax.

(*Enter Gwendolen. Exit Merriman.*)

CECILY (*advancing to meet her*). Pray let me introduce myself to you. My name is Cecily Cardew.

GWENDOLEN. Cecily Cardew? (*Moving to her and shaking hands.*) What a very sweet name! Something tells me that we are going to be great friends. I like you already more than I can say. My first impressions of people are never wrong.

CECILY. How nice of you to like me so much after we have known each other such a comparatively short time. Pray sit down.

GWENDOLEN (*still standing up*). I may call you Cecily, may I not?

CECILY. With pleasure!

GWENDOLEN. And you will always call me Gwendolen, won't you?

CECILY. If you wish.

GWENDOLEN. Then that is all quite settled, is it not?

CECILY. I hope so. (*A pause. They both sit down together.*)

GWENDOLEN. Perhaps this might be a favourable opportunity for my mentioning who I am. My father is Lord Bracknell. You have never heard of papa, I suppose?

CECILY. I don't think so.

GWENDOLEN. Outside the family circle, papa, I am glad to say, is entirely unknown. I think that is quite as it should be. The home seems to me to be the proper sphere for the man. And certainly once a man begins to neglect his domestic duties he becomes painfully effeminate, does he not? And I don't like that. It makes men so very attractive. Cecily, mamma, whose views on education are remarkably strict, has brought me up to be extremely short-sighted; it is part of her system; so do you mind my looking at you through my glasses?

CECILY. Oh, not at all, Gwendolen. I am very fond of being looked at.

GWENDOLEN (*after examining Cecily carefully through a lorgnette*). You are here on a short visit, I suppose.

CECILY. Oh, no, I live here.

GWENDOLEN (*severely*). Really? Your mother, no doubt, or some female relative of advanced years, resides here also?

CECILY. Oh, no. I have no mother, nor, in fact, any relations.

GWENDOLEN. Indeed?

CECILY. My dear guardian, with the assistance of Miss Prism, has the arduous task of looking after me.

GWENDOLEN. Your guardian?

CECILY. Yes, I am Mr. Worthing's ward.

GWENDOLEN. Oh! It is strange he never mentioned to me that he had a ward. How secretive of him! He grows more interesting hourly. I am not sure, however, that the news inspires me with feelings of unmixed delight. (*Rising and going to her.*) I am very fond of you, Cecily; I have liked you ever since I met you. But I am bound to state that now that I know that you are Mr. Worthing's ward, I cannot help expressing a wish you were—well, just a little older than you seem to be—and not quite so very alluring in appearance. In fact, if I may speak candidly—

CECILY. Pray do! I think that whenever one has anything unpleasant to say, one should always be quite candid.

GWENDOLEN. Well, to speak with perfect candour, Cecily, I wish that you were fully forty-two, and more than usually plain for your age. Ernest has a strong upright nature. He is the very soul of truth and honour. Disloyalty would be as impossible to him as deception. But even men of the noblest possible moral character are extremely susceptible to the influence of the physical charms of others. Modern, no less than Ancient History, supplies us with many most painful examples of what I refer to. If it were not so, indeed, History would be quite unreadable.

CECILY. I beg your pardon, Gwendolen, did you say Ernest?

GWENDOLEN. Yes.

CECILY. Oh, but it is not Mr. Ernest Worthing who is my guardian. It is his brother—his elder brother.

GWENDOLEN (*sitting down again*). Ernest never mentioned to me that he had a brother.

CECILY. I am sorry to say they have not been on good terms for a long time.

GWENDOLEN. Ah! that accounts for it. And now that I think of it I have never heard any man mention his brother. The subject seems distasteful to most men. Cecily, you have lifted a load from my mind. I was growing almost anxious. It would have been terrible if any cloud had come across a friendship like ours, would it not? Of course you are quite, quite sure that it is not Mr. Ernest Worthing who is your guardian?

CECILY. Quite sure. (*A pause.*) In fact, I am going to be his.

GWENDOLEN (*enquiringly*). I beg your pardon?

CECILY (*rather shy and confidingly*). Dearest Gwendolen, there is no reason why I should make a secret of it to you. Our little county newspaper is sure to chronicle the fact next week. Mr. Ernest Worthing and I are engaged to be married.

GWENDOLEN (*quite politely, rising*). My darling Cecily, I think there must be some slight error. Mr. Ernest Worthing is engaged to me. The announcement will appear in the *Morning Post* on Saturday at the latest.

CECILY (*very politely, rising*). I am afraid you must be under some misconception. Ernest proposed to me exactly ten minutes ago. (*Shows diary.*)

GWENDOLEN (*examines diary through her lorgnette carefully*). It is certainly very curious, for he asked me to be his wife yesterday afternoon at 5.30. If you would care to verify the incident, pray do so. (*Produces diary of her own.*) I never travel without my diary. One should always have something sensational to read in the train. I am so sorry, dear Cecily, if it is any disappointment to you, but I am afraid I have the prior claim.

CECILY. It would distress me more than I can tell you, dear Gwendolen, if it caused you any mental or physical anguish, but I feel bound to point out that since Ernest proposed to you he clearly has changed his mind.

GWENDOLEN (*meditatively*). If the poor fellow has been entrapped into any foolish promise I shall consider it my duty to rescue him at once, and with a firm hand.

CECILY (*thoughtfully and sadly*). Whatever unfortunate entanglement my dear boy may have got into, I will never reproach him with it after we are married.

GWENDOLEN. Do you allude to me, Miss Cardew, as an entanglement? You are presumptuous. On an occasion of this kind it becomes more than a moral duty to speak one's mind. It becomes a pleasure.

CECILY. Do you suggest, Miss Fairfax, that I entrapped Ernest into an engagement? How dare you? This is no time for wearing the shallow mask of manners. When I see a spade I call it a spade.

GWENDOLEN (*satirically*). I am glad to say that I have never seen a spade. It is obvious that our social spheres have been widely different.

(*Enter Merriman, followed by the footman. He carries a salver, tablecloth, and plate-stand. Cecily is about to retort. The presence of the servants exercises a restraining influence, under which both girls chafe.*)

MERRIMAN. Shall I lay tea here as usual, miss?

CECILY (*sternly, in a calm voice*). Yes, as usual. (*Merriman begins to clear and lay cloth. A long pause. Cecily and Gwendolen glare at each other.*)

GWENDOLEN. Are there many interesting walks in the vicinity, Miss Cardew?

CECILY. Oh, yes, a great many. From the top of one of the hills quite close one can see five counties.

GWENDOLEN. Five counties! I don't think I should like that. I hate crowds.

CECILY (*sweetly*). I suppose that is why you live in town? (*Gwendolen bites her lip, and beats her foot nervously with her parasol.*)

GWENDOLEN (*looking round*). Quite a well-kept garden this is, Miss Cardew.

CECILY. So glad you like it, Miss Fairfax.

GWENDOLEN. I had no idea there were any flowers in the country.

CECILY. Oh, flowers are as common here, Miss Fairfax, as people are in London.

GWENDOLEN. Personally I cannot understand how anybody manages to exist in the country, if anybody who is anybody does. The country always bores me to death.

CECILY. Ah! This is what the newspapers call agricultural depression, is it not? I believe the aristocracy are suffering very much from it just at present. It is almost an epidemic amongst them, I have been told. May I offer you some tea, Miss Fairfax?

GWENDOLEN (*with elaborate politeness*). Thank you. (*Aside.*) Detestable girl! But I require tea!

CECILY (*sweetly*). Sugar?

GWENDOLEN (*superciliously*). No, thank you. Sugar is not fashionable any more. (*Cecily looks angrily at her, takes up the tongs and puts four lumps of sugar into the cup.*)

CECILY (*severely*). Cake or bread and butter?

GWENDOLEN (*in a bored manner*). Bread and butter, please. Cake is rarely seen at the best houses nowadays.

CECILY (*cuts a very large slice of cake, and puts it on the tray*). Hand that to Miss Fairfax. (*Merriman does so, and goes out with footman. Gwendolen drinks the tea and makes a grimace. Puts down cup at once, reaches out her hand to the bread and butter, looks at it, and finds it is cake. Rises in indignation.*)

GWENDOLEN. You have filled my tea with lumps of sugar, and though I asked most distinctly for bread and butter, you have given me cake. I am known for the gentleness of my disposition, and the extraordinary sweetness of my nature, but I warn you, Miss Cardew, you may go too far.

CECILY (*rising*). To save my poor, innocent, trusting boy from the machinations of any other girl there are no lengths to which I would not go.

GWENDOLEN. From the moment I saw you I distrusted you. I felt that you were false and deceitful. I am never deceived in such matters. My first impressions of people are invariably right.

CECILY. It seems to me, Miss Fairfax, that I am trespassing on your valuable time. No doubt you have many other calls of a similar character to make in the neighbourhood.

(*Enter Jack.*)

GWENDOLEN (*catching sight of him*). Ernest! My own Ernest!

JACK. Gwendolen! Darling! (*Offers to kiss her.*)

GWENDOLEN (*drawing back*). A moment! May I ask if you are engaged to be married to this young lady? (*Points to Cecily.*)

JACK (*laughing*). To dear little Cecily! Of course not! What could have put such an idea into your pretty little head?

GWENDOLEN. Thank you. You may. (*Offers her cheek.*)

CECILY (*very sweetly*). I knew there must be some misunderstanding, Miss Fairfax. The gentleman whose arm is at present around your waist is my dear guardian, Mr. John Worthing.

GWENDOLEN. I beg your pardon?

CECILY. This is Uncle Jack.

GWENDOLEN (*receding*). Jack! Oh!

(*Enter Algernon.*)

CECILY. Here is Ernest.

ALGERNON (*goes straight over to Cecily without noticing anyone else*). My own love! (*Offers to kiss her.*)

CECILY (*drawing back*). A moment, Ernest! May I ask you— are you engaged to be married to this young lady?

ALGERNON (*looking round*). To what young lady? Good heavens! Gwendolen!

CECILY. Yes, to good heavens, Gwendolen, I mean to Gwendolen.

ALGERNON (*laughing*). Of course not! What could have put such an idea into your pretty little head?

CECILY. Thank you. (*Presenting her cheek to be kissed.*) You may. (*Algernon kisses her.*)

GWENDOLEN. I felt there was some slight error, Miss Cardew. The gentleman who is now embracing you is my cousin, Mr. Algernon Moncrieff.

CECILY (*breaking away from Algernon*). Algernon Moncrieff! Oh! (*The two girls move towards each other and put their arms round each other's waists as if for protection.*)

CECILY. Are you called Algernon?

ALGERNON. I cannot deny it.

CECILY. Oh!

GWENDOLEN. Is your name really John?

JACK (*standing rather proudly*). I could deny it if I liked. I could deny anything if I liked. But my name certainly is John. It has been John for years.

CECILY (*to Gwendolen*). A gross deception has been practised on both of us.

GWENDOLEN. My poor wounded Cecily!

CECILY. My sweet, wronged Gwendolen!

GWENDOLEN (*slowly and seriously*). You will call me sister, will you not? (*They embrace. Jack and Algernon groan and walk up and down.*)

CECILY (*rather brightly*). There is just one question I would like to be allowed to ask my guardian.

GWENDOLEN. An admirable idea! Mr. Worthing, there is just one question I would like to be permitted to put to you. Where is your brother Ernest? We are both engaged to be married to your brother Ernest, so it is a matter of some importance to us to know where your brother Ernest is at present.

JACK (*slowly and hesitatingly*). Gwendolen—Cecily—it is very painful for me to be forced to speak the truth. It is the first time in my life that I have ever been reduced to such a painful position, and I am really quite inexperienced in doing anything of the kind. However I will tell you quite frankly that I have no brother Ernest. I have no brother at all. I never had a brother in my life, and I certainly have not the smallest intention of ever having one in the future.

CECILY (*surprised*). No brother at all?

JACK (*cheerily*). None!

GWENDOLEN (*severely*). Had you never a brother of any kind?

JACK (*pleasantly*). Never. Not even of any kind.

GWENDOLEN. I am afraid it is quite clear, Cecily, that neither of us is engaged to be married to anyone.

CECILY. It is not a very pleasant position for a young girl suddenly to find herself in. Is it?

GWENDOLEN. Let us go into the house. They will hardly venture to come after us there.

CECILY. No, men are so cowardly, aren't they? (*They retire into the house with scornful looks.*)

JACK. This ghastly state of things is what you call Bunburying, I suppose?

ALGERNON. Yes, and a perfectly wonderful Bunbury it is. The most wonderful Bunbury I have ever had in my life.

JACK. Well, you've no right whatsoever to Bunbury here.

ALGERNON. That is absurd. One has a right to Bunbury anywhere one chooses. Every serious Bunburyist knows that.

JACK. Serious Bunburyist! Good heavens!

ALGERNON. Well, one must be serious about something, if one wants to have any amusement in life. I happen to be serious about Bunburying. What on earth you are serious about I haven't got the remotest idea. About everything, I should fancy. You have such an absolutely trivial nature.

JACK. Well, the only small satisfaction I have in the whole of this wretched business is that your friend Bunbury is quite exploded. You won't be able to run down to the country quite so often as you used to do, dear Algy. And a very good thing, too.

ALGERNON. Your brother is a little off colour, isn't he, dear Jack? You won't be able to disappear to London quite so frequently as your wicked custom was. And not a bad thing, either.

JACK. As for your conduct towards Miss Cardew, I must say that your taking in a sweet, simple, innocent girl like that is quite inexcusable. To say nothing of the fact that she is my ward.

ALGERNON. I can see no possible defence at all for your deceiving a brilliant, clever, thoroughly experienced young lady like Miss Fairfax. To say nothing of the fact that she is my cousin.

JACK. I wanted to be engaged to Gwendolen, that is all. I love her.

ALGERNON. Well, I simply wanted to be engaged to Cecily. I adore her.

JACK. There is certainly no chance of your marrying Miss Cardew.

ALGERNON. I don't think there is much likelihood, Jack, of you and Miss Fairfax being united.

JACK. Well, that is no business of yours.

ALGERNON. If it was my business, I wouldn't talk about it. (*Begins to eat muffins.*) It is very vulgar to talk about one's business. Only people like stock-brokers do that, and then merely at dinner parties.

JACK. How you can sit there, calmly eating muffins, when we are in this horrible trouble, I can't make out. You seem to me to be perfectly heartless.

ALGERNON. Well, I can't eat muffins in an agitated manner. The butter would probably get on my cuffs. One should always eat muffins quite calmly. It is the only way to eat them.

JACK. I say it's perfectly heartless your eating muffins at all, under the circumstances.

ALGERNON. When I am in trouble, eating is the only thing that consoles me. Indeed, when I am in really great trouble, as anyone who knows me intimately will tell you, I refuse everything except food and drink. At the present moment I am eating muffins because I am unhappy. Besides, I am particularly fond of muffins. (*Rising.*)

JACK (*rising*). Well, that is no reason why you should eat them all in that greedy way. (*Takes muffin from Algernon.*)

ALGERNON (*offering tea-cake*). I wish you would have tea-cake instead. I don't like tea-cake.

JACK. Good heavens! I suppose a man may eat his own muffins in his own garden.

ALGERNON. But you have just said it was perfectly heartless to eat muffins.

JACK. I said it was perfectly heartless of you, under the circumstances. That is a very different thing.

ALGERNON. That may be. But the muffins are the same. (*He seizes the muffin dish from Jack.*)

JACK. Algy, I wish to goodness you would go.

ALGERNON. You can't possibly ask me to go without having some dinner. It's absurd. I never go without my dinner. No one ever does, except vegetarians and people like that. Besides I have just made arrangements with Dr.

Chasuble to be christened at a quarter to six under the name of Ernest.

JACK. My dear fellow, the sooner you give up that nonsense the better. I made arrangements this morning with Chasuble to be christened myself at 5:30, and I naturally will take the name of Ernest. Gwendolen would wish it. We can't both be christened Ernest. It's absurd. Besides, I have a perfect right to be christened if I like. There is no evidence at all that I ever have been christened by anybody. I should think it extremely probable I never was, and so does Dr. Chasuble. It is entirely different in your case. You have been christened already.

ALGERNON. Yes, but I have not been christened for years.

JACK. Yes, but you have been christened. That is the important thing.

ALGERNON. Quite so. So I know my constitution can stand it. If you are not quite sure about your ever having been christened, I must say I think it rather dangerous your venturing on it now. It might make you very unwell. You can hardly have forgotten that someone very closely connected with you was very nearly carried off this week in Paris by a severe chill.

JACK. Yes, but you said yourself that a severe chill was not hereditary.

ALGERNON. It usedn't to be, I know—but I daresay it is now. Science is always making wonderful improvements in things.

JACK (*picking up the muffin-dish*). Oh, that is nonsense; you are always talking nonsense.

ALGERNON. Jack, you are at the muffins again! I wish you wouldn't. There are only two left. (*Takes them.*) I told you I was particularly fond of muffins.

JACK. But I hate tea-cake.

ALGERNON. Why on earth then do you allow tea-cake to be served up for your guests? What ideas you have of hospitality!

JACK. Algernon! I have already told you to go. I don't want you here. Why don't you go?

ALGERNON. I haven't quite finished my tea yet, and there is still one muffin left. (*Jack groans, and sinks into a chair. Algernon still continues eating.*)

CURTAIN

ACT 3

SCENE: *Morning-room at the Manor House. Gwendolen and Cecily are at the window, looking out into the garden.*

GWENDOLEN. The fact that they did not follow us at once into the house, as anyone else would have done, seems to me to show that they have some sense of shame left.

CECILY. They have been eating muffins. That looks like repentance.

GWENDOLEN (*after a pause*). They don't seem to notice us at all. Couldn't you cough?

GWENDOLEN. They're looking at us. What effrontery!

CECILY. They're approaching. That's very forward of them.

GWENDOLEN. Let us preserve a dignified silence.

CECILY. Certainly, it's the only thing to do now.

(*Enter Jack, followed by Algernon. They whistle some dreadful popular air from a British opera.*)

GWENDOLEN. This dignified silence seems to produce an unpleasant effect.

CECILY. A most distasteful one.

GWENDOLEN. But we will not be the first to speak.

CECILY. Certainly not.

GWENDOLEN. Mr. Worthing, I have something very particular to ask you. Much depends on your reply.

CECILY. Gwendolen, your common sense is invaluable. Mr. Moncrieff, kindly answer me the following question. Why did you pretend to be my guardian's brother?

ALGERNON. In order that I might have an opportunity of meeting you.

CECILY (*to Gwendolen*). That certainly seems a satisfactory explanation, does it not?

GWENDOLEN. Yes, dear, if you can believe him.

CECILY. I don't. But that does not affect the wonderful beauty of his answer.

GWENDOLEN. True. In matters of grave importance, style, not sincerity, is the vital thing. Mr. Worthing, what explanation can you offer to me for pretending to have a brother? Was it in order that you might have an opportunity of coming up to town to see me as often as possible?

JACK. Can you doubt it, Miss Fairfax?

GWENDOLEN. I have the gravest doubts upon the subject. But I intend to crush them. This is not the moment for German scepticism. (*Moving to Cecily.*) Their explanations appear to be quite satisfactory, especially Mr. Worthing's. That seems to me to have the stamp of truth upon it.

CECILY. I am more than content with what Mr. Moncrieff said. His voice alone inspires one with absolute credulity.

GWENDOLEN. Then you think we should forgive them?

CECILY. Yes. I mean no.

GWENDOLEN. True! I had forgotten. There are principles at stake that one cannot surrender. Which of us should tell them? The task is not a pleasant one.

CECILY. Could we not both speak at the same time?

GWENDOLEN. An excellent idea! I nearly always speak at the same time as other people. Will you take the time from me?

CECILY. Certainly. (*Gwendolen beats time with uplifted finger.*)

GWENDOLEN and CECILY (*speaking together*). Your Christian names are still an insuperable barrier. That is all!

JACK and ALGERNON (*speaking together*). Our Christian names! Is that all? But we are going to be christened this afternoon.

GWENDOLEN (*to Jack*). For my sake you are prepared to do this terrible thing?

JACK. I am.

CECILY (*to Algernon*). To please me you are ready to face this fearful ordeal?

ALGERNON. I am!

GWENDOLEN. How absurd to talk of the equality of the sexes! Where questions of self-sacrifice are concerned, men are infinitely beyond us.

JACK. We are. (*Clasps hands with Algernon.*)

CECILY. They have moments of physical courage of which we women know absolutely nothing.

GWENDOLEN (*to Jack*). Darling!

ALGERNON (*to Cecily*). Darling! (*They fall into each other's arms.*)

(*Enter Merriman. When he enters he coughs loudly, seeing the situation.*)

MERRIMAN. Ahem! Ahem! Lady Bracknell!

JACK. Good heavens!

(*Enter Lady Bracknell. The couples separate in alarm. Exit Merriman.*)

LADY BRACKNELL. Gwendolen! What does this mean?

GWENDOLEN. Merely that I am engaged to be married to Mr. Worthing, Mamma.

LADY BRACKNELL. Come here. Sit down. Sit down immediately. Hesitation of any kind is a sign of mental decay in the young, of physical weakness in the old. (*Turns to Jack.*) Apprised, sir, of my daughter's sudden flight by her trusty maid, whose confidence I purchased by means of a small coin, I followed her at once by a luggage train. Her unhappy father is, I am glad to say, under the impression that she is attending a more than usually lengthy lecture by the University Extension Scheme on the Influence of a Permanent Income on Thought. I do not propose to undeceive him. Indeed I have never undeceived him on any question. I would consider it wrong. But of course, you will clearly understand that all communication between yourself and my daughter must cease immediately from this moment. On this point, as indeed on all points, I am firm.

JACK. I am engaged to be married to Gwendolen, Lady Bracknell!

LADY BRACKNELL. You are nothing of the kind, sir. And now, as regards Algernon! . . . Algernon!

ALGERNON. Yes, Aunt Augusta.

LADY BRACKNELL. May I ask if it is in this house that your invalid friend Mr. Bunbury resides?

ALGERNON (*stammering*). Oh no! Bunbury doesn't live here. Bunbury is somewhere else at present. In fact, Bunbury is dead.

LADY BRACKNELL. Dead! When did Mr. Bunbury die? His death must have been extremely sudden.

ALGERNON (*airily*). Oh, I killed Bunbury this afternoon. I mean poor Bunbury died this afternoon.

LADY BRACKNELL. What did he die of?

ALGERNON. Bunbury? Oh, he was quite exploded.

LADY BRACKNELL. Exploded! Was he the victim of a revolutionary outrage? I was not aware that Mr. Bunbury was interested in social legislation. If so, he is well punished for his morbidity.

ALGERNON. My dear Aunt Augusta, I mean he was found out! The doctors found out that Bunbury could not live, that is what I mean—so Bunbury died.

LADY BRACKNELL. He seems to have had great confidence in the opinion of his physicians. I am glad, however, that he made up his mind at the last to some definite course of action, and acted under proper medical advice. And now that we have finally got rid of this Mr. Bunbury, may I ask, Mr. Worthing, who is that young person whose hand my nephew Algernon is now holding in what seems to me a peculiarly unnecessary manner?

JACK. That lady is Miss Cecily Cardew, my ward. (*Lady Bracknell bows coldly to Cecily.*)

ALGERNON. I am engaged to be married to Cecily, Aunt Augusta.

LADY BRACKNELL. I beg your pardon?

CECILY. Mr. Moncrieff and I are engaged to be married, Lady Bracknell.

LADY BRACKNELL (*with a shiver, crossing to the sofa and sitting down*). I do not know whether there is anything peculiarly exciting in the air of this particular part of Hertfordshire, but the number of engagements that go on seems to me considerably above the proper average that statistics have laid down for our guidance. I think some preliminary enquiry on my part would not be out of place. Mr. Worthing, is Miss Cardew at all connected with any of the larger railway stations in London? I merely desire information. Until yesterday I had no idea that there were any families or persons whose origin was a Terminus. (*Jack looks perfectly furious, but restrains himself.*)

JACK (*in a clear, cold voice*). Miss Cardew is the granddaughter of the late Mr. Thomas Cardew of 149, Belgrave Square, S.W.; Gervase Park, Dorking, Surrey; and the Sporran, Fifeshire, N.B.

LADY BRACKNELL. That sounds not unsatisfactory. Three addresses always inspire confidence, even in tradesmen. But what proof have I of their authenticity?

JACK. I have carefully preserved the Court Guide of the period. They are open to your inspection, Lady Bracknell.

LADY BRACKNELL (*grimly*). I have known strange errors in that publication.

JACK. Miss Cardew's family solicitors are Messrs. Markby, Markby, and Markby.

LADY BRACKNELL. Markby, Markby, and Markby? A firm of the very highest position in their profession. Indeed I am told that one of the Mr. Markbys is occasionally to be seen at dinner parties. So far I am satisfied.

JACK (*very irritably*). How extremely kind of you, Lady Bracknell! I have also in my possession, you will be pleased to hear, certificates of Miss Cardew's birth, baptism, whooping cough, registration, vaccination, confirmation, and the measles; both the German and the English variety.

LADY BRACKNELL. Ah! A life crowded with incident, I see; though perhaps somewhat too exciting for a young girl. I am not myself in favor of premature experiences. (*Rises, looks at her watch.*) Gwendolen! the time approaches for our departure. We have not a moment to lose. As a matter of form, Mr. Worthing, I had better ask you if Miss Cardew has any little fortune?

JACK. Oh, about a hundred and thirty thousand pounds in the Funds. That is all. Good-bye, Lady Bracknell. So pleased to have seen you.

LADY BRACKNELL (*sitting down again*). A moment, Mr. Worthing. A hundred and thirty thousand pounds! And in the Funds! Miss Cardew seems to me a most attractive young lady, now that I look at her. Few girls of the present day have any really solid qualities, any of the qualities that last, and improve with time. We live, I regret to say, in an age of surfaces. (*To Cecily.*) Come over here, dear. (*Cecily goes across.*) Pretty child! your dress is sadly simple, and your hair seems almost as Nature might have left it. But we can soon alter all that. A thoroughly experienced French maid produces a really marvellous result in a very brief space of time. I remember recommending one to young Lady Lancing, and after three months her own husband did not know her.

JACK (*aside*). And after six months nobody knew her.

LADY BRACKNELL (*glares at Jack for a few moments. Then bends, with a practised smile, to Cecily*). Kindly turn round, sweet child. (*Cecily turns completely round.*) No, the side view is what I want. (*Cecily presents her profile.*) Yes, quite as I expected. There are distinct social possibilities in your profile. The two weak points in our age are its want of principle and its want of profile. The chin a little higher, dear. Style largely depends on the way the chin is worn. They are worn very high, just at present. Algernon!

ALGERNON. Yes, Aunt Augusta!

LADY BRACKNELL. There are distinct social possibilities in Miss Cardew's profile.

ALGERNON. Cecily is the sweetest, dearest, prettiest girl in the whole world. And I don't care twopence about social possibilities.

LADY BRACKNELL. Never speak disrespectfully of society, Algernon. Only people who can't get into it do that. (*To Cecily.*) Dear child, of course you know that Algernon has nothing but his debts to depend upon. But I do not approve of mercenary marriages. When I married Lord Bracknell I had no fortune of any kind. But I never dreamed for a moment of allowing that to stand in my way. Well, I suppose I must give my consent.

ALGERNON. Thank you, Aunt Augusta.

LADY BRACKNELL. Cecily, you may kiss me!

CECILY (*kisses her*). Thank you, Lady Bracknell.

LADY BRACKNELL. You may also address me as Aunt Augusta for the future.

CECILY. Thank you, Aunt Augusta.

LADY BRACKNELL. The marriage, I think, had better take place quite soon.

ALGERNON. Thank you, Aunt Augusta.

CECILY. Thank you, Aunt Augusta.

LADY BRACKNELL. To speak frankly, I am not in favour of long engagements. They give people the opportunity of finding out each other's character before marriage, which I think is never advisable.

JACK. I beg your pardon for interrupting you, Lady Bracknell, but this engagement is quite out of the question. I am Miss Cardew's guardian, and she cannot marry without my consent until she comes of age. That consent I absolutely decline to give.

LADY BRACKNELL. Upon what grounds, may I ask? Algernon is an extremely, I may almost say an ostentatiously, eligible young man. He has nothing, but he looks everything. What more can one desire?

JACK. It pains me very much to have to speak frankly to you, Lady Bracknell, about your nephew, but the fact is that I do not approve at all of his moral character. I suspect him of being untruthful. (*Algernon and Cecily look at him in indignant amazement.*)

LADY BRACKNELL. Untruthful! My nephew Algernon? Impossible! He is an Oxonian.

JACK. I fear there can be no possible doubt about the matter. This afternoon, during my temporary absence in London on an important question of romance, he obtained admission to my house by means of the false pretence of being my brother. Under an assumed name he drank, I've just been informed by my butler, an entire pint bottle of my Perrier-Jouet, Brut, '89; a wine I was specially reserving for myself. Continuing his disgraceful deception, he succeeded in the course of the afternoon in alienating the affections of my only ward. He subsequently stayed to tea, and devoured every single muffin. And what makes his conduct all the more heartless is, that he was perfectly well aware from the first that I have no brother, that I never had a brother, and that I don't intend to have a brother, not even of any kind. I distinctly told him so myself yesterday afternoon.

LADY BRACKNELL. Ahem! Mr. Worthing, after careful consideration I have decided entirely to overlook my nephew's conduct to you.

JACK. That is very generous of you, Lady Bracknell. My own decision, however, is unalterable. I decline to give my consent.

LADY BRACKNELL (*to Cecily*). Come here, sweet child. (*Cecily goes over.*) How old are you, dear?

CECILY. Well, I am really only eighteen, but I always admit to twenty when I go to evening parties.

LADY BRACKNELL. You are perfectly right in making some slight alteration. Indeed, no woman should ever be quite accurate about her age. It looks so calculating. . . . (*In meditative manner.*) Eighteen, but admitting to twenty at evening parties. Well, it will not be very long before you are of age and free from the restraints of tutelage. So I don't think your guardian's consent is, after all, a matter of any importance.

JACK. Pray excuse me, Lady Bracknell, for interrupting you again, but it is only fair to tell you that according to the terms of her grandfather's will Miss Cardew does not come legally of age till she is thirty-five.

LADY BRACKNELL. That does not seem to me to be a grave objection. Thirty-five is a very attractive age. London society is full of women of the very highest birth who have, of their own free choice, remained thirty-five for years. Lady Dumbleton is an instance in point. To my own knowledge she had been thirty-five ever since she arrived at the age of forty, which was many years ago now. I see no reason why our dear Cecily should not be even still more attractive at the age you mention than she is at present. There will be a large accumulation of property.

CECILY. Algy, could you wait for me till I was thirty-five?

ALGERNON. Of course I could, Cecily. You know I could.

CECILY. Yes, I felt it instinctively, but I couldn't wait all that time. I hate waiting even five minutes for anybody. It always makes me rather cross. I am not punctual myself, I know, but I do like punctuality in others, and waiting, even to be married, is quite out of the question.

ALGERNON. Then what is to be done, Cecily?

CECILY. I don't know, Mr. Moncrieff.

LADY BRACKNELL. My dear Mr. Worthing, as Miss Cardew states positively that she cannot wait till she is thirty-five—a remark which I am bound to say seems to me to show a somewhat impatient nature—I would beg of you to reconsider your decision.

JACK. But my dear Lady Bracknell, the matter is entirely in your own hands. The moment you consent to my marriage with Gwendolen, I will most gladly allow your nephew to form an alliance with my ward.

LADY BRACKNELL (*rising and drawing herself up*). You must be quite aware that what you propose is out of the question.

JACK. Then a passionate celibacy is all that any of us can look forward to.

LADY BRACKNELL. That is not the destiny I propose for Gwendolen. Algernon, of course, can choose for himself. (*Pulls out her watch.*) Come, dear, (*Gwendolen rises*) we have already missed five, if not six, trains. To miss any more might expose us to comment on the platform.

(*Enter Dr. Chasuble.*)

CHASUBLE. Everything is quite ready for the christenings.

LADY BRACKNELL. The christenings, sir! Is not that somewhat premature?

CHASUBLE (*looking rather puzzled, and pointing to Jack and Algernon*). Both these gentlemen have expressed a desire for immediate baptism.

LADY BRACKNELL. At their age? The idea is grotesque and irreligious! Algernon, I forbid you to be baptised. I will not hear of such excesses. Lord Bracknell would be highly displeased if he learned that that was the way in which you wasted your time and money.

CHASUBLE. Am I to understand then that there are to be no christenings at all this afternoon?

JACK. I don't think that, as things are now, it would be of much practical value to either of us, Dr. Chasuble.

CHASUBLE. I am grieved to hear such sentiments from you, Mr. Worthing. They savour of the heretical views of the Anabaptists, views that I have completely refuted in four of my unpublished sermons. However, as your present mood seems to be one peculiarly secular, I will return to the church at once. Indeed, I have just been informed by the pew-opener that for the last hour and a half Miss Prism has been waiting for me in the vestry.

LADY BRACKNELL (*starting*). Miss Prism! Did I hear you mention a Miss Prism?

CHASUBLE. Yes, Lady Bracknell. I am on my way to join her.

LADY BRACKNELL. Pray allow me to detain you for a moment. This matter may prove to be one of vital importance to Lord Bracknell and myself. Is this Miss Prism a female of repellent aspect, remotely connected with education?

CHASUBLE (*somewhat indignantly*). She is the most cultivated of ladies, and the very picture of respectability.

LADY BRACKNELL. It is obviously the same person. May I ask what position she holds in your household?

CHASUBLE (*severely*). I am a celibate, madam.

JACK (*interposing*). Miss Prism, Lady Bracknell, has been for the last three years Miss Cardew's esteemed governess and valued companion.

LADY BRACKNELL. In spite of what I hear of her, I must see her at once. Let her be sent for.

CHASUBLE (*looking off*). She approaches; she is nigh.

(*Enter Miss Prism hurriedly.*)

MISS PRISM. I was told you expected me in the vestry, dear Canon. I have been waiting for you there for an hour and three-quarters. (*Catches sight of Lady Bracknell, who has fixed her with a stony glare. Miss Prism grows pale and quails. She looks anxiously round as if desirous to escape.*)

LADY BRACKNELL (*in a severe, judicial voice*). Prism! (*Miss Prism bows her head in shame.*) Come here, Prism! (*Miss Prism approaches in a humble manner.*) Where is that baby? (*General consternation. The Canon starts back in horror. Algernon and Jack pretend to be anxious to shield Cecily and Gwendolen from hearing the details of a terrible public scandal.*) Twenty-eight years ago, Prism, you left Lord Bracknell's house, Number 104, Upper Grosvenor Street, in charge of a perambulator that contained a baby, of the male sex. You never returned. A few weeks later, through the elaborate investigations of the Metropolitan police, the perambulator was discovered at midnight, standing by itself in a remote corner of Bayswater. It contained the manuscript of a three-volume novel of more than usually revolting sentimentality. (*Miss Prism starts in involuntary indignation.*) But the baby was not there! (*Everyone looks at Miss Prism.*) Prism, where is that baby? (*A pause.*)

MISS PRISM. Lady Bracknell, I admit with shame that I do not know. I only wish I did. The plain facts of the case are these. On the morning of the day you mention, a day that is forever branded on my memory, I prepared as usual to take the baby out in its perambulator. I had also with me a somewhat old but capacious hand-bag in which I had intended to place the manuscript of a work of fiction that I had written during my few unoccupied hours. In a moment of mental abstraction, for which I never can forgive myself, I deposited the manuscript in the bassinette, and placed the baby in the hand-bag.

JACK (*who had been listening attentively*). But where did you deposit the hand-bag?

MISS PRISM. Do not ask me, Mr. Worthing.

JACK. Miss Prism, this is a matter of no small importance to me. I insist on knowing where you deposited the handbag that contained that infant.

MISS PRISM. I left it in the cloak-room of one of the larger railway stations in London.

JACK. What railway station?

MISS PRISM (*quite crushed*). Victoria. The Brighton line. (*Sinks into a chair.*)

JACK. I must retire to my room for a moment. Gwendolen, wait here for me.

GWENDOLEN. If you are not too long, I will wait here for you all my life.

(*Exit Jack in great excitement.*)

CHASUBLE. What do you think this means, Lady Bracknell?

LADY BRACKNELL. I dare not even suspect, Dr. Chasuble. I need hardly tell you that in families of high position strange coincidences are not supposed to occur. They are hardly considered the thing. (*Noises heard overhead as if someone was throwing trunks about. Everybody looks up.*)

CECILY. Uncle Jack seems strangely agitated.

CHASUBLE. Your guardian has a very emotional nature.

LADY BRACKNELL. This noise is extremely unpleasant. It sounds as if he was having an argument. I dislike arguments of any kind. They are always vulgar, and often convincing.

CHASUBLE (*looking up*). It has stopped now. (*The noise is redoubled.*)

LADY BRACKNELL. I wish he would arrive at some conclusion.

GWENDOLEN. The suspense is terrible. I hope it will last.

(*Enter Jack with a hand-bag of black leather in his hand.*)

JACK (*rushing over to Miss Prism*). Is this the hand-bag, Miss Prism? Examine it carefully before you speak. The happiness of more than one life depends on your answers.

MISS PRISM (*calmly*). It seems to be mine. Yes, here is the injury it received through the upsetting of a Gower Street omnibus in younger and happier days. Here is the stain on the lining caused by the explosion of a temperance beverage, an incident that occurred at Leamington. And here, on the lock, are my initials. I had forgotten that in an extravagant mood I had had them placed there. The bag is undoubtedly mine. I am delighted to have it so unexpectedly restored to me. It has been a great inconvenience being without it all these years.

JACK (*in a pathetic voice*). Miss Prism, more is restored to you than this hand-bag. I was the baby you placed in it.

MISS PRISM (*amazed*). You?

JACK (*embracing her*). Yes . . . mother!

MISS PRISM (*recoiling in indignant astonishment*). Mr. Worthing! I am unmarried!

JACK. Unmarried! I do not deny that is a serious blow. But after all, who has the right to cast a stone against one who has suffered? Cannot repentance wipe out an act of folly? Why should there be one law for men and another for women? Mother, I forgive you. (*Tries to embrace her again.*)

MISS PRISM (*still more indignant*). Mr. Worthing, there is some error. (*Pointing to Lady Bracknell.*) There is the lady who can tell you who you really are.

JACK (*after a pause*). Lady Bracknell, I hate to seem inquisitive, but would you kindly inform me who I am?

LADY BRACKNELL. I am afraid that the news I have to give you will not altogether please you. You are the son of my poor sister, Mrs. Moncrieff, and consequently Algernon's elder brother.

JACK. Algy's elder brother! Then I have a brother after all. I knew I had a brother! I always said I had a brother! Cecily,—how could you have ever doubted that I had a brother? (*Seizes hold of Algernon.*) Dr. Chasuble, my unfortunate brother. Miss Prism, my unfortunate brother. Gwendolen, my unfortunate brother. Algy, you young scoundrel, you will have to treat me with more respect in the future. You have never behaved to me like a brother in all your life.

ALGERNON. Well, not till to-day, old boy, I admit. I did my best, however, though I was out of practice. (*Shakes hands.*)

GWENDOLEN (*to Jack*). My own! But what own are you? What is your Christian name, now that you have become someone else?

JACK. Good heavens! . . . I had quite forgotten that point. Your decision on the subject of my name is irrevocable, I suppose?

GWENDOLEN. I never change, except in my affections.

CECILY. What a noble nature you have, Gwendolen!

JACK. Then the question had better be cleared up at once. Aunt Augusta, a moment. At the time when Miss Prism left me in the hand-bag, had I been christened already?

LADY BRACKNELL. Every luxury that money could buy, including christening, had been lavished on you by your fond and doting parents.

JACK. Then I was christened! That is settled. Now, what name was I given? Let me know the worst.

LADY BRACKNELL. Being the eldest son you were naturally christened after your father.

JACK (*irritably*). Yes, but what was my father's Christian name?

LADY BRACKNELL (*meditatively*). I cannot at the present moment recall what the General's Christian name was. But I have no doubt he had one. He was eccentric, I admit. But only in later years. And that was the result of the Indian climate, and marriage, and indigestion, and other things of that kind.

JACK. Algy! Can't you recollect what our father's Christian name was?

ALGERNON. My dear boy, we were never even on speaking terms. He died before I was a year old.

JACK. His name would appear in the Army Lists of the period, I suppose, Aunt Augusta?

LADY BRACKNELL. The general was essentially a man of peace, except in his domestic life. But I have no doubt his name would appear in any military directory.

JACK. The Army Lists of the last forty years are here. These delightful records should have been my constant study. (*Rushes to bookcase and tears the books out.*) M. Generals . . . Mallham, Maxbohm, Magley, what ghastly names they have—Markby, Migsby, Mobbs, Moncrieff! Lieutenant 1840, Captain, Lieutenant-Colonel, Colonel, General 1869, Christian names, Ernest John. (*Puts book very quietly down and speaks quite calmly.*) I always told you, Gwendolen, my name was Ernest, didn't I? Well, it is Ernest after all, I mean it naturally is Ernest.

LADY BRACKNELL. Yes, I remember the General was called Ernest. I knew I had some particular reason for disliking the name.

GWENDOLEN. Ernest! My own Ernest! I felt from the first that you could have no other name!

JACK. Gwendolen, it is a terrible thing for a man to find out suddenly that all his life he has been speaking nothing but the truth. Can you forgive me?

GWENDOLEN. I can. For I feel sure that you are sure to change.

JACK. My own one!

CHASUBLE (*to Miss Prism*). Lætitia! (*Embraces her.*)

MISS PRISM (*enthusiastically*). Frederick! At last!

ALGERNON. Cecily! (*Embraces her.*) At last!

JACK. Gwendolen! (*Embraces her.*) At last!

LADY BRACKNELL. My nephew, you seem to be displaying signs of triviality.

JACK. On the contrary, Aunt Augusta, I've now realized for the first time in my life the vital Importance of Being Earnest.

TABLEAU

CURTAIN

TOPICS FOR CRITICAL THINKING AND WRITING

The Play on the PAGE

1. Speaking of this play, Wilde said in an interview: "It has as its philosophy . . . that we should treat all the trivial things of life seriously, and all the serious things of life with sincere and studied triviality." Was he kidding? To what extent does the play dramatize such a view?

2. Can it be argued that the play presents a fanciful world utterly remote from the real world, and that attempts to see it as in any way related to our world do it an injustice? If this is the case, what value does the play have?

3. Describe some of Wilde's chief devices of verbal humor. One such device, for instance, is to turn a proverb inside out, as with the proverbial "Marriages are made in heaven." What other examples of this device do you find? And what other kinds of humor?

4. What are Lady Bracknell's values? What is your response to her—not to her values, but to her? Why?

The Play on the STAGE

5. Take one part of one act—Lady Bracknell's examination of Jack in Act I would be a good choice—and indicate what stage business you would use if you were directing the play. A simple example: When Lady Bracknell finishes questioning Jack about his finances and his social standing, she might close her notebook and invitingly pat the seat beside her as she says, "Now to minor matters. Are your parents living?" A little later, when Jack confesses that he cannot identify his parents, she might tear the page out of her notebook.

6. If you were directing a production, what suggestions would you offer the actors for the first fifteen lines of the play? Consider, for instance, "Did you hear what I was playing, Lane?" Which word(s) should be stressed? What facial movements are appropriate, what gestures, what voice qualities? What sort of eye contact? Would you aim for the maximum humorous effect? For delineation of social class? Or what?

7. List all of Miss Prism's appearances, and then put into writing the advice you would give to an actress playing the role. For each appearance indicate how she might stand, how her face should be set, at

whom she should look, when she should show emotion, and so forth. Suggest an actress—either well known or known within the class or college—whom you would nominate for the role, and give your reasons.

8. Should Cecily and Gwendolen seem interchangeable—that is, are they both sweet, young, vain, spoiled? If so, point to evidence supporting your view. If not, indicate the ways in which they differ, and point to the supporting evidence.

9. As costume designer, what colors would you choose for each of the young women? What accessories?

10. Wilde's opening instructions merely call for the sound of a piano. If you were the sound designer for *The Importance of Being Earnest*, what musical piece (specific title and composer) would you propose for a production set in the 1890s? For a production set in the 1990s? Explain your choices.

11. The original production (1895) used a contemporary setting. What arguments might you advance for and against the idea of setting the play in a period other than the original, for instance in the 1920s, or the 1990s?

The Play in PERFORMANCE

When *The Importance of Being Earnest* had its premiere performance in London in 1895 it was an immediate hit with audiences and with critics. Three months later, when the author was convicted of indecency and was sentenced to two years of hard labor, the play was withdrawn from the stage. In 1899 Wilde arranged for the publication of the play, but, such was his disgrace, reviewers ignored the book.

There were revivals in London in 1898 and 1902, but not until the revival of 1909 did the play have a long run. By the 1920s it was a staple of the theater, and probably not a week now goes by that it is not produced somewhere. Between the 1920s and the 1970s most productions probably were set in the 1890s, and they were more or less in the tradition of museum theater, that is, they sought to perform the play in the way that (in the director's view) it was originally performed. The set, for instance, recreated an elegant Victorian bachelor's apartment. Such productions are often still seen today, though there are variations. In 1982 Sir Peter Hall staged *Earnest* with minimal sets—two white cane chairs and a few pots of roses for the garden in Act II, for instance—and the production was well received.

But the difference between *Earnest* in 1895 and *Earnest* today is something larger than the set. The original audience knew that Wilde was a dandy—a man who pays too much attention to his clothes and too little attention to bourgeois morality—but until the trial they did not know that he was a homosexual. Dandyism, it should be mentioned, was by no means associated with homosexuality. It was associated with the idle rich, or the would-be idle rich, and the hard-working middle-class male regarded it with disapproval because Victorian men were supposed to work hard and leave such things as attention to clothing to women, who (in the common view) were not suited for serious work. When Wilde's homosexuality became public knowledge, for a while his name could scarcely be mentioned in decent society, and the play could not be staged. With the passage of a few years, however, the play could be staged so long as one did not mention homosexuality. And this was not hard to do, because in fact the two young men in the play are in love with women.

But since homosexuality has come out of the closet (around the 1970s), today it is common to read discussions of the play as a gay play (which we can define as a play about gay life), a sort of closet revelation of homosexuality. One reads, for example, that *bunburying* is a thinly veiled pun on *burying in the buns*, that is, on penetrating the buttocks. At the risk of being spoilsports, we must mention that no one has bothered to offer evidence that in Wilde's day the word *buns* was used in England to refer to buttocks. (In fact, the earliest recorded use of *buns* in this sense is in mid-twentieth-century American English.) The published critical interpretations of course are paralleled by an occasional gay production, and so we have been given versions in which Algy and Jack are presented as lovers (they kiss) who only pretend to be interested in women. There has also been at least one all-male production of the play (the Berlin Actors, in New York in 1987), and many productions in which Lady Bracknell is played by a man in drag.

Was Wilde in fact setting forth his secret life in a code that the initiate could read? Was he saying that *The Importance of Being Earnest* is autobiographical when, writing from prison to his former lover, he said, "I took the drama, the most objective form known to art, and made it as personal a mode of expression as the lyric or the sonnet?" In the play was he talking in code about his secret double life when he had Cecily say, "I hope you have not been leading a double life, pretending to be wicked and being really good all the time. That would be hypocrisy"? Conceivably. Even so, one can ask if a "gay" production makes sense. And one can ask if it does not lose more than it gains. Gay productions usually strike audiences as unfunny, or at least as far less funny than versions that are done straight.

One last point about the play in production: Wilde wrote a four-act version, but his director insisted that it be cut to three acts. Wilde protested, but the director prevailed. One might ask, then, if Wilde's "real" play is the four-act version rather than the three-act version. The answer probably is no. When Wilde published the play, he published the three-act version, and so we can assume that he ultimately decided that the revised version was indeed preferable. The four-act version is occasionally produced out of academic piety, but audiences familiar with the three-act version regard the longer version as less successful.

ANTON Chekhov

Anton Chekhov (1860–1904) received his medical degree from the University of Moscow in 1884, but he had already published some stories. His belief that his medical training assisted him in writing about people caused some people to find him cold, but on the whole the evidence suggests that he was a genial, energetic young man with considerable faith in reason and (as befitted a doctor) in science, and with very little faith in religion and in heroics. His major plays are *The Seagull* (1896), *Uncle Vanya* (1899), *Three Sisters* (1901), and, finally, *The Cherry Orchard* (1903), written during his last illness.

◼◼◼◼◼◼◼◼◼◼◼◼◼◼

COMMENTARY ON *THE CHERRY ORCHARD*

At the end of *The Cherry Orchard*, the old servant Firs, forgotten by the family he has long served, wanders onto the stage, locked within the house that is no longer theirs. Is he comic, in his mutterings, in his old-maidish frettings about Leonid Andreevich's inadequate coat, and in his implicit realization that although he is concerned about the aristocrats the aristocrats are unconcerned about him? Or is he tragic, dying in isolation? Or neither? The comedy is scarcely uproarious; if there is humor in his realization that his life has been trivial, this humor is surely tinged with melancholy. And the "tragic" reading is also ambiguous: First, the text does not say that he dies; second, if it can be assumed that he dies, the death of an ill eighty-seven-year-old man can scarcely seem untimely; and third, Firs does not seem particularly concerned about dying.

If this play ends with a death, then, it is not the sort of death that Byron had in mind when he said, "All tragedies are finished by a death, / All comedies are ended by a marriage." We are in the dramatic world that Shaw spoke of when he said that "the curtain no longer comes down on a hero slain or married: it comes down when the audience has seen enough of the life presented to it, . . . and must either leave the theatre or miss its last train."

Chekhov insisted that *The Cherry Orchard* was a comedy, but what sort of comedy? In the latter part of the last act there is almost a proposal of marriage, but, typically, it never gets made. For two years everyone has joked about the anticipated marriage between Lopakhin and Varya, but when these two are thrust together they are overcome by embarrassment, and the interview is dissipated in small talk. Not that (of course) a comedy must end with a marriage; marriage is only the conventional way of indicating a happy union, or reunion, that symbolizes the triumph of life. But in this play we *begin* with a reunion—the family is reunited in the ancestral home—and we end with a separation, the inhabitants scattering when the home is sold.

Another way of getting at *The Cherry Orchard* is to notice that in this play, although there are innumerable references to time between the first speech, when Lopakhin says "Train's in, thank God! What's the time?" and the last act, where there is much talk about catching the outbound train, Time does not function as it usually functions either in tragedy or in comedy. In tragedy we usually feel: if there had only been more time. . . . For example, in *Romeo and Juliet* Friar Laurence writes a letter to Romeo, explaining that Juliet will take a potion that will put her in a temporary, deathlike trance, but the letter is delayed, Romeo mistakenly hears that Juliet is dead, and he kills himself. A few moments after his suicide Juliet revives. Had Friar Laurence's message arrived on schedule, or had Romeo not been so quick to commit suicide, no great harm would have been done. In *King Lear*, Edmund repents that he has ordered a soldier to kill Cordelia, and a messenger hurries out to change the order, but he is too late.

If in tragedy we usually feel the pressure of time, in comedy there is usually a sense of leisure. Things are difficult now, but in the course of time they will work themselves out. Sooner or later people will realize that the strange goings-on are due to the existence of identical twins; sooner or later the stubborn parents will realize that they cannot forever stand in the way of young lovers; sooner or later the money will turn up and all will be well. In the world of comedy, one is always safe in relying on time. In *The Cherry Orchard*, Lopakhin insists, correctly enough, that the family must act *now* if it is to save the orchard: "You've got to decide once and for all—time won't stand still." There is ample time to act on Lopakhin's suggestion that the orchard be leased for summer houses, and the play covers a period from May to October; but the plan is not acted on because to the aristocrats any sort of selling is unthinkable, and although one Pishchik is in the course of time miraculously redeemed from financial ruin by some Englishmen who discover and buy "some kind of white clay" on *his* land, time brings Mme. Ranevskaya and her brother Gaev no such good fortune. So far as the main happenings in the play are concerned, time neither presses nor preserves; it only passes.

During the passage of time in this play, the orchard is lost (tragic?) and the characters reveal themselves to be funny (comic?). The loss of the orchard is itself a happening of an uncertain kind. It stands, partly, for the end of an old way of life. But if that way once included intelligent and gracious aristocrats, it also included slavery, and in any case it now is embodied in the irresponsible heirs we see on the stage—Mme. Ranevskaya and her brother Gaev, along with their deaf and near-senile servant Firs. For Gaev the orchard is important chiefly because it lends prestige, since it is mentioned in the encyclopedia. Mme. Ranevskaya sees more to it. For her it is "all white" and it is "young again, full of happiness"; we are momentarily touched by her vision, but there is yet another way of seeing the orchard: For Trofimov, a student who envisions a new society as an orchard for all people, the ancestral cherry orchard is haunted by the serfs of the bad old days. Moreover, although the orchard is much talked about, it seems to have decayed to a trivial ornament. Long ago its crop was regularly harvested, pickled, and sold, thus providing food and income, but now "nobody remembers" the pickling formula and nobody buys the crop. There seems to be some truth to Lopakhin's assertion that "the only remarkable thing about this cherry orchard is that it's very big," and although one must point out that this remark is made by a despised merchant, Lopakhin is neither a fool nor the "money grubber" that Gaev thinks he is. Lopakhin delights in nature put to use. He "cleared forty thousand net" from poppies, "And when my poppies bloomed, it was like a picture!" His enthusiasm for the flowers is undercut for us only a little, if at all, by the fact that they were of use to him and to others.

Lopakhin's serious concern, whether for his poppies or for the future of the cherry orchard, contrasts interestingly with Mme. Ranevskaya's and with Gaev's sporadic passion for the orchard. Mme. Ranevskaya says, "Without the cherry orchard, I couldn't make sense of my life," and she doubtless means what she says; but that her words have not much relation to reality is indicated by her meaningless addition, "If it really has to be sold, then sell me along with the orchard." After the orchard has been sold, Gaev confesses, "everything's fine now. Until the sale of the cherry orchard, we were all upset, distressed, but then, when the dilemma was settled, finally, irrevocably, everyone calmed down, even became cheerful . . . I'm a bank employee. . . . Lyuba, anyway, you're looking better, that's for sure." His sister agrees: "Yes. My nerves are better, that's true. . . . I'm sleeping well. Carry my things out, Yasha. It's time." She returns to her lover in Paris, Gaev goes off to a job in the bank, and though we can imagine that the orchard will continue to be an occasional topic of conversation, we cannot imagine that the loss has in any way changed them. The play ends, but things will go on in the same way; neither a tragic nor a comic action has been completed.

The characters no less than the action are tragicomic. Their longings would touch the heart if only these people did not so quickly digress or engage in little actions that call their depth into doubt. Charlotta laments that she had no proper passport and that her deceased parents may not have been married: "Where I came from and who I am I don't know." And then, having touched on the mighty subject of one's identity, the subject that is the stuff of tragedy in which heroes endure the worst in order to know who they are, she begins to eat a cucumber, and somehow that simple and entirely necessary act diminishes her dignity—though it does not totally dissipate our glimpse of her alienation. In the same scene, when Yepikhodov confesses that although he reads "all kinds of remarkable books" he "cannot discover [his] own inclinations," we hear another echo of the tragic hero's quest for self-knowledge, but we also hear an echo from the world of comedy, say of the pedant who guides his life by a textbook. Yepikhodov, perhaps like a tragic hero, is particularly concerned with whether to live or to shoot himself; but this racking doubt is diminished by his prompt explanation that since he may someday decide on suicide, he always carries a revolver, which he proceeds to show to his listeners. Almost all of the characters bare their souls, but their slightly addled minds and their hungry bodies expose them to a gentle satirical treatment so that they evoke a curious amused pathos. One can, for example, sympathize with Mme. Ranevskaya's despair—but one cannot forget that she is scatterbrained and that domestic duties and local pieties occupy her mind only occasionally and that her disreputable lover in Paris means as much as the orchard she thinks she cannot live without. And when Gaev says, "Word of honor I'll swear, by whatever you like, that the estate won't be sold," we know that he has very little honor and even less ability to focus on the problem (mostly he takes refuge in thoughts about billiards, and somehow his habit of eating candy does not enhance his status in our eyes) and that the estate will be sold.

Finally, something must be said about the ambiguous treatment of the future. We know, from his correspondence, that Chekhov looked forward to a new and happier society. Russia, like much of the rest of Europe, was ceasing to be an agrarian society, but if the death throes were evident, one could not be so confident about the birth pangs. Something of the presence of two worlds is hinted at in the stage direction at the beginning of the second act, where we see the estate with its orchard, and also "Further off are telegraph poles, and way in the distance, dimly sketched on the horizon, is a large town." The telegraph poles and the town silently represent the new industrial society, but Trofimov the student speaks at length of the glorious possibilities of the future, and his speeches were suffi-

ciently close to the bone for the censor to delete two passages sharply critical of the present. But we cannot take Trofimov's speeches quite at face value. He is a student, but he is almost thirty and still has not received his degree. His speeches in Act 2 are moving, especially those on the need to work rather than to talk if the future is to be better than the past, but we cannot quite rid ourselves of the suspicion that Trofimov talks rather than works. Certainly he is contemptuous of the merchant Lopakhin, who delights in work. And, worse, Trofimov frets too much about his overshoes, thinks he is "above love," and is so confounded by Mme. Ranevskaya's remark, "At your age, not to have a mistress!" that he falls down a flight of stairs. None of these personal failings invalidates his noble view of the future; certainly none of them turns this view into a comic pipedream, and yet all of these things, along with a certain nostalgia that we feel for the past, do suffuse even his noblest statements about the future with a delicate irony that puts them, along with the much praised but totally neglected cherry orchard, firmly in the tragicomic world. One understands why Chekhov called the play a comedy, and one understands why Stanislavsky (who directed the first production and played the part of Gaev) told Chekhov, "It is definitely not a comedy . . . but a tragedy." Perhaps neither of the men fully wanted to see the resonant ambiguities in the play.

THE CHERRY ORCHARD
Anton Chekhov

Translated by Laurence Senelick

LIST OF CHARACTERS[1]

RANEVSKAYA, LYUBOV ANDREEVNA, *a landowner* (*Lyoo-BAWFF Ahn-DRAY-eff-nah Rahn-YEHFF-skei-ah*)

ANYA, *her daughter, age 17* (*AHN-yah*)

VARYA, *her adopted daughter, age 24* (*VAHR-yah*)

GAEV, LEONID ANDREEVICH, *Ranevskaya's brother* (*Lyaw-NEED Ahn-DRAY-eech GEI-ehff*)

LOPAKHIN, YERMOLAI ALEKSEICH, *a businessman* (*Yehr-mah-LEI Ah-lihk-SAY-eech Lah-PAH-kheen*)

TROFIMOV, PYOTR SERGEEVICH, *a student* (*PYAW-tr Ser-GAY-veech Trah-FEE-mawff*)

SIMEONOV-PISHCHIK, BORIS BORISOVICH, *a landowner* (*Seem-YAWN-awff PEESH-cheek*)

CHARLOTTA IVANOVNA, *a governess* (*Sharh-LAW-tah Ee-VAHN-awff-nah*)

YEPIKHODOV, SEMYON PANTELEEVICH, *a bookkeeper* (*Sim-YAHN Pahn-til-YAY-eech Ippy-KHAW-dawff*)

DUNYASHA, *a parlor-maid* (*Doon-YAH-shah*)

FIRS NIKOLAEVICH, *a footman, an old fellow of 87* (*FEERRSS Nee-kaw-LEI-yeh-veech*)

YASHA, *a young manservant* (*YAH-shah*)

A TRAMP

THE STATIONMASTER

A POSTAL CLERK

GUESTS, SERVANTS

The action takes place on Madam Ranevskaya's estate.

ACT 1

A room, which is still known as the Nursery. One of the doors opens into Anya's bedroom. Dawn, soon the sun will be up. It is already May, the cherry trees are in blossom, but it is chilly in the orchard, there is a frost. The windows in the room are shut.

(Enter Dunyasha carrying a candle, and Lopakhin holding a book.)

LOPAKHIN. Train's in, thank God. What's the time?

DUNYASHA. Almost two. (*Blows out the candle.*) Daylight already.

LOPAKHIN. But just how late was the train? Must have been two hours at least. (*Yawns and stretches.*) I'm a fine one, made quite a fool of myself! Drove over here on purpose, so as to meet them at the station, and fell asleep just like

that . . . dozed off in a chair. Annoying . . . but you should have woken me up.

DUNYASHA. I thought you'd gone. (*Listening.*) Listen, it sounds like they're coming.

LOPAKHIN (*listening*). No . . . the luggage has to be brought in, and what-have-you. . . . (*Pause.*) Lyubov Andreevna's been living abroad five years now. I wonder what she's like these days. . . . She's a good sort of person. An easygoing, unpretentious person. I remember, when I was a lad of about fifteen, my late father—at that time he kept a shop here in the village—punched me in the face with his fist, blood was pouring from my nose. . . . We'd come into the yard for some reason or other, and he was tipsy. Lyubov Andreevna, I remember as if it were yesterday, she was still a young lady, so slender, led me to the washbasin, right here in this very room, the nursery. "Don't cry," says she "peasant boy, it'll heal in time for your wedding . . . " (*Pause.*) Peasant boy. . . . My father, it's true, was a peasant, and here am I in a white waistcoat and tan shoes. Like a pig rooting in a pastry shop. . . . Now here am I, rich, plenty of money, but if you think it over and consider, once a peasant, always a peasant. . . . (*Leafs through the book.*) I was reading this book and couldn't make head or tail of it. Reading and dozed off.

(Pause.)

DUNYASHA. The dogs didn't sleep all night, they sense the mistress coming home.

LOPAKHIN. What's got into you, Dunyasha, you're such a . . .

[1]Unlike earlier dramatists like Gogol or Ostrovsky, Chekhov seldom resorts to word play in naming the characters in his full-length pieces, but to a Russian ear, certain associations can be made. *Lyubov* means "love" (perhaps Amy is the English equivalent), and a kind of indiscriminate love is indeed the soul of Ranevskaya's character. *Gaev* suggests *gaer*, buffoon, while *Lopakhin* may be derived from either *lopata*, a shovel, or *lopat'*, to shovel food down one's gullet—both words of the earth, earthy. *Simeonov-Pishchik* is a Dickensian combination of a noble boyar name and a silly one reminiscent of *pishchat'*, to chirp. A similar English appellation might be Montmorency-Tweet. [All notes are by the translator.]

The premiere production of *The Cherry Orchard* in 1904 was highly realistic, but recent productions usually mix realistic costumes—to evoke the period—with stylized or symbolic elements, as in this photograph of a 1990 production by the Seattle Repertory company, where, behind and above the characters, a miniature of the house stands for the world that is being lost.

DUNYASHA. My hands are trembling. I'm going to swoon.

LOPAKHIN. You're much too delicate, Dunyasha. Dressing up like a lady, fixing your hair like one too. Mustn't do that. Mustn't forget who you are.

(*Yepikhodov enters with a bouquet; he is wearing a jacket and brightly polished boots, which squeak noisily. On entering, he drops the bouquet.*)

YEPIKHODOV (*picks up the bouquet*). Here, the gardener sent them, he says to stick 'em in the dining room. (*He hands Dunyasha the bouquet.*)

LOPAKHIN. And bring me some beer.

DUNYASHA. Very good. (*She exits.*)

YEPIKHODOV. Three degrees of frost this morning, but the cherries are all in bloom. I can't condone our climate. (*He sighs.*) I can't. I mean, it doesn't seem to make an effort. Look, Yermolai Alekseich, allow me to append, I bought myself some boots the day before yesterday, and they, I make bold to assert, squeak so much, it's quite out of the question. What should I grease them with?

LOPAKHIN. Leave me alone. You're a pest.

YEPIKHODOV. Every day something unlucky happens to me. But I don't complain, I'm used to it. I even smile.

(*Dunyasha enters and gives Lopakhin some beer.*)

YEPIKHODOV. I'm on my way. (*Bumps into a chair which falls over.*) There. . . . (*As if triumphant*) You see, pardon the

expression, what a circumstance, incidentally. . . . It's simply, you might say conspicuous! (*He exits.*)

DUNYASHA. Just let me tell you, Yermolai Alekseich, Yepikhodov proposed to me.

LOPAKHIN. Ah!

DUNYASHA. I don't know what to do. . . . He's a quiet sort, but sometimes he starts talking away, and you can't understand a thing. It's nice and it's sensitive, only you can't understand it. I kind of like him. He's madly in love with me. He's an unlucky sort of fellow, something happens every day. So we've nicknamed him: twenty-two troubles. . . .

LOPAKHIN (*hearkening*). Listen, I think they're coming. . . .

DUNYASHA. Coming! What's the matter with me . . . I'm all over chills.

LOPAKHIN. They are coming. Let's go meet them. Will she recognize me? We haven't set eyes on one another for five years.

DUNYASHA (*in a flurry*). I'll faint this minute. . . . Ach, I'll faint!

(*We hear the sounds of two carriages drawing up to the house. Lopakhin and Dunyasha exeunt quickly. The stage is empty. Noises begin in the adjoining rooms. Firs, leaning on a stick, hurries across the stage; he has just been to meet Lyubov Andreevna: he is wearing an old suit of livery and a top hat; he mutters something to himself but no words can be made out. The offstage noises keep growing*)

*louder. A voice: "Let's go through here." Lyubov An-
dreevna, Anya, and Charlotta Ivanovna with a lapdog on
a leash, the three dressed in travelling clothes, Varya in an
overcoat and kerchief, Gaev, Simeonov-Pishchik,
Lopakhin, Dunyasha with a bundle and a parasol, servants carrying suitcases—all pass through the room.)*

ANYA. Let's go through here. Mama, do you remember what
room this was?

LYUBOV ANDREEVNA (*joyously, through tears*). The nursery!

VARYA. It's cold, my hands are numb. (*To Lyubov Andreevna*)
Your rooms, the white and the violet, are still the same as
ever, Mama dear.

LYUBOV ANDREEVNA. The nursery, my darling, beautiful
room. . . . I slept here when I was a little girl. . . . (*She
weeps.*) And now I'm like a little girl. . . . (*She kisses her
brother and Varya and then her brother again.*) And Varya is
just the same as before, looks like a nun. And I recognized Dunyasha. . . . (*Kisses Dunyasha.*)

GAEV. The train was two hours late. What's going on? What
kind of organization is that?

CHARLOTTA (*to Pishchik*). My dog, he even eats nuts.

PISHCHIK (*astounded*). Can you imagine!

(They all go out, except for Anya and Dunyasha.)

DUNYASHA. We've been waiting and waiting. (*Helps to remove Anya's overcoat and hat.*)

ANYA. I couldn't sleep the four nights on the train . . . now
I'm so frozen.

DUNYASHA. You left during Lent, then there was snow, frost,
and now? My darling! (*She laughs and kisses her.*) We kept
waiting for you, my sweet, my precious . . . I'll tell you
now, I can't keep it back another minute. . . .

ANYA (*weary*). Now what . . .

DUNYASHA. Yepikhodov the bookkeeper proposed to me
right after Easter.

ANYA. You've got a one-track mind. . . . (*Setting her hair to
rights.*) I've lost all my hair-pins. . . . (*She is very tired,
practically staggering.*)

DUNYASHA. I just don't know what to think. He loves me,
loves me so much!

ANYA (*peering through the door to her room, tenderly*). My
room, my windows, as if I'd never gone away. I'm home!
Tomorrow morning I'll get up, I'll run through the orchard. . . . Oh, if only I could get some sleep! I couldn't
sleep the whole way. I was worried to death.

DUNYASHA. Day before yesterday, Pyotr Sergeich arrived.

ANYA (*joyfully*). Petya!

DUNYASHA. Sleeping in the bathhouse, practically lives
there. "I'm afraid," says he, "of being a bother." (*Looking
at her pocket watch*) Somebody ought to wake him up, but
Varvara Mikhailovna gave the order not to. "You mustn't
wake him up," she says.

(Enter Varya, with a key-ring on her belt.)

VARYA. Dunyasha, coffee immediately. . . . Mama dear is asking for coffee.

DUNYASHA. Right this minute. (*She exits.*)

VARYA. Well, thank God, you've come back. You're home
again. (*Caressing her.*) My darling's come back! My
beauty's come back!

ANYA. I've had so much to put up with.

VARYA. I can imagine!

ANYA. I left during Holy Week, it was so cold then. Charlotta kept on talking the whole way, performing card
tricks. Why you stuck me with Charlotta. . . .

VARYA. You couldn't have travelled by yourself, precious.
Seventeen years old!

ANYA. We got to Paris, it was cold there too, snowing. I speak
awful French. Mama was living on a fifth floor walkup,
she had all sorts of French visitors, ladies, some old
Catholic priest with a little book, so smoky and tawdry.
And all of a sudden I started pitying Mama, pitying her
so, I took her head between my hands and couldn't let go.
Then Mama kept hugging me, crying. . . .

VARYA (*through tears*). Don't talk about it, don't talk about
it . . .

ANYA. The villa near Menton she'd already sold, she had
nothing left, nothing. And I hadn't a kopek left either,
we barely got this far. And Mama doesn't understand!
We sit down to dine at a station, and she orders the most
expensive meal and gives each waiter a ruble tip. Charlotta's the same way. And Yasha insists on his share too,
it's simply horrible. Of course Mama has her own valet
Yasha, we brought him back. . . .

VARYA. I saw the loafer. . . .

ANYA. Well, how is everything? Have we paid off the interest?

VARYA. What with?

ANYA. Oh dear, oh dear. . . .

VARYA. In August the estate's to be auctioned off. . . .

ANYA. Oh dear. . . .

LOPAKHIN (*sticking his head in the door and bleating*).
Me-e-eh. . . . (*Exits.*)

VARYA (*through tears*). I'd like to smack him one. . . . (*Shakes
her fist.*)

ANYA (*embraces Varya, quietly*). Varya, has he proposed?
(*Varya shakes her head.*) He *does* love you. . . . Why don't you
talk it over, what are you waiting for?

VARYA. I don't think anything will come of it for us. He's got
so much work, no time for me . . . and pays me no attention. May he go with God, it's hard for me even to get to
see him . . . Everybody talks about our wedding, everybody's congratulating us, but as a matter of fact, there's
nothing to it, it's all like a dream. . . . (*In a different tone*)
You've got a new brooch like a bumble-bee.

ANYA (*sadly*). Mama bought it. (*Goes to her room, speaks merrily, like a child.*) And in Paris I went up in a balloon!

VARYA. My darling's come back! My beauty's come back!

(*Dunyasha has returned with a coffee-pot and is making coffee.*)

VARYA (*stands near the door*). I go about the whole day, darling, with my household chores and dream and dream. If only there were a rich man for you to marry, I'd be at peace too, I'd go to a hermitage, then to Kiev . . . to Moscow, and so I'd keep on going to holy places . . . I'd go on and on. Glorious! . . .

ANYA. Birds are singing in the orchard. What's the time now?

VARYA. Must be three. Time for you to be asleep, dearest. (*Going into Anya's room.*) Glorious!

(*Yasha enters with a lap rug, and a travelling bag.*)

YASHA (*crosses the stage; affectedly*). May I pass through here?

DUNYASHA. A body'd hardly recognize you, Yasha. How you've changed abroad.

YASHA. Mm. . . . Who are you?

DUNYASHA. When you left here, I was so high. . . . (*Measures from the floor.*) Dunyasha, Fyodor Kozoedov's daughter. You don't remember!

YASHA. Mm . . . some tomato! (*Glances around, embraces her; she shrieks and drops a saucer. Yasha hurriedly exits.*)

VARYA (*in the doorway, crossly*). Now what was that?

DUNYASHA (*through tears*). I broke a saucer. . . .

VARYA. That's good luck.

ANYA (*entering from her room*). We ought to warn Mama that Petya's here. . . .

VARYA. I gave orders not to wake him.

ANYA (*pensively*). Six years ago, a month after father died, brother Grisha drowned in the river, a sweet little boy, seven years old. Mama couldn't stand it, she went away, went away without looking back. . . . (*Shivers.*) How I understand her, if she only knew! (*Pause.*) And Petya Trofimov was Grisha's tutor, he might remind . . .

(*Enter Firs in a jacket and white vest.*)

FIRS (*goes to the coffee pot; preoccupied*). The mistress will take her coffee in here. . . . (*Putting on white gloves*) Coffee ready? (*Sternly to Dunyasha*) You! where's the cream?

DUNYASHA. Ach, my God. . . . (*Exits hurriedly.*)

FIRS (*fussing with the coffee-pot*). Ech, you're half-baked. . . . (*Mumbles to himself*) Come home from Paris. . . . And the master went to Paris once upon a time . . . by coach. . . . (*Laughs.*)

VARYA. Firs, what are you on about?

FIRS. What's wanted? (*Joyfully*) My mistress has come home! I've been waiting! Now I can die. . . . (*Weeps with joy.*)

(*Enter Lyubov Andreevna, Gaev, and Simeonov-Pishchik, the last in a peasant coat of excellent cloth and wide trousers. Gaev, on entering, moves his arms and torso as if he were playing billiards.*)

LYUBOV ANDREEVNA. How does it go? Let me remember. . . . Yellow to the corner! Doublet to the center!

GAEV. Red to the corner! Once upon a time, sister we used to sleep together in this very room, and now I'm already fifty-one years old, strange as it seems. . . .

LOPAKHIN. Yes, time flies.

GAEV. How's that?

LOPAKHIN. Time, I say, flies.

GAEV. It smells of cheap perfume in here.

ANYA. I'm going to bed. Good night, Mama. (*Kisses her mother.*)

LYUBOV ANDREEVNA. My precious little princess. (*Kisses her hands.*) Are you glad you're home? I can't pull myself together.

ANYA. Good night, Uncle.

GAEV (*kisses her face, hands*). God bless you. How like your mother you are! (*To his sister*) Lyuba, you were just the same at her age.

(*Anya gives her hand to Lopakhin and Pishchik, exits, and shuts the door behind her.*)

LYUBOV ANDREEVNA. She's very tired.

PISHCHIK. Must be a long trip.

VARYA (*to Lopakhin and Pishchik*). Well, gentlemen? Three o'clock, by this time you've worn out your welcome.

LYUBOV ANDREEVNA (*laughing*). You never change, Varya. (*Draws Varya to her and kisses her.*) First I'll have some coffee, then everybody will go. (*Firs puts a cushion under her feet.*) Thank you, dear. I've grown accustomed to coffee. I drink it night and day. Thank you, old dear. (*Kisses Firs.*)

VARYA. I'll see if all the luggage was brought in. . . . (*Exits.*)

LYUBOV ANDREEVNA. Can I really be sitting here? (*Laughs.*) I feel like jumping up and down and swinging my arms. (*Hides her face in her hands.*) But suppose I'm dreaming! God knows, I love my country, love it tenderly. I couldn't look at it from the carriage, couldn't stop crying. (*Through tears*) However, must drink some coffee. Thank you, Firs, thank you, my old dear. I'm so glad you're still alive.

FIRS. Day before yesterday.

GAEV. He doesn't hear well.

LOPAKHIN. I've got to leave for Kharkov around five. What a nuisance! I wanted to have a look at you, to talk. . . . You're still as lovely as ever.

PISHCHIK (*breathing hard*). Even gotten prettier. . . . Dressed in Parisian fashions. . . . "Lost my cart with all four wheels. Lost my heart head over heels."

LOPAKHIN. Your brother, Leonid Andreich here, says that I'm a boor, a money-grubbing peasant, but it doesn't make the least bit of difference to me. Let him talk. The only thing I want is for you to believe in me as you once did, for your wonderful, heart-breaking eyes to look at me as they once did. Merciful God! My father was your grandfather's serf and your father's, but you, you personally, did so much for me once that I forgot it all and love you like my own kin—more than my own kin.

LYUBOV ANDREEVNA. I can't sit still. I just can't. . . . (*Leaps up and walks about in great excitement.*) I won't survive the joy. . . . Laugh at me, I'm silly. . . . My dear bookcase! (*Kisses the bookcase.*) My little table.

GAEV. While you were away, Nanny died.

LYUBOV ANDREEVNA (*sits and drinks coffee*). Yes, may she rest in peace. They wrote me.

GAEV. And Anastasy died. Cross-eyed Petrusha left me and now he's working in town for the police. (*Takes a box from his pocket and eats caramels out of it.*)

PISHCHIK. My dear daughter Dashenka . . . says to say hello. . . .

LOPAKHIN. I'd like to tell you something very enjoyable, cheery. (*Looking at his watch.*) I have to go now, never time for a chat . . . well, here it is in two or three words. As you already know, the cherry orchard will be sold to pay your debts, the auction is set for August 22nd but don't you fret, dear lady, don't lose any sleep, there's a way out. . . . Here's my plan. Please pay attention! Your estate lies only thirteen miles from town, the railroad runs alongside it, and if the cherry orchard were divided into building lots and then leased out for summer cottages, you'd be making at the very least twenty-five thousand a year.

GAEV. Excuse me, what poppycock!

LYUBOV ANDREEVNA. I don't quite understand you, Yermolai Alekseich.

LOPAKHIN. You'll get out of the tenants about twenty-five rubles a year per two-and-a-half acres at the very least, and if you advertise now, I'll willingly bet anything that by fall there won't be a single unoccupied plot, it'll all be grabbed up. In a word, congratulations, you're saved. Wonderful location, deep river. Only, of course, we'll have to put it to rights, fix it up . . . for example, say, pull down all the old sheds, and this house, which is absolutely worthless, chop down the old cherry orchard.

LYUBOV ANDREEVNA. Chop it down? My dear, forgive me, but you don't understand anything. If there's one thing of interest in the entire district, even outstanding, it's none other than our cherry orchard.

LOPAKHIN. The only outstanding thing about this orchard is that it's enormous. The cherries grow once in two years, and there's no way of getting rid of them, nobody buys them.

GAEV. This orchard is cited in the Encyclopedia.

LOPAKHIN (*glancing at his watch*). If we don't think up something and come to some decision, then on the twenty-second of August the cherry orchard and the whole estate will be sold at auction. Make up your mind! There's no other way out, I promise you. Absolutely none!

FIRS. In the old days, some forty–fifty years back—cherries were dried, preserved, pickled, made into jam, and sometimes . . .

GAEV. Be quiet, Firs.

FIRS. And sometimes whole cartloads of dried cherries were sent to Moscow and Kharkov. Then there was money! And in those days the dried cherries were soft, juicy, sweet, tasty. . . . They knew a recipe then. . . .

LYUBOV ANDREEVNA. And where's that recipe today?

FIRS. Forgotten. Nobody remembers.

PISHCHIK (*to Lyubov*). What's going on in Paris? How was it? You ate frogs?

LYUBOV ANDREEVNA. I ate crocodiles.

PISHCHIK. Can you imagine . . .

LOPAKHIN. Up till now there were only gentry and peasants in the country, but now the summer tourists have sprung up. Every town, even the smallest, is surrounded these days by summer cottages. And I'll bet that during the next twenty-odd years the summer tourist will multiply fantastically. Now he only drinks tea on his veranda, but it might just happen that on his puny two-and-a-half acres, he goes in for farming and then your cherry orchard will become happy, rich, lush. . . .

GAEV (*getting indignant*). What poppycock!

(*Enter Varya and Yasha.*)

VARYA. Mama dear, here are two telegrams for you. (*Selects a key; with a jangle opens the old bookcase.*) Here they are.

LYUBOV ANDREEVNA. This is from Paris. (*Tears up the telegrams, without reading them.*) I'm through with Paris.

GAEV. Lyuba, do you know how old that bookcase is? A week ago I pulled out the bottom drawer, and I looked, and there were numbers burnt into it. This bookcase was built exactly one hundred years ago. How do you like that? Maybe we ought to celebrate its anniversary. An inanimate object, but all the same, any way you look at it, a case to hold books.

PISHCHIK (*astounded*). A hundred years. . . . Can you imagine! . . .

GAEV. Yes. . . . This thing. . . . (*Clasping the bookcase*) Dear, venerable bookcase! I salute your existence, which for over a century has been dedicated to the enlightened idealism of virtue and justice. Your mute appeal to constructive endeavor has not faltered in the course of a century, upholding (*through tears*) in generations of our line, courage, faith in a better future and nurturing within us ideals of decency and social consciousness.

(*Pause.*)

LOPAKHIN. Yes. . . .

LYUBOV ANDREEVNA. You're still the same, Lyonya.

GAEV (*somewhat embarrassed*). Carom to the right corner! Red to the center!

LOPAKHIN (*glancing at his watch*). Well, my time's up.

YASHA (*handing medicine to Lyubov*). Maybe you'll take your pills now. . . .

PISHCHIK. Shouldn't take medicine, dearest lady. . . . It does no good, or harm. . . . Give that here . . . most respected lady. (*He takes the pills, shakes them into his palm, blows on them, pops them into his mouth and drinks some beer.*) There!

LYUBOV ANDREEVNA (*alarmed*). You've gone crazy!

PISHCHIK. I took all the pills.

LOPAKHIN. What a glutton!

(*They all laugh.*)

FIRS. The gentleman stayed with us during Holy Week, ate half-a-bucket of cucumbers. . . . (*Mumbles.*)

LYUBOV ANDREEVNA. What is he on about?

VARYA. For three years now he's been mumbling like that. We're used to it.

YASHA. Senility.

(*Charlotta Ivanovna crosses the stage in a white dress. She is very slender, tightly laced, with a pair of pincenez on a cord at her belt.*)

LOPAKHIN. Excuse me, Charlotta Ivanovna, I haven't yet had time to say hello to you. (*Tries to kiss her hand.*)

CHARLOTTA (*pulling her hand away*). If I let you kiss a hand, then next you'd be after a elbow, then a shoulder. . . .

LOPAKHIN. My unlucky day. (*Everybody laughs.*) Charlotta Ivanovna, show us a trick!

LYUBOV ANDREEVNA. Charlotta, show us a trick!

CHARLOTTA. No reason. I want to go to bed. (*Exits.*)

LOPAKHIN. We'll see each other again in three weeks. (*Kisses Lyubov Andreevna's hand.*) Meanwhile good-bye. It's time. (*To Gaev*) Be seeing you. (*Exchanges kisses with Pishchik*) Be seeing you. (*Gives his hand to Varya, then to Firs and Yasha*) I don't want to go. (*To Lyubov Andreevna*) If you think over this business of the cottages and decide, then let me know, I'll arrange a loan of fifty thousand or so. Give it some serious thought.

VARYA (*angrily*). Well, go once and for all!

LOPAKHIN. I'm going, I'm going. . . . (*He leaves.*)

GAEV. Boor. However, I apologize. . . . Varya's going to marry him, that's Varya's little fiancé!

VARYA. Don't say anything uncalled for, Uncle dear.

LYUBOV ANDREEVNA. Anyway, Varya, I shall be delighted. He's a good man.

PISHCHIK. A man, you've got to tell the truth . . . most worthy. . . . And my Dashenka . . . also says that . . . says all sorts of things. (*Snores but immediately wakes up.*) But by the way, most respected lady, will you lend me . . . two hundred forty rubles . . . tomorrow I've got to pay the interest on the mortgage.

VARYA (*alarmed*). We haven't got any, we haven't got any!

LYUBOV ANDREEVNA. As a matter of fact, I haven't a thing.

PISHCHIK. It'll turn up. (*Laughs.*) I never lose hope. There, I think, all is lost, I'm ruined, lo and behold!—the railroad runs across my land and . . . pays me for it. And then, watch, something else will happen, if not today, tomorrow . . . Dashenka will win two hundred thousand . . . she's got a lottery ticket.

LYUBOV ANDREEVNA. The coffee's finished, now we can go to bed.

FIRS (*brushes Gaev's clothes, scolding*). You didn't put on them trousers again. What am I going to do with you!

VARYA (*quietly*). Anya's asleep. (*Quietly opens a window.*) The sun's up already, it's not so cold. Look, Mama dear: what wonderful trees! My God, the air! The starlings are singing.

GAEV (*opens another window*). The orchard's all white. You haven't forgotten, Lyuba? There's that long pathway leading straight on, straight on, like a stretched ribbon, it glistens on moonlit nights. You remember? You haven't forgotten?

LYUBOV ANDREEVNA (*looks through the window at the orchard*). O my childhood, my innocence! I slept in this nursery, gazed out at the orchard, happiness awoke with me every morning, and it was just the same then, nothing has changed. (*Laughs with joy.*) All, all white! O my orchard! After the dark, drizzly autumn and the cold winter, you're young again, full of happiness, the heavenly angels haven't forsaken you. . . . If only I could lift this heavy stone from off my chest and shoulders, if only I could forget my past!

GAEV. Yes, and the orchard will be sold for debts, strange as it seems.

LYUBOV ANDREEVNA. Look, our poor Mama is walking through the orchard . . . in a white dress! (*Laughs with joy.*) There she is.

GAEV. Where?

VARYA. God be with you, Mama dear.

LYUBOV ANDREEVNA. There's nobody there, it just seemed so to me. At the right, by the turning to the summerhouse, a white sapling is bent over, looking like a woman. . . . (*Enter Trofimov in a shabby student's uniform and eyeglasses.*) What a marvelous orchard! White bunches of blossoms, blue sky . . .

TROFIMOV. Lyubov Andreevna! (*She stares round at him.*) I'll only pay my respects and then leave at once. (*Kisses her hand fervently.*) They told me to wait till morning, but I didn't have the patience. . . .

(*Lyubov Andreevna stares in bewilderment.*)

VARYA (*through tears*). This is Petya Trofimov.

TROFIMOV. Petya Trofimov, one-time tutor to your Grisha. . . . Can I have changed so much?

(*Lyubov Andreevna embraces him and weeps quietly.*)

GAEV (*embarrassed*). Come, come, Lyuba.

VARYA (*weeps*). Didn't I tell you, Petya, to wait till tomorrow.

LYUBOV ANDREEVNA. My Grisha . . . my little boy . . . Grisha . . . son. . . .

VARYA. There's no help for it, Mama dear. God's will be done.

TROFIMOV (*gently, through tears*). All right, all right. . . .

LYUBOV ANDREEVNA (*quietly weeping*). A little boy lost, drowned. . . . What for? What for, my friend? (*More quietly*) Anya's asleep in there, and I'm shouting . . . making noise. . . . Well now, Petya? Why have you become so homely? Why have you aged so?

TROFIMOV. On the train an old peasant woman called me "the mangy gent."

LYUBOV ANDREEVNA. You were just a boy in those days, a dear little student, but now your hair is thinning, eyeglasses. Are you really still a student? (*Goes to the door.*)

TROFIMOV. I suppose I'll be a perpetual student.

LYUBOV ANDREEVNA (*kisses her brother, then Varya*). Well, let's go to bed. . . . You've aged too, Leonid.

PISHCHIK (*follows her*). That means it's time for bed. . . . Och, my gout. I'll stay over with you. . . . And if you would, Lyubov Andreevna, my soul, tomorrow morning early . . . two hundred forty rubles. . . .

GAEV. He never gives up.

PISHCHIK. Two hundred forty rubles . . . to pay the interest on the mortgage.

LYUBOV ANDREEVNA. I haven't any money, dovie.

PISHCHIK. We'll pay it back, dear lady. . . . A trifling sum. . . .

LYUBOV ANDREEVNA. Well, all right, Leonid will let you have it. . . . You give it to him, Leonid.

GAEV. I'll give it to him all right, hold out your pockets.

LYUBOV ANDREEVNA. What can we do, give it to him. . . . He needs it. . . . He'll pay it back.

(*Lyubov Andreevna, Trofimov, Pishchik, and Firs exeunt. Gaev, Varya and Yasha remain.*)

GAEV. My sister still hasn't outgrown the habit of squandering money. (*To Yasha.*) Out of the way, my good man, you smell like a chicken-coop.

YASHA (*with a sneer*). But you're just the same as you always were, Leonid Andreich.

GAEV. Hows that? (*To Varya*) What did he say?

VARYA (*to Yasha*). Your mother's come from the village, ever since yesterday she's been sitting in the servant's hall, wanting to see you. . . .

YASHA. To hell with her!

VARYA. Ach, disgraceful!

YASHA. That's all I need. She might have come tomorrow. (*Exits.*)

VARYA. Mama dear is just as she was before, she hasn't changed a bit. If it were in her power, she'd give away everything.

GAEV. Yes. . . . (*Pause.*) If a large number of cures is suggested for a particular disease, that means the disease is incurable. I think, wrack my brains, I've come up with all sorts of solutions, all sorts, and that means, actually, none. It would be nice to inherit a fortune from somebody, nice if

we married off our Anya to a very rich man, nice to go off to Yaroslavl and try our luck with our auntie the Countess. Auntie's really very, very wealthy.

VARYA (*weeps*). If only God would help us.

GAEV. Stop snivelling. Auntie's very wealthy, but she isn't fond of us. In the first place, Sister married a courtroom lawyer, not a nobleman. . . . (*Anya appears in the doorway.*) Married a commoner and behaved herself, well, you can't say very virtuously. She's a good, kind, splendid person, I love her very much, but, no matter how much you consider the extenuating circumstances, even so, it must be admitted she's depraved. You can feel it in her slightest movement.

VARYA (*whispering*). Anya's standing in the doorway.

GAEV. Hows that? (*Pause.*) Extraordinary, something's got in my right eye. . . . My sight's beginning to fail. And Thursday, when I was at the County Court . . .

(*Anya enters.*)

VARYA. Why aren't you asleep, Anya?

ANYA. I can't fall asleep. I can't.

GAEV. My little tadpole. (*Kisses Anya's face, hands.*) My little girl. . . . (*Through tears*) You're not my niece, you're my angel, you're everything to me. Believe me, believe . . .

ANYA. I believe you, Uncle. Everybody loves you, respects you . . . but, dear Uncle, you must keep still, simply keep still. What were you saying just now about my Mama, your own sister? Why did you say that?

GAEV. Yes, yes. . . . (*Hides his face in his hands.*) In fact, it was terrible! My God! God, save me! And today I made a speech to the bookcase . . . like a fool! And as soon as I'd finished, I realized what a fool I'd been.

VARYA. True, Uncle dear, you ought to keep still. Just keep still. That's all.

ANYA. If you keep still, you'll be more at peace with yourself.

GAEV. I'll keep still. (*Kisses Anya's and Varya's hands.*) I'll keep still. Only this is business. Thursday I was at the County Court, well, some friends gathered around, started a conversation about this and that, six of one, half a dozen of the other, and it turns out it's possible to borrow money on an I.O.U. to pay the interest to the bank.

VARYA. If only God would help us!

GAEV. I'll go there on Tuesday and have another talk. (*To Varya*) Stop snivelling. (*To Anya*) Your Mama will talk to Lopakhin, he won't refuse her, of course. . . . And you, when you're rested up, will go to Yaroslavl to your grandmother the Countess. That way we'll have action in three directions—and our business is in the bag! We'll pay off the interest. I'm positive. . . . (*Pops a caramel into his mouth.*) Word of honor. I'll swear by whatever you like, the estate won't be sold! (*Excited*) I swear by my happiness! Here's my hand on it, call me a trashy, dishonorable man if I permit that auction! I swear with all my heart!

ANYA (*a more peaceful mood comes over her, she is happy*). You're so good, Uncle, so clever! (*Embraces her uncle.*) Now I feel calm! I'm calm! I'm happy!

(*Enter Firs.*)

FIRS (*scolding*). Leonid Andreich, have you no fear of God? When are you going to bed?

GAEV. Right now, right now. Go along, Firs. I'll even undress myself, how about that. Well, children, beddy-bye. . . . Details tomorrow, but for now go to bed. (*Kisses Anya and Varya.*) I'm a man of the 'eighties.[2] . . . People don't put much stock in that period, but all the same I can say I've suffered considerably for my convictions in my time. It's not for nothing I'm loved by the peasant. You've got to know the peasant! You've got to know with what . . .

ANYA. You're at it again, Uncle!

VARYA. You must keep still, Uncle dear.

FIRS (*angrily*). Leonid Andreich!

GAEV. Coming, coming. . . . Go to bed. Two cushion carom to the center! I pocket the white . . . (*Exits followed by Firs, hobbling.*)

ANYA. Now I'm calm. I don't want to go to Yaroslavl. I don't like Grandmama, but just the same, I'm calm. Thanks to Uncle. (*Sits down.*)

VARYA. I must get some sleep. I'm off. Oh, there was some unpleasantness while you were away. As you probably know, only the old servants live in the old quarters; Yefimushka, Polya, Yevstignei, oh, and Karp. They started letting certain tramps spend the night with them—I held my peace. Only then, I hear they're spreading the rumor that I gave orders to feed them nothing but peas. Out of stinginess, you see. . . . And this was all Yevstignei's doing. . . . Fine, thinks I. If that's how things are, thinks I, then just you wait. I send for Yevstignei. . . . (*Yawns.*) Up he trots. . . . What's wrong with you, I say, Yevstignei . . . you're such a nincompoop. . . . (*Glancing at Anya.*) Anechka! (*Pause.*) Fallen asleep! . . . (*Takes Anya by the arm.*) Let's go to bed. . . . Let's go! . . . (*Leads her.*) My darling has fallen asleep! Let's go. . . .

(*They exeunt. Far beyond the orchard a shepherd is playing his pipes. Trofimov crosses the stage and, seeing Anya and Varya, stops short.*)

[2]**A man of the 'eighties** The 1880s, when Russia was ruled by the reactionary Alexander III, was a period of intensive political repression. Revolutionary movements were forcibly suppressed, as were the more liberal journals, and social activism virtually ceased. The intelligentsia took refuge in the passive resistance of Tolstoyanism and a tame dabbling in "art for art's sake" (which explains Gaev's chatter about the decadents, mentioned in Act 2). The feeling of social and political impotence led to the torpid aimlessness that is a common theme in Chekhov's works.

VARYA. Ssh. . . . She's asleep . . . asleep. . . . Let's go, dearest.

ANYA (*softly, half-asleep*). I'm so tired. . . . all the bells. . . . Uncle . . . dear . . . and mama and uncle . . .

VARYA. Let's go, dearest, let's go. . . . (*Exits into Anya's room.*)

TROFIMOV (*moved*). My sunshine! My springtime!

ACT 2

A field. An old, long-abandoned shrine leaning to one side. Beside it a well, large stones which were once, obviously, tombstones, and an old bench. At one side, towering poplars cast their shadows; here the cherry orchard begins. Further off are telegraph poles, and way in the distance, dimly sketched on the horizon, is a large town, which can be seen only in the best and clearest weather. A road to Gaev's estate can be seen. Soon the sun will set. Charlotta, Yasha, and Dunyasha are sitting on the bench. Yepikhodov stands nearby and strums a guitar; everyone sits rapt in thought. Charlotta is wearing an old peaked cap; she has taken a rifle off her shoulder and is adjusting a buckle on the strap.

CHARLOTTA (*pensively*). I haven't got a proper passport. I don't know how old I am, and I always have the impression I'm still a young thing. When I was a little girl, my father and Mama used to go from fairground to fairground, giving performances, rather good ones. And I would jump the *salto mortale*[3] and do all sorts of different stunts. And when Papa and Mama died, a German lady took me to her house and started teaching me. Fine. I grew up, then turned into a governess. But where I'm from and who I am—I don't know. . . . Who my parents were, maybe they weren't married. . . . I don't know. (*Pulls a cucumber from her pocket and eats it.*) I don't know anything. (*Pause.*) I would so like to talk, but there's no one to talk with. . . . No one.

YEPIKHODOV (*strums his guitar and sings*). "What care I for the noisy world, what are friends and foes to me. . . . " How pleasant to play the mandolin!

DUNYASHA. That's a guitar, not a mandolin. (*Looks in a hand-mirror and powders her nose.*)

YEPIKHODOV. To a lovesick lunatic, this is a mandolin. . . . (*Sings quietly*) "Were but my heart aflame with the spark of requited love. . . . "

(*Yasha joins in.*)

CHARLOTTA. These people are rotten singers. . . . Fooey! A pack of hyenas.

DUNYASHA (*to Yasha*). Anyway, how lucky you were to live abroad.

YASHA. Yes, of course. I can't disagree with you there. (*Yawns, then lights a cigar.*)

[3]**salto mortale** death-defying leap

YEPIKHODOV. Stands to reason. Abroad everything has long since attained its complete maturation point.

YASHA. Goes without saying.

YEPIKHODOV. I'm a cultured fellow, I read all kinds of remarkable books, but somehow I can't figure out my own inclinations, what I personally want, to live or to shoot myself, strictly speaking, but nevertheless I always carry a revolver on my person. Here it is. . . . (*Displays a revolver.*)

CHARLOTTA. I'm done. Now I'll go. (*Slips the gun over her shoulder.*) Yepikhodov, you're a very clever fellow and a very frightening one; the women ought to love you madly. Brr! (*Exiting*) These clever people are all so stupid there's no one for me to talk to. . . . No one. . . . All alone, alone, I've got no one and . . . who I am, why I am, I don't know. (*Exits.*)

YEPIKHODOV. Strictly speaking, not flying off on tangents, I must declare concerning myself, by the way, that Fate treats me ruthlessly, as a storm does a rowboat. If, suppose, I'm wrong about this, then why when I woke up this morning, to give but a single example, I look and there on my chest is a terrifically huge spider. . . . This big. (*Uses both hands to show.*) Or then again, I'll take some beer, so as to drink it, and there, lo and behold, is something in the highest degree improper, such as a cockroach. . . . (*Pause.*) Have you read Buckle?[4] (*Pause.*) I should like to trouble you with a couple of words, Avdotya Fyodorovna.

DUNYASHA. Go ahead.

YEPIKHODOV. I'm desirous of seeing you in private. . . . (*Sighs.*)

DUNYASHA (*embarrassed*). All right . . . only first bring me my shawl . . . It's next to the cupboard . . . it's getting damp.

YEPIKHODOV. All right, ma'am . . . I'll fetch it, ma'am. . . . Now I know what I must do with my revolver. . . . (*Takes the guitar and exits playing it.*)

YASHA. Twenty-two troubles! Pretty stupid, take it from me. (*Yawns.*)

DUNYASHA. God forbid he should shoot himself. (*Pause.*) I've gotten jittery, always worrying. When I was still a little girl, they took me to the master's house, now I'm out of touch with the simple life, and my hands are white, as white as can be, like a young lady's. I've gotten sensitive, so delicate, ladylike, afraid of everything. . . . Awfully so.

---

[4] **Buckle** Henry Thomas Buckle—pronounced Bucklee—(1821–62), whose *History of Civilization in England* (1857, 1861) posited that skepticism was the handmaiden of progress and that credulity (for which, read religion) retarded civilization's advance. He enjoyed immense popularity among progressive Russians in the 1860s, but by the end of the century seemed outmoded. Chekhov himself had read Buckle when a youth and quoted him approvingly in his early correspondence; as the years wore on, however, he began to take issue with many of Buckle's contentions. In *The Cherry Orchard*, he uses the reference to indicate that Yepikhodov's attempts at self-education are jejune and far behind the times.

And, Yasha, if you deceive me, then I don't know what'll happen to my nerves.

YASHA (*kisses her*). Some tomato! Of course, every girl ought to know just how far to go, and if there's one thing I hate, it's a girl who misbehaves herself.

DUNYASHA. I love you ever so much, you're educated, you can discuss anything.

(*Pause.*)

YASHA (*yawns*). Yes'm. . . . The way I look at it, it's like this: if a girl loves somebody, that means she's immoral. (*Pause.*) Nice smoking a cigar in the fresh air. . . . (*Listening*) Someone's coming this way. . . . The gentry. . . . (*Dunyasha impulsively embraces him.*) Go home, as if you'd been to the river for a swim, take this road or you'll run into them and they'll think I've been going out with you. I couldn't stand that.

DUNYASHA (*coughs quietly*). I've got a headache from your cigar. . . . (*Exits.*)

(*Yasha remains sitting beside the shrine. Enter Lyubov Andreevna, Gaev, and Lopakhin.*)

LOPAKHIN. You've got to decide once and for all—time won't stand still. It's really quite a dead issue. Do you agree to rent land for cottages or not? Answer in one word: yes or no? Just one word!

LYUBOV ANDREEVNA. Who's been smoking those revolting cigars here? . . . (*Sits.*)

GAEV. Now that the railroad's in operation it's become convenient. (*Sits.*) You ride to town and have lunch . . . yellow to the center! I ought to stop off at home, play one game. . . .

LYUBOV ANDREEVNA. You'll have time.

LOPAKHIN. Just one word! (*Pleading.*) Give me an answer!

GAEV (*yawning*). How's that?

LYUBOV ANDREEVNA (*looking into her purse*). Yesterday I had lots of money, but today there's very little. My poor Varya for economy's sake feeds everybody milk soup, in the kitchen the old people get nothing but peas, and somehow I'm spending recklessly. . . . (*Drops the purse, scattering gold coins.*) Oh dear, spilled all over the place. . . . (*Annoyed.*)

YASHA. Allow me, I'll pick them up at once. (*Gathers the money.*)

LYUBOV ANDREEVNA. That's sweet of you, Yasha. And why did I go into town for lunch. . . . That shabby restaurant of yours with its music, the tablecloths smelt of soap. . . . Why drink so much, Lyonya? Why eat so much? Why talk so much? Today in the restaurant you started in talking a lot again and all off the subject. About the 'seventies, about the decadents. And who to? Talking to waiters about the decadents!

LOPAKHIN. Yes.

GAEV (*waves his hands*). I'm incorrigible, it's obvious. . . . (*Irritably, to Yasha*) What's the matter, forever whirling around in front of us. . . .

YASHA (*laughing*). I can't hear your voice without laughing.

GAEV (*to his sister*). Either he goes, or I do. . . .

LYUBOV ANDREEVNA. Go away, Yasha, run along.

YASHA (*handing the purse to Lyubov Andreevna*). I'll go right now. (*Barely restraining his laughter.*) This very minute. . . . (*Exits.*)

LOPAKHIN. Rich old Deriganov intends to purchase your estate. They say he's coming to the auction.

LYUBOV ANDREEVNA. Where did you hear that?

LOPAKHIN. They were discussing it in town.

GAEV. Our aunt in Yaroslavl promised to send something, but when and how much she'll send I don't know.

LOPAKHIN. How much is she sending? A hundred thousand? Two hundred?

LYUBOV ANDREEVNA. Well . . . ten or fifteen thousand—and we're grateful for that much.

LOPAKHIN. Excuse me, but such frivolous people as you, my friends, such unbusinesslike, peculiar people I never encountered before. Somebody tells you in plain Russian your estate is going to be sold, but you simply refuse to understand.

LYUBOV ANDREEVNA. But what are we going to do? Inform us, what?

LOPAKHIN. I inform you every day. Every day I tell you one and the same thing. Both the cherry orchard and the land have got to be leased as lots for cottages, do it right now, immediately—the auction is staring you in the face! Will you understand! Decide once and for all that there'll be cottages, they'll lend you as much money as you want, and then you'll be saved.

LYUBOV ANDREEVNA. Summer cottages and summer tourists—it's so vulgar, excuse me.

GAEV. I agree with you wholeheartedly.

LOPAKHIN. I'll either burst into tears or scream or fall down in a faint. It's too much for me! You're wearing me out! (*To Gaev*) You old woman!

GAEV. How's that?

LOPAKHIN. Old woman! (*Starts to exit.*)

LYUBOV ANDREEVNA (*frightened*). No, don't go, stay, dovie. Please! Maybe we'll think of something.

LOPAKHIN. What's there to think about?

LYUBOV ANDREEVNA. Don't go, please. With you here somehow it's jollier. . . . (*Pause.*) I keep anticipating something, as if the house were about to collapse on top of us.

GAEV (*in deep meditation*). Off the cushion to the corner . . . double to the center. . . .

LYUBOV ANDREEVNA. We've sinned so very much. . . .

LOPAKHIN. What kind of sins have you got. . . .

GAEV (*pops a caramel into his mouth*). They say I've eaten up my whole estate in caramels. . . . (*Laughs*)

LYUBOV ANDREEVNA. Oh, my sins. . . . I've always thrown money around recklessly, like a maniac, and married a man who produced nothing but debts. My husband died of champagne—he drank frightfully—and then, to my misfortune, I fell in love with another man, had an affair, and just at that time—this was my first punishment, dropped right on my head—the river over there . . . my little boy drowned, and I went abroad, went for good, so as never to return, never see that river again . . . I shut my eyes, ran away, beside myself, and *he* came after me . . . cruelly, brutally. I bought a villa near Menton, because *he* fell ill there, and for three years I didn't know what it was to rest day or night: the invalid exhausted me, my heart shrivelled up. But the next year, when the villa was sold for debts, I went to Paris, and there he robbed me, ran off and had an affair with another woman, I tried to poison myself . . . so silly, so shameful . . . and suddenly I had a longing for Russia, for my country, my little girl. . . . (*Wipes away her tears.*) Lord, Lord, be merciful, forgive me my sins! Don't punish me anymore! (*Takes a telegram out of her pocket.*) I received this today from Paris. . . . He begs my forgiveness, implores me to come back. . . . (*Tears up telegram.*) Sounds like music somewhere. (*Listens.*)

GAEV. That's our famous Jewish orchestra. You remember, four fiddles, a flute and a double bass.

LYUBOV ANDREEVNA. Does it still exist? We ought to hire them sometime and throw a party.

LOPAKHIN (*listening*). I don't hear it. . . . (*Sings softly*) "And for cash the Prussians will Frenchify the Russians." (*Laughs.*) What a play I saw at the theatre yesterday, very funny.

LYUBOV ANDREEVNA. And most likely there was nothing funny about it. It's not for you to look at plays, you should look at yourselves more. You all lead such gray lives, you talk such utter nonsense.

LOPAKHIN. That's true. I've got to admit, our life is idiotic. . . . (*Pause.*) My daddy was a peasant, an ignoramus, he didn't understand anything, didn't teach me but kept getting drunk and beating me with a stick. When you come down to it, I'm the same kind of idiot and ignoramus. I never studied anything, my handwriting is terrible, I write, I'm ashamed to show it to people, like a pig.

LYUBOV ANDREEVNA. You ought to get married, my friend.

LOPAKHIN. Yes . . . that's true.

LYUBOV ANDREEVNA. You should marry our Varya; she's a good girl.

LOPAKHIN. Yes.

LYUBOV ANDREEVNA. I adopted her from the common folk, she works the livelong day, but the main thing is she loves you. Yes and you've cared for her for a long time.

LOPAKHIN. Why not? I'm not against it. . . . She's a good girl.

(*Pause.*)

GAEV. They've offered me a position at the bank. Six thousand a year. . . . Did you hear?

LYUBOV ANDREEVNA. You indeed! Stay where you are. . . .

(*Firs enters; he is carrying an overcoat.*)

FIRS (*to Gaev*). Please, sir, put it on, it's damp here.

GAEV (*putting on the overcoat*). You're a pest, my man.

FIRS. Never you mind. . . . You went out this morning, didn't tell me. (*Inspects him.*)

LYUBOV ANDREEVNA. How old you're getting, Firs!

FIRS. What's wanted?

LOPAKHIN. The mistress says, you're getting very old!

FIRS. I've lived a long time. They were planning my wedding, long before your daddy was even born. . . . (*Laughs.*) And when the serfs was freed,[5] I was already head valet. Those days I didn't hanker to be freed, I stayed by the masters. . . . (*Pause.*) And I remember, everybody was glad, but what they was glad about, they didn't know themselves.

LOPAKHIN. It used to be nice all right. For instance, you got flogged.

FIRS (*not having heard*). I'll say. The peasants stood by the masters, the masters stood by the peasants, but now everything is topsy-turvy, can't figure out nothing.

GAEV. Keep quiet, Firs. Tomorrow I have to go to town. They promised to introduce me to some general, who might make us a loan on an I.O.U.

LOPAKHIN. Nothing'll come of it. And you won't pay the interest, you can be sure.

LYUBOV ANDREEVNA. He's raving. There are no such generals.

(*Enter Trofimov, Anya, and Varya.*)

GAEV. And here comes our crowd.

ANYA. Mama's sitting down.

LYUBOV ANDREEVNA (*tenderly*). Come, come. . . . My darlings. . . . (*kissing Anya and Varya.*) If only you both knew how much I love you. Sit beside me, that's right.

(*Everyone sits down.*)

LOPAKHIN. Our perpetual student is always stepping out with the ladies.

TROFIMOV. None of your business.

LOPAKHIN. Soon he'll be fifty and he'll still be a student.

TROFIMOV. Stop your idiotic jokes.

LOPAKHIN. What are you getting angry about, you crank?

TROFIMOV. Stop pestering me.

---

[5]**When the serfs was freed** The serfs were emancipated by Alexander II in 1861, two years before Lincoln followed suit. Under the terms of the Emancipation Act, peasants were allotted land but had to pay back the government in annual installments, the sum used to indemnify former landowners. House serfs, on the other hand, were allotted no land. Both these conditions caused tremendous hardship and were responsible for great unrest among the newly manumitted. So there is more than a grain of truth in Firs's jeremiad.

LOPAKHIN (*laughs*). May I ask, what's your opinion of me?

TROFIMOV. Here's my opinion, Yermolai Alekseich. You're a rich man, soon you'll be a millionaire. And in the same way a wild beast that devours everything that crosses its path is necessary to the conversion of matter, *you're* necessary.

(*Everyone laughs.*)

VARYA. Petya, tell us about the planets instead.

LYUBOV ANDREEVNA. No, let's go with yesterday's conversation.

TROFIMOV. What was that about?

GAEV. About human pride.

TROFIMOV. Yesterday we talked for quite a while, but we didn't get anywhere. In a proud man, according to you, there's something mystical. It may be your viewpoint's the right one, but if we reason it out simply, without frills, what pride can there be, is there any sense to it, if Man is poorly constructed physiologically, if the vast majority is crude, unthinking, profoundly wretched? We ought to stop admiring ourselves. We should just work.

GAEV. You'll die nonetheless.

TROFIMOV. Who knows? What does that mean—you'll die? Maybe Man has a hundred senses and with death only five, the ones known to us, perish, but the remaining ninety-five live on.

LYUBOV ANDREEVNA. Aren't you clever, Petya. . . .

LOPAKHIN (*ironically*). Awfully!

TROFIMOV. Mankind moves forward, perfecting its powers. Everything that's unattainable for us now will some day come within our grasp and our understanding, only we've got to work to help the Truth seekers with all our might. Here in Russia very few people do any work at the moment. The vast majority of educated people, as I know them, are searching for nothing, do nothing, and so far aren't capable of work. They call themselves intellectuals, but they refer to their servants by pet names, treat the peasants like animals, are poorly informed, read nothing serious, do absolutely nothing, just talk about science, barely understand art. They're all intense, they all have glum faces, and all they talk about is major concerns, they philosophize, but meanwhile anybody can see that the working class is abominably fed, sleeps without pillows, thirty or forty to a single room, everywhere bedbugs, foul odors, dampness, moral filth. . . . And obviously all our nice chitchat serves only to shut our own eyes and other people's. Show me, where are the day-care centers we do so much talking about so often, where are the reading rooms? People only write about them in novels, in fact there aren't any. There's only dirt, vulgarity, Asiatic bestiality. . . . I distrust and don't care for very intense faces, I distrust intense conversations. It's better to keep still!

LOPAKHIN. Take me, I get up before five every morning, I work from dawn to dusk, well, I always have money on hand, my own and other people's, and I notice what the people around me are like. You only have to start in business to find out how few honest, decent people there are. Sometimes, when I can't sleep, I think: "Lord, you gave us vast forests, boundless fields, the widest horizons, and living here, we ourselves ought to be regular giants."

LYUBOV ANDREEVNA. What do you need giants for? . . . They're only useful in fairy tales, anywhere else they're scary.

(*Far upstage Yepikhodov crosses and plays his guitar.*)

LYUBOV ANDREEVNA (*dreamily*). There goes Yepikhodov. . . .

ANYA (*dreamily*). There goes Yepikhodov. . . .

GAEV. The sun is setting ladies and gentlemen.

TROFIMOV. Yes.

GAEV (*quietly, as if declaiming*). Oh, Nature, wondrous creature, aglow with eternal radiance, beautiful yet impassive, you, whom we call Mother, merging within yourself Life and Death, you vitalize and you destroy. . . .

VARYA (*pleading*). Uncle dear!

ANYA. Uncle, you're at it again!

TROFIMOV. You'd better bank the yellow to the center doublet.

GAEV. I'll keep still, keep still.

(*Everyone sits down, absorbed in thought. The only sound is Firs softly muttering. Suddenly a distant sound is heard, as if from the sky, the sound of a snapped string, dying away, mournfully.*)

LYUBOV ANDREEVNA. What's that?

LOPAKHIN. I don't know. Somewhere far off in a mineshaft a bucket dropped. But somewhere very far off.

GAEV. Or perhaps it was some kind of bird . . . such as a heron.

TROFIMOV. Or an owl . . .

LYUBOV ANDREEVNA (*shivers*). Unpleasant anyway.

(*Pause.*)

FIRS. Before the disaster it was the same: the screech-owl hooted and the samovar hummed non-stop.

GAEV. Before what disaster?

FIRS. Before the serfs were freed.

(*Pause.*)

LYUBOV ANDREEVNA. Come everyone, let's go home. Evening's coming on. (*To Anya*) You've got tears in your eyes. . . . What is it, my little girl? (*Kisses her.*)

ANYA. Nothing special, Mama. Never mind.

TROFIMOV. Someone's coming.

(*A Tramp appears, in a shabby white peaked cap, and an overcoat; he's tipsy.*)

TRAMP. Allow me to inquire, can I reach the station straight on from here?

GAEV. You can. Follow that road.

TRAMP. I'm extremely obliged to you. (*Coughs.*) Splendid weather. . . . (*Declaiming*) "Brother mine, suffering brother. . . . come to Volga, whose laments . . . " (*To Varya*) Mademoiselle, bestow some thirty kopeks on a famished fellow Russian. . . .

(*Varya is alarmed, screams.*)

LOPAKHIN (*angrily*). That'll be enough of that!

LYUBOV ANDREEVNA (*flustered*). Take this . . . here you are. . . . (*Looks in her purse.*) No silver. . . . Never mind, here's a gold-piece for you. . . .

TRAMP. Extremely obliged to you! (*Exits.*)

(*Laughter.*)

VARYA (*frightened*). I'm going. . . . I'm going. . . . Ach, Mama dear, there's nothing in the house for people to eat, and you gave him a gold-piece.

LYUBOV ANDREEVNA. What can you do with a silly like me! I'll let you have everything I've got when we get home. Yermolai Alekseich, lend me some more!

LOPAKHIN. Gladly.

LYUBOV ANDREEVNA. Come along, ladies and gentlemen, it's time. And look, Varya, we've made quite a match for you, congratulations.

VARYA (*through tears*). You mustn't joke about this, Mama.

LOPAKHIN. Oldphelia, get thee to a nunnery.[6] . . .

GAEV. My hands are trembling: it's been a long time since I played billiards.

LOPAKHIN. Oldphelia, oh nymph, in thy horizons be all my sins remembered!

LYUBOV ANDREEVNA. Come along, ladies and gentlemen. Almost time for supper.

VARYA. He scared me. My heart's pounding so.

LOPAKHIN. I remind you, ladies and gentlemen, on the twenty-second of August the estate will be auctioned off. Think about that! . . . Think! . . .

(*Exeunt everyone except Trofimov and Anya.*)

ANYA (*laughing*). Thank the tramp, he scared off Varya, now we're alone.

TROFIMOV. Varya's afraid we'll suddenly fall in love with one another, so she hangs around us all day long. Her narrow mind can't comprehend that we're above love. Avoiding the petty and specious that keeps us from being free and happy, that's the goal and meaning of our life. Forward! We march irresistibly toward the shining star, glowing there in the distance! Forward! No dropping behind, friends!

[6]**Oldphelia** Lopakhin is apparently an avid theatre-goer and misquotes from one of the many bad Russian translations of Shakespeare. The reference is to Hamlet's admonition to Ophelia.

ANYA (*stretching up her arms*). You speak so well! (*Pause.*) It's wonderful here today.

TROFIMOV. Yes, superb weather.

ANYA. What you have done to me, Petya, why have I stopped loving the cherry orchard as I did? I loved it so tenderly, there seemed to me no finer place on earth than our orchard.

TROFIMOV. All Russia is our orchard. The world is wide and beautiful and there are many wonderful places in it. (*Pause.*) Just think, Anya: your grandfather, great-grandfather and all your ancestors were slave-owners, owners of living souls, and from every cherry in the orchard, every leaf, every tree trunk there must be human beings watching you, you must hear voices. . . . To own living souls—it's really corrupted all of you, those who lived before and those living now, so that your mother, you, your uncle, no longer notice that you're living in debt, at other peoples' expense, at the expense of those people whom you wouldn't even let beyond your front hall. . . . We're at least two hundred years behind the times, we've still got absolutely nothing, no definite attitude to the past, we just philosophize, complain we're depressed or drink vodka. Yet it's so clear that before we start living in the present, we must first atone for our past, finish with it, and we can atone for it only through suffering, only through extraordinary, incessant labor. Understand that, Anya.

ANYA. The house we live in hasn't been our house for a long time, and I'll go away, I give you my word.

TROFIMOV. If you have the housekeeper's keys, throw them down the well and go away. Be free as the wind.

ANYA (*enraptured*). You speak so well!

TROFIMOV. Believe me, Anya, believe! I'm not yet thirty, I'm young. I'm still a student, but I've already undergone so much! When winter comes, I'm starved, sick, worried, poor as a beggar, and—where haven't I been chased by Fate, where haven't I been! And yet, always, every moment of the day and night, my soul has been full of inexplicable presentiments. I foresee happiness, Anya, I can see it already. . . .

ANYA (*dreamily*). The moon's on the rise.

(*We can hear Yepikhodov playing the same gloomy tune as before on his guitar. The moon comes up. Somewhere near the poplars Varya is looking for Anya and calling: "Anya! Where are you?"*)

TROFIMOV. Yes, the moon's on the rise. (*Pause.*) Here's happiness, here it comes, drawing closer and closer, I can already hear its footsteps. And if we don't see it, can't recognize it, what's wrong with that? Others will see it!

VARYA'S VOICE. Anya! Where are you?

TROFIMOV. That Varya again! (*Angrily*) Appalling!

ANYA. So what? Let's go down to the river. It's nice there.

TROFIMOV. Let's go. (*They exit.*)

VARYA'S VOICE. Anya! Anya!

ACT 3

The drawing room, separated from the ballroom by an arch. A chandelier is alight. We can hear, as if in the hallway, a Jewish orchestra, the same mentioned in Act 2. Evening. Grand-rond is being played in the ballroom. Simeonov-Pishchik's voice: "Promenade à une paire!" Enter the drawing room: in the first couple Pishchik and Charlotta Ivanovna, in the second Trofimov and Lyubov Andreevna, in the third Anya and the Postal Clerk, in the fourth Varya and the Stationmaster, etc. Varya is weeping quietly and while dancing, wipes away the tears. In the last couple Dunyasha. They go through the drawing-room. Pishchik calls out: "Grand-rond balancez!" and "Les cavaliers à genoux et remerciez vos dames!" Firs in a tail-coat crosses the room with seltzer bottle on a tray. Pishchik and Trofimov enter the room.

PISHCHIK. I've got high blood pressure, I've already had two strokes, it's tough dancing, but as the saying goes, when you run with the pack, bark or don't bark, but keep on wagging your tail. Actually I've got the constitution of a horse. My late father, what a cut-up, rest in peace, used to talk of our ancestry as if our venerable line, the Simeonov-Pishchiks, were descended from the very horse Caligula made a Senator. . . . (*Sits down.*) But here's my problem: no money! A hungry dog believes only in meat. . . . (*Snores and immediately wakes up.*) Just like me. . . . I can't think of anything but money. . . .

TROFIMOV. As a matter of fact, there is something horsey about your build.

PISHCHIK. So what . . . a horse is a fine beast . . . you could sell a horse. . . .

(*We hear billiards played in the next room. Varya appears under the arch in the ballroom.*)

TROFIMOV (*teasing*). Madam Lopakhin! Madam Lopakhin!

VARYA (*angrily*). Mangy gent!

TROFIMOV. Yes, I'm a mangy gent and proud of it!

VARYA (*brooding bitterly*). Here we've hired musicians and what are we going to pay them with? (*Exits.*)

TROFIMOV (*to Pishchik*). If the energy you've wasted in the course of a lifetime tracking down money to pay off interest had gone into something else, then you probably could have turned the world upside-down.

PISHCHIK. Nietzsche[7] . . . a philosopher . . . the greatest, most famous . . . a man of immense intellect, says in his works it's justifiable to counterfeit money.

TROFIMOV. So you've read Nietzsche?

---

[7]**Nietzsche** Friedrich Wilhelm Nietzsche (1844–1900), whose philosophy encourages a new "master" morality for Supermen and instigates revolt against the conventional constraints of Western civilization

PISHCHIK. Well . . . Dashenka told me. But now I'm in such straits that if it came to counterfeiting money . . . Day after tomorrow three hundred rubles to pay . . . I've already borrowed a hundred and thirty. . . . (*Feeling his pockets, alarmed.*) The money's gone! I've lost the money! (*Through tears*) Where's the money? (*Gleefully*) Here it is, in the lining. . . . I was really sweating for a minute.

(*Enter Lyubov Andreevna and Charlotta Ivanovna.*)

LYUBOV ANDREEVNA (*humming a lively dance*). Why is Lyonya taking so long? What's he doing in town? (*To Dunyasha*) Dunyasha, offer the musicians some tea. . . .
TROFIMOV. The auction didn't come off, in all likelihood.
LYUBOV ANDREEVNA. And the musicians arrived at the wrong time and we started the ball at the wrong time. . . . Well, never mind. . . . (*Sits down and hums softly.*)
CHARLOTTA (*hands Pishchik a deck of cards*). Here's a deck of cards for you, think of one particular card.
PISHCHIK. I've got one.
CHARLOTTA. Now shuffle the deck. Very good. Hand it over. O my dear Mister Pishchik. Ein, zwei, drei! Now look at it, it's in your breast pocket. . . .
PISHCHIK (*pulling a card from his breast pocket*). Eight of spades, absolutely right! (*Astounded*) Can you imagine!
CHARLOTTA (*holds deck of cards on her palm, to Trofimov*). Tell me quick, which card's on top.
TROFIMOV. What? Well, the queen of spades.
CHARLOTTA. Right! (*To Pishchik*) Well? Which card's on top?
PISHCHIK. The ace of hearts.
CHARLOTTA. Right! (*Claps her hand over her palm, the deck of cards disappears.*) Isn't it lovely weather today! (*She is answered by a mysterious feminine voice, as if from beneath the floor: "Oh yes, marvellous weather, Madam."*) You're so nice, my ideal. . . .
VOICE. Madam, I been liking you ferry much.
STATIONMASTER (*applauding*). Lady ventriloquist, bravo!
PISHCHIK (*astounded*). Can you imagine! Bewitching Charlotta Ivanovna. . . . I'm simply in love with you. . . .
CHARLOTTA. In love? (*Shrugging*) What do you know about love? *Guter Mensch, aber schlechter Musikant.*[8]
TROFIMOV (*claps Pishchik on the shoulder*). Good old horse. . . .
CHARLOTTA. Please pay attention, one more trick. (*Takes a rug from a chair.*) Here is a very nice rug. I'd like to sell it . . . (*Shakes it out.*) What am I offered?
PISHCHIK (*astounded*). Can you imagine!
CHARLOTTA. Ein, zwei, drei! (*Quickly lifts the lowered rug.*)

(*Behind the rug stands Anya, who curtsies, runs to her mother, embraces her, and runs back to the ballroom amid the general delight.*)

LYUBOV ANDREEVNA (*applauding*). Bravo, bravo!

---

[8]*Guter Mensch, aber schlechter Musikant* a good man, but a poor musician

CHARLOTTA. One more! Ein, zwei, drei! (*Raises the rug.*)

(*Behind the rug stands Varya, who bows.*)

PISHCHIK (*astounded*). Can you imagine!
CHARLOTTA. The end! (*Throws the rug at Pishchik, curtsies, and runs into the ballroom.*)
PISHCHIK (*scurrying after her*). You little rascal! . . . How do you like that! How do you like that! (*Exits.*)
LYUBOV ANDREEVNA. And Leonid still isn't back. I don't understand what he can be doing in town all this time! Everything must be over there, either the estate is sold or the auction didn't take place, but why keep us in suspense so long?
VARYA (*trying to solace her*). Uncle dear bought it, I'm sure of it.
TROFIMOV (*sarcastically*). Sure.
VARYA. Granny sent him power of attorney, so he could buy it in her name and transfer the debt. She did it for Anya. And I'm sure, God willing, that Uncle dear bought it.
LYUBOV ANDREEVNA. Granny in Yaroslavl sent fifty thousand to buy the estate in her name—she doesn't trust us—but that money won't even manage to pay off the interest. (*Hides her face in her hands.*) Today my fate will be decided, my fate. . . .
TROFIMOV (*teases Varya*). Madam Lopakhin!
VARYA (*angrily*). Perpetual student! Twice already you've been expelled from the university.
LYUBOV ANDREEVNA. Why are you getting angry, Varya? He teases you about Lopakhin, what of it? You want to—then marry Lopakhin, he's a good man, an interesting person. You don't want to—don't get married; nobody's forcing you, sweetheart. . . .
VARYA. I regard this as a serious matter, Mama dear, I've got to speak frankly. He's a good man, I like him.
LYUBOV ANDREEVNA. Then marry him. I don't understand what you're waiting for!
VARYA. Mama dear, I can't propose to him myself. It's been two years now they've talked about him, everyone's talking, but he either keeps still or makes jokes. I understand. He's getting rich, involved in business, no time for me. If only I'd had some money, even a little, just a hundred rubles, I'd have dropped everything and gone far away. I'd have gone to a convent.
TROFIMOV. Glorious!
VARYA (*to Trofimov*). A student ought to act intelligent! (*In a soft voice, tearfully*) How homely you've become, Petya. How old you've grown! (*To Lyubov Andreevna, no longer weeping*) Only I can't do without work, Mama dear. I have to do something every minute.

(*Enter Yasha.*)

YASHA (*barely restraining his laughter*). Yepikhodov broke a billiard cue!

(*He exits.*)

VARYA. What's Yepikhodov doing here? Who allowed him to play billiards? I don't understand these people. (*She exits.*)

LYUBOV ANDREEVNA. Don't tease her, Petya, can't you see she's sad enough without that?

TROFIMOV. She's just too officious, poking her nose in other people's business. All summer long she couldn't leave us alone, me or Anya. She was afraid a romance might spring up between us. What concern is it of hers? And anyway, I didn't show any signs of it, I'm so removed from banality. We're above love!

LYUBOV ANDREEVNA. Well then, I must be beneath love. (*Extremely upset*) Why isn't Leonid back? If only I knew whether the estate were sold or not. Calamity seems so incredible to me that I don't even know what to think, I'm at a loss. . . . I could scream right this minute. . . . I could do something absurd. Save me, Petya. Say something, tell me. . . .

TROFIMOV. Whether the estate's sold today or not—what's the difference? It's been over and done with for a long time now, no turning back, the bridges are burnt. Calm down, dear lady. You mustn't deceive yourself, for once in your life you've got to look the truth straight in the eye.

LYUBOV ANDREEVNA. What truth? You can see where truth is and where falsehood is, but I seem to have lost my sight. I can't see anything. You boldly settle all the important questions, but tell me, dovie, isn't that because you're young, because you haven't had time to suffer through any of your problems? You boldly look forward, but isn't that because you don't see and don't expect anything awful, because life is still concealed from your young eyes? You're more courageous and more sincere and more profound than we are, but stop and think, be indulgent if only in your fingertips, spare me. Why, I was born here, here lived my father and my mother, my grandfather, I love this house, without the cherry orchard, I couldn't make sense of my life, and if it really has to be sold, then sell me along with the orchard. . . . (*Embraces Trofimov, kisses him on the forehead.*) Why, my son was drowned here. . . . (*Weeps.*) Show me some pity, dear, kind man.

TROFIMOV. You know I sympathize wholeheartedly.

LYUBOV ANDREEVNA. But you should say so differently, differently. . . . (*Takes out a handkerchief, a telegram falls to the floor.*) My heart is so heavy today, you can't imagine. Here it's too noisy for me, my soul shudders at every sound, I shudder all over, but I can't go off by myself, it would terrify me to be alone in silence. Don't blame me, Petya . . . I love you like my own flesh-and-blood. I'd gladly have given you Anya's hand, believe me, only, dovie, you've got to study, got to finish your course. You don't do anything, Fate simply hustles you from place to place, it's so odd. . . . Isn't that right? Isn't it? And some-thing's got to be done about your beard, to make it grow somehow. . . . (*Laughs.*) You look funny!

TROFIMOV (*picks up telegram*). I've no desire to be a fashion-plate.

LYUBOV ANDREEVNA. This telegram's from Paris. Every day I get one. Yesterday too and today. That wild man has fallen ill again, something's wrong with him again. . . . He begs my forgiveness, implores me to come back, and actually I feel I ought to go to Paris, stay with him for a while. You look so stern, Petya, but what's to be done, dove, what am I to do, he's ill, he's lonely, unhappy, and who's there to look after him, who'll keep him out of mischief, who'll give him his medicine at the right time? And what's there to hide or keep mum about, I love him, it's obvious. I love him, I love him. . . . It's a millstone around my neck, it's dragging me to the depths, but I love that stone and I can't live without it. (*Presses Trofimov's hand.*) Don't think harshly of me, Petya, don't say anything, don't talk. . . .

TROFIMOV (*through tears*). Forgive my frankness, for God's sake: but he robbed you blind!

LYUBOV ANDREEVNA. No, no, no, don't talk that way. . . . (*Puts her hands over her ears.*)

TROFIMOV. Why, he's a scoundrel, you're the only one who doesn't realize it! He's an insignificant scoundrel, a nonentity. . . .

LYUBOV ANDREEVNA (*getting angry, but restraining herself*). You're twenty-six or twenty-seven, but you're still a sophomoric schoolboy!

TROFIMOV. So what!

LYUBOV ANDREEVNA. You should act like a man, at your age you should understand people in love. And you should be in love yourself . . . you should fall in love! (*Angrily*) Yes, yes! And there's no purity in you, you're simply "puritanical," a ridiculous crank, a freak. . . .

TROFIMOV (*horrified*). What is she saying!

LYUBOV ANDREEVNA. "I am above love!" You're not above love, but simply, as our Firs here says, you're half-baked. At your age not to have a mistress! . . .

TROFIMOV (*horrified*). This is horrible! What is she saying! (*Rushes to the ballroom clutching his head.*) This is horrible . . . I can't stand it, I'm going. . . . (*Exits, but immediately returns.*) All is over between us! (*Exits into the hall.*)

LYUBOV ANDREEVNA (*shouting after him*). Petya, wait! You funny man, I was joking! Petya!

(*We hear in the hallway, someone running up the stairs and suddenly falling back down with a crash. Anya and Varya shriek, but immediately laughter is heard.*)

LYUBOV ANDREEVNA. What's going on in there?

(*Anya runs in.*)

ANYA (*laughing*). Petya fell down the stairs! (*Runs out.*)

LYUBOV ANDREEVNA. What a character that Petya is! . . .

(*The Stationmaster stops in the center of the ballroom and recites Aleksei Tolstoi's "The Fallen Woman." The guests listen, but barely has he recited a few lines, when the strains of a waltz reach them from the hallway, and the recitation breaks off. Everyone dances. Enter from the hall, Trofimov, Anya, Varya, and Lyubov Andreevna.*)

LYUBOV ANDREEVNA. Well, Petya. . . . well, my pure-in-heart. I apologize . . . let's go dance. . . . (*Dances with Trofimov.*)

(*Anya and Varya dance.*)

(*Firs enters, leaves his stick by the side-door. Yasha also enters the drawing room, watching the dancers.*)

YASHA. How're you doing, Gramps?
FIRS. I'm none too well. In the old days we had generals, barons, admirals dancing at our parties, but now we send for the postal clerk and the stationmaster, yes and they don't come a-running. Somehow I've gotten weak. The late master, the grandfather, doctored everybody with sealing wax for every ailment. I've took sealing wax every day now for twenty-odd years, and maybe more; maybe that's why I'm still alive.
YASHA. You bore me stiff, Gramps. (*Yawns.*) How about dropping dead.
FIRS. Ech, you're . . . half-baked! (*Mutters.*)

(*Trofimov and Lyubov Andreevna dance in the ballroom, then in the drawing-room.*)

LYUBOV ANDREEVNA. Merci, I'm going to sit down a bit. . . . (*Sits down.*) I'm tired.

(*Enter Anya.*)

ANYA (*agitated*). Just now in the kitchen some man was saying that the cherry orchard has already been sold.
LYUBOV ANDREEVNA. Sold to whom?
ANYA. He didn't say. He left. (*Dances with Trofimov.*)

(*They both exeunt into the ballroom.*)

YASHA. It was some old coot babbling away there. A stranger.
FIRS. And Leonid Andreich still isn't back, still not returned. He's got on a light topcoat, for between seasons, see if he don't catch cold. Ech, these striplings!
LYUBOV ANDREEVNA. I'll die this instant. Yasha, go and find out whom it's been sold to.
YASHA. He went away a long time ago, that old man. (*Laughs.*)
LYUBOV ANDREEVNA (*somewhat annoyed*). Well, what are you laughing about? What's made you so happy?

YASHA. Yepikhodov's awfully funny. Empty-headed fellow. Twenty-two troubles.
LYUBOV ANDREEVNA. Firs, if the estate is sold, then where will you go?
FIRS. Wherever you order, there I'll go.
LYUBOV ANDREEVNA. Why do you look like that? Aren't you well? You know you ought to go to bed. . . .
FIRS. Yes—(*With a grin*) I go to bed, and with me gone, who'll serve, who'll take care of things? I'm the only one in the whole house.
YASHA (*to Lyubov Andreevna*). Lyubov Andreevna! Let me ask you a favor, be so kind! If you go off to Paris again, take me with you, please. For me to stay around here is absolutely out of the question. (*Glances around, lowers his voice*) Why bring it up, you see for yourself, an uncivilized country, immoral people, besides it's boring, in the kitchen they feed us disgusting stuff and there's that Firs going around, muttering all sorts of uncalled-for remarks. Take me with you, be so kind!

(*Enter Pishchik.*)

PISHCHIK. Allow me to request . . . a little waltz, loveliest of ladies. . . . (*Lyubov Andreevna goes with him.*) Enchanting lady, I'll borrow that hundred and eighty rubles off you just the same . . . I'll borrow . . . (*Dances*) a hundred and eighty rubles. . . .

(*They pass into the ballroom.*)

YASHA (*singing softly*). "Wilt thou learn my soul's unrest . . ."

(*In the ballroom a figure in a gray top-hat and checked trousers waves its arms and jumps up and down; shouts of "Bravo, Charlotta Ivanovna!"*)

DUNYASHA (*stops to powder her nose*). The young mistress orders me to dance—lots of gentlemen and few ladies—but dancing makes my head swim, my heart pound. Firs Nikolaevich, just now the clerk from the post-office told me something that took my breath away.

(*The music subsides.*)

FIRS. Well, what did he tell you?
DUNYASHA. You, he says, are like a flower.
YASHA (*yawns*). Ignorance. . . . (*Exits.*)
DUNYASHA. Like a flower. . . . I'm such a sensitive girl, I'm frightfully fond of compliments.
FIRS. You'll get your head turned.

(*Enter Yepikhodov.*)

YEPIKHODOV. Avdotya Fyodorovna, you refuse to see me . . . as if I were some sort of bug. (*Sighs.*) Ech, life!
DUNYASHA. What can I do for you?

YEPIKHODOV. No doubt you may be right. (*Sighs.*) But, of course, if it's considered from a standpoint, then you, I venture to express myself thus, pardon my outspokenness, positively drove me into a state of mind. I know my fate, every day something unlucky happens to me, and I've grown accustomed to that long ago, so that I look upon my destiny with a smile. You gave me your word, and although I . . .

DUNYASHA. Please, we'll talk later on, but now leave me alone. I'm dreaming now. (*Plays with her fan.*)

YEPIKHODOV. I suffer misfortune every day, and I, I venture to express myself thus, merely smile, even laugh.

(*Enter Varya from the ballroom.*)

VARYA. Haven't you gone yet, Semyon? What a really disrespectful person you are. (*To Dunyasha.*) Clear out of here, Dunyasha. (*To Yepikhodov.*) First you play billiards and break the cue, and now you're strolling around the drawing room like a guest.

YEPIKHODOV. To make demands on me, allow me to inform you, you can't.

VARYA. I'm not making demands on you, I'm just telling you. The only thing you know is walking from place to place, instead of attending to business. We keep a bookkeeper but nobody knows what for.

YEPIKHODOV (*offended*). Whether I work or whether I walk or whether I eat or whether I play billiards may only be discussed by people of understanding, my elders.

VARYA. You dare to talk to me that way? (*Flying into a rage*) You dare? You mean I don't understand anything? Get out of here! This minute!

YEPIKHODOV (*alarmed*). I request you to express yourself in a tactful fashion.

VARYA (*beside herself*). This very minute, out of here! Out! (*He goes to the door, she follows him.*) Twenty-two troubles! Don't draw another breath here! Don't let me set eyes on you! (*Yepikhodov exits, behind the door his voice:*)

YEPIKHODOV'S VOICE. I'm going to complain about you.

VARYA. So, you're coming back? (*Seizes the stick, left near the door by Firs.*) Come on . . . come on . . . come on, I'll show you. . . . Well, are you coming? Are you coming? So take this. . . . (*Swings the stick.*)

(*At the same moment, Lopakhin enters.*)

LOPAKHIN. My humble thanks.

VARYA (*angrily and sarcastically*). My fault!

LOPAKHIN. Don't mention it. Thank you kindly for the pleasant surprise.

VARYA. It's not worth thanks. (*Starts out, then looks back and asks gently.*) I didn't hurt you?

LOPAKHIN. No, it's nothing. Raised an enormous bump though.

(*Voices in the ballroom: "Lopakhin's arrived! Yermolai Alekseich!"*)

PISHCHIK. Sights to be seen, sounds to be heard. . . . (*He and Lopakhin kiss.*) You smell a little of cognac, my dear boy, my bucko. But we were making merry here too.

(*Enter Lyubov Andreevna.*)

LYUBOV ANDREEVNA. Is that you, Yermolai Alekseich? Why so long? Where's Leonid?

LOPAKHIN. Leonid Andreich returned with me, he's on his way. . . .

LYUBOV ANDREEVNA (*agitated*). Well, what? Was there an auction? Tell me!

LOPAKHIN (*embarrassed, afraid to display his joy*). The auction was over by four o'clock. . . . We missed the train, had to wait till half-past nine. (*Sighs heavily.*) Oof! My head's in a bit of a whirl. . . .

(*Enter Gaev; his right hand is holding packages, his left is wiping away tears.*)

LYUBOV ANDREEVNA. Lyonya, what? Well, Lyonya? (*Impatiently, tearfully*) Hurry up, for God's sake. . . .

GAEV (*not answering her, only waves his hand, to Firs, weeping*). Here, take this. . . . There's anchovies, Kerch herring. . . . I didn't eat a thing all day. . . . What I've been through!

(*The door to the billiard room opens. We hear the sounds of the balls and Yasha's voice: "Seven and Eighteen!" Gaev's expression shifts, he stops crying.*)

GAEV. I'm awfully tired. Firs, help me change. (*Exits through the ballroom, followed by Firs.*)

PISHCHIK. What happened at the auction? Tell us!

LYUBOV ANDREEVNA. Is the cherry orchard sold?

LOPAKHIN. Sold.

LYUBOV ANDREEVNA. Who bought it?

LOPAKHIN. I bought it.

(*Pause. Lyubov Andreevna is overcome; she would fall, were she not standing beside an armchair and a table. Varya takes the keys from her belt, throws them on the floor in the middle of the drawing room and exits.*)

LOPAKHIN. I bought it! Wait, ladies and gentlemen, please for a minute, my head's in a muddle, I can't talk. . . . (*Laughs.*) We showed up at the auction, Deriganov was there already. Leonid Andreich only had fifty thousand, and Deriganov right off bid thirty over and above the mortgage. I get the picture, I pitched into him, bid forty. He forty-five. I fifty-five. I mean, he kept adding by fives, I by tens. . . . Well, it ended. Over and above the mortgage I bid ninety thousand, it was knocked down to me. Now the cherry orchard's mine. Mine! (*Chuckling.*) My God, Lord, the cherry orchard's mine! Tell me I'm drunk, out of my mind, that I'm imagining it all. . . . (*Stamps his feet.*) Don't laugh at me! If only my father and grandfather could rise up from their graves and see all that's happened, how their Yermolai, beaten, half-literate Yermolai, who used to run around barefoot in the wintertime;

how this same Yermolai bought the estate, the most beautiful thing in the world. I bought the estate where grandfather and father were slaves, where they weren't even allowed in the kitchen. I'm asleep, this is only one of my dreams, it only looks this way. . . . This is a figment of your imagination, hidden by the shadows of ignorance. . . . (*Picks up the keys, smiles gently.*) She threw down the keys, she wants to show that she's no longer mistress here. . . . (*Jingles the keys.*) Well, it's all the same. (*We hear the orchestra tuning up.*) Hey, musicians, play, I want to hear you! Come on, everybody, see how Yermolai Lopakhin will swing an axe in the cherry orchard, how the trees'll come tumbling to the ground!! We'll build cottages, and our grandchildren and great-grandchildren will see a new life here. . . . Music, play! (*The music plays, Lyubov Andreevna has sunk into a chair, crying bitterly.*) (*Reproachfully*) Why, oh, why didn't you listen to me? My poor, dear lady, you can't undo it now. (*Tearfully*) Oh, if only this were all over quickly, if somehow our clumsy, unhappy life could be changed quickly.

PISHCHIK (*takes him by the arm; in an undertone*). She's crying. Let's go into the ballroom, leave her alone. . . . Let's go. . . . (*Drags him by the arm and leads him into the ballroom.*)

LOPAKHIN. So what? Music, play louder! Let everything be the way I want it! (*Ironically*) Here comes the new landlord, the owner of the cherry orchard! (*He accidentally bumps into a small table and almost knocks over the candelabrum.*) I can pay for everything! (*Exits with Pishchik.*)

(*No one is left in the ballroom or drawing room except Lyubov Andreevna, who is sitting, all bunched up, weeping bitterly. The music is playing, softly. Anya and Trofimov hurry in. Anya goes up to her mother and kneels before her. Trofimov remains at the entrance to the ballroom.*)

ANYA. Mama! . . . Mama, you're crying? Dear, kind, good Mama, my own, my beautiful, I love you . . . I bless you. The cherry orchard's sold, there isn't any more, that's true, true, true, but don't cry, Mama, you've got your life ahead of you, you've got your good, pure heart . . . Come with me, come, dearest, away from here, come! . . . We'll plant a new orchard, more splendid than this one, you'll see it, you'll understand, and joy, peaceful, profound joy will sink into your heart, like the sun at nightfall, and you'll smile, Mama! Come, dearest! Come! . . .

ACT 4

First act set. Neither curtains on the windows, nor pictures on the walls, a few sticks of furniture remain, piled up in a corner, as if for sale. A feeling of emptiness. Near the door to the outside and at the back of the stage are piled suitcases, travelling bags, etc. At the left the door is open, and through it we can hear the voices of Varya and Anya. Lopakhin stands waiting. Yasha is holding a tray of champagne glasses. In the hallway, Yepikhodov is tying up a carton.

Offstage, at the back, a hum. It's the peasants come to say good-bye. Gaev's voice: "Thank you, friends, thank you."

YASHA. The common folk have come to say good-bye. I'm of the opinion, Yermolai Alekseich, they're decent enough people, but they aren't too bright.

(*The hum subsides. Enter through the hall Lyubov Andreevna and Gaev. She isn't crying, but is pale, her face twitches, she can't talk.*)

GAEV. You gave them your purse, Lyuba. You mustn't! You mustn't!

LYUBOV ANDREEVNA. I couldn't help it! I couldn't help it!

(*Both exit.*)

LOPAKHIN (*through the door, after them*). Please, I humbly beseech you! A little drink at parting. It didn't occur to me to bring any from town, and at the station I only found one bottle. Please! (*Pause.*) How about it, ladies and gentlemen? Don't you want any? (*Walks away from the door.*) Had I known, I wouldn't have bought it. Well, I won't drink any either. (*Yasha carefully sets the tray on a chair.*) You drink up, Yasha, anyway.

YASHA. To those departing! And happy days to the stay-at-homes! (*Drinks.*) This champagne isn't the genuine article, you can take it from me.

LOPAKHIN. Eight rubles a bottle. (*Pause.*) It's cold as hell in here.

YASHA. They didn't stoke up today, it doesn't matter, we're leaving. (*Laughs.*)

LOPAKHIN. What's that for?

YASHA. Sheer satisfaction.

LOPAKHIN. Outside it's October, but sunny and mild, like summer. Good building weather. (*Glances at his watch, at the door.*) Ladies and gentlemen, remember, until the train leaves, there's forty-seven minutes in all! Which means, in twenty minutes we start for the station. Get a move on.

(*Enter from outdoors Trofimov in an overcoat.*)

TROFIMOV. Seems to me it's time to go now. The horses are at the door. Where the hell are my galoshes? Disappeared. (*Through the door*) Anya, my galoshes aren't here! I can't find them!

LOPAKHIN. And I have to be in Kharkov. I'll accompany you on the same train. I'm staying all winter in Kharkov. I've been hanging around here with you, I'm worn out doing nothing. I can't be without work, I don't even know what to do with my hands. They dangle something strange, like somebody else's.

TROFIMOV. We'll be going soon, and you can return to your productive labor.

LOPAKHIN. Do have a little drink.

TROFIMOV. None for me.

LOPAKHIN. Looks like off to Moscow now?

TROFIMOV. Yes, I'll see them as far as town, but tomorrow off to Moscow.

LOPAKHIN. Yes. . . . Hey, the professors are holding off on lectures, I'll bet they're waiting for your arrival!

TROFIMOV. None of your business.

LOPAKHIN. How many years have you been studying at the University?

TROFIMOV. Think up something fresher. That's old and stale. (*Looks for his galoshes.*) By the way, we probably won't see each other again, so let me give you a piece of advice as a farewell: don't wave your arms! Break yourself of that habit—arm-waving. And also cottage-building, figuring that eventually tourists will turn into private householders, figuring in that way is just the same as arm-waving. . . . When you come down to it, I'm fond of you anyhow. You've got delicate, gentle fingers, like an artist, you've got a delicate, gentle soul. . . .

LOPAKHIN (*embraces him*). Good-bye, dear boy. Thanks for everything. If you need it, borrow some money from me for the road.

TROFIMOV. What for? No need.

LOPAKHIN. But you've got none!

TROFIMOV. I do. Thank you. I received some for a translation. Here it is, in my pocket. (*Anxiously*) But my galoshes are gone!

VARYA (*from the next room*). Take your nasty things! (*She flings a pair of rubber galoshes on stage.*)

TROFIMOV. What are you upset about, Varya? Hm. . . . But these aren't *my* galoshes!

LOPAKHIN. Last spring I planted twenty-seven hundred acres of poppies, and now I've cleared forty thousand net. And when my poppies bloomed, it was like a picture! Here's what I'm driving at, I cleared forty thousand, which means I offer you a loan because I'm able to. Why turn up your nose? I'm a peasant . . . plain and simple.

TROFIMOV. Your father was a peasant, mine, a druggist, but from that absolutely nothing follows. (*Lopakhin pulls out his wallet.*) Don't bother, don't bother. . . . Even if you gave me two hundred thousand, I wouldn't take it. I'm a free man. And everything that's valued so highly and fondly by all of you, rich men and beggars, hasn't the slightest sway over me, it's like fluff floating in the air. I can manage without you, I can pass you by. I'm strong and proud. Humanity is moving toward the most exalted truth, the most exalted happiness possible on earth, and I'm in the front ranks!

LOPAKHIN. Will you get there?

TROFIMOV. I'll get there. (*Pause.*) I'll get there, or I'll show others the way to get there.

(*We hear in the distance an axe striking a tree.*)

LOPAKHIN. Well, good-bye, my boy. Time to go. We turn up our noses at each other, but life keeps slipping by. When I work a long time nonstop, then my thoughts are sharper, and even I seem to know why I exist. But, brother, how many people there are in Russia who have no reason to exist. Well, what's the difference, that's not what makes the world go round. Leonid Andreich, they say, took a

position, he'll be in the bank, six thousand a year. . . . Only he won't keep at it, too lazy. . . .

ANYA (*in the doorway*). Mama begs you: until she's gone, not to chop down the orchard.

TROFIMOV. I mean really, haven't you got any tact. . . . (*Exits through the hall.*)

LOPAKHIN. Right away, right away. . . . These people, honestly! (*Exits after him.*)

ANYA. Did they take Firs to the hospital?

YASHA. I told them to this morning. They took him, I should think.

ANYA (*to Yepikhodov, who is crossing through the ballroom*). Semyon Panteleich, please find out whether Firs was taken to the hospital.

YASHA (*offended*). I told Yegor this morning. Why ask ten times?

YEPIKHODOV. Superannuated Firs, in my conclusive opinion, is past all repairing, he should be gathered to his fathers. And I can only envy him. (*Sets a suitcase on top of a cardboard hatbox and crushes it.*) Well, look at that, naturally. I should have known. (*Exits.*)

YASHA (*mocking*). Twenty-two troubles. . . .

YEPIKHODOV. Well, it could have happened to anybody.

VARYA (*from behind door*). Have they sent Firs to the hospital?

ANYA. They have.

VARYA. Then why didn't they take the letter to the doctor?

ANYA. We'll have to send someone after them. . . . (*Exits.*)

VARYA (*from the adjoining room*). Where's Yasha? Tell him his mother's arrived, wants to say good-bye to him.

YASHA (*waves his hand*). They simply try my patience.

(*Dunyasha in the meantime has been fussing with the luggage; now that Yasha is alone, she comes up to him.*)

DUNYASHA. If only you'd take one little look at me, Yasha. You're going away . . . you're leaving me behind. . . . (*Weeps and throws herself around his neck.*)

YASHA. What's to cry about? (*Drinks champagne.*) In six days I'll be in Paris again. Tomorrow we'll board an express train and dash away, just try and spot us. Somehow I can't believe it. Vive la France! . . . It doesn't suit me, here, I can't live . . . nothing going on. I've seen enough ignorance—fed up. (*Drinks champagne.*) What's there to cry about? Behave respectably, then you won't have to cry.

DUNYASHA (*powdering her nose, looks in a hand-mirror*). Drop me a line from Paris. I really loved you, Yasha, loved you so! I'm a soft-hearted creature, Yasha!

YASHA. Someone's coming in here. (*Fusses around with the luggage, humming softly.*)

(*Enter Lyubov Andreevna, Gaev, Anya, and Charlotta Ivanovna.*)

GAEV. We should be off. Not much time left. (*Looking at Yasha*) Who's that smelling of herring?

LYUBOV ANDREEVNA. In about ten minutes we ought to be getting into the carriages . . . (*Casting a glance around the room*.) Good-bye, dear old house, old grandfather. Winter will pass, spring will come again, but you won't be here anymore, they'll tear you down. How much these walls have seen! (*Kissing her daughter ardently*.) My precious, you're radiant, your eyes are sparkling like two diamonds. Are you glad? Very?

ANYA. Very! A new life is beginning, Mama!

GAEV. As a matter of fact, everything's fine now. Until the sale of the cherry orchard, we were all upset, distressed, but then, when the dilemma was settled, finally, irrevocably, everyone calmed down, even became cheerful. . . . I'm a bank employee, now; I'm a financier . . . yellow to the center, and you, Lyuba, anyway, you're looking better, that's for sure.

LYUBOV ANDREEVNA. Yes. My nerves are better, that's true. (*They help her on with her hat and coat*.) I'm sleeping well. Carry my things out, Yasha. It's time. (*To Anya*) My little girl, we'll see each other soon. . . . I'm off to Paris, I'll live there on that money your granny in Yaroslavl sent us to buy the estate—hurray for Granny!—but that money won't last long.

ANYA. Mama, you'll come back soon . . . won't you? I'll study, pass the examination at the high school, and then I'll work to help you. Mama, we'll be together and read all sorts of books . . . won't we? (*Kisses her mother's hand*.) We'll read in the autumn evenings, we'll read lots of books, and before us a new, wonderful world will open up. . . . (*Dreaming*) Mama, come back. . . .

LYUBOV ANDREEVNA. I'll come back, my treasure. (*Embraces her daughter*.)

(*Enter Lopakhin. Charlotta is quietly singing a song.*)

GAEV. Charlotta's happy! She's singing.

CHARLOTTA (*picks up a bundle that looks like a swaddled baby*). Rock-a-bye, baby, on-the-tree-top. (*We hear a baby crying: "Waa! Waa!"*) Hush, my sweet, my dear little boy. ("*Waa! Waa!*") I'm so sorry for you! (*Tossing back the bundle*.) Will you please find me a position! I can't keep on this way.

LOPAKHIN. We'll find one, Charlotta Ivanovna, don't worry.

GAEV. Everyone's dropping us, Varya's leaving . . . we've suddenly become superfluous.

CHARLOTTA. There's no place to live in town. Have to go away. . . . (*Hums*.) It doesn't matter.

(*Enter Pishchik.*)

LOPAKHIN. The freak of nature! . . .

PISHCHIK (*out of breath*). Oy, let me catch my breath. . . . I'm winded . . . my most honored. . . . Give me some water. . . .

GAEV. After money, I suppose? Your humble servant, I'll keep out of temptation's way. . . . (*Exits*.)

PISHCHIK (*out of breath*). I haven't been to see you for a long time . . . loveliest of ladies. . . . (*To Lopakhin*) You here . . . glad to see you . . . a man of the widest intellect . . . take . . . go on. . . . (*Hands money to Lopakhin*.) Four hundred rubles. . . . I still owe you eight hundred and forty. . . .

LOPAKHIN (*bewildered, shrugs*). It's like a dream. . . . Where did you get this?

PISHCHIK. Wait. . . . Hot. . . . Most amazing thing happened. Some Englishmen stopped by my place and found some kind of white clay on the land. . . . (*To Lyubov Andreevna*) And four hundred for you . . . beautiful lady, divine. . . . (*Hands her money*.) The rest later. (*Drinks water*.) Just now some young man on the train was relating that a certain . . . great philosopher recommends jumping off roofs . . . "Jump!"—he says, and in that lies the whole problem. (*Astounded*.) Can you imagine! Water! . . .

LOPAKHIN. Who were these Englishmen?

PISHCHIK. I leased them the lot with the clay for twenty-four years. . . . But now, excuse me, no time. . . . Have to run along . . . I'm going to Znoikov's . . . Kardamonov's . . . I owe everybody. . . . (*Drinks*.) I wish you health. . . . On Thursday I'll drop by. . . .

LYUBOV ANDREEVNA. We're just about to move to town, and tomorrow I'll be abroad.

PISHCHIK. What? (*Agitated*) Why to town? Goodness, look at the furniture . . . the suitcases . . . well, never mind. . . . (*Through tears*) Never mind. Persons of the highest intelligence . . . those Englishmen. . . . Never mind. . . . Be happy. . . . God will aid you. . . . Never mind. . . . Everything in this world comes to an end. . . . (*Kisses Lyubov Andreevna's hand*.) And should rumor reach you that my end has come, just remember this very thing—a horse, and say: "There was on earth thus-and-such . . . Simeonov-Pishchik . . . rest in peace." . . . Incredible weather . . . yes. . . . (*Exits, overcome with emotion, but immediately reappears in the doorway and says*) Dashenka says to say hello! (*Exits*.)

LYUBOV ANDREEVNA. Now we can go. I'm leaving with two things on my mind. First—that Firs is ill. (*Glancing at her watch*.) There's still five minutes. . . .

ANYA. Mama, they've already sent Firs to the hospital. Yasha sent him this morning.

LYUBOV ANDREEVNA. My second anxiety is Varya. She's used to early rising and working, and now without work, she's like a fish out of water. She's got thin, she's got pale, she cries, poor thing. . . . (*Pause*.) You know this perfectly well, Yermolai Alekseich: I had dreamt . . . of marrying her to you, yes and it certainly looked as if you were ready to get married. (*Whispers to Anya, who nods to Charlotta, and both leave*.) She loves you, you're fond of her, I don't know, I just don't know why you seem to avoid each other. I don't understand.

LOPAKHIN. Personally I don't understand either, I admit. It's all sort of strange. . . . If there's still time, then I'm ready right now. . . . Let's settle it right away—and there's an end to it, but if it weren't for you I feel I wouldn't propose.

LYUBOV ANDREEVNA. That's excellent. All it takes is one little minute. I'll call her right now. . . .

LOPAKHIN. And there's champagne for the occasion. (*Looks in the glasses*.) Empty, somebody drank it already. (*Yasha coughs*.) I should say, lapped it up. . . .

LYUBOV ANDREEVNA (*lively*). Fine! We'll leave . . . Yasha, allez! I'll call her. . . . (*In the doorway*) Varya, drop everything, come here. Come on! (*Exits with Yasha.*)

LOPAKHIN (*glancing at his watch*). Yes. . . . (*Pause. Behind the door a stifled laugh, whispering, finally Varya enters.*)

VARYA (*scrutinizes the luggage for a long time*). That's odd, I just can't find it. . . .

LOPAKHIN. What are you looking for?

VARYA. I packed it myself and can't remember. (*Pause.*)

LOPAKHIN. Where are you off to now, Varvara Mikhailovna?

VARYA. Me? To the Ragulins'. . . . I've agreed to take charge of their household . . . as a housekeeper, or something.

LOPAKHIN. That's in Yashnevo? On to seventy miles from here. (*Pause.*) So ends life in this house. . . .

VARYA (*examining the luggage*). Where in the world is it. . . . Or maybe I packed it in the trunk. . . . Yes, life in this house is ended . . . there won't be any more.

LOPAKHIN. And I'll be riding to Kharkov soon . . . by the same train. Lots of business. But I'm leaving Yepikhodov on the grounds . . . I hired him.

VARYA. That so!

LOPAKHIN. Last year by this time it was snowing already, if you remember, but now it's mild, sunny. Except that it's cold. . . . About three degrees of frost.

VARYA. I haven't noticed. (*Pause.*) And besides our thermometer is broken. . . .

(*Pause. Voice from the yard through the door: "Yermolai Alekseich!"*)

LOPAKHIN (*as if expecting this call for a long time*). Right away! (*Rushes out.*)

(*Varya, sitting on the floor, laying her head on a pile of dresses, quietly sobs. The door opens, Lyubov Andreevna enters cautiously.*)

LYUBOV ANDREEVNA. Well? (*Pause.*) We've got to go.

VARYA (*has stopped crying, wipes her eyes*). Yes, it's time, Mama dear. I'll get to the Ragulins today, if only I don't miss the train. . . .

LYUBOV ANDREEVNA (*in the doorway*). Anya, put your things on!

(*Enter Anya, then Gaev, Charlotta Ivanovna. Gaev has on a heavy overcoat with a hood. The servants and coachman foregather. Yepikhodov fusses around with the luggage.*)

LYUBOV ANDREEVNA. Now we can be on our way.

ANYA (*joyously*). On our way!

GAEV. My friends, beloved friends! Leaving this house forever, can I be silent, can I restrain myself from expressing at parting those feelings which now fill my whole being . . .

ANYA (*entreating*). Uncle!

VARYA. Uncle dear, you mustn't!

GAEV (*depressed*). Bank the yellow to the center . . . I'll keep still. . . .

(*Enter Trofimov, then Lopakhin.*)

TROFIMOV. Well, ladies and gentlemen, time to go!

LOPAKHIN. Yepikhodov, my overcoat!

LYUBOV ANDREEVNA. I'll sit just one more minute. It's as if I'd never before seen what the walls are like in this house, what the ceilings are like, and now I gaze at them greedily, with such tender love. . . .

GAEV. I remember when I was six, on Trinity Sunday I sat in this window and watched my father driving to church. . . .

LYUBOV ANDREEVNA. Is all the luggage loaded?

LOPAKHIN. Everything, I think. (*Putting on his overcoat, to Yepikhodov*) You there, Yepikhodov, see that everything's in order.

YEPIKHODOV (*talks in a hoarse voice*). Don't worry, Yermolai Alekseich!

LOPAKHIN. What's the matter with your voice?

YEPIKHODOV. I just drank some water, swallowed something.

YASHA (*contemptuously*). Ignorance. . . .

LYUBOV ANDREEVNA. We're leaving—and not a soul will be left here. . . .

LOPAKHIN. Until next spring.

VARYA (*pulls a parasol out of a bundle, looking as if she were about to hit somebody. Lopakhin pretends to be scared*). What are you . . . what are you doing . . . it never crossed my mind. . . .

TROFIMOV. Ladies and gentlemen, let's get into the carriages. . . . It's high time! The train'll be here any minute!

VARYA. Petya, here they are, your galoshes, next to the suitcase. (*Tearfully*) And yours are so muddy, so old. . . .

TROFIMOV (*putting on his galoshes*). Let's go, ladies and gentlemen! . . .

GAEV (*overcome with emotion, afraid he'll cry*). The train . . . the station. . . . Followshot to the center, white doublet to the corner. . . .

LYUBOV ANDREEVNA. Let's go!

LOPAKHIN. Everybody here? Nobody there? (*Locking the side door on the left.*) Things stored here, have to lock up. Let's go! . . .

ANYA. Good-bye, house! Good-bye, old life!

TROFIMOV. Hello, new life! (*Exits with Anya.*)

(*Varya casts a glance around the room and exits unhurriedly. Exeunt Yasha and Charlotta with a lapdog.*)

LOPAKHIN. Which means, till spring. Come along, ladies and gentlemen. . . . Till we meet again! . . . (*Exits.*)

(*Lyubov Andreevna and Gaev are left alone. As if they had been waiting for this, they throw themselves around one another's neck and sob with restraint, quietly, afraid of someone hearing them.*)

GAEV (*in despair*). Sister dear, sister dear. . . .

LYUBOV ANDREEVNA. Oh, my darling, my sweet, beautiful orchard! . . . My life, my youth, my happiness, good-bye! . . . Good-bye! . . .

(*Anya's voice, gaily, appealing: "Mama!" Trofimov's voice, gaily, excited: "Yoo-hoo!"*)

LYUBOV ANDREEVNA. One last look at the walls, the windows. . . . Our poor mother loved to walk about in this room. . . .

GAEV. Sister dear, sister dear! . . .

ANYA'S VOICE. Mama! . . .

TROFIMOV'S VOICE. Yoo-hoo! . . .

LYUBOV ANDREEVNA. We're coming!

(*They exeunt. The stage is empty. We hear the doors being locked with a key, then the carriages driving off. It grows quiet. In the silence there is the dull thud of the axe against a tree, sounding forlorn and doleful. We hear footsteps. From the door at right Firs appears. He's dressed as always, in a jacket and white vest, slippers on his feet. He is ill.*)

FIRS (*crosses to the door, tries the knob*). Locked. They've gone. . . . (*Sits on the sofa.*) Forgot about me. . . . Never mind. . . . I'll sit here a bit. . . . And I guess Leonid Andreich didn't put on his fur-coat, went out in his topcoat. . . . (*Sighs, anxiously.*) I didn't see to it. . . . Young striplings! (*Mutters something that cannot be understood.*) This life's gone by like I hadn't lived. (*Lies down.*) I'll lie down a bit. . . . Ain't no strength in you, nothing left, nothing. . . . Ech, you're . . . half-baked! . . . (*Lies immobile.*)

(*We hear the distant sound, as if from the sky, the sound of a snapped string, dying away mournfully. Silence ensues, and all we hear far away in the orchard is the thud of an axe on a tree.*)

TOPICS FOR CRITICAL THINKING AND WRITING

 ## The Play on the PAGE

1. What do you make of the fact that the opening stage directions specify that the setting for the first act is a room that "is still known as the Nursery"?
2. Characterize Lyubov Andreevna.
3. Can some of the characters clearly be called comic? Do some of these characters help to make Lyubov Andreevna less comic?
4. How might the theme of the play be stated?

5. Chekhov said that he wrote "a comedy, in places even a farce." But the director, Stanislavsky, replied, "This is not a comedy or a farce. . . . It is a tragedy." What can be said for each of these views? Try to specify speeches or scenes that can be used to support these judgments. For instance, when Trofimov falls downstairs, is the episode farcical?

 ## The Play on the STAGE

6. What do the costumes, as specified by Chekhov, communicate? (Consider, for example, the brief description of Lopakhin's costume, page 640.)
7. In a letter to his wife, Olga Knipper, who was preparing to play the role of Mme. Ranevskaya, Chekhov wrote, "It's not hard to play Ranevskaya. It's only necessary to strike the right note from the very beginning. It's necessary to invent a smile and a way of smiling, and it's necessary to know how to dress." How would you dress her?
8. In at least one production, Firs was played with great dignity, providing a contrast to the frantic and absurd behavior of the others. What do you think of this interpretation of the character?

9. What do you make of the sound of the broken string at the end of the play?
10. Do you think the setting of the play might effectively be transferred to the United States? One production, for instance, set it in the South in the late nineteenth century. What might be gained or lost by such a transfer?
11. Imagine that you are casting *The Cherry Orchard*. For three or four roles, choose several well-known actors, and explain why you are choosing them. (Incidentally, directors often succeed with surprising choices. For the role of Lopakhin, Peter Brook chose Brian Dennehy, a bearish man known for his work in cop dramas on television.)

The Play in PERFORMANCE

Our introduction mentions that although Chekhov said *The Cherry Orchard* was a comedy, Constantin Stanislavsky (cofounder of the Moscow Art Theatre in 1898, the first director of Chekhov's plays, and the performer of the role of Gaev) insisted it was a tragedy. With the productions of Stanislavsky, we are in the world of "director's theater"—theater in which the director rather than the author is the dominant voice.

The director, it should be mentioned, is a relatively recent invention. There is no sign of the director in Shakespeare's day, for instance; presumably the company of actors—Shakespeare was himself an actor—put on the play in accordance with what the author told them. But of course in a theater such as today's, which offers modern productions of classic plays, it is impossible to consult the author, and we are rarely certain about the author's intentions. Chekhov, however, though dying, *was* available for consultation. Still, one can argue that even if the author is alive, the author's views are by no means definitive. The creator of a play may not be consciously aware of what he or she is including in it, and artists—however independent they may think they are—to some degree unconsciously participate in the ideological conflicts of their age. (In the terminology of modern critical theory, to accept the artist's statements about his or her intentions in the work is "to privilege intentionalism.") The idea that the seeming creator of the work cannot comment definitively on it is especially associated with Roland Barthes (1915–80), author of "The Death of the Author," in *Image-Music-Text* (1977), and with Michel Foucault (1926–84), author of "What Is an Author?," in *The Foucault Reader* (1984). For example, Foucault assumes that the concept of the author (we can say the playwright) is a repressive invention designed to impede the free circulation of ideas. In Foucault's view, the work does not belong to the alleged maker; rather, it belongs—or ought to belong—to the *perceivers*, who of course interpret it variously, according to their historical, social, and psychological circumstances. These ideas are especially relevant to drama, particularly for a live performance.

How has *The Cherry Orchard* been perceived? If one reads the several dozen reviews of early productions (from 1911 to 1944) reprinted in *Chekhov: The Critical Heritage,* ed. Victor Emeljanow (1981), one notices that most of the productions have leaned toward tragedy, or toward an emphasis on a tragic mood. This is true not only of the Moscow Art Theatre productions at home and abroad (the company made several visits to London and New York, performing in Russian) but it is true also of most later productions. Inevitably the Russian Revolution—the overthrow of the czarist government and the old aristocracy in 1917—gave the play a meaning it had not had in Chekhov's day; after the revolution the play had to be seen in the light of history. Most productions emphasized the melancholy implicit in the fate that the unwitting characters were about to undergo. But even putting aside the historical developments, the characters' present situation was seen as melancholy. Here is Edmund Wilson commenting on the Moscow Art Theatre's production in New York in 1923:

> In *The Cherry Orchard*, for example, not only is a whole complex of social relations presented with the most convincing exactitude, but *The Cherry Orchard* itself, the sort of beauty which Mme Ranevskaya represents, the charm which hangs about the Russian gentry even in decay is somehow put upon the stage in a way that their futility is never dreary, but moving, their ineptitude touched with the tragedy of all human failure.
>
> (CHEKHOV: *THE CRITICAL HERITAGE*, 236)

Or consider a statement made by a reviewer of a 1925 London production: "A sense of beauty now and again steals through the miasma of misery." Remember, these remarks are made about a play that Chekhov insisted was a comedy.

True, occasional productions—notably those of Tyrone Guthrie in 1933 and again in 1941—labored hard to emphasize the comic aspects of the play, but, judging from the reviews, most audiences were not much entertained, partly because the productions were not what audiences expected of Chekhov. A 1977 production in New York, directed by Andrei Serban, however, did emphasize the comedy, and did play to enthusiastic audiences. This production was very much an example of "director's theater"; for instance, in the third act Chekhov tells us that a dance is going on, and we hear the offstage music, but in Serban's version the dance was elaborately staged, eclipsing the actors.

The most recent professional production to achieve national attention was by Peter Brook, a director known for his unconventional presentations. Thus,

Brook's *King Lear* was in large measure *Lear* as Samuel Beckett might have conceived it, a Lear of the Absurd. And Brook's *Midsummer Night's Dream* was not the usual amiable play about the delightful tribulations of engaging lovers, but was a disturbing play about deep sexual and class conflicts. To take a single example: In *A Midsummer Night's Dream* the set representing the forest is usually a pretty thing showing realistic or pleasantly stylized greenery, but in Brook's production

it consisted of jangling coils. Not surprisingly, then, Brook's production of *The Cherry Orchard* dispensed with the usual realistic box set filled with furniture. The rear wall was not the wall of a room, with pictures, windows, draperies, and so forth, but was the dilapidated real wall of the theater, and the characters sat not on chairs but on a rug on the floor. (We reprint, on page 664, a review of Brook's production.)

ALAN MacVEY
Directing The Cherry Orchard

Alan MacVey is a member of the theater department at the University of Iowa. In 1991 he directed a production of *The Cherry Orchard* at the Bread Loaf School of English. The cast included Equity actors, staff, and students from the school.

In the course of directing the play, did your conception change?

It deepened. Going into rehearsal I considered the play to be about change. As the social and political world alters around them, the characters face changes in their relationships and in themselves. A director may decide that the lives of the characters are quite different at the end than they were at the beginning, or that their lives are really much the same; either way, however, the characters are dealing with change all around them. This is where I began.

Well, you said "going into rehearsal." So your ideas did change?

I'm getting there. The first act takes place in a nursery, so our set contained a large toy box. When the lid was opened a tune played as if from a music box; when the lid closed the tune stopped. Planning the production, I thought it would be good to open the box at one point and have music play beneath the action for perhaps five minutes. In the course of rehearsal, though, I found myself closing the box earlier and earlier because the music provided too coherent a mood; though it was quite soft, the music subtly forced all the action and dialogue to fit into a certain tone. This didn't

work because we were discovering that things did not fit together—characters were in very different psychological states, much of the time they hardly heard each other, and they changed their actions and moods very quickly. We discovered that the play was indeed about change, but at a microscopic level: Nothing lasts longer than a few seconds. Internal stimulation (from thoughts, memories, etc.) combined with external stimulation (the other characters, the set, the music, etc.) so that each character's internal landscape changed very quickly. Thus "mood music" was an imposition on the scene. By the first performance we simply opened the toy box, listened to its music for five seconds and closed it again. Nothing lasts long in the world of this play.

I heard your staging of the end of the play was especially effective. What did you do?

You'll recall that at the end of Act 4 Firs is left alone on stage. Chekhov has beautifully created the sounds of the scene, which include the cutting of cherry trees and the famous breaking string. We took a hint from Chekhov and added something of our own. The set made use of real French doors that opened west, out to the Vermont mountains. As Firs was left alone on stage, a workman passed by the doors outside and locked them all, just as Chekhov suggests. But our theater also had doors behind the audience, opening to the east. As the last stage door to the west was locked and Firs sat alone, forgotten, a second workman slowly locked the remaining doors behind the audience. We were all locked in the abandoned old house with Firs. The string broke for us as it did for him. Something had happened—but like Firs we could hardly say when or how.

FRANK RICH
Review of Peter Brook's The Cherry Orchard

It is not until the final act of *The Cherry Orchard* that the malevolent thud of an ax signals the destruction of a family's ancestral estate and, with it, the traumatic uprooting of a dozen late-nineteenth-century Russian lives. But in Peter Brook's production of Chekhov's play, the landscape seems to have been cleared before Act I begins. Mr. Brook has stripped *The Cherry Orchard* of its scenery, its front curtain, its intermissions. Even the house in which the play unfolds—the Brooklyn Academy of Music's semirestored Majestic Theater—looks half-demolished, a once-genteel palace of gilt and plush now a naked, faded shell of crumbling brick, chipped paint and forgotten hopes.

What little decorative elegance remains can be found on the vast stage floor, which Mr. Brook has covered, as is his wont, with dark Oriental rugs. And that—plus an extraordinary international cast, using a crystalline new translation by Elisaveta Lavrova—proves to be all that's needed. On this director's magic carpets, *The Cherry Orchard* flies. By banishing all forms of theatrical realism except the only one that really matters—emotional truth—Mr. Brook has found the pulse of a play that its author called "not a drama but a comedy, in places almost a farce." That pulse isn't to be confused with the somber metronomic beat of the Act IV ax—the Stanislavskian gloom that Chekhov so despised—and it isn't the kinetic, too frequently farcical gait of Andrei Serban's fascinating 1977 production at Lincoln Center. The real tone of *The Cherry Orchard* is that of a breaking string—that mysterious unidentifiable offstage sound that twice interrupts the action, unnerving the characters and audience alike with the sensation that unfathomable life is inexorably rushing by.

We feel that strange tingle, an exquisite pang of joy and suffering, again and again. When the beautiful Natasha Parry, as the bankrupt landowner Lyubov, returns to her estate from Paris, her brimming eyes take in the vast reaches of the auditorium in a single sweeping glance of nostalgic longing. But when she says, "I feel like a little girl again," the husky darkness of her voice fills in the scarred decades since childhood, relinquishing the girlishness even as it is reclaimed. Later, Miss Parry will simply sit in a chair, quietly crying, as Brian Dennehy, in the role of the merchant

Lopakhin, announces that he has purchased her estate at auction. Lopakhin, whose ancestors were serfs on the land he now owns, can't help celebrating his purchase, but his half-jig of victory is slowly tempered by the realization that he has forfeited any chance of affection from the aristocratic woman he has just bought out. A bear of a man, Mr. Dennehy ends up prostrate on the floor behind Miss Parry's chair, tugging ineffectually at her hem. We're left with an indelible portrait of not one but two well-meaning souls who have lost what they most loved by recognizing their own desires too late.

That Lopakhin is as sympathetic and complex a figure as Lyubov, rather than a malicious arriviste, is a tribute not just to Mr. Dennehy's performance but also to Mr. Brook's entire approach to the play. When Trofimov (Zeljko Ivanek), the eternal student, angrily tells Miss Parry to "face the truth" for once in her life, she responds rhetorically, "What truth?" The director, like Chekhov, recognizes that there is no one truth. Each character must be allowed his own truth—a mixture of attributes and convictions that can't easily be typed or judged. Mr. Dennehy gives us both sides (and more) of the man whom Trofimov variously calls a "beast of prey" and "a fine, sensitive soul." Mr. Ivanek does the same with Trofimov, providing a rounded view of the sometimes foolish but fundamentally idealistic young man whose opinions swing so wildly. Though the student may look immature telling off Lyubov or Lopakhin, his vision of a happier future is so stirring that Mr. Ivanek quite rightly prompts the moon to rise while proclaiming it ("I can feel my happiness coming—I can see it!") at the end of Act II.

Miss Parry, Mr. Dennehy and Mr. Ivanek are all brilliant under Mr. Brook's guidance, and they're not alone. As Lyubov's brother, Gaev—a forlorn representative of Czarist Russia's obsolete, decaying nobility—the Swedish actor Erland Josephson embodies the fossilized remains of a civilization. Elegant of bearing yet fuzzy of expression, his voice mellifluous yet childlike, he snaps into focus only when drifting into imaginary billiard games. One of the evening's comic high points is his absurdly gratuitous tribute to a century-old family bookcase, but the hilarity of his futility is matched by the poignance of his Act III entrance, in which his exhausted posture and sad, dangling bundle of anchovy and herring tins announce the estate's sale to his sister well before Lopakhin does.

As Firs, the octogenarian family retainer, Roberts Blossom is a tall, impish, bearded figure in formal black, stooping over his cane—a spindly, timeless ghost from the past, as rooted to the soil as the trees we never see. Stephanie Roth is a revelation as Varya, whose fruitless religious piety is balanced by a bravery that saves her from despair when her last prayer for happiness, a marriage proposal from Lopakhin, flickers and then dies in Mr. Dennehy's eyes. Linda Hunt (Charlotta), Jan Triska (Yepikhodov) and Mike Nussbaum (Pishchik) find the melancholy humor of true Old World clowns in their subsidiary, more broadly conceived roles. If the play's younger generation—Rebecca Miller (Anya), Kate Mailer (Dunyasha) and David Pierce (Yasha)—is not of the same class, holding one's own with a company of this stature is no small achievement in itself.

In keeping with his work with the actors, Mr. Brook's staging has a supple, airy flow that avoids cheap laughs or sentimentality yet is always strikingly theatrical. In Act III, the reveling dancers twirl around velvet screens in choreographic emulation of the ricocheting rumors of the estate's sale. Throughout the evening, the transitions of mood are lightning fast. In an instant, Miss Parry's reminiscence of her son's drowning can be dispelled by the jaunty strains of a nearby band. Neither Lyubov nor anyone else is allowed the self-pity that would plunge *The Cherry Orchard* from the flickering tearfulness of regret into the maudlin sobs of phony high drama.

The mood that is achieved instead, though not tragic, recalls Mr. Brook's *Endgame*-inspired *King Lear* of the 1960s. Beckett is definitely on the director's mind, as is evident not just from the void in which he sets the play but also by his explicit evocation of the Beckett humor in several scenes. When Miss Hunt's governess gives her monologue describing her utter lack of identity—she doesn't know who she is or where she came from—it's a cheeky, center-stage effusion of existential verbal slapstick, with a vegetable for a prop, right out of *Waiting for Godot* or *Happy Days*. When, at evening's end, old Firs is locked by accident in the mansion, we're keenly aware of the repetition of the word "nothing" in his final speech. As Mr. Blossom falls asleep in his easy chair, illuminated by a bare shaft of light and accompanied by the far-off sound of the ax, one can't be blamed for thinking of Krapp reviewing his last tape.

But the delicate connections Mr. Brook draws between Beckett and Chekhov are inevitable and to the point, not arch and pretentious, and they help explain why this *Cherry Orchard* is so right. Though Chekhov was dying when he wrote this play, he didn't lose his perspective on existence and the people who endure it. Horrible, inexplicable things happen to the characters in *The Cherry Orchard*—the shadow of death is always cloaking their shoulders, as it does Beckett's lost souls—but, as Mr. Brook writes in the program, "they have not given up." They simply trudge on, sometimes with their senses of humor intact, sometimes with a dogged faith in the prospects for happiness.

That's the human comedy, and, if it isn't riotously funny, one feels less alone in the solitary plight, indeed exhilarated, watching it unfold on stage as honestly and buoyantly and poetically as a dream. This is a *Cherry Orchard* that pauses for breath only when life does, for people to recoup after dying a little. I think Mr. Brook has given us the Chekhov production that every theatergoer fantasizes about but, in my experience, almost never finds.

BERNARD Shaw

Bernard Shaw (1856–1950) was born in Dublin of Anglo-Irish stock. His father drank too much, his mother—something of an Ibsenite "new woman"—went to London to make her way as singer and voice teacher. Shaw worked in a Dublin real estate office for a while (he did not attend a college or university), and then followed his mother to London, where he wrote critical reviews, and five novels (1879–83) before turning playwright. His first play, begun with William Archer (playwright and translator of Ibsen), was abandoned in 1885, and then entirely revised by Shaw into *Widowers' Houses* (1892). He had already shown, in a critical study entitled *The Quintessence of Ibsenism* (1891), that he regarded the stage as a pulpit and soapbox; before the nineteenth century was over, he wrote nine more plays, in order (he said) to espouse socialism effectively. *Major Barbara* (1905) is his comic masterpiece, but at least a dozen of his plays have established themselves in the repertoire, including one tragedy, *Saint Joan* (1924).

■■■■■■■■■■■■■■■

COMMENTARY ON *MAJOR BARBARA*

One of the earliest English remarks about comedy, Sir Philip Sidney's written about 1580, runs thus:

> Comedy is an imitation of the common errors of our life, which [the writer] representeth in the most ridiculous and scornful sort that may be; so that it is impossible that any beholder can be content to be such a one.

Sidney is indebted to Italian commentators, who in turn are indebted to Roman commentators, and behind them are the Greeks, notably Aristotle. Along the way there are lots of variations, but the basic ideas may fairly be said to constitute the "classical" theory of comedy:

1. The characters are ignoble
2. Their actions arouse derision (rather than, say, terror or pity)
3. The spectators, if they have resembled the *dramatis personae*, leave the theater morally improved after seeing the absurdity of such behavior.

The "classical" theory, often stated before Sidney, has since been restated at least as often. Almost every comic dramatist who has commented on his work has offered it as his justification. Shaw, in a preface to his *Complete Plays*, put it thus:

> If I make you laugh at yourself, remember that my business as a classic writer of comedies is "to chasten morals with ridicule"; and if I sometimes make you feel like a fool, remember that I have by the same ac-

tion cured your folly, just as the dentist cures your toothache by pulling out your tooth. And I never do it without giving you plenty of laughing gas.

To begin with the laughing gas in *Major Barbara*: The first act suggests that the play is a drawing-room comedy, full of aristocratic people bouncing elegant lines off each other. (Lady Brit, of course, affects innocence, but she is accomplished at getting what she wants.) Sample:

> I am not a Pharisee, I hope; and I should not have minded his merely doing wrong things: we are none of us perfect. But your father didnt exactly do wrong things: he said them and thought them: that was what was so dreadful. He really had a sort of religion of wrongness. Just as one doesnt mind men practising immorality so long as they own that they are in the wrong by preaching morality; so I couldnt forgive Andrew for preaching immorality while he practised morality.

Another sample:

> CUSINS. Let me advise you to study Greek, Mr. Undershaft. Greek scholars are privileged men. Few of them know Greek; and none of them know anything else; but their position is unchallengeable. Other languages are the qualifications of waiters and commercial travellers: Greek is to a man of position what the hallmark is to silver.

If Shaw had been content to write a comedy in the classical tradition, he would have contrived a plot that would probably have involved an unsuitable wooer of

Barbara, maybe a rich old aristocrat, maybe a parvenu, maybe a fortune hunter, who would finally be unmasked and then displaced by an appropriately young and charming and socially acceptable bridegroom. But Shaw turned to comedy as a propagandist. He had been deeply impressed by Ibsen's plays, and he saw in the drama an opportunity to preach his economic ideas to a wider audience than is normally reached by the pamphleteer. For Shaw, the heart of Ibsen's plays lies in such a "discussion" as the one in *A Doll's House*, in which Nora explains to her husband that things are all wrong in their apparently happy marriage. (The interested reader is advised to look at Shaw's *The Quintessence of Ibsenism*, especially the next to the last chapter, "The Technical Novelty," which insists that post-Ibsen plays must replace the old formula of exposition-situation-unraveling with "exposition, situation, and discussion; and the discussion is the test of the playwright. . . . The serious playwright recognizes not only the main test of his highest powers, but also the real center of his play's interest.")

What Shaw does, then, is introduce massive discussions into a comedy that at first seems to be doing little more than spoofing Lady Brit and holding her son Stephen up to rather obvious ridicule. Stephen is not merely an ass; he is made to serve as a sort of straightman for Undershaft, who expounds at length unconventional ideas about munitions, sin, power, and poverty. These ideas require discussion because Shaw, unlike most comic writers, is not content with the traditional views. Comic playwrights usually criticize eccentric behavior, and at least implicitly suggest that there is a reasonable norm, known to all men of sense, from which fools depart. But because Shaw believed that society's norm is itself foolish, he devotes much of his play to expounding a new creed. Shaw reverses the old joke about the entire platoon being out of step except Johnny; for Shaw, the deviant, Johnny, *is* in step, and the rest of the platoon is laughably out of step.

During the central part of *Major Barbara*, then, Undershaft, the eccentric, is for Shaw the least laughable character. Even Barbara, the heroine, is exposed as a fool, though with great tenderness, and is forced to shed her conventional illusions. So great is the tenderness that as we see her world collapse, she seems almost a tragic figure:

> I stood on the rock I thought eternal; and without a word of warning it reeled and crumbled under me.

But Undershaft dispels the tragedy, harshly but necessarily, with, "Come, come, my daughter! dont make too much of your little tinpot tragedy. . . . Dont persist in that folly. If your old religion broke down yesterday, get a newer and a better one for tomorrow."

Enough has been said to give some idea of the novelty of Shaw's comic practice, however conventional his theory. But one should note, too, that in one important way his practice is conventional: His plays have the stock quack doctors, pompous statesmen, dragonlike matrons, and young lovers of traditional comedy. And in *Major Barbara* he even uses the ancient motif of the foundling who proves to be a suitable husband for the heroine.

Something more, however, must be said of Undershaft. Having allowed Undershaft to triumph over Barbara, Shaw does not stop; very late in the play Undershaft himself is threatened with the loss of *his* illusions when Barbara and Adolphus Cusins will make their presence felt in the munitions factory. The play ends with the usual marriage, joy, and promise of a newly organized society; in its suggestion, however, that this new society is not a return to a sensible world that was lost before the play began (think, for example, of the end of *As You Like It*, where the duke is restored to his realm), but rather is the beginning of a totally new sort of world, it marks a departure from comic practice. Maybe that is why the end of the play has seemed to most audiences the least amusing part.

MAJOR BARBARA*
Bernard Shaw

ACT 1

It is after dinner in January 1906, in the library in Lady Britomart Undershaft's house in Wilton Crescent. A large and comfortable settee is in the middle of the room, upholstered in dark leather. A person sitting on it (it is vacant at present) would have, on his right, Lady Britomart's writing table, with the lady herself busy at it; a smaller writing table behind him on his left; the door behind him on Lady Britomart's side; and a window with a window seat directly on his left. Near the window is an armchair.

Lady Britomart is a woman of fifty or thereabouts, well dressed and yet careless of her dress, well bred and quite reckless of her breeding, well mannered and yet appallingly outspoken and indifferent to the opinion of her interlocutors, amiable and yet peremptory, arbitrary, and high-tempered to the last bearable degree, and withal a very typical managing matron of the upper class, treated as a naughty child until she grew into a scolding mother, and finally settling down with plenty of practical ability and worldly experience, limited in the oddest way with domestic and class limitations, conceiving the universe exactly as if it were a large house in Wilton Crescent, though handling her corner of it very effectively on that assumption, and being quite enlightened and liberal as to the books in the library, the pictures on the walls, the music in the portfolios, and the articles in the papers.

Her son, Stephen, comes in. He is a gravely correct young man under 25, taking himself very seriously, but still in some awe of his mother, from childish habit and bachelor shyness rather than from any weakness of character.

STEPHEN. Whats the matter?

LADY BRITOMART. Presently, Stephen.

Stephen submissively walks to the settee and sits down. He takes up a Liberal weekly called The Speaker.

LADY BRITOMART. Dont begin to read, Stephen. I shall require all your attention.

STEPHEN. It was only while I was waiting—

*N.B. The Euripidean verses in the second act of *Major Barbara* are not by me, nor even directly by Euripides. They are by Professor Gilbert Murray, whose English version of *The Bacchae* came into our dramatic literature with all the impulsive power of an original work shortly before *Major Barbara* was begun. The play, indeed, stands indebted to him in more ways than one.—G.B.S.

LADY BRITOMART. Dont make excuses, Stephen. (*He puts down The Speaker.*) Now! (*She finishes her writing; rises; and comes to the settee.*) I have not kept you waiting very long, I think.

STEPHEN. Not at all, mother.

LADY BRITOMART. Bring me my cushion. (*He takes the cushion from the chair at the desk and arranges it for her as she sits down on the settee.*) Sit down. (*He sits down and fingers his tie nervously.*) Dont fiddle with your tie, Stephen: there is nothing the matter with it.

STEPHEN. I beg your pardon. (*He fiddles with his watch chain instead.*)

LADY BRITOMART. Now are you attending to me, Stephen?

STEPHEN. Of course, mother.

LADY BRITOMART. No: it's not of course. I want something much more than your everyday matter-of-course attention. I am going to speak to you very seriously, Stephen. I wish you would let that chain alone.

STEPHEN (*hastily relinquishing the chain*). Have I done anything to annoy you, mother? If so, it was quite unintentional.

LADY BRITOMART (*astonished*). Nonsense! (*With some remorse.*) My poor boy, did you think I was angry with you?

STEPHEN. What is it, then, mother? You are making me very uneasy.

LADY BRITOMART (*squaring herself at him rather aggressively*). Stephen: may I ask how soon you intend to realize that you are a grown-up man, and that I am only a woman?

STEPHEN (*amazed*). Only a—

LADY BRITOMART. Dont repeat my words, please: it is a most aggravating habit. You must learn to face life seriously, Stephen. I really cannot bear the whole burden of our family affairs any longer. You must advise me; you must assume the responsibility.

STEPHEN. I!

LADY BRITOMART. Yes, you, of course. You were 24 last June. Youve been at Harrow and Cambridge. Youve been to India and Japan. You must know a lot of things, now; unless you have wasted your time most scandalously. Well, advise me.

STEPHEN (*much perplexed*). You know I have never interfered in the household—

LADY BRITOMART. No: I should think not. I dont want you to order the dinner.

STEPHEN. I mean in our family affairs.

LADY BRITOMART. Well, you must interfere now; for they are getting quite beyond me.

STEPHEN (*troubled*). I have thought sometimes that perhaps I ought; but really, mother, I know so little about them;

and what I do know is so painful! it is so impossible to mention some things to you—(*He stops, ashamed.*)

LADY BRITOMART. I suppose you mean your father.

STEPHEN (*almost inaudibly*). Yes.

LADY BRITOMART. My dear: we cant go on all our lives not mentioning him. Of course you were quite right not to open the subject until I asked you to; but you are old enough now to be taken into my confidence, and to help me to deal with him about the girls.

STEPHEN. But the girls are all right. They are engaged.

LADY BRITOMART (*complacently*). Yes: I have made a very good match for Sarah. Charles Lomax will be a millionaire at 35. But that is ten years ahead; and in the meantime his trustees cannot under the terms of his father's will allow him more than £800 a year.

STEPHEN. But the will says also that if he increases his income by his own exertions, they may double the increase.

LADY BRITOMART. Charles Lomax's exertions are much more likely to decrease his income than to increase it. Sarah will have to find at least another £800 a year for the next ten years; and even then they will be as poor as church mice. And what about Barbara? I thought Barbara was going to make the most brilliant career of all of you. And what does she do? Joins the Salvation Army; discharges her maid; lives on a pound a week; and walks in one evening with a professor of Greek whom she has picked up in the street, and who pretends to be a Salvationist, and actually plays the big drum for her in public because he has fallen head over ears in love with her.

STEPHEN. I was certainly rather taken aback when I heard they were engaged. Cusins is a very nice fellow, certainly: nobody would ever guess that he was born in Australia; but—

LADY BRITOMART. Oh, Adolphus Cusins will make a very good husband. After all, nobody can say a word against Greek: it stamps a man at once as an educated gentleman. And my family, thank Heaven, is not a pig-headed Tory one. We are Whigs, and believe in liberty. Let snobbish people say what they please: Barbara shall marry, not the man they like, but the man *I* like.

STEPHEN. Of course I was thinking only of his income. However, he is not likely to be extravagant.

LADY BRITOMART. Dont be too sure of that, Stephen. I know your quiet, simple, refined, poetic people like Adolphus: quite content with the best of everything! They cost more than your extravagant people, who are always as mean as they are second rate. No: Barbara will need at least £2000 a year. You see it means two additional households. Besides, my dear, you must marry soon. I dont approve of the present fashion of philandering bachelors and late marriages; and I am trying to arrange something for you.

STEPHEN. It's very good of you, mother; but perhaps I had better arrange that for myself.

LADY BRITOMART. Nonsense! you are much too young to begin matchmaking: you would be taken in by some pretty little nobody. Of course I dont mean that you are not to

be consulted: you know that as well as I do. (*Stephen closes his lips and is silent.*) Now dont sulk, Stephen.

STEPHEN. I am not sulking, mother. What has all this got to do with—with—with my father?

LADY BRITOMART. My dear Stephen: where is the money to come from? It is easy enough for you and the other children to live on my income as long as we are in the same house; but I cant keep four families in four separate houses. You know how poor my father is: he has barely seven thousand a year now; and really, if he were not the Earl of Stevenage, he would have to give up society. He can do nothing for us. He says, naturally enough, that it is absurd that he should be asked to provide for the children of a man who is rolling in money. You see, Stephen, your father must be fabulously wealthy, because there is always a war going on somewhere.

STEPHEN. You need not remind me of that, mother. I have hardly ever opened a newspaper in my life without seeing our name in it. The Undershaft torpedo! The Undershaft quick firers! The Undershaft ten inch! the Undershaft disappearing rampart gun! the Undershaft submarine! and now the Undershaft aerial battleship! At Harrow they called me the Woolwich Infant. At Cambridge it was the same. A little brute at King's who was always trying to get up revivals, spoilt my Bible—your first birthday present to me—by writing under my name, "Son and heir to Undershaft and Lazarus, Death and Destruction Dealers: address, Christendom and Judea." But that was not so bad as the way I was kowtowed to everywhere because my father was making millions by selling cannons.

LADY BRITOMART. It is not only the cannons, but the war loans that Lazarus arranges under cover of giving credit for the cannons. You know, Stephen, it's perfectly scandalous. Those two men, Andrew Undershaft and Lazarus, positively have Europe under their thumbs. That is why your father is able to behave as he does. He is above the law. Do you think Bismarck or Gladstone or Disraeli could have openly defied every social and moral obligation all their lives as your father has? They simply wouldnt have dared. I asked Gladstone to take it up. I asked The Times to take it up. I asked the Lord Chamberlain to take it up. But it was just like asking them to declare war on the Sultan. They wouldnt. They said they couldnt touch him. I believe they were afraid.

STEPHEN. What could they do? He does not actually break the law.

LADY BRITOMART. Not break the law! He is always breaking the law. He broke the law when he was born: his parents were not married.

STEPHEN. Mother! Is that true?

LADY BRITOMART. Of course it's true: that was why we separated.

STEPHEN. He married without letting you know this!

LADY BRITOMART (*rather taken aback by this inference*). Oh no. To do Andrew justice, that was not the sort of thing he did. Besides, you know the Undershaft motto: Unashamed. Everybody knew.

STEPHEN. But you said that was why you separated.

LADY BRITOMART. Yes, because he was not content with being a foundling himself: he wanted to disinherit you for another foundling. That was what I couldnt stand.

STEPHEN (*ashamed*). Do you mean for—for—for—

LADY BRITOMART. Dont stammer, Stephen. Speak distinctly.

STEPHEN. But this is so frightful to me, mother. To have to speak to you about such things!

LADY BRITOMART. It's not pleasant for me, either, especially if you are still so childish that you must make it worse by a display of embarrassment. It is only in the middle classes, Stephen, that people get into a state of dumb helpless horror when they find that there are wicked people in the world. In our class, we have to decide what is to be done with wicked people; and nothing should disturb our self-possession. Now ask your question properly.

STEPHEN. Mother: have you no consideration for me? For Heaven's sake either treat me as a child, as you always do, and tell me nothing at all; or tell me everything and let me take it as best I can.

LADY BRITOMART. Treat you as a child! What do you mean? It is most unkind and ungrateful of you to say such a thing. You know I have never treated any of you as children. I have always made you my companions and friends, and allowed you perfect freedom to do and say whatever you liked, so long as you liked what I could approve of.

STEPHEN (*desperately*). I daresay we have been the very imperfect children of a very perfect mother; but I do beg you to let me alone for once, and tell me about this horrible business of my father wanting to set me aside for another son.

LADY BRITOMART (*amazed*). Another son! I never said anything of the kind. I never dreamt of such a thing. This is what comes of interrupting me.

STEPHEN. But you said—

LADY BRITOMART (*cutting him short*). Now be a good boy, Stephen, and listen to me patiently. The Undershafts are descended from a foundling in the parish of St Andrew Undershaft in the city. That was long ago, in the reign of James the First. Well, this foundling was adopted by an armorer and gun-maker. In the course of time the foundling succeeded to the business; and from some notion of gratitude, or some vow or something, he adopted another foundling, and left the business to him. And that foundling did the same. Ever since that, the cannon business has always been left to an adopted foundling named Andrew Undershaft.

STEPHEN. But did they never marry? Were there no legitimate sons?

LADY BRITOMART. Oh yes: they married just as your father did; and they were rich enough to buy land for their own children and leave them well provided for. But they always adopted and trained some foundling to succeed them in the business; and of course they always quar-relled with their wives furiously over it. Your father was adopted in that way; and he pretends to consider himself bound to keep up the tradition and adopt somebody to leave the business to. Of course I was not going to stand that. There may have been some reason for it when the Undershafts could only marry women in their own class, whose sons were not fit to govern great estates. But there could be no excuse for passing over my son.

STEPHEN (*dubiously*). I am afraid I should make a poor hand of managing a cannon foundry.

LADY BRITOMART. Nonsense! you could easily get a manager and pay him a salary.

STEPHEN. My father evidently had no great opinion of my capacity.

LADY BRITOMART. Stuff, child! you were only a baby: it had nothing to do with your capacity. Andrew did it on principle, just as he did every perverse and wicked thing on principle. When my father remonstrated, Andrew actually told him to his face that history tells us of only two successful institutions: one the Undershaft firm, and the other the Roman Empire under the Antonines. That was because the Antonine emperors all adopted their successors. Such rubbish! The Stevenages are as good as the Antonines, I hope; and you are a Stevenage. But that was Andrew all over. There you have the man! Always clever and unanswerable when he was defending nonsense and wickedness: always awkward and sullen when he had to behave sensibly and decently!

STEPHEN. Then it was on my account that your home life was broken up, mother. I am sorry.

LADY BRITOMART. Well, dear, there were other differences. I really cannot bear an immoral man. I am not a Pharisee, I hope; and I should not have minded his merely doing wrong things: we are none of us perfect. But your father didnt exactly do wrong things: he said them and thought them: that was what was so dreadful. He really had a sort of religion of wrongness. Just as one doesnt mind men practising immorality so long as they own that they are in the wrong by preaching morality; so I couldnt forgive Andrew for preaching immorality while he practised morality. You would all have grown up without principles, without any knowledge of right and wrong, if he had been in the house. You know, my dear, your father was a very attractive man in some ways. Children did not dislike him; and he took advantage of it to put the wickedest ideas into their heads, and make them quite unmanageable. I did not dislike him myself: very far from it; but nothing can bridge over moral disagreement.

STEPHEN. All this simply bewilders me, mother. People may differ about matters of opinion, or even about religion; but how can they differ about right and wrong? Right is right; and wrong is wrong; and if a man cannot distinguish them properly, he is either a fool or a rascal: thats all.

LADY BRITOMART (*touched*). Thats my own boy! (*She pats his cheek.*) Your father never could answer that: he used to laugh and get out of it under cover of some affectionate nonsense. And now that you understand the situation, what do you advise me to do?

STEPHEN. Well, what can you do?

LADY BRITOMART. I must get the money somehow.

STEPHEN. We cannot take money from him. I had rather go and live in some cheap place like Bedford Square or even Hampstead[1] than take a farthing of his money.

LADY BRITOMART. But after all, Stephen, our present income comes from Andrew.

STEPHEN (*shocked*). I never knew that.

LADY BRITOMART. Well, you surely didnt suppose your grandfather had anything to give me. The Stevenages could not do everything for you. We gave you social position. Andrew had to contribute something. He had a very good bargain, I think.

STEPHEN (*bitterly*). We are utterly dependent on him and his cannons, then?

LADY BRITOMART. Certainly not: the money is settled. But he provided it. So you see it is not a question of taking money from him or not: it is simply a question of how much. I dont want any more for myself.

STEPHEN. Nor do I.

LADY BRITOMART. But Sarah does; and Barbara does. That is, Charles Lomax and Adolphus Cusins will cost them more. So I must put my pride in my pocket and ask for it, I suppose. That is your advice, Stephen, is it not?

STEPHEN. No.

LADY BRITOMART (*sharply*). Stephen!

STEPHEN. Of course if you are determined—

LADY BRITOMART. I am not determined: I ask your advice; and I am waiting for it. I will not have all the responsibility thrown on my shoulders.

STEPHEN (*obstinately*). I would die sooner than ask him for another penny.

LADY BRITOMART (*resignedly*). You mean that *I* must ask him. Very well, Stephen: it shall be as you wish. You will be glad to know that your grandfather concurs. But he thinks I ought to ask Andrew to come here and see the girls. After all, he must have some natural affection for them.

STEPHEN. Ask him here!!!

LADY BRITOMART. Do not repeat my words, Stephen. Where else can I ask him?

STEPHEN. I never expected you to ask him at all.

LADY BRITOMART. Now dont tease, Stephen. Come! you see that it is necessary that he should pay us a visit, dont you?

STEPHEN (*reluctantly*). I suppose so, if the girls cannot do without his money.

LADY BRITOMART. Thank you, Stephen: I knew you would give me the right advice when it was properly explained to you. I have asked your father to come this evening.

---

[1]**Bedford Square . . . Hampstead** Good neighborhoods but not at the very top.

(*Stephen bounds from his seat.*) Dont jump, Stephen: it fidgets me.

STEPHEN (*in utter consternation*). Do you mean to say that my father is coming here tonight—that he may be here at any moment?

LADY BRITOMART (*looking at her watch*). I said nine. (*He gasps. She rises.*) Ring the bell, please. (*Stephen goes to the smaller writing table; presses a button on it; and sits at it with his elbows on the table and his head in his hands, outwitted and overwhelmed.*) It is ten minutes to nine yet; and I have to prepare the girls. I asked Charles Lomax and Adolphus to dinner on purpose that they might be here. Andrew had better see them in case he should cherish any delusions as to their being capable of supporting their wives. (*The butler enters: Lady Britomart goes behind the settee to speak to him.*) Morrison: go up to the drawing room and tell everybody to come down here at once. (*Morrison withdraws. Lady Britomart turns to Stephen.*) Now remember, Stephen: I shall need all your countenance and authority. (*He rises and tries to recover some vestige of these attributes.*) Give me a chair, dear. (*He pushes a chair forward from the wall to where she stands, near the smaller writing table. She sits down; and he goes to the armchair, into which he throws himself.*) I dont know how Barbara will take it. Ever since they made her a major in the Salvation Army she has developed a propensity to have her own way and order people about which quite cows me sometimes. It's not ladylike: I'm sure I dont know where she picked it up. Anyhow, Barbara shant bully me; but still it's just as well that your father should be here before she has time to refuse to meet him or make a fuss. Dont look nervous, Stephen: it will only encourage Barbara to make difficulties. *I* am nervous enough, goodness knows; but I dont shew it.

Sarah and Barbara come in with their respective young men, Charles Lomax and Adolphus Cusins. Sarah is slender, bored, and mundane. Barbara is robuster, jollier, much more energetic. Sarah is fashionably dressed: Barbara is in Salvation Army uniform. Lomax, a young man about town, is like many other young men about town. He is afflicted with a frivolous sense of humor which plunges him at the most inopportune moments into paroxysms of imperfectly suppressed laughter. Cusins is a spectacled student, slight, thin haired, and sweet voiced, with a more complex form of Lomax's complaint. His sense of humor is intellectual and subtle, and is complicated by an appalling temper. The lifelong struggle of a benevolent temperament and a high conscience against impulses of inhuman ridicule and fierce impatience has set up a chronic strain which has visibly wrecked his constitution. He is a most implacable, determined, tenacious, intolerant person who by mere force of character presents himself as—and indeed actually is—considerate, gentle, explanatory, even mild and apologetic, capable possibly of murder, but not of cruelty or coarseness. By the operation of some instinct which is not merciful enough to blind him with the illusions of love, he is obstinately bent on marrying Barbara. Lomax likes Sarah and thinks it will be rather a lark to marry her. Consequently he has not attempted to resist Lady Britomart's arrangements to that end.

All four look as if they had been having a good deal of fun in the drawing room. The girls enter first, leaving the swains outside. Sarah comes to the settee. Barbara comes in after her and stops at the door.

BARBARA. Are Cholly and Dolly to come in?

LADY BRITOMART (*forcibly*). Barbara: I will not have Charles called Cholly: the vulgarity of it positively makes me ill.

BARBARA. It's all right, mother: Cholly is quite correct nowadays. Are they to come in?

LADY BRITOMART. Yes, if they will behave themselves.

BARBARA (*through the door*). Come in, Dolly; and behave yourself.

Barbara comes to her mother's writing table. Cusins enters smiling, and wanders towards Lady Britomart.

SARAH (*calling*). Come in, Cholly. (*Lomax enters, controlling his features very imperfectly, and places himself vaguely between Sarah and Barbara.*)

LADY BRITOMART (*peremptorily*). Sit down, all of you. (*They sit. Cusins crosses to the window and seats himself there. Lomax takes a chair. Barbara sits at the writing table and Sarah on the settee.*) I dont in the least know what you are laughing at, Adolphus. I am surprised at you, though I expected nothing better from Charles Lomax.

CUSINS (*in a remarkably gentle voice*). Barbara has been trying to teach me the West Ham Salvation March.

LADY BRITOMART. I see nothing to laugh at in that; nor should you if you are really converted.

CUSINS (*sweetly*). You were not present. It was really funny, I believe.

LOMAX. Ripping.

LADY BRITOMART. Be quiet, Charles. Now listen to me, children. Your father is coming here this evening.

General stupefaction. Lomax, Sarah, and Barbara rise: Sarah scared, and Barbara amused and expectant.

LOMAX (*remonstrating*). Oh I say!

LADY BRITOMART. You are not called on to say anything, Charles.

SARAH. Are you serious, mother?

LADY BRITOMART. Of course I am serious. It is on your account, Sarah, and also on Charles's. (*Silence. Sarah sits, with a shrug. Charles looks painfully unworthy.*) I hope you are not going to object, Barbara.

BARBARA. I! why should I? My father has a soul to be saved like anybody else. He's quite welcome as far as I am concerned. (*She sits on the table, and softly whistles 'Onward, Christian Soldiers.'*)

LOMAX (*still remonstrant*). But really, dont you know! Oh I say!

LADY BRITOMART (*frigidly*). What do you wish to convey, Charles?

LOMAX. Well, you must admit that this is a bit thick.

LADY BRITOMART (*turning with ominous suavity to Cusins*). Adolphus: you are a professor of Greek. Can you translate Charles Lomax's remarks into reputable English for us?

CUSINS (*cautiously*). If I may say so, Lady Brit, I think Charles has rather happily expressed what we all feel. Homer, speaking of Autolycus, uses the same phrase. πυκινὸν δόμον ἐλθεῖν[2] means a bit thick.

LOMAX (*handsomely*). Not that I mind, you know, if Sarah dont. (*He sits.*)

LADY BRITOMART (*crushingly*). Thank you. Have I your permission, Adolphus, to invite my own husband to my own house?

CUSINS (*gallantly*). You have my unhesitating support in everything you do.

LADY BRITOMART. Tush! Sarah: have you nothing to say?

SARAH. Do you mean that he is coming regularly to live here?

LADY BRITOMART. Certainly not. The spare room is ready for him if he likes to stay for a day or two and see a little more of you; but there are limits.

SARAH. Well, he cant eat us, I suppose. I dont mind.

LOMAX (*chuckling*). I wonder how the old man will take it.

LADY BRITOMART. Much as the old woman will, no doubt, Charles.

LOMAX (*abashed*). I didn't mean—at least—

LADY BRITOMART. You didnt think, Charles. You never do; and the result is, you never mean anything. And now please attend to me, children. Your father will be quite a stranger to us.

LOMAX. I suppose he hasnt seen Sarah since she was a little kid.

LADY BRITOMART. Not since she was a little kid, Charles, as you express it with that elegance of diction and refinement of thought that seem never to desert you. Accordingly—er—(*impatiently*). Now I have forgotten what I was going to say. That comes of your provoking me to be sarcastic, Charles. Adolphus: will you kindly tell me where I was.

CUSINS (*sweetly*). You were saying that as Mr Undershaft has not seen his children since they were babies, he will form his opinion of the way you have brought them up from their behavior tonight, and that therefore you wish us all to be particularly careful to conduct ourselves well, especially Charles.

LADY BRITOMART (*with emphatic approval*). Precisely.

LOMAX. Look here, Dolly: Lady Brit didnt say that.

LADY BRITOMART (*vehemently*). I did, Charles. Adolphus's recollection is perfectly correct. It is most important that

---

[2]πυκινὸν δόμον ἐλθεῖν "Pukinon domon elthein." In Homer, the phrase refers to a fortified house.

you should be good; and I do beg you for once not to pair off into opposite corners and giggle and whisper while I am speaking to your father.

BARBARA. All right, mother. We'll do you credit. (*She comes off the table, and sits in her chair with ladylike elegance.*)

LADY BRITOMART. Remember, Charles, that Sarah will want to feel proud of you instead of ashamed of you.

LOMAX. Oh I say! theres nothing to be exactly proud of, dont you know.

LADY BRITOMART. Well, try and look as if there was.

Morrison, pale and dismayed, breaks into the room in unconcealed disorder.

MORRISON. Might I speak a word to you, my lady?

LADY BRITOMART. Nonsense! Shew him up.

MORRISON. Yes, my lady. (*He goes.*)

LOMAX. Does Morrison know who it is?

LADY BRITOMART. Of course. Morrison has always been with us.

LOMAX. It must be a regular corker for him, dont you know.

LADY BRITOMART. Is this a moment to get on my nerves, Charles, with your outrageous expressions?

LOMAX. But this is something out of the ordinary, really—

MORRISON (*at the door*). The—er—Mr Undershaft. (*He retreats in confusion.*)

Andrew Undershaft comes in. All rise. Lady Britomart meets him in the middle of the room behind the settee.

Andrew is, on the surface, a stoutish, easygoing elderly man, with kindly patient manners, and an engaging simplicity of character. But he has a watchful, deliberate, waiting, listening face, and formidable reserves of power, both bodily and mental, in his capacious chest and long head. His gentleness is partly that of a strong man who has learnt by experience that his natural grip hurts ordinary people unless he handles them very carefully, and partly the mellowness of age and success. He is also a little shy in his present very delicate situation.

LADY BRITOMART. Good evening, Andrew.

UNDERSHAFT. How d'ye do, my dear.

LADY BRITOMART. You look a good deal older.

UNDERSHAFT (*apologetically*). I am somewhat older. (*Taking her hand with a touch of courtship.*) Time has stood still with you.

LADY BRITOMART (*throwing away his hand*). Rubbish! This is your family.

UNDERSHAFT (*surprised*). Is it so large? I am sorry to say my memory is failing very badly in some things. (*He offers his hand with paternal kindness to Lomax.*)

LOMAX (*jerkily shaking his hand*). Ahdedoo.

UNDERSHAFT. I can see you are my eldest. I am very glad to meet you again, my boy.

LOMAX (*remonstrating*). No, but look here dont you know—(*Overcome.*) Oh I say!

LADY BRITOMART (*recovering from momentary speechlessness*). Andrew: do you mean to say that you dont remember how many children you have?

UNDERSHAFT. Well, I am afraid I—. They have grown so much—er. Am I making any ridiculous mistake? I may as well confess: I recollect only one son. But so many things have happened since, of course—er—

LADY BRITOMART (*decisively*). Andrew: you are talking nonsense. Of course you have only one son.

UNDERSHAFT. Perhaps you will be good enough to introduce me, my dear.

LADY BRITOMART. That is Charles Lomax, who is engaged to Sarah.

UNDERSHAFT. My dear sir, I beg your pardon.

LOMAX. Notatall. Delighted, I assure you.

LADY BRITOMART. This is Stephen.

UNDERSHAFT (*bowing*). Happy to make your acquaintance, Mr Stephen. Then (*going to Cusins*) you must be my son. (*Taking Cusins' hands in his.*) How are you, my young friend? (*To Lady Britomart.*) He is very like you, my love.

CUSINS. You flatter me, Mr Undershaft. My name is Cusins: engaged to Barbara. (*Very explicitly.*) That is Major Barbara Undershaft, of the Salvation Army. That is Sarah, your second daughter. This is Stephen Undershaft, your son.

UNDERSHAFT. My dear Stephen, I beg your pardon.

STEPHEN. Not at all.

UNDERSHAFT. Mr Cusins: I am much indebted to you for explaining so precisely. (*Turning to Sarah.*) Barbara, my dear—

SARAH (*prompting him*). Sarah.

UNDERSHAFT. Sarah, of course. (*They shake hands. He goes over to Barbara.*) Barbara—I am right this time, I hope?

BARBARA. Quite right. (*They shake hands.*)

LADY BRITOMART (*resumimg command*). Sit down, all of you. Sit down, Andrew. (*She comes forward and sits on the settee. Cusins also brings his chair forward on her left. Barbara and Stephen resume their seats. Lomax gives his chair to Sarah and goes for another.*)

UNDERSHAFT. Thank you, my love.

LOMAX (*conversationally, as he brings a chair forward between the writing table and the settee, and offers it to Undershaft*). Takes you some time to find out exactly where you are, dont it?

UNDERSHAFT (*accepting the chair, but remaining standing*). That is not what embarrasses me, Mr Lomax. My difficulty is that if I play the part of a father, I shall produce the effect of an intrusive stranger; and if I play the part of a discreet stranger, I may appear a callous father.

LADY BRITOMART. There is no need for you to play any part at all, Andrew. You had much better be sincere and natural.

UNDERSHAFT (*submissively*). Yes, my dear: I daresay that will be best. (*He sits down comfortably.*) Well, here I am. Now what can I do for you all?

LADY BRITOMART. You need not do anything, Andrew. You are one of the family. You can sit with us and enjoy yourself.

A painfully conscious pause. Barbara makes a face at Lomax, whose too long suppressed mirth immediately explodes in agonized neighings.

LADY BRITOMART (*outraged*). Charles Lomax: if you can behave yourself, behave yourself. If not, leave the room.

LOMAX. I'm awfully sorry, Lady Brit; but really you know, upon my soul! (*He sits on the settee between Lady Britomart and Undershaft, quite overcome.*)

BARBARA. Why dont you laugh if you want to, Cholly? It's good for your inside.

LADY BRITOMART. Barbara: you have had the education of a lady. Please let your father see that; and dont talk like a street girl.

UNDERSHAFT. Never mind me, my dear. As you know, I am not a gentleman; and I was never educated.

LOMAX (*encouragingly*). Nobody'd know it, I assure you. You look all right, you know.

CUSINS. Let me advise you to study Greek, Mr Undershaft. Greek scholars are privileged men. Few of them know Greek; and none of them know anything else; but their position is unchallengeable. Other languages are the qualifications of waiters and commercial travellers: Greek is to a man of position what the hallmark is to silver.

BARBARA. Dolly: dont be insincere. Cholly: fetch your concertina and play something for us.

LOMAX (*jumps up eagerly, but checks himself to remark doubtfully to Undershaft*). Perhaps that sort of thing isnt in your line, eh?

UNDERSHAFT. I am particularly fond of music.

LOMAX (*delighted*). Are you? Then I'll get it. (*He goes upstairs for the instrument.*)

UNDERSHAFT. Do you play, Barbara?

BARBARA. Only the tambourine. But Cholly's teaching me the concertina.

UNDERSHAFT. Is Cholly also a member of the Salvation Army?

BARBARA. No: he says it's bad form to be a dissenter. But I dont despair of Cholly. I made him come yesterday to a meeting at the dock gates, and take the collection in his hat.

UNDERSHAFT (*looks whimsically at his wife*)!!

LADY BRITOMART. It is not my doing, Andrew. Barbara is old enough to take her own way. She has no father to advise her.

BARBARA. Oh yes she has. There are no orphans in the Salvation Army.

UNDERSHAFT. Your father there has a great many children and plenty of experience, eh?

BARBARA (*looking at him with quick interest and nodding*). Just so. How did you come to understand that? (*Lomax is heard at the door trying the concertina.*)

LADY BRITOMART. Come in, Charles. Play us something at once.

LOMAX. Righto! (*He sits down in his former place, and preludes.*)

UNDERSHAFT. One moment, Mr Lomax. I am rather interested in the Salvation Army. Its motto might be my own: Blood and Fire.

LOMAX (*shocked*). But not your sort of blood and fire, you know.

UNDERSHAFT. My sort of blood cleanses: my sort of fire purifies.

BARBARA. So do ours. Come down tomorrow to my shelter—the West Ham shelter—and see what we're doing. We're going to march to a great meeting in the Assembly Hall at Mile End. Come and see the shelter and then march with us: it will do you a lot of good. Can you play anything?

UNDERSHAFT. In my youth I earned pennies, and even shillings occasionally, in the streets and in public house parlors by my natural talent for stepdancing. Later on, I became a member of the Undershaft orchestral society, and performed passably on the tenor trombone.

LOMAX (*scandalized—putting down the concertina*). Oh I say!

BARBARA. Many a sinner has played himself into heaven on the trombone, thanks to the Army.

LOMAX (*to Barbara, still rather shocked*). Yes; but what about the cannon business, dont you know? (*To Undershaft.*) Getting into heaven is not exactly in your line, is it?

LADY BRITOMART. Charles!!!

LOMAX. Well; but it stands to reason, dont it? The cannon business may be necessary and all that: we cant get on without cannons; but it isnt right, you know. On the other hand, there may be a certain amount of tosh about the Salvation Army—I belong to the Established Church myself—but still you cant deny that it's religion; and you cant go against religion, can you? At least unless youre downright immoral, dont you know.

UNDERSHAFT. You hardly appreciate my position, Mr Lomax—

LOMAX (*hastily*). I'm not saying anything against you personally—

UNDERSHAFT. Quite so, quite so. But consider for a moment. Here I am, a profiteer in mutilation and murder. I find myself in a specially amiable humor just now because, this morning, down at the foundry, we blew twenty-seven dummy soldiers into fragments with a gun which formerly destroyed only thirteen.

LOMAX (*leniently*). Well, the more destructive war becomes, the sooner it will be abolished, eh?

UNDERSHAFT. Not at all. The more destructive war becomes the more fascinating we find it. No, Mr Lomax: I am obliged to you for making the usual excuse for my trade; but I am not ashamed of it. I am not one of those men who keep their morals and their business in water-tight compartments. All the spare money my trade rivals spend on hospitals, cathedrals, and other receptacles for conscience money, I devote to experiments and researches in improved methods of destroying life and property. I have always done so; and I always shall. Therefore your Christmas card moralities of peace on earth and goodwill among men are of no use to me. Your Christianity, which enjoins you to resist not evil, and to turn the other cheek, would make me a bankrupt. My morality—my religion—must have a place for cannons and torpedoes in it.

STEPHEN (*coldly—almost sullenly*). You speak as if there were half a dozen moralities and religions to choose from, instead of one true morality and one true religion.

UNDERSHAFT. For me there is only one true morality; but it might not fit you, as you do not manufacture aerial battleships. There is only one true morality for every man; but every man has not the same true morality.

LOMAX (*overtaxed*). Would you mind saying that again? I didnt quite follow it.

CUSINS. It's quite simple. As Euripides says, one man's meat is another man's poison morally as well as physically.

UNDERSHAFT. Precisely.

LOMAX. Oh, that! Yes, yes, yes. True. True.

STEPHEN. In other words, some men are honest and some are scoundrels.

BARBARA. Bosh! There are no scoundrels.

UNDERSHAFT. Indeed? Are there any good men?

BARBARA. No. Not one. There are neither good men nor scoundrels: there are just children of one Father; and the sooner they stop calling one another names the better. You neednt talk to me: I know them. Ive had scores of them through my hands: scoundrels, criminals, infidels, philanthropists, missionaries, county councillors, all sorts. Theyre all just the same sort of sinner; and theres the same salvation ready for them all.

UNDERSHAFT. May I ask have you ever saved a maker of cannons?

BARBARA. No. Will you let me try?

UNDERSHAFT. Well, I will make a bargain with you. If I go to see you tomorrow in your Salvation Shelter, will you come the day after to see me in my cannon works?

BARBARA. Take care. It may end in your giving up the cannons for the sake of the Salvation Army.

UNDERSHAFT. Are you sure it will not end in your giving up the Salvation Army for the sake of the cannons?

BARBARA. I will take my chance of that.

UNDERSHAFT. And I will take my chance of the other. (*They shake hands on it.*) Where is your shelter?

BARBARA. In West Ham. At the sign of the cross. Ask anybody in Canning Town. Where are your works?

UNDERSHAFT. In Perivale St Andrews. At the sign of the sword. Ask anybody in Europe.

LOMAX. Hadnt I better play something?

BARBARA. Yes. Give us Onward, Christian Soldiers.

LOMAX. Well, thats rather a strong order to begin with, dont you know. Suppose I sing Thourt passing hence, my brother. It's much the same tune.

BARBARA. It's too melancholy. You get saved, Cholly; and youll pass hence, my brother, without making such a fuss about it.

LADY BRITOMART. Really, Barbara, you go on as if religion were a pleasant subject. Do have some sense of propriety.

UNDERSHAFT. I do not find it an unpleasant subject, my dear. It is the only one that capable people really care for.

LADY BRITOMART (*looking at her watch*). Well, if you are determined to have it, I insist on having it in a proper and respectable way. Charles: ring for prayers.

General amazement. Stephen rises in dismay.

LOMAX (*rising*). Oh I say!

UNDERSHAFT (*rising*). I am afraid I must be going.

LADY BRITOMART. You cannot go now, Andrew: it would be most improper. Sit down. What will the servants think?

UNDERSHAFT. My dear: I have conscientious scruples. May I suggest a compromise? If Barbara will conduct a little service in the drawing room, with Mr Lomax as organist, I will attend it willingly. I will even take part, if a trombone can be procured.

LADY BRITOMART. Dont mock, Andrew.

UNDERSHAFT (*shocked—to Barbara*). You dont think I am mocking, my love, I hope.

BARBARA. No, of course not; and it wouldnt matter if you were: half the Army came to their first meeting for a lark. (*Rising.*) Come along. (*She throws her arm round her father and sweeps him out, calling to the others from the threshold.*) Come, Dolly. Come, Cholly.

Cusins rises.

LADY BRITOMART. I will not be disobeyed by everybody. Adolphus: sit down. (*He does not.*) Charles: you may go. You are not fit for prayers: you cannot keep your countenance.

LOMAX. Oh I say! (*He goes out.*)

LADY BRITOMART (*continuing*). But you, Adolphus, can behave yourself if you choose to. I insist on your staying.

CUSINS. My dear Lady Brit: there are things in the family prayer book that I couldnt bear to hear you say.

LADY BRITOMART. What things, pray?

CUSINS. Well, you would have to say before all the servants that we have done things we ought not to have done, and left undone things we ought to have done, and that there is no health in us. I cannot bear to hear you doing yourself such an injustice, and Barbara such an injustice. As for myself, I flatly deny it: I have done my best. I shouldnt dare to marry Barbara—I couldnt look you in the face—if it were true. So I must go to the drawing room.

LADY BRITOMART (*offended*). Well, go. (*He starts for the door.*) And remember this, Adolphus: (*He turns to listen.*) I have a very strong suspicion that you went to the Salvation Army to worship Barbara and nothing else. And I quite appreciate the very clever way in which you systematically humbug me. I have found you out. Take care Barbara doesnt. Thats all.

CUSINS (*with unruffled sweetness*). Dont tell on me. (*He steals out.*)

LADY BRITOMART. Sarah: if you want to go, go. Anything's better than to sit there as if you wished you were a thousand miles away.

SARAH (*languidly*). Very well, mamma. (*She goes.*)

Lady Britomart, with a sudden flounce, gives way to a little gust of tears.

STEPHEN (*going to her*). Mother: whats the matter?

LADY BRITOMART (*swishing away her tears with her handkerchief*). Nothing. Foolishness. You can go with him, too, if you like, and leave me with the servants.

STEPHEN. Oh, you mustnt think that, mother. I—I dont like him.

LADY BRITOMART. The others do. That is the injustice of a woman's lot. A woman has to bring up her children; and that means to restrain them, to deny them things they want, to set them tasks, to punish them when they do wrong, to do all the unpleasant things. And then the father, who has nothing to do but pet them and spoil them, comes in when all her work is done and steals their affection from her.

STEPHEN. He has not stolen our affection from you. It is only curiosity.

LADY BRITOMART (*violently*). I wont be consoled, Stephen. There is nothing the matter with me. (*She rises and goes towards the door.*)

STEPHEN. Where are you going, mother?

LADY BRITOMART. To the drawing room, of course. (*She goes out. Onward, Christian Soldiers, on the concertina, with tambourine accompaniment, is heard when the door opens.*) Are you coming, Stephen?

STEPHEN. No. Certainly not. (*She goes. He sits down on the settee, with compressed lips and an expression of strong dislike.*)

ACT 2

The yard of the West Ham shelter of the Salvation Army is a cold place on a January morning. The building itself, an old warehouse, is newly whitewashed. Its gabled end projects into the yard in the middle, with a door on the ground floor, and another in the loft above it without any balcony or ladder, but with a pulley rigged over it for hoisting sacks. Those who come from this central gable end into the yard have the gateway leading to the street on their left, with a stone horse-trough just beyond it, and, on the right, a penthouse shielding a table from the weather. There are forms at the table; and on them are seated a man and a woman, both much down on their luck, finishing a meal of bread (one thick slice each, with margarine and golden syrup) and diluted milk.

The man, a workman out of employment, is young, agile, a talker, a poser, sharp enough to be capable of anything in reason except honesty or altruistic considerations of any kind. The woman is a commonplace old bundle of poverty and hard-worn humanity. She looks sixty and probably is forty-five. If they were rich people, gloved and muffed and well wrapped up in furs and overcoats, they would be numbed and miserable; for it is a grindingly cold raw January day; and a glance at the background of grimy warehouses and leaden sky visible over the whitewashed walls of the yard would drive any idle rich person straight to the Mediterranean. But these two, being no more troubled with visions of the Mediterranean than of the moon, and being compelled to keep more of their clothes in the pawnshop, and less on their persons, in winter than in summer, are not depressed by the cold: rather are they stung into vivacity, to which their meal has just now given an almost jolly turn. The man takes a pull at his mug, and then gets up and moves about the yard with his hands deep in his pockets, occasionally breaking into a stepdance.

THE WOMAN. Feel better arter your meal, sir?

THE MAN. No. Call that a meal! Good enough for you, praps; but wot is it to me, an intelligent workin man.

THE WOMAN. Workin man! Wot are you?

THE MAN. Painter.

THE WOMAN (*sceptically*). Yus, I dessay.

THE MAN. Yus, you dessay! I know. Every loafer that cant do nothink calls isself a painter. Well, I'm a real painter: grainer, finisher, thirty-eight bob a week when I can get it.

THE WOMAN. Then why dont you go and get it?

THE MAN. I'll tell you why. Fust: I'm intelligent—fffff! it's rotten cold here—(*He dances a step or two.*) yes: intelligent beyond the station o life into which it has pleased the capitalists to call me; and they dont like a man that sees through em. Second, an intelligent bein needs a doo share of appiness; so I drink somethink cruel when I get the chawnce. Third, I stand by my class and do as little as I can so's to leave arf the job for me fellow workers. Fourth, I'm fly enough to know wots inside the law and wots outside it; and inside it I do as the capitalists do: pinch wot I can lay me ands on. In a proper state of society I am sober, industrious and honest: in Rome, so to speak, I do as the Romans do. Wots the consequence? When trade is bad—and it's rotten bad just now—and the employers az to sack arf their men, they generally start on me.

THE WOMAN. Whats your name?

THE MAN. Price. Bronterre O'Brien Price. Usually called Snobby Price, for short.

THE WOMAN. Snobby's a carpenter, aint it? You said you was a painter.

PRICE. Not that kind of snob, but the genteel sort. I'm too uppish, owing to my intelligence, and my father being a Chartist[3] and a reading, thinking man: a stationer, too. I'm none of your common hewers of wood and drawers of water; and dont you forget it. (*He returns to his seat at the table, and takes up his mug.*) Wots your name?

THE WOMAN. Rummy Mitchens, sir.

PRICE (*quaffing the remains of his milk to her*). Your elth, Miss Mitchens.

RUMMY (*correcting him*). Missis Mitchens.

PRICE. Wot! Oh Rummy, Rummy! Respectable married woman, Rummy, gittin rescued by the Salvation Army by pretendin to be a bad un. Same old game!

RUMMY. What am I to do? I cant starve. Them Salvation lasses is dear good girls; but the better you are, the worse they likes to think you were before they rescued you. Why shouldnt they av a bit o credit, poor loves? theyre worn to rags by their work. And where would they get the money to rescue us if we was to let on we're no worse than other people? You know what ladies and gentlemen are.

PRICE. Thievin swine! Wish I ad their job, Rummy, all the same. Wot does Rummy stand for? Pet name praps?

RUMMY. Short for Romola.[4]

PRICE. For wot!?

RUMMY. Romola. It was out of a new book. Somebody me mother wanted me to grow up like.

PRICE. We're companions in misfortune, Rummy. Both on us got names that nobody cawnt pronounce. Consequently I'm Snobby and youre Rummy because Bill and Sally wasnt good enough for our parents. Such is life!

RUMMY. Who saved you, Mr Price? Was it Major Barbara?

PRICE. No: I come here on my own. I'm going to be Bronterre O'Brien Price, the converted painter. I know wot they like. I'll tell em how I blasphemed and gambled and wopped my poor old mother—

RUMMY (*shocked*). Used you to beat your mother?

PRICE. Not likely. She used to beat me. No matter: you come and listen to the converted painter, and youll hear how she was a pious woman that taught me me prayers at er knee, an how I used to come home drunk and drag her out o bed be er snow white airs, an lam into er with the poker.

RUMMY. That whats so unfair to us women. Your confessions is just as big lies as ours: you dont tell what you really done no more than us; but you men can tell your lies right out at the meetins and be made much of for it; while the sort o confessions we az to make az to be wis-pered to one lady at a time. It aint right, spite of all their piety.

PRICE. Right! Do you spose the Army'd be allowed if it went and did right? Not much. It combs out air and makes us good little blokes to be robbed and put upon. But I'll play the game as good as any of em. I'll see somebody struck by lightnin, or hear a voice sayin "Snobby Price: where will you spend eternity?" I'll av a time of it, I tell you.

RUMMY. You wont be let drink, though.

PRICE. I'll take it out in gorspellin, then. I dont want to drink if I can get fun enough any other way.

Jenny Hill, a pale, overwrought, pretty Salvation lass of 18, comes in through the yard gate, leading Peter Shirley, a half hardened, half worn-out elderly man, weak with hunger.

JENNY (*supporting him*). Come! pluck up. I'll get you something to eat. Youll be all right then.

PRICE (*rising and hurrying officiously to take the old man off Jenny's hands*). Poor old man! Cheer up, brother: youll find rest and peace and appiness ere. Hurry up with the food, miss: e's fair done (*Jenny hurries into the shelter.*) Ere, buck up, daddy! she's fetchin y'a thick slice o breadn treacle,[5] an a mug o skyblue. (*He seats him at the corner of the table.*)

RUMMY (*gaily*). Keep up your old art! Never say die!

SHIRLEY. I'm not an old man. I'm only 46. I'm as good as ever I was. The grey patch come in my hair before I was thirty. All it wants is three pennorth o hair dye: am I to be turned on the streets to starve for it? Holy God! Ive worked ten to twelve hours a day since I was thirteen, and paid my way all through; and now am I to be thrown into the gutter and my job given to a young man that can do it better than me because Ive black hair that goes white at the first change?

PRICE (*cheerfully*). No good jawrin about it. Youre ony a jumped-up, jerked-off, orspittle-turned-out incurable of an ole workin man: who cares about you? Eh? Make the thievin swine give you a meal: theyve stole many a one from you. Get a bit o your own back (*Jenny returns with the usual meal.*) There you are, brother. Awsk a blessin an tuck that into you.

SHIRLEY (*looking at it ravenously but not touching it, and crying like a child*). I never took anything before.

JENNY (*petting him*). Come, come! the Lord sends it to you: he wasnt above taking bread from his friends; and why should you be? Besides, when we find you a job you can pay us for it if you like.

SHIRLEY (*eagerly*). Yes, yes: thats true. I can pay you back: it's only a loan. (*Shivering.*) Oh Lord! oh Lord! (*He turns to the table and attacks the meal ravenously.*)

---

[3]**Chartist** a member of an English workers' reform movement of the 1840's. [4]**Romola** the idealistic heroine of George Eliot's novel, 1863.

[5]**treacle** molasses.

JENNY. Well, Rummy, are you more comfortable now?

RUMMY. God bless you, lovey! youve fed my body and saved my soul, havnt you? (*Jenny, touched, kisses her.*) Sit down and rest a bit: you must be ready to drop.

JENNY. Ive been going hard since morning. But theres more work than we can do. I mustnt stop.

RUMMY. Try a prayer for just two minutes. Youll work all the better after.

JENNY (*her eyes lighting up*). Oh isnt it wonderful how a few minutes prayer revives you! I was quite lightheaded at twelve o'clock, I was so tired; but Major Barbara just sent me to pray for five minutes; and I was able to go on as if I had only just begun. (*To Price.*) Did you have a piece of bread?

PRICE (*with unction*). Yes, miss; but Ive got the piece that I value more; and thats the peace that passeth hall hannerstennin.

RUMMY (*fervently*). Glory Hallelujah!

Bill Walker, a rough customer of about 25, appears at the yard gate and looks malevolently at Jenny.

JENNY. That makes me so happy. When you say that, I feel wicked for loitering here. I must get to work again.

She is hurrying to the shelter, when the new-comer moves quickly up to the door and intercepts her. His manner is so threatening that she retreats as he comes at her truculently, driving her down the yard.

BILL. Aw knaow you. Youre the one that took away maw girl. Youre the one that set er agen me. Well, I'm gowin to ev er aht. Not that Aw care a carse for er or you: see? Bat Aw'll let er knaow; and Aw'll let you knaow. Aw'm gowing to give her a doin thatll teach er to cat awy from me. Nah in wiv you and tell er to cam aht afore Aw cam in and kick er aht. Tell er Bill Walker wants er. She'll knaow wot thet means; and if she keeps me witin itll be worse. You stop to jawr beck at me; and Aw'll stawt on you: d'ye eah? Theres your wy. In you gow. (*He takes her by the arm and slings her towards the door of the shelter. She falls on her hand and knee. Rummy helps her up again.*)

PRICE (*rising, and venturing irresolutely towards Bill*). Easy there, mate. She aint doin you no arm.

BILL. Oo are you callin mite? (*Standing over him threateningly.*) Youre gowin to stend ap for er, aw yer? Put ap your ends.

RUMMY (*running indignantly to him to scold him*). Oh, you great brute—(*He instantly swings his left hand back against her face. She screams and reels back to the trough, where she sits down, covering her bruised face with her hands and rocking herself and moaning with pain.*)

JENNY (*going to her*). Oh, God forgive you! How could you strike an old woman like that?

BILL (*seizing her by the hair so violently that she also screams, and tearing her away from the old woman*). You Gawd forgimme again an Aw'll Gawd forgive you one on the jawr thetll stop you pryin for a week. (*Holding her and turning fiercely on Price.*) Ev you ennything to sy agen it?

PRICE (*intimidated*). No, matey: she aint anything to do with me.

BILL. Good job for you! Aw'd pat two meals into you and fawt you with one finger arter, you stawved cur. (*To Jenny.*) Nah are you gowin to fetch aht Mog Ebbijem; or em Aw to knock your fice off you and fetch her meself?

JENNY (*writhing in his grasp*). Oh please someone go in and tell Major Barbara—(*She screams again as he wrenches her head down; and Price and Rummy flee into the shelter.*)

BILL. You want to gow in and tell your Mijor of me, do you?

JENNY. Oh please dont drag my hair. Let me go.

BILL. Do you or downt you? (*She stifles a scream.*) Yus or nao?

JENNY. God give me strength—

BILL (*striking her with his fist in the face*). Gow an shaow her thet, and tell her if she wants one lawk it to cam and interfere with me. (*Jenny, crying with pain, goes into the shed. He goes to the form and addresses the old man.*) Eah: finish your mess; an git aht o maw wy.

SHIRLEY (*springing up and facing him fiercely, with the mug in his hand*). You take a liberty with me, and I'll smash you over the face with the mug and cut your eye out. Aint you satisfied—young whelps like you—with takin the bread out o the mouths of your elders that have brought you up and slaved for you, but you must come shovin and cheekin and bullyin in here, where the bread o charity is sickenin in our stummicks?

BILL (*contemptuously, but backing a little*). Wot good are you, you aold palsy mag?[6] Wot good are you?

SHIRLEY. As good as you and better. I'll do a day's work agen you or any fat young soaker of your age. Go and take my job at Horrockses, where I worked for ten year. They want young men there: they cant afford to keep men over forty-five. Theyre very sorry—give you a character and happy to help you to get anything suited to your years—sure a steady man wont be long out of a job. Well, let em try you. Theyll find the differ. What do you know? Not as much as how to beeyave yourself—layin your dirty fist across the mouth of a respectable woman!

BILL. Downt provowk me to ly it acrost yours: d'ye eah?

SHIRLEY (*with blighting contempt*). Yes: you like an old man to hit, dont you, when youve finished with the women. I aint seen you hit a young one yet.

BILL (*stung*). You loy, you aold soupkitchener, you. There was a yang menn eah. Did Aw offer to itt him or did Aw not?

SHIRLEY. Was he starvin or was he not? Was he a man or only a crosseyed thief an a loafer? Would you hit my son-in-law's brother?

[6]**palsy mag** drunkard.

BILL. Oo's ee?

SHIRLEY. Todger Fairmile o Balls Pond. Him that won £20 off the Japanese wrastler at the music hall by standin out 17 minutes 4 seconds agen him.

BILL (*sullenly*). Aw'm nao music awl wrastler. Ken he box?

SHIRLEY. Yes: an you cant.

BILL. Wot! Aw cawnt, cawnt Aw? Wots thet you sy? (*Threatening him.*)

SHIRLEY (*not budging an inch*). Will you box Todger Fairmile if I put him on to you? Say the word.

BILL (*subsiding with a slouch*). Aw'll stend ap to enny menn alawv, if he was ten Todger Fairmawls. But Aw dont set ap to be a perfeshnal.

SHIRLEY (*looking down on him with unfathomable disdain*). You box! Slap an old woman with the back o your hand! You hadnt even the sense to hit her where a magistrate couldnt see the mark of it, you silly young lump of conceit and ignorance. Hit a girl in the jaw and ony make her cry! If Todger Fairmile'd done it, she wouldnt a got up inside o ten minutes, no more than you would if he got on to you. Yah! I'd set about you myself if I had a week's feedin in me instead o two months' starvation. (*He turns his back on him and sits down moodily at the table.*)

BILL (*following him and stooping over him to drive the taunt in*). You loy! youve the bread and treacle in you that you cam eah to beg.

SHIRLEY (*bursting into tears*). Oh God! it's true: I'm only an old pauper on the scrap heap. (*Furiously.*) But youll come to it yourself; and then youll know. Youll come to it sooner than a teetotaller like me, fillin yourself with gin at this hour o the mornin!

BILL. Aw'm nao gin drinker, you oald lawr; bat wen Aw want to give my girl a bloomin good awdin Aw lawk to ev a bit o devil in me: see? An eah Aw emm, talkin to a rotten aold blawter like you sted o givin her wot for. (*Working himself into a rage.*) Aw'm gowin in there to fetch her aht. (*He makes vengefully for the shelter door.*)

SHIRLEY. Youre goin to the station on a stretcher, more likely; and theyll take the gin and the devil out of you there when they get you inside. You mind what youre about: the major here is the Earl o Stevenage's granddaughter.

BILL (*checked*). Garn!

SHIRLEY. Youll see.

BILL (*his resolution oozing*). Well, Aw aint dan nathin to er.

SHIRLEY. Spose she said you did! who'd believe you?

BILL (*very uneasy, skulking back to the corner of the penthouse*). Gawd! theres no jastice in this cantry. To think wot them people can do! Aw'm as good as er.

SHIRLEY. Tell her so. It's just what a fool like you would do.

Barbara, brisk and businesslike, comes from the shelter with a note book, and addresses herself to Shirley. Bill, cowed, sits down in the corner on a form, and turns his back on them.

BARBARA. Good morning.

SHIRLEY (*standing up and taking off his hat*). Good morning, miss.

BARBARA. Sit down: make yourself at home. (*He hesitates; but she puts a friendly hand on his shoulder and makes him obey.*) Now then! since youve made friends with us, we want to know all about you. Names and addresses and trades.

SHIRLEY. Peter Shirley. Fitter. Chucked out two months ago because I was too old.

BARBARA (*not at all surprised*). Youd pass still. Why didnt you dye your hair?

SHIRLEY. I did. Me age come out at a coroner's inquest on me daughter.

BARBARA. Steady?

SHIRLEY. Teetotaller. Never out of a job before. Good worker. And sent to the knackers[7] like an old horse!

BARBARA. No matter: if you did your part God will do his.

SHIRLEY (*suddenly stubborn*). My religion's no concern of anybody but myself.

BARBARA (*guessing*). I know. Secularist?[8]

SHIRLEY (*hotly*). Did I offer to deny it?

BARBARA. Why should you? My own father's a Secularist, I think. Our Father—yours and mine—fulfils himself in many ways; and I daresay he knew what he was about when he made a Secularist of you. So buck up, Peter! we can always find a job for a steady man like you. (*Shirley, disarmed and a little bewildered, touches his hat. She turns from him to Bill.*) Whats your name?

BILL (*insolently*). Wots thet to you?

BARBARA (*calmly making a note*). Afraid to give his name. Any trade?

BILL. Oo's afride to give is nime? (*Doggedly, with a sense of heroically defying the House of Lords in the person of Lord Stevenage.*) If you want to bring a chawge agen me, bring it. (*She waits, unruffled.*) Moy nime's Bill Walker.

BARBARA (*as if the name were familiar: trying to remember how*). Bill Walker? (*Recollecting.*) Oh, I know: youre the man that Jenny Hill was praying for inside just now. (*She enters his name in her note book.*)

BILL. Oo's Jenny Ill? And wot call as she to pry for me?

BARBARA. I dont know. Perhaps it was you that cut her lip.

BILL (*defiantly*). Yus, it was me that cat her lip. Aw aint afride o you.

BARBARA. How could you be, since youre not afraid of God? Youre a brave man, Mr Walker. It takes some pluck to do our work here; but none of us dare lift our hand against a girl like that, for fear of her father in heaven.

BILL (*sullenly*). I want nan o your kentin jawr. I spowse you think Aw cam eah to beg from you, like this demmiged lot eah. Not me. Aw downt want your bread and scripe

---

[7]**Knackers** buyers and slaughterers of old animals.   [8]**Secularist** an atheist.

and ketlep.[9] Aw dont blieve in your Gawd, no more than you do yourself.

BARBARA (*sunnily apologetic and ladylike, as on a new footing with him*). Oh, I beg your pardon for putting your name down, Mr Walker. I didnt understand. I'll strike it out.

BILL (*taking this as a slight, and deeply wounded by it*). Eah! you let maw nime alown. Aint it good enaff to be in your book?

BARBARA (*considering*). Well, you see, theres no use putting down your name unless I can do something for you, is there? Whats your trade?

BILL (*still smarting*). Thets nao concern o yours.

BARBARA. Just so. (*Very businesslike.*) I'll put you down as (*writing*) the man who—struck—poor little Jenny Hill—in the mouth.

BILL (*rising threateningly*). See eah. Awve ed enaff o this.

BARBARA (*quite sunny and fearless*). What did you come to us for?

BILL. Aw cam for maw gel, see? Aw cam to tike her aht o this and to brike er jawr for er.

BARBARA (*complacently*). You see I was right about your trade. (*Bill, on the point of retorting furiously, finds himself, to his great shame and terror, in danger of crying instead. He sits down again suddenly.*) Whats her name?

BILL (*dogged*). Er nime's Mog Ebbijem: thets wot her nime is.

BARBARA. Mog Habbijam! Oh, she's gone to Canning Town, to our barracks there.

BILL (*fortified by his resentment of Mog's perfidy*). Is she? (*Vindictively.*) Then Aw'm gowin to Kennintahn arter her. (*He crosses to the gate; hesitates; finally comes back at Barbara.*) Are you loyin to me to git shat o me?

BARBARA. I dont want to get shut of you. I want to keep you here and save your soul. Youd better stay: youre going to have a bad time today, Bill.

BILL. Oo's gowin to give it to me? You, preps?

BARBARA. Someone you dont believe in. But youll be glad afterwards.

BILL (*slinking off*). Aw'll gow to Kennintahn to be aht o reach o your tangue. (*Suddenly turning on her with intense malice.*) And if Aw downt fawnd Mog there, Aw'll cam beck and do two years for you, selp me Gawd if Aw downt!

BARBARA (*a shade kindlier, if possible*). It's no use, Bill. She's got another bloke.

BILL. Wot!

BARBARA. One of her own converts. He fell in love with her when he saw her with her soul saved, and her face clean, and her hair washed.

BILL (*surprised*). Wottud she wash it for, the carroty slat? It's red.

BARBARA. It's quite lovely now, because she wears a new look in her eyes with it. It's a pity youre too late. The new bloke has put your nose out of joint, Bill.

BILL. Aw'll put his nowse aht o joint for him. Not that Aw care a carse for er, mawnd thet. But Aw'll teach her to drop me as if Aw was dirt. And Aw'll teach him to meddle with maw judy. Wots iz bleedin nime?

BARBARA. Sergeant Todger Fairmile.

SHIRLEY (*rising with grim joy*). I'll go with him, miss. I want to see them two meet. I'll take him to the infirmary when it's over.

BILL (*to Shirley, with undissembled misgiving*). Is thet im you was speakin on?

SHIRLEY. Thats him.

BILL. Im that wrastled in the music awl?

SHIRLEY. The competitions at the National Sportin Club was worth nigh a hundred a year to him. He's gev em up now for religion; so he's a bit fresh for want of the exercise he was accustomed to. He'll be glad to see you. Come along.

BILL. Wots is wight?

SHIRLEY. Thirteen four.[10] (*Bill's last hope expires.*)

BARBARA. Go and talk to him, Bill. He'll convert you.

SHIRLEY. He'll convert your head into a mashed potato.

BILL (*sullenly*). Aw aint afride of im. Aw aint afride of ennybody. Bat e can lick me. She's dan me. (*He sits down moodily on the edge of the horse trough.*)

SHIRLEY. You aint goin. I thought not. (*He resumes his seat.*)

BARBARA (*calling*). Jenny!

JENNY (*appearing at the shelter door with a plaster on the corner of her mouth*). Yes, Major.

BARBARA. Send Rummy Mitchens out to clear away here.

JENNY. I think she's afraid.

BARBARA (*her resemblance to her mother flashing out for a moment*). Nonsense! she must do as she's told.

JENNY (*calling into the shelter*). Rummy: the Major says you must come.

Jenny comes to Barbara, purposely keeping on the side next Bill, lest he should suppose that she shrank from him or bore malice.

BARBARA. Poor little Jenny! Are you tired? (*Looking at the wounded cheek.*) Does it hurt?

JENNY. No: it's all right now. It was nothing.

BARBARA (*critically*). It was as hard as he could hit, I expect. Poor Bill! You dont feel angry with him, do you?

JENNY. Oh no, no, no: indeed I dont, Major, bless his poor heart! (*Barbara kisses her; and she runs away merrily into the shelter. Bill writhes with an agonizing return of his new and alarming symptoms, but says nothing. Rummy Mitchens comes from the shelter.*)

BARBARA (*going to meet Rummy*). Now Rummy, bustle. Take in those mugs and plates to be washed; and throw the crumbs about for the birds.

Rummy takes the three plates and mugs; but Shirley takes back his mug from her, as there is still some milk left in it.

---

[9]**Scripe and ketlep** "scrape," that is, thinly spread butter, and "catlap," a diluted drink.

[10]**Thirteen four** Thirteen stone, four pounds, i.e. 186 pounds.

RUMMY. There aint any crumbs. This aint a time to waste good bread on birds.

PRICE (*appearing at the shelter door*). Gentleman come to see the shelter, Major. Says he's your father.

BARBARA. All right. Coming. (*Snobby goes back into the shelter, followed by Barbara.*)

RUMMY (*stealing across to Bill and addressing him in a subdued voice, but with intense conviction*). I'd av the lor of you, you flat eared pignosed potwalloper,[11] if she'd let me. Youre no gentleman, to hit a lady in the face. (*Bill, with greater things moving in him, takes no notice.*)

SHIRLEY (*following her*). Here! in with you and dont get yourself into more trouble by talking.

RUMMY (*with hauteur*). I aint ad the pleasure o being hintroduced to you, as I can remember. (*She goes into the shelter with the plates.*)

SHIRLEY. Thats the—

BILL (*savagely*). Downt you talk to me, d'ye eah? You lea me alown, or Aw'll do you a mischief. Aw'm not dirt under your feet, ennywy.

SHIRLEY (*calmly*). Dont you be afeerd. You aint such prime company that you need expect to be sought after. (*He is about to go into the shelter when Barbara comes out, with Undershaft on her right.*)

BARBARA. Oh, there you are, Mr Shirley! (*Between them.*) This is my father: I told you he was a Secularist, didnt I? Perhaps youll be able to comfort one another.

UNDERSHAFT (*startled*). A Secularist! Not the least in the world: on the contrary, a confirmed mystic.

BARBARA. Sorry, I'm sure. By the way, papa, what is your religion? in case I have to introduce you again.

UNDERSHAFT. My religion? Well, my dear, I am a Millionaire. That is my religion.

BARBARA. Then I'm afraid you and Mr Shirley wont be able to comfort one another after all. Youre not a Millionaire, are you, Peter?

SHIRLEY. No; and proud of it.

UNDERSHAFT (*gravely*). Poverty, my friend, is not a thing to be proud of.

SHIRLEY (*angrily*). Who made your millions for you? Me and my like. Whats kep us poor? Keepin you rich. I wouldnt have your conscience, not for all your income.

UNDERSHAFT. I wouldnt have your income, not for all your conscience, Mr Shirley. (*He goes to the penthouse and sits down on a form.*)

BARBARA (*stopping Shirley adroitly as he is about to retort*). You wouldnt think he was my father, would you, Peter? Will you go into the shelter and lend the lasses a hand for a while: we're worked off our feet.

SHIRLEY (*bitterly*). Yes: I'm in their debt for a meal, aint I?

BARBARA. Oh, not because youre in their debt, but for love of them, Peter, for love of them. (*He cannot understand,*

---

[11]**potwalloper** a pot-washer, a menial servant.

and is rather scandalized.) There! dont stare at me. In with you; and give that conscience of yours a holiday (*bustling him into the shelter*).

SHIRLEY (*as he goes in*). Ah! it's a pity you never was trained to use your reason, miss. Youd have been a very taking lecturer on Secularism.

Barbara turns to her father.

UNDERSHAFT. Never mind me, my dear. Go about your work; and let me watch it for a while.

BARBARA. All right.

UNDERSHAFT. For instance, whats the matter with that outpatient over there?

BARBARA (*looking at Bill, whose attitude has never changed, and whose expression of brooding wrath has deepened*). Oh, we shall cure him in no time. Just watch. (*She goes over to Bill and waits. He glances up at her and casts his eyes down again, uneasy, but grimmer than ever.*) It would be nice to just stamp on Mog Habbijam's face, wouldnt it, Bill?

BILL (*starting up from the trough in consternation*). It's a loy: Aw never said so. (*She shakes her head.*) Oo taold you wot was in moy mawnd?

BARBARA. Only your new friend.

BILL. Wot new friend?

BARBARA. The devil, Bill. When he gets round people they get miserable, just like you.

BILL (*with a heartbreaking attempt at devil-may-care cheerfulness*). Aw aint miserable. (*He sits down again, and stretches his legs in an attempt to seem indifferent.*)

BARBARA. Well, if youre happy, why dont you look happy, as we do?

BILL (*his legs curling back in spite of him*). Aw'm eppy enaff, Aw tell you. Woy cawnt you lea me alown? Wot ev I dan to you? Aw aint smashed y o u r fice, ev Aw?

BARBARA (*softly: wooing his soul*). It's not me thats getting at you, Bill.

BILL. Oo else is it?

BARBARA. Somebody that doesn't intend you to smash women's faces, I suppose. Somebody or something that wants to make a man of you.

BILL (*blustering*). Mike a menn o m e! Aint Aw a menn? eh? Oo sez Aw'm not a menn?

BARBARA. Theres a man in you somewhere, I suppose. But why did he let you hit poor little Jenny Hill? That wasnt very manly of him, was it?

BILL (*tormented*). Ev dan wiv it, Aw tell you. Chack it. Aw'm sick o your Jenny Ill and er silly little fice.

BARBARA. Then why do you keep thinking about it? Why does it keep coming up against you in your mind? Youre not getting converted, are you?

BILL (*with conviction*). Not ME. Not lawkly.

BARBARA. Thats right, Bill. Hold out against it. Put out your strength. Dont lets get you cheap. Todger Fairmile said he wrestled for three nights against his salvation harder than he ever wrestled with the Jap at the music hall. He gave in to the Jap when his arm was going to break. But he didnt give in to his salvation until his heart was going to break. Perhaps youll escape that. You havnt any heart, have you?

BILL. Wot d'ye mean? Woy aint Aw got a awt the sime as ennybody else?

BARBARA. A man with a heart wouldnt have bashed poor little Jenny's face, would he?

BILL (almost crying). Ow, will you lea me alown? Ev Aw ever offered to meddle with you, that you cam neggin and provowkin me lawk this? (He writhes convulsively from his eyes to his toes.)

BARBARA (with a steady soothing hand on his arm and a gentle voice that never lets him go). It's your soul thats hurting you, Bill, and not me. Weve been through it all ourselves. Come with us, Bill. (He looks wildly round.) To brave manhood on earth and eternal glory in heaven. (He is on the point of breaking down.) Come. (A drum is heard in the shelter; and Bill, with a gasp, escapes from the spell as Barbara turns quickly. Adolphus enters from the shelter with a big drum.) Oh! there you are, Dolly. Let me introduce a new friend of mine, Mr Bill Walker. This is my bloke, Bill: Mr Cusins. (Cusins salutes with his drumstick.)

BILL. Gowin to merry im?

BARBARA. Yes.

BILL (fervently). Gawd elp im! Gaw-aw-aw-awd elp im!

BARBARA. Why? Do you think he wont be happy with me?

BILL. Awve aony ed to stend it for a mawnin: e'll ev to stend it for a lawftawm.

CUSINS. That is a frightful reflection, Mr Walker. But I cant tear myself away from her.

BILL. Well, Aw ken. (To Barbara.) Eah! do you knaow where Aw'm gowin to, and wot Aw'm gowin to do?

BARBARA. Yes: youre going to heaven; and youre coming back here before the week's out to tell me so.

BILL. You loy. Aw'm gowin to Kennintahn, to spit in Todger Fairmawl's eye. Aw beshed Jenny Ill's fice; an nar Aw'll git me aown fice beshed and cam beck and shaow it to er. Ee'll itt me ardern Aw itt er. Thatll mike us square. (To Adolphus.) Is thet fair or is it not? Youre a genlmn: you oughter knaow.

BARBARA. Two black eyes wont make one white one, Bill.

BILL. Aw didnt awst you. Cawnt you never keep your mahth shat? Oy awst the genlmn.

CUSINS (reflectively). Yes: I think youre right, Mr Walker. Yes: I should do it. It's curious: it's exactly what an ancient Greek would have done.

BARBARA. But what good will it do?

CUSINS. Well, it will give Mr Fairmile some exercise; and it will satisfy Mr Walker's soul.

BILL. Rot! there aint nao such a thing as a saoul. Ah kin you tell wevver Awve a saoul or not? You never seen it.

BARBARA. Ive seen it hurting you when you went against it.

BILL (with compressed aggravation). If you was maw gel and took the word aht o me mahth lawk thet, Aw'd give you sathink youd feel urtin, Aw would. (To Adolphus.) You tike maw tip, mite. Stop er jawr; or youll doy afoah your tawm (With intense expression.) Wore aht: thets wot youll be: wore aht. (He goes away through the gate.)

CUSINS (looking after him). I wonder!

BARBARA. Dolly! (Indignant, in her mother's manner.)

CUSINS. Yes, my dear, it's very wearing to be in love with you. If it lasts, I quite think I shall die young.

BARBARA. Should you mind?

CUSINS. Not at all. (He is suddenly softened, and kisses her over the drum, evidently not for the first time, as people cannot kiss over a big drum without practice. Undershaft coughs.)

BARBARA. It's all right, papa, weve not forgotten you. Dolly: explain the place to papa: I havnt time. (She goes busily into the shelter.)

Undershaft and Adolphus now have the yard to themselves. Undershaft, seated on a form, and still keenly attentive, looks hard at Adolphus. Adolphus looks hard at him.

UNDERSHAFT. I fancy you guess something of what is in my mind, Mr Cusins. (Cusins flourishes his drumsticks as if in the act of beating a lively rataplan, but makes no sound.) Exactly so. But suppose Barbara finds you out!

CUSINS. You know, I do not admit that I am imposing on Barbara. I am quite genuinely interested in the views of the Salvation Army. The fact is, I am a sort of collector of religions; and the curious thing is that I find I can believe them all. By the way, have you any religion?

UNDERSHAFT. Yes.

CUSINS. Anything out of the common?

UNDERSHAFT. Only that there are two things necessary to Salvation.

CUSINS (disappointed, but polite). Ah, the Church Catechism. Charles Lomax also belongs to the Established Church.

UNDERSHAFT. The two things are—

CUSINS. Baptism and—

UNDERSHAFT. No. Money and gunpowder.

CUSINS (surprised, but interested). That is the general opinion of our governing classes. The novelty is in hearing any man confess it.

UNDERSHAFT. Just so.

CUSINS. Excuse me: is there any place in your religion for honor, justice, truth, love, mercy and so forth?

UNDERSHAFT. Yes: they are the graces and luxuries of a rich, strong, and safe life.

CUSINS. Suppose one is forced to choose between them and money or gunpowder?

UNDERSHAFT. Choose money and gunpowder; for without enough of both you cannot afford the others.

CUSINS. That is your religion?

UNDERSHAFT. Yes.

The cadence of this reply makes a full close in the conversation. Cusins twists his face dubiously and contemplates Undershaft. Undershaft contemplates him.

CUSINS. Barbara wont stand that. You will have to choose between your religion and Barbara.

UNDERSHAFT. So will you, my friend. She will find out that that drum of yours is hollow.

CUSINS. Father Undershaft: you are mistaken: I am a sincere Salvationist. You do not understand the Salvation Army. It is the army of joy, of love, of courage: it has banished the fear and remorse and despair of the old hell-ridden evangelical sects: it marches to fight the devil with trumpet and drum, with music and dancing, with banner and palm, as becomes a sally from heaven by its happy garrison. It picks the waster out of the public house and makes a man of him: it finds a worm wriggling in a back kitchen, and lo! a woman! Men and women of rank too, sons and daughters of the Highest. It takes the poor professor of Greek, the most artificial and self-suppressed of human creatures, from his meal of roots, and lets loose the rhapsodist in him; reveals the true worship of Dionysos to him; sends him down the public street drumming dithyrambs. (*He plays a thundering flourish on the drum.*)

UNDERSHAFT. You will alarm the shelter.

CUSINS. Oh, they are accustomed to these sudden ecstasies. However, if the drum worries you—(*He pockets the drumsticks; unhooks the drum; and stands it on the ground opposite the gateway.*)

UNDERSHAFT. Thank you.

CUSINS. You remember what Euripides says about your money and gunpowder?

UNDERSHAFT. No.

CUSINS (*declaiming*).

> One and another
> In money and guns may outpass his brother;
> And men in their millions float and flow
> And seethe with a million hopes as leaven;
> And they win their will; or they miss their will;
> And their hopes are dead or are pined for still;
> But who'er can know
> As the long days go
> That to live is happy, has found his heaven.

My translation: what do you think of it?

UNDERSHAFT. I think, my friend, that if you wish to know, as the long days go, that to live is happy, you must first acquire money enough for a decent life, and power enough to be your own master.

CUSINS. You are damnably discouraging. (*He resumes his declamation.*)

> Is it so hard a thing to see
> That the spirit of God—whate'er it be—

> The law that abides and changes not, ages long,
> The Eternal and Nature-born: these things be strong?
> What else is Wisdom? What of Man's endeavor,
> Or God's high grace so lovely and so great?
> To stand from fear set free? to breathe and wait?
> To hold a hand uplifted over Fate?
> And shall not Barbara be loved for ever?

UNDERSHAFT. Euripides mentions Barbara, does he?

CUSINS. It is a fair translation. The word means Loveliness.

UNDERSHAFT. May I ask—as Barbara's father—how much a year she is to be loved for ever on?

CUSINS. As Barbara's father, that is more your affair than mine. I can feed her by teaching Greek: that is about all.

UNDERSHAFT. Do you consider it a good match for her?

CUSINS (*with polite obstinacy*). Mr Undershaft: I am in many ways a weak, timid, ineffectual person; and my health is far from satisfactory. But whenever I feel that I must have anything, I get it, sooner or later. I feel that way about Barbara. I dont like marriage: I feel intensely afraid of it; and I dont know what I shall do with Barbara or what she will do with me. But I feel that I and nobody else must marry her. Please regard that as settled.—Not that I wish to be arbitrary; but why should I waste your time in discussing what is inevitable?

UNDERSHAFT. You mean that you will stick at nothing: not even the conversion of the Salvation Army to the worship of Dionysos.

CUSINS. The business of the Salvation Army is to save, not to wrangle about the name of the pathfinder. Dionysos or another: what does it matter?

UNDERSHAFT (*rising and approaching him*). Professor Cusins: you are a young man after my own heart.

CUSINS. Mr Undershaft: you are, as far as I am able to gather, a most infernal old rascal; but you appeal very strongly to my sense of ironic humor.

Undershaft mutely offers his hand. They shake.

UNDERSHAFT (*suddenly concentrating himself*). And now to business.

CUSINS. Pardon me. We are discussing religion. Why go back to such an uninteresting and unimportant subject as business?

UNDERSHAFT. Religion is our business at present, because it is through religion alone that we can win Barbara.

CUSINS. Have you, too, fallen in love with Barbara?

UNDERSHAFT. Yes, with a father's love.

CUSINS. A father's love for a grown-up daughter is the most dangerous of all infatuations. I apologize for mentioning my own pale, coy, mistrustful fancy in the same breath with it.

UNDERSHAFT. Keep to the point. We have to win her; and we are neither of us Methodists.

CUSINS. That doesnt matter. The power Barbara wields here—the power that wields Barbara herself—is not Calvinism, not Presbyterianism, not Methodism—

UNDERSHAFT. Not Greek Paganism either, eh?

CUSINS. I admit that. Barbara is quite original in her religion.

UNDERSHAFT (*triumphantly*). Aha! Barbara Undershaft would be. Her inspiration comes from within herself.

CUSINS. How do you suppose it got there?

UNDERSHAFT (*in towering excitement*). It is the Undershaft inheritance. I shall hand on my torch to my daughter. She shall make my converts and preach my gospel—

CUSINS. What! Money and gunpowder!

UNDERSHAFT. Yes, money and gunpowder. Freedom and power. Command of life and command of death.

CUSINS (*urbanely: trying to bring him down to earth*). This is extremely interesting, Mr Undershaft. Of course you know that you are mad.

UNDERSHAFT (*with redoubled force*). And you?

CUSINS. Oh, mad as a hatter. You are welcome to my secret since I have discovered yours. But I am astonished. Can a madman make cannons?

UNDERSHAFT. Would anyone else than a madman make them? And now (*with surging energy*) question for question. Can a sane man translate Euripides?

CUSINS. No.

UNDERSHAFT (*seizing him by the shoulder*). Can a sane woman make a man of a waster or a woman of a worm?

CUSINS (*reeling before the storm*). Father Colossus—Mammoth Millionaire—

UNDERSHAFT (*pressing him*). Are there two mad people or three in this Salvation shelter today?

CUSINS. You mean Barbara is as mad as we are?

UNDERSHAFT (*pushing him lightly off and resuming his equanimity suddenly and completely*). Pooh, Professor! let us call things by their proper names. I am a millionaire; you are a poet; Barbara is a savior of souls. What have we three to do with the common mob of slaves and idolaters? (*He sits down again with a shrug of contempt for the mob.*)

CUSINS. Take care! Barbara is in love with the common people. So am I. Have you never felt the romance of that love?

UNDERSHAFT (*cold and sardonic*). Have you ever been in love with Poverty, like St Francis? Have you ever been in love with Dirt, like St Simeon! Have you ever been in love with disease and suffering, like our nurses and philanthropists? Such passions are not virtues, but the most unnatural of all the vices. This love of the common people may please an earl's granddaughter and a university professor; but I have been a common man and a poor man; and it has no romance for me. Leave it to the poor to pretend that poverty is a blessing: leave it to the coward to make a religion of his cowardice by preaching humility: we know better than that. We three must stand together above the common people: how else can we help their children to climb up beside us? Barbara must belong to us, not to the Salvation Army.

CUSINS. Well, I can only say that if you think you will get her away from the Salvation Army by talking to her as you have been talking to me, you dont know Barbara.

UNDERSHAFT. My friend: I never ask for what I can buy.

CUSINS (*in a white fury*). Do I understand you to imply that you can buy Barbara?

UNDERSHAFT. No; but I can buy the Salvation Army.

CUSINS. Quite impossible.

UNDERSHAFT. You shall see. All religious organizations exist by selling themselves to the rich.

CUSINS. Not the Army. That is the Church of the poor.

UNDERSHAFT. All the more reason for buying it.

CUSINS. I dont think you quite know what the Army does for the poor.

UNDERSHAFT. Oh yes I do. It draws their teeth: that is enough for me as a man of business.

CUSINS. Nonsense! It makes them sober—

UNDERSHAFT. I prefer sober workmen. The profits are larger.

CUSINS. —honest—

UNDERSHAFT. Honest workmen are the most economical.

CUSINS. —attached to their homes—

UNDERSHAFT. So much the better: they will put up with anything sooner than change their shop.

CUSINS. —happy—

UNDERSHAFT. An invaluable safeguard against revolution.

CUSINS. —unselfish—

UNDERSHAFT. Indifferent to their own interests, which suits me exactly.

CUSINS. —with their thoughts on heavenly things—

UNDERSHAFT (*rising*). And not on Trade Unionism nor Socialism. Excellent.

CUSINS (*revolted*). You really are an infernal old rascal.

UNDERSHAFT (*indicating Peter Shirley, who has just come from the shelter and strolled dejectedly down the yard between them*). And this is an honest man!

SHIRLEY. Yes; and what av I got by it? (*He passes on bitterly and sits on the form, in the corner of the penthouse.*)

Snobby Price, beaming sanctimoniously, and Jenny Hill, with a tambourine full of coppers, come from the shelter and go to the drum, on which Jenny begins to count the money.

UNDERSHAFT (*replying to Shirley*). Oh, your employers must have got a good deal by it from first to last. (*He sits on the table, with one foot on the side form. Cusins, overwhelmed, sits down on the same form nearer the shelter. Barbara comes from the shelter to the middle of the yard. She is excited and a little overwrought.*)

BARBARA. Weve just had a splendid experience meeting at the other gate in Cripps's lane. Ive hardly ever seen them so much moved as they were by your confession, Mr Price.

PRICE. I could almost be glad of my past wickedness if I could believe that it would elp to keep hathers stright.

BARBARA. So it will, Snobby. How much, Jenny?

JENNY. Four and tenpence, Major.

BARBARA. Oh Snobby, if you had given your poor mother just one more kick, we should have got the whole five shillings!

PRICE. If she heard you say that, miss, she'd be sorry I didnt. But I'm glad. Oh what a joy it will be to her when she hears I'm saved!

UNDERSHAFT. Shall I contribute the odd twopence, Barbara? The millionaire's mite, eh? (*He takes a couple of pennies from his pocket.*)

BARBARA. How did you make that twopence?

UNDERSHAFT. As usual. By selling cannons, torpedoes, submarines, and my new patent Grand Duke hand grenade.

BARBARA. Put it back in your pocket. You cant buy your salvation here for twopence: you must work it out.

UNDERSHAFT. Is twopence not enough? I can afford a little more, if you press me.

BARBARA. Two million millions would not be enough. There is bad blood on your hands; and nothing but good blood can cleanse them. Money is no use. Take it away. (*She turns to Cusins.*) Dolly: you must write another letter for me to the papers. (*He makes a wry face.*) Yes: I know you dont like it; but it must be done. The starvation this winter is beating us: everybody is unemployed. The General says we must close this shelter if we cant get more money. I force the collections at the meetings until I am ashamed: dont I, Snobby?

PRICE. It's a fair treat to see you work it, miss. The way you got them up from three-and-six to four-and-ten with that hymn, penny by penny and verse by verse, was a caution. Not a Cheap Jack on Mile End Waste[12] could touch you at it.

BARBARA. Yes; but I wish we could do without it. I am getting at last to think more of the collection than of the people's souls. And what are those hatfuls of pence and halfpence? We want thousands! tens of thousands! hundreds of thousands! I want to convert people, not to be always begging for the Army in a way I'd die sooner than beg for myself.

UNDERSHAFT (*in profound irony*). Genuine unselfishness is capable of anything, my dear.

BARBARA (*unsuspectingly, as she turns away to take the money from the drum and put it in a bag she carries*). Yes, isnt it? (*Undershaft looks sardonically at Cusins.*)

CUSINS (*aside to Undershaft*). Mephistopheles! Machiavelli!

BARBARA (*tears coming into her eyes as she ties the bag and pockets it*). How are we to feed them? I cant talk religion to a man with bodily hunger in his eyes. (*Almost breaking down.*) It's frightful.

JENNY (*running to her*). Major, dear—

[12]**Cheap Jack . . . Waste** a peddler at fairs.

BARBARA (*rebounding*). No: dont comfort me. It will be all right. We shall get the money.

UNDERSHAFT. How?

JENNY. By praying for it, of course. Mrs Baines says she prayed for it last night; and she has never prayed for it in vain: never once. (*She goes to the gate and looks out into the street.*)

BARBARA (*who has dried her eyes and regained her composure*). By the way, dad, Mrs Baines has come to march with us to our big meeting this afternoon; and she is very anxious to meet you, for some reason or other. Perhaps she'll convert you.

UNDERSHAFT. I shall be delighted, my dear.

JENNY (*at the gate: excitedly*). Major! Major! heres that man back again.

BARBARA. What man?

JENNY. The man that hit me. Oh, I hope he's coming back to join us.

Bill Walker, with frost on his jacket, comes through the gate, his hands deep in his pockets and his chin sunk between his shoulders, like a cleaned-out gambler. He halts between Barbara and the drum.

BARBARA. Hullo, Bill! Back already!

BILL (*nagging at her*). Bin talkin ever sence, ev you?

BARBARA. Pretty nearly. Well, has Todger paid you out for poor Jenny's jaw?

BILL. Nao e aint.

BARBARA. I thought your jacket looked a bit snowy.

BILL. Sao it is snaowy. You want to knaow where the snaow cam from, downt you?

BARBARA. Yes.

BILL. Well, it cam from orf the grahnd in Pawkinses Corner in Kennintahn. It got rabbed orf be maw shaoulders: see?

BARBARA. Pity you didnt rub some off with your knees, Bill! That would have done you a lot of good.

BILL (*with sour mirthless humor*). Aw was sivin anather menn's knees at the tawm. E was kneelin on moy ed, e was.

JENNY. Who was kneeling on your head?

BILL. Todger was. E was pryin for me: pryin camfortable wiv me as a cawpet. Sow was Mog. Sao was the aol bloomin meetin. Mog she sez "Ow Lawd brike is stabborn sperrit; bat downt urt is dear art." Thet was wot she said. "Downt urt is dear art"! An er blowk—thirteen stun four!—kneelin wiv all is wight on me. Fanny, aint it?

JENNY. Oh no. We're sorry, Mr Walker.

BARBARA (*enjoying it frankly*). Nonsense! of course it's funny. Served you right, Bill! You must have done something to him first.

BILL (*doggedly*). Aw did wot Aw said Aw'd do. Aw spit in is eye. E looks ap at the skoy and sez, "Ow that Aw should be fahnd worthy to be spit upon for the gospel's sike!" e sez; an Mog sez "Glaory Allelloolier!"; an then e called me Braddher, an dahned me as if Aw was a kid and e was me mather worshin me a Setterda nawt. Aw ednt jast nao shaow wiv im at all. Arf the street pryed; an the tather arf larfed fit to split theirselves. (*To Barbara.*) There! are you settisfawd nah?

BARBARA (*her eyes dancing*). Wish I'd been there, Bill.

BILL. Yus: youd a got in a hextra bit o talk on me, wouldnt you?

JENNY. I'm so sorry, Mr Walker.

BILL (*fiercely*). Downt you gow bein sorry for me: youve no call. Listen eah. Aw browk your jawr.

JENNY. No, it didn't hurt me: indeed it didnt, except for a moment. It was only that I was frightened.

BILL. Aw downt want to be forgive be you, or be ennybody. Wot Aw did Aw'll py for. Aw trawd to gat me aown jawr browk to settisfaw you—

JENNY (*distressed*). Oh no—

BILL (*impatiently*). Tell y Aw did: cawnt you listen to wots bein taold you? All Aw got be it was being mide a sawt of in the pablic street for me pines. Well, if Aw cawnt settisfaw you one wy, Aw ken anather. Listen eah! Aw ed two quid[13] sived agen the frost; an Awve a pahnd of it left. A mite o mawn last week ed words with the judy e's gowin to merry. E give er wot-for; an e's bin fawnd fifteen bob.[14] E ed a rawt to itt er cause they was gowin to be merrid; but Aw ednt nao rawt to itt you; sao put anather fawv bob on an call it a pahnd's worth. (*He produces a sovereign.*)[15] Eahs the manney. Tike it; and lets ev no more o your forgivin an pryin and your Mijor jawrin me. Let wot Aw dan be dan an pide for; and let there be a end of it.

JENNY. Oh, I couldnt take it, Mr Walker. But if you would give a shilling or two to poor Rummy Mitchens! you really did hurt her; and she's old.

BILL (*contemptuously*). Not lawkly. Aw'd give her another as soon as look at er. Let her ev the lawr o me as she threatened! She aint forgiven me: not mach. Wot Aw dan to er is not on me mawnd—wot she (*indicating Barbara*) mawt call on me conscience—no more than stickin a pig. It's this Christian gime o yours that Aw wownt ev plyed agen me: this bloomin forgivin an neggin an jawrin that mikes a menn thet sore that iz lawf's a burdn to im. Aw wownt ev it, Aw tell you; sao tike your manney and stop thraowin your silly beshed fice hap agen me.

JENNY. Major: may I take a little of it for the Army?

BARBARA. No: the Army is not to be bought. We want your soul, Bill; and we'll take nothing less.

BILL (*bitterly*). Aw knaow. Me an maw few shillins is not good enaff for you. Youre a earl's grendorter, you are. Nathink less than a andered pahnd for you.

UNDERSHAFT. Come, Barbara! you could do a great deal of good with a hundred pounds. If you will set this gentleman's mind at ease by taking his pound, I will give the other ninety-nine.

Bill, dazed by such opulence, instinctively touches his cap.

BARBARA. Oh, youre too extravagant, papa. Bill offers twenty pieces of silver. All you need offer is the other ten.[16] That will make the standard price to buy anybody who's for sale. I'm not; and the Army's not. (*To Bill.*) Youll never have another quiet moment, Bill, until you come round to us. You cant stand out against your salvation.

BILL (*sullenly*). Aw cawnt stand aht agen music awl wrastlers and awtful tangued women. Awve offered to py. Aw can do no more. Tike it or leave it. There it is. (*He throws the sovereign on the drum, and sits down on the horse-trough. The coin fascinates Snobby Price, who takes an early opportunity of dropping his cap on it.*)

Mrs Baines comes from the shelter. She is dressed as a Salvation Army Commissioner. She is an earnest looking woman of about 40, with a caressing, urgent voice, and an appealing manner.

BARBARA. This is my father, Mrs Baines (*Undershaft comes from the table, taking his hat off with marked civility.*) Try what you can do with him. He wont listen to me, because he remembers what a fool I was when I was a baby. (*She leaves them together and chats with Jenny.*)

MRS BAINES. Have you been shewn over the shelter Mr Undershaft? You know the work we're doing, of course.

UNDERSHAFT (*very civilly*). The whole nation knows it, Mrs Baines.

MRS BAINES. No, sir: the whole nation does not know it, or we should not be crippled as we are for want of money to carry our work through the length and breadth of the land. Let me tell you that there would have been rioting this winter in London but for us.

UNDERSHAFT. You really think so?

MRS BAINES. I know it. I remember 1886, when you rich gentlemen hardened your hearts against the cry of the poor. They broke the windows of your clubs in Pall Mall.

UNDERSHAFT (*gleaming with approval of their method*). And the Mansion House Fund went up next day from thirty thousand pounds to seventy-nine thousand! I remember quite well.

MRS BAINES. Well, wont you help me to get at the people? They wont break windows then. Come here, Price. Let me shew you to this gentleman. (*Price comes to be inspected.*) Do you remember the window breaking?

PRICE. My ole father thought it was the revolution, maam.

MRS BAINES. Would you break windows now?

PRICE. Oh no, maam. The windows of eaven av bin opened to me. I know now that the rich man is a sinner like myself.

RUMMY (*appearing above at the loft door*). Snobby Price!

SNOBBY. Wot is it?

---

[13] **quid** slang for a pound note.   [14] **bob** a shilling, or one-twentieth of a pound.   [15] **sovereign** a gold coin worth a pound.

[16] Bill's sovereign is twenty silver shillings; the thirty "pieces of silver" was Judas's reward for betraying Jesus.

RUMMY. Your mother's askin for you at the other gate in Cripps's Lane. She's heard about your confession. (*Price turns pale.*)

MRS BAINES. Go, Mr Price; and pray with her.

JENNY. You can go through the shelter, Snobby.

PRICE (*to Mrs. Baines*). I couldnt face her now, maam, with all the weight of my sins fresh on me. Tell her she'll find her son at ome, waitin for her in prayer. (*He skulks off through the gate, incidentally stealing the sovereign on his way out by picking up his cap from the drum.*)

MRS BAINES (*with swimming eyes*). You see how we take the anger and the bitterness against you out of their hearts, Mr Undershaft.

UNDERSHAFT. It is certainly most convenient and gratifying to all large employers of labor, Mrs Baines.

MRS BAINES. Barbara: Jenny: I have good news: most wonderful news. (*Jenny runs to her.*) My prayers have been answered. I told you they would, Jenny, didnt I?

JENNY. Yes, yes.

BARBARA (*moving nearer to the drum*). Have we got money enough to keep the shelter open?

MRS BAINES. I hope we shall have enough to keep all the shelters open. Lord Saxmundham has promised us five thousand pounds—

BARBARA. Hooray!

JENNY. Glory!

MRS BAINES. —if—

BARBARA. "If!" If what?

MRS BAINES. —if five other gentlemen will give a thousand each to make it up to ten thousand.

BARBARA. Who is Lord Saxmundham? I never heard of him.

UNDERSHAFT (*who has pricked up his ears at the peer's name, and is now watching Barbara curiously*). A new creation, my dear. You have heard of Sir Horace Bodger?

BARBARA. Bodger! Do you mean the distiller? Bodger's whisky!

UNDERSHAFT. That is the man. He is one of the greatest of our public benefactors. He restored the cathedral at Hakington. They made him a baronet for that. He gave half a million to the funds of his party: they made him a baron for that.

SHIRLEY. What will they give him for the five thousand?

UNDERSHAFT. There is nothing left to give him. So the five thousand, I should think, is to save his soul.

MRS BAINES. Heaven grant it may! Oh Mr Undershaft, you have some very rich friends. Cant you help us towards the other five thousand? We are going to hold a great meeting this afternoon at the Assembly Hall in the Mile End Road. If I could only announce that one gentleman had come forward to support Lord Saxmundham, others would follow. Dont you know somebody? couldnt you? wouldnt you? (*Her eyes fill with tears.*) oh, think of those poor people, Mr Undershaft: think of how much it means to them, and how little to a great man like you.

UNDERSHAFT (*sardonically gallant*). Mrs Baines: you are irresistible. I cant disappoint you; and I cant deny myself the satisfaction of making Bodger pay up. You shall have your five thousand pounds.

MRS BAINES. Thank God!

UNDERSHAFT. You dont thank me?

MRS BAINES. Oh sir, dont try to be cynical: dont be ashamed of being a good man. The Lord will bless you abundantly; and our prayers will be like a strong fortification round you all the days of your life. (*With a touch of caution.*) You will let me have the cheque to shew at the meeting, wont you? Jenny: go in and fetch a pen and ink. (*Jenny runs to the shelter door.*)

UNDERSHAFT. Do not disturb Miss Hill: I have a fountain pen. (*Jenny halts. He sits at the table and writes the cheque. Cusins rises to make room for him. They all watch him silently.*)

BILL (*cynically, aside to Barbara, his voice and accent horribly debased*). Wot prawce selvytion nah?

BARBARA. Stop. (*Undershaft stops writing: they all turn to her in surprise.*) Mrs Baines: are you really going to take this money?

MRS BAINES (*astonished*). Why not, dear?

BARBARA. Why not! Do you know what my father is? Have you forgotten that Lord Saxmundham is Bodger the whisky man? Do you remember how we implored the County Council to stop him from writing Bodger's Whisky in letters of fire against the sky; so that the poor drink-ruined creatures on the Embankment could not wake up from their snatches of sleep without being reminded of their deadly thirst by that wicked sky sign? Do you know that the worst thing I have had to fight here is not the devil, but Bodger, Bodger, Bodger, with his whisky, his distilleries, and his tied houses?[17] Are you going to make our shelter another tied house for him, and ask me to keep it?

BILL. Rotten dranken whisky it is too.

MRS BAINES. Dear Barbara: Lord Saxmundham has a soul to be saved like any of us. If heaven has found the way to make a good use of his money, are we to set ourselves up against the answer to our prayers?

BARBARA. I know he has a soul to be saved. Let him come down here; and I'll do my best to help him to his salvation. But he wants to send his cheque down to buy us, and go on being as wicked as ever.

UNDERSHAFT (*with a reasonableness which Cusins alone perceives to be ironical*). My dear Barbara: alcohol is a very necessary article. It heals the sick—

BARBARA. It does nothing of the sort.

UNDERSHAFT. Well, it assists the doctor: that is perhaps a less questionable way of putting it. It makes life bearable to millions of people who could not endure their existence if they were quite sober. It enables Parliament to do things at eleven at night that no sane person would do at eleven in the morning. Is it Bodger's fault that this inestimable gift is deplorably abused by less than one per cent

---

[17]**tied houses** taverns owned by brewing firms.

of the poor? (*He turns again to the table; signs the cheque; and crosses it.*)

MRS BAINES. Barbara: will there be less drinking or more if all those poor souls we are saving come tomorrow and find the doors of our shelters shut in their faces? Lord Saxmundham gives us the money to stop drinking—to take his own business from him.

CUSINS (*impishly*). Pure self-sacrifice on Bodger's part, clearly! Bless dear Bodger! (*Barbara almost breaks down as Adolphus, too, fails her.*)

UNDERSHAFT (*tearing out the cheque and pocketing the book as he rises and goes past Cusins to Mrs Baines*). I also, Mrs Baines, may claim a little disinterestedness. Think of my business! think of the widows and orphans! the men and lads torn to pieces with shrapnel and poisoned with lyddite![18] (*Mrs Baines shrinks; but he goes on remorselessly*) the oceans of blood, not one drop of which is shed in a really just cause! the ravaged crops! the peaceful peasant forced, women and men, to till their fields, under the fire of opposing armies on pain of starvation! the bad blood of the fierce little cowards at home who egg on others to fight for the gratification of their national vanity! All this makes money for me: I am never richer, never busier than when the papers are full of it. Well, it is your work to preach peace on earth and goodwill to men. (*Mrs Baines's face lights up again.*) Every convert you make is a vote against war. (*Her lips move in prayer.*) Yet I give you this money to help you to hasten my own commercial ruin. (*He gives her the cheque.*)

CUSINS (*mounting the form in an ecstasy of mischief*). The millennium will be inaugurated by the unselfishness of Undershaft and Bodger. Oh be joyful! (*He takes the drumsticks from his pocket and flourishes them.*)

MRS BAINES (*taking the cheque*). The longer I live the more proof I see that there is an Infinite Goodness that turns everything to the work of salvation sooner or later. Who would have thought that any good could have come out of war and drink? And yet their profits are brought today to the feet of salvation to do its blessed work. (*She is affected to tears.*)

JENNY (*running to Mrs Baines and throwing her arms around her*). Oh dear! how blessed, how glorious it all is!

CUSINS (*in a convulsion of irony*). Let us seize this unspeakable moment. Let us march to the great meeting at once. Excuse me just an instant. (*He rushes into the shelter. Jenny takes her tambourine from the drum head.*)

MRS BAINES. Mr Undershaft: have you ever seen a thousand people fall on their knees with one impulse and pray? Come with us to the meeting. Barbara shall tell them that the Army is saved, and saved through you.

CUSINS (*returning impetuously from the shelter with a flag and a trombone, and coming between Mrs Baines and Undershaft*). You shall carry the flag down the first street, Mrs Baines. (*He gives her the flag.*) Mr Undershaft is a gifted trombon-

ist: he shall intone an Olympian diapason to the West Ham Salvation March. (*Aside to Undershaft, as he forces the trombone on him.*) Blow, Machiavelli, blow.

UNDERSHAFT (*aside to him, as he takes the trombone*). The trumpet in Zion! (*Cusins rushes to the drum, which he takes up and puts on. Undershaft continues, aloud.*) I will do my best. I could vamp a bass if I knew the tune.

CUSINS. It is a wedding chorus from one of Donizetti's operas; but we have converted it. We convert everything to good here, including Bodger. You remember the chorus. "For thee immense rejoicing—immenso giubilo—immenso giubilo." (*With drum obbligato.*) Rum tum ti tum, tum tum ti ta—

BARBARA. Dolly: you are breaking my heart.

CUSINS. What is a broken heart more or less here? Dionysos Undershaft has descended. I am possessed.

MRS BAINES. Come, Barbara: I must have my dear Major to carry the flag with me.

JENNY. Yes, yes, Major darling.

CUSINS (*snatches the tambourine out of Jenny's hand and mutely offers it to Barbara*).

BARBARA (*coming forward a little as she puts the offer behind her with a shudder, whilst Cusins recklessly tosses the tambourine back to Jenny and goes to the gate*). I cant come.

JENNY. Not come!

MRS BAINES (*with tears in her eyes*). Barbara: do you think I am wrong to take the money?

BARBARA (*impulsively going to her and kissing her*). No, no: God help you, dear, you must: you are saving the Army. Go; and may you have a great meeting!

JENNY. But arnt you coming?

BARBARA. No. (*She begins taking off the silver S brooch from her collar.*)

MRS BAINES. Barbara: what are you doing?

JENNY. Why are you taking your badge off? You cant be going to leave us, Major.

BARBARA (*quietly*). Father: come here.

UNDERSHAFT (*coming to her*). My dear! (*Seeing that she is going to pin the badge on his collar, he retreats to the penthouse in some alarm.*)

BARBARA (*following him*). Dont be frightened. (*She pins the badge on and steps back towards the table, shewing him to the others.*) There! It's not much for £5000, is it?

MRS BAINES. Barbara: if you wont come and pray with us, promise me you will pray for us.

BARBARA. I cant pray now. Perhaps I shall never pray again.

MRS BAINES. Barbara!

JENNY. Major!

BARBARA (*almost delirious*). I cant bear any more. Quick march!

CUSINS (*calling to the procession in the street outside*). Off we go. Play up, there! I m m e n s o g i u b i l o . (*He gives the time with his drum; and the band strikes up the march, which rapidly becomes more distant as the procession moves briskly away.*)

[18]**lyddite** an explosive.

MRS BAINES. I must go, dear. Youre overworked: you will be all right tomorrow. We'll never lose you. Now Jenny: step out with the old flag. Blood and Fire! (*She marches out through the gate with her flag.*)

JENNY. Glory Hallelujah! (*Flourishing her tambourine and marching.*)

UNDERSHAFT (*to Cusins, as he marches out past him easing the slide of his trombone*). "My ducats and my daughter"!

CUSINS (*following him out*). Money and gunpowder!

BARBARA. Drunkenness and Murder! My God: why hast thou forsaken me?

She sinks on the form with her face buried in her hands. The march passes away into silence. Bill Walker steals across to her.

BILL (*taunting*). Wot prawce selvytion nah?

SHIRLEY. Dont you hit her when she's down.

BILL. She itt me wen aw wiz dahn. Waw shouldnt Aw git a bit o me aown beck?

BARBARA (*raising her head*). I didnt take your money, Bill. (*She crosses the yard to the gate and turns her back on the two men to hide her face from them.*)

BILL (*sneering after her*). Naow, it warnt enaff for you. (*Turning to the drum, he misses the money.*) Ellow! If you aint took it sammun else ez. Weres it gorn? Bly me if Jenny Ill didnt tike it arter all!

RUMMY (*screaming at him from the loft*). You lie, you dirty blackguard! Snobby Price pinched it off the drum when he took up his cap. I was up here all the time an see im do it.

BILL. Wot! Stowl maw manney! Waw didnt you call thief on him, you silly aold macker you?

RUMMY. To serve you aht for ittin me across the fice. It's cost y'pahnd, that az. (*Raising a paean of squalid triumph.*) I done you. I'm even with you. Ive ad it aht o y—(*Bill snatches up Shirley's mug and hurls it at her. She slams the loft door and vanishes. The mug smashes against the door and falls in fragments.*)

BILL (*beginning to chuckle*). Tell us, aol menn, wot o'clock this mawnin was it wen im as they call Snobby Prawce was sived?

BARBARA (*turning to him more composedly, and with unspoiled sweetness*). About half past twelve, Bill. And he pinched your pound at a quarter to two. I know. Well, you cant afford to lose it. I'll send it to you.

BILL (*his voice and accent suddenly improving*). Not if Aw wiz to stawve for it. Aw aint to be bought.

SHIRLEY. Aint you? Youd sell yourself to the devil for a pint o beer; only there aint no devil to make the offer.

BILL (*unshamed*). Sao Aw would, mite, and often ev, cheerful. But she cawnt baw me. (*Approaching Barbara.*) You wanted maw saoul, did you? Well, you aint got it.

BARBARA. I nearly got it, Bill. But weve sold it back to you for ten thousand pounds.

SHIRLEY. And dear at the money!

BARBARA. No, Peter: it was worth more than money.

BILL (*salvationproof*). It's nao good: you cawnt get rahnd me nah. Aw downt blieve in it; and Awve seen tody that Aw was rawt. (*Going.*) Sao long, aol soupkitchener! Ta, ta, Mijor Earl's Grendorter! (*Turning at the gate.*) Wot prawce selvytion nah? Snobby Prawce! Ha! ha!

BARBARA (*offering her hand*). Goodbye, Bill.

BILL (*taken aback, half plucks his cap off; then shoves it on again defiantly*). Git aht. (*Barbara drops her hand, discouraged. He has a twinge of remorse.*) But thets aw rawt, you knaow. Nathink pasnl. Naow mellice. Sao long, Judy. (*He goes.*)

BARBARA. No malice. So long, Bill.

SHIRLEY (*shaking his head*). You make too much of him, miss, in your innocence.

BARBARA (*going to him*). Peter: I'm like you now. Cleaned out, and lost my job.

SHIRLEY. Youve youth an hope. Thats two better than me.

BARBARA. I'll get you a job, Peter. Thats hope for you: the youth will have to be enough for me. (*She counts her money.*) I have just enough left for two teas at Lockharts, a Rowton doss[19] for you, and my tram and bus home. (*He frowns and rises with offended pride. She takes his arm.*) Dont be proud, Peter: it's sharing between friends. And promise me youll talk to me and not let me cry. (*She draws him towards the gate.*)

SHIRLEY. Well, I'm not accustomed to talk to the like of you—

BARBARA (*urgently*). Yes, yes: you must talk to me. Tell me about Tom Paine's books and Bradlaugh's lectures.[20] Come along.

SHIRLEY. Ah, if you would only read Tom Paine in the proper spirit, miss! (*They go out through the gate together.*)

ACT 3

Next day after lunch Lady Britomart is writing in the library in Wilton Crescent. Sarah is reading in the armchair near the window. Barbara, in ordinary fashionable dress, pale and brooding, is on the settee. Charles Lomax enters. He starts on seeing Barbara fashionably attired and in low spirits.

LOMAX. Youve left off your uniform!

Barbara says nothing; but an expression of pain passes over her face.

LADY BRITOMART (*warning him in low tones to be careful*). Charles!

LOMAX (*much concerned, coming behind the settee and bending sympathetically over Barbara*). I'm awfully sorry, Barbara. You know I helped you all I could with the concertina and so forth. (*Momentously.*) Still, I have never shut my

---

[19]**a Rowton doss** a bed in one of Rowton's cheap rooming houses.
[20]**Charles Bradlaugh,** a secularist, died in 1891.

eyes to the fact that there is a certain amount of tosh about the Salvation Army. Now the claims of the Church of England—

LADY BRITOMART. Thats enough, Charles. Speak of something suited to your mental capacity.

LOMAX. But surely the Church of England is suited to all our capacities.

BARBARA (*pressing his hand*). Thank you for your sympathy, Cholly. Now go and spoon with Sarah.

LOMAX (*dragging a chair from the writing table and seating himself affectionately by Sarah's side*). How is my ownest today?

SARAH. I wish you wouldnt tell Cholly to do things, Barbara. He always comes straight and does them. Cholly: we're going to the works this afternoon.

LOMAX. What works?

SARAH. The cannon works.

LOMAX. What? your governor's shop!

SARAH. Yes.

LOMAX. Oh I say!

Cusins enters in poor condition. He also starts visibly when he sees Barbara without her uniform.

BARBARA. I expected you this morning, Dolly. Didn't you guess that?

CUSINS (*sitting down beside her*). I'm sorry. I have only just breakfasted.

SARAH. But weve just finished lunch.

BARBARA. Have you had one of your bad nights?

CUSINS. No: I had rather a good night: in fact, one of the most remarkable nights I have ever passed.

BARBARA. The meeting?

CUSINS. No: after the meeting.

LADY BRITOMART. You should have gone to bed after the meeting. What were you doing?

CUSINS. Drinking.

LADY BRITOMART. ⎫ Adolphus!
SARAH. ⎪ Dolly!
BARBARA. ⎬ Dolly!
LOMAX. ⎭ Oh I say!

LADY BRITOMART. What were you drinking, may I ask?

CUSINS. A most devilish kind of Spanish burgundy, warranted free from added alcohol: a Temperance burgundy in fact. Its richness in natural alcohol made any addition superfluous.

BARBARA. Are you joking, Dolly?

CUSINS (*patiently*). No. I have been making a night of it with the nominal head of this household: that is all.

LADY BRITOMART. Andrew made you drunk!

CUSINS. No: he only provided the wine. I think it was Dionysos who made me drunk. (*To Barbara.*) I told you I was possessed.

LADY BRITOMART. Youre not sober yet. Go home to bed at once.

CUSINS. I have never before ventured to reproach you, Lady Brit; but how could you marry the Prince of Darkness?

LADY BRITOMART. It was much more excusable to marry him than to get drunk with him. That is a new accomplishment of Andrew's, by the way. He usent to drink.

CUSINS. He doesnt now. He only sat there and completed the wreck of my moral basis, the rout of my convictions, the purchase of my soul. He cares for you, Barbara. That is what makes him so dangerous to me.

BARBARA. That has nothing to do with it, Dolly. There are larger loves and diviner dreams than the fireside ones. You know that, dont you?

CUSINS. Yes: that is our understanding. I know it. I hold to it. Unless he can win me on that holier ground he may amuse me for a while; but he can get no deeper hold, strong as he is.

BARBARA. Keep to that; and the end will be right. Now tell me what happened at the meeting?

CUSINS. It was an amazing meeting. Mrs Baines almost died of emotion. Jenny Hill simply gibbered with hysteria. The Prince of Darkness played his trombone like a madman: its brazen roarings were like the laughter of the damned. 117 conversions took place then and there. They prayed with the most touching sincerity and gratitude for Bodger, and for the anonymous donor of the £5000. Your father would not let his name be given.

LOMAX. That was rather fine of the old man, you know. Most chaps would have wanted the advertisement.

CUSINS. He said all the charitable institutions would be down on him like kites on a battle-field if he gave his name.

LADY BRITOMART. Thats Andrew all over. He never does a proper thing without giving an improper reason for it.

CUSINS. He convinced me that I have all my life been doing improper things for proper reasons.

LADY BRITOMART. Adolphus: now that Barbara has left the Salvation Army, you had better leave it too. I will not have you playing that drum in the streets.

CUSINS. Your orders are already obeyed, Lady Brit.

BARBARA. Dolly: were you ever really in earnest about it? Would you have joined if you had never seen me?

CUSINS (*disingenuously*). Well—er—well, possibly, as a collector of religions—

LOMAX (*cunningly*). Not as a drummer, though, you know. You are a very clearheaded brainy chap, Dolly; and it must have been apparent to you that there is a certain amount of tosh about—

LADY BRITOMART. Charles: if you must drivel, drivel like a grown-up man and not like a schoolboy.

LOMAX (*out of countenance*). Well, drivel is drivel, dont you know, whatever a man's age.

LADY BRITOMART. In good society in England, Charles, men drivel at all ages by repeating silly formulas with an air of wisdom. Schoolboys make their own formulas out of slang, like you. When they reach your age, and get political private secretaryships and things of that sort, they drop slang and get their formulas out of The Spectator or The Times. You had better confine yourself to The

Times. You will find that there is a certain amount of tosh about The Times; but at least its language is reputable.

LOMAX (*overwhelmed*). You are so awfully strong-minded, Lady Brit—

LADY BRITOMART. Rubbish! (*Morrison comes in.*) What is it?

MORRISON. If you please, my lady, Mr Undershaft has just drove up to the door.

LADY BRITOMART. Well, let him in. (*Morrison hesitates.*) Whats the matter with you?

MORRISON. Shall I announce him, my lady; or is he at home here, so to speak, my lady?

LADY BRITOMART. Announce him.

MORRISON. Thank you, my lady. You wont mind my asking, I hope. The occasion is in a manner of speaking new to me.

LADY BRITOMART. Quite right. Go and let him in.

MORRISON. Thank you, my lady. (*He withdraws.*)

LADY BRITOMART. Children: go and get ready. (*Sarah and Barbara go upstairs for their out-of-door wraps.*) Charles: go and tell Stephen to come down here in five minutes: you will find him in the drawing room. (*Charles goes.*) Adolphus: tell them to send round the carriage in about fifteen minutes. (*Adolphus goes.*)

MORRISON (*at the door*). Mr Undershaft.

Undershaft comes in. Morrison goes out.

UNDERSHAFT. Alone! How fortunate!

LADY BRITOMART (*rising*). Dont be sentimental, Andrew. Sit down. (*She sits on the settee: he sits beside her, on her left. She comes to the point before he has time to breathe.*) Sarah must have £800 a year until Charles Lomax comes into his property. Barbara will need more, and need it permanently, because Adolphus hasnt any property.

UNDERSHAFT (*resignedly*). Yes, my dear: I will see to it. Anything else? for yourself, for instance?

LADY BRITOMART. I want to talk to you about Stephen.

UNDERSHAFT (*rather wearily*). Dont, my dear. Stephen doesnt interest me.

LADY BRITOMART. He does interest me. He is our son.

UNDERSHAFT. Do you really think so? He has induced us to bring him into the world; but he chose his parents very incongruously, I think. I see nothing of myself in him, and less of you.

LADY BRITOMART. Andrew: Stephen is an excellent son, and a most steady, capable, highminded young man. You are simply trying to find an excuse for disinheriting him.

UNDERSHAFT. My dear Biddy: the Undershaft tradition disinherits him. It would be dishonest of me to leave the cannon foundry to my son.

LADY BRITOMART. It would be most unnatural and improper of you to leave it to anyone else, Andrew. Do you suppose this wicked and immoral tradition can be kept up for ever? Do you pretend that Stephen could not carry on the foundry just as well as all the other sons of the big business houses?

UNDERSHAFT. Yes: he could learn the office routine without understanding the business, like all the other sons; and

the firm would go on by its own momentum until the real Undershaft—probably an Italian or a German—would invent a new method and cut him out.

LADY BRITOMART. There is nothing that any Italian or German could do that Stephen could not do. And Stephen at least has breeding.

UNDERSHAFT. The son of a foundling! Nonsense!

LADY BRITOMART. My son, Andrew! And even you may have good blood in your veins for all you know.

UNDERSHAFT. True. Probably I have. That is another argument in favor of a foundling.

LADY BRITOMART. Andrew: dont be aggravating. And dont be wicked. At present you are both.

UNDERSHAFT. This conversation is part of the Undershaft tradition, Biddy. Every Undershaft's wife has treated him to it ever since the house was founded. It is a mere waste of breath. If the tradition be ever broken it will be for an abler man than Stephen.

LADY BRITOMART (*pouting*). Then go away.

UNDERSHAFT (*deprecatory*). Go away!

LADY BRITOMART. Yes: go away. If you will do nothing for Stephen, you are not wanted here. Go to your foundling, whoever he is; and look after him.

UNDERSHAFT. The fact is, Biddy—

LADY BRITOMART. Dont call me Biddy. I dont call you Andy.

UNDERSHAFT. I will not call my wife Britomart: it is not good sense. Seriously, my love, the Undershaft tradition has landed me in a difficulty. I am getting on in years; and my partner Lazarus has at last made a stand and insisted that the succession must be settled one way or the other; and of course he is quite right. You see, I havnt found a fit successor yet.

LADY BRITOMART (*obstinately*). There is Stephen.

UNDERSHAFT. Thats just it: all the foundlings I can find are exactly like Stephen.

LADY BRITOMART. Andrew!!

UNDERSHAFT. I want a man with no relations and no schooling: that is, a man who would be out of the running altogether if he were not a strong man. And I cant find him. Every blessed foundling nowadays is snapped up in his infancy by Barnardo homes, or School Board officers, or Boards of Guardians; and if he shews the least ability he is fastened on by schoolmasters; trained to win scholarships like a racehorse; crammed with secondhand ideas; drilled and disciplined in docility and what they call good taste; and lamed for life so that he is fit for nothing but teaching. If you want to keep the foundry in the family, you had better find an eligible foundling and marry him to Barbara.

LADY BRITOMART. Ah! Barbara! Your pet! You would sacrifice Stephen to Barbara.

UNDERSHAFT. Cheerfully. And you, my dear, would boil Barbara to make soup for Stephen.

LADY BRITOMART. Andrew: this is not a question of our likings and dislikings: it is a question of duty. It is your duty to make Stephen your successor.

UNDERSHAFT. Just as much as it is your duty to submit to your husband. Come, Biddy! these tricks of the governing class are of no use with me. I am one of the governing class myself; and it is a waste of time giving tracts to a missionary. I have the power in this matter; and I am not to be humbugged into using it for your purposes.

LADY BRITOMART. Andrew: you can talk my head off; but you cant change wrong into right. And your tie is all on one side. Put it straight.

UNDERSHAFT (*disconcerted*). It wont stay unless it's pinned— (*He fumbles at it with childish grimaces.*)

Stephen comes in.

STEPHEN (*at the door*). I beg your pardon. (*About to retire.*)

LADY BRITOMART. No: come in, Stephen. (*Stephen comes forward to his mother's writing table.*)

UNDERSHAFT (*not very cordially*). Good afternoon.

STEPHEN (*coldly*). Good afternoon.

UNDERSHAFT (*to Lady Britomart*). He knows all about the tradition, I suppose?

LADY BRITOMART. Yes. (*To Stephen.*) It is what I told you last night, Stephen.

UNDERSHAFT (*sulkily*). I understand you want to come into the cannon business.

STEPHEN. *I* go into trade! Certainly not.

UNDERSHAFT (*opening his eyes, greatly eased in mind and manner*). Oh! in that case—

LADY BRITOMART. Cannons are not trade, Stephen. They are enterprise.

STEPHEN. I have no intention of becoming a man of business in any sense. I have no capacity for business and no taste for it. I intend to devote myself to politics.

UNDERSHAFT (*rising*). My dear boy: this is an immense relief to me. And I trust it may prove an equally good thing for the country. I was afraid you would consider yourself disparaged and slighted. (*He moves towards Stephen as if to shake hands with him.*)

LADY BRITOMART (*rising and interposing*). Stephen: I cannot allow you to throw away an enormous property like this.

STEPHEN (*stiffly*). Mother: there must be an end of treating me as a child, if you please. (*Lady Britomart recoils, deeply wounded by his tone.*) Until last night I did not take your attitude seriously, because I did not think you meant it seriously. But I find now that you left me in the dark as to matters which you should have explained to me years ago. I am extremely hurt and offended. Any further discussion of my intentions had better take place with my father, as between one man and another.

LADY BRITOMART. Stephen! (*She sits down again, her eyes filling with tears.*)

UNDERSHAFT (*with grave compassion*). You see, my dear, it is only the big men who can be treated as children.

STEPHEN. I am sorry, mother, that you have forced me—

UNDERSHAFT (*stopping him*). Yes, yes, yes, yes: thats all right, Stephen. She wont interfere with you any more: your independence is achieved: you have won your latchkey. Dont rub it in; and above all, dont apologize. (*He resumes his seat.*) Now what about your future, as between one man and another—I beg your pardon, Biddy: as between two men and a woman.

LADY BRITOMART (*who has pulled herself together strongly*). I quite understand, Stephen. By all means go your own way if you feel strong enough. (*Stephen sits down magisterially in the chair at the writing table with an air of affirming his majority.*)

UNDERSHAFT. It is settled that you do not ask for the succession to the cannon business.

STEPHEN. I hope it is settled that I repudiate the cannon business.

UNDERSHAFT. Come, come! dont be so devilishly sulky: it's boyish. Freedom should be generous. Besides, I owe you a fair start in life in exchange for disinheriting you. You cant become prime minister all at once. Havnt you a turn for something? What about literature, art, and so forth?

STEPHEN. I have nothing of the artist about me, either in faculty or character, thank Heaven!

UNDERSHAFT. A philosopher, perhaps? Eh?

STEPHEN. I make no such ridiculous pretension.

UNDERSHAFT. Just so. Well, there is the army, the navy, the Church, the Bar. The Bar requires some ability. What about the Bar?

STEPHEN. I have not studied law. And I am afraid I have not the necessary push—I believe that is the name barristers give to their vulgarity—for success in pleading.

UNDERSHAFT. Rather a difficult case, Stephen. Hardly anything left but the stage, is there? (*Stephen makes an impatient movement.*) Well, come! is there anything you know or care for?

STEPHEN (*rising and looking at him steadily*). I know the difference between right and wrong.

UNDERSHAFT (*hugely tickled*). You dont say so! What! no capacity for business, no knowledge of law, no sympathy with art, no pretension to philosophy; only a simple knowledge of the secret that has puzzled all the philosophers, baffled all the lawyers, muddled all the men of business, and ruined most of the artists: the secret of right and wrong. Why, man, youre a genius, a master of masters, a god! At twentyfour, too!

STEPHEN (*keeping his temper with difficulty*). You are pleased to be facetious. I pretend to nothing more than any honorable English gentleman claims as his birthright (*He sits down angrily.*)

UNDERSHAFT. Oh, thats everybody's birthright. Look at poor little Jenny Hill, the Salvation lassie! she would think you were laughing at her if you asked her to stand up in the street and teach grammar or geography or mathematics or even drawing room dancing; but it never occurs to her to doubt that she can teach morals and religion. You are all alike, you respectable people. You cant tell me the bursting strain of a ten-inch gun, which is a very simple matter; but you all think you can tell me the bursting strain of a man under temptation. You darent handle high explosives; but youre all ready to handle honesty and truth and justice and the whole duty of man, and kill one another at that game. What a country! What a world!

LADY BRITOMART (*uneasily*). What do you think he had better do, Andrew?

UNDERSHAFT. Oh, just what he wants to do. He knows nothing and he thinks he knows everything. That points clearly to a political career. Get him a private secretaryship to someone who can get him an Under Secretaryship; and then leave him alone. He will find his natural and proper place in the end on the Treasury Bench.

STEPHEN (*springing up again*). I am sorry, sir, that you force me to forget the respect due to you as my father. I am an Englishman and I will not hear the Government of my country insulted. (*He thrusts his hands in his pockets, and walks angrily across to the window.*)

UNDERSHAFT (*with a touch of brutality*). The government of your country! *I* am the government of your country: I, and Lazarus. Do you suppose that you and half a dozen amateurs like you, sitting in a row in that foolish gabble shop, can govern Undershaft and Lazarus? No, my friend: you will do what pays *us*. You will make war when it suits us, and keep peace when it doesnt. You will find out that trade requires certain measures when we have decided on those measures. When I want anything to keep my dividends up, you will discover that my want is a national need. When other people want something to keep my dividends down, you will call out the police and military. And in return you shall have the support and applause of my newspapers, and the delight of imagining that you are a great statesman. Government of your country! Be off with you, my boy, and play with your caucuses and leading articles and historic parties and great leaders and burning questions and the rest of your toys. *I* am going back to my counting-house to pay the piper and call the tune.

STEPHEN (*actually smiling, and putting his hand on his father's shoulder with indulgent patronage*). Really, my dear father, it is impossible to be angry with you. You dont know how absurd all this sounds to *me*. You are very properly proud of having been industrious enough to make money; and it is greatly to your credit that you have made so much of it. But it has kept you in circles where you are valued for your money and deferred to for it, instead of in the doubtless very old-fashioned and behind-the-times public school and university where I formed my habits of mind. It is natural for you to think that money governs England; but you must allow me to think I know better.

UNDERSHAFT. And what does govern England, pray?

STEPHEN. Character, father, character.

UNDERSHAFT. Whose character? Yours or mine?

STEPHEN. Neither yours nor mine, father, but the best elements in the English national character.

UNDERSHAFT. Stephen: Ive found your profession for you. Youre a born journalist. I'll start you with a high-toned weekly review. There!

Before Stephen can reply Sarah, Barbara, Lomax, and Cusins come in ready for walking. Barbara crosses the room to the window and looks out. Cusins drifts amiably to the armchair. Lomax remains near the door, whilst Sarah comes to her mother.

Stephen goes to the smaller writing table and busies himself with his letters.

SARAH. Go and get ready, mama: the carriage is waiting. (*Lady Britomart leaves the room.*)

UNDERSHAFT (*to Sarah*). Good day, my dear. Good afternoon, Mr Lomax.

LOMAX (*vaguely*). Ahdedoo.

UNDERSHAFT (*to Cusins*). Quite well after last night, Euripides, eh?

CUSINS. As well as can be expected.

UNDERSHAFT. Thats right. (*To Barbara.*) So you are coming to see my death and devastation factory, Barbara?

BARBARA (*at the window*). You came yesterday to see my salvation factory. I promised you a return visit.

LOMAX (*coming forward between Sarah and Undershaft*). Youll find it awfully interesting. Ive been through the Woolwich Arsenal; and it gives you a ripping feeling of security, you know, to think of the lot of beggars we could kill if it came to fighting. (*To Undershaft, with sudden solemnity.*) Still, it must be rather an awful reflection for you, from the religious point of view as it were. Youre getting on, you know, and all that.

SARAH. You dont mind Cholly's imbecility, papa, do you?

LOMAX (*much taken aback*). Oh I say!

UNDERSHAFT. Mr Lomax looks at the matter in a very proper spirit, my dear.

LOMAX. Just so. Thats all I meant, I assure you.

SARAH. Are you coming, Stephen?

STEPHEN. Well, I am rather busy—er—(*Magnanimously.*) Oh well, yes: I'll come. That is, if there is room for me.

UNDERSHAFT. I can take two with me in a little motor I am experimenting with for field use. You wont mind its being rather unfashionable. It's not painted yet; but it's bullet proof.

LOMAX (*appalled at the prospect of confronting Wilton Crescent in an unpainted motor*). Oh I say!

SARAH. The carriage for me, thank you. Barbara doesnt mind what she's seen in.

LOMAX. I say, Dolly, old chap: do you really mind the car being a guy? Because of course if you do I'll go in it. Still—

CUSINS. I prefer it.

LOMAX. Thanks awfully, old man. Come, my ownest. (*He hurries to secure his seat in the carriage. Sarah follows him.*)

CUSINS (*moodily walking across to Lady Britomart's writing table*). Why are we two coming to this Works Department of Hell? that is what I ask myself.

BARBARA. I have always thought of it as a sort of pit where lost creatures with blackened faces stirred up smoky fires and were driven and tormented by my father? Is it like that, dad?

UNDERSHAFT (*scandalized*). My dear! It is a spotlessly clean and beautiful hillside town.

CUSINS. With a Methodist chapel? Oh do say theres a Methodist chapel.

UNDERSHAFT. There are two: a Primitive one and a sophisticated one. There is even an Ethical Society; but it is not much patronized, as my men are all strongly religious. In the High Explosives Sheds they object to the presence of Agnostics as unsafe.

CUSINS. And yet they dont object to you!

BARBARA. Do they obey all your orders?

UNDERSHAFT. I never give them any orders. When I speak to one of them it is "Well, Jones, is the baby doing well? and has Mrs Jones made a good recovery?" "Nicely, thank you, sir." And thats all.

CUSINS. But Jones has to be kept in order. How do you maintain discipline among your men?

UNDERSHAFT. I dont. They do. You see, the one thing Jones wont stand is any rebellion from the man under him, or any assertion of social equality between the wife of the man with 4 shillings a week less than himself, and Mrs Jones! Of course they all rebel against me, theoretically. Practically, every man of them keeps the man just below him in his place. I never meddle with them. I never bully them. I dont even bully Lazarus. I say that certain things are to be done; but I dont order anybody to do them. I dont say, mind you, that there is no ordering about and snubbing and even bullying. The men snub the boys and order them about; the carmen snub the sweepers; the artisans snub the unskilled laborers; the foremen drive and bully both the laborers and artisans; the assistant engineers find fault with the foremen; the chief engineers drop on the assistants; the departmental managers worry the chiefs; and the clerks have tall hats and hymnbooks and keep up the social tone by refusing to associate on equal terms with anybody. The result is a colossal profit, which comes to me.

CUSINS (*revolted*). You really are a—well, what I was saying yesterday.

BARBARA. What was he saying yesterday?

UNDERSHAFT. Never mind, my dear. He thinks I have made you unhappy. Have I?

BARBARA. Do you think I can be happy in this vulgar silly dress? I! who have worn the uniform. Do you understand what you have done to me? Yesterday I had a man's soul in my hand. I set him in the way of life with his face to salvation. But when we took your money he turned back to drunkenness and derision. (*With intense conviction.*) I will never forgive you that. If I had a child, and you destroyed its body with your explosives—if you murdered Dolly with your horrible guns—I could forgive you if my forgiveness would open the gates of heaven to you. But to take a human soul from me, and turn it into the soul of a wolf! that is worse than any murder.

UNDERSHAFT. Does my daughter despair so easily? Can you strike a man to the heart and leave no mark on him?

BARBARA (*her face lighting up*). Oh, you are right: he can never be lost now: where was my faith?

CUSINS. Oh, clever clever devil!

BARBARA. You may be a devil; but God speaks through you sometimes (*She takes her father's hands and kisses them.*) You have given me back my happiness: I feel it deep down now, though my spirit is troubled.

UNDERSHAFT. You have learnt something. That always feels at first as if you had lost something.

BARBARA. Well, take me to the factory of death; and let me learn something more. There must be some truth or other behind all this frightful irony. Come, Dolly. (*She goes out.*)

CUSINS. My guardian angel! (*To Undershaft.*) Avaunt! (*He follows Barbara.*)

STEPHEN (*quietly, at the writing table*). You must not mind Cusins, father. He is a very amiable good fellow; but he is a Greek scholar and naturally a little eccentric.

UNDERSHAFT. Ah, quite so. Thank you, Stephen. Thank you. (*He goes out.*)

Stephen smiles patronizingly; buttons his coat responsibly; and crosses the room to the door. Lady Britomart, dressed for out-of-doors, opens it before he reaches it. She looks round for the others; looks at Stephen; and turns to go without a word.

STEPHEN (*embarrassed*). Mother—

LADY BRITOMART. Dont be apologetic, Stephen. And dont forget that you have outgrown your mother. (*She goes out.*)

Perivale St Andrews lies between two Middlesex hills, half climbing the northern one. It is an almost smokeless town of white walls, roofs of narrow green slates or red tiles, tall trees, domes, campaniles, and slender chimney shafts, beautifully situated and beautiful in itself. The best view of it is obtained from the crest of a slope about half a mile to the east, where the high explosives are dealt with. The foundry lies hidden in the depths between, the tops of its chimneys sprouting like huge skittles into the middle distance. Across the crest runs an emplacement of concrete, with a firestep, and a parapet which suggests a fortification, because there is a huge cannon of the obsolete Woolwich Infant pattern peering across it at the town. The can-

non is mounted on an experimental gun carriage: possibly the original model of the Undershaft disappearing rampart gun alluded to by Stephen. The firestep, being a convenient place to sit, is furnished here and there with straw disc cushions; and at one place there is the additional luxury of a fur rug.

Barbara is standing on the firestep, looking over the parapet towards the town. On her right is the cannon; on her left the end of a shed raised on piles, with a ladder of three or four steps up to the door, which opens outwards and has a little wooden landing at the threshold, with a fire bucket in the corner of the landing. Several dummy soldiers more or less mutilated, with straw protruding from their gashes, have been shoved out of the way under the landing. A few others are nearly upright against the shed; and one has fallen forward and lies, like a grotsque corpse, on the emplacement. The parapet stops short of the shed, leaving a gap which is the beginning of the path down the hill through the foundry to the town. The rug is on the firestep near this gap. Down on the emplacement behind the cannon is a trolley carrying a huge conical bombshell with a red band painted on it. Further to the right is the door of an office, which, like the sheds, is of the lightest possible construction.

Cusins arrives by the path from the town.

BARBARA. Well?

CUSINS. Not a ray of hope. Everything perfect! wonderful! real! It only needs a cathedral to be a heavenly city instead of a hellish one.

BARBARA. Have you found out whether they have done anything for old Peter Shirley?

CUSINS. They have found him a job as gatekeeper and timekeeper. He's frightfully miserable. He calls the time-keeping brainwork, and says he isnt used to it; and his gate lodge is so splendid that he's ashamed to use the rooms, and skulks in the scullery.

BARBARA. Poor Peter!

Stephen arrives from the town. He carries a fieldglass.

STEPHEN (*enthusiastically*). Have you two seen the place? Why did you leave us?

CUSINS. I wanted to see everything I was not intended to see; and Barbara wanted to make the men talk.

STEPHEN. Have you found anything discreditable?

CUSINS. No. They call him Dandy Andy and are proud of his being a cunning old rascal; but it's all horribly, frightfully, immorally, unanswerably perfect.

Sarah arrives.

SARAH. Heavens! what a place! (*She crosses to the trolley.*) Did you see the nursing home!? (*She sits down on the shell.*)

STEPHEN. Did you see the libraries and schools!?

SARAH. Did you see the ball room and the banqueting chamber in the Town Hall!?

STEPHEN. Have you gone into the insurance fund, the pension fund, the building society, the various applications of cooperation!?

Undershaft comes from the office, with a sheaf of telegrams in his hand.

UNDERSHAFT. Well, have you seen everything? I'm sorry I was called away. (*Indicating the telegrams.*) Good news from Manchuria.

STEPHEN. Another Japanese victory?

UNDERSHAFT. Oh, I dont know. Which side wins does not concern us here. No: the good news is that the aerial battleship is a tremendous success. At the first trial it has wiped out a fort with three hundred soldiers in it.

CUSINS (*from the platform*). Dummy soldiers?

UNDERSHAFT (*striding across to Stephen and kicking the prostrate dummy brutally out of his way*). No: the real thing.

Cusins and Barbara exchange glances. Then Cusins sits on the step and buries his face in his hands. Barbara gravely lays her hand on his shoulder. He looks up at her in whimsical desperation.

UNDERSHAFT. Well, Stephen, what do you think of the place?

STEPHEN. Oh, magnificent. A perfect triumph of modern industry. Frankly, my dear father, I have been a fool: I had no idea of what it all meant: of the wonderful forethought, the power of organization, the administrative capacity, the financial genius, the colossal capital it represents. I have been repeating to myself as I came through your streets "Peace hath her victories no less renowned than War." I have only one misgiving about it all.

UNDERSHAFT. Out with it.

STEPHEN. Well, I cannot help thinking that all this provision for every want of your workmen may sap their independence and weaken their sense of responsibility. And greatly as we enjoyed our tea at that splendid restaurant—how they gave us all that luxury and cake and jam and cream for threepence I really cannot imagine!—still you must remember that restaurants break up home life. Look at the continent, for instance! Are you sure so much pampering is really good for the men's characters?

UNDERSHAFT. Well you see, my dear boy, when you are organizing civilization you have to make up your mind whether trouble and anxiety are good things or not. If you decide that they are, then, I take it, you simply dont organize civilization; and there you are, with trouble and anxiety enough to make us all angels! But if you decide the other way, you may as well go through with it. However, Stephen, our characters are safe here. A sufficient dose of anxiety is always provided by the fact that we may be blown to smithereens at any moment.

SARAH. By the way, papa, where do you make the explosives?

UNDERSHAFT. In separate little sheds, like that one. When one of them blows up, it costs very little; and only the people quite close to it are killed.

Stephen, who is quite close to it, looks at it rather scaredly, and moves away quickly to the cannon. At the same moment the door of the shed is thrown abruptly open; and a foreman in overalls and list slippers[21] comes out on the little landing and holds the door for Lomax, who appears in the doorway.

LOMAX (*with studied coolness*). My good fellow: you neednt get into a state of nerves. Nothing's going to happen to you; and I suppose it wouldnt be the end of the world if anything did. A little bit of British pluck is what you want, old chap. (*He descends and strolls across to Sarah.*)

UNDERSHAFT (*to the foreman*). Anything wrong, Bilton?

BILTON (*with ironic calm*). Gentleman walked into the high explosives shed and lit a cigaret, sir: thats all.

UNDERSHAFT. Ah, quite so. (*Going over to Lomax.*) Do you happen to remember what you did with the match?

LOMAX. Oh come! I'm not a fool. I took jolly good care to blow it out before I chucked it away.

BILTON. The top of it was red hot inside, sir.

LOMAX. Well, suppose it was! I didn't chuck it into any of your messes.

UNDERSHAFT. Think no more of it, Mr Lomax. By the way, would you mind lending me your matches.

LOMAX (*offering his box*). Certainly.

UNDERSHAFT. Thanks. (*He pockets the matches.*)

LOMAX (*lecturing to the company generally*). You know, these high explosives dont go off like gunpowder, except when theyre in a gun. When theyre spread loose, you can put a match to them without the least risk: they just burn quietly like a bit of paper. (*Warming to the scientific interest of the subject.*) Did you know that, Undershaft? Have you ever tried?

UNDERSHAFT. Not on a large scale, Mr Lomax. Bilton will give you a sample of gun cotton when you are leaving if you ask him. You can experiment with it at home. (*Bilton looks puzzled.*)

SARAH. Bilton will do nothing of the sort, papa. I suppose it's your business to blow up the Russians and Japs; but you might really stop short of blowing up poor Cholly. (*Bilton gives it up and retires into the shed.*)

LOMAX. My ownest, there is no danger. (*He sits beside her on the shell.*)

Lady Britomart arrives from the town with a bouquet.

LADY BRITOMART (*impetuously*). Andrew: you shouldnt have let me see this place.

UNDERSHAFT. Why, my dear?

LADY BRITOMART. Never mind why: you shouldnt have: thats all. To think of all that (*indicating the town*) being yours! and that you have kept it to yourself all these years!

UNDERSHAFT. It does not belong to me. I belong to it. It is the Undershaft inheritance.

LADY BRITOMART. It is not. Your ridiculous cannons and that noisy banging foundry may be the Undershaft inheritance; but all that plate and linen, all that furniture and those houses and orchards and gardens belong to us. They belong to me: they are not a man's business. I wont give them up. You must be out of your senses to throw them all away; and if you persist in such folly, I will call in a doctor.

UNDERSHAFT (*stooping to smell the bouquet*). Where did you get the flowers, my dear?

LADY BRITOMART. Your men presented them to me in your William Morris Labor Church.[22]

CUSINS. Oh! It needed only that. A Labor Church! (*He mounts the firestep distractedly, and leans with his elbows on the parapet, turning his back to them.*)

LADY BRITOMART. Yes, with Morris's words in mosaic letters ten feet high round the dome. NO MAN IS GOOD ENOUGH TO BE ANOTHER MAN'S MASTER. The cynicism of it!

UNDERSHAFT. It shocked the men at first, I am afraid. But now they take no more notice of it than of the ten commandments in church.

LADY BRITOMART. Andrew: you are trying to put me off the subject of the inheritance by profane jokes. Well, you shant. I dont ask it any longer for Stephen: he has inherited far too much of your perversity to be fit for it. But Barbara has rights as well as Stephen. Why should not Adolphus succeed to the inheritance? I could manage the town for him; and he can look after the cannons, if they are really necessary.

UNDERSHAFT. I should ask nothing better if Adolphus were a foundling. He is exactly the sort of new blood that is wanted in English business. But he's not a foundling; and theres an end of it. (*He makes for the office door.*)

CUSINS (*turning to them*). Not quite. (*They all turn and stare at him.*) I think—Mind! I am not committing myself in any way as to my future course—but I think the foundling difficulty can be got over. (*He jumps down to the emplacement.*)

UNDERSHAFT (*coming back to him*). What do you mean?

CUSINS. Well, I have something to say which is in the nature of a confession.

---

[21]**list slippers** cloth overshoes.

[22]**Labor church** the Labor church, founded in 1891, was part of an attempt to transform the Labor movement into a kind of religious organization.

SARAH.
LADY BRITOMART. } Confession!
BARBARA.
STEPHEN.

LOMAX. Oh I say!

CUSINS. Yes, a confession. Listen, all. Until I met Barbara I thought myself in the main an honorable, truthful man, because I wanted the approval of my conscience more than I wanted anything else. But the moment I saw Barbara, I wanted her far more than the approval of my conscience.

LADY BRITOMART. Adolphus!

CUSINS. It is true. You accused me yourself, Lady Brit, of joining the Army to worship Barbara; and so I did. She bought my soul like a flower at a street corner; but she bought it for herself.

UNDERSHAFT. What! Not for Dionysos or another?

CUSINS. Dionysos and all the others are in herself. I adored what was divine in her, and was therefore a true worshipper. But I was romantic about her too. I thought she was a woman of the people, and that a marriage with a professor of Greek would be far beyond the wildest social ambitions of her rank.

LADY BRITOMART. Adolphus!!

LOMAX. Oh I say!!!

CUSINS. When I learnt the horrible truth—

LADY BRITOMART. What do you mean by the horrible truth, pray?

CUSINS. That she was enormously rich; that her grandfather was an earl; that her father was the Prince of Darkness—

UNDERSHAFT. Chut!

CUSINS. —and that I was only an adventurer trying to catch a rich wife, then I stooped to deceive her about my birth.

BARBARA (rising). Dolly!

LADY BRITOMART. Your birth! Now Adolphus, dont dare to make up a wicked story for the sake of these wretched cannons. Remember: I have seen photographs of your parents; and the Agent General for South Western Australia knows them personally and has assured me that they are most respectable married people.

CUSINS. So they are in Australia; but here they are outcasts. Their marriage is legal in Australia, but not in England. My mother is my father's deceased wife's sister; and in this island I am consequently a foundling.[23] (Sensation.)

BARBARA. Silly! (She climbs to the cannon, and leans, listening, in the angle it makes with the parapet.)

CUSINS. Is the subterfuge good enough, Machiavelli?

UNDERSHAFT (thoughtfully). Biddy: this may be a way out of the difficulty.

LADY BRITOMART. Stuff! A man cant make cannons any the better for being his own cousin instead of his proper self.

[23]**The Deceased Wife's Sister Act,** later repealed, forbade marriage of a widower with his late wife's sister.

(She sits down on the rug with a bounce that expresses her downright contempt for their casuistry.)

UNDERSHAFT (to Cusins). You are an educated man. That is against the tradition.

CUSINS. Once in ten thousand times it happens that the schoolboy is a born master of what they try to teach him. Greek has not destroyed my mind: it has nourished it. Besides, I did not learn it at an English public school.

UNDERSHAFT. Hm! Well, I cannot afford to be too particular: you have cornered the foundling market. Let it pass. You are eligible, Euripides: you are eligible.

BARBARA. Dolly: yesterday morning, when Stephen told us all about the tradition, you became very silent; and you have been strange and excited ever since. Were you thinking of your birth then?

CUSINS. When the finger of Destiny suddenly points at a man in the middle of his breakfast, it makes him thoughtful.

UNDERSHAFT. Aha! You have had your eye on the business, my young friend, have you?

CUSINS. Take care! There is an abyss of moral horror between me and your accursed aerial battleships.

UNDERSHAFT. Never mind the abyss for the present. Let us settle the practical details and leave your final decision open. You know that you will have to change your name. Do you object to that?

CUSINS. Would any man named Adolphus—any man called Dolly!—object to be called something else?

UNDERSHAFT. Good. Now, as to money! I propose to treat you handsomely from the beginning. You shall start at a thousand a year.

CUSINS (with sudden heat, his spectacles twinkling with mischief). A thousand! You dare offer a miserable thousand to the son-in-law of a millionaire! No, by Heavens, Machiavelli! you shall not cheat me. You cannot do without me; and I can do without you. I must have two thousand five hundred a year for two years. At the end of that time, if I am a failure, I go. But if I am a success, and stay on, you must give me the other five thousand.

UNDERSHAFT. What other five thousand?

CUSINS. To make the two years up to five thousand a year. The two thousand five hundred is only half pay in case I should turn out a failure. The third year I must have ten per cent on the profits.

UNDERSHAFT (taken aback). Ten per cent! Why, man, do you know what my profits are?

CUSINS. Enormous, I hope: otherwise I shall require twenty-five per cent.

UNDERSHAFT. But, Mr Cusins, this is a serious matter of business. You are not bringing any capital into the concern.

CUSINS. What! no capital! Is my mastery of Greek no capital? Is my access to the subtlest thought, the loftiest poetry yet attained by humanity, no capital? My character! my intellect! my life! my career! what Barbara calls my soul! are these no capital? Say another word; and I double my salary.

UNDERSHAFT. Be reasonable—

CUSINS (*permptorily*). Mr Undershaft: you have my terms. Take them or leave them.

UNDERSHAFT (*recovering himself*). Very well. I note your terms; and I offer you half.

CUSINS (*disgusted*). Half!

UNDERSHAFT (*firmly*). Half.

CUSINS. You call yourself a gentleman; and you offer me half!!

UNDERSHAFT. I do not call myself a gentleman; but I offer you half.

CUSINS. This to your future partner! your successor! your son-in-law!

BARBARA. You are selling your own soul, Dolly, not mine. Leave me out of the bargain, please.

UNDERSHAFT. Come! I will go a step further for Barbara's sake. I will give you three fifths; but that is my last word.

CUSINS. Done!

LOMAX. Done in the eye! Why, *I* get only eight hundred, you know.

CUSINS. By the way, Mac, I am a classical scholar, not an arithmetical one. Is three fifths more than half or less?

UNDERSHAFT. More, of course.

CUSINS. I would have taken two hundred and fifty. How you can succeed in business when you are willing to pay all that money to a University don who is obviously not worth a junior clerk's wages!—well! What will Lazarus say?

UNDERSHAFT. Lazarus is a gentle romantic Jew who cares for nothing but string quartets and stalls at fashionable theatres. He will be blamed for your rapacity in money matters, poor fellow! as he has hitherto been blamed for mine. You are a shark of the first order, Euripides. So much the better for the firm!

BARBARA. Is the bargain closed, Dolly? Does your soul belong to him now?

CUSINS. No: the price is settled: that is all. The real tug of war is still to come. What about the moral question?

LADY BRITOMART. There is no moral question in the matter at all, Adolphus. You must simply sell cannons and weapons to people whose cause is right and just, and refuse them to foreigners and criminals.

UNDERSHAFT (*determinedly*). No: none of that. You must keep the true faith of an Armorer, or you dont come in here.

CUSINS. What on earth is the true faith of an Armorer?

UNDERSHAFT. To give arms to all men who offer an honest price for them, without respect of persons or principles: to aristocrat and republican, to Nihilist and Tsar, to Capitalist and Socialist, to Protestant and Catholic, to burglar and policeman, to black man, white man and yellow man, to all sorts and conditions, all nationalities, all faiths, all follies, all causes and all crimes. The first Undershaft wrote up in his shop IF GOD GAVE THE HAND, LET NOT MAN WITHHOLD THE SWORD. The second wrote up ALL HAVE THE RIGHT TO FIGHT: NONE HAVE THE RIGHT TO JUDGE. The third wrote up TO MAN THE WEAPON: TO HEAVEN THE VICTORY. The fourth had no literary turn; so

he did not write up anything; but he sold cannons to Napoleon under the nose of George the Third. The fifth wrote up PEACE SHALL NOT PREVAIL SAVE WITH A SWORD IN HER HAND. The sixth, my master, was the best of all. He wrote up NOTHING IS EVER DONE IN THIS WORLD UNTIL MEN ARE PREPARED TO KILL ONE ANOTHER IF IT IS NOT DONE. After that, there was nothing left for the seventh to say. So he wrote up, simply, UNASHAMED.

CUSINS. My good Machiavelli, I shall certainly write something up on the wall; only, as I shall write it in Greek, you wont be able to read it. But as to your Armorer's faith, if I take my neck out of the noose of my own morality I am not going to put it into the noose of yours. I shall sell cannons to whom I please and refuse them to whom I please. So there!

UNDERSHAFT. From the moment when you become Andrew Undershaft, you will never do as you please again. Dont come here lusting for power, young man.

CUSINS. If power were my aim I should not come here for it. You have no power.

UNDERSHAFT. None of my own, certainly.

CUSINS. I have more power than you, more will. You do not drive this place: it drives you. And what drives the place?

UNDERSHAFT (*enigmatically*). A will of which I am a part.

BARBARA (*startled*). Father! Do you know what you are saying; or are you laying a snare for my soul?

CUSINS. Dont listen to his metaphysics, Barbara. The place is driven by the most rascally part of society, the money hunters, the pleasure hunters, the military promotion hunters; and he is their slave.

UNDERSHAFT. Not necessarily. Remember the Armorer's Faith. I will take an order from a good man as cheerfully as from a bad one. If you good people prefer preaching and shirking to buying my weapons and fighting the rascals, dont blame me. I can make cannons: I cannot make courage and conviction. Bah! you tire me, Euripides, with your morality mongering. Ask Barbara: she understands. (*He suddenly reaches up and takes Barbara's hands, looking powerfully into her eyes.*) Tell him, my love, what power really means.

BARBARA (*hypnotized*). Before I joined the Salvation Army, I was in my own power; and the consequence was that I never knew what to do with myself. When I joined it, I had not time enough for all the things I had to do.

UNDERSHAFT (*approvingly*). Just so. And why was that, do you suppose?

BARBARA. Yesterday I should have said, because I was in the power of God. (*She resumes her self-possession, withdrawing her hands from his with a power equal to his own.*) But you came and shewed me that I was in the power of Bodger and Undershaft. Today I feel—oh! how can I put it into words? Sarah: do you remember the earthquake at Cannes, when we were little children?—how little the surprise of the first shock mattered compared to the dread and horror of waiting for the second? That is how I feel in this place today. I stood on the rock I thought eternal;

and without a word of warning it reeled and crumbled under me. I was safe with an infinite wisdom watching me, an army marching to Salvation with me; and in a moment, at a stroke of your pen in a cheque book, I stood alone; and the heavens were empty. That was the first shock of the earthquake: I am waiting for the second.

UNDERSHAFT. Come, come, my daughter! dont make too much of your little tinpot tragedy. What do we do here when we spend years of work and thought and thousands of pounds of solid cash on a new gun or an aerial battleship that turns out just a hairsbreadth wrong after all? Scrap it. Scrap it without wasting another hour or another pound on it. Well, you have made for yourself something that you call a morality or a religion or what not. It doesnt fit the facts. Well, scrap it. Scrap it and get one that does fit. That is what is wrong with the world at present. It scraps its obsolete steam engines and dynamos; but it wont scrap its old prejudices and its old moralities and its old religions and its old political constitutions. Whats the result? In machinery it does very well; but in morals and religion and politics it is working at a loss that brings it nearer bankruptcy every year. Dont persist in that folly. If your old religion broke down yesterday, get a newer and a better one for tomorrow.

BARBARA. Oh how gladly I would take a better one to my soul! But you offer me a worse one. (*Turning on him with sudden vehemence.*) Justify yourself: shew me some light through the darkness of this dreadful place, with its beautifully clean workshops, and respectable workmen, and model homes.

UNDERSHAFT. Cleanliness and respectability do not need justification, Barbara: they justify themselves. I see no darkness here, no dreadfulness. In your Salvation shelter I saw poverty, misery, cold and hunger. You gave them bread and treacle and dreams of heaven. I give them thirty shillings a week to twelve thousand a year. They find their own dreams; but I look after the drainage.

BARBARA. And their souls?

UNDERSHAFT. I save their souls just as I saved yours.

BARBARA (*revolted*). You saved my soul! What do you mean?

UNDERSHAFT. I fed you and clothed you and housed you. I took care that you should have money enough to live handsomely—more than enough; so that you could be wasteful, careless, generous. That saved your soul from the seven deadly sins.

BARBARA (*bewildered*). The seven deadly sins!

UNDERSHAFT. Yes, the deadly seven. (*Counting on his fingers.*) Food, clothing, firing, rent, taxes, respectability and children. Nothing can lift those seven millstones from Man's neck but money; and the spirit cannot soar until the millstones are lifted. I lifted them from your spirit. I enabled Barbara to become Major Barbara; and I saved her from the crime of poverty.

CUSINS. Do you call poverty a crime?

UNDERSHAFT. The worst of crimes. All the other crimes are virtues beside it: all the other dishonors are chivalry itself by comparison. Poverty blights whole cities; spreads horrible pestilences; strikes dead the very souls of all who come within sight, sound, or smell of it. What you call crime is nothing: a murder here and a theft there, a blow now and a curse then: what do they matter? they are only the accidents and illnesses of life: there are not fifty genuine professional criminals in London. But there are millions of poor people, abject people, dirty people, ill fed, ill clothed people. They poison us morally and physically: they kill the happiness of society: they force us to do away with our own liberties and to organize unnatural cruelties for fear they should rise against us and drag us down into their abyss. Only fools fear crime: we all fear poverty. Pah! (*Turning on Barbara.*) you talk of your half-saved ruffian in West Ham: you accuse me of dragging his soul back to perdition. Well, bring him to me here; and I will drag his soul back again to salvation for you. Not by words and dreams; but by thirtyeight shillings a week, a sound house in a handsome street, and a permanent job. In three weeks he will have a fancy waistcoat; in three months a tall hat and a chapel sitting; before the end of the year he will shake hands with a duchess at a Primrose League meeting, and join the Conservative Party.

BARBARA. And will he be the better for that?

UNDERSHAFT. You know he will. Dont be a hypocrite, Barbara. He will be better fed, better housed, better clothed, better behaved; and his children will be pounds heavier and bigger. That will be better than an American cloth mattress in a shelter, chopping firewood, eating bread and treacle, and being forced to kneel down from time to time to thank heaven for it: knee drill, I think you call it. It is cheap work converting starving men with a Bible in one hand and a slice of bread in the other. I will undertake to convert West Ham to Mahometanism on the same terms. Try your hand on my men: their souls are hungry because their bodies are full.

BARBARA. And leave the east end to starve?

UNDERSHAFT (*his energetic tone dropping into one of bitter and brooding remembrance*). I was an east ender. I moralized and starved until one day I swore that I would be a full-fed free man at all costs; that nothing should stop me except a bullet, neither reason nor morals nor the lives of other men. I said "Thou shalt starve ere I starve"; and with that word I became free and great. I was a dangerous man until I had my will: now I am a useful, beneficent, kindly person. That is the history of most self-made millionaires, I fancy. When it is the history of every Englishman we shall have an England worth living in.

LADY BRITOMART. Stop making speeches, Andrew. This is not the place for them.

UNDERSHAFT (*punctured*). My dear: I have no other means of conveying my ideas.

LADY BRITOMART. Your ideas are nonsense. You got on because you were selfish and unscrupulous.

UNDERSHAFT. Not at all. I had the strongest scruples about poverty and starvation. Your moralists are quite unscrupulous about both: they make virtues of them. I had rather be a thief than a pauper. I had rather be a murderer than a slave. I dont want to be either; but if you force the alternative on me, then, by Heaven, I'll choose the braver and more moral one. I hate poverty and slavery worse than any other crimes whatsoever. And let me tell you this. Poverty and slavery have stood up for centuries to your sermons and leading articles: they will not stand up to my machine guns. Dont preach at them: dont reason with them. Kill them.

BARBARA. Killing. Is that your remedy for everything?

UNDERSHAFT. It is the final test of conviction, the only lever strong enough to overturn a social system, the only way of saying Must. Let six hundred and seventy fools loose in the streets; and three policemen can scatter them. But huddle them together in a certain house in Westminster; and let them go through certain ceremonies and call themselves certain names until at last they get the courage to kill; and your six hundred and seventy fools become a government. Your pious mob fills up ballot papers and imagines it is governing its masters; but the ballot paper that really governs is the paper that has a bullet wrapped up in it.

CUSINS. That is perhaps why, like most intelligent people, I never vote.

UNDERSHAFT. Vote! Bah! When you vote, you only change the names of the cabinet. When you shoot, you pull down governments, inaugurate new epochs, abolish old orders and set up new. Is that historically true, Mr Learned Man, or is it not?

CUSINS. It is historically true. I loathe having to admit it. I repudiate your sentiments. I abhor your nature. I defy you in every possible way. Still, it is true. But it ought not to be true.

UNDERSHAFT. Ought! ought! ought! ought! ought! Are you going to spend your life saying ought, like the rest of our moralists? Turn your oughts into shalls, man. Come and make explosives with me. Whatever can blow men up can blow society up. The history of the world is the history of those who had courage enough to embrace this truth. Have you the courage to embrace it, Barbara?

LADY BRITOMART. Barbara: I positively forbid you to listen to your father's abominable wickedness. And you, Adolphus, ought to know better than to go about saying that wrong things are true. What does it matter whether they are true if they are wrong?

UNDERSHAFT. What does it matter whether they are wrong if they are true?

LADY BRITOMART (rising). Children: come home instantly. Andrew: I am exceedingly sorry I allowed you to call on us. You are wickeder than ever. Come at once.

BARBARA (shaking her head). It's no use running away from wicked people, mamma.

LADY BRITOMART. It is every use. It shews your disapprobation of them.

BARBARA. It does not save them.

LADY BRITOMART. I can see that you are going to disobey me. Sarah: are you coming home or are you not?

SARAH. I daresay it's very wicked of papa to make cannons; but I dont think I shall cut him on that account.

LOMAX (pouring oil on the troubled waters). The fact is, you know, there is a certain amount of tosh about this notion of wickedness. It doesnt work. You must look at facts. Not that I would say a word in favor of anything wrong; but then, you see, all sorts of chaps are always doing all sorts of things; and we have to fit them in somehow, dont you know. What I mean is that you cant go cutting everybody; and thats about what it comes to. (Their rapt attention to his eloquence makes him nervous.) Perhaps I dont make myself clear.

LADY BRITOMART. You are lucidity itself, Charles. Because Andrew is successful and has plenty of money to give to Sarah, you will flatter him and encourage him in his wickedness.

LOMAX (unruffled). Well, where the carcase is, there will the eagles be gathered, dont you know. (To Undershaft.) Eh? What?

UNDERSHAFT. Precisely. By the way, may I call you Charles?

LOMAX. Delighted. Cholly is the usual ticket.

UNDERSHAFT (to Lady Britomart). Biddy—

LADY BRITOMART (violently). Dont dare call me Biddy. Charles Lomax: you are a fool. Adolphus Cusins: you are a Jesuit. Stephen: you are a prig. Barbara: you are a lunatic. Andrew: you are a vulgar tradesman. Now you all know my opinion; and my conscience is clear, at all events. (She sits down with a vehemence that the rug fortunately softens.)

UNDERSHAFT. My dear: you are the incarnation of morality. (She snorts.) Your conscience is clear and your duty done when you have called everybody names. Come, Euripides! it is getting late; and we all want to go home. Make up your mind.

CUSINS. Understand this, you old demon—

LADY BRITOMART. Adolphus!

UNDERSHAFT. Let him alone, Biddy. Proceed, Euripides.

CUSINS. You have me in a horrible dilemma. I want Barbara.

UNDERSHAFT. Like all young men, you greatly exaggerate the difference between one young woman and another.

BARBARA. Quite true, Dolly.

CUSINS. I also want to avoid being a rascal.

UNDERSHAFT (with biting contempt). You lust for personal righteousness, for self-approval, for what you call a good conscience, for what Barbara calls salvation, for what I call patronizing people who are not so lucky as yourself.

CUSINS. I do not: all the poet in me recoils from being a good man. But there are things in me that I must reckon with. Pity—

UNDERSHAFT. Pity! The scavenger of misery.

CUSINS. Well, love.

UNDERSHAFT. I know. You love the needy and the outcast: you love the oppressed races, the negro, the Indian ryot,[24] the underdog everywhere. Do you love the Japanese? Do you love the French? Do you love the English?

CUSINS. No. Every true Englishman detests the English. We are the wickedest nation on earth; and our success is a moral horror.

UNDERSHAFT. That is what comes of your gospel of love, is it?

CUSINS. May I not love even my father-in-law?

UNDERSHAFT. Who wants your love, man? By what right do you take the liberty of offering it to me? I will have your due heed and respect, or I will kill you. But your love! Damn your impertinence!

CUSINS (*grinning*). I may not be able to control my affections, Mac.

UNDERSHAFT. You are fencing, Euripides. You are weakening: your grip is slipping. Come! try your last weapon. Pity and love have broken in your hand: forgiveness is still left.

CUSINS. No: forgiveness is a beggar's refuge. I am with you there: we must pay our debts.

UNDERSHAFT. Well said. Come! you will suit me. Remember the words of Plato.

CUSINS (*starting*). Plato! You dare quote Plato to me!

UNDERSHAFT. Plato says, my friend, that society cannot be saved until either the Professors of Greek take to making gunpowder, or else the makers of gunpowder become Professors of Greek.

CUSINS. Oh, tempter, cunning tempter!

UNDERSHAFT. Come! choose, man, choose.

CUSINS. But perhaps Barbara will not marry me if I make the wrong choice.

BARBARA. Perhaps not.

CUSINS (*desperately perplexed*). You hear!

BARBARA. Father: do you love nobody?

UNDERSHAFT. I love my best friend.

LADY BRITOMART. And who is that, pray?

UNDERSHAFT. My bravest enemy. That is the man who keeps me up to the mark.

CUSINS. You know, the creature is really a sort of poet in his way. Suppose he is a great man, after all!

UNDERSHAFT. Suppose you stop talking and make up your mind, my young friend.

CUSINS. But you are driving me against my nature. I hate war.

UNDERSHAFT. Hatred is the coward's revenge for being intimidated. Dare you make war on war? Here are the means: my friend Mr. Lomax is sitting on them.

LOMAX (*springing up*). Oh I say! You dont mean that this thing is loaded, do you? My ownest: come off it.

SARAH (*sitting placidly on the shell*). If I am to be blown up, the more thoroughly it is done the better. Dont fuss, Cholly.

LOMAX (*to Undershaft, strongly remonstrant*). Your own daughter, you know!

UNDERSHAFT. So I see. (*To Cusins.*) Well, my friend, may we expect you here at six tomorrow morning?

CUSINS (*firmly*). Not on any account. I will see the whole establishment blown up with its own dynamite before I will get up at five. My hours are healthy, rational hours: eleven to five.

UNDERSHAFT. Come when you please: before a week you will come at six and stay until I turn you out for the sake of your health. (*Calling.*) Bilton! (*He turns to Lady Britomart, who rises.*) My dear: let us leave these two young people to themselves for a moment. (*Bilton comes from the shed.*) I am going to take you through the gun cotton shed.

BILTON (*barring the way*). You cant take anything explosive in here, sir.

LADY BRITOMART. What do you mean? Are you alluding to me?

BILTON (*unmoved*). No, maam. Mr Undershaft has the other gentleman's matches in his pocket.

LADY BRITOMART (*abruptly*). Oh! I beg your pardon. (*She goes into the shed.*)

UNDERSHAFT. Quite right, Bilton, quite right: here you are. (*He gives Bilton the box of matches.*) Come, Stephen. Come, Charles. Bring Sarah. (*He passes into the shed.*)

Bilton opens the box and deliberately drops the matches into the fire-bucket.

LOMAX. Oh! I say. (*Bilton stolidly hands him the empty box.*) Infernal nonsense! Pure scientific ignorance! (*He goes in.*)

SARAH. Am I all right, Bilton?

BILTON. Youll have to put on list slippers, miss: thats all. Weve got em inside. (*She goes in.*)

STEPHEN (*very seriously to Cusins*). Dolly, old fellow, think. Think before you decide. Do you feel that you are a sufficiently practical man? It is a huge undertaking, an enormous responsibility. All this mass of business will be Greek to you.

CUSINS. Oh, I think it will be much less difficult than Greek.

STEPHEN. Well, I just want to say this before I leave you to yourselves. Dont let anything I have said about right and wrong prejudice you against this great chance in life. I have satisfied myself that the business is one of the highest character and a credit to our country. (*Emotionally.*) I am very proud of my father. I—(*Unable to proceed, he presses Cusins' hand and goes hastily into the shed, followed by Bilton.*)

Barbara and Cusins, left alone together, look at one another silently.

CUSINS. Barbara: I am going to accept this offer.

BARBARA. I thought you would.

CUSINS. You understand, dont you, that I had to decide without consulting you. If I had thrown the burden of the choice on you, you would sooner or later have despised me for it.

[24]**ryot** tenant farmer.

BARBARA. Yes; I did not want you to sell your soul for me any more than for this inheritance.

CUSINS. It is not the sale of my soul that troubles me: I have sold it too often to care about that. I have sold it for a professorship. I have sold it for an income. I have sold it to escape being imprisoned for refusing to pay taxes for hangmen's ropes and unjust wars and things that I abhor. What is all human conduct but the daily and hourly sale of our souls for trifles? What I am now selling it for is neither money nor position nor comfort, but for reality and for power.

BARBARA. You know that you will have no power, and that he has none.

CUSINS. I know. It is not for myself alone. I want to make power for the world.

BARBARA. I want to make power for the world too; but it must be spiritual power.

CUSINS. I think all power is spiritual: these cannons will not go off by themselves. I have tried to make spiritual power by teaching Greek. But the world can never be really touched by a dead language and a dead civilization. The people must have power; and the people cannot have Greek. Now the power that is made here can be wielded by all men.

BARBARA. Power to burn women's houses down and kill their sons and tear their husbands to pieces.

CUSINS. You cannot have power for good without having power for evil too. Even mother's milk nourishes murderers as well as heroes. This power which only tears men's bodies to pieces has never been so horribly abused as the intellectual power, the imaginative power, the poetic, religious power that can enslave men's souls. As a teacher of Greek I gave the intellectual man weapons against the common man. I now want to give the common man weapons against the inellectual man. I love the common people. I want to arm them against the lawyers, the doctors, the priests, the literary men, the professors, the artists, and the politicians, who, once in authority, are more disastrous and tyrannical than all the fools, rascals, and impostors. I want a power simple enough for common men to use, yet strong enough to force the intellectual oligarchy to use its genius for the general good.

BARBARA. Is there no higher power than that? (*Pointing to the shell.*)

CUSINS. Yes; but that power can destroy the higher powers just as a tiger can destroy a man: therefore Man must master that power first. I admitted this when the Turks and Greeks were last at war. My best pupil went out to fight for Hellas. My parting gift to him was not a copy of Plato's Republic, but a revolver and a hundred Undershaft cartridges. The blood of every Turk he shot—if he shot any—is on my head as well as on Undershaft's. That act committed me to this place for ever. Your father's challenge has beaten me. Dare I make war on war? I dare. I must. I will. And now, is it all over between us?

BARBARA (*touched by his evident dread of her answer*). Silly baby Dolly! How could it be!

CUSINS (*overjoyed*). Then you—you—you—Oh for my drum! (*He flourishes imaginary drumsticks.*)

BARBARA (*angered by his levity*). Take care, Dolly, take care. Oh, if only I could get away from you and from father and from it all! if I could have the wings of a dove and fly away to heaven!

CUSINS. And leave me!

BARBARA. Yes, you, and all the other naughty mischievous children of men. But I cant. I was happy in the Salvation Army for a moment. I escaped from the world into a paradise of enthusiasm and prayer and soul saving; but the moment our money ran short, it all came back to Bodger: it was he who saved our people: he, and the Prince of Darkness, my papa. Undershaft and Bodger: their hands stretch everywhere: when we feed a starving fellow creature, it is with their bread, because there is no other bread; when we tend the sick, it is in the hospitals they endow; if we turn from the churches they build, we must kneel on the stones of the streets they pave. As long as that lasts, there is no getting away from them. Turning our backs on Bodger and Undershaft is turning our backs on life.

CUSINS. I thought you were determined to turn your back on the wicked side of life.

BARBARA. There is no wicked side: life is all one. And I never wanted to shirk my share in whatever evil must be endured, whether it be sin or suffering. I wish I could cure you of middle-class ideas, Dolly.

CUSINS (*gasping*). Middle cl—! A snub! A social snub to me! from the daughter of a foundling!

BARBARA. That is why I have no class, Dolly: I come straight out of the heart of the whole people. If I were middle-class I should turn my back on my father's business; and we should both live in an artistic drawing room, with you reading the reviews in one corner, and I in the other at the piano, playing Schumann: both very superior persons, and neither of us a bit of use. Sooner than that, I would sweep out the guncotton shed, or be one of Bodger's barmaids. Do you know what would have happened if you had refused papa's offer?

CUSINS. I wonder!

BARBARA. I should have given you up and married the man who accepted it. After all, my dear old mother has more sense than any of you. I felt like her when I saw this place—felt that I must have it—that never, never, never could I let it go; only she thought it was the houses and the kitchen ranges and the linen and china, when it was really all the human souls to be saved: not weak souls in starved bodies, sobbing with gratitude for a scrap of bread and treacle, but fullfed, quarrelsome, snobbish, uppish creatures, all standing on their little rights and dignities, and thinking that my father ought to be greatly obliged to them for making so much money for him—and so he ought. That is where salvation is really wanted. My father shall never throw it in my teeth again that my converts were bribed with bread. (*She is transfigured.*) I have got rid of the bribe of bread. I have got rid of the bribe of heaven. Let God's work be done for its own sake: the work he had to create us to do because it cannot be done except by living men and women. When I die, let him be in my debt, not I in his; and let me forgive him as becomes a woman of my rank.

CUSINS. Then the way of life lies through the factory of death?

BARBARA. Yes, through the raising of hell to heaven and of man to God, through the unveiling of an eternal light in the Valley of The Shadow. (*Seizing him with both hands.*) Oh, did you think my courage would never come back? did you believe that I was a deserter? that I, who have stood in the streets, and taken my people to my heart, and talked of the holiest and greatest things with them, could ever turn back and chatter foolishly to fashionable people about nothing in a drawing room? Never, never, never, never: Major Barbara will die with the colors. Oh! and I have my dear little Dolly boy still; and he has found me my place and my work. Glory Hallelujah! (*She kisses him.*)

CUSINS. My dearest: consider my delicate health. I cannot stand as much happiness as you can.

BARBARA. Yes: it is not easy work being in love with me, is it? But it's good for you. (*She runs to the shed, and calls, childlike.*) Mamma! Mamma! (*Bilton comes out of the shed, followed by Undershaft.*) I want Mamma.

UNDERSHAFT. She is taking off her list slippers, dear. (*He passes on to Cusins.*) Well? What does she say?

CUSINS. She has gone right up into the skies.

LADY BRITOMART (*coming from the shed and stopping on the steps, obstructing Sarah, who follows with Lomax. Barbara clutches like a baby at her mother's skirt*). Barbara: when will you learn to be independent and to act and think for yourself? I know as well as possible what that cry of "Mamma, Mamma," means. Always running to me!

SARAH (*touching Lady Britomart's ribs with her finger tips and imitating a bicycle horn*). Pip! pip!

LADY BRITOMART (*highly indignant*). How dare you say Pip! pip! to me, Sarah? You are both very naughty children. What do you want, Barbara?

BARBARA. I want a house in the village to live in with Dolly. (*Dragging at the skirt.*) Come and tell me which one to take.

UNDERSHAFT (*to Cusins*). Six o'clock tomorrow morning, Euripides.

THE END

TOPICS FOR CRITICAL THINKING AND WRITING

The Play on the PAGE

1. What is the basic comic situation in Lady Britomart's dialogue with Stephen at the beginning of the play? Do we laugh with her or at her, or both? Explain.

2. When Undershaft is confused about which persons are his children, do we laugh with him or at him, or both? Explain. What sort of man had we expected? What sort of man does he seem to be in this scene?

3. In a paragraph characterize Barbara on the basis of her lines in Act 1.

4. The opening dialogue in Act 2, between Snobby Price and Rummy Mitchens, suggests that those who seek help from the Salvation Army are hypocrites. How does Shaw make Rummy likeable, and how does he prevent us from seeing Jenny and Barbara as mere dupes?

5. Is it a defect that Stephen, who was prominent in Act 1, plays only a small part in Act 3? Should his rebellion against his mother, in a way foreshad-owed in the first act, have been made more of? Or did Shaw rightly move to bigger game? Explain.

6. What arguments can be offered to support the view that Cusins, and not Barbara or Undershaft, is the central figure in the play? Do these arguments convince us that Cusins is as successfully created as Barbara and Undershaft, or do we find him less memorable?

7. Aristotle's terms *peripeteia* (reversal) and *anagnorisis* (recognition) are commonly used in discussions of tragedy (see page 34), but they can also be useful in discussions of comedy. What reversals and recognitions occur in *Major Barbara*? When Bill Walker says, "Wot prawce selvytion nah?" is this recognition the point toward which the play has been moving? Has he a point? The whole point?

8. Shaw once said, "It is the business of a writer of comedy to wound the susceptibilities of his audience. The classic definition of his function is 'the

chastening of morals by ridicule.'" Does *Major Barbara* wound susceptibilities? If so, to any purpose? Is the play a serious examination of capitalism, charity, and religion, or does the clowning (e.g., Lady Britomart's "I know your quiet, simple, refined, poetic people like Adolphus: quite content with the best of everything,") obliterate the ideological content? Explain. Consider Undershaft's speeches on power on pages 694 and 698. Are they contradictory? If so, do they indicate that Shaw is writing amusing speeches but is not seriously concerned with the development of an idea? Consider, too, Cusins' assertion (page 702) that he wishes to help the common man by arming him against the lawyer, the doctor, the priest, the literary man, the professor, and so on. How will the manufacture of weapons help the common man?

9. One of the chief theories of laughter is neatly stated in Thomas Hobbes's *Leviathan* (1651):

> *Sudden Glory,* is the passion which maketh those *Grimaces* called Laughter; and is caused either by some sudden act of their own, that pleaseth them; or by the apprehension of some deformed thing in another, in comparison whereof they suddenly applaud themselves.

If *Major Barbara* evokes laughter, is the laughter of Hobbes's sort? Does Hobbes's theory cover any or all laughable occurrences?

The Play on the STAGE

10. Shaw is known for his detailed stage directions, but of course he can specify only a relatively few of a performer's actions. Take the first fifteen or so speeches, and prepare a detailed commentary on how you would hope the actors would deliver them.

11. On one occasion Shaw said that the scene in which Barbara pits herself against Bill is a love scene. Reread the scene and think about staging it in a way that would bring out Shaw's view.

12. At the beginning of the final act, attention is drawn to the fact that Barbara is not wearing the Salvation Army uniform. Nothing is said of Cusins's garment. If you were directing the play, would you have him wear the uniform? Explain.

13. What actors—or persons known to your classmates—would you cast in the chief roles in the play?

A Context for *MAJOR BARBARA*

Selections from Shaw's Preface

[Shaw usually equipped the published versions of his plays with lengthy prefaces, not so much discussing the plays themselves as discussing issues associated with the plays. His preface to *Major Barbara* was no exception. We reprint here some of the most relevant comments.]

The Gospel of St. Andrew Undershaft

In the millionaire Undershaft I have represented a man who has become intellectually and spiritually as well as practically conscious of the irresistible natural truth which we all abhor and repudiate; to wit, that the greatest of our evils, and the worst of our crimes is poverty, and that our first duty, to which every other consideration should be sacrificed, is not to be poor. "Poor but honest," "the respectable poor," and such phrases are as intolerable and as immoral as "drunken but amiable," "fraudulent but a good after-dinner speaker," "splendidly criminal," or the like. Security, the chief pretense of civilization, cannot exist where the worst of dangers, the danger of poverty, hangs over everyone's head, and where the alleged protection of our persons from violence is only an accidental result of the existence of a police force whose real business is to force the poor man to see his children starve whilst idle people overfeed pet dogs with the money that might feed and clothe them.

. . .

Now what does this Let Him Be Poor mean? It means let him be weak. Let him be ignorant. Let him become a nucleus of disease. Let him be a standing exhibition and example of ugliness and dirt. Let him have rickety children. Let him be cheap, and drag his fellows down to his own price by selling himself to do their work. Let his habitations turn our cities into poisonous congeries of slums. Let his daughters infect our young men with the diseases of the streets, and his sons revenge him by turning the nation's manhood into scrofula, cowardice, cruelty, hypocrisy, political imbecility, and all the other fruits of oppression and malnutrition. Let the undeserving become still less deserving; and let the deserving lay up for himself, not treasures in heaven, but horrors in hell upon earth. This being so, is it really wise to let him be poor? Would he not do ten times less harm as a prosperous burglar, incendiary, ravisher or murderer, to the utmost limits of humanity's comparatively negligible impulses in these directions? Suppose we were to abolish all penalties for such activities, and decide that poverty is the one thing we will not tolerate—that every adult with less than, say, £365 a year, shall be painlessly but inexorably killed, and every hungry half naked child forcibly fattened and clothed, would not that be an enormous improvement on our existing system, which has already destroyed so many civilizations, and is visibly destroying ours in the same way?

Is there any radicle of such legislation in our parliamentary system? Well, there are two measures just sprouting in the political soil, which may conceivably grow to something valuable. One is the institution of a Legal Minimum Wage. The other, Old Age Pensions. But there is a better plan than either of these. Some time ago I mentioned the subject of Universal Old Age Pensions to my fellow Socialist Cobden-Sanderson, famous as an artist-craftsman in bookbinding and printing. "Why not Universal Pensions for Life?" said Cobden-Sanderson. In saying this, he solved the industrial problem at a stroke. At present we say callously to each citizen "If you want money, earn it" as if his having or not having it were a matter that concerned himself alone. We do not even secure for him the opportunity of earning it: on the contrary, we allow our industry to be organized in open dependence on the maintenance of "a reserve army of unemployed" for the sake of "elasticity." The sensible course would be Cobden-Sanderson's: that is, to give every man enough to live well on, so as to guarantee the community against the possibility of a case of the malignant disease of poverty, and then (necessarily) to see that he earned it.

Undershaft, the hero of Major Barbara, is simply a man who, having grasped the fact that poverty is a crime, knows that when society offered him the alternative of poverty or a lucrative trade in death and destruction, it offered him, not a choice between opulent villainy and humble virtue, but between energetic enterprise and cowardly infamy. His conduct stands the Kantian test, which Peter Shirley's does not. Peter Shirley is what we call the honest poor man. Undershaft is what we call the wicked rich one: Shirley is Lazarus, Undershaft Dives. Well, the misery of the world is due to the fact that the great mass of men act and believe as Peter Shirley acts and believes. If they acted and believed as Undershaft acts and believes, the immediate result would be a revolution of incalculable beneficence. To be wealthy, says Undershaft, is with me a point of honor for which I am prepared to kill at the risk of my own life. This preparedness is, as he says, the final test of sincerity. Like Froissart's medieval hero, who saw that "to rob and pill was a good life," he is not the dupe of that public sentiment against killing which is propagated and endowed by people who would otherwise be killed themselves, or of the mouth-honor paid to poverty and obedience by rich and insubordinate do-nothings who want to rob the poor without courage and command them without superiority. Froissart's knight, in placing the achievement of a good life before all the other duties—which indeed are not duties at all when they conflict with it, but plain wickedness—behaved bravely, admirably, and, in the final analysis, public-spiritedly. Medieval society, on the other hand, behaved very badly indeed in organizing itself so stupidly that a good life could be achieved by robbing and pilling. If the knight's contemporaries had been all as resolute as he, robbing and pilling would have been the shortest way to the gallows, just as, if we were all as resolute and clearsighted as Undershaft, an attempt to live by means of what is called "an independent income" would be the shortest way to the lethal chamber. But as, thanks to our political imbecility and personal cowardice (fruits of poverty, both), the best imitation of a good life now procurable is life on an independent income, all sensible people aim at securing such an income, and are, of course, careful to legalize and moralize both it and all the actions and sentiments which lead to it and support it as an institution. What else can they do? They know, of course, that they are rich because others are poor. But they cannot help that: it is for the poor to repudiate poverty when they have had enough of it. The thing can be done easily enough: the demonstrations to the contrary made by the economists, jurists, moralists and sentimentalists hired by the rich to defend them, or even doing the work gratuitously out of sheer folly and abjectness, impose only on those who want to be imposed on.

. . .

The Salvation Army

When *Major Barbara* was produced in London, the second act was reported in an important northern newspaper as a withering attack on the Salvation Army, and the despairing ejaculation of Barbara deplored by a London daily as a tasteless blasphemy. And they were set right, not by the professed critics of the theater, but by religious and philosophical publicists like Sir Oliver Lodge and Dr. Stanton Coit, and strenuous Nonconformist journalists like William Stead, who not only understood the act as well as the Salvationists themselves, but also saw it in its relation to the religious life of the nation, a life which seems to lie not only outside the sympathy of many of our theater critics, but actually outside their knowledge of society. Indeed nothing could be more ironically curious than the confrontation Major Barbara effected of the theater enthusiasts with the religious enthusiasts. On the one hand was the playgoer, always seeking pleasure, paying exorbitantly for it, suffering unbearable discomforts for it, and hardly ever getting it. On the other hand was the Salvationist, repudiating gaiety and courting effort and sacrifice, yet always in the wildest spirits, laughing, joking, singing, rejoicing, drumming, and tambourining: his life flying by in a flash of excitement, and his death arriving as a climax of triumph. And, if you please, the playgoer despising the Salvationist as a joyless person, shut out from the heaven of the theater, self-condemned to a life of hideous gloom; and the Salvationist mourning over the playgoer as over a prodigal with vine leaves in his hair, careering outrageously to hell amid the popping of champagne corks and the ribald laughter of sirens! Could misunderstanding be more complete, or sympathy worse misplaced?

Fortunately, the Salvationists are more accessible to the religious character of the drama than the playgoers to the gay energy and artistic fertility of religion. They can see, when it is pointed out to them, that a theater, as a place where two or three are gathered together, takes from that divine presence an inalienable sanctity of which the grossest and profanest farce can no more deprive it than a hypocritical sermon by a snobbish bishop can desecrate Westminster Abbey. But in our professional playgoers this indispensable preliminary conception of sanctity seems wanting. They talk of actors as mimes and mummers, and I fear, think of dramatic authors as liars and pandars, whose main business is the voluptuous soothing of the tired city speculator when what he calls the serious business of the day is over. Passion, the life of drama, means nothing to them but primitive sexual excitement: such phrases as "impassioned poetry" or "passionate love of truth" have fallen quite out of their vocabulary and been replaced by "passional crime" and the like. They assume, as far as I can gather, that people in whom passion has a larger scope are passionless and therefore uninteresting. Consequently they come to think of religious people as people who are not interesting and not amusing. And so, when Barbara cuts the regular Salvation Army jokes, and snatches a kiss from her lover across his drum, the devotees of the theater think they ought to appear shocked, and conclude that the whole play is an elaborate mockery of the Army. And then either hypocritically rebuke me for mocking, or foolishly take part in the supposed mockery!

Even the handful of mentally competent critics got into difficulties over my demonstration of the economic deadlock in which the Salvation Army finds itself. Some of them thought that the Army would not have taken money from a distiller and a cannon founder: others thought it should not have taken it: all assumed more or less definitely that it reduced itself to absurdity or hypocrisy by taking it. On the first point the reply of the Army itself was prompt and conclusive. As one of its officers said, they would take money from the devil himself and be only too glad to get it out of his hands and into God's. They gratefully acknowledged that publicans not only give them money but allow them to collect it in the bar—sometimes even when there is a Salvation meeting outside preaching teetotalism. In fact, they questioned the verisimilitude of the play, not because Mrs Baines took the money, but because Barbara refused it.

On the point that the Army ought not to take such money, its justification is obvious. It must take the money because it cannot exist without money, and there is no other money to be had. Practically all the spare money in the country consists of a mass of rent, interest, and profit, every penny of which is bound up with crime, drink, prostitution, disease, and all the evil fruits of poverty, as inextricably as with enterprise, wealth, commercial probity, and national prosperity. The notion that you can earmark certain coins as tainted is an unpractical individualist superstition. Nonetheless the fact that all our money is tainted gives a very severe shock to earnest young souls when some dramatic instance of the taint first makes them conscious of it.

. . .

Weaknesses of the Salvation Army

For the present, however, it is not my business to flatter the Salvation Army. Rather must I point out to it that it has almost as many weaknesses as the Church of England itself. It is building up a business organization which will compel it eventually to see that its present staff of enthusiast-commanders shall be succeeded by a bureaucracy of men of business who will be no better than bishops, and perhaps a good deal more unscrupulous. That has always happened sooner or later to great orders founded by saints; and the order founded by St William Booth is not exempt from the same danger. It is even more dependent than the Church on rich people who would cut off supplies at once if it began to preach that indispensable revolt against poverty which must also be a revolt against riches. It is hampered by a heavy contingent of pious elders who are not really Salvationists at all, but Evangelicals of the old school. It still, as Commissioner Howard affirms, "sticks to Moses," which is flat nonsense at this time of day if the Commissioner means, as I am afraid he does, that the Book of Genesis contains a trustworthy scientific account of the origin of species, and that the god to whom Jephthah sacrificed his daughter is any less obviously a tribal idol than Dagon or Chemosh.

Further, there is still too much other-worldliness about the Army. Like Frederick's grenadier, the Salvationist wants to live forever (the most monstrous way of crying for the moon); and though it is evident to anyone who has ever heard General Booth and his best officers that they would work as hard for human salvation as they do at present if they believed that death would be the end of them individually, they and their followers have a bad habit of talking as if the Sal-

vationists were heroically enduring a very bad time on earth as an investment which will bring them in dividends later on in the form, not of a better life to come for the whole world, but of an eternity spent by themselves personally in a sort of bliss which would bore any active person to a second death. Surely the truth is that the Salvationists are unusually happy people. And is it not the very diagnostic of true salvation that it shall overcome the fear of death? Now the man who has come to believe that there is no such thing as death, the change so called being merely the transition to an exquisitely happy and utterly careless life, has not overcome the fear of death at all: on the contrary, it has overcome him so completely that he refuses to die on any terms whatever. I do not call a Salvationist really saved until he is ready to lie down cheerfully on the scrap heap, having paid scot and lot and something over, and let his eternal life pass on to renew its youth in the battalions of the future.

Then there is the nasty lying habit called confession, which the Army encourages because it lends itself to dramatic oratory, with plenty of thrilling incident. For my part, when I hear a convert relating the violences and oaths and blasphemies he was guilty of before he was saved, making out that he was a very terrible fellow then and is the most contrite and chastened of Christians now, I believe him no more than I believe the millionaire who says he came up to London or Chicago as a boy with only three halfpence in his pocket.

. . .

And here my disagreement with the Salvation Army, and with all propagandists of the Cross (which I loathe as I loathe all gibbets) becomes deep indeed. Forgiveness, absolution, atonement, are figments: punishment is only a pretense of canceling one crime by another; and you can no more have forgiveness without vindictiveness than you can have a cure without a disease. You will never get a high morality from people who conceive that their misdeeds are revocable and pardonable, or in a society where absolution and expiation are officially provided for us all. The demand may be very real; but the supply is spurious. Thus Bill Walker, in my play, having assaulted the Salvation Lass, presently finds himself overwhelmed with an intolerable conviction of sin under the skilled treatment of Barbara. Straightway he begins to try to unassault the lass and deruffianize his deed, first by getting punished for it in kind, and, when that relief is denied him, by fining himself a pound to compensate the girl.

He is foiled both ways. He finds the Salvation Army is inexorable as fact itself. It will not punish him: it will not take his money. It will not tolerate a redeemed ruffian: it leaves him no means of salvation except ceasing to be a ruffian. In doing this, the Salvation Army instinctively grasps the central truth of Christianity, and discards its central superstition: that central truth being the vanity of revenge and punishment, and that central superstition the salvation of the world by the gibbet.

For, be it noted, Bill has assaulted an old and starving woman also; and for this worse offense he feels no remorse whatever, because she makes it clear that her malice is as great as his own. "Let her have the law of me, as she said she would," says Bill: "what I done to her is no more on what you might call my conscience than sticking a pig." This shows a perfectly natural and wholesome state of mind on his part. The old woman, like the law she threatens him with, is perfectly ready to play the game of retaliation with him: to rob him if he steals, to flog him if he strikes, to murder him if he kills. By example and precept the law and public opinion teach him to impose his will on others by anger, violence, and cruelty, and to wipe off the moral score by punishment. That is sound Crosstianity. But his Crosstianity has got entangled with something which Barbara calls Christianity, and which unexpectedly causes her to refuse to play the hangman's game of Satan casting out Satan. She refuses to prosecute a drunken ruffian; she converses on equal terms with a blackguard to whom no lady should be seen speaking in the public street: in short, she imitates Christ. Bill's conscience reacts to this just as naturally as it does to the old woman's threats. He is placed in a position of unbearable moral inferiority, and strives by every means in his power to escape from it, whilst he is still quite ready to meet the abuse of the old woman by attempting to smash a mug on her face. And that is the triumphant justification of Barbara's Christianity as against our system of judicial punishment and the vindictive villain-thrashings and "poetic justice" of the romantic stage.

. . .

In short, when Major Barbara says that there are no scoundrels, she is right: there are no absolute scoundrels, though there are impracticable people of whom I shall treat presently. Every reasonable man (and woman) is a potential scoundrel and a potential good citizen. What a man is depends on his character; but what he does, and what we think of what he does, depends on his circumstances. The characteristics that ruin a man in one class make him eminent in another. The characters that behave differently in different circumstances behave alike in similar circumstances. Take a common English character like that of Bill Walker. We meet Bill everywhere: on the judicial bench, on the episcopal bench, in the Privy Council, at the War Office and Admiralty, as well as in the Old Bailey dock or in the ranks of casual unskilled labor. And the morality of Bill's characteristics varies with these various circumstances. The faults of the burglar are the qualities of the financier: the manners and habits of a duke would cost a city clerk his situation. In short, though character is independent of circumstances, conduct is not; and our moral judgments of character are not: both are circumstantial. Take any condition of life in which the circumstances are for a mass of men practically alike: felony, the House of Lords, the factory, the stables, the gipsy encampment or where you please! In spite of diversity of character and temperament, the conduct and morals of the individuals in each group are as predicable and as alike in the main as if they were a flock of sheep, morals being mostly only social habits and circumstantial necessities.

The Play in PERFORMANCE

When *Major Barbara* opened in London in 1905, Shaw was a well-known dramatist and the play inevitably attracted much comment. The reviews were mixed—a good deal of praise for its brilliance, a good deal of regret for its talkiness, and a good deal of anger at its message, sometimes all in a single review. The reviewer in the *Daily Telegraph*, for instance, spoke of the play's "desolating cleverness . . . that is purely destructive and never constructive."

Throughout his life Shaw heard pretty much the same kinds of judgements. He was willing to accept the praise for his "cleverness," but he customarily replied to charges that he was destructive by arguing that his critics were stuck in some sort of old-fashioned thinking and simply could not bring themselves to see that the destructiveness was a prelude to a new way of thinking and of living. As for the common complaint that his plays were all talk, he replied that of course his plays were full of talk, "just as Raphael's pictures are all paint, Michael Angelo's statues all marble, Beethoven's symphonies all noise." (This particular witty response, much later than *Major Barbara*, comes from "The Play of Ideas," an essay of 1950.) But the talk, Shaw insisted, has ideas behind it. Further, the talk *is* highly dramatic he argued, but in a special way. Here we quote again from the essay of 1950:

> Opera taught me to shape my plays into recitatives, arias, duets, trios, ensemble finales, and bravura pieces to display the technical accomplishments of the executants. . . .

Consider, as an example, this duet from *Major Barbara*. Undershaft has offered to take into his business Cusins, and in the course of bargaining Cusins demands ten percent of the profit:

UNDERSHAFT (*taken aback*). Ten per cent! Why, man, do you know what my profits are?
CUSINS. Enormous, I hope: otherwise I shall require twenty-five per cent.
UNDERSHAFT. But, Mr. Cusins, this is a serious matter of business. You are not bringing any capital into the concern.

CUSINS. What! No capital! Is my mastery of Greek no capital? Is my access to the subtlest thought, the loftiest poetry yet attained by humanity, no capital? My character! my intellect! my life! my career! what Barbara calls my soul! are these no capital? say another word, and I double my salary.
UNDERSHAFT. Be reasonable—
CUSINS. Mr. Undershaft: you have my terms. Take them or leave them.
UNDERSHAFT (*recovering himself*). Very well. I note your terms; and I offer you half.
CUSINS (*disgusted*). Half!
UNDERSHAFT (*firmly*). Half.
CUSINS. You call yourself a gentleman; and you offer me half!!
UNDERSHAFT. I do not call myself a gentleman; but I offer you half.

Given dialogue like this, it is easy to see the truth of Shaw's statement that he learned from opera, and hard to see how anyone can regard the play as undramatic or talky.

The fact, however, is (as we have said) that the play received mixed reviews. But even the most negative critics and spectators—chiefly those who were deeply offended by the shocking ideas—recognized its brilliance, and the play has had a very strong stage history. It is often staged in colleges and universities, and perhaps every eight or ten years it receives a major professional production. A film version in 1941 starred Wendy Hiller and Rex Harrison.

American Theater Comes of Age

Death of a Salesman is widely regarded as the indispensible American play. Pictured here are Kevin Anderson as Biff (left) and Brian Dennehy as Willy (right and in detail) in the 1999 production that opened on February 10, 1999—fifty years to the day from the landmark play's world premiere.

At the height of his fame in the late 1920s, Eugene O'Neill was asked what the theater was like at the beginning of the century when his father was barnstorming in the ever-popular Romantic melodrama *The Count of Monte Cristo*. O'Neill felt no duty to defend his father's era; he called it "the dark age, closed shop, star system, amusement racket. . . . It's difficult in these days, when the native playwright can function in comparative freedom, to realize that in that benighted period a play of any imagination, originality or integrity by an American was almost automatically barred from a hearing in our theater." Almost every serious nineteenth-century writer who spoke to the issue shared O'Neill's judgment. In *Democratic Vistas* (1871), Walt Whitman wryly noted, "Of what is called the drama or dramatic presentation in the United States . . . I would say it deserves to be treated with the same gravity, and on a par with the questions of ornamental confectionary at public dinners, or the arrangements of curtains and hangings in a ballroom—nor more, nor less."

Nowadays scholars tend to be a bit less harsh, primarily because they have widened the net of "dramatic presentations." True, one cannot name a major nineteenth-century American play, but between the two Irishmen Sheridan and Shaw who bookend the century, can we find much in the British theater to earn our admiration? The history of drama in the century, a wag remarked, was itself a tragedy. American playwrights followed British and French models (largely melodramas and sentimental comedies) because they had to struggle so hard to be allowed to exist. We were, after all, a nation founded by Puritans who saw the theater as "the devil's playhouse." Although the British troops during the Revolutionary War conducted amateur theatricals, the fledging American Congress passed a law stating that "any person holding any office under the United States, who shall act, promote, encourage or attend plays, shall be deemed unworthy to hold such office and shall be accordingly dismissed" (1778). Ironically, the best native play written between the eighteenth and twentieth centuries is the very first professional production after American nationhood: Royall Tyler's *The Contrast*, (1787) built on the solid dramatic armature of Sheridan's *School for Scandal*.

But if we examine the range of nineteenth-century American *theater*, we find more of interest than is initially apparent. With no inhibiting model of "legitimate" theater, Americans develop a unique variety of theatrical performances and entertainments: minstrel shows, showboat extravaganzas, wild west shows, street processions, vaudeville. And they naturalize melodrama (a French import), developing a fiercely simplistic pictorial form that then and now appeals to simple emotions and American egalitarianism. These performance forms move right into mass art in the twentieth century and hence begin to claim scholarly interest. But Whitman and O'Neill's dour assessments remain valid: There is no serious nineteenth-century dramatic art to contemplate.

When the new drama of Europe erupts at century's end, American artists and intellectuals are aware of what's happening. The doctrines of Realism and Modernism soon find American champions and disciples in fiction—William Dean Howells, Henry James, Edith Wharton, later Stephen Crane, Theodore Dreiser, Willa Cather—but drama stands back because the Little Theater revolution that had created venues for the new European drama finds no fertile ground here. A fascinating case in point concerns a play written by a successful actor/playwright, James A. Herne, who had established himself within the popular boundaries of the theater of his time. Deeply influenced by the new radical currents, Herne decided to write an Ibsenite play that would attack the double standard whereby a man is socially permitted to sow his wild oats while a woman is morally condemned and ostracized for doing the same. All of Herne's attempts to produce the resulting play, *Margaret Fleming,* ended in bitter disappointment. No theater manager would produce so radical a play. Finally, on the advice of William Dean Howells, Herne rented a small auditorium in Boston, and with support from the local artistic community, put on *Margaret Fleming* for three performances. Indeed, the play created a stir among the Boston *literati,* but it clearly would have no professional afterlife, despite Herne's own production of the play some years later in New York. Herne ironically assessed audience response: "The public doesn't want a good play. They say, 'Write a bad play, Jim. Not too bad, but bad enough.'" He returned professionally to the world of common taste.

But gradually things began to change: In 1907 the actress Alla Nazimova gave a season of Ibsen plays in New York. Later, O'Neill recalled the profound impact it created in giving him his "first conception of a theater where truth might live." Four years later he was similarly impressed by the visit of the Irish Abbey Players with their productions of plays by his ethnic compatriots Yeats, Synge, and Lady Gregory. Meanwhile, the texts of the new drama were coming available: From 1906 to 1908 Everyman brought out an eleven-volume edition of Ibsen's works. The year 1912 saw the publication of cheap editions of Ibsen and Strindberg, and Synge's plays were published. But, most importantly, the Little Theater movement finally began to strike American roots. In 1910 Chicago—which for a time led American literary innovation with Harriett Monroe's *Poetry Magazine*—saw the founding of the Chicago Little Theatre, committed to the production of new European plays. In 1915, as a downtown area of Manhattan began to define itself as a Bohemian enclave—Greenwich Village—a group called the Washington Square Players was established. (In the 1920s it was to transform itself into the influential Theatre Guild.) And in 1916 Sheldon Cheney founded a periodical called *Theatre Arts Magazine,* which in its first issue lamented the absence of an American Yeats or Bernard Shaw. Its second issue welcomed a new little theater dedicated to new American drama that had been founded the previous year in Provincetown, Massachusetts by young radicals such as George Cram ("Jig") Cook, Susan Glaspell, John Reed, and Marguerite Zorach; at their new New York base on MacDougal Street in Greenwich Village, the Provincetown Players were presenting a play there by a young Irishman who had been vacationing on the Cape.

Déjà vu: It was like the Moscow Art finding Chekhov. Eugene O'Neill provided the Provincetown with what it desperately needed: an original, distinctive voice that helped shape the theater's vision of itself. At first, this dramatic voice was naturalistic: The first O'Neill productions were short, gritty, atmospheric, autobiographical plays about the sea based on O'Neill's earlier years as a merchant seaman. (Four of the plays, set on the same merchant ship, are often presented as an evening's bill under the fictional name of that ship, *S.S. Glencairn.*) But when asked whether he considered his lightly plotted (by contemporary standards) plays "realistic," O'Neill replied, "That term is used loosely on the stage, where most of the so-called realistic plays deal only with the appearance of things, while a truly realistic play deals with what might be called the soul of the character, . . . a thing which makes the character that person and no other. Strindberg's *Dance of Death* is an example of that real realism."

Late Strindberg as a model of realism? What had happened was this: Twenty years separate the realistic *Miss Julie* from the antinaturalist *Ghost Sonata.* In Europe, antirealism arose in dialectical response to a realism that had established itself. (André Antoine was made head of one branch of the *Comédie Française.*) But because of the generation-long delay in America's entry into modern theater, realistic and counter-realistic texts arrived *at the same time,* and the European experience was telescoped.

So, paradoxically, realism in America began to be attacked by would-be renovators *before* a serious realistic theater had been created. And, indeed, O'Neill was soon to provide the Provincetown with its greatest successes in the famous antirealistic plays *The Emperor Jones* and *The Hairy Ape*.

But perhaps the greatest sign that a new dramatic and theatrical era had begun was the fact that the pessimistic young Irish-American playwright was not only accepted on Broadway without sentimental compromise but was hailed as a potential dramatic savior. In the years 1920 and 1921 O'Neill received consecutive Pulitzer Prizes (no Tonys yet) for *Beyond the Horizon* and *Anna Christie*. A dying James O'Neill managed to see the former, and, true to the values of *his* theater, asked his now celebrated son, "Do you think people go to the theater to be *depressed?*" Soon, O'Neill was to be joined by a host of young playwrights—Elmer Rice, Maxwell Anderson, Sidney Howard, George Kelly, Sophie Treadwell, S.N. Berhman, Robert Sherwood—who weren't afraid to take the risk.

EUGENE O'Neill

Eugene O'Neill (1888–1953), the son of an actor, was born in a hotel room near New York City's Broadway and spent his early years traveling with his parents throughout the United States. He entered Princeton University in 1906 but left before the end of the first year. In 1909 he traveled to Honduras looking for gold, contracted malaria, and returned to the United States in 1910. After touring briefly with his father's company, he shipped to Buenos Aires, jumped ship there, did odd jobs, shipped to South Africa, and returned to the United States in 1911. The following year he learned that he had tuberculosis. In a sanatorium he began seriously reading plays, and in 1916 he joined the Provincetown Players, who put on some of his one-act plays. *The Emperor Jones* (1920), produced by the Provincetown Players in New York City, was his first major play. In time he was awarded four Pulitzer Prizes (one, given posthumously was for *A Long Day's Journey into Night*, written in 1940 but not produced until 1955), and a Nobel Prize.

■■■■■■■■■■■■■■■

COMMENTARY ON *THE EMPEROR JONES*

The gist of the story of *The Emperor Jones* is simply this: Jones, a black fugitive from a chain gang, has turned up on an island in the West Indies and established himself as emperor. By his own admission he has tyrannized his subjects, and he was able to get away with it because they believed that he could be killed only by a silver bullet. (This is the *antecedent action;* we learn it during the play, but it reports what happened before the play begins.) At the beginning of the play, hearing that a rebellion is in progress, Jones confidently sets out to leave the island; he becomes increasingly terrified, and at the end of the play he is shot with a silver bullet.

This is moderately interesting and not totally different from some historical episodes. For example, President Guillaume Sam of Haiti boasted he would kill himself with a silver bullet, but he was hacked to pieces by his oppressed subjects in 1915, only five years before O'Neill wrote *The Emperor Jones*. A century earlier, Henri Christophe, a slave who had become the merciless ruler of part of Haiti, shot himself when confronted with an insurrection. O'Neill knew these bits of history and used them to shape *The Emperor Jones*. However, even if he had not changed some facts, a play about Sam or Christophe inevitably would—if it were any good—be very different from an encyclopedia entry on them because, in Ezra Pound's words, a play is made not out of words but out of "persons moving about on a stage using words."

Let's begin with the stage and its setting. When the curtain goes up on a performance of *The Emperor Jones*, the audience sees "the audience chamber in the palace of the Emperor." It is furnished solely with "one huge chair. . . . painted a dazzling, eye-smiting scarlet," a cushion that serves as a footstool, and two scarlet mats that go "from the foot of the throne to the two entrances." This stage, at least in the context of what follows, "says" a lot. It conveys Jones's dominance, for he alone can sit in the room, and it conveys something of his bloody career, for if the scarlet throne on which Jones sits at first suggests royalty, it also (in retrospect) suggests the blood that surrounds his career. Whether or not O'Neill was conscious of the fact when he was writing the play, the huge scarlet chair, which at the start is boldly emblematic of Jones both as Emperor and as murderer, makes a notable contrast to the "little reddish-purple hole under his left breast" when his corpse is brought onstage at the end of the play. The imperial murderer has diminished to this.

The play uses only two other sets, and these are almost one: the edge of the Great Forest and within the Great Forest. The Forest, in the context of the action, says something. O'Neill tells us, in his first description of it, that it gives an impression of "relentless immobility" and of "brooding, implacable silence." Fleeing through the forest Jones becomes terrified, and we see that the dark forest is, in part at least, the jungle of the human mind, the world of inarticulate, elemental passions that seethe beneath the fragile surface of reason. (*The Emperor Jones* belongs, at least roughly, to the movement called **expressionism,** in which scenery is commonly used not to present an image of the external world but, rather, to convey a character's state of mind. (See the Glossary.) The darkness of the jungle, a strong contrast to the brightly illuminated throne room where Jones was the confident master, provides us with an example of the way in which a dramatist uses lighting—or, rather, darkness—symbolically.

Among the stock dramatic types of the black man available to O'Neill in 1920, the chief were the Tom (faithful black retainer), the Buffoon (clownish lazy servant), the Bull (villain who wants to rape white women), and the Tragic Mulatto (hovering between two races.) Almost all depictions of blacks on the American stage of the time fell into these classifications. O'Neill, in a remarkable step forward in the history of American drama and, therefore, in the history of American thought, used none of these stereotypes. (In *The Emperor Jones* the lazy man is not the black, who has diligently learned the language of the islanders and who for two years worked hard and efficiently at his job of robbing his subjects; the lazy man is the white man, Smithers, who in ten years has not bothered to learn the language.)

Today, some seventy years after O'Neill wrote the play, inevitably we are disturbed by some of its racist implications, especially by what seems to be the implication that a black more quickly than a white reverts to the condition of the "primitive" human being. Indeed, we can find traces of racism in the play. For instance, O'Neill's first description of Jones says that "his features are typically negroid, yet there is something decidedly distinctive about his face—an underlying strength of will, a hardy, self-reliant confidence in himself that inspires respect." The "yet" is very troublesome, and we can all wish that O'Neill had written "and" instead of "yet." Nevertheless, the actor Paul Robeson, the African American who knew O'Neill best, never suggested that O'Neill was a racist. On the contrary, Robeson had nothing but praise for O'Neill, whom he called his "dear friend," and who, in *Paul Robeson Speaks,* says that O'Neill "has had many Negro friends and appreciated them for their true worth" (p. 71). Langston Hughes and W. E. B. Du Bois were among the other African Americans who praised O'Neill.

In fact, O'Neill was far ahead of most whites of his time in presenting a black whose face showed "an underlying strength of will, a hardy, self-reliant confidence," and whose eyes showed "a keen, cunning in-

telligence." If these words put us in mind of any type, it is, paradoxically, the rugged white individualist who was so worshiped in the nineteenth and early twentieth centuries. O'Neill gives us not a stereotypical black man (and none of the stereotypes was flattering) but a fresh conception, a black who has the virtues and faults of white society, of America as it was and is, and perhaps of mankind. (The very name *Jones* suggests Everyman—though *Brutus* adds to it a sense of high Roman dignity, a sense of grotesque incongruity, as well as a hint of the "brute" that is beneath the clothes of every person, white or black.) Jones is quite explicit about his code: His aim is to get rich in the great white man's way by hard work and by cunning immorality on a grand scale.

JONES. . . . You heah what I tells you, Smithers. Dere's little stealin' like you does, and dere's big stealin' like I does. For de little stealin' dey gits you in jail soon or late. For de big stealin' dey makes you Emperor and puts you in de Hall o' Fame when you croaks. (*Reminiscently.*) If dey's one thing I learns in ten years on de Pullman ca's listenin' to de white quality talk, it's dat same fact. And when I gits a chance to use it I winds up Emperor in two years.

Smithers is no less unscrupulous or cruel than Jones is, but he simply does not have Jones's courage, perseverance, intelligence, and vision. In short, O'Neill gives us a fresh, fully realized picture of believable human beings, and we should not be deceived by the funny spelling into thinking that Jones is the conventional black man that existed on the stage up to O'Neill's time.

It should be mentioned, too, that O'Neill strongly and successfully urged that the role be played by Charles Gilpin, a black actor who had played only minor parts in essentially white plays. For instance, he had played the small role of a slave in John Drinkwater's *Abraham Lincoln.* O'Neill somehow became acquainted with him, and Gilpin became the first Emperor Jones—and the first black man to play a major role in an integrated cast. Today, when all casts are integrated, we can hardly imagine how astounding it was not to use a white actor in blackface, but even as late as 1943, when Paul Robeson was playing Othello, there were surprised murmurs about a black man doing the role.

In any case—and this is perhaps the central point—although it sounds astounding to say so, O'Neill did not see the play as essentially about a black man. He was deeply influenced by the psychology of C. G. Jung, who in *Psychology of the Unconscious* (1912, translated 1917) argued that "each individual inherits a residue from the significant memories of the human race." The operative words are "the human race." Of course, Jung granted that the individual is also influenced by his or her particular culture, but essentially, he said, we all share an instinctual life. We draw, he claimed, on some sort of human collective memory, hence, the communal fear of night and the need for a god. In Jones's case the memory of a god takes the form of a crocodile god (not surprising for someone of African origin), but in someone else it would take a different form, such as a storm god for an Icelander. In short, O'Neill was writing about what he considered to be a universal condition, though of course to set forth this condition he had to use individuals. It should be mentioned that the idea that *all* of us, under certain kinds of conditions, will revert to our "primitive" origins was fairly widespread from the late nineteenth century and can be seen in the white man Kurtz's degeneration in Joseph Conrad's *Heart of Darkness* and in many works by Jack London, most notably in *Call of the Wild*.

Finally, something should be said about O'Neill's use of Black English Vernacular, or, rather, about his use of spelling to indicate Jones's pronunciation, for instance "dat" for "that" and "dis" for "this." Today such spelling offends many readers, but in O'Neill's day it was regularly used by African American writers as well as by white writers. One has only to look at the works of Charles Waddell Chestnutt, Paul Laurence Dunbar, Zora Neale Hurston, and Langston Hughes to verify this assertion. O'Neill's spelling, like the spelling of these black authors, was an effort at realism—an effort to catch distinctive speech.

THE EMPEROR JONES
Eugene O'Neill

CHARACTERS

BRUTUS JONES, *emperor*
HENRY SMITHERS, *a Cockney trader*
AN OLD NATIVE WOMAN
LEM, *a native chief*
SOLDIERS, *adherents of Lem*
THE LITTLE FORMLESS FEARS
JEFF
THE NEGRO CONVICTS
THE PRISON GUARD

THE PLANTERS
THE AUCTIONEER
THE SLAVES
THE CONGO WITCH-DOCTOR
THE CROCODILE GOD

The action of the play takes place on an island in the West Indies as yet not self-determined by white Marines. The form of native government is, for the time being, an empire.

SCENE 1

SCENE: *The audience chamber in the palace of the Emperor—a spacious, high-ceilinged room with bare, white-washed walls. The floor is of white tiles. In the rear, to the left of center, a wide archway giving out on a portico with white pillars. The palace is evidently situated on high ground for beyond the portico nothing can be seen but a vista of distant hills, their summits crowned with thick groves of palm trees. In the right wall, center, a smaller arched doorway leading to the living quarters of the palace. The room is bare of furniture with the exception of one huge chair made of uncut wood which stands at center, its back to rear. This is very apparently the Emperor's throne. It is painted a dazzling, eye-smiting scarlet. There is a brilliant orange cushion on the seat and another smaller one is placed on the floor to serve as a footstool. Strips of matting, dyed scarlet, lead from the foot of the throne to the two entrances.*

It is late afternoon but the sunlight still blazes yellowly beyond the portico and there is an oppressive burden of exhausting heat in the air.

As the curtain rises, a native Negro woman sneaks in cautiously from the entrance on the right. She is very old, dressed in cheap calico, bare-footed, a red bandana handkerchief covering all but a few stray wisps of white hair. A bundle bound in colored cloth is carried over her shoulder on the end of a stick. She hesitates beside the doorway, peering back as if in extreme dread of being discovered. Then she begins to glide noiselessly, a step at a time, toward the doorway in the rear. At this moment, Smithers appears beneath the portico.

Smithers is a tall, stoop-shouldered man about forty. His bald head, perched on a long neck with an enormous Adam's apple, looks like an egg. The tropics have tanned his naturally pasty face with its small, sharp features to a sickly yellow, and native rum has painted his pointed nose to a startling red. His little, washy-blue eyes are red-rimmed and dart about him like a ferret's. His expression is one of unscrupulous meanness, cowardly and dangerous. He is dressed in a worn riding suit of dirty white drill, puttees, spurs, and wears a white cork helmet. A cartridge belt with an automatic revolver is around his waist. He carries a riding whip in his hand. He sees the woman and stops to watch her suspiciously. Then, making up his mind, he steps quickly on tiptoe into the room. The woman, looking back over her shoulder continually, does not see him until it is too late. When she does Smithers springs forward and grabs her firmly by the shoulder. She struggles to get away, fiercely but silently.

SMITHERS (*tightening his grasp—roughly*). Easy! None o' that, me birdie. You can't wriggle out now. I got me 'ooks on yer.

WOMAN (*seeing the uselessness of struggling, gives way to frantic terror, and sinks to the ground, embracing his knees supplicatingly*). No tell him! No tell him, Mister!

SMITHERS (*with great curiosity*). Tell 'im? (*Then scornfully.*) Oh, you mean 'is bloomin' Majesty. What's the gaime, any 'ow? What are you sneakin' away for? Been stealin' a bit, I s'pose. (*He taps her bundle with his riding whip significantly.*)

WOMAN (*shaking her head vehemently*). No, me no steal.

SMITHERS. Bloody liar! But tell me what's up. There's somethin' funny goin' on. I smelled it in the air first thing I

Paul Robeson was not the first actor to play Brutus Jones in O'Neill's The Emperor Jones—that honor goes to another African-American actor, Charles Gilpin—but Robeson was the first to play it on Broadway. For a picture of Robeson as Othello, see page 923.

got up this mornin'. You blacks are up to some devilment. This palace of 'is is like a bleedin' tomb. Where's all the 'ands?

(*The woman keeps sullenly silent. Smithers raises his whip threateningly.*)

Ow, yer won't, won't yer? I'll show yer what's what.

WOMAN (*coweringly*). I tell, Mister. You no hit. They go—all go. (*She makes a sweeping gesture toward the hills in the distance.*)

SMITHERS. Run away—to the 'ills?

WOMAN. Yes, Mister. Him Emperor—Great Father. (*She touches her forehead to the floor with a quick mechanical jerk.*) Him sleep after eat. Then they go—all go. Me old woman. Me left only. Now me go too.

SMITHERS (*his astonishment giving way to an immense, mean satisfaction*). Ow! So that's the ticket! Well, I know bloody well wot's in the air—when they runs orf to the 'ills. The tom-tom 'll be thumping out there bloomin' soon. (*With extreme vindictiveness.*) And I'm bloody glad of it, for one! Serve 'im right! Puttin' on airs, the stinkin' nigger! 'Is Majesty! Gawd blimey! I only 'opes I'm there when they takes 'im out to shoot 'im. (*Suddenly.*) 'E's still 'ere all right, ain't 'e?

WOMAN. Yes. Him sleep.

SMITHERS. 'E's bound to find out soon as 'e wakes up. 'E's cunnin' enough to know when 'is time's come.

(*He goes to the doorway on right and whistles shrilly with his fingers in his mouth. The old woman springs to her feet and runs out of the doorway, rear. Smithers goes after her, reaching for his revolver.*)

Stop or I'll shoot! (*Then stopping—indifferently.*) Pop orf then, if yer like, yer black cow. (*He stands in the doorway, looking after her.*)

(*Jones enters from the right. He is a tall, powerfully-built, full-blooded Negro of middle age. His features are typically negroid, yet there is something decidedly distinctive about his face—an underlying strength of will, a hardy, self-reliant confidence in himself that inspires respect. His eyes are alive with a keen, cunning intelligence. In manner he is shrewd, suspicious, evasive. He wears a light blue uniform coat, sprayed with brass buttons, heavy gold chevrons on his shoulders, gold braid on the collar, cuffs, etc. His pants are bright red with a light blue stripe down the side. Patent-leather laced boots with brass spurs, and a belt with a long-barreled, pearl-handled revolver in a holster complete his make up. Yet there is something not altogether ridiculous about his grandeur. He has a way of carrying it off.*)

JONES (*not seeing anyone—greatly irritated and blinking sleepily—shouts*). Who dare whistle dat way in my palace? Who dare wake up de Emperor? I'll git de hide fravled off some o' you niggers sho'!

SMITHERS (*showing himself—in a manner half-afraid and half-defiant*). It was me whistled to yer. (*As Jones frowns angrily.*) I got news for yer.

JONES (*putting on his suavest manner, which fails to cover up his contempt for the white man*). Oh, it's you, Mister Smithers. (*He sits down on his throne with easy dignity.*) What news you got to tell me?

SMITHERS (*coming close to enjoy his discomfiture*). Don't yer notice nothin' funny today?

JONES (*coldly*). Funny? No. I ain't perceived nothin' of de kind!

SMITHERS. Then yer ain't so foxy as I thought yer was. Where's all your court? (*Sarcastically.*) The Generals and the Cabinet Ministers and all?

JONES (*imperturbably*). Where dey mostly runs de minute I closes my eyes—drinkin' rum and talkin' big down in de town. (*Sarcastically.*) How come you don't know dat? Ain't you sousin' with 'em most every day?

SMITHERS (*stung but pretending indifference—with a wink*). That's part of the day's work. I got ter—ain't I—in my business?

JONES (*contemptuously*). Yo' business!

SMITHERS (*imprudently enraged*). Gawd blimey, you was glad enough for me ter take yer in on it when you landed here first. You didn' 'ave no 'igh and mighty airs in them days!

JONES (*his hand going to his revolver like a flash—menacingly*). Talk polite, white man! Talk polite, you heah me! I'm boss heah now, is you fergettin'? (*The Cockney seems about to challenge this last statement with the facts but something in the other's eyes holds and cows him.*)

SMITHERS (*in a cowardly whine*). No 'arm meant, old top.

JONES (*condescendingly*). I accepts yo' apology. (*Lets his hand fall from his revolver.*) No use'n you rakin' up ole times. What I was den is one thing. What I is now 's another. You didn't let me in on yo' crooked work out o' no kind feelin's dat time. I done de dirty work fo' you—and most o' de brain work, too, fo' dat matter—and I was wu'th money to you, dat's de reason.

SMITHERS. Well, blimey, I give yer a start, didn't I—when no one else would. I wasn't afraid to 'ire yer like the rest was—'count of the story about your breakin' jail back in the States.

JONES. No, you didn't have no s'cuse to look down on me fo' dat. You been in jail you'self more'n once.

SMITHERS (*furiously*). It's a lie! (*Then trying to pass it off by an attempt at scorn.*) Garn! Who told yer that fairy tale?

JONES. Dey's some tings I ain't got to be tole. I kin see 'em in folk's eyes. (*Then after a pause—meditatively.*) Yes, you sho' give me a start. And it didn't take long from dat time to git dese fool, woods' niggers right where I wanted dem.

(*With pride.*) From stowaway to Emperor in two years! Dat's goin' some!

SMITHERS (*with curiosity*). And I bet you got yer pile o' money 'id safe some place.

JONES (*with satisfaction*). I sho' has! And it's in a foreign bank where no pusson don't ever git it out but me no matter what come. You didn't s'pose I was holdin' down dis Emperor job for de glory in it, did you? Sho'! De fuss and glory part of it, dat's only to turn de heads o' de low-flung, bush niggers dat's here. Dey wants de big circus show for deir money. I gives it to 'em an' I gits de money. (*With a grin.*) De long green, dat's me every time! (*Then rebukingly.*) But you ain't got no kick agin me, Smithers. I'se paid you back all you done for me many times. Ain't I pertected you and winked at all de crooked tradin' you been doin' right out in de broad day? Sho' I has—and me makin' laws to stop it at de same time! (*He chuckles.*)

SMITHERS (*grinning*). But, meanin' no 'arm, you been grabbin' right and left yourself, ain't yer? Look at the taxes you've put on 'em! Blimey! You've squeezed 'em dry!

JONES (*chuckling*). No, dey ain't *all* dry yet. I'se still heah, ain't I?

SMITHERS (*smiling at his secret thought*). They're dry right now, you'll find out. (*Changing the subject abruptly.*) And as for me breakin' laws, you've broke 'em all yerself just as fast as yer made 'em.

JONES. Ain't I de Emperor? De laws don't go for him. (*Judicially.*) You heah what I tells you, Smithers. Dere's little stealin' like you does, and dere's big stealin' like I does. For de little stealin' dey gits you in jail soon or late. For de big stealin' dey makes you Emperor and puts you in de Hall o' Fame when you croaks. (*Reminiscently.*) If dey's one thing I learns in ten years on de Pullman ca's listenin' to de white quality talk, it's dat same fact. And when I gits a chance to use it I winds up Emperor in two years.

SMITHERS (*unable to repress the genuine admiration of the small fry for the large*). Yes, yer turned the bleedin' trick, all right. Blimey, I never seen a bloke 'as 'ad the bloomin' luck you 'as.

JONES (*severely*). Luck? What you mean—luck?

SMITHERS. I suppose you'll say as that swank about the silver bullet ain't luck—and that was what first got the fool blacks on yer side the time of the revolution, wasn't it?

JONES (*with a laugh*). Oh, dat silver bullet! Sho' was luck! But I makes dat luck, you heah? I loads de dice! Yessuh! When dat murderin' nigger ole Lem hired to kill me takes aim ten feet away and his gun misses fire and I shoots him dead, what you heah me say?

SMITHERS. You said yer'd got a charm so's no lead bullet'd kill yer. You was so strong only a silver bullet could kill yer, you told 'em. Blimey, wasn't that swank for yer—and plain, fat-'eaded luck?

JONES (*proudly*). I got brains and I uses 'em quick. Dat ain't luck.

SMITHERS. Yer know they wasn't 'ardly liable to get no silver bullets. And it was luck 'e didn't 'it you that time.

JONES (*laughing*). And dere all dem fool, bush niggers was kneelin' down and bumpin' deir heads on de ground like I was a miracle out o' de Bible. Oh Lawd, from dat time on I has dem all eatin' out of my hand. I cracks de whip and dey jumps through.

SMITHERS (*with a sniff*). Yankee bluff done it.

JONES. Ain't a man's talkin' big what makes him big—long as he makes folks believe it? Sho', I talks large when I ain't got nothin' to back it up, but I ain't talkin' wild just de same. I knows I kin fool 'em—I *knows* it—and dat's backin' enough fo' my game. And ain't I got to learn deir lingo and teach some of dem English befo' I kin talk to 'em? Ain't dat wuk? You ain't never learned ary word er it, Smithers, in de ten years you been heah, dough yo' knows it's money in yo' pocket tradin' wid 'em if you does. But you'se too shiftless to take de trouble.

SMITHERS (*flushing*). Never mind about me. What's this I've 'eard about yer really 'avin' a silver bullet moulded for yourself?

JONES. It's playin' out my bluff. I has de silver bullet moulded and I tells 'em when de time comes I kills myself wid it. I tells 'em dat's 'cause I'm de on'y man in de world big en-uff to git me. No use'n deir tryin'. And dey falls down and bumps deir heads. (*He laughs.*) I does dat so's I kin take a walk in peace widout no jealous nigger gunnin' at me from behind de trees.

SMITHERS (*astonished*). Then you 'ad it made—'onest?

JONES. Sho' did. Heah she be. (*He takes out his revolver, breaks it, and takes the silver bullet out of one chamber.*) Five lead an' dis silver baby at de last. Don't she shine pretty? (*He holds it in his hand, looking at it admiringly, as if strangely fascinated.*)

SMITHERS. Let me see. (*Reaches out his hand for it.*)

JONES (*harshly*). Keep yo' hands whar dey b'long, white man. (*He replaces it in the chamber and puts the revolver back on his hip.*)

SMITHERS (*snarling*). Gawd blimey! Think I'm a bleedin' thief, you would.

JONES. No, 'tain't dat. I knows you'se scared to steal from me. On'y I ain't 'lowin' nary body to touch dis baby. She's my rabbit's foot.

SMITHERS (*sneering*). A bloomin' charm, wot? (*Venomously.*) Well, you'll need all the bloody charms you 'as before long, s' 'elp me!

JONES (*judicially*). Oh, I'se good for six months yit 'fore dey gits sick o' my game. Den, when I sees trouble comin', I makes my getaway.

SMITHERS. Ho! You got it all planned, ain't yer?

JONES. I ain't no fool. I knows dis Emperor's time is sho't. Dat why I make hay when de sun shine. Was you thinkin' I'se aimin' to hold down dis job for life? No, suh! What good is gittin' money if you stays back in dis raggedy country? I wants action when I spends. And when I sees dese niggers gittin' up deir nerve to tu'n me out, and I'se got all de money in sight, I resigns on de spot and beats it quick.

SMITHERS. Where to?

JONES. None o' yo' business.

SMITHERS. Not back to the bloody States, I'll lay my oath.

JONES (*suspiciously*). Why don't I? (*Then with an easy laugh.*) You mean 'count of dat story 'bout me breakin' from jail back dere? Dat's all talk.

SMITHERS (*skeptically*). Ho, yes!

JONES (*sharply*). You ain't 'sinuatin' I'se a liar, is you?

SMITHERS (*hastily*). No, Gawd strike me! I was only thinkin' o' the bloody lies you told the blacks 'ere about killin' white men in the States.

JONES (*angered*). How come dey're lies?

SMITHERS. You'd 'ave been in jail if you 'ad, wouldn't yer then? (*With venom.*) And from what I've 'eard, it ain't 'ealthy for a black to kill a white man in the States. They burns 'em in oil, don't they?

JONES (*with cool deadliness*). You mean lynchin' 'd scare me? Well, I tells you, Smithers, maybe I does kill one white man back dere. Maybe I does. And maybe I kills another right heah 'fore long if he don't look out.

SMITHERS (*trying to force a laugh*). I was on'y spoofin' yer. Can't yer take a joke? And you was just sayin' you'd never been in jail.

JONES (*in the same tone—slightly boastful*). Maybe I goes to jail dere for gettin' in an argument wid razors ovah a crap game. Maybe I gits twenty years when dat colored man die. Maybe I gits in 'nother argument wid de prison guard was overseer ovah us when we're wukin' de roads. Maybe he hits me wid a whip and I splits his head wid a shovel and runs away and files de chain off my leg and gits away safe. Maybe I does all dat an' maybe I don't. It's a story I tells you so's you knows I'se de kind of man dat if you evah repeats one word of it, I ends yo' stealin' on dis yearth mighty damn quick!

SMITHERS (*terrified*). Think I'd peach on yer? Not me! Ain't I always been yer friend?

JONES (*suddenly relaxing*). Sho' you has—and you better be.

SMITHERS (*recovering his composure—and with it his malice*). And just to show yer I'm yer friend, I'll tell yer that bit o' news I was goin' to.

JONES. Go ahead! Shoot de piece. Must be bad news from de happy way you look.

SMITHERS (*warningly*). Maybe it's gettin' time for you to re-sign—with that bloomin' silver bullet, wot? (*He finishes with a mocking grin.*)

JONES (*puzzled*). What's dat you say? Talk plain.

SMITHERS. Ain't noticed any of the guards or servants about the place today, I 'aven't.

JONES (*carelessly*). Dey're all out in de garden sleepin' under de trees. When I sleeps, dey sneaks a sleep, too, and I pre-tends I never suspicions it. All I got to do is to ring de bell and dey come flyin', makin' a bluff dey was wukin' all de time.

SMITHERS (*in the same mocking tone*). Ring the bell now an' you'll bloody well see what I means.

JONES (*startled to alertness, but preserving the same careless tone*). Sho' I rings. (*He reaches below the throne and pulls out a big, common dinner bell which is painted the same vivid scarlet as the throne. He rings this vigorously—then stops to listen. Then he goes to both doors, rings again, and looks out.*)

SMITHERS (*watching him with malicious satisfaction, after a pause—mockingly*). The bloody ship is sinkin' an' the bleedin' rats 'as slung their 'ooks.

JONES (*in a sudden fit of anger flings the bell clattering into a corner*). Low-flung, woods' niggers! (*Then catching Smithers' eye on him, he controls himself and suddenly bursts into a low chuckling laugh.*) Reckon I overplays my hand dis once! A man can't take de pot on a bob-tailed flush all de time. Was I sayin' I'd sit in six months mo'? Well, I'se changed my mind den. I cashes in and resigns de job of Emperor right dis minute.

SMITHERS (*with real admiration*). Blimey, but you're a cool bird, and no mistake.

JONES. No use'n fussin'. When I knows de game's up I kisses it good-bye widout no long waits. Dey've all run off to de hills, ain't dey?

SMITHERS. Yes—every bleedin' man jack of 'em.

JONES. Den de revolution is at de post. And de Emperor better git his feet smokin' up de trail. (*He starts for the door in rear.*)

SMITHERS. Goin' out to look for your 'orse? Yer won't find any. They steals the 'orses first thing. Mine was gone when I went for 'im this mornin'. That's wot first give me a suspicion of wot was up.

JONES (*alarmed for a second, scratches his head, then philosophically*). Well, den I hoofs it. Feet, do yo' duty! (*He pulls out a gold watch and looks at it.*) Three-thuty. Sundown's at six-thuty or dereabouts. (*Puts his watch back—with cool confidence.*) I got plenty o' time to make it easy.

SMITHERS. Don't be so bloomin' sure of it. They'll be after you 'ot and 'eavy. Ole Lem is at the bottom o' this business an' 'e 'ates you like 'ell. 'E'd rather do for you than eat 'is dinner, 'e would!

JONES (*scornfully*). Dat fool no-count nigger! Does you think I'se scared o' him? I stands him on his thick head more'n once befo' dis, and I does it again if he come in my way . . . (*Fiercely.*) And dis time I leave him a dead nigger fo' sho'!

SMITHERS. You'll 'ave to cut through the big forest—an' these blacks 'ere can sniff and follow a trail in the dark like 'ounds. You'd 'ave to 'ustle to get through that forest in twelve hours even if you knew all the bloomin' trails like a native.

JONES (*with indignant scorn*). Look-a-heah, white man! Does you think I'se a natural bo'n fool? Give me credit fo'

havin' some sense, fo' Lawd's sake! Don't you s'pose I'se looked ahead and made sho' of all de chances? I'se gone out in dat big forest, pretendin' to hunt, so many times dat I knows it high an' low like a book. I could go through on dem trails wid my eyes shut. (*With great contempt.*) Think dese ign'rent bush niggers dat ain't got brains enuff to know deir own names even can catch Brutus Jones? Huh, I s'pects not! Not on yo' life! Why, man, de white men went after me wid bloodhounds where I come from an' I jes' laughs at 'em. It's a shame to fool dese black trash around heah, dey're so easy. You watch me, man! I'll make dem look sick, I will. I'll be 'cross de plain to de edge of de forest by time dark comes. Once in de woods in de night, dey got a swell chance o' findin' dis baby! Dawn tomorrow I'll be out at de oder side and on de coast whar dat French gunboat is stayin'. She picks me up, take me to Martinique when she go dar, and dere I is safe wid a mighty big bankroll in my jeans. It's easy as rollin' off a log.

SMITHERS (*maliciously*). But s'posin' somethin' 'appens wrong an' they do nab yer?

JONES (*decisively*). Dey don't—dat's de answer.

SMITHERS. But, just for argyment's sake—what'd you do?

JONES (*frowning*). I'se got five lead bullets in dis gun good enuff fo' common bush niggers—and after dat I got de silver bullet left to cheat 'em out o' gittin' me.

SMITHERS (*jeeringly*). Ho, I was fergettin' that silver bullet. You'll bump yourself orf in style, won't yer? Blimey!

JONES (*gloomily*). You kin bet yo' whole roll on one thing, white man. Dis baby plays out his string to de end and when he quits, he quits wid a bang de way he ought. Silver bullet ain't none too good for him when he go, dat's a fac'! (*Then shaking off his nervousness—with a confident laugh.*) Sho'! What is I talkin' about? Ain't come to dat yit and I never will—not wid trash niggers like dese yere. (*Boastfully.*) Silver bullet bring me luck anyway. I kin outguess, outrun, outfight, an' outplay de whole lot o' dem all ovah de board any time o' de day er night! You watch me!

(*From the distant hills comes the faint, steady thump of a tom-tom, low and vibrating. It starts at a rate exactly corresponding to normal pulse beat—72 to the minute—and continues at a gradually accelerating rate from this point uninterruptedly to the very end of the play.*

Jones starts at the sound. A strange look of apprehension creeps into his face for a moment as he listens. Then he asks, with an attempt to regain his most casual manner.)

What's dat drum beatin' fo'?

SMITHERS (*with a mean grin*). For you. That means the bleedin' ceremony 'as started. I've 'eard it before and I knows.

JONES. Cer'mony? What cer'mony?

SMITHERS. The blacks is 'oldin' a bloody meetin', 'avin' a war dance, gettin' their courage worked up b'fore they starts after you.

JONES. Let dem! Dey'll sho' need it!

SMITHERS. And they're there 'oldin' their 'eathen religious service—makin' no end of devil spells and charms to 'elp 'em against your silver bullet. (*He guffaws loudly.*) Blimey, but they're balmy as 'ell!

JONES (*a tiny bit awed and shaken in spite of himself*). Huh! Takes more'n dat to scare dis chicken!

SMITHERS (*scenting the other's feeling—maliciously*). Ternight when it's pitch black in the forest, they'll 'ave their pet devils and ghosts 'oundin' after you. You'll find yer bloody 'air 'll be standin' on end before termorrow mornin'. (*Seriously.*) It's a bleedin' queer place, that stinkin' forest, even in daylight. Yer don't know what might 'appen in there, it's that rotten still. Always sends the cold shivers down my back minute I gets in it.

JONES (*with a contemptuous sniff*). I an't no chicken-liver like you is. Trees an' me, we'se friends, and dar's a full moon comin' bring me light. And let dem po' niggers make all de fool spells dey'se a min' to. Does yo' s'pect I'se silly enuff to b'lieve in ghosts an' ha'nts an' all dat ole woman's talk? G'long, white man! You ain't talkin' to me. (*With a chuckle.*) Doesn't you know dey's got to do wid a man was member in good standin' o' de Baptist Church? Sho' I was dat when I was porter on de Pullmans, befo' I gits into my little trouble. Let dem try deir heathen tricks. De Baptist Church done pertect me and land dem all in hell. (*Then with more confident satisfaction.*) And I'se got little silver bullet o' my own, don't forgit.

SMITHERS. Ho! You 'aven't give much 'eed to your Baptist Church since you been down 'ere. I've 'eard myself you 'ad turned yer coat an' was takin' up with their blarsted witch-doctors, or whatever the 'ell yer calls the swine.

JONES (*vehemently*). I pretends to! Sho' I pretends! Dat's part o' my game from de fust. If I finds out dem niggers believes dat black is white, den I yells it out louder 'n deir loudest. It don't git me nothin' to do missionary work for de Baptist Church. I'se after de coin, an' I lays my Jesus on de shelf for de time bein'. (*Stops abruptly to look at his watch—alertly.*) But I ain't got de time to waste no more fool talk wid you. I'se gwine away from heah dis secon'. (*He reaches in under the throne and pulls out an expensive Panama hat with a bright multi-colored band and sets it jauntily on his head.*) So long, white man! (*With a grin.*) See you in jail sometime, maybe!

SMITHERS. Not me, you won't. Well, I wouldn't be in yer bloody boots for no bloomin' money, but 'ere's wishin' yer luck just the same.

JONES (*contemptuously*). Yo're de frightenedest man evah I see! I tells you I'se safe's 'f I was in New York City. It takes dem niggers from now to dark to git up de nerve to start somethin'. By dat time, I'se got a head start dey never kotch up wid.

SMITHERS (*maliciously*). Give my regards to any ghosts yer meets up with.

JONES (*grinning*). If dat ghost got money, I'll tell him never ha'nt you less'n he wants to lose it.

SMITHERS (*flattered*). Garn! (*Then curiously.*) Ain't yer takin' no luggage with yer?

JONES. I travels light when I wants to move fast. And I got tinned grub buried on de edge o' de forest. (*Boastfully.*) Now say dat I don't look ahead an' use my brains! (*With a wide, liberal gesture.*) I will all dat's left in de palace to you—and you better grab all you kin sneak away wid befo' dey gits here.

SMITHERS (*gratefully*). Righto—and thanks ter yer. (*As Jones walks toward the door in rear—cautioningly.*) Say! Look 'ere, you ain't goin' out that way, are yer?

JONES. Does you think I'd slink out de back door like a common nigger? I'se Emperor yit, ain't I? And de Emperor Jones leaves de way he comes, and dat black trash don't dare stop him—not yit, leastways. (*He stops for a moment in the doorway, listening to the far-off but insistent beat of the tom-tom.*) Listen to dat roll-call, will you? Must be mighty big drum carry dat far. (*Then with a laugh.*) Well, if dey ain't no whole brass band to see me off, I sho' got de drum part of it. So long, white man. (*He puts his hands in his pockets and with studied carelessness, whistling a tune, he saunters out of the doorway and off to the left.*)

SMITHERS (*looks after him with a puzzled admiration*). 'E's got 'is bloomin' nerve with 'im, s'elp me! (*Then angrily.*) Ho—the bleedin' nigger—puttin' on 'is bloody airs! I 'opes they nabs 'im an' gives 'im what's what! (*Then putting business before the pleasure of this thought, looking around him with cupidity.*) A bloke ought to find a 'ole lot in this palace that'd go for a bit of cash. Let's take a look, 'Arry, me lad. (*He starts for the doorway on right as*

THE CURTAIN FALLS

SCENE 2

SCENE: *Nightfall. The end of the plain where the Great Forest begins. The foreground is sandy, level ground dotted by a few stones and clumps of stunted bushes covering close against the earth to escape the buffeting of the trade wind. In the rear the forest is a wall of darkness dividing the world. Only when the eye becomes accustomed to the gloom can the outlines of separate trunks of the nearest trees be made out, enormous pillars of deeper blackness. A somber monotone of wind lost in the leaves moans in the air. Yet this sound serves but to intensify the impression of the forest's relentless immobility, to form a background throwing into relief its brooding, implacable silence.*

Jones enters from the left, walking rapidly. He stops as he nears the edge of the forest, looks around him quickly, peering into the dark as if searching for some familiar landmark. Then, apparently, satisfied that he is where he ought to be, he throws himself on the ground, dog-tired.

Well, heah I is. In de nick o' time, too! Little mo' an' it'd be blacker'n de ace of spades heahabouts. (*He pulls a bandana handkerchief from his hip pocket and mops off his perspiring face.*) Sho'! Gimme air! I'se tuckered out sho' nuff. Dat soft Emperor job ain't no trainin' fo' a long hike ovah dat plain in de brilin' sun. (*Then with a chuckle.*) Cheah up, nigger, de worst is yet to come. (*He lifts his head and stares at the forest. His chuckle peters out abruptly. In a tone of awe.*) My goodness, look at dem woods, will you? Dat no-count Smithers said dey'd be black an' he sho' called de turn. (*Turning away from them quickly and looking down at his feet, he snatches at a chance to change the subject—solicitously.*) Feet, you is holdin' up yo' end fine an' I sutinly hopes you ain't blisterin' none. It's time you git a rest. (*He takes off his shoes, his eyes studiously avoiding the forest. He feels of the soles of his feet gingerly.*) You is still in de pink—on'y a little mite feverish. Cool yo'selfs. Remember you done got a long journey yit befo' you. (*He sits in a weary attitude, listening to the rhythmic beating of the tom-tom. He grumbles in a loud tone to cover up a growing uneasiness.*) Bush niggers! Wonder dey wouldn' get sick o' beatin' dat drum. Sound louder, seem like. I wonder if dey's startin' after me? (*He scrambles to his feet, looking back across the plain.*) Couldn't see dem now, nohow, if dey was hundred feet away. (*Then shaking himself like a wet dog to get rid of these depressing thoughts.*) Sho', dey's miles an' miles behind. What you gittin' fidgety about? (*But he sits down and begins to lace up his shoes in great haste, all the time muttering reassuringly.*) You know what? Yo' belly is empty, dat's what's de matter wid you. Come time to eat! Wid nothin' but wind on yo' stumach, o' course you feels jiggedy. Well, we eats right heah an' now soon's I gits dese pesky shoes laced up! (*He finishes lacing up his shoes.*) Dere! Now le's see. (*Gets on his hands and knees and searches the ground around him with his eyes.*) White stone, white stone, where is you? (*He sees the first white stone and crawls to it—with satisfaction.*) Heah you is! I knowed dis was de right place. Box of grub, come to me. (*He turns over the stone and feels in under it—in a tone of dismay.*) Ain't heah! Gorry, is I in de right place or isn't I? Dere's 'nother stone. Guess dat's it. (*He scrambles to the next stone and turns it over.*) Ain't heah, neither! Grub, whar is you? Ain't heah. Gorry, has I got to go hungry into dem woods—all de night? (*While he is talking he scrambles from one stone to another, turning them over in frantic haste. Finally, he jumps to his feet excitedly.*) Is I lost de place? Must have! But how dat happen when I was followin' de trail across de plain in broad daylight? (*Almost plaintively.*) I'se hungry, I is! I gotta git my feed. Whar's my strength gonna come from if I doesn't? Gorry, I gotta find dat grub high an' low somehow! Why it come dark so quick like dat? Can't see nothin'. (*He scratches a match on his trousers and peers about him. The rate of the beat of the far-off tom-tom increases perceptibly as he does so. He mutters in a bewildered voice.*) How come all dese white stones come heah when I only remembers one? (*Suddenly, with a frightened gasp, he flings the match on the ground and stamps on it.*) Nigger, is you gone crazy mad? Is you lightin' matches to show dem whar you is? Fo' Lawd's sake, use yo' haid. Gorry, I'se got to be careful! (*He stares at the plain behind him apprehensively, his hand on his revolver.*) But how come all dese white stones? And whar's dat tin box o' grub I had all wrapped up in oil cloth?

(*While his back is turned, the Little Formless Fears creep out from the deeper blackness of the forest. They are black, shapeless, only their glittering little eyes can be seen. If they have any describable form at all it is that of a grubworm about the size of a creeping child. They move noiselessly, but with deliberate, painful effort, striving to raise themselves on end, failing and sinking prone again. Jones turns about to face the forest. He stares up at the tops of the trees, seeking vainly to discover his whereabouts by their conformation.*)

Can't tell nothin' from dem trees! Gorry, nothin' 'round heah look like I evah seed it befo'. I'se done lost de place sho' 'nuff! (*With mournful foreboding.*) It's mighty queer! It's mighty queer! (*With sudden forced defiance—in an angry tone.*) Woods, is you tryin' to put somethin' ovah on me?

(*From the formless creatures on the ground in front of him comes a tiny gale of low mocking laughter like a rustling of leaves. They squirm upward toward him in twisted attitudes. Jones looks down, leaps backward with a yell of terror, yanking out his revolver as he does so—in a quavering voice.*)

What's dat? Who's dar? What is you? Git away from me befo' I shoots you up! You don't? . . .

(*He fires. There is a flash, a loud report, then silence broken only by the far-off, quickened throb of the tom-tom. The formless creatures have scurried back into the forest. Jones remains fixed in his position, listening intently. The sound of the shot, the reassuring feel of the revolver in his hand, have somewhat restored his shaken nerve. He addresses himself with renewed confidence.*)

Dey're gone. Dat shot fix 'em. Dey was only little animals—little wild pigs, I reckon. Dey've maybe rooted out yo' grub an' eat it. Sho', you fool nigger, what you think dey is—ha'nts? (*Excitedly.*) Gorry, you give de game away when you fire dat shot. Dem niggers heah dat fo' su'tin! Time you beat it in de woods widout no long waits. (*He starts for the forest—hesitates before the plunge—then urging himself in with manful resolution.*) Git in, nigger! What you skeered at? Ain't nothin' dere but de trees! Git in! (*He plunges boldly into the forest.*)

SCENE 3

SCENE: *Nine o'clock. In the forest. The moon has just risen. Its beams, drifting through the canopy of leaves, make a barely perceptible, suffused, eerie glow. A dense low wall of underbrush and creepers is in the nearer foreground, fencing in a small triangular clearing. Beyond this* is the massed blackness of the forest like an encompassing barrier. A path is dimly discerned leading down to the clearing from left, rear, and winding away from it again toward the right. As the scene opens nothing can be distinctly made out. Except for the beating of the tom-tom, which is a trifle louder and quicker than in the previous scene, there is silence, broken every few seconds by a queer, clicking sound. Then gradually the figure of the Negro, Jeff, can be discerned crouching on his haunches at the rear of the triangle. He is middle-aged, thin, brown in color, is dressed in a Pullman porter's uniform, cap, etc. He is throwing a pair of dice on the ground before him, picking them up, shaking them, casting them out with the regular, rigid, mechanical movements of an automaton. The heavy, plodding footsteps of someone approaching along the trail from the left are heard and Jones' voice, pitched in a slightly higher key and strained in a cheering effort to overcome its own tremors.

De moon's rizen. Does you heah dat, nigger? You gits more light from dis out. No mo' buttin' yo' fool head agin' de trunks an' scratchin' de hide off yo' legs in de bushes. Now you sees whar yo'se gwine. So cheer up! From now on you has a snap. (*He steps just to the rear of the triangular clearing and mops off his face on his sleeve. He has lost his Panama hat. His face is scratched, his brilliant uniform shows several large rents.*) What time's it gittin' to be, I wonder? I dassent light no match to find out. Phoo'. It's wa'm an' dat's a fac'! (*Wearily.*) How long I been makin' tracks in dese woods? Must be hours an' hours. Seems like fo'evah! Yit can't be, when de moon's jes' riz. Dis am a long night fo' yo', yo' Majesty! (*With a mournful chuckle.*) Majesty! Der ain't much majesty 'bout dis baby now. (*With attempted cheerfulness.*) Never min'. It's all part o' de game. Dis night come to an end like everything else. And when you gits dar safe and has dat bankroll in yo' hands you laughs at all dis. (*He starts to whistle but checks himself abruptly.*) What yo' whistlin' for, you po' dope! Want all de worl' to heah you? (*He stops talking to listen.*) Heah dat ole drum! Sho' gits nearer from de sound. Dey're packin' it along wid 'em. Time fo' me to move. (*He takes a step forward, then stops—worriedly.*) What's dat odder queer clickety sound I heah? Dere it is! Sound close! Sound like—sound like—Fo' God sake, sound like some nigger was shootin' crap! (*Frightenedly.*) I better beat it quick when I gits dem notions. (*He walks quickly into the clear space—then stands transfixed as he sees Jeff—in a terrified gasp.*) Who dar? Who dat? Is dat you, Jeff? (*Starting toward the other, forgetful for a moment of his surroundings and really believing it is a living man that he sees—in a tone of happy relief.*) Jeff! I'se sho' mighty glad to see you! Dey tol' me you done died from dat razor cut I gives you. (*Stopping suddenly, bewilderedly.*) But how you come to be heah, nigger? (*He stares fascinatedly at the other who continues his mechanical

play with the dice. Jones' eyes begin to roll wildly. He stutters.*) Ain't you gwine—look up—can't you speak to me? Is you—is you—a ha'nt? (*He jerks out his revolver in a frenzy of terrified rage.*) Nigger, I kills you dead once. Has I got to kill you again? You take it den. (*He fires. When the smoke clears away Jeff has disappeared. Jones stands trembling—then with a certain reassurance.*) He's gone, anyway. Ha'nt or no ha'nt, dat shot fix him. (*The beat of the far-off tom-tom is perceptibly louder and more rapid. Jones becomes conscious of it—with a start, looking back over his shoulder.*) Dey's gittin' near! Dey's comin' fast! And heah I is shootin' shots to let 'em know jes' whar I is. Oh, Gorry, I'se got to run. (*Forgetting the path he plunges wildly into the underbrush in the rear and disappears in the shadow.*)

SCENE 4

SCENE: *Eleven o'clock. In the forest. A wide dirt road runs diagonally from right, front, to left, rear. Rising sheer on both sides the forest walls it in. The moon is now up. Under its light the road glimmers ghastly and unreal. It is as if the forest had stood aside momentarily to let the road pass through and accomplish its veiled purpose. This done, the forest will fold in upon itself again and the road will be no more. Jones stumbles in from the forest on the right. His uniform is ragged and torn. He looks about him with numbed surprise when he sees the road, his eyes blinking in the bright moonlight. He flops down exhaustedly and pants heavily for a while. Then with sudden anger.*

I'm meltin' wid heat! Runnin' an' runnin' an' runnin'! Damn dis heah coat! Like a strait-jacket! (*He tears off his coat and flings it away from him, revealing himself stripped to the waist.*) Dere! Dat's better! Now I kin breathe! (*Looking down at his feet, the spurs catch his eye.*) And to hell wid dese high-fangled spurs. Dey're what's been a-trippin' me up an' breakin' my neck. (*He unstraps them and flings them away disgustedly.*) Dere! I gits rid o' dem frippety Emperor trappin's an' I travels lighter. Lawd! I'se tired! (*After a pause, listening to the insistent beat of the tom-tom in the distance.*) I must 'a put some distance between myself an' dem—runnin' like dat—and yit—dat damn drum sound jes' de same—nearer, even. Well, I guess I a'most holds my lead anyhow. Dey won't never catch up. (*With a sigh.*) If on'y my fool legs stands up. Oh, I'se sorry I evah went in for dis. Dat Emperor job is sho' hard to shake. (*He looks around him suspiciously.*) How'd dis road evah git heah? Good level road, too. I never remembers seein' it befo'. (*Shaking his head apprehensively.*) Dese woods is sho' full o' de queerest things at night. (*With a sudden terror.*) Lawd God, don't let me see no more o' dem ha'nts! Dey gits my goat! (*Then trying to talk himself into confidence.*) Ha'nts! You fool nigger, dey ain't no such things! Don't de Baptist parson tell you dat many time? Is you civilized, or is you like dese ign'rent black niggers heah? Sho'! Dat was all in yo' own head. Wasn't nothin' dere. Wasn't no Jeff! Know what? You jus' get seein' dem things 'cause yo' belly's empty and you's sick wid hunger inside. Hunger 'fects yo' head and yo' eyes. Any fool know dat. (*Then pleading fervently.*) But bless God, I don't come across no more o' dem, whatever dey is! (*Then cautiously.*) Rest! Don't talk! Rest! You needs it. Den you gits on yo' way again. (*Looking at the moon.*) Night's half gone a'most. You hits de coast in de mawning! Den you'se all safe.

(*From the right forward a small gang of Negroes enter. They are dressed in striped convict suits, their heads are shaven, one leg drags limpingly, shackled to a heavy ball and chain. Some carry picks, the others shovels. They are followed by a white man dressed in the uniform of a prison guard. A Winchester rifle is slung across his shoulders and he carries a heavy whip. At a signal from the Guard they stop on the road opposite where Jones is sitting. Jones, who has been staring up at the sky, unmindful of their noiseless approach, suddenly looks down and sees them. His eyes pop out, he tries to get to his feet and fly, but sinks back, too numbed by fright to move. His voice catches in a choking prayer.*)

Lawd Jesus!

(*The Prison Guard cracks his whip—noiselessly—and at that signal all the convicts start to work on the road. They swing their picks, they shovel, but not a sound comes from their labor. Their movements, like those of Jeff in the preceding scene, are those of automatons,—rigid, slow, and mechanical. The Prison Guard points sternly at Jones with his whip, motions him to take his place among the other shovelers. Jones gets to his feet in a hypnotized stupor. He mumbles subserviently.*)

Yes, suh! Yes, suh! I'se comin'.

(*As he shuffles, dragging one foot, over to his place, he curses under his breath with rage and hatred.*)

God damn yo' soul, I gits even wid you yit, sometime.

(*As if there were a shovel in his hands he goes through weary, mechanical gestures of digging up dirt, and throwing it to the roadside. Suddenly the Guard approaches him angrily, threateningly. He raises his whip and lashes Jones viciously across the shoulders with it. Jones winces with pain and cowers abjectly. The Guard turns his back on him and walks away contemptuously. Instantly Jones straightens up. With arms upraised as if his shovel were a club in his hands he springs murderously at the unsuspecting Guard. In the act of crashing down his shovel on the white man's skull, Jones suddenly becomes aware that his hands are empty. He cries despairingly.*)

Whar's my shovel? Gimme my shovel till I splits his damn head! (*Appealing to his fellow convicts.*) Gimme a shovel, one o' you, fo' God's sake!

(*They stand fixed in motionless attitudes, their eyes on the ground. The Guard seems to wait expectantly, his back turned to the attacker. Jones bellows with baffled, terrified rage, tugging frantically at his revolver.*)

I kills you, you white debil, if it's de last thing I evah does! Ghost or debil, I kill you again!

(*He frees the revolver and fires point blank at the Guard's back. Instantly the walls of the forest close in from both sides, the road and the figures of the convict gang are blotted out in an enshrouding darkness. The only sounds are a crashing in the underbrush as Jones leaps away in mad flight and the throbbing of the tom-tom, still far distant, but increased in volume of sound and rapidity of beat.*)

SCENE 5

SCENE: *One o'clock. A large circular clearing, enclosed by the serried ranks of gigantic trunks of tall trees whose tops are lost to view. In the center is a big dead stump worn by time into a curious resemblance to an auction block. The moon floods the clearing with a clear light. Jones forces his way in through the forest on the left. He looks wildly about the clearing with hunted, fearful glances. His pants are in tatters, his shoes cut and misshapen, flapping about his feet. He slinks cautiously to the stump in the center and sits down in a tense position, ready for instant flight. Then he holds his head in his hands and rocks back and forth, moaning to himself miserably.*

Oh Lawd, Lawd! Oh Lawd, Lawd! (*Suddenly he throws himself on his knees and raises his clasped hands to the sky—in a voice of agonized pleading.*) Lawd Jesus, heah my prayer! I'se a po' sinner, a po' sinner! I knows I done wrong, I knows it! When I cotches Jeff cheatin' wid loaded dice my anger overcomes me and I kills him dead! Lawd, I done wrong! When dat guard hits me wid de whip, my anger overcomes me, and I kills him dead. Lawd, I done wrong! And down heah whar dese fool bush niggers raises me up to de seat o' de mighty, I steals all I could grab. Lawd, I done wrong! I knows it! I'se sorry! Forgive me, Lawd! Forgive dis po' sinner! (*Then beseeching terrifiedly.*) And keep dem away, Lawd! Keep dem away from me! And stop dat drum soundin' in my ears! Dat begin to sound ha'nted, too. (*He gets to his feet, evidently slightly reassured by his prayer—with attempted confidence.*) De Lawd'll preserve me from dem ha'nts after dis. (*Sits down on the stump again.*) I ain't skeered o' real men. Let dem come. But dem odders . . . (*He shudders—then looks down at his feet, working his toes inside the shoes—with a groan.*) Oh, my po' feet! Dem shoes ain't no use no more 'ceptin' to hurt. I'se better off widout dem. (*He un-laces them and pulls them off—holds the wrecks of the shoes in his hands and regards them mournfully.*) You was real, A-one patin' leather, too. Look at you now. Emperor, you'se gittin' mighty low!

(*He sits dejectedly and remains with bowed shoulders, staring down at the shoes in his hands as if reluctant to throw them away. While his attention is thus occupied, a crowd of figures silently enter the clearing from all sides. All are dressed in Southern costumes of the period of the fifties of the last century. There are middle-aged men who are evidently well-to-do planters. There is one spruce, au-thoritative individual—the Auctioneer. There is a crowd of curious spectators, chiefly young belles and dandies who have come to the slave-market for diversion. All exchange courtly greetings in dumb show and chat silently together. There is something stiff, rigid, unreal, marionettish about their movements. They group themselves about the stump. Finally a batch of slaves are led in from the left by an at-tendant—three men of different ages, two women, one with a baby in her arms, nursing. They are placed to the left of the stump, beside Jones.*

The white planters look them over appraisingly as if they were cattle, and exchange judgments on each. The dandies point with their fingers and make witty remarks. The belles titter bewitchingly. All this in silence save for the ominous throb of the tom-tom. The Auctioneer holds up his hand, taking his place at the stump. The group strain forward at-tentively. He touches Jones on the shoulder peremptorily, motioning for him to stand on the stump—the auction block.

Jones looks up, sees the figures on all sides, looks wildly for some opening to escape, sees none, screams and leaps madly to the top of the stump to get as far away from them as possible. He stands there, cowering, para-lyzed with horror. The Auctioneer begins his silent spiel. He points to Jones appeals to the planters to see for them-selves. Here is a good field hand, sound in wind and limb as they can see. Very strong still in spite of his being mid-dle-aged. Look at that back. Look at those shoulders. Look at the muscles in his arms and his sturdy legs. Capa-ble of any amount of hard labor. Moreover, of a good dis-position, intelligent and tractable. Will any gentleman start the bidding? The Planters raise their fingers, make their bids. They are apparently all eager to posses Jones. The bidding is lively, the crowd interested. While this has been going on, Jones has been seized by the courage of desperation. He dares to look down and around him. Over his face abject terror gives way to mystification, to gradual realization—stutteringly.)

What you all doin', white folks? What's all dis? What you all lookin' at me fo'? What you doin' wid me, any-how? (*Suddenly convulsed with raging hatred and fear.*) Is dis a auction? Is you sellin' me like dey uster befo' de war?

(*Jerking out his revolver just as the Auctioneer knocks him down to one of the planters—glaring from him to the pur-chaser.*) And *you* sells me? And *you* buys me? I shows you I'se a free nigger, damn yo' souls!

(*He fires at the Auctioneer and at the Planter with such rapidity that the two shots are almost simultaneous. As if this were a signal the walls of the forest fold in. Only blackness remains and silence broken by Jones as he rushes off, crying with fear—and by the quickened, ever louder beat of the tom-tom.*)

SCENE 6

SCENE: *Three o'clock. A cleared space in the forest. The limbs of the trees meet over it forming a low ceiling about five feet from the ground. The interlocked ropes of creepers reaching upward to entwine the tree trunks give an arched appearance to the sides. The space thus enclosed is like the dark, noisome hold of some ancient vessel. The moonlight is almost completely shut out and only a vague, wan light filters through. There is the noise of someone approaching from the left, stumbling and crawling through the under-growth. Jones' voice is heard between chattering moans.*

Oh, Lawd, what I gwine do now? Ain't got no bullet left on'y de silver one. If mo' o' dem ha'nts come after me, how I gwine skeer dem away? Oh, Lawd, on'y de sil-ver one left—an' I gotta save dat fo' luck. If I shoots dat one I'm a goner sho'! Lawd, it's black heah! Whar's de moon? Oh, Lawd, don't dis night evah come to an end? (*By the sounds, he is feeling his way cautiously forward.*) Dere! Dis feels like a clear space. I gotta lie down an' rest. I don't care if dem niggers does cotch me. I gotta rest.

(*He is well forward now where his figure can be dimly made out. His pants have been so torn away that what is left of them is no better than a breech cloth. He flings him-self full length, face downward on the ground, panting with exhaustion. Gradually it seems to grow lighter in the enclosed space and two rows of seated figures can be seen behind Jones. They are sitting in crumpled, despairing atti-tudes, hunched, facing one another with their backs touch-ing the forest walls as if they were shackled to them. All are Negroes, naked save for loin cloths. At first they are silent and motionless. Then they begin to sway slowly for-ward toward each other and back again in unison, as if they were laxly letting themselves follow the long roll of a ship at sea. At the same time, a low, melancholy murmur rises among them, increasing gradually by rhythmic de-grees which seem to be directed and controlled by the throb of the tom-tom in the distance, to a long, tremulous wail of despair that reaches a certain pitch, unbearably acute, then falls by slow gradations of tone into silence and is taken up again. Jones starts, looks up, sees the figures, and throws himself down again to shut out the sight. A shudder of terror shakes his whole body as the wail rises up about him again. But the next time, his voice, as if under some uncanny compulsion, starts with the others. As their chorus lifts he rises to a sitting posture similar to the others, swaying back and forth. His voice reaches the highest pitch of sorrow, of desolation. The light fades out, the other voices cease, and only darkness is left. Jones can be heard scrambling to his feet and running off, his voice sinking down the scale and receding as he moves farther and farther away in the forest. The tom-tom beats louder, quicker, with a more insistent, triumphant pulsation.)*

SCENE 7

SCENE: *Five o'clock. The foot of a gigantic tree by the edge of a great river. A rough structure of boulders, like an altar, is by the tree. The raised river bank is in the nearer background. Beyond this the surface of the river spreads out, brilliant and unruffled in the moonlight, blotted out and merged into a veil of bluish mist in the distance. Jones' voice is heard from the left rising and falling in the long, despairing wail of the chained slaves, to the rhythmic beat of the tom-tom. As his voice sinks into silence, he enters the open space. The expression of his face is fixed and stony, his eyes have an obsessed glare, he moves with a strange deliberation like a sleepwalker or one in a trance. He looks around at the tree, the rough stone altar, the moonlit surface of the river beyond, and passes his hand over his head with a vague gesture of puzzled bewilderment. Then, as if in obedience to some obscure impulse, he sinks into a kneeling, devotional posture before the altar. Then he seems to come to himself partly, to have an uncertain realization of what he is doing, for he straightens up and stares about him horrifiedly—in an incoherent mumble.*

What—what is I doin'? What is—dis place? Seems like—seems like I know dat tree—an' dem stones—an' de river. I remember—seems like I been heah befo'. (*Tremblingly.*) Oh, Gorry, I'se skeered in dis place! I'se skeered! Oh, Lawd, pertect dis sinner!

(*Crawling away from the altar, he cowers close to the ground, his face hidden, his shoulders heaving with sobs of hysterical fright. From behind the trunk of the tree, as if he had sprung out of it, the figure of the Congo Witch-doctor appears. He is wizened and old, naked except for the fur of some small animal tied about his waist, its bushy tail hanging down in front. His body is stained all over a bright red. Antelope horns are on each side of his head, branching upward. In one hand he carries a bone rattle, in the other a charm stick with a bunch of white cockatoo feathers tied to the end. A great number of glass beads and bone ornaments are about his neck, ears, wrists, and ankles. He*

struts noiselessly with a queer prancing step to a position in the clear ground between Jones and the altar. Then with a preliminary, summoning stamp of his foot on the earth, he begins to dance and to chant. As if in response to his summons the beating of the tom-tom grows to a fierce, exultant boom whose throbs seem to fill the air with vibrating rhythm. Jones looks up, starts to spring to his feet, reaches a half-kneeling, half-squatting position and remains rigidly fixed there, paralyzed with awed fascination by this new apparition. The Witch-doctor sways, stamping with his foot, his bone rattle clicking the time. His voice rises and falls in a weird, monotonous croon, without articulate word divisions. Gradually his dance becomes clearly one of a narrative in pantomime, his croon is an incantation, a charm to allay the fierceness of some implacable deity demanding sacrifice. He flees, he is pursued by devils, he hides, he flees again. Ever wilder and wilder becomes his flight, nearer and nearer draws the pursuing evil, more and more the spirit of terror gains possession of him. His croon, rising to intensity, is punctuated by shrill cries. Jones has become completely hypnotized. His voice joins in the incantation, in the cries, he beats time with his hands and sways his body to and fro from the waist. The whole spirit and meaning of the dance has entered into him, has become his spirit. Finally the theme of the pantomime halts on a howl of despair, and is taken up again in a note of savage hope. There is a salvation. The forces of evil demand sacrifice. They must be appeased. The Witch-doctor points with his wand to the sacred tree, to the river beyond, to the altar, and finally to Jones with a ferocious command. Jones seems to sense the meaning of this. It is he who must offer himself for sacrifice. He beats his forehead abjectly to the ground, moaning hysterically.)

Mercy, Oh Lawd! Mercy! Mercy on dis po' sinner.

(*The Witch-doctor springs to the river bank. He stretches out his arms and calls to some god within its depths. Then he starts backward slowly, his arms remaining out. A huge head of a crocodile appears over the bank and its eyes, glittering greenly, fasten upon Jones. He stares into them fascinatedly. The Witch-doctor prances up to him, touches him with his wand, motions with hideous command toward the waiting monster. Jones squirms on his belly nearer and nearer, moaning continually.*)

Mercy, Lawd! Mercy!

(*The crocodile heaves more of his enormous bulk onto the land. Jones squirms toward him. The Witch-doctor voice shrills out in furious exultation, the tom-tom beats madly. Jones cries out in a fierce, exhausted spasm of anguished pleading.*)

Lawd, save me! Lawd Jesus, heah my prayer!

(*Immediately, in answer to his prayer, comes the thought of the one bullet left him. He snatches at his hip, shouting defiantly.*)

De silver bullet! You don't git me yit!

(*He fires at the green eyes in front of him. The head of the crocodile sinks back behind the river bank, the Witch-doctor springs behind the sacred tree and disappears. Jones lies with his face to the ground, his arms outstretched, whimpering with fear as the throb of the tom-tom fills the silence about him with a somber pulsation, a baffled but revengeful power.*)

SCENE 8

SCENE: *Dawn. Same as Scene II, the dividing line of forest and plain. The nearest tree trunks are dimly revealed but the forest behind them is still a mass of glooming shadows. The tom-tom seems on the very spot, so loud and continuously vibrating are its beats. Lem enters from the left, followed by a small squad of his soldiers, and by the Cockney trader, Smithers. Lem is a heavy-set, ape-faced old savage of the extreme African type, dressed only in a loin cloth. A revolver and cartridge belt are about his waist. His soldiers are in different degrees of rag-concealed nakedness. All wear broad palm-leaf hats. Each one carries a rifle. Smithers is the same as in Scene I. One of the soldiers, evidently a tracker, is peering about keenly on the ground. He grunts and points to the spot where Jones entered the forest. Lem and Smithers come to look.*

SMITHERS (*after a glance, turns away in disgust*). That's where 'e went in right enough. Much good it'll do yer. 'E's miles orf by this an' safe to the Coast, damn 'is 'ide! I tole yer yer'd lose 'im, didn't I?—wastin' the 'ole bloomin' night beatin' yer bloody drum and castin' yer silly spells! Gawd blimey, wot a pack!

LEM (*gutturally*). We cotch him. You see. (*He makes a motion to his soldiers who squat down on their haunches in a semicircle.*)

SMITHERS (*exasperatedly*). Well, ain't yer goin' in an' 'unt 'im in the woods? What the 'ell's the good of waitin'?

LEM (*imperturbably—squatting down himself*). We cotch him.

SMITHERS (*turning away from him contemptuously*). Aw! Garn! 'E's a better man than the lot o' you put together. I 'ates the sight o' 'im but I'll say that for 'im.

(*A sound of snapping twigs comes from the forest. The soldiers jump to their feet, cocking their rifles alertly. Lem remains sitting with an imperturbable expression, but listening intently. The sound from the woods is repeated. Lem makes a quick signal with his hand. His followers creep quickly but noiselessly into the forest, scattering so that each enters at a different spot.*)

SMITHERS (*in the silence that follows—in a contemptuous whisper*). You ain't thinkin' that would be 'im, I 'ope?

LEM (*calmly*). We cotch him.

SMITHERS. Blarsted fat 'eads! (*Then after a second's thought—wonderingly.*) Still an' all, it might 'appen. If 'e lost 'is bloody way in these stinkin' woods 'e'd likely turn in a circle without 'is knowin' it. They all does.

LEM (*peremptorily*). Sssh!

(*The reports of several rifles sound from the forest, followed a second later by savage, exultant yells. The beating of the tom-tom abruptly ceases. Lem looks up at the white man with a grin of satisfaction.*)

We cotch him. Him dead.

SMITHERS (*with a snarl*). 'Ow d'yer know it's 'im an' 'ow d'yer know 'e's dead?

LEM. My mens dey got 'um silver bullets. Dey kill him shore.

SMITHERS (*astonished*). They got silver bullets?

LEM. Lead bullet no kill him. He got um strong charm. I cook um money, make um silver bullet, make um strong charm, too.

SMITHERS (*light breaking upon him*). So that's wot you was up to all night, wot? You was scared to put after 'im till you'd moulded silver bullets, eh?

LEM (*simply stating a fact*). Yes. Him got strong charm. Lead no good.

SMITHERS (*slapping his thigh and guffawing*). Haw-haw! If yer don't beat all 'ell! (*Then recovering himself—scornfully.*) I'll bet yer it ain't 'im they shot at all, yer bleedin' looney!

LEM (*calmly*). Dey come bring him now.

(*The soldiers come out of the forest, carrying Jones' limp body. There is a little reddish-purple hole under his left breast. He is dead. They carry him to Lem, who examines his body with great satisfaction. Smithers over his shoulder—in a tone of frightened awe.*)

Well, they did for yer right enough, Jonsey, me lad! Dead as a 'erring! (*Mockingly.*) Where's yer 'igh an' mighty airs now, yer bloomin' Majesty? (*Then with a grin.*) Silver bullets! Gawd blimey, but yer died in the 'eighth o' style, any'ow!

(*Lem makes a motion to the soldiers to carry the body out left. Smithers speaks to him sneeringly.*)

SMITHERS. And I s'pose you think it's yer bleedin' charms and yer silly beatin' the drum that made 'im run in a circle when 'e'd lost 'imself, don't yer?

(*But Lem makes no reply, does not seem to hear the question, walks out left after his men. Smithers looks after him with contemptuous scorn.*)

Stupid as 'ogs, the lot of 'em! Blarsted niggers!

CURTAIN FALLS

TOPICS FOR CRITICAL THINKING AND WRITING

The Play on the PAGE

1. Smithers is essentially a coward. Why, then, does he talk impudently and even angrily to Jones at the start of the play?

2. Discuss the organization of the six scenes in the jungle. (O'Neill gives us, first, the "little formless fears," then the memory of the murder of Jeff, the memory of the murder of the prison guard, the slave auction, the slave ship, and the African ceremony.) How are the last three of these fundamentally different from the first three? Dramatically speaking, could the last three be given before the first three? Explain.

3. Jones runs in a circle. Smithers sees in this only a simple fact, but can one say that the symmetry is meaningful? Do you think it is appropriate, for instance, to see in it a return to our inarticulate and mysterious origin? Explain.

4. If you don't recall the time scheme of the play, look again to see at what time of day the play begins and at what time it ends. What do you make out of this structure?

5. How relevant to the play do you find the concepts of *hybris* and *hamartia* (see pages 33–34 and Glossary)? Explain.

6. The play was enthusiastically received in 1920. Heywood Broun, however, writing in the *New York Tribune* (see page 732), offered one objection in an otherwise ecstatic review: "We cannot understand just why he [O'Neill] has allowed the Emperor to die to the sound of off-stage shots. It is our idea that he should come crawling to the very spot where he meets his death and that the natives should be molding silver bullets there and waiting without so much as stretching out a finger for him." What do you think of Broun's suggestion?

The Play on the STAGE

7. O'Neill's stage direction concerning the tom-tom is inaccurate. He says that it "continues . . . uninterruptedly to the very end of the play," but in the middle of Scene 8 O'Neill writes, "The beating of the tom-tom abruptly ceases." Why does O'Neill stop the tom-tom here? Would it be more effective if it continued until the end of the play? Explain.

8. In addition to the tom-tom, other sound effects are used. What are they, and how effective do you think they are?

9. *The Emperor Jones* has eight scenes, a large number for a short play. What is the effect of so large a number? After all, the six central, expressionistic scenes between the realistic opening and closing scenes could, with a little rewriting, have been one long scene, but O'Neill chose to put the material into six scenes. Why? Hint: Expressionistic drama (see Glossary) often uses a lot of scenes—but why?

10. Some years after the original production, O'Neill said, "All the figures in Jones's flight through the forest should be masked. Masks would dramatically stress their phantasmal quality, as contrasted with the unmasked Jones, intensify the supernatural menace of the tom-tom, give the play a more complete and vivid expression." If you were staging the play, would you use masks, as O'Neill suggests? Why?

The Play in PERFORMANCE

The Emperor Jones opened on November 4, 1920, at the Provincetown Playhouse, in Greenwich Village, New York. (The theater derived its name from a town on Cape Cod, Massachusetts, where in the summer of 1915 a group of amateurs staged some of their own plays. In the following year—the year that O'Neill joined them—they moved to Greenwich Village, in New York City, but they kept their original name.) Although not every review was highly favorable, several reviewers were extremely enthusiastic, and on the whole the reviews were good. Early in the run the play moved to a larger theater, and what was scheduled for a run of two weeks turned into a run of two hundred four performances.

For the first run, O'Neill and the other members of the company selected an African American actor, Charles Gilpin (1878–1930). The choice of a black seems unexceptional now (indeed, any other choice is almost unthinkable), but in 1920, when blacks played only minor roles in plays with white companies, the choice was highly daring. Ordinarily, the role would have gone to a white actor who would play it in blackface. O'Neill himself had acted in blackface in an earlier play. Gilpin was immensely successful, and many years later O'Neill said that Gilpin was the only actor who ever performed an O'Neill role to O'Neill's fullest satisfaction. However, a strain developed during the course of the run. Gilpin felt uneasy speaking the word *nigger,* and so he began to substitute words such as *colored man* and *Negro* for *nigger.* O'Neill was furious and insisted that Gilpin follow the text.

When the play was revived in 1924, O'Neill turned with some relief to Paul Robeson (1898–1976), who also played in the London production of 1925. In later years Robeson performed in revivals in Europe and the United States until 1940. Robeson also played Jones in a film version of 1933 and in a concert version of an opera (1933), though in the full production of the opera the baritone Lawrence Tibbett sang Jones in blackface.

In 1964 *The Emperor Jones* was performed at the Boston Arts Festival, starring James Earl Jones, in a production that used no scenery other than a few platforms and some backing flats. A dozen dancers were used for the phantoms. On the whole, the play was rarely seen in the 1960s and 1970s, doubtless because the advanced thinking of 1920 seemed to be racist thinking forty or fifty years later, but an off-Broadway revival in 1977 was greeted favorably. A revival in the 1990s was offered in New York by the Wooster Group, which is known for its utterly untraditional methods. Any description of one of its productions (especially a brief description) is bound to sound puzzling and more than a little eccentric, but audiences who experience the plays find the productions exciting. Kate Valk, a white woman, played Jones in blackface. More precisely, in the opening sequence her head appeared on a large television screen, in blackface, but because a negative was projected, her face was white and her lips were dark. In the dialogue with Smithers, she addressed the audience, not Smithers; Smithers, offstage, spoke to a video camera, and his image was reproduced on an up-center stage screen. Again, we can say only that the production caught the *excitement* that (judging from the original reviews) animated the Provincetown Players when they produced the play in 1920. Something of the Wooster production can be ascertained from a discussion in *The Eugene O'Neill Review* 16.2 (1992): 114–22.

We have already mentioned that Robeson starred in a film version of 1933. The film is a very free adaptation, apparently constructed chiefly to allow Robeson to show his talents as a singer. Louis Gruenberg's opera (1933) had a very limited success in New York, Los Angeles, and San Francisco when it was first done and probably has not been heard since. José Limon, the Mexican-born dancer and choreographer who grew up in the United States, choreographed the play in 1956 and often performed it in later years. The play also exists as a recording. In 1971 Caedmon issued an album of two long-playing records starring James Earl Jones. The records include comments by Jones, who expresses the suspicion that O'Neill was a racist and that he used "Niggerisms" in order to make the play acceptable to a white audience of the 1920s. Jones does grant that younger blacks, seeing the play as a "study of power," may find it acceptable. We should add that Jones's performance on the recording is extremely effective.

HEYWOOD BROUN
A Review of The Emperor Jones

Heywood Broun (1888–1939), a newspaper columnist and critic, wrote a syndicated column, "It Seems to Me." We reprint his influential review of the first production of *The Emperor Jones*.

Subject to later reservations and revisions, when all the missing districts are in, Eugene O'Neill's *The Emperor Jones* seems to us just about the most interesting play which has yet come from the most promising playwright in America. Perhaps we ought to be a little more courageous and say right out the best of American playwrights, but somehow or other a superlative carries the implication of a certain static quality. We never see a play by O'Neill without feeling that something of the sort will be done better within a season or so, and that O'Neill will do it.

As gorgeous a piece as *The Emperor Jones* has loose ends fluttering here and there as they trail along with the clouds of glory. This is a play of high trajectory and up above the country stores and the lobby of the Palace Hotel, Wuppinger Falls, ten months later and Yvette's boudoir there is a rarer atmosphere which makes it difficult to avoid an occasional slip this way and that.

The Emperor Jones tells of an American negro, a Pullman porter, who, by some chance or other, comes to an island in the West Indies, "not yet self-determined by white marines." In two years Jones has made himself emperor. Luck has played a part, but he has been quick to take advantage of it. Once a native tried to shoot him at point-blank range, but the gun missed fire, whereupon Jones announced that he was protected by a charm and that only silver bullets could harm him. When the play begins he has been emperor long enough to amass a fortune by imposing heavy taxes on the islanders and carrying on all sorts of large-scale graft. Rebellion is brewing. When Emperor Jones rings the bell which should summon his servants no one appears. The palace is deserted, but from deep in the jungle there comes the sound of the steady beat of a big drum. The islanders are whipping up their courage to the fighting point by calling on the local gods and demons of the forest.

Jones, realizing that his reign is over, starts to make his escape to the coast where a French gunboat is anchored. First it is necessary for him to travel through the jungle and as time presses he must go through at night. Back in the States he was a good Baptist and he begins the journey through the dark places unafraid. But under the dim moonlight he cannot recognize any familiar landmarks and, hard as he runs, the continuous drumbeat never grows any less in his ears. Then demons and apparitions begin to torment him. First it is the figure of a negro he killed back in the States. He fires and the dim thing vanishes, but immediately he reproaches himself, for in his revolver now he has only five shots left. Four are lead bullets and the fifth is a silver one which he has reserved for himself, if by any chance capture seems imminent.

Other little "formless fears" creep in upon him. As his panic increases the fears become not things in his own life, but old race fears. He sees himself being sold in a slave market and then, most horrible of all, a Congo witch doctor tries to lure him to death in a river where a crocodile god is waiting. It is at this point that he fires his last bullet, the silver one.

During the night he has discarded his big patent leather boots and most of his clothes in order to run faster from the drumbeat. But it is louder now than ever and in the last scene we find the natives sitting about in a circle weaving spells and molding bullets. And it is to this spot that the defenseless and exhausted emperor crawls, having made a complete circle in the jungle as his panic whipped him on.

The play is of eight scenes and it is largely a monologue by one character, the Emperor Jones. Unfortunately, production in the tiny Provincetown Theatre is difficult and the waits between these scenes are often several minutes in length. Each wait is a vulture which preys upon the attention. With the beginning of each new scene, contact must again be established and all this unquestionably hurts. Still we have no disposition to say, "If only the play had been done in 'the commercial theatre'!" This is a not infrequent comment whenever a little theatre does a fine piece of work and it seems to us to have in it something of the spirit of a man standing on the deck of a great liner who should remark, "Wasn't Columbus a bally ass to come over in such a little tub!"

The Emperor Jones is so unusual in its technique that it might wait in vain for a production anywhere except in so adventurous a playhouse as the Provincetown Theatre. As a matter of fact, the setting of the play on the little stage is fine and imaginative and the lighting effects uncommonly beautiful. There is nothing for complaint but the delays. Also, if *The Emperor Jones* were taken elsewhere we have little doubt that the manager would engage a white man with a piece of burnt cork to play Brutus Jones. They have done better in Macdougal Street. The Emperor is played by a negro actor named Charles S. Gilpin, who gives the most thrilling performance we have seen any place this season. He sustains the succession of scenes in monologue not only because his voice is one of gorgeous natural quality, but because he knows just what to do with it. All the notes are there and he has also the extraordinary facility for being in the right place at the right time. Generally he seems fairly painted into the scenic design. One performance is not enough to entitle a player to the word great even from a not too careful critic, but there can be no question whatever that in *The Emperor Jones* Gilpin is great. It is a performance

of heroic stature. It is so good that the fact that it is enormously skillful seems only incidental.

Aside from difficulties of production there are some faults in O'Neill's play. He has almost completely missed the opportunities of his last scene, which should blaze with a vast tinder spark of irony. Instead, he rounds it off with a snap of the fingers, a little O. Henry dido. We cannot understand just why he has allowed the Emperor to die to the sound of off-stage shots. It is our idea that he should come crawling to the very spot where he meets his death and that the natives should be molding silver bullets there and waiting without so much as stretching out a finger for him. Of course all this goes to show that *The Emperor Jones* is truly a fine play. It is only such which tempt the spectator to leap in himself as a collaborator.

SOPHIE Treadwell

Sophie Treadwell (1885–1970) was born in Northern California and studied at the University of California, Berkeley, from which she graduated in 1906. During the course of her studies, she found an outlet for her considerable creativity, acting in university theater productions, writing plays, and working for the school newspaper. After a brief stint as a vaudeville performer, she joined the *San Francisco Bulletin*, covering everything from play premieres to baseball games and steadily gaining a reputation as a first-class reporter. Her assignments included undercover reporting of homeless women, a European tour as one of the first women war correspondents (1916–18), and a period of time in Mexico where she had an exclusive interview with the Mexican revolutionary, Pancho Villa. Her world travels often served as inspiration for her plays, such as her first New York–produced work, *Gringo* (1922). Her most famous play, *Machinal* (French for "mechanical"), was produced on Broadway in 1928. In the course of her prolific career, Treadwell, who died at age eighty-four, had completed hundreds of newspaper stories, four novels, and forty plays on a variety of subjects and in a variety of styles. Seven of the plays were produced in New York City.

COMMENTARY ON *MACHINAL*

The inspiration for *Machinal* was a sensational murder trial that filled the newspapers and tabloids during 1927. The Ruth Snyder-Judd Gray case centered on a Long Island housewife and her lover, a traveling corset salesman, who murdered the housewife's husband. Treadwell, fascinated and horrified by the trial and its attendant publicity, attended the full trial proceedings and the execution. The writing of *Machinal* gave Treadwell the opportunity to create a female character with a mental and emotional background that leads her to commit such a crime.

As a woman herself, Treadwell had a long and abiding interest in the position of women in society. She had been active in the suffrage movement, taking part in a long march from New York City to Albany to present a suffrage petition to the state legislature in 1914. Her writing consistently examines the social and cultural conditions that inhibit women from obtaining independence and equality. With *Machinal* she was able to explore these issues in an innovative and experimental way. Although the Snyder case was the springboard for her inquiry into her gender critique of contemporary life, Treadwell begins her play with the following: "The Plot [is] the story of a woman who murders her husband—an ordinary young woman, any woman." This sense of "any woman" is stressed in the script by identifying the characters generically such as "Young Woman," "Filing Clerk," "Mother." The point

for Treadwell was not about the specific case of Ruth Snyder, but the pervasive and oppressive way in which male-created laws and society stifle the voices and emotional needs of women.

Opportunely for Treadwell, New York theater in the 1920s was a hotbed for new forms of nonrealistic playwriting, directing, and designing. European expressionism had made a particular impact on American writers, resulting in plays on Broadway such as Eugene O'Neill's *The Emperor Jones* (1920, also in this volume), Susan Glaspell's *The Verge* (1921), and Elmer Rice's *The Adding Machine* (1923). After the U.S. release in 1921 of the German innovative expressionist film *The Cabinet of Dr. Caligari*, a fair number of European plays were produced in translation, including Georg Kaiser's *From Morn to Midnight* (1924), August Strindberg's *The Ghost Sonata* (1924) and *A Dream Play* (1926), and Franz Werfel's *Goat Song* (1926).

Expressionism, an early twentieth-century movement that encompassed all the arts, began in Germany before World War I and was characterized as a revolt against the industrialization of society. Through a variety of stylizations—such as angled distortions, exaggerated facial expressions or movement, dreamlike action, fragmentation—expressionist artists eschewed representations of surface reality and, instead, depicted inner, subjective states of emotion and experience. (For further details, see the Glossary.)

In *Machinal* Sophie Treadwell achieved an innovative fusion between American realism and European expressionism. She is one of the first American women playwrights to experiment with nonrealistic innovations in style and plot, and, no less significant, she is one of the first playwrights to pursue a feminist aesthetic in theater. As Jerry Dickey says in "The Expressionist Moment: Sophie Treadwell":

> Treadwell presents the action of *Machinal* in an episodic, fragmented manner. The action unfolds in fits and starts and appears noteworthy especially for what it does not present on stage. *Machinal* avoids the type of confrontational scenes normally found in both realistic and expressionist dramas: there is no scene in which the jealous husband accuses his wife of infidelity, no emotionally contrived scene in which the Young Woman's daughter appears for sentimental affect, no tearful farewell episode between the Young Woman and Roe when he returns to Mexico, and most obviously no scene depicting the actual murder or subsequent arrest. Instead, Treadwell augments her short, suggestive scenes with a wide variety of expressionist devices to encourage audiences to project into the skeletal action the motivations and factors affecting the behavior of the characters. (in Murphy 74)

MACHINAL
Sophie Treadwell

CHARACTERS

YOUNG WOMAN
TELEPHONE GIRL
STENOGRAPHER
FILING CLERK
ADDING CLERK
MOTHER
HUSBAND
BELLBOY
NURSE
DOCTOR
YOUNG MAN
GIRL
MAN
BOY
MAN
ANOTHER MAN
WAITER
JUDGE
LAWYER FOR DEFENSE
LAWYER FOR PROSECUTION
COURT REPORTER
BAILIFF
REPORTER
SECOND REPORTER
THIRD REPORTER
JAILER
MATRON
PRIEST

EPISODE I, *To Business*
EPISODE II, *At Home*
EPISODE III, *Honeymoon*
EPISODE IV, *Maternal*
EPISODE V, *Prohibited*
EPISODE VI, *Intimate*
EPISODE VII, *Domestic*
EPISODE VIII, *The Law*
EPISODE IX, *A Machine*

The Plot: The story of a woman who murders her husband—an ordinary young woman, any woman.

The Plan: To tell this story by showing the different phases of life that the woman comes in contact with, and in none of which she finds any place, any peace. The woman is essentially soft, tender, and the life around her is essentially hard, mechanized.

Business, home, marriage, having a child, seeking pleasure—all are difficult for her—mechanical, nerve nagging. Only in an illicit love does she find anything with life in it for her, and when she loses this, the desperate effort to win free to it again is her undoing.

The story is told in nine scenes. In the dialogue of these scenes there is the attempt to catch the rhythm of our common city speech, its brassy sound, its trick of repetition, etc.

Then there is, also, the use of many different sounds chosen primarily for their inherent emotional effect (steel riveting, a priest chanting, a Negro singing, jazz band, etc.), but contributing also to the creation of a background, an atmosphere.

The Hope: To create a stage production that will have 'style,' and at the same time, by the story's own innate drama, by the directness of its telling, by the variety and quick changingness of its scenes, and the excitement of its sounds, to create an interesting play.

Scenically: This play is planned to be handled in two basic sets (or in one set with two backs).

The first division—the first Four Episodes—needs an entrance at one side, and a back having a door and a large window. The door gives, in

Episode 1—to Vice President's office.
Episode 2 – to hall.
Episode 3 – to bathroom.
Episode 4 – to corridor.

And the window shows, in

Episode 1 – An opposite office.
Episode 2 – An inner apartment court.
Episode 3 – Window of a dance casino opposite.
Episode 4 – Steel girders. (Of these, only the casino window is important. Sky could be used for the others.)

The second division—the last Five Episodes—has the same side entrance, but the back has only one opening—for a small window (barred).

Episode 5, window is masked by electric piano.
Episode 6, window is disclosed (sidewalk outside).
Episode 7, window is curtained.
Episode 8, window is masked by Judge's bench.
Episode 9, window is disclosed (sky outside).

There is a change of furniture, and props for each episode—only essential things, full of character. For Episode 9, the room is closed in from the sides, and there is a place with bars and a door *in it, put straight across stage down front (back far enough to leave a clear passageway in front of it).*

    Lighting concentrated and intense.—Light and shadow— bright light and darkness.—This darkness, already in the scene, grows and blacks out the light for dark stage when the scene changes are made.

Offstage Voices: *Characters in the Background Heard, but Unseen:*

> *A Janitor*
> *A Baby*
> *A Boy and a Girl*
> *A Husband and Wife*
> *A Husband and Wife*
> *A Radio Announcer*
> *A Negro Singer*

Mechanical Offstage Sounds:
> *A small jazz band*

> *A hand organ*
> *Steel riveting*
> *Telegraph instruments*
> *Aeroplane engine*

Mechanical Onstage Sounds:
> *Office Machines (typewriters, telephones, etc.)*
> *Electric piano.*

Characters: *in the Background Seen, Not Heard (Seen, off the main set; i.e., through a window or door)*

> *Couples of men and women dancing*
> *A Woman in a bathrobe*
> *A Woman in a wheel chair*
> *A Nurse with a covered basin*
> *A Nurse with a tray*
> *The feet of men and women passing in the street*

EPISODE ONE

TO BUSINESS

    SCENE: *An office: a switchboard, filing cabinet, adding machine, typewriter and table, manifold machine.*
    SOUNDS: *Office machines: typewriters, adding machine, manifold, telephone bells, buzzers.*
    CHARACTERS AND THEIR MACHINES: *A Young Woman (typewriter); A Stenographer (typewriter); A Filing Clerk (filing cabinet and manifold); An Adding Clerk (adding machine); Telephone Operator (switchboard); Jones*

BEFORE THE CURTAIN: *Sounds of machines going. They continue throughout the scene, and accompany the Young Woman's thoughts after the scene is blacked out.*

AT THE RISE OF THE CURTAIN: *All the machines are disclosed, and all the characters with the exception of the Young Woman.*
    Of these characters, the Young Woman, going any day to any business. Ordinary. The confusion of her own inner thoughts, emotions, desires, dreams cuts her off from any actual adjustment to the routine of work. She gets through this routine with a very small surface of her consciousness. She is not homely and she is not pretty. She is preoccupied with herself—with her person. She has well kept hands, and a trick of constantly arranging her hair over her ears.
    The Stenographer is the faded, efficient woman office worker. Drying, dried.

The Adding Clerk is her male counterpart.
The Filing Clerk is a boy not grown, callow adolescence.
The Telephone Girl, young, cheap and amorous.
Lights come up on office scene. Two desks right and left.
Telephone booth back right center. Filing cabinet back of center, Adding machine back left center.

ADDING CLERK (*in the monotonous voice of his monotonous thoughts; at his adding machine*). 2490, 28, 76, 123, 36842, 1, 1/4, 37, 804, 23 1/2, 982.

FILING CLERK (*in the same way—at his filing desk*). Accounts— A. Bonds—B. Contracts—C. Data—D. Earnings—E.

STENOGRAPHER (*in the same way—left*). Dear Sir—in re— your letter—recent date—will state—

TELEPHONE GIRL. Hello—Hello—George H. Jones Company good morning—hello hello—George H. Jones Company good morning—hello.

FILING CLERK. Market—M. Notes—N. Output—O. Profits— P.—! (*Suddenly.*) What's the matter with Q?

TELEPHONE GIRL. Matter with it—Mr. J.—Mr. K. wants you—What you mean matter? Matter with what?

FILING CLERK. Matter with Q.

TELEPHONE GIRL. Well—what is? Spring 1726?

FILING CLERK. I'm asking yuh—

TELEPHONE GIRL. Well?

FILING CLERK. Nothing filed with it—

TELEPHONE GIRL. Well?

FILING CLERK. Look at A. Look at B. What's the matter with Q?

TELEPHONE GIRL. Ain't popular. Hello—Hello—George H. Jones Company

FILING CLERK. Hot dog! Why ain't it?

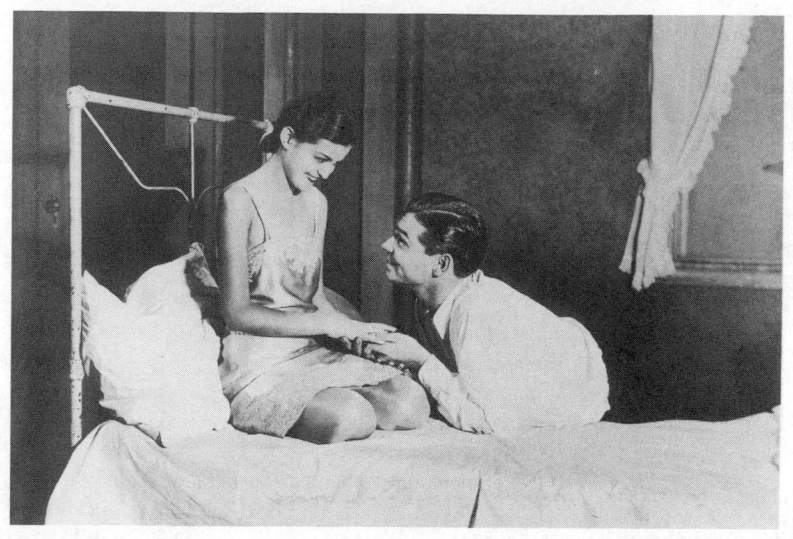

In the original 1928 Broadway production of Tread-well's *Machinal*, Zita Johann plays a young woman and the young lover is played by Clark Gable in his first appearance on Broadway. Arthur Hopkins directed this production with expressionistic sets by Robert Edmond Jones.

ADDING CLERK. Has it personality?
STENOGRAPHER. Has it Halitosis?
TELEPHONE GIRL. Has it got it?
FILING CLERK. Hot dog!
TELEPHONE GIRL. What number do you want? (*Recognizing but not pleased.*) Oh—hello—sure I know who it is—tonight? Uh, uh—(*Negative, but each with a different inflection.*) You heard me—No!
FILING CLERK. Don't you like him?
STENOGRAPHER. She likes 'em all.
TELEPHONE GIRL. I do not!
STENOGRAPHER. Well—pretty near all!
TELEPHONE GIRL. What number do you want? Wrong number. Hello—hello—George H. Jones Company. Hello, hello—
STENOGRAPHER. Memorandum—attention Mr. Smith—at a conference of—
ADDING CLERK. 125—83 3/4—22—908—34—1/4—28593.
FILING CLERK. Report—R, Sales—S, Trade—T.
TELEPHONE GIRL. Shh—! Yes, Mr. J.—? No—Miss A. ain't in yet—I'll tell her, Mr. J.—just the minute she gets in.
STENOGRAPHER. She's late again, huh?
TELEPHONE GIRL. Out with her sweetie last night, huh?
FILING CLERK. Hot dog.
ADDING CLERK. She ain't got a sweetie.
STENOGRAPHER. How do you know?
ADDING CLERK. I know.
FILING CLERK. Hot dog.
ADDING CLERK. She lives alone with her mother.
TELEPHONE GIRL. Spring 1876? Hello—Spring 1876. Spring! Hello, Spring 1876? 1876! Wrong number! Hello! Hello!
STENOGRAPHER. Director's meeting semi-annual report card.
FILING CLERK. Shipments—Sales—Schedules—S.
ADDING CLERK. She doesn't belong in an office.
TELEPHONE GIRL. Who does?

STENOGRAPHER. I do!
ADDING CLERK. You said it!
FILING CLERK. Hot dog!
TELEPHONE GIRL. Hello—hello—George H. Jones Company—hello—hello—
STENOGRAPHER. I'm efficient. She's inefficient.
FILING CLERK. She's inefficient.
TELEPHONE GIRL. She's got J. going.
STENOGRAPHER. Going?
TELEPHONE GIRL. Going and coming.
FILING CLERK. Hot dog.

Enter Jones.

JONES. Good morning, everybody.
TELEPHONE GIRL. Good morning.
FILING CLERK. Good morning.
ADDING CLERK. Good morning.
STENOGRAPHER. Good morning, Mr. J.
JONES. Miss A. isn't in yet?
TELEPHONE GIRL. Not yet, Mr. J.
FILING CLERK. Not yet.
ADDING CLERK. Not yet.
STENOGRAPHER. She's late.
JONES. I just wanted her to take a letter.
STENOGRAPHER. I'll take the letter.
JONES. One thing at a time and that done well.
ADDING CLERK (*yessing*). Done well.
STENOGRAPHER. I'll finish it later.
JONES. Hew to the line.
ADDING CLERK. Hew to the line.
STENOGRAPHER. Then I'll hurry.
JONES. Haste makes waste.
ADDING CLERK. Waste.
STENOGRAPHER. But if you're in a hurry.

JONES. I'm never in a hurry—That's how I get ahead! (*Laughs. They all laugh.*) First know you're right—then go ahead.

ADDING CLERK. Ahead.

JONES (*to Telephone Girl*). When Miss A. comes in tell her I want her to take a letter. (*Turns to go in—then.*) It's important.

TELEPHONE GIRL (*making a note*). Miss A.—important.

JONES (*starts up—then*). And I don't want to be disturbed.

TELEPHONE GIRL. You're in conference?

JONES. I'm in conference. (*Turns—then.*) Unless it's A.B.—of course.

TELEPHONE GIRL. Of course—A.B.

JONES (*starts—turns again; attempts to be facetious*). Tell Miss A. the early bird catches the worm.

Exit Jones.

TELEPHONE GIRL. The early worm gets caught.

ADDING CLERK. He's caught.

TELEPHONE GIRL. Hooked.

ADDING CLERK. In the pan.

FILING CLERK. Hot dog.

STENOGRAPHER. We beg leave to announce—

Enter Young Woman. Goes behind telephone booth to desk right.

STENOGRAPHER. You're late!

FILING CLERK. You're late.

ADDING CLERK. You're late.

STENOGRAPHER. And yesterday!

FILING CLERK. The day before.

ADDING CLERK. And the day before.

STENOGRAPHER. You'll lose your job.

YOUNG WOMAN. No!

STENOGRAPHER. No?

Workers exchange glances.

YOUNG WOMAN. I can't!

STENOGRAPHER. Can't?

Same business.

FILING CLERK. Rent—bills—installments—miscellaneous.

ADDING CLERK. A dollar ten—ninety-five—3.40—35—12.60.

STENOGRAPHER. Then why are you late?

YOUNG WOMAN. Why?

STENOGRAPHER. Excuse!

ADDING CLERK. Excuse!

FILING CLERK. Excuse.

TELEPHONE GIRL. Excuse it, please.

STENOGRAPHER. Why?

YOUNG WOMAN. The subway?

TELEPHONE GIRL. Long distance?

FILING CLERK. Old stuff!

ADDING CLERK. That stall!

STENOGRAPHER. Stalled?

YOUNG WOMAN. No—

STENOGRAPHER. What?

YOUNG WOMAN. I had to get out!

ADDING CLERK. Out!

FILING CLERK. Out?

STENOGRAPHER. Out where?

YOUNG WOMAN. In the air!

STENOGRAPHER. Air?

YOUNG WOMAN. All those bodies pressing.

FILING CLERK. Hot dog!

YOUNG WOMAN. I thought I would faint! I had to get out in the air!

FILING CLERK. Give her the air.

ADDING CLERK. Free air—

STENOGRAPHER. Hot air.

YOUNG WOMAN. Like I'm dying.

STENOGRAPHER. Same thing yesterday. (*Pause.*) And the day before.

YOUNG WOMAN. Yes—what am I going to do?

ADDING CLERK. Take a taxi! (*They laugh.*)

FILING CLERK. Call a cop!

TELEPHONE GIRL. Mr. J. wants you.

YOUNG WOMAN. Me?

TELEPHONE GIRL. You!

YOUNG WOMAN (*rises*). Mr. J.!

STENOGRAPHER. Mr. J.

TELEPHONE GIRL. He's bellowing for you!

Young Woman gives last pat to her hair—goes off into door—back.

STENOGRAPHER (*after her*). Get it just right.

FILING CLERK. She's always doing that to her hair.

TELEPHONE GIRL. It gives a line—it gives a line—

FILING CLERK. Hot dog.

ADDING CLERK. She's artistic.

STENOGRAPHER. She's inefficient.

FILING CLERK. She's inefficient.

STENOGRAPHER. Mr. J. knows she's inefficient.

ADDING CLERK. 46—23—84—2—2—2—1,492—678.

TELEPHONE GIRL. Hello—hello—George H. Jones Company—hello—Mr. Jones? He's in conference.

STENOGRAPHER (*sarcastic*). Conference!

ADDING CLERK. Conference.

FILING CLERK. Hot dog!

TELEPHONE GIRL. Do you think he'll marry her?

ADDING CLERK. If she'll have him.

STENOGRAPHER. If she'll have him!

FILING CLERK. Do you think she'll have him?

TELEPHONE GIRL. How much does he get?

ADDING CLERK. Plenty—5,000—10,000—15,000—20,000—25,000.

STENOGRAPHER. And plenty put away.

ADDING CLERK. Gas Preferred—4's—steel—5's—oil—6's.

FILING CLERK. Hot dog.

STENOGRAPHER. Will she have him? Will she have him? This agreement entered into—party of the first part—party of the second part—will he have her?

TELEPHONE GIRL. Well, I'd hate to get into bed with him. (*Familiar melting voice.*) Hello—humhum—hum—hum—hold the line a minute—will you—hum hum. (*Professional voice.*) Hell, hello—A.B., just a minute, Mr. A.B.—Mr. J.? Mr. A.B.—go ahead, Mr. A.B. (*Melting voice.*) We were interrupted—huh—huh—huh—huh-huh—hum—hum.

Enter Young Woman—she goes to her chair, sits with folded hands.

FILING CLERK. That's all you ever say to a guy—

STENOGRAPHER. Hum—hum—or uh huh—(*Negative.*)

TELEPHONE GIRL. That's all you have to. (*To phone.*) Hum—hum—hum hum—hum hum—

STENOGRAPHER. Mostly hum hum.

ADDING CLERK. You've said it!

FILING CLERK. Hot dog.

TELEPHONE GIRL. Hum hum huh hum humhumhum—tonight? She's got a date—she told me last night—humhumhuh—hum—all right. (*Disconnects.*) Too bad—my boy friend's got a friend—but my girl friend's got a date.

YOUNG WOMAN. You have a good time.

TELEPHONE GIRL. Big time.

STENOGRAPHER. Small time.

ADDING CLERK. A big time on the small time.

TELEPHONE GIRL. I'd ask you, kid, but you'd be up to your neck!

STENOGRAPHER. Neckers!

ADDING CLERK. Petters!

FILING CLERK. Sweet papas.

TELEPHONE GIRL. Want to come?

YOUNG WOMAN. Can't.

TELEPHONE GIRL. Date?

YOUNG WOMAN. My mother.

STENOGRAPHER. Worries?

TELEPHONE GIRL. Nags—hello—George H. Jones Company—Oh hello—

Young Woman sits before her machine—hands in lap, looking at them.

STENOGRAPHER. Why don't you get to work?

YOUNG WOMAN (*dreaming*). What?

ADDING CLERK. Work!

YOUNG WOMAN. Can't.

STENOGRAPHER. Can't?

YOUNG WOMAN. My machine's out of order.

STENOGRAPHER. Well, fix it!

YOUNG WOMAN. I can't—got to get somebody.

STENOGRAPHER. Somebody! Somebody! Always somebody! Here, sort the mail, then!

YOUNG WOMAN (*rises*). All right.

STENOGRAPHER. And hurry! You're late.

YOUNG WOMAN (*sorting letters*). George H. Jones and Company—George H. Jones Inc. George H. Jones—

STENOGRAPHER. You're always late.

ADDING CLERK. You'll lose your job.

YOUNG WOMAN (*hurrying*). George H. Jones—George H. Jones Personal—

TELEPHONE GIRL. Don't let 'em get your goat, kid—tell 'em where to get off.

YOUNG WOMAN. What?

TELEPHONE GIRL. Ain't it all set?

YOUNG WOMAN. What?

TELEPHONE GIRL. You and Mr. J.

STENOGRAPHER. You and the boss.

FILING CLERK. You and the big chief.

ADDING CLERK. You and the big cheese.

YOUNG WOMAN. Did he tell you?

TELEPHONE GIRL. I told you!

ADDING CLERK. I told you!

STENOGRAPHER. I don't believe it.

ADDING CLERK. 5,000—10,000—15,000.

FILING CLERK. Hot dog.

YOUNG WOMAN. No—it isn't so.

STENOGRAPHER. Isn't it?

YOUNG WOMAN. No.

TELEPHONE GIRL. Not yet.

ADDING CLERK. But soon.

FILING CLERK. Hot dog.

Enter Jones.

TELEPHONE GIRL (*busy*). George H. Jones Company—Hello—Hello.

STENOGRAPHER. Awaiting your answer—

ADDING CLERK. 5,000—10,000—15,000—

JONES (*crossing to Young Woman—puts hand on her shoulder, all stop and stare*). That letter done?

YOUNG WOMAN. No. (*She pulls away.*)

JONES. What's the matter?

STENOGRAPHER. She hasn't started.

JONES. O.K.—want to make some changes.

YOUNG WOMAN. My machine's out of order.

JONES. O.K.—use the one in my room.

YOUNG WOMAN. I'm sorting the mail.

STENOGRAPHER (*sarcastic*). One thing at a time!

JONES (*retreating—goes back center*). O.K. (*To Young Woman.*) When you're finished. (*Starts back to his room.*)

STENOGRAPHER. Haste makes waste.

JONES (*at door*). O.K.—don't hurry.

Exits.

STENOGRAPHER. Hew to the line!

TELEPHONE GIRL. He's hewing.

FILING CLERK. Hot dog.

TELEPHONE GIRL. Why did you flinch, kid?

YOUNG WOMAN. Flinch?

TELEPHONE GIRL. Did he pinch?

YOUNG WOMAN. No!

TELEPHONE GIRL. Then what?

YOUNG WOMAN. Nothing!—Just his hand.

TELEPHONE GIRL. Oh—just his hand—(*Shakes her head thoughtfully.*) Uhhuh. (*Negative.*) Uhhuh. (*Decisively.*) No! Tell him no.

STENOGRAPHER. If she does she'll lose her job.

ADDING CLERK. Fired.

FILING CLERK. The sack!

TELEPHONE GIRL (*on the defensive*). And if she doesn't?

ADDING CLERK. She'll come to work in a taxi!

TELEPHONE GIRL. Work?

FILING CLERK. No work.

STENOGRAPHER. No worry.

ADDING CLERK. Breakfast in bed.

STENOGRAPHER (*sarcastic*). Did Madame ring?

FILING CLERK. Lunch in bed!

TELEPHONE GIRL. A double bed! (*In phone.*) Yes, Mr. J. (*To Young Woman.*) J. wants you.

YOUNG WOMAN (*starts to get to her feet—but doesn't*). I can't—I'm not ready—in a minute. (*Sits staring ahead of her.*)

ADDING CLERK. 5,000—10,000—15,000—

FILING CLERK. Profits—plans—purchase—

STENOGRAPHER. Call your attention our prices are fixed.

TELEPHONE GIRL. Hello—hello—George H. Jones Company—hello—hello—

YOUNG WOMAN (*thinking her thoughts aloud—to the subdued accompaniment of the office sounds and voices*). Marry me—wants to marry me—George H. Jones—George H. Jones and Company—Mrs. George H. Jones—Mrs. George H. Jones. Dear Madame—marry—do you take this man to be your wedded husband—I do—to love honor and to love—kisses—no—I can't—George H. Jones—How would you like to marry me—What do you say—Why Mr. Jones I—let me look at your little hands—you have such pretty little hands—let me hold your pretty little hands—George H. Jones—Fat hands—flabby hands—don't touch me—please—fat hands are never weary—please don't—married—all girls—most girls—married—babies—a baby—curls—little curls all over its head—George H. Jones—straight—thin—bald—don't touch me—please—no—can't—must—somebody—something—no rest—must rest—no rest—must rest—no rest—late today—yesterday—before—late—subway—air—pressing—bodies pressing—bodies—trembling—air—stop—air—late—job—no job—fired—late—alarm clock—alarm clock—alarm clock—hurry—job—ma—nag—nag—nag—ma—hurry—job—no job—no money—installments due—no money—money—George H. Jones—money—Mrs. George H. Jones—money—no work—no worry—free!—rest—sleep till nine—sleep till ten—sleep till noon—now you take a good rest this morning—don't get up till you want to—thank you—oh thank you—oh don't!—please don't touch me—I want to rest—no rest—earn—got to earn—married—earn—no—yes—earn—all girls—most girls—ma—pa—ma—all women—most women—I can't—must—maybe—must—somebody—something—ma—pa—ma—can I, ma? Tell me, ma—something—somebody.

The scene blacks out. The sounds of the office machines continue until the scene lights into Episode Two—and the office sounds become the sound of a radio, offstage.

EPISODE TWO

AT HOME

SCENE: *A kitchen: table, chairs, plates and food, garbage can, a pair of rubber gloves. The door at the back now opens on a hall—the window, on an apartment house court.*

SOUNDS: *Buzzer, radio (voice of announcer; music and singer).*

CHARACTERS: *Young Woman; Mother*

OUTSIDE VOICES: *characters heard, but not seen: A Janitor; A Baby; A Mother and a Small Boy; A Young Boy and Young Girl; A Husband and a Wife; Another Husband and a Wife*

AT RISE: *Young Woman and Mother eating—radio offstage—radio stops.*

YOUNG WOMAN. Ma—I want to talk to you.

MOTHER. Aren't you eating a potato?

YOUNG WOMAN. No.

MOTHER. Why not?

YOUNG WOMAN. I don't want one.

MOTHER. That's no reason. Here! Take one.

YOUNG WOMAN. I don't want it.

MOTHER. Potatoes go with stew—here!

YOUNG WOMAN. Ma, I don't want it!

MOTHER. Want it! Take it!

YOUNG WOMAN. But I—oh, all right. (*Takes it—then.*) Ma, I want to ask you something.

MOTHER. Eat your potato.

YOUNG WOMAN (*takes a bite—then*). Ma, there's something I want to ask you—something important.

MOTHER. Is it mealy?

YOUNG WOMAN. S'all right. Ma—tell me.

MOTHER. Three pounds for a quarter.

YOUNG WOMAN. Ma—tell me—(*Buzzer.*)

MOTHER (*her dull voice brightening*). There's the garbage. (*Goes to door—or dumbwaiter—opens it. Stop radio.*)

JANITOR'S VOICE (*offstage*). Garbage.

MOTHER (*pleased—busy*). All right. (*Gets garbage can—puts it out. Young Woman walks up and down.*) What's the matter now?

YOUNG WOMAN. Nothing.

MOTHER. That jumping up from the table every night the garbage is collected! You act like you're crazy.

YOUNG WOMAN. Ma, do all women—

MOTHER. I suppose you think you're too nice for anything so common! Well, let me tell you, my lady, that it's a very important part of life.

YOUNG WOMAN. I know, but, Ma, if you—

MOTHER. If it weren't for garbage cans where would we be? Where would we all be? Living in filth—that's what! Filth! I should think you'd be glad! I should think you'd be grateful!

YOUNG WOMAN. Oh, Ma!

MOTHER. Well, are you?

YOUNG WOMAN. Am I what?

MOTHER. Glad! Grateful.

YOUNG WOMAN. Yes!

MOTHER. You don't act like it!

YOUNG WOMAN. Oh, Ma, don't talk!

MOTHER. You just said you wanted to talk.

YOUNG WOMAN. Well now—I want to think. I got to think.

MOTHER. Aren't you going to finish your potato?

YOUNG WOMAN. Oh, Ma!

MOTHER. Is there anything the matter with it?

YOUNG WOMAN. No—

MOTHER. Then why don't you finish it?

YOUNG WOMAN. Because I don't want it.

MOTHER. Why don't you?

YOUNG WOMAN. Oh, Ma! Let me alone!

MOTHER. Well, you've got to eat! If you don't eat—

YOUNG WOMAN. Ma! Don't nag!

MOTHER. Nag! Just because I try to look out for you—nag! Just because I try to care for you—nag! Why, you haven't sense enough to eat! What should become of you I'd like to know—if I didn't nag!

Offstage—a sound of window opening—all these offstage sounds come in through the court window at the back.

WOMAN'S VOICE. Johnny—Johnny—come in now!

A SMALL BOY'S VOICE. Oh, Ma!

WOMAN'S VOICE. It's getting cold.

A SMALL BOY'S VOICE. Oh, Ma!

WOMAN'S VOICE. You heard me! (*Sound of window slamming.*)

YOUNG WOMAN. I'm grown up, Ma.

MOTHER. Grown up! What do you mean by that?

YOUNG WOMAN. Nothing much—I guess. (*Offstage sound of baby crying. Mother rises, clatters dishes.*) Let's not do the dishes right away, Ma. Let's talk—I gotta.

MOTHER. Well, I can't talk with dirty dishes around—you may be able to but—(*Clattering—clattering.*)

YOUNG WOMAN. Ma! Listen! Listen!—There's a man wants to marry me.

MOTHER (*stops clattering—sits*). What man?

YOUNG WOMAN. He says he fell in love with my hands.

MOTHER. In love! Is that beginning again! I thought you were over that!

Offstage Boy's voice—whistles—Girls's voice answers.

BOY'S VOICE. Come on out.

GIRL'S VOICE. Can't.

BOY'S VOICE. Nobody'll see you.

GIRL'S VOICE. I can't.

BOY'S VOICE. It's dark now—come on.

GIRL'S VOICE. Well—just for a minute.

BOY'S VOICE. Meet you round the corner.

YOUNG WOMAN. I got to get married, Ma.

MOTHER. What do you mean?

YOUNG WOMAN. I gotta.

MOTHER. You haven't got in trouble, have you?

YOUNG WOMAN. Don't talk like that!

MOTHER. Well, you say you got to get married—what do you mean?

YOUNG WOMAN. Nothing.

MOTHER. Answer me!

YOUNG WOMAN. All women get married, don't they?

MOTHER. Nonsense!

YOUNG WOMAN. You got married, didn't you?

MOTHER. Yes, I did!

Offstage voices.

WOMAN'S VOICE. Where you going?

MAN'S VOICE. Out.

WOMAN'S VOICE. You were out last night.

MAN'S VOICE. Was I?

WOMAN'S VOICE. You're always going out.

MAN'S VOICE. Am I?

WOMAN'S VOICE. Where you going?

MAN'S VOICE. Out

End of offstage voices.

MOTHER. Who is he? Where did you come to know him?

YOUNG WOMAN. In the office.

MOTHER. In the office!

YOUNG WOMAN. It's Mr. J.

MOTHER. Mr. J.?

YOUNG WOMAN. The Vice-President.

MOTHER. Vice-President! His income must be—Does he know you've got a mother to support?

YOUNG WOMAN. Yes.

MOTHER. What does he say?

YOUNG WOMAN. All right.

MOTHER. How soon you going to marry him?

YOUNG WOMAN. I'm not going to.

MOTHER. Not going to!

YOUNG WOMAN. No! I'm not going to.

MOTHER. But you just said—

YOUNG WOMAN. I'm not going to.

MOTHER. Are you crazy?

YOUNG WOMAN. I can't, Ma! I can't!

MOTHER. Why can't you?

YOUNG WOMAN. I don't love him.

MOTHER. Love!—what does that amount to! Will it clothe you? Will it feed you? Will it pay the bills?

YOUNG WOMAN. No! But it's real just the same!

MOTHER. Real!

YOUNG WOMAN. If it isn't—what can you count on in life?

MOTHER. I'll tell you what you can count on! You can count that you've got to eat and sleep and get up and put clothes on your back and take 'em off again—that you got to get old—and that you got to die. That's what you can count on! All the rest is in your head!

YOUNG WOMAN. But Ma—didn't you love Pa?

MOTHER. I suppose I did—I don't know—I've forgotten—what difference does it make—now?

YOUNG WOMAN. But then!—oh Ma, tell me!

MOTHER. Tell you what?

YOUNG WOMAN. About all that—love!

Offstage voices.

WIFE'S VOICE. Don't.

HUSBAND'S VOICE. What's the matter—don't you want me to kiss you?

WIFE'S VOICE. Not like that.

HUSBAND'S VOICE. Like what?

WIFE'S VOICE. That silly kiss!

HUSBAND'S VOICE. Silly kiss?

WIFE'S VOICE. You look so silly—oh I know what's coming when you look like that—and kiss me like that—don't—go away—

End of offstage voices.

MOTHER. He's a decent man, isn't he?

YOUNG WOMAN. I don't know. How should I know—yet.

MOTHER. He's a Vice-President—of course he's decent.

YOUNG WOMAN. I don't care whether he's decent or not. I won't marry him.

MOTHER. But you just said you wanted to marry—

YOUNG WOMAN. Not him.

MOTHER. Who?

YOUNG WOMAN. I don't know—I don't know—I haven't found him yet!

MOTHER. You talk like you're crazy!

YOUNG WOMAN. Oh, Ma—tell me!

MOTHER. Tell you what?

YOUNG WOMAN. Tell me—(*Words suddenly pouring out.*) Your skin oughtn't to curl—ought it—when he just comes near you—ought it? That's wrong, ain't it? You don't get over that, do you—ever, do you or do you? How is it, Ma—do you?

MOTHER. Do you what?

YOUNG WOMAN. Do you get used to, it—so after a while it doesn't matter? Or don't you? Does it always matter? You ought to be in love, oughtn't you, Ma? You must be in love, mustn't you, Ma? That changes everything, doesn't

it—or does it? Maybe if you just like a person it's all right—is it? When he puts a hand on me, my blood turns cold. But your blood oughtn't to run cold, ought it? His hands are—his hands are fat, Ma—don't you see—his hands are fat—and they sort of press—and they're fat—don't you see?—Don't you see?

MOTHER (*stares at her bewildered*). See what?

YOUNG WOMAN (*rushing on*). I've always thought I'd find somebody—somebody young—and—and attractive—with wavy hair—wavy hair—I always think of children with curls—little curls all over their head—somebody young—and attractive—that I'd like—that I'd love—But I haven't found anybody like that yet—I haven't found anybody—I've hardly known anybody—you'd never let me go with anybody and—

MOTHER. Are you throwing it up to me that—

YOUNG WOMAN. No—let me finish, Ma! No—let me finish! I just mean I've never found anybody—anybody—nobody's ever asked me—till now—he's the only man that's ever asked me—And I suppose I got to marry somebody—all girls do—

MOTHER. Nonsense.

YOUNG WOMAN. But, I can't go on like this, Ma—I don't know why—but I can't—it's like I'm all tight inside—sometimes I feel like I'm stifling!—You don't know—stifling. (*Walks up and down.*) I can't go on like this much longer—going to work—coming home—going to work—coming home—I can't—Sometimes in the subway I think I'm going to die—sometimes even in the office if something don't happen—I got to do something—I don't know—it's like I'm all tight inside.

MOTHER. You're crazy.

YOUNG WOMAN. Oh, Ma!

MOTHER. You're crazy.

YOUNG WOMAN. Ma—if you tell me that again I'll kill you! I'll kill you!

MOTHER. If that isn't crazy!

YOUNG WOMAN. I'll kill you—Maybe I am crazy—I don't know. Sometimes I think I am—the thoughts that go on in my mind—sometimes I think I am—I can't help it if I am—I do the best I can—I do the best I can and I'm nearly crazy! (*Mother rises and sits.*) Go away! Go away! You don't know anything about anything! And you haven't got any pity—no pity—you just take it for granted that I go to work every day—and come home every night and bring my money every week—you just take it for granted—you'd let me go on forever—and never feel any pity—

Offstage radio—a voice singing a sentimental mother song or popular home song. Mother begins to cry—crosses to chair left—sits.

Oh Ma—forgive me! Forgive me!

MOTHER. My own child! To be spoken to like that by my own child!

YOUNG WOMAN. I didn't mean it, Ma—I didn't mean it! (*She goes to her mother—crosses to left.*)

MOTHER (*clinging to her hand*). You're all I've got in the world—and you don't want me—you want to kill me.

YOUNG WOMAN. No—no, I don't, Ma! I just said that!

MOTHER. I've worked for you and slaved for you!

YOUNG WOMAN. I know, Ma.

MOTHER. I brought you into the world.

YOUNG WOMAN. I know, Ma.

MOTHER. You're flesh of my flesh and—

YOUNG WOMAN. I know, Ma, I know.

MOTHER. And—

YOUNG WOMAN. You rest, now, Ma—you rest—

MOTHER (*struggling*). I got to do the dishes.

YOUNG WOMAN. I'll do the dishes—You listen to the music, Ma—I'll do the dishes.

Ma sits. Young Woman crosses to behind screen. Takes a pair of rubber gloves and begins to put them on. The Mother sees them—they irritate her—there is a return of her characteristic mood.

MOTHER. Those gloves! I've been washing dishes for forty years and I never wore gloves! But my lady's hands! My lady's hands!

YOUNG WOMAN. Sometimes you talk to me like you're jealous, Ma.

MOTHER. Jealous?

YOUNG WOMAN. It's my hands got me a husband.

MOTHER. A husband? So you're going to marry him now!

YOUNG WOMAN. I suppose so.

MOTHER. If you ain't the craziest—

The scene blacks out. In the darkness, the mother song goes into jazz—very faint—as the scene lights into

EPISODE THREE

HONEYMOON

SCENE: *Hotel bedroom: bed, chair, mirror. The door at the back now opens on a bathroom; the window, on a dancing casino opposite.*

SOUNDS: *A small jazz band (violin, piano, saxophone—very dim, at first, then louder).*

CHARACTERS: *Young Woman; Husband; Bellboy*

OFFSTAGE: *Seen but not heard, Men and Women dancing in couples.*

AT RISE: *Set dark Bellboy, Husband, and Young Woman enter. Bellboy carries luggage. He switches on light by door. Stop music.*

HUSBAND. Well, here we are. (*Throws hat on bed; Bellboy puts luggage down, crosses to window; raises shade three inches. Opens window three inches. Sounds of jazz music louder. Offstage.*)

BELLBOY (*comes to man for tip*). Anything else, Sir? (*Receives tip. Exits.*)

HUSBAND. Well, here we are.

YOUNG WOMAN. Yes, here we are.

HUSBAND. Aren't you going to take your hat off—stay a while? (*Young Woman looks around as though looking for a way out, then takes off her hat, pulls the hair automatically around her ears.*) This is all right, isn't it? Huh? Huh?

YOUNG WOMAN. It's very nice.

HUSBAND. Twelve bucks a day! They know how to soak you in these pleasure resorts. Twelve bucks! (*Music.*) Well—we'll get our money's worth out of it all right. (*Goes toward bathroom.*) I'm going to wash up. (*Stops at door.*) Don't you want to wash up?

Young Woman shakes head 'No'.

I do! It was a long trip! I want to wash up!

Goes off—closes door; sings in bathroom. Young Woman goes to window—raises shade—sees the dancers going round and round in couples. Music is louder. Re-enter Husband.

Say, pull that blind down! They can see in!

YOUNG WOMAN. I thought you said there'd be a view of the ocean!

HUSBAND. Sure there is.

YOUNG WOMAN. I just see people—dancing.

HUSBAND. The ocean's beyond.

YOUNG WOMAN (*desperately*). I was counting on seeing it!

HUSBAND. You'll see it tomorrow—what's eating you? We'll take in the boardwalk—Don't you want to wash up?

YOUNG WOMAN. No!

HUSBAND. It was a long trip. Sure you don't? (*Young Woman shakes her head 'No'. Husband takes off his coat—puts it over chair.*) Better make yourself at home. I'm going to. (*She stares at him—moves away from the window.*) Say, pull down that blind! (*Crosses to chair down left—sits.*)

YOUNG WOMAN. It's close—don't you think it's close?

HUSBAND. Well—you don't want people looking in, do you? (*Laughs.*) Huh—huh?

YOUNG WOMAN. No.

HUSBAND (*laughs*). I guess not. Huh? (*Takes off shoes. Young Woman leaves the window, and crosses down to the bed.*) Say—you look a little white around the gills! What's the matter?

YOUNG WOMAN. Nothing.

HUSBAND. You look like you're scared.

YOUNG WOMAN. No.

HUSBAND. Nothing to be scared of. You're with your husband, you know. (*Takes her to chair, left.*)

YOUNG WOMAN. I know.

HUSBAND. Happy?

YOUNG WOMAN. Yes.

HUSBAND (*sitting*). Then come here and give us a kiss. (*He puts her on his knee.*) That's the girlie. (*He bends her head *down, and kisses her along the back of her neck.)* Like that? *(She tries to get to her feet.)* Say—stay there! What you moving for?—You know—you got to learn to relax, little girl—*(Dancers go off. Dim lights. Pinches her above knee.)* Say, what you got under there?

YOUNG WOMAN. Nothing.

HUSBAND. Nothing! *(Laughs.)* That's a good one! Nothing, huh? Huh? That reminds me of the story of the pullman porter and the—what's the matter—did I tell you that one? *(Music dims off and out.)*

YOUNG WOMAN. I don't know.

HUSBAND. The pullman porter and the tart?

YOUNG WOMAN. No.

HUSBAND. It's a good one—well—the train was just pulling out and the tart—

YOUNG WOMAN. You did tell that one!

HUSBAND. About the—

YOUNG WOMAN. Yes! Yes! I remember now!

HUSBAND. About the—

YOUNG WOMAN. Yes!

HUSBAND. All right—if I did. You're sure it was the one about the—

YOUNG WOMAN. I'm sure.

HUSBAND. When he asked her what she had underneath her seat and she said—

YOUNG WOMAN. Yes! Yes! That one!

HUSBAND. All right—But I don't believe I did. *(She tries to get up again, and he holds her.)* You know you have got something under there—what is it?

YOUNG WOMAN. Nothing—just—just my garter.

HUSBAND. Your garter! Your garter! Say did I tell you the one about—

YOUNG WOMAN. Yes! Yes!

HUSBAND *(with dignity).* How do you know which one I mean?

YOUNG WOMAN. You told me them all!

HUSBAND *(pulling her back to his knee).* No, I didn't! Not by a jugful! I got a lot of 'em up my sleeve yet—that's part of what I owe my success to—my ability to spring a good story—You know—you got to learn to relax, little girl—haven't you?

YOUNG WOMAN. Yes.

HUSBAND. That's one of the biggest things to learn in life. That's part of what I owe my success to. Now you go and get those heavy things off—and relax.

YOUNG WOMAN. They're not heavy.

HUSBAND. You haven't got much on—have you? But you'll feel better with 'em off. *(Gets up.)* Want me to help you?

YOUNG WOMAN. No.

HUSBAND. I'm your husband, you know.

YOUNG WOMAN. I know.

HUSBAND. You aren't afraid of your husband, are you?

YOUNG WOMAN. No—of course not—but I thought maybe—can't we go out for a little while?

HUSBAND. Out? What for?

YOUNG WOMAN. Fresh air—walk—talk.

HUSBAND. We can talk here—I'll tell you all about myself. Go along now. *(Young Woman goes toward bathroom door. Gets bag.)* Where are you going?

YOUNG WOMAN. In here.

HUSBAND. I thought you'd want to wash up.

YOUNG WOMAN. I just want to—get ready.

HUSBAND. You don't have to go in there to take your clothes off!

YOUNG WOMAN. I want to.

HUSBAND. What for?

YOUNG WOMAN. I always do.

HUSBAND. What?

YOUNG WOMAN. Undress by myself.

HUSBAND. You've never been married till now—have you? *(Laughs.)* Or have you been pulling something over on me?

YOUNG WOMAN. No.

HUSBAND. I understand—kind of modest—huh? Huh?

YOUNG WOMAN. Yes.

HUSBAND. I understand women—*(Indulgently.)* Go along.

She goes off—starts to close door. Young Woman exits.

Don't close the door—thought you wanted to talk.

He looks around the room with satisfaction—after a pause—rises—takes off his collar.

You're awful quiet—what are you doing in there?

YOUNG WOMAN. Just—getting ready—

HUSBAND *(still in his mood of satisfaction).* I'm going to enjoy life from now on—I haven't had such an easy time of it. I got where I am by hard work and self denial—now I'm going to enjoy life—I'm going to make up for all I missed—aren't you about ready?

YOUNG WOMAN. Not yet.

HUSBAND. Next year maybe we'll go to Paris. You can buy a lot of that French underwear—and Switzerland—all my life I've wanted a Swiss watch—that I bought right there—I coulda' got a Swiss watch here, but I always wanted one that I bought right there—Isn't that funny—huh? Isn't it? Huh? Huh?

YOUNG WOMAN. Yes.

HUSBAND. All my life I've wanted a Swiss watch that I bought right there. All my life I've counted on having that some day—more than anything—except one thing—you know what?

YOUNG WOMAN. No.

HUSBAND. Guess.

YOUNG WOMAN. I can't.

HUSBAND. Then I'm coming in and tell you.

YOUNG WOMAN. No! Please! Please don't.

HUSBAND. Well hurry up then! I thought you women didn't wear much of anything these days—huh? Huh? I'm coming in!

YOUNG WOMAN. No—no! Just a minute!

HUSBAND. All right. Just a minute. (*Young Woman is silent. Husband laughs and takes out watch.*) 13—14—I'm counting the seconds on you—that's what you said, didn't you—just a minute!—49—50—51—52—53—

Enter Young Woman.

YOUNG WOMAN (*at the door*). Here I am. (*She wears a little white gown that hangs very straight. She is very still, but her eyes are wide with a curious, helpless, animal terror.*)

HUSBAND (*starts toward her—stops. The room is in shadow except for one dim light by the bed. Sound of girl weeping*). You crying? (*Sound of weeping.*) What you crying for? (*Crosses to her.*)

YOUNG WOMAN (*crying out*). Ma! Ma! I want my mother!

HUSBAND. I thought you were glad to get away from her.

YOUNG WOMAN. I want her now—I want somebody.

HUSBAND. You got me, haven't you?

YOUNG WOMAN. Somebody—somebody—

HUSBAND. There's nothing to cry about. There's nothing to cry about.

The scene blacks out. The music continues until the lights go up for Episode Four. Rhythm of the music is gradually replaced by the sound of steel riveting for Episode Four.

EPISODE FOUR

MATERNAL

SCENE: *A room in a hospital: bed, chair. The door in the back now opens on a corridor; the window on a tall building going up.*

SOUNDS: *Outside window—riveting.*

CHARACTERS IN THE SCENE: *Young Woman; Doctors; Nurses; Husband*

CHARACTERS SEEN BUT NOT HEARD: *Woman in Wheel Chair; Woman in Bathrobe; Stretcher Wagon; Nurse with Tray; Nurse with Covered Basin*

AT RISE: *Young Woman lies still in bed. The door is open. In the corridor, a stretcher wagon goes by. Enter Nurse.*

NURSE. How are you feeling today? (*No response from Young Woman.*) Better? (*No response.*) No Pain? (*No response. Nurse takes her watch in one hand, Young Woman's wrist in the other—stands, then goes to chart at foot of bed—writes.*) You're getting along fine. (*No response.*) Such a sweet baby you have, too. (*No response.*) Aren't you glad it's a girl? (*Young Woman makes sign with her head 'No'.*) You're not! Oh, my! That's no way to talk! Men want boys—woman ought to want girls. (*No response.*) Maybe you didn't want either, eh? (*Young Woman signs 'No'. Riveting machine.*) You'll feel different when it begins to nurse. You'll just love it then. Your milk hasn't come yet—has it? (*Sign—'No'.*) It will! (*Sign—'No'.*) Oh, you don't know Doctor! (*Goes to door—turns.*) Anything else you want? (*Young Woman points to window.*) Draft? (*Sign—'No'.*) The noise? (*Young Woman signs 'Yes'.*) Oh, that can't be helped. Hospital's got to have a new wing. We're the biggest Maternity Hospital in the world. I'll close the window, though. (*Young Woman signs 'No'.*) No?

YOUNG WOMAN (*whispers*). I smell everything then.

NURSE (*starting out the door—riveting machine.*) Here's your man!

Enter Husband with large bouquet. Crosses to bed.

HUSBAND. Well, how are we today? (*Young Woman—no response.*)

NURSE. She's getting stronger!

HUSBAND. Of course she is!

NURSE (*taking flowers*). See what your husband brought you.

HUSBAND. Better put 'em in water right away. (*Exit nurse.*) Everything O.K.? (*Young Woman signs 'No'.*) Now see here, my dear, you've got to brace up, you know! And—and face things! Everybody's got to brace up and face things! That's what makes the world go round. I know all you've been through but—(*Young Woman signs 'No'.*) Oh, yes I do! I know all about it! I was right outside all the time! (*Young Woman makes violent gestures of 'No'. Ignoring.*) Oh yes! But you've got to brace up now! Make an effort! Pull yourself together! Start the up-hill climb! Oh I've been down—but I haven't stayed down. I've been licked but I haven't stayed licked! I've pulled myself up by my own bootstraps, and that's what you've go to do! Will power! That's what conquers! Look at me! Now you've got to brace up! Face the music! Stand the gaff! Take life by the horns! Look it in the face!—Having a baby's natural! Perfectly natural thing—why should—

Young Woman chokes—points wildly to door. Enter Nurse with flowers in a vase.

NURSE. What's the matter?

HUSBAND. She's got that gagging again—like she had the last time I was here.

Young Woman gestures him out.

NURSE. Better go, sir.

HUSBAND (*at door*). I'll be back.

Young Woman gasping and gesturing.

NURSE. She needs rest.

HUSBAND. Tomorrow then. I'll be back tomorrow—tomorrow and every day—goodbye. (*Exits.*)

NURSE. You got a mighty nice husband, I guess you know that? (*Writes on chart.*) Gagging.

Corridor life—Woman in a Bathrobe passes door. Enter Doctor, Young Doctor, Nurse, wheeling surgeon's wagon with bottles, instruments, etc.

DOCTOR. How's the little lady today? (*Crosses to bed.*)

NURSE. She's better, Doctor.

DOCTOR. Of course she's better! She's all right—aren't you? (*Young Woman does not respond.*) What's the matter? Can't you talk? (*Drops her hand. Takes chart.*)

NURSE. She's a little weak yet, Doctor.

DOCTOR (*at chart*). Milk hasn't come yet?

NURSE. No, Doctor.

DOCTOR. Put the child to breast. (*Young Woman—'No-no'!—Riveting machine.*) No? Don't you want to nurse your baby? (*Young Woman signs 'No'.*) Why not? (*No response.*) These modern neurotic women, eh, Doctor. What are we going to do with 'em? (*Young Doctor laughs. Nurse smiles.*) Bring the baby!

YOUNG WOMAN. No!

DOCTOR. Well—that's strong enough. I thought you were too weak to talk—that's better. You don't want your baby?

YOUNG WOMAN. No.

DOCTOR. What do you want?

YOUNG WOMAN. Let alone—let alone.

DOCTOR. Bring the baby.

NURSE. Yes, Doctor—she's behaved very badly every time, Doctor—very upset—maybe we better not.

DOCTOR. I decide what we better and better not here, Nurse!

NURSE. Yes, Doctor.

DOCTOR. Bring the baby.

NURSE. Yes, Doctor.

DOCTOR (*with chart*). Gagging—you mean nausea.

NURSE. Yes, Doctor, but—

DOCTOR. No buts, nurse.

NURSE. Yes, Doctor.

DOCTOR. Nausea!—Change the diet!—What is her diet?

NURSE. Liquids.

DOCTOR. Give her solids.

NURSE. Yes, Doctor. She says she can't swallow solids.

DOCTOR. Give her solids.

NURSE. Yes, Doctor. (*Starts to go—riveting machine.*)

DOCTOR. Wait—I'll change her medicine. (*Takes pad and writes prescription in Latin. Hands it to Nurse.*) After meals. (*To door.*) Bring her baby.

Exit Doctor, followed by Young Doctor and Nurse with surgeon's wagon.

NURSE. Yes, Doctor.

Exits.

YOUNG WOMAN (*alone*). Let me alone—let me alone—let me alone—I've submitted to enough—I won't submit to any more—crawl off—crawl off in the dark—Vixen crawled under the bed—way back in the corner under the bed—they were all drowned—puppies don't go to heaven—heaven—golden stairs—long stairs—long—too long—long golden stairs—climb those golden stairs—stairs—stairs—climb—tired—too tired—dead—no matter—nothing matters—dead—stairs—long stairs—all

the dead going up—going up—to be in heaven—heaven—golden stairs—all the children coming down—coming down to be born—dead going up—children coming down—going up—coming down—going up—coming down—going up—coming down—going up—stop—stop—no—no traffic cop—no—no traffic cop in heaven—traffic cop—traffic cop—can't you give us a smile—tired—too tired—no matter—it doesn't matter—St. Peter—St. Peter at the gate—you can't come in—no matter—it doesn't matter—I'll rest—I'll lie down—down—all written down—down in a big book—no matter—it doesn't matter—I'll lie down—it weighs me—it's over me—it weighs—weighs—it's heavy—it's a heavy book—no matter—lie still—don't move—can't move—rest—forget—they say you forget—a girl—aren't you glad it's a girl—a little girl—with no hair—none—little curls all over his head—a little bald girl—curls—curls all over his head—what kind of hair had God? No matter—it doesn't matter—everybody loves God—they've got to—got to—got to love God—God is love—even if he's bad they got to love him—even if he's got fat hands—fat hands—no no—he wouldn't be God—His hands make you well—He lays on his hands—well—and happy—no matter—doesn't matter—far—too far—tired—too tired Vixen crawled off under bed—eight—there were eight—a woman crawled off under the bed—a woman has one—two three four—one two three four—one two three four—two plus two is four—two times two is four—two times four is eight Vixen had eight—one two three four five six seven eight—eight—Puffie had eight—all drowned—drowned—drowned in blood—blood—Oh God! God—God never had one—Mary had one—in a manger—the lowly manger—God's on a high throne—far—too far—no matter—it doesn't matter—God Mary Mary God Mary—Virgin Mary—Mary had one—the Holy Ghost—the Holy Ghost—George H. Jones—oh don't—please don't! Let me rest—now I can rest—the weight is gone—inside the weight is gone—it's only outside—outside—all around—weight—I'm under it—Vixen crawled under the bed—there were eight—I'll not submit any more—I'll not submit—I'll not submit—

The scene blacks out. The sound of riveting continues until it goes into the sound of an electric piano and the scene lights up for Episode Five.

EPISODE FIVE

PROHIBITED

SCENE: *Bar: bottles, tables, chairs, electric piano.*
SOUND: *Electric piano.*
CHARACTERS: *Man behind the bar; Policeman at bar; Waiter; At Table 1: a Man and a Woman; At Table 2: a Man and a Boy; At Table 3: Two Men waiting for Two Girls, who are; Telephone Girl of Episode One and Young Woman.*

AT RISE: *Everyone except the Girls on. Of the characters, the Man and Woman at Table 1 are an ordinary man and woman. The Man at Table 2 is a middle-aged fairy; the Boy is young, untouched. At Table 3, First Man is pleasing, common, vigorous. He has coarse wavy hair. Second Man is an ordinary salesman type.*

At Table 3.

FIRST MAN. I'm going to beat it.
SECOND MAN. Oh, for the love of Mike.
FIRST MAN. They ain't going to show.
SECOND MAN. Sure they'll show.
FIRST MAN. How do you know they'll show?
SECOND MAN. I tell you you can't keep that baby away from me—just got to—(*Snaps fingers.*)—She comes running.
FIRST MAN. Looks like it.
SECOND MAN (*to Waiter makes sign '2' with his fingers*). The same. (*Waiter goes to the bar.*)

At Table 2.

MAN. Oh, I'm sorry I brought you here.
BOY. Why?
MAN. This Purgatory of noise! I brought you here to give you pleasure—let you taste pleasure. This sherry they have here is bottled—heaven. Wait till you taste it.
BOY. But I don't drink.
MAN. Drink! This isn't drink! Real amontillado is sunshine and orange groves—it's the Mediterranean and blue moonlight and—love? Have you ever been in love?
BOY. No.
MAN. Never in love with—a woman?
BOY. No—not really.
MAN. What do you mean really?
BOY. Just—that.
MAN. Ah! (*Makes sign to Waiter.*) Two—you know what I want—Two. (*Waiter goes to the bar.*)

At Table 1.

MAN. Well, are you going through with it, or ain't you?
WOMAN. That's what I want to do—go through with it.
MAN. But you can't.
WOMAN. Why can't I?
MAN. How can yuh? (*Silence.*) It's nothing—most women don't think anything about it—they just—Bert told me a doctor to go to—gave me the address—
WOMAN. Don't talk about it!
MAN. Got to talk about it—you got to get out of this. (*Silence—Man makes sign to Waiter.*) What you having?
WOMAN. Nothing—I don't want anything. I had enough.
MAN. Do you good. The same?
WOMAN. I suppose so.
MAN (*makes sign '2' to Waiter*). The same. (*Waiter goes to the bar.*)

At Table 3.

FIRST MAN. I'm going to beat it.
SECOND MAN. Oh say, listen! I'm counting on you to take the other one off my hands.
FIRST MAN. I'm going to beat it.
SECOND MAN. For the love of Mike have a heart! Listen—as a favor to me—I got to be home by six—I promised my wife—sure. That don't leave me no time at all if we got to hang around—entertain some dame. You got to take her off my hands.
FIRST MAN. Maybe she won't fall for me.
SECOND MAN. Sure she'll fall for you! They all fall for you— even my wife likes you—tries to kid herself it's your brave exploits, but I know what it is—sure she'll fall for you.

Enter two girls—Telephone Girl and Young Woman.

GIRL (*coming to table*). Hello—
SECOND MAN (*grouch*). Good night.
GIRL. Good night? What's eatin' yuh?
SECOND MAN (*same*). Nothin's eatin' me—thought somethin' musta swallowed you.
GIRL. Why?
SECOND MAN. You're late!
GIRL (*unimpressed*). Oh—(*Brushing it aside.*) Mrs. Jones—Mr. Smith.
SECOND MAN. Meet my friend, Mr. Roe. (*They all sit. To the Waiter.*) The same and two more. (*Waiter goes.*)
GIRL. So we kept you waiting, did we?
SECOND MAN. Only about an hour.
YOUNG WOMAN. Was it that long?
SECOND MAN. We been here that long—ain't we Dick?
FIRST MAN. Just about, Harry.
SECOND MAN. For the love of God what delayed yuh?
GIRL. Tell Helen that one.
SECOND MAN (*to Young Woman*). The old Irish woman that went to her first race? Bet on the skate that came in last—she went up to the jockey and asked him, 'For the love of God, what delayed yuh'.

All laugh.

YOUNG WOMAN. Why, that's kinda funny!
SECOND MAN. Kinda!—What do you mean kinda?
YOUNG WOMAN. I just mean there are not many of 'em that are funny at all.
SECOND MAN. Not if you haven't heard the funny ones.
YOUNG WOMAN. Oh I've heard 'em all.
FIRST MAN. Not a laugh in a carload, eh?
GIRL. Got a cigarette?
SECOND MAN (*with package*). One of these?
GIRL (*taking one*). Uhhuh.

He offers the package to Young Woman.

YOUNG WOMAN (*taking one*). Uhhuh.
SECOND MAN (*to First Man*). One of these?
FIRST MAN (*showing his own package*). Thanks—I like these.

He lights Young Woman's cigarette.

SECOND MAN (*lighting Girl's cigarette*). Well—baby—how they comin', huh?

GIRL. Couldn't be better.

SECOND MAN. How's every little thing?

GIRL. Just great.

SECOND MAN. Miss me?

GIRL. I'll say so—when did you get in?

SECOND MAN. Just a coupla hours ago.

GIRL. Miss me?

SECOND MAN. Did I? You don't know the half of it.

YOUNG WOMAN (*interrupting restlessly*). Can we dance here?

SECOND MAN. Not here.

YOUNG WOMAN. Where do we go from here?

SECOND MAN. Where do we go from here! You just got here!

FIRST MAN. What's the hurry?

SECOND MAN. What's the rush?

YOUNG WOMAN. I don't know.

GIRL. Helen wants to dance.

YOUNG WOMAN. I just want to keep moving.

FIRST MAN (*smiling*). You want to keep moving, huh?

SECOND MAN. You must be one of those restless babies! Where do we go from here!

YOUNG WOMAN. It's only some days—I want to keep moving.

FIRST MAN. You want to keep moving, huh? (*He is staring at her smilingly.*)

YOUNG WOMAN (*nods*). Uhhuh.

FIRST MAN (*quietly*). Stick around a while.

SECOND MAN. Where do we go from here! Say, what kind of a crowd do you run with, anyway?

GIRL. Helen don't run with any crowd—do you, Helen?

YOUNG WOMAN (*embarrassed*). No.

FIRST MAN. Well, I'm not a crowd—run with me.

SECOND MAN (*gratified*). All set, huh?—Dick was about ready to beat it.

FIRST MAN. That's before I met the little lady.

Waiter serves drinks.

FIRST MAN. Here's how.

SECOND MAN. Here's to you.

GIRL. Here's looking at you.

YOUNG WOMAN. Here's—happy days.

They all drink.

FIRST MAN. That's good stuff!

SECOND MAN. Off a boat.

FIRST MAN. Off a boat?

SECOND MAN. They get all their stuff here—off a boat.

GIRL. That's what *they* say.

SECOND MAN. No! Sure! Sure they do! Sure!

GIRL. It's all right with me.

SECOND MAN. But they do! Sure!

GIRL. I believe you, darling!

SECOND MAN. Did you miss me?

GIRL. Uhhuh. (*Affirmative.*)

SECOND MAN. Any other daddies?

GIRL. Uhhuh. (*Negative.*)

SECOND MAN. Love any daddy but daddy?

GIRL. Uhhuh. (*Negative.*)

SECOND MAN. Let's beat it!

GIRL (*a little self-conscious before Young Woman*). We just got here.

SECOND MAN. Don't I know it—Come on!

GIRL. But—(*Indicates Young Woman.*)

SECOND MAN (*not understanding*). They're all set—aren't you?

FIRST MAN (*to Young Woman*). Are we? (*She doesn't answer.*)

SECOND MAN. I got to be out to the house by six—come on—(*Rising—to Girl.*) Come on, kid—let's us beat it! (*Girl indicates Young Woman. Now understanding—very elaborate.*) Business is business, you know! I got a lot to do yet this afternoon—thought you might go along with me—help me out—how about it?

GIRL (*rising, her dignity preserved*). Sure—I'll go along with you—help you out. (*Both rise.*)

SECOND MAN. All right with you folks?

FIRST MAN. All right with me.

SECOND MAN. All right with you? (*To Young Woman.*)

YOUNG WOMAN. All right with me.

SECOND MAN. Come on, kid. (*They rise.*) Where's the damage?

FIRST MAN. Go on!

SECOND MAN. No!

FIRST MAN. Go on!

SECOND MAN. I'll match you.

YOUNG WOMAN. Heads win!

GIRL. Heads I win—tails you lose.

SECOND MAN (*impatiently*). He's matching me.

FIRST MAN. Am I matching you or you matching me?

SECOND MAN. I'm matching you. (*They match.*) You're stung!

FIRST MAN (*contentedly*). Not so you can notice it. (*Smiles at Young Woman.*)

GIRL. That's for you, Helen.

SECOND MAN. She ain't dumb! Come on.

GIRL (*to First Man*). You be nice to her now. She's very fastidious.—Goodbye.

Exit Second Man and Girl.

YOUNG WOMAN. I know what business is like.

FIRST MAN. You do—do yuh?

YOUNG WOMAN. I used to be a business girl myself before—

FIRST MAN. Before what?

YOUNG WOMAN. Before I quit.

FIRST MAN. What did you quit for?

YOUNG WOMAN. I just quit.

FIRST MAN. You're married, huh?

YOUNG WOMAN. Yes—I am.

FIRST MAN. All right with me.

YOUNG WOMAN. Some men don't seem to like a woman after she's married—

Waiter comes to the table.

FIRST MAN. What's the difference?

YOUNG WOMAN. Depends on the man, I guess.

FIRST MAN. Depends on the woman, I guess. (*To Waiter, makes sign of '2'.*) The same. (*Waiter goes to the bar.*)

At Table 1.

MAN. It don't amount to nothing. God! Most women just—

WOMAN. I know—I know—I know.

MAN. They don't think nothing of it. They just—

WOMAN. I know—I know—I know.

Re-enter Second Man and Girl. They go to Table 3.

SECOND MAN. Say, I forgot—I want you to do something for me, will yuh?

FIRST MAN. Sure—what is it?

SECOND MAN. I want you to telephone me out home tomorrow—and ask me to come into town—will yuh?

FIRST MAN. Sure—why not?

SECOND MAN. You know—business—get me?

FIRST MAN. I get you.

SECOND MAN. I've worked the telegraph gag to death—and my wife likes you.

FIRST MAN. What's your number?

SECOND MAN. I'll write it down for you. (*Writes.*)

FIRST MAN. How is your wife?

SECOND MAN. She's fine.

FIRST MAN. And the kid?

SECOND MAN. Great. (*Hands him the card. To girl.*) Come on, kid. (*Turns back to Young Woman.*) Get this bird to tell you about himself.

GIRL. Keep him from it.

SECOND MAN. Get him to tell you how he killed a couple of spig down in Mexico.

GIRL. You been in Mexico?

SECOND MAN. He just came up from there.

GIRL. Can you teach us the tango?

YOUNG WOMAN. You killed a man?

SECOND MAN. Two of 'em! With a bottle! Get him to tell you—with a bottle. Come on, kid. Goodbye.

Exit Second Man and Girl.

YOUNG WOMAN. Why did you?

FIRST MAN. What?

YOUNG WOMAN. Kill 'em?

FIRST MAN. To get free.

YOUNG WOMAN. Oh.

At Table 2.

MAN. You really must taste this—just taste it. It's a real amontillado, you know.

BOY. Where do they get it here?

MAN. It's always down the side streets one finds the real pleasures, don't you think?

BOY. I don't know.

MAN. Learn. Come, taste this! Amontillado! Or don't you like amontillado?

BOY. I don't know. I never had any before.

MAN. Your first taste! How I envy you! Come, taste it! Taste it! And die.

Boy tastes wine—finds it disappointing.

MAN (*gliding it*). Poe was a lover of amontillado. He returns to it continually, you remember—or are you a lover of Poe?

BOY. I've read a lot of him.

MAN. But are you a lover?

At Table 3.

FIRST MAN. There were a bunch of bandidos—bandits, you know, took me into the hills—holding me there—what was I to do? got the two birds that guarded me drunk one night, and then I filled the empty bottle with small stones—and let 'em have it!

YOUNG WOMAN. Oh!

FIRST MAN. I had to get free, didn't I? I let 'em have it—

YOUNG WOMAN. Oh—then what did you do?

FIRST MAN. Then I beat it.

YOUNG WOMAN. Where to—?

FIRST MAN. Right here. (*Pause.*) Glad?

YOUNG WOMAN (*nods*). Yes.

FIRST MAN (*makes sign to Waiter of '2'*). The same. (*Waiter goes to the bar.*)

At Table 1.

MAN. You're just scared because this is the first time and—

WOMAN. I'm not scared.

MAN. Then what are you for Christ's sake?

WOMAN. I'm not scared. I want it—I want to have it—that ain't being scared, is it?

MAN. It's being goofy.

WOMAN. I don't care.

MAN. What about your folks?

WOMAN. I don't care.

MAN. What about your job? (*Silence.*) You got to keep your job, haven't you? (*Silence.*) Haven't you?

WOMAN. I suppose so.

MAN. Well—there you are!

WOMAN (*silence—then*). All right—let's go now—You got the address?

MAN. Now you're coming to.

They get up and go off. Exit Man and Woman.

At Table 3.

YOUNG WOMAN. A bottle like that? (*She picks it up.*)

FIRST MAN. Yeah—filled with pebbles.

YOUNG WOMAN. What kind of pebbles?

FIRST MAN. Pebbles! Off the ground.

YOUNG WOMAN. Oh.

FIRST MAN. Necessity, you know, mother of invention. (*As Young Woman handles the bottle.*) Ain't a bad weapon—first you got a sledge hammer—then you got a knife.

YOUNG WOMAN. Oh. (*Puts bottle down.*)

FIRST MAN. Women don't like knives, do they? (*Pours drink.*)

YOUNG WOMAN. No.

FIRST MAN. Don't mind a hammer so much, though, do they?

YOUNG WOMAN. No—

FIRST MAN. I didn't like it myself—any of it—but I had to get free, didn't I? Sure I had to get free, didn't I? (*Drinks.*) Now I'm damn glad I did.

YOUNG WOMAN. Why?

FIRST MAN. You know why. (*He puts his hand over hers.*)

At Table 2.

MAN. Let's go to my rooms—and I'll show them to you—I have a first edition of Verlaine that will simply make your mouth water. (*They stand up.*) Here—there's just a sip at the bottom of my glass—

Boy takes it.

That last sip's the sweetest—Wasn't it?

BOY (*laughs*). And I always thought that was dregs. (*Exit Man followed by Boy.*)

At Table 3.

The Man is holding her hand across the table.

YOUNG WOMAN. When you put your hand over mine! When you just touch me!

FIRST MAN. Yeah? (*Pause.*) Come on, kid, let's go!

YOUNG MAN. Where?

FIRST MAN. You haven't been around much, have you, kid?

YOUNG WOMAN. No.

FIRST MAN. I could tell that just to look at you.

YOUNG WOMAN. You could?

FIRST MAN. Sure I could, What are you running around with a girl like that other one for?

YOUNG WOMAN. I don't know. She seems to have a good time.

FIRST MAN. So that's it?

YOUNG WOMAN. Don't she?

FIRST MAN. Don't you?

YOUNG WOMAN. No.

FIRST MAN. Never?

YOUNG WOMAN. Never.

FIRST MAN. What's the matter?

YOUNG WOMAN. Nothing—just me, I guess.

FIRST MAN. You're all right.

YOUNG WOMAN. Am I?

FIRST MAN. Sure. You just haven't met the right guy—that's all—girl like you—you got to meet the right guy.

YOUNG WOMAN. I know.

FIRST MAN. You're different from girls like that other one—any guy'll do her. You're different.

YOUNG WOMAN. I guess I am.

FIRST MAN. You didn't fall for that business gag—did you—when they went off?

YOUNG WOMAN. Well, I thought they wanted to be alone probably, but—

FIRST MAN. And how!

YOUNG WOMAN. Oh—so that's it.

FIRST MAN. That's it. Come along—let's go—

YOUNG WOMAN. Oh, I couldn't! Like this?

FIRST MAN. Don't you like me?

YOUNG WOMAN. Yes.

FIRST MAN. Then what's the matter?

YOUNG WOMAN. Do—you—like me?

FIRST MAN. Like yuh? You don't know the half of it—listen—you know what you seem like to me?

YOUNG WOMAN. What?

FIRST MAN. An angel. Just like an angel.

YOUNG WOMAN. I do?

FIRST MAN. That's what I said! Let's go!

YOUNG WOMAN. Where?

FIRST MAN. Where do you live?

YOUNG WOMAN. Oh, we can't go to my place.

FIRST MAN. Then come to my place.

YOUNG WOMAN. Oh I couldn't—is it far?

FIRST MAN. Just a step—come on—

YOUNG WOMAN. Oh I couldn't—what is it—a room?

FIRST MAN. No—an apartment—a one room apartment.

YOUNG WOMAN. That's different.

FIRST MAN. On the ground floor—no one will see you—coming or going.

YOUNG WOMAN (*getting up*). I couldn't.

FIRST MAN (*rises*). Wait a minute—I got to pay the damage—and I'll get a bottle of something to take along.

YOUNG WOMAN. No—don't.

FIRST MAN. Why not?

YOUNG WOMAN. Well—don't bring any pebbles.

FIRST MAN. Say—forget that! Will you?

YOUNG WOMAN. I just meant I don't think I'll need anything to drink.

FIRST MAN (*leaning to her eagerly*). You like me—don't you, kid?

YOUNG WOMAN. Do you me?

FIRST MAN. Wait!

He goes to the bar. She remains, her hands outstretched on the table, staring ahead. Enter a Man and a Girl. They go to one of the empty tables. The Waiter goes to them.

MAN (*to Girl*). What do you want?

GIRL. Same old thing.

MAN (*to the Waiter*). The usual. (*Makes a sign '2'.*)

The First Man crosses to Young Woman with a wrapped bottle under his arm. She rises and starts out with him. As they pass the piano, he stops and puts in a nickel—the music starts as they exit. The scene blacks out.

The music of the electric piano continues until the lights go up for Episode Six, and the music has become the music of a hand organ, very very faint.

EPISODE SIX

INTIMATE

SCENE: *A dark room.*
SOUNDS: *A hand organ; footbeats, of passing feet.*
CHARACTERS: *Man; Young Woman*
AT RISE: *Darkness. Nothing can be discerned. From the outside comes the sound of a hand organ, very faint, and the irregular rhythm of passing feet. The hand organ is playing* Cielito Lindo, *that Spanish song that has been on every hand organ lately.*

MAN. You're awful still, honey. What you thinking about?
WOMAN. About sea shells. (*The sound of her voice is beautiful.*)
MAN. Sheshells? Gee! I can't say it!
WOMAN. When I was little my grandmother used to have a big pink sea shell on the mantle behind the stove. When we'd go to visit her they'd let me hold it, and listen. That's what I was thinking about now.
MAN. Yeah?
WOMAN. You can hear the sea in 'em, you know.
MAN. Yeah, I know.
WOMAN. I wonder why that is?
MAN. Search me. (*Pause.*)
WOMAN. You going? (*He has moved.*)
MAN. No. I just want a cigarette.
WOMAN (*glad, relieved*). Oh.
MAN. Want one?
WOMAN. No. (*Taking the match.*) Let me light it for you.
MAN. You got mighty pretty hands, honey. (*The match is out.*) This little pig went to market. This little pig stayed home. This little pig went—
WOMAN (*laughs*). Diddle diddle dee. (*Laughs again.*)
MAN. You got awful pretty hands.
WOMAN. I used to have. But I haven't taken much care of them lately. I will now—(*Pause. The music gets clearer.*) What's that?
MAN. What?
WOMAN. That music?
MAN. A dago hand organ. I gave him two bits the first day I got here—so he comes every day.
WOMAN. I mean—what's that he's playing?
MAN. *Cielito Lindo.*
WOMAN. What does that mean?
MAN. Little Heaven.
WOMAN. Little Heaven?
MAN. That's what lovers call each other in Spain.
WOMAN. Spain's where all the castles are, ain't it?
MAN. Yeah.
WOMAN. Little Heaven—sing it!
MAN (*singing to the music of the hand organ*). Da la sierra morena viene, bajando viene, bajando; un par de ojitos negros—cielito lindo—da contrabando.
WOMAN. What does it mean?

MAN. From the high dark mountains.
WOMAN. From the high dark mountains—?
MAN. Oh it doesn't mean anything. It doesn't make sense. It's love. (*Taking up the song.*) Ay-ay-ay-ay.
WOMAN. I know what that means.
MAN. What?
WOMAN. Ay-ay-ay-ay. (*They laugh.*)
MAN (*taking up the song*). Canta non llores—Sing don't cry—
WOMAN (*taking up song*). La-la-la-la-la-la-la-la-la-la—Little Heaven!
MAN. You got a nice voice, honey.
WOMAN. Have I? (*Laughs—tickles him.*)
MAN. You bet you have—hey!
WOMAN (*laughing*). You ticklish?
MAN. Sure I am! Hey! (*They laugh.*) Go on, honey, sing something.
WOMAN. I couldn't.
MAN. Go on—you got a fine voice.
WOMAN (*laughs and sings*). Hey, diddle, diddle, the cat and the fiddle, The cow jumped over the moon, The little dog laughed to see the sport, And the dish ran away with the spoon—

Both laugh.

I never thought that had any sense before—now I get it.
MAN. You got me beat.
WOMAN. It's you and me—La-lalalalalala—lalalalalalala—Little Heaven. You're the dish and I'm the spoon.
MAN. You're a little spoon all right.
WOMAN. And I guess I'm the little cow that jumped over the moon. (*A pause.*) Do you believe in sorta guardian angels?
MAN. What?
WOMAN. Guardian angels?
MAN. I don't know. Maybe.
WOMAN. I do. (*Taking up the song again.*) Lalalalala—lalalalala—lalalala—Little Heaven. (*Talking.*) There must be something that looks out for you and brings you your happiness, at last—look at us! How did we both happen to go to that place today if there wasn't something!
MAN. Maybe you're right.
WOMAN. Look at us!
MAN. Everything's us to you, kid—ain't it?
WOMAN. Ain't it?
MAN. All right with me.
WOMAN. We belong together! We belong together! And we're going to stick together, ain't we?
MAN. Sing something else.
WOMAN. I tell you I can't sing!
MAN. Sure you can!
WOMAN. I tell you I hadn't thought of singing since I was a little bit of a girl.
MAN. Well sing anyway.
WOMAN (*singing*). And every little wavelet had its night cap on—its night cap on—its night cap on—and every little wave had its night cap on—so very early in the morning.

(*Talking.*) Did you used to sing that when you were a little kid?

MAN. Nope.

WOMAN. Didn't you? We used to—in the first grade—little kids—we used to go round and round in a ring—and flop our hands up and down—supposed to be the waves. I remember it used to confuse me—because we did just the same thing to be little angels.

MAN. Yeah?

WOMAN. You know why I came here?

MAN. I can make a good guess.

WOMAN. Because you told me I looked like an angel to you! That's why I came.

MAN. Jeez, honey, all women look like angels to me—all white women. I ain't been seeing nothing but Indians, you know for the last couple a years. Gee, when I got off the boat here the other day—and saw all the women—gee I pretty near went crazy—talk about looking like angels—why—

WOMAN. You've had a lot of women, haven't you?

MAN. Not so many—real ones.

WOMAN. Did you—like any of 'em—better than me?

MAN. Nope—there wasn't one of 'em any sweeter than you, honey—not as sweet—no—not as sweet.

WOMAN. I like to hear you say it. Say it again—

MAN (*protesting good humoredly*). Oh—

WOMAN. Go on—tell me again!

MAN. Here! (*Kisses her.*) Does that tell you?

WOMAN. Yes. (*Pause.*) We're going to stick together—always—aren't we?

MAN (*honestly*). I'll have to be moving on, kid—some day, you know.

WOMAN. When?

MAN. Quien sabe?

WOMAN. What does that mean?

MAN. Quien sabe? You got to learn that, kid, if you're figuring on coming with me. It's the answer to everything—below the Rio Grande.

WOMAN. What does it mean?

MAN. It means—who knows?

WOMAN. Keen sabe?

MAN. Yep—don't forget it—now.

WOMAN. I'll never forget it!

MAN. Quien sabe.

WOMAN. And I'll never get used to it.

MAN. Quien sabe.

WOMAN. I'll never get—below the Rio Grande—I'll never get out of here.

MAN. Quien sabe.

WOMAN (*change of mood*). That's right! Keen sabe? Who knows?

MAN. That's the stuff.

WOMAN. You must like it down there.

MAN. I can't live anywhere else—for long.

WOMAN. Why not?

MAN. Oh—you're free down there! You're free!

A street light is lit outside. The outlines of a window take form against this light. There are bars across it, and from outside it, the sidewalk cuts across almost at the top. It is a basement room. The constant going and coming of passing feet, mostly feet of couples, can be dimly seen. Inside, on the ledge, there is a lily blooming in a bowl of rocks and water.

WOMAN. What's that?

MAN. Just the street light going on.

WOMAN. Is it as late as that?

MAN. Late as what?

WOMAN. Dark.

MAN. It's been dark for hours—didn't you know that?

WOMAN. No!—I must go! (*Rises.*)

MAN. Wait—the moon will be up in a little while—full moon.

WOMAN. It isn't that! I'm late! I must go!

She comes into the light. She wears a white chemise that might be the tunic of a dancer, and as she comes into the light she fastens about her waste a little skirt. She really wears almost exactly the clothes that women wear now, but the finesse of their cut, and the grace and ease with which she puts them on, must turn this episode of her dressing into a personification, an idealization of a woman clothing herself. All her gestures must be unconscious, innocent, relaxed, sure and full of natural grace. As she sits facing the window pulling on a stocking.

What's that?

MAN. What?

WOMAN. On the window ledge.

MAN. A flower.

WOMAN. Who gave it to you?

MAN. Nobody gave it to me. I bought it.

WOMAN. For yourself?

MAN. Yeah—Why not?

WOMAN. I don't know.

MAN. In Chinatown—made me think of Frisco where I was a kid—so I bought it.

WOMAN. Is that where you were born—Frisco?

MAN. Yep. Twin Peaks.

WOMAN. What's that?

MAN. A couple of hills—together.

WOMAN. One for you and one for me.

MAN. I bet you'd like Frisco.

WOMAN. I know a woman went out there once!

MAN. The bay and the hills! Jeez, that's the life! Every Saturday we used to cross the Bay—get a couple nags and just ride—over the hills. One would have a blanket on the saddle—the other, the grub. At night, we'd make a little fire and eat—and then roll up in the old blanket and—

WOMAN. Who? Who was with you?

MAN (*indifferently*). Anybody. (*Enthusiastically.*) Jeez, that dry old grass out there smells good at night—full of tar weed—you know—

WOMAN. Is that a good smell?

MAN. Tar weed? Didn't you ever smell it? (*She shakes her head 'No'.*) Sure it's a good smell! The Bay and the hills.

She goes to the mirror of the dresser, to finish dressing. She has only a dress to put on that is in one piece—with one fastening on the side. Before slipping it on, she stands before the mirror and stretches. Appreciatively but indifferently.

You look in good shape, kid. A couple of months riding over the mountains with me, you'd be great.

WOMAN. Can I?

MAN. What?

WOMAN. Some day—ride mountains with you?

MAN. Ride mountains? Ride donkeys!

WOMAN. It's the same thing!—with you!—Can I—some day? The high dark mountains?

MAN. Who knows?

WOMAN. It must be great!

MAN. You ever been off like that, kid?—high up? On top of the world?

WOMAN. Yes.

MAN. When?

WOMAN. Today.

MAN. You're pretty sweet.

WOMAN. I never knew anything like this way! I never knew that I could feel like this! So,—so purified! Don't laugh at me!

MAN. I ain't laughing, honey.

WOMAN. Purified.

MAN. It's a hell of a word—but I know what you mean. That's the way it is—sometimes.

WOMAN (*she puts on a little hat, then turns to him*). Well—goodbye.

MAN. Aren't you forgetting something? (*Rises.*)

She looks toward him, then throws her head slowly back, lifts her right arm—this gesture that is in so many statues of women—Volupte. He comes out of the shadow, puts his arm around her, kisses her. Her head and arm go further back—then she brings her arm around with a wide encircling gesture, her hand closes over his head, her fingers spread. Her fingers are protective, clutching. When he releases her, her eyes are shining with tears. She turns away. She looks back at him—and the room—and her eyes fasten on the lily.

WOMAN. Can I have that?

MAN. Sure—why not?

She takes it—goes. As she opens the door, the music is louder. The scene blacks out.

WOMAN. Goodbye. And—(*Hesitates.*) And—thank you.

CURTAIN

The music continues until the curtain goes up for Episode Seven. It goes up on silence.

EPISODE SEVEN

DOMESTIC

SCENE: *A sitting room: a divan, a telephone, a window.*
CHARACTERS: *Husband; Young Woman*

They are seated on opposite ends of the divan. They are both reading papers—to themselves.

HUSBAND. Record production.

YOUNG WOMAN. Girl turns on gas.

HUSBAND. Sale hits a million—

YOUNG WOMAN. Woman leaves all for love—

HUSBAND. Market trend steady—

YOUNG WOMAN. Young wife disappears—

HUSBAND. Owns a life interest—

Phone rings. Young Woman looks toward it.

That's for me. (*In phone.*) Hello—oh hello, A.B. It's all settled?—Everything signed? Good. Good! Tell R.A. to call me up. (*Hangs up phone—to Young Woman.*) Well, it's all settled. They signed!—aren't you interested? Aren't you going to ask me?

YOUNG WOMAN (*by rote*). Did you put it over?

HUSBAND. Sure I put it over.

YOUNG WOMAN. Did you swing it?

HUSBAND. Sure I swung it.

YOUNG WOMAN. Did they come through?

HUSBAND. Sure they came through.

YOUNG WOMAN. Did they sign?

HUSBAND. I'll say they signed.

YOUNG WOMAN. On the dotted line?

HUSBAND. On the dotted line.

YOUNG WOMAN. The property's yours?

HUSBAND. The property's mine. I'll put a first mortgage. I'll put a second mortgage and the property's mine. Happy?

YOUNG WOMAN (*by rote*). Happy.

HUSBAND (*going to her*). The property's mine! It's not all that's mine! (*Pinching her cheek—happy and playful.*) I got a first mortgage on her—I got a second mortgage on her—and she's mine!

Young Woman pulls away swiftly.

What's the matter?

YOUNG WOMAN. Nothing—what?

HUSBAND. You flinched when I touched you.

YOUNG WOMAN. No.

HUSBAND. You haven't done that in a long time.

YOUNG WOMAN. Haven't I?

HUSBAND. You used to do it every time I touched you.

YOUNG WOMAN. Did I?

HUSBAND. Didn't know that, did you?

YOUNG WOMAN (*unexpectedly*). Yes. Yes, I know it.

HUSBAND. Just purity.

YOUNG WOMAN. No.

HUSBAND. Oh, I liked it. Purity.

YOUNG WOMAN. No.

HUSBAND. You're one of the purest women that ever lived.

YOUNG WOMAN. I'm just like anybody else only—(*Stops.*)

HUSBAND. Only what?

YOUNG WOMAN (*pause*). Nothing.

HUSBAND. It must be something.

Phone rings. She gets up and goes to window.

HUSBAND (*in phone*). Hello—hello, R.A.—well, I put it over—yeah, I swung it—sure they came through—did they sign? On the dotted line! The property's mine. I made the proposition. I sold them the idea. Now watch me. Tell D.D. to call me up. (*Hangs up.*) That was R.A. What are you looking at?

YOUNG WOMAN. Nothing.

HUSBAND. You must be looking at something.

YOUNG WOMAN. Nothing—the moon.

HUSBAND. The moon's something, isn't it?

YOUNG WOMAN. Yes.

HUSBAND. What's it doing?

YOUNG WOMAN. Nothing.

HUSBAND. It must be doing something.

YOUNG WOMAN. It's moving—moving—(*She comes down restlessly.*)

HUSBAND. Pull down the shade, my dear.

YOUNG WOMAN. Why?

HUSBAND. People can look in.

Phone rings.

Hello—hello D.D.—Yes—I put it over—they came across—I put it over on them—yep—yep—yep—I'll say I am—yep—on the dotted line—Now you watch me—yep. Yep yep. Tell B.M. to phone me. (*Hangs up.*) That was D.D. (*To Young Woman who has come down to davenport and picked up a paper.*) Aren't you listening?

YOUNG WOMAN. I'm reading.

HUSBAND. What you reading?

YOUNG WOMAN. Nothing.

HUSBAND. Must be something. (*He sits and picks up his paper.*)

YOUNG WOMAN (*reading*). Prisoner escapes—lifer breaks jail—shoots way to freedom—

HUSBAND. Don't read that stuff—listen—here's a first rate editorial. I agree with this. I agree absolutely. Are you listening?

YOUNG WOMAN. I'm listening.

HUSBAND (*importantly*). All men are born free and entitled to the pursuit of happiness. (*Young Woman gets up.*) My, you're nervous tonight.

YOUNG WOMAN. I try not to be.

HUSBAND. You inherit that from your mother. She was in the office today.

YOUNG WOMAN. Was she?

HUSBAND. To get her allowance.

YOUNG WOMAN. Oh—

HUSBAND. Don't you know it's the *first*.

YOUNG WOMAN. Poor Ma.

HUSBAND. What would she do without me?

YOUNG WOMAN. I know. You're very good.

HUSBAND. One thing—she's grateful.

YOUNG WOMAN. Poor Ma—poor Ma.

HUSBAND. She's got to have care.

YOUNG WOMAN. Yes. She's got to have care.

HUSBAND. A mother's a very precious thing—a good mother.

YOUNG WOMAN (*excitedly*). I try to be a good mother.

HUSBAND. Of course you're a good mother.

YOUNG WOMAN. I try! I try!

HUSBAND. A mother's a very precious thing—(*Resuming his paper.*) And a child's a very precious thing. Precious jewels.

YOUNG WOMAN (*reading*). Sale of jewels and precious stones.

Young Woman puts her hand to throat.

HUSBAND. What's the matter?

YOUNG WOMAN. I feel as though I were drowning.

HUSBAND. Drowning?

YOUNG WOMAN. With stones around my neck.

HUSBAND. You just imagine that.

YOUNG WOMAN. Stifling.

HUSBAND. You don't breathe deep enough—breathe now—look at me. (*He breathes.*) Breath is life. Life is breath.

YOUNG WOMAN (*suddenly*). And what is death?

HUSBAND (*smartly*). Just—no breath!

YOUNG WOMAN (*to herself*). Just no breath.

Takes up paper.

HUSBAND. All right?

YOUNG WOMAN. All right.

HUSBAND (*reads as she stares at her paper. Looks up after a pause.*) I feel cold air, my dear.

YOUNG WOMAN. Cold air?

HUSBAND. Close the window, will you?

YOUNG WOMAN. It isn't open.

HUSBAND. Don't you feel cold air?

YOUNG WOMAN. No—you just imagine it.

HUSBAND. I never imagine anything. (*Young Woman is staring at the paper.*) What are you reading?

YOUNG WOMAN. Nothing.

HUSBAND. You must be reading something.

YOUNG WOMAN. Woman finds husband dead.

HUSBAND (*uninterested*). Oh. (*Interested.*) Here's a man says 'I owe my success to a yeast cake a day—my digestion is good—I sleep very well—and—(*His wife gets up, goes toward door.*) Where you going?

YOUNG WOMAN. No place.

HUSBAND. You must be going some place.

YOUNG WOMAN. Just—to bed.

HUSBAND. It isn't eleven yet. Wait.

YOUNG WOMAN. Wait?

HUSBAND. It's only ten-forty-six—wait! (*Holds out his arms to her.*) Come here!

YOUNG WOMAN (*takes a step toward him—recoils*). Oh—I want to go away!

HUSBAND. Away? Where?

YOUNG WOMAN. Anywhere—away.

HUSBAND. Why, what's the matter?

YOUNG WOMAN. I'm scared.

HUSBAND. What of?

YOUNG WOMAN. I can't sleep—I haven't slept.

HUSBAND. That's nothing.

YOUNG WOMAN. And the moon—when it's full moon.

HUSBAND. That's nothing.

YOUNG WOMAN. I can't sleep.

HUSBAND. Of course not. It's the light.

YOUNG WOMAN. I don't see it! I feel it! I'm afraid.

HUSBAND (*kindly*). Nonsense—come here.

YOUNG WOMAN. I want to go away.

HUSBAND. But I can't get away now.

YOUNG WOMAN. Alone!

HUSBAND. You've never been away alone.

YOUNG WOMAN. I know.

HUSBAND. What would you do?

YOUNG WOMAN. Maybe I'd sleep.

HUSBAND. Now you wait.

YOUNG WOMAN (*desperately*). Wait?

HUSBAND. We'll take a trip—we'll go to Europe—I'll get my watch—I'll get my Swiss watch—I've always wanted a Swiss watch that I bought right there—isn't that funny? Wait—wait. (*Young Woman comes down to davenport—sits. Husband resumes his paper.*) Another revolution below the Rio Grande.

YOUNG WOMAN. Below the Rio Grande?

HUSBAND. Yes—another—

YOUNG WOMAN. Anyone—hurt?

HUSBAND. No.

YOUNG WOMAN. Any prisoners?

HUSBAND. No.

YOUNG WOMAN. All free?

HUSBAND. All free.

He resumes his paper. Young Woman sits, staring ahead of her. The music of the hand organ sounds off very dimly, playing Cielito Lindo. Voices begin to sing it—'Ay-ay-ay-ay'—and then the words—the music and voices get louder.

THE VOICE OF HER LOVER. They were a bunch of bandidos—bandits you know—holding me there—what was I to do—I had to get free—didn't I? I had to get free—

VOICES. Free—free—free—

LOVER. I filled an empty bottle with small stones—

VOICES. Stones—stones—precious   stones—millstones—stones—stones—millstones

LOVER. Just a bottle with small stones.

VOICES. Stones—stones—small stones—

LOVER. You only need a bottle with small stones.

VOICES. Stones—stones—small stones—

VOICE OF A HUCKSTER. Stones for sale—stones—stones—small stones—precious stones—

VOICES. Stones—stones—precious stones—

LOVER. Had to get free, didn't I? Free?

VOICES. Free? Free?

LOVER. Quien sabe? Who knows? Who knows?

VOICES. Who'd know? Who'd know? Who'd know?

HUCKSTER. Stones—stones—small   stones—big   stones—millstones—cold stones—head stones—

VOICES. Head stones—head stones—head stones.

The music—the voices—mingle—increase—the Young Woman flies from her chair and cries out in terror.

YOUNG WOMAN. Oh! Oh!

The scene blacks out—the music and the dim voices, 'Stones—stones—stones,' continue until the scene lights for Episode Eight.

EPISODE EIGHT
THE LAW

SCENE: *Courtroom*

SOUNDS: *Clicking of telegraph instruments offstage.*

CHARACTERS: *Judge; Jury; Lawyers; Spectators; Reporters; Messenger Boys; Law Clerks; Bailiff; Court Reporter; Young Woman*

The words and movements of all these people except the Young Woman are routine—mechanical. Each is going through the motions of his own game.

AT RISE: *All assembled, except Judge.*

Enter Judge

BAILIFF (*mumbling*). Hear ye—hear ye—! (*All rise. Judge sits. All sit. Lawyer for Defense gets to his feet—He is the verbose, 'eloquent' typical criminal defense lawyer. Judge signs to him to wait—turns to Law Clerks, grouped at foot of the bench.*)

FIRST CLERK (*handing up a paper—routine voice*). State versus Kling—stay of execution.

JUDGE. Denied.

First Clerk goes.

SECOND CLERK. Bing vs. Ding—demurrer.

Judge signs. Second Clerk goes.

THIRD CLERK. Case of John King—habeas corpus.

Judge signs. Third Clerk goes. Judge signs to Bailiff.

BAILIFF (*mumbling*). People of the State of ————versus Helen Jones.

JUDGE (*to Lawyer for Defense*). Defense ready to proceed?

LAWYER FOR DEFENSE. We're ready, your Honor.

JUDGE. Proceed.

LAWYER FOR DEFENSE. Helen Jones.

BAILIFF. Helen Jones!

Young Woman rises.

LAWYER FOR DEFENSE. Mrs. Jones, will you take the stand?

Young Woman goes to witness stand.

FIRST REPORTER (*writing rapidly*). The defense sprang a surprise at the opening of court this morning by putting the accused woman on the stand. The prosecution was swept off its feet by this daring defense strategy and—(*Instruments get louder.*)

SECOND REPORTER. Trembling and scarcely able to stand, Helen Jones, accused murderess, had to be almost carried to the witness stand this morning when her lawyer—

BAILIFF (*mumbling—with Bible*). Do you swear to tell the truth, the whole truth and nothing but the truth—so help you God?

YOUNG WOMAN. I do.

JUDGE. You may sit.

She sits in witness chair.

COURT REPORTER. What is your name?

YOUNG WOMAN. Helen Jones.

COURT REPORTER. Your age?

YOUNG WOMAN (*hesitates—then*). Twenty-nine.

COURT REPORTER. Where do you live?

YOUNG WOMAN. In prison.

LAWYER FOR DEFENSE. This is my client's legal address.

Hands a scrap of paper.

LAWYER FOR PROSECUTION (*jumping to his feet*). I object to this insinuation on the part of counsel of any illegality in the holding of this defendant in jail when the law—

LAWYER FOR DEFENSE. I made no such insinuation.

LAWYER FOR PROSECUTION. You implied it—

LAWYER FOR DEFENSE. I did not!

LAWYER FOR PROSECUTION. You're a—

JUDGE. Order!

BAILIFF. Order!

LAWYER FOR DEFENSE. Your Honor, I object to counsel's constant attempt to—

LAWYER FOR PROSECUTION. I protest—I—

JUDGE. Order!

BAILIFF. Order!

JUDGE. Proceed with the witness.

LAWYER FOR DEFENSE. Mrs. Jones, you are the widow of the late George H. Jones, are you not?

YOUNG WOMAN. Yes.

LAWYER FOR DEFENSE. How long were you married to the late George H. Jones before his demise?

YOUNG WOMAN. Six years.

LAWYER FOR DEFENSE. Six years! And it was a happy marriage, was it not? (*Young Woman hesitates.*) Did you quarrel?

YOUNG WOMAN. No, sir.

LAWYER FOR DEFENSE. Then it was a happy marriage, wasn't it?

YOUNG WOMAN. Yes, sir.

LAWYER FOR DEFENSE. In those six years of married life with your late husband, the late George H. Jones, did you EVER have a quarrel?

YOUNG WOMAN. No, sir.

LAWYER FOR DEFENSE. Never one quarrel?

LAWYER FOR PROSECUTION. The witness has said—

LAWYER FOR DEFENSE. Six years without one quarrel! Six years! Gentlemen of the jury, I ask you to consider this fact! Six years of married life without a quarrel. (*The Jury grins.*) I ask you to consider it seriously! Very seriously! Who of us—and this is not intended as any reflection on the sacred institution of marriage—no—but!

JUDGE. Proceed with your witness.

LAWYER FOR DEFENSE. You have one child—have you not, Mrs. Jones?

YOUNG WOMAN. Yes, sir.

LAWYER FOR DEFENSE. A little girl, is it not?

YOUNG WOMAN. Yes, sir.

LAWYER FOR DEFENSE. How old is she?

YOUNG WOMAN. She's five—past five.

LAWYER FOR DEFENSE. A little girl of past five. Since the demise of the late Mr. Jones you are the only parent she has living, are you not?

YOUNG WOMAN. Yes, sir.

LAWYER FOR DEFENSE. Before your marriage to the late Mr. Jones, you worked and supported your mother, did you not?

LAWYER FOR PROSECUTION. I object, your honor! Irrelevant—immaterial—and—

JUDGE. Objection sustained!

LAWYER FOR DEFENSE. In order to support your mother and yourself as a girl, you worked, did you not?

YOUNG WOMAN. Yes, sir.

LAWYER FOR DEFENSE. What did you do?

YOUNG WOMAN. I was a stenographer.

LAWYER FOR DEFENSE. And since your marriage you have continued as her sole support, have you not?

YOUNG WOMAN. Yes, sir.

LAWYER FOR DEFENSE. A devoted daughter, gentlemen of the jury! As well as a devoted wife and a devoted mother!

LAWYER FOR PROSECUTION. Your Honor!

LAWYER FOR DEFENSE (*quickly*). And now, Mrs. Jones, I will ask you—the law expects me to ask you—it demands that I ask you—did you—or did you not—on the night of June 2nd last or the morning of June 3rd last—kill your husband, the late George H. Jones—did you, or did you not?

YOUNG WOMAN. I did not.

LAWYER FOR DEFENSE. You did not?

YOUNG WOMAN. I did not.

LAWYER FOR DEFENSE. Now, Mrs. Jones, you have heard the witnesses for the State—They were not many—and they did not have much to say—

LAWYER FOR PROSECUTION. I object.

JUDGE. Sustained.

LAWYER FOR DEFENSE. You have heard some police and you have heard some doctors. None of whom was present! The prosecution could not furnish any witness to the crime—not one witness!

LAWYER FOR PROSECUTION. Your Honor!

LAWYER FOR DEFENSE. Nor one motive.

LAWYER FOR PROSECUTION. Your Honor—I protest! I—

JUDGE. Sustained.

LAWYER FOR DEFENSE. But such as these witnesses were, you have heard them try to accuse you of deliberately murdering your own husband, this husband with whom, by your own statement, you had never had a quarrel—not one quarrel in six years of married life, murdering him, I say, or rather—they say, while he slept, by brutally hitting him over the head with a bottle—a bottle filled with small stones—Did you, I repeat this, or did you not?

YOUNG WOMAN. I did not.

LAWYER FOR DEFENSE. You did not! Of course you did not! (*Quickly.*) Now, Mrs. Jones, will you tell the jury in your own words exactly what happened on the night of June 2nd or the morning of June 3rd last, at the time your husband was killed.

YOUNG WOMAN. I was awakened by hearing somebody—something—in the room, and I saw two men standing by my husband's bed.

LAWYER FOR DEFENSE. Your husband's bed—that was also your bed, was it not, Mrs. Jones?

YOUNG WOMAN. Yes.

LAWYER FOR DEFENSE. You hadn't the modern idea of separate beds, had you, Mrs. Jones?

YOUNG WOMAN. Mr. Jones objected.

LAWYER FOR DEFENSE. I mean you slept in the same bed, did you not?

YOUNG WOMAN. Yes.

LAWYER FOR DEFENSE. Then explain just what you mean by saying 'my husband's bed'.

YOUNG WOMAN. Well—I—

LAWYER FOR DEFENSE. You meant his side of the bed, didn't you?

YOUNG WOMAN. Yes. His side.

LAWYER FOR DEFENSE. That is what I thought, but I wanted the jury to be clear on that point. (*To the Jury.*) Mr. and Mrs. Jones slept in the same bed. (*To her.*) Go on, Mrs. Jones. (*As she is silent.*) You heard a noise and—

YOUNG WOMAN. I heard a noise and I awoke and saw two men standing beside my husband's side of the bed.

LAWYER FOR DEFENSE. Two men?

YOUNG WOMAN. Yes.

LAWYER FOR DEFENSE. Can you describe them?

YOUNG WOMAN. Not very well—I couldn't see them very well.

LAWYER FOR DEFENSE. Could you say whether they were big or small—light or dark, thin or—

YOUNG WOMAN. They were big dark looking men.

LAWYER FOR DEFENSE. Big dark looking men?

YOUNG WOMAN. Yes.

LAWYER FOR DEFENSE. And what did you do, Mrs. Jones, when you suddenly awoke and saw two big dark looking men standing beside your bed?

YOUNG WOMAN. I didn't do anything!

LAWYER FOR DEFENSE. You didn't have time to do anything—did you?

YOUNG WOMAN. No. Before I could do anything—one of them raised—something in his hand and struck Mr. Jones over the head with it.

LAWYER FOR DEFENSE. And what did Mr. Jones do?

Spectators laugh.

JUDGE. Silence.

BAILIFF. Silence.

LAWYER FOR DEFENSE. What did Mr. Jones do, Mrs. Jones?

YOUNG WOMAN. He gave a sort of groan and tried to raise up.

LAWYER FOR DEFENSE. Tried to raise up!

YOUNG WOMAN. Yes!

LAWYER FOR DEFENSE. And then what happened?

YOUNG WOMAN. The man struck him again and he fell back.

LAWYER FOR DEFENSE. I see. What did the men do then? The big dark looking men.

YOUNG WOMAN. They turned and ran out of the room.

LAWYER FOR DEFENSE. I see. What did you do then, Mrs. Jones?

YOUNG WOMAN. I saw Mr. Jones was bleeding from the temple. I got towels and tried to stop it, and then I realized he had—passed away.

LAWYER FOR DEFENSE. I see. What did you do then?

YOUNG WOMAN. I didn't know what to do. But I thought I'd better call the police. So I went to the telephone and called the police.

LAWYER FOR DEFENSE. What happened then?

YOUNG WOMAN. Nothing. Nothing happened.

LAWYER FOR DEFENSE. The police came, didn't they?

YOUNG WOMAN. Yes—they came.

LAWYER FOR DEFENSE (*quickly*). And that is all you know concerning the death of your husband in the late hours of June 2nd or the early hours of June 3rd last, isn't it?

YOUNG WOMAN. Yes sir.

LAWYER FOR DEFENSE. All?

YOUNG WOMAN. Yes sir.

LAWYER FOR DEFENSE (to Lawyer for Prosecution). Take the witness.

FIRST REPORTER (writing). The accused woman told a straightforward story of—

SECOND REPORTER. The accused woman told a rambling, disconnected story of—

LAWYER FOR PROSECUTION. You made no effort to cry out, Mrs. Jones, did you, when you saw those two big dark men standing over your helpless husband, did you?

YOUNG WOMAN. No sir. I didn't. I—

LAWYER FOR PROSECUTION. And when they turned and ran out of the room, you made no effort to follow them or cry out after them, did you?

YOUNG WOMAN. No sir.

LAWYER FOR PROSECUTION. Why didn't you?

YOUNG WOMAN. I saw Mr. Jones was hurt.

LAWYER FOR PROSECUTION. Ah! You saw Mr. Jones was hurt! You saw this—how did you see it?

YOUNG WOMAN. I just saw it.

LAWYER FOR PROSECUTION. Then there was a light in the room?

YOUNG WOMAN. A sort of light.

LAWYER FOR PROSECUTION. What do you mean—a sort of light? A bed light?

YOUNG WOMAN. No. No, there was no light on.

LAWYER FOR PROSECUTION. Then where did it come from—this sort of light?

YOUNG WOMAN. I don't know.

LAWYER FOR PROSECUTION. Perhaps—from the window.

YOUNG WOMAN. Yes—from the window.

LAWYER FOR PROSECUTION. Oh, the shade was up!

YOUNG WOMAN. No—no, the shade was down.

LAWYER FOR PROSECUTION. You're sure of that?

YOUNG WOMAN. Yes. Mr. Jones always wanted the shade down.

LAWYER FOR PROSECUTION. The shade was down—there was no light in the room—but the room was light—how do you explain this?

YOUNG WOMAN. I don't know.

LAWYER FOR PROSECUTION. You don't know!

YOUNG WOMAN. I think where the window was open—under the shade—light came in

LAWYER FOR PROSECUTION. There is a street light there?

YOUNG WOMAN. No—there's no street light.

LAWYER FOR PROSECUTION. Then where did this light come from—that came in under the shade?

YOUNG WOMAN (desperately). From the moon!

LAWYER FOR PROSECUTION. The moon!

YOUNG WOMAN. Yes! It was bright moon!

LAWYER FOR PROSECUTION. It was bright moon—you are sure of that!

YOUNG WOMAN. Yes.

LAWYER FOR PROSECUTION. How are you sure?

YOUNG WOMAN. I couldn't sleep—I never can sleep in the bright moon. I never can.

LAWYER FOR PROSECUTION. It was bright moon. Yet you could not see two big dark looking men—but you could see your husband bleeding from the temple.

YOUNG WOMAN. Yes sir.

LAWYER FOR PROSECUTION. And did you call a doctor?

YOUNG WOMAN. No.

LAWYER FOR PROSECUTION. Why didn't you?

YOUNG WOMAN. The police did.

LAWYER FOR PROSECUTION. But you didn't?

YOUNG WOMAN. No.

LAWYER FOR PROSECUTION. Why didn't you? (No answer.) Why didn't you?

YOUNG WOMAN (whispers). I saw it was—useless.

LAWYER FOR PROSECUTION. Ah! You saw that! You saw that—very clearly.

YOUNG WOMAN. Yes.

LAWYER FOR PROSECUTION. And you didn't call a doctor.

YOUNG WOMAN. It was—useless.

LAWYER FOR PROSECUTION. What did you do?

YOUNG WOMAN. It was useless—there was no use of anything.

LAWYER FOR PROSECUTION. I asked you what you did?

YOUNG WOMAN. Nothing.

LAWYER FOR PROSECUTION. Nothing!

YOUNG WOMAN. I just sat there.

LAWYER FOR PROSECUTION. You sat there! A long while, didn't you?

YOUNG WOMAN. I don't know.

LAWYER FOR PROSECUTION. You don't know? (Showing her the neck of a broken bottle.) Mrs. Jones, did you ever see this before?

YOUNG WOMAN. I think so.

LAWYER FOR PROSECUTION. You think so.

YOUNG WOMAN. Yes.

LAWYER FOR PROSECUTION. What do you think it is?

YOUNG WOMAN. I think it's the bottle that was used against Mr. Jones.

LAWYER FOR PROSECUTION. Used against him—yes—that's right. You've guessed right. This neck and these broken pieces and these pebbles were found on the floor and scattered over the bed. There were no fingerprints, Mrs. Jones, on this bottle. None at all. Doesn't that seem strange to you?

YOUNG WOMAN. No.

LAWYER FOR PROSECUTION. It doesn't seem strange to you that this bottle held in the big dark hand of one of those big dark men left no mark! No print! That doesn't seem strange to you?

YOUNG WOMAN. No.

LAWYER FOR PROSECUTION. You are in the habit of wearing rubber gloves at night, Mrs. Jones—are you not? To protect—to soften your hands—are you not?

YOUNG WOMAN. I used to.

LAWYER FOR PROSECUTION. Used to—when was that?

YOUNG WOMAN. Before I was married.

LAWYER FOR PROSECUTION. And after your marriage you gave it up?

YOUNG WOMAN. Yes.

LAWYER FOR PROSECUTION. Why?

YOUNG WOMAN. Mr. Jones did not like the feeling of them.

LAWYER FOR PROSECUTION. You always did everything Mr. Jones wanted?

YOUNG WOMAN. I tried to—Anyway I didn't care any more—so much—about my hands.

LAWYER FOR PROSECUTION. I see—so after your marriage you never wore gloves at night any more?

YOUNG WOMAN. No.

LAWYER FOR PROSECUTION. Mrs. Jones, isn't it true that you began wearing your rubber gloves again—in spite of your husband's expressed dislike—about a year ago—a year ago this spring?

YOUNG WOMAN. No.

LAWYER FOR PROSECUTION. You did not suddenly begin to care particularly for your hands again—about a year ago this spring?

YOUNG WOMAN. No.

LAWYER FOR PROSECUTION. You're quite sure of that?

YOUNG WOMAN. Yes.

LAWYER FOR PROSECUTION. Quite sure?

YOUNG WOMAN. Yes.

LAWYER FOR PROSECUTION. Then you did not have in your possession, on the night of June 2nd last, a pair of rubber gloves?

YOUNG WOMAN (*shakes her head*). No.

LAWYER FOR PROSECUTION (*to Judge*). I'd like to introduce these gloves as evidence at this time, your Honor.

JUDGE. Exhibit 24.

LAWYER FOR PROSECUTION. I'll return to them later—now, Mrs. Jones—this nightgown—you recognize it, don't you?

YOUNG WOMAN. Yes.

LAWYER FOR PROSECUTION. Yours, is it not?

YOUNG WOMAN. Yes.

LAWYER FOR PROSECUTION. The one you were wearing the night your husband was murdered, isn't it?

YOUNG WOMAN. The night he died—yes.

LAWYER FOR PROSECUTION. Not the one you wore under your peignoir—I believe that it's what you call it, isn't it? A peignoir? When you received the police—but the one you wore before that—isn't it?

YOUNG WOMAN. Yes.

LAWYER FOR PROSECUTION. This was found—not where the gloves were found—no—but at the bottom of the soiled clothes hamper in the bathroom—rolled up and wet— why was it wet, Mrs. Jones?

YOUNG WOMAN. I had tried to wash it.

LAWYER FOR PROSECUTION. Wash it? I thought you had just sat?

YOUNG WOMAN. First—I tried to make things clean.

LAWYER FOR PROSECUTION. Why did you want to make this—clean—as you say?

YOUNG WOMAN. There was blood on it.

LAWYER FOR PROSECUTION. Spattered on it?

YOUNG WOMAN. Yes.

LAWYER FOR PROSECUTION. How did that happen?

YOUNG WOMAN. The bottle broke—and the sharp edge cut.

LAWYER FOR PROSECUTION. Oh, the bottle broke and the sharp edge cut!

YOUNG WOMAN. Yes. That's what they told me afterwards.

LAWYER FOR PROSECUTION. Who told you?

YOUNG WOMAN. The police—that's what they say happened.

LAWYER FOR PROSECUTION. Mrs. Jones, why did you try so desperately to wash that blood away—before you called the police?

LAWYER FOR DEFENSE. I object!

JUDGE. Objection overruled.

LAWYER FOR PROSECUTION. Why, Mrs. Jones?

YOUNG WOMAN. I don't know. It's what anyone would have done, wouldn't they?

LAWYER FOR PROSECUTION. That depends, doesn't it? (*Suddenly taking up bottle.*) Mrs. Jones—when did you first see this?

YOUNG WOMAN. The night my husband was—done away with.

LAWYER FOR PROSECUTION. Done away with! You mean killed?

YOUNG WOMAN. Yes.

LAWYER FOR PROSECUTION. Why don't you say killed?

YOUNG WOMAN. It sounds so brutal.

LAWYER FOR PROSECUTION. And you never saw this before then?

YOUNG WOMAN. No sir.

LAWYER FOR PROSECUTION. You're quite sure of that?

YOUNG WOMAN. Yes.

LAWYER FOR PROSECUTION. And these stones—when did you first see them?

YOUNG WOMAN. The night my husband was done away with.

LAWYER FOR PROSECUTION. Before that night your husband was murdered—you never saw them? Never before then?

YOUNG WOMAN. No sir.

LAWYER FOR PROSECUTION. You are quite sure of that!

YOUNG WOMAN. Yes.

LAWYER FOR PROSECUTION. Mrs. Jones, do you remember about a year ago, a year ago this spring, bringing home to your house—a lily, a Chinese water lily?

YOUNG WOMAN. No—I don't think so.

LAWYER FOR PROSECUTION. You don't think you remember bringing home a water lily growing in a bowl filled with small stones?

YOUNG WOMAN. No—No I don't.

LAWYER FOR PROSECUTION. I'll show you this bowl, Mrs. Jones. Does that refresh your memory?

YOUNG WOMAN. I remember the bowl—but I don't remember—the lily.

LAWYER FOR PROSECUTION. You recognize the bowl then?

YOUNG WOMAN. Yes.

LAWYER FOR PROSECUTION. It is yours, isn't it?

YOUNG WOMAN. It was in my house—yes.

LAWYER FOR PROSECUTION. How did it come there?

YOUNG WOMAN. How did it come there?

LAWYER FOR PROSECUTION. Yes—where did you get it?

YOUNG WOMAN. I don't remember.

LAWYER FOR PROSECUTION. You don't remember?

YOUNG WOMAN. No.

LAWYER FOR PROSECUTION. You don't remember about a year ago bringing this bowl into your bedroom filled with small stones and some water and a lily? You don't remember tending very carefully that lily till it died? And when it died you don't remember hiding the bowl full of little stones away on the top shelf of your closet—and keeping it there until—you don't remember?

YOUNG WOMAN. No, I don't remember.

LAWYER FOR PROSECUTION. You may have done so?

YOUNG WOMAN. No—no—I didn't! I didn't! I don't know anything about all that.

LAWYER FOR PROSECUTION. But you do remember the bowl?

YOUNG WOMAN. Yes. It was in my house—you found it in my house.

LAWYER FOR PROSECUTION. But you don't remember the lily or the stones?

YOUNG WOMAN. No—No I don't!

(*Lawyer for Prosecution turns to look among his papers in a brief case.*)

FIRST REPORTER (*writing*). Under the heavy artillery fire of the State's attorney's brilliant cross-questioning, the accused woman's defense was badly riddled. Pale and trembling she—

SECOND REPORTER (*writing*). Undaunted by the Prosecution's machine-gun attack, the defendant was able to maintain her position of innocence in the face of rapid-fire questioning that threatened, but never seriously menaced her defense. Flushed but calm she—

LAWYER FOR PROSECUTION (*producing paper*). Your Honor, I'd like to introduce this paper in evidence at this time.

JUDGE. What is it?

LAWYER FOR PROSECUTION. It is an affidavit taken in the State of Guanajato, Mexico.

LAWYER FOR DEFENSE. Mexico? Your Honor, I protest. A Mexican affidavit! Is this the United States of America or isn't it?

LAWYER FOR PROSECUTION. It's properly executed—sworn to before a notary—and certified to by an American Consul.

LAWYER FOR DEFENSE. Your Honor! I protest! In the name of this great United States of America—I protest—are we to permit our sacred institutions to be thus—

JUDGE. What is the purpose of this document—who signed it?

LAWYER FOR PROSECUTION. It is signed by one Richard Roe, and its purpose is to refresh the memory of the witness on the point at issue—and incidentally supply a motive for

this murder—this brutal and cold-blooded murder of a sleeping man by—

LAWYER FOR DEFENSE. I protest, your Honor! I object!

JUDGE. Objection sustained. Let me see the document. (*Takes paper which is handed to him—looks at it.*) Perfectly regular. Do you offer this affidavit as evidence at this time for the purpose of refreshing the memory of the witness at this time?

LAWYER FOR PROSECUTION. Yes, your Honor.

JUDGE. You may introduce the evidence.

LAWYER FOR DEFENSE. I object! I object to the introduction of this evidence at this time as irrelevant, immaterial, illegal, biased, prejudicial, and—

JUDGE. Objection overruled.

LAWYER FOR DEFENSE. Exception.

JUDGE. Exception noted. Proceed.

LAWYER FOR PROSECUTION. I wish to read the evidence to the jury at this time.

JUDGE. Proceed.

LAWYER FOR DEFENSE. I object.

JUDGE. Objection overruled.

LAWYER FOR DEFENSE. Exception.

JUDGE. Noted.

LAWYER FOR DEFENSE. Why is this witness himself not brought into court—so he can be cross-questioned?

LAWYER FOR PROSECUTION. The witness is a resident of the Republic of Mexico and as such not subject to subpoena as a witness to this court.

LAWYER FOR DEFENSE. If he was out of the jurisdiction of this court how did you get this affidavit out of him?

LAWYER FOR PROSECUTION. This affidavit was made voluntarily by the deponent in the furtherance of justice.

LAWYER FOR DEFENSE. I suppose you didn't threaten him with extradition on some other trumped-up charge so that—

JUDGE. Order!

BAILIFF. Order!

JUDGE. Proceed with the evidence.

LAWYER FOR PROSECUTION (*reading*). In the matter of the State of ——— vs. Helen Jones, I Richard Roe, being of sound mind, do herein depose and state that I know the accused, Helen Jones, and have known her for a period of over one year immediately preceding the date of the signature on this affidavit. That I first met the said Helen Jones in a so-called speak-easy somewhere in the West 40s in New York City. That on the day I met her, she went with me to my room, also somewhere in the West 40s in New York City, where we had intimate relations—

YOUNG WOMAN (*moans*). Oh!

LAWYER FOR PROSECUTION (*continues reading*). —and where I gave her a bowl filled with pebbles, also containing a flowering lily. That from the first day we met until I departed for Mexico in the Fall, the said Helen Jones was an almost daily visitor to my room where we continued to—

YOUNG WOMAN. No! No! (*Moans.*)

LAWYER FOR PROSECUTION. What is it, Mrs. Jones—what is it?

YOUNG WOMAN. Don't read any more! No more!

LAWYER FOR PROSECUTION. Why not!

YOUNG WOMAN. I did it! I did it! I did it!

LAWYER FOR PROSECUTION. You confess?

YOUNG WOMAN. Yes—I did it!

LAWYER FOR DEFENSE. I object, your Honor.

JUDGE. You confess you killed your husband?

YOUNG WOMAN. I put him out of the way—yes.

JUDGE. Why?

YOUNG WOMAN. To be free.

JUDGE. To be free? Is that the only reason?

YOUNG WOMAN. Yes.

JUDGE. If you just wanted to be free—why didn't you divorce him?

YOUNG WOMAN. Oh I couldn't do that!! I couldn't hurt him like that!

Burst of laughter from all in the court. The Young Woman stares out at them, and then seems to go rigid.

JUDGE. Silence!

BAILIFF. Silence!

(*There is a gradual silence.*)

JUDGE. Mrs. Jones, why—

Young Woman begins to moan—suddenly—as though the realization of the enormity of her isolation had just come upon her. It is a sound of desolation, of agony, of human woe. It continues until the end of the scene.

Why—?

(*Young Woman cannot speak.*)

LAWYER FOR DEFENSE. Your Honor, I ask a recess to—

JUDGE. Court's adjourned.

Spectators begin to file out. The Young Woman continues in the witness box, unseeing, unheeding.

FIRST REPORTER. Murderess confesses.

SECOND REPORTER. Paramour brings confession.

THIRD REPORTER. I did it! Woman cries!

There is a great burst of speed from the telegraphic instruments. They keep up a constant accompaniment to the Woman's moans. The scene blacks out as the courtroom empties, and two policemen go to stand by the woman. The sound of the telegraph instruments continues until the scene lights into Episode Nine—and the prayers of the Priest.

EPISODE NINE

A MACHINE

SCENE: *A prison room. The front bars face the audience. They are set back far enough to permit a clear passageway across the stage.*

SOUNDS: *The voice of a Negro singing; the whir of an aeroplane flying.*

CHARACTERS: *Young Woman; A Priest; A Jailer; Two Barbers; A Matron; Mother; Two Guards*

AT RISE: *In front of the bars, at one side, sits a Man; at the opposite side, a Woman—the Jailer and the Matron.*

Inside the bars, a Man and a Woman—the Young Woman and a Priest. The Young Woman sits still with folded hands. The Priest is praying.

PRIEST. Hear, oh Lord, my prayer; and let my cry come to Thee. Turn not away Thy face from me; in the day when I am in trouble, incline Thy ear to me. In what day soever I shall call upon Thee, hear me speedily. For my days are vanished like smoke; and my bones are grown dry, like fuel for the fire. I am smitten as grass, and my heart is withered; because I forgot to eat my bread. Through the voice of my groaning, my bone hath cleaved to my flesh. I am become like to a pelican of the wilderness. I am like a night raven in the house. I have watched and become as a sparrow all alone on the housetop. All the day long my enemies reproach me; and they that praised me did swear against me. My days have declined like a shadow, and I am withered like grass. But Thou, oh Lord, end rest forever. Thou shalt arise and have mercy, for it is time to have mercy. The time is come.

Voice of Negro offstage—begins to sing a Negro spiritual.

PRIEST. The Lord hath looked upon the earth, that He might hear the groans of them that are in fetters, that He might release the children of—

Voice of Negro grown louder.

JAILER. Stop that nigger yelling.

YOUNG WOMAN. No, let him sing. He helps me.

MATRON. You can't hear the Father.

YOUNG WOMAN. He helps me.

PRIEST. Don't I help you, daughter?

YOUNG WOMAN. I understand him. He is condemned. I understand him.

The voice of the Negro goes on louder, drowning out the voice of the Priest.

PRIEST (*chanting in Latin*). Gratiam tuum, quaesumus, Domine, metibus nostris infunde, ut qui, angelo nuntiante, Christifilii tui incarnationem cognovimus, per passionem eius et crucem ad ressurectionis gloriam perducamus. Per eudem Christum Dominum nostrum.

Enter Two Barbers. There is a rattling of keys.

FIRST BARBER. How is she?

MATRON. Calm.

JAILER. Quiet.

YOUNG WOMAN (*rising*). I am ready.

FIRST BARBER. Then sit down.

YOUNG WOMAN (*in a steady voice*). Aren't you the death guard come to take me?

FIRST BARBER. No, we ain't the death guard. We're the barbers.

YOUNG WOMAN. The barbers.

MATRON. You hair must be cut.

JAILER. Must be shaved.

BARBER. Just a patch

The Barbers draw near her.

YOUNG WOMAN. No!

PRIEST. Daughter, you're ready. You know you are ready.

YOUNG WOMAN (*crying out*). Not for this! Not for this!

MATRON. The rule.

JAILER. Regulations.

BARBER. Routine.

The Barbers take her by the arms.

YOUNG WOMAN. No! No! Don't touch me—touch me!

(*They take her and put her down in the chair, cut a patch from her hair.*)

I will not be submitted—this indignity! No! I will not be submitted!—Leave me alone! Oh my God am I never to be let alone! Always to have to submit—to submit! No more—not now—I'm going to die—I won't submit! Not now!

BARBER (*finishing cutting a patch from her hair*). You'll submit, my lady. Right to the end, you'll submit! There, and a neat job too.

JAILER. Very neat.

MATRON. Very neat.

Exit Barbers.

YOUNG WOMAN (*her calm shattered*). Father, Father! Why was I born?

PRIEST. I came forth from the Father and have come into the world—I leave the world and go into the Father.

YOUNG WOMAN (*weeping*). Submit! Submit! Is nothing mine? The hair on my head! The very hair on my head—

PRIEST. Praise God.

YOUNG WOMAN. Am I never to be let alone! Never to have peace! When I'm dead, won't I have peace?

PRIEST. Ye shall indeed drink of my cup.

YOUNG WOMAN. Won't I have peace tomorrow?

PRIEST. I shall raise Him up at the last day.

YOUNG WOMAN. Tomorrow! Father! Where shall I be tomorrow?

PRIEST. Behold the hour cometh. Yea, is now come. Ye shall be scattered every man to his own.

YOUNG WOMAN. In Hell! Father! Will I be in Hell!

PRIEST. I am the Resurrection and the Life.

YOUNG WOMAN. Life has been hell to me, Father!

PRIEST. Life has been hell to you, daughter, because you never knew God! Gloria in excelsis Deo.

YOUNG WOMAN. How could I know Him, Father? He never was around me.

PRIEST. You didn't seek Him, daughter. Seek and ye shall find.

YOUNG WOMAN. I sought something—I was always seeking something.

PRIEST. What? What were you seeking?

YOUNG WOMAN. Peace. Rest and peace. Will I find it tonight, Father? Will I find it?

PRIEST. Trust in God.

A shadow falls across the passage in the front of the stage—and there is a whirring sound.

YOUNG WOMAN. What is that? Father! Jailer! What is that?

JAILER. An aeroplane.

MATRON. Aeroplane.

PRIEST. God in his Heaven.

YOUNG WOMAN. Look, Father! A man flying! He has wings! But he is not an angel!

JAILER. Hear his engine.

MATRON. Hear the engine.

YOUNG WOMAN. He has wings—but he isn't free! I've been free, Father! For one moment—down here on earth—I have been free! When I did what I did I was free! Free and not afraid! How is that, Father? How can that be? A great sin—a mortal sin—for which I must die and go to hell—but it made me free! One moment I was free! How is that, Father? Tell me that?

PRIEST. Your sins are forgiven.

YOUNG WOMAN. And that other sin—that other sin—that sin of love—That's all I ever knew of Heaven—heaven on earth! How is that, Father? How can that be—a sin—a mortal sin—all I know of heaven?

PRIEST. Confess to Almighty God.

YOUNG WOMAN. Oh, Father, pray for me—a prayer—that I can understand!

PRIEST. I will pray for you, daughter, the prayer of desire. Behind the King of Heaven, behold Thy Redeemer and God, Who is even now coming; prepare thyself to receive Him with love, invite him with the ardor of thy desire; come, oh my Jesus, come to thy soul which desires Thee! Before Thou givest Thyself to me, I desire to give Thee my miserable heart. Do Thou accept it, and come quickly to take possession of it! Come my God, hasten! Delay no longer! My only and Infinite Good, my Treasure, my Life, my Paradise, my Love, my all, my wish is to receive Thee with the love with which—

Enter the Mother. She comes along the passageway and stops before the bars.

YOUNG WOMAN (*recoiling*). Who's that woman?

JAILER. Your Mother.

MATRON. Your Mother.

YOUNG WOMAN. She's a stranger—take her away—she's a stranger.

JAILER. She's come to say goodbye to you—

MATRON. To say goodbye.

YOUNG WOMAN. But she's never known me—never known me—ever—(*To the Mother.*) Go away! You're a stranger! Stranger! Stranger! (*Mother turns and starts away. Reaching out her hands to her.*) Oh Mother! Mother! (*They embrace through the bars.*)

Enter Two Guards.

PRIEST. Come, daughter.

FIRST GUARD. It's time.

SECOND GUARD. Time.

YOUNG WOMAN. Wait! Mother, my child; my little strange child! I never knew her! She'll never know me! Let her live, Mother. Let her live! Live! Tell her—

PRIEST. Come, daughter.

YOUNG WOMAN. Wait! Wait! Tell her—

The Jailer takes the Mother away.

GUARD. It's time.

YOUNG WOMAN. Wait! Wait! Tell her! Wait! Just a minute more! There's so much I want to tell her—Wait—

The Jailer takes the Mother off. The Two Guards take the Young Woman by the arms, and start through the door in the bars and down the passage, across stage and off: the Priest follows; the Matron follows the Priest; the Priest is praying. The scene blacks out. The voice of the Priest gets dimmer and dimmer.

PRIEST. Lord have mercy—Christ have mercy—Lord have mercy—Christ hear us! God the Father of Heaven! God the Son, Redeemer of the World, God the Holy Ghost—Holy Trinity one God—Holy Mary—Holy Mother of God—Holy Virgin of Virgins—St. Michael—St. Gabriel—St. Raphael—

His voice dies out. Out of the darkness come the voices of Reporters.

FIRST REPORTER. What time is it now?

SECOND REPORTER. Time now.

THIRD REPORTER. Hush.

FIRST REPORTER. Here they come.

THIRD REPORTER. Hush.

PRIEST (*his voice sounds dimly—gets louder—continues until the end*). St. Peter pray for us—St. Paul pray for us—St. James pray for us—St. John pray for us—all ye holy Angels and Archangels—all ye blessed orders of holy spirits—St. Joseph—St. John the Baptist—St. Thomas—

FIRST REPORTER. Here they are!

SECOND REPORTER. How little she looks! She's gotten smaller.

THIRD REPORTER. Hush.

PRIEST. St. Phillip pray for us. All you Holy Patriarchs and prophets—St. Phillip—St. Matthew—St. Simon—St. Thaddeus—All ye holy apostles—all ye holy disciples—all ye holy innocents—Pray for us—Pray for us—Pray for us—

FIRST REPORTER. Suppose the machine shouldn't work!

SECOND REPORTER. It'll work!—It always works!

THIRD REPORTER. Hush!

PRIEST. Saints of God make intercession for us—Be merciful—Spare us, oh Lord—be merciful—

FIRST REPORTER. Her lips are moving—what is she saying?

SECOND REPORTER. Nothing.

THIRD REPORTER. Hush!

PRIEST. Oh Lord deliver us from all evil—from all sin—from Thy wrath—from the snares of the devil—from anger and hatred and every evil will—from—

FIRST REPORTER. Did you see that? She fixed her hair under the cap—pulled her hair out under the cap.

THIRD REPORTER. Hush!

PRIEST. —Beseech Thee—hear us—that Thou would'st spare us—that Thou would'st pardon us—Holy Mary—pray for us—

SECOND REPORTER. There—

YOUNG WOMAN (*calling out*). Somebody! Somebod—

Her voice is cut off.

PRIEST. Christ have mercy—Lord have mercy—Christ have mercy—

CURTAIN

TOPICS FOR CRITICAL THINKING AND WRITING

The Play on the PAGE

1. The title of the play, *Machinal*, is French for "mechanical" or "automated." What is the significance of the play's title?

2. Critics of the original 1928 production praised Treadwell for her sensitive treatment of the scene with the Man and Young Woman in his bedroom, stating that she refrained from pointing a moral finger at the couple, as would other playwrights of the time. How would today's critics respond to this scene?

3. Treadwell writes lengthy interior monologues for the central character, the Young Woman. What is the purpose of these passages of personal introspection?

4. Susan Glaspell in *Trifles* (page 18) also uses the plot of a woman murdering her husband. What are the similarities between Glaspell's play and Treadwell's? The differences?

The Play on the STAGE

5. How can the expressionist elements of the play be fully realized on the stage? Discuss how scenery and lighting design would address this.

6. At the beginning of each episode, Treadwell gives clear stage directions for sounds. Why are sounds especially important to the performance of the piece?

7. The play works best with no intermission. Why is this so? How would a break in the play have an impact on the audience?

8. Contemporary productions of *Machinal* usually employ a movement specialist to work with the director. Why is movement especially important to this play?

The Play in PERFORMANCE

Machinal opened in New York at the Plymouth Theater on September 7, 1928. It was directed by Arthur Hopkins, who was known for previous productions that emphasized a subtle form of psychological realism and had developed his own style of eliminating what he termed the "nonessentials," referring to any extraneous action, self-conscious stage business, or acting tricks. He had already successfully tackled productions with an expressionist style. Robert Edmond Jones, celebrated stage designer who advocated for a style of design that evoked the underlying feeling for the play as opposed to detailed, specified realism, was the scenic designer. The production launched the Broadway career of Clark Gable, who played the lover of the Young Woman. *Machinal* had a successful 91-performance run and was credited with revitalizing the fading interest in expressionism on the American commercial stage.

The play was selected by Burns Mantle to appear in the volume *Best Plays of 1928–29*. It was widely reviewed receiving extremely favorable press. Brooks Atkinson of the *New York Times* was so intrigued by the play he reviewed it twice, stating that the play was "a triumph of individual distinction, gleaming with intangible beauty . . . an illuminating measured drama such as we are not likely to see again."

In 1931 *Machinal* was produced in London under the title *The Life Machine*. It received its longest run, however, in the stunning 1933 production in Moscow's Kamerny Theater under the direction of Alexander Tairov. *Machinal* has had recent prominent revivals: in 1990 by the New York Shakespeare Festival and in 1993 at the Royal National Theater in London.

CLIFFORD Odets

Born in Philadelphia, Clifford Odets (1906–63) dropped out of high school to pursue a career as an actor in New York. By the late 1920s he was sufficiently well known to be invited by Harold Clurman to become a charter member of a serious new theater company to be called the Group Theatre. In its early years (1931–33) neither the Group nor Odets made much of an impact. When, with the success of Sidney Kingsley's *Men in White* (1933), the Group began to be noticed, they searched for another original new play to produce; overriding the objections of its then artistic director, Lee Strasberg, the company decided to put on a play written by the under-utilized young Odets, *Awake and Sing!* to be directed by Clurman, the Group's literary adviser. But a month before *Awake and Sing!* opened on Broadway, Odets became notorious for a short play he had written for a benefit for the magazine of the New Theatre League, the umbrella group for experimental radical theater companies. The euphoric debut of *Waiting for Lefty* was followed by the smash success of *Awake and Sing!* and, after *Lefty* transferred to Broadway, both Odets's reputation and the reputation of the Group Theatre were made.

For the rest of the life of the Group, Odets was, in essence, its house playwright, writing, among other plays, *Paradise Lost* (1935), *Golden Boy* (1937), and *Rocket to the Moon* (1938), with varying degrees of success. But despite his loyalty to the Group, Odets—like many of his generation—as early as 1936 had begun a tortured love affair with Hollywood that lasted until his death there in 1963. Despite some excellent film credits as both screenwriter and director—*None But the Lonely Heart* (1944), *The Country Girl* (1954), and *The Sweet Smell of Success* (1957)—he was never able to lose a sense of self-loathing at betraying his socially committed theater and taking "my filthy salary every week." In both the late 1930s and 1940s he returned to New York repentantly with plays attacking Hollywood values: *Golden Boy* (1937), and, most corrosively, *The Big Knife* (1949), which exposed a duplicity by all members of the film colony that was soon exacerbated by Hollywood's abject surrender to McCarthyism. Falsely accused of being "active in communist work in the film colony," Odets was blacklisted, along with many of his Group colleagues. For whatever combination of personal or political reasons, Odets responded by becoming a "friendly witness" for the House Committee on Un-American Activities, and "named names," taking pains to announce to the committee that "I did not learn my hatred of poverty, sir, out of communism." In 1955 he returned to Hollywood for good and resumed his career as filmmaker. He had not, however, completely abandoned his vocation as playwright: His later years produced *The Country Girl* (1950) and *The Flowering Peach* (1954), plays that were, for the most part, critically well received.

■ ■ ■ ■ ■ ■ ■ ■ ■ ■ ■ ■ ■

COMMENTARY ON *WAITING FOR LEFTY*

In the middle of the Great Depression that had idled one-quarter of America's laboring force, Clifford Odets scrawled his name across the page marked 1935 in American dramatic history. In the course of that year he had five plays produced, four of them on Broadway: *Waiting for Lefty*, *Till the Day I Die*, *Awake and Sing!*, and *Paradise Lost*. His short monologue, *I Can't Sleep*, was produced at a union benefit, and the aforementioned *Lefty* began a theatrical career that was to carry it, not only from one end of the United States to the other, but all over the world. The name of Odets became the number one topic of literary conversation,

and the hitherto unknown and struggling young actor became one of the foremost celebrities of the day. The *Literary Digest* described his emergence: "In less than ninety days, toiling with the unrest of his times as a central theme, a young actor in the New York theatre . . . has become the most exciting spokesman the world of workers yet has produced, and he has become perhaps the most articulate dramatist available in the theatre."

The plays just listed were written with a specific political agenda, for Odets had been recruited by the small core of radical leftists in the Group Theatre. Years later, in the familiar purgative drama of the 1950s, Odets testified to the House Committee on

Un-American Activities that for less than a year, from late 1934 to late 1935, he was a member of the Communist party. During this period of militancy he accepted the view that "the truth followed to its logical conclusion is inevitably revolutionary" (Odets, quoted in the New York *World Telegram*, March 19, 1935), and with *Waiting for Lefty* he made good the Marxist slogan that "drama is a weapon" in the war against capitalism. *Lefty* was not written for the Group but for a specific political occasion—a benefit for *New Theatre*, the magazine of the radical New Theatre League. Written at white heat in three days, the play was based on a contemporary event, a recent taxicab strike that had inconvenienced New York. But rather than document the actual labor disturbance Odets used the *idea* of a strike as a theatrical metaphor. Set in the union hall of a corrupt taxi union where members are deciding whether or not to go out on strike, Odets focuses on the members of the strike committee sitting on stage. He then flashes back to the conditions that moved each to take a militant stance.

Odets succeeded where radical dramatists before him had failed because he had written a militant "agitprop" (agitation/propaganda) drama that appealed to unaffiliated liberals as well as to convinced Marxists. He had done so by humanizing a then familiar form of political drama whose avowed purpose was to present doctrine directly to the audience by means of broadly theatrical playlets. Some titles of these leftist morality plays reveal the thematic simplicity of the form: *Work or Wages, Unemployment, The Miners Are Striking, Vote Communist*. In essentials, *Waiting for Lefty* sticks to traditional agitprop guidelines: It is overtly didactic in its political affirmations; it is episodic in structure, cartoonlike in its character delineation, directly presentational in technique, and replete with slogans and political comment; it ends with an effort to merge actors and audience in a collective affirmation leading to specific action. But *Lefty* does something more. Most agitprops ended with a call for direct action on some real current issue; *Lefty*'s final plea to strike is not real; it is a dramatic device because this strike is fictional. The answer and response of actor and audience is not designed to achieve an immediate goal as in the case, say, of the play it was originally presented with: Elia Kazan and Art Smith's *Dimitroff*, which demanded the release of the Bulgarian communist leader who stood up to the Nazis at the Reichstag fire trial. *Lefty* is, rather, a sym-

bolic call to arms, a demonstration of unity and achieved class consciousness. *Lefty*'s success lay in the fact that it appealed to the unconverted as well as to the committed; it swept all of a liberal persuasion into militant participation, at least in the theater, by virtue of the precision with which Odets enunciated the Depression malaise. Odets's achievement lay in his ability to humanize the agitprop without forgoing its theatricality and didacticism.

He succeeded not only in presenting the conversion to militancy of a series of taxicab workers, but in forcing the audience to see in the plight of these characters a reflection of their own social predicament. Several Marxist critics, among them John Howard Lawson, objected to the designation of *Lefty* as a proletarian play because "the militant strike committee is made up largely of declassed members of the middle class. One cannot reasonably call these people 'stormbirds of the working class.'" But *Lefty*'s strength as a conversion drama lay precisely in Odets's appeal, not to workers, but to the class to which he belonged, the middle class. Of the principal characters on the strike committee, only two, Joe and Sid, are proletarians; the others represent various members of the declassed bourgeoisie: a lab assistant who refuses to become an informer, an actor who cannot find work on the Broadway flesh market, a medical intern who is fired because of the anti-Semitism of his superiors. All are forced into activism by social circumstances. "Don't call me red," shouts Joe. "You know what we are? The black and blue boys! We've been kicked around so long we're black and blue from head to toes!" But Joe had not always been as adamant as he is now. He had been goaded to militancy by his wife's threat to leave him unless he organized and fought for his rights: "Get those hack boys together! . . . Stand up like men and fight for the crying kids and wives. Goddamnit! I'm tired of slavery and sleepless nights!"

Joe's social awakening is but one in the series of conversations that structure *Waiting for Lefty*. Each episode presents the road to commitment of the several members of the strike committee against the backdrop of various capitalist evils: labor spying, informing, anti-semitism, economic aggression, and so on. One by one the dramas of conversion are enacted: The intern finds that Jewish and Gentile capitalists are cut from the same cloth; the lab assistant recognizes that the logic of capitalism sees profit in war; the workers, Sid and Joe, realize the cards are stacked against the proletariat; and the young actor, turned down by a producer who cares more for his pet dog than for human beings, is taken in hand by a radical stenographer who undertakes his ideological enlightenment:

> One dollar buys ten loaves of bread, Mister. Or one dollar buys nine loaves of bread and one copy of the Communist Manifesto. Learn while you eat. Read while you run. . . . From Genesis to Revelation. . . . the meek shall not inherit the earth! . . . THE MILITANT! Come out in the light, Comrade!

All roads lead to Agate's final peroration, his cry for solidarity when it is discovered that Lefty, the head of the strike committee, has not shown up at the meeting because he has been murdered: "It's war! Working class, unite and fight! Tear down the slaughter house of our old lives!" The lesson of the play is, of course, the futility of waiting for something that may never come, the hope that somehow conditions may be alleviated by other than direct action. Fatt, the personification of corrupt capitalism, had counseled the workers to put their faith in "the man in the White House" in his attempt to dissuade them from striking. But halfway measures are doomed to failure. Salvation must be earned; Lefty never comes because he has suffered the ritual martyrdom of political art. No, the act of waiting must be replaced by *collective action*. "Hello America! Hello! We're Stormbirds of the Working Class. . . . And when we die they'll know what we did to make a new world! Christ, cut us up into little pieces. We'll die for what is right! Put fruit trees where our ashes are!" This radical faith, soon lost, left a personal and artistic void that Odets—and many of his generation—was never able to replace.

WAITING FOR LEFTY
Clifford Odets

CHARACTERS

FATT

JOE

EDNA

MILLER

FAYETTE

IRV

FLORRIE

SID

CLAYTON

AGATE KELLER

HENCHMAN

SECRETARY

ACTOR

REILLY

DR. BARNES

DR. BENJAMIN

A MAN

As the curtain goes up we see a bare stage. On it are sitting six or seven men in a semi-circle. Lolling against the proscenium down left is a young man chewing a toothpick: a gunman. A fat man of porcine appearance is talking directly to the audience. In other words he is the head of a union and the men ranged behind him are a committee of workers. They are now seated in interesting different attitudes and present a wide diversity of type, as we shall soon see. The fat man is hot and heavy under the collar, near the end of a long talk, but not too hot: he is well fed and confident. His name is Harry Fatt.

FATT. You're so wrong I ain't laughing. Any guy with eyes to read knows it. Look at the textile strike—out like lions and in like lambs. Take the San Francisco tie-up—starvation and broken heads. The steel boys wanted to walk out too, but they changed their minds. It's the trend of the times, that's what it is. All we workers got a good man behind us now. He's top man of the country—looking out for our interests—the man in the White House is the one I'm referrin' to. That's why the times ain't ripe for a strike. He's working day and night—

VOICE FROM THE AUDIENCE. For who?

(*The Gunman stirs himself.*)

FATT. For you! The records prove it. If this was the Hoover regime, would I say don't go out, boys? Not on your tin-type! But things is different now. You read the papers as well as me. You know it. And that's why I'm against the strike. Because we gotta stand behind the man who's standin' behind us! The whole country——

ANOTHER VOICE. Is on the blink!

(*The Gunman looks grave.*)

FATT. Stand up and show yourself, you damn red! Be a man, let's see what you look like! (*Waits in vain*) Yellow from the word go! Red and yellow makes a dirty color, boys. I got my eyes on four or five of them in the union here.

What the hell'll they do for you? Pull you out and run away when trouble starts. Give those birds a chance and they'll have your sisters and wives in the whore houses, like they done in Russia. They'll tear Christ off his bleeding cross. They'll wreck your homes and throw your babies in the river. You think that's bunk? Read the papers! Now listen, we can't stay here all night. I gave you the facts in the case. You boys got hot suppers to go to and——

ANOTHER VOICE. Says you!

GUNMAN. Sit down, Punk!

ANOTHER VOICE. Where's Lefty? (*Now this question is taken up by the others in unison. Fatt pounds with gavel.*)

FATT. That's what I wanna know. Where's your pal, Lefty? You elected him chairman—where the hell did he disappear?

VOICES. We want Lefty! Lefty! Lefty!

FATT (*pounding*). What the hell is this—a circus? You got the committee here. This bunch of cowboys you elected. (*Pointing to man on extreme right end.*)

MAN. Benjamin.

FATT. Yeah, Doc Benjamin. (*Pointing to other men in circle in seated order*) Benjamin, Miller, Stein, Mitchell, Phillips, Keller. It ain't my fault Lefty took a run-out powder. If you guys——

A GOOD VOICE. What's the committee say?

Elia Kazan as Agate exhorts his fellow cab drivers to "Strike! Strike! Strike!" in the Group Theater's production of Odets's *Waiting for Lefty*.

OTHERS. The committee! Let's hear from the committee!

(*Fatt tries to quiet the crowd, but one of the seated men suddenly comes to the front. The Gunman moves over to center stage, but Fatt says*):

FATT. Sure, let him talk. Let's hear what the red boys gotta say!

(*Various shouts are coming from the audience. Fatt insolently goes back to his seat in the middle of the circle. He sits on his raised platform and relights his cigar. The Gunman goes back to his post. Joe, the new speaker, raises his hand for quiet. Gets it quickly. He is sore.*)

JOE. You boys know me. I ain't a red boy one bit! Here I'm carryin' a shrapnel that big I picked up in the war. And maybe I don't know it when it rains! Don't tell me red! You know what we are? The black and blue boys! We been kicked around so long we're black and blue from head to toes. But I guess anyone who says straight out he don't like it, he's a red boy to the leaders of the union. What's this crap about goin' home to hot suppers? I'm asking to your faces how many's got hot suppers to go home to? Anyone who's sure of his next meal, raise your hand! A certain gent sitting behind me can raise them both. But not in front here! And that's why we're talking strike—to get a living wage!

VOICE. Where's Lefty?

JOE. I honest to God don't know, but he didn't take no run-out powder. That Wop's got more guts than a slaughter house. Maybe a traffic jam got him, but he'll be here. But don't let this red stuff scare you. Unless fighting for a living scares you. We gotta make up our minds. My wife made up my mind last week, if you want the truth. It's plain as the nose on Sol Feinberg's face we need a strike. There's us comin' home every night—eight, ten hours on the cab. "God," the wife says, "eighty cents ain't money—don't buy beans almost. You're workin' for the company," she says to me, "Joe! you ain't workin' for me or the family no more!" She says to me, "If you don't start. . . ."

I. JOE AND EDNA

The lights fade out and a white spot picks out the playing space within the space of seated men. The seated men are very dimly visible in the outer dark, but more prominent is Fatt smoking his cigar and often blowing the smoke in the lighted circle.

A tired but attractive woman of thirty comes into the room, drying her hands on an apron. She stands there sullenly as Joe comes in from the other side, home from work. For a moment they stand and look at each other in silence.

JOE. Where's all the furniture, honey?

EDNA. They took it away. No installments paid.

JOE. When?

EDNA. Three o'clock.

JOE. They can't do that.

EDNA. Can't? They did it.

JOE. Why, the palookas, we paid three-quarters.

EDNA. The man said read the contract.

JOE. We must have signed a phony. . . .

EDNA. It's a regular contract and you signed it.

JOE. Don't be so sour, Edna. . . . (*Tries to embrace her.*)

EDNA. Do it in the movies, Joe—they pay Clark Gable big money for it.

JOE. This is a helluva house to come home to. Take my word!

EDNA. Take MY word! Whose fault is it?

JOE. Must you start that stuff again?

EDNA. Maybe you'd like to talk about books?

JOE. I'd like to slap you in the mouth!

EDNA. No, you won't.

JOE (*sheepish*). Jeez, Edna, you get me sore some time. . . .

EDNA. But just look at me—I'm laughing all over!

JOE. Don't insult me. Can I help it if times are bad? What the hell do you want me to do, jump off a bridge or something?

EDNA. Don't yell. I just put the kids to bed so they won't know they missed a meal. If I don't have Emmy's shoes soled tomorrow, she can't go to school. In the meantime let her sleep.

JOE. Honey, I rode the wheels off the chariot today. I cruised around five hours without a call. It's conditions.

EDNA. Tell it to the A & P!

JOE. I booked two-twenty on the clock. A lady with a dog was lit . . . she gave me a quarter tip by mistake. If you'd only listen to me—we're rolling in wealth.

EDNA. Yeah? How much?

JOE. I had "coffee and—" in a beanery. (*Hands her silver coins*) A buck four.

EDNA. The second month's rent is due tomorrow.

JOE. Don't look at me that way, Edna.

EDNA. I'm looking through you, not at you. . . . Everything was gonna be so ducky! A cottage by the waterfall, roses in Picardy. You're a four-star-bust! If you think I'm standing for it much longer, you're crazy as a bedbug.

JOE. I'd get another job if I could. There's no work—you know it.

EDNA. I only know we're at the bottom of the ocean.

JOE. What can I do?

EDNA. Who's the man in the family, you or me?

JOE. That's no answer. Get down to brass tacks. Christ, gimme a break, too! A coffee cake and java all day. I'm hungry, too, Babe. I'd work my fingers to the bone if—

EDNA. I'll open a can of salmon.

JOE. Not now. Tell me what to do!

EDNA. I'm not God!

JOE. Jeez, I wish I was a kid again and didn't have to think about the next minute.

EDNA. But you're not a kid and you do have to think about the next minute. You got two blonde kids sleeping in the next room. They need food and clothes. I'm not mentioning anything else—But we're stalled like a flivver in the snow. For five years I laid awake at night listening to my heart pound. For God's sake, do something, Joe, get wise. Maybe get your buddies together, maybe go on strike for better money. Poppa did it during the war and they won out. I'm turning into a sour old nag.

JOE (*defending himself*). Strikes don't work!

EDNA. Who told you?

JOE. Besides that means not a nickel a week while we're out. Then when it's over they don't take you back.

EDNA. Suppose they don't! What's to lose?

JOE. Well, we're averaging six-seven dollars a week now.

EDNA. That just pays for the rent.

JOE. That is something, Edna.

EDNA. It isn't. They'll push you down to three and four a week before you know it. Then you'll say, "That's somethin'," too!

JOE. There's too many cabs on the street, that's the whole damn trouble.

EDNA. Let the company worry about that, you big fool! If their cabs didn't make a profit, they'd take them off the streets. Or maybe you think they're in business just to pay Joe Mitchell's rent!

JOE. You don't know a-b-c, Edna.

EDNA. I know this—your boss is making suckers outa you boys every minute. Yes, and suckers out of all the wives and the poor innocent kids who'll grow up with crooked spines and sick bones. Sure, I see it in the papers, how good orange juice is for kids. But dammit our kids get colds one on top of the other. They look like little ghosts. Betty never saw a grapefruit. I took her to the store last week and she pointed to a stack of grapefruits. "What's that!" she said. My God, Joe—the world is supposed to be for all of us.

JOE. You'll wake them up.

EDNA. I don't care, as long as I can maybe wake you up.

JOE. Don't insult me. One man can't make a strike.

EDNA. Who says one? You got hundreds in your rotten union!

JOE. The Union ain't rotten.

EDNA. No? Then what are they doing? Collecting dues and patting your back?

JOE. They're making plans.

EDNA. What kind?

JOE. They don't tell us.

EDNA. It's too damn bad about you. They don't tell little Joey what's happening in his bitsie witsie union. What do you think it is—a ping pong game?

JOE. You know they're racketeers. The guys at the top would shoot you for a nickel.

EDNA. Why do you stand for that stuff?

JOE. Don't you wanna see me alive?

EDNA (*after a deep pause*). No . . . I don't think I do, Joe. Not if you can lift a finger to do something about it, and don't. No, I don't care.

JOE. Honey, you don't understand what—

EDNA. And any other hackie that won't fight . . . let them all be ground to hamburger!

JOE. It's one thing to—

EDNA. Take your hand away! Only they don't grind me to little pieces! I got different plans. (*Starts to take off her apron.*)

JOE. Where are you going?

EDNA. None of your business.

JOE. What's up your sleeve?

EDNA. My arm'd be up my sleeve, darling, if I had a sleeve to wear. (*Puts neatly folded apron on back of chair.*)

JOE. Tell me!

EDNA. Tell you what?

JOE. Where are you going?

EDNA. Don't you remember my old boy friend?

JOE. Who?

EDNA. Bud Haas. He still has my picture in his watch. He earns a living.

JOE. What the hell are you talking about.

EDNA. I heard worse than I'm talking about.

JOE. Have you seen Bud since we got married?

EDNA. Maybe.

JOE. If I thought . . . (*He stands looking at her.*)

EDNA. See much? Listen, boy friend, if you think I won't do this it just means you can't see straight.

JOE. Stop talking bull!

EDNA. This isn't five years ago, Joe.

JOE. You mean you'd leave me and the kids?

EDNA. I'd leave *you* like a shot!

JOE. No. . . .

EDNA. Yes!

(*Joe turns away, sitting on a chair with his back to her. Outside the lighted circle of the playing stage we hear the other seated members of the strike committee. "She will . . . she will . . . it happens that way," etc. This group should be used throughout for various comments, political, emotional and as general chorus. Whispering. . . . The fat boss now blows a heavy cloud of smoke into the scene.*)

JOE (*finally*). Well, I guess I ain't got a leg to stand on.

EDNA. No?

JOE (*suddenly mad*). No, you lousy tart, no! Get the hell out of here. Go pick up that bull-thrower on the corner and stop at some cushy hotel downtown. He's probably been coming here every morning and laying you while I hacked my guts out!

EDNA. You're crawling like a worm!

JOE. You'll be crawling in a minute.

EDNA. You don't scare me that much! (*Indicates a half inch on her finger.*)

JOE. This is what I slaved for!

EDNA. Tell it to your boss!

JOE. He don't give a damn for you or me!

EDNA. That's what I say.

JOE. Don't change the subject!

EDNA. This is the subject, the EXACT SUBJECT! Your boss makes this subject. I never saw him in my life, but he's putting ideas in my head a mile a minute. He's giving your kids that fancy disease called the rickets. He's making a jelly-fish outa you and putting wrinkles in my face. This is the subject every inch of the way! He's throwing me into Bud Haas' lap. When in hell will you get wise——

JOE. I'm not so dumb as you think! But you are talking like a Red.

EDNA. I don't know what that means. But when a man knocks you down you get up and kiss his fist! You gutless piece of boloney.

JOE. One man can't——

EDNA (*with great joy*). I don't say one man! I say a hundred, a thousand, a whole million, I say. But start in your own union. Get those hack boys together! Sweep out those racketeers like a pile of dirt! Stand up like men and fight for the crying kids and wives. Goddammit! I'm tired of slavery and sleepless nights.

JOE (*with her*). Sure, sure! . . .

EDNA. Yes. Get brass toes on your shoes and know where to kick!

JOE (*suddenly jumping up and kissing his wife full on the mouth*). Listen, Edna. I'm goin' down to 174th Street to look up Lefty Costello. Lefty was saying the other day. . . . (*He suddenly stops*). How about this Haas guy?

EDNA. Get out of here!

JOE. I'll be back! (*Runs out.*)

(*For a moment Edna stands triumphant. There is a black-out and when the regular lights come up, Joe Mitchell is concluding what he has been saying.*)

JOE. You guys know this stuff better than me. We gotta walk out! (*Abruptly he turns and goes back to his seat and blackout.*)

BLACKOUT

II. LAB ASSISTANT EPISODE

Discovered: Miller, a lab assistant, looking around; and Fayette, an industrialist.

FAY. Like it?

MILLER. Very much. I've never seen an office like this outside the movies.

FAY. Yes, I often wonder if interior decorators and bathroom fixture people don't get all their ideas from Hollywood. Our country's extraordinary that way. Soap, cosmetics, electric refrigerators—just let Mrs. Consumer know they're used by the Crawfords and Garbos—more volume of sale than one plant can handle!

MILL. I'm afraid it isn't that easy, Mr. Fayette.

FAY. No, you're right—gross exaggeration on my part. Competition is cut-throat today. Markets up flush against a stone wall. The astronomers had better hurry—open Mars to trade expansion.

MILL. Or it will be just too bad!

FAY. Cigar?

MILL. Thank you, don't smoke.

FAY. Drink?

MILL. Ditto, Mr. Fayette.

FAY. I like sobriety in my workers . . . the trained ones, I mean. The Pollacks and niggers, they're better drunk—

keeps them out of mischief. Wondering why I had you come over?

MILL. If you don't mind my saying—very much.

FAY (*patting him on the knee*). I like your work.

MILL. Thanks.

FAY. No reason why a talented young man like yourself shouldn't string along with us—a growing concern. Loyalty is well repaid in our organization. Did you see Siegfried this morning?

MILL. He hasn't been in the laboratory all day.

FAY. I told him yesterday to raise you twenty dollars a month. Starts this week.

MILL. You don't know how happy my wife'll be.

FAY. Oh, I can appreciate it. (*He laughs.*)

MILL. Was that all, Mr. Fayette?

FAY. Yes, except that we're switching you to laboratory A tomorrow. Siegfried knows about it. That's why I had you in. The new work is very important. Siegfried recommended you very highly as a man to trust. You'll work directly under Dr. Brenner. Make you happy?

MILL. Very. He's an important chemist!

FAY (*leaning over seriously*). We think so, Miller. We think so to the extent of asking you to stay within the building throughout the time you work with him.

MILL. You mean sleep and eat in?

FAY. Yes. . . .

MILL. It can be arranged.

FAY. Fine. You'll go far, Miller.

MILL. May I ask the nature of the new work?

FAY (*looking around first*). Poison gas. . . .

MILL. Poison!

FAY. Orders from above. I don't have to tell you from where. New type poison gas for modern warfare.

MILL. I see.

FAY. You didn't know a new war was that close, did you?

MILL. I guess I didn't.

FAY. I don't have to stress the importance of absolute secrecy.

MILL. I understand!

FAY. The world is an armed camp today. One match sets the whole world blazing in forty-eight hours. Uncle Sam won't be caught napping!

MILL (*addressing his pencil*). They say 12 million men were killed in the last one and 20 million more wounded or missing.

FAY. That's not our worry. If big business went sentimental over human life there wouldn't be big business of any sort!

MILL. My brother and two cousins went in the last one.

FAY. They died in a good cause.

MILL. My mother says "no!"

FAY. She won't worry about you this time. You're too valuable behind the front.

MILL. That's right.

FAY. All right, Miller. See Siegfried for further orders.

MILL. You should have seen my brother—he could ride a bike without hands. . . .

FAY. You'd better move some clothes and shaving tools in tomorrow. Remember what I said—you're with a growing organization.

MILL. He could run the hundred yards in 9:8 flat. . . .

FAY. Who?

MILL. My brother. He's in the Meuse-Argonne Cemetery. Momma went there in 1926. . . .

FAY. Yes, those things stick. How's your handwriting, Miller, fairly legible?

MILL. Fairly so.

FAY. Once a week I'd like a little report from you.

MILL. What sort of report?

FAY. Just a few hundred words once a week on Dr. Brenner's progress.

MILL. Don't you think it might be better coming from the Doctor?

FAY. I didn't ask you that.

MILL. Sorry.

FAY. I want to know what progress he's making, the reports to be purely confidential—between you and me.

MILL. You mean I'm to watch him?

FAY. Yes!

MILL. I guess I can't do that. . . .

FAY. Thirty a month raise . . .

MILL. You said twenty. . . .

FAY. Thirty!

MILL. Guess I'm not built that way.

FAY. Forty. . . .

MILL. Spying's not in my line, Mr. Fayette!

FAY. You use ugly words, Mr. Miller!

MILL. For ugly activity? Yes!

FAY. Think about it, Miller. Your chances are excellent. . . .

MILL. No.

FAY. You're doing something for your country. Assuring the United States that when those goddam Japs start a ruckus we'll have offensive weapons to back us up! Don't you read your newspapers, Miller?

MILL. Nothing but Andy Gump.

FAY. If you were on the inside you'd know I'm talking cold sober truth! Now, I'm not asking you to make up your mind on the spot. Think about it over your lunch period.

MILL. No. . . .

FAY. Made up your mind already?

MILL. Afraid so.

FAY. You understand the consequences?

MILL. I lose my raise——

	MILL. And my job!
(*Simulta-*	FAY. And your job!
neously)	MILL. You misunder-
	stand——

MILL. Rather dig ditches first!

FAY. That's a big job for foreigners.

MILL. But sneaking—and making poison gas—that's for Americans?

FAY. It's up to you.

MILL. My mind's made up.

FAY. No hard feelings?

MILL. Sure hard feelings! I'm not the civilized type, Mr. Fayette. Nothing suave or sophisticated about me. Plenty of hard feelings! Enough to want to bust you and all your kind square in the mouth! (*Does exactly that.*)

BLACKOUT

III. THE YOUNG HACK AND HIS GIRL

Opens with girl and brother. Florence waiting for Sid to take her to a dance.

FLOR. I gotta right to have something out of life. I don't smoke, I don't drink. So if Sid wants to take me to a dance, I'll go. Maybe if you was in love you wouldn't talk so hard.

IRV. I'm saying it for your good.

FLOR. Don't be so good to me.

IRV. Mom's sick in bed and you'll be worryin' her to the grave. She don't want that boy hanging around the house and she don't want you meeting him in Crotona Park.

FLOR. I'll meet him anytime I like!

IRV. If you do, yours truly'll take care of it in his own way. With just one hand, too!

FLOR. Why are you all so set against him?

IRV. Mom told you ten times—it ain't him. It's that he ain't got nothing. Sure, we know he's serious, that he's stuck on you. But that don't cut no ice.

FLOR. Taxi drivers used to make good money.

IRV. Today they're makin' five and six dollars a week. Maybe you wanta raise a family on that. Then you'll be back here living with us again and I'll be supporting two families in one. Well . . . over my dead body.

FLOR. Irv, I don't care—I love him!

IRV. You're a little kid with half-baked ideas!

FLOR. I stand there behind the counter the whole day. I think about him—

IRV. If you thought more about Mom it would be better.

FLOR. Don't I take care of her every night when I come home? Don't I cook supper and iron your shirts and . . . you give me a pain in the neck, too. Don't try to shut me up! I bring a few dollars in the house, too. Don't you see I want something else out of life? Sure, I want romance, love, babies. I want everything in life I can get.

IRV. You take care of Mom and watch your step!

FLOR. And if I don't?

IRV. Yours truly'll watch it for you!

FLOR. You can talk that way to a girl. . . .

IRV. I'll talk that way to your boy friend, too, and it won't be with words! Florrie, if you had a pair of eyes you'd see it's for your own good we're talking. This ain't no time to get married. Maybe later—

FLOR. "Maybe Later" never comes for me, though. Why don't we send Mom to a hospital? She can die in peace there instead of looking at the clock on the mantelpiece all day.

IRV. That needs money. Which we don't have!

FLOR. Money, money, money!

IRV. Don't change the subject.

FLOR. This is the subject!

IRV. You gonna stop seeing him? (*She turns away*) Jesus, kiddie, I remember when you were a baby with curls down your back. Now I gotta stand here yellin' at you like this.

FLOR. I'll talk to him, Irv.

IRV. When?

FLOR. I asked him to come here tonight. We'll talk it over.

IRV. Don't get soft with him. Nowadays is no time to be soft. You gotta be hard as a rock or go under.

FLOR. I found that out. There's the bell. Take the egg off the stove I boiled for Mom. Leave us alone, Irv.

(*Sid comes in—the two men look at each other for a second. Irv exits.*)

SID (*enters*). Hello, Florrie.

FLOR. Hello, Honey. You're looking tired.

SID. Naw, I just need a shave.

FLOR. Well, draw your chair up to the fire and I'll ring for brandy and soda . . . like in the movies.

SID. If this was the movies I'd bring a big bunch of roses.

FLOR. How big?

SID. Fifty or sixty dozen—the kind with long, long stems—big as that. . . .

FLOR. You dope. . . .

SID. Your Paris gown is beautiful.

FLOR. (*acting grandly*). Yes, Percy, velvet panels are coming back again. Madame La Farge told me today that Queen Marie herself designed it.

SID. Gee . . . !

FLOR. Every princess in the Balkans is wearing one like this. (*Poses grandly.*)

SID. Hold it. (*Does a nose camera—thumbing nose and imitating grinding of camera with other hand. Suddenly she falls out of the posture and swiftly goes to him, to embrace him, to kiss him with love. Finally.*)

SID. You look tired, Florrie.

FLOR. Naw, I just need a shave. (*She laughs tremorously.*)

SID. You worried about your mother?

FLOR. No.

SID. What's on your mind?

FLOR. The French and Indian War.

SID. What's on your mind?

FLOR. I got us on my mind, Sid. Night and day, Sid!

SID. I smacked a beer truck today. Did I get hell! I was driving along thinking of *us*, too. You don't have to say it—I know what's on your mind. I'm rat poison around here.

FLOR. Not to me. . . .

SID. I know to who . . . and I know why. I don't blame them. We're engaged now for three years. . . .

FLOR. That's a long time. . . .

SID. My brother Sam joined the navy this morning—to get a break that way. They'll send him down to Cuba with the hootchy-kootchy girls. He don't know from nothing, that dumb basket ball player!

FLOR. Don't you do that.

SID. Don't you worry, I'm not the kind who runs away. But I'm so tired of being a dog, Baby, I could choke. I don't even have to ask what's going on in your mind. I know from the word go, 'cause I'm thinking the same things, too.

FLOR. It's yes or no—nothing in between.

SID. The answer is no—a big electric sign looking down on Broadway!

FLOR. We wanted to have kids. . . .

SID. But that sort of life ain't for the dogs which is us. Christ, Baby! I get like thunder in my chest when we're together. If we went off together I could maybe look the world straight in the face, spit in its eye like a man should do. Goddamit, it's trying to be a man on the earth. Two in life together.

FLOR. But something wants us to be lonely like that—crawling alone in the dark. Or they want us trapped.

SID. Sure, the big shot money men want us like that.

FLOR. Highly insulting us——

SID. Keeping us in the dark about what is wrong with us in the money sense. They got the power and mean to be damn sure they keep it. They know if they give in just an inch, all the dogs like us will be down on them together—an ocean knocking them to hell and back and each singing cuckoo with stars coming from their nose and ears. I'm not raving, Florrie——

FLOR. I know you're not, I know.

SID. I don't have the words to tell you what I feel. I never finished school. . . .

FLOR. I know. . . .

SID. But it's relative, like the professors say. We worked like hell to send him to college—my kid brother Sam, I mean—and look what he done—joined the navy! The damn fool don't see the cards is stacked for all of us. The money man dealing himself a hot royal flush. Then giving you and me a phony hand like a pair of tens or something. Then keep on losing the pots 'cause the cards is stacked against you. Then he says, what's the matter you can't win—no stuff on the ball, he says to you. And kids like my brother believe it 'cause they don't know better. For all their education, they don't know from nothing.

But wait a minute! Don't he come around and say to you—this millionaire with a jazz band—listen Sam or Sid or what's-your-name, you're no good, but here's a chance. The whole world'll know who you are. Yes sir, he says, get up on that ship and fight those bastards who's making the world a lousy place to live in. The Japs, the Turks, the Greeks. Take this gun—kill the slobs like a real hero, he says, a real American. Be a hero!

And the guy you're poking at? A real louse, just like you, 'cause they don't let him catch more than a pair of tens, too. On that foreign soil he's a guy like me and Sam, a guy who wants his baby like you and hot sun on his face! They'll teach Sam to point the guns the wrong way, that dumb basket ball player!

FLOR. I got a lump in my throat, Honey.

SID. You and me—we never even had a room to sit in somewhere.

FLOR. The park was nice . . .

SID. In Winter? The hallways . . . I'm glad we never got together. This way we don't know what we missed.

FLOR (in a burst). Sid, I'll go with you—we'll get a room somewhere.

SID. Naw . . . they're right. If we can't climb higher than this together—we better stay apart.

FLOR. I swear to God I wouldn't care.

SID. You would, you would—in a year, two years, you'd curse the day. I seen it happen.

FLOR. Oh, Sid. . . .

SID. Sure, I know. We got the blues, Babe—the 1935 blues. I'm talkin' this way 'cause I love you. If I didn't, I wouldn't care. . . .

FLOR. We'll work together, we'll—

SID. How about the backwash? Your family needs your nine bucks. My family——

FLOR. I don't care for them!

SID. You're making it up, Florrie. Little Florrie Canary in a cage.

FLOR. Don't make fun of me.

SID. I'm not, Baby.

FLOR. Yes, you're laughing at me.

SID. I'm not.

(*They stand looking at each other, unable to speak. Finally, he turns to a small portable phonograph and plays a cheap, sad, dance tune. He makes a motion with his hand; she comes to him. They begin to dance slowly. They hold each other tightly, almost as though they would merge into each other. The music stops, but the scratching record continues to the end of the scene. They stop dancing. He finally unlooses her clutch and seats her on the couch, where she sits, tense and expectant.*)

SID. Hello, Babe.

FLOR. Hello. (*For a brief time they stand as though in a dream.*)

SID (*finally*). Good-by, Babe. (*He waits for an answer, but she is silent. They look at each other.*)

SID. Did you ever see my Pat Rooney imitation? (*He whistles Rosy O'Grady and soft shoes to it. Stops. He asks:*)

SID. Don't you like it?

FLOR (*finally*). No. (*Buries her face in her hands.*)

(*Suddenly he falls on his knees and buries his face in her lap.*)

BLACKOUT

IV. LABOR SPY EPISODE

FATT. You don't know how we work for you. Shooting off your mouth won't help. Hell, don't you guys ever look at the records like me? Look in your own industry. See what happened when the hacks walked out in Philly three months ago! Where's Philly? A thousand miles away? An hour's ride on the train.

VOICE. Two hours!!

FATT. Two hours . . . what the hell's the difference. Let's hear from someone who's got the practical experience to back him up. Fellers, there's a man here who's seen the whole parade in Philly, walked out with his pals, got knocked down like the rest—and blacklisted after they went back. That's why he's here. He's got a mighty interestin' word to say. (*Announces:*) TOM CLAYTON! (*As Clayton starts up from the audience, Fatt gives him a hand which is sparsely followed in the audience. Clayton comes forward*) Fellers, this is a man with practical strike experience—Tom Clayton from little ole Philly.

CLAYTON (*a thin, modest individual*). Fellers, I don't mind your booing. If I thought it would help us hacks get better living conditions, I'd let you walk all over me, cut me up to little pieces. I'm one of you myself. But what I wanna say is that Harry Fatt's right. I only been working here in the big town five weeks, but I know conditions just like the rest of you. You know how it is—don't take long to feel the sore spots, no matter where you park.

CLEAR VOICE (*from audience*). Sit down!

CLAYTON. But Fatt's right. Our officers is right. The time ain't ripe. Like a fruit don't fall off the tree until it's ripe.

CLEAR VOICE. Sit down, you fruit!

FATT (*on his feet*). Take care of him, boys.

VOICE (*in audience, struggling*). No one takes care of me.

(*Struggle in house and finally the owner of the voice runs up on stage, says to speaker:*)

SAME VOICE. Where the hell did you pick up that name! Clayton! This rat's name is Clancy, from the old Clancys, way back! Fruit! I almost wet myself listening to that one!

FATT (*gunman with him*). This ain't a barn! What the hell do you think you're doing here!

SAME VOICE. Exposing a rat!

FATT. You can't get away with this. Throw him the hell outa here.

VOICE (*preparing to stand his ground*). Try it yourself. . . . When this bozo throws that slop around. You know who he is? That's a company spy.

FATT. Who the hell are you to make—

VOICE. I paid dues in this union for four years, that's who's me! I gotta right and this pussy-footed rat ain't coming in here with ideals like that. You know his record. Lemme say it out——

FATT. You'll prove all this or I'll bust you in every hack outfit in town!

VOICE. I gotta right. I gotta right. Looka *him*, he don't say boo!

CLAYTON. You're a liar and I never seen you before in my life!

VOICE. Boys, he spent two years in the coal fields breaking up any organization he touched. Fifty guys he put in jail. He's ranged up and down the east coast—shipping, textiles, steel—he's been in everything you can name. Right now——

CLAYTON. That's a lie!

VOICE. Right now he's working for that Bergman outfit on Columbus Circle who furnishes rats for any outfit in the country before, during, and after strikes.

(*The man who is the hero of the next episode goes down to his side with other committee men.*)

CLAYTON. He's trying to break up the meeting, fellers!

VOICE. We won't search you for credentials. . . .

CLAYTON. I got nothing to hide. Your own secretary knows I'm straight.

VOICE. Sure. Boys, you know who this sonovabitch is?

CLAYTON. I never seen you before in my life!!

VOICE. Boys, I slept with him in the same bed sixteen years. HE'S MY OWN LOUSY BROTHER!!

FATT (*after pause*). Is this true? (*No answer from Clayton.*)

VOICE to CLAYTON. Scram, before I break your neck!

(*Clayton scrams down center aisle.*)

VOICE (*says watching him*). Remember his map—he can't change that—Clancy! (*Standing in his place says:*) Too bad you didn't know about this, Fatt! (*After a pause*) The Clancy family tree is bearing nuts!

(*Standing isolated clear on the stage is the hero of the next episode.*)

BLACKOUT

V. THE YOUNG ACTOR*

A New York theatrical producer's office. Present are a stenographer and a young actor. She is busy typing; he, waiting with card in hand.

STEN. He's taking a hot bath . . . says you should wait.

PHILIPS (*the actor*). A bath did you say? Where?

STEN. See that door? Right through there—leads to his apartment.

PHIL. Through there?

---

*For whatever reason, this episode—the most radical in the play—which was originally performed and included in the first edition of Odets' collected plays, *Three Plays* (published by Random House in 1935), was omitted from the most widely disseminated collection of his plays, the Modern Library edition of *Six Plays of Clifford Odets*, also published by Random House in 1939. [Editor's note]

STEN. Mister, he's laying there in a hot perfumed bath. Don't say I said it.

PHIL. You don't say!

STEN. An oriental den he's got. Can you just see this big Irishman burning Chinese punk in the bedroom? And a big old rose canopy over his casting couch. . . .

PHIL. What's that—casting couch?

STEN. What's that? You from the sticks?

PHIL. I beg your pardon?

STEN (*rolls up her sleeves, makes elaborate deaf and dumb signs*). No from side walkies of New Yorkie . . . savvy?

PHIL. Oh, you're right. Two years of dramatic stock out of town. One in Chicago.

STEN. Don't tell him, Baby Face. He wouldn't know a good actor if he fell over him in the dark. Say you had two years with the Group, two with the Guild.

PHIL. I'd like to get with the Guild. They say——

STEN. He won't know the difference. Don't say I said it!

PHIL. I really did play with Watson Findlay in "Early Birds."

STEN (*withering him*). Don't tell him!

PHIL. He's a big producer, Mr. Grady. I wish I had his money. Don't you?

STEN. Say, I got a clean heart, Mister. I love my fellow man! (*About to exit with typed letters*) Stick around—Mr. Philips. You might be the type. If you were a woman——

PHIL. Please. Just a minute . . . please . . . I need the job.

STEN. Look at him!

PHIL. I mean . . . I don't know what buttons to push, and you do. What my father used to say—we had a gas station in Cleveland before the crash—"Know what buttons to push," Dad used to say, "and you'll go far."

STEN. You can't push me, Mister! I don't ring right these last few years!

PHIL. We don't know where the next meal's coming from. We——

STEN. Maybe . . . I'll lend you a dollar?

PHIL. Thanks very much: it won't help.

STEN. One of the old families of Virginia? Proud?

PHIL. Oh, not that. You see, I have a wife. We'll have our first baby next month . . . so . . . a dollar isn't much help.

STEN. Roped in?

PHIL. I love my wife!

STEN. Okay, you love her! Excuse me! You married her. Can't support her. No . . . not blaming you. But you're fools, all you actors. Old and young! Watch you parade in and out all day. You still got apples in your cheeks and pins for buttons. But in six months you'll be like them—putting on an act: Phony strutting "pishers"—that's French for dead codfish! It's not their fault. Here you get like that or go under. What kind of job is this for an adult man!

PHIL. When you have to make a living——

STEN. I know, but——

PHIL. Nothing else to do. If I could get something else——

STEN. You'd take it!

PHIL. Anything!

STEN. Telling me! With two brothers in my hair! (*Mr. Grady now enters; played by Fatt*) Mr. Brown sent this young man over.

GRADY. Call the hospital: see how Boris is. (*She assents and exits.*)

PHIL. Good morning, Mr. Grady. . . .

GRADY. The morning is lousy!

PHIL. Mr. Brown sent me. (*Hands over card.*)

GRADY. I heard that once already.

PHIL. Excuse me. . . .

GRADY. What experience?

PHIL. Oh, yes. . . .

GRADY. Where?

PHIL. Two years in stock, sir. A year with the Goodman Theatre in Chicago. . . .

GRADY. That all?

PHIL (*abashed*). Why, no . . . with the Theatre Guild . . . I was there. . . .

GRADY. Never saw you in a Guild show!

PHIL. On the road, I mean . . . understudying Mr. Lunt . . .

GRAY. What part? (*Philips can not answer*) You're a lousy liar, son.

PHIL. I did. . . .

GRADY. You don't look like what I want. Can't understand that Brown. Need a big man to play a soldier. Not a lousy soldier left on Broadway! All in pictures, and we get the nannces! (*Turns to work on desk.*)

PHIL (*immediately playing the soldier*). I was in the ROTC in college . . . Reserve Officers' Training Corps. We trained twice a week. . . .

GRADY. Won't help.

PHIL. With real rifles. (*Waits*) Mr. Grady, I weigh a hundred and fifty-five!

GRADY. How many years back? Been eating regular since you left college?

PHIL (*very earnestly*). Mr. Grady, I could act this soldier part. I could build it up and act it. Make it up——

GRADY. Think I run a lousy acting school around here?

PHIL. Honest to God I would! I need the job—that's why I could do it! I'm strong. I know my business! You'll get an A-1 performance. Because I need this job! My wife's having a baby in a few weeks. We need the money. Give me a chance!

GRADY. What do I care if you can act it! I'm sorry about your baby. Use your head, son. Tank Town stock is different. Here we got investments to be protected. When I sink fifteen thousand in a show I don't take chances on some youngster. We cast to type!

PHIL. I'm an artist! I can——

GRADY. That's your headache. Nobody interested in artists here. Get a big bunch for a nickel on any corner. Two flops in a row on this lousy street nobody loves you—only God, and He don't count. We protect investments: we cast to type. Your face and height we want, not your soul, son. And Jesus Christ himself couldn't play a soldier in this show . . . with all his talent. (*Crosses himself in quick repentance for this remark.*)

PHIL. Anything . . . a bit, a walk-on?

GRADY. Sorry: small cast. (*Looking at papers on his desk*) You try Russia, son. I hear it's hot stuff over there.

PHIL. Stage manager? Assistant?

GRADY. All filled, sonny. (*Stands up; crumples several papers from the desk*) Better luck next time.

PHIL. Thanks. . . .

GRADY. Drop in from time to time. (*Crosses and about to exit*) You never know when something—(*The Stenographer enters with papers to put on desk*) What did the hospital say?

STEN. He's much better, Mr. Grady.

GRADY. Resting easy?

STEN. Dr. Martel said Boris is doing even better than he expected.

GRADY. A damn lousy operation!

STEN. Yes. . . .

GRADY (*belching*). Tell the nigger boy to send up a bromo seltzer.

STEN. Yes, Mr. Grady. (*He exits*) Boris wanted lady friends.

PHIL. What?

STEN. So they operated . . . poor dog!

PHIL. A dog?

STEN. His Russian wolf hound! They do the same to you, but you don't know it! (*Suddenly*) Want advice? In the next office, don't let them see you down in the mouth. They don't like it—makes them shiver.

PHIL. You treat me like a human being. Thanks.

STEN. You're human!

PHIL. I used to think so.

STEN. He wants a bromo for his hangover. (*Goes to door*) Want that dollar?

PHIL. It won't help much.

STEN. One dollar buys ten loaves of bread, Mister. Or one dollar buys nine loaves of bread and one copy of The Communist Manifesto. Learn while you eat. Read while you run. . . .

PHIL. Manifesto? What's that? (*Takes dollar*) What is that, what you said. . . . Manifesto?

STEN. Stop off on your way out—I'll give you a copy. From Genesis to Revelation, Comrade Philips! "And I saw a new earth and a new heaven; for the first earth and the first heaven were passed away; and there was no more sea."

PHIL. I don't understand that. . . .

STEN. I'm saying the meek shall not inherit the earth!

PHIL. No?

STEN. The MILITANT! Come out in the light, Comrade.

BLACKOUT

VI. INTERNE EPISODE

Dr. Barnes, an elderly distinguished man, is speaking on the telephone. He wears a white coat.

DR. BARNES. No, I gave you my opinion twice. You outvoted me. You did this to Dr. Benjamin yourself. That is why you can tell him yourself. (*Hangs up phone, angrily. As he is about to pour himself a drink from a bottle on the table, a knock is heard.*)

BARNES. Who is it?

BENJAMIN (*without*). Can I see you a minute, please?

BARNES (*hiding the bottle*). Come in Dr. Benjamin, come in.

BENJ. It's important—excuse me—they've got Leeds up there in my place—He's operating on Mrs. Lewis—the hysterectomy—it's my job. I washed up, prepared . . . they told me at the last minute. I don't mind being replaced, Doctor, but Leeds is a damn fool! He shouldn't be permitted—

BARNES (*dryle*). Leeds is the nephew of Senator Leeds.

BENJ. He's incompetent as hell.

BARNES (*obviously changing subject, picks up lab jar*). They're doing splendid work in brain surgery these days. This is a very fine specimen. . . .

BENJ. I'm sorry, I thought you might be interested.

BARNES (*still examining jar*). Well, I am, young man, I am! Only remember it's a charity case!

BENJ. Of course. They wouldn't allow it for a second, otherwise.

BARNES. Her life is in danger?

BENJ. Of course! You know how serious the case is!

BARNES. Turn your gimlet eyes elsewhere, Doctor. Jigging around like a cricket on a hot grill won't help. Doctors don't run these hospitals. He's the Senator's nephew and there he stays.

BENJ. It's too bad.

BARNES. I'm not calling you down either. (*Plopping down jar suddenly*) Goddammit, do you think it's my fault?

BENJ (*about to leave*). I know . . . I'm sorry.

BARNES. Just a minute. Sit down.

BENJ. Sorry, I can't sit.

BARNES. Stand then!

BENJ (*sits*). Understand, Dr. Barnes, I don't mind being replaced at the last minute this way, but . . . well, this flagrant bit of class distinction—because she's poor—

BARNES. Be careful of words like that—"class distinction." Don't belong here. Lots of energy, you brilliant young men, but idiots. Discretion! Ever hear that word?

BENJ. Too radical?

BARNES. Precisely. And some day like in Germany, it might cost you your head.

BENJ. Not to mention my job.

BARNES. So they told you?

BENJ. Told me what?

BARNES. They're closing Ward C next month. I don't have to tell you the hospital isn't self supporting. Until last year that board of trustees met deficits. . . . You can guess the rest. At a board meeting Tuesday, our fine feathered friends discovered they couldn't meet the last quarter's deficit—a neat little sum well over $100,000. If the hospital is to continue at all, its damn—

BENJ. Necessary to close another charity ward!

BARNES. So they say. . . . (*A wait.*)

BENJ. But that's not all?

BARNES (*ashamed*). Have to cut down on staff too. . . .

BENJ. That's too bad. Does it touch me?

BARNES. Afraid it does.

BENJ. But after all I'm top man here. I don't mean I'm better than others, but I've worked harder.

BARNES. And shown more promise. . . .

BENJ. I always supposed they'd cut from the bottom first.

BARNES. Usually.

BENJ. But in this case?

BARNES. Complications.

BENJ. For instance?

(*Barnes hesitant.*)

BARNES. I like you, Benjamin. It's one ripping shame.

BENJ. I'm no sensitive plant—what's the answer?

BARNES. An old disease, malignant, tumescent. We need an anti-toxin for it.

BENJ. I see.

BARNES. What?

BENJ. I met that disease before—at Harvard first.

BARNES. You have seniority here, Benjamin.

BENJ. But I'm a Jew!

(*Barnes nods his head in agreement. Benj. stands there a moment and blows his nose*).

BARNES (*blows his nose*). Microbes!

BENJ. Pressure from above?

BARNES. Don't think Kennedy and I didn't fight for you!

BENJ. Such discrimination, with all those wealthy brother Jews on the board?

BARNES. I've remarked before—doesn't seem to be much difference between wealthy Jews and rich Gentiles. Cut from the same piece!

BENJ. For myself I don't feel sorry. My parents gave up an awful lot to get me this far. They ran a little dry goods shop in the Bronx until their pitiful savings went in the crash last year. Poppa's peddling neckties. . . . Saul Ezra Benjamin—a man who's read Spinoza all his life.

BARNES. Doctors don't run medicine in this country. The men who know their jobs don't run anything here, except the motormen on trolley cars. I've seen medicine change—plenty—anesthesia, sterilization—but not becaucse of rich men—in *spite* of them! In a rich man's country your true self's buried deep. Microbes! Less. . . . Vermin! See this ankle, this delicate sensitive hand? Four hundred years to breed that. Out of a revolutionary background! Spirit of '76! Ancestors froze at Valley Forge! What's it all mean! Slops! The honest workers were sold out then, in '76. The Constitution's for rich men then and now. Slops! (*The phone rings.*)

BARNES (*angrily*). Dr. Barnes. (*Listens a moment, looks at Benjamin*). I see. (*Hangs up, turns slowly to the younger Doctor*) They lost your patient.

BENJ. (*stands solid with the shock of this news but finally hurls his operation gloves to the floor*).

BARNES. That's right . . . that's right. Young, hot, go and do it! I'm very ancient, fossil, but life's ahead of you, Dr. Benjamin, and when you fire the first shot say, "This one's for old Doc Barnes!" Too much dignity—bullets. Don't shoot vermin! Step on them! If I didn't have an invalid daughter— (*Barnes goes back to his seat, blows his nose in silence*) I have said my piece, Benjamin.

BENJ. Lots of things I wasn't certain of. Many things these radicals say . . . you don't believe theories until they happen to you.

BARNES. You lost a lot today, but you won a great point.

BENJ. Yes, to know I'm right? To really begin believing in something? Not to say, "What a world!" but to say, "Change the world!" I wanted to go to Russia. Last week I was thinking about it—the wonderful opportunity to do good work in their socialized medicine—

BARNES. Beautiful, beautiful!

BENJ. To be able to work—

BARNES. Why don't you go? I might be able—

BENJ. Nothing's nearer what I'd like to do!

BARNES. Do it!

BENJ. No! Our work's here—America! I'm scared. . . . What future's ahead, I don't know. Get some job to keep alive—maybe drive a cab—and study and work and learn my place—

BARNES. And step down hard!

BENJ. Fight! Maybe get killed, but goddam! We'll go ahead! (*Benjamin stands with clenched fist raised high.*)

BLACKOUT

AGATE. LADIES AND GENTLEMEN, and don't let anyone tell you we ain't got some ladies in this sea of upturned faces! Only they're wearin' pants. Well, maybe I don't know a thing; maybe I fell outa the cradle when I was a kid and ain't been right since—you can't tell!

VOICE. Sit down, cockeye!

AGATE. Who's paying you for those remarks, Buddy?—Moscow Gold? Maybe I got a *glass eye*, but it come from working in a factory at the age of eleven. They hooked it out because they didn't have a shield on the works. But I wear it like a medal 'cause it tells the world where I belong—deep down in the working class! We had delegates in the union there—all kinds of secretaries and treasurers . . . walkin' delegates, but not with blisters on their feet! Oh no! On their fat little ass from sitting on cushions and raking in mazuma. (*Secretary and Gunman remonstrate in words and actions here*) Sit down, boys. I'm just sayin' that about unions in general. I know it ain't true here! Why no, our officers is all aces. Why, I seen our own secretary Fatt walk outa his way not to step on a cockroach. No, boys, don't think—

FATT (*breaking in*). You're out of order!

AGATE (*to audience*). Am I outa order?

ALL. No, no. Speak. Go on, etc.

AGATE. Yes, our officers is all aces. But I'm a member here—and no experience in Philly either! Today I couldn't wear my union button. The damnedest thing happened. When I take the old coat off the wall, I see she's smoking. I'm a sonovagun if the old union button isn't on fire! Yep, the old celluloid was makin' the most god-awful stink: the landlady come up and give me hell! You know what happened?—that old union button just blushed itself to death! Ashamed! Can you beat it?

FATT. Sit down, Keller! Nobody's interested!

AGATE. Yes, they are!

GUNMAN. Sit down like he tells you!

AGATE (*continuing to audience*). And when I finish—(*His speech is broken by Fatt and Gunman who physically handle him. He breaks away and gets to other side of stage. The two are about to make for him when some of the committee men come forward and get in between the struggling parties. Agate's shirt has been torn.*)

AGATE (*to audience*). What's the answer, boys? The answer is, if we're reds because we wanna strike, then we take over their salute too! Know how they do it? (*Makes Communist salute*). What is it? An uppercut! The good old uppercut to the chin! Hell, some of us boys ain't even got a shirt to our backs. What's the boss class tryin' to do—make a nudist colony outa us?

(*The audience laughs and suddenly Agate comes to the middle of the stage so that the other cabmen back him up in a strong clump.*)

AGATE. Don't laugh! Nothing's funny! This is your life and mine! It's skull and bones every incha the road! Christ, we're dyin' by inches! For what? For the debutant-ees to have their sweet comin' out parties in the Ritz! Poppa's got a daughter she's gotta get her picture in the papers. Christ, they make 'em with our blood. Joe said it. Slow death or fight. It's war! (*Throughout this whole speech Agate*

is backed up by the other six workers, so that from their activity it is plain that the whole group of them are saying these things. Several of them may take alternate lines out of this long last speech) You Edna, God love your mouth! Sid and Florrie, the other boys, old Doc Barnes—fight with us for right! It's war! Working class, unite and fight! Tear down the slaughter house of our old lives! Let freedom really ring. These slick slobs stand here telling us about bogeymen. That's a new one for the kids—the reds is bogeymen! But the man who got me food in 1932, he called me Comrade! The one who picked me up where I bled—he called me Comrade too! What are we waiting for. . . . Don't wait for Lefty! He might never come. Every minute—

(*This is broken into by a man who has dashed up the center aisle from the back of the house. He runs up on stage, says*)

MAN. Boys, they just found Lefty!

OTHERS. What? What? What?

SOME. Shhh. . . . Shhh. . . .

MAN. They found Lefty. . . .

AGATE. Where?

MAN. Behind the car barns with a bullet in his head!

AGATE (*crying*). Hear it, boys, hear it? Hell, listen to me! Coast to coast! HELLO AMERICA! HELLO! WE'RE STORMBIRDS OF THE WORKING-CLASS. WORKERS OF THE WORLD. . . . OUR BONES AND BLOOD! And when we die they'll know what we did to make a new world! Christ, cut us up to little pieces. We'll die for what is right! Put fruit trees where our ashes are! (*To audience*). Well, what's the answer?

ALL. STRIKE!

AGATE. LOUDER!

ALL. STRIKE!

AGATE and OTHERS (*on Stage*). AGAIN!

ALL. STRIKE, STRIKE, STRIKE!!!

CURTAIN

ODETS'S NOTES FOR PRODUCTION

The background of the episodes, a strike meeting, is not an excuse. Each of the committeemen shows in his episode the crucial moment of his life which brought him to this very platform. The dramatic structure on which the play has been built is simple but highly effective. The form used is the old black-face minstrel form of chorus, end men, specialty men and interlocutor.

In Fatt's scenes before the "Spy Exposé," mention should again be made of Lefty's tardiness. Sitting next to Fatt in the center of the circle is a little henchman

who sits with his back to the audience. On the other side of Fatt is Lefty's empty chair. This is so indicated by Fatt when he himself asks: "Yeah, where's your chairman?"

Fatt, of course, represents the capitalist system throughout the play. The audience should constantly be kept aware of him, the ugly menace which hangs over the lives of all the people who act out their own dramas. Perhaps he puffs smoke into the spotted playing space; perhaps during the action of a playlet he might insolently walk in and around the unseeing players. It is possible that some highly gratifying results can be achieved by the imaginative use of this character.

The strike committee on the platform during the acting out of the playlet should be used as chorus. Emotional, political, musical, they have in them possibilities of various comments on the scenes. This has been indicated once in the script in the place where

Joe's wife is about to leave him. In the climaxes of each scene, slogans might very effectively be used—a voice coming out of the dark. Such a voice might announce at the appropriate moments in the "Young Interne's" scene that the USSR is the only country in the world where Anti-Semitism is a crime against the State.

Do not hesitate to use music wherever possible. It is very valuable in emotionally stirring an audience.

TOPICS FOR CRITICAL THINKING AND WRITING

The Play on the PAGE

1. What arguments does Fatt offer to try to convince the union members *not* to strike?
2. What does the play tell us about the attitude of the communists to FDR's New Deal in 1935?
3. Odets wrote at this time: "The artist never gives the thing or the person; he gives only the trend

represented by the thing or the person." Interpret this and discuss whether or not, and why, you agree or disagree.
4. Given his premises, is Agate convincing, or does he overstate his case?

The Play on the STAGE

5. Discuss a possible production. Which elements in the play would you affirm? Which would you downplay?
6. What do you think about plays that deliberately engage the audience?

7. Could one—should one—update the play? If so, what contemporary issues would *you* stress?

The Play in PERFORMANCE

Within weeks of its initial production, *Waiting for Lefty* became the public property of the left, and groups were organized all over the country to perform it. Odets later doubted he had earned a thousand dollars out of the play: "People just did it. . . . It has been done all over the world . . . and I have not received five cents of royalties. . . . It was at one time a kind of light machine gun that you wheeled in to use whenever there was any kind of strike trouble." A storm of censorship accompanied its production in many different cities: It was banned in New Haven; in Boston, the actors were arrested for language that was "extremely blasphe-

mous"; in Philadelphia, the theater in which the play was to be produced was suddenly called "unsafe," and the performance was canceled; in Newark, New Jersey, some of the cast were jailed; Will Geer produced the play in Hollywood despite threats and was severely beaten by hoodlums. In general, the stridency of conservative outrage revealed that Odets's "machine gun" was indeed a formidable weapon.

Lefty's great success at the New Theatre League benefit opened the Group Theatre's eyes, and it decided to present the play as one of its scheduled productions. In moving to Broadway, however, a new companion piece was needed to fill out the bill, since *Dimitroff* was clearly too parochially leftist to succeed uptown, and to fill out the bill Odets wrote a new play based on contemporary life in Nazi Germany called *Till the Day I Die*. The program enjoyed a substantial run even as *Lefty* continued to expand its wide-ranging role of radical consciousness raiser. It enjoyed particular success when done by the left-wing Unity Theater in London. For by turning a real strike into a symbolic strike, Odets had freed his piece from journalistic particularity, and it could be thrown into any political breach; indeed, through the years *Lefty* has shown up in the strangest places. One such was Madrid in the 1970s after the death of Franco and the beginning of the democratization of Spain. Another place was Greece after the Colonels' junta collapsed.

It has frequently been revived under amateur and professional circumstances. We may note its last major revival in 1997 at La MaMa Experimental Theatre Club, New York City, by the Blue Light Theater Company directed by Joanne Woodward with actors such as Marisa Tomei and Greg Naughton. Although it evoked the 1930s through costumes and music, the production was hardly an exercise in nostalgia. As Woodward told the *New York Times*, "We still haven't figured out how to pay people a living wage. To me this play is not just about the Depression. It's about changing people's minds. Which is what theater is for."

HAROLD CLURMAN
*Our Youth Had Found Its Voice**

Sunday night, January 5, 1935, at the old Civic Repertory Theatre on Fourteenth Street, an event took place to be noted in the annals of the American theatre. The evening had opened with a mildly amusing one-act play by Paul Green. The audience, though attracted by the guest appearance of a good part of the Group company, had no idea of what was to follow.

The first scene of *Lefty* had not played two minutes when a shock of delighted recognition struck the audience like a tidal wave. Deep laughter, hot assent, a kind of joyous fervor seemed to sweep the audience toward the stage. The actors no longer performed; they were being carried along as if by an exultancy of communication such as I had never witnessed in the theatre before. Audience and actors had become one.

Line after line brought applause, whistles, bravos, and heartfelt shouts of kinship.

The taxi strike of February 1934 had been a minor incident in the labor crisis of this period. There were very few taxi-drivers in that first audience, I am sure; very few indeed who had ever been directly connected with such an event as the union meeting that provided the play its pivotal situation. When the audience at the end of the play responded to the militant question from the stage: "Well, what's the answer?" with a spontaneous roar of "Strike! Strike!" it was something more than a tribute to the play's effectiveness, more even than a testimony of the audience's hunger for constructive social action. It was the birth cry of the thirties. Our youth had found its voice. It was a call to join the good fight for a greater measure of life in a world free of economic fear, falsehood, and craven servitude to stupidity and greed. "Strike!" was *Lefty*'s lyric message, not alone for a few extra pennies of wages or for shorter hours of work, strike for greater dignity, strike for a bolder humanity, strike for the full stature of man.

The audience, I say, was delirious. It stormed the stage, which I persuaded the stunned author to mount. People went from the theatre dazed and happy: a new awareness and confidence had entered their lives.

*Excerpt from Harold Clurman, *The Fervent Years* (New York: Hill & Wang, 1957) 138–39.

GERTRUDE Stein

Gertrude Stein (1874–1946), experimental poet, novelist, essayist, autobiographer, and playwright, was born into a prosperous American family of German-Jewish background living in Allegheny, Pennsylvania (now part of Pittsburgh). From 1875 to 1879 the family lived in Europe, then returned to the United States and settled in Oakland, California. (Of Oakland she later said, "There is no there there.")

Stein graduated from Radcliffe College, and then, on the recommendation of the philosopher and psychologist William James, she studied medicine at Johns Hopkins, intending to become a physiological psychologist, but she dropped out before completing her last semester. Financially independent (her parents had died and left her with adequate resources), in 1902 she moved to London, and then in 1903 she joined her brother Leo in Paris, where she spent the rest of her life except for a period in the French countryside when the Germans occupied Paris during World War II. "America is my country," she said, "and Paris is my home town and it is as it has come to be." She and Leo promoted and collected such modern French painters as Cézanne, Renoir, Gauguin, and Manet, and especially two younger painters, Picasso and Matisse, though in time she and Leo went their separate ways. Gertrude Stein is also known for offering hospitality and abundant advice (not all of it welcome) to Americans in Paris, including Hemingway, Paul Robeson, and Richard Wright.

Stein's best-known works are *Three Lives* (1909), three stories about women, and a memoir of her early years in Paris entitled *The Autobiography of Alice B. Toklas* (1933). Toklas moved into Stein's apartment in 1909 and remained her housekeeper, typist, editor, and lover until Stein's death 37 years later. Stein wrote about 70 works that she called plays—some no longer than a few lines—but only one, *Yes Is for a Very Young Man*, comes at all near to being a conventional play. Her best-known dramatic works are *Four Saints in Three Acts* (1927, 1934) and *The Mother of Us All* (1945–46), both of which were set to music by Virgil Thomson.

■■■■■■■■■■■■■

COMMENTARY ON *THE MOTHER OF US ALL*

An opera is a dramatic text set to music. One can make distinctions between grand opera (an opera on a serious theme, with the whole text set to music), comic opera (a story that ends happily, set to music but usually with some spoken dialogue), operetta (an amusing dramatic performance with songs and spoken dialogue), and a play with incidental music; but for our purposes we need say only that in 1945–46 Gertrude Stein wrote a play called *The Mother of Us All* with the understanding that the composer Virgil Thomson (who had previously set to music Stein's *Four Saints in Three Acts*) would compose the music. Stein completed the text but died before she could hear any of the music that Thomson wrote for it.

Stein was not interested in what we might think of as drama of the conventional sort, that is, plays in which characters speak realistically and engage in an action that ultimately comes to a resolution—an action of the sort that Aristotle had in mind when he said that a dramatic plot has a beginning, a middle, and an end. In an essay called "Plays," originally delivered as a lecture in 1934, she says that when she was a child she liked to read a play by Shakespeare because "there were so many little bits in it that were lively words." She goes on to make two distinctions, first between dramatic poetry and other kinds of poetry, and then between poetic drama and prose drama:

> In the poetry of plays words are more lively words than in any other kind of poetry and if one naturally liked lively words and I naturally did one likes to read plays in poetry. I always as a child read all the plays I could get hold of that were in poetry. Plays in prose do not read so well. The words in prose are livelier when they are not a play. I am not saying anything about why, it is just a fact.

As to the first assertion, that words are more "lively" in a poetic play than in a nondramatic poem such as a sonnet, for instance, perhaps an explanation (assuming that one thinks Stein may have a point) might go as follows: A nondramatic poem is usually the utterance of a single speaker (for instance, a man lamenting the death of his beloved), whereas a drama plays many voices against each other, so that in a drama there is, so to speak, a music of harmonizing (even if conflicting) voices. As to Stein's belief that "Plays in prose do not read so well" and that "The words in prose are livelier when they are not in a play," one can easily grasp her point. In short stories and novels—even those that can be called highly realistic—the prose often has an intensity that much of the language of prose drama does not have. For instance, the narrator of a story can quickly and even movingly describe the setting, whereas the dramatist ploddingly tells us that at the left of the stage are two chairs, etc., etc. Similarly, the writer of fiction can give us a scrap of dialogue and can then enter the mind of the speaker, perhaps describing that character's state of mind with effective metaphors, whereas the playwright will have to give extensive dialogue if we are to know the speaker's thoughts.

Later in her talk on "Plays" Stein tells us how she came to write plays while living in Paris. (Stein's language and thinking here, as always, are unusual, as you doubtless have recognized from the few passages that we have already quoted.)

> I had just come home from a pleasant dinner party and I realized then as anybody can know that something is always happening.
>
> Something is always happening, anybody knows a quantity of stories of people's lives that are always happening, there are always plenty for the newspapers and there are always plenty in private life. Everybody knows so many stories and what is the use of telling another story. What is the use of telling a story since there are so many and everybody knows so many and tells so many. In the country it is perfectly extraordinary how many complicated dramas go on all the time. And everybody knows them, so why tell another one. There is always a story going on.
>
> So naturally what I wanted to do in my play was what everybody did not always know nor always tell. By everybody I do of course include myself by always I do of course include myself.
>
> And so I wrote, What Happened. A Play.

For the nominal subject of her last play—really an opera, because Stein knew that Virgil Thomson would set it to music—Stein chose Susan B. Anthony (1820–1906), the American reformer and advocate of women's rights, notably the right to control property and wages, the right to coeducation, and the right to vote. More than any other single person Anthony was responsible for extending the vote to women, though it was not until 14 years after her death that the Nineteenth Amendment, giving women the right to vote—the "Anthony Amendment"—was passed. (Anthony had energetically worked for The Fourteenth Amendment, which in 1868 extended the vote to black males, but she had been unsuccessful in her effort to have that amendment include women. In 1872 she registered and voted in order to test the legality of the Fourteenth Amendment. She was arrested, tried, found guilty, and fined, but she refused to pay on the grounds that the law was unfair. The case went to the Supreme Court of the United States, where it was decided against Anthony and her followers.)

One might think that the events of Susan B. Anthony's life might afford the material for a play, but Stein was not interested in writing a biographical or conventional historical drama. In fact, she flouts history by including characters who were not contemporaries; for instance, Stein includes a young friend, Donald Gallup, who was not born until seven years after Anthony's death, and another friend, Joseph Barry (called Jo the Loiterer in the play), who was not born until eleven years after Anthony's death. Even some of the characters whose lives did overlap Anthony's, such as Stein and Virgil Thomson, to say nothing of John Adams and Daniel Webster, never met her. In one of her novels, *Lucy Church Amiably*, Stein says, "Supposing everyone lived at the same time what would they say?" *The Mother of Us All* provides an answer to that question; Stein brings together people from different periods, and lets them converse, or, perhaps more accurately, lets them express their thoughts in the presence of others. Although she carefully read *History of Women's Suffrage*, a work by Anthony and others, as well as documents about Daniel Webster, Stein's chief interest apparently is not history; rather, it is the play—the music, we might say—of voices in conversation. Stein's Susan B. Anthony is less an historic figure than an heroic, mythic (and thus properly operatic) figure, the Mother of Us All.

The Susan B. Anthony who is the Mother of Us All is an archetypal figure, but she is also an individual, a real person, not simply the creation of society. Perhaps something of her individuality and her emphasis on the individuality of each person is suggested when she says to Jo the Loiterer, "A crowd is never allowed but each one of you can come in." Anthony is a "one," a distinctive personality. Interestingly, unlike most protagonists, she does not develop, and we might therefore think of her as something of a symbol, a static representation of, say, anti-patriarchal thinking, especially since the last scene shows us a statue of Susan B. Anthony. Does this lifeless monument at the end indicate what she has been all along, an idea rather than a human being? On the contrary, the Anthony of the play is never so abstract or heroic that she ceases to be profoundly human, a distinctive voice that holds our ear.

Gertrude Stein must have felt some sense of identity with Susan B. Anthony. Like Stein, Anthony was unmarried, and like Stein she had a close female companion, Anna Howard Shaw, who for 18 years worked closely with Anthony. *The Mother of Us All* is Stein's last work, and one can easily think that in part she used Anthony as a way of talking about herself, a way of summing up her own career as an anti-establishment figure, a person dedicated to individuality. Further, Stein may also have felt that just as Anthony died without seeing her ideals fulfilled, so Stein, dying of cancer, would not live to see her goals (and her reputation) solidly established.

Still, for the reader, or for the hearer and viewer of the opera, the work is not about Gertrude Stein but about Susan B. Anthony, or rather about Anthony and her Americas as imagined by Stein. In particular it is about Anthony's dedication to the idea of female independence and her resistance to patriarchal authority of the sort that is comically embodied in John Adams and Daniel Webster, men who put women on a pedestal so that they will not be troubled by women as real people. Stein is true to Anthony in emphasizing not the matter of the vote for women but marriage as an oppressive social institution that reduced women to poverty. This point is made, for instance, in a comic bit of dialogue when Jo the Loiterer speaks of buying something and a listener thinks he is speaking of buying a wife.

We hope that what we have said thus far is true, but we know that it is too solemn. *The Mother of Us All*, however serious a comment on nineteenth- and early twentieth-century society, is for the most part highly amusing, most notably in the debates between Webster and Susan B. (The debates are imaginary; Webster died in 1852, just as Susan B. began to give herself full time to her causes.) In contrast to Susan B.'s direct speech ("I am not married and the reason why is that I have had to do what I have had to do") is the grotesque rhetoric of Webster and the VIP's. Here, for instance, is a typical passage of political hot air: "When the mariner has been tossed for many days, in thick weather, and on an unknown sea, he naturally avails himself of the first pause in the storm." A second example: "Mr. President I shall enter on no encomium upon Massachusetts she need none. There she is behold her and judge for yourself." This is the language of nineteenth-century public oratory, but today it strikes us as lifeless—a way of *not* communicating—especially in comparison with the language of Susan. Webster is so bound by parliamentary conventions that he addresses Susan B. in the third person ("the honorable member") and he uses the masculine pronoun "he" when speaking of her. (One can almost say that for Webster, women do not exist.) We are not surprised to hear that Webster has slept through the speeches of others (a comic touch), but perhaps we are surprised to hear Susan B.'s comment: "The right to sleep is given to no woman" (a comic touch, but one that makes a telling point). Or, again, Webster orates, "I resist it today and always. Who ever falters or whoever flies I continue the contest." Constance Fletcher (born after Webster had died) comments approvingly, "Dear man, he can make us glad that we have had so great so dear a man," but Susan B. cuts through the nonsense with, "Hush, this is slush."

Most of the critical commentaries on Gertrude Stein concentrate on her experiments with language, for instance her attempt in *Tender Buttons* (1914) to achieve in words the effects of abstract painting. But we can make a case that the essential, enduring Gertrude Stein is to be found not in these experiments but in her understanding of American society and especially in her efforts to show the role of women in American life.

A Note on the Characters: As the preceding comment indicates, the play includes historical characters from the nineteenth century and also persons of

Stein's acquaintance in the twentieth century, as well as imaginary characters.

The chief historical figures are Susan B. Anthony (1820–1906), social reformer; Anna Howard Shaw (1847–1919), woman-suffrage leader; Daniel Webster (1782–1852), American statesman and orator; John Adams (1735–1826), second president of the United States; Andrew Johnson (1808–75), seventeenth president of the United States; Ulysses S. Grant (1822–85), eighteenth president of the United States; Thaddeus Stevens (1792–1868), statesman and aboli-

tionist; Anthony Comstock (1844–1915), self-appointed censor of books and plays; Lillian Russell (1861–1922), American singer and actress.

Among the people whom Stein knew were: Constance Fletcher, (1858–1938), the author of novels and plays; Donald Gallup (1913–2000), an American soldier who met Stein when the war ended in 1945 and who later edited some of her work; Joseph Barry (b. 1917), a journalist who is called "the loiterer" because in his student days he had been arrested while picketing and was charged with loitering.

THE MOTHER OF US ALL
Gertrude Stein

ACT 1

(Prologue sung by Virgil T.)

> Pity the poor persecutor.
>   Why,
> If money is money isn't money money,
>   Why,
> Pity the poor persecutor,
>   Why,
> Is money money or isn't money money.
> Why.
> Pity the poor persecutor.
> Pity the poor persecutor because the poor persecutor
>   always gets to be poor
>   Why,
> Because the persecutor gets persecuted
> Because is money money or isn't money money,
>   That's why,
> When the poor persecutor is persecuted he has to cry,
> Why,
> Because the persecutor always ends by being perse-
>   cuted,
>   That is the reason why.

(Virgil T. after he has sung his prelude begins to sit.)

VIRGIL T. Begins to sit. Begins to sit. He begins to sit. That's why. Begins to sit. He begins to sit. And that is the reason why.

SCENE 1

DANIEL WEBSTER. He digged a pit, he digged it deep he digged it for his brother.
Into the pit he did fall in the pit he digged for tother.
ALL THE CHARACTERS. Daniel was my father's name,
My father's name was Daniel.
JO THE LOITERER. Not Daniel.
CHRIS THE CITIZEN. Not Daniel in the lion's den.
ALL THE CHARACTERS. My father's name was Daniel.
G.S. My father's name was Daniel, Daniel and a bear, a bearded Daniel,
   not Daniel in the lion's den not Daniel, yes Daniel my father had
   a beard my father's name was Daniel,
DANIEL WEBSTER. He digged a pit he digged it deep he digged it for his brother,

Into the pit he did fall in the pit he digged for tother.
INDIANA ELLIOT. Choose a name.
SUSAN B. ANTHONY. Susan B. Anthony is my name to choose a name is feeble, Susan B. Anthony is my name, a name can only be a name my name can only be my name, I have a name, Susan B. Anthony is my name, to choose a name is feeble.
INDIANA ELLIOT. Yes, that's easy, Susan B. Anthony is that kind of a name but my name Indiana Elliot. What's in a name.
SUSAN B. ANTHONY. Everything.
G.S. My father's name was Daniel he had a black beard he was not tall not at all tall, he had a black beard his name was Daniel.
ALL THE CHARACTERS. My father had a name his name was Daniel.
JO THE LOITERER. Not Daniel
CHRIS THE CITIZEN. Not Daniel not Daniel in the lion's den not Daniel.
SUSAN B. ANTHONY. I had a father, Daniel was not his name.
INDIANA ELLIOT. I had no father no father.
DANIEL WEBSTER. He digged a pit he digged it deep he digged it for his brother, into the pit he did fall in the pit he digged for tother.

SCENE 2

JO THE LOITERER. I want to tell
CHRIS THE CITIZEN. Very well
JO THE LOITERER. I want to tell oh hell.
CHRIS THE CITIZEN. Oh very well.
JO THE LOITERER. I want to tell oh hell I want to tell about my wife.
CHRIS THE CITIZEN. And have you got one.
JO THE LOITERER. No not one.
CHRIS THE CITIZEN. Two then
JO THE LOITERER. No not two.
CHRIS. How many then
JO THE LOITERER. I haven't got one. I want to tell oh hell about my wife I haven't got one.
CHRIS THE CITIZEN. Well.
JO THE LOITERER. My wife, she had a garden.
CHRIS THE CITIZEN. Yes
JO THE LOITERER. And I bought one.
CHRIS THE CITIZEN. A wife.
   No said Jo I was poor and I bought a garden. And then said Chris. She said, said Jo, she said my wife said one

Under a great deal of playful language, and under exuberant costumes and scenery, Stein sets forth the story of a lonely woman fighting for her rights in a paternalistic world.

tree in my garden was her tree in her garden. And said Chris, Was it. Jo, We quarreled about it. And then said Chris. And then said Jo, we took a train and we went where we went. And then said Chris. She gave me a little package said Jo. And was it a tree said Chris. No it was money said Jo. And was she your wife said Chris, yes said Jo when she was funny, How funny said Chris. Very funny said Jo. Very funny said Jo. To be funny you have to take everything in the kitchen and put it on the floor, you have to take all your money and all your jewels and put them near the door you have to go to bed then and leave the door ajar. That is the way you do when you are funny.

CHRIS THE CITIZEN. Was she funny.

JO THE LOITERER. Yes she was funny.

(*Chris and Jo put their arms around each other.*)

ANGEL MORE. Not any more I am not a martyr any more, not any more.

Be a martyr said Chris.

ANGEL MORE. Not any more. I am not a martyr any more. Surrounded by sweet smelling flowers I fell asleep three times.

Darn and wash and patch, darn and wash and patch, darn and wash and patch darn and wash and patch.

JO THE LOITERER. Anybody can be accused of loitering.

CHRIS BLAKE A CITIZEN. Any loiterer can be accused of loitering.

HENRIETTA M. Daniel Webster needs an artichoke.

ANGEL MORE. Susan B. is cold in wet weather.

HENRY B. She swore an oath she'd quickly come to any one to any one.

ANTHONY COMSTOCK. Caution and curiosity, oil and obligation, wheels and appurtenances, in the way of means.

VIRGIL T. What means.

JOHN ADAMS. I wish to say I also wish to stay, I also wish to go away, I also wish I endeavor to also wish.

ANGEL MORE. I wept on a wish.

JOHN ADAMS. Whenever I hear any one say of course, do I deny it, yes I do deny it whenever I hear any one say of course I deny it, I do deny it.

THADDEUS S. Be mean.

DANIEL WEBSTER. Be there.

HENRIETTA M. Be where.

CONSTANCE FLETCHER. I do and I do not declare that roses and wreaths, wreaths and roses around and around, blind as a bat, curled as a hat and a plume, be mine when I die, farewell to a thought, he left all alone, be firm in despair dear dear never share, dear dear, dear dear, I Constance Fletcher dear dear, I am a dear, I am dear dear I am a dear, here there everywhere. I bow myself out.

INDIANA ELLIOT. Anybody else would be sorry.

SUSAN B. ANTHONY. Hush, I hush, you hush, they hush, we hush. Hush.

GLOSTER HEMING AND ISABEL WENTWORTH. We, hush, dear as we are, we are very dear to us and to you we hush, we hush you say hush, dear hush. Hush dear.

ANNA HOPE. I open any door, that is the way that any day is today, any day is today I open any door every door a door.

LILLIAN RUSSELL. Thank you.

ANTHONY COMSTOCK. Quilts are not crazy, they are kind.

JENNY REEFER. My goodness gracious me.

ULYSSES S. GRANT. He knew that his name was not Eisenhower. Yes he knew it. He did know it.

HERMAN ATLAN. He asked me to come he did ask me.

DONALD GALLUP. I chose a long time, a very long time, four hours are a very long time, I chose, I took a very long time, I took a very long time. Yes I took a very long time to choose, yes I did.

T.T. AND A.A. They missed the boat yes they did they missed the boat.

JO A LOITERER. I came again but not when I was expected, but yes when I was expected because they did expect me.

CHRIS THE CITIZEN. I came to dinner.

(*They all sit down.*)

CURTAIN

SCENE 3

(*Susan B. Anthony and Daniel Webster seated in two straight-backed chairs not too near each other. Jo the Loiterer comes in.*)

JO THE LOITERER. I don't know where a mouse is I don't know what a mouse is. What is a mouse.

ANGEL MORE. I am a mouse

JO THE LOITERER. Well

ANGEL MORE. Yes Well

JO THE LOITERER. All right well. Well what is a mouse

ANGEL MORE. I am a mouse

JO THE LOITERER. Yes well, And she.

(*Susan B. dressed like a Quakeress turns around.*)

SUSAN B. I hear a sound.

JO THE LOITERER. Yes well

DANIEL WEBSTER. I do not hear a sound. When I am told.

SUSAN B. ANTHONY. Silence.

(*Everybody is silent.*)

SUSAN B. ANTHONY. Youth is young, I am not old.

DANIEL WEBSTER. When the mariner has been tossed for many days, in thick weather, and on an unknown sea, he naturally avails himself of the first pause in the storm.

SUSAN B. ANTHONY. For instance. They should always fight. They should be martyrs. Some should be martyrs. Will they. They will.

DANIEL WEBSTER. We have thus heard sir what a resolution is.

SUSAN B. ANTHONY. I am resolved.

DANIEL WEBSTER. When this debate sir was to be resumed on Thursday it so happened that it would have been convenient for me to be elsewhere.

SUSAN B. I am here, ready to be here. Ready to be here. Ready to be here. It is my habit.

DANIEL WEBSTER. The honorable member complained that I had slept on his speech.

SUSAN B. The right to sleep is given to no woman.

DANIEL WEBSTER. I did sleep on the gentleman's speech; and slept soundly.

SUSAN B. I too have slept soundly when I have slept, yes when I have slept I too have slept soundly.

DANIEL WEBSTER. Matches and over matches.

SUSAN B. I understand you undertake to overthrow my undertaking.

DANIEL WEBSTER. I can tell the honorable member once for all that he is greatly mistaken, and that he is dealing with one of whose temper and character he has yet much to learn.

SUSAN B. I have declared that patience is never more than patient. I too have declared, that I who am not patient am patient.

DANIEL WEBSTER. What interest asks he has South Carolina in a canal in Ohio.

SUSAN B. What interest have they in me, what interest have I in them, who holds the head of whom, who can bite their lips to avoid a swoon.

DANIEL WEBSTER. The harvest of neutrality had been great, but we had gathered it all.

SUSAN B. Near hours are made not by shade not by heat not by joy, I always know that not now rather not now, yes and I do not stamp but I know that now yes now is now. I have never asked any one to forgive me.

DANIEL WEBSTER. On yet another point I was still more unaccountably misunderstood.

SUSAN B. Do we do what we have to do or do we have to do what we do. I answer.

DANIEL WEBSTER. Mr. President I shall enter on no encomium upon Massachusetts she need none. There she is behold her and judge for yourselves.

SUSAN B. I enter into a tabernacle I was born a believer in peace, I say fight for the right, be a martyr and live, be a coward and die, and why, because they, yes they, sooner or later go away. They leave us here. They come again. Don't forget, they come again.

DANIEL WEBSTER. So sir I understand the gentleman and am happy to find I did not misunderstand him.

SUSAN B. I should believe, what they ask, but they know, they know.

DANIEL WEBSTER. It has been to us all a copious fountain of national, social and personal happiness.

SUSAN B. Shall I protest, not while I live and breathe, I shall protest, shall I protest, shall I protest while I live and breathe.

DANIEL WEBSTER. When my eyes shall be turned to behold for the last time the sun in heaven.

SUSAN B. Yes.

JO THE LOITERER. I like a mouse

ANGEL MORE. I hate mice.

JO THE LOITERER. I am not talking about mice, I am talking about a mouse. I like a mouse.

ANGEL MORE. I hate a mouse.

JO THE LOITERER. Now you do.

CURTAIN

INTERLUDE

(*Susan B. A Short Story.*)

Yes I was said Susan.

You mean you are, said Anne.

No said Susan no.

When this you see remember me said Susan B.

I do said Anne.

After a while there was education. Who is educated said Anne.

Susan began to follow, she began to follow herself. I am not tired said Susan. No not said Anne. No I am not said Susan. This was the beginning. They began to travel not to travel you know but to go from one place to another place. In each place Susan B. said here I am I am here. Well said Anne. Do not let it trouble you said Susan politely. By the time she was there she was polite. She often thought about politeness. She said politeness was so agreeable. Is it said Anne. Yes said Susan yes I think so that is to say politeness is agreeable that is to say it could be agreeable if everybody were polite but when it is only me, ah me, said Susan B.

Anne was reproachful why do you not speak louder she said to Susan B. I speak as loudly as I can said Susan B. I even speak louder I even speak louder than I can. Do you really said Anne. Yes I really do said Susan B. it was dark and as it was dark it was necessary to speak louder or very softly, very softly. Dear me said Susan B., if it was not so early I would be sleepy. I myself said Anne never like to look at a newspaper. You are entirely right said Susan B. only I disagree with you. You do said Anne. You know very well I do said Susan B.

Men said Susan B. are so conservative, so selfish, so boresome and said Susan B. they are so ugly, and said Susan B. they are gullible, anybody can convince them, listen said Susan B. they listen to me. Well said Anne anybody would. I know said Susan B. I know anybody would I know that.

Once upon a time any day was full of occupation. You were never tired said Anne. No I was never tired said Susan B. And now, said Anne. Now I am never tired said Susan B. Let us said Anne let us think about everything. No said Susan B. no, no no, I know, I know said Susan B. no, said Susan B. No. But said Anne. But me no buts said Susan B. I know, now you like every one, every one and you each one and you they all do, they all listen to me, utterly unnecessary to deny, why deny, they themselves will they deny that they listen to me but let them deny it, all the same they do they do, listen to me all the men do, see them said Susan B., do see them, see them, why not, said Susan B., they are men, and men, well of course they know that they cannot either see or hear unless I tell them so, poor things said Susan B. I do not pity them. Poor things. Yes said Anne they are poor things. Yes said Susan B. they are poor things. They are poor things said Susan B. men are poor things. Yes they are said Anne. Yes they are said Susan B. and nobody pities them. No said Anne no, nobody pities them. Very likely said Susan B. More than likely, said Anne. Yes said Susan B. yes.

It was not easy to go away but Susan B. did go away. She kept on going away and every time she went away she went away again. Oh my said Susan B. why do I go away, I go away because if I did not go away I would stay. Yes of course said Anne yes of course, if you did not go away you would stay. Yes of course said Susan B. Now said Susan B., let us not forget that in each place men are the same just the same, they are conservative, they are selfish and they listen to me. Yes they do said Anne. Yes they do said Susan B.

Susan B. was right, she said she was right and she was right. Susan B. was right. She was right because she was right. It is easy to be right, everybody else is wrong so it is easy to be right, and Susan B. was right, of course she was right, it is easy to be right, everybody else is wrong it is easy to be right. And said Susan B., in a way yes in a way yes really in a way, in a way really it is useful to be right. It does what it does, it does do what it does, if you are right, it does do what it does. It is very remarkable said Anne. Not very remarkable said Susan B. not very remarkable, no not very remarkable. It is not very remarkable really not very remarkable said Anne. No said Susan B. no not very remarkable.

And said Susan B. that is what I mean by not very remarkable.

Susan B. said she would not leave home. No said Susan B. I will not leave home. Why not said Anne. Why not said Susan B. all right I will I will always have I always will. Yes you always will said Anne. Yes I always will said Susan B. In a little while anything began again and Susan B. said she did not mind. Really and truly said Susan B. really and truly I do not mind. No said Anne you do not mind, no said Susan B. no really and truly truly and really I do not mind. It was very necessary never to be cautious said Susan B. Yes said Anne it is very necessary.

In a little while they found everything very mixed. It is not really mixed said Susan B. How can anything be really mixed when men are conservative, dull, monotonous, deceived, stupid, unchanging and bullies, how said Susan B. how when men are men can they be mixed. Yes said Anne, yes men are men, how can they when men are men how can they be mixed yes how can they. Well said Susan B. let us go on they always listen to me. Yes said Anne yes they always listen to you. Yes said Susan B. yes they always listen to me.

ACT 2

ANDREW J. It is cold weather.

HENRIETTA M. In winter.

ANDREW J. Wherever I am

(*Thaddeus S. comes in singing a song.*)

THADDEUS S. I believe in public school education, I do not believe in free masons I believe in public school education, I do not believe that every one can do whatever he likes because (a pause) I have not always done what I liked, but, I would, if I could, and so I will, I will do what I will, I will have my will, and they, when the they, where are they, beside a poll, Gallup the poll. It is remarkable that there could be any nice person by the name of Gallup, but there is, yes there is, that is my decision.

ANDREW J. Bother your decision, I tell you it is cold weather.

HENRIETTA M. In winter.

ANDREW J. Wherever I am.

CONSTANCE FLETCHER. Antagonises is a pleasant name, antagonises is a pleasant word, antagonises has occurred, bless you all and one.

JOHN ADAMS. Dear Miss Constance Fletcher, it is a great pleasure that I kneel at your feet, but I am Adams, I kneel at the feet of none, not any one, dear Miss Constance Fletcher dear dear Miss Constance Fletcher I kneel at your feet, you would have ruined my father if I had had one but I have had one and you had ruined him, dear Miss Constance Fletcher if I had not been an Adams I would have kneeled at your feet.

CONSTANCE FLETCHER. And kissed my hand.

J. ADAMS (*shuddering*). And kissed your hand.

CONSTANCE FLETCHER. What a pity, no not what a pity it is better so, but what a pity what a pity it is what a pity.

J. ADAMS. Do not pity me kind beautiful lovely Miss Constance Fletcher do not pity me, no do not pity me, I am an Adams and not pitiable.

CONSTANCE FLETCHER. Dear dear me if he had not been an Adams he would have kneeled at my feet and he would have kissed my hand. Do you mean that you would have kissed my hand or my hands, dear Mr. Adams.

J. ADAMS. I mean that I would have first kneeled at your feet and then I would have kissed one of your hands and then I would still kneeling have kissed both of your hands, if I had not been an Adams.

CONSTANCE FLETCHER. Dear me Mr. Adams dear me.

ALL THE CHARACTERS. If he had not been an Adams he would have kneeled at her feet and he would have kissed one of her hands, and then still kneeling he would have kissed both of her hands still kneeling if he had not been an Adams.

ANDREW J. It is cold weather.

HENRIETTA M. In winter.

ANDREW J. Wherever I am.

THADDEUS S. When I look at him I fly, I mean when he looks at me he can cry.

LILLIAN RUSSELL. It is very naughty for men to quarrel so.

HERMAN ATLAN. They do quarrel so.

LILLIAN RUSSELL. It is very naughty of them very naughty.

(*Jenny Reefer begins to waltz with Herman Atlan.*)

A SLOW CHORUS:
Naughty men, they quarrel so
Quarrel about what.
About how late the moon can rise.
About how soon the earth can turn.
About how naked are the stars.
About how black are blacker men.

About how pink are pinks in spring.
About what corn is best to pop.
About how many feet the ocean has dropped.
Naughty men naughty men, they are always always quarrelling.

JENNY REEFER. Ulysses S. Grant was not the most earnest nor the most noble of men, but he was not always quarrelling.

DONALD GALLUP. No he was not.

JO THE LOITERER. Has everybody forgotten Isabel Wentworth. I just want to say has everybody forgotten Isabel Wentworth.

CHRIS THE CITIZEN. Why shouldn't everybody forget Isabel Wentworth.

JO THE LOITERER. Well that is just what I want to know I just want to know if everybody has forgotten Isabel Wentworth. That is all I want to know I just want to know if everybody has forgotten Isabel Wentworth.

SCENE 2

SUSAN B. Shall I regret having been born, will I regret having been born, shall and will, will and shall, I regret having been born.

ANNE. Is Henrietta M. a sister of Angel More.

SUSAN B. No, I used to feel that sisters should be sisters, and that sisters prefer sisters, and I.

ANNE. Is Angel More the sister of Henrietta M. It is important that I know important.

SUSAN B. Yes important.

ANNE. An Indiana Elliott are there any other Elliots beside Indiana Elliot. It is important that I should know, very important.

SUSAN B. Should one work up excitement, or should one turn it low so that it will explode louder, should one work up excitement should one.

ANNE. Are there any other Elliots beside Indiana Elliott, had she sisters or even cousins, it is very important that I should know, very important.

SUSAN B. A life is never given for a life, when a life is given a life is gone, if no life is gone there is no room for more life, life and strife, I give my life, that is to say, I live my life every day.

ANNE. And Isabel Wentworth, is she older or younger than she was it is very important very important that I should know just how old she is. I must have a list I must of how old every one is, it is very important.

SUSAN B. I am ready.

ANNE. We have forgotten we have forgotten Jenny Reefer, I don't know even who she is, it is very important that I know who Jenny Reefer is very important.

SUSAN B. And perhaps it is important to know who Lillian Russell is, perhaps it is important.

ANNE. It is not important to know who Lillian Russell is.

SUSAN B. Then you do know.

ANNE. It is not important for me to know who Lillian Russell is.

SUSAN B. I must choose I do choose, men and women women and men I do choose. I must choose colored or white white or colored I must choose, I must choose, weak or strong, strong or weak I must choose.

(*All the men coming forward together.*)

SUSAN B. I must choose

JO THE LOITERER. Fight fight fight, between the nigger and the white.

CHRIS THE CITIZEN. And the women.

ANDREW J. I wish to say that little men are bigger than big men, that they know how to drink and to get drunk. They say I was a little man next to that big man, nobody can say what they do say nobody can.

CHORUS OF ALL THE MEN. No nobody can, we feel that way too, no nobody can.

ANDREW JOHNSON. Begin to be drunk when you can so be a bigger man than a big man, you can.

CHORUS OF MEN. You can.

ANDREW J. I often think, I am a bigger man than a bigger man. I often think I am.

(*Andrew J. moves around and as he moves around he sees himself in a mirror.*)

Nobody can say little as I am I am not bigger than anybody bigger bigger bigger (and then in a low whisper) bigger than him bigger than him.

JO THE LOITERER. Fight fight between the big and the big never between the little and the big.

CHRIS THE CITIZEN. They don't fight.

(*Virgil T. makes them all gather around him.*)

VIRGIL T. Hear me he says hear me in every way I have satisfaction, I sit I stand I walk around and I am grand, and you all know it.

CHORUS OF MEN. Yes we all know it. That's that.

And Said VIRGIL T. I will call you up one by one and then you will know which one is which, I know, then you will be known. Very well, Henry B.

HENRY B. (*comes forward*). I almost thought that I was Tommy I almost did I almost thought I was Tommy W. but if I were Tommy W. I would never come again, not if I could do better no not if I could do better.

VIRGIL T. Useless. John Adams. (*John Adams advances.*) Tell me are you the real John Adams you know I sometimes doubt it not really doubt it you know but doubt it.

JOHN ADAMS. If you were silent I would speak.

JO THE LOITERER. Fight fight fight between day and night.

CHRIS THE CITIZEN. Which is day and which is night.

JO THE LOITERER. Hush, which.

JOHN ADAMS. I ask you Virgil T. do you love women, I do. I love women but I am never subdued by them never.

VIRGIL T. He is no good. Andrew J. and Thaddeus S. better come together.

JO THE LOITERER. He wants to fight fight fight between.

CHRIS. Between what.

JO THE LOITERER. Between the dead.

ANDREW J. I tell you I am bigger bigger is not biggest is not bigger. I am bigger and just to the last minute, I stick, it's better to stick than to die, it's better to itch than to cry, I have tried them all.

VIRGIL T. You bet you have.

THADDEUS S. I can be carried in dying but I will never quit trying.

JO THE LOITERER. Oh go to bed when all is said oh go to bed, everybody, let's hear the women.

CHRIS THE CITIZEN. Fight fight between the nigger and the white and the women.

(*Andrew J. and Thaddeus S. begin to quarrel violently.*)

Tell me said Virgil T. tell me I am from Missouri.

(*Everybody suddenly stricken dumb.*)

(*Daniel advances holding Henrietta M. by the hand.*)

DANIEL. Ladies and gentlemen let me present you let me present to you Henrietta M. it is rare in this troubled world to find a woman without a last name rare delicious and troubling, ladies and gentlemen let me present Henrietta M.

CURTAIN

SCENE 3

SUSAN B. I do not know whether I am asleep or awake, awake or asleep, asleep or awake. Do I know.

JO THE LOITERER. I know, you are awake Susan B.

(*A snowy landscape. A negro man and a negro woman.*)

SUSAN B. Negro man would you vote if you only can and not she.

NEGRO MAN. You bet.

SUSAN B. I fought for you that you could vote would you vote if they would not let me.

NEGRO MAN. Holy gee.

SUSAN B.(*moving down in the snow*). If I believe that I am right and I am right if they believe that they are right and they are not in the right, might, might, might there be what might be.

NEGRO MAN AND WOMAN (*following her*). All right Susan B. all right.

SUSAN B. How then can we entertain a hope that they will act differently, we may pretend to go in good faith but there will be no faith in us.

DONALD GALLUP. Let me help you Susan B.

SUSAN B. And if you do and I annoy you what will you do.

DONALD GALLUP. But I will help you Susan B.

SUSAN B. I tell you if you do and I annoy you what will you do.

DONALD GALLUP. I wonder if I can help you Susan B.

SUSAN B. I wonder.

(*Andrew G., Thaddeus and Daniel Webster come in together.*)

We are the chorus of the V.I.P. Very important persons to every one who can hear and see, we are the chorus of the V.I.P.

SUSAN B. Yes, so they are. I am important but not that way, not that way.

THE THREE V.I.P.'S. We you see we V.I.P. very important to any one who can hear or you can see, just we three, of course lots of others but just we three, just we three we are the chorus of V.I.P. Very important persons to any one who can hear or can see.

SUSAN B. My constantly recurring thought and prayer now are that no word or act of mine may lessen the might of this country in the scale of truth and right.

THE CHORUS OF V.I.P.

DANIEL WEBSTER. When they all listen to me.

THADDEUS S. When they all listen to me.

ANDREW J. When they all listen to him, by him I mean me.

DANIEL WEBSTER. By him I mean me.

THADDEUS S. It is not necessary to have any meaning I am he, he is me I am a V.I.P.

THE THREE. We are the V.I.P. the very important persons, we have special rights, they ask us first and they wait for us last and wherever we are well there we are everybody knows we are there, we are the V.I.P. Very important persons for everybody to see.

JO THE LOITERER. I wished that I knew the difference between rich and poor, I used to think I was poor, now I think I am rich and I am rich, quite rich not very rich quite rich, I wish I knew the difference between rich and poor.

CHRIS THE CITIZEN. Ask her, ask Susan B. I always ask, I find they like it and I like it, and if I like it, and if they like it, I am not rich and I am not poor, just like that Joe just like that.

JO THE LOITERER. Susan B. listen to me, what is the difference between rich and poor poor and rich no use to ask the V.I.P., they never answer me but you Susan B. you answer, answer me.

SUSAN B. Rich, to be rich, is to be so rich that when they are rich they have it to be that they do not listen and when they do they do not hear, and to be poor to be poor, is to be so poor they listen and listen and what they hear well what do they hear, they hear that they listen, they listen to hear, that is what it is to be poor, but I, I Susan B., there is no wealth nor poverty, there is no wealth, what is wealth, there is no poverty, what is poverty, has a pen ink, has it.

JO THE LOITERER. I had a pen that was to have ink for a year and it only lasted six weeks.

SUSAN B. Yes I know Jo. I know.

CURTAIN

SCENE 4

(*A Meeting.*)

SUSAN B. (*on the platform*). Ladies there is no neutral position for us to assume. If we say we love the cause and then sit down at our ease, surely does our action speak the lie.
And now will Daniel Webster take the platform as never before.

DANIEL WEBSTER. Coming and coming alone, no man is alone when he comes, when he comes when he is coming he is not alone and now ladies and gentlemen I have done, remember that remember me remember each one.

SUSAN B. And now Virgil T. Virgil T. will bow and speak and when it's necessary they will know that he is he.

VIRGIL T. I make what I make, I make a noise, there is a poise in making a noise.

(*An interruption at the door.*)

JO THE LOITERER. I have behind me a crowd, are we allowed.

SUSAN B. A crowd is never allowed but each one of you can come in.

CHRIS THE CITIZEN. But if we are allowed then we are a crowd.

SUSAN B. No, this is the cause, and a cause is a pause. Pause before you come in.

JO THE LOITERER. Yes ma'am.

(*All the characters crowd in. Constance Fletcher and Indiana Elliot leading*).

DANIEL WEBSTER. I resist it today and always. Who ever falters or whoever flies I continue the contest.

(*Constance Fletcher and Indiana Elliot bowing low say*).

Dear man, he can make us glad that we have had so great so dear a man here with us now and now we bow before him here, this dear this dear great man.

SUSAN B. Hush, this is slush. Hush.

JOHN ADAMS. I cannot be still when still and until I see Constance Fletcher dear Constance Fletcher noble Constance Fletcher and I spill I spill over like a thrill and a trill, dear Constance Fletcher there is no cause in her presence, how can there be a cause. Women what are women. There is Constance Fletcher, men what are men, there is Constance Fletcher, Adams, yes, Adams, I am John Adams, there is Constance Fletcher, when this you see listen to me, Constance, no I cannot call her Constance I can only call her Constance Fletcher.

INDIANA ELLIOT. And how about me.

JO THE LOITERER. Whist shut up I have just had an awful letter from home, shut up.

INDIANA ELLIOT. What did they say.

JO THE LOITERER. They say I must come home and not marry you.

INDIANA. Who ever said we were going to marry.

JO THE LOITERER. Believe me I never did.

INDIANA. Disgrace to the cause of women, out. (*And she shoves him out.*)

JO THE LOITERER. Help Susan B. help me.

SUSAN B. I know that we suffer, and as we suffer we grow strong, I know that we wait and as we wait we are bold, I know that we are beaten and as we are beaten we win, I know that men know that this is not so but it is so, I know, yes I know.

JO THE LOITERER. There didn't I tell you she knew best, you just give me a kiss and let me alone.

DANIEL WEBSTER. I who was once old am now young, I who was once weak am now strong, I who have left every one behind am now overtaken.

SUSAN B. I undertake to overthrow your undertaking.

JO THE LOITERER. You bet.

CHRIS THE CITIZEN. I always repeat everything I hear.

JO THE LOITERER. You sure do.

(*While all this is going on, all the characters are crowding up on the platform.*)

(THEY SAY).

Now we are all here there is nobody down there to hear, now if it is we're always like that there would be no reason why anybody should cry, because very likely if at all it would be so nice to be the head, we are the head we have all the bread.

JO THE LOITERER. And the butter too.

CHRIS THE CITIZEN. And Kalamazoo.

SUSAN B. (*advancing*). I speak to those below who are not there who are not there who are not there. I speak to those below to those below who are not there to those below who are not there.

CURTAIN

SCENE 5

SUSAN B. Will they remember that it is true that neither they that neither you, will they marry will they carry, aloud, the right to know that even if they love them so, they are alone to live and die, they are alone to sink and swim they are alone to have what they own, to have no idea but that they are here, to struggle and thirst to do everything first, because until it is done there is no other one.

(*Jo the Loiterer leads in Indiana Elliot in wedding attire, followed by John Adams and Constance Fletcher and followed by Daniel Webster and Angel More. All the other characters follow after. Anne and Jenny Reefer come and*

stand by Susan B. Ulysses S. Grant sits down in a chair right behind the procession.)

ANNE. Marriage.

JENNY REEFER. Marry marriage.

SUSAN B. I know I know and I have told you so, but it no one marries how can there be women to tell men, women to tell men.

ANNE. What.

JENNY REEFER. Women should not tell men.

SUSAN B. Men can not count, they do not know that two and two make four if women do not tell them so. There is a devil creeps into men when their hands are strengthened. Men want to be half slave half free. Women want to be all slave or all free, therefore men govern and women know, and yet.

ANNE. Yet.

JENNY REEFER. There is no yet in paradise.

SUSAN B. Let them marry.

(*The marrying commences.*)

JO THE LOITERER. I tell her if she marries me do I marry her.

INDIANA ELLIOT. Listen to what he says so you can answer, have you the ring.

JO THE LOITERER. You did not like the ring and mine is too large.

INDIANA ELLIOT. Hush.

JO THE LOITERER. I wish my name was Adams.

INDIANA ELLIOT. Hush.

JOHN ADAMS. I never marry I have been twice divorced but I have never married, fair Constance Fletcher fair Constance Fletcher do you not admire me that I never can married be. I who have been twice divorced. Dear Constance Fletcher dear dear Constance Fletcher do you not admire me.

CONSTANCE FLETCHER. So beautiful. It is so beautiful to meet you here, so beautiful, so beautiful to meet you here dear, dear John Adams, so beautiful to meet you here.

DANIEL WEBSTER. When I have joined and not having joined have separated and not having separated have led, and not having led have thundered, when I having thundered have provoked and having provoked have dominated, may I dear Angel More not kneel at your feet because I cannot kneel my knees are not kneeling knees but dear Angel More be my Angel More for evermore.

ANGEL MORE. I join the choir that is visible, because the choir that is visible is as visible.

DANIEL WEBSTER. As what Angel More.

ANGEL MORE. As visible as visible, do you not hear me, as visible.

DANIEL WEBSTER. You do not and I do not.

ANGEL MORE. What.

DANIEL WEBSTER. Separate marriage from marriage.

ANGEL MORE. And why not.

DANIEL WEBSTER. And.

(*Just as this moment Ulysses S. Grant makes his chair pound on the floor.*)

ULYSSES S. GRANT. As long as I sit I am sitting, silence again as you were, you were all silent, as long as I sit I am sitting.

ALL TOGETHER. We are silent, as we were.

SUSAN B. We are all here to celebrate the civil and religious marriage of Jo the Loiterer and Indiana Elliot.

JO THE LOITERER. Who is civil and who is religious.

ANNE. Who is, listen to Susan B. She knows.

(*The Brother of Indiana Elliot rushes in.*)

Nobody knows who I am but I forbid the marriage, do we know whether Jo the Loiterer is a bigamist or a grandfather or an uncle or a refugee. Do we know, no we do not know and I forbid the marriage, I forbid it, I am Indiana Elliot's brother and I forbid it, I am known as Herman Atlan and I forbid it, I am known as Anthony Comstock and I forbid it. I am Indiana Elliot's brother and I forbid it.

JO THE LOITERER. Well well well, I knew that ring of mine was too large, It could not fall off an account of my joints but I knew it was too large.

INDIANA ELLIOT. I renounce my brother.

JO THE LOITERER. That's right my dear that's all right.

SUSAN B. What is marriage, is marriage protection or religion, is marriage renunciation or abundance, is marriage a stepping-stone or an end. What is marriage.

ANNE. I will never marry.

JENNY REEFER. If I marry I will divorce but I will not marry because if I did marry, I would be married.

(*Ulysses S. Grant pounds his chair.*)

ULYSSES S. GRANT. Didn't I say I do not like noise, I do not like cannon balls, I do not like storms, I do not like talking, I do not like noise. I like everything and everybody to be silent and what I like I have. Everybody be silent.

JO THE LOITERER. I know I was silent, everybody can tell just by listening to me just how silent I am, dear General, dear General Ulysses, dear General Ulysses Simpson dear General Ulysses Simpson Grant, dear dear sir, am I not a perfect example of what you like, am I not silent.

(*Ulysses S. Grant's chair pounds and he is silent.*)

SUSAN B. I am not married and the reason why is that I have had to do what I have had to do, I have had to be what I have had to be, I could never be one of two I could never be two in one as married couples do and can, I am but one all one, one and all one, and so I have never been married to any one.

ANNE. But I have been, I have been married to what you have been to that one.

SUSAN B. No no, no, you may be married to the past one, the one that is not the present one, no one can be married to the present one, the one, the one, the present one.

JENNY REEFER. I understand you undertake to overthrow their undertaking.

SUSAN B. I love the sound of these, one over two, two under one, three under four, four over more.

ANNE. Dear Susan B. Anthony thank you.

JOHN ADAMS. All this time I have been lost in my thoughts in my thoughts of thee beautiful thee, Constance Fletcher, do you see, I have been lost in my thoughts of thee.

CONSTANCE FLETCHER. I am blind and therefore I dream.

DANIEL WEBSTER. Dear Angel More, dear Angel More, there have been men who have stammered and stuttered but not, not I.

ANGEL MORE. Speak louder.

DANIEL WEBSTER. Not I.

THE CHORUS. Why the hell don't you all get married, why don't you, we want to go home, why don't you.

JO THE LOITERER. Why don't you.

INDIANA ELLIOT. Why don't you.

INDIANA ELLIOT'S BROTHER. Why don't you because I am here.

The crowd remove him forcibly

SUSAN B. ANTHONY(*suddenly*). They are married all married and their children women as well as men will have the vote, they will they will, they will have the vote.

CURTAIN

SCENE 6

(*Susan B. doing her housework in her house.*)

Enter ANNE. Susan B. they want you.

SUSAN B. Do they

ANNE. Yes. You must go.

SUSAN B. No.

JENNY REEFER (*Comes in*). Oh yes they want to know if you are here.

SUSAN B. Yes still alive. Painters paint and writers write and soldiers drink and fight and I am still alive.

ANNE. They want you.

SUSAN B. And when they have me.

JENNY REEFER. Then they will want you again.

SUSAN B. Yes I know, they love me so, they tell me so and they tell me so, but I, I do not tell them so because I know, they will not do what they could do and I I will be left alone to die but they will not have done what I need to have done to make it right that I live lived my life and fight.

JO THE LOITERER (*at the window*). Indiana Elliot wants to come in, she will not take my name she says it is not all the same, she says that she is Indiana Elliot and that I am Jo, and that she will not take my name and that she will always tell me so. Oh yes she is right of course she is right it is not all the same Indiana Elliot is her name, she is only married to me, but there is no difference that I can see, but all the same there she is and she will not change her name, yes it is all the same.

SUSAN B. Let her in.

INDIANA ELLIOT. Oh Susan B. they want you they have to have you, can I tell them you are coming I have not changed my name can I tell them you are coming and that you will do everything.

SUSAN B. No but there is no use in telling them so, they won't vote my laws, there is always a clause, there is always a pause, they won't vote my laws.

(*Andrew Johnson puts his head in at the door.*)

ANDREW JOHNSON. Will the good lady come right along.

THADDEUS STEVENS (*behind him*). We are waiting, will the good lady not keep us waiting, will the good lady not keep us waiting.

SUSAN B. You you know so well that you will not vote my laws.

STEVENS. Dear lady remember humanity comes first.

SUSAN B. You mean men come first, women, you will not vote my laws, how can you dare when you do not care, how can you dare, there is no humanity in humans, there is only law, and you will not because you know so well that there is no humanity there are only laws, you know it so well that you will not you will not vote my laws.

(*Susan B. goes back to her housework. All the characters crowd in.*)

CHORUS. Do come Susan B. Anthony do come nobody no nobody can make them come the way you make them come, do come do come Susan B. Anthony, it is your duty, Susan B. Anthony, you know you know your duty, you come, do come, come.

SUSAN B. ANTHONY. I suppose I will be coming, is it because you flatter me, is it because if I do not come you will forget me and never vote my laws, you will never vote my laws even if I do come but if I do not come you will never vote my laws, come or not come it always comes to the same thing it comes to their not voting my laws, not voting my laws, tell me all you men tell me you know you will never vote my laws.

ALL THE MEN. Dear kind lady we count on you, and as we count on you so can you count on us.

SUSAN B. ANTHONY. Yes but I work for you I do, I say never again, never again, never never, and yet I know I do say no but I do not mean no, I know I always hope that if I go that if I go and go and go, perhaps then you men will vote my laws but I know how well I know, a little this way a little that way you steal away, you steal a piece away you steal yourselves away, you do not intend to stay and vote my laws, and still when you call I go, I go, I go, I say no, no, no, and I go, but no, this time no, this time

you have to do more than promise, you must write it down that you will vote my laws, but no, you will pay no attention to what is written, well then swear by my hearth, as you hope to have a home and hearth, swear after I work for you swear that you will vote my laws, but no, no oaths, no thoughts, no decisions, no intentions, no gratitude, no convictions, no nothing will make you pass my laws. Tell me can any of you be honest now, and say you will not pass my laws.

JO THE LOITERER. I can I can be honest I can say I will not pass your laws, because you see I have no vote, no loiterer has a vote so it is easy Susan B. Anthony easy for one man among all these men to be honest and to say I will not pass your laws. Anyway Susan B. Anthony what are your laws. Would it really be all right to pass them, if you say so it is all right with me. I have no vote myself but I'll make them as long as I don't have to change my name don't have to don't have to change my name.

T. STEVENS. Thanks dear Susan B. Anthony, thanks we all know that whatever happens we all can depend upon you to do your best for any cause which is a cause, and any cause is a cause and because any cause is a cause therefore you will always do your best for any cause, and now you will be doing your best for this cause our cause the cause.

SUSAN B. Because. Very well is it snowing.

CHORUS. Not just now.

SUSAN B. ANTHONY. It is cold.

CHORUS. A little.

SUSAN B. ANTHONY. I am not well

CHORUS. But you look so well and once started it will be all right.

SUSAN B. ANTHONY. All right.

CURTAIN

SCENE 7

(*Susan B. Anthony busy with her housework.*)

ANNE (*comes in*). Oh it was wonderful, wonderful, they listen to nobody the way they listen to you.

SUSAN B. Yes it is wonderful as the result of my work for the first time the word male has been written into the constitution of the United States concerning suffrage. Yes it is wonderful.

ANNE. But.

SUSAN B. Yes but, what is man, what are they. I do not say that they haven't kind hearts, if I fall down in a faint, they will rush to pick me up, if my house is on fire, they will rush in to put the fire out and help me, yes they have kind hearts but they are afraid, afraid, they are afraid, they are afraid. They fear women, they fear each other, they fear their neighbor, they fear other countries and then they hearten themselves in their fear by crowding together and following each other, and when they crowd together and follow each other they are brutes, like animals who stampede, and so they have written in the name male into the United States constitution, because they are afraid of black men because they are afraid of women, because they are afraid afraid. Men are afraid.

ANNE (*timidly*). And women.

SUSAN B. Ah women often have not any sense of danger, after all a hen screams pitifully when she sees an eagle but she is only afraid for her children, men are afraid for themselves, that is the real difference between men and women.

ANNE. But Susan B. why do you not say these things out loud.

SUSAN B. Why not, because if I did they would not listen they not alone would not listen they would revenge themselves. Men have kind hearts when they are not afraid but they are afraid afraid afraid. I say they are afraid, but if I were to tell them so their kindness would turn to hate. Yes the Quakers are right, they are not afraid because they do not fight, they do not fight.

ANNE. But Susan B. you fight and you are not afraid.

SUSAN B. I fight and I am not afraid, I fight but I am not afraid.

ANNE. And you will win.

SUSAN B. Win what, win what.

ANNE. Win the vote for women.

SUSAN B. Yes some day some day the women will vote and by that time.

ANNE. By that time oh wonderful time.

SUSAN B. By that time it will do them no good because having the vote they will become like men, they will be afraid, having the vote will make them afraid, oh I know it, but I will fight for the right, for the right to vote for them even though they become like men, become afraid like men, become like men.

(*Anne bursts into tears, Jenny Reefer rushes in.*)

JENNY REEFER. I have just converted Lillian Russell to the cause of woman's suffrage, I have converted her, she will give all herself and all she earns oh wonderful day I know you will say, here she comes isn't she beautiful.

(*Lillian Russell comes in followed by all the women in the chorus. Women crowding around, Constance Fletcher in the background.*)

LILLIAN RUSSELL. Dear friends, it is so beautiful to meet you all, so beautiful, so beautiful to meet you all.

(*John Adams comes in and sees Constance Fletcher.*)

JOHN ADAMS. Dear friend beautiful friend, there is no beauty where you are not.

CONSTANCE FLETCHER. Yes dear friend but look look at real beauty look at Lillian Russell look at real beauty.

JOHN ADAMS. Real beauty real beauty is all there is of beauty and why should my eye wander where no eye can look

without having looked before. Dear friend I kneel to you because dear friend each time I see you I have never looked before, dear friend you are an open door.

(*Daniel Webster strides in, the women separate.*)

DANIEL WEBSTER. What what is it, what is it, what is the false and the true and I say to you you Susan B. Anthony, you know the false from the true and yet you will not wait you will not wait, I say you will you will wait. When my eyes, and I have eyes when my eyes, beyond that I seek not to penetrate the veil, why should you want what you have chosen, when mine eyes, why do you want that the curtain may rise, why when mine eyes, why should the vision be opened to what lies behind, why, Susan B. Anthony fight the fight that is the fight, what any fight may be a fight for the right. I hear that you say that the word male should not be written into the constitution of the United States of America, but I say, I say, that so long that the gorgeous ensign of the republic, still full high advanced, its arms and trophies streaming in their original luster not a stripe erased or polluted not a single star obscured.

JO THE LOITERER. She has decided to change her name.

INDIANA ELLIOT. Not because it is his name but it is such a pretty name, Indiana Loiterer is such a pretty name I think all the same he will have to change his name, he must be Jo Elliot, yes he must, it is what he has to do, he has to be Jo Elliot and I am going to be Indiana Loiterer, dear friends, all friends is it not a lovely name, Indiana Loiterer all the same.

JO THE LOITERER. All right I never fight, nobody will know it's men, but what can I do, if I am not she and I am not me, what can I do, if a name is not true, what can I do but do as she tells me.

ALL THE CHORUS. She is quite right, Indiana Loiterer is so harmonious, so harmonious, Indiana Loiterer is so harmonious.

(*All the men come in.*)

What did she say.

JO. I was talking not she but nobody no nobody every wants to listen to me.

ALL THE CHORUS (*men and women*). Susan B. Anthony was very successful we are all very grateful to Susan B. Anthony because she was so successful, she worked for the votes for women and she worked for the vote for colored men and she was so successful, they wrote the word male into the constitution of the United States of America, dear Susan B. Anthony. Dear Susan B., whenever she wants to be and she always wants to be she is always so successful so very successful.

SUSAN B. So successful.

CURTAIN

SCENE 8

(*The Congressional Hall, the replica of the statue of Susan B. Anthony and her comrades in the suffrage fight.*)

ANNE (*alone in front of the statuary*). The Vote. Women have the vote. They have it each and every one, it is glorious glorious glorious.

SUSAN B. ANTHONY (*behind the statue*). Yes women have the vote, all my long life of strength and strife, all my long life, women have it, they can vote, every man and every woman have the vote, the word male is not there any more, that is to say, that is to say.

(*Silence. Virgil T. comes in very nicely, he looks around and sees Anne.*)

VIRGIL T. Very well indeed, very well indeed, you are looking very well indeed, have you a chair anywhere, very well indeed, as we sit, we sit, some day very soon some day they will vote sitting and that will be a very successful day any day, every day.

(*Henry comes in. He looks all around at the statue and then he sighs.*)

HENRY B. Does it really mean that women are as white and cold as marble does it really mean that.

(*Angel More comes in and bows gracefully to the sculptured group.*)

ANGEL MORE. I can always think of dear Daniel Webster daily.

(*John Adams comes in and looks around, and then carefully examines the statue.*)

JOHN ADAMS. I think that they might have added dear delicate Constance Fletcher I do think they might have added her wonderful profile. I do think they might have, I do, I really do. (*Andrew Johnson shuffles in.*)

ANDREW JOHNSON. I have no hope in black or white in white or black in black or black or white or white, no hope.

(*Thaddeus Stevens comes in, he does not address anybody, he stands before the statue and frowns.*)

THADDEUS S. Rob the cradle, rob it, rob the robber, rob him, rob whatever there is to be taken, rob, rob the cradle, rob it.

DANIEL WEBSTER (*he sees nothing else*). Angel More, more more Angel More, did you hear me, can you hear shall you hear me, when they come and they do come; when they go and they do go, Angel More can you will you shall you may you might you would you hear me, when they have lost and won, when they have won and lost, when words are bitter and snow is white. Angel More come to me and we will leave together.

ANGEL MORE. Dear sir, not leave, stay.

HENRIETTA M. I have never been mentioned again. (*She curtseys.*)

CONSTANCE FLETCHER. Here I am, I am almost blind but here I am, dear dear here I am, I cannot see what is so white, here I am.

JOHN ADAMS (*kissing her hand*). Here you are, blind as a bat and beautiful as a bird, here you are, white and cold as marble, beautiful as marble, yes that is marble but you you are the living marble dear Constance Fletcher, you are.

CONSTANCE FLETCHER. Thank you yes I am here, blind as a bat, I am here.

INDIANA ELLIOT. I am sorry to interrupt so sorry to interrupt but I have a great deal to say about marriage, either one or the other married must be economical, either one or the other, if either one or the other of a married couple are economical then a marriage is successful, if not not, I have a great deal to say about marriage, and dear Susan B. Anthony was never married, how wonderful it is to be never married how wonderful. I have a great deal to say about marriage.

SUSAN B. ANTHONY (*voice from behind the statue*). It is a puzzle, I am not puzzled but it is a puzzle, if there are no children there are no men and women, and if there are men and women, it is rather horrible, and if it is rather horrible, then there are children, I am not puzzled but it is very puzzling, women and men vote and children, I am not puzzled but it is very puzzling.

GLOSTER HEMING. I have only been a man who has a very fine name, and it must be said I made it up yes I did, so many do why not I, so many do, so many do, and why not two, when anybody might, and you can vote and you can dote with any name. Thank you.

ISABEL WENTWORTH. They looked for me and they found me, I like to talk about it. It is very nearly necessary not to be noisy not to be noisy and hope, hope and hope, no use in enjoying men and women no use, I wonder why we are all happy, yes.

ANNIE HOPE. There is another Anne and she believes. I am hopey hope and I do not believe I have been in California and Kalamazoo, and I do not believe I burst into tears and I do not believe.

(*They all crowd closer together and Lillian Russell who comes in stands quite alone.*)

LILLIAN RUSSELL. I can act so drunk that I never drink, I can drink so drunk that I never act, I have a curl I was a girl and I am old and fat but very handsome for all that.

(*Anthony Comstock comes in and glares at her.*)

ANTHONY COMSTOCK. I have heard that they have thought that they would wish that one like you could vote a vote and help to let the ones who want do what they like, I have heard that even you, and I am through, I cannot hope that there is dope, oh yes a horrid word. I have never heard, short.

JENNY REEFER. I have hope and faith, not charity no not charity, I have hope and faith, no not, not charity, no not charity.

ULYSSES S. GRANT. Women are women, soldiers are soldiers, men are not men, lies are not lies, do, and then a dog barks, listen to him and then a dog barks, a dog barks a dog barks any dog barks, listen to him any dog barks. (*He sits down.*)

HERMAN ATLAN. I am not loved any more, I was loved oh yes I was loved but I am not loved any more. I am not, was I not, I knew I would refuse what a woman would choose and so I am not loved any more, not loved any more.

DONALD GALLUP. Last but not least, first and not best, I am tall as a man, I am firm as a clam, and I never change, from day to day.

(*Jo the Loiterer and Chris a Citizen.*)

JO THE LOITERER. Let us dance and sing, Chrissy Chris, wet and not in debt, I am a married man and I know how I show I am a married man. She votes, she changes her name and she votes.

(*They all crowd together in front of the statue, there is a moment of silence and then a chorus.*)

CHORUS. To vote the vote, the vote we vote, can vote do vote will vote could vote, the vote the vote.

JO THE LOITERER. I am the only one who cannot vote, no loiterer can vote.

INDIANA ELLIOT. I am a loiterer Indiana Loiterer and I can vote.

JO THE LOITERER. You only have the name, you have not got the game.

CHORUS. The vote the vote we will have the vote.

LILLIAN RUSSELL. It is so beautiful to meet you all here so beautiful.

ULYSSES S. GRANT. Vote the vote, the army does not vote, the general generals, there is no vote, bah vote.

THE CHORUS. The vote we vote we note the vote.

(*They all bow and smile to the statue. Suddenly Susan B.'s voice is heard.*)

SUSAN B.'S VOICE. We cannot retrace our steps, going forward may be the same as going backwards. We cannot retrace our steps, retrace our steps. All my long life, all my life, we do not retrace our steps, all my long life, but.

(*A silence a long silence.*)

But—we do not retrace our steps, all my long life, and here; here we are here, in marble and gold, did I say gold, yes I said gold, in marble and gold and where—

(*A silence.*)

Where is where, in my long life of effort and strife, dear life; life is strife, in my long life, it will not come and go, I tell you so, it will stay it will pay but

(*A long silence.*)

But do I want what we have got, has it not gone, what made it live, has it not gone because now it is had, in my long life in my long life

(*Silence.*)

Life is strife, I was a martyr all my life not to what I won but to what was done.

(*Silence.*)

Do you know because I tell you so, or do you know, do you know.

(*Silence.*)

My long life, my long life.

CURTAIN

TOPICS FOR CRITICAL THINKING AND WRITING

 ### The Play on the STAGE

1. Virgil Thomson suggested that the 1948 production at Western Reserve University might use a set and staging that were "visually a sort of evocation of a 19th-century photograph album." (See Thomson's letter to Nadine Miles, page 801, for further details.) What do you think of the idea? Why?

2. Is the opera anti-male, or on the contrary simply anti-patriarchal?

3. In Stein's libretto, in the last scene of the last act (2.8), Susan B. Anthony sings only from behind a statue of herself. In the first production, however, at Columbia University in 1947, during this scene she twice crossed the stage before taking her place on the pedestal, that is, before becoming a statue. What, if anything, can be said on behalf of this staging?

4. Richard Bridgman, in *Gertrude Stein in Pieces*, says that the opera ends bleakly in the recognition of SBA's failure. To what extent, if any, do you agree?

Contexts for *The Mother of Us All*

VIRGIL THOMSON
Letters and Other Writings

Virgil Thomson (1896–1989), music critic and composer, met Gertrude Stein in Paris in 1926 and later collaborated with her on two operas, *Four Saints in Three Acts* and *The Mother of Us All*. In the following selections (an essay, letters, and a passage from his autobiography) he discusses *The Mother of Us All*.

How *The Mother of Us All* Was Created*

The Mother of Us All is an opera about American public and private life in the nineteenth century. That was a time, rare in history, when great issues were debated in great language. As in the Greece of Pericles and Demosthenes, in the Rome of Caesar and Cicero, in the England of Pitt and Burke, historical changes of the utmost gravity were argued in noble prose by Webster, Clay and Calhoun in the Senate, by Beecher and Emerson in the pulpit, by Douglas and Lincoln on the partisan political platform.

These changes, which became burning issues after the Missouri Compromise of 1820, dealt with political, economic, racial and sexual equality. And the advocated reforms—excepting woman suffrage—were all embodied in the Constitution by 1870. In fifty glorious and tragic years the United States grew up. We ceased to be an eighteenth-century country and became a twentieth-century one. Surely, it had long seemed to me, surely somewhere in this noble history and in its oratory there must be the theme, and perhaps even the words, of a musico-dramatic spectacle that would be a pleasure to compose.

So it came about that in 1945, when Douglas Moore, for the Alice M. Ditson Fund of Columbia University, asked me to write an opera, I turned with this theme to my old friend and former operatic collaborator, Gertrude Stein. She liked it and began at once to read and reread the words of the period. She exhausted the American Library in Paris and the librarian obtained more books for her from the New York Public Library. She asked me if I minded her making feminism

the central theme and Susan B. Anthony the heroine. I did not. And so she began to write.

She showed me the first two scenes in October, 1945. In March, 1946, she sent me the whole libretto. It was her last completed work. In May and June we talked about it, agreed on some transpositions in the order of the scenes and on the possibility of certain cuts, these to be left eventually to my discretion. She obtained also the promise of the painter, Maurice Grosser, who had added to our earlier opera, *Four Saints in Three Acts*, a workable scenario for staging, that he would do the same for *The Mother of Us All*. In July she died. I had not yet composed any of the music.

The composing was begun Oct. 12, 1946, and seven of the eight scenes that make up the opera were finished by Dec. 10. Then I played and sang them to my friends—tried them out, so to speak. And in January, 1947, I composed the epilogue, in which Susan B. Anthony, dead and turned to marble, sings as a statue from her pedestal her own (and Gertrude Stein's own) funeral oration. The opera was orchestrated during February and March; and it was produced, beginning May 9, at the Brander Mathews Theatre at Columbia.

Since then it has been given in Cleveland, Denver, New Orleans and other cities, and just last month at Sanders Theatre in Cambridge, Mass. The Phoenix Theatre performances tomorrow and on April 23 will mark its first revival in New York and its first performance anywhere by a wholly professional cast.

The libretto deals with real persons and invented persons, with historical celebrities and with their friends and neighbors. The celebrities speak in the style of their historic utterances, sometimes even in quotations from them. The others speak straight American.

There is little in the libretto that is not directly comprehensible. All the same, its dialogue is far more an expression of the characters themselves than a vehicle for advancing the plot. As in real life, the people of the play, especially when more than two are present, rarely answer one another or even listen. They tend rather to say what is urgently on their own minds.

In Shakespeare and Shaw the characters talk mostly about what they have done or are going to do, defending their past and future actions with argument, poetry and wit. In Gertrude Stein's plays they rarely defend their actions. They merely give you their own emotional and character background. The language of

*Virgil Thomson, the *New York Times*, April 15, 1956. Copyright 1956 by the New York Times Company.

Stein's later plays is the essence of American English, but their story-line is that of Corneille and Racine and the court ballets of Molière. They are French classical theatre in the American dialect.

The music of *The Mother of Us All* is an evocation of nineteenth-century America, with its gospel hymns and cocky marches, its sentimental ballads, waltzes, darn-fool ditties and intoned sermons. Only in descriptions of weather, which has no period, does it engage the dissonant elements. Like the libretto, which deals with the attitudes and speeches, the playgames and the passions of our Victorian forebears, it is a memory book. It is a souvenir of all those sounds and kinds of tunes that were once the music of rural American and that are still the basic idiom of our country because they are the oldest vernacular still remembered here and used.

Virgil Thomson: Three Letters*

To a Correspondent   March 21, 1947
I am not too happy at seeing my score called whimsical. Also, I think the idea that Miss Stein and I are primarily wits is, if you will permit me, both antiquated and inaccurate. I should appreciate it if you could refer to *The Mother of Us All*—both the words and the music—as a serious work on a serious theme. That theme is not "the war between the sexes" but woman suffrage. There is comedy in it, of course; but referring to it as witty, whimsical, and charming does not give a resembling picture of it any more than those same adjectives would of *Hamlet*. I am sorry to be so critical, because I know you have spent a great deal of thought on the paragraph which you sent me. But since you have asked for my cooperation, I should be most grateful, and so would Miss Stein if she were living, for some word that would not place us quite so definitely with the amusers.
                                Always cordially yours,

To Nadine Miles   December 22, 1948
Dear Miss Miles:
Mr. Shepherd tells me that you are in charge of the production of my opera *The Mother of Us All*, and I am delighted to hear it. If I can be of any help to you, please do not hesitate to write me about anything that bothers you. You are certain to run into a nasty set change just before the final scene of the opera. The

music at this point is not long enough, and a silent wait is not desirable dramatically. I should like to write a rather noisy intermezzo to cover this change. Will two minutes be enough, or do you need three? I shall try to make it adjustable, so that cuts or repetitions can be operated to make it fit your stagehands' timing.

Mr. Shepherd asked me to tell you about a production idea which we were not able to put into execution at Columbia University but which I have always hoped could be realized. That is to make the opera visually a sort of evocation of a 19th-century photograph album. A permanent frame for the stage would be helpful in this regard, and so would a special curtain designed somewhat like the cover of such an album. Since 19th-century photographs were often hand-colored, one would not need to limit the sets and costumes to gray or sepia tints. Grays and warm browns could give the chief tone to the color composition of the stage but a whole range of pinks, red, purples, and other bright colors could be added in the costumes. In this way a variety of color could be achieved while keeping the spectacle at all times in harmony. The stage movement could be regulated, with or without aid of a choreographer, to suggest photographic poses. I do not mean a series of motionless tableaux vivants, though certain moments might be impressive if held a little. I see the whole rather as a series of such motionless tableaux but with the singers moving constantly from one to another. Each character could move in a different and characteristic way, since each speaks and sings in a different way and since the costumes are also intended to accentuate contrasts of character and decade. All these contrasts risk turning the opera into a costume party unless there is some deliberate overall stylization. It has long seemed to me that the photograph album idea could solve this problem effectively and that the addition of regulated movement would help. Any movement or histrionic effort of a naturalistic character would, of course, interfere.

Do not hesitate to add dances to any of the scenes where these may seem appropriate to you. Real dancing can only heighten the effect of the movements executed by the singers. . . .

The V.I.P. scene can be pointed up perhaps by vaudeville routines of a pseudo-military character. In general, heightening the spectacle by choreographic means seems to me thoroughly desirable. I have even thought of adding a ballet to the opera but I don't know exactly where I could put it.
                                Most sincerely yours,

*From *Selected Letters of Virgil Thomson* by Virgil Thomson. © Copyright 1988 by Virgil Thomson.

To Arthur Shepherd   January 12, 1949

Dear Mr. Shepherd:

The idea of using a subject from 19th-century American political history was mine; also that of using direct quotation from the oratory of the period. The selection of the characters and their arrangement into a play I left to Miss Stein. She transformed my proposal about the oratory of the period into a method whereby Susan B. Anthony, Daniel Webster, and others speak as they really spoke.

I suggested my ideas to her in the fall of 1945 in Paris, and she wrote the first two scenes immediately. The libretto was finished during the course of the winter and sent to me in the early spring of '46, I being then in New York. In the late spring we discussed it in Paris. She died in July of that year before I had begun the actual composition, which was done during the early and middle part of the following winter.

The Mother of Us All was Miss Stein's last completed work. It represents an attempt to revivify history, to show historical movements and personalities as these appeared to those personalities themselves and to others living at the time. That time, of course, was not a specific moment but a whole epoch in the life of our country, the last epoch about which any of us can have, through his own memories or through those of persons he has known in his lifetime, a feeling of having been there.

Always faithfully yours,

Virgil Thomson: from *Virgil Thomson* by Virgil Thomson*

I began *The Mother of Us All* on October 10 of 1946. On December 10 the voice-and-piano score was complete up to the last scene. I waited a month before composing that, feeling that I must back off and view the rest. In order to find out what the rest was like, I invited friends to hear me play and sing it. Through performing it for others, as I had done for seven years with *Four Saints*, I could find out how it moved and learn its ways. In January, I composed the final scene; by this time a partial cast was learning roles, with Jack Beeson as *répétiteur*. Otto Leuning, who was to conduct, had as yet no orchestral score; but that was not urgent, since we were not opening till May.

*Excerpt from *Virgil Thomson* by Virgil Thomson. Copyright © 1966 by Virgil Thomson.

The production was for Columbia University's Brander Matthews Theatre, where the house was small but the pit commodious. The cast was part professionals and part students; no one was paid for working in the show. The scenery and costumes were by Paul du Pont; staging was by the choreographer John Taras to a scenario, as before, by Maurice Grosser. I cast all the roles myself, holding auditions in my Hotel Chelsea drawing room. For minor parts we used Columbia students and trained them for understudying the leads. Among the finer singers who took part were Dorothy Dow (later of La Scala) and Teresa Stich-Randall (Mozart specialist and *Kammersängerin*, who now sings everywhere). The names of Belva Kibler, Hazel Gravell, Jean Handzlik, and Alice Howland are remembered by many in the music world, those too of William Horne and Everett Anderson. The stage was beautiful for sight and sound, though not to be compared to my Negroes-and-cellophane *Four Saints*.

The student orchestral players were pretty poor; and Leuning, an experienced opera man, was patient, to prevent nervousness on stage. The instrumental textures, therefore, which I had laid out with transparency in mind, were likely to come out on any night with holes in them. Nevertheless, after the fourth or fifth performance, when I felt the players knew their parts as well as they ever would, I asked Leuning to speed up the pacing. "Can you take twenty minutes off the running time?" I said. "Can do," he answered. And with no cuts made, the next performance came out shorter by that much.

Everybody up-to-date came to hear the new opera, and the press was receptive. The Music Critics' Circle, though reluctant to honor a member, even voted it a special award. Koussevitzky, still angry over criticisms, said to his neighbor (textually), "I do not like it to say it, but I like it." And wrote me to offer a commission for another opera. My colleague Samuel Barber, perhaps also smarting, remarked of my plain-as-Dick's-hatband harmony, "I hope you won't mind my stealing a few of your chords."

From its beginning, *The Mother of Us All* has often been produced by colleges, though it was never designed for amateurs and is difficult for young voices. I have not seen all these productions by any means; but in all that I have seen some charm has come through, for there is in both text and music a nostalgia for nineteenth-century rural America which makes any presentation warm and touching. Western Reserve gave it in Cleveland at elegant Severance Hall; and the orchestra, Cleveland's Philharmonia, was first class. Harvard performances in the Civil War memorial Sanders Theater, with only students singing (and not vocal students either), were so perfectly paced by their conductor, Victor Yellin, then a graduate student, that audiences laughed and applauded, wept at the end. Even at the University of Denver, with everything else precarious, an ingenious stage direction gave the spectacle security, enough at least for Stravinsky to comprehend. But it was not till eighteen years after its birth that it got interesting scenery. Then in 1965, at the University of California, Los Angeles, with Jan Popper conducting, an impressive young soprano, Barbara Gordon (my discovery), singing the role of Susan B., and with myself having coached everybody, including the choreographer, a visual investiture was created by David Hilberman which was an original, evocative, and appropriate as what Florine Stettheimer had created in 1934 for *Four Saints*.

The originality of this scenery lay in its representing neither buildings nor landscapes, but, of all things,

people. It consisted of a set of giant cutouts painted to illustrate nineteenth-century ladies and gentlemen, for all the world like colored prints from some Victorian magazine. And all these flats could be moved horizontally to closed-in or to open stage-positions. They were dark blue in color, a tone rarely effective in painted scenery but one which, when lightly rubbed with red, can take light in glowing vibrant ways. And to the profiled figures slight additions of flowering branches, brief cases, flags, gave to outdoor scenes, to a departure, to a political meeting complete evocation. Moreover, the gigantic proportions of these pictured people reduced our singing actors to human size, a desideratum in not overlarge Schoenberg Hall, where any smaller scaling of the scenery tends to make giants of the actors and to trivialize them. The *Mother* sets were, in addition, airy. For all their largeness and somber color, they did not weigh on the spirit or box-in the play, but gave it space and lightness, as if great distances lay all about and the stage were just the segment of a continent.

Arthur Miller (1915–) was born in New York. In 1938 he graduated from the University of Michigan, where he won several prizes for drama. Six years later he had his first Broadway production, *The Man Who Had All the Luck,* but the play was unlucky and closed after four days. By the time of his first commercial success, *All My Sons* (1947), he had already written eight or nine plays. In 1949 he won a Pulitzer Prize with *Death of a Salesman* and achieved an international reputation. Among his other works are an adaptation (1950) of Ibsen's *Enemy of the People* and a play about the Salem witch trials, *The Crucible* (1953), both containing political implications, and *The Misfits* (1961, a screenplay), *After the Fall* (1964), and *Incident at Vichy* (1965).

COMMENTARY ON *DEATH OF A SALESMAN*

For the ancient Greeks, at least for Aristotle, *pathos* was the destructive or painful act common in tragedy. In English, however, *pathos* refers to an element in art or life that evokes tenderness or sympathetic pity. Modern English critical usage distinguishes between tragic figures and pathetic figures by recognizing some element either of strength or of regeneration in the former that is not in the latter. The tragic protagonists perhaps act so that they bring their destruction upon themselves, or if their destruction comes from outside, they resist it. In either case, they come to at least a partial understanding of the causes of their suffering. Pathetic figures, however, are largely passive, unknowing, and unresisting innocents. In such a view, Macbeth is tragic, but Duncan pathetic. Lear is tragic; Cordelia pathetic. Othello is tragic; Desdemona pathetic. Hamlet is tragic (the situation is not of his making, but he does what he can to alter it); Ophelia pathetic. (Note, by the way, that of the four pathetic figures named, the first is old and the remaining three are women. Pathos is more likely to be evoked by persons assumed to be relatively defenseless than by those who are able-bodied.)

That the spectators were not themselves heroic figures seems to have been assumed by the Greeks and by the Elizabethans; the lesser choral figures or nameless citizens interpret the action and call attention to the fact that even highly placed great heroes are not exempt from pain. Indeed, high place and strenuous activity invite pain: the lofty pine tree or the mariner who ventures far from the coast is more likely to meet destruction than the lowly shrub or the fair-weather sailor. For Greeks of the fifth century B.C.E. and for Elizabethans, high place was not a mere matter of rank, but of worth. In both ages, it was of course known that a king may be unkingly, but it was assumed that kingship required a special nature—though that nature was not always forthcoming. In other words, tragedy deals with kings, not because they are men with a certain title (though of course the title does give them special power), but because they are men with a certain nature. This nature is an extraordinary capacity for action and for feeling; when they make an error, its consequences are enormous, and they themselves feel it as lesser people would not. When Oedipus is polluted, all of Thebes feels it. Arthur Miller is somewhat misleading when he argues (page 843) that because Oedipus has given his name to a complex that the common man may have, the common man is therefore "as apt a subject for tragedy." It is not Oedipus's "complex" but his unique importance that is the issue in the play. Moreover, even if one argues that a person of no public importance may suffer as much as one of public importance (and surely nobody doubts this), one may be faced with the fact that unimportant people by their ordinariness are not particularly good material for drama, and we are here concerned with drama rather than with life. In *Death of a Salesman* Willy Loman's wife says, rightly, "A small man can be just as exhausted as a great man." Yes, but is his exhaustion itself interesting, and do his activities (and this includes the words he utters) before his exhaustion have interesting dramatic possibilities? Isn't there a colorlessness that may weaken the play, an impoverishment of what John Milton called "gorgeous tragedy"?

Inevitably, the rise of the bourgeoisie brought about the rise of bourgeois drama, and in the eighteenth century we get a fair number of tragedies with prologues that insist that characters like ourselves deserve our *pity*:

No fustian hero rages here tonight,
No armies fall, to fix a tyrant's right.
From lower life we draw our scene's distress:
—Let not your equals move your pity less.
GEORGE LILLO, FATAL CURIOSITY (1733)

Note the deflation of older tragedy, the implication that its heroes were "fustian" (bombastic, pretentious) rather than genuinely heroic persons of deep feelings and high aspirations. Put differently, in the bourgeois view older tragedy dealt with persons of high rank, but rank (in this view) is not significant; therefore one may as well show persons of middle rank with whom the middle-class audience may readily identify. At the same time, the dismissal of heroic activities ("no fustian hero *rages*," "no armies *fall*") and the substitution of "distress" indicates that we are well on the road to the hero as victim.

And we have kept on that road. As early as the sixteenth century Copernicus had shown that humanity and its planet were not the center of the universe, but the thought did not distress most people until much later. In 1859 Darwin published *The Origin of Species*, arguing that human beings are not a special creation but creatures that have evolved because "accidental variations" have aided them in the struggle for survival. At about the same time, Marx (who wished to dedicate *Capital* to Darwin) argued that economic forces guide our lives. Early in the twentieth century Freud seemed to argue that we are conditioned by infantile experiences and are enslaved by the dark forces of the id. All in all, by the time of the depression of the 1930s, it was difficult to have much confidence in our ability to shape our destiny. The human condition was a sorry one; we were insignificant, lust-ridden, soulless creatures in a terrifying materialistic universe. A human being was no Oedipus whose moral pollution infected a great city, no Brutus whose deed might bring civil war to Rome. A human being was really not much of anything, except perhaps to a few immediate dependents.

Arthur Miller accurately noted (*Theatre Arts*, October 1953) that American drama "has been a steady year by year documentation of the frustration of man," and it is evident that Miller has set out to restore a sense of importance if not greatness to the individual. In "Tragedy and the Common Man" (see page 843), published in the same year that *Death of a Salesman* was produced and evidently a defense of the play, he argues on behalf of the common man as a tragic figure and he insists that tragedy and pathos are very different: "Pathos truly is the mode of the pessimist. . . . [T]he plays we revere, century after century, are the tragedies. In them, and in them alone, lies the belief—optimistic, if you will—in the perfectibility of man."

Curiously, however, many spectators and readers find that by Miller's own terms Willy Loman fails to be a tragic figure; he seems to them pathetic rather than tragic, a victim rather than a man who acts and who wins our esteem. True, he is partly the victim of his own actions (although he could have chosen to be a carpenter, he chose to live by the bourgeois code that values a white collar), but he seems in larger part to be a victim of the system itself, a system of ruthless competition that has no place for the man who can no longer produce. (Here is an echo of the social-realist drama of the thirties.) Willy had believed in this system. Although his son Biff comes to the realization that Willy "had the wrong dreams," Willy himself seems not to achieve this insight. Of course he knows that he is out of a job, that the system does not value him any longer, but he still seems not to question the values he had subscribed to. Even in the last minutes of the play, when he is planning his suicide in order to provide money for his family—really for Biff—he says such things as, "Can you imagine his magnificence with twenty thousand dollars in his pocket?" and "When the mail comes he'll be ahead of Bernard again." In the preface to his *Collected Plays*, Miller comments on the "exultation" with which Willy faces the end, but it is questionable whether an audience shares it. Many people find that despite the gulf in rank, they can share Hamlet's feelings more easily than Willy's.

Perhaps, however, tradition has been too arbitrary in its use of the word *tragedy*. Perhaps we should be as liberal as the ancient Greeks who did not withhold it from any play that was serious and dignified.

DEATH OF A SALESMAN
Arthur Miller

Certain Private Conversations in Two Acts and a Requiem

LIST OF CHARACTERS

WILLY LOMAN

LINDA

BIFF

HAPPY

BERNARD

THE WOMAN

CHARLEY

UNCLE BEN

HOWARD WAGNER

JENNY

STANLEY

MISS FORSYTHE

LETTA

SCENE

The action takes place in Willy Loman's house and yard and in various places he visits in the New York and Boston of today.

ACT 1

SCENE: *A melody is heard, played upon a flute. It is small and fine, telling of grass and trees and the horizon. The curtain rises.*

Before us is the Salesman's house. We are aware of towering, angular shapes behind it, surrounding it on all sides. Only the blue light of the sky falls upon the house and forestage; the surrounding area shows an angry glow of orange. As more light appears, we see a solid vault of apartment houses around the small, fragile-seeming home. An air of the dream clings to the place, a dream rising out of reality. The kitchen at center seems actual enough, for there is a kitchen table with three chairs, and a refrigerator. But no other fixtures are seen. At the back of the kitchen there is a draped entrance, which leads to the living room. To the right of the kitchen, on a level raised two feet, is a bedroom furnished only with a brass bedstead and a straight chair. On a shelf over the bed a silver athletic trophy stands. A window opens onto the apartment house at the side.

Behind the kitchen, on a level raised six and a half feet, is the boys' bedroom, at present barely visible. Two beds are dimly seen, and at the back of the room a dormer window. (This bedroom is above the unseen living room.) At the left a stairway curves up to it from the kitchen.

The entire setting is wholly or, in some places, partially transparent. The roof-line of the house is one-dimensional; under and over it we see the apartment buildings. Before the house lies an apron, curving beyond the forestage into the orchestra. This forward area serves as the back yard as well as the locale of all Willy's imaginings and of his city scenes. Whenever the action is in the present the actors observe the imaginary wall-lines, entering the house only through its door at the left. But in the scenes of the past these boundaries are broken, and characters enter or leave a room by stepping "through" a wall onto the forestage.

From the right, Willy Loman, the Salesman, enters, carrying two large sample cases. The flute plays on. He hears but is not aware of it. He is past sixty years of age, dressed quietly. Even as he crosses the stage to the doorway of the house, his exhaustion is apparent. He unlocks the door, comes into the kitchen, and thankfully lets his burden down, feeling the soreness of his palms. A word-sigh escapes his lips—it might be "Oh, boy, oh, boy." He closes the door, then carries his cases out into the living room, through the draped kitchen doorway.

Linda, his wife, has stirred in her bed at the right. She gets out and puts on a robe, listening. Most often jovial, she has developed an iron repression of her exceptions to Willy's behavior—she more than loves him, she admires him, as though his mercurial nature, his temper, his massive dreams and little cruelties, served her only as sharp reminders of the turbulent longings within him, longings which she shares but lacks the temperament to utter and follow to their end.

LINDA [*hearing Willy outside the bedroom, calls with some trepidation*]. Willy!

WILLY. It's all right. I came back.

LINDA. Why? What happened? (*Slight pause.*) Did something happen, Willy?

WILLY. No, nothing happened.

LINDA. You didn't smash the car, did you?

WILLY (*with casual irritation*). I said nothing happened. Didn't you hear me?

LINDA. Don't you feel well?

WILLY. I'm tired to the death. (*The flute has faded away. He sits on the bed beside her, a little numb.*) I couldn't make it. I just couldn't make it, Linda.

LINDA (*very carefully, delicately*). Where were you all day? You look terrible.

WILLY. I got as far as a little above Yonkers. I stopped for a cup of coffee. Maybe it was the coffee.

LINDA. What?

WILLY (*after a pause*). I suddenly couldn't drive any more. The car kept going off onto the shoulder, y'know?

LINDA (*helpfully*). Oh. Maybe it was the steering again. I don't think Angelo knows the Studebaker.

WILLY. No, it's me, it's me. Suddenly I realize I'm goin' sixty miles an hour and I don't remember the last five minutes. I'm—I can't seem to—keep my mind to it.

LINDA. Maybe it's your glasses. You never went for your new glasses.

WILLY. No, I see everything. I came back ten miles an hour. It took me nearly four hours from Yonkers.

LINDA (*resigned*). Well, you'll just have to take a rest, Willy, you can't continue this way.

WILLY. I just got back from Florida.

LINDA. But you didn't rest your mind. Your mind is overactive, and the mind is what counts, dear.

WILLY. I'll start out in the morning. Maybe I'll feel better in the morning. (*She is taking off his shoes.*) These goddam arch supports are killing me.

LINDA. Take an aspirin. Should I get you an aspirin? It'll soothe you.

WILLY (*with wonder*). I was driving along, you understand? And I was fine. I was even observing the scenery. You can imagine, me looking at scenery, on the road every week of my life. But it's so beautiful up there, Linda, the trees are so thick, and the sun is warm. I opened the windshield and just let the warm air bathe over me. And then all of a sudden I'm goin' off the road! I'm tellin' ya, I absolutely forgot I was driving. If I'd've gone the other way over the white line I might've killed somebody. So I went on again—and five minutes later I'm dreamin' again, and I nearly . . . (*He presses two fingers against his eyes.*) I have such thoughts, I have such strange thoughts.

LINDA. Willy, dear. Talk to them again. There's no reason why you can't work in New York.

WILLY. They don't need me in New York. I'm the New England man. I'm vital in New England.

LINDA. But you're sixty years old. They can't expect you to keep traveling every week.

WILLY. I'll have to send a wire to Portland. I'm supposed to see Brown and Morrison tomorrow morning at ten o'clock to show the line. Goddammit, I could sell them! (*He starts putting on his jacket.*)

LINDA (*taking the jacket from him*). Why don't you go down to the place tomorrow and tell Howard you've simply got to work in New York? You're too accommodating, dear.

WILLY. If old man Wagner was alive I'd a been in charge of New York now! That man was a prince, he was a masterful man. But that boy of his, that Howard, he don't appreciate. When I went north the first time, the Wagner Company didn't know where New England was!

LINDA. Why don't you tell those things to Howard, dear?

WILLY (*encouraged*). I will, I definitely will. Is there any cheese?

LINDA. I'll make you a sandwich.

WILLY. No, go to sleep. I'll take some milk. I'll be up right away. The boys in?

LINDA. They're sleeping. Happy took Biff on a date tonight.

WILLY (*interested*). That so?

LINDA. It was so nice to see them shaving together, one behind the other, in the bathroom. And going out together. You notice? The whole house smells of shaving lotion.

WILLY. Figure it out. Work a lifetime to pay off a house. You finally own it, and there's nobody to live in it.

LINDA. Well, dear, life is a casting off. It's always that way.

WILLY. No, no, some people—some people accomplish something. Did Biff say anything after I went this morning?

LINDA. You shouldn't have criticized him, Willy, especially after he just got off the train. You mustn't lose your temper with him.

WILLY. When the hell did I lose my temper? I simply asked him if he was making any money. Is that a criticism?

LINDA. But, dear, how could he make any money?

WILLY (*worried and angered*). There's such an undercurrent in him. He became a moody man. Did he apologize when I left this morning?

LINDA. He was crestfallen, Willy. You know how he admires you. I think if he finds himself, then you'll both be happier and not fight any more.

WILLY. How can he find himself on a farm? Is that a life? A farm hand? In the beginning, when he was young, I thought, well, a young man, it's good for him to tramp around, take a lot of different jobs. But it's more than ten years now and he has yet to make thirty-five dollars a week!

LINDA. He's finding himself, Willy.

WILLY. Not finding yourself at the age of thirty-four is a disgrace!

LINDA. Shh!

WILLY. The trouble is he's lazy, goddammit!

LINDA. Willy, please!

WILLY. Biff is a lazy bum!

LINDA. They're sleeping. Get something to eat. Go on down.

WILLY. Why did he come home? I would like to know what brought him home.

LINDA. I don't know. I think he's still lost, Willy. I think he's very lost.

WILLY. Biff Loman is lost. In the greatest country in the world a young man with such—personal attractiveness, gets lost. And such a hard worker. There's one thing about Biff—he's not lazy.

LINDA. Never.

WILLY (*with pity and resolve*). I'll see him in the morning; I'll have a nice talk with him. I'll get him a job selling. He could be big in no time. My God! Remember how they used to follow him around in high school? When he smiled at one of them their faces lit up. When he walked down the street . . . (*He loses himself in reminiscences.*)

LINDA (*trying to bring him out of it*). Willy, dear, I got a new kind of American-type cheese today. It's whipped.

WILLY. Why do you get American when I like Swiss?

LINDA. I just thought you'd like a change . . .

WILLY. I don't want a change! I want Swiss cheese. Why am I always being contradicted?

LINDA (*with a covering laugh*). I thought it would be a surprise.

WILLY. Why don't you open a window in here, for God's sake?

LINDA (*with infinite patience*). They're all open, dear.

WILLY. The way they boxed us in here. Bricks and windows, windows and bricks.

LINDA. We should've bought the land next door.

WILLY. The street is lined with cars. There's not a breath of fresh air in the neighborhood. The grass don't grow any more, you can't raise a carrot in the back yard. They should've had a law against apartment houses. Remember those two beautiful elm trees out there? When I and Biff hung the swing between them?

LINDA. Yeah, like being a million miles from the city.

WILLY. They should've arrested the builder for cutting those down. They massacred the neighborhood. (*Lost.*) More and more I think of those days, Linda. This time of year it was lilac and wisteria. And then the peonies would come out, and the daffodils. What fragrance in this room!

LINDA. Well, after all, people had to move somewhere.

WILLY. No, there's more people now.

LINDA. I don't think there's more people. I think . . .

WILLY. There's more people! That's what's ruining this country! Population is getting out of control. The competition is maddening! Smell the stink from that apartment house! And another one on the other side . . . How can they whip cheese?

On Willy's last line, Biff and Happy raise themselves up in their beds, listening.

LINDA. Go down, try it. And be quiet.

WILLY (*turning to Linda, guiltily*). You're not worried about me, are you, sweetheart?

BIFF. What's the matter?

HAPPY. Listen!

LINDA. You've got too much on the ball to worry about.

WILLY. You're my foundation and my support, Linda.

LINDA. Just try to relax, dear. You make mountains out of molehills.

WILLY. I won't fight with him any more. If he wants to go back to Texas, let him go.

LINDA. He'll find his way.

WILLY. Sure. Certain men just don't get started till later in life. Like Thomas Edison, I think. Or B. F. Goodrich. One of them was deaf. (*He starts for the bedroom doorway.*) I'll put my money on Biff.

LINDA. And Willy—if it's warm Sunday we'll drive in the country. And we'll open the windshield, and take lunch.

WILLY. No, the windshields don't open on the new cars.

LINDA. But you opened it today.

WILLY. Me? I didn't. (*He stops.*) Now isn't that peculiar! Isn't that a remarkable . . . (*He breaks off in amazement and fright as the flute is heard distantly.*)

LINDA. What, darling?

WILLY. That is the most remarkable thing.

LINDA. What, dear?

WILLY. I was thinking of the Chevvy. (*Slight pause.*) Nineteen twenty-eight . . . when I had that red Chevvy . . . (*Breaks off:*) That funny? I coulda sworn I was driving that Chevvy today.

LINDA. Well, that's nothing. Something must've reminded you.

WILLY. Remarkable. Ts. Remember those days? The way Biff used to simonize that car? The dealer refused to believe there was eighty thousand miles on it. (*He shakes his head.*) Heh! (*To Linda.*) Close your eyes, I'll be right up. (*He walks out of the bedroom.*)

HAPPY (*to Biff*). Jesus, maybe he smashed up the car again!

LINDA (*calling after Willy*). Be careful on the stairs, dear! The cheese is on the middle shelf. (*She turns, goes over to the bed, takes his jacket, and goes out of the bedroom.*)

Light has risen on the boys' room. Unseen, Willy is heard talking to himself; "Eighty thousand miles," and a little laugh. Biff gets out of bed, comes downstage a bit, and stands attentively. Biff is two years older than his brother Happy, well built, but in these days bears a worn air and seems less self-assured. He has succeeded less, and his dreams are stronger and less acceptable than Happy's. Happy is tall, powerfully made. Sexuality is like a visible color on him, or a scent that many women have discovered. He, like his brother, is lost, but in a different way, for he has never allowed himself to turn his face toward defeat and is thus more confused and hard-skinned, although seemingly more content.

HAPPY (*getting out of bed*). He's going to get his license taken away if he keeps that up. I'm getting nervous about him, y'know, Biff?

BIFF. His eyes are going.

HAPPY. No, I've driven with him. He sees all right. He just doesn't keep his mind on it. I drove into the city with him last week. He stops at a green light and then it turns red and he goes. (*He laughs.*)

BIFF. Maybe he's color-blind.

HAPPY. Pop? Why he's got the finest eye for color in the business. You know that.

BIFF (*sitting down on his bed*). I'm going to sleep.

HAPPY. You're not still sour on Dad, are you, Biff?

BIFF. He's all right, I guess.

WILLY (*underneath them, in the living room*). Yes, sir, eighty thousand miles—eighty-two thousand!

BIFF. You smoking?

HAPPY (*holding out a pack of cigarettes*). Want one?

BIFF (*taking a cigarette*). I can never sleep when I smell it.

WILLY. What a simonizing job, heh!

HAPPY (*with deep sentiment*). Funny, Biff, y'know? Us sleeping in here again? The old beds. (*He pats his bed affectionately.*) All the talk that went across those beds, huh? Our whole lives.

BIFF. Yeah. Lotta dreams and plans.

HAPPY (*with a deep and masculine laugh*). About five hundred women would like to know what was said in this room. (*They share a soft laugh.*)

BIFF. Remember that big Betsy something—what the hell was her name—over on Bushwick Avenue?

HAPPY (*combing his hair*). With the collie dog!

BIFF. That's the one. I got you in there, remember?

HAPPY. Yeah, that was my first time—I think. Boy, there was a pig. (*They laugh, almost crudely.*) You taught me everything I know about women. Don't forget that.

BIFF. I bet you forgot how bashful you used to be. Especially with girls.

HAPPY. Oh, I still am, Biff.

BIFF. Oh, go on.

HAPPY. I just control it, that's all. I think I got less bashful and you got more so. What happened, Biff? Where's the old humor, the old confidence? (*He shakes Biff's knee. Biff gets up and moves restlessly about the room.*) What's the matter?

BIFF. Why does Dad mock me all the time?

HAPPY. He's not mocking you, he . . .

BIFF. Everything I say there's a twist of mockery on his face. I can't get near him.

HAPPY. He just wants you to make good, that's all. I wanted to talk to you about Dad for a long time, Biff. Something's—happening to him. He—talks to himself.

BIFF. I noticed that this morning. But he always mumbled.

HAPPY. But not so noticeable. It got so embarrassing I sent him to Florida. And you know something? Most of the time he's talking to you.

BIFF. What's he say about me?

HAPPY. I can't make it out.

BIFF. What's he say about me?

HAPPY. I think the fact that you're not settled, that you're still kind of up in the air . . .

BIFF. There's one or two other things depressing him, Happy.

HAPPY. What do you mean?

BIFF. Never mind. Just don't lay it all to me.

HAPPY. But I think if you just got started—I mean—is there any future for you out there?

BIFF. I tell ya, Hap, I don't know what the future is. I don't know—what I'm supposed to want.

HAPPY. What do you mean?

BIFF. Well, I spent six or seven years after high school trying to work myself up. Shipping clerk, salesman, business of one kind or another. And it's a measly manner of existence. To get on that subway on the hot mornings in summer. To devote your whole life to keeping stock, or making phone calls, or selling or buying. To suffer fifty weeks of the year for the sake of a two-week vacation, when all you really desire is to be outdoors, with your shirt off. And always to have to get ahead of the next fella. And still—that's how you build a future.

HAPPY. Well, you really enjoy it on a farm? Are you content out there?

BIFF (*with rising agitation*). Hap, I've had twenty or thirty different kinds of jobs since I left home before the war, and it always turns out the same. I just realized it lately. In Nebraska when I herded cattle, and the Dakotas, and Arizona, and now in Texas. It's why I came home now, I guess, because I realized it. This farm I work on, it's spring there now, see? And they've got about fifteen new colts. There's nothing more inspiring or—beautiful than the sight of a mare and a new colt. And it's cool there now, see? Texas is cool now, and it's spring. And whenever spring comes to where I am, I suddenly get the feeling, my God, I'm not gettin' anywhere! What the hell am I doing, playing around with horses, twenty-eight dollars a week! I'm thirty-four years old, I oughta be makin' my future. That's when I come running home. And now, I get here, and I don't know what to do with myself. (*After a pause.*) I've always made a point of not wasting my life, and everytime I come back here I know that all I've done is to waste my life.

HAPPY. You're a poet, you know that, Biff? You're a—you're an idealist!

BIFF. No, I'm mixed up very bad. Maybe I oughta get married. Maybe I oughta get stuck into something. Maybe that's my trouble. I'm like a boy. I'm not married, I'm not in business, I just—I'm like a boy. Are you content, Hap? You're a success, aren't you? Are you content?

HAPPY. Hell, no!

BIFF. Why? You're making money, aren't you?

HAPPY (*moving about with energy, expressiveness*). All I can do now is wait for the merchandise manager to die. And suppose I get to be merchandise manager? He's a good friend of mine, and he just built a terrific estate on Long Island. And he lived there about two months and sold it, and now he's building another one. He can't enjoy it once it's finished. And I know that's just what I would do. I don't know what the hell I'm workin' for. Sometimes I sit in my apartment—all alone. And I think of the rent I'm paying. And it's crazy. But then, it's what I always wanted. My own apartment, a car, and plenty of women. And still, goddammit, I'm lonely.

BIFF (*with enthusiasm*). Listen, why don't you come out West with me?

HAPPY. You and I, heh?

BIFF. Sure, maybe we could buy a ranch. Raise cattle, use our muscles. Men built like we are should be working out in the open.

HAPPY (*avidly*). The Loman Brothers, heh?

BIFF (*with vast affection*). Sure, we'd be known all over the counties!

HAPPY (*enthralled*). That's what I dream about, Biff. Sometimes I want to just rip my clothes off in the middle of the store and outbox that goddam merchandise manager. I mean I can outbox, outrun, and outlift anybody in that store, and I have to take orders from those common, petty sons-of-bitches till I can't stand it any more.

BIFF. I'm tellin' you, kid, if you were with me I'd be happy out there.

HAPPY (*enthused*). See, Biff, everybody around me is so false that I'm constantly lowering my ideals . . .

BIFF. Baby, together we'd stand up for one another, we'd have someone to trust.

HAPPY. If I were around you . . .

BIFF. Hap, the trouble is we weren't brought up to grub for money. I don't know how to do it.

HAPPY. Neither can I!

BIFF. Then let's go!

HAPPY. The only thing is—what can you make out there?

BIFF. But look at your friend. Builds an estate and then hasn't the peace of mind to live in it.

HAPPY. Yeah, but when he walks into the store the waves part in front of him. That's fifty-two thousand dollars a year coming through the revolving door, and I got more in my pinky finger than he's got in his head.

BIFF. Yeah, but you just said . . .

HAPPY. I gotta show some of those pompous, self-important executives over there that Hap Loman can make the grade. I want to walk into the store the way he walks in. Then I'll go with you, Biff. We'll be together yet, I swear. But take those two we had tonight. Now weren't they gorgeous creatures?

BIFF. Yeah, yeah, most gorgeous I've had in years.

HAPPY. I get that any time I want, Biff. Whenever I feel disgusted. The only trouble is, it gets like bowling or something. I just keep knockin' them over and it doesn't mean anything. You still run around a lot?

BIFF. Naa. I'd like to find a girl—steady, somebody with substance.

HAPPY. That's what I long for.

BIFF. Go on! You'd never come home.

HAPPY. I would! Somebody with character, with resistance! Like Mom, y'know? You're gonna call me a bastard when I tell you this. That girl Charlotte I was with tonight is engaged to be married in five weeks. (*He tries on his new hat.*)

BIFF. No kiddin'!

HAPPY. Sure, the guy's in line for the vice-presidency of the store. I don't know what gets into me, maybe I just have an overdeveloped sense of competition or something, but I went and ruined her, and furthermore I can't get rid of her. And he's the third executive I've done that to. Isn't that a crummy characteristic? And to top it all, I go to their weddings! (*Indignantly, but laughing.*) Like I'm not supposed to take bribes. Manufacturers offer me a hundred-dollar bill now and then to throw an order their way. You know how honest I am, but it's like this girl, see. I hate myself for it. Because I don't want the girl, and, still, I take it and—I love it!

BIFF. Let's go to sleep.

HAPPY. I guess we didn't settle anything, heh?

BIFF. I just got one idea that I think I'm going to try.

HAPPY. What's that?

BIFF. Remember Bill Oliver?

HAPPY. Sure, Oliver is very big now. You want to work for him again?

BIFF. No, but when I quit he said something to me. He put his arm on my shoulder, and he said, "Biff, if you ever need anything, come to me."

HAPPY. I remember that. That sounds good.

BIFF. I think I'll go to see him. If I could get ten thousand or even seven or eight thousand dollars I could buy a beautiful ranch.

HAPPY. I bet he'd back you. 'Cause he thought highly of you, Biff. I mean, they all do. You're well liked, Biff. That's why I say to come back here, and we both have the apartment. And I'm tellin' you, Biff, any babe you want . . .

BIFF. No, with a ranch I could do the work I like and still be something. I just wonder though. I wonder if Oliver still thinks I stole that carton of basketballs.

HAPPY. Oh, he probably forgot that long ago. It's almost ten years. You're too sensitive. Anyway, he didn't really fire you.

BIFF. Well, I think he was going to. I think that's why I quit. I was never sure whether he knew or not. I know he thought the world of me, though. I was the only one he'd let lock up the place.

WILLY (*below*). You gonna wash the engine, Biff?

HAPPY. Shh!

Biff looks at Happy, who is gazing down, listening. Willy is mumbling in the parlor.

HAPPY. You hear that?

They listen. Willy laughs warmly.

BIFF (*growing angry*). Doesn't he know Mom can hear that?

WILLY. Don't get your sweater dirty, Biff!

A look of pain crosses Biff's face.

HAPPY. Isn't that terrible? Don't leave again, will you? You'll find a job here. You gotta stick around. I don't know what to do about him, it's getting embarrassing.

WILLY. What a simonizing job!

BIFF. Mom's hearing that!

WILLY. No kiddin', Biff, you got a date? Wonderful!

HAPPY. Go on to sleep. But talk to him in the morning, will you?

BIFF (*reluctantly getting into bed*). With her in the house. Brother!

HAPPY (*getting into bed*). I wish you'd have a good talk with him.

The light on their room begins to fade.

BIFF (*to himself in bed*). That selfish, stupid . . .

HAPPY. Sh . . . Sleep, Biff.

Their light is out. Well before they have finished speaking, Willy's form is dimly seen below in the darkened kitchen. He opens the refrigerator, searches in there, and takes out a bottle of milk. The apartment houses are fading out, and the entire house and surroundings become covered with leaves. Music insinuates itself as the leaves appear.

WILLY. Just wanna be careful with those girls, Biff, that's all. Don't make any promises. No promises of any kind. Because a girl, y'know, they always believe what you tell 'em, and you're very young, Biff, you're too young to be talking seriously to girls.

Light rises on the kitchen. Willy, talking, shuts the refrigerator door and comes downstage to the kitchen table. He pours milk into a glass. He is totally immersed in himself, smiling faintly.

WILLY. Too young entirely, Biff. You want to watch your schooling first. Then when you're all set, there'll be plenty of girls for a boy like you. (*He smiles broadly at a kitchen chair.*) That so? The girls pay for you? (*He laughs.*) Boy, you must really be makin' a hit.

Willy is gradually addressing—physically—a point offstage, speaking through the wall of the kitchen, and his voice has been rising in volume to that of a normal conversation.

WILLY. I been wondering why you polish the car so careful. Ha! Don't leave the hubcaps, boys. Get the chamois to the hubcaps. Happy, use newspaper on the windows, it's the easiest thing. Show him how to do it, Biff! You see, Happy? Pad it up, use it like a pad. That's it, that's it, good work. You're doin' all right, Hap. (*He pauses, then nods in approbation for a few seconds, then looks upward.*) Biff, first thing we gotta do when we get time is clip that big branch over the house. Afraid it's gonna fall in a

storm and hit the roof. Tell you what. We get a rope and sling her around, and then we climb up there with a couple of saws and take her down. Soon as you finish the car, boys, I wanna see ya. I got a surprise for you, boys.

BIFF (*offstage*). Whatta ya got, Dad?

WILLY. No, you finish first. Never leave a job till you're finished—remember that. (*Looking toward the "big trees."*) Biff, up in Albany I saw a beautiful hammock. I think I'll buy it next trip, and we'll hang it right between those two elms. Wouldn't that be something? Just swingin' there under those branches. Boy, that would be . . .

Young Biff and Young Happy appear from the direction Willy was addressing. Happy carries rags and a pail of water. Biff, wearing a sweater with a block "S," carries a football.

BIFF (*pointing in the direction of the car offstage*). How's that, Pop, professional?

WILLY. Terrific. Terrific job, boys. Good work, Biff.

HAPPY. Where's the surprise, Pop?

WILLY. In the back seat of the car.

HAPPY. Boy! (*He runs off.*)

BIFF. What is it, Dad? Tell me, what'd you buy?

WILLY (*laughing, cuffs him*). Never mind, something I want you to have.

BIFF (*turns and starts off*). What is it, Hap?

HAPPY (*offstage*). It's a punching bag!

BIFF. Oh, Pop!

WILLY. It's got Gene Tunney's signature on it!

Happy runs onstage with a punching bag.

BIFF. Gee, how'd you know we wanted a punching bag?

WILLY. Well, it's the finest thing for the timing.

HAPPY (*lies down on his back and pedals with his feet*). I'm losing weight, you notice, Pop?

WILLY (*to Happy*). Jumping rope is good too.

BIFF. Did you see the new football I got?

WILLY (*examining the ball*). Where'd you get a new ball?

BIFF. The coach told me to practice my passing.

WILLY. That so? And he gave you the ball, heh?

BIFF. Well, I borrowed it from the locker room. (*He laughs confidentially.*)

WILLY (*laughing with him at the theft*). I want you to return that.

HAPPY. I told you he wouldn't like it!

BIFF (*angrily*). Well, I'm bringing it back!

WILLY (*stopping the incipient argument, to Happy*). Sure, he's gotta practice with a regulation ball, doesn't he? (*To Biff.*) Coach'll probably congratulate you on your initiative!

BIFF. Oh, he keeps congratulating my initiative all the time, Pop.

WILLY. That's because he likes you. If somebody else took that ball there'd be an uproar. So what's the report, boys, what's the report?

BIFF. Where'd you go this time, Dad? Gee we were lonesome for you.

WILLY (*pleased, puts an arm around each boy and they come down to the apron*). Lonesome, heh?

BIFF. Missed you every minute.

WILLY. Don't say? Tell you a secret, boys. Don't breathe it to a soul. Someday I'll have my own business, and I'll never have to leave home any more.

HAPPY. Like Uncle Charley, heh?

WILLY. Bigger than Uncle Charley! Because Charley is not—liked. He's liked, but he's not—well liked.

BIFF. Where'd you go this time, Dad?

WILLY. Well, I got on the road, and I went north to Providence. Met the Mayor.

BIFF. The Mayor of Providence!

WILLY. He was sitting in the hotel lobby.

BIFF. What'd he say?

WILLY. He said, "Morning!" And I said, "Morning!" And I said, "You got a fine city here, Mayor." And then he had coffee with me. And then I went to Waterbury. Waterbury is a fine city. Big clock city, the famous Waterbury clock. Sold a nice bill there. And then Boston—Boston is the cradle of the Revolution. A fine city. And a couple of other towns in Mass., and on to Portland and Bangor and straight home!

BIFF. Gee, I'd love to go with you sometime, Dad.

WILLY. Soon as summer comes.

HAPPY. Promise?

WILLY. You and Hap and I, and I'll show you all the towns. America is full of beautiful towns and fine, upstanding people. And they know me, boys, they know me up and down New England. The finest people. And when I bring you fellas up, there'll be open sesame for all of us, 'cause one thing, boys: I have friends. I can park my car in any street in New England, and the cops protect it like their own. This summer, heh?

BIFF AND HAPPY (*together*). Yeah! You bet!

WILLY. We'll take our bathing suits.

HAPPY. We'll carry your bags, Pop!

WILLY. Oh, won't that be something! Me comin' into the Boston stores with you boys carryin' my bags. What a sensation!

Biff is prancing around, practicing passing the ball.

WILLY. You nervous, Biff, about the game?

BIFF. Not if you're gonna be there.

WILLY. What do they say about you in school, now that they made you captain?

HAPPY. There's a crowd of girls behind him everytime the classes change.

BIFF (*taking Willy's hand*). This Saturday, Pop, this Saturday—just for you, I'm going to break through for a touchdown.

HAPPY. You're supposed to pass.

BIFF. I'm takin' one play for Pop. You watch me, Pop, and when I take off my helmet, that means I'm breakin' out. Then you watch me crash through that line!

WILLY (*kisses Biff*). Oh, wait'll I tell this in Boston!

Bernard enters in knickers. He is younger than Biff, earnest and loyal, a worried boy.

BERNARD. Biff, where are you? You're supposed to study with me today.

WILLY. Hey, looka Bernard. What're you lookin' so anemic about, Bernard?

BERNARD. He's gotta study, Uncle Willy. He's got Regents next week.

HAPPY (*tauntingly, spinning Bernard around*). Let's box, Bernard!

BERNARD. Biff! (*He gets away from Happy.*) Listen, Biff, I heard Mr. Birnbaum say that if you don't start studyin' math he's gonna flunk you, and you won't graduate. I heard him!

WILLY. You better study with him, Biff. Go ahead now.

BERNARD. I heard him!

BIFF. Oh, Pop, you didn't see my sneakers! (*He holds up a foot for Willy to look at.*)

WILLY. Hey, that's a beautiful job of printing!

BERNARD (*wiping his glasses*). Just because he printed University of Virginia on his sneakers doesn't mean they've got to graduate him, Uncle Willy!

WILLY (*angrily*). What're you talking about? With scholarships to three universities they're gonna flunk him?

BERNARD. But I heard Mr. Birnbaum say . . .

WILLY. Don't be a pest, Bernard! (*To his boys.*) What an anemic!

BERNARD. Okay, I'm waiting for you in my house, Biff.

Bernard goes off. The Lomans laugh.

WILLY. Bernard is not well liked, is he?

BIFF. He's liked, but he's not well liked.

HAPPY. That's right, Pop.

WILLY. That's just what I mean. Bernard can get the best marks in school, y'understand, but when he gets out in the business world, y'understand, you are going to be five times ahead of him. That's why I thank Almighty God you're both built like Adonises. Because the man who makes an appearance in the business world, the man who creates personal interest, is the man who gets ahead. Be liked and you will never want. You take me, for instance. I never have to wait in line to see a buyer. "Willy Loman is here!" That's all they have to know, and I go right through.

BIFF. Did you knock them dead, Pop?

WILLY. Knocked 'em cold in Providence, slaughtered 'em in Boston.

HAPPY (*on his back, pedaling again*). I'm losing weight, you notice, Pop?

Linda enters as of old, a ribbon in her hair, carrying a bas-
ket of washing.

LINDA (*with youthful energy*). Hello, dear!

WILLY. Sweetheart!

LINDA. How'd the Chevvy run?

WILLY. Chevrolet, Linda, is the greatest car ever built. (*To the*
boys.) Since when do you let your mother carry wash up
the stairs?

BIFF. Grab hold there, boy!

HAPPY. Where to, Mom?

LINDA. Hang them up on the line. And you better go down
to your friends, Biff. The cellar is full of boys. They don't
know what to do with themselves.

BIFF. Ah, when Pop comes home they can wait!

WILLY (*laughs appreciatively*). You better go down and tell
them what to do. Biff.

BIFF. I think I'll have them sweep out the furnace room.

WILLY. Good work, Biff.

BIFF (*goes through wall-line of kitchen to doorway at back and*
calls down). Fellas! Everybody sweep out the furnace
room! I'll be right down!

VOICES. All right! Okay, Biff.

BIFF. George and Sam and Frank, come out back! We're
hangin' up the wash! Come on, Hap, on the double! (*He*
and Happy carry out the basket.)

LINDA. The way they obey him!

WILLY. Well, that's training, the training. I'm tellin' you, I was
sellin' thousands and thousands, but I had to come home.

LINDA. Oh, the whole block'll be at that game. Did you sell
anything?

WILLY. I did five hundred gross in Providence and seven hundred gross in Boston.

LINDA. No! Wait a minute. I've got a pencil. (*She pulls pencil*
and paper out of her apron pocket.) That makes your commission . . . Two hundred—my God! Two hundred and
twelve dollars!

WILLY. Well, I didn't figure it yet, but . . .

LINDA. How much did you do?

WILLY. Well, I—I did—about a hundred and eighty gross in
Providence. Well, no—it came to—roughly two hundred
gross on the whole trip.

LINDA (*without hesitation*). Two hundred gross. That's . . . (*She*
figures.)

WILLY. The trouble was that three of the stores were half-
closed for inventory in Boston. Otherwise I woulda broke
records.

LINDA. Well, it makes seventy dollars and some pennies.
That's very good.

WILLY. What do we owe?

LINDA. Well, on the first there's sixteen dollars on the refrigerator . . .

WILLY. Why sixteen?

LINDA. Well, the fan belt broke, so it was a dollar eighty.

WILLY. But it's brand new.

LINDA. Well, the man said that's the way it is. Till they work
themselves in, y'know.

They move through the wall-line into the kitchen.

WILLY. I hope we didn't get stuck on that machine.

LINDA. They got the biggest ads of any of them!

WILLY. I know, it's a fine machine. What else?

LINDA. Well, there's nine-sixty for the washing machine.
And for the vacuum cleaner there's three and a half due
on the fifteenth. Then the roof, you got twenty-one dollars remaining.

WILLY. It don't leak, does it?

LINDA. No, they did a wonderful job. Then you owe Frank
for the carburetor.

WILLY. I'm not going to pay that man! That goddam Chevrolet, they ought to prohibit the manufacture of that car!

LINDA. Well, you owe him three and a half. And odds and
ends, comes to around a hundred and twenty dollars by
the fifteenth.

WILLY. A hundred and twenty dollars! My God, if business
don't pick up I don't know what I'm gonna do!

LINDA. Well, next week you'll do better.

WILLY. Oh, I'll knock 'em dead next week. I'll go to Hartford.
I'm very well liked in Hartford. You know, the trouble is,
Linda, people don't seem to take to me.

They move onto the forestage.

LINDA. Oh, don't be foolish.

WILLY. I know it when I walk in. They seem to laugh at me.

LINDA. Why? Why would they laugh at you? Don't talk that
way, Willy.

Willy moves to the edge of the stage. Linda goes into the
kitchen and starts to darn stockings.

WILLY. I don't know the reason for it, but they just pass me
by. I'm not noticed.

LINDA. But you're doing wonderful, dear. You're making seventy to a hundred dollars a week.

WILLY. But I gotta be at it ten, twelve hours a day. Other
men—I don't know—they do it easier. I don't know
why—I can't stop myself—I talk too much. A man
oughta come in with a few words. One thing about
Charley. He's a man of few words, and they respect him.

LINDA. You don't talk too much, you're just lively.

WILLY (*smiling*). Well, I figure, what the hell, life is short, a
couple of jokes. (*To himself:*) I joke too much! (*The smile*
goes.)

LINDA. Why? You're . . .

WILLY. I'm fat. I'm very—foolish to look at, Linda. I didn't
tell you, but Christmas time I happened to be calling on
F. H. Stewarts, and a salesman I know, as I was going in to

see the buyer I heard him say something about—walrus. And I—I cracked him right across the face. I won't take that. I simply will not take that. But they do laugh at me. I know that.

LINDA. Darling . . .

WILLY. I gotta overcome it. I know I gotta overcome it. I'm not dressing to advantage, maybe.

LINDA. Willy, darling, you're the handsomest man in the world . . .

WILLY. Oh, no, Linda.

LINDA. To me you are. (*Slight pause.*) The handsomest.

From the darkness is heard the laughter of a woman. Willy doesn't turn to it, but it continues through Linda's lines.

LINDA. And the boys, Willy. Few men are idolized by their children the way you are.

Music is heard as behind a scrim, to the left of the house; The Woman, dimly seen, is dressing.

WILLY (*with great feeling*). You're the best there is. Linda, you're a pal, you know that? On the road—on the road I want to grab you sometimes and just kiss the life outa you.

The laughter is loud now, and he moves into a brightening area at the left, where The Woman has come from behind the scrim and is standing, putting on her hat, looking into a "mirror" and laughing.

WILLY. 'Cause I get so lonely—especially when business is bad and there's nobody to talk to. I get the feeling that I'll never sell anything again, that I won't make a living for you, or a business, a business for the boys. (*He talks through The Woman's subsiding laughter; The Woman primps at the "mirror."*) There's so much I want to make for . . .

THE WOMAN. Me? You didn't make me, Willy. I picked you.

WILLY (*pleased*). You picked me?

THE WOMAN (*who is quite proper-looking, Willy's age*). I did. I've been sitting at that desk watching all the salesmen go by, day in, day out. But you've got such a sense of humor, and we do have such a good time together, don't we?

WILLY. Sure, sure. (*He takes her in his arms.*) Why do you have to go now?

THE WOMAN. It's two o'clock . . .

WILLY. No, come on in! (*He pulls her.*)

THE WOMAN. . . . my sisters'll be scandalized. When'll you be back?

WILLY. Oh, two weeks about. Will you come up again?

THE WOMAN. Sure thing. You do make me laugh. It's good for me. (*She squeezes his arm, kisses him.*) And I think you're a wonderful man.

WILLY. You picked me, heh?

THE WOMAN. Sure. Because you're so sweet. And such a kidder.

WILLY. Well, I'll see you next time I'm in Boston.

THE WOMAN. I'll put you right through to the buyers.

WILLY (*slapping her bottom*). Right. Well, bottoms up!

THE WOMAN (*slaps him gently and laughs*). You just kill me, Willy. (*He suddenly grabs her and kisses her roughly.*) You kill me. And thanks for the stockings. I love a lot of stockings. Well, good night.

WILLY. Good night. And keep your pores open!

THE WOMAN. Oh, Willy!

The Woman bursts out laughing, and Linda's laughter blends in. The Woman disappears into the dark. Now the area at the kitchen table brightens. Linda is sitting where she was at the kitchen table, but now is mending a pair of her silk stockings.

LINDA. You are, Willy. The handsomest man. You've got no reason to feel that . . .

WILLY (*coming out of The Woman's dimming area and going over to Linda*). I'll make it all up to you, Linda, I'll . . .

LINDA. There's nothing to make up, dear. You're doing fine, better than . . .

WILLY (*noticing her mending*). What's that?

LINDA. Just mending my stockings. They're so expensive . . .

WILLY (*angrily, taking them from her*). I won't have you mending stockings in this house! Now throw them out!

Linda puts the stockings in her pocket.

BERNARD (*entering on the run*). Where is he? If he doesn't study!

WILLY (*moving to the forestage, with great agitation*). You'll give him the answers!

BERNARD. I do, but I can't on a Regents! That's a state exam! They're liable to arrest me!

WILLY. Where is he? I'll whip him, I'll whip him!

LINDA. And he'd better give back that football, Willy, it's not nice.

WILLY. Biff! Where is he? Why is he taking everything?

LINDA. He's too rough with the girls, Willy. All the mothers are afraid of him!

WILLY. I'll whip him!

BERNARD. He's driving the car without a license!

The Woman's laugh is heard.

WILLY. Shut up!

LINDA. All the mothers . . .

WILLY. Shut up!

BERNARD (*backing quietly away and out*). Mr. Birnbaum says he's stuck up.

WILLY. Get outa here!

BERNARD. If he doesn't buckle down he'll flunk math! (*He goes off.*)

LINDA. He's right, Willy, you've gotta . . .

WILLY (*exploding at her*). There's nothing the matter with him! You want him to be a worm like Bernard? He's got spirit, personality . . .

As he speaks, Linda, almost in tears, exits into the living room. Willy is alone in the kitchen, wilting and staring. The leaves are gone. It is night again, and the apartment houses look down from behind.

WILLY. Loaded with it. Loaded! What is he stealing? He's giving it back, isn't he? Why is he stealing? What did I tell him? I never in my life told him anything but decent things.

Happy in pajamas has come down the stairs; Willy suddenly becomes aware of Happy's presence.

HAPPY. Let's go now, come on.

WILLY (*sitting down at the kitchen table*). Huh! Why did she have to wax the floors herself? Everytime she waxes the floors she keels over. She knows that!

HAPPY. Shh! Take it easy. What brought you back tonight?

WILLY. I got an awful scare. Nearly hit a kid in Yonkers. God! Why didn't I go to Alaska with my brother Ben that time! Ben! That man was a genius, that man was success incarnate! What a mistake! He begged me to go.

HAPPY. Well, there's no use in . . .

WILLY. You guys! There was a man started with the clothes on his back and ended up with diamond mines!

HAPPY. Boy, someday I'd like to know how he did it.

WILLY. What's the mystery? The man knew what he wanted and went out and got it! Walked into a jungle, and comes out, the age of twenty-one, and he's rich! The world is an oyster, but you don't crack it open on a mattress!

HAPPY. Pop, I told you I'm gonna retire you for life.

WILLY. You'll retire me for life on seventy goddam dollars a week? And your women and your car and your apartment, and you'll retire me for life! Christ's sake, I couldn't get past Yonkers today! Where are you guys, where are you? The woods are burning! I can't drive a car!

Charley has appeared in the doorway. He is a large man, slow of speech, laconic, immovable. In all he says, despite what he says, there is pity, and, now, trepidation. He has a robe over pajamas, slippers on his feet. He enters the kitchen.

CHARLEY. Everything all right?

HAPPY. Yeah, Charley, everything's . . .

WILLY. What's the matter?

CHARLEY. I heard some noise. I thought something happened. Can't we do something about the walls? You sneeze in here, and in my house hats blow off.

HAPPY. Let's go to bed, Dad. Come on.

Charley signals to Happy to go.

WILLY. You go ahead, I'm not tired at the moment.

HAPPY (*to Willy*). Take it easy, huh? (*He exits.*)

WILLY. What're you doin' up?

CHARLEY (*sitting down at the kitchen table opposite Willy*). Couldn't sleep good. I had a heartburn.

WILLY. Well, you don't know how to eat.

CHARLEY. I eat with my mouth.

WILLY. No, you're ignorant. You gotta know about vitamins and things like that.

CHARLEY. Come on, let's shoot. Tire you out a little.

WILLY (*hesitantly*). All right. You got cards?

CHARLEY (*taking a deck from his pocket*). Yeah, I got them. Someplace. What is it with those vitamins?

WILLY (*dealing*). They build up your bones. Chemistry.

CHARLEY. Yeah, but there's no bones in a heartburn.

WILLY. What are you talkin' about? Do you know the first thing about it?

CHARLEY. Don't get insulted.

WILLY. Don't talk about something you don't know anything about.

They are playing. Pause.

CHARLEY. What're you doin' home?

WILLY. A little trouble with the car.

CHARLEY. Oh. (*Pause.*) I'd like to take a trip to California.

WILLY. Don't say.

CHARLEY. You want a job?

WILLY. I got a job, I told you that. (*After a slight pause.*) What the hell are you offering me a job for?

CHARLEY. Don't get insulted.

WILLY. Don't insult me.

CHARLEY. I don't see no sense in it. You don't have to go on this way.

WILLY. I got a good job. (*Slight pause.*) What do you keep comin' in here for?

CHARLEY. You want me to go?

WILLY (*after a pause, withering*). I can't understand it. He's going back to Texas again. What the hell is that?

CHARLEY. Let him go.

WILLY. I got nothin' to give him, Charley, I'm clean, I'm clean.

CHARLEY. He won't starve. None a them starve. Forget about him.

WILLY. Then what have I got to remember?

CHARLEY. You take it too hard. To hell with it. When a deposit bottle is broken you don't get your nickel back.

WILLY. That's easy enough for you to say.

CHARLEY. That ain't easy for me to say.

WILLY. Did you see the ceiling I put up in the living room?

CHARLEY. Yeah, that's a piece of work. To put up a ceiling is a mystery to me. How do you do it?

WILLY. What's the difference?

CHARLEY. Well, talk about it.

WILLY. You gonna put up a ceiling?

CHARLEY. How could I put up a ceiling?

WILLY. Then what the hell are you bothering me for?

CHARLEY. You're insulted again.

WILLY. A man who can't handle tools is not a man. You're disgusting.

CHARLEY. Don't call me disgusting, Willy.

Uncle Ben, carrying a valise and an umbrella, enters the forestage from around the right corner of the house. He is a stolid man, in his sixties, with a mustache and an authoritative air. He is utterly certain of his destiny, and there is an aura of far places about him. He enters exactly as Willy speaks.

WILLY. I'm getting awfully tired, Ben.

Ben's music is heard. Ben looks around at everything.

CHARLEY. Good, keep playing; you'll sleep better. Did you call me Ben?

Ben looks at his watch.

WILLY. That's funny. For a second there you reminded me of my brother Ben.

BEN. I only have a few minutes. (*He strolls, inspecting the place. Willy and Charley continue playing.*)

CHARLEY. You never heard from him again, heh? Since that time?

WILLY. Didn't Linda tell you? Couple of weeks ago we got a letter from his wife in Africa. He died.

CHARLEY. That so.

BEN (*chuckling*). So this is Brooklyn, eh?

CHARLEY. Maybe you're in for some of his money.

WILLY. Naa, he had seven sons. There's just one opportunity I had with that man . . .

BEN. I must make a train, William. There are several properties I'm looking at in Alaska.

WILLY. Sure, sure! If I'd gone with him to Alaska that time, everything would've been totally different.

CHARLEY. Go on, you'd froze to death up there.

WILLY. What're you talking about?

BEN. Opportunity is tremendous in Alaska, William. Surprised you're not up there.

WILLY. Sure, tremendous.

CHARLEY. Heh?

WILLY. There was the only man I ever met who knew the answers.

CHARLEY. Who?

BEN. How are you all?

WILLY (*taking a pot, smiling*). Fine, fine.

CHARLEY. Pretty sharp tonight.

BEN. Is Mother living with you?

WILLY. No, she died a long time ago.

CHARLEY. Who?

BEN. That's too bad. Fine specimen of a lady, Mother.

WILLY (*to Charley*). Heh?

BEN. I'd hoped to see the old girl.

CHARLEY. Who died?

BEN. Heard anything from Father, have you?

WILLY (*unnerved*). What do you mean, who died?

CHARLEY (*taking a pot*). What're you talkin' about?

BEN (*looking at his watch*). William, it's half-past eight!

WILLY (*as though to dispel his confusion he angrily stops Charley's hand*). That's my build!

CHARLEY. I put the ace . . .

WILLY. If you don't know how to play the game I'm not gonna throw my money away on you!

CHARLEY (*rising*). It was my ace, for God's sake!

WILLY. I'm through, I'm through!

BEN. When did Mother die?

WILLY. Long ago. Since the beginning you never knew how to play cards.

CHARLEY (*picks up the cards and goes to the door*). All right! Next time I'll bring a deck with five aces.

WILLY. I don't play that kind of game!

CHARLEY (*turning to him*). You ought to be ashamed of yourself!

WILLY. Yeah?

CHARLEY. Yeah! (*He goes out.*)

WILLY (*slamming the door after him*). Ignoramus!

BEN (*as Willy comes toward him through the wall-line of the kitchen*). So you're William.

WILLY (*shaking Ben's hand*). Ben! I've been waiting for you so long! What's the answer? How did you do it?

BEN. Oh, there's a story in that.

Linda enters the forestage, as of old, carrying the wash basket.

LINDA. Is this Ben?

BEN (*gallantly*). How do you do, my dear.

LINDA. Where've you been all these years? Willy's always wondered why you . . .

WILLY (*pulling Ben away from her impatiently*). Where is Dad? Didn't you follow him? How did you get started?

BEN. Well, I don't know how much you remember.

WILLY. Well, I was just a baby, of course, only three or four years old . . .

BEN. Three years and eleven months.

WILLY. What a memory, Ben!

BEN. I have many enterprises, William, and I have never kept books.

WILLY. I remember I was sitting under the wagon in—was it Nebraska?

BEN. It was South Dakota, and I gave you a bunch of wild flowers.

WILLY. I remember you walking away down some open road.

BEN (*laughing*). I was going to find Father in Alaska.

WILLY. Where is he?

BEN. At that age I had a very faulty view of geography, William. I discovered after a few days that I was heading due south, so instead of Alaska, I ended up in Africa.

LINDA. Africa!

WILLY. The Gold Coast!

BEN. Principally diamond mines.

LINDA. Diamond mines!

BEN. Yes, my dear. But I've only a few minutes . . .

WILLY. No! Boys! Boys! (*Young Biff and Happy appear.*) Listen to this. This is your Uncle Ben, a great man! Tell my boys, Ben!

BEN. Why, boys, when I was seventeen I walked into the jungle, and when I was twenty-one I walked out. (*He laughs.*) And by God I was rich.

WILLY (*to the boys*). You see what I been talking about? The greatest things can happen!

BEN (*glancing at his watch*). I have an appointment in Ketchikan Tuesday week.

WILLY. No, Ben! Please tell about Dad. I want my boys to hear. I want them to know the kind of stock they spring from. All I remember is a man with a big beard, and I was in Mamma's lap, sitting around a fire, and some kind of high music.

BEN. His flute. He played the flute.

WILLY. Sure, the flute, that's right!

New music is heard, a high, rollicking tune.

BEN. Father was a very great and a very wild-hearted man. We would start in Boston, and he'd toss the whole family into the wagon, and then he'd drive the team right across the country; through Ohio, and Indiana, Michigan, Illinois, and all the Western states. And we'd stop in the towns and sell the flutes that he'd made on the way. Great inventor, Father. With one gadget he made more in a week than a man like you could make in a lifetime.

WILLY. That's just the way I'm bringing them up, Ben—rugged, well liked, all-around.

BEN. Yeah? (*To Biff.*) Hit that, boy—hard as you can. (*He pounds his stomach.*)

BIFF. Oh, no, sir!

BEN (*taking boxing stance*). Come on, get to me! (*He laughs.*)

WILLY. Go to it. Biff! Go ahead, show him!

BIFF. Okay! (*He cocks his fists and starts in.*)

LINDA (*to Willy*). Why must he fight, dear?

BEN (*sparring with Biff*). Good boy! Good boy!

WILLY. How's that, Ben, heh?

HAPPY. Give him the left, Biff!

LINDA. Why are you fighting?

BEN. Good boy! (*Suddenly comes in, trips Biff, and stands over him, the point of his umbrella poised over Biff's eye.*)

LINDA. Look out, Biff!

BIFF. Gee!

BEN (*patting Biff's knee*). Never fight fair with a stranger, boy. You'll never get out of the jungle that way. (*Taking Linda's hand and bowing.*) It was an honor and a pleasure to meet you, Linda.

LINDA (*withdrawing her hand coldly, frightened*). Have a nice—trip.

BEN (*to Willy*). And good luck with your—what do you do?

WILLY. Selling.

BEN. Yes. Well . . . (*He raises his hand in farewell to all.*)

WILLY. No, Ben, I don't want you to think . . . (*He takes Ben's arm to show him.*) It's Brooklyn, I know, but we hunt too.

BEN. Really, now.

WILLY. Oh, sure, there's snakes and rabbits and—that's why I moved out here. Why, Biff can fell any one of these trees in no time! Boys! Go right over to where they're building the apartment house and get some sand. We're gonna rebuild the entire front stoop right now! Watch this, Ben!

BIFF. Yes, sir! On the double, Hap!

HAPPY (*as he and Biff run off*). I lost weight, Pop, you notice?

Charley enters in knickers, even before the boys are gone.

CHARLEY. Listen, if they steal any more from that building the watchman'll put the cops on them!

LINDA (*to Willy*). Don't let Biff . . .

Ben laughs lustily.

WILLY. You shoulda seen the lumber they brought home last week. At least a dozen six-by-tens worth all kinds a money.

CHARLEY. Listen, if that watchman . . .

WILLY. I gave them hell, understand. But I got a couple of fearless characters there.

CHARLEY. Willy, the jails are full of fearless characters.

BEN (*clapping Willy on the back, with a laugh at Charley*). And the stock exchange, friend!

WILLY (*joining in Ben's laughter*). Where are the rest of your pants?

CHARLEY. My wife bought them.

WILLY. Now all you need is a golf club and you can go upstairs and go to sleep. (*To Ben.*) Great athlete! Between him and his son Bernard they can't hammer a nail!

BERNARD (*rushing in*). The watchman's chasing Biff!

WILLY (*angrily*). Shut up! He's not stealing anything!

LINDA (*alarmed, hurrying off left*). Where is he? Biff, dear! (*She exits.*)

WILLY (*moving toward the left, away from Ben*). There's nothing wrong. What's the matter with you?

BEN. Nervy boy. Good!

WILLY (*laughing*). Oh, nerves of iron, that Biff!

CHARLEY. Don't know what it is. My New England man comes back and he's bleedin', they murdered him up there.

WILLY. It's contacts, Charley, I got important contacts!

CHARLEY (*sarcastically*). Glad to hear it, Willy. Come in later, we'll shoot a little casino. I'll take some of your Portland money. (*He laughs at Willy and exits.*)

WILLY (*turning to Ben*). Business is bad, it's murderous. But not for me, of course.

BEN. I'll stop by on my way back to Africa.

WILLY (*longingly*). Can't you stay a few days? You're just what I need, Ben, because I—I have a fine position here, but

I—well, Dad left when I was such a baby and I never had a chance to talk to him and I still feel—kind of temporary about myself.

BEN. I'll be late for my train.

They are at opposite ends of the stage.

WILLY. Ben, my boys—can't we talk? They'd go into the jaws of hell for me, see, but I . . .

BEN. William, you're being first-rate with your boys. Outstanding, manly chaps!

WILLY (*hanging on to his words*). Oh, Ben, that's good to hear! Because sometimes I'm afraid that I'm not teaching them the right kind of—Ben, how should I teach them?

BEN (*giving great weight to each word, and with a certain vicious audacity*). William, when I walked into the jungle, I was seventeen. When I walked out I was twenty-one. And, by God, I was rich! (*He goes off into darkness around the right corner of the house.*)

WILLY. . . . was rich! That's just the spirit I want to imbue them with! To walk into a jungle! I was right! I was right! I was right!

Ben is gone, but Willy is still speaking to him as Linda, in nightgown and robe, enters the kitchen, glances around for Willy, then goes to the door of the house, looks out and sees him. Comes down to his left. He looks at her.

LINDA. Willy, dear? Willy?

WILLY. I was right!

LINDA. Did you have some cheese? (*He can't answer.*) It's very late, darling. Come to bed, heh?

WILLY (*looking straight up*). Gotta break your neck to see a star in this yard.

LINDA. You coming in?

WILLY. Whatever happened to that diamond watch fob? Remember? When Ben came from Africa that time? Didn't he give me a watch fob with a diamond in it?

LINDA. You pawned it, dear. Twelve, thirteen years ago. For Biff's radio correspondence course.

WILLY. Gee, that was a beautiful thing. I'll take a walk.

LINDA. But you're in your slippers.

WILLY (*starting to go around the house at the left*). I was right! I was! (*Half to Linda, as he goes, shaking his head.*) What a man! There was a man worth talking to. I was right!

LINDA (*calling after Willy*). But in your slippers, Willy!

Willy is almost gone when Biff, in his pajamas, comes down the stairs and enters the kitchen.

BIFF. What is he doing out there?

LINDA. Sh!

BIFF. God Almighty, Mom, how long has he been doing this?

LINDA. Don't, he'll hear you.

BIFF. What the hell is the matter with him?

LINDA. It'll pass by morning.

BIFF. Shouldn't we do anything?

LINDA. Oh, my dear, you should do a lot of things, but there's nothing to do, so go to sleep.

Happy comes down the stair and sits on the steps.

HAPPY. I never heard him so loud, Mom.

LINDA. Well, come around more often; you'll hear him. (*She sits down at the table and mends the lining of Willy's jacket.*)

BIFF. Why didn't you ever write me about this, Mom?

LINDA. How would I write to you? For over three months you had no address.

BIFF. I was on the move. But you know I thought of you all the time. You know that, don't you, pal?

LINDA. I know, dear, I know. But he likes to have a letter. Just to know that there's still a possibility for better things.

BIFF. He's not like this all the time, is he?

LINDA. It's when you come home he's always the worst.

BIFF. When I come home?

LINDA. When you write you're coming, he's all smiles, and talks about the future, and—he's just wonderful. And then the closer you seem to come, the more shaky he gets, and then, by the time you get here, he's arguing, and he seems angry at you. I think it's just that maybe he can't bring himself to—to open up to you. Why are you so hateful to each other? Why is that?

BIFF (*evasively*). I'm not hateful, Mom.

LINDA. But you no sooner come in the door than you're fighting!

BIFF. I don't know why. I mean to change. I'm tryin', Mom, you understand?

LINDA. Are you home to stay now?

BIFF. I don't know. I want to look around, see what's doin'.

LINDA. Biff, you can't look around all your life, can you?

BIFF. I just can't take hold, Mom. I can't take hold of some kind of a life.

LINDA. Biff, a man is not a bird, to come and go with the spring time.

BIFF. Your hair . . . (*He touches her hair.*) Your hair got so gray.

LINDA. Oh, it's been gray since you were in high school. I just stopped dyeing it, that's all.

BIFF. Dye it again, will ya? I don't want my pal looking old. (*He smiles.*)

LINDA. You're such a boy! You think you can go away for a year and . . . You've got to get it into your head now that one day you'll knock on this door and there'll be strange people here . . .

BIFF. What are you talking about? You're not even sixty, Mom.

LINDA. But what about your father?

BIFF (*lamely*). Well, I meant him too.

HAPPY. He admires Pop.

LINDA. Biff, dear, if you don't have any feeling for him, then you can't have any feeling for me.

BIFF. Sure I can, Mom.

LINDA. No. You can't just come to see me, because I love him. (*With a threat, but only a threat, of tears.*) He's the dearest man in the world to me, and I won't have anyone making him feel unwanted and low and blue. You've got to make up your mind now, darling, there's no leeway any more. Either he's your father and you pay him that respect, or else you're not to come here. I know he's not easy to get along with—nobody knows that better than me—but . . .

WILLY (*from the left, with a laugh*). Hey, hey, Biffo!

BIFF (*starting to go out after Willy*). What the hell is the matter with him? (*Happy stops him.*)

LINDA. Don't—don't go near him!

BIFF. Stop making excuses for him! He always, always wiped the floor with you. Never had an ounce of respect for you.

HAPPY. He's always had respect for . . .

BIFF. What the hell do you know about it?

HAPPY (*surlily*). Just don't call him crazy!

BIFF. He's got no character—Charley wouldn't do this. Not in his own house—spewing out that vomit from his mind.

HAPPY. Charley never had to cope with what he's got to.

BIFF. People are worse off than Willy Loman. Believe me, I've seen them!

LINDA. Then make Charley your father, Biff. You can't do that, can you? I don't say he's a great man. Willy Loman never made a lot of money. His name was never in the paper. He's not the finest character that ever lived. But he's a human being, and a terrible thing is happening to him. So attention must be paid. He's not to be allowed to fall into his grave like an old dog. Attention, attention must be finally paid to such a person. You called him crazy . . .

BIFF. I didn't mean . . .

LINDA. No, a lot of people think he's lost his—balance. But you don't have to be very smart to know what his trouble is. The man is exhausted.

HAPPY. Sure!

LINDA. A small man can be just as exhausted as a great man. He works for a company thirty-six years this March, opens up unheard-of territories to their trademark, and now in his old age they take his salary away.

HAPPY (*indignantly*). I didn't know that, Mom.

LINDA. You never asked, my dear! Now that you get your spending money someplace else you don't trouble your mind with him.

HAPPY. But I gave you money last . . .

LINDA. Christmas time, fifty dollars! To fix the hot water it cost ninety-seven fifty! For five weeks he's been on straight commission, like a beginner, an unknown!

BIFF. Those ungrateful bastards!

LINDA. Are they any worse than his sons? When he brought them business, when he was young, they were glad to see him. But now his old friends, the old buyers that loved him so and always found some order to hand him in a pinch—they're all dead, retired. He used to be able to make six, seven calls a day in Boston. Now he takes his valises out of the car and puts them back and takes them out again and he's exhausted. Instead of walking he talks now. He drives seven hundred miles, and when he gets there no one knows him any more, no one welcomes him. And what goes through a man's mind, driving seven hundred miles home without having earned a cent? Why shouldn't he talk to himself? Why? When he has to go to Charley and borrow fifty dollars a week and pretend to me that it's his pay? How long can that go on? How long? You see what I'm sitting here and waiting for? And you tell me he has no character? The man who never worked a day but for your benefit? When does he get the medal for that? Is this his reward—to turn around at the age of sixty-three and find his sons, who he loved better than his life, one a philandering bum . . .

HAPPY. Mom!

LINDA. That's all you are, my baby! (*To Biff.*) And you! What happened to the love you had for him? You were such pals! How you used to talk to him on the phone every night! How lonely he was till he could come home to you!

BIFF. All right, Mom. I'll live here in my room, and I'll get a job. I'll keep away from him, that's all.

LINDA. No, Biff. You can't stay here and fight all the time.

BIFF. He threw me out of this house, remember that.

LINDA. Why did he do that? I never knew why.

BIFF. Because I know he's a fake and he doesn't like anybody around who knows!

LINDA. Why a fake? In what way? What do you mean?

BIFF. Just don't lay it all at my feet. It's between me and him—that's all I have to say. I'll chip in from now on. He'll settle for half my paycheck. He'll be all right. I'm going to bed. (*He starts for the stairs.*)

LINDA. He won't be all right.

BIFF (*turning on the stairs, furiously*). I hate this city and I'll stay here. Now what do you want?

LINDA. He's dying, Biff.

Happy turns quickly to her, shocked.

BIFF (*after a pause*). Why is he dying?

LINDA. He's been trying to kill himself.

BIFF (*with great horror*). How?

LINDA. I live from day to day.

BIFF. What're you talking about?

LINDA. Remember I wrote you that he smashed up the car again? In February?

BIFF. Well?

LINDA. The insurance inspector came. He said that they have evidence. That all these accidents in the last year—weren't—weren't—accidents.

HAPPY. How can they tell that? That's a lie.

LINDA. It seems there's a woman . . . (*She takes a breath as:*)

{ BIFF (*sharply but contained*). What woman?

{ LINDA (*simultaneously*). . . . and this woman . . .

LINDA. What?

BIFF. Nothing. Go ahead.

LINDA. What did you say?

BIFF. Nothing. I just said what woman?

HAPPY. What about her?

LINDA. Well, it seems she was walking down the road and saw his car. She says that he wasn't driving fast at all, and that he didn't skid. She says he came to that little bridge, and then deliberately smashed into the railing, and it was only the shallowness of the water that saved him.

BIFF. Oh, no, he probably just fell asleep again.

LINDA. I don't think he fell asleep.

BIFF. Why not?

LINDA. Last month . . . (*With great difficulty.*) Oh, boys, it's so hard to say a thing like this! He's just a big stupid man to you, but I tell you there's more good in him than in many other people. (*She chokes, wipes her eyes.*) I was looking for a fuse. The lights blew out, and I went down the cellar. And behind the fuse box—it happened to fall out—was a length of rubber pipe—just short.

HAPPY. No kidding!

LINDA. There's a little attachment on the end of it. I knew right away. And sure enough, on the bottom of the water heater there's a new little nipple on the gas pipe.

HAPPY (*angrily*). That—jerk.

BIFF. Did you have it taken off?

LINDA. I'm—I'm ashamed to. How can I mention it to him? Every day I go down and take away that little rubber pipe. But, when he comes home, I put it back where it was. How can I insult him that way? I don't know what to do. I live from day to day, boys. I tell you, I know every thought in his mind. It sounds so old-fashioned and silly, but I tell you he put his whole life into you and you've turned your backs on him. (*She is bent over in the chair, weeping, her face in her hands.*) Biff, I swear to God! Biff, his life is in your hands!

HAPPY (*to Biff*). How do you like that damned fool!

BIFF (*kissing her*). All right, pal, all right. It's all settled now. I've been remiss. I know that, Mom. But now I'll stay, and I swear to you, I'll apply myself. (*Kneeling in front of her, in a fever of self-reproach.*) It's just—you see, Mom, I don't fit in business. Not that I won't try. I'll try, and I'll make good.

HAPPY. Sure you will. The trouble with you in business was you never tried to please people.

BIFF. I know, I . . .

HAPPY. Like when you worked for Harrison's. Bob Harrison said you were tops, and then you go and do some damn fool thing like whistling whole songs in the elevator like a comedian.

BIFF (*against Happy*). So what? I like to whistle sometimes.

HAPPY. You don't raise a guy to a responsible job who whistles in the elevator!

LINDA. Well, don't argue about it now.

HAPPY. Like when you'd go off and swim in the middle of the day instead of taking the line around.

BIFF (*his resentment rising*). Well, don't you run off? You take off sometimes, don't you? On a nice summer day?

HAPPY. Yeah, but I cover myself!

LINDA. Boys!

HAPPY. If I'm going to take a fade the boss can call any number where I'm supposed to be and they'll swear to him that I just left. I'll tell you something that I hate to say, Biff, but in the business world some of them think you're crazy.

BIFF (*angered*). Screw the business world!

HAPPY. All right, screw it! Great, but cover yourself!

LINDA. Hap, Hap!

BIFF. I don't care what they think! They've laughed at Dad for years, and you know why? Because we don't belong in this nuthouse of a city! We should be mixing cement on some open plain or—or carpenters. A carpenter is allowed to whistle!

Willy walks in from the entrance of the house, at left.

WILLY. Even your grandfather was better than a carpenter. (*Pause. They watch him.*) You never grew up. Bernard does not whistle in the elevator, I assure you.

BIFF (*as though to laugh Willy out of it*). Yeah, but you do, Pop.

WILLY. I never in my life whistled in an elevator! And who in the business world thinks I'm crazy?

BIFF. I didn't mean it like that, Pop. Now don't make a whole thing out of it, will ya?

WILLY. Go back to the West! Be a carpenter, a cowboy, enjoy yourself!

LINDA. Willy, he was just saying . . .

WILLY. I heard what he said!

HAPPY (*trying to quiet Willy*). Hey, Pop, come on now . . .

WILLY (*continuing over Happy's line*). They laugh at me, heh? Go to Filene's, go to the Hub, go to Slattery's, Boston. Call out the name Willy Loman and see what happens! Big shot!

BIFF. All right, Pop.

WILLY. Big!

BIFF. All right!

WILLY. Why do you always insult me?

BIFF. I didn't say a word. (*To Linda.*) Did I say a word?

LINDA. He didn't say anything, Willy.

WILLY (*going to the doorway of the living room*). All right, good night, good night.

LINDA. Willy, dear, he just decided . . .

WILLY (*to Biff*). If you get tired hanging around tomorrow, paint the ceiling I put up in the living room.

BIFF. I'm leaving early tomorrow.

HAPPY. He's going to see Bill Oliver, Pop.

WILLY (*interestedly*). Oliver? For what?

BIFF (*with reserve, but trying; trying*). He always said he'd stake me. I'd like to go into business, so maybe I can take him up on it.

LINDA. Isn't that wonderful?

WILLY. Don't interrupt. What's wonderful about it? There's fifty men in the City of New York who'd stake him. (*To Biff.*) Sporting goods?

BIFF. I guess so. I know something about it and . . .

WILLY. He knows something about it! You know sporting goods better than Spalding, for God's sake! How much is he giving you?

BIFF. I don't know, I didn't even see him yet, but . . .

WILLY. Then what're you talkin' about?

BIFF (*getting angry*). Well, all I said was I'm gonna see him, that's all!

WILLY (*turning away*). Ah, you're counting your chickens again.

BIFF (*starting left for the stairs*). Oh, Jesus, I'm going to sleep!

WILLY (*calling after him*). Don't curse in this house!

BIFF (*turning*). Since when did you get so clean?

HAPPY (*trying to stop them*). Wait a . . .

WILLY. Don't use that language to me! I won't have it!

HAPPY (*grabbing Biff, shouts*). Wait a minute! I got an idea. I got a feasible idea. Come here, Biff, let's talk this over now, let's talk some sense here. When I was down in Florida last time, I thought of a great idea to sell sporting goods. It just came back to me. You and I, Biff—we have a line, the Loman Line. We train a couple of weeks, and put on a couple of exhibitions, see?

WILLY. That's an idea!

HAPPY. Wait! We form two basketball teams, see? Two water-polo teams. We play each other. It's a million dollars' worth of publicity. Two brothers, see? The Loman Brothers. Displays in the Royal Palms—all the hotels. And banners over the ring and the basketball court: "Loman Brothers." Baby, we could sell sporting goods!

WILLY. That is a one-million-dollar idea!

LINDA. Marvelous!

BIFF. I'm in great shape as far as that's concerned.

HAPPY. And the beauty of it is, Biff, it wouldn't be like a business. We'd be out playin' ball again.

BIFF (*enthused*). Yeah, that's . . .

WILLY. Million-dollar . . .

HAPPY. And you wouldn't get fed up with it, Biff. It'd be the family again. There'd be the old honor, and comradeship, and if you wanted to go off for a swim or somethin'—well, you'd do it! Without some smart cooky gettin' up ahead of you!

WILLY. Lick the world! You guys together could absolutely lick the civilized world.

BIFF. I'll see Oliver tomorrow. Hap, if we could work that out . . .

LINDA. Maybe things are beginning to . . .

WILLY (*widely enthused, to Linda*). Stop interrupting! (*To Biff.*) But don't wear sport jacket and slacks when you see Oliver.

BIFF. No, I'll . . .

WILLY. A business suit, and talk as little as possible, and don't crack any jokes.

BIFF. He did like me. Always liked me.

LINDA. He loved you!

WILLY (*to Linda*). Will you stop! (*To Biff.*) Walk in very serious. You are not applying for a boy's job. Money is to pass. Be quiet, fine, and serious. Everybody likes a kidder, but nobody lends him money.

HAPPY. I'll try to get some myself, Biff. I'm sure I can.

WILLY. I see great things for you kids, I think your troubles are over. But remember, start big and you'll end big. Ask for fifteen. How much you gonna ask for?

BIFF. Gee, I don't know . . .

WILLY. And don't say "Gee." "Gee" is a boy's word. A man walking in for fifteen thousand dollars does not say "Gee!"

BIFF. Ten, I think, would be top though.

WILLY. Don't be so modest. You always started too low. Walk in with a big laugh. Don't look worried. Start off with a couple of your good stories to lighten things up. It's not what you say, it's how you say it—because personality always wins the day.

LINDA. Oliver always thought the highest of him . . .

WILLY. Will you let me talk?

BIFF. Don't yell at her, Pop, will ya?

WILLY (*angrily*). I was talking, wasn't I?

BIFF. I don't like you yelling at her all the time, and I'm tellin' you, that's all.

WILLY. What're you, takin' over this house?

LINDA. Willy . . .

WILLY (*turning to her*). Don't take his side all the time, god-dammit!

BIFF (*furiously*). Stop yelling at her!

WILLY (*suddenly pulling on his cheek, beaten down, guilt ridden*). Give my best to Bill Oliver—he may remember me. (*He exits through the living room doorway.*)

LINDA (*her voice subdued*). What'd you have to start that for? (*Biff turns away.*) You see how sweet he was as soon as you talked hopefully? (*She goes over to Biff.*) Come up and say good night to him. Don't let him go to bed that way.

HAPPY. Come on, Biff, let's buck him up.

LINDA. Please, dear. Just say good night. It takes so little to make him happy. Come. (*She goes through the living room doorway, calling upstairs from within the living room.*) Your pajamas are hanging in the bathroom, Willy!

HAPPY (*looking toward where Linda went out*). What a woman! They broke the mold when they made her. You know that, Biff.

BIFF. He's off salary. My God, working on commission!

HAPPY. Well, let's face it: he's no hot-shot selling man. Except that sometimes, you have to admit, he's a sweet personality.

BIFF (*deciding*). Lend me ten bucks, will ya? I want to buy some new ties.

HAPPY. I'll take you to a place I know. Beautiful stuff. Wear one of my striped shirts tomorrow.

BIFF. She got gray. Mom got awful old. Gee, I'm gonna go in to Oliver tomorrow and knock him for a . . .

HAPPY. Come on up. Tell that to Dad. Let's give him a whirl. Come on.

BIFF (*steamed up*). You know, with ten thousand bucks, boy!

HAPPY (*as they go into the living room*). That's the talk, Biff, that's the first time I've heard the old confidence out of you! (*From within the living room, fading off*) You're gonna live with me, kid, and any babe you want just say the word . . . (*The last lines are hardly heard. They are mounting the stairs to their parents' bedroom.*)

LINDA (*entering her bedroom and addressing Willy, who is in the bathroom. She is straightening the bed for him*). Can you do anything about the shower? It drips.

WILLY (*from the bathroom*). All of a sudden everything falls to pieces. Goddam plumbing, oughta be sued, those people. I hardly finished putting it in and the thing . . . (*His words rumble off.*)

LINDA. I'm just wondering if Oliver will remember him. You think he might?

WILLY (*coming out of the bathroom in his pajamas*). Remember him? What's the matter with you, you crazy? If he'd've stayed with Oliver he'd be on top by now! Wait'll Oliver gets a look at him. You don't know the average caliber any more. The average young man today—(*he is getting into bed*)—is got a caliber of zero. Greatest thing in the world for him was to bum around.

Biff and Happy enter the bedroom. Slight pause.

WILLY (*stops short, looking at Biff*). Glad to hear it, boy.

HAPPY. He wanted to say good night to you, sport.

WILLY (*to Biff*). Yeah. Knock him dead, boy. What'd you want to tell me?

BIFF. Just take it easy, Pop. Good night. (*He turns to go.*)

WILLY (*unable to resist*). And if anything falls off the desk while you're talking to him—like a package or something—don't you pick it up. They have office boys for that.

LINDA. I'll make a big breakfast . . .

WILLY. Will you let me finish? (*To Biff.*) Tell him you were in the business in the West. Not farm work.

BIFF. All right, Dad.

LINDA. I think everything . . .

WILLY (*going right through her speech*). And don't undersell yourself. No less than fifteen thousand dollars.

BIFF (*unable to bear him*). Okay. Good night, Mom. (*He starts moving.*)

WILLY. Because you got a greatness in you, Biff, remember that. You got all kinds of greatness . . . (*He lies back, exhausted. Biff walks out.*)

LINDA (*calling after Biff*). Sleep well, darling!

HAPPY. I'm gonna get married, Mom. I wanted to tell you.

LINDA. Go to sleep, dear.

HAPPY (*going*). I just wanted to tell you.

WILLY. Keep up the good work. (*Happy exits.*) God . . . remember that Ebbets Field game? The championship of the city?

LINDA. Just rest. Should I sing to you?

WILLY. Yeah. Sing to me. (*Linda hums a soft lullaby.*) When that team came out—he was the tallest, remember?

LINDA. Oh, yes. And in gold.

Biff enters the darkened kitchen, takes a cigarette, and leaves the house. He comes downstage into a golden pool of light. He smokes, staring at the night.

WILLY. Like a young god. Hercules—something like that. And the sun, the sun all around him. Remember how he waved to me? Right up from the field, with the representatives of three colleges standing by? And the buyers I brought, and the cheers when he came out—Loman, Loman, Loman! God Almighty, he'll be great yet. A star like that, magnificent, can never really fade away!

The light on Willy is fading. The gas heater begins to glow through the kitchen wall, near the stairs, a blue flame beneath red coils.

LINDA (*timidly*). Willy dear, what has he got against you?

WILLY. I'm so tired. Don't talk any more.

Biff slowly returns to the kitchen. He stops, stares toward the heater.

LINDA. Will you ask Howard to let you work in New York?

WILLY. First thing in the morning. Everything'll be all right.

Biff reaches behind the heater and draws out a length of rubber tubing. He is horrified and turns his head toward Willy's room, still dimly lit, from which the strains of Linda's desperate but monotonous humming rise.

WILLY (*staring through the window into the moonlight*). Gee, look at the moon moving between the buildings!

Biff wraps the tubing around his hand and quickly goes up the stairs.

ACT 2

SCENE: *Music is heard, gay and bright. The curtain rises as the music fades away. Willy, in shirt sleeves, is sitting at the kitchen table, sipping coffee, his hat in his lap. Linda is filling his cup when she can.*

WILLY. Wonderful coffee. Meal in itself.

LINDA. Can I make you some eggs?

WILLY. No. Take a breath.

LINDA. You look so rested, dear.

WILLY. I slept like a dead one. First time in months. Imagine, sleeping till ten on a Tuesday morning. Boys left nice and early, heh?

LINDA. They were out of here by eight o'clock.

WILLY. Good work!

LINDA. It was so thrilling to see them leaving together. I can't get over the shaving lotion in this house!

WILLY (*smiling*). Mmm . . .

LINDA. Biff was very changed this morning. His whole attitude seemed to be hopeful. He couldn't wait to get downtown to see Oliver.

WILLY. He's heading for a change. There's no question, there simply are certain men that take longer to get—solidified. How did he dress?

LINDA. His blue suit. He's so handsome in that suit. He could be a—anything in that suit!

Willy gets up from the table. Linda holds his jacket for him.

WILLY. There's no question, no question at all. Gee, on the way home tonight I'd like to buy some seeds.

LINDA (*laughing*). That'd be wonderful. But not enough sun gets back there. Nothing'll grow any more.

WILLY. You wait, kid, before it's all over we're gonna get a little place out in the country, and I'll raise some vegetables, a couple of chickens . . .

LINDA. You'll do it yet, dear.

Willy walks out of his jacket. Linda follows him.

WILLY. And they'll get married, and come for a weekend. I'd build a little guest house. 'Cause I got so many fine tools, all I'd need would be a little lumber and some peace of mind.

LINDA (*joyfully*). I sewed the lining . . .

WILLY. I could build two guest houses, so they'd both come. Did he decide how much he's going to ask Oliver for?

LINDA (*getting him into the jacket*). He didn't mention it, but I imagine ten or fifteen thousand. You going to talk to Howard today?

WILLY. Yeah. I'll put it to him straight and simple. He'll just have to take me off the road.

LINDA. And Willy, don't forget to ask for a little advance, because we've got the insurance premium. It's the grace period now.

WILLY. That's a hundred . . . ?

LINDA. A hundred and eight, sixty-eight. Because we're a little short again.

WILLY. Why are we short?

LINDA. Well, you had the motor job on the car . . .

WILLY. That goddam Studebaker!

LINDA. And you got one more payment on the refrigerator . . .

WILLY. But it just broke again!

LINDA. Well, it's old, dear.

WILLY. I told you we should've bought a well-advertised machine. Charley bought a General Electric and it's twenty years old and it's still good, that son-of-a-bitch.

LINDA. But, Willy . . .

WILLY. Whoever heard of a Hastings refrigerator? Once in my life I would like to own something outright before it's broken! I'm always in a race with the junkyard! I just finished paying for the car and it's on its last legs. The refrigerator consumes belts like a goddam maniac. They time those things. They time them so when you finally paid for them, they're used up.

LINDA (*buttoning up his jacket as he unbuttons it*). All told, about two hundred dollars would carry us, dear. But that includes the last payment on the mortgage. After this payment, Willy, the house belongs to us.

WILLY. It's twenty-five years!

LINDA. Biff was nine years old when we bought it.

WILLY. Well, that's a great thing. To weather a twenty-five year mortgage is . . .

LINDA. It's an accomplishment.

WILLY. All the cement, the lumber, the reconstruction I put in this house! There ain't a crack to be found in it any more.

LINDA. Well, it served its purpose.

WILLY. What purpose? Some stranger'll come along, move in, and that's that. If only Biff would take this house, and raise a family . . . (*He starts to go.*) Good-by, I'm late.

LINDA (*suddenly remembering*). Oh, I forgot! You're supposed to meet them for dinner.

WILLY. Me?

LINDA. At Frank's Chop House on Forty-eighth near Sixth Avenue.

WILLY. Is that so! How about you?

LINDA. No, just the three of you. They're gonna blow you to a big meal!

WILLY. Don't say! Who thought of that?

LINDA. Biff came to me this morning, Willy, and he said, "Tell Dad, we want to blow him to a big meal." Be there six o'clock. You and your two boys are going to have dinner.

WILLY. Gee whiz! That's really somethin'. I'm gonna knock Howard for a loop, kid. I'll get an advance, and I'll come home with a New York job. Goddammit, now I'm gonna do it!

LINDA. Oh, that's the spirit, Willy!

WILLY. I will never get behind a wheel the rest of my life!

LINDA. It's changing, Willy, I can feel it changing!

WILLY. Beyond a question. G'by, I'm late. (*He starts to go again.*)

LINDA (*calling after him as she runs to the kitchen table for a handkerchief*). You got your glasses?

WILLY (*feels for them, then comes back in*). Yeah, yeah, got my glasses.

LINDA (*giving him the handkerchief*). And a handkerchief.

WILLY. Yeah, handkerchief.

LINDA. And your saccharine?

WILLY. Yeah, my saccharine.

LINDA. Be careful on the subway stairs.

She kisses him, and a silk stocking is seen hanging from her hand. Willy notices it.

WILLY. Will you stop mending stockings? At least while I'm in the house. It gets me nervous. I can't tell you. Please.

Linda hides the stocking in her hand as she follows Willy across the forestage in front of the house.

LINDA. Remember, Frank's Chop House.

WILLY (*passing the apron*). Maybe beets would grow out there.

LINDA (*laughing*). But you tried so many times.

WILLY. Yeah. Well, don't work hard today. (*He disappears around the right corner of the house.*)

LINDA. Be careful!

As Willy vanishes, Linda waves to him. Suddenly the phone rings. She runs across the stage and into the kitchen and lifts it.

LINDA. Hello? Oh, Biff! I'm so glad you called, I just . . . Yes, sure, I just told him. Yes, he'll be there for dinner at six o'clock, I didn't forget. Listen, I was just dying to tell you. You know that little rubber pipe I told you about? That he connected to the gas heater? I finally decided to go down the cellar this morning and take it away and destroy it. But it's gone! Imagine? He took it away himself, it isn't there! (*She listens.*) When? Oh, then you took it. Oh—nothing, it's just that I'd hoped he'd taken it away himself. Oh, I'm not worried, darling, because this morning he left in such high spirits, it was like the old days! I'm not afraid any more. Did Mr. Oliver see you? . . . Well, you wait there then. And make a nice impression on him, darling. Just don't perspire too much before you see him. And have a nice time with Dad. He may have big news too! . . . That's right, a New York job. And be sweet to him tonight, dear. Be loving to him. Because he's only a little boat looking for a harbor. (*She is trembling with sorrow and joy.*) Oh, that's wonderful, Biff, you'll save his life. Thanks, darling. Just put your arm around him when he comes into the restaurant. Give him a smile. That's the boy . . . Good-by, dear. . . . You got your comb? . . . That's fine. Good-by, Biff dear.

In the middle of her speech, Howard Wagner, thirty-six, wheels in a small typewriter table on which is a wire-recording machine and proceeds to plug it in. This is on the left forestage. Light slowly fades on Linda as it rises on Howard. Howard is intent on threading the machine and only glances over his shoulder as Willy appears.

WILLY. Pst! Pst!

HOWARD. Hello, Willy, come in.

WILLY. Like to have a little talk with you, Howard.

HOWARD. Sorry to keep you waiting. I'll be with you in a minute.

WILLY. What's that, Howard?

HOWARD. Didn't you ever see one of these? Wire recorder.

WILLY. Oh. Can we talk a minute?

HOWARD. Records things. Just got delivery yesterday. Been driving me crazy, the most terrific machine I ever saw in my life. I was up all night with it.

WILLY. What do you do with it?

HOWARD. I bought it for dictation, but you can do anything with it. Listen to this. I had it home last night. Listen to what I picked up. The first one is my daughter. Get this. (*He flicks the switch and "Roll Out the Barrel" is heard being whistled.*) Listen to that kid whistle.

WILLY. That is lifelike, isn't it?

HOWARD. Seven years old. Get that tone.

WILLY. Ts, ts. Like to ask a little favor if you . . .

The whistling breaks off, and the voice of Howard's daughter is heard.

HIS DAUGHTER. "Now you, Daddy."

HOWARD. She's crazy for me! (*Again the same song is whistled.*) That's me! Ha! (*He winks.*)

WILLY. You're very good!

The whistling breaks off again. The machine runs silent for a moment.

HOWARD. Sh! Get this now, this is my son.

HIS SON. "The capital of Alabama is Montgomery; the capital of Arizona is Phoenix; the capital of Arkansas is Little Rock; the capital of California is Sacramento . . ." (*and on, and on.*)

HOWARD (*holding up five fingers*). Five years old, Willy!

WILLY. He'll make an announcer some day!

HIS SON (*continuing*). "The capital . . ."

HOWARD. Get that—alphabetical order! (*The machine breaks off suddenly.*) Wait a minute. The maid kicked the plug out.

WILLY. It certainly is a . . .

HOWARD. Sh, for God's sake!

HIS SON. "It's nine o'clock, Bulova watch time. So I have to go to sleep."

WILLY. That really is . . .

HOWARD. Wait a minute! The next is my wife.

They wait.

HOWARD'S VOICE. "Go on, say something." (*Pause.*) "Well, you gonna talk?"

HIS WIFE. "I can't think of anything."

HOWARD'S VOICE. "Well, talk—it's turning."

HIS WIFE (*shyly, beaten*). "Hello." (*Silence.*) "Oh, Howard, I can't talk into this . . ."

HOWARD (*snapping the machine off*). That was my wife.

WILLY. That is a wonderful machine. Can we . . .

HOWARD. I tell you, Willy, I'm gonna take my camera, and my bandsaw, and all my hobbies, and out they go. This is the most fascinating relaxation I ever found.

WILLY. I think I'll get one myself.

HOWARD. Sure, they're only a hundred and a half. You can't do without it. Supposing you wanna hear Jack Benny, see? But you can't be at home at that hour. So you tell the maid to turn the radio on when Jack Benny comes on, and this automatically goes on with the radio . . .

WILLY. And when you come home you . . .

HOWARD. You can come home twelve o'clock, one o'clock, any time you like, and you get yourself a Coke and sit yourself down, throw the switch, and there's Jack Benny's program in the middle of the night!

WILLY. I'm definitely going to get one. Because lots of times I'm on the road, and I think to myself, what I must be missing on the radio!

HOWARD. Don't you have a radio in the car?

WILLY. Well, yeah, but who ever thinks of turning it on?

HOWARD. Say, aren't you supposed to be in Boston?

WILLY. That's what I want to talk to you about, Howard. You got a minute? (*He draws a chair in from the wing.*)

HOWARD. What happened? What're you doing here?

WILLY. Well . . .

HOWARD. You didn't crack up again, did you?

WILLY. Oh, no. No . . .

HOWARD. Geez, you had me worried there for a minute. What's the trouble?

WILLY. Well, tell you the truth, Howard. I've come to the decision that I'd rather not travel any more.

HOWARD. Not travel! Well, what'll you do?

WILLY. Remember, Christmas time, when you had the party here? You said you'd try to think of some spot for me here in town.

HOWARD. With us?

WILLY. Well, sure.

HOWARD. Oh, yeah, yeah. I remember. Well, I couldn't think of anything for you, Willy.

WILLY. I tell ya, Howard. The kids are all grown up, y'know. I don't need much any more. If I could take home—well, sixty-five dollars a week, I could swing it.

HOWARD. Yeah, but Willy, see I . . .

WILLY. I tell ya why, Howard. Speaking frankly and between the two of us, y'know—I'm just a little tired.

HOWARD. Oh, I could understand that, Willy. But you're a road man, Willy, and we do a road business. We've only got a half-dozen salesmen on the floor here.

WILLY. God knows, Howard. I never asked a favor of any man. But I was with the firm when your father used to carry you in here in his arms.

HOWARD. I know that, Willy, but . . .

WILLY. Your father came to me the day you were born and asked me what I thought of the name Howard, may he rest in peace.

HOWARD. I appreciate that, Willy, but there just is no spot here for you. If I had a spot I'd slam you right in, but I just don't have a single solitary spot.

He looks for his lighter. Willy has picked it up and gives it to him. Pause.

WILLY (*with increasing anger*). Howard, all I need to set my table is fifty dollars a week.

HOWARD. But where am I going to put you, kid?

WILLY. Look, it isn't a question of whether I can sell merchandise, is it?

HOWARD. No, but it's business, kid, and everybody's gotta pull his own weight.

WILLY (*desperately*). Just let me tell you a story, Howard . . .

HOWARD. 'Cause you gotta admit, business is business.

WILLY (*angrily*). Business is definitely business, but just listen for a minute. You don't understand this. When I was a boy—eighteen, nineteen—I was already on the road. And there was a question in my mind as to whether selling had a future for me. Because in those days I had a yearning to go to Alaska. See, there were three gold strikes in one month in Alaska, and I felt like going out. Just for the ride, you might say.

HOWARD (*barely interested*). Don't say.

WILLY. Oh, yeah, my father lived many years in Alaska. He was an adventurous man. We've got quite a little streak of self-reliance in our family. I thought I'd go out with my older brother and try to locate him, and maybe settle in the North with the old man. And I was almost decided to go, when I met a salesman in the Parker House. His name was Dave Singleman. And he was eighty-four years old, and he'd drummed merchandise in thirty-one states. And old Dave, he'd go up to his room, y'understand, put on his green velvet slippers—I'll never forget—and pick up his phone and call the buyers, and without ever leaving his room, at the age of eighty-four, he made his living. And when I saw that, I realized that selling was the greatest career a man could want. 'Cause what could be more satisfying than to be able to go, at the age of eighty-four, into twenty or thirty different cities, and pick up a phone, and be remembered and loved and helped by so many different people? Do you know? when he died— and by the way he died the death of a salesman, in his green velvet slippers in the smoker of the New York, New Haven and Hartford, going into Boston—when he died, hundreds of salesmen and buyers were at his funeral. Things were sad on a lotta trains for months after that. (*He stands up, Howard has not looked at him.*) In those days there was personality in it, Howard. There was respect, and comradeship, and gratitude in it. Today, it's all cut and dried, and there's no chance for bringing friendship to bear—or personality. You see what I mean? They don't know me any more.

HOWARD (*moving away, to the right*). That's just the thing, Willy.

WILLY. If I had forty dollars a week—that's all I'd need. Forty dollars, Howard.

HOWARD. Kid, I can't take blood from a stone, I . . .

WILLY (*desperation is on him now*). Howard, the year Al Smith was nominated, your father came to me and . . .

HOWARD (*starting to go off*). I've got to see some people, kid.

WILLY (*stopping him*). I'm talking about your father! There were promises made across this desk! You mustn't tell me you've got people to see—I put thirty-four years into this firm, Howard, and now I can't pay my insurance! You can't eat the orange and throw the peel away—a man is not a piece of fruit! (*After a pause.*) Now pay attention. Your father—in 1928 I had a big year. I averaged a hundred and seventy dollars a week in commissions.

HOWARD (*impatiently*). Now, Willy, you never averaged . . .

WILLY (*banging his hand on the desk*). I averaged a hundred and seventy dollars a week in the year of 1928! And your father came to me—or rather, I was in the office here—it was right over this desk—and he put his hand on my shoulder . . .

HOWARD (*getting up*). You'll have to excuse me, Willy, I gotta see some people. Pull yourself together. (*Going out.*) I'll be back in a little while.

On Howard's exit, the light on his chair grows very bright and strange.

WILLY. Pull myself together! What the hell did I say to him? My God, I was yelling at him! How could I? (*Willy breaks off, staring at the light, which occupies the chair, animating it. He approaches this chair, standing across the desk from it.*) Frank, Frank, don't you remember what you told me that time? How you put your hand on my shoulder, and Frank . . . (*He leans on the desk and as he speaks the dead man's name he accidentally switches on the recorder, and instantly*)

HOWARD'S SON. " . . . of New York is Albany. The capital of Ohio is Cincinnati, the capital of Rhode Island is . . . " (*The recitation continues.*)

WILLY (*leaping away with fright, shouting*). Ha! Howard! Howard! Howard!

HOWARD (*rushing in*). What happened?

WILLY (*pointing at the machine, which continues nasally, child-ishly, with the capital cities*). Shut it off! Shut it off!

HOWARD (*pulling the plug out*). Look, Willy . . .

WILLY (*pressing his hands to his eyes.*) I gotta get myself some coffee. I'll get some coffee . . .

Willy starts to walk out. Howard stops him.

HOWARD (*rolling up the cord*). Willy, look . . .

WILLY. I'll go to Boston.

HOWARD. Willy, you can't go to Boston for us.

WILLY Why can't I go?

HOWARD. I don't want you to represent us. I've been mean-ing to tell you for a long time now.

WILLY. Howard, are you firing me?

HOWARD. I think you need a good long rest, Willy.

WILLY. Howard . . .

HOWARD. And when you feel better, come back, and we'll see if we can work something out.

WILLY. But I gotta earn money, Howard. I'm in no position to . . .

HOWARD. Where are your sons? Why don't your sons give you a hand?

WILLY. They're working on a very big deal.

HOWARD. This is no time for false pride, Willy. You go to your sons and you tell them that you're tired. You've got two great boys, haven't you?

WILLY. Oh, no question, no question, but in the meantime . . .

HOWARD. Then that's that, heh?

WILLY. All right, I'll go to Boston tomorrow.

HOWARD. No, no.

WILLY. I can't throw myself on my sons. I'm not a cripple!

HOWARD. Look, kid, I'm busy this morning.

WILLY (*grasping Howard's arm*). Howard, you've got to let me go to Boston!

HOWARD (*hard, keeping himself under control*). I've got a line of people to see this morning. Sit down, take five min-utes, and pull yourself together, and then go home, will ya? I need the office, Willy. (*He starts to go, turns, remem-bering the recorder, starts to push off the table holding the recorder.*) Oh, yeah. Whenever you can this week, stop by and drop off the samples. You'll feel better, Willy, and then come back and we'll talk. Pull yourself together, kid, there's people outside.

Howard exits, pushing the table off left. Willy stares into space, exhausted. Now the music is heard—Ben's mu-sic—first distantly, then closer, closer. As Willy speaks, Ben enters from the right. He carries valise and umbrella.

WILLY. Oh, Ben, how did you do it? What is the answer? Did you wind up the Alaska deal already?

BEN. Doesn't take much time if you know what you're doing. Just a short business trip. Boarding ship in an hour. Wanted to say good-by.

WILLY. Ben, I've got to talk to you.

BEN (*glancing at his watch*). Haven't the time, William.

WILLY (*crossing the apron to Ben*). Ben, nothing's working out. I don't know what to do.

BEN. Now, look here, William. I've bought timberland in Alaska and I need a man to look after things for me.

WILLY. God, timberland! Me and my boys in those grand out-doors!

BEN. You've a new continent at your doorstep, William. Get out of these cities, they're full of talk and time payments and courts of law. Screw on your fists and you can fight for a fortune up there.

WILLY. Yes, yes! Linda, Linda!

Linda enters as of old, with the wash.

LINDA. Oh, you're back?

BEN. I haven't much time.

WILLY. No, wait! Linda, he's got a proposition for me in Alaska.

LINDA. But you've got . . . (*To Ben.*) He's got a beautiful job here.

WILLY. But in Alaska, kid, I could . . .

LINDA. You're doing well enough, Willy!

BEN (*to Linda*). Enough for what, my dear?

LINDA (*frightened of Ben and angry at him*). Don't say those things to him! Enough to be happy right here, right now. (*To Willy, while Ben laughs.*) Why must everybody conquer the world? You're well liked, and the boys love you, and someday—(*To Ben*)—why, old man Wagner told him just the other day that if he keeps it up he'll be a member of the firm, didn't he, Willy?

WILLY. Sure, sure. I am building something with this firm, Ben, and if a man is building something he must be on the right track, mustn't he?

BEN. What are you building? Lay your hand on it. Where is it?

WILLY (*hesitantly*). That's true, Linda, there's nothing.

LINDA. Why? (*To Ben.*) There's a man eighty-four years old . . .

WILLY. That's right, Ben, that's right. When I look at that man I say, what is there to worry about?

BEN. Bah!

WILLY. It's true, Ben. All he has to do is go into any city, pick up the phone, and he's making his living and you know why?

BEN (*picking up his valise*). I've got to go.

WILLY (*holding Ben back*). Look at this boy!

Biff, in his high school sweater, enters carrying suitcase. Happy carries Biff's shoulder guards, gold helmet, and football pants.

WILLY. Without a penny to his name, three great universities are begging for him, and from there the sky's the limit, because it's not what you do, Ben. It's who you know and the smile on your face! It's contacts, Ben, contacts! The whole wealth of Alaska passes over the lunch table at the Commodore Hotel, and that's the wonder, the wonder of this country, that a man can end with diamonds here on the basis of being liked! (*He turns to Biff.*) And that's why when you get out on that field today it's important. Because thousands of people will be rooting for you and loving you. (*To Ben, who has again begun to leave.*) And Ben! when he walks into a business office his name will sound

out like a bell and all the doors will open to him! I've seen it, Ben, I've seen it a thousand times! You can't feel it with your hand like timber, but it's there!

BEN. Good-by, William.

WILLY. Ben, am I right? Don't you think I'm right? I value your advice.

BEN. There's a new continent at your doorstep, William. You could walk out rich. Rich! (*He is gone.*)

WILLY. We'll do it here, Ben! You hear me? We're gonna do it here!

Young Bernard rushes in. The gay music of the Boys is heard.

BERNARD. Oh, gee, I was afraid you left already!

WILLY. Why? What time is it?

BERNARD. It's half-past one!

WILLY. Well, come on, everybody! Ebbets Field next stop! Where's the pennants? (*He rushes through the wall-line of the kitchen and out into the living room.*)

LINDA (*to Biff*). Did you pack fresh underwear?

BIFF (*who has been limbering up*). I want to go!

BERNARD. Biff, I'm carrying your helmet, ain't I?

HAPPY. No, I'm carrying the helmet.

BERNARD. Oh, Biff, you promised me.

HAPPY. I'm carrying the helmet.

BERNARD. How am I going to get in the locker room?

LINDA. Let him carry the shoulder guards. (*She puts her coat and hat on in the kitchen.*)

BERNARD. Can I, Biff? 'Cause I told everybody I'm going to be in the locker room.

HAPPY. In Ebbets Field it's the clubhouse.

BERNARD. I meant the clubhouse. Biff!

HAPPY. Biff!

BIFF (*grandly, after a slight pause*). Let him carry the shoulder guards.

HAPPY (*as he gives Bernard the shoulder guards*). Stay close to us now.

Willy rushes in with the pennants.

WILLY (*handing them out*). Everybody wave when Biff comes out on the field. (*Happy and Bernard run off.*) You set now, boy?

The music has died away.

BIFF. Ready to go, Pop. Every muscle is ready.

WILLY (*at the edge of the apron*). You realize what this means?

BIFF. That's right, Pop.

WILLY (*feeling Biff's muscles*). You're comin' home this afternoon captain of the All-Scholastic Championship Team of the City of New York.

BIFF. I got it, Pop. And remember, pal, when I take off my helmet, that touchdown is for you.

WILLY. Let's go! (*He is starting out, with his arm around Biff, when Charley enters, as of old, in knickers.*) I got no room for you, Charley.

CHARLEY. Room? For what?

WILLY. In the car.

CHARLEY. You goin' for a ride? I wanted to shoot some casino.

WILLY (*furiously*). Casino! (*Incredulously.*) Don't you realize what today is?

LINDA. Oh, he knows, Willy. He's just kidding you.

WILLY. That's nothing to kid about!

CHARLEY. No, Linda, what's goin' on?

LINDA. He's playing in Ebbets Field.

CHARLEY. Baseball in this weather?

WILLY. Don't talk to him. Come on, come on! (*He is pushing them out.*)

CHARLEY. Wait a minute, didn't you hear the news?

WILLY. What?

CHARLEY. Don't you listen to the radio? Ebbets Field just blew up.

WILLY. You go to hell! (*Charley laughs. Pushing them out.*) Come on, come on! We're late.

CHARLEY (*as they go*). Knock a homer, Biff, knock a homer!

WILLY (*the last to leave, turning to Charley*). I don't think that was funny, Charley. This is the greatest day of his life.

CHARLEY. Willy, when are you going to grow up?

WILLY. Yeah, heh? When this game is over, Charley, you'll be laughing out of the other side of your face. They'll be calling him another Red Grange. Twenty-five thousand a year.

CHARLEY (*kidding*). Is that so?

WILLY. Yeah, that's so.

CHARLEY. Well, then, I'm sorry, Willy. But tell me something.

WILLY. What?

CHARLEY. Who is Red Grange?

WILLY. Put up your hands. Goddam you, put up your hands!

Charley, chuckling, shakes his head and walks away, around the left corner of the stage. Willy follows him. The music rises to a mocking frenzy.

WILLY. Who the hell do you think you are, better than everybody else? You don't know everything, you big, ignorant, stupid . . . Put up your hands!

Light rises, on the right side of the forestage, on a small table in the reception room of Charley's office. Traffic sounds are heard. Bernard, now mature, sits whistling to himself. A pair of tennis rackets and an old overnight bag are on the door beside him.

WILLY (*offstage*). What are you walking away for? Don't walk away! If you're going to say something say it to my face! I

know you laugh at me behind my back. You'll laugh out of the other side of your goddam face after this game. Touchdown! Touchdown! Eighty thousand people! Touchdown! Right between the goal posts.

Bernard is a quiet, earnest, but self-assured young man. Willy's voice is coming from right upstage now. Bernard lowers his feet off the table and listens. Jenny, his father's secretary, enters.

JENNY (*distressed*). Say, Bernard, will you go out in the hall?

BERNARD. What is that noise? Who is it?

JENNY. Mr. Loman. He just got off the elevator.

BERNARD (*getting up*). Who's he arguing with?

JENNY. Nobody. There's nobody with him. I can't deal with him any more, and your father gets all upset every time he comes. I've got a lot of typing to do, and your father's waiting to sign it. Will you see him?

WILLY (*entering*). Touchdown! Touch—(*He sees Jenny.*) Jenny, Jenny, good to see you. How're ya? Workin'? Or still honest?

JENNY. Fine. How've you been feeling?

WILLY. Not much any more, Jenny. Ha, ha! (*He is surprised to see the rackets.*)

BERNARD. Hello, Uncle Willy.

WILLY (*almost shocked*). Bernard! Well, look who's here! (*He comes quickly, guiltily, to Bernard and warmly shakes his hand.*)

BERNARD. How are you? Good to see you.

WILLY. What are you doing here?

BERNARD. Oh, just stopped by to see Pop. Get off my feet till my train leaves. I'm going to Washington in a few minutes.

WILLY. Is he in?

BERNARD. Yes, he's in his office with the accountant. Sit down.

WILLY (*sitting down*). What're you going to do in Washington?

BERNARD. Oh, just a case I've got there, Willy.

WILLY. That so? (*Indicating the rackets.*) You going to play tennis there?

BERNARD. I'm staying with a friend who's got a court.

WILLY. Don't say. His own tennis court. Must be fine people, I bet.

BERNARD. They are, very nice. Dad tells me Biff's in town.

WILLY (*with a big smile*). Yeah, Biff's in. Working on a very big deal, Bernard.

BERNARD. What's Biff doing?

WILLY. Well, he's been doing very big things in the West. But he decided to establish himself here. Very big. We're having dinner. Did I hear your wife had a boy?

BERNARD. That's right. Our second.

WILLY. Two boys! What do you know!

BERNARD. What kind of a deal has Biff got?

WILLY. Well, Bill Oliver—very big sporting-goods man—he wants Biff very badly. Called him in from the West. Long distance, carte blanche, special deliveries. Your friends have their own private tennis court?

BERNARD. You still with the old firm, Willy?

WILLY (*after a pause*). I'm—I'm overjoyed to see how you made the grade, Bernard, overjoyed. It's an encouraging thing to see a young man really—really . . . Looks very good for Biff—very . . . (*He breaks off, then.*) Bernard . . . (*He is so full of emotion, he breaks off again.*)

BERNARD. What is it, Willy?

WILLY (*small and alone*). What—what's the secret?

BERNARD. What secret?

WILLY. How—how did you? Why didn't he ever catch on?

BERNARD. I wouldn't know that, Willy.

WILLY (*confidentially, desperately*). You were his friend, his boyhood friend. There's something I don't understand about it. His life ended after that Ebbets Field game. From the age of seventeen nothing good ever happened to him.

BERNARD. He never trained himself for anything.

WILLY. But he did, he did. After high school he took so many correspondence courses. Radio mechanics; television; God knows what, and never made the slightest mark.

BERNARD (*taking off his glasses*). Willy, do you want to talk candidly?

WILLY (*rising, faces Bernard*). I regard you as a very brilliant man, Bernard. I value your advice.

BERNARD. Oh, the hell with the advice, Willy. I couldn't advise you. There's just one thing I've always wanted to ask you. When he was supposed to graduate, and the math teacher flunked him . . .

WILLY. Oh, that son-of-a-bitch ruined his life.

BERNARD. Yeah, but, Willy, all he had to do was go to summer school and make up that subject.

WILLY. That's right, that's right.

BERNARD. Did you tell him not to go to summer school?

WILLY. Me? I begged him to go. I ordered him to go!

BERNARD. Then why wouldn't he go?

WILLY. Why? Why! Bernard, that question has been trailing me like a ghost for the last fifteen years. He flunked the subject, and laid down and died like a hammer hit him!

BERNARD. Take it easy, kid.

WILLY. Let me talk to you—I got nobody to talk to. Bernard, Bernard, was it my fault? Y'see? It keeps going around in my mind, maybe I did something to him. I got nothing to give him.

BERNARD. Don't take it so hard.

WILLY. Why did he lay down? What is the story there? You were his friend!

BERNARD. Willy, I remember, it was June, and our grades came out. And he'd flunked math.

WILLY. That son-of-a-bitch!

BERNARD. No, it wasn't right then. Biff just got very angry, I remember, and he was ready to enroll in summer school.

WILLY (*surprised*). He was?

BERNARD. He wasn't beaten by it at all. But then, Willy, he disappeared from the block for almost a month. And I got the idea that he'd gone up to New England to see you. Did he have a talk with you then?

Willy stares in silence.

BERNARD. Willy?

WILLY (*with a strong edge of resentment in his voice*). Yeah, he came to Boston. What about it?

BERNARD. Well, just that when he came back—I'll never forget this, it always mystifies me. Because I'd thought so well of Biff, even though he'd always taken advantage of me. I loved him, Willy, y'know? And he came back after that month and took his sneakers—remember those sneakers with "University of Virginia" printed on them? He was so proud of those, wore them every day. And he took them down in the cellar, and burned them up in the furnace. We had a fist fight. It lasted at least half an hour. Just the two of us, punching each other down the cellar, and crying right through it. I've often thought of how strange it was that I knew he'd given up his life. What happened in Boston, Willy?

Willy looks at him as at an intruder.

BERNARD. I just bring it up because you asked me.

WILLY (*angrily*). Nothing. What do you mean, "What happened?" What's that got to do with anything?

BERNARD. Well, don't get sore.

WILLY. What are you trying to do, blame it on me? If a boy lays down is that my fault?

BERNARD. Now, Willy, don't get . . .

WILLY. Well, don't—don't talk to me that way! What does that mean, "What happened?"

Charley enters. He is in his vest, and he carries a bottle of bourbon.

CHARLEY. Hey, you're going to miss that train. (*He waves the bottle.*)

BERNARD. Yeah, I'm going. (*He takes the bottle.*) Thanks, Pop. (*He picks up his rackets and bag.*) Good-by, Willy, and don't worry about it. You know, "If at first you don't succeed . . ."

WILLY. Yes, I believe in that.

BERNARD. But sometimes, Willy, it's better for a man just to walk away.

WILLY. Walk away?

BERNARD. That's right.

WILLY. But if you can't walk away?

BERNARD (*after a slight pause*). I guess that's when it's tough. (*Extending his hand.*) Good-by, Willy.

WILLY (*shaking Bernard's hand*). Good-by, boy.

CHARLEY (*an arm on Bernard's shoulder*). How do you like this kid? Gonna argue a case in front of the Supreme Court.

BERNARD (*protesting*). Pop!

WILLY (*genuinely shocked, pained, and happy*). No! The Supreme Court!

BERNARD. I gotta run. 'By, Dad!

CHARLEY. Knock 'em dead, Bernard!

Bernard goes off.

WILLY (*as Charley takes out his wallet*). The Supreme Court! And he didn't even mention it!

CHARLEY (*counting out money on the desk*). He don't have to—he's gonna do it.

WILLY. And you never told him what to do, did you? You never took any interest in him.

CHARLEY. My salvation is that I never took any interest in anything. There's some money—fifty dollars. I got an accountant inside.

WILLY. Charley, look . . . (*with difficulty.*) I got my insurance to pay. If you can manage it—I need a hundred and ten dollars.

Charley doesn't reply for a moment; merely stops moving.

WILLY. I'd draw it from my bank but Linda would know, and I . . .

CHARLEY. Sit down, Willy.

WILLY (*moving toward the chair*). I'm keeping an account of everything, remember. I'll pay every penny back. (*He sits.*)

CHARLEY. Now listen to me, Willy.

WILLY. I want you to know I appreciate . . .

CHARLEY (*sitting down on the table*). Willy, what're you doin'? What the hell is going on in your head?

WILLY. Why? I'm simply . . .

CHARLEY. I offered you a job. You make fifty dollars a week. And I won't send you on the road.

WILLY. I've got a job.

CHARLEY. Without pay? What kind of a job is a job without pay? (*He rises.*) Now, look, kid, enough is enough. I'm no genius but I know when I'm being insulted.

WILLY. Insulted!

CHARLEY. Why don't you want to work for me?

WILLY. What's the matter with you? I've got a job.

CHARLEY. Then what're you walkin' in here every week for?

WILLY (*getting up*). Well, if you don't want me to walk in here . . .

CHARLEY. I'm offering you a job.

WILLY. I don't want your goddam job!

CHARLEY. When the hell are you going to grow up?

WILLY (*furiously*). You big ignoramus, if you say that to me again I'll rap you one! I don't care how big you are! (*He's ready to fight.*)

Pause.

CHARLEY (*kindly, going to him*). How much do you need, Willy?

WILLY. Charley, I'm strapped. I'm strapped. I don't know what to do. I was just fired.

CHARLEY. Howard fired you?

WILLY. That snotnose. Imagine that? I named him. I named him Howard.

CHARLEY. Willy, when're you gonna realize that them things don't mean anything? You named him Howard, but you can't sell that. The only thing you got in this world is what you can sell. And the funny thing is that you're a salesman, and you don't know that.

WILLY. I've always tried to think otherwise, I guess. I always felt that if a man was impressive, and well liked, that nothing . . .

CHARLEY. Why must everybody like you? Who liked J. P. Morgan? Was he impressive? In a Turkish bath he'd look like a butcher. But with his pockets on he was very well liked. Now listen, Willy, I know you don't like me, and nobody can say I'm in love with you, but I'll give you a job because—just for the hell of it, put it that way. Now what do you say?

WILLY. I—I just can't work for you, Charley.

CHARLEY. What're you, jealous of me?

WILLY. I can't work for you, that's all, don't ask me why.

CHARLEY (*angered, takes out more bills*). You been jealous of me all your life, you damned fool! Here, pay your insurance. (*He puts the money in Willy's hand.*)

WILLY. I'm keeping strict accounts.

CHARLEY. I've got some work to do. Take care of yourself. And pay your insurance.

WILLY (*moving to the right*). Funny, y'know? After all the highways, and the trains, and the appointments, and the years, you end up worth more dead than alive.

CHARLEY. Willy, nobody's worth nothin' dead. (*After a slight pause.*) Did you hear what I said?

Willy stands still, dreaming.

CHARLEY. Willy!

WILLY. Apologize to Bernard for me when you see him. I didn't mean to argue with him. He's a fine boy. They're all fine boys, and they'll end up big—all of them. Someday they'll all play tennis together. Wish me luck, Charley. He saw Bill Oliver today.

CHARLEY. Good luck.

WILLY (*on the verge of tears*). Charley, you're the only friend I got. Isn't that a remarkable thing? (*He goes out.*)

CHARLEY. Jesus!

Charley stares after him a moment and follows. All light blacks out. Suddenly raucous music is heard, and a red glow rises behind the screen at right. Stanley, a young waiter, appears, carrying a table, followed by Happy, who is carrying two chairs.

STANLEY (*putting the table down*). That's all right, Mr. Loman, I can handle it myself. (*He turns and takes the chairs from Happy and places them at the table.*)

HAPPY (*glancing around*). Oh, this is better.

STANLEY. Sure, in the front there you're in the middle of all kinds of noise. Whenever you got a party, Mr. Loman, you just tell me and I'll put you back here. Y'know, there's a lotta people they don't like it private, because when they go out they like to see a lotta action around them because they're sick and tired to stay in the house by theirself. But I know you, you ain't from Hackensack. You know what I mean?

HAPPY (*sitting down*). So how's it coming, Stanley?

STANLEY. Ah, it's a dog life. I only wish during the war they'd a took me in the Army. I coulda been dead by now.

HAPPY. My brother's back, Stanley.

STANLEY. Oh, he come back, heh? From the Far West.

HAPPY. Yeah, big cattle man, my brother, so treat him right. And my father's coming too.

STANLEY. Oh, your father too!

HAPPY. You got a couple of nice lobsters?

STANLEY. Hundred per cent, big.

HAPPY. I want them with the claws.

STANLEY. Don't worry, I don't give you no mice. (*Happy laughs.*) How about some wine? It'll put a head on the meal.

HAPPY. No. You remember, Stanley, that recipe I brought you from overseas? With the champagne in it?

STANLEY. Oh, yeah, sure. I still got it tacked up yet in the kitchen. But that'll have to cost a buck apiece anyways.

HAPPY. That's all right.

STANLEY. What'd you, hit a number or somethin'?

HAPPY. No, it's a little celebration. My brother is—I think he pulled off a big deal today. I think we're going into business together.

STANLEY. Great! That's the best for you. Because a family business, you know what I mean?—that's the best.

HAPPY. That's what I think.

STANLEY. 'Cause what's the difference? Somebody steals? It's in the family. Know what I mean? (*Sotto voce.*) Like this bartender here. The boss is goin' crazy what kinda leak he's got in the cash register. You put it in but it don't come out.

HAPPY (*raising his head*). Sh!

STANLEY. What?

HAPPY. You notice I wasn't lookin' right or left, was I?

STANLEY. No.

HAPPY. And my eyes are closed.

STANLEY. So what's the . . . ?

HAPPY. Strudel's comin'.

STANLEY (*catching on, looks around*). Ah, no, there's no . . .

He breaks off as a furred, lavishly dressed Girl enters and sits at the next table. Both follow her with their eyes.

STANLEY. Geez, how'd ya know?

HAPPY. I got radar or something. (*Staring directly at her profile.*) Oooooooo . . . Stanley.

STANLEY. I think that's for you, Mr. Loman.

HAPPY. Look at that mouth. Oh, God. And the binoculars.

STANLEY. Geez, you got a life, Mr. Loman.

HAPPY. Wait on her.

STANLEY (*going to the Girl's table*). Would you like a menu, ma'am?

GIRL. I'm expecting someone, but I'd like a . . .

HAPPY. Why don't you bring her—excuse me, miss, do you mind? I sell champagne, and I'd like you to try my brand. Bring her a champagne, Stanley.

GIRL. That's awfully nice of you.

HAPPY. Don't mention it. It's all company money. (*He laughs.*)

GIRL. That's a charming product to be selling, isn't it?

HAPPY. Oh, gets to be like everything else. Selling is selling, y'know.

GIRL. I suppose.

HAPPY. You don't happen to sell, do you?

GIRL. No, I don't sell.

HAPPY. Would you object to a compliment from a stranger? You ought to be on a magazine cover.

GIRL (*looking at him a little archly*). I have been.

Stanley comes in with a glass of champagne.

HAPPY. What'd I say before, Stanley? You see? She's a cover girl.

STANLEY. Oh, I could see, I could see.

HAPPY (*to the Girl*). What magazine?

GIRL. Oh, a lot of them. (*She takes the drink.*) Thank you.

HAPPY. You know what they say in France, don't you? "Champagne is the drink of the complexion"—Hya, Biff!

Biff has entered and sits with Happy.

BIFF. Hello, kid. Sorry I'm late.

HAPPY. I just got here. Uh, Miss . . . ?

GIRL. Forsythe.

HAPPY. Miss Forsythe, this is my brother.

BIFF. Is Dad here?

HAPPY. His name is Biff. You might've heard of him. Great football player.

GIRL. Really? What team?

HAPPY. Are you familiar with football?

GIRL. No, I'm afraid I'm not.

HAPPY. Biff is quarterback with the New York Giants.

GIRL. Well, that is nice, isn't it? (*She drinks.*)

HAPPY. Good health.

GIRL. I'm happy to meet you.

HAPPY. That's my name. Hap. It's really Harold, but at West Point they called me Happy.

GIRL (*now really impressed*). Oh, I see. How do you do? (*She turns her profile.*)

BIFF. Isn't Dad coming?

HAPPY. You want her?

BIFF. Oh, I could never make that.

HAPPY. I remember the time that idea would never come into your head. Where's the old confidence, Biff?

BIFF. I just saw Oliver . . .

HAPPY. Wait a minute. I've got to see that old confidence again. Do you want her? She's on call.

BIFF. Oh, no. (*He turns to look at the Girl.*)

HAPPY. I'm telling you. Watch this. (*Turning to the Girl.*) Honey? (*She turns to him.*) Are you busy?

GIRL. Well, I am . . . but I could make a phone call.

HAPPY. Do that, will you, honey? And see if you can get a friend. We'll be here for a while. Biff is one of the greatest football players in the country.

GIRL (*standing up*). Well, I'm certainly happy to meet you.

HAPPY. Come back soon.

GIRL. I'll try.

HAPPY. Don't try, honey, try hard.

The Girl exits. Stanley follows, shaking his head in bewildered admiration.

HAPPY. Isn't that a shame now? A beautiful girl like that? That's why I can't get married. There's not a good woman in a thousand. New York is loaded with them, kid!

BIFF. Hap, look . . .

HAPPY. I told you she was on call!

BIFF (*strangely unnerved*). Cut it out, will ya? I want to say something to you.

HAPPY. Did you see Oliver?

BIFF. I saw him all right. Now look, I want to tell Dad a couple of things and I want you to help me.

HAPPY. What? Is he going to back you?

BIFF. Are you crazy? You're out of your goddam head, you know that?

HAPPY. Why? What happened?

BIFF (*breathlessly*). I did a terrible thing today, Hap. It's been the strangest day I ever went through. I'm all numb, I swear.

HAPPY. You mean he wouldn't see you?

BIFF. Well, I waited six hours for him, see? All day. Kept sending my name in. Even tried to date his secretary so she'd get me to him, but no soap.

HAPPY. Because you're not showin' the old confidence, Biff. He remembered you, didn't he?

BIFF (*stopping Happy with a gesture*). Finally, about five o'clock, he comes out. Didn't remember who I was or anything. I felt like such an idiot, Hap.

HAPPY. Did you tell him my Florida idea?

BIFF. He walked away. I saw him for one minute. I got so mad I could've torn the walls down! How the hell did I ever get the idea I was a salesman there? I even believed myself that I'd been a salesman for him! And then he gave me one look and—I realized what a ridiculous lie my whole life has been! We've been talking in a dream for fifteen years. I was a shipping clerk.

HAPPY. What'd you do?

BIFF (*with great tension and wonder*). Well, he left, see. And the secretary went out. I was all alone in the waiting room. I don't know what came over me, Hap. The next thing I know I'm in his office—paneled walls, everything. I can't explain it. I—Hap. I took his fountain pen.

HAPPY. Geez, did he catch you?

BIFF. I ran out. I ran down all eleven flights. I ran and ran and ran.

HAPPY. That was an awful dumb—what'd you do that for?

BIFF (*agonized*). I don't know, I just—wanted to take something, I don't know. You gotta help me, Hap. I'm gonna tell Pop.

HAPPY. You crazy? What for?

BIFF. Hap, he's got to understand that I'm not the man somebody lends that kind of money to. He thinks I've been spiting him all these years and it's eating him up.

HAPPY. That's just it. You tell him something nice.

BIFF. I can't.

HAPPY. Say you got a lunch date with Oliver tomorrow.

BIFF. So what do I do tomorrow?

HAPPY. You leave the house tomorrow and come back at night and say Oliver is thinking it over. And he thinks it over for a couple of weeks, and gradually it fades away and nobody's the worse.

BIFF. But it'll go on forever!

HAPPY. Dad is never so happy as when he's looking forward to something!

Willy enters.

HAPPY. Hello, scout!

WILLY. Gee, I haven't been here in years!

Stanley has followed Willy in and sets a chair for him. Stanley starts off but Happy stops him.

HAPPY. Stanley!

Stanley stands by, waiting for an order.

BIFF (*going to Willy with guilt, as to an invalid*). Sit down, Pop. You want a drink?

WILLY. Sure, I don't mind.

BIFF. Let's get a load on.

WILLY. You look worried.

BIFF. N-no. (*To Stanley.*) Scotch all around. Make it doubles.

STANLEY. Doubles, right. (*He goes.*)

WILLY. You had a couple already, didn't you?

BIFF. Just a couple, yeah.

WILLY. Well, what happened, boy? (*Nodding affirmatively, with a smile.*) Everything go all right?

BIFF (*takes a breath, then reaches out and grasps Willy's hand*). Pal . . . (*He is smiling bravely, and Willy is smiling too.*) I had an experience today.

HAPPY. Terrific, Pop.

WILLY. That so? What happened?

BIFF (*high, slightly alcoholic, above the earth*). I'm going to tell you everything from first to last. It's been a strange day. (*Silence. He looks around, composes himself as best he can, but his breath keeps breaking the rhythm of his voice.*) I had to wait quite a while for him, and . . .

WILLY. Oliver?

BIFF. Yeah, Oliver. All day, as a matter of cold fact. And a lot of—instances—facts, Pop, facts about my life came back to me. Who was it, Pop? Who ever said I was a salesman with Oliver?

WILLY. Well, you were.

BIFF. No, Dad, I was a shipping clerk.

WILLY. But you were practically . . .

BIFF (*with determination*). Dad, I don't know who said it first, but I was never a salesman for Bill Oliver.

WILLY. What're you talking about?

BIFF. Let's hold on to the facts tonight, Pop. We're not going to get anywhere bullin' around. I was a shipping clerk.

WILLY (*angrily*). All right, now listen to me . . .

BIFF. Why don't you let me finish?

WILLY. I'm not interested in stories about the past or any crap of that kind because the woods are burning, boys, you understand? There's a big blaze going on all around. I was fired today.

BIFF (*shocked*). How could you be?

WILLY. I was fired, and I'm looking for a little good news to tell your mother, because the woman has waited and the woman has suffered. The gist of it is that I haven't got a story left in my head, Biff. So don't give me a lecture about facts and aspects. I am not interested. Now what've you got to say to me?

Stanley enters with three drinks. They wait until he leaves.

WILLY. Did you see Oliver?

BIFF. Jesus, Dad!

WILLY. You mean you didn't go up there?

HAPPY. Sure he went up there.

BIFF. I did. I—saw him. How could they fire you?

WILLY (*on the edge of his chair*). What kind of a welcome did he give you?

BIFF. He won't even let you work on commission?

WILLY. I'm out! (*Driving.*) So tell me, he gave you a warm welcome?

HAPPY. Sure, Pop, sure!

BIFF (*driven*). Well, it was kind of . . .

WILLY. I was wondering if he'd remember you. (*To Happy.*) Imagine, man doesn't see him for ten, twelve years and gives him that kind of a welcome!

HAPPY. Damn right!

BIFF (*trying to return to the offensive*). Pop, look . . .

WILLY. You know why he remembered you, don't you? Because you impressed him in those days.

BIFF. Let's talk quietly and get this down to the facts, huh?

WILLY (*as though Biff had been interrupting*). Well, what happened? It's great news, Biff. Did he take you into his office or'd you talk in the waiting room?

BIFF. Well, he came in, see, and . . .

WILLY (*with a big smile*). What'd he say? Betcha he threw his arm around you.

BIFF. Well, he kinda . . .

WILLY. He's a fine man. (*To Happy.*) Very hard man to see, y'know.

HAPPY (*agreeing*). Oh, I know.

WILLY (*to Biff*). Is that where you had the drinks?

BIFF. Yeah, he gave me a couple of—no, no!

HAPPY (*cutting in*). He told him my Florida idea.

WILLY. Don't interrupt. (*To Biff.*) How'd he react to the Florida idea?

BIFF. Dad, will you give me a minute to explain?

WILLY. I've been waiting for you to explain since I sat down here! What happened? He took you into his office and what?

BIFF. Well—I talked. And—and he listened, see.

WILLY. Famous for the way he listens, y'know. What was his answer?

BIFF. His answer was—(*He breaks off, suddenly angry.*) Dad, you're not letting me tell you what I want to tell you!

WILLY (*accusing, angered*). You didn't see him, did you?

BIFF. I did see him!

WILLY. What'd you insult him or something? You insulted him, didn't you?

BIFF. Listen, will you let me out of it, will you just let me out of it!

HAPPY. What the hell!

WILLY. Tell me what happened!

BIFF (*to Happy*). I can't talk to him!

A single trumpet note jars the ear. The light of green leaves stains the house, which holds the air of night and a dream. Young Bernard enters and knocks on the door of the house.

YOUNG BERNARD (*frantically*). Mrs. Loman, Mrs. Loman!

HAPPY. Tell him what happened!

BIFF (*to Happy.*) Shut up and leave me alone!

WILLY. No, no! You had to go and flunk math!

BIFF. What math? What're you talking about?

YOUNG BERNARD. Mrs. Loman, Mrs. Loman!

Linda appears in the house, as of old.

WILLY (*wildly*). Math, math, math!

BIFF. Take it easy, Pop!

YOUNG BERNARD. Mrs. Loman!

WILLY (*furiously*). If you hadn't flunked you'd've been set by now!

BIFF. Now, look, I'm gonna tell you what happened, and you're going to listen to me.

YOUNG BERNARD. Mrs. Loman!

BIFF. I waited six hours . . .

HAPPY. What the hell are you saying?

BIFF. I kept sending in my name but he wouldn't see me. So finally he . . . (*He continues unheard as light fades low on the restaurant.*)

YOUNG BERNARD. Biff flunked math!

LINDA. No!

YOUNG BERNARD. Birnbaum flunked him! They won't graduate him!

LINDA. But they have to. He's gotta go to the university. Where is he? Biff! Biff!

YOUNG BERNARD. No, he left. He went to Grand Central.

LINDA. Grand—You mean he went to Boston!

YOUNG BERNARD. Is Uncle Willy in Boston?

LINDA. Oh, maybe Willy can talk to the teacher. Oh, the poor, poor boy!

Light on house area snaps out.

BIFF (*at the table, now audible, holding up a gold fountain pen*). . . . so I'm washed up with Oliver, you understand? Are you listening to me?

WILLY (*at a loss*). Yeah, sure. If you hadn't flunked . . .

BIFF. Flunked what? What're you talking about?

WILLY. Don't blame everything on me! I didn't flunk math—you did! What pen?

HAPPY. That was awful dumb, Biff, a pen like that is worth—

WILLY (*seeing the pen for the first time*). You took Oliver's pen?

BIFF (*weakening*). Dad, I just explained it to you.

WILLY. You stole Bill Oliver's fountain pen!

BIFF. I didn't exactly steal it! That's just what I've been explaining to you!

HAPPY. He had it in his hand and just then Oliver walked in, so he got nervous and stuck it in his pocket!

WILLY. My God, Biff!

BIFF. I never intended to do it, Dad!

OPERATOR'S VOICE. Standish Arms, good evening!

WILLY (*shouting*). I'm not in my room!

BIFF (*frightened*). Dad, what's the matter? (*He and Happy stand up.*)

OPERATOR. Ringing Mr. Loman for you!

WILLY. I'm not there, stop it!

BIFF (*horrified, gets down on one knee before Willy*). Dad, I'll make good, I'll make good. (*Willy tries to get to his feet. Biff holds him down.*) Sit down now.

WILLY. No, you're no good, you're no good for anything.

BIFF. I am, Dad, I'll find something else, you understand? Now don't worry about anything. (*He holds up Willy's face.*) Talk to me, Dad.

OPERATOR. Mr. Loman does not answer. Shall I page him?

WILLY (*attempting to stand, as though to rush and silence the Operator*). No, no, no!

HAPPY. He'll strike something, Pop.

WILLY. No, no . . .

BIFF (*desperately, standing over Willy*). Pop, listen! Listen to me! I'm telling you something good. Oliver talked to his partner about the Florida idea. You listening? He—he talked to his partner, and he came to me . . . I'm going to be all right, you hear? Dad, listen to me, he said it was just a question of the amount!

WILLY. Then you . . . got it?

HAPPY. He's gonna be terrific, Pop!

WILLY (*trying to stand*). Then you got it, haven't you? You got it! You got it!

BIFF (*agonized, holds Willy down*). No, no. Look, Pop. I'm supposed to have lunch with them tomorrow. I'm just telling you this so you'll know that I can still make an impression, Pop. And I'll make good somewhere, but I can't go tomorrow, see.

WILLY. Why not? You simply . . .

BIFF. But the pen, Pop!

WILLY. You give it to him and tell him it was an oversight!

HAPPY. Sure, have lunch tomorrow!

BIFF. I can't say that . . .

WILLY. You were doing a crossword puzzle and accidentally used his pen!

BIFF. Listen, kid, I took those balls years ago, now I walk in with his fountain pen? That clinches it, don't you see? I can't face him like that! I'll try elsewhere.

PAGE'S VOICE. Paging Mr. Loman!

WILLY. Don't you want to be anything?

BIFF. Pop, how can I go back?

WILLY. You don't want to be anything, is that what's behind it?

BIFF (*now angry at Willy for not crediting his sympathy*). Don't take it that way! You think it was easy walking into that office after what I'd done to him? A team of horses couldn't have dragged me back to Bill Oliver!

WILLY. Then why'd you go?

BIFF. Why did I go? Why did I go! Look at you! Look at what's become of you!

Off left, The Woman laughs.

WILLY. Biff, you're going to go to that lunch tomorrow, or . . .

BIFF. I can't go. I've got no appointment!

HAPPY. Biff, for . . . !

WILLY. Are you spiting me?

BIFF. Don't take it that way! Goddammit!

WILLY (*strikes Biff and falters away from the table*). You rotten little louse! Are you spiting me?

THE WOMAN. Someone's at the door, Willy!

BIFF. I'm no good, can't you see what I am?

HAPPY (*separating them*). Hey, you're in a restaurant! Now cut it out, both of you! (*The girls enter.*) Hello, girls, sit down.

The Woman laughs, off left.

MISS FORSYTHE. I guess we might as well. This is Letta.

THE WOMAN. Willy, are you going to wake up?

BIFF (*ignoring Willy*). How're ya, miss, sit down. What do you drink?

MISS FORSYTHE. Letta might not be able to stay long.

LETTA. I gotta get up very early tomorrow. I got jury duty. I'm so excited! Were you fellows ever on a jury?

BIFF. No, but I been in front of them! (*The girls laugh.*) This is my father.

LETTA. Isn't he cute? Sit down with us, Pop.

HAPPY. Sit him down, Biff!

BIFF (*going to him*). Come on, slugger, drink us under the table. To hell with it! Come on, sit down, pal.

On Biff's last insistence, Willy is about to sit.

THE WOMAN (*now urgently*). Willy, are you going to answer the door!

The Woman's call pulls Willy back. He starts right, befuddled.

BIFF. Hey, where are you going?

WILLY. Open the door.

BIFF. The door?

WILLY. The washroom . . . the door . . . where's the door?

BIFF (*leading Willy to the left*). Just go straight down.

Willy moves left.

THE WOMAN. Willy, Willy, are you going to get up, get up, get up, get up?

Willy exits left.

LETTA. I think it's sweet you bring your daddy along.

MISS FORSYTHE. Oh, he isn't really your father!

BIFF (*at left, turning to her resentfully*). Miss Forsythe, you've just seen a prince walk by. A fine, troubled prince. A hardworking, unappreciated prince. A pal, you understand? A good companion. Always for his boys.

LETTA. That's so sweet.

HAPPY. Well, girls, what's the program? We're wasting time. Come on, Biff. Gather round. Where would you like to go?

BIFF. Why don't you do something for him?

HAPPY. Me!

BIFF. Don't you give a damn for him, Hap?

HAPPY. What're you talking about? I'm the one who . . .

BIFF. I sense it, you don't give a good goddam about him. (*He takes the rolled-up hose from his pocket and puts it on the table in front of Happy.*) Look what I found in the cellar, for Christ's sake. How can you bear to let it go on?

HAPPY. Me? Who goes away? Who runs off and . . .

BIFF. Yeah, but he doesn't mean anything to you. You could help him—I can't! Don't you understand what I'm talking about? He's going to kill himself, don't you know that?

HAPPY. Don't know it! Me!

BIFF. Hap, help him! Jesus . . . help him . . . Help me, help me, I can't bear to look at his face! (*Ready to weep, he hurries out, up right.*)

HAPPY (*starting after him*). Where are you going?

MISS FORSYTHE. What's he so mad about?

HAPPY. Come on, girls, we'll catch up with him.

MISS FORSYTHE (*as Happy pushes her out*). Say, I don't like that temper of his!

HAPPY. He's just a little overstrung, he'll be all right!

WILLY (*off left, as The Woman laughs*). Don't answer! Don't answer!

LETTA. Don't you want to tell your father . . .

HAPPY. No, that's not my father. He's just a guy. Come on, we'll catch Biff, and, honey, we're going to paint this town! Stanley, where's the check! Hey, Stanley!

They exit. Stanley looks toward left.

STANLEY (*calling to Happy indignantly*). Mr. Loman! Mr. Loman!

Stanley picks up a chair and follows them off. Knocking is heard off left. The Woman enters, laughing. Willy follows her. She is in a black slip; he is buttoning his shirt. Raw, sensuous music accompanies their speech:

WILLY. Will you stop laughing? Will you stop?

THE WOMAN. Aren't you going to answer the door? He'll wake the whole hotel.

WILLY. I'm not expecting anybody.

THE WOMAN. Whyn't you have another drink, honey, and stop being so damn self-centered?

WILLY. I'm so lonely.

THE WOMAN. You know you ruined me, Willy? From now on, whenever you come to the office, I'll see that you go right through to the buyers. No waiting at my desk anymore, Willy. You ruined me.

WILLY. That's nice of you to say that.

THE WOMAN. Gee, you are self-centered! Why so sad? You are the saddest, self-centeredest soul I ever did see-saw. (*She laughs. He kisses her.*) Come on inside, drummer boy. It's silly to be dressing in the middle of the night. (*As knocking is heard.*) Aren't you going to answer the door?

WILLY. They're knocking on the wrong door.

THE WOMAN. But I felt the knocking. And he heard us talking in here. Maybe the hotel's on fire!

WILLY (*his terror rising*). It's a mistake.

THE WOMAN. Then tell him to go away!

WILLY. There's nobody there.

THE WOMAN. It's getting on my nerves, Willy. There's somebody standing out there and it's getting on my nerves!

WILLY (*pushing her away from him*). All right, stay in the bathroom here, and don't come out. I think there's a law in Massachusetts about it, so don't come out. It may be that new room clerk. He looked very mean. So don't come out. It's a mistake, there's no fire.

The knocking is heard again. He takes a few steps away from her, and she vanishes into the wing. The light follows him, and now he is facing Young Biff, who carries a suit-case. Biff steps toward him. The music is gone.

BIFF. Why didn't you answer?

WILLY. Biff! What are you doing in Boston?

BIFF. Why didn't you answer? I've been knocking for five minutes, I called you on the phone . . .

WILLY. I just heard you. I was in the bathroom and had the door shut. Did anything happen home?

BIFF. Dad—I let you down.

WILLY. What do you mean?

BIFF. Dad . . .

WILLY. Biffo, what's this about? (*Putting his arm around Biff.*) Come on, let's go downstairs and get you a malted.

BIFF. Dad, I flunked math.

WILLY. Not for the term?

BIFF. The term. I haven't got enough credits to graduate.

WILLY. You mean to say Bernard wouldn't give you the answers?

BIFF. He did, he tried, but I only got a sixty-one.

WILLY. And they wouldn't give you four points?

BIFF. Birnbaum refused absolutely. I begged him, Pop, but he won't give me those points. You gotta talk to him before they close the school. Because if he saw the kind of man you are, and you just talked to him in your way, I'm sure he'd come through for me. The class came right before practice, see, and I didn't go enough. Would you talk to him? He'd like you, Pop. You know the way you could talk.

WILLY. You're on. We'll drive right back.

BIFF. Oh, Dad, good work! I'm sure he'll change it for you!

WILLY. Go downstairs and tell the clerk I'm checkin' out. Go right down.

BIFF. Yes, sir! See, the reason he hates me, Pop—one day he was late for class so I got up at the blackboard and imitated him. I crossed my eyes and talked with a lithp.

WILLY (*laughing*). You did? The kids like it?

BIFF. They nearly died laughing!

WILLY. Yeah? What'd you do?

BIFF. The thquare root of thixthy twee is . . . (*Willy bursts out laughing; Biff joins.*) And in the middle of it he walked in!

Willy laughs and The Woman joins in offstage.

WILLY (*without hesitation*). Hurry downstairs and . . .

BIFF. Somebody in there?

WILLY. No, that was next door.

The Woman laughs offstage.

BIFF. Somebody got in your bathroom!

WILLY. No, it's the next room, there's a party . . .

THE WOMAN (*enters, laughing; she lisps this*). Can I come in? There's something in the bathtub, Willy, and it's moving!

Willy looks at Biff; who is staring open-mouthed and horrified at The Woman.

WILLY. Ah—you better go back to your room. They must be finished painting by now. They're painting her room so I let her take a shower here. Go back, go back . . . (*He pushes her.*)

THE WOMAN (*resisting*). But I've got to get dressed, Willy, I can't . . .

WILLY. Get out of here! Go back, go back . . . (*Suddenly striving for the ordinary.*) This is Miss Francis, Biff, she's a buyer. They're painting her room. Go back, Miss Francis, go back . . .

THE WOMAN. But my clothes, I can't go out naked in the hall!

WILLY (*pushing her offstage*). Get outa here! Go back, go back!

Biff slowly sits down on his suitcase as the argument continues offstage.

THE WOMAN. Where's my stockings? You promised me stockings, Willy!

WILLY. I have no stockings here!

THE WOMAN. You had two boxes of size nine sheers for me, and I want them!

WILLY. Here, for God's sake, will you get outa here!

THE WOMAN (*enters holding a box of stockings*). I just hope there's nobody in the hall. That's all I hope. (*To Biff.*) Are you football or baseball?

BIFF. Football.

THE WOMAN (*angry, humiliated*). That's me too. G'night. (*She snatches her clothes from Willy, and walks out.*)

WILLY (*after a pause*). Well, better get going. I want to get to the school first thing in the morning. Get my suits out of the closet. I'll get my valise. (*Biff doesn't move.*) What's the matter! (*Biff remains motionless, tears falling.*) She's a buyer. Buys for J. H. Simmons. She lives down the hall—they're painting. You don't imagine—(*He breaks off. After a pause.*) Now listen, pal, she's just a buyer. She sees merchandise in her room and they have to keep it looking just so . . . (*Pause. Assuming command.*) All right, get my suits. (*Biff doesn't move.*) Now stop crying and do as I say. I gave you an order. Biff, I gave you an order! Is that what you do when I give you an order? How dare you cry! (*Putting his arm around Biff.*) Now look, Biff, when you grow up you'll understand about these things. You mustn't—you mustn't overemphasize a thing like this. I'll see Birnbaum first thing in the morning.

BIFF. Never mind.

WILLY (*getting down beside Biff.*) Never mind! He's going to give you those points. I'll see to it.

BIFF. He wouldn't listen to you.

WILLY. He certainly will listen to me. You need those points for the U. of Virginia.

BIFF. I'm not going there.

WILLY. Heh? If I can't get him to change that mark you'll make it up in summer school. You've got all summer to . . .

BIFF (*his weeping breaking from him*). Dad . . .

WILLY (*infected by it*). Oh, my boy . . .

BIFF. Dad . . .

WILLY. She's nothing to me, Biff. I was lonely, I was terribly lonely.

BIFF. You—you gave her Mama's stockings! (*His tears break through and he rises to go.*)

WILLY (*grabbing for Biff*). I gave you an order!

BIFF. Don't touch me, you—liar!

WILLY. Apologize for that!

BIFF. You fake! You phony little fake! You fake! (*Overcome, he turns quickly and weeping fully goes out with his suitcase. Willy is left on the floor on his knees.*)

WILLY. I gave you an order! Biff, come back here or I'll beat you! Come back here! I'll whip you!

Stanley comes quickly in from the right and stands in front of Willy.

WILLY (*shouts at Stanley*). I gave you an order . . .

STANLEY. Hey, let's pick it up, pick it up, Mr. Loman. (*He helps Willy to his feet.*) Your boys left with the chippies. They said they'll see you home.

A second waiter watches some distance away.

WILLY. But we were supposed to have dinner together.

Music is heard, Willy's theme.

STANLEY. Can you make it?

WILLY. I'll—sure, I can make it. (*Suddenly concerned about his clothes.*) Do I—I look all right?

STANLEY. Sure, you look all right. (*He flicks a speck off Willy's lapel.*)

WILLY. Here—here's a dollar.

STANLEY. Oh, your son paid me. It's all right.

WILLY (*putting it in Stanley's hand*). No, take it. You're a good boy.

STANLEY. Oh, no, you don't have to . . .

WILLY. Here—here's some more, I don't need it any more. (*After a slight pause.*) Tell me—is there a seed store in the neighborhood?

STANLEY. Seeds? You mean like to plant?

As Willy turns, Stanley slips the money back into his jacket pocket.

WILLY. Yes. Carrots, peas . . .

STANLEY. Well, there's hardware stores on Sixth Avenue, but it may be too late now.

WILLY (*anxiously*). Oh, I'd better hurry. I've got to get some seeds. (*He starts off to the right.*) I've got to get some seeds, right away. Nothing's planted. I don't have a thing in the ground.

Willy hurries out as the light goes down. Stanley moves over to the right after him, watches him off. The other waiter has been staring at Willy.

STANLEY (*to the waiter*). Well, whatta you looking at?

The waiter picks up the chairs and moves off right. Stanley takes the table and follows him. The light fades on this area. There is a long pause, the sound of the flute coming over. The light gradually rises on the kitchen, which is empty. Happy appears at the door of the house, followed by Biff. Happy is carrying a large bunch of long-stemmed roses. He enters the kitchen, looks around for Linda. Not seeing her, he turns to Biff, who is just outside the house door, and makes a gesture with his hands, indicating "Not here, I guess." He looks into the living room and freezes. Inside, Linda, unseen, is seated, Willy's coat on her lap. She rises ominously and quietly and moves toward Happy, who backs up into the kitchen, afraid.

HAPPY. Hey, what're you doing up? (*Linda says nothing but moves toward him implacably.*) Where's Pop? (*He keeps backing to the right, and now Linda is in full view in the doorway to the living room.*) Is he sleeping?

LINDA. Where were you?

HAPPY (*trying to laugh it off*). We met two girls, Mom, very fine types. Here, we brought you some flowers. (*Offering them to her.*) Put them in your room, Ma.

She knocks them to the floor at Biff's feet. He has now come inside and closed the door behind him. She stares at Biff, silent.

HAPPY. Now what'd you do that for? Mom, I want you to have some flowers . . .

LINDA (*cutting Happy off, violently to Biff*). Don't you care whether he lives or dies?

HAPPY (*going to the stairs*). Come upstairs, Biff.

BIFF (*with a flare of disgust, to Happy*). Go away from me! (*To Linda.*) What do you mean, lives or dies? Nobody's dying around here, pal.

LINDA. Get out of my sight! Get out of here!

BIFF. I wanna see the boss.

LINDA. You're not going near him!

BIFF. Where is he? (*He moves into the living room and Linda follows.*)

LINDA (*shouting after Biff.*) You invite him for dinner. He looks forward to it all day—(*Biff appears in his parents' bedroom, looks around, and exits*)—and then you desert him there. There's no stranger you'd do that to!

HAPPY. Why? He had a swell time with us. Listen, when I—(*Linda comes back into the kitchen*)—desert him I hope I don't outlive the day!

LINDA. Get out of here!

HAPPY. Now look, Mom . . .

LINDA. Did you have to go to women tonight? You and your lousy rotten whores!

Biff re-enters the kitchen.

HAPPY. Mom, all we did was follow Biff around trying to cheer him up! (*To Biff.*) Boy, what a night you gave me!

LINDA. Get out of here, both of you, and don't come back! I don't want you tormenting him any more. Go on now, get your things together! (*To Biff.*) You can sleep in his apartment. (*She starts to pick up the flowers and stops herself.*) Pick up this stuff, I'm not your maid any more. Pick it up, you bum, you!

Happy turns his back to her in refusal. Biff slowly moves over and gets down on his knees, picking up the flowers.

LINDA. You're a pair of animals! Not one, not another living soul would have had the cruelty to walk out on that man in a restaurant!

BIFF (*not looking at her*). Is that what he said?

LINDA. He didn't have to say anything. He was so humiliated he nearly limped when he came in.

HAPPY. But, Mom, he had a great time with us . . .

BIFF (*cutting him off violently*). Shut up!

Without another word, Happy goes upstairs.

LINDA. You! You didn't even go in to see if he was all right!

BIFF (*still on the floor in front of Linda, the flowers in his hand; with self-loathing*). No. Didn't. Didn't do a damned thing. How do you like that, heh? Left him babbling in a toilet.

LINDA. You louse. You . . .

BIFF. Now you hit it on the nose! (*He gets up, throws the flowers in the wastebasket.*) The scum of the earth, and you're looking at him!

LINDA. Get out of here!

BIFF. I gotta talk to the boss, Mom. Where is he?

LINDA. You're not going near him. Get out of this house!

BIFF (*with absolute assurance, determination*). No. We're gonna have an abrupt conversation, him and me.

LINDA. You're not talking to him.

Hammering is heard from outside the house, off right. Biff turns toward the noise.

LINDA (*suddenly pleading*). Will you please leave him alone?

BIFF. What's he doing out there?

LINDA. He's planting the garden!

BIFF (*quietly*). Now? Oh, my God!

Biff moves outside, Linda following. The light dies down on them and comes up on the center of the apron as Willy walks into it. He is carrying a flashlight, a hoe, and a handful of seed packets. He raps the top of the hoe sharply to fix it firmly, and then moves to the left, measuring off the distance with his foot. He holds the flashlight to look at the seed packets, reading off the instructions. He is in the blue of night.

WILLY. Carrots . . . quarter-inch apart. Rows . . . one-foot rows. (*He measures it off.*) One foot. (*He puts down a package and measures off.*) Beets. (*He puts down another package and measures again.*) Lettuce. (*He reads the package, puts it down.*) One foot—(*He breaks off as Ben appears at the right and moves slowly down to him.*) What a proposition, ts, ts. Terrific, terrific. 'Cause she's suffered, Ben, the woman has suffered. You understand me? A man can't go out the way he came in, Ben, a man has got to add up to something. You can't, you can't—(*Ben moves toward him as though to interrupt.*) You gotta consider now. Don't answer so quick. Remember, it's a guaranteed twenty-thousand-dollar proposition. Now look, Ben, I want you to go through the ins and outs of this thing with me. I've got nobody to talk to, Ben, and the woman has suffered, you hear me?

BEN (*standing still, considering*). What's the proposition?

WILLY. It's twenty thousand dollars on the barrelhead. Guaranteed, gilt-edged, you understand?

BEN. You don't want to make a fool of yourself. They might not honor the policy.

WILLY. How can they dare refuse? Didn't I work like a coolie to meet every premium on the nose? And now they don't pay off? Impossible!

BEN. It's called a cowardly thing, William.

WILLY. Why? Does it take more guts to stand here the rest of my life ringing up a zero?

BEN (*yielding*). That's a point, William. (*He moves, thinking, turns.*) And twenty thousand—that is something one can feel with the hand, it is there.

WILLY (*now assured, with rising power*). Oh, Ben, that's the whole beauty of it! I see it like a diamond, shining in the dark, hard and rough, that I can pick up and touch in my hand. Not like—like an appointment! This would not be another damned-fool appointment, Ben, and it changes all the aspects. Because he thinks I'm nothing, see, and so he spites me. But the funeral . . . (*Straightening up.*) Ben, that funeral will be massive! They'll come from Maine, Massachusetts, Vermont, New Hampshire! All the old-timers with the strange license plates—that boy will be thunderstruck, Ben, because he never realized—I am known! Rhode Island, New York, New Jersey—I am known, Ben, and he'll see it with his eyes once and for all. He'll see what I am, Ben! He's in for a shock, that boy!

BEN (*coming down to the edge of the garden*). He'll call you a coward.

WILLY (*suddenly fearful*). No, that would be terrible.

BEN. Yes. And a damned fool.

WILLY. No, no, he mustn't, I won't have that! (*He is broken and desperate.*)

BEN. He'll hate you, William.

The gay music of the Boys is heard.

WILLY. Oh, Ben, how do we get back to all the great times? Used to be so full of light, and comradeship, the sleigh-riding in winter, and the ruddiness on his cheeks. And always some kind of good news coming up, always something nice coming up ahead. And never even let me carry the valises in the house, and simonizing, simonizing that little red car! Why, why can't I give him something and not have him hate me?

BEN. Let me think about it. (*He glances at his watch.*) I still have a little time. Remarkable proposition, but you've got to be sure you're not making a fool of yourself.

Ben drifts off upstage and goes out of sight. Biff comes down from the left.

WILLY (*suddenly conscious of Biff, turns and looks up at him, then begins picking up the packages of seeds in confusion*). Where the hell is that seed? (*Indignantly.*) You can't see nothing out here! They boxed in the whole goddam neighborhood!

BIFF. There are people all around here. Don't you realize that?

WILLY. I'm busy. Don't bother me.

BIFF (*taking the hoe from Willy*). I'm saying good-by to you, Pop. (*Willy looks at him, silent, unable to move.*) I'm not coming back any more.

WILLY. You're not going to see Oliver tomorrow?

BIFF. I've got no appointment, Dad.

WILLY. He put his arm around you, and you've got no appointment?

BIFF. Pop, get this now, will you? Everytime I've left it's been a—fight that sent me out of here. Today I realized something about myself and I tried to explain it to you and I—I think I'm just not smart enough to make any sense out of it for you. To hell with whose fault it is or anything like that. (*He takes Willy's arm.*) Let's just wrap it up, heh? Come on in, we'll tell Mom. (*He gently tries to pull Willy to left.*)

WILLY (*frozen, immobile, with guilt in his voice*). No, I don't want to see her.

BIFF. Come on! (*He pulls again, and Willy tries to pull away.*)

WILLY (*highly nervous*). No, no, I don't want to see her.

BIFF (*tries to look into Willy's face, as if to find the answer there*). Why don't you want to see her?

WILLY (*more harshly now*). Don't bother me, will you?

BIFF. What do you mean, you don't want to see her? You don't want them calling you yellow, do you? This isn't your fault; it's me, I'm a bum. Now come inside! (*Willy strains to get away.*) Did you hear what I said to you?

Willy pulls away and quickly goes by himself into the house. Biff follows.

LINDA (*to Willy*). Did you plant, dear?

BIFF (*at the door, to Linda*). All right, we had it out. I'm going and I'm not writing any more.

LINDA (*going to Willy in the kitchen*). I think that's the best way, dear. 'Cause there's no use drawing it out, you'll just never get along.

Willy doesn't respond.

BIFF. People ask where I am and what I'm doing, you don't know, and you don't care. That way it'll be off your mind and you can start brightening up again. All right? That clears it, doesn't it? (*Willy is silent, and Biff goes to him.*) You gonna wish me luck, scout? (*He extends his hand.*) What do you say?

LINDA. Shake his hand, Willy.

WILLY (*turning to her, seething with hurt*). There's no necessity—to mention the pen at all, y'know.

BIFF (*gently*). I've got no appointment, Dad.

WILLY (*erupting fiercely*). He put his arm around . . . ?

BIFF. Dad, you're never going to see what I am, so what's the use of arguing? If I strike oil I'll send you a check. Meantime forget I'm alive.

WILLY (*to Linda*). Spite, see?

BIFF. Shake hands, Dad.

WILLY. Not my hand.

BIFF. I was hoping not to go this way.

WILLY. Well, this is the way you're going. Good-by.

Biff looks at him a moment, then turns sharply and goes to the stairs.

WILLY (*stops him with*). May you rot in hell if you leave this house!

BIFF (*turning*). Exactly what is it that you want from me?

WILLY. I want you to know, on the train, in the mountains, in the valleys, wherever you go, that you cut down your life for spite!

BIFF. No, no.

WILLY. Spite, spite, is the word of your undoing! And when you're down and out, remember what did it. When you're rotting somewhere beside the railroad tracks, remember, and don't you dare blame it on me!

BIFF. I'm not blaming it on you!

WILLY. I won't take the rap for this, you hear?

Happy comes down the stairs and stands on the bottom step, watching.

BIFF. That's just what I'm telling you!

WILLY (*sinking into a chair at a table, with full accusation*). You're trying to put a knife in me—don't think I don't know what you're doing!

BIFF. All right, phony! Then let's lay it on the line. (*He whips the rubber tube out of his pocket and puts it on the table.*)

HAPPY. You crazy . . .

LINDA. Biff! (*She moves to grab the hose, but Biff holds it down with his hand.*)

BIFF. Leave it there! Don't move it!

WILLY (*not looking at it*). What is that?

BIFF. You know goddam well what that is.

WILLY (*caged, wanting to escape*). I never saw that.

BIFF. You saw it. The mice didn't bring it into the cellar! What is this supposed to do, make a hero out of you? This supposed to make me sorry for you?

WILLY. Never heard of it.

BIFF. There'll be no pity for you, you hear it? No pity!

WILLY (*to Linda*). You hear the spite!

BIFF. No, you're going to hear the truth—what you are and what I am!

LINDA. Stop it!

WILLY. Spite!

HAPPY (*coming down toward Biff*). You cut it now!

BIFF (*to Happy*). The man don't know who we are! The man is gonna know! (*To Willy.*) We never told the truth for ten minutes in this house!

HAPPY. We always told the truth!

BIFF (*turning on him*). You big blow, are you the assistant buyer? You're one of the two assistants to the assistant, aren't you?

HAPPY. Well, I'm practically . . .

BIFF. You're practically full of it! We all are! and I'm through with it. (*To Willy.*) Now hear this, Willy, this is me.

WILLY. I know you!

BIFF. You know why I had no address for three months? I stole a suit in Kansas City and I was in jail. (*To Linda, who is sobbing.*) Stop crying. I'm through with it.

Linda turns away from them, her hands covering her face.

WILLY. I suppose that's my fault!

BIFF. I stole myself out of every good job since high school!

WILLY. And whose fault is that?

BIFF. And I never got anywhere because you blew me so full of hot air I could never stand taking orders from anybody! That's whose fault it is!

WILLY. I hear that!

LINDA. Don't, Biff!

BIFF. It's goddam time you heard that! I had to be boss big shot in two weeks, and I'm through with it!

WILLY. Then hang yourself! For spite, hang yourself!

BIFF. No! Nobody's hanging himself, Willy! I ran down eleven flights with a pen in my hand today. And suddenly I stopped, you hear me? And in the middle of that office building, do you hear this? I stopped in the middle of that building and I saw—the sky. I saw the things that I love in this world. The work and the food and time to sit and smoke. And I looked at the pen and said to myself, what the hell am I grabbing this for? Why am I trying to become what I don't want to be? What am I doing in an office, making a contemptuous, begging fool of myself, when all I want is out there, waiting for me the minute I say I know who I am! Why can't I say that, Willy? (*He tries to make Willy face him, but Willy pulls away and moves to the left.*)

WILLY (*with hatred, threateningly*). The door of your life is wide open!

BIFF. Pop! I'm a dime a dozen, and so are you!

WILLY (*turning on him now in an uncontrolled outburst*). I am not a dime a dozen! I am Willy Loman, and you are Biff Loman!

Biff starts for Willy, but is blocked by Happy. In his fury, Biff seems on the verge of attacking his father.

BIFF. I am not a leader of men, Willy, and neither are you. You were never anything but a hard-working drummer who landed in the ash can like all the rest of them! I'm one dollar an hour, Willy! I tried seven states and couldn't raise it. A buck an hour! Do you gather my meaning? I'm not bringing home any prizes any more, and you're going to stop waiting for me to bring them home!

WILLY (*directly to Biff*). You vengeful, spiteful mutt!

Biff breaks from Happy. Willy, in fright, starts up the stairs. Biff grabs him.

BIFF (*at the peak of his fury*). Pop! I'm nothing! I'm nothing, Pop. Can't you understand that? There's no spite in it any more. I'm just what I am, that's all.

Biff's fury has spent itself and he breaks down, sobbing, holding on to Willy, who dumbly fumbles for Biff's face.

WILLY (*astonished*). What're you doing? What're you doing? (*To Linda.*) Why is he crying?

BIFF (*crying, broken*). Will you let me go, for Christ's sake? Will you take that phony dream and burn it before something happens? (*Struggling to contain himself, he pulls away and moves to the stairs.*) I'll go in the morning. Put him—put him to bed. (*Exhausted, Biff moves up the stairs to his room.*)

WILLY (*after a long pause, astonished, elevated*). Isn't that—isn't that remarkable? Biff—he likes me!

LINDA. He loves you, Willy!

HAPPY (*deeply moved*). Always did, Pop.

WILLY. Oh, Biff! (*Staring wildly.*) He cried! Cried to me. (*He is choking with his love, and now cries out his promise.*) That boy—that boy is going to be magnificent!

Ben appears in the light just outside the kitchen.

BEN. Yes, outstanding, with twenty thousand behind him.

LINDA (*sensing the racing of his mind, fearfully, carefully*). Now come to bed, Willy. It's all settled now.

WILLY (*finding it difficult not to rush out of the house*). Yes, we'll sleep. Come on. Go to sleep, Hap.

BEN. And it does take a great kind of a man to crack the jungle.

In accents of dread, Ben's idyllic music starts up.

HAPPY (*his arm around Linda*). I'm getting married, Pop, don't forget it. I'm changing everything. I'm gonna run that department before the year is up. You'll see, Mom. (*He kisses her.*)

BEN. The jungle is dark but full of diamonds, Willy.

Willy turns, moves, listening to Ben.

LINDA. Be good. You're both good boys, just act that way, that's all.

HAPPY. 'Night, Pop. (*He goes upstairs.*)

LINDA (*to Willy*). Come, dear.

BEN (*with greater force*). One must go in to fetch a diamond out.

WILLY (*to Linda, as he moves slowly along the edge of the kitchen, toward the door*). I just want to get settled down, Linda. Let me sit alone for a little.

LINDA (*almost uttering her fear*). I want you upstairs.

WILLY (*taking her in his arms*). In a few minutes, Linda. I couldn't sleep right now. Go on, you look awful tired. (*He kisses her.*)

BEN. Not like an appointment at all. A diamond is rough and hard to the touch.

WILLY. Go on now. I'll be right up.

LINDA. I think this is the only way, Willy.

WILLY. Sure, it's the best thing.

BEN. Best thing!

WILLY. The only way. Everything is gonna be—go on, kid, get to bed. You look so tired.

LINDA. Come right up.

WILLY. Two minutes.

Linda goes into the living room, then reappears in her bedroom. Willy moves just outside the kitchen door.

WILLY. Loves me. (*Wonderingly.*) Always loved me. Isn't that a remarkable thing? Ben, he'll worship me for it!

BEN (*with promise*). It's dark there, but full of diamonds.

WILLY. Can you imagine that magnificence with twenty thousand dollars in his pocket?

LINDA (*calling from her room*). Willy! Come up!

WILLY (*calling into the kitchen*). Yes! Yes. Coming! It's very smart, you realize that, don't you, sweetheart? Even Ben sees it. I gotta go, baby. 'By! 'By! (*Going over to Ben, almost dancing.*) Imagine? When the mail comes he'll be ahead of Bernard again!

BEN. A perfect proposition all around.

WILLY. Did you see how he cried to me? Oh, if I could kiss him, Ben!

BEN. Time, William, time!

WILLY. Oh, Ben, I always knew one way or another we were gonna make it, Biff and I.

BEN (*looking at his watch*). The boat. We'll be late. (*He moves slowly off into the darkness.*)

WILLY (*elegiacally, turning to the house*). Now when you kick off, boy, I want a seventy-yard boot, and get right down the field under the ball, and when you hit, hit low and hit hard, because it's important, boy. (*He swings around and faces the audience.*) There's all kinds of important people in the stands, and the first thing you know . . . (*Suddenly realizing he is alone.*) Ben! Ben, where do I . . . ? (*He makes a sudden movement of search.*) Ben, how do I . . . ?

LINDA (*calling*). Willy, you coming up?

WILLY (*uttering a gasp of fear, whirling about as if to quiet her*). Sh! (*He turns around as if to find his way; sounds, faces, voices, seem to be swarming in upon him and he flicks at them, crying.*) Sh! Sh! (*Suddenly music, faint and high, stops him. It rises in intensity, almost to an unbearable scream. He goes up and down on his toes, and rushes off around the house.*) Shhh!

LINDA. Willy?

There is no answer. Linda waits. Biff gets up off his bed. He is still in his clothes. Happy sits up. Biff stands listening.

LINDA (*with real fear*). Willy, answer me! Willy!

There is the sound of a car starting and moving away at full speed.

LINDA. No!

BIFF (*rushing down the stairs*). Pop!

As the car speeds off the music crashes down in a frenzy of sound, which becomes the soft pulsation of a single cello string. Biff slowly returns to his bedroom. He and Happy gravely don their jackets. Linda slowly walks out of her room. The music has developed into a dead march. The leaves of day are appearing over everything. Charley and Bernard, somberly dressed, appear and knock on the kitchen door. Biff and Happy slowly descend the stairs to the kitchen as Charley and Bernard enter. All stop a moment when Linda, in clothes of mourning, bearing a little bunch of roses, comes through the draped doorway into the kitchen. She goes to Charley and takes his arm. Now all move toward the audience, through the wall-line of the kitchen. At the limit of the apron, Linda lays down the flowers, kneels, and sits back on her heels. All stare down at the grave.

REQUIEM

CHARLEY. It's getting dark, Linda.

Linda doesn't react. She stares at the grave.

BIFF. How about it, Mom? Better get some rest, heh? They'll be closing the gate soon.

Linda makes no move. Pause.

HAPPY (*deeply angered*). He had no right to do that. There was no necessity for it. We would've helped him.

CHARLEY (*grunting*). Hmmm.

BIFF. Come along, Mom.

LINDA. Why didn't anybody come?

CHARLEY. It was a very nice funeral.

LINDA. But where are all the people he knew? Maybe they blame him.

CHARLEY. Naa. It's a rough world, Linda. They wouldn't blame him.

LINDA. I can't understand it. At this time especially. First time in thirty-five years we were just about free and clear. He only needed a little salary. He was even finished with the dentist.

CHARLEY. No man only needs a little salary.

LINDA. I can't understand it.

BIFF. There were a lot of nice days. When he'd come home from a trip; or on Sundays, making the stoop; finishing the cellar; putting on the new porch; when he built the extra bathroom; and put up the garage. You know something, Charley, there's more of him in that front stoop than in all the sales he ever made.

CHARLEY. Yeah. He was a happy man with a batch of cement.

LINDA. He was so wonderful with his hands.

BIFF. He had the wrong dreams. All, all, wrong.

HAPPY (*almost ready to fight Biff*). Don't say that!

BIFF. He never knew who he was.

CHARLEY (*stopping Happy's movement and reply; to Biff*). Nobody dast blame this man. You don't understand: Willy was a salesman. And for a salesman, there is no rock bottom to the life. He don't put a bolt to a nut, he don't tell you the law or give you medicine. He's a man way out there in the blue, riding on a smile and a shoeshine. And when they start not smiling back—that's an earthquake. And then you get yourself a couple of spots on your hat, and you're finished. Nobody dast blame this man. A salesman is got to dream, boy. It comes with the territory.

BIFF. Charley, the man didn't know who he was.

HAPPY (*infuriated*). Don't say that!

BIFF. Why don't you come with me, Happy?

HAPPY. I'm not licked that easily. I'm staying right in this city, and I'm gonna beat this racket! (*He looks at Biff, his chin set.*) The Loman Brothers!

BIFF. I know who I am, kid.

HAPPY. All right, boy. I'm gonna show you and everybody else that Willy Loman did not die in vain. He had a good dream. It's the only dream you can have—to come out number-one man. He fought it out here, and this is where I'm gonna win it for him.

BIFF (*with a hopeless glance at Happy, bends toward his mother*). Let's go, Mom.

LINDA. I'll be with you in a minute. Go on, Charley. (*He hesitates.*) I want to, just for a minute. I never had a chance to say good-by.

Charley moves away, followed by Happy. Biff remains a slight distance up and left of Linda. She sits there, summoning herself. The flute begins, not far away, playing behind her speech.

LINDA. Forgive me, dear. I can't cry. I don't know what it is, but I can't cry. I don't understand it. Why did you ever do that? Help me, Willy, I can't cry. It seems to me that you're just on another trip. I keep expecting you. Willy, dear, I can't cry. Why did you do it? I search and search and I search, and I can't understand it, Willy. I made the last payment on the house today. Today, dear. And there'll be nobody home. (*A sob rises in her throat.*) We're free and clear. (*Sobbing mournfully, released.*) We're free. (*Biff comes slowly toward her.*) We're free . . . We're free . . .

Biff lifts her to her feet and moves out up right with her in his arms. Linda sobs quietly. Bernard and Charley come together and follow them, followed by Happy. Only the music of the flute is left on the darkening stage as over the house the hard towers of the apartment buildings rise into sharp focus and the curtain falls.

TOPICS FOR CRITICAL THINKING AND WRITING

The Play on the PAGE

1. Miller said in the *New York Times* (February 27, 1949, Sec. II, p. 1) that tragedy shows man's struggle to secure "his sense of personal dignity" and that "his destruction in the attempt posits a wrong or an evil in his environment." Does this make sense when applied to some earlier tragedy (for example, *Oedipus Rex* or *Hamlet*), and does it apply convincingly to *Death of a Salesman*? Is this the tragedy of an individual's own making? Or is society at fault for corrupting and exploiting Willy? Or both?

2. Is Willy pathetic rather than tragic? If pathetic, does this imply that the play is less worthy than if he is tragic?

3. Do you feel that Miller is straining too hard to turn a play about a little man into a big, impressive play? For example, do the musical themes, the unrealistic setting, the appearances of Ben, and the speech at the grave seem out of keeping in a play about the death of a salesman?

4. We don't know what Willy sells, and we don't know whether or not the insurance will be paid after his death. Do you consider these uncertainties to be faults in the play?

5. Is Howard a villain?

6. Characterize Linda.

 ## The Play on the STAGE

7. It is sometimes said that in this realistic play that includes symbolic and expressionistic elements (on expressionism, see page 716 and the Glossary), Biff and Happy can be seen as two aspects of Willy. In this view, Biff more or less represents Willy's spiritual needs, and Happy represents his materialism and his sexuality. If you were directing the play, would you adopt this point of view? Whatever your interpretation, how would you costume the brothers?

8. As we indicate on page 846, although Miller envisioned Willy as a small man (literally small), the role was first performed by Lee J. Cobb, a large man. If you were casting the play, what actor would you select? Why? Whom would you choose for Linda, Biff, Happy, Bernard, and Charley?

9. Select roughly thirty lines of dialogue, and discuss the movements (gestures and blocking) that as a director you would suggest to the performers.

Contexts for *DEATH OF A SALESMAN*

ARTHUR MILLER
Tragedy and the Common Man

In this age few tragedies are written. It has often been held that the lack is due to a paucity of heroes among us, or else that modern man has had the blood drawn out of his organs of belief by the skepticism of science, and the heroic attack on life cannot feed on an attitude of reserve and circumspection. For one reason or another, we are often held to be below tragedy—or tragedy above us. The inevitable conclusion is, of course, that the tragic mode is archaic, fit only for the very highly placed, the kings or the kingly, and where this admission is not made in so many words it is most often implied.

I believe that the common man is as apt a subject for tragedy in its highest sense as kings were. On the face of it this ought to be obvious in the light of modern psychiatry, which bases its analysis upon classic formulations, such as the Oedipus and Orestes complexes, for instances, which were enacted by royal beings, but which apply to everyone in similar emotional situations.

More simply, when the question of tragedy in art is not at issue, we never hesitate to attribute to the well-placed and the exalted the very same mental processes as the lowly. And finally, if the exaltation of tragic action were truly a property of the high-bred character alone, it is inconceivable that the mass of mankind should cherish tragedy above all other forms, let alone be capable of understanding it.

As a general rule, to which there may be exceptions unknown to me, I think the tragic feeling is evoked in us when we are in the presence of a character who is ready to lay down his life, if need be, to secure one thing—his sense of personal dignity. From Orestes to Hamlet, Medea to Macbeth, the underlying struggle is that of the individual attempting to gain his "rightful" position in his society.

Sometimes he is one who has been displaced from it, sometimes one who seeks to attain it for the first time, but the fateful wound from which the inevitable events spiral is the wound of indignity, and its dominant force is indignation. Tragedy, then, is the consequence of a man's total compulsion to evaluate himself justly.

In the sense of having been initiated by the hero himself, the tale always reveals what has been called his "tragic flaw," a failing that is not peculiar to grand or elevated characters. Nor is it necessarily a weakness. The flaw, or crack in the character, is really nothing—and need be nothing, but his inherent unwillingness to remain passive in the face of what he conceives to be a challenge to his dignity, his image of his rightful status. Only the passive, only those who accept their lot without active retaliation, are "flawless." Most of us are in that category.

But there are among us today, as there always have been, those who act against the scheme of things that degrades them, and in the process of action everything we have accepted out of fear or insensitivity or ignorance is shaken before us and examined, and from this total onslaught by an individual against the seemingly stable cosmos surrounding us—from this total examination of the "unchangeable" environment—comes the terror and the fear that is classically associated with tragedy.

More important, from this total questioning of what has previously been unquestioned, we learn. And such a process is not beyond the common man. In revolutions around the world, these past thirty years, he has demonstrated again and again this inner dynamic of all tragedy.

Insistence upon the rank of the tragic hero, or the so-called nobility of his character, is really but a clinging to the outward forms of tragedy. If rank or nobility of character was indispensable, then it would follow that the problems of those with rank were the particular problems of tragedy. But surely the right of one monarch to capture the domain from another no longer raises our passions, nor are our concepts of justice what they were to the mind of an Elizabethan king.

The quality in such plays that does shake us, however, derives from the underlying fear of being displaced, the disaster inherent in being torn away from our chosen image of what and who we are in this world. Among us today this fear is as strong, and perhaps stronger, than it ever was. In fact, it is the common man who knows this fear best.

Now, if it is true that tragedy is the consequence of a man's total compulsion to evaluate himself justly, his destruction in the attempt posits a wrong or an evil in his environment. And this is precisely the morality of tragedy and its lesson. The discovery of the moral law, which is what the enlightenment of tragedy consists of, is not the discovery of some abstract or metaphysical quantity.

The tragic right is a condition of life, a condition in which the human personality is able to flower and realize itself. The wrong is the condition which suppresses man, perverts the flowing out of his love and creative instinct. Tragedy enlightens—and it must, in that it points the heroic finger at the enemy of man's freedom. The thrust for freedom is the quality in tragedy which exalts. The revolutionary questioning of the stable environment is what terrifies. In no way is the common man debarred from such thoughts or such actions.

Seen in this light, our lack of tragedy may be partially accounted for by the turn which modern literature has taken toward the purely psychiatric view of life, or the purely sociological. If all our miseries, our indignities, are born and bred within our minds, then all action, let alone the heroic action, is obviously impossible.

And if society alone is responsible for the cramping of our lives, then the protagonist must needs be so pure and faultless as to force us to deny his validity as a character. From neither of these views can tragedy derive, simply because neither represents a balanced concept of life. Above all else, tragedy requires the finest appreciation by the writer of cause and effect.

No tragedy can therefore come about when its author fears to question absolutely everything, when he regards any institution, habit or custom as being either everlasting, immutable or inevitable. In the tragic view the need of man to wholly realize himself is the only fixed star, and whatever it is that hedges his nature and lowers it is ripe for attack and examination. Which is not to say that tragedy must preach revolution.

The Greeks could probe the very heavenly origin of their ways and return to confirm the rightness of laws. And Job could face God in anger, demanding his right, and end in submission. But for a moment everything is in suspension, nothing is accepted, and in this stretching and tearing apart of the cosmos, in the very action of so doing, the character gains "size," the tragic stature which is spuriously attached to the royal or the high-born in our minds. The commonest of men may take on that stature to the extent of his willingness to throw all he has into the contest, the battle to secure his rightful place in his world.

There is a misconception of tragedy with which I have been struck in review after review, and in many conversations with writers and readers alike. It is the idea that tragedy is of necessity allied to pessimism. Even the dictionary says nothing more about the word than that it means a story with a sad or unhappy ending. This impression is so firmly fixed that I almost hesitate to claim that in truth tragedy implies more optimism in its author than does comedy, and that its final result ought to be the reinforcement of the onlooker's brightest opinions of the human animal.

For, if it is true to say that in essence the tragic hero is intent upon claiming his whole due as a personality, and if this struggle must be total and without reservation, then it automatically demonstrates the indestructible will of man to achieve his humanity.

The possibility of victory must be there in tragedy. Where pathos rules, where pathos is finally derived, a character has fought a battle he could not possibly have won. The pathetic is achieved when the protagonist is, by virtue of his witlessness, his insensitivity or the very air he gives off, incapable of grappling with a much superior force.

Pathos truly is the mode for the pessimist. But tragedy requires a nicer balance between what is possible and what is impossible. And it is curious, although edifying, that the plays we revere, century after century, are the tragedies. In them, and in them alone, lies the belief—optimistic, if you will—in the perfectibility of man.

It is time, I think, that we who are without kings, took up this bright thread of our history and followed it to the only place it can possibly lead in our time—the heart and spirit of the average man.

ARTHUR MILLER
Willy Loman's Ideals

[In 1958 Arthur Miller made these comments during the course of a symposium on *Death of a Salesman*.]

Miller. The trouble with Willy Loman is that he has tremendously powerful ideals. We're not accustomed to speaking of ideals in his terms; but, if Willy Loman, for instance, had not had a very profound sense that his life as lived had left him hollow, he would have died contentedly polishing his car on some Sunday afternoon at a ripe old age. The fact is he has values. The fact that they cannot be realized is what is driving him mad—just as, unfortunately, it's driving a lot of other people mad. The truly valueless man, a man without ideals, is always perfectly at home anywhere . . . because there

cannot be a conflict between nothing and something. Whatever negative qualities there are in the society or in the environment don't bother him, because they are not in conflict with what positive sense one may have. I think Willy Loman, on the other hand, is seeking for a kind of ecstasy in life, which the machine-civilization deprives people of. He's looking for his selfhood, for his immortal soul, so to speak. People who don't know the intensity of that quest, possibly, think he's odd. Now an extraordinarily large number of salesmen particularly, who are in a line of work where a large measure of ingenuity and individualism are required, have a very intimate understanding of this problem. More so, I think, than literary critics who probably need strive less after a certain point. A salesman is a kind of creative person (it's possibly idiotic to say so on a literary program, but they are), they have to get up in the morning and conceive a plan of attack and use all kinds of ingenuity all day long, just the way a writer does.

The Play in PERFORMANCE

When Miller began working on the play that became *Death of a Salesman,* he tells us in his introduction to *Collected Plays* (1957) that he tentatively thought of calling it *The Inside of His Head*. The audience would see "an enormous face the height of the proscenium arch which would appear and then open up, and we would see the inside of a man's head . . . It was conceived half in laughter, for the inside of his head was a mass of contradictions." However, as he worked on the play, he reports in his autobiography *Timebends* (1987), he toyed with using only "three bare platforms and only the minimum necessary furniture for a kitchen and two bedrooms, with the Boston hotel room as well as Howard's office to be played in open space" (188).

Miller found a producer relatively quickly. Elia Kazan directed the play, Joel Mielziner designed the set, and the rest is history. (The set, depicted on page 13, combined realism—for instance the period-piece refrigerator—along with expressionistic elements, such as the skeletal roof that suggests vulnerability. The opening stage direction clearly indicates some expressionistic elements, that is, elements that express the states of mind of the characters. The house, we are told, is surrounded by an "angry glow of orange," and as the light increases "we see a solid vault of apartment houses around the small, fragile-seeming house." In the second act, in the restaurant scene, "a red glow rises behind the screen at right," and still later in the act "[a] single trumpet note jars the ear. The light of green leaves stains the house, which holds the air of night and a dream.") In January 1949 *Death of a Salesman* was enthusiastically received by reviewers and by the general public in its pre-Broadway run in Philadelphia, and it was received with at least equal enthusiasm when it opened in New York City in February. In the autumn a touring company visited cities throughout the United States, and by 1950 it had played in a dozen countries in Europe, the Middle East, and South America. It has been said that since its first performance in Philadelphia in 1949, there probably has not been a single day when *Death of a Salesman* has not been produced somewhere in the world. As early as 1959 it was produced in the Soviet Union, where it was taken as a condemnation of American capitalism, and in 1983 it was produced in Beijing under Miller's own direction, where, of course, the play was seen through Marxist eyes. The Chinese audiences (and the actors, too) expected to find a hero and a villain—not a man of mingled qualities. In his account of the production, in *Salesman in Beijing* (1983), Miller says that he had considerable difficulty getting the actor who played Willy to think of Willy sympathetically, since Willy is not a symbol of the virtuous man. Furthermore, Miller had trouble getting the actors, who were trained in a Chinese style of operatic acting, to act realistically. For instance, in the Chinese theater, characters may address the audience rather than each other. Similarly, the Chinese actors wanted to wear the light-colored wigs and white makeup that they customarily used when playing Caucasians. Miller felt, however, that these devices made the play seem *un*real, and he persuaded them to perform the play in a more Western manner. The result, he reports, was that the spectators, seeing Asian faces instead of Asians made up to look like whites, were able to identify with the actors and thus with the Westerners for whom the actors stood.

In the early days most productions of *Death of a Salesman* used the highly praised set (or an adaptation of it) that Jo Mielziner had designed for the original production. However, at least as early as 1963 grumblings were heard. Mielziner's set was now said (by some) to be too elaborate, too attention getting, and it was argued that the play would benefit from a stripped-down set, perhaps just some multilevel platforms and a few pieces of furniture. Most sets continue, however, to be realistic and, at the same time, at least mildly expressionistic.

The first Willy Loman was Lee J. Cobb, a large man (he is usually described as "bearish"). Miller was at first uncertain about this choice, because he had envisioned the role as being played by a small man, but Cobb was enormously successful. Over the years, there have been two kinds of Willy Lomans—big men such as Cobb, George C. Scott, and Brian Dennehy and small men (almost always described as "feisty bantams") such as Dustin Hoffman and Hume Cronyn. Actors of both sorts have received favorable reviews, and, in fact, it is a rare production that does stir an audience.

For a readable history of the play on the stage and screen, see Brenda Murphy, *Miller: Death of a Salesman* (1995).

THE AMERICAN MUSICAL

Music has been part of theater from the very beginning. In Aristotle's *Poetics*, "song" is listed as one of the six constituent parts of tragedy. We may have lost the music and choreography of Greek tragedy, but we know they were there. In the classical Japanese drama called Noh (see the introduction to *Dôjôji*), the Japanese performance tradition has preserved much of the form's musical heritage and made us aware that it is as important as the verbal element. Indeed, as we look back at theater history we can see that the separation of music and dance into individual performance traditions is a very late European development, a little more than two centuries old. Opera and ballet are post–seventeenth-century creations that grew out of medieval liturgical drama and Renaissance interludes and *intermezzi*. As opera matured as an art form in the eighteenth and nineteenth centuries, it differentiated itself into subgenres distinguished by subject matter, theme, and form: *opera seria* (serious opera), *opera buffa* (comic opera), *opéra-comique* (opera that uses spoken dialogue rather than Grand Opera's recitative).

In the mid-nineteenth century a light form of opera developed, called appropriately "little opera," or *operetta*. The father of the form is generally considered to be Jacques Offenbach (1819–80), who moved to Paris to attend the conservatoire, remained there, and wrote over a hundred light musical plays including *Orpheus in the Underworld* and *La Belle Hélène*. (His most famous piece remains his most serious: the posthumously produced *Tales of Hoffmann*.) Once established, the tradition of operetta flourished in Vienna at the hands of Johann Strauss II (1825–99), who had been convinced by Offenbach to write for the stage. His most famous work remains evergreen: *Die Fledermaus* (1874). After Strauss, Viennese-style operetta proliferated with such figures as Franz Lehar (*The Merry Widow*) and Oscar Strauss (*The Chocolate Soldier*). It is this tradition more than any other which, through emigration, fuels what might be called the first wave of American musical comedy. (Interestingly enough, the operetta composers best known in the English-speaking world—W.S. Gilbert and Arthur Sullivan—do not directly influence the development of the form.)

The immigrants who helped create the American musical comedy were: Victor Herbert (1859–1924), born in Dublin but half German, who started out as a cellist for the Metropolitan Opera. His well-known operettas (many made into movies in the 1930) include *Babes in Toyland, Naughty Marietta*, and *Sweetheart;* Rudolf Friml (1879–1972), born in Prague, toured the States as a pianist and decided to stay. *The Firefly, Rose-Marie*, and *The Vagabond King* also became film vehicles for MGM's Jeanette MacDonald and Nelson Eddie; Sigmund Romberg (1887–1951) moved to the United States from Hungary and became a pianist and bandleader. He is remembered for *Maytime, The New Moon, The Desert Song*, and *The Student Prince*—the latter filmed as late as 1954 with Mario Lanza.

The native-born New Yorker who represents the transition from the world of European operetta to the world of American musical comedy is Jerome Kern (1885–1946), who studied for a while in Germany. Starting out as a rehearsal pianist, he moved quickly to song plugger and composer. At first he wrote songs mainly to be added to operetta imports from Europe. Soon, however, he developed his own indigenous style, and by 1915 was represented by several Broadway shows. By the 1920s he incorporated contemporary dance music into his show *Sally* (which gave us "Look for the Silver Lining"); by 1925 he had teamed up with Oscar Hammerstein II for *Sunny*, a collaboration that was to result next in the musical play which, more than any other, established the form as we know it: *Show Boat* (1927). Kern and Hammerstein both felt that Broadway musical theater did not have to be mindlessly escapist. So they radically chose for their subject Edna Ferber's sprawling novel of life on the Mississippi, a story replete with broken marriages and racial prejudice. The work has achieved almost classic status, being frequently revived (as recently as 1994) and having been filmed twice.

But if *Show Boat* established the bona fides of the American musical, it did not initiate the form. Others besides Kern were already on the scene: Indeed, a native popular musical tradition existed that went back to nineteenth-century burlesque and minstrel shows. Historians often cite an 1866 improvisation at Niblo's Garden in New York City as the beginning of musical comedy: A stranded group of French ballet dancers were placed in a melodrama called *The Black Crook* that included songs by a local composer. The result was a surprising musical success. Nor should we forget

George M. Cohan, that Yankee Doodle Dandy who wrote the book, words, and music for *Forty-five Minutes from Broadway* as early as 1906. In 1915 a young immigrant who renamed himself Irving Berlin wrote songs for a musical revue called *Watch Your Step*. And in 1919 a musical called *La, La Lucille* opened with a score by a young George Gershwin. By the time of *Show Boat*'s opening, the Gershwins had collaborated on *Lady Be Good* (1924) and *Funny Face* (1927) as vehicles for Fred and Adele Astaire. But *Show Boat* ushered in a new era of more serious and ambitious musical works. The Gershwins turned to political subjects in *Strike Up the Band* (1930) and *Of Thee I Sing* (1931). Irving Berlin acknowledged the Depression in *Face the Music* (1932) and *As Thousands Cheer* (1933). *The Boys from Syracuse* by Richard Rodgers and Lorenz Hart (1938) was the first musical based on Plautus and Shakespeare. And two years later the same pair based a musical on hard-boiled, unsentimental stories by John O'Hara, *Pal Joey*. Moss Hart and Kurt Weill explored psychoanalysis in *Lady in the Dark* (1941).

The next formal innovation occurred in 1943 when Rodgers and his new partner Hammerstein (Larry Hart having died that year) debuted *Oklahoma!* Abandoning such traditions as the opening chorus and comic routines, the work integrated book and music more thoroughly than had been done before, and permitted much of the narrative to be carried by the unfamiliar (for musicals) form of ballet as choreographed by Agnes de Mille. Rodgers and Hammerstein followed with a string of musical triumphs that includes *South Pacific*, *Carousel*, *The King and I*, and *The Sound of Music*.

The other ground-breaking musical that demands mention is *West Side Story* (1957). Initially conceived by Jerome Robbins as *East Side Story*, in which *Romeo and Juliet* would be contemporized into a star-crossed romance between a Jewish boy and an Italian Catholic girl, the project was shelved for other commitments for six years. By the time Robbins and his major collaborators—Arthur Laurents and Leonard Bernstein—returned to the project (with the addition of lyricist Stephen Sondheim) the ethnic balance in New York had shifted, and they decided to make the fated lovers native-born Polish and immigrant Puerto Rican. The result pushed the musical comedy form to its limits on all fronts: In essentials, the book was faithful to its source and ended tragically; the music achieved the enviable balance of being classically complex without sacrificing melodic accessibility; the lyrics were street-smart and clever; and the dancing—like Bernstein's score—was venacular but classically rigorous; startlingly vital, Robbins's choreography radically raised the bar for Broadway dancing—a bar already rather high, given the fact that George Balanchine was active in the 1930s and the 1940s choreographing musicals such as *On Your Toes*, *Cabin in the Sky*, and *Where's Charley?*

Space limitations preclude discussing the outpouring of musical artistry that flourished in the post–*Show Boat* period that historians designate as the Golden Age of the American musical. It is an era that is clearly over, even if all do not agree when it ended. (Many would cite the closing of *Gypsy* in 1961.) Other major talents that must at least be remembered, however, include Cole Porter, Frank Loesser, Harold Arlen, Alan Jay Lerner and Frederick Loewe, Jule Styne, and John Kander and Fred Ebb. But like Grand Opera and the movie musical, Broadway musical comedy has recently fallen on hard times *as an original creative contemporary form*. (A critic recently remarked that given the preponderance of musical revival it feels like 1948 again.) Sondheim and Kander and Ebb soldier on in a desolated landscape dominated since the 1970s by revivals and spectacles patterned after the megahits *Cats* and *Les Miserables*. The pendulum of influence has swung back to Europe with the commercial success of Andrew Lloyd-Webber and Alain Boubil and Claude-Michel Schönberg. The troubled nature of the form is revealed by the awarding of the 1999–2000 season's best musical award to *Contact*, a piece with no new music and no live music. Despite its continued popularity as a form of entertainment, the American musical awaits a new infusion of creative energy.

For further study, please see the following:

Gottfried, Martin. *Broadway Musicals* (1979).

Joblonski, Edward. *Irwin Berlin: American Troubador* (1999).

Mordden, Ethan. *Beautiful Mornin': The Broadway Musical in the 1940s* (1999).

Myers, Paul. *Leonard Bernstein* (1998).

Rosenberg, Deena. *Fascinating Rhythm: The Collaboration of George and Ira Gershwin* (1993).

Steyn, Mark. *Broadway Babies Say Goodnight: Musicals Then and Now* (2000).

Thelen, Lawrence. *The Show Makers: Great Directors of the American Musical Theatre* (2000).

ARTHUR Laurents

Arthur Laurents (librettist), born in 1918 in Brooklyn, was unhappy at Cornell until an English professor encouraged him to write anything he wanted. Drawn to dialogue, Laurents discovered that "writing plays was happiness." Drafted into the army before Pearl Harbor, he was assigned to writing training films, one of which was directed by erstwhile Hollywood director Pvt. George Cukor. One afternoon on leave, he attended the ballet *Fancy Free*, about three sailors on leave. The music, by a young man named Leonard Bernstein, and the choreography, by a young man named Jerome Robbins, enthralled him, and he made the acquaintance of both of them. After the war Laurents made an impact with *Home of the Brave*, a play about anti-Semitism in the army. In 1949 Robbins came to Laurents and Bernstein with an idea for a contemporary musical based on *Romeo and Juliet*. The enormous success of their collaboration, *West Side Story* (1957), definitively launched Laurents's prolific career on both stage and screen.

He went on to write the books for the musicals *Gypsy* (1959), *Anyone Can Whistle* (1965), and *Do I Hear a Waltz?* (1965). He also began a long directorial career with *I Can Get It for You Wholesale* (1962) in which he cast an unknown Barbra Streisand. (He subsequently directed two revivals of *Gypsy* and won the 1984 Tony award in directing for *La Cage aux Folles*.) And he kept on writing plays: *The Time of the Cuckoo* (1952), *A Clearing in the Woods* (1957), *Invitation to the March* (1963), and others. His film career was equally distinguished. He wrote the screenplays for *The Snake Pit, Rope, Anastasia, Bonjour Tristesse, The Way We Were,* and *The Turning Point.* He has also written for radio and television, and has been honored by awards from many organizations, among them the National Institute of Arts and Letters, Writers Guild of America, Drama Desk, and the National Board of Review. He is a member of the Theatre Hall of Fame, P.E.N., the Screenwriter's Guild, the Motion Picture Academy of Arts and Sciences, and an emeritus member of the Council of the Dramatist Guild.

■■■■■■■■■■■■■■

STEPHEN Sondheim

One of America's most successful lyricists and composers—the winner of Grammy, Tony, and New York Drama Critics awards as well as a Pulitzer prize—Stephen Sondheim (lyricist) was born on March 22, 1930, in New York City to Herbert Sondheim, a dress manufacturer, and his wife, Janet, a fashion designer and interior decorator. His infatuation with music began early when his father took him to his first Broadway musical, *Very Warm for May* (1939). Unfortunately, it would be one of their last outings; Sondheim's parents divorced shortly thereafter and his mother forbade him to see his father. Sondheim eventually found a surrogate father and musical mentor in his friend Jamie's father, the famous lyricist Oscar Hammerstein II. Their relationship had a profound influence on Sondheim throughout his adolescence and in later years. Sondheim wrote his first musical at age fifteen and presented it to Hammerstein, who promptly panned it while assuring the young composer he had talent nonetheless.

Sondheim graduated from Williams College in 1950 and proceeded to embark on a career in show business. One of his early jobs was writing scripts in Hollywood for the television comedy series *Topper.* The turning point in Sondheim's career came when he was given the opportunity to write the lyrics for Leonard Bernstein's songs in *West Side Story* (1957), whose triumph established the twenty-seven-year-old Sondheim's reputation. It was confirmed by his next outing as a lyricist: *Gypsy* (1959), another huge success.

Over the succeeding years, Sondheim has written music and lyrics—usually both—for many Broadway shows, including *A Funny Thing Happened on the Way to the Forum* (1962), *Anyone Can Whistle* (1964), and *Do I Hear a Waltz?* (1965) with Richard Rodgers, the last time he would write lyrics for another composer's show, except for a small lyrical contribution to Bernstein's *Candide* (1973). Other shows include *Company* (1970); *Follies* (1971); *A Little Night Music* (1973), which featured his Grammy award-winning song "Send in the Clowns"; *Pacific Overtures* (1976); *Sweeney Todd* (1979); *Merrily We Roll Along* (1981); *Sunday in the Park with George* (1984), which earned him a Pulitzer prize; *Into the Woods* (1989); and *Assassins* (1991). Stephen Sondheim's music plays are frequently revived, particularly in England, where they are almost in constant repertory. He was Oxford University's first visiting professor of contemporary theater.

■■■■■■■■■■■■■■

JULE Styne

With the score of such long-running Broadway classics as *High Button Shoes* (1947), *Gentlemen Prefer Blondes* (1949), *Gypsy* (1959), *The Bells Are Ringing* (1956), and *Funny Girl* (1964) to his credit, composer Jule Styne (1905–94) ranks as a major architect of the American musical theater. From 1949 through 1974, nearly every new Broadway season saw the opening of a show with a Jule Styne score, many of them in partnership with Betty Comden and Adolph Green. Some years two or three Styne hits ran simultaneously.

Born Julius Kerwin Styne on December 31, 1905, in London's East End, Styne's family emigrated to the United States in 1912, where young Julius showed such a talent for the piano that he performed with the Chicago, St. Louis, and Detroit symphonies before age ten. In 1921, a sixteen-year-old Styne was commissioned to write a song by a teenaged Mike Todd for a musical act he was creating, and a successful career was launched—more than 1500 published songs over three-quarters of a century. In Hollywood Styne found a champion in Frank Sinatra, the beneficiary of many great songs from Styne's fruitful collaboration with Sammy Cahn. Styne's memorable songs for Broadway—including "Diamonds Are a Girl's Best Friend," "The Party's Over," "Let Me Entertain You," and "People"—helped spark the theatrical careers of Carol Channing, Judy Holliday, Mary Martin, Ethel Merman, Carol Burnett, Phil Silvers, and Barbra Streisand. He was elected to the Songwriters Hall of Fame in 1972 and the Theater Hall of Fame in 1981. On the occasion of his 25th anniversary in show business in 1959, the following tribute was read into the Congressional Record: "The lives of Americans throughout our land as well as the lives of people throughout the corners of the world have been enriched by the artistry and genius of Jule Styne."

■ ■ ■ ■ ■ ■ ■ ■ ■ ■ ■ ■ ■ ■ ■

COMMENTARY ON *GYPSY*

The creative team behind the enormous success of *West Side Story*—Laurents, Bernstein, Sondheim, and Robbins—was eager to work together again, but Leonard Bernstein had other commitments. So the other three invited composer Jule Styne (*High Button Shoes, Gentlemen Prefer Blondes, The Bells Are Ringing*) to join on their next project, a musical adaptation of the memoirs of the performer who had made the striptease respectable: Gypsy Rose Lee. Lee had made herself a major celebrity of the time by the atypical refinement of her act and the conscious cultivation of the persona of a *very* unusual stripper who spoke French and loved books and the arts. Indeed, in their acerbic musical *Pal Joey* (1940) Rodgers and Hart wrote a song called "Zip" (the sound of unzipping a garment) that comically exploited the contrast between the high and the low: "I interviewed Leslie Howard / I interviewed Noël Coward / I interviewed the great Stravinsky / But my greatest achievement / Is the interview I had / With the star who worked for Minsky"—the latter being the operator of New York City's premier burlesque house. And—zip!—into her strip: "Zip! I was reading Schopenhauer last night / Zip! And I think that Schopenhauer was right." Lee

(and her sister "Baby" June Havoc as well) lived up to her image and had a respectable literary career after her stripping days had ended. Her memoirs, which focused on her hardscrabble show-biz upbringing in the 1920s and early 1930s under the demanding eye of her quintessential Stage Mother, became the basis for the musical comedy many vote for as the best of all.

Arthur Laurents never wrote a tighter work than his book for *Gypsy*. It tells a not unfamiliar but archetypically American tale: Rose, the overbearing mother who will not settle for "living life in a living room," pushes her younger daughter June into the wandering, gypsy life of vaudeville in the search for the dream of big-time success. Finally finding her mother's single-minded manipulations intolerable, June elopes, which forces Rose to redirect her attentions toward her elder, less talented daughter, Louise. The dream becomes reality with Louise's improvised reincarnation as stripper Gypsy Rose Lee, but she, like her sister before her, gathers the strength to distance herself from her impossible mother. The piece works toward a dark conclusion with Rose, alone on stage, abandoned by all those (including her agent-lover) she felt she had sacrificed everything for. Her last big number—"Rose's Turn"—is a tour de force of musical theater as Rose laments, "One quick look at each of 'em leaves you / All your life and what does it get you?" and asks fiercely, "Somebody tell me, when is it my turn? / Don't I get a dream for myself?" This number is so devastating that its creators obviously felt the play could not end on this note. So it is followed by a scene of reconciliation between Gypsy and her mother that rings as hollow as Eliza returning to Higgins to bring him his slippers at the end of both *My Fair Lady* and the film version of *Pygmalion*. Since Bernard Shaw wrote his own screenplay for the 1939 film, we can only assume that contrary to his postscript to the play in which he states that a union between Eliza and Higgins is impossible, he was persuaded by that seductive producer, Gabriel Pascal, to provide a romantic curtain. Laurents and Co. must have responded to similar overt or covert pressures to not leave us with an image of a daughter rejecting her own mother, even if they've provided us with plenty of reasons to do so. In any case, Rose is never hateful; she is a complex character whose vices spring from a desperate, unyielding determination to make a mark on life. And Styne and Sondheim have provided her with some of the most expressive songs in musical comedy history. No wonder that so many major performers—from Rose's creator Ethel Merman to Bette Midler—have triumphed in the role.

But theater or show business is more than the subject of *Gypsy*; it is the metaphor on which the entire production rests. The play is presented as a performance in old vaudeville style: When the curtain rises, on either side of the proscenium illuminated placards identify and define place and/or action: "Home Sweet Home. / Seattle," "Baby June and Her Newsboys. / Los Angeles," or "The Bottom. / Wichita." Many scenes take place on stage or backstage. The play's climax— the transformation of duckling Louise into swan Gypsy—brilliantly combines the reality of live performance with the shifting point of view of film:

> [Louise] . . . turns from the mirror [in the dressing room] and begins to walk away from it, as though she were going in the direction of the "stage." The mirror moves off, the lights come up and we are "on the stage." The curtain is upstage; strip music can be heard . . . Louise . . . stands alone before the curtain. A roll of the drum and lights reveal the curtain as a scrim. Through it we can see the glow of the stripper's runway. Another drum roll: the curtains part and Louise steps forward. Another drum roll: a spotlight

hits her and her head goes back as though she has been blinded. Blinding floodlights then shine directly into the eyes of the audience; then a total blackout. When the lights go on again, Louise is downstage, facing the audience before a curtain the exact replica of the one upstage . . . the small burlesque band in the pit begins "Let Me Entertain You." . . .

And with us as the entranced audience, the metamorphosis begins. After this "reverse shot," Gypsy's rapid rise to stardom is communicated through another quasi-filmic convention: Instead of pages peeling off a calendar, the passage of time is communicated by a montage of changing placards ("Philadelphia," "Boston," "Minsky's / New York") and overlapping voices—until a voice introduces "the Queen of the Strip Tease, the incomparable Gypsy Rose Lee."

How much of this is Laurents's invention and how much is the invention of director/choreographer James Robbins, it is futile to try to quantify. The musical is inherently a collaborative medium. But Robbins's creative contribution must be strongly acknowledged; indeed, as one of *Gypsy*'s primary "authors," his biography might well have joined those of Laurents, Sondheim, and Styne that introduce this section. Born Jerome Rabinowitz in 1918, Robbins choreographed his first ballet, *Fancy Free*, in 1942 to music by Leonard Bernstein. This led to his first musical comedy, *On the Town* (1945), which launched an extraordinary career as a choreographer and director. From *High Button Shoes* (1947), through *Call Me Madam* (1953), *The King and I* (1956), *The Pajama Game* (1957), to *West Side Story* (1961), *Gypsy*, and *Fiddler on the Roof* (1964), Robbins for a quarter century dominated Broadway musical theatrical production.* He had revealed himself as a choreographer superbly capable of taking popular dance forms—contemporary *or* past—and enfusing them with balletic rigor (the Keystone Kops sequence in *High Button Shoes*, the street dances in *West Side Story*).

Rose and family's decade-long tour of American vaudeville and burlesque was tailor-made to Robbins's

---

*Leaving Broadway behind, he returned to his first love, ballet, after 1964. In his career with the New York City Ballet he created some fifty ballets that testify to the diversity of his talent, from *Afternoon of a Faun* (1953) to *The Concert* (1956) to *Dances at a Gathering* (1969) and *Watermill* (1972). After the death of Balanchine in 1983, he shared the post of artistic director of the New York City Ballet with Peter Martins until 1990. He died in New York City in 1998.

skills, and he lovingly recreated bygone forms in the detailed versions of the awful acts that Rose concocted for June to star in. But despite the acts' dependence on clichéd devices like blatant flag-waving, Robbins pulled off the difficult trick of making these kitschy routines entertaining by virtue of the loving authenticity with which they were presented. "Let Me Enter-

tain You" —which modulates from Baby June's early perky Shirley-Templish rendition to Gypsy's seductive burlesque come-on, was Robbins's credo; it was the credo of all the talented artists who in *Gypsy* collaborated to fulfill this imperative as well as has ever been done in the history of the musical comedy form.

Almost as much as the music, spectacle plays a part in the modern American musical. Here, the spectacle is Rose's name in lights—that most significant indicator of fame—as Linda Lavin belts out "Rose's Turn" in the final scene of this 1989 Broadway revival of *Gypsy*.

GYPSY
A MUSICAL

Book by Arthur Laurents
Lyrics by Stephen Sondheim
Music by Jule Styne

Suggested by The Memoirs of Gypsy Rose Lee

MUSICAL NUMBERS

ACT ONE

1. "May We Entertain You" BABY JUNE AND BABY LOUISE
2. "Some People" ROSE
3. Traveling
4. "Small World" ROSE AND HERBIE
5. Baby June and Her Newsboys
6. "Mr. Goldstone, I Love You" ROSE AND ENSEMBLE
7. "Little Lamb" LOUISE
8. "You'll Never Get Away from Me" ROSE AND HERBIE
9. Dainty June and Her Farmboys
10. "If Momma Was Married" LOUISE AND JUNE
11. "All I Need Is the Girl" TULSA AND LOUISE
12. "Everything's Coming Up Roses" ROSE

ACT TWO

1. "Madame Rose's Toreadorables" LOUISE AND THE HOLLYWOOD BLONDES
2. "Together, Wherever We Go" ROSE, LOUISE AND HERBIE
3. "You Gotta Get a Gimmick" TESSIE, MAZEPPA AND ELECTRA
4. "Small World" —Reprise ROSE
5. "Let Me Entertain You" LOUISE AND COMPANY
6. "Rose's Turn" ROSE

The action of the play covers a period from the early twenties to the early thirties, and takes place in various cities throughout the country.

ACT ONE

SCENE ONE

On either side of the proscenium, there are illuminated placards—as in the days of vaudeville. After the overture, the placards light up to read:

UNCLE JOCKO'S KIDDIE SHOW

SEATTLE

The light illuminating the placards fades slowly as the curtain rises on the stage of a tacky vaudeville theatre.

The stage is half-set for the rehearsal of a kiddie show. "Uncle Jocko"—the nervous, oily master of ceremonies—is surrounded by a pack of babbling kids and their tigress mothers. The kids are in horrible, homemade costumes; the mothers wear clothes of the very early twenties; Jocko wears a tartan cap and fake horn-rimmed glasses as a concession to his name.

JOCKO. Everybody—SHUT UP! . . . All mothers—*out. (To his assistant)* Georgie, I don't want them in the wings, I don't want them in the theatre, I want them OUT!

GEORGIE. It's a pleasure. O.K., mothers—this way. Move it! *(He herds them out as—)*

JOCKO. All right, kids, get in a straight line along here and come forward one at a time. The doors open at seven and Uncle Jocko doesn't have enough time to rehearse your darlin' acts. *(He takes a simpering little girl completely covered with balloons out of line and moves her down, apart from the others)* You wait here, girly-girl. *(Calling out front to the Spot Man)* Oh, Gus! Hit this doll with a surprise pink when she does her turn. *(To the girl)* Uncle Jocko promised the wee bairn would be a winner and she will. *(The kid kisses him coyly. To Georgie)* Chip off her sister's block. And you ought to see them balloons! O.K. Let's have the first wee laddie in Uncle Jocko's Kiddie Show.

(As a little boy with a big accordion comes forward, Jocko speaks to the actual Conductor in the pit)

Take each of them from the top and then cut to the last eight. Every Friday night, ya ta ta, ya ta ta, Uncle Jocko dinna ken there were so many talented bairns right here in Seattle and the rest of the crap—ARNOLD AND HIS ACCORDION! (*As Arnold plays—indicating the kid*) Georgie, that's what's gonna kill vaudeville. All right, Arnold, cut to the end. The end, kiddo.

(*He signals the Conductor for a sick chord; Georgie pushes Arnold off. Jocko speaks to two little girls dressed as a Dutch boy and girl*)

And who does Uncle Jocko have here? Who the hell does he—BABY JUNE AND COMPANY? . . . (*To the Conductor*) Half of the song, half of the dance, and off.

CONDUCTOR. Got ya.

(*A small band starts the introduction*)

JUNE (*Singing*).
    May we entertain you?
    May we see you smile?
    I will do some kicks—

LOUISE (*Singing*).
    I will do some tricks.

ROSE (*From out front*). Sing out, Louise—sing out!

JOCKO. Who said that?

JUNE (*Singing*).
    I'll tell you a story.

LOUISE (*Singing*).
    I'll dance when she's done.

ROSE (*From front*). You're behind, Louise! Catch up, honey, catch up!

JOCKO. Who let in one of them mothers?

JUNE, LOUISE.
    By the time we're through
    Entertaining you—

(*Coming down the aisle and onto the stage, carrying a little dog and a big handbag is—momma!*)

ROSE. Hold it, please, hold it! Save your strength, June. Louise, dear, if you don't count—

JOCKO. Madam, do you realize you are absolutely—

ROSE. I do, Uncle Jocko, but I want to save your very valuable time for you.

JOCKO. In that case—

ROSE. When I saw your sensitive face at the Odd Fellows Hall—my first husband was an Odd Fellow—

JOCKO. I am not an Odd Fellow!

ROSE. I meant a Knight of Pythias. My second husband was—

JOCKO. I'm not a Knight of Pythias!

ROSE. Then where *did* you catch our act?

JOCKO. At the Elks.

ROSE. My father is an Elk! I have his tooth here someplace. (*She dumps the dog into Jocko's arms as she rummages in her handbag*) If you'll just hold Chowsie for me—that's short

for chow mein. (*Baby talk*) Mommy just loves chow mein, doesn't she, Chowsie Wowsie? Stop sucking your thumb, Louise. (*To the Conductor*) Professor, I just marvel how you can make a performer into an artist.

JOCKO (*Following her as she gads about*). What is going on here??

ROSE. Now if you could help my little girls by giving them a good loud la da *da* de da da *da*—(*To Jocko, whom she delicately shoves back as he moves to intervene*) God helps him who helps himself. (*To the Drummer*) Mr. Zipser—when the girls do their specialty would you please ad lick it? Show him, girls.

JOCKO. Is this really happening?!

ROSE. Oh, Gus? Gus, would you please slap Baby June with something pink? She's the star. Smile, Baby dear!

JOCKO. I have seen all kinds of mothers—

ROSE. Do you know of a really good agent—don't hang on the baby, Louise, you're rumpling her dress—who could book a professional act like ours?

JOCKO. A professional act! Hey, Georgie! Get a load of this crazy—

ROSE (*Suddenly grabbing him*). Don't you laugh! *Don't you dare laugh!* . . . That child is going to be a star.

JOCKO. That's what they all say. All right—(*He shoves the dog back into her arms*)

ROSE. But we're not finished!

JOCKO. You are as far as I'm concerned.

ROSE. Because you're trying to play favorites!

JOCKO (*Stops*). What?

ROSE. How dare you let that rotten, untalented fat balloon block up my babies? I won't leave this stage till she does!

JOCKO. That child—

ROSE. Have you no loyalty to the Elks?

JOCKO. I'm not an Elk!

ROSE. Well, the editor of the *Gazette* is! I happen to know because at the last meeting he showed my father a letter he got—complaining some contest was fixed . . . I guess desperate people do desperate things.

(*Jocko stares at her, then motions the Balloon Girl to go. Rose looks at the Conductor, and signals him as before*)

La da *da* de da *da*!

(*Music starts and the girls begin their act*)

Thank you, Professor. Thank you, Uncle Jocko. (*She gives him the dog*) Thank you, Gus! Thank you, Mr. Zipser! Smile, girls, smile!

(*She is singing along with her girls when she sees the Balloon Girl, who has edged out from the wings. Still singing gaily, Rose removes her hatpin. The Balloon Girl backs into the wings as Rose marches after her, the hatpin extended like Joan of Arc's sword. Her dancing daughters watch, grin and finish to a blare of music.*)

(*The lights black out*)

SCENE TWO

The illuminated placards change to read:

"HOME SWEET HOME"
SEATTLE

The scene is the kitchen of a frame house. Later that night.
We see an icebox, a sink overflowing with dishes, calendars and timetables on the walls, a rocker, etc.
Louise and June enter yawning, and take off the coats they wear over their costumes as Rose slams in, throws her coat on a chair and heads for the icebox. She gives Chowsie, the little dog, to Louise as she gets a can of dog food from the icebox. As usual, she is talking all the time.

ROSE. That rotten little Uncle Jocko! He's as cheap as your grandpa. (*To June*) Ten bucks for a talent like yours! Well, we're through with Kiddie Shows. *And* with your grandpa's lodge hall. It's time we moved on anyway! I'm gonna get us an agent to book the act on the Orpheum Circuit.

LOUISE. That's dog food, Momma.

ROSE. That's what she thinks. I'm hungry.

LOUISE. Then why didn't you eat some of our chow mein after the show?

ROSE. Because you two did the work and we gotta save every cent. (*To June, who brings her a hair brush—as she brushes June's hair*) I had a dream last night: a whole new act for you! Baby June and Her Newsboys!

JUNE. How are you going to get the boys, Momma?

ROSE. Louise can be a boy—

(*Louise exits*)

—and I'll find three others.

JUNE. How are you going to pay them?

ROSE. The experience'll be their pay. I've got just enough saved up for scenery and costumes. If I can squeeze a few bucks out of Grandpa, we can head for Los Angeles and the Orpheum Circuit . . .

(*Pop enters. He is a crusty old man, holding the Bible he is eternally reading. A short pause*)

JUNE (*Tactfully*). Good night, Momma. Good night, Grandpa. (*She exits*)

POP. You oughta be ashamed: fooling your kids with those dreams!

ROSE. They're real dreams and I'm gonna make 'em *come* real for my kids!

POP. What are you, Rose, a crazy woman?! God put you down right here because He meant for you to stay right here!

ROSE. God's like me, Pop: we both need outside assistance.

POP. You've squeezed the last penny outa me that you're ever gonna get!

ROSE. It ain't for me! It's for my girls. It's too late for me.

POP. It ain't too late for you to get a husband to support you.

ROSE. After three husbands, I'm through with marriage. I want to enjoy myself. I want my girls to enjoy themselves and travel like Momma does!

POP. And you'll leave them just like your mother left you!

ROSE. Never! (*She turns to see Louise, who has entered behind her*) Why aren't you ready for bed, Louise?

LOUISE. June says you said she can sleep with you tonight.

ROSE. You know how high-strung the baby is after a performance.

LOUISE. I performed.

ROSE. It ain't the same. Now say good night and go to bed.

LOUISE. Good night, Grandpa. (*She kisses him*)

POP. Good night, Plug. You're a good girl.

ROSE. You *are* a good girl and I was proud of you tonight.

(*Louise runs to her and hugs her*)

LOUISE. Momma, how come I have three fathers?

ROSE. Because you're lucky. . . . You were born with a caul. That means you got powers to read palms and tell fortunes and wonderful things are going to happen for you!

(*Louise goes*)

POP. Why do you fill her with such bunk?

ROSE. It ain't bunk!

POP. Nothin' wonderful is going to happen to her or June— or to you.

ROSE. Maybe not to me, but they're gonna have a marvelous time! I'll be damned if I'm gonna let them sit away their lives like I did. And like you do—with only that calendar to tell you one day is different from the next! And that plaque—

(*Pointing to a gold plaque on the wall*)

—from your rotten railroad company to say congratulations: for fifty years, you did the same dull thing every dull day!

POP. That plaque is a great tribute! It's solid gold!

ROSE. How much could you get for it?

POP. Rose, if you—

ROSE. What good's it doin' sittin' there?!

POP. That plaque belongs there like you belong home—instead of running around the country like a Gypsy!

ROSE. Anybody that stays home is dead! If I die, it won't be from sittin'! It'll be from fightin' to get up and get out!

(*She sings*)

Some people can get a thrill
Knitting sweaters and sitting still—
    That's okay for some people who don't know
    they're alive;

Some people can thrive and bloom,
Living life in a living room—
    That's perfect for some people of one hundred and
    five!

But I
At least gotta try,
When I think of all the sights that I gotta see yet,
All the places I gotta play,
All the things that I gotta be yet—
   Come on, Poppa, whaddaya say?

Some people can be content
Playing bingo and paying rent—
   That's peachy for some people,
   For some humdrum people
To be,
But some people ain't me!

I had a dream,
A wonderful dream, Poppa,
   All about June and the Orpheum Circuit—
   Give me a chance and I know I can work it!
I had a dream,
Just as real as can be, Poppa—
There I was in Mr. Orpheum's office
And he was saying to me,
"Rose!
Get yourself some new orchestrations,
New routines and red velvet curtains,
Get a feathered hat for the Baby,
Photographs in front of the theatre,
Get an agent—and in jig time
You'll be being booked in the big time!"
Oh, what a dream,
A wonderful dream, Poppa,
And all that I need
Is eighty-eight bucks, Poppa!
That's what he said, Poppa,
Only eighty-eight bucks, Poppa . . .

POP. You ain't getting eighty-eight cents from me, Rose! (*He goes*)

ROSE (*Shouting after him*). Then I'll get it someplace else—but I'll get it and get my kids out!

(*She sings*)

Goodbye
To blueberry pie!
Good riddance to all the socials I had to go to,
All the lodges I had to play,
All the Shriners I said hello to—
Hey, L.A., I'm coming your way!
Some people sit on their butts,
Got the dream—yeah, but not the guts!
   That's living for some people,
   For some humdrum people,
I suppose.
   Well, they can stay and rot—

(*She starts out, takes the plaque from the wall, dumps it in her purse, then finishes her song*)

But not
Rose!

(*And she strides out*)

(*The lights black out*)

SCENE THREE

A road.

   In front of the curtain, June and Louise—wearing their coats and hats and carrying suitcases—stand trying to thumb a ride. The music of "Some People" is continuous underneath. The cut-out of a fancy old touring car "driven" by a rich man and his little son comes on and stops to pick up the children. But as they get in, June signals—and Rose comes running out carrying a suitcase and Chowsie.

   She sings as the car "drives" across. Behind it, boys cross carrying signs indicating the lessening distance between Seattle and Rose's goal: Los Angeles.

   They pass an urchin tap dancing, his hat held out for money. Rose puts some pennies in his cap, then, impressed by his dancing, she yanks him into the car and they move on.

   A troop of boy scouts passes, singing. Rose hears the last little boy hold a good high note—and yanks him into the car.

   At last, they, they reach a welcome banner: LOS ANGELES. *The car stops. Rose gets out with her daughters and the dog and the suitcases and the two stolen boys. The car drives away and as the little band marches off gaily, Rose brings up the rear—with the rich man's tearful little boy, whom she has also stolen.*

SCENE FOUR

The illuminated placards change to read:

"DON'T CALL US"
LOS ANGELES

The backstage of a vaudeville house. There are odds and ends of scenery, crates, trunks, lights, etc.

   Mr. Weber, the theatre manager, rushes on, followed by Rose and her exhausted brood, who collapse near the wings.

WEBER. No, Madam Rose, no!

ROSE. Now listen, Mr. Weber, I did not come all the way from Seattle to Los Angeles to take "No" for an answer.

WEBER. You'll take it from me.

ROSE. Because you don't know how to run your theatre. Your business is slipping. You need youth, fresh young talent.

WEBER. Madam Rose, I told you this morning, I told you this afternoon and I am telling you now: if there is anything I hate worse than kids, it's kids on stage!

ROSE. Children, go play in the alley. (*As they go*) Mr. Weber, that was a rotten remark. If you were a gentleman, you'd apologize and book my act.

WEBER. I am not a gentleman.

(*A nice-looking man carrying a suitcase enters. He has a sweetly sad, tired quality*)

ROSE. Oh, deep down, you are. And if you—

WEBER (*To the man*). Herbie! I been looking for you to get your opinion of the show.

HERBIE. I doubled your crackerjack order, Ed.

WEBER. That bad?

HERBIE. Except for a coupla acts. I left a memo on your desk.

(*A sexual look between Herbie and Rose*)

ROSE. Mr. Weber, you left me right in the middle of a sentence.

WEBER. Madam Rose, you're always in the middle of a sentence.

ROSE. But if your show is as bad as this intelligent gentleman says, you could certainly try my act for a few nights. (*To Herbie*) Couldn't he?

HERBIE. Yeah, he could. You could, Ed.

WEBER. What??

HERBIE. Your theatre gets a family audience. They love kids.

ROSE. And my kids are great!

HERBIE. They sure are.

(*Rose and Weber gape*)

WEBER. How do you know?

HERBIE. I've seen 'em.

WEBER. Where?

HERBIE. In—Seattle. They'd give your show a lift, Ed.

WEBER. Well . . .

ROSE. Listen—

WEBER. Stop pushing. Let me think it over. (*He goes*)

ROSE. Gee—it's hard for me to say thanks!

HERBIE. You just said it.

ROSE. Why'd he listen to you?

HERBIE. Everybody in show business listens to anybody. Besides, I used to book acts into this theatre.

ROSE. Are you an agent?

HERBIE. I was but I'm in the candy business now: I sell to vaudeville houses all over the West.

ROSE. How could you ever leave show business?

HERBIE. When the acts I handled had too little talent, I got sick to my stomach. Ulcers.

ROSE. You're too sympathetic.

HERBIE. Also I went bust. I was always giving them my commission and telling them they got a raise.

ROSE. The good Lord says charity begins at home.

HERBIE. I don't have a home.

ROSE (*Eyes him*). You're not married?

HERBIE. I had five sisters, and the ugly one didn't get married until a year ago.

ROSE. . . . Why'd you help me just now?

HERBIE. I love kids.

ROSE. Oh.

HERBIE. Also—I saw you before.

ROSE. Where?

HERBIE. Waiting outside Weber's office. You looked like a pioneer woman without a frontier.

ROSE. I don't suppose you'd consider being an agent again.

HERBIE. Would you consider marrying again?

ROSE. How do you know I'm not married now?

HERBIE. I asked your kids about you.

ROSE. Oh. Well, after three husbands, it takes a lot of butter to get you back in the frying pan.

HERBIE. After twenty years of show business—(*Picks up bag*)—you kinda breathe better in the real world.

ROSE. Funny.

(*Music starts*)

HERBIE. What?

ROSE. Us. I like you—but I don't want marriage. You like me—but you don't want show business.

HERBIE. That seems to leave you there—and me here.

ROSE. Oh, that depends on how you look at it. You look at what we don't have, I look at what we do have.

(*She sings*)

> Funny, you're a stranger who's come here,
>   Come from another town.
> Funny, I'm a stranger myself here—
>   Small world, isn't it?
> Funny, you're a man who goes traveling
>   Rather than settling down.
> Funny, 'cause I'd love to go traveling—
>   Small world, isn't it?
>
> We have much in common,
>   It's a phenomenon.
> We could pool our resources
> By joining forces
>   From now on.
> Lucky, you're a man who likes children—
>   That's an important sign.
> Lucky, I'm a woman with children—
>   Small world, isn't it?
> Funny, isn't it?
>   Small, and funny, and fine.

(*Music continues as Weber returns*)

WEBER. Well, I'm not gonna pay you much money.

ROSE. Oh, you'll have to talk about money to Herbie.

WEBER. You handling her act?!

HERBIE. Well—no, I—

(*Looks at her. She moves suggestively and he laughs*)

—yeah, I guess I am.

WEBER (*As he goes*). I'll be in the office.
ROSE (*Singing happily*).

> We have so much in common,
>   It's a phenomenon.
> We could pool our resources
> By joining forces
> From now on.

HERBIE. Rose . . . is that act of yours any good?
ROSE. Good? It's great—and June is absolutely sensational!
Wait till you see it!

(*Singing*)

> Lucky, you're a man who likes children—
>   That's an important sign.
> Lucky, I'm a woman with children—
> Small world, isn't it?
> Funny, isn't it?
>   Small, and funny, and fine.

(*The lights fade out*)

SCENE FIVE

The illuminated placards change to read:

BABY JUNE AND HER NEWSBOYS
LOS ANGELES

The curtains part to show a street drop typical of vaudeville; before it, a newspaper kiosk. The orchestra is a tacky, rickety vaudeville combination that tears into the screeching musical introduction for Baby June and Her Newsboys. The Boys, of course, are Louise and the three little kids Rose stole en route to L.A. Their costumes are cheap representations of newsboy outfits, and they wave papers wildly as they sing.

NEWSBOYS (*Singing*).

> Extra! Extra! Hey, look at the headline!
> Historical news is being made!
> Extra! Extra! They're drawing a red line
> Around the biggest scoop of the decade!
> A barrel of charm, a fabulous thrill!
> The biggest little headline in vaud-e-ville:

(*Spoken—to ecstatic drum rolls*) Presenting—in person—that three-foot-three bundle of dynamite: BABY JUNE!

(*There is the greatest drum roll of them all, and crashing through the "front page" plastered across the kiosk comes June, wearing the gaudiest, fanciest, richest costume Rose has been able to whip up. She whirls madly to the footlights, does a split and coyly screeches—*)

JUNE. Hello, everybody! My name is June. What's yours!

(*Then, assisted by the Newsboys, June sings a ragtime version of "Let Me Entertain You"*)

> Let me entertain you,
> Let me make you smile,
>   Let me do a few tricks,
>   Some old and then some new tricks—
> I'm very versatile!
>   And if you're real good,
>   I'll make you feel good—
> I want your spirits to climb.
> So let me entertain you
> And we'll have a real good time—yessir!
> We'll have a real good time!

(*After that, she tap dances wildly about the stage and does every trick Rose has been able to teach, steal and think up. She has a big finish—with the Boys offstage, of course. She squeals as she does high kicks for her bows and then, breathing as though each gasp were her last, she trips daintily to the footlights and says—*)

Thank you so much, ladies and gentlemen. You're very kind . . . You know, everybody has someone to thank for their success. Usually, it's their mother; sometimes, it's their father. But tonight, I'd like you all to join me in giving thanks to an uncle of mine—and an uncle of yours. The Greatest Uncle of Them All: OUR—UNCLE—SAM!

(*A crash from the orchestra and, as June darts behind the kiosk to change her costume, the Newsboys and Louise return—in military costumes. Each of the three Boys represents a wing of our armed forces; Louise is Uncle Sam. Each child does whatever he can for a specialty; Louise does a trick step—which she also did in the opening. The pièce de résistance is, naturally, June. This time she is dressed like a red, white and blue Statue of Liberty and she is on point, twirling batons for all she is worth. Behind her, the American eagle pops up over the kiosk; the band plays "The Stars and Stripes." But Rose takes no chances. As June twirls herself into a split, Louise and the Boys fire the rifles they are carrying—and American flags pop up. Wild applause, stopped by June, breathing harder than ever*)

Mr. Conductor, if you please.

(*The orchestra strikes up again and June and her Newsboys start a traveling step. As the music builds and gets faster, the name of the city on the illuminated placard changes. It goes from one town to another, finally winding up with AKRON. During this, however, the lights on the performers begin to flicker faster and faster—and as June and her Boys seem to dance faster and faster, they appear to be flying through space and growing. Actually, through the flickering dissolve they are replaced by another June, another Louise, and other Boys—all in the same costumes as the originals, but all older and bigger. Time has passed. The act is the same, but the cast is older and the placard has changed to read:*)

DAINTY JUNE AND HER NEWSBOYS
AKRON

The music ends with a flourish. The older June blows the same coy kiss and squeals with the same high-kick bow that the Baby June did, and—thank heaven—the lights black out)

SCENE SIX

The placards read:

> "HAPPY BIRTHDAY"
> AKRON

Two plaster-cracked hotel rooms.
    An alarm clock is ringing wildly as the light comes up on the smaller room. It is festooned with clotheslines hung with winter underwear, costumes, etc. On the bare bed-springs of the one bed lies Louise, wrapped up in a blanket of a very distinct pattern. The mattress has been put on the floor and on it, wrapped in another blanket of the same pattern, are three of the boys in the act. Asleep on two chairs pushed together is the oldest, best-looking and brightest boy in the act: Tulsa. He is also wrapped in one of the blankets. There is one small window with the shade down.
    As the alarm keeps ringing, Louise reaches out and shuts it off. A moment, then she bolts upright and looks around. Carefully then, she reaches out, sets the alarm off again and lies back quickly.

YONKERS (*From the floor. A wiseguy*). Awright, awright!

L.A. (*Sweet-ass*). We're up, Madam Rose!

YONKERS (*Looks at clock*). Hey, it ain't even ten o'clock! Turn it off!

L.A. Louise!

TULSA (*Quietly*). Turn it off, Plug.

LOUISE (*Sits up and turns off the alarm. Yawns elaboratively*). Was that the alarm?

YONKERS. No, it was your mother singing! Shut up!

LOUISE. I was having the loveliest dream. About a special day—My dream book says you dream about a day like that because it maybe really is your—

ANGIE. We wanna sleep!

LOUISE. I just wanted to say—

(She catches Tulsa's eye. He shakes his head)

I'm sorry. (*Silence. She watches them return to sleep. Then she gets out of bed with a great clomping. No reaction. She goes to the window and considers the shade, finally yanking it up quickly. It rolls up with a tremendous clatter—but not a drop of light comes in: the window is smack up against a brick wall. She sticks her head out, craning her neck like mad to see the sky)* How can you all sleep on such a beautiful day!!

YONKERS. Easy—if you shut up.

LOUISE. Do you suppose that sun is so bright because—

(June enters from the other room. Her hair is in curlers; she wears a frilly nightgown and robe)

JUNE. You woke up Mother.

LOUISE (*Whispering*). I didn't mean to, June. But today is a . . . well, you know.

JUNE. Today is one day we don't have to travel and we don't have to rehearse.

YONKERS. Which means we could sleep!

LOUISE. Is Momma mad?

JUNE. She's in the bathroom—making coffee. (*To the Boys*) She says as long as *she's* up, everybody come have breakfast.

LOUISE. June—

JUNE. Honest, Louise!

(June goes out as the Boys groan. Louise groans back at them)

LOUISE. I said I was sorry!

(A moment, then she timidly goes into the other room. The light comes up just a trifle as she enters, but the room is very dim. It is much larger than the other room. Louise speaks, wistfully)

Momma? . . . Momma?

ROSE (*Calling*). Happy birthday!

(The bathroom door bursts open and out comes Rose in a battered bathrobe, carrying a small birthday cake with lighted candles. She, June and the Boys—who pop up and come crashing through the doorway—sing "Happy Birthday" to Louise, who is startled and cries happily. One of the boys turns on the lights and the room is bright and gay. There is a big bed and a table near it. Little dogs run about yapping; there are June's cat, a monkey chained to the bed and bird cages suspended from the chandelier, etc. There are yells of "Surprise! Surprise!" "Blow out the candles," "Make a wish," hugs and kisses, etc.)

Make a wish!

LOUISE. I wish . . . oh, Momma, I wish—

ROSE. Oh! That rotten monkey ate a piece outa the cake! (*Going to the monkey*) Gigolo! Bad, Gigolo, bad bad! (*Then, looking at the blanket Louise has draped over her pajamas*) Say, that would make a good coat.

(Louise blows out the candles)

YONKERS. Hey, there's only ten candles on this cake!

ROSE. What do you care? You ain't gonna eat candles.

YONKERS. But she only had ten candles last year.

L.A. And the year before that.

YONKERS. Come to think of it, she's had ten candles for the last—

ROSE. STOP RIGHT THERE! As long as we have this act, nobody is over twelve and you all know it! Excepting of course me and—where's Herbie? I had a dream— Tulsa, go across the hall and see what's keeping Herbie. The rest of you can give Louise her presents while I see if the chow mein is warmed up.

YONKERS. Chow mein?

LOUISE. It's my birthday!

YONKERS. But chow mein for breakfast??

ROSE. Why not? There's egg roll, ain't there? (*She exits into the bathroom*)

YONKERS. If Madam Rose paid us a salary, we coulda *bought* you presents, Louise—(*He has picked up a box from under the bed*) But it's more fun to clip from the five and dime anyway. (*Hands her the box proudly*). It's a catcher's mitt and a big-league baseball.

LOUISE. Thank you, Yonkers.

L.A. Here's a real stuffed cat.

ANGIE. I clipped a bowl of goldfish. But they caught me, so I drew a fish instead.

LOUISE. I love it. Oh, June, what a beautiful package!

JUNE. It's a complete sewing set in a velvet-lined basket.

(*They embrace. Tulsa, who has come back into the room, picks up his present—three second-hand books tied with cord—and puts it into Louise's hands*)

TULSA. I should have wrapped them.

LOUISE. (*Very touched*). You don't have to wrap books.

TULSA. Well—happy birthday, Plug.

LOUISE. Happy birthday, Tulsa. I mean, you're welcome.

(*Rose comes out of the bathroom carrying food. During the following, the others help by arranging the plates and food*)

ROSE. All right, one egg roll apiece and no more.

TULSA. Herbie wasn't in his room, Madam Rose.

ROSE (*Stops dead*). He wasn't?

TULSA. No.

ROSE. Where could he be?

LOUISE. Momma, can I see my present from you, please?

ROSE. It's from Herbie and me.

LOUISE. It's not from Herbie. He's an agent. It's from *you*.

ROSE. Well, I picked it out, but Herbie paid for it—with his commission for a whole month.

YONKERS. Old Herb makes the same salary we do!

ROSE. Inside, you, and get the coffee! (*Serving food*) Here I am, busting to tell Herbie the dream I had—

LOUISE. Momma—

ROSE. It's really in your honor, coming on the very evening of your birthday. (*To June*) Oh, Baby! You'll love it. You all will. It's— (*Looks toward door, then makes a gesture of dismissal*) —children, it's a *new act*!

YONKERS. That ain't a dream, it's a miracle!

ROSE. In this dream, I saw June singing a song in like a barnyard. And then—a cow came on stage.

TULSA. A cow??

YONKERS. That's pretty sexy.

ROSE. Not a real cow. Sort of a dancing cow—with a great big smile. And that cow—that cow leaned right over my bed and spoke to me!

JUNE (*Cynically*). What did the cow say?

(*A knocking on the door*)

KRINGELEIN (*Offstage*). Madame Rose—

ROSE. I am *not* cooking in here, Mr. Kringelein. That cow—

KRINGELEIN. Open this door!

ROSE. I'm dressing. That cow—

KRINGELEIN. Madame Rose—

ROSE. I'll call you tomorrow when I'm finished. That dear fat cow looked me right in the eye and said: "Rose, if you want to get on the Orpheum Circuit, put *me* in your act." Children, you know what I'm going to do?

YONKERS. You're going to pay that crummy cow and not us!

ROSE. I'm not paying anybody but I am going to take that cow's advice! I'm going to call the new act: Dainty June and Her Farmboys. I'm going to get more boys. I'm going to put that cow in the act—

(*Kringelein—a pompous hotel manager—quietly opens the door of the other room, shuts it behind him and tiptoes to the doorway between the two rooms*)

—and Chowsie and the monkey. And Louise's present— if you don't mind, honey—

LOUISE. But, Momma, I don't even know what it is!

KRINGELEIN (*Coming into the room. Haughtily*). No cooking, Madame Rose?

ROSE. How dare you enter a lady's boudoir without knocking?

KRINGELEIN (*Advancing*). Where's your hot plate?

ROSE. Where's your search warrant?

KRINGELEIN (*Heading toward the bathroom*). In all the years I have been running a theatrical hotel—

ROSE (*Opening the corridor door*). If you don't leave, I'm going to scream!

(*One of the boys darts to block the bathroom door*)

KRINGELEIN (*Pointing toward a sign*). You know the rules. No cooking. No electrical appliances. No—no pets other than small— (*Pushes the kid out of the way*) —dogs or—

(*He opens the bathroom door. A little lamb in rubber drawers runs out between his legs and over to Louise*)

ROSE. Happy birthday, darling!

KRINGELEIN. It's a GODDAM ZOO!

ROSE. Profanity in front of my babies! June, get the Bible! Get the Bible!

(*People in bathrobes and wrappers begin to appear in the doorway, flowing into the room*)

KRINGELEIN. You pack up this dirty menagerie and get out!

ROSE. You'll have to throw me out, you rotten ANIMAL HATER! (*To the others*) That's what he is! Send for the SPCA!

KRINGELEIN. Send for the police! I rented these two rooms to one adult and three children! Now I see one adult! Five pets and one, two, three, four—

ROSE (*Points to one of the boys*). You counted him twice! (*The kids are running in and out. She turns to the others*) It's a simple little birthday party for my baby—

KRINGELEIN. One, two, three four—STAND STILL!

ROSE. Chow mein. I'd offer you some but there's only one egg roll—

KRINGELEIN. One, two, three, four, five—how many are sleeping in that room?

ROSE. What room?

KRINGELEIN (*In the doorway between the two rooms*). THIS room, madam, THIS room!

ROSE (*Pushing him in*). There isn't a soul in this room. (*Closing the door behind them*) Except you and me. (*She lets out a scream as she shoves him down onto the mattress on the floor*) Mr. Kringelein, what are you trying to do?!! (*Throws pillows and blankets on him*) Mr. Kringelein! Stop! Help! Rape!

(*She wrenches her robe open and staggers back into the other room, where the people get a chair for her and ad lib their concern as Rose continues*)

My babies! My babies! MONSTER! Thank you, Gladys. A little birthday party—chow mein—a tiny little cake—

(*Louise, with her lamb, goes into other room during this. Kringelein gets out of the snarl of blankets and exits*)

HERBIE'S VOICE (*From the hall*). Rose! Rose! Are you all right? (*He enters the room and pushes his way to Rose's side*) Rose! What's happened? Are you O.K., honey?

ROSE (*Straightening herself*). Sure! Where have you— (*Then, remembering*) Herbie. Mr. Kringelein, the hotel manager, he—tried to—to—

HERBIE (*A cynical eye*). Again? (*He starts for the other room*)

ROSE. Well, I had to do something, Herbie, don't you dare apologize to him!

HERBIE. Where's Louise?

ROSE. A fat lot you care. The child has a birthday—

HERBIE. Does she like her present?

ROSE. I'm surprised you remembered, where've you been? That's what I want to know.

HERBIE (*Bringing forward a mild little man*). Rose, this is Mr. Goldstone.

ROSE. I ask you, Mr. Goldstone. The child has a birthday once a year. We plan a little party—I'm sorry it's such a small cake and—

HERBIE. Mr. Goldstone is from the Orpheum Circuit.

ROSE. There's only one egg roll and some fried . . . rice . . . and sub . . . gum . . . chow . . .

HERBIE. The act is booked on the Orpheum Circuit.

(*A long pause. Rose stares, numb with a growing happiness. Mechanically, she picks up a plate from the trunk and holds it out*)

ROSE (*Singing*).

Have an egg, roll, Mr. Goldstone,
Have a napkin, have a chopstick, have a chair!
Have a sparerib, Mr. Goldstone—
Any sparerib that I can spare, I'd be glad to share!
Have a dish, have a fork,
Have a fish, have a pork,
Put your feet up, feel at home.
Have a smoke, have a coke,
Would you like to hear a joke?
I'll have June recite a poem!
Have a lichee, Mr. Goldstone,
Tell me any little thing that I can do.
Ginger-peachy, Mr. Goldstone,
Have a kumquat—have two!
Everybody give a cheer—
Santa Claus is sittin' here—
Mr. Goldstone, I love you!

(*Hysterical with excitement*)

Have a goldstone, Mr. Egg Roll,
Tell me any little thing that I can do.
Have some fried rice, Mr. Soy Sauce,
Have a cookie, have a few!
What's the matter, Mr. G.?
Have another pot of tea!
Mr. Goldstone, I love you!

There are good stones and bad stones
And curbstones and Gladstones
And touchstones and such stones as them!
There are big stones and small stones
And grindstones and gallstones,
But Goldstone is a gem.

There are milestones, there are millstones,
There's a cherry, there's a yellow, there's a blue!
But we don't want any old stone,
Only Goldstone will do!

ALL (*Singing*).

Moonstone, sunstone—we all scream for one stone!
Mervyn Goldstone, we love you!
Goldstone!

(*The lights black out in the larger bedroom and fade in slowly on the small room, where a forgotten Louise sits with the lamb*)

LOUISE (*Singing softly*).

Little lamb, little lamb,
My birthday is here at last.

Little lamb, little lamb,
A birthday goes by so fast.
Little bear, little bear,
You sit on my right, right there.
Little hen, little hen,
What game shall we play, and when?
Little cat, little cat,
Ah, why do you look so blue?
Did somebody paint you like that,
Or is it your birthday, too?
Little fish, little fish,
Do you think I'll get my wish?
Little lamb, little lamb,
I wonder how old I am.
I wonder how old I am . . .

(*The lights dim out*)

SCENE SEVEN

The placards change to read:

"TABLE FOR TWO"
NEW YORK

The scene is a section of a gaudy Chinese restaurant. Herbie sits at a table with June. Rose is scraping leftovers from the plates into cartons which she eventually gathers into a paper sack. She hums happily.

ROSE. Hand me Louise's plate, June.

JUNE (*Embarrassed*). Mother—

ROSE. We're paying for it, ain't we? You'll get an ulcer like Herbie. Besides, what the dogs don't eat, we will.

HERBIE. Rose, did it ever occur to you there might be somebody in this world who *doesn't* like Chinese food?

ROSE. Don't be silly. Who? (*Hums, scrapes; then softly*) Don't you like it, Herbie?

HERBIE (*A beat, then he smiles*). Sure Rose. I love it.

(*Louise enters wearing a coat made of the hotel blanket and holding a little dog that is also wearing a blanket-coat*)

ROSE. Did she?

LOUISE. Yes.

ROSE (*Baby talk to the dog*). 'Atsa healthy-wealthy lady-wadie.

HERBIE. Oh, God!

JUNE. Herbie's angry: he's chain smoking.

ROSE. Herbie's never angry, it's bad for his stomach. Come on, girls, beddie-bye.

(*She and June put on their blanket-coats*)

JUNE. It's so early!

ROSE. You're going to audition for Mr. T. T. Grantziger and his Palace Theatre tomorrow and you have to look *young*.

LOUISE. Can I wear a dress?

ROSE. You'd look old in a dress. Besides you haven't got one.

JUNE. Good night, Uncle Herbie. (*She kisses him*)

HERBIE. Good night, June. (*Stands up to kiss Louise, who stiff-arms him*) Good night, Louise.

LOUISE. Good night, Herbie. (*She exits with June*)

ROSE. I'll cold-cream their faces and be right back.

HERBIE. The hotel is two doors away! Honestly, you behave as though those girls—Rose!

(*This because she is collecting silverware and is about to put it in her bag*)

ROSE. We need new silverware. (*Stops, then puts down the silver*) Herbie, how long is it going to take you to get used to me?

HERBIE. How long did it take me to get used to those coats?

ROSE. What's the matter with them? They're real stylish! Louise is very talented with a needle. Herbie, as the good Lord says: an eye for an eye, a tooth for a tooth— (*On this, she sweeps the silver into her bag*) And it serves them right for overcharging.

(*Starts to go. Herbie hands her a knife, which she also takes, but she stops and returns*)

They can skip the cold cream *for one night*.

(*Automatically, he gets up and helps her off with her coat. Rose, admiringly:*)

All this time we've been together, and you still stand up for me!

HERBIE. It's instead of standing up *to* you.

ROSE. O.K., you say we're never alone. I wanted to have dinner tonight, just the two of us, but what was I going to do with the girls? They're babies.

HERBIE. Rose, no matter how you dress 'em, no matter how you smother 'em, they're big girls. They're almost young women—

ROSE. They're not and they never will be!

HERBIE. I'm embarrassed in front of them! When are you going to marry me, Rose?

ROSE. Don't forget to take our scrapbooks to Mr. Grantziger's tomorrow.

HERBIE. When are you going to quite stalling? Honey, don't you know there's a depression?

ROSE. Of course I know! I read *Variety*.

HERBIE. Don't you know what it's doing to vaudeville? Don't you know what the talkies are doing to vaudeville? Don't you know I love you?

ROSE. You think I'd be unfaithful to my husbands if you didn't? But I have to think of my girls and their happiness.

HERBIE. Louise is very happy being the front end of a cow!

ROSE. It's better than being the rear end! Anyway, she loves animals.

HERBIE. She and June should both be in school—

ROSE. And be just like other girls; cook and clean and sit and die! (*To a passing waitress, sweetly*) Honey, could I have a spoon to stir my tea? . . . Herbie, I promised June I'd make her a star and I will. I promised I'd get her on the Pantages Circuit and I did. I promised I'd get her on the Orpheum Circuit and I did.

HERBIE. *I did!* And you promised me that after I did, you'd marry me.

ROSE. I promised her she'd headline on Broadway and—

HERBIE. Didn't you hear what I said?

ROSE. Yes, but I'm ignoring it. (*To the waitress, for the spoon*) Thanks, honey. Herbie, it isn't very polite for a gentleman to remind a lady that she welched. There was no date on that promise—

HERBIE. ROSE, STOP HANDING ME—

ROSE. Your stomach! (*Quickly handing him a pill*) Herbie, why don't you get angry outside, instead of letting it settle in your stomach?

HERBIE. I'm afraid.

ROSE. Of me?

HERBIE. Of me.

ROSE. What do you mean?

HERBIE. If I ever let loose, it'll end with me picking up and walking.

ROSE. Only around the block.

HERBIE. No.

ROSE. Don't say that.

(*Sings*)

> You'll never get away from me.
> You can climb the tallest tree,
>   I'll be there somehow.
> True, you could say, "Hey, here's your hat,"
> But a little thing like that
>   Couldn't stop me now.
> I couldn't get away from you
> Even if you told me to,
>   So go on and try!
> Just try,
> And you're gonna see
> How you're gonna not at all get away from me!

HERBIE. What is it? What do you want? There are better agents.

ROSE. Not for me.

HERBIE. And even weaker men.

ROSE. Not for me.

HERBIE. Then what?

ROSE. You. Oh, Herbie, just help me like you been helping. Just let me get June's name up in lights so big, they'll last my whole life.

HERBIE. Rose, what you expect—

ROSE. I'll *get!* And after I get it, I promise I'll marry you.

(*Herbie moves away from the table*)

I even promise to keep my promise. (*Silence*) Please, Herbie. I don't want to upset anything before the audition tomorrow. Including your stomach.

HERBIE (*Singing*).

> Rose, I love you,
> But don't count your chickens.

ROSE (*Singing*).

> Come dance with me.

HERBIE.

> I warn you
> That I'm no Boy Scout.

ROSE.

> Relax a while—come dance with me.

HERBIE.

> So don't think
> That I'm easy pickin's—

ROSE.

> The music's so nice—

HERBIE.

> Rose!
> 'Cause I just may
> Some day
> Pick up and pack out.

ROSE.

> Oh no, you won't.
> No, not a chance.
> No arguments,
> Shut up and dance.

BOTH.

> You'll never get away from me,
> You can climb the tallest tree—
> I'll be there somehow!
> True, you could say "Hey, here's your hat,"
> But a little thing like that
> Couldn't stop me now.
> I couldn't get away from you
> Even if I wanted to—

ROSE.

> Well, go on and try!
> Just try—

HERBIE.

> Ah, Rose—

ROSE.

> And you're gonna see—

HERBIE.

> Ah, Rose—

ROSE.

> How you're gonna not at all
> Get away from me!

(*The lights fade*)

SCENE EIGHT

The placards change to read:

GRANTZIGER'S PALACE
NEW YORK

The scene is the stage of a good theatre.

A telephone is ringing as the lights come up on the gold theatre curtains. An attractive, smartly groomed secretary—Cratchitt—hurries on, signals toward the top of the theatre, pulls out a telephone attached on a bracket to the proscenium and answers.

CRATCHITT. Yes, Mr. Grantziger . . . I know, but they're having a little difficulty with their scenery. Well, wait till you see it . . .

(Rose appears wearing a hat and coat)

ROSE. *(To the Conductor)* Now keep the tempo bright. Keep it up.
CRATCHITT *(On phone)*. That's the mother . . . I *have* told her!
ROSE *(Peering out front)*. Hello, Mr. Grantziger. Where is he?
CRACHITT *(Pointing)*. In his office at the top of the theater.
ROSE *(Waving—neighborly)*. Hi!
HERBIE *(Runs on to try to get Rose off)*. It's a privilege to audition for you, Mr. Grantziger!
ROSE *(Just before Herbie drags her off)*. You're going to love us!

(They exit)

CRATCHITT *(Into the phone)*. That's the agent. *He's* nice.
HERBIE *(Returning)*. We're ready now.
CRATCHITT *(Into the phone)*. They're ready now, Mr. Grantziger. *(To Herbie)* Good luck.
HERBIE. Thank you.

(They both go off, the lights dim and the curtains part to reveal a corny set of a vaudeville barnyard, complete with haystack. Rose's Newsboys are now Farmboys, and they stand with rakes, hoes, etc., in a picturesque tableau (!) as birds and music twitter the approach of dawn—which comes up violently. The music crashes into the introduction for the Newsboys' song—sung, this time, by the Farmboys—and on cue, the haystack parts for Dainty June to whirl out and down front, where she ends in that same split. This time, she sings and dances with a COW, however. During the dance, the front end of the COW does a familiar trick step: Louise is still doing her big specialty)

FARMBOYS *(Singing)*.

Extra! Extra! Hey look at the headline!
Historical news is being made!
Extra! Extra! They're drawing a red line
Around the biggest scoop of the decade!
A barrel of charm, a fabulous thrill!

The biggest little headline in vaud-e-ville!

(Spoken) Presenting—in person—that five-foot-two bundle of dynamite: DAINTY JUNE!
JUNE. Hello, everybody! My name is June. What's yours?

(She sings)

I have a moo cow, a new cow, a true cow
Named Caroline.

COW. Moo moo moo moo—
JUNE.

She's an extra special friend of mine.

COW. Moo moo moo moo—
JUNE.

I like everything about her fine.

COW. Moo moo moo moo—
JUNE.

She likes to moo in the moonlight
When the moody moon appears.
And when she moos in the moonlight,
Gosh, it's moosic to my ears!
She's so moosical . . .
She loves a man cow, a tan cow who can cow
Her with a glance.

(The Cow recites, "Moo moo moo moo," following this and the next two lines)

When he winks at her, she starts to dance,
It's what grownups call a real romance,
But if we moved to the city
Or we settled by the shore,
She'd make the mooooooooove,
'Cause she loves me more!

(June and the Cow continue the dance to the end and exit. The phone rings. Cratchitt comes on to answer)

CRATCHITT *(Into the phone)*. Yes, Mr. Grantziger. Dainty June, will you come out please?

(June comes on)

Face front, dear. Profile.

(Rose appears in the other wing)

Yes, Mr. Grantziger. Thank you. That's all.
ROSE. But we have a great dramatic finale!
CRATCHITT. I'm sure. But he's seen quite enough.
ROSE. Ahh— *(To the Conductor)* Hit it!
CRATCHITT. But Mr. Grantziger does not want to see any—

(But even while she is talking, the music crashes in and the Farmboys—directed by Rose—dance on in Eton suits with high hats and canes, frightening Cratchitt off. They launch into the song and tap dance that always built up to the entrance of the blond star. And it does this time, for June comes on, dazzling, glamorous, singing and dancing for all she—and Rose—are worth. During the Boys' number,

one of the high hats falls off, and Rose dashes out from the wings to retrieve and replace it. At the end of June's song-and-dance with the Boys, Rose helps the stagehands get the haystack offstage. Behind it is the front of a train which puffs smoke)

FARMBOYS (*Singing*).

> Broadway, Broadway! We've missed it so!
> We're going soon and taking June
> To star her in a show!
> Bright lights! White lights!
> Rhythm and romance!
> The train is late so while we wait
> We're gonna do a little dance!

(*And they do—as a prelude to June's song*)

JUNE (*Singing*).

> Broadway! Broadway! How great you are!
> I'll leave the farm with all its charm
> To be a Broadway star!
> Bright lights! White lights!
> Where the neons glow!
> My bag is packed, I've got my act.
> So all aboard, come on, let's go!

YONKERS (*Calls*). All aboard!

ROSE. Woo woo . . . Watch this! It's a train.

FARMBOYS. Let's go!

(*Waving and "goodbyes" from everybody. A train effect; the Cow tries to run after the train*)

JUNE (*To the Cow*). Goodbye, Caroline. I'll write to you.

COW. Moo!

JUNE. Goodbye, Caroline—take care. Don't forget to write! . . . Wait! Stop the train! (*A chord*) Stop everything! I can't go to Broadway with you!

TULSA. Why not, Dainty June?

JUNE (*To soupy music*). Because everything in life that really matters is right here! What care I for tinsel and glamour when I have friendship and true love? I'm staying here with Caroline!

(*She runs off the train platform and embraces the Cow to general cheering. A chord from the orchestra—which launches once again into "The Stars and Stripes"; this time the American Eagle—and a big one—pops up over the train; June grabs batons from the platform and twirls them madly as she marches downstage to end in a triumphant split while the Farmboys fire American flags from their canes. Rose has done it again. The light changes to work light and the phone is ringing loudly. Crachitt comes out to answer it. Rose and Herbie come out from the opposite wing to hear the verdict*)

CRATCHITT. Yes, Mr. Grantziger . . . What? (*To Rose and Herbie, in astonishment*) He liked it! (*On the phone again*) Yes, sir. Yes, sir, if that's what you want. (*Hangs up and turns to Rose*) If you and your tribe will come up to the office—I'll make out the contracts.

(*She shoots a peculiar look up to Mr. Grantziger's office and exits as Rose shouts up*)

ROSE. You won't be sorry, Mr. Grantziger! (*Herbie yanks her off, but she is right back to add*) This is gonna make ya!

(*The lights black out*)

SCENE NINE

An ornately Gothic office with a door center. Louise and June are seated on a bench. Crachitt is at a desk, answering the phone.

CRATCHITT. Yes? . . . No. Mr. Grantziger's busy. He's gone down to the stage. (*Hangs up*) Your mother and her friend are just reading over the contract. They won't be much longer. She's gotta eat *sometime* . . . Say, woman to woman, how old are you?

JUNE. Nine.

CRATCHITT. Nine *what*?

JUNE. Nine going on ten.

CRATCHITT. How long has that been going on?

(*Herbie comes in carrying a contract, followed by Rose*)

HERBIE. Miss Cratchitt, I think Mr. Grantziger made a mistake in this contract.

CRATCHITT (*Gaily*). So do I.

(*The phone rings. Cratchitt picks it up*)

Yes?

ROSE. Happy, girls?

LOUISE. Yes, Momma.

CRATCHITT. No. (*She hangs up*)

HERBIE. Miss Cratchitt, we were auditioning for Grantziger's Palace. This contract is for Grantziger's Variety.

CRATCHITT. That's right.

HERBIE. But the Variety is way down on Twelfth Street.

CRATCHITT. He'll give you a visa to get there.

(*The phone rings again*)

Yes?

HERBIE. I'd like to talk to Mr. Grantziger.

CRATCHITT (*Hangs up quickly*). No. Listen, I told you: He's down on the stage.

HERBIE (*Going toward the second door*). This the way?

CRATCHITT. You can't disturb him. He's still holding auditions.

HERBIE. Then I'll wait.

CRATCHITT. Look, friend. Strictly between us, if I were you I'd sign that contract. There's only one item in that act of yours that the Boss likes: Dainty Little June. He thinks she can be an actress.

ROSE (*As June stands up*). He's right.

CRATCHITT. Can be—*if*.

HERBIE. If what?

CRATCHITT. If she goes to school for a solid year and takes lessons. He's ready to pay for everything—on one condition. (*To Rose*) You stay away.

ROSE. Stay away? I'm her mother!

CRATCHITT. You said it, I didn't.

HERBIE. What about the act?

CRATCHITT (*Shrugs*). One week at the Variety.

ROSE. But June *is* the act! How is it suppose to go on without her?

HERBIE. Rose, we could—

ROSE (*To Cratchitt*). How are Louise and I supposed to live?

CRATCHITT. You might get a job, dear.

ROSE. I have a job, dear, and I do it damn well! My daughters are my job and I have two of them!

LOUISE. Momma, if June—

ROSE. June is my baby! I'm her mother!

(*The phone rings*)

CRATCHITT (*Answering*). Yes—

ROSE (*Taking it away and slamming the receiver down on the table*). Don't you dare answer the phone when I'm yelling at you! Nobody knows June like I do and nobody can do for her what I can!

JUNE. Momma, this is my chance to be an actress. Mr. Grantziger can make me a star!

ROSE. You *are* a star! And I made you one! Who's got clippings like she has? Books full of 'em! She don't need lessons any more than she needs Mr. T. T. Grantziger!

CRATCHITT. There isn't a person in show business who doesn't need Mr. Grantziger!

ROSE. Take a good look at *this* person!

HERBIE. Rose—

ROSE. They're so smart in New York!

CRATCHITT. New York is the center of everything.

ROSE. New York is the center of New York! There's a whole country full of people who *know* people!—who know what a mother means to her daughter! It's hicks like you who don't know! And you want to know something else? Grantziger's a hick. He'll get no place!

HERBIE. Rose—

ROSE. He's trying to take my baby away from me, that's what he's trying to do! Well, over my dead body, he will!

(*And she storms out the door to the "stage," with Herbie and Cratchitt calling and running out after her. A pause, then Louise picks up the phone left off the hook*)

LOUISE (*Quietly*). No. (*Hangs up*) Momma's just talking big, June. She won't really—

JUNE. Yes, she will.

LOUISE. Maybe Mr. Grantziger will—

JUNE. No, he won't . . . Well, that's show business.

LOUISE. Aren't you happy someone like Mr. T. T. Grantziger thinks you can be a star?

JUNE. You're funny.

LOUISE. Why?

JUNE. You're never jealous.

LOUISE. Oh. Well, I don't have any talent. I don't really mind—except Momma would like it better if I did.

JUNE. I guess that's what she likes about me. Momma's no fool. I'm not a star.

LOUISE. You are.

JUNE. *I'm not!* Mr. Grantziger could make me one.

LOUISE. Momma can make you a star, too.

JUNE (*Ice*). Momma can do one thing: She can make herself believe anything she makes up. Like with that rhinestone finale dress *you* sewed for me. Momma wants publicity so she makes up a story that three nuns went blind sewing it! Now she believes it. She even believes the act is good.

LOUISE. Isn't it?

JUNE (*Cold anger*). It's a terrible act and I hate it. I've hated it from the beginning and I hate it more now. I hate pretending I'm two years old. I hate singing those same awful songs, doing those same awful dances, wearing those same awful costumes—I didn't mean it about the costumes.

LOUISE. No. You just meant you're too big for them now.

JUNE. . . . Do you ever feel like you didn't have a sister?

LOUISE. . . . Sometimes.

JUNE. It's Momma's fault.

LOUISE. You can't blame everything on Momma.

JUNE. *You* can't maybe. I wish she'd marry Herbie and let me alone.

LOUISE. Herbie doesn't want to marry her. All he cares about is the act.

JUNE. Honest, Louise.

LOUISE. Well, he's an agent!

HERBIE (*Enters and tosses the contract back on the desk*). Your mother isn't feeling well. I'm going to take her back to the hotel . . . Don't worry, I'll get you a good booking. (*He kisses June, looks at Louise who looks away and exits*)

LOUISE. I wish Momma would marry a plain man . . . so we'd all be together.

(*She sings*)

> If Momma was married we'd live in a house,
> As private as private can be:
> Just Momma, three ducks, five canaries, a mouse,
> Two monkeys, one father, six turtles and me . . .
> If Momma was married.

JUNE (*Singing*).

> If Momma was married, I'd jump in the air
> And give all my toeshoes to you.
> I'd get all these hair ribbons out of my hair,
> And once and for all, I'd get Momma out, too . . .
> If Momma was married.

LOUISE.

> Momma, get out your white dress!
> You've done it before—

JUNE.

Without much success—

BOTH.

Momma, God speed and God bless,
We're not keeping score—
What's one more or less?
Oh, Momma, say yes
And waltz down the aisle while you may.

LOUISE.

I'll gladly support you,
I'll even escort you—

JUNE.

And I'll gladly give you away!

BOTH.

Oh, Momma, get married today!

JUNE.

If Momma was married there wouldn't be any more—
"Let me entertain you,
Let me make you smile.
I will do some kicks."

LOUISE.

"I will do some tricks.

JUNE.

Sing out, Louise!

LOUISE.

Smile, baby!
Momma, please take our advice:
We aren't the Lunts.

JUNE.

I'm not Fanny Brice.
Momma, we'll buy you the rice,
If only this once

BOTH.

You wouldn't think twice!
It could be so nice
If Momma got married to stay.

LOUISE.

But Momma gets married—

JUNE.

And—

LOUISE.

Married—

JUNE.

And—

LOUISE.

Married

BOTH.

And never gets carried away.

Oh, Momma,
Oh, Momma,
Oh, Momma, get married today!

(*The lights dim out.*)

SCENE 10

The placards change to read:

"DREAMS OF GLORY"
BUFFALO

A theatre alley, with steps that lead up to the stage door.
Without music, Tulsa is dancing, rehearsing a routine with a broom for a partner. Herbie comes out the stage door and watches until Tulsa sees him and stops in embarrassment.

HERBIE. That's pretty fancy footwork, Tulsa. Why don't you show it to Madam Rose?

TULSA. I'm not that good, Herbie. It's just foolin' around.

HERBIE (*As, unseen by him, Louise enters*). You started "foolin' around" about three months ago. Just after Mr. Grantziger canceled our booking.

TULSA. Well . . .

HERBIE. Why, Tulsa?

LOUISE. He's just had more time, that's all. Like that two-week layoff in Albany.

TULSA. And the layoff in Rochester.

LOUISE. And the layoff in Niagara Falls.

HERBIE. Oh. I thought you were maybe worried about the act.

TULSA. Oh, no, Herbie.

HERBIE. Because the way things are pickin' up—why, I wouldn't be surprised if you kids got paid! (*To Louise*) Matter of fact, they're good enough right now for me to treat you to an icecream soda.

LOUISE. No, thank you.

HERBIE. Chow mein?

LOUISE. Momma doesn't like us to eat just before a show.

HERBIE (*After a moment, strong*). Louise—there's one thing your momma knows that I wish you did: I like her. (*He starts toward the stage door*)

LOUISE. Herbie . . . (*He stops. A moment, then she shakes her head*) Nothing.

HERBIE. Tulsa, if you or any of the boys have any problems, you bring 'em to me.

TULSA. Sure, Herbie.

(*Herbie exits*)

LOUISE. You didn't tell him, did you? I mean that you're rehearsing a dance-team act?

TULSA. How'd you know I was?

LOUISE. I saw you practicing Monday after the matinée, with your broom for a partner. I was up in the flies.

TULSA. Louise—

LOUISE. Oh, I won't tell anybody, Tulsa! I'm very secretive. Just like you. (*Takes his hand*) See? That's what this means in your palm. And this means you make up dreams—just like me.

TULSA. What do you make up dreams about, Louise?

LOUISE. . . . People.

TULSA. Oh, I do that too.

LOUISE. Yes, but yours are about a partner for your act.

TULSA. She's gonna be more than a partner, I hope. I mean I dream . . . well, you know . . . (*He starts to dance around*)

LOUISE. What would she have to be like, Tulsa? A wonderful singer and dancer, I guess.

TULSA. No. I'm going to do most of that. I don't mean I'm going to hog it but—they always look at the girl . . . in a dance team. Especially if she's pretty.

LOUISE. Makeup can help. And costumes.

TULSA. I've got the costumes all figured out. A blue satin tux for me—

LOUISE. With rhinestone lapels—

TULSA. You think?

LOUISE. I'll sew them on.

(*Music*)

TULSA (*As the music starts*). O.K. Thanks. Well, I pretend I'm home getting ready for a date. I'm combing my hair. I take a flower. Put it in my lapel. Then I spot the audience.

(*He sings*)

> Once my clothes were shabby,
> Tailors called me "Cabbie,"
>   So I took a vow,
>   Said "This bum'll
>   Be Beau Brummel."
> Now I'm smooth and snappy,
> Now my tailor's happy.
>   I'm the cat's meow,
>   My wardrobe is a wow:
> Paris silk, Harris tweed,
> There's only one thing I need.
> Got my tweed pressed,
> Got my best vest,
>   All I need now is the girl!
> Got my striped tie,
> Got my hopes high,
>   Got the time and the place, and I got rhythm—
> Now all I need's the girl to go with 'em!
> If she'll
> Just appear, we'll
>   Take this big town for a whirl,
> And if she'll say, "My
> Darling, I'm yours," I'll throw away my
>   Striped tie and my best-pressed tweed—
>   All I really need
>   Is the girl!

(*Louise has been watching with yearning and now, as Tulsa begins to dance, the yearning increases. He explains his dance to her as he goes along*)

I start easy . . . Now I'm more—debonair . . . Break! And I sell it here . . . I start this step—double it—and she appears! All in white!

(*He reaches out his hand to the invisible partner, and Louise—who has gotten up—holds out her hand, tentatively. He is unaware of her, unaware of her hopes, unaware she is following him about, visualizing herself as the partner for him*)

I take her hand—kiss it—and lead her out on the floor . . . This step is good for the costumes . . . Now we waltz. Strings come in. And I lift her! . . . Again! . . . Once more! . . . Now the tempo changes; all the lights come up; and I build for the finale!

(*At last, he starts a step that Louise knows, and, clumsily, she starts to do it with him. At last, he notices and shouts*)

That's it, Louise! But do it over here! Give me your hand! Faster! Now Charleston right! Again! Again! Turn!

(*She is dancing joyously, her happiness making up for her awkwardness. They end together—in triumph. L.A. runs in from the stage door in costume for the Cow Act and whistles to them. They get up and race into the theatre*)

(*The lights dim out*)

SCENE ELEVEN

The placards change to read:

> "TERMINAL"
> OMAHA

The scene is a railroad platform. It is a misty night. Baggage is piled near Rose and Herbie. Yonkers and Angie are there.

ROSE. Don't lower yourself to argue, Herbie. If those rats want to quit the act, let them quite. If they want their train tickets home, give them their bus tickets home. (*Crossing*) What's keeping those girls?

HERBIE. There's plenty of time, Rose,

ROSE (*Going to the end of the platform, peering out*). And you say they're big enough to take care of themselves.

HERBIE. Look, fellas, I know we've had a couple of layoffs in the—

YONKERS. It ain't that, Herbie.

HERBIE. Then what is it?

YONKERS. We're—too old.

HERBIE (*Sotto voce*). Would you be too old if Madame Rose and I could see our way clear to increasing your salary?

ROSE (*A bellow from clear across the stage*). Increase what salary?!

ANGIE. Herbie's been paying us—

YONKERS (*Kicks him*). Moron!

ROSE (*Coming back*). Herbie . . .

HERBIE. How long is it going to take you to get used to me, Rose?

ROSE. Button your coat. (*To the Boys*) Ingrates! You take the bread out of that man's mouth and spit it in his face! Well, as the good Lord says, "Good riddance to bad rubbish." Give 'em their tickets, Herbie. They were both rotten in the act anyway.

HERBIE. O.K. (*He takes out tickets as she peers out for the girls*)

YONKERS. Thanks, Herbie. Only we'd like tickets for all the fellows.

HERBIE. . . . All the fellows?

YONKERS. Well, they asked us.

HERBIE. You're all leaving?

ANGIE. Yes, sir, Herbie.

ROSE. Something's funny. Something's very funny here.

HERBIE. Why, Angie? (*Silence*)

ROSE. What's this all about? (*Silence*)

HERBIE. O.K. If you're all going, you're all going. But why, Yonkers—

(*Louise runs on, a note in her hand*)

ROSE. Where've you been? Where's June? (*Silence*) Louise, where's June?

(*Louise holds out the note*)

Don't give me any of your poems to read now. Answer me!

LOUISE. June wrote this. To you.

ROSE. Wrote what? What's she writing me for?

LOUISE. Momma, *read it!*

(*Rose looks at her, then takes the letter. She reads it, then sits and stares at it, not moving, looking like a dead woman through the following*)

ANGIE (*To Herbie*). She eloped.

YONKERS. She didn't elope, stupid. They got married three weeks ago.

HERBIE. Who got married?

YONKERS. June and Tulsa. Only they hadda wait till their act was ready before they took off.

ANGIE. It's a keen act. Ain't it, Louise?

LOUISE. I didn't see it.

YONKERS. We ain't rats, Herbie. We just knew that without June—

HERBIE. Where'd they go?

ANGIE. Well, first they got a club date in Kansas City . . .

YONKERS (*Kicks him*). Big mouth! Could we have the tickets now, please, Herbie? We gotta get moving. See, we fixed up an act of our own and—

HERBIE. Get moving!

L.A. Don't be sore, Herbie. Geez, it ain't our fault the act's washed up.

(*He and Angie start off*)

HERBIE. Hey, fellas. Good Luck!

YONKERS (*Brightens*). Thanks. Good luck to you, Herbie.

ANGIE. Good luck, Louise.

LOUISE. Good luck.

YONKERS. Good luck, Madame Rose. (*Silence*) Come on, Angie.

(*They go off. Louise stands a good distance from Rose, who has not moved. Herbie goes to Rose and speaks with growing passion*)

HERBIE. Rose . . . Honey, listen. I can go back in the candy business. It's steady: fifty-two weeks all year every year. I'll work my fingers to the bone; I'll do twice what I did before and that was pretty fair. Rose, I could be a district manager and we could stay put in one place. We could have our own house. Louise could go to school. Rose? Rose, honey, you still got Herbie. You can marry me and I promise you, you won't have one single worry the rest of your life. Rose, don't you want that?

LOUISE (*A burst*). Yes! Momma, say yes!

(*Herbie turns and looks at her. A moment, then she runs across the platform into his arms. He holds her tight and rocks her*)

Herbie . . .

HERBIE. You read palms, I read minds. It's O.K. (*Going back to Rose, brighter*) It's going to be fine now, honey. Everything happens for the best. O.K., the act's finished. But you and me and our daughter, we're going to have a home—say, we got a cow for the backyard! Why, we are going to be the best damn—

(*During the last, Rose slowly gets up and brushes Herbie aside as though she has not heard a word. The letter hangs from her hand as she walks—as though in a trance—to Louise. Her voice is flat and deadly calm*)

ROSE. I'm used to people walking out. When my own mother did it, I cried for a week. Your father did it, and then the man I married after him did it, and now— (*Unaware, she tears the letter in half*) Well this time, I'm not crying. This time, I'm apologizing. To you. I pushed you aside for her. I made everything only for her.

LOUISE. No, Momma.

ROSE. But she says I can't make her an actress like she wants to be. The boys walk because they think the act's finished. They think we're nothing without her. (*Now going over the edge*) Well, she's nothing without me! (*Throws the pieces of the letter in the air*) I'm her mother and I made her! And I can make you now! And I will, my baby, I swear I will! I'm going to *make* you a star! I'm going to build a whole new act—all around you! It's going to be better than anything we ever did before! Better than anything we even dreamed!

HERBIE. Rose!

ROSE (*An express train out of control*). You're right, Herbie! It *is* for the best! The old act was getting stale and tired! But the new one?! Look at the new star, Herbie! She's going to be beautiful. She *is* beautiful! Finished?! We're just beginning and there's no stopping us this time!

I had a dream,
A dream about you, Baby!
It's gonna come true, Baby!
They think that we're through,
But,
Baby,
You'll be swell, you'll be great,
Gonna have the whole world on a plate!
Starting here, starting now,
    Honey, everything's coming up roses!
Clear the decks, clear the tracks,
You got nothing to do but relax
Blow a kiss, take a bow—
    Honey, everything's coming up roses!
Now's your inning—
    Stand the world on its ear!
Set it spinning,
'N that'll be just the beginning!
Curtain up, light the lights,
You got nothing to hit but the heights!
You'll be swell,
    You'll be great,
I can tell—
    Just you wait!
That lucky star I talk about is due!
Honey, everything's coming up roses for me and for you!

You can do it,
    All you need is a hand.
We can do it,
Momma is gonna see to it!

(*Herbie and Louise stand silent, numb, as she plows on, singing triumphantly*)

Curtain up, light the lights,
We got nothing to hit but the heights!
I can tell,
    Wait and see!
There's the bell,
    Follow me.
And nothing's gonna stop us till we're through!
Honey, everything's coming up roses and daffodils,
Everything's coming up sunshine and Santa Claus,
Everything's gonna be bright lights and lollipops,
Everything's coming up roses for me and for you!

(*The curtain falls*)

ACT TWO

SCENE ONE

Before the curtain, the illuminated placards read:

MME. ROSE'S TOREADORABLES
TEXAS

It is desert country. Late afternoon. The rear end of a touring car sticks out from one side. From the other, part of a tent.

ROSE (*Calling*). Are you ready, Louise?

LOUISE (*Off*). Yes, Momma.

ROSE. Ready, girls?

GIRLS (*Off*). Yes, Madame Rose.

ROSE. Now don't let the past discourage you. Remember: you're artists of the theatre! (*She imitates a trumpet call*) Madame Rose's Toreadorables!

(*A crash of Spanish-type music and an assortment of Girls lurches on in ghastly, homemade señorita costumes. What they lack in talent—everything—they make up for in enthusiasm. And what do they sing? The same opening as the Newsboys and Farmboys, their predecessors*)

GIRLS (*As Rose yells for them to "Sing out!"*).

Extra! Extra! Hey, look at the headline!
Historical news is being made!
Extra! Extra! They're drawing a red line
Around the biggest scoop of the decade!
A barrel of charm, a fabulous thrill!
The biggest little headline in vaud-e-ville!

ROSE. Now sell it! Sell it! And give it atmosphere!

GIRLS. Presenting—in person—that five-foot-four bundle of dynamite: SEÑORITA LOUISE!

ROSE. Come on, Louise, come on!

(*Louise comes on in a glittering, gaudy toreador costume—and a blond wig. She makes a pathetic attempt to twirl and do a split like June before saying—*)

LOUISE. Olé, everybody! My name's Louise. What's yours?

(*She looks up at Rose in appeal. A pause. Then—*)

ROSE. Well—it's coming along.

LOUISE. Momma, I'm just no good at it.

ROSE. Don't be silly. Let's try the finale. If you have a good strong finish, they'll forgive anything!

(*The Cow runs on*)

You're late . . . Now, girls, make it stirring!

(*She again imitates a trumpet call—and the music launches into—surprise—"The Stars and Stripes." Louis tries vainly to twirl that same baton*)

Pick your feet up, Louise, pick 'em up!

(*Herbie strolls on wearily in time for the finale: the Girls remove their Spanish shawls and turn them around to form an American flag. But the stars are on bottom, there is much switching and when the last note is ended, the stars are in place but some of the stripes go the wrong way. Rose look at Herbie's face*)

They're tired. Up to your tent, girls. Get ready for bed.

AGNES (*One of the girls*). Good night, Madame Rose.

ROSE. Good night, Louise. (*Rose takes the blond wig from Louise and kisses her good night. Then she calls to the others*) Don't forget to write your mothers. For money! (*To Herbie*) How'd you make out in town?

HERBIE. Not even a lodge hall.

ROSE. They're too damn un-American down here, that's the trouble. (*Starts to brush the wig*). We better talk about heading up north after I tell the girls their bedtime story.

HERBIE. Once upon a time, there was a prince named Ziegfeld—

ROSE. It could happen! . . . Anyway, everybody needs something impossible to hope for.

HERBIE. Rose . . . Why do you make Louise wear that wig in the act?

ROSE. It makes her look more like—a star.

HERBIE. And why do you keep that cow?

ROSE. Herbie, if that cow goes, I go! (*As Louise enters behind them in pajamas*) The act can be fixed. If I was doing it for June, I'd have it all set.

LOUISE. But you're not, and I'm not June.

HERBIE. Now, Plug, nobody expects you to—

LOUISE (*Quietly*). Herbie, I love you very much but you always let everything slide.

ROSE. He does not!

LOUISE (*Quietly*). Momma, I love you so much I've tried hard as I could. The act is rotten and I'm rotten in it.

ROSE. How do you like that? Typical of a kid!

LOUISE. I've been wanting to say this—

ROSE. Always impatient!

LOUISE. Momma—

ROSE. A few break-in dates don't go too hot so she—

LOUISE (*Grabs the wig out of Rose's hand and throws it away*). Momma, I am not June! I am not a blonde! I can't do what she did!

HERBIE. She's not asking you to.

LOUISE. Maybe you want to stay in show business—

ROSE. Maybe??

LOUISE. Well, I thought—

ROSE. That's our whole life! What've we been working for ever since you were a baby? . . . Maybe I've been on the wrong track with you and the material, but like the good Lord says, you gotta take the rough with the smooth, Baby. And like I always said, you're lucky—because you don't have to take it alone. Right, Herbie?

HERBIE. Right.

ROSE. You got Herbie for brains; we got you for talent; and you both got me—to yell at.

(*She sings*)

Wherever we go,
Whatever we do,
We're gonna go through it together.
We may not go far.
But sure as a star,
Wherever we are, it's together!

Wherever I go, I know he goes.
Wherever I go, I know she goes.
No fits, no fights, no feuds and no egos—
Amigos, together!

Through thick and through thin,
All out or all in,
And whether it's win, place, or show,
With you for me and me for you
We'll muddle through whatever we do
Together, wherever we go!

(*Rose holds out her hands to them. They start to sway together*)

ALL.

Wherever we go,
Whatever we do,
We're gonna go through it together.

ROSE.

Wherever we sleep—

LOUISE.

If prices are steep—

HERBIE.

We'll always sleep cheaper together.

ROSE.

Whatever the boat I row, you row—

HERBIE.

A duo!

ROSE.

Whatever the row I hoe, you hoe—

LOUISE.

A trio!

ROSE.

And any IOU I owe, you owe—

HERBIE.

Who me? Oh,
No, you owe!

LOUISE.

>No, we owe—

ALL.

>Together!
>We all take the bow,

ROSE.

>Including the cow,

ALL.

>Though business is lousy and slow.

ROSE.

>With Herbie's vim, Louise's verve—

HERBIE, LOUISE.

>Now all we need is someone with nerve—

ROSE. (*Giving them a look*).

>Together—

HERBIE, LOUISE.

>Together—

ROSE.

>Wherever—

HERBIE, LOUISE.

>Wherever—

ALL.

>Together wherever we go!

ROSE.

>If I start to dance,

HERBIE, LOUISE.

>We both start to dance,

ALL.

>And sometimes by chance we're together.

ROSE.

>If I sing B flat—ohhhh—

LOUISE.

>We both sing B flat—ohhhh—

HERBIE.

>We all can be flat—ohhhh—

ALL.

>Together!

HERBIE (*Twirling a pie plate*).

>Whatever the trick, we can do it!

LOUISE (*Twirling a pie plate*).

>With teamwork we're bound to get through it!

ROSE (*Twirling a third pie plate*).

>There really isn't anything to it—
>You do it.

(*They toss the plates in the air as if to catch them—the trick is a disaster*)

>I knew it—

ALL.

>We blew it—
>Together!
>We go in a group,
>We tour in a troupe,
>We land in the soup
>But we know:
>The things we do, we do by threes,
>A perfect team—

(*Louise heads off in the wrong direction*)

ROSE.

>No, this way, Louise!
>Together—

HERBIE, LOUISE.

>Wherever—

ALL.

>Together wherever we go!

(*Agnes enters with letters*)

AGNES. Here are the letters, Madam Rose.

ROSE. That's a good girl. Now go to bed, Agnes.

AGNES. Now that I'm an actress, it's Amanda.

ROSE. Whatever it is, go to bed.

AGNES. Could I please ask Herbie a question first?

HERBIE. Sure.

AGNES. Herbie . . . do you think we'll ever work again?

ROSE. Of course we will!

HERBIE. I'll get us a booking, Amanda.

AGNES. Thank you, Herbert. (*Turns to go, then sees the wig*) Oh, Louise, your hair!

LOUISE. It's yours if you want it.

AGNES. Gee, I always wanted to be a blonde!

ROSE (*Taking the wig from her*). Then get some peroxide and a toothbrush. Wigs are expensive.

(*Agnes goes off. Rose looks at the wig*)

You know, we could get a nice refund on this—if we'd ever paid for it.

HERBIE. How about getting a gallon of peroxide and a carton of toothbrushes?

ROSE. What for?

HERBIE. Make 'em all blondes!

ROSE. I was only joking, Herbie.

HERBIE. So was I, honey.

LOUISE. But why not do it?

ROSE. They're children, Louise!

LOUISE. They're young girls, Momma. With blond hair, they could be pretty young girls.

HERBIE. With a stretch of imagination, they might be. It'd sure jazz up the act and make it easier to sell. We could all it, Madam Rose's Blonde Babies.

ROSE. Baby Blondes!

LOUISE. Nothing with babies.

HERBIE. Hollywood Blondes.

LOUISE. Yes!

ROSE. All blondes except you—because you're the star!

LOUISE. If I'm the star, it should be: *Louise and Her Hollywood Blondes.*

ROSE. (*Looks at her—then*). *Rose Louise and Her Hollywood Blondes.*

LOUISE. O.K.

ALL (*Singing*).

> Throught thick and through thin,
> All out or all in
> And whether it's win, place or show,
> With you for me and me for you
> We'll muddle through whatever we do
> Together, wherever we go!

(*The lights dim out*)

SCENE TWO

The placards change to read:

"THE BOTTOM"
WICHITA

Backstage. At one side, there is a theatre dressing room. Upstage is the back of the curtain on the stage of the burlesque theatre.

During the scene, snatches of brassy music come from the "stage." Right now, Agnes and three or four other Girls in the act come in. Each is awed; each carries bags, props, part of the cow; and each has hair of the same, exact hideous shrieking shade of white blonde.

AGNES (*In happy awe*). It's a real live theatre!

MAN'S VOICE (*Off*). Let in the traveler!

MARJORIE MAY (*Looking off*). With a real live stage! Don't you love it?

AGNES. Oh, Marjorie May, we've arrived at last!

(*They squeal and hug each other as Louise—in slacks—enters from the alley, also carrying bags, props and the cow's head*)

DOLORES. Louise, look!

AGNES. A real live theatre!

MAN (*Off*). Will you kill them floods?

LOUISE (*Happily*). It's just like opening day rehearsals used to be! Oh, Momma's going to love it!

PASTEY (*Off*). Will you shut your hole?

AGNES (*Shocked*). She isn't going to love that!

MARJORIE MAY (*Pointing to the silhouette of a stripper behind the upstage curtain*). Or that!

AGNES. What kind of a act is that?

PASTEY (*Off*). O.K., jailbait! (*He enters: a young snot, with clipboard and pencil*) You the Hollywood Blondes?

LOUISE. Yes. I'm—

PASTEY. You're late.

LOUISE. Well, our car broke down and—

PASTEY. Skip it. Some of you dogs can use this dressing room, and the rest of you the one past it. The first one you share with Tessie Tura, the Texas Twirler—

LOUISE. My mother doesn't—

PASTEY. The second with Mazeppa, Revolution in Dance. Shake it up. (*Starts to go, then turns back*) So you're the act that's supposed to keep the cops out. Boy, you must be lousy!

(*He exits. A moment of deflation. Then—*)

LOUISE. It's a real live theatre, all right.

AGNES. He reminds me of my brother.

LOUISE. Don't start sniveling, Amanda. Take the cow and anything else you can carry in there. Marjorie May, you take the other girls into the second room and start unpacking.

(*She starts with props and bags for the dressing room. The others pick up their stuff and exist upstage. Thus, all their backs are turned and they do not see two girls who enter to get a gilded spear from a stack leaning against the corridor wall. Each of these bored females wears a gladiator helmet, gladiator boots and carries a large shield in front of her. As they cross up to go to the "stage," we see that the shield is the only thing that covers them. They are nude. In the dressing room, Louise and Agnes have started to hang up costumes*)

AGNES. Oooh, look at this! (*She is holding up a jeweled G-string, which she proceeds to try on as a necklace*) That Tessie Tura must be a very fancy lady!

LOUISE. (*Trying to clean a messy dressing table*). She must also be a pig!

(*Rose enters through the alley door, carrying more bags and props*)

ROSE. Louise?

LOUISE. In here, Momma. (*Goes to the door*) Let me help you.

ROSE (*Looking around*). Baby, we're back in a theatre! We're back in a real theater!

LOUISE. Momma, where's Herbie?

ROSE. He went around front to check our billing. Louise, I need you here to help me with the rest of the things. (*To the Stagehand, who crosses*) Good morning!

STAGEHAND. Jesus. (*Exits*)

(*Rose turns back, stops dead and her mouth drops open. Louise turns and she gapes too. One hand on the edge of the dressing room, throwing wild bumps savagely, is Tessie Tura, a blowsy stripper wearing almost nothing besides a G-string, which does not bump with her. She looks up, during her exercises*)

TESSIE. It ain't weighted right, goddamit.

(*Mazeppa—a pseudo-exotic grand stripper dressed as Queen of the Gladiators—writhes past Tessie to get her spear from the wall*)

It scratches hell outa me and it just don't bump when I do.

MAZEPPA. Maybe there's something wrong with your bumper. (*She exits*)

TESSIE. Big joke. (*To Rose*) I'm out there bumpin' my brains off with no action and she's bein' witty! (*To Agnes, who is gaping at her from the dressing room doorway*) Hey you with the neck! I paid six bucks for that G-string. Back where you found it!

AGNES. Yes, ma'am.

(*She curtsies and scurries back in as Tessie goes off. Rose looks at Louise*)

ROSE (*Low*). Get the bags. Get the cow. Get the props.

LOUISE. Now, Momma—

ROSE. You don't know what kind of people are out there on that stage. You don't know what kind of a theatre this is.

LOUISE. Yes I do. It's a house of burlesque.

ROSE. A house of burlesque. Do you know what that is? Filth, that's what! I tell you, when your friend Herbie shows his face—

LOUISE. Momma, I'm sure Herbie didn't know—

ROSE (*Picking up the props, etc., which keep dropping*). Not much, he didn't know! Agnes!

LOUISE. He got the booking over the telephone—

ROSE. Agnes!

LOUISE. We were all so happy—

ROSE (*Storming to the dressing-room door*). AGNES, DAMMIT!

AGNES. Madame Rose, you know my name is—

ROSE. Your name is Agnes and I want you and the other girls out of this hell hole in two seconds flat.

AGNES. But, Madam—

ROSE. March!

AGNES. Yes, ma'am.

(*She comes out. Rose goes inside and starts to pack up what has been unpacked*)

LOUISE (*To Agnes*). Wait in the other room.

(*Agnes disappears behind the dressing room as Louise goes in*)

ROSE. You take the rear end of the cow, I'll take the front and what bags we can't carry, your friend Herbie can damn well pick up and carry himself.

(*Louise shuts the door. Rose turns and looks at Louise leaning against it. Her voice is low and cold*)

Now you listen to me, Louise. Just because you think your friend Herbie can do no wrong—

LOUISE. This has nothing to do with Herbie.

ROSE. You don't know what burlesque is.

LOUISE. Yes I—

ROSE. NO YOU DON'T. No daughter of mine is going to work in burlesque. And no daughter of any woman I know—

LOUISE. Then where *are* we going to work?

ROSE. I'd rather starve!

LOUISE. Momma, how much money do we have? Including what's left of their allowances, how much money do we have?

ROSE. Something'll turn up.

LOUISE. It *has* turned up and *this is it!* We're flat broke, Momma. We've *got* to take this job . . . Even if you wanted to quit and go home, we'd have to take it.

(*Rose stops in the act of taking a costume off a hook. A pause. Then abruptly, heavily, she sits*)

ROSE. I had a dream . . .

LOUISE. Momma . . .

ROSE. You'll like this one. I had it over a week ago, only I didn't want to tell. I was home in Seattle, and the cow came into my room. But she wasn't dancing and smiling this time. She was wheezing and sad-like. She came over to the bed and looked at me and she said: "Rose, move over."

LOUISE. I'm sorry, Momma.

ROSE (*Smiles*). Why? She didn't ask you to move over.

LOUISE. I mean I'm sorry I'm not good enough. In the act.

ROSE. Oh, it's the act that ain't good enough, Baby. Or something.

(*Herbie hurries in through the alley door*)

HERBIE. Rose?

LOUISE (*Opens the dressing-room door*). In here, Herbie.

HERBIE (*Runs in*). Rose, I didn't know, believe me.

ROSE. I do, honey. What the hell! The money's good, it's only two weeks, and maybe by that time, something'll turn up. Right.

LOUISE. Right.

HERBIE. You're a nice girl, Rose. Thank you.

ROSE. Well—that's show business. (*She starts to unpack again*)

LOUISE. One good thing: I'll bet we got top billing.

HERBIE. Well—actually they kind of had us lost in the middle. I thought last was better, so it says: "*And Rose Louise and Her Hollywood Blondes.*" And I'm making them put a box around it.

ROSE. Forget the box, Herbie.

LOUISE. But, Momma, if—

ROSE. You don't know what they say in the business. But Herbie does. They say when a vaudeville act plays in burlesque, that means it's all washed up. (*Pause*) Herbie . . . nothin's gonna turn up for us, is it?

HERBIE. No.

ROSE. I guess it is a pretty rotten act.

HERBIE. It ain't the act, honey. I been telling you, vaudeville's dead . . . stone cold dead.

ROSE. Well—we sure as hell tried!

HERBIE. You sure as hell did. Right?

LOUISE. Right.

HERBIE. Well, I better get the cues ready. (*He goes to the door*)

ROSE. Herbie—how about marrying me?

HERBIE (*Turns around. A moment. Then, casually*). Sure!

ROSE. I love you, you know.

HERBIE. I know.

LOUISE. Do it today!

ROSE. Not while we're in burlesque!

HERBIE. The day we close.

ROSE. It's a deal. (*They shake hands and suddenly kiss*) I do, Herbie, I do.

HERBIE. So do I, Rose.

(*Pastey barges in. During the following, Tessie appears in the corridor*)

PASTEY. Hey, Rose Louise, where the hell's your music and light cues?

HERBIE. I'll be right with you.

PASTEY (*Snotty*). You Rose Louise?

HERBIE. Yeah, I'm Rose Louise.

PASTEY. Things're looking up. Well, I got a show to open, Rose Louise, so move your ass.

(*Before Pastey can get out, Herbie has grabbed him, whirled him around and cracked him in the face. Then, holding him by the scruff of his neck—*)

HERBIE. Listen, you little punk. For the next two weeks, you're gonna speak like a Sunday School teacher. You have something in this theatre you probably never saw before. A lady. (*Points him toward Rose*) Look at her. That is a lady. (*Points him toward Louise*) That is also a lady. Every girl in this damn act is a lady, you understand?

PASTEY. Yes, sir.

HERBIE. Now get on stage and I'll give you those cues when I'm ready.

PASTEY. Yes, sir. Excuse me, ma'am.

(*He goes out and off. Rose kisses Herbie. He goes out but is stopped in the corridor by Tessie*)

TESSIE. Oh, sir? Won't you give *me* your protection? I'm a lady, too! (*On the last, a vivacious grind and bump. The bumper flips*) Hey! The goddam thing worked! (*She goes into the dressing room as Herbie goes off*) If you ladies will excuse me—

ROSE. We're very busy.

TESSIE. In *my* dressing room.

ROSE. In *your* dress—

LOUISE (*Overlapping*). Momma—

TESSIE. You're damn right. And I don't like sharing it any more than you do. Particularly with a troupe of professional virgins.

ROSE. We are not—

TESSIE. All right, so you're acrobats.

ROSE. We happen to be headliners from the Orpheum Circuit. We were booked into this theatre by mistake.

TESSIE. Weren't we all! (*Reaching for a costume Rose has unpacked*) Say! Who made that?

LOUISE. I did. I make all our costumes.

TESSIE. My! Look at them ladylike little stitches! That miserable broad who makes my gowns must be usin' a fish hook!

LOUISE. What do you pay her?

TESSIE. Twenty-five bucks a gown and I provide the material.

ROSE. Thirty.

TESSIE. She's new in the business!

ROSE. Thirty.

TESSIE. Who're you? Her mother?

ROSE. Yes.

TESSIE. Thirty. I'll get the material after the matinée.

ROSE. It's a deal. (*To Louise*) Where's your toreador costume?

LOUISE. The girls must have it in the dressing room with them.

ROSE. God knows that else they've got in there with them! (*She exits*)

TESSIE. You know, from the way that dame walks, she would have made a damn good stripper in her day.

(*A burly man, Cigar, the manager, enters*)

CIGAR. Hey, Tessie, I'm short a talking woman.

TESSIE. Tough titty.

CIGAR. The new comic won't use a chorus girl.

TESSIE. Then let him use Mazeppa. (*To Louise*) Everyone else has. (*She laughs at her joke*)

CIGAR. Now you know Mazeppa's got her Gladiator Ballet just before his spot.

TESSIE. Cut the ballet. It stinks anyway.

CIGAR. Be a sport. I'm in a bind.

TESSIE. You're always in a bind in this flea-bitten trap. I'm a strip woman, slob. I don't do no scenes. Now screw! (*To Louise*) You ever hear of a strip woman playing scenes? Well, you play stock in a dump like this, you gotta expect to be insulted.

CIGAR. The work is steady, ain't it?

TESSIE. But you bring in a new star for each show, don't you?

CIGAR. Tessie, it's just a few lines—

TESSIE. Fat boy, save your bad breath.

CIGAR. I'll give you ten bucks extra.

TESSIE. Nay.

LOUISE (*As Rose returns*). I can read lines.

CIGAR. Who're you?

LOUISE. Rose Louise. Of Rose Louise and Her Hollywood Blondes

ROSE. Wait a minute. What kind of lines?

CIGAR. You in her act?

ROSE. Well, not exactly.

CIGAR. Shut up. (*To Louise*) How are your legs?

TESSIE. Great! And I'll learn her the scenes.

CIGAR. O.K. Ten bucks. (*He goes*)

LOUISE. It's money, Momma.

ROSE (*Going to Tessie*). What is she going to be saying out there on that stage?

TESSIE. The same burlesque crap that's been said since the Year One. Say, where you been all your life?

ROSE (*Proudly*). Playing vaudeville.

TESSIE. Where? In the Vatican?

ROSE. You name a big city and we've played it!

LOUISE. My grandpa says we've covered the country like Gypsies!

TESSIE. Yeah? Well, you may be a Gypsy, Rose Louise—say, that ain't a bad name if you ever take up stripping—

ROSE. She won't!

TESSIE. No! But you'll let her feed lines to a bum comic for a lousy ten bucks a week!

ROSE. That's training: she's going to be an actress! This is only temporary! After we finish here, she goes right back to vaudeville! (*She turns away—and sees Louise's look. Embarrassed, she exits*)

TESSIE (*Quietly*). Back to vaudeville, my eye. There ain't any vaudeville left except burlesque.

LOUISE. We know.

TESSIE. *You* know. You better wise *her* up.

LOUISE (*Sudden burst*). She's wise! She's a damn sight wiser than any of you!

TESSIE (*Shrugs*). Like mother, like daughter. O.K. Say, whose feelings did I hurt? Yours or hers?

LOUISE (*Smiles*). Neither. We'll both be fine.

TESSIE. I hope so, because sharing a dressing room is like sleeping together. And if you don't get along with—

(*Mazeppa comes storming on with Electra, another stripper*)

MAZEPPA. Miss Tura, I'll thank you not to give the boss any notion that I would ever play scenes. And one more disparaging remark about my ballet will find this bugle right up your—

TESSIE. Please: there's a lady present!

MAZEPPA. Where?

TESSIE. Open your eyes instead of your mouth. Gypsy, meet Miss Mazeppa—and Miss Electra.

ELECTRA. Say, you're even younger than I was when I began stripping.

LOUISE. I'm not going to strip.

MAZEPPA (*Belligerent*). Something wrong with stripping?

LOUISE. No. I just meant I don't have any talent.

TESSIE. You think they have? I myself of course was a ballerina. But take it from me, to be a stripper all you need to have is no talent.

MAZEPPA. You'll pardon me, but to have no talent is not enough. What you need is an idea that makes your strip special.

(*During the following number, each of the three strippers demonstrates the gimmick that has made her a "star." Mazeppa sings*)

> You can pull all the stops out
> Till they call the cops out,
> Grind your behind till you're banned,
> But you gotta get a gimmick
> If you wanna get a hand.
> You can sacrifice your sacro
> Workin' in the back row,
> Bump in a dump till you're dead.
> Kid, you gotta get a gimmick
> If you wanna get ahead.
> You can—!, you can—!, you can—!!!
> That's how burlesque was born.
> So I—! and I—! and I—!!!
> But I do it with a horn!

(*She demonstrates: bumping and grinding like mad while she blows army calls on her bugle*)

> Once I was a schlepper,
> Now I'm Miss Mazeppa

> With my Revolution in Dance.
> You gotta have a gimmick
> If you wanna have a chance!!!

ELECTRA (*Singing*).

> She can—!, she can—!, she can—!!!
> They'll never make her rich.
> Me, I—! and I—! and I—!!!
> But I do it with a switch!

(*She demonstrates: punctuating her bumps and grinds with electric lights which illuminate her strategic points*)

> I'm electrifying,
> And I'm not even trying.
> I never have to sweat to get paid.
> 'Cause if you got a gimmick,
> Gypsy girl, you've got it made.

TESSIE (*Singing*).

> All them—!s and them—!s and them—!!!s
> Ain't gonna spell success.
> Me, I—! and! I—! and I—!!!
> But I do it with finesse!

(*And she demonstrates: a broken-down version of ballet climaxed with the same eternal bumps and grinds*)

> Dressy Tessie Tura
> Is so much demurer
> Than all them other ladies because
> You gotta got a gimmick
> If you wanna get applause!

ALL.

> Do somethin' special;
> Anything that's fresh'll
> Earn you a big fat cigar.
> You're more than just a mimic
> When you get a gimmick—
> Take a look how different we are!

(*They bump and grind: what else?*)

ELECTRA.

> If you wanna make it,
> Shake it till you break it.

TESSIE.

> If you wanna grind it,
> Wait till you've refined it.

MAZEPPA.

> If you wanna bump it,
> Bump it with a trumpet!

ALL.

> Get yourself a gimmick
> And you too
> Can be a star!

(*The lights black out*)

SCENE THREE

The scene is backstage.

STAGEHAND (*To Pastey, who is crossing*). Kill the floods and bring in number four!

PASTEY. I tole ya we ain't usin' number four this show, ya pinhead!

HERBIE (*Runs on with a little bouquet*). Hey, you seen Amanda?

PASTEY. She must be packin'. Ain't your act through today?

HERBIE (*Joyously*). You bet it is! Through—finished—over!

(*Agnes comes on with a suitcase. Herbie crosses to her*)

PASTEY (*To the Stagehand*). Will you kill number four? (*He exits*)

HERBIE (*To Agnes*). I've been hunting for you. Here. (*He gives her the bouquet*)

AGNES. Oh, Herbie, it's like for a funeral!

HERBIE. It's for the wedding! Madame Rose and I want you to be bridesmaid, Amanda.

AGNES. It's Agnes again.

HERBIE (*Hugs her*) You'll be happier as Agnes, Amanda. (*Dashing off*) See you out front.

TESSIE (*Runs on*). Oh, you're leaving!

ANGES. I have to go home and let my hair grow out.

TESSIE. Ya poor kid.

PASTEY (*Off*). Tessie!

TESSIE. Well—for the last time: (*Doing a grind*) Meet ya round the corner (*Agnes joins in*) in a half-hour.

(*Agnes breaks down on Tessie's bosom*)

PASTEY. TESSIE!

TESSIE. TESSIE! I'm coming, ya creep!

(*She hurries to the wings leading to the "stage." A farewell wave to Agnes, a lift to her sagging bosoms—and she floats off like a ballerina*)

(*The lights black out*)

SCENE FOUR

The dressing room looks emptier. Most of Rose's belongings have been packed.

The lights are different. The corridor is darker but streaked with colored light coming from the "stage," where the show is on. Herbie—in a different suit—Rose and Louise—in coats—are finishing packing. Rose is very subdued; Herbie is very up; Louise keeps watching Rose.

HERBIE (*To Rose*). Why aren't you nervous? I've never been so nervous in my whole life!

LOUISE (*Hands Rose a baton*). You've never been married before.

HERBIE. Well, your mother's never been married like she's going to be this time. For keeps and forever—to me! Ain't you a *little* nervous, honey!

ROSE. Sure.

HERBIE (*Admiring the marriage license*). Say, the minister doesn't keep this, does he? I want to have it framed. Framed and hanging in our living room.

LOUISE (*Holding the cow head*). What about this Momma?

ROSE. Take it.

HERBIE. Rose—

LOUISE (*Putting the cow head on the suitcase*). We can hang her up in the living room, too, Herbie. Over the mantelpiece.

HERBIE. Rose honey, it ain't that I don't know what you're feeling. Or that I don't know I oughta shut up. But I'm so goddam happy, I can't!

(*Cigar and Pastey enter the corridor. Their dialogue and Herbie's are simultaneous. Rose listens to Herbie*)

I'm finally getting everything I wanted! Even a fancy ceremony with bridesmaids. Of course, what the minister's going to say when he gets a load of all that hair, I don't know. But the hell with him!

(*Rose's attention shifts to the hall*)

All he's gotta say is, Do you, Rose, take him, Herbie?

CIGAR. I don't know why the hell I stay in this business. If it ain't one damn headache, it's another!

PASTEY. Ssh! They'll hear you out front.

CIGAR. It's my theatre, ain't it? Let 'em! Last show, no talking woman. Show before that, no second banana. If that crazy broad wasn't here, why did you start the performance?

PASTEY. She don't go on till next to closing, and she said she was only goin' next door to the drugstore.

(*Herbie and then Louise become aware that Rose is standing dead still, listening. They stand, watching her, tense, afraid*)

CIGAR. What'd they arrest her for? Shoplifting?

PASTEY. No, soliciting.

CIGAR. She always was greedy. Well, cut the spot.

HERBIE. Honey, do you think we can invite the minister for a drink after?

PASTEY. It's the star strip!

CIGAR. Cut it.

PASTEY. They'll yell murder if it's only the same bags they've been seeing the last eight weeks. The star's the novelty!

CIGAR. Whaddya want me to do? Let you strip?

(*Rose throws down whatever she is holding and runs out of the dressing room into the corridor*)

ROSE. My daughter can do it. (*They look at her. She steps back, as though afraid of herself*) Rose Louise.

PASTEY. Since when?

ROSE. Since she's been here to see how little there is to it.
CIGAR. She didn't look bad in them scenes.
ROSE. She'll look great in her own gowns.
PASTEY. What's the gimmick?
CIGAR. She's young. And you got any better ideas?
PASTEY (*As he exits*). Well, she better get ready right damn now.
ROSE. It's the star spot.
CIGAR. You telling me?
ROSE. That means the star salary.
CIGAR. If we keep her.
ROSE. You will. She's going to be wonderful.

(*Cigar goes off as Rose runs excitedly into the dressing room and begins opening a suitcase. Herbie and Louise stand dead still, watching*)

I knew something would turn up? Where's that dress you were gonna make for Tessie? It'll work perfect for you! . . . (*Gets the dress out*) Well, get your makeup on, there ain't much time! . . . Oh, silly, you're not really gonna strip! All you'll do is walk around the stage in time to the music and drop a shoulder strap at the end. (*Takes out the makeup*) You're a lady—like Herbie says you are! You just parade so grand they'll think it's a favor if you even show them your knee—Louise, it's the star spot! I promised my daughter we'd be a star! (*Still, Louise just stands*) Baby, it's all right to walk out when they *want* you. But you can't walk out when after all these rotten years, we're still a flop. That's quitting. We can't quit because we're a flop! Louise (*A burst*) don't be like June. Just do this, and then we can walk away proud because we made it! Maybe only in burlesque, maybe only in second-rate burlesque at that—but let's walk away a star!

(*Louise unbuttons her coat. Rose hugs her, then rummages for the dress as Louise begins quickly to get ready*)

I guess there ain't time to finish the dress, but we can pin it easy. Hey, here's some material for extra panels! Didn't I always say you were born lucky? You can unpin the panels and drop 'em every once in a while so they'll think you're taking something off.

(*Slowly, Herbie folds up the license and walks out of the room, and disappears in the corridor. Louise is making up feverishly*)

Not too much makeup, Baby. Young and girlish. Pure. Don't smear that junk all over your face like they do. You just keep your mouth the way the Lord made it . . . No rouge. No beauty marks. You be a lady: grand, elegant . . . with a classy, ladylike walk. My God! Shoes! . . . Well, we can use the old silver ones we borrowed from Tessie. (*She takes them from her own suitcase*) They'll do for this performance . . . Come on. Get into 'em. (*As Louise does*) Oh, no—your hair's wrong. You can't let it just hang like spaghetti. Put it up! Like Momma's! It's got to have class! Puff it out in front. Thank God, the Lord gave us good color—and that you washed it

this morning . . . Say, do you think we should put a couple of feathers in? (*Tries some*) No, that's what they all do. (*Tosses them aside*) Jewelry? No. Let Tessie and the others wear all the vulgar junk they want.

PASTEY (*Rushes in*). She almost ready? She goes on in five minutes.
ROSE (*Pushing him out*). She'll be there—she'll be there! Come on, get into the dress.

(*Louise exits through another door, presumably leading into a bathroom, to change into the strip dress. Rose picks up a pair of long white gloves*)

Whose are these? Oh—my wedding present from Tessie. Good for a lady. Wear 'em . . . Now, what else? . . . Music! (*Flips through sheet music in the suitcase*) "Spanish"—"Cow"? (*Shakes her head*) No. Say, you can do June's "Let Me Entertain You" number! I'll mark it for the conductor to repeat two choruses slow—no, two and a half choruses, and sing out, Louise! You just walk and dip . . . you're a lady; you make 'em beg for more—and then *don't* give it to them! . . . Now—have I forgotten anything? Anything else?

(*On the last, Herbie enters the dressing room. He is almost shaking with anger and his effort to control it*)

Where you been? Out front?
HERBIE. No, I got sick to my stomach, and threw up.
ROSE. But you feel better now.
HERBIE. No.
ROSE. Herbie—I just had to.
HERBIE. That's why I'm leaving.
ROSE. I apologize.
HERBIE. No, let me. For my resemblance to a mouse. No: to a worm—the way I've crawled after you. No more, Rose. I won't. I was even going to crawl away from you—because my stomach started to turn over at the idea of coming back and telling you we're finished.
ROSE. Tell me tomorrow—after we're married.
HERBIE. We're never getting married, Rose.
ROSE. We certainly are! First thing in the morning, we'll—
HERBIE. *Never!* Not if you went down on your knees and begged. I still love you—but all the vows from here to doomsday . . . they couldn't make you a wife. I want a wife, Rose. I'm going to be a man if it kills me.
ROSE (*Angrily*). So you're killing *me!*
HERBIE. Nobody can kill you.
ROSE. You're jealous, that's what you are! Like every man I've ever known! Jealous—because my girls come first. Well, they always did and they always will!
HERBIE. Then why did June leave?
ROSE. I don't wanna hear her name!
HERBIE. She didn't want the act any more than Louise wants this!
ROSE. Louise does!
HERBIE. She'll leave like June did!
ROSE. Never! She's gonna be a star.

HERBIE. She's gonna be a star! If it kills *you and her*, she's gonna be a star *someplace!* She's gonna be a star. Where are *you* gonna be, Rose? Where are you gonna be when *she* gets married?

ROSE. She won't be getting married for years—she's a baby!

HERBIE. Sure!

ROSE. Anyway, her career will always come first. (*She sits, looks over the music defiantly*)

HERBIE. That's right. That-is-right. (*He picks up his suitcase, and starts out*)

ROSE. Herbie . . . what does everybody walk out?

HERBIE. Maybe Louise won't.

ROSE. Don't leave, Herbie . . . I need you.

HERBIE. . . . What for?

ROSE. A millions things.

HERBIE. Just one would be better. Goodbye, honey. Be a good girl.

(*He goes out the door. Music starts*)

ROSE. You go to hell!

(*Rose sits starting and Pastey runs in*)

PASTEY. Get her music to the conductor and you better stand by me for the light cues. I just hope you know what you're doing.

(*Pastey races out*)

ROSE (*Singing*).

Lucky, you're a man who likes children—
    That's an important sign.
Lucky, I'm a woman with children—
Funny,
    Small and funny—

(*Rose gets up and slowly walks to the white gloves. She has them in her hand, and is staring at them as Louise comes out and takes the gloves from her. Rose watches her start to put them on, then speaks quietly, as though dazed*)

ROSE. I'll get the music to the conductor. Just remember—you're a lady (*With anguished determination*) And you-are-going-to-be-a-star!

(*Music in hand, she walks out, leaving Louise alone before a long mirror in the dressing room. As she draws on the white gloves, the music ends and the light in the corridor goes very dark. There is a soft glow on the mirror as dark figures scurrying through the corridor outside saying: "Let's watch from the wings." "No, I'm going out front." "What's she gonna do?" "She isn't the type." "She'll quit halfway through." "How do you know?" "She'll never make it." "Come on, let's get a good place." "I'm scared for her." During this, the dressing room has been rolling off, leaving only the mirror. The only light on the stage is the glow of the mirror bulbs; the only figure is Louise. She looks at herself, goes close to the mirror to check her*

makeup, then suddenly stops. She touches her body lightly, moves back, straightens up and stares at her reflection. Very softly—)

LOUISE. Momma . . . I'm pretty . . . I'm a pretty girl, Momma!

(*Very grand, very proud, very beautiful, she turns from the mirror and begins to walk away from it, as though she were going in the direction of the "stage." The mirror moves off, the lights come up and we are "on the stage." The curtain is upstage; strip music can be heard, a dim stripper can be seen through the curtain. Rose, who is peering through, turns around and sees Louise*)

ROSE. (*Softly*). You look beautiful!

TESSIE (*Runs on with an old fur stole which she wraps around Louise*). For luck, honey!

ROSE. Are you nervous, Baby?

LOUISE. . . . What?

ROSE. I said, are you nervous?

LOUISE. No, Mother.

(*The offstage music ends; there is applause as the weary stripper comes on from behind the curtain, looks at Louise and goes off. Pastey grabs a microphone*)

PASTEY. Wichita's one and only Burlesque Theatre presents—

LOUISE (*Nervous after all*). Momma—

PASTEY. Miss—Gypsy—Rose—Lee!

TESSIE (*Correcting him angrily*). Louise!

(*But he shrugs. Everyone exits but Louise, who stands alone before the curtain. A roll of the drum and lights reveal the curtain as a scrim. Through it, we can see the glow of the strippers' runway. Another drum roll: the curtains part and Louise steps forward. Another drum roll: a spotlight hits her and her head goes back as though she has been blinded. Blinding floodlights then shine directly into the eyes of the audience; then a total blackout. When the lights go on again, Louise is downstage, facing the audience before a curtain the exact replica of the one upstage. Her head is back a bit, her eyes closed, the spotlight bright on her. The small burlesque band in the pit begins "Let Me Entertain You." Louise can barely start singing. Rose, from the wings, calls out*)

ROSE. Sing out, Louise!

(*Louise sings a little louder, a little truer. She looks around at the men out front: They like her. Her voice is stronger as she finishes. What now? She begins to walk around a little awkwardly*)

CIGAR (*From the wings*). Do something!

(*Louise shoots a panicky look to Rose in the wings*)

ROSE. Dip! Dip!

(*Louise does. But that's not enough*)

CIGAR. Take something off!

ROSE. A glove! Give 'em a glove!

(*Louise does. But now what?*)

Say something!

LOUISE. Hello—

(*A nice laugh from out front. She smiles*)

—everybody. My name is—Gypsy—Rose—Lee! (*She's enjoying this now. A sexy look to a man out front*) What's yours—sir? (*Now she has it*) Mr. Conductor—if you please! (*And from the way she walks, it is clear she is on her way. A dropped shoulder strap just before she exits is her confirming punctuation*)

(*The lights on the curtain change. The placards scroll to read*

DETROIT

and an announcer's voice comes over)

ANNOUNCER. Detroit's Diamond Burlesque is happy to present a new jewel in its glittering crown—Miss Gypsy—Rose—Lee!

(*And out she comes in a glittering, revealing dress and a rose in her hair. She is poised now and her humor is beginning to shine through. As she walks downstage:*)

LOUISE. I'm beginning to like this! (*She stops and begins to toy with her dress and her body. She speaks in a syncopated rhythm*) My mother—who got me into this business—

(*She is pulling up her dress*)

Always told me
Make them beg for more—

(*Drops the dress*)

And then, don't give it to them!
But I'm not my mothah!
Beg!

(*Change of lights and music for a montage of changing placards and overlapping voices:*

PHILADELPHIA
BOSTON

and last):

MINSKY'S
NEW YORK

ANNOUNCER. Philadelphia, the city of Brotherly Love, brings all you brothers a sister to make you leave home!

SECOND ANNOUNCER. Boston's World Famous Howard Burlesque has no need of Paul Revere to announce the arrival at the home of Liberty of the Belle that rings out for one and all—

THIRD ANNOUNCER. Minsky's World Famous Burlesque takes great pride and pleasure in presenting the Queen of the Strip Tease, the incomparable Miss Gypsy Rose Lee in our Salute to the Garden of Eden!

(*The curtain opens on a garish version of the garden with semi-nudes who come down from sequined trees, grinding away like mad and singing—along with multi-dubbed additional angel voices—as they throw apples to the audience. At the peak, two almost nude satyrs bring on a big jeweled apple out of which steps Gypsy: elegant, mischievous, glittering like a real diamond in the Five and Dime. Crescendo, then:*)

LOUISE. Pack up your apples, girls, and back to the trees.

(*As the girls depart, the curtain closes in front of them and Louise chatters to the audience as, accompanied by percussion only, she walks around the stage, stripping off gloves, etc.*)

Bonsoir, messieurs—et messieurs Je m'appelle Gypsy Rose Lee et je suis dans le jardin de ma mère, Eve. And that concludes my entire performance—in French. I've been too busy learning Greek. Some man called me an ecdysiast. Do you know what that means? Do you? Do you?

(*Spot hits man in audience*)

Oh, he does. Where were you last night? He's embarrassed. Don't be embarrassed. I like men without hair. An ecdysiast is one who—or that which—sheds its skin. In vulgar parlance, a stripper. But I'm not a stripper. At these prices, I'm an ecdysiast!

(*She has seemingly taken everything off and now grabs the curtain to cover herself as she drags it across the stage, singing the last eight bars of "Let Me Entertain You." On the last note, the light go out except for a blue spot on Louise. She drops the curtain and throws a bump and a kiss. Blackout*)

SCENE FIVE

The placards change to read:

"MOTHER'S DAY"
MINSKY'S

A dressing room.

The basic crumminess of the room is all but hidden by the trappings its occupant has installed: gleaming bottles; a nude statue festooned with feathers and a rhinestone G-string; souvenirs; costumes, etc.

Rose is hammering a spike into the wall, as she talks to Renée, the maid, who barely listens. During the following, Rose hangs the cow's head up on the spike.

ROSE. Sure I saw that sign! If I can read the fine print in our contracts, I can certainly read letters two feet high: "THE MOTHER OF MISS GYPSY ROSE LEE IS NOT ALLOWED BACKSTAGE AT THIS THEATRE." You know what I did with that sign? (*Puts a string of beads on the cow's horn*) I tore it off the wall, spread it on the floor, and set Chowsie III down on it. That dog's a trouper: *she* knew what to do! . . . It'll take more than signs to keep me out of a theatre.

(*The door opens and Louise enters in a negligée. She is singing until she sees Rose. And the cow head*)

LOUISE. That comes down. (*She sits at the dressing table and swiftly sets about repairing her makeup*)

ROSE. You need *something* to remind you your goal was to be a great actress, not a cheap stripper.

LOUISE. June's the actress, Mother. And I'm not a cheap stripper. I'm the highest paid in the business.

ROSE. You won't be ready when vaudeville comes back.

LOUISE. No, I'll be dead. (*Then, indicating the furs she has thrown on a chair*) Renée, tell Sam he can lock up the animals for the night.

ROSE. I'll do it.

LOUISE. Mother, please. (*To Renée*) And bring my press agent in as soon as he gets here.

RENÉE. *Oui, madame.* (*She goes out with the furs and the cow head*)

ROSE. Since when do you fix your face before you take your bath?

LOUISE. A photographer's coming.

ROSE. Where's he going to photograph you? In the tub?

LOUISE. Eventually.

ROSE (*Shocked*). Louise!

LOUISE. It's for *Vogue*.

ROSE (*Elated*). Louise!! Think I ought to freshen up?

LOUISE. They only want me in the tub, Mother.

(*The telephone rings*)

ROSE. I've got it.

LOUISE (*Beating Rose to it*). Hello? . . . (*Intimately*) Hello. No, it's difficult right now.

ROSE. I'm not leaving.

LOUISE. Let's meet at the party . . . Yes, I promise. À *bientôt*. (*She hangs up*)

ROSE. À *bien* what?

LOUISE. I guess I am being a little much—but, Momma, I love it.

ROSE. Who's giving the party?

LOUISE. Some friends.

ROSE. In the old days, I was always invited first.

LOUISE. Mother—

ROSE (*Very grandly*). I wouldn't go even if I *did* have something to wear. I got more important things to do—like thinking up an idea for a new strip for us.

LOUISE. Mother, we're still stuck with that wind machine you bought to *blow* my clothes off. Actually—I'm putting in a new number on Saturday.

ROSE. What is it?

LOUISE. You'll see.

ROSE. I'll see.

LOUISE. Let me surprise you.

ROSE. These days, you're just one big surprise after another.

Well, we better go shopping tomorrow for the material for the gown.

LOUISE. I've a got a French lesson tomorrow.

ROSE. Oh. Well, I'll go alone. Got any particular color in mind?

LOUISE. Mother—I've already started to make the gown.

ROSE. Oh. Well. I better run your bath for you.

LOUISE. You don't have to. That's what I've got a maid for.

ROSE. LET ME DO SOMETHING, DAMMIT!

LOUISE (*Very quietly*). What, Mother?

ROSE. A million things. I'm not a baby.

LOUISE. Neither am I.

ROSE. Don't you take that tone to me. Your sister used to get that edge to her voice—

LOUISE. I am not June!

ROSE. You're not Louise, either!

LOUISE. And neither are you!

ROSE. Oh, yes I am! More than you, Miss Gypsy Rose Lee— with your dirty pictures for *Vogue*!

LOUISE. Mother—

ROSE. And your maids and your press agents and your fancy friends with their fancy parties!

LOUISE. They happen—

ROSE. Your loud-mouth mother ain't invited to those goddam parties. They laugh at her!

LOUISE. They don't—

ROSE. THEY DO! And don't think I don't know that's one reason why you don't want me backstage: so I won't hear 'em laugh. Well, it's *them* you oughta keep out, not me! Because they're laughing at you, too! The burlesque queen who speaks lousy French and reads book reviews like they was books!

LOUISE. Turn it off, Mother.

ROSE. You know what you are to them? A circus freak! This year's novelty act! And when the bill is changed—

LOUISE. I SAID TURN IT OFF! *Nobody laughs at me*—because I laugh first! At me! ME—from Seattle; me—with no education; me, with no talent—as you've kept reminding me my whole life. Look at me now: a star! Look how I live! Look at my friends! Look where I'm going! I'm not staying in burlesque. I'm moving—maybe up, maybe down—but wherever it is, I'm *enjoying* it! I'm having the time of my life, because for the first time, it *is* my life! I love it! I love every second of it and I'll be damned if you're going to take it away from me! I *am* Gypsy Rose Lee! I love her—and if you don't you can clear out *now*!

(*A moment: Rose stares at her stunned. Then a knocking on the door and Renée enters*)

RENÉE. You press agent is here with the photographer.

LOUISE. Tell him I'll be ready in a minute. (*Softly*) Momma, we can't go shouting seven performances of this a week.

ROSE. The whole family shouts: it comes from our living so near the railroad tracks.

LOUISE. I'm getting an ulcer.

ROSE. You think I'm not?

LOUISE. Yes, I think you're not. And if you want an ulcer, Momma, get one of your own. You can't have mine.

ROSE. Everyone has stomach trouble but me!

LOUISE. Mother, you fought your whole life. I wish you could relax now—

ROSE. You need more mascara on your left eye.

LOUISE. *Momma, you have got to let go of me!*

ROSE. Let go?

LOUISE. I'll give you anything you want—

ROSE. You *need* me!

LOUISE. A house, a farm, a school—a dramatic school for kids? You were always great with kids!

ROSE (*Cutting in*). *I'm a pro!* Not an old work horse you can turn out to pasture just because you think you're riding high on your own.

LOUISE. Momma, no kid does it all on his own but *I am not a kid anymore!* From now on, even if I flop, I flop on my own!

(*A knock on the door*)

PHIL (*Off*). Hey, Gyps, what do you say?

ROSE. "So long, Rose," that's what she says. "Don't slam the door as you leave." (*She starts to go, but is pushed aside by the press agent and the photographer who come in. She stands watching*)

PHIL (*As he enters*). Hi, Rose. Gyps, baby, may I present Monsieur Bougeron-Cochon.

LOUISE. *Enchanté, monsieur.*

BOUGERON-CHOCHON. *Enchanté.*

PHIL. Let's make with the *oiseau*, kiddies. One before you take the plunge, Gyps. All set . . .

(*Louise takes a cheesecake pose*)

Fine!

ROSE. All right, miss. But just one thing I want to know. All the working and pushing and fenagling. All the scheming and scrimping and lying awake nights figuring: How do we get from one town to the next? How do we all eat on a buck? How do I make an act out of nothing? What'd I do it for? You say I fought my whole life. I fought *your* whole life. So now tell me: *What'd I do it for?*

LOUISE (*Quietly, after a long moment*). I thought you did it for me, Momma.

(*Rose stares. Her hands drop to her sides. She turns and quietly goes out*)

PHIL. Come on, smile, Gyps. Show us your talent!

(*She bares a leg*)

That's it!

(*The flashbulb explodes*)

(*The lights black out*)

SCENE SIX

A lone spot picks up Rose as she moves down front.

ROSE. "I thought you did it for me, Momma." "I thought you did it for me, Momma . . ." I thought you made a no-talent ox into a star because you like doing things the hard way, Momma. (*Louder*) And you *haven't* got any talent! Not what *I* call talent, Miss Gypsy Rose Lee!

(*The lights now begin to come up*)

I made you! And you wanna know why? You wanna know what I did it for?! (*Louder*) *Because I was born too soon and started too late, that's why!* With what I have in me, I could've been better than ANY OF YOU! What I got in me—what I been holding down inside of me—if I ever let it out, there wouldn't be signs big enough! There wouldn't be lights bright enough! (*Shouting right out to everyone now*) HERE SHE IS, BOYS! HERE SHE IS, WORLD! HERE'S ROSE!!

(*She sings*)

CURTAIN UP!!!
LIGHT THE LIGHTS!!!

(*Speaking as the lights come up on the strippers' runway*)

Play it, boys.

(*Singing*)

> You either got it,
> or you ain't—
> And, boys, I got it!
> You like it?

ORCHESTRA. Yeah!

ROSE.

> Well, I got it!
> Some people got it
>   And make it pay,
> Some people can't even
>   Give it away.
> This people's got it
>   And this people's spreadin' it around.
> You either have it
>   Or you've had it.

(*Speaking*)

Hello, everybody. My name's Rose. What yours?
(*Bumps*) How d'ya like them egg rolls, Mr. Goldstone?

(*Singing*)

> Hold your hats,
>   And hallelujah,
> Momma's gonna show it to ya!

((*Speaking*)

Ready or not, here comes Momma!

(*Singing*)

> Momma's takin' loud,
> Momma's doin' fine,

Momma's getting' hot,
Momma's goin' strong,
Momma's movin' on,
Momma's all alone,
Momma's doesn't care,
Momma's lettin' loose,
Momma's got the stuff,
Momma's lettin' go—

(*Stopping dead as the words hit her*)

Momma—
Momma's—

(*Shaking off the mood*)

Momma's got the stuff,
Momma's got to move,
Momma's got to go—

(*Stopping dead again, trying to recover*)

Momma—
Momma's—
Momma's gotta let go!

(*Stops; after a moment she begins to pace*)

Why did I do it?
    What did it get me?
Scrapbooks full of me in the background.
Give 'em love and what does it get you?
What does it get you?
One quick look as each of 'em leaves you.
All your life and what does it get you?
Thanks a lot—and out with the garbage.
They take bows and you're battin' zero.
I had a dream—
I dreamed it for you,
    June,
It wasn't for me, Herbie.
And if it wasn't for me
Then where would you be,
Miss Gypsy Rose Lee!
Well, someone tell me, when is it my turn?
Don't I get a dream for myself?
Startin' now it's gonna be my turn!
Gangway, world,
    Get offa my runway!
Startin' now I bat a thousand.
This time, boys, I'm takin' the bows and
Everything's coming up Rose—
Everything's coming up Roses—
Everything's coming up Roses
This time for me!
For me—
For me—
For me—
For me—
FOR ME!

(*She takes her bows. The runway lights go out, the applause dies out, but Rose is still bowing to the triumph in her head. Louise comes on applauding, tall and beautiful in a mink coat over a perfect evening gown. Rose turns, and with an embarrassed smile says—*)

Just trying out a few ideas you might want to use . . .
LOUISE (*Quietly*). You'd really have been something, Mother.
ROSE. Think so?
LOUISE. If you had had someone to push you like I had . . .
ROSE. If I could've been, I would've been. And *that's* show business . . . I guess I did do it for me.
LOUISE. Why, Mother?
ROSE. Just wanted to be noticed.
LOUISE. Like I wanted you to notice me.

(*Rose turns and looks at her*)

I still do, Momma. (*She holds out her arms to Rose, who hesitates, then goes into Louise's arms*) O.K., Momma . . . O.K., Rose.

(*Rose clutches her, then moves away. She forces a smile as she turns back*)

ROSE. Say, you look like you should speak French!
LOUISE. You're coming to that party with me.
ROSE. No.
LOUISE. Come on.
ROSE. Like this?
LOUISE. Here. You wear my mink. I've got a stole in the box office.
ROSE. Well—just for an hour or two. Say, this looks better on me than on you! . . . Funny how we can wear the same size.
LOUISE (*A knowing look*). Especially in mink.
ROSE. You know, I had a dream last night. It was a big poster of a mother and daughter—you know, like the cover of that ladies' magazine.
LOUISE (*Warningly*). Yes, Mother?
ROSE (*Stops moving*). Only it was you and me, wearing exactly the same gown. It was an ad for Minsky—and the headline said: (*She traces the name in the air*) MADAME ROSE—

(*Louise gives her a look; Rose catches it and, moving her hand up to give Louise top billing, says*)

AND HER DAUGHTER, GYPSY!

(*Louise laughs and starts off. Rose starts to follow, then turns back: The runway lights come on. She takes an eager step toward them, they go out in her face. A moment, then she turns and goes off*)

(*The curtain falls*)

TOPICS FOR CRITICAL THINKING AND WRITING

The Play on the PAGE

1. How sympathetic or unsympathetic do you find Rose to be?
2. Do you agree or disagree with the assertion that the ending of the play is sentimental? Could the play end with the conclusion of "Rose's Turn"?
3. Why do you think the transformation of Louise into Gypsy occurs so late in the play, in fact just before the end?

4. Discuss Herbie's relationship with Rose. Why does he finally abandon her?
5. In our postfeminist era how do you assess Rose's prefeminist situation?

The Play on the STAGE

6. Gypsy is a theater work that seems to demand only one style of presentation. But use your imagination to conjure up alternative ways of staging it. Can you conceive of an inexpensive, minimalist production?

The Play in PERFORMANCE

Gypsy opened at the Broadway Theater on May 21, 1959, and closed on March 25, 1961, after 702 performances. A great success, it gave Ethel Merman the triumph of her late career. But since Merman was not considered a big enough film star, when Gypsy was filmed in 1963 the role of Rose was given to Rosalind Russell (Natalie Wood played Louise). The film, although competent, necessarily lost the productional metaphor of theater. Through the years, the musical has frequently been revived on many levels: from school and dinner theater productions to full-scale professional revival. A London production with Angela Lansbury as Rose transferred to Broadway in 1974. Tyne Daly starred in a 1989 revival (to be replaced by Linda Lavin late in the run). And in 1993 it became a television movie with Bette Midler. Its enduring popularity can be gleaned from this review of a dinner theater production in Boca Raton, Florida:

> On the Royal Palm stage, a bite-size theater-in-the-round with difficult sight lines, the musical unfolds, or rather unravels, without the benefit of anything approaching the elan of the Jerome Robbins choreography for which it is famous; the acting skills necessary to illuminate its convoluted main character; or the high spirits that propelled this gem to its permanent place in the Broadway canon. . . . But even mediocre

production values can't undermine the genius of Gypsy's score. When [Rose] . . . sings "Goodbye to Blueberry Pie," the haunting refrain from "Some People," the song inspires chills at the thought that in 1959, Broadway offered us a woman who wanted more than a clean kitchen and a reliable husband. (In fact, Arthur Laurents' book paints a world that's more psychologically complicated than any Broadway musical from the past two decades.) This lone collaboration between Jule Styne and Stephen Sondheim, each of whom would go on to compose entirely disparate bodies of work, is one of the last musicals to create a coherent universe with its songs alone. From gentle ballads ("Little Lamb,"), and novelty songs ("Mr. Goldstone, I Love You," in which Mama Rose delivers the last word on egg rolls) to its showcase, reality-defying anthem ("Everything's Coming Up Roses"), there's not a clunker among them. Given the likable voices at the Royal Palm, it's too bad the production falls so far from the grace notes of the score.*

Even mediocre productions can't mar Gypsy's charms. As Rose sagaciously noted, "Some people got it / And make it pay / Some people can't even / Give it away."

*Robin Dougherty, "Stripped of Spirit" Miami News Times 7 Jan. 1999 (www.miaminewstimes.com/issues/1999-01-07/theater).

TENNESSEE Williams

Not Tennessee (where his father was born), but Mississippi is the state—Columbus is the city—in which Thomas Lanier Williams was born in 1911. He was the first son—the second child—of a troubled misalliance between a shoe salesman and a genteel minister's daughter who overprotected and dandified her young boy. The family lived for several years in the town of Clarksdale before moving to St. Louis in 1918 where his father had accepted a job. In 1929 young Tom (who had already won a literary prize from *Smart Set* magazine) entered the University of Missouri where a college production of *Ghosts* so moved him that he determined to become a playwright. But a deteriorating family situation forced him in 1931 to withdraw from college and work in a shoe company. Six years later his first play, *Cairo, Shanghai, Bombay,* was produced in Memphis, an experience he built on to submit two later plays to the Mummers, a group in St. Louis. He returned to college, first to Washington University in St. Louis, then to the University of Iowa from which he graduated in 1938. After graduation he continued to write plays assiduously, as he supported himself with menial jobs. A breakthrough finally occurred when he won the Group Theater prize for a series of short plays called *American Blues.* This in turn led to a major Rockefeller grant of $1000, and to the chance of a Broadway production.

The play, *Battle of Angels,* closed in Boston tryouts, but it did not die, resurfacing—with revision—years later as *Orpheus Descending* (1957). But near the end of the war, Williams *did* make it to Broadway with a play that won universal critical acclaim and immediately established him as a playwright of note. A "memory" play, consciously autobiographical, it distilled the experience of his family in St. Louis and offered indelible portraits of his mother and troubled sister: *The Glass Menagerie* (1944–45) remains his most universally popular play. And two years later he was to follow this success with an even greater one: *A Streetcar Named Desire* became—like *Death of a Salesman* for Arthur Miller—Williams's signature work, a contemporary classic frequently revived.

For the next decade Williams was at the height of his creativity: Almost every year saw a substantial achievement, from *The Rose Tattoo* in 1951 to *Night of the Iguana* in 1961. Williams was clearly our most productive and commercially successful serious playwright. (Most of his 1950s plays, including *Suddenly Last Summer* [1958], were turned into films.) But then a combination of factors combined to diminish his dramatic reputation: Personal problems and addictions sapped his energy and productivity, and a new decade had given rise to new concerns and new aesthetics that found Williams's new work wanting. But however rejected or reviled, Williams kept writing and revising to the end when he choked to death on a bottle cap in a New York City hotel in 1983. His stature since restored, he remains, with O'Neill and Miller, among our most frequently produced playwrights.

■■■■■■■■■■■■■

COMMENTARY ON *SUDDENLY LAST SUMMER*

In Tennessee Williams's most productive decade—the 1950s—even the plays that received negative or mixed reviews are now accepted as important and have recently been revived: *Camino Real* (1953), *Orpheus Descending* (1957), and *Suddenly Last Summer* (1958). *Orpheus*—Williams's revision of his failed early play *Battle of Angels*—was a dark fable of the triumph of the impotent and brutal over the sexually vital and sensitive. It transposes the Orpheus/Eurydice myth (in which a husband attempts to rescue his wife from the realm of the dead) to a small southern town steeped in the racism and bigotry that Williams had fled. A guitar-playing drifter, Val, falls in love and tries to rescue Lady, the trapped wife of an evil storekeeper, from this dead land. Val faces a dilemma that often confronts Williams's characters: to cease wandering and accept a possibly redemptive experience, or to take off fast as usual to avoid being destroyed by powerful forces of evil. The play's central image is premonitory: A bird born without legs that can survive only so long as it continues to fly. Val waits too long (like Chance Wayne after him in *Sweet Bird of Youth*) and is blowtorched to death as Lady is shot dead by her husband, the Lord of the Dead. But their legend remains: "Wild things leave skins behind them, they leave clean skins and teeth and white bones behind them, and these are tokens passed from one to another, so that the fugitive kind can always follow their kind."

As Sidney Lumet's brilliant 1960 film (with Marlon Brando and Anna Magnani) and Peter Hall's powerful 1988 stage revival (with Vanessa Redgrave) both revealed, *Orpheus Descending* is as emotionally wrenching as anything Williams has written. But its message was *too* bleak and despairing for audiences at mid-century to accept. The play's Broadway failure, the rejection of what he knew to be a major work, so depressed Williams that he entered psychoanalysis, which perhaps explains why the analyst in one of his next plays is a figure of benign authority. In January 1958 Williams opened two short plays Off-Broadway under the general title *Garden District* (a section of New Orleans). The longer and more substantial of the plays, *Suddenly Last Summer*, is as dark, in its own way, as *Orpheus Descending*. Its plot concerns a wealthy New Orleans matron, Violet Venable, who is determined to have her niece Catharine undergo radical brain surgery because of the girl's "slanders" about the death of her son Sebastian who she was accompanying on a holiday abroad. The wealthy dowager urges (to the point of trying to bribe) a young doctor to "cure" Catharine by performing a lobotomy, thus excising the horror from her brain. The doctor wants first to probe the causes of Catharine's "derangement." In doing so, a story of lust and cannibalism is unflinchingly revealed.

For what we discover is that Sebastian was a poet of coterie reputation who wrote one poem a year—every summer when he traveled abroad with his doting mother. They were, Violet insists, "a famous couple" known in all the fashionable places. But *last* summer Violet could not accompany her son on his travels because she had suffered what she insists was a minor aneurysm, but which clearly was a stroke. So Sebastian asked Catharine to go in her place. Watching and listening "with calm detachment," the doctor extracts the whole, horrifying tale, which came to a deadly climax in a Spanish town symbolically named Cabeza de Lobo (Wolf's Head). Far from being chaste, as his mother insists he was, Sebastian was sexually gluttonous, his objects being impoverished young boys whose favors were easily purchasable. And far from adoring his glamorous mother as his one true soul companion, Sebastian used her as a come-on to attract his prey, a role he transferred to Catharine when his mother was no longer available. His death—whose shocking description is the play's climax—comes

about because he makes the fatal error of allowing irritation caused by illness to order waiters to drive off a trailing horde of "little monsters," a band of ragged children who were Sebastian's customary sexual objects. But the band of children pursues and engulfs Sebastian. When Catharine returns with the police, they find Sebastian's mutilated body, parts of which had been devoured: "They had torn bits of him away and stuffed them into those gobbling fierce little empty black mouths of theirs. . . . What was left of him . . . looked like a big white-paper-wrapped bunch of red roses that had been *torn, thrown, crushed!*—against that blazing white wall. . . ."

It is characteristic Williams that this sundered corpse be described in a floral metaphor. "*Flores, flores, para los muertos!*" That cry ("Flowers, flowers for the dead") from *A Streetcar Named Desire* catches the symbiotic union of beauty and death that runs through all of his work. All that is natural, all that is human are governed by contradiction, ambivalence, and impermanence: the no-legged bird in constant fugitive flight, the beautiful cats on hot tin roofs, the inky rose tattoo, the ugly but free iguana, the not-so-royal road of the camino real, the sweet birds of youth succumbing to the ravages of time, the nightingale's eccentricities, the lovely glass menagerie that breaks just like a little girl. And nowhere in his work is the dialect of desire and death more sharply contrasted than in *Suddenly Last Summer* in whose world the governing instinct is predatory consumption. In one of his short stories, "Desire and the Black Masseur"* (in which he could be more sexually explicit than he could in the theater of his day), Williams more fully explores the subject of eater and eaten—how sexual appetite transforms itself into the desire to be physically consumed. In *Suddenly Last Summer* Williams bends all resources to establish this image theatrically and anticipate what is to come: The set is a fantastic garden that resembles a tropical forest. "The colors of this jungle-garden are violent. . . . There are massive tree-flowers that suggest organs of a body, torn out, still glistening with undried blood; here are harsh cries and sibilant hissings and thrashing sounds in the garden as if it were inhabited by beasts, serpents and birds, all of savage nature." At crucial moments as the narrative unfolds the garden emits ominous predatory sounds.

But if *Suddenly Last Summer* writes large Williams's perennial vision of natural violence, it also includes a

---

One Arm, and Other Stories. (New York: New Directions, 1967).

fascinating thematic variation. For usually in Williams's dramatic world, victims and victimizers are arrayed consistently: On one side, the victims: hustlers, deviants, marginal losers, outsiders, people on the edge or on the run; if they are not artists they possess the sensitivity of artists. On the other side are the forces that have power or aspire to it: the sheriffs, politicians, small-town bigots, vengeful fathers and brothers, macho defenders of racist and reactionary orthodoxy, greedy relatives: anti-art, anti-culture, anti-"deviance." All of them—from Stanley Kowalski to Jabe Torrance to Boss Finley—are governed by the dominating quality of corruption, what Big Daddy calls "mendacity."

But in *Suddenly Last Summer* Williams alters the balance, for here the artist is not exempt from mendacity; on the contrary, he is its primary source. Three years later, in *Night of the Iguana* (1961), Williams would return to his traditional redemptive affirmation of the creative act as Hannah's spiritually pure old grandfather, Nonno, dies after reciting the "perfect poem" he has struggled all his life to compose; but Sebastian's annual poems issue from the corrupt vessel of a man who was the opposite of what he pretended to be, a man who *used* people for personal and artistic ends. If Violet and Catharine are to be sacrificed to his poetry, so be it. As Williams's biography reveals, his own life offers occasional disquieting glimpses of this malign tendency. Perhaps due to his psychoanalytic initiation, Williams in *Suddenly Last Summer* examines for one of the very few times the artist's own complicity in the world's corruption.

SUDDENLY LAST SUMMER
Tennessee Williams

CAST OF CHARACTERS

MRS. VENABLE

DR. CUKROWICZ

MISS FOXHILL

MRS. HOLLY

GEORGE HOLLY

CATHARINE HOLLY

SISTER FELICITY

SCENE ONE

The set may be as unrealistic as the decor of a dramatic ballet. It represents part of a mansion of Victorian Gothic style in the Garden District of New Orleans on a late afternoon, between late summer and early fall. The interior is blended with a fantastic garden which is more like a tropical jungle, or forest, in the prehistoric age of giant fern-forests when living creatures had flippers turning to limbs and scales to skin. The colors of this jungle-garden are violent, especially since it is steaming with heat after rain. There are massive tree-flowers that suggest organs of a body, torn out, still blistering with undried blood; there are harsh cries and sibilant hissings and thrashing sounds in the garden as if it were inhabited by beasts, serpents and birds, all of savage nature. . . .

The jungle tumult continues a few moments after the curtain rises; then subsides into relative quiet, which is occasionally broken by a new outburst.

A lady enters with the assistance of a silver-knobbed cane. She has light orange or pink hair and wears a lavender lace dress, and over her withered bosom is pinned a starfish of diamonds.

She is followed by a young blond Doctor, all in white, glacially brilliant, very, very good-looking, and the old lady's manner and eloquence indicate her undeliberate response to his icy charm.

MRS. VENABLE. Yes, this was Sebastian's garden. The Latin names of the plants were printed on tags attached to them but the print's fading out. Those ones there—(*She draws a deep breath*)—are the oldest plants on earth, survivors from the age of the giant fern-forests. Of course in this semitropical climate—(*She takes another deep breath*)—some of the rarest plants, such as the Venus fly-trap—you know what this is, Doctor? The Venus flytrap?

DOCTOR. An insectivorous plant?

MRS. VENABLE. Yes, it feeds on insects. It has to be kept under glass from early fall to late spring and when it went under glass, my son, Sebastian, had to provide it with fruit flies flown in at great expense from a Florida laboratory that used fruit flies for experiments in genetics. Well, I can't do that, Doctor. (*She takes a deep breath.*) I can't, I just can't do it! It's not the expense but the—

DOCTOR. Effort.

MRS. VENABLE. Yes. So goodbye, Venus flytrap!—like so much else . . . Whew! . . . (*She draws breath.*)—I don't know why, but—! I already feel I can lean on your shoulder, Doctor—Cu? —Cu?

DOCTOR. Cu-kro-wicz. It's a Polish word that mean sugar, so let's make it simple and call me Doctor Sugar.

(*He returns her smile.*)

MRS. VENABLE. Well, now, Doctor Sugar, you've seen Sebastian's garden.

(*They are advancing slowly to the patio area.*)

DOCTOR. It's like a well-groomed jungle. . . .

MRS. VENABLE. That's how he meant it to be, nothing was accidental, everything was planned and designed in Sebastian's life and his—(*She dabs her forehead with her handkerchief which she had taken from her reticule*)—work!

DOCTOR. What was your son's work, Mrs. Venable?—besides this garden?

MRS. VENABLE. As many times as I've had to answer that question! D'you know it still shocks me a little?—to realize that Sebastian Venable, the poet is still unknown outside of a small coterie of friends, including his mother.

DOCTOR. Oh.

MRS. VENABLE. You see, strictly speaking, his *life* was his occupation.

DOCTOR. I see.

MRS. VENABLE. No, you *don't* see, yet, but before I'm through, you will.—Sebastian was a poet! That's what I meant when I said his life was his work because the work of a poet is the life of a poet and—vice versa, the life of a poet is the work of a poet, I mean you can't separate them, I mean—well, for instance, a salesman's work is one thing and his life is another—or can be. The same thing's true of—doctor, lawyer, merchant, *thief!*—But a poet's life is his work and his work is his life in a special sense because—oh, I've already talked myself breathless and dizzy.

(*The Doctor offers his arm.*)

Thank you.

DOCTOR. Mrs. Venable, did your doctor okay this thing?

MRS. VENABLE (*breathless*). What thing?

DOCTOR. Your meeting this girl that you think is responsible for your son's death?

MRS. VENABLE. I've waited months to face her because I couldn't get to St. Mary's to face her—I've had her brought here to my house. I won't collapse! She'll collapse! I mean her lies will collapse—not my truth—not the truth. . . . *Forward march, Doctor Sugar!*

(*He conducts her slowly to the patio.*)

Ah, we've *made* it, *ha ha!* I didn't know that I was so weak on my pins! Sit down, Doctor. I'm not afraid of using every last ounce and inch of my little, leftover strength in doing just what I'm doing. I'm devoting all that's left of my life, Doctor, to the defense of a dead poet's reputation. Sebastian had no public name as a poet, he didn't want one, he refused to have one. He *dreaded, abhorred!*—false values that come from being publicly known, from fame, from personal—exploitation. . . . Oh, he'd say to me: "Violet? Mother?—You're going to outlive me!!"

DOCTOR. What made him think that?

MRS. VENABLE. Poets are always clairvoyant!—And he had rheumatic fever when he was fifteen and it affected a heart-valve and he wouldn't stay off horses and out of water and so forth. . . . "Violet? Mother? You're going to live longer than me, and then, when I'm gone, it will be yours, in your hands, to do whatever you please with!"— Meaning, of course, his future recognition!—That he *did* want, he wanted it after his death when it couldn't disturb him; then he did want to offer his work to the world. All right. Have I made my point, Doctor? Well, here is my son's work, Doctor, here's his life going *on!*

(*She lifts a thin gilt-edged volume from the patio table as if elevating the Host before the altar. Its gold leaf and lettering catch the afternoon sun. It says* Poem of Summer. *Her face suddenly has a different look, the look of a visionary, an exalted religieuse. At the same instant a bird sings*

clearly and purely in the garden and the old lady seems to be almost young for a moment.*)

DOCTOR (*reading the title*). Poem of Summer?

MRS. VENABLE. *Poem of Summer*, and the date of the summer, there are twenty-five of them, he wrote one poem a year which he printed himself on an eighteenth-century hand-press at his—atelier in the—French—Quarter—so no one but he could see it. . . .

(*She seems dizzy for a moment.*)

DOCTOR. He wrote one poem a year?

MRS. VENABLE. One for each summer that we traveled together. The other nine months of the year were really only a preparation.

DOCTOR. Nine months?

MRS. VENABLE. The length of a pregnancy, yes. . . .

DOCTOR. The poem was hard to deliver?

MRS. VENABLE. Yes, even with me. *Without* me, *impossible*, Doctor!—he wrote no poem last summer.

DOCTOR. He died last summer?

MRS. VENABLE. Without me he died last summer, that was his last summer's poem.

(*She staggers; he assists here toward a chair. She catches her breath with difficulty.*)

One long-ago summer—now, why am I thinking of this?—my son, Sebastian, said, "Mother?—Listen to this!"—He read me Herman Millville's description of the Encantadas, the Galapagos Islands. Quote—take five and twenty heaps of cinders dumped here and there in an outside city lot. Imagine some of them magnified into mountains, and the vacant lot, the sea. And you'll have a fit idea of the general aspect of the Encantadas, the Enchanted Isles—extinct volcanos, looking much as the world at large might look—after a last conflagration— end quote. He read me that description and said that we had to go there. And so we did go there that summer on a chartered boat, a four-masted schooner, as close as possible to the sort of a boat that Melville must have sailed on. . . . We saw the Encantadas, but on the Encantadas we saw something Melville *hadn't* written about. We saw the great sea-turtles crawl up out of the sea for their annual egg-laying. . . . Once a year the female of the sea-turtle crawls up out of the equatorial sea onto the blazing sand-beach of a volcanic island to dig a pit in the sand and deposit her eggs there. It's a long and dreadful thing, the depositing of the eggs in the sand-pits, and when it's finished the exhausted female turtle crawls back to the sea half-dead. She never sees her offspring, but we did. Sebastian knew exactly when the sea-turtles eggs would be hatched out and we returned in time for it. . . .

DOCTOR. You went back to the—?

MRS. VENABLE. Terrible Encantadas, those heaps of extinct volcanoes, in time to witness the hatching of the sea-turtles and their desperate flight to the sea!

(*There is a sound of harsh bird-cries in the air. She looks up.*)

—The narrow beach, the color of caviar, was all in motion! But the sky was in motion, too. . . .

DOCTOR. The sky was in motion, too?

MRS. VENABLE. —Full of flesh-eating birds and the noise of the birds, the horrible savage cries of the—

DOCTOR. Carnivorous birds?

MRS. VENABLE. Over the narrow black beach of the Encantadas as the just hatched sea-turtles scrambled out of the sandpits and started their race to the sea. . . .

DOCTOR. Race to the sea?

MRS. VENABLE. To escape the flesh-eating birds that made the sky almost as black as the beach!

(*She gazes up again: we hear the wild, ravenous, harsh cries of the birds. The sound comes in rhythmic waves like a savage chant.*)

And the sand all alive, all alive, as the hatched sea-turtles made their dash for the sea, while the birds hovered and swooped to attack and hovered and—swooped to attack! They were diving down on the hatched sea-turtles, turning them over to expose their soft undersides, tearing the undersides open and rendering and eating their flesh. Sebastian guessed that possibly only a hundredth of one percent of their number would escape to the sea. . . .

DOCTOR. What was it about this that fascinated your son?

MRS. VENABLE. My son was looking for—(*She stops short with a slight gasp.*)—Let's just say he was interested in sea-turtles!

DOCTOR. That isn't what you started to say.

MRS. VENABLE. I stopped myself just in time.

DOCTOR. Say what you started to say.

MRS. VENABLE. I started to say that my son was looking for God and I stopped myself because I thought you'd think 'Oh, a pretentious young crackpot!'—which Sebastian was *not!*

DOCTOR. Mrs. Venable, doctors look for God, too.

MRS. VENABLE. Oh?

DOCTOR. I think they have to look harder for him than priests since they don't have the help of such well-known guidebooks and well-organized expeditions as the priests have with their scriptures and—churches. . . .

MRS. VENABLE. You mean they go on a solitary safari like a poet?

DOCTOR. Yes. Some do. I do.

MRS. VENABLE. I believe, I *believe* you! (*She laughs, startled.*)

DOCTOR. Let me tell you something—the first operation I performed at Lion's View.—You can image how anxious and nervous I was about the outcome.

MRS. VENABLE. Yes.

DOCTOR. The patient was a young girl regarded as hopeless and put in the Drum—

MRS. VENABLE. Yes.

DOCTOR. The name for the violent ward at Lion's View because it looks like the inside of a drum with very bright lights burning all day and night.—So the attendants can see any change of expression or movement among the inmates in time to grab them if they're about to attack. After the operation I stayed with the girl, as if I'd delivered a child that might stop breathing.—When they finally wheeled her out of surgery, I still stayed with her. I walked along by the rolling table holding onto her hand—with my heart in my throat. . . .

(*We hear faint music.*)

—It was a nice afternoon, as fair as this one. And the moment we wheeled her outside, she whispered something, she whispered: "Oh, how blue the sky is!"—And I felt proud, I felt proud and relieved, because up till then her speech, everything that she'd babbled, was a torrent of obscenities!

MRS. VENABLE. Yes, well, now, I can tell you without any hesitation that my son *was* looking for God, I mean for a clear image of him. He spent that whole blazing equatorial day in the crow's nest of the schooner watching this thing on the beach till it was too dark to see it, and when he came down the rigging he said "Well, now I've seen Him!," and he meant God.—And for several weeks after that he had a fever, he was delirious with it.—

(*The Encantadas music then fades in again, briefly, at a lower level, a whisper.*)

DOCTOR. I can see how he *might* be, I think he *would* be disturbed if he thought he'd seen God's image, an equation of God, in that spectacle you watched in the Encantadas: creatures of the air hovering over and swooping down to devour creatures of the sea that had had the bad luck to be hatched on land and weren't able to scramble back into the sea fast enough to escape that massacre you witnessed, yes, I can see how such a spectacle could be equated with a good deal of—*experience, existence!*—but not with *God! Can you?*

MRS. VENABLE. Dr. Sugar, I'm a reasonably loyal member of the Protestant Episcopal Church, but I understood what he meant.

DOCTOR. Did he mean we must rise above God?

MRS. VENABLE. He meant that God shows a savage face to people and shouts some fierce things at them, it's all we see or hear of Him. Isn't it all we ever really see and hear of Him, now?—Nobody seems to know why. . . .

(*Music fades out again.*)

Shall I go on from there?

DOCTOR. Yes, do.

MRS. VENABLE. Well, next?—India—China—

(*Miss Foxhill appears with the medicine. Mrs. Venable sees her.*)

MISS FOXHILL. Mrs. Venable.

MRS. VENABLE. Oh, God—elixir—of—. (*She takes the glass.*) Isn't it kind of the drugstore to keep me alive. Where was I, Doctor?

DOCTOR. In the Himalayas.

MRS. VENABLE. Oh yes, that long-ago summer. . . . In the Himalayas he almost entered a Buddhist monastery, had gone so far as to shave his head and eat just rice out of a wood bowl on a grass mat. He'd promised those sly Buddhist monks that he would give up the world and himself and all his wordly possessions to their mendicant order.—Well, I cabled his father, "For God's sake notify bank to freeze Sebastian's accounts!"—I got back this cable from my late husband's lawyer: "Mr. Venable critically ill Stop Wants you Stop Needs you Stop Immediate return advised most strongly. Stop. Cable time of arrival. . . ."

DOCTOR. Did you go back to your husband?

MRS. VENABLE. I made the hardest decision of my life I stayed with my son. I got him through that crisis too. In less than a month he got up off the filthy grass mat and threw the rice bowl away—and booked us into Shepheard's Hotel in Cairo and the Ritz in Paris—. And from then on, oh, we—still lived in a—world of light and shadow. . . .

(*She turns vaguely with empty glass. He rises and takes it from her.*)

But the shadow was almost as luminous as the light.

DOCTOR. Don't you want to sit down now?

MRS. VENABLE. Yes, indeed I do, before I fall down.

(*He assists her into wheelchair.*)

—Are your hind-legs still on you?

DOCTOR (*still concerned over her agitation*). —My what? Oh—hind legs!—Yes . . .

MRS. VENABLE. Well, then you're not a donkey, you're certainly not a donkey because I've been talking the hind-legs off a donkey—several donkeys. . . . But I had to make it clear to you that the world lost a great deal too when I lost my son last summer. . . . You would have liked my son, he would have been charmed by you. My son, Sebastian, was not a family snob or a money snob but he was a

snob, all right. He was a snob about personal charm in people, he insisted upon good looks in people around him, and, oh, he had a perfect little court of young and beautiful people around him always, wherever he was, here in New Orleans or New York or on the Riviera or in Paris and Venice, he always had a little entourage of the beautiful and the talented and the young!

DOCTOR. Your son was young, Mrs. Venable?

MRS. VENABLE. Both of us were young, and stayed young, Doctor.

DOCTOR. Could I see a photograph of your son, Mrs. Venable?

MRS. VENABLE. Yes, indeed you could, Doctor. I'm glad that you asked to see one. I'm going to show you not one photograph but two. Here. Here is my son, Sebastian, in a Renaissance pageboy's costume at a masked ball in Cannes. Here is my son, Sebastian, in the same costume at a masked ball in Venice. These two pictures were taken twenty years apart. Now which is the older one, Doctor?

DOCTOR. This photograph looks older.

MRS. VENABLE. The photograph looks older but not the subject. It takes character to refuse to grow old, Doctor—successfully to refuse to. It calls for discipline, abstention. One cocktail before dinner, not two, four, six—a single lean chop and lime juice on a salad in restaurants famed for rich dishes.

(*Foxhill comes from the house.*)

MISS FOXHILL. Mrs. Venable, Miss Holly's mother and brother are—

(*Simultaneously Mrs. Holly and George appear in the window.*)

GEORGE Hi, Aunt Vi!

MRS. FOXHILL. Violet, dear, we're here.

MISS FOXHILL. They're here.

MRS. VENABLE. Wait upstairs in my upstairs living room for me.

(*To Miss Foxhill:*)

Get them upstairs. I don't want them at that window during this talk.

(*To the Doctor:*)

Let's get away from the window.

(*He wheels her to stage center.*)

DOCTOR. Mrs. Venable? Did your son have a—well—what kind of a *personal*, well, *private* life did—

MRS. VENABLE. That's a question I wanted you to ask me.

MISS FOXHILL. Why?

MRS. VENABLE. I haven't heard the girl's story except indirectly in a watered-down version, being too ill to go to hear it directly, but I've gathered enough to know that it's a hideous attack on my son's moral character which, being dead, he can't defend himself from. I have to be the defender. Now. Sit down. Listen to me . . .

(*The Doctor sits.*)

. . . before you hear whatever you're going to hear from the girl when she gets here. My son, Sebastian, was chaste. Not c-h-a-s-e-d! Oh, he was chased in that way of spelling it, too, we had to be very fleet-footed I can tell you, with his looks and his charm, to keep ahead of pursuers, every kind of pursuer!—I mean he was c-h-a-s-t-e!—Chaste. . . .

DOCTOR. I understood what you meant, Mrs. Venable.

MRS. VENABLE. And you *believe* me, don't you?

DOCTOR. Yes, but—

MRS. VENABLE. But *what*?

DOCTOR. Chastity at—what age was your son last summer?

MRS. VENABLE. *Forty*, maybe. We really didn't count birthdays. . . .

DOCTOR. He lived a celibate life?

MRS. VENABLE. As strictly as if he'd *vowed* to! This sounds like vanity, Doctor, but really I was actually the only one in his life that satisfied the demands he made of people. Time after time my son would let people go, dismiss them!—because their, their, their!—*attitude* toward him was—

DOCTOR. Not pure as—

MRS. VENABLE. My son, Sebastian, demanded! We were a famous couple. People didn't speak to Sebastian and his mother or Mrs. Venable and her son, they said "Sebastian and Violet, Violet and Sebastian are staying at the Lido, they're at the Ritz in Madrid. Sebastian and Violet, Violet and Sebastian have taken a house at Biarritz for the season," and every appearance, every time we appeared, attention was centered on *us*!—everyone else! Eclipsed! Vanity? Ohhhh, no, Doctor, you can't call it that—

DOCTOR. I didn't call it that.

MRS. VENABLE. —It wasn't *folie de grandeur*, it was grandeur.

DOCTOR. I see.

MRS. VENABLE. An attitude toward life that's hardly been known in the world since the great Renaissance princes were crowded out of their palaces and gardens by successful shopkeepers!

DOCTOR. I see.

MRS. VENABLE. Most people's lives—what are they but trails of debris, each day more debris, more debris, long, long trails of debris with nothing to clean it all up but, finally, death. . . .

(*We hear lyric music.*)

My son, Sebastian, and I constructed our days, each day, we would—carve out each day of our lives like a piece of sculpture.—Yes, we left behind us a trail of days like a gallery of sculpture! But, last summer—

(*Pause: the music continues.*)

I can't forgive him for it, not even now that he's paid for it with his life!—he let in this—*vandal!* This—

DOCTOR. The girl that—?

MRS. VENABLE. That you're going to meet here this afternoon! Yes. He admitted this vandal and with her tongue for a hatchet she's gone about smashing our legend, the memory of—

DOCTOR. Mrs. Venable, what do you think is her reason?

MRS. VENABLE. Lunatics don't have reason.

DOCTOR. I mean what do you think is her—motive?

MRS. VENABLE. What a question!—We put the bread in her mouth and the clothes on her back. People that like you for that or even forgive you for it are, are—*hen's teeth*, Doctor. The role of the benefactor is worse than thankless, it's the role of a victim, Doctor, a sacrificial victim, yes, they want your blood, Doctor, they want your blood on the altar steps of their *outraged, outrageous* egos!

DOCTOR. Oh. You mean she resented the—

MRS. VENABLE. Loathed!—They can't shut her up at St. Mary's.

DOCTOR. I thought she'd been there for months.

MRS. VENABLE. I mean keep her *still* there. She *babbles!* They couldn't shut her up in Cabeza de Lobo or at the clinic in Paris—she babbled, babbled!—smashing my son's reputation.—On the Berengaria bringing her back to the States she broke out of the stateroom and babbled, babbled; even at the airport when she was flown down here, she babbled a bit of her story before they could whisk her into an ambulance to St. Mary's. This is a reticule, doctor. (*She raises a cloth bag.*) A catch-all, carry-all bag for an elderly lady which I turned into last summer. . . . Will you open it for me, my hands are stiff, and fish out some cigarettes and a cigarette holder.

(*He does.*)

DOCTOR. I don't have matches.

MRS. VENABLE. I think there's a table-lighter on the table.

DOCTOR. Yes, there is.

(*He lights it, it flames up high.*)

My Lord, what a torch!

MRS. VENABLE (*with a sudden, sweet smile*). "So shines a good deed in a naughty world," Doctor—Sugar. . . .

(*Pause. A bird sings sweetly in the garden.*)

DOCTOR. Mrs. Venable?

MRS. VENABLE. Yes?

DOCTOR. In your letter last week you made some reference to a, to a—fund of some kind, an endowment fund of—

MRS. VENABLE. I wrote you that my lawyers and bankers and certified public accountants were setting up the Sebastian Venable Memorial Foundation to subsidize the work of young people like you that are pushing out the frontiers of art and science but have a financial problem. You have a financial problem, don't you, Doctor?

DOCTOR. Yes, we do have that problem. My work is such a *new* and *radical* thing that people in charge of state funds are naturally a little scared of it and keep us on a small budget, so small that—. We need a separate ward for my patients, I need trained assistants, I'd like to marry a girl I can't afford to marry!—But there's also the problem of getting right patients, not just—criminal psychopaths that the State turns over to us for my operation!—because it's—well—risky. . . . I don't want to turn you against my work at Lion's View but I have to be honest with you. There is a good deal of risk in my operation. Whenever you enter the brain with a foreign object . . .

MRS. VENABLE. Yes.

DOCTOR. —Even a needle-thin knife . . .

MRS. VENABLE. Yes.

DOCTOR. —In a skilled surgeon's fingers . . .

MRS. VENABLE. Yes.

DOCTOR. —There is a good deal of risk involved in—the operation. . . .

MRS. VENABLE. You said that it pacifies them, it quiets them down, it suddenly makes them peaceful.

DOCTOR. Yes. It does that, that much we already know, but—

MRS. VENABLE. What?

DOCTOR. Well, it will be ten years before we can tell if the immediate benefits of the operation will be lasting or—passing or even if there'd still be—and this is what haunts me about it!—any possibility, afterwards, of reconstructing a—totally sound person, it may be that the person will always be limited afterwards, relieved of acute disturbances but—*limited,* Mrs. Venable. . . .

MRS. VENABLE. Oh, but what a blessing to them, Doctor, to be just peaceful, to be just suddenly—peaceful. . . .

(*A bird sings sweetly in the garden.*)

After all that horror, after those nightmares: just to be able to lift up their eyes and see—(*She looks up and raises a hand to indicate the sky*)—a sky not as black with savage, devouring birds as the sky that we saw in the Encantadas, Doctor.

DOCTOR. —Mrs. Venable? I can't guarantee that a lobotomy would stop her—*babbling!!*

MRS. VENABLE. That may be, maybe not, but after the operation, who would *believe* her, Doctor?

(*Pause: faint jungle music.*)

DOCTOR (*quietly*). My God. (*Pause.*)—Mrs. Venable, suppose after meeting the girl and observing the girl and hearing this story she babbles—I still shouldn't feel that her condition's—intractable enough! to justify the risks of—suppose I shouldn't feel that non-surgical treatment such as insulin shock and electric shock and—

MRS. VENABLE. SHE'S HAD ALL THAT AT SAINT MARY'S!! Nothing else is left for her.

DOCTOR. But if I disagreed with you? (*Pause.*)

MRS. VENABLE. That's just part of a question: finish the question, Doctor.

DOCTOR. Would you still be interested in my work at Lion's View? I mean would the Sebastian Venable Memorial Foundation still be interested in it?

MRS. VENABLE. Aren't we always more interested in a thing that concerns us personally, Doctor?

DOCTOR. Mrs. Venable!!

(*Catharine Holly appears between the lace window curtains.*)

You're such an innocent person that it doesn't occur to you, it obviously hasn't even occurred to you that anybody less innocent than you are could possibly interpret this offer of a subsidy as—well, as sort of a *bribe?*

MRS. VENABLE (*laughs throwing her head back*). Name it that—I don't care—. There's just two things to remember. She's a destroyer. My son was a *creator!*—Now if my honesty's shocked you—pick up your little black bag without the subsidy in it, and run away from this garden!—Nobody's heard our conversation but you and I, Doctor Sugar. . . .

(*Miss Foxhill comes out of the house and calls.*)

MISS FOXHILL. Mrs. Venable?

MRS. VENABLE. What is it, what do you want, Miss Foxhill?

MISS FOXHILL. Mrs. Venable? Miss Holly is here, with—

(*Mrs. Venable sees Catharine at the window.*)

MRS. VENABLE. Oh, my God. There she is, in the window!—I told you I didn't want her to enter my house again, I told you to meet them at the door and lead them around the side of the house to the garden and you didn't listen. I'm not ready to face her. I have to have my five o'clock cocktail first, to fortify me. Take my chair inside. Doctor? Are you still here? I thought you'd run out of the garden. I'm going back through the garden to the other entrance. Doctor Sugar? You may stay in the garden if you wish to or run out of the garden if you wish to or go in this way if you wish to or do anything that you wish to but I'm going to have my five o'clock daiquiri, *frozen!*—before I face her. . . .

(*All during this she has been sailing very slowly off through the garden like a stately vessel at sea with a fair wind in her* sails, a pirate's frigate or a treasure-laden galleon. The young Doctor stares at Catharine framed by the lace window curtains. Sister Felicity appears beside her and draws her away from the window. Music: an ominous fanfare. Sister Felicity holds the door open for Catharine as the Doctor starts quickly forward. He starts to pick up his bag but doesn't. Catharine rushes out, they almost collide with each other.)

CATHARINE. *Excuse me.*
DOCTOR. I'm sorry. . . .

(*She looks after him as he goes into the house.*)

SISTER FELICITY. Sit down and be still till your family come outside.

DIM OUT

SCENE TWO

Catharine removes a cigarette from a lacquered box on the table and lights it. The following quick, cadenced lines are accompanied by quick, dancelike movement, almost formal, as the Sister in her sweeping white habit, which should be starched to make a crackling sound, pursues the girl about the white wicker patio table and among the wicker chairs: this can be accompanied by quick music.

SISTER. What did you take out of that box on the table?
CATHRAINE. Just a cigarette, sister.
SISTER. Put it back in the box.
CATHARINE. Too late, it's already lighted.
SISTER. Give it here.
CATHARINE. Oh, please, let me smoke, Sister!
SISTER. Give it here.
CATHARINE. *Please,* Sister Felicity.
SISTER. Catharine, give it here. You know that you're not allowed to smoke at Saint Mary's.
CATHARINE. We're not at Saint Mary's, this is an afternoon out.
SISTER. You're still in my charge. I can't permit you to smoke because the last time you smoked you dropped a lighted cigarette on your dress and started a fire.
CATHARINE. Oh, I did not start a fire. I just burned a hole in my skirt because I was half unconscious under medication.

(*She is now back of a white wicker chair.*)

SISTER (*overlapping her*). Catharine, give it here.
CATHARINE. Don't be such a bully!
SISTER. Disobedience has to be paid for later.
CATHARINE. All right, I'll pay for it later.
SISTER (*overlapping*). Give me that cigarette or I'll make a report that'll put you right back on the violent ward, if you don't.

(*She claps her hands twice and holds one hand out across the table.*)

CATHARINE (*overlapping*). I'm not being violent, sister.
SISTER (*overlapping*). Give me that cigarette, I'm holding my hand out for it!
CATHARINE. All right, take it, here, take it!

(*She thrusts the lighted end of the cigarette into the palm of the Sister's hand. The Sister cries out and sucks her burned hand*).

SISTER. *You burned me with it!*
CATHARINE. I'm sorry, I didn't mean to.
SISTER (*shocked, hurt*). You deliberately burned me!
CATHARINE (*overlapping*). You said give it to you and so I gave it to you.
SISTER (*overlapping*). You stuck the lighted end of that cigarette in my hand!
CATHARINE (*overlapping*). I'm sick, I'm sick—of being *bossed* and *bullied!*
SISTER (*commandingly*). Sit down!

(*Catharine sits down stiffly in a white wicker chair on forestage, facing the audience. The sister resumes sucking the burned palm of her hand. Ten beats. Then from inside the house the whirr of a mechanical mixer.*)

CATHARINE. There goes the Waring Mixer, Aunt Violet's about to have her five o'clock frozen daiquiri, you could set a watch by it! (*She almost laughs. Then she draws a deep, shuddering breath and leans back in her chair, but her hands remain clenched on the white wicker arms.*)—We're in Sebastian's garden. My God, I can still cry!
SISTER. Did you have any medication before you went out?
CATHARINE. No. I didn't have any. Will you give me some, Sister?
SISTER (*almost gently*). I can't. I wasn't told to. However, I think the doctor will give you something.
CATHARINE. The young blond man I bumped into?
SISTER. Yes. The young doctor's a specialist from another hospital.
CATHARINE. What hospital?
SISTER. A word to the wise is sufficient. . . .

(*The Doctor has appeared in the window.*)

CATHARINE (*rising abruptly*). I knew I was being watched, he's in the window, staring out at me!
SISTER. Sit down and be still. Your family's coming outside.
CATHARINE (*overlapping*). LION'S VIEW, IS IT! DOCTOR?

(*She has advanced toward the bay window. The Doctor draws back, letting the misty white gauze curtains down to obscure him.*)

SISTER (*rising with a restraining gesture which is almost pitying*). Sit down, dear.
CATHARINE. IS IT LION'S VIEW? DOCTOR?!

SISTER. Be still. . . .

CATHARINE. WHEN CAN I STOP RUNNING DOWN THAT STEEP WHITE STREET IN CABEZA DE LOBO?

SISTER. Catharine, dear, sit down.

CATHARINE. I loved him, Sister! Why wouldn't he let me save him? I tried to hold onto his hand but he struck me away and ran, ran, ran in the wrong direction, Sister!

SISTER. Catharine, dear—be still.

(*The Sister sneezes.*)

CATHARINE. Bless you, Sister. (*She says this absently, still watching the window*).

SISTER. Thank you.

CATHARINE. The Doctor's still at the window but he's too blond to hide behind window curtains, he catches the light, he shines through them. (*She turns from the window.*)—We were *going* to blonds, blonds were next on the menu.

SISTER. Be still now. Quiet, dear.

CATHARINE. Cousin Sebastian said he was famished for blonds, he was fed up with the dark ones and was famished for blonds. All the travel brochures he picked up were advertisements of the blond northern countries. I think he'd already booked us to—Copenhagen or—Stockholm.—Fed up with dark ones, famished for light ones: that's how he talked about people, as if they were—items on a menu.—"That one's delicious-looking, that one is appetizing," or "that one is *not* appetizing"—I think because he was really nearly half-starved from living on pills and salads. . . .

SISTER. *Stop it!*—Catharine, be still.

CATHARINE. He liked me and so I loved him. . . . (*She cries a little again.*) If he'd kept hold of my hand I could have saved him!—Sebastian suddenly said to me last summer: "Let's fly north, little bird—I want to walk under those radiant, cold northern lights—I've never *seen* the aurora borealis!"—Somebody said once or wrote, once: "We're all of us children in a vast kindergarten trying to spell God's name with the wrong alphabet blocks!"

MRS. HOLLY (*offstage*). Sister?

(*The Sister rises.*)

CATHARINE (*rising*). I think it's *me* they're calling, they call me "Sister," Sister!

SCENE THREE

The Sister resumes her seat impassively as the girl's mother and younger brother appear from the garden. The mother, Mrs. Holly, is a fatuous Southern lady who requires no other description. The brother, George, is typically good-looking, he has the best "looks" of the family, tall and elegant of figure. They enter.

MRS. FOXHILL. Catharine, dear! Catharine—

(*They embrace tentatively.*)

Well, well! Doesn't she look fine, George?

GEORGE Un huh.

CATHARINE. They send you to the beauty parlor whenever you're going to have a family visit. Other times you look awful, you can't have a compact or lipstick or anything made out of metal because they're afraid you'll swallow it.

MRS. HOLLY (*giving a tinkly little laugh*). I think she looks just splendid, don't you, George?

GEORGE Can't we talk to her without the nun for a minute?

MRS. HOLLY. Yes, I'm sure it's all right to. Sister?

CATHARINE. Excuse me, Sister Felicity, this is my mother, Mrs. Holly, and my brother, George.

SISTER. How do you do.

GEORGE. How d'ya do.

CATHARINE. This is Sister Felicity. . . .

MRS. HOLLY. We're so happy that Catharine's at Saint Mary's! So very grateful for all you're doing for her.

SISTER (*sadly, mechanically*). We do the best we can for her, Mrs. Holly.

MRS. HOLLY. I'm sure you do. Yes, well—I wonder if you would mind if we had a little private chat with our Cathie?

SISTER. I'm not supposed to let her out of my sight.

MRS. HOLLY. It's just for a minute. You can sit in the hall or the garden and we'll call you right back here the minute the private part of the little talk is over.

(*Sister Felicity withdraws with an uncertain nod and a swish of starched fabric.*)

GEORGE (*to Catharine*). *Jesus! What are you up to? Huh? Sister? Are you trying to RUIN us?!*

MRS. HOLLY. GAWGE! WILL YOU BE QUIET. You're upsetting your sister!

(*He jumps up and stalks off a little, rapping his knee with his zipper-covered tennis racket.*)

CATHARINE. How elegant George looks.

MRS. HOLLY. George inherited Cousin Sebastian's wardrobe but everything else is in probate! Did you know that? That everything else is in probate and Violet can keep it in probate just as long as she wants to?

CATHARINE. Where is Aunt Violet?

MRS. HOLLY. *George, come back here!*

(*He does, sulkily.*)

Violet's on her way down.

GEORGE Yeah. Aunt Violet has an elevator now.

MRS. HOLLY. Yais, she has, she's had an elevator installed where the back stairs were, and, Sister, it's the cutest little thing you ever did see! It's paneled in Chinese lacquer, black an' gold Chinese lacquer, with lovely bird-pictures on it. But there's only room for two people at a time in it. George and I came down on foot.—I think she's havin' her frozen daiquiri now, she still has a frozen daiquiri promptly at five o'clock ev'ry afternoon in the world . . . in warm weather. . . . Sister, the horrible death of Sebastian just about *killed* her!—She's now slightly better . . . but it's a question of time.—Dear, you know, I'm sure that you understand, why we haven't been out to see you at Saint Mary's. They said you were too disturbed, and a family visit might disturb you more. But I want you to know that nobody, absolutely nobody in the city, knows a thing about what you've been through. Have they, George? Not a thing. Not a soul even knows that you've come back from Europe. When people enquire, when they question us about you, we just say that you've stayed abroad to study something or other. (*She catches her breath.*) Now. Sister?—I want you to please be *very* careful what you say to your Aunt Violet about what happened to Sebastian in Cabeza de Lobo.

CATHARINE. What do you want me to say about what—?

MRS. HOLLY. Just don't repeat that same fantastic story! For my sake and George's sake, the sake of your brother and mother, don't repeat that horrible story again! Not to Violet! Will you?

CATHARINE. Then I am going to have to tell Aunt Violet what happened to her son in Cabeza de Lobo?

MRS. HOLLY. Honey, that's why you're here. She has IN-SISTED on hearing it straight from YOU!

GEORGE You were the only witness to it, Cathie.

CATHARINE. No, there were others. That *ran*.

MRS. HOLLY. Oh, Sister, you've just had a little sort of a—*nightmare* about it! Now, listen to me, will you, Sister? Sebastian has left, has BEQUEATHED!—to you an' Gawge in his *will*—

GEORGE (*religiously*). *To each of us, fifty grand, each!*—AF-TER! TAXES!—GET IT?

CATHARINE. Oh, yes, but if they give me an injection—I won't have any choice but to tell exactly what happened in Cabeza de Lobo last summer. Don't you see? I won't have any choice but to tell the truth. It makes you tell the because it shuts something off that might make you able not to and *everything* comes out, decent or *not* decent, you have no control, but always, always the truth!

MRS. HOLLY. Catharine, darling. I don't know the full story, but surely you're not too sick in your *head* to know in your *heart* that the story you've been telling is just—too—

GEORGE (*cutting in*). Cathie, Cathie, you got to forget that story! Can'tcha? For *your* fifty grand?

MRS. HOLLY. Because if Aunt Vi contests the will, and we know she'll contest it, she'll keep it in the courts forever!—We'll be—

GEORGE It's in PROBATE NOW! And'll never get out of probate until you drop that story—we can't afford to hire lawyers good enough to contest it! So if you don't stop telling that crazy story, we won't have a pot to—cook greens in!

(*He turns away with a fierce grimace and a sharp, abrupt wave of his hand, as if slapping down something. Catharine stares at his tall back for a moment and laughs wildly.*)

MRS. HOLLY. Catharine, don't laugh like that, it scares me, Catharine.

(*Jungle birds scream in the garden.*)

GEORGE (*turning his back on his sister*). Cathie, the money is all tied up.

(*He stoops over sofa, hands on flannel knees, speaking directly into Catharine's face as if she were hard of hearing. She raises a hand to touch his cheek affectionately; he seizes the hand and removes it but holds it tight.*)

If Aunt Vi decided to contest Sebastian's will that leaves us all of this cash?!—Am I coming through to you?

CATHARINE. Yes, little brother, you are.

GEORGE You see, Mama, she's crazy like a coyote!

(*He gives her a quick cold kiss*)

We won't get a single damn penny, honest t' God we won't! So you've just GOT to stop tellin' that story about what you say happened to Cousin Sebastian in Cabeza de Lobo, even if it's what it *couldn't* be, TRUE!—You got to drop it, Sister, you can't tell such a story to civilized people in a civilized up-to-date country!

MRS. HOLLY. Cathie, why, why, why!—did you invent such a tale?

CATHARINE. But, Mother, I DIDN'T invent it. I know it's a hideous story but it's a true story of our time and the world we live in and what did truly happen to Cousin Sebastian in Cabeza de Lobo. . . .

GEORGE Oh, then you are going to tell it. Mama, she IS going to tell it! Right to Aunt Vi, and lose us a hundred thousand!—Cathie? You are a BITCH!

MRS. HOLLY. GAWGE!

GEORGE. I repeat it, a bitch! She ain't crazy, Mama, she's no more crazy than I am, she's just, just—PERVERSE! Was ALWAYS!—perverse. . . .

(*Catharine turns away and breaks into quiet sobbing.*)

MRS. HOLLY. Gawge, Gawge, apologize to Sister, this is no way for you to talk to your sister. You come right back over here and tell your sweet little sister you're sorry you spoke like that to her!

GEORGE (*turning back to Catharine*). I'm sorry, Cathie, but you know we NEED that money! Mama and me, we—Cathie? I got *ambitions*! And, Cathie, I'm YOUNG!—I *want* things, I *need* them, Cathie! So will you please think about ME? Us?

MISS FOXHILL (*offstage*). Mrs. Holly? Mrs. Holly?

MRS. HOLLY. Somebody's callin' fo' me. Catharine, Gawge put it very badly but you know that it's TRUE! WE DO HAVE TO GET WHAT SEBASTIAN HAS LEFT US IN HIS WILL, DEAREST! AND YOU WON'T LET US DOWN? PROMISE? YOU WON'T? LET US DOWN?

GEORGE (*fiercely shouting*). HERE COMES AUNT VI! Mama, Cathie, Aunt Violet's—here is Aunt Vi!

SCENE FOUR

Mrs. Venable enters downstage area. Entrance music.

MRS. HOLLY. *Cathie! Here's Aunt Vi!*

MRS. VENABLE. She sees me and I see her. That's all that's necessary. Miss Foxhill, put my chair in this corner. Crank the back up a little.

(*Miss Foxhill does this business.*)

More. More. Not that much!—Let it back down a little. All right. Now, then. I'll have my frozen daiquiri, now. . . . Do any of you want coffee?

GEORGE. I'd like a chocolate malt.

MRS. HOLLY. Gawge!

MRS. VENABLE. This isn't a drugstore.

MRS. HOLLY. Oh, Gawge is just being Gawge.

MRS. VENABLE. That's what I *thought* he was being!

(*An uncomfortable silence falls. Miss Foxhill creeps out like a burglar. She speaks in a breathless whisper, presenting a cardboard folder toward Mrs. Venable.*)

MISS FOXHILL. Here's the portfolio marked Cabeza de Lobo. It has all your correspondence with the police there and the American consul.

MRS. VENEABLE. I asked for the *English transcript!* It's in a separate—

MISS FOXHILL. Separate, yes, here it is!

MRS. VENABLE. Oh . . .

MISS FOXHILL. And here's the report of the private investigators and here's the report of—

MRS. VENABLE. Yes, yes, yes! Where's the doctor?

MISS FOXHILL. On the phone in the library!

MRS. VENABLE. Why does he choose such a moment to make a phone-call?

MISS FOXHILL. He didn't make a phone-call, he received a phone-call from—

MRS. VENABLE. Miss Foxhill, why are you talking to me like a burglar!?

(*Miss Foxhill giggles a little desperately.*)

CATHARINE. Aunt Violet, she's frightened.—Can I move? Can I get up and move around till it starts?

MRS. HOLLY. Cathie, Cathie, dear, did Gawge tell you that he received bids from every good fraternity on the Tulane campus and went Phi Delt because Paul Junior did?

MRS. VENABLE. I see that he had the natural tact and good taste to come here this afternoon outfitted from head to foot in clothes that belonged to my son!

GEORGE. You gave 'em to me, Aunt Vi.

MRS. VENABLE. I didn't know you'd parade them in front of me, George.

MRS. HOLLY (*quickly*). Gawge, tell Aunt Violet how grateful you are for—

GEORGE. I found a little Jew tailor on Britannia Street that makes alterations so good you'd never guess that they weren't cut *out* for me to *begin* with!

MRS. HOLLY. *AND* so reasonable!—Luckily, since it seems that Sebastian's wonderful, wonderful bequest to Gawge an' Cathie is going to be tied up a while!?

GEORGE. Aunt Vi? About the will?

(*Mrs. Holly coughs.*)

I was just wondering if we can't figure out some way to, to—

MRS. HOLLY. Gawge means to EXPEDITE it! To get through the red tape quicker?

MRS. VENABLE. I understand his meaning. Foxhill, get the doctor.

(*She has risen with her cane and hobbled to the door.*)

MISS FOXHILL (*exits calling*). Doctor!

MRS. HOLLY. Gawge, no more about money.

GEORGE. How do we know we'll ever see her again?

(*Catharine gasps and rises; she moves downstage, followed quickly by Sister Felicity.*)

SISTER (*mechanically*). What's wrong, dear?

CATHARINE. I think I'm just dreaming this, it doesn't seem real!

(*Miss Foxhill comes back out, saying:*)

MISS FOXHILL. He had to answer an urgent call from Lion's View.

(*Slight, tense pause.*)

MRS. HOLLY. Violet! *Not* Lion's View!

(*Sister Felicity had started conducting Catharine back to the patio; she stops her, now.*)

SISTER. Wait, dear.

CATHARINE. What for? I know what's coming.

MRS. VENABLE (*at same time*). Why? are you all prepared to put out a thousand a month plus extra charge for treatments to keep the girl at St. Mary's?

MRS. HOLLY. Cathie, Cathie, dear?

(*Catharine has returned with the sister.*)

Tell Aunt Violet how grateful you are for her makin' it possible for you to rest an' recuperate at such a sweet, sweet place as St. Mary's!

CATHARINE. No place for lunatics is a sweet, sweet place.

MRS. HOLLY. But the food's good there. Isn't the food good there?

CATHARINE. Just give me written permission not to eat fried grits. I had yard privileges till I refused to eat fried grits.

SISTER. She lost yard privileges because she couldn't be trusted in the yard without constant supervision or even with it because she'd run to the fence and make signs to cars on the highway.

CATHARINE. Yes, I did, I did that because I've been trying for weeks to get a message out of that "sweet, sweet place."

MRS. HOLLY. What message, dear?

CATHARINE. I got panicky, Mother.

MRS. HOLLY. Sister, I don't understand.

GEORGE. What're you scared of, Sister?

CATHARINE. What they might do to me now, after they've done all the rest!—That man in the window's a specialist from Lion's View! We get newspapers. I know what they're . . .

(*The Doctor comes out.*)

MRS. VENABLE. Why, Doctor, I thought you'd left us with just that little black bag to remember you by!

DOCTOR. Oh, no: Don't you remember our talk? I had to answer a call about a patient that—

MRS. VENABLE. This is Dr. Cukrowicz He says it means "sugar" and we can call him "Sugar"—

(*George laughs.*)

He's a specialist from Lion's View.

CATHARINE (*cutting in*). WHAT DOES HE SPECIALIZE IN?

MRS. VENABLE. Something new. When other treatments have failed.

(*Pause. The jungle clamor comes up and subsides again.*)

CATHARINE. *Do you want to bore a hole in my skull and turn a knife in my brain?* Everything else was done to me!

(*Mrs. Holly sobs. George raps his knee with the tennis racket.*)

You'd have to have my mother's permission for that.

MRS. VENABLE. I'm paying to keep you in a private asylum.

CATHARINE. You're not my legal guardian.

MRS. VENABLE. Your mother's dependent on me. All of you are!—Financially. . . .

CATHARINE. I think the situation is—clear to me, now. . . .

MRS. VENABLE. Good! In that case. . . .

DOCTOR. I think a quiet atmosphere will get us the best results.

MRS. VENABLE. I don't know what you mean by a quiet atmosphere. She shouted, I didn't.

DOCTOR. Mrs. Venable, let's try to keep things on a quiet level, now. Your niece seems to be disturbed.

MRS. VENABLE. She has every reason to be. She took my son from me, and then she—

CATHARINE. Aunt Violet, you're not being fair.

MRS. VENABLE. Oh, aren't I?

CATHARINE (*to the others*). She's not being fair.

(*Then back to Mrs. Venable:*)

Aunt Violet, you know why Sebastian asked me to travel with him.

MRS. VENABLE. Yes, I *do* know why!

CATHARINE. You weren't able to travel. You'd had a—(*She stops short.*)

MRS. VENABLE. Go on! *What* had I had? Are you afraid to say it in front of the Doctor? She meant that I had a stroke.—I DID NOT HAVE A STROKE!—I had a slight aneurysm. You know what that is, Doctor? A little vascular convulsion! Not a hemorrhage, just a little convulsion of a blood-vessel. I had it when I discovered that she was trying to take my son away from me. Then I had it. It gave a little temporary—muscular—contraction.—To one side of my face. . . . (*She crosses back into main acting area.*) These people are not blood-relatives of mine, they're my dead husband's relations. I always detested these people, my dead husband's sister and—her two worthless children. But I did more than my duty to keep their heads above water. To please my son, whose weakness was being excessively softhearted, I went to the expense and humiliation, yes, public humiliation, of giving this girl a debut which was a fiasco. Nobody liked her when I brought her out. Oh, she had some kind of—notoriety! She had a sharp tongue that some people mistook for wit. A habit of laughing in the faces of decent people which would infuriate them, and also reflected adversely on me and Sebastian, too. But, he, Sebastian, was amused by this girl. While I was disgusted, sickened. And halfway through the season, she was dropped off the party lists, yes, dropped off the lists in spite of my position. Why? Because she'd lost her head over a young married man, made a scandalous scene at a Mardi Gras ball, in the middle of the ballroom. Then everybody dropped her like a hot—rock, but—(*She loses her breath.*) My son, Sebastian, still felt sorry for her and took her with him last summer instead of me. . . .

CATHARINE (*springing up with a cry*). I can't change truth, I'm not God! I'm not even sure that He could, I don't think God can change truth! How can I change the story of what happened to her son in Cabeza de Lobo?

MRS. VENABLE (*at the same time*). She was in love with my son!

CATHARINE (*overlapping*). Let me go back to Saint Mary's. Sister Felicity, let's go back to Saint—

MRS. VENABLE (*overlapping*). Oh, no! That's not where you'll go!

CATHARINE (*overlapping*). All right, *Lion's View* but don't ask me to—

MRS. VENABLE (*overlapping*). You *know* that you were!

CATHARINE (*overlapping*). That I was *what*, Aunt Violet?

MRS. VENABLE (*overlapping*). Don't call me "Aunt," you're the niece of my dead husband, not me!

MRS. HOLLY (*overlapping*). Catharine, Catharine, don't upset your—Doctor? Oh, Doctor!

(*But the Doctor is calmly observing the scene, with detachment. The jungle garden is loud with the sounds of its feathered and scaled inhabitants.*)

CATHARINE. I don't want to, I didn't want to come here! I know what she thinks, she thinks I murdered her son, she thinks that I was responsible for his death.

MRS. VENABLE. That's right. I told him when he told me that he was going with you in my place last summer that I'd never see him again and I never did. And only you know why!

CATHARINE. Oh, my God, I—

(*She rushes out toward garden, followed immediately by the Sister.*)

SISTER. Miss Catharine, Miss Catharine—

DOCTOR (*overlapping*). Mrs. Venable?

SISTER (*overlapping*). Miss Catharine?

DOCTOR (*overlapping*). Mrs. Venable?

MRS. VENABLE. What?

DOCTOR. I'd like to be left alone with Miss Catharine for a few minutes.

MRS. HOLLY. George, talk to her, George.

(*George crouches appealingly before the old lady's chair, peering close into her face, a hand on her knee.*)

GEORGE Aunt Vi? Cathie can't go to Lion's View. Everyone in the Garden District would know you'd put your niece in a state asylum, Aunt Vi.

MRS. VENABLE. Foxhill!

GEORGE What do you want, Aunt Vi?

MRS. VENABLE. Let go of my chair. Foxhill? Get me away from these people!

GEORGE Aunt Vi, listen, think of the talk it—

MRS. VENABLE. I can't get up! Push me, push me away!

GEORGE (*rising but holding chair*). I'll push her, Miss Foxhill.

MRS. VENABLE. Let go of my chair or—

MISS FOXHILL. Mr. Holly, I—

GEORGE. I got to talk to her.

(*He pushes her chair downstage*)

MRS. VENABLE. Foxhill!

MISS FOXHILL. Mr. Holly, she doesn't want you to push her.

GEORGE. I know what I'm doing, leave me alone with Aunt Vi!

MRS. VENABLE. Let go me or I'll *strike* you!

GEORGE. Oh, Aunt Vi!

MRS. VENABLE. Foxhill!

MRS. HOLLY. George—

GEORGE Aunt Vi?

(*She strikes at him with her cane. He releases the chair and Miss Foxhill pushes her off. He trots after her a few steps, then he returns to Mrs. Holly, who is sobbing into a handkerchief. He sighs, and sits down beside her, taking her hand. The scene fades as light is brought up on Catharine and the Sister in the garden. The Doctor comes up to them. Mrs. Holly stretches her arms out to George, sobbing, and he crouches before her chair and rests his head in her lap. She strokes his head. During this: the Sister has stood beside Catharine, holding onto her arm.*)

CATHARINE. You don't have to hold onto me. I can't run away.

DOCTOR. Miss Catharine?

CATHARINE. What?

DOCTOR. Your aunt is a very sick woman. She had a stroke last spring?

CATHARINE. Yes, she did, but she'll never admit it. . . .

DOCTOR. You have to understand why.

CATHARINE. I do, I understand why. I didn't want to come here.

DOCTOR. Miss Catharine, do you hate her?

CATHARINE. I don't understand what hate is. How can you hate anybody and still be sane? You see, I still think I'm sane!

DOCTOR. You think she did have a stroke?

CATHARINE. She had a slight stroke in April. It just affected one side, the left side, of her face . . . but it was disfiguring, and after that, Sebastian couldn't use her.

DOCTOR. Use her? Did you say use her?

(*The sounds of the jungle garden are not loud but ominous.*)

CATHARINE. Yes, we all use each other and that's what we think of as love, and not being able to use each other is what's—*hate*. . . .

DOCTOR. Do you hate her, Miss Catharine?

CATHARINE. Didn't you ask me that, once? And didn't I say that I didn't understand hate. A ship struck an iceberg at sea—everyone sinking—

DOCTOR. Go on, Miss Catharine!

CATHARINE. But that's no reason for everyone drowning for hating everyone drowning! Is it, Doctor?

DOCTOR. Tell me: what was your feeling for your cousin Sebastian?

CATHARINE. He liked me and so I loved him.

DOCTOR. In what way did you love him?

CATHARINE. The only way he'd accept—a sort of motherly way. I tried to save him, Doctor.

DOCTOR. From what? Save him from what?

CATHARINE. Completing—a sort of!—*image!*—he had of himself as a sort of!—*sacrifice* to a!—*terrible* sort of a—

DOCTOR. —God?

CATHARINE. Yes, a—*cruel* one, Doctor!

DOCTOR. How did you feel about that?

CATHARINE. Doctor, my feelings are the sort of feelings that you have in a dream. . . .

DOCTOR. Your life doesn't seem real to you?

CATHARINE. Suddenly last winter I began to write my journal in the third person.

(*He grasps her elbow and leads her out upon forestage. At the same time Miss Foxhill wheels Mrs. Venable off, Mrs. Holly weeps into a handkerchief and George rises and shrugs and turns his back to the audience.*)

DOCTOR. Something happened last winter?

CATHARINE. At a Mardi Gras ball some—some boy that took me to it got too drunk to stand up! (*A short, mirthless note of laughter.*) I wanted to go home. My coat was in the cloakroom, they couldn't find the check for it in his pockets. I said, "Oh, hell, let it go!"—I started out for a taxi. Somebody took my arm and said, "I'll drive you home." He took off his coat as we left the hotel and put over my shoulders, and then I looked at him and—I don't think I'd ever seen him before then, really!—He took me home in his car but took me another place first. We stopped near the Duelling Oaks at the end of Esplanade Street. . . . Stopped!—I said, "What for?"—He didn't answer, just struck a match in the car to light a cigarette in the car and I looked at him in the car and I knew "what for"!—I think I got out of the car before he got out of the car, and we walked through the wet grass to the great misty oaks as if somebody was calling us for help there!

(*Pause. The subdued, toneless bird-cries in the garden turn to a single bird-song.*)

DOCTOR. After that?

CATHARINE. I lost him.—He took me home and said an awful thing to me. "We'd better forget it," he said, "my wife's expecting a child and—."—I just entered the house and sat there thinking a little and then I suddenly called a taxi and went right back to the Roosevelt Hotel ballroom. The ball was still going on. I thought I'd gone back to pick up my borrowed coat but that wasn't what I'd gone back for. I'd gone back to make a scene on the floor of the ballroom, yes, I didn't stop at the cloakroom to pick Aunt Violet's old mink stole, no, I rushed right into the ballroom and spotted him on the floor and ran up to him and beat him as hard as I could in the face and chest with my fists till—Cousin Sebastian took me away.—After that, the next morning, I started writing my diary in the third person, singular, such as "She's still living this morning," meaning that *I* was. . . . —"WHAT'S NEXT

FOR HER? GOD KNOWS!"—I couldn't go out any more.—However one morning my Cousin Sebastian came in my bedroom and said: "Get up!"—Well . . . if you're still alive after dying, well then, you're obedient, Doctor.—I got up. He took me downtown to a place for passport photos. Said: "Mother can't go abroad with me this summer. You're going to go with me this summer instead of Mother."—If you don't believe me, read my journal of Paris!—"She woke up at daybreak this morning, had her coffee and dressed and took a brief walk—"

DOCTOR. *Who* did?

CATHARINE. *She* did. *I* did—from the Hotel Plaza Athénée to the Place de l'Étoile as if pursued by a pack of Siberian wolves! (*She laughs her tired, helpless laugh.*)—Went right through all stop signs—couldn't wait for green signals.— "Where did she think she was going? Back to the Duelling Oaks?"—Everything chilly and dim but his hot, ravenous mouth! on—

DOCTOR. Miss Catharine, let me give you something.

(*The others go out, leaving Catharine and the Doctor onstage.*)

CATHARINE. Do I have to have the injection again, this time? What am I going to be stuck with this time, Doctor? I don't care. I've been stuck so often that if you connected me with a garden hose I'd make a good sprinkler.

DOCTOR (*preparing needle*). Please take off your jacket.

(*She does. The Doctor gives her an injection.*)

CATHARINE. I didn't feel it.

DOCTOR. That's good. Now sit down.

(*She sits down.*)

CATHARINE. Shall I start counting backwards from a hundred?

DOCTOR. Do you like counting backwards?

CATHARINE. Love it! Just love it! One hundred! Nine-nine! Ninety-eight! Ninety-seven. Ninety-six. Ninety—five.— Oh!—I already feel it! How funny!

DOCTOR. That's right. Close your eyes for a minute.

(*He moves his chair closer to hers. Half a minute passes.*)

Miss Catharine? I want you to give me something.

CATHARINE. Name it and it's yours, Doctor Sugar.

DOCTOR. Give me all your resistance.

CATHARINE. Resistance to what?

DOCTOR. The truth. Which you're going to tell me.

CATHARINE. The truth's the one thing I have never resisted!

DOCTOR. Sometimes people just think they don't resist it, but still do.

CATHARINE. They say it's at the bottom of a bottomless well, you know.

DOCTOR. Relax.

CATHARINE. Truth.

DOCTOR. Don't talk.
CATHARINE. Where was I, now? At ninety?
DOCTOR. You don't have to count backwards.
CATHARINE. At ninety something?
DOCTOR. You can open your eyes.
CATHARINE. Oh, I do feel funny!

(*Silence, pause.*)

You know what I think you're doing? I think you're trying to hypnotize me. Aren't you? You're looking so straight at me and doing something to me with your eyes and your—eyes. . . . Is that what you're doing to me?
DOCTOR. Is that what you *feel* I'm doing?
CATHARINE. Yes! I feel so peculiar. And it's not just the drug.
DOCTOR. Give me all your resistance. See. I'm holding my hand out. I want you to put yours in mind and give me all your resistance. Pass all of your resistance out of your hand to mine.
CATHARINE. Here's my hand. But there's no resistance in it.
DOCTOR. You are totally passive.
CATHARINE. Yes, I am.
DOCTOR. You will do what I ask.
CATHARINE. Yes, I will try.
DOCTOR. You will tell the true story.
CATHARINE. Yes, I will.
DOCTOR. The absolutely true story. No lies, nothing not spoken. Everything told, exactly.
CATHARINE. Everything. Exactly. Because I'll have to. Can I—can I stand up?
DOCTOR. Yes, but be careful. You might feel a little bit dizzy.

(*She struggles to rise, then falls back.*)

CATHARINE. I can't get up! Tell me to. Then I think I could do it.
DOCTOR. Stand up.

(*She rises unsteadily.*)

CATHARINE. How funny! Now I can! Oh, I do feel dizzy! Help me, I'm—

(*He rushes to support her.*)

—about to fall over. . . .

(*He holds her. She looks out vaguely toward the brilliant, steaming garden. Looks back at him. Suddenly sways toward him, against him.*)

DOCTOR. You see, you lost your balance.
CATHARINE. No, I didn't. I did what I wanted to do without you telling me to.

(*She holds him tight against her.*)

Let me! Let! Let! Let me! Let me, let me, oh, let me. . . .

(*She crushes her mouth to his violently. He tries to disengage himself. She presses her lips to his fiercely, clutching his body against her. Her brother George enters.*)

Please hold me! I've been so lonely. It's lonelier than death, if I've gone mad, it's lonelier than death!
GEORGE (*shocked, disgusted*). Cathie!—you've got a hell of a nerve.

(*She falls back, panting, covers her face, runs a few paces and grabs the back of a chair. Mrs. Holly enters.*)

MRS. HOLLY. What's the matter, George? Is Catharine ill?
GEORGE. No.
DOCTOR. Miss Catharine had an injection that made her a little unsteady.
MRS. HOLLY. What did he say about Catharine?

(*Catharine has gone out into the dazzling jungle of the garden.*)

SISTER (*returning*). She's gone into the garden.
DOCTOR. That's all right, she'll come back when I call her.
SISTER. It may be all right for you. You're not responsible for her.

(*Mrs. Venable has re-entered.*)

MRS. VENABLE. Call her now!
DOCTOR. Miss Catharine! Come back.

(*To the Sister:*)

Bring her back, please, Sister!

(*Catharine enters quietly, a little unsteady.*)

Now, Miss Catharine, you're going to tell the true story.
CATHARINE. Where do I start the story?
DOCTOR. Wherever you think it started.
CATHARINE. I think it started the day he was born in this house.
MRS. VENABLE. Ha! You see!
GEORGE. Cathie.
DOCTOR. Let's start later than that. (*Pause.*) Shall we begin with last summer?
CATHARINE. Oh. Last summer.
DOCTOR. Yes. Last summer.

(*There is a long pause. The raucous sounds in the garden fade into a bird-song which is clear and sweet. Mrs. Holly coughs. Mrs. Venable stirs impatiently. George crosses downstage to catch Catharine's eye as he lights a cigarette.*)

CATHARINE. Could I—?
MRS. VENABLE. Keep that boy away from her!
GEORGE. She wants to smoke, Aunt Vi.
CATHARINE. Something helps in the—hands. . . .
SISTER. Unh unh!

DOCTOR. It's all right, Sister. (*He lights her cigarette.*) About last summer: how did it begin?

CATHARINE. It began with his kindness and the six days at sea that took me so far away from the—Duelling Oaks that I forgot them, nearly. He was affectionate with me, so sweet and attentive to me, that some people took us for a honeymoon couple until they noticed that we had—separate staterooms, and—then in Paris, he took me to Patou and Schiaparelli's—*this* is from Schiaparelli's! (*Like a child, she indicates her suit.*)—bought me so many new clothes that I gave away my old ones to make room for my new ones in my new luggage to—travel. . . . I turned into a peacock! Of course, so was *he* one, too. . . .

GEORGE. *Ha Ha!*

MRS. VENABLE. Shh!

CATHARINE. But then I made the mistake of responding too much to his kindness, of taking hold of his hand before he'd take hold of mine, of holding onto his arm and leaning on his shoulder, of appreciating his kindness more than he wanted me to, and, suddenly, last summer, he began to be restless, and—oh!

DOCTOR. Go on.

CATHARINE. The Blue Jay notebook!

DOCTOR. Did you say notebook?

MRS. VENABLE. I know what she means by that, she's talking about the school composition book with a Blue Jay trademark that Sebastian used for making notes and revisions on his *"Poem of Summer."* It went with him everywhere that he went, in his jacket pocket, even his dinner jacket. I have the one that he had with him last summer. *Foxhill! The Blue Jay notebook!*

(*Miss Foxhill rushes in with a gasp.*)

It came with his personal effects shipped back from Cabeza de Lobo.

DOCTOR. I don't quite get the connection between new clothes and so forth and the Blue Jay notebook.

MRS. VENABLE. I HAVE IT!—Doctor, tell her I've found it.

(*Miss Foxhill hears this as she comes back out of house: gasps with relief, retires.*)

DOCTOR. With all these interruptions it's going to be awfully hard to—

MRS. VENABLE. This is important. I don't know why she mentioned the Blue Jay notebook but I want you to see it. Here it is, here! (*She holds up a notebook and leafs swiftly through the pages.*) Title? *"Poems of Summer,"* and the date of the summer—1935. After that: *what? Blank pages, blank pages,* nothing but *nothing!*—last summer. . . .

DOCTOR. What's that got to do with—?

MRS. VENABLE. His destruction? I'll tell you. A poet's vocation is something that rests on something as thin and fine as the web of a spider, Doctor. That's all that holds him

over!—out of destruction. . . . Few, very few are able to do it alone! Great help is needed! I *did* give it! She *didn't.*

CATHARINE. She's right about that. I failed him. I wasn't able to keep the web from—breaking. . . . I saw it breaking but couldn't save or—repair it!

MRS. VENABLE. There now, the truth's coming out. We had an agreement between us, a sort of contract or covenant between us which he broke last summer when he broke away from me and took her with him, not me! When he was frightened and I knew when and what of, because his hands would shake and his eyes looked in, not out, I'd reach across a table and touch his hands and say not a word, just look, and touch his hands with my hand until his hands stopped shaking and his eyes looked out, not in, and in the morning, the poem would be continued. *Continued until it was finished!*

(*The following ten speeches are said very rapidly, overlapping*).

CATHARINE. I—couldn't!

MRS. VENABLE. *Naturally* not! He was *mine!* I *knew* how to help him, I *could!* You didn't, you couldn't!

DOCTOR. These interruptions—

MRS. VENABLE. I would say, "You *will*" and he *would,* I—!

CATHARINE. Yes, you see, I failed him! And so, last summer, we went to Cabeza de Lobo, we flew down there from where he gave up writing his poem last summer. . . .

MRS. VENABLE. Because he'd broken our—

CATHARINE. Yes! Yes, something had broken, that string of pearls that old mothers hold their sons by like a—sort of a—sort of—*umbilical* cord, *long—after . . .*

MRS. VENABLE. She means that I held him back from—

DOCTOR. *Please!*

MRS. VENABLE. *Destruction!*

CATHARINE. All I know is that suddenly, last summer, he wasn't young any more, and we went to Cabeza de Lobo, and he suddenly switched from the evenings to the beach. . . .

DOCTOR. From evenings? To beach?

CATHARINE. I mean from the evenings to the afternoons and from the fa—fash—

(*Silence: Mrs. Holly draws a long, long painful breath. George stirs impatiently.*)

DOCTOR. Fashionable! Is that the word you—?

CATHARINE. Yes. Suddenly, last summer Cousin Sebastian changed to the afternoons and the beach.

DOCTOR. What beach?

CATHAINE. In Cabeza de Lobo there is a beach that's named for Sebastian's name saint, it's known as La Playa San Sebastian, and that's where we started spending all afternoon, every day.

DOCTOR. What kind of beach was it?

CATHARINE. It was a big city beach near the harbor.

DOCTOR. It was a big public beach?

CATHARINE. Yes, public.

MRS. VENABLE. It's little statements like that that give her away.

(*The Doctor rises and crosses to Mrs. Venable without breaking his concentration on Catharine.*)

After all I've told you about his fastidiousness, can you accept such a statement?

DOCTOR. You mustn't interrupt her.

MRS. VENABLE (*overlapping him*). That Sebastian would go every day to some dirty free public beach near a harbor? A man that had to go out a mile in a boat to find water to swim in?

DOCTOR. Mrs. Venable, no matter what she says you have to let her say it without any more interruptions or this interview will be useless.

MRS. VENABLE. I won't speak again. I'll keep still, if it kills me.

CATHARINE. I don't want to go on. . . .

DOCTOR. Go on with the story. Every afternoon last summer your Cousin Sebastian and you went out to this free public beach?

CATHARINE. No, it wasn't the free one, the free one was right next to it, there was a fence between the free beach and the one that we went to that charged a small charge of admission.

DOCTOR. Yes, and what did you do there?

(*He still stands beside Mrs. Venable and the light gradually changes as the girl gets deeper into her story: the light concentrations on Catharine, the other figures sink into shadow.*)

Did anything happen there that disturbed you about it?

CATHARINE. Yes!

DOCTOR. What?

CATHARINE. He bought me a swim-suit I didn't want to wear. I laughed. I said, "I can't wear that, it's a scandal to the jay-birds!"

DOCTOR. What did you mean by that? That the suit was immodest?

CATHARINE. My God, yes! It was a one-piece suit made of white lisle, the water made it transparent! (*She laughs sadly at the memory of it.*)—I didn't want to swim in it, but he'd grab my hand and drag me into the water, all the way in, and I'd come out looking naked!

DOCTOR. Why did he do that? Did you understand why?

CATHARINE. —Yes! To attract!—Attention.

DOCTOR. He wanted you to attract attention, did he, because he felt you were moody? Lonely? He wanted to shock you out of your depression last summer?

CATHARINE. Don't you understand? I was PROCURING for him!

(*Mrs. Venable's gasp is like the sound that a great hooked fish might make*)

She used to do it, too.

(*Mrs. Venable cries out.*)

Not consciously! She didn't *know* that she was procuring for him in the smart, the fashionable places they used to go to before last summer! Sebastian was shy with people. She wasn't. Neither was I. We both did the same thing for him, made contacts for him, but she did it in nice places and in decent ways and I had to do it the way that I just told you!—Sebastian was lonely, Doctor, and the empty Blue Jay notebook got bigger and bigger, so big it was big and empty as that big empty blue sea and sky. . . . I knew what I was doing. I came out in the French Quarter years before I came out in the Garden District. . . .

MRS. HOLLY. Oh, Cathie! Sister . . .

DOCTOR. Hush!

CATHARINE. And before long, when the weather got warmer and the beach so crowded, he didn't need me any more for that purpose. The ones on the free beach began to climb over the fence or swim around it, bands of homeless young people that lived on the free beach like scavenger dogs, hungry children. . . . So now he let me wear a decent dark suit. I'd go to a faraway empty end of the beach, write postcards and letters and keep up my— third-person journal till it was—five o'clock and time to meet him outside the bathhouses, on the street. . . . He would come out, *followed.*

DOCTOR. Who would follow him out?

CATHARINE. The homeless, hungry young people that had climbed over the fence from the free beach that they lived on. He'd pass out tips among them as if they'd all— shined his shoes or called taxis for him. . . . Each day the crowd was bigger, noisier, greedier!—Sebastian began to be frightened.—At last we stopped going out there. . . .

DOCTOR. And then? After that? After you quit going out to the public beach?

CATHARINE. Then one day, a few days after we stopped going out to the beach—it was one of those white blazing days in Cabeza de Lobo, not a blazing hot *blue* one but a blazing hot *white* one.

DOCTOR. Yes?

CATHARINE. We had a late lunch at one of those open-air restaurants on the sea there.—Sebastian was white as the weather. He had on a spotless white silk Shantung suit and a white silk tie and a white panama and white shoes, white—white lizard skin—pumps! He—(*She throws back her head in a startled laugh at the recollection*)—kept touching his face and his throat here and there with a white silk handkerchief and popping little white pills in his mouth, and I knew he was having a bad time with his heart and was frightened about it and that was the reason we hadn't gone out to the beach. . . .

(*During the monologue the lights have changed, the surrounding area has dimmed out and a hot white spot is focused on Catharine.*)

"I think we ought to go north," he kept saying, "I think we've done Cabeza de Lobo, I think we've done it, don't you?" *I thought we'd done it!*—but I had learned it was better not to seem to have an opinion because if I did, well, Sebastian, well, you know Sebastian, he always preferred to do what no one else wanted to do, and I always tried to give the impression that I was agreeing reluctantly to his wishes . . . it was a—game. . . .

SISTER. She's dropped her cigarette.

DOCTOR. I've got it, Sister.

(*There are whispers, various movements in the penumbra. The Doctor fills a glass for her from the cocktail shaker.*)

CATHARINE. Where was I? Oh, yes, that five o'clock lunch at one of those fish-places along the harbor of Cabeza de Lobo, it was between the city and the sea, and there were naked children along the beach which was fenced off with barbed wire from the restaurant and we had our tables less than a yard from the barbed wire fence that held the beggars at bay. . . . There were naked children along the beach, a band of frightfully thin and dark naked children that looked like a flock of plucked birds, and they would come darting up to the barbed wire fence as if blown there by the wind, the hot white wind from the sea, all crying out, "*Pan, pan, pan!*"

DOCTOR (*quietly*). What's *pan*?

CATHARINE. The word for bread, and they made gobbling noises with their little black mouths, stuffing their little black fists to their mouths and making those gobbling noises, with frightful grins!—Of course we were sorry that we had come to this place but it was too late to go. . . .

DOCTOR (*quietly*). Why was it "too late to go"?

CATHARINE. I told you Cousin Sebastian wasn't well. He was popping those little white pills in his mouth. I think he had popped in so many of them that they had made him feel weak. . . . His, his!—eyes looked—dazed, but he said: "Don't look at those little monsters. Beggars are a social disease in this country. If you look at them, you get sick of the country, it spoils the whole country for you. . . ."

DOCTOR. Go on.

CATHARINE. I'm going on. I have to wait now and then till it gets clearer. Under the drug it has to be a vision, or nothing comes. . . .

DOCTOR. All right?

CATHARINE. Always when I was with him I did what he told me. I didn't look at the band of naked children, not even when the waiters drove them away from the barbed wire fence with sticks!—Rushing out through a wicket gate like an assault party in war!—and beating them screaming away from the barbed wire fence with the sticks. . . . Then! (*Pause.*)

DOCTOR. Go on, Miss Catherine, what comes next in the vision?

CATHARINE. The, the the!—band of children began to—serenade us. . . .

DOCTOR. Do what?

CATHARINE. Play for us! On instruments! Make music!—if you could call it music. . . .

DOCTOR. Oh?

CATHARINE. Their, their—instruments were—instruments of percussion! —Do you know what I mean?

DOCTOR (*making a note*). Yes. Instruments of percussion such as—*drums*?

CATHARINE. I stole glances at them when Cousin Sebastian wasn't looking, and as well as I could make out in the white blaze of the sand-beach, the instruments were tin cans strung together.

DOCTOR (*slowly, writing*). *Tin—cans—strung—together.*

CATHARINE. *And, and, and, and—and!—bits of metal, other bits of metal that had been flattened out, made into—*

DOCTOR. What?

CATHARINE. *Cymbals! You know? Cymbals?*

DOCTOR. Yes. Brass plates hit together.

CATHARINE. That's right, Doctor.—Tin cans flattened out and clashed together!—Cymbals. . . .

DOCTOR. Yes. I understand. What's after that, in the vision?

CATHARINE (*rapidly, panting a little*). And others had paper bags, bags made out of—coarse paper!—with something on a string inside the bags which they pulled up and down, back and forth, to make a sort of a—

DOCTOR. Sort of a—?

CATHARINE. Noise like—

DOCTOR. Noise like?

CATHARINE (*rising stiffly from chair*). Ooompa! Oompa! Oooooooompa!

DOCTOR. Ahhh . . . a sound like a *tuba*?

CATHARINE. That's right!—they made a sound like a tuba. . . .

DOCTOR. Oompa, oompa, oompa, like a tuba.

(*He is making a note of the description*).

CATHARINE. Oompa, oompa, oompa, like a—

(*Short pause.*)

DOCTOR. —Tuba. . . .

CATHARINE. All during lunch they stayed at a—a fairly *close—distance*. . . .

DOCTOR. Go on with the vision, Miss Catharine.

CATHARINE (*striding about the table*). *Oh, I'm going on, nothing could stop it now!!*

DOCTOR. Your Cousin Sebastian was *entertained* by this—concert?

CATHARINE. I think he was *terrified* of it!

DOCTOR. Why was he terrified of it?

CATHARINE. I think he recognized some of the musicians, some of the boys, between childhood and—older. . . .

DOCTOR. What did he do? Did he do anything about it, Miss Catharine?—Did he complain to the manager about it?

CATHARINE. *What* manager? *God?* Oh, *no!*—The manager of the fishplace on the beach? Haha!—No!—You don't understand my cousin!

DOCTOR. What do you mean?

CATHARINE. *He!*—accepted!—*all!*—as—how! —things!—are!—And thought nobody had any right to complain or interfere in any way whatsoever, and even though he knew that what was awful was awful, that what was wrong was wrong, and my Cousin Sebastian was certainly never sure that anything was wrong!—He thought it unfitting to ever take any action about anything whatsoever!—except to go on doing as something in him directed. . . .

DOCTOR. What did something in him direct him to do?—I mean on this occasion in Cabeza de Lobo.

CATHARINE. After the salad, before they brought the coffee, he suddenly pushed himself away from the table, and said, "They've got to stop that! Waiter, make them stop that. I'm not a well man, I have a heart condition, it's making me sick!"—This was the first time that Cousin Sebastian had ever attempted to correct a human situation!—I think perhaps that *that* was his fatal error. . . . It was then that the waiters, all eight or ten of them, charged out of the barbed wire wicket gate and beat the little musicians away with clubs and skillets and anything hard that they could snatch from the kitchen!—Cousin Sebastian left the table. He stalked out of the restaurant after throwing a handful of paper money on the table and he fled from the place. I followed. It was all white outside. White hot, a blazing white hot, hot blazing white, at five o'clock in the afternoon in the city of—Cabeza de Lobo. It looked as if—

DOCTOR. It looked as if?

CATHARINE. As if a huge white bone had caught on fire in the sky and blazed so bright it was white and turned the sky and everything under the sky white with it!

DOCTOR. —White . . .

CATHARINE. Yes—white . . .

DOCTOR. You followed your cousin Sebastian out of the restaurant onto the hot white street?

CATHARINE. Running up and down hill. . . .

DOCTOR. You ran up and down hill?

CATHARINE. No, no! *Didn't!*—move either *way!*—at first, we were—

(*During this recitation there are various sound effects. The percussive sounds described are very softly employed.*)

I rarely made any suggestion but *this* time I *did*. . . .

DOCTOR. What did you suggest?

CATHARINE. Cousin Sebastian seemed to be paralyzed near the entrance of the café, so I said, "Let's go." I remember that it was a very wide and steep white street, and I said, "Cousin Sebastian, down that way is the waterfront and we are more likely to find a taxi near there. . . . Or why don't we go back in?—and have them *call* us a taxi! Oh,

let's do! Let's do *that*, that's better!" And he said, "*Mad*, are you *mad?* Go back in that filthy place? Never! That gang of kids shouted vile things about me to the waiters!" "Oh," I said, "then let's go down toward the docks, down there at the bottom of the hill, let's not try to climb the hill in this dreadful heat." And Cousin Sebastian shouted, "Please shut up, let me handle this situation, will you? I want to handle this thing." And he started up the steep street with a hand stuck in his jacket where I knew he was having a pain in his chest from his palpitations. . . . But he walked faster and faster, in panic, but the faster he walked the louder and closer it got!

DOCTOR. What got louder?

CATHARINE. The music.

DOCTOR. The music again.

CATHARINE. The oompa-oompa of the—following band.—They'd somehow gotten through the barbed wire and out on the street, and they were following, following!—up the blazing white street. The band of naked children pursued us up the steep white street in the sun that was like a great white bone of a giant beast that had caught on fire in the sky!—Sebastian started to run and they all screamed at once and seemed to fly in the air, they outran him so quickly. I screamed. I heard Sebastian scream, he screamed just once before this flock of black plucked little birds that pursued him and overtook him halfway up the white hill.

DOCTOR. And you, Miss Catharine, what did *you* do, then?

CATHARINE. Ran!

DOCTOR. Ran where?

CATHARINE. Down! Oh, I ran down, the easier direction to run was down, down, down!—The hot, white, blazing street, screaming out "Help" all the way, till—

DOCTOR. What?

CATHARINE. —Waiters, police, and others—ran out of buildings and rushed back up the hill with me. When we got back to where my Cousin Sebastian had disappeared in the flock of featherless little black sparrows, he—he was lying naked as they had been naked against a white wall, and this you won't believe, nobody *has* believed it, nobody *could* believe it, nobody, nobody on earth could possible believe it, and I don't *blame* them!—They had *devoured* parts of him.

(*Mrs. Venable cries out softly.*)

Torn or cut parts of him away with their hands or knives or maybe those jagged tin cans they made music with, they had torn bits of him away and stuffed them into those gobbling fierce little empty black mouths of theirs. There wasn't a sound any more, there was nothing to see but Sebastian, what was left of him, that looked like a big white-paper-wrapped bunch of red roses had been *torn, thrown, crushed!* —against that blazing white wall. . . .

(*Mrs. Venable springs with amazing power from her wheelchair, stumbles erratically but swiftly toward the girl and tries to strike her with her cane. The Doctor snatches it from her and catches her as she is about to fall. She gasps hoarsely several times as he leads her toward the exit.*)

MRS. VENABLE (*offstage*). *Lion's View! State asylum, cut this hideous story out of her brain!*

(*Mrs. Holly sobs and crosses to George, who turns away from her, saying:*)

GEORGE. Mom, I'll quit school, I'll get a job, I'll—
MRS. HOLLY. Hush son! Doctor, can't you say something?

(*Pause. The Doctor comes downstage. Catherine wanders out into the garden followed by the Sister.*)

DOCTOR (*after a while, reflectively, into space*). I think we ought at least to consider the possibility that the girl's story could be true. . . .

TOPICS FOR CRITICAL THINKING AND WRITING

The Play on the PAGE

1. Describe the relationship with her son as perceived by Violet.
2. Describe Sebastian's view of his relationship with his mother. How consciously is he exploiting her? How deep is his Oedipus complex?
3. What is Catharine's view of Sebastian *before* their vacation last summer?

4. What do you think of the play's violent ending? Williams was accused of writing something "morally objectionable." Do you find this accusation fair or unfair?
5. What do you feel about Williams's vision of reality?

The Play on the STAGE

6. How far would you go in stressing the nonrealistic elements that Williams requests in his stage directions?
7. How would you stage the end of the play?
8. What would you tell your actors in helping them work on their roles? Would you, or would you not,

tell them to watch the movie with Elizabeth Taylor and Katherine Hepburn and/or the videotape with Natasha Richardson and Maggie Smith?

The Play in PERFORMANCE

Tennessee Williams rose to prominence as a playwright just after the Second World War, a period that saw the widespread dissemination of an Americanized version of Stanislavski's theories about acting and the theater. The Group Theater had ended in 1940 and its members dispersed into the profession as actors, directors, master teachers. The growing reputation of the Actors' Studio (founded in 1947 by Elia Kazan, Robert Lewis, and Cheryl Crawford) perpetuated the realistically based style that had been developed by the Group. In a very few years the "method"—the emen-

dation by Lee Strasberg, Sanford Meisner, Stella Adler, and others of Stanislavski's "system"—became *the* dominant, distinctive American acting style, not only on Broadway but in Hollywood as well. The accolades received by Elia Kazan as the director of postwar theater triumphs A *Streetcar Named Desire* and Arthur Miller's *Death of a Salesman* reinforced the realistic triumph.

All this is to note a paradox in the staging of Tennessee Williams's plays. Apart from the director and cast of his first success, *The Glass Menagerie*, his brilliant interpreters were all schooled in the Method: young actors like Marlon Brando, Kim Hunter, Karl Malden, Geraldine Page, Paul Newman, Ben Gazzara, Eli Wallach, Maureen Stapleton, and, above all, director Kazan. So desperate was Williams to have Kazan continue to direct his plays in the early 1950s that against his better judgment he acquiesced to major revision of the last act of *Cat on a Hot Tin Roof* to meet Kazan's specifications—a decision he later tried to amend by including both the original *and* the Broadway versions in the published text of the play. Undeniably Kazan and Company provided Williams with many powerful, visceral interpretations of his plays, and helped create a distinctive style that might be called "lyrical realism." But the very success of this style obscured the fact that right from the outset of his writing career Williams announced himself as an *anti*realist. Before the adjective "Brechtian" had any currency, Williams had requested literary titles be projected to highlight themes in *The Glass Menagerie* (a request almost never followed in production). A note to the play reads: "Everyone should know nowadays the unimportance of the photographic in art; that truth, life or reality, is an organic thing which the poetic imagination can represent or suggest in essence only through transformation, through changing into other forms than those which merely present appearances." The consistent, consciously metaphoric titles of Williams's plays clearly reveal their poetic reach.

In certain plays, where the playwright clearly feels a stylized productional approach is essential, he explicitly states his antirealistic intentions. *Suddenly Last Summer* is such a play. The fantastic predatory tropical garden/jungle with its tree flowers that suggest body organs (which I have described earlier) "may be as unrealistic," Williams states in his stage directions, "as the decor of a dramatic ballet." Again, neither in the original production, nor in subsequent revivals on stage and television, have directors, designers, and actors taken the productional style as far as Williams suggests. Similarly in *Sweet Bird of Youth* he requests this scene: "The stage is backed by a cyclorama that should give a poetic unity of mood to the several specific settings. There are nonrealistic projections on this "cyc," the most important and constant being a grove of royal palm trees . . . during the daytime scenes the cyclorama projection is a poetic abstraction of semitropical sea and sky. . . . At night it is a palm garden with its branches among the stars." And Williams is equally precise about the importance of aural effects: In the text of *Night of the Iguana* he writes, "This part of the scene, which is played in a 'scherzo' mood, has an accompanying windy obligato on the hilltop . . ." Or this from *Sweet Bird:* "There is nearly always a wind among these tall palm trees, sometimes loud, sometimes just a whisper, and sometimes it blends into a thematic music which will be identified, when it occurs, as 'The Lament.'" And so "the harsh cries and sibilant hissings and thrashing sounds in the garden" called for in *Suddenly Last Summer* reveal Williams's continual sensitivity to the arsenal of nonverbal theatrical tools through which the playwright can intensify his dramatic vision *nonrealistically*.

Recently, some young directors have begun to explore more fully than ever before nonrealistic approaches to staging Williams's plays. One example is the 1999 production at New York Theater Workshop of *A Streetcar Named Desire* directed by Ivo van Hove. Remember when Stanley "clears the table" at Blanche's birthday party by hurling his plate, cup, and saucer to the floor? In this production, Stanley rose from his chair (there was no table, no food, no cake) walked upstage to where a props person had placed a pile of plates and methodically smashed them one after the other. In the famous poker game Mitch, Stanley, Pablo, and Steve played with no table, no cards, no beers, no chips—only words flew back and forth furiously. "My production is an X-ray of what's going on underneath," said the young Flemish director. "Props and furniture to convey the illusion of realism would only distract."

This is not to suggest that this how one should approach staging Williams. On the contrary, one moves away from Williams's theatrical specifications at one's risk. But it does counterbalance the dominant realism we invariably expect from a Williams's production because of the accident of the time of his emergence. Perhaps the answer is given by Hannah in *Night of the Iguana:* Shannon asks, "Yeah, well, you know we—live on two levels, Miss Jelkes, the realistic level and the fantastic level, and which is the real one, really?" To which Hannah replies, "I would say both, Mr. Shannon."

The Unkindest Cut*
or
"I'd rather have a bottle in front of me than a frontal lobotomy."

Jackie Curtis, The Francis Farmer Story

The first consistent technique for psychosurgery was developed by Portuguese neurologist Dr. Antônio Egas Moniz and performed for the first time in 1935, with his colleague, Almeida Lima. Moniz based his operation on the finding, made a few years before, that certain neurotic symptoms induced in chimpanzees could be decreased by cutting the nerve fibers connecting the prefrontal cortex to the rest of the brain. He then developed a technique, called leucotomy, or lobotomy which consisted in severing fiber tracts between the thalamus and the frontal lobes, using a special knife, which he called a leucotome.

His results were considered so good that lobotomy started to be used in several countries as a radical, last-ditch attempt at reducing psychosis and severe depression or violent behavior in patients who could not be treated by any other means (at the time insulin-induced shock and electro-convulsive shock were also in their beginning stages, and drugs were still not available). Thus, lobotomy was used mostly on institutionalized patients who showed chronic agitation, distress, and obsessive-impulsive behavior. Moniz was awarded the Nobel Prize in 1949 for his discovery.

Two American surgeons, Walter Freeman and Watts [no first name given], enthusiastically adopted Moniz's procedure, and improved it. They developed a quick and easy surgical procedure called "trans-orbital leucotomy," which could be done in a few minutes under local anesthesia in a medical office. It consisted of inserting with a slight blow of a hammer, an ice pick instrument through the roof of the orbits, and a rapid sideway movement to sever the fibers. Freeman operated, lectured and taught extensively, popularizing leucotomy as a tool to control undesirable behavior in the nation's insane asylums, hospitals, reformatories, and psychiatric clinics. Thus, in the 1940s and 50s, more than 50,000 persons were subjected to lobotomy all over the world based on very scanty scientific evidence. [Among them: Rosemary Kennedy, JFK's sister; Frances Farmer, Hollywood actress; Rose Williams, Tennessee's sister]. It soon became apparent, however, that although lobotomy was able to curtail several agitated and violent behavior, there were many undesirable effects. Prefrontal lobotomy produced persons without emotions, with reduced drive and initiative, apathetic to everything. Several important higher mental functions were lost, such as socially adequate behavior and the capability to plan actions. With this evidence of widespread abuse and collateral effects, and with the appearance of effective drugs against anxiety and depression, in the 1950s lobotomy and other forms of leucotomy were abandoned and are no longer performed.

. . .

Rose Williams, the once gentle, slender, and beautiful sister of noted American playwright Tennessee Williams, had several nervous breakdowns and was diagnosed as a schizophrenic (some biographers believe that Blanche DuBois, the unforgettable character in *A Streetcar Named Desire* was created after her).[†] After many unsuccessful attempts at therapy, she was finally subjected to a prefrontal lobotomy in 1943, in Washington DC. As in the case of Rosemary Kennedy, the surgery was botched, and Rose was disabled for life. This was a great shock for Tennessee Williams, who was very attached to her, and was probably one of the factors which made him into an alcoholic. The topic of lobotomy became the subject of one of his important plays, *Suddenly Last Summer,* which also had great success as a 1959 film directed by Joseph L. Mankiewicz, and starring Elizabeth Taylor.

In the plot, an aging and domineering Southern matriarch named Violet Venable (played in the film by Katharine Hepburn) hires a young doctor named Cukrowicz (played by Montgomery Clift) whom she wishes to perform a frontal lobotomy on the brain of her niece, Catharine Holly (played by Elizabeth Taylor), because she supposedly has become insane due to her witnessing the mysterious death of Mrs. Venable's son, a decadent poet named Sebastian. In her madness, according to Mrs. Venable, Catharine is telling horrifying stories about her son's death. Dr. Cukrowicz has been asked to observe the girl, in order to deter-

---

*Excerpts from R. M. E. Sabbatini, "The History of Psychosurgery," *Brain & Mind Magazine* July-Aug. 1997.

[†][editor's note] It is, of course, Laura in *The Glass Menagerie,* and not Blanche, that is Williams's most exact portrait of his sister.

mine whether she needs a lobotomy. Mrs. Venable proposes to establish a foundation to finance his work in brain surgery if he complies. At the end of the play, we know the truth, told by Catharine to the physician under the influence of a drug. A dark story of cannibalism and horrible death emerges, but Mrs. Venable still wants to "cut this hideous story out of her brain."

In this play, lobotomy is clearly shown by Williams as a device to suppress the truth and repress weaker people. Influenced by his sister's lobotomy in 1943, Williams expresses a pessimistic view of the voracious-

ness of the universe. The play explores many of the themes which haunted Williams all his life: madness, death, desire, savagery, and the indifference of God. A new social dimension was added to the film (written by Williams himself and Gore Vidal) by showing the awful conditions of the sanatorium, portraying the violence of patient against patient, and the indifference of the staff. Elizabeth Taylor won an Oscar nomination for Best Actress, and the Golden Globe Award for Best Actress for her performance.

EDWARD Albee

Edward Albee (b. 1928) in infancy was adopted by the multimillionaires who owned the chain of Albee theaters. Though surrounded by material comfort, he was an unhappy child who disliked his adoptive parents. The only member of his family with whom he seems to have had an affectionate relationship was his grandmother. His work at school and in college was poor, but he wrote a good deal even as an adolescent; when in 1960 he achieved sudden fame with *The Zoo Story* (written in 1958), he had already written plays for more than a decade. Among his other plays are *The Death of Bessie Smith* (1960), *The Sandbox* (1960), *The American Dream* (1961), *Who's Afraid of Virginia Woolf?* (1962), *A Delicate Balance* (1966), *Seascape* (1975), *The Man Who Had Three Arms* (1983), and *Three Tall Women* (written in 1991 but not performed in the United States until 1994). Three of his plays (*A Delicate Balance, Seascape,* and *Three Tall Women*) have won Pulitzer Prizes. A fourth play, *Who's Afraid of Virginia Woolf?,* was so highly regarded that when the committee refused to give it the Pulitzer Prize, two members of the Pulitzer committee resigned in protest.

COMMENTARY ON *THE SANDBOX*

In the middle of the twentieth century, the dominant American playwrights were Tennessee Williams and Arthur Miller, both of whom wrote plays that were basically realistic. Although Williams's dialogue was sometimes a bit "poetic" and Miller's *Death of a Salesman* included unrealistic, expressionistic elements (chiefly in staging Willy's memories), both of these playwrights were in the line of the great realists of the end of the nineteenth century, Ibsen and Chekhov. Their characters moved in settings (usually living rooms or kitchens) that resembled those in which we live, and the characters themselves were believable.

In 1958 Edward Albee arrived on the dramatic scene with *The Zoo Story,* a very different sort of play. He was indebted to Beckett and Ionesco, the dramatists of the theater of the absurd (see Glossary) and continued in the new mode. For instance, in *The Sandbox* the set does not allow us to pretend that we are eavesdropping on life, peeking through a window into someone's living room. Here is Albee's opening description:

> THE SCENE: *A bare stage, with only the following: Near the footlights, far stage-right, two simple chairs set side by side, facing the audience; near the footlights, far stage-left, a chair facing stage-right with a music stand before it; farther back, and stage-center, slightly elevated and raked, a large child's sandbox with a toy pail and shovel; the background is the sky, which alters from brightest day to deepest night.*

Conceivably this *could* be a realistic setting, for example, the backyard of a house belonging to a musician who has a small child. However, even if when we first saw the set we drew such an improbable conclusion, the first line of the dialogue would force us to revise our view: "Well, here we are; this is the beach." And as we read the play, encountering characters who are called only "the Musician," "the Young Man," "Mommy," "Daddy," and "Grandma," we realize that Albee is not much interested in giving us complex people responding to each other believably. For one thing, what sort of family is this that transacts its business in the presence of the Musician, who clearly is not a member of the family?

Moreover, Albee seems to go out of his way to tell us (as Ibsen and Chekhov and, for that matter, Williams and Miller would not) that we are witnessing *a play,* not life. Thus, Mommy is a sort of theatrical director, telling the Musician when to play and when to stop, and Grandma on occasion speaks directly to the audience and also to a stagehand. One of Grandma's speeches includes the following passage:

> GRANDMA. I'm not complaining. (*She looks up at the sky, shouts to someone off stage.*) Shouldn't it be getting dark now, dear? . . .

As the time for Grandma's death approaches, Albee tells us that "there is an off-stage rumble," almost a parody of the theatrical hokum that one might find in a melodrama.

Our point is simply this: With Albee, America saw the Americanization of a kind of drama that in the preceding decade had been available only in the imported work of such Europeans as Beckett and Ionesco or the English playwright Harold Pinter. Albee, however, differs notably from his European and English predecessors, if for no other reason than that he is partly the dramatist of American life, or, more accurately, the satirist of American life. To say that he is a satirist is another way of saying his characters are unrealistic. One does not encounter realistic characters in the work of, for example, Garry Trudeau or, to go beyond the contemporary, Jonathan Swift. One finds caricature, which is to say that one finds such qualities as a delight in exaggeration and in improbability.

Are we saying that unreality, exaggeration, and improbability are characteristic of Albee's work or are characteristic of the theater of the absurd? We will let Albee have the last word. When the *New York Times Magazine* ran an article about Albee (February 25, 1962), the subject of the theater of the absurd came up. Albee talked about his sort of drama. He dismissed the traditional fare of Broadway as inane and suggested that the truly absurd theater was the popular theater of New York. Unlike the Broadway trash, genuine theater, he said, including the new drama that had come to be called the theater of the absurd, seeks to make us "face up to the human condition as it really is."

THE SANDBOX
Edward Albee

THE PLAYERS

THE YOUNG MAN, 25, *a good looking, well-built boy in a bathing suit*

MOMMY, 55, *a well-dressed, imposing woman*

DADDY, 60, *a small man; gray, thin*

GRANDMA, 86, *a tiny, wizened woman with bright eyes*

THE MUSICIAN, *no particular age, but young would be nice*

NOTE

When, in the course of the play, Mommy and Daddy call each other by these names, there should be no suggestion of regionalism. These names are of empty affection and point up the pre-senility and vacuity of their characters.

THE SCENE

A bare stage, with only the following: Near the footlights, far stage-right, two simple chairs set side by side, facing the audience; near the footlights, far stage-left, a chair facing stage-right with a music stand before it; farther back, and stage-center, slightly elevated and raked, a large child's sandbox with a toy pail and shovel; the background is the sky, which alters from brightest day to deepest night.

At the beginning, it is brightest day, the Young Man is alone on stage, to the rear of the sandbox, and to one side. He is doing calisthenics; he does calisthenics until quite at the very end of the play. These calisthenics, employing the arms only, should suggest the beating and fluttering of wings. The Young Man is, after all, the Angel of Death.

Mommy and Daddy enter from the stage-left, Mommy first.

MOMMY (*motioning to Daddy*). Well, here we are; this is the beach.

DADDY (*whining*). I'm cold.

MOMMY (*dismissing him with a little laugh*). Don't be silly; it's as warm as toast. Look at that nice young man over there: he doesn't think it's cold. (*Waves to the Young Man.*) Hello.

YOUNG MAN (*with an endearing smile*). Hi!

MOMMY (*looking about*). This will do perfectly . . . don't you think so, Daddy? There's sand there . . . and the water beyond. What do you think, Daddy?

DADDY (*vaguely*). Whatever you say, Mommy.

MOMMY (*with the same little laugh*). Well, of course . . . whatever I say. Then, it's settled, is it?

DADDY (*shrugs*). She's *your* mother, not mine.

MOMMY. I know she's my mother. What do you take me for? (*A pause.*) All right, now; let's get on with it. (*She shouts into the wings, stage-left.*) You! Out there! You can come in now.

The Musician enters, seats himself in the chair, stage-left, places music on the music stand, is ready to play. Mommy nods approvingly.

MOMMY. Very nice; very nice. Are you ready, Daddy? Let's go get Grandma.

DADDY. Whatever you say, Mommy.

MOMMY (*leading the way out, stage-left*). Of course, whatever I say. (*To the Musician.*) You can begin now.

The Musician begins playing; Mommy and Daddy exit; the Musician, all the while playing nods to the Young Man.

YOUNG MAN (*with the same endearing smile*). Hi!

After a moment, Mommy and Daddy re-enter, carrying Grandma. She is borne in by their hands under her armpits; she is quite rigid; her legs are drawn up; her feet do not touch the ground; the expression on her ancient face is that of puzzlement and fear.

DADDY. Where do we put her?

MOMMY (*the same little laugh*). Wherever I say, of course. Let me see . . . well . . . all right, over there . . . in the sandbox. (*Pause.*) Well, what are you waiting for Daddy? . . . The sandbox!

Together they carry Grandma over to the sandbox and more or less dump her in.

GRANDMA (*righting herself to a sitting position; her voice a cross between a baby's laugh and cry*). Ahhhhhh! Graaaaa!

DADDY (*dusting himself*). What do we do now?

MOMMY (*to the Musician*). You can stop now. (*The Musician stops.*) (*Back to Daddy.*) What do you mean, what do we do now? We go over there and sit down, of course. (*To the Young Man.*) Hello there.

YOUNG MAN (*again smiling*). Hi!

Mommy and Daddy move to the chairs, stage-right, and sit down. A pause.

GRANDMA (*same as before*). Ahhhhhh! Ahhaaaaaa! Graaaaaa!

DADDY. Do you think . . . do you think she's . . . comfortable?

MOMMY (*impatiently*). How would I know?

DADDY (*pause*). What do we do now?

MOMMY (*as if remembering*). We . . . wait. We . . . sit here . . . and we wait . . . that's what we do.

DADDY (*after a pause*). Shall we talk to each other?

MOMMY (*with that little laugh; picking something off her dress*). Well, *you* can talk, if you want to . . . if you can think of anything to *say* . . . if you can think of anything *new*.

DADDY (*thinks*). No . . . I suppose not.

MOMMY (*with a triumphant laugh*). Of course not!

GRANDMA (*banging the toy shovel against the pail*). Haaaaaa! Ah-haaaaaa!

MOMMY (*out over the audience*). Be quiet, Grandma . . . just be quiet, and wait.

Grandma throws a shovelful of sand at Mommy.

MOMMY (*still out over the audience*). She's throwing sand at me! You stop that, Grandma; you stop throwing sand at Mommy! (*To Daddy.*) She's throwing sand at me.

Daddy looks around at Grandma, who screams at him.

GRANDMA. GRAAAAA!

MOMMY. Don't look at her. Just . . . sit here . . . be very still . . . and wait. (*To the Musician.*) You . . . uh . . . you go ahead and do whatever it is you do.

The Musician plays.
  Mommy and Daddy are fixed, staring out beyond the audience.
  Grandma looks at them, looks at the Musician, looks at the sandbox, throws down the shovel.

GRANDMA. Ah-haaaaaa! Graaaaaa! (*Looks for reaction; gets none. Now . . . directly to the audience.*) Honestly! What a way to treat an old woman! Drag her out of the house . . . stick her in a car . . . bring her out here from the city . . . dump her in a pile of sand . . . and leave her here to set. I'm eighty-six years old! I was married when I was seventeen. To a farmer. He died when I was thirty. (*To the Musician.*) Will you stop that, please?

The Musician stops playing.

I'm a feeble old woman . . . how do you expect anybody to hear me over that peep! peep! peep! (*To herself.*)

There's no respect around here. (*To the Young Man.*) There's no respect around here!

YOUNG MAN (*same smile*). Hi!

GRANDMA (*after a pause, a mild double-take, continues, to the audience*). My husband died when I was thirty (*indicates Mommy*), and I had to raise that big cow over there all by my lonesome. You can imagine what *that* was like. Lordy! (*To the Young Man.*) Where'd they get *you*?

YOUNG MAN. Oh . . . I've been around for a while.

GRANDMA. I'll bet you have! Heh, heh, heh. Will you look at you!

YOUNG MAN (*flexing his muscles*). Isn't that something? (*Continues his calisthenics.*)

GRANDMA. Boy, oh boy; I'll say. Pretty good.

YOUNG MAN (*sweetly*). I'll say.

GRANDMA. Where ya from?

YOUNG MAN. Southern California.

GRANDMA (*nodding*). Figgers, figgers. What's your name, honey?

YOUNG MAN. I don't know . . .

GRANDMA (*to the audience*). Bright, too!

YOUNG MAN. I mean . . . I mean, they haven't given me one yet . . . the studio . . .

GRANDMA (*giving him the once-over*). You don't say . . . you don't say. Well . . . uh, I've got to talk some more . . . don't you go 'way.

YOUNG MAN. Oh, no.

GRANDMA (*turning her attention back to the audience*). Fine; fine. (*Then, once more, back to the Young Man.*) You're . . . you're an actor, hunh?

YOUNG MAN (*beaming*). Yes. I am.

GRANDMA (*to the audience again; shrugs*). I'm smart that way. Anyhow, I had to raise . . . *that* over there all by my lonesome; and what's next to her there . . . that's what she married. Rich? I tell you . . . money, money, money. They took me off the *farm* . . . which was real decent of them . . . and they moved me into the big town house with *them* . . . fixed a nice place for me under the stove . . . gave me an army blanket . . . and my own dish . . . my very own dish! So, what have I got to complain about? Nothing, of course. I'm not complaining. (*She looks up at the sky, shouts to someone offstage.*) Shouldn't it be getting dark now, dear?

The lights dim; night comes on. The Musician begins to play; it becomes deepest night. There are spots on all the players, including the Young Man, who is, of course, continuing his calisthenics.

DADDY (*stirring*). It's nighttime.

MOMMY. Shhhh. Be still . . . wait.

DADDY (*whining*). It's so hot.

MOMMY. Shhhhhh. Be still . . . wait.

GRANDMA (*to herself*). That's better. Night. (*To the Musician.*) Honey, do you play all through this part?

The Musician nods.

Well, keep it nice and soft; that's a good boy.

The Musician nods again; plays softly.

That's nice.

There is an off-stage rumble.

DADDY (*starting*). What was that?

MOMMY (*beginning to weep*). It was nothing.

DADDY. It was . . . it was . . . thunder . . . or a wave breaking . . . or something.

MOMMY (*whispering, through her tears*). It was an off-stage rumble . . . and you know what *that* means . . .

DADDY. I forget. . . .

MOMMY (*barely able to talk*). It means the time has come for poor Grandma . . . and I can't bear it!

DADDY (*vacantly*). I . . . I suppose you've got to be brave.

GRANDMA (*mocking*). That's right, kid; be brave. You'll bear up; you'll get over it.

(*Another off-stage rumble . . . louder.*)

MOMMY. Ohhhhhhhhhh . . . poor Grandma . . . poor Grandma. . . .

GRANDMA (*to Mommy*). I'm fine! I'm all right! It hasn't happened yet!

A violent off-stage rumble. All the lights go out, save the spot on the Young Man; the Musician stops playing.

MOMMY. Ohhhhhhhhhh. . . . Ohhhhhhhhhh. . . .

Silence.

GRANDMA. Don't put the lights up yet . . . I'm not ready; I'm not quite ready. (*Silence.*) All right, dear . . . I'm about done.

The lights come up again, to brightest day; the Musician begins to play. Grandma is discovered, still in the sandbox, lying on her side, propped up on an elbow, half covered, busily shoveling sand over herself.

GRANDMA (*muttering*). I don't know how I'm supposed to do anything with this goddam toy shovel. . . .

DADDY. Mommy! It's daylight!

MOMMY (*brightly*). So it is! Well! Our long night is over. We must put away our tears, take off our mourning . . . and face the future. It's our duty.

GRANDMA (*still shoveling; mimicking*). . . . take off our mourning . . . face the future. . . . Lordy!

Mommy and Daddy rise, stretch. Mommy waves to the young man.

YOUNG MAN (*with that smile*). Hi!

Grandma plays dead. (!) Mommy and Daddy go over to look at her; she is a little more than half buried in the sand; the toy shovel is in her hands, which are crossed on her breast.

MOMMY (*before the sandbox; shaking her head*). Lovely! It's . . . it's hard to be sad . . . she looks . . . so happy. (*With pride and conviction.*) It pays to do things well. (*To the Musician.*) All right, you can stop now, if you want to. I mean, stay around for a swim, or something; it's all right with us. (*She sighs heavily.*) Well, Daddy . . . off we go.

DADDY. Brave Mommy!

MOMMY. Brave Daddy!

They exit, stage-left.

GRANDMA (*after they leave; lying quite still*). It pays to do things well. . . . Boy, oh boy! (*She tries to sit up*) . . . well, kids . . . (*but she finds she can't*) . . . I . . . I can't get up, I . . . I can't move. . . .

The Young Man stops his calisthenics, nods to the Musician, walks over to Grandma, kneels down by the sandbox.

GRANDMA. I . . . can't move. . . .

YOUNG MAN. Shhhhh . . . be very still. . . .

GRANDMA. I . . . I can't move. . . .

YOUNG MAN. Uh . . . ma'am; I . . . I have a line here.

GRANDMA. Oh, I'm sorry, sweetie; you go right ahead.

YOUNG MAN. I am . . . uh . . .

GRANDMA. Take your time, dear.

YOUNG MAN (*prepares; delivers the line like a real amateur*). I am the Angel of Death. I am . . . uh . . . I am come for you.

GRANDMA. What . . . wha . . . (*Then, with resignation.*) . . . ohhhh . . . ohhhh, I see.

The Young Man bends over, kisses Grandma gently on the forehead.

GRANDMA (*her eyes closed, her hands folded on her breast again, the shovel between her hands, a sweet smile on her face*). Well . . . that was very nice, dear . . .

YOUNG MAN (*still kneeling*). Shhhhhh . . . be still. . . .

GRANDMA. What I mean was . . . you did that very well, dear. . . .

YOUNG MAN (*blushing*) . . . oh . . .

GRANDMA. No; I mean it. You've got that . . . you've got a quality.

YOUNG MAN (*with his endearing smile*). Oh . . . thank you; thank you very much . . . ma'am.

GRANDMA (*slowly; softly—as the Young Man puts his hands on top of Grandma's*). You're . . . you're welcome . . . dear.

Tableau. The Musician continues to play as the curtain slowly comes down.

CURTAIN

TOPICS FOR CRITICAL THINKING AND WRITING

The Play on the PAGE

1. In a sentence, characterize Mommy, and in another sentence characterize Daddy. By the way, why doesn't Albee give them names?

2. Of the four speaking characters in the play, which do you find the most sympathetic? Exactly why? Set forth your answer, with supporting evidence, in a paragraph, or perhaps in two paragraphs—the first devoted to the three less sympathetic characters and the second devoted to the most sympathetic character.

3. What do you make of the sandbox? Is it an image of the grave, with suggestions that life is meaningless and sterile? Alternatively, is it an image only of the sterility of life in the United States in the second half of the twentieth century? Does the fact that Grandma was married to a farmer suggest an alternative way of life? Explain.

4. In a longer play, *The American Dream*, Albee uses the same four characters that he uses in *The Sandbox*. Of *The American Dream* he wrote,

   > The play . . . is a condemnation of complacency, cruelty, emasculation and vacuity; it is a stand against the fiction that everything in this slipping land of ours is peachy-keen.

   To what extent does this statement help you to understand (and to enjoy) *The Sandbox*?

5. In the *New York Times Magazine* (February 25, 1962), Albee protested against the view that his plays, and others of the so-called theater of the absurd, are depressing. He includes a quotation from Martin Esslin's book *The Theatre of the Absurd*:

   > Ultimately . . . the Theatre of the Absurd does not reflect despair or a return to dark irrational forces but expresses modern man's endeavor to come to terms with the world in which he lives. It attempts to make him face up to the human condition as it really is, to free him from illusions that are bound to cause constant maladjustment and disappointment. . . . For the dignity of man lies in his reality in all its senselessness; to accept it freely, without fear, without illusions—and to laugh at it.

   In what ways do you find this statement helpful? In what ways do you find it not helpful? Explain.

6. In an interview in 1979, Albee said,

   > I like to think people are forced to rethink some things as a result of the experience of seeing some of my plays, that they are not left exactly the way they came in.

   Has reading *The Sandbox* forced you to rethink anything? If so, what?

The Play on the STAGE

7. Why, in your opinion, does Albee insist in the first stage direction that the scene be "a bare stage"? Do you think a realistic setting would in some way diminish the play? Explain.

8. Albee specifies in the opening stage direction that the Young Man "is doing calisthenics; he does calisthenics until quite at the very end of the play." Some viewers and readers who visualize the play find that the calisthenics distract from the lines of the play. If you were directing the play, might you neglect Albee's instruction? If you did omit the calisthenics, what would you have the Young Man do?

9. The Musician plays under two circumstances—when he is asked by Mommy and when he plays unasked. Would you distinguish between these two circumstances by using different kinds of music? What kind or kinds of music would you use?

10. In a stage direction Albee tells us that when the Young Man delivers his big line ("I am the Angel of Death"), he "delivers the line like a real amateur." Furthermore, the Young Man muffs his next line ("I am . . . uh . . . I come for you"). Exactly how would you speak these two sentences and with what (if any) gestures?

A Context for *THE SANDBOX*

EDWARD ALBEE
Interview

[William Flanagan conducted this interview with Albee. It was originally published in *Paris Review*.]

Flanagan: One of your most recent plays was an adaptation of James Purdy's novel Malcolm. *It had as close to one hundred percent bad notices as a play could get. The resultant commercial catastrophe and quick closing of the play apart, how does this affect your own feeling about the piece itself?*

Albee: I see you're starting with the hits. Well, I retain for all my plays, I suppose, a certain amount of enthusiasm. I don't feel intimidated by either the unanimously bad press that *Malcolm* got or the unanimously good press that some of the other plays have received. I haven't changed my feeling about *Malcolm*. I liked doing the adaptation of Purdy's book. I had a number of quarrels with the production, but then I usually end up with quarrels about all of my plays. With the possible exception of the little play *The Sandbox*, which takes thirteen minutes to perform, I don't think anything I've done has worked out to perfection.

While it doesn't necessarily change your feeling, does the unanimously bad critical response open questions in your mind?

I imagine that if we had a college of criticism in this country whose opinions more closely approximated the value of the works of art inspected, it might; but as often as not, I find relatively little relationship between the work of art and the immediate critical response it gets. Every writer's got to pay some attention, I suppose, to what his critics say because theirs is a re-

flection of what the audience feels about his work. And a playwright, especially a playwright whose work deals very directly with an audience, perhaps he should pay some attention to the nature of the audience response—not necessarily to learn anything about his craft, but as often as not merely to find out about the temper of the time, what is being tolerated, what is being permitted.

. . .

Actually, the final evaluation of a play has nothing to do with immediate audience or critical response. The playwright, along with any writer, composer, painter in this society, has got to have a terribly private view of his own value, of his own work. He's got to listen to his own voice primarily. He's got to watch out for fads, for what might be called the critical aesthetics.

. . .

Since I guess it's fairly imbecilic to ask a writer what he considers to be his best work or his most important work, perhaps I could ask you this question: which of all of your plays do you feel closest to?

Well, naturally the one I'm writing right now.

Well, excepting that.

I don't know.

There's no one that you feel any special fondness for?

I'm terribly fond of *The Sandbox*. I think it's an absolutely beautiful, lovely, perfect play.

AFRICAN AMERICAN THEATER

African American drama has its roots both in Africa and in America. In Africa, public performances of dance, mime, and ritual served specific functions, including political satire, a celebration of social events, and an observance of religious ceremonies. Africans have traditionally celebrated life and death in theater ritual. In the nineteenth century, when Africans were transported to North America as slaves, they brought with them a range of songs and oral drama. Entertainments comprising song, dance, folktales, and music were often performed for white masters and grew into the minstrel shows, which remained popular for many decades. In these shows, both white and black actors appeared in blackface with exaggerated features, and black personalities were stereotyped. Although post–civil rights thinking criticizes minstrel characterizations as demeaning to blacks, these shows provided a venue for black performers and writers. The audiences were blacks as well as whites, although in the South audiences were segregated, blacks being confined to the balconies or back rows of theaters.

The first African American drama company, the African Theatre, was founded in 1821 in New York City by a former West Indian sailor named William Henry Brown. Most of the scripts were adaptations of existing plays. For example, the company opened with a cut version of Shakespeare's *Richard III*. However, Brown was also a playwright, and his *The Drama of King Shotoway* (1823), concerning a rebellion by the Caribs on the Island of St. Vincent, is believed to be the first play written and performed by African Americans. From the African Theatre, too, came the internationally praised Shakespearean actor, Ira Aldridge.

William Wells Brown (no relation to William Henry Brown) was an escaped slave who wrote two antislavery plays, *Experience: Or How to Give a Northern Man a Backbone* (1856) and *The Escape: Or a Leap for Freedom* (1858). *Experience* is chiefly a satire on a northern preacher, and *The Escape* is a melodrama indicting slavery and exposing the South as a corrupt society. Brown read the plays on northern Abolitionist platforms, but they did not receive production in his lifetime. Other serious drama written by blacks includes William Edgar Easton's plays on the Haitian revolution and Scott Joplin's opera *Treemonisha* (written in 1911 but unproduced until 1972). W.E.B. Du Bois—the civil rights leader who cofounded the NAACP and who edited an important journal, *The Crisis*—urged the formation of theater companies to present plays "about us, for us, and near us." *The Crisis* and other influential black journals sponsored playwriting contests and published prizewinning entries. Willis Richardson's one-act *The Chip Woman's Fortune* (1923) was the earliest nonmusical black play seen on Broadway. The play celebrates the black family, but it represents hypocritical blacks as well as racist whites as obstacles to black happiness. By the early twentieth century, a number of black theater companies had been established around the nation and black actors began appearing in Broadway plays, but only in roles calling for blacks. Several plays by white writers offered strong black characters, most notably Eugene O'Neill's *The Emperor Jones* (see page 715).

A list of black playwrights from the late nineteenth and early twentieth centuries includes Angelina Weld Grimke, Alice Dunbar-Nelson, Bob Cole, Bert Williams, Joseph Seamon Cotter, Wallace Thurman, and Mary Burrill. Much of their output protested racism, violence against black communities, difficult working conditions for blacks, and the economic disparities between white and black workers. On the other hand, *Shuffle Along* (1921), with music and lyrics by Noble Sissle and Eubie Blake, was a genial musical that aimed chiefly to entertain, not to protest. Still, it is important in the history of drama because it presented to a largely white audience images of blacks who were human beings with feelings, not just comic stereotypes. It played to great acclaim in Washington, D.C., Philadelphia, and New York.

The years 1920–1930, now called the Harlem Renaissance, brought an exciting flowering of black literature extending well beyond the physical boundaries of Harlem. Of special note are plays by Langston Hughes, Theodore Ward, May Miller, Hall Johnson, Maritia Bonner, Eulalie Spence, and Georgia Douglas Johnson.

The American Negro Theater (A.N.T.), established in New York in 1940 by Abram Hill, Frederick O'Neal, and other writer/directors, emphasized training and production. A.N.T. nurtured much talent, including Harry Belafonte, Sidney Poitier, Ruby Dee, and Ossie Davis. After World War II, as the civil rights movement began to gain momentum, many black playwrights found recognition. Among a list too long to cite here, we call special attention to Louis Peterson, Alice Childress, Loften Mitchell, Lorraine Hansberry (*A Raisin in the Sun,* 1959, won the New York Drama Critics' Circle Award), Amiri Baraka, James Baldwin, Lonnie Elder, Charles Gordone, Ed Bullins, Adrienne Kennedy (see page 925), Douglas Turner Ward (who founded the Negro Ensemble Company in 1968), Barbara Ann Tear, and Ron Milner. The most talented black dramatists of the militant 1960s largely turned their backs on white audiences and, in effect, wrote plays aimed at showing blacks that they—not their white oppressors—must change in the sense that they must cease to accept the myths that whites had created. Among many strong scripts in this category are *Dutchman* (1964), a one-act play by LeRoi Jones (Imamu Amiri Baraka), and *The Electronic Nigger* (1968) by Ed Bullins.

By the mid-1970s, black dramatists were exploring a full range of modes and themes. As Bullins stated, "the literature has changed from a social-protest oriented form to one of a dialectical nature among black people—Black dialectics—and this new thrust has two main branches, the dialectic of change and the dialectic of experience." In general, more and more opportunities for black writers, actors, and directors became available. For example, Joseph Papp, founder of the New York Shakespeare Festival, cast black performers in roles previously taken by whites. Notable playwrights of the contemporary period include Ntozake Shange, Charles Fuller (who won the Pulitzer Prize for his 1981 *A Soldier's Play*), Sonia Sanchez, Kathleen Collins, August Wilson (see p. 1313—two of Wilson's plays have won Pulitzer Prizes), and Anna Deavere Smith (see p. 1359). Students will find a number of excellent references and anthologies for continuing an investigation of African American drama. To start, we recommend:

Bigsby, W. E. *A Critical Introduction to Twentieth-Century American Drama.* Volume I (1982).

Brown-Guillory, Elizabeth. *Their Place on the Stage: Black Women Playwrights in America* (1988).

Bullins, Ed, ed. *The New Lafayette Theatre Presents: Plays with Aesthetic Comments by 6 Black Playwrights* (1974).

Hatch, James V., and Ted Shine. *Black Theater, U.S.A.: Forty-five Plays by Black Americans, 1847–1974* (1974).

Hay, Samuel A. *African-American Theatre: A Historical and Critical Analysis* (1994).

Hill, Earl, ed. *The Theater of Black Americans* (1980).

Keyssar, Helene. *The Curtain and the Veil: Strategies in Black Drama* (1981).

Oliver, Clinton, ed. *Contemporary Black Drama* (1971).

Sanders, Leslie Catherine. *The Development of Black Theatre in America* (1988).

Wilkerson, Margaret B., ed. *Nine Plays by Black Women* (1986).

Photo Essay:
African Americans on the Stage

In the section on "African American Theater" (pages 917–18), we sketch a history of some black theater companies and we mention some major black dramatists, and in the Commentary on Eugene O'Neill's *The Emperor Jones*, we mention the stereotypical roles that white dramatists presented of blacks. Otherwise, we have not discussed black performers. In the following pages we look briefly at blacks in black roles and in white roles.

Many thick (in two senses of the word) books have been written about race. In the late nineteenth century, one finds talk about "the Germanic race," "the Irish race," and so forth. In that context, race is perceived as some sort of complex of distinctive mental traits inherited by members of a group. Today race is usually regarded as a matter of the color of the skin, the color and form of hair, and the shape of the nose. Given this view, there are three races, Caucasoid (pinkish skin, light blond to dark brown hair, high nosebridge); Mongoloid (skin saffron to reddish brown, hair dark and straight, nosebridge usually low or medium); Negroid (skin brown to brown-black, dark hair, usually kinky, nosebridge low and nostrils broad). The genes accounting for any hereditary distinctions among these three races are very few compared to the number of genes common to all human beings. Race, then, is yet another social construction of reality, a way of making sense of the world around us. It has been a very harmful construction, yet it has also been a source of pride. Much depends on who is defining and constructing the category and for what purposes.

In the United States, to talk of race in connection with theater has chiefly been to talk of white and black theater, though in the last few decades we have all be-

come increasingly aware of Asian American theater. Earlier in the book we comment briefly on the history of African American theater (pages 917–18) and on images of African Americans presented in the dramas of whites (page 716). Here we talk chiefly about black actors and the roles that have been available to them.

First, we want to mention that unless you are attending a predominantly black institution, you probably will not see many black actors or black plays. Whites have become increasingly uneasy about directing productions of plays by and about blacks, and many schools do not have a black director on the faculty. Occasionally, an outside director is invited to direct a campus production, but some black directors will not accept invitations to direct a black play. Stanley Williams, director of the Lorraine Hansberry Theatre in San Francisco, says of such invitations, "That's colonization. I'm the field nigger, and I'm being called up to the big house. I'm not interested in that" (quoted in *American Theatre*, March 1996, p. 16).

Whether or not you get to see black plays on your campus, there is a thriving black drama, and there are talented black actors who perform not only in roles that call for blacks but also in other roles.

Ira Aldridge (c. 1806–1867), an African American actor who began his theatrical career with the African Grove Theatre in New York, soon found he could not get adequate roles in the United States, and at the age of seventeen or so he went to England, where he achieved fame, especially as a Shakespearean actor. He played Othello (see page 923), as well as another black part that Shakespeare wrote, Aaron (the Moor in *Titus Andronicus*), but Aldridge also played white roles, notably Lear, Macbeth, and Shylock, in white-face.

Despite Aldridge's fame in England and in Europe, he had no successors. For decades after his death, the role of Othello in England as well as in the United States was almost always played by a white actor. In 1930, however, Paul Robeson (1898–1976) made theatrical history when he played Othello in London (see page 923). The reviews were highly favorable, and there was some talk about bringing the production to the United States, but there was more talk about whether American audiences would tolerate the sight of a black man—a real black man, not a white man wearing blackface—kissing and then killing a white woman. Not until 1942 did Robeson play Othello in the United States, and then it was only in a summer stock production in Cambridge, Boston, and Providence. The reviews again were enthusiastic, and no unpleasant noises were heard, so in 1943 Robeson opened on Broadway in a production that ran an astounding 296 performances. The previous record for a New York Othello was 57 performances. It should be added that several reviewers said that Robeson was the first black to play Othello in the United States. In fact, he had been preceded by at least six performers in the late nineteenth century and the early twentieth, but between 1910 and 1943 blacks had been so absent from Broadway—except in minor stereotyped roles—that all memory of serious black performers had been erased.

Despite Robeson's success in the role, Othello was played chiefly by whites for the next twenty years or so. The civil rights movement, however, heightened everyone's awareness of discrimination against blacks, and in the 1960s blacks increasingly played Othello, though whites continued to play it, too. For instance, Laurence Olivier played the part on stage in 1964 and then in a film version (1966) of his stage performance. Although most white actors had played the role pretty much as a white man with a dark skin, Olivier—perhaps responding to the period's emphasis on negritude—gave Othello a distinctive behavior, a sway in his walk and a lilt in his voice. The reviews were mixed, but today (judging from classroom responses) most viewers are disturbed by what they see as racial stereotyping. In any case, Olivier may have been the last white to play the role, at least in the English-speaking world.

African American actors, of course, cannot subsist on the relatively few available black roles. All or virtually all black theater departments in colleges and universities agree that their students should be immersed in classical drama—let's say the Greeks through Tennessee Williams and Arthur Miller—but questions arise as to whether at least some plays should be interpreted in a distinctive black way. To begin dealing with this issue, we give a quotation from an article in which Philip Kolin discusses black productions of a white play, Tennessee Williams's The Glass Menagerie. Most of the productions made no changes in the text, but a few made some small changes, for instance, altering Amanda's membership in the DAR to membership in a black sorority, the Delta Club. Kolin says that "these nontraditional productions address four key issues":

1. Williams's play, as done by African American companies, renegotiates the question of universality as a team of Western aesthetics.
2. The language of ownership, often used in relation to plays and playwrights is also problematized. As Ruby Dee affirms, "I feel Tennessee belongs to me, too."
3. Black and multi-ethnic productions of The Glass Menagerie . . . liberate the subtext from racially-imposed constraints. . . .
4. . . . White theatre history has been, a priori, the standard by which Williams's productions are measured. . . . All Amandas are held up to the performances of Laurette Taylor—the original Amanda—or Helen Hayes, or Maureen Stapleton, or Joanne Woodward. Black productions of The Glass Menagerie, therefore, free the play from restrictive so-called "prototypical" or "seminal" interpretations of individual roles by white actors.

"BLACK AND MULTI-RACIAL PRODUCTIONS OF TENNESSEE WILLIAMS'S THE GLASS MENAGERIE," JOURNAL OF DRAMATIC THEORY AND CRITICISM 9 (1995): 97–98.

According to Kolin, the first black production of the play was given at Howard University in 1947, less than two years after the Broadway premiere, and a second black production was given in 1950 at the University of Iowa. The first interracial production was given in 1965 at the Karamu Theatre in Cleveland, Ohio, where the Wingfields were played by African Americans and Jim (the Gentleman Caller) was played by a white (see page 923). (Karamu House—Swahili for "a place of enjoyment for all"—holds a distinguished place in the history of multiracial theatrical activity. The adult theater group, formed in 1921, originally was called the Gilpin Players, in honor of Charles Gilpin, the African American who created the title role in Eugene O'Neill's The Emperor Jones. See page 716.)

According to Kolin, none of the reviewers of the Karamu production of *The Glass Menagerie* addressed the issue of a white man calling on a black woman. A question: Should the reviewers have addressed this issue, or were they right to ignore it?

The next interracial production was performed by the Inner City Cultural Center in Los Angeles in 1987, but the audience was unaware that the production was interracial. All of the characters were white, but Jim O'Connor was played by a black actor (Paul Winfield) with "light-skin make-up with an uplifted Irish nose and a red wig" (see page 924). Reviewers praised Winfield and did raise the issue of the makeup. Kolin remarks, interestingly, "Even in such a disguise Winfield earned high honors." What is interesting about the remark is this: No one would have said of a white actor performing Othello in blackface that "even in such a disguise" he was effective. It has always been assumed that whites would put on the makeup appropriate to the role, whether the role was Othello or Charlie Chan.

In a moment we will continue this brief discussion of makeup, but before we leave productions of *The Glass Menagerie*, we should say that (judging from Kolin's article) black productions are prompted by people who believe that the play speaks to blacks as well as to whites. Very few black directors sought to give a special black twist to the play, but one twist is so interesting that it should be mentioned. When Whitney J. LeBlanc directed it at the Lorraine Hansberry Theatre in 1991, the picture of the missing father was of a white man. LeBlanc used the picture in order to say something about the historic relationship between whites and blacks: "We've always been abandoned by fathers ever since miscegenation" (113).

We can now briefly return to the question of African American actors in roles that are identifiably white, such as a king of England. Can we have a black King Lear with, for example, a white daughter and two black daughters? If open casting (also called nontraditional casting or colorblind casting) is taken seriously, what effect is produced by having a Lear with, for example, an Asian daughter, a black daughter, and a white or Latino daughter? When the great black actor Canada Lee in 1946 played Bosola in a Jacobean tragedy, *The Duchess of Malfi* (c. 1613), he wore whiteface (really a sort of pinkish greasepaint) and gloves, working within the traditional idea that acting is a matter of impersonation, and theatrical impersonation usually involves makeup. (See page 924.) If Lee had appeared without makeup, critics doubtless would have said that he shattered the dramatic illusion. On the other hand, the concept of dramatic illusion is very fragile—the audience of course always knows that the actor is an actor, not the role he or she is playing. Stage actors perform chiefly with their voices and their bodies (as opposed to movie actors, who perform chiefly with their faces), and most theatergoers know that with a great actor, costume and makeup are relatively unimportant. On several occasions we have seen performers—John Gielgud, Laurence Olivier, and Michael Redgrave come to mind—in street clothes perform scenes from Shakespeare, and the effect was staggering. No hearer could have wished for costumes and makeup. On the other hand, we are talking about actors of the highest rank, speaking lines that have endured for centuries. Whether lesser actors can be as compelling when they speak lesser lines is another question. With a major actress such as Ruby Dee, who played Amanda in a black production, the color or the makeup probably doesn't matter, but, again, with less skilled actors makeup may be useful. Still, it is now an established convention that actors of color not whiten their faces, and audiences seem able to accept the convention of, for example, a black King Henry V of England (see page 924) or a black Cordelia, even if the actor playing Lear is white. Just as Desdemona "saw Othello's visage in his mind," if we are properly attuned we can probably ignore a mere matter of pigmentation. Certainly an audience that is used to seeing multicultural productions, such as those that Joseph Papp staged in New York, grew accustomed to color-blind casting. Especially in plays that are not essentially realistic, experience indicates that an audience can disregard race in the casting.

However, what about casting African Americans in a play that is largely realistic, specifically in *Death of a Salesman*? Henry Louis Gates, rejecting the idea that today black artists must work with distinctively black material, in 1994 said in an interview in *Time*, "Discarding the anxieties of a bygone era, [black artists today] presume the universality of the black experience." One understands what Gates means, and one is not calling into question the competence of black actors, but when black actors perform in *Death of a Salesman*, do they somehow transform the play? Alternatively, does the play somehow overwhelm them?

According to Brenda Murphy in *Miller: Death of a Salesman* (1995), an all-black production at the Center Stage, in Baltimore in 1972, left the critics rather cool.

"Willy Loman's values," Mel Gussow wrote in the *New York Times*, "are white values—the elevation of personality, congeniality, conformity, salesmanship in the sense of selling oneself." In the all-black production, Gussow said, "Willy becomes a black man embracing the white world as an example to be emulated" (quoted in Murphy, page 86). Two years later an integrated production was scheduled for the Circle in the Square Theatre in New York, with Charley played by a black. Miller was uneasy when he learned of the plan. He cautioned that color-blind casting might work if, for example, Biff were black and Happy were white—that is, if it were evident that race was irrelevant. However, in an essentially realistic play, Miller thought that to cast Charley as the sole black would lead the audience to assume that Willy dares to have a black man for his best friend in the 1930s. The critics were cool toward the production, which was staged in 1975.

The question, again, seems to be this: If the play is chiefly realistic, can a theater audience ignore the pigmentation of the actors? We hope so. However, if not yet, perhaps theater can play a role in helping to bring about a society in which pigmentation is scarcely noticed.

■ SUGGESTED REFERENCES

Most of the titles listed at the end of "African American Theater" (page 918) are relevant here. In addition, see Martin B. Duberman, *Paul Robeson* (1989); Herbert Marshall and Mildred Stock, *Ira Aldridge, The Negro Tragedian* (1958); and Kenneth Tynan, *Othello by William Shakespeare: The National Theatre Production* (1966, on Olivier's Othello).

Ira Aldridge, unable to find sufficient work as a Shakespearean actor in the United States, left for England and spent the rest of his life there and in Europe. He was especially famous for his Othello (shown here), but he performed other roles, too, including Shylock, Macbeth, and Lear. When performing white roles, in keeping with the prevailing realism of the theater of the period, he wore white makeup and a wig.

Paul Robeson, an African American who had achieved fame as an athlete, as a singer, and as an actor—notably in Eugene O'Neill's *The Emperor Jones*—was invited to play the role of Othello at Stratford-upon-Avon in 1930. His performance was enthusiastically received—the reviewer in the London *Morning Post* said, "There has been no Othello on our stage for forty years to compare with his dignity, simplicity, and true passion"—but American producers were unsure about how American audiences would respond to the sight of a black actor kissing a white woman. Not until 1942 could they be persuaded to let Robeson play the role in the United States. The favorable response to the 1942 production led to another production with Robeson in 1943, which was immediately successful.

In 1965 the Karamu Theatre in Cleveland, Ohio staged Tennessee Williams's *The Glass Menagerie* with an integrated cast: The Wingfield family was black and Jim O'Connor (the Gentleman Caller) was white. The play had been done fairly often by all-black companies, but the use of one white player made the production unusual.

Paul Winfield, an African American actor, played the role of Jim O'Connor in whiteface in a 1967 production by the Inner City Cultural Center in Los Angeles. Audiences apparently were unaware that the cast was integrated. The Inner City Cultural Center has been an early innovator in the area now known as "nontraditional" casting. It is highly unusual, however, for a black actor today to perform in whiteface.

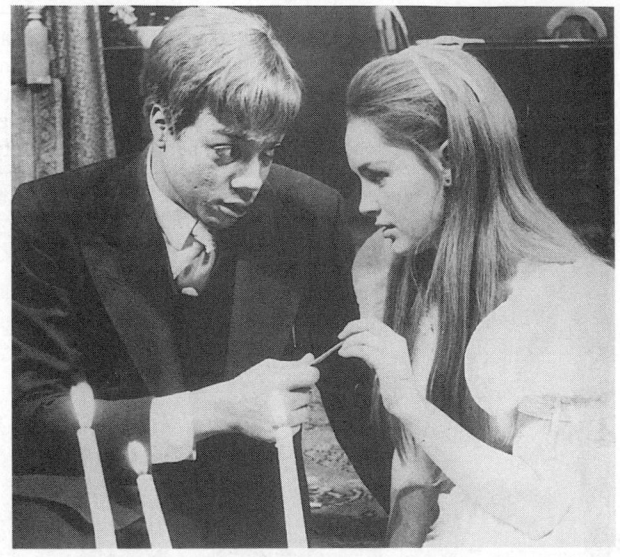

Canada Lee, a black actor (at the left), in 1946 played the villainous Bosola in John Webster's tragedy, *The Duchess of Malfi.* Doubtless the chief reason for the makeup was the idea that in appearance performers should resemble their roles, but a second reason may possibly have been that if Lee had appeared without white makeup the audience might have mistakenly assumed that the character in the play was black, or that the director was sending a message suggesting that blacks are villainous.

Robert Hooks played Henry V in Joseph Papp's production at the New York Shakespeare Festival's Mobile Theatre in 1965. As the founder of a theatrical enterprise in a highly multicultural city, Papp could hardly ignore the talent of people of color. His principle was to choose the best actors he could find, regardless of color. Although a few reviewers objected that spectators cannot ignore the incongruity of, say, a black actor in a decidedly white role, most viewers did not share the objection.

ADRIENNE Kennedy

Adrienne Hawkins Kennedy, born into a middle-class family in 1931, grew up in an integrated neighborhood in Cleveland, Ohio, enjoying the rich cultural heritage of African Americans, Italians, Jews, and Poles. During her childhood she made frequent trips to visit her grandparents in rural Georgia. Her father, the executive secretary of the YMCA, took her to a performance of the great singer-actor Paul Robeson, and he read her poems from the celebrated black poet Paul Laurence Dunbar. Her mother, a teacher, taught her to read at age three and told her stories of her life in Georgia. When she was sixteen she saw a production of Williams's *The Glass Menagerie* at Karamu Playhouse in Cleveland, which instilled in her a fascination with theater. She loved literature in high school and received her bachelor's degree from Ohio State University, majoring in education but chiefly interested in English. She married Joseph Kennedy in 1953, moved to New York with him when he went there for graduate study, and used this opportunity to study creative writing at Columbia University, the American Theater Wing, and at the Circle-in-the-Square School with Edward Albee. The 1964 production of *Funnyhouse of a Negro* launched a prolific career in theater including the plays *The Owl Answers* (1965), *A Rat's Mass* (1966), *Sun* (commissioned by the Royal Court Theater in London, 1968), *A Lesson in Dead Language* (1970), *A Movie Star Has to Star in Black and White* (1976), and adaptations of Euripides's *Electra* and *Orestes* (1980). In 1987 she published an experimental autobiography entitled *People Who Led to My Plays;* through journal entries and photographs Kennedy explores the rich, eclectic influences on her life as a writer. In it she recalls moments of discrimination she experienced in her youth: riding the train to Georgia in Jim Crow cars, a teacher telling her she could not become a journalist because of her color, and the dorms at Ohio State where white dorm mates "were determined to subjugate the Negro girls." Her plays have been produced in major theaters in the United States and Europe and several have been translated into Spanish, French, Danish, German, and Portuguese. Known for her imagistic, symbolic plays, Kennedy offers unusual insights into the human, particularly American, experience and examines how that experience has been informed by the history of race in this country. Her more recent plays include *The Alexander Plays* (1992) and *Sleep Deprivation Chamber* (1966), which she co-wrote with her son, Adam P. Kennedy. In 1990 she published her first novel, *Deadly Triplets: A Theater and Mystery Journal.*

■■■■■■■■■■■■■■

COMMENTARY ON *FUNNYHOUSE OF A NEGRO*

The inspiration for *Funnyhouse of a Negro* came from an extensive trip Kennedy and her husband took through Europe and Africa. She was confronted for the first time by the remnants of the British Empire, epitomized for her by an enormous statue of Queen Victoria at Buckingham Palace and the legacy of colonialism in West Africa. During her visit, Patrice Lumumba, the first premier of the Republic of Congo, was murdered. She began writing the play while in West Africa, integrating and juxtaposing various events and images into the text.

The play's title comes from the funnyhouse of Euclid Beach, an old-style amusement park in Cleveland, which featured two life-size white clownlike figures in large glass boxes perched on either side of a hall of mirrors. The figures, arms outstretched, laughed hysterically while they bounced and bobbed in a menacing fashion. Patrons walked through the hall, seeing their images as distorted giants, figures with enormous torsos and tiny legs, or grotesquely overweight figures while the sound of cruel laughter played in the background.

Unlike most of the plays in this anthology, *Funnyhouse of a Negro* has no conventional plot, but is instead a dreamlike rendering of the identity crisis and confusion of a young, impressionable African American woman named Sarah. Her internal conflict is personified by multiple selves that appear and disappear in the course of the play, much as the self-images of someone in a hall of mirrors come into focus and fade from view as one moves through the reflective maze.

Kennedy was greatly influenced by the time she spent in West Africa. In a statement published in *Inter-*

view with Contemporary Women Playwrights (edited by Kathleen Betsko and Rachel Koenig), Kennedy says,

> It was a tremendous turning point. I was exactly twenty-nine when I wrote *Funnyhouse of a Negro* . . . I would say almost every image in *Funnyhouse* took form while I was in West Africa where I became aware of masks. I lived in Ghana at a most fortunate time. Ghana had just won its freedom. It was wonderful to see that liberation. . . . I think the main thing was that I discovered a strength in being a black person and a connection to West Africa.

Most of Kennedy's writing is grounded in personal autobiography. She draws on subconscious dream imagery, employs a language that is rhythmic and deliberately repetitious, and fills her work with metaphor and symbols. The multiple-personaed Sarah is torn between her loyalty and guilt, not knowing which way to turn in her black/white world. On one level she is full of self-loathing because of her racially mixed heritage. On another the play shows us the disturbing, shocking consequences of repression stemming from the history of colonialism.

Funnyhouse of a Negro is full of violence—fear of rape, suicide, multiple images of death, and a stage curtain that Kennedy describes in her graphic stage directions as "gnawed by rats." The play allows the audience to confront this violence, to come to terms with the painful and damaging history of race in our culture. Part of this confrontation of violence includes dealing with the violence inherent in the racist word *nigger*. Kennedy has documented her own personal struggle in dealing with this word. In the copy of the script she gave to the play's first director, Michael Kahn, she had deleted it. Late in the rehearsal process, Kahn asked her for the original script and permission to deal with the word in performance. Edward Albee, who ran the writing workshop in which Kennedy developed the play, encouraged her to put the difficult word back in the script. He stated, "A playwright is someone who lets her guts hang out on the stage and that's what you've done in this play" (Bryant-Jackson). Thus violence is apparent in its language as well as its imagery, creating a vivid, tortuous dream world for readers and audiences alike.

FUNNYHOUSE OF A NEGRO
Adrienne Kennedy

CHARACTERS

SARAH, *Negro*
DUCHESS OF HAPSBURG, *one of herselves*
QUEEN VICTORIA, *one of herselves*
PATRICE LUMUMBA, *one of herselves*
JESUS, *one of herselves*
THE MOTHER
LANDLADY, *Funnylady*
RAYMOND, *Funnyman*

BEGINNING

Before the closed curtain a woman dressed in a white night-gown walks across the stage carrying before her a bald head. She moves as one in a trance and is mumbling something in-audible to herself. She appears faceless, wearing a yellow whitish mask over her face, with no apparent eyes. Her hair is wild, straight and black and falls to her waist. As she moves, holding her hands before her, she gives the effect of one in a dream. She crosses the stage from right to left. Before she has barely vanished, the curtain opens. It is a white satin curtain of a cheap material and a ghastly white, a material that brings to mind the interior of a cheap casket; parts of it are frayed and it looks as if it has been gnawed by rats.

THE SCENE

Two women are sitting in what appears to be a queen's cham-ber. It is set in the middle of the stage in a strong white light while the rest of the stage is in strong unnatural blackness. The quality of the white light is unreal and ugly. The queen's cham-ber consists of a dark monumental bed resembling an ebony tomb, a low dark chandelier with candles and wine-colored walls. Flying about are great black ravens. Queen Victoria is standing before her bed, holding a small mirror in her hand. On the white pillow of her bed is a dark indistinguishable object. The Duchess of Hapsburg is standing at the foot of her bed. Her back is to us as is the Queen's. Throughout the entire scene they do not move. Both women are dressed in royal gowns of white, a white similar to the white of the curtain, the material cheap satin. Their headpieces are white and of a net that falls over their faces. From beneath both their headpieces springs a headful of wild kinky hair. Although in this scene we do not see their faces, they look exactly alike and will wear masks or be made up to appear a whitish yellow. It is an alabaster face, the skin drawn tightly over the high cheekbones, great dark eyes that seem gouged out of the head, a high forehead, a full red mouth and a head of frizzy hair. If the characters do not wear a mask, the face must be highly powdered and possess a hard expression-less quality and a stillness as in the face of death.

(We hear a knocking.)

VICTORIA *(listening to the knocking).* It is my father. He is ar-riving again for the night.

(The Duchess makes no reply.)

He comes through the jungle to find me. He never tires of his journey.

DUCHESS. How dare he enter the castle, he who is the dark-est of them all, the darkest one. My mother looked like a white woman, hair as straight as any white woman's. And at least I am yellow, but he is black, the blackest one of them all. I hoped he was dead. Yet he still comes through the jungle to find me.

(The knocking is louder.)

VICTORIA. He never tires of the journey, does he, Duchess?

(Looking at herself in the mirror.)

DUCHESS. How dare he enter the castle of Queen Victoria Regina, Monarch of England. It is because of him that my mother died. The wild black beast put his hands on her. She died.

VICTORIA. Why does he keep returning? He keeps returning forever, coming back ever and keeps coming back for-ever. He is my father.

DUCHESS. He is a black Negro.

Ellen Bethea as "Negro Sarah" and Cleve Lamison as "Jesus" in a scene from the Signature Theatre Company production of Adrienne Kennedy's *Funnyhouse of a Negro.* This production was part of the company's retrospective of Kennedy's work for their 1995–96 season in New York City.

VICTORIA. He is my father. I am tied to the black Negro. He came when I was a child in the south, before I was born he haunted my conception, diseased by birth.

DUCHESS. Killed my mother.

VICTORIA. My mother was the light. She was the lightest one. She looked like a white woman.

DUCHESS. We are tied to him unless, of course, he should die.

VICTORIA. But he is dead.

DUCHESS. And he keeps returning.

(*The knocking is louder.*)

BLACKOUT

The lights go out in the chamber. Onto the stage from the left comes the figure in the white nightgown carrying the bald head. This time we hear her speak.

MOTHER. Black man, black man, I never should have let a black man put his hands on me. The wild black beast raped me and now my skull is shining.

(*She disappears to the right. Now the light is focused on a single white square wall that is to the left of the stage that is suspended and stands alone, of about five feet in dimension and width. It stands with the narrow part facing the audience. A character steps through. She is a faceless dark character with a hangman's rope about her neck and red blood on the part that would be her face. She is the Negro. On first glance she might be a young person but at a closer look the impression of an ancient character is given. The*

most noticeable aspect of her looks is her wild kinky hair, part of which is missing. It is a ragged head with a crown which the Negro carries in her hand. She is dressed in black. She steps slowly through the wall, stands still before it and begins her monologue.)

NEGRO. Part of the time I live with Raymond, part of the time with God, Prince Charles and Albert Saxe Coburg. I live in my room. It is a small room on the top floor of a brownstone in the West Nineties in New York, a room filled with my dark old volumes, a narrow bed and on the wall old photographs of castles and monarchs of England. It is also Victoria's chamber, Queen Victoria Regina's. Partly because it is consumed by a gigantic plaster statue of Queen Victoria, who is my idol, and partly for other reasons; three steps that I contrived out of boards lead to the statue which I have placed opposite the door as I enter the room. It is a sitting figure, a replica of one in London, and a thing of astonishing whiteness. I found it in a dusty shop on Morningside Heights. Raymond says it is a thing of terror, possessing the quality of nightmares, suggesting large and probable deaths. And of course he is right. When I am the Duchess of Hapsburg, I sit opposite Victoria in my headpiece and we talk. The other time I wear the dress of a student, dark clothes and dark stockings. Victoria always wants me to tell her of whiteness. She wants me to tell her of a royal world where everything and everyone is white and there are no unfortunate black ones. For as we of royal blood know, black is evil and has been from the beginning. Even before my mother's hair started to fall out. Before she was raped by a wild black beast. Black was evil.

When I am not the Duchess of Hapsburg I am myself. As for myself, I long to become even a more pallid Negro than I am now, pallid like Negroes on the covers of American Negro magazines; soulless, educated and irreligious. I want to possess no moral value, particularly value as to my being. I want not to be. I ask nothing except anonymity.

I am an English major, as my mother was when she went to school in Atlanta. My father majored in social work. I am graduated from a city college and have occasional work in libraries, but mostly spend my days preoccupied with the placement and geometric position of words on paper. I write poetry, filling white page after white page with imitations of Edith Sitwell. It is my dream to live in rooms with European antiques and my Queen Victoria, photographs of Roman ruins, walls of books, a piano, oriental carpets, and to eat my meals on a white glass table. I will visit my friends' apartments which will contain books, photographs of Roman ruins, pianos and oriental carpets. My friends will be white. I need them as an embankment to keep me from reflecting too much upon the fact that I am a Negro. For, like all educated Negroes—out of life and death essential—I find it necessary to maintain a stark fortress against recognition of myself. My white friends like myself will be shrewd, intellectual and anxious for death. Anyone's death. I will mistrust them, as I do myself. But if I had not wavered in my opinion of myself then my hair would never have fallen out. And if my hair hadn't fallen out, I wouldn't have bludgeoned my father's head with an ebony mask.

In appearance I am good-looking in a boring way, no glaring Negroid features, medium nose, medium mouth and pale yellow skin. My one defect is that I have a head of frizzy hair, unmistakably Negro kinky hair; and is indisguisable. I would like to lie and say I love Raymond. But I do not. He is a poet and is Jewish. He is very interested in Negroes.

(*The Negro stands by the wall and throughout her following speech, the following characters come through the wall, disappearing off into the varying directions in the darkened night of the stage—Duchess, Queen Victoria, Jesus, Patrice Lumumba. Jesus is a hunchback, yellow-skinned dwarf, dressed in white rags and sandals. Patrice Lumumba is a black man. His head appears to be split in two with blood and tissue in eyes. He carries an ebony mask.*)

The characters are myself; the Duchess of Hapsburg, Queen Victoria Regina, Jesus, Patrice Lumumba. The rooms are my rooms; a Hapsburg chamber, a chamber in a Victorian castle, the hotel where I killed my father, the jungle. These are the places myselves exist in. I know no places. That is I cannot believe in places. To believe in places is to know hope and to know the emotion of hope is to know beauty. It links us across a horizon and connects us to the world. I find there are no places, only my funnyhouse. Streets are rooms, cities are rooms, eternal rooms. I try to create a space for myselves in cities. New York, the midwest, a southern town but it becomes a lie. I try to give myselves a logical relationship but that too is a lie. For relationships was one of my last religions. I clung loyally to the lie of relationships, again and again seeking to establish a connection between my characters. Jesus is Victoria's son. Mother loved my father before her hair fell out. A loving relationship exists between myself and Jesus but they are lies. You will assume I am trifling with you, teasing your intellect, dealing in subtleties, denying connection then suddenly at a point reveal a startling heartbreaking connection. You are wrong. For the days are past when there are places and characters with connections with themes as in stories you pick up on the shelves of public libraries.

Too, there is no theme. No statements, I might borrow a statement, struggle to fabricate a theme, borrow one from my contemporaries, renew one from the master, hawkishly scan other stories searching for statements, consider the theme then deceive myself that I held such a statement within me, refusing to accept the fact that a statement has to come from an ordered force. I might try to join horizontal elements such as dots on a horizontal line, or create a centrifugal force, or create causes and effects so that they would equal a quantity but it would be a lie. For the statement is the characters and the characters are myself.

BLACKOUT

Then to the right front of the stage comes the white light. It goes to a suspended stairway. At the foot of it stands the Landlady. She is a tall, thin woman dressed in a black hat with red and appears to be talking to someone in a suggested open doorway in a corridor of a rooming house. She laughs like a mad character in a funnyhouse throughout her speech.

LANDLADY (*looking up the stairway*). Ever since her father hung himself in a Harlem hotel when Patrice Lumumba was murdered, she hides in her room. Each night she repeats; he keeps returning. How dare he enter the castle walls, he who is the darkest of them all, the darkest one. My mother looked like a white woman, hair as straight as any white woman's. And I am yellow but he, he is black, the blackest one of them all. I hoped he was dead. Yet still he comes through the jungle.

I tell her: Sarah, honey, the man hung himself. It's not your blame. But, no, she stares at me: No, Mrs. Conrad, he did not hang himself, that is only the way they understand it, they do, but the truth is that I bludgeoned his head with an ebony skull that he carries about with him. Wherever he goes, he carries out black masks and heads.

She's suffering so till her hair has fallen out. But then she did always hide herself in that room with the walls of books and her statues. I always did know she thought she was somebody else, a Queen or something, somebody else.

BLACKOUT

FUNNYMAN'S PLACE: *The next scene is enacted with the Duchess and Raymond. Raymond's place is suggested as being above the Negro's room, and is etched in with a prop of blinds and a bed . . . behind the blinds are mirrors and when the blinds are opened and closed by Raymond, this is revealed. Raymond turns out to be the Funnyman of the funnyhouse. He is tall, white and ghostly thin and dressed in a black shirt and black trousers in attire suggesting an artist. Throughout his dialogue he laughs. The Duchess is partially disrobed and it is implied from their attitudes of physical intimacy—he is standing and she is sitting before him clinging to his leg. During the scene, Raymond keeps opening and closing the blinds. His face has black sores on it and he is wearing a black hat. Throughout the scene he strikes her as in affection when he speaks to her.*

DUCHESS (*carrying a red paper bag*). My father is arriving, and what am I to do?

(*Raymond walks about the place opening the blinds and laughing.*)

FUNNYMAN. He is arriving from Africa, is he not?

DUCHESS. Yes, yes, he is arriving from Africa.

FUNNYMAN. I always knew your father was African.

DUCHESS. He is an African who lives in the jungle. He is an African who has always lived in the jungle. Yes, he is a nigger who is an African, who is a missionary teacher and is now dedicating his life to the erection of a Christian mission in the middle of the jungle. He is a black man.

FUNNYMAN. He is a black man who shot himself when they murdered Patrice Lumumba.

DUCHESS (*goes on wildly*). Yes, my father is a black man who went to Africa years ago as a missionary teacher, got mixed up in politics, was reviled and is now devoting his foolish life to the erection of a Christian mission in the middle of the jungle in one of those newly freed countries. Hide me.

(*Clinging to his knees.*)

Hide me here so the nigger will not find me.

FUNNYMAN (*laughing*). Your father is in the jungle dedicating his life to the erection of a Christian mission.

DUCHESS. Hide me here so the jungle will not find me. Hide me.

FUNNYMAN. Isn't it cruel of you?

DUCHESS. Hide me from the jungle.

FUNNYMAN. Isn't it cruel?

DUCHESS. No, no.

FUNNYMAN. Isn't it cruel of you?

DUCHESS. No.

(*She screams and opens her red paper bag and draws from it her fallen hair. It is a great mass of dark wild. She holds it up to him. He appears not to understand. He stares at it.*)

It is my hair.

(*He continues to stare at her.*)

When I awakened this morning it had fallen out, not all of it but a mass from the crown of my head that lay on the center of my pillow. I rose and in the greyish winter morning light of my room I stood staring at my hair, dazed by my sleeplessness, still shaken by nightmares of my mother. Was it true, yes, it was my hair. In the mirror

I saw that, although my hair remained on both sides, clearly on the crown and at my temples my scalp was bare.

(*She removes her black crown and shows him the top of her head.*)

RAYMOND (*Funnyman*). (*Staring at her.*) Why would your hair fall out? Is it because you are cruel? How could a black father haunt you so.

DUCHESS. He haunted my very conception. He was a black wild beast who raped my mother.

RAYMOND (*Funnyman*). He is a black Negro. (*Laughing.*)

DUCHESS. Ever since I can remember he's been in a nigger pose of agony. He is the wilderness. He speaks niggerly, grovelling about wanting to touch me with his black hand.

FUNNYMAN. How tormented and cruel you are.

DUCHESS (*as if not comprehending*). Yes, yes, the man's dark, very dark skinned. He is the darkest, my father is the darkest, my mother is the lightest. I am between. But my father is the darkest. My father is a nigger who drives me to misery. Any time spent with him evolves itself into suffering. He is a black man and the wilderness.

FUNNYMAN. How tormented and cruel you are.

DUCHESS. He is a nigger.

FUNNYMAN. And your mother, where is she?

DUCHESS. She is in the asylum. In the asylum bald. Her father was a white man. And she is the asylum.

(*He takes her in his arms. She responds wildly.*)

BLACKOUT
Knocking is heard, it continues, then somewhere near the center of stage a figure appears in the darkness, a large dark faceless Man carrying a mask in his hand.

MAN. It begins with the disaster of my hair. I awaken. My hair has fallen out, not all of it, but a mass from the crown of my head that lies on the center of my white pillow. I arise and in the greyish winter morning light of my room I stand staring at my hair, dazed by sleeplessness, still shaken by nightmares of my mother. Is it true? Yes. It is my hair. In the mirror I see that although my hair remains on both sides, clearly on the crown and at my temples my scalp is bare. And in my sleep I had been visited by my bald crazy mother who comes to me crying, calling me to her bedside. She lies on the bed watching the strands of her own hair fall out. Her hair fell out after she married and she spent her days lying on the bed watching the strands fall from her scalp, covering the bedspread until she was bald and admitted to the hospital. Black man, black man, my mother says I never should have let a black man put his hands on me. She comes to me, her bald skull shining.

Black diseases, Sarah, she says. Black diseases. I run. She follows me, her bald skull shining. That is the beginning.

(*Several Women with white nightgowns on, waistlength black hair, all identical, emerge from the sides of the stage and run into the darkness, toward him shouting—black man, black man. They are carrying bald heads.*)

BLACKOUT

Queen's Chamber. Her hair is in a small pile on the bed and in a small pile on the floor, several other piles of hair are scattered about her and her white gown is covered with fallen out hair.

Queen Victoria acts out the following scene: She awakens (in pantomime) and discovers her hair has fallen. It is on her pillow. She arises and stands at the side of the bed with her back towards us staring at her hair. She opens the red paper bag that she is carrying and takes out her hair, attempting to place it back on her head (for unlike Victoria, she does not wear her headpiece now). Suddenly the women in white gowns come running from the rear of the stage carrying their skulls before them screaming.

(*The unidentified man returns out of the darkness and speaks. He carries the mask.*)

MAN (*Patrice Lumumba*). I am a nigger of two generations. I am Patrice Lumumba. I am a nigger of two generations. I am the black shadow that haunted my mother's conception. I belong to the generation born at the turn of the century and the generation born before the depression. At present I reside in New York City in a brownstone in the West Nineties. I am an English major at a city college. My nigger father majored in social work, so did my mother. I am a student and have occasional work in libraries. But mostly I spend my vile days preoccupied with the placement and geometric position of words on paper. I write poetry filling white page after white page with imitations of Sitwell. It is my vile dream to live in rooms with European antiques and my statues of Queen Victoria, photographs of Roman ruins, walls of books, a piano and oriental carpets and to eat my meals on a white glass table. It is also my nigger dreams for my friends to eat their meals on white glass tables and to live in rooms with European antiques, photographs of Roman ruins, pianos and oriental carpets. My friends will be white. I need them as an embankment to keep me from reflecting too much upon the fact that I am Patrice Lumumba who haunted my mother's conception. They are necessary for me to maintain recognition against myself. My white friends, like myself, will be shrewd intellectuals and anxious for death. Anyone's death. I will despise them as I do myself. For if I did not despise myself then my hair would not have fallen and if my hair had not fallen then I would

not have bludgeoned my father's face with the ebony mask.

(*Then another wall is dropped, larger than the first one was. This one is near the front of the stage facing thus. Throughout the following monologue the characters Duchess, Victoria, Jesus go back and forth. As they go in their backs are to us but the Negro faces us speaking.*)

NEGRO. I always dreamed of a day when my mother would smile at me. My father—his mother wanted him to be Christ. From the beginning in the lamp of their dark room she said—I want you to be Jesus, to walk in Genesis and save the race. You must return to Africa, find revelation in the midst of golden savannas, nim and white frankopenny trees, white stallions roaming under a blue sky, you must walk with a white dove and heal the race, heal the misery, take us off the cross. She stared at him anguished in the kerosene light . . . at dawn he watched her rise, kill a hen for him to eat at breakfast, then go to work down at the big house till dusk, till she died.

His father told him the race was no damn good. He hated his father and adores his mother. His mother didn't want him to marry my mother and sent a dead chicken to the wedding. I DON'T want you marrying that child, she wrote, she's not good enough for you, I want you to go to Africa. When they first married they lived in New York.

Then they went to Africa where my mother fell out of love with my father. She didn't want him to save the black race and spent her days combing her hair. She would not let him touch her in their wedding bed and called him black. He is black of skin with dark eyes and a great dark square brow. Then in Africa he started to drink and came home drunk one night and raped my mother. The child from the union is me. I clung to my mother. Long after she went to the asylum I wove long dreams of her beauty, her straight hair and fair skin and gray eyes, so identical to mine. How it anguished him. I turned from him, nailing him to the cross, he said, dragging him through grass and nailing him on a cross until he bled. He pleaded with me to help him find Genesis, search for Genesis in the minds of golden savannas, nim and white frankopenny trees and white stallions roaming under a blue sky, help him search for the white dove; he wanted the black man to make a pure statement, he wanted the black man to rise from colonialism. But I sat in the room with my mother, sat by her bedside and helped her comb her straight black hair and wove long dreams of her beauty. She had long since began to curse the place and spoke of herself trapped in blackness. She preferred the company of night owls. Only at night did she rise, walking in the garden among the trees with the owls. When I spoke to her she saw I was a black man's child and she preferred speaking to owls. Nights my father came from his school in the village struggling to embrace me. But I fled and hid under my mother's bed while she screamed of remorse. Her hair was falling badly and after a while we had to return to this country.

He tried to hang himself once. After my mother went to the asylum he had hallucinations, his mother threw a dead chicken at him, his father laughed and said the race was no damn good, my mother appeared in her nightgown screaming she had trapped herself in blackness. No white doves flew. He had left Africa and was again in New York. We lived in Harlem and no white doves flew. Sarah, Sarah, he would say to me, the soldiers are coming and a cross they are placing high on a tree and are dragging me through the grass and nailing me upon the cross. My blood is gushing. I wanted to live in Genesis in the midst of golden savannas, nim and white frankopenny trees and white stallions roaming under a blue sky. I wanted to walk with a white dove. I wanted to be a Christian. Now I am Judas, I betrayed my mother. I sent your mother to the asylum. I created a yellow child who hates me. And he tried to hang himself in a Harlem hotel.

BLACKOUT

(A bald head is dropped on a string. We hear laughing.)

DUCHESS'S PLACE: *The next scene is done in the Duchess of Hapsburg's place which is a chandelier ballroom with snow falling, a black and white marble floor, a bench decorated with white flowers, all of this can be made of obviously fake materials as they would be in a funnyhouse. The Duchess is wearing a white dress and as in the previous scene a white headpiece with her kinky hair springing out from under it. In the scene are the Duchess and Jesus. Jesus enters the room which is at first dark, then suddenly brilliant, he starts to cry out at the Duchess who is seated on a bench under the chandelier, and pulls his hair from the red paper bag holding it up for the Duchess to see.*

JESUS. My hair!

(*The Duchess does not speak, Jesus again screams.*)

My hair.

(*Holding the hair up, waiting for a reaction from the Duchess.*)

DUCHESS.

(*As if oblivious.*)

I have something I must show you.

(*She goes quickly to shutters and darkens the room, returning standing before Jesus. She then slowly removes her headpiece and from under it takes a mass of her hair.*)

When I awakened I found it fallen out, not all of it but a mass that lay on my white pillow. I could see, although my hair hung down at the sides, clearly on my white scalp it was missing.

(*Her baldness is identical to Jesus's.*)

BLACKOUT

The light comes back up. They are both sitting on the bench examining each other's hair, running it through their fingers, then slowly the Duchess disappears behind the shutters and returns with a long red comb. She sits on the bench next to Jesus and starts to comb her remaining hair over her baldness. This is done slowly. Jesus then takes the comb and proceeds to do the same to the Duchess of Hapsburg's hair. After they finish they place the Duchess's headpiece back on and we can see the strands of their hair falling to the floor. Jesus then lays down across the bench while the Duchess walks back and forth, the knocking does not cease. They speak in unison as the Duchess walks and Jesus lays on the bench in the falling snow, staring at the ceiling.

DUCHESS and JESUS (*Their hair is falling more now, they are both hideous*). My father isn't going to let us alone.

(*Knocking.*)

Our father isn't going to let us alone, our father is the darkest of us all, my mother was the fairest, I am in between, but my father is the darkest of them all. He is a black man. Our father is the darkest of them all. He is a black man. My father is a dead man.

(*Then they suddenly look up at each other and scream, the lights go to their heads and we see that they are totally bald. There is a knocking. Lights go to the stairs and the Landlady.*)

LANDLADY. He wrote to her saying he loved her and asked for forgiveness. He begged her to take him off the cross. (He had dreamed she would.) Stop them from tormenting him, the one with the chicken and his cursing father. Her mother's hair fell out, the race's hair fell out because he left Africa, he said. He had tried to save them. She must embrace him. He said his existence depended on her embrace. He wrote her from Africa where he is creating his Christian center in the jungle and that is why he came here. I know that he wanted her to return there with him and not desert the race. He came to see her once before he tried to hang himself, appearing in the corridor of my apartment. I had let him in. I found him sitting on a bench in the hallway. He put out his hand to her, tried to take her in his arms, crying out—Forgiveness, Sarah. Is it that you will never forgive me for being black? I know you were a child of torment. But forgiveness. That was before his breakdown. Then, he wrote her and repeated that his mother hoped he would be Christ but he failed. He had married his mother because he could not resist the light. Yet, his mother from the beginning in the kerosene lamp of their dark rooms in Georgia said—I want you to be Jesus, to walk in Genesis and save the race, return to Africa, find revelation in the black. He went away.

But Easter morning, she got to feeling badly and went into Harlem to see him; the streets were filled with vendors selling lilies. He had checked out of that hotel. When she arrived back at my brownstone he was here, dressed badly, rather drunk. I had let him in again. He sat on a bench in the dark hallway, put out his hand to her, trying to take her in his arms, crying out—Forgiveness, Sarah. Forgiveness for my being black, Sarah. I know you are a child of torment. I know on dark winter afternoons you sat alone, weaving stories of your mother's beauty. But, Sarah, answer me, don't turn away, Sarah. Forgive my blackness. She would not answer. He put out his hand to her. She ran past him on the stairs, left him there with his hands out to me, repeating his past, saying his mother hoped he would be Christ. From the beginning in the kerosene lamp of their dark rooms, she said—Wally, I want you to be Jesus, to walk in Genesis and save the race. You must return to Africa, Wally, find revelation in the midst of golden savannas, nim and white franko-penny trees and white stallions roaming under a blue sky. Wally, you must find the white dove and heal the pain of the race, heal the misery of the black man, Wally, take us off the cross, Wally. In the kerosene light she stared at him anguished from her old Negro face . . . but she ran past him leaving him. And now he is dead, she says, now he is dead. He left Africa and now Patrice Lumumba is dead.

(*The next scene is enacted back in the Duchess of Haps-burg's place. Jesus is still in the Duchess's chamber, apparently he has fallen asleep and we see him as he awakes with the Duchess by his side, and sits here as in a trance. He rises terrified and speaks.*)

JESUS. Through my apocalypses and my raging sermons I have tried so to escape him, through God Almighty I have tried to escape being black.

(*He then appears to rouse himself from his thoughts and calls.*)

Duchess, Duchess.

(*He looks about for her, there is no answer. He gets up slowly, walks back into the darkness and there we see that she is hanging on the chandelier, her bald head suddenly drops to the floor and she falls upon Jesus. He screams.*)

I am going to Africa and kill this black man named Patrice Lumumba. Why? Because all my life I believed my Holy Father to be God, but now I know that my father is a black man. I have no fear for whatever I do, I will do in the name of God, I will do in the name of Albert Saxe Godburg, in the name of Victoria, Queen Victoria Regina, the monarch of England, I will.

BLACKOUT

NEXT SCENE: *In the jungle, red run, flying things, wild black grass. The effect of the jungle is that it, unlike the other scenes, is over the entire stage. In time this is the longest scene in the play and is played the slowest as the slow, almost standstill stages of a dream. By lighting the desired effect would be—suddenly the jungle has overgrown the chambers and all the other places with a violence and a dark brightness, a grim yellowness.*

Jesus is the first to appear in the center of the jungle darkness. Unlike in previous scenes, he has a nimbus above his head. As they each successively appear, they all too have nimbuses atop their heads in a manner to suggest that they are saviours.

JESUS. I always believed my father to be God.

(*Suddenly they all appear in various parts of the jungle. Patrice Lumumba, the Duchess, Victoria, wandering about speaking at once. Their speeches are mixed and repeated by one another.*)

ALL. He never tires of the journey, he who is the darkest one, the darkest one of them all. My mother looked like a white woman, hair as straight as any white woman's. I am yellow but he is black, the darkest of us all. How I hoped he was dead, yet he never tires of the journey. It was because of him that my mother died because she let a black man put his hands on her. Why does he keep returning? He keeps returning forever, keeps returning and returning and he is my father. He is a black Negro. They told me my father was God but my father is black. He is my father. I am tied to a black Negro. He returned when I lived in the south back in the twenties, when I was a child, he returned. Before I was born at the turn of the century, he haunted my conception, diseased my birth . . . killed my mother. He killed the light. My mother was the lightest one. I am bound to him unless, of course, he should die.

But he is dead.

And he keeps returning. Then he is not dead.

Then he is not dead.

Yes, he is dead, but dead he comes knocking at my door.

(*This is repeated several times, finally reaching a loud pitch and then all rushing about the grass. They stop and stand perfectly still. All speaking tensely at various times in a chant.*)

I see him. The black ugly thing is sitting in his hallway, surrounded by his ebony masks, surrounded by the blackness of himself. My mother comes into the room. He is there with his hand out to me, groveling, saying—Forgiveness, Sarah, is it that you will never forgive me for being black.

Forgiveness, Sarah. I know you are a nigger of torment. Why? Christ would not rape anyone.

You will never forgive me for being black.

Wild beast. Why did you rape my mother? Black beast, Christ would not rape anyone.

He is in grief from that black anguished face of his. Then at once the room will grow bright and my mother will come toward me smiling while I stand before his face and bludgeon him with an ebony head.

Forgiveness, Sarah, I know you are a nigger of torment.

(*Silence—Victory: Then they suddenly begin to laugh and shout as though they are in. They continue for some minutes running about laughing and shouting.*)

BLACKOUT

Another wall drops. There is a white plaster of Queen Victoria which represents the Negro's room in the brownstone, the room appears near the staircases highly lit and small. The main prop is the statue but a bed could be suggested. The figure of Victoria is a sitting figure, one of astonishing repulsive whiteness, possessing the quality of nightmares and terror. Sarah's room could be further suggested by dusty volumes of books and old yellowed walls.

The Negro, Sarah, is standing perfectly still, we hear the knocking, the lights come on quickly, her father's black figures with bludgeoned hands rush upon her, the lights black and we see her hanging in the room.

Lights come on the laughing Landlady. And at the same time remain on the hanging figure of the Negro.

LANDLADY. The poor bitch has hung herself.

(*Funnyman, Raymond, appears from his room at the commotion.*)

LANDLADY. The poor bitch has hung herself.

RAYMOND (*observing her hanging figure*). She was a funny little liar.

LANDLADY (*informing him*). Her father hung himself in a Harlem hotel when Patrice Lumumba died.

RAYMOND. She was a funny little liar.

LANDLADY. Her father hung himself in a Harlem hotel when Patrice Lumumba died.

RAYMOND. Her father never hung himself in a Harlem hotel when Patrice Lumumba was murdered.

I know the man. He is a doctor, married to a white whore. He lives in the city in a room with European antiques, photographs of Roman ruins, walls of books and oriental carpets. Her father is a nigger who eats his meals on a white glass table.

TOPICS FOR CRITICAL THINKING AND WRITING

The Play on the PAGE

1. Kennedy's plays are often described as surreal and dreamlike. Referring to the definition of *surrealism* given in the Glossary in this book, select a moment from the script you think is surreal and discuss the justification for your choice.

2. An aspect of the surreal quality of the play is captured through the multiple Sarahs that appear in the script. What do Sarah's different "selves" represent in the play?

3. Compare and contrast Kennedy's characterization of Sarah with the character Jones in O'Neill's *The Emperor Jones*.

4. Three writers in this anthology with African ancestry (Walcott, Soyinka, and Kennedy) use metaphors of theater or performance to inform their work. What is the significance of this metaphor, and how does each playwright treat it differently?

5. "Nonlinear" is a term used to describe Kennedy's work, particularly her early plays. What does the term mean and how does it apply to this play?

The Play on the STAGE

6. Most of the productions of *Funnyhouse of a Negro* use masks. Why is this important to the staging of the production? Would you maintain the convention in a production that you staged today? Why or why not?

7. Because of its surreal, dense poetic style, lighting design plays a major role in any production of *Funnyhouse of a Negro*. Select one of the sequences and describe and sketch how you would use light in a production of the play.

8. Michael Kahn, the director of the 1964 production, has stated in an interview, "The plays are symbolic, and the working out is a clash of symbols, and there is a strong emotional connection. There is a real story in those plays [he directed both *Funnyhouse* and *The Owls Answers*] that actually can be talked about—a woman who lives in a walk-up flat with a white Jewish boyfriend kills herself—that's the story. Then it is all transformed like a dream into this other story. And I always had both stories working" (Bryant-Jackson 192). How is it possible in a stage production to get "both stories working"? If you were to direct *Funnyhouse of a Negro*, how would you approach the doubled stories that Kahn describes?

The Play in PERFORMANCE

Funnyhouse of a Negro premiered in 1964 at the East End Theater in New York City. Directed by Michael Kahn and co-produced by Edward Albee and Joseph Papp, it received an Obie Distinguished Play Award in the same year and established Kennedy as one of the leading African American theater artists of the late twentieth century. The play went on to have numerous productions including the Theater Company of Boston (1965), the Petit Odéon in Paris (1968), and the Royal Court Theater in London (1968). Most recently it was produced by the Signature Theater Company in New York as part of their retrospecive of Kennedy's work for their 1995–96 season.

Billie Allen, a classically trained dancer and performer who has appeared on Broadway and in television specials, concerts, and opera, was the first actress to play the role of Sarah in the original production. In an interview with Allen (published in *Intersecting Boundaries: The Theater of Adrienne Kennedy* edited by Paul Bryant-Jackson and Lois More Overlook), she offers insights into her personal connections to the play:

> In the play, *Funnyhouse of a Negro*, Adrienne Kennedy delves into the black psyche, exposing our universal demons to the scrutiny of the light. She forces us to look at them and deal with them.
>
> Hair, for example, had not been dealt with in the theater. Our hair, that grows from us and is a part of us, has always been an ongoing battle: too curly, too straight, too kinky, too thin, too thick.
>
> Sarah, in *Funnyhouse*, says "My one defect is that I have a head of frizzy hair—unmistakably Negro kinky hair—and it is undisguisable." I felt this way about my own hair at that time. Creating the role of Sarah . . . I wore my hair long—brushed back and clamped tightly. At a certain point in the play I unleashed it: it sprang forth, gushing from my head like a fountain, alive and visible to the public. Many black women and men were ashamed of my doing this and wondered what "possessed" me. I was possessed by the rhythm, the ancient rituals called up from the depths by Adrienne. I began to love my hair; for me this was a catharsis for life.
>
> Adrienne Kennedy dared to step into the avant-garde surrealistic theater, her strong images, poetry, repetition of phrases, and nonlinear form soaring to new heights.

HISPANIC AMERICAN THEATER

First we must acknowledge that the word *Hispanic* is unsatisfactory. Although it is commonly used to refer to persons who traced their origins to a Spanish-speaking country (*Hispania* was the Latin name for Spain), many people object that the word overemphasizes the European influence on ethnic identity and neglects the indigenous and black heritages. *Latino* and *Latina* are sometimes used, partly because they are Spanish words, but many people object that these words obscure the unique cultural heritages of, for example, Mexican Americans (Chicanos), Cuban Americans, and Puerto Ricans, just as *Hispanic* does. In particular, a single term misleadingly blends Chicano theater, Cuban American theater, and Nuyorican theater (theater of Puerto Rican migrants in New York). Furthermore, even within these kinds of theater there are differences. For instance, although men have produced most of the plays, women (e.g., Estela Portillo Trambley) have produced important plays that differ in theme and technique from the plays written by men.

Drama in Spanish is nothing new in the New World. As we point out in our comment on the stage history of *The Second Shepherds' Play* (page 179), Spanish friars performed a play in what is now Mexico City as early as 1526. There are records, too, of a Spanish language play being performed near what is now El Paso, Texas, in 1598; in fact, the entire area of what we think of as the Southwest of the United States saw a good deal of Spanish-language dramatic activity at least until Mexico was forced to surrender it in the mid-nineteenth century. Even when this region became part of the United States, dramatic activity in Spanish continued, ranging from religious plays to melodramas and musicals. For an eyewitness account of a late-nineteenth-century religious folk play in Texas, along with generous quotations from the play, see an essay reprinted (originally from the *Journal of American Folklore*, 1893) in *Folklore in America*, edited by Tristram P. Coffin and Hennig Cohen (1966), pages 197–204. Furthermore, visiting theatrical companies from Cuba and Mexico helped to keep Spanish-language drama alive in the United States.

Still, in the first half of the twentieth century, despite the persistence of what we can call folkloric drama and of visiting companies, drama in Spanish was thought of as an endangered species. In the 1960s, however, it gained new life when, influenced by the civil rights movement, it became highly political. (See the Commentary on Luis Valdez's play, *Los Vendidos,* page 939.) It must be understood, however, that although Hispanic theater in the 1960s and later sought to effect political and economic changes (for instance, better working conditions for Chicanos), it also sought to reaffirm cultural identity. Leaders in the movement stressed a dual heritage, for example, Chicanos are rooted in Mexican culture as well as in European or Anglo culture. In Valdez's words:

> We have to rediscover ourselves. There are years and years of discoveries we have to make up for our people. People ask me: What is Mexican history in the United States? There is no textbook of the history of La Raza. Yet the history of the Mexican in this country is four hundred years old. We know we predate the landing of the Pilgrims and the American Revolution. But, beyond that? What really happened? No one can tell you. Our history has been lost. . . . Our generation says, Wait! Stop! Let's reconsider our roots.

QUOTED BY SUSAN BASSINETT-MCGUIRE IN *THEATRE QUARTERLY* 9 (SUMMER 1979):20.

At least a hundred *teatros* (groups devoted to dramatic representations of Hispanic experience), such as Jorge Huerta's Teatro de la Esperanza (Theater of Hope) in Santa Barbara and Joe Rosenberg's Teatro Bilingüe (Bilingual Theater) in Kingsville, Texas, were active in the late 1960s and 1970s. Many of these theaters continue today. In 1971 a national group, TENAZ (El Teatro Nacional de Aztlan, i.e., the National Theater of Aztlan), was established to sponsor theater festivals across the country. Not surprisingly, given the diversity of the Hispanic theater, this national organization does not speak with one voice.

For further comments on Hispanic theater, see the Commentary on Luis Valdez (page 937).

For detailed studies, we recommend:

Antush, John. *Puerto Rican Theater: Five Plays from New York* (1991).

Chávez, Denise, and Linda Feyder. *Shattering the Myth: Plays by Hispanic Women* (1992).

Huerta, Jorge. *Chicano Theater: Themes and Forms* (1982).

Kanellos, Nicolás. *A History of Hispanic Theatre in the United States: The Origins to 1940* (1990).

———, ed. *Mexican American Theatre Then and Now* (1983).

LUIS Valdez

Luis Valdez was born into a family of migrant farm workers in Delano, California, in 1940. After completing high school, he entered San Jose State College on a scholarship. He wrote his first plays while still an undergraduate, and after receiving his degree (in English and drama) from San Jose in 1964, he joined the San Francisco Mime Troupe, a left-wing group that performed in parks and streets. Revolutionary in technique as well as in political content, the Mime Troupe rejected the traditional forms of drama and instead drew on the traditions of the circus and the carnival.

In 1965 Valdez returned to Delano, California, where Cesar Chavez had organized a strike of farm workers and a boycott against grape growers. It was here, under the wing of the United Farm Workers, that he established El Teatro Campesino (the Farm Workers' Theater), which at first specialized in doing short, improvised, satirical skits called *actos*. When the *teatro* moved to Del Rey, California, it expanded its repertoire beyond farm issues and became part of a cultural center that gave workshops (in English and Spanish) in such subjects as history, drama, and politics.

The *actos*, performed by amateurs on college campuses and on flatbed trucks and at the edges of vineyards, were highly political. Making use of stereotypes (for example, the boss, the scab), the *actos* sought not to present the individual thoughts of a gifted playwright but to present the social vision of ordinary people—the *pueblo*—though it was acknowledged that in an oppressive society the playwright might have to help guide the people to see their own best interests.

Valdez moved from *actos* to *mitos* (myths)—plays that drew on Aztec mythology, Mexican folklore, and Christianity—and then to *Zoot Suit*, a play that ran for many months in California and that became the first Mexican American play to be produced on Broadway. More recently he wrote and directed a hit movie, *La Bamba*, and in 1991 received an award from the A.T.&T. Foundation for his musical, *Bandido*, to be presented by El Teatro Campesino.

Los Vendidos was written in 1967, when Ronald Reagan was governor of California.

■■■■■■■■■■■■■■■

COMMENTARY ON *LOS VENDIDOS*

As the preceding biographical note indicates, Valdez has not stood still as a dramatist. However, one thread that runs through his career is his vision of drama as politics, a form of art that may be used to help shape society. Such a view is scarcely modern; it can be found as early as Aristophanes (c. 450–c. 385 B.C.E.), who used comedy as a way of scolding Athens on a variety of matters, from its schools of philosophy to its destructive colonial politics. Closer to our own age, we find Bernard Shaw (1856–1950) and Bertolt Brecht (1898–1956) insisting that they seek not to please us by showing the surface of reality but to change our ways of thinking and, especially, to change the structure of our society.

One form of political theater, *agitprop*, developed in the Soviet Union in the 1920s by the Department of Agitation and Propaganda, consisted of short episodic plays (skits or sketches, we might call them) with a strong Marxist thrust. The playwrights were not interested in presenting rounded, plausible characters, and they were not interested in developing a complicated plot. In short, these works were not at all like the realistic drama of late nineteenth-century Europe, which is still the dominant form of drama in the commercial American theater. Rather, they used stereotypical characters—the worker (good), the boss (bad), the Marxist journalist (good), and so on—and they juxtaposed them in simple (and strong) conflicts. These skits were performed not in well-equipped theaters but in bare halls and in the streets. In the United States agitprop influenced the work of some dramatists in the 1930s, for instance Clifford Odets and Langston Hughes, but probably the closest thing to it in this country was the guerrilla theater of the 1960s, which aimed to use theater as a working-class weapon against the bourgeoisie.

Valdez was deeply influenced by both the leftist politics and the improvisatory methods of guerilla theater.

His *actos*, performed in streets, on flatbed trucks at the edges of vineyards, in meeting halls, and on campuses, were developed with and for the striking workers in the California vineyards. The plays are, he says, "collaborative work," sketches that took shape as he worked with his actors. These actors were not professionals or even trained amateurs; rather, they were unemployed farm workers who were persuaded that they could help their cause by taking roles in the *actos*. Their lack of theatrical training, along with the audience's lack of theatrical experience, meant that the roles had to be drawn fairly broadly, but this was not necessarily a disadvantage, any more than the exaggeration of a caricature is a disadvantage. A caricature (in a newspaper, for instance) can offer us enjoyment, and it may even stimulate us to think and to act in a certain way—it may move us (at least in a tiny degree) to vote against a particular candidate. Such a picture is not to be judged by its realism or, for that matter, by its subtlety.

The stereotypes that Valdez employs in the *actos* are political realities as he perceives them. According to this view, the essence of a person might be, for example, an exploited farm worker or an exploiting grower. Subtle distinctions are unimportant. Thus, a boss may be shown wearing a pig mask and (in pantomime) driving a big car. The facts that few bosses really look like pigs and that many do not drive big cars are said to be irrelevant. The pig-boss, the play implies, is the essence of boss. It should be mentioned, too, that the plays were intended not only to instill political ideas but also to entertain and to keep up the spirits of his audience (chiefly striking workers).

In short, Valdez sought to produce a revolutionary theater for and by workers. A truly revolutionary theater, he believed, could be produced *without* the use of traditional theatrical methods and *with* the aid of workers. In 1966 he wrote:

> If you want unbourgeois theater, find unbourgeois people to do it. Your head could burst open at the simplicity of the *acto* . . . but that's the way it is in Delano. Real theater lies in the excited laughter (or silence) of recognition in the audience, not in all the paraphernalia on the stage. Minus actors, the entire Teatro can be packed into one trunk, and when the Teatro goes on tour, the spirit of the Delano grape strikers goes with it.

Although *Los Vendidos* ("The Sellouts") is no less political than the earlier *actos*, the focus is no longer on striking farm laborers. It is on the Chicano's relationship to Anglo culture. Furthermore, *Los Vendidos* departs from earlier *actos* in not offering a solution to a condition that it reveals. Earlier *actos* had in effect said "Strike" or "Join the union," but *Los Vendidos* seems less concerned with proposing a solution than with showing contrasting kinds of Chicanos, although it is clear where Valdez's sympathies lie.

LOS VENDIDOS*
Luis Valdez

LIST OF CHARACTERS

HONEST SANCHO
SECRETARY
FARM WORKER
JOHNNY
REVOLUCIONARIO
MEXICAN-AMERICAN

SCENE

Honest Sancho's Used Mexican Lot and Mexican Curio Shop. Three models are on display in Honest Sancho's shop: to the right, there is a Revolucionario, complete with sombrero, carrilleras[1] and carabina 30-30. At center, on the floor, there is the Farm Worker, under a broad straw sombrero. At stage left is the Pachuco,[2] filero[3] in hand.

(Honest Sancho is moving among his models, dusting them off and preparing for another day of business.)

SANCHO. Bueno, bueno, mis monos, vamos a ver a quien vendemos ahora, ¿no?[4] [*To audience.*] ¡Quihubo! I'm Honest Sancho and this is my shop. Antes fui contratista pero ahora logré tener mi negocito[5] All I need now is a customer. (*A bell rings offstage.*) Ay, a customer!

SECRETARY (*entering*). Good morning, I'm Miss Jiménez from—

SANCHO. ¡Ah, una chicana! Welcome, welcome Señorita Jiménez.

SECRETARY (*Anglo pronunciation*). JIM-enez.

SANCHO. ¿Qué?

SECRETARY. My name is Miss JIM-enez. Don't you speak English? What's wrong with you?

SANCHO. Oh, nothing, Señorita JIM-enez. I'm here to help you.

SECRETARY. That's better. As I was starting to say, I'm a secretary from Governor Reagan's office, and we're looking for a Mexican type for the administration.

SANCHO. Well, you come to the right place, lady. This is Honest Sancho's Used Mexican lot, and we got all types here. Any particular type you want?

SECRETARY. Yes, we were looking for somebody suave—

SANCHO. Suave.

SECRETARY. Debonair.

SANCHO. De buen aire.

SECRETARY. Dark.

SANCHO. Prieto.

SECRETARY. But of course not too dark.

SANCHO. No muy prieto.

SECRETARY. Perhaps, beige.

SANCHO. Beige, just the tone. Así como cafecito con leche,[6] ¿no?

SECRETARY. One more thing. He must be hard-working.

SANCHO. That could only be one model. Step right over here to the center of the shop, lady. (*They cross to the Farm Worker.*) This is our standard farm worker model. As you can see, in the words of our beloved Senator George Murphy, he is "built close to the ground." Also take special notice of his four-ply Goodyear huaraches, made from the rain tire. This wide-brimmed sombrero is an extra added feature—keeps off the sun, rain, and dust.

SECRETARY. Yes, it does look durable.

SANCHO. And our farmworker model is friendly. Muy amable.[7] Watch. (*Snaps his fingers.*)

---

*__Los Vendidos__ the sellouts [1]__carrilleras__ cartridge belts. [2]__Pachuco__ an urban tough guy [3]__filero__ blade [4]__Bueno . . . no?__ Well, well, darlings, let's see who we can sell now, O.K.? [5]__Antes . . . negocito__ I used to be a contractor, but now I've succeeded in having my little business.

[6]__Así . . . leche__ like coffee with milk [7]__Muy amable__ very friendly

This photograph is from the 1988 spring tour, in California and in Europe, of El Teatro Ensemble de U.C.S.D. The production, like the text of the play, was highly stylized: here, for instance, stereotypical characters bear labels indicating the stereotypes. On page 945 we include an interview with Professor Jorge A. Huerta of the University of California, San Diego, who directed the play.

FARM WORKER (*lifts up head*). Buenos días, señorita. (*His head drops.*)

SECRETARY. My, he's friendly.

SANCHO. Didn't I tell you? Loves his patrones! But his most attractive feature is that he's hard working. Let me show you. (*Snaps fingers. Farm Worker stands.*)

FARM WORKER. ¡El jale!⁸ (*He begins to work.*)

SANCHO. As you can see, he is cutting grapes.

SECRETARY. Oh, I wouldn't know.

SANCHO. He also picks cotton. (*Snap. Farm Worker begins to pick cotton.*)

SECRETARY. Versatile isn't he?

SANCHO. He also picks melons. (*Snap. Farm Worker picks melons.*) That's his slow speed for late in the season. Here's his fast speed. (*Snap. Farm Worker picks faster.*)

SECRETARY. ¡Chihuahua! . . . I mean, goodness, he sure is a hard worker.

SANCHO (*pulls the Farm Worker to his feet*). And that isn't the half of it. Do you see these little holes on his arms that appear to be pores? During those hot sluggish days in the field, when the vines or the branches get so entangled, it's almost impossible to move; these holes emit a certain grease that allow our model to slip and slide right through the crop with no trouble at all.

SECRETARY. Wonderful. But is he economical?

SANCHO. Economical? Señorita, you are looking at the Volkswagen of Mexicans. Pennies a day is all it takes. One plate of beans and tortillas will keep him going all day. That, and chile. Plenty of chile. Chile jalapeños, chile verde, chile colorado. But, of course, if you do give him chile (*Snap. Farm Worker turns left face. Snap. Farm*

Worker bends over.) then you have to change his oil filter once a week.

SECRETARY. What about storage?

SANCHO. No problem. You know these new farm labor camps our Honorable Governor Reagan has built out by Parlier or Raisin City? They were designed with our model in mind. Five, six, seven, even ten in one of those shacks will give you no trouble at all. You can also put him in old barns, old cars, river banks. You can even leave him out in the field overnight with no worry!

SECRETARY. Remarkable.

SANCHO. And here's an added feature: Every year at the end of the season, this model goes back to Mexico and doesn't return, automatically, until next Spring.

SECRETARY. How about that. But tell me: does he speak English?

SANCHO. Another outstanding feature is that last year this model was programmed to go out on STRIKE! (*Snap.*)

FARM WORKER. ¡HUELGA! ¡HUELGA! Hermanos, sálganse de esos files.⁹ (*Snap. He stops.*)

SECRETARY. No! Oh no, we can't strike in the State Capitol.

SANCHO. Well, he also scabs. (*Snap.*)

FARM WORKER. Me vendo barato, ¿y qué?¹⁰ (*Snap.*)

SECRETARY. That's much better, but you didn't answer my question. Does he speak English?

SANCHO. Bueno . . . no, pero¹¹ he has other—

SECRETARY. No.

SANCHO. Other features.

SECRETARY. NO! He just won't do!

---

⁸**El jale** The job

⁹**Huelga . . . files.** Strike! Strike! Brothers, leave those rows.   ¹⁰**Me . . . qué** I come cheap. So what?   ¹¹**Bueno . . . no, pero** Well, no but

SANCHO. Okay, okay pues. We have other models.

SECRETARY. I hope so. What we need is something a little more sophisticated.

SANCHO. Sophisti—¿qué?

SECRETARY. An urban model.

SANCHO. Ah, from the city! Step right back. Over here in this corner of the shop is exactly what you're looking for. Introducing our new 1969 JOHNNY PACHUCO model! This is our fast-back model. Streamlined. Built for speed, low-riding, city life. Take a look at some of these features. Mag shoes, dual exhausts, green chartreuse paint-job, dark-tint windshield, a little poof on top. Let me just turn him on. (*Snap. Johnny walks to stage center with a pachuco bounce.*)

SECRETARY. What was that?

SANCHO. That, señorita, was the Chicano shuffle.

SECRETARY. Okay, what does he do?

SANCHO. Anything and everything necessary for city life. For instance, survival: He knife fights. (*Snap. Johnny pulls out switch blade and swings at Secretary.*)

(*Secretary screams.*)

SANCHO. He dances. (*Snap.*)

JOHNNY (*singing*). "Angel Baby, my Angel Baby . . . " (*Snap.*)

SANCHO. And here's a feature no city model can be without. He gets arrested, but not without resisting, of course. (*Snap.*)

JOHNNY. ¡En la madre, la placa!12 I didn't do it! I didn't do it! (*Johnny turns and stands up against an imaginary wall, legs spread out, arms behind his back.*)

SECRETARY. Oh no, we can't have arrests! We must maintain law and order.

SANCHO. But he's bilingual!

SECRETARY. Bilingual?

SANCHO. Simón que yes.13 He speaks English! Johnny, give us some English. (*Snap.*)

JOHNNY (*comes downstage*). Fuck-you!

SECRETARY (*gasps*). Oh! I've never been so insulted in my whole life!

SANCHO. Well, he learned it in your school.

SECRETARY. I don't care where he learned it.

SANCHO. But he's economical!

SECRETARY. Economical?

SANCHO. Nickels and dimes. You can keep Johnny running on hamburgers, Taco Bell tacos, Lucky Lager beer, Thunderbird wine, yesca—

SECRETARY. Yesca?

SANCHO. Mota.

SECRETARY. Mota?

SANCHO. Leños14 . . . Marijuana. (*Snap; Johnny inhales on an imaginary joint.*)

SECRETARY. That's against the law!

JOHNNY (*big smile, holding his breath*). Yeah.

SANCHO. He also sniffs glue. (*Snap. Johnny inhales glue, big smile.*)

JOHNNY. That's too much man, ése.15

SECRETARY. No, Mr. Sancho, I don't think this—

SANCHO. Wait a minute, he has other qualities I know you'll love. For example, an inferiority complex. (*Snap.*)

JOHNNY (*to Sancho*). You think you're better than me, huh ése? (*Swings switchblade.*)

SANCHO. He can also be beaten and he bruises, cut him and he bleeds; kick him and he—(*He beats, bruises and kicks Pachuco.*) would you like to try it?

SECRETARY. Oh, I couldn't.

SANCHO. Be my guest. He's a great scapegoat.

SECRETARY. No, really.

SANCHO. Please.

SECRETARY. Well, all right. Just once. (*She kicks Pachuco.*) Oh, he's so soft.

SANCHO. Wasn't that good? Try again.

SECRETARY (*kicks Pachuco*). Oh, he's so wonderful! (*She kicks him again.*)

SANCHO. Okay, that's enough, lady. You ruin the merchandise. Yes, our Johnny Pachuco model can give you many hours of pleasure. Why, the L.A.P.D. just bought twenty of these to train their rookie cops on. And talk about maintenance. Señorita, you are looking at an entirely self-supporting machine. You're never going to find our Johnny Pachuco model on the relief rolls. No, sir, this model knows how to liberate.

SECRETARY. Liberate?

SANCHO. He steals. (*Snap. Johnny rushes the Secretary and steals her purse.*)

JOHNNY. ¡Dame esa bolsa, vieja!16 (*He grabs the purse and runs. Snap by Sancho. He stops.*)

(*Secretary runs after Johnny and grabs purse away from him, kicking him as she goes.*)

SECRETARY. No, no, no! We can't have any *more* thieves in the State Administration. Put him back.

SANCHO. Okay, we still got other models. Come on, Johnny, we'll sell you to some old lady. (*Sancho takes Johnny back to his place.*)

SECRETARY. Mr. Sancho, I don't think you quite understand what we need. What we need is something that will attract the women voters. Something more traditional, more romantic.

SANCHO. Ah, a lover. (*He smiles meaningfully.*) Step right over here, señorita. Introducing our standard Revolucionario and/or Early California Bandit type. As you can see he is well-built, sturdy, durable. This is the International Harvester of Mexicans.

12¡**En . . . la placa!** Wow, the cops!   13**Simón que yes.** Yea, sure.   14**Leños** joints (marijuana)

15**ése** fellow   16**Dame . . . vieja** Give me that bag, old lady!

SECRETARY. What does he do?

SANCHO. You name it, he does it. He rides horses, stays in the mountains, crosses deserts, plains, rivers, leads revolutions, follows revolutions, kills, can be killed, serves as a martyr, hero, movie star—did I say movie star? Did you ever see *Viva Zapata? Viva Villa? Villa Rides? Pancho Villa Returns? Pancho Villa Goes Back? Pancho Villa Meets Abbott and Costello—*

SECRETARY. I've never seen any of those.

SANCHO. Well, he was in all of them. Listen to this. (*Snap.*)

REVOLUCIONARIO (*Scream*). ¡VIVA VILLAAAAA!

SECRETARY. That's awfully loud.

SANCHO. He has a volume control. (*He adjusts volume. Snap.*)

REVOLUCIONARIO (*mousey voice*). ¡Viva Villa!

SECRETARY. That's better.

SANCHO. And even if you didn't see him in the movies, perhaps you saw him on TV. He makes commercials. (*Snap.*)

REVOLUCIONARIO. Is there a Frito Bandito in your house?

SECRETARY. Oh yes, I've seen that one!

SANCHO. Another feature about this one is that he is economical. He runs on raw horsemeat and tequila!

SECRETARY. Isn't that rather savage?

SANCHO. Al contrario,[17] it makes him a lover. (*Snap.*)

REVOLUCIONARIO (*to Secretary*). ¡Ay, mamasota, cochota, ven pa'ca![18] (*He grabs Secretary and folds her back—Latin-Lover style.*)

SANCHO (*Snap. Revolucionario goes back upright*). Now wasn't that nice?

SECRETARY. Well, it was rather nice.

SANCHO. And finally, there is one outstanding feature about this model I KNOW the ladies are going to love: He's a GENUINE antique! He was made in Mexico in 1910!

SECRETARY. Made in Mexico?

SANCHO. That's right. Once in Tijuana, twice in Guadalajara, three times in Cuernavaca.

SECRETARY. Mr. Sancho, I thought he was an American product.

SANCHO. No, but—

SECRETARY. No, I'm sorry. We can't buy anything but American-made products. He just won't do.

SANCHO. But he's an antique!

SECRETARY. I don't care. You still don't understand what we need. It's true we need Mexican models such as these, but it's more important that he be *American.*

SANCHO. American?

SECRETARY. That's right, and judging from what you've shown me, I don't think you have what we want. Well, my lunch hour's almost over: I better—

SANCHO. Wait a minute! Mexican but American?

SECRETARY. That's correct.

---

[17]**Al contrario** On the contrary   [18]**Ay . . . pa'ca!** —, get over here!

SANCHO. Mexican but . . . (*A sudden flash.*) AMERICAN! Yeah, I think we've got exactly what you want. He just came in today! Give me a minute. (*He exits. Talks from backstage.*) Here he is in the shop. Let me just get some papers off. There. Introducing our new 1970 Mexican-American! Ta-ra-ra-ra-ra-ra-RA-RAAA!

(*Sancho brings out the Mexican-American model, a clean-shaven middle-class type in a business suit, with glasses.*)

SECRETARY (*impressed*). Where have you been hiding this one?

SANCHO. He just came in this morning. Ain't he a beauty? Feast your eyes on him! Sturdy US STEEL frame, streamlined, modern. As a matter of fact, he is built exactly like our Anglo models except that he comes in a variety of darker shades: naugahyde, leather, or leatherette.

SECRETARY. Naugahyde.

SANCHO. Well, we'll just write that down. Yes, señorita, this model represents the apex of American engineering! He is bilingual, college educated, ambitious! Say the word "acculturate" and he accelerates. He is intelligent, well-mannered, clean—did I say clean? (*Snap. Mexican-American raises his arm.*) Smell.

SECRETARY (*smells*). Old Sobaco, my favorite.

SANCHO (*Snap. Mexican-American turns toward Sancho*). Eric! (*To Secretary.*) We call him Eric García. (*To Eric.*) I want you to meet Miss JIM-enez, Eric.

MEXICAN-AMERICAN. Miss JIM-enez, I am delighted to make your acquaintance. (*He kisses her hand.*)

SECRETARY. Oh, my, how charming!

SANCHO. Did you feel the suction? He has seven especially engineered suction cups right behind his lips. He's a charmer all right!

SECRETARY. How about boards? Does he function on boards?

SANCHO. You name them, he is on them. Parole boards, draft boards, school boards, taco quality control boards, surf boards, two-by-fours.

SECRETARY. Does he function in politics?

SANCHO. Señorita, you are looking at a political MACHINE. Have you ever heard of the OEO, EOC, COD, WAR ON POVERTY? That's our model! Not only that, he makes political speeches.

SECRETARY. May I hear one?

SANCHO. With pleasure. (*Snap.*) Eric, give us a speech.

MEXICAN-AMERICAN. Mr. Congressman, Mr. Chairman, members of the board, honored guests, ladies and gentlemen. (*Sancho and Secretary applaud.*) Please, please. I come before you as a Mexican-American to tell you about the problems of the Mexican. The problems of the Mexican stem from one thing and one thing alone: He's stupid. He's uneducated. He needs to stay in school. He needs to be ambitious, forward-looking, harder-working. He needs to think American, American, American, AMERICAN, AMERICAN, AMERICAN. GOD

BLESS AMERICA! GOD BLESS AMERICA! GOD BLESS AMERICA!! (*He goes out of control.*)

(*Sancho snaps frantically and the Mexican-American finally slumps forward, bending at the waist.*)

SECRETARY. Oh my, he's patriotic too!

SANCHO. Sí, señorita, he loves his country. Let me just make a little adjustment here. (*Stands Mexican-American up.*)

SECRETARY. What about upkeep? Is he economical?

SANCHO. Well, no, I won't lie to you. The Mexican-American costs a little bit more, but you get what you pay for. He's worth every extra cent. You can keep him running on dry Martinis, Langendorf bread.

SECRETARY. Apple pie?

SANCHO. Only Mom's. Of course, he's also programmed to eat Mexican food on ceremonial functions, but I must warn you: an overdose of beans will plug up his exhaust.

SECRETARY. Fine! There's just one more question: HOW MUCH DO YOU WANT FOR HIM?

SANCHO. Well, I tell you what I'm gonna do. Today and today only, because you've been so sweet, I'm gonna let you steal this model from me! I'm gonna let you drive him off the lot for the simple price of—let's see taxes and license included—$15,000.

SECRETARY. Fifteen thousand DOLLARS? For a MEXICAN!

SANCHO. Mexican? What are you talking, lady? This is a Mexican-AMERICAN! We had to melt down two pachucos, a farm worker and three gabachos[19] to make this model! You want quality, but you gotta pay for it! This is no cheap run-about. He's got class!

SECRETARY. Okay, I'll take him.

SANCHO. You will?

SECRETARY. Here's your money.

SANCHO. You mind if I count it?

SECRETARY. Go right ahead.

SANCHO. Well, you'll get your pink slip in the mail. Oh, do you want me to wrap him up for you? We have a box in the back.

SECRETARY. No, thank you. The Governor is having a luncheon this afternoon, and we need a brown face in the crowd. How do I drive him?

SANCHO. Just snap your fingers. He'll do anything you want.

(*Secretary snaps. Mexican-American steps forward.*)

MEXICAN-AMERICAN. RAZA QUERIDA, ¡VAMOS LEVANTANDO ARMAS PARA LIBERARNOS DE ESTOS DESGRACIADOS GABACHOS QUE NOS EXPLOTAN! VAMOS.[20]

SECRETARY. What did he say?

SANCHO. Something about lifting arms, killing white people, etc.

SECRETARY. But he's not supposed to say that!

SANCHO. Look, lady, don't blame me for bugs from the factory. He's your Mexican-American; you bought him, now drive him off the lot!

SECRETARY. But he's broken!

SANCHO. Try snapping another finger.

(*Secretary snaps. Mexican-American comes to life again.*)

MEXICAN-AMERICAN. ¡ESTA GRAN HUMANIDAD HA DICHO BASTA! Y SE HA PUESTO EN MARCHA! ¡BASTA! ¡BASTA! ¡VIVA LA RAZA! ¡VIVA LA CAUSA! ¡VIVA LA HUELGA! ¡VIVAN LOS BROWN BERETS! ¡VIVAN LOS ESTUDIANTES![21] ¡CHICANO POWER!

(*The Mexican-American turns toward the Secretary, who gasps and backs up. He keeps turning toward the Pachuco, Farm Worker, and Revolucionario, snapping his fingers and turning each of them on, one by one.*)

PACHUCO (*Snap. To Secretary*). I'm going to get you, baby! ¡Viva La Raza!

FARM WORKER (*Snap. To Secretary*). ¡Viva la huelga! ¡Viva la Huelga! ¡VIVA LA HUELGA!

REVOLUCIONARIO (*Snap. To Secretary*). ¡Viva la revolución! ¡VIVA LA REVOLUCIÓN!

(*The three models join together and advance toward the Secretary who backs up and runs out of the shop screaming. Sancho is at the other end of the shop holding his money in his hand. All freeze. After a few seconds of silence, the Pachuco moves and stretches, shaking his arms and loosening up. The Farm Worker and Revolucionario do the same. Sancho stays where he is, frozen to his spot.*)

JOHNNY. Man, that was a long one, ése.[22] (*Others agree with him.*)

FARM WORKER. How did we do?

JOHNNY. Perty good, look at all that lana,[23] man! (*He goes over to Sancho and removes the money from his hand. Sancho stays where he is.*)

REVOLUCIONARIO. En la madre, look at all the money.

JOHNNY. We keep this up, we're going to be rich.

FARM WORKER. They think we're machines.

REVOLUCIONARIO. Burros.

JOHNNY. Puppets.

[19]**gabachos** whites   [20]**Raza . . . Vamos.** Beloved Raza [persons of Mexican descent], let's take up arms to liberate ourselves from those damned whites who exploit us. Let's get going.

[21]**¡Esta . . . Estudiantes!** This great mass of humanity has said enough! And it has begun to march. Enough! Enough! Long live La Raza! Long live the Cause! Long live the strike! Long live the Brown Berets! Long live the students!   [22]**ése** man   [23]**lana** money

MEXICAN-AMERICAN. The only thing I don't like is—how come I always got to play the goddamn Mexican-American?

JOHNNY. That's what you get for finishing high school.

FARM WORKER. How about our wages, ése?

JOHNNY. Here it comes right now. $3,000 for you, $3,000 for you, $3,000 for you, and $3,000 for me. The rest we put back into the business.

MEXICAN-AMERICAN. Too much, man. Heh, where you vatos[24] going tonight?

FARM WORKER. I'm going over to Concha's. There's a party.

JOHNNY. Wait a minute, vatos. What about our salesman? I think he needs an oil job.

[24] **vatos** guys

REVOLUCIONARIO. Leave him to me.

(*The Pachuco, Farm Worker, and Mexican-American exit, talking loudly about their plans for the night. The Revolucionario goes over to Sancho, removes his derby hat and cigar, lifts him up and throws him over his shoulder. Sancho hangs loose, lifeless.*)

REVOLUCIONARIO (*to audience*). He's the best model we got! ¡Ajua![25]

(*Exit.*)

THE END

[25] **Ajua!** Wow!

TOPICS FOR CRITICAL THINKING AND WRITING

The Play on the PAGE

1. If you are an Anglo (shorthand for a Caucasian with traditional Northern European values), do you find the play deeply offensive? Why, or why not? If you are a Mexican American, do you find the play entertaining or do you find parts of it offensive? What might Anglos enjoy in the play, and what might Mexican Americans find offensive?

2. What stereotypes of Mexican Americans are presented here? At the end of the play, what image of the Mexican American is presented? How does it compare with the stereotypes?

3. Putting aside the politics of the play (and your own politics), what do you think are the strengths of *Los Vendidos*? What do you think are the weaknesses?

4. The play was written in 1967. Putting aside a few specific references, for instance to Governor Reagan, do you find it dated? If not, why not?

5. In his short essay, "The Actos," Valdez says that *actos* achieve the following: "Inspire the audience to social action. Illuminate specific points about social problems. Satirize the opposition. Show or hint at a solution. Express what people are feeling." How much of this do you think *Los Vendidos* does?

6. Many people assume that politics gets in the way of serious art. That is, they assume that artists ought to be concerned with issues that transcend politics. Does this point make any sense to you? Why or why not?

The Play on the STAGE

7. In 1971 when *Los Vendidos* was produced by El Teatro de la Esperanza, the group altered the ending by having the men decide to use the money to build a community center. (See the interview with the director, Jorge Huerta, that follows.) Evaluate this ending.

8. On page 945, Jorge Huerta suggests that it was a mistake for Jane Fonda to be cast as Miss Jimenes in the videotape. "Something is lost," he says, "in the realization that this woman is not pretending to be white. . . . " Do you agree? Explain.

9. When the play was videotaped by KNBC in Los Angeles for broadcast in 1973, Valdez changed the ending. In the revised version we discover that a scientist (played by Valdez) masterminds the operation, placing Mexican American models wherever there are persons of Mexican descent. These models soon will become Chicanos (as opposed to persons with Anglo values) and will aid rather than work against their fellows. Evaluate this ending.

The Play in PERFORMANCE

JORGE HUERTA
Directing Los Vendidos

Jorge Huerta is a professor at the University of California, San Diego; a director; critic (among his books is *Chicano Theater: Themes and Forms*); and a founding member of several theatrical groups. In this interview he responds to questions about his production of *Los Vendidos*.

Interviewer: What sort of stage did you use? A proscenium stage? A theater-in-the-round? Do you think that the play works best on one kind of stage?

Huerta: The beauty of *Los Vendidos*, and indeed, any good *acto*, is that it can be performed virtually anywhere. In a classroom, a theater, outdoors. I have directed this *acto* on several occasions, under every conceivable condition, touring it to the Southwestern U.S. as well as Western Europe with equal success, regardless of the performance situation.

Do you find that the responses of Anglos differ greatly from the responses of Chicanos?

Definitely. The humor of the piece often comes from the recognition of the stereotypes and if an audience member does not "connect" with a particular type, such as the *pachuco*, because s/he has no reference point, the humor is diminished. The farce, a vital element of any *acto*, is a universal comic device, however, and there is enough of that (physicality) in this *acto* to generate laughter from most audiences. In Europe (Spain, France and what in 1988 was West Germany) our audiences were mostly university students who had been studying the Chicanos and they were therefore familiar with the types. Some of the satire, such as equating the farmworker with the (then economical) Volkswagen, crosses cultures as well.

I have heard that some Chicanos find the acto *demeaning. What would you say to them?*

If I could dialogue with those people who are offended by the stereotypes, I would explain to them that this *acto* is exposing the stereotypes, and, in fact, appropriating them for the Chicanos' own purposes, which is to educate them about themselves. *Los Vendidos* is about a very particular Mexican American who denies her or his Mexican heritage and attempts to "pass." If people are offended by this, perhaps the message is hitting too close to home.

Have you ever used Anglo performers in the play?

Actually, no.

Is this a matter of chance or of principle?

Not chance, and not necessarily "principle." I believe that some theatrical pieces are "ethno-specific" and lose part of their impact if the wrong "type" is cast. However, the Teatro Campesino has a videotape, or film, of this *acto* with none other than Jane Fonda as Miss Jimenes. But something is lost in the realization that this woman is not pretending to be white; she is white. I have always cast a dark-skinned actress as Miss Jimenes, because the audience can see the irony in her denial. Mexican and Chicano audiences love to see the "vendida/o" type ridiculed and always have, as evidenced in early twentieth-century sketches performed in the Southwest, according to the research of Nicolás Kanellos.

In the 1971 production by El Teatro de la Esperanza, the ending was changed—the men decide to use the money to build a community center. How do you personally feel about this change?

We (Teatro de la Esperanza) felt that the original ending/solution was superfluous. We had just become the theatrical arm of a community-based organization, La Casa de la Raza (The Home of the People) in Santa Barbara's Mexican/Chicano community, and we hoped to use the *acto* as an example to the audiences there. When the characters talked about a community center, they and the audiences were in that very center. The ending should not be about "partying," but, rather, about building communities. By the way, as you know, even Valdez altered the ending for the NBC version of his *acto*.

In directing the play, did any special problems arise that you had not anticipated? If so, what were they, and how did you handle them?

The 1971 production at La Casa de la Raza generated some discussion among the Mexican American audience members who felt that we should not be revealing this negative image of our people to non-Chicano audiences. They felt that it was like hanging out one's dirty laundry. At the universities, however, nobody questioned this exposure. It is usually the case that community-based audiences will be less progressive than the younger, student audiences. Other than this minor problem, which did not deter us from performing the play, by the way, I have not encountered any problems with *Los Vendidos*.

Los Vendidos was first written and produced in 1967. Do you think that it is still valid today?

Definitely. It is a classic of the genre and is as successful today as it was when first produced in 1967. Every one of the types illustrated still exists. However, as you have noted, some of the contemporary references, such as "Governor Reagan," would have to be updated. The Revolucionario's line, "Is there a Frito Bandito in the house?" may no longer resonate, since the television commercial was discontinued long ago, but there are plenty of current equivalents. And the major theme, the problems of assimilation and denial of one's culture, are still with us.

Can other culture adapt and perform this acto?

The setup of a "Used Mexican Lot" is universally understood to mean a used car lot and anybody can buy and sell "cars." A Filipino student of mine adapted *Los Vendidos* to his community, substituting the Mexican and Chicano types with similar models from his own community. I do not know if he ever produced it for his intended audience, but it was quite funny to me. Great fun.

Can anybody write an acto?

Absolutely. All the creator(s) need is a passionate need to educate an audience with their message. If the *acto* is being created by a group of individuals, they have to have the same agenda. You cannot create a good *acto* if you do believe in the *acto's* conclusion or solutions. Once the writer or writers have decided which issue they wish to expose, they need only improvise the conflicts, with clearly delineated heroes and villains and they will have a ready-to-perform *acto*. Most essential to a good *acto*, however, is a very clear understanding of the issues involved. This means understanding the enemy as well as the hero. You can-

not ridicule your enemy unless you know the enemy very, very well. Finally, the creators of an *acto* must have fun as they ridicule and expose the enemy's weaknesses. Also, study other *actos* as well as radical theater of the 1960s for good models.

What are issues that students might want to dramatize in an acto?

I have never given a student an issue to dramatize as an *acto*. I can't. The idea has to come from the creators. They have to be passionate about something in order to effectively create an *acto*.

As we point out in our introduction to this acto, *Chicano theater is and has been political, leaning particularly to the left. Do the actos have to be radical-left or even liberal?*

Not at all. I had an Anglo male student who disliked affirmative action and wanted to write an *acto* against this concept because of a bad experience he had had with a potential employer. Regardless of how I felt about affirmative action (and he knew how I felt!), I urged him to "Let it all hang out." He did, and although I disagreed with the message philosophically, the writer captured the essence of the *acto* quite well. I laughed all the way through this *acto* because the writer knew the situation and had grasped the major features of the *acto* as expressed in *Los Vendidos* and other *actos* by Valdez and his Teatro Campesino.

What other issues does the creator of an acto *have to consider?*

The audience for whom the *acto* is written. The anti–affirmative action *acto* would be embraced at the Republican National Convention; a gun-control *acto* might not be so welcome. *Actos* are meant to educate and entertain but do not expect an audience of detractors to sit through your *acto*. Remember that the original *actos* were created by striking farmworkers for striking farmworkers. They were meant to remind their audiences of the goals of their struggles while also giving them some much-needed comic relief, portraying the boss with a pig-faced mask, etc. Laughter is a very healthy tool and a mediating device as well. So have fun and laugh at your enemy with an acto.

The World Stage in
the Twentieth Century

Punctuated with pop songs, Tom Stoppard's *The Real Thing* asks fundamental questions about the validity of the modern romantic relationship. Henry (played by John Feltch) and Charlotte (played by Elizabeth Heflin) quarrel in this 2000 production at the Alley Theater in Houston, Texas.

Even as recently as a few decades ago, if a book of this sort contained a unit called "The World Stage," the unit would have included examples of highly distinctive national dramas, for instance the ancient dance-drama of Bali (*barong*), or the seventeenth-century puppet plays of Japan (*bunraku*). These forms continue to exist, partly as antique curiosities, partly as entertainments for tourists, but partly also because they unquestionably have an inherent power. They remain living forces in their own countries, and when troupes perform them abroad, let's say (courtesy of the airlines) today in Boston, tomorrow in Atlanta, and the day after tomorrow in Columbus, Ohio, new audiences are moved in new ways.

Modern technology (film and video of course, but also digital media, radio, airplanes, and countless other forces) has made the theater of even the most remote culture readily available to us, and has made Western culture readily available to what once were remote cultures. The classical Greek playwrights are performed throughout the world in different languages and in different performance styles. In 1994 at the Festival of Avignon in southern France, one of the largest international theater festivals in the world, Euripides's *Andromache* was performed in French outdoors in front of an immense medieval building. The costumes, a mixture of classical Greek robes and contemporary military uniforms, pointedly reminded the audience of the ongoing civil war in Bosnia-Herzegovnia. At the same festival, a Japanese company performed a Noh play (we include an example in our text) in Japanese, to a predominantly French audience, who were assisted in understanding the story by following detailed program notes. In 1956 Ibsen's *A Doll's House* was performed for the first time in the People's Republic of China, with the Chinese actress Ji Shuping in the role of Nora. In 1996, in recognition of her stellar performance, this Chinese Nora was flown to Oslo by the National Theater of Norway for an Ibsen commemoration. Norway and China are far apart geographically and culturally but the text of the play, brought to life by the performers, provides an example of how theater brings people together. Yet another example, if one is needed, is Arthur Miller's enormously successful production in China—he directed it himself—of that quintessentially American play, *Death of a Salesman*. We will return to the issue of live performances in a moment, but first we want to talk about another aspect of "The World Stage."

Although the focus of *Types of Drama* is the Western theater tradition, or, rather, traditions, this unit in the book demonstrates the international context of theater. Yeats's *Purgatory* shows an Irish playwright drawing on a Japanese dramatic tradition, the Noh play. Elizabeth Robins, author of *Votes for Women*, was an American, but she spent most of her life in England. Samuel Beckett, author of *Krapp's Last Tape*, was an Irishman who spent most of his life in Paris. Bertolt Brecht, a German, spent a good deal of his adult life in political exile in Denmark, Finland, and the United States, and he drew on Chinese dramatic traditions. Tom Stoppard is known as a British dramatist, yet his style and material is greatly influenced by his birthplace in what was previously known as Czechoslovakia. The Nigerian writer Wole Soyinka received a British-style education at University College, Ibadan, and then for further education went to Leeds University in England, and later to London, where he worked for the Royal Court Theatre. Soyinka returned to Nigeria, was imprisoned, and after his release lived for a while in Ghana and then again in England, though he eventually returned to Nigeria. He writes chiefly in English, but also occasionally in his native language, Yoruba. Dario Fo, by contrast, seems essentially Italian, but his works are performed throughout the world. Derek Walcott acknowledges his West Indian roots (he was born in St. Lucia), but he lives half the year in Boston and half the year in the Caribbean.

And yet if "The World Stage" seems—no, not "seems" but *is*—especially vigorous, we should remember too that live theater is a notably perishable form. True, the texts that we reprint in *Types of Drama* receive their fullest life only through live performance, when the words are spoken by costumed actors moving before us, but theater is ephemeral. Anyone who has seen a live performance and then tried to remember it in some detail knows the truth of this comment on the brevity of the actor's art:

> Nor pen nor pencil can the actor save,
> The art and artist share one common grave.

When we witness a live performance, we witness an unrepeatable experience. The play may be staged again tomorrow, but the audience will be different and the actors will give different performances, for better or worse. We have all seen performances that did not fulfill our expectations. That's life. Samuel Beckett kept at his desk a note to himself that every writer, including every student and every instructor, might also tack up: "Fail. Fail again. Fail better." Let's end with some words spoken by Robin Goodfellow ("Puck") in the epilogue to *A Midsummer Night's Dream*. Robin speaks of himself and his fellow performers as "shadows," earlier in the play he speaks of Oberon, the king of the fairies, as "the king of shadows," but in the epilogue "shadows" applies to the actors who fleetingly impersonate the figures in the play and who, when the play is over, put off their temporary roles and return to their ordinary lives.

> If we shadows have offended,
> Think but this, and all is mended:
> That you have but slumb'red here,
> While these visions did appear.
> And this weak and idle theme,
> No more yielding but a dream.
> Gentles, do not reprehend:
> If you pardon, we will mend.
> ⋯
> Give me your hands, if we be friends,
> And Robin shall restore amends.

When Robin says "Give me your hands," Shakespeare (through the shadowy Robin) is—not too subtly—asking the audience to applaud. Peter Brook had the inspired idea, in his now-classic production of *A Midsummer Night's Dream*, of having Puck deliver the epilogue with the house lights up, and when Robin said "Give me your hands" the actors left the stage, entered the space of the audience, and shook hands with the spectators, as players and spectators alike left the theater. It is hard to think of an equally memorable image of the living theater, with the strong and yet fleeting effect that players have on spectators, and spectators have on players when, after (so to speak) having been joined in the performance, they go their separate ways.

WOMEN'S THEATER

The earliest surviving plays in Western dramatic literature, written in the fifth century B.C.E., are from ancient Greece. They of course include female characters, some of whom (for instance, Antigone) are heroic, but all of the plays were written by men and the female roles were acted by men. It is even possible that the plays were seen only by men, since the evidence that women attended the Greek dramatic festivals is inconclusive. Not until the tenth century C.E. do we find dramatic work written by a woman, six Latin plays by Hrotsvit of Gandersheim (also called Hrotswitha and Roswith, c. 935–973), a German noblewoman who imitated the Roman dramatist Terence. In the preface she says that her "object is to glorify to the best of [her] poor ability the praiseworthy chastity of Christian virgins in the same form [i.e., in dramatic form] that has been used to describe the indecent acts of licentious women." It is not known whether her plays were performed in her lifetime, though at least some of them have been performed recently in academic surroundings.

Until about 1960 most people probably thought it was "natural" that there were not many plays by women. In fact, there *were* many plays by women, but the older ones had been forgotten. For instance, in England Aphra Behn (1640–89), a professional writer, had written at least sixteen plays, one of which, *The Rover* (1677), held the stage for almost a century. (We reprint it on page 500.) In the mid-nineteenth century another woman, Anna Cora Mowatt (1819–1870), wrote an immensely popular play, *Fashion* (1845), spoofing the infatuation of the *nouveaux riches* with English and European culture. Somewhat closer to our own time are two figures represented in *Types of Drama*, Elizabeth Robins (1862–1952) and Susan Glaspell (1876–1948). Robins, whose important *Votes for Women* (1906) we reprint, was not only an actress and a playwright but was also a theatrical manager. It would be easy to add at least a dozen comparable names—Lillian Hellman (1906–84) and Lorraine Hansberry (1930–65) for starters—but it is also true that however notable the achievements of all of these women as playwrights were, they were not seen as forming a distinctive "women's theater." Similarly, those relatively few women who were active in the theater in other capacities—for instance, as directors (Margo Jones [1913–55] and Eva Le Gallienne [1899–1991] are the best-known examples) or producers—worked in an essentially male world.

Honor Moore, in *The New Women's Theatre* (1977), suggests an explanation: Theater (unlike writing fiction or poetry) is a communal activity, and men have not welcomed women into this community. "Male exclusion of women," she says, "perhaps more than any other single factor, has been responsible for the lack of a female tradition in playwriting similar to that which exists in both fiction and poetry." Then, too, working for the theater requires larger chunks of time (for instance, whole days at early rehearsals) than most women in the past were able to spare, because they were tied to households. (Nevertheless, performers—that is, actresses—managed to find the time, and so one must conclude that it was not simply domestic obligations that kept women from serving as directors in the theater.)

Feminist critics looked at the past, noticed that the dramatic canon assumed that the spectator was male and that the subject matter often concerned fathers and sons (for example, *Oedipus, Hamlet, Death of a Salesman*). Was this pattern "natural," or was there a further explanation? Elaine Showalter, writing in *Signs* 1:2 (Winter 1975) put it this way, "Feminist criticism has allowed us to see meaning in what previously has been empty space" (435). The most obvious meaning of the emptiness was, of course, that the theater reinforced the ideals of patriarchal cultures.

In any case, despite the achievements of the women we have already mentioned, it was not until the late 1960s, as part of the women's movement, that a substantial number of women began to set forth on the stage a drama of feminine sensibility. These plays are not just plays by women; they are plays about the experiences of women, especially about the difficult business of surviving as a woman in a man's world. As Eve Merriam said in 1976, surveying the plays written by women since 1960, "First you had to write an Arthur Miller play, then you had to write an absurd play. Now there is a new freedom—you can write empathetic women characters."

Once alerted to political realities, what sorts of theatrical activities would enlightened women engage in and what kinds of plays would women write? In the 1960s, seeing the gains made by the civil rights movement, many women engaged in consciousness-raising sessions: Women were the equals of men, and they should have the rights that men had long enjoyed. In the 1970s, a shift in thinking occurred: Women should, of course, have the opportunities that men have had, but women and men are *different*—not only biologically but also by virtue of their life experiences. Why, then, should the art of women resemble the art of men? Men might engage in painting and sculpture, but women might (for instance) use their bodies as their medium and as their subject, and this they did in a form now called performance art. Although performance art uses language and sometimes music and pictures, an equally important medium is the performer's body. For instance, in *Sally's Rape*, an episode in a longer work called *Confessions of a Black Working-Class Woman*, Robbie McCauley, an African American woman, strips off all of her clothing and stands on a bench, representing a slave on the auction block. Her white partner urges the audience to participate by chanting, "Bid em in, bid em in." While the audience chants, McCauley says,

> They take off my sack dress
> and order me onto the block with my socks
>   rolled down.
> On the auction block, they put
> their hands all down yr body
> the men smell ya, feel ya. . . .

Raewyn Whyte, who describes the performance in *Acting Out: Feminist Performances*, edited by Lynda Hart and Peggy Phelan (1993), goes on to say that

> [a]s she speaks, she flinches at the invisible, probing fingers, which assess her soundness for childbearing. . . . For the onlooker there is an awe-ful fascination in this representation of the slave auction, this scene of victimage. The pleasure of looking at the naked body of the black woman caught in the spotlight is made guilty by the awareness of being inescapably positioned as a potential buyer in the slave market, yet the urge to look away is countered by the seductive intensity of the scene. Similarly, whether or not you join the chanting you are trapped by the sympathetic magic of sound, which reanimates the past, and, no matter how much you tell yourself you had nothing to do with this scene, you are made vicariously complicit in the auction system that McCauley's staging represents. (278)

Clearly this sort of performance is a kind of drama that is remote from such canonical dramas as *Oedipus the King* and *Death of a Salesman*. Broadly speaking, feminists have characterized canonical drama as Aristotelian, male, and linear. In canonical drama, a plot is developed—we might say the plot advances—in a fairly consistent way. Most critics, from Aristotle to the present, have held that a plot should be unified, the actions of the characters should be convincingly motivated, and the end should be implicit in the beginning, that is, the end should not be arbitrary but should (at least in retrospect) seem inevitable. Some feminist critics, as we have said, characterize this view of plot as masculine. Sue-Ellen Case in *Feminism and Theatre* (1988) puts it this way:

> Within the study of the theatre, several versions of masculine and feminine morphology have taken hold. For example, some feminist critics have described the form of tragedy as a replication of the male sexual experience. Tragedy is composed of foreplay, excitation and ejaculation (catharsis). The broader organization of plot—complication, crisis and resolution—is also tied to this phallic experience. The central focus in male forms is labelled phallocentric, reflecting the nature of the male's sexual physiology. A female form might embody her sexual mode, aligned with multiple orgasms, with no dramatic focus on ejaculation or necessity to build to a single climax. The contiguous organization would replace this ejaculatory form. The feminist critic might analyze the plays of Adrienne Kennedy, women's performance-art pieces or witches' cyclic rituals using this notion. (129)

If you have read Kennedy's *Funnyhouse of a Negro* (page 925), you know that the episodes in her play are indeed better described as "contiguous" than as interdependent and leading to a single climax. However, Case does not suggest that the feminist view she has just sketched is incontestable. She goes on to point out that other feminists, objecting to this "biologizing" or "essentializing" of gender, argue that this particular "feminine morphology" neglects the enormous influence of social forces. Proponents of this counterview of course recognize biological distinctions between the sexes, but they distinguish between "sex" and "gender." Gender, they argue, concerns such qualities as masculinity and femininity, and these are largely a matter of cultural practice. In this view, the biological material is shaped by human intervention. If at first this sounds odd, perhaps it will become convincing when you consider Susan Brownmiller's witty formulation, "Women are all female impersonators to some degree." From this it is an easy step to seeing that men are male impersonators to some degree. Some feminists argue, Case points out, that the biological or essentialist approach may discount the products of women who chose to work in what is alleged to be a male form. And, to complicate matters, Adrienne Kennedy herself, a woman working in what is characterized as a woman's mode, seems to think that playwriting is essentially a masculine form. This is supported by her comment (*New York Times*, May 13, 1973, section 2, page 3) that playwriting is "an arena of glory and power like bullfighting, like boxing."

Kennedy's provocative statement forces us to realize that no single formulation of drama, or of feminist drama, can be entirely satisfactory. Certainly it is now evident that the feminism of the 1960s, which most often asserted the equality of men with women, yielded to a much more radical feminism in the 1970s and 1980s, which emphasized the distinctiveness of women, even to the extent of banishing *man* from *woman* and *men* from *women*, by adopting such spellings as *womon*, *wimmin*, and *womyn*. The radical feminists held the view that gender roles—created not by nature but by patriarchal oppression—can be changed only by a revolutionary restructuring of power. Plays, or, better, performances, created in this spirit tend *not* to use the linear structure of canonical plays but find some precedent in the work of Bertolt Brecht's "epic drama" (see page 1006). As in the plays of Brecht, the actors do not seek to generate dramatic illusion, but rather they break through the proscenium and confront the audience directly.

Interestingly, at the very time that radical feminist theater was perhaps at its height, women were winning prizes on Broadway with plays that from a radical feminist point of view left much to be desired. In the 1980s three plays by women were awarded Pulitzer Prizes: Beth Henley's *Crimes of the Heart* (1981), Marsha Norman's *'night, Mother* (1983), and Wendy Wasserstein's *The Heidi Chronicles* (1989). All are fairly traditional in form and in content, and in fact some feminist critics took issue with the images of women in Marsha Norman's play.

In short, not all women are willing to welcome as "women's theater" a prize-winning play by a woman. Furthermore, in the last twenty years or so, it has become evident that one cannot speak about "women" as though they constitute a group with a single vision. Perhaps the first great division in the feminist movement occurred around 1970, when women of color, especially African Americans, pointed out that the feminist movement at that time was chiefly white and middle class. The movement, falsely assuming a uniformity of experience, did not speak for the poor or for blacks, Asian Americans, or Latinas. Nor (it was soon pointed out) did it speak for lesbians; in fact, with its middle-class values, its celebration of the achievements of Aphra Behn and Virginia Woolf and other notable white women, it seemed almost as narrow and as self-satisfied as the patriarchal structure that it opposed.

Looking back on the years since 1970, then, one should speak not of women's theater but of women's theaters. There can be no doubt that women are now playing much more active roles in the theater than they did in the past, partly because we now all recognize that indeed there are many mansions in the house of the drama; the Aristotelian dramatists may still occupy the royal suite, but the achievements of other kinds of dramatists, as well as the achievements of producers, directors, and actors in these other kinds of play have enriched not only women's theater but (and here we slip into universalizing) all theater.

A recommended reading list includes the following:

Aston, Elaine. *An Introduction to Feminism and Theatre* (1995).

Austin, Gayle *Feminist Theories for Drama Criticism* (1990).

Betsko, Kathleen, and Rachel Koenig. *Interviews with Contemporary Women Playwrights* (1987).

Brown-Guillory, Elizabeth. *Their Place on the Stage: Black Women Playwrights in America* (1988).

Canning, Charlotte. *Feminist Theaters in the U.S.A.* (1996).

Chinoy, Helen Krich, and Lynda Walsh Jenkins, eds., *Women in American Theatre*, rev. ed. (1981).

Dolan, Jill. *The Feminist Spectator as Critic* (1988).

Goodman, Lizbeth. ed. *The Routledge Reader in Gender and Performance* (1998).

Hart, Lynda, ed. *Making a Spectacle: Feminist Essays on Contemporary Women's Theatre* (1989).

Keyssar, Helene. *Feminist Theatre*, rev. ed. (1990).

Murphy, Brenda. *The Cambridge Companion to American Women Playwrights* (1999).

Yarbro-Bejarano, Yvonne. "The Female Subject in Chicano Theatre," in Sue-Ellen Case, *Performing Feminisms* (1990).

For anthologies of plays, see *Plays by Women* (ten volumes, with various editors, 1983). See also *Women's Work: Five New Plays from The Women's Project*, edited by Julia Miles (1989); two collections by Honor Moore, *Women's Theatre* (1972), and *The New Women's Theatre: Ten Plays by Contemporary American Women* (1977); and *Black Female Playwrights: An Anthology of Plays before 1950*, edited by Kathy A. Perkins (1989).

ELIZABETH Robins

Elizabeth Robins (1862–1952), playwright, novelist, actress, political activist, was born in Louisville, Kentucky, went to Vassar College to study medicine, but ran away when she was eighteen to become an actress. She achieved considerable fame in America, and then in 1888 she set sail for England. She soon established herself as one of the leading actresses on the London scene but was frustrated and angered by the limited opportunities and stereotyped roles for women in theater. Challenging the status quo she joined a small group of women who were actor-managers and who therefore could control the plays selected for production. In 1891 she formed the Robins-Lea Joint Management with fellow American expatriate actress Marion Lea. One of their first acts was to produce a play by a woman playwright. They also championed the plays of Henrik Ibsen and worked to get him produced in London by translating *Hedda Gabler* in 1891. Robins played the title role, and two years later she performed the role of Hilda Wangel in Ibsen's *The Master Builder.* At this time she published her first novel anonymously but she soon adopted the sexually ambiguous pen name of C. E. Raimond. In 1906 she turned her hand to suffrage drama; *Votes for Women,* produced in 1907, inaugurated a rich array of plays by women and men dedicated to such issues. After the success of *Votes for Women,* Robins continued to write plays and novels, remaining a politically active feminist throughout her life.

■■■■■■■■■■■■■■

COMMENTARY ON *VOTES FOR WOMEN*

As an actress and a theater manager, Elizabeth Robins was already actively involved in supporting opportunities for women in theater. When she was commissioned to write a play for a London actress she turned her hand to suffrage drama. In the course of writing and researching the play, she attended a suffrage meeting in Trafalgar Square where she was galvanized by the commitment and political acuity of the women speakers. She had also witnessed the terrifying act of mounted police riding down small bands of women walking to one of their political meetings. Robins herself was driven off the sidewalk three times and at one point was in danger of being trampled. Such experiences changed her from someone in broad agreement on women's right to vote to a committed suffragist who was publicly identified with the cause.

The height of the suffrage campaign in Britain was 1907 to 1914. The conservative Victorian view that women should not be involved in the rough, worldly activity of political life dominated British life despite the fact that for decades a queen had held the British Empire together. Another older prejudice held fast as well, that women were not emotionally stable enough to deal with the harsh realities of politics.

In 1907, the same year that *Votes for Women* premiered, the first street procession organized to support

women's suffrage took place in London. Although it rained the day of the march, thus giving it the name of the Mud March, the event was reported in all the newspapers and considered successful. For the first time a variety of women from different walks of life were taking to the street as a political statement. Such action flew in the face of social convention, which dictated that respectable women should stay at home and remain silent.

While the Mud March gave impetus to the development of a new kind of political spectacle that dramatically realized the cause of women's suffrage, plays were being staged in theaters all around the country that spotlighted the issue as well. A year after the successful staging of *Votes for Women,* the Woman Writers' Suffrage League (WWSL) was formed with Elizabeth Robins serving as its first president. Its objective was "to obtain the vote for women on the same terms as it is or may be granted to men. Its methods are proper to writers—the use of the pen" (Stowell 40). Later in the same year the Actresses' Franchise League (AFL) was formed. It recruited a wide range of well-known performers, and it created a play department that oversaw the writing, collection, and publication of suffrage drama. Following the example of Robins's play, the AFL recognized that theater productions offered the opportunity for a new way of conducting propaganda beyond speeches, pamphlets, and essays. For them "one play is worth a hundred speeches" (Stowell 40). It must be pointed out here that the term "suffrage drama" refers to the specific time and historical moment in which these plays were written and produced, not to the subject matter and content of the plays, which in fact varied widely. Together the WWSL and AFL collaborated until the beginning of World War I in 1914 to promote and produce plays concerned with feminist issues.

Other suffrage drama produced during this time included *How the Vote Was Won* (1908) by Cicely Hamilton and Christopher St. John, *Diana of Dobson's* (1908) by Cicely Hamilton, *The Apple* (1909) by Ines Bensusan (the head of the AFL's play department), *In the Workhouse* (1911) by Margaret Nevison, *A Chat with Mrs. Chicky* (1912) by Evelyn Glover, and *The*

First Actress (1911) by Christopher St. John. In addition to these works a new translation of *Paphnutius* by Hrotswitha was produced in 1912. Hrotswitha, a tenth-century Benedictine nun in Germany, wrote six plays; the revival of her work demonstrated that women had a history of writing and creating, and the retrieval of this "lost" woman playwright was part of the women's movement goals to find and reclaim women of achievement.

Although the issue of women's right to vote is central to Robbins's play, it cannot be divorced from other themes she pursues, such as the hardships and poverty of women's lives and the double sexual standard that condemns women for the same actions that men are permitted with impunity.

VOTES FOR WOMEN
Elizabeth Robins

CHARACTERS

LORD JOHN WYNNSTAY
LADY JOHN WYNNSTAY, *his wife*
MRS HERIOT, *sister of Lady John*
MISS JEAN DUNBARTON, *niece to Lady John and Mrs Heriot*
THE HON. GEOFFREY STONOR, *Unionist M.P. affianced to Jean Dunbarton*
MR ST JOHN GREATOREX, *Liberal M.P.*
THE HON. RICHARD FARNBOROUGH
MR FREDDY TUNBRIDGE
MRS FREDDY TUNBRIDGE
MR ALLEN TRENT

MISS ERNESTINE BLUNT, *a Suffragette*
MR PILCHER, *a working man*
A WORKING WOMAN
MISS VIDA LEVERING
PERSONS IN THE CROWD: SERVANTS IN THE TWO HOUSES

ACT I, *Wynnstay House in Hertfordshire*
ACT II, *Trafalgar Square, London*
ACT III, *Eaton Square, London*

The Entire Action of the Play takes place between Sunday noon and six o'clock in the evening of the same day.

ACT ONE

Hall of Wynnstay House.

    Twelve o'clock, Sunday morning, end of June. With the rising of the curtain, enter the Butler. As he is going, with majestic port, to answer the door, enter briskly from the garden, by the lower French window, Lady John Wynnstay, flushed, and flapping a garden hat to fan herself. She is a pink-cheeked woman of fifty-four, who has plainly been a beauty, keeps her complexion, but is 'gone to fat.'

LADY JOHN. Has Miss Levering come down yet?
BUTLER (*pausing*). I haven't seen her, m'lady
LADY JOHN (*almost sharply as Butler turns*). I won't have her disturbed if she's resting. (*To herself as she goes to the writing table.*) She certainly needs it.
BUTLER. Yes, m'lady.
LADY JOHN (*sitting at the writing table, her back to the front door*). But I want her to know the moment she comes down that the new plans arrived by the morning post.
BUTLER (*pausing nearly at the door*). Plans, m'la—
LADY JOHN. She'll understand. There they are. (*Glancing at the clock.*) It's very important she should have them in time to look over before she goes—

(*Butler opens the door.*)

(*Over her shoulder.*) Is that Miss Levering?
BUTLER. No, m'lady. Mr. Farnborough.

(*Exit Butler.*)

(*Enter the Hon. R. Farnborough. He is twenty-six; reddish hair, high-coloured, sanguine, self-important.*)

FARNBOROUGH. I'm afraid I'm scandalously early. It didn't take me nearly as long to motor over as Lord John said.
LADY JOHN (*shaking hands*). I'm afraid my husband is no authority on motoring—and he's not home yet from church.
FARNBOROUGH. It's the greatest luck finding *you*. I thought Miss Levering was the only person under this roof who was ever allowed to observe Sunday as a real Day of Rest.
LADY JOHN. If you've come to see Miss Levering—
FARNBOROUGH. Is she here? I give you my word I didn't know it.
LADY JOHN (*unconvinced*). Oh?
FARNBOROUGH. Does she come every weekend?
LADY JOHN. Whenever we can get her to. But we've only known her a couple of months.
FARNBOROUGH. And I have only known her three weeks! Lady John, I've come to ask you to help me.
LADY JOHN (*quickly*). With Miss Levering? I can't do it!
FARNBOROUGH. No, no—all that's no good. She only laughs.
LADY JOHN (*relieved*). Ah!—she looks upon you as a boy.
FARNBOROUGH (*firing up*). Such rot! What do you think she said to me in London the other day?
LADY JOHN. That she was four years older than you?
FARNBOROUGH. Oh, I knew that. No. She said she knew she was all the charming things I'd been saying, but there was only one way to prove it—and that was to marry some one young enough to be her son. She'd noticed that was what the *most* attractive women did—and she named names.

LADY JOHN (*laughing*). *You* were too old!

FARNBOROUGH (*nods*). Her future husband, she said, was probably just entering Eton.

LADY JOHN. Just like her!

FARNBOROUGH (*waving the subject away*). No. I wanted to see you about the Secretaryship.

LADY JOHN. You didn't get it, then?

FARNBOROUGH. No. It's the grief of my life.

LADY JOHN. Oh, if you don't get one you'll get another.

FARNBOROUGH. But there *is* only one.

LADY JOHN. Only one vacancy?

FARNBOROUGH. Only one man I'd give my ears to work for.

LADY JOHN (*smiling*). I remember.

FARNBOROUGH (*quickly*). Do I always talk about Stonor? Well, it's a habit people have got into.

LADY JOHN. I forget, do you know Mr. Stonor personally, or (*smiling*) are you just dazzled from afar?

FARNBOROUGH. Oh, I know him. The trouble is he doesn't know me. If he did he'd realise he can't be sure of winning his election without my valuable services.

LADY JOHN. Geoffrey Stonor's re-election is always a foregone conclusion.

FARNBOROUGH. That the great man shares that opinion is precisely his weak point. (*Smiling.*) His only one.

LADY JOHN. You think because the Liberals swept the country the last time—

FARNBOROUGH. How can we be sure any Conservative seat is safe after—(*As Lady John smiles and turns to her papers:*) Forgive me, I know you're not interested in politics *qua* politics. But this concerns Geoffrey Stonor.

LADY JOHN. And you count on my being interested in him like all the rest of my sex.

FARNBOROUGH (*leans forward*). Lady John, I've heard the news.

LADY JOHN. What news?

FARNBOROUGH. That your little niece—the Scotch heiress—is going to become Mrs. Geoffrey Stonor.

LADY JOHN. Who told you that?

FARNBOROUGH. Please don't mind my knowing.

LADY JOHN (*visibly perturbed*). She had set her heart upon having a few days with just her family in the secret, before the flood of congratulations breaks loose.

FARNBOROUGH. Oh, that's all right. I always hear things before other people.

LADY JOHN. Well, I must ask you to be good enough to be very circumspect. I wouldn't have my niece think that I—

FARNBOROUGH. Oh, of course not.

LADY JOHN. She will be here in an hour.

FARNBOROUGH (*jumping up delighted*). What? Today? The future Mrs. Stonor!

LADY JOHN (*harassed*). Yes. Unfortunately we had one or two people already asked for the weekend—

FARNBOROUGH. And I go and invite myself to luncheon! Lady John, you can buy me off. I'll promise to remove myself in five minutes if you'll—

LADY JOHN. No, the penalty is you shall stay and keep the others amused between church and luncheon, and so leave me free. (*Takes up the plan.*) Only *remember*—

FARNBOROUGH. Wild horses won't get a hint out of me! I only mentioned it to you because—since we've come back to live in this part of the world you've been so awfully kind—I thought, I hoped maybe you—you'd put in a word for me.

LADY JOHN. With—?

FARNBOROUGH. With your nephew that is to be. Though I'm *not* the slavish satellite people make out, you can't doubt—

LADY JOHN. Oh, I don't doubt. But you know Mr. Stonor inspires a similar enthusiasm in a good many young—

FARNBOROUGH. They haven't studied the situation as I have. They don't know what's at stake. They don't go to that hole Dutfield as I did just to hear his Friday speech.

LADY JOHN. Ah! But you were rewarded. Jean—my niece—wrote me it was 'glorious.'

FARNBOROUGH (*judicially*). Well, you know, *I* was disappointed. He's too content just to criticise, just to make his delicate pungent fun of the men who are grappling—very inadequately, of course—still *grappling* with the big questions. There's a carrying power (*gets up and faces an imaginary audience*)—some of Stonor's friends ought to point it out—there's a driving power in the poorest construction policy that makes the most brilliant criticism look barren.

LADY JOHN (*with good-humoured malice*). Who told you that?

FARNSBOROUGH. You think there's nothing in it because *I* say it. But now that's he's coming into the family, Lord John or somebody really ought to point out—Stonor's overdoing his role of magnificent security.

LADY JOHN. I don't see even Lord John offering to instruct Mr. Stonor.

FARNBOROUGH. Believe me, that's just Stonor's danger! Nobody saying a word, everybody hoping he's on the point of adopting some definite line, something strong and original that's going to fire the public imagination and bring the Tories back into power.

LADY JOHN. So he will.

FARNBOROUGH (*hotly*). Not if he disappoints meetings—goes calmly up to town—and leaves the field to the Liberals.

LADY JOHN. When did he do anything like that?

FARNBOROUGH. Yesterday! (*With a harassed air.*) And now that he's got this other preoccupation—

LADY JOHN. You mean—

FARNBOROUGH. Yes, your niece—that spoilt child of Fortune. Of course! (*Stopping suddenly*). She kept him from the meeting last night. Well! (*Sits down.*) If that's the effect she's going to have it's pretty serious!

LADY JOHN (*Smiling*). *You* are!

FARNBOROUGH. I can assure you the election agent's more so. He's simply tearing his hair.

LADY JOHN (*more gravely and coming nearer*). How do you know?

FARNBOROUGH. He told me so himself—yesterday. I scraped acquaintance with the agent just to see if—if—

LADY JOHN. It's not only here that you manœuvre for that Secretaryship!

FARNBOROUGH (*confidentially*). You can never tell when your chance might come! That election chap's promised to keep me posted.

(*The door flies open and Jean Dunbarton rushes in.*)

JEAN. Aunt Ellen—here I—

LADY JOHN (*astonished*). My dear child!

(*They embrace. Enter Lord John from the garden—a benevolent, silver-haired despot of sixty-two.*)

LORD JOHN. I thought that was you running up the avenue.

(*Jean greets her uncle warmly, but all the time she and her aunt talk together. 'How did you get here so early?' 'I knew you'd be surprised—wasn't it clever of me to manage it? I don't deserve all the credit.' 'But there isn't any train be- tween—' 'Yes, wait till I tell you.' 'You walked in the broiling sun—' 'No, no.' 'You must be dead. Why didn't you tele- graph? I ordered the carriage to meet the 1.10. Didn't you say the 1.10? Yes, I'm sure you did—here's your letter.'*)

LORD JOHN (*has shaken hands with Farnborough and speaks through the torrent*). Now they'll tell each other for ten minutes that she's an hour earlier than we expected.

(*Lord John leads Farnborough towards the garden.*)

FARNBOROUGH. The Freddy Tunbridges said *they* were com- ing to you this week.

LORD JOHN. Yes, they're dawdling through the park with the Church Brigade.

FARNBOROUGH. Oh! (*With a glance back at Jean.*) I'll go and meet them.

(*Exit Farnborough.*)

LORD JOHN (*as he starts back*). That discreet young man will get on.

LADY JOHN (*to Jean*). But *how* did you get here?

JEAN (*breathless*). 'He' motored me down.

LADY JOHN. Geoffrey Stonor? (*Jean nods.*) Why, where is he, then?

JEAN. He dropped me at the end of the avenue and went on to see a supporter about something.

LORD JOHN. You let him go off like that without—

LADY JOHN (*taking Jean's two hands*). Just tell me, my child, is it all right?

JEAN. My engagement? (*Radiantly.*) Yes, absolutely.

LADY JOHN. Geoffrey Stonor isn't going to be—a little too old for you?

JEAN (*laughing*). Bless me, am I such a chicken?

LADY JOHN. Twenty-four used not to be so young—but it's become so.

JEAN. Yes, we don't grow up so quick. (*Gaily.*) But on the other hand we *stay* up longer.

LORD JOHN. You've got what's vulgarly called 'looks,' my dear, and that will help to *keep* you up!

JEAN (*smiling*). I know what Uncle John's thinking. But I'm not the only girl who's been left 'what's vulgarly called' money.

LORD JOHN. You're the only one of our immediate circle who's been left so beautifully much.

JEAN. Ah, but remember Geoffrey could—everybody *knows* he could have married any one in England.

LADY JOHN (*faintly ironic*). I'm afraid everybody does know it—not excepting Mr. Stonor.

LORD JOHN. Well, how spoilt is the great man?

JEAN. Not the least little bit in the world. You'll see! He so wants to know my best-loved relations better. (*Another embrace.*) An orphan has so few belongings, she has to make the most of them.

LORD JOHN (*smiling*). Let us hope he'll approve of us on more intimate acquaintance.

JEAN (*firmly*). He will. He's an angel. Why, he gets on with my grandfather!

LADY JOHN. *Does* he? (*Teasing.*) You mean to say Mr. Geof- frey Stonor isn't just a tiny bit—'superior' about Dis- senters.

JEAN (*stoutly*). Not half as much as Uncle John and all the rest of you! My grandfather's been ill again, you know, and rather difficult—bless him! (*Radiantly.*) But Geof- frey—(*Clasps her hands.*)

LADY JOHN. He must have powers of persuasion!—to get that old Covenanter to let you come in an abhorred motor car—on Sunday, too!

JEAN (*half whispering*). Grandfather didn't know!

LADY JOHN. Didn't know?

JEAN. I honestly meant to come by train. Geoffrey met me on the way to the station. We had the most glorious run. Oh, Aunt Ellen, we're so happy! (*Embracing her.*) I've so looked forward to having you to myself the whole day just to talk to you about—

LORD JOHN (*turning away with affected displeasure*). Oh, very well—

JEAN (*catches him affectionately by the arm*). You'd find it dr- effly dull to hear me talk about Geoffrey the whole blessed day!

LADY JOHN. Well, till luncheon, my dear, you mustn't mind if I—(*To Lord John, as she goes to the writing table.*) Miss Levering wasn't only tired last night, she was ill.

LORD JOHN. I thought she looked very white.

JEAN. Who is Miss—You don't mean to say there are other people?

LADY JOHN. One or two. Your uncle's responsible for asking that old cynic, St. John Greatorex, and I—

JEAN (*gravely*). Mr. Greatorex—he's a Radical, isn't he?

LORD JOHN (*laughing*). *Jean!* Beginning to 'think in parties'!

LADY JOHN. It's very natural now that she should—

JEAN. I only meant it was odd he should be here. Naturally at my grandfather's—

LORD JOHN. It's all right, my child. Of course we expect now that you'll begin to think like Geoffrey Stonor, and to feel like Geoffrey Stonor, and to talk like Geoffrey Stonor. And quite proper too.

JEAN (*smiling*). Well, if I do think with my husband and feel with him—as, of course, I shall—it will surprise me if I ever find myself talking a tenth as well—(*Following her uncle to the French window.*) You should have heard him at Dutfield—(*Stopping short, delighted.*) Oh! The Freddy Tunbridges. What? Not Aunt Lydia! Oh-h! (*Looking back reproachfully at Lady John, who makes a discreet motion 'I couldn't help it.'*)

(*Enter the Tunbridges. Mr. Freddy, of no profession and of independent means. Well-groomed, pleasant-looking; of few words. A 'nice man' who likes 'nice women', and has married one of them. Mrs. Freddy is thirty. An attractive figure, delicate face, intelligent grey eyes, over-sensitive mouth, and naturally curling dust-coloured hair.*)

MRS FREDDY. What a delightful surprise!

JEAN (*Shaking hands warmly*). I'm so glad. How d'ye do, Mr Freddy?

(*Enter Lady John's sister, Mrs Heriot—smart, pompous, fifty—followed by Farnborough.*)

MRS HERIOT. My dear Jean! My darling child!

JEAN. How do you do, aunt?

MRS HERIOT (*sotto voce*). I wasn't surprised. I always prophe-sied—

JEAN. Sh! *Please!*

FARNBOROUGH. We haven't met since you were in short skirts. I'm Dick Farnborough.

JEAN. Oh, I remember.

(*They shake hands.*)

MRS FREDDY (*looking round*). Not down yet—the Elusive One?

JEAN. Who is the Elusive One?

MRS FREDDY. Lady John's new friend.

LORD JOHN (*to Jean*). Oh, I forgot you hadn't seen Miss Levering; such a nice creature! (*To Mrs Freddy.*)—don't you think?

MRS FREDDY. Of course I do. You're lucky to get her to come so often. She won't go to other people.

LADY JOHN. She knows she can rest here.

FREDDY (*who has joined Lady John near the writing table*). What does she do to tire her?

LADY JOHN. She's been helping my sister and me with a scheme of ours.

MRS HERIOT. She certainly knows how to inveigle money out of the men.

LADY JOHN. It would sound less equivocal, Lydia, if you added that the money is to build baths in our Shelter for Homeless Women.

MRS FREDDY. Homeless women?

LADY JOHN. Yes, in the most insanitary part of Soho.

FREDDY. Oh—a—really.

FARNBOROUGH. It doesn't sound quite in Miss Levering's line!

LADY JOHN. My dear boy, you know as little about what's in a woman's line as most men.

FREDDY (*laughing*). Oh, I say!

LORD JOHN (*indulgently to Mr. Freddy and Farnborough*). Phil-anthropy in a woman like Miss Levering is a form of rest-lessness. But she's a *nice* creature; all she needs is to get some 'nice' fella to marry her.

MRS FREDDY (*laughing as she hangs on her husband's arm*). Yes, a woman needs a balance wheel—if only to keep her from flying back to town on a hot day like this.

LORD JOHN. Who's proposing anything so—

MRS FREDDY. The Elusive One.

LORD JOHN. Not Miss—

MRS FREDDY. Yes, before luncheon!

(*Exit Farnborough to the garden.*)

LADY JOHN. She must be in London by this afternoon, she says.

LORD JOHN. What for in the name of—

LADY JOHN. Well, *that* I didn't ask her. But (*consults her watch*) I think I'll just go up and see if she's changed her plans.

(*Exit Lady John.*)

LORD JOHN. Oh, she must be *made* to. Such a nice creature! All she needs—

(*Voices outside. Enter fussily, talking and gesticulating. St John Greatorex, followed by Miss Levering and Farnbor-ough. Greatorex is sixty, wealthy, a county magnate, and Liberal MP. He is square, thick-set, square-bearded. His shining bald pate has two strands of coal-black hair trained across his crown from left ear to right and securely pasted there. He has small, twinkling eyes and a reputation for telling good stories after dinner when ladies have left the room. He is carrying a little book for Miss Levering. She (parasol over shoulder), an attractive, essentially feminine, and rather 'smart' woman of thirty-two, with a somewhat foreign grace; the kind of whom men and women alike say, 'What's her story? Why doesn't she marry?'*)

GREATOREX. I protest! Good Lord! what are the women of this country coming to? I *protest* against Miss Levering being carried off to discuss anything so revolting. Bless my soul! what can a woman like you *know* about it?

MISS LEVERING (*smiling*). Little enough. Good morning.

GREATOREX (*relieved*). I should think so indeed!

LORD JOHN (*aside*). You aren't serious about going—

GREATOREX (*waggishly breaking in*). We were so happy out there in the summer-house, weren't we?

MISS LEVERING. Ideally.

GREATOREX. And to be haled out to talk about Public *Sanitation* forsooth! (*Hurries after Miss Levering as she advances to speak to the Freddys & co.*) Why, God bless my soul, do you realise that's *drains*?

MISS LEVERING. I'm dreadfully afraid it is! (*Holds out her hand for the small book Greatorex is carrying.*)

(*Greatorex returns Miss Levering's book open; he has been keeping the place with his finger. She opens it and shuts her handkerchief in.*)

GREATOREX. And we in the act of discussing Italian literature! Perhaps you'll tell me that isn't a more savoury topic for a lady.

MISS LEVERING. But for the tramp population less conducive to saviouriness, don't you think, than—baths?

GREATOREX. No, I can't understand this morbid interest in vagrants. *You're* much too—leave it to the others.

JEAN. What others?

GREATOREX (*with smiling impertinence*). Oh, the sort of woman who smells of indiarubber. The typical English spinster. (*To Miss Levering.*) *You* know—Italy's full of her. She never goes anywhere without a mackintosh and a collapsible bath—rubber. When you look at her, it's borne in upon you that she doesn't only smell of rubber. *She's* rubber too.

LORD JOHN (*laughing*). This is my neice, Miss Jean Dunbarton, Miss Levering.

JEAN. How do you do? (*The shake hands.*)

GREATOREX (*to Jean*). I'm sure *you* agree with me.

JEAN. About Miss Levering being too—

GREATOREX. For that sort of thing—*much* too—

MISS LEVERING. What a pity you've exhausted the more eloquent adjectives.

GREATOREX. But I haven't!

MISS LEVERING. Well, you can't say to me as you did to Mrs Freddy: 'You're too young and too happily married—and too—(*Glances round smiling at Mrs Freddy, who, oblivious, is laughing and talking to her husband and Mrs Heriot.*)

JEAN. For what was Mrs Freddy too happily married and all the rest?

MISS LEVERING (*lightly*). Mr Greatorex was repudiating the horrid rumour that Mrs Freddy had been speaking in public; about Women's Trade Unions—wasn't that what you said, Mrs Heriot?

LORD JOHN (*chuckling*). Yes, it isn't made up as carefully as your aunt's parties usually are. Here we've got Greatorex (*takes his arm*) who hates political women, and we've got in that mild and inoffensive looking little lady—(*Motion over his shoulder towards Mrs Freddy.*)

GREATOREX (*shrinking down stage in comic terror*). You don't mean she's *really*—

JEAN (*simultaneously and gaily rising*). Oh, and you've got me!

LORD JOHN (*with genial affection*). My dear child, he doesn't hate the charming wives and sweethearts who help to win seats.

(*Jean makes her uncle a discreet little signal of warning.*)

MISS LEVERING. Mr Greatorex objects only to the unsexed creatures who—a—

LORD JOHN (*hastily to cover up his slip*). Yes, yes, who want to act independently of men.

MISS LEVERING. Vote, and do silly things of that sort.

LORD JOHN (*with enthusiasm*). Exactly.

MRS HERIOT. It will be a long time before we hear any more of *that* nonsense.

JENA. You mean that rowdy scene in the House of Commons?

MRS HERIOT. Yes. No decent woman will be able to say 'Suffrage' without blushing for another generation, thank Heaven!

MISS LEVERING (*smiling*). Oh? I understood that so little I almost imagined people were more stirred up about it than they'd ever been before.

GREATOREX (*with a quizzical affectation of gallantry*). Not people like you.

MISS LEVERING (*teasingly*). How do you know?

GREATOREX (*with a start*). God bless my soul!

LORD JOHN. She's saying that only to get a rise out of you.

GREATOREX. Ah, yes, your frocks aren't serious enough.

MISS LEVERING. I'm told it's an exploded notion that the Suffrage women are all dowdy and dull.

GREATOREX. Don't you believe it!

MISS LEVERING. Well, of course we know you've been an authority on the subject for—let's see, how many years is it you've kept the House in roars whenever Woman's Rights are mentioned?

GREATOREX (*flattered but not entirely comfortable*). Oh, as long as I've known anything about politics there have been a few discontented old maids and hungry widows—

MISS LEVERING. 'A few!' That's really rather forbearing of you, Mr Greatorex. I'm afraid the number of the discontented and the hungry was 96,000—among the mill operatives alone. (*Hastily.*) At least the papers said so, didn't they?

GREATOREX. Oh, don't ask me; that kind of woman doesn't interest me, I'm afraid. Only I am able to point out to the people who lose their heads and seem inclined to treat the phenomenon seriously that there's absolutely nothing new in it. There have been women for the last forty years who haven't had anything more pressing to do than petition Parliament.

MISS LEVERING (*reflectively*). And that's as far as they've got.

LORD JOHN (*turning on his heel*). It's as far as they'll ever get.

(*Meets the group coming down.*)

MISS LEVERING (*chaffing Greatorex*). Let me see, wasn't a deputation sent to you not long ago? (*Sits.*)

GREATOREX. H'm! (*Irritably.*) Yes, yes.

MISS LEVERING (*as though she has just recalled the circumstances*). Oh, yes, I remember. I thought at the time, in my modest way, it was nothing short of heroic of them to go asking audience of their arch opponent.

GREATOREX (*stoutly*). It didn't come off.

MISS LEVERING (*innocently*). Oh! I thought they insisted on bearding the lion in his den.

GREATOREX. Of course I wasn't going to be bothered with a lot of—

MISS LEVERING. You don't mean you refused to go out and face them!

GREATOREX (*with a comic look of terror*). I wouldn't have done it for worlds. But a friend of mine went and had a look at 'em.

MISS LEVERING (*smiling*). Well, did he get back alive?

GREATOREX Yes, but he advised me not to go. 'You're quite right,' he said. 'Don't you think of bothering,' he said. 'I've looked over the lot,' he said, 'and there isn't a weekender among 'em.'

JEAN (*gaily precipitates herself into the conversation*). You remember Mrs Freddy's friend who came to tea here in the winter? (*To Greatorex.*) He was a member of Parliament too—quite a little young one—he said women would never be respected till they had the vote!

(*Greatorex snorts, the other men smile and all the women except Mrs Heriot.*)

MRS HERIOT (*sniffing*). I remember telling him that he was too young to know what he was talking about.

LORD JOHN. Yes, I'm afraid you all sat on the poor gentleman.

LADY JOHN (*entering*). Oh, *there* you are! (*Greets Miss Levering.*)

JEAN. It was such fun. He was flat as a pancake when we'd done with him. Aunt Ellen told him with her most distinguished air she didn't want to be 'respected.'

MRS FREDDY (*with a laugh of remonstrance*). My *dear* Lady John!

FARNBOROUGH. Quite right! Awful idea to think you're respected!

MISS LEVERING (*smiling*). Simply revolting.

LADY JOHN (*at writing-tablet*). Now, you frivolous people, go away. We've only got a few minutes to talk over the terms of the late Mr Soper's munificence before the carriage come for Miss Levering—

MRS FREDDY (*to Farnborough*). Did you know she'd got that old horror to give Lady John £8,000 for her charity before he died?

MRS FREDDY. Who got him to?

LADY JOHN. Miss Levering. He wouldn't do it for me, but she brought him round.

FREDDY. Yes, Bah-ee Jove! I expect so.

MRS FREDDY (*turning enthusiastically to her husband*). Isn't she wonderful?

LORD JOHN (*aside*). Nice creature. All she needs is—

Mr and Mrs Freddy and Farnborough stroll off to the garden. Lady John is on the far side of the writing-table. Mrs Heriotis at the top. Jean and Lord John on the left.

GREATOREX (*on divan centre, aside, to Miss Levering*). Too 'wonderful' to waste your time on the wrong people.

MISS LEVERING. I shall waste less of my time after this.

GREATOREX. I'm relieved to hear it. I can't see you wheedling money for shelters and rot of that sort out of retired grocers.

MISS LEVERING. You see, you call it rot. We couldn't have got £8,000 out of *you*.

GREATOREX (*very low*). I'm not sure.

(*Miss Levering looks at him.*)

GREATOREX. If I gave you that much—for your little projects—what would you give me?

MISS LEVERING (*speaking quietly*). Soper didn't ask that.

GREATOREX (*horrified*). Soper! I should think not!

LORD JOHN (*turning to Miss Levering*). Soper? You two still talking Soper. How flattered the old beggar'd be!

LORD JOHN (*lower*). Did you hear what Mrs Heriot said about him? 'So kind; so munificent—*so vulgar,* poor soul, we couldn't know him in London—*but we shall meet him in heaven*'.

(*Greatorex and Lord John go off laughing.*)

LADY JOHN (*to Miss Levering*). Sit over there, my dear. (*Indicating chair in front of the writing table.*) You needn't stay, Jean. This won't interest you.

MISS LEVERING (*in the tone of one agreeing*). It's only an effort to meet the greatest evil in the world?

JEAN (*pausing as she's following the others*). What do you call the greatest evil in the world?

(*Looks pass between Mrs Heriot and Lady John.*)

MISS LEVERING (*without emphasis*). The helplessness of women.

(*Jean stands still.*)

LADY JOHN (*rising and putting her arm about the girl's shoulder*). Jean, darling, I know you can think of nothing but (*aside*) *him*—so just go and—

JEAN (*brightly*). Indeed, indeed, I can think of everything better than I ever did before. He has lit up everything for me—made everything vivider, more—more significant.

MISS LEVERING (*turning round*). Who has?

JEAN. Oh, yes. I don't care about other things less but a thousand times more.

LADY JOHN. You *are* in love.

MISS LEVERING. Oh, that's it! (*Smiling at Jean.*) I congratulate you.

LADY JOHN (*returning to the outspread plan*). Well—this, you see, obviates the difficulty you raised.

MISS LEVERING. Yes, quite.

MRS HERIOT. But it's going to cost a great deal more.

MISS LEVERING. It's worth it.

MRS HERIOT. We'll have nothing left for the organ at St Pilgrim's.

LADY JOHN. My dear Lydia, we're putting the organ aside.

MRS HERIOT (*with asperity*). We can't afford to 'put aside' the elevating effect of music.

LADY JOHN. What we must make for, first, is the cheap and humanely conducted lodging-house.

MRS HERIOT. There are several of those already, but poor St Pilgrim's—

MISS LEVERING. There are none for the poorest women.

LADY JOHN. No, even the excellent Soper was for multiplying Rowton Houses. You can never get men to realise—you can't always get women—

MISS LEVERING. It's the work least able to wait.

MRS HERIOT. I don't agree with you, and I happen to have spent a great deal of my life in works of charity.

MISS LEVERING. Ah, then you'll be interested in the girl I saw dying in a Tramp Ward a little while ago. *Glad* her cough was worse—only she mustn't die before her father. Two reasons. Nobody but her to keep the old man out of the workhouse—and 'father is so proud.' If she died first, he would starve; worse of all he might hear what had happened up in London to his girl.

MRS HERIOT. She didn't say, I suppose, how she happened to fall so low.

MISS LEVERING. Yes, she had been in service. She lost the train back one Sunday night and was too terrified of her employer to dare ring him up after hours. The wrong person found her crying on the platform.

MRS HERIOT. She should have gone to one of the Friendly Societies.

MISS LEVERING. At eleven at night?

MRS HERIOT. And there are the Rescue Leagues. I myself have been connected with one for twenty years—

MISS LEVERING (*reflectively*). 'Twenty years!' Always arriving 'after the train's gone'—after the girl and the Wrong Person have got to the journey's end.

(*Mrs Heriot's eyes flash.*)

JEAN. Where is she now?

LADY JOHN. Never mind.

MISS LEVERING. Two nights ago she was waiting at a street corner in the rain.

MRS HERIOT. Near a public-house, I suppose.

MISS LEVERING. Yes, a sort of 'public house.' She was plainly dying—she was told she shouldn't be out in the rain. 'I mustn't go in yet,' she said. 'This is what he gave me,' and she began to cry. In her hand were two pennies silvered over to look like half-crowns.

MRS HERIOT. I don't believe that story. It's just the sort of thing some sensation-monger trumps up—now, who tells you such—

MISS LEVERING. Several credible people. I didn't believe them till—

JEAN. Till—?

MISS LEVERING. Till last week I saw for myself.

LADY JOHN. *Saw?* Where?

MISS LEVERING. In a low lodging-house not a hundred yards from the church you want a new organ for.

MRS HERIOT. How did *you* happen to be there?

MISS LEVERING. I was on a pilgrimage.

JEAN. A pilgrimage?

MISS LEVERING. Into the Underworld.

LADY JOHN. *You* went?

JEAN. How *could* you?

MISS LEVERING. I put on an old gown and a tawdry hat—(*Turns to Lady John.*) You'll never know how many things are hidden from a woman in good clothes. The bold, free look of a man at a woman he believes to be destitute—you must feel that look on you before you can understand—a good half of history.

MRS HERIOT (*rises*). Jean!—

JEAN. But where did you go—dressed like that?

MISS LEVERING. Down among the homeless women—on a wet night looking for shelter.

LADY JOHN (*hastily*). No wonder you've been ill.

JEAN (*under her breath*). And it's like that?

MISS LEVERING. No.

JEAN. No?

MISS LEVERING. It's so much worse I dare not tell about it—even if you weren't here I couldn't.

MRS HERIOT (*to Jean*). You needn't suppose, darling, that those wretched creatures feel it as we would.

MISS LEVERING. The girls who need shelter and work aren't all serving-maids.

MRS HERIOT (*with an involuntary flash*). We know that all the women who—*make mistakes* aren't.

MISS LEVERING (*steadily*). That is why *every* woman ought to take an interest in this—every girl too.

JEAN.   Yes—oh, yes!

LADY (*simultaneously*).   No. This is a

JOHN.   matter for us older—

MRS HERIOT (*with an air of sly challenge*). Or for a person who has some special knowledge. (*Significantly.*) We can't pretend to have access to such sources of information as Miss Levering.

MISS LEVERING (*meeting Mrs. Heriot's eye steadily*). Yes, for I can give you access. As you seem to think, I have some first-hand knowledge about homeless girls.

LADY JOHN (*cheerfully turning it aside*). Well, my dear, it will all come in convenient. (*Tapping the plan.*)

MISS LEVERING. It once happened to me to take offence at an ugly thing that was going on under my father's roof. Oh, *years* ago! I was an impulsive girl. I turned my back on my father's house—

LADY JOHN (*for Jean's benefit*). That was ill-advised.

MRS HERIOT. Of course, if a girl does *that*—

MISS LEVERING. That was what all my relations said (*with a glance at Jean*), and I couldn't explain.

JEAN. Not to your mother?

MISS LEVERING. She was dead. I went to London to a small hotel and tried to find employment. I wandered about all day and every day from agency to agency. I was supposed to be educated. I'd been brought up partly in Paris; I could play several instruments, and sing little songs in four different tongues. (*Slight pause.*)

JEAN. Did nobody want you to teach French or sing the little songs?

MISS LEVERING. The heads of schools thought me too young. There were people ready to listen to my singing but the terms—they were too hard. Soon my money was gone. I began to pawn my trinkets. *They* went.

JEAN. And still no work?

MISS LEVERING. No; but by that time I had some real education—an unpaid hotel bill, and not a shilling in the world. (*Slight pause.*) Some girls think it hardship to have to earn their living. The horror is not to be allowed to—

JEAN (*bending forward*). What happened?

LADY JOHN (*rises*). My dear (*to Miss Levering:*) have your things been sent down? Are you quite ready?

MISS LEVERING. Yes, all but my hat.

JEAN. Well?

MISS LEVERING. Well, by chance I met a friend of my family.

JEAN. That was lucky.

MISS LEVERING. I thought so. He was nearly ten years older than I. He said he wanted to help me. (*Pause.*)

JEAN. And didn't he?

(*Lady John lays her hand on Miss Levering's shoulder.*)

MISS LEVERING. Perhaps after all he did. (*With sudden change of tone.*) Why do I waste time over myself? I belonged to the little class of armed women. My body wasn't born weak, and my spirit wasn't broken by the *habit* of slavery. But, as Mrs Heriot was kind enough to hint, I do know something about the possible fate of homeless girls. I found there were pleasant parks, museums, free libraries in our great rich London—and not one single place where destitute women can be sure of work that isn't killing or food that isn't worse than prison fare. That's why women ought not to sleep o' nights till this Shelter stands spreading out wide arms.

JEAN. No, no—

MRS HERIOT (*gathering up her gloves, fan, prayer-book, etc.*). Even when it's built—you'll see! Many of those creatures will prefer the life they lead. They *like* it.

MISS LEVERING. A woman told me—one of the sort that knows—told me many of them 'like it' so much that they are indifferent to the risk of being set to prison. '*It gives them a rest,*' she said.

LADY JOHN. A rest!

(*Miss Levering glances at the clock as she rises to go upstairs.*)

(*Lady John and Mrs Heriot bend their heads over the plan, covertly talking.*)

JEAN (*intercepting Miss Levering*). I want to begin to understand something of—I'm horribly ignorant.

MISS LEVERING (*Looks at her searchingly*). I'm a rather busy person—

JEAN (*interrupting*). I have quite a special reason for wanting *not* to be ignorant. (*Impulsively.*) I'll go to town tomorrow, if you'll come and lunch with me.

MISS LEVERING. Thank you—I (*catches Mrs Heriot's eye*)—I must go and put my hat on.

(*Exit upstairs.*)

MRS HERIOT (*aside*). How little she minds all these horrors!

LADY JOHN. They turn me cold. Ugh. (*Rising, harassed.*) I wonder if she's signed the visitor's book!

MRS HERIOT. For all her Shelter schemes, she's a hard woman.

JEAN. Miss Levering is?

MRS HERIOT. Oh, of course *you* won't think so. She has angled very adroitly for your sympathy.

JEAN. She doesn't look hard.

LADY JOHN (*glancing at Jean and taking alarm*). I'm not sure but what she does. Her mouth—always like this . . . as if she were holding back something by main force!

MRS HERIOT (*half under her breath*). Well, so she is.

(*Exit Lady John into the lobby to look at the visitors' book.*)

JEAN. Why haven't I seen her before?

MRS HERIOT. Oh, she's lived abroad. (*Debating with herself.*) You don't know about her, I suppose?

JEAN. I don't know how Aunt Ellen came to know her.

MRS HERIOT. That was my doing. But I didn't bargain for her being introduced to you.

JEAN. She seems to go everywhere. And why shouldn't she?

MRS HERIOT (*quickly*). You mustn't ask her to Eaton Square.

JEAN. I have.

MRS HERIOT. Then you'll have to get out of it.

JEAN (*with a stubborn look*). I must have a reason. And a very good reason.

MRS HERIOT. Well, it's not a thing I should have preferred to tell you, but I know how difficult you are to guide . . . so I suppose you'll have to know. (*Lowering her voice.*) It was ten or twelve years ago. I found her horribly ill in a lonely Welsh farmhouse. We had taken the Manor for that August. The farmer's wife was frightened, and begged me to go and see what I thought. I soon saw how it was—I thought she was dying.

JEAN. *Dying!* What was the—

MRS HERIOT. I got no more out of her than the farmer's wife did. She had had no letters. There had been no one to see her except a man down from London, a shady-looking doctor—nameless, of course. And then this result. The farmer and his wife, highly respectable people, were incensed. They were for turning the girl out.

JEAN. *Oh!* but—

MRS HERIOT. Yes. Pitiless some of these people are! I insisted they should treat the girl humanely, and we became friends . . . that is, 'sort of'. In spite of all I did for her—

JEAN. What did you do?

MRS HERIOT. I—I've told you, and I lent her money. No small sum either.

JEAN. Has she never paid it back?

MRS HERIOT. Oh, yes, after a time. But I *always* kept her secret—as much as I knew of it.

JEAN. But you've been telling me!

MRS HERIOT. That was my duty—and I *never* had her full confidence.

JEAN. Wasn't it natural she—

MRS HERIOT. Well, all things considered, she might have wanted to tell me who was responsible.

JEAN. Oh! Aunt Lydia!

MRS HERIOT. All she ever said was that she was ashamed—(*losing her temper and her fine feeling for the innocence of her auditor*)—ashamed that she 'hadn't had the courage to resist'—not the original temptation but the pressure brought to bear on her 'not to go through with it,' as she said.

JEAN (*wrinkling her brows*). You are being so delicate—I'm not sure I understand.

MRS HERIOT (*irritably*). The only thing you need understand is that she's not a desirable companion for a young girl.

(*Pause.*)

JEAN. When did you see her after—after—

MRS HERIOT (*with a slight grimace*). I met her last winter at the Bishop's. (*Hurriedly.*) She's a connection of his wife's. They'd got her to help with some of their work. Then she took hold of ours. Your aunt and uncle are quite foolish about her, and I'm debarred from taking any steps, at least till the Shelter is out of hand.

JEAN. I do rather wonder she can bring herself to talk about—the unfortunate women of the world.

MRS HERIOT. The effrontery of it!

JEAN. Or . . . the courage! (*Puts her hand up to her throat as if the sentence had caught there.*)

MRS HERIOT. Even presumes to set *me* right! Of course I don't *mind* in the least, poor soul . . . but I feel I owe it to your dead mother to tell you about her, especially as you're old enough now to know something about life—

JEAN (*slowly*). —and since a girl needn't be very old to suffer for her ignorance. (*Moves a little away.*) I *felt* she was rather wonderful.

MRS HERIOT. *Wonderful!*

JEAN (*pausing*) . . . To have lived through *that* when she was . . . how old?

MRS HERIOT (*rising*). Oh, nineteen or thereabouts.

JEAN. Five years younger than I. To be abandoned and to come out of it like this!

MRS HERIOT (*laying her hand on the girl's shoulder*). It was too bad to have to tell you such a sordid story today of all days.

JEAN. It is a very terrible story, but this wasn't a bad time. I feel very sorry today for women who aren't happy.

(*Motor horn heard faintly.*)

(*Jumping up.*) That's Geoffrey!

MRS HERIOT. Mr. Stonor! What makes you think . . . ?

JEAN. Yes, yes. I'm sure, I'm sure—

(*Checks herself as she is flying off. Turns and sees Lord John entering from the garden.*)

(*Motor horn louder.*)

LORD JOHN. Who do you think is motoring up the drive?

JEAN (*catching hold of him*). Oh, dear! How am I ever going to be able to behave like a girl who isn't engaged to the only man in the world worth marrying?

MRS HERIOT. You were expecting Mr Stonor all the time!

JEAN. He promised he'd come to luncheon if it was humanly possible; but I was afraid to tell you for fear he'd be prevented.

LORD JOHN (*laughing as he crosses to the lobby*). You felt we couldn't have borne the disappointment.

JEAN. I felt I couldn't.

(*The lobby door opens. Lady John appears radiant, followed by a tall figure in a dustcoat, etc., no goggles. He has straight, firm features, a little blunt; fair skin, high coloured; fine, straight hair, very fair; grey eyes, set somewhat prominently and heavy when not interested; lips full, but firmly moulded, Geoffrey Stonor is heavier than a man of forty should be, but otherwise in the pink of physical condition. The Footman stands waiting to help him off with his motor coat.*)

LADY JOHN. Here's an agreeable surprise!

(*Jean has gone forward only a step, and stands smiling at the approaching figure.*)

LORD JOHN. How do you do? (*As he comes between them and briskly shakes hands with Stonor.*)

(*Farnborough appears at the French window.*)

FARNBOROUGH. Yes, by Jove! (*Turning to the others clustered round the window.*) What gigantic luck!

(*Those outside crane and glance, and then elaborately turn their backs and pretend to be talking among them-*

selves, but betray as far as manners permit the enormous sensation the arrival has created.)

STONOR. How do you do?

(Shakes hands with Mrs Heriot, who has rushed up to him with both hers outstretched. He crosses to Jean, who meets him half way; they shake hands, smiling into each other's eyes.)

JEAN. Such a long time since we met!

LORD JOHN *(to Stonor)*. You're growing very enterprising. I could hardly believe my ears when I heard you'd motored all the way from town to see a supporter on Sunday.

STONOR. I don't know how we covered the ground in the old days. *(To Lady John.)* It's no use to stand for your borough any more. The American, you know, he 'runs' for Congress. By and by we shall all be flying after the thing we want. *(Smiles at Jean.)*

JEAN. Sh! *(Smiles and then glances over her shoulder and speaks low.)* All sorts of irrelevant people here.

FARNBOROUGH *(unable to resist the temptation, comes forward)*. How do you do, Mr. Stonor?

STONOR. Oh—how d'you do.

FARNBOROUGH. Some of them were arguing in the smoking-room last night whether it didn't hurt a man's chances going about in a motor.

LORD JOHN. Yes, we've been hearing a lot of stories about the unpopularity of motor cars—among the class that hasn't got 'em, of course. What do you say?

LADY JOHN. I'm sure you gain more votes by being able to reach so many more of your constituency than we used—

STONOR. Well, I don't know—I've sometimes wondered whether the charm of our presence wasn't counterbalanced by the way we tear about smothering our fellow-beings in dust and running down their pigs and chickens, not to speak of their children.

LORD JOHN *(anxiously)*. What on the whole are the prospects?

(Farnborough cranes forward.)

STONOR *(gravely)*. We shall have to work harder than we realised.

FARNBOROUGH. Ah! *(Retires towards group.)*

JEAN *(in a half-aside as she slips her arm in her uncle's and smiles at Geoffrey)*. He says he believes I'll be able to make a real difference to his chances. Isn't it angelic of him?

STONOR *(in a jocular tone)*. Angelic? Macchiavelian. I pin all my hopes on your being able to counteract the pernicious influence of my opponent's glib wife.

JEAN. You want me to have a *real* share in it all, don't you, Geoffrey?

STONOR *(smiling into her eyes)*. Of course I do.

(Farnborough drops down again on pretence of talking to Mrs Heriot.)

LORD JOHN. I don't gather you're altogether sanguine. Any complication?

(Jean and Lady John stand close together, the girl radiant, following Stonor with her eyes and whispering to the sympathetic elder woman.)

STONOR. Well, *(taking Sunday paper out of pocket)* there's this agitation about the Woman Question. Oddly enough, it seems likely to affect the issue.

LORD JOHN. Why should it? Can't you do what the other four hundred have done?

STONOR *(laughs)*. Easily. But, you see, the mere fact that four hundred and twenty members have been worried into promising support—and then once in the House have left the matter severely alone—

LORD JOHN *(to Stonor)*. Let is alone! Bless my soul, I should think so indeed.

STONOR. Of course. Only it's a device that's somewhat worn.

(Enter Miss Levering, with hat on; gloves and veil in her hand.)

LORD JOHN. Still if they think they're getting a future Cabinet Minister on their side—

STONOR. . . . . it will be sufficiently embarassing for the Cabinet Minister.

(Stonor turns to speak to Jean. He stops dead seeing Miss Levering.)

JEAN *(smiling)*. You know one another?

MISS LEVERING *(looking at Stonor with intentness but quite calmly)*. Everybody in this part of the world knows Mr Stonor, but he doesn't know me.

LORD JOHN. Miss Levering.

(They bow.)

(Enter Greatorex, sidling in with an air of giving Mrs Freddy a wide berth.)

JEAN *(to Miss Levering with artless enthusiasm)*. Oh, have you been hearing him speak?

MISS LEVERING. Yes, I was visiting some relations near Dutfield. They took me to hear you.

STONOR. Oh—the night the Suffragettes made their customary row.

MISS LEVERING. The night they asked you—

STONOR *(flying at the first chance of distraction, shakes hands with Mrs. Freddy)*. Well, Mrs Freddy, what do you think of your friends now?

MRS FREDDY. My friends?

STONOR *(offering her the Sunday paper)*. Yes, the disorderly women.

MRS FREDDY *(with dignity)*. They are not my friends, but I don't think you must call them—

STONOR. Why not? *(Laughs.)* I can forgive them for worrying the late Government. But they *are* disorderly.

MISS LEVERING *(quietly)*. Isn't the phrase consecrated to a different class?

GREATOREX *(who has got hold of the Sunday paper)*. He's perfectly right. How do you do? Disorderly women! That's what they are!

FARNBOROUGH (*reading over his shoulder*). Ought to be locked up! Every one of 'em.

GREATOREX (*assenting angrily*). Public nuisances! Going about with dog whips and spitting in policemen's faces.

FREDDY (*with a harassed air*). I wonder if they did spit?

GREATOREX (*exulting*). Of *course* they did.

MRS FREDDY (*turns on him*). You're no authority on what they do. *You* run away.

GREATOREX (*trying to turn the laugh*). Run away? Yes. (*Backing a few paces.*) And if ever I muster up courage to come back, it will be to vote for better manners in public life, not worse than we have already.

MRS FREDDY (*meekly*). So should I. Don't think that *I* defend the Suffragette methods.

JEAN (*with cheerful curiosity*). Still, you *are* an advocate of the Suffrage, aren't you?

MRS FREDDY. Here? (*Shrugs.*) I don't beat the air.

GREATOREX (*mocking*). Only policemen.

MRS FREDDY (*plaintively*). If you cared to know the attitude of the real workers in the reform, you might have noticed in any paper last week we lost no time in dissociating ourselves from the little group of hysterical— (*Catches her husband's eye, and instantly checks her flow of words.*)

MRS HERIOT. They have lowered the whole sex in the eyes of the entire world.

JEAN (*joining Geoffrey Stonor*). I can't quite see what they want—those Suffragettes.

GREATOREX. Notoriety.

FARNBOROUGH. What they want? A good thrashin'—that's what I'd give 'em.

MRS HERIOT (*murmurs*). Spirited fellow!

LORD JOHN. Well, there's one sure thing—they've dished their goose. (*Greatorex chuckles, still reading the account.*) I believe these silly scenes are a pure joy to you.

GREATOREX. Final death-blow to the whole silly business!

JEAN (*mystified, looking from one to the other*). The Suffragettes don't seem to *know* they're dead.

GREATOREX. They will keep up a sort of death-rattle. But they've done for themselves.

JEAN (*clasping her hands with a fervour*). Oh, I hope they'll last till the election's over.

FARNBOROUGH (*stares*). Why?

JEAN. Oh, we want them to get the working men to—(*stumbling and a little confused*) —to vote for . . . the Conservative candidate. Isn't that so?

(*Looking round for help. General laughter.*)

LORD JOHN. Fancy, Jean—!

GREATOREX. The working man's a good deal of an ass, but even he won't listen to—

JEAN (*again appearing to the silent Stonor*). But he *does* listen like anything! I asked why there were so few at the Long Mitcham meeting, and I was told, 'Oh, they've all gone to hear Miss—'

STONOR. Just for a lark, that was.

LORD JOHN. It has no real effect on the vote.

GREATOREX. Not the smallest.

JEAN (*wide-eyed to Stonor*). Why, I thought you said—

STONOR (*hastily, rubbing his hand over the lower part of his face and speaking quickly*). I've a notion a little soap and water wouldn't do me any harm.

LORD JOHN. I'll take you up. You know Freddy Tunbridge.

(*Stonor pauses to shake hands. Exeunt all three.*)

JEAN (*perplexed, as Stonor turns away, says to Greatorex*). Well, if women are of no importance in politics, it isn't for the reason you gave. There is now and then a week-ender among them.

GREATOREX (*shuffles about uneasily*). Hm—Hm. (*Finds himself near Mrs Freddy.*) Lord! The perils that beset the feet of man! (*With an air of comic caution, moves away, left.*)

JEAN (*to Farnborough, aside, laughing*). Why does he behave like that?

FARNBOROUGH. His moral sense is shocked.

JEAN. Why, I saw him and Mrs Freddy together at the French Play the other night—as thick as thieves.

MISS LEVERING. Ah, that was before he knew her revolting views.

JEAN. What revolting views?

GREATOREX. Sh! Sunday.

(*As Greatorex sidles cautiously further away.*)

JEAN (*laughing in spite of herself*). I can't believe women are so helpless when I see men so afraid of them.

GREATOREX. The great mistake was in teaching them to read and write.

JEAN (*over Miss Levering's shoulder, whispers*). *Say* something.

MISS LEVERING (*to Greatorex, smiling*). Oh no, that wasn't the worst mistake.

GREATOREX. Yes, it was.

MISS LEVERING. No. Believe me. The mistake was in letting women learn to talk.

GREATOREX. Ah! (*Wheels about with sudden rapture.*) I see now what's to be the next great reform.

MISS LEVERING (*holding up the little volume*). When women are all dumb, no more discussions of the 'Paradiso.'

GREATOREX (*with a gesture of mock rapture*). The thing itself! (*Aside.*) That's a great deal better than talking about it, as I'm sure *you* know.

MISS LEVERING. Why do you think I know?

GREATOREX. Only the plain women are in any doubt.

(*Jean joins Miss Levering.*)

GREATOREX. Wait for me, Farnborough. I cannot go about unprotected.

(*Exeunt Farnborough and Greatorex.*)

MRS FREDDY. It's true what that old cynic says. The scene in the House has put back the reform a generation.

JEAN. I wish I'd been there.

MRS FREDDY. I *was*.

JEAN. Oh, was it like the papers said?

MRS FREDDY. Worse. I've never been so moved in public. No tragedy, no great opera ever gripped an audience as the situation in the House did that night. There we all sat breathless—with everything more favourable to us than it had been within the memory of women. Another five minutes and the Resolution would have passed. Then . . . all in a moment—

LORD JOHN (*to Mrs Heriot*). Listen—they're talking about the female hooligans.

MRS HERIOT. No, thank you! (*Sits apart with the 'Church Times'.*)

MRS FREDDY (*excitedly*). All in a moment a horrible dingy little flag was poked through the grille of the Woman's Gallery—cries—insults—scuffling—the police—the ignominious turning out of the women—*us* as well as the—Oh, I can't *think* of it without—(*Jumps up and walks to and fro. Pauses.*) Then the next morning! The people gloating. Our friends antigonised—people who were wavering—nearly won over—all thrown back—heart breaking! Even my husband! Freddy's been an angel about letting me take my share when I felt I must—but of course I've always known he doesn't really like it. It makes him shy. I'm sure it gives him a horrid twist inside when he sees my name among the speakers on the placards. But he's always been an angel about it before this. After the disgraceful scene he said, 'It just shows how unfit women are for any sort of coherent thinking or concerted action.

JEAN. To think that it should be women who've given the Cause the worst blow it ever had!

MRS FREDDY. The work of forty years destroyed in five minutes!

JEAN. They must have felt pretty sick when they woke up the next morning—the Suffragettes.

MRS FREDDY. I don't waste any sympathy on *them*. I'm thinking of the penalty *all* women have to pay because a handful of hysterical—

JEAN. Still I think I'm sorry for them. It must be dreadful to find you've done such a lot of harm to the thing you care most about in the world.

MISS LEVERING. Do you picture the Suffragettes sitting in sackcloth?

MRS FREDDY. Well, they can't help realising *now* what they've done.

MISS LEVERING (*quietly*). Isn't it just possible they realise they've waked up interest in the Woman Question so that it's advertised in every paper and discussed in every house from Land's End to John O'Groats? Don't you think *they* know there's been more said and written about it in these ten days since the scene, than in the ten years before it?

MRS FREDDY. You aren't saying you think it was a good way to get what they wanted?

MISS LEVERING (*shrugs*). I'm only pointing out that it seems not such a bad way to get it known they *do* want something—and (*smiling*) 'want it bad'.

JEAN (*getting up*). Didn't Mr Greatorex say women had been politely petitioning Parliament for forty years?

MISS LEVERING. And men have only laughed.

JEAN. But they'd come round. (*She looks from one to the other.*) Mrs Tunbridge says, before that horrid scene, everything was favourable at last.

MISS LEVERING. At last? Hadn't it been just as 'favourable' before?

MRS FREDDY. No. We'd never had so many members pledged to our side.

MISS LEVERING. I thought I'd heard somebody say the Bill had got as far as that, time and time again.

JEAN. Oh no. Surely not—

MRS FREDDY (*reluctantly*). Y-yes. This was only a Resolution. The Bill passed a second reading thirty-seven years ago.

JEAN (*with wide eyes*). And what difference did it make?

MISS LEVERING. The men laughed rather louder.

MRS FREDDY. Oh, it's got as far as a second reading several times—but we never had so many friends in the House before—

MISS LEVERING (*with a faint smile*). 'Friends!'

JEAN. Why do you say it like that?

MISS LEVERING. Perhaps because I was thinking of a funny story—he said it was funny—a Liberal Whip told me the other day. A Radical Member went out of the House after his speech in favour of the Woman's Bill, and as he came back half an hour later, he heard some Members talking in the Lobby about the astonishing number who were going to vote for the measure. And the Friend of Woman dropped his jaw and clutched the man next to him: 'My God!' he said, 'you don't mean to say they're going to give it to them!'

JEAN. Oh!

MRS FREDDY. You don't think all men in Parliament are like that!

MISS LEVERING. I don't think all men are burglars, but I lock my doors.

JEAN (*below her breath*). You think that night of the scene—you think the men didn't *mean* to play fair?

MISS LEVERING (*her coolness in contrast to the excitement of the others*). Didn't the women sit quiet till ten minutes to closing time?

JEAN. Ten minutes to settle a question like that!

MISS LEVERING (*quietly to Mrs Freddy*). Couldn't you see the men were at their old game?

LADY JOHN (*coming forward*). You think they were just putting off the issue till it was too late?

MISS LEVERING (*in detached tone*). I wasn't there, but I haven't heard anybody deny that the women waited till ten minutes to eleven. Then they discovered the policeman who'd been sent up at the psychological moment to the back of the gallery. Then, I'm told, when the women saw they were betrayed once more, they utilised the few minutes left, to impress on the country at large the fact of their demands—did it in the only way left them. (*Sits leaning for-*

ward reflectively smiling, chin in hand.) It does rather look to the outside as if the well-behaved women had worked for forty years and made less impression on the world then those fiery young women made in five minutes.

MRS FREDDY. Oh, come, be fair!

MISS LEVERING. Well, you must admit that, next day, every newspaper reader in Europe and America knew there were women in England in such dead earnest about the Suffrage that the men had stopped laughing at last, and turned them out of the House. Men even advertised how little they appreciated the fun by sending the women to gaol in pretty sober earnest. And all the world was talking about it.

(*Mrs Heriot lays down the 'Church Times' and joins the others.*)

LADY JOHN. I have noticed, whenever the men aren't there, the women sit and discuss that scene.

JEAN (*cheerfully*). I shan't have to wait till the men are gone. (*Leans over Lady John's shoulder and says half aside*) He's in sympathy.

LADY JOHN. How do you know?

JEAN. He told the interrupting women so.

(*Mrs Freddy looks mystified. The others smile.*)

LADY JOHN. Oh!

(*Mr. Freddy and Lord John appear by the door they went out of. They stop to talk.*)

MRS FREDDY. Here's Freddy! (*Lower, hastily to Miss Levering*). You're judging from the outside. Those of us who have been working for years—we all realise it was a perfectly lunatic proceeding. Why, think! The only chance of our getting what we want is by *winning over* the men. (*Her watchful eye, leaving her husband for a moment, catches Miss Levering's little involuntary gesture.*) What's the matter?

MISS LEVERING. 'Winning over the men' has been the woman's way for centuries. Do you think the result should make us proud of our policy? Yes? Then go and walk in Piccadilly at midnight. (*The older women glance at Jean.*) No, I forgot—

MRS HERIOT (*with majesty*). Yes, it's not the first time you've forgotten.

MISS LEVERING. I forgot the magistrate's ruling. He said no decent woman had any business to be in London's main thoroughfare at night unless she has *a man with her*. I heard that in Nine Elms, too. 'You're obliged to take up with a chap!' was what the woman said.

MRS HERIOT (*rising*). Jean! Come!

(*She takes Jean by her arm and draws her to the window, where she signals Greatorex and Farnborough. Mrs Freddy joins her husband and Lord John.*)

LADY JOHN (*kindly, aside to Miss Levering*). My dear, I think Lydia Heriot's right. We oughtn't to do anything or *say*

anything to encourage this ferment of feminism, and I'll tell you why: it's like to bring a very terrible thing in its train.

MISS LEVERING. What terrible thing?

LADY JOHN. Sex antagonism.

MISS LEVERING (*rising*). It's here.

LADY JOHN (*very gravely*). Don't say that.

(*Jean has quietly disengaged herself from Mrs Heriot, and the group at the window returns and stands behind Lady John, looking up into Miss Levering's face.*)

MISS LEVERING (*to Lady John*). You're so conscious it's here, you're afraid to have it mentioned.

LADY JOHN (*turning and seeing Jean. Rising hastily*). If it's here, it is the fault of those women agitators.

MISS LEVERING (*gently*). No woman *begins* that way. (*Leans forward with clasped hands looking into vacancy.*) Every woman's in a state of natural subjection (*smiles at Jean*)— no, I'd rather say allegiance to her idea of romance and her hope of motherhood. They're embodied for her in man. They're the strongest things in life—till man kills them. (*Rousing herself and looking into Lady John's face.*) Let's be fair. Each woman knows why that allegiance died.

(*Lady John turns hastily, sees Lord John coming down with Mr Freddy and meets them at the foot of the stairs. Miss Levering has turned to the table looking for her gloves, etc., among the papers; unconsciously drops the handkerchief she had in her little book.*)

JEAN (*in a low voice to Miss Levering*). All this talk against the wicked Suffragettes—it makes me want to go and hear what they've got to say for themselves.

MISS LEVERING (*smiling with a non-committal air as she finds the veil she's been searching for*). Well, they're holding a meeting in Trafalgar Square at three o'clock.

JEAN. This afternoon? But that's no use to people out of town—Unless I could invent some excuse . . .

LORD JOHN (*benevolently*). Still talking over the Shelter plans?

MISS LEVERING. No. We left the Shelter some time ago.

LORD JOHN (*to Jean*). Then what's all the chatterment about?

(*Jean, a little confused, looks at Miss Levering.*)

MISS LEVERING. The latest thing in veils. (*Ties hers round her hat.*)

GREATOREX. The invincible frivolity of woman!

LORD JOHN (*genially*). Don't scold them. It's a very proper tonic.

MISS LEVERING (*whimsically*). Oh, I was afraid you'd despise us for it.

BOTH MEN (*with condescension*). Not at all—not at all.

JEAN (*to Miss Levering as Footman appears*). Oh, they're coming for you. Don't forget your book. (*Footman holds out a salver with a telegram on it for Jean.*) Why, it's for me!

MISS LEVERING. But it's time I was—

(*She crosses to the table.*)

JEAN (*opening the telegram*). May I? (*Reads, and glances over the paper at Miss Levering.*) I've got your book. (*Crosses to Miss Levering, and, looking at the back of the volume*) Dante! Wereabouts are you? (*Opening at the marker.*) Oh, the 'Inferno'.

MISS LEVERING. No: I'm in a worse place.

JEAN. I didn't know there was a worse.

MISS LEVERING. Yes: it's worse with the Vigliacchi.

JEAN. I forget. Were they Guelf or Ghibelline?

MISS LEVERING (*smiling*). They weren't either, and that was why Dante couldn't stand them. (*more gravely.*) He said there was not place in Heaven nor in Purgatory—not even a corner in Hell—for the souls who had stood aloof from strife. (*Looking steadily into the girl's eyes.*) He called them 'wretches who never lived,' Dante did, because they'd never felt the pangs of partizanship. And so they wander homeless on the skirts of limbo among the abortions and off-scourings of Creation.

JEAN (*a long breath after a long look. When Miss Levering has turned away to make her leisurely adieux Jean's eyes fall on the open telegram*). Aunt Ellen, I've got to go to London.

(*Stonor, re-entering, hears this, but pretends to talk to Mr. Freddy, etc.*)

LADY JOHN. My dear child!

MRS HERLIOT. Nonsense! Is your grandfather worse?

JEAN (*folding the telegram*). No-o. I don't think so. But it's necessary I should go, all the same.

MRS HERIOT. Go away when Mr Stonor—

JEAN. He said he'd have to leave directly after luncheon.

LADY JOHN. I'll just see Miss Levering off, and then I'll come back and talk about it.

LORD JOHN (*to Miss Levering*). Why are you saying goodbye as if you were never coming back?

MISS LEVERING (*smiling*). One never knows. Maybe I shan't come back. (*To Stonor.*) Goodbye.

(*Stonor bows ceremoniously. The others go up laughing. Stonor comes down.*)

JEAN (*impulsively*). There mayn't be another train! Miss Levering—

STONOR (*standing in front of her*). What if there isn't? I'll take you back in the motor.

JEAN (*rapturously*). Will you? (*Inadvertently drops the telegram.*) I must be there by three!

STONOR (*picks up the telegram ad a handkerchief lying near, glances at the message*). Why, it's only an invitation to dine—Wednesday!

JEAN. Sh! (*Takes the telegram and puts it in her pocket.*)

STONOR. Oh, I see! (*Lower, smiling.*) It's rather dear of you to arrange our going off like that. You *are* a clever little girl!

JEAN. It's not that I was arranging. I want to hear those women in Trafalgar Square—the Suffragettes.

STONOR (*incredulous, but smiling*). How perfectly absurd! (*Looking after Lady John.*) Besides, I expect she wouldn't like my carrying you off like that.

JEAN. Then she'll have to make an excuse and come too.

STONOR. Ah, it wouldn't be quite the same—

JEAN (*rapidly thinking it out*). We could get back here in time for dinner.

(*Geoffrey Stonor glances down at the handkerchief still in his hand, and turns it half mechanically from corner to corner.*)

JEAN (*absent-mindedly*). Mine?

STONOR (*hastily, without reflection*). No. (*He hands it to Miss Levering as she passes*). Yours.

(*Miss Levering, on her way to the lobby with Lord John seems not to notice.*)

JEAN (*takes the handkerchief to give it to her, glancing down at the embroidered corner; stops*). But that's not an L! It's Vi—!

(*Geoffrey Stonor suddenly turns his back and takes up the newspaper.*)

LADY JOHN (*from the lobby*). Come, Vida, since you will go.

MISS LEVERING. Yes; I'm coming.

(*Exit Miss Levering.*)

JEAN. *I didn't know her name was Vida: how did you?*

(*Stonor stares silently over the top of his paper.*)

ACT TWO

SCENE: *The north side of the Nelson Column in Trafalgar Square. The curtain rises on an uproar. The crowd, which momentarily increases, is composed chiefly of weedy youths and wastrel old men. There are a few decent artisans; three or four 'beery' out-o'-works; three or four young women of the domestic servant or Strand restaurant cashier class; one aged woman in rusty black peering with faded, wondering eyes, consulting the faces of men and laughing nervously and apologetically from time to time; one or two quiet-looking, business-like women, thirty to forty; two middle-class men, who stare and whisper and smile. A quiet old man with a lot of unsold Sunday papers under one arm stands in an attitude of rapt attention, with the free hand round his deaf ear. A brisk-looking woman of forty-five or so, wearing pince-nez, goes round with a pile of propagandist literature on her arm. Many of the men smoking cigarettes—the old ones pipes. On the outskirts of this crowd, of several hundred, a couple of smart men in tall shining hats hover a few moments, single eyeglass up, and then saunter off. Against the middle of the Column, where it rises above the stone platform, is a great red banner, one supporting pole upheld by a grimy sandwichman, the other by a small, dirty boy of eight. If practicable only the lower portion of the banner need be seen, bearing the final words of the legend—* 'VOTES FOR WOMEN!' *in immense white letters. It will be well to get, to the full, the effect of the height above the crowd of the straggling group of speakers on the pedestal platform. These are, as the Curtain rises, a working-class woman who is waving her arms and talking very earnestly, her voice for the moment blurred in the uproar. She is dressed in brown serge and looks pinched and sallow. At her side is the Chairman urging that she be given a fair hearing. Allen Trent is a tall, slim, brown-haired man of twenty-eight, with a slight stoop, an agreeable aspect, well-bred voice, and the gleaming brown eye of the visionary. Behind these two, looking on or talking among themselves, are several other carelessly dressed women; one, better turned out than the rest, is quite young, very slight and gracefully built, with round, very pink cheeks, full, scarlet lips, naturally waving brown hair, and an air of childish gravity. She looks at the unruly mob with imperturbable calm. The Chairman's voice is drowned.*

WORKING WOMAN (*with lean, brown finger out and voice raised shriller now above the tumult*). I've got boys o' me own and we laugh at all sorts o' things, but I should be ashymed and so would they if ever they was to be'yve as you're doin' to-d'y.

(*In laughter the noise dies.*)

People 'ave been sayin' this is a middle-class woman's movement. It's a libel. I'm a workin' woman myself, the wife of a working man. (*Voice:* 'Pore devil!') I'm a Poor Law Guardian and a—

NOISY, YOUNG MAN. Think of that, now—gracious me!

(*Laughter and interruption.*)

OLD NEWSVENDOR (*to the noisy young man near him*). Oh, shut up, cawn't yer?

NOISY YOUNG MAN. Not for *you!*

VOICE. Go 'ome and darn yer old man's stockens!

VOICE. Just clean yer *own* doorstep!

WORKING WOMAN. It's a pore sort of 'ousekeeper that leaves 'er doorstep till Sunday afternoon. Maybe that's when you would do *your* doorstep. I do mine in the mornin' before you men are awake.

OLD NEWSVENDOR. It's true, wot she says!—every word.

WORKING WOMAN. You say we women 'ave got no business servin' on boards and thinkin' about policits. Wot's *politics?*

(*A derisive roar.*)

It's just 'ousekeepin' on a big scyle. 'Oo among you workin' men 'as the most comfortable 'omes? Those of you that gives yer wives yer wyges.

(*Loud laughter and jeers.*)

VOICES. {
That's it!
Wantin' our money.
Lord 'Igh 'Ousekeeper of England.

WORKING WOMAN. If it wus only to use fur *our* comfort, d'ye think many o' you workin' men would be found turnin' over their wyges to their wives? No! Wot's the reason thousands do—and the best and the soberest? Because the workin' man knows that wot's a pound to 'im is twenty shillin's to 'is wife. And she'll myke every penny in every one o' them shillin's *tell*. She gets more fur 'im out of 'is wyges than wot 'e can! Some o' you know wot the 'omes is like where the men don't let the women manage. Well, the Poor Laws and the 'ole Government is just in the same muddle because the men 'ave tried to do the national 'ousekeepin' without the women.

(*Roars.*)

But, like I told you before, it's a libel to say it's only the well-off women wot's wantin' the vote. Wot about the 96,000 textile workers? Wot about the Yorkshire tailoresses? I can tell you wot plenty o' the poor women think about it. I'm one of them, and I can tell you we see there's reforms needed. *We ought to 'ave the vote* (jeers), and we know 'ow to appreciate the other women 'oo go to prison fur tryin' to get fur us!

(*With a little final bob of emphasis and a glance over shoulder at the old woman and the young one behind her, she seems about to retire, but pauses as the murmur in the crowd grows into distinct phrases.* 'They get their 'air cut free . . .' 'Naow they don't, that's only us!' 'Silly Suffragettes!' 'Stop at 'ome!' ''Inderin' policemen—mykin' rows in the streets!'*)

VOICE (*louder than the others*). They sees yer ain't fit t'ave—

OTHER VOICES. 'Ha, ha!' 'Shut up!' 'Keep quiet, cawn't yer?' (*General uproar.*)

CHAIRMAN. You evidently don't know what had to be done by *men* before the extension of the Suffrage in '67. If it hadn't been for demonstrations of violence. (*His voice is drowned.*)

WORKING WOMAN (*coming forward again, her shrill note rising clear*). You s'y woman's plyce is 'ome! Don't you know there's a third of the women o' this country can't afford the luxury of stayin' in their 'omes. They *got* to go out and 'elp make money to p'y the rent and keep the 'ome from bein' sold up. Then there's all the women that 'aven't got even miseerable 'omes. They 'aven't got any 'omes *at all*.

NOISY YOUNG MAN. You said *you* got one. W'y don't you stop in it?

WORKING WOMAN. Yes, that's like a man. If one o' you is all right, he thinks the rest don't matter. We women—

NOISY YOUNG MAN. The lydies! God bless 'em!

(*Voices drown her and the Chairman.*)

OLD NEWSVENDOR (*to Noisy, Young Man*). Oh, take that extra 'alf pint 'ome and *sleep it off!*

WORKING WOMAN. P'r'aps *your* 'omes are all right. P'r'haps you aren't livin', old and young, married and single, in one room. I come from a plyce where many fam'lies 'ave to live like that if they're to go on livin' *at all.* If you don't believe me, come and let me show you! (*She spreads out her lean arms*) Come with me to Canning Town!—come with me to Bromley—come to Poplar and to Bow! No. You won't even *think* about the overworked women and the underfed children and the 'ovels they live in. And you want that we shouldn't think neither—

A VAGRANT. We'll do the thinkin'. You go 'ome and nuss the byby.

WORKING WOMAN. I do nurse my byby! I've nursed seven. What 'ave you done for yours? P'r'aps your children never goes 'ungry, and maybe you're satisfied—though I must say I wouldn't a' thought it from the *look* o' you.

VOICE. Oh, I s'y!

WORKING WOMAN. But we women are not satisfied. We don't only want better things for our own children. We want better things for all. *Every* child is our child. We know in our 'earts we oughtn't to rest till we've mothered 'em every one.

VOICE. 'Women'—'children'—wot about the *men?* Are *they* all 'appy?

(*Derisive laughter and 'No! no!' 'Not precisely.' 'Appy? Lord!'*)

WORKING WOMAN. No, there's lots o' you men I'm sorry for (*Shrill Voice: 'Thanks awfully!'*), an' we'll 'elp you if you let us.

VOICE. 'Elp us? You tyke the bread out of our mouths. You women are black-leggin' the men!

WORKING WOMAN. W'y does any woman tyke less wyges than a man for the same work? Only because we can't get anything better. That's part the reason w'y we're yere to-d'y. Do you reely think we tyke them there low wyges because we got a *lykin'* for low wyges? No. We're just like you. We want as much as ever we can get. (*'Ear! 'Ear!' and laughter.*) We got a gryte deal to do with our wyges, we women has. We got the children to think about. And w'en we got our rights, a woman's flesh and blood won't be so much cheaper than a man's that employers can get rich on keepin' you out o' work, and sweatin' us. If you men could see it, we got the *syme* cause, and if you 'elped us you'd be 'elpin yerselves.

VOICES. 'Rot!' 'Drivel.'

OLD NEWSVENDOR. True as gospel!

(*She retires against the banner with the others. There is some applause.*)

A MAN (*patronisingly*). Well, now, that wusn't so bad—fur a woman.

ANOTHER. Nnaw. *Not fur a woman.*

CHAIRMAN (*speaking through this last*). Miss Ernestine Blunt will now address you.

(*Applause, chiefly ironic, laughter, a general moving closer and knitting up of attention. Ernestine Blunt is about twenty-four, but looks younger. She is very downright, not to say pugnacious—the something amusing and attractive about her is there, as it were, against her will, and the more fetching for that. She has no conventional gestures, and none of any sort at first. As she warms to her work she uses her slim hands to enforce her emphasis, but as though unconsciously. Her manner of speech is less monotonous than that of the average woman-speaker, but she, too, has a fashion of leaning all her weight on the end of the sentence. She brings out the final word or two with an effort of underscoring, and makes a forward motion of the slim body as if the better to drive the last nail in. She evidently means to be immensely practical—the kind who is pleased to think she hasn't a grain of sentimentality in her composition, and whose feeling, when it does all but master her, communicates itself magnetically to others.*)

MISS ERNESTINE BLUNT. Perhaps I'd better begin by explaining a little about our 'tactics'.

(*Cries of 'Tactics! We know!' 'Mykin' troble!' 'Public scandal!'*)

To make you understand what we've done, I must remind you of what others have done. Perhaps you don't know that women first petitioned Parliament for the Franchise as long ago as 1866.

VOICE. How do *you* know?

(*She pauses a moment, taken off her guard by the suddenness of the attack.*)

VOICE. You wasn't there!

VOICE. That was the trouble. Haw! haw!

MISS ERNESTINE BLUNT. And the petition was presented—

VOICE. Give 'er a 'earin' now she 'as got out of 'er crydle.

MISS ERNESTINE BLUNT. —presented to the House of Commons by that great Liberal, John Stewart Mill. (*Voice: 'Mill? Who is he when he's at home?'*) Bills or Resolutions have been before the House on and off for the last thirty-six years. That, roughly, is our history. We found ourselves, towards the close of the year 1905, with no assurance that if we went on in the same way any girl born into the world in this generation would live to exercise the rights of citizenship, though she lived to be a hundred. So we said all this has been in vain. We must try some other way. How did the working man get the Suffrage, we asked ourselves? Well, we turned up the records, and we *saw*—

VOICES. 'Not by scratching people's faces!' . . . 'Disraeli give it 'em!' 'Dizzy? Get out!' "Cahnty Cahncil scholarships!'

'Oh, Lord, this education!' 'Chartists riots, she's thinkin' of!' (*Noise in the crowd.*)

MISS ERNESTINE BLUNT. But we don't *want* to follow such a violent example. We would much rather *not*—but if that's the only way we can make the country see we're in earnest, we are prepared to show them.

VOICE. An' they'll show you!—Give you another month 'ard.

MISS ERNESTINE BLUNT. Don't think that going to prison has any fears for us. We'd go *for life* if by doing that we could get freedom for the rest of the women.

VOICES. 'Hear, hear!' 'Rot!' 'W'ye don't the men 'elp ye to get your rights?'

MISS ERNESTINE BLUNT. Here's some one asking why the men don't help. It's partly they don't understand yet—they *will* before we've done! (*Laughter.*) Partly they don't understand yet what's at stake—

RESPECTABLE OLD MAN (*chuckling*). Lord, they're a 'educatin' of us!

VOICE. Wot next?

MISS ERNESTINE BLUNT. —and partly that the bravest man is afraid of ridicule. Oh, yes; we've heard a great deal all our lies about the timidity and the sensitiveness of women. And it's true. We *are* sensitive. But I tell you, ridicule crumples a man up. It steels a woman. We've come to know the value of ridicule. We've educated ourselves so that we welcome ridicule. We owe our sincerest thanks to the comic writers. The cartoonist is our unconscious friend. Who cartoons people who are of no importance? What advertisement is so sure of being remembered?

POETIC YOUNG MAN. I admit that.

MISS ERNESTINE BLUNT. If we didn't know it by any other sign, the comic papers would tell us *we've arrived!* But our greatest debt of gratitude we owe, to the man who called us female hooligans.

(*The crowd bursts into laughter.*)

We aren't hooligans, but we hope the fact will be overlooked. If everybody said we were nice, well-behaved women, who'd come to hear us? *Not the men.*

(*Roars.*)

Men tell us it isn't womanly for us to care about politics. How do they know what's womanly? It's for women to decide that. Let the men attend to being manly. It will take them all their time.

VOICE. Are we down-'earted? Oh no!

MISS ERNESTINE BLUNT. And they say it would be dreadful if we got the vote, because then we'd be pitted against men in the economic struggle. But that's come about already. Do you know that out of every hundred women in this country eight-two are wage-earning women? It used to be thought unfeminine for women to be students and to aspire to the arts—that bring fame and fortune. But nobody has ever said it was unfeminine for women to do the heavy drudgery that's badly paid. That kind of work had to be done by *somebody*—and the men didn't hanker after it. Oh, no.

(*Laughter and interruption.*)

A MAN ON THE OUTER FRINGE. She can talk—the little one can.

ANOTHER. Oh, they can all 'talk'.

A BEERY, DIRTY FELLOW OF FIFTY. I wouldn't like to be 'er 'usban'. Think o' comin' 'ome to *that*!

HIS PAL. I'd soon learn 'er!

MISS ERNESTINE BLUNT (*speaking through the noise*). Oh, no! *Let* the women scrub and cook and wash. That's all right! But if they want to try their hand at the better paid work of the liberal professions—oh, very unfeminine indeed! Then there's another thing. Now I want you to listen to this, because it's *very* important. Men say if we persist in competing with them for the bigger prizes, they're dreadfully afraid we'd lose the beautiful protecting chivalry that—Yes, I don't wonder you laugh. *We* laugh. (*Bending forward with lit eyes.*) But the women I found at the Ferry Tin Works working for five shillings a week—I didn't see them laughing. The beautiful chivalry of the employers of women doesn't prevent them from paying women tenpence a day for sorting coal and loading and unloading carts—doesn't prevent them from forcing women to earn bread in ways worse still. So we won't talk about chivalry. It's being over-sarcastic. We'll just let this poor ghost of chivalry go—in exchange for a little plain justice.

VOICE. If the House of Commons won't give you justice, why don't you go to the House of Lords?

MISS ERNESTINE BLUNT. What?

VOICE. Better 'urry up. Case of early closin'.

(*Laughter. A man at the back asks the speaker something.*)

MISS ERNESTINE BLUNT (*unable to hear*). You'll be allowed to ask any question you like at the end of the meeting.

NEWCOMER (*boy of eighteen*). Oh, is it question time? I s'y, Miss, 'oo killed cock robin?

(*She is about to resume, but above the general noise the voice of a man at the back reaches her indistinct but insistent. She leans forward trying to catch what he says. While the indistinguishable murmur has been going on Geoffrey Stonor has appeared on the edge of the crowd, followed by Jean and Lady John in motor veils.*)

JEAN (*pressing forward eagerly and raising her veil*). Is she one of them? That little thing!

STONOR (*doubtfully*). I—I suppose so.

JEAN. Oh, ask some one, Geoffrey. I'm so disappointed. I did so hope we'd hear one of the—the worst.

MISS ERNESTINE BLUNT (*to the interrupter—on the other side*). What? What do you say? (*She screws up her eyes with the effort to hear, and puts a hand up to her ear. A few indistinguishable words between her and the man.*)

LADY JOHN (*who has been studying the figures on the platform through her lorgnon, turns to a working man beside her*). Can you tell me, my man, which are the ones that—a—that make the disturbances?

WORKING MAN. Don't you be took in, Miss.

MISS ERNESTINE BLUNT. Oh, yes—I see. There's a man over here asking—

A YOUNG MAN. *I've* got a question, too. Are—you—married?

ANOTHER (*sniggering*). Quick! There's yer chawnce. 'E's a bachelor.

(*Laughter.*)

MISS ERNESTINE BLUNT (*goes straight on as if she not heard*). —man asking: if the women get full citizenship, and a war is declared, will the women fight?

POETIC YOUNG MAN: No, really—no, really, now!

(*The Crowd: 'Haw! Haw!' 'Yes!' 'Yes, how about that?'*)

MISS ERNESTINE BLUNT (*smiling*). Well, you know, some people say the whole trouble about us is that we *do* fight. But it is only hard necessity makes us do that. We don't *want* to fight—as men seem to—just for fighting's sake. Women are for peace.

VOICE. Hear, hear.

MISS ERNESTINE BLUNT. And when we have a share in public affairs there'll be less likelihood of war. But that's not to say women can't fight. The Boer women did. The Russian women face conflicts worse than any battlefield can show. (*Her voice shakes a little, and her eyes fill, but she controls her emotion gallantly, and dashes on.*) But we women know all that is evil, and we're for peace. Our part—we're proud to remember it—our part has been to go about after you men in war time, and—*pick up the pieces!*

(*A great shout.*)

Yes—seems funny, doesn't it? You men blow them to bits, and then we come along and put them together again. If you know anything about military nursing, you know a good deal of our work has been done in the face of danger—*but it's always been done.*

OLD NEWSVENDOR. That's so. That's so.

MISS ERNESTINE BLUNT. You complain that more and more we're taking away from you men the work that's always been yours. You can't any longer keep women out of the industries. The only question is upon what terms shall she continue to be in? As long as she's in on bad terms, she's not only hurting herself—she's hurting you. But if you're being discouraged about our competing with you, we're willing to leave you your trade in war. *Let* the men take life! We *give* life! (*Her voice is once more moved and proud.*) No one will pretend ours isn't one of the dangerous trades either. I won't say any more to you now, be-

cause we've got others to speak to you, and a new woman helper that I want you to hear.

(*She retires to the sound of clapping. There's a hurried consultation between her and the Chairman. Voices in the Crowd: 'The little 'un's all right' 'Ernestine's a corker,' etc.*)

JEAN (*looking at Stonor to see how he's taken it*). Well?

STONOR (*smiling down at her*). Well—

JEAN. Nothing reprehensible in what *she* said, was there?

STONOR (*shrugs*). Oh, reprehensible!

JEAN. It makes me rather miserable all the same.

STONOR (*draws her hand protectingly through his arm*). You mustn't take it as much to hear as all that.

JEAN. I can't help it—I can't indeed, Geoffrey. I shall *never* be able to make a speech like that!

STONOR (*taken aback*). I hope not, indeed.

JEAN. Why, I thought you said you wanted me—?

STONOR (*smiling*). To make nice little speeches with composure—so I did! So I—(*Seems to lose his thread as he looks at her.*)

JEAN (*with a little frown*): You *said*—

STONOR. That you have very pink cheeks? Well, I stick to that.

JEAN (*smiling*). Sh! Don't tell everybody.

STONOR. And you're the only female creature I ever say who didn't look a fright in motor things.

JEAN (*melted and smiling*). I'm glad you don't think me a fright.

CHAIRMAN. I will now ask (*name indistinguishable*) to address the meeting.

JEAN (*as she sees Lady John moving to one side*). Oh, don't go yet, Aunt Ellen!

LADY JOHN. Go? Certainly not. I want to hear another. (*Craning her neck.*) I can't believe, you know, she was really one of the worst.

(*A big, sallow Cockney has come forward. His scanty hair grows in wisps on a great bony skull.*)

VOICE. That's Pilcher.

ANOTHER. 'Oo's Pilcher?

ANOTHER. If you can't afford a bottle of Tatcho, w'y don't you get yer 'air cut.

MR PILCHER (*not in the least discomposed*). I've been addressin' a big meetin' at 'Ammersmith this morning, and we'en I told 'em I was comin' 'ere this awfternoon to speak fur the women—well—then the usual thing began!

(*An appreciative roar from the crowd.*)

In these times if you want peace and quiet at a public meetin'—

(*The crowd fills in the hiatus with laughter.*)

There was a man at 'Ammersmith, too, talkin' about women's sphere bein' 'ome. 'Ome do you call it? You've got a kennel w'ere you can munch your tommy. You've got a corner w'ere you can curl up fur a few hours till you go out to work again. No, my man, there's too many of you ain't able to *give* the women 'omes —fit to live in, too many of you in that fix fur you to go on jawin' at those o' the women 'oo want to myke the 'omes a little decenter.

VOICE. If the vote ain't done us any good, 'ow'll it do the women any good?

MR PILCHER. Looke 'ere! Any men here belongin' to the Labour Party?

(*Shouts and applause.*)

Well, I don't need to tell these men the vote 'as done us *some* good. They know it. And it'll do us a lot more good w'en you know 'ow to use the power you got in your 'and.

VOICE. Power! It's those fellers at the bottom o' the street that's got the power.

MR PILCHER. It's you, and men like you, that gave it to 'em. You carried the Liberals into Parliament Street on your own shoulders.

(*Complacent applause.*)

You believed all their fine words. You never asked yourselves, 'Wot's a Liberal, anyw'y?'

A VOICE. He's a jolly good fellow.

(*Cheers and booing.*)

MR PILCHER. No, 'e ain't, or if 'e is jolly, it's only because 'e thinks you're such silly codfish you'll go swellin' his majority again. (*Laughter, in which Stonor joins.*) It's enough to make any Liberal jolly to see sheep like you lookin' on, proud and 'appy, while you see Liberal leaders desertin' Liberal principles.

(*Voices in agreement and protest.*)

You show me a Liberal, and I'll show you a Mr Fycing-both-W'ys. Yuss.

(*Stonor moves closer with an amused look.*)

'E sheds the light of 'is warm and 'andsome smile on the working man, and round on the other side 'e's tippin' a wink to the great landowners. That's to let 'em know 'e's standin' between them and the Socialists. Huh! Socialists. Yuss, *Socialists.*

(*General laughter, in which Stonor joins.*)

The Liberal, e's the judicial sort o'chap that sits in the middle—

VOICE. On the fence!

MR PILCHER. Tories one side—Socialists the other. Well it ain't always so comfortable in the middle. You're like to get squeezed. Now, I s'y to the women, the Conservatives don't promise they *do*!

STONOR (*to Jean*). This fellow isn't half bad.

MR PILCHER. The liberals—they'll promise you the earth, and give yer . . . the whole o' nothing.

(*Roars of approval.*)

JEAN. *Isn't* it fun? Now, aren't you glad I brought you?

STONOR (*laughing*). This chap's rather amusing!

MR. PILCHER. We men 'ave seen it 'appen over and over. But the women can tyke a 'int quicker 'n what we can. They won't stand the nonsense men do. Only they 'aven't got a fair chawnce even to agitate fur their rights. As I wus comin' up 'ere I 'eard a man sayin', 'Look at this big crowd. W'y, we're all *men!* If the women want the vote w'y ain't they 'ere to s'y so? Well, I'll tell you w'y. It's because they've 'ad to get the dinner fur you and me, and now they're washin' up the dishes.

A VOICE. D'you think *we* ought to st'y 'ome and wash the dishes?

MR PILCHER (*laughs good-naturedly*). If they'd leave it to us once or twice per'aps we'd understand a little more about the Woman Question. I know w'y *my* wife isn't here. It's because she *knows* I ain't much use round the 'ouse, and she's 'opin' I can talk to some purpose. Maybe she's mistaken. Any'ow, here I am to vote for her and all the other women.

VOICES. 'Hear! hear!', 'Oh-h!'

MR PILCHER. And to tell you men what improvements you can expect to see when a women 'as the share in public affairs they *ought* to 'ave!

VOICE. What do you know about it? You can't even talk grammar.

MR PILCHER (*is dashed a fraction of a moment, for the first and only time*). I'm not 'ere to talk grammar but to talk Reform. I ain't defendin' my grammar—but I'll say in pawssing that if my mother 'ad 'ad 'er rights, maybe my grammar would have been better.

(*Stonor and Jean exchange smiles. He takes her arm again and bends his head to whisper something in her ear. She listens with lowered eyes and happy face. The discreet love-making goes on during the next few sentences. Interruption. One voice insistent but not clear. The speaker waits only a second and they resumes. 'Yes, if the women,' but he cannot instantly makes himself heard. The boyish Chairman looks harassed and anxious. Miss Ernestine Blunt alert, watchful.*)

MR PILCHER. Wait a bit—'arf a minute, my man!

VOICE. 'Oo yer talkin' to? I ain't your man.

MR PILCHER. Lucky for me! There seems to be a *gentleman* 'ere who doesn't think women ought to 'ave the vote.

VOICE. *One?* Oh-h!

(*Laughter.*)

MR PILCHER. Per'aps 'e doesn't know much about women?

(*Indistinguishable repartee.*)

Oh, the gentleman says 'e's married. Well, then, fur the syke of 'is wife we mustn't be too sorry 'e's 'ere. No doubt she s'ying: "'Eaven by prysed those women are mykin' a Demonstrytion in Trafalgar Square, and I'll 'ave a little peace and quiet at 'ome for one Sunday in my life.'

(*The crowd laughs and there are jeers for the interruptor—and at the speaker.*)

(*Pointing.*) Why, *you're* like the man at Ammersmith this morning. 'E was awskin' me. "'Ow would you like men to st'y at 'ome and do the family washin'?'

(*Laughter.*)

I told 'im I wouldn't advise it. I 'ave too much respect fur—me clo'es.

VAGRANT. It's their palce—the women ought to do the washin'.

MR PILCHER. I'm not sure you ain't right. For a good many o' you fellas, from the look o' you—you cawn't even wash yerselves.

(*Laughter.*)

VOICE (*threatening*). 'Oo are you talkin' to?

(*Chairman more anxious than before—movement in the crowd.*)

THREATENING VOICE. Which of us d'you mean?

MR PILCHER (*coolly looking down*). Well, it takes about ten of your sort to myke a man, so you may take it I mean the lot of you.

(*Angry indistinguishable retorts and the crowd sways. Miss Ernestine Blunt, who has been watching the fray with serious face, turns suddenly catching sight of someone just arrived at the end of the platform. Miss Blunt goes right with alacrity, saying audibly to Pilcher as she passes, 'Here she is,' and proceeds to offer her hand helping some one to get up the improvised steps. Laughter and interruption in the crowd.*)

LADY JOHN. Now, there's another woman going to speak.

JEAN. Oh, is she? Who? Which? I do hope she'll be one of the wild ones.

MR PILCHER (*speaking through this last. Glancing at the new arrival whose hat appears above the platform.*) That's all right, then. (*Turns to the left.*) When I've attended to this microbe that's vitiating the air on my right—

(*Laughter and interruption from the crowd.*)

(*Stonor stares, one dazed instant, at the face of the new arrival; his own changes.*)

(*Jean withdraws her arm from his and quite suddenly presses a shade nearer the platform. Stonor moves forward and takes her by the arm.*)

STONOR. We're going now.

JEAN. Not yet—oh, please not yet. (*Breathless, looking back.*). Why I—I do believe—

STONOR (*to Lady John, with decision*). I'm going to take Jean out of this mob. Will you come?

LADY JOHN. What? Oh yes, if you think—(*Another look through her glasses.*) But isn't that—surely it's—!!!

(*Vida Levering comes forward. She wears a long, plain, dark green dustcloak. Stands talking to Ernestine Blunt and glancing a little apprehensively at the crowd.*)

JEAN. Geoffrey!

STONOR (*trying to draw Jean away*). Lady John's tired—

JEAN. But you don't see who it is, Geoffrey—! (*Looks into his face, and is arrested by the look she finds there.*)

(*Lady John has pushed in front of them amazed, transfixed, with glass up.*)

(*Geoffrey Stonor restrains a gesture of annoyance, and withdraws behind two big policemen. Jean from time to time turns to look at him with a face of perplexity.*)

MR PHILCHER (*resuming through a fire of indistinct interruption*). I'll come down and attend to that microbe while a lady will say a few words to you (*raises his voice*) —if she can myke 'erself 'eard.

(*Pilcher retires in the midst of booing and cheers.*)

CHAIRMAN (*harassed and trying to create a diversion*). Some one suggests—and it's such a good idea I'd like you to listen to it—

(*Noise dies down.*)

that a clause shall be inserted in the next Suffrage Bill that shall expressly reserve to each Cabinet Minister, and to any respectable man, the power to prevent the Franchise being given to the female members of his family on his public declaration of their lack of sufficient intelligence to entitle them to vote.

VOICES. Oh! oh.

CHAIRMAN. Now, I ask you to listen, as quietly as you can, to a lady who is not accustomed to speaking—a—in Trafalgar Square—or a . . . as a matter of fact, at all.

VOICES. 'A dumb lady.' 'Hooray!'
    'Three cheers for the dumb lady!'

CHAIRMAN. A lady who, as I've said, will tell you, if you'll behave yourselves, her impressions of the administration of police court justice in this country.

(*Jean looks wondering at Stonor's sphinx-like face as Vida Levering comes to the edge of the platform.*)

MISS LEVERING. Mr Chairman, men and women—

VOICES (*off*). Speak up.

(*Miss Levering flushes, comes quite to the edge of the platform and raises her voice a little.*)

MISS LEVERING. I just wanted to tell you that I was—I was—present in the police court when the women were charged for creating a disturbance.

VOICE. Y' oughtn't t' get mixed up in wot didn't concern you.

MISS LEVERING. I—I—(*Stumbles and stops.*)

(*Talking and laughing increases. 'Wot's 'er name?' 'Mrs or Miss?' 'Ain't seen this one before.'*)

CHAIRMAN (*anxiously*). Now, see here, men: don't interrupt—

A GIRL (*shrilly*). I don't like this one's 'at. Ye can see she ain't one of 'em.

MISS LEVERING (*trying to recommence*). I—

VOICE. They're a disgrace—them women be'ind yer.

A MAN WITH A FATHERLY AIR. It's the w'y they goes on as mykes the Government keep ye from getting' yer rights.

CHAIRMAN (*losing his temper*). It's the way *you* go on that—

(*Noise increases. Chairman drowned, waves his arms and moves his lips. Miss Levering discouraged, turns and looks at Ernestine Blunt and pantomimes 'It's no good. I can't go on. Ernestine Blunt comes forward, says a word to the Chairman, who ceases gyrating, and nods.*)

MISS ERNESTINE BLUNT (*facing the crowd*). Look here. If the Government withhold the vote because they don't like the way some of us ask for it—*let them give it to the Quiet Ones.* Does the Government want to punish *all* women because they don't like the manners of a handful? Perhaps that's you men's notion of justice. It isn't women's.

VOICES. Haw! haw!

MISS LEVERING. Yes. Thi-this is the first time I've ever 'gone on,' as you call it, but they never gave me a vote.

MISS ERNESTINE BLUNT (*with energy*). NO! And there are one—two—three—four women on this platform. Now, we all want the vote, as you know. Well, we'd agree to be disfranchised all our lives, if they'd give the vote to all the other women.

VOICE. Look here, you made one speech, give a lady a chawnce.

MISS ERNESTINE BLUNT (*retires smiling*). That's *just* what I wanted *you* to do!

MISS LEVERING. Perhaps you—you don't know—you don't know—

VOICE (*sarcastic*). 'Ow 're we goin' to know if you can't tell us?

MISS LEVERING (*flushing and smiling*). Thank you for that. We couldn't have a better motto. How *are* you to know if we can't somehow manage to tell you? (*With a visible effort she goes on.*) Well, I certainly didn't know before that the sergeants and policemen are instructed to deceive the people as to the time such cases are heard. You ask, and you're sent to Marlborough Police Court instead of to Marylebone.

VOICE. They ought ter sent yer to 'Olloway—do y' good.

OLD NEWSVENDOR. You go on, Miss, don't mind 'im.

VOICE. Wot d'you expect from a pig but a grunt?

MISS LEVERING. You're told the case will be at two o'clock, and it's really called for eleven. Well, I took a great deal of trouble, and I didn't believe what I was told—

(*Warming a little to her task.*)

Yes, that's almost the first thing we have to learn—to get over our touching faith that, because a man tells us something, it's true. I got to the right court, and I was so anxious not to be late, I was too early. The case before the women's was just coming on. I heard a noise. At the door I saw the helmets of two policemen, and I said to myself: 'What sort of crime shall I have to sit and hear about? Is this a burglar coming along between the two big policemen, or will it be a murderer? What sort of felon is to stand in the dock before the women whose crime is they ask for the vote?' But, try as I would, I couldn't see the prisoner. My heart misgave me. Is it a woman, I wondered? Then the policemen got nearer, and I saw—(*she waits an instant*)—a little, thin, half-starved boy. What do you think he was charged with? Stealing. What had he been stealing—that small criminal? *Milk*. It seemed to me as I sat there looking on, that the men who had the affairs of the world in their hands from the beginning, and who've made so poor a business of it—

VOICES. Oh! oh! Pore benighted man! Are we down-'earted? Oh, no!

MISS LEVERING. —so poor a business of it as to have the poor and the unemployed in the condition they're in today—when your own remedy for a starving child is to hale him off to the police court—because he had managed to get a little milk—well, I *did* wonder that the men refuse to be helped with a problem they've so notoriously failed at. I began to say to myself: 'Isn't it time the women lent a hand?'

A VOICE. Would you have women magistrates?

(*She is stumped by the suddenness of the demand.*)

VOICES. Haw! Haw! Magistrates!

ANOTHER. Women! Let 'em prove first they deserve—

A SHABBY ART STUDENT. (*his hair longish, soft hat, and flowing tie*). They study music by thousands; where's their Beethoven? Where's their Plato? Where's the woman Shakespeare?

ANOTHER. Yes—what 'a' they ever *done*.

(*The speaker clenches her hands, and is recovering her presence of mind, so that by the time the Chairman can makes himself heard with, 'Now men, give this lady a fair hearing—don't interrupt'—she, with the slightest of gestures, waves him aside with a low 'It's all right.'*)

MISS LEVERING (*steadying and raising her voice*). These questions are quite proper! They are often asked elsewhere; and I would like to ask in return: Since when was human society held to exist for its handful of geniuses? How many Platos are there here in this crowd?

A VOICE (*very loud and shrill*). Divil a wan!

(*Laughter.*)

MISS LEVERING. Not one. Yet that doesn't keep you men off the register. How many Shakespeares are there in all England today? Not one. Yet the State doesn't tumble to pieces. Railroads and ships are built—homes are kept going, and babies are born. The world goes on! (*Bending over the crowd.*) It goes on *by virtue of its common people.*

VOICES (*subdued*). Hear! hear!

MISS LEVERING. I am not concerned that you should think we women can paint great pictures, or compose immortal music, or write good books. I am content that we should be classed with the common people—who keep the world going. But (*Straightening up and taking a fresh start.*) I'd like the world to go a great deal better. We were talking about justice. I have been inquiring into the kind of lodging the poorest class of homeless women can get in this town of London. I find that only the men of that class are provided for. Some measure to establish Rowton Houses for women has been before the London County Council. They looked into the question 'very carefully,' so their apologists say. And what did they decide? They decided that *they could do nothing.*

LADY JOHN (*having forced her way to Stonor's side*). Is that true?

STONOR (*speaking through Miss Levering's next words*). I don't know.

MISS LEVERING. Why could that great, all-powerful body do nothing? Because, if these cheap and decent houses were opened, they said, the homeless women in the streets would make use of them! You'll think I'm not in earnest. But that was actually the decision and the reason given for it. Women that the bitter struggle for existence has forced into a life of horror—

STONOR (*sternly to Lady John*). You think this is the kind of thing—(*A motion of the head towards Jean.*)

MISS LEVERING.—the outcast women might take advantage of the shelter these decent, cheap places offered. But the *men*, I said! Are all who avail themselves of Lord Rowton's hostels, are *they* all angels? Or does wrong-doing in a man not matter? Yet women are recommended to depend on the chivalry of men.

(*The two policemen, who at first had been strolling about, have stood during this scene in front of Geoffrey Stonor. They turn now and walk away, leaving Stonor exposed. He, embarrassed, moves uneasily, and Vida Levering's eye falls upon his big figures. He still has the collar of his motor coat turned up in his ears. A change passes over her face, and her nerve fails her an instant.*)

MISS LEVERING. Justice and chivalry!! (*She steadies her voice and hurries on.*)—they both remind me of what those of you who read the police court news—(I have begun only lately to do that)—but you've seen the accounts of the girl who's been tried in Manchester lately for the murder of her child. Not pleasant reading. Even if we'd noticed it, we wouldn't speak of it in my world. A few months ago I should have turned away my eyes and forgotten even the headline as quickly as I could. But since that morning in the police court, I read these things. This, as you'll remember, was about a little working girl—an orphan of eighteen—who crawled with the dead body of her new born child to her master's back door, and left the baby there. She dragged herself a little way off and fainted. A few days later she found herself in court, being tried for the murder of her child. Her master—a married man—had of course reported the 'find' at his back door to the police, and he had been summoned to give evidence. The girl cried out to him in the open court, 'You are the father!' He couldn't deny it. The Coroner at the jury's request censured the man, and regretted that the law didn't make him responsible. But he went scot-free. And that girl is now serving her sentence in Strangeways Gaol.

(*Murmuring and scraps of indistinguishable comment in the crowd, through which only Jean's voice is clear.*)

JEAN (*who has wormed her way in Stonor's side*). Why do you dislike her so?

STONOR. I? Why should you think—

JEAN (*with a vaguely frightend air*). I never saw you look as you did—as you do.

CHAIRMAN. Order, please—give the lady a fair—

MISS LEVERING (*signing to him 'It's all right'*). Men make boast that an English citizen is tried by his peers. What woman is tried by hers?

(*A sombre passion strengthens her voice and hurries her on.*)

A woman is arrested by a man, brought before a man judge, tried by a jury of men, condemned by men, taken to prison by a man, and by a man she's hanged! Where in all this were *her* 'peers'? Why did men so long ago insist on trial by 'a jury of their peers'? 'So that justice shouldn't miscarry—wasn't it'? A man's peers would best understand his circumstances, his temptation, the degree of his guilt. Yet there's no such unlikeness between different classes of men as exists between man and woman. What man has the knowledge that makes him a fit judge of woman's deeds at that time of anguish—that hour—(*lowers her voice and bends over the crowd*)—that hour that some woman struggled through to put each man here into the world. I noticed when a previous speaker quoted the Labour Party you applauded. Some of you here—I gather—call yourselves Labour men. Every woman who has borne a child is a Labour woman. No man among you can judge what she goes through in her hour of darkness—

JEAN (*with frightened eyes on her lover's set, white face, whispers*). Geoffrey—

MISS LEVERING (*catching her fluttering breath, goes on very low*)—in that great agony when, even under the best conditions that money and devotion can buy, many a woman falls into temporary mania, and not a few go down to death. In the case of this poor little abandoned working girl, what man can be the fit judge of her deeds in that awful moment of half-crazed temptation? Women know of these things as those know burning who have walked through fire.

(*Stonor makes a motion towards Jean and she turns away fronting the audience. Her hands go up to her throat as though she suffered a choking sensation. It is in her face that she 'knows'. Miss Levering leans over the platform and speaks with a low and thrilling earnestness.*)

I would say in conclusion to the women here, it's not enough to be sorry for these unfortunate sisters. We must get the conditions of life made fairer. We women must organise. We must learn to work together. We have all (rich and poor, happy and unhappy) worked so long and so exclusively for men, we hardly know how to work for one another. But we must learn. Those who can, may give money—

VOICES (*grumbling*). Oh, yes—Money! Money!

MISS LEVERING. Those who haven't pennies to give—even those people aren't so poor they can't give some part of their labour—some share of their sympathy and support. (*Turns to hear something the Chairman is whispering to her.*)

JEAN (*low to Lady John*). Oh, I'm glad I've got power!

LADY JOHN (*bewildered*). Power!—*you*?

JEAN. Yes, all that money—

(*Lady John tries to make her way to Stonor.*)

MISS LEVERING (*suddenly turning from the Chairman to the crowd*). Oh, yes, I hope you'll all join the Union. Come up after the meeting and give your names.

LOUD VOICE. You won't get many men.

MISS LEVERING (*with fire*). Then it's to the women I appeal!

(*She is about to retire when, with a sudden gleam in her lit eyes, she turns for the last time to the crowd, silencing the general murmur and holding the people by the sudden concentration of passion in her face.*)

I don't mean to say it wouldn't be better if men and women did this work together—shoulder to shoulder. But the mass of men won't have it so. I only hope they'll realise in time the good they've renounced and the spirit they've aroused. For I know as well as any man could tell me, it would be a bad day for England if all women felt about all men *as I do*.

(*She retires in a tumult. The others on the platform close about her. The Chairman tries in vain to get a hearing from the excited crowd.*)

(*Jean tries to make her way through the knot of people surging round her.*)

STONOR (*calls*). Here—follow me!

JEAN. No—no—I—

STONOR. You're going the wrong way.

JEAN. *This* is the way I must go.

STONOR. You can get out quicker on this side.

JEAN. I don't *want* to get out.

STONOR. What? Where are you going?

JEAN. To ask that woman to let me have the honour of working with her.

(*She disappears in the crowd.*)

(*Curtain.*)

ACT THREE

SCENE: *The drawing room at old Mr Dunbarton's house in Eaton Square. Six o'clock the same evening. As the Curtain rises the door opens and Jean appears on the threshold. She looks back into her own sitting room, then crosses the drawing room, treading softly on the parquet spaces between the rugs. She goes to the window and is in the act of parting the lace curtains when the folding doors are opened by the Butler.*

JEAN (*to the Servant*). Sh!

(*She goes softly back to the door she has left open and closes it carefully. When she turns, the Butler has stepped aside to admit Geoffrey Stonor, and departed, shutting the folding doors. Stonor comes rapidly forward.*)

(*Before he gets a word out.*) Speak low, please.

STONOR (*angrily*). I waited about a whole hour for you to come back.

(*Jean turns away as though vaguely looking for the nearest chair.*)

If you don't mind leaving *me* like that you might have considered Lady John.

JEAN (*pausing*). Is she here with you?

STONOR. No. My place was nearer than this, and she was very tired. I left her to get some tea. We couldn't tell whether you'd be here, or *what* had become of you.

JEAN. Mr Trent got us a hansom.

STONOR. Trent?

JEAN. The Chairman of the meeting.

STONOR. 'Got us—'?

JEAN. Miss Levering and me.

STONOR (*incensed*). Miss L—

BUTLER (*opens the door and announces*). Mr Farnborough.

(*Enter Mr Richard Farnborough—more flurried than ever.*)

FARNBOROUGH (*seeing Stonor*). At last! You'll forgive this incursion, Miss Dunbarton, when you hear—(*Turns abruptly back to Stonor.*) They've been telegraphing you all over London. In despair they set me on your track.

STONOR. Who did? What's up.

FARNBOROUGH (*lays down his hat and fumbles agitatedly in his breast pocket*). There was the devil to pay at Dutfield last night. The Liberal chap tore down from London and took over your meeting.

STONOR. Oh?—Nothing about it in the Sunday paper *I* saw.

FARNBOROUGH. Wait till you see the Press tomorrow morning! There was a great rally and the beggar made a rousing speech.

STONOR. What about?

FARNBOROUGH. Abolition of the Upper House—

STONOR. They were at that when I was at Eton!

FARNBOROUGH. Yes. But this new man has got a way of putting things!—the people went mad. (*Pompously.*) The Liberal platform as defined at Dutfield is going to make a big difference.

STONOR (*drily*). You think so.

FARNBOROUGH. Well, your agent says as much. (*Opens telegram.*)

STONOR. My—(*Taking telegram.*) 'Try find Stonor'—Hm! Hm!

FARNBOROUGH (*pointing*). —'tremendous effect of last night's Liberal manifesto ought to be counteracted in tomorrow's papers.' (*Very earnestly.*) You see, Mr. Stonor, it's a battle cry we want.

STONOR (*turns on his heel*). Claptrap!

FARNBOROUGH (*a little dashed*). Well, they've been saying we have nothing to offer but personal popularity. No practical reform. No—

STONOR. No trucking to the masses, I suppose. (*Walks impatiently away.*)

FARNBOROUGH (*snubbed*). Well, in these democratic days— (*Turns to Jean for countenance.*) I hope you'll forgive my bursting in like this. (*Struck by her face.*) But I can see you realise the gravity—(*Lowering his voice with an air of speaking for her ear alone.*) It isn't as if he were going to be a mere private member. Everybody knows he'll be in the Cabinet.

STONOR (*drily*). It may be a Liberal Cabinet.

FARNBOROUGH. Nobody thought so up to last night. Why, even your brother—but I am afraid I'm seeming officious. (*Takes up his hat.*)

STONOR (*coldly*). What about my brother?

FARNBOROUGH. I met Lord Windlesham as I rushed out of the Carlton.

STONOR. Did he say anything?

FARNBOROUGH. I told him the Dutfield news.

STONOR (*impatiently*). Well?

FARNBOROUGH. He said it only confirmed his fears.

STONOR (*half under his breath*). Said that, did he?

FARNBOROUGH. Yes. Defeat is inevitable, he thinks, unless— (*Pause.*)

(*Geoffrey Stonor who has been pacing the floor, stops but doesn't raise his eyes.*)

unless you can 'manufacture some political dynamite within the next few hours.' Those were his words.

STONOR (*resumes his walking to and fro, raises his head and catches sight of Jean's white, drawn face. Stops short*). You are very tired.

JEAN. No. No.

STONOR (*to Farnborough*). I'm obliged to you for taking so much trouble. (*Shakes hands by way of dismissing Farnborough.*) I'll see what can be done.

FARNBOROUGH (*offering the reply-paid form*). If you'd like to wire I'll take it.

STONOR (*faintly amused*). You don't understand, my young friend. Moves of this kind are not rushed at by responsible politicians. I must have time for consideration.

FARNBOROUGH (*disappointed*). Oh, well, I only hope someone else won't jump into the breach before you—(*Watch in hand.*) I tell you. (*To Jean.*) I'll find out what time the newspapers go to press on Sunday. Goodbye (*To Stonor.*) I'll be at the Club just *in case* I can be of any use.

STONOR (*firmly*). No, don't do that. If I should have anything new to say—

FARNBOROUGH (*feverishly*). B-b-but with our party, as your brother said—'heading straight for a vast electoral disaster—'

STONOR. If I decide on a counterblast I shall simply telegraph to headquarters. Goodbye.

FARNBOROUGH. Oh—a—g-goodbye. (*A gesture of 'The country's going to the dogs.'*)

(*Jean rings the bell. Exit Farnborough.*)

STONOR (*studying the carpet*). 'Political dynamite,' eh? (*Pause.*) After all . . . women are much more conservative than men—aren't they?

(*Jean looks straight in front of her, making no attempt to reply.*)

Especially the women the property qualification would bring in. (*He glances at Jean as though for the first time conscious of her silence.*) You see now (*He throws himself into the chair by the table.*) one reason why I've encouraged you to take an interest in public affairs. Because people like us don't go screaming about it, is no sign we don't (some of us) see what's on the way. However little they want to, women of our class will have to come into line. All the best things in the world—everything that civilisation has won will be in danger if—when this change comes—the only women who have practical political training are the women of the lower classes. Women of the lower classes, and (*His brows knit heavily.*)—women inoculated by the Socialist virus.

JEAN. Geoffrey.

STONOR (*draws the telegraph form towards him*). Let us see, how we shall put it—when the time comes—shall we? (*He detaches a pencil from his watch chain and bends over the paper, writing.*)

(*Jean opens her lips to speak, moves a shade nearer the table and then falls back upon her silent, half-incredulous misery.*)

STONOR (*holds the paper off, smiling*). Enough dynamite in that! Rather too much, isn't there, little girl?

JEAN. Geoffrey. I know her story.

STONOR. Whose story?

JEAN. Miss Levering's

STONOR. *Whose?*

JEAN. Vida Levering's

(*Stonor stares speechless. Slight pause.*)

(*The words escaping from her in a miserable cry.*) Why did you desert her?

STONOR (*staggered*). I! *I?*

JEAN. Oh, why did you do it?

STONOR (*bewildered*). What in the name of—What has she been saying to you?

JEAN. Someone else told me part. Then the way you looked when you saw her at Aunt Ellen's—Miss Levering's saying you didn't know her—then your letting out that you knew, even the curious name on the handkerchief—Oh, I pieced it together—

STONOR (*with recovered self-possession*). Your ingenuity is undeniable!

JEAN. —and then, when she said that at the meeting about 'the dark hour' and I looked at your face—it flashed over me—Oh, *why* did you desert her?

STONOR. I *didn't* desert her.

JEAN. Ah-h! (*Puts her hands before her eyes.*)

(*Stonor makes a passionate motion towards her, is checked by her muffled voice saying.*)

I'm glad—I'm glad!

(*He stares bewildered. Jean drops her hands in her lap and steadies her voice.*)

She went away from you, then?

STONOR. You don't expect me to enter into—

JEAN. She went away from you?

STONOR (*with a look of almost uncontrollable anger*). Yes!

JEAN. Was that because you wouldn't marry her?

STONOR. I couldn't marry her—and she knew it.

JEAN. Did you want to?

STONOR (*an instant's angry scrutiny and then turning away his eyes*). I thought I did—*then.* It's a long time ago.

JEAN. And why 'couldn't' you?

STONOR (*a movement of strong irritation cut short*). Why are you catechising me? It's a matter that concerns another woman.

JEAN. If you're saying that it doesn't concern me, you're saying—(*her lip trembles*)—that *you* don't concern me.

STONOR (*commanding his temper with difficulty*). In those days I—I was absolutely dependent on my father.

JEAN. Why, you must have been thirty, Geoffrey.

STONOR (*slight pause*). What? Oh—thereabouts.

JEAN. And everybody says you're so clever.

STONOR. Well, everybody's mistaken.

JEAN (*drawing nearer*). It must have been terribly hard—

(*Stonor turns towards her.*)

for you both—

(*He arrests his movement and stands stonily.*)

that a man like you shouldn't have had the freedom that even the lowest seem to have.

STONOR. Freedom?

JEAN. To marry the woman they choose.

STONOR. She didn't break off our relations because I couldn't marry her.

JEAN. Why was it, then?

STONOR. You're too young to discuss such a story. (*Half turns away.*)

JEAN. I'm not so young as she was when—

STONOR (*wheeling upon her*). Very well, then, if you will have it! The truth is, it didn't seem to weigh upon her, as it seems to on you, that I wasn't able to marry her.

JEAN. Why are you so sure of that?

STONOR. Because she didn't so much as hint such a thing when she wrote that she meant to break off the—the—

JEAN. What made her write like that?

STONOR (*with suppressed rage*). Why *will* you go on talking of what's so long over and ended?

JEAN. What reason did she give?

STONOR. If your curiosity has so got the upper hand—*ask her.*

JEAN (*her eyes upon him*). You're afraid to tell me.

STONOR (*putting pressure on himself to answer quietly*). I still hoped—at *that* time—to win my father over. She blamed me because (*goes to the window and looks blindly out and speaks in a low tone.*) if the child had lived it wouldn't have been possible to get my father to—overlook it.

JEAN (*faintly*). You wanted it *overlooked?* I don't underst—

STONOR (*turning passionately back to her*). Of course you don't. (*He seizes her hand and tries to draw her to him.*) If you did, you wouldn't be the beautiful, tender, innocent child you are—

JEAN (*has withdrawn her hand and shrunk from him with an impulse—slight as is its expression—so tragically eloquent, that fear for the first time catches hold of him*). I am glad you didn't mean to desert her, Geoffrey. It wasn't your fault after all—only some misunderstanding that can be cleared up.

STONOR. *Cleared up?*

JEAN. Yes. Cleared up.

STONOR (*aghast*). You aren't thinking that this miserable old affair I'd as good as forgotten—

JEAN (*in a horror struck whisper, with a glance at the door which he doesn't see*). Forgotten!

STONOR. No, no. I don't mean exactly forgotten. But you're torturing me so I don't know what I'm saying. (*He goes closer.*) You aren't—Jean! you—you aren't going to let it come between you and me!

JEAN (*presses her handkerchief to her lips, and then, taking it away, answers steadily*). I can't make or unmake what's past. But I'm glad, at least, that you didn't *mean* to desert her in her trouble. You'll remind her of that first of all, won't you? (*Moves to the door.*)

STONOR. Where are you going? (*Raising his voice.*) Why should I remind anybody of what I want only to forget?

JEAN (*finger on lip*). Sh!

STONOR (*with eyes on the door*). You don't mean that *she's*—

JEAN. Yes. I left her to get a little rest.

(*He recoils in an access of uncontrollable rage. She follows him. Speechless, he goes to get his hat.*)

Geoffrey, don't go before you hear me. I don't know if what I think matters to you now—but I hope it does. (*With tears.*) You can still make me think of you without shrinking—if you will.

STONOR (*fixes her a moment with his eyes. Then sternly*). What is it you are asking of me?

JEAN. To make amends, Geoffrey.

STONOR (*with an outburst*). You poor little innocent!

JEAN. I'm poor enough. But (*locking her hands together.*) I'm not so innocent but what I know you must right that old wrong now, if you're ever to right it.

STONOR. You aren't insane enough to think I would turn round in these few hours and go back to something that ten years ago was ended for ever! Why, it's stark, staring madness!

JEAN. No. (*Catching on his arm*). What you did ten years ago—*that* was mad. This is paying a debt.

STONOR. Look here, Jean, you're dreadfully wrought up and excited—tired too—

JEAN. No, not tired—though I've travelled so far today. I know you smile at sudden conversions. You think they're hysterical—worse—vulgar. But people must get their revelation how they can. And, Geoffrey, if I can't make you see this one of mine—I shall know your love could never mean strength to me. Only weakness. And I shall be afraid. So afraid I'll never dare to give you the *chance* of making me loathe myself. I shall never see you again.

STONOR. How right *I* was to be afraid of that vein of fascination in you. (*Moves towards the door.*)

JEAN. Certainly, you couldn't make a greater mistake than to go away now and think it any good ever to come back. (*He turns.*) Even if I came to feel different, I couldn't *do* anything different. I should know all this couldn't be forgotten. I should know that it would poison my life in the end. Yours too.

STONOR (*with suppressed fury*). She has made good use of her time! (*With a sudden thought.*) What has changed her? Has *she* been seeing visions too?

JEAN. What do you mean?

STONOR. Why is she intriguing to get hold of a man that, ten years ago, she flatly refused to see, or hold any communication with?

JEAN. 'Intriguing to get hold of.' She hasn't mentioned you!

STONOR. *What!* Then how in the name of Heaven do you know—that she wants—what you ask?

JEAN (*firmly*). There can't be any doubt about that.

STONOR (*with immense relief*). You absurd, ridiculous child! Then all this is just your own unaided invention. Well— I could thank God! (*Falls into the nearest chair and passes his handkerchief over his face.*)

JEAN (*perplexed, uneasy*). For what are you thanking God?

STONOR (*trying to think out his plan of action*). Suppose, (I'm not going risk it) —but suppose—(*He looks up and at the sight of Jean's face a new tenderness comes into his own. He rises suddenly.*) Whether I deserve to suffer or not—it's quite certain *you* don't. Don't cry, dear one. It never was the real thing. I had to wait till I knew you before I understood.

JEAN (*lifts her eyes brimming*). Oh, is that true? (*Checks her movement towards him.*) Loving you has made things clear to me I didn't dream of before. If I could think that because of me you were able to do this—

STONOR (*seizes her by the shoulders and says hoarsely*). Look here! Do you seriously ask me to give up the girl I love— to go and offer to marry a woman that even to think of—

JEAN. You cared for her once. You'll care about her again. She is beautiful and brilliant—everything. I've heard she could win any man she set herself to—

STONOR (*pushing Jean from him*). She's bewitched you!

JEAN. Geoffrey, Geoffrey, you aren't going away like that. This isn't *the end!*

STONOR (*darkly—hesitating*). I suppose even if she refused me, you'd—

JEAN. She won't refuse you.

STONOR. She did once.

JEAN. She didn't refuse to *marry* you—

(*Jean is going to the door.*)

STONOR (*catches her by the arm*). Wait!—a—(*Hunting for some means of gaining time.*) Lady John is waiting all this while for the car to go back with a message.

JEAN. *That's* not a matter of life and death—

STONOR. All the same—I'll go down and give the order.

JEAN (*stopping quite still on a sudden*). Very well. (*Sits.*) You'll come back if you're the man I pray you are. (*Breaks into a flood of silent tears, her elbows on the table, her face in her hands.*)

STONOR (*returns, bends over her, about to take her in his arms*). Dearest of all the world—

(*Door opens softly and Vida Levering appears. She is arrested at the sight of Stonor, and is in the act of drawing back when, upon the slight noise, Stonor looks round. His face darkens, he stands staring at her and then with a look of speechless anger goes silently out. Jean, hearing him shut the door, drops her head on the table with a sob. Vida Levering crosses slowly to her and stands a moment silent at the girl's side.*)

MISS LEVERING. What is the matter?

JEAN (*lifting her head and drying her eyes*). I—I've been seeing Geoffrey.

MISS LEVERING (*with an attempt at lightness*). Is this the effect seeing Geoffrey has?

JEAN. You see, I know now (*as Miss Levering looks quite uncomprehending*)—how he (*drops her eyes*)—how he spoiled some one else's life.

MISS LEVERING (*quickly*). Who tells you that?

JEAN. Several people have told me.

MISS LEVERING. Well, you should be very careful how you believe what you hear.

JEAN (*passionately*). You *know* it's true.

MISS LEVERING. I know that it's possible to be mistaken.

JEAN. I see! You're trying to shield him—

MISS LEVERING. Why should I—what is it to me?

JEAN (*with tears*). Oh-h, how you must love him!

MISS LEVERING. Listen to me—

JEAN (*rising*). What's the use of your going on denying it? (*Miss Levering, about to break in, is silenced.*) Geoffrey doesn't.

(*Jean, struggling to command her feelings, goes to window. Vida Levering relinquishes an impulse to follow, and sits left centre. Jean comes slowly back with her eyes bent on the floor, does not lift them till she is quite near Vida. Then the girl's self-absorbed face changes.*)

Oh, don't look like that! I shall bring him back to you! (*Drops on her knees beside the other's chair.*)

MISS LEVERING. You would be impertinent (*softening*) if you weren't a romantic child. You can't bring him back.

JEAN. Yes, he—

MISS LEVERING. But there's something you *can* do—

JEAN. What?

MISS LEVERING. Bring him to the point where he recognises that he's in our debt.

JEAN. In *our* debt?

MISS LEVERING. In debt to women. He can't repay the one he robbed—

JEAN (*wincing and rising from her knees*). Yes, yes.

MISS LEVERING (*sternly*). No, he can't repay the dead. But there are the living. There are the thousands with hope still in their hearts and youth in their blood. Let him help *them*. Let him be a friend to Women.

JEAN (*rising on a wave of enthusiasm*). Yes, yes—I understand. That too!

(*The door opens. As Stonor enters, with Lady John, he makes a slight gesture towards the two as much as to say, 'You see.'*)

JEAN (*catching sight of him*). Thank you!

LADY JOHN (*in a clear, commonplace tone to Jean*). Well, you rather gave us the slip. Vida, I believe Mr. Stonor wants to see you for a few minutes (*glances at watch*)—but I'd like a word with you first, as I must get back. (*To Stonor.*) Do you think the car—your man said something about re-charging.

STONOR (*hastily*). Oh, did he? I'll see about it.

(*As Stonor is going out he encounters the Butler. Exit Stonor.*)

BUTLER. Mr Trent has called, Miss, to take Miss Levering to the meeting.

JEAN. Bring Mr Trent into my sitting room. I'll tell him—you can't go tonight.

(*Exeunt Butler centre, Jean left.*)

LADY JOHN (*hurriedly*). I know, my dear, *you're* not aware of what that impulsive girl wants to insist on.

MISS LEVERING. Yes, I am aware of it.

LADY JOHN. But it isn't with your sanction, surely, that she goes on making this extraordinary demand.

MISS LEVERING (*slowly*). I didn't sanction it at first, but I've been thinking it over.

LADY JOHN. Then all I can say is I am greatly disappointed in you. You threw this man over years ago for reasons—whatever they were—that seemed to you good and sufficient. And now you come between him and a younger woman—just to play Nemesis, so far as I can make out!

MISS LEVERING. Is that what he says?

LADY JOHN. He says nothing that isn't fair and considerate.

MISS LEVERING. I can see he's changed.

LADY JOHN. And you're unchanged—is that it?

MISS LEVERING. I've changed even more than he.

LADY JOHN. But (*pity and annoyance blended in her tone*)—you care about him still, Vida?

MISS LEVERING. No.

LADY JOHN. I see. It's just that you wish to marry somebody—

MISS LEVERING. Oh, Lady John, there are no men listening.

LADY JOHN (*surprised*). No, I didn't suppose there were.

MISS LEVERING. Then why keep up that old pretence?

LADY JOHN. What pre—

MISS LEVERING. That to marry *at all costs* is every woman's dearest ambition till the grave closes over her. You and I *know* it isn't true.

LADY JOHN. Well. but—Oh! it was just the unexpected sight of him bringing it back—*That* was what fired you this afternoon! (*With an honest attempt at sympathetic understanding.*) Of course. The memory of a thing like that can never die—can never even be dimmed—*for the woman.*

MISS LEVERING. I mean her to think so.

LADY JOHN (*bewildered*). Jean!

MISS LEVERING. *nods.*

LADY JOHN. And it *isn't* so?

MISS LEVERING. You don't seriously believe a woman with anything else to think about, comes to the end of ten years still *absorbed* in a memory of that sort?

LADY JOHN (*astonished*). You've got over it, then!

MISS LEVERING. If the newspapers didn't remind me I shouldn't remember once a twelvemonth that there was ever such a person as Geoffrey Stonor in the world.

LADY JOHN (*with unconscious rapture*). Oh, I'm *so* glad!

MISS LEVERING (*smiles grimly*). Yes. I'm glad too.

LADY JOHN. And if Geoffrey Stonor offered you—what's called 'reparation'—you'd refuse it?

MISS LEVERING (*smiles a little contemptuously*). Geoffrey Stonor! For me he's simply one of the far back links in a chain of evidence. It's certain I think a hundred times of other women's present unhappiness, to once that I remember that old unhappiness of mine that's past. I think of the nail and chain makers of Cradley Heath. The sweated girls of the slums. I think of the army of ill-used women whose very existence I mustn't mention—

LADY JOHN (*interrupting hurriedly*). Then why in Heaven's name do you let poor Jean imagine—

MISS LEVERING (*bending forward*). Look—I'll trust you, Lady John. I don't suffer from that old wrong as Jean thinks I do, but I shall coin her sympathy into gold for a greater cause than mine.

LADY JOHN. I don't understand you.

MISS LEVERING. Jean isn't old enough to be able to care as much about a principle as about a person. But if my half-forgotten pain can turn her generosity into the common treasury—

LADY JOHN. What do you propose she shall do, poor child?

MISS LEVERING. Use her hold over Geoffrey Stonor to make him help us!

LADY JOHN. Help you?

MISS LEVERING. The man who served one woman—God knows how many more—very ill, shall serve hundreds of thousands well. Geoffrey Stonor shall make it harder for his son, harder still for his grandson, to treat any woman as he treated me.

LADY JOHN. How will he do that?

MISS LEVERING. By putting an end to the helplessness of women.

LADY JOHN (*ironically*). You must think he has a great deal of power—

MISS LEVERING. Power? Yes, men have too much over penniless and frightened women.

LADY JOHN (*impatiently*). What nonsense! You talk as though the women hadn't their share of human nature. *We* aren't made of ice any more than the men.

MISS LEVERING. No, but all the same we have more self-control.

LADY JOHN. Than men?

MISS LEVERING. You know we have.

LADY JOHN (*shrewdly*). I know we mustn't admit it.

MISS LEVERING. For fear they'd call us fishes!

LADY JOHN (*evasively*). They talk of our lack of self-control—but it's the last thing they *want* women to have.

MISS LEVERING. Oh, we know what they want us to have. So we make shift to have it. If we don't, we go without hope—sometimes we go without bread.

LADY JOHN (*shocked*). Vida—do you mean to say that you—

MISS LEVERING. I mean to say that men's vanity won't let them see it, but the thing's largely a question of economics.

LADY JOHN (*shocked*). You *never* loved him, then!

MISS LEVERING. Oh yes, I loved him—*once*. It was my helplessness turned the best thing life can bring, into a curse for both of us.

LADY JOHN. I don't understand you—

MISS LEVERING. Oh, being 'understood!'—that's too much to expect. When people come to know I've joined the Union—

LADY JOHN. But you won't—

MISS LEVERING. —who is there who will resist the temptation to say, 'Poor Vida Levering! What a pity she hasn't got a husband and a baby to keep her quiet'? The few who know about me, they'll be equally sure that it's not the larger view of life I've gained—my own poor little story is responsible for my new departure. (*Leans forward and looks into Lady John's face.*) My best friend, she will be surest of all, that it's a private sense of loss, or, lower yet, a grudge—! But I tell you the only difference between me and thousands of women with husbands and babies is that I'm free to say what I think. *They aren't.*

LADY JOHN (*rising and looking at her watch*). I must get back—my poor ill-used guests.

MISS LEVERING (*rising*). I won't ring. I think you'll find Mr Stonor downstairs waiting for you.

LADY JOHN (*embarrassed*). Oh—a—he will have left word about the car in any case.

(*Miss Levering has opened the door. Allen Trent is in the act of saying goodbye to Jean in the hall.*)

MISS LEVERING. Well, Mr. Trent, I didn't expect to see you this evening.

TRENT (*comes and stands in the doorway*). Why not? Have I ever failed?

MISS LEVERING. Lady John, this is one of our allies. He is good enough to squire me through the rabble from time to time.

LADY JOHN. Well, I think it's very handsome of you, after what she said today about men. (*Shakes hands.*)

TRENT. I've no great opinion of most men myself. I might add—or of most women.

LADY JOHN. Oh! Well, at any rate I shall go away relieved to think that Miss Levering's plain speaking hasn't alienated *all* masculine regard.

TRENT. Why should it?

LADY JOHN. That's right, Mr. Trent! Don't believe all she says in the heat of propaganda.

TRENT. I do believe all she says. But I'm not cast down.

LADY JOHN (*smiling*). Not when she says—

TREND (*interrupting*). Was there never a misogynist of my sex who ended by deciding to make an exception?

LADY JOHN (*smiling significantly*). Oh, if *that's* what you build on!

TRENT. Well, why shouldn't a man-hater on your side prove equally open to reason?

MISS LEVERING. That part of the question doesn't concern me. I've come to a place where I realise that the first battles of this new campaign must be fought by women alone. The only effective help men could give—amendment of the law—they refuse. The rest is nothing.

LADY JOHN. Don't be ungrateful, Vida. Here's Mr. Trent ready to face criticism in publicly championing you.

MISS LEVERING. It's an illusion that I as an individual need Mr Trent. I am quite safe in the crowd. Please don't wait for me, and don't come for me again.

TREND (*flushes*). Of course if you'd rather—

MISS LEVERING. And that reminds me I was asked to thank you and to tell you, too, that they—the women of the Union—they won't need your chairmanship any more—though that, I beg you to believe, has nothing to do with any feeling of mine.

TREND (*hurt*). Of course, I know there must be other men ready—better known men—

MISS LEVERING. It isn't that. It's simply that they find a man can't keep a rowdy meeting in order as well as a woman.

(*He stares.*)

LADY JOHN. You aren't serious?

MISS LEVERING (*to Trent*). Haven't you noticed that all their worst disturbances come when men are in charge?

TRENT. Well—a—(*laughs a little ruefully as he moves to the door.*) I hadn't connected the two ideas. Goodbye.

MISS LEVERING. Goodbye.

(*Jean takes him downstairs, right centre.*)

LADY JOHN (*as Trent disappears*). That nice boy's in love with you.

(*Miss Levering simply looks at her.*)

Goodbye. (*They shake hands.*) I wish you hadn't been so unkind to that nice boy!

MISS LEVERING. Do you?

LADY JOHN. Yes, for then I would be more certain of your telling Geoffrey Stonor that intelligent women don't nurse their wrongs and lie in wait to punish them.

MISS LEVERING. You are *not* certain?

LADY JOHN (*goes close up to Vida*). Are you?

(*Vida stand with her eyes on the ground, silent, motionless. Lady John, with a nervous glance at her watch and a gesture of extreme perturbation, goes hurried out. Vida shuts the door. She comes slowly back, sits down and covers her face with her hands. She rises and begins to walk up and down, obviously trying to master her agitation. Enter Geoffrey Stonor.*)

MISS LEVERING. Well, have they primed you? Have you got your lesson (*with a little broken laugh*) by heart at last?

STONOR (*looking at her from immeasurable distance*). I am not sure I understand you. (*Pause.*) However unpropitious your mood may be—I shall discharge my errand. (*Pause. Her silence irritates him.*) I have promised to offer you what I believe is called 'amends.'

MISS LEVERING (*quickly*). You've come to realise, then—after all these years—that you owed me something?

STONOR (*on the brink of protest, checks himself*). I am not here to deny it.

MISS LEVERING (*fiercely*). Pay, then—*pay*.

STONOR (*a moment's dread as he looks at her, his lips set. Then stonily*). I have promised that, if you exact it, I will.

MISS LEVERING. Ah! If I insist you'll 'make it all good'! (*Quite low.*) Then don't you know you must pay me in kind?

STONOR. What do you mean?

MISS LEVERING. Give me back what you took from me: my old faith. Give me that.

STONOR. Oh, if you mean to make phrases—(*A gesture of scant patience.*)

MISS LEVERING (*going closer*). Or give me back mere kindness—or even tolerance. Oh, I don't mean *your* tolerance. Give me back the power to think fairly of my brothers—not as mockers—thieves.

STONOR. I have not mocked you. And I have asked you—

MISS LEVERING. Something you knew I should refuse! Or (*her eyes blaze*) did you dare to be afraid I wouldn't?

STONOR. I suppose, if we set our teeth, we could—

MISS LEVERING. I couldn't—not even if I set my teeth. And you wouldn't dream of asking me, if you thought there was the smallest chance.

STONOR. I can do no more than make you an offer of such reparation as is in my power. If you don't accept it—(*He turns with an air of 'That's done.'*)

MISS LEVERING. Accept it? No! . . . Go away and live in debt! Pay and pay and pay—and find yourself still in debt!—for a thing you'll never be able to give me back. (*Lower.*) And when you come to die, say to yourself, "I paid all creditors but one."

STONOR. I'm rather tired, you know, of this talk of debt. If I hear that you persist in it I shall have to—

MISS LEVERING. What? (*She faces him.*)

STONOR. No. I'll keep to my resolution. (*Turning to the door.*)

MISS LEVERING (*intercepting him*). What resolution?

STONOR. I came here, under considerable pressure, to speak of the future, not to re-open the past.

MISS LEVERING. The Future and the Past are one.

STONOR. You talk as if that old madness was mine alone. It is the woman's way.

MISS LEVERING. I know. And it's not fair. Men suffer as well as we by the woman's starting wrong. We are taught to think the man a sort of demigod. If he tells her: 'go down into Hell'—down into Hell she goes.

STONOR. Make no mistake. Not the woman alone. *They go down together.*

MISS LEVERING. Yes, they go down together, but the man comes up alone. As a rule. It is more convenient so—for him. And for the Other Woman.

(*The eyes of both go to Jean's door.*)

STONOR (*angrily*). My conscience is clear. I know—and so do you—that most men in my position wouldn't have troubled themselves. I gave myself endless trouble.

MISS LEVERING (*with wondering eyes*). So you've gone about all these years feeling that you'd discharged every obligation.

STONOR. Not only that. I stood by you with a fidelity that was nothing short of Quixotic. If, woman like, you *must* recall the Past—I insist on your recalling it correctly.

MISS LEVERING (*very low*). You think I don't recall it correctly.

STONOR. Not when you make—other people believe that I deserted you. (*With gathering wrath.*) It's a curious enough charge when you stop to consider—(*Checks himself, and with a gesture of impatience sweeps the whole thing out of his way.*)

MISS LEVERING. Well, when we *do*—just for five minutes out of ten years—when we do stop to consider—

STONOR. We remember it was *you* who did the deserting! Since you had to rake the story up, you might have had the fairness to tell the facts.

MISS LEVERING. You think 'the facts' would have excused you! (*She sits.*)

STONOR. No doubt you've forgotten them, since Lady John tells me you wouldn't remember my existence once a year if the newspapers didn't—

MISS LEVERING. Ah, you minded that!

STONOR (*with many spirit*). I minded your giving false impressions. (*She is about to speak, he advances on her.*) Do you deny that you returned my letters unopened?

MISS LEVERING (*quietly*). No.

STONOR. Do you deny that you refused to see me—and that, when I persisted, you vanished?

MISS LEVERING. I don't deny any of those things.

STONOR. Why, I had no trace of you for years!

MISS LEVERING. I suppose not.

STONOR. Very well, then. What *could* I do?

MISS LEVERING. Nothing. It was too late to do anything.

STONOR. It wasn't too late! You knew since you 'read the papers'—that my father died that same year. There was no longer any barrier between us.

MISS LEVERING. Oh yes, there was a barrier.

STONOR. Of your own making, then.

MISS LEVERING. I had my guilty share in it—but the barrier (*her voice trembes*)—the barrier was your invention.

STONOR. It was no 'invention'. If you had ever know my father—

MISS LEVERING. Oh, the echoes! The echoes! How often you used to say, if I 'knew your father!' But you said, too (*lower*)—you called the greatest barrier by another name.

STONOR. What name?

MISS LEVERING (*very low*). The child that was to come.

STONOR (*hastily*). That was before my father died. While I still hoped to get his consent.

MISS LEVERING (*nods*). How the thought of that all-powerful personage used to terrorise me? What chance had a little unborn child against 'the last of the great feudal lords', as you called him.

STONOR. You *know* the child would have stood between you and me!

MISS LEVERING. I know the child *did* stand between you me!

STONOR (*with vague uneasiness*). It *did* stand—

MISS LEVERING. Happy mothers teach their children. Mine had to teach me.

STONOR. You talk as if—

MISS LEVERING. —teach me that a woman may do a thing for love's sake that shall kill love.

(*A silence.*)

STONOR (*fearing and putting from him fuller comprehension, rises with an air of finality*). You certainly made it plain you had no love left for me.

MISS LEVERING. I had need of it all for the child.

STONOR (*stares—comes closer, speaks hurriedly and very low*). Do you mean then that, after all—it lived?

MISS LEVERING. No; I mean that it was sacrificed. But it showed me no barrier is so impassible as the one a little child can raise.

STONOR (*a light dawning*). Was that why you . . . was *that* why?

MISS LEVERING (*nods, speechless a moment*). Day and night there it was!—between my thought of you and me. (*He sits again, staring at her.*) When I was most unhappy I would wake, thinking I heard a cry. It was my own crying

I heard, but I seemed to have it in my arms. I suppose I was mad. I used to lie there in that lonely farmhouse pretending to hush it. It was so hushed myself.

STONOR. I never knew—

MISS LEVERING. I didn't blame you. You couldn't risk being with me.

STONOR. You agreed that for both our sakes—

MISS LEVERING. Yes, you had to be very circumspect. You were so well known. Your autocratic father—your brilliant political future—

STONOR. Be fair. *Our* future—as I saw it then.

MISS LEVERING. Yes, it all hung on concealment. It must have looked quite simple to you. You didn't know that the ghost of child that had never seen the light, the frail thing you meant to sweep aside and forget—*have* swept aside and forgotten—you didn't know it was strong enough to push you out of my life. (*Lower with an added intensity.*) It can do more. (*Leans over him and whispers.*) It can push that girl out. (*Stoner's face changes.*) It can do more still.

STONOR. Are you threatening me?

MISS LEVERING. No, I am preparing you.

STONOR. For what?

MISS LEVERING. For the work that must be done. Either with *your* help—or *that girl's.*

(*Stonor lifts his eyes a moment.*)

One of two things. Either her life and all she has, given to this new service—or a Ransom, if I give her up to you.

STONOR. I see. A price. Well—?

MISS LEVERING (*looks searchingly in his face, hesitates and shakes her head*). Even if I could trust you to pay—no. It would be a poor bargain to give her up for anything you could do.

STONOR (*rising*). In spite of your assumption—she may not be your tool.

MISS LEVERING. You are horribly afraid she is! But you are wrong. Don't think it's merely I that have got hold of Jean Dumbarton.

STONOR (*angrily*). Who else?

MISS LEVERING. The New Spirit that's abroad.

(*Stonor turns away with an exclamation and begins to pace, sentinel-like, up and down before Jean's door.*)

How else should that inexperienced girl have felt the new loyalty and responded as she did!

STONOR (*under his breath*). 'New' indeed—however little loyal.

MISS LEVERING. Loyal above all. But no newer than electricity was when it first lit up the world. It had been there since the world began—waiting to do away with the dark. *So has the thing you're fighting.*

STONOR (*his voice held down to its lowest register*). The thing I'm fighting is nothing more than one person's hold on a

highly sensitive imagination. I consented to this interview with the hope—(*A gesture of impotence.*) It only remains for me to show her your true motive is revenge.

MISS LEVERING. Once say that to her and you are lost!

(*Stonor motionless; his look is the look of a man who sees happiness slipping away.*)

I know what it is that men fear. It even seems as if it must be through fear that your enlightenment will come. That is why I see a value in Jean Dunbarton far beyond her fortune.

(*Stonor lifts his eyes dully and fixes them on Vida's face.*)

More than any girl I know—if I keep her from you—that gentle, inflexible creature could rouse in men the old half-superstitious fear—

STONOR. 'Fear?' I believe you are made.

MISS LEVERING. 'Mad.' 'Unsexed.' These are the words of today. In the Middle Ages men cried out 'Witch!' and burnt her—the woman who served no man's bed or board.

STONOR. You want to make that poor child believe—

MISS LEVERING. She sees for herself we've come to a place where we find there's a value men see in them. You teach us not to look to you for some of the things we need most. If women must be freed by women, we have need of such as—(*Her eyes go to Jean's door.*)—who knows? She may be the new Joan of Arc.

STONOR (*aghast*). That *she* should be the sacrifice!

MISS LEVERLING. You have taught us to look very calmly on the sacrifice of women. Men tell us in every tongue it's 'a necessary evil'.

(*Stonor stands rooted, staring at the ground.*)

One girl's happiness—against a thing nobler than happiness for thousands—who can hesitate?—*Not Jean.*

STONOR. Good God! Can't you see that this crazed campaign you'd start her on—even if its successful, it can only be so through the help of men? What excuse shall you make your own soul for not going straight to the goal?

MISS LEVERING. You think we wouldn't be glad to go straight to the goal?

STONOR. I do. I see you'd much rather punish me and see her revel in a morbid self-sacrifice.

MISS LEVERING. You say I want to punish you only because, like most men, you won't take the trouble to understand what we do want—or how determined we are to have it. You can't kill this new spirit among women. (*Going nearer.*) And you couldn't make a greater mistake than to think it finds a home only in the exceptional, or the unhappy. It's so strange, Geoffrey, to see a man like you as much deluded as the Hyde Park loafers who say to Ernestine Blunt. 'Who's hurt *your* feelings?' Why not realise (*Going quite close to him.*) this is a thing that goes deeper than personal experience? And yet (*Lowering her voice and glancing at the door.*) if you take only the narrowest personal view, a good deal depends on what you and I agree upon in the next five minutes.

STONOR (*bringing her farther away from the door*). You recommend my realising the larger issues. But in your ambition to attach that girl to the chariot wheels of 'Progress,' you quite ignore the fact that people fitter for such work—the men you look to enlist in the end are ready waiting to give the thing a chance.

MISS LEVERING. Men are ready! What men?

STONOR (*avoiding her eyes, picking his words*). Women have themselves to blame that the question has grown so delicate that responsible people shrink—for the moment—from being implicated in it.

MISS LEVERING. We have seen the 'shrinking'.

STONOR. Without quoting any one else, I might point out that the New Antagonism seems to have blinded you to the small fact that I, for one, am not an opponent.

MISS LEVERING. The phrase *has* a familiar ring. We have heard it from four hundred and twenty others.

STONOR. I spoke, if I may say so, of some one who would count. Some one who can carry his party along with him—or risk a seat in the Cabinet.

MISS LEVERING (*quickly*). Did you mean you are ready to do that?

STONOR. An hour ago I was.

MISS LEVERING. Ah! . . . an hour ago.

STONOR. Exactly. You don't understand men. They can be led. They can't be driven. Ten minutes before you came into the room I was ready to say I would throw in my political lot with this Reform.

MISS LEVERING. And now . . . ?

STONOR. Now you block my way by an attempt at coercion. By forcing my hand you give my adherence an air of bargain-driving for a personal end. Exactly the mistake of the ignorant agitators of your 'Union,' as you call it. You have a great deal to learn. This movement will go forward, not because of the agitation, but in spite of it. There are men in Parliament who would have been actively serving the Reform today . . . as actively as so vast a constitutional change—

MISS LEVERING (*smiles faintly*). And they haven't done it because—

STONOR. Because it would have put a premium on breaches of decent behaviour. (*He takes a crumpled piece of paper out of his pocket.*) Look here!

MISS LEVERING (*flushes with excitement as she reads the telegram*). This is very good. I see only one objection.

STONOR. Objection!

MISS LEVERING. You haven't sent it.

STONOR. *That* is your fault.

MISS LEVERING. When did you write this?

STONOR. Just before you came in—when—(*He glances at the door.*)

MISS LEVERING. Ah! It must have pleased Jean—that message. (*Offers him back the paper.*)

(*Stonor astonished at her yielding it up so lightly, and remembering Jean had not so much as read it. He throws himself heavily into a chair and drops his head in his hands.*)

I could drive a hard-and-fast bargain with you, but I think I won't. If *both* love and ambition urge you on, perhaps—(*She gazes at the slack, hopeless figure with its sudden look of age—goes over silently and stands by his side.*) After all, life hasn't been quite fair to you—

(*He raises his heavy eyes.*)

You fall out of one ardent woman's dreams into another's.

STONOR. You may as well tell me—do you mean to—?

MISS LEVERING. To keep you and her apart? No.

STONOR (*for the first time tears come into his eyes. After a moment he holds out his hand*). What can I do for you?

(*Miss Levering shakes her head—speechless.*)

For the real you. Not the Reformer, or the would-be politician—for the woman I so unwillingly hurt. (*As she turns away, struggling with her feelings, he lays a detaining hand on her arm.*) You may not believe it, but now that I understand, there is almost nothing I wouldn't do to right that old wrong.

MISS LEVERING. There's nothing to be done. You can never give me back my child.

STONOR (*at the anguish in Vida's face his own has changed*). Will that ghost give you no rest?

MISS LEVERING. Yes, oh, yes. I see life is nobler than I knew. There is work to do.

STONOR (*stopping her as she goes towards the folding doors*). Why should you think that it's only you, these ten years have taught something to? Why not give even a man credit for a willingness to learn something of life, and for being sorry—profoundly sorry—for the pain his instruction has cost others? You seem to think I've taken it all quite lightly. That's not fair. All my life, ever since you disappeared, the thought of you has hurt. I would give anything I possess to know you—were happy again.

MISS LEVERING. Oh, happiness!

STONOR (*significantly*). Why shouldn't you find it still.

MISS LEVERING (*stares an instant*). I see! She couldn't help telling about Allen Trent—Lady John couldn't.

STONOR. You're one of the people the years have not taken from, but given more to. You are more than ever . . . You haven't lost your beauty.

MISS LEVERING. The gods saw it was so little effectual, it wasn't worth taking away. (*She stands looking out into the void.*) One woman's mishap?—what is that? A thing as trivial to the great world as it's sordid in most eyes. But the time has come when a woman may look about her, and say, 'What general significance has my secret pain? Does it "join on" to anything.' And I find it does. I'm no longer merely a woman who has stumbled on the way. I'm one (*She controls with difficulty the shake in her voice.*) who has got up bruised and bleeding, wiped the dust from her hands and the tears from her face, and said to herself not merely, 'Here's one luckless woman! but—here is a stone of stumbling to many. Let's see if it can't be moved out of other women's ways.' And she calls people to come and help. No mortal man, let alone a woman, by herself, can make a rock of offence. But (*With a sudden sombre flame of enthusiasm.*) if many help. Geoffrey, the thing can be done.

STONOR (*looks at her with wondering pity*). Lord! how you care!

MISS LEVERING (*touched by his moved face*). Don't be so sad. Shall I tell you a secret? Jean's ardent dreams needn't frighten you, if she has a child. *That*—from the begin-

ning, it was not the strong arm—it was the weakest—the little, little arms that subdued the fiercest of us.

(*Stonor puts out a pitying hand uncertainly towards her. She does not take it, but speaks with great gentleness.*)

You will have other children. Geoffrey for me there was to be only one. Well, well—(*She brushes her tears away.*) since men alone have tried and failed to make a decent world for the little children to live in—it's as well some of us are childless. (*Quietly taking up her hat and cloak.*) Yes, *we* are the ones who have no excuse for standing aloof from the fight.

STONOR. Vida!

MISS LEVERING. What?

STONOR. You've forgotten something (*As she looks back he is signing the message.*) *This.*

(*She goes out silently with the 'political dynamite' in her hand.*)

CURTAIN

TOPICS FOR CRITICAL THINKING AND WRITING

The Play on the PAGE

1. Much of the plot depends on unspoken clues, such as when Bee notices the look on Levering's face when she sees Stonor. Does Robins's reliance on nonverbal communication make it difficult for a reader to understand the play? Why or why not?

2. Critics have commented on the importance of the character descriptions. Select one of these and discuss its importance to the action of the play.

3. How is *Votes for Women* a critique of people with power?

4. Does Vida lose her credibility as a strong woman when she marries Stonor at the end of the play?

The Play on the STAGE

5. Robins's construction of the Trafalgar Square scene at the beginning of Act 2 and Granville Barker's staging of it was considered a tour de force of stage composition, realistically capturing the passing of a political demonstration. Discuss what elements of the script make this possible. How could this scene be staged today?

6. During its many productions around England after its premiere, *Votes for Women* needed to be staged

with a minimum of set and props. How would you plan such a staging?

7. Act 3 is the emotional climax of the play, but the dialogue between Vida and Stonor may seem melodramatic today. What can actors do to make this act work for a contemporary audience?

The Play in PERFORMANCE

Directed by the well-known theater artist Harley Granville-Barker, *Votes for Women* opened on April 9, 1907, at the Court Theater in London and ran for eight matinee performances. Because these matinees were sold out, it was given additional performances including thirteen evenings. The original title of the play was *The Friend of Woman,* but Granville-Barker suggested to Robbins that she rename it. The play was subsequently produced in New York and Rome in 1909.

Once it was clear that the bold and risk-taking Court Theater under the Vedrenne-Barker management would produce the play, a great deal of support and advice came Robins's way. Her friend the American novelist Henry James was impressed with the work but suggested she reduce the number of characters, thus ridding the script of the large cast scene at Trafalgar Square. Robins refused to depoliticize it, saying "I have *got* to have as much of the woman movement as shall put the ignorant in possession of its main facts" (in John 147). Playwrights J. M. Barrie and George Bernard Shaw, as well as Granville-Barker himself, gave positive feedback to Robins before the play opened. After its successful London run, Robins donated the royalties she received to two British suffrage societies.

The play annoyed some people who did not like theater being used for such political reasons. For many others, however, the play was a powerful, realistic indictment of a male-dominated world that stifles the voice and autonomy of women. Some contemporaries criticized the British suffrage movement as being too single-minded and focused on the vote. *Votes for Women* opened up wider issues about motherhood, sexuality, and work and demonstrated how these were bound to women's right to a political voice.

WILLIAM Butler Yeats

W. B. Yeats (1865–1939) is chiefly known as a lyric poet, but he played an important role in helping found the Abbey Theatre in Dublin, and, partly to keep the theater going, he wrote twenty-six plays, which in his *Collected Plays* run to 705 pages. The number of manuscript pages is in the thousands. He also wrote important essays on the theater, collected in two volumes, *Explorations* and *Essays and Introductions*.

Yeats was born in Dublin but spent a good part of his early years in Sligo, a romantic western county of Ireland where the peasants' talk was full of fairies and ghosts, and his experiences in Sligo furnished him with much of his material. His father was a professional painter, and in 1883 the young Yeats was enrolled not in a college but in the Metropolitan School of Art, but he stayed there only briefly. In 1885 he published his first poems and also his first play, *The Island of Statues,* though this work is really a poem in dramatic form. In 1888 he published two books of Irish folklore, drawing especially on the material he had collected in Sligo, and in the following year he became a co-founder, with Lady August Gregory, Edward Martyn, and George Moore, of the Irish Literary Theatre. Martyn's interest was chiefly in realistic Ibsenite plays dealing with social issues, whereas the other co-founders were chiefly concerned with what they thought were more enduring issues, and by 1902 Martyn withdrew, with George Moore. In 1904 Annie Horniman, a wealthy British theater-manager, bought a theater in Abbey Street and allowed Yeats and Lady Gregory to present plays, rent free. At this point the group officially changed its name to the Irish National Theatre Society, but became known throughout the English-speaking world as the Abbey Theatre. Although Yeats played an active role in running the theater, and in writing plays for it, the success of the theater depended chiefly on prose plays by others, including distinguished works by Lady Gregory, John Millington Synge, and (until Yeats quarreled with him) Sean O'Casey.

In 1922 Yeats was appointed a senator in the newly established Irish Free State, and he served in that office until 1928. In 1933 he was awarded the Nobel Prize for Literature. *Purgatory,* staged at the Abbey in 1938, was Yeats's last play for the theater.

■■■■■■■■■■■■■■

COMMENTARY ON *PURGATORY*

Much of the world's great drama has been written in verse—but not lately. Ancient Greek and Roman plays are poetic drama, and so is medieval drama, much of Japanese Noh drama, much of Shakespeare, Molière, Corneille, and—well, one can give a long list of major dramatists who wrote in verse. Nevertheless, it is now easy to see that by the end of the seventeenth century the days of verse drama in Europe and England were numbered.

Of course some people continued to write plays in verse; in nineteenth-century England, Coleridge, Wordsworth, Tennyson, and Browning were among the many poets who tried their hand at verse plays. Given Shakespeare's success on—indeed, his dominance of—the stage, these writers tended to imitate Shakespeare, using blank verse (iambic pentameter, often with Elizabethan diction) for the characters of high rank and prose for the low characters. Their plays, alas,

are lifeless, in part because they are so clearly derived from Shakespeare and are so removed from the life of their own time. Of course many of Shakespeare's plays, for instance *Julius Caesar* and *Hamlet,* are remote from Elizabethan England in time and place, but Shakespeare was writing in the language of his day, not in a remote literary language. In France, at the end of the nineteenth century, Edmund Rostand wrote *Cyrano de Bergerac* (1897), perhaps the only verse play of the nineteenth century that has a substantial stage-history in the twentieth. If there is an exception to this statement it is that Ibsen's verse plays *Brand* (1865) and *Peer Gynt* (1867) are occasionally performed, but one can wonder if they would be staged if Ibsen had not gone on to establish himself as a master of drama—in prose.

In the twentieth century, several English, Irish, and American poets wrote plays—for instance T. S. Eliot, W. B. Yeats, Wallace Stevens, William Carlos Williams, W. H. Auden, and Archibald MacLeish. MacLeish's *J.B.* (1958), a retelling of the story of Job in a modern setting, won a Pulitzer prize, and the work of all of these people is of interest, especially to readers interested in poetry, but only Yeats can be said to have devoted much of his life to the theater, and only Yeats can be said to have produced notable dramatic work. Despite the apparent lack of an audience for poetic drama, a few playwrights of course continue to use verse: In our own time, the Nigerian playwright Wole Soyinka used it for his adaptation of Euripides's *The Bacchae* (we reprint Soyinka's 1973 play in this book), in England Caryl Churchill used varying meters in *Serious Money* (1987), and the Trinidadian poet and playwright Derek Walcott (resident in Boston) continues to write verse plays that have attracted serious attention from readers.

Yeats was first and last a great lyric poet, but he had a lifelong interest in the theater. In his early work, in the late 1880s and the 1990s, he is very much in the romantic tradition of Blake and Shelley. Years later he summarized his early career and that of his fellows:

> We were the last romantics—chose for theme
> Traditional sanctity and loveliness

In "The Lake Isle of Innisfree" (1893), Yeats the lyric poet longs to go to a place where "midnight's all a glimmer, and noon a purple glow, / And evening full of linnet's wings"; this poet is not much different from the early dramatic Yeats, who concludes one of his early plays, *The Land of Heart's Desire* (1894), with a speech describing a place where

> the lonely of heart is withered away;
> While the faeries dance in a place apart,
> Shaking their milk-white feet in a ring,
> Tossing their milk-white arms in the air;
> For they hear the wind laugh and murmur and sing
> Of a land where even the old are fair. . . .

But Yeats soon came to see that drama had to be closer to life, both in subject matter and in language. We will talk about his language in a moment, when we look at *Purgatory*, but first it may be best to glance at his ideas about drama. Some short quotations will show his lack of interest in, even his hostility to, the realistic drama of Ibsen, and his commitment to a poetic drama. His early plays draw on Irish folklore and heroic legend, not surprising since in 1888 he had published *Poems and Ballads of Young Ireland* and *Fairy and Folk Tales of the Irish Peasantry*, though in some of his later plays

(including *Purgatory*) he turned from Irish mythology to contemporary life. On page 908 we reprint several extended statements by Yeats about the theater, but here are five short passages. The first four of these quotations (1904–05) come from material he wrote for a theater movement in Dublin that he had co-founded with Lady Augusta Gregory; the fifth comes from a note he wrote for one of his later plays (1916), when he had developed a new style under the influence of Japanese Noh theater.

I was at the first performance of an Ibsen play given in England. It was *A Doll's House*. . . . Ibsen has sincerity and logic beyond any writer of our time, and we are all seeking to learn them at his hands; but is he not a good deal less than the greatest of all times, because he lacks beautiful and vivid language? (1904)

At the first performance of [Ibsen's] *Ghosts* I could not escape from an illusion unaccountable to me at the time. All the characters seemed to be less than life-size; the stage, though it was but the little Royalty stage, seemed larger than I had ever seen it. Little whimpering puppets moved here and there in the middle of that great abyss. Why did they not speak out with louder voices or move with freer gestures? What was it that weighed upon their souls perpetually? Certainly they were all in prison, yet there was no prison. (1904)

What attracts me to drama is that it is, in the most obvious way, what all the arts are upon a last analysis. A farce and a tragedy are alike in this, that they are a moment of immense life. An action is taken out of all other actions; it is reduced to its simplest form, or at any rate to as simple a form as it can be brought to without our losing the sense of its place in the world. The characters that are involved in it are freed from everything that is not a part of that action; and whether it is, as in the less important kinds of drama, a mere bodily activity, a hairbreadth escape or the like, or as it is in the more important kinds, an activity of the souls of the characters, it is an energy, an eddy of life purified from everything but itself. (1904)

The more carefully the [realistic] play [of our times] reflected the surface of life the more would the elements be limited to those that naturally display themselves during so many minutes of our ordinary affairs. It is [on the other hand] only by extravagance, by an emphasis far greater than that of life as we observe it, that we can crowd into a few minutes the knowledge of years. Shakespeare or Sophocles can so quicken, as it were, the circles of the clock, so heighten the expression of life, that many years can unfold themselves in a few minutes, and it is always Shakespeare or Sophocles, and not Ibsen, that makes us say, "How true, how often I have felt as that man feels"; or "How intimately I have come to know those people on the stage." (1905)

But if Yeats wanted the heightened expression of Shakespeare, he nevertheless knew that a playwright of the twentieth century could not try to write Elizabethan blank verse:

If our modern poetical drama has failed, it is mainly because, always dominated by the example of Shakespeare, it would restore an irrevocable past. (1916)

What was needed in the English-speaking world was a break with the tradition of poetic drama, the tradition of Shakespeare. And Yeats was assisted in making this break by encountering, in 1913–14, the Noh drama of Japan through Ezra Pound, who at that time was editing the manuscripts of Ernest Fenollosa, an American who had gone to Japan to teach economics and had become deeply interested in the arts of Japan. Fenollosa never got around to publishing his translations of Noh, but Pound, who inherited them and showed them to Yeats, did publish them in 1916, under the title of *"Noh" or Accomplishment*, with an introductory essay by Yeats, "Certain Noble Plays of Japan." We reprint a Noh play on page 206, and we say something about the genre in our introductory comment, but here it is enough to say that the plays are short, they are in verse, they employ few characters—often only two, plus a chorus—some actors are masked, the plays use no scenery other than a painted pine tree at the rear of the stage, the properties are minimal and stylized (a gesture with a fan may indicate rain, or a breeze), the plays often deal with the supernatural (especially with ghosts or apparitions who are drawn to a place where they have lived intensely, or have died), and a common theme is the need for the main character to be freed from the burden of the past. (When you have read *Purgatory*, which includes an apparition, you will see Yeats's indebtedness; Of course supernatural figures are common in Irish folklore too, but in one of his books, *A Vision*, Yeats specifically mentions the apparitions in Noh drama.) In a way, Japanese drama was for Yeats what Japanese prints had been forty or even fifty years earlier for painters such as Manet, Whistler, and van Gogh. That is, just as the Japanese prints with their areas of flat color and their lack of perspective and lack of modeling helped European painters to see there was another way of looking at reality, or another way of representing it—a way other than what seemed

to progressive painters of the period to be a worn-out tradition of realism—so the Noh drama helped Yeats to see a non-Shakespearean alternative to the realistic drama with social content of Ibsen. In his essay on Noh plays Yeats said, "With the help of Japanese plays 'translated by Ernest Fenollosa and finished by Ezra Pound,' I have invented a form of drama, distinguished, indirect, and symbolic . . . an aristocratic form." The plays Yeats wrote around the time of his essay (notably *At the Hawk's Well*, in which he employed a Japanese dancer) show very obviously the use of Noh, but by the time he wrote *Purgatory*, more than twenty years later, Yeats had assimilated the form and was able to use it less self-consciously.

A brief summary of the plot of *Purgatory* will allow us in a moment to offer some comments about Yeats's poetic styles. An aristocratic woman fell in love with a disreputable groom and married him. The couple had a son who, when he was sixteen, killed his father because by drinking and prodigality the father had despoiled the mother's heritage and while drunk had burned down the great house. The son, now an old man with a son of his own, returns to the dilapidated house, and there sees his mother's ghost. According to the Old Man, the dead "come back / To habitations and familiar spots" where they "Re-live their transgressions, and that not once / But many times. . . ." Thus his mother's remorseful soul forces her to reenact the shameful, passionate, tragic moment when she abandoned her aristocratic heritage and brought ruin to her family:

> She must live
> Through everything in exact detail,
> Driven to it by remorse, and yet
> Can she renew the sexual act
> And find no pleasure in it, and if not,
> If pleasure and remorse must both be there,
> Which is the greater?

If the mother finds pleasure in the act, her remorse is diminished and she therefore is not purging herself. The Old Man kills the boy in an attempt to end the consequences of his mother's indiscretion, but, on hearing the ghostly hoofbeats of his father's horse, he knows he has failed to free the ghost of his mother from its memories, and so he prays to God that his mother's ghost will someday be released from its memories and will find peace.

This summary of the plot proceeds chronologically, but the play does not. The play begins with the Old

Man and the Boy, and only gradually do we learn about the lady and the groom. But even if we were to recount the happenings in the sequence in which Yeats presents them, our recounting would still be far from the play. For one thing, the play is in verse, and our prose summary would lose (among other things) the incantatory effect of its rhythmic language. Look at the opening speech:

> Half-door, hall door,
> Hither and thither day and night,
> Hill or hollow, shouldering this pack,
> Hearing you talk.

Not only are we told that the boy and the Old Man have been wandering, and not only do we see that the Boy is irritable, but also we are immediately given a sense of ritual: The repeated "h's," the echo of "half-door" in "hall door," the rhyme of "hither and thither," the consonance of "hill" and "hollow," make this speech almost a magic chant. These lines take us out of our everyday world, make us focus on the dark scene before us, and communicate to us a sense of mystery.

The whole of the play, of course, is not in this same incantatory style. As an instance, note that the Boy's fourth speech (line 27) is a flat "There's nobody here." But even this statement verges on ritual because the Old Man's response is a variation: "There's somebody there." Still further removed from incantation is what may be the most memorable line in the play: "Twice a murderer and all for nothing" (line 234). In short, Yeats varies his style as the occasion warrants, just as Shakespeare varies his style in *Hamlet* from

> But look, the morn in russet mantle clad
> Walks o'er the dew of yon high eastward hill,

to

> O villain, villain, smiling, damned villain!

or from

> Ay, so, goodbye to you

to

> Absent thee from felicity awhile,
> And in this harsh world draw thy breath in pain
> To tell my story.

In *Purgatory* Yeats tends to use a four-stressed line (tetrameter) line, as opposed to the five-stressed (pen-

tameter) line typical of Shakespeare and of all later verse drama in English, but you will notice, as you read the play, that the lines are remarkably varied. Still, the lines are rhythmic, and rhythm, Yeats once said, is "to keep us in that state of perhaps real trance, in which the mind liberated from the pressure of the will is unfolded in symbols." Certainly the opening lines of *Purgatory* liberate us from the world of ordinary conversation, and prepare us for the mysteries that follow. The appeal that rhythm makes to the ear is reinforced by the appeal that the scenery makes to the eye. It is dark, but moonlight illuminates a ruined house and tree. The Old Man says,

> The moonlight falls upon the path,
> The shadow of a cloud upon the house,
> And that's symbolical; study that tree,
> What is it like?

The Old Man's explicit reference to symbolism is almost unnecessary; the dark house and tree themselves force on us an awareness that they are rich with suggestions or meanings. Take the tree. The Old Man says he saw it fifty years ago:

> Before the thunderbolt had riven it,
> Green leaves, ripe leaves, leaves thick as butter,
> Fat, greasy life.

And the decayed house was once a noble structure:

> Great people lived and died in this house;
> Magistrates, colonels, members of Parliament,
> Captains and Governors, and long ago
> Men that had fought at Aughrim and the Boyne.

(Yeats was of Irish Protestant stock, and the battles he mentions here were the sites of Protestant victories.) In the next few lines the two symbols come together:

> They had loved the trees that he cut down
> To pay what he had lost at cards
> Or spent on horses, drink and women;
> Had loved the house, had loved all
> The intricate passages of the house,
> But he killed the house.

The physical house surely is suggestive of the old aristocratic way of life, with its magistrates, colonels, and members of Parliament, brought to darkness and ruin by vulgar upstarts who have no respect for tradition and for heroic behavior. And the tree, riven by a thunderbolt, seems almost to proclaim that a divine hand can be discerned in the present ruin; the aristocracy was doomed to be destroyed when it yielded to the pressure of the lowest classes. In the play, the house and tree are sufficiently insisted on so we can not help but feel they are loaded with significance. In fact, the Old Man, after he has killed his son, calls attention to the tree's resemblance (in the white night) to "a purified soul." We are not surprised to learn that Yeats said, in a speech he made after the opening performance, that the play had a significance extending beyond the footlights: "In my play a spirit suffers because of its share, when alive, in the destruction of an honored house. That destruction is taking place all over Ireland today."

Sometimes the Old Man is so caught up in his narrative that he is speaking more to himself than to his son, and his narrative is in some measure a lyric meditation, but there is no mere lyric indulgence on Yeats's part. *Purgatory* has none of the tacked-on decorative lines that are found in some of his other plays, plays written, he said, for the sake of the lyrics. The Old Man's meditative narration of the house's history is dramatically perfect; it not only reveals his state of mind, but it also tells us something we need to know about the past. When his son interrupts with a vulgar comment more or less justifying the groom, the Old Man ignores him, partly because such a comment is beneath attention, partly because he is rapt in his memories and in his outrage. Similarly, the interruption to lines 84–85 is unnoticed. But the next interruption (line 94) demands notice, for here the Boy comments not only on the ghostly past but on his own immediate past and on his father's recent behavior. The interruption provokes an abusive burst, preventing us from sentimentalizing the Old Man. In short, the conflict and the subsequent tension are to be seen not only in such episodes as the squabble over the bag of money and the stabbing, but also in the words with which the characters attack each other and the silences by which they ignore each other. *Purgatory*, not surprisingly, was greatly admired by Yeats's fellow countryman, Samuel Beckett, whose plays have much of the desolation and yet the richness (for instance in their allusiveness) of *Purgatory*. It is not going too far to suggest that the leafless tree at the start of Beckett's *Waiting for Godot* may come from a seed of Yeats's "bare tree" in *Purgatory*.

PURGATORY
William Butler Yeats

PERSONS IN THE PLAY

A BOY,
AN OLD MAN

SCENE

A ruined house and a bare tree in the background.

BOY.
    Half-door, hall door,°
    Hither and thither day and night,
    Hill or hollow, shouldering this pack.
    Hearing you talk.
OLD MAN.   Study that house.
5   I think about its jokes and stories;
    I try to remember what the butler
    Said to a drunken gamekeeper
    In mid-October, but I cannot.
    If I cannot, none living can.
10   Where are the jokes and stories of a house,
    Its threshold gone to patch a pig-sty?
BOY.
    So you have come this path before?
OLD MAN.
    The moonlight falls upon the path,
    The shadow of a cloud upon the house,
15   And that's symbolical; study that tree,
    What is it like?
BOY.   A silly old man.
OLD MAN.
    It's like—no matter what it's like.
    I saw it a year ago stripped bare as now,
    So I chose a better trade.
20   I saw it fifty years ago
    Before the thunderbolt had riven it,
    Green leaves, ripe leaves, leaves thick as butter,
    Fat, greasy life. Stand there and look,
    Because there is somebody in that house.

    (*The Boy puts down pack and stands in the doorway.*)

BOY.
    There's nobody here.

---

1 Half-door, hall door Irish cottages had a door made in two parts, the upper half being left open for ventilation. A **hall door** presumably is the door not to a peasant's cottage but to a great house belonging to the gentry.

OLD MAN.   There's somebody there.   25
BOY.
    The floor is gone, the window's gone,
    And where there should be roof there's sky,
    And here's a bit of an egg-shell thrown
    Out of jackdaw's nest.
OLD MAN.   But there are some
    That do not care what's gone, what's left: 30
    The souls of Purgatory that come back
    To habitations and familiar spots.
BOY.
    Your wits are out again.
OLD MAN.   Re-live
    Their transgressions, and that not once
    But many times; they know at last   35
    The consequence of those transgressions
    Whether upon others or upon themselves;
    Upon others, others may bring help,
    For when the consequence is at an end
    The dream must end; if upon themselves,   40
    There is no help but in themselves
    And in the mercy of God.
BOY.   I have had enough!
    Talk to the jackdaws, if talk you must.
OLD MAN.
    Stop! Sit there upon that stone.
    That is the house where I was born.   45
BOY.
    The big old house that was burnt down?
OLD MAN.
    My mother that was your grand-dam owned it,
    This scenery and this countryside,
    Kennel and stable, horse and hound—
    She had a horse at the Curragh,° and there met   50
    My father, a groom in a training stable,

---

50 Curragh in County Kildare, noted for training race horses.

Looked at him and married him.
Her mother never spoke to her again,
And she did right.

BOY.   What's right and wrong?
55   My grand-dad got the girl and the money.

OLD MAN.
Looked at him and married him,
And he squandered everything she had.
She never knew the worst, because
She died in giving birth to me,
60   But now she knows it all, being dead.
Great people lived and died in this house;
Magistrates, colonels, members of Parliament,
Captains and Governors, and long ago
Men that had fought at Aughrim and the Boyne.°
65   Some that had gone on Government work
To London or to India came home to die,
Or came from London every spring
To look at the may-blossom in the park.
They had loved the trees that he cut down
70   To pay what he had lost at cards
Or spent on horses, drink and women;
Had loved the house, had loved all
The intricate passages of the house,
But he killed the house; to kill a house
75   Where great men grew up, married, died,
I here declare a capital offense.

BOY.
My God, but you had luck! Grand clothes,
And maybe a grand horse to ride.

OLD MAN.
That he might keep me upon his level
80   He never sent me to school, but some
Half-loved me for my half of her:
A gamekeeper's wife taught me to read,
A Catholic curate taught me Latin.
There were old books and books made fine
85   By eighteenth-century French binding, books
Modern and ancient, books by the ton.

BOY.
What education have you given me?

OLD MAN.
I gave the education that befits
A bastard that a pedlar got
90   Upon a tinker's daughter in a ditch.
When I had come to sixteen years old
My father burned down the house when drunk.

BOY.
But that is my age, sixteen years old,
At the Puck Fair.°

OLD MAN.   And everything was burnt;
Books, library, all were burnt.   95

BOY.
Is what I have heard upon the road the truth,
That you killed him in the burning house?

OLD MAN.
There's nobody here but our two selves?

BOY.
Nobody, Father.

OLD MAN.   I stuck him with a knife,
The knife that cuts my dinner now,   100
And after that I left him in the fire.
They dragged him out, somebody saw
The knife-wound but could not be certain
Because the body was all black and charred.
Then some that were his drunken friends   105
Swore they would put me upon trial,
Spoke of quarrels, a threat I had made.
The gamekeeper gave me some old clothes,
I ran away, worked here and there
Till I became a pedlar on the roads,   110
No good trade, but good enough
Because I am my father's son,
Because of what I did or may do.
Listen to the hoof-beats! Listen, listen!

BOY.
I cannot hear a sound.

OLD MAN.   Beat! Beat!   115
This night is the anniversary
Of my mother's wedding night,
Or of the night wherein I was begotten.
My father is riding from the public-house,
A whiskey-bottle under his arm.   120

(A window is lit showing a young girl.)

Look at the window; she stands there
Listening, the servants are all in bed,
She is alone, he has stayed late
Bragging and drinking in the public-house.

BOY.
There's nothing but an empty gap in the wall.   125
You have made it up. No, you are mad!
You are getting madder every day.

OLD MAN.
It's louder now because he rides

---

64 Aughrim and the Boyne sites of victories by the Protestant
forces of William III over the Catholic forces of James II in, respectively, 1691 and 1960. Presumably the Old Man's ancestors fought
on the Protestant side.

94 Puck Fair an annual fair held in Killorglin, County Kerry,
doubtless ultimately derived from pagan fertility rites, in which a
white male goat is crowned.

Upon a graveled avenue
130 All grass to-day. The hoof-beat stops,
He has gone to the other side of the house,
Gone to the stable, put the horse up.
She has gone down to open the door.
This night she is no better than her man
135 And does not mind that he is half-drunk,
She is mad about him. They mount the stairs.
She brings him into her own chamber.
And that is the marriage-chamber now.

(*The window is dimly lit again.*)

Do not let him touch you! It is not true
140 That drunken men cannot beget
And if he touch he must beget
And you must bear his murderer,
Deaf! Both deaf! If I should throw
A stick or a stone they would not hear;
145 And that's a proof my wits are out.
But there's a problem: she must live
Through everything in exact detail,
Driven to it by remorse, and yet
Can she renew the sexual act
150 And find no pleasure in it, and if not,
If pleasure and remorse must both be there,
Which is the greater?
⠀⠀⠀⠀⠀⠀⠀⠀⠀⠀I lack schooling.
Go fetch Tertullian°; he and I
Will ravel all that problem out
155 Whilst those two lie upon the mattress
Begetting me.
⠀⠀⠀⠀⠀⠀⠀⠀⠀Come back! Come back!
And so you thought to slip away,
My bag of money between your fingers,
And that I could not talk and see!
160 You have been rummaging in the pack.

(*The light in the window has faded out.*)

BOY.
You never gave me my right share.
OLD MAN.
And had I given it, young as you are,
You would have spent it upon drink.
BOY.
What if I did? I had a right
165 To get it and spend it as I chose.
OLD MAN.
Give me that bag and no more words.
BOY.
I will not.
OLD MAN.⠀⠀I will break your fingers.

153 Tertullian Quintus Septimus Floreus Tertullian (c. 160–c. 220), a convert to Christianity, in a treatise called *De Anima* (On the Soul) argued that the souls of the dead experience pleasure and remorse.

(*They struggle for the bag. In the struggle it drops, scattering the money. The Old Man staggers but does not fall. They stand looking at each other. The window is lit up. A man is seen pouring whiskey into a glass.*)

BOY.
What if I killed you? You killed my grand-dad,
Because you were young and he was old.
Now I am young and you are old.
OLD MAN (*staring at window*).⠀⠀⠀⠀⠀⠀⠀⠀170
Better-looking, those sixteen years—
BOY.
What are you muttering?
OLD MAN.⠀⠀⠀⠀⠀⠀⠀⠀⠀⠀⠀⠀Younger—and yet
She should have known he was not her kind.
BOY.
What are you saying? Out with it!

(*Old Man points to window.*)

My God! The window is lit up⠀⠀⠀⠀⠀⠀⠀⠀175
And somebody stands there, although
The floorboards are all burnt away.
OLD MAN.
The window is lit up because my father
Has come to find a glass for his whiskey.
He leans there like some tired beast.⠀⠀⠀⠀180
BOY.
A dead, living, murdered man!
OLD MAN.
"Then the bride-sleep fell upon Adam":
Where did I read those words?
⠀⠀⠀⠀⠀⠀⠀⠀⠀⠀⠀⠀⠀⠀⠀⠀And yet
There's nothing leaning in the window
But the impression upon my mother's mind;⠀185
Being dead she is alone in her remorse.
BOY.
A body that was a bundle of old bones
Before I was born. Horrible! Horrible!

(*He covers his eyes.*)

OLD MAN.
That beast there would know nothing, being nothing,
If I should kill a man under the window⠀⠀190
He would not even turn his head.

(*He stabs the Boy.*)

My father and my son on the same jack-knife!
That finishes—there—there—there—

(*He stabs again and again. The window grows dark.*)

"Hush-a-bye baby, thy father's a knight,
Thy mother a lady, lovely and bright."⠀⠀⠀195
No, that is something that I read in a book,
And if I sing it must be to my mother,
And I lack rhyme.

(*The stage has grown dark except where the tree stands in white light.*)

Study that tree.
It stands there like a purified soul,
200 All cold, sweet, glistening light.
Dear mother, the window is dark again,
But you are in the light because
I finished all that consequence.
I killed that lad because had he grown up
205 He would have struck a woman's fancy,
Begot, and passed pollution on.

I am a wretched foul old man
And therefore harmless. When I have stuck
This old jack-knife into a sod
210 And pulled it out all bright again,
And picked up all the money that he dropped,
I'll to a distant place, and there

Tell my old jokes among new men.

(*He cleans the knife and begins to pick up money.*)

Hoof-beats! Dear God,
How quickly it returns—beat—beat—!   215
Her mind cannot hold up that dream.
Twice a murderer and all for nothing,
And she must animate that dead night
Not once but many times!

       O God,
Release my mother's soul from its dream!   220
Mankind can do no more. Appease
The misery of the living and the remorse of the dead.

THE END

TOPICS FOR CRITICAL THINKING AND WRITING

The Play on the PAGE

1. Is the Old Man a one-sided character—black or white or a fixed shade of gray? Substantiate your response by specific references to the text.
2. Characterize the boy. What is his background? What are his values? How much moral sense does he have? Can you say something like, "The Boy stands for . . ."?
3. The Boy can see the ghost of his grandfather but not of his grandmother. Why?
4. Exactly why does the Old Man kill the Boy? On rereading the play, what lines and happenings in particular make the murder plausible?

5. Which lines prepare us for the prayer at the end?
6. The Old Man prays that God will release the "mother's soul from its dream." Should he perhaps pray that God will release him from his hatred of his parents?
7. T. S. Eliot said of Yeats's *Purgatory*, "I wish he had not given it this title, because I cannot accept a purgatory in which there is no hint, or at least no emphasis upon, purgation." Evaluate Eliot's comment.
8. How relevant to this play are Aristotle's concepts of *hamartia* and *hybris?*

The Play on the STAGE

9. The ruined house is pretty clearly a symbol. If you were staging the play would the house be realistic? If not, how would you represent it? Note: Although Yeats specifies the scene as "A ruined house and a bare tree in the background," the play has been staged with no scenery at all. What is your view?
10. If you were staging the play, when the Old Man hears the sound of hoofbeats while he is cleaning

his knife, would you have the audience hear the hoofbeats?
11. The play ends with the Old Man speaking a prayer, asking God to free his mother from her crime. Ordinarily a remorseful spirit, reenacting its offense, would be moving toward purgation, but in this instance the woman is not engaged in purgation because she finds renewed pleasure in the offense. If

you were staging the play, what gestures and what lighting effects would you use?

12. In some of his Japanese-influenced plays, Yeats prescribes the use of masks or of faces painted like masks. Why do you suppose he does not use these devices in *Purgatory*?

A Context for *Purgatory*

YEATS ON THE DRAMA
Poetic Drama

[These extracts come from an essay entitled "The Theater," first published in 1899.]

A common opinion is that the poetic drama has come to an end, because modern poets have no dramatic power; and Mr. Binyon seems to accept this opinion when he says: 'It has been too often assumed that it is the manager who bars the way to poetic plays. But it is much more probable that the poets have failed the managers. If poets mean to serve the stage, their dramas must be dramatic.' I find it easier to believe that audiences, who have learned, as I think, from the life of crowded cities to live upon the surface of life, and actors and managers, who study to please them, have changed, than that imagination, which is the voice of what is eternal in man, has changed. The arts are but one Art; and why should all intense painting and all intense poetry have become not merely unintelligible but hateful to the greater number of men and women, and intense drama move them to pleasure? The audiences of Sophocles and of Shakespeare and of Calderón were not unlike the audiences I have heard listening in Irish cabins to songs in Gaelic about 'an old poet telling his sins,' and about 'five young men who were drowned last year,' and about 'the lovers that were drowned going to America,' or to some tale of Oisin and his three hundred years in Tir na nOg. . . .

When the first day of the drama had passed by, actors found that an always larger number of people were more easily moved through the eyes than through the ears. The emotion that comes with the music of words is exhausting, like all intellectual emotions, and few people like exhausting emotions; and therefore actors began to speak as if they were reading something out of the newspapers. They forgot the noble art of oratory, and gave all their thought to the poor art of acting, that is content with the sympathy of our nerves; until at last those who love poetry found it better to read alone in their rooms what they had once delighted to hear sitting friend by friend, lover by beloved. I once asked Mr. William Morris if he had thought of writing a play, and he answered that he had, but would not write one, because actors did not know how to speak poetry with the half-chant men spoke it with in old times. . . .

As audiences and actors changed, managers learned to substitute meretricious landscapes, painted upon wood and canvas, for the descriptions of poetry, until the painted scenery, which had in Greece been a charming explanation of what was least important in the story, became as important as the story. It needed some imagination, some gift for day-dreams, to see the horses and the fields and flowers of Colonus as one listened to the elders gathered about Oedipus, or to see 'the pendent bed and procreant cradle' of the 'martlet' as one listened to Banquo before the castle of Macbeth; but it needs no imagination to admire a painting of one of the more obvious effects of nature painted by somebody who understands how to show everything to the most hurried glance. At the same time the managers made the costumes of the actors more and more magnificent, that the mind might sleep in peace, while the eye took pleasure in the magnificence of velvet and silk and in the physical beauty of women. These changes gradually perfected the theatre of commerce, the masterpiece of that movement towards externality in life and thought and art against which the criticism of our day is learning to protest.

Even if poetry were spoken as poetry, it would still seem out of place in many of its highest moments upon a stage where the superficial appearances of nature are so closely copied; for poetry is founded upon convention, and becomes incredible the moment painting or a gesture reminds us that people do not speak verse when they meet upon the highway. The theatre of art, when it comes to exist, must therefore discover grave and decorative gestures, such as delighted Rossetti and Madox Brown, and grave and decorative scenery that will be forgotten the moment an actor has said, 'It is dawn,' or 'It is raining,' or 'The wind is shaking the trees'; and dresses of so little irrelevant magnificence that the mortal actors and actresses may change without much labour into the immortal people of romance. The theatre began in ritual, and it cannot come to its greatness again without recalling words to their ancient sovereignty.

It will take a generation, and perhaps generations, to restore the theatre of art; for one must get one's actors, and perhaps one's scenery, from the theatre of commerce, until new actors and new painters have come to help one; and until many failures and imperfect successes have made a new tradition, and perfected in detail the ideal that is beginning to float before our eyes. If one could call one's painters and one's actors from where one would, how easy it would be! . . .

The Reform of the Theater

[This piece was published in 1903 in Samhain, a journal that served as the official organ of the Irish National Theatre Society, published from 1901–06, and 1908. The name is that of an ancient Celtic festival celebrated in early November, marking the end of the summer.]

I think the theatre must be reformed in its plays, its speaking, its acting, and its scenery. That is to say, I think there is nothing good about it at present.

First. We have to write or find plays that will make the theatre a place of intellectual excitement—a place where the mind goes to be liberated as it was liberated by the theatres of Greece and England and France at certain great moments of their history, and as it is liberated in Scandinavia to-day. If we are to do this we must learn that beauty and truth are always justified of themselves, and that their creation is a greater service to our country than writing that compromises either in the seeming service of a cause. We will, doubtless, come more easily to truth and beauty because we love some cause with all but all our heart; but we must remember when truth and beauty open their mouths to speak, that all other mouths should be as silent as Finn bade the son of Lugaidh be in the houses of the great. Truth and beauty judge and are above judgment. They justify and have no need of justification.

Such plays will require, both in writers and audiences, a stronger feeling for beautiful and appropriate language than one finds in the ordinary theatre. Sainte-Beuve has said that there is nothing immortal in literature except style, and it is precisely this sense of style, once common among us, that is hardest for us to recover. I do not mean by style words with an air of literature about them, what is ordinarily called eloquent writing. The speeches of Falstaff are as perfect in their style as the soliloquies of Hamlet. One must be able to make a king of Faery or an old countryman or a modern love speak that language which is his and nobody else's, and speak it with so much of emotional subtlety that the hearer may find it hard to know whether it is the thought or the word that has moved him, or whether these could be separated at all.

If we do not know how to construct, if we cannot arrange much complicated life into a single action, our work will not hold the attention or linger in the memory, but if we are not in love with words it will lack the delicate movement of living speech that is the chief garment of life; and because of this lack the great realists seem to the lovers of beautiful art to be wise in this generation, and for the next generation, perhaps, but not for all generations that are to come.

Second. But if we are to restore words to their sovereignty we must make speech even more important than gesture upon the stage.

I have been told that I desire a monotonous chant, but that is not true, for though a monotonous chant may be a safer beginning for an actor than the broken and prosaic speech of ordinary recitation, it puts me to sleep none the less. The sing-song in which a child says a verse is a right beginning, though the child grows out of it. An actor should understand how so to discriminate cadence from cadence, and so to cherish the musical lineaments of verse or prose that he delights the ear with a continually varied music. Certain passages of lyrical feeling, or where one wishes, as in the Angel's part in *The Hour-Glass*, to make a voice sound like the voice of an Immortal, may be spoken upon pure notes which are carefully recorded and learned as if they were notes of a song. Whatever method one adopts, one must always be certain that the work of art, as a whole, is masculine and intellectual, in its sound as in its form.

Third. We must simplify acting, especially in poetical drama, and in prose drama that is remote from real life like my *Hour-Glass*. We must get rid of everything that is restless, everything that draws the attention away from the sound of the voice, or from the few moments of intense expression, whether that expression is through the voice or through the hands; we must from time to time substitute for the movements that the eye sees the nobler movements that the heart sees, the rhythmical movements that seem to flow up into the imagination from some deeper life than that of the individual soul.

Fourth. Just as it is necessary to simplify gesture that it may accompany speech without being its rival, it is necessary to simplify both the form and colour of scenery and costume. As a rule the background should be but a single colour, so that the persons in the play, wherever they stand, may harmonise with it and preoccupy our attention. In other words, it should be thought out not as one thinks out a landscape, but as if it were the background of a portrait, and this is especially necessary on a small stage where the moment the stage is filled, the painted forms of the background are broken up and lost. Even when one has to represent trees or hills they should be treated in most cases decoratively, they should be little more than an unobtrusive pattern. There must be nothing unnecessary, nothing that will distract the attention from speech and movement. An art is always at its greatest when it is most human. Greek acting was great because it did all but everything with the voice, and modern acting may be great when it does everything with voice and movement. But an art which smothers these things with bad painting, with innumerable garish colours, with continual restless mimicries of the surface of life, is an art of fading humanity, a decaying art.

Remarks about Purgatory

[Father Connolly, an American Jesuit, asked Yeats to comment on the play. Yeats's response was printed in the *Irish Independent* on August 13, 1938]

Father Connolly said that my plot is perfectly clear but that he does not understand my meaning. My plot is my meaning. I think the dead suffer remorse and re-create their old lives just as I have described. There are mediaeval Japanese plays about it, and much in the folklore of all countries.

In my play, a spirit suffers because of its share, when alive, in the destruction of an honoured house; that destruction is taking place all over Ireland today.

Sometimes it is the result of poverty, but more often because a new individualistic generation has lost interest in the ancient sanctities.

I know of old houses, old pictures, old furniture that have been sold without apparent regret. In some few cases a house has been destroyed by a *mésalliance*. I have founded my play on this exceptional case, partly because of my interest in certain problems of eugenics, partly because it enables me to depict more vividly than would otherwise be possible the tragedy of the house.

In Germany there is special legislation to enable old families to go on living where their fathers lived. The problem is not Irish, but European, though it is perhaps more acute here than elsewhere.

Tragic Joy

[This paragraph—the title is our own—is taken from Yeats's pamphlet entitled *On the Boiler* (1938). "On the boiler" is approximately equivalent to "on a soapbox," or "spouting off." *On the Boiler* contains six essays and *Purgatory*.]

The arts are all the bridal chambers of joy. No tragedy is legitimate unless it leads some great character to his final joy. Polonius may go out wretchedly, but I can hear the dance music in 'Absent thee from felicity awhile', or in Hamlet's speech over the dead Ophelia, and what of Cleopatra's last farewells, Lear's rage under the lightning, Oedipus sinking down at the story's end into an earth 'riven' by love? Some Frenchman has said that farce is the struggle against a ridiculous object, comedy against a movable object, tragedy against an immovable; and because the will, or energy, is greatest in tragedy, tragedy is the more noble; but I add that 'will or energy is eternal delight', and when its limit is reached it may become a pure, aimless joy, though the man, the shade, still mourns his lost object.

The Play in PERFORMANCE

Purgatory, written in the last year of his life, was Yeats's last play for the Abbey Theatre, the Dublin theatrical group with which he had a love-hate relationship. The social dramas that some of his fellow directors at the Abbey wanted to do, and the sentimental and romantic comedies that were among the Abbey's most successful (financially speaking) plays, were not the plays

that Yeats valued. His own plays, however, rarely gained enthusiastic audiences.

In 1938 Lennox Robinson, who had been one of the Abbey's chief directors of plays, conceived the idea of a dramatic festival that would immediately follow the Dublin Horse Show, an important annual event. Lectures on drama were given on the mornings of August 8 through August 20, and plays—old and new— were staged in the evenings. *Purgatory* was given its premiere production on August 10, with a set designed by the author's daughter, Anne Butler Yeats. The festival was successful enough, but *Purgatory*, or rather its title, caused a fuss. At the end of the first performance Yeats made a short speech, to the effect that the play contained his views of this world and the next. He did not amplify his view of purgatory, but even a very casual reading of the play reveals that Yeats's purgatory, in which souls revisit places of importance in their lives, and relive experiences, is very different from the Roman Catholic view of purgatory as a state in which the souls of those who die in God's grace may make

satisfaction for unrepented or minor sins and thus become fit for heaven. The day after the premiere, F. R. Higgins, an Anglo-Irish lyric poet and a director of the Abbey Theatre, gave a lecture on Yeats, in which, responding to a question by a Jesuit priest, he admitted that he did not know what Yeats's *Purgatory* meant. Lennox Robinson, who was chairing the meeting, said that only Yeats could explain, but Yeats was not present. Later Yeats was interviewed—we print the published summary of the interview on page 1000—but his remarks only set off a flurry of angry letters in the press, the gist of most being that Yeats had no right to use this word as the title of a play that had nothing to do with the Catholic concept of purgatory.

JEFFERY JONES
Directing Purgatory

Jeffery Jones, an adjunct faculty member of the English Department at Boston College, directed *Purgatory* as the inaugural production of the Boston-based Bridge Theatre Company. The original production, paired with company playwright Todd Hearon's *That Room*, was staged in close adherence to Yeats's stage directions. In 1995 Jones and company staged a revised traveling production, employing many of the stagecraft techniques Yeats had developed for his dance plays inspired by Japanese Noh drama.

What made you want to stage Purgatory? *Why direct a verse play written by an Irish poet for a contemporary American audience?*

This play was produced and The Bridge Theatre Company itself was formed because a group of scholars wanted to connect theory with practice, the page with the stage. What better way to christen a company dedicated to word-focused, imaginative drama, than to tackle a verse tragedy written by perhaps the greatest twentieth-century poet writing in English?

As director of the Bridge's production, I approached the script with three goals in mind. First, I wanted to make this a collaborative experience, one in which actors and directors were involved in all stages of the process. During rehearsals, all four of us were involved in script analysis, discussion, and decision making.

My second goal was to implement Yeats's ideas for a word-focused theater, a theater in which every aspect

of production would support the script's words and meaning. In keeping with Yeats's ideas, we worked to keep the actors' gestures and movements few, but powerful. We also chose simple, suggestive costumes, music, lighting, and setting—sparse and symbolic, like the actors' movements and gestures.

Finally, I wanted to make Yeats's script and stagecraft ideas work on the modern stage. This meant constantly reminding myself that *Purgatory* is not simply a text to be read and analyzed—it's also a script to be performed. Yeats said that the key to understanding *Purgatory* lies in its plot, that in this play, his plot is his meaning; so, to make *Purgatory* work meant making its plot and meaning work on the stage, making both intelligible to a modern audience.

For a play to be intelligible—accessible to an audience—there has to be a unified production concept. Although there were several possible concepts to choose from—among them a sociopolitical interpretation or a contemporized staging—I decided that my production concept would hinge upon the ghost story itself and the conflict between the supernatural world of the Old Man's vision and the ruined natural world of the setting. I wanted to relate Yeats's "ideas about this world and the next."

You mention the supernatural—this is in many ways a ghost story written for adults. Can a ghost story, particularly a staged ghost story, work for adults?

I believe it can. Most of us still seem fascinated by the supernatural. And, while film's special effects can offer realistic-appearing ghosts, Yeats relies chiefly upon the script's poetic language to conjure not only symbols, but also spirits. I think the most real, the most horrifying ghosts are the ones that we ourselves imagine, rather than the ones we are actually shown—on film, in the novel. Remember, for instance, Nathaniel Hawthorne never shows us what's beneath the minister's black veil—to show us what's there can never approach the horror our own imaginations can conjure. So, while Yeats's ghosts could not be effective if presented realistically—by "realistically" I mean by actors walking onto the stage—when represented by poetic language and, in the case of our initial production, silhouettes, they are extremely effective.

I suppose one of the questions one must ask is *Why did Yeats choose to tell a ghost story?* I think telling, staging this ghost story serves a very practical purpose for Yeats: to meld the two theatrical traditions in which he was working, namely the subjective theater of his Noh-inspired dance and drawing room dramas and the objective, realistic theater with which the Abbey Theater had come to be associated. In *Purgatory*, Yeats employs realistic conventions such as a ruined house and bare tree, but he infuses them with symbolic, supernatural significance. Yeats was also able to fuse realism and symbolism by telling a realistic tale with a twist. This is not simply a story about an old man and his young son visiting the remains of the family house; it is about the ghosts who also visit that house in order to reexperience and repent past sins. Through the telling of a ghost story, Yeats can embody his "ideas about this world and the next"—ideas shaped by Irish folklore, Eastern philosophy, and occultism—in a plot which is accessible to a Western audience. I say it is accessible because we are already familiar with dramatic tragedy and spiritual purgation. As Yeats himself said about this play, "My plot is my meaning." In *Purgatory*, Yeats succeeds in combining Eastern and Western dramatic and philosophic traditions—quite a tour de force for a man who's been striving to do this throughout much of his life.

This is a play with only two characters, "An Old Man" and "A Boy." Are these characters merely allegorical stereotypes? Do they "work" on the contemporary stage?

Theoretically speaking, Yeats believed comedy was built upon *character*—the individualized figure—while tragedy was built upon a sort of archetypal or universal figure. He believed that audience members would recognized themselves in the tragic figure, thus allowing all audience members to experience a shared identification. In an essay called "The Tragic Theatre," Yeats says comedy is based on a separation between the spectator and the characters, but tragedy is "a drowning and breaking of the dykes that separate [individuals]"—what Yeats calls "tragic ecstasy."

Practically speaking, I felt it was important to take *Purgatory's* characters (and here I use "characters" in the traditional, not in the Yeatsian sense of the word) a step beyond the archetypes they represent. Because most of us have been raised assuming that good theater is psychologically realistic theater, I felt it important to make the characters believable, human. This seemed to be the best way to create a link between stage characters and audience members and, I hoped, to dissolve the dykes separating individuals.

Because the Boy's language is largely colloquial and, therefore, familiar, and because he is, like the audience, largely an observer of the strange tale that unfolds, I felt the Boy was "the way in" for the audience. He makes the plot and meaning accessible. He needs to be a character with whom the audience can to some extent sympathize, a character whose realistic representation provides the audience with a stable viewpoint from which to observe the unstable Old Man and the play's supernaturalism.

I was fortunate to cast an actor (Dan Koughan) whose strength is natural reaction. I encouraged him to move and gesture in a natural manner. I also allowed him to downplay the verse—I asked him to find a natural, colloquial delivery. We exchanged the Boy's naturalistic acting and delivery style for a more heightened, poetic style at only one point, when the Boy sees the ghostly figure of "A dead, living, murdered man!" Immediately, reality was suspended for the Boy, as well as for the audience, and his acting style lapsed from a naturalistic manner into something more ritualistic and symbolic. Both his words and movements slowed—as if his horror had frozen his ability to react.

In contrast to the Boy's naturalism, the Old Man initially appears to be a supernatural character. His words introduce the Boy and the audience to the supernatural world, conjuring up visions and memories. However, this is too simplistic an analysis of the Old Man's characterization. Within him a conflict between the natural and supernatural worlds is raging. Standing on the brink of insanity, the Old Man is both a rough beast and a refined gentleman. He is having an identity crisis: Is he the last remnant of a dying race of country gentility or one of the "Base-born products of a base-bed"? The conflict that rages within the Old Man dri-ves the play's plot. The Old Man's conflict also mirrors the conflict that the play's meaning seeks to resolve: How are the natural and supernatural worlds related?

To convince the audience that the Old Man stands on the rift of two worlds, the actor must be able to shift between two predominant styles of delivery. First, he must portray a bitter old man whose delivery, move-ment, and gestures suggest someone ruined by time, someone growing insane. Like the Boy, this half of the Old Man's character is natural, realistic. Second, the actor must be able to sweep the audience up in his su-pernatural vision, attaining lofty, powerful vocal deliv-ery, fluid movement, and grand gesture. Again, I was fortunate to have an actor (Todd Hearon) who could shift from poetic recitation and philosophic musing to guilt-ridden simpering and angry outburst.

You keep touching upon the importance of the words themselves. This play is written in verse. Did you stress this? Can American actors speak verse drama? What were the techniques you used to get the verse delivery from your actors?

Because Yeats is a poet and because we were all at that time formal students of literature, we were keenly aware of the challenges of the verse. I think this could have become constrictive. Often we tend to think of verse drama as the realm of Shakespeare and, there-fore, the past and the British. Although they have be-come increasingly rare, verse plays continues to be written and not only in the U.K. As for speaking verse, if the verse is "good," which it certainly is in Yeats, of course American actors can speak it. If you let the verse do its job, it will direct you as an actor—it gives hints about delivery, pronunciation, movement.

We spent probably the first week or longer working through the language and ideas of the script; even once we were on our feet, we kept engaging the verse. We noticed passages in the script that call for height-ened line delivery, such as when the Old Man invokes the memory of the house or his mother or when the Boy is transformed by the horror of seeing "a dead, liv-ing, murdered man." We also discovered passages that appear to emphasize a more natural delivery as when the Old Man angrily confronts the Boy about sneaking away with the moneybag.

One of the techniques we used was one I adapted from something Yeats said. He thought that actors moved and gestured too much; he wished he could put

actors in barrels to restrict their movements, forcing them to rely solely on their voices for emphasis. While I didn't go to this extreme, I did stress the importance of words over gesture and movement. In one exercise, I had the two actors sit next to but not facing each other. I asked them to rest their hands on their knees, as if their hands were weighed down. They were to ges-ture only when their speech could no longer contain the power that was driving it. We tried this exercise several times, and I think it was helpful.

Another technique we used let us explore the range of possible line deliveries. First, we asked the actors to speak through the script, focusing on the verse's sense, its meaning. They were to speak as themselves in a re-laxed, colloquial manner. We then had them speak through the script again, this time focusing entirely on the sound of the verse, feeling the rolling (largely) iambic line, speaking in a nearly singsong manner. This second sounding of the verse was particularly use-ful later in the rehearsal process as a way to revisit, to re-hear and re-see the verse line.

One important thing to note: We chose not to have the actors speak in an Irish dialect. We didn't want this to be just an Irish play. And, while the play cer-tainly contains many Irish references, the themes Yeats explores are not confined to the Irish experience.

This raises some other important questions: Is this play about the decline of Ireland? Does this play appeal to a non-Irish audience?

Sure, on one level this play certainly is about the de-cline of Ireland as Yeats saw it. In his book *W.B. Yeats & Georgian Ireland*, Donald Torchiana offers a sophisti-cated reading of the play as sociopolitical history of modern Ireland. I don't doubt that what Torchiana sees is there; however, one of the things that interests me and, I would guess, most audience members, is the tragedy contained within the play itself. Yeats may have begun writing an inherently Irish political play, but—as sometimes happens in Yeats's work—he ended up offering us something much more universal or hu-man. The tragedy doesn't merely lie in Yeats's percep-tion that modern Ireland was falling into a state of de-cay; the play's tragedy lies in its plot, in the horror of the action that unfolds between a father and son. In many ways, this is a play about cyclical violence—and I don't think Yeats saw this occurring in Ireland alone. His poem "The Second Coming" is very much about the entire world being engulfed in a deluge of anarchic violence in which "The ceremony of innocence is drowned."

The height of the play's violence is the Old Man's stabbing of the Boy. How did you stage this?

For the much of the play, we kept the two characters physically separated—either they were on opposite sides of the stage or on different levels (the Boy seated, the Old Man standing). We did choose, however, three moments to allow the two to come together physically in order to reveal a kind of psychological intimacy. First, the characters were brought together by their common past—as the Old Man told the story of his education, he hovered over the Boy, inviting him to enter this remembered world. This intimacy was broken for a moment as the Old Man burst forth: "I gave the education that befits/A bastard that a pedlar got/Upon a tinker's daughter in a ditch." Immediately, however, the Old Man was "pulled" back to the Boy. He resumed telling his tale, relating how his father had burnt down the house and how he, fifty years ago, had stabbed his father with a jack knife—"That knife that cuts my dinner now." This seemed to us a kind of invitation for the two characters to sit down and, literally, break bread together. Using the murder weapon to slice the bread created an odd, yet effective moment.

The other two moments of intimacy were caused by more immediate violence. The struggle over the moneybag brought the characters together in a moment that was both physically and emotionally intimate, though cruel. We echoed this intimacy as the Old Man murdered the Boy. Horrified by the vision he sees in the window of a "dead, living, murdered man," the Boy turns to his father for explanation and protection. The Old Man, while offering the mixed comfort of a half-hearted embrace, stabbed this seemingly willing sacrifice. As the Boy died, the Old Man lowered him to the ground, cradling him in a passionless pietà, gently rocking him and singing a tuneless lullaby.

What are some of the differences in staging that you made between your original and traveling productions?

In keeping with Yeats's stage directions, our original production used a minimalistic setting. Upstage center was a cinder block that served as the stone for the Boy to sit on ("Sit there upon that stone"). The bare tree, situated upstage left, was composed of a burlap tree trunk cleft in two and several branches suspended over the stage. At the points when the tree takes on supernatural meaning, it was bathed in green light. The house itself was situated along the stage right edge of the playing area. All that was shown of the house was its face: Vertical boards framed its exterior, including its door frame; two windows—one on the first, another on the second floor—were suspended freely, appearing to float in midair. The entire structure was draped in dirtied burlap. The entryway porch was composed of two stacked platforms, a decaying set of wooden stairs, and crumbling cinder block pillars. The house was specially lighted on only one occasion: As the Old Man stood on the porch expressing his love of the house and all its "intricate passages," the house was bathed in a barely perceptible golden glow.

We followed Yeats's stage direction regarding the ghostly figures. They were only visible to the audience at two moments: The Old Man's mother appeared as the Old Man conjured her ("Look at the window; she stands there"); the father became visible after the violent struggle over the moneybag, disappearing following the Boy's murder. Our window was just a wooden frame upon which we'd stretched translucent fabric and could project the silhouettes of a woman freeing her long tresses from their genteel confinement and a man slowly raising a whiskey glass to his lips.

Since we wanted the play to be as adaptable (and portable) as possible, our travelling production exchanged minimalism for imagination. We borrowed and adapted some of the stagecraft conventions that Yeats employed in his Noh-inspired dance- and drawing-room plays, most notably his use of Musicians to set the scene and mood. The production began with the ceremonial unfolding of a cloth by the two Musicians dressed in black on a bare stage (except for the cinder block stone, which we kept). They placed the unfolded cloth upstage right to represent the ruined house. While the female Musician (assistant director, Sharon Tinney) lifted her eyes and meditated on an imagined second-floor window, the male Musician (I was the male Musician, as well as the director) placed a second cloth stage left to represent the tree. Then, using two tree branches which would later serve as drum sticks, the male Musician pantomimed the growth of a tree, showing midway through the tree's growth that it had been riven in two. At this point, the two Musicians took their places on opposite sides of the proscenium, and the play's scripted action began.

Yeats's text doesn't say that the hoofbeats are actually to be heard by the audience, so probably in the original production there were no audible hoofbeats. But because we left so much to the audience's imagination in the drawing-room style version, we felt we had to add the sound of hoofbeats. Hoping to heighten the play's ritual and supernatural mood, the male Musician struck an African drum to a slow, steady rhythm. We also used sound to replace lighting effects—at the two moments when the tree would have been bathed in green light, the female Musician struck a wind chime, effecting the voice of the mother in conversation with her now aged son.

I wanted to retain the figures in the window, but couldn't, of course, replicate the same silhouette effect. What I chose to do was again use the Musicians. At the time when the silhouetted figure of the ghostly mother would have appeared, the female Musician—seated stage right—passionlessly rose and stood frozen, facing the audience; she sat at the time when the window's light would have faded. Similarly, when the silhouetted figure of the ghostly father would have appeared, the male Musician stood, staring blankly at the audience until the window light would have faded at the Boy's death.

BERTOLT Brecht

Bertolt Brecht (1898–1956) was born in Germany of middle-class parents, attended public schools, and then entered the University of Munich to study medicine. However, after one year he was drafted for military service in World War I and served as a medical orderly for about a year. At the end of the war, he returned to a shattered Germany, and during most of the twenties he seems to have been more or less an anarchist. His earliest poems and plays (e.g., *The Threepenny Opera*, 1928) cannot be called communist, although around 1928 he seems to have become a believer in communism. With the rise of Hitler, Brecht left Germany (1933), spending most of the years 1933 to 1939 in Denmark, 1940 in Finland, and 1941 to 1948 in the United States. Most of his best-known plays (including *The Good Woman of Setzuan*, 1938–1941) were written during these fifteen years of exile. His return in 1948 to Germany—to East Berlin—was somewhat equivocal, for he obtained Austrian citizenship (1950) and arranged for the copyright to his work to be held by a publisher in West Berlin. He died suddenly, of a thrombosis, in 1956.

■■■■■■■■■■■■■■

COMMENTARY ON *THE GOOD WOMAN OF SETZUAN*

Earlier drama interested Brecht enormously. However, he believed it was obsolete and devoted a fair amount of his time to trying to adapt it to the twentieth century. (His most popular play, *The Threepenny Opera*, is an adaptation of John Gay's *The Beggar's Opera*, and at the time of his death Brecht was working on an adaptation of Shakespeare's *Coriolanus*. Accused of plagiarism, he replied that in literature as in life he did not recognize the idea of private property.)

Roughly speaking, Brecht saw early forms of tragedy as depicting a hero who, inevitably driven to the wall, performs some terrible deed and then becomes aware of all of its implications, thus achieving full understanding of himself and his fate. Interpreting Aristotle's comments on tragedy, Brecht went on to say that early tragedy customarily seeks to cause the audience to identify itself with the tragic hero, thereby undergoing an emotional cleansing, or catharsis. Here is one of Brecht's characteristically earthy and acerbic comments:

> The drama of our time still follows Aristotle's recipe for achieving what he calls catharsis (the spiritual cleansing of the spectator). In Aristotelian drama the plot leads the hero into situations where he reveals his innermost being. All the incidents shown have the object of driving the hero into spiritual conflicts. It is a possibly blasphemous but quite useful comparison if one turns one's mind to the burlesque shows on Broadway, where the public, with yells of "Take it off!"

forces the girls to expose their bodies more and more. The individual whose innermost being is thus driven into the open then of course comes to stand for Man with a capital M. Everyone (including every spectator) is then carried away by the momentum of the events portrayed, so that in a performance of *Oedipus* one has for all practical purposes an auditorium full of little Oedipuses, an auditorium full of Emperor Joneses for a performance of *The Emperor Jones*.[1]

In opposition to what he called "Aristotelian drama," Brecht, drawing partly on German critical theories about the difference between drama and epic, developed the idea of "non-Aristotelian drama," or "epic drama." Whereas the usual play is set in the present and implies that what is happening on the stage happens *now*, to all of us, the epic drama traditionally is set in the past and is quite frankly about how things *used to be*. The readers of an epic, the argument goes, are detached individuals capable of using their minds critically, but the spectators at a performance of an Aristotelian drama are part of a mob, their reason having been subordinated to a communal emotion. Epic drama, then, in opposition to traditional Aristotelian drama, seeks to create a detachment comparable to that which the epic creates.

---

[1]*Brecht on Theatre*, translated by John Willett (New York: Hill and Wang; London: Methuen & Co., 1964), p. 87.

Brecht's word for this quality is *Verfremdung*, that is, detachment, estrangement, alienation. The reason for estranging the dramatic action from the audience is to make the audience regard it critically and thus see it more clearly, unobscured by emotional prejudices. To induce this estrangement, to shatter a sense of community between actors and audience, Brecht interrupted the action of his plays with such devices as songs, addresses to the audience, and slogans projected onto the stage, and he insisted on highly stylized acting (Chaplin was one of his heroes) and unrealistic scenery. Brecht's ideal audience at an epic drama is critically aware of—not emotionally overcome by—what it sees on the stage. Brecht thus rejected tragedy of the sort that Yeats characterized as "a drowning and breaking of the dykes that separate man from man," and he insisted, in contrast to Yeats, that detachment is not limited to the spectator at a comedy.

Every play gives some image of the world. According to Brecht, the Aristotelian play shows a static world, for in the hero's agony it claims to reveal with increasing clarity how things inevitably are. The epic play, however, shows a dynamic, or changing, world—a world that can be, must be, changed. (The direction in which Brecht wanted the change to go is clear enough; he was a communist.)

> The dramatic [i.e., Aristotelian] theatre's spectator says: Yes, I have felt like that too—Just like me—It's only natural—It'll never change—The sufferings of this man appall me, because they are inescapable—That's great art; it all seems the most obvious thing in the world—I weep when they weep, I laugh when they laugh.
>
> The epic theatre's spectator says: I'd never have thought it—That's not the way—That's extraordinary, hardly believable—It's got to stop—The sufferings of this man appall me, because they are unnecessary—That's great art: nothing obvious in it—I laugh when they weep, I weep when they laugh.[2]

Brecht put the distinctions between the two kinds of drama into the following tabular form, but one should keep in mind that he was talking about emphases, not utter opposites:[3]

DRAMATIC THEATRE	EPIC THEATRE
plot	narrative
implicates the spectator in a stage situation	turns the spectator into an observer, but
wears down his capacity for action	arouses his capacity for action
provides him with sensations	forces him to take decisions
experience	picture of the world
the spectator is involved in something	he is made to face something
suggestion	argument
instinctive feelings are preserved	brought to the point of recognition
the spectator is in the thick of it, shares the experience	the spectator stands outside, studies
the human being is taken for granted	the human being is the object of the inquiry
he is unalterable	he is alterable and able to alter
eyes on the finish	eyes on the race
one scene makes another	each scene for itself
growth	montage
linear development	in curves
evolutionary determinism	jumps
man as a fixed point	man as a process
thought determines being	social being determines thought
feeling	reason

It was with this scaffolding that Brecht built his plays. His interest was not in passionate tragic heroes who reveal their greatness when they assert themselves and do a deed of horror that affronts a mysterious metaphysical order that demands their life in expiation. Nevertheless, Brecht dealt with no less momentous issues than these: How do we survive? Must little people be imposed on? Above all, What is to be done?

Such plays do not seek to evoke the "woe or wonder" that Shakespeare spoke of in connection with tragedy, for these emotions induce a sense of the inevitability of guilt and suffering and send us out of the theater reconciled to the naturalness of our present condition. For Brecht, what is "natural" is not guilty actions but generous actions. (Brecht would argue that

---

[2]*Brecht on Theatre*, p. 71.

[3]The list is reprinted from *Brecht on Theatre*, translated by John Willett, p. 37. Copyright © 1957, 1963 and 1964 by Suhrkamp Verlag, Frankfurt am Main.

the following speech is counterbalanced by many other speeches, because epic drama shows several sides, but it seems evident that the speech represents Brecht's own thinking.) Shen Te, the charitable prostitute, says in another version of *The Good Woman of Setzuan:*

> Why are you so bad?
> You tread on your fellow man.
> Isn't it a strain?
> Your veins swell with your efforts to be greedy.
> Extended naturally, a hand gives and receives with
>   equal ease.

Somehow, according to Brecht, in our present (i.e., capitalistic) society, we find that we are forced into unnatural postures. For example, Shen Te finds that she cannot continue to be charitable without the aid of a cruel "cousin" (she is so torn by the problem that she invents this person in order to protect herself from her own generous impulses). Moreover, in our society love itself must become savage. For instance, Shen Te so loves her child and so fears that he may encounter a life of poverty that she determines for his sake to be ruthless in her business dealings, and she determines also (further irony) to shield the child from knowledge of her activities so that he will grow up to be good—in a world in which goodness cannot survive.

These life-and-death issues are treated tragicomically. First, and least importantly, the play mingles gods and mortals, as does Plautus's *Amphitryon*, a mixture which caused Plautus to introduce the word *tragicomedy*. And what gods they are, mouthing amiable pieties; getting a black eye when they intervene in a mortal quarrel; and, finally, in a concluding scene that is funny and terrible, ascending to heaven on a cloud, singing, smiling, and waving to Shen Te, who is crying for help. More importantly, in this immensely earnest play that seeks to face some of the darkest facts of our life as it is, there are a good many comic figures and there is a good deal of wry wit. One example will have to suffice. Yang Sun wants to be sure that his wife will be frugal.

YANG SUN. Can you sleep on a straw mattress the size of that book?
SHEN TE. The two of us?
YANG SUN. The one of you.
SHEN TE. In that case, no.

More broadly, *The Good Woman of Setzuan*, like all comedies, calls attention to incongruity, but here the incongruity is not from some sort of unlovely behavior needlessly adopted in a smiling world where things will work out all right; rather, the incongruity is generosity in a corrupt world. Shen Te is funny in her persistent innocence and goodness—but she is not only funny, she is also compelling (despite Brecht's theories?) and deeply sympathetic, as when she persists in loving the deceitful Yang Sun:

SHEN TE.
> When I heard his cunning laugh, I was afraid
> But when I saw the holes in his shoes, I loved him
>   dearly.

At the end, the play does not let us rest content, as tragedy and comedy in their different ways traditionally do. An epilogue invites us to work out a sequel:

> We feel deflated too. We too are nettled
> To see the curtain down and nothing settled.
> How could a better ending be arranged?
> Could one change people? Can the world be
>   changed?
> Would new gods do the trick? Will atheism?
> Moral rearmament? Materialism?
> It is for you to find a way, my friends,
> To help good men arrive at happy ends.
> *You* write the happy ending to the play!
> There must, there must, there's got to be a way!

Probably Brecht assumed that Marx had shown us the way out: Change the economic basis of society, and you will find a new human nature. Still, at rehearsals of his plays Brecht sometimes quoted his own Galileo: "I'm not trying to show that I'm in the right, but to find out whether."

THE GOOD WOMAN OF SETZUAN
Bertolt Brecht

Translated by Eric Bentley

LIST OF CHARACTERS

WONG, *a water seller*
THREE GODS
SHEN TE, *a prostitute, later a shopkeeper*
MRS. SHIN, *former owner of Shen Te's shop*
A FAMILY OF EIGHT *(husband, wife, brother, sister-in-law, grand-father, nephew, niece, boy)*
AN UNEMPLOYED MAN
A CARPENTER

MRS. MI TZU, *Shen Te's landlady*
YANG SUN, *an unemployed pilot, later a factory manager*
AN OLD WHORE
A POLICEMAN
AN OLD MAN
AN OLD WOMAN, *his wife*
MR. SHU FU, *a barber*
MRS. YANG, *mother of Yang Sun*
GENTLEMEN, VOICES, CHILDREN *(three)*, etc.

PROLOGUE

(*At the gates of the half-westernized city of Setzuan.* Evening. Wong the Water Seller introduces himself to the audience.*)

WONG. I sell water here in the city of Setzuan. It isn't easy. When water is scarce, I have long distances to go in search of it, and when it is plentiful, I have no income. But in our part of the world there is nothing unusual about poverty. Many people think only the gods can save the situation. And I hear from a cattle merchant—who travels a lot—that some of the highest gods are on their way here at this very moment. Informed sources have it that heaven is quite disturbed at all the complaining. I've been coming out here to the city gates for three days now to bid these gods welcome. I want to be the first to greet them. What about those fellows over there? No, no, they *work*. And that one there has ink on his fingers, he's no god, he must be a clerk from the cement factory. *Those* two are another story. They look as though they'd like to beat you. But gods don't need to beat you, do they? (*Enter Three Gods.*) What about those three? Old-fashioned clothes—dust on their feet—they *must* be gods! (*He throws himself at their feet.*) Do with me what you will, illustrious ones!

*"So Brecht's first manuscript. Brecht must later have learned that Setzuan (usually spelled Szechwan) is not a city but a province, and he adjusted the printed German text. I have kept the earlier reading since such mythology seems to me more Brechtian than Brecht's own second thoughts."—E.B.

FIRST GOD (*with an ear trumpet*). Ah! (*He is pleased.*) So we were expected?
WONG (*giving them water*). Oh, yes. And I *knew* you'd come.
FIRST GOD. We need somewhere to stay the night. You know of a place?
WONG. The whole town is at your service, illustrious ones! What sort of a place would you like?

(*The Gods eye each other.*)

FIRST GOD. Just try the first house you come to, my son.
WONG. That would be Mr. Fo's place.
FIRST GOD. Mr. Fo.
WONG. One moment! (*He knocks at the first house.*)
VOICE FROM MR. FO'S. No!

(*Wong returns a little nervously.*)

WONG. It's too bad. Mr. Fo isn't in. And his servants don't dare do a thing without his consent. He'll have a fit when he finds out who they turned away, won't he?
FIRST GOD (*smiling*). He will, won't he?
WONG. One moment! The next house is Mr. Cheng's. Won't he be thrilled?
FIRST GOD. Mr. Cheng.

(*Wong knocks.*)

VOICE FROM MR. CHENG'S. Keep your gods. We have our own troubles!
WONG (*back with the Gods*). Mr. Cheng is very sorry, but he has a houseful of relations. I think some of them are a bad lot, and naturally, he wouldn't like you to see them.
THIRD GOD. Are we so terrible?

WONG. Well, only with bad people, of course. Everyone knows the province of Kwan is always having floods.

SECOND GOD. Really? How's *that*?

WONG. Why, because they're so irreligious.

SECOND GOD. Rubbish. It's because they neglected the dam.

FIRST GOD (*to Second*). Sh! (*To Wong.*) You're still in hopes, aren't you, my son?

WONG. Certainly. All Setzuan is competing for the honor! What happened up to now is pure coincidence. I'll be back. (*He walks away, but then stands undecided.*)

SECOND GOD. What did I tell you?

THIRD GOD. It *could* be pure coincidence.

SECOND GOD. The same coincidence in Shun, Kwan, and Setzuan? People just aren't religious any more, let's face the fact. Our mission has failed!

FIRST GOD. Oh come, we might run into a good person any minute.

THIRD GOD. How did the resolution read? (*Unrolling a scroll and reading from it.*) "The world can stay as it is if enough people are found living lives worthy of human beings." Good people, that is. Well, what about this Water Seller himself? *He's* good, or I'm very much mistaken.

SECOND GOD. You're very much mistaken. When he gave us a drink, I had the impression there was something odd about the cup. Well, look! (*He shows the cup to the First God.*)

FIRST GOD. A false bottom!

SECOND GOD. The man is a swindler.

FIRST GOD. Very well, count *him* out. That's one man among millions. And as a matter of fact, we only need one on *our* side. These atheists are saying, "The world must be changed because no one can *be* good and *stay* good." No one, eh? I say: let us find one—just one—and we have those fellows where we want them!

THIRD GOD (*to Wong*). Water Seller, is it so hard to find a place to stay?

WONG. Nothing could be easier. It's just me. I don't go about it right.

THIRD GOD. Really? (*He returns to the others. A Gentleman passes by.*)

WONG. Oh dear, they're catching on. (*He accosts the Gentleman.*) Excuse the intrusion, dear sir, but three Gods have just turned up. Three of the very highest. They need a place for the night. Seize this rare opportunity—to have real gods as your guests!

GENTLEMAN (*laughing*). A new way of finding free rooms for a gang of crooks.

(*Exit Gentleman.*)

WONG (*shouting at him*). Godless rascal! Have you no religion, gentlemen of Setzuan? (*Pause.*) Patience, illustrious ones! (*Pause.*) There's only one person left. Shen Te, the prostitute. She *can't* say no. (*Calls up to a window.*) Shen Te!

(*Shen Te opens the shutters and looks out.*)

WONG. *They're* here, and nobody wants them. Will you take them?

SHEN TE. Oh, no, Wong, I'm expecting a gentleman.

WONG. Can't you forget about him for tonight?

SHEN TE. The rent has to be paid by tomorrow or I'll be out on the street.

WONG. This is no time for calculation, Shen Te.

SHEN TE. Stomachs rumble even on the Emperor's birthday, Wong.

WONG. Setzuan is one big dung hill!

SHEN TE. Oh, very well! I'll hide till my gentleman has come and gone. Then I'll take them. (*She disappears.*)

WONG. They mustn't see her gentleman or they'll know what she is.

FIRST GOD (*who hasn't heard any of this*). I think it's hopeless.

(*They approach Wong.*)

WONG (*jumping, as he finds them behind him*). A room has been found, illustrious ones! (*He wipes sweat off his brow.*)

SECOND GOD. Oh, good.

THIRD GOD. Let's see it.

WONG (*nervously*). Just a minute. It has to be tidied up a bit.

THIRD GOD. Then we'll sit down here and wait.

WONG (*still more nervous*). No, no! (*Holding himself back.*) Too much traffic, you know.

THIRD GOD (*with a smile*). Of course, if you *want* us to move.

(*They retire a little. They sit on a doorstep. Wong sits on the ground.*)

WONG (*after a deep breath*). You'll be staying with a single girl—the finest human being in Setzuan!

THIRD GOD. That's nice.

WONG (*to the audience*). They gave me such a look when I picked up my cup just now.

THIRD GOD. You're worn out, Wong.

WONG. A little, maybe.

FIRST GOD. Do people here have a hard time of it?

WONG. The good ones do.

FIRST GOD. What about yourself?

WONG. You mean I'm not good. That's true. And I don't have an easy time either!

(*During this dialogue, a Gentleman has turned up in front of Shen Te's house, and has whistled several times. Each time Wong has given a start.*)

THIRD GOD (*to Wong, softly*). Psst! I think he's gone now.

WONG (*confused and surprised*). Ye-e-es.

(*The Gentleman has left now, and Shen Te has come down to the street.*)

SHEN TE (*softly*). Wong!

(*Getting no answer, she goes off down the street. Wong arrives just too late, forgetting his carrying pole.*)

WONG (*softly*). Shen Te! Shen Te! (*To himself.*) So she's gone off to earn the rent. Oh dear, I can't go to the gods *again* with no room to offer them. Having failed in the service of the gods, I shall run to my den in the sewer pipe down by the river and hide from their sight!

(*He rushes off. Shen Te returns, looking for him, but finding the gods. She stops in confusion.*)

SHEN TE. You are the illustrious ones? My name is Shen Te. It would please me very much if my simple room could be of use to you.

THIRD GOD. Where is the Water Seller, Miss . . . Shen Te?

SHEN TE. I missed him, somehow.

FIRST GOD. Oh, he probably thought you weren't coming, and was afraid of telling us.

THIRD GOD (*picking up the carrying pole*). We'll leave this with you. He'll be needing it.

(*Led by Shen Te, they go into the house. It grows dark, then light. Dawn. Again escorted by Shen Te, who leads them through the half-light with a little lamp, the Gods take their leave.*)

FIRST GOD. Thank you, thank you, dear Shen Te, for your elegant hospitality! We shall not forget! And give our thanks to the Water Seller—he showed us a good human being.

SHEN TE. Oh, *I'm* not good. Let me tell you something: when Wong asked me to put you up, I hesitated.

FIRST GOD. It's all right to hesitate if you then go ahead! And in giving us that room you did much more than you knew. You proved that good people still exist, a point that has been disputed of late—even in heaven. Farewell!

SECOND GOD. Farewell!

THIRD GOD. Farewell!

SHEN TE. Stop, illustrious ones! I'm not sure you're right. I'd like to be good, it's true, but there's the rent to pay. And that's not all: I sell myself for a living. Even so I can't make ends meet, there's too much competition. I'd like to honor my father and mother and speak nothing but the truth and not covet my neighbor's house. I should love to stay with one man. But how? How is it done? Even breaking only a *few* of your commandments, I can hardly manage.

FIRST GOD (*clearing his throat*). These thoughts are but, um, the misgivings of an unusually good woman!

THIRD GOD. Goodbye, Shen Te! Give our regards to the Water Seller!

SECOND GOD. And above all: be good! Farewell!

FIRST GOD. Farewell!

THIRD GOD. Farewell!

(*They start to wave good-bye.*)

SHEN TE. But everything is so expensive, I don't feel sure I can do it!

SECOND GOD. That's not in our sphere. We never meddle with economics.

THIRD GOD. One moment.

(*They stop.*)

Isn't it true she might do better if she had more money?

SECOND GOD. Come, come! How could we ever account for it Up Above?

FIRST GOD. Oh, there are ways.

(*They put their heads together and confer in dumb show.*)

(*To Shen Te, with embarrassment.*) As you say you can't pay your rent, well, um, we're not paupers, so of course we *insist* on paying for our room. (*Awkwardly thrusting money into her hands.*) There! (*Quickly.*) But don't tell anyone! The incident is open to misinterpretation.

SECOND GOD. It certainly is!

FIRST GOD (*defensively*). But there's no law against it! It was never decreed that a god mustn't pay hotel bills!

(*The Gods leave.*)

SCENE 1

(*A small tobacco shop. The shop is not as yet completely furnished and hasn't started doing business.*)

SHEN TE (*to the audience*). It's three days now since the gods left. When they said they wanted to pay for the room, I looked down at my hand, and there was more than a thousand silver dollars! I bought a tobacco shop with the money, and moved in yesterday. I don't own the building, of course, but I can pay the rent, and I hope to do a lot of good here. Beginning with Mrs. Shin, who's just coming across the square with her pot. She had the shop before me, and yesterday she dropped in to ask for rice for her children.

(*Enter Mrs. Shin. Both women bow.*)

How do you do, Mrs. Shin.

MRS. SHIN. How do you do, Miss Shen Te. You like your new home?

SHEN TE. Indeed, yes. Did your children have a good night?

MRS. SHIN. In that hovel? The youngest is coughing already.

SHEN TE. Oh, dear!

MRS. SHIN. You're going to learn a thing or two in these slums.

SHEN TE. Slums? That's not what you said when you sold me the shop!

MRS. SHIN. Now don't start nagging! Robbing me and my innocent children of their home and then calling it a slum! That's the limit! (*She weeps.*)

SHEN TE (*tactfully*). I'll get your rice.

MRS. SHIN. And a little cash while you're at it.

SHEN TE. I'm afraid I haven't sold anything yet.

MRS. SHIN (*screeching*). I've got to have it. Strip the clothes from my back and then cut my throat, will you? I know what I'll do: I'll leave my children on your doorstep! (*She snatches the pot out of Shen Te's hands.*)

SHEN TE. Please don't be angry. You'll spill the rice.

(*Enter an elderly Husband and Wife with their shabbily-dressed Nephew.*)

WIFE. Shen Te, dear! You've come into money, they tell me. And we haven't a roof over our heads! A tobacco shop. We had one too. But it's gone. Could we spend the night here, do you think?

NEPHEW (*appraising the shop*). Not bad!

WIFE. He's our nephew. We're inseparable!

MRS. SHIN. And who are these . . . ladies and gentlemen?

SHEN TE. They put me up when I first came in from the country. (*To the audience.*) Of course, when my small purse was empty, they put me out on the street, and they may be afraid I'll do the same to them. (*To the newcomers, kindly.*) Come in, and welcome, though I've only one little room for you—it's behind the shop.

HUSBAND. That'll do. Don't worry.

WIFE (*bringing Shen Te some tea*). We'll stay over here, so we won't be in your way. Did you make it a tobacco shop in memory of your first real home? We can certainly give you a hint or two! That's one reason we came.

MRS. SHIN (*to Shen Te*). Very nice! As long as you have a few customers too!

HUSBAND. Sh! A customer!

(*Enter an Unemployed Man, in rags.*)

UNEMPLOYED MAN. Excuse me. I'm unemployed.

(*Mrs. Shin laughs.*)

SHEN TE. Can I help you?

UNEMPLOYED MAN. Have you any damaged cigarettes? I thought there might be some damage when you're unpacking.

WIFE. What nerve, begging for tobacco! (*Rhetorically.*) Why don't they ask for bread?

UNEMPLOYED MAN. Bread is expensive. One cigarette butt and I'll be a new man.

SHEN TE (*giving him cigarettes*). That's very important—to be a new man. You'll be my first customer and bring me luck.

(*The Unemployed Man quickly lights a cigarette, inhales, and goes off, coughing.*)

WIFE. Was that right, Shen Te, dear?

MRS. SHIN. If this is the opening of a shop, you can hold the closing at the end of the week.

HUSBAND. I bet he had money on him.

SHEN TE. Oh, no, he said he hadn't!

NEPHEW. How d'you know he wasn't lying?

SHEN TE (*angrily*). How do you know he was?

WIFE (*wagging her head*). You're too good, Shen Te, dear. If you're going to keep this shop, you'll have to learn to say No.

HUSBAND. Tell them the place isn't yours to dispose of. Belongs to . . . some relative who insists on all accounts being strictly in order . . .

MRS. SHIN. That's right! What do you think you are—a philanthropist?

SHEN TE (*laughing*). Very well, suppose I ask you for my rice back, Mrs. Shin?

WIFE (*combatively, at Mrs. Shin*). So that's *her* rice?

(*Enter the Carpenter, a small man.*)

MRS. SHIN (*who, at the sight of him, starts to hurry away*). See you tomorrow, Miss Shen Te! (*Exit Mrs. Shin.*)

CARPENTER. Mrs. Shin, it's you I want!

WIFE (*to Shen Te*). Has she some claim on you?

SHEN TE. She's hungry. That's a claim.

CARPENTER. Are you the new tenant? And filling up the shelves already? Well, they're not yours, till they're paid for, ma'am. I'm the carpenter, so I should know.

SHEN TE. I took the shop "furnishings included."

CARPENTER. You're in league with that Mrs. Shin, of course. All right: I demand my hundred silver dollars.

SHEN TE. I'm afraid I haven't got a hundred silver dollars.

CARPENTER. Then you'll find it. Or I'll have you arrested.

WIFE (*whispering to Shen Te*). That relative: make it a cousin.

SHEN TE. Can't it wait till next month?

CARPENTER. No!

SHEN TE. Be a little patient, Mr. Carpenter, I can't settle all claims at once.

CARPENTER. Who's patient with me? (*He grabs a shelf from the wall.*) Pay up—or I take the shelves back!

WIFE. Shen Te! Dear! Why don't you let your . . . cousin settle this affair? (*To Carpenter.*) Put your claim in writing. Shen Te's cousin will see you get paid.

CARPENTER (*derisively*). Cousin, eh?

HUSBAND. Cousin, yes.

CARPENTER. I know these cousins!

NEPHEW. Don't be silly. He's a personal friend of mine.

HUSBAND. What a man! Sharp as a razor!

CARPENTER. All right. I'll put my claim in writing. (*Puts shelf on floor, sits on it, writes out bill.*)

WIFE (*to Shen Te*). He'd tear the dress off your back to get his shelves. Never recognize a claim! That's my motto.

SHEN TE. He's done a job, and wants something in return. It's shameful that I can't give it to him. What will the gods say?

HUSBAND. You did your bit when you took *us* in.

(*Enter the Brother, limping, and the Sister-in-Law, pregnant.*)

BROTHER (*to Husband and Wife*). So this is where you're hiding out! There's family feeling for you! Leaving us on the corner!

WIFE (*embarrassed, to Shen Te*). It's my brother and his wife. (*To them.*) Now stop grumbling, and sit quietly in that corner. (*To Shen Te.*) It can't be helped. She's in her fifth month.

SHEN TE. Oh, yes. Welcome!

WIFE (*to the couple*). Say thank you.

(*They mutter something.*)

The cups are there. (*To Shen Te.*) Lucky you bought this shop when you did!

SHEN TE (*laughing and bringing tea*). Lucky indeed!

(*Enter Mrs. Mi Tzu, the landlady.*)

MRS. MI TZU. Miss Shen Te? I am Mrs. Mi Tzu, your landlady. I hope our relationship will be a happy one? I like to think I give my tenants modern, personalized service. Here is your lease. (*To the others, as Shen Te reads the lease.*) There's nothing like the opening of a little shop, is there? A moment of true beauty! (*She is looking around.*) Not very much on the shelves, of course. But everything in the gods' good time! Where are your references, Miss Shen Te?

SHEN TE. Do I *have* to have references?

MRS. MI TZU. After all, I haven't a notion who you are!

HUSBAND. Oh, *we'd* be glad to vouch for Miss Shen Te! We'd go through fire for her!

MRS. MI TZU. And who may *you* be?

HUSBAND (*stammering*). Ma Fu, tobacco dealer.

MRS. MI TZU. Where is your shop, Mr. . . . Ma Fu?

HUSBAND. Well, um, I haven't a shop—I've just sold it.

MRS. MI TZU. I see. (*To Shen Te.*) Is there no one else that knows you?

WIFE (*whispering to Shen Te*). Your cousin! Your cousin!

MRS. MI TZU. This is a respectable house, Miss Shen Te. I never sign a lease without certain assurances.

SHEN TE (*slowly, her eyes downcast*). I have . . . a cousin.

MRS. MI TZU. On the square? Let's go over and see him. What does he do?

SHEN TE (*as before*). He lives . . . in another city.

WIFE (*prompting*). Didn't you say he was in Shung?

SHEN TE. That's right. Shung.

HUSBAND (*prompting*). I had his name on the tip of my tongue. Mr. . . .

SHEN TE (*with an effort*). Mr. . . . Shui . . . Ta.

HUSBAND. That's it! Tall, skinny fellow!

SHEN TE. Shui Ta!

NEPHEW (*to Carpenter*). You were in touch with him, weren't you? About the shelves?

CARPENTER (*surlily*). Give him this bill. (*He hands it over.*) I'll be back in the morning. (*Exit Carpenter.*)

NEPHEW (*calling after him, but with his eyes on Mrs. Mi Tzu*). Don't worry! Mr. Shui Ta pays on the nail!

MRS. MI TZU (*looking closely at Shen Te*). I'll be happy to make his acquaintance, Miss Shen Te. (*Exit Mrs. Mi Tzu.*)

(*Pause.*)

WIFE. By tomorrow morning she'll know more about you than you do yourself.

SISTER-IN-LAW (*to Nephew*). This thing isn't built to last.

(*Enter Grandfather.*)

WIFE. It's Grandfather! (*To Shen Te.*) Such a good old soul!

(*The Boy enters.*)

BOY (*over his shoulder*). Here they are!

WIFE. And the boy, how he's grown! But he always could eat enough for ten.

(*Enter the Niece.*)

WIFE (*to Shen Te*). Our little niece from the country. There are more of us now than in your time. The less we had, the more there were of us; the more there were of us, the less we had. Give me the key. We must protect ourselves from unwanted guests. (*She takes the key and locks the door.*) Just make yourself at home. I'll light the little lamp.

NEPHEW (*a big joke*). I hope her cousin doesn't drop in tonight! The strict Mr. Shui Ta!

(*Sister-in-Law laughs.*)

BROTHER (*reaching for a cigarette*). One cigarette more or less . . .

HUSBAND. One cigarette more or less.

(*They pile into the cigarettes. The Brother hands a jug of wine round.*)

NEPHEW. Mr. Shui Ta'll pay for it!

GRANDFATHER (*gravely, to Shen Te*). How do you do?

(*Shen Te, a little taken aback by the belatedness of the greeting, bows. She has the Carpenter's bill in one hand, the landlady's lease in the other.*)

WIFE. How about a bit of a song? To keep Shen Te's spirits up?

NEPHEW. Good idea. Grandfather: you start!

SONG OF THE SMOKE

GRANDFATHER.

> I used to think (before old age beset me)
> That brains could fill the pantry of the poor.
> But where did all my cerebration get me?
> I'm just as hungry as I was before.
> So what's the use?
> See the smoke float free
> Into ever colder coldness!
> It's the same with me.

HUSBAND.

> The straight and narrow path leads to disaster
> And so the crooked path I tried to tread.
> That got me to disaster even faster.
> (They say we shall be happy when we're dead.)
>   So what's the use, etc.

NIECE.

> You older people, full of expectation,
> At any moment now you'll walk the plank!
> The future's for the younger generation!
> Yes, even if that future is a blank.
>   So what's the use, etc.

NEPHEW (*to the Brother*). Where'd you get that wine?

SISTER-IN-LAW (*answering for the Brother*). He pawned the sack of tobacco.

HUSBAND (*stepping in*). What? That tobacco was all we had to fall back on! You pig!

BROTHER. *You'd* call a man a pig because your wife was frigid! Did you refuse to drink it?

(*They fight. The shelves fall over.*)

SHEN TE (*imploringly*). Oh, don't! Don't break everything! Take it, take it all, but don't destroy a gift from the gods!

WIFE (*disparagingly*). This shop isn't big enough. I should never have mentioned it to Uncle and the others. When *they* arrive, it's going to be disgustingly overcrowded.

SISTER-IN-LAW. And did you hear our gracious hostess? She cools off quick!

(*Voices outside. Knocking at the door.*)

UNCLE'S VOICE. Open the door!

WIFE. Uncle? Is that you, Uncle?

UNCLE'S VOICE. Certainly, it's me. Auntie says to tell you she'll have the children here in ten minutes.

WIFE (*to Shen Te*). I'll have to let him in.

SHEN TE (*who scarcely hears her*).

> The little lifeboat is swiftly sent down
> Too many men too greedily
> Hold on to it as they drown.

SCENE 1A

(*Wong's den in a sewer pipe.*)

WONG (*crouching there*). All quiet! It's four days now since I left the city. The gods passed this way on the second day. I heard their steps on the bridge over there. They must be a long way off by this time, so I'm safe.

(*Breathing a sigh of relief, he curls up and goes to sleep. In his dream the pipe becomes transparent, and the Gods appear.*)

(*Raising an arm, as if in self-defense.*) I know, I know, illustrious ones! I found no one to give you a room—not in all Setzuan! There, it's out. Please continue on your way!

FIRST GOD (*mildly*). But you did find someone. Someone who took us in for the night, watched over us in our sleep, and in the early morning lighted us down to the street with a lamp.

WONG. It was . . . Shen Te, that took you in?

THIRD GOD. Who else?

WONG. And I ran away! "She isn't coming," I thought, "she just can't afford it."

GODS (*singing*).

> O you feeble, well-intentioned, and yet feeble chap!
> Where there's need the fellow thinks there is no goodness!
> When there's danger he thinks courage starts to ebb away!
> Some people only see the seamy side!
> What hasty judgment! What premature desperation!

WONG. I'm *very* ashamed, illustrious ones.

FIRST GOD. Do us a favor, Water Seller. Go back to Setzuan. Find Shen Te, and give us a report on her. We hear that she's come into a little money. Show interest in her goodness—for no one can be good for long if goodness is not in demand. Meanwhile we shall continue the search, and find other good people. After which, the idle chatter about the impossibility of goodness will stop!

(*The Gods vanish.*)

SCENE 2

(*A knocking.*)

WIFE. Shen Te! Someone at the door. Where is she anyway?

NEPHEW. She must be getting the breakfast. Mr. Shui Ta will pay for it.

(*The Wife laughs and shuffles to the door. Enter Mr. Shui Ta and the Carpenter.*)

WIFE. Who is it?

SHUI TA. I am Miss Shen Te's cousin.

WIFE. What?

SHUI TA. My name is Shui Ta.

WIFE. Her cousin?

NEPHEW. Her cousin?

NIECE. But that was a joke. She hasn't got a cousin.

HUSBAND. So early in the morning?

BROTHER. What's all the noise?

SISTER-IN-LAW. This fellow says he's her cousin.

BROTHER. Tell him to prove it.

NEPHEW. Right. If you're Shen Te's cousin, prove it by getting the breakfast.

SHUI TA (*whose regime begins as he puts out the lamp to save oil. Loudly, to all present, asleep or awake*). Would you all please get dressed! Customers will be coming! I wish to open my shop!

HUSBAND. *Your* shop? Doesn't it belong to our good friend Shen Te?

(Shui Ta shakes his head.)

SISTER-IN-LAW. So we've been cheated. Where *is* the little liar?

SHUI TA. Miss Shen Te has been delayed. She wishes me to tell you there will be nothing she can do—now I am here.

WIFE *(bowled over)*. I thought she was *good!*

NEPHEW. Do you have to believe *him?*

HUSBAND. *I* don't.

NEPHEW. Then do something.

HUSBAND. Certainly! I'll send out a search party at once. You, you, you, and you, go out and look for Shen Te.

(As the Grandfather rises and makes for the door.)

Not you, Grandfather, you and I will hold the fort.

SHUI TA. You won't find Miss Shen Te. She has suspended her hospitable activity for an unlimited period. There are too many of you. She asked me to say: this is a tobacco shop, not a gold mine.

HUSBAND. Shen Te never said a thing like that. Boy, food! There's a bakery on the corner. Stuff your shirt full when they're not looking!

SISTER-IN-LAW. Don't overlook the raspberry tarts.

HUSBAND. And don't let the policeman see you.

(The Boy leaves.)

SHUI TA. Don't you depend on this shop now? Then why give it a bad name, by stealing from the bakery?

NEPHEW. Don't listen to him. Let's find Shen Te. She'll give him a piece of her mind.

SISTER-IN-LAW. Don't forget to leave us some breakfast.

(Brother, Sister-in-Law, and Nephew leave.)

SHUI TA *(to the Carpenter)*. You see, Mr. Carpenter, nothing has changed since the poet, eleven hundred years ago, penned these lines:

> A governor was asked what was needed
> To save the freezing people in the city.
> He replied:
> "A blanket ten thousand feet long
> To cover the city and all its suburbs."

(He starts to tidy up the shop.)

CARPENTER. Your cousin owes me money. I've got witnesses. For the shelves.

SHUI TA. Yes, I have your bill. *(He takes it out of his pocket.)* Isn't a hundred silver dollars rather a lot?

CARPENTER. No deductions! I have a wife and children.

SHUI TA. How many children?

CARPENTER. Three.

SHUI TA. I'll make you an offer. Twenty silver dollars.

(The Husband laughs.)

CARPENTER. You're crazy. Those shelves are real walnut.

SHUI TA. Very well. Take them away.

CARPENTER. What?

SHUI TA. They cost too much. Please take them away.

WIFE. Not bad! *(And she, too, is laughing.)*

CARPENTER *(a little bewildered)*. Call Shen Te, someone! *(To Shui Ta.)* She's good!

SHUI TA. Certainly. She's ruined.

CARPENTER *(provoked into taking some of the shelves)*. All right, you can keep your tobacco on the floor.

SHUI TA *(to the Husband)*. Help him with the shelves.

HUSBAND *(grins and carries one shelf over to the door where the Carpenter now is)*. Goodbye, shelves!

CARPENTER *(to the Husband)*. You dog! You want my family to starve?

SHUI TA. I repeat my offer. I have no desire to keep my tobacco on the floor. Twenty silver dollars.

CARPENTER *(with desperate aggressiveness)*. One hundred!

(Shui Ta shows indifference, looks through the window. The Husband picks up several shelves.)

(To Husband.) You needn't smash them against the doorpost, you idiot! *(To Shui Ta.)* These shelves were made to measure. They're no use anywhere else!

SHUI TA. Precisely.

(The Wife squeals with pleasure.)

CARPENTER *(giving up, sullenly)*. Take the shelves. Pay what you want to pay.

SHUI TA *(smoothly)*. Twenty silver dollars.

(He places two large coins on the table. The Carpenter picks them up.)

HUSBAND *(brings the shelves back in)*. And quite enough too!

CARPENTER *(slinking off)*. Quite enough to get drunk on.

HUSBAND *(happily)*. Well, we got rid of *him!*

WIFE *(weeping with fun, gives a rendition of the dialogue just spoken)*. "Real walnut," says he. "Very well, take them away," says his lordship. "I have children," says he. "Twenty silver dollars," says his lordship. "They're no use anywhere else," says he. "Precisely," said his lordship! *(She dissolves into shrieks of merriment.)*

SHUI TA. And now: go!

HUSBAND. What's that?

SHUI TA. You're thieves, parasites. I'm giving you this chance. Go!

HUSBAND *(summoning all his ancestral dignity)*. That sort deserves no answer. Besides, one should never shout on an empty stomach.

WIFE. Where's that boy?

SHUI TA. Exactly. The boy. I want no stolen goods in this shop. *(Very loudly.)* I strongly advise you to leave! *(But they remain seated, noses in the air. Quietly.)* As you wish.

(Shui Ta goes to the door. A Policeman appears. Shui Ta bows.)

I am addressing the officer in charge of this precinct?

POLICEMAN. That's right, Mr., um . . . what was the name, sir?

SHUI TA. Mr. Shui Ta.

POLICEMAN. Yes, of course, sir.

(*They exchange a smile.*)

SHUI TA. Nice weather we're having.

POLICEMAN. A little on the warm side, sir.

SHUI TA. Oh, a little on the warm side.

HUSBAND (*whispering to the Wife*). If he keeps it up till the boy's back, we're done for. (*Tries to signal Shui Ta.*)

SHUI TA (*ignoring the signal*). Weather, of course, is one thing indoors, another out on the dusty street!

POLICEMAN. Oh, quite another, sir!

WIFE (*to the Husband*). It's all right as long as he's standing in the doorway—the boy will see him.

SHUI TA. Step inside for a moment! It's quite cool indoors. My cousin and I have just opened the place. And we attach the greatest importance to being on good terms with the, um, authorities.

POLICEMAN (*entering*). Thank you, Mr. Shui Ta. It *is* cool!

HUSBAND (*whispering to the Wife*). And now the boy *won't* see him.

SHUI TA (*showing Husband and Wife to the Policeman*). Visitors, I think my cousin knows them. They were just leaving.

HUSBAND (*defeated*). Ye-e-es, we were . . . just leaving.

SHUI TA. I'll tell my cousin you couldn't wait.

(*Noise from the street. Shouts of "Stop, thief!"*)

POLICEMAN. What's that?

(*The Boy is in the doorway with cakes and buns and rolls spilling out of his shirt. The Wife signals desperately to him to leave. He gets the idea.*)

No, you don't! (*He grabs the Boy by the collar.*) Where's all this from?

BOY (*vaguely pointing*). Down the street.

POLICEMAN (*grimly*). So that's it. (*Prepares to arrest the Boy.*)

WIFE (*stepping in*). And *we* knew nothing about it. (*To the Boy.*) Nasty little thief!

POLICEMAN (*dryly*). Can you clarify the situation, Mr. Shui Ta?

(*Shui Ta is silent.*)

POLICEMAN (*who understands silence*). Aha. You're all coming with me—to the station.

SHUI TA. I can hardly say how sorry I am that *my* establishment . . .

WIFE. Oh, he saw the boy leave not ten minutes ago!

SHUI TA. And to conceal the theft asked a policeman in?

POLICEMAN. Don't listen to her, Mr. Shui Ta, I'll be happy to relieve you of their presence one and all! (*To all three.*) Out! (*He drives them before him.*)

GRANDFATHER (*leaving last. Gravely*). Good morning!

POLICEMAN. Good morning!

(*Shui Ta, left alone, continues to tidy up. Mrs. Mi Tzu breezes in.*)

MRS. MI TZU. *You're* her cousin, are you? Then have the goodness to explain what all this means—police dragging people from a respectable house! By what right does your Miss Shen Te turn my property into a house of assignation?—Well, as you see, I know all!

SHUI TA. Yes. My cousin has the worst possible reputation: that of being poor.

MRS. MI TZU. No sentimental rubbish, Mr. Shui Ta. Your cousin was a common . . .

SHUI TA. Pauper. Let's use the uglier word.

MRS. MI TZU. I'm speaking of her conduct, not her earnings. But there must have *been* earnings, or how did she buy all this? Several elderly gentlemen took care of it, I suppose. I repeat: this is a respectable house! I have tenants who prefer not to live under the same roof with such a person.

SHUI TA (*quietly*). How much do you want?

MRS. MI TZU (*he is ahead of her now*). I beg your pardon.

SHUI TA. To reassure yourself. To reassure your tenants. How much will it cost?

MRS. MI TZU. You're a cool customer.

SHUI TA (*picking up the lease*). The rent is high. (*He reads on.*) I assume it's payable by the month?

MRS. MI TZU. Not in her case.

SHUI TA (*looking up*). What?

MRS. MI TZU. Six months rent payable in advance. Two hundred silver dollars.

SHUI TA. Six . . . ! Sheer usury! And where am I to find it?

MRS. MI TZU. You should have thought of that before.

SHUI TA. Have you no heart, Mrs. Mi Tzu? It's true Shen Te acted foolishly, being kind to all those people, but she'll improve with time. I'll see to it she does. She'll work her fingers to the bone to pay her rent, and all the time be as quiet as a mouse, as humble as a fly.

MRS. MI TZU. Her social background . . .

SHUI TA. Out of the depths! She came out of the depths! And before she'll go back there, she'll work, sacrifice, shrink from nothing. . . . Such a tenant is worth her weight in gold, Mrs. Mi Tzu.

MRS. MI TZU. It's silver we were talking about, Mr. Shui Ta. Two hundred silver dollars or . . .

(*Enter the Policeman.*)

POLICEMAN. Am I intruding, Mr. Shui Ta?

MRS. MI TZU. This tobacco shop is well-known to the police, I see.

POLICEMAN. Mr. Shui Ta has done us a service, Mrs. Mi Tzu. I am here to present our official felicitations!

MRS. MI TZU. That means less than nothing to me, sir. Mr. Shui Ta, all I can say is: I hope your cousin will find my terms acceptable. Good day, gentlemen. (*Exit.*)

SHUI TA. Good day, ma'am.

(*Pause.*)

POLICEMAN. Mrs. Mi Tzu a bit of a stumbling block, sir?

SHUI TA. She wants six months' rent in advance.

POLICEMAN. And you haven't got it, eh?

(*Shui Ta is silent.*)

But surely you can get it, sir? A man like you?

SHUI TA. What about a woman like Shen Te?

POLICEMAN. You're not staying, sir?

SHUI TA. No, and I won't be back. Do you smoke?

POLICEMAN (*taking two cigars, and placing them both in his pocket*). Thank you, sir—I see your point. Miss Shen Te—let's mince no words—Miss Shen Te lived by selling herself. "What else could she have done?" you ask. "How else was she to pay the rent?" True. But the fact remains, Mr. Shui Ta, it is not respectable. Why not? A very deep question. But, in the first place, love—love isn't bought and sold like cigars, Mr. Shui Ta. In the second place, it isn't respectable to go waltzing off with someone that's paying his way, so to speak—it must be for love! Thirdly and lastly, as the proverb has it: not for a handful of rice but for love! (*Pause. He is thinking hard.*) "Well," you may say, "and what good is all this wisdom if the milk's already spilt?" Miss Shen Te is what she is. Is *where* she is. We have to face the fact that if she doesn't get hold of six months' rent pronto, she'll be back on the streets. The question then as I see it—everything in this world is a matter of opinion—the question as I see it is: *how* is she to get hold of this rent? How? Mr. Shui Ta: I don't know. (*Pause.*) I take that back, sir. It's just come to me. A husband. We must find her a husband!

(*Enter a little Old Woman.*)

OLD WOMAN. A good cheap cigar for my husband, we'll have been married forty years tomorrow and we're having a little celebration.

SHUI TA. Forty years? And you still want to celebrate?

OLD WOMAN. As much as we can afford to. We have the carpet shop across the square. We'll be good neighbors, I hope?

SHUI TA. I hope so too.

POLICEMAN (*who keeps making discoveries*). Mr. Shui Ta, you know what we need? We need capital. And how do we acquire capital? We get married.

SHUI TA (*to Old Woman*). I'm afraid I've been pestering this gentleman with my personal worries.

POLICEMAN (*lyrically*). We can't pay six months' rent, so what do we do? We marry money.

SHUI TA. That might not be easy.

POLICEMAN. Oh, I don't know. She's a good match. Has a nice, growing business. (*To the Old Woman.*) What do you think?

OLD WOMAN (*undecided*). Well—

POLICEMAN. Should she put an ad in the paper?

OLD WOMAN (*not eager to commit herself*). Well, if *she* agrees—

POLICEMAN. I'll write it for her. *You* lend us a hand, and *we* write an ad for you! (*He chuckles away to himself, takes out his notebook, wets the stump of a pencil between his lips, and writes away.*)

SHUI TA (*slowly*). Not a bad idea.

POLICEMAN. "What . . . *respectable* . . . man . . . with small capital . . . widower . . . not excluded . . . desires . . . marriage . . . into flourishing . . . tobacco shop?" And now let's add: "am . . . pretty . . . " No! . . . "Prepossessing appearance."

SHUI TA. If you don't think that's an exaggeration?

OLD WOMAN. Oh, not a bit. I've seen her.

(*The Policeman tears the page out of his notebook, and hands it over to Shui Ta.*)

SHUI TA (*with horror in his voice*). How much luck we need to keep our heads above water! How many ideas! How many friends! (*To the Policeman.*) Thank you, sir. I think I see my way clear.

SCENE 3

(*Evening in the municipal park. Noise of a plane overhead. Yang Sun, a young man in rags, is following the plane with his eyes: one can tell that the machine is describing a curve above the park. Yang Sun then takes a rope out of his pocket, looking anxiously about him as he does so. He moves toward a large willow. Enter Two Prostitutes, one old, the other the Niece whom we have already met.*)

NIECE. Hello. Coming with me?

YANG SUN (*taken aback*). If you'd like to buy me a dinner.

OLD WHORE. Buy you a dinner! (*To the Niece.*) Oh, we know him—it's the unemployed pilot. Waste no time on him!

NIECE. But he's the only man left in the park. And it's going to rain.

OLD WHORE. Oh, how do you know?

(*And they pass by. Yang Sun again looks about him, again takes his rope, and this time throws it round a branch of the willow tree. Again he is interrupted. It is the Two Prostitutes returning—and in such a hurry they don't notice him.*)

NIECE. It's going to pour!

(*Enter Shen Te.*)

OLD WHORE. There's that *gorgon* Shen Te! That *drove* your family out into the cold!

NIECE. It wasn't her. It was that cousin of hers. She offered to *pay* for the cakes. I've nothing against her.

OLD WHORE. I have, though. (*So that Shen Te can hear.*) Now where could the little lady be off to? She may be rich now but that won't stop her snatching our young men, will it?

SHEN TE. I'm going to the tearoom by the pond.

NIECE. Is it true what they say? You're marrying a widower—with three children?

SHEN TE. Yes. I'm just going to see him.

YANG SUN (*his patience at breaking point*). Move on there! This is a park, not a whorehouse!

OLD WHORE. Shut your mouth!

(*But the Two Prostitutes leave.*)

YANG SUN. Even in the farthest corner of the park, even when it's raining, you can't get rid of them! (*He spits.*)

SHEN TE (*overhearing this*). And what right have you to scold them? (*But at this point she sees the rope.*) Oh!

YANG SUN. Well, what are you staring at?

SHEN TE. That rope. What is it for?

YANG SUN. Think! Think! I haven't a penny. Even if I had, I wouldn't spend it on you. I'd buy a drink of water.

(*The rain starts.*)

SHEN TE (*still looking at the rope*). What is the rope for? You mustn't!

YANG SUN. What's it to you? Clear out!

SHEN TE (*irrelevantly*). It's raining.

YANG SUN. Well, don't try to come under this tree.

SHEN TE. Oh, no. (*She stays in the rain.*)

YANG SUN. Now go away. (*Pause.*) For one thing, I don't like your looks, you're bow-legged.

SHEN TE (*indignantly*). That's not true!

YANG SUN. Well, don't show 'em to me. Look, it's raining. You better come under this tree.

(*Slowly, she takes shelter under the tree.*)

SHEN TE. Why did you want to do it?

YANG SUN. You really want to know? (*Pause.*) To get rid of you! (*Pause.*) You know what a flyer is?

SHEN TE. Oh yes, I've met a lot of pilots. At the tearoom.

YANG SUN. You call *them* flyers? Think they know what a machine *is*? Just 'cause they have leather helmets? They gave the airfield director a bribe, that's the way *those* fellows got up in the air! Try one of them out sometime. "Go up to two thousand feet," tell him, "then let it fall, then pick it up again with a flick of the wrist at the last moment." Know what he'll say to that? "It's not in my contract." Then again, there's the landing problem. It's like landing on your own backside. It's no different, planes are human. Those fools don't understand. (*Pause.*) And I'm the biggest fool for reading the book on flying in the Peking school and skipping the page where it says: "we've got enough flyers and we don't need you." I'm a mail pilot and no mail. You understand that?

SHEN TE (*shyly*). Yes. I do.

YANG SUN. No, you don't. You'd never understand that.

SHEN TE. When we were little we had a crane with a broken wing. He made friends with us and was very good-natured about our jokes. He would strut along behind us

and call out to stop us going too fast for him. But every spring and autumn when the cranes flew over the villages in great swarms, he got quite restless. (*Pause.*) I understood that. (*She bursts out crying.*)

YANG SUN. Don't!

SHEN TE (*quieting down*). No.

YANG SUN. It's bad for the complexion.

SHEN TE (*sniffing*). I've stopped.

(*She dries her tears on her big sleeve. Leaning against the tree, but not looking at her, he reaches for her face.*)

YANG SUN. You can't even wipe your own face. (*He is wiping it for her with his handkerchief. Pause.*)

SHEN TE (*still sobbing*). I don't know *anything*!

YANG SUN. You interrupted me! What for?

SHEN TE. It's such a rainy day. You only wanted to do . . . *that* because it's such a rainy day.

(*To the audience.*)

> In our country
> The evenings should never be somber
> High bridges over rivers
> The grey hour between night and morning
> And the long, long winter:
> Such things are dangerous
> For, with all the misery,
> A very little is enough
> And men throw away an unbearable life.

(*Pause.*)

YANG SUN. Talk about yourself for a change.

SHEN TE. What about me? I have a shop.

YANG SUN (*incredulous*). You have a shop, do you? Never thought of walking the streets?

SHEN TE. I *did* walk the streets. Now I have a shop.

YANG SUN (*ironically*). A gift of the gods, I suppose!

SHEN TE. How did you know?

YANG SUN (*even more ironical*). One fine evening the gods turned up saying: here's some money!

SHEN TE (*quickly*). One fine morning.

YANG SUN (*fed up*). This isn't much of an entertainment.

(*Pause.*)

SHEN TE. I can play the zither a little. (*Pause.*) And I can mimic men. (*Pause.*) I got the shop, so the first thing I did was to give my zither away. I can be as stupid as a fish now, I said to myself, and it won't matter.

> I'm rich now, I said
> I walk alone, I sleep alone
> For a whole year, I said
> I'll have nothing to do with a man.

YANG SUN. And now you're marrying one! The one at the tearoom by the pond?

(*Shen Te is silent.*)

YANG SUN. What do you know about love?

SHEN TE. Everything.

YANG SUN. Nothing. (*Pause.*) Or d'you just mean you enjoyed it?

SHEN TE. No.

YANG SUN (*again without turning to look at her, he strokes her cheek with his hand*). You like that?

SHEN TE. Yes.

YANG SUN (*breaking off*). You're easily satisfied, I must say. (*Pause.*) What a town!

SHEN TE. You have no friends?

YANG SUN (*defensively*). Yes, I have! (*Change of tone.*) But they don't want to hear I'm still unemployed. "What?" they ask. "Is there still water in the sea?" You have friends?

SHEN TE (*hesitating*). Just a . . . cousin.

YANG SUN. Watch him carefully.

SHEN TE. He only came once. Then he went away. He won't be back.

(*Yang Sun is looking away.*)

But to be without hope, they say, is to be without goodness!

(*Pause.*)

YANG SUN. Go on talking. A voice is a voice.

SHEN TE. Once, when I was a little girl, I fell, with a load of brushwood. An old man picked me up. He gave me a penny too. Isn't it funny how people who don't have very much like to give some of it away? They must like to show what they can do, and how could they show it better than by being kind? Being wicked is just like being clumsy. When we sing a song, or build a machine, or plant some rice, we're being kind. You're kind.

YANG SUN. You make it sound easy.

SHEN TE. Oh, no. (*Little pause.*) Oh! A drop of rain!

YANG SUN. Where'd you feel it?

SHEN TE. Between the eyes.

YANG SUN. Near the right eye? Or the left?

SHEN TE. Near the left eye.

YANG SUN. Oh, good. (*He is getting sleepy.*) So you're through with men, eh?

SHEN TE (*with a smile*). But I'm not bow-legged.

YANG SUN. Perhaps not.

SHEN TE. Definitely not.

(*Pause.*)

YANG SUN (*leaning wearily against the willow*). I haven't had a drop to drink all day, I haven't eaten anything for *two* days. I couldn't love you if I tried.

(*Pause.*)

SHEN TE. I like it in the rain.

(*Enter Wong the Water Seller, singing.*)

THE SONG OF THE WATER SELLER IN THE RAIN
   "Buy my water," I am yelling

And my fury restraining
For no water I'm selling
'Cause it's raining, 'cause it's raining!
   I keep yelling: "Buy my water!"
   But no one's buying
   Athirst and dying
   And drinking and paying!
   Buy water!
   Buy water, you dogs!

Nice to dream of lovely weather!
Think of all the consternation
Were there no precipitation
Half a dozen years together!
Can't you hear them shrieking: "Water!"
Pretending they adore me!
They all would go down on their knees before me!
Down on your knees!
Go down on your knees, you dogs!

What are lawns and hedges thinking?
What are fields and forests saying?
"At the cloud's breast we are drinking!
And we've no idea who's paying!"
   I keep yelling: "Buy my water!"
   But no one's buying
   Athirst and dying
   And drinking and paying!
   Buy water!
   Buy water, you dogs!

(*The rain has stopped now. Shen Te sees Wong and runs toward him.*)

SHEN TE. Wong! You're back! Your carrying pole's at the shop.

WONG. Oh, thank you, Shen Te. And how is life treating *you*?

SHEN TE. I've just met a brave and clever man. And I want to buy him a cup of your water.

WONG (*bitterly*). Throw back your head and open your mouth and you'll have all the water you need—

SHEN TE (*tenderly*).

I want *your* water, Wong
The water that has tired you so
The water that you carried all this way
The water that is hard to sell because it's been raining
I need it for the young man over there—he's a flyer!
   A flyer is a bold man:
   Braving the storms
   In company with the clouds
   He crosses the heavens
   And brings to friends in far-away lands
   The friendly mail!

(*She pays Wong, and runs over to Yang Sun with the cup. But Yang Sun is fast asleep.*)

(*Calling to Wong, with a laugh.*) He's fallen asleep! Despair and rain and I have worn him out!

SCENE 3A

(*Wong's den. The sewer pipe is transparent, and the Gods again appear to Wong in a dream.*)

WONG (*radiant*). I've seen her, illustrious ones! And she hasn't changed!

FIRST GOD. That's good to hear.

WONG. She loves someone.

FIRST GOD. Let's hope the experience gives her the strength to stay good!

WONG. It does. She's doing good deeds all the time.

FIRST GOD. Ah? What sort? What sort of good deeds, Wong?

WONG. Well, she has a kind word for everybody.

FIRST GOD (*eagerly*). And then?

WONG. Hardly anyone leaves her shop without tobacco in his pocket—even if he can't pay for it.

FIRST GOD. Not bad at all. Next?

WONG. She's putting up a family of eight.

FIRST GOD (*gleefully, to the Second God*). Eight! (*To Wong.*) And that's not all, of course!

WONG. She bought a cup of water from me even though it was raining.

FIRST GOD. Yes, yes, yes, all these smaller good deeds!

WONG. Even they run into money. A little tobacco shop doesn't make so much.

FIRST GOD (*sententiously*). A prudent gardener works miracles on the smallest plot.

WONG. She hands out rice every morning. That eats up half her earnings.

FIRST GOD (*a little disappointed*). Well, as a beginning . . .

WONG. They call her the Angel of the Slums—whatever the Carpenter may say!

FIRST GOD. What's this? A carpenter speaks ill of her?

WONG. Oh, he only says her shelves weren't paid for in full.

SECOND GOD (*who has a bad cold and can't pronounce his n's and m's*). What's this? Not paying a carpenter? Why was that?

WONG. I suppose she didn't have the money.

SECOND GOD (*severely*). One pays what one owes, that's in our book of rules! First the letter of the law, then the spirit!

WONG. But it wasn't Shen Te, illustrious ones, it was her cousin. She called *him* in to help.

SECOND GOD. Then her cousin must never darken her threshold again!

WONG. Very well, illustrious ones! But in fairness to Shen Te, let me say that her cousin is a businessman.

FIRST GOD. Perhaps we should inquire what is customary? I find business quite unintelligible. But everybody's doing it. Business! Did the Seven Good Kings do business? Did Kung the Just sell fish?

SECOND GOD. In any case, such a thing must not occur again!

(*The Gods start to leave.*)

THIRD GOD. Forgive us for taking this tone with you, Wong, we haven't been getting enough sleep. The rich recom-

mend us to the poor, and the poor tell us they haven't enough room.

SECOND GOD. Feeble, feeble, the best of them!

FIRST GOD. No great deeds! No heroic daring!

THIRD GOD. On such a *small* scale!

SECOND GOD. Sincere, yes, but what is actually *achieved*?

(*One can no longer hear them.*)

WONG (*calling after them*). I've thought of something, illustrious ones: Perhaps you shouldn't ask—too—much—all—at—once!

SCENE 4

(*The square in front of Shen Te's tobacco shop. Beside Shen Te's place, two other shops are seen: the carpet shop and a barber's. Morning. Outside Shen Te's the Grandfather, the Sister-in-Law, the Unemployed Man, and Mrs. Shin stand waiting.*)

SISTER-IN-LAW. She's been out all night again.

MRS. SHIN. No sooner did we get rid of that crazy cousin of hers than Shen Te herself starts carrying on! Maybe she does give us an ounce of rice now and then, but can you depend on her? Can you depend on her?

(*Loud voices from the Barber's.*)

VOICE OF SHU FU. What are you doing in my shop? Get out—at once!

VOICE OF WONG. But sir. They all let me sell . . .

(*Wong comes staggering out of the barber's shop pursued by Mr. Shu Fu, the barber, a fat man carrying a heavy curling iron.*)

SHU FU. Get out, I said! Pestering my customers with your slimy old water! Get out! Take your cup!

(*He holds out the cup. Wong reaches out for it. Mr. Shu Fu strikes his hand with the curling iron, which is hot. Wong howls.*)

You had it coming, my man!

(*Puffing, he returns to his shop. The Unemployed Man picks up the cup and gives it to Wong.*)

UNEMPLOYED MAN. You can report that to the police.

WONG. My hand! It's smashed up!

UNEMPLOYED MAN. Any bones broken?

WONG. I can't move my fingers.

UNEMPLOYED MAN. Sit down. I'll put some water on it.

(*Wong sits.*)

MRS. SHIN. The water won't cost you anything.

SISTER-IN-LAW. You might have got a bandage from Miss Shen Te till she took to staying out all night. It's a scandal.

MRS. SHIN (*despondently*). If you ask me, she's forgotten we ever existed!

(*Enter Shen Te down the street, with a dish of rice.*)

SHEN TE (*to the audience*). How wonderful to see Setzuan in the early morning! I always used to stay in bed with my dirty blanket over my head afraid to wake up. This morning I saw the newspapers being delivered by little boys, the streets being washed by strong men, and fresh vegetables coming in from the country on ox carts. It's a long walk from where Yang Sun lives, but I feel lighter at every step. They say you walk on air when you're in love, but it's even better walking on the rough earth, on the hard cement. In the early morning, the old city looks like a great rubbish heap. Nice, though—with all its little lights. And the sky, so pink, so transparent, before the dust comes and muddies it! What a lot you miss if you never see your city rising from its slumbers like an honest old craftsman pumping his lungs full of air and reaching for his tools, as the poet says! (*Cheerfully, to her waiting guests.*) Good morning, everyone, here's your rice! (*Distributing the rice, she comes upon Wong.*) Good morning, Wong, I'm quite lightheaded today. On my way over, I looked at myself in all the shop windows. I'd love to be beautiful.

(*She slips into the carpet shop. Mr. Shu Fu has just emerged from his shop.*)

SHU FU (*to the audience*). It surprises me how beautiful Miss Shen Te is looking today! I never gave her a passing thought before. But now I've been gazing upon her comely form for exactly three minutes! I begin to suspect I am in love with her. She is overpoweringly attractive! (*Crossly, to Wong.*) Be off with you, rascal!

(*He returns to his shop. Shen Te comes back out of the carpet shop with the Old Man, its proprietor, and his wife—whom we have already met—the Old Woman. Shen Te is wearing a shawl. The Old Man is holding up a looking glass for her.*)

OLD WOMAN. Isn't it lovely? We'll give you a reduction because there's a little hole in it.

SHEN TE (*looking at another shawl on the Old Woman's arm*). The other one's nice too.

OLD WOMAN (*smiling*). Too bad there's no hole in that!

SHEN TE. That's right. My shop doesn't make very much.

OLD WOMAN. And your good deeds eat it all up! Be more careful, my dear . . .

SHEN TE (*trying on the shawl with the hole*). Just now, I'm lightheaded! Does the color suit me?

OLD WOMAN. You'd better ask a man.

SHEN TE (*to the Old Man*). Does the color suit me?

OLD MAN. You'd better ask your young friend.

SHEN TE. I'd like to have your opinion.

OLD MAN. It suits you, very well. But wear it this way: the dull side out.

(*Shen Te pays up.*)

OLD WOMAN. If you decide you don't like it, you can exchange it. (*She pulls Shen Te to one side.*) Has he got money?

SHEN TE (*with a laugh*). Yang Sun? Oh, no.

OLD WOMAN. Then how're you going to pay your rent?

SHEN TE. I'd forgotten about that.

OLD WOMAN. And next Monday is the first of the month! Miss Shen Te, I've got something to say to you. After we (*indicating her husband*) got to know you, we had our doubts about that marriage ad. We thought it would be better if you'd let *us* help you. Out of our savings. We reckon we could lend you two hundred silver dollars. We don't need anything in writing—you could pledge us your tobacco stock.

SHEN TE. You're prepared to lend money to a person like me?

OLD WOMAN. It's folks like you that need it. We'd think twice about lending anything to your cousin.

OLD MAN (*coming up*). All settled, my dear?

SHEN TE. I wish the gods could have heard what your wife was just saying, Mr. Ma. They're looking for good people who're happy—and helping me makes you happy because you know it was love that got me into difficulties!

(*The old couple smile knowingly at each other.*)

OLD MAN. And here's the money, Miss Shen Te.

(*He hands her an envelope. Shen Te takes it. She bows. They bow back. They return to their shop.*)

SHEN TE (*holding up her envelope*). Look, Wong, here's six months' rent! Don't you believe in miracles now? And how do you like my new shawl?

WONG. For the young fellow I saw you with in the park?

(*Shen Te nods.*)

MRS. SHIN. Never mind all that. It's time you took a look at his hand!

SHEN TE. Have you hurt your hand?

MRS. SHIN. That barber smashed it with his hot curling iron. Right in front of our eyes.

SHEN TE (*shocked at herself*). And I never noticed! We must get you to a doctor this minute or who knows what will happen?

UNEMPLOYED MAN. It's not a doctor he should see, it's a judge. He can ask for compensation. The barber's filthy rich.

WONG. You think I have a chance?

MRS. SHIN (*with relish*). If it's really good and smashed. But is it?

WONG. I think so. It's very swollen. Could I get a pension?

MRS. SHIN. You'd need a witness.

WONG. Well, you all saw it. You could all testify.

(*He looks round. The Unemployed Man, the Grandfather, and the Sister-in-Law are all sitting against the wall of the shop eating rice. Their concentration on eating is complete.*)

SHEN TE (*to Mrs. Shin*). You saw it yourself.

MRS. SHIN. I want nothin' to do with the police. It's against my principles.

SHEN TE (*to Sister-in-Law*). What about you?

SISTER-IN-LAW. Me? I wasn't looking.

SHEN TE (*to the Grandfather, coaxingly*). Grandfather, *you'll* testify, won't you?

SISTER-IN-LAW. And a lot of good that will do. He's simple-minded.

SHEN TE (*to the Unemployed Man*). You seem to be the only witness left.

UNEMPLOYED MAN. My testimony would only hurt him. I've been picked up twice for begging.

SHEN TE. Your brother is assaulted, and you shut your eyes?

> He is hit, cries out in pain, and you are silent?
> The beast prowls, chooses and seizes his victim, and you say:
> "Because we showed no displeasure, he has spared us."

If no one present will be a witness, I will. I'll say I saw it.

MRS. SHIN (*solemnly*). The name for that is perjury.

WONG. I don't know if I can accept that. Though maybe I'll have to. (*Looking at his hand.*) Is it swollen enough, do you think? The swelling's not going down?

UNEMPLOYED MAN. No, no, the swelling's holding up well.

WONG. Yes. It's *more* swollen if anything. Maybe my wrist is broken after all. I'd better see a judge at once.

(*Holding his hand very carefully, and fixing his eyes on it, he runs off. Mrs. Shin goes quickly into the barber's shop.*)

UNEMPLOYED MAN (*seeing her*). She is getting on the right side of Mr. Shu Fu.

SISTER-IN-LAW. You and I can't change the world, Shen Te.

SHEN TE. Go away! Go away all of you!

(*The Unemployed Man, the Sister-in-Law, and the Grandfather stalk off, eating and sulking.*)

(*To the audience.*)

> They've stopped answering
> They stay put
> They do as they're told
> They don't care
> Nothing can make them look up
> But the smell of food.

(*Enter Mrs. Yang, Yang Sun's mother, out of breath.*)

MRS. YANG. Miss. Shen Te. My son has told me everything. I am Mrs. Yang, Sun's mother. Just think. He's got an offer. Of a job as a pilot. A letter has just come. From the director of the airfield in Peking!

SHEN TE. So he can fly again? Isn't that wonderful!

MRS. YANG (*less breathlessly all the time*). They won't give him the job for nothing. They want five hundred silver dollars.

SHEN TE. We can't let money stand in his way, Mrs. Yang!

MRS. YANG. If only you could help him out!

SHEN TE. I have the shop. I can try! (*She embraces Mrs. Yang.*) I happen to have two hundred with me now. Take it. (*She gives her the old couple's money.*) It was a loan but they said I could repay it with my tobacco stock.

MRS. YANG. And they were calling Sun the Dead Pilot of Setzuan! A friend in need!

SHEN TE. *We* must find another three hundred.

MRS. YANG. How?

SHEN TE. Let me think. (*Slowly.*) I know someone who can help. I didn't want to call on his services again, he's hard and cunning. But a flyer must fly. And I'll make this the last time.

(*Distant sound of a plane.*)

MRS. YANG. If the man you mentioned can do it. . . . Oh, look, there's the morning mail plane, heading for Peking!

SHEN TE. The pilot can see us, let's wave!

(*They wave. The noise of the engine is louder.*)

MRS. YANG. You know that pilot up there?

SHEN TE. Wave, Mrs. Yang! I know the pilot who *will* be up there. He gave up hope. But he'll do it now. One man to raise himself above the misery, above us all.

(*To the audience.*)

> Yang Sun, my lover:
> Braving the storms
> In company with the clouds
> Crossing the heavens
> And bringing to friends in far-away lands
> The friendly mail!

SCENE 4A

(*In front of the inner curtain. Enter Shen Te, carrying Shui Ta's mask. She sings.*)

THE SONG OF DEFENSELESSNESS
> In our country
> A useful man needs luck
> Only if he finds strong backers can he prove himself useful
> The good can't defend themselves and
> Even the gods are defenseless.
>
> Oh, why don't the gods have their own ammunition
> And launch against badness their own expedition
> Enthroning the good and preventing sedition
> And bringing the world to a peaceful condition?
>
> Oh, why don't the gods do the buying and selling

Injustice forbidding, starvation dispelling
Give bread to each city and joy to each dwelling?
Oh, why don't the gods do the buying and selling?

(*She puts on Shui Ta's mask and sings in his voice.*)

You can only help one of your luckless brothers
By trampling down a dozen others

Why is it the gods do not feel indignation
And come down in fury to end exploitation
Defeat all defeat and forbid desperation
Refusing to tolerate such toleration?

Why is it?

SCENE 5

(*Shen Te's tobacco shop. Behind the counter, Mr. Shui Ta, reading the paper. Mrs. Shin is cleaning up. She talks and he takes no notice.*)

MRS. SHIN. And when certain' rumors get about, what *happens* to a little place like this? It goes to pot. *I* know. So, if you want my advice, Mr. Shui Ta, find out just what exactly has been going on between Miss Shen Te and that Yang Sun from Yellow Street. And remember: a certain interest in Miss Shen Te has been expressed by the barber next door, a man with twelve houses and only one wife, who, for that matter, is likely to drop off at any time. A certain interest has been expressed. (*She relishes the phrase.*) He was even inquiring about her means and, if *that* doesn't prove a man is getting serious, what would? (*Still getting no response, she leaves with her bucket.*)

YANG SUN'S VOICE. Is that Miss Shen Te's tobacco shop?

MRS. SHIN'S VOICE. Yes, it is, but it's Mr. Shui Ta who's here today.

(*Shui Ta runs to the looking glass with the short, light steps of Shen Te, and is just about to start primping, when he realizes his mistake, and turns away, with a short laugh. Enter Yang Sun. Mrs. Shin enters behind him and slips into the back room to eavesdrop.*)

YANG SUN. I am Yang Sun.

(*Shui Ta bows.*)

Is Miss Shen Te in?

SHUI TA. No.

YANG SUN. I guess you know our relationship? (*He is inspecting the stock.*) Quite a place! And I thought she was just talking big. I'll be flying again, all right. (*He takes a cigar, solicits and receives a light from Shui Ta.*) You think we can squeeze the other three hundred out of the tobacco stock?

SHUI TA. May I ask if it is your intention to sell at once?

YANG SUN. It was decent of her to come out with the two hundred but they aren't much use with the other three hundred still missing.

SHUI TA. Shen Te was overhasty promising so much. She might have to sell the shop itself to raise it. Haste, they say, is the wind that blows the house down.

YANG SUN. Oh, she isn't a girl to keep a man waiting. For one thing or the other, if you take my meaning.

SHUI TA. I take your meaning.

YANG SUN (*leering*). Uh, huh.

SHUI TA. Would you explain what the five hundred silver dollars are for?

YANG SUN. Trying to sound me out? Very well. The director of the Peking airfield is a friend of mine from flying school. I give him five hundred: he gets me the job.

SHUI TA. The price is high.

YANG SUN. Not as these things go. He'll have to fire one of the present pilots—for negligence. Only the man he has in mind isn't negligent. Not easy, you understand. You needn't mention that part of it to Shen Te.

SHUI TA (*looking intently at Yang Sun*). Mr. Yang Sun, you are asking my cousin to give up her possessions, leave her friends, and place her entire fate in your hands. I presume you intend to marry her?

YANG SUN. I'd be prepared to.

(*Slight pause.*)

SHUI TA. Those two hundred silver dollars would pay the rent here for six months. If you were Shen Te wouldn't you be tempted to continue in business?

YANG SUN. What? Can you imagine Yang Sun the Flyer behind a counter? (*In an oily voice.*) "A strong cigar or a mild one, worthy sir?" Not in this century!

SHUI TA. My cousin wishes to follow the promptings of her heart, and, from her own point of view, she may even have what is called the right to love. Accordingly, she has commissioned me to help you to this post. There is nothing here that I am not empowered to turn immediately into cash. Mrs. Mi Tzu, the landlady, will advise me about the sale.

(*Enter Mrs. Mi Tzu.*)

MRS. MI TZU. Good morning, Mr. Shui Ta, you wish to see me about the rent? As you know it falls due the day after tomorrow.

SHUI TA. Circumstances have changed, Mrs. Mi Tzu: my cousin is getting married. Her future husband here, Mr. Yang Sun, will be taking her to Peking. I am interested in selling the tobacco stock.

MRS. MI TZU. How much are you asking, Mr. Shui Ta?

YANG SUN. Three hundred sil—

SHUI TA. Five hundred silver dollars.

MRS. MI TZU. How much did she pay for it, Mr. Shui Ta?

SHUI TA. A thousand. And very little has been sold.

MRS. MI TZU. She was robbed. But I'll make you a special offer if you'll promise to be out by the day after tomorrow. Three hundred silver dollars.

YANG SUN (*shrugging*). Take it, man, take it.

SHUI TA. It is not enough.

YANG SUN. Why not? Why not? Certainly, it's enough.

SHUI TA. Five hundred silver dollars.

YANG SUN. But why? We only need three!

SHUI TA (to Mrs. Mi Tzu). Excuse me. (Takes Yang Sun on one side.) The tobacco stock is pledged to the old couple who gave my cousin the two hundred.

YANG SUN. Is it in writing?

SHUI TA. No.

YANG SUN (to Mrs. Mi Tzu). Three hundred will do.

MRS. MI TZU. Of course, I need an assurance that Miss Shen Te is not in debt.

YANG SUN. Mr. Shui Ta?

SHUI TA. She is not in debt.

YANG SUN. When can you let us have the money?

MRS. MI TZU. The day after tomorrow. And remember: I'm doing this because I have a soft spot in my heart for young lovers! (Exit.)

YANG SUN (calling after her). Boxes, jars and sacks—three hundred for the lot and the pain's over! (To Shui Ta.) Where else can we raise money by the day after tomorrow?

SHUI TA. Nowhere. Haven't you enough for the trip and the first few weeks?

YANG SUN. Oh, certainly.

SHUI TA. How much, exactly?

YANG SUN. Oh, I'll dig it up, if I have to steal it.

SHUI TA. I see.

YANG SUN. Well, don't fall off the roof. I'll get to Peking somehow.

SHUI TA. Two people can't travel for nothing.

YANG SUN (not giving Shui Ta a chance to answer). I'm leaving her behind. No millstones round my neck!

SHUI TA. Oh.

YANG SUN. Don't look at me like that!

SHUI TA. How precisely is my cousin to live?

YANG SUN. Oh, you'll think of something.

SHUI TA. A small request, Mr. Yang Sun. Leave the two hundred silver dollars here until you can show me two tickets for Peking.

YANG SUN. You learn to mind your own business, Mr. Shui Ta.

SHUI TA. I'm afraid Miss Shen Te may not wish to sell the shop when she discovers that . . .

YANG SUN. You don't know women. She'll want to. Even then.

SHUI TA (a slight outburst). She is a human being, sir! And not devoid of common sense!

YANG SUN. Shen Te is a woman: she is devoid of common sense. I only have to lay my hand on her shoulder, and church bells ring.

SHUI TA (with difficulty). Mr. Yang Sun!

YANG SUN. Mr. Shui Whatever-it-is!

SHUI TA. My cousin is devoted to you . . . because . . .

YANG SUN. Because I have my hands on her breasts. Give me a cigar. (He takes one for himself, stuffs a few more in his pocket, then changes his mind and takes the whole box.) Tell her I'll marry her, then bring me the three hundred. Or let her bring it. One or the other. (Exit.)

MRS. SHIN (sticking her head out of the back room). Well, he has your cousin under his thumb, and doesn't care if all Yellow Street knows it!

SHUI TA (crying out). I've lost my shop! And he doesn't love me! (He runs berserk through the room, repeating these lines incoherently. Then stops suddenly, and addresses Mrs. Shin.) Mrs. Shin, you grew up in the gutter, like me. Are we lacking in hardness? I doubt it. If you steal a penny from me, I'll take you by the throat till you spit it out! You'd do the same to me. The times are bad, this city is hell, but we're like ants, we keep coming, up and up the walls, however smooth! Till bad luck comes. Being in love, for instance. One weakness is enough, and love is the deadliest.

MRS. SHIN (emerging from the back room). You should have a little talk with Mr. Shu Fu the Barber. He's a real gentleman and just the thing for your cousin. (She runs off.)

SHUI TA.

A caress becomes a stranglehold
A sigh of love turns to a cry of fear
Why are there vultures circling in the air?
A girl is going to meet her lover.

(Shui Ta sits down and Mr. Shu Fu enters with Mrs. Shin.)

Mr. Shu Fu?

SHU FU. Mr. Shui Ta.

(They both bow.)

SHUI TA. I am told that you have expressed a certain interest in my cousin Shen Te. Let me set aside all propriety and confess: she is at this moment in grave danger.

SHU FU. Oh, dear!

SHUI TA. She has lost her shop, Mr. Shu Fu.

SHU FU. The charm of Miss Shen Te, Mr. Shui Ta, derives from the goodness, not of her shop, but of her heart. Men call her the Angel of the Slums.

SHUI TA. Yet her goodness has cost her two hundred silver dollars in a single day: we must put a stop to it.

SHU FU. Permit me to differ, Mr. Shui Ta. Let us rather, open wide the gates to such goodness! Every morning, with pleasure tinged by affection, I watch her charitable ministrations. For they are hungry, and she giveth them to eat! Four of them, to be precise. Why only four? I ask. Why not four hundred? I hear she has been seeking shelter for the homeless. What about my humble cabins behind the cattle run? They are at her disposal. And so forth. And so on. Mr. Shui Ta, do you think Miss Shen Te could be persuaded to listen to certain ideas of mine? Ideas like these?

SHUI TA. Mr. Shu Fu, she would be honored.

(*Enter Wong and the Policeman. Mr. Shu Fu turns abruptly away and studies the shelves.*)

WONG. Is Miss Shen Te here?

SHUI TA. No.

WONG. I am Wong the Water Seller. You are Mr. Shui Ta?

SHUI TA. I am.

WONG. I am a friend of Shen Te's.

SHUI TA. An intimate friend, I hear.

WONG (*to the Policeman*). You see? (*To Shui Ta.*) It's because of my hand.

POLICEMAN. He hurt his hand, sir, that's a fact.

SHUI TA (*quickly*). You need a sling, I see. (*He takes a shawl from the back room, and throws it to Wong.*)

WONG. But that's her new shawl!

SHUI TA. She has no more use for it.

WONG. But she bought it to please someone!

SHUI TA. It happens to be no longer necessary.

WONG (*making the sling*). She is my only witness.

POLICEMAN. Mr. Shui Ta, your cousin is supposed to have seen the Barber hit the Water Seller with a curling iron.

SHUI TA. I'm afraid my cousin was not present at the time.

WONG. But she was, sir! Just ask her! Isn't she in?

SHUI TA (*gravely*). Mr. Wong, my cousin has her own troubles. You wouldn't wish her to add to them by committing perjury?

WONG. But it was she that told me to go to the judge!

SHUI TA. Was the judge supposed to heal your hand?

(*Mr. Shu Fu turns quickly around. Shui Ta bows to Shu Fu, and vice versa.*)

WONG (*taking the sling off, and putting it back*). I see how it is.

POLICEMAN. Well, I'll be on my way. (*To Wong.*) And you be careful. If Mr. Shu Fu wasn't a man who tempers justice with mercy, as the saying is, you'd be in jail for libel. Be off with you!

(*Exit Wong, followed by Policeman.*)

SHUI TA. Profound apologies, Mr. Shu Fu.

SHU FU. Not at all, Mr. Shui Ta. (*Pointing to the shawl.*) The episode is over?

SHUI TA. It may take her time to recover. There are some fresh wounds.

SHU FU. We shall be discreet. Delicate. A short vacation could be arranged . . .

SHUI TA. First, of course, you and she would have to talk things over.

SHU FU. At a small supper in a small, but high-class, restaurant.

SHUI TA. I'll go and find her. (*Exit into back room.*)

MRS. SHIN (*sticking her head in again*). Time for congratulations, Mr. Shu Fu?

SHU FU. Ah, Mrs. Shin! Please inform Miss Shen Te's guests they may take shelter in the cabins behind the cattle run!

(*Mrs. Shin nods, grinning.*)

(*To the audience.*) Well? What do you think of me, ladies and gentlemen? What could a man do more? Could he be less selfish? More farsighted? A small supper in a small but . . . Does that bring rather vulgar and clumsy thoughts into your mind? Ts, ts, ts. Nothing of the sort will occur. She won't even be touched. Not even accidentally while passing the salt. An exchange of ideas only. Over the flowers on the table—white chrysanthemums, by the way (*He writes down a note of this.*)—yes, over the white chrysanthemums, two young souls will . . . shall I say "find each other"? We shall NOT exploit the misfortune of others. Understanding? Yes. An offer of assistance? Certainly. But quietly. Almost inaudibly. Perhaps with a single glance. A glance that could also—mean more.

MRS. SHIN (*coming forward*). Everything under control, Mr. Shu Fu?

SHU FU. Oh, Mrs. Shin, what do you know about this worthless rascal Yang Sun?

MRS. SHIN. Why, he's the most worthless rascal . . .

SHU FU. Is he really? You're sure? (*As she opens her mouth.*) From now on, he doesn't exist! Can't be found anywhere!

(*Enter Yang Sun.*)

YANG SUN. What's been going on here?

MRS. SHIN. Shall I call Mr. Shui Ta, Mr. Shu Fu? He wouldn't want strangers in here!

SHU FU. Mr. Shui Ta is in conference with Miss Shen Te. Not to be disturbed!

YANG SUN. Shen Te here? I didn't see her come in. What kind of conference?

SHU FU (*not letting him enter the back room*). Patience, dear sir! And if by chance I have an inkling who you are, pray take note that Miss Shen Te and I are about to announce our engagement.

YANG SUN. What?

MRS. SHIN. You didn't expect that, did you?

(*Yang Sun is trying to push past the barber into the back room when Shen Te comes out.*)

SHU FU. My dear Shen Te, ten thousand apologies! Perhaps you . . .

YANG SUN. What is it, Shen Te? Have you gone crazy?

SHEN TE (*breathless*). My cousin and Mr. Shu Fu have come to an understanding. They wish me to hear Mr. Shu Fu's plans for helping the poor.

YANG SUN. Your cousin wants to part us.

SHEN TE. Yes.

YANG SUN. And you've agreed to it?

SHEN TE. Yes.

YANG SUN. They told you I was bad.

(*Shen Te is silent.*)

And suppose I am. Does that make me need you less? I'm low, Shen Te, I have no money, I don't do the right thing but at least I put up a fight! (*He is near her now, and speaks in an undertone.*) Have you no eyes? Look at him. Have you forgotten already?

SHEN TE. No.

YANG SUN. How it was raining?

SHEN TE. No.

YANG SUN. How you cut me down from the willow tree? Bought me water? Promised me money to fly with?

SHEN TE (*shakily*). Yang Sun, what do you want?

YANG SUN. I want you to come with me.

SHEN TE (*in a small voice*). Forgive me, Mr. Shu Fu, I want to go with Mr. Yang Sun.

YANG SUN. We're lovers you know. Give me the key to the shop.

(*Shen Te takes the key from around her neck. Yang Sun puts it on the counter. To Mrs. Shin.*)

Leave it under the mat when you're through. Let's go, Shen Te.

SHU FU. But this is rape! Mr. Shui Ta!!

YANG SUN (*to Shen Te*). Tell him not to shout.

SHEN TE. Please don't shout for my cousin, Mr. Shu Fu. He doesn't agree with me, I know, but he's wrong. (*To the audience.*)

I want to go with the man I love
I don't want to count the cost
I don't want to consider if it's wise
I don't want to know if he loves me
I want to go with the man I love.

YANG SUN. That's the spirit.

(*And the couple leave.*)

SCENE 5A

(*In front of the inner curtain. Shen Te in her wedding clothes, on the way to her wedding.*)

SHEN TE. Something terrible has happened. As I left the shop with Yang Sun, I found the old carpet dealer's wife waiting in the street, trembling all over. She told me her husband had taken to his bed—sick with all the worry and excitement over the two hundred silver dollars they lent me. She said it would be best if I gave it back now. Of course, I had to say I would. She said she couldn't quite trust my cousin Shui Ta or even my fiancé Yang Sun. There were tears in her eyes. With my emotions in an uproar, I threw myself into Yang Sun's arms, I couldn't resist him. The things he'd said to Shui Ta had taught Shen Te nothing. Sinking into his arms, I said to myself:

To let no one perish, not even oneself
To fill everyone with happiness, even oneself
Is so good

How could I have forgotten those two old people? Yang Sun swept me away like a small hurricane. But he's not a bad man, and he loves me. He'd rather work in the cement factory than owe his flying to a crime. Though, of course, flying *is* a great passion with Sun. Now, on the way to my wedding, I waver between fear and joy.

SCENE 6

(*The "private dining room" on the upper floor of a cheap restaurant in a poor section of town. With Shen Te: the Grandfather, the Sister-in-Law, the Niece, Mrs. Shin, the Unemployed Man. In a corner, alone, a Priest. A Waiter pouring wine. Downstage, Yang Sun talking to his mother. He wears a dinner jacket.*)

YANG SUN. Bad news, Mamma. She came right out and told me she can't sell the shop for me. Some idiot is bringing a claim because he lent her the two hundred she gave you.

MRS. YANG. What did *you* say? Of course, you can't marry her now.

YANG SUN. It's no use saying anything to *her*. I've sent for her cousin, Mr. Shui Ta. He said there was nothing in writing.

MRS. YANG. Good idea. I'll go out and look for him. Keep an eye on things.

(*Exit Mrs. Yang. Shen Te has been pouring wine.*)

SHEN TE (*to the audience, pitcher in hand*). I wasn't mistaken in him. He's bearing up well. Though it must have been an awful blow—giving up flying. I do love him so. (*Calling across the room to him.*) Sun, you haven't drunk a toast with the bride!

YANG SUN. What do we drink to?

SHEN TE. Why, to the future!

YANG SUN. When the bridegroom's dinner jacket won't be a hired one!

SHEN TE. But when the bride's dress will still get rained on sometimes!

YANG SUN. To everything we ever wished for!

SHEN TE. May all our dreams come true!

(*They drink.*)

YANG SUN (*with loud conviviality*). And now, friends, before the wedding gets under way, I have to ask the bride a few questions. I've no idea what kind of a wife she'll make, and it worries me. (*Wheeling on Shen Te.*) For example. Can you make five cups of tea with three tea leaves?

SHEN TE. No.

YANG SUN. So I won't be getting very much tea. Can you sleep on a straw mattress the size of that book? (*He points to the large volume the Priest is reading.*)

SHEN TE. The two of us?

YANG SUN. The one of you.

SHEN TE. In that case, no.

YANG SUN. What a wife! I'm shocked!

(*While the audience is laughing, his mother returns. With a shrug of her shoulders, she tells Yang Sun the expected guest hasn't arrived. The Priest shuts the book with a bang, and makes for the door.*)

MRS. YANG. Where are *you* off to? It's only a matter of minutes.

PRIEST (*watch in hand*). Time goes on, Mrs. Yang, and I've another wedding to attend to. Also a funeral.

MRS. YANG (*irately*). D'you think we planned it this way? I was hoping to manage with one pitcher of wine, and we've run through two already. (*Points to empty pitcher. Loudly.*) My dear Shen Te, I don't know where your cousin can be keeping himself!

SHEN TE. My cousin?

MRS. YANG. Certainly. I'm old fashioned enough to think such a close relative should attend the wedding.

SHEN TE. Oh, Sun, is it the three hundred silver dollars?

YANG SUN (*not looking her in the eye*). Are you deaf? Mother says she's old fashioned. And I say I'm considerate. We'll wait another fifteen minutes.

HUSBAND. Another fifteen minutes.

MRS. YANG (*addressing the company*). Now you all know, don't you, that my son is getting a job as a mail pilot?

SISTER-IN-LAW. In Peking, too, isn't it?

MRS. YANG. In Peking, too! The two of us are moving to Peking!

SHEN TE. Sun, tell your mother Peking is out of the question now.

YANG SUN. Your cousin'll tell her. If he agrees. I don't agree.

SHEN TE (*amazed, and dismayed*). Sun!

YANG SUN. I hate this godforsaken Setzuan. What people! Know what they look like when I half close my eyes? Horses! Whinnying, fretting, stamping, screwing their necks up! (*Loudly.*) And what is it the thunder says? They are su-per-flu-ous! (*He hammers out the syllables.*) They've run their last race! They can go trample themselves to death! (*Pause.*) I've got to get out of here.

SHEN TE. But I've promised the money to the old couple.

YANG SUN. And since you always do the wrong thing, it's lucky your cousin's coming. Have another drink.

SHEN TE (*quietly*). My cousin can't be coming.

YANG SUN. How d'you mean?

SHEN TE. My cousin can't be where I am.

YANG SUN. Quite a conundrum!

SHEN TE (*desperately*). Sun, I'm the one that loves you. Not my cousin. He was thinking of the job in Peking when he promised you the old couple's money—

YANG SUN. Right. And that's why he's bringing the three hundred silver dollars. Here—to my wedding.

SHEN TE. He is not bringing the three hundred silver dollars.

YANG SUN. Huh? What makes you think that?

SHEN TE (*looking into his eyes*). He says you only bought one ticket to Peking.

(*Short pause.*)

YANG SUN. That was yesterday. (*He pulls two tickets part way out of his inside pocket, making her look under his coat.*) Two tickets. I don't want Mother to know. She'll get left behind. I sold her furniture to buy these tickets, so you see . . .

SHEN TE. But what's to become of the old couple?

YANG SUN. What's to become of me? Have another drink. Or do you believe in moderation? If I drink, I fly again. And if you drink, you may learn to understand me.

SHEN TE. You want to fly. But I can't help you.

YANG SUN. "Here's a plane, my darling—but it's only got one wing!"

(*The Waiter enters.*)

WAITER. Mrs. Yang! Mrs. Yang!

MRS. YANG. Yes?

WAITER. Another pitcher of wine, ma'am?

MRS. YANG. We have enough, thanks. Drinking makes me sweat.

WAITER. Would you mind paying, ma'am?

MRS. YANG (*to everyone*). Just be patient a few moments longer, everyone, Mr. Shui Ta is on his way over! (*To the Waiter.*) Don't be a spoilsport.

WAITER. I can't let you leave till you've paid your bill, ma'am.

MRS. YANG. But they know me here!

WAITER. That's just it.

PRIEST (*ponderously getting up*). I humbly take my leave. (*And he does.*)

MRS. YANG (*to the others, desperately*). Stay where you are, everybody! The priest says he'll be back in two minutes!

YANG SUN. It's no good, Mamma. Ladies and gentlemen, Mr. Shui Ta still hasn't arrived and the priest has gone home. We won't detain you any longer.

(*They are leaving now.*)

GRANDFATHER (*in the doorway, having forgotten to put his glass down*). To the bride! (*He drinks, puts down the glass, and follows the others.*)

(*Pause.*)

SHEN TE. Shall I go too?

YANG SUN. You? Aren't you the bride? Isn't this your wedding? (*He drags her across the room, tearing her wedding dress.*) If we can wait, you can wait. Mother calls me her falcon. She wants to see me in the clouds. But I think it may be St. Nevercome's Day before she'll go to the door and see my plane thunder by. (*Pause. He pretends the guests are still present.*) Why such a lull in the conversation, ladies and gentlemen? Don't you like it here? The

ceremony is only slightly postponed—because an important guest is expected at any moment. Also because the
bride doesn't know what love is. While we're waiting, the
bridegroom will sing a little song. (*He does so.*)

THE SONG OF ST. NEVERCOME'S DAY
> On a certain day, as is generally known,
>   One and all will be shouting: Hooray, hooray!
> For the beggar maid's son has a solid-gold throne
>   And the day is St. Nevercome's Day
> On St. Nevercome's, Nevercome's, Nevercome's Day
>   He'll sit on his solid-gold throne
>
> Oh, hooray, hooray! That day goodness will pay!
>   That day badness will cost you your head!
> And merit and money will smile and be funny
>   While exchanging salt and bread
> On St. Nevercome's, Nevercome's, Nevercome's Day
>   While exchanging salt and bread
>
> And the grass, oh, the grass will look down at the sky
>   And the pebbles will roll up the stream
> And all men will be good without batting an eye
>   They will make of our earth a dream
> On St. Nevercome's, Nevercome's, Nevercome's Day
>   They will make of our earth a dream
>
> And as for me, that's the day I shall be
>   A flyer and one of the best
> Unemployed man, you will have work to do
>   Washerwoman, you'll get your rest
> On St. Nevercome's, Nevercome's, Nevercome's Day
>   Washerwoman, you'll get your rest.

MRS. YANG. It looks like he's not coming.

(*The three of them sit looking at the door.*)

SCENE 6A

(*Wong's den. The sewer pipe is again transparent and
again the Gods appear to Wong in a dream.*)

WONG. I'm so glad you've come, illustrious ones. It's Shen
Te. She's in great trouble from following the rule about
loving thy neighbor. Perhaps she's *too* good for this
world!
FIRST GOD. Nonsense! You are eaten up by lice and doubts!
WONG. Forgive me, illustrious one, I only meant you might
deign to intervene.
FIRST GOD. Out of the question! My colleague here intervened in some squabble or other only yesterday. (*He
points to the Third God who has a black eye.*) The results
are before us!
WONG. She had to call on her cousin again. But not even he
could help. I'm afraid the shop is done for.
THIRD GOD (*a little concerned*). Perhaps we should help after
all?
FIRST GOD. The gods help those that help themselves.

WONG. What if we *can't* help ourselves, illustrious ones?

(*Slight pause.*)

SECOND GOD. Try, anyway! Suffering ennobles!
FIRST GOD. Our faith in Shen Te is unshaken!
THIRD GOD. We certainly haven't found any *other* good peo-
ple. You can see where we spend our nights from the
straw on our clothes.
WONG. You might help her find her way by—
FIRST GOD. The good man finds his own way here below!
SECOND GOD. The good woman too.
FIRST GOD. The heavier the burden, the greater her strength!
THIRD GOD. We're only onlookers, you know.
FIRST GOD. And everything will be all right in the end, O ye
of little faith!

(*They are gradually disappearing through these last lines.*)

SCENE 7

(*The yard behind Shen Te's shop. A few articles of furniture on a cart. Shen Te and Mrs. Shin are taking the
washing off the line.*)

MRS. SHIN. If you ask me, you should fight tooth and nail to
keep the shop.
SHEN TE. How can I? I have to sell the tobacco to pay back
the two hundred silver dollars today.
MRS. SHIN. No husband, no tobacco, no house and home!
What are you going to live on?
SHEN TE. I can work. I can sort tobacco.
MRS. SHIN. Hey, look, Mr. Shui Ta's trousers! He must have
left here stark naked!
SHEN TE. Oh, he may have another pair, Mrs. Shin.
MRS. SHIN. But if he's gone for good as you say, why has he
left his pants behind?
SHEN TE. Maybe he's thrown them away.
MRS. SHIN. Can I take them?
SHEN TE. Oh, no.

(*Enter Mr. Shu Fu, running.*)

SHU FU. Not a word! Total silence! I know all. You have sacrificed your own love and happiness so as not to hurt a dear
old couple who had put their trust in you! Not in vain
does this district—for all its malevolent tongues!—call
you the Angel of the Slums! That young man
couldn't rise to your level, so you left him. And now,
when I see you closing up the little shop, that veritable
haven of rest for the multitude, well, I cannot, I cannot
let it pass. Morning after morning I have stood watching
in the doorway not unmoved—while you graciously
handed out rice to the wretched. Is that never to happen
again? Is the good woman of Setzuan to disappear? If only
you would allow *me* to assist you! Now don't say anything!
No assurances, no exclamations of gratitude! (*He has
taken out his check book.*) Here! A blank check. (*He places

it on the cart.) Just my signature. Fill it out as you wish. Any sum in the world. I herewith retire from the scene, quietly, unobtrusively, making no claims, on tiptoe, full of veneration, absolutely selflessly . . . (*He has gone.*)

MRS. SHIN. Well! You're saved. There's always some idiot of a man . . . Now hurry! Put down a thousand silver dollars and let me fly to the bank before he comes to his senses.

SHEN TE. I can pay you for the washing without any check.

MRS. SHIN. What? You're not going to cash it just because you might have to marry him? Are you crazy? Men like him *want* to be led by the nose! Are you still thinking of that flyer? All Yellow Street knows how he treated you!

SHEN TE.

When I heard his cunning laugh, I was afraid
But when I saw the holes in his shoes, I loved him
   dearly.

MRS. SHIN. Defending that good for nothing after all that's happened!

SHEN TE (*staggering as she holds some of the washing*). Oh!

MRS. SHIN (*taking the washing from her, dryly*). So you feel dizzy when you stretch and bend? There couldn't be a little visitor on the way? If that's it, you can forget Mr. Shu Fu's blank check: it wasn't meant for a christening present!

(*She goes to the back with a basket. Shen Te's eyes follow Mrs. Shin for a moment. Then she looks down at her own body, feels her stomach, and a great joy comes into her eyes.*)

SHEN TE. O joy! A new human being is on the way. The world awaits him. In the cities the people say: he's got to be reckoned with, this new human being! (*She imagines a little boy to be present, and introduces him to the audience.*)

This is my son, the well-known flyer!
Say: Welcome
To the conqueror of unknown mountains and
   unreachable regions
Who brings us our mail across the impassable deserts!

(*She leads him up and down by the hand.*) Take a look at the world, my son. That's a tree. Tree, yes. Say: "Hello, tree!" And bow. Like this. (*She bows.*) Now you know each other. And, look, here comes the Water Seller. He's a friend, give him your hand. A cup of fresh water for my little son, please. Yes, it *is* a warm day. (*Handing the cup.*) Oh dear, a policeman, we'll have to make a circle round *him.* Perhaps we can pick a few cherries over there in the rich Mr. Pung's garden. But we mustn't be seen. You want cherries? Just like children with fathers. No, no, you can't go straight at them like that. Don't pull. We must learn to be reasonable. Well, have it your own way. (*She has let him make for the cherries.*) Can you reach? Where to put them? Your mouth is the best place. (*She tries one herself.*) Mmm, they're good. But the policeman, we must run! (*They run.*) Yes, back to the street. Calm now, so no one will notice us. (*Walking the street with her child, she sings.*)

Once a plum—'twas in Japan—

Made a conquest of a man
But the man's turn soon did come
For he gobbled up the plum

(*Enter Wong, with a Child by the hand. He coughs.*)

SHEN TE. Wong!

WONG. It's about the Carpenter, Shen Te. He's lost his shop, and he's been drinking. His children are on the streets. This is one. Can you help?

SHEN TE (*to the child*). Come here, little man. (*Takes him down to the footlights. To the audience.*)

You there! A man is asking you for shelter!
A man of tomorrow says: what about today?
His friend the conqueror, whom you know,
Is his advocate!

(*To Wong.*) He can live in Mr. Shu Fu's cabins. I may have to go there myself. I'm going to have a baby. That's a secret—don't tell Yang Sun—we'd only be in his way. Can you find the Carpenter for me?

WONG. I knew you'd think of something. (*To the Child.*) Goodbye, son, I'm going for your father.

SHEN TE. What about your hand, Wong? I wanted to help, but my cousin . . .

WONG. Oh, I can get along with one hand, don't worry. (*He shows how he can handle his pole with his left hand alone.*)

SHEN TE. But your right hand! Look, take this cart, sell everything that's on it, and go to the doctor with the money . . .

WONG. She's still good. But first I'll bring the Carpenter. I'll pick up the cart when I get back. (*Exit Wong.*)

SHEN TE (*to the Child*). Sit down over here, son, till your father comes.

(*The Child sits crosslegged on the ground. Enter the Husband and Wife, each dragging a large, full sack.*)

WIFE (*furtively*). You're alone, Shen Te, dear?

(*Shen Te nods. The Wife beckons to the Nephew offstage. He comes on with another sack.*)

Your cousin's away?

(*Shen Te nods.*)

He's not coming back?

SHEN TE. No. I'm giving up the shop.

WIFE. That's why we're here. We want to know if we can leave these things in your new home. Will you do us this favor?

SHEN TE. Why, yes, I'd be glad to.

HUSBAND (*cryptically*). And if anyone asks about them, say they're yours.

SHEN TE. Would anyone ask?

WIFE (*with a glance back at her Husband*). Oh, someone might. The police, for instance. They don't seem to like us. Where can we put it?

SHEN TE. Well, I'd rather not get in any more trouble . . .

WIFE. Listen to her! The good woman of Setzuan!

(*Shen Te is silent.*)

HUSBAND. There's enough tobacco in those sacks to give us a new start in life. We could have our own tobacco factory!

SHEN TE (*slowly*). You'll have to put them in the back room.

(*The sacks are taken offstage, where the Child is left alone. Shyly glancing about him, he goes to the garbage can, starts playing with the contents, and eating some of the scraps. The others return.*)

WIFE. We're counting on you, Shen Te!

SHEN TE. Yes. (*She sees the Child and is shocked.*)

HUSBAND. We'll see you in Mr. Shu Fu's cabins.

NEPHEW. The day after tomorrow.

SHEN TE. Yes. Now, go. Go! I'm not feeling well.

(*Exeunt all three, virtually pushed off.*)

He is eating the refuse in the garbage can!
Only look at his little grey mouth!

(*Pause. Music.*)

As this is the world my son will enter
I will study to defend him.
To be good to you, my son,
I shall be a tigress to all others
If I have to.
And I shall have to.

(*She starts to go.*) One more time, then. I hope really the last.

(*Exit Shen Te, taking Shui Ta's trousers. Mrs. Shin enters and watches her with marked interest. Enter the Sister-in-Law and the Grandfather.*)

SISTER-IN-LAW. So it's true, the shop has closed down. And the furniture's in the back yard. It's the end of the road!

MRS. SHIN (*pompously*). The fruit of high living, selfishness, and sensuality! Down the primrose path to Mr. Shu Fu's cabins—with you!

SISTER-IN-LAW. Cabins? Rat holes! He gave them to us because his soap supplies only went mouldy there!

(*Enter the Unemployed Man.*)

UNEMPLOYED MAN. Shen Te is moving?

SISTER-IN-LAW. Yes. She was sneaking away.

MRS. SHIN. She's ashamed of herself, and no wonder!

UNEMPLOYED MAN. Tell her to call Mr. Shui Ta or she's done for this time!

SISTER-IN-LAW. Tell her to call Mr. Shui Ta or we're done for this time!

(*Enter Wong and Carpenter, the latter with a Child on each hand.*)

CARPENTER. So we'll have a roof over our heads for a change!

MRS. SHIN. Roof? Whose roof?

CARPENTER. Mr. Shu Fu's cabins. And we have little Feng to thank for it. (*Feng, we find, is the name of the child already there; his Father now takes him. To the other two.*) Bow to your little brother, you two! (*The Carpenter and the two new arrivals bow to Feng.*)

(*Enter Shui Ta.*)

UNEMPLOYED MAN. Sst! Mr. Shui Ta!

(*Pause.*)

SHUI TA. And what is this crowd here for, may I ask?

WONG. How do you do, Mr. Shui Ta? This is the Carpenter. Miss Shen Te promised him space in Mr. Shu Fu's cabins.

SHUI TA. That will not be possible.

CARPENTER. We can't go there after all?

SHUI TA. All the space is needed for other purposes.

SISTER-IN-LAW. You mean we have to get out? But we've got nowhere to go.

SHUI TA. Miss Shen Te finds it possible to provide employment. If the proposition interests you, you may stay in the cabins.

SISTER-IN-LAW (*with distaste*). You mean work? Work for Miss Shen Te?

SHUI TA. Making tobacco, yes. There are three bales here already. Would you like to get them?

SISTER-IN-LAW (*trying to bluster*). We have our own tobacco! We were in the tobacco business before you were born!

SHUI TA (*to the Carpenter and the Unemployed Man*). You don't have your own tobacco. What about you?

(*The Carpenter and the Unemployed Man get the point, and go for the sacks. Enter Mrs. Mi Tzu.*)

MRS. MI TZU. Mr. Shui Ta? I've brought you your three hundred silver dollars.

SHUI TA. I'll Sign your lease instead. I've decided not to sell.

MRS. MI TZU. What? You don't need the money for that flyer?

SHUI TA. No.

MRS. MI TZU. And you can pay six months' rent?

SHUI TA (*takes the barber's blank check from the cart and fills it out*). Here is a check for ten thousand silver dollars. On Mr. Shu Fu's account. Look! (*He shows her the signature on the check.*) Your six months' rent will be in your hands by seven this evening. And now, if you'll excuse me.

MRS. MI TZU. So it's Mr. Shu Fu now. The flyer has been given his walking papers. These modern girls! In my day they'd have said she was flighty. That poor, deserted Mr. Yang Sun!

(*Exit Mrs. Mi Tzu. The Carpenter and the Unemployed Man drag the three sacks back on the stage.*)

CARPENTER (*to Shui Ta*). I don't know why I'm doing this for you.

SHUI TA. Perhaps your children want to eat, Mr. Carpenter.

SISTER-IN-LAW (*catching sight of the sacks*). Was my brother-in-law here?

MRS. SHIN. Yes, he was.

SISTER-IN-LAW. I thought as much. I know those sacks! That's our tobacco!

SHUI TA. Really? I thought it came from my back room? Shall we consult the police on the point?

SISTER-IN-LAW (*defeated*). No.

SHUI TA. Perhaps you will show me the way to Mr. Shu Fu's cabins?

(*Shui Ta goes off, followed by the Carpenter and his two older children, the Sister-in-Law, the Grandfather, and the Unemployed Man. Each of the last three drags a sack. Enter Old Man and Old Woman.*)

MRS. SHIN. A pair of pants—missing from the clothes line one minute—and next minute on the honorable backside of Mr. Shui Ta!

OLD WOMAN. We thought Miss Shen Te was here.

MRS. SHIN (*preoccupied*). Well, she's not.

OLD MAN. There was something she was going to give us.

WONG. She was going to help me too. (*Looking at his hand.*) It'll be too late soon. But she'll be back. This cousin has never stayed long.

MRS. SHIN (*approaching a conclusion*). No, he hasn't, has he?

SCENE 7A

(*The sewer pipe: Wong asleep. In his dream, he tells the Gods his fears. The Gods seem tired from all their travels. They stop for a moment and look over their shoulders at the Water Seller.*)

WONG. Illustrious ones, I've been having a bad dream. Our beloved Shen Te was in great distress in the rushes down by the rivers—the spot where the bodies of suicides are washed up. She kept staggering and holding her head down as if she was carrying something and it was dragging her down into the mud. When I called out to her, she said she had to take your Book of Rules to the other side, and not get it wet, or the ink would all come off. You had talked to her about the virtues, you know, the time she gave you shelter in Setzuan.

THIRD GOD. Well, but what do you suggest, my dear Wong?

WONG. Maybe a little relaxation of the rules, Benevolent One, in view of the bad times.

THIRD GOD. As for instance?

WONG. Well, um, good-will, for instance, might do instead of love?

THIRD GOD. I'm afraid that would create new problems.

WONG. Or, instead of justice, good sportsmanship?

THIRD GOD. That would only mean more work.

WONG. Instead of honor, outward propriety?

THIRD GOD. Still more work! No, no! The rules will have to stand, my dear Wong!

(*Wearily shaking their heads, all three journey on.*)

SCENE 8

(*Shui Ta's tobacco factory in Shu Fu's cabins. Huddled together behind bars, several families, mostly women and children. Among these people the Sister-in-Law, the Grandfather, the Carpenter, and his three children. Enter Mrs. Yang followed by Yang Sun.*)

MRS. YANG (*to the audience*). There's something I just *have* to tell you: strength and wisdom are wonderful things. The strong and wise Mr. Shui Ta has transformed my son from a dissipated good-for-nothing into a model citizen. As you may have heard, Mr. Shui Ta opened a small tobacco factory near the cattle runs. It flourished. Three months ago—I shall never forget it—I asked for an appointment, and Mr. Shui Ta agreed to see us—me and my son. I can see him now as he came through the door to meet us . . .

(*Enter Shui Ta, from a door.*)

SHUI TA. What can I do for you, Mrs. Yang?

MRS. YANG. This morning the police came to the house. We find you've brought an action for breach of promise of marriage. In the name of Shen Te. You also claim that Sun came by two hundred silver dollars by improper means.

SHUI TA. That is correct.

MRS. YANG. Mr. Shui Ta, the money's all gone. When the Peking job didn't materialize, he ran through it all in three days. I know he's a good-for-nothing. He sold my furniture. He was moving to Peking without me. Miss Shen Te thought highly of him at one time.

SHUI TA. What do *you* say, Mr. Yang Sun?

YANG SUN. The money's gone.

SHUI TA (*to Mrs. Yang*). Mrs. Yang, in consideration of my cousin's incomprehensible weakness for your son, I am prepared to give him another chance. He can have a job—here. The two hundred silver dollars will be taken out of his wages.

YANG SUN. So it's the factory or jail?

SHUI TA. Take your choice.

YANG SUN. May I speak with Shen Te?

SHUI TA. You may not.

(*Pause.*)

YANG SUN (*sullenly*). Show me where to go.

MRS. YANG. Mr. Shui Ta, you are kindness itself: the gods will reward you! (*To Yang Sun.*) And honest work will make a man of you, my boy.

(*Yang Sun follows Shui Ta into the factory. Mrs. Yang comes down again to the footlights.*)

Actually, honest work didn't agree with him—at first. And he got no opportunity to distinguish himself till—in the third week—when the wages were being paid. . . .

(*Shui Ta has a bag of money. Standing next to his foreman—the former Unemployed Man—he counts out the wages. It is Yang Sun's turn.*)

UNEMPLOYED MAN (*reading*). Carpenter, six silver dollars. Yang Sun, six silver dollars.

YANG SUN (*quietly*). Excuse me, sir. I don't think it can be more than five. May I see? (*He takes the foreman's list.*) It says six working days. But that's a mistake, sir. I took a day off for court business. And I won't take what I haven't earned, however miserable the pay is!

UNEMPLOYED MAN. Yang Sun. Five silver dollars. (*To Shui Ta.*) A rare case, Mr. Shui Ta!

SHUI TA. How is it the book says six when it should say five?

UNEMPLOYED MAN. I must've made a mistake, Mr. Shui Ta. (*With a look at Yang Sun.*) It won't happen again.

SHUI TA (*taking Yang Sun aside*). You don't hold back, do you? You give your all to the firm. You're even honest. Do the foreman's mistakes always favor the workers?

YANG SUN. He does have . . . friends.

SHUI TA. Thank you. May I offer you any little recompense?

YANG SUN. Give me a trial period of one week, and I'll prove my intelligence is worth more to you than my strength.

MRS. YANG (*still down at the footlight*). Fighting words, fighting words! That evening, I said to Sun: "If you're a flyer, then fly, my falcon! Rise in the world!" And he got to be foreman. Yes, in Mr. Shui Ta's tobacco factory, he worked real miracles.

(*We see Yang Sun with his legs apart standing behind the workers who are handing along a basket of raw tobacco above their heads.*)

YANG SUN. Faster! Faster! You there, d'you think you can just stand around now you're not foreman any more? It'll be your job to lead us in song. Sing!

(*Unemployed Man starts singing. The others join in the refrain.*)

SONG OF THE EIGHTH ELEPHANT

Chang had seven elephants—all much the same—
    But then there was Little Brother
The seven, they were wild, Little Brother, he was tame
    And to guard them Chang chose Little Brother
        Run faster!
        Mr. Chang has a forest park
        Which must be cleared before tonight
        And already it's growing dark!

When the seven elephants cleared that forest park
    Mr. Chang rode high on Little Brother
While the seven toiled and moiled till dark
    On his big behind sat Little Brother
        Dig faster!
        Mr. Chang has a forest park
        Which must be cleared before tonight
        And already it's growing dark!

And the seven elephants worked many an hour
    Till none of them could work another
Old Chang, he looked sour, on the seven, he did glower
    But gave a pound of rice to Little Brother
        What was that?
        Mr. Chang has a forest park
        Which must be cleared before tonight
        And already it's growing dark!

And the seven elephants hadn't any tusks
    The one that had the tusks was Little Brother!
Seven are no match for one, if the one has a gun!
    How old Chang did laugh at Little Brother!
        Keep on digging!
        Mr. Chang has a forest park
        Which must be cleared before tonight
        And already it's growing dark!

(*Smoking a cigar, Shui Ta strolls by. Yang Sun, laughing, has joined in the refrain of the third stanza and speeded up the tempo of the last stanza by clapping his hands.*)

MRS. YANG. And that's why I say: strength and wisdom are wonderful things. It took the strong and wise Mr. Shui Ta to bring out the best in Yang Sun. A real superior man is like a bell. If you ring it, it rings, and if you don't, it don't, as the saying is.

SCENE 9

(*Shen Te's shop, now an office with club chairs and fine carpets. It is raining. Shui Ta, now fat, is just dismissing the Old Man and Old Woman. Mrs. Shin, in obviously new clothes, looks on, smirking.*)

SHUI TA. No! I can NOT tell you when we expect her back.

OLD WOMAN. The two hundred silver dollars came today. In an envelope. There was no letter, but it must be from Shen Te. We want to write and thank her. May we have her address?

SHUI TA. I'm afraid I haven't got it.

OLD MAN (*pulling Old Woman's sleeve*). Let's be going.

OLD WOMAN. She's got to come back some time! (*They move off, uncertainly, worried. Shui Ta bows.*)

MRS. SHIN. They lost the carpet shop because they couldn't pay their taxes. The money arrived too late.

SHUI TA. They could have come to me.

MRS. SHIN. People don't like coming to you.

SHUI TA (*sits suddenly, one hand to his head*). I'm dizzy.

MRS. SHIN. After all, you *are* in your seventh month. But old Mrs. Shin will be there in your hour of trial! (*She cackles feebly.*)

SHUI TA (*in a stifled voice*). Can I count on that?

MRS. SHIN. We all have our price, and mine won't be too high for the great Mr. Shui Ta! (*She opens Shui Ta's collar.*)

SHUI TA. It's for the child's sake. All of this.

MRS. SHIN. "All for the child," of course.

SHUI TA. I'm so fat. People must notice.

MRS. SHIN. Oh no, they think it's 'cause you're rich.

SHUI TA (*more feelingly*). What will happen to the child?

MRS. SHIN. You ask that nine times a day. Why, it'll have the best that money can buy!

SHUI TA. He must never see Shui Ta.

MRS. SHIN. Oh, no. Always Shen Te.

SHUI TA. What about the neighbors? There are rumors, aren't there?

MRS. SHIN. As long as Mr. Shu Fu doesn't find out, there's nothing to worry about. Drink this.

(*Enter Yang Sun in a smart business suit, and carrying a businessman's brief case. Shui Ta is more or less in Mrs. Shin's arms.*)

YANG SUN (*surprised*). I seem to be in the way.

SHUI TA (*ignoring this, rises with an effort*). Till tomorrow, Mrs. Shin.

(*Mrs. Shin leaves with a smile, putting her new gloves on.*)

YANG SUN. Gloves now! She couldn't be fleecing you? And since when did *you* have a private life? (*Taking a paper from the brief case.*) You haven't been at your best lately, and things are getting out of hand. The police want to close us down. They say that at the most they can only permit twice the lawful number of workers.

SHUI TA (*evasively*). The cabins are quite good enough.

YANG SUN. For the workers maybe, not for the tobacco. They're too damp. We must take over some of Mrs. Mi Tzu's buildings.

SHUI TA. Her price is double what I can pay.

YANG SUN. Not unconditionally. If she has me to stroke her knees she'll come down.

SHUI TA. I'll never agree to that.

YANG SUN. What's wrong? Is it the rain? You get so irritable whenever it rains.

SHUI TA. Never! I will never . . .

YANG SUN. Mrs. Mi Tzu'll be here in five minutes. *You* fix it. And Shu Fu will be with her. . . . What's all that noise?

(*During the above dialogue, Wong is heard off stage calling: "The good Shen Te, where is she? Which of you has seen Shen Te, good people? Where is Shen Te?" A knock. Enter Wong.*)

WONG. Mr. Shui Ta, I've come to ask when Miss Shen Te will be back, it's six months now . . . There are rumors. People say something's happened to her.

SHUI TA. I'm busy. Come back next week.

WONG (*excited*). In the morning there was always rice on her doorstep—for the needy. It's been there again lately!

SHUI TA. And what do people conclude from this?

WONG. That Shen Te is still in Setzuan! She's been . . . (*He breaks off.*)

SHUI TA. She's been what? Mr. Wong, if you're Shen Te's friend, talk a little less about her, that's my advice to you.

WONG. I don't want your advice! Before she disappeared, Miss Shen Te told me something very important—she's pregnant!

YANG SUN. What? What was that?

SHUI TA (*quickly*). The man is lying.

WONG. A good woman isn't so easily forgotten. Mr. Shui Ta.

(*He leaves. Shui Ta goes quickly into the back room.*)

YANG SUN (*to the audience*). Shen Te pregnant? So that's why. Her cousin sent her away, so I wouldn't get wind of it. I have a son, a Yang appears on the scene, and what happens? Mother and child vanish into thin air! That scoundrel, that unspeakable . . . (*The sound of sobbing is heard from the back room.*) What was that? Someone sobbing? Who was it? Mr. Shui Ta the Tobacco King doesn't weep his heart out. And where does the rice come from that's on the doorstep in the morning?

(*Shui Ta returns. He goes to the door and looks out into the rain.*)

Where is she?

SHUI TA. Sh! It's nine o'clock. But the rain's so heavy, you can't hear a thing.

YANG SUN. What do you want to hear?

SHUI TA. The mail plane.

YANG SUN. What?

SHUI TA. I've been told *you* wanted to fly at one time. Is that all forgotten?

YANG SUN. Flying mail is night work. I prefer the daytime. And the firm is very dear to me—after all it belongs to my ex-fiancée, even if she's not around. And she's not, is she?

SHUI TA. What do you mean by that?

YANG SUN. Oh, well, let's say I haven't altogether—lost interest.

SHUI TA. My cousin might like to know that.

YANG SUN. I might not be indifferent—if I found she was being kept under lock and key.

SHUI TA. By whom?

YANG SUN. By you.

SHUI TA. What could you do about it?

YANG SUN. I could submit for discussion—my position in the firm.

SHUI TA. You are now my Manager. In return for a more appropriate position, you might agree to drop the enquiry into your ex-fiancée's whereabouts?

YANG SUN. I might.

SHUI TA. What position *would* be more appropriate?

YANG SUN. The one at the top.

SHUI TA. My own? (*Silence.*) And if I preferred to throw you out on your neck?

YANG SUN. I'd come back on my feet. With suitable escort.

SHUI TA. The police?

YANG SUN. The police.

SHUI TA. And when the police found no one?

YANG SUN. I might ask them not to overlook the back room. (*Ending the pretense.*) In short, Mr. Shui Ta, my interest in this young woman has not been officially terminated. I should like to see more of her. (*Into Shui Ta's face.*) Besides, she's pregnant and needs a friend. (*He moves to the door.*) I shall talk about it with the Water Seller. (*Exit.*)

(*Shui Ta is rigid for a moment, then he quickly goes into the back room. He returns with Shen Te's belongings: underwear, etc. He takes a long look at the shawl of the previous scene. He then wraps the things in a bundle which, upon hearing a noise, he hides under the table. Enter Mrs. Mi Tzu and Mr. Shu Fu. They put away their umbrellas and galoshes.*)

MRS. MI TZU. I thought your manager was here, Mr. Shui Ta. He combines charm with business in a way that can only be to the advantage of all of us.

SHU FU. You sent for us, Mr. Shui Ta?

SHUI TA. The factory is in trouble.

SHU FU. It always is.

SHUI TA. The police are threatening to close us down unless I can show that the extension of our facilities is imminent.

SHU FU. Mr. Shui Ta, I'm sick and tired of your constantly expanding projects. I place cabins at your cousin's disposal; you make a factory of them. I hand your cousin a check; you present it. Your cousin disappears and you find the cabins too small and talk of yet more . . .

SHUI TA. Mr. Shu Fu, I'm authorized to inform you that Miss Shen Te's return is now imminent.

SHU FU. Imminent? It's becoming his favorite word.

MRS. MI TZU. Yes, what does it mean?

SHUI TA. Mrs. Mi Tzu, I can pay you exactly half what you asked for your buildings. Are you ready to inform the police that I am taking them over?

MRS. MI TZU. Certainly, if I can take over your manager.

SHU FU. What?

MRS. MI TZU. He's so efficient.

SHUI TA. I'm afraid I need Mr. Yang Sun.

MRS. MI TZU. So do I.

SHUI TA. He will call on you tomorrow

SHU FU. So much the better. With Shen Te likely to turn up at any moment, the presence of that young man is hardly in good taste.

SHUI TA. So we have reached a settlement. In what was once the good Shen Te's little shop we are laying the foundations for the great Mr. Shui Ta's twelve magnificent super tobacco markets. You will bear in mind that though they call me the Tobacco King of Setzuan, it is my cousin's interests that have been served . . .

VOICES (*off*). The police, the police! Going to the tobacco shop! Something must have happened! (*et cetera.*)

(*Enter Yang Sun, Wong, and the Policeman.*)

POLICEMAN. Quiet there, quiet, quiet! (*They quiet down.*) I'm sorry, Mr. Shui Ta, but there's a report that you've been depriving Miss Shen Te of her freedom. Not that I believe all I hear, but the whole city's in an uproar.

SHUI TA. That's a lie.

POLICEMAN. Mr. Yang Sun has testified that he heard someone sobbing in the back room.

SHU FU. Mrs. Mi Tzu and myself will testify that no one here has been sobbing.

MRS. MI TZU. We have been quietly smoking our cigars.

POLICEMAN. Mr. Shui Ta, I'm afraid I shall have to take a look at that room. (*He does so. The room is empty.*) No one there, of course, sir.

YANG SUN. But I hear sobbing. What's that? (*He finds the clothes.*)

WONG. Those are Shen Te's things. (*To crowd.*) Shen Te's clothes are here!

VOICES (*Off. In sequence*). Shen Te's clothes! They've been found under the table! Body of murdered girl still missing! Tobacco King suspected!

POLICEMAN. Mr. Shui Ta, unless you can tell us where the girl is, I'll have to ask you to come along.

SHUI TA. I do not know.

POLICEMAN. I can't say how sorry I am, Mr. Shui Ta. (*He shows him the door.*)

SHUI TA. Everything will be cleared up in no time. There are still judges in Setzuan.

YANG SUN. I heard sobbing!

SCENE 9A

(*Wong's den. For the last time, the Gods appear to the Water Seller in his dream. They have changed and show signs of a long journey, extreme fatigue, and plenty of mishaps. The First no longer has a hat; the Third has lost a leg; all Three are barefoot.*)

WONG. Illustrious ones, at last you're here. Shen Te's been gone for months and today her cousin's been arrested. They think he murdered her to get the shop. But I had a dream and in this dream Shen Te said her cousin was keeping her prisoner. You must find her for us, illustrious ones!

FIRST GOD. We've found very few good people anywhere, and even they didn't keep it up. Shen Te is still the only one that stayed good.

SECOND GOD. If she *has* stayed good.

WONG. Certainly she has. But she's vanished.

FIRST GOD. That's the last straw. All is lost!

SECOND GOD. A little moderation, dear colleague!

FIRST GOD (*plaintively*). What's the good of moderation now? If she can't be found, we'll have to resign! The world is a terrible place! Nothing but misery, vulgarity, and waste! Even the countryside isn't what it used to be. The trees are getting their heads chopped off by telephone wires, and there's such a noise from all the gunfire, and I can't stand those heavy clouds of smoke, and—

THIRD GOD. The place is absolutely unlivable! Good intentions bring people to the brink of the abyss, and good deeds push them over the edge. I'm afraid our book of rules is destined for the scrap heap—

SECOND GOD. It's people! They're a worthless lot!

THIRD GOD. The world is too cold!

SECOND GOD. It's people! They are too weak!

FIRST GOD. Dignity, dear colleagues, dignity! Never despair! As for this world, didn't we agree that we only have to find one human being who can stand the place? Well, we found her. True, we lost her again. We must find her again, that's all! And at once!

(*They disappear.*)

SCENE 10

(*Courtroom. Groups: Shu Fu and Mrs. Mi Tzu; Yang Sun and Mrs. Yang; Wong, the Carpenter, the Grandfather, the Niece, the Old Man, the Old Woman; Mrs. Shin, the Policeman; the Unemployed Man, the Sister-in-Law.*)

OLD MAN. So much power isn't good for one man.

UNEMPLOYED MAN. And he's going to open twelve super tobacco markets!

WIFE. One of the judges is a friend of Mr. Shu Fu's.

SISTER-IN-LAW. Another one accepted a present from Mr. Shui Ta only last night. A great fat goose.

OLD WOMAN (*to Wong*). And Shen Te is nowhere to be found.

WONG. Only the gods will ever know the truth.

POLICEMAN. Order in the court! My lords the judges!

(*Enter the Three Gods in judges' robes. We overhear their conversation as they pass along the footlights to their bench.*)

THIRD GOD. We'll never get away with it, our certificates were so badly forged.

SECOND GOD. My predecessor's "sudden indigestion" will certainly cause comment.

FIRST GOD. But he *had* just eaten a whole goose.

UNEMPLOYED MAN. Look at that! *New* judges!

WONG. New judges. And what good ones!

(*The Third God hears this, and turns to smile at Wong. The Gods sit. The First God beats on the bench with his gavel. The Policeman brings in Shui Ta who walks with lordly steps. He is whistled at.*)

POLICEMAN (*to Shui Ta*). Be prepared for a surprise. The judges have been changed.

(*Shui Ta turns quickly round, looks at them, and staggers.*)

NIECE. What's the matter now?

WIFE. The great Tobacco King nearly fainted.

HUSBAND. Yes, as soon as he saw the new judges.

WONG. Does *he* know who they are?

(*Shui Ta picks himself up, and the proceedings open.*)

FIRST GOD. Defendant Shui Ta, you are accused of doing away with your cousin Shen Te in order to take possession of her business. Do you plead guilty or not guilty?

SHUI TA. Not guilty, my lord.

FIRST GOD (*thumbing through the documents of the case*). The first witness is the Policeman. I shall ask him to tell us something of the respective reputations of Miss Shen Te and Mr. Shui Ta.

POLICEMAN. Miss Shen Te was a young lady who aimed to please, my lord. She liked to live and let live, as the saying goes. Mr. Shui Ta, on the other hand, is a man of principle. Though the generosity of Miss Shen Te forced him at times to abandon half measures, unlike the girl, he was always on the side of the law, my lord. One time, he even unmasked a gang of thieves to whom his too trustful cousin had given shelter. The evidence, in short, my lord, proves that Mr. Shui Ta was *incapable* of the crime of which he stands accused!

FIRST GOD. I see. And are there others who could testify along, shall we say, the same lines?

(*Shu Fu rises.*)

POLICEMAN (*whispering to Gods*). Mr. Shu Fu—a very important person.

FIRST GOD (*inviting him to speak*). Mr. Shu Fu!

SHU FU. Mr. Shui Ta is a businessman, my lord. Need I say more?

FIRST GOD. Yes.

SHU FU. Very well, I will. He is Vice President of the Council of Commerce and is about to be elected a Justice of the Peace. (*He returns to his seat.*)

WONG. Elected! He gave him the job!

(*With a gesture the First God asks who Mrs. Mi Tzu is.*)

POLICEMAN. Another very important person. Mrs. Mi Tzu.

FIRST GOD (*inviting her to speak*). Mrs. Mi Tzu!

MRS. MI TZU. My lord, as Chairman of the Committee on Social Work, I wish to call attention to just a couple of eloquent facts: Mr. Shui Ta not only has erected a model factory with model housing in our city, he is a regular contributor to our home for the disabled. (*She returns to her seat.*)

POLICEMAN (*whispering*). And she's a great friend of the judge that ate the goose!

FIRST GOD (*to the* Policeman). Oh, thank you. What next? (*To the Court, genially.*) Oh, yes. We should find out if any of the evidence is less favorable to the Defendant.

(*Wong, the Carpenter, the Old Man, the Old Woman, the Unemployed Man, the Sister-in-Law, and the Niece come forward.*)

POLICEMAN (*whispering*). Just the riff raff, my lord.

FIRST GOD (*addressing the "riff raff"*). Well, um, riff raff—do you know anything of the Defendant, Mr. Shui Ta?

WONG. Too much, my lord.

UNEMPLOYED MAN. What don't we know, my lord?

CARPENTER. He ruined us.

SISTER-IN-LAW. He's a cheat.

NIECE. Liar.

WIFE. Thief.

BOY. Blackmailer.

BROTHER. Murderer.

FIRST GOD. Thank you. We should now let the Defendant state his point of view.

SHUI TA. I only came on the scene when Shen Te was in danger of losing what I had understood was a gift from the gods. Because I did the filthy jobs which someone had to do, they hate me. My activities were held down to the minimum, my lord.

SISTER-IN-LAW. He had us arrested!

SHUI TA. Certainly. You stole from the bakery!

SISTER-IN-LAW. Such concern for the bakery! You didn't want the shop for yourself, I suppose!

SHUI TA. I didn't want the shop overrun with parasites.

SISTER-IN-LAW. We had nowhere else to go.

SHUI TA. There were too many of you.

WONG. What about this old couple: Were *they* parasites?

OLD MAN. We lost our shop because of you!

SISTER-IN-LAW. And we gave your cousin money!

SHUI TA. My cousin's fiancé was a flyer. The money had to go to *him*.

WONG. Did you care whether he flew or not? Did you care whether she married him or not? You wanted her to marry someone else! (*He points at Shu Fu.*)

SHUI TA. The flyer unexpectedly turned out to be a scoundrel.

YANG SUN (*jumping up*). Which was the reason you made him your Manager?

SHUI TA. Late on he improved.

WONG. And when he improved, you sold him to her? (*He points out Mrs. Mi Tzu.*)

SHUI TA. She wouldn't let me have her premises unless she had him to stroke her knees!

MRS. MI TZU. What? The man's a pathological liar. (*To him.*) Don't mention my property to me as long as you live! Murderer! (*She rustles off, in high dudgeon.*)

YANG SUN (*pushing in*). My lord, I wish to speak for the Defendant.

SISTER-IN-LAW. Naturally. He's your employer.

UNEMPLOYED MAN. And the worst slave driver in the country.

MRS. YANG. That's a lie! My lord, Mr. Shui Ta is a great man. He . . .

YANG SUN. He's this and he's that, but he is not a murderer, my lord. Just fifteen minutes before his arrest I heard Shen Te's voice in his own back room.

FIRST GOD. Oh? Tell us more!

YANG SUN. I heard sobbing, my lord!

FIRST GOD. But lots of women sob, we've been finding.

YANG SUN. Could I fail to recognize her voice?

SHU FU. No, you made her sob so often yourself, young man!

YANG SUN. Yes. But I also made her happy. Till he (*pointing at Shui Ta*) decided to sell her to you!

SHUI TA. Because you didn't love her.

WONG. Oh, no: it was for the money, my lord!

SHUI TA. And what was the money for, my lord? For the poor! And for Shen Te so she could go on being good!

WONG. For the poor? That he sent to his sweatshops? And why didn't you let Shen Te be good when you signed the big check?

SHUI TA. For the child's sake, my lord.

CARPENTER. What about *my* children? What did he do about them?

(*Shui Ta is silent.*)

WONG. The shop was to be a fountain of goodness. That was the gods' idea. You came and spoiled it!

SHUI TA. If I hadn't, it would have run dry!

MRS. SHIN. There's a lot in that, my lord.

WONG. What have you done with the good Shen Te, bad man? She *was* good, my lords, she was, I swear it! (*He raises his hand in an oath.*)

THIRD GOD. What's happened to your hand, Water Seller?

WONG (*pointing to Shui Ta*). It's all his fault, my lord, *she* was going to send me to a doctor—(*To Shui Ta.*) You were her worst enemy!

SHUI TA. I was her only friend!

WONG. Where is she then? Tell us where your good friend is!

(*The excitement of this exchange has run through the whole crowd.*)

ALL. Yes, where is she? Where is Shen Te? (*et cetera.*)

SHUI TA. Shen Te had to go.

WONG. Where? Where to?

SHUI TA. I cannot tell you! I cannot tell you!

ALL. Why? Why did she have to go away? (*et cetera.*)

WONG (*into the din with the first words, but talking on beyond the others*). Why not, why not? Why did she have to go away?

SHUI TA (*shouting*). Because you'd all have torn her to shreds, that's why! My lords, I have a request. Clear the court! When only the judges remain, I will make a confession.

ALL (*except Wong, who is silent, struck by the new turn of events*). So he's guilty? He's confessing! (*et cetera.*)

FIRST GOD (*using the gavel*). Clear the court!

POLICEMAN. Clear the court!

WONG. Mr. Shui Ta has met his match this time.

MRS. SHIN (*with a gesture toward the judges*). You're in for a little surprise.

(*The court is cleared. Silence.*)

SHUI TA. Illustrious ones!

(*The Gods look at each other, not quite believing their ears.*)

SHUI TA. Yes, I recognize you!

SECOND GOD (*taking matters in hand, sternly*). What have you done with our good woman of Setzuan?

SHUI TA. I have a terrible confession to make: I am she! (*He takes off his mask, and tears away his clothes. Shen Te stands there.*)

SECOND GOD. Shen Te!

SHEN TE. Shen Te, yes. Shui Ta *and* Shen Te. Both.

> Your injunction
> To be good and yet to live
> Was a thunderbolt:
> It has torn me in two
> I can't tell how it was
> But to be good to others
> And myself at the same time
> I could not do it
> Your world is not an easy one, illustrious ones!
> When we extend our hand to a beggar, he tears it off
>   for us
> When we help the lost, we are lost ourselves.
> And so
> Since not to eat is to die
> Who can long refuse to be bad?
> As I lay prostrate beneath the weight of good
>   intentions
> Ruin stared me in the face
> It was when I was unjust that I ate good meat
> And hobnobbed with the mighty
> Why?
> Why are bad deeds rewarded?
> Good ones punished?
> I enjoyed giving
> I truly wished to be the Angel of the Slums
> But washed by a foster-mother in the water of the
>   gutter
> I developed a sharp eye
> The time came when pity was a thorn in my side
> And, later, when kind words turned to ashes in my
>   mouth
> And anger took over
> I became a wolf
> Find me guilty, then, illustrious ones,
> But know:
> All that I have done I did
> To help my neighbor
> To love my lover

> And to keep my little one from want
> For your great, godly deeds, I was too poor, too small.

(*Pause.*)

FIRST GOD (*shocked*). Don't go on making yourself miserable, Shen Te! We're overjoyed to have found you!

SHEN TE. I'm telling you I'm the bad man who committed all those crimes!

FIRST GOD (*using—or failing to use—his ear trumpet*). The good woman who did all those good deeds?

SHEN TE. Yes, but the bad man too!

FIRST GOD (*as if something had dawned*). Unfortunate coincidences! Heartless neighbors!

THIRD GOD (*shouting in his ear*). But how is she to continue?

FIRST GOD. Continue? Well, she's a strong, healthy girl . . .

SECOND GOD. You didn't hear what she said!

FIRST GOD. I heard every word! She is confused, that's all! (*He begins to bluster.*) And what about this book of rules—we can't renounce our rules, can we? (*More quietly.*) Should the world be changed? How? By whom? The world should *not* be changed! (*At a sign from him, the lights turn pink, and music plays.*)

> And now the hour of parting is at hand.
> Dost thou behold, Shen Te, yon fleecy cloud?
> It is our chariot. At a sign from me
> 'Twill come and take us back from whence we came
> Above the azure vault and silver stars . . .

SHEN TE. No! Don't go, illustrious ones!

FIRST GOD.

> Our cloud has landed now in yonder field
> From whence it will transport us back to heaven.
> Farewell, Shen Te, let not thy courage fail thee . . .

(*Exeunt Gods.*)

SHEN TE. What about the old couple? They've lost their shop! What about the Water Seller and his hand? And I've got to defend myself against the barber, because I don't love him! And against Sun, because I do love him! How? How?

(*Shen Te's eyes follow the Gods as they are imagined to step into a cloud which rises and moves forward over the orchestra and up beyond the balcony*)

FIRST GOD (*from on high*). We have faith in you, Shen Te!

SHEN TE. There'll be a child. And he'll have to be fed. I can't stay here. Where shall I go?

FIRST GOD. Continue to be good, good woman of Setzuan!

SHEN TE. I need my bad cousin!

FIRST GOD. But not very often!

SHEN TE. Once a week at least!

FIRST GOD. Once a month will be quite enough!

SHEN TE (*shrieking*). No, no! Help!

(*But the cloud continues to recede as the Gods sing.*)

VALEDICTORY HYMN

What rapture, oh, it is to know
  A good thing when you see it
And having seen a good thing, oh,
  What rapture 'tis to flee it

Be good, sweet maid of Setzuan
  Let Shui Ta be clever
Departing, we forget the man
  Remember your endeavor

Ò Because through all the length of days
  Her goodness faileth never
Sing hallelujah! May Shen Te's
  Good name live on forever!

SHEN TE. Help!

EPILOGUE

You're thinking, aren't you, that this is no right
Conclusion to the play you've seen tonight?
After a tale, exotic, fabulous,
A nasty ending was slipped up on us.
We feel deflated too. We too are nettled
To see the curtain down and nothing settled.
How could a better ending be arranged?
Could one change people? Can the world be changed?
Would new gods do the trick? Will atheism?
Moral rearmament? Materialism?
It is for you to find a way, my friends,
To help good men arrive at happy ends.
You write the happy ending to the play!
There must, there must, there's got to be a way!

TOPICS FOR CRITICAL THINKING AND WRITING

The Play on the PAGE

1. It has been said that Brecht's "characters are social types without a private psychological side." Do you agree? If so, do you think this is a shortcoming in his work? Explain.

2. In your opinion, why does Shen Te assume the mask of Shui Ta?

3. It has been said that drama is the art of preparation—meaning that speeches and scenes generate suspense that is interestingly fulfilled. How important would you say suspense is in *The Good Woman*?

4. Brecht was a didactic writer, unashamed of preaching. What would you say is his message in this play? How acceptable to you is the message? Why? Would you say that Brecht presents the message interestingly? Explain.

5. Originally Brecht set the play in the Berlin of the 1920s. What do you think is gained or lost by setting it in a rather mythical China?

6. What do the gods stand for? What do you think Brecht's attitude is toward them?

7. Is Shui Ta bad or merely realistic? Explain.

8. What, if anything, is Brecht saying about the causes of evil?

The Play on the STAGE

9. Imagine that you are directing a production of the play. Select a passage of some fifty to one hundred lines, such as the interlude that follows Scene 6, and indicate what instructions you would give about how to deliver the lines.

10. Select one of the songs, for instance "The Song of St. Nevercome's Day" in Scene 6, and explain what sort of music you would want it set to. Jazz? Rock? Country? What?

11. How would you costume the gods? Would they wear the same costumes throughout, or might they change costumes?

12. In some productions almost all of the lines are delivered in a sort of a chant. What do you think of this idea? Why?

The Play in PERFORMANCE

First, it must be mentioned that because Brecht kept tinkering with the play, it exists in several versions. The translations, too, differ not only because different translators inevitably translated speeches somewhat differently (for example, titles include *The Good Woman of Setzuan*, *The Good Person of Setzuan*, and *The Good Soul of Setzuan*) but also because they may draw on different manuscripts. Furthermore, Brecht sometimes told a translator to omit this speech or that for political reasons.

The play had its world premiere in Zurich in 1943; the American premiere was at Carleton College in Northfield, Minnesota, in the spring of 1948; and the first professional American production was at the Hedgerow Theatre, near Philadelphia, in the summer of 1948. It was not performed by the Berliner Ensemble (a company established in the Soviet section of Berlin to promote Brecht's works) until 1957, a year after Brecht's death.

Because of his leftist politics, the commercial theater has been leery of producing Brecht, but he has been popular on campuses, and *The Good Woman* is probably the Brecht play most often staged. Perhaps because Brecht himself did not hesitate to adapt plays freely, modern productions of Brecht often are very free. A 1984 production at Indiana University Theatre, for instance, dared to turn the gods into Jesus Christ look-alikes. A production in Santa Monica had the gods enter on roller skates. And Brecht left it up to the director to decide who should speak the Epilogue. It is usually spoken by the actress who plays Shen Te, or by the actor who plays Wong. In any case, in most productions whichever actor speaks it usually drops the role and appears as an actor rather than as a character in the play.

HAROLD Pinter

Harold Pinter (1930–) was born in London, the son of tailor. He attended the Royal Academy of Dramatic Art, and from 1949 until 1957 he acted in a touring repertory company throughout the British Isles. In 1957 he wrote his first play; later in the same year he wrote *The Dumb Waiter*—though it was not produced until 1960. Another play, *The Birthday Party*, was produced in 1958. He won critical acclaim finally with *The Caretaker* in 1960. Besides *The Homecoming* (1965), he has written radio and television scripts, and several films, most notably *The Servant* and *The Go-Between*. His as yet unproduced film adaptation of Marcel Proust's *Remembrance of Things Past* was published in 1977.

■■■■■■■■■■■■■■

COMMENTARY ON *THE DUMB WAITER*

I've never started a play from any kind of abstract idea or theory and never envisaged my own characters as messengers of death, doom, heaven or the milky way or, in other words, as allegorical representations of any particular force, whatever that may mean. When a character cannot be comfortably defined or understood in terms of the familiar, the tendency is to perch him on a symbolic shelf, out of harm's way. Once there, he can be talked about but not lived with.*

Probably most or even all of the dramatists represented in this book could say the same thing: It is impossible to believe that (for example) Shakespeare began *Hamlet* with "any kind of abstract idea"—in fact, he must have begun it with seeing the old (now lost) play *Hamlet*, and felt that he could do it much better, make the characters breathe and make the story move us. And probably every dramatist in this book would be distressed if, because we could not find a character familiar, we turned the character into a tidy symbol and talked about it but did not live with it in all its unfamiliarity.

Still, when we read or see a good play we inevitably feel that it has some meaning, that it adds up to something. That's what makes any work of art different from, say, a story in a newspaper. If we read on page 1 of *The Daily Record* that a gunman killed another, we don't bother to think of the meaning; the story is in the paper simply because it happened, not because the happening has any significance. But a work of art has

*Harold Pinter, "Writing for the Theatre," in *The New British Drama*, ed. Henry Popkin (New York: Grove, 1964), pp. 575–76.

not only the concrete immediacy of experience—the sort of thing that newspapers and history books are full of; it has something of the distillation or significance of experience that we find (usually in a highly abstract form) in philosophy.

The meaning of a good play, however, is not usually to be found in a philosophical or preachy speech; rather, it is diffused throughout the play, from the first line to the last, or, rather, from our first view of the stage to the last. In "The Language of Drama" (pages 6–15) we call attention to the meaning of Ibsen's set in *A Doll's House*, and to the meanings of the costumes and gestures, as well as of the dialogue and even of the sound of the door slamming at the end of the play. If we were similarly analyzing *The Dumb Waiter* we would, for example, call attention to the fact that near the end of the play, when he is probably about to be murdered by his partner Ben, Gus "is stripped of his jacket, waistcoat, tie, holster, and revolver." Here, as when Nora in *A Doll's House* takes off her fancy costume, or when O'Neill's Emperor Jones's splendid uniform becomes "ragged and torn," we see the stripping away of those accoutrements that conceal humanity's essential vulnerability.

We might consider, too, the characterization in the play (What sort of people are Gus and Ben? Why is it that we learn almost nothing of their background, nothing about why they do what they do?), or we might consider the setting (What is implied by "a basement room"?), but instead we shall briefly glance at the structure of the play. The germ of the play—two hit-men wait to do a job—probably owes something to Ernest Hemingway's short story "The Killers," in which two hired assassins engage in flat small talk while waiting for their victim; but it owes something also to gangster films and suspense films. The gangster film, however, usually has a plot, with what Aristotle calls a beginning, a middle, and an end: it begins with a situation that is fairly stable, fairly understandable (for instance, a young hood joins an organization of gangsters); the film proceeds to a middle—the consequences of the beginning and the causes of the end (the middle of the gangster film may show the youngster pushing his way to the top of the mob); and it concludes with the end, which is caused by the middle and which does not seem to lead to anything further (having rubbed out the apparent opposition, the new boss is now himself rubbed out by a younger contender or by the police, or—as in *The Godfather, Part II*—the central figure finds that his success has brought him nothing, for he cannot share it with his family). A suspense film, too, usually has an easily perceptible structure, for example, the scary hunt for the criminals, the forces of evil waiting behind closed doors for the good guy who pursues them, mysterious messages, and finally a resolution in which (usually) virtue is rewarded.

In *The Dumb Waiter* we get suspense and mystery (the sudden clatter of the previously unnoticed dumb waiter, the envelope with matches that is slipped under the door, the erratic flushing of the toilet, the whistling of the speaking-tube, and, of course, the mysterious orders from above), but we are not given the satisfaction of witnessing a story unfold episode by episode. Gus and Ben are waiting for their victim, and near the end of the play, when Gus goes to the toilet, Ben learns that the victim will be "coming in straight away." He levels his revolver at the door—and Gus walks in. The two stare at each other, there is "a long silence," and the play ends. Anton Chekhov, talking about the importance of foreshadowing and of inevitability in drama, said that if there is a gun on the wall in the first act, it must go off in the last act—but here no gun goes off.

Has Pinter, then, merely written an hour's worth of small talk with no shape to it? Not quite. First, although at the start of the drama we see two men waiting, we do not clearly understand until about the middle that they are hired murderers waiting for their victim. And it is not until the end of the play that we learn (as the two men themselves learn) who the victim is. Ben does not

kill Gus in the play, but it seems almost certain that he will kill Gus, for Ben has been consistently presented (in contrast to Gus) as a mindless hood who unthinkingly follows the orders given to him. Or, to put it a little differently, we come to understand that Gus, by the very doubts he has expressed throughout the play, is doomed to be eradicated (the toilet flushes, just before the end) by a system that brooks no questions. The play is not mere chitchat; it progresses, in the sense that *we* come to an understanding.

Second, and more obvious as a structural pattern, at the start of the play we hear Ben recount two newspaper stories of death—one of an eighty-seven-year-old man who was killed while crawling under a lorry (i.e., a truck), and the other of an eight-year-old girl who killed a cat. The first story, then, introduces the motif of the unpredictability of death (at the end of the play, Gus, who thinks he is the killer, finds that he is the victim); the second news story, too, introduces a note of surprise, but now the surprise is tinged with the mystery of the suspense story, for Gus doubts the accuracy of the newspaper report and he conjectures that in fact the girl's eleven-year-old brother was the real killer of the cat. Whether or not Gus is right, then, the seemingly trivial dialogue at the beginning of the play is preparation for the dialogue and the action at the end of the play. Or, rather, for the silence and the inaction. We are left wondering, just as at the start we wonder which child did in fact kill the cat.

At the end of the play, then, Pinter leaves us with an ambiguity, but the play has been ambiguous from the start. If we are annoyed by the uncertainty of the resolution of the plot, we may be even more annoyed by the uncertainty of the meaning, but this is perhaps because we mistakenly expect playwrights to be philosophers who answer our largest questions. Perhaps we should recall that in *King Lear* we get no answer to Lear's agonized question, asked over the body of his beloved daughter Cordelia, "Why should a dog, a horse, a rat, have life, / And thou no breath at all?" The question is unforgettable; the answer is not forthcoming. In *A Midsummer Night's Dream*, Lear's question is asked comically, when Pyramus laments the seeming death, at the jaws of a lion, of his beloved Thisby: "O wherefore, Nature, didst thou lions frame?" Not answers, but an experience of life, is what the best playwrights offer.

THE DUMB WAITER
Harold Pinter

CHARACTERS

BEN
GUS

SCENE

A basement room. Two beds, flat against the back wall. A serving hatch, closed, between the beds. A door to the kitchen and lavatory, left. A door to a passage, right.

Ben is lying on a bed, left, reading a paper. Gus is sitting on a bed, right, tying his shoe laces, with difficulty. Both are dressed in shirts, trousers and braces.

Silence.

Gus ties his laces, rises, yawns and begins to walk slowly to the door, left. He stops, looks down, and shakes his foot.

Ben lowers his paper and watches him. Gus kneels and unties his shoe-lace and slowly takes off the shoe. He looks inside it and brings out a flattened matchbox. He shakes it and examines it. Their eyes meet. Ben rattles his paper and reads. Gus puts the matchbox in his pocket and bends down to put on his shoe. He ties his lace, with difficulty. Ben lowers his paper and watches him. Gus walks to the door, left, stops, and shakes the other foot. He kneels, unties his shoelace, and slowly takes off the shoe. He looks inside it and brings out a flattened cigarette packet. He shakes it and examines it. Their eyes meet. Ben rattles his paper and reads. Gus puts the packet in his pocket, bends down, puts on his shoe and ties the lace.

He wanders off, left.

Ben slams the paper down on the bed and glares after him. He picks up the paper and lies on his back, reading.

Silence.

A lavatory chain is pulled twice off, but the lavatory does not flush.

Silence.

Gus re-enters, left, and halts at the door, scratching his head. Ben slams down the paper.

BEN. Kaw!

(*He picks up the paper.*)

What about this? Listen to this!

(*He refers to the paper.*)

A man of eighty-seven wanted to cross the road. But there was a lot of traffic, see? He couldn't see how he was going to squeeze through. So he crawled under a lorry.
GUS. He what?
BEN. He crawled under a lorry. A stationary lorry.
GUS. No?
BEN. The lorry started and ran over him.
GUS. Go on!
BEN. That's what it says here.
GUS. Get away.
BEN. It's enough to make you want to puke, isn't it?
GUS. Who advised him to do a thing like that?
BEN. A man of eighty-seven crawling under a lorry!
GUS. It's unbelievable.
BEN. It's down here in black and white.
GUS. Incredible.

(*Silence.*)

Gus shakes his head and exists. Ben lies back and reads. The lavatory chain is pulled once off left, but the lavatory does not flush.

Ben whistles at an item in the paper.

Gus re-enters.

I want to ask you something.
BEN. What are you doing out there?
GUS. Well, I was just—
BEN. What about the tea?
GUS. I'm just going to make it.
BEN. Well, go on, make it.
GUS. Yes, I will. (*He sits in a chair. Ruminatively*) He's laid on some very nice crockery this time. I'll say that. It's sort of striped. There's a white stripe.

(*Ben reads.*)

It's very nice. I'll say that.

(*Ben turns the page.*)

You know, sort of round the cup. Round the rim. All the rest of it's black, you see. Then the saucer's black, except for right in the middle, where the cup goes, where it's white.

(*Ben reads.*)

Then the plates are the same, you see. Only they've got a black stripe—the plates—right across the middle. Yes, I'm quite taken with the crockery.

BEN (*still reading*). What do you want plates for? You're not going to eat.

GUS. I've brought a few biscuits.

BEN. Well, you'd better eat them quick.

GUS. I always bring a few biscuits. Or a pie. You know I can't drink tea without anything to eat.

BEN. Well, make the tea then, will you? Time's getting on.

(*Gus brings out the flattened cigarette packet and examines it.*)

GUS. You got any cigarettes? I think I've run out.

(*He throws the packet high up and leans forward to catch it.*)

I hope it won't be a long job, this one.

(*Aiming carefully, he flips the packet under his bed.*)

Oh, I wanted to ask you something.

BEN (*slamming his paper down*). Kaw!

GUS. What's that?

BEN. A child of eight killed a cat!

GUS. Get away.

BEN. It's a fact. What about that, eh? A child of eight killing a cat!

GUS. How did he do it?

BEN. It was a girl.

GUS. How did she do it?

BEN. She—

(*He picks up the paper and studies it.*)

It doesn't say.

GUS. Why not?

BEN. Wait a minute. It just says—Her brother, aged eleven, viewed the incident from the toolshed.

GUS. Go on!

BEN. That's bloody ridiculous.

(*Pause.*)

GUS. I bet he did it.

BEN. Who?

GUS. The brother.

BEN. I think you're right.

(*Pause.*)

(*Slamming down the paper*) What about that, eh? A kid of eleven killing a cat and blaming it on his little sister of eight! It's enough to—

(*He breaks off in disgust and seizes the paper. Gus rises.*)

GUS. What time is he getting in touch?

(*Ben reads.*)

What time is he getting in touch?

BEN. What's the matter with you? It could be any time. Any time.

GUS (*moves to the foot of Ben's bed*). Well, I was going to ask you something.

BEN. What?

GUS. Have you noticed the time that tank takes to fill?

BEN. What tank?

GUS. In the lavatory.

BEN. No. Does it?

GUS. Terrible.

BEN. Well, what about it?

GUS. What do you think's the matter with it?

BEN. Nothing.

GUS. Nothing?

BEN. It's got a deficient ballcock, that's all.

GUS. A deficient what?

BEN. Ballcock.

GUS. No? Really?

BEN. That's what I should say.

GUS. Go on! That didn't occur to me.

(*Gus wanders to his bed and presses the mattress.*)

I didn't have a very restful sleep today, did you? It's not much of a bed. I could have done with another blanket, too. (*He catches sight of a picture on the wall.*) Hello, what's this? (*Peering at it*) "The First Eleven." Cricketers. You seen this, Ben?

BEN (*reading*). What?

GUS. The first eleven.

BEN. What?

GUS. There's a photo here of the first eleven.

BEN. What first eleven?

GUS (*studying the photo*). It doesn't say.

BEN. What about that tea?

GUS. They all look a bit old to me.

(*Gus wanders downstage, looks out front, then all about the room.*)

I wouldn't like to live in this dump. I wouldn't mind if you had a window, you could see what it looked like outside.

BEN. What do you want a window for?

GUS. Well, I like to have a bit of a view, Ben. It whiles away the time.

(*He walks around the room.*)

I mean, you come into a place when it's still dark, you come into a room you've never seen before, you sleep all day, you do your job, and then you go away in the night again.

(*Pause.*)

I like to get a look at the scenery. You never get the chance in this job.

BEN. You get your holidays, don't you?

GUS. Only a fortnight.

BEN (*lowering the paper*). You kill me. Anyone would think you're working every day. How often do we do a job? Once a week? What are you complaining about?

GUS. Yes, but we've got to be on tap though, haven't we? You can't move out of the house in case a call comes.

BEN. You know what your trouble is?

GUS. What?

BEN. You haven't got any interests.

GUS. I've got interests.

BEN. What? Tell me one of your interests.

(*Pause.*)

GUS. I've got interests.

BEN. Look at me. What have I got?

GUS. I don't know. What?

BEN. I've got my woodwork. I've got my model boats. Have you ever seen me idle? I'm never idle. I know how to occupy my time, to its best advantage. Then when a call comes, I'm ready.

GUS. Don't you ever get a bit fed up?

BEN. Fed up? What with?

(*Silence.*

Ben reads. Gus feels in the pocket of his jacket, which hangs on the bed.*)

GUS. You got any cigarettes? I've run out.

(*The lavatory flushes off left.*)

There she goes.

(*Gus sits on the bed.*)

No, I mean, I say the crockery's good. It is. It's very nice. But that's about all I can say for this place. It's worse than the last one. Remember that last place we were in? Last time, where was it? At least there was a wireless there. No, honest. He doesn't seem to bother much about our comfort these days.

BEN. When are you going to stop jabbering?

GUS. You'd get rheumatism in a place like this, if you stay long.

BEN. We're not staying long. Make the tea, will you? We'll be on the job in a minute.

(*Gus picks up a small bag by his bed and brings out a packet of tea. He examines it and looks up.*)

GUS. Eh, I've been meaning to ask you.

BEN. What the hell is it now?

GUS. Why did you stop the car this morning, in the middle of that road?

BEN (*lowering the paper*). I thought you were asleep.

GUS. I was, but I woke up when you stopped. You did stop, didn't you?

(*Pause.*)

In the middle of that road. It was still dark, don't you remember? I looked out. It was all misty. I thought perhaps you wanted to kip, but you were sitting up dead straight, like you were waiting for something.

BEN. I wasn't waiting for anything.

GUS. I must have fallen asleep again. What was all that about then? Why did you stop?

BEN (*picking up the paper*). We were too early.

GUS. Early? (*He rises.*) What do you mean? We got the call, didn't we, saying we were to start right away. We did. We shoved out on the dot. So how could we be too early?

BEN (*quietly*). Who took the call, me or you?

GUS. You.

BEN. We were too early.

GUS. Too early for what?

(*Pause.*)

You mean someone had to get out before we got in?

(*He examines the bedclothes.*)

I thought these sheets didn't look too bright. I thought they ponged a bit. I was too tired to notice when I got in this morning. Eh, that's taking a bit of a liberty, isn't it? I don't want to share my bedsheets. I told you things were going down the drain. I mean, we've always had clean sheets laid on up till now. I've noticed it.

BEN. How do you know those sheets weren't clean?

GUS. What do you mean?

BEN. How do you know they weren't clean? You've spent the whole day in them, haven't you?

GUS. What, you mean it might be my pong? (*He sniffs sheets.*) Yes. (*He sits slowly on bed.*) It could be my pong, I suppose. It's difficult to tell. I don't really know what I pong like, that's the trouble.

BEN (*referring to the paper*). Kaw!

GUS. Eh, Ben.

BEN. Kaw!

GUS. Ben.

BEN. What?

GUS. What town are we in? I've forgotten.

BEN. I've told you. Birmingham.

GUS. Go on!

(*He looks with interest about the room.*)

That's in the Midlands. The second biggest city in Great Britain. I'd never have guessed.

(*He snaps his fingers.*)

Eh, it's Friday today, isn't it? It'll be Saturday tomorrow.

BEN. What about it?

GUS (*excited*). We could go and watch the Villa.

BEN. They're playing away.

GUS. No, are they? Caarr! What a pity.

BEN. Anyway, there's no time. We've got to get straight back.

GUS. Well, we have done in the past, haven't we? Stayed over and watched a game, haven't we? For a bit of relaxation.

BEN. Things have tightened up, mate. They've tightened up.

(*Gus chuckles to himself.*)

GUS. I saw the Villa get beat in a cup tie once. Who was it against now? White shirts. It was one-all at half-time. I'll never forget it. Their opponents won by a penalty. Talk about drama. Yes, it was a disputed penalty. Disputed. They got beat two-one, anyway, because of it. You were there yourself.

BEN. Not me.

GUS. Yes, you were there. Don't you remember that disputed penalty?

BEN. No.

GUS. He went down just inside the area. Then they said he was just acting. I don't think the other bloke touched him myself. But the referee had the ball on the spot.

BEN. Didn't touch him! What are you talking about? He laid him out flat!

GUS. Not the Villa. The Villa don't play that sort of game.

BEN. Get out of it.

(*Pause.*)

GUS. Eh, that must have been here, in Birmingham.

BEN. What must?

GUS. The Villa. That must have been here.

BEN. They were playing away.

GUS. Because you know who the other team was? It was the Spurs. It was Tottenham Hotspur.

BEN. Well, what about it?

GUS. We've never done a job in Tottenham.

BEN. How do you know?

GUS. I'd remember Tottenham.

(*Ben turns on his bed to look at him.*)

BEN. Don't make me laugh, will you?

(*Ben turns back and reads. Gus yawns and speaks through his yawn.*)

GUS. When's he going to get in touch!

(*Pause.*)

Yes, I'd like to see another football match. I've always been an ardent football fan. Here, what about coming to see the Spurs tomorrow?

BEN (*tonelessly*). They're playing away.

GUS. Who are?

BEN. The Spurs.

GUS. Then they might be playing here.

BEN. Don't be silly.

GUS. If they're playing away they might be playing here. They might be playing the Villa.

BEN (*tonelessly*). But the Villa are playing away.

(*Pause. An envelope slides under the door, right, Gus sees it. He stands, looking at it.*)

GUS. Ben.

BEN. Away. They're all playing away.

GUS. Ben, look here.

BEN. What?

GUS. Look.

(*Ben turns his head and sees the envelope. He stands.*)

BEN. What's that?

GUS. I don't know.

BEN. Where did it come from?

GUS. Under the door.

BEN. Well, what is it?

GUS. I don't know.

(*They stare at it.*)

BEN. Pick it up.

GUS. What do you mean?

BEN. Pick it up!

(*Gus slowly moves towards it, bends and picks it up.*)

What is it?

GUS. An evelope.

BEN. Is there any thing on it?

GUS. No.

BEN. Is it sealed?

GUS. Yes.

BEN. Open it.

GUS. What?

BEN. Open it!

(*Gus opens it and looks inside.*)

What's in it?

(*Gus empties twelve matches into his hand.*)

GUS. Matches.

BEN. Matches?

GUS. Yes.

BEN. Show it to me.

(*Gus passes the envelope. Ben examines it.*)

Nothing on it. Not a word.

GUS. That's funny, isn't it?

BEN. It came under the door?

GUS. Must have done.

BEN. Well, go on.

GUS. Go on where?

BEN. Open the door an see if you can catch anyone outside.

GUS. Who, me?

BEN. Go on!

(*Gus stares at him, puts the matches in his pocket, goes to his bed and brings a revolver from under the pillow. He goes to the door, opens it, looks out and shuts it.*)

GUS. No one.

(*He replaces the revolver.*)

BEN. What did you see?

GUS. Nothing.

BEN. They must have been pretty quick.

(*Gus takes the matches from pocket and looks at them.*)

GUS. Well, they'll come in handy.

BEN. Yes.

GUS. Won't they?

BEN. Yes, you're always running out, aren't you?

GUS. All the time.

BEN. Well, they'll come in handy then.

GUS. Yes.

BEN. Won't they?

GUS. Yes, I could do with them. I could do with them, too.

BEN. You could, eh?

GUS. Yes.

BEN. Why?

GUS. We haven't got any.

BEN. Well, you've got some now, haven't you?

GUS. I can light the kettle now.

BEN. Yes, you're always cadging matches. How many have you got there?

GUS. About a dozen.

BEN. Well, don't lose them. Red, too. You don't even need a box.

(*Gus probes his ear with a match.*)

(*Slapping his hand*). Don't waste them! Go on, go and light it.

GUS. Eh?

BEN. Go and light it.

GUS. Light what?

BEN. The kettle.

GUS. You mean the gas.

BEN. Who does?

GUS. You do.

BEN (*his eyes narrowing*). What do you mean, I mean the gas?

GUS. Well, that's what you mean, don't you? The gas.

BEN (*powerfully*). If I say go and light the kettle I mean go and light the kettle.

GUS. How can you light a kettle?

BEN. It's a figure of speech! Light the kettle. It's a figure of speech!

GUS. I've never heard it.

BEN. Light the kettle! It's common usage!

GUS. I think you've got it wrong.

BEN (*menacing*). What do you mean?

GUS. They say put on the kettle.

BEN (*taut*). Who says?

(*They stare at each other, breathing hard.*)

(*Deliberately*) I have never in all my life heard anyone say put on the kettle.

GUS. I bet my mother used to say it.

BEN. Your mother! When did you last see your mother?

GUS. I don't know, about—

BEN. Well, what are you talking about your mother for?

(*They stare.*)

Gus, I'm not trying to be unreasonable. I'm just trying to point out something to you.

GUS. Yes, but—

BEN. Who's the senior partner here, me or you?

GUS. You.

BEN. I'm only looking after your interests, Gus. You've got to learn, mate.

GUS. Yes, but I've never heard—

BEN (*vehemently*). Nobody says light the gas! What does the gas light?

GUS. What does the gas—?

BEN (*grabbing him with two hands by the throat, at arm's length*). THE KETTLE, YOU FOOL!

(*Gus takes the hands from his throat.*)

GUS. All right, all right.

(*Pause.*)

BEN. Well, what are you waiting for?

GUS. I want to see if they light.

BEN. What?

GUS. The matches.

(*He takes out the flattened box and tries to strike.*)

No.

(*He throws the box under the bed. Ben stares at him Gus raises his foot.*)

Shall I try it on here?

(*Ben stares. Gus strikes a match on his shoe. It lights.*)

Here we are.

BEN (*wearily*). Put on the bloody kettle, for Christ's sake.

(*Ben goes to his bed, but, realising what he has said, stops and half turns. They look at each other. Gus slowly exists, left. Ben slams his paper down on the bed and sits on it, head in hands.*)

GUS (*entering*). It's going.

BEN. What?

GUS. The stove.

(*Gus goes to his bed and sits.*)

I wonder who it'll be tonight.

(*Silence.*)

Eh, I've been wanting to ask you something.

BEN (*putting his legs on the bed*). Oh, for Christ's sake.

GUS. No. I was going to ask you something.

(*He rises and sits on Ben's bed.*)

BEN. What are you sitting on my bed for?

(*Gus sits.*)

What's the matter with you? You're always asking me questions. What's the matter with you?

GUS. Nothing.

BEN. You never used to ask me so many damn questions. What's come over you?

GUS. No, I was just wondering.

BEN. Stop wondering. You've got a job to do. Why don't you just do it and shut up?

GUS. That's what I was wondering about.

BEN. What?

GUS. The job.

BEN. What job?

GUS (*tentatively*). I thought perhaps you might know something.

(*Ben looks at him.*)

I thought perhaps you—I mean—have you got any idea—who it's going to be tonight?

BEN. Who what's going to be?

(*They look at each other.*)

GUS (*at length*). Who it's going to be.

(*Silence.*)

BEN. Are you feeling all right?

GUS. Sure.

BEN. Go and make the tea.

GUS. Yes, sure.

(*Gus exits, left, Ben looks after him. He then takes his revolver from under the pillow and checks it for ammunition. Gus re-enters.*)

The gas has gone out.

BEN. Well, what about it?

GUS. There's a meter.

BEN. I haven't got any money.

GUS. Nor have I.

BEN. You'll have to wait.

GUS. What for?

BEN. For Wilson.

GUS. He might no come. He might just send a message. He doesn't always come.

BEN. Well, you'd have to do with it, won't you?

GUS. Blimey.

BEN. You'll have a cup of tea afterwards. What's the matter with you?

GUS. I like to have one before.

(*Ben holds the revolver up to the light and polishes it.*)

BEN. You'd better get ready anyway.

GUS. Well, I don't know, that's a bit much, you know, for my money.

(*He picks up a packet of tea from the bed and throws it into the bag.*)

I hope he's got a shilling, anyway, if he comes. He's entitled to have. After all, it's his place, he could have seen there was enough gas for a cup of tea.

BEN. What do you mean, it's his place?

GUS. Well, isn't it?

BEN. He's probably only rented it. It doesn't have to be his place.

GUS. I know it's his place. I bet the whole house is. He's not even laying on any gas now either.

(*Gus sits on his bed.*)

It's his place all right. Look at all the other places. You go to this address, there's a key there, there's a teapot, there's never a soul in sight—(*He pauses.*) Eh, nobody ever hears a thing, have you ever thought of that? We never get any complaints, do we, too much noise or anything like that? You never see a soul, do you?—except the bloke who comes. You ever noticed that? I wonder if the walls are sound-proof. (*He touches the wall above his head.*) Can't tell. All you do is wait, eh? Half the time he doesn't even bother to put in an appearance, Wilson.

BEN. Why should he? He's a busy man.

GUS (*thoughtfully*). I find him hard to talk to, Wilson. Do you know that, Ben?

BEN. Scrub round it, will you?

(*Pause.*)

GUS. There are a number of things I want to ask him. But I can never get round to it, when I see him.

(*Pause.*)

I've been thinking about the last one.

BEN. What last one?

GUS. That girl.

(*Ben grabs the paper, which he reads.*)

(*Rising, looking down at Ben*) How many times have you read that paper?

(*Ben slams the paper down and rises.*)

BEN (*angrily*). What do you mean?

GUS. I was just wondering how many times you'd—

BEN. What are you doing, criticising me?

GUS. No, I was just—

BEN. You'll get a swipe round your earhole if you don't watch your step.

GUS. Now look here, Ben—

BEN. I'm not looking anywhere! (*He addresses the room.*) How many times have I—! A bloody liberty!

GUS. I didn't mean that.

BEN. You just get on with it, mate. Get on with, that's all.

(*Ben gets back on the bed.*)

GUS. I was just thinking about that girl, that's all.

(*Gus sits on his bed.*)

She wasn't much to look at, I know, but still. It was a mess though, wasn't it? What a mess. Honest, I can't remember a mess like that one. They don't seem to hold together like men, women. A looser texture, like. Didn't she spread, eh? She didn't half spread. Kaw! But I've been meaning to ask you.

(*Ben sits up and clenches his eyes.*)

Who clears up after we've gone? I'm curious about that. Who does the clearing up? Maybe they don't clear up. Maybe they just leave them there, eh? What do you think? How many jobs have we done? Blimey, I can't count them. What if they never clear anything up after we've gone.

BEN (*pityingly*). You mutt. Do you think we're the only branch of this organisation? Have a bit of common. They got departments for everything.

GUS. What cleaners and all?

BEN. You birk!

GUS. Not, it was that girl made me start to think—

(*There is a loud clatter and racket in the bulge of wall between the beds, of something descending. They grab their revolvers, jump up and face the wall. The noise comes to a stop. Silence. They look at each other. Ben gestures sharply towards the wall. Gus approaches the wall slowly. He bangs it with his revolver. It is hollow. Ben moves to the head of his bed, his revolver cocked. Gus puts his revolver on his bed and pats along the bottom of the centre panel. He finds a rim. He lifts the panel. Disclosed is a serving-hatch, a "dumb waiter." A wide box is held by pulleys. Gus peers into the box. He brings out a piece of paper.*)

BEN. What is it?

GUS. You have a look at it.

BEN. Read it.

GUS (*reading*). Two braised steak and chips. Two sago puddings. Two teas without sugar.

BEN. Let me see that. (*He takes the paper.*)

GUS (*to himself*). Two teas without sugar.

BEN. Mmmnn.

GUS. What do you think of that?

BEN. Well—

(*The box goes up. Ben levels his revolver.*)

GUS. Give us a chance! They're in a hurry, aren't they?

(*Ben re-reads the note. Gus looks over his shoulder.*)

That's a bit—that's a bit funny, isn't it?

BEN (*quickly*). No. It's not funny. It probably used to be a café here, that's all. Upstairs. These places change hands very quickly.

GUS. A café?

BEN. Yes.

GUS. What, you mean this was the kitchen down there?

BEN. Yes, they change hands overnight, these places. Go into liquidation. The people who run it, you know, they don't find it a going concern, they move out.

GUS. You mean the people who ran this place didn't find it a going concern and moved out?

BEN. Sire.

GUS. WELL, WHO'S GOT IT NOW?

(*Silence.*)

BEN. What do you mean, who's got it now?

GUS. Who's got it now? If they moved out, who moved in?

BEN. Well, that all depends—

(*The box descends with a clatter and bang. Ben levels his revolver. Gus goes to the box and brings out a piece of paper.*)

GUS (*reading*). Soup of the day. Liver and onions. Jam tart.

(*A pause. Gus looks at Ben. Ben takes the note and reads it. He walks slowly to the hatch. Gus follows. Ben looks into the hatch but not up it. Gus puts his hand on Ben's shoulder. Ben throws it off. Gus puts his finger to his mouth. He leans on the hatch and swiftly looks up it. Ben flings him away in alarm. Ben looks at the note. He throws his revolver on the bed and speaks with decision.*)

BEN. We'd better send something up.

GUS. Eh?

BEN. We'd better send something up.

GUS. Oh! Yes. Yes. Maybe you're right.

(*They are both relieved at the decision.*)

BEN (*purposefully*). Quick! What have you got in that bag?

GUS. Not much.

(*Gus goes to the hatch and shouts up it.*)

Wait a minute!

BEN. Don't do that!

(*Gus examines the contents of the bag and brings them out, one by one.*)

GUS. Biscuits. A bar of chocolate. Half a pint of milk.

BEN. That all?

GUS. Packet of tea.

BEN. Good.

GUS. We can't send the tea. That's all the tea we've got.

BEN. Well, there's no gas. You can't do anything with it, can you?

GUS. Maybe they can send us down a bob.

BEN. What else is there?

GUS (*reaching into bag*). One Eccles cake.

BEN. One Eccles cake?

GUS. Yes.

BEN. You never told me you had an Eccles cake.

GUS. Didn't I?

BEN. Why only one? Didn't you bring one for me?

GUS. I didn't think you'd be keen.

BEN. Well, you can't send up one Eccles cake, anyway.

GUS. Why not?

BEN. Fetch one of those plates.

GUS. All right.

(*Gus goes towards the door, left, and stops.*)

Do you mean I can keep the Eccles cake then?

BEN. Keep it?

GUS. Well, they don't know we've got it, do they?

BEN. That's not the point.

GUS. Can't I keep it?

BEN. No, you can't. Get the plate.

(*Gus exits, left. Ben looks in the bag. He brings out a packet of crisps. Enter Gus with a plate.*)

(*Accusingly, holding up the crisps*) Where did these come from?

GUS. What?

BEN. Where did these crisps come from?

GUS. Where did you find them?

BEN (*hitting him on the shoulder*). You're playing a dirty game, my lad!

GUS. I only eat those with beer!

BEN. Well, where were you going to get the beer?

GUS. I was saving them till I did.

BEN. I'll remember this. Put everything on the plate.

(*They pile everything on the plate. The box goes up with the plate.*)

Wait a minute!

(*They stand.*)

GUS. It's gone up.

BEN. It's all your stupid fault, playing about?

GUS. What do we do now?

BEN. We'll have to wait till it comes down.

(*Ben puts the plate on the bed, puts on his shoulder holster, and starts to put on his tie.*)

You'd better get ready.

(*Gus goes to his bed, puts on his tie, and starts to fix his holster.*)

GUS. Hey, Ben.

BEN. What?

GUS. What's going on here?

(*Pause.*)

BEN. What do you mean?

GUS. How can this be a café?

BEN. It used to be a café.

GUS. Have you seen the gas stove?

BEN. What about it?

GUS. It's only got three rings.

BEN. So what?

GUS. Well, you couldn't cook much on three rings, not for a busy place like this.

BEN (*irritably*). That's why the service is slow!

(*Ben puts on his waistcoat.*)

GUS. Yes, but what happens when we're not here? What do they do then? All these menus coming down and nothing going up. It might have been going on like this for years.

(*Ben brushes his jacket.*)

What happens when we go?

(*Ben puts on his jacket.*)

They can't do much business.

(*The box descends. They turn about. Gus goes to the hatch and brings out a note.*)

GUS (*reading*). Macaroni Pastitsio. Ormitha Macarounada.
BEN. What was that?
GUS. Mararoni Pastitsio. Ormitha Macarounada.
BEN. Greek dishes.
GUS. No.
BEN. That's right.
GUS. That's pretty high class.
BEN. Quick before it goes up.

(*Gus puts the plate in the box.*)

GUS (*calling up the hatch*). Three McVitie and Price! One Lyons Red Label! One Smith's Crisps! One Eccle's cake! One Fruit and Nut!
BEN. Cadbury's.
GUS (*up the hatch*). Cadbury's!
BEN (*handing the milk*). One bottle of milk.
GUS (*up the hatch*). One bottle of milk! Half a pint! (*He looks at the label.*) Express Dairy! (*He puts the bottle in the box.*)

(*The box goes up.*)

Just did it.
BEN. You shouldn't shout like that.
GUS. Why not?
BEN. It isn't done.

(*Ben goes to his bed.*)

Well, that should be all right, anyway, for the time being.
GUS. You think so, eh?
BEN. Get dressed, will you? It'll be any minute now.

(*Gus puts on his waistcoat. Ben lies down and looks up at the ceiling.*)

GUS. This is some place. No tea and no biscuits.
BEN. Eating makes you lazy, mate. You're getting lazy, you know that? You don't want to get slack on your job.
GUS. Who me?
BEN. Slack, mate, slack.
GUS. Who me? Slack?
BEN. Have you checked your gun? You haven't even checked your gun. It looks disgraceful, anyway. Why don't you ever polish it?

(*Gus rubs his revolver on the sheet. Ben takes out a pocket mirror and straightens his tie.*)

GUS. I wonder where the cook is. They must have had a few, to cope with that: Maybe they had a few more gas stoves. Eh! Maybe there's another kitchen along the passage.
BEN. Of course there is! Do you know what is takes to make an Ormitha Macarounada?

GUS. No, what?
BEN. An Ormitha—! Buck your ideas up, will you?
GUS. Takes a few cooks, eh?

(*Gus puts his revolver in his holster.*)

The sooner we're out of this place the better.

(*He puts on his jacket.*)

Why doesn't he get in touch? I feel like I've been here years. (*He takes his revolver out of its holster to check the ammunition.*) We've never let him down though, have we? We've never let him down. I was thinking only the other day, Ben. We're reliable, aren't we?

(*He puts his revolver back in its holster.*)

Still, I'll be glad when it's over tonight.

(*He brushes his jacket.*)

I hope the bloke's not going to get excited tonight, or anything. I'm feeling a bit off. I've got a splitting headache.

(*Silence. The box descends. Ben jumps up. Gus collects the note.*)

(*Reading.*) One Bamboo Shoots, Water Chestnuts and Chicken. One Char Siu and Beansprouts.
BEN. Beansprouts?
GUS. Yes.
BEN. Blimey.
GUS. I wouldn't know where to begin.

(*He looks back at the box. The packet of tea is inside it. He picks it up.*)

They've sent back the tea.
BEN (*anxious*). What'd they do that for?
GUS. Maybe it isn't tea-time.

(*The box goes up. Silence.*)

BEN (*throwing the tea on the bed, and speaking urgently*). Look here. We'd better call them.
GUS. Tell them what?
BEN. That we can't do it, we haven't got it.
GUS. All right then.
BEN. Lend us your pencil. We'll write a note.

(*Gus, turning for a pencil, suddenly discovers the speaking-tube, which hangs on the right wall of the hatch facing his bed.*)

GUS. What's this?
BEN. What?
GUS. This.
BEN (*examining it*). This? It's a speaking-tube.

GUS. How long has that been there?

BEN. Just the job. We should have used it before, instead of shouting up there.

GUS. Funny, I never noticed it before.

BEN. Well, come on.

GUS. What do you do?

BEN. See that? That's a whistle?

GUS. What, this?

BEN. Yes, take it out. Pull it out.

(*Gus does so.*)

That's it.

GUS. What do we do now?

BEN. Blow into it?

GUS. Blow?

BEN. It whistles up there if you blow. Then they know you want to speak. Blow.

(*Gus blows. Silence.*)

GUS (*tube at mouth*). I can't hear a thing.

BEN. Now you speak! Speak into it!

(*Gus looks at Ben, then speaks into the tube.*)

GUS. The larder's bare!

BEN. Give me that!

(*He grabs the tube and puts it to his mouth.*)

(*Speaking with great deference*). Good evening. I'm sorry to—bother you, but we just though we'd better let you know that we haven't got anything left. We sent up all we had. There's no more food down here.

(*He brings the tube slowly to his ear.*)

What?

(*To mouth.*)

What?

(*To ear. He listens. To mouth.*)

No, all we had we sent up.

(*To ear. He listens. To mouth.*)

Oh, I'm very sorry to hear that.

(*To ear. He listens. To Gus.*)

The Eccles cake was stale.

(*He listens. To Gus.*)

The chocolate was melted.

(*He listens. To Gus.*)

The milk was sour.

GUS. What about the crisps?

BEN (*listening*). The biscuits were mouldy.

(*He glares at Gus. Tube to mouth.*)

Well, we're very sorry about that.

(*Tube to ear.*)

What?

(*To mouth.*)

What?

(*To ear.*)

Yes. Yes.

(*To mouth.*)

Yes certainly. Certainly. Right away.

(*To ear. The voice has ceased. He hangs up the tube.*)

(*Excitedly.*) Did you hear that?

GUS. What?

BEN. You know what he said? Light the kettle! Not put on the kettle! Not light the gas! But light the kettle!

GUS. How can we light the kettle?

BEN. There's no gas.

BEN (*clapping hand to head*). Now what do we do?

GUS. What did he want us to light the kettle for?

BEN. For tea. He wanted a cup of tea! What about me? I've been wanting a cup of tea all night!

BEN (*despairingly*). What do we do now?

GUS. What are we supposed to drink?

(*Ben sits on his bed, staring.*)

What about us?

(*Ben sits.*)

I'm thirsty, too. I'm starving. And he wants a cup of tea. That beats the band, that does.

(*Ben lets his head sink on to his chest.*)

I could do with a bit of sustenance myself. What about you? You look as if you could do with something too.

(*Gus sits on his bed.*)

We send him up all we've got and he's not satisfied. No, honest, it's enough to make the cat laugh. Why did you send him up all that stuff? (*Thoughtfully*). Why did I send it up?

(*Pause.*)

Who knows what he's got upstairs? He's probably got a salad bowl. They must have something up there. They won't get much from down here. You notice they didn't ask for any salads? They've probably got a salad bowl up there. Cold meat, radishes, cucumbers. Watercress. Roll mops.

(*Pause.*)

Hardboiled eggs.

(*Pause.*)

The lot. They've probably got a crate of beer too. Probably eating my crisps with a pint of beer now. Didn't have anything to say about those crisps, did he? They do all right, don't worry about that. You don't think they're just going to sit there and wait for stuff to come up from down here, do you? That's get them nowhere.

(*Pause.*)

They do all right.

(*Pause.*)

And he wants a cup of tea.

(*Pause.*)

That's past a joke, in my opinion.

(*He looks over at Ben, rises, and goes to him.*)

What's the matter with you? You don't look too bright. I feel like an Alka-Seltzer myself.

(*Ben sits up.*)

BEN (*in a low voice*). Time's getting on.
GUS. I know. I don't like doing a job on an empty stomach.
BEN (*wearily*). Be quiet a minute. Let me give you your instructions.
GUS. What for? We always do it the same way, don't we?
BEN. Let me give you your instructions.

(*Gus sighs and sits next to Ben on the bed. The instructions are stated and repeated automatically.*)

When we get the call, you go over and stand behind the door.
GUS. Stand behind the door.
BEN. If there's a knock on the door you don't answer it.
GUS. If there's a knock on the door I don't answer it.
BEN. But there won't be a knock on the door.
GUS. So I won't answer it.
BEN. When the bloke comes in—
GUS. When the bloke comes in—
BEN. Shut the door behind him.
GUS. Shut the door behind him.
BEN. Without divulging your presence.
GUS. Without divulging my presence.
BEN. He'll see me and come towards me.
GUS. He'll see you and come towards you.

BEN. He won't see you.
GUS (*absently*) Eh?
BEN. He won't see you.
GUS. He won't see me.
BEN. But he'll see me.
GUS. He'll see you.
BEN. He won't know you're there.
GUS. He won't know you're there.
BEN. He won't know *you're* there.
GUS. He won't know I'm there.
BEN. I take out my gun.
GUS. You take out your gun.
BEN. He stops in his tracks.
GUS. He stops in his tracks.
BEN. If he turns round—
GUS. If he turns round—
BEN. You're there.
GUS. I'm here.

(*Ben frowns and presses his forehead.*)

You've missed something out.
BEN. I know. What?
GUS. I haven't taken my gun out, according to you.
BEN. You take you gun out—
GUS. After I've closed the door.
BEN. After you've closed the door.
GUS. You've never missed that out before, you know that?
BEN. When he sees you behind him—
GUS. Me behind him—
BEN. And me in front of him—
GUS. And you in front of him—
BEN. He'll feel uncertain—
GUS. Uneasy.
BEN. He won't know what to do.
GUS. So what will he do?
BEN. He'll look at me and he'll look at you.
GUS. We won't say a word.
BEN. We'll look at him.
GUS. He won't say a word.
BEN. He'll look at us.
GUS. And we'll look at him.
BEN. Nobody says a word.

(*Pause.*)

GUS. What do we do if it's a girl?
BEN. We do the same.
GUS. Exactly the same?
BEN. Exactly.

(*Pause.*)

GUS. We don't do anything different?
BEN. We do exactly the same.
GUS. Oh.

(*Gus rises, and shivers.*)

Excuse me.

(*He exits through the door on the left. Ben remains sitting on the bed, still.*
The lavatory chain is pulled once off left, but the lavatory does not flush.
Silence.
Gus re-enters and stops inside the door, deep in thought. He looks at Ben, then walks slowly across to his own bed. He is troubled. He stands, thinking. He turns and looks at Ben. He moves a few paces towards him.)

(*Slowly in a low, tense voice*) Why did he send us matches if he knew there was no gas?

(*Silence.*
Ben stares in front of him. Gus crosses to the left side of Ben, to the foot of his bed, to get to his other ear.)

BEN. Why did he send us matches if he knew there was no gas?

(*Ben looks up.*)

Why did he do that?

BEN. Who?

GUS. Who sent us those matches?

BEN. What are you talking about?

(*Gus stares down at him.*)

GUS (*thickly*). Who is it upstairs?

BEN (*nervously*). What's one thing to do with another?

GUS. Who is it, though?

BEN. What's one thing to do with the another?

(*Ben fumbles for his paper on the bed.*)

GUS. I asked you a question.

BEN. Enough!

GUS (*with growing agitation*). I asked you before. Who moved in? I asked you. You said the people who had it before moved out. Well, who moved in?

BEN (*hunched*). Shut up.

GUS. I told you, didn't I?

BEN (*standing*). Shut up!

GUS (*feverishly*). I told you before who owned this place, didn't I? I told you.

(*Ben hits him viciously on the shoulder.*)

I told you who ran this place, didn't I?

(*Ben hits him viciously on the shoulder.*)

(*Violently*) Well, what's he playing all these games for? That's what I want to know? What's he doing it for?

BEN. What games?

GUS (*passionately, advancing*). What's he doing it for? We've been through our tests, haven't we? We got right through

our tests, years ago, didn't we? We took them together, don't you remember, didn't we? We've proved ourselves before now, haven't we? We've always done our job. What's he doing all this for? What's the idea? What's he playing these games for?

(*The box in the shaft comes down behind them. The noise is this time accompanied by a shrill whistle, as it falls. Gus rushes to the hatch and seizes the note.*)

(*Reading.*) Scampi!

(*He crumples the note, picks up the tube, takes out the whistle, blows and speaks.*)

WE'VE GOT NOTHING LEFT! NOTHING! DO YOU UNDER-STAND?

(*Ben seizes the tube and flings Gus away. He follows Gus and slaps him hard, back-handed, across the chest.*)

BEN. Stop it! You maniac!

GUS. But you heard!

BEN (*savagely*). That's enough! I'm warning you!

(*Silence.*
Ben hangs the tube. He goes to his bed and lies down. He picks up his paper and reads.
Silence.
The box goes up.
They turn quickly, their eyes meet. Ben turns to his paper.
Slowly Gus goes back to his bed, and sits.
Silence.
The hatch falls back into place.
They turn quickly, their eyes meet. Ben turns back to his paper.
Silence.
Ben throws his paper down.)

BEN. Kaw!

(*He picks up the paper and looks at it.*)

Listen to this!

(*Pause.*)

What about that, eh?

(*Pause.*)

Kaw!

(*Pause.*)

Have you ever heard such a thing?

GUS (*dully*). Go on!

BEN. It's true.

GUS. Get away.

BEN. It's down here in black and white.
GUS (*very low*). Is that a fact?
BEN. You can imagine it.
GUS. It's unbelievable.
BEN. It's enough to make you want to puke, isn't it?
GUS (*almost inaudible*). Incredible.

(*Ben shakes his head. He puts the paper down and rises. He fixes the revolver in his holster.*

Gus stands up. He goes towards the door on the left.)

BEN. Where are you going?
GUS. I'm going to have a glass of water.

(*He exits. Ben brushes dust off his clothes and shoes. The whistle in the speaking-tube blows. He goes to it, takes the whistle out and puts the tube to his ear. He listens. He puts it to his mouth.*)

BEN. Yes.

(*To ear. He listens. To mouth.*)

Straight away. Right.

(*To ear. He listens. To mouth.*)

Sure we're ready.

(*To ear. He listens. To mouth.*)

Understood. Repeat. He has arrived and will be coming in straight away. The normal method to be employed. Understood.

(*To ear. He listens. To mouth.*)

Sure we're ready.

(*To ear. He listens. To mouth.*)

Right.

(*He hangs up the tube up.*)

Gus!

(*He takes out a comb and combs his hair, adjusts his jacket to diminish the bulge of the revolver. The lavatory flushes off left. Ben goes quickly to the door, left*).

Gus!

(*The door right opens sharply. Ben turns, his revolver levelled at the door.*
Gus stumbles in.
He is stripped of his jacket, waistcoat, tie, holster and revolver.
He stops, body stooping, his arms at his sides.
He raises his head and looks at Ben.
A long silence.
they stare at each other.)

CURTAIN

Topics for Critical Thinking and Writing

The Play on the PAGE

1. Is *The Dumb Waiter* a menacing play about a terrifying absurdity, or is it largely an entertaining comedy with a puzzling ending? Take, for instance, the debate over "Light the kettle" and "Light the gas." Are we to take this seriously or just as a comic bit?
2. How certain or uncertain are we about Gus's fate?
3. In an interview published in Mel Gussow's *Conversations with Pinter* (1994), Pinter says that *The Dumb Waiter* is a "political play" (p. 69). Does this make sense to you? Is Pinter perhaps talking about power and victimization? Explain.
4. What do you make of the title? Do you think it can reasonably be said to refer not only to the machine but also to Gus? To Ben? To us?

The Play on the STAGE

5. *The Dumb Waiter* begins with a long stage direction that in effect calls for substantial pantomime before any words are spoken. Why do you suppose Pinter begins thus?
6. Think about exactly how you would stage this opening pantomime. Would the gestures indicate to the audience that one of the two men is brighter than the other?

The Play in PERFORMANCE

The Dumb Waiter, written in 1957, was first produced in 1959, in Frankfurt, Germany. The first English production was in 1960 at the Hampstead Theatre Club, and the reviews were sufficiently favorable so that it soon moved to the more convenient Royal Court Theatre. On the whole the reviewers found the play engaging, but many of them expressed uncertainty about its meaning or theme. In November 1962 it opened in New York, off-Broadway, to reviews that generally were favorable, though again critics expressed uncertainty about the meaning, and an occasional critic expressed some uneasiness with the director. For instance, in *The-*atre Arts (Jan. 1963: 10), Alan Pryce-Jones wrote, "It is arguable . . . that Alan Schneider's otherwise perceptive direction has set the pitch of the talk too high. In the original London production a still more menacing atmosphere was created by the ominous quietness which filled the room throughout."

The play has been staged fairly often, especially by amateur and semiprofessional groups. Among the more ingenious locales was a room above a pub in London, 1982, where, during the performance, the spectators could order some of the dishes mentioned in the play.

SAMUEL Beckett

Samuel Beckett was born on Good Friday, April 13, 1906, near Dublin, Ireland. Raised in a middle-class Protestant home, the son of a quantity surveyor and a nurse, he was sent at the age of fourteen to the same school Oscar Wilde had attended. Looking back on his childhood, he once remarked, "I had little talent for happiness." In 1928 he moved to Paris, and the city quickly won his heart. Shortly after he arrived, a mutual friend introduced him to James Joyce to whom he became a disciple. A year later, he won his first literary prize for a poem entitled *Whoroscope,* which dealt with the philosopher Descartes meditating on the subject of time and the transiency of life. After writing a study of Proust, Beckett came to the conclusion that habit and routine were the "cancer of time," and he resigned a post at Trinity College to set out on a nomadic journey across Europe.

After five years of wandering, Beckett finally settled in Paris in 1937. Shortly thereafter, he was approached in the street by a man who asked for money and stabbed him, perforating a lung. After his recovery, he went to visit his assailant in prison. When asked why he had attacked Beckett, the prisoner replied, "*Je ne sais pas, Monsieur,*" a phrase hauntingly reminiscent of some of the lost souls that would populate the writer's later works.

During World War II, Beckett remained in Paris after it had become occupied by the Germans. He joined the underground movement and fought for the Resistance until 1942 when several members of his group were arrested and he was forced to flee with his French-born wife, Suzanne Deschevaux-Dumesnil, to the unoccupied zone. In 1945, after it had been liberated from the Germans, he return to Paris and began his most prolific period as a writer. In the five years that followed, he wrote the novels *Molloy, Malone Dies, The Unnamable,* and *Mercier et Camier,* two books of short stories, a book of criticism—and the plays *Eleutheria, Waiting for Godot,* and *Endgame.*

Samuel Beckett's first play, *Eleutheria* (1947, unproduced), mirrors his own search for freedom, revolving around a young man's efforts to cut himself loose from his family and social obligations. His first real triumph, however, came on January 5, 1953, when *En attendant Godot* premiered at the Théâtre de Babylone. The strange play in which "nothing happens"—in fact, it has been said that "nothing happens twice"—became an instant success, running for four hundred performances in Paris and as *Waiting for Godot* was soon given controversial, attention-getting productions in London and New York. Beckett secured his position as a major dramatist on April 3, 1957, when his second play, *Endgame,* premiered (in French, as *Fin de partie*) at the Royal Court Theatre in London. His subsequent plays, of which *Krapp's Last Tape* (1958), *Happy Days* (1961), and *Play* (1963) are best known, became more and more minimalist as time went on (*Not I,* 1972, and *Rockaby,* 1981, were short intense monologues). Numerous other works, including scripts for radio and television, and even for a movie entitled *Film,* starring Buster Keaton, complete what John Updike called "a single holy book." Beckett was awarded the Nobel Prize for literature in 1969; he died in Paris in 1989.

COMMENTARY ON *KRAPP'S LAST TAPE*

In Samuel Beckett's trilogy of novels, *Molloy, Malone Dies,* and *The Unnamable,* as in *Waiting for Godot,* the protagonists glimpse their pasts through a glass darkly. The octogenarian Malone, in *Malone Dies,* like Molloy before him, does not know how he reached the room where he is entombed. He has a blood-stained club by his bed and the faintest of memories of a forest and a blow on his head, but Beckett, only interested in the process of Malone's dying, gives us no further clues. Similarly, in *Waiting for Godot,* despite Didi and Gogo's occasional allusions to something or someplace ("the Macon country") elsewhere, there is no reality beyond this place where they are waiting and which they cannot leave. Starting with *Endgame,* however, Beckett begins to be concerned with personal histories; after all, Hamm's progenitors, his crippled parents Nag and Nell, are present in the play in garbage cans on stage. In *Krapp's Last Tape,* Beckett's next important play after *Endgame,* the past—accessible through the modern technology of the tape recorder—overwhelms a dismal present.

Krapp is a short play, and like *Godot* and *Endgame* it couches serious themes in comic garb. It is a one-character play but it is not a monologue; there are two voices: the voice of the character we see—a "wearish" old man described almost as a clown: "rusty black trousers too short for him. Rusty black sleeveless waist-coat, . . . white face. Purple nose. Disordered grey hair. Unshaven . . . Hard of hearing. Cracked voice"—and, on tape, his voice of many years ago when he was thirty-nine—a "strong voice, rather pompous." The meager plot of the brief play consists of the old man, after a farcical introductory section in which he eats a banana, slips on its discarded skin, and guzzles a drink in an offstage room, lovingly taking out a spool of tape, loading it on his machine, and listening to his younger self. He brusquely stops the tape at times to bypass or replay a salient section. Then he takes out a virgin tape and acidly records comments on the earlier recording. Finally, he replays a section of the first tape as he stares motionlessly before him as the tape runs on in silence.

This first tape is a retrospect of the year just then past that records the death of his mother mixed with memories of a beautiful nursemaid, a dog, and a rubber ball. It describes a moment of revelation never fully revealed, made at night by the sea during a storm, in which the younger Krapp made a decision that changed his life. "What I suddenly saw was this, that the belief I had been going on all my life, namely—" The old Krapp impatiently stops the tape here to wind it forward and avoid hearing the confession. When he turns the tape back on, his younger self is in mid-account of a love encounter on a river: "We lay there without moving. But under us all moved, and moved us, gently, up and down, and from side to side." It is to this recorded blissful moment that the old man returns at play's end.

Though it is not necessary to the appreciation of the play, much of the narrative detail revealed here, it is interesting to note, is for the first time in Beckett's writing, autobiographical (Miss McGlone and her dog are based on a Miss Beamish of his childhood; the "house on the canal where mother lay a-dying in the late autumn" is his first literary reference to his own mother's death). And the "vision" here described echoes an early mystical revelation he experienced in Ireland that committed Beckett to the life of an artist. Even his lover in the boat is identifiable. Perhaps the most transparent biographical indebtedness occurs when old Krapp angrily shuts off the tape because of his irritation at "that stupid bastard I took myself for thirty years ago" to ironically reflect on his career accomplishments: "Seventeen copies sold, of which eleven at trade price to free circulating libraries beyond the seas. Getting known." Pre-*Godot* commercial failure—particularly the dismal sales of *Murphy*—is here sarcastically addressed.

But no biographical knowledge is necessary to make accessible the play's major theme: the contrast between the dreams of youth and the realities of age. It is not only a nostalgia for a body that worked, that was not beset by hobbling infirmities. The greater contrast is between hope and resignation, between a vision of a future of infinite possibility compounded of "storm and night with the light of the understanding and the fire" and a deteriorated present reality: "What's a year now? The sour cud and the iron stool." At least he still has a love life, if not a very satisfactory one: "Fanny came in a couple of times. Bony old ghost of a whore. Couldn't do much." What's happiness now? A moment's sensuous pleasure from a banana or a drink; even a word, "spool"—which he lovingly elongates into "spooool!"—becomes his "happiest moment of the last half million." Earlier in the play the younger man, who despite his announced optimism always had his self-doubts, had asked, "Did I sing as a boy? No. Did I ever sing? No." But that is precisely what he did in the description of the love scene to which the failed old codger returns hypnotically: "Under us all moved, and moved us gently, up and down, and from side to side." That's music. Most of us have been lucky enough in the inexorable passage of our lives to perhaps once or twice experience such an epiphany, when we are one with our bodies, with the other, with the world, beyond time, beyond death. It never lasts, but our memories retain its magic. And so the play ends with fierce irony: After recounting his epiphanic moment, the younger man self-doubtingly ends the recording. "Perhaps my best years are gone. When there was a chance of happiness." He pulls himself together: "But I wouldn't want them back. Not with the fire in me now. No, I wouldn't want them back." As the old man stares motionlessly before him, we nod ironically: not much, not much.

KRAPP'S LAST TAPE
A PLAY IN ONE ACT
Samuel Beckett

A late evening in the future.

Krapp's den.

Front centre a small table, the two drawers of which open towards audience.

Sitting at the table, facing front, i.e. across from the drawers, a wearish old man: Krapp.

Rusty black narrow trousers too short for him. Rusty black sleeveless waistcoat, four capacious pockets. Heavy silver watch and chain. Grimy white shirt open at neck, no collar. Surprising pair of dirty white boots, size ten at least, very narrow and pointed.

White face. Purple nose. Disordered grey hair. Unshaven.

Very near-sighted (but unspectacled). Hard of hearing.

Cracked voice. Distinctive intonation.

Laborious walk.

On the table a tape-recorder with microphone and a number of cardboard boxes containing reels of recorded tapes.

Table and immediately adjacent area in strong white light. Rest of stage in darkness.

Krapp remains a moment motionless, heaves a great sigh, looks at his watch, fumbles in his pockets, takes out an envelope, puts it back, fumbles, takes out a small bunch of keys, raises it to his eyes, chooses a key, gets up and moves to front of table. He stoops, unlocks first drawer, peers into it, feels about inside it, takes out a reel of tape, peers at it, puts it back, locks drawer, unlocks second drawer, peers into it, feels about inside it, takes out a large banana, peers at it, locks drawer, puts keys back in his pocket. He turns, advances to edge of stage, halts, strokes banana, peels it, drops skin at his feet, puts end of banana in his mouth and remains motionless, staring vacuously before him. Finally he bites off the end, turns aside and begins pacing to and fro at edge of stage, in the light, i.e. not more than four or five paces either way, meditatively eating banana. He treads on skin, slips, nearly falls, recovers himself, stoops and peers at skin and finally pushes it, still stooping, with his foot over the edge of stage into pit. He resumes his pacing, finishes banana, returns to table, sits down, remains a moment motionless, heaves a great sigh, takes keys from his pockets, raises them to his eyes, chooses key, gets up and moves to front of table, unlocks second drawer, takes out a second large banana, peers at it, locks drawer, puts back keys in

his pocket, turns, advances to edge of stage, halts, strokes banana, peels it, tosses skin into pit, puts end of banana in his mouth and remains motionless, staring vacuously before him. Finally he has an idea, puts banana in his waistcoat pocket, the end emerging, and goes with all the speed he can muster backstage into darkness. Ten seconds. Loud pop of cork. Fifteen seconds. He comes back into light carrying an old ledger and sits down at table. He lays ledger on table, wipes his mouth, wipes his hands on the front of his waistcoat, brings them smartly together and rubs them.

KRAPP (*briskly*). Ah! (*He bends over ledger, turns the pages, finds the entry he wants, reads.*) Box . . . three . . . spool . . . five. (*He raises his head and stares front. With relish.*) Spool! (*Pause.*) Spooool!. (*Happy smile. Pause. He bends over table, starts peering and poking at the boxes.*) Box . . . thrree . . . thrree . . . four . . . two . . . (*with surprise*) nine! good God! . . . seven . . . ah! the little rascal! (*He takes up box, peers at it.*) Box thrree. (*He lays it on table, opens it and peers at spools inside.*) Spool . . . (*he peers at ledger*) . . . five . . . (*he peers at spools*) . . . five . . . five . . . ah! the little scoundrel! (*He takes out a spool, peers at it.*) Spool five. (*He lays it on table, closes box three, puts it back with the other, takes up the spool.*) Box thrree, spool five. (*He bends over the machine, looks up. With relish.*) Spooool! (*Happy smile. He bends, loads spool on machine, rubs his hands.*) Ah! (*He peers at ledger, reads entry at foot of page.*) Mother at rest at last . . . Hm . . . The black ball . . . (*He raises his head, stares blankly front. Puzzled.*) Black ball? . . . (*He peers again at ledger, reads.*) The dark nurse . . . (*He raises his head, broods, peers again at ledger, reads.*) Slight improvement in bowel condition . . . Hm . . . Memorable . . . what? (*He peers closer.*) Equinox, memorable equinox. (*He raises his head, stares blankly front. Puzzled.*) Memorable equinox? . . . (*Pause. He shrugs his shoulders, peers again at ledger, reads.*) Farewell to—(*he turns the page*)—love.

He raises his head, broods, bends over machine, switches on and assumes listening posture, i.e. leaning forward, elbows on table, hand cupping ear towards machine, face front.

TAPE (*strong voice, rather pompous, clearly Krapp's at a much earlier time*). Thirty-nine today, sound as a—(*Settling him-*

self more comfortably he knocks one of the boxes off the table, curses, switches off, sweeps boxes and ledger violently to the ground, winds tape back to beginning, switches on, resumes posture.) Thirty-nine today, sound as a bell, apart from my old weakness, and intellectually I have now every reason to suspect at the . . . *(hesitates)* . . . crest of the wave—or thereabouts. Celebrated the awful occasion, as in recent years, quietly at the Winehouse. Not a soul. Sat before the fire with closed eyes, separating the grain from the husks. Jotted down a few notes, on the back of an envelope. Good to be back in my den, in my old rags. Have just eaten I regret to say three bananas and only with difficulty refrained from a fourth. Fatal things for a man with my condition. *(Vehemently.)* Cut 'em out! *(Pause.)* The new light above my table is a great improvement. With all this darkness round me I feel less alone. *(Pause.)* In a way. *(Pause.)* I love to get up and move about in it, then back here to . . . *(hesitates)* . . . me. *(Pause.)* Krapp.

Pause.

The grain, now what I wonder do I mean by that, I mean . . . *(hesitates)* . . . I suppose I mean those things worth having when all the dust has—when all *my* dust has settled. I close my eyes and try and imagine them.

Pause. Krapp closes his eyes briefly.

Extraordinary silence this evening, I strain my ears and do not hear a sound. Old Miss McGlome always sings at this hour. But not tonight. Songs of her girlhood, she says. Hard to think of her as a girl. Wonderful woman though. Connaught, I fancy. *(Pause.)* Shall I sing when I am her age, if I ever am? No. *(Pause.)* Did I sing as a boy? No. *(Pause.)* Did I ever sing? No.

Pause.

Just been listening to an old year, passages at random. I did not check in the book, but it must be at least ten or twelve years ago. At that time I think I was still living on and off with Bianca in Kedar Street. Well out of that, Jesus yes! Hopeless business. *(Pause.)* Not much about her, apart from a tribute to her eyes. Very warm. I suddenly saw them again. *(Pause.)* Incomparable! *(Pause.)* Ah well . . . *(Pause.)* These old P.M.s are gruesome, but I often find them—*(Krapp switches off, broods, switches on)*—a help before embarking on a new . . . *(hesitates)* . . . retrospect. Hard to believe I was ever that young whelp. The voice! Jesus! And the aspirations! *(Brief laugh in which Krapp joins.)* And the resolutions! *(Brief laugh in which Krapp joins.)* To drink less, in particular. *(Brief laugh of Krapp alone.)* Statistics. Seventeen hundred hours, out of the preceding eight thousand odd, consumed on licensed premises alone. More than 20%, say 40% of his waking life. *(Pause.)* Plans for a less . . . *(hesitates)* . . . engrossing sexual life. Last illness of his father. Flagging pursuit of happiness. Un-

attainable laxation. Sneers at what he calls his youth and thanks to God that it's over. *(Pause.)* False ring there. *(Pause.)* Shadows of the opus . . . magnum. Closing with a—*(brief laugh)*—yelp to Providence. *(Prolonged laugh in which Krapp joins.)* What remains of all that misery? A girl in a shabby green coat, on a railway-station platform? No?

Pause.

When I look—

(Krapp switches off, broods, looks at his watch, gets up, goes backstage into darkness. Ten seconds. Pop of cork. Ten seconds, Second cork. Tens seconds. Third cork. Ten seconds. Brief burst of quavering song.)

KRAPP *(sings)*. Now the day is over.
   Night is drawing nigh-igh,
   Shadows—

Fit of coughing. He comes back into light, sits down, wipes his mouth, switches on, resumes his listening posture.

TAPE —back on the year that is gone, with what I hope is perhaps a glint of the old eye to come, there is of course the house on the canal where mother lay a-dying, in the late autumn, after her long viduity *(Krapp gives a start)*, and the—*(Krapp switches off, winds back tape a little, bends his ear closer to machine, switches on)*—a-dying, after her long viduity, and the—

Krapp switches off, raises his head, stares blankly before him. His lips move in the syllables of "viduity." No sound. He gets up, goes backstage into darkness, comes back with an enormous dictionary, lays it on table, sits down and looks up the word.

KRAPP *(reading from dictionary)*. State—or condition of being—or remaining—a widow—or widower. *(Looks up. Puzzled.)* Being—or remaining? . . . *(Pause. He peers again at dictionary. Reading.)* "Deep weeds of viduity" . . . Also of an animal, especially a bird . . . the vidua or weaver-bird . . . Black plumage of male . . . *(He looks up. With relish.)* The vidua-bird!

Pause. He closes dictionary, switches on, resumes listening posture.

TAPE —bench by the weir from where I could see her window. There I sat, in the biting wind, wishing she were gone. *(Pause.)* Hardly a soul, just a few regulars, nursemaids, infants, old men, dogs. I got to know them quite well—oh by appearance of course I mean! One dark young beauty I recollect particularly, all white and starch, incomparable bosom, with a big black hooded perambulator, most funereal thing. Whenever I looked in her direction she had her eyes on me. And yet when I was bold enough to speak to her—not having been introduced—she threatened to call a policeman. As if I had designs on her virtue! (*Laugh. Pause.*) The face she had! The eyes! Like . . . (*hesitates*) . . . chrysolite! (*Pause.*) Ah well . . . (*Pause.*) I was there when—(*Krapp switches off, broods, switches on again*)—the blind went down, one of those dirty brown roller affairs, throwing a ball for a little white dog, as chance would have it. I happened to look up and there it was. All over and done with, at last. I sat on for a few moments with the ball in my hand and the dog yelping and pawing at me. (*Pause.*) Moments. Her moments, my moments. (*Pause.*) The dog's moments. (*Pause.*) In the end I held it out to him and he took it in his mouth, gently, gently. A small, old, black, hard, solid rubber ball. (*Pause.*) I shall feel it, in my hand, until my dying day. (*Pause.*) I might have kept it. (*Pause.*) But I gave it to the dog.

Pause.

Ah well . . .

Pause.

Spiritually a year of profound gloom and indigence until that memorable night in March, at the end of the jetty, in the howling wind, never to be forgotten, when suddenly I saw the whole thing. The vision, at last. This I fancy is what I have chiefly to record this evening, against the day when my work will be done and perhaps no place left in my memory, warm or cold, for the miracle that . . . (*hesitates*) . . . for the fire that set it alight. What I suddenly saw then was this, that the belief I had been going on all my life, namely—(*Krapp switches off impatiently, winds tape forward, switches on again*)—great granite rocks the foam flying up in the light of the lighthouse and the wind-gauge spinning like a propellor, clear to me at last that the dark I have always struggled to keep under is in reality my most—(*Krapp curses, switches off, winds tape forward, switches on again*)—unshatterable association until my dissolution of storm and night with the light of the understanding and the fire—(*Krapp curses louder, switches off, winds tape forward, switches on again*)—my face in her breasts and my hand on her. We lay there without moving. But under us all moved, and moved us, gently, up and down, and from side to side.

Pause.

Past midnight. Never knew such silence. The earth might be uninhabited.

Pause.

Here I end—

Krapp switches off, winds tape back, switches on again.

—upper lake, with the punt, bathed off the bank, then pushed out into the stream and drifted. She lay stretched out on the floorboards with her hands under her head and her eyes closed. Sun blazing down, bit of a breeze, water nice and lively. I noticed a scratch on her thigh and asked her how she came by it. Picking gooseberries, she said. I said again I thought it was hopeless and no good going on, and she agreed, without opening her eyes. (*Pause.*) I asked her to look at me and after a few moments—(*pause*)—after a few moments she did, but the eyes just slits, because of the glare. I bent over her to get them in the shadow and they opened. (*Pause. Low.*) Let me in. (*Pause.*) We drifted in among the flags and stuck. The way they went down, sighing, before the stem! (*Pause.*) I law down across her with my face in her breasts and my hand on her. We lay there without moving. But under us all moved, and moved us, gently, up and down, and from side to side.

Pause.

Past midnight. Never knew—

Krapp switches off, broods. Finally he fumbles in his pockets, encounters the banana, takes it out, peers at it, puts it back, fumbles, brings out the envelope, fumbles, puts back envelope, looks at his watch, gets up and goes backstage into darkness. Ten seconds. Sound of bottle against glass, then brief siphon. Ten seconds. Bottle against glass alone. Ten seconds. He comes back a little unsteadily into light, goes to front of table, takes out keys, raises them to his eyes, chooses key, unlocks first drawer, peers into it, feels about inside, takes out reel, peers at it, locks drawer, puts keys back in his pocket, goes and sits down, takes reel off machine, lays it on dictionary, loads virgin reel on machine, takes envelope form his pocket, consults back of it, lays it on table, switches on, clears his throat and begins to record.

KRAPP. Just been listening to that stupid bastard I took myself for thirty years ago, hard to believe I was ever as bad as that. Thank God that's all done with anyway. (*Pause.*) The eyes she had! (*Broods, realizes he is recording silence, switches off, broods. Finally.*) Everything there, everything, all the—(*Realizes this is not being recorded, switches on.*) Everything there, everything on this old muckball, all the light and dark and famine and feasting of . . . (*hesitates*) . . . the ages! (*In a shout.*) Yes! (*Pause.*) Let that go! Jesus! Take his mind off his homework! Jesus! (*Pause. Weary.*) Ah well, maybe he was right. (*Pause.*) Maybe he was right. (*Broods. Realizes. Switches off. Consults envelope.*) Pah! (*Crumples it and throws it away. Broods. Switches on.*) Nothing to say, not a squeak. What's a year now? The sour cud and the iron stool. (*Pause.*) Revelled in the word spool. (*With relish.*) Spooool! Happiest moment of the past half million. (*Pause.*) Seventeen copies sold, of which eleven at trade price to free circulating libraries beyond the seas. Getting known. (*Pause.*) One pound six and something, eight I have little doubt. (*Pause.*) Crawled out once or twice, before the summer was cold. Sat shivering in the park, drowned in dreams and burning to be gone. Not a soul. (*Pause.*) Last fancies.

(*Vehemently.*) Keep 'em under? (*Pause.*) Scalded the eyes out of me reading *Effie* again, a page a day, with tears again. Effie . . . (*Pause.*) Could have been happy with her, up there on the Baltic, and the pines, and the dunes. (*Pause.*) Could I? (*Pause.*) And she? (*Pause.*) Pah! (*Pause.*) Fanny came in a couple of times. Bony old ghost of a whore. Couldn't do much, but I suppose better than a kick in the crutch. The last time wasn't so bad. How do you manage it, she said, at your age? I told here I'd been saving up for her all my life. (*Pause.*) Went to Vespers once, like when I was in short trousers. (*Pause. Sings.*)

> Now the day is over,
> Night is drawing nigh-igh,
> Shadows—(*coughing, then almost inaudible*)—of the
>   evening
> Steal across the sky.

(*Gasping.*) Went to sleep and fell off the pew. (*Pause.*) Sometimes wondered in the night if a last effort mightn't —(*Pause.*) Ah finish your booze now and get to your bed. Go on with this drivel in the morning. Or leave it at that. (*Pause.*) Leave it at that. (*Pause.*) Lie propped up in the dark—and wander. Be again in the dingle on a Christmas Eve, gathering holly, the red-berried. (*Pause.*) Be again on Croghan on a Sunday morning, in the haze, with the bitch, stop and listen to the bells. (*Pause.*) And so on. (*Pause.*) Be again, be again. (*Pause.*) All that old misery. (*Pause.*) Once wasn't enough for you. (*Pause.*) Lie down across her.

Long pause. He suddenly bends over machine, switches off, wrenches off tape, throws it away, puts on the other, winds it forward to the passage he wants, switches on, listens staring front.

TAPE —gooseberries, she said. I said again I thought it was hopeless and no good going on, and she agreed, without opening her eyes. (*Pause.*) I asked her to look at me and after a few moments—(*pause*)—after a few moments she did, but the eyes just slits, because of the glare. I bent over her to get them in the shadow and they opened. (*Pause. Low.*) Let me in. (*Pause.*) We drifted in among the flags and stuck. The way they went down, sighing, before the stem! (*Pause.*) I lay down across her with my face in her breasts and my hand on her. We lay there without moving. But under us all moved, and moved us, gently, up and down, and from side to side.

Pause. Krapp's lips move. No sound.

Past midnight. Never knew such silence. The earth might be uninhabited.

Pause.

Here I end this reel. Box—(*pause*)—three, spool—(*pause*)—five. (*Pause.*) Perhaps my best years are gone. When there was a chance of happiness. But I wouldn't want them back. Not with the fire in me now. No, I wouldn't want them back.

Krapp motionless staring before him. The tape runs on in silence.

CURTAIN

TOPICS FOR CRITICAL THINKING AND WRITING

The Play on the PAGE

1. Why do you think Beckett makes Krapp so farcical a character, particularly at the outset?
2. Why do you think he gives him a quasi-obscene name?
3. How would you describe the character of Krapp as a younger man?
4. Discuss the themes of memory and desire as revealed in the play.

The Play on the STAGE

5. How clownish should Krapp be played?
6. How would you handle the scenes where he just listens to his recorded voice?
7. What mood would you (as director) try to establish in the play?
8. How much would you stress the play's comedy?
9. The text calls only for a table, a chair, a tape recorder, a microphone, and a box of tapes. A film version with John Hurt, however, is set in a cramped private library packed with books, files, and papers. Do you approve the change? Why or why not?

The Play in PERFORMANCE

When, in 1957, a radio play by Beckett, *All That Fall*, was broadcast by the BBC, he met several of the actors, among them Patrick Magee, a boisterous Irishman with a mellifluous voice. Beckett told the actor that he was astonished when he first heard Magee speak because the voice was one that Beckett heard in his own head. And so he thought about writing another radio play specifically for Magee. But as he worked on the text that was to become *Krapp's Last Tape*, he decided to reconceive it for the stage. He realized it might well be an excellent companion piece for *Endgame*, which had not yet been performed in English and was then in rehearsal under the direction of George Devine (who was also playing Hamm). Beckett did not want to interfere with Devine's production (though what he saw at a rehearsal worried him a lot), but with this new piece for Magee, to be directed by Donald McWhinnie, he was heavily involved from the very beginning. Magee and McWhinnie were heavy drinkers, and Beckett spent many late alcoholic nights with them pub crawling and going over his text. He worked particularly on getting them to distinguish between Krapp's two voices—the voices of youth and age—and on the rhythms of the recordings. He attended every rehearsal. He was fascinated by the old box tape recorder with its large spools. All in all, he found it an exhilarating experience.

The British critical response to the opening of the bill was mixed, but largely disheartening. Even critics who did not dismiss the plays as "weird and wanton drivel" found them, particularly the production of *Endgame*, wanting. Devine felt that he had failed Beckett, and that his own performance as Hamm was inadequate. Even Harold Hobson, who had championed *Godot*, felt that the members of the *Endgame* cast "simply have not that element that will radiate through the language, giving it body and soul." The shorter play fared somewhat better but not much. Although Magee's "brilliant tour de force" performance was admired by several critics, the "depressing" play was not to the liking of many of them. Kenneth Tynan was particularly dismissive in a parody review:

Slamm's Last Knock
(Foreground figure a blind and lordly cripple with superficial mannerisms. Sawn-off parents in bins, stage right, and shuffling servant over the stage)

SLAMM. Is that all the review he's getting?
SECK. That's all the play he's written.

SLAMM. But a genius. Could you do as much?
SECK. Not as much. But as little.

Beckett, however, was very pleased. He loved the meticulousness of McWhinnie's production, the way he moved Magee in and out of a single spotlight, exactly as Beckett had envisioned it. He wrote a friend: "Terrific performance by Magee, pitilessly directed by McWhinnie. Best experience in the theater yet."

When *Krapp* opened two years later in New York City (the Provincetown Playhouse, January 14, 1960), the initial bad notices did not surprise Beckett at all because he expected misunderstanding and misinterpretation from American critics and audiences. But as more information about the production reached Beckett in France, he was pleasantly surprised by what he heard. He had met with and discussed the play with the American director, Alan Schneider, and now found that reports indicated that Schneider had followed his advice thoroughly. "The staging sounds very remarkable," he wrote, "and the director seems to have done all I asked of him." Still the negative reviews rankled. Schneider explained critical reaction to Beckett's plays in terms of a domino theory: "First [the critics] . . . say *Godot* was terrible, but when I do *Endgame*, they say, Well, *Godot* was really good but what happened to *Endgame*? And *Krapp* was really lousy. As each new play comes along, the previous ones get better while the current one is awful." But then the tide began to turn. The reviews from the weeklies were singing a different tune from that of the daily newspapers. Tom Driver called the play "the best theater now visible in New York," and Robert Brustein in *The New Republic* described *Krapp* as "the perfect realization of Beckett's idea of human isolation." The critical war had been won, and Beckett was never treated contemptuously again. Through the years, *Krapp's Last Tape* has become one of Beckett's most frequently produced plays (even on public television). Actors who have distinguished themselves in the role include Jack MacGowan, Albert Finney, and Hume Cronyn.

Beckett Directs *Krapp*

The special affection that Beckett had for *Krapp's Last Tape* is confirmed by the fact that he directed the play three times. Beckett was not predominantly a man of the theater and came to directing relatively late in his career. He did so because he saw his plays as more than words to be brought alive by others; they were part of a total image involving eye, ear, and mind. Because of his strong vision of how his plays should be staged, Beckett was involved in several controversies regarding the interpretation of his work. One such occurred at the American Repertory Theatre in Cambridge, Massachusetts, in 1984, when director Joanne Akalaitis staged an *Endgame* that disregarded Beckett's laconic scenic instructions for "a bare interior . . . two small windows . . . a door." Akalaitis set the play in a desolate length of subway tunnel replete with derelict cars and technological junk. Barney Rosset, Beckett's American agent, informed him of this change and a flurry of letters and threats of lawsuits flew between Paris, New York, and Cambridge, with Beckett and Rosset insisting that the contract ART signed demanded fidelity to the play's complete text—*including the stage directions*. Akalaitis, ART artistic director Robert Brustein, and several critics insisted on the director's right to what Brustein called "the normal rights of interpretation . . . in order to free the full energy and meaning of the play." The controversy never made it to court: A compromise was reached whereby the production went forward with a condemnatory comment by Beckett included in the program. But when Beckett himself turned to directing his plays he did not hesitate to stray occasionally from the literal wordings of his texts, nor to approach different productions of the same play differently depending on whom he was working with. Of course, these were his plays to begin with, and yet his practice often confirmed Brustein's point about the freedom of directorial interpretation.

Always generous with advice to his interpreters, Beckett assumed full directorial responsibility in the late 1960s when he accepted an invitation to direct first *Endgame,* then his other plays in Berlin. He liked the idea of directing his plays through the prism of German translations he respected. After *Endgame* in 1967 he staged *Krapp* in 1969. The actor he chose to play Krapp was Martin Held, a large, ponderous man, who had a quality Beckett liked but was physically very different from the sprightly Pat Magee. Beckett saw something particularly sexually needy in Held, for in the production notebook he kept listing matters needing directorial attention, he designates the tape recorder as a masturbatory agent. Beckett instructed Held to hold the box erotically, to almost caress it. He sharpened other details: He wanted a starker contrast between still listening and agitated nonlistening. He expanded stage business and simplified the stage picture. He min-

imized Krapp's clown component, excising comic business with keys and envelope and introduced rheumatic fingers. He suggested to Held a gesture in which Krapp hugs himself in a gesture of self-love. All these changes moved the piece away from comedy toward pathos. Was it a reconsideration of his play by Beckett, or a response to a quality possessed by Held?

Beckett returned to *Krapp* in 1975—in his French translation (*La Dernière bande*) to accompany the French premier of *Not I*. Krapp was now played by Pierre Chabert, an actor Beckett had worked with ten years before in a play by Robert Pinget called *Hypothèse*. Because of Chabert's relative youth, Beckett dressed him in a frayed dressing gown to hide his tall frame, a toque to hide his abundant hair, and black half-gloves to cover his unwrinkled hands. Tall, pale, and thin, Chabert shivered with an old man's cold; he stretched to listen to compensate for deafness, his hand curled listlessly around the recorder handle. Immobile, he sucked in his cheeks, and maladroitly bumped into the overhead light when he rose from the table. All this created a Krapp almost the opposite of the stolid Held. Moreover, Beckett revised stage business: When Krapp goes backstage to drink he now leaves a curtain open so his guzzling shadow is visible in a long triangle projected by a Chinese lantern on a screen. Another new touch: At play's end, after the lights go out, the tape recorder light continues to glow symbolically in the dark.

Beckett's last *Krapp* occurred two years later again in Berlin at the Art Academy, but in English, not German, for an American theater workshop. The productional circumstances were amateur—no proper theater, lights, sound—but Beckett assumed the task out of loyalty to his friend Rick Cluchey who was playing Krapp. This time around Beckett (sensing the American's verbal inadequacies) stressed rhythm, occasionally beating time, and precisely choreographing movements (seven steps to and from the table, thirteen steps to and from the alcove). Again, he adjusted details: In contrast to Held's erotic recorder, Cluchey's was both friend and foe, alternately caressed *and* cursed. To get the precise shuffling sound he wanted, Beckett made Cluchey wear Beckett's own worn slippers. He now focused more on the play's structure: His notebook divides the play into four distinct scenes, and more starkly than in his earlier productions, he here stressed oppositions: stillness / movement, silence / noise, dark / light. Clearly, the evidence of his various approaches to *Krapp*—as that of his several productions of *Godot* and *Endgame*—reveals Beckett as a most practical, resourceful, and adaptable director unafraid to change his mind.

WOLE Soyinka

Akinwande Oluwole Soyinka (known as Wole Soyinka, pronounced *shoy-ING-ka*) was born in 1934 in Aké, Abe-outa, in what was then called the Western Region of Nigeria. Soyinka's parents belonged to the Yoruba tribe but converted to Christianity, and his father was a canon in the Anglican church. He studied at University College in Ibadan and at Leeds University in England, where he worked with the Shakespeare scholar G. Wilson Knight, graduating with an English degree in 1957. Between 1957 and 1959 he worked as a script reader for the Royal Court Theater in London, acknowledged breeding ground of new drama. Over the next decade he produced an impressive body of plays. In 1958 his play *The Swamp Dwellers* was presented at the University of London Drama Festival. In 1960 Nigeria gained independence and he returned home and founded The 1960 Masks, a theater company that produced his first major play, *A Dance of the Forests.* During the 1960s several of his plays were produced, including *The Strong Breed* (1963), and his first novel, *The Interpreters* (1965), was published. Also in 1965 he was arrested for allegedly seizing a radio station in Nigeria and making a politically charged broadcast. He was acquitted, but as Nigeria slid into civil war, known as the Nigerian-Biafran war, he was detained without a trial in 1967. Soyinka was imprisoned for twenty-seven months in solitary confinement for his outspoken criticism of human-rights violations and political corruption in Nigeria. Upon his release in 1969 he went into exile and wrote a memoir of his incarceration, *The Man Died* (1972), as well as numerous plays including *Madmen and Specialists* (1970), *Death and the King's Horseman* (1975), *The Bacchae of Euripides* (1973), *Opera Wonyosi* (1977, a Nigerian version of Brecht's *Three Penny Opera*), and *A Play of Giants* (1985). While visiting at Cambridge University he wrote an influential collection of essays entitled *Myth, Literature, and the African World* (1976), which theorizes an African aesthetic. He returned to Nigeria in 1976 to teach. In 1981 he published an autobiography of his childhood entitled *Aké: The Years of Childhood,* in which he examines the tension between his Christian home life and Yoruba tribal worship. In 1986 Wole Soyinka was awarded the Nobel Prize, the first African writer to receive the prize for literature. He is a staunch defender of human rights, and when he was threatened by the Nigerian government in 1994 he went into exile for a second time during which time he was charged with treason by the military dictatorship. When the political climate in Nigeria changed he was able to return to his country in 1998.

■ ■ ■ ■ ■ ■ ■ ■ ■ ■ ■ ■ ■

COMMENTARY ON *THE BACCHAE OF EURIPIDES: A COMMUNION RITE*

Soyinka is known for creating a fusion between African and Western themes, stories, and imagery. He is greatly interested in ritual—African and Western—and has written about the connection between ritual and theater. *The Bacchae*, written in the fifth century B.C.E. by the Greek playwright Euripides (whose play *Medea* is found earlier in this volume), focuses on ritual ceremonies and is sometimes used as an example to support Aristotle's assertion that Greek drama arose from ritual performances linked to the Greek god Dionysus, also known as Bacchus. The title of Euripides's play refers to the women followers, or priestesses, of the god, whose worship included a riotous, frenzied ceremony in which the women are possessed by the spirit of the god. Dionysus is said to have taught the

cultivation of the grape and creation of wine to the Greeks.

Using Euripides's play gives Soyinka the opportunity to explore the similarity between Dionysus and the Yoruban god, Ogun. In Yoruban thought, Ogun, patron god of craftworkers and god of iron, war, and fire, is a sacrificial figure who was so distressed by the separation between gods and mortals that he threw himself into the dividing abyss between gods and mortals to build a bridge toward humanity. Dionysus, the Greek god of wine, marriage, and theater, also embodies the link between mortals and gods because he is half-human, half-divine.

A theme to which Soyinka often returns in his plays is the death of a sacrificial victim, or a scapegoat. This idea is found in *The Strong Breed, Death and the King's Horseman,* and *The Bacchae of Euripides: A Communion Rite.* The word *scapegoat* was given currency by the King James Version of the Bible (1611) where it appears in Leviticus 16.8. The idea of a scapegoat is that the sins of a community are transferred to a goat, which is then sacrificed or driven into the wilds. Evidence suggests the goat was a substitution for a human sacrifice. The essence of the ritual was widespread in the ancient Near East, and judging from Soyinka's plays, it was practiced by the Yoruba people in Nigeria.

Soyinka's version of *The Bacchae* stresses the political nature of the myth by pointing out the class allegiance to Dionysus. Slaves and women are the ones who see a liberating potential in the worship of Dionysus; the aristocratic leader, Pentheus, sees such worship as threatening to his power and ability to control events. Soyinka explains his class-conscious exploration in his program note for the first production of *The Bacchae of Euripides*:

> *The Bacchae* is not a play of accommodation but of group challenge and conflict. The Dionysiac religion had a powerful social impact on the slave-sustained economy of Greece. Punishment for economic sabotage—malingering, rebelliousness, quota failure, etc—was, in a sense, a disciplinary perversion of the nature propitiation principle in traditional religion. At least it must have appeared to the classes who provided the scapegoat in times of plague or famine. The selected sacrifice was ritualistically tied, whipped on the genitals, and led on a procession through the city. He was then burnt to death and his ashes were scattered to the winds. This effort to stimulate growth must have struck the oppressed groups as hardly different from the "public deterrent"—flogging, breaking on the wheel, etc—meted out to the mine-worker who had ruined a piece of machinery, attempted to foment labor unrest or reduced the week's profit in some other

way. Both forms of imposed penance were designed to stimulate greater productivity. What the class-conscious myth of Dionysus achieved was to shift the privilege of supplying scapegoats to the class that had already monopolized all other privileges. The magnificence of Nature requires both challenge and sacrifice in all Nature renewal myths. Pentheus, the aristocrat, provides both in the highly seditious version of the myth of Euripides.

I see *The Bacchae*, finally, as a prodigious barbaric banquet, a manifestation of man's universal need to match himself against Nature. The more-than-hinted-at cannibalism corresponds to the periodic need of humans to swill, gorge and copulate on a scale as huge as Nature in her monstrous cycle of regeneration. The Dionysiac cult is both social therapy and reaffirmation of group solidarity. It is a celebration of life, bloody and tumultuous, an extravagant rite of the human and communal psyche.

Other African writers have criticized Soyinka for being too oriented toward Europe in his work. He writes chiefly in English, the language of colonial power, instead of his native Yoruba, and some of his plays are reworkings or adaptations of Western plays, such as the one printed here. On the other hand, the friction Soyinka creates when he brings the two worlds together—African and European—serves as a springboard for the rich and powerful poetry and dramatic invention that characterizes his work. When he was awarded the Nobel Prize, his acceptance speech, entitled "The Past Must Address Its Present," was a restatement of his artistic beliefs and a call for African writers to use the past, including the evils of colonialism, as a cultural and historical legacy for literature.

THE BACCHAE OF EURIPIDES*
A COMMUNION RITE
Wole Soyinka

CHARACTERS

DIONYSOS

Chorus of Slaves
LEADER
OLD SLAVE
HERDSMAN
OTHERS

Procession of Eleusis
MASTER OF REVELS
VESTALS
PRIESTS
FLOGGERS
KADMOS
PENTHEUS
OFFICER
AGAVE

The Bacchantes
1ST BACCHANTE
WEEPING BACCHANTE
OTHERS

The Wedding Scenes
1. IN-LAWS
   BRIDEGROOM
   BESTMAN
   BRIDE
2. SEATED FIGURE
   THREE WOMEN

The Slaves, and the Bacchantes should be as mixed a cast as is possible, testifying to their varied origins. Solely because of the 'hollering' style suggested for the Slave Leader's solo in the play it is recommended that this character be fully negroid.

To one side, a road dips steeply into lower background, lined by the bodies of crucified slaves mostly in the skeletal stage. The procession that comes later along this road appears to rise almost from the bowels of earth. The tomb of Semele, smoking slightly is to one side, behind the shoulder of this rise. Green vines cling to its charred ruins.

In the foreground, the main gate to the palace of Pentheus. Further down and into the wings, a lean-to built against the wall, a threshing-floor. A cloud of chaff, and through it, dim figures of slaves flailing and treading. A smell and sweat of harvest. Ripeness. A spotlight reveals Dionysos just behind the rise, within the tomb of Semele. He is a being of calm rugged strength, of a rugged beauty, not of effeminate prettiness. Relaxed, as becomes divine self-assurance but equally tensed as if for action, an arrow drawn in readiness for flight.

*Acknowledgement:

A twenty-year rust on my acquaintanceship with classical Greek made it necessary for me to rely heavily on previous translations in this adaptation of *The Bacchae*. Two versions which deserve especial mention in that I have not hesitated to borrow phrases and even lines from them are those by Gilbert Murray, published by Allen & Unwin, London, and Oxford University Press, New York, and by William Arrowsmith, in *Euripides Five: Three Tragedies*, The Complete Greek Tragedies, edited by David Grene and Richard Lattimore, published by University of Chicago Press, ©1959 by the University of Chicago. My publishers and I gratefully acknowledge the publishers concerned for the use I have made of these translations. I must also mention the debt to my own *Idanre*, a Passion poem of Ogun, elder brother to Dionysos. From this long poem I have also lifted entire lines especially in the praise chants. Finally, thanks to the National Theatre of Great Britain who commissioned this adaptation of *The Bacchae*.

Wole Soyinka

DIONYSOS. Thebes taints me with bastardy. I am turned into an alien, some foreign outgrowth of her habitual tyranny. My followers daily pay forfeit for their faith. Thebes blasphemes against me, makes me a scapegoat of a god.

It is time to state my patrimony—even here in Thebes.

I am the gentle, jealous joy. Vengeful and kind. An essence that will not exclude, not be excluded. If you are Man or Woman, I am Dionysos. Accept.

A seed of Zeus was sown in Semele my mother earth, here on this spot. It has burgeoned through the cragged rocks of far Afghanistan, burst the banks of fertile Tmolus, sprung oases through the red-eyed sands of Arabia, flowered in hill and gorge of dark Ethiopia. It pounds in the blood and breasts of my wild-haired women, long companions on this journey home through Phrygia and the isles of Crete. It beats on the walls of Thebes, bringing vengeance on all who deny my holy origin and call my mother—slut.

Here, in Soyinka's *The Bacchae of Euripides*, the Old Slave, standing left, addresses the chorus of slaves and the Bacchantes, decked with flowers in their hair. The Old Slave tries to convince them that Dionysus is a "trickster," a "windbag," but in the moments after this scene the followers of the god refuse to listen and engulf the stage in ecstatic chants and dancing that succeed in calling Dionysus forth from the prison cell where Pentheus has imprisoned him.

(*He looks down on the clouds of smoke wrapped round his feet, rising from the tomb. He scuffs the ground with a foot, scattering ashes and sparks.*)

Something lives yet, there is smoke among the rubble. Live embers. The phoenix rises and that is life—wings from cooling cinders, tendrils from putrefaction, motion from what was petrified. . . . There are green vines on the slag of ruin. Mine. As on the mountain slopes, clustering and swelling. They flush, they flood the long-parched throats of men and release their joy. This sacrament of earth is life. Dionysos.

(*From the direction of the 'crucifixion slope' comes a new sound, a liturgical drone—lead and refrain—a dull, thin monotone, still at some distance. A Herdsman carrying a jar darts across the stage to the threshers. Dionysos stands still, statuesque.*)

HERDSMAN. I think I hear them coming.

SLAVE LEADER (*eagerly seizes the jug and takes a swig.*). What did you say?

HERDSMAN. The Masters of Eleusis. They've begun the revels.

(*The slaves gather round and listen. The jug is passed round.*)

LEADER (*spits.*). Revels!

HERDSMAN. Which of us is the victim this year?

SLAVE. That old man of the king's household. The one who looks after the dogs.

HERDSMAN (*shrugs.*). He's old enough to die.

LEADER. He had better survive!

HERSDMAN (*fearfully.*). Sh-sh!

LEADER. I have said it before. If another of us dies under the lash . . . !

(*The jug is passed to him again. He takes a long draught, sighs.*)

There is heaven in this juice. It flows through my lips and I say, now I roll the sun upon my tongue and it neither burns nor scorches. And a scent-laden breeze fills the cavern of my mouth, pressing for release. I know that scent. I mean, I knew it once. I live to know it once again.

HERDSMAN. I think I understand you. Forget it friend.

LEADER. A scent of freedom is not easily forgotten. Have you ever slept, dreamt, and woken up with the air still perfumed with the fragrance of grapes?

HERDSMAN. There is no other smell at this time of the year. If you live in the hills that is. It gets oppressive sometimes, to tell the truth. You know, rather cloying.

LEADER. Surrounded by walls one can only dream. But one day . . . one day . . .

HERDSMAN. Not you. No one will ever trust you outside of the city walls. Dissimulation is an art you will never master. You need the sly humility, the downcast eye. Yes Sire, King Pentheus, no Sir Honourable Eunuch of the Queen's Bedchamber . . .

LEADER. Let's speak of better things. Tell me of those hidden vineyards. They are like my buried longings: I know each precious acre of the forbidden terrain, inch by inch. And I know I envy you. The air of Thebes is sterile. Nothing breathes in it. Nothing—really—lives. Come closer . . . distend your nostrils . . . now breathe in, deeply . . . smell!

HERDSMAN. Look, if every time I bring you wine you have to . . .

LEADER. Do you smell anything? Anything at all? After the hills and the vines and the wind can you smell me? Do I live?

HERDSMAN. You promised . . .

LEADER (*He makes an effort, takes a deep breath.*). What does it matter anyway. An open-air slave or a walled-up slave . . . we all fold our arms and thank the gods for a generous harvest.

HERDSMAN. Generous is not the word for it. The vines went mad so to speak; they were not themselves. Something seemed to have got under the soil and was feeding them nectar. The weight that hung on the vines even from the scrubbiest patch, each cluster . . . (*his hands shape them.*) pendulous breasts of the wives of Kronos, bursting all over with giant nipples.

LEADER. I felt it on my tongue. The sun has left the heavens and made a home within the grapes of Boetia.

HERDSMAN. You may say that. It was a joy to tread them.

(*The liturgical drone is now very close.*)

They are nearly here. I must go.

LEADER. Wait. (*Takes hold of him.*) Suppose the old man dies?

HERDSMAN. We all have to die sometime.

LEADER. Flogged to death? In the name of some unspeakable rites?

HERDSMAN. Someone must cleanse the new year of the rot of the old or, the world will die. Have you ever known famine? Real famine?

LEADER. Why us? Why always us?

HERDSMAN. Why not?

LEADER. Because the rites bring us nothing! Let those who profit bear the burden of the old year dying.

HERDSMAN. Careful. (*Points to the row of crosses.*) The palace does not need the yearly Feast of Eleusis to deal with rebellious slaves.

(*He takes the jug and turns to go.*)

LEADER. Look, tell them on the hills, tell your fellows up there . . .

HERDSMAN (*instantly rigid.*). What?

LEADER (*hesitates, sighs.*). Nothing. Tell them—we also are waiting.

(*The Herdsman goes off the same way as he entered. Led by a solemn figure who is the Master of Revels, a procession emerges and proceeds over the rise.*

First, the Master of Revels, next black-robed priests intoning a liturgy, punctuated by hand-bells. After them comes a group of vestals in white. The first pair carry fresh branches, the middle section garlands and flowers, the last pair carry bowls. The vestals are followed by an Old Man, completely white-bearded, dressed in what might approximate to sackcloth-and-ashes, who carries a bunch of used twigs. Behind him are four stalwart figures in red, armed with strong, supple lashes. At every three or four paces the priests ring their bell, upon which the two maidens in front of the Old Man turn and sprinkle him with what might be ashes or chaff, while the four men lay into him from all sides with their whips. A straggle of crowd follows. This sedate procession passes through and around Dionysos without seeing him and proceeds downstage towards the gates of the palace. The slaves have stopped work and are watching. A small ceremony of 'cleansing' is performed on the palace gate. The priests take branches from a bundle borne by the two leading girls, symbolically scour the gates with them, then pile the used twigs on the bunch already borne by the Old Man. He is sprinkled and flogged as before.

At the sight of the Old Man, there is distinct surprise and agitation among the slaves.

Suddenly the Old Man appears to wilt, collapse. A further stroke of the lash brings him to his knees. The intoning continues without stopping, and the lashes. As he falls prone, a bright flash reveals Dionysos on the tomb of Semele. All action ceases. The music of Dionysos.)

DIONYSOS (*smiling.*). Sing Death of the Old Year, and—welcome the new—god.

(*A prolonged, confused silence. In the threshing-hut the slaves forcefully restrain their Leader who seems bent on giving immediate vocal acknowledgement to the god.*)

SLAVE. You'll get us killed. We'll be wiped out to a man.

ANOTHER. Remember the helots. Don't be rash.

(*Dionysos comes down among the procession. The priests retreat in terror as he turns towards the vestals.*)

DIONYSOS. And the vestals of Eleusis?

VESTALS (*hesitant and fearful.*). We . . . welcome the new . . . god.

DIONYSOS. Oh, but joyfully, joyfully! Welcome the new god. joyfully. Sing death of the old year passing.

VESTALS (*liturgical, lifeless.*). Welcome the new god. Joyfully. Sing death . . .

(*They stop, look at one another foolishly. One or two begin to titter and Dionysos bellows with laughter. The venals regain some relaxation.*)

DIONYSOS. And now try again. Together, with joy.

VESTALS (*courageously*). We . . .

(*A vestal detaches herself from the group, her eyes riveted on the face of Dionysos. She scoops up a garland as she passes the flower-bearers and comes up to the stranger. He bows his head and she garlands him.*)

THE VESTAL. Welcome the new . . .

(*Keels over in a faint and is caught by Dionysos. Carrying her he moves towards the priests.*)

DIONYSOS. And now the priests of Eleusis?

PRIEST. We welcome . . .

ANOTHER. . . . a miracle, a miracle.

(*They hurriedly edge their way out and flee in the direction from which they made their entry. The floggers also retreat a little way, watchful.*)

LEADER (*breaking loose after the priests' retreat.*). Welcome the new god! Thrice welcome the new order! (*hands cupped to his mouth, he yodels.*) Evohe-e-e-e! Evohe-e-e-e!

(*The sound is taken up by echoes from the hills. It roves round and round and envelops the scene. All heads turn outwards in different directions, listening. A mixture of excitement and unease as the sound continues, transformed beyond the plain echo to an eerie response from vast distances.*

From the same responsive source, intermingled strains of the music of Dionysos. It swells inwards to the attentive listeners. The vestal in the arms of Dionysos stirs, responding. She lowers herself to the ground slowly, moves into a dance to the music. As the dance takes her close to the Slave Leader he moves away with her; the dance soon embraces all the vestals and slaves.

Dionysos, smiling, slips off as they become engrossed in the dance. The music stops, the enchantment is cut off. The fainting vestal looks round her in growing panic.)

VESTAL. Don't leave us!

(*She runs out in pursuit, the other vestals following.*)

LEADER. Let's follow.

(*The slaves hang back. The euphoria has melted rapidly.*)

SLAVE. I think we've gone too far already.

LEADER.
You hesitant fools! Don't you understand?
Don't you *know*? We are no longer alone—
Slaves, helots, the near and distant dispossessed!
This master race, this much vaunted dragon spawn
Have met their match. Nature has joined forces with us.
Let them reckon now, not with mere men, not with

The scapegoat bogey of a slave uprising
But with a new remorseless order, forces
Unpredictable as molten fire in mountain wombs.
To doubt, to hesitate is to prove undeserving.

SLAVE. There is such a fault as rashness.

LEADER. When the present is intolerable, the unknown harbours no risks.

ANOTHER. I don't know . . . why make ourselves conspicuous. Let the free citizens of Thebes declare for this stranger or against him.

LEADER. Whose interest will direct their choice? Ours?

SLAVE. No, but . . .

(*The slaves look away from one another, uncomfortable but afraid. After an awkward silence, the Leader sighs in defeat.*)

LEADER. Let us go as far as the gates then. We should know at least how the Thebans receive him. In our own interest.

(*They follow him out, guiltily.*)
(*The Old Man is left alone with the floggers. As he begins to pick himself up painfully, they rush forward to help him up. He brushes them off angrily.*)

TIRESIAS. Take your hands off!

(*He rises, tries to dust himself and winces.*)

1ST MAN. Were you hurt?

TIRESIAS. Animals!

1ST MAN. Oh. We . . . didn't mean to.

TIRESIAS. You never do.

2ND MAN. Who was he?

1ST MAN. Yes who was he? Where did he spring from?

TIRESIAS (*snorts.*). Who was he? Where did he spring from? Fools! Blind, stupid, bloody brutes! Can you see how you've covered me in weals? Can't you bastards ever tell the difference between ritual and reality.

1ST MAN. *I* was particularly careful. I pulled my blows.

TIRESIAS. Symbolic flogging, that is what I keep trying to drum into your thick heads.

4TH MAN. I could have sworn I only tapped you gently from time to time.

3RD MAN. It's all that incantation. It soaks in your brain and you can't feel yourself anymore.

TIRESIAS. I suppose you would have carried on like you do year after year. Flogged the last breath out of my body.

3RD MAN (*among shocked protests.*). How could you think such a thing? You are not a slave. I mean, we do have some control.

TIRESIAS. Yah, you showed it. Anyway what are you standing there for?

1ST MAN. Well . . . we . . . I mean, we don't quite know what to do.

3RD MAN. I mean, it's a bit of a departure isn't it? Never known anything like this happen before. Well damn it, who was he?

4TH MAN. And the vestals, gone with him.

TIRESIAS. Go after them. You've been cheated of your blood this time so your throats are a little parched. Go up in the mountains and you'll find other juices to quench your thirst.

1ST MAN (*irritated.*). You will speak in riddles!

TIRESIAS. The feast has shifted to the mountains—is that simple enough?

1ST MAN (*wearily.*). Just tell us what we are now expected to do when we get there?

TIRESIAS. Whatever you wish. Just take your violent presences away from me!

3RD MAN. Well, that's plain enough.

1ST MAN. You know who he was.

TIRESIAS (*draws himself up.*). Since when has it been the custom for common no-brain wrestlers to cross-examine the seer of Thebes.

1ST MAN. Let's go. (*They exit.*)

TIRESIAS. Swine! (*He feels his body tenderly, then shouts.*) Wait! Which of you kept my staff?

DIONYSOS (*re-enters.*). Borrow my thyrsus.

TIRESIAS. Thank you. Dionysos I presume?

DIONYSOS. You see too well Tiresias.

TIRESIAS. As if the gentlest emanations from the divine *maestro* would not penetrate the thickest cataract.

DIONYSOS. Yet there is one here who has no defect in his eyes but will not see.

TIRESIAS. I know. Handle him gently Dionysos, if only for his grandfather's sake.

DIONYSOS. Kadmos was pious. Consecrating this ground in memory of my mother at least kept her alive in the heart of Thebes . . . but that is Kadmos. Let every man's actions save or damn him. We shall see what Pentheus chooses to do.

TIRESIAS (*shrugs.*). I knew that would be the answer. Anyway, thank you for stepping in just now. You were just in time.

DIONYSOS. Were you really in trouble?

TIRESIAS. I was. One can never tell how far the brutes will go. Mind you, I took the precaution of wearing your fawn-skin under my gown. You see how the sack-cloth has been flogged to ribbons. I had to collapse to remind them they were getting carried away again.

DIONYSOS. But what made the high priest of Thebes elect to play flagellant?

TIRESIAS. The city must be cleansed. Filth, pollution, cruelties, secret abominations—a whole year's accumulation.

DIONYSOS. Why you? Are you short of lunatics, criminals, or slaves?

TIRESIAS. A mere favour to Kadmos whom I love like a brother. Kadmos is Thebes. He has yielded all power to Pentheus but I know he still rejoices or weeps with Thebes. And Thebes—well, let's just say the situation is touch and go. If one more slave had been killed at the cleansing rites, or sacrificed to that insatiable altar of nation-building . . .

DIONYSOS. Quite a politician eh Tiresias?

TIRESIAS. A priest is not much use without a following, and that's soon washed away in what social currents he fails to sense or foresee. As priest and sage and prophet and I know not how else I am regarded in Thebes, I must see for the blind young man who is king and even sometimes—act for him.

DIONYSOS. And if you have been flogged to pieces at the end, like an effigy?

TIRESIAS. Then I shall pass into the universal energy of renewal . . . like some heroes or gods I could name.

DIONYSOS. Go on.

TIRESIAS. Isn't that it? Is that not why Dionysos?

DIONYSOS. Is that not what?

TIRESIAS. Why you all seem to get torn to pieces at some point or the other?

DIONYSOS. Don't change the subject. Go on about you.

TIRESIAS. I've said it all. What more do you want me to say?

DIONYSOS (*He moves close to Tiresias, tugs gently at his beard.*). Poor Tiresias, poor neither-nor, eternally tantalized psychic intermediary, poor agent of the gods through whom everything passes but nothing touches, what happened to you in the midst of the crowd, dressed and powdered by the hands of ecstatic women, flagellated by sap-swollen birches? What sensations coursed your withered veins as the whips drew blood, as the skin of the birches broke against yours and its fragrant sap mingled with your blood. You poor starved votary at the altar of soul, what deep hunger unassuaged by a thousand lifelong surrogates drove you to this extreme self-sacrifice. Don't lie to a god Tiresias.

TIRESIAS. I never lie. I told you the truth.

DIONYSOS. Yes, but only a half-truth, like your prophesies. Tell me the rest.

TIRESIAS (*cornered. Finally.*). Yes, there was a hunger. Thirst. In this job one lives half a life, neither priest nor man. Neither man nor woman. I have longed to know what flesh is made of. What suffering is. Feel the taste of blood instead of merely foreseeing it. Taste the ecstasy of rejuvenation after long organizing its ritual. When the slaves began to rumble I saw myself again playing that futile role, pouring my warnings on deaf ears. An uprising would come, bloodshed, and I would watch, untouched, merely vindicated as before—as prophet. I approach death and dissolution, without having felt life . . . its force . . .

DIONYSOS. And just now?

TIRESIAS. You forget. That goes by role. Ecstasy is too elusive a quarry for such tricks. Even if I did shed a few drops of blood.

DIONYSOS (*lays his hands gently on the Old Man's shoulders.*).

Thebes shall have its full sacrifice. And Tiresias will know ecstasy.

TIRESIAS. Something did begin. Perhaps those lashes did begin something. I feel . . . a small crack in the dead crust of the soul. Listen! Can you hear women's voices? Strange, just then I almost felt my veins race.

DIONYSOS (*drawing back.*). Dance for me Tiresias, Dance for Dionysos.

TIRESIAS. That's like asking the elephant to fly. I've never danced in all my life.

(*The music of Dionysos is heard. Tiresias stands entranced for some moments, then moves naturally into the rhythm, continues to dance, rapt.*

Dionysos watches for a while, then slips off. Enter Kadmos, stands amazed and watches. Tiresias senses his presence after a while and stops, clutching his thyrsus defensively.)

TIRESIAS. It's someone else. Who is it?

KADMOS. Your good friend, Kadmos of the royal house. How goes it with you Tiresias? Are you well?

TIRESIAS. You must be blind to need ask such a question.

KADMOS. Well I confess I do not believe my eyes.

TIRESIAS. Oh Kadmos Kadmos, how I wish you were still king of Thebes.

KADMOS. That's not like you to wish undone what is already done. What's biting you?

TIRESIAS. Your grandson, the foolish, blind, headstrong, suicide-bent king.

KADMOS. Not suicide-bent I hope. His faults I readily admit. But what's he done now?

TIRESIAS. Nothing yet. It's what he's going to do. I know how it will all end. Oh Kadmos, wisdom is what we need in a king at this moment, a sense of balance and proportion.

KADMOS. You didn't seem a model of proportion when I came on you a moment ago. What did you think you were doing?

TIRESIAS. Saving Thebes again, though I fear that it is too late. It is far far easier to save Thebes from the anger of disgruntled classes than from the vengeance of a spited god. Neither your piety nor my new-found ecstasy can help him now.

KADMOS. Tiresias, you know I have no head for conundrums . . .

TIRESIAS. Yes, your son takes after you there. But at least you don't go at every riddle with sledgehammer and pitchfork.

KADMOS. Is there yet another danger that threatens Thebes?

TIRESIAS. None that you or I could help. (*Sounds in the distance.*) Listen to them! Can you hear that? Can you feel the power of it Kadmos?

KADMOS (*The significance dawns on him.*). But you are not with them. You promised me Tiresias. You promised Thebes.

TIRESIAS. What you hear is another sound, a new order. Your *other* grandson took my place. The wanderer has come home. He's here.

(*The Bacchantes enter to shouts of Bromius! Evohe-e! Zagreus!*)

Quickly. Stand aside and be silent. They sound already possessed.

(*They hide themselves.*)

BACCHANTE. Where?
BACCHANTE. Where?
BACCHANTE. Where?
BACCHANTE. Where?

(*That cry is taken up, repeated fast from mouth to mouth, ending with a long, impassioned communal cry.*)

BACCHANTES. Bro-o-o-o-o-mius!
BACCHANTE. Bromius . . .
BACCHANTE. Bromius . . .
BACCHANTE. Bromius . . .

(*Again the name is tossed from tongue to tongue, beginning as a deep audible breath and accompanied by spasmodic, scenting movements. It swells in volume and breaks suddenly into another passionate scream by the leader of the Bacchantes.*)

1ST BACCHANTE.
Bro-o-o-o-o-mius! Be Manifest! Be manifest Bromius,
your Bacchantes have taken the field. You've led us.
Lead us now.
ANOTHER.
We've journeyed together. Through Lydia and Phrygia . . .
ANOTHER.
Over rivers of gold, Bactrian fastness . . .
ANOTHER.
Through slopes of the clustering vine.
ANOTHER.
Companion of forest and towered cities,
Of the steppes of Persia and wastes of Media.
ANOTHER.
Through the dance of the sun on Ethiopia's rivers,
Lakes, seas, emerald oases.
ANOTHER.
Rooting deep, ripeness and mysteries
Rooting as vine in the most barren of soils.
1ST BACCHANTE.
The silvering firs have trembled, we have seen rockhills
Shudder, earth awaken, ramparts of heaven cave
Beasts answer from their lairs, sap rise in the trees
And the sevenfold bars on the gates of Thebes
Splinter—at the Maenads' cry of BROMIUS!
BACCHANTES.
Evohe-e-e-e-e-e!

(*Re-enter the slaves.*)

LEADER (*in a ringing voice.*). Bacchantes, fellow strangers, to this land!

(*A gradual hush. They turn towards the sound.*)

LEADER. Fellow aliens, let me ask you—do you know Bromius?

(*The women turn to one another, still in a haze of possession, but astonished at such ridiculous question. One or two continue to moan, completely oblivious to the interruption.*)

1ST BACCHANTE. Do we *know* Bromius?
LEADER. Bromius. Zagreus. Offspring of Zeus as the legend goes.
1ST BACCHANTE (*over a general peal of laughter.*). Stranger, do *you* know Bromius?
LEADER. A god goes by many names. I have long been a spokesman for the god.
1ST BACCHANTE. And yet you ask, do we know Bromius. Who led us down from the mountains of Asia, down holy Tmolus, through the rugged bandit-infested hills of the Afgans, the drugged Arabian sands, whose call have we followed through the great delta? Who opened our eyes to the freedom of sands, to the liberation of waters? Do we know Bromius?
LEADER. Do you love his worship?
1ST BACCHANTE.
Hard are the labours of a god
Hard, but his service is sweet fulfillment.
LEADER (*coming forward.*). Then make way. (*They part and he comes among them.*)
WEEPING BACCHANTE (*the Fainting Vestal*). What is it? What does the slave want with us? I want my god, the son of Zeus.
ANOTHER. Where shall we seek him? Where find him?
LEADER. Fall back a little. Seal up the streets and let no one intrude. There is a human all believers know.

(*Pause. The Bacchante sizes him up, decides for him.*)

1ST BACCHANTE. Let every mouth be silent. Let no ill-omened words profane your tongues.
LEADER.
It is the hour we have long awaited.
What is hidden must some day come to light
Now, raise with me the old old hymn to godhead.

(*The Chorus intone beneath the prayer.*)

1ST BACCHANTE.
Blessed are they who know the mysteries of god
Blessed all who hallow their life in worship of god
Whom the spirit of god possesses, who are one
With earth, leaves and vine in the holy body of god.
Blessed are the dancers whose hearts are purified
Who tread on the hill in the holy dance of god.
Blessed are they who keep the rites of the Earth-Mother

Who bear the thyrsus, who wield the holy wand of god
Blessed are all who wear the ivy crown of god
Blessed, blessed are they: Dionysos is their god.
CHORUS.
Blessed, blessed, thrice blessed are we:
Dionysos is our god.

(*The first chords of music, oriental strings and timbrels.*)

WEEPING BACCHANTE.
Bromius, Bromius . . .
LEADER.
Blessed are they who bathe in the seminal river
Who merge in harmony with earth's eternal seeding
Blessed they whose hands are cupped to heaven
Their arms shall be funnel for the rain of understanding
Blessed are all whose feet have trodden the dance of grapes
Whose hands have nursed the vine, earth's gentlest binding
Blessed their joys in the common sacrament, whose beings
Open to intuitions in the liberation of the grape
Blessed, thrice blessed the innocence of acceptance
The arms that reach to a welcome of god
Blessed, thrice blessed, the moment of recognition
Of god without as the essence within.
CHORUS.
Blessed, blessed, thrice blessed are we:
Dionysos is our god.
LEADER.
For he is the living essence of whom, said heaven
The seed is mine, this seminal germ
Earthed in sublimation of the god in flesh
The flesh in god. I bind my seed in hoops of iron
And though all seek him, safe I hold him
Safe in the loins wherefrom he sprang.
Let all revere the gracious earth,
Womb of the infant deity.
WEEPING BACCHANTE.
Bromius, Bromius . . .
LEADER.
Tribute to the holy hills of Ethiopia
Caves of the unborn, and the dark ancestral spirits. Home
Of primal drums round which the dead and living
Dance. I praise the throbbing beat of the hide
The squeal and the wail of flutes . . .
MORE BACCHANTES (*moaning.*).
Oh Bromius, Bromius.
1ST BACCHANTE.
It is fallen to me at last, fallen
All fallen to me from the raving satyrs
Fallen at last to me to celebrate his name:
Dionysos! Stranger, honey-voiced
Spokesman of my god. Tell us tales of what you know,
Sing to me again of Dionysos.

(Music. It has the strange quality—the nearest familiar example is the theme-song of Zorba the Greek—with its strange mixture of nostalgia, violence, and death. The scene which follows needs the following quality: extracting the emotional colour and temperature of a European pop scene without degenerating into that tawdry commercial manipulation of teenage mindlessness. The lines are chanted not sung, to musical accompaniment. The Slave Leader is not a gyrating pop drip. His control emanates from the self-contained force of his person, a progressively deepening spiritual presence. His style is based on the lilt and energy of the black hot gospellers who themselves are often first to become physically possessed. The effect on his crowd is however, the same—physically—as would be seen in a teenage pop audience. From orgasmic moans the surrogate climax is achieved. A scream finds its electric response in others and a rush begins for the person of the preacher. Handfuls of his clothes are torn, his person is endangered but he never 'loses his cool'. As his chant approaches climax a sudden human wave engulfs him and he is completely submerged under screaming, 'possessed' lungs and bodies.

As with such scenes there is always something of an overall ugliness about the manifested emotion. But the radiant isolated votive or two, or even the few faces of intensely energized spiritual rapture that stand out in the mêlée indicate something of the awesome depths of this self-release.)

LEADER.
Then listen Thebes, nurse of Semele,
Crown your hair with ivy
Turn your fingers green with bryony
Redden your walls with berries,
Decked with boughs of oak and fir
Come dance the dance of god.
Fringe your skins of dappled fawn
With wool from the shuttle and loom
For the looms are abandoned by throngs of women
They run to the mountains and Bromius before
They follow the violent wand of the bringer of life
The violent wand,
Of the gentle, jealous, joy!

BACCHANTES *(like a wail.).*
Bromius, Bromius . . .

LEADER *(progressively radiant.).*
He . . . is . . .
Sweet upon the mountains, such sweetness
As afterbirth, such sweetness as death.
His hand strap wildness, and breed it gentle
He infuses tameness with savagery.
I have seen him on the mountains, in vibrant fawn-skin
I have seen his smile in the red flash of blood
I have seen the raw heart of a mountain-lion
Yet pulsing in his throat.
In the mountains of Eritrea, in the deserts of Libya

In Phrygia whose copper hills ring with cries of
Bromius, Zagreus, Dionysos,
I know he is the awaited, the covenant, promise,
Restorer of fullness to Nature's lean hours.
As milk he flows in the earth, as wine
In the hills. He runs in the nectar of bees, and
In the duct of their sting lurks—Bromius.
Oh let his flames burn gently in you, gently,
Or else—consume you it must—consume you . . .

CHORUS.
Bromius . . . Bromius . . .

LEADER.
His hair a bush of foxfires in the wind
A streak of lightning his thyrsus.
He runs, he dances,
Kindling the tepid
Spurring the stragglers
And the women are like banks to his river—
A stream of gold from beyond the desert—
They cradle the path of his will.

CHORUS.
Come, come Dionysos . . .

LEADER.
Oh Thebes, Thebes, flatten your walls.
Raise your puny sights
To where the heights of Kithairon await you.

CHORUS.
Yes, yes . . .

LEADER.
On the slopes where Dionysos will come
Run free with you in your labour of song
Your dancing drudgery, your chores of dreaming—
In the truth of night descends his secret—
Hold, embrace it.

CHORUS.
Yes, yes . . . set me free . . . set me free.

LEADER.
The sun touches the vines on the slopes
And *that* is godhead. Dew falls on the grass
And *that* is godhead. The sap awakens—
A birth
A dawn
A spring
Pure dewdrops down the mountain
That is godhead. And you
Nestled in earth's womb are
Green leaves in winter, woodsap in snow
You are the eternal ivy on the wand of life
Emerald pines that defy the winter
Dates of the oases in drought of deserts.

BACCHANTES.
Bromius . . . Bromius . . .

LEADER.
Seek him in your breasts with love, within

Your hidden veins, in the quiet murmur of your blood
Seek him in the marrow, in wombstone, he is fount
Of life. He makes an anvil of the mountain-peaks
Hammers forth a thunderous will, he farms the slopes
And the vine tempers his will. In plains and valleys
Nest his joyful Bacchae, his mesh of elements
Reconciles a warring universe.

BACCHANTES.
Come Bromius, come . . .

LEADER.
He is the new life, the new breath, creative flint
Flood earth with his blood, let your shabby streets
Flow with his life, his light, drum him into the heart
Like thunder. He is the storehouse of life
His bull horns empower him
A bud on the autumn bough, he blossoms in you
His green essence fills your womb of earth. . . .

BACCHANTES.
Bromius . . . Bromius . . .

LEADER.
There is power in his thyrsus, feel!
It pulses. Feel! It quivers and races with sap.
Throat, tongue, breast, calling forth the powers of life
Hold him, embrace him. His dance covers you
His drums envelop you, your skin is one with his
    drum
Tuning and straining tight. Spindle and shuttle
In your hand—behold—the wand of god
The hearthstone his thyrsus, thrusting from earth
The fire is tamed in new greenery of life,
In fawn-skin and ivy, and the thorn of life comes
Piercing your blood . . . !

(*A long scream from a Bacchante snaps the last restraint
of the women. They rush the Leader and engulf him. He
disappears under. From under the mêlée of limbs, the wild,
desperate chant of 'Where? Where? Where?' recom-
mences, diminishing as the mass of flesh unravels, dispersed in different directions, groping unseeing. Other
slaves drag their Leader to safety. The chant continues
faintly off for some time after they have all disappeared.*

    *Cautiously, the two Old Men emerge. Kadmos is in a
high state of excitement.*)

KADMOS.
Why are we waiting. Let's go, let's go.

TIRESIAS. Where?

KADMOS. To the mountains where else? Let's go and do him
honour.

TIRESIAS. But are you dressed?

(*Kadmos flings off his cloak, revealing the Dionysian
fawn-skin under it.*)

KADMOS. Aren't I? (*Takes Tiresias's hand.*) Here, feel that.

You won't find finer foreskin except on Dionysos
himself.

TIRESIAS. He isn't circumcised?

KADMOS. Who? Who isn't circumcised?

TIRESIAS. Dionysos. What you said about his foreskin.

KADMOS. Did I? Slip of the tongue.

TIRESIAS (*considers it quite seriously.*). I wonder how many of
that you'd need to make a Bacchic smock.

KADMOS. If that was what Dionysos demanded . . . a couple
of thousand slaves forcibly circumcised . . . Pentheus
could arrange it.

TIRESIAS. Not for Dionysos.

KADMOS. I suppose not. Anyway how come you to think of
such things in the first place?

TIRESIAS. You said it, not me.

KADMOS. Alright, alright. I said it was a slip of tongue. Quite
natural at my age.

TIRESIAS. It's not natural at your age, that's the point. I found
that significant. It's not natural at all.

KADMOS. When you start on significances you lose me.

TIRESIAS. You are a wily one. Fancy hiding your Bacchic togs
under a cloak. You shook me when you first came in, all
that pretence, as if you were shocked at the sight of me
dancing.

KADMOS. Oh that. I was merely tasting my own resolve. Kadmos, Kadmos, it doesn't befit your age and rank—so I
kept telling myself. I was on my way to find you. When I
saw you dancing by yourself I said, I'll make a display of
my doubts before Tiresias, and watch his reactions. He is
old enough to be considered wise.

TIRESIAS (*preening.*). Enough of that old Tiresias bit.
Dionysos has knocked years off my back.

KADMOS. It's going round, it's catching Thebes on the re-
bound. Thebes has fallen out of love with our fossilized
past and needs to embrace a new vitality. Come on, I am
rearing to go.

TIRESIAS. Have you a crown?

KADMOS. Have I a crown? Ho ho. (*He reaches into a side-
pouch and brings an ivy wreath. Sets it on his head at a rakish
angle.*) If only you knew how my head has itched all day
to put this on. Here, feel it. What do you think? Not too
. . . dashing is it?

TIRESIAS. A bit fanciful for your age.

KADMOS. Now now, no more of that age nonsense. A man is
as young as he feels and I feel thirty.

TIRESIAS. Well we'll just say you've set a new fashion then.
Under divine inspiration.

KADMOS. Hey, have I told you about my daughters? They've
got it really bad you know. They are all up in the mountains frisking around in the very madness of spring.

TIRESIAS. Ah yes, look around and see if those other women
dropped bits of ivy while they were prancing about.

KADMOS. Yes, plenty around. What do you . . . ah of course.
Hold on, I'll soon wreathe you a crown.

(*Picks up a good bit of ivy and begins to weave a crown for Tiresias.*)

What a relief to find one's innermost doubts banished once for all. What shall I do when I meet him Tiresias? He's my grandson after all, but still one must be careful with gods mustn't one?

TIRESIAS. Will you know him?

KADMOS. Why not? My own flesh and blood.

TIRESIAS. You've never seen him.

KADMOS. Doesn't matter. Flesh will call to flesh. I already sense his nearness.

TIRESIAS. Pentheus doesn't know his own flesh. And when he does he'll think he's duty-bound to cut it out of himself. If you held out the mirror of longing to him, he will utterly fail to recognize his own image or else he'll smash the mirror in anger.

KADMOS. There you go again talking in riddles. Here's your crown. Trad or trendy. (*He holds it poised over Tiresias's head.*)

TIRESIAS. We-e-e-ell, one is madness two is fashion. I don't like to see you mad.

KADMOS. Done. (*He stands some distance away and returns to adjust the angle.*) Perfect. Fawn-skin and ivy crowns. Oh Tiresias, do you think we've aged before our time?

TIRESIAS. You at least have lived, sower of dragon's teeth.

KADMOS. True. But then I wonder. Perhaps I retired too soon. It is wrong to wait for death isn't it? Simply to do nothing except wait for death. That's hardly a befitting end for a man. Suddenly I wonder about the past. From a life which constantly rejuvenated my bones I sat down and became an administrator. An administrator Tiresias! Then an old-age pensioner—on the court list. I who slew the dragon and bred a race of warriors from his teeth.

TIRESIAS. It is good to rest sometimes.

KADMOS. Then will you tell me why suddenly I feel grape-skins under my feet?

TIRESIAS. Oh come on let's go. Give me your hand.

KADMOS. Here, hold on to me. Where shall we go? Where shall we tread this dance of life, tossing our white heads to the drums of Dionysos. Shall I lead the way to the mountains.

TIRESIAS. Lead the way.

KADMOS. I don't understand it. I am restless with a thousand schemes. Why should I keep thinking now I should never have left the throne to Pentheus? I know he will do something wrong. Shall I arrest him for his own good do you think? There are still soldiers loyal to me. We could stage a *coup d'état*.

TIRESIAS. To the mountains Kadmos. The god awaits us.

KADMOS. Ah well, maybe you're right. It is this new surge of life, I can't explain it. I feel I could even solve any of these riddles you are so fond of. I could dance all night

without tiring, simply beating earth with my thyrsus. Hey, where is that anyway?

(*He rummages inside his pouch and brings out a blunt-ended telescoped object which he proceeds to pull out into a thyrsus. The following exchange is done music-hall style.*)

Oh, what a shame you can't see to admire this Tiresias. Here, hold it in both hands, one hand at each end— that's it. Now pull out slowly. See how it works? First collapsible thyrsus in Attica, in the whole world maybe. Made it myself. Couldn't trust the palace joiner not to talk. Shows you how nervous I was, going all that length to disguise the obvious.

(*Plants it on the ground meaning to use it as a walking stick. It collapses and he falls. Tiresias helps him up.*)

The damned thing collapsed.

TIRESIAS. You can't expect it to be as strong as the joiner's.

KADMOS (*straightens it out.*). Why not? It works doesn't it. Forgot to put a lock on it that's all. (*The thyrsus collapses again.*) Damn!

TIRESIAS. No good? (*As it fails again.*)

KADMOS. I can't walk through the streets with this. Let's go up in my chariot.

TIRESIAS. Walking is better. It shows more honour to the god.

KADMOS. With the shortest thyrsus in Thebes? I'll be a laughing-stock.

TIRESIAS. Let's go. Put it back in your trousers.

KADMOS (*morosely replacing it in the pouch.*). I should have let the joiner show me how. But it would only make him cocky.

(*They both guffaw.*)

TIRESIAS. Give me your hand? When you step into the dance you'll lose all your silly notions. You accept, and that's the real stature of man. You are immersed in the richest essence of all—you inner essence. This is what the dance of Dionysos brings forth from you, this is the meaning of the dance. Follow the motion of my feet and dance Kadmos. We will dance all the way to the hills. One—Two—Back, One—Two—Back.

KADMOS (*obeys him.*). I am a man, nothing more. I do not scoff at the will of heaven.

TIRESIAS. No, only fools trifle with divinity. People will say, Aren't you ashamed? At your age, dancing, wreathing your head with ivy? . . . Have you caught it? One—Two—Back, One—Two—Back

KADMOS. I am not ashamed. Damn them, did the god declare that just the young or women must dance? They mean to kill us off before our time.

TIRESIAS. He has broken the barrier of age, the barrier of sex or slave and master. It is the will of Dionysos that no one be excluded from his worship.

KADMOS. Except those who exclude themselves. Like this one who approaches us Tiresias.

(*He stops dancing, makes Tiresias stop.*)

TIRESIAS. Who is it?

KADMOS. The man to whom I left the throne. He seems excited and disturbed. Let us keep out of his way for a while.

(*Enter Pentheus, straight, militaristic in bearing and speech. His attendants have to run to keep up with him. Once on stage he strides angrily up and down.*)

PENTHEUS.

I shall have order! Let the city know at once
Pentheus is here to give back order and sanity.
To think those reports which came to us abroad are true!
Not padded or strained. Disgustingly true in detail.
If anything reality beggars the report. It's *disgusting!*
I leave the country, I'm away only a moment
Campaigning to secure our national frontiers. And what
    happens?
Behind me—chaos! The city in uproar. Let everyone
Know I've returned to re-impose order. Order!
And tell it to the women especially, those
Promiscuous bearers of this new disease.
They leave their home, desert their children
Follow the new fashion and join the Bacchae
Flee the hearth to mob the mountains—those contain
Deep shadows of course, secret caves to hide
Lewd games for this new god—Dionysos!
That's the holy spirit newly discovered—
Dionysos! Their ecstasy is flooded down
In brimming bowls of wine—so much for piety!
Soused, with all the senses aroused, they crawl
Into the bushes and there of course a man
Awaits them. All part of the service for this
Mysterious deity. The hypocrisy! All that concerns them
    is
Getting serviced. We netted a few.
The rest escaped into the mountains. I want them
Hunted down. Chained and caged behind bars of iron.
I want an end to the drunken dancing
The filth, the orgies, the rot and creeping
Poison in the body of state. I want Order and—
I want immediate results. Go!

(*An officer salutes and exits.*)

And this stranger, who is he? A sorcerer?
Hypnotist? Some such kind of faker I'm sure, vomited
From Lydia, or Media, those decadent lands where
They wear their hair long, ribboned, and curled,
Stink of scent and their cheeks are perpetually
Flushed with wine, their eyes full of furtive

Messages. So goes the report on this intruder.
The charlatan spends his days and nights only
In the company of our women. Calls it initiation.
I'll initiate his balls from his thighs once
We have him safely bound. I'll initiate
That head away from his body. I'll end his
Thumping, jumping, hair-tossing snaking game.
He claims Dionysos lives? Some nerve!
A likely story for a brat who got roasted
Right in his mother's womb, blasted by the bolt
Of Zeus. The slut! Slandered Zeus by proclaiming
The bastard's divine paternity. That myth he instantly
Exploded in her womb, a fiery warning against all pro
    fanity.
You'd think my own relations would have learnt
From that family history but no, Ino and Autonoe,
My own mother Agave are principals at the obscenities!
I'll teach them myself. I have woven
Iron nets to trap them. I'll bring an end
To the cunning subversion. . . .

(*He sees Tiresias and Kadmos for the first time.*)

                                No . . . it's not true!
I won't believe it. Tiresias, seer of Thebes
Tricked out in a dappled fawn-skin? No.
And you, my own grandfather, surely not you!
Not playing at bacchant with wand and ivy!
How awful to witness such foolishness in age.
Oh you disgust me, you, playing with infant toys.
I beg you now, shake off that ivy, drop
The wand of shame. Drop it I say!

(*He wheels back on Tiresias.*)

This is your doing Tiresias; I know
You talked him into it, and I know why.
Another god revealed is a new way opened
Into men's pockets, profits from offerings.
Power over private lives—and state affairs—
Don't deny it! I've known your busy priesthood
Manipulations. You try all you can, cleverly
To influence matters which belong to better trained
Heads than yours. It's all read in the entrails
Of fowls and goats of course. A new god!
Soon we'll have state policies revealed
In brimming cups of wine—by heaven!—
If you were not such a mouldering old ruin
You'd soon be rattling chains with others
Caged for smuggling in this lecherous gospel.
I warn you, presume too far on that protection and
I'll convince you Thebes is wide awake.
Thebes shall stop at nothing to preserve her good name
Faced with anarchy and indecency.

KADMOS.

    Do not blaspheme son. Have some respect
    For heaven. Or at least for your elders.
    I am still Kadmos, I sowed the dragon's teeth
    And brought forth a race of supermen.
    You are born of earth yourself—remember that.
    Will the son of Ichion now disgrace his house?

TIRESIAS.

    Oh it's so easy for some to make speeches.
    They pick a soft target and the words rush out.
    Now listen you. Your tongue runs loose
    Makes a plausible sound and might
    Almost be taken for sense. But you have none.
    Your glibness flows from sheer conceit.
    Arrogant, over-confident and a gift—yes—
    A gift for phrases, and that makes you a great
    Danger to your fellow men. For your mind
    Is closed. Dead. Imprisoned in words. A new life
    Comes into our midst, so vast, so potent
    Soon it will be powerful all over Greece, but
    You cannot feel it. Wake up Pentheus, open your heart.
    Shall I tell you what to look for in this being?
    Think of two principles, two supreme
    Principles in life. First, the principle
    Of earth, Demeter, goddess of soil or what you will.
    This nourishes man, yields him grain. Bread. Womb-like
    It earths him as it were, anchors his feet.
    Second, the opposite, and complementary principle—
    Ether, locked in the grape until released by man.
    For after Demeter came the son of Semele
    And matched her present with the juice of grapes.
    Think of it as more than drug for pain
    Though it is that. We wash our souls, our parched and
    Aching souls in streams of wine and enter
    Sleep and oblivion. Filled with this good gift
    Mankind forgets its grief. But wine is more!
    It is the sun that comes after winter, the power
    That nudges earth awake. Dionysos comes alive in us.
    We soar, we fly, we shed the heavy clods of earth
    That weigh down the ethereal man
    To that first principle. Balance is the key.
    Now take this answer for your smear of bastardy
    Though Dionysos needs no advocate. Too soon alas
    You'll find that he can speak—and act—on his own
      behalf.
    You ridicule the story men commonly repeat, that
    This god was sewn into the thigh of Zeus?
    Why do men quibble and clutch the literal for the sense?
    If I should say to you Pentheus, you sprang from the loins
    Of Kadmos here, full-formed, even to the teeth you so
    Irreverently snap at me, what would it mean? Is the man
    Not fully present in the seed? And the offspring
    Of the son of Ichion, are they not even now ensconced
    Within that dangling pouch between your thighs?

    Offspring whose genesis you now endanger
    By a sharp tongue wagging impiously?
    It's not for me to say if Zeus had his scrotum
    Sewn to one side of his thighs or
    In-between like—presumably—yours.
    Let's leave mythology aside. Think only of
    And come to terms with what we know.

PENTHEUS.

    And what do we know—apart from your casuistry?

TIRESIAS.

    Our human condition, made of those two principles.

PENTHEUS.

    I said, apart from your quibbling.

TIRESIAS.

    Use your eyes Pentheus. I cannot see but I do
    Know. And feel. And so do you, though you will not
    Accept. You see this power made manifest
    Yet you deny it. Think again of human fate—
    What is this but a journey toward death.
    Extinction. But visions open up another world, give
    Strength and consolation. Through Dionysos we
    Transcend that putrefaction of the flesh that begins
    From the instant of our drawing breath.
    This is a god of prophecy. His worshippers
    Like seers, are endowed with mantic powers.
    Reason is cluttered by too much matter, details,
    Cravings, acquisitions, anxieties. When he invades the
      mind
    Reason is put to sleep. He frees the mind
    Expands and fills it with uplifting visions.
    Flesh is transcended. What else? Where else?
    At war you'll find him, confounding the enemy
    With the unnatural courage of his followers.
    And at Delphi too, home of Apollo, sanctuary
    Of reason. How else does the priestess enter
    The oracular state?

PENTHEUS (*angry.*).

    That's blasphemy!

TIRESIAS.

    Slander perhaps, or heresy. A priestess is no god.
    You are the blasphemer.

PENTHEUS.

    I warn you . . .

TIRESIAS.

    Is it not customary to pour libations
    At the altar of Apollo? This is
    To pour the body of god itself and through
    His intercession win the favour of heaven.

PENTHEUS.

    You are quibbling again, you are trying
    To wriggle out of the smear you laid upon
    Apollo's priesthood.

TIRESIAS.

    What Apollo does not reject cannot harm

His servant. A drop for the altar, the rest
To smooth the passage of prayers down the throat.

PENTHEUS.
You go too far Tiresias!

TIRESIAS.
Not so far as Dionysos means to go. Oh
Accept him Pentheus. Look up at the rockhills.
Whom do you see bounding
Over the high plateau among the peaks?
Who is the rustle of wind in pine forests, shaking
Winter into life with green branches? It's he.
Dionysos is here.
In your state. He is at work
All over the world.
Accept him
Pour wine for him
Put vine leaves in your hair for him
Dance for him.

PENTHEUS.
You would love that: Madness and folly
Ever seek company. Licentiousness requires
The stamp of approval from a head of state
To break the last barriers of restraint.
Then power passes into the hands of those
Who prove the most self-abandoned.

TIRESIAS.
If only you would lose this notion that power
Is all that matters in the life of man.
Do not mistake for wisdom these fantasies
Of your sick mind. Abandonment? Dionysos, I admit
Will not restrain desire in man or woman.
Yet if a woman is chaste in nature she stays
Uncorrupted in the rites of Dionysos.
Restraint is something people must practise
Themselves. It cannot be imposed. Those
Who have learnt self-discipline—the greatest
Guarantee of human will and freedom—
Will not then lose it for losing themselves
To Dionysos. Answer me, is control not built
Upon self-knowledge?

PENTHEUS.
What if it is?

TIRESIAS.
Dionysos grants self-knowledge. With that thought
I leave you. There is still time.
Save yourself if you can: look inwards, ask—
Does Pentheus truly know himself?

KADMOS.
Son, you are pleased to have men crowd
Around the city gates to welcome you,
And every street rings with the name—
'Pentheus! Pentheus!' A god deserves no less.

TIRESIAS.
Come, we have done our duty.

We shall dance you and I, partner each other
An ancient foolish pair perhaps, but—dance we must
Not fight this power. I pity Pentheus
His terrible madness. There is no cure,
No relief from potions. Nor from preaching.

KADMOS.
Wait. His mind is surely distracted,
His thoughts sheer delirium. Son, remember
That dreadful death your cousin Actaeon died
When those man-eating hounds reared
By his own hands savaged him, tore him
Limb from limb for boasting that his prowess
In the hunt surpassed the skill of Aretmis.
Do not let his fate be yours.

PENTHEUS (grimly.). It won't. But I thank you for suggesting a
most befitting fate for that sorcerer when we find him.

KADMOS.
Not sorcerer. God. And even if your mind
Will not accept his person—I know appearances
Do more than prejudice even men of reason—
Since you must know within yourself, secretly
In the silence of your heart, this force exists
Take him simply as high priest of the rites, and
Semele is at least mother of a seer
Conferring great distinction on your family.

(Misjudging the thoughtful mood of Pentheus, he thinks he
has at least mollified his stand. He removes the wreath
from his own head.)

KADMOS.
Here, take mine. Let me wreathe
Your head with leaves of ivy. Come with us,
Glorify the god!

PENTHEUS (knocks it off.).
Take your hands off me! Get out!
Go and play Bacchae, but don't wipe
Your drooling idiocy off on me. Don't you dare
Touch my person again. As for you Tiresias,
Your punishment need not wait
One moment longer. I'll make you pay
Dearly for this folly of yours.

(turns to his attendants.)

                                    Go, this instant!
Find the place where this prophet sits
Faking revelations out of birdsong. Go.
Pry it up with crowbars, heave it over
Upside down. Demolish everything you see.
Throw his fillets out to wind and weather.
That will teach you! The rest of you,
Go scour the city, bring me this foreigner
This thing of doubtful gender who infects

Our women with his strange disease and pollutes
Our marriage beds. Find him. Clap him in chains.
Drag him here. He'll suffer stoning to death
The nearest fate I can devise to Actaeon's
Piecemeal death at the jaws of his hunting hounds.
He'll find Thebes a harder bed than he had
Bargained for with his Bacchic jigs.

(*The attendants hesitate. They move as far as the exit, stop.*)

TIRESIAS.
You are mad. Do you realize what you're saying?
You made little enough sense before but now—
You are raving! Lead me out of here Kadmos.
It's almost an impiety to stay beside such folly.
We must no longer think of him, only of us,
Pray that for the sake of Thebes, this folly
Is overlooked. We must harness this great force
For our common good.

(*as they exit.*)

Kadmos, in Greek the name Pentheus signifies
Sorrow. Does that mean anything? Let's hope not.

PENTHEUS (*turns round, attracted by whispering. He is surprised to see his attendants still there.*). Are you still here?

(*An Old Man comes forward.*)

OLD SLAVE. We wondered . . . about the hut of the holy man
. . . you would not . . . really want it destroyed?

(*For reply Pentheus fetches him a slap which knocks him flat.*)

PENTHEUS. Slave! Is that language simple enough even for a slave? Something is wrong with the old men of this city. It affects freemen and slaves alike.

LEADER. Back! Keep away!

VARIOUS.
Keep away!
—This is filth, stain
—Smear, decay.
—Abomination

LEADER.
Back! Leave him there
Let him lie there and accuse him!

VARIOUS.
—With the scorn that dripped
Scathing, corroding from his mouth
Fouling Dionysos, child of his own city.
—I am a stranger, but I think
—Now I know Dionysos.

PENTHEUS (*his hand on his sword.*).
Do you slaves defy me?

VARIOUS.
We are strangers but we know the meaning of madness
—To hit an old servant
With frost on his head
Such a one as has stood
At the gateway of Mysteries.

LEADER.
You know it. This
Was the body of the Old Year Dying
The choice of the priests of Eleusis
Till good Tiresias stepped in his place.

SLAVE.
And now you'll pull down the Old Seer's hut.

LEADER.
You said to the Master of Revels
Take him—perhaps he'll live, or the gods
Will claim him—he's old enough.
Is such a one to be violated by you?

VARIOUS.
Oh the scorn on his lips. Such
Inhuman indifference. Corrosive
As his hate for Dionysos.
—Age is holy
To hit an old man
Or demolish the roof of a sage?
Yet we are the barbarians
And Greece the boast of civilization.
We are slaves and have no souls.

LEADER.
No one will touch him where he lies
The world must see it.
Dionysos shall avenge this profanity.
I live to share
The feast of the vengeance of joy. O-oh
I have heard earth turn at the tramp
Of dancing Bacchantes, and my heart
Has leapt. At the sound of flutes, whole
Galaxies have fallen in my cupped hands
I have drunk the stars . . .

(*He bows his head suddenly and intones, the others repeating each line after him, as if this is a practised liturgy. Pentheus's face registers horror and disbelief as he recognizes the implications of this.*)

And yielded to the power of life, the god in me
To the seminal flood that courses earth and me
The alliance of blood to wine, the bond
Of ether and flesh, earth, and the breath in me.
And this is what this day we celebrate
Our feet at the dance are the feet of men
Grape-pressing, grain-winnowing, our joy
Is the great joy of union with mother earth
And the end of separation between man and man.

LEADER (*alone.*).

Said Bromius,
I am the gentle comb of breezes on the slope of vines
The autumn flush on clustered joy of grapes
I am the autumn sacrament, the bond, word, pledge
The blood rejuvenated from a dying world
I am the life that's trodden by the dance of joy
My flesh, my death, my re-birth is the song
That rises from men's lips, they know not how.
But also,
The wild blood of the predator that's held in leash
The fearful flames that prowl the thicket of the night
I melt as wax the willful barriers of the human mind
Gently even in this, except to the tyrant mind
That thinks to dam the flood-tide from the hills.
I am Dionysos.

(*A pause of an instant, then, powerfully.*)

                                    Lead us Bromius!

SLAVES. Lead us—!
PENTHEUS (*He has snatched out his sword.*). Shut up! (*dead silence.*) I'll cut out the tongue of the next man that utters that name Bromius. Or Dionysos!

(*Enter Dionysos, captive, surrounded by soldiers. Three or four Bacchae are with him, their hands similarly tied.*)

DIONYSOS. Who calls on Dionysos? You, Pentheus?

(*Freeze. Hold for between thirty and forty-five seconds, sixty if possible.*)

(*Pentheus moves first, approaches the prisoner and inspects him in silence. The officer begins his report. Pentheus continues his inspection.*)

OFFICER.
We found him Pentheus. The hunt is over.
Here is the animal you sent us after.
And not so dangerous after all, quite docile
To tell the truth. We had no trouble over him.
Handed himself over without a murmur
Held out his arms for the chains, no attempt
To run or hide, or escape our dragnet.
To confess the truth, that bothered me.
I was—well—quite embarrassed. It seemed
Not quite playing the game. For a professional—
Code of conflict and all that—well—I felt
Quite ashamed. I said to him, Stranger,
I am not here by choice. I take orders and
My orders were to bring you live to Pentheus.
He seemed to understand. Oh, another thing—
The women you locked up in gaol are free.
They've shed their chains, they're up and away
In the forests and mountains, running like deer,
Calling on their god Bromius. He seems to be
Their master, governs them completely.

Naturally, I probed the matter. I am
Compelled to report the truth. It was
No human hands that snapped those chains, no
Human cunning picked the locks on those
Iron gates. The thing is beyond me. Thebes
Is suddenly full of miracles—I say no more.
The rest is your affair.
PENTHEUS.
Untie his hands. He is fast within our net
And cannot escape.

(*They untie him. Dionysos and Pentheus stand face to face.*)

So. You are not at all bad-looking
Quite attractive I am sure, to women.
Perhaps it was this that brought you to Thebes—
Our women have a reputation for being easy game . . .
Long hair, all nicely curled. Hold out your hands.

(*Dionysos obeys.*)

I thought so. You have never wrestled
Or done a day's work in the fields. The arts
Of war must be just as strange to you. Your skin
Is smooth. You cultivate the shadows, the dark
For the larks of Aphrodite. Ah yes,
And what they call a handsome profile, quite
An asset in your style of life. Now answer straight:
Who are you? Where do you come from?
DIONYSOS.
I am . . .
Nothing of note, nothing to boast of.
As for where—have you heard of a river
Called Tmolus. It runs
Through fields of flowers.
PENTHEUS.
Yes, I know that river.
It circles the city of Sardis.
DIONYSOS.
I come from there.
My country is Lydia.
PENTHEUS.
Hm, that fits with my reports.
And who is this new god whose worship
You have brought to us in Hellas?
DIONYSOS.
Dionysos, the son of Zeus. The god himself
Initiated me.
PENTHEUS.
You have some local Zeus there
Who spawns new gods?
DIONYSOS.
He is the same as yours.
The Zeus who sowed his seed

In earth.

PENTHEUS.
And he initiated you. Was it
In truth-defining day, or was it by night
This 'inspiration' came to you.

DIONYSOS.
Will you reduce it all to a court
Of inquiry? A fact-finding commission such as
One might set up to decide the cause
Of a revolt in your salt-mines, or a slave uprising?
These matters are beyond the routine machinery of state.

PENTHEUS.
Answer me!

DIONYSOS.
How does the earth take seed? By night
Or day? When heaven opens forth and,
Swarms and probes earth's thirsty womb, do you ask
Did her 'inspiration' come by night or day?
And when the grape begins to swell, its purple juice
Pounding on the tender skin or, at the sight
Of the bursting udder of a cow
Do you wait to date and time
Her 'inspiration' or simply fetch the milk-pail?
Do you demand of earth the secret of the vine or
Tread the grapes and say a prayer of thanks to heaven?

PENTHEUS.
So it is all, and must remain a secret?

DIONYSOS.
To those in whom Dionysos is not born.
To others there are no secrets for
Their minds are open.

PENTHEUS.
You are clever, but not clever enough.
If there were no shameful acts in this
New worship, you would hardly wait to speak.

DIONYSOS.
Mysteries are only for the initiates.
And in this worship all, even you Pentheus
May enter into the Mysteries.

PENTHEUS.
Very clever. Your answers are designed
To make me curious. Tell me this at least
What benefits do the initiates derive,
The followers of this god?

DIONYSOS.
Again I am forbidden to say. But they are
Well worth knowing.

PENTHEUS.
I see your game, it is so transparent.
You think to play on my curiosity.

DIONYSOS.
Our Mysteries abhor an unbelieving man.

PENTHEUS.
You say you saw the god? What form

Did he assume?

DIONYSOS.
The form of all men, all beasts
And all nature. He chose at will.

PENTHEUS.
You evade my question.

DIONYSOS.
Talk truth to a deaf man and he
Begs your pardon.

PENTHEUS.
You grow bold stranger. In a moment
You shall learn how unwise that is.
Now, are we the first to suffer your visitation
Or have you spread your dirt in other cities?

DIONYSOS.
The world everywhere now dances for Dionysos.

PENTHEUS.
We have more sense than barbarians.
Greece has a culture.

DIONYSOS.
Just how much have you traveled Pentheus?
I have seen even among your so-called
Barbarian slaves, natives of lands whose cultures
Beggar yours.

PENTHEUS.
Don't try to wander off the subject.
These sacred practices of your god, this worship
The rites of great devotion, do they
Hold at night, or in the day?

DIONYSOS. (kindly, very gently and without scorn or attack.).
Poor Pentheus, how you must suffer, tying
So rigidly the hour of day and night with sin or virtue.
We hold our rites mostly at night, but only
Because it is cooler. And the lamps
Lend atmosphere and feeling to the heart in worship.
The lighting of a lamp is in itself
A votive act. Oil is an offering. A woman
Bears a lamp and the ring of light that falls
Around her frame is magic, holy,
A secretive and tender kind of grace. Think of a dark
    mountain
Pierced by myriads of tiny flames, then see
The human mind as that dark mountain whose caves
Are filled with self-inflected fears. Dionysos
Is the flame that puts such fears to flight, a flame
That must be gently lit or else consume you.

PENTHEUS (violently.). And I say night hours are dangerous
    Lascivious hours, lechery . . .

DIONYSOS. You'll find debauchery in daylight too.

PENTHEUS. You wrestle well—with words. You will regret
    Your ill-timed cleverness.

DIONYSOS (wearily.). And you, your stupid blasphemies.

PENTHEUS. Enough! You, bring me the shears!

DIONYSOS. Shears? What terrible fate am I to undergo?

PENTHEUS. First, we shall rid you of your girlish curls.

DIONYSOS. My hair is holy. My curls belong to god.

(*Pentheus shears off his hair.*)

PENTHEUS. Next, you will surrender the wand.

DIONYSOS. You will have to take it. It belongs to Dionysos.

PENTHEUS (*snatching it.*).
You think I fear a common
Conjurer's wand? And now we will place you
Under guard and confine you to the palace.

DIONYSOS.
Dionysos will set me free whenever I request it.

PENTHEUS.
Yes, when you get your followers round you
And 'summon his presence'!

DIONYSOS.
He sees. He is here. This minute he knows
What is being done to me.

PENTHEUS.
Where is he then? Is he always invisible?
Why doesn't he show himself?

DIONYSOS.
He does. But you being crass and insensitive
You can see nothing.

PENTHEUS.
You insult me? You must be raving!
(*to the Guards.*)
He insults your king. He insults Thebes.
Load him with chains! The man is insane.

DIONYSOS.
I am sane, but you are not. I warn you,
Set me free.

PENTHEUS.
Chain him I say! Weight him down with chains.
I'll show you who has the power here.

DIONYSOS.
You do not know what life is. You do not know
What you do. You do not know the limits
Of your power. You will not be forgiven.

PENTHEUS.
What are you all waiting for. Chain him I said.

(*The Guards with obvious reluctance approach him with chains.*)

DIONYSOS.
I give you sober warning Pentheus.
Place no chains on me.

(*The Guards chain him quickly, move away as if from a distasteful job.*)

PENTHEUS.
I am Pentheus, son of Ichion.
You are—nothing.

DIONYSOS.
Pentheus. The name befits a doomed man.

PENTHEUS.
Oh take him away. Get him out of my sight.
He talks and talks. Lock him up somewhere near—
In the stables—yes, leave him in the stables
Let him thrash in the hay and light up his darkness
With the flame of Dionysos. Dance in there.
And the creatures you brought with you, your
Accomplices in subversion, I shall have them
Sold to slavery. They'll work at the looms or carry
Water for the troops, day and night—that
Will silence their drums.   (*Exit Pentheus.*)

(*As Dionysos is chained, his Bacchantes begin a noise, a kind of ululating which is found among some African and Oriental peoples and signifies great distress, warning, or agitation. Sometimes all combined. It increases in volume. As Dionysos is led away it spreads towards the Chorus of Slaves, swelling into deafening proportions.*)

DIONYSOS.
I leave you now. I go, not to suffer
For that cannot be. But Dionysos whose
Godhead you deny will call you to account.
When you set chains on me, you manacle the god.

(*From within the shrieking intensity of sound protesting the sacrilege, a Bacchante's voice rises.*)

BACCHANTE.
He ranges. He is full of the mad wind
Of rage. Pentheus, son of Ichion and Agave
I know now you are mad. You have chained
The messenger of god.

SLAVE.
Why am I rejected? Why am I a second time
Rejected O blessed Nile. First, banished
From your banks into this city, a slave. And now to see
The promise broken, the messenger of Bromius in chains
Heavier than mine! Rejected? Pentheus!
By the clustered grapes on the hills I swear
You shall come to know the name of Bromius!

BACCHANTE.
He, a second time rejected, sweet Dirce
Life-stream to these fields! Again
Rejected from your sweet breast, from
Banks that were a cradle for the new-born child.

BACCHANTE.
I head the voice of Zeus in thunder
Saying, Welcome my son,
Welcome to the world, spirit of all
That lives and moves. . . .

SLAVE.
Free spirit, soul of liberty, seed of the new order.

BACCHANTE.
Yet this river spurns the god a second time!
Come not near. No ivy crowns on my banks
No gatherings, no dances, no flutes
To ruffle flowers on my beds.

BACCHANTE.
Oh some day you'll thirst, ache
Parched, long for this immortal
Communion.
Yes, some day, you'll crave
Dionysos.

SLAVES.
Such fury from his eyes, yet not he
Violated, outraged. But the fury!
With spite with hate he rages. No, not a man.
A beast run wild. A crop of dragon's teeth
That earth has never tamed with nursing.
A freak, a monster
Gorged and rank with pestilence . . .

BACCHANTE.
A fiend, murderous to the bone. And this
This thing means to shut me up, to
Plunge me in the darkness of his mind!
I am not his. I belong
To Dionysos!

BACCHANTE.
In a dungeon, in a sightless pit
He buries our leader.

OLD SLAVE.
He is nothing. A trickster. Windbag. A commonplace
Illusionist. Beyond that, nothing.
Briefly I dreamt I saw salvation. Now
The breeder of false cravings lies
Bound in the net of his own spinning,
Crushed.

1ST BACCHANTE.
CRUSHED?

SEVERAL.
NO! NO! NO!

1ST BACCHANTE.
Chained, but like a tower of gold.

BACCHANTE.
A column of the sun that touches
Earth from Olympus.

ALL.
Come Dionysos!

BACCHANTE.
With a tree in his hand, the rockhills
Of his brow are drawn, they frown . . .

BACCHANTE.
Down on the palace walls of Pentheus—
Come Dionysos!

LEADER.
Pentheus! Retribution lowers

From the brow of a prisoner.

SLAVES.
Come Dionysos!

LEADER.
Prestidigitator god.

1ST BACCHANTE.
Apocalyptic utterance.

LEADER.
Bromius, come, COME! Be manifest!

VARIOUS.
—Come from the mountain forests
—Glide from the wild beast's lair
—Spring from a cruel peak
—Leap from a whirlwind dance
—Burst from a thousand oaks
—Rise from the silent valley
  A tree-leafed menace
  Like the end of Orpheus' spell
  On the hounds of death
—Breaking the forest netting
  On limbs of mahogany
—From out of mountain torrents
  Heralded on drumming feet
—Surge over waves towards us
  Over green plains, a raging stallion

SLAVE.
Break interminable shackles
Break bonds of oppressors
Break the beast of blood
Break bars that sprout
In travesty of growth

1ST BACCHANTE.
Wounding the farmlands
Bruising the grapes
Lashing the late buds
Ploughing the hills
Watering the fields
In torrents of wine
Spirit of motion
Quickener of life
Oh let your sweet grape burst in me
Come Dionysos!

ALL (*ecstatically.*).
Bromius! Bromius! BROMIUS!

(*a loud rumble, as of thunder. A hush falls on the scene.*)

1ST BACCHANTE.
It is happening. Do you hear it? I know it is happening.

CHORUS (*a whisper.*).
Bromius?

1ST BACCHANTE.
It is happening. I hear him
In footsteps of the earthquake.

CHORUS.
Bromius?
1ST BACCHANTE.
In the chords that Orpheus fingered
In the hunger of women
CHORUS.
Bromius?
1ST BACCHANTE.
In the terror of children
And the anger of slaves.
CHORUS.
Now. Now is the time. Bromius
Be manifest! Come, the new order!
BACCHANTE.
Shatter the floor of the world!
SLAVE LEADER.
It's happening. The palace of Pentheus
Totters, bulges, quivers. Rot gapes
In the angry light of lightning. Roots
Long trapped in evil crevices have burgeoned
Their strength empowers me, the strength
Of a Master. . . . Join him! Power his will!
CHORUS.
Come BROMIUS!

(*Again, another rending as of deep thunder rolling off into a distance. Like heavy breathing—In—Out.*)

1ST BACCHANTE. Earth—
CHORUS.   —Shake!
1ST BACCHANTE. Earth—
CHORUS.   —Retch!
1ST BACCHANTE. Earth—
CHORUS.   —Melt!
1ST BACCHANTE. Earth—
CHORUS.   —Swarm!
1ST BACCHANTE. Earth—
CHORUS.   —Take!
1ST BACCHANTE. Earth—
CHORUS.   —Swell!
1ST BACCHANTE. Earth—
CHORUS.   —Grow!
1ST BACCHANTE. Earth—
CHORUS.   —Move!
1ST BACCHANTE. Earth—
CHORUS.   —Strain!
1ST BACCHANTE. Earth—
CHORUS.   —Groan!
1ST BACCHANTE. Earth—
CHORUS.   —Clutch!
1ST BACCHANTE. Earth—
CHORUS.   —Thrust!
1ST BACCHANTE. Earth—
CHORUS.   —Burst!
1ST BACCHANTE. Earth—

CHORUS.   —TAKE!
1ST BACCHANTE. Earth—
CHORUS.   —Breathe! Live! Blow upon the walls
                            of darkness. Melt marble, pillars,
                            take! Take! TAKE!
1ST BACCHANTE. Adore him!
CHORUS. We adore him.

(*Darkness, thunder, flames. Roar of collapsing masonry. From among it all, the music of Dionysos.*)

1ST BACCHANTE.
Flames! The fevered flames around the grave
Of Semele, charred earth that no one walks upon
Except . . .
DIONYSOS.
Dionysos.

(*He is revealed as first seen standing on the charred ruin of the grave of Semele. The flames are higher round his feet. The Bacchantes and the Chorus are down on their faces.*)

BACCHANTE.
We do not move, or look, or breathe.
DIONYSOS.
Afraid, my companions from distant lands?
Look at you, hugging the earth, terror struck.
You saw the house of darkness split and sundered—
For Dionysos was there. You willed him,
Summoned him, your needs
Invoked his presence. Why do you tremble?
Look up. Look up at me. The mortal ribs of Pentheus
Crumble, sundered by the presence
Of the eternal. Look up. All is well.
BACCHANTE.
The dawn we know, our life-light departed
When you left in chains.
DIONYSOS.
Did you think I would be buried in those
Death cells of Pentheus' darkness, and so
Settle down to despair?
OLD SLAVE.
You are free?
DIONYSOS.
You willed my freedom. I could not resist.
SLAVE.
How did you do it? How did you escape?
DIONYSOS.
With ease. No effort was required.
SLAVE.
With manacles on your wrists? That man
Had blood-lust in his eyes.
DIONYSOS.
Oh, but there I fooled him. It was my turn
To humiliate the godless fool, serve him
Outrage for outrage. I made the sick desires
Of his mind and his goal, and he pursued them.

He fed on vapours of his own malignant
Hate, pursued and roped mirages in the stable—
Manacled hooves and horns of a docile bull,
Stumbled on pails, wrestled beams, lost his way
In collapsing hay, slipped on manure
Then sat in a lather of sweat, chewing his lips
Cursing the stranger from Phrygia.
I sat nearby, quietly watching. Untouched.
That moment came Dionysos.
He shook the roof of the palace of Pentheus
Touched the living grave and cradle of his being
And up leapt ribbons of fire. Pentheus looked up
He saw—only his palace, possessions, his high estate
Menaced by passionate flames. From end to end
Of his palace he rushed, screaming at servants
To pour water, more water on water till every slave
Was working—over nothing. The fire existed
Only in his unquiet mind. He left it suddenly—
A fear had crept upon him that I might escape—
Snatched up a long steel sword and hurled himself
Back into the stables. His prisoner was gone,
But there was bright, gleaming air where Dionysos
Had been. At this emanation in the stable gloom
Pentheus charged, stabbing and lunging, thinking
To slake his vengeance in my blood. More folly.
And it brought more havoc in its wake. For now
      Dionysos
Razed the palace to the ground, reduced it
To utter ruins. At that bitter sight
Pentheus, spent and limp, threw away his sword
Broken by the struggle. Well, he is only a man
He exceeded himself, tried to fight a god.
Quietly I left the house, came back to you.
He never touched me.
                    Listen. I hear footsteps
That would be him. He'll come out and rave and
    swear . . .
But what can he say now? Let him bluster.
I'll manage him easily. The secret of life is
Balance, tolerance . . . perhaps he's learnt that now.

(*Enter Pentheus.*)

PENTHEUS.
I had him trussed up. He could not move.
Still, he got away. I have been tricked.

(*He sees Dionysos.*)

                    What! You?
How did you escape? Answer me!
DIONYSOS.
Tread lightly. Let your anger drain off . . .
Slowly . . . slowly . . .
PENTHEUS (*even more peremptorily.*).
How did you escape?

DIONYSOS.
Have you forgotten? Someone, I said
Would set me free.
PENTHEUS.
Who? Spell out his name.
DIONYSOS.
He who tends the grape for mankind.
PENTHEUS.
He who sows drunkenness and disorder.
DIONYSOS.
Poor Pentheus. He has learnt nothing.
PENTHEUS (*to the Guards.*).
Surround the palace. Close every gate in the city.
Seal up every nook and cranny. I want the city
Bolted tight.
DIONYSOS.
You are truly incurable. These powers
That you dispute move on a higher plane
Than towers and city walls.
PENTHEUS.
Very clever talk, as usual. This time
It will not help you.
DIONYSOS.
No. I use it thinking to help *you*. As usual
It is futile. You are a doomed man Pentheus.
Look, here comes someone with a message.
Listen to him first. Carefully. Don't hurry anything.
We are in no hurry. We'll wait for you.
Hear what he has to say; he comes from the
    mountains.
HERDSMAN.
Pentheus, I am one of your subjects here
In Thebes. I am just from Kithairon. The snow
Is there still and white hills dazzle you. . . .
PENTHEUS. Get to the point man! What is your news?
HERDSMAN.   Sire, I have seen
Miracles. The very stuff of ballads. You cannot . . .
No, wait. If I must report faithfully . . .
You see, it has to do with the Maenads, these
Women who run barefoot from city to city . . .
I have witnessed weird, fantastic things, but . . .
Can I speak freely, and in my own way?
Master, you have a cruel temper. We, your subjects
Know it to our cost. And all too often.
PENTHEUS.
You may speak freely. Do your duty and nothing
Will happen to you. You have my promise.
Tell me the worst things they've done, the worse
It shall be for the man who began it.
But you are safe—speak.
HERDSMAN.
Well then—and may the god of oaths protect me—
Our herds of cattle had just climbed a hill
Grazing as they went—the dew was wet upon the grass,

The sun being hardly warmed up that early hour—
Well, by chance I stumble on this meadow, and in it
Find a scene just like a painting on a vase—motion
    less—
Three rings of women—fast asleep. One brief look
Is enough. I say to myself—it's *them*.
One is grouped round Autonoe—that would be your
Auntie I think. The second I was more sure of—Agave
Your mother. The third had to be Ino. Each ring
Is formed around the leader, in a kind of
Magic circle to my thinking. They were *still*,
So peaceful it seemed a shame they had to wake.
Some you'd find propped against the pine-tree trunks
Others, curled up on a pile of oak leaves
A few were simply pillowed on earth. I found there
None of that drunkenness we'd heard so much about,
None of the obscene abandon, or the wild music.
No topping among the bushes. If I may describe it—
A kind of radiant peace, like the sacred grove of a deity.
Well, our cattle soon put an end to that. Their lowing
Wakes up your mother, she leaps up, cries out
And wakes the rest of the women. Her voice was clear
And strangely tuneful in those echoing hills, I heard her
Warn the others men and cattle were close by.
They shook off sleep from their eyes, yet even awake
That air of peace still controlled their actions . . .
And such beauties! We do have some treasures in Thebes.
Young supple limbs, maidens who have yet to know
    man—
Such jet and gold flew through the air when they let fall
Their hair. They brushed their clothes, then
Fastened them at the waist with . . . well, tell me I'm ly-
    ing—
Snakes! *Live* snakes! I see their tongues still flickering
Clearly as I see you now! But that was nothing.
There was still more live wonder to come.
Have you ever seen a woman nurse a fawn
Exactly like a child? Or a wild wolf cub? I mean
To the point where she gives it suck? From—her—
    own—breast!
Heavy of breast those were, newly delivered,
Left their own babes at home—you know, the breast
Can get painful with milk—but to suckle a wild cub!
Again, that is nothing, for now rushed one miracle
After another. From weaving strands of ivy,
Oak-leaves, and flowering bryony to dress their hair,
One turned to twining leaves around a branch,
Like the most natural act you could conceive. She
Tapped a rock and—tell me I'm lying—out of that rock
Spouts—water! Clear, spring water, fresh as dew.
Another drove her fennel in the ground, and, where
The earth was wounded—another spring! But this time—
Wine! A wine-spring! Two women on their knees
Scrape the soil with fingers and out flows

Milk, creamier than the morning yield from a champion
    cow.
From all their ivy-covered branches, sweet honey
Dripped in golden cascades . . . Oh sire, if you had been
    there
If you had witnessed but a part you would be
On bended knees, giving thanks, praying the heavens
For help and guidance.
                          We met, shepherds and cowherds
Gathered in small groups to argue, comparing rumours
With this real event, for these were fantastic
Deeds! We could hardly believe our eyes. Now,
Up gets a city fellow, a great one for speeches,
Seizes his chance and addresses our group:
'Friends from the meadows of these mountains'—
Majestic meadows he said—I'll give him his due—
'Allow me to suggest a judicious and expedient hunt
One not without great expectations. Let us pursue
Agave the Queen-mother, rescue and bear her from
    these
Unmajestic orgiastics. Indubitably I declare
Pentheus will most royally reward us.' That did it.
Who would turn his back on such a profit? Straightway we
Devised an ambush for the women. We hid
Among the undergrowth, covered in leaves. We waited.
The hour for their ritual soon approached
Their ivy-covered staves were beating earth in rhythm—
It gets in your blood, that rhythm, it really does—
The chanting began—'Iacchos' 'Dionysos'
'Bromius!' 'Son of Zeus!'
                          Everything—
The very mountain seemed to sway to that one beat.
A beat like the hearts of a thousand men in unison.
The beasts moved with them, they seemed
Touched by a savage divinity,
                          It quickened,
The Maenads were swift upon their feet, rapt, unseeing,
Blind to all except the vision of their god.
Agave raced towards me, she flew close
Her arms were flashing like blades but I leapt,
My hands hot on the quarry. That scream!
I never will forget that screaming summons from her lips
To her swift hounds—for so she termed them—
Exhorting them to follow and turn hunter.
And they obeyed her. We changed roles and became the
    hunted,
Fleeing for sweet life. Another moment and
We would have been shredded like chaff.
Balked of their prey, the Maenads turned upon our herd.
Unarmed, they swooped down on our heifers grazing
In the meadows, nothing in their hands, nothing.
Their bare arms sufficed. They rent young, stocky
Heifers in two—you should have heard their death bel-
    lows,

Seen these frail-built creatures wrench
Full-grown cattle limb from limb, ribs, hooves
Spiral in the air, fall in torrents of blood,
Seen our dismembered livestock hang from branches
Blood spattering the leaves, seen wild bulls
With surging horns, unapproachable till now
Tripped, sprawled full-length on the ground
Bellow in unaccustomed terror as girlish limbs
Tore them apart, flayed them living.
There was a force within them; it drove them
Uphill, their feet hardly touching the ground.
Like invaders they swooped into Hysiae
Sacked Erythrae in the foothills of Kithairon.
Nothing withstood them, they pillaged and raided
Snatched children from homes, razed walls to the
    ground.
And all this plunder they piled on their backs,
Nothing held it, nothing. Yet neither bronze nor iron
Fell to the ground. Flames flickered in their curls but
Their hair remained unsinged.

                    Until at last,
Mad at these monstrosities, some villagers
Foolishly took to arms and made to attack them.
It was a terrible sight my masters. The men's
Spears and swords are lethal and sharp but,
They draw no blood, while the wands of the women . . . !
The men ran, yes, *ran*! Routed by women!
Master, it is not for me to say, but
Some god was surely with them. I watched them
Transformed in an instant, troop peacefully back
To where they had started, by those springs magically
Bestowed by their god, wash stains from their bodies
And the snakes licking the drops of blood
That clung to their hair.

                  Whoever this god may be
Sire, welcome him to Thebes. He is great
In other ways I hear. Didn't he make us
Mortal men the gift of wine? If that is true
You have much to thank him for—wine makes
Our labours bearable. Take wine away
And the world is without joy, tolerance or love.

(*Pentheus remains as he is for some moments.*)

PENTHEUS.
It spreads. The craze, the violence,
Like a blazing fire. It comes close, close,
It comes too close. It contaminates even by report.
As a people we are disgraced, humiliated.
It's firmness now, no more hesitation.

(*To the Officer.*)

Go to the gates of Electra, order out
All the heavy-armoured infantry.
Call out the fastest troops of the cavalry

The mobile squadrons and the archers.
Issue a general call-up—all able-bodied men
Who can hold shield and spear. Set in motion
The standard drill for a state of emergency—
I have reasons for that—these restive dogs
Might see their chance to stage a slave uprising,
I have seen signs, so see to it!
I want the troops massed here directly.
We attack the Bacchae at once.
DIONYSOS.
Pentheus . . .
PENTHEUS.
Shut up! (*turns to a Guard.*) You. Give me the map of
Thebes.
DIONYSOS.
Pentheus, you've done me wrong, Still
I warn you yet again, do not take arms
Against a god.

(*Pentheus begins to plot the attack.*)

PENTHEUS.
You escaped from prison, let that suffice you.
Or else I'll take you first, before your women.
DIONYSOS.
Stay quite. Safe. Bromius will not let you
Drive his women from the hills.
PENTHEUS.
If you had ever borne responsibility for
Law and order anywhere you might be worth
Attention. Since you have not
Be less glib with your advice.
DIONYSOS.
And yet I offer only sane advice.
Sacrifice to this god. It is futile
To rage and kick against such power.
You are a man.
PENTHEUS.
All the sacrifice your god will have already
Lies in the glades of Kithairon. His women
Have been lavish. The state has nothing more to offer.
DIONYSOS.
And for this you raise the army of Thebes—
Against women?
PENTHEUS.
Those are not women. They are alien monsters
Who have invaded Thebes. I have a duty to preserve
The territorial integrity of Thebes.
DIONYSOS.
You will actually *attack* them Pentheus?
Draw sword, bow, cast spears, drive
Your armoured chariots into—women?
PENTHEUS.
They will have a chance to surrender
Peacefully. If not—think who began the violence.

Thebes must take measures for her own safety.

DIONYSOS.
Thebes' well-being lies in acceptance
Of this god. Your way leads to defeat,
An ignominious rout. Bronze shields are no match
For women's hands.

PENTHEUS.
Will no man rid me of this pestilential tongue?
All it does is wag. Whatever I do or say
It's all the same. Yakkity-yak-yak-yak!

DIONYSOS.
But there is a better way than yours. I ask
Only for a chance to prove it.

(*Pentheus ignores him, concentrates on plotting his campaign.*)

I will bring the women here.
Without use of force.

PENTHEUS.
Brilliant. This is the great
Master plan. The grand deception.

DIONYSOS.
You are too distrustful. I wish you well.
I want you, and Thebes, to keep whole.

(*Pentheus has finished. He looks satisfied, prepared. Turns to the Guards.*)

PENTHEUS.
Bring out my armour. And you—(*to Dionysos.*)
Be quiet. I am not a simpleton.

DIONYSOS (*stops the Guards*).
Wait! (*He moves close to Pentheus.*) You could see them.
I mean, there, up in the hills.

PENTHEUS.
Your mind is always busy, but I thought you
Cleverer. Any fool can see through that trap.

DIONYSOS.
Why do you fear me Pentheus?

PENTHEUS.
Fear? I, son of Ichion?

DIONYSOS.
Yes, you are afraid of me.

PENTHEUS.
Because I will not follow you into a trap?

DIONYSOS.
No. It goes deeper. I saw it from our first encounter.

PENTHEUS.
If you refer to your cheap conjurer tricks
Don't let that swell your head. I have seen
Greater spectacles in market-places, greater feats
Of illusion. But now my mind is clear. I know you
For a charlatan. Perhaps a spy, an agent
Of subervsion for some foreign power. Certainly

A degenerate, quite contemptible. Fear you?
Rid your mind of such conceit.

DIONYSOS.
But you do fear me. You fear my presence here
May set you free.

PENTHEUS. Me? Who is the prisoner—You or I?

DIONYSOS. You Pentheus, because you are a man of chains. You love chains. Have you uttered one phrase today that was not hyphenated by chains? You breathe chains, talk chains, eat chains, dream chains, think chains. Your world is bound in manacles. Even in repose you are a cow chewing the cud, but for you it is molten iron issuing from the furnace of your so-called kingly will. It has replaced your umbilical cord and issues from this point . . .

(*He touches him on the navel, commences to turn Pentheus round and round, gently. In spite of himself Pentheus is quite submissive.*)

                    . . . and winds about you all the way back into your throat where it issues forth again in one unending cycle.

(*He holds out his hand before Pentheus's eyes, like a mirror.*)

                    Look well in the mirror Pentheus. What beast is it? Do you recognize it? Have you ever seen the like? In all your wanderings have your eyes been affronted by a creature so gross, so unnatural, so obscene?

(*With a superhuman effort Pentheus shakes off his hypnotic state, tries to snatch the 'mirror' but clutches at nothing. He backs off, his face livid.*)

PENTHEUS. Try that trick again! Touch our person once more and it won't be mere chains for you. How dare you!

DIONYSOS. Again chains. You are so scared I shall cut through that chain and set you at liberty.

PENTHEUS (*to the Guard.*). Has no one brought my armour? (*to Dionysos.*) Better keep your hacksaw for yourself. You shall need it before long.

DIONYSOS. Hacksaw. Your thoughts are so metallic. Dionysos loosens chains by gentler means.

PENTHEUS. I know what those are.

DIONYSOS. Tell me Pentheus, wouldn't you give a lot to know the future—not yours, you have none—but the future of this god Dionysos. It's a short cut, but . . . would you? Would you like to see something of his fate, the past and future legends of Dionysos—don't talk—look!

(*In the direction in which he points, a scene lights up. Wedding scene. Music. The bridal procession enters, masked. The mask is the half-mask. The bridal retinue registers variations of hauteur, their clothes and attitude denote sixty-carat nobility, probably trade.*)

The bride is veiled.

An altar to Aphrodite is set at the entrance. The bride's father pauses by it, is handed a jug by a servant and pours libation at its base. He hands the jug to the bride who also pours libation, makes a silent prayer. They proceed on to an elevated throne. A servant-girl brings wine, is waved away by the aristocratic front-liners. She finds takers in the very rear.

By the time she gets there the bridegroom arrives. His retinue is one, a sort of bestman. The bridegroom is clumsy, awkwardly dressed for the occasion in what must be his Sunday best. Bestman makes last-minute adjustments to groom's attire, pulls him back in time to the altar, where the jug has been left. In his nervousness he takes a swig, then hastily pours a libation.

In the hall the bridegroom is waved unceremoniously to a seat almost at the feet of the bridal group. He sweats, his collar (or whatever) is too tight. This is a creature who is not comfortable in clothes. The masks from on high turn on him and inspect him coldly. We can almost hear the sigh of resignation as they turn away.

Guests arrive, perfunctorily spilling a little libation. The wedding feast begins. Dancers perform. The bridegroom grows more and more uncomfortable. The serving-girl carries on a quiet flirtation with him, doesn't wait for his cup to empty before refilling it. The bridegroom visibly responds to both charm and blandishments.

A sudden clash of cymbals. All movements stop. Ceremonially the father rises, unveils the bride. From all the guests, hands and faces are lifted in unmistakable gestures of rapture. Except the bridegroom. On his face and on the face of his bestman are expressions of horror. The bride (also masked) is a picture of horrendous, irredeemable ugliness.

A movement (of light?) turns our attention to the bust of Aphrodite. The face is coming off. Underneath, the mocking face of Dionysos. He beams on the scene.

The wine-girl is almost never away from the bridegroom. The performing dancers resume their jigs. The bridegroom drinks. The bride transfers to and fro between devastating glares at the wine-girl and loving smirks at her groom. Her groom drinks more and more. Suddenly he leaps up, brushing aside the restraining arm of his bestman, He strides among the dancers, stops the musicians and gives them instructions. He begins to dance. Already, a transformation has commenced. The music quickens. He stops, flings off his mask and garments. Underneath, the Dionysian fawn-skin. The bridal group registers predictable shock at the scantiness. He begins to dance. He DANCES!

The dance ends with a leap on to the bridal table, upside down, his back to the shocked 'high table'. The bride screams, the father rises in fury. His lips move and over an amplified system, the historic exchange:)

FATHER-IN-LAW. Hippoclides, you have danced your wife away.

BRIDEGROOM (*a melon-sized grin on his face.*). Hippoclides— does-not-care! οὐ φροντὶς 'Ιπποχλείδη

(*A snap black-out, except on the altar of Aphronysos.*)

DIONYSOS (*voice.*). Look Pentheus!

(*A new scene to another side. Again a wedding scene, but a huge contrast. All the noise—music, revellers, snatches of drunken singing comes from Off. What we see is the traditional Christ-figure, seated. But his halo is an ambiguous thorn-ivy-crown of Dionysos. At his feet a woman kneels, anointing them. Behind him, embroidering is a slightly more elderly woman. Her mask is beautiful, radiates an internal peace.*

A woman enters, irate, with a pitcher under her arm. She frowns on this scene and points angrily to the kneeling woman. Turns the pitcher upside down to indicate the problem. Her angry gestures include the feminine logic (pace Fem. Lib.) that the wine shortage is related to the idle foot-anointer. The Christ-figure makes peace, indicates that the pitcher should be filled with the contents of a pot in a corner. Water is poured into the pitcher. He raises his hand, blesses it. Takes a cup and invites her to fill it from the pitcher. Tastes, nods, passes the cup to the irate woman. Her expression changes to rapture. She passes the cup to the kneeling woman, embraces the man. All taste, all are full of wonder, love and forgiveness. General embraces. She hurries out. Noise from Off indicates the success of this wine. The figure looks up, smiles beatifically in the direction of the sound.

The scene fades slowly, as lights come up on Dionysos and Pentheus. Dionysos is holding out a cup (the same as last seen) to Pentheus.)

PENTHEUS (*taking it*). Was that . . . he? Your god?

DIONYSOS. Does it matter? Drink!

PENTHEUS. Can I see some more? (*Slowly, dreamily, Pentheus raises the cup to his lips.*)

DIONYSOS.
You are a king. You have to administer.
Don't take the shadows too seriously. Reality
Is your only safety. Continue to reject illusion.

PENTHEUS.
I do.

DIONYSOS.
You found me out. I have the gift
Of magic, conjuring. But reality
Awaits you on the mountains.
Are you still afraid?

PENTHEUS.
No. What do you suggest?

DIONYSOS.
Come with me to the mountains. See for yourself.
Watch the Maenads, unseen. There are risks
A king must take for his own people.

PENTHEUS.
    Yes, yes, that is true.
DIONYSOS.
    You are king. Your blood provides its own
    Immunity. Just the same, if I may suggest it—
    It is foolhardiness to take avoidable risks. . . .
PENTHEUS.
    Go on. I am interested in your scheme. I find
    Somehow, you are trustworthy. Your ways
    Are strange, but . . . go on.
DIONYSOS.
    You must not be recognized. Cunning proves
    Always more successful than a show of force. You must
    Wear a disguise.
PENTHEUS.
    Yes, yes, I could dress as a common soldier,
    Or a peasant, a herdsman . . . where is that cowherd?
    I'll borrow his clothes.
DIONYSOS.
    You forget. He and his sycophantic companions
    Fomented this trouble. The sight of a herdsman
    now . . .
PENTHEUS.
    True, true. How shall I go then? I long
    To see them at their revels.
DIONYSOS.
    Do you? Then trust me. I shall lead you there
    Safely.
PENTHEUS.
    And stay to bring me back? I may get lost.
    I know so little of Thebes beyond the city.
    Almost nothing of the country, come to think of it.
DIONYSOS.
    Your mother will bring you back, in triumph,
    Leading a great procession. You will make your peace
    With Dionysos.
PENTHEUS.
    Oh, oh, not so fast. But I'll come with you.
    I shall do as you say—short of surrender
    To your priest of sly subversion.
DIONYSOS.
    Then come disguised as one of those we go
    To spy upon.
PENTHEUS.
    What! Dress myself as a Maenad? A woman?
    Make the throne a laughing-stock in Thebes?
DIONYSOS.
    Suppose the madness has not left them?
PENTHEUS.
    Don't mention it again. It is too undignified.
DIONYSOS.
    Even more undignified it is to be severed
    Limb from limb.
PENTHEUS.
    Forget it, I will not bring myself

Down to such a mockery of the throne.
    I shall go as I am, or not at all.
DIONYSOS.
    As you wish. But wear your armour at least.
    It may deflect a stone or two. Why seek bruises
    From foolhardiness.

(*Turns to the Old Slave, speaking with emphasis.*)

Bring the king his armour. Bring out
    His only protection against the Bacchae.
PENTHEUS.
    Yes, I shall go up the mountains as a king.
    Alone. Except for you as guide.
DIONYSOS.   In your royal armour.
PENTHEUS.
    Yes, I shall go with you in the battledress
    Of a worthy king of Thebes.
DIONYSOS.
    It is by far the best plan. And if the Maenads
    Spy you out, your royal presence will recall
    Your mother and her sisters back to their
    True heritage.

(*The slave returns—with a female Bacchic costume.*)

Here. I'll help you dress.

(*Dionysos begins to dress him. Pentheus strikes the customary stance for when he is being armed by a retainer.
The contrast is pathetic.*)

PENTHEUS (*as the first piece is slipped on.*).
    Strange, it feels so soft today. Hardly
    Like bronze and steel.
DIONYSOS.
    It is the wine. It does create that effect.
PENTHEUS.
    And lighter. It has hardly any weight.
DIONYSOS.
    Wine lightens all burdens. You will discover
    How lightly you walk, how your steps quicken
    And turn to dance.
PENTHEUS.
    I feel it already. Hurry. You must restrain me
    As we go. I feel I shall hardly conduct myself
    As becomes a soldier and a king.
DIONYSOS.
    Trust me. I shall be your guide. There is a force
    That blinds all men to diadems, swords and sceptres.
    You feel the beginnings of it.
PENTHEUS (*as Dionysos fastens a jewelled brooch.*).
    You are a dark horse, full of hidden talents
    To look at you, one would hardly think you knew those
    Intricacies of an armour's chains and buckles
    Yet you handle them like a practised armourer.
    Is there anything you don't know?

DIONYSOS.
Dionysos taught me all I know.

PENTHEUS (*chuckles, in very good humour.*).
It is instructive to meet a fanatic. I could use
Such loyalty. Whatever I say is turned
And exploited by you to glorify Dionysos.

(*He tilts the cup.*)

Is there more of this nectar? I feel
A great thirst within me.

DIONYSOS (*stretching his hand.*).
Your cup is full.

PENTHEUS (*looks.*).
Ah. (*Takes a prolonged draught.*)

1ST BACCHANTE.
Look! He stands at the gate of the trap
He'll find the Bacchae and with his life
He'll answer. He thrashes in the net
Of Dionysos, his wits are distracted.
Though he fought with the will of a Titan
Yet, for all that, he's a man.

DIONYSOS.
Some hair still shows beneath your head-piece
Not very soldierly—I'll tuck it in.

(*Places a wig on his head and ties it with a ribbon.*)

OLD SLAVE.
He stands at the gate of retribution,
The tyrant. Shall I pity him? I do not know.
His thoughts are dislodged, his reason slithers.
What sane mind struts in woman's clothing
And thinks it an armour of bronze.

BACCHANTE.
He'll raise a howl of derision all through Thebes
Mincing like a camp-follower.

DIONYSOS.
Dionysos will admit he's met his match
To see such a figure of Ares walking the earth.

BACCHANTE.
Once he mouthed fearsome threats. Now,
He is dressed, a docile lamb, for a descent
Into Hades. A rough caress by his mother
Will ease him there.

SLAVE.
A jealous joy, a ferocious, gentle joy
Is my Dionysos.

BACCHANTE.
Consummate god, most terrible, most gentle
To mankind.

PENTHEUS.
Mind you, I shall not forgive Tiresias,
Or my grandfather. They should have set
A good example and saved me all this bother.

DIONYSOS.
You will meet them on your way. Your grandfather
Shall be cruelly punished. And Agave . . .

PENTHEUS.
She most especially. My own mother,
What a disgrace! I hope we don't find her
Doing something really disgusting at those revels
I would be forced to kill her—for the honour
Of the house of Kadmos—you understand?

DIONYSOS.
Of course. Keep still while I fix this stubborn—
There, it's in . . . About Agave, set your mind
At rest. I shall bring reconciliation to
Mother and son. You shall return, Pentheus
Cradled in your mother's arms.

(*A gradual commencement of light changes.*)

1ST BACCHANTE.
Night—will it ever come
When what we know is done?
I seek release to a calm
Of green hills, white thighs
Flashing in the grass
The dew-soaked air kissing my throat.

LEADER.
Night, night set me free
Sky of a million roe, highway of eyes
Dust on mothwing, let me ride
On ovary silences, freely
Drawn on the reins of dreams.

BACCHANTE.   . . . the dance of night
Where darkness is deepest.

SLAVE LEADER.
Come, dawn, in the dance of the sun.
Come, dawn, herald of the new order.

1ST BACCHANTE.
But gently, as the dance of the young deer, swathed
In emerald meadow, when the terror of the hunt is past,
The leap over knotted nets, the hunter's shrieks
Forgotten. Let the new order bring peace,
Repose, plentitude. . . .

BACCHANTE.   . . . the lull
Of a sweet mothering copse, a timeless shade
Where no danger lurks . . .

DIONYSOS (*still tucking in and tricking out Pentheus, his mouth is full of pins and clips.*).
Is your wish still white-hot for a peep
At the forbidden? I would hate to take this trouble
Over nothing. Is your resolve as strong as ever?

PENTHEUS (*with just a touch of tipsiness.*).
Yes, but listen. I seem to see two suns
Blazing in the heavens. And now two Thebes
Two cities, each with seven gates. And you—
Are you a bull? There are horns newly
Sprouted from your head. Have you always been

A bull? Were you . . .

(*He searches foggily in his brain.*)

           . . . yes, that bull, in there?
Was it you?

DIONYSOS.
Now you see what you ought to see. Dionysos
Has been good to you with his gift of wine.

PENTHEUS.
Funny. Inside, I went this way with my head
Then, that way—back, forward—back. It was
Almost a kind of trance. I dreamed I stabbed
A bull. A minotaur. Was that you?

DIONYSOS.
I am whole. There—all that agitation has made
Your cuirass come loose. And the knee-guard.
Keep still till they are strapped in position.

(*He adjusts his sash, dolls out the pleats of his dress.*)

PENTHEUS.
I shall make you my armourer, after this campaign.

OLD SLAVE.
What does it mean life? Dare one
Hope for better than merely warring, seeking
Change, seeking the better life? Can we
Control what threatens before the eruption?
Defeat what oppresses by anticipation? Can we?
Dare we surrender to what comes after, embrace
The ambiguous face of the future? It is enough
To concede awareness of the inexplicable, to wait
And watch the unfolding. . . .

SLAVE.
For there are forces not ruled by us
And we obey them
Trust them. Though they travel inch by inch
They arrive.

OLD SLAVE.
Dionysos? or—Nothing.
Not even a word for these forces.
They lack a name. We will call them
Spirits.
Gods.

SLAVE.
Principles,
Elements,

SLAVE.
Currents,
Laws, Eternal Causes.

SLAVE.
But they are born in the blood
Unarguable, observed and preserved before time . . .

LEADER.
As freedom. No teaching implants it

No divine revelation at the altar.
It is knotted in the blood, a covenant from birth.

DIONYSOS (*hands Pentheus a thyrsus.*).
Your sword. (*Pentheus sticks it through the sash.*) Perfect. If
your mind matches your appearance,
Then the enemies of Thebes have surprises to come.

PENTHEUS (*straighter than ever, conscious militaristic preening.*).
I feel superhuman. I could hoist the whole of Kithairon
On one shoulder—with valleys full of women
Despite their dancing and madness . . . yes?

DIONYSOS.
I do not doubt it. We'll find a hiding place
That suits you best.

PENTHEUS.
Take me right through Thebes
Right through the centre. I am the only man here
With dare and courage.

DIONYSOS.
Yes, you alone
Make sacrifices for your people, you alone.
The role belongs to a king. Like those gods, who yearly
Must be rent to spring anew, that also
Is the fate of heroes.

PENTHEUS.
We'll march through Thebes. I lately imported
A famed drill-master for the troops. An expert.
He hails, I think, from . . . Phrygia! Hey, that's you.
Do you know him? Is he your countryman?

DIONYSOS.
It is possible.

PENTHEUS.
He's taught a new march to the household cavalry
A masterpiece of precision. We'll prance through
Thebes like those splendid horsemen. Wait,
I'll teach you the movements. It's simple—
Watch my feet!

(*He draws his 'sword', performs a brief salute forwards
and sideways, then strikes a dance pose.*)

           Here we go—
One-Two-Back, One-Two-Back, One-Two-Back . . .

(*exactly like Tiresias. The music of Dionysos accompanies
him, welling in volume as Pentheus throws himself passionately into the dance, exhorting Dionysos's efforts.*)

That's it. Very good. A little higher at the knees.
You're light on your feet I must say, quite
An accomplished dancer. Well, shall we advance?

DIONYSOS.
Forward Pentheus!

PENTHEUS (*lets off a loud yodel.*).
Death to the Bacchae!
One-Two-Back! One-Two-Back! One-Two-Back!

(*His voice dies off in the distance, punctuated to the last by fierce yodels. Dionysos stands and speaks with more than a suspicion of weariness from this now concluding conflict. It is not entirely a noble victory.*)

DIONYSOS.

At last he comes, my Bacchantes
Prepare, you sisters, daughters of Kadmos
Agave, open your mothering arms—
Take him. Mother him. Smother him with joy.

(*Exit Dionysos. As his speech ends, part of the Chorus of Slaves set up a dog-howl, a wail of death. Instantly a section separate themselves, move throughout the next speeches until they are joined with the Bacchantes. They form, for this last part, a solid fanatic front with the followers of Dionysos. The progress across should not be a dance, but a terse series of dramatic motions which takes its motif from the following invocation, the decisive gesture of throwing their lot with the Bacchae, the casting off of the long vassalage in the House of Pentheus.*)

LEADER.

A self-swollen and calloused soul
Tumoured and hard.
All your malignant growths of thought
Level now, pare, and crop
They move in the dark with a fading glimmer
The ruler is overruled
You countered and strove at your peril
Seeking Dionysos. Death follows your finding.

BACCHANTE.

Go, track to the mountains
Swift hounds of madness
Run, dogs run,
Find the daughters of Kadmos

SLAVE (*separating.*).

Snap at their dancing heels
Sink your fangs into their brains
Then turn them loose
Turn them loose on the foolhardy
Ruler, who spies in flapping skirts.

ANOTHER.

He's mad for the secret
He spies on the faithful possessed
His mother shall see him first
She'll cry to the Maenads:

BACCHANTE.

LOOK! See what creeps across the hillside

(*begins a stylized mime of the hunt. It ends just before the 'coup de grace' at the entry of the Officer. Only three or four of the Bacchae take part.*)

What creature is this?
What monstrous obscenity!

It surely was born of no woman
It took life from a rotting foetus
That heaved from a dying gorgon.

SLAVE.

Watch him sniffing up our mountains
Watch him drag like the spawn of a reptile.

ANOTHER.

Now we shall see the balance restored
O Justice! O Spirit of Equity, Restitution
Be manifest! A sharp clear sword
With blood on its edge—drive
To the gullet of Pentheus.

BACCHANTE.

Intent with sick passion
His mind is a sewer rat
Rooting and sniffing to the living heart
Madly assailing, profaning
The rites of the mother of god.

(*A steady beat of the chant 'Bromius Bromius' by the Bacchantes commences as counterpoint to the dog-howl of the remnant Slave Chorus, gradually gaining ascendancy until the arrival of the Messenger.*)

LEADER.

Come, god
Of seven paths: oil, wine, blood, spring, rain
Sap and sperm, O dirge of shadows, dark-shod feet
Seven-ply crossroads, hands of camwood
Breath of indigo, O god of the seven roads
Farm, hill, forge, breath, field of battle
Death and the recreative flint . . .

SLAVE.

He runs, against the unassailable.
Runs with violence against his, my
Forever-free spirit, unchainable,
He runs, with chains in his hand
With manacles for the encounter—
Death will counter his inventions
Death will end him!

OLD SLAVE (*he remains with the Slave Chorus.*).

Headlong he runs to his death
The gods do humble us with death
Lest we forget
We are not such as gods are made of.
I say accept, accept.
Humility is wise, is blessed
There are great things unfathomable
The mind cannot grasp them.

SLAVE.

Where do we seek him? Where find him?
Where conflict rages, where sweat
Is torrents of rain, where flesh springs
Of blood fill him with longing as the rush
Of wine. There seek the hunter god.

LEADER.

    Justice! Restitution! O Spirit of Equity
    Be manifest! Bright clear sword, a gleam
    Of blood on its edge—drive!
    Destroy the earth-spurning evil spawn of Ichion.

1ST BACCHANTE.

    Reveal yourself Dionysos! Be manifest!
    O Bacchus come! Come with your killing smile!
    Come, a dragon with swarming heads, vomiting flames!
    Come hunter, cast your noose.
    Bring him down. Trample him
    Underfoot with the heard of justice, your Maenads!
    Bromius come! Master! Lover! Bull with horns
    Of fire. Serpent with fangs of love. Lion
    At my breasts, Eternal Ember in my hearth
    Hunt this game to ground, Come Bromius!

(*Enter the Officer just as the arm of the miming Bacchante
is raised to strike the 'quarry'.*)

OFFICER.

    What is this? Has this god not done enough
    That you still call here on Bromius?

(*Gradual silence. They turn to him.*)

    In this house lived people who were once
    The envy of all Greece—once—a family begun
    In dragon's teeth, that summer harvest reaped
    By Kadmos. It is winter now for this great race
    I see no future spring.

CHORUS.   What is it?

    Have you news? Were you in the hills

OFFICER.

    I am only a soldier, nothing more, yet
    I mourn the fortunes of this fallen house.
    King Pentheus, son of Ichion, is dead.

BACCHANTE.

    All power to Bromius: Victory on this first day
    Of his homecoming. Quickly, how did he die?

OFFICER.

    What is this? You dare rejoice
    At the disasters of this house? My master
    Is—DEAD!

SLAVE.

    Your master not mine.
    I have another home, another life.
    Nor will the fear of dungeons stop me
    Manifesting my joy.

OFFICER.

    Your feelings can be forgiven. But this,
    This exultation over terrible misfortune—
    It's ugly.

BACCHANTE.

    Was it truly terrible? Tell us. Were you there?

OFFICER.

    There were three of us in all: Pentheus, I
    Attending the king, and that stranger who offered
    His services as guide. We soon left behind us
    The last outlying farms of Thebes, forded
    The Aesopus, then struck into the barren scrubland
    Of Kithairon.

                There, we halted in a grassy glen
    Unmoving, wordless, taking all precausiton
    Not to be discovered. It was there we saw them,
    In a sudden meadow carved in rockface of the cliffs
    Water ran freely there, and the pines grew dense
    With shade—there the Maenads rested, their hands
    Busy with their normal tasks, singing. They were
    Weird, disturbing tunes

                But our king, Pentheus
    Unhappy man, found his view obscured by springy
    Undergrowth. 'Stranger' he said, 'from here I can see
    Little of these counterfeiting worshippers.
    What if I climbed that towering fir that overhangs
    The banks, do you think I might see them better at
    Their shameless orgies?'

                And now the stranger worked a miracle!
    He reached up to the highest branch of a great fir
    Bent it down, down to the dark earth
    Till it was curved, a drawn bow in giant hands
    A wooden rim bent to encase a wheel for the chariot
    Of the sun. I was awed. No mortal could have done this.
    He seated Pentheus on the highest tip and,
    With great control he eased aloft the trunk
    Slowly, gently, most careful not to throw our king
    From his new throne among the leaves.
    And that fir rose, towering back to heaven
    With my master proudly seated at the top.
    You know that saying?—A man the whole world seeks to
    roast
    Rubs himself in oil, crouches beside an open fire
    Moaning, I have a chill: the rest is soon told.
    The stranger had vanished. Only his voice, a bull's roar
    Filled the mountains, stayed to set his doom in train.
    'Maenads, look up!' it bellowed. They obeyed. The
    women
    Saw King Pentheus stark against the sky
    Clearer than he could see them. Hell broke loose.
    Like startled doves, through grove and torrent
    Over jagged rocks they flew, their feet excited
    By the breath of god.

                His mother took the lead
    I heard the voice of Agave calling on her Maenads
    To make a circle, shouting, 'This climbing beast
    Must not escape lest he reveal the secrets
    Of our god.' They made a ring. A hundred hands
    A hundred supple arms heaved and strained. King
    Pentheus

Clutched at futile anchors on his naked nest
Hoping to keep death at bay. I heard the wrench of roots
From their long bed of earth and rocks. The fir was
Lifted out, it rose from earth, tilted, and down
From his high perch fell Pentheus, tumbling
Down to earth, sobbing and screaming as he fell.
He knew the end was near. His mother
First at the sacrifice of her own son
Fell upon him, angry priestess at the rites of death.
Pentheus, still miraculously alive, tore off wig
And snood, touched her face and hoped for recognition.
He mouthed a last despairing plea in silence, his voice
Broken from the fall.   She foamed at the mouth, her eyes
Rolled with frenzy. Agave was mad, stark mad
Possessed by Bacchus, blind to all plea for pity.
She seized the waving arm by the wrist, then
Planted her foot upon his chest and pulled,
Tore the arm clean off the shoulder. The tongue
Of Pentheus stretched out in agony, his mouth ran blood
But no sound came. Ino, on the other side of him
Began to peel his flesh. The Autonoe, the swarming
Horde of Maenads homed on him, his other arm
Was torn, a foot flew up in the air, still encased
Within its sandal. The last I saw, his rib-case
Dragged, clawed clean of flesh. They played
With lumps of flesh, tossed from hand to blood-stained
Hand until the hills and valleys of Kithairon
Were strewn with fragments of his body.
                The pitiful remains lie scattered
One piece among sharp rocks, others
Lost among the leaves in forest depths.
His mother seized the head, impaled it on a wand
And seems to think it is a mountain lion's head
She bears in triumph through the thickness of
Kithairon. She calls on Bromius: he is her 'fellow-hunts-
man'
'Comrade of the chase', she is 'crowned with victory'.
All the victory you will find on her is that grisly prize
And her own loss.
                I must go. Best to flee
This place before the caryatid of grief returns and,
Proves flesh and blood in the hour of truth.
Let who can console the house of Kadmos.

                                                (*Exit.*)

OLD SLAVE.
  The ways of god are hard to understand
  We know full well that some must die, chosen
  To bear the burden of decay, lest we all die—
  The farms, the wheatfields, cattle, even the
  Vineyards up on the hills. And yet, this knowledge
  Cannot blunt the edge of pain, the cruel
  Nature of this death. Oh this is a heartless

Deity, bitter, unnatural in his revenge.
To make a mother rip her son like bread
Across a banqueting board! I pity her.
LEADER.
  Who pities us? When the mine-prop falls and pulps
  Our bones with mud, who pities us? When harvest
  Fails, who goes without? And you, if you had
  Died at the feast of Eleusis, would Thebes
  Have remembered you with pity?
OLD SLAVE.
  I pity her. But I fear she'll prove
  Beyond mortal consolation.
1ST BACCHANTE.
  Look! Here she comes, the priestess
  Of hunting rites. Take her, enfold the new triumphant
  Bride of Bromius.

  (*Agave runs in with her trophy stuck on a thyrsus but invisible under gold ribbons. She raises the stave and the ribbons flow around her as she runs once round the stage.*)

AGAVE.
  Women of the hills . . . Bacchae!
CHORUS.
  Speak Agave! Welcome!
AGAVE.
  Do you see this bough, this fresh-cut
  Spray from the mountains? Observe
  How it streams. Can you see it?
CHORUS.
  We see it Agave.
1ST BACCHANTE.
  We know it Agave and for this
  We sing your praise. Tell us of the hunt.
  We've heard of the snarling beast whose towering
  Pride was humbled by the might of Bromius.
AGAVE.
  Have you know a mountain lion
  Wild-fanged, red-eyed indomitable whelp.
  Have you known such savagery ever
  Trapped without net or noose? Without
  Weapons, without beaters or other
  Time-consuming subterfuge. Answer me.
CHORUS.
  It is unheard-of.
AGAVE.
  Then look on this? Look at the prize.
  Is it noble?
OLD SLAVE.
  It is royal, Agave. Where did you find it?
AGAVE.
  On the mountains of Kithairon. Happy,
  Happy was the hunting!
OLD SLAVE.
  Who killed him?

AGAVE.

I, Agave. I struck first, tore off
A limb that launched its unsheathed claws
Against my face. Thus—my foot was planted
Crushing its rib-case! I heard sweet sounds of sinews
Yielding at the socket as I tugged. The beast's snarl
Turned to agony. I swung its lifeless limb
Up in the air, the first taste of the hunt
To Dionysos. The Maenads call me
Agave the Blest.

BACCHANTE.

Blessed Agave, thrice blessed daughter of
Kadmos!

OLD SLAVE.

Tell the rest Agave.

AGAVE.

All the daughters of Kadmos are blest.
Ino, Autonoe came after. But mine was the first
Hand on the quarry. I struck the death-blow.
Later, we rested. My sisters wove a worthy
Garland for the noble prize. See how it flows.
A god-like mane for a royal beast. It flows bountifully
Like my golden joy.

OLD SLAVE.

Joy indeed. Joyful Kadmos. Joyful Thebes.

AGAVE.

All must share in my glory. I summon you all
To a feast of celebration.

OLD SLAVE.

A feast . . . ? Oh Agave.

SLAVE LEADER.

To eat of this—lion, Agave?

AGAVE.

This bull, lion, this swift mountain-goat
This flash of the wind in grassland,
This dew-skinned deer . . .
                        Oh, our god is generous
Cunningly, cleverly, Bacchus the hunter
Launched the Maenads on his prey.

OLD SLAVE.

Yes, he is a great hunter. He knows
The way to a death-hunt of the self.

AGAVE.

Ah, you praise him now.

CHORUS.

We praise Dionysos.

AGAVE.

And the blessed Agave?

CHORUS.

We praise the blessed Mother.

OLD SLAVE.

And your son?

AGAVE.

Will praise the Mother who caught

And offered the sacrifice.
                        Oh he'll wear his pride
As palpably as mine, his joy will mount
In full flood-tide higher than mine.
I feel a strength in me like the purity
Of Dionysos. And here is the proof—
This boon of our chase, this golden gift
Of Dionysos.

OLD SLAVE.

Then poor woman, unshroud this great prize
Show the citizens of Thebes, this trophy
Of the god of joy.

AGAVE.

Why? Can't they see it?

(*She looks up at the thyrsus.*)

                        Ah! The shroud of gold
Obscures him. Maenads! Catch this billowing mane.

(*She takes the thyrsus in both hands and whirls it. The Maenads chase and catch the ribbons as they unfurl and float outwards. With Agave in the centre, a Maypole dance evolves naturally from their positions. It is a soft graceful dance.*)

Men and women of Thebes, the city of high
Towers, impregnable, behold the trophy of your—
Women, captured in the hunt. Behold our offering
To this year of Dionysos. We tracked him down
Not with nets nor spears forged in workshops
Of Thessaly, but with the untried, delicate hands
That give birth. What are they worth, those clumsy
Tools you fabricate, your armour and swords?
We caught this beast, we brought him to the altar,
Our fair mothers' hands our only weapons. Tell me
Do you know of any greater than the power
Of our creative wombs?
                        But . . . where is father?
He should be here. And my son, Pentheus?
Fetch them someone. And bring a ladder too.
I want it set against the wall. This masthead must
Fly high upon our palace walls.

(*Exit the Slave Leader. A Bacchante relieves Agave at the Maypole and she takes her place. Instantly the dance grows frenzied and works up to a high pitch. The Slave Leader re-enters with a ladder, stands watching for some moments. He sets the ladder in position and shouts above the music.*)

SLAVE LEADER (*a mock-bow.*)

The Ladder, Queen Mother Agave!

(*She looks up, rushes back and snatches the thyrsus and 'flies' up the ladder with it. Enter Kadmos supported by*

Tiresias followed by attendants who carry a covered bier, the remnants of Pentheus.)

KADMOS.

This way . . . follow me. Is the burden heavy?
My grief is heavier. Set him down, there
Before the palace.
Pentheus has come home.
It was a long, weary search, there was so much
Of my dismembered son, and set so wide apart
Through the forest. No two pieces in a single place.
Tiresias and I, we had paid our tribute to Dionysos
And were back in the city. The news found us here
Of this unseasonable harvest reaped upon the
mountains.
Oh the mountains of Kithairon boast a gory crop!
Unlucky house . . . I saw them at the mountainside
Aristaus' wife, mother of Actaeon, Autonoe and Ino
All still stung with madness. Agave I hear
Is still possessed . . . what was in their minds?
What moved them to do this thing? Why couldn't . . .
(*violently.*) She should have known him!

(*Raising his head, he sees her.*)

No . . . no . . .

I don't want to see!
TIRESIAS.

What is it Kadmos?
AGAVE (*turning from her task.*).

Did I hear . . . ? Ah, you at last. No! Don't look.
Turn around. Wait until this silken mane is
Fully displayed in all its splendour. Then you can tell me
How it looks from there? No royal wall
Ever boasted ornament to equal this.
Have rumours reached you yet? If not
I have such news for you. You are the proud
Father of brave daughters. I tell you, nowhere
Can such prowess be excelled. We have left our
Shuttle in the loom, raised our sights
To higher things. We hunt. We kill. Now, look!
A royal masthead! Look Father. Turn around!
Glory in my kill, my new-found prowess, invite
All Thebes to a great celebration. You are blessed father
By this great deed of mine.
KADMOS.

Oh gods, can I measure grief like this?
I cannot look. This is awful murder, child.
This, this is the noble victim you have slaughtered
To the gods? To share this *glory* you invite
All Thebes and me.

Oh gods!

How terribly I pity you and then myself.
The things you've done, the horror, the abomination,
Oh fling your thanksgiving before what deity you please

Not ask my grief to come and celebrate!
Celebrate . . .

(*He breaks down.*)

Dioynsos is just. But he is not fair!
Though he had right on his side, he lacks
Compassion, the deeper justice. And he was born
Here. This . . . is his home . . . this soil gave him breath.

(*Agave comes down slowly, right up to him.*)

AGAVE.

Oh look at him, old sourpuss. Monopoly
Of the sacrificial knife passes
Into women's hands
And turns him crabbed and sour.
I hope Pentheus takes after me, and wins as I
The laurels of the hunt when he goes hunting
With the younger men of Thebes. Alas, all he does
Is quarrel with god. You should talk to him.
You're the one to do it. Yes, someone call him out
Let him witness his mother's triumph.
KADMOS (*anguished.*).

You'll know. You must! You'll see the horror
In your deed, then pain will wring blood from your eyes
Though, if I could grant . . . a boon . . . I would
You never woke up from your present state until
You die. It won't be happiness, but . . .
You'll feel no pain.
AGAVE. Why do you reproach me? Is something wrong?
KADMOS. Look up at the sky.

(*Agave obeys.*)

AGAVE. So? What do you expect me to see.
KADMOS. Does it look the same to you? Or has it changed?
AGAVE. It seems . . . somehow . . . clearer, brighter than
before. There is red glow of sunset, a colour of blood.
KADMOS.

And inside you, do you still
Feel the same sense of floating?
AGAVE.

Floating? No. And it's quieter . . . restful.
I feel . . . a sense of changing. The world
No longer heaves as if within my womb.
There was a wind too but . . . I think . . . it's . . . dropped.
KADMOS. Can you still hear me? Do you know what I'm
saying? Do you remember what you said before?
AGAVE. I . . . no. What were we talking about?
KADMOS. Who was your husband?
AGAVE. Ichion, born they say of the dragon seed.
KADMOS. And the name of the child you bore him?
AGAVE. Pentheus?
KADMOS. Is he living?
AGAVE. Assuredly.

KADMOS.
Now look up at the face you've set
Upon that wall. Whose head is it?

AGAVE.
Whose . . . ? (*violently.*) It's a lion!
It's . . . I . . . think . . .

KADMOS.
Look at it. Look directly at it.

AGAVE.
No. What is it? First tell me what it is.

KADMOS.
You must look. Look closely and carefully.

(*She brings herself to obey him.*)

AGAVE.
Oh. Another slave? But why did I nail it
Right over the entrance?

KADMOS.
Closer. Move closer. Go right up to it.

(*She moves closer until she is standing almost directly under it, looking up. She stiffens suddenly, her body shudders and she whirls round screaming.*)

AGAVE.
Bring him down! Bring him down! Bring him . . .

(*Kadmos has moved closer, and she collapses into his shoulders sobbing.*)

KADMOS (*to the Slaves.*).
Bring down the head.

(*But they all retreat and look down, as if they dare not touch him. After a while Kadmos realizes that no one has moved to obey him.*)

Did no one hear me? Take down my son!

AGAVE (*suddenly calmer.*).
Let no hand but mine be laid on him.
I am his mother. I brought him out to life
I shall prepare him for his grave.

(*She turns towards the ladder, stops.*)

How did he die!

KADMOS.
He mocked the god Dionysos, spied on his Mysteries.

(*Goes towards the bier and lifts a corner of the cover.*)

Here is his body. A long weary search.
I gathered him together, piece by piece
On the mountains of Kithairon.

AGAVE.
Kithairon . . . but . . .

KADMOS.
Where Actaeon was torn to pieces.

AGAVE.
And Pentheus?

KADMOS.
The whole city was possessed by Dionysos.
He drove you mad. You rushed to the mountains . . .

AGAVE.
Of Kithairon? Yes . . . was I not there?

KADMOS.
You killed him.

AGAVE.
I?

KADMOS.
You and your sisters. You were possessed.

AGAVE (*a soft sigh.*).
A-ah.

(*She stands stock-still. Then turns towards the ladder.*)

It is time to bring him down. (*Begins to climb, slowly.*)

KADMOS.
Console her Tiresias. I no longer understand
The ways of god. I may blaspheme.

TIRESIAS.
Understanding of these things is far beyond us.
Perhaps . . . perhaps our life-sustaining earth
Demands . . . a little more . . . sometimes, a more
Than token offering for her own needful renewal.
And who, more than we should know it? For all too many
The soil of Thebes has proved a most unfeeling
Host, harsh, unyielding, as if the dragon's teeth
That gave it birth still farms its subsoil.
They feel this, same as I, even through calloused soles.
O Kadmos, it was a cause beyond madness, this
Scattering of his flesh to the seven winds, the rain
Of blood that streamed out endlessly to soak
Our land. Remember when I said, Kadmos, we seem to be upon
Sheer rockface, yet moisture oozes up at every
Step? Blood you replied, blood. His blood
Is everywhere. The leaves of Kithairon have turned red with it.

KADMOS (*The cry is wrung from him.*).
Why us?

AGAVE (*Her hands are on Pentheus's head, about to lift it. Quietly.*).
Why not?

(*The theme music of Dionysos begins, welling up and filling the stage with the god's presence.*

A powerful red glow shines suddenly as if from within the head of Pentheus, rendering it near-luminous. The stage is bathed in it and, instantly, from every orifice of the impaled head spring red jets, spurting in every direction. Reactions of horror and panic. Agave screams and flattens herself below the head, hugging the ladder.)

TIRESIAS.
What is it Kadmos? What is it?
KADMOS.
Again blood Tiresias. Nothing but blood.
TIRESIAS (*He feels his way nearer the fount. A spray hits him and he holds out a hand, catches some of the fluid and sniffs. Tastes it.*).
No. It's wine.

(*Slowly, dream-like, they all move towards the fountain, cup their hands and drink. Agave raises herself at last to observe them, then tilts her head backwards to let a jet flush full in her face and flush her mouth. The light contracts to a final glow around the heads of Pentheus and Agave.*)

THE END

TOPICS FOR CRITICAL THINKING AND WRITING

The Play on the PAGE

1. Soyinka includes a chorus of male slaves in addition to Euripides's original chorus of female Bacchantes. Why do you think he felt that was necessary? What is the relationship of these two choruses to each other? What do they share and how do they differ from each other?
2. Sometimes the main character of a tragedy will have a single tragic flaw that leads to his or her downfall. Does Pentheus have a tragic flaw? If so, what is it?
3. In many cultures, the scapegoat is a sacred figure whose sacrifice purges the ills of that culture. In this story, why must Pentheus serve as the scapegoat?
4. Soyinka wrote the subtitle "A Communion Rite" for the play. What is its significance?

The Play on the STAGE

5. How would you stage the combination of African and Greek elements written into the play? In terms of costumes? In terms of set design? In terms of movement and sound?
6. A major visual image that Soyinka uses at the end of the play is the fountain of red wine spurting from the head of Pentheus. How would you stage this?
7. Identify the ritual elements in the script and describe how you would create these on the stage.

The Play in PERFORMANCE

The Bacchae of Euripides: A Communion Rite was commissioned by the National Theater in London and produced there in 1973 at the Old Vic Theatre. In the program notes from that production, Soyinka refers to himself as an "adapter," and although the narrative of Soyinka's script is close to Euripides's original, Soyinka's version is clearly a reworking of the material in a vibrant, powerful poetic rendering. Soyinka has acknowledged the Yoruban god Ogun as the personal source for his artistic vision, and this work gave him the opportunity to explore the close relationship between Ogun and Dionysus. The work was influenced by Nigeria's political turmoil at the time that Soyinka was writing the play.

EZEKIEL KOFOWOROLA
Directing The Bacchae of Euripides

Ezekiel Kofoworola, theater professor and director from Nigeria, was a guest artist in the Department of Theatre at Ohio State University, where he directed *The Bacchae of Euripides* in 1998. In this interview he discusses the themes and ideas in the play.

Soyinka incorporates qualities of the Yoruba deity Ogun into his portrayal of Dionysos. What is the relationship between these two gods in the play?

Now among the Yorubas, Ogun is regarded as god of wine, god of fertility, also god of iron and god of the road. Soyinka could not fail to see that Dionysus was a similar god, if not the same god.

The way the Yoruban mythology thinks about Ogun is that, as a god of iron, there is an equation between him and creativity. Any work, any skill connected with iron is inspired by Ogun. His spirit infuses his followers with a "fertility" of body and spirit. Among the Yorubas it is believed that even the farmers who use hoes—hoes are made of metal—have to pay some kind of homage to Ogun, who gives them the skill to use this hoe, this tool—as must hunters, warriors, blacksmiths, surgeons, woodcarvers, and even poets.

And because Ogun is regarded as the god of fertility, there is the concept that the fertility of the soil is equated with the fertility of mankind. In other words there are two levels of the idea of fertility. The fertility of the soil is manifested when the seed is planted in order to produce bountiful harvests. There is also the fertility of procreation, that comes out of the copulation between man and woman, and is manifested with the production of children. And it is believed that the physical and the spiritual must always be kept in balance.

We also believe that Ogun is god of wine; wine if used properly can transport you to a state of otherness that will give you a kind of transportation, transportation to the spiritual realm. And once that has been achieved you will then be able to assert your energy in whatever you want to do.

We also use words to make things happen. The priests and the adherents perform rituals that are essentially like the clearing away of obstacles in one's mind.

In order to avoid these obstacles, to clear the mind, the priest transports himself with the use of words or incantations. And so Soyinka uses words—words that are chanted, dense and powerful to provide the actor, the audience with a clear path to see the contest of wills that play out before you. Words become like arrows, like bullets, before the real arrow and the real bullet. For Ogun, something has to happen in the spiritual level before it is manifested in the physical.

So it is believed that Ogun, the god of creativity, the god of iron, incorporates all these qualities, the abilities of hunters, warriors, pilots, travelers, blacksmiths, woodcarvers, poets, dancers, and so forth. And so the adherents believe they can use the potent power of words to make things happen.

There seem to be two central characters in the play, Dionysos and Pentheus. What is the relationship of these two characters?

Pentheus—we may want to consider him a kind of heroic representation of authority in its secular essence. Dionysos, on the other hand, represents the unwritten laws, a nonsecular essence.

But from the conceptual point of view—that is from the African cosmology—the two extremes are supposed to operate in balance, just like we have the day following the darkness. At the dawn of every day the cock will crow. There will be fresh, cool air, a singing through the system of everybody and tickling you to an awakening new day, and making you feel (*breathes in a deep breath*) I have gone through a passage. But in Soyinka's play the two men are not in balance, they are in opposition with each other, they confront each other. The world of letting go, the world of release clashes with the world of control, the world of repression. Pentheus also represents the force of reality, but there is reality beyond the reality. This is what Dionysos represents. Pentheus is the power of science. Testing, assessing, examining and reexamining, making sure or making certain. Dionysos represents the force that says testing is not enough. Rules, regulations are not enough. The more you do, the less you see. You may examine and reexamine, but certain things cannot be tested or measured. So these are the things I see between Pentheus and Dionysus.

You chose to have perpetual live music behind the action of the production. During rehearsals, you spoke of the drums as the "heartbeat" of the play. What did you mean by this?

THE PLAY IN PERFORMANCE   1101

There are signs around us, vibrations, all about the place, and these vibrations, these signs have some kind of influence and effect over us.

Now why is it that music when it is played is like a tonic? There is healing power in different connections of sound, sounds and vibrations.

I believe the music will entwine with whatever the character is saying, entwine with it and create a vehicle, not only for the character, but also for the audience. I also believe the music will create some kind of rhythm, the rhythm that will energize and stimulate the actors, and by energizing and stimulating them, since actors are now vehicles in artistic experience, artistic experience which the audience is going through, so the artists will now be turned into a vehicle of these positive impressions. Or even negative impressions when they want to register in the psyche of the audience. . . .

And it seems that it could be transformed into a kind of special game by which the actor on stage, if he renders his lines appropriately, will get you mesmerized as you drum behind him, and if you render your own drumming appropriately, you will get him mesmerized. And so the two of you, if you have a harmonious balance drumming and acting, may find yourself in a kind of euphoria, lifted, you are lifted up. You at the backstage, giving him the pulse, the rhythm, the sound, the vibration, he taking it on to energize himself and giving it back to you, not only you but even to the audience. So it is like getting two forces. The negative, the positive, just like you have in electricity, and charging the audience with the light, the real light of the message.

In his adaptation of Euripides's drama, Wole Soyinka alters the ending, having wine spurt from the severed head of Pentheus. In your opinion, why is this important?

I think that it's a kind of poetic justice, because at the end of the play the audience becomes traumatized; the tragedy is too much: Pentheus's mother discovers the havoc she has wreaked on herself without actually knowing what she did. And the damnation of the tragedy cannot be contained, because why would Dionysos allow a faithful follower to murder her own son? Could not Dionysos use any other person, any other character to commit the murder?

And we know what happens in the end is that the power of reality as we see it on this earthly plane is broken. Pentheus represents that power of reality. The reality of the father. There are certain things you just have to do, and you must do them, because that's what regulations say, otherwise you will not be part and parcel of whatever organization you belong to.

But that reality was broken. It was broken, and it was turned into a fountain of wine. There is another reality which infuses in us the spiritual essence, that makes us do things which we may not be capable of doing.

There are things that make us escape, that make us fly without growing any wings. And the symbolism of that reality is the breaking of this reality that is seemingly unbreakable. And the essence of it comes in the fountain of wine, which gives a spiritual freedom, in which the world is a large place full of possibility, in which nothing is impossible. Wine is used in many religions as a holy drink, a drink that blesses. Here, for Soyinka, the wine douses the tragedy, we in the audience and on stage partake of the red drink. We come together in this brief moment of spiritual communion. At one level: Pentheus was murdered, the mother felt shocked. But at another, we must come together to regain our balance, to start down the path of life renewed.

DARIO FO

Born of working class parents in northern Italy in 1926, Dario Fo moved to Milan when still a teenager in order to study art at the Brera Academy. In Milan he began performing improvised comic sketches in amateur theaters. Between 1943 and 1945 Fo returned home to help his father smuggle people across the Italian/Swiss border as part of the Resistance. After World War II, he returned to Milan to study set design and architecture, but left just before completing his degree in 1951. He launched his own solo radio series in 1951, the same year he met the actress Franca Rame, whom he married in 1953. Rame has not only interpreted many of the roles he has written, but she has also co-written several plays with Fo. Together in the 1950s they worked in film; then in 1958 they founded the Compagnia Fo-Rame and started producing Fo's early farces. Fo and Rame wrote, produced, and acted in numerous plays and are known throughout Italy because of Fo's popular TV programs. Disturbed by censorship of some of their work, they left television to continue their theater work with a stronger, more focused political edge. In 1970 Fo wrote one of his most produced works, *Accidental Death of an Anarchist,* and four years later the popular *We Won't Pay! We Won't Pay!* By 1978 Dario Fo was the most widely performed Italian playwright outside of Italy. His other plays include *Archangels Don't Play Pinball* (1959), *Mistero Buffo* (1969), *Trumpets and Raspberries* (1981), *Elizabeth* (1984), *Hellequin, Harilekin, Arlecchino* (1985), *The Pope and the Witch* (1989), and *Free Marino! Marino Is Innocent* (1998). During the late 1970s Fo witnessed a triumphant television comeback when a retrospective of seven of his plays was aired on Italian television and seen by more than five million viewers. It was also during this period that his plays started to appear outside Italy in translation. In addition to writing over seventy plays, Dario Fo is acknowledged to be one of the world's great comic actors. In 1997 Dario Fo was awarded the Nobel Prize for literature.

COMMENTARY ON *WE WON'T PAY! WE WON'T PAY!*

Dario Fo's prolific career in theater is inseparable from two important facts. First, he is committed to direct engagement with Italian political life. Second, his work as a writer and an actor goes back to the venerable traditions of popular performance. Fo uses stage techniques from the knock-about farces of the ancient Roman, the medieval *giullare* (juster, buffoon), the circus, burlesque, satire, and *commedia dell'arte*. In particular Fo characterizes himself as a *giullare*.

Giullari were traveling performers mostly from the lower classes who worked within the oral tradition. The term emerged sometime during the ninth century to describe players who busked in the streets, often fleeing censorship or persecution from authorities. They included a wide range of performers such as acrobats, musicians, storytellers, and mimes. In many ways *giullari* are like the stand-up comedians of today. Some theater historians believe that the comic characters of *commedia dell'arte* developed from the *giullare*.

Although Fo acknowledges the importance of the *commedia* tradition in his work, he uses the *commedia* precursor, the *giullarie*, as the source for much of his work. In Fo's view, this peasant performer was, in his satire, more subversive and disruptive and less institutionalized than *commedia* actors. Furthermore, whereas *commedia* performers worked in companies, *giullari* were usually solo performers who devised acting techniques to play multiple roles. One of Fo's celebrated solo scripts, written in 1969 but which he continues to perform with great success, is *Mistero Buffo* (literally a "comical mystery"). The piece is a series of monologues in which Fo uses his incredible skills as a mime, actor, and improviser to highlight the people's struggle against the oppression of the Catholic church and wealthy classes. One of the monologues is based on the New Testament story of Lazarus, requiring Fo to play an entire crowd of people straining to see Christ's miracle of raising Lazarus (John 11.1–44) from the dead. Fo explains:

> The text of "The Resurrection of Lazarus" is a text for a virtuoso because the *giullare* often found himself having to play as many as 15 or 16 characters one after the other, with no way of indicating the changes except with his body—by striking a posture, without even changing his voice. It's the kind of piece which calls on the performer to improvise according to the audience's laughter, cadences, and silences. In practice, it's an improvisation which requires occasional ad-libbing. (Mitchell 24)

A trademark of Dario Fo's work is his use of real political events as the impetus for writing his plays. *Accidental Death of an Anarchist* was written in response to audience demands for a play about the "accidental" death in Milan of an anarchist who was in police custody. *We Won't Pay! We Won't Pay!* was inspired by the *autoriduzione di prezzi*, a consumer revolt in which people refused to pay inflated prices. This form of mass

civil disobedience was carried out mainly by working-class people in several towns in southern Italy. In the mid-1970s Italy was going through a severe economic crisis: Prices were rising and unemployment was rife. Inspired by this grassroots, collective political action, Fo wrote a wildly farcical comedy that focused on the problems of working women in running a household during times of economic crisis. Once the play opened in Milan, similar political action took place in northern Italian supermarkets, and Fo was accused of fomenting civil unrest.

Many critics have commented on the festive, carnivalesque nature of the comedy, the ways in which hunger and pregnancy underscore the notions of fat and lean bellies. Carnival, or mardi gras, is an ancient religious festival that celebrates life's chaos and excess. Fo draws on a central conceit of carnival: the world turned upside down. In Fo's play, people of the lower classes (housewives, factory workers) rise up—if only momentarily—to take power into their own hands.

WE WON'T PAY! WE WON'T PAY!
Dario Fo

Translated by Ron Jenkins

CHARACTERS

ANTONIA
GIOVANNI
MARGHERITA
LUIGI

STATE TROOPER
POLICE SARGENT
GRAVEDIGGER
GRANDFATHER
SEVERAL TROOPERS AND POLICEMEN

ACT ONE

A modest working class home. On the right side of the stage is a dresser and a bed. On the left side of the stage is a hat rack and a wardrobe. In the center is a table. In the background is a set of shelves with plates. A refrigerator, a gas stove, and a little further back two gas tanks hooked together for welding. The lights go up on the entrance of Antonia (this is her home) followed by Margherita (her younger friend). They are loaded down with numerous plastic bags overflowing with merchandise that they set down on the table.

ANTONIA. It's a good thing I ran into you, or I don't know how I ever could have carried all this stuff.

MARGHERITA. Can I ask you where you found the money to pay for it all.

ANTONIA. I won it . . . in a lottery . . . the church was raffling off scratch tickets . . . mine had a portrait of the Pope, in silhouette, in the Pope-mobile.

MARGHERITA. The Pope-mobile . . . come on!

ANTONIA. Why, you don't believe it?

MARGHERITA. No!

ANTONIA. Okay, then I'll tell you the truth.

MARGHERITA (*sitting*). Go on. Tell me.

ANTONIA. This morning I had to go grocery shopping, but I didn't know how I could buy anything, because I didn't have any money. So I walked into the supermarket, and I see a crowd of women. They're all raising hell because the prices are higher than they were just the day before. (*As she talks she looks into the sacks and goes back and forth putting things into the kitchen shelves*) The manager's trying to calm them down. 'Well, there's nothing I can do about it,' he said. 'The distributors set the prices, and they've decided

to raise them.' "They decided? With whose permission?" "With nobody's permission. It's the free market. Free competition." "Free competition against who? Against us? And we're supposed to give in? . . . While they fire our husbands . . . and keep raising prices . . . " So I yelled, "You're the thieves!," . . . and then I hid, because I was really scared.

MARGHERITA. Good for you!

ANTONIA. Then one of the women said, "We've had enough! This time, we're setting the prices. We'll pay what we paid last month. And if you don't like it, we won't pay nothing. Understand?" You should have seen the manager. He turned white as a sheet. "You're out of your minds. I'm calling the police." He runs for the telephone behind the cash register, but the phone doesn't work. Somebody cut the line. "Excuse me. I've got to get to my office. Excuse me . . . " But he can't get through . . . not with all the women around him . . . so he pushes them . . . they push him . . . and while we were pushing a woman pretended he'd punched her in the belly, and fell down on the ground as if she'd fainted.

MARGHERITA. Ah . . . nice move!

ANTONIA. You should have seen what an artist she was! Just like the real thing . . . And there was a fat old woman there, she was huge, waving her finger like it was a machine gun . . . she pointed it at the manager and said, "Coward! Picking a fight with a defenseless woman, and she's pregnant. And now if she loses her baby, what's going to happen to you! They'll throw you in jail. Murderer." And then we all started chanting together: "BABY-KILLER! BABY-KILLER! BABY-KILLER!" (*She bursts out laughing*) It was great.

MARGHERITA. And then . . . what happened?

ANTONIA. Well, that prick of a manager was so scared he caved in completely . . . we paid whatever we wanted to pay.

Marisa Tomei as Antonia and Thomas Derrah as Giovanni in the American Repertory Theatre production of Dario Fo's comedy *We Won't Pay! We Won't Pay!* in 1999, which featured Ron Jenkins's new translation printed here.

MARGHERITA (*laughing*). Ah! Ah!

ANTONIA. "The cops are coming," someone shouts. We all start running. We're dropping our bags on the ground. We're crying with fear. It's a false alarm. Some truckers came to help when they heard us shouting—"Hey. Calm down. What's there to be afraid of. Don't get your panties in a wad worrying about the police. You're within your rights to pay a fair price. Let 'em have it!" So this is the payback for all the money they've stolen from us in all years we've been shopping there. And then a woman yelled, "We won't pay anything. We won't pay? We won't Pay. We won't pay. We won't pay!" We went back and started shopping all over again. We shopped and we shopped and we shopped. You don't know how good it feels to shop without spending money.

MARGHERITA. Ah, how beautiful! What a shame I wasn't there!

ANTONIA. But in the meantime, the police actually did show up, for real . . . in riot gear . . . I can't tell you how scared I was! I was shaking, we were all shaking, our bags were shaking . . . the noise from the plastic was deafening! But this time, none of the women ran away. We walked calmly out of the supermarket with decisive faces, . . . so firm, so honest . . . we looked like Hillary Clinton defending her man . . . and we said to the cops, "Oh, thank God you're here. Finally! Go in there and arrest those thieves!"

MARGHERITA. How beautiful!

ANTONIA. It was thrilling! It was a shopping spree to end all shopping sprees! Not because we didn't pay for the stuff, but because suddenly we were all there together with the courage to stand up for ourselves. And we caught the bastards off balance. Now they're the ones who are afraid. Soon supermarkets will have to put those plastic theft protection devices on every onion.

MARGHERITA. But what are you going to tell your husband? You're not going to try sell him the story about the Popemobile . . .

ANTONIA. Why, don't you think he'll buy it?

MARGHERITA. Not a chance.

ANTONIA. Yeah . . . maybe it's a bit much. The problem is, he's a man. You know how men are. They can't see the big picture. He's a law and order freak. Who knows what kind of tantrum he'll throw! "How could you do such a thing?," he'll say. "My father built a good life for his children by following the rules. I follow the rules. We're poor, but we're honest!" He doesn't know that I've spent everything, that there's nothing left to pay the gas, the electric, or the rent. . . . I don't even know how many months behind we are . . .

MARGHERITA. I haven't paid the rent for five months! And I didn't manage to get in on the shopping spree like you did . . .

ANTONIA. There's enough stuff here to feed a day care center. Take some home.

MARGHERITA. No, no, please. Thanks, but I don't have any money to pay for it.

ANTONIA (*serious*). Well, if you can't pay for it . . . (*changes tone*) Are you crazy! I donated this stuff to myself . . . Go on, take it home. Take it!

MARGHERITA. Sure, and then what am I going to tell my husband? He'd murder me!

ANTONIA (*while she speaks, she takes cans of varying sizes out of a bag*). Mine would just lock himself in the closet.

MARGHERITA (*astonished*). In the closet?

ANTONIA (*points at wardrobe*). Yeah! For ten years. . . every time we have an argument . . . he locks himself in that wardrobe. He's very organized about it! He has his little flashlight, his little chair. And he reads Dante's "Inferno." He's trying to memorize it. (*Looks at can in her hand*) What's this? (*Reads*) Meat compost for cats and dogs?

MARGHERITA (*reads*). Homogenized for the beefy flavor your pet can't resist! But why did you take this?

ANTONIA. In the confusion . . I just grabbed what was there . . . (*she takes another can*) Look at this one?!

MARGHERITA (*reads*). Bird seed for canaries?

ANTONIA. Well, it's a good thing I didn't pay for this stuff, or I'd be eating . . . (*reads*) "Frozen rabbit heads!"

MARGHERITA. Frozen heads?

ANTONIA. That's what it says: "To enrich the meals of your chickens . . . five rabbit heads for twenty cents." At least it's cheap. (*Disappointed*) But I can't return this stuff . . . they'll just arrest me.

MARGHERITA (*laughing*). And you wanted me to bring this junk home to my Luigi?

ANTONIA. Ah, no! I'm much too attached to my rabbit heads . . . You take home the bad stuff: the oil, the pasta . . . go on, get moving. You husband's on the night shift, so you'll have time to hide it all.

MARGHERITA. Yeah, . . . and what if the police start searching house to house?

ANTONIA. Don't be silly! The whole neighborhood was at the supermarket . . . you think the police are going to come and search every house . . . (*Opens a window*) Oh dammit, my husband! He's coming up. Quick, get this stuff out of here . . .

MARGHERITA (*frightened*). Where should I put it?

ANTONIA. Under your coat! (*Margherita stuffs some of the bags under her coat*) Help me get it under the bed . . . (*she takes all the bags on the table and stuffs them under the bed. She puts the animal food on the counter behind her.*) If Giovanni finds out, he'll call the police. "Officer, arrest my wife. She's an enemy of the people! Come on, run . . . and keep it quiet! Tell him some fairy tale. (*Margherita goes to the door and bumps into Antonia's husband, Giovanni, entering the house*)

MARGHERITA (*in a hurry, very embarrassed*). Good morning, Giovanni.

GIOVANNI. Oh, good morning, Margherita . . . how are you?

MARGHERITA. Fine, thank you . . . Bye, Antonia, see you later . . . (*she leaves*)

(*Giovanni remains perplexed and looks at Margherita's belly as she leaves*)

ANTONIA. So, Giovanni, why are you standing there? It's about time you came home. Where have you been? (*She prepares the table for dinner, plastic plates, napkins, etc.*)

GIOVANNI. What's up with Margherita?

ANTONIA. Why, what should be up?

GIOVANNI. Well . . . she's all fat up front: there's a belly!

ANTONIA. So? Is that the first time you ever saw a married woman with a belly?

GIOVANNI. You mean she's pregnant?

ANTONIA. Well, it's one of those things that can happen when you make love.

GIOVANNI. But, how many months is it? I just saw her last Sunday and it didn't seem like . . .

ANTONIA. What do you know about these things? It's already been a week since last Sunday . . . and in a week, who knows what could happen!

GIOVANNI. Listen, I'm not that stupid . . . Luigi, her husband, works next to me on the assembly line. He tells me everything . . . and he never said anything about having a baby . . .

ANTONIA. Well . . . there are some things . . . people don't bother to talk about.

GIOVANNI. What are you talking about? Is it too embarrassing? "Oh, God, I made my wife pregnant!"

ANTONIA (*searching*). Maybe . . . he hasn't said anything . . . because he doesn't know yet. (*Giovanni looks at her dumbfounded. She continues unperturbed.*) And if he doesn't know, how could he tell you.

GIOVANNI. What do you mean he doesn't know?

ANTONIA. Eh, yes. It's obvious. She doesn't want to tell him.

GIOVANNI. What do you mean she doesn't want to tell him?

ANTONIA. Eh, yes, because she . . . that girl . . . is very shy. And he, Luigi . . . is always saying it's too soon, it's not the right time, they have to get organized first . . . and if she gets pregnant the company where she works will fire her. He's so worried about it that he makes her take the pill.

GIOVANNI. And if he makes her take the pill, how come she's pregnant?

ANTONIA. Well, obviously, it had no effect. It happens, you know!

GIOVANNI. And if it happens, then why does she have to hide it from her husband. It's not her fault, is it?

ANTONIA. Well, maybe the pill had no effect, because of the fact . . . that she didn't take it . . . if you don't take the pill . . . (*doesn't know what to say*) . . . it can happen that the pill . . . has no effect.

GIOVANNI. But what are you saying?

ANTONIA. Eh . . . yes . . . she's very Catholic. And since the Pope has declared the pill to be a mortal sin . . .

GIOVANNI. You're crazy! The Pope! Her with a nine month belly and her husband hasn't noticed?

ANTONIA (*getting in deeper difficulty*). Maybe Luigi hasn't noticed . . . because Margherita . . . binds herself up!

GIOVANNI. Binds herself up!?

ANTONIA. Yes, yes. She ties it all in tight . . . very tight . . . so no one can see! It got to the point where today I just had to say, "You're crazy. Do you want to lose the baby? Unbind yourself immediately, and who cares if they fire you! The baby's more important!" Was I right?

GIOVANNI. Of course you were right. You were right, yes!

ANTONIA. Did I do the right thing?

GIOVANNI. Yes, yes . . . the right thing.

ANTONIA. And so she . . . Margherita . . . decided to unbind herself and: ploff!!! A big belly!! You should have seen it, Giovanni!

GIOVANNI. I saw it!

ANTONIA. And I also said, "If your husband gives you any trouble, tell him to come to my house, and my Giovanni will teach him a thing or two." Was I right?

GIOVANNI. Of course you were right?

ANTONIA. Did I do the right thing?

GIOVANNI. Yes, yes . . .

ANTONIA. Listen to you: "Yes, yes . . ." Is that any way to answer? Are you holding something against me? Tell me, what have I done now? (*Takes a broom and starts sweeping the house*)

GIOVANNI. No, I'm not holding anything against you. If I'm upset it's because of what happened today at work.

ANTONIA. Why, what happened?

GIOVANNI. There's all this tension in the air. . . All this talk about downsizing . . . yesterday the company fired four dead men . . . Yes, four dead men! Died two months ago . . . four welders . . . and they fired them . . . for absenteeism. There's so much mistrust floating around that you can never relax. And then today in the cafeteria some guys . . . five of them, started raising hell about the food: "It's disgusting. Pig slop. Right out of the dumpster!"

ANTONIA. When it was really fine cuisine cooked with farm fresh ingredients?

GIOVANNI. No, no . . . it was absolutely disgusting . . . but that's no reason to whip everyone up into a mass frenzy.

ANTONIA. A mass frenzy? You said there were only five of them.

GIOVANNI. At first! But then everyone got into it . . . they all ate and left without paying!

ANTONIA. Them too?

GIOVANNI. What do you mean, them too?

ANTONIA. I mean, not only those five, but all the others too . . .

GIOVANNI. Yes, everybody got into the act.

ANTONIA (*feigning indignation*). How shocking!

GIOVANNI. But that's not all: I passed by a bunch of women at the supermarket, the one near work . . . and they were all shouting . . . maybe three hundred of them . . . loaded down with bags of stuff. So I asked what was going on . . . and they told me that they had only paid what they decided they wanted to pay!

ANTONIA (*still more indignant*). Oh, what a thing to do!

GIOVANNI. And what's worse, they stormed the checkout counter, and most of them left without paying anything at all.

ANTONIA. Them too?!

GIOVANNI. What do you mean, them too?

ANTONIA. Eh, I mean . . . like those bums from your factory who didn't pay for their lunches.

GIOVANNI. Eh, yes, them too!

ANTONIA. Oh, what a thing to do! Look at me, I'm standing here in shock.

GIOVANNI. I don't know what kind of husbands those women have, but if my wife ever did anything like that I'd make her eat every tin can she stole and the can opener too. And I hope you don't get it into your head to pull a stunt like that, because, if I find out you've been ripping off supermarkets, or even paying one penny less than what is marked on those little stickers, I'll . . . I'll . . .

ANTONIA. I know . . . you'll make me eat every tin can I stole and the can opener too.

GIOVANNI. No, worse! . . . I'd pack my bags and you'd never see me again. And what's more, I'd murder you first, and divorce you later!

ANTONIA (*furious*). Listen, with that attitude you can leave now . . . without a divorce. How dare you even insinuate that I? . . . Look, before I'd bring home anything that was not bought at a legal price, I'd . . . I'd . . . I'd let you starve to death!

GIOVANNI. That's more like it . . . And speaking of starving, what's for dinner? (*He sits at the table*)

ANTONIA. This! (*Angrily, she throws on the table a can of meat for cats and dogs*)

GIOVANNI. What's this?

ANTONIA. Can't you read? It's a meat compost for cats and dogs?

GIOVANNI. Meat compost for cats and dogs?

ANTONIA. It's delicious!

GIOVANNI. Delicious for dogs maybe!

ANTONIA. That's all I could afford. Besides, it's cheap, and nutritious . . . and full of protein . . . estrogen free . . . so it won't make you fat! It's exquisite! Look, it says so right here.

GIOVANNI. Are you kidding?

ANTONIA. Who's kidding? You don't' know what it's like to go grocery shopping without any money.

GIOVANNI. Come on, I'm not a dog. You eat it!

ANTONIA. Oh, yes. I'll eat it, yes! (*She starts barking*)

GIOVANNI. Isn't there anything else?

ANTONIA. Yes, I can make you a little soup.

GIOVANNI. What kind?

ANTONIA (*pulling out the package from the shelf*). Bird seed for canaries.

GIOVANNI. Bird seed!

ANTONIA. Yes, it's delicious, . . . and you know it helps fight diabetes!

GIOVANNI. But I don't have diabetes!

ANTONIA. Well, it's not my fault you don't have it yet . . . and besides, it's half the price of rice.

GIOVANNI. Listen, you've got to make up your mind. Am I a dog or a canary?

ANTONIA. Oh, don't be silly . . . Angela next door makes it every morning for her husband . . . and he loves it . . .

GIOVANNI. Yeah, I noticed he's been growing a few feathers lately! And this morning when we were waiting for the bus his foot started going like this. Then his neck went like this. (*Mimes chicken walk*) And when the bus came he . . . (*imitates rooster*) "Cockadoodledoo" (*Mimes a rooster flapping wings*) "I think I'll be getting to work on my own today."

ANTONIA. Stop joking around. This bird seed is a blessing! The secret is in the broth . . . see, I also got some frozen rabbit heads. (*She puts the package with the rabbit heads under his nose*)

GIOVANNI. Rabbit heads?

ANTONIA. Sure! Bird seed soup is always made with rabbit! Only the heads, though . . . frozen.

GIOVANNI (*puts on his jacket and goes towards the door*). Okay, okay . . . I get it . . . see you later!

ANTONIA. Where are you going?

GIOVANNI. Where do you want me to go? I'm going out for dinner.

ANTONIA. And what are you going to do for money?

GIOVANNI. Right, give me some money.

ANTONIA. From where?

GIOVANNI. What do you mean, from where? Don't tell me there's none left . . .

ANTONIA. No, but maybe you forgot that tomorrow we have to pay the gas, electricity, and rent. Or do you want them to evict us, and cut off the gas and lights.

GIOVANNI. Dammit! We'll starve to death, but at least we'll be illuminated. (*Antonia puts on her coat*) Where are you going?

ANTONIA. To Margherita's. She did a lot of shopping today, and I'm going to borrow a few things. I'll be right back.

GIOVANNI. Don't come back with any rabbit heads.

ANTONIA. No, I'll just bring the feet. (*She leaves*)

GIOVANNI. Yeah, very funny . . . while I'm here hungry as a . . . I could even eat a . . . (*he takes a can in his hand and turns it as he reads the label*) "A gourmet treat for your dogs and cats! Homogenized, tasty . . ." Well, maybe I'll just see what it smells like. How do you open it? Look at that. Typical. They forget to give you the key. Oh, look, it's self-opening. For dogs and cats who are self starters. (*Opens the can and sniffs it*) Ah, doesn't smell too bad . . . kind of like ground kidney with pickled marmalade and a dash of cod liver oil. (*He puts the can next to his ear and laughs*) You can hear the ocean! (*Laughs in disgust*) (*Changes tone*) Who knows, maybe I'll try just a taste! (*From outside there are the sounds of police sirens, shouting crowds, and military orders*) What's going on out there? (*He goes to the imaginary window in the middle of the proscenium and makes signs to a neighbor across the street*) Aldo! Hey, Aldo! What's happening? Yes, I can see it's the police . . . but what do they want? Oh, stolen merchandise! From where? What, the supermarket? Which

supermarket? Oh, here too? The one in the neighborhood? But when did it happen? Today? Who did it? What do you mean, everyone? Stop exaggerating! A thousand women! No, my wife wasn't there, I'm sure. She's so set against that kind of stuff that she'd rather eat frozen rabbit heads! No, just the heads . . . you throw the rest away. They're delicious. You crack them in half with a few drops of lemon and . . . (*mimes eating one*) . . . like an oyster! No, no. No way . . . My wife didn't even leave the house today. She had to unbind her best friend's belly. No, no, it doesn't hurt . . . she just took off the wrapping that she tied herself up with so her husband Luigi wouldn't know she was pregnant . . . because he was making her take the pill . . . but she had orders from the Pope, so the pill had no effect, and it only took a week for her belly to blow up like a beach ball . . . what!! What do you mean, you don't understand? (*He looks down on the street and hears the shouts and orders*) What's that? A house to house search? Well if they try to come in here, I'll teach them a thing or two! Because that's an out and out provocation!

(*There's a knock at the door*)

VOICE FROM THE OUTSIDE. Can I come in?

GIOVANNI. Who is it?

VOICE FROM OUTSIDE. Open up. Police!

GIOVANNI (*opening the door*). Police? What do you want?

(*Enter a police officer. A local cop on the beat*)

SARGENT. This is a search. Here's the warrant. We're searching the whole building.

GIOVANNI. For what?

SARGENT. There was an assault on the supermarket today. A thousand women, and men too, removed a large quantity of merchandise at reduced prices . . . and some of them didn't pay anything at all. We're looking for the stolen goods, or if you prefer, the merchandise acquired at deep discount.

GIOVANNI. So you come here looking for it at my house. That's like calling me a thief, a looter, a hooligan!

SARGENT. Listen. This is not my choice. I get my orders and I have to carry them out.

GIOVANNI. Just following orders, eh . . . but I'm warning you . . . this is a provocation . . . You come here insulting people dying of hunger . . . Look at what we're reduced to eating: homogenized meat compost for cats and dogs! (*Thrusts the can towards the officer*)

SARGENT. What?!

GIOVANNI. Yeah! We can't afford decent food . . . We've got to be creative. Use our heads . . . rabbit heads! (*He puts the bag of frozen rabbit heads under the officer's nose*)

SARGENT. You really eat this stuff?

GIOVANNI. It's not bad, you know! Do you want to try some? No kidding . . . a few drops of lemon and it goes down like cat shit! Taste it. It's good for the nerves.

SARGENT. No thanks . . . I never vomit before dinner.

GIOVANNI. I understand . . . Maybe you'd prefer me to fix you a nice soup made from bird seed for canaries?

SARGENT. Bird seed?

GIOVANNI. Yeah! Look it's right here: costs only ten cents a pound . . . eat a little bit . . . and before you know it. . . a few feathers . . . and then . . . then your wings start to flutter . . . (*imitates a rooster*) and you become a chicken. Or maybe you'd prefer another barnyard animal. A pig perhaps. (*He snorts*) After all you are a cop. (*Snorts again*)

SARGENT. I can see you've been reduced to hard times here. And to tell you the truth, on a policeman's salary, my family's not doing much better. My wife has to perform miracles in the kitchen too! Listen, I understand what you're going through . . . and, I shouldn't say this, but I understand why the neighborhood women had to do what they did today. Personally I sympathize with them completely: the only defense against thieves is confiscation.

GIOVANNI (*astonished, looks at the officer incredulously*). You mean, you mean . . . you think they were right.

SARGENT. Sure they were . . . they couldn't put up with all this for much longer. You might not believe me, but sometimes it disgusts me to be a policeman . . . to have to rob people of their dignity. And for who . . . for the politicians and slum lords who steal them blind and leave them homeless and hungry . . . Those bastards are the real thieves. (*He takes off his hat*)

GIOVANNI. Are you really a cop?

SARGENT. Yes, I'm a cop.

GIOVANNI. You've got some pretty strange ideas for a policeman.

SARGENT. I'm just a guy who thinks things out, and gets pissed off about them! You've got to stop looking at us policemen as a bunch of idiots who salivate when we hear a whistle and: "follow orders, jump, bark, bite" like a bunch of guard dogs! As if we didn't have minds of our own.

GIOVANNI. If that's how you feel, may I ask why you chose to join the police force?

SARGENT. Did you choose to eat that dog food or those rabbit heads?

GIOVANNI. No! It was my nutritionists idea. (*Becomes serious*) No, of course not.

SARGENT. See. I didn't make this choice on my own either. It was sign up or die hungry. And "inter nos," I've got a college degree, dear sir.

GIOVANNI. Oh, college? Is that where you learned to say "inter nos"?

MALE VOICE (*from outside*). Sargent . . . we've finished out here . . . what should we do . . . keep looking?

SARGENT (*towards the door, to the man outside*). Don't stand around busting my balls . . . Search the other goddamn floors you scumbag . . . (*Continues his discussion with Giovanni*) Anyway, I was saying that I've got a degree. My father tightened his belt for years so I could go to

college . . . and in the end what did it get me? Nothing: I had no choice . . . dear, sir! "Join the police force and see the world." I've seen the world. It's a world of bastards, thieves and con-men!

GIOVANNI. But not all policemen think like you. Some of them like being police.

SARGENT. Sure, some guys buy into it. They get off on giving orders. They need to oppress somebody else to feel good about themselves.

GIOVANNI. This is amazing! Excuse me, but are you really a cop. Because now I feel it's my turn to defend the police. We need police, don't we? Without them, we'd have chaos . . . someone has to lay down the law!

SARGENT. And what if the law is wrong? What if it's just a cover-up for robbery?

GIOVANNI. Well, uh, then there's the political parties . . . the democratic system . . . laws can be reformed.

SARGENT. But who's going to do the reforming? Where are the reforms? What is reform! Lies, that's what reforms are! They've been promising us reforms for umpteen years, but has that gotten us better health care, or less homeless people on the streets. Believe me, the only real reform will come when people start thinking for themselves and reforming things on their own. Because until the day that people have faith in each other, with trust, patience, a sense of responsibility, and self-discipline . . . and move on . . . nothing is going to change! And now, if you'll excuse me, I have to do my job. (*He puts his hat on and goes towards the door*)

GIOVANNI (*snickering*). I was waiting for that. The utopian subversive puts his hat on back on and turns into a policeman again.

SARGENT. You're right. I'm all words . . . I vent and I'm gone.

GIOVANNI. Without even conducting a little search? Come on! You're insulting me! Do a little snooping just to humor me . . . anywhere, under the bed, in the cupboard . . .

SARGENT. Thanks, but I'll pass. Goodbye and good eating! (*He leaves*)

GIOVANNI. That guy was an undercover agent. He was trying to trick me into talking. And if I had agreed with him he'd be: "Stop right there! You're under arrest."

(*Antonia comes in out of breath*)

ANTONIA. Have they been here too?

GIOVANNI. Who?

ANTONIA. They're searching the neighborhood, house to house.

GIOVANNI. Yes, I know.

ANTONIA. They've already arrested the Mambettis and the Fossanis . . . they've found groceries in lots of houses, and confiscated everything!

GIOVANNI. It serves them right. That's what they get for breaking the law.

ANTONIA. But they've also taken away things people paid for legitimately.

GIOVANNI. Of course, it always happens that way. When looters go wild, people who have nothing to do with it always end up suffering. For example when they came here . . .

ANTONIA. They came here?

GIOVANNI. Of course.

ANTONIA. And what did they find?

GIOVANNI (*surprised*). Why, what should they find?

ANTONIA (*trying to divert him, changes tone*). Nothing. No, I was just saying . . . you never know . . . sometimes you're convinced that you don't have anything in the house, and then out of nowhere . . .

GIOVANNI. And then out of nowhere?

ANTONIA. And then out of nowhere the police plant stuff in your house . . . to trap you! It wouldn't be the first time . . .

GIOVANNI. You mean you think they'd actually put bags of pasta and sugar under the bed? I'd better take a look.

ANTONIA (*grabs him from behind, stopping him with a violent jerk*). No!

GIOVANNI. What are you doing? Are you crazy? You displaced a vertebra!

ANTONIA. I forbid you to touch my bedcover! I just washed it . . . I'll give a look myself . . . meanwhile, you go and let in Margherita.

GIOVANNI. Margherita? Where is she?

ANTONIA. She's there, behind the door. (*Pretends to look under the bed*) No, there's nothing's there.

GIOVANNI (*goes to the door*). Are you losing your mind, letting a poor pregnant woman stand out in the hall? Oh, my God, Margherita, what are you doing there. Come inside, come in. (*Margherita enters trying to stop herself from laughing*) What's wrong. Why are you crying?

ANTONIA (*goes to Margherita and sits her down on the bed*). Come here Margherita . . . (*to her husband*) Oh, the poor girl was home alone . . . and with all those police sniffing around, she was terrified! Can you believe that one of the officers wanted to squeeze her belly?

GIOVANNI. What for?

ANTONIA. Because he got it in his head that instead of a baby, she had bags of pasta and fine herbs in there.

GIOVANNI. The son of a bitch!

ANTONIA. Yeah, you said it . . . And so I told her to come over here to our house. Did I do the right thing?

GIOVANNI. Of course you did the right thing! (*He approaches Margherita and tries to help her take off her coat*) Stay here and relax, Margherita . . . take off your coat . . .

MARGHERITA (*frightened*). No!

GIOVANNI. Make yourself comfortable . . .

MARGHERITA. NO!

(*Antonia intercepts Giovanni and grabs him by the shoulder*)

GIOVANNI (*lets out a scream, then turns toward Antonia, furiously*). If you keep smacking around my vertebra every five minutes, I'm going to go into the wardrobe and never come out again.

ANTONIA. She told you she'd rather keep her coat on! She's cold!

GIOVANNI. But it's hot in here!

ANTONIA. It's hot for you, but pregnant women are always cold! Maybe she's got a fever!

GIOVANNI. A fever! Is she sick!

ANTONIA. She's in labor!

GIOVANNI. Already.

ANTONIA. What do you mean, already? What do you know about it? A half hour ago you didn't even know she was pregnant and now you're amazed that she's in labor!

GIOVANNI. Well, it seems to me, you might say . . . maybe it's a little premature!

ANTONIA. You think you know better than her?

GIOVANNI. But if she's in labor, maybe we should call the doctor, or an ambulance.

ANTONIA (*goes to the cupboard and takes out two pillows that she places on the bed so that Margherita can lie down comfortably*). Oh sure, an ambulance. There's not a chance in hell we'd find a vacant bed! You have no idea what it's like in those hospitals. You have to make reservations a month in advance!

GIOVANNI. So why didn't she reserve a place?

ANTONIA. That's right, we run the errands, we make the babies, and you want us to make the reservations too! And why didn't her husband do it?

GIOVANNI. But her husband didn't know about it. How could he think of it?

ANTONIA. Very convenient! Just give us the pay checks and then it's, "Pay the bills!" You make us pregnant and then, "Take care of it yourself! Take the pill." And who cares if the poor wife, who's a strict Catholic, dreams all night of the Pope saying, "It's a sin, you must procreate!"

GIOVANNI. Apart from the Pope . . . how long has Margherita been pregnant?

ANTONIA. What do you care?

GIOVANNI. No, I was just saying . . . because she hasn't even been married five months yet . . .

ANTONIA. So what? Isn't it possible that they might have made love before they got married . . . or are you turning moralistic on us . . . you're worse than the Pope!

GIOVANNI. Luigi told me that they only made love after they were married.

MARGHERITA. My Luigi talks to you about those things?!!

GIOVANNI (*embarrassed*). We were playing pool . . .

ANTONIA. Jesus, Mary and Joseph!!! What a bum! Margherita, that's grounds for divorce!

GIOVANNI. Let's not get carried away . . .

ANTONIA. What do you mean? Going around talking about private, personal moments . . . to just anyone out on the street.

GIOVANNI (*insulted*). I'm not "just anyone out on the street." I'm his friend! His best friend! He tells me everything. He asks my advice . . . because I'm older, and I've got more experience!

ANTONIA (*shoots him a look full of irony*). Oh, oh, he's got more experience! (*Giovanni is about to respond when there is a knock at the door*) Who's there?

VOICE FROM OUTSIDE. Police. Open up!

GIOVANNI. Again?

MARGHERITA. Oh, God!

(*Giovanni goes to open the door, and there appears the same actor who played the part of the police sargent. Now he's wearing the uniform of a state trooper and wearing a moustache. Two other troopers enters behind him*)

GIOVANNI. Well, hello . . . you again?

TROOPER. What do you mean, you again?

GIOVANNI. Sorry, I thought you were the one from before.

TROOPER. Which one from before?

GIOVANNI. The police sargent.

TROOPER. But I'm a state trooper.

GIOVANNI. I see. And you've got a moustache too. So you must be someone else. What can I do for you?

TROOPER. We have to conduct a search.

GIOVANNI. Your colleague from the Police force just did that a little while ago.

TROOPER. That doesn't matter. We'll do it again ourselves.

GIOVANNI. So you don't trust them . . . You've come to make sure they haven't botched things up! Then I guess the National Guard will come to check up on you. Next it'll be the CIA . . . and then frog men from the Marines will show up in our bathtub . . . (*he mimes a grotesque frogman*).

TROOPER (*angry*). Listen, cut the comedy. Just show us around and let us do our job.

ANTONIA (*bursts out*). Sure, your job is to make sure we comply with orders. (*The troopers open the wardrobe and cupboards*) Why don't you ever check to make sure that management is honoring our contracts, that the air in our workplaces is breathable, that they're not downsizing our jobs so that they can exploit child workers in third world countries, that they're not evicting us from our homes, and starving us to death! (*Giovanni tries to calm his wife*).

GIOVANNI. No, no. You shouldn't talk like that, because they're disgusted by all those things themselves. Isn't that true, officer, that you're fed up with robbing people in the name of authority. Tell my wife how you police officers are sick and tired of salivating when the whistle blows: "Follow orders! Jump. Bark! Bite like a bunch of guard dogs . . . " (*howls like a dog on a chain*).

TROOPER. Could you say that again, please? (*Giovanni barks*) No, the part about the guard dogs?

GIOVANNI. Yes, I was just saying that you're just bought and sold by the politicians to help them can get re-elected!

TROOPER. Is that right?

GIOVANNI. Yes, I was just . . .

TROOPER (*turns to the two troopers*). Cuff him!

(*The two troopers move to put handcuffs on Giovanni*)

GIOVANNI. Handcuffs? Excuse me, but why?

TROOPER. For insulting a public official.

GIOVANNI. What insult? I'm just saying what your colleague the police sargent told me a few minutes ago . . . he's the one who told me that you feel like servants of the politicians, slaves of the system.

TROOPER. Who's you? . . . us state troopers?

GIOVANNI. No, he was talking about them . . . the city cops on the street.

TROOPER. Oh, the city cops. (*laughs derisively at the insult to city cops*) Okay, take off the handcuffs. But watch what you say about us State Troopers.

GIOVANNI. Okay, okay. I'm watching, I'm watching.

(*The troopers continue their search. Now one of them begins searching near the bed*)

ANTONIA (*to Margherita*). Moan, go on, cry!

MARGHERITA. Aihoooaooo!

ANTONIA. Louder.

MARGHERITA (*agonizing cries*). Ahiouua! Ahiaaooioo!

TROOPER. What is it? What's wrong with her?

ANTONIA. Pain, a lot of pain . . . she's in labor.

GIOVANNI. She's five months premature!

ANTONIA. She was traumatized a little while ago . . . the police tried to squeeze her belly . . .

TROOPER. Squeeze her belly?

GIOVANNI. Yeah, to see if, maybe, instead of a baby, she had rice or pasta in there. Go on, why don't you help yourselves while you're here: squeeze her to make sure! Go ahead, squeeze away! (*Margherita continues screaming hysterically*)

TROOPER. Have you called an ambulance?

ANTONIA. An ambulance? Why?

TROOPER. Do you want her to die right here? Besides, if she's premature like you say, she might lose the baby.

GIOVANNI. He's right! I told you we should have called an ambulance.

ANTONIA. And I told you already that without a reservation, the hospital won't admit her. They'll send her driving around to every hospital in town. She'll die in the car!

(*From outside there is the sound of a siren*)

TROOPER (*going to look out the window*). Look, it's the ambulance that we called for the sick woman downstairs. (*He turns to the two troopers*) Come on, give me a hand. We can take her too.

ANTONIA (*stopping them*). No, for God's sake . . . don't disturb her.

MARGHERITA (*crying in fear*). No, I don't want to go to the hospital.

ANTONIA. See, she doesn't want to go.

MARGHERITA. I want my husband, my husband . . . Ahio! Ahiuaaoo!

ANTONIA. Hear that? She wants her husband . . . and he's not around because he works the night shift. I'm sorry, but without her husband's consent, we can't take this responsibility.

GIOVANNI. Eh, no, we can't take it.

TROOPER. Oh, you can't take it, can you. You'd rather take responsibility for having her die right here?

ANTONIA. What difference does it make?

TROOPER. In the hospital they might be able to save her, and maybe the baby too!

GIOVANNI. But it's premature. I already told you!

ANTONIA. Yes, it's premature! And with all those potholes in the road, the baby will pop out right in the car. How could a five month baby survive that?

TROOPER. Obviously, you have no idea of the progress that modern medicine has made in our times. Haven't you heard about test tube babies.

ANTONIA. Yes, I've heard about them, but what's this got to do with test tubes? The baby's five months old. You can't stuff it in a test tube . . . you can't even put it in an oxygen tent.

GIOVANNI. Of course not, such a little baby under a tent . . . what's he going to do, go camping?

TROOPER. You people are completely ignorant! Haven't you ever seen the hospital equipment they're using these days . . . at the gynecological centers? I work a shift there five months ago, and I actually saw the doctors perform a transplant.

GIOVANNI AND ANTONIA. What kind of transplant?

TROOPER. A premature baby transplant. They took a four and a half month old fetus from a woman who couldn't hold it any longer and put it in the belly of another woman.

GIOVANNI. In her belly?

TROOPER. Yes, a cesarean. They put it in there with the placenta and everything . . . and four months later . . . just last month, it was born again, healthy as a fish!

GIOVANNI (incredulous). A fish . . . ?

TROOPER. Yes!

GIOVANNI. I think it was some kind of a trick.

TROOPER. What do you mean trick? I saw it myself. Sure it's hard to believe: a baby that's born twice . . . a baby with two mothers!

MARGHERITA. I don't want to do it. I don't want to do it. I won't give my consent.

ANTONIA. See . . . she won't give her consent . . . so we can't make her go.

TROOPER. I'll give the consent. I'll take responsibility.

ANTONIA. This is complete and utter arrogance! You come into our home, you search everywhere, put us in handcuffs . . . and now you want to drag us into an ambulance! We know you won't leave us alone to live our lives, but at least you can let us die in peace wherever we want to.

TROOPER. No, you can't die in peace whereever you want to.

GIOVANNI. Of course not, we have to die according to the law! (He goes towards the wardrobe)

TROOPER. And you, enough with the jokes. I already told you once . . . Where's he going?

GIOVANNI (opens the wardrobe door, enters, and sticks his head out). I'm in my office . . .

ANTONIA. Come out. Stop it! Now's not the time. Come on, let's bring her downstairs.

TROOPER. Should we get a stretcher?

ANTONIA. No, she'll go down on her own . . . You can walk, can't you?

MARGHERITA. Yes, yes . . . (she gets up. She suddenly puts her hands on her belly to arrange the stolen goods) Oh, no, no, it's slipping out . . .

ANTONIA. Dammit! Could you please step outside a moment . . .

TROOPER. Why?

ANTONIA. It's a woman's thing! (All the men leave. To Margherita, angrily) Idiot! (Imitates her) It's slipping out! . . . (changes tone) This trooper's going to hang us!

MARGHERITA. If it's slipping out, it's slipping out!

ANTONIA. Oh, shut up! And another thing, is that any way to walk? Haven't you ever seen the way pregnant women walk. Do they walk like this? (Imitates grotesquely Margherita) Who are you kidding! When a pregnant woman walks . . . think of the Virgin Mary! (Advances majestically)

MARGHERITA. I knew it would end up like this! What's going to happen at the hospital when they realize I'm pregnant with rice and tin cans?

ANTONIA. Nothing's going to happen, because we're never going to get to the hospital.

MARGHERITA. Sure, because they're going to arrest us first.

ANTONIA. Stop whining! As soon as we get into the ambulance, we'll tell the driver where things stand . . . I'm sure he'll help us.

MARGHERITA. What if he turns us in instead?

ANTONIA. Stop it, he's not going to turn us in! And pull up your belly! (She helps her)

MARGHERITA. Another bag's slipping out. I'm falling apart!

ANTONIA. Hold onto it! Oh what a mess!

MARGHERITA. No, don't press there . . . Oh, my God, you ripped the packet of olives in pickle juice. Ahhhhhh!!!!

(Giovanni and the troopers return, alarmed by her shouting)

GIOVANNI. Now what happened?

MARGHERITA. It's coming out! It's all coming out!

GIOVANNI. The baby's coming out! The baby's coming out! Quick, officers, help me, grab her arms!

(They follow his lead)

TROOPER (supporting Margherita's back with his arm). She's all wet! What is it?

ANTONIA. She's breaking her water!

GIOVANNI. Ohhh! Look at that water! . . . (mimes being in a swamp) Quick, or she'll have the baby right here!

MARGHERITA. It's coming out! It's coming out!

(*The woman is carried off the stage. Giovanni returns immediately.*)

GIOVANNI. Wait for me. I'll get my jacket and be right there.

ANTONIA. Where are you going?

GIOVANNI. To see the premature baby get born . . .

ANTONIA. No, you stay home! This is a woman's thing. I'll go! (*She puts on her coat*) Get a rag and clean all that water off the floor. (*She leaves*)

GIOVANNI. I see, okay . . . I'll get a rag and start cleaning . . . because that's a man's thing! (*He grabs a rag and leans against the window*). What a mess! Who knows how Luigi will take it when he comes home tomorrow and all of the sudden finds out he's a father . . . he'll have a stroke! And then what if he finds his kid transplanted into the belly of another woman . . . he'll have a double stroke . . . and drop dead on the spot! I've got to talk to him first. Prepare him for it, little by little . . . give him the big picture . . . yeah, that's it . . . I'll start with the Pope . . . (*he's down on his hands and knees wiping up the floor*) Ohhh!! All that water! But what a funny odor . . . it smells like vinegar . . . (*sniffs the rag*) It's pickle juice. (*Taken aback*) Pickle juice? I never knew! Before we're born, we spend nine months floating in pickle juice? (*Continues to wash the pavement*) Oh, look at that . . . what's that? An olive? We float in pickle juice with olives? Oh, that's how it . . . No! No! Olives have nothing to do with it. (*He hears another siren and gets up to go to the window*) Well, they're on their way. I hope it all turns out okay. But where did this olive come from? Oh, look, another one! Two olives? If I wasn't so unsure about where they came from I'd eat 'em . . . I'm starving! (*He puts the two olives on a plate on the table*). Maybe I'll try cooking up a little of that bird seed soup. At least it's organic. The water's already boiling. I'll put in a bouillon cube, some onion . . . (*opens the refrigerator*) Look at that. I knew it . . . there's no bouillon . . not even an onion . . . All I've got to put in is this rabbit head! Goddammit! (*Without thinking he leans against the welding cannister*) How many times do I have to tell that dopey Antonia that this is a welding gun, not a lighter for the gas stove. It's dangerous! One day it'll blow up the house!

(*Luigi, Margherita's husband, opens the door*)

LUIGI. Can I come in? Anybody home?

GIOVANNI. Oh, Luigi! But what are you doing here at this hour? You don't get off work until tomorrow morning.

LUIGI. Something happened . . . I'll explain later . . . but what I want to know is, where's my wife? I went home and the doors were open, but nobody was there.

GIOVANNI. Oh yeah, your wife was just here a few minutes ago. She went out with Antonia.

LUIGI. Where'd she go? What for?

GIOVANNI. Well, you know, it's a woman's thing.

LUIGI. And what would that be, that woman's thing.

GIOVANNI. It would be a thing that we wouldn't be interested in. We should only be interested in men's things.

LUIGI. What do you mean I shouldn't be interested? I'm very interested!

GIOVANNI. Ah, now you're interested, are you? And how come you weren't interested last month when you were supposed to reserve a bed like everyone else does?

LUIGI. A bed? For what?

GIOVANNI. Oh sure, that's woman's work, huh? It's the same old story! We give they our pay checks, and then we say, "Pay the bills" We make love to 'em and say "Take the pill." We make them pregnant and it's "You take care of it." They're the ones who nurse the babies.

LUIGI. What are you saying?

GIOVANNI. I'm saying that they're right. We're just a bunch of good-for-nothing loafers.

LUIGI. But what does all this have to do with the fact that my Margherita, went off with the doors open and didn't even leave me a note, just disappeared like . . .

GIOVANNI. And why should she leave you a note. Weren't you supposed to be working the night shift? Which reminds me, how come you're home so early?

LUIGI. Work stoppage.

GIOVANNI. What do you mean?

LUIGI. We were protesting because they wanted to raise the price of our commuter passes thirty percent!

GIOVANNI. Christ! With all the tension there already, why would you want to screw things up even more?

LUIGI. Sure, sure, I agree it was a screwed up thing to do. I even told the other guys, "Guys! It's useless trying to get them to bring down the price of our commuter passes."

GIOVANNI. Good for you!

LUIGI. "We should get our commuter passes for free!

GIOVANNI. Are you out of your mind. We shouldn't pay anything?

LUIGI. Sure, the company should pay for our commute. And they should also pay us for the time we're on the train. Because we lose those hours, and believe you me, it ain't no vacation . . .

GIOVANNI. Who put this stuff in your head? Have you been talking to that police sargent without the moustache who looks like the state trooper with the moustache?

LUIGI (*tastes the contents of the open can*). Hey, this pate is great . . . what kind is it?

GIOVANNI. Did you eat the stuff in that can?

LUIGI. Yeah, it's not bad. Sorry, I was hungry.

GIOVANNI. Without any lemon?

LUIGI. Why? Are you supposed to eat it with lemon?

GIOVANNI. Uh . . . I don't know . . . but are you sure it tastes all right?

LUIGI. Yeah, it's delicious.

GIOVANNI. Let me taste. Oh, that's not bad! Go open that other can on the sink.

(*They feast on the animal food at the table making appreciative sounds of satisfaction*)

LUIGI. Hey, what is this stuff?

GIOVANNI. It's a kind of pate . . . for rich cats and dogs.

LUIGI. Pate for cats and dogs? Come on, are you crazy?

GIOVANNI. No, I'm a gourmet! And while you're at it, taste this. (*Pours him some of the soup*) Taste it. Taste it!

LUIGI. Hey, this isn't bad! What's in it?

GIOVANNI. It's one of my specialities: bird seed soup; . . . with broth from frozen rabbit heads!

LUIGI (*spits soup in Giovanni's face from the shock*). Bird seed soup with rabbit heads?

GIOVANNI. Yeah, it's a Chinese delicacy. Over there they call it 'consumme du Won Ton Dim Sum Hang Yan Lo.' When Nixon went to China, he was nuts about it. "I'll never go back to America. I'm gonna stay here and eat this soup forever." It's in the tapes.

LUIGI. But the bird seed's a little crunchy . . .

GIOVANNI. That's because it's bird seed Pilaff . . . you've got to serve it 'al dente.' The bird seed is always 'al dente' and the rabbit heads are medium rare . . . (*Alarmed*) Did you eat those olives?

LUIGI. Yeah. Why. Shouldn't I have?

GIOVANNI (*almost hysterical*). Eh, no, no you shouldn't have! They were your wife's olives, you boob! You'd even stoop to eating fetus!

LUIGI. My wife's olives . . . fetus?

GIOVANNI. Yeah. Don't you know that when a baby's born, . . . the woman loses her pickle juice? First there's the slipping part . . . well, we'll leave that out for now . . . then there's the problem of the pill that has no effect . . . and that's because the Pope never stays put . . . he's always running all over the place . . . he doesn't even know what day it is anymore . . . night . . . day . . . now he's in Africa . . . then he's in Brazil . . . next stop India . . . kisses the ground . . . then a little dip in the Papal pool, filled with holy water! Some skiing! Always the steep slopes . . . scvum . . . Scvum! And that's without the ski poles . . . so his arms are free to bless people on the way down. (*Mimes ski-borne benedictions*). Dominus Pacem. Dominus Pacem. Dominus Pacem. (*Mimes high speed blessings*)

LUIGI. Giovanni, what kind of talk is that? The Pope . . . olives . . . fetus . . . ?

GIOVANNI. Yeah, you're the voice of reason, aren't you? The company should pay our train fare and gives us wages for commuting time. Next you'll want them to pay a bonus to our wives when they make love with us . . . because sex regenerates us, and makes us more productive!

LUIGI. That's right. You said it! We need some relief from this life of shit we're forced to live.

GIOVANNI. Well, let's not get carried away. It's not exactly a life of shit, is it . . . we're better off than we used to be. We've got a house, maybe a little run down, but it has what we need . . . of course some of us have to work overtime . . .

LUIGI. So what if I've got a stove and a refrigerator, if I'm disgusted by my life . . . goddammit . . . with a job that could be done by a trained monkey (*mimes the assembly line*)

Weld! Hammer! Drill! Weld! Hammer! One piece finished, here comes the next. Weld! (*Mechanically, Giovanni joins the movement without thinking*) Hammer! Faster! Weld . . .

GIOVANNI. Hammer, drill, weld . . . weld (*stops himself suddenly*) For God's sake, what have you got me doing. You're making me crazy too!

LUIGI. No, I'm not the one making you crazy. It's the way we live. Everything's going down the drain . . . look at all the factories closing, toxic dumping, ethnic cleansing all over the world. Earthquakes. Hurricanes. The Pope.

GIOVANNI. Yeah, scaring all the women in the world to make sure they get pregnant!

LUIGI. What were you saying about the Pope getting pregnant! (*Laughs*)

GIOVANNI. No, he's not pregnant. I was talking about your wife.

LUIGI. What's my wife got to do with the Pope?

GIOVANNI. Ah, you're pretending you don't know about it?

LUIGI. No. It's just that I don't know! What's this story about the Pope?

GIOVANNI. Look, if you spent less time stirring up trouble at work and paid more attention to your wife, you'd know what she was dreaming about at night when the Pope comes to her and says, "Don't take the pill for Christ's sake!"

LUIGI. Actually . . . Margherita doesn't take the pill.

GIOVANNI. Oh, so you know. Who told you?

LUIGI. Who do you think told me? She doesn't have to take the pill because she can't have babies. She's got a malformation down there in the whattayacallit . . .

GIOVANNI. You're the one with the malformation! In your head! Your wife is very healthy, and has no problem with having babies, in fact she's having one.

LUIGI. Having a baby? When?

GIOVANNI. Now. In fact she could be giving birth this minute: five months premature!

LUIGI. Don't be silly. Five months. She doesn't even have a belly.

GIOVANNI. She doesn't have one because she tied it up . . . and then Antonia untied it and . . . plaff . . . a belly big enough to be nine months . . maybe even eleven.!

LUIGI. Come on, are you kidding me?

GIOVANNI. My wife, if you must know, took her in an ambulance to the hospital . . . because she just about gave birth to the kid here on the floor.

LUIGI. Here on the floor?

GIOVANNI. She broke her water here . . . I cleaned it up myself!

LUIGI. You cleaned up her water?

GIOVANNI. Well, it wasn't exactly water . . . "Pickle juice" . . . with a few olives . . . the ones you just ate.

LUIGI. Listen, stop joking around. Where's my wife?

GIOVANNI. I told you. At the hospital.

LUIGI. Which hospital?

GIOVANNI. Who knows. If you'd have reserved a room a month ago like you're supposed to, we'd know. But no . . .

now the baby's going to be born in the car . . . poor kid, in the middle of all those olives!

LUIGI. Come on, stop this nonsense! Tell me what hospital she's in or I'll punch you out.

GIOVANNI. Hey, calm down. I already told you that I don't know . . . No, wait, maybe they went to that Gyne . . . Gyneca . . . that Gynecological place.

LUIGI. The Gynecological Place?

GIOVANNI. Yeah, the place where they do the premature baby transplants.

LUIGI. The premature baby transplants?

GIOVANNI. Where have you been living? At the Gynecological place, there's a machine with a tent full of oxygen . . . they take woman with the baby that's premature by four and half, or even five months . . . then they take another woman to be the second mother . . . they do a cesarean . . . put the baby in the new belly, stuff in the placenta and everything . . . and then four months later . . . (*pause*) . . . a fish!

LUIGI. Cut it out. I don't give a damn about your transplant machines, and cesareans . . . I want to know where the hell is this gynecological place. Get the telephone book and we can look it up.

GIOVANNI. I don't have a phone. What would I do with a phone book: read up on who lives in the neighborhood?

LUIGI. Come on, we can go to the bar downstairs. They've got a phone . . .

GIOVANNI. I just remembered. It's next to the new mall.

LUIGI. The new mall? Why would they go so far away?

GIOVANNI. I told you! It's the only place where they do the transplants! They'd find another woman. A healthy woman who happens to be near by. (*He stops. He has an idea*) Another woman? (*He screams*) Antonia! (*Luigi screams in response*) She's going to be right there . . . She'll be the first one they ask . . . and she's crazy enough to do it! She's going to have a transplant, and come home pregnant. Quick! Let's go! (*They exit, running*)

END OF ACT ONE

ACT TWO

The two women are returning. Margherita still has a big belly; she is sniffling.

ANTONIA (*Calling*). Giovanni. Giovanni! He's not here. He went to work. What time is it? (*Looks at the alarm clock on the shelves*) Five-thirty. Can you believe it? We've been out playing this charade for more than four hours. (*Peeks into the other room*)

MARGHERITA. I should never have listened to you! Look at the mess we're in now!

ANTONIA. You're such a complainer. It all worked out, didn't it? All we had to say to the ambulance team was, "Careful, this girl's not pregnant . . ., but she's got a gut full of stolen goods," and they couldn't wait to give us a hand.

They wanted to throw a party for us! And you were so worried . . . for nothing . . . you have to have faith in people! Me, I have faith in people! (*She looks into the refrigerator*) Where's the butter. Who stole my butter? Ah, no, there it is. Now I'll make you some soup. Ah, the rice. Give me a packet of rice. (*Margherita pulls a packet of rice out from the bag hidden under her coat. Antonia goes to the stove. She sees the pot.*) But what's this stuff? The bird seed? Don't tell me that dopey Giovanni really cooked up a bird seed soup with rabbit heads! All you have to do is feed him a story and he swallows the whole thing. Let's see what I can whip up for you.

MARGHERITA. If you're making the soup just for me, don't bother. I'm not hungry. My stomach's all blocked up.

ANTONIA (*Margherita unpacks her 'belly'*). What are you doing?

MARGHERITA. Did you think I was going to carry this stuff around the rest of my life?

ANTONIA. I don't want any stolen goods in my house! Is that clear? And while you're at it, could you help me get rid of the stuff under the bed. I'll make myself a little belly too. (*She takes some pillowcases from a drawer*)

MARGHERITA. And where will we put it all?

ANTONIA. We'll carry it out to my father-in-law's little shed behind the railroad tracks. He grows vegetables there. It will be a great hiding-place.

MARGHERITA. That's enough. I can't take this any more . . . I've had it to here with your hare-brained schemes. I'm going home.

ANTONIA. You're a loser.

MARGHERITA. Well, if you're so smart, tell me what I say to my husband when he sees me without a belly . . . or a baby?

ANTONIA. Oh, I thought of that already. We'll tell him that you had a hysterical pregnancy.

MARGHERITA. Hysterical?

ANTONIA. Yes, it happens all the time . . . a woman thinks she's pregnant, her belly blows up, and then, when she's ready to give birth, all that comes out is air. Just air!

MARGHERITA. And how would I have gotten this hysterical pregnancy?

ANTONIA. From the Pope. He kept coming to you in your dreams and saying, "Make a baby! Make a baby!" So you obeyed him: you made a baby . . . of air. Just the soul of a baby!

MARGHERITA. Now we drag the Pope into the story.

ANTONIA. Look at all the times he's dragged us into his stories. (*Margherita has removed her bundles, while Antonia has re-stuffed her coat*) I'll be back in ten minutes . . .

MARGHERITA. But why don't you just get a cart and carry it all over there at once, instead of playing this pregnant mother game?

ANTONIA. Because we'd be caught right away. See those police wagons down there. They're waiting to catch you in the act! (*She brings the welding tanks to the stove*)

MARGHERITA. What are you doing? Won't you ruin it.

ANTONIA. No. It's Giovanni's welding cannister. It's made of iron . . . it's special stuff called animonio . . . it can heat up to 2000 degrees without even turning red . . . (*She lights the gas stove with it*)

MARGHERITA (*standing by the window so she can peek out*). Look, it's Maria from the third floor. She's pregnant too.

ANTONIA. Stealing all my ideas. Before you know it there'll be pregnant dogs walking by . . . pregnant men . . .

MARGHERITA. Listen, I thought it over. I'm coming with you. (*Starts re-inserting the bags in her belly.*)

ANTONIA. Brava! I knew you'd change your mind. Let's go. Today is the day of the mammas!

(*Scene change. A half-curtain runs the length of the proscenium. The two workers enter as if walking on the street. Luigi pulls out a beret and puts it on his head. Giovanni does the same.*)

LUIGI. Listen. I want to tell you something.

GIOVANNI. What.

LUIGI (*he can't bring himself to say it*). Look, it's raining. Like the saying goes, "When it rains, the government is stealing something."

GIOVANNI. Well, that's just to remind you that when it's sunny, the government is murdering somebody.

LUIGI. Goddammit, do you still have the energy to make jokes and keep laughing?

GIOVANNI. Me, no! But my feet, yes. They're dying for a good laugh! You and your bright idea of checking every hospital in town on foot. I've had enough. I'm going back to the station and get a train to work. I'll already be docked an hour's pay as it is.

(*Two stagehands walk by as the sound effect of a truck plays on the lousdspeaker. The stagehands/truck drop several sacks in front of Luigi and Giovanni as they pass by and exit*)

GIOVANNI. Look! Those sacks must have fallen off that . . . truck. They're filled with coffee.

LUIGI. Yeah, Ethiopian. Kenyan. French Vanilla. Let's take some home.

GIOVANNI. Are you crazy. Do you want to lower yourself to the level of thieves and looters. I don't take stuff that's not mine. I work for what I have.

LUIGI. Listen. What I was trying to tell you before is . . . starting tomorrow we're all being downsized.

GIOVANNI. Downsized?

LUIGI. Yeah. I heard it on the train. Six thousand out of twenty six thousand employees are being downsized now. And the rest of the plant closes in the next few months.

GIOVANNI. They're closing the plant?

LUIGI. Not only that. We won't get paid for our last two weeks.

GIOVANNI. Come on. Help me load up this stuff. Let's take it all.

(*As they leave the State Trooper enters*)

TROOPER. Drop those sacks or I'll shoot.

LUIGI. Look. He's got a gun.

TROOPER. Stop or I'll shoot.

GIOVANNI. Go ahead and shoot.

TROOPER (*as he chases them offstage*). Those bastards.

(*Dark. Change of scene. The curtain stays down. Only the lights change to indicate another street. From the left side, the two workers re-enter with their sacks*)

GIOVANNI. You can do it. We're almost there. Wait. There's a police van . . . in front of my house . . .

LUIGI. Look at those two women crossing the street. Aren't they our wives?

GIOVANNI. No, it can't be them.

LUIGI. Sure, they're standing there in front of the building you live in. And one of them's pregnant.

GIOVANNI. No, take a better look . . . they're both pregnant.

LUIGI. Oh, I guess it's not them.

GIOVANNI (*grabbing his shoulder*). Goddammit, we're trapped. Look across the street. It's the State Trooper who was chasing us!

LUIGI. Why not? He knows where you live . . . he'll head straight to your house to find us!

GIOVANNI. So we'll go to your house!

LUIGI. Right. Keep moving. Let's go this way and shake him off. (*They exit through the curtain*)

(*The trooper crosses the entire stage and exist to the left*)

TROOPER. You can't get away . . . I know where you live! I know the streets! . . . I know hot to read too!

(*In the dark the curtain rises and we find ourselves again in the house of Giovanni and Antonia. The two women are entering with big bellies. They are overwhelmed and exhausted*)

ANTONIA. I want to die . . . I want to die. . .

MARGHERITA. Load, unload, I feel like I'm turning into a truck!

ANTONIA (*goes to sit on the bed*). I want to die . . . Oh, God, the exhaustion of pregnancy . . .

MARGHERITA (*she loosens her coat and removes some leaves of lettuce and a few cabbages*). Look, look at all the vegetables we have here from your father's farm. There's enough to make salads for a year!

ANTONIA. At this rate we'll never get the stuff out of here . . . With the cops down there we can't go out with big bellies, and come home with no bellies . . . and go out again with big bellies . . . no bellies . . . big bellies . . . no bellies. The soup! (*Runs to the oven*). I forgot about the soup . . . it'll be all burned up! My God, the hunger's gone to my brain . . . (*lifts pot cover*) That's a relief. It didn't even boil . . . but why? It's been on four hours? The gas! Those bastards cut off the gas! Disgusting creeps, murderers, thieves . . . just because I didn't pay the gas bill. And they cut off the electricity too . . .

MARGHERITA. They cut off the gas?

ANTONIA. Yes. The man was here yesterday to check up on it . . . (*There's a knock at the door*) Who is it?

VOICE (*from outside*). Friends.

ANTONIA. What friends?

VOICE. I'm a friend of your husband's from work. He asked me to come and tell you something.

ANTONIA. Oh, my God! What could it be? (*Goes to open the door*)

MARGHERITA. Wait a second. Let me hide the lettuce. (*She puts it in her coat*)

ANTONIA. Just a moment please . . . I'm not dressed. (*She opens the door and sees the State Trooper*) You again? What kind of joke is this?

TROOPER. Stop right there, where you are! This time I've got you! Look at that. Now you're both pregnant! My how those bellies grow! I knew all along it was a trick!

ANTONIA. What kind of trick are you talking about?

MARGHERITA (*letting herself flop on the bed in exhaustion*). Now we're in for it. I knew it. I knew it.

TROOPER (*to Margherita*). Glad to see you haven't lost your little bundle of joy. And you, madam . . . congratulations! In five hours you've made love, become a mommy, and arrived at your ninth month!

ANTONIA. Look, officer, you're making a mistake . . .

TROOPER. No, I made the mistake last time. . . when I fell for your little act with the labor pains and premature birth! But I'm not going to fall for it again. Out with the stolen goods!

ANTONIA. But what stolen goods are you talking about?

TROOPER. Let's stop playing games. Your scam's an open book: the husbands go out to commit the robberies, pass the bags to the wives, and all day long I see nothing but pregnant women! Now why is it that all the women in this neighborhood got buns in their ovens at the same time! Mature women, teenagers, little girls . . . Today I even saw an eighty year old woman who was pregnant . . . with twins.

ANTONIA. That's because . . . because of the festival . . . the festival of the Patron Saint . . .

TROOPER. The Patron Saint?

ANTONIA. You don't know about her? What a Saint! The holiest of Saints! A good woman . . . who . . . who wanted to have children . . . she was obsessed . . . she wanted to get pregnant . . . but she couldn't do it . . . she just couldn't do it! Poor saint. Hard as she tried, she never succeeded . . . up to the point where the Heavenly Father Above took pity on her and: Pscium! She was pregnant! . . . at sixty years old! A miracle!

TROOPER. Sixty years old?

ANTONIA. Yes, you can imagine, and her husband was over eighty!

TROOPER. But . . .

ANTONIA. The power of faith! They say, though, that the husband died immediately. Anyway, in memory of this miracle all the women in the neighborhood go around for three days with false bellies.

TROOPER. Oh, what a wonderful tradition. And is that why they empty out the supermarkets, to put stuff in their bellies? Come on! Enough with the fairy tales! Let me see what you have under there, or I'll lose my patience!

ANTONIA. And do what? Rip off our clothes? I warn you, that if you lay even a finger on us . . . a . . . a . . . a curse . . . will befall you!

TROOPER. Don't make me laugh. What curse?

ANTONIA. The same thing that happened to the incredulous husband of Santa Eulalia! The old man was a skeptic and he didn't believe her: "Santa Eulalia, come here right away. Open your blouse and let me see what you have in your belly, and I warn you, if you really are pregnant, I'll strangle you, because that baby's not mine." And then she, Santa Eulalia, opened her blouse, and a second miracle: out of her stomach . . . out of her stomach . . . came roses . . . roses . . . a cascade of roses.

TROOPER. Roses?

ANTONIA. Yes, but that's not all . . . all of a sudden the old man's eyes went black: "I can't see any more. I can't see any more," he shouted. "I'm blind! God has punished me!"— "Oh, skeptic, now you believe," said Santa Eulalia. —"Yes, I believe!" —and then, third miracle: out of the roses sprang a ten month old baby boy who could already speak, and he said, "Papa, Papa, the Lord forgives you. Now you can die in peace." The baby put his little hand on the old man's head, and he dropped dead just like that.

TROOPER. Okay, story time's over. Now show me the roses . . . I mean . . . the goods. Hurry up!

ANTONIA. So you don't believe in miracles?

TROOPER. Not at all.

ANTONIA. You're not afraid of the curse?

TROOPER. No, I said so already!

ANTONIA. Okay. Have it your way! Don't say I didn't warn you. (*To Margherita*) Come on. Get up and we'll show him together:

> Santa Eulalia of the big belly
> On whomever does not believe in the miracle
> Let fall the curse
> To whomever does not believe the oracle
> Let come the evil black bastard
> To darken his sight
> Santa Eulalia, Santa Pia
> Unleash your curse
> And so be it!!!!! (*The two women open their coats*)

TROOPER. What's all that stuff in there?

ANTONIA. What stuff? (*They shout in amazement*) Oh, look at that! It's a salad!

TROOPER. Salad?

ANTONIA. Yes, an apparition of a salad: chicory, endive, fennel, and even a cabbage!

MARGHERITA. Me too, me too, I have a cabbage!

TROOPER. What's going on here? Why are you hiding all these vegetables in your stomach?

ANTONIA. But we didn't hide anything. Can't you see? It's a miracle!?

TROOPER. Yeah, the miracle of Our Lady of the Cabbage!

ANTONIA. Well, these days you make a miracle with whatever vegetable you can get your hands on. But whether you believe or not, there's nothing wrong with it, is there? Is there some law that says a citizen is not allowed to carry chicory, endive, and cabbage in her belly? Is it prohibited?

TROOPER. No.

ANTONIA. Is there a law against it?

TROOPER. No.

ANTONIA. Then goodbye! (*Begins to usher him out*)

TROOPER. What do you mean, goodbye! (*The trooper grabs the vegetable and presses the nozzle of his gun against the head of the cabbage, as if holding it hostage.*) All right! That's it! Tell me why you put all this stuff under your clothes . . . or else!

ANTONIA. I told you already. To make a belly in honor of the miracle of Santa Eulalia! And anyone who doesn't believe in it is cursed!

(*Slowly the lights dim*)

ANTONIA AND MARGHERITA.

Santa Eulalia of the big belly
On whomever does not believe in the miracle
Let fall the curse . . .

(*The women repeat the 'prayer' to Santa Eulalia, noticing with anxiety the dimming of the lights*)

TROOPER. What's happening now? The lights are going out.

ANTONIA (*very calmly*). What are you talking about, officer?

TROOPER. Can't you see . . . (*Worried*) It's getting dark . . .

ANTONIA. No, you must be mistaken . . . I can see just fine. (*To Margherita*) Can you see?

MARGHERITA (*Antonia kicks her*). Yes, yes . . . I can see . . .

ANTONIA. We can see. Maybe your eyesight is fading.

MARGHERITA (*moves close to Antonia and whispers*). They cut off the electricity.

ANTONIA. Quiet!

TROOPER. Come on, stop kidding around. The light switch. Where's the light switch?

ANTONIA (*Moving comfortably, in spite of the darkness*). It's right here. Can't you see it? Wait, I'll try it . . . (*she clicks the switch audibly*) There, you see. Not it's off. Now it's on. There's an awful lot of light in my house! Don't you see it?

TROOPER. No, I can't see.

ANTONIA. Oh, my God. He's gone blind! It's the curse!

TROOPER. Cut it out! Open the window . . . I want to see outside!

ANTONIA. But the window is open!

MARGHERITA. Yes, the window's open. Can't you see?

ANTONIA. Come on, come and look. (*Leads him to a chair*) Look, over here. Watch out for the chair!

TROOPER (*bumps into the chair*). Ahhiaa . . . owww. That hurt!

ANTONIA. Pay attention when you walk!

TROOPER. How can I, if I can't see?

ANTONIA. Oh, I forgot, you're blind.

TROOPER (*scared and angry*). Blind!!!!!!!!!!

ANTONIA. Come on . . . there's the window . . . (*takes him to the shelf and opens the two glass cabinet doors on top*) Careful now . . . look, we're opening the window . . . feel the glass? (*The officer touches the glass tentatively*) Look out there . . . what a panorama! Sometimes I forget myself how beautiful it is. Let's hope the landlord doesn't realize what a great view this is, or he'll raise the rent!

TROOPER (*desperate*). No I don't see it. I can't see anything. Dammit, what happened to me? A match . . . Light a match!

ANTONIA (*worried*). A match? . . . I have something better than a match (*Goes and gets the welding tank*) Stay there. Don't move. You don't know the house, and you might hurt yourself . . . I'll bring it over . . . it's a welding torch . . . (*she lights it*) Look, look . . . what a beautiful red flame!

TROOPER. I don't see any flame . . . let me touch it.

ANTONIA. No, no, can't you see it's red hot . . .

TROOPER (*arrogant*). I said let me touch it. That's an order! (*Antonia obeys*) Ah, ah, iaohoo! My hand! I burned my hand! Oh, God, that hurts! What a burn!

ANTONIA. I tried to warn you.

TROOPER (*cries desperately*). I'm blind!

ANTONIA. Don't cry . . . it's going to be alright . . . come on . . . at the end of the day what happened . . . it's nothing . . . so you've gone a little blind . . .

TROOPER. I want to get out of here . . . I've got to get out! (*Becoming more desperate*) I want to get out of this house . . . to my superiors . . .

ANTONIA. Wait, wait, I'll help you to the door . . . Here it is . . . there's the door . . . (*opens door to wardrobe*)

(*The state trooper rushes into it like a madman, smashes his head on the interior, falls back staggering, and collapses on the floor*)

MARGHERITA. He hit his head!

TROOPER. Ahhii! Who punched me?

ANTONIA (*searching*). The baby . . . It's Santa Eulalia's baby. He's touched your forehead with his little hand!

TROOPER. That's some little hand! (*Collapses on the floor*)

ANTONIA. Officer . . . Officer! Dammit, he fainted. (*She gets down on her knees by the officer*)

MARGHERITA. Maybe he's dead!

ANTONIA. Always the optimist! What do you mean, dead . . . get a pillow . . . (*Margherita obeys*) No, he's not dead. He's just having some faintness . . . a slight case of faintness . . . he's fine . . . he's breathing . . .

MARGHERITA. He's dead, he's dead . . . he's not breathing any more!

ANTONIA. He's breathing . . . he's breathing . . . no . . . he's not breathing! And his heart's not beating either!

MARGHERITA. Oh, God! We killed a cop!

ANTONIA. Oh, yeah! Maybe I got a little carried away. What do we do now?

MARGHERITA. Ah, you're asking me? What do I have to do with it? It was all your idea . . . I'm sorry but I'm going home . . . The keys! Where did I put the keys to my house?

ANTONIA. Some friend you are. Walking out on me just like that.

MARGHERITA (*finds keys on the shelf*). Ah, here they are! But I have another pair in my pocket. Two sets of keys! These are my husband's! So he was here . . . he came looking for me . . . and he forgot them!

ANTONIA. What do I care about that! I'm here with a dead cop and you're talking to me about keys! . . .

MARGHERITA. That means that Luigi met Giovanni and he must have told him that I was pregnant, and now what am I supposed to say? You've got to think up something to get me out of this mess . . .

ANTONIA. I'm desperate. (*Crying, she speaks to the unconscious officer*) Officer . . . don't be that way . . . let's make up . . . It was just a little bump on the head . . . officer . . . wake up (*Lifts the officer's arm and lets it go. The arm falls heavily without life*) He's dead! He's really dead!

MARGHERITA. See what happens when you make fun of miracles?

ANTONIA. No, he was the one making fun of them . . . I even warned him: watch out for the curse, because Santa Eulalia is an awesome Saint! (*She grabs him by the shoulders, lifts him up and drops him*)

MARGHERITA. And now what are you doing?

ANTONIA. Artificial respiration.

MARGHERITA. No. You have to use mouth to mouth resuscitation like they do when people drown.

ANTONIA. Now you want me to kiss a cop! With my political background! No, . . . you kiss him . . .

MARGHERITA. No. I can't do it! Maybe we should get him an oxygen tank.

ANTONIA (*thinks a moment*). I've got one. It's with Giovanni's welding equipment. One valve's for hydrogen, and the other's for oxygen. Come here and help me . . . close the hydrogen valve . . . like that . . . and open the one for oxygen. Stay calm . . . you'll see. As soon as he gets the oxygen, he'll come around! He'll even feel better than before! Like he spent a month in the mountains!

MARGHERITA. Are you sure it's going to work?

ANTONIA. No problem. You'll see . . . (*she puts the tube from the welding cannister in the trooper's mouth*) The oxygen's going to his stomach . . . you see, his chest is rising . . . and then it falls . . . look . . . he's waking up . . . he's breathing . . . see how nicely that chest rises . . . and how it falls.

MARGHERITA. It looks to me like it's only rising . . . and his stomach too . . . stop . . . you're going to blow him up.

(*The two women try frantically to turn off the infernal machine*)

ANTONIA (*lifts the tube up to the officer's mouth*). Oh no. I gave

him hydrogen instead of oxygen . . . Oh, God, what a belly . . . what a belly! I made a policeman pregnant!

(*Blackout. Curtain falls. Onstage, Giovanni and Luigi pretend to be outside Luigi's apartment*)

GIOVANNI. Well, we can't keep on sitting outside your place like a couple of bums. I'm going to see if I can break down the door down with my shoulder.

LUIGI. No, you saw what happened when I tried. I couldn't get past the two locks.

GIOVANNI. Why do you have all that hardware?

LUIGI. My wife made me install it. She's terrified of thieves.

GIOVANNI. We're screwed.

LUIGI. Son of a bitch! Now I remember where I left the keys. At your house . . . yeah . . . on the table.

GIOVANNI. Are you sure?

LUIGI. Absolutely. Come on. Give me the keys to your house and I'll go get them.

GIOVANNI. Yeah, with that State Trooper waiting outside my place! Trac . . . You're under arrest!

LUIGI. No, after all this time, he must be gone.

GIOVANNI. Don't kid yourself. That guy's a bloodhound. We can't even think of going back there. (*They hear noises*) Dammit, someone's coming . . .

LUIGI. Calm down, it's probably just a neighbor.

GIOVANNI. What do you mean, neighbor. It's that cop . . . (*he tries to hide the bags*)

VOICE (*offstage*). Excuse me, I need some information.

GIOVANNI. Dammit, we're screwed.

LUIGI. No, it's not him. It looks like him, but it's not him.

GIOVANNI. You're right. It's not him.

GRAVEDIGGER (*enters the stage*). What were you saying? Who do I look like?

GIOVANNI. Damn, he looks just like him. Ah, I'm sorry for laughing, but you are the spitting image of the Sargent without the moustache who looks like the state trooper with the moustache. I feel like I'm in a play that I saw when I was a kid . . . you know, one of those theater companies where they can't afford to pay more than a few actors, so one of them has to play the parts of all the cops.

GRAVEDIGGER. But, really, I'm not a policeman.

GIOVANNI. Ah no, and what do you do?

GRAVEDIGGER. I'm an undertaker.

GIOVANNI AND LUIGI. Oh, Mother of God! (*With rapid gestures, the two of them touch their testicles*)

GIOVANNI (*explains to the audience*). This is an Italian gesture expressing the fear of death. (*He demonstrates the gesture again and then turns to the Gravedigger*) Sorry, it was just an instinct.

GRAVEDIGGER. Oh, don't worry . . . I understand . . . everyone does that when they meet me . . . I do it myself whenever I look in the mirror.

GIOVANNI. How nice.

GRAVEDIGGER. Can you tell me if a certain Sergio Prampolini lives around here.

LUIGI. Sure, he's upstairs on the third floor. But I'm sure he's not home. He's in the hospital. The poor guy is always sick . . . !

GRAVEDIGGER. He's dead. But do you know if any one in his family is coming home today? I've got to get someone to sign for the casket I've got out there.

GIOVANNI. Oh well, just leave it in the hall . . . with a little note on it . . . and when the son comes home: "Oh, it's Dad!" (*Mimes the action of carrying the casket on his shoulder*)

GRAVEDIGGER. A casket in the hallway? Abandoned? . . . With all the people passing by . . . little kids jumping in to play Indians paddling their canoe? No, I can't do that. I have to have the papers signed by someone who's responsible. You live here, don't you?

LUIGI. Yes, I live right there.

GRAVEDIGGER. Good, then it's all set. I'll leave the casket with you, you keep it in your house . . . and this evening when the son of the deceased . . .

GIOVANNI (*shocked*). A dead man's coffin in my house?

GRAVEDIGGER. It doesn't take up much space, you know . . . and if you overlook it's macabre function, it's actually quite decorative.

GIOVANNI. Sure, put a little doily on top, and it's a portable bar!

GRAVEDIGGER. Be serious.

GIOVANNI. I'm dead serious.

LUIGI. The fact is, you see . . . we locked ourselves out.

GRAVEDIGGER. Oh, what a shame! Then, I'll have to return it to the warehouse.

GIOVANNI. No . . . maybe we can take it to my house. I live just down the street . . . I'll take care of everything. But you'd have to let us load these sacks into the casket . . . so our stuff won't get wet in the rain. The casket has a lid I hope?

GRAVEDIGGER. Yes, yes, it's a regulation casket. it's cheap, but even so we never make them without the lid.

GIOVANNI. What a great country we live in! Every coffen has a lid!

GRAVEDIGGER. Okay, let's go: I'll go ahead so you can load up the casket. (*He leaves*)

(*They gather the bags*)

GIOVANNI. I'd like to see a cop who's got the guts to stick his nose into a dead man's casket. I'll be the corpse, and you can be the undertaker making a delivery to the house. Come on. Let's get the sacks and go. (*They leave*)

(*Blackout. The curtain rises on the women in the house. Trooper is still stretched out on the floor. Antonia is filling up her bag with food from under the bed. Margherita is furious.*)

MARGHERITA. You're crazy. We're here with a dead man in the house and you're still worried about smuggling out rice and pasta.

ANTONIA. Well, it's the last trip. And besides, if he's dead, he's dead. Just come over here and help me lift the guy up . . . so we can get rid of him.

MARGHERITA. Where are we going to put him?

ANTONIA. In the wardrobe.

MARGHERITA. In the wardrobe?

ANTONIA. Where else? Haven't you ever seen a detective movie? They always put the body in the wardrobe.

(*They lift the policeman's feet. Antonia lifts him over her shoulders.*)

MARGHERITA (*struggling*). He's heavy.

ANTONIA. What do you expect? He's a cop! (*manipulates him as if he were a puppet and stows him away in the cupboard*). There, he's in. Now let's put a coat-hanger under his jacket so we can suspend him from this hook . . . (*they do it*). Perfect! Dammit, the door won't close. Let's push . . . come on. There! Look how nicely he fits in now! Just like Baby Jesus in the manger! (*closes wardrobe door*)

MARGHERITA. Well, that's that. (*Mimes opening the window*) The rain's coming down by the bucketful.

ANTONIA. I'll be right back . . . I'm going in there for a minute . . . load up your belly . . . just one more trip and we're done . . . so exhausting! (*She goes out to go to the bathroom*)

(*The door opens. Luigi enters. He's wearing the cap of the gravedigger*)

LUIGI (*barely peeking in, whispers*). Hey, is anybody home?

MARGHERITA. Who's there? . . . (*frightened*) Luigi, is that you? What are you doing dressed up like that?

LUIGI. Margherita, my sweetie pie, finally . . . How are you? . . . Let me look at you! But don't you have a belly? The baby? Where's the baby? Did you lose it?

MARGHERITA. No, no . . . don't worry . . . everything's fine . . .

LUIGI. Really, everything's fine? And you're okay? Tell me . . .

MARGHERITA. Later, later . . . it's better if Antonia tells you . . .

LUIGI. Why Antonia?

GRAVEDIGGER (*voice from outside*). Hey this casket's heavy, are we coming in or not?

LUIGI. Yes, yes, come on in . . . (*At that moment the door of the cupboard opens so that the Sargent can be seen hanging inside. Margherita closes it quickly and runs into the other room*) Come on, Giovanni, get out of the casket . . .

GIOVANNI (*from outside*). Too bad, I was just getting comfortable in here . . . (*door opens again. Without seeing what's inside, Giovanni closes door. They put the coffin on the table*).

VOICE OF MARGHERITA (*from the other room*). Antonia, Antonia, come here . . . hurry.

ANTONIA. What is it . . . can't I even pee in peace?

GIOVANNI. They're both back?

LUIGI. Yes, yes, and everything's fine . . . they're all doing fine.

GIOVANNI. That's good . . . Close it, close the lid . . . (*to the gravedigger*) Thank you. Thanks for everything.

GRAVEDIGGER. Don't mention it. (*he leaves*)

LUIGI. Listen, I have an idea. Let's close the door and lock ourselves in here until we unload everything. Then we can hide the stuff under the bed, and stand up the casket in the closet.

GIOVANNI. All right, go lock the door. (*They take the bags out of the casket and put them under the bed*)

MARGHERITA (*from the other room*). Hurry up, Antonia. I have to tell you something.

ANTONIA. I'm coming. I'm fixing my clothes. Everything's fallin out.

GIOVANNI. There, it's done . . the bags are all out of sight. Push, push them further under.

LUIGI. Look at that! We push the bags in on one side and they come out the other . . . (*bends over to look under the bed*) It didn't seem like that much in the casket! It looks like twice as much!

GIOVANNI. Of course it does, if you look at it with your head upside down . . . everything seems exaggerated that way . . . they call it the yoga effect . . . Come on, help me lift up the casket . . . No, wait, first let's take off the lid so it won't be too thick.

(*They lift the casket and insert it into the wardrobe, after resting the lid up against the wall*)

LUIGI. You're right . . . But what was that yoga effect you were talking about?

GIOVANNI. Oh, that was discovered in India . . . people there are so poor that when their hunger gets too much to bear . . . they stand on their heads . . . and while they're upside down they imagine whatever they want . . . all kinds of things to eat and drink . . .

LUIGI. And that makes the hunger go away?

GIOVANNI. No, but it keeps people off the streets. Come on, we've almost got it in . . . push.

(*They manage to squeeze in the coffin so that the trooper fits into it when they close the door*)

LUIGI. Ah, so the illusion is enough to satisfy them . . . is that it?

GIOVANNI. Yeah, that's it . . . (*tries to close the door of the cupboard*)

LUIGI. You know I had an illusion too.

GIOVANNI. Yeah, you told me.

LUIGI. No, no, another one . . . I thought I saw the State Trooper in the closet.

GIOVANNI. State Trooper? (*opens the wardrobe door*) Good thing it was an illusion . . . Don't let me catch you standing on your head again, okay . . . Dammit, it won't close. (*pushes, but the door stays open*)

MARGHERITA (*voice from outside*). Listen, Antonia, I'm getting tired of this . . . Just let me wait in there . . .

GIOVANNI. Go open the door. I can't move . . .

(*Luigi runs to open the door. Margherita enters*)

MARGHERITA. Oh, thanks, that's better . . . (*sees Giovanni*) Oh, Giovanni, hello.

GIOVANNI. Hello. Your husband told me everything went well . . . So did you have the baby or not?

ANTONIA (*enters suddenly*). So what did you have to tell me that was so urgent? (*She tries to hide her belly as much as possible and slowly, bent over double, she goes towards the exit door*)

GIOVANNI (*blocks her with a shout*). Antonia! Your belly! You had the transplant?!

LUIGI. The transplant?!

ANTONIA. Well . . .

GIOVANNI (*starts to walk into the cupboard, but turns suddenly to block her*). Did you get the cesarean?

ANTONIA. A little.

GIOVANNI. What do you mean, a little?

ANTONIA. Well, in the end . . . it was the right thing.

LUIGI (*to Margherita*). Did you have a Cesarean too?

MARGHERITA. Uh, yes, well, I don't know . . . Antonia, did I have one?

LUIGI. Why are you asking her . . . don't you know?

ANTONIA. Uh, no, poor thing. They put her to sleep. And since she was asleep, how could she know?

GIOVANNI. You mean they operated on you while you were awake?

ANTONIA. What's with this interrogation? Why the third degree. I take the fifth. (*At a certain point, almost out of sympathy, the cupboard shelf doors and the front door of the house start opening, setting off an absurd merry-go-round of activity*) You could have asked how our health is, if we're living or dying. What do you care that we dragged ourselves out of bed like idiots against the doctors orders to that you wouldn't worry about us. And what do you think I should have done . . . she was going to lose her baby . . . I was in a position to save it . . . how could I say no . . . Aren't you always telling me that we have to help one another . . .

GIOVANNI. Yes, yes, you're right . . . I'm sorry . . . maybe you did the right thing . . . yes, of course you did . . .

LUIGI. Thank you, Antonia. Thank you, Antonia, for all you did. You are truly a remarkable woman.

GIOVANNI. Yes, truly a remarkable woman.

LUIGI (*to Margherita*). You tell her too. Come on.

MARGHERITA. Yes, Antonia. You are a remarkable woman.

GIOVANNI. Come . . . come here . . . you shouldn't be standing up . . . (*sits her on the bed*) not with that cesarean, you know . . . maybe it would have been better for you to stay there at the hospital.

ANTONIA. Don't be silly . . . I'm fine . . . didn't even notice it!

GIOVANNI. Yes, you look absolutely great . . . And look at that great big belly! (*He caresses her stomach*) It's moving already!

LUIGI. It's moving? Excuse me, Antonia, can I touch it too?

MARGHERITA. No, you're not touching a damn thing!

LUIGI. Eh, but it's my son too, you know?

GIOVANNI. Yeah . . . we're all related now.

MARGHERITA. What about me. All this cheering for Antonia . . .

ANTONIA. Yeah. Do some cheering for Margherita. Go lift

her up on your shoulders. I have to go. (*She gets up and rushes towards the door*)

GIOVANNI (*blocking her way*). Go? Are you crazy? You're not going anywhere . . . except to bed . . . to stay warm . . . in fact we'll move the bed next to the heater. (*Begins to move the bed*)

LUIGI. Stop, what are you doing!? (*All look at him*)

GIOVANNI. You're right . . . it's too dangerous to move it, too dangerous . . . the gas tanks are there . . . (*puts Antonia back on the bed*)

ANTONIA (*stops him; she's seen the cover of the coffin inside the wardrobe door*). Giovanni . . . what's that?

GIOVANNI (*talks to distract her while he tries to come up with a plausible response*). The gas tanks . . . are there . . . But you could at least have warned me . . . instead of letting me worry . . . all it would have taken was a phone call . . .

ANTONIA. Giovanni, what's that?

GIOVANNI. All it takes is a dime . . . a quarter . . . you could have asked a nurse . . . you could have said: "Look, call my house . . . no, call the bar downstairs from my house . . . and say . . . 'listen, tell my husband . . .'"

ANTONIA (*trying to interrupt him*). Excuse me, Giovanni, what is that thing . . .

GIOVANNI (*desperate, doesn't know what to say*). Hello, could you tell my husband that everything's fine . . .

ANTONIA. Giovanni, what is that brown wooden object?

GIOVANNI. Don't change the subject! How come, instead of calling me . . . about the baby . . . you keep talking to me about that disgusting piece of wood . . . I'll burn it . . . I don't know why I ever bought the thing . . . it's . . . it's . . .

ANTONIA (*exasperated*). Giovanni, what is it?

GIOVANNI. You still don't get it do you? Don't you ever watch TV? A child . . . would understand right away, even a child . . . watching TV . . . the commercials . . . especially when you see the foam . . . the waves . . .

ANTONIA. But what is it, Giovanni?

GIOVANNI. It's a surf board! They sell them at the factory . . . in front of the gate . . .

LUIGI. The gate.

GIOVANNI. Yeah. We're going to be laid off until January . . . so what are we going to do in December? Surf the Atlantic. I know, I know . . . you don't believe it . . . in fact it's something else entirely . . .

ANTONIA. What is it? . . .

GIOVANNI. You have such a limited imagination! It's a cradle! When I said to Luigi, "Look, Luigi, you're wife's expecting a baby," right away he said, "A cradle, a cradle!"

LUIGI. A cradle.

GIOVANNI. So I went into the first cradle store I could find. And got the most modern cradle on the market. From Japan. It's a Toyota. (*Luigi and Giovanni grab the cover the rock it*) You see, it's got four holes here, two on each side, . . . so you can suspend it from the ceiling with two steel cables . . . you put the baby in . . . you barely have to touch it and look how the cradle swings for hours . . .

then, when the baby cries, just give it a slap and zac! The spin of death! And the baby (*mimes baby's terror*) frozen stiff. Doesn't make a peep for a week!

ANTONIA (*noticing the size of the lid*). It looks a little big to me . . .

GIOVANNI. But babies are always growing!

(*Antonia stretches out on the bed, unconvinced. An old man comes to the door. It's the same actor with a white wig and his face covered in a cobweb of wrinkles.*)

OLD MAN. Excuse me. Am I disturbing you?

GIOVANNI. Oh, Papa, what a pleasure. Come in. Come in.

ANTONIA. Hi, Papa!

GIOVANNI. Do you know my friends? This is my father.

OLD MAN. My pleasure.

LUIGI. Giovanni, have you noticed that your father . . . looks a lot like the State Trooper and the Police Sargent?

GIOVANNI. Don't tell him, because he's already getting a little senile . . .

OLD MAN. I am not senile . . . (*turns to Margherita*) How is my Antonia . . . oh, how beautiful you look . . . you're getting so much younger all the time.

GIOVANNI. No, Papa, she's not Antonia. That's Antonia.

OLD MAN. Is that so?

ANTONIA. Yes, Papa, it's me.

OLD MAN. What are you doing in bed? Are you sick?

GIOVANNI. No, she's expecting a baby.

OLD MAN. Oh, is that so? And where has he gone? Don't worry . . . you'll see, he'll come back. (*Looks at Luigi and confuses him for his nephew*) Oh, look, he's come back already. And he's all grown up . . . You shouldn't keep your mamma waiting like that . . .

GIOVANNI. Dad, this is a friend.

OLD MAN. That's good! You should always be friends with your children. But I came here to tell you that they're throwing you out of your house.

GIOVANNI. Who?

OLD MAN. Your landlord. He sent the eviction letter to my house by mistake. Look here. It says that you haven't paid the rent for four months.

GIOVANNI. Don't be silly. It must be a mistake. Let me see that. Antonia always pays the rent on time, isn't that true Antonia?

ANTONIA. Yes, of course.

OLD MAN. In any case, they're going to clear out the whole building, because for months hardly anybody has been paying . . .

GIOVANNI. Who told you that?

OLD MAN. The Sheriff . . . who's clearing people out apartment by apartment . . . a nice man!

(*Almost imperceptibly, voices are heard shouting orders outside*)

LUIGI. Take a look out there on the street. There's a whole squadron of police cars . . .

GIOVANNI. Yeah . . . look at that formation. It's like a war out there. And look at all those trucks.

OLD MAN. Sure, to carry away the furniture and everything else. All for free.

(*The noise outside increases. Voices of woman and children mixed with the shouting of orders*)

VOICE OF A POLICEMAN (*from outside*). Come on . . . keep it moving . . . carry that stuff out . . . don't leave anything behind!

GIOVANNI. So I guess this eviction letter really is for us. Antonia, for God's sake! How did this happen?

ANTONIA. Don't shout. You'll scare the baby!

GIOVANNI. Okay, I'll speak softly. Antonia, is this true. Answer me.

ANTONIA. Okay: yes, it's true. I haven't paid the rent for four months, and I haven't paid the gas or electricity either . . . that's why they cut our service.

GIOVANNI. They cut off our gas and electric? Because you didn't' pay the bill?

ANTONIA. Because with everything we earn between the two of us, there's barely enough to eat.

MARGHERITA. Luigi, I have something to tell you: I haven't paid the rent either.

LUIGI. No!

ANTONIA. See, see, we all have the same problem . . . everyone else who lives in our building, and the people across the street too . . . and over there . . . everybody.

GIOVANNI. For God's sake, why didn't you tell me that you were short of money?

ANTONIA. But what could you have done . . . go out and commit a robbery?

GIOVANNI. Ah, no, of course not . . . but in the end . . .

ANTONIA. In the end, you would have had a fit and cursed the day you married me. (*Sniffles*)

LUIGI (*to Margherita*). And you, did you at least pay the gas and electricity?

MARGHERITA. Yes, yes, the gas and the electric, yes!

LUIGI. That's a relief.

GIOVANNI. Come on, don't cry. It's not good for the baby.

OLD MAN. That's right, that's right, everything will be all right. Oh, I just remembered. I came by to bring you something. Wait, I left it outside in the hall. (*He gets a bag and puts it on the table*) Sometimes I'm just not all here. There, look at this. I found it in my shed. It must be yours.

LUIGI (*goes to the bag and looks inside*). What's this? Butter, flour, tomatoes?

ANTONIA. I've got nothing to do with it.

GIOVANNI. No, papa, this isn't our stuff.

OLD MAN. Sure it is. I saw Antonia come out of my shed this morning?

ANTONIA. All right, yes, it's the stuff I bought yesterday at reduced prices . . .

GIOVANNI. At the supermarket?

ANTONIA. Yes, but I only paid for half of it, the rest I stole . . .

GIOVANNI. Stole? You've become a robber?

ANTONIA. Yes!

LUIGI (*to Margherita*). You too?

MARGHERITA. Yes, me too . . .

ANTONIA. No, it's not true . . . she had nothing to do with it! She was just helping me out.

(*The two policemen from earlier enter*)

POLICEMAN. Excuse me? The Bardi family . . . is that you?

GIOVANNI. Yes . . .

POLICEMAN. I've got an eviction notice here. You've got a half hour to get ready. We'll be back in a few minutes to give you a hand . . . (*They leave*)

GIOVANNI. This is really unbelievable . . . I'm losing my mind!

LUIGI. Calm down, Giovanni . . . when it comes to talking about stealing, we should keep our mouths shut.

GIOVANNI. What do you mean keep our mouths shut! What's that got to do with it? We were in the middle of the street, don't you understand the difference . . . she's a disgrace, a dishonest criminal.

ANTONIA. Sure, you're right . . . I'm nothing but a criminal who throws mud on your poor but honorable name . . . and who also toys with your delicate sentiments of fatherhood . . . because you should know . . . (*removes packages from belly*) all I've got in my belly is sugar, rice, and pasta.

LUIGI. The baby, the transplant . . . (*to his wife*) Margherita?

GIOVANNI. I'm going to murder her . . . I'll murder her! (*Goes towards Antonia but is blocked by Luigi*)

OLD MAN. Well, now that I've done what I came for . . . I'll bid you children goodbye. Have a nice day. (*He leaves*)

(*The noises outside keep getting louder. Women and men yelling. Orders shouted. Sirens*)

GIOVANNI. You dirty liar. How dare you joke about the story of our son! (*To Luigi*) Let me go.

ANTONIA. Let him kill me! Go ahead. I'm sick of this lousy life! And I'm fed up with your sermonizing . . . about law and order, and how you follow the rules, rules, rules . . . with such pride. Bullshit! You swallow your pride every day. And then when other people try to find a little dignity by breaking free of rules you call them looters, bums, terrorists. Terrorism . . . Terrorism is being held hostage by a minimum wage job. But you don't want to know how things really are.

GIOVANNI. I know how things are. And I can see. I'm mad as hell and I'm frustrated and I'm not the only one. Nobody can make ends meet. There's Aldo across the street whose wife left him when he lost his job. And how about our neighbors next door. They sleep four to a bed. People are hungry. And when they ask for help nobody listens. And the rage I feel isn't at you . . . it's at myself, and at the impotence I feel . . . when I'm being screwed over every day . . . because I don't see a way out. And it seems there's nobody out there who gives a shit about the people who end up on the street with no place to live. And you know what. I'm starting to take it personally. Because in just a few minutes the homeless are us.

ANTONIA. What happened, Giovanni, is that really you talking? Is your head screwed on straight?

GIOVANNI. I've felt like this for a long time . . . I just never had the courage to say it before. And there's something else you should know about me. I'm a thief too. Look under here. Luigi and I stole these: bags of coffee!

ANTONIA (*truly astonished*). You stole!

LUIGI (*going to the rescue*). Yes, but he only did it after he got mad about getting laid off our jobs.

GIOVANNI. No, that was just the last straw . . . because I'd already been mad enough to scream for a long time . . . (*to Antonia*) And one more thing, Antonia . . . This is not a cradle. It's the lid to a dead man's coffin! (*Antonia makes the sign of reaching for her crotch to express the fear of death*) Look in here. (*He goes to the wardrobe. Antonia and Margherita try to stop him.*).

ANTONIA. No, stop, what are you doing?

GIOVANNI. I'm doing what I have to do . . . you should know everything . . . (*Luigi helps him pull out of the casket*)

(*The State Trooper that was inside is revealed*)

STATE TROOPER. I can see! (*Comes out of wardrobe*) I can see! Santa Eulalia forgave me . . . she blessed me! (*He notices his belly*) I'm pregnant! God bless Santa Eulalia! . . . I'm a mother . . . I'm a mother! (*Exits running*) I'm a mother.

GIOVANNI. What day is it today? (*He hears shots and shouts from outside and runs to the window*) Look, the women are pulling their stuff off of the trucks. The police are shooting!

LUIGI. Yeah, and look at those kid on the rooftops . . . they're throwing things . . . tiles . . . bricks!

GIOVANNI. The police are shooting to kill. One kid's already down.

MARGHERITA. They're firing for keeps!

(*The four of them go to the window and shout insults*)

ALL. Murderers . . . bastards . . . cowards . . .

LUIGI. They're running away . . . the police are running away!

ANTONIA. And the women are taking their things down from the trucks.

LUIGI. It's happening.

GIOVANNI. Of course it's happening. People have been putting up with things out of fear. But fear can turn into rage when you can't see any way out and you watch your bills piling up and up and up and you've got nothing in the bank. And you keep getting downsized and downsized and downsized until no one can even see you anymore.

MARGHERITA. There's a limit to what people can take.

ANTONIA. People are hungry. They're not just hungry for food. They're hungry for dignity. They're hungry for justice, for a chance.

GIOVANNI. Desperation's funny, isn't it. Especially when it's somebody else's. Then it's really funny. It's a scream. It's a riot. Remember the Los Angeles riots. Nobody expected them. You're smiling, aren't you. Sure, we all know that the poor people just burned down their own neighborhoods, and left themselves flat on their asses with nothing to show for all their rage. But just wait, because it might turn out that, little by little, they're going to get up off their asses onto their knees. And then they just might drag themselves up off the ground and onto their feet. And that's when we better start paying attention, because when people stand up for themselves, they can always find a way to make things happen.

(*The lights are dimmed during the last speech until the darkness is complete*)

MUSIC. BLACKOUT.

TOPICS FOR CRITICAL THINKING AND WRITING

The Play on the PAGE

1. Who is the more politically committed in the play, Antonia or Giovanni? How does the script make this clear?
2. Fo has the same actor play four roles: the Inspector, the Sergeant, the Undertaker, and the Old Man. What is the significance of this choice?
3. Ron Jenkins's translation of the script includes some contemporary American references. What are these, and will they work in the context of the whole script?
4. Direct addresses and asides to the audience are a trademark of many of Dario Fo's scripts. What is the function of these devices in this script, and how do they add to the overall comic tone?

The Play on the STAGE

5. A great deal of the physical comedy relies on the slapstick tradition of *commedia dell'arte*. Select an example and describe how you would stage it.
6. Fo has the same actor play the Inspector, the Sergeant, the Undertaker, and the Old Man. If you were casting the show today, would you maintain this convention? If so, why? If not, why not?
7. The first London production of the play made links between the events in the play that related to the Thatcher administration in Britain. If you staged

the play today, are there current events to which you could link the production? What staging choices would you make to highlight those connections?

8. Fo's use of the *giullare* is important to much of his work. Are you able to distinguish moments in this script that can be attributed to his fascination with this medieval clown figure?

The Play in PERFORMANCE

We Won't Pay! We Won't Pay! (*Non Si Paga! Non Si Paga!*) premiered in Milan in 1974, directed by Dario Fo. In 1978 it was his first play to receive a production in the United Kingdom, under the title *We Can't Pay! We Won't Pay!* This production began in the Half Moon Theater, a small fringe theater is the East End of London, but after a sold-out run it moved to the commercial West End where it remained for an impressive two years. It has had numerous English-language productions in Britain, Ireland, Australia, and the United States. Because of the play's popularity abroad, which included several years in the repertoire of the Berliner Ensemble, Fo produced a revised, updated version in 1980. In that year 24,000 Fiat workers were laid off, so

Fo made the male characters in the play Fiat workers. He also included topical references to the political situation in Poland and Afghanistan and made jokes about Pope John Paul II. The play is considered his most comic and entertaining work in terms of the plot reversals and complications and in terms of its fusion of political points and farce. By 1990 *We Won't Pay! We Won't Pay!* had been performed in thirty-five countries. The most recent American version, produced in 1999 by the American Repertory Theater in Cambridge, Massachusetts with the Oscar-winning performer Marisa Tomei in the role of Antonia, used Ron Jenkins translation, which we reprint here. We include a review of this production.

ED SIEGEL
Fo's Farce Works: Pay *Is Reward**

By the end of "We Won't Pay! We Won't Pay!" you might still not agree that Dario Fo deserved the Nobel Prize for Literature, but you would have no trouble if the American Comedy Awards gave the Italian playwright a statue for his contributions to theater.

Or if they gave one to everyone who contributed to the slaphappy American Repertory Theatre production.

By the time translator Ron Jenkins, director Andrei Belgrader, and the ART ensemble with guest Marisa Tomei are done, the term "hysterical pregnancies" has an entirely different meaning from the technical one, particularly during the riotous first-act conclusion. For those of you unfamiliar with the commie clown, Fo's plays are a fusion of commedia dell'arte and radical politics. Such a union is not always a marriage made in theatrical heaven, but here the knot is tied with such gusto that it really doesn't matter what Fo is selling. The audience is buying—at least at Sunday's press opening.

It takes a while to seal the deal, though. As you walk in, there's a pregame Vegas lounge act—a crooner and pianist—traipsing through "Fly Me to the Moon," "Our Love Is Here to Stay," "Santa Lucia," and even going through the audience looking for a birthday boy or girl. Even if you're an ART regular, you may not realize it's Thomas Derrah singing and Will LeBow tickling the ivories until Derrah delivers the tongue-in-cheek preamble that the hunger and homelessness we are about to see in the play could never happen in 1990s America.

Enter Tomei and Caroline Hall onto Anita Stewart's set, which looks like an Italian version of "The Honeymooners," with dingy appliances and a backdrop of crowded tenements. In fact, Jenkins and/or Belgrader must have had 1950s American television in mind, as the production is "The Honeymooners" (Derrah as Ralph and Ken Cheeseman and Ed) meets "I Love Lucy" (Tomei as Lucy and Hall as Ethel). LeBow adds more comedic fuel to the fire as two different Keystone Kops, among other roles.

Tomei had been out shopping and because of hyperinflation, none of the housewives could afford groceries. They start chanting the title of the play and just walk out with the groceries. The problems are that not only are the police going door to door, but her husband, Derrah, is a law-and-order guy who would rather eat birdseed than break the law. She convinces Hall to hide some of the food under her coat and the fun begins, as Tomei invents stranger and stranger explanations for her friend's sudden pregnancy—and Hall has to go through stranger and stranger contortions to make it convincing.

Derrah is, as always, a great comedian who here makes the lunkheadedness of his character delightfully ludicrous. There's also a farcical precision here that is the best I've seen on an ART stage—or perhaps any other in the area. Of course, this is farce with a message, as Tomei plays off a credulity that wouldn't be possible if Derrah, Cheeseman, and LeBow weren't so ignorant of reproductive reality or if they weren't so superstitious about religion, miracles, curses, and capitalism. Although Tomei has the Lucy part, she's more a straight woman or ringmaster for the hilarity when Hall goes into labor and for the myopic menfolk. You might not have known it from her last appearance in the area, "Wait Until Dark," but the "My Cousin Vinny" Oscar winner is a gifted and versatile stage actress. Tomei ties the story up in knots, but it's Derrah and LeBow who are likely to leave you in stitches.

Belgrader's direction doesn't force the pace, which starts out a bit slow, but he makes the wait worth it. I can't pretend to be an expert on Fo, but Jenkins seems to have done a superlative job staying true to his hero while updating his work so that it doesn't seem stuck in the 1970s. Fo's clunky ending remains, where Derrah steps out of character to deliver the message, or sermon, to the audience. But Belgrader gets it back on track, and squares the circle with the lounge act by having the characters lip-synch "Stand By Me" in Italian. You may not rise to your feet yelling "Vive La Revolution" at the end, but that would have been the wrong language anyway. A simple "Bravo! Brava!" would be entirely appropriate.

DEREK Walcott

Born in 1930 on the island of St. Lucia in the West Indies, Derek Walcott is from a mixed-race, English-speaking middle-class Protestant family. At the time of his birth the island was still a British colony, though the majority of the population was Catholic and French speaking. Walcott studied French, Latin, and Spanish at the University College of the West Indies in Jamaica and graduated with a degree in 1953. He then taught at several different schools in Grenada, St. Lucia, and Jamaica while writing poetry and plays. Before his thirtieth birthday he published three volumes of poetry and saw twelve of his plays produced in the Caribbean. In 1958 a Rockefeller Foundation grant allowed him to study with the director José Quintero and the Phoenix Theater Company in New York City. In the following year Walcott settled in Trinidad and founded the Trinidad Theater Workshop. Derek Walcott's work has often been characterized as embodying equally his Caribbean cultural roots, his love of English literature, and the tensions of his African and European heritage. He is the author of seventeen volumes of poetry and ten volumes of drama. His plays include *Ti-Jean and His Brothers* (1958), *Dream on Monkey Mountain* (1967), *Pantomine* (1978), an adaptation of the *Odyssey* (1993), and the recent book for the Broadway musical *The Capeman* (1998) with Paul Simon. In 1981 Walcott was named professor of creative writing at Boston University and founded the Boston Playwrights' Theater. He now divides his time between Boston and his native Caribbean. In 1992 the Swedish Academy awarded him the Nobel Prize for Literature.

COMMENTARY ON *PANTOMIME*

The word *pantomime* has two connotations, both theatrical. The first is generic: action or gestures without words as a means of expression. The second is a specific type of dramatic entertainment found in England, usually performed during the Christmas season. Based on popular stories or fairy tales, pantomimes include music, dancing, farcical tricks, and often include traditional characters, such as a clown figure. Walcott clearly draws on the second meaning by having his two characters rehearse a pantomime in which the "popular" story is *Robinson Crusoe* (1719). Like Daniel Defoe's novel, *Pantomime* has two male characters: one white, one black. In the play a mutually defining relationship unfolds between a representative of the colonizer and a representative of the colonized. This relationship is consciously depicted by Walcott through the pantomime that his characters, Trewe and Philip, rehearse and perform.

Walcott drew his inspiration for the play from the lively conversation he witnessed one night between a white English hotel manager and a local black employee. He was struck by the "equality in the exchange of repartee that dissolved racial, class, and economic differences" (King 295). This relationship is haunted, however, by the colonial history of the West Indies. The Crusoe-Friday relationship from Defoe's novel is an enduring metaphor in Western literature concerned with colony and race. It appears in other works as diverse as Shakespeare's *The Tempest* (1611), Aphra Behn's novel *Oroonoko* (1688), Herman Melville's *Moby Dick* (1851), and Mark Twain's *Adventures of Huckleberry Finn* (1884).

Shortly before the close of Act 1, Philip announces to Trewe (and to the audience): "This is the story. . . . This is history. This moment that we are now acting here is the history of imperialism; it's nothing less than that." *Pantomime* is a microcosm of the predicament of colony. While Philip and Trewe negotiate their roles in the pantomime, they are also negotiating their roles in the postcolony. Through a series of role reversals and a shifting locus of power, their identities are constantly being redefined by their relationship. The critic Patrick Taylor in his essay "Myth and Reality in Caribbean Narrative: Derek Walcott's *Pantomime*" states,

> The mythical form, the Prospero-Caliban archetype, is transformed by the content of the play, the reality of man in history. *Pantomime is a mimesis* or creative imitation of a social drama structured in terms of mimicry. Walcott's play takes this Pantomime form (the Crusoe drama) as its content and opens it to the possibilities of liberating narrative. We are challenged to appropriate the text in terms of our own reality, in terms of the faithful overthrow of myth, in terms, we might want to add, of the content of neocolonialism *today*.

The play is Walcott's testament to reconciliation and renegotiation and remains a major statement about the West Indies in his body of drama.

PANTOMIME
Derek Walcott

For Wilbert Holder

CHARACTERS

HARRY TREWE, *English, mid-forties, owner of the Castaways Guest House, retired actor*

JACKSON PHILIP, *Trinidadian, forty, his factotum, retired calypsonian*

The action takes place in a gazebo on the edge of a cliff, part of a guest house on the island of Tobago, West Indies.

ACT ONE

A small summerhouse or gazebo, painted white, with a few plants and a table set for breakfast. Harry Trewe enters—in white, carrying a tape recorder, which he rests on the table. He starts the machine.

HARRY (*Sings and dances*).

> It's our Christmas panto,
> it's called: Robinson Crusoe.
> We're awfully glad that you've shown up,
> it's for kiddies as well as for grown-ups.
> Our purpose is to please:
> so now with our magic wand . . .

(*Dissatisfied with the routine, he switches off the machine. Rehearses his dance. Then presses the maching again*)

> Just picture a lonely island
> and a beach with its golden sand.
> There walks a single man
> in the beautiful West Indies!

(*He turns off the machine. Stands, staring out to sea. Then exits with the tape recorder. Stage empty for a few beats, then Jackson, in an open, white waiter's jacket and black trousers, but barefoot, enters with a breakfast tray. He puts the tray down, looks around*)

JACKSON. Mr. Trewe?

(*English accent*)

Mr. Trewe, your scramble eggs is here! *are* here!

(*Creole accent*)

You hear, Mr. Trewe? I here wid your eggs!

(*English accent*)

Are you in there?

(*To himself*)

And when the eggs get cold, is I to catch.

(*He fans the eggs with one hand*)

What the hell I doing? That ain't go heat them. It go make them more cold. Well, he must be leap off the ledge. At long last. Well, if he ain't dead, he could call.

(*He exits with tray. Stage bare. Harry returns, carrying a hat made of goatskin and a goatskin parasol. He puts on the hat, shoulders the parasol, and circles the table. Then he recoils, looking down at the floor*)

HARRY (*Sings and dances*).

> Is this the footpring of a naked man,
> or is it the naked footprint of a man,
> that startles me this morning on this bright and golden
>   sand.

(*To audience*)

> There's no one here but I,
> just the sea and lonely sky . . .

(*Pauses*)

Yes . . . and how the hell did it go on?

(*Jackson enters, without the tray. Studies Harry*)

JACKSON. Morning, Mr. Trewe. Your breakfast ready.
HARRY. So how're you this morning, Jackson?
JACKSON. Oh, fair to fine, with seas moderate, with waves three to four feet in open water, and you, sir?
HARRY. Overcast with sunny periods, with the possibility of heavy showers by mid-afternoon, I'd say, Jackson.
JACKSON. Heavy showers, Mr. Trewe?
HARRY. Heavy showers. I'm so bloody bored I could burst into tears.

JACKSON. I bringing in breakfast.

HARRY. You do that, Friday.

JACKSON. Friday? It ain't go keep.

HARRY (*Gesturing*). Friday, you, bring Crusoe, me, breakfast now. Crusoe hungry.

JACKSON. Mr. Trewe, you come back with that same rake again? I tell you, I ain't no actor, and I ain't walking in front a set of tourists naked playing cannibal. Carnival, but not canni-bal.

HARRY. What tourists? We're closed for repairs. We're the only ones in the guest house. Apart from the carpenter, if he ever shows up.

JACKSON. Well, you ain't seeing him today, because he was out on a heavy lime last night . . . Saturday, you know? And with the peanuts you does pay him for overtime.

HARRY. All right, then. It's goodbye!

(*He climbs onto the ledge between the uprights, teetering, walking slowly*)

JACKSON. Get offa that ledge, Mr. Trewe! Is a straight drop to them rocks!

(*Harry kneels, arms extended, Jolson-style*)

HARRY. Hold on below there, sonny boooy! Daddy's a-coming. Your papa's a-coming, Sonnnnneee Boooooooy! (*To Jackson*) You're watching the great Harry Trewe and his high-wire act.

JACKSON. You watching Jackson Phillip and his disappearing act.

(*Turning to leave*)

HARRY (*Jumping down*). I'm not a suicide, Jackson. It's a good act, but you never read the reviews. It would be too exasperating, anyway.

JACKSON. What, sir?

HARRY. Attempted suicide in a Third World country. You can't leave a note because the pencils break, you can't cut your wrist with the local blades . . .

JACKSON. We trying we best, sir, since all you gone.

HARRY. Doesn't matter if we're a minority group. Suicides are taxpayers, too, you know, Jackson.

JACKSON. Except it ain't going be suicide. They go say I push you. So, now the fun and dance done, sir, breakfast now?

HARRY. I'm rotting from insomnia, Jackson. I've been up since three, hearing imaginary guests arriving in the rooms, and I haven't slept since. I nearly came around the back to have a little talk. I started thinking about the same bloody problem, which is, What entertainment can we give the guests?

JACKSON. They ain't guests, Mr. Trewe. They's casualties.

HARRY. How do you mean?

JACKSON. This hotel like a hospital. The toilet catch asthma, the air-condition got ague, the front-balcony rail missing four teet', and every minute the fridge like it dancing the Shango . . . brrgudup . . . jukjuk . . . brrugudup. Is no wonder that the carpenter collapse. Termites jumping like steel band in the foundations.

HARRY. For fifty dollars a day they want Acapulco?

JACKSON. Try giving them the basics: Food. Water. Shelter. They ain't shipwrecked, they pay in advance for their vacation.

HARRY. Very funny. But the ad says, "Tours" and "Nightly Entertainment." Well, Christ, after they've seen the molting parrot in the lobby and the faded sea fans, they'll be pretty livid if there's no "nightly entertainment," and so would you, right? So, Mr. Jackson, it's your neck and mine. We open next Friday.

JACKSON. Breakfast, sir. Or else is overtime.

HARRY. I kept thinking about this panto I co-authored, man. *Robinson Crusoe*, and I picked up this old script. I can bring it all down to your level, with just two characters. Crusoe, Man Friday, maybe even the parrot, if that horny old bugger will remember his lines . . .

JACKSON. Since we on the subject, Mr. Trewe, I am compelled to report that parrot again.

HARRY. No, not again, Jackson?

JACKSON. Yes.

HARRY (*Imitating parrot*). Heinegger, Heinegger. (*In his own voice*) Correct?

JACKSON. Wait, wait! I know your explanation: that a old German called Herr Heinegger used to own this place, and that when that maquereau of a macaw keep cracking: "Heinegger, Heinegger," he remembering the Nazi and not heckling me, but it playing a little havoc with me nerves. This is my fifth report. I am marking them down. Language is ideas, Mr. Trewe. And I think that this pre-colonial parrot have the wrong idea.

HARRY. It's his accent, Jackson. He's a Creole parrot. What can I do?

JACKSON. Well, I am not saying not to give the bird a fair trial, but I see nothing wrong in taking him out the cage at dawn, blindfolding the bitch, giving him a last cigarette if he want it, lining him up against the garden wall, and perforating his arse by firing squad.

HARRY. The war's over, Jackson! And how can a bloody parrot be prejudiced?

JACKSON. The same damn way they corrupt a child. By their upbringing. That parrot survive from a pre-colonial epoch, Mr. Trewe, and if it want to last in Trinidad and Tobago, then it go have to adjust.

(*Long pause*)

HARRY (*Leaping up*). Do you think we could work him into the panto? Give him something to do? Crusoe had a parrot, didn't he? You're right, Jackson, let's drop him from the show.

JACKSON. Mr. Trewe, you are a truly, truly stubborn man. I am *not* putting that old goatskin hat on my head and making an ass of myself for a million dollars, and I have said so already.

HARRY. You got it wrong. I put the hat on, I'm . . . Wait, wait a minute. *Cut! Cut!* You know what would be a heavy twist, heavy with irony?

JACKSON. What, Mr. Trewe?

HARRY. We reverse it.

(*Pause*)

JACKSON. You mean you prepared to walk round naked as your mother make you, in your jockstrap, playing a white cannibal in front of your own people? You're a real actor! And you got balls, too, excuse me, Mr. Trewe, to even consider doing a think like that! Good. Joke finish. Breakfast now, eh? Because I ha' to fix the sun deck since the carpenter ain't reach.

HARRY. All right, breakfast. Just heat it a little.

JACKSON. Right, sir. The coffee must be warm still. But I best do some brand-new scramble eggs.

HARRY. Never mind the eggs, then. Slip in some toast, butter, and jam.

JACKSON. How long you in this hotel business, sir? No butter. Marge. No sugar. Big strike. Island-wide shortage. We down to half a bag.

HARRY. Don't forget I've heard you sing calypsos, Jackson. Right back there in the kitchen.

JACKSON. Mr. Trewe, every day I keep begging you to stop trying to make a entertainer out of me. I finish with show business. I finish with Trinidad. I come to Tobago for peace and quiet. I quite satisfy. If you ain't want me to resign, best drop the topic.

(*Exits. Harry sits at the table, staring out to sea. He is reciting softly to himself, then more audibly*)

HARRY.

"Alone, alone, all, all alone,
Alone on a wide wide sea . . .
I bit my arm, I sucked the blood,
And cried, A sail! a sail!"

(*He removes the hat, then his shirt, rolls up his trousers, removes them, puts them back on, removes them again*)

Mastah . . . Mastah . . . Friday sorry. Friday never do it again. Master.

(*Jackson enters with breakfast tray, groans, turns to leave. Returns*)

JACKSON. Mr. Trewe, what it is going on on this blessed Sunday morning, if I may ask?

HARRY. I was feeling what it was like to be Friday.

JACKSON. Well, Mr. Trewe, you ain't mind putting back on your pants?

HARRY. Why can't I eat breakfast like this?

JACKSON. Because I am here. I happen to be here. I am the one serving you, Mr. Trewe.

HARRY. There's nobody here.

JACKSON. Mr. Harry, you putting on back your pants?

HARRY. You're frightened of something?

JACKSON. You putting on back your pants?

HARRY. What're you afraid of? Think I'm bent? That's such a corny interpretation of the Crusoe-Friday relationship, boy. My son's been dead three years, Jackson, and I'vn't had much interest in women since, but I haven't gone queer, either. And to be a flasher, you need an audience.

JACKSON. Mr. Trewe, I am trying to explain that I myself feel like a ass holding this tray in my hand while you standing up there naked, and that if anybody should happen to pass, my name is immediately mud. So, when you put back on your pants, I will serve your breakfast.

HARRY. Actors do this sort of thing. I'm getting into a part.

JACKSON. Don't bother getting into the part, get into the pants. Please.

HARRY. Why? You've got me worried now, Jackson.

JACKSON (*Exploding*). *Put on your blasted pants, man! You like a blasted child, you know!*

(*Silence. Harry puts on his pants*)

HARRY. Shirt, too?

(*Jackson sucks his teeth*)

There.

(*Harry puts on his shirt*)

You people are such prudes, you know that? What's it in you, Jackson, that gets so Victorian about a man in his own hotel deciding to have breakfast in his own underwear, on a totally deserted Sunday morning?

JACKSON. Manners, sir. Manners.

(*He puts down the tray*)

HARRY. Sit.

JACKSON. Sit? Sit where? How you mean, sit?

HARRY. Sit, and I'll serve breakfast. You can teach me manners. There's more manners in serving than in being served.

JACKSON. I ain't know what it is eating you this Sunday morning, you hear, Mr. Trewe, but I don't feel you have any right to mama-guy me, because I is a big man with three children, all outside. Now, being served by a white man ain't no big deal for me. It happen to me every day in New York, so it's not going to be any particularly thrilling experience. I would like to get breakfast finish with, wash up, finish my work, and go for my sea bath. Now I have worked here six months and never lost my temper, but it wouldn't take much more for me to fling this whole fucking tray out in that sea and get somebody more to your sexual taste.

HARRY (*Laughs*). Aha!

JACKSON. Not aha, oho!

HARRY (*Drawing out a chair*). Mr. Phillips . . .

JACKSON. Phillip. What?

HARRY. Your reservation.

JACKSON. You want me to play this game, eh? (*He walks around, goes to a corner of the gazebo*)

I'll tell you something, you hear, Mr. Trewe? And listen to me good, good. Once and for all. My sense of humor can stretch so far. Then it does snap. You see that sea out there? You know where I born? I born over there. Trinidad. I was a very serious steel-band man, too. And where I come from is a very serious place. I used to get into some serious trouble. A man keep bugging my arse once. A bad john called Boysie. Indian fellow, want to play nigger. Every day in that panyard he would come making joke with nigger boy this, and so on, and I used to just laugh and tell him stop, but he keep laughing and I keep laughing and he going on and I begging him to stop and two of us laughing, until . . .

(*He turns, goes to the tray, and picks up a fork*)

one day, just out of the blue, I pick up a ice pick and walk over to where he and two fellers was playing card, and I nail that ice pick through his hand to the table, and I laugh, and I walk away.

HARRY. Your table, Mr. Phillip.

(*Silence, Jackson shrugs, sits at the table*)

JACKSON. Okay, then. Until.

HARRY. You know, if you want to exchange war experiences, lad, I could bore you with a couple of mine. Want to hear?

JACKSON. My shift is seven-thirty to one.

(*He folds his arms. Harry offers him a cigarette*)

I don't smoke on duty.

HARRY. We put on a show in the army once. Ground crew. RAF. In what used to be Palestine. A Christmas panto. Another one. And yours truly here was the dame. The dame in a panto is played by a man. Well, I got the part. Wrote the music, the book, everything, whatever original music there was. *Aladdin and His Wonderful Vamp.* Very obscene, of course, I was the Wonderful Vamp. Terrific reaction all around. Thanks to me music-hall background. Went down great. Well, there was a party afterward. Then a big sergeant in charge of maintenance started this very boring business of confusing my genius with my life. Kept pinching my arse and so on. It got kind of boring after a while. Well, he was the size of a truck, mate. And there wasn't much I could do but keep blushing and pretending to be liking it. But the Wonderful Vamp was waiting outside for him, the Wonderful Vamp and a wrench this big, and after that, laddie, it took all of maintenance to put him back again.

JACKSON. That is white-man fighting. Anyway, Mr. Trewe, I feel the fun finish; I would like, with your permission, to get up now and fix up the sun deck. 'Cause when rain fall . . .

HARRY. Forget the sun deck. I'd say, Jackson, that we've come closer to a mutual respect, and that things need not get that hostile. Sit, and let me explain what I had in mind.

JACKSON. I take it that's an order?

HARRY. You want it to be an order? Okay, it's an order.

JACKSON. It didn't sound like no order.

HARRY. Look, I'm a liberal, Jackson. I've done the whole routine. Aldermaston, Suez, Ban the Bomb, Burn the Bra, Pity the Poor Pakis, et cetera. I've even tried jumping up to the steel band at Notting Hill Gate, and I'd no idea I'd wind up in this ironic position of giving orders, but if the new script I've been given says: HARRY TREWE, HOTEL MANAGER, then I'm going to play Harry Trewe, Hotel Manager, to the hilt, damnit. So *sit* down! Please. Oh, goddamnit, *sit . . . down . . .*

(*Jackson sits. Nods*)

Good. Relax. Smoke. Have a cup of tepid coffee. I sat up from about three this morning, working out this whole skit in my head.

(*Pause*)

Mind putting that hat on for a second, it will help my point. Come on. It'll make things clearer.

(*He gives Jackson the goatskin hat. Jackson, after a pause, puts it on*)

JACKSON. I'll take that cigarette.

(*Harry hands over a cigarette*)

HARRY. They've seen that stuff, time after time. Limbo, dancing girls, fire-eating . . .

JACKSON. Light.

HARRY. Oh, sorry.

(*He lights Jackson's cigarette*)

JACKSON. I listening.

HARRY. We could turn this little place right here into a little cabaret, with some very witty acts. Build up the right audience. Get an edge on the others. So, I thought, Suppose I get this material down to two people. Me and . . . well, me and somebody else. Robinson Crusoe and Man Friday. We could work up a good satire, you know, on the master-servant—no offense—relationship. Labor-management, white-black, and so on . . . Making some trenchant points about topical things, you know. Add that show to the special dinner for the price of one ticket . . .

JACKSON. You have to have music.

HARRY. Pardon?

JACKSON. A show like that should have music. Just a lot of talk is very boring.

HARRY. Right. But I'd have to have somebody help me, and that's where I thought . . . Want to take the hat off?

JACKSON. It ain't bothering me. When you going make your point?

HARRY. We had that little Carnival contest with the staff and you knocked them out improvising, remember that? You had the bloody guests in stitches . . .

JACKSON. You ain't start to talk money yet, Mr. Harry.

HARRY. Just improvising with the quatro. And not the usual welcome to Port of Spain, I am glad to see you again, but I'll tell you, artist to artist, I recognized a real pro, and this is the point of the hat. I want to make a point about the hotel industry, about manners, conduct, to generally improve relations all around. So, whoever it is, you or whoever, plays Crusoe, and I, or whoever it is, get to play Friday, and imagine first of all the humor and then the impact of that. What you think?

JACKSON. You want my honest, professional opinion?

HARRY. Fire away.

JACKSON. I think it is shit.

HARRY. I've never been in shit in my life, my boy.

JACKSON. It sound like shit to me, but I could be wrong.

HARRY. You could say things in fun about this place, about the whole Caribbean, that would hurt while people laughed. You get half the gate.

JACKSON. Half?

HARRY. What do you want?

JACKSON. I want you to come to your senses, let me fix the sun deck and get down to the beach for my sea bath. So, I put on this hat, I pick up this parasol, and I walk like a mama-poule up and down this stage and you have a black man playing Robinson Crusoe and then a half-naked, white, fish-belly man playing Friday, and you want to tell me it ain't shit?

HARRY. It could be hilarious!

JACKSON. Hilarious, Mr. Trewe? Supposing I wasn't a waiter, and instead of breakfast I was serving you communion, this Sunday morning on this tropical island, and I turn to you, Friday, to teach you my faith, and I tell you, kneel down and eat this man. Well, kneel, nuh! What you think you would say, eh?

(*Pause*)

You, this white savage?

HARRY. No, that's cannibalism.

JACKSON. Is no more cannibalism than to get a god. Suppose I make you tell me: For three hundred years I have made you my servant. For three hundred years . . .

HARRY. It's pantomime, Jackson, just keep it light . . . Make them laugh.

JACKSON. Okay. (*Giggling*) For three hundred years I served you. Three hundred years I served you breakfast in . . . in my white jacket on a white veranda, boss, bwana, effendi, bacra, sahib . . . in that sun that never set on your empire I was your shadow, I did what you did, boss, bwana, ef-

fendi, bacra, sahib . . . that was my pantomime. Every movement you made, your shadow copied . . .

(*Stops giggling*)

and you smiled at me as a child does smile at his shadow's helpless obedience, boss, bwana, effendi, bacra, sahib, Mr. Crusoe. Now . . .

HARRY. Now?

(*Jackson's speech is enacted in a trance-like drone, a zombie*)

JACKSON. But after a while the child does get frighten of the shadow he make. He say to himself, That is too much obedience, I better hads stop. But the shadow don't stop, no matter if the child stop playing that pantomime, and the shadow does follow the child everywhere; when he praying, the shadow pray too, when he turn round frighten, the shadow turn round too, when he hide under the sheet, the shadow hiding too. He cannot get rid of it, no matter what, and that is the power and black magic of the shadow, boss, bwana, effendi, bacra, sahib, until it is the shadow that start dominating the child, it is the servant that start dominating the master . . .

(*Laughs maniacally, like The Shadow*)

and that is the victory of the shadow, boss.

(*Normally*)

And that is why all them Pakistani and West Indians in England, all them immigrant Fridays driving all you so crazy. And they go keep driving you crazy till you go mad. In that sun that never set, they's your shadow, you can't shake them off.

HARRY. Got really carried away that time, didn't you? It's pantomime, Jackson, keep it light. Improvise!

JACKSON. You mean we making it up as we go along?

HARRY. Right!

JACKSON. Right! I in dat!

(*He assumes a stern stance and points stiffly*)

Robinson obey Thursday now. Speak Thursday language. Obey Thursday gods.

HARRY. Jesus Christ!

JACKSON (*Inventing language*). Amaka nobo sakamaka khaki pants kamaluma Jesus Christ! Jesus Christ kamalogo!

(*Pause. Then with a violent gesture*)

Kamalongo kaba!

(*Meaning: Jesus is dead!*)

HARRY. Sure.

(*Pause. Peers forward. Then speaks to an imaginary projectionist, while Jackson stands, feet apart, arms folded, frowning, in the usual stance of the Noble Savage*)

Now, could you run it with the subtitles, please?

(*He walks over to Jackson, who remains rigid. Like a movie director*)

Let's have another take, Big Chief.

(*To imaginary camera*)

Roll it. Sound!

(*Jackson shoves Harry aside and strides to the table. He bangs the heel of his palm on the tabletop*)

JACKSON. Patamba! Patamba! Yes?

HARRY. You want us to strike the prop? The patamba?

(*To cameraman*)

Cut!

JACKSON (*To cameraman*). Rogoongo! Rogoongo!

(*Meaning: Keep it rolling*)

HARRY. Cut!

JACKSON. Rogoongo, damnit!

(*Defiantly, furiously, Jackson moves around, first signaling the camera to follow him, then pointing out the objects which he rechristens, shaking or hitting them violently. Slams table*)

Patamba!

(*Rattles beach chair*)

Backaraka! Backaraka!

(*Holds up cup, points with other hand*)

Banda!

(*Drops cup*)

Banda karan!

(*Puts his arm around Harry; points at him*)

Subu!

(*Faster, pointing*)

Masz!

(*Stamping the floor*)

Zohgooooor!

(*Rests his snoring head on his closed palms*)

Oma! Omaaaa!

(*Kneels, looking skyward. Pauses; eyes closed*)

Booora! Booora!

(*Meaning the world. Silence. He rises*)

Cut!

And dat is what it was like, before you come here with your table this and cup that.

HARRY. All right. Good audition. You get twenty dollars a day without dialogue.

JACKSON. But why?

HARRY. You never called anything by the same name twice. What's a table?

JACKSON. I forget.

HARRY. I remember: patamba!

JACKSON. Patamba?

HARRY. Right. You fake.

JACKSON. That's a breakfast table. *Ogushi*. That's a dressing table. *Amanga ogushi*. I remember now.

HARRY. I'll tell you one thing, friend. If you want me to learn your language, you'd better have a gun.

JACKSON. You best play Crusoe, chief. I surrender. All you win.

(*Points wearily*)

Table. Chair. Cup. Man. Jesus. I accept. I accept. All you win. Long time.

(*Smiles*)

HARRY. All right, then. Improvise, then. Sing us a song. In your new language, mate. In English. Go ahead. I challenge you.

JACKSON. You what?

(*Rises, takes up parasol, handling it like a guitar, and strolls around the front row of the audience*)

(*Sings*)

> I want to tell you 'bout Robinson Crusoe.
> He tell Friday, when I do so, do so.
> Whatever I do, you must do like me.
> He make Friday a Good Friday Bohbolee;*
> That was the first example of slavery,
> 'Cause I am still Friday and you ain't me.
> Now Crusoe he was this Christian and all,
> And Friday, his slave, was a cannibal,
> But one day things bound to go in reverse,
> With Crusoe the slave and Friday the boss.

HARRY. Then comes this part where Crusoe sings to the goat. Little hint of animal husbandry:

(*Kneels, embraces an imaginary goat, to the melody of "Swanee"*)

(*Sings*)
> Nanny, how I love you,
> How I love you,
> My dear old nanny . . .

---

*A Judas effigy beaten at Easter in Trinidad and Tobago.

JACKSON. Is a li'l obscene.

HARRY (*Music-hall style*). Me wife thought so. Know what I used to tell her? Obscene? Well, better to be obscene than not heard. How's that? Harry Trewe, I'm telling you again, the music hall's loss is calypso's gain.

(*Stops*)

(*Jackson pauses. Stares upward, muttering to himself. Harry turns. Jackson is signaling in the air with a self-congratulatory smile*)

HARRY. What is it? What've we stopped for?

(*Jackson hisses for silence from Harry, then returns to his reverie. Miming*)

Are you feeling all right, Jackson?

(*Jackson walks some distance away from Harry. An imaginary guitar suddenly appears in his hand. Harry circles him. Lifts one eyelid, listens to his heartbeat. Jackson revolves, Harry revolves with him. Jackson's whole body is now silently rocking in rhythm. He is laughing to himself. We hear, very loud, a calypso rhythm*)

Two can play this game, Jackson.

(*He strides around in imaginary straw hat, twirling a cane. We hear, very loud, music hall. It stops. Harry peers at Jackson*)

JACKSON. You see what you start?

(*Sings*)

> Well, a Limey name Trewe came to Tobago.
> He was in show business but he had no show,
> so in desperation he turn to me
> and said: "Mister Phillip" is the two o' we,
> one classical actor, and one Creole . . .

HARRY. Wait! Hold it, hold it, man! Don't waste that. Try and remember it. I'll be right back.

JACKSON. Where you going?

HARRY. Tape. Repeat it, and try and keep it. That's what I meant, you see?

JACKSON. You start to exploit me already?

HARRY. That's right. Memorize it.

(*Exits quickly. Jackson removes his shirt and jacket, rolls up his pants above the knee, clears the breakfast tray to one side of the floor, overturns the table, and sits in it, as if it were a boat, as Harry returns with the machine*)

What's all this? I'm ready to tape. What're you up to?

(*Jackson sits in the upturned table, rowing calmly, and from time to time surveying the horizon. He looks up toward the sky, shielding his face from the glare with one hand; then he gestures to Harry*)

What?

(*Jackson flaps his arms around leisurely, like a large sea bird, indicating that Harry should do the same*)

What? What about the song? You'll forget the bloody song. It was a fluke.

JACKSON (*Steps out from the table, crosses to Harry, irritated*). If I suppose to help you with this stupidness, we will have to cool it and collaborate a little bit. Now, I was in that boat, rowing, and I was looking up to the sky to see a storm gathering, and I wanted a big white sea bird beating inland from a storm. So what's the trouble, Mr. Trewe?

HARRY. Sea bird? What sea bird? I'm not going to play a fekking sea bird.

JACKSON. Mr. Trewe, I'm only asking you to play a white sea bird because I am supposed to play a black explorer.

HARRY. Well, I don't want to do it. Anyway, that's the silliest acting I've seen in a long time. And Robinson Crusoe wasn't *rowing* when he got shipwrecked; he was a huge boat. I didn't come here to play a sea bird, I came to tape the song.

JACKSON. Well, then, is either the sea bird or the song. And I don't see any reason why you have to call my acting silly. We suppose to improvise.

HARRY. All right, Jackson, all right. After I do this part, I hope you can remember the song. Now you just tell me, before we keep stopping, what I am supposed to do, how many animals I'm supposed to play, and . . . you know, and so on, and so on, and then when we get all that part fixed up, we'll tape the song, all right?

JACKSON. That suits me. Now, the way I see it here: whether Robinson Crusoe was on a big boat or not, the idea is that he got . . .

(*Pause*)

shipwrecked. So I . . . if I am supposed to play Robinson Crusoe my way, then I will choose the way in which I will get shipwrecked. Now, as Robinson Crusoe is rowing, he looks up and he sees this huge white sea bird, which is making loud sea-bird noises, because a storm is coming. And Robinson Crusoe looks up toward the sky and sees that there is this storm. Then, there is a large wave, and Robinson Crusoe finds himself on the beach.

HARRY. Am I supposed to play the beach? Because that's white . . .

JACKSON. Hilarious! Mr. Trewe. Now look, you know, I am doing *you* a favor. On this beach, right? Then he sees a lot of goats. And because he is naked and he needs clothes, he kills a goat, he takes off the skin, and he makes this parasol here and this hat, so he doesn't go around naked for everybody to see. Now I *know* that there is nobody there, but there is an audience, so the sooner Robinson Crusoe puts on his clothes, then the better and happier we will all be. I am going to go back in the boat. I am going to look up toward the sky. You will, *please*, make the sea-bird noises. I will do the wave, I will crash onto the sand, you will come down like a goat, and I will kill you, take off your skin, make a parasol *and* a hat, and after that, then I promise you that I will remember the song. And I will sing it to the best of my ability.

(*Pause*)

However shitty that is.

HARRY. I said "silly." Now listen . . .

JACKSON. Yes, Mr. Trewe?

HARRY. Okay, if you're a black explorer . . . Wait a minute . . . wait a minute. If you're really a white explorer but you're black, shouldn't I play a black sea bird because I'm white?

JACKSON. Are you . . . going to extend . . . the limits of prejudice to include . . . the flora and fauna of this island? I am entering the boat.

(*He is stepping into the upturned table or boat, as Harry halfheartedly imitates a bird, waving his arms*)

HARRY. Kekkkk, kekkkk, kekkk, kekkkk!

(*Stops*)

What's wrong?

JACKSON. What's wrong? Mr. Trewe, that is not a sea gull . . . that is some kind of . . . well, I don't know what it is . . . some kind of *jumbie* bird or something.

(*Pause*)

I am returning to the boat.

(*He carefully enters the boat, expecting an interrupting bird cry from Harry, but there is none, so he begins to row*)

HARRY. Kekk! Kekkk.

(*He hangs his arms down. Pause*)

Er. Jackson, wait a minute. Hold it a second. Come here a minute.

(*Jackson patiently gets out of the boat, elaborately pantomiming lowering his body into shallow water, releasing his hold on the boat, swimming a little distance toward shore, getting up from the shallows, shaking out his hair and hands, wiping his hands on his trousers, jumping up and down on one foot to unplug water from his clogged ear, seeing Harry, then walking wearily, like a man who has swum a tremendous distance, and collapsing at Harry's feet*)

Er, Jackson. This is too humiliating. Now, let's just forget it and please don't continue, or you're fired.

(*Jackson leisurely wipes his face with his hands*)

JACKSON. It don't go so, Mr. Trewe. You know me to be a meticulous man. I didn't want to do this job. I didn't even want to work here. You convinced me to work here. I have worked as meticulously as I can, until I have been promoted. This morning I had no intention of doing what I am doing now; you have always admired the fact that whatever I begin, I finish. Now, I will accept my resignation, if you want me to, *after* we have finished this thing. But I am not leaving in the middle of a job, that has never been my policy. So you can sit down, as usual, and watch me work, but until I have finished this whole business of Robinson Crusoe being in the boat

(*He rises and repeats the pantomime*)

looking at an imaginary sea bird, being shipwrecked, killing a goat, making this hat *and* this parasol, walking up the beach and finding a naked footprint, which should take me into about another ten or twelve minutes, at the most, I will pack my things and I will leave, and you can play *Robinson Crusoe* all by yourself. My plans were, after this, to take the table like this . . .

(*He goes to the table, puts it upright*)

Let me show you: take the table, turn it all around, go under the table . . .

(*He goes under the table*)

and this would now have become Robinson Crusoe's hut.

(*Emerges from under the table and, without looking at Harry, continues to talk*)

Now, you just tell me if you think I am overdoing it, or if you think it's more or less what we agreed on?

(*Pause*)

Okay, But I am not resigning.

(*Turns to Harry slowly*)

You see, it's your people who introduced us to this culture: Shakespeare, *Robinson Crusoe*, the classics, and so on, and when we start getting as good as them, you can't leave halfway. So, I will continue? Please?

HARRY. No, Jackson. You will *not* continue. You will straighten this table, put back the tablecloth, take away the breakfast things, give me back the hat, put your jacket back on, and we will continue as normal and forget the whole matter. Now, I'm very serious, I've had enough of this farce. I would like to stop.

JACKSON. May I say what I think, Mr. Trewe? I think it's a matter of prejudice. I think that you cannot believe: one: that I can act, and two: that any black man should play Robinson Crusoe. A little while aback, I came out here quite calmly and normally with the breakfast things and find you almost stark naked, kneeling down, and you told me you were getting into your part. Here am I getting into *my* part and you object. This is the story . . . this is history. This moment that we are now acting here is the history of imperialism; it's nothing less than that. And I don't think that I can—should—concede my getting into a part halfway and abandoning things, just because you, as my superior, give me orders. People become independent. Now, I could go down to that beach by myself with this hat, and I could play Robinson Crusoe, I could play Columbus, I could play Sir Francis Drake, I could play anybody discovering anywhere, but I don't want you to tell me when and where to draw the line!

(*Pause*)

Or what to discover and when to discover it. All right?

HARRY. Look, I'm sorry to interrupt you again, Jackson, but as I—you know—was watching you, I realized it's much more profound than that; that it could get offensive. We're trying to do something light, just a little pantomime, a little satire, a little picong. But if you take this thing seriously, we might commit Art, which is a kind of crime in this society . . . I mean, there'd be a lot of things there that people . . . well, it would make them think too much, and well, we don't want that . . . we just want a little . . . entertainment.

JACKSON. How do you mean, Mr. Trewe?

HARRY. Well, I mean if you . . . well, I mean. If you did the whole thing in reverse . . . I mean, okay, well, all right . . . you've got this black man . . . no, no . . . all right. You've got this man who is black, Robinson Crusoe, and he discovers this island on which there is this white cannibal, all right?

JACKSON. Yes. That is, after he has killed the goat . . .

HARRY. Yes, I know, I know. After he has killed the goat and made a . . . the hat, the parasol, and all of that . . . and, anyway, he comes across this man called Friday.

JACKSON. How do you know I mightn't choose to call him Thursday? Do I have to copy every . . . I mean, are we improvising?

HARRY. All right, so it's Thursday. He comes across this naked white cannibal called Thursday, you know. And then look at what would happen. He would have to start to . . . well, he'd have to, sorry . . . This cannibal, who is a Christian, would have to start unlearning his Christianity. He would have to be taught . . . I mean . . . he'd have to be taught by this—African . . . that everything was wrong, that what he was doing . . . I mean, for nearly two thousand years . . . was wrong. That his civilization, his culture, his whatever, was . . . *horrible*. Was all . . . wrong. Barbarous, I mean, you know. And Crusoe would then have to teach him things like, you know, about . . . Africa, his gods, patamba, and so on . . . and it would get very, very complicated, and I suppose ultimately it would be very boring, and what we'd have on our hands would be . . . would be a play and not a little pantomime . . .

JACKSON. I'm too ambitious?

HARRY. No, no, the whole thing would have to be reversed; white would become black, you know . . .

JACKSON. (*Smiling*) You see, Mr. Trewe, I don't see anything wrong with that, up to now.

HARRY. Well, I do. It's not the sort of thing I want, and I think you'd better clean up, and I'm going inside, and when I come back I'd like this whole place just as it was. I mean, just before everything started.

JACKSON. You mean you'd like it returned to its primal state? Natural? Before Crusoe finds Thursday? But, you see, that is not history. That is not the world.

HARRY. No, no, I don't give an Eskimo's fart about the world, Jackson. I just want this little place here *cleaned up,* and I'd like you to get back to fixing the sun deck. Let's forget the whole matter. Righto. Excuse me.

(*He is leaving. Jackson's tone will stop him*)

JACKSON. Very well. So I take it you don't want to hear the song, neither?

HARRY. No, no, I'm afraid not. I think really it was a silly idea, it's all my fault, and I'd like things to return to where they were.

JACKSON. The story of the British Empire, Mr. Trewe. However, it is too late. The history of the British Empire.

HARRY. Now, how do you get that?

JACKSON. Well, you come to a place, you find that place as God make it; like Robinson Crusoe, you civilize the natives; they try to do something, you turn around and you say to them: "You are not good enough, let's call the whole thing off, return things to normal, you go back to your position as slave or servant, I will keep mine as master, and we'll forget the whole thing ever happened." Correct? You would like me to accept this.

HARRY. You're really making this very difficult, Jackson. Are you hurt? Have I offended you?

JACKSON. Hurt? No, no, no. I didn't expect any less. I am not hurt.

(*Pause*)

I am just . . .

(*Pause*)

HARRY. You're just what?

JACKSON. I am just ashamed . . . of making such a fool of myself.

(*Pause*)

I expected . . . a little respect. That is all.

HARRY. I respect you . . . I just, I . . .

JACKSON. No. It's perfectly all right.

(*Harry goes to the table, straightens it*)

I . . . no . . . I'll fix the table myself.

(*He doesn't move*)

I am all right, thank you. Sir.

(*Harry stops fixing the table*)

(*With the hint of a British accent*)

Thank you very much.

HARRY (*Sighs*). I . . . am sorry . . . er . . .

(*Jackson moves toward the table*)

JACKSON. It's perfectly all right, sir. It's perfectly all . . . right.

(*Almost inaudibly*)

Thank you.

(*Harry begins to straighten the table again*)

No, thank you very much, don't touch anything.

(*Jackson is up against the table. Harry continues to straighten the table*)

Don't touch anything . . . Mr. Trewe. Please.

(*Jackson rests one arm on the table, fist closed. They watch each other for three beats*)

Now that . . . is MY order . . .

(*They watch each other for several beats as the lights fade*)

ACT TWO

Noon. White glare. Harry, with shirt unbuttoned, in a deck chair reading a paperback thriller. Sound of intermittent hammering from stage left, where Jackson is repairing the sun-deck slats. Harry rises, decides he should talk to Jackson about the noise, decides against it, and leans back in the deck chair, eyes closed. Hammering has stopped for a long while. Harry opens his eyes, senses Jackson's presence, turns suddenly, to see him standing quite close, shirtless, holding a hammer. Harry bolts from his chair.

JACKSON. You know something, sir? While I was up there nailing the sun deck, I just stay so and start giggling all by myself.

HARRY. Oh, yes? Why?

JACKSON. No, I was remembering a feller, you know . . . ahhh, he went for audition once for a play, you know, and the way he, you know, the way he prop . . . present himself to the people, said . . . ahmm, "You know, I am an actor, you know. I do all kind of acting, classical acting, Creole acting." That's when I laugh, you know?

(*Pause*)

I going back and fix the deck, then.

(*Moves off. Stops, turns*)

The . . . the hammering not disturbing you?

HARRY. No, no, it's fine. You have to do it, right? I mean, you volunteered, the carpenter didn't come, right?

JACKSON. Yes. Creole acting. I wonder what kind o' acting dat is.

(*Spins the hammer in the air and does or does not catch it*)

Yul Brynner. *Magnificent Seven.* Picture, papa! A kind of Western Creole acting. It ain't have no English cowboys, eh, Mr. Harry? Something wrong, boy, something wrong.

(*He exits. Harry lies back in the deck chair, the book on his chest, arms locked behind his head. Silence. Hammering violently resumes*)

(*Off*)

Kekkk, kekkkekk, kekk!
Kekkekk, kekkkekk, ekkek!

(*Harry rises, moves from the deck chair toward the sun deck*)

HARRY. Jackson. What the hell are you doing? What's that noise?

JACKSON (*Off; loud*). I doing like a black sea gull, suh!

HARRY. Well, it's very distracting.

JACKSON (*Off*). Sorry, sir.

(*Harry returns. Sits down on the deck chair. Waits for the hammering. Hammering resumes. Then stops. Silence. Then we hear*)

(*Singing loudly*)

I want to tell you 'bout Robinson Crusoe.
He tell Friday, when I do so, do so.
Whatever I do, you must do like me,
He make Friday a Good Friday Bohbolee

(*Spoken*)

And the chorus:

(*Sings*)

Laide-die
Laidie, lay-day, de-day-de-die,
Laidee-doo-day-dee-day-dee-die
Laidee-day-doh-dee-day-dee-die

Now that was the first example of slavery,
'Cause I am still Friday and you ain't me,
Now Crusoe he was this Christian and all,
Friday, his slave, was a cannibal,
But one day things bound to go in reverse,
With Crusoe the slave and Friday the boss . . .
Caiso, boy! Caiso!

(*Harry rises, goes toward the sun deck*)

HARRY. Jackson, man! Jesus!

(*He returns to the deck chair, is about to sit*)

JACKSON (*Off*). Two more lash and the sun deck finish, sir!

(*Harry waits*)

Stand by . . . here they come . . .
First lash . . .

(*Sound*)

Pow!
Second lash:

(*Two sounds*)

Pataow! Job complete! Lunch, Mr. Trewe? You want your lunch now? Couple sandwich or what?

HARRY (*Shouts without turning*). Just bring a couple beers from the icebox, Jackson. And the Scotch.

(*To himself*)

What the hell, let's all get drunk.

(*To Jackson*)

Bring some beer for yourself, too, Jackson!

JACKSON (*Off*). Thank you, Mr. Robinson . . . Thank you, Mr. Trewe, sir! *Cru-soe, Trewe-so!*

(*Faster*)

Crusoe-Trusoe, Robinson Trewe-so!

HARRY. Jesus, Jackson; cut that out and just bring the bloody beer!

JACKSON (*Off*). Right! A beer for you and a beer for me! Now, what else is it going to be? A sandwich for you, but none for me.

(*Harry picks up the paperback and opens it, removing a folded sheet of paper. He opens it and is reading it carefully, sometimes lifting his head, closing his eyes, as if remembering its contents, then reading again. He puts it into a pocket quickly as Jackson returns, carrying a tray with two beers, a bottle of Scotch, a pitcher of water, and two glasses. Jackson sets them down on the table*)

I'm here, sir. At your command.

HARRY. Sit down. Forget the sandwiches, I don't want to eat. Let's sit down, man to man, and have a drink. That was the most sarcastic hammering I've ever heard, and I know you were trying to get back at me with all those noises and that Uncle Tom crap. So let's have a drink, man to man, and try to work out what happened this morning, all right?

JACKSON. I've forgotten about this morning, sir.

HARRY. No, no, no, I mean, the rest of the day it's going to bother me, you know?

JACKSON. Well, I'm leaving at half-past one.

HARRY. No, but still . . . Let's . . . Okay. Scotch?

JACKSON. I'll stick to beer, sir, thank you.

(*Harry pours a Scotch and water, Jackson serves himself a beer. Both are still standing*)

HARRY. Sit over there, please, Mr. Phillip. On the deck chair.

(*Jackson sits on the deck chair, facing Harry*)

Cheers?

JACKSON. Cheers. Cheers. Deck chair and all.

(*They toast and drink*)

HARRY. All right. Look, I think you misunderstood me this morning.

JACKSON. Why don't we forget the whole thing, sir? Let me finish this beer and go for my sea bath, and you can spend the rest of the day all by yourself.

(*Pause*)

Well. What's wrong? What happen, sir? I said something wrong just now?

HARRY. This place isn't going to drive me crazy, Jackson. Not if I have to go mad preventing it. Not physically crazy; but you just start to think crazy thoughts, you know? At the beginning it's fine; there's the sea, the palm trees, monarch of all I survey and so on, all that postcard stuff. And then it just becomes another back yard. God, is there anything deadlier than Sunday afternoons in the tropics when you can't sleep? The horor and stillness of the heat, the shining, godforsaken sea, the bored and boring clouds? Especially in an empty boarding house. You sit by the stagnant pool counting the dead leaves drifting to the edge. I daresay the terror of emptiness made me want to act. I wasn't trying to humiliate you. I meant nothing by it. Now, I don't usually apologize to people. I don't do things to apologize for. When I do them, I mean them, but, in your case, I'd like to apologize.

JACKSON. Well, if you find here boring, go back home. Do something else, nuh?

HARRY. It's not that simple. It's a little more complicated than that. I mean, everything I own is sunk here, you see? There's a little matter of a brilliant actress who drank too much, and a car crash at Brighton after a panto . . . Well. That's neither here nor there now. Right? But I'm determined to make this place work. I gave up the theater for it.

JACKSON. Why?

HARRY. Why? I wanted to be the best. Well, among other things; oh, well, that's neither here nor there. Flopped at too many things, though. Including classical and Creole acting. I just want to make this place work, you know. And a desperate man'll try anything. Even at the cost of his sanity, maybe. I mean, I'd hate to believe that under everything else I was also prejudiced, as well. I wouldn't have any right here, right?

JACKSON. 'Tain't prejudice that bothering you, Mr. Trewe; you ain't no parrot to repeat opinion. No, is loneliness that sucking your soul as dry as the sun suck a crab shell. On a Sunday like this, I does watch you. The whole staff does study you. Walking round restless, staring at the sea. You remembering your wife and your son, not right? You ain't get over that yet?

HARRY. Jackson . . .

JACKSON. Is none of my business. But it really lonely here out of season. Is summer, and your own people gone, but come winter they go flock like sandpipers all down that beach. So you lonely, but I could make you forget all o' that. I could make H. Trewe, Esquire, a brand-new man. You come like a challenge.

HARRY. Think I keep to myself too much?

JACKSON. If! You would get your hair cut by phone. You drive so careful you make your car nervous. If you was in charge of the British Empire, you wouldn'ta lose it, you'da misplace it.

HARRY. I see, Jackson.

JACKSON. But all that could change if you do what I tell you.

HARRY. I don't want a new life, thanks.

JACKSON. Same life. Different man. But that stiff upper lip goin' have to quiver a little.

HARRY. What's all this? Obeah? "That old black magic"?

JACKSON. Nothing. I could have the next beer?

HARRY. Go ahead. I'm drinking Scotch.

(*Jackson takes the other beer, swallows deep, smacks his lips, grins at Harry*)

JACKSON. Nothing. We will have to continue from where we stop this morning. You will have to be Thursday.

HARRY. Aha, you bastard! It's a thrill giving orders, hey? But I'm not going through all that rubbish again.

JACKSON. All right. Stay as you want. But if you say yes, it go have to be man to man, and none of this boss-and-Jackson business, you see, Trewe . . . I mean, I just call you plain Trewe, for example, and I notice that give you a slight shock. Just a little twitch of the lip, but a shock all the same, eh, Trewe? You see? You twitch again. It would be just me and you, all right? You see, two of we both acting a role here we ain't really really believe in, you know. I ent think you strong enough to give people orders, and I know I ain't the kind who like taking *them*. So both of we doesn't have to *improvise* so much as *exaggerate*. We faking, faking all the time. But, man to man, I mean . . .

(*Pause*)

that could be something else. Right, Mr. Trewe?

HARRY. Aren't we man to man now?

JACKSON. No, no. We having one of them "playing man-to-man" talks, where a feller does look a next feller in the eye and say, "Le' we settle this thing, man to man," and this time the feller who smiling and saying it, his whole honest intention is to take that feller by the crotch and rip out he stones, and dig out he eye and leave him for corbeaux to pick.

(*Silence*)

HARRY. You know, that thing this morning had an effect on me, man to man now. I didn't think so much about the comedy of *Robinson Crusoe*, I thought what we were getting into was a little sad. So, when I went back to the room, I tried to rest before lunch, before you began all that vindictive hammering . . .

JACKSON. Vindictive?

HARRY. Man to man: that vindictive hammering and singing, and I thought, Well, maybe we could do it straight. Make a real straight thing out of it.

JACKSON. You mean like a tradegy. With one joke?

HARRY. Or a codemy, with none. You mispronounce words on purpose, don't you, Jackson?

(*Jackson smiles*)

Don't think for one second that I'm not up on your game, Jackson. You're playing the stage nigger with me. I'm an actor, you know. It's a smile in front and a dagger behind your back, right? Or the smile itself is the bloody dagger. I'm aware, chum. I'm aware.

JACKSON. The smile kinda rusty, sir, but it goes with the job. Just like the water in this hotel:

(*Demonstrates*)

I turn it on at seven and lock it off at one.

HARRY. Didn't hire you for the smile; I hired you for your voice. We've the same background. Old-time calypso, old-fashioned music hall:

(*Sings*)

> Oh, me wife can't cook and she looks like a horse
> And the way she makes coffee is grounds for divorce . . .

(*Does a few steps*)

> But when love is at stake she's my Worcester sauce . . .

(*Stops*)

Used to wow them with that. All me own work. Ah, the lost glories of the old music hall, the old provincials, grimy brocade, the old stars faded one by one. The brassy pantomimes! Come from an old music-hall family, you know, Jackson. Me mum had this place she ran for broken-down actors. Had tea with the greats as a tot.

(*Sings softly, hums*)

> Oh, me wife can't cook . . .

(*Silence*)

You married, Jackson?

JACKSON. I not too sure, sir.

HARRY. You're not sure?

JACKSON. That's what I said.

HARRY. I know what you mean. I wasn't sure I was when I was. My wife's remarried.

JACKSON. You showed me her photo. And the little boy own.

HARRY. But I'm not. Married. So there's absolutely no hearth for Crusoe to go home to. While you were up there, I rehearsed this thing.

(*Presents a folded piece of paper*)

Want to read it?

JACKSON. What . . . er . . . what is it . . . a poetry?

HARRY. No, no, not a poetry. A thing I wrote. Just a speech in the play . . . that if . . .

JACKSON. Oho, we back in the play again?

HARRY. Almost. You want to read it?

(*He offers the paper*)

JACKSON. All right.

HARRY. I thought—no offense, now. Man to man. If you were doing Robinson Crusoe, this is what you'd read.

JACKSON. You want me to read this, right?

HARRY. Yeah.

JACKSON (*Reads slowly*). "O silent sea, O wondrous sunset that I've gazed on ten thousand times, who will rescue me from this complete desolation? . . ."

(*Breaking*)

All o' this?

HARRY. If you don't mind. Don't act it. Just read it.

(*Jackson looks at him*)

No offense.

JACKSON (*Reads*). "Yes, this is paradise, I know. For I see around me the splendors of nature . . . "

HARRY. Don't act it . . .

JACKSON (*Pauses; then continues*). "How I'd like to fuflee this desolate rock."

(*Pauses*)

Fuflee? Pardon, but what is a fuflee, Mr. Trewe?

HARRY. A fuflee? I've got "fuflee" written there?

JACKSON (*Extends paper, points at word*). So, how you does fuflee, Mr. Harry? Is Anglo-Saxon English?

(*Harry kneels down and peers at the word. He rises*)

HARRY. It's F . . . then F-L-E-E—flee to express his hesitation. It's my own note as an actor. He quivers, he hesitates . . .

JACKSON. He quivers, he hesitates, but he still can't fuflee?

HARRY. Just leave that line out, Jackson.

JACKSON. I like it.

HARRY. *Leave it out!*

JACKSON. No fuflee?

HARRY. I said no.

JACKSON. Just because I read it wrong. I know the word "flee," you know. Like to take off. Flee. Faster than run.

Is the extra *F* you put in there so close to flee that had me saying fuflee like a damn ass, but le' we leave it in, nuh? One fuflee ain't go kill anybody. Much less bite them.

(*Silence*)

Get it?

HARRY. Don't take this personally . . .

JACKSON. No fuflees on old Crusoe, boy . . .

HARRY. But, if you're going to do professional theater, Jackson, don't take this personally, more discipline is required. All right?

JACKSON. You write it. Why you don't read it?

HARRY. I wanted to hear it. Okay, give it back . . .

JACKSON (*Loudly, defiantly*). "The ferns, the palms like silent sentinels, the wide and silent lagoons that briefly hold my passing, solitary reflection. The volcano . . . "

(*Stops*)

"The volcano." What?

HARRY. . . . "wreathed" . . .

JACKSON. Oho, oho . . . like a wreath? "The volcano *wreathed* in mist. But what is paradise without a woman? Adam in paradise!"

HARRY. Go ahead.

JACKSON (*Restrained*). "Adam in paradise had his woman to share this loneliness, but I miss the voice of even one consoling creature, the touch of a hand, the look of kind eyes. Where is the wife from whom I vowed never to be sundered? How old is my little son? If he could see his father like this, mad with memories of them . . . Even Job had his family. But I am alone, alone, I am all alone."

(*Pause*)

Oho. You write this?

HARRY. Yeah.

JACKSON. Is good. Very good.

HARRY. Thank you.

JACKSON. Touching. Very sad. But something missing.

HARRY. What?

JACKSON. Goats. You leave out the goats.

HARRY. The goats. So what? What've you got with goats, anyway?

JACKSON. Very funny. Very funny, sir.

HARRY. Try calling me Trewe.

JACKSON. Not yet. That will come. Stick to the point. You ask for my opinion and I *gave* you my opinion. No doubt I don't have the brains. But *my* point is that this man ain't facing reality. *There are goats* all around him.

HARRY. You're full of shit.

JACKSON. The man is not facing reality. He is not a practical man *shipwrecked*.

HARRY. I suppose that's the difference between classical and Creole acting?

(*He pours a drink and downs it furiously*)

JACKSON. If he is not practical, he is not Robinson Crusoe. And yes, is Creole acting, yes. Because years afterward his little son could look at the parasol and the hat and look at a picture of Daddy and boast: "My daddy smart, boy. He get shipwreck and first thing he do is he build a hut, then he kill a goat or two and make clothes, a parasol and a hat." That way Crusoe *achieve* something, and his son could boast . . .

HARRY. Only his son is dead.

JACKSON. Whose son dead?

HARRY. Crusoe's.

JACKSON. No, pardner. *Your* son dead. Crusoe wife and child waiting for him, and he is a practical man and he know somebody go come and save him . . .

HARRY (*Almost inaudibly*).

"I bit my arm, I sucked the blood,
And cried, 'A sail! a sail!'"

How the hell does he know "somebody go come and save him"? That's shit. That's not in his character at that moment. How the hell can he know? You're a cruel bastard . . .

JACKSON (*Enraged*). *Because, you fucking ass, he has faith!*

HARRY (*Laughing*). Faith? What faith?

JACKSON. He not sitting on his shipwrecked arse bawling out . . . what it is you have here?

(*Reads*)

"O . . ." Where is it?

(*Reads*)

"O silent sea, O wondrous sunset," and all that shit. No. He shipwrecked. He desperate, he hungry. He look up and he see this fucking goat with its fucking beard watching him and smiling, this goat with its forked fucking beard and square yellow eye just like the fucking devil, standing up there . . .

(*Pantomimes the goat and Crusoe in turn*)

smiling at him, and putting out its tongue and letting go one fucking *bleeeeeh*! And Robbie ent thinking 'bout his wife and son and O silent sea and O wondrous sunset; no, Robbie is the First True Creole, so he watching the goat with his eyes narrow, narrow, and he say: *blehhh*, eh? You muther-fucker, I go show you *blehhh* in your goat-ass, and vam, vam, next thing is Robbie and the goat, *mano a mano*, man to man, man to goat, goat to man, wrestling on the sand, and next thing we know we hearing one last faint, feeble *bleeeeeehhhhhhhhhhhhhhhh*, and Robbie is next seen walking up the beach with a goatskin hat and a goatskin umbrella, feeling like a million dollars because *he have faith*!

HARRY (*Applauds*). Bravo! You're the Christian. I am the cannibal. Bravo!

JACKSON. If I does hammer sarcastic, you does clap sarcastic. Now I want to pee.

HARRY. I think I'll join you.

JACKSON. So because I go and pee, you must pee, too?

HARRY. Subliminal suggestion.

JACKSON. Monkey see, monkey do.

HARRY. You're the bloody ape, mate. You people just came down from the trees.

JACKSON. Say that again, please.

HARRY. I'm going to keep that line.

JACKSON. Oho! Rehearse you rehearsing? I thought you was serious.

HARRY. You go have your pee. I'll turn over my monologue.

JACKSON. No, you best do it now, sir. Or it going to be on my mind while we rehearsing that what you really want to do is take a break and pee. We best go together, then.

HARRY. We'll call it the pee break. Off we go, then. How long will you be, then? You people take forever.

JACKSON. Maybe you should hold up a sign, sir, or give some sort of signal when you serious or when you joking, so I can know not to react. I would say five minutes.

HARRY. Five minutes? What is this, my friend, Niagara Falls?

JACKSON. It will take me . . . look, you want me to time it? I treat it like a ritual, I don't just pee for peeing's sake. It will take me about forty to fifty seconds to walk to the servants' toilets . . .

HARRY. Wait a second . . .

JACKSON. No, you wait, please, sir. That's almost one minute, take another fifty seconds to walk back, or even more, because after a good pee a man does be in a mood, both ruminative and grateful that the earth has received his libation, so that makes . . .

HARRY. Hold on, please.

JACKSON (*Voice rising*). Jesus, sir, give me a break, nuh? That is almost two minutes, and in between those two minutes it have such solemn and ruminative behavior as opening the fly, looking upward or downward, the ease and relief, the tender shaking, the solemn tucking in, like you putting a little baby back to sleep, the reverse zipping or buttoning, depending on the pants, then, with the self-congratulating washing of the hands, looking at yourself for at least half a minute in the mirror, then the drying of hands as if you were a master surgeon just finish a major operation, and the walk back . . .

HARRY. You said that. Any way you look at it, it's under five minutes, and I interrupted you because . . .

JACKSON. I could go and you could time me, to see if I on a go-slow, or wasting up my employer's precious time, but I know it will take at least five, unless, like most white people, you either don't flush it, a part I forgot, or just wipe your hands fast fast or not at all . . .

HARRY. Which white people, Jackson?

JACKSON. I was bathroom attendant at the Hilton, and I know men and races from their urinary habits, and most Englishmen . . .

HARRY. Most Englishmen . . . Look, I was trying to tell you, instead of going all the way round to the servants' lavatories, pop into my place, have a quick one, and that'll be under five bloody minutes in any circumstances and regardless of the capacity. Go on. I'm all right.

JACKSON. Use your bathroom, Mr. Harry?

HARRY. Go on, will you?

JACKSON. I want to get this. You giving me permission to go through your living room, with all your valuables lying about, with the picture of your wife watching me in case I should leave the bathroom open, and you are granting me the privilege of taking out my thing, doing my thing right there among all those lotions and expensive soaps, and . . . after I finish, wiping my hands on a clean towel?

HARRY. Since you make it so vividly horrible, why don't you just walk around to the servants' quarters and take as much time as you like? Five minutes won't kill me.

JACKSON. I mean, equality is equality and art is art, Mr. Harry, but to use those clean, rough Cannon towels . . . You mustn't rush things, people have to slide into independence. They give these islands independence so fast that people still ain't recover from the shock, so they pissing and wiping their hands indiscriminately. You don't want that to happen in this guest house, Mr. Harry. Let me take my little five minutes, as usual, and if you have to go, you go to your place, and I'll go to mine, and let's keep things that way until I can feel I can use your towels without a profound sense of gratitude, and you could, if you wanted, a little later maybe, walk round the guest house in the dark, put your foot in the squelch of those who missed the pit by the outhouse, that charming old-fashioned outhouse so many tourists take Polaroids of, without feeling degraded, and we can then respect each other as artists. So, I appreciate the offer, but I'll be back in five. Kindly excuse me.

(*He exits*)

HARRY. You've got logorrhea, Jackson. You've been running your mouth like a parrot's arse. But don't get sarcastic with me, boy!

(*Jackson returns*)

JACKSON. You don't understand, Mr. Harry. My problem is, I really mean what I say.

HARRY. You've been pretending indifference to this game, Jackson, but you've manipulated it your way, haven't you? Now you can spew out all that bitterness in fun, can't you? Well, we'd better get things straight around here, friend. You're still on duty. And if you stay out there too long, your job is at stake. It's . . .

(*Consulting his watch*)

five minutes to one now. You've got exactly three minutes to get in there and back, and two minutes left to finish straightening this place. It's a bloody mess.

(*Silence*)

JACKSON. Bloody mess, eh?

HARRY. That's correct.

JACKSON (*In exaggerated British accent*). I go try and make it back in five, bwana. If I don't, the mess could be bloodier. I saw a sign once in a lavatory in Mobile, Alabama. COLORED. But it didn't have no time limit. Funny, eh?

HARRY. Ape! Mimic! Three bloody minutes!

(*Jackson exits, shaking his head. Harry recovers the sheet of paper from the floor and puts it back in his pants pocket. He pours a large drink, swallows it all in two large gulps, then puts the glass down. He looks around the gazebo, wipes his hands briskly. He removes the drinks tray with Scotch, the two beer bottles, glasses, water pitcher, and sets them in a corner of the gazebo. He lifts up the deck chair and sets it, sideways, in another corner. He turns the table carefully over on its side; then, when it is on its back, he looks at it. He changes his mind and carefully tilts the table back upright. He removes his shirt and folds it and places it in another corner of the gazebo. He rolls up his trouser cuffs almost to the knee. He is now half-naked. He goes over to the drinks tray and pours the bowl of melted ice, now tepid water, over his head. He ruffles his hair, his face dripping; then he sees an ice pick. He picks it up*)

JACKSON'S VOICE. "One day, just out of the blue, I pick up a ice pick and walk over to where he and two fellers was playing cards, and I nail that ice pick through his hand to the table, and I laugh . . ."

(*Harry drives the ice pick hard into the tabletop, steps back, looking at it. Then he moves up to it, wrenches it out, and gets under the table, the ice pick at his feet. A few beats, then Jackson enters, pauses*)

JACKSON (*Laughs*). What you doing under the table, Mr. Trewe?

(*Silence. Jackson steps nearer the table*)

Trewe? You all right?

(*Silence. Jackson crouches close to Harry*)

Harry, boy, you cool?

(*Jackson rises. Moves away some distance. He takes in the space. An arena. Then he crouches again*)

Ice-pick time, then?
Okay. "Fee fi fo fum,
I smell the blood of an Englishman . . ."

(*Jackson exits quickly. Harry waits a while, then crawls from under the table, straightens up, and places the ice pick gently on the tabletop. He goes to the drinks tray and has a sip from the Scotch; then replaces the bottle and takes up a position behind the table. Jackson returns dressed as Crusoe—goatskin hat, open umbrella, the hammer stuck in the waistband of his rolled-up trousers. He throws something across the room to Harry's feet. The dead parrot, in a carry-away box. Harry opens it*)

One parrot, to go! Or you eating it here?

HARRY. You son of a bitch.

JACKSON. Sure.

(*Harry picks up the parrot and hurls it into the sea*)

First bath in five years.

(*Jackson moves toward the table, very calmly*)

HARRY. You're a bloody savage. Why'd you strangle him?

JACKSON (*As Friday*). Me na strangle him, bwana. Him choke from prejudice.

HARRY. Prejudice? A bloody parrot. The bloody thing can't reason.

(*Pause. They stare at each other. Harry crouches, tilts his head, shifts on his perch, flutters his wings like the parrot, squawks*)

Heinegger. Heinegger.

(*Jackson stands over the table and folds the umbrella*)

You people create nothing. You imitate everything. It's all been done before, you see, Jackson. The parrot. Think that's something? It's from *The Seagull*. It's from *Miss Julie*. You can't ever be original, boy. That's the trouble with shadows, right? They can't think for themselves.

(*Jackson shrugs, looking away from him*)

So you take it out on a parrot. Is that one of your African sacrifices, eh?

JACKSON. Run your mouth, Harry, run your mouth.

HARRY (*Squawks*). Heinegger . . . Heinegger . . .

(*Jackson folds the parasol and moves to enter the upturned table*)

I wouldn't go under there if I were you, Jackson.

(*Jackson reaches into the back of his waistband and removes a hammer*)

JACKSON. The first English cowboy.

(*He turns and faces Harry*)

HARRY. It's my property. Don't get in there.

JACKSON. The hut. That was my idea.

HARRY. The table's mine.

JACKSON. What else is yours, Harry?

(*Gestures*)

This whole fucking island? Dem days gone, boy.

HARRY. The costume's mine, too.

(*He crosses over, almost nudging Jackson, and picks up the ice pick*)

I'd like them back.

JACKSON. Suit yourself.

(*Harry crosses to the other side, sits on the edge of the wall or leans against a post. Jackson removes the hat and throws it into the arena, then the parasol*)

HARRY. The hammer's mine.

JACKSON. I feel I go need it.

HARRY. If you keep it, you're a bloody thief.

(*Jackson suddenly drops to the floor on his knees, letting go of the hammer, weeping and cringing, and advancing on his knees toward Harry*)

JACKSON. Pardon, master, pardon! Friday bad boy! Friday wicked nigger. Sorry. Friday nah t'ief again. Mercy, master. Mercy.

(*He rolls around on the floor, laughing*)

Oh, Jesus, I go dead! I go dead. Ay-ay.

(*Silence. Jackson on the floor, gasping, lying on his back. Harry crosses over, picks up the parasol, opens it, after a little difficulty, then puts on the goatskin hat. Jackson lies on the floor, silent*)

HARRY. I never hit any goddamned maintenance sergeant on the head in the service. I've never hit anybody in my life. Violence makes me sick. I don't believe in ownership. If I'd been more possessive, more authoritative, I don't think she'd have left me. I don't think you ever drove an ice pick through anybody's hand, either. That was just the two of us acting.

JACKSON. Creole acting?

(*He is still lying on the floor*)

Don't be too sure about the ice pick.

HARRY. I'm sure. You're a fake. You're a kind man and you think you have to hide it. A lot of other people could have used that to their own advantage. That's the difference between master and servant.

JACKSON. That master-and-servant shit finish. Bring a beer for me.

(*He is still on his back*)

HARRY. There's no more beer. You want a sip of Scotch?

JACKSON. Anything.

(*Harry goes to the Scotch, brings over the bottle, stands over Jackson*)

HARRY. Here. To me bloody wife! (*Jackson sits up, begins to move off*) What's wrong, you forget to flush it?

JACKSON. I don't think you should bad-talk her behind her back.

(*He exits*)

HARRY. Behind her back? She's in England. She's a star. Star? She's a bloody planet.

(*Jackson returns, holding the photograph of Harry's wife*)

JACKSON. If you going bad-talk, I think she should hear what you going to say, you don't think so, darling?

(*Addressing the photograph, which he puts down*)

If you have to tell somebody something, tell them to their face.

(*Addressing the photograph*)

Now, you know all you women, eh? Let the man talk his talk and don't interrupt.

HARRY. You're fucking bonkers, you know that? Before I hired you, I should have asked for a medical report.

JACKSON. Please tell your ex-wife good afternoon or something. The dame in the pantomime is always played by a man, right?

HARRY. Bullshit.

Jackson sits close to the photograph, wiggling as he ventriloquizes)

JACKSON (*In an Englishwoman's voice*). Is not bullshit at all, Harold. Everything I say you always saying bullshit, bullshit. How can we conduct a civilized conversation if you don't give me a chance? What have I done, Harold, oh, Harold, for you to treat me so?

HARRY. Because you're a silly selfish bitch and you *killed our son!*

JACKSON (*crying*). There, there, you see . . . ?

(*He wipes the eyes of the photograph*)

You're calling me names, it wasn't my fault, and you're calling me names. Can't you ever forgive me for that, Harold?

HARRY. Ha! You never told him that, did you? You neglected to mention that little matter, didn't you, love?

JACKSON (*Weeping*). I love you, Harold. I love you, and I loved him, too. Forgive me, O God, please, please forgive me . . .

(*As himself*)

So how it happen? Murder? A accident?

HARRY (*To the photograph*). Love me? You loved me so much you get drunk and you . . . ah, ah, what's the use? What's the bloody use?

(*Wipes his eyes. Pause*)

JACKSON (*As wife*). I'm crying too, Harold. Let bygones be bygones . . .

(*Harry lunges for the photograph, but Jackson whips it away*)

(*As himself*)

You miss, Harold.

(*Pause; as wife*)

Harold . . .

(*Silence*)

Harold . . . speak to me . . . please.

(*Silence*)

What do you plan to do next?

(*Sniffs*)

What'll you do now?

HARRY. What difference does it make? . . . All right. I'll tell you what I'm going to do next, Ellen: you're such a big star, you're such a luminary, I'm going to leave you to shine by yourself. I'm giving up this blood rat race and I'm going to take up Mike's offer. I'm leaving "the theatuh," which destroyed my confidence, screwed up my marriage, and made you a star. I'm going somewhere where I can get pissed every day and watch the sun set, like Robinson bloody Crusoe. That's what I'm going to bloody do. You always said it's the only part I could play.

JACKSON (*As wife*). Take me with you, then. Let's get away together. I always wanted to see the tropics, the palm trees, the lagoons . . .

(*Harry grabs the photograph from Jackson; he picks up the ice pick and puts the photograph on the table, pressing it down with one palm*)

HARRY. All right, Ellen, I'm going to . . . You can scream all you like, but I'm going to . . .

(*He raises the ice pick*)

JACKSON (*As wife*). My face is my fortune.

(*He sneaks up behind Harry, whips the photograph away while Harry is poised with the ice pick*)

HARRY. Your face is your fortune, eh? I'll kill her, Jackson, I'll maim that smirking bitch . . .

(*He lunges toward Jackson, who leaps away, holding the photograph before his face, and runs around the gazebo, shrieking*)

JACKSON (*As wife*). Help! Help! British police! My husband trying to kill me! Help, somebody, help!

(*Harry chases Jackson with the ice pick, but Jackson nimbly avoids him*)

(*As wife*)

Harry! Have you gone mad?

(*He scrambles onto the ledge of the gazebo. He no longer holds the photograph to his face, but his voice is the wife's*)

HARRY. Get down off there, you melodramatic bitch. You're too bloody conceited to kill yourself. Get down from there, Ellen! Ellen, it's a straight drop to the sea!

JACKSON (*As wife*). Push me, then! Push me, Harry! You hate me so much, why you don't come and push me?

HARRY. Push yourself, then. You never needed my help. Jump!

JACKSON (*As wife*). Will you forgive me now, or after I jump?

HARRY. Forgive you? . . .

JACKSON (*As wife*). All right, then. Goodbye!

(*He turns, teetering, about to jump*)

HARRY (*Shouts*). *Ellen! Stop! I forgive you!*

(*Jackson turns on the ledge. Silence. Harry is now sitting on the floor*)

That's the real reason I wanted to do the panto. To do it better than you ever did. You played Crusoe in the panto, Ellen. I was Friday. Black bloody greasepaint that made you howl. You wiped the stage with me . . . Ellen . . . well. Why not? I was no bloody good.

JACKSON (*As himself*). Come back to the play, Mr. Trewe. Is Jackson. We was playing Robinson Crusoe, remember?

(*Silence*)

Master, Friday here . . .

(*Silence*)

You finish with the play? The panto? Crusoe must get up, he must make himself get up. He have to face a next day again.

(*Shouts*)

I tell you: man must live! Then, after many years, he see this naked footprint that is the mark of his salvation . . .

HARRY (*Recites*).

   "The self-same moment I could pray;
   and . . . tata tee-tum-tum
   The Albatross fell off and sank
   Like lead into the sea."
   God, my memory . . .

JACKSON. That ain't Crusoe, that is "The Rime of the Ancient Mariner."

(*He pronounces it "Marina"*)

HARRY. Mariner.

JACKSON. Marina.

HARRY. Mariner.

JACKSON. "The Rime of the Ancient Marina." So I learn it in Fourth Standard.

HARRY. It's your country, mate.

JACKSON. Is your language, pardner. I stand corrected. Now, you ain't see English crazy? I could sit down right next to you and tell you I *stand* corrected.

HARRY. Sorry. Where were we, Mr. Phillip?

JACKSON. Tobago. Where are you? It was your cue, Mr. Trewe.

HARRY. Where was I, then?

JACKSON. Ahhm . . . That speech you was reading . . . that speech . . .

HARRY. Speech?

JACKSON. "O silent sea and so on . . . wreathed in mist . . ." Shall we take it from there, then? The paper.

HARRY. I should know it. After all, I wrote it. But prompt . . .

(*Harry gives Jackson his copy of the paper, rises, walks around, looks toward the sea*)

Creole or classical?

JACKSON. Don't make joke.

(*Silence. Sea-gull cries*)

HARRY. Then Crusoe, in his desolation, looks out to the sea, for the ten thousandth time, and remembers England, his wife, his little son, and speaks to himself:

(*As Crusoe*)

"O silent sea, O wondrous sunset that I've gazed on ten thousand times, who will rescue me from this complete desolation? Yes, this is paradise, I know. For I see around me the splendors of nature. The ferns, the palms like silent sentinels, the wide and silent lagoons that briefly hold my passing, solitary reflection. The volcano wreathed in mist. But what is paradise without a woman? Adam in paradise had his woman to share his loneliness . . . loneliness . . .

JACKSON (*Prompts*). . . . but I miss the voice . . .

HARRY (*Remembering*). "But I miss the voice . . .

(*Weeping, but speaking clearly*)

of even one consoling creature, the touch . . . of a hand . . . the look of kind eyes . . . Where is the wife from whom I vowed . . . never to be sundered? How old is my little son? If he could see his father like this . . . dressed in goatskins and mad with memories of them?"

(*He breaks down, quietly sobbing. A long pause*)

JACKSON. You crying or you acting?

HARRY. Acting.

JACKSON. I think you crying. Nobody could act that good.

HARRY. How would you know? You an actor?

JACKSON. Maybe not. But I cry a'ready.

HARRY. Okay, I was crying.

JACKSON. For what?

HARRY (*Laughs*). For what? I got carried away. I'm okay now.

JACKSON. But you laughing now.

HARRY. It's the same sound. You can't tell the difference if I turn my back.

JACKSON. Don't make joke.

HARRY. It's an old actor's trick. I'm going to cry now, all right?

(*He turns, then sobs with laughter, covering and uncovering his face with his hands. Jackson stalks around, peers at him, then begins to giggle. They are now both laughing*)

JACKSON (*Through laughter*). So . . . so . . . next Friday . . . when the tourists come . . . Crusoe . . . Crusoe go be ready for them . . . Goat race . . .

HARRY (*Laughing*). Goat-roti!

JACKSON (*Laughing*). Gambling.

HARRY (*Baffled*). Gambling?

JACKSON. Goat-to-pack. Every night . . .

HARRY (*Laughing*). Before they goat-to-bed!

JACKSON (*Laughing*). So he striding up the beach with his little goat-ee . . .

HARRY (*Laughing*). E-goat-istical, again.

(*Pause*)

JACKSON. You get the idea. So, you okay, Mr. Trewe?

HARRY. I'm fine, Mr. Phillip. You know . . .

(*He wipes his eyes*)

An angel passes through a house and leaves no imprint of his shadow on its wall. A man's life slowly changes and he does not understand the change. Things like this have happened before, and they can happen again. You understand, Jackson? You see what it is I'm saying?

JACKSON. You making a mole hill out of a mountain, sir. But I think I follow you. You know what all this make me decide, pardner?

HARRY. What?

(*Jackson picks up the umbrella, puts on the goatskin hat*)

JACKSON. I going back to the gift that's my God-given calling. I benignly resign, you fire me. With inspiration. Caiso is my true work, caiso is my true life.

(*Sings*)

> Well, a Limey name Trewe come to Tobago.
> He was in show business but he had no show,
> so in desperation he turn to me
> and said: "Mr. Phillip" is the two o' we,
> one classical actor and one Creole,
> let we act together with we heart and soul.
> It go be man to man, and we go do it fine,
> and we go give it the title of pantomime.
> La da dee da da da
> Dee da da da da da . . .

(*He is singing as if in a spotlight. Music, audience applause. Harry joins in*)

Wait! Wait! Hold it!

(*Silence: walks over to Harry*)

Starting from Friday, Robinson, we could talk 'bout a raise?

(*Fadeout*)

TOPICS FOR CRITICAL THINKING AND WRITING

The Play on the PAGE

1. How many ways is *Pantomime* a play within a play? Why do you think the playwright makes the choice to focus the play on the notion of performance?

2. What does Philip mean when he says, "We're faking, faking all the time"?

3. What happened to Harry Trewe's son? Why does Philip "play" Trewe's wife at the end of the play?

4. The out-of-season hotel is located on the island of Tobago in the Caribbean. How does this location add to the meaning of the play?

5. Is *Pantomime* a comedy? If so, how does that affect the social messages many critics have ascribed to it?

The Play on the STAGE

6. How might a minimalist production of the play be different from one with a realistic design? How would the tension of the cliff-top location be affected? How does that tension affect the play?

7. Derek Walcott has expressed concern about American actors playing characters who were raised in a very different culture of race relations. Do you think a Caribbean actor could play Jackson Philip better than an African American actor? Why or why not?

8. How would you stage the play-within-a-play elements of the script to clearly indicate to the audience these important dramatic changes?

The Play in PERFORMANCE

Pantomime premiered on April 12, 1978, under the auspices of All Theater productions at the Little Carib Theater, Port of Spain, Trinidad, with William Holder as a particularly aggressive Philip. It was subsequently revived in December of the same year with the classically trained Horace James in the role of Philip. This second production tried to shift the balance from Holder's racial attacks in the earlier production toward more what Walcott intended: the development of a

nervous sustained tension between the two men that shifts and fluctuates in the course of the play. Since its premiere, the play has had numerous productions. The play's minimal casting and scenic requirements have helped make it a popular one for production, and it may well be Walcott's most frequently performed play.

The following is a review from the 1986 production in Boston.

FREDERICK H. GUIDRY
Oft-staged Walcott Play Reaches Playwright's Neighborhood*

Derek Walcott, West Indian poet and playwright, has been living in the Boston area for four years, but his play *Pantomime* is just now having its first performances in this city. The production at the Boston Shakespeare Theater is putting Mr. Walcott's talent before appreciative audiences, who may have been unacquainted with his presence as a creative-writing teacher at Boston University.

The theater organization itself has reason to be pleased at having a potential hit on its hands, since its stage is reportedly a candidate for destruction as part of a remodeling project. The building in which the Boston Shakespeare Company is a tenant is to be turned into residential condominiums in 1987.

Pantomime came well recommended by a history of productions ranging from New York to Seattle, as well as abroad. Its staging in Boston is benefitting from strong performances by actors with Broadway as well as regional theater credentials.

The two-character play involves a white Briton, in self-imposed Caribbean exile, and a black Trinidadian, seeking peace and quiet on Tobago island. The former, Harry Trewe, a former London music-hall entertainer, now runs a guest house on Tobago. The Trinidadian, Jackson Phillip, works for him, serving in a white coat

that symbolizes their mutual attempt to uphold a high standard of manners amid the chosen remoteness.

As the action unfolds off-season, there are no guests, and the action consists entirely of the frequently abrasive but generally congenial interaction between the resort owner and his servant. Harry fights the tropical torpor and pictures himself making a success of the guest house by devising an entertainment for the expected tourist trade. He proposes that he and Jackson improvise a turnabout sketch in which the black will play Robinson Crusoe and the white man the cannibal, Friday. Jackson at first ridicules the idea but later throws himself into the project with a fervor that frightens Harry.

In the course of their discussions, *Pantomime* ranges thoughtfully and entertainingly over considerations of race relations as well as theater. Although Jackson protests, in preparations for the Crusoe skit, that "Just a lot of talk is boring," the Walcott play engages in little else and the opening-night audience found "a lot of talk"—unfortunately spiced with considerable crudity—could be totally engaging.

Terry Alexander plays the Trinidadian with a fine command of calypso rhythms in speech and song—even shows a surprising skill at getting music out of a steel drum. In what is obviously the juicier of the two roles—wider-ranging, more showy, more appealing in its sentiments—Mr. Alexander has a marvelous time and gives the audience one, too. Chuck Stransky, as Harry, anchors the production with a prevailing moodiness, broken chiefly by flashes of anger and apprehension. The company's present small auditorium enforces an intimacy that heightens the threatening aspects of the play and puts nuances of performance into agreeably sharp focus.

---

*Review of *Pantomime, Christian Science Monitor* 17 June 1986: 33.

CARYL Churchill

Caryl Churchill was born in London in 1938; when she was ten years old her family moved to Canada. In 1957 she returned to Britain to study at Oxford, graduating in 1960 with a degree in English. While at the university she began writing plays for student drama groups. She married a barrister in 1961 and three sons were born during the 1960s, a decade in which her highly acclaimed first radio dramas were broadcast on BBC. In 1972 the Royal Court Theatre presented in its experimental space, Theater Upstairs, her first professionally produced play, *Owners*. In 1975 she became a founding member of the Theatre Writer's Group, which later became the Theatre Writer's Union. In 1976 she joined a workshop with Joint Stock Theater, a company known for an innovative work method based on close collaboration among writers, director, and actors. Her first play for Joint Stock was *Light Shining in Buckinghamshire* (1976), and other notable works followed with the company: *Cloud Nine* (1979, for which she won an Obie in its New York production), *Fen* (1983), *A Mouthful of Birds* (1986). In 1976 the feminist company Monstrous Regiment staged her play, *Vinegar Tom,* about seventeenth-century witchcraft. In 1980 she began writing *Top Girls,* widely regarded as one of the most powerful plays of the late twentieth century. *Top Girls* was produced at the Royal Court Theatre in 1982 and after a successful run transferred to the Public Theater in New York where it was presented by the New York Shakespeare Festival. Churchill, known for rejecting the conventions of realism in favor of theatrical invention and subversive comedy, in her best-known works focuses on a social criticism and philosophical questioning of gender issues. Motherhood as a political issue is central in *Top Girls* and this issue appears again in several of her works. Her other plays include *Serious Money* (1987), *Mad Forest* (1990, about the revolution in Romania), *Lives of the Great Poisoners* (1991), *The Skriker* (1994), and *Blue Heart* (1997).

■■■■■■■■■■■■■

COMMENTARY ON *TOP GIRLS*

Top Girls is grounded in a very specific time and place, the political and social climate in Britain in the late 1970s and early 1980s. However, by offering us a range of women from the past as well as contemporary society, Churchill stages connections for us to see how the specific can speak to the larger issues of our culture. In the opening scene, Churchill conjures up a fantasy dinner party in a restaurant with a group of women from history, hosted by the central character, Marlene. Marlene, a woman of the present, is celebrating her recent promotion. Like Margaret Thatcher, she is a "top girl," the first woman to be selected for her position.

Churchill's decision to use the image of a dinner party is particularly redolent with meaning. At the time Churchill was researching her material for *Top Girls,* a major art work created by the American feminist artist Judy Chicago was being exhibited in London. The work, titled *The Dinner Party,* consisted of three oblong, linking tables that formed a large triangle. Each table was set with thirteen place settings; each dinner plate represented a woman from history, from early goddesses to the biblical Judith, to the Greek classical poet Sappho, to early women's rights advocate and author Mary Wollstonecraft, to artist Georgia O'Keeffe. The thirty-nine dinner plates and the tablecloth were individually designed to represent the accomplishments of the women. Women together at a dinner party made a statement about making connections from women of one century or country to women of another. Women normally serve at dinner parties and have historically been responsible for washing up. With Chicago's work, these "dinners," served as works of art, provide nourishment through the rewriting of history.

Whereas Chicago's dinner party celebrates the continuous and reclaimed history of women of achievement, Churchill's party questions the kinds of success some contemporary women have achieved. Compared to the accomplishments of Chicago's women from history, Marlene celebrates a much more mundane event: her promotion to head an employment agency. The dinner party scene ends with Lady Nijo laughing and crying simultaneously, Pope Joan getting sick, and Marlene tipsy, drinking brandy. The sense of confusion and emotionally high stakes that end the scene fore-ground the rest of the play with a sense of historical struggle and resilience on the part of these women. It is against this background that Marlene starts running the employment agency, interviews the women who come to her for work, and deals with her working-class family that she has left behind. By celebrating and embracing the new morality of Thatcher and Reagan, Marlene isolates herself from her family and loses any sense of compassion and humanity. Churchill describes her ideas about *Top Girls* in *Interviews with Contemporary Women Playwrights* edited by Kathleen Betsko and Rachel Koenig:

> When I wrote *Top Girls* . . . I wanted to write about women doing different kinds of work and didn't feel I knew enough about it. Then I thought, this is ridiculous, if you were with a [theater] company you'd go out and talk to people, so I did. Which is how I came up with the employment agency . . .

What I was intending to do was make it first look as though it was celebrating the achievements of women and then—by showing the main character, Marlene, being successful in a very competitive, destructive, capitalist way—ask, what kind of achievement is that? The idea is that it would start out looking like a feminist play and turn into a socialist one, as well. And I think on the whole it's mostly been understood like that. A lot of people have latched on to Marlene leaving her child, which interestingly was something that came very late. Originally the idea was just that Marlene was "writing off" her niece, Angie, because she'd never make it; I didn't yet have the plot idea that Angie was actually Marlene's own child. Of course women are pressured to make choices between working and having children in a way that men aren't, so it *is* relevant, but it isn't the main point of it. (81–82)

TOP GIRLS
Caryl Churchill

CHARACTERS

MARLENE

ISABELLA BIRD }*
JOYCE
MRS. KIDD

LADY NIJO }
WIN

DULL GRET }
ANGIE

POPE JOAN }
LOUISE

PATIENT GRISELDA }
NELL
JEANINE

WAITRESS }
KITT
SHONA

*Indicates multiple roles played by a single performer.

ACT ONE

Scene One, Restaurant. Saturday night.
Scene Two, 'Top Girls' Employment agency. Monday morning.
Scene Three, Joyce's back yard. Sunday afternoon.

ACT TWO

Scene One, Employment agency. Monday morning.
Scene Two, Joyce's kitchen. Sunday evening, a year earlier.

NOTE ON CHARACTERS

ISABELLA BIRD *(1831–1904) lived in Edinburgh, travelled extensively between the ages of 40 and 70.*
LADY NIJO *(b. 1258) Japanese, was an Emperor's courtesan and later a Buddhist nun who travelled on foot through Japan.*
DULL GRET *is the subject of the Brueghel painting, Dulle Griet, in which a woman in an apron and armour leads a crowd of women charging through hell and fighting the devils.*
POPE JOAN, *disguised as a man, is thought to have been Pope between 854–856.*

PATIENT GRISELDA *is the obedient wife whose story is told by Chaucer in The Clerk's Tale of The Canterbury Tales.*

NOTE ON LAYOUT

A speech usually follows the one immediately before it BUT:
1 when one character starts speaking before the other has finished, the point of interruption is marked / .

eg. ISABELLA. This is the Emperor of Japan? / I once met the Emperor of Morocco.
    NIJO. In fact he was the ex-Emperor.

2 a character sometimes continues speaking right through another's speech:

eg. ISABELLA. When I was forty I thought my life was over. / Oh I was pitiful. I was
    NIJO. I didn't say I felt it for twenty years. Not every minute.
    ISABELLA. sent on a cruise for my health and I felt even worse. Pains in my bones, pins and needles . . . etc.

3 sometimes a speech follows on from a speech earlier than the one immediately before it, and continuity is marked*.

eg. GRISELDA. I'd seen him riding by, we all had. And he'd seen me in the fields with the sheep*.
    ISABELLA. I would have been well suited to minding sheep.
    NIJO. And Mr. Nugent riding by.
    ISABELLA. Of course not, Nijo, I mean a healthy life in the open air.
    JOAN. *He just rode up while you were minding the sheep and asked you to marry him?

where 'in the fields with the sheep' is the cue to both 'I would have been' and 'He just rode up'.

The author gratefully acknowledges use of the following books: *The Confessions of Lady Nijo*, translated from the Japanese by Karen Brazell, and published by Peter Owen Ltd, London *A Curious Life for a Lady* (about Isabella Bird) by Pat Barr, originally published by Macmillan, London

ACT ONE

SCENE ONE

Restaurant: Table set for dinner with white tablecloth. Six places. Marlene and Waitress.

MARLENE. Excellent, yes, table for six. One of them's going to be late but we won't wait. I'd like a bottle of Frascati straight away if you've got one really cold.

(The Waitress goes.)
(Isabella Bird arrives.)

Distinguished women of the past gather for dinner in Caryl Churchill's *Top Girls.* Seated L.R. Carole Hayman as Dull Gret and Lindsay Duncan as Lady Nijo; Standing L.R. Gwen Taylor as Marlene and Selina Cadell as Pope Joan.

here we are, Isabella.

ISABELLA. Congratulations, my dear.

MARLENE. Well, it's a step. It makes for a party. I haven't time for a holiday. I'd like to go somewhere exotic like you but I can't get away. I don't know how you could bear to leave Hawaii. / I'd like to lie in the sun forever, except of course I

ISABELLA. I did think of settling.

MARLENE. can't bear sitting still.

ISABELLA. I sent for my sister Hennie to come and join me. I said, Hennie we'll live here forever and help the natives. You can buy two sirloins of beef for what a pound of chops costs in Edinburgh. And Hennie wrote back, the dear, that yes, she would come to Hawaii if I wished, but I said she had far better stay where she was. Hennie was suited to life in Tobermory.

MARLENE. Poor Hennie.

ISABELLA. Do you have a sister?

MARLENE. Yes in fact.

ISABELLA. Hennie was happy. She was good. I did miss its face, my own pet. But I couldn't stay in Scotland. I loathed the constant murk.

MARLENE. Ah! Nijo!

(She sees Lady Nijo arrive.)
(The Waitress enters with wine.)

NIJO. Marlene!

MARLENE. I think a drink while we wait for the others. I think a drink anyway. What a week.

(The Waitress pours wine.)

NIJO. It was always the men who used to get so drunk. I'd be one of the maidens, passing the sake.

ISABELLA. I've had sake. Small hot drink. Quite fortifying after a day in the wet.

NIJO. One night my father proposed three rounds of three cups, which was normal, and then the Emperor should have said three rounds of three cups, but he said three rounds of nine cups, so you can imagine. Then the Emperor passed his sake cup to my father and said, 'Let the wild goose come to me this spring.'

MARLENE. Let the what?

NIJO. It's a literary allusion to a tenth-century epic, / His Majesty was very cultured.

ISABELLA. This is the Emperor of Japan? / I once met the Emperor of Morocco.

NIJO. In fact he was the ex-Emperor.

MARLENE. But he wasn't old? / Did you, Isabella?

NIJO. Twenty-nine.

ISABELLA. Oh it's a long story.

MARLENE. Twenty-nine's an excellent age.

NIJO. Well I was only fourteen and I knew he meant something but I didn't know what. He sent me an eight-layered gown and I sent it back. So when the time came I did nothing but cry. My thin gowns were badly ripped. But even that morning when he left / —he'd a green robe with a scarlet lining and

MARLENE. Are you saying he raped you?

NIJO. very heavily embroidered trousers, I already felt different about him. It made me uneasy. No, of course not, Marlene, I belonged to him, it was what I was brought up for from a baby. I soon found I was sad if he stayed away. It was depressing day after day not knowing when he would come. I never enjoyed taking other women to him.

ISABELLA. I certainly never saw my father drunk. He was a clergyman. / And I didn't get married till I was fifty.

(*The Waitress brings menus.*)

NIJO. Oh, my father was a very religious man. Just before he died he said to me, 'Serve His Majesty, be respectful, if you lose his favour enter holy orders.'

MARLENE. But he meant stay in a convent, not go wandering round the country.

NIJO. Priests were often vagrants, so why not a nun? You think I shouldn't? / I still did what my father wanted.

MARLENE. No no, I think you should. / I think it was wonderful.

(*Dull Gret arrives.*)

ISABELLA. I tried to do what my father wanted.

MARLENE. Gret, good. Nijo. Gret. / I know Griselda's going to be late, but should we wait for Joan? / Let's get you a drink.

ISABELLA. Hello Gret! (*Continues to Nijo:*) I tried to be a clergyman's daughter. Needlework, music, charitable schemes. I had a tumour removed from my spine and spent a great deal of time on the sofa. I studied the metaphysical poets and hymnology. / I thought I enjoyed intellectual pursuits.

NIJO. Ah, you like poetry. I come of a line of eight generations of poets. Father had a poem / in the anthology.

ISABELLA. My father taught me Latin although I was a girl. / But

MARLENE. They didn't have Latin at my school.

ISABELLA. really I was more suited to manual work. Cooking, washing, mending, riding horses. / Better than reading books,

NIJO. Oh but I'm sure you're very clever.

ISABELLA. eh Gret? A rough life in the open air.

NIJO. I can't say I enjoyed my rough life. What I enjoyed most was being the Emperor's favourite / and wearing thin silk.

ISABELLA. Did you have any horses, Gret?

GRET. Pig.

(*Pope Joan arrives.*)

MARLENE. Oh Joan, thank God, we can order. Do you know everyone? We were just talking about learning Latin and being clever girls. Joan was by way of an infant prodigy. Of course you were. What excited you when you were ten?

JOAN. Because angels are without matter they are not individuals. Every angel is a species.

MARLENE. There you are.

(*They laugh. They look at menus.*)

ISABELLA. Yes, I forgot all my Latin. But my father was the mainspring of my life and when he died I was so grieved. I'll have the chicken, please, / and the soup.

NIJO. Of course you were grieved. My father was saying his prayers and he dozed off in the sun. So I touched his knee to rouse him. 'I wonder what will happen,' he said, and then he was dead before he finished the sentence. / If he'd died saying

MARLENE. What a shock.

NIJO. his prayers he would have gone straight to heaven. / Waldorf salad.

JOAN. Death is the return of all creatures to God.

NIJO. I shouldn't have woken him.

JOAN. Damnation only means ignorance of the truth. I was always attracted by the teachings of John the Scot, though he was inclined to confuse / God and the world.

ISABELLA. Grief always overwhelmed me at the time.

MARLENE. What I fancy is a rare steak. Gret?

ISABELLA. I am of course a member of the / Church of England*

GRET. Potatoes.

MARLENE. *I haven't been to church for years. / I like Christmas carols.

ISABELLA. Good works matter more than church attendance.

MARLENE. Make that two steaks and a lot of potatoes. Rare. But I don't do good works either.

JOAN. Canelloni, please, / and a salad.

ISABELLA. Well, I tried, but oh dear. Hennie did good works.

NIJO. The first half of my life was all sin and the second / all repentance.*

MARLENE. Oh what about starters?

GRET. Soup.

JOAN. *and which did you like best?

MARLENE. Were your travels just a penance? Avocado vinaigrette. Didn't you / enjoy yourself?

JOAN. Nothing to start with for me, thank you.

NIJO. Yes, but I was very unhappy. / It hurt to remember

MARLENE. And the wine list.

NIJO. the past. I think that was repentance.

MARLENE. Well I wonder.

NIJO. I might have just been homesick.

MARLENE. Or angry.

NIJO. Not angry, no, / why angry?

GRET. Can we have some more bread?

MARLENE. Don't you get angry? I get angry.

NIJO. But what about?

MARLENE. Yes let's have two more Frascati. And some more bread, please.

(*The waitress exits.*)

ISABELLA. I tried to understand Buddhism when I was in Japan but all this birth and death succeeding each other through eternities just filled me with the most profound melancholy. I do like something more active.

NIJO. You couldn't say I was inactive. I walked every day for twenty years.

ISABELLA. I don't mean walking. / I mean in the head.

NIJO. I vowed to copy five Mahayana sutras. / Do you know how

MARLENE. I don't think religious beliefs are something we have in common. Activity yes.

NIJO. long they are? My head was active. / My head ached.

JOAN. It's no good being active in heresy.

ISABELLA. What heresy? She's calling the Church of England / a heresy.

JOAN. There are some very attractive / heresies.

NIJO. I had never heard of Christianity. Never / heard of it. Barbarians.

MARLENE. Well I'm not a Christian. / And I'm not a Buddhist.

ISABELLA. You have heard of it?

MARLENE. We don't all have to believe the same.

ISABELLA. I knew coming to dinner with a pope we should keep off religion.

JOAN. I always enjoy a theological argument. But I won't try to convert you, I'm not a missionary. Anyway I'm a heresy myself.

ISABELLA. There are some barbaric practices in the east.

NIJO. Barbaric?

ISABELLA. Among the lower classes.

NIJO. I wouldn't know.

ISABELLA. Well theology always made my head ache.

MARLENE. Oh good, some food.

(*Waitress is bringing the first course.*)

NIJO. How else could I have left the court if I wasn't a nun? When father died I had only His Majesty. So when I fell out of favour I had nothing. Religion is a kind of nothing / and I dedicated what was left of me to nothing.

ISABELLA. That's what I mean about Buddhism. It doesn't brace.

MARLENE. Come on, Nijo, have some wine.

NIJO. Haven't you ever felt like that? Nothing will ever happen again. I am dead already. You've all felt / like that.

ISABELLA. You thought your life was over but it wasn't.

JOAN. You wish it was over.

GRET. Sad.

MARLENE. Yes, when I first came to London I sometimes . . . and when I got back from America I did. But only for a few hours. Not twenty years.

ISABELLA. When I was forty I thought my life was over. / Oh I

NIJO. I didn't say I felt it for twenty years. Not every minute.

ISABELLA. was pitiful. I was sent on a cruise for my health and I felt even worse. Pains in my bones, pins and needles in my hands, swelling behind the ears, and—oh, stupidity. I shook all over, indefinable terror. And Australia seemed to me a hideous country, the acacias stank like drains. / I had a

NIJO. You were homesick.

ISABELLA. photograph for Hennie but I told her I wouldn't send it, my hair had fallen out and my clothes were crooked, I looked completely insane and suicidal.

NIJO. So did I, exactly, dressed as a nun. I was wearing walking shoes for the first time.

ISABELLA. I longed to go home, / but home to what? Houses

NIJO. I longed to go back ten years.

ISABELLA. are so perfectly dismal.

MARLENE. I thought travelling cheered you both up.

ISABELLA. Oh it did / of course. It was on the trip from

NIJO. I'm not a cheerful person, Marlene. I just laugh a lot.

ISABELLA. Australia to the Sandwich Isles, I fell in love with the sea. There were rats in the cabin and ants in the food but suddenly it was like a new world. I woke up every morning happy, knowing there would be nothing to annoy me. No nervousness. No dressing.

NIJO. Don't you like getting dressed? I adored my clothes. / When I was chosen to give sake to His Majesty's brother,

MARLENE. You had prettier colours than Isabella.

NIJO. the Emperor Kameyana, on his formal visit, I wore raw silk pleated trousers and a seven-layered gown in shades of red, and two outer garments, / yellow lined with green and a light

MARLENE. Yes, all that silk must have been very . . .

(*The Waitress starts to clear the first course.*)

JOAN. I dressed as a boy when I left home.*

NIJO. green jacket. Lady Betto had a five-layered gown in shades of green and purple.

ISABELLA. *You dressed as a boy?

MARLENE. Of course, / for safety.

JOAN. It was easy, I was only twelve. / Also women weren't allowed in the library. We wanted to study in Athens.

MARLENE. You ran away alone?

JOAN. No, not alone, I went with my friend. / He was sixteen

NIJO. Ah, an elopement.

JOAN. but I thought I knew more science than he did and almost as much philosophy.

ISABELLA. Well I always travelled as a lady and I repudiated strongly any suggestion in the press that I was other than feminine.

MARLENE. I don't wear trousers in the office. / I could but I don't.

ISABELLA. There was no great danger to a woman of my age and appearance.

MARLENE. And you got away with it, Joan?

JOAN. I did then.

(*The Waitress starts to bring the main course.*)

MARLENE. And nobody noticed anything?

JOAN. They noticed I was a very clever boy. / And when I

MARLENE. I couldn't have kept pretending for so long.

JOAN. shared a bed with my friend, that was ordinary—two poor students in a lodging house. I think I forgot I was pretending.

ISABELLA. Rocky Mountain Jim, Mr. Nugent, showed me no disrespect. He found it interesting, I think, that I could make scones and also lasso cattle. Indeed he declared his love for me, which was most distressing.

NIJO. What did he say? / We always sent poems first.

MARLENE. What did you say?

ISABELLA. I urged him to give up whisky, / but he said it was too late.

MARLENE. Oh Isabella.

ISABELLA. He had lived alone in the mountains for many years.

MARLENE. But did you—?

(*The Waitress goes.*)

ISABELLA. Mr. Nugent was a man that any woman might love but none could marry. I came back to England.

NIJO. Did you write him a poem when you left? / Snow on the

MARLENE. Did you never see him again?

ISABELLA. No, never.

NIJO. mountains. My sleeves are wet with tears. In England no tears, no snow.

ISABELLA. Well, I say never. One morning very early in Switzerland, it was a year later, I had a vision of him as I last saw him / in his trapper's clothes with his hair round his face,

NIJO. A ghost!

ISABELLA. and that was the day, / I learnt later, he died with a

NIJO. Ah!

ISABELLA. bullet in his brain. / He just bowed to me and vanished.

MARLENE. Oh Isabella.

NIJO. When your lover dies—One of my lovers died. / The priest Ariake.

JOAN. My friend died. Have we all got dead lovers?

MARLENE. Not me, sorry.

NIJO (*to Isabella*). I wasn't a nun, I was still at court, but he was a priest, and when he came to me he dedicated his whole life to hell. / He knew that when he died he would fall into one of the three lower realms. And he died, he did die.

JOAN (*to Marlene*). I'd quarrelled with him over the teachings of John the Scot, who held that our ignorance of God is the same as his ignorance of himself. He only knows what he creates because he creates everything he knows but he himself is above being—do you follow?

MARLENE. No, but go on.

NIJO. I couldn't bear to think / in what shape would he be reborn.*

JOAN. St. Augustine maintained that the Neo-Platonic Ideas are indivisible from God, but I agreed with John that the created

ISABELLA. *Buddhism is really most uncomfortable.

JOAN. world is essences derived from Ideas which derived from God. As Denys the Areopagite said—the pseudo-Denys—first we give God a name, then deny it / then reconcile the

NIJO. In what shape would he return?

JOAN. contradiction by looking beyond / those terms—

MARLENE. Sorry, what? Denys said what?

JOAN. Well we disagreed about it, we quarrelled. And next day he was ill, / I was so annoyed with him, all the time I was

NIJO. Misery in this life and worse in the next, all because of me.

JOAN. nursing him I kept going over the arguments in my mind. Matter is not a means of knowing the essence. The source of the species is the Idea. But then I realised he'd never understand my arguments again, and that night he died. John the Scot held that the individual disintegrates / and there is no personal immortality.

ISABELLA. I wouldn't have you think I was in love with Jim Nugent. It was yearning to save him that I felt.

MARLENE (*to Joan*). So what did you do?

JOAN. First I decided to stay a man. I was used to it. And I wanted to devote my life to learning. Do you know why I went to Rome? Italian men didn't have beards.

ISABELLA. The loves of my life were Hennie, my own pet, and my dear husband the doctor, who nursed Hennie in her last illness. I knew it would be terrible when Hennie died but I didn't know how terrible. I felt half of myself had gone. How could I go on my travels without that sweet soul waiting at home for my letters? It was Doctor Bishop's devotion to her in her last illness that made me decide to marry him. He and Hennie had the same sweet character. I had not.

NIJO. I thought his majesty had sweet character because when he found out about Ariake he was so kind. But really it was because he no longer cared for me. One night he even sent me out to a man who had been pursuing me. / He lay awake on the other side of the screens and listened.

ISABELLA. I did wish marriage had seemed more of a step. I tried very hard to cope with the ordinary drudgery of life. I was ill again with carbuncles on the spine and nervous prostration. I ordered a tricycle, that was my idea of adventure then. And John himself fell ill, with erysipelas and anaemia. I began to love him with my whole heart but it was too late. He was a skeleton with transparent white hands. I wheeled him on various seafronts in a bathchair. And he faded and left me. There was nothing in my life. The doctors said I had gout / and my heart was much affected.

NIJO. There was nothing in my life, nothing, without the Emperor's favour. The Empress had always been my enemy, Marlene, she said I had no right to wear three-layered gowns. / But I was the adopted daughter of my grandfather the Prime Minister. I had been publicly granted permission to wear thin silk.

JOAN. There was nothing in my life except my studies. I was obsessed with pursuit of the truth. I taught at the Greek School in Rome, which St. Augustine had made famous. I was poor, I worked hard. I spoke apparently brilliantly, I was still very young. I was a stranger; suddenly I was quite famous, I was everyone's favourite. Huge crowds came to hear me. The day after they made me cardinal I fell ill and lay two weeks without speaking, full of terror and regret. / But then I got up

MARLENE. Yes, success is very . . .

JOAN. determined to go on. I was seized again / with a desperate longing for the absolute.

ISABELLA. Yes, yes, to go on. I sat in Tobermory among Hennie's flowers and sewed a complete outfit in Jaeger flannel. / I was fifty-six years old.

NIJO. Out of favour but I didn't die. I left on foot, nobody saw me go. For the next twenty years I walked through Japan.

GRET. Walking is good.

(The Waitress enters.)

JOAN. Pope Leo died and I was chosen. All right then. I would be Pope. I would know God. I would know everything.

ISABELLA. I determined to leave my grief behind and set off for Tibet.

MARLENE. Magnificent all of you. We need some more wine, please, two bottles I think, Griselda isn't even here yet, and I want to drink a toast to you all.

ISABELLA. To yourself surely, / we're here to celebrate your success.

NIJO. Yes, Marlene.

JOAN. Yes, what is it exactly, Marlene?

MARLENE. Well it's not Pope but it is managing director.*

JOAN. And you find work for people.

MARLENE. Yes, an employment agency.

NIJO. *Over all the women you work with. And the men.

ISABELLA. And very well deserved too. I'm sure it's just the beginning of something extraordinary.

MARLENE. Well it's worth a party.

ISABELLA. To Marlene.*

MARLENE. And all of us.

JOAN. *Marlene.

NIJO. Marlene.

GRET. Marlene.

MARLENE. We've all come a long way. To our courage and the way we changed our lives and our extraordinary achievements.

(They laugh and drink a toast.)

ISABELLA. Such adventures. We were crossing a mountain pass at seven thousand feet, the cook was all to pieces,

the muleteers suffered fever and snow blindness. But even though my spine was agony I managed very well.

MARLENE. Wonderful.

NIJO. Once I was ill for four months lying alone at an inn. Nobody to offer a horse to Buddha. I had to live for myself, and I did live.

ISABELLA. Of course you did. It was far worse returning to Tobermory. I always felt dull when I was stationary. / That's why I could never stay anywhere.

NIJO. Yes, that's it exactly. New sights. The shrine by the beach, the moon shining on the sea. The goddess had vowed to save all living things. / She would even save the fishes. I was full of hope.

JOAN. I had thought the Pope would know everything. I thought God would speak to me directly. But of course he knew I was a woman.

MARLENE. But nobody else even suspected?

(The Waitress brings more wine.)

JOAN. In the end I did take a lover again.*

ISABELLA. In the Vatican?

GRET. *Keep you warm.

NIJO. *Ah, lover.

MARLENE. *Good for you.

JOAN. He was one of my chamberlains. There are such a lot of servants when you're a Pope. The food's very good. And I realised I did know the truth. Because whatever the Pope says, that's true.

NIJO. What was he like, the chamberlain?*

GRET. Big cock.

ISABELLA. Oh Gret.

MARLENE. *Did he fancy you when he thought you were a fella?

NIJO. What was he like?

JOAN. He could keep a secret.

MARLENE. So you did know everything.

JOAN. Yes, I enjoyed being Pope. I consecrated bishops and let people kiss my feet. I received the King of England when he came to submit to the church. Unfortunately there were earthquakes, and some village reported it had rained blood, and in France there was a plague of giant grasshoppers, but I don't think that can have been my fault, do you?*

(Laughter.)

The grasshoppers fell on the English Channel / and were

NIJO. I once went to sea. It was very lonely. I realised it made very little difference where I went.

JOAN. washed up on shore and their bodies rotted and poisoned the air and everyone in those parts died.

(Laughter.)

ISABELLA. *Such superstition! I was nearly murdered in China by a howling mob. They thought the barbarians are babies and put them under railway sleepers to make the tracks steady, and ground up their eyes to make the lenses of cameras. / So

MARLENE. And you had a camera!

ISABELLA. they were shouting, 'child-eater, child-eater.' Some people tried to sell girl babies to Europeans for cameras or stew!

(*Laughter.*)

MARLENE. So apart from the grasshoppers it was a great success.

JOAN. Yes, if it hadn't been for the baby I expect I'd have lived to an old age like Theodora of Alexandria, who lived as a monk. She was accused by a girl / who fell in love with her of being the father of her child and—

NIJO. But tell us what happened to your baby. I had some babies.

MARLENE. Didn't you think of getting rid of it?

JOAN. Wouldn't that be a worse sin than having it? / But a Pope with a child was about as bad as possible.

MARLENE. I don't know, you're the Pope.

JOAN. But I wouldn't have known how to get rid of it.

MARLENE. Other Popes had children, surely.

JOAN. They didn't give birth to them.

NIJO. Well you were a woman.

JOAN. Exactly and I shouldn't have been a woman. Women, children and lunatics can't be Pope.

MARLENE. So the only thing to do / was to get rid of it somehow.

NIJO. You had to have it adopted secretly.

JOAN. But I didn't know what was happening. I thought I was getting fatter, but then I was eating more and sitting about, the life of a Pope is quite luxurious. I don't think I'd spoken to a woman since I was twelve. The chamberlain was the one who realised.

MARLENE. And by then it was too late.

JOAN. Oh I didn't want to pay attention. It was easier to do nothing.

NIJO. But you had to plan for having it. You had to say you were ill and go away.

JOAN. That's what I should have done I suppose.

MARLENE. Did you want them to find out?

NIJO. I too was often in embarrassing situations, there's no need for a scandal. My first child was His Majesty's, which unfortunately died, but my second was Akebono's. I was seventeen. He was in love with me when I was thirteen, he was very upset when I had to go to the Emperor, it was very romantic, a lot of poems. Now His Majesty hadn't been near me for two months so he thought I was four months pregnant when I was really six, so when I reached the ninth month / I

JOAN. I never knew what month it was.

NIJO. announced I was seriously ill, and Akebono announced he had gone on a religious retreat. He held me round the waist and lifted me up as the baby was born. He cut the cord with a short sword, wrapped the baby in white and took it away. It was only a girl but I was sorry to lose it. Then I told the Emperor that the baby had miscarried because of my illness, and there you are. The danger was past.

JOAN. But Nijo, I wasn't used to having a woman's body.

ISABELLA. So what happened?

JOAN. I didn't know of course that it was near the time. It was Rogation Day, there was always a procession. I was on the horse dressed in my robes and a cross was carried in front of me, and all the cardinals were following, and all the clergy of Rome, and a huge crowd of people. / We set off from

MARLENE. Total Pope.

JOAN. St. Peter's to go to St. John's. I had felt a slight pain earlier, I thought it was something I'd eaten, and then it came back, and came back more often. I thought when this is over I'll go to bed. There were still long gaps when I felt perfectly all right and I didn't want to attract attention to myself and spoil the ceremony. Then I suddenly realised what it must be. I had to last out till I could get home and hide. Then something changed, my breath started to catch, I couldn't plan things properly any more. We were in a little street that goes between St. Clement's and the Colosseum, and I just had to get off the horse and sit down for a minute. Great waves of pressure were going through my body. I heard sounds like a cow lowing, they came out of my mouth. Far away I heard people screaming, 'The Pope is ill, the Pope is dying.' And the baby just slid out onto the road.*

MARLENE. The cardinals / won't have known where to put themselves.

NIJO. Oh dear, Joan, what a thing to do! In the street!

ISABELLA. *How embarrassing.

GRET. In a field, yah.

(*They are laughing.*)

JOAN. One of the cardinals said, "The Antichrist!" and fell over in a faint.

(*They all laugh.*)

MARLENE. So what did they do? They weren't best pleased.

JOAN. They took me by the feet and dragged me out of town and stoned me to death.

(*They stop laughing.*)

MARLENE. Joan, how horrible.

JOAN. I don't really remember.

NIJO. And the child died too?

JOAN. Oh yes, I think so, yes.

(*Pause.*)
(*The Waitress enters to clear the plates. They start talking quietly.*)

ISABELLA. (*to Joan*). I never had any children. I was very fond of horses.

NIJO (*to Marlene*). I saw my daughter once. She was three years old. She wore a plum-red / small-sleeved gown. Akebono's

ISABELLA. Birdie was my favourite. A little Indian bay mare I rode in the Rocky Mountains.

NIJO. wife had taken the child because her own died. Everyone thought I was just a visitor. She was being brought up carefully so she could be sent to the palace like I was.

ISABELLA. Legs of iron and always cheerful, and such a pretty face. If a stranger led her she reared up like a bronco.

NIJO. I never saw my third child after he was born, the son of Ariake the priest. Ariake held him on his lap the day he was born and talked to him as if he could understand, and cried. My fourth child was Ariake's too. Ariake died before he was born. I didn't want to see anyone, I stayed alone in the hills. It was a boy again, my third son. But oddly enough I felt nothing for him.

MARLENE. How many children did you have, Gret?

GRET. Ten.

ISABELLA. Whenever I came back to England I felt I had so much to atone for. Hennie and John were so good. I did no good in my life. I spent years in self-gratification. So I hurled myself into committees, I nursed the people of Tobermory in the epidemic of influenza, I lectured the Young Women's Christian Association on Thrift. I talked and talked explaining how the East was corrupt and vicious. My travels must do good to someone beside myself. I wore myself out with good causes.

MARLENE. Oh God, why are we all so miserable?

JOAN. The procession never went down that street again.

MARLENE. They rerouted it specially?

JOAN. Yes they had to go all round to avoid it. And they introduced a pierced chair.

MARLENE. A pierced chair?

JOAN. Yes, a chair made out of solid marble with a hole in the seat / and it was in the Chapel of the Saviour, and after he was

MARLENE. You're not serious.

JOAN. elected the Pope had to sit in it.

MARLENE. And someone looked up his skirts? / Not really?

ISABELLA. What an extraordinary thing.

JOAN. Two of the clergy / made sure he was a man.

NIJO. On their hands and knees!

MARLENE. A pierced chair!

GRET. Balls!

(*Griselda arrives unnoticed.*)

NIJO. Why couldn't he just pull up his robe?

JOAN. He had to sit there and look dignified.

MARLENE. You could have made all your chamberlains sit in it.*

GRET. Big one, small one.

NIJO. Very useful chair at court.

ISABELLA. *Or the laird of Tobermory in his kilt.

(*They are quite drunk. They get the giggles.*)
(*Marlene notices Griselda.*)

MARLENE. Griselda! / There you are. Do you want to eat?

GRISELDA. I'm sorry I'm so late. No, no, don't bother.

MARLENE. Of course it's no bother. / Have you eaten?

GRISELDA. No really, I'm not hungry.

MARLENE. Well have some pudding.

GRISELDA. I never eat pudding.

MARLENE. Griselda, I hope you're not anorexic. We're having pudding. I am, and getting nice and fat.

GRISELDA. Oh if everyone is. I don't mind.

MARLENE. Now who do you know? This is Joan who was Pope in the ninth century, and Isabella Bird, the Victorian traveller, and Lady Nijo from Japan, Emperor's concubine and Buddhist nun, thirteenth century, nearer your own time, and Gret who was painted by Brueghel. Griselda's in Boccaccio and Petrarch and Chaucer because of her extraordinary marriage. I'd like profiteroles because they're disgusting.

JOAN. Zabaglione, please.

ISABELLA. Apple pie / and cream.

NIJO. What's this?

MARLENE. Zabaglione, it's Italian, it's what Joan's having, / it's delicious.

NIJO. A Roman Catholic / dessert? Yes please.

MARLENE. Gret?

GRET. Cake.

GRISELDA. Just cheese and biscuits, thank you.

MARLENE. yes, Griselda's life is like a fairy-story, except it starts with marrying the prince.

GRISELDA. He's only a marquis, Marlene.

MARLENE. Well everyone for miles around is his liege and he's absolute lord of life and death and you were the poor but beautiful peasant girl and he whisked you off. / Near enough a prince.

NIJO. How old were you?

GRISELDA. Fifteen.

NIJO. I was brought up in court circles and it was still a shock. Had you ever seen him before?

GRISELDA. I'd seen him riding by, we all had. And he'd seen me in the fields with the sheep.*

ISABELLA. I would have been well suited to minding sheep.

NIJO. And Mr. Nugent riding by.

ISABELLA. Of course not, Nijo, I mean a healthy life in the open air.

JOAN. *He just rode up while you were minding the sheep and asked you to marry him?

GRISELDA. No, no, it was on the wedding day. I was waiting outside the door to see the procession. Everyone wanted him to get married so there'd be an heir to look after us when he died, / and at last he announced a day for the wedding but

MARLENE. I don't think Walter wanted to get married. It is Walter? Yes.

GRISELDA. nobody knew who the bride was, we thought it must be a foreign princess, we were longing to see her. Then the carriage stopped outside our cottage and we couldn't see the bride anywhere. And he came and spoke to my father.

NIJO. And your father told you to serve the Prince.

GRISELDA. My father could hardly speak. The Marquis said it wasn't an order, I could say no, but if I said yes I must always obey him in everything.

MARLENE. That's when you should have suspected.

GRISELDA. But of course a wife must obey her husband. / And of course I must obey the Marquis.*

ISABELLA. I swore to obey dear John, of course, but it didn't seem to arise. Naturally I wouldn't have wanted to go abroad while I was married.

MARLENE. *Then why bother to mention it at all? He'd got a thing about it, that's why.

GRISELDA. I'd rather obey the Marquis than a boy from the village.

MARLENE. Yes, that's a point.

JOAN. I never obeyed anyone. They all obeyed me.

NIJO. And what did you wear? He didn't make you get married in your own clothes? That would be perverse.*

MARLENE. Oh, you wait.

GRISELDA. *He had ladies with him who undressed me and they had a white silk dress and jewels for my hair.

MARLENE. And at first he seemed perfectly normal?

GRISELDA. Marlene, you're always so critical of him. / Of course he was normal, he was very kind.

MARLENE. But Griselda, come on, he took your baby.

GRISELDA. Walter found it hard to believe I loved him. He couldn't believe I would always obey him. He had to prove it.

MARLENE. I don't think Walter likes women.

GRISELDA. I'm sure he loved me, Marlene, all the time.

MARLENE. He just had a funny way / of showing it.

GRISELDA. It was hard for him too.

JOAN. How do you mean he took away your baby?

NIJO. Was it a boy?

GRISELDA. No, the first one was a girl.

NIJO. Even so it's hard when they take it away. Did you see it at all?

GRISELDA. Oh yes, she was six weeks old.

NIJO. Much better to do it straight away.

ISABELLA. But why did your husband take the child?

GRISELDA. He said all the people hated me because I was just one of them. And now I had a child they were restless. So he had to get rid of the child to keep them quiet. But he said he wouldn't snatch her, I had to agree and obey and give her up. So when I was feeding her a man came in an took her away. I thought he was going to kill her even before he was out of the room.

MARLENE. But you let him take her? You didn't struggle?

GRISELDA. I asked him to give her back so I could kiss her. And I asked him to bury her where no animals could dig her up. / It

ISABELLA. Oh my dear.

GRISELDA. was Walter's child to do what he liked with.*

MARLENE. Walter was bonkers.

GRET. Bastard.

ISABELLA. *But surely, murder.

GRISELDA. I had promised.

MARLENE. I can't stand this. I'm going for a pee.

(Marlene goes out.)
(The Waitress brings dessert.)

NIJO. No, I understand. Of course you had to, he was your life. And were you in favour after that?

GRISELDA. Oh yes, we were very happy together. We never spoke about what had happened.

ISABELLA. I can see you were doing what you thought was your duty. But didn't it make you ill?

GRISELDA. No, I was very well, thank you.

NIJO. And you had another child?

GRISELDA. Not for four years, but then I did, yes, a boy.

NIJO. Ah a boy. / So it all ended happily.

GRISELDA. Yes he was pleased. I kept my son till he was two years old. A peasant's grandson. It made the people angry. Walter explained.

ISABELLA. But surely he wouldn't kill his children / just because—

GRISELDA. Oh it wasn't true. Walter would never give in to the people. He wanted to see if I loved him enough.

JOAN. He killed his children / to see if you loved him enough?

NIJO. Was it easier the second time or harder?

GRISELDA. It was always easy because I always knew I would do what he said.

(Pause. They start to eat.)

ISABELLA. I hope you didn't have any more children.

GRISELDA. Oh no, no more. It was twelve years till he tested me again.

ISABELLA. So whatever did he do this time? / My poor John, I never loved him enough, and he would never have dreamt . . .

GRISELDA. He sent me away. He said the people wanted him to marry someone else who'd give him an heir and he'd got special permission from the Pope. So I said I'd go home to my father. I came with nothing / so I went with nothing. I

NIJO. Better to leave if your master doesn't want you.

GRISELDA. took off my clothes. He let me keep a slip so he wouldn't be shamed. And I walked home barefoot. My father came out in tears. Everyone was crying except for me.

NIJO. At least your father wasn't dead. / I had nobody.

ISABELLA. Well it can be a relief to come home. I loved to see Hennie's sweet face again.

GRISELDA. Oh yes, I was perfectly content. And quite soon he sent for me again.

JOAN. I don't think I would have gone.

GRISELDA. But he told me to come. I had to obey him. He wanted me to help prepare his wedding. He was getting married to a young girl from France / and nobody except me knew how to arrange things the way he liked them.

NIJO. It's always hard taking him another woman.

(*Marlene comes back.*)

JOAN. I didn't live a woman's life. I don't understand it.

GRISELDA. The girl was sixteen and far more beautiful than me. I could see why he loved her. / She had her younger brother with her as a page.

(*The waitress enters.*)

MARLENE. Oh God, I can't bear it. I want some coffee. Six coffees. Six brandies. / Double brandies. Straightaway.

GRISELDA. They all went in to the feast I'd prepared. And he stayed behind and put his arms round me and kissed me. / I felt half asleep with the shock.

NIJO. Oh, like a dream.

MARLENE. And he said, 'This is your daughter and your son.'

GRISELDA. Yes.

JOAN. What?

NIJO. Oh. Oh I see. You got them back.

ISABELLA. I did think it was remarkably barbaric to kill them but you learn not to say anything. / So he had them brought up secretly I suppose.

MARLENE. Walter's a monster. Weren't you angry? What did you do?

GRISELDA. Well I fainted. Then I cried and kissed the children. / Everyone was making a fuss of me.

NIJO. But did you feel anything for them?

GRISELDA. What?

NIJO. Did you feel anything for the children?

GRISELDA. Of course, I loved them.

JOAN. So you forgave him and lived with him?

GRISELDA. He suffered so much all those years.

ISABELLA. Hennie had the same sweet nature.

NIJO. So they dressed you again?

GRISELDA. Cloth of gold.

JOAN. I can't forgive anything.

MARLENE. You really are exceptional, Griselda.

NIJO. Nobody gave me back my children.

(*Nijo cries. The Waitress brings brandies.*)

ISABELLA. I can never be like Hennie. I was always so busy in England, a kind of business I detested. The very presence of people exhausted my emotional reserves. I could not be like Hennie however I tried. I tried and was as ill as could be. The doctor suggested a steel net to support my head, the weight of my own head was too much for my diseased spine. / It is dangerous to put oneself in depressing circumstances. Why should I do it?

JOAN. Don't cry.

NIJO. My father and the Emperor both died in the autumn. So much pain.

JOAN. Yes, but don't cry.

NIJO. They wouldn't let me into the palace when he was dying. I hid in the room with his coffin, then I couldn't find where I'd left my shoes, I ran after the funeral procession in bare feet, I couldn't keep up. When I got there it was over, a few wisps of smoke in the sky, that's all that was left of him. What I want to know is, if I'd still been at court, would I have been allowed to wear full mourning?

MARLENE. I'm sure you would.

NIJO. Why do you say that? You don't know anything about it. Would I have been allowed to wear full mourning?

ISABELLA. How can people live in this dim pale island and wear our hideous clothes? I cannot and will not live the life of a lady.

NIJO. I'll tell you something that made me angry. I was eighteen, at the Full Moon Ceremony. They make a special rice gruel and stir it with their sticks, and then they beat their women across the loins so they'll have sons and not daughters. So the Emperor beat us all / very hard as usual—that's not it,

MARLENE. What a sod.

NIJO. Marlene, that's normal, what made us angry, he told his attendants they could beat us too. Well they had a wonderful time. / So Lady Genki and I made a plan, and the ladies all hid

(*The Waitress has entered with coffees.*)

MARLENE. I'd like another brandy please. Better make it six.

NIJO. in his rooms, and Lady Mashimizu stood guard with a stick at the door, and when His Majesty came in Genki seized him and I beat him till he cried out and promised he would never order anyone to hit us again. Afterwards there was a terrible fuss. The nobles were horrified. 'We wouldn't even dream of stepping on your Majesty's shadow.' And I had hit him with a stick. Yes, I hit him with a stick.

JOAN. Suave, mari magno turbantibus aequora ventis,
e terra magnum alterius spectare laborem;
non quia vexari quemquamst iucunda voluptas,
sed quibus ipse malis careas quia cernere suave est.
Suave etiam belli certamina magna tueri
per campos instructa tua sine parte pericli.
Sed nil dulcius est, bene quam munita tenere
edita doctrina sapientum templa serena, /
despicere unde queas alios passimque videre
errare atque viam palantis quaerere vitae,

GRISELDA. I do think—I do wonder—it would have been nicer if Walter hadn't had to.

ISABELLA. Why should I? Why should I?

MARLENE. Of course not.

NIJO. I hit him with a stick.

JOAN. certare ingenio, contendere nobilitate,

noctes atque dies niti praestante labore
ad summas emergere opes retumque potiri.
O miseras / hominum mentis, o pectora caeca!*

ISABELLA. Oh miseras!

NIJO. *Pectora caeca.

JOAN. qualibus in tenebris vitae quantisque periclis
degitur hoc aevi quodcumquest! / nonne videre
nil aliud sibi naturam latrare, nisi utqui
corpore seiunctus dolor absit, mente fruatur

(*Joan subsides.*)

GRET. We come into hell through a big mouth. Hell's black
and red. / It's like the village where I come from. There's
a river and

MARLENE (*to Joan*). Shut up, pet.

ISABELLA. Listen, she's been to hell.

GRET. a bridge and houses. There's places on fire like when
the soldiers come. There's a big devil sat on a roof with a
big hole in his arse and he's scooping stuff out of it with a
big ladle and it's falling down on us, and it's money, so a
lot of the women stop and get some. But most of us is
fighting the devils. There's lots of little devils, our size,
and we get them down all right and give them a beating.
There's lots of funny creatures round your feet, you don't
like to look, like rats and lizards, and nasty things, a bum
with a face, and fish with legs, and faces on things that
don't have faces on. But they don't hurt, you just keep
going. Well we'd had worse, you see, we'd had the Spanish. We'd all had family killed. My big son die on a
wheel. Birds eat him. My baby, a soldier run her through
with a sword. I'd had enough, I was mad, I hate the bastards. I come out my front door that morning and shout
till my neighbours come out and I said, 'Come on, we're
going where the evil come from and pay the bastards out.'
And they all come out just as they was / from baking or
washing in their

NIJO. All the ladies come.

GRET. aprons, and we push down the street and the ground
opens up and we go through a big mouth into a street
just like ours but in hell. I've got a sword in my hand
from somewhere and I fill a basket with gold cups they
drink out of down there. You just keep running on and
fighting / you didn't stop for nothing. Oh we give them
devils such a beating.

NIJO. Take that, take that.

JOAN. Something something something mortisque timores
tum vacuum pectus—damn.
Quod si ridicula—
something something on and on and on and something
splendorem purpureai.

ISABELLA. I thought I would have a last jaunt up the west
river in China. Why not? But the doctors were so very
grave. I just went to Morocco. The sea was so wild I had
to be landed by ship's crane in a coal bucket. / My horse
was a terror to me a

GRET. Coal bucket, good.

JOAN. nos in luce timemus
something
terrorem.

ISABELLA. powerful black charger.

(*Nijo is laughing and crying.*)
(*Joan gets up and is sick in a corner.*)
(*Marlene is drinking Isabella's brandy.*)

So off I went to visit the Berber sheikhs in full blue
trousers and great brass spurs. I was the only European
woman ever to have seen the Emperor of Morocco. I was
seventy years old. What lengths to go to for a last chance
of joy. I knew my return of vigour was only temporary, but
how marvellous while it lasted.

SCENE TWO

Employment Agency: Marlene and Jeanine.

MARLENE. Right Jeanine, you are Jeanine aren't you? Let's
have a look. Os and As. / No As, all those Os you probably

JEANINE. Six Os.

MARLENE. could have got an A. / Speeds, not brilliant, not
too bad.

JEANINE. I wanted to go to work.

MARLENE. Well, Jeanine, what's your present job like?

JEANINE. I'm a secretary.

MARLENE. Secretary or typist?

JEANINE. I did start as a typist but the last six months I've
been a secretary.

MARLENE. To?

JEANINE. To three of them, really, they share me. There's Mr
Ashford, he's the office manager, and Mr Philby / is sales,
and—

MARLENE. Quite a small place?

JEANINE. A bit small.

MARLENE. Friendly?

JEANINE. Oh it's friendly enough.

MARLENE. Prospects?

JEANINE. I don't think so, that's the trouble. Miss Lewis is
secretary to the managing director and she's been there
forever, and Mrs Bradford / is—

MARLENE. So you want a job with better prospects?

JEANINE. I want a change.

MARLENE. So you'll take anything comparable?

JEANINE. No, I do want prospects. I want more money.

MARLENE. You're getting—

JEANINE. Hundred.

MARLENE. It's not bad you know. You're what? Twenty?

JEANINE. I'm saving to get married.

MARLENE. Does that mean you don't want a long-term job,
Jeanine?

JEANINE. I might do.

MARLENE. Because where do the prospects come in? No kids for a bit?

JEANINE. Oh no, not kids, not yet.

MARLENE. So you won't tell them you're getting married?

JEANINE. Had I better not?

MARLENE. It would probably help.

JEANINE. I'm not wearing a ring. We thought we wouldn't spend on a ring.

MARLENE. Saves taking it off.

JEANINE. I wouldn't take it off.

MARLENE. There's no need to mention it when you go for an interview. / Now Jeanine do you have a feel for any particular

JEANINE. But what if they ask?

MARLENE. kind of company?

JEANINE. I thought advertising.

MARLENE. People often do think advertising. I have got a few vacancies but I think they're looking for something glossier.

JEANINE. You mean how I dress? / I can dress different. I

MARLENE. I mean experience.

JEANINE. dress like this on purpose for where I am now.

MARLENE. I have a marketing department here of a knitwear manufacturer. / Marketing is near enough advertising. Secretary

JEANINE. Knitwear?

MARLENE. to the marketing manager, he's thirty-five, married, I've sent him a girl before and she was happy, left to have a baby, you won't want to mention marriage there. He's very fair I think, good at his job, you won't have to nurse him along. Hundred and ten, so that's better than you're doing now.

JEANINE. I don't know.

MARLENE. I've a fairly small concern here, father and two sons, you'd have more say potentially, secretarial and reception duties, only a hundred but the job's going to grow with the concern and then you'll be in at the top with new girls coming in underneath you.

JEANINE. What is it they do?

MARLENE. Lampshades. / This would be my first choice for you.

JEANINE. Just lampshades?

MARLENE. There's plenty of different kinds of lampshade. So we'll send you there, shall we, and the knitwear second choice. Are you free to go for an interview any day they call you?

JEANINE. I'd like to travel.

MARLENE. We don't have any foreign clients. You'd have to go elsewhere.

JEANINE. Yes I know. I don't really . . . I just mean . . .

MARLENE. Does your fiancé want to travel?

JEANINE. I'd like a job where I was here in London and with him and everything but now and then—I expect it's silly. Are there jobs like that?

MARLENE. There's personal assistant to a top executive in a multinational. If that's the idea you need to be planning ahead. Is that where you want to be in ten years?

JEANINE. I might not be alive in ten years.

MARLENE. Yes but you will be. You'll have children.

JEANINE. I can't think about ten years.

MARLENE. You haven't got the speeds anyway. So I'll send you to these two shall I? You haven't been to any other agency? Just so we don't get crossed wires. Now Jeanine I want you to get one of these jobs, all right? If I send you that means I'm putting myself on the line for you. Your presentation's OK, you look fine, just be confident and go in there convinced that this is the best job for you and you're the best person for the job. If you don't believe it they won't believe it.

JEANINE. Do you believe it?

MARLENE. I think you could make me believe it if you put your mind to it.

JEANINE. Yes, all right.

SCENE THREE

Joyce's back yard: The house with back door is upstage. Downstage a shelter made of junk, made by children. Two girls, Angie and Kit, are in it, squashed together. Angie is 16, Kit is 12. They cannot be seen from the house. Joyce calls from the house.

JOYCE. Angie. Angie are you out there?

(Silence. They keep still and wait. When nothing else happens they relax.)

ANGIE. Wish she was dead.

KIT. Wanna watch *The Exterminator*?

ANGIE. You're sitting on my leg.

KIT. There's nothing on telly. We can have an ice cream. Angie?

ANGIE. Shall I tell you something?

KIT. Do you wanna watch *The Exterminator*?

ANGIE. It's X, innit.

KIT. I can get into Xs.

ANGIE. Shall I tell you something?

KIT. We'll go to something else. We'll go to Ipswich. What's on the Odeon?

ANGIE. She won't let me, will she?

KIT. Don't tell her.

ANGIE. I've no money.

KIT. I'll pay.

ANGIE. She'll moan though, won't she?

KIT. I'll ask her for you if you like.

ANGIE. I've no money, I don't want you to pay.

KIT. I'll ask her.

ANGIE. She don't like you.

KIT. I still got three pounds birthday money. Did she say she don't like me? I'll go by myself then.

ANGIE. Your mum don't let you. I got to take you.

KIT. She won't know.

ANGIE. You'd be scared who'd sit next to you.

KIT. No I wouldn't.

She does like me anyway.

Tell me then.

ANGIE. Tell you what?

KIT. It's you she doesn't like.

ANGIE. Well I don't like her so tough shit.

JOYCE (off). Angie. Angie. Angie. I know you're out there. I'm not coming out after you. You come in here.

(Silence. Nothing happens.)

ANGIE. Last night when I was in bed. I been thinking yesterday could I make things move. You know, make things move by thinking about them without touching them. Last night I was in bed and suddenly a picture fell down off the wall.

KIT. What picture?

ANGIE. My gran, that picture. Not the poster. The photograph in the frame.

KIT. Had you done something to make it fall down?

ANGIE. I must have done.

KIT. But were you thinking about it?

ANGIE. Not about it, but about something.

KIT. I don't think that's very good.

ANGIE. You know the kitten?

KIT. Which one?

ANGIE. There only is one. The dead one.

KIT. What about it?

ANGIE. I heard it last night.

KIT. Where?

ANGIE. Out here. In the dark. What if I left you here in the dark all night?

KIT. You couldn't. I'd go home.

ANGIE. You couldn't.

KIT. I'd / go home.

ANGIE. No you couldn't, not if I said.

KIT. I could.

ANGIE. Then you wouldn't see anything. You'd just be ignorant.

KIT. I can see in the daytime.

ANGIE. No you can't. You can't hear it in the daytime.

KIT. I don't want to hear it.

ANGIE. You're scared that's all.

KIT. I'm not scared of anything.

ANGIE. You're scared of blood.

KIT. It's not the same kitten anyway. You just heard an old cat, / you just heard some old cat.

ANGIE. You don't know what I heard. Or what I saw. You don't know nothing because you're a baby.

KIT. You're sitting on me.

ANGIE. Mind my hair / you silly cunt.

KIT. Stupid fucking cow, I hate you.

ANGIE. I don't care if you do.

KIT. You're horrible.

ANGIE. I'm going to kill my mother and you're going to watch.

KIT. I'm not playing.

ANGIE. You're scared of blood.

(Kit puts her hand under her dress, brings it out with blood on her finger.)

KIT. There, see, I got my own blood, so.

(Angie takes Kit's hand and licks her finger.)

ANGIE. Now I'm a cannibal. I might turn into a vampire now.

KIT. That picture wasn't nailed up right.

ANGIE. You'll have to do that when I get mine.

KIT. I don't have to.

ANGIE. You're scared.

KIT. I'll do it, I might do it. I don't have to just because you say. I'll be sick on you.

ANGIE. I don't care if you are sick on me, I don't mind sick. I don't mind blood. If I don't get away from here I'm going to die.

KIT. I'm going home.

ANGIE. You can't go through the house. She'll see you.

KIT. I won't tell her.

ANGIE. Oh great, fine.

KIT. I'll say I was by myself. I'll tell her you're at my house and I'm going there to get you.

ANGIE. She knows I'm here, stupid.

KIT. Then why can't I go through the house?

ANGIE. Because I said not.

KIT. My mum don't like you anyway.

ANGIE. I don't want her to like me. She's a slag.

KIT. She is not.

ANGIE. She does it with everyone.

KIT. She does not.

ANGIE. You don't even know what it is.

KIT. Yes I do.

ANGIE. Tell me then.

KIT. We get it all at school, cleverclogs. It's on television. You haven't done it.

ANGIE. How do you know?

KIT. Because I know you haven't.

ANGIE. You know wrong then because I have.

KIT. Who with?

ANGIE. I'm not telling you / who with.

KIT. You haven't anyway.

ANGIE. How do you know?

KIT. Who with?

ANGIE. I'm not telling you

KIT. You said you told me everything.

ANGIE. I was lying wasn't I?

KIT. Who with? You can't tell me who with because / you never—

ANGIE. Sh.

(*Joyce has come out of the house. She stops half way across the yard and listens. They listen.*)

JOYCE. You there Angie? Kit? You there Kitty? Want a cup of tea? I've got some chocolate biscuits. Come on now I'll put the kettle on. Want a choccy biccy, Angie?

(*They all listen and wait.*)

Fucking rotten little cunt. You can stay there and die. I'll lock the back door.

(*They all wait.*)
(*Joyce goes back to the house.*)
(*Angie and Kit sit in silence for a while.*)

KIT. When there's a war, where's the safest place?

ANGIE. Nowhere.

KIT. New Zealand is, my mum said. Your skin's burned right off. Shall we go to New Zealand?

ANGIE. I'm not staying here.

KIT. Shall we go to New Zealand?

ANGIE. You're not old enough.

KIT. You're not old enough.

ANGIE. I'm old enough to get married.

KIT. You don't want to get married.

ANGIE. No but I'm old enough.

KIT. I'd find out where they were going to drop it and stand right in the place.

ANGIE. You couldn't find out.

KIT. Better than walking round with your skin dragging on the ground. Eugh. / Would you like walking round with your skin dragging on the ground?

ANGIE. You couldn't find out, stupid, it's a secret.

KIT. Where are you going?

ANGIE. I'm not telling you.

KIT. Why?

ANGIE. It's a secret.

KIT. But you tell me all your secrets.

ANGIE. Not the true secrets.

KIT. Yes you do.

ANGIE. No I don't.

KIT. I want to go somewhere away from the war.

ANGIE. Just forget the war.

KIT. I can't.

ANGIE. You have to. It's so boring.

KIT. I'll remember it at night.

ANGIE. I'm going to do something else anyway.

KIT. What? Angie come on. Angie.

ANGIE. It's a true secret.

KIT. It can't be worse than the kitten. And killing your mother. And the war.

ANGIE. Well I'm not telling you so you can die for all I care.

KIT. My mother says there's something wrong with you playing with someone my age. She says why haven't you got friends your own age. People your own age know there's something funny about you. She says you're a bad influence. She says she's going to speak to your mother.

(*Angie twists Kit's arm till she cries out.*)

ANGIE. Say you're a liar.

KIT. She said it not me.

ANGIE. Say you eat shit.

KIT. You can't make me.

(*Angie lets go.*)

ANGIE. I don't care anyway. I'm leaving.

KIT. Go on then.

ANGIE. You'll all wake up one morning and find I've gone.

KIT. Good.

ANGIE. I'm not telling you when.

KIT. Go on then.

ANGIE. I'm sorry I hurt you.

KIT. I'm tired.

ANGIE. Do you like me?

KIT. I don't know.

ANGIE. You do like me.

KIT. I'm going home.

(*Kit gets up.*)

ANGIE. No you're not.

KIT. I'm tired.

ANGIE. She'll see you.

KIT. She'll give me a chocolate biscuit.

ANGIE. Kitty.

KIT. Tell me where you're going.

ANGIE. Sit down.

(*Kit sits in the hut again.*)

KIT. Go on then.

ANGIE. Swear?

KIT. Swear.

ANGIE. I'm going to London. To see my aunt.

KIT. And what?

ANGIE. That's it.

KIT. I see my aunt all the time.

ANGIE. I don't see my aunt.

KIT. What's so special?

ANGIE. It is special. She's special.

KIT. Why?

ANGIE. She is.

KIT. Why?

ANGIE. She is.

KIT. Why?

ANGIE. My mother hates her.

KIT. Why?

ANGIE. Because she does.

KIT. Perhaps she's not very nice.

ANGIE. She is nice.

KIT. How do you know?

ANGIE. Because I know her.

KIT. You said you never see her.

ANGIE. I saw her last year. You saw her.

KIT. Did I?

ANGIE. Never mind.

KIT. I remember her. That aunt. What's so special?

ANGIE. She gets people jobs.

KIT. What's so special?

ANGIE. I think I'm my aunt's child. I think my mother's really my aunt.

KIT. Why?

ANGIE. Because she goes to America, now shut up.

KIT. I've been to London.

ANGIE. Now give us a cuddle and shut up because I'm sick.

KIT. You're sitting on my arm.

(*Silence.*)
(*Joyce comes out and comes up to them quietly.*)

JOYCE. Come on.

KIT. Oh hello.

JOYCE. Time you went home.

KIT. We want to go to the Odeon.

JOYCE. What time?

KIT. Don't know.

JOYCE. What's on?

KIT. Don't know.

JOYCE. Don't know much do you?

KIT. That all right then?

JOYCE. Angie's got to clean her room first.

ANGIE. No I don't.

JOYCE. Yes you do, it's a pigsty.

ANGIE. Well I'm not.

JOYCE. Then you're not going. I don't care.

ANGIE. Well I am going.

JOYCE. You've no money, have you?

ANGIE. Kit's paying anyway.

JOYCE. No she's not.

KIT. I'll help you with your room.

JOYCE. That's nice.

ANGIE. No you won't. You wait here.

KIT. Hurry then.

ANGIE. I'm not hurrying. You just wait.

(*Angie goes into the house. Silence.*)

JOYCE. I don't know.

(*Silence.*)

How's school then?

KIT. All right.

JOYCE. What are you now? Third year?

KIT. Second year.

JOYCE. Your mum says you're good at English.

(*Silence.*)

Maybe Angie should've stayed on.

KIT. She didn't like it.

JOYCE. I didn't like it. And look at me. If your face fits at school it's going to fit other places too. It wouldn't make no difference to Angie. She's not going to get a job when jobs are hard to get. I'd be sorry for anyone in charge of her. She'd better get married. I don't know who'd have her, mind. She's one of those girls might never leave home. What do you want to be when you grow up, Kit?

KIT. Physicist.

JOYCE. What?

KIT. Nuclear physicist.

JOYCE. Whatever for?

KIT. I could, I'm clever.

JOYCE. I know you're clever, pet.

(*Silence.*)

I'll make a cup of tea.

(*Silence.*)

Looks like it's going to rain.

(*Silence.*)

Don't you have friends your own age?

KIT. Yes.

JOYCE. Well then.

KIT. I'm old for my age.

JOYCE. And Angie's simple is she? She's not simple.

KIT. I love Angie.

JOYCE. She's clever in her own way.

KIT. You can't stop me.

JOYCE. I don't want to.

KIT. You can't, so.

JOYCE. Don't be cheeky, Kitty. She's always kind to little children.

KIT. She's coming so you better leave me alone.

(*Angie comes out. She has changed into an old best dress, slightly small for her.*)

JOYCE. What you put that on for? Have you done your room? You can't clean your room in that.

ANGIE. I looked in the cupboard and it was there.

JOYCE. Of course it was there, it's meant to be there. Is that why it was a surprise, finding something in the right place? I should think she's surprised, wouldn't you Kit, to find something in her room in the right place.

ANGIE. I decided to wear it.

JOYCE. Not today, why? To clean your room? You're not going to the pictures till you've done your room. You can put your dress on after if you like.

(*Angie picks up a brick.*)

Have you done your room? You're not getting out of it, you know.

KIT. Angie, let's go.

JOYCE. She's not going till she's done her room.

KIT. It's starting to rain.

JOYCE. Come on, come on then. Hurry and do your room, Angie, and then you can go to the cinema with Kit. Oh it's wet, come on. We'll look up the time in the paper. Does your mother know, Kit, it's going to be a late night for you, isn't it? Hurry up, Angie. You'll spoil your dress. You make me sick.

(*Joyce and Kit run in.*)
(*Angie stays where she is. Sound of rain.*)
(*Kit comes out of the house and shouts.*)

KIT. Angie. Angie, come on, you'll get wet.

(*Kit comes back to Angie.*)

ANGIE. I put on this dress to kill my mother.

KIT. I suppose you thought you'd do it with a brick.

ANGIE. You can kill people with a brick.

KIT. Well you didn't, so.

ACT TWO

SCENE ONE

Office of 'top girls' employment agency: Three desks and a small interviewing area. Monday morning. Win and Nell have just arrived for work.

NELL. Coffee coffee coffee coffee / coffee.

WIN. The roses were smashing. / Mermaid.

NELL. Ohhh.

WIN. Iceberg. He taught me all their names.

(*Nell has some coffee now.*)

NELL. Ah. Now then.

WIN. He has one of the finest rose gardens in West Sussex. He exhibits.

NELL. He what?

WIN. His wife was visiting her mother. It was like living together.

NELL. Crafty, you never said.

WIN. He rang on Saturday morning.

NELL. Lucky you were free.

WIN. That's what I told him.

NELL. Did you hell.

WIN. Have you ever seen a really beautiful rose garden?

NELL. I don't like flowers. / I like swimming pools.

WIN. Marilyn. Esther's Baby. They're all called after birds.

NELL. Our friend's late. Celebrating all weekend I bet you.

WIN. I'd call a rose Elvis. Or John Conteh.

NELL. Is Howard in yet?

WIN. If he is he'll be bleeping us with a problem.

NELL. Howard can just hang onto himself.

WIN. Howard's really cut up.

NELL. Howard thinks because he's a fella the job was his as of right. Our Marlene's got far more balls than Howard and that's that.

WIN. Poor little bugger.

NELL. He'll live.

WIN. He'll move on.

NELL. I wouldn't mind a change of air myself.

WIN. Serious?

NELL. I've never been a staying put lady. Pastures new.

WIN. So who's the pirate?

NELL. There's nothing definite.

WIN. Inquiries?

NELL. There's always inquiries. I'd think I'd got bad breath if there stopped being inquiries. Most of them can't afford me. Or you.

WIN. I'm all right for the time being. Unless I go to Australia.

NELL. There's not a lot of room upward.

WIN. Marlene's filled it up.

NELL. Good luck to her. Unless there's some prospects moneywise.

WIN. You can but ask.

NELL. Can always but ask.

WIN. So what have we got? I've got a Mr Holden I saw last week.

NELL. Any use?

WIN. Pushy. Bit of a cowboy.

NELL. Good-looker?

WIN. Good dresser.

NELL. High flyer?

WIN. That's his general idea certainly but I'm not sure he's got it up there.

NELL. Prestel wants six high flyers and I've only seen two and a half.

WIN. He's making a bomb on the road but he thinks it's time for an office. I sent him to IBM but he didn't get it.

NELL. Prestel's on the road.

WIN. He's not overbright.

NELL. Can he handle an office?

WIN. Provided his secretary can punctuate he should go far.

NELL. Bear Prestel in mind then, I might put my head round the door. I've got that poor little nerd I should never have said I could help. Tender heart me.

WIN. Tender like old boots. How old?

NELL. Yes well forty-five.

WIN. Say no more.

NELL. He knows his place, he's not after calling himself a manager, he's just a poor little bod wants a better commission and a bit of sunshine.

WIN. Don't we all.

NELL. He's just got to relocate. He's got a bungalow in Dymchurch.

WIN. And his wife says.

NELL. The lady wife wouldn't care to relocate. She's going through the change.

WIN. It's his funeral, don't waste your time.

NELL. I don't waste a lot.

WIN. Good weekend you?

NELL. You could say.

WIN. Which one?

NELL. One Friday, one Saturday.

WIN. Aye — aye.

NELL. Sunday night I watched telly.

WIN. Which of them do you like best really?

NELL. Sunday was best, I liked the Ovaltine.

WIN. Holden, Barker, Gardner, Duke.

NELL. I've a lady here thinks she can sell.

WIN. Taking her on?

NELL. She's had some jobs.

WIN. Services?

NELL. No, quite heavy stuff, electric.

WIN. Tough bird like us.

NELL. We could do with a few more here.

WIN. There's nothing going here.

NELL. No but I always want the tough ones when I see them. Hang onto them.

WIN. I think we're plenty.

NELL. Derek asked me to marry him again.

WIN. He doesn't know when he's beaten.

NELL. I told him I'm not going to play house, not even in Ascot.

WIN. Mind you, you could play house.

NELL. If I chose to play house I would play house ace.

WIN. You could marry him and go on working.

NELL. I could go on working and not marry him.

(*Marlene arrives.*)

MARLENE. Morning ladies.

(*Win and Nell cheer and whistle.*)

    Mind my head.

NELL. Coffee coffee coffee.

WIN. We're tactfully not mentioning you're late.

MARLENE. Fucking tube.

WIN. We've heard that one.

NELL. We've used that one.

WIN. It's the top executive doesn't come in as early as the poor working girl.

MARLENE. Pass the sugar and shut your face, pet.

WIN. Well I'm delighted.

NELL. Howard's looking sick.

WIN. Howard is sick. He's got ulcers and heart. He told me.

NELL. He'll have to stop then won't he?

WIN. Stop what?

NELL. Smoking, drinking, shouting. Working.

WIN. Well, working.

NELL. We're just looking through the day.

MARLENE. I'm doing some of Pam's ladies. They've been piling up while she's away.

NELL. Half a dozen little girls and an arts graduate who can't type.

WIN. I spent the whole weekend at his place in Sussex.

NELL. She fancies his rose garden.

WIN. I had to lie down in the back of the car so the neighbours wouldn't see me go in.

NELL. You're kidding.

WIN. It was funny.

NELL. Fuck that for a joke.

WIN. It was funny.

MARLENE. Anyway they'd see you in the garden.

WIN. The garden has extremely high walls.

NELL. I think I'll tell the wife.

WIN. Like hell.

NELL. She might leave him and you could have the rose garden.

WIN. The minute it's not a secret I'm out on my ear.

NELL. Don't know why you bother.

WIN. Bit of fun.

NELL. I think it's time you went to Australia.

WIN. I think it's pushy Mr Holden time.

NELL. If you've any really pretty bastards, Marlene, I want some for Prestel.

MARLENE. I might have one this afternoon. This morning it's all Pam's secretarial.

NELL. Not long now and you'll be upstairs watching over us all.

MARLENE. Do you feel bad about it?

NELL. I don't like coming second.

MARLENE. Who does?

WIN. We'd rather it was you than Howard. We're glad for you, aren't we Nell.

NELL. Oh yes. Aces.

Interview

(*Win and Louise.*)

WIN. Now Louise, hello, I have you details here. You've been very loyal to the one job I see.

LOUISE. Yes I have.

WIN. Twenty-one years is a long time in one place.

LOUISE. I feel it is. I feel it's time to move on.

WIN. And you are what age now?

LOUISE. I'm in my early forties.

WIN. Exactly?

LOUISE. Forty-six.

WIN. It's not necessarily a handicap, well it is of course we have to face that, but it's not necessarily a disabling handicap, experience does count for something.

LOUISE. I hope so.

WIN. Now between ourselves is there any trouble, any reason why you're leaving that wouldn't appear on the form?

LOUISE. Nothing like that.

WIN. Like what?

LOUISE. Nothing at all.

WIN. No long term understandings come to a sudden end, making for an insupportable atmosphere?

LOUISE. I've always completely avoided anything like that at all.

WIN. No personality clashes with your immediate superiors or inferiors?

LOUISE. I've always taken care to get on very well with everyone.

WIN. I only ask because it can affect the reference and it also affects your motivation, I want to be quite clear why you're moving on. So I take it the job itself no longer satisfies you. Is it the money?

LOUISE. It's partly the money. It's not so much the money.

WIN. Nine thousand is very respectable. Have you dependants?

LOUISE. No, no dependants. My mother died.

WIN. So why are you making a change?

LOUISE. Other people make changes.

WIN. But why are you, now, after spending most of your life in the one place?

LOUISE. There you are, I've lived for that company, I've given my life really you could say because I haven't had a great deal of social life, I've worked in the evenings. I haven't had office entanglements for the very reason you just mentioned and if you are committed to your work you don't move in many other circles. I had management status from the age of twenty-seven and you'll appreciate what that means. I've built up a department. And there it is, it works extremely well, and I feel I'm stuck there. I've spent twenty years in middle management. I've seen young men who I trained go on, in my own company or elsewhere, to higher things. Nobody notices me, I don't expect it, I don't attract attention by making mistakes, everybody takes it for granted that my work is perfect. They will notice me when I go, they will be sorry I think to lose me, they will offer me more money of course, I will refuse. They will see when I've gone what I was doing for them.

WIN. If they offer you more money you won't stay?

LOUISE. No I won't.

WIN. Are you the only woman?

LOUISE. Apart from the girls of course, yes. There was one, she was my assistant, it was the only time I took on a young woman assistant, I always had my doubts. I don't care greatly for working with women, I think I pass as a man at work. But I did take on this young woman, her qualifications were excellent, and she did well, she got a department of her own, and left the company for a competitor where she's now on the board and good luck to her. She has a different style, she's a new kind of attractive well-dressed—I don't mean I don't dress properly. But there is a kind of woman who is thirty now who grew up in a different climate. They are not so careful. They take themselves for granted. I have had to justify my existence every minute, and I have done so, I have proved—well.

WIN. Let's face it, vacancies are going to be ones where you'll be in competition with younger men. And there are companies that will value your experience enough you'll be in with a chance. There are also fields that are easier for a woman, there is a cosmetic company here where your experience might be relevant. It's eight and a half, I don't know if that appeals.

LOUISE. I've proved I can earn money. It's more important to get away. I feel it's now or never. I sometimes / think—

WIN. You shouldn't talk too much at an interview.

LOUISE. I don't. I don't normally talk about myself. I know very well how to handle myself in an office situation. I only talk to you because it seems to me this is different, it's your job to understand me, surely. You asked the questions.

WIN. I think I understand you sufficiently.

LOUISE. Well good, that's good.

WIN. Do you drink?

LOUISE. Certainly not. I'm not a teetotaller, I think that's very suspect, it's seen as being an alcoholic if you're teetotal. What do you mean? I don't drink. Why?

WIN. I drink.

LOUISE. I don't.

WIN. Good for you.

Main office

(*Marlene and Angie.*)
(*Angie arrives.*)

ANGIE. Hello.

MARLENE. Have you an appointment?

ANGIE. It's me. I've come.

MARLENE. What? It's not Angie?

ANGIE. It was hard to find this place. I got lost.

MARLENE. How did you get past the receptionist? The girl on the desk, didn't she try to stop you?

ANGIE. What desk?

MARLENE. Never mind.

ANGIE. I just walked in. I was looking for you.

MARLENE. Well you found me.

ANGIE. Yes.

MARLENE. So where's your mum? Are you up in town for the day?

ANGIE. Not really.

MARLENE. Sit down. Do you feel all right?

ANGIE. Yes thank you.

MARLENE. So where's Joyce?

ANGIE. She's at home.

MARLENE. Did you come up on a school trip then?

ANGIE. I've left school.

MARLENE. Did you come up with a friend?

ANGIE. No. There's just me.

MARLENE. You came up by yourself, that's fun. What have you been doing? Shopping? Tower of London?

ANGIE. No, I just come here. I come to you.

MARLENE. That's very nice of you to think of paying your aunty a visit. There's not many nieces make that the first port of call. Would you like a cup of coffee?

ANGIE. No thank you.

MARLENE. Tea, orange?

ANGIE. No thank you.

MARLENE. Do you feel all right?

ANGIE. Yes thank you.

MARLENE. Are you tired from the journey?

ANGIE. Yes, I'm tired from the journey.

MARLENE. You sit there for a bit then. How's Joyce?

ANGIE. She's all right.

MARLENE. Same as ever.

ANGIE. Oh yes.

MARLENE. Unfortunately you've picked a day when I'm rather busy, if there's ever a day when I'm not, or I'd take you out to lunch and we'd go to Madame Tussaud's. We could go shopping. What time do you have to be back? Have you got a day return?

ANGIE. No.

MARLENE. So what train are you going back on?

ANGIE. I came on the bus.

MARLENE. So what bus are you going back on? Are you staying the night?

ANGIE. Yes.

MARLENE. Who are you staying with? Do you want me to put you up for the night, is that it?

ANGIE. Yes please.

MARLENE. I haven't got a spare bed.

ANGIE. I can sleep on the floor.

MARLENE. You can sleep on the sofa.

ANGIE. Yes please.

MARLENE. I do think Joyce might have phoned me. It's like her.

ANGIE. This is where you work is it?

MARLENE. It's where I have been working the last two years but I'm going to move into another office.

ANGIE. It's lovely.

MARLENE. My new office is nicer than this. There's just the one big desk in it for me.

ANGIE. Can I see it?

MARLENE. Not now, no, there's someone else in it now. But he's leaving at the end of next week and I'm going to do his job.

ANGIE. Is that good?

MARLENE. Yes, it's very good.

ANGIE. Are you going to be in charge?

MARLENE. Yes I am.

ANGIE. I knew you would be.

MARLENE. How did you know?

ANGIE. I knew you'd be in charge of everything.

MARLENE. Not quite everything.

ANGIE. You will be.

MARLENE. Well we'll see.

ANGIE. Can I see it next week then?

MARLENE. Will you still be here next week?

ANGIE. Yes.

MARLENE. Don't you have to go home?

ANGIE. No.

MARLENE. Why not?

ANGIE. It's all right.

MARLENE. Is it all right?

ANGIE. Yes, don't worry about it.

MARLENE. Does Joyce know where you are?

ANGIE. Yes of course she does.

MARLENE. Well does she?

ANGIE. Don't worry about it.

MARLENE. How long are you planning to stay with me then?

ANGIE. You know when you came to see us last year?

MARLENE. Yes, that was nice wasn't it?

ANGIE. That was the best day of my whole life.

MARLENE. So how long are you planning to stay?

ANGIE. Don't you want me?

MARLENE. Yes yes, I just wondered.

ANGIE. I won't stay if you don't want me.

MARLENE. No, of course you can stay.

ANGIE. I'll sleep on the floor. I won't be any bother.

MARLENE. Don't get upset.

ANGIE. I'm not, I'm not. Don't worry about it.

(*Mrs Kidd comes in.*)

MRS. KIDD. Excuse me.

MARLENE. Yes.

MRS. KIDD. Excuse me.

MARLENE. Can I help you?

MRS. KIDD. Excuse me bursting in on you like this but I have to talk to you.

MARLENE. I am engaged at the moment. / If you could go to reception—

MRS. KIDD. I'm Rosemary Kidd, Howard's wife, you don't recognise me but we did meet, I remember you of course / but you wouldn't—

MARLENE. Yes of course, Mrs Kidd, I'm sorry, we did meet. Howard's about somewhere I expect, have you looked in his office?

MRS. KIDD. Howard's not about, no. I'm afraid it's you I've come to see if I could have a minute or two.

MARLENE. I do have an appointment in five minutes.

MRS. KIDD. This won't take five minutes. I'm very sorry. It is a matter of some urgency.

MARLENE. Well of course. What can I do for you?

MRS. KIDD. I just wanted a chat, an informal chat. It's not something I can simply—I'm sorry if I'm interrupting your work. I know office work isn't like housework / which is all interruptions.

MARLENE. No no, this is my niece. Angie. Mrs Kidd.

MRS. KIDD. Very pleased to meet you.

ANGIE. Very well thank you.

MRS. KIDD. Howard's not in today.

MARLENE. Isn't he?

MRS. KIDD. He's feeling poorly.

MARLENE. I didn't know. I'm sorry to hear that.

MRS. KIDD. The fact is he's in a state of shock. About what's happened.

MARLENE. What has happened?

MRS. KIDD. You should know if anyone. I'm referring to you being appointed managing director instead of Howard. He hasn't been at all well all weekend. He hasn't slept for three nights. I haven't slept.

MARLENE. I'm sorry to hear that, Mrs. Kidd. Has he thought of taking sleeping pills?

MRS. KIDD. It's very hard when someone has worked all these years.

MARLENE. Business life is full of little setbacks. I'm sure Howard knows that. He'll bounce back in a day or two. We all bounce back.

MRS. KIDD. If you could see him you'd know what I'm talking about. What's it going to do to him working for a woman? I think if it was a man he'd get over it as something normal.

MARLENE. I think he's going to have to get over it.

MRS. KIDD. It's me that bears the brunt. I'm not the one that's been promoted. I put him first every inch of the way. And now what do I get? You women this, you women that. It's not my fault. You're going to have to be very careful how you handle him. He's very hurt.

MARLENE. Naturally I'll be tactful and pleasant to him, you don't start pushing someone round. I'll consult him over any decisions affecting his department. But that's no different, Mrs. Kidd, from any of my other colleagues.

MRS. KIDD. I think it is different, because he's a man.

MARLENE. I'm not quite sure why you came to see me.

MRS. KIDD. I had to do something.

MARLENE. Well you've done it, you've seen me. I think that's probably all we've time for. I'm sorry he's been taking it out on you. He really is a shit, Howard.

MRS. KIDD. But he's got a family to support. He's got three children. It's only fair.

MARLENE. Are you suggesting I give up the job to him then?

MRS. KIDD. It had crossed my mind if you were unavailable after all for some reason, he would be the natural second choice I think, don't you? I'm not asking.

MARLENE. Good

MRS. KIDD. You mustn't tell him I came. He's very proud.

MARLENE. If he doesn't like what's happening here he can go and work somewhere else.

MRS. KIDD. Is that a threat?

MARLENE. I'm sorry but I do have some work to do.

MRS. KIDD. It's not that easy, a man of Howard's age. You don't care. I thought he was going too far but he's right. You're one of these ballbreakers / that's what you are. You'll end up

MARLENE. I'm sorry but I do have some work to do.

MRS. KIDD. miserable and lonely. You're not natural.

MARLENE. Could you please piss off?

MRS. KIDD. I thought if I saw you at least I'd be doing something.

(*Mrs. Kidd goes.*)

MARLENE. I've got to go and do some work now. Will you come back later?

ANGIE. I think you were wonderful.

MARLENE. I've got to go and do some work now.

ANGIE. You told her to piss off.

MARLENE. Will you come back later?

ANGIE. Can't I stay here?

MARLENE. Don't you want to go sightseeing?

ANGIE. I'd rather stay here.

MARLENE. You can stay here I suppose, if it's not boring.

ANGIE. It's where I most want to be in the world.

MARLENE. I'll see you later then.

(*Marlene goes.*)
(*Angie sits at Win's desk*)

Interview

(*Nell and Shona.*)

NELL. Is this right? You are Shona?

SHONA. Yeh.

NELL. It says here you're twenty-nine.

SHONA. Yeh.

NELL. Too many late nights, me. So you've been where you are for four years, Shona, you're earning six basic and three commission. So what's the problem?

SHONA. No problem.

NELL. Why do you want a change?

SHONA. Just a change.

NELL. Change of product, change of area?

SHONA. Both.

NELL. But you're happy on the road?

SHONA. I like driving.

NELL. You're not after management status?

SHONA. I would like management status.

NELL. You'd be interested in titular management status but not come off the road?

SHONA. I want to be on the road, yeh.

NELL. So how many calls have you been making a day?

SHONA. Six.

NELL. And what proportion of those are successful?

SHONA. Six.

NELL. That's hard to believe.

SHONA. Four.

NELL. You find it easy to get the initial interest do you?

SHONA. Oh yeh, I get plenty of initial interest.

NELL. And what about closing?

SHONA. I close, don't I?

NELL. Because that's what an employer is going to have doubts about with you a lady as I needn't tell you, whether she's got the guts to push through a closing situation. They think we're too nice. They think we listen to the buyer's doubts. They think we consider his needs and feelings.

SHONA. I never consider people's feelings.

NELL. I was selling for six years, I can sell anything, I've sold in three continents, and I'm jolly as they come but I'm not very nice.

SHONA. I'm not very nice.

NELL. What sort of time do you have on the road with the other reps? Get on all right? Handle the chat?

SHONA. I get on. Keep myself to myself.

NELL. Fairly much of a loner are you?

SHONA. Sometimes.

NELL. So what field are you interested in?

SHONA. Computers.

NELL. That's a top field as you know and you'll be up against some very slick fellas there, there's some very pretty boys in computers, it's an American-style field.

SHONA. That's why I want to do it.

NELL. Video systems appeal? That's a high-flying situation.

SHONA. Video systems appeal OK.

NELL. Because Prestel have half a dozen vacancies I'm looking to fill at the moment. We're talking in the area of ten to fifteen thousand here and upwards.

SHONA. Sounds OK.

NELL. I've half a mind to go for it myself. But it's good money here if you've got the top clients. Could you fancy it do you think?

SHONA. Work here?

NELL. I'm not in a position to offer, there's nothing officially going just now, but we're always on the lookout. There's not that many of us. We could keep in touch.

SHONA. I like driving.

NELL. So the Prestel appeals?

SHONA. Yeh.

NELL. What about ties?

SHONA. No ties.

NELL. So relocation wouldn't be a problem.

SHONA. No problem.

NELL. So just fill me in a bit more could you about what you've been doing.

SHONA. What I've been doing. It's all down there.

NELL. The bare facts are down here but I've got to present you to an employer.

SHONA. I'm twenty-nine years old.

NELL. So it says here.

SHONA. We look young. Youngness runs in the family in our family.

NELL. So just describe your present job for me.

SHONA. My present job at present. I have a car. I have a Porsche. I go up the M1 a lot. Burn up the M1 a lot. Straight up the M1 in the fast lane to where the clients are, Staffordshire, Yorkshire, I do a lot in Yorkshire. I'm selling electric things. Like dishwashers, washing machines, stainless steel tubs are a feature and the reliability of the programme. After sales service, we offer a very good after sales service, spare parts, plenty of spare parts. And fridges, I sell a lot of fridges specially in the summer. People want to buy fridges in the summer because of the heat melting the butter and you get fed up standing the milk in a basin of cold water with a cloth over, stands to reason people don't want to do that in this day and age. So I sell a lot of them. Big ones with big freezers. Big freezers. And I stay in hotels at night when I'm away from home. On my expense account. I stay in various hotels. They know me, the ones I go to. I check in, have a bath, have a shower. Then I go down to the bar, and have a gin and tonic, have a chat. Then I go into the dining room and have dinner. I usually have fillet steak and mushrooms, I like mushrooms. I like smoked salmon very much. I like having a salad on the side. Green salad. I don't like tomatoes.

NELL. Christ what a waste of time.

SHONA. Beg your pardon?

NELL. Not a word of this is true is it?

SHONA. How do you mean?

NELL. You just filled in the form with a pack of lies.

SHONA. Not exactly.

NELL. How old are you?

SHONA. Twenty-nine.

NELL. Nineteen?

SHONA. Twenty-one.

NELL. And what jobs have you done? Have you done any?

SHONA. I could though, I bet you.

Main office

(*Angie sitting as before.*)
(*Win comes in.*)

WIN. Who's sitting in my chair?

ANGIE. What? Sorry.

WIN. Who's been eating my porridge?

ANGIE. What?

WIN. It's all right, I saw Marlene. Angie isn't it? I'm Win. And I'm not going out for lunch because I'm knackered. I'm going to set me down here and have a yoghurt. Do you like yoghurt?

ANGIE. No.

WIN. That's good because I've only got one. Are you hungry?

ANGIE. No.

WIN. There's a café on the corner.

ANGIE. No thank you. Do you work here?

WIN. How did you guess?

ANGIE. Because you look as if you might work here and you're sitting at the desk. Have you always worked here?

WIN. No I was headhunted. That means I was working for another outfit like this and this lot came and offered me more money. I broke my contract, there was a hell of a stink. There's not many top ladies about. Your aunty's a smashing bird.

ANGIE. Yes I know.

MARLENE. Fan are you? Fan of your aunty's?

ANGIE. Do you think I could work here?

WIN. Not at the moment.

ANGIE. How do I start?

WIN. What can you do?

ANGIE. I don't know. Nothing.

WIN. Type?

ANGIE. Not very well. The letters jump up when I do capitals. I was going to do a CSE in commerce but I didn't.

WIN. What have you got?

ANGIE. What?

WIN. CSE's, O's.

ANGIE. Nothing, none of that. Did you do all that?

WIN. Oh yes, all that, and a science degree funnily enough. I started out dong medical research but there's no money in it. I thought I'd go abroad. Did you know they sell Coca-Cola in Russia and Pepsi-cola in China? You don't have to be qualified as much as you might think. Men are awful bullshitters, they like to make out jobs are harder than they are. Any job I ever did I started doing it better than the rest of the crowd and they didn't like it. So I'd get unpopular and I'd have a drink to cheer myself up. I lived with a fella and supported him for four years, he couldn't get work. After that I went to California. I like the sunshine. Americans know how to live. This country's too slow. Then I went to Mexico, still in sales, but it's no country for a single lady. I came home, went bonkers for a bit, thought I was five different people, got over that all right, the psychiatrist said I was perfectly sane and highly intelligent. Got married in a moment of weakness and he's inside now, he's been inside four years, and I've not been to see him too much this last year. I like this better than sales, I'm not really that aggressive. I started thinking sales was a good job if you want to meet people, but you're meeting people that don't want to meet you. It's no good if you like being liked. Here your clients want to meet you because you're the one doing them some good. They hope.

(*Angie has fallen asleep. Nell comes in.*)

NELL. You're talking to yourself, sunshine.

WIN. So what's new?

NELL. Who is this?

WIN. Marlene's little niece.

NELL. What's she got, brother, sister? She never talks about her family.

WIN. I was telling her my life story.

NELL. Violins?

WIN. No, success story.

NELL. You've heard Howard's had a heart attack?

WIN. No, when?

NELL. I heard just now. He hadn't come in, he was at home, he's gone to hospital. He's not dead. His wife was here, she rushed off in a cab.

WIN. Too much butter, too much smoke. We must send him some flowers.

(*Marlene comes in.*)

You've heard about Howard?

MARLENE. Poor sod.

NELL. Lucky he didn't get the job if that's what his health's like.

MARLENE. Is she asleep?

WIN. She wants to work here.

MARLENE. Packer in Tesco more like.

WIN. She's a nice kid. Isn't she?

MARLENE. She's a bit thick. She's a bit funny.

WIN. She thinks you're wonderful.

MARLENE. She's not going to make it.

SCENE TWO

(*A year earlier. Sunday evening. Joyce's kitchen. Joyce, Angie, Marlene. Marlene is taking presents out of a bright carrier bag. Angie has already opened a box of chocolates.*)

MARLENE. Just a few things. / I've no memory for

JOYCE. There's no need.

MARLENE. birthdays have I, and Christmas seems to slip by. So I think I owe Angie a few presents.

JOYCE. What do you say?

ANGIE. Thank you very much. Thank you very much, Aunty Marlene.

(*She opens a present. It is the dress from Act One, new.*)

ANGIE. Oh look, Mum, isn't it lovely?

MARLENE. I don't know if it's the right size. She's grown up since I saw her. / I knew she was always tall for her age.

ANGIE. Isn't it lovely?

JOYCE. She's a big lump.

MARLENE. Hold it up, Angie, let's see.

ANGIE. I'll put it on, shall I?

MARLENE. Yes, try it on.

JOYCE. Go on to your room then, we don't want / a strip show thank you.

ANGIE. Of course I'm going to my room, what do you think? Look Mum, here's something for you. Open it, go on. What is it? Can I open it for you.

JOYCE. Yes, you open it, pet.

ANGIE. Don't you want to open it yourself? / Go on.

JOYCE. I don't mind, you can do it.

ANGIE. It's something hard. It's—what is it? A bottle. Drink is it? No, it's what? Perfume, look. What a lot. Open it, look, let's smell it. Oh it's strong. It's lovely. Put it on me. How do you do it? Put it on me.

JOYCE. You're too young.

ANGIE. I can play wearing it like dressing up.

JOYCE. And you're too old for that. Here, give it here, I'll do it, you'll tip the whole bottle over yourself / and we'll have you smelling all summer.

ANGIE. Put it on you. Do I smell? Put it on Aunty too. Put it on Aunty too. Let's all smell.

MARLENE. I didn't know what you'd like.

JOYCE. There's no danger I'd have it already, / that's one thing.

ANGIE. Now we all smell the same.

MARLENE. It's a bit of nonsense.

JOYCE. It's very kind of you Marlene, you shouldn't.

ANGIE. Now I'll put on the dress and then we'll see.

Angie goes.

JOYCE. You've caught me on the hop with the place in a mess. / If you'd let me know you was coming I'd have got

MARLENE. That doesn't matter.

JOYCE. something in to eat. We had our dinner dinnertime. We're just going to have a cup of tea. You could have an egg.

MARLENE. No, I'm not hungry. Tea's fine.

JOYCE. I don't expect you take sugar.

MARLENE. Why not?

JOYCE. You take care of yourself.

MARLENE. How do you mean you didn't know I was coming?

JOYCE. You could have written. I know we're not on the phone but we're not completely in the dark ages, / we do have a postman.

MARLENE. But you asked me to come.

JOYCE. How did I ask you to come?

MARLENE. Angie said when she phoned up.

JOYCE. Angie phoned up, did she?

MARLENE. Was it just Angie's idea?

JOYCE. What did she say?

MARLENE. She said you wanted me to come and see you. / It was a couple of weeks ago. How was I to know that's a

JOYCE. Ha.

MARLENE. ridiculous idea? My diary's always full a couple of weeks ahead so we fixed it for this weekend. I was meant to get here earlier but I was held up. She gave me messages from you.

JOYCE. Didn't you wonder why I didn't phone you myself?

MARLENE. She said you didn't like using the phone. You're shy on the phone and can't use it. I don't know what you're like, do I.

JOYCE. Are there people who can't use the phone?

MARLENE. I expect so.

JOYCE. I haven't met any.

MARLENE. Why should I think she was lying?

JOYCE. Because she's like what she's like.

MARLENE. How do I know / what she's like?

JOYCE. It's not my fault you don't know what she's like. You never come and see her.

MARLENE. Well I have now / and you don't seem over the moon*

JOYCE. Good.

    *Well I'd have got a cake if she'd told me.

(*Pause.*)

MARLENE. I did wonder why you wanted to see me.

JOYCE. I didn't want to see you.

MARLENE. Yes, I know. Shall I go?

JOYCE. I don't mind seeing you.

MARLENE. Great, I feel really welcome.

JOYCE. You can come and see Angie any time you like, I'm not stopping you. / You know where we are. You're the

MARLENE. Ta ever so.

JOYCE. one went away, not me. I'm right here where I was. And will be a few years yet I shouldn't wonder.

MARLENE. All right. All right.

(*Joyce gives Marlene a cup of tea.*)

JOYCE. Tea.

MARLENE. Sugar?

(*Joyce passes Marlene the sugar.*)

    It's very quiet down here.

JOYCE. I expect you'd notice it.

MARLENE. The air smells different too.

JOYCE. That's the scent.

MARLENE. No, I mean walking down the lane.

JOYCE. What sort of air you get in London then?

(*Angie comes in, wearing the dress. It fits.*)

MARLENE. Oh, very pretty. / You do look pretty, Angie.

JOYCE. That fits all right.

MARLENE. Do you like the colour?

ANGIE. Beautiful. Beautiful.

JOYCE. You better take it off, / you'll get it dirty.

ANGIE. I want to wear it. I want to wear it.

MARLENE. It is for wearing after all. You can't just hang it up and look at it.

ANGIE. I love it.

JOYCE. Well if you must you must.

ANGIE. If someone asks me what's my favourite colour I'll tell them it's this. Thank you very much, Aunty Marlene.

MARLENE. You didn't tell your mum you asked me down.

ANGIE. I wanted it to be a surprise.

JOYCE. I'll give you a surprise / one of these days.

ANGIE. I thought you'd like to see her. She hasn't been here since I was nine. People do see their aunts.

MARLENE. Is it that long? Doesn't time fly?

ANGIE. I wanted to.

JOYCE. I'm not cross.

ANGIE. Are you glad?

JOYCE. I smell nicer anyhow, don't I?

(*Kit comes in without saying anything, as if she lived there.*)

MARLENE. I think it was a good idea, Angie, about time. We are sisters after all. It's a pity to let that go.

JOYCE. This is Kitty, / who lives up the road. This is Angie's Aunty Marlene.

KIT. What's that?

ANGIE. It's a present. Do you like it?

KIT. It's all right. / Are you coming out?*

MARLENE. Hello, Kitty.

ANGIE. *No.

KIT. What's that smell?

ANGIE. It's a present.

KIT. It's horrible. Come on*

MARLENE. Have a chocolate.

ANGIE. *No, I'm busy.

KIT. Coming out later?

ANGIE. No.

KIT (*to Marlene*). Hello.

(*Kit goes without a chocolate.*)

JOYCE. She's a little girl Angie sometimes plays with because she's the only child lives really close. She's like a little sister to her really. Angie's good with little children.

MARLENE. Do you want to work with children, Angie? / Be a teacher or a nursery nurse?

JOYCE. I don't think she's ever thought of it.

MARLENE. What do you want to do?

JOYCE. She hasn't an idea in her head what she wants to do. / Lucky to get anything.

MARLENE. Angie?

JOYCE. She's not clever like you.

(*Pause.*)

MARLENE. I'm not clever, just pushy.

JOYCE. True enough.

(*Marlene takes a bottle of whisky out of the bag.*)

I don't drink spirits.

ANGIE. You do at Christmas.

JOYCE. It's not Christmas, is it?

ANGIE. It's better than Christmas.

MARLENE. Glasses?

JOYCE. Just a small one then.

MARLENE. Do you want some, Angie?

ANGIE. I can't, can I?

JOYCE. Taste it if you want. You won't like it.

MARLENE. We got drunk together the night your grandfather died.

JOYCE. We did not get drunk.

MARLENE. I got drunk. You were just overcome with grief.

JOYCE. I still keep up the grave with flowers.

MARLENE. Do you really?

JOYCE. Why wouldn't I?

MARLENE. Have you seen Mother?

JOYCE. Of course I've seen Mother.

MARLENE. I mean lately.

JOYCE. Of course I've seen her lately, I go every Thursday.

MARLENE (*to Angie*). Do you remember your grandfather?

ANGIE. He got me out of the bath one night in a towel.

MARLENE. Did he? I don't think he ever gave me a bath. Did he give you a bath, Joyce? He probably got soft in his old age. Did you like him?

ANGIE. Yes of course.

MARLENE. Why?

ANGIE. What?

MARLENE. So what's the news? How's Mrs. Paisley? Still going crazily? / And Dorothy. What happened to Dorothy?*

ANGIE. Who's Mrs. Paisley?

JOYCE. *She went to Canada.

MARLENE. Did she? What to do?

JOYCE. I don't know. She just went to Canada.

MARLENE. Well / good for her.

ANGIE. Mr. Connolly killed his wife.

MARLENE. What, Connolly at Whitegates?

ANGIE. They found her body in the garden. / Under the cabbages.

MARLENE. He was always so proper.

JOYCE. Stuck up git. Connolly. Best lawyer money could buy but he couldn't get out of it. She was carrying on with Matthew.

MARLENE. How old's Matthew then?

JOYCE. Twenty-one. / He's got a motorbike.

MARLENE. I think he's about six.

ANGIE. How can he be six? He's six years older than me. / If he was six I'd be nothing, I'd be just born this minute.

JOYCE. Your aunty knows that, she's just being silly. She means it's so long since she's been here she's forgotten about Matthew.

ANGIE. You were here for my birthday when I was nine. I had a pink cake. Kit was only five then, she was four, she hadn't started school yet. She could read already when she went to school. You remember my birthday? / You remember me?

MARLENE. Yes, I remember the cake.

ANGIE. You remember me?

MARLENE. Yes, I remember you.

ANGIE. And Mum and Dad was there, and Kit was.

MARLENE. Yes, how is your dad? Where is he tonight? Up the pub?

JOYCE. No, he's not here.

MARLENE. I can see he's not here.

JOYCE. He moved out.

MARLENE. What? When did he? / Just recently?*

ANGIE. Didn't you know that? You don't know much.

JOYCE. *No, it must be three years ago. Don't be rude, Angie.

ANGIE. I'm not, am I Aunty? What else don't you know?

JOYCE. You was in America or somewhere. You sent a postcard.

ANGIE. I've got that in my room. It's the Grand Canyon. Do you want to see it? Shall I get it? I can get it for you.

MARLENE. Yes, all right.

(*Angie goes.*)

JOYCE. You could be married with twins for all I know. You must have affairs and break up and I don't need to know about any of that so I don't see what the fuss is about.

MARLENE. What fuss?

(*Angie comes back with the postcard.*)

ANGIE. 'Driving across the states for a new job in L.A. It's a long way but the car goes very fast. It's very hot. Wish you were here. Love from Aunty Marlene.'

JOYCE. Did you make a lot of money?

MARLENE. I spent a lot.

ANGIE. I want to go to America. Will you take me?

JOYCE. She's not going to America, she's been to America, stupid.

ANGIE. She might go again, stupid. It's not something you do once. People who go keep going all the time, back and forth on jets. They go on Concorde and Laker and get jet lag. Will you take me?

MARLENE. I'm not planning a trip.

ANGIE. Will you let me know?

JOYCE. Angie, / you're getting silly.

ANGIE. I want to be American.

JOYCE. It's time you were in bed.

ANGIE. No it's not. / I don't have to go to bed at all tonight.

JOYCE. School in the morning.

ANGIE. I'll wake up.

JOYCE. Come on now, you know how you get.

ANGIE. How do I get? / I don't get anyhow.

JOYCE. Angie.
    Are you staying the night?

MARLENE. Yes, if that's all right. / I'll see you in the morning.

ANGIE. You can have my bed. I'll sleep on the sofa.

JOYCE. You will not, you'll sleep in your bed. / Think I can't

ANGIE. Mum.

JOYCE. see through that? I can just see you going to sleep / with us talking.

ANGIE. I would, I would go to sleep, I'd love that.

JOYCE. I'm going to get cross, Angie.

ANGIE. I want to show her something.

JOYCE. Then bed.

ANGIE. It's a secret.

JOYCE. Then I expect it's in your room so off you go. Give us a shout when you're ready for bed and your aunty'll be up and see you.

ANGIE. Will you?

MARLENE. Yes of course.

(*Angie goes.*)
(*Silence.*)

It's cold tonight.

JOYCE. Will you be all right on the sofa? You can / have my bed.

MARLENE. The sofa's fine.

JOYCE. Yes the forecast said rain tonight but it's held off.

MARLENE. I was going to walk down to the estuary but I've left it a bit late. Is it just the same?

JOYCE. They cut down the hedges a few years back. Is that since you were here?

MARLENE. But it's not changed down the end, all the mud? And the reeds? We used to pick them when they were bigger than us. Are there still lapwings, yes.

JOYCE. You get strangers walking there on a Sunday. I expect they're looking at the mud and the lapwings?

MARLENE. You could have left.

JOYCE. Who says I wanted to leave?

MARLENE. Stop getting at me then, you're really boring.

JOYCE. How could I have left?

MARLENE. Did you want to?

JOYCE. I said how, / how could I?

MARLENE. If you'd wanted to you'd have done it.

JOYCE. Christ.

MARLENE. Are we getting drunk?

JOYCE. Do you want something to eat?

MARLENE. No, I'm getting drunk.

JOYCE. Funny time to visit, Sunday evening.

MARLENE. I came this morning. I spent the day.

ANGIE (*off*). Aunty! Aunty Marlene!

MARLENE. I'd better go.

JOYCE. Go on then.

MARLENE. All right.

ANGIE (*off*). Aunty! Can you hear me? I'm ready.

(*Marlene goes.*)
(*Joyce goes on sitting.*)
(*Marlene comes back.*)

JOYCE. So what's the secret?

MARLENE. It's a secret.

JOYCE. I know what it is anyway.

MARLENE. I bet you don't. You always said that.

JOYCE. It's her exercise book.

MARLENE. Yes, but you don't know what's in it.

JOYCE. It's some game, some secret society she has with Kit.

MARLENE. You don't know the password. You don't know the code.

JOYCE. You're really in it, aren't you. Can you do the handshake?

MARLENE. She didn't mention a handshake.

JOYCE. I thought they'd have a special handshake. She spends hours writing that but she's useless at school. She copies things out of books about black magic, and politicians out of the paper. It's a bit childish.

MARLENE. I think it's a plot to take over the world.

JOYCE. She's been in the remedial class the last two years.

MARLENE. I came up this morning and spent the day in Ipswich. I went to see mother.

JOYCE. Did she recognise you?

MARLENE. Are you trying to be funny?

JOYCE. No, she does wander.

MARLENE. She wasn't wandering at all, she was very lucid thank you.

JOYCE. You were very lucky then.

MARLENE. Fucking awful life she's had.

JOYCE. Don't tell me.

MARLENE. Fucking waste.

JOYCE. Don't talk to me.

MARLENE. Why shouldn't I talk? Why shouldn't I talk to you? / Isn't she my mother too?

JOYCE. Look, you've left, you've gone away, / we can do without you.

MARLENE. I left home, so what, I left home. People do leave home / it is normal.

JOYCE. We understand that, we can do without you.

MARLENE. We weren't happy. Were you happy?

JOYCE. Don't come back.

MARLENE. So it's just your mother is it, your child, you never wanted me round, / you were jealous of me because I was the

JOYCE. Here we go.

MARLENE. little one and I was clever.

JOYCE. I'm not clever enough for all this psychology / if that's what it is.

MARLENE. Why can't I visit my own family / without all this?*

JOYCE. Aah.

Just don't go on about Mum's life when you haven't been to see her for how many years. / I go and see her every week.

MARLENE. It's up to me.

*Then don't go and see her every week.

JOYCE. Somebody has to.

MARLENE. No they don't. / Why do they?

JOYCE. How would I feel if I didn't go?

MARLENE. A lot better.

JOYCE. I hope you feel better.

MARLENE. It's up to me.

JOYCE. You couldn't get out of here fast enough.

MARLENE. Of course I couldn't get out of here fast enough. What was I going to do? Marry a dairyman who'd come home pissed? / Don't you fucking this fucking that fucking bitch

JOYCE. Christ.

MARLENE. fucking tell me what to fucking do fucking.

JOYCE. I don't know how you could leave your own child.

MARLENE. You were quick enough to take her.

JOYCE: What does that mean?

MARLENE: You were quick enough to take her.

JOYCE. Or what? Have her put in a home? Have some stranger / take her would you rather?

MARLENE. You couldn't have one so you took mine.

JOYCE. I didn't know that then.

MARLENE. Like hell, / married three years.

JOYCE. I didn't know that. Plenty of people / take that long.

MARLENE. Well it turned out lucky for you, didn't it?

JOYCE. Turned out all right for you by the look of you. You'd be getting a few less thousand a year.

MARLENE. Not necessarily.

JOYCE. You'd be stuck here / like you said.

MARLENE. I could have taken her with me.

JOYCE. You didn't want to take her with you. It's no good coming back now, Marlene, / and saying—

MARLENE. I know a managing director who's got two children, she breast feeds in the board room, she pays a hundred pounds a week on domestic help alone and she can afford that because she's an extremely high-powered lady earning a great deal of money.

JOYCE. So what's that got to do with you at the age of seventeen?

MARLENE. Just because you were married and had somewhere to live—

JOYCE. You could have lived at home. / Or live with me

MARLENE. Don't be stupid.

JOYCE. and Frank. / You said you weren't keeping it. You

MARLENE. You never suggested.

JOYCE. shouldn't have had it / if you wasn't going to keep it.

MARLENE. Here we go.

JOYCE. You was the most stupid, / for someone so clever you was the most stupid, get yourself pregnant, not go to the doctor, not tell.

MARLENE. You wanted it, you said you were glad, I remember the day, you said I'm glad you never got rid of it, I'll look after it, you said that down by the river. So what are you saying, sunshine, you don't want her?

JOYCE. Course I'm not saying that.

MARLENE. Because I'll take her, / wake her up and pack now.

JOYCE. You wouldn't know how to begin to look after her.

MARLENE. Don't you want her?

JOYCE. Course I do, she's my child.

MARLENE. Then what are you going on about / why did I have her?

JOYCE. You said I got her off you / when you didn't—

MARLENE. I said you were lucky / the way it—

JOYCE. Have a child now if you want one. You're not old.

MARLENE. I might do.

JOYCE. Good.

(*Pause.*)

MARLENE. I've been on the pill so long / I'm probably sterile.

JOYCE. Listen when Angie was six months I did get pregnant and I lost it because I was so tired looking after your fucking baby / because she cried so much—yes I did tell

MARLENE. You never told me.

JOYCE. you— / and the doctor said if I'd sat down all day with

MARLENE. Well I forgot.

JOYCE. my feet up I'd've kept it / and that's the only chance I ever had because after that—

MARLENE. I've had two abortions, are you interested? Shall I tell you about them? Well I won't, it's boring, it wasn't a problem. I don't like messy talk about blood / and what a bad

JOYCE. If I hadn't had your baby. The doctor said.

MARLENE. time we all had. I don't want a baby. I don't want to talk about gynaecology.

JOYCE. Then stop trying to get Angie off of me.

MARLENE. I come down here after six years. All night you've been saying I don't come often enough. If I don't come for another six years she'll be twenty-one, will that be OK?

JOYCE. That'll be fine, yes, six years would suit me fine.

(*Pause.*)

MARLENE. I was afraid of this.
I only came because I thought you wanted . . .
I just want . . .

(*Marlene cries.*)

JOYCE. Don't grizzle, Marlene, for God's sake.
Marly? Come on, pet. Love you really. Fucking stop it, will you?

MARLENE. No, let me cry. I like it.

(*They laugh, Marlene begins to stop crying.*)

I knew I'd cry if I wasn't careful.

JOYCE. Everyone's always crying in this house. Nobody takes any notice.

MARLENE. You've been wonderful looking after Angie.

JOYCE. Don't get carried away.

MARLENE. I can't write letters but I do think of you.

JOYCE. You're getting drunk. I'm going to make some tea.

MARLENE. Love you.

(*Joyce gets up to make tea.*)

JOYCE. I can see why you'd want to leave. It's a dump here.

MARLENE. So what's this about you and Frank?

JOYCE. He was always carrying on, wasn't he? And if I wanted to go out in the evening he'd go mad, even if it was nothing, a class, I was going to go to an evening class. So he had this girlfriend, only twenty-two poor cow, and I said go on, off you go, hoppit. I don't think he even likes her.

MARLENE. So what about money?

JOYCE. I've always said I don't want your money.

MARLENE. No, does he send you money?

JOYCE. I've got four different cleaning jobs. Adds up. There's not a lot round here.

MARLENE. Does Angie miss him?

JOYCE. She doesn't say.

MARLENE. Does she see him?

JOYCE. He was never that fond of her to be honest.

MARLENE. He tried to kiss me once. When you were engaged.

JOYCE. Did you fancy him?

MARLENE. No, he looked like a fish.

JOYCE. He was lovely then.

MARLENE. Ugh.

JOYCE. Well I fancied him. For about three years.

MARLENE. Have you got someone else?

JOYCE. There's not a lot round here. Mind you, the minute you're on your own, you'd be amazed how your friends' husbands drop by. I'd sooner do without.

MARLENE. I don't see why you couldn't take my money.

JOYCE. I do, so don't bother about it.

MARLENE. Only got to ask.

JOYCE. So what about you? Good job?

MARLENE. Good for a laugh. / Got back from the US of A a bit

JOYCE. Good for more than a laugh I should think.

MARLENE. wiped out and slotted into this speedy employment agency and still there.

JOYCE. You can always find yourself work then.

MARLENE. That's right.

JOYCE. And men?

MARLENE. Oh there's always men.

JOYCE. No one special?

MARLENE. There's fellas who like to be seen with a high-flying lady. Shows they've got something really good in their pants. But they can't take the day to day. They're waiting for me to turn into the little woman. Or maybe I'm just horrible of course.

JOYCE. Who needs them?

MARLENE. Who needs them? Well I do. But I need adventures more. So on on into the sunset. I think the eighties are going to be stupendous.

JOYCE. Who for?

MARLENE. For me. / I think I'm going up up up.

JOYCE. Oh for you. Yes, I'm sure they will.

MARLENE. And for the country, come to that. Get the economy back on its feet and whoosh. She's a tough lady, Maggie. I'd give her a job. / She just needs to hang in there. This country

JOYCE. You voted for them, did you?

MARLENE. needs to stop whining. / Monetarism is not stupid.

JOYCE. Drink your tea and shut up, pet.

MARLENE. It takes time, determination. No more slop. / And

JOYCE. Well I think they're filthy bastards.

MARLENE. who's got to drive it on? First woman prime minister. Terrifico. Aces. Right on. / You must admit. Certainly gets my vote.

JOYCE. What good's first woman if it's her? I suppose you'd have liked Hitler if he was a woman. Ms Hitler. Got a lot done, Hitlerina. / Great adventures.

MARLENE. Bosses still walking on the workers' faces? Still Dadda's little parrot? Haven't you learned to think for yourself? I believe in the individual. Look at me.

JOYCE. I am looking at you.

MARLENE. Come on, Joyce, we're not going to quarrel over politics.

JOYCE. We are though.

MARLENE. Forget I mentioned it. Not a word about the slimy unions will cross my lips.

(*Pause.*)

JOYCE. You say Mother had a wasted life.

MARLENE. Yes I do. Married to that bastard.

JOYCE. What sort of life did he have? / Working in the fields like

MARLENE. Violent life?

JOYCE. an animal. / Why wouldn't he want a drink?

MARLENE. Come off it.

JOYCE. You want a drink. He couldn't afford whisky.

MARLENE. I don't want to talk about him.

JOYCE. You started, I was talking about her. She had a rotten life because she had nothing. She went hungry.

MARLENE. She was hungry because he drank the money. / He used to hit her.

JOYCE. It's not all down to him. / Their lives were rubbish. They

MARLENE. She didn't hit him.

JOYCE. were treated like rubbish. He's dead and she'll die soon and what sort of life / did they have?

MARLENE. I saw him one night. I came down.

JOYCE. Do you think I didn't? / They didn't get to America and

MARLENE. I still have dreams.

JOYCE. drive across it in a fast car. / Bad nights, they had bad days.

MARLENE. America, America, you're jealous. / I had to get out,

JOYCE. Jealous?

MARLENE. I knew when I was thirteen, out of their house, out of them, never let that happen to me, / never let him, make my own way, out.

JOYCE. Jealous of what you've done, you're ashamed of me if I came to your office, your smart friends, wouldn't you, I'm ashamed of you, think of nothing but yourself, you've got on, nothing's changed for most people / has it?

MARLENE. I hate the working class / which is what you're going

JOYCE. Yes you do.

MARLENE. to go on about now, it doesn't exist any more, it means lazy and stupid. / I don't like the way they talk. I don't

JOYCE. Come on, now we're getting it.

MARLENE. like beer guts and football vomit and saucy tits / and brothers and sisters—

JOYCE. I spit when I see a Rolls Royce, scratch it with my ring / Mercedes it was.

MARLENE. Oh very mature—

JOYCE. I hate the cows I work for / and their dirty dishes with blanquette of fucking veau.

MARLENE. and I will not be pulled down to their level by a flying picket and I won't be sent to Siberia / or a loony bin

JOYCE. No, you'll be on a yacht, you'll be head of Coca-Cola and you wait, the eighties is going to be stupendous all right because we'll get you lot off our backs—

MARLENE. just because I'm original. And I support Reagan even if he is a lousy movie star because the reds are

swarming up his map and I want to be free in a free world—

JOYCE. What? / What?

MARLENE. I know what I mean / by that—not shut up here.

JOYCE. So don't be round here when it happens because if someone's kicking you I'll just laugh.

(*Silence.*)

MARLENE. I don't mean anything personal. I don't believe in class. Anyone can do anything if they've got what it takes.

JOYCE. And if they haven't?

MARLENE. If they're stupid or lazy or frightened, I'm not going to help them get a job, why should I?

JOYCE. What about Angie?

MARLENE. What about Angie?

JOYCE. She's stupid, lazy and frightened, so what about her?

MARLENE. You run her down too much. She'll be all right.

JOYCE. I don't expect so, no. I expect her children will say what a wasted life she had. If she has children. Because nothing's changed and it won't with them in.

MARLENE. Them, them. / Us and them?

JOYCE. And you're one of them.

MARLENE. And you're us, wonderful us, and Angie's us / and Mum and Dad's us.

JOYCE. Yes, that's right, and you're them.

MARLENE. Come on, Joyce, what a night. You've got what it takes.

JOYCE. I know I have.

MARLENE. I didn't really mean all that.

JOYCE. I did.

MARLENE. But we're friends anyway.

JOYCE. I don't think so, no.

MARLENE. Well it's lovely to be out in the country. I really must make the effort to come more often.

I want to go to sleep.

I want to go to sleep.

(*Joyce gets blankets for the sofa.*)

JOYCE. Goodnight then. I hope you'll be warm enough.

MARLENE. Goodnight. Joyce—

JOYCE. No, pet. Sorry.

(*Joyce goes.*)

(*Marlene sits wrapped in a blanket and has another drink.*)

(*Angie comes in.*)

ANGIE. Mum?

MARLENE. Angie? What's the matter?

ANGIE. Mum?

MARLENE. No, she's gone to bed. It's Aunty Marlene.

ANGIE. Frightening.

MARLENE. Did you have a bad dream? What happened in it? Well you're awake now, aren't you pet?

ANGIE. Frightening.

END

TOPICS FOR CRITICAL THINKING AND WRITING

The Play on the PAGE

1. The overlapping dialogue in *Top Girls* is a signature element of Churchill's plays. Apart from causing some frustration or confusion in readers unfamiliar with her style, what is the purpose of what one reviewer calls "precisely organized cross babble" of the characters?

2. Marlene is the central character in this play, but is she a likable character? Do you think Churchill intended her to be viewed as such? Why or why not? Find examples in the text to support your view. What does she represent?

3. The first act of *Top Girls* is a nonrealistic fantasy scene, whereas Act 2 is grounded in a realistic portrayal of women of various ages, backgrounds, and class. What is the purpose of juxtaposing the real with the nonreal in the play?

4. How does the structure of the play add to the major theme that Churchill explores: The success achieved by women like Marlene is bitter if it means appropriating "male" behavior and positions traditionally held by men? Why not structure the play chronologically?

5. The "willful woman" is a central female image in the Western theater canon. Female characters such as Medea and Miss Julie have been called willful, and Churchill's character of Marlene could potentially fit this image. Compare and contrast these three female roles and agree or disagree with the concept of describing them as "willful."

6. Many scholars and critics have said out that Churchill writes the roles of children better than anyone. Using the role of Angie, agree or disagree with this. Elaborate by drawing on specific examples from the script.

The Play on the STAGE

7. Churchill has said that when she began working on *Top Girls* she envisioned it being performed by a large cast of women without the use of doubling roles. What do you think would be lost in performance if the play were staged in this way? Would anything be gained?

8. The play is set in four different locations. If you were to produce *Top Girls,* how would you design the setting? Sketch some examples using the text to support your answers.

9. Select a short sequence of overlapping dialogue. Cast yourself and some others in the roles in the sequence and read it aloud, following Churchill's directions. Experiment with volume, rhythm, and speed. What effect does the scene produce?

10. Churchill uses a nonlinear narrative in the play. How does Angie's "old best dress," which she puts on at the end of Act 1, Scene 3, serve as a visual clue for the audience? How would you stage this scene to highlight the importance of the dress?

The Play in PERFORMANCE

Top Girls premiered at the Royal Court Theatre in August 1982 directed by Max Stafford-Clark. It transferred to the Public Theater in New York in December 1982 and won an Obie award. It enjoyed a second run at the Royal Court in 1983 and a revival in 1991 also directed by Stafford-Clark. It has had numerous productions around the world including productions in Australia, Sweden, Japan, West Germany, Greece, Switzerland, Denmark, Norway, Finland, Holland, Peru, New Zealand, and Yugoslavia. *Top Girls* established Churchill as a major contemporary playwright. The following is a review of the production when it opened in New York by Erika Munk, theater critic of *The Village Voice.*

ERIKA MUNK
*Making It**

My companion at *Top Girls* said that though it was a pleasure to find Caryl Churchill an even better writer than she'd thought from *Cloud 9*, there wasn't a feminist moment on stage at the Public. The young woman who takes care of my daughter said she enjoyed the play immensely, but had qualms about its attitude toward women. A friend was amazed that the cruelty of the mother-daughter scenes didn't bother me. And a critic colleague was reduced to a huff: *East Lynne!* Odets! Sentimental proletarian rhetoric! They are all quite mad. I'd say the play is, among other things, a critique of bourgeois feminism; that the motor of its harshness is compassion; that Churchill writes mothers and children better than anyone around; and that sentimentality has rarely been so remote.

Top Girls opens in a medium-fancy London restaurant called La Prima Donna. Picked for that, no doubt, by Marlene, who has just been appointed managing director of an employment agency, and wishes to celebrate. Her guests arrive: Isabella Bird, Scots Victorian explorer of exotic places; Nijo, an Emperor's courtesan from 13th century Japan, later a wandering Buddhist nun; Dull Gret, Breughel's devil-chasing peasant, who led an army of women; Joan, a ninth century pope; and Griselda, the poor girl who married a marquis. Boundary breakers all: Isabella and Nijo unfemininely traveled alone, Gret fought hell itself, Joan disguised her sex to reach God, even Griselda's obedient patience took her, after all, above her class.

The meal is a wildly heightened variation on the wine-and-confidences part of a '70s consciousness-raising group: competitive storytelling, bragging and pain-mongering, lurches of friendship and antagonism. But isn't Marlene a little high-falutin' to think these women are her spiritual ancestors? Every time she opens her mouth a thin brassy contemporaneity obtrudes: as Joan tells of how after being made cardinal she lay ill for two weeks full of terror and regret. Marlene interrupts, beginning a sentence about success that surely would have ended as a banality out of *The Cinderella Complex*. The scene moves from a happy exploration of eccentric character through revelations of the price each paid: Joan stoned to death when she

*Review of *Top Girls*, *The Village Voice* 11 Jan. 1983.

gave birth; Nijo's children given away, so when she finally could keep one she had no feeling for him; Gret impelled to action when her children are tortured and killed by soldiers. Only Isabella, in her restless self-centerdness, rode off for a last joyous adventure at 70. And Griselda, who allowed her husband to take away her children in order, she thought, to kill them, smugly enjoyed her dress of gold.

This beginning can be parsed a multitude of ways; before its meaning starts to unfold in relationship to the rest of the play, it opens us to particularity and history, the power of individual will and the limits of that power—which can be seized only by living disguised as a man, by leaving one's society, by obeying absolutely, by taking arms and disobeying absolutely. Drastic courses. These characters are parables: in women's history, you can't get what you want in an ordinary, simple, humane way, if you want anything much.

The second scene shows Marlene in her agency, interviewing a mediocre young woman who wants to change employers, to get married, to travel. Basically she doesn't know what she wants, and probably has neither the will nor the skill to get it if she did. An ordinary person, unfit to make extraordinary decisions in a world which discounts her. She does, however, go ahead with looking for a new job.

Next we are in a scruffy backyard. Two girls, 12 and 16 years old, huddle in a makeshift playhouse, hiding from Angie's, the older's, mother. Angie is odd, "slow," a drop-out, frightening the younger one with the ghosts of dead kittens, twisting her arm, tasting her blood. A heavy, miserable child whose mother, Joyce, can neither control nor comfort her: she offers her biscuits, then calls her a cunt. My mother-self winced away from their dialogue's foreordained meanness, its too recognizable fury and frustration. Angie has an aunt in London whom she's running away to: Marlene.

In the second act she arrives at the employment agency. A different Angie, easily hurt but determined, worshiping Marlene's toughness. This is interrupted by an interview between one of the agency employees, Win, and Louise, 46 years old. After 20 years in one firm as a corporate middle-management "man," she is consumed by her grievance at being passed over, at seeing younger women take such employment as a right, at the blankness of her life. Back, with Angie and Marlene, we reach the chronological last lines of the play—though not the final ones—when Win says to Marlene about Angie, whom she likes, "She thinks you're wonderful," and Marlene replies, "She's not going to make it." Marlene's idea of making it can never include Angie; other women's futures don't interest her. In Marlene's scheme of things, Angie is what gets left behind.

Quite literally, as it turns out. In the final part, which occurs a year earlier in Joyce's kitchen—the opposite sort of place from La Prima Donna—we discover that Marlene is actually Angie's mother. This moment briefly filled me with dismay. Pure soap, claiming with regressive bluntness that in order to get ahead a woman has to dump all ties, feel sisterhood with Margaret Thatcher, leave the kiddie with sis—who stays behind, holds four cleaning jobs at once, pays a weekly visit to decrepit mum, loses her man to a younger woman, and never finds or gives a moment's affection. As family naturalism this is trite tripe. But pushed to such an extreme, the plot is no plot, it's a deliberate model of an entire world of women, frozen in sterile polarity. Joyce, joyless, is class resentment made flesh, she's trapped, she's almost as mean as Marlene; and Angie at least for a while chooses Marlene.

For her own freedom, and every woman's, that's no choice at all. The last word of the play is "Frightening." Indeed. If Churchill means that you and your children have to choose Marlene or Joyce, bleakness is

all. I do not think she means only this; at least, it is certainly possible to find something more in the script: these two, these sisters, are trapped not only by their circumstances but by their acceptance of society as it is. Joyce's resentment and Marlene's ambition are equally unrebellious. The way Marlene climbs the ladder and the way Joyce raises Angie go by the rules. And so, in varying eccentric degrees, bending them and evading them, but changing just their own lives, and just for a moment, did Isabella, Nijo, Joan and Griselda. Only Dull Gret went further.

Gret is performed by the same actress (Carole Hayman) who plays Angie, so maybe there's a frail hope. I am afraid of reading too much into the doubling of parts, but as it works out, whether intrinsic to the play's conception or not, the doubling adds connective tissue. Thus Selina Cadell, a radiantly intelligent and truehearted Pope Joan, becomes, as Louise, a commentary on the diminished returns of imitating a "man" not for theology but for capital. At other times, there's no such nuance to the multiple roles, only the immense pleasure of seeing actresses who can illuminate different parts totally. All the performances are splendid—moving, precise, and deep. As is the play.

TOM Stoppard

Born Tomáš Straussler in Zlin, Czechoslovakia, on July 3, 1937, Tom Stoppard was taken by his family to Singapore in 1939 to escape the Nazis. Shortly before the Japanese invasion of Singapore two years later, young Tom, with his mother and brother, fled again to Darjeeling, India. His father, who remained behind, was killed in the invasion. At the end of the war, the family emigrated to England where Tom's mother met and married Kenneth Stoppard, a major in the British army.

At the age of seventeen, Stoppard left school to become a journalist in Bristol, working for several local newspapers as a jack-of-all-trades: news reporter, feature writer, gossip columnist, and theater and film critic. After six years of such work, he became drama critic for a London-based magazine, *Scene*. It was during this time (1962–66) that he began writing seriously, at first largely radio and television plays, most of which were produced. But his first major success came when he turned to the stage. *Rosencrantz and Guildenstern Are Dead*, which opened in London in 1967, catapulted him instantly into the front ranks of British playwrights. Inspired by the plays of Samuel Beckett, it cleverly retold the story of *Hamlet* from the worm's-eye view of Shakespeare's minor characters.

Some milestones in Stoppard's productive theater career are as follows: *Enter a Free Man* (1967)—an adaptation of an early television play; *The Real Inspector Hound* (1968)—a farcical whodunit in which drama critics are pulled into the play they are witnessing; *Jumpers* (1972)—an intellectual circus that scrutinizes modern philosophy; *Travesties* (1974)—an audacious conflation of the lives and ideas of James Joyce, Tristan Tzara, and Nikolai Lenin; *The Real Thing* (1988)—an elegant comedy of love and infidelity recently revived with great success; *Hapgood* (1988)—a seriocomic espionage thriller; *Arcadia* (1993)—an ambitious exercise in time travel which mixes elements of literature, history, and science; and *The Invention of Love* (1997)—a celebration of scholarship and a disquisition on love focused on the figure of the poet A.E. Housman.

In the late 1970s, after visiting the then Soviet Union as a member of Amnesty International, Stoppard's work became more overtly political. Plays of this period—*Every Good Boy Deserves Favour* (1977), *Professional Foul* (1977), *Dogg's Hamlet, Cahoot's Macbeth* (1979)—championed human rights, directly attacking the suppression of dissent in the then Eastern bloc, particularly in Stoppard's native Czechoslovakia.

In addition to writing for the stage, radio, and television, Stoppard has also established a major career in film with screenplays for such films as *Empire of the Sun* (1987) and *Billy Bathgate* (1991). In 1985 he was nominated for an Academy Award for the screenplay for *Brazil* (with Terry Gilliam), an award he won in 1998 for *Shakespeare in Love* (with Marc Norman).

■■■■■■■■■■■■■

COMMENTARY ON *THE REAL THING*

None of Tom Stoppard's more than a dozen stage plays—not even his most familiar work, *Rosencrantz and Guildenstern Are Dead*—has achieved the popularity of *The Real Thing*, which has enjoyed not one, but two commercially successful runs in London's West End and New York's Broadway. (See "The Play in Performance.") At first glance, the reason seems obvious: Of all Stoppard's major plays it makes the least demands of the audience's cultural and intellectual baggage. It does not, like *Rosencrantz and Guildenstern*, assume a familiarity (a strong familiarity) with (a) *Hamlet*, (b) Samuel Beckett and absurdist drama, and

(c) T.S. Eliot's "The Love Song of J. Alfred Prufrock." It does not, like *Arcadia*, assume at least a nodding acquaintance with (a) Lord Byron, (b) mathematical theory, (c) landscape gardening, (d) neoclassicism and romanticism; it does not, like *Travesties*, assume *some* historical knowledge about Lenin, dadaism, and James Joyce. It does not like . . . well you get the idea: Stoppard, that ferocious autoddact, loves to couch his dramatic conceits—usually abstract oppositions—in learned garb.

This has always been characteristic of his dialectical dramatic method. From *Rosencrantz and Guildenstern* onward, Stoppard has loved radical contrast: "My ambition has always been to combine a play of ideas with farce," he stated when his first play was performed; low comedy became a vehicle for complex intellectual ideas. But Stoppard's concept of a play of ideas has rarely been the exposition of a singular point of view; only when attacking totalitarian repression has Stoppard mounted a platform. On the contrary, it is the interplay of *competing* ideas that invariably inspires him: He loves an arena where opposite intellectual positions and systems duke it out. "What I'm always saying," he explained in a 1974 interview, "is, firstly, A. Secondly Not A." And so he loves to construct plays on the armatures of opposed ideas gleaned from his voracious reading. *Arcadia*, for example, is built on proliferating pairs of oppositions: present/past; lust/love; art/science; rationalism/romanticism; randomness/predetermination; Newtonian order/fractal chaos. *Travesties* plays revolutionary determinism against revolutionary meaninglessness. With such intellectual structures in hand, Stoppard the crafty dramatist constructs an ingenious plot to bring the ideas to theatrical life: the worm's eye view of *Hamlet*, the meeting of Lenin, Tzara, Joyce in 1913 Zurich, the time traveling between the present and the early nineteenth century in the same room in an English country house.

But the plot of *The Real Thing* avoids this trademark cleverness: it is set in contemporary times, with allusions only those unfamiliar with old pop music will find esoteric (all right, class, identify Procul Harum and the Monkees). True, it does allude sarcastically to certain incidents bred by the "politically correct" propensities of the British literary establishment, but Americans can easily supply their own examples. No, its plot—how un-Stoppardian!—derives from its protagonist's romantic entanglements, from his attempt to come to terms with his life and loves. Stoppard usually distances himself radically from his characters through time, place, occupation. But here he chooses a protagonist not unlike himself. Briefly, the play centers on Henry, a successful playwright trying to balance his personal and professional life and finding it increasingly difficult to do so. Married to an actress, Charlotte (who, we will learn, has her own history of infidelity), Henry has initiated a passionate affair with another one, Annie, the sensual, unpredictable wife of one of his actors, Max. Both marriages come apart and Henry and Annie move into new "digs." Reading from Strindberg's *Miss Julie*, Henry muses that despite his passion he can't write believable romantic dialogue: "Loving and being loved is very unliterary. It's happiness expressed in banality and lust."

Eventually, Annie betrays Henry with a young actor she's performing with. Henry, however, loves her too much to end what has become more than an affair: "It's no trick loving somebody at their *best*. Love is loving them at their worst." The play ends ambiguously. The last scene is largely devoted to introducing and savaging Brodie, the loutish political martyr whose incompetent play Henry has been coerced by the leftish Annie into rewriting. We work to try to discern the state of Henry and Annie's relationship through the banal torrent of Brodie's meanderings. But Stoppard refuses to end things neatly. For his final curtain he indeed gives us a new beginning—announced over the phone to Henry—*not* for Annie and Henry but for the cuckolded Max! He's getting married again. Henry offers congratulations: "Isn't love wonderful?" As Annie retires to the bedroom, Henry, still chatting with the new fiancé, absent-mindedly switches on the radio. The song quickly wins his attention. It's the Monkees singing "I'm a Believer." Despite everything, Henry is.

But to say that *The Real Thing* has an atypically accessible plot is not to say it is a conventionally naturalistic play. Far from it; Stoppard has more than a few of his customary tricks up his sleeve. The play's first scene, for example, opens with Max sitting at home building a house of cards while he awaits the return of his wife from a presumed trip abroad. When she arrives he accuses her of adultery based on the fact that he found her passport in a drawer at home. The second scene reveals that what we've just seen is in fact a play within a play, one written by Henry in which Max is a character. But *that* Max is soon contrasted with the *real* Max who now makes an entrance with his faithless wife. Stoppard later again uses the play-within-a-play device to allow us to experience directly the utter banality of Brodie's cliché-ridden script. As always in Stoppard's works, even at their most accessible, ideas lurk behind the playfulness. There is only one major operative dialectic in this play: real/false. The question is, Can we always tell the real thing from the fake? Annie defends Brodie's amateurish writing: "You write because you're a writer. . . . Then somebody who isn't in on the game comes along, like Brodie, who really has something to write about, something real, and you can't get through it. Well, he couldn't get through yours, so where are you? To you, he can't write. To him, write is all you do." Henry retaliates: "Maybe Brodie got a raw deal, maybe he didn't . . . [But] he's a lout with language. I can't help somebody who thinks that throwing bricks is a demonstration while building tower blocks is social violence. Words don't deserve that kind of malarkey. They're innocent, neutral, precise . . . but when they get their corners knocked off, they're no good anymore, and Brodie knocks their corners off."

But it's in the private not the public arena where the attempt to separate the real from the fake carries greatest consequences. The play's restless major characters weigh in on the problem. Charlotte (to Henry's statement that, "I thought we had a commitment."): "There are no commitments, only bargains. And they have to be made again every day. You think a commit-

ment is *it*. Finished." Annie: "You have to find a part of yourself where I'm not important or you won't be worth loving." Henry: "The trouble is, I can't *find* a part of myself where you're not important. I write in order to be worth your while and to finance the way I want to live with you. Not the way *you* want to live. The way *I* want to live with *you*." As Stoppard's articulate surrogates struggle with separating love's true nuggets from its fool's gold, they'll make the best of their situations. As another old pop song puts it: "If this isn't love / It'll have to do / Until the real thing comes along."

THE REAL THING
Tom Stoppard

CHARACTERS

MAX, *40-ish*
CHARLOTTE, *35-ish*
HENRY, *40-ish*

ANNIE, *30-ish*
BILLY, *22-ish*
DEBBIE, *17*
BRODIE, *25*

ACT ONE

SCENE ONE

MAX *and* CHARLOTTE.

Max doesn't have to be physically impressive, but you wouldn't want him for an enemy. Charlotte doesn't have to be especially attractive, but you instantly want her for a friend.

Living-room. Architect's drawing board, perhaps. A partly open door leads to an unseen hall and an unseen front door. One or two other doors to other rooms.

Max is alone, sitting in a comfortable chair, with a glass of wine and an open bottle to hand. He is using a pack of playing cards to build a pyramidical, tiered viaduct on the coffee table in front of him. He is a about to add a pair of playing cards (leaning against each other to hold each other up), and the pyramid is going well. Beyond the door to the hall, the front door is heard being opened with a key. The light from there changes as the unseen front door is opened.

Max does not react to the opening of the door, which is more behind him than in front of him.

MAX. Don't slam—

(The front door slams, not violently. The viaduct of cards collapses.)

(Superfluously, philosophically) . . . the door.

(Charlotte, in the hall, wearing a topcoat, looks round the door just long enough to say two words and disappears again.)

CHARLOTTE. It's me.

(Max leaves the cards where they have fallen. He takes a drink from the glass. He doesn't look up at all.

Charlotte, without the topcoat, comes back into the room carrying a small suitcase and a plastic duty-free airport bag. She puts the case down and comes up behind Max's chair and kisses the top of his head.)

CHARLOTTE. Hello.
MAX. Hello, lover.
CHARLOTTE. That's nice. You used to call me lover.

(She drops the airport bag on his lap and returns towards the suitcase.)

MAX. Oh, it's you. I thought it was my lover. *(He doesn't look at his present. He puts the bag on the floor by his chair.)* Where is it you've been?

(The question surprises her. She is deflected from picking up her suitcase—presumably to take it into the bedroom—and the case remains where it is.)

CHARLOTTE. Well, Switzerland, of course. Weren't you listening?

(Max finally looks at her.)

MAX. You look well. Done you good.
CHARLOTTE. What, since yesterday?
MAX. Well, something has. How's Ba'l?
CHARLOTTE. Who?

(Max affects to puzzle very briefly over her answer.)

MAX. I meant Ba'l.
Do you say 'Basel'?
I say Ba'l.
CHARLOTTE. Oh . . . yes. I say Basel.
MAX *(Lilts)*. 'Let's call the whole thing *off* . . .'

(Charlotte studies him briefly, quizzically.)

CHARLOTTE. Fancy a drink?

(*She notes the glass, the bottle and his behaviour.*)

(*Pointedly, but affectionately*) Another drink?

(*He smiles at her, empties his glass and holds it up for her. She takes the glass, finds a second glass, pours wine into both glasses and gives Max his own glass.*)

MAX. How's old Basel, then? Keeping fit?
CHARLOTTE: Are you a tiny bit sloshed?
MAX. Certainly.
CHARLOTTE. I didn't go to Basel.

(*Max is discreetly but definitely interested by that.*)

MAX. No? Where did you go, then?
CHARLOTTE. Geneva.

(*Max is surprised. He cackles.*)

MAX. Geneva!

(*He drinks from his glass.*)

How's old Geneva, then? Franc doing well?
CHARLOTTE. Who?

(*He affects surprise.*)

MAX. The Swiss franc. Is it doing well?
CHARLOTTE. Are you all right?
MAX. Absolutely.
CHARLOTTE. How have you got on?
MAX. Not bad. My best was eleven pairs on the bottom row, but I ran out of cards.
CHARLOTTE. What about the thing you were working on? . . . What is it?
MAX. An hotel.
CHARLOTTE. Yes. You were two elevators short.
MAX. I've cracked it.
CHARLOTTE. Good.
MAX. I'm turning the whole place on its side and making it a bungalow. I still have a problem with the rooftop pool. As far as I can see, all the water is going to fall into the shallow end. How's the lake, by the way?
CHARLOTTE. What lake?

(*He affects surprise.*)

MAX. Lake Geneva. You haven't been to Loch Ness, have you? Lake Geneva. It is at Geneva? It must be. They wouldn't call it Lake Geneva if it was at Ba'l or Basel. They'd call it Lake Ba'l or Basel. You know the Swiss. Utterly reliable. And they've done it without going digital, that's what I admire so much. They know it's all a snare and a delusion. I can remember digitals when they first came out. You had to give your wrist a vigorous shake like bringing down a thermometer, and the only place you could buy one was Tokyo. But it looked all over for the fifteen-jewelled movement. Men ran through the market

place shouting, 'The cog is dead.' But still the Swiss didn't panic. In fact, they made a few digitals themselves, as a feint to draw the Japanese further into the mire, and got on with numbering the bank accounts. And now you see how the Japs are desperately putting hands on their digital watches. It's yodelling in the dark. They can yodel till the cows come home. The days of the digitals are numbered. The metaphor is built into them like a self-destruct mechanism. Mark my words, I was right about the skate-board, I was right about *nouvelle cuisine*, and I'll be proved right about the digital watch. Digitals have got no class, you see. They're science and technology. Makes nonsense of a decent pair of cufflinks, as the Swiss are the first to understand. Good sale?

(*Charlotte stares at him.*)

CHARLOTTE. What?

(*He affects surprise.*)

MAX. Good sale. Was the sale good? The sale in Geneva, how was it? Did it go well in Geneva, the sale?
CHARLOTTE. What's the matter?
MAX. I'm showing an interest in your work. I thought you liked me showing an interest in your work. My showing. Save the gerund and screw the whale. Yes, I'm sure you do. I remember how cross you got when I said to someone, 'My wife works for Sotheby's or Christie's, I forget which.' You misjudged me, as it happens. You thought I was being smart at your expense. In fact, I had forgotten. How's old Christie, by the way? (*Strikes his forehead.*) There I go. How's old Sothers, by the way? Happy with the Geneva sale, I trust?

(*Charlotte puts her glass down and moves to stand facing him.*)

CHARLOTTE (*To call a halt*). All right.
MAX. Just all right? Well, that's the bloody Swiss for you. Conservative, you see. The Japs could show them a thing or two. They'd have a whaling fleet in Lake Geneva by now. How's the skiing, by the way? Plenty of snow?
CHARLOTTE. Stop it—stop it—*stop it*.
What have I done?
MAX. You forgot your passport.
CHARLOTTE. I did what?
MAX. You went to Switzerland without your passport.
CHARLOTTE. What makes you think that?
MAX. I found it in your recipe drawer.
CHARLOTTE (*Quietly*). Jesus God.
MAX. Quite.

(*Charlotte moves away and looks at him with some curiosity.*)

CHARLOTTE. What were you looking for?
MAX. Your passport.

CHARLOTTE. It's about the last place I would have looked.

MAX. It was.

CHARLOTTE. Why were you looking for it?

MAX. I didn't know it was going to be your passport. If you see what I mean.

CHARLOTTE. I think I do. You go through my things when I'm away? (*Pause. Puzzled.*) Why?

MAX. I liked it when I found nothing. You should have just put it in your handbag. We'd still be an ideal couple. So to speak.

CHARLOTTE. Wouldn't you have checked to see if it had been stamped?

MAX. That's a very good point. I notice that you never went to Amsterdam when you went to Amsterdam. I must say I take my hat off to you, coming home with Rembrandt place mats for your mother. It's those little touches that lift adultery out of the moral arena and make it a matter of style.

CHARLOTTE. I wouldn't go on, if I were you.

MAX. Rembrandt place mats! I wonder who's got the originals. Some Arab, is it? 'Dinner's ready, Abdul, put the Rembrandts on the table.'

CHARLOTTE. It's like when we were burgled. The same violation. Worse.

MAX. I'm not a burglar. I'm your husband.

CHARLOTTE. As I said. Worse.

MAX. Well, I'm sorry.

I think I just apologized for finding out that you've deceived me.

Yes, I did.

How does she do it?

(*She moves away, to leave the room.*)

Are you going somewhere?

CHARLOTTE. I'm going to bed.

MAX. Aren't you going to tell me who it is?

CHARLOTTE. Who what is?

MAX. Your lover, lover.

CHARLOTTE. Which lover?

MAX. I assumed there'd only be the one.

CHARLOTTE. Did you?

MAX. Well, do you see them separately or both together?

Sorry, that's not fair.

Well, tell you what, nod your head if it's separately.

(*She looks at him.*)

Heavens.

If you have an opening free, I'm not doing much at the moment. Or is the position taken?

It is only two, is it?

Nod your head.

(*She looks at him.*)

Golly, you are a dark horse. How do they all three get away at the same time? Do they work together, like the Marx Brothers?

I'm not upsetting you, I hope?

CHARLOTTE. You underestimate me.

MAX (*Interested*). Do I? A string quartet, you mean? That sort of thing?

(*He ponders for a moment.*)

What does the fourth one do?

(*She raises her hand.*)

Got it. Plays by himself.

You can slap me if you like. I won't slap you back. I abhor cliché. It's one of the things that has kept me faithful.

(*Charlotte returns to the hall and reappears wearing her topcoat.*)

CHARLOTTE. If you don't mind, I think I will go out after all.

(*She moves to close the door behind her.*)

MAX. You've forgotten your suitcase.

(*Pause. She comes back and picks up the suitcase. She takes the case to the door.*)

CHARLOTTE. I'm sorry if you've had a bad time. But you've done everything wrong. There's a right thing to say if you can think what it is.

(*She waits a moment while Max thinks.*)

MAX. Is it anyone I know?

CHARLOTTE. You aren't anyone I know.

(*She goes out, closing the door, and then the front door is heard opening and closing.*

Max remains seated. After a moment he reaches down for the airport bag, puts it back on his lap and looks inside it. He starts to laugh. He withdraws from the bag a miniature Alp in a glass bowl. He gives the bowl a shake and creates a snowstorm within it. Then the snowstorm envelops the stage. Music—a pop record—makes a bridge into the next scene.)

SCENE TWO

HENRY, CHARLOTTE, MAX *and* ANNIE.

Henry is amiable but can take care of himself. Charlotte is less amiable and can take even better care of herself. Max is nice, seldom assertive, conciliatory. Annie is very much like the woman whom Charlotte has ceased to be.

A living-room. a record player and shelves of records. Sunday newspapers.

The music is coming from the record player.

Henry, with several record sleeves around him, is searching for a particular piece of music.

There are doors to hall, kitchen, bedroom. Charlotte enters barefoot, wearing Henry's dressing-gown which is too big for her. She is unkempt from sleep and seems generally disordered.

Henry looks up briefly.

HENRY. Hello.

(Charlotte moves forward without answering, sits down and looks around in a hopeless way.)

CHARLOTTE. Oh, God.

HENRY. I thought you'd rather lie in. Do you want some coffee?

CHARLOTTE. I don't know. *(Possibly referring to the litter of record sleeves, wanly.)* What a mess.

HENRY. Don't worry . . . don't worry . . .

(Henry continues to search among the records.)

CHARLOTTE. I think I'll just stay in bed.

HENRY. Actually, I phoned Max.

CHARLOTTE. What? Why?

HENRY. He was on my conscience. He's coming round.

CHARLOTTE *(Quite strongly).* I don't want to see *him.*

HENRY. Sorry.

CHARLOTTE. Honestly, Henry.

HENRY. Hang on—I think I've found it.

(He removes the pop record, which might have come to its natural end by now, from the record player and puts a different record on. Meanwhile—)

CHARLOTTE. Are you still doing your list?

HENRY. Mmm.

CHARLOTTE. Have you got a favourite book?

HENRY. *Finnegans Wake.*

CHARLOTTE. Have you read it?

HENRY. Don't be silly.

(He lowers the arm on to the record and listens to a few bars of alpine Strauss—or sub-Strauss. Then he lifts the arm again.)

No . . . No . . . Damnation.

(He starts to put the record away.)

Do you remember when we were in some place like Bournemouth or Deauville, and there was an open-air dance floor right outside our window?

CHARLOTTE. No.

HENRY. Yes you do, I was writing my Sartre play, and there was this bloody orchestra which kept coming back to the same tune every twenty minutes, so I started shouting out of the window and the hotel manager—

CHARLOTTE. That was St. Moritz. *(Scornfully)* Bournemouth.

HENRY. Well, what was it?

CHARLOTTE. What was what?

HENRY. What was the tune called? It sounded like Strauss or somebody.

CHARLOTTE. How does it go?

HENRY. I don't know, do I?

CHARLOTTE. Who were you with in Bournemouth?

HENRY. Don't mess about. I'm supposed to give them my eight records tomorrow, and so far I've got five and *Finnegans Wake.*

CHARLOTTE. Well, if you don't know what it's called and you can't remember how it goes, why in Christ's name do you want it on your desert island?

HENRY. It's not supposed to be eight records you love and adore.

CHARLOTTE. Yes, it is.

HENRY. It is not. It's supposed to be eight records you associate with turning-points in your life.

CHARLOTTE. Well, I'm a turning-point in your life, and when you took me to St. Moritz your favourite record was the Ronettes doing 'Da Doo Ron Ron'.

HENRY. The Crystals. *(Scornfully)* The Ronettes.

(Charlotte gets up and during the following searches, successfully, for a record, which she ends up putting on the machine.)

CHARLOTTE. You're going about this the wrong way. Just pick your eight all-time greats and then remember what you were doing at the time. What's wrong with that?

HENRY. I'm supposed to be one of your intellectual playwrights. I'm going to look a total prick, aren't I, going on the radio to announce that while I was telling Jean-Paul Sartre that he was essentially superficial, I was spending the whole time listening to the Crystals singing 'Da Doo Ron Ron'. Look, ages ago, Debbie put on one of those classical but not too classical records—she must have been about ten or eleven, it was before she dyed her hair—and I said to you, 'That's that bloody tune they were driving me mad with when I was trying to write "Jean-Paul is up the Wall" in that hotel in Switzerland. Maybe *she'll* remember.

CHARLOTTE. Where is she?

(Charlotte has placed the record on the machine, which now starts to play the Skater's Waltz.)

HENRY. Riding stables.

That's it! *(Triumphant and pleased, examining the record sleeve.)* Skater's Waltz! How did you know?

CHARLOTTE. They don't have open-air dance floors in the Alps in mid-winter. They have skating rinks. Now you've got six.

HENRY. Oh, I can't use that. It's so banal.

(*The doorbell rings. Henry goes to take the record off the machine.*)

That's Max. Do you want to let him in?

CHARLOTTE. No. Say I'm not here.

HENRY. He knows perfectly well you're here. Where else would you be? I'll say you don't want to see him because you've seen quite enough of him. How's that?

CHARLOTTE (*Giving up*). Oh, I'll get dressed.

(*She goes out the way she came in, towards the bedroom. Henry goes out through another door into the hall. His voice and Max's voice are heard, and the two men come in immediately afterwards.*)

HENRY. Hello, Max. Come in.

MAX. Hello, Henry.

HENRY (*Entering*). It's been some time.

(*Max enters unassertively.*)

MAX. Well, you've rather been keeping out of the way, haven't you?

HENRY. Yes. I'm sorry, Max. (*Indicating the bedroom*) Charlotte's not here. How are you?

MAX. I'm all right.

HENRY. Good.

MAX. And you?

HENRY. I'm all right.

MAX. Good.

HENRY. Well, we all seem to be all right.

MAX. Is Charlotte all right?

HENRY. I don't think she's terribly happy. Well, is it coffee or open a bottle?

MAX. Bottle, I should think.

HENRY. Hang on, then.

(*Henry goes out through the door to the kitchen. Max turns aside and looks at a paper without interest. Charlotte enters from the bedroom, having dressed without trying hard. She regards Max, who then notices her.*)

MAX. Hello, darling.

CHARLOTTE. Don't I get a day off?

MAX (*Apologetically*). Henry phoned . . .

CHARLOTTE (*More kindly*). It's all right, Max.

(*Henry enters busily from the kitchen, carrying an open champagne bottle and a jug of orange juice. Wine glasses are available in the living-room. Henry puts himself in charge of arranging the drinks.*)

HENRY. Hello, Charlotte. I was just telling Max you weren't here. So nice to see you, Max. What are you doing with yourself?

MAX. Is he joking?

HENRY. I mean apart from that. Actors are so sensitive. They feel neglected if one isn't constantly going round to the theatre to check up on them.

MAX. I was just telling Henry off for keeping out of the way.

CHARLOTTE. You'd keep out of the way if you'd written it. (*To Henry.*) If that orange juice is for me, you can forget it.

HENRY. No, no—buck's fizz all round. I feel reckless, extravagant, famous, in love, and I'm next week's castaway on *Desert Island Discs*.

MAX. Are you really?

HENRY. Head over heels. Here you are, lover. How was last night, by the way?

(*He hands Max and Charlotte their glasses.*)

CHARLOTTE. Hopeless. I had to fake it again.

HENRY. Very witty woman, my present wife. Actually, I was talking about my play.

CHARLOTTE. Actually, so was I. I've decided it's a mistake appearing in Henry's play.

MAX. Not for me, it isn't.

CHARLOTTE. Well, of course not for you, you idiot, you're not his wife.

MAX. Oh, I see what you mean.

CHARLOTTE. Max sees what I mean. You're right, Max.

MAX. I never said anything!

HENRY. How was it really?—last night.

CHARLOTTE. Not good. The stalls had a deserted look, about two-thirds, I should think. (*With false innocence.*) Oh, sorry, darling, is that what you meant?

MAX (*Disapproving*). Honestly, Charlotte, it was all right, Henry, *really*. All the laughs were in place, for a Saturday night anyway, and I had someone who came round afterwards who said the reconciliation scene was extremely moving. Actually, that reminds me. They *did* say—I mean, it's a tiny thing but I thought I'd pass it on because I do feel rather the same way . . . I mean all that stuff about the Japanese and digital watches—they suddenly have no idea what I'm talking about, you see, and I thought if we could just try it one night without—

(*Henry halts him, like a traffic policeman.*)

HENRY. Excuse me, Max.

(*Henry turns to Charlotte.*)

Two-thirds empty or two-thirds full?

(*Charlotte laughs brazenly.*)

CHARLOTTE. Hard luck, Max. (*She toasts.*) Well, here's to closing night. To the collapse of *House of Cards*.

MAX (*Shocked*). Charlotte!

CHARLOTTE. Well, you try playing the feed one night instead of acting Henry after a buck's fizz and two rewrites. All *his* laughs are in place all right. So's my groan. Groan, groan, they all go when they find out. Oh, *groan*, so she hasn't got a lover at all, eh? And they lose interest in me totally. I'm a victim of Henry's fantasy—a quiet, faithful bird with an interesting job, and a recipe drawer, and a stiff upper lip, and two semi-stiff lower ones all trembling for him—I'm sorry if you've had a bad time . . . There's a right thing to say now . . .

MAX. Jesus, Charlotte—

CHARLOTTE (*Quite genially*). Oh, shut up, Max. If he'd given her a lover instead of a temporary passport, we'd be in a play.

HENRY. It's a little early in the day for all this.

CHARLOTTE. No, darling, it's a little late.

MAX. Er, where's young Deborah today?

CHARLOTTE. Who?

MAX. Debbie.

CHARLOTTE (*Baffled*). Debbie?

MAX. Your daughter.

CHARLOTTE. Oh, daughter.

HENRY. Riding school.

CHARLOTTE. Must be some mistake. Smart talk, that's the thing. Having children is so unsmart. Endless dialogue about acne. Henry couldn't do that. He doesn't like research.

HENRY. True.

MAX (*To Charlotte*). Lots of people don't have children, in real life. Me and Annie . . .

Henry: Oh, don't—I told her once that lots of women were only good for fetching drinks, and she became quite unreasonable.

(*Blithely, knowing what he is doing, Henry holds his empty glass towards Charlotte.*)

Is there any more of that?

(*Max glances at Charlotte and hastily tries to defuse the bomb.*)

MAX. Let me . . .

(*Max takes Henry's glass and fills it from the bottle and the jug.*)

CHARLOTTE. Lots of *men* are only good for fetching drinks— why don't you write about *them*?

(*Max hands the glass back to Henry.*)

HENRY (*Smiling up at Max*). Terribly pleased you could come round.

CHARLOTTE. Oh, yes, you owe him a drink. What an ego trip! Having all the words to come back with just as you need them. That's the difference between plays and real life—thinking time. You don't really think that if Henry caught me out with a lover, he'd sit around being witty about Rembrandt place mats? Like hell he would. He'd come apart like a pick-a-sticks. His sentence structure would go to pot, closely followed by his sphincter. You know that, don't you, Henry? Henry? No answer. Are you there, Henry? Say something witty.

(*Henry turns his head to her.*)

HENRY. Is it anyone I know?

MAX (*Starting to rise*). Well, look, thanks for the drink—

CHARLOTTE. Oh, sit down, Max, for God's sake, or he'll think it's you.

HENRY. It isn't you, is it, Max?

MAX. Oh, for Christ's sake . . .

(*Max subsides unhappily.*)

HENRY. Just kidding, Max. Badinage. You know, *dialogue*.

(*The doorbell rings.*)

See what I mean?

MAX. Annie said she'd come round if her committee finished early. She's on this Justice for Brodie Committee . . . you know . . . (*Pause*) I'll go, should I?

HENRY. I'll go.

MAX. No, stay where you are, I'll see if it's her.

(*Max goes out to the front door.*)

CHARLOTTE. Thanks very much. Anyone else coming?

HENRY. Just give them a cheese stick. They won't stay.

CHARLOTTE. What did you phone him for in the first place?

HENRY. Well, I only have to write it once. He has to show up every night. I had a conscience.

CHARLOTTE. Do you have a conscience about me too?

HENRY. Absolutely. You can have a cheese stick.

CHARLOTTE. Well, don't ask her about Brodie.

HENRY. Right.

CHARLOTTE. If she starts on about scapegoats and cover-ups, she'll get a cheese stick up her nostril.

HENRY. Right.

CHARLOTTE (*Enthusiastically*). Darling! It's been ages!

(*Annie has entered, followed by Max. Annie is carrying a carrier bag loaded with greengrocery.*)

ANNIE. Hello, Charlotte. This is jolly nice of you.

MAX. We can only stay a minute.

ANNIE. How are you, Henry?

HENRY. Fine.

MAX. Annie's stewarding at the protest meeting this afternoon, so we can't—

HENRY. Oh, do shut up. Don't take any notice of Max. I made him nervous.

ANNIE. What did you do to him?

HENRY. Nothing at all. I asked him if he was having an affair with Charlotte, and he was offended.

ANNIE. Was he?

HENRY. Apparently not. Been shopping?

ANNIE. Not exactly. I saw a place open on my way back and . . . Anyway, you might as well take it as an offering.

CHARLOTTE (*Taking the bag from her and investigating it*). Darling, there was absolutely no need to bring . . . mushrooms?

ANNIE. Yes.

CHARLOTTE (*Not quite behaving well*) And a turnip . . .

ANNIE (*Getting unhappy*). And carrots . . . Oh, dear, it must look as if—

HENRY. Where's the meat?

CHARLOTTE. Shut up.

ANNIE. I wish I'd brought flowers now.

CHARLOTTE. This is much nicer.

HENRY. So original. I'll get a vase.

ANNIE. It's supposed to be crudités.

HENRY. Crudités! Perfect title for a pornographic revue.

CHARLOTTE. I'll make a dip.

MAX. We're not staying to eat, for heaven's sake.

HENRY. Just a quick dip.

ANNIE. Would you like *me* to?

CHARLOTTE. No, no. I know where everything is.

HENRY. Yes, Charlotte will provide dips for the crudity. She knows where everything is.

(*Charlotte takes charge of the vegetables. Henry gets a fourth glass.*)

Sit down, have some buck's fizz. I feel reckless, extravagant, famous, and I'm next week's castaway on *Desert Island Discs*. You can be my luxury if you like.

ANNIE. I'm not sure I'm one you can afford.

MAX. What are your eight records?

HENRY. This is the problem. I hate music.

CHARLOTTE. He likes pop music.

HENRY. You don't have to repeat everything I say.

MAX. I don't understand the problem.

CHARLOTTE. The problem is he's a snob without being an inverted snob. He's *ashamed* of liking pop music.

(*Charlotte takes the vegetables out into the kitchen, closing the door.*)

HENRY. This is true. The trouble is I don't like the pop music which it's all right to like. You can have a bit of Pink Floyd shoved in between your symphonies and your Dame Janet Baker—that shows a refreshing breadth of taste or at least a refreshing candour—but *I* like Wayne Fontana and the Mindbenders doing 'Um Um Um Um Um Um'.

MAX. Doing what?

HENRY. That's the title. (*He demonstrates it.*) 'Um-Um-Um-Um-Um-Um'. I like Neil Sedaka. Do you remember 'Oh, Carol'?

MAX. For God's sake.

HENRY (*Cheerfully*). Yes, I'm not very up to date. I like Herman's Hermits, and the Hollies, and the Everly Brothers, and Brenda Lee, and the Supremes . . . I don't mean everything they did. I don't like *artists*. I like singles.

MAX. This is sheer pretension.

HENRY (*Insistently*). No. It *moves* me, the way people are supposed to be moved by *real* music. I was taken once to Covent Garden to hear a woman called Callas in a sort of foreign musical with no dancing which people were donating kidneys to get tickets for. The idea was that I would be cured of my strange disability. As though the place were a kind of Lourdes for the musically disadvantaged. My illness at the time took the form of believing that the Righteous Brothers' recording of 'You've Lost that Lovin' Feelin'' on the London label was possibly the most haunting, the most deeply moving noise ever produced by the human spirit, and this female vocalist person was going to set me right.

MAX. No good?

HENRY. Not even close. That woman would have had a job getting into the top thirty if she were *hyped*.

MAX. You preferred the Brothers.

HENRY. I did. Do you think there's something wrong with me?

MAX. Yes. I'd say you were a moron.

HENRY. What can I do?

MAX. There's nothing you can do.

HENRY. I mean about *Desert Island Discs*.

ANNIE. You know damned well what you should do.

HENRY. Cancel?

MAX. Actually, I remember it. (*He sings, badly.*) 'You've lost that lovin' feeling . . .'

HENRY. That's an idea—aversion therapy.

MAX (*Sings*). '. . . that lovin' feeling . . . You've lost that lovin' feeling . . .'

HENRY. I think it's working.

MAX (*Sings*). '. . . it's gorn, gorn, gorn . . . oh—oh—oh—yeah . . .'

HENRY (*Happily*). God, it's *rubbish*! You've cracked it. Now do 'Oh, Carol'.

MAX. I don't know that one.

HENRY. I'll play it for you.

MAX. I think I'll go and help Charlotte.

ANNIE. I should go.

MAX. No. I thought of it first.

(*Charlotte enters, carrying a bowl.*)

CHARLOTTE. One dip.

MAX. I was coming to help.

CHARLOTTE. All right, you can chop.

MAX. Fine. Chop . . .

(*Max goes out into the kitchen. Charlotte places the bowl and is about to follow Max out. Henry dips his finger into the bowl and tastes the dip.*)

HENRY. It needs something.

CHARLOTTE. I beg your pardon?

HENRY. It needs something. A bit of interest. Garlic? Lemon juice? I don't know.

CHARLOTTE (*Coldly*). Perhaps you should employ a cook.

HENRY. Surely that would be excessive—a cook who spends all her time emptying jars of mayonnaise and adding lemon juice? What we we do with the surplus?

CHARLOTTE. Presumably put it on stage with the rest of your stuff.

(*Charlotte goes out into the kitchen, closing the door. Pause.*)

HENRY. Are you all right?

(*Annie nods.*)

ANNIE. Are you all right?

(*Henry nods.*)

Touch me.

(*Henry shakes his head.*)

Touch me.

HENRY. No.

ANNIE. Come on, touch me.
Help yourself.
Touch me anywhere you like.

HENRY. No.

ANNIE. Touch me.

HENRY. No.

ANNIE. Coward.

HENRY. I love you anyway.

ANNIE. Yes, say that.

HENRY. I love you.

ANNIE. Go on.

HENRY. I love you.

ANNIE. That's it.

HENRY. I love you.

ANNIE. Touch me then. They'll come in or they won't. Take a chance. Kiss me.

HENRY. For Christ's sake.

ANNIE. Quick one on the carpet then.

HENRY. You're crackers.

ANNIE. I'm not interested in your mind.

HENRY. Yes, you are.

ANNIE. No, I'm not, I lied to you.

(*Pause. Henry smiles at her.*)

I hate Sunday.

HENRY. Thought I'd cheer you up with an obscene phone call, but Max got to it first, so I improvised.

ANNIE. I might have come round anyway. 'Hello, Henry, Charlotte, just passing, long time no see.'

HENRY. That would have been pushing it.

ANNIE. I'm in a mood to push it. Let's go while they're chopping turnips.

HENRY. You *are* crackers.

ANNIE. We'll go, and then it will be done. Max will suffer. Charlotte will make you suffer and get custody. You'll see

Debbie on Sundays, and in three years she'll be at university not giving a damn either way.

HENRY. It's not just Debbie.

ANNIE. No, you want to give it time—

HENRY. Yes—

ANNIE. . . . time to go wrong, change, spoil. Then you'll know it wasn't the real thing.

HENRY. I don't steal other men's wives.

ANNIE. Thanks a lot.

HENRY. You know what I mean.

ANNIE. Yes, you mean you love me but you don't want it to get around. Me and the Righteous Brothers. Well, thanks a lot.

(*The kitchen door is flung open and Max enters rather dramatically, bleeding from a cut finger.*)

MAX. Don't panic! Have you got a hankie?

ANNIE. Max?

(*Annie and Henry respond appropriately, each searching for a handkerchief. Henry produces one first, a clean white one, from his pocket.*)

HENRY. Here—

MAX. Thanks. No, let me—

ANNIE. Let me see.

MAX. It's all right, it's not as bad as it looks. (*To Henry.*) Typical of your bloody kitchen—all champagne and no paper towels.

ANNIE. Poor love, just hold the cut for a while.

MAX. I think I'll put it back under the tap.

(*He moves towards the kitchen.*)

HENRY. Sorry about this, Max. She tried to do it to me once.

(*Max leaves, leaving the door open. Henry and Annie's conversation is in no way furtive but pitched to acknowledge the open door.*)

ANNIE. I'm sorry.

HENRY. No, I'm sorry.

ANNIE. It's all right. Anything's all right.

(*Henry moves forward and kisses her lightly.*)

HENRY. It'll get better.

ANNIE. How?

HENRY. Maybe we'll get found out.

ANNIE. Better to tell them. Whoever comes in first, eh? If it's Max, I'll tell him. If it's Charlotte, you start.
All right.
It's easy. Like Butch Cassidy and the Sundance Kid jumping off the cliff.
It's only a couple of marriages and a child.
All right?

(*Charlotte enters from the kitchen, carrying a tray of chopped-up vegetables.*)

(*To Henry.*) All right?

(*This is bold as brass and, consequently, safe as houses: in this way Annie and Henry continue to speak quite privately to each other in the interstices of the general conversation, under or over the respective preoccupations of Charlotte and Max.*)

CHARLOTTE. Did Max tell you? It's red cabbage. I've taken him off the knives. He's making another dip. He says it's Hawaiian. It's supposed to be served in an empty pineapple. We haven't got a pineapple. He's going to serve it in an empty tin of pineapple chunks. I do envy you being married to a man with a sense of humour. Henry thinks he has a sense of humour, but what he has is a joke reflex. Eh, Henry? His mind is racing. Pineapple, pineapple . . . Come on, darling.

HENRY (*To Annie*). No. Sorry.

ANNIE. It's all right.

CHARLOTTE (*Busy with cutlery*). Is Debbie expecting lunch?

HENRY (*To Annie*). Not really.

CHARLOTTE. What?

HENRY. No. She wants to stay out.

(*Annie drinks what remains in her glass.*)

ANNIE. Where is Debbie?

HENRY. Riding school. Drink?

(*Henry takes her empty glass out of her hand.*)

ANNIE. Love you.

CHARLOTTE. She used to eat like a horse, till she had one.

(*Henry refills Annie's glass.*)

HENRY. I'm picking her up this afternoon.

(*He returns Annie's glass.*)

Buck's fizz all right?

CHARLOTTE. Picking her up?

ANNIE. I don't care.

(*Max enters with the Hawaiian dip in the pineapple tin.*)

MAX. Here we are.

ANNIE. Anything's all right.

MAX. It's Hawaiian.

HENRY. You're a lovely feller.

CHARLOTTE. Well done, Max.

ANNIE. So are you.

(*She meets Max, dips her finger into the tin and tastes the dip.*)

MAX. I hope I've got it right. What do you think?

(*In his other hand Max has Henry's somewhat blood-stained handkerchief, which he now offers back.*)

(*To Henry.*) Thanks. What should I do with it?

HENRY (*Taking it*). It's okay, I'll take it.

(*Henry puts the handkerchief in his pocket.*)

ANNIE (*To Max*). Not bad. (*To Charlotte.*) May I?

CHARLOTTE. Feel free.

ANNIE. Hang on a sec.

(*She takes the tin from Max and leaves the room with it, going to the kitchen.*)

CHARLOTTE (*To Henry*). You're over-protective. She could walk it in half an hour.

MAX. Who, what?

CHARLOTTE. Debbie.

HENRY. By the time she finished mucking out, whatever they call it . . .

CHARLOTTE. Grooming the mount, mounting the groom . . .

HENRY (*Unamused*). Hilarious.

MAX. *I* wouldn't let her walk. Someone got murdered on the common not long ago. Mustn't put temptation in the way.

CHARLOTTE. Debbie wouldn't murder anyone. She'd just duff them up a little bit. I can't make her out at all.

(*Annie re-enters with the dip.*)

Some people have daughters who love ponies.

(*Passing Henry, Annie casually puts her finger in his mouth, without pausing.*)

ANNIE. What do you think?

CHARLOTTE. Some people have daughters who go punk. We've got one who goes riding on Barnes Common looking like the Last of the Mohicans.

HENRY. Crackers.

(*Annie delivers the dip to Charlotte.*)

CHARLOTTE (*To Annie*). Is yours a case of sperm count or twisted tubes? Or is it that you just can't stand the little buggers?

MAX. Charlotte!

HENRY. What business is that of yours?

CHARLOTTE. He's in love with his, you know.

ANNIE. Isn't that supposed to be normal?

CHARLOTTE. No, dear, normal is the other way round.

HENRY. I say, Annie, what's this Brodie Committee all about? Charlotte was asking.

MAX. You know, Private Brodie.

ANNIE. It's all right.

MAX. Annie knows him.

ANNIE. I don't know him.

MAX. Tell them about meeting him on the train.

ANNIE. Yes. I met him on a train.

(*Pause. But Henry, exhibiting avid interest, disobliges her.*)

HENRY. Yes?

ANNIE (*Laughs uncomfortably*). I seem to have told this story before.

HENRY. But we haven't seen you for ages.

MAX. Annie was travelling up to London from our cottage, weren't you?

HENRY. *Were you?*

ANNIE. Yes.

HENRY (*Fascinated*). You have a cottage in . . . ?

ANNIE. Norfolk.

HENRY. Norfolk! What, up in the hills there?

ANNIE (*Testily*) *What* hills? Norfolk is absolutely—

(*She brings herself up short.*)

CHARLOTTE. Oh, very funny. Stop it, Henry.

HENRY. I have no idea what you are talking about. So, you were coming up to London from your Norfolk flat—*cottage*—and you met this Private Brodie on the train.

ANNIE. Yes.

MAX. It was quite remarkable. Brodie was on his way to the anti-missiles demonstration, just like Annie.

HENRY. *Really?*

ANNIE. Yes.

HENRY. How did you know?
    Was he wearing a 'Missiles Out' badge on his uniform?

ANNIE. He wasn't in uniform.

MAX. The guts of it, the sheer moral courage. An ordinary soldier using his weekend pass to demonstrate against their bloody missiles.

HENRY. *Their?* I thought they were ours.

MAX. No, they're American.

HENRY. Oh, yes—*their* . . .

MAX. Pure moral conscience, you see—I mean, he didn't have our motivation.

HENRY. *Our?*

MAX. Mine and Annie's.

(*Henry appears not to understand.*)

    Owning property in Little Barmouth.

HENRY. Yes, of course. Private Brodie didn't own a weekend cottage in Little Barmouth, you mean.

MAX. No, he's a Scots lad. He was stationed at the camp down the road. He was practically guarding the base where these rockets are making Little Barmouth into a sitting duck for the Russian counter-attack, should it ever come to that.

HENRY (*To Annie*). I see what you mean.

ANNIE. Do you?

HENRY. Well, yes. Little Barmouth isn't going to declare war on Russia, so why should Little Barmouth be wiped out in a war not of Little Barmouth's making?

MAX. Quite.

CHARLOTTE. Shut up, Henry.

MAX. Is he being like that?

CHARLOTTE. Yes, he's being like that.

MAX. I don't see what he's got to be like that about.

HENRY (*Capitulating enthusiastically*). Absolutely! So you met this Private Brodie on the train, and Brodie said, 'I see you're going to the demo down Whitehall.' Right?

ANNIE. No. He recognized me from my children's serial. He used to watch *Rosie of the Royal Infirmary* when he was a kid.

MAX. How *about* that? It seems like the day before yesterday Annie was doing *Rosie of the Royal Infirmary*. He's *still* a kid.

ANNIE. Yes. Twenty-one.

MAX. He's a child.

HENRY. He kicked two policemen inside out, didn't he?

MAX. Piss off.
    (*To Charlotte.*) If you want to know what it's all about, you should come to the meeting.

CHARLOTTE. I know I should, but I like to keep my Sundays free. For entertaining friends, I mean. Fortunately, there are people like Annie to make up for people like me.

HENRY. Perhaps I'll go.

CHARLOTTE. No, you're people like me. You tell him, Annie.

ANNIE. You're picking up Debbie from riding school.

HENRY. Actually, I think I'll join the Justice for Brodie Committee. I should have thought of that before.

CHARLOTTE. They don't want dilettantes. You have to be properly motivated, like Annie.

HENRY. Brodie just wants to get out of jail. What does he care if we're motivated by the wrong reasons.

MAX. Like what?

HENRY. Perhaps one of us is worried that his image is getting a bit too right-of-centre. Another is in love with a committee member and wishes to gain her approbation . . .

CHARLOTTE. Which one are you?

HENRY. You think I'm kidding, but I'm not. Public postures have the configuration of private derangement.

MAX. Who said that?

HENRY. I did, you fool.

MAX. I mean first.

HENRY. Oh, first. (*To Annie.*) Take him off to your meeting, I'm sick of him.

ANNIE. He's not coming.

HENRY (*Savouring it*). You are not going to the meeting?

MAX. No, actually. Not that I wouldn't, but it would mean letting down my squash partner.

HENRY. Squash partner? An interesting moral dilemma. I wonder what Saint Augustine would have done?

MAX. I don't think Saint Augustine had a squash partner.

HENRY. I know that. Nobody would play with him. Even so. I put myself in his place. I balance a pineapple chunk on my carrot. I ponder. On the one hand, Max's squash partner. Decent chap but not a deprivation of the first magnitude. And on the other hand, Brodie, an out-and-out thug, an arsonist, vandalizer of a national shrine, *but* mouldering in jail for years to come owing, *perhaps*, to society's inability to comprehend a man divided against himself, a pacifist hooligan.

MAX. I don't condone vandalism, however idealistic. I just—

HENRY. Yes, well, as acts of vandalism go, starting a fire on a war memorial using the wreath to the Unknown Soldier as kindling scores very low on discretion. I assumed he was trying to be provocative.

MAX. Of course he was, you idiot. But he got hammered by an emotional backlash.

HENRY. No, no, you *can't*—

MAX. Yes, he bloody was!

HENRY. I mean 'hammer' and 'backlash'. You can't *do it!*

MAX. Oh, for Christ's sake. This is your house, and I'm drinking your wine, but if you don't mind me saying so, Henry—

HENRY. My saying, Max.

MAX. Right.

(*He puts down his glass definitively and stands up.*)

Come on, Annie.
There's something wrong with you.
You've got something missing. You may have all the words, but having all the words is not what life's about.

HENRY. I'm sorry, but it actually *hurts*.

MAX. Brodie may be no intellectual, like you, but he did march for a cause, and now he's got six years for a stupid piece of bravado and a punch-up, and he'd have been forgotten in a week if it wasn't for Annie. That's what life's about—messy bits of good and bad luck, and people caring and not necessarily having all the answers. Who the hell are you to patronize Annie? She's worth ten of you.

HENRY. I know that.

MAX. I'm sorry, Charlotte.

CHARLOTTE. Well done, Henry.

(*Max leaves towards the front door. Charlotte, with a glance at Henry, rolling her eyes in rebuke, follows him out of the room. Annie stands up. For the rest of the scene she is moving, hardly looking at Henry, perhaps fetching her handbag.*)

HENRY. It was just so I could look at you without it looking funny.

ANNIE. What time are you going for Debbie?

HENRY. Four o'clock. Why?

ANNIE. Three o'clock. Look for my car.

HENRY. What about Brodie?

ANNIE. Let him rot.

(*Annie leaves, closing the door. Pop music: Herman's Hermits, I'm Into Something Good'.*)

SCENE THREE

MAX *and* ANNIE.

A living-room.
    Max is alone, listening to a small radio, from which Herman's Hermits continue to be heard, at an adjusted level. The disposition of furniture and doors makes the scene immediately reminiscent of the beginning of Scene I. The front door, off stage, is heard being opened with a key. The door closes. Annie, wearing a topcoat, appears briefly round the door to the hall. She is in a hurry.

ANNIE. Have you got it on?

(*She disappears and reappears without the coat.*)

How much have I missed?

MAX. Five or ten minutes.

ANNIE. Damn. If I'd had the car, I'd have caught the beginning.

MAX. Where have you been?

ANNIE. You know where I've been. Rehearsing.

(*The music ends and is followed by Henry being interviewed on Desert Island Discs, but the radio dialogue, during the few moments before Max turns the sound down, is meaningless under the stage dialogue.*)

MAX. How's Julie?

ANNIE. Who?

MAX. Julie. Miss Julie. Strindberg's Miss Julie. Miss Julie by August Strindberg, how is she?

ANNIE. Are you all right?

MAX. This probably—

ANNIE. Shush up.

MAX. This probably isn't anything, but—

ANNIE. *Max*, can I *listen?*

(*Max turns the radio sound right down.*)

What's up? Are you cross?

MAX. This probably isn't anything, but I found this in the car, between the front seats.

(*He shows her a soiled and blood-stained white handkerchief.*)

ANNIE. What is it?

MAX. Henry's handkerchief.

ANNIE. Well, give it back to him.

(*She reaches for it.*)

Here, I'll wash it and you can give it to Charlotte at the theatre.

MAX. I did give it back to him.

When was he in the car?

(*Pause*)

It was a clean handkerchief, apart from my blood. Have you got a cold? It looks filthy. It's dried filthy. You're filthy. You filthy cow. You rotten filthy—

(*He starts to cry, barely audible, immobile. Annie waits. He recovers his voice.*)

It's not true, is it?

ANNIE. Yes.

MAX. Oh, God.

(*He stands up.*)

Why did you?

ANNIE. I'm awfully sorry, Max—

MAX (*Interrupting, suddenly pulled together*). All right. It happened. All right. It didn't mean anything.

ANNIE. I'm awfully sorry, Max, but I love him.

MAX. Oh, no.

ANNIE. Yes.

MAX. Oh, *no*. You don't.

ANNIE. Yes, I do. And he loves me. That's that, isn't it? I'm sorry it's awful. But it's better really. All that lying.

MAX (*Breaking up again*). Oh, Christ, Annie, stop it. I love you. Please don't—

ANNIE. Come on, please—it doesn't have to be like this.

MAX. How long for? And *him*—oh, God.

(*He kicks the radio savagely. The radio has gone into music again—the Righteous Brothers singing 'You've Lost That Lovin' Feelin''—and Max's kick has the effect of turning up the volume rather loud. He flings himself upon Annie in something like an assault which turns immediately into an embrace. Annie does no more than suffer the embrace, looking over Max's shoulder, her face blank.*)

SCENE FOUR

HENRY and ANNIE.

Living-room. Obviously temporary and makeshift quarters, divided Left and Right by a clothes rail, making two areas, 'his' and 'hers'.

Henry is alone, writing at a desk.

The disposition of door and furniture makes the scene immediately reminiscent of Scene 2. On the floor are a number of cardboard boxes containing files, papers, let-

ters, scripts, bills . . . The pillage of a filing system. There is also a couch. The Sunday newspapers and a bound script are on or near the couch.

A radio plays pop music quietly while Henry writes.

Annie enters from the bedroom door, barefoot and wearing Henry's robe, which is too big for her. Henry, in mid-sentence, looks up briefly and looks down again.

ANNIE. I'm not here. Promise.

(*She goes to the couch and carefully opens a newspaper. Henry continues to write. Annie glances towards him once or twice. He takes no notice. She stands up and goes behind his chair, looking over his shoulder as he works. He takes no notice. She goes round the desk and stands in front of him. He takes no notice. She flashes open the robe for his benefit. He takes no notice. She moves round behind him again and looks over his shoulder. He turns and grabs her with great suddenness, causing her to scream and laugh. The assault turns into a standing embrace.*)

HENRY. You're a bloody nuisance.

ANNIE. Sorry, sorry, sorry. I'll be good. I'll sit and learn my script.

HENRY. No, you won't.

ANNIE. I'll go in the other room.

HENRY. This room will do.

ANNIE. No, you've got to do my play.

HENRY. I can't write it. Let me off.

ANNIE. No, you promised. It's my gift.

HENRY: All right. Stay and talk a minute. (*He turns off the radio.*) Raw material, then I'll do this page, then I'll rape you, then I'll do the page again, then I'll—Oh (*happily*), are you all right?

(*Annie nods.*)

ANNIE. Yeah. Are you all right?

(*He nods.*)

(*Gleefully, self-reproachful.*) Isn't it awful? Max is so unhappy while I feel so . . . *thrilled*. His misery just seems . . . not in very good taste. Am I awful? He leaves letters for me at rehearsal, you know, and gets me to come to the phone by pretending to be my agent and people. He loves me, and he wants to punish me with his pain, but I can't come up with the proper guilt. I'm sort of irritated by it. It's so *tiring* and so *uninteresting*. You never write about that, you lot.

HENRY. What?

ANNIE. Gallons of ink and miles of typewriter ribbon expended on the misery of the unrequited lover; not a word about the utter tedium of the unrequiting. It's a very interesting . . .

HENRY. Lacuna?

ANNIE. What? No, I mean it's a very interesting sort of . . .

HENRY. Prejudice?

ANNIE. It's a very interesting . . . thing.

HENRY. Yes, thing.

ANNIE. No, I mean it shows—never mind—I've lost it now.

HENRY. How are you this morning?

ANNIE. One behind. Where were you?

HENRY. You were flat out.

ANNIE. Your own fault. When I take a sleeping pill, I'm on the downhill slope. You should have come to bed when you said.

HENRY (*Indicating his desk*). It wasn't where I could leave it. I would have gone to sleep depressed.

ANNIE. Well, I thought, the honeymoon is over. Fifteen days and fuckless to bye-byes.

HENRY. No, actually, I managed.

ANNIE. You did not.

HENRY. Yes, I did. You were totally zonked. Only your reflexes were working.

ANNIE. Liar.

HENRY. Honestly.

ANNIE. Why didn't you wake me?

HENRY. I thought I'd try it without you talking.

Look, I'm not doing any good, why don't we—?

ANNIE. You rotter. Just for that I'm going to learn my script.

HENRY. I'll read in for you.

(*She glowers at him but finds a page in the script and hands the script to him.*)

ANNIE. You didn't really, did you?

HENRY. Yes.

(*She 'reads' without inflection.*)

ANNIE. 'Très gentil, Monsieur Jean, très gentil!'

HENRY (*Reading*). 'Vous voulez plaisanter, madame!'

ANNIE. 'Et vous voulez parler français? Where did you pick that up?'

HENRY. 'In Switzerland. I worked as a waiter in one of the best hotels in Lucerne.'

ANNIE. 'You're quite the gentleman in that coat . . . *charmant*.'

You rotter.

HENRY. 'You flatter me, Miss Julie.'

ANNIE. 'Flatter? I flatter?'

HENRY. 'I'd like to accept the compliment, but modesty forbids. And, of course, my modesty entails your insincerity. Hence, you flatter me.'

ANNIE. 'Where did you learn to talk like that? Do you spend a lot of time at the theatre?'

HENRY. 'Oh yes. I get about, you know.'

ANNIE. Oh, Hen. Are you all right?

HENRY. Not really. I can't do mine. I don't know how to write love. I try to write it properly, and it just comes out embarrassing. It's either childish or it's rude. And the rude bits are absolutely juvenile. I can't use any of it. My cred-

ibility is already hanging by a thread after *Desert Island Discs*. Anyway, I'm too prudish. Perhaps I should write it completely artificial. Blank verse. Poetic imagery. Not so much of the 'Will you still love me when my tits are droopy?' 'Of course I will, darling, it's your bum I'm mad for', and more of the 'By my troth, thy beauty makest the moon hide her radiance', do you think?

ANNIE. Not really, no.

HENRY. No. Not really. I don't know. Loving and being loved is unliterary. It's happiness expressed in banality and lust. It makes me nervous to see three-quarters of a page and no *writing* on it. I mean, I *talk* better than this.

ANNIE. You'll have to learn to do sub-text. My Strindberg is steaming with lust, but there is nothing rude on the page. We just talk round it. Then he sort of bites my finger and I do the heavy breathing and he gives me a quick feel, kisses me on the neck . . .

HENRY. Who does?

ANNIE. Gerald. It's all very exciting.

(*Henry laughs, immoderately, and Annie continues coldly.*)

Or amusing, of course.

HENRY. We'll do that bit . . . you breathe, I'll feel . . . (*She pushes him away.*)

ANNIE. Go away. You'll just get moody afterwards.

HENRY. When was I ever moody?

ANNIE. Whenever you get seduced from your work.

HENRY. You mean the other afternoon?

ANNIE. What other afternoon? No, I don't mean *seduced*, for God's sake. Can't you think about anything else?

HENRY. Certainly. Like what?

ANNIE. I mean 'seduced', like when you're seduced by someone on the television.

HENRY. I've never been seduced on the television.

ANNIE. You were seduced by Miranda Jessop on the television.

HENRY. Professional duty.

ANNIE. If she hadn't been in it, you wouldn't have watched that play if they'd come round and done it for you on your carpet.

HENRY. Exactly. I had a postcard from her agent, would I be sure to watch her this week in *Trotsky Playhouse* or whatever they call it.

ANNIE. You only looked up when she stripped off. Think I can't see through you? That's why I took my pill. Screw you, I thought, feel free.

HENRY. You're daft. I've got to watch her if she's going to do my telly. It's just good manners.

ANNIE. *Her* tits are droopy already.

HENRY. I'm supposed to have an opinion, you see.

ANNIE. I think she's bloody overrated, as a matter of fact

HENRY. I have to agree. I wouldn't give them more than six out of ten.

(*She clouts him with her script.*)

Four.

(*She clouts him again.*)

Three.

ANNIE. You think you're so bloody funny.

HENRY. What's up with you? I hardly know the woman.

ANNIE. You'll like her. She wears leopard-skin pants.

HENRY. How do you know?

ANNIE. I shared a dressing-room with her.

HENRY. I don't suppose she wears them all the time.

ANNIE. I'm bloody sure she doesn't.

HENRY. 'By my troth thy beauty makest the moon—'

ANNIE. Oh, shut up.

HENRY. What are you jealous about?

ANNIE. I'm not jealous.

HENRY. All right, what are you cross about?

ANNIE. I'm not cross. Do your work.

(*She makes a show of concentrating on her script. Henry makes a show of resuming work. Pause.*)

HENRY. I'm sorry.

ANNIE. What for?

HENRY. I don't know.
   I'll have to be going out to pick up Debbie. I don't want to go if we're not friends.
   Will you come, then?

ANNIE. No. It was a mistake last time. It spoils it for her, being nervous.

HENRY. She wasn't nervous.

ANNIE. Not her. You.

(*Pause*)

HENRY. Well, I'll be back around two.

ANNIE. I won't be here.

(*Pause*)

HENRY (*Remembering*). Oh, yes. Is it today you're going prison-visiting? You're being very—um—faithful to Brodie.

ANNIE. That surprises you, does it?

HENRY. I only mean that you haven't got much time for good causes. You haven't got a weekend cottage either.

ANNIE. You think I'm more like you.

HENRY. Yes.

ANNIE. It's just that I happen to know him.

HENRY. You don't know him. You met him on a train.

ANNIE. Well, he's the only political prisoner I've ever met on a train. He's lucky.

HENRY. Political?

ANNIE. It was a political act which got him jumped on by the police in the first place so it's . . .

HENRY. A priori?

ANNIE. No, it's—

HENRY. De facto?

ANNIE. It's common sense that resisting arrest isn't the same as a criminal doing it.

HENRY. Arson is a criminal offence.

ANNIE. Arson is burning down buildings. Setting fire to the wreath on the war memorial is a symbolic act. Surely you can see the difference?

HENRY (*Carefully*). Oh, yes . . . That's . . . easy to see.

(*Not carefully enough. Annie looks at him narrowly.*)

ANNIE. And, of course, he did get hammered by an emotional backlash.

(*Pause*)

HENRY. Do you mean real leopard skin or just printed nylon?

(*She erupts and assails him, shouting.*)

ANNIE. You don't love me the way I love you. I'm just a relief after Charlotte, and a novelty.

HENRY. You're a novelty all right. I never *met* anyone so silly. I love you. I don't know why you're behaving like this.

ANNIE. I'm behaving normally. It's you who's abnormal. You don't care enough to *care*. Jealousy is normal.

HENRY. I thought you said you *weren't* jealous.

ANNIE. Well, why aren't *you* ever jealous?

HENRY. Of whom?

ANNIE. Of anybody. You don't care if Gerald Jones sticks his tongue in my ear—which, incidentally, he does whenever he gets the chance.

HENRY. Is that what this is all about?

ANNIE. It's insulting the way you just laugh.

HENRY. But you've got no interest in him.

ANNIE. I know that, but why should you assume it?

HENRY. Because you haven't. This is stupid.

ANNIE. But why don't you *mind*?

HENRY. I do.

ANNIE. No, you don't.

HENRY. That's true, I don't.
   Why *is* that?
   It's because I feel superior. There he is, poor bugger, picking up the odd crumb of ear wax from the rich man's table. You're right. I don't mind. I like it. I like the way his presumption admits his poverty. I like him, knowing that that's all there is, because you're coming home to me and we don't want anyone else.
   I love love. I love having a lover and being one. The insularity of passion. I love it. I love the way it blurs the distinction between everyone who isn't one's lover.
   Only two kinds of presence in the world. There's you and there's them.
   I love you so.

ANNIE. I love you so, Hen.

(*They kiss. The alarm on Henry's wristwatch goes off. They separate.*)

HENRY. Sorry.
ANNIE. Don't get kicked by the horse.
HENRY. Don't get kicked by Brodie.

(*He goes to the door to leave. At the door he looks at her and nods. She nods at him. He leaves.*

Annie goes slowly to Henry's desk and looks at the pages on it.

She turns on the radio and turns it from pop to Bach. She goes back to the desk and, almost absently, opens one of the drawers. Leaving it open, she goes to the door and disappears briefly into the hall, then reappears, closing the door. She goes to one of the cardboard boxes on the floor. She removes the contents from the box. She places the pile of papers on the floor. Squatting down, she starts going through the pile, methodically and unhurriedly. The radio plays on.)

ACT TWO

SCENE FIVE

HENRY *and* ANNIE.

Living-room-study. Three doors.
Two years later. A different house. The two years ought to show on Henry and on Annie. Perhaps he now uses glasses when he is reading, as he is at the beginning of the scene, or he may even have grown a moustache. Annie may have cut her hair short. Opera (Verdi) is playing on the record player. There is a TV and video and a small radio on Henry's desk, on which there is also a typewriter. Henry is alone, reading a script which consists of a sheaf of typed pages.
Henry reads for a few moments.
Annie enters from bedroom or kitchen and glances at Henry, not casually, then sits down and watches him read for a moment. Then she looks away and listens to the music for a moment. Henry glances up at her.
Annie looks at him.

ANNIE. Well?
HENRY. Oh—um—Strauss.
ANNIE. What?
HENRY. Not Strauss.
ANNIE. I meant the play.
HENRY (*Indicating the script*). Ah. The play.
ANNIE (*Scornfully*). Strauss. How can it be Strauss? It's in Italian.
HENRY. Is it? (*He listens.*) So it is.
Italian opera.
One of the Italian operas.

Verdi.
ANNIE. Which one?
HENRY. Giuseppe.

(*He judges from her expression that this is not the right answer.*)

Monty?
ANNIE. I mean which *opera*.
HENRY. Ah. (*Confidently*) *Madame Butterfly*.
ANNIE. You're doing it on purpose.

(*She goes to the record player and stops it playing.*)

HENRY. I promise you.
ANNIE. You'd think that *something* would have sunk in after two years and a bit.
HENRY. I like it—I really do like it—quite, it's just that I can't tell them apart. Two years and a bit isn't very long when they're all going for the same sound. Actually, I've got a better ear than you—*you* can't tell the difference between the Everly Brothers and the Andrews Sisters.
ANNIE. There isn't any difference.
HENRY. Or we could split up. Can we have something decent on now?
ANNIE. No.
HENRY. All right. Put on one of your instrumental numbers. The big band sound. (*He does the opening of Beethoven's Fifth.*) Da—da—da—dah . . .
ANNIE. Get on.
HENRY. Right.

(*He turns his attention to the script.*)

Stop me if anybody has said this before, but it's interesting how many of the all time greats begin with B: Beethoven, the Big Bopper . . .
ANNIE. That's all they have in common.
HENRY. I wouldn't say that. They're both dead. The Big Bopper died in the same plane crash that killed Buddy Holly and Richie Valens, you know.
ANNIE. No, I didn't know. Have you given up on the play or what?
HENRY. Buddy Holly was twenty-two. Think of what he might have gone on to achieve. I mean, if Beethoven had been killed in a plane crash at twenty-two, the history of music would have been very different. As would the history of aviation, of course.
ANNIE. *Henry.*
HENRY. The play.

(*He turns his attention back to the script.*)

ANNIE. How far have you got?
HENRY. Do you have a professional interest in this or is it merely personal?
ANNIE. Merely?

(*Pause*)

HENRY. Do you have a personal interest in this or is it merely professional?

ANNIE. Which one are you dubious about?

(Pause)

HENRY. Pause.

ANNIE. I could do her, couldn't I?

HENRY. Mary? Oh, sure—without make-up.

ANNIE. Well, then. *Three Sisters* is definitely off.

HENRY. Nothing's definite with that lot.

ANNIE. The other two are pregnant.

HENRY. Half a dozen new lines could take care of that.

ANNIE. If this script could be in a fit state, say, a month from now—

HENRY. Anyway, I thought you were committing incest in Glasgow.

ANNIE. I haven't said I'll do it.

HENRY. I think you should. It's classy stuff, Webster. I love all that Jacobean sex and violence.

ANNIE. It's Ford, not Webster. *And* it's Glasgow.

HENRY. Don't you work north of the West End, then?

ANNIE. I was thinking you might miss me—pardon my mistake.

HENRY. I was thinking you might like me to come with you—pardon mine.

ANNIE. You hadn't the faintest intention of coming to Glasgow for five weeks.

HENRY. That's true. I answered out of panic. Of course I'd miss you.

ANNIE. Also, it *is* somewhat north.

(*Henry 'shoots' her between the eyes with his forefinger.*)

HENRY. Got you. Is it rehearsing in Glasgow?

ANNIE (*Nods*). After the first week. (*Indicating the script.*) Where've you got to?

HENRY. They're on the train.

'You're a strange boy, Billy. How old are you?'

'Twenty. But I've lived more than you'll ever live.'

Should I read out loud?

ANNIE. If you like.

HENRY. Give you the feel of it.

ANNIE. All right.

HENRY. I'll go back a bit . . . where they first meet. All right?

(*Annie nods. Henry makes train noises. She is defensive, not quite certain whether he is being wicked or not.*)

(*Reading*) 'Excuse me, is this seat taken?'

'No.'

'Mind if I sit down?'

'It's a free country.'

'Thank you.'

(*He sits down opposite her. Mary carries on with reading her book.*)

'Going far?'

'To London.'

'So, you were saying . . . So you think it's a free country.'

'Don't you?'

'This is it, we're all free to do as we're told. My name's Bill, by the way. What's yours?'

'Mary.'

'I'm glad to make your acquaintance, Mary.'

'I'm glad to make yours, Bill.'

'Do you know what time this train is due to arrive in London?'

'At about half-past one, I believe, if it is on time.'

'You put me in mind of Mussolini, Mary. Yes, you look just like him, you've got the same eyes.'

ANNIE. If you're not going to read it properly, don't bother.

HENRY. Sorry.

'At about half-past one, I believe, if it is on time.'

'You put me in mind of Mussolini, Mary. People used to say about Mussolini, he may be a Fascist, but at least the trains run on time. Makes you wonder why British Rail isn't totally on time, eh?'

'What do you mean?'

'I mean it's a funny thing. The Fascists are in charge but the trains are late often as not.'

'But this isn't a Fascist country.'

'Are you quite sure of that, Mary? Take the army—' You're not going to do this, are you?

ANNIE. Why not?

HENRY. It's no good.

ANNIE. You mean it's not literary.

HENRY. It's not literary, and it's no good. He can't write.

ANNIE. You're a snob.

HENRY. I'm a snob, and he can't write.

ANNIE. I know it's raw, but he's got something to say.

HENRY. He's got something to say. It happens to be something extremely silly and bigoted. But leaving that aside, there is still the problem that he can't write. He can burn things down, but he can't write.

ANNIE. Give it back. I shouldn't have asked you.

HENRY. For God's sake, Annie, if it wasn't Brodie you'd never have got through it.

ANNIE. But it *is* Brodie. That's the point. Two and a half years ago he could hardly put six words together.

HENRY. He still can't.

ANNIE. You *pig*.

HENRY. I'm a pig, and he can't—

ANNIE. I'll smash you one. It's you who's bigoted. You're bigoted about what writing is supposed to be like. You judged everything as though everyone starts off from the same place, aiming at the same prize. English Lit. Shakespeare out in front by a mile, and the rest of the field strung out behind trying to close the gap. You all write for people who would like to write like you if only they could write. Well, screw you, and screw English Lit.!

HENRY. Right.

ANNIE. Brodie isn't writing to compete like you. He's writing to be heard.

HENRY. Right.

ANNIE. And he's done it on his own.

HENRY. Yes. Yes . . . I can see he's done a lot of reading.

ANNIE. You can't expect it to be English Lit.

HENRY. No.

ANNIE. He's a prisoner shouting over the wall.

HENRY. Quite. Yes, I see what you mean.

ANNIE. Oh shut up! I'd rather have your sarcasm.

HENRY. Why a play? Did you suggest it?

ANNIE. Not exactly.

HENRY. Why did you?

ANNIE. The committee, what's left of it, thought . . . I mean, people have got bored with Brodie. People get bored with anything after two or three years. The campaign needs . . .

HENRY. A shot in the arm?

ANNIE. No, it needs . . .

HENRY. A kick up the arse?

ANNIE (*Flares*). For Christ's sake, will you stop finishing my sentences for me!

HENRY. Sorry.

ANNIE. I've lost it now.

HENRY. The campaign needs . . .

ANNIE. A writer is harder to ignore. I thought, TV plays get talked about, make some impact. Get his case reopened. Do you think? I mean, Henry, what *do* you think?

HENRY. I think it makes a lot of sense.

ANNIE. No, what do you *really* think?

HENRY. Oh, *really* think. Well, I *really* think writing rotten plays is not in itself proof of rehabilitation. Still less of wrongful conviction. But even if it were, I think that anyone who thinks that they're bored with Brodie won't know what boredom is till they've sat through his apologia. Not that anyone will get the chance, because it's half as long as *Das Kapital* and only twice as funny. I also think you should know better.

ANNIE. You arrogant bastard.

HENRY. You swear too much.

ANNIE. Roger is willing to do it, in principle.

HENRY. What Roger? Oh *Roger*. Why the hell would Roger do it?

ANNIE. He's on the committee.

(*Henry looks at the ceiling.*)

It just needs a bit of work.

HENRY. You're all bent.

ANNIE. You're jealous.

HENRY. Of Brodie?

ANNIE. You're jealous of the idea of the writer. You want to keep it sacred, special, not something anybody can do. Some of us have it, some of us don't. *We* write, *you* get written about. What gets you about Brodie is he doesn't

know his place. You say he can't write like a head waiter saying you can't come in here without a tie. Because he can't put words together. What's so good about putting words together?

HENRY. It's traditionally considered advantageous for a writer.

ANNIE. He's not a writer. He's a convict. *You're* a writer. You write *because* you're a writer. Even when you write *about* something, you have to think up something to write about just so you can keep writing. More well chosen words nicely put together. So what? Why should that be *it*? Who says?

HENRY. Nobody says. It just works best.

ANNIE. Of *course* it works. You teach a lot of people what to expect from good writing, and you end up with a lot of people saying you write well. Then somebody who isn't in on the game comes along, like Brodie, who really has something to write about, something real, and you can't get through it. Well, *he* couldn't get through *yours*, so where are you? To you, he can't write. To him, write is all you *can* do.

HENRY: Jesus, Annie, you're beginning to appal me. There's something scary about stupidity made coherent. I can deal with idiots, and I can deal with sensible argument, but I don't know how to deal with you. Where's my cricket bat?

ANNIE. Your cricket bat?

HENRY. Yes. It's a new approach.

(*He heads out into the hall.*)

ANNIE. Are you trying to be funny?

HENRY. No, I'm serious.

(*He goes out while she watches in wary disbelief. He returns with an old cricket bat.*)

ANNIE. You better not be.

HENRY. Right, you silly cow—

ANNIE. Don't you bloody dare—

HENRY. Shut up and listen. This thing here, which looks like a wooden club, is actually several pieces of particular wood cunningly put together in a certain way so that the whole thing is sprung, like a dance floor. It's for hitting cricket balls with. If you get it right, the cricket ball will travel two hundred yards in four seconds, and all you've done is give it a knock like knocking the top off a bottle of stout, and it makes a noise like a trout taking a fly . . . (*He clucks his tongue to make the noise.*) What we're trying to do is to write cricket bats, so that when we throw up an idea and give it a little knock, it might . . . *travel* . . . (*He clucks his tongue again and picks up the script.*) Now, what we've got here is a lump of wood of roughly the same shape trying to be a cricket bat, and if you hit a ball with it, the ball will travel about ten feet and you will drop the bat and dance about shouting 'Ouch!' with your hands stuck into your armpits. (*Indicating the cricket bat.*) This isn't better because someone says it's better, or because there's a conspiracy by the MCC to keep cudgels off the field. It's better because it's better. You don't believe me, so I suggest you go out to bat with this and see how you get on. 'You're a strange boy, Billy, how old are you?' 'Twenty, but I've lived more than you'll ever live.' Ooh, ouch!

(*He drops the script and hops about with his hands in his armpits, going 'Ouch!' Annie watches him expressionlessly until he desists.*)

ANNIE. I hate you.

HENRY. I love you. I'm your pal. I'm your best mate. I look after you. You're the only chap.

ANNIE. Oh, Hen . . . Can't you help?

HENRY. What did you expect me to do?

ANNIE. Well . . . cut it and shape it . . .

HENRY. Cut it and shape it. Henry of Mayfair. Look—he can't write. I would have to write it for him.

ANNIE. Well, write it for him.

HENRY. I can't.

ANNIE. Why?

HENRY. Because it's *balls*. Announcing every stale revelation of the newly enlightened like stout Cortez coming upon the Pacific—war is profits, politicians are puppets, Parliament is a farce, justice is a fraud, property is theft . . . It's all here: pages and pages of it. It's like being run over very slowly by a travelling freak show of favourite simpletons, the india rubber pedagogue, the midget intellectual, the human panacea . . .

ANNIE. It's his view of the world. Perhaps from where he's standing you'd see it the same way.

HENRY. Or perhaps I'd realize where I'm standing. Or at least that I'm standing *somewhere*. There is, I suppose, a world of objects which have a certain form, like this coffee mug. I turn it, and it has no handle. I tilt it, and it has no cavity. But there is something real here which is always a mug with a handle. I suppose. But politics, justice, patriotism—they aren't even like coffee mugs. There's nothing real there separate from our perception of them. So if you try to change them as though there were something there to change, you'll get frustrated, and frustration will finally make you violent. If you know this and proceed with humility, you may perhaps alter people's perceptions so that they behave a little differently at that axis of behaviour where we locate politics or justice; but if you don't know this, then you're acting on a mistake. Prejudice is the expression of this mistake.

ANNIE. Or such is your perception.

HENRY. All right.

ANNIE. And who wrote it, why he wrote it, *where* he wrote it—none of these things count with you?

HENRY. Leave me out of it. They don't count. Maybe Brodie got a raw deal, maybe he didn't. I don't know. It doesn't count. He's a lout with language. I can't help somebody who thinks, or thinks he thinks, that editing a newspaper is censorship, or that throwing bricks is a demonstration while building tower blocks is social violence, or that unpalatable statement is provocation while disrupting the speaker is the exercise of free speech . . . Words don't deserve that kind of malarkey. They're innocent, neutral, precise, standing for this, describing that, meaning the other, so if you look after them you can build bridges across incomprehension and chaos. But when they get their corners knocked off, they're no good any more, and Brodie knocks their corners off. I don't think writers are sacred, but words are. They deserve respect. If you get the right ones in the right order, you can nudge the world a little or make a poem which children will speak for you when you're dead.

(*Annie goes to the typewriter, pulls out the page from the machine and reads it.*)

ANNIE. 'Seventy-nine. Interior. Commander's capsule. From Zadok's p.o.v. we see the green glow of the laser strike-force turning towards us. BCU Zadok's grim smile. *Zadok:* "I think it's going to work. Here they come!" *Kronk,* voice over: "Hold your course!" *Zadok:*—'

HENRY (*Interrupts*). That's not words, that's pictures. The movies. Anyway, alimony doesn't count. If Charlotte made it legal with that architect she's shacked up with, I'd be writing the real stuff.

(*Annie lets the page drop on to the typewriter.*)

ANNIE. You never wrote mine.

HENRY. That's true. I didn't. I tried.

I can't remember when I last felt so depressed.

Oh yes. Yesterday.

Don't be rotten to me. I'll come to Glasgow and I'll sit in your dressing-room and I'll write Kronk and Zadok every night while you're doing '*Tis Pity She's a Whore*.

ANNIE. I'm not going to Glasgow.

HENRY. Yes, you bloody are.

ANNIE. No I'm bloody not. We'll get Brodie's play off the ground. I want to do it. *I* want to do it. Don't *I* count? Hen? (*Pause*) Well, I can see it's difficult for a man of your fastidious tastes. Let's have some literacy. Something decent.

(*Annie stabs her finger on to the small radio on Henry's desk. Quietly it starts playing pop. She starts to go out of the room.*)

HENRY (*Exasperated*). *Why Brodie?* Do you fancy him or what?

(*She looks back at him and he sees that he has made a mistake.*)

I take it back.

ANNIE. Too late.

(*She leaves the room.*)

SCENE SIX

ANNIE *and* BILLY.

Annie is sitting by the window of a moving train. She is immersed in a paperback book.

Billy walks into view and pauses, looking at her for a moment. She is unaware of his presence. He carries a zipped grip bag. He speaks with a Scottish accent.

BILLY. Excuse me, is this seat taken?

(*Annie hardly raises her eyes.*)

ANNIE. No.

(*Billy sits down next to or opposite her. He puts the grip on the seat next to him. He looks at her. She doesn't look up from her book. He looks at his watch and then out of the window and then back at her.*)

BILLY. You'd think with all these Fascists the trains would be on time.

(*Annie looks up at him and jumps a mile. She gives a little squeal.*)

ANNIE. Jesus, you gave me a shock.

(*She looks at him, pleased and amused.*)

You fool.

(*Billy drops the accent.*)

BILLY. Hello.

ANNIE. I didn't know you were on the train.

BILLY. Yes, well, there you are. How are you?

ANNIE. All right. I gather you read it, then.

BILLY. Brodie's play? Yes, I read it.

ANNIE. And?

BILLY. He can't write.

(*Small pause.*)

ANNIE. I know.
  I just thought it was something you'd do well.

BILLY. Oh, yes. I could do a job on it.
  Are you going to do it?

ANNIE. I hope so. Not as it is, I suppose. Thank you for reading it anyway.

BILLY. Do you mind me coming to sit with you?

ANNIE. No, not at all.

BILLY. It doesn't mean we have to talk.

ANNIE. It's all right.

BILLY. How do you feel?

ANNIE. Scared. I'm always scared. I think, this is the one where I get found out.

BILLY. Well, better in Glasgow.

ANNIE. Is anyone else on this train?

BILLY. No, we're completely alone.

ANNIE. I mean any of *us*, the others.

BILLY. I don't know. Some of them are flying up, on the shuttle.

ANNIE. I fancied the train.

BILLY. I fancied it with you.

(*Annie meets his look.*)

ANNIE. Billy . . .

BILLY. What did you think when you saw me?

ANNIE. Just now?

BILLY. No. On the first day.

ANNIE. I thought God, he's so *young*.

BILLY (*Scottish*). I've lived more than you'll ever live.

ANNIE. All right, all right.

BILLY. I'm the one who should be scared. You're smashing.

ANNIE. I don't feel right.

BILLY. You seem right to me.

ANNIE. I'm older than you.

BILLY. That doesn't matter.

ANNIE. I'm a lot older. I'm going to look more like your mother than your sister.

BILLY. That's all right, so long as it's incest. Anyway, I like older women.

ANNIE. Billy, you mustn't keep flirting with me.

BILLY. Why not?

ANNIE. Well, because there's no point. Will you stop?

BILLY. No. Is that all right?

(*Pause*)

ANNIE. Did you know I was going to be on this train?

BILLY (*Nods*). Watched you get on. I thought I'd come and find you when it got started.

ANNIE. You certainly thought about it.

BILLY. I had to wait until the inspector came round. I haven't got a first-class ticket.

ANNIE. What will you do if he comes back?

BILLY. I'll say you're my mum. How come you get a first-class ticket?

ANNIE. I don't really. I'm afraid I upped it myself.

BILLY. You approve of the class system?

ANNIE. You mean on trains or in general?

BILLY. In general. Travelling first-class.

ANNIE. There's no system. People group together when they've got something in common. Sometimes it's religion and sometimes it's, I don't know, breeding budgies or being at Eton. Big and small groups overlapping. You can't blame them. It's a cultural thing; it's not *classes* or *system*.

(*She makes a connection.*)

There's nothing really *there*—it's just the way you see it. Your perception.

BILLY. Bloody brilliant. There's people who's spent their lives trying to get rid of the class system, and you've done it without leaving your seat.

ANNIE. Well . . .

BILLY. The only problem with your argument is that you've got to be travelling first-class to really appreciate it.

ANNIE. I . . .

BILLY. Where do you get all that from? Did you just make it up? It's daft. I prefer Brodie. He sounds like rubbish, but you know he's right. You sound all right, but you know it's rubbish.

ANNIE. Why won't you do his play, then?

BILLY. I didn't say I wouldn't. I'll do it if you're doing it.

ANNIE. You shouldn't do it for the wrong reasons.

BILLY. Why not? Does he care?

ANNIE. You said he can't write.

BILLY. He can't write like your husband. But your husband's a first-class writer.

ANNIE. Are you being nasty about Henry?

BILLY. No. I saw *House of Cards*. I thought it was quite good.

ANNIE. He'll be relieved to hear that.

(*Pause*)

BILLY. Don't go off me.

ANNIE. If you weren't a child, you'd know that you won't get anywhere with a married woman if you're snotty about her husband. Remember that with the next one.

BILLY. I'faith, I mean no harm, sister. I'm just scared sick of you. How is't with ye?

ANNIE. I am very well, brother.

BILLY. Trust me, but I am sick; I fear so sick 'twill cost my life.

ANNIE. Mercy forbid it! 'Tis not so, I hope.

BILLY. I think you love me, sister.

ANNIE. Yes, you know I do.

BILLY. I know't, indeed. You're very fair.

ANNIE. Nay, then, I see you have a merry sickness.

BILLY. That's as it proves. The poets feign, I read,
    That Juno for her forehead did exceed
    All other goddesses; but I durst swear
    Your forehead exceeds hers, as hers did theirs.

ANNIE. 'Troth, this is pretty!

BILLY. Such a pair of stars
    As are thine eyes would, like Promethean fire,
    If gently glanced, give life to senseless stones.

ANNIE. Fie upon ye!

BILLY. The lily and the rose, most sweetly strange,
    Upon your dimpled cheeks do strive for change:
    Such lips would tempt a saint; such hands as those
    Would make an anchorite lascivious.

ANNIE. Oh, you are a trim youth!

BILLY. Here!

(*His 'reading' has been getting less and less discreet. Now he stands up and opens his shirt.*)

ANNIE. (*Giggling*) Oh, leave off.

(*She looks around nervously.*)

BILLY (*Starting to shout*). And here's my breast; strike home!
    Rip up my bosom; there thou shalt behold
    A heart in which is writ the truth I speak.

ANNIE. You daft idiot.

BILLY. Yes, most earnest. You cannot love?

ANNIE. Stop it.

BILLY. My tortured soul
    Hath felt affliction in the heat of death.
    Oh, Annabella, I am quite undone!

ANNIE. Billy!

SCENE SEVEN

HENRY *and* CHARLOTTE *and* DEBBIE.

The living-room of Scene 2, without all the records. Charlotte is searching through a file of newspaper cuttings and programmes. A large, loaded ruck-sack is sitting by the door. Debbie is smoking.

HENRY. Since when did you smoke?

DEBBIE. I don't know. Years. At school. Me and Terry used to light up in the boiler room.

HENRY. I and Terry.

DEBBIE. I and Terry. Are you sure?

HENRY. It doesn't sound right but it's correct. I paid school fees so that you wouldn't be barred by your natural disabilities from being taught Latin and learning to speak English.

CHARLOTTE. I thought it was that she'd be a virgin a bit longer.

HENRY. It was also so that she'd speak English. *Virgo syntacta*.

DEBBIE. You were done, Henry. Nobody left the boiler room virgo with Terry.

HENRY. I wish you'd stop celebrating your emancipation by flicking it at me like a wet towel. Did the staff know about this lout, Terry.

DEBBIE. He was on the staff. He taught Latin.

HENRY. Oh well, that's all right then.

CHARLOTTE. Apparently she'd already lost it riding anyway.

HENRY. That doesn't count.

CHARLOTTE. In the tackroom.

HENRY. God's truth. The groom.

CHARLOTTE. That's why he was bow-legged.

HENRY. I told you—I said you've got to warn her about being carried away.

DEBBIE. You don't get carried away in jodhpurs. It needs absolute determination.

HENRY. Will you stop this.

CHARLOTTE. No. I can't find it. It was yonks ago. I mean, not being catty, I was nearer the right age.

HENRY. Does it really matter who played Giovanni to your Annabella in 'Tis Pity She's a Whore?

CHARLOTTE. I just think it's awful to have forgotten his name.

DEBBIE. Perhaps he's forgotten yours.

CHARLOTTE. But it was *my* virginity, not his.

DEBBIE. Was it actually on stage?

CHARLOTTE. Don't be silly—it was a British Council tour. No, it was in a boarding house in Zagreb.

DEBBIE. A bawdy house?

CHARLOTTE. The British Council has a lot to answer for.

HENRY. Look, we're supposed to be discussing a family crisis.

CHARLOTTE. What's that?

HENRY. Our daughter going on the streets.

DEBBIE. On the *road*, not the streets.

CHARLOTTE. Stop being so dramatic.

HENRY. I have a right to be dramatic.

CHARLOTTE. I see what you mean.

HENRY. I'm her father.

CHARLOTTE. Oh, I see what you mean.

HENRY. She's too young to go off with a man.

CHARLOTTE. She's certainly too young to go off without one. It's all right. He's nice.

(*Charlotte has given up her search of the file and now leaves carrying the file.*)

(*To Debbie.*) If I'm in the bath when he comes I want to see you both before you disappear.

(*Charlotte goes out.*)

HENRY. What does he play? (*Debbie looks blank.*) Ma said he's a musician.

DEBBIE. Oh—um—steam organ . . .

HENRY. A traveling steam organist? (*Pause*) He's not a musician.

DEBBIE. Fairground.

HENRY. Well, swings and roundabouts.

DEBBIE. Tunnel of love. How's Annie?

HENRY. In Glasgow.

DEBBIE. Don't worry, Henry. I'll be happy.

HENRY. Happy? What do you mean happy?

DEBBIE. Happy! Like a warm puppy.

HENRY. Dear Christ, is that what it's all come down to?—no philosophy that can't be printed on a T-shirt. You don't get visited by happiness like being lucky with the weather. The weather is the weather.

DEBBIE. And happiness?

HENRY. Happiness is . . . equilibrium. Shift your weight.

DEBBIE. Are you happy, Henry?

HENRY. I don't much like your calling me Henry. I liked being called Fa. Fa and Ma. How're the Everlys getting on? And the Searchers. How's old Elvis?

HENRY. He's dead.

DEBBIE. I did know that. I mean how's he holding up apart from that?

HENRY. I never went for him much. 'All Shook Up' was the last good one. However, I suppose that's the fate of all us artists.

DEBBIE. Death?

HENRY. People saying they preferred the early stuff.

DEBBIE. Well, maybe you were better then.

HENRY. Didn't you like the last one?

DEBBIE. What, *House of Cards*? Well, it wasn't about anything, except did she have it off or didn't she? What a crisis. Infidelity among the architect class. Again.

HENRY. It was about self-knowledge through pain.

DEBBIE. No, it was about did she have it off or didn't she. As if having it off is infidelity.

HENRY. Most people think it is.

DEBBIE. Most people think *not* having it off is *fidelity*. They think all relationships hinge in the middle. Sex or no sex. What a fantastic range of possibilities. Like an on/off switch. Did she or didn't she. By Henry Ibsen. Why would you want to make it such a crisis?

HENRY. I don't know, why would I?

DEBBIE. It's what comes of making such a mystery of it. When I was twelve I was obsessed. Everything was sex. Latin was sex. The dictionary fell open at *meretrix*, a harlot. You could feel the mystery coming off the word like musk. *Meretrix*! This was none of your *amo, amas, amat*, this was a flash from the forbidden planet, and it was everywhere. History was sex, French was sex, art was sex, the Bible, poetry, penfriends, games, music, everything was sex except biology which was obviously sex but obviously not *really* sex, not the one which was secret and ecstatic and wicked and a sacrament and all the things it was supposed to be but couldn't be at one and the same time—I got that in the boiler room and it turned out to be biology after all. That's what free love is free of—propaganda.

HENRY. Don't get too good at that.

DEBBIE. What?

HENRY. Persuasive nonsense. Sophistry in a phrase so neat you can't see the loose end that would unravel it. It's flawless but wrong. A perfect dud. You can do that with words, bless 'em. How about 'What free love is free of, is love'? Another little gem. You could put a 'what' on the end of it, like Bertie Wooster, 'What free love is free of is love, what?'—and the words would go on replicating themselves like a spiral of DNA . . . 'What love is free of love?—*free* love is what love, what?—'

DEBBIE (*Interrupting*). *Fa*. You're going on.

HENRY. Yes. Well, I remember, the first time I succumbed to the sensation that the universe was dispensable minus one lady—

DEBBIE. Don't write it, Fa. Just say it. The first time you fell in love. What?

HENRY. It's to do with knowing and being known. I remember how it stopped seeming odd that in biblical Greek knowing was used for making love. Whosit knew so-and-so. Carnal knowledge. It's what lovers trust each other with. Knowledge of each other, not of the flesh but through the flesh, knowledge of self, the real him, the real her, *in extremis*, the mask slipped from the face. Every other version of oneself is on offer to the public. We share our vivacity, grief, sulks, anger, joy . . . we hand it out to anybody who happens to be standing around, to friends and family with a momentary sense of indecency perhaps, to strangers without hesitation. Our lovers share us with the passing trade. But in pairs we insist that we give ourselves to each other. What selves? What's left? What else is there that hasn't been dealt out like a deck of cards? Carnal knowledge. Personal, final, uncompromised. Knowing, being known. I revere that. Having that is being rich, you can be generous about what's shared— she walks, she talks, she laughs, she lends a sympathetic ear, she kicks off her shoes and dances on the tables, she's everybody's and it don't mean a thing, let them eat cake; knowledge is something else, the undealt card, and while it's held it makes you free-and-easy and nice to know, and when it's gone everything is pain. Every single thing. Every object that meets the eye, a pencil, a tangerine, a travel poster. As if the physical world has been wired up to pass a current back to the part of your brain where imagination glows like a filament in a lobe no bigger than a torch bulb. Pain.

(*Pause*)

DEBBIE. Has Annie got someone else then?
HENRY. Not as far as I know, thank you for asking.
DEBBIE. Apologies.
HENRY. Don't worry.
DEBBIE. Don't you. Exclusive rights isn't love, it's colonization.
HENRY. Christ almighty. Another *ersatz* masterpiece. Like Michelangelo working in polystyrene.
DEBBIE. Do you know what your problem is, Henry?
HENRY. What?
DEBBIE. Your Latin mistress never took you into the boiler room.
HENRY. Well, at least I passed.
DEBBIE. Only in Latin.

(*Doorbell*)

Do me a favour.
HENRY. What?
DEBBIE. Stay here.
HENRY. That bad, is he?
DEBBIE. He's frightened of you.
HENRY. Jesus.

(*Charlotte enters in a bath robe, a towel round her hair perhaps. She carries a bunch of postcards.*)

CHARLOTTE. Ten postcards—stamped and addressed. Every week I get a postcard you get ten quid. No postcards, no remittance.

(*She gives Debbie the postcards.*)

DEBBIE. Oh—Charley—(*kisses Charlotte*).
See you, Henry.
HENRY. There; my blessing with thee. And these few precepts in thy memory . . .
DEBBIE. Too late, Fa. Love you. (*Kisses him.*)

(*Debbie leaves with the ruck-sack followed by Charlotte. Henry waits until Charlotte returns.*)

CHARLOTTE. What a good job we sold the pony.
HENRY. Musician is he? She's hardly seventeen.
CHARLOTTE. I was in Zagreb when I was seventeen. (*Pause*) How's Annie? Are you going to Glasgow for the first night?
HENRY. They don't open for a couple of weeks.
CHARLOTTE. Who's playing Giovanni?
HENRY. I don't know.
CHARLOTTE. Aren't you interested?
HENRY. Should I be?
CHARLOTTE. There's something touching about you, Henry. Everybody should be like you. Not interested. It used to bother me that you were never bothered. Even when I got talked into that dreadful nudie film because it was in Italian and Italian films were supposed to be art . . . God, that dates me, doesn't it? Debbie's into Australian films. *Australian*. Not Chips Rafferty—actual *films*.
HENRY. You've gone off again.
CHARLOTTE. Yes, well, it didn't bother you so I decided it meant you were having it off right left and centre and it wasn't supposed to matter. By the time I realized you were the last romantic it was too late. I found it *didn't* matter.
HENRY. Well, now that it doesn't . . . How many—um—roughly how many—?
CHARLOTTE. Nine.

(*Pause*)

HENRY. Gosh.
CHARLOTTE. And look what your one did compared to my nine.
Henry: Nine?
CHARLOTTE. Feel betrayed?
HENRY. Surprised. I thought we'd made a commitment.
CHARLOTTE. There are no commitments, only bargains. And they have to be made again every day. You think making a commitment is *it*. Finish. You think it sets like a concrete platform and it'll take any strain you want to put on it. You're committed. You don't have to prove anything. In fact you can afford a little neglect, indulge in a little bit of sarcasm here and there, isolate yourself when you want to. Underneath it's concrete for life. I'm a cow in some ways, but you're an idiot. *Were* an idiot.
HENRY. Better luck next time.
CHARLOTTE. You too.
Have a drink?

HENRY. I don't think so, thank you.

How are things with your friend? An architect, isn't he?

CHARLOTTE. I had to give him the elbow. Well, he sort of left. I called him the architect of my misfortune.

HENRY. What was the matter with him?

CHARLOTTE. Very possessive type. I came home from a job, I'd been away only a couple of days, and he said, why did I take my diaphragm? He'd been through my bathroom cabinet, would you believe? And then, not finding it, he went through everything else. Can't have that.

HENRY. What did you say?

CHARLOTTE. I said, I didn't *take* my diaphragm, it just went with me. So he said, what about the tube of Duragel? I must admit he had me there.

HENRY. You should have said, 'Duragel!—no wonder the bristles fell out of my toothbrush.'

CHARLOTTE (*Laughs*). Cheers.

HENRY (*Toasting with an empty hand*). Cheers.

(*Henry stands up.*)

CHARLOTTE. Do you have to go?

HENRY. Yes, I ought to.

CHARLOTTE. You don't fancy one for the road?

HENRY. No, really.

CHARLOTTE. Or a drink?

HENRY (*Smiles*). No offence.

CHARLOTTE. Remember what I said.

HENRY. What was that? (*Pause*) Oh . . . yes. No commitments. Only bargains. The trouble is I don't really believe it. I'd rather be an idiot. It's a kind of idiocy I like. 'I use you because you love me. I love you so use me. Be indulgent, negligent, preoccupied, premenstrual . . . your credit is infinite, I'm yours, I'm committed . . .

It's no trick loving somebody at their *best*. Love is loving them at their worst. Is that romantic? Well, good. Everything should be romantic. Love, work, music, literature, virginity, loss of virginity . . .

CHARLOTTE. You've still got one to lose, Henry.

(*Quiet music begins, continuing without break to the end of Scene eight.*)

SCENE EIGHT*

ANNIE *and* BILLY.

An empty space.
They are kissing, embracing: wearing rehearsal clothes.

BILLY. Come, Annabella,—no more sister now,
But love, a name more gracious—do not blush,

*In order to accommodate a scene change, Scene 8 was spoken twice, once as a 'word rehearsal' and then again as an 'acting rehearsal'.

Beauty's sweet wonder, but be proud to know
That yielding thou hast conquered, and inflamed
A heart whose tribute is thy brother's life.

ANNIE: And mine is his. O, how these stol'n contents
Would print a modest crimson on my cheeks,
Had any but my heart's delight prevailed!

BILLY. I marvel why the chaster of your sex
Should think this pretty toy called maidenhead
So strange a loss, when, being lost, 'tis nothing,
And you are still the same.

ANNIE. 'Tis well for you;
Now you can talk.

BILLY. Music as well consists
In the ear as in the playing.

ANNIE. O, you're wanton!
Tell on't you're best; do.

BILLY. Thou wilt chide me, then.
Kiss me:—

(*He kisses her lightly.*)

ANNIE (*Quietly*). Billy . . .

(*She returns the kiss in earnest.*)

SCENE NINE

HENRY *and* ANNIE.

The living-room. Henry is alone, sitting in a chair, doing nothing.
It's like the beginning of Scene 1 and Scene 3.
Annie is heard letting herself in through the front door. Then she comes in from the hall.
Annie enters wearing a topcoat and carrying a suitcase and a small travelling bag.

ANNIE. Hello, I'm back.

(*She puts down the suitcase and the bag and goes to kiss Henry.*)

HENRY. Hello.

(*She starts taking off her coat.*)

How was it?

ANNIE. We had a good finish—a woman in the audience was sick. Billy came on with my heart skewered on his dagger and—ugh—whoops!

(*She takes her coat out into the hall, reappears and goes to the travelling bag.*)

HENRY. I thought you were coming back overnight.

(*From the travelling bag Annie takes a small, smart-looking carrier bag with handles, a purchase from a boutique.*)

ANNIE. What have you been doing? How's the film?

(*She gives the present to Henry, kissing him lightly.*)

HENRY. I thought you were on the sleeper.

ANNIE. What's the matter?

HENRY. I was wondering what happened to you.

ANNIE. Nothing happened to me. Have you had lunch?

HENRY. No. Did you catch the early train this morning, then?

ANNIE. Yes. Scratch lunch, all right?

(*She goes into the kitchen and returns after a moment.*)

My God, it's all gone downhill since Sunday. Hasn't Mrs. Chamberlain been?

HENRY. I phoned the hotel.

ANNIE. When?

HENRY. Last night. They said you'd checked out.

ANNIE. Did they?

(*She picks up her suitcase and goes out into the bedroom. Henry doesn't move. A few moments later Annie reappears, without the suitcase and almost walking backwards.*)

Oh God, Hen. Have we had burglars? What were you doing?

HENRY. Where were you?

ANNIE. On the sleeper. I don't know why I said I came down this morning. It just seemed easier. I wasn't there last night because I caught the train straight from the theatre.

HENRY. Was the train late arriving?

ANNIE. Do you want to see my ticket?

HENRY. Well, have you been to the zoo?

(*She meets his look expressionlessly.*)

Who were you with?

ANNIE. Don't be like this, Hen. You're not like this.

HENRY. Yes, I am.

ANNIE. I don't want you to. It's humiliating.

HENRY. I really am not trying to humiliate you.

ANNIE. For you, I mean. It's humiliating for you. (*Pause*) I travelled down with one of the company. We had breakfast at Euston Station. He was waiting for a train. I stayed talking. Then I came home, not thinking that suddenly after two and a half years I'd be asked to account for my movements.

HENRY. You got off the sleeper and spent the morning sitting at Euston Station?

ANNIE. Yes.

HENRY. You and this actor.

ANNIE. Yes. Can I go now?

(*She turns away.*)

HENRY. How did you sleep?

(*She turns to look at him blankly.*)

Well did you?

ANNIE. Did I what?

What's the point? You'd only wonder if I was lying.

HENRY. Would you lie?

ANNIE. I might.

HENRY. Did you?

ANNIE. No. You see? I'm going to tidy up and put everything back.

HENRY. Do you want to know what I was looking for?

ANNIE: No. Did you find it?

HENRY. No.

(*She turns towards the bedroom.*)

HENRY. Was it Billy?

(*She turns back.*)

ANNIE. Why Billy?

HENRY. I know it's him. Billy, Billy, Billy, the name keeps dropping, each time without significance, but it can't help itself. Hapless as a secret in a computer. Blip, blip. Billy, Billy. Talk to me.

I'm sorry about the bedroom.

ANNIE. You should have put everything back. Everything would be the way it was.

HENRY. You can't put things back. They won't go back. Talk to me.

I'm your chap. I know about this. We start off like one of those caterpillars designed for a particular leaf. The exclusive voracity of love. And then not. How strange that the way of things is not suspended to meet our special case. But it never is. I don't want anyone else but sometimes, surprisingly, there's someone, not the prettiest or the most available, but you know that in another life it would be her. Or him, don't you find? A small quickening. The room responds slightly to being entered. Like a raised blind. Nothing intended, and a long way from doing anything, but you catch the glint of being someone else's possibility, and it's a sort of politeness to show you haven't missed it, so you push it a little, well within safety, but there's that sense of a promise being made in the touching and kissing without which no one can seem to say good morning in this poncy business and one more push would do it. Billy. Right?

ANNIE. Yes.

HENRY. I love you.

ANNIE. And I you. I wouldn't be here if I didn't.

HENRY. Tell me, then.

ANNIE. I love you.

HENRY. Not that.

ANNIE. Yes, that. That's all I'd need to know.

HENRY. You'd need more.

ANNIE. No.

HENRY. I need it. I can manage knowing if you did but I can't manage not knowing if you did or not. I won't be able to work.

ANNIE. Don't blackmail.

HENRY. You'd ask me.

ANNIE. I never have.

HENRY. There's never *been* anything.

ANNIE. Dozens.

HENRY. In your head.

ANNIE. What's the difference? For the first year at least, every halfway decent looking woman under fifty you were ever going to meet.

HENRY. But you learned better.

ANNIE. No, I just learned not to care. There was nothing to keep you here so I assumed you wanted to stay. I stopped caring about the rest of it.

HENRY. I care. Tell me.

ANNIE (*Hardening*). I did tell you. I spent the morning talking to Billy in a station cafeteria instead of coming straight home to you and I fibbed about the train because *that* seemed like infidelity—but all you want to know is did I sleep with him first?

HENRY. Yes. Did you?

ANNIE. No.

HENRY. Did you want to?

ANNIE. Oh, for God's sake!

HENRY. You can ask me.

ANNIE. I prefer to respect your privacy.

HENRY. I have none. I disclaim it. Did you?

ANNIE. What about your dignity, then?

HENRY. Yes, you'd behave better than me. I don't believe in behaving well. I don't believe in debonair relationships. 'How's your lover today, Amanda?' 'In the pink, Charles. How's yours?' I believe in mess, tears, pain, self-abasement, loss of self-respect, nakedness. Not caring doesn't seem much different from not loving. Did you? You did, didn't you?

ANNIE. This isn't caring. If I had an affair, it would be out of need. Care about that. You won't play on my guilt or my remorse. I'd have none.

HENRY. Need?

What did you talk about?

ANNIE. Brodie mostly.

HENRY. Yes. I had it coming.

ANNIE. Billy wants to do Brodie's play.

HENRY. When are you going to see Billy again?

ANNIE. He's going straight into another show. I promised to see him. I want to see him.

HENRY. Fine, when should we go? It's all right to come with you, is it?

ANNIE. Why not? Don't let me out of your sight, eh, Hen?

HENRY. When were you thinking of going?

ANNIE. I thought the weekend.

HENRY. And where is it?

ANNIE. Well, Glasgow.

HENRY. Billy travelled down with you from Glasgow and then took a train back?

ANNIE. Yes.

HENRY. And I'm supposed to score points for dignity. I don't think I can. It'll become my only thought. It'll replace thinking.

ANNIE. You mustn't do that. You have to find a part of yourself where I'm not important or you won't be worth loving. It's awful what you did to my clothes and everything. I mean what you did to yourself. It's not you. And it's you I love.

HENRY. Actually I don't think I can manage the weekend. I hope it goes well.

ANNIE. Thank you. (*She moves towards the bedroom.*)

HENRY. What does Billy think of Brodie's play?

ANNIE. He says he can't write.

(*She leaves. Henry takes his present out of its bag. It is a tartan scarf.*)

SCENE TEN

BILLY *and* ANNIE.

Annie sits reading on the train.
    Billy approaches the seat next to Annie. He speaks with a Scottish accent. He carries a grip.
    The dialogue is amplified through a mike.

BILLY. Excuse me, is this seat taken?

ANNIE. No.

BILLY. Mind if I sit down?

ANNIE. It's a free country.

(*Billy sits down.*)

BILLY. D'you reckon?

ANNIE. Sorry?

BILLY. You reckon it's a free country?

(*Annie ignores him.*)

    Going far?

ANNIE. To London.

BILLY. All the way.

(*Annie starts to move to an empty seat.*)

    I'll let you read.

ANNIE. Thank you.

(*She sits in the empty seat.*)

BILLY. My name's Bill.

(*She ignores him.*)

    Can I just ask you one question?

ANNIE. Mary.

BILLY. Can I just ask you one question, Mary?

ANNIE. One.

BILLY. Do you know what time this train is due to arrive in London?

ANNIE. At about half-past one, I believe, if it's on time.

BILLY. You put me in mind of Mussolini, Mary. People used to say about Mussolini, he may be a Fascist, but—

ANNIE. No—that's wrong—that's the old script—

BILLY (*Swears under his breath*). Sorry, Roger . . .

ROGER (*Voice off*). Okay, cut the tape.

ANNIE. From the top, Roger?

ROGER (*Voice off*). Give us a minute.

(*A light change reveals that the setting is a fake, in a TV studio. Annie gets up and moves away. Billy joins her. They exchange a few words, and she moves back to her seat, leaving him estranged, an unhappy feeling between them.*

After a moment the scene fades out.)

SCENE ELEVEN

HENRY *and* ANNIE.

Henry is alone listening to the radio, which is playing Bach's Air on a G String.

Annie enters from the bedroom, dressed to go out, and she is in a hurry.

HENRY (*Urgently, on seeing her*). Listen—

ANNIE. I can't. I'm going to be late now.

HENRY. It's important. *Listen.*

ANNIE. What?

HENRY. *Listen.*

(*She realizes that he means the radio. She listens for a few moments.*)

What is it?

ANNIE (*Pleased*). Do you like it?

HENRY. I *love* it.

ANNIE (*Congratulating him*). It's Bach.

HENRY. The cheeky beggar.

ANNIE. What?

HENRY. He's stolen it.

ANNIE. *Bach?*

HENRY. Note for note. Practically a straight lift from Procul Harum. And he can't even get it right. Hang on. I'll play you the original.

(*He moves to get the record. She, pleased by him but going, moves to him.*)

ANNIE. Work well.

(*She kisses him quickly and lightly but he forces the kiss into a less casual one. His voice, however, keeps its detachment.*)

HENRY. You too.

ANNIE. Last day. Why don't you come?

(*Henry shrugs.*)

No, all right.

HENRY. I'm only the ghost writer anyway.

(*The phone rings.*)

ANNIE. If that's them, say I've left.

HENRY (*Into the phone*). She's left . . . Oh . . .

(*To Annie.*) It's your friend.

(*She hesitates.*)

Just go.

(*Annie takes the phone.*)

ANNIE (*Into phone*). Billy . . . ? Yes—what?—yes, of course— I'm just late—yes—goodbye—all right . . . Yes, fine. (*She hangs up.*) I love you. Do you understand?

HENRY. No.

ANNIE. Do you think it's unfair?

HENRY. No. It's as though I've been careless, left a door open somewhere while preoccupied.

ANNIE. I'll stop.

HENRY. Not for me. I won't be the person who stopped you. I can't be that. When I got upset you said you'd stop so I try not to get upset. I don't get pathetic because when I get pathetic I could feel how tedious it was, how unattractive. Like Max, your ex. Remember Max? Love me because I'm in pain. No good. Not in very good taste.

So.

Dignified cuckoldry is a difficult trick, but it can be done. Think of it as modern marriage. We have got beyond hypocrisy, you and I. Exclusive rights isn't love, it's colonization.

ANNIE. Stop it—please stop it.

(*Pause*)

HENRY. The trouble is, I can't *find* a part of myself where you're not important. I write in order to be worth your while and to finance the way I want to live with you. Not the way *you* want to live. The way *I* want to live with *you*. Without you I wouldn't care. I'd eat tinned spaghetti and put on yesterday's clothes. But as it is I change my socks, and make money, and tart up Brodie's unspeakable drivel into speakable drivel so he can be an author too, like me. Not that it seems to have done him much good. Perhaps the authorities saw that it was a touch meretricious. *Meretrix, meretricis.* Harlot.

ANNIE. You shouldn't have done it if you didn't think it was right.

HENRY. You think it's right. I can't cope with more than one moral system at a time. Mine is that what you think is right is right. What you do is right. What you want is right. There was a tribe, wasn't there, which worshipped Charlie Chaplin. It worked just as well as any other theology, apparently. They loved Charlie Chaplin. I love you.

ANNIE. So you'll forgive me anything, is that it, Hen? I'm a selfish cow but you love me so you'll overlook it, is that right? Thank you, but that's not it. I wish I felt selfish, everything would be easy. Goodbye Billy. I don't need him. How can I need someone I spend half my time telling to grow up? I'm . . . —what's a petard?, I've often wondered.

HENRY. What?

ANNIE. A petard. Something you hoist, is it, piece of rope?

HENRY. I don't think so.

ANNIE. Well, anyway. All right?

HENRY. All right what? I keep marrying people who suddenly lose a wheel.

ANNIE. I don't feel selfish, I feel hoist. I send out waves, you know. Not free. Not interested. He sort of got in under the radar. Acting daft on a train. Next thing I'm looking round for him, makes the day feel better, it's like love or something: no—love, absolutely, how can I say it wasn't? You weren't replaced, or even replaceable. But I liked it, being older for once, in charge, my pupil. And it was a long way north. And so on. I'm sorry I hurt you. But I meant it. It meant something. And now that it means less than I thought and I feel silly, I won't drop him as if it was nothing, a pick-up, it wasn't that, I'm not that. I just want him to stop needing me so I stop behaving well. This is me behaving well. I have to choose who I hurt and I choose you because I'm yours. (*Pause. The phone rings.*) Maybe it's just me.

HENRY (*Into phone*). Roger—? She's left, about ten minutes ago—yes, I know, dear, but—don't talk to me about unprofessional, Roger—you lost half a day shooting the war memorial with a boom shadow all over it—okay, scream at me if it makes you feel better—

(*Annie takes the phone out of his hand.*)

ANNIE (*Into phone*). Keep your knickers on, it's only a bloody play.

(*She hangs up and starts to go.*)

    (*Going*) Bye.

HENRY. Annie. (*Pause*) Yes, all right.

ANNIE. I need you.

HENRY. Yes, I know.

ANNIE. Please don't let it wear away what you feel for me. It won't, will it?

HENRY. No, not like that. It will go on or it will flip into its opposite.

    What time will you be back?

ANNIE. Not late.

(*He nods at her. She nods back and leaves. Henry sits down in his chair. Then he gets up and starts the record playing—Procul Harum's 'A Whiter Shade of Pale', which is indeed a version of Air on a G String.*

    He stands listening to it, smiling at its Bach, until the vocals start. Then the smile gets overtaken.)

HENRY. Oh, please, please, please, please, *don't.*

(*Then blackout, but the music continues.*)

SCENE TWELVE

HENRY, ANNIE *and* BRODIE.

In the blackout the music gives way to recorded dialogue between Annie and Billy, who speaks with a Scottish accent.

BILLY (*Voice*). Wait for me.

ANNIE (*Voice*). Yes, I will.

BILLY (*Voice*). Everything's got to change. Except you. Don't you change.

ANNIE (*Voice*). No. I won't. I'll wait for you and for everything to change.

BILLY (*Voice*). That could take longer. (*Laughs*) I might have to do it myself.

(*By this time, light has appeared starting with the faint glow from the television screen.*

    Brodie, alone in the living-room, is twenty-five, wearing a cheap suit. He is holding a tumbler of neat scotch, his attention engaged by the television set and particularly by the accompanying video machine. From the television the dialogue has been followed by the echoing clang of a cell door, footsteps, credit music . . . Brodie turns the volume down.

    Henry enters from the kitchen carrying a small jug of water for Brodie's scotch. In the room there is wine for Henry and another glass for Annie.

    Brodie speaks with a Scottish accent.)

BRODIE. Very handy, these machines. When did they come out?

HENRY. Well, I suppose they were coming out about the time you were going in.

BRODIE. You can set them two weeks ahead.

HENRY. Yes.

BRODIE. How much?

HENRY. A few hundred. They vary.

BRODIE. I'll have to pinch one sometime.

HENRY. If you leave it a bit, they'll probably improve them so that you can have it recording concurrently with your sentence.

(*Brodie looks at Henry without expression.*)

BRODIE. Annie looked nice. She's come on a bit since *Rosie of the Royal Infirmary*. A good-looking woman.

(*Henry doesn't answer. Annie enters from the kitchen with a dip, peanuts, etc. on a tray. She puts the tray down. Henry pours wine into a third glass.*)

Just saying you looked nice.

ANNIE. Oh, yes?

BRODIE. The pretty one was supposed to be me, was he?

ANNIE. Well . . .

BRODIE. He's not a pansy, is he?

ANNIE. I don't think so.

(*Henry hands her the glass of wine.*)

Thank you.

HENRY (*To Brodie, indicating the TV*). What did you think?

BRODIE. I liked it better before. You don't mind me saying?

HENRY. No.

ANNIE. It did work.

BRODIE. You mean getting me sprung?

ANNIE. No, I didn't mean that.

BRODIE. That's right. I got sprung by the militarists.

HENRY. I don't think I follow that.

BRODIE. Half a billion pounds for defence, nothing left for prisons. So you get three, four to a cell. First off, they tell the magistrates, for God's sake go easy, *fine* the bastards. But still they keep coming—four, five to a cell. Now they're frightened it's going to blow up. Even the warders are going on strike. So: 'Give us the money to build more prisons!' 'Can't be done, laddie, we're spending the money to keep the world free, not in prison.' So they start freeing the prisoners. Get it? I'm out because the missiles I was marching against are using up the money they need for a prison to put me in. Beautiful. Can I have another?

(*He holds up his empty glass for Annie. Slight pause. Henry stays still.*)

ANNIE. Please help yourself.

(*Brodie does so.*)

BRODIE. Early release. There was eight of us just on my corridor. (*To Henry.*) Not one of them a controversial TV author. I don't owe you.

HENRY. Is it against your principles to say thank you for *anything*, even a drink?

BRODIE. Fair enough. You had a go. You did your best. It probably needed something, to work in with their prejudices.

HENRY. Yes, they are a bit prejudiced, these drama producers. They don't like plays which go 'clunk' every time someone opens his mouth. They gang up against soap-box bigots with no idea that everything has a length. They think TV is a visual medium. (*To Annie, puzzled.*) Is this *him*?

BRODIE. Don't be clever with me, Henry, like you were clever with my play. I lived it and put my guts into it, and you

came along and wrote it clever. Not for me. For her. I'm not stupid.

ANNIE (*To Henry*). No, this isn't him.

BRODIE. Yes, it bloody is. That was me on the train, and this is me again, and I don't think you're that different either.

ANNIE. And *that* wasn't him. (*She points at the TV.*) He was helpless, like a three-legged calf, nervous as anything. A boy on the train. Chatting me up. Nice. He'd been in some trouble at the camp, some row, I forget, he was going absent without leave. He didn't know anything about a march. He didn't know anything about anything, except *Rosie of the Royal Infirmary*. By the time we got to London he would have followed me into the Ku Klux Klan. He tagged on. And when we were passing the war memorial he got his lighter out. It was one of those big chrome Zippos—click, snap. Private Brodie goes over the top to the slaughter, not an idea in his head except to impress me. What else could I do? He was my recruit.

HENRY. You should have told me. That one I would have known how to write.

ANNIE. Yes.

BRODIE. Listen—I'm still here.

ANNIE. So you are, Bill. Finish your drink, will you?

BRODIE. Why not?

(*Brodie finishes his drink and stands up.*)

I can come back for some dip another time.

ANNIE. No time like the present.

(*Annie picks up the bowl of dip and smashes it into his face. She goes to the hall door, leaving it open while she briefly disappears to get Brodie's coat.*
  Henry has stood up, but Brodie isn't going to do anything. He carefully wipes his face with his handkerchief.)

HENRY. Well, it was so interesting to meet you. I'd heard so much about you.

BRODIE. I don't really blame you, Henry. The price was right. I remember the time she came to visit me. She was in a blue dress, and there was a thrill coming off her like she was back on the box, but there was no way in. It was the first time I felt I was in prison. You know what I mean.

(*Annie stands at the door holding Brodie's coat. He takes it from her, ignoring her as he walks out. She follows him, and the front door is heard closing. Annie returns.*)

HENRY. I don't know what it did to him, but it scared the hell out of me. Are you all right?

(*She nods.*)

ANNIE. Are you all right?

(*The phone rings. Henry picks it up.*)

HENRY. Hello.
(*Into the phone, suddenly uncomfortable.*) Oh, hello. Did you want to speak to Annie?
ANNIE. No.
HENRY (*Suddenly relaxes*). Well, that's fantastic, Max!
(*To Annie.*) It's your ex. He's getting married.
(*To phone*) Congratulations. Who is she?

(*Henry ferries this over to Annie with an expressive look, which she returns. Annie moves to Henry and embraces his shoulders from behind. She leans on him tiredly while he deals with the phone.*)

Oh, I think you're very wise. To marry one actress is unfortunate, to marry two is simply asking for it.

(*Annie kisses him. He covers the mouthpiece with his hand.*)

(*Into phone*) Really? Across a crowded room, eh?
ANNIE. I've had it. Look after me.

(*He covers the mouthpiece.*)

HENRY. Don't worry. I'm your chap.
(*Into phone*) Well, it's very decent of you to say so, Max.

(*To Annie.*) 'No hard feelings?' What does he mean? If it wasn't for me, he wouldn't be engaged *now*.

(*Annie disengages herself from him with a smile and goes around turning out the lights until the only light is coming from the bedroom door.*)

(*Into phone*) No. I'm afraid she isn't . . . She'll be so upset when I tell her . . . No, I mean when I tell her she missed you . . . No, she'll be delighted. I'm delighted, Max. Isn't love wonderful?

(*Annie finishes with the lights and goes out into the bedroom.*
Henry is being impatiently patient with Max on the phone, trying to end it.)

HENRY. Yes, well, we look forward to meeting her. What? Oh, yes?

(*Absently he clicks on the little radio, which starts playing, softly, 'I'm a Believer' by the Monkees. He is immediately beguiled. He forgets Max until the phone crackle gets back through to him.*)

Sorry. Yes, I'm still here.

(*He turns the song up slightly.*)

TOPICS FOR CRITICAL THINKING AND WRITING

The Play on the PAGE

1. How many contrasts can you find in the play between "real" and "fake" things?
2. Is Stoppard fair to Brodie? Or is he attacking Brodie's character because he doesn't like his politics?
3. Do you find these characters sympathetic despite their infidelities?
4. Is this a comedy? What makes it so?
5. What do you think explains the play's great popularity through the years?

The Play on the STAGE

6. The 1980s production of the play evoked elegant drawing-room comedy; the 2000 version was jaggedly contemporary. Discuss how these productional decisions alter the meaning of the play.
7. What advice/instructions would you give to the leading actors to guide them through the interpretations of their characters?
8. If you were directing the play, what would you want the audience to come away with?

The Play in PERFORMANCE

The Real Thing opened at the Strand Theatre, London, on November 16, 1982. The production was directed by Peter Wood and featured Roger Rees as Henry and Felicity Kendal as Annie. It was uniformly well received and won the *Evening Standard* Best Play award for 1982. In 1984 it opened in New York—in a new production directed by Mike Nichols with Jeremy Irons as Henry, Glenn Close as Annie, and Christine Baranski as Charlotte—to even more acclaim than it received in London: It won Tony Awards for all the individuals just named for Best Director, Best Actor (Play), Best Actress (Play), Best Featured Actress (Play), and for Tom Stoppard for Best Play. It also won the best play award from the New York Drama Critics' Circle, Drama Desk, and the Outer Critics' Circle. It played for 566 performances at the Plymouth Theater.

Twenty-seven years after its premiere, *The Real Thing* was revived triumphantly in London at the innovative small theater the Donmar Warehouse. The sold-out production transferred to the West End in January 2000. From there, the entire production—including the full British cast—was brought to the Barrymore Theater in New York where American Actors Equity permitted a limited engagement of twenty weeks. Once again it conquered the field at awards time: this time for Best Revival (Play) and for Best Actor and Best Actress (Stephen Dillane as Henry and Jennifer Ehle as Annie).

Despite their equal successes, the three above-mentioned versions—the 1982 British, the 1984 American, and the 2000 transferred Donmar production—differed in revealing ways. The recent Donmar version was scenically more severe than its predecessors; it evoked a very contemporary, revved-up modernity whose jagged rhythms were aurally enhanced by amplified rock transitions. But neither scenic variations nor directorial readings of the play have been as significant as the differences in the actors' physical presences and interpretations. The character of Henry is the core of the play. In the early 1980s versions, London's Roger Rees was much more harried than New York's more sarcastic Jeremy Irons. Many of those who have seen all the versions agree that Stephen Dillane—decidedly less "U," upper class—than his predecessors, brought a new level of understanding to his most recent incarnation as Henry. As Clive Barnes noted,

> Dillane gives us insight to the real Stoppard. Wry and painfully charming, Dillane (give that man his Tony right now!*) embues the beleaguered dramatist Henry with seemingly everything we've read about Stoppard himself. He brings utter conviction, for example, to his character's love of cricket—a passion that Stoppard shares with the likes of Harold Pinter. Dillane's convincing and natural performance also reminds me of a powerful irony, that Stoppard himself left his own wife for Felicity Kendal, the actress who was so marvelous as the tempting Annie in the original *Real Thing* in London. But it is not only Dillane's performance that makes this *The Real Thing* so much better on Broadway the second time around. Director David Leveaux, unlike his predecessors Peter Wood (1982) in London and Mike Nichols on Broadway (1984), brings a rueful brilliance to its theater box of plays within plays, or art within life and life within art. And he gives the play's roaring comedy a hollow after-laugh of truth. And while Dillane's Henry III is superior to the flamboyant version from Jeremy Irons, . . . his Cressida-like heroine is here played by the succulently sensual Jennifer Ehle, a sumptuous far cry from the sexless Glenn Close. The whole cast, including Sarah Woodward and Nigel Lindsay, is for a playwright to die for. If you have only one show to see in New York, make it real and make it *The Real Thing*.

*They did.

ERIKA MUNK
The Real *Stops Here**

"There's something scary about stupidity made coherent," says Henry, hero of Tom Stoppard's *The Real Thing,* after one of his lover Annie's trendy-lefty effusions. There's something scarier about stupidity made a hit precisely because of its trendy-conservative aeffusions. If it weren't being praised without limit as a serious, indeed brilliant comedy by a writer who after years of cool and flashy wit finally has mastered character and feeling, *The Real Thing's* stupidity—that of a clever writer in the grip of commerce—could be dismissed with dispatch. The play is shallowly reactionary in its art and its politics, crudely subservient to a wealthy, aging audience, and self-pitying in its psychology—though funny, line by line, for those of us who are easy laughs. But when critics are urging their readers to see the play twice and are themselves going twice (e.g., John Simon), dismissiveness isn't enough; however false it may be, the thing is a cultural event.

Stoppard's comedy enmeshes a love-and-adultery-among-theater-folk story with an argument about literature and politics. It's so deeply enmeshed that the moment when working-class antinuclear politics, in the form of one Brodie, is thrown out of Henry and Annie's living room is the moment when true love is affirmed, and Annie, freed of her radical burden, truly becomes Henry's real thing and he hers. Henry, hand-

Village Voice (Jan. 17, 1984), p. 101.

some and successful writer of amusing, but superficial plays, was married to Charlotte, with whom he has a daughter, Debbie, now 16, but fell in love with Annie, who was married to Max. Charlotte, Annie, and Max are actors—which makes it easy for Henry to win arguments—and so is Billy, a young man with whom Annie has an affair after she marries Henry. Brodie, an offstage presence until the end, was jailed for torching a monument during an antimissile rally, and has written a play, a real stinker, which Annie talks Henry into rewriting—a bit of unprincipled hackwork he completes while disclaiming his respect for language and his hatred of Brodie's immoral politics. When Annie finally meets Brodie he turns out to be a crass, gross, thuggish sexist, and Annie's moment of truth comes when she custard-pies him with a bowl of dip.

The Real Thing isn't stupid because its politics are right-wing and its form a regressive combination of drawing-room mannerism and sentimental cliché; the one could be a matter of conviction, the other an ironic aesthetic tactic. What goes against the grain is Stoppard's avoidance of any discussion of the issue he raises. Shaw's obviously not one of his models. Then there's the philistinism of the play's underlying statement that eloquence and complexity are incompatible with emotional truth. Not to mention the crude way the psychological course of events is stacked in Henry's favor. Intellectually, no one ever gives him a run for his money; emotionally, he never really hurts anyone. . . . The limits of Henry's self-knowledge, the cramped boundaries of his love, could make him a deeply comic figure. Instead, he's a hero, which gives his lines a thin, whining edge.

BEN BRANTLEY
*Poor Henry! He's So Clever, So Glib . . . So Vulnerable**

Now here is a man you would surely love to have at your table at one of those insufferably self-important dinner parties. He speaks in sentences that might have been cut by a jeweler; he banishes conversational clichés by merely cocking an eyebrow, and he has somehow turned undergraduate self-consciousness into

The New York Times 18 Apr. 2000: B1, 5.

a highly evolved form of charm. What's more, when he describes himself as a romantic, you believe him, just as you believe that he suffers for it. That makes him easier to take when he seems a little, well, superior. There is much to be said for the aesthetic value of shadow in a bright presence.

Such are the attributes of Henry, the playwright who wrote that West End hit *House of Cards,* or at least Henry as he is represented by Stephen Dillane, the immensely appealing center of the immensely appealing revival of Tom Stoppard's *Real Thing,* which opened last night at the Ethel Barrymore Theater. Under the accomplished direction of David Leveaux, this is a production that should lure those New Yorkers who say they rarely go to the theater because it's too juvenile or too vulgar or too ponderous, usually opting instead for yet another dinner party. And with the delectable Jennifer Ehle playing self-confident body to Mr. Dillane's self-questioning mind, the show has a sensual sparkle that was less evident in the fine Tony-winning New York incarnation of 1984 with Jeremy Irons and Glenn Close.

The Real Thing—an import from the Donmar Warehouse, the current epicenter of theatrical glamour in London (*Cabaret, The Blue Room*)—is a rare thing even in what has been an exceptionally strong season for straight plays on Broadway: an elegant comedy of infidelity filled with the sort of comebacks that people only wish they were capable of themselves. True, this 1982 play from the author of *Jumpers* and *Arcadia* is also always subverting itself, pointing out how some things, love among them, defy glib articulation. But, ah, how articulately it manages to say so. If its structural game-playing seems a tad too clever this time around and its second act weaker than its first, the fact remains that few comedies have ever managed to have it so successfully both ways.

When *The Real Thing* first opened, it was greeted with the kind of exclamations that heralded Garbo's debut in talking pictures: "Stoppard feels!" was the delighted implication of most of the reviews, a sense that the most dizzyingly cerebral of British playwrights had at last led with his heart instead of his head. What gave the play an extra savory twist was the fact that it was about a dizzyingly cerebral playwright who confesses at one point that he just doesn't know how to "write love." The title itself seemed a charming admission of the same defeat, using the sort of non-specific noun that was anathema to its main character. Which isn't to say that Mr. Stoppard had forsaken his playful intellectualism or sure hand for form.

The Real Thing begins with a sort of literary *trompe l'oeil*: a scene in which a husband confronts his wife with her presumed infidelity. This turns out to be a scene in a London play by Henry, performed by Charlotte (Sarah Woodward), an actress who is Henry's wife in real life, and Max (Nigel Lindsay), who is married to another actress, Annie (Ms. Ehle), with whom Henry is having an affair. The scene becomes a reference point for the rest of the evening, as two real-life marriages shatter, echoing and diverging from the play within the play. . . . Although Charlotte early on observes that the difference between dialogue onstage and in life is that life demands "thinking time" between epigrams, the characters are still remarkably quick on the uptake: Henry, especially, of course, but so are Charlotte and Henry's teenage daughter, Debbie (Charlotte Parry), and Charlotte herself.

It is a testament to the arbitrariness of love that Henry and Charlotte seem to be more naturally matched than Henry and Annie, who while obviously intelligent is less deft with the *mot juste*. She is also unswervingly headstrong and gets involved politically with an imprisoned Scottish soldier (Joshua Henderson) and sexually with a younger actor (Oscar Pearce). The distress these events cause Henry lead him to lively disquisitions on the virtues and limitations of language. . . .

Throughout the evening, vintage pop songs are played, numbers like "Do Wah Diddy Diddy" and "Will You Still Love Me Tomorrow?" It's a running joke that this is the only kind of music to which Henry responds. But the play takes the emotional pull of such music, and the varied feelings it addresses, seriously. As I was leaving *The Real Thing,* I noticed a middle aged member of the audience singing the Monkees' hit "I'm a Believer," a recording of which ends the production. It's an upbeat song, but the man looked puzzled and just a bit melancholy. Mr. Stoppard, one imagines, would have been pleased by the response.

Contemporary American Visions

Although there remains a strong naturalistic segment in contemporary theater, the last 40 years have seen exciting experiments in theatrical performance. Pictured here, (from left to right) Shami Chaikin, Raymond Barry, and Paul Zimet perform the Open Theatre's *Terminal*.

In periodizing art, it is almost as difficult to pin down the concept of the "contemporary" as that of the "modern." The contemporary is not just what's happening today; it's trying to find the point in the recent past where the forms and ideas that preoccupy us today began. This can never be done with absolute precision. In discussing contemporary theater, first of all we have to agree on what constitutes the most important working being done *now*. All would not agree what this is. But most scholars and critics might agree—whatever their judgments about the artistic consequences—that much of what we call serious theater, as well as most of that theater we call "experimental," expresses values that have their roots in the turbulent decade of the 1960s, a period in which domestic and international political trauma bred new attitudes that engage us today, primarily feminism and multiculturalism. So it is there that we initiate our discussion.

The first half of the decade saw the climax of the civil rights movement begun in the 1950s: in sit-ins, Freedom Rides, southern police violence, the march on Washington, the murder of three activists in Mississippi, the civil rights bill of 1964 following the traumatic assassination of President Kennedy in 1963. The civil rights movement inspired the free speech movement (begun in Berkeley in 1964) that aroused many students to protest the impersonality of the giant university. As the decade progressed, this activism was fueled by the steady growth of American involvement in Vietnam and the reinstitution of the draft. The climax of the decade was the year of the barricades, 1968. The Tet offensive belied the government's insistence that there was "light at the end of the [Vietnam] tunnel." Martin Luther King, Jr., and Robert Kennedy were assassinated. Youth and student rebellions broke out around the world: in even elite colleges in the United States and Britain, in Chicago at the Democratic convention, in Mexico City, and, preeminently, in Paris, where the Sorbonne was occupied by students and all civil society was disrupted. This extraordinary revolutionary moment did not last, but it placed its indelible mark on the decade.

These political events inevitably found expression in the arts, particularly in theater, which is, after all, preeminently a social art. Social and aesthetic protest were linked. A new generation sought new answers. In theater, a burst of energy subsumed by the name "off-off Broadway" arose, not primarily in existing little theaters, but in alternate spaces such as coffee shops, lofts, and churches. The 1950s movement known as off-Broadway—supposedly as much in recognition of its alternative to the commercial theater as to its geography—was seen as insufficiently radical. It was time for new dramatic and theatrical voices. The key words were "alternative" and "new"—and even, for a while, "underground." Aesthetics and ideology might vary widely, but there was a common, unifying energy of dissent. Most of the young playwrights whose plays graced such new venues as Caffé Cino, Café La MaMa, and Theater Genesis (in St. Mark's Church in-the-Bowery) had voices that have become silent. But several continue to be heard, preeminently, Maria Irene Fornes, Lanford Wilson, and Sam Shepard, who survived the dispersion of the energy of the period of their emergence to create sustained bodies of dramatic work. Each of these playwrights accepted a model of close collaboration with their theatrical interpreters that was followed by many playwrights of the next generation like David Mamet.

As in another turbulent decade, the 1930s, political and social imperatives bred collective responses politically and artistically. It was an era of group activity in theater as in life. Ensemble groups such as the Open Theater, the Performance Group, and the Bread and Puppet Theater arose dedicated to some form of social commitment. At its most overtly political, protest assumed the form of street and guerrilla theater, another flank in the Theater of Demonstration of Abbie Hoffman and the Yippies (who, among other public actions, attempted to levitate the Pentagon). Usually, protest was more obliquely expressed in the search for communal alternatives and in the rejection of prevailing sexual orthodoxies (the "Ridiculous" theater movement started demolishing male and female stereotypes by cross-gender casting *before* the Stonewall rebellion of 1969). Stylistically, the new experimental groups rejected the prevailing authority of the realistic Stanislavski-derived Method, seeking alternative artistic paths derived from non-Western and avant-garde traditions—even if many of the historically challenged young were unaware of their indebtedness.

The year that marked the political climax of the decade, 1968, also marked its apogee of theater experiment. The year saw the Radical Theater Festival's gathering at San Francisco State College of street and guerrilla theaters; the two Ridiculous theaters' gender-bending productions of *The Moke-Eater* and *Turds in Hell*; the premiere of the Open Theater's *The Serpent* in Rome (see the section on *Terminal*); and the debut of Richard Schechner's Performance Group with its radical improvisation on *The Bacchae*, *Dionysus in '69*. In London, Peter Brook directed an innovative *Tempest*, a piece that contained the seeds of his subsequent investigatory work in Paris; that remarkable Polish theater ensemble, Jerzy Grotowski's Theatre Laboratory of Wroclaw, triumphed from Edinburgh to Aix-en-Provence and was soon to triumph in the United States. The modern black theater movement effectively started in 1968 with the founding of the Negro Ensemble Company. And recall the impact of Joseph Papp's Public Theater, which followed its debut offerings of *Hair* and a radical *Hamlet* in 1967 with Václav Havel's *The Memorandum* in 1968. And 1968 saw the triumphant, if controversial, return from European exile of Julan Beck and Judith Malina's Living Theatre—the precursor and fount of so much then current theater experiment—which filled auditoriums, gymnasiums, churches, and theaters from Berkeley to Brooklyn. It was also the year that Richard Foreman founded his Ontological-Hysteric Theater.

But if 1968 was an *annus mirabilis* for radical performance, it was also, in a way, a last hurrah. The triumphs of a community of dissent were soured by the crushing of the student rebellions; the assassinations of Dr. King and Robert Kennedy, the Soviet extinction of the Prague Spring. Activism abated, and countercultural unity dissipated into individual agendas, political and artistic. As the barricades fell, experimental theater increasingly turned away from political commitment toward more introspective concerns. Richard Foreman's first production, *Angelface*, was a harbinger of this change. The play's opaque language, its accumulation of mysterious images without social referents, its inward turn toward questions of consciousness and perception, the very name of Foreman's theater—Ontologic-Hysteric—suggested that something new was afoot. Soon, Foreman would be joined (albeit in their own individualistic ways) by Robert Wilson, the Mabou Mines collective, and others, a disparate coupling that Bonnie Marranca subsumed under the rubric "Theatre of Images." In 1968 Wilson was conducting dance/theater experiments with the Byrd Hoffman School of Byrds in preparation for his first major work, *The Life and Times of Sigmund Freud*, performed the following year; and Mabou Mines was founded the year after that, in 1970. Mabou Mines created a new experimental synthesis that suffused the ideal of the artistic collective with both the surrounding innovation of new art, music, dance (an energy

creating the conceptual synthesis called performance art) and more traditional concerns of motivational acting. Thirty years later, in the dawn of the twenty-first century, Foreman, Wilson, and Mabou Mines remain active theatrically.

In the early years of counter-culture experiment, notions of collective identity had begun to form in groups that had been excluded or marginalized. The new "underground" theater became a means of expressing these shared identities. The homage/parodies of the "ridiculous" theater companies gave voice to a hitherto closeted gay sensibility that was to flower after Stonewall (see later). But by far the fount of identity theater was the rise of a black theater movement that became the model for later ethnic and feminist identity theaters. The civil rights movement had given way to a new separatist black nationalism, and its cultural expression necessarily followed. The integrationist model of the pioneering Negro Ensemble Company would no longer do. An early crucial transitional figure in this regard was the African American poet and playwright LeRoi Jones who left "beat" Bohemia to journey "home" and reemerge as Amiri Imamu Baraka.

His rediscovery of his black identity begins with his early visceral indictment of American racism in *Dutchman* (1964), in which a seductive white woman kills a young black man on a New York subway train. It won a *Village Voice* Obie that year for best new play, but caused considerable controversy for what some perceived as stridency. When Jones became Baraka, he felt it was essential to create a space where black theater artists could produce new work and not depend on the white liberal arts establishment for productional support. In 1965 he founded the Black Arts Repertory Theater and School in Harlem and started a program to encourage a radical cultural and political awakening in the black community. In 1968, after being arrested in urban riots in Newark, New Jersey, he created a black arts center there called Spirit-House.

By the early 1970s, African American voices were increasingly heard, both in conventional theaters and in new groups in new venues in inner cities throughout the country—groups encouraged by the growth of governmental and arts foundation funding. A host of new Afrocentrist theaters arose. New York saw many, including the National Black Theater (1968) and the New Federal Theater (1970). Other prominent new groups or venues were New Orleans's Free Southern Theater, and Los Angeles's Inner City Cultural Center. As black nationalism waned, many black arts institutions—particularly the smaller theaters—did not survive. But several—like the New Federal Theater and Crossroads Theater (New Brunswick, New Jersey)—continue to produce significant work. And Black dramatic voices like those of August Wilson, Anna Deavere Smith, and Susan-Lori Parks are among the most resonant in new American drama.

The opportunity offered a new generation of African American theater artists by the black theater movement had parallels in the experience of other marginalized ethnic groups. In 1966 New York City's growing Latino/Latina community founded INTAR (International Arts Relations/Hispanic American Arts Center) to provide a place where new Hispanic voices could be heard; it supported writing workshops, such as those taught by Maria Irene Fornes, and began producing plays. The Hispanic community has a complex, interrupted history in this country due to erratic patterns of immigration and the different countries of origin from which its diverse population hails. There is also the fact that while it usually expresses itself in English, it sometimes expresses itself in its native Spanish (and sometimes bilingually in both languages). Its theater activity is, then, diverse: The dominant strands hail from opposite sides of the country: Chicano/Chicana and Nuyorican. The former is the elder and politically linked to the politics of migrant farming in the West and Southwest.

In 1965 San Francisco Mime Troupe member Luis Valdez founded El Teatro Campesino (The Farmworker's Theater) to dramatize the issues in the Delano grape strike in which migrant workers from Mexico and other Latin American countries joined the United Farm Workers to alleviate their exploitative working conditions. Using Mexican *mitos* (myths, legends) and elements of Chicano (American-born Mexican) culture to collectively create works like *La Carpa de los Rasquachis* (*The Tent of the Underdogs*), El Teatro was a theater of activist politics, as when the group accompanied the striking workers in pilgrimage from Delano in central California to the northern capital of Sacramento. By 1967 they were touring nationally, playing schools, lofts, and festivals. El Teatro Campesino became the model for numerous Chicano *teatros* founded in the late 1960s and 1970s.

Meanwhile, on the other side of the country, New York Puerto Ricans—Nuyoricans—also began to express themselves theatrically. As it began to be formed, Nuyorican theater particularly followed black models,

a natural indebtedness, since Puerto Ricans and blacks share the bitter realities of the urban ghetto. But Nuyorican culture began to find its own voice in its own experience and musical heritage: in the pulse of *salsa,* Spanish and West Indian rhythms, the urban beat of rock. The Nuyorican Poet's Cafe on Loisada (Lower East Side) became its artistic center, and in Miguel Piñero, whose visceral *Short Eyes* stunned audiences in 1974, they found a powerful playwright silenced by premature death. Other Hispanic groups in America—Dominicans, South Americans, and so on—have added their own voices. Mention should also be made of Cuban American theater—yet another important strand of Latino/a identity in this country. A most recent example is Alina Troyana, Cuban American theater artist, who has created an outrageous character, Carmelita Tropicana, to perform comic monologues exploring issues of ethnic and sexual identity.

The same year that Baraka and Valdez founded their identity-focused theaters, 1965, saw the founding of the first Asian American theater company: the East-West Players of Los Angeles. But Asian American theater has, by and large, been the least visible of the ethnic-based theaters. Compared to the black and Latino/a theater movements, it started with certain disadvantages: It did not share a common political catalyst (the civil rights crisis) nor a common language. Nevertheless, Asian Americans developed a strong and vibrant theater on the West Coast. One of the scripts from a playwriting competition sponsored by East-West Players, Frank Chin's *The Chickencoop Chinaman,* became the first Asian American play to be performed in New York City in 1972. A year later Chin helped form the Asian-American Theater Workshop (1973–78) as part of the American Conservatory Theater in San Francisco. Other West Coast theaters followed: San Diego's Pacific Asian Actors Ensemble and Seattle's Asian Multimedia Center. In 1977 it was New York's turn: Tisa Chang, known for her advocacy for Asian American performers on Broadway, founded the influential—then and now—Pan Asian Repertory.

We have noted that the 1960s climate of dissent widened to challenge traditional gender and sexual roles. Greenwich Village, the home base of artistic experimentation, had, since the days of Louise Bryant, John Reed, and Eugene O'Neill, long accepted social behavior the larger the society considered "deviant." The new café and experimental theaters that arose in the 1960s increasingly and outspokenly began to give voice to gay concerns. Pioneers in this regard include the Caffé Cino (1960–67) where Joe Cino gave new young gay playwrights like Lanford Wilson (*The Madness of Lady Bright*) and Robert Patrick (*Camera Oscura*) their first public platforms. In 1965 John Vaccaro founded the Play-House of the Ridiculous out of the contemporary energy of the pop art movement and presented plays like Kenneth Bernard's *The Moke Eater* (1968) in which men played women and vice versa. In 1967 Charles Ludlam (1943–87) broke away from this company to found the Ridiculous Theatrical Company, which produced high camp parodies of classic plays, operas, and films, such as *Camille, Galas,* and *Der Ring Gott Farblonjet.*

Ludlam pioneered a new kind of drag performance in which female impersonation went beyond mere burlesque to serious acting. But as it has proliferated in gay theater since the late 1960s, the theatrical practice of cross-dressing continues to be riddled with dissension and controversy: Many see contemporary drag as the core of a viable gay aesthetic, but others find that the act of a man playing a women promulgates misogynist stereotypes. Nevertheless, none deny that gay drag was at the fount of the contemporary gay rights movement. In 1969 police officers, in a familiar ritual of harassment, raided a gay bar in Greenwich Village called the Stonewall Inn. The camel's back broke, and the drag queens who were habitués in the bar uneffeminately resisted being carted away. The ensuing riot that erupted ignited the flames of a gay liberation movement that claimed the same civil rights being granted to people of color. Since Stonewall, issues of gay rights have entered mainstream politics, and the "love that dare not speak its name" has been anything but tongue-tied. Gay playwrights like Williams and Albee could never write explicitly about their sexuality in their plays, but since Stonewall the Berlin Wall of puritanism has crumbled in the theater. When Harvey Fierstein made the crossover from off-off Broadway to off-Broadway to Broadway with his *Torch Song Trilogy* (1982 Broadway), the stage door was wide open for playwrights like Tony Kushner (see discussion of *Angels in America*), Robin Baitz, Terrence McNally and many other gay *and* lesbian playwrights.

The 1960s also saw the resurgence of feminism after its postsuffrage dormancy. Inevitably it would have theatrical consequences. As experimental ensembles proliferated, feminine theater companies were formed. One of the earliest was the It's All Right to Be a Woman Theater, founded in New York City in 1969. Women, who had traditionally been marginalized across race and ethnic lines, found coming together to create theater self-empowering. One of the hallmarks of this early feminist theater was the nonhierarchical model of collective creation established by ensembles like the Open Theater. Two women from this group went on to help found feminist theaters: Megan Terry helped create the Omaha Magic Theatre in Nebraska and Roberta Sklar (with Sondra Segal and Clare Coss) co-founded Women's Experimental Theater in New York (1977–86).

Women's companies emerged across the country, including At the Foot of the Mountain, Minneapolis (1974–91), Lilith, San Francisco (1974–86), and Rhode Island Feminist Theater (1973–86). Subject matter during the 1970s focused on issues of violence against women, mother/daughter relationships, and the ways cultural images define and control women. Two early companies that remain active are Spiderwoman Theater (1975–), named after the Hopi goddess of creation and dedicated to Native American and feminist concerns, and Split Britches, a feminist/lesbian company, founded in 1981. In 1982 the WOW (Women's One World) Café was created in New York City as a venue committed to cultivating feminist/lesbian performance in the manner that the earlier Caffée Cino had supported gay male performance. During the late 1980s and into the 1990s, solo performance, such as Rachel Rosenthal's *My Brazil*, which appears earlier in this volume, became an important new model.

In 1991, Split Britches collaborated with the British gay company Bloo Lips to create *Belle Reprieve*, an innovative excursion into the politics of gender and cross-dressing through a parodic deconstruction of Williams's *A Streetcar Named Desire*. A stunning critique of masculinity and femininity, at the same time enormously entertaining, *Belle Reprieve*, in its disruption of dominant ideology, through laughter, proved Brecht's point that "theater remains theater even when it is instructive theater, and in so far as it is good theater it will amuse."*

---

*For further discussion of the history of the various forms of identity theater, see individual sections on African American theater, Hispanic American theater, Asian American theater, and women's theater.

SAM Shepard

Sam Shepard Rogers, Jr., was born on an army base near Chicago in 1943 where his father—who had returned from World War II greatly disturbed by his experiences—was stationed. After several years of moving around (including Guam and the Philippines), the family finally settled in Duarte in Southern California's San Gabriel Valley, east of Los Angeles. Here the young Shepard—at first called Steve to distinguish him from his father—grew up in familiar all-American rebel style: He disdained school, played drums in a garage band, engaged in petty delinquency, read Kerouac and the beats, and had violent fights with his alcoholic father. After high school he enrolled in a local junior college where he only lasted three semesters. As his family situation worsened, he decided to go east to try a musical career while he shared the East Village cold-water flat of a high school friend, Charles Mingus, Jr., the son of the famous jazz bassist.

Arriving in New York in 1963 just as an era of "alternative" experimental art was burgeoning, "Steve" Shepard Rogers became Sam Shepard "because it was shorter." Exploring all the increasingly intertwined arts, fascinated by the new café-theaters such as Caffé Cino and La MaMa, young Shepard remembered Beckett's *Waiting for Godot,* which he had read in Duarte, and determined to write plays that had the improvisational fluidity of jazz. In the fall of 1964 a new theater group, Theater Genesis, inaugurated its first season with two short plays by Shepard: *Cowboys* and *The Rock Garden,* a play about leaving home and rejecting a culture of sexual repressiveness. Within a very few years the newly prolific young writer had won two *Village Voice* Obie awards for off-Broadway theater, and was acknowledged as a (some would say "the") major playwright on the avant-garde theater scene. In the mid–1960s Shepard realized his musical dream and became the drummer for a rock group called the Holy Modal Rounders, wrote several rock-influenced plays, and wrote his first full-length play, *La Turista* (1967), which was extravagantly praised by many critics. But the pressures of an increasing drug problem and his dislike of notoriety caused him in 1970 to flee New York, first for California, then for London.

With the perspective of distance, Shepard wrote one of his most enduring plays about the warfare of generations in America, *The Tooth of Crime* (1972), which blended rock history with American genre archetypes from science fiction, westerns, and gangster films. But permanent expatriation was not in his blood, and in 1974 he and his family returned to California—*Northern* California—"to find our roots." Shortly after his return he found a theater of his own and a director who proved to be his perfect interpreter: For the better part of a decade he became the resident playwright at the Magic Theatre, a small experimental company in San Francisco. The plays for which he is best known—his domestic "trilogy" *Curse of the Starving Class, Buried Child,* and *True West*—originated at the Magic in the late 1970s and were directed by Robert Woodruff, for a time his exclusive director, until Shepard himself started directing his plays in the mid–1980s. In the last two decades his output has slowed, but he has continued to produce such plays of distinction as *Fool for Love* (1983), *A Lie of the Mind* (1985), and *Simpatico* (1994).

■■■■■■■■■■■■■■■

COMMENTARY ON *TRUE WEST*

In the radical experimentation of his early, fragmented short plays, Sam Shepard seemed at first glance to have completely jettisoned traditional dramaturgy and subject matter. Starting not with plot, character, or theme, but with an image—"a picture of a guy in a bathtub, or of two guys on stage with a sign blinking"—Shepard, partly out of a genuine theatrical naïveté, unleashed a stream of what seemed to be au-

tomatic writing in the surrealist tradition. Yet, despite their ambiguities, the evocative, often outrageous visual and verbal changes that Shepard rang on his original images in his short plays always pulsated with thematic resonances and undeniable theatrical energy. Shepard's later move toward longer, more conventional, quasi-realistic modes stylistically departed from his early imagism; but a close look at these early plays reveals (if obliquely) themes present in his work from the very beginning. In *The Rock Garden* (1964), for example, the titular image becomes a denial of fecundity; the son's tirade launches an obscene assault against the sterility of the father and the family.

But Shepard's dissent from American repressiveness is more than the familiar exorcising of the close-minded puritanism of the American heartland. Growing up in California—the last frontier where it's still common faith that lives and values can be made new—Shepard is all too aware that he belongs to a culture "where nothing is permanent, where everything could be knocked down and it wouldn't be missed." There's no doubt that his plays capture, better than those of any other American playwright, our shifting spiritual landscape shaped by the detritus of popular culture and inhabited by the ghosts of old solitary myths: the pioneer, the cowboy, the Indian, the gangster. Contemporary anxiety, charged with a fear of deviance, is challenged by the myth—both optimistic and despairing—of forever striking out for new territory on one's own.

In the late 1970s, secure in his new theatrical collaboration at the Magic Theatre in San Francisco, Shepard returned to the family as subject in the trio of plays that established him as the foremost American playwright he was so long on the verge of becoming. Beginning with *The Curse of the Starving Class* in 1977, and following with *Buried Child* (1978) and *True West* (1980), Shepard developed a new dramatic strategy that did not abandon his individual, eccentric style; he strengthened it with an intrusion of the narrative power and accessible realism of American domestic tragedy—the tradition running from O'Neill through Odets and Miller and beyond that takes as its text the destruction of the family by the mendacious illusions of the American dream. *Curse* recounts the dispossession from their home of a family of deluded but not unsympathetic eccentrics victimized by a culture polluted with greed and consumerism. The disordered home they inhabit somewhere in the western desert is the target of grasping land developers, lawyers, and criminals—to Shepard one breed of despoilers who will stop at nothing to turn a profit.

In *Buried Child*, the destruction of the family—one just as eccentric but less sympathetic—is rooted not merely in its acceptance of false values, but in a common guilt its members share, a dreadful secret they try in vain to keep buried. Shepard suggests that American guilt is so deep-rooted that the evil it generates will inevitably destroy all that is built on it. In a farmhouse ostensibly in Illinois (Shepard's birthplace) but really in Shepard Country—a landscape of fragmented images from all regions of American life—this family enacts hostile rituals of contentiousness and incomprehension. As the patriarch of the clan lies festering and decomposing on the couch, impotent but still pugnacious, the arrival of newcomers (the family grandson and his girlfriend) sets in motion a confrontation threatening the delicate balance of mutual guilt that sustains the strange clan. A struggle for territorial and patriarchal authority ensues, one which ends with the dreadful family secret uncovered and the power and the guilt passed on to the younger generation.

True West is the third in a trilogy of domestic disintegration. In each of the plays the spiritual death of the family becomes a metaphor for larger themes: the death of community, the death of the dream of freedom promised by the wilderness. What makes Shepard so archetypally American is that he so desperately wants to believe in this dream, even though he cannot fail to recognize betrayals by history. The very idea of a "true west" contains a fierce irony. The brothers in the play seem to have opposite dreams: Austin, the screenwriter, yearns to make it commercially; Lee, the drifter, lives by the tenets of an anarchic, antisocial individualism. But by play's end each steals the other's dream and is victimized by his theft. Lee undercuts his brother's movie deal by successfully proposing to Austin's producer a dumb, conventional western whose banalities unwittingly parody the old heroic virtues. And Austin, after reverting to an orgy of petty thievery in which he fills the house with pilfered toasters, reluctantly helps him write it, begging his brother in payment to take him away to the desert. Because "I can't make it here. . . . There's no such thing as the West anymore! It's a dead issue! It's dried up!"

This seeming character reversal reveals a deeper truth: The two brothers represent two sides of one complex sensibility. As Shepard told a reporter when the play first opened, "I wanted to write a play about double nature, one that wouldn't be symbolic or metaphorical or any of that stuff. I just wanted to give a taste of what it feels like to be two-sided. . . . I think we're split in a much more devastating way than psychology can ever reveal." That Shepard should "violate" the wholeness of character reveals his faithfulness to the shifting aesthetic with which he began writing: "Instead of the idea of a 'whole character' with logical motives behind his behavior which the actor submerges himself into, he should consider instead a fractured whole with bits and pieces of character flying off the central theme." In *True West* that central theme explores a variety of dualisms that are all paradoxical: family/self; brother/enemy; brother/savior; city/desert; settler/nomad; the frontier is gone/long live the frontier! one man's kitsch/another man's passion; hold your dream fast/kill it and be born again.

It's ironic that Shepard should deny so powerfully the possibility of healthy community in an art that sprang from a time of collaborative affirmation in his artistic life. But as the ritual exchange/blending of identities in *True West* (and so many other of his plays) reveals, Shepard not only *sees* paradox, he *is* a paradoxical, dialectical artist. As a bitter social critic he excoriates America's power brokers, the consumerist "curse" that afflicts the "starving class." ("Buy refrigerators. Buy cars, homes, lots. Invest."), the buried child of collective guilt that refuses to stay buried, the search for a "true west" that no longer exists. Americans are members of a cursed family, all victims: Fathers (invariably modeled on Shepard senior) are drunken misfits, mothers are disassociated observers, brothers are mortal enemies. But all are symbiotically connected by ineradicable blood ties. The final verbal image of *Curse of the Starving Class* is of predator and victim—an eagle that has picked up a tomcat in its talons—destroying each other in midair and crashing to earth "like one whole thing." The final visual image of *True West* is the perpetual struggle of two brothers under an indifferent desert moon. The vision is apocalyptic, but the dream of the true west remains indelible. Shepard shares that very American hope—affirmed so defiantly in the 1960s—that against all the denials recorded in his art, somehow the dream can become a reality.

TRUE WEST
Sam Shepard

CHARACTERS

AUSTIN: *Early thirties, light blue sports shirt, light tan cardigan sweater, clean blue jeans, white tennis shoes*

LEE: *His older brother, early forties, filthy white t-shirt, tattered brown overcoat covered with dust, dark blue baggy suit pants from the Salvation Army, pink suede belt, pointed black forties dress shoes scuffed up, holes in the soles, no socks, no hat, long pronounced sideburns, "Gene Vincent" hairdo, two days' growth of bead, bad teeth*

SAUL KIMMER: *Late forties, Hollywood producer, pink and white flower print sports shirt, white sports coat with matching polyester slacks, black and white loafers*

MOM: *Early sixties, mother of the brothers, small woman, conservative white skirt and matching jacket, red shoulder bag, two pieces of matching red luggage*

SCENE

All nine scenes take place on the same set; a kitchen and adjoining alcove of an older home in a Southern California suburb, about 40 miles east of Los Angeles. The kitchen takes up most of the playing area to stage left. The kitchen consists of a sink, upstage center, surrounded by counter space, a wall telephone, cupboards, and a small window just above it bordered by neat yellow curtains. Stage left of sink is a stove. Stage right, a refrigerator. The alcove adjoins the kitchen to stage right. There is no wall division or door to the alcove. It is open and easily accessible from the kitchen and defined only by the objects in it: a small round glass breakfast table mounted on white iron legs, two matching white iron chairs set across from each other. The two exterior walls of the alcove which prescribe a corner in the upstage right are composed of many small windows, beginning from a solid wall about three feet high and extending to the ceiling. The windows look out to bushes and citrus trees. The alcove is filled with all sorts of house plants in various pots, mostly Boston ferns hanging in planters at different levels. The floor of the alcove is composed of green synthetic grass.

All entrances and exits are made stage left from the kitchen. There is no door. The actors simply go off and come onto the playing area.

NOTE ON SET AND COSTUME

The set should be constructed realistically with no attempt to distort its dimensions, shapes, objects, or colors. No objects should be introduced which might draw special attention to themselves other than the props demanded by the script. If a stylistic "concept" is grafted onto the set design it will only serve to confuse the evolution of the character's situation, which is the most important focus of the play.

Likewise, the costumes should be exactly representative of who the characters are and not added onto for the sake of making a point to the audience.

NOTE ON SOUND

The Coyote of Southern California has a distinct yapping, dog-like bark, similar to a Hyena. This yapping grows more intense and maniacal as the pack grows in numbers, which is usually the case when they lure and kill pets from suburban yards. The sense of growing frenzy in the pack should be felt in the background, particularly in Scenes 7 and 8. In any case, these Coyotes never make the long, mournful, solitary howl of the Hollywood stereotype.

The sound of Crickets can speak for itself.

These sounds should also be treated realistically even though they sometimes grow in volume and numbers.

ACT ONE
SCENE 1

Night. Sound of crickets in dark. Candlelight appears in alcove, illuminating Austin, seated at glass table hunched over a writing notebook, pen in hand, cigarette burning in ashtray, cup of coffee, typewriter on table, stacks of paper, candle burning on table.

Soft moonlight fills kitchen illuminating Lee, beer in hand, six-pack on counter behind him. He's leaning against the sink, mildly drunk; takes a slug of beer.

LEE. So, Mom took off for Alaska, huh?
AUSTIN. Yeah.
LEE. Sorta' left you in charge.
AUSTIN. Well, she knew I was coming down here so she offered me the place.

John Malkovich as Lee (right) gives his brother Austin (Gary Sinese) some advice on screenwriting in the acclaimed 1982 Steppenwolf production of Shepard's *True West.*

LEE. You keepin' the plants watered?

AUSTIN. Yeah.

LEE. Keepin' the sink clean? She don't like even a single tea leaf in the sink ya' know.

AUSTIN (*trying to concentrate on writing*). Yeah, I know.

(*Pause*)

LEE. She gonna' be up there a long time?

AUSTIN. I don't know.

LEE. Kinda' nice for you, huh? Whole place to yourself.

AUSTIN. Yeah, it's great

LEE. Ya' got crickets anyway. Tons a' crickets out there. (*looks around kitchen*) Ya' got groceries? Coffee?

AUSTIN (*looking up from writing*). What?

LEE. You got coffee?

AUSTIN. Yeah.

LEE. At's good. (*short pause*) Real coffee? From the bean?

AUSTIN. Yeah. You want some?

LEE. Naw. I brought some uh— (*motions to beer*)

AUSTIN. Help yourself to whatever's— (*motions to refrigerator*)

LEE. I will. Don't worry about me. I'm not the one to worry about. I mean I can uh— (*pause*) You always work by candlelight?

AUSTIN. No—uh— Not always.

LEE. Just sometimes?

AUSTIN (*puts pen down, rubs his eyes*). Yeah. Sometimes it's soothing.

LEE. Isn't that what the old guys did?

AUSTIN. What old guys?

LEE. The Forefathers. You know.

AUSTIN. Forefathers?

LEE. Isn't that what they did? Candlelight burning into the night? Cabins in the wilderness.

AUSTIN (*rubs hand through his hair*). I suppose.

LEE. I'm not botherin' you am I? I mean I don't wanna break into yer uh—concentration or nothin'.

AUSTIN. No, it's all right.

LEE. That's good. I mean I realize that yer line a' work demands a lota' concentration.

AUSTIN. It's okay.

LEE. You probably think that I'm not fully able to comprehend somethin' like that, huh?

AUSTIN. Like what?

LEE. That stuff yer doin'. That art. You know. Whatever you call it.

AUSTIN. It's just a little research.

LEE. You may not know it but I did a little art myself once.

AUSTIN. You did?

LEE. Yeah! I did some a' that. I fooled around with it. No future in it.

AUSTIN. What'd you do?

LEE. Never mind what I did! Just never mind about that. (*pause*) It was ahead of its time.

(*Pause*)

AUSTIN. So, you went out to see the old man, huh?

LEE. Yeah, I seen him.

AUSTIN. How's he doing?

LEE. Same. He's doin' just about the same.

AUSTIN. I was down there too, you know.

LEE. What d'ya' want, an award? You want some kinda' medal? You were down there. He told me all about you.

AUSTIN. What'd he say?

LEE. He told me. Don't worry.

(*Pause*)

AUSTIN. Well—

LEE. You don't have to say nothin'.

AUSTIN. I wasn't.

LEE. Yeah, you were gonna' make somethin' up. Somethin' brilliant.

(*Pause*)

AUSTIN. You going to be down here very long, Lee?

LEE. Might be. Depends on a few things.

AUSTIN. You got some friends down here?

LEE (*laughs*). I know a few people. Yeah.

AUSTIN. Well, you can stay here as long as I'm here.

LEE. I don't need your permission do I?

AUSTIN. No.

LEE. I mean she's my mother too, right?

AUSTIN. Right.

LEE. She might've just as easily asked me to take care of her place as you.

AUSTIN. That's right.

LEE. I mean I know how to water plants.

(*Long pause*)

AUSTIN. So you don't know how long you'll be staying then?

LEE. Depends mostly on houses, ya' know.

AUSTIN. Houses?

LEE. Yeah. Houses. Electric devices. Stuff like that. I gotta' make a little tour first.

(*Short pause*)

AUSTIN. Lee, why don't you just try another neighborhood, all right?

LEE (*laughs*). What'sa' matter with this neighborhood? This is a great neighborhood. Lush. Good class a' people. Not many dogs.

AUSTIN. Well, our uh— Our mother just happens to live here. That's all.

LEE. Nobody's gonna' know. All they know is somethin's missing. That's all. She'll never even hear about it. Nobody's gonna' know.

AUSTIN. You're going to get picked up if you start walking around here at night.

LEE. Me? I'm gonna' git picked up? What about you? You stick out like a sore thumb. Look at you. You think yer regular lookin'?

AUSTIN. I've got too much to deal with here to be worrying about—

LEE. Yer not gonna' have to worry about me! I've been doin' all right without you. I haven't been anywhere near you for five years! Now isn't that true?

AUSTIN. Yeah.

LEE. So you don't have to worry about me. I'm a free agent.

AUSTIN. All right.

LEE. Now all I wanna' do is borrow yer car.

AUSTIN. No!

LEE. Just fer a day. One day.

AUSTIN. No!

LEE. I won't take it outside a twenty mile radius. I promise ya'. You can check the speedometer.

AUSTIN. You're not borrowing my car! That's all there is to it.

(*Pause*)

LEE. Then I'll just take the damn thing.

AUSTIN. Lee, look—I don't want any trouble, all right?

LEE. That's a dumb line. That is a dumb fuckin' line. You git paid fer dreamin' up a line like that?

AUSTIN. Look, I can give you some money if you need money.

(*Lee suddenly lunges at Austin, grabs him violently by the shirt and shakes him with tremendous power*)

LEE. Don't you say that to me! Don't you ever say that to me! (*just as suddenly he turns him loose, pushes him away and backs off*) You may be able to git away with that with the Old Man. Git him tanked up for a week! Buy him off with yer Hollywood blood money, but not me! I can git my own money my own way. Big money!

AUSTIN. I was just making an offer.

LEE. Yeah, well keep it to yourself!

(*Long pause*)

Those are the most monotonous fuckin' crickets I ever heard in my life.

AUSTIN. I kinda' like the sound.

LEE. Yeah. Supposed to be able to tell the temperature by the number a' pulses. You believe that?

AUSTIN. The temperature?

LEE. Yeah. The air. How hot it is.

AUSTIN. How do you do that?

LEE. I don't know. Some woman told me that. She was a Botanist. So I believed her.

AUSTIN. Where'd you meet her?

LEE. What?

AUSTIN. The woman Botanist?

LEE. I met her on the desert. I been spendin' a lota' time on the desert.

AUSTIN. What were you going out there?

LEE (*pause, stares in space*). I forgit. Had me a Pit Bull there for a while but I lost him.

AUSTIN. Pit Bull?

LEE. Fightin' dog. Damn I made some good money off that little dog. Real good money.

(*Pause*)

AUSTIN. You could come up north with me, you know.

LEE. What's up there?

AUSTIN. My family.

LEE. Oh, that's right, you got the wife and kiddies now don't ya'. The house, the car, the whole slam. That's right.

AUSTIN. You could spend a couple days. See how you like it. I've got an extra room.

LEE. Too cold up there.

(*Pause*)

AUSTIN. You want to sleep for a while?

LEE (*pause, stares at Austin*). I don't sleep.

(*Lights to black*)

SCENE 2

Morning. Austin is watering plants with a vaporizer. Lee sits at glass table in alcove drinking beer.

LEE. I never realized the old lady was so security-minded.

AUSTIN. How do you mean?

LEE. Made a little tour this morning. She's got locks on everything. Locks and double-locks and chain locks and—What's she got that's so valuable?

AUSTIN. Antiques I guess. I don't know.

LEE. Antiques? Brought everything with her from the old place, huh. Just the same crap we always had around. Plates and spoons.

AUSTIN. I guess they have personal value to her.

LEE. Personal value. Yeah. Just a lota' junk. Most of it's phony anyway. Idaho decals. Now who in the hell wants to eat offa' plate with the State of Idaho starin' ya' in the face. Every time ya' take a bite ya' get to see a little bit more.

AUSTIN. Well it must mean something to her or she wouldn't save it.

LEE. Yeah, well personally I don't wann' be invaded by Idaho when I'm eatin'. When I'm eatin' I'm home. Ya' know what I'm sayin'? I'm not driftin', I'm home. I don't need my thoughts swept off to Idaho. I don't need that!

(*Pause*)

AUSTIN. Did you go out last night?

LEE. Why?

AUSTIN. I thought I head you go out.

LEE. Yeah, I went out. What about it?

AUSTIN. Just wondered.

LEE. Damn coyotes kept me awake.

AUSTIN. Oh yeah, I heard them. They must've killed somebody's dog or something.

LEE. Yappin' their fool heads off. They don't yap like that on the desert. They howl. These are city coyotes here.

AUSTIN. Well, you don't sleep anyway do you?

(*Pause, Lee stares at him*)

LEE. You're pretty smart aren't ya?

AUSTIN. How do you mean?

LEE. I mean you never had any more on the ball than I did. But here you are getting' invited into prominent people's houses. Sittin' around talkin' like you know somethin'.

AUSTIN. They're not so prominent.

LEE. They're a helluva' lot more prominent than the houses I get invited into.

AUSTIN. Well you invite yourself.

LEE. That's right. I do. In fact I probably got a wider range a' choices than you do, come to think of it.

AUSTIN. I wouldn't doubt it.

LEE. In fact I been inside some pretty classy places in my time. And I never even went to an Ivy League school either.

AUSTIN. You want some breakfast or something?

LEE. Breakfast?

AUSTIN. Yeah. Don't you eat breakfast?

LEE. Look, don't worry about me pal. I can take care a' myself. You just go ahead as though I wasn't even here, all right?

(*Austin goes into kitchen, makes coffee*)

AUSTIN. Where'd you walk to last night?

(*Pause*)

LEE. I went up in the foothills there. Up in the San Gabriels. Heat was drivin' me crazy.

AUSTIN. Well, wasn't it hot out on the desert?

LEE. Different kinda' heat. Out there it's clean. Cools off at night. There's a nice little breeze.

AUSTIN. Where were you, the Mojave?

LEE. Yeah. The Mojave. That's right.

AUSTIN. I haven't been out there in years.

LEE. Out past Needles there.

AUSTIN. Oh yeah.

LEE. Up here it's different. This country's real different.

AUSTIN. Well, it's built up.

LEE. Built up? Wiped out is more like it. I don't even hardly recognize it.

AUSTIN. Yeah. Foothills are the same though, aren't they?

LEE. Pretty much. It's funny goin' up in there. The smells and everything. Used to catch snakes up there, remember?

AUSTIN. You caught snakes.

LEE. Yeah. And you'd pretend you were Geronimo or some damn thing. You used to go right out to lunch.

AUSTIN. I enjoyed my imagination.

LEE. That what you call it? Looks like yer still enjoyin' it.

AUSTIN. So you just wandered around up there, huh?

LEE. Yeah. With a purpose.

AUSTIN. See any houses?

(*Pause*)

LEE. Couple. Couple a' real nice ones. One of 'em didn't even have a dog. Walked right up and stuck my head in the window. Not a peep. Just a sweet kinda' suburban silence.

AUSTIN. What kind of a place was it?

LEE. Like a paradise. Kinda' place that sorta' kills ya' inside. Warm yellow lights. Mexican tile all around. Copper pots hangin' over the stove. Ya' know like they got in the magazines. Blonde people movin' in and outa' the rooms, talkin' to each other. (*pause*) Kinda' place you wish you sorta' grew up in, ya' know.

AUSTIN. That's the kind of place you wish you'd grown up in?

LEE. Yeah, why not?

AUSTIN. I thought you hated that kind of stuff.

LEE. Yeah, well you never knew too much about me did ya'?

(*Pause*)

AUSTIN. Why'd you go out to the desert in the first place?

LEE. I was on my way to see the old man.

AUSTIN. You mean you just passed through there?

LEE. Yeah. That's right. Three months of passin' through.

AUSTIN. Three months?

LEE. Somethin' like that. Maybe more. Why?

AUSTIN. You lived on the Mojave for three months?

LEE. Yeah. What'sa' matter with that?

AUSTIN. By yourself?

LEE. Mostly. Had a couple a' visitors. Had that dog for a while.

AUSTIN. Didn't you miss people?

LEE (*laughs*). People?

AUSTIN. Yeah. I mean I go crazy if I have to spend three nights in a motel by myself.

LEE. Yer not in a motel now.

AUSTIN. No, I know. But sometimes I have to stay in motels.

LEE. Well, they got people in motels don't they?

AUSTIN. Strangers.

LEE. Yer friendly aren't ya'? Aren't you the friendly type?

(*Pause*)

AUSTIN. I'm going to have somebody coming by here later, Lee.

LEE. Ah! Lady friend?

AUSTIN. No, a producer.

LEE. Aha! What's he produce?

AUSTIN. Film. Movies. You know.

LEE. Oh, movies. Motion Pictures! A Big Wig huh?

AUSTIN. Yeah.

LEE. What's he comin' by here for?

AUSTIN. We have to talk about a project.

LEE. Whadya' mean, "a project"? What's "a project"?

AUSTIN. A script.

LEE. Oh. That's what yer doin' with all these papers?

AUSTIN. Yeah.

LEE. Well, what's the project about?

AUSTIN. We're uh—it's a period piece.

LEE. What's "a period piece?"

AUSTIN. Look, it doesn't matter. The main thing is we need to discuss this alone. I mean—

LEE. Oh, I get it. You want me outa' the picture.

AUSTIN. Not exactly. I just need to be alone with him for a couple of hours. So we can talk.

LEE. Yer afraid I'll embarrass ya' huh?

AUSTIN. I'm not afraid you'll embarrass me!

LEE. Well, I tell ya' what— Why don't you just gimme the keys to yer car and I'll be back here around six o'clock or so. That give ya' enough time?

AUSTIN. I'm not loaning you may car, Lee.

LEE. You want me to just git lost huh? Take a hike? Is that it? Pound the pavement a few hours while you bullshit yer way into a million bucks.

AUSTIN. Look, it's going to be hard enough for me to face this character on my own without—

LEE. You don't know this guy?

AUSTIN. No I don't know—He's a producer. I mean I've been meeting with him for months but you never get to know a producer.

LEE. Yer tryin' to hustle him? Is that it?

AUSTIN. I'm not trying to hustle him! I'm trying to work out a deal! It's not easy.

LEE. What kinda' deal?

AUSTIN. Convince him it's a worthwhile story.

LEE. He's not convinced? How come he's coming over here if he's not convinced? I'll convince him for ya'.

AUSTIN. You don't understand the way things work down here.

LEE. How do things work down here?

(*Pause*)

AUSTIN. Look, if I loan you my car will you have it back here by six?

LEE. On the button. With a full tank a' gas.

AUSTIN (*digging in his pocket for keys*). Forget about the gas.

LEE. Hey, these days gas is gold, old buddy.

(*Austin hands the keys to Lee*)

You remember that car I used to loan you?

AUSTIN. Yeah.

LEE. Forty Ford. Flathead.

AUSTIN. Yeah.

LEE. Sucker hauled ass didn't it?

AUSTIN. Lee, it's not that I don't want to loan you my car—

LEE. You are loanin' me yer car.

(*Lee gives Austin a pat on the shoulder, pause*)

AUSTIN. I know. I just wish—

LEE. What? You wish what?

AUSTIN. I don't know. I wish I wasn't— I wish I didn't have to be doing business down here. I'd like to just spend some time with you.

LEE. I though it was "Art" you were doin'.

(*Lee moves across kitchen toward exist, tosses keys in his hand*)

AUSTIN. Try to get it back here by six, okay?

LEE. No sweat. Hey, ya' know, if that uh—story of yours doesn't go over with the guy—tell him I got a couple a' "projects" he might be interested in. Real commercial. Full a' suspense. True-to-life stuff.

(*Lee exits, Austin stares after Lee then turns, goes to papers at table, leafs through pages, lights fade to black*)

SCENE 3

Afternoon. Alcove. Saul Kimmer and Austin seated across from each other at table.

SAUL. Well, to tell you the truth Austin, I have never felt so confident about a project in quite a long time.

AUSTIN. Well, that's good to hear, Saul.

SAUL. I am absolutely convinced we can get this thing off the ground. I mean we'll have to make a sale to television and that means getting a major star. Somebody bankable. But I think we can do it. I really do.

AUSTIN. Don't you think we need a first draft before we approach a star?

SAUL. No, no, not at all. I don't think it's necessary. Maybe a brief synopsis. I don't want you to touch the typewriter until we have some seed money.

AUSTIN. That's fine with me.

SAUL. I mean it's a great story. Just the story alone. You've really managed to capture something this time.

AUSTIN. I'm glad you like it, Saul.

(*Lee enters abruptly into kitchen carrying a stolen television set, short pause*)

LEE. Aw shit, I'm sorry about that. I am really sorry Austin.

AUSTIN (*standing*). That's all right.

LEE (*moving toward them*). I mean I thought it was way past six already. You said to have it back here by six.

AUSTIN. We were just finishing up. (*to Saul*) This is my, uh—brother, Lee.

SAUL (*standing*). Oh, I'm very happy to meet you.

(*Lee sets T.V. on sink counter, shakes hands with Saul*)

LEE. I can't tell ya' how happy I am to meet you sir.

SAUL. Saul Kimmer.

LEE. Mr. Kipper.

SAUL. Kimmer.

AUSTIN. Lee's been living out on the desert and he just uh—

SAUL. Oh, that's terrific! (*to Lee*) Palm Springs?

LEE. Yeah. Yeah, right. Right around in that area. Near uh—Bob Hope Drive there.

SAUL. Oh, I love it out there. I just love it. The air is wonderful.

LEE. Yeah. Sure is, Healthy.

SAUL. And the golf. I don't know if you play golf, but the golf is just about the best.

LEE. I play a lota' golf.

SAUL. Is that right?

LEE. Yeah. In fact I was hoping I'd run into somebody out here who played a little golf. I've been lookin' for a partner.

SAUL. Well, I uh—

AUSTIN. Lee's just down for a visit while our mother's in Alaska.

SAUL. Oh, your mother's in Alaska?

AUSTIN. Yes. She went up there on a little vacation. This is her place.

SAUL. I see. Well isn't that something, Alaska.

LEE. What kinda' handicap do ya' have, Mr. Kimmer?

SAUL. Oh I'm just a Sunday duffer really. You know.

LEE. That's good 'cause I haven't swung a club for months.

SAUL. Well we ought to get together sometime and have a little game. Austin, do you play?

(*Saul mimes a Johnny Carson golf swing for Austin*)

AUSTIN. No. I don't uh—I've watched it on T.V.

LEE (*to Saul*). How 'bout tomorrow morning? Bright and early. We could get out there and put in eighteen holes before breakfast.

SAUL. Well, I've got uh—I have several appointments—

LEE. No, I mean real early. Crack a'dawn. While the dew's still thick on the fairway.

SAUL. Sounds really great.

LEE. Austin could be our caddie.

SAUL. Now that's an idea. (*laughs*)

AUSTIN. I don't know the first thing about golf.

LEE. There's nothin' to it. Isn't that right, Saul? He'd pick it up in fifteen minutes.

SAUL. Sure. Doesn't take long. 'Course you have to play for years to find your true form. (*chuckles*)

LEE (*to Austin*). We'll give ya' a quick run-down on the club faces. The irons, the woods. Show ya' a couple pointers on the basic swing. Might even let ya' hit the ball a couple times. Whadya' think, Saul?

SAUL. Why not. I think it'd be great. I haven't had any exercise in weeks.

LEE. 'At's the spirit! We'll have a little orange juice right afterwards.

(*Pause*)

SAUL. Orange juice?

LEE. Yeah! Vitamin C! Nothin' like a shot a' orange juice after a round a' golf. Hot shower. Snappin' towels at each others' privates. Real sense a' fraternity.

SAUL (*smiles at Austin*). Well, you make it sound very inviting, I must say. It really does sound great.

LEE. Then it's a date.

SAUL. Well, I'll call the country club and see if I can arrange something.

LEE. Great! Boy, I sure am sorry that I busted in on ya' all in the middle of yer meeting.

SAUL. Oh that's quite all right. We were just about finished anyway.

LEE. I can wait out in the other room if you want.

SAUL. No really—

LEE. Just got Austin's color T.V. back from the shop. I can watch a little amateur boxing now.

(*Lee and Austin exchange looks*)

SAUL. Oh—Yes.

LEE. You don't fool around in Television, do you Saul?

SAUL. Uh— I have in the past. Produced some T.V. Specials. Network stuff. But it's mainly features now.

LEE. That's where the big money is, huh?

SAUL. Yes. That's right.

AUSTIN. Why don't I call you tomorrow, Saul and we'll get together. We can have lunch or something.

SAUL. That'd be terrific.

LEE. Right after the golf.

(*Pause*)

SAUL. What?

LEE. You can have lunch right after the golf.

SAUL. Oh, right.

LEE. Austin was tellin' me that yer interested in stories.

SAUL. Well, we develop certain projects that we feel have commercial potential.

LEE. What kinda' stuff do ya' go in for?

SAUL. Oh, the usual. You know. Good love interests. Lots of action. (*chuckles at Austin*)

LEE. Westerns?

SAUL. Sometimes.

AUSTIN. I'll give you a ring, Saul.

(*Austin tries to move Saul across the kitchen but Lee blocks their way*)

LEE. I got a Western that'd knock yer lights out.

SAUL. Oh, really?

LEE. Yeah. Contemporary Western. Based on a true story. 'Course I'm not a writer like my brother here. I'm not a man of the pen.

SAUL. Well—

LEE. I mean I can tell ya' a story off the tongue but I can't put it down on paper. That don't make any difference though does it?

SAUL. No, not really.

LEE. I mean plenty a' guys have stories don't they? True-life stories. Musta' been a lota' movies made from real life.

SAUL. Yes. I suppose so.

LEE. I haven't seen a good Western since "Lonely Are the Brave." You remember that movie?

SAUL. No, I'm afraid I—

LEE. Kirk Douglas. Helluva' movie. You remember that movie, Austin.

AUSTIN. Yes.

LEE (*to Saul*). The man dies for the love of a horse.

SAUL. Is that right.

LEE. Yeah. Ya' hear the horse screamin' at the end of it. Rain's comin' down. Horse is screamin'. Then there's a shot. BLAM! Just a single shot like that. Then nothin' but the sound of rain. And Kirk Douglas is ridin' in the ambulance. Ridin' away from the scene of the accident. And when he hears that shot he knows that his horse has died. He knows. And you see his eyes. And his eyes die. Right inside his face. And then his eyes close. And you know that he's died too. You know that Kirk Douglas has died from the death of his horse.

SAUL (*eyes Austin nervously*). Well, it sounds like a great movie. I'm sorry I missed it.

LEE. Yeah, you shouldn't a' missed that one.

SAUL. I'll have to try to catch it some time. Arrange a screening or something. Well, Austin, I'll have to hit the freeway before rush hour.

AUSTIN (*ushers him toward exit*). It's good seeing you, Saul.

(*Austin and Saul shake hands*)

LEE. So ya' think there's room for a real Western these days? A true-to-life Western?

SAUL. Well, I don't see why not. Why don't you uh—tell the story to Austin and have him write a little outline.

LEE. You'd take a look at it then?

SAUL. Yes. Sure. I'll give it a read-through. Always eager for new material. (*smiles at Austin*)

LEE. That's great! You'd really read it then huh?

SAUL. It would just be my opinion of course.

LEE. That's all I want. Just an opinion. I happen to think it has a lota' possibilities.

SAUL. Well, it was great meeting you and I'll—

(*Saul and Lee shake*)

LEE. I'll call you tomorrow about the golf.

SAUL. Oh. Yes, right.

LEE. Austin's got your number, right?

SAUL. Yes.

LEE. So long Saul. (*gives Saul a pat on the back*)

(*Saul exits, Austin turns to Lee, looks at T.V. then back to Lee*)

AUSTIN. Give me the keys.

(*Austin extends his hand toward Lee. Lee doesn't move, just stares at Austin, smiles, lights to black*)

SCENE 4

Night. Coyotes in distance, fade, sound of typewriter in dark, crickets, candlelight in alcove, dim light in kitchen, lights reveal Austin at glass table typing, Lee sits across from him, foot on table, drinking beer and whiskey, the

T.V. is still on sink counter, Austin types for a while, then stops.

LEE. All right, now read it back to me.

AUSTIN. I'm not reading it back to you, Lee. You can read it when we're finished. I can't spend all night on this.

LEE. You got better things to do?

AUSTIN. Let's just go ahead. Now what happens when he leaves Texas?

LEE. Is he ready to leave Texas yet? I didn't know we were that far along. He's not ready to leave Texas.

AUSTIN. He's right at the border.

LEE (*sitting up*). No, see this is one a' the crucial parts. Right here. (*taps paper with beer can*) We can't rush through this. He's not right at the border. He's a good fifty miles form the border. A lot can happen in fifty miles.

AUSTIN. It's only an outline. We're not writing an entire script now.

LEE. Well ya' can't leave things out even if it is an outline. It's one a' the most important parts. Ya' can't go leavin' it out.

AUSTIN. Okay, okay. Let's just—get it done.

LEE. All right. Now. He's in the truck and he's got his horse trailer and his horse.

AUSTIN. We've already established that.

LEE. And he sees this other guy comin' up behind him in another truck. And that truck is pullin' a gooseneck.

AUSTIN. What's a gooseneck?

LEE. Cattle trailer. You know the kind with a gooseneck, goes right down in the bed a' the pick-up.

AUSTIN. Oh. All right. (*types*)

LEE. It's important.

AUSTIN. Okay. I got it.

LEE. All these details are important.

(*Austin types as they talk*)

AUSTIN. I've got it.

LEE. And this other guy's got his horse all saddled up in the back a' the gooseneck.

AUSTIN. Right.

LEE. So both these guys have got their horses right along with 'em, see.

AUSTIN. I understand.

LEE. Then this first guy suddenly realizes two things.

AUSTIN. The guy in front?

LEE. Right. The guy in front realizes two things almost at the same time. Simultaneous.

AUSTIN. What were the two things?

LEE. Number one, he realizes that the guy behind him is the husband of the woman he's been—

(*Lee makes gesture of screwing by pumping his arm*)

AUSTIN (*see Lee's gesture*). Oh. Yeah.

LEE. And number two, he realizes he's in the middle of Tornado Country.

AUSTIN. What's "Tornado Country"?

LEE. Panhandle.

AUSTIN. Panhandle?

LEE. Sweetwater. Around in that area. Nothin'. Nowhere. And number three—

AUSTIN. I thought there was only two.

LEE. There's three. There's a third unforeseen realization.

AUSTIN. And what's that?

LEE. That's he's runnin' outa' gas.

AUSTIN (*stops typing*). Come on, Lee.

(*Austin gets up, moves to kitchen, gets a glass of water*)

LEE. Whadya' mean, "come on"? That's what it is. Write it down! He's runnin' outa' gas.

AUSTIN. It's too—

LEE. What? It's too what? It's too real! That's what ya' mean isn't it. It's too much like real life!

AUSTIN. It's not like real life! It's not enough like real life. Things don't happen like that.

LEE. What! Men don't fuck other men's women?

AUSTIN. Yes. But they don't end up shading each other across the Panhandle. Through "Tornado Country."

LEE. They do in this movie!

AUSTIN. And they don't have horses conveniently along with them when they run out of gas! And they don't run out of gas either!

LEE. These guys run outa' gas! This is my story and one a' these guys runs outa' gas!

AUSTIN. It's just a dumb excuse to get them into a chase scene. It's contrived.

LEE. It is a chase scene! It's already a chase scene. They been chasin' each other fer days.

AUSTIN. So now they're supposed to abandon their trucks, climb on their horses and chase each other into the mountains?

LEE (*standing suddenly*). There aren't any mountains in the Panhandle. It's flat!

(*Lee turns violently toward windows in alcove and throws beer can at them*)

LEE. Goddamn these crickets (*yells at crickets*) Shut up out there! (*pause, turns back toward table*) This place is like a fuckin' rest home here. How're you supposed to think!

AUSTIN. You wanna' take a break?

LEE. No, I don't wanna' take a break! I wanna' get this done! This is my last chance to get this done.

AUSTIN (*moves back into alcove*). All right. Take it easy.

LEE. I'm gonna' be leavin' this area. I don't have time to mess around here.

AUSTIN. Where are you going?

LEE. Never mind where I'm goin'! That's got nothin' to do with you. I just gotta' get this done. I'm not like you. Hangin' around bein' a parasite offa' other fools. I gotta' do this thing and get out.

(*Pause*)

AUSTIN. A parasite? Me?

LEE. Yeah, you!

AUSTIN. After you break into people's houses and take their televisions?

LEE. They don't need their televisions! I'm doin' them a service.

AUSTIN. Give me back my keys, Lee.

LEE. Not until you write this thing! You're gonna' write this outline thing for me or that car's gonna' wind up in Arizona with a different paint job.

AUSTIN. You think you can force me to write this? I was doing you a favor.

LEE. Git off yer high horse will ya'! Favor! Big favor. Handin' down favors from the mountain top.

AUSTIN. Let's just write it, okay? Let's sit down and not get upset and see if we can just get through this.

(*Austin sits at typewriter*)

(*Long pause*)

LEE. Yer not gonna' even show it to him, are ya'?

AUSTIN. What?

LEE. This outline. You got no intention of showin' it to him. Yer just doin' this 'cause yer afraid a' me.

AUSTIN. You can show it to him yourself.

LEE. I will, boy! I'm gonna' read it to him on the golf course.

AUSTIN. And I'm not afraid of you either.

LEE. Then how come yer doin' it?

AUSTIN (*pause*). So I can get my keys back.

(*pause as Lee takes keys out of his pocket slowly and throws them on table, long pause, Austin stares at keys*)

LEE. There. Now you got yer keys back.

(*Austin looks up at Lee but doesn't take keys*)

LEE. Go ahead. There's yer keys.

(*Austin slowly takes keys off table and puts them back in his own pocket*)

Now what're you gonna' do? Kick me out?

AUSTIN. I'm not going to kick you out, Lee.

LEE. You couldn't kick me out, boy.

AUSTIN. I know.

LEE. So you can't even consider that one. (*pause*) You could call the police. That'd be the obvious thing.

AUSTIN. You're my brother.

LEE. That don't mean a thing. You go down to the L.A. Police Department there and ask them what kinda' people kill each other the most. What do you think they'd say?

AUSTIN. Who said anything about killing?

LEE. Family people. Brothers. Brothers-in-law. Cousins. Real American-type people. They kill each other in the heat mostly. In the Smog-Alerts. In the Brush Fire Season. Right about this time a' year.

AUSTIN. This isn't the same.

LEE. Oh no? What makes it different?

AUSTIN. We're not insane. We're not driven to acts of violence like that. Not over a dumb movie script. Now sit down.

(*Long pause, Lee considers which way to go with it*)

LEE. Maybe not. (*he sits back down at table across from Austin*) Maybe you're right. Maybe we're too intelligent, huh? (*pause*) We got our heads on our shoulders. One of us has even got a Ivy League diploma. Now that means somethin' don't it? Doesn't that mean somethin'?

AUSTIN. Look, I'll write this thing for you, Lee. I don't mind writing it. I just don't want to get all worked up about it. It's not worth it. Now, come on. Let's just get through it, okay?

LEE. Nah. I think there's easier money. Lotsa' places I could pick up thousands. Maybe millions. I don't need this shit. I could go up to Sacramento Valley and steal me a diesel. Ten thousand a week dismantling one a' those suckers. Ten thousand a week!

(*Lee opens another beer, puts his foot back up on table*)

AUSTIN. No, really, look, I'll write it out for you. I think it's a great idea.

LEE. Nah, you got yer own work to do. I don't wanna' interfere with yer life.

AUSTIN. I mean it'd be really fantastic if you could sell this. Turn it into a movie. I mean it.

(*Pause*)

LEE. Ya' think so huh?

AUSTIN. Absolutely. You could really turn your life around, you know. Change things.

LEE. I could get me a house maybe.

AUSTIN. Sure you could get a house. You could get a whole ranch if you wanted to.

LEE (*laughs*). A ranch? I could get a ranch?

AUSTIN. 'Course you could. You know what a screenplay sells for these days?

LEE. No. What's it sell for?

AUSTIN. A lot. A whole lot of money.

LEE. Thousands?

AUSTIN. Yeah. Thousands.

LEE. Millions?

AUSTIN. Well—

LEE. We could get the old man outa' hock then.

AUSTIN. Maybe.

LEE. Maybe? Whadya' mean, maybe?

AUSTIN. I mean it might take more than money.

LEE. You were just tellin' me it'd change my whole life around. Why wouldn't it change his?

AUSTIN. He's different.

LEE. Oh, he's of a different ilk huh?

AUSTIN. He's not gonna' change. Let's leave the old man out of it.

LEE. That's right. He's not gonna' change but I will. I'll just turn myself right inside out. I could be just like you then, huh? Sittin' around dreamin' stuff up. Gettin' paid to dream. Ridin' back and forth on the freeway just dreamin' my fool head off.

AUSTIN. It's not all that easy.

LEE. It's not, huh?

AUSTIN. No. There's a lot of work involved.

LEE. What's the toughest part? Deciding whether to jog or play tennis?

(*Long pause*)

AUSTIN. Well, look. You can stay here—do whatever you want to. Borrow the car. Come in and out. Doesn't matter to me. It's not my house. I'll help you write this thing or—not. Just let me know what you want? You tell me.

LEE. Oh. So now suddenly you're at my service. Is that it?

AUSTIN. What do you want to do Lee?

(*Long pause, Lee stares at him then turns and dreams at windows*)

LEE. I tell ya' what I'd do if I still had that dog. Ya' wanna' know what I'd do?

AUSTIN. What?

LEE. Head out to Ventura. Cook up a little match. God that little dog could bear down. Lota' money in dog fightin'. Big money.

(*Pause*)

AUSTIN. Why don't we try to see this through, Lee. Just for the hell of it. Maybe you've really got something here. What do you think?

(*Pause, Lee considers*)

LEE. Maybe so. No harm in tryin' I guess. You think' it's such a hot idea. Besides, I always wondered what'd be like to be you.

AUSTIN. You did?

LEE. Yeah, sure. I used to picture you walkin' around some campus with yer arms fulla' books. Blondes chasin' after ya'.

AUSTIN. Blondes? That's funny.

LEE. What's funny about it?

AUSTIN. Because I always used to picture you somewhere.

LEE. Where'd you picture me?

AUSTIN. Oh, I don't know. Different places. Adventures. You were always on some adventure.

LEE. Yeah.

AUSTIN. And I used to say to myself, "Lee's got the right idea. He's out there in the world and here I am. What am I doing?"

LEE. Well you were settin' yourself up for somethin'.

AUSTIN. I guess.

LEE. We better get started on this thing then.

AUSTIN. Okay.

(*Austin sits up at typewriter, puts new paper in*)

LEE. Oh. Can I get the keys back before I forget?

(*Austin hesitates*)

You said I could borrow the car if I wanted, right? Isn't that what you said?

AUSTIN. Yeah. Right.

(*Austin takes keys out of his pocket, sets them on table, Lee takes keys slowly, plays with them in his hand*)

LEE. I could get a ranch, huh?

AUSTIN. Yeah. We have to write it first though.

LEE. Okay. Let's write it.

(*Lights start dimming slowly to end of scene as Austin types, Lee speaks*)

So they take off after each other straight into an endless black prairie. The sun is just comin' down and they can feel the night on their backs. What they don't know is that each one of 'em is afraid, see. Each one separately thinks that he's the only one that's afraid. And they keep ridin' like that straight into the night. Not knowing. And the one who's chasin' doesn't know where the other one is taking him. And the one who's being chased doesn't know where's he's going.

(*Lights to black, typing stops in the dark, crickets fade*)

ACT TWO

SCENE 5

Morning. Lee at the table in alcove with a set of golf clubs in a fancy leather bag, Austin at sink washing a few dishes.

AUSTIN. He really liked it, huh?

LEE. He wouldn't a' gave me these clubs if he didn't like it.

AUSTIN. He gave you the clubs?

LEE. Yeah. I told ya' he gave me the clubs. The bag too.

AUSTIN. I thought he just loaned them to you.

LEE. He said it was part a' the advance. A little gift like. Gesture of his good faith.

AUSTIN. He's giving you an advance?

LEE. Now what's so amazing about that? I told ya' it was a good story. You even said it was a good story.

AUSTIN. Well that is really incredible Lee. You know how many guys spend their whole lives down here trying to break into this business? Just trying to get in the door?

LEE (*pulling clubs out of bag, testing them*). I got no idea. How many?

(*Pause*)

AUSTIN. How much of an advance is he giving you?

LEE. Plenty. We were talkin' big money out there. Ninth hole is where I sealed the deal.

AUSTIN. He made a firm commitment?

LEE. Absolutely.

AUSTIN. Well, I know Saul and he doesn't fool around when he says he likes something.

LEE. I thought you said you didn't know him.

AUSTIN. Well, I'm familiar with his tastes.

LEE. I let him get two up on me goin' into the back nine. He was sure he had me cold. You shoulda' seen his face when I pulled out the old pitching wedge and plopped it pin-high, two feet from the cup. He 'bout shit his pants. "Where'd a guy like you ever learn how to play golf like that?" he says.

(*Lee laughs, Austin stares at him*)

AUSTIN. 'Course there's no contract yet. Nothing's final until it's on paper.

LEE. It's final, all right. There's no way he's gonna' back out of it now. We gambled for it.

AUSTIN. Saul, gambled?

LEE. Yeah, sure. I mean he liked the outline already so he wasn't risking that much. I just guaranteed it with my short game.

(*Pause*)

AUSTIN. Well, we should celebrate or something. I think Mom left a bottle of champagne in the refrigerator. We should have a little toast.

(*Austin gets glasses from cupboard, goes to refrigerator, pulls out bottle of champagne*)

LEE. You shouldn't oughta' take her champagne, Austin. She's gonna' miss that.

AUSTIN. Oh, she's not going to mind. She'd be glad we put it to good use. I'll get her another bottle. Besides it's perfect for the occasion.

(*Pause*)

LEE. Yer gonna' get a nice fee fer writin' the script a' course. Straight fee.

(*Austin stops, stares at Lee, puts glasses and bottle on table, pause*)

AUSTIN. I'm writing the script?

LEE. That's what he said. Said we couldn't hire a better screenwriter in the whole town.

AUSTIN. But I'm already working on a script. I've got my own project. I don't have time to write two scripts.

LEE. No, he said he was gonna' drop that other one.

(*Pause*)

AUSTIN. What? You mean mine? He's going to drop mine and do yours instead?

LEE. (*smiles*). Now look Austin. it's jest beginner's luck ya' know. I mean I sank a fifty foot putt for this deal. No hard feelings.

(*Austin goes to phone on wall, grabs it, starts dialing*)

He's not gonna' be in, Austin. Told me he wouldn't be in 'till late this afternoon.

AUSTIN (*stays on phone, dialing, listens*). I can't believe this. I just can't believe it. Are you sure he said that? Why would he drop mine?

LEE. That's what he told me.

AUSTIN. He can't do that without telling me first. Without talking to me at least. He wouldn't just make a decision like that without talking to me!

LEE. Well I was kinda' surprised myself. But he was real enthusiastic about my story.

(*Austin hangs up phone violently, paces*)

AUSTIN. What'd he say! Tell me everything he said!

LEE. I been tellin' ya'! He said he liked the story a whole lot. It was the first authentic Western to come along in a decade.

AUSTIN. He liked that story! Your story?

LEE. Yeah! What so surprisin' about that?

AUSTIN. It's stupid! It's the dumbest story I ever heard in my life.

LEE. Hey, hold on! That's my story yer takin' about!

AUSTIN. It's a bullshit story! It's idiotic. Two lamebrains chasing each other across Texas! Are you kidding? Who do you think's going to go see a film like that.

LEE. It's not a film! It's a movie. There's a big difference. That's somethin' Saul told me.

AUSTIN. Oh he did, huh?

LEE. Yeah, he said, "In this business we make movies, American movies. Leave the films to the French."

AUSTIN. So you got real intimate with old Saul huh? He started pouring forth his vast knowledge of Cinema.

LEE. I think he liked me a lot, to tell ya' the truth. I think he felt I was somebody he could confide in.

AUSTIN. What'd you do, beat him up or something?

LEE. (*stands fast*) Hey, I've about had it with the insults buddy! You think yer the only one in the brain department here? Yer the only one that can sit around and cook things up? There's other people got ideas too, ya' know!

AUSTIN. You must've done something. Threatened him or something. Now what'd you do Lee?

LEE. I convinced him!

(*Lee makes sudden menacing lunge toward Austin, wielding golf club above his head, stops himself, frozen moment, long pause, Lee lowers club*)

AUSTIN. Oh, Jesus. You didn't hurt him did you?

(*Long silence, Lee sits back down at table*)

Lee! Did you hurt him?

LEE. I didn't do nothin' to him! He liked my story. Pure and simple. He said it was the best story he's come across in a long, long time.

AUSTIN. That's what he told me about my story! That's the same thing he said to me.

LEE. Well, he musta' been lyin'. He musta' been lyin' to one of us anyway.

AUSTIN. You can't come into this town and start pushing people around. They're gonna' put you away!

LEE. I never pushed anybody around! I beat him fair and square. (*pause*) They can't touch me anyway. They can't put a finger on me. I'm gone. I can come in through the window and go out through the door. They never knew what hit 'em. You, yer stuck. Yer the one that's stuck. Not me. So don't be warnin' me what to do in this town.

(*Pause, Austin crosses to table, sits at typewriter, rests*)

AUSTIN. Lee, come on, level with me will you? It doesn't make any sense that suddenly he'd throw my idea out the window. I've been talking to him for months. I've got too much at stake. Everything's riding on this project.

LEE. What's yer idea?

AUSTIN. It's just a simple love story.

LEE. What kinda' love story?

AUSTIN (*stands, crosses into kitchen*). I'm not telling you!

LEE. Ha! 'Fraid I'll steal it huh? Competition's gettin' kinda' close to home isn't it?

AUSTIN. Where did Saul say he was going?

LEE. He was gonna' take my story to a couple studios.

AUSTIN. That's *my* outline you know! I wrote that outline! You've got no right to be peddling it around.

LEE. You weren't ready to take credit for it last night.

AUSTIN. Give me my keys!

LEE. What?

AUSTIN. The keys! I want my keys back!

LEE. Where you goin'?

AUSTIN. Just give me my keys! I gotta' take a drive. I gotta' get out of here for a while.

LEE. Where you gonna' go, Austin?

AUSTIN (*pause*). I might just drive out to the desert for a while. I gotta' think.

LEE. You can think here just as good. This is the perfect setup for thinkin'. We got some writin' to do here, boy. Now let's just have us a little toast. Relax. We're partners now.

(*Lee pops the cork of the champagne bottle, pours two drinks as the lights fade to black*)

SCENE 6

Afternoon. Lee and Saul in kitchen, Austin in alcove

LEE. Now you tell him. You tell him, Mr. Kipper.

SAUL. Kimmer.

LEE. Kimmer. You tell him what you told me. He don't believe me.

AUSTIN. I don't want to hear it.

SAUL. It's really not a big issue, Austin. I was simply amazed by your brother's story and—

AUSTIN. Amazed? You lost a bet! You gambled with my material!

SAUL. That's really beside the point, Austin. I'm ready to go all the way with your brother's story. I think it has a great deal of merit.

AUSTIN. I don't want to hear about it, okay? Go tell it to the executives! Tell it to somebody who's going to turn it into a package deal or something. A T.V. series. Don't tell it to me.

SAUL. But I want to continue with your project too, Austin. It's not as though we can't do both. We're big enough for that aren't we?

AUSTIN. "We"? *I* can't do both! I don't know about "we."

LEE (*to Saul*). See, what'd I tell ya'. He's totally unsympathetic.

SAUL. Austin, there's no point in our going to another screenwriter for this. It just doesn't make sense. You're brothers. You know each other. There's a familiarity with the material that just wouldn't be possible otherwise.

AUSTIN. There's no familiarity with the material! None! I don't know what "Tornado Country" is. I don't know what a "gooseneck" is. And I don't want to know! (*pointing to Lee*) He's a hustler! He's a bigger hustler than you are! If you can't see that, then—

LEE (*to Austin*). Hey, now hold on. I didn't have to bring this bone back to you, boy. I persuaded Saul here that you were the right man for the job. You don't have to go throwin' up favors in my face.

AUSTIN. Favors! I'm the one who wrote the fuckin' outline! You can't even spell.

SAUL (*to Austin*). Your brother told me about the situation with your father.

(*Pause*)

AUSTIN. What? (*looks at Lee*)

SAUL. That's right. Now we have a clear-cut deal here, Austin. We have big studio money standing behind this thing. Just on the basis of your outline.

AUSTIN (*to Saul*). What'd he tell you about my father?

SAUL. Well—that he's destitute. He needs money.

LEE. That's right. He does.

(*Austin shakes his head, stares at them both*)

AUSTIN (*to Lee*). And this little assignment is supposed to go toward the old man? A charity project? Is that what this is? Did you cook this up on the ninth green too?

SAUL. It's a big slice, Austin.

AUSTIN (*to Lee*). I give him money! I already gave him money. You know that. He drank it all up!

LEE. This is a different deal here.

SAUL. We can set up a trust for your father. A large sum of money. It can be doled out to him in parcels so he can't misuse it.

AUSTIN. Yeah, and who's doing the doling?

SAUL. Your brother volunteered.

(*Austin laughs*)

LEE. That's right. I'll make sure he uses it for groceries.

AUSTIN (*to Saul*). I'm not doing this script! I'm not writing this crap for you or anybody else. You can't blackmail me into it. You can't threaten me into it. There's no way I'm doing it. So just give it up. Both of you.

(*Long pause*)

SAUL. Well, that's it then. I mean this is an easy three hundred grand. Just for a first draft. It's incredible, Austin. We've got three different studios all trying to cut each other's throats to get this material. In one morning. That's how hot it is.

AUSTIN. Yeah, well you can afford to give me a percentage on the outline then. And you getter get the genius here an agent before he gets burned.

LEE. Saul's gonna' be my agent. Isn't that right, Saul?

SAUL. That's right. (*to Austin*) Your brother has really got something, Austin. I've been around too long not to recognize it. Raw talent.

AUSTIN. He's got a lota' balls is what he's got. He's taking you right down the river.

SAUL. Three hundred thousand, Austin. Just for a first draft. Now you've never been offered that kind of money before.

AUSTIN. I'm not writing it.

(*Pause*)

SAUL. I see. Well—

LEE. We'll just go to another writer then. Right, Saul? Just hire us somebody with some enthusiasm. Somebody who can recognize the value of a good story.

SAUL. I'm sorry about this, Austin.

AUSTIN. Yeah.

SAUL. I mean I was hoping we could continue both things but now I don't see how it's possible.

AUSTIN. So you're dropping my idea altogether. Is that it? Just trade horses in midstream? After all these months of meetings.

SAUL. I wish there was another way.

AUSTIN. I've got everything riding on this, Saul. You know that. It's my only shot. If this falls through—

SAUL. I have to go with what my instincts tell me—

AUSTIN. Your instincts!

SAUL. My gut reaction.

AUSTIN. You lost! That's your gut reaction. You lost a gamble. Now you're trying to tell me you like his story? How could you possibly fall for that story? It's as phony as Hoppalong Cassidy. What do you see in it. I'm curious.

SAUL. It has the ring of truth, Austin.

AUSTIN (*laughs*). Truth?

LEE. It is true.

SAUL. Something about the real West.

AUSTIN. Why? Because it's got horses? Because it's got grown men acting like little boys?

SAUL. Something about the land. Your brother is speaking from experience.

AUSTIN. So am I!

SAUL. But nobody's interested in love these days, Austin. Let's face it.

LEE. That's right.

AUSTIN (*to Saul*). He's been camped out on the desert for three months. Talking to cactus. What's he know about what people wanna' see on the screen! I drive on the freeway ever day. I swallow the smog. I watch the news in color. I shop in the Safeway. I'm the one who's in touch! Not him!

SAUL. I have to go now, Austin.

(*Saul starts to leave*)

AUSTIN. There's no such thing as the West anymore! It's a dead issue! It's dried up, Saul, and so are you.

(*Saul stops and turns to Austin*)

SAUL. Maybe you're right. But I have to take the gamble, don't I?

AUSTIN. You're a fool to do this, Saul.

SAUL. I've always gone on my hunches. Always. And I've never been wrong. (*to Lee*) I'll talk to you tomorrow, Lee.

LEE. All right, Mr. Kimmer.

SAUL. Maybe we could have some lunch.

LEE. Fine with me. (*smiles at Austin*)

SAUL. I'll give you a ring.

(*Saul exits, lights to black as brothers look at each other from a distance*)

SCENE 7

Night. Coyotes, crickets, sound of typewriter in dark, candlelight up on Lee at typewriter struggling to type with one finger system. Austin sits sprawled out on kitchen floor with whiskey bottle, drunk.

AUSTIN (*singing, from floor*).

> "*Red sails in the sunset*
> *Way out on the blue*
> *Please carry my loved one*
> *Home safely to me*
>
> *Red sails in the sunset—*"

LEE (*slams fist on table*). Hey! Knock it off will ya'! I'm tryin' to concentrate here.

AUSTIN (*laughs*). You're tryin' to concentrate?

LEE. Yeah. That's right.

AUSTIN. Now you're tryin' to concentrate.

LEE. Between you, the coyotes and the crickets a thought don't have much of a chance.

AUSTIN. "Between me, the coyotes and the crickets." What a great title.

LEE. I don't need a title! I need a thought.

AUSTIN (*laughs*). A thought! Here's a thought for ya'—

LEE. I'm not askin' fer yer thoughts! I got my own. I can do this thing on my own.

AUSTIN. You're going to write an entire script on your own?

LEE. That's right.

(*Pause*)

AUSTIN. Here's a thought. Saul Kimmer—

LEE. Shut up will ya'!

AUSTIN. He thinks we're the same person.

LEE. Don't get cute.

AUSTIN. He does! He's lost his mind. Poor old Saul. (*giggles*) Thinks we're one and the same.

LEE. Why don't you ease up on that champagne.

AUSTIN (*holding up bottle*). This isn't champagne anymore. We went through the champagne a long time ago. This is serious stuff. The days of champagne are long gone.

LEE. Well, go outside and drink it.

AUSTIN. I'm enjoying your company, Lee. For the first time since your arrival I am finally enjoying your company. And now you want me to go outside and drink alone?

LEE. That's right.

(*Lee reads through paper in typewriter, makes an erasure*)

AUSTIN. You think you'll make more progress if you're alone? You might drive yourself crazy.

LEE. I could have this thing done in a night if I had a little silence.

AUSTIN. Well you'd still have the crickets to contend with. The coyotes. The sounds of the Police Helicopters prowling above the neighborhood. Slashing their searchlights down through the streets. Hunting for the likes of you.

LEE. I'm a screenwriter now! I'm legitimate.

AUSTIN (*laughing*). A screenwriter!

LEE. That's right. I'm on salary. That's more'n I can say for you. I got an advance coming.

AUSTIN. This is true. This is very true. An advance. (*pause*) Well, maybe I oughta' go out and try my hand at your trade. Since you're doing so good at mine.

LEE. Ha!

(*Lee attempts to type some more but gets the ribbon tangled up, starts trying to re-thread it as they continue talking*)

AUSTIN. Well why not? You don't think I've got what it takes to sneak into people's houses and steal their T.V.s?

LEE. You couldn't steal a toaster without losin' yer lunch.

(*Austin stands with a struggle, supports himself by the sink.*)

AUSTIN. You don't think I could sneak into somebody's house and steal a toaster?

LEE. Go take a shower or somethin' will ya!

(*Lee gets more tangled up with the typewriter ribbon, pulling it out of the machine as though it was fishing line*)

AUSTIN. You really don't think I could steal a crumby toaster? How much you wanna' bet I can't steal a toaster! How much? Go ahead! You're a gambler aren't you? Tell me how much yer willing to put on the line. Some part of your big advance? Oh, you haven't got that yet have you. I forgot.

LEE. All right. I'll bet you your car that you can't steal a toaster without gettin' busted.

AUSTIN. You already got my car!

LEE. Okay, your house then.

AUSTIN. What're you gonna' give me! I'm not talkin' about my house and my car. I'm talkin' about what are you gonna' give me. You don't have nothin' to give me.

LEE. I'll give you—shared screen credit. How 'bout that? I'll have it put in the contract that this was written by the both of us.

AUSTIN. I don't want my name on that piece of shit! I want something of value. You got anything of value? You got any tidbits from the desert? Any Rattlesnake bones? I'm not a greedy man. Any little personal treasure will suffice.

LEE. I'm gonna' just kick yer ass out in a minute.

AUSTIN. Oh, so now you're gonna' kick me out! Now I'm the intruder. I'm the one who's invading your precious privacy.

LEE. I'm trying to do some screenwriting here!!

(*Lee stands, picks up typewriter, slams it down hard on table, pause, silence except for crickets*)

AUSTIN. Well, you got everything you need. You got plenty a' coffee? Groceries. You got a car. A contract. (*pause*) Might need a new typewriter ribbon but other than that you're pretty well fixed. I'll just leave ya' alone for a while.

(*Austin tries to steady himself to leave, Lee makes a move toward him*)

LEE. Where you goin'?

AUSTIN. Don't worry about me. I'm not the one to worry about.

(*Austin weaves toward exit, stops*)

LEE. What're you gonna' do? Just go wander out into the night?

AUSTIN. I'm gonna' make a little tour.

LEE. Why don't ya' just go to bed for Christ's sake. Yer makin' me sick.

AUSTIN. I can take care a' myself. Don't worry about me.

(*Austin weaves badly in another attempt to exit, he crashes to the floor, Lee goes to him but remains standing*)

LEE. You want me to call your wife for ya' or something?

AUSTIN (*from floor*). My wife?

LEE. Yeah. I mean maybe she can help ya' out. Talk to ya' or somethin.'

AUSTIN (*struggles to stand again*). She's five hundred miles away. North. North of here. Up in the North country where things are calm. I don't need any help. I'm gonna' go outside and I'm gonna' steal a toaster. I'm gonna' steal some other stuff too. I might even commit bigger crimes. Bigger than you ever dreamed of. Crimes beyond the imagination!

(*Austin manages to get himself vertical, tries to head for exit again*)

LEE. Just hang on a minute, Austin.

AUSTIN. Why? What for? You don't need my help, right? You got a handle on the project. Besides, I'm lookin' forward to the smell of the night. The bushes. Orange blossoms. Dust in the driveways. Rain bird sprinklers. Lights in people's houses. You're right about the lights, Lee. Everybody else is livin' the life. Indoors. Safe. This is a Paradise down here. You know that? We're livin' in a Paradise. We've forgotten about that.

LEE. You sound just like the old man now.

AUSTIN. Yeah, well we all sound alike when we're sloshed. We just sorta' echo each other.

LEE. Maybe if we could work on this together we could bring him back out here. Get him settled down some place.

(*Austin turns violently toward Lee, takes a swing at him, misses and crashes to the floor again, Lee stays standing*)

AUSTIN. I don't want him out here! I've had it with him! I went all the way out there! I went out of my way. I gave him money and all he did was play Al Jolson records and spit at me! I gave him money!

(*Pause*)

LEE. Just help me a little with the characters, all right? You know how to do it, Austin.

AUSTIN (*on floor, laughs*). The characters!

LEE. Yeah. You know. The way they talk and stuff. I can hear it in my head but I can't get it down on paper.

AUSTIN. What characters?

LEE. The guys. The guys in the story.

AUSTIN. Those aren't characters.

LEE. Whatever you call 'em then. I need to write somethin' out.

AUSTIN. Those are illusions of characters.

LEE. I don't give a damn what ya' call 'em! You know what I'm talkin' about!

AUSTIN. Those are fantasies of a long lost boyhood.

LEE. I gotta' write somethin' out on paper!!

(*Pause*)

AUSTIN. What for? Saul's gonna' get you a fancy screenwriter isn't he?

LEE. I wanna' do it myself!

AUSTIN. Then do it! Yer on your own now, old buddy. You bulldogged yer way into contention. Now you gotta' carry it through.

LEE. I will but I need some advice. Just a couple a' things. Come on, Austin. Just help me get 'em talkin' right. It won't take much.

AUSTIN. Oh, now you're having a little doubt huh? What happened? The pressure's on, boy. This is it. You gotta' come up with it now. You don't come up with a winner on your first time out they just cut your head off. They don't give you a second chance ya' know.

LEE. I got a good story! I know it's a good story. I just need a little help is all.

AUSTIN. Not from me. Not from yer little old brother. I'm retired.

LEE. You could save this thing for me, Austin. I'd give ya' half the money. I would. I only need half anyway. With this kinda' money I could be a long time down the road. I'd never bother ya' again. I promise. You'd never even see me again.

AUSTIN (*still on floor*). You'd disappear?

LEE. I would for sure.

AUSTIN. Where would you disappear to?

LEE. That don't matter. I got plenty a' places.

AUSTIN. Nobody can disappear. The old man tried that. Look where it got him. He lost his teeth.

LEE. He never had any money.

AUSTIN. I don't mean that. I mean his teeth! His real teeth. First he lost his real teeth, then he lost his false teeth. You never knew that did ya'? He never confided in you.

LEE. Nah, I never knew that.

AUSTIN. You wanna' drink?

(*Austin offers bottle to Lee, Lee takes it, sits down on kitchen floor with Austin, they share the bottle*)

Yeah, he lost his real teeth one at a time. Woke up every morning with another tooth lying on the mattress. Finally, he decides he's gotta' get 'em all pulled out but he doesn't have any money. Middle of Arizona with no money and no insurance and every morning another tooth is lying on the mattress. (*takes a drink*) So what does he do?

LEE. I dunno'. I never knew about that.

AUSTIN. He begs the government, G.I. Bill or some damn thing. Some pension plan he remembers in the back of his head. And they send him out the money.

LEE. They did?

(*They keep trading the bottle between them, taking drinks*)

AUSTIN. Yeah, They send him the money but it's not enough money. Costs a lot to have all yer teeth yanked. They charge by the individual tooth, ya' know. I mean one tooth isn't equal to another tooth. Some are more expensive. Like the big ones in the back—

LEE. So what happened?

AUSTIN. So he locates a Mexican dentist in Juarez who'll do the whole thing for a song. And he takes off hitchhiking to the border.

LEE. Hitchhiking?

AUSTIN. Yeah. So how long you think it takes him to get to the border? A man his age.

LEE. I dunno.

AUSTIN. Eight days it takes him. Eight days in the rain and the sun and every day he's droppin' teeth on the blacktop and nobody'll pick him up 'cause his mouth's full a' blood.

(*Pause, they drink*)

So finally he stumbles into the dentist. Dentist takes all his money and all his teeth. And there he is, in Mexico, with his gums sewed up and his pockets empty.

(*Long silence, Austin drinks*)

LEE. That's it?

AUSTIN. Then I go out to see him, see. I go out there and I take him out for a nice Chinese dinner. But he doesn't eat. All he wants to do is drink Martinis outa' plastic cups. And he takes his teeth out and lays 'em on the table 'cause he can't stand the feel of 'em. And we ask the waitress for one a' those doggie bags to take the Chop Suey home in. So he drops his teeth in the doggie bag along with the Chop Suey. And then we go out to hit all the bars up and down the highway. Says he wants to introduce me to all his buddies. And in one a' those bars, in one a' those bars up and down the highway, he left that doggie bag with his teeth laying in the Chop Suey.

LEE. You never found it?

AUSTIN. We went back but we never did find it. (*pause*) Now that's a true story. True to life.

(*They drink as lights fade to black*)

SCENE 8

Very early morning, between night and day. No crickets, coyotes yapping feverishly in distance before light comes up, a small fire blazes up in the dark from alcove area, sound of Lee smashing typewriter with a golf club, lights coming up, Lee seen smashing typewriter methodically then dropping pages of his script into a burning bowl set on the floor of alcove, flames leap up, Austin has a whole bunch of stolen toasters lined up on the sink counter along with Lee's stolen T.V., the toasters are of a wide variety of models, mostly chrome, Austin goes up and down the line of toasters, breathing on them and polishing them with a dish towel, both men are drunk, empty whiskey bottles and

beer cans litter floor of kitchen, they share a half empty bottle on one of the chairs in the alcove, Lee keeps periodically taking deliberate ax-chops at the typewriter using a nine-iron as Austin speaks, all of their mother's house plants are dead and drooping.

AUSTIN (*polishing toasters*). There's gonna' be a general lack of toast in the neighborhood this morning. Many, many unhappy, bewildered breakfast faces. I guess it's best not to even think of the victims. Not to even entertain it. Is that the right psychology?

LEE (*pauses*). What?

AUSTIN. Is that the correct criminal psychology? Not to think of the victims?

LEE. What victims?

(*Lee takes another swipe at typewriter with nine-iron, adds pages to the fire*)

AUSTIN. The victims of crime. Of breaking and entering. I mean is it a prerequisite for a criminal not to have a conscience?

LEE. Ask a criminal.

(*Pause, Lee stares at Austin*)

What're you gonna' do with all those toasters? That's the dumbest thing I ever saw in my life.

AUSTIN. I've got hundreds of dollars worth of household appliances here. You may not realize that.

LEE. Yeah, and how many hundreds of dollars did you walk right past?

AUSTIN. It was toasters you challenged me to. Only toasters. I ignored every other temptation.

LEE. I never challenged you! That's no challenge. Anybody can steal a toaster.

(*Lee smashes typewriter again*)

AUSTIN. You don't have to take it out on my typewriter ya' know. It's not the machine's fault that you can't write. It's a sin to do that to a good machine.

LEE. A sin?

AUSTIN. When you consider all the writers who never even had a machine. Who would have given an eyeball for a good typewriter. Any typewriter.

(*Lee smashes typewriter again*)

AUSTIN (*polishing toasters*). All the ones who wrote on matchbook covers. Paper bags. Toilet paper. Who had their writing destroyed by their jailers. Who persisted beyond all odds. Those writers would find it hard to understand your actions.

(*Lee comes down on typewriter with one final crushing blow of the nine-iron then collapses in one of the chairs, takes a drink from bottle, pause*)

AUSTIN (*after pause*). Not to mention demolishing a perfectly good golf club. What about all the struggling golfers? What about Lee Trevino? What do you think he would've said when he was batting balls around with broomsticks at the age of nine. Impoverished.

(*Pause*)

LEE. What time is it anyway?

AUSTIN. No idea. Time stands still when you're havin' fun.

LEE. Is it too late to call a woman? You know any women?

AUSTIN. I'm a married man.

LEE. I mean a local woman.

(*Austin looks out at light through window above sink*)

AUSTIN. It's either too late or too early. You're the nature enthusiast. Can't you tell the time by the light in the sky? Orient yourself around the North Star or something?

LEE. I can't tell anything.

AUSTIN. Maybe you need a little breakfast. Some toast! How 'bout some toast?

(*Austin goes to cupboard, pulls out loaf of bread and starts dropping slices into every toaster, Lee stays sitting, drinks, watches Austin*)

LEE. I don't need toast. I need a woman.

AUSTIN. A woman isn't the answer. Never was.

LEE. I'm not talkin' about permanent. I'm talkin' about temporary.

AUSTIN (*putting toast in toasters*). We'll just test the merits of these little demons. See which brands have a tendency to burn. See which one can produce a perfectly golden piece of fluffy toast.

LEE. How much gas you got in yer car?

AUSTIN. I haven't driven my car for days now. So I haven't had the opportunity to look at the gas gauge.

LEE. Take a guess. You think there's enough to get me to Bakersfield?

AUSTIN. Bakersfield? What's in Bakersfield?

LEE. Just never mind what's in Bakersfield! You think there's enough goddamn gas in the car!

AUSTIN. Sure.

LEE. Sure. You could care less, right. Let me run outa' gas on the Grapevine. You could give a shit.

AUSTIN. I'd say there was enough gas to get you just about anywhere, Lee. With your determination and guts.

LEE. What the hell time is it anyway?

(*Lee pulls out his wallet, starts going through dozens of small pieces of paper with phone numbers written on them, drops some on the floor, drops others in the fire*)

AUSTIN. Very early. This is the time of morning when the coyotes kill people's cocker spaniels. Did you hear them? That's what they were doing out there. Luring innocent pets away form their homes.

LEE. (*searching through his papers*) What's the area code for Bakersfield? You know?

AUSTIN. You could always call the operator.

LEE. I can't stand that voice they give ya'.

AUSTIN. What voice?

LEE. That voice that warns you that if you'd only tried harder to find the number in the phone book you wouldn't have to be calling the operator to begin with.

(*Lee gets up, holding a slip of paper from his wallet, stumbles toward phone on wall, yanks receiver, starts dialing*)

AUSTIN. Well I don't understand why you'd want to talk to anybody else anyway. I mean you can talk to me. I'm your brother.

LEE (*dialing*). I wanna' talk to a woman. I haven't heard a woman's voice in a long time.

AUSTIN. Not since the Botanist?

LEE. What?

AUSTIN. Nothing. (*starts singing as he tends toast*)

> "Red sails in the sunset
> Way out on the blue
> Please carry my loved one
> Home safely to me"

LEE. Hey, knock it off will ya'! This is long distance here.

AUSTIN. Bakersfield?

LEE. Yeah, Bakersfield. It's Kern County.

AUSTIN. Well, what County are *we* in?

LEE. You better get yourself a 7-Up, boy.

AUSTIN. One County's as good as another.

(*Austin hums "Red Sails" softly as Lee talks on phone*)

LEE (*to phone*). Yeah, operator look—first off I wanna' know the area code for Bakersfield. Right. Bakersfield! Okay. Good. Now I wanna' know if you can help me track somebody down. (*pause*) No, no I mean a phone number. Just a phone number. Okay. (*holds a piece of paper up and reads it*) Okay, the name is Melly Ferguson. Melly. (*pause*) I dunno'. Melly. Maybe. Yeah. Maybe Melanie. Yeah. Melanie Ferguson. Okay. (*pause*) What? I can't hear ya' so good. Sounds like yer under the ocean. (*pause*) You got ten Melanie Fergusons? How could that be? Ten Melanie Fergusons in Bakersfield? Well gimme all of 'em then. (*pause*) What d'ya' mean? Gimme all ten Melanie Fergusons! That's right. Just a second. (*to Austin*) Gimme a pen.

AUSTIN. I don't have a pen.

LEE. Gimme a pencil then!

AUSTIN. I don't have a pencil.

LEE (*to phone*). Just a second, operator. (*to Austin*) Yer a writer and ya' don't have a pen or a pencil!

AUSTIN. I'm, not a writer. You're a writer.

LEE. I'm on the phone here! Get me a pen or a pencil.

AUSTIN. I gotta' watch the toast.

LEE (*to phone*). Hang on a second, operator.

(*Lee lets the phone drop then starts pulling all the drawers in the kitchen out on the floor and dumping the contents, searching for a pencil, Austin watches him casually*)

LEE (*crashing through drawers, throwing contents around kitchen*). This is the last time I try to live with people, boy! I can't believe it. Here I am! Here I am again in a desperate situation! This would never happen out on the desert. I would never be in this kinda' situation out on the desert. Isn't there a pen or a pencil in this house! Who lives in this house anyway!

AUSTIN. Our mother.

LEE. How come she don't have a pen or a pencil! She's a social person isn't she? Doesn't she have to make shopping lists? She's gotta' have a pencil. (*finds a pencil*) Aaha! (*he rushes back to phone, picks up receiver*) All right operator. Operator? Hey! Operator! Goddamnit!

(*Lee rips the phone off the wall and throws it down, goes back to chair and falls into it, drinks, long pause*)

AUSTIN. She hung up?

LEE. Yeah, she hung up. I knew she was gonna' hang up. I could hear it in her voice.

(*Lee starts going through his slips of paper again*)

AUSTIN. Well, you're probably better off staying here with me anyway. I'll take care of you.

LEE. I don't need takin' care of! Not by you anyway.

AUSTIN. Toast is almost ready.

(*Austin starts buttering all the toast as it pops up*)

LEE. I don't want any toast!

(*Long pause*)

AUSTIN. You gotta' eat something. Can't just drink. How long have we been drinking, anyway?

LEE (*looking through slips of paper*). Maybe it was Fresno. What's the area code for Fresno? How could I have lost that number! She was beautiful.

(*Pause*)

AUSTIN. Why don't you just forget about that, Lee. Forget about that woman.

LEE. She had green eyes. You know what green eyes do to me?

AUSTIN. I know but you're not gonna' get in on with her now anyway. It's dawn already. She's in Bakersfield for Christ's sake.

(*Long pause, Lee considers the situation*)

LEE. Yeah. (*looks at windows*) It's dawn?

AUSTIN. Let's just have some toast and—

LEE. What is this bullshit with the toast anyway! You make it sound like salvation or something. I don't want any god-damn toast! How many times I gotta' tell ya'! (*Lee gets up, crosses upstage to windows in alcove, looks out, Austin butters toast*)

AUSTIN. Well it is like salvation sort of. I mean the smell. I love the smell of toast. And the sun's coming up. It makes me feel like anything's possible. Ya' know?

LEE (*back to Austin, facing windows upstage*). So go to church why don't ya'.

AUSTIN. Like a beginning. I love beginnings.

LEE. Oh, yeah. I've always been kinda' partial to endings myself.

AUSTIN. What if I come with you, Lee?

LEE (*pause as Lee turns toward Austin*). What?

AUSTIN. What if I come with you out to the desert?

LEE. Are you kiddin'?

AUSTIN. No. I'd just like to see what it's like.

LEE. You wouldn't last a day out there pal.

AUSTIN. That's what you said about the toasters. You said I couldn't steal a toaster either.

LEE. A toaster's got nothin' to do with the desert.

AUSTIN. I could make it, Lee. I'm not that helpless. I can cook.

LEE. Cook?

AUSTIN. I can.

LEE. So what! You can cook. Toast.

AUSTIN. I can make fires. I know how to get fresh water from condensation.

(*Austin stacks buttered toast up in a tall stack on plate*)

(*Lee slams table*)

LEE. It's not somethin' you learn out of a Boy Scout handbook!

AUSTIN. Well how do you learn it then! How're are you supposed to learn it!

(*Pause*)

LEE. Ya' just learn it, that's all. Ya' learn it 'cause ya' have to learn it. You don't *have* to learn it.

AUSTIN. You could teach me.

LEE (*stands*). What're you, crazy or somethin'? You went to college. Here, you are down here, rollin' in bucks. Floatin' up and down in elevators. And you wanna' learn how to live on the desert!

AUSTIN. I do, Lee. I really do. There's nothin' down here for me. There never was. When we were kids here it was different. There was a life here then. But now—I keep comin' down here thinkin' it's the fifties or somethin'. I keep finding myself getting off the freeway at familiar landmarks that turn out to be unfamiliar. On the way to appointments. Wandering down streets I thought I recognized that turn out to be replicas of streets I remember. Streets I misremember. Streets I can't tell if I lived on or saw in a postcard. Fields that don't even exist anymore.

LEE. There's no point cryin' about that now.

AUSTIN. There's nothin' real down here, Lee! Least of all me!

LEE. Well I can't save you from that!

AUSTIN. You can let me come with you.

LEE. No dice, pal.

AUSTIN. You could let me come with you, Lee!

LEE. Hey, do you actually think I chose to live out in the middle a' nowhere? Do ya'? Ya' think it's some kinda' philosophical decision I took or somethin'? I'm livin' out there 'cause I can't make it here! And yer bitchin' to me about all yer success!

AUSTIN. I'd cash it all in in a second. That's the truth.

LEE (*pause, shakes his head*). I can't believe this.

AUSTIN. Let me go with you.

LEE. Stop sayin' that will ya'! Yer worse than a dog.

(*Austin offers out the plate of neatly stacked toast to Lee*)

AUSTIN. You want some toast?

(*Lee suddenly explodes and knocks the plate out of Austin's hand, toast goes flying, long frozen moment where it appears Lee might go all the way this time when Austin breaks it by slowly lowering himself to his knees and begins gathering the scattered toast from the floor and stacking it back on the plate, Lee begins to circle Austin in a low, predatory way, crushing pieces of toast in his wake, no words for a while, Austin keeps gathering toast, even the crushed pieces*)

LEE. Tell ya' what I'll do, little brother. I might just consider makin' you a deal. Little trade. (*Austin continues gathering toast as Lee circles him through this*) You write me up this screenplay thing just like I tell ya'. I mean you can use all yer usual tricks and stuff. Yer fancy language. Yer artistic hocus pocus. But ya' gotta' write everything like I say. Every move. Every time they run outa' gas, they run outa' gas. Every time they wanna' jump on a horse, they do just that. If they wanna' stay in Texas, by God they'll stay in Texas! (*Keeps circling*) And you finish the whole thing up for me. Top to bottom. And you put my name on it. And I own all the rights. And every dime goes in my pocket. You do that and I'll sure enough take ya' with me to the desert. (*Lee stops, pause, looks down at Austin*) How's that sound?

(*Pause as Austin stands slowly holding plate of demolished toast, their faces are very close, pause*)

AUSTIN. It's a deal.

(*Lee stares straight into Austin's eyes, then he slowly takes a piece of toast off the plate, raises it to his mouth and takes a huge crushing bite never taking his eyes off Austin's, as Lee crunches into the toast the lights black out*)

SCENE 9

Mid-day. No sound, blazing heat, the stage is ravaged; bottles, toasters, smashed typewriter, ripped out telephone, etc. All the debris from previous scene is now starkly visi- *ble in intense yellow light, the effect should be like a desert junkyard at high noon, the coolness of the preceding scenes is totally obliterated. Austin is seated at table in alcove, shirt open, pouring with sweat, hunched over a writing notebook, scribbling notes desperately with a ballpoint pen. Lee with no shirt, beer in hand, sweat pouring down his chest, is walking a slow circle around the table, picking his way through the objects, sometimes kicking them aside.*

LEE (*as he walks*). All right, read it back to me. Read it back to me!

AUSTIN (*scribbling at top speed*). Just a second.

LEE. Come on, come on! Just read what ya' got.

AUSTIN. I can't keep up! It's not the same as if I had a typewriter.

LEE. Just read what we got so far. Forget about the rest.

AUSTIN. All right. Let's see—okay—(*wipes sweat from his face, reads as Lee circles*) Luke says uh—

LEE. Luke?

AUSTIN. Yeah.

LEE. His name's Luke? All right, all right—we can change the names later. What's he say? Come on, come on.

AUSTIN. He says uh— (*reading*) "I told ya' you were a fool to follow me in here. I know this prairie like the back a' my hand."

LEE. No, no, no! That's not what I said. I never said that.

AUSTIN. That's what I wrote.

LEE. It's not what I said. I never said "like the back a' my hand." That's stupid. That's one a' those—whadya' call it? Whadya' call that?

AUSTIN. What?

LEE. Whadya' call it when somethin's been said a thousand times before. Whadya' call that?

AUSTIN. Um—a cliché?

LEE. Yeah. That's right. Cliché. That's what that is. A cliché. "The back a' my hand." That's stupid.

AUSTIN. That's what you said.

LEE. I never said that! And even if I did, that's where yer supposed to come in. That's where yer suppose to change it to somethin' better.

AUSTIN. Well how am I supposed to do that and write down what you say at the same time?

LEE. Ya' just do, that's all! You hear a stupid line you change it. That's yer job.

AUSTIN. All right. (*makes more notes*)

LEE. What're you changin' it to?

AUSTIN. I'm not changing it. I'm just trying to catch up.

LEE. Well change it! We gotta' change that, we can't leave that in there like that. ". . . the back a' my hand." That's dumb.

AUSTIN (*stops writing, sits back*). All right.

LEE (*pacing*). So what'll we change it to?

AUSTIN. Um—How 'bout —"I'm on intimate terms with this prairie."

LEE (*to himself considering line as he walks*). "I'm on intimate terms with this prairie." Intimate terms, intimate terms. Intimate—that means like uh—sexual right?

AUSTIN. Well—yeah—or—

LEE. He's on sexual terms with the prairie? How dya' figure that?

AUSTIN. Well it doesn't necessarily have to mean sexual.

LEE. What's it mean then?

AUSTIN. It means uh—close—personal—

LEE. All right. How's it sound? Put it into the uh—the line there. Read it back. Let's see how it sounds. (*to himself*) "Intimate terms."

AUSTIN (*scribbles in notebook*). Okay. It'd go something like this: (*reads*) "I told ya' you were a fool to follow me in here. I'm on intimate terms with this prairie."

LEE. That's good. I like that. That's real good.

AUSTIN. You do?

LEE. Yeah. Don't you?

AUSTIN. Sure.

LEE. Sounds original now. "Intimate terms." That's good. Okay. Now we're cookin! That has a real ring to it.

(*Austin makes more notes, Lee walks around, pours beer on his arms and rubs it over his chest feeling good about the new progress, as he does this Mom enters unobtrusively down left with her luggage, she stops and stares at the scene still holding luggage as the two men continue, un- aware of her presence, Austin absorbed in his writing, Lee cooling himself off with beer*)

LEE (*continues*). "He's on intimate terms with this prairie." Sounds real mysterious and kinda' threatening at the same time.

AUSTIN (*writing rapidly*). Good.

LEE. Now—(*Lee turns and suddenly sees Mom, he stares at her for a while, she stares back, Austin keeps writing feverishly, not noticing, Lee walks slowly over to Mom and takes a closer look, long pause*)

LEE. Mom?

(*Austin looks up suddenly from his writing, sees Mom, stands quickly, long pause, Mom surveys the damage*)

AUSTIN. Mom. What're you doing back?

MOM. I'm back.

LEE. Here, lemme take those for ya.

(*Lee sets beer on counter then takes both her bags but doesn't know where to set them down in the sea of junk so he just keeps holding them*)

AUSTIN. I wasn't expecting you back so soon. I thought uh— How was Alaska?

MOM. Fine.

LEE. See any igloos?

MOM. No. Just glaciers.

AUSTIN. Cold huh?

MOM. What?

AUSTIN. It must've been cold up there?

MOM. Not really.

LEE. Musta' been colder than this here. I mean we're havin' a real scorcher here.

MOM. Oh? (*she looks at damage*)

LEE. Yeah. Must be in the hundreds.

AUSTIN. You wanna' take your coat off, Mom?

MOM. No. (*pause, she surveys space*) What happened in here?

AUSTIN. Oh um—Me and Lee were just sort of celebrating and uh—

MOM. Celebrating?

AUSTIN. Yeah. Uh—Lee sold a screenplay. A story, I mean.

MOM. Lee did?

AUSTIN. Yeah.

MOM. Not you?

AUSTIN. No. Him.

MOM (*to Lee*). You sold a screenplay?

LEE. Yeah. That's right. We're just sorta' finishing it up right now. That's what we're doing here.

AUSTIN. Me and Lee are going out to the desert to live.

MOM. You and Lee?

AUSTIN. Yeah. I'm taking off with Lee.

MOM (*she looks back and forth at each of them, pause*). You gonna go live with your father?

AUSTIN. No. We're going to a different desert Mom.

MOM. I see. Well, you'll probably wind up on the same desert sooner or later. What're all these toasters doing here?

AUSTIN. Well—we had kind of a contest.

MOM. Contest?

LEE. Yeah.

AUSTIN. Lee won.

MOM. Did you win a lot of money, Lee?

LEE. Well not yet. It's comin' in any day now.

MOM (*to Lee*). What happened to your shirt?

LEE. Oh. I was sweatin' like a pig and I took it off.

(*Austin grabs Lee's shirt off the table and tosses it to him, Lee sets down suitcases and puts his shirt on*)

MOM. Well it's one hell of a mess in here isn't it?

AUSTIN. Yeah, I'll clean it up for you, Mom. I just didn't know you were coming back so soon.

MOM. I didn't either.

AUSTIN. What happened?

MOM. Nothing. I just started missing all my plants.

(*She notices dead plants*)

AUSTIN. Oh.

MOM. Oh, they're all dead aren't they. (*she crosses toward them, examines them closely*) You didn't get a chance to water I guess.

AUSTIN. I was doing it and then Lee came and—

LEE. Yeah I just distracted him a whole lot here, Mom. It's not his fault.

(*Pause, as Mom stares at plants*)

MOM. Oh, well, one less thing to take care of I guess. (*turns toward brothers*) Oh, that reminds me— You boys will probably never guess who's in town. Try and guess.

(*Long pause, brothers stare at her*)

AUSTIN. Whadya' mean, Mom?

MOM. Take a guess. Somebody very important has come to town. I read it, coming down on the Greyhound.

LEE. Somebody very important?

MOM. See if you can guess. You'll never guess.

AUSTIN. Mom—we're trying to uh—(*points to writing pad*)

MOM. Picasso. (*pause*) Picasso's in town. Isn't that incredible? Right now.

(*Pause*)

AUSTIN. Picasso's dead, Mom.

MOM. No, he's not dead. He's visiting the museum. I read it on the bus. We have to go down there and see him.

AUSTIN. Mom—

MOM. This is a chance of a lifetime. Can you imagine? We could all go down and meet him. All three of us.

LEE. Uh—I don't think I'm really up fer meetin' anybody right now. I'm uh— What's his name?

MOM. Picasso! Picasso! You've never heard of Piccaso? Austin, you've heard of Picasso.

AUSTIN. Mom, we're not going to have time.

MOM. It won't take long. We'll just hop in the car and go down there. An opportunity like this doesn't come along every day.

AUSTIN. We're gonna' be leavin' here, Mom!

(*Pause*)

MOM. Oh.

LEE. Yeah.

(*Pause*)

MOM. You're both leaving?

LEE (*looks at Austin*). Well we were thinkin' about that before but now I—

AUSTIN. No, we are! We're both leaving. We've got it all planned.

MOM (*to Austin*). Well you can't leave. You have a family.

AUSTIN. I'm leaving. I'm getting out of here.

LEE (*to Mom*). I don't really think Austin's cut out for the desert do you?

MOM. No. He's not.

AUSTIN. I'm going with you, Lee!

MOM. He's too thin.

LEE. Yeah, he'd just burn up out there.

AUSTIN (*to Lee*). We just gotta' finish this screenplay and then we're gonna' take off. That's the plan. That's what you said. Come on, let's get back to work, Lee.

LEE. I can't work under these conditions here. It's too hot.

AUSTIN. Then we'll do it on the desert.

LEE. Don't be tellin' me what we're gonna do!

MOM. Don't shout in the house.

LEE. We're just gonna' have to postpone the whole deal.

AUSTIN. I can't postpone it! It's gone past postponing! I'm doing everything you said. I'm writing down exactly what you tell me.

LEE. Yeah, but you were right all along see. It is a dumb story. "Two lamebrains chasin' each other across Texas." That's what you said, right?

AUSTIN. I never said that.

(*Lee sneers in Austin's face then turns to Mom*)

LEE. I'm gonna just borrow some a' your antiques, Mom. You don't mind do ya'? Just a few plates and things. Silverware.

(*Lee starts going through all the cupboards in kitchen pulling out plates and stacking them on counter as Mom and Austin watch*)

MOM. You don't have any utensils on the desert?

LEE. Nah, I'm fresh out.

AUSTIN (*to Lee*). What're you doing?

MOM. Well some of those are very old. Bone China.

LEE. I'm tired of eatin' outa' my bare hands, ya' know. It's not civilized.

AUSTIN (*to Lee*). What're you doing? We made a deal!

MOM. Couldn't you borrow the plastic ones instead? I have plenty of plastic ones.

LEE (*as he stacks plates*). It's not the same. Plastic's not the same at all. What I need is somethin' authentic. Somethin' to keep me in touch. It's easy to get outa' touch out there. Don't worry I'll get em' back to ya'.

(*Austin rushes up to Lee, grabs him by shoulders*)

AUSTIN. You can't just drop the whole thing, Lee!

(*Lee turns, pushes Austin in the chest knocking him backwards into the alcove, Mom watches numbly, Lee returns to collecting the plates, silverware, etc.*)

MOM. You boys shouldn't fight in the house. Go outside and fight.

LEE. I'm not fightin'. I'm leavin'.

MOM. There's been enough damage done already.

LEE (*his back to Austin and Mom, stacking dishes on counter*). I'm clearin' outa' here once and for all. All this town does is drive a man insane. Look what it's done to Austin there. I'm not lettin' that happen to me. Sell myself down the river. No sir. I'd rather be a hundred miles from nowhere than let that happen to me.

(*During this Austin has picked up the ripped-out phone from the floor and wrapped the cord tightly around both his*

*hands, he lunges at Lee whose back is still to him, wraps
the cord around Lee's neck, plants a foot in Lee's back and
pulls back on the cord, tightening it, Lee chokes desperately, can't speak and can't reach Austin with his arms,
Austin keeps applying pressure on Lee's back with his foot,
bending him into the sink, Mom watches)*

AUSTIN (*tightening cord*). You're not goin' anywhere! You're
not takin' anything with you. You're not takin' my car!
You're not takin' the dishes! You're not takin' anything!
You're stayin' right here!

MOM. You'll have to stop fighting in the house. There's
plenty of room outside to fight. You've got the whole outdoors to fight in.

*(Lee tries to tear himself away, he crashes across the stage
like an enraged bull dragging Austin with him, he snorts
and bellows but Austin hangs on and manages to keep
clear of Lee's attempts to grab him, they crash into the
table, to the floor, Lee is face down thrashing wildly and
choking, Austin pulls cord tighter, stands with one foot
planted on Lee's back and the cord stretched taut)*

AUSTIN (*holding cord*). Gimme back my keys, Lee! Take the
keys out! Take 'em out!

*(Lee desperately tries to dig in his pockets, searching for
the car keys, Mom move closer)*

MOM (*calmly to Austin*). You're not killing him are you?

AUSTIN. I don't know. I don't know if I'm killing him. I'm
stopping him. That's all. I'm just stopping him.

(Lee thrashes but Austin is relentless)

MOM. You oughta' let him breathe a little bit.

AUSTIN. Throw the keys out, Lee!

*(Lee finally gets keys out and throws them on floor but out
of Austin's reach, Austin keeps pressure on cord, pulling
Lee's neck back, Lee gets one hand to the cord, but can't
relieve the pressure)*

Reach me those keys would ya' Mom.

MOM (*not moving*). Why are you doing this to him?

AUSTIN. Reach me the keys!

MOM. Not until you stop choking him.

AUSTIN. I can't stop choking him! He'll kill me if I stop
choking him!

MOM. He won't kill you. He's your brother.

AUSTIN. Just get me the keys would ya'!

*(Pause. Mom picks keys up off floor, hands them to
Austin)*

AUSTIN (*to Mom*). Thanks.

MOM. Will you let him go now?

AUSTIN. I don't know. He's not gonna' let me get outa' here.

MOM. Well you can't kill him.

AUSTIN. I can kill him! I can easily kill him. Right now.
Right here. All I gotta' do is just tighten up. See? (*he
tightens cord, Lee thrashes wildly, Austin releases pressure a
little, maintaining control*) Ya' see that?

MOM. That's a savage thing to do.

AUSTIN. Yeah well don't tell me I can't kill him because I
can. I can just twist. I can just keep twisting. (*Austin
twists the cord tighter, Lee weakens, his breathing changes to a
short rasp*)

MOM. Austin!

*(Austin relieves pressure, Lee breathes easier but Austin
keeps him under control)*

AUSTIN (*eyes on Lee, holding cord*). I'm goin' to the desert.
There's nothing stopping me. I'm going by myself to the
desert.

(Mom moving toward her luggage)

MOM. Well, I'm going to check into a motel. I can't stand
this anymore.

AUSTIN. Don't go yet!

(Mom pauses)

MOM. I can't stay here. This is worse than being homeless.

AUSTIN. I'll get everything fixed up for you, Mom. I promise.
Just stay for a while.

MOM (*picking up luggage*). You're going to the desert.

AUSTIN. Just wait!

*(Lee thrashes, Austin subdues him, Mom watches holding
luggage, pause)*

MOM. It was the worst feeling being up there. In Alaska.
Staring out a window. I never felt so desperate before.
That's why when I saw that article on Picasso I
thought—

AUSTIN. Stay here, Mom. This is where you live.

(She looks around the stage)

MOM. I don't recognize it at all.

*(She exits with luggage, Austin makes a move toward her
but Lee starts to struggle and Austin subdues him again
with cord, pause)*

AUSTIN (*holding cord*). Lee? I'll make ya' a deal. You let me
get outa' here. Just let me get to my car. All right, Lee?
Gimme a little headstart and I'll turn you loose. Just
gimme a little headstart. All right?

(*Lee makes no response, Austin slowly releases tension cord, still nothing from Lee*)

AUSTIN. Lee?

(*Lee is motionless, Austin very slowly begins to stand, still keeping a tenuous hold on the cord and his eyes riveted to Lee for any sign of movement, Austin slowly drops the cord and stands, he stares down at Lee who appears to be dead*)

AUSTIN (*whispers*). Lee?

(*Pause, Austin considers, looks toward exit, back to Lee, then makes a small movement as if to leave. Instantly Lee is on his feet and moves toward exit, blocking Austin's escape. They square off to each other, keeping a distance between them. Pause, a single coyote heard in distance, lights fade softly into moonlight, the figures of the brothers now appear to be caught in a vast desert-like landscape, they are very still but watchful for the next move, lights go slowly to black as the after-image of the brothers pulses in the dark, coyote fades*)

TOPICS FOR CRITICAL UNDERSTANDING AND WRITING

The Play on the PAGE

1. Discuss the relationship of each brother to their father.
2. What do you make of the strange behavior of their mother when she returns at the end of the play?
3. Is it credible that Lee would so easily win over the Hollywood producer, or is the satire too broad?
4. Analyze the metaphorical power of the desert.
5. What do you make of the ambiguous ending of the play?

The Play on the STAGE

6. Having actors switch roles in the same production is nothing new: In O'Neill's autobiographical *Long Day's Journey into Night*, James Tyrone (O'Neill's father) euphorically remembers switching Othello and Iago with the great actor Edwin Booth. Whether or not you've seen the Warhus production (see "The Play in Performance"), discuss the larger theatrical implications of actors exchanging the roles of the brothers. Shouldn't a director strive for the *best* actor in each role? Would Stanislavsky—who taught that actors must believe in the given circumstances that establish their characters—sanction switching roles in Moscow Art Theater productions?

7. Shepard has maintained that this play challenges the idea of masculinity. And yet Shepard himself is often accused of creating a womanless world of macho posturing. Discuss.

The Play in PERFORMANCE

The stage history of *True West* tells a cautionary tale: In judging a new play, how much of its success or failure lies in the play itself, and how much in the production it is accorded? Indeed, can one always clearly differentiate between the contribution of the playwright and that of the director? *True West* was originally performed at the tiny Magic Theatre in San Francisco in July 1980 where it was well received by a small loyal audience. Following the pattern of transfer to a major venue, the play was scheduled to move to Joseph Papp's Public Theater later that year. The Public had enjoyed some success with its production of *Curse of the Starving Class* two years before. (*Buried Child* did *not* open at the Public, but rather at the off-off Broadway

Theater for a New City, a very successful production that subsequently transferred to off-Broadway.*) Shepard and director Robert Woodruff wanted to retain the lead actors from their Magic Theater production. But producer Papp did not think they were good enough; indeed, he had his doubts about Woodruff, who had directed *Curse* for him two years previous. He realized, however, that he had no choice: No Woodruff meant no Shepard at all.

Papp finally convinced his reluctant playwright and director to accept two excellent established actors—Peter Boyle and Tommy Lee Jones—as replacements. As rehearsals progressed, Papp's misgivings (the set was cluttered and badly lit, the play was "half-directed," etc.)—and his interference—proliferated. Relations deteriorated to the point where Woodruff resigned and requested that his name be removed from the program, a move Papp refused. From California, Shepard went public with a statement that called Papp a divisive force who had taken "artistic control . . . out of the hands of the playwright and the director." He never worked with Papp again. Finally, the production opened in late December 1980 to mixed reviews: To some critics it was something to rush to see; to others something was missing—it was not major Shepard. Frank Rich, the *New York Times* critic wrote, "This play hasn't been misdirected; it really looks as if it hasn't been directed at all."

Then two years later a new version of the play arrived in New York via the Midwest. An innovative Chicago company called Steppenwolf transferred to off-Broadway a production of *True West* that was a revelation. Two young actors—John Malkovich and Gary Sinise—gave electrifying performances as the warring brothers and launched major acting careers in the process. The play was directed by Sinise with subtle

variations of mood between psychological insight and thematic urgency, between comedy and danger. And everyone said, Why didn't we see it before? This play isn't just average Shepard; it's *great* Shepard! Malkovich, in particular, in the more explosive role, projected a ferocious vitality that was in turns ingratiating and terrifying and totally irresistible. And so thanks to the Steppenwolf production (which was recorded by PBS and, with some work, is available), *True West* joined that short list of major plays underappreciated until the second time around—plays such as *The Iceman Cometh*, *Summer and Smoke*, and *The Birthday Party*.

Almost twenty years further down the road, in early 2000 another production of *True West* surfaces, and this time *on* Broadway. Ironically, despite being recognized as one of America's leading playwrights for a quarter of a century, until the new millennium Shepard had never had a Broadway production of any of his plays. The off-Broadway transfer of *Buried Child* in 1979 came closest and, indeed, won Shepard the Pulitzer Prize that year. The new version that opened in February 2000 was directed by an Englishman, Matthew Warhus, who had directed the French play *Art* on Broadway, and had a most novel performance idea at its core. Seizing on the "double-natured" theme in the play, two young actors who had caused some stir in offbeat films—Philip Seymour Hoffman and John C. Reilly—decided to alternate as *each* of the brothers (three performances in one role, then switch). The result was enormously successful artistically and commercially. Even if one saw only one performance one saw a well-crafted, intelligent reading of the play; if one was fortunate enough to see the actors play *both* roles, one discovered something at the heart of the play: Individual autonomy stands on shaky ground. As Shepard has stated, "At its heart [the play is about] this conflict between the intellect and the emotions, the physical wild man part and the reasonable intellectual side [of] . . . what it really means to be a man. . . . American men haven't resolved this; the American male is in conflict, uniquely in conflict in the cultures of the West."

*From a pragmatic point of view, the distinctions between Broadway, off-Broadway, and off-off Broadway are rooted in legal and contractual considerations concerning the size of the playhouse and the nature of the actors' contracts—union or nonunion.

BRUCE WEBER
Sam Shepard on True West*

In 1980, before *True West* his play about the contorted reunion of two estranged brothers, opened at the Magic Theater in San Francisco, Sam Shepard was asked by a reporter why he wrote it. "I wanted to write a play about double nature, one that wouldn't be symbolic or metaphorical or any of that stuff," Mr. Shepard replied in an interview in the *New York Times Magazine*. "I just wanted to give a taste of what it feels like to be two-sided. . . . It's not so cute. Not some little thing we can get over. It's something we've got to live with."

Twenty years later, there is something prescient-sounding in that; the third of three family-nightmare plays Mr. Shepard wrote in the 1970's (*Curse of the Starving Class* and *Buried Child* are the others), *True West* has lingered, a favorite of student productions and small theater companies, as a work of impact and influence. As a new revival gets set to open on March 9, at Circle in the Square with two rising film actors, John C. Reilly and Philip Seymour Hoffman, alternating in the brothers' roles, it comes to Broadway for the first time as perhaps Mr. Shepard's most resonant and famous play. That is partly because the fraternal duel to near death that takes place in an unassuming suburban home is the hyperbolic reflection of the kind of family conflict that almost anyone can find, well, familiar. And it is partly because, Mr. Shepard's demurral notwithstanding, there is something metaphorical in the struggle between Austin, the college-educated, conventionally ambitious screenwriter, and Lee, the slightly unhinged renegade who supports himself as a burglar.

The brothers' battle, an increasingly antic squabble over whose idea for a screenplay describes a more authentic Western story, sends up Hollywood's appropriation of Americana. Though it devolves into a mutual primal scream, the conflict that live within each of them—intellect versus loins, dream versus actual experience, obedience to the code of civilization versus impulse to rebel—live within the culture as well as in the individual. Set on the periphery of the Los Angeles suburban sprawl, the play quite consciously evokes the image of a spoiled and even perverted American frontier that seems, if anything, more spoiled and perverted today. Even to the playwright.

"The struggle with the land is finished," Mr. Shepard, now 56, said in a recent telephone interview from his home in rural Minnesota. He acknowledged he might well have said the same thing twenty years ago, when the movie-fed celebrity culture was burgeoning—*True West*, predated Broadway's most well-known Hollywood sendups, David Rabe's *Hurleyburly* and David Mamet's *Speed-the-Plow*—but he said *True West* was never meant as an assault on Hollywood: "It's absolutely futile to criticize Hollywood, not that it doesn't deserve it," Mr. Shepard said. "It simply doesn't care what your attitude toward it is. The machinery is too powerful, too awesome. But the seduction of the place is unbelievable, an extraordinary American thing. Like Las Vegas, it's all about winning and losing. The play deals with that—the success and failure and power. Nobody's ever going to turn that system around; this is not a Buddhist culture."

In any case, he went on, "now the frontier is the computer, so it has become an internal thing. Computers cause protracted dreaming about what might be, and the frontier everyone is seeking is how in the imagination. That means everything—relationships, families—has taken on a new dimension. We don't even need a family anymore; you can have an imaginary family. To even talk about the structure of the family anymore is ridiculous. . . . Theme is really a bad word, but there's a current in the play about what's true and what isn't, what is reality and what's fantasy. The scripts being concocted are the fantasy, but in the course of it all, the two guys come up with stories about their father, simple, defined stories about him losing his teeth, going to Mexico, that are the real stories. That's the dichotomy I wanted to set up. Where is the actual experience? Is it in something you hope will come true? Or is it what is happening to you, moment by moment? I was writing about how that has lost its meaning."

. . .

Mr. Shepard said that all he did during the rehearsals was stay out of the way and talk a bit about his personal connection to the play. Mr. Shepard grew up mostly in Duarte, Calif., on an avocado ranch at the edge of the Mojave desert. He had two sisters, but no brother; like Lee and Austin, however, he had a wayward father. He said he told the actors, neither of whom is from the West (Mr. Reilly grew up in Chicago, Mr. Hoffman outside Rochester), about the

---

*Excerpts from "An Unusual Case of Role Reversal," *New York Times* 27 Feb. 2000, Arts & Leisure section: 10.

desert's strange and eerie allure. "It's a pretty strong influence," Mr. Shepard said, "this vast empty thing out there, the heat and all the rest of it, on temperament and things like longing—as in longing to get the hell out of there."

He understood, he said, why Mr. Hoffman and Mr. Reilly were so drawn to their work. "It's the kind of play actors love to handle," Mr. Shepard said. "There's a lot of stuff in there that men, in particular, love to grapple with. At its heart is this conflict between the intellect and the emotions, the physical wild man part and the reasonable intellectual side. You know, what it really means to be a man. It sounds a little trite, but

there's not a whole lot of men who know what a man is, and I always thought it was weird that American men haven't resolved this; the American male is in conflict. . . . You're either a rassler or you're a book guy, and I think they're getting farther and farther apart; there's a bigger gap between the macho man and the other one."

Mr. Shepard said he had just finished a new play, *The Late Henry Moss,* which he described as "a fatherand-son kind of deal." Asked what it was about, he laughed.

"Same stuff," he said. "Same old stuff."

DAVID Mamet

Certain dominating themes in David Mamet's work—a sense of not belonging, a conviction that authority is betrayal—are clearly rooted in a childhood, which, in his words, "was not a bundle of laughs." The firstborn son of two intelligent first-generation Jewish Americans, Mamet was born in Chicago in 1947. In 1958 his parents divorced bitterly, and the fractured childhood shuttling between them had disturbing psychological consequences for Mamet and his sister, consequences he has increasingly tried to face in such plays as *The Cryptogram* (1994) and *The Old Neighborhood* (1997). Mamet studied at Goddard College in Vermont and at the Neighborhood Playhouse in New York, where he was introduced by its director, Sanford Meisner, to the theater philosophy that "acting is doing." One repetition exercise in particular has proved basic to forging Mamet's distinctive style of dialogue.

In the early 1970s, he became intensively involved in what was becoming a vital, original Chicago theater milieu: "The air feels new," he said, "and all things seem possible." It was not long before he turned to writing plays, the first of which, *Sexual Perversity in Chicago* and *Duck Variations,* garnered critical attention first in Chicago and then off Broadway in New York. Soon he was to achieve major success with a play set in a Chicago junk shop: *American Buffalo* (1977), which established Mamet as a playwright of note and won the New York Drama Critics Award. Unlike many of his contemporary playwright colleagues, Mamet has been consistently prolific ever since, building an impressive body of work. In 1984 he was awarded the Pulitzer Prize for *Glengarry Glen Ross.* Other important plays are *The Water Engine* (1976, 1978), *A Life in the Theatre* (1977), *Edmond* (1982), *Prairie du Chien* and *The Shawl* (1986), *Speed-the-Plow* (1988), *Oleanna* (1993), *The Cryptogram* (1994), and *The Old Neighborhood* (1997).

In the early 1980s Mamet turned his attention to film with distinction, first as screenwriter, then as screenwriter/director. Critically acclaimed screenplays include *The Postman Always Rings Twice* (1981), *The Verdict* (1982), *The Untouchables* (1987), and *Wag the Dog* (1998). Films he has directed as well as written include *House of Games* (1987), *Things Change* (1988), *Homicide* (1991), and *The Spanish Prisoner* (1997). He has also written fiction and nonfiction: *Writing in Restaurants* (1986), *Cabin* (1992), *Make-Believe Town* (1996), and *True and False: Heresy and Common Sense for the Actor* (1997). The recognition of his lost Jewish roots, evidenced in the play *The Old Neighborhood,* can also be seen in such books as *The Village: A Novel* (1994), *Passover* (1995), and *The Old Religion* (1997).

▪▪▪▪▪▪▪▪▪▪▪▪▪

COMMENTARY ON *GLENGARRY GLEN ROSS*

After graduating from Goddard College in Vermont, David Mamet returned to Chicago to try to find work as an actor. He quickly discovered that paying work was scarce, and with no credits to his name he was "virtually unemployable." Needing money, he registered with an employment agency that sent him out for a two-day job as a typist in a real estate office. He stayed more than a year, working up to assistant office manager. The fly-by-night concern sold tracts of undeveloped land in Arizona and Florida to gullible Chicagoans. It was, Mamet wrote later, "one of those companies . . . [with] an ad on television that says 'Interested in the Arizona way of life? No salesman will

call,' and the next thing that happens is that a salesman calls." This is Mamet's description of how the firm worked:

> Interested viewers would telephone in for the brochure and their names and numbers were given to me. My job was to call back, assess their income and sales susceptibility, and arrange an appointment with them for one of the office salesmen. . . . This appointment was called a lead—in the same way that a clue in a criminal case is called a lead, i.e., it may lead to the suspect, the suspect in this case being a prospect. It was my job to assess the relative worth of these leads and assign them to the salesforce. The salesmen would then take their assigned leads and go out on the appointments, which were called *sits, i.e.,* a meeting where one actually sits down with the prospects.

With minor changes, this is the world of *Glengarry Glen Ross*, whose euphonic title with its exotic Scottish connotations names a parcel of drab Florida real estate. It is a Darwinian world where the battle to survive is at its most intense. To underline this struggle, Mamet ups the ante in his fictional company: The bosses have organized a sales competition in which the salesman with the highest grosses wins a Cadillac and is automatically guaranteed the best leads. The rewards drop precipitously: The runners-up win a set of steak knives, and the losers get nothing. The system, then, is deliberately geared to penalize the weak at the expense of the strong; those who need it least—the successful—are rewarded with the good leads; the others have little choice but to accept the inferior leads if they want to save their jobs. Mamet defines the world succinctly: The "play is about a society based on business, a society with only one bottom line: How much money you make." The driven salesmen define themselves totally in terms of their sales. There are few moments when they use any language that is not expressly concerned with business, and when they do it's clearly a ploy to con a customer. The office the salesmen share is as all-confining a world as Hamm's room in Beckett's *Endgame*.

Mamet is not primarily thought of as a political playwright, and yet no American playwright is more intensely critical of American free enterprise and the price it exacts, not even the play that *Glengarry* invariably evokes: Arthur Miller's *Death of a Salesman*. At the time of the play's opening Mamet gave an interview in which he did not hesitate to declare that capitalism was "obviously an idea whose time has come and gone. . . . The idea to go West and make your fortune . . . was an idea promulgated for the storekeepers in the gold rush and the railroads in the westward expansion as a way of enslaving the common man and woman . . . [by] playing on their greed." Americans are fundamentally dishonest about our aspiration to get something for nothing, and that's why we're enslaved by the idea of the "happy capitalist" instead of observing that "the operative maxim is 'Hurrah for me and fuck you.' Familiar American pieties are always linked to criminality. That's why they're familiar American pieties."

This linking of capitalism and criminality is a theme Mamet has pursued in other plays. If the world of commerce in *Glengarry* inevitably leads to crime, in Mamet's breakthrough play, *American Buffalo*, its hapless main characters—a fence, a thief, a recovering junkie—see themselves as business entrepreneurs. As they concoct—badly—a scheme to rob a customer of a buffalo head nickel he had bought in the junkshop where the play is set, they talk business talk, laced with obscenity. Teach, who wheedles his way into the scheme and then acts like its inventor, continually refers to himself as "a businessman. I am here to do business." Much of the humor in the play lies in the irony that these marginal losers identify with the values of a competitive society that has relegated them to the junk heap, as this exchange reveals:

TEACH. You know what is free enterprise?
DON. No. What?
TEACH. The freedom . . .
DON. . . . yeah?
TEACH. Of the *Individual* . . .
DON. . . . yeah?
TEACH. To Embark on Any Fucking Course that he sees fit.
DON. Uh huh . . .
TEACH. In order to secure his honest chance to make a profit. Am I so out of line on this?
DON. No.
TEACH. The country's *founded* on this, Don. You know this . . . Without this we're just savage shitheads in the wilderness.

But the play's real irony lies in the fact that no business gets done; the scheme implodes as Teach's paranoia pushes the situation to disaster. They talk the talk but they can't walk the walk. In several of Mamet's other plays, however, business *does* get done, and if illegality or even violence springs inevitably from the M.O.—modus operandi—so be it. In *The Water Engine*, for example (which Mamet had written as a radio play in 1976 and then revised for the stage in 1978 retaining the scenic metaphor of a 1930s radio drama), a young man invents an engine that runs on water and finds himself caught in a web woven by corrupt businessmen who want so suppress his invention. It's no contest and his fate is not a happy one; Mamet has no sentimental illusions of where real power lies. Similarly in *Speed-the-Plow* (1988), an evisceration of Hollywood corruption, everything and everyone's a commodity, betrayal is normative behavior, and legal constrains are malleable. His Hollywood "players" are cagey predators who differ from Mamet's lower-class characters only in their cosmetic sleekness and seeming self-irony. No word is trustworthy. "It's only words," says a producer, "unless they're true."

Glengarry Glen Ross, then, merely carries Mamet's cynicism to its logical conclusion. The play opens with a slipping salesman, Levene, desperately trying to fast-talk the office manager into meatier leads. The manager seems stonily resistant until a bribe is offered. Others respond to their subordination more defiantly: The aggressive Moss proposes to his hapless colleague Aaranow that they (i.e., he, Aaranow) break into the office after hours and steal the good leads. The appalled Aaranow, who thought he was only going out for a drink, suddenly finds himself an accessory to a crime. As Moss points out, pressing his advantage: "You listened." The subsequent robbery and trashing of the office and the solution of the mystery of its perpetrator occupies the second act of the play. As in an Agatha Christie mystery everyone is a suspect because everyone has a motive. From top to bottom, the only ethical consideration is self-interest, the only goal to win.

Despite the consistent intensity of his social critique, however, Mamet refuses to posit any alternative political solution; indeed, he is doubtful that one exists. But beneath the surface corruption that he compulsively documents, Mamet does at times reveal the seed of an idealism struggling to grow. It is, however, always expressed in individual, not collective, terms: *Edmond*—his harrowing portrait of a middle-class man's frenzied decent into the lower depths of murder—ends at the bottom but on a note of personal acceptance. In *Speed-the-Plow*, the hustlewise producer, prompted by his temporary secretary, rejects a surefire blockbuster in favor of an unconventional project because he glimpses the possibility that the blockbuster may well be an exercise in "degradation, rage, sex, violence." In *American Buffalo*, a genuine affection links Donny and Bobby, and the only real action in the play is a gratuitous one: Bobby buys a buffalo nickel for $50 just to please his surrogate father. But no gratuitous unselfishness marks the pitiless world of *Glengarry Glen Ross*, which remains Mamet's most uncompromising, unconsoling play.

GLENGARRY GLEN ROSS
David Mamet

THE CHARACTERS

WILLIAMSON, BAYLEN, ROMA, LINGK—Men *in their early forties.*

LEVENE, MOSS, AARONOW—*Men in their fifties.*

THE SCENE

The three scenes of Act One take place in a Chinese restaurant.

Act Two takes place in a real estate office.

ACT ONE

SCENE 1

A booth at a Chinese restaurant, Williamson and Levene are seated at the booth.

LEVENE. John . . . John . . . John. Okay. John. John. Look: (*pause*) The Glengarry Highland's leads, you're sending Roma out. Fine. He's a good man. We know what he is. He's fine. All I'm saying, you look at the *board,* he's throwing . . . wait, wait, wait, he's throwing them *away,* he's throwing the leads away. All that I'm saying, that you're wasting leads. I don't want to tell you your *job.* All that I'm saying, things get *set,* I know they do, you get a certain *mindset.* . . . A guy gets a reputation. We know how this . . . all I'm saying, put a *closer* on the job. There's more than one man for the . . . Put a . . . wait a second, put a *proven man out* . . . and you watch, now *wait* a second—and you watch your *dollar* volumes. . . . Your start closing them for *fifty* 'stead of *twenty-five* . . . you put a *closer* on the . . .

WILLIAMSON. Shelly, you blew the last . . .

LEVENE. No. John. No. Let's wait, let's back up here, I did . . . will you please? Wait a second. Please. I didn't "blow" them. No. I didn't "blow" them. No. One kicked *out,* one I closed . . .

WILLIAMSON. . . . you didn't close . . .

LEVENE. . . . I, if you'd *listen* to me. Please. I *closed* the cocksucker. His *ex,* John, his *ex, I* didn't know he was married . . . he, the *judge* invalidated the . . .

WILLIAMSON. Shelly.

LEVENE. . . . and what is that, John? What? Bad *luck.* That's all it is. I pray in your *life* you will never find it runs in streaks. That's what it does, that's all it's doing. Streaks. I pray it misses you. That's all I want to say.

WILLIAMSON (*pause*). What about the other two?

LEVENE. What two?

WILLIAMSON. Four. You had four leads. One kicked out, one the *judge,* you say . . .

LEVENE. . . . you want to see the court records? John? Eh? You want to go down . . .

WILLIAMSON. . . . no . . .

LEVENE. . . . do you want to go down*town* . . . ?

WILLIAMSON. . . . no . . .

LEVENE. . . . then . . .

WILLIAMSON. . . . I only . . .

LEVENE. . . . then what is this "you *say*" shit, what is that? (*pause*) What is that . . . ?

WILLIAMSON. All that I'm saying . . .

LEVENE. What is this "you *say*"? A deal kicks out . . . I got to *eat. Shit,* Williamson, *shit.* You . . . Moss . . . Roma . . . look at the *sheets* . . . look at the *sheets.* Nineteen *eighty,* eighty-*one* . . . eighty-*two* . . . six months of eighty-two . . . who's there? Who's up there?

WILLIAMSON. Roma.

LEVENE. Under him?

WILLIAMSON. Moss.

LEVENE. Bullshit. John. Bull*shit.* April, September 1981. It's *me.* It isn't fucking *Moss.* Due respect, he's an *order* taker, John. He *talks,* he talks a good game, look at the *board,* and it's *me,* John, it's me . . .

WILLIAMSON. Not lately it isn't.

LEVENE. Lately kiss my ass lately. That isn't how you build an org . . . talk, talk to Murray. Talk to Mitch. When we were on Peterson, who paid for his fucking *car?* You talk to him. The *Seville* . . . ? He came in, "You bought that for me Shelley." Out of *what?* Cold *calling. Nothing.* Sixty-*five,* when we were there, with Glen *Ross* Farms? You call 'em downtown. What was that? *Luck?* That was "luck"? *Bullshit,* John. You're burning my ass, I can't get a fucking *lead* . . . you think that was luck. My stats for those

David Mamet "regulars" Mike Nussbaum as Aaranow (left) and Joe Mantegna as Roma in the Goodman Theater of Chicago's American premiere performance of *Glengarry Glen Ross*.

years? Bull*shit* . . . over that period of time . . . ? Bull*shit*. It wasn't luck. It was *skill*. You want to throw that away, John . . . ? You want to throw that away?

WILLIAMSON. It isn't me . . .

LEVENE. . . . it isn't you . . . ? Who *is* it? Who is this I'm talking to? I need the *leads* . . .

WILLIAMSON. . . . after the thirtieth . . .

LEVENE. Bull*shit* the thirtieth. I don't get on the board the thirtieth, they're going to can my ass. I need the leads. I need them now. Or I'm gone, and you're going to miss me, John, I swear to you.

WILLIAMSON. Murray . . .

LEVENE. . . . you *talk* to Murray . . .

WILLIAMSON. I have. And my job is to marshal those leads . . .

LEVENE. Marshal the leads . . . marshal the leads? What the fuck, what bus did *you* get off of, we're here to fucking *sell*. *Fuck* the marshaling the leads. What the fuck talk is that? What the fuck talk is that? Where did you learn that? In school? (*pause*) That's "talk," my friend, that's "talk." Our job is to *sell*. I'm the *man* to sell. I'm getting garbage. (*pause*) You're giving it to me, and what I'm saying is it's *fucked*.

WILLIAMSON. You're saying that I'm fucked.

LEVENE. Yes. (*pause*) I am. I'm sorry to antagonize you.

WILLIAMSON. Le me . . .

LEVENE. . . . And I'm going to get bounced and you're . . .

WILLIAMSON. . . . let me . . . are you listening to me . . . ?

LEVENE. Yes.

WILLIAMSON. Let me tell you something, Shelly. I do what I'm hired to do. I'm . . . wait a second. I'm *hired* watch the leads. I'm given . . . hold on, I'm given a *policy*. My job is to *do that*. What I'm *told*. That's it. You, wait a second,

anybody falls below a certain mark I'm not *permitted* to give them the premium leads.

LEVENE. Then how do they come up above that mark? With *dreck* . . . ? That's *nonsense*. Explain this me. 'Cause it's a waste, and it's a stupid waste. I want to tell you something . . .

WILLIAMSON. You know what those leads cost?

LEVENE. The premium leads. Yes. I know what they cost. John. Because I, *I* generated the dollar revenue sufficient to *buy* them. Nineteen senny-*nine*, you know what I made? Senny-*nine*? Ninety-six thousand dollars. John? For *Murray* . . . For *Mitch* . . . look at the sheets . . .

WILLIAMSON. Murray said . . .

LEVENE. *Fuck* him. *Fuck* Murray. John? You know? You tell him I said so. What does *he* fucking know? He's going to have a "sales" contest . . . you know what our sales contest used to be? *Money. A fortune.* Money lying on the ground, Murray? When was the last time he went out on a sit? Sales contest? It's *laughable*. It's cold out there now, John. It's tight. Money is *tight*. This ain't sixty-five. It ain't. It just ain't. See? See? Now, I'm a good *man*—but I need a . . .

WILLIAMSON. Murray said . . .

LEVENE. John. John. . . .

WILLIAMSON. Will you please wait a second. Shelly. Please. Murray told me: the hot leads . . .

LEVENE. . . . ah, *fuck* this . . .

WILLIAMSON. The . . . Shelly? (*pause*) The hot leads are assigned according to the board. During the contest. *Period*. Anyone who beats fifty per . . .

LEVENE. That's fucked. That's fucked. You don't look at the fucking *percentage*. You look at the *gross*.

WILLIAMSON. Either way. You're out.

LEVENE. I'm out.

WILLIAMSON. Yes.

LEVENE. I'll tell you why I'm out. I'm *out*, you're giving me toilet paper. John, I've *seen* those leads. I saw them when I was at Homestead, we pitched those cocksuckers Rio Rancho nineteen sixty-*nine* they wouldn't buy. They couldn't buy a fucking *toaster*. They're *broke*, John. They're cold. They're deadbeats, you can't judge on that. Even so. Even so. Alright. Fine. Fine. Even so. I go in, FOUR FUCKING LEADS they got their money in a *sock*. They're fucking *Polacks*, John. Four leads. I close two. *Two*. Fifty per . . .

WILLIAMSON. . . . *they* kicked out.

LEVENE. They *all* kick out. You run in *streaks*, pal. *Streaks*. I'm . . . I'm . . . don't look at the *board*, look at me. Shelly Levene. *Anyone*. Ask them on Western. Ask Getz at Homestead. Go ask Jerry Graff. You know who I am . . . I NEED A SHOT. I got to get on the fucking board. Ask them. *Ask* them. Ask them who ever picked up a check I was flush. Moss, Jerry Graff, Mitch himself . . . Those buys *lived* on the business I brought it. They *lived* on it . . . and so did Murray, John. You were here you'd of benefited from it too. And now I'm saying this. Do I want charity? Do I want *pity*? I want *sits*. I want leads don't come right out of a *phone book*. Give me a lead hotter than that, I'll go in and close it. Give me a chance. That's all I want. I'm going to *get* up on that fucking board and all I want is a chance. It's a *streak* and I'm going to turn it around. (*pause*) I need your help. (*pause*)

WILLIAMSON. I can't do it, Shelly. (*pause*)

LEVENE. Why?

WILLIAMSOM. The leads are assigned randomly . . .

LEVENE. *Bullshit, bullshit*, you assign them. . . . What are you *telling* me?

WILLIAMSON. . . . apart from the top men on the contest board.

LEVENE. Then put me on the board.

WILLIAMSON. You start closing again, you'll *be* on the board.

LEVENE. I can't close these leads, John. No one can. It's a joke. John, look, just give me a hot lead. Just give me two of the premium leads. As a "test," alright? As a "test" and I promise you . . .

WILLIAMSON. I can't do it, Shel. (*pause*)

LEVENE. I'll give you ten percent. (*pause*)

WILLIAMSON. Of what?

LEVENE. Of my end what I close.

WILLIAMSON. And what if you don't close.

LEVENE. I *will* close.

WILLIAMSON. What if you *don't* close . . . ?

LEVENE. I *will* close.

WILLIAMSON. What if you *don't*? Then *I'm* fucked. You see . . . ? Then it's *my* job. That's what I'm *telling* you.

LEVEN. I *will* close. John, John, ten percent. I can get hot. You *know* that . . .

WILLIAMSON. Not lately you can't . . .

LEVENE. Fuck that. That's defeatist. Fuck that. Fuck it. . . . Get on my side. Go with me. Let's *do* something. You want to run this office, *run* it.

WILLIAMSON. Twenty percent. (*pause*)

LEVENE. Alright.

WILLIAMSON. And fifty bucks a lead.

LEVENE. John (*pause*). Listen. I want to talk to you. Permit me to do this a second. I'm older than you. A man acquires a reputation. On the street. What he does when he's *up*, what he does otherwise. . . . I said "ten," you said "no." You said "twenty." I said "fine," I'm not going to fuck with you, how can I beat that, you tell me? . . . Okay. Okay. We'll . . . Okay. Fine. We'll . . . Alright, twenty percent, and fifty bucks a lead. That's fine. For now. That's fine. A month or two we'll talk. A month from now. Next month. After the thirtieth. (*pause*) We'll talk.

WILLIAMSON. What are we going to say?

LEVENE. No. You're right. That's for later. We'll talk in a month. What have you got? I want two sits. Tonight.

WILLIAMSON. I'm not sure I have two.

LEVENE. I saw the board. You've got *four* . . .

WILLIAMSON. I've got *Roma*. Then I've got Moss . . .

LEVENE. *Bullshit*. They ain't been in the office yet. Give 'em some stiff. We have a deal or not? Eh? Two sits. The Des Plaines. Both of 'em, six and ten, you can do it . . . six and ten . . . eight and eleven, I don't give a shit, you set 'em up? Alright? The two sits in Des Plaines.

WILLIAMSON. Alright.

LEVENE. Good. Now we're talking. (*pause*)

WILLIAMSON. A hundred bucks. (*pause*)

LEVENE. Now? (*pause*) *Now*?

WILLIAMSON. Now. (*pause*) Yes . . . *When*?

LEVENE. Ah, *shit*, John. (*pause*)

WILLIAMSON. I wish I could.

LEVENE. You fucking asshole. (*pause*) I haven't got it. (*pause*) I haven't got it, John. (*pause*) I'll pay you tomorrow. (*pause*) I'm coming in here with the sales, I'll pay you tomorrow. (*pause*) I haven't *got* it, when I pay, the gas . . . I get back the hotel, I'll bring it in tomorrow.

WILLIAMSON. Can't do it.

LEVENE. I'll give you thirty on them now, I'll bring the rest tomorrow. I've got it at the hotel. (*pause*) John? (*pause*) We do that, for crissake?

WILLIAMSON. No.

LEVENE. I'm asking you. As a favor to me? (*pause*) John. (*long pause*) John: my *daughter* . . .

WILLIAMSON. I can't do it, Shelly.

LEVENE. Well, I want to tell you something, fella, wasn't long I could pick up the phone, call *Murray* and I'd have your job. You know that? Not too *long* ago. For what? For *nothing*. "Mur, this new kid burns my ass." "Shelley, he's out." You're gone before I'm back from lunch. I bought him a trip to Bermuda once . . .

WILLIAMSON. I have to go . . . (*gets up*)

LEVENE. Wait. Alright. Fine. (*starts going in pocket for money*) The one. Give me the lead. Give me the one lead. The best one you have.

WILLIAMSON. I can't split them. (*pause*)

LEVENE. Why?

WILLIAMSON. Because I say so.

LEVENE. (*pause*) Is that it? Is that *it*? You want to do business that way . . . ? (*Williamson gets up, leaves money on the table.*) You want to do business that way . . . ? Alright. Alright. Alright. Alright. What is there on the other list . . . ?

WILLIAMSON. You want something off the B list?

LEVENE. *Yeah.* Yeah.

WILLIAMSON. Is that what you're saying?

LEVENE. That's what I'm saying. Yeah. (*pause*) I'd like something off the other list. Which, very least, that I'm entitled to. If I'm still *working* here, which for the moment I guess that I am. (*pause*) What? I'm sorry I spoke harshly to you.

WILLIAMSON. That's alright.

LEVENE. The deal still stands, our other thing. (*Williamson shrugs. Starts out of the booth.*) Good. Mmm. I, you know, I left my wallet back at the hotel.

SCENE 2

A booth at the restaurant. Moss and Aaronow seated. After the meal.

MOSS. Polacks and deadbeats.

AARONOW. . . . Polacks . . .

MOSS. Deadbeats *all.*

AARONOW. . . . they hold on to their money . . .

MOSS. All of 'em. They, *hey*: it happens to us all.

AARONOW. Where am I going to work?

MOSS. You have to cheer up, George, you aren't out yet.

AARONOW. I'm not?

MOSS. You missed a fucking sale. Big deal. A deadbeat Polack. Big deal. How you going to sell 'em in the *first* place . . . ? Your mistake, you shoun'a took the lead.

AARONOW. I had to.

MOSS. You had to, yeah. Why?

AARONOW. To get on the . . .

MOSS. To get on the board. Yeah. How you goan'a get on the board sell'n a Polack? And I'll tell you, I'll tell you what *else*. You listening? I'll tell you what else: don't ever try to sell an Indian.

AARONOW. I'd never try to sell an Indian.

MOSS. You get those names come up, you ever get 'em, "Patel"?

AARONOW. Mmm . . .

MOSS. You ever get 'em?

AARONOW. Well, I think I had one once.

MOSS. You did?

AARONOW. I . . . I don't know.

MOSS. You had one you'd know it. *Patel.* They keep coming up. I don't know. They like to talk to salesmen. (*pause*) They're *lonely*, something. (*pause*) They like to feel *superior*, I don't know. Never bought a fucking thing. You're sitting down "The Rio Rancho *this*, the blah blah blah," "The Mountain View—" "Oh yes. My brother told me that. . . ." They got a grapevine. Fuckin' Indians, George. Not my cup of tea. Speaking of which I want to tell you something (*pause*) I never got a cup of tea with them. You see them in the restaurants. A supercilious race. What is this *look* on their face all the time? I don't know. (*pause*) I don't know. Their broads all look like they just got fucked with a dead *cat*, I don't know. (*pause*) I don't know. I don't like it. Christ . . .

AARONOW. What?

MOSS. The whole fuckin' thing . . . The pressure's just too great. You're ab . . . you're absolu . . . they're too important. All of them. You go in the door. I . . . "I got to *close* this fucker, or I don't eat lunch," "or I don't win the *Cadillac*. . . ." We fuckin' work too hard. You work too hard. We all, I remember when we were at Platt . . . huh? Glen Ross Farms . . . *didn't* we sell a bunch of that . . .

AARONOW. They came in and they, you know . . .

MOSS. Well, they fucked it up.

AARONOW. They did.

MOSS. They killed the goose.

AARONOW. They did.

MOSS. And now . . .

AARONOW. We're stuck with *this* . . .

MOSS. We're stuck with *this* fucking shit . . .

AARONOW. . . . *this* shit . . .

MOSS. It's too . . .

AARONOW. It is.

MOSS. Eh?

AARONOW. It's too . . .

MOSS. You get a bad month, all of a . . .

AARONOW. You're on this . . .

MOSS. All of, they got you on this "board . . . "

AARONOW. I, I . . . I . . .

MOSS. Some *contest* board . . .

AARONOW. I . . .

MOSS. It's not right.

AARONOW. It's not.

MOSS. No. (*pause*)

AARONOW. And it's not right to the *customers.*

MOSS. I know it's not. I'll tell you, you got, you know, you got . . . what did I learn as a kid on Western? Don't sell a guy one car? Sell him *five* cars over fifteen years.

AARONOW. That's right.

MOSS. Eh . . . ?

AARONOW. That's right.

MOSS. Goddamn right, that's right. Guys come on: "Oh, the blah blah blah, *I* know what I'll do: I'll go in and rob everyone blind and go to Argentina cause nobody ever *thought* of this before."

AARONOW. . . . that's right . . .

MOSS. Eh?

AARONOW. No. That's absolutely right.

MOSS. And so they kill the goose . . . and, and a fuckin' *man*, worked all his *life* has got to . . .

AARONOW. . . . that's right . . .

MOSS. . . . cower in his boots . . .

AARONOW (*simultaneously with "boots"*). Shoes, boots, yes . . .

MOSS. For some fuckin' "Sell ten thousand and you win the steak knives . . ."

AARONOW. For some *sales* pro . . .

MOSS. . . . sale promotion, "You *lose*, then we fire your . . ." No. It's *medieval* . . . it's wrong. "Or we're going to fire your ass." It's wrong.

AARONOW. Yes.

MOSS. Yes, it is. And you know whose responsible?

AARONOW. Who?

MOSS. Look at Jerry Graff. He's *clean*, he's doing business for *himself*, he's got his, that *list* of his with the *nurses* . . . see? You see? That's *thinking*. Why take ten percent. A ten percent comm . . . why are we giving the rest away? What are we giving ninety per . . . for *nothing*. For some jerk sit in the office tell you "Get out there and close." "Go win the Cadillac." Graff. He goes out and *buys*. He pays top dollar for the . . . you see?

AARONOW. Yes.

MOSS. That's *thinking*. Now, he's got the leads, he goes in business for *himself*. He's . . . that's what I . . . that's *thinking*! "Who? Who's got a steady *job*, a couple bucks nobody's touched, who?"

AARONOW. Nurses.

MOSS. So Graff buys a fucking list of nurses, one grand—if he paid two I'll eat my hat—four, five thousand nurses, and he's going *wild* . . .

AARONOW. He is?

MOSS. He's doing *very* well.

AARONOW. I heard that they were running cold.

MOSS. The nurses?

AARONOW. Yes.

MOSS. You hear a *lot* of things. . . . He's doing very well. He's doing *very* well.

AARONOW. With River Oaks?

MOSS. River Oaks, Brook Farms. *All* of that shit. Somebody told me, you know what he's clearing *himself*? Fourteen, fifteen grand a *week*.

AARONOW. Himself?

MOSS. That's what I'm *saying*. Why? The *leads*. He's got the good leads . . . what are we, we're sitting in the shit here. Why? We have to go to *them* to *get* them. Huh. Ninety percent our sale, we're *paying* to the *office* for the *leads*.

AARONOW. The leads, the overhead, the telephones, there's *lots* of things.

MOSS. What do you need? A *telephone*, some broad to say "Good morning," nothing . . . nothing . . .

AARONOW. No, it's not that simple, Dave . . .

MOSS. *Yes*. It *is*. It *is* simple, and you know what the hard part is?

AARONOW. What?

MOSS. Starting up.

AARONOW. What hard part?

MOSS. Of doing the thing. The dif . . . the difference. Between me and Jerry Graff. Going to business for yourself. The hard part is . . . you know what it is?

AARONOW. What?

MOSS. Just the *act*.

AARONOW. What act?

MOSS. To say "I'm going on my own." 'Cause what you do, George, let me tell you what you do: you find yourself in *thrall* to someone else. And we *enslave* ourselves. To *please*. To win some fucking *toaster* . . . to . . . to . . . and the guy who got there first made *up* those . . .

AARONOW. That's right . . .

MOSS. He made *up* those rules, and we're working for *him*.

AARONOW. That's the truth . . .

MOSS. That's the *God's* truth. And it gets me depressed. I *swear* that it does. At MY AGE. To see a goddamn: "Somebody wins the Cadillac this month. P.S. Two guys get fucked."

AARONOW. Huh.

MOSS. You don't *ax* your sales force.

AARONOW. No.

MOSS. You . . .

AARONOW. You . . .

MOSS. You *build* it!

AARONOW. That's what I . . .

MOSS. You fucking *build* it! Men come . . .

AARONOW. Men come *work* for you . . .

MOSS. . . . you're absolutely right.

AARONOW. They . . .

MOSS. They have . . .

AARONOW. When they . . .

MOSS. Look look look look, when they *build* your business, then you can't fucking turn around, *enslave* them, treat them like *children*, fuck them up the ass, leave them to fend for themselves . . . no. (*pause*) No. (*pause*) You're absolutely right, and I want to tell you something.

AARONOW. What?

MOSS. I want to tell you what somebody should do.

AARONOW. What?

MOSS. Someone should stand up and strike *back*.

AARONOW. What do you mean?

MOSS. *Somebody* . . .

AARONOW. Yes . . . ?

MOSS. Should do something to *them*.

AARONOW. What?

MOSS. Something. To pay the back. (*pause*) Someone, someone should hurt them. Murray and Mitch.

AARONOW. Someone should hurt them.

MOSS. Yes.

AARONOW (*pause*). How?

MOSS. How? Do something to hurt them. Where they live.

AARONOW. What? (*pause*)

MOSS. Someone should rob the office.

AARONOW. Huh.

MOSS. That's what I'm *saying*. We were, if we were that kind of guys, to knock it off, and *trash* the joint, it looks like robbery, and *take* the fuckin' leads out of the files . . . go to Jerry Graff. (*long pause*)

AARONOW. What could somebody get for them?

MOSS. What could we *get* for them? I don't know. Buck a *throw* . . . buck-a-half a throw . . . I don't know. . . . Hey, who knows what they're worth, what do they *pay* for them? All told . . . must be, I'd . . . three bucks a throw . . . *I* don't know.

AARONOW. How many leads have we got?

MOSS. The *Glengarry* . . . the premium leads . . . ? I'd say we got five thousand. Five. Five thousand leads.

AARONOW. And you're saying a fella could take and sell these leads to Jerry Graff.

MOSS. Yes.

AARONOW. How do you know he'd buy them?

MOSS. Graff? Because I worked for him.

AARONOW. You haven't talked to him.

MOSS. No. What do you mean? Have I talked to him about *this*? (*pause*)

AARONOW. Yes. I mean are you actually *talking* about this, or are we just . . .

MOSS. No, we're just . . .

AARONOW. We're just "*talking*" about it.

MOSS. We're just *speaking* about it. (*pause*) As an *idea*.

AARONOW. As an idea.

MOSS. Yes.

AARONOW. We're not actually *talking* about it.

MOSS. No.

AARONOW. Talking about it as a . . .

MOSS. No.

AARONOW. As a *robbery*.

MOSS. As a "robbery"?! No.

AARONOW. *Well*. Well . . .

MOSS. *Hey*. (*pause*)

AARONOW. So all this, um, you didn't, actually, you didn't actually go talk to Graff.

MOSS. Not actually, no. (*pause*)

AARONOW. You didn't?

MOSS. No. Not actually.

AARONOW. Did you?

MOSS. What did I say?

AARONOW. What did you say?

MOSS. Yes. (*pause*) I said, "Not actually." The fuck *you* care, George? We're just *talking* . . .

AARONOW. We are?

MOSS. Yes. (*pause*)

AARONOW. Because, because, you know, it's a *crime*.

MOSS. That's right. It's a crime. It is a crime. It's also very safe.

AARONOW. You're actually *talking* about this?

MOSS. That's right. (*pause*)

AARONOW. You're going to steal the leads?

MOSS. Have I said that? (*pause*)

AARONOW. Are you? (*pause*)

MOSS. Did I say that?

AARONOW. Did you talk to Graff?

MOSS. Is that what I said?

AARONOW. What did he say?

MOSS. What did he say? He'd *buy* them. (*pause*)

AARONOW. You're going to steal the leads and sell the leads to him? (*pause*)

MOSS. Yes.

AARONOW. What will he pay?

MOSS. A buck a shot.

AARONOW. For five thousand?

MOSS. However they are, that's the deal. A buck a throw. Five thousand dollars. Split it half and half.

AARONOW. You're saying "me."

MOSS. Yes. (*pause*) Twenty-five hundred apiece. One night's work, and the job with Graff. Working the premium leads. (*pause*)

AARONOW. A job with Graff.

MOSS. Is that what I said?

AARONOW. He'd give me a job.

MOSS. He would take you on. Yes. (*pause*)

AARONOW. Is that the truth?

MOSS. Yes. It is, George. (*pause*) Yes. It's a big decision. (*pause*) And it's a big reward. (*pause*) It's a big reward. For one night's work. (*pause*) But it's got to be tonight.

AARONOW. What?

MOSS. What? What? The *leads*.

AARONOW. You have to steal the leads tonight?

MOSS. That's *right*, the guys are moving them downtown. After the thirtieth. Murray and Mitch. After the contest.

AARONOW. You're, you're saying so you have to go in there tonight and . . .

MOSS. You.

AARONOW. I'm sorry?

MOSS. You (*pause*)

AARONOW. Me?

MOSS. *You* have to go in. (*pause*) *You* have to get the leads. (*pause*)

AARONOW. I do?

MOSS. Yes.

AARONOW. I . . .

MOSS. It's not something for nothing, George, I took you in on this, you have to go. That's your thing. I've made the deal with Graff. I can't go. I can't go in, I've spoken on this too much. I've got a big mouth. (*pause*) "The fucking leads" et cetera, "blah blah blah" . . . "the fucking tight ass company . . ."

AARONOW. They'll know when you go over to Graff . . .

MOSS. What will they know? That I stole the leads? I *didn't* steal the leads. I'm going to the *movies* tonight with a friend, and then I'm going to the Como Inn. Why did I go to Graff? I got a better deal. *Period.* Let 'em prove something. They can't prove anything that's not the case. (*pause*)

AARONOW. *Dave.*

MOSS. Yes.

AARONOW. You want me to break into the office tonight and *steal* the leads?

MOSS. Yes. (*pause*)

AARONOW. No.

MOSS. Oh, yes, George.

AARONOW. What does that mean?

MOSS. Listen to this. I have an alibi, I'm going to the Como Inn. Why? The place gets robbed, they're going to come looking for *me*. Why? Because I probably did it. Are you going to turn me in? (*pause*) George? Are you going to turn me in?

AARONOW. What if you don't get caught?

MOSS. They come to you, you going to turn me in?

AARONOW. Why would they come to me?

MOSS. They're going to come to *everyone*.

AARONOW. Why would I *do* it?

MOSS. You wouldn't, George, that's why I'm talking to you. Answer me. They come to you. You going to turn me in?

AARONOW. No.

MOSS. Are you sure?

AARONOW. Yes. I'm sure.

MOSS. Then listen to this: I have to get those leads tonight. That's something I have to do. If I'm not at the *movies* . . . if I'm not eating over at the inn . . . If you don't do this, then *I* have to come in here . . .

AARONOW. . . . you don't have to come in . . .

MOSS. . . . and *rob* the place . . .

AARONOW. . . . I thought that we were only talking . . .

MOSS. . . . they *take* me, then. They're going to ask me who were my accomplices.

AARONOW. *Me?*

MOSS. Absolutely.

AARONOW. That's ridiculous.

MOSS. Well, to the law, you're an accessory. Before the fact.

AARONOW. I didn't ask to be.

MOSS. Then tough luck, George, because you are.

AARONOW. Why? *Why*, because you only *told* me about it?

MOSS. That's right.

AARONOW. Why are you doing this to me, Dave. Why are you talking this way to me? I don't understand. Why are you doing this at *all* . . . ?

MOSS. That's none of your fucking business . . .

AARONOW. Well, well, well, *talk* to me, we sat down to eat *dinner*, and here I'm a *criminal* . . .

MOSS. You *went* for it.

AARONOW. In the abstract . . .

MOSS. So I'm making it concrete.

AARONOW. Why?

MOSS. Why? *You* going to give me five grand?

AARONOW. Do you need five grand?

MOSS. Is that what I just said?

AARONOW. You need money? Is that the . . .

MOSS. Hey, hey, let's just keep it simple, what I need is not the . . . what do *you* need . . . ?

AARONOW. What is the five grand? (*pause*) What is the, you said that we were going to *split* five . . .

MOSS. I lied. (*pause*) Alright. My end is *my* business. Your end's twenty-five. In or out. You tell me, you're out you take the consequences.

AARONOW. I do?

MOSS. Yes. (*pause*)

AARONOW. And why is that?

MOSS. Because you listened.

SCENE 3

The restaurant. Roma is seated alone at the booth. Lingk is at the booth next to him. Roma is talking to him.

ROMA. . . . all train compartments smell vaguely of shit. It gets so you don't mind it. That's the worst thing that I can confess. You know how long it took me to get there? A long time. When you *die* you're going to regret the things you don't do. You think you're *queer* . . . ? I'm going to tell you something: we're *all* queer. You think that you're a *thief*? So *what*? You get befuddled by a middle-class morality . . . ? Get *shut* of it. Shut it out. You cheated on your wife . . . ? You *did* it, *live* with it. (*pause*) You fuck little girls, so *be* it. There's an absolute morality? May *be*. And *then* what? If you *think* there is, then *be* that thing. Bad people go to hell? I don't *think* so. If you think that, act that way. A hell exists on earth? Yes. I won't live in it. That's *me*. You ever take a dump made you feel you'd just slept for twelve hours . . . ?

LINGK. Did I . . . ?

ROMA. Yes.

LINGK. I don't know.

ROMA. Or a *piss* . . . ? A great meal fades in reflection. Everything else gains. You know why? 'Cause it's only food. This shit we eat, it keeps us going. But it's only food. The great fucks that you may have had. What do you remember about them?

LINGK. What do I . . . ?

ROMA. Yes.

LINGK. Mmmm . . .

ROMA. I don't know. For *me*, I'm saying, what it is, it's probably not the orgasm. Some broads, forearms on your neck, something her *eyes* did. There was a *sound* she made . . . or, me, lying, in the, I'll tell you: me lying in bed; the next day she brought me café au lait. She gives me a cigarette, my balls feel like concrete. Eh? What I'm saying, what is our life? (*pause*) It's looking forward or its looking back. And that's our life. That's *it*. Where is the *moment*? (*pause*) And what is it that we're afraid of? Loss. What else? (*pause*) The *bank* closes. We get *sick,* my wife died on a plane, the stock market collapsed. . . . the house burnt down . . . what of these happen . . . ? None of 'em. We worry anyway. What does this mean? I'm not *secure.* How can I be secure? (*pause*) Through amassing wealth beyond all measure? No. And what's beyond all measure? That's a sickness. That's a trap. There is no measure. Only greed. How can we act? The right way, we would say, to deal with this: "There is a one-in-a-million chance that so and so will happen. . . . *Fuck* it, it won't happen to *me*. . . ." No. We know that's not the right way I think. (*pause*) We say the *correct* way to deal with this is "There is a one-in-so-and-so chance this will happen . . . God *protect* me. I am powerless, let it not happen to me. . . . But no to *that.* I say. There's something else. What is it? "If it happens, AS IT MAY for that is not within our powers, I will *deal* with it, just as I do *today* with what draws my concern today." I say *this* is how *we* must act. I do these things which seem correct to me *today.* I trust myself. And if security concerns me, I do that which *today* I think will make me secure. And every day I *do* that, when that day *arrives* that I need a reserve, (a) odds are that I have it, and (b) the *true* reserve that I have is the strength that I have of *acting each day* without fear. (*pause*) According to the dictates of my mind. (*pause*) Stocks, bonds, objects of art, real estate. Now: what are they? (*pause*) An opportunity. To what? To make money? Perhaps. To lose money? Perhaps. To "indulge" and to "learn" about ourselves? Perhaps. So *fucking what?* What *isn't?* They're an *opportunity.* That's all. They're an *event.* A guy comes up to you, you make a call, you send in a brochure, it doesn't matter. "There're these *properties* I'd like for you to see." What does it mean? What you *want* it to mean. (*Pause*) Money? (*pause*) If that's what it signifies to you. Security? (*pause*) Comfort? (*pause*) All it is is THINGS THAT HAPPEN TO YOU. (*pause*) That's all it is. How are they different? (*pause*) Some poor newly married guy gets run down by a cab. Some *busboy* wins the lottery. (*pause*) All it is, it's a carnival. What's special . . . what *draws* us? (*pause*) We're all different. (*pause*) We're not the same. (*pause*) We are not the same. (*pause*) Hmmm. (*pause, sighs*) It's been a long day. (*pause*) What are you drinking?

LINGK. Gimlet.

ROMA. Well, let's have a couple more. My name is Richard Roma, what's yours?

LINGK. Lingk, James Lingk.

ROMA. James. I'm glad to meet you. (*They shake hands.*) I'm glad to meet you. James. (*pause*) I want to show you something. (*pause*) It might mean *nothing* to you . . . and it might not. I don't know. I don't know anymore. (*Pause. He takes out a small map and spreads it on the table.*) What is that? Florida. Glengarry Highlands, Florida. "Florida. *Bullshit.*" And maybe that's true; and that's what *I* said: but look *here*: what is this? This is a piece of land. Listen to what I'm going to tell you now:

The real estate office. Ransacked. A broken plateglass window boarded up, glass all over the floor. Aaronow and Williamson standing around, smoking. Pause.

AARONOW. People used to say that there are numbers of such magnitude that multiplying them by two made no difference. (*pause*)

WILLIAMSON. Who used to say that?

AARONOW. In school. (*pause*)

(*Baylen, a detective, comes out of the inner office.*)

BAYLEN. Alright . . . ?

(*Roma enters from the street.*)

ROMA. *Williamson . . . Williamson,* they stole the *contracts* . . . ?

BAYLEN. Excuse me, sir . . .

ROMA. Did they get my contracts?

WILLIAMSON. They got . . .

BAYLEN. Excuse me, fella.

ROMA. . . . did they . . .

BAYLEN. Would you excuse us, please . . . ?

ROMA. Don't *fuck* with me, fella. I'm talking about a fuckin' Cadillac car that you owe me . . .

WILLIAMSON. They didn't get your contract. I filed it before I left.

ROMA. They didn't get my contracts?

WILLIAMSON. They—excuse me . . . (*He goes back into inner room with the detective.*)

ROMA. Oh, *fuck. Fuck.* (*He starts kicking the desk.*) FUCK FUCK FUCK! WILLIAMSON!!! WILLIAMSON!!! (*Goes to the door Williamson went into, tries the door; it's locked.*) OPEN THE FUCKING . . . WILLIAMSON . . .

BAYLEN. (*coming out*) Who are you? (*Williamson comes out.*)

WILLIAMSON. They didn't get the contracts.

ROMA. Did they . . .

WILLIAMSON. They got, listen to me . . .

ROMA. Th . . .

WILLIAMSON. Listen to me: They got *some* of them.

ROMA. Some of them . . .

BAYLEN. Who told you . . . ?

ROMA. Who told me wh . . . ? You've got a fuckin', you've . . . a . . . who is this . . . ? You've got a board up on the window. . . . Moss told me.

BAYLEN (*looking back toward the inner office*). Moss . . . Who told him?

ROMA. How the fuck do *I* know? (*to Williamson*) What . . . *talk* to me.

WILLIAMSON. They took *some* of the con . . .

ROMA. . . . some of the contracts . . . Lingk. James Lingk. I closed . . .

WILLIAMSON. You closed him yesterday.

ROMA. Yes.

WILLIAMSON. It went down. I filed it.

ROMA. You did?

WILLIAMSON. Yes.

ROMA. Then I'm over the fucking top and you owe me a Cadillac.

WILLIAMSON. I . . .

ROMA. And I don't want any fucking shit and I don't give a shit, Lingk puts me over the top, you filed it, that's fine, any other shit kicks out *you* go back. You . . . *you* reclose it, 'cause I *closed* it and you . . . you owe me the car.

BAYLEN. Would you excuse us, please.

AARONOW. I, um, and may . . . maybe they're in . . . they're in . . . you should, John, if we're ins . . .

WILLIAMSON. I'm sure that we're insured, George . . . (*going back inside*)

ROMA. Fuck insured. You owe me a car.

BAYLEN (*stepping back into the inner room*). Please don't leave. I'm going to talk to you. What's your name?

ROMA. Are you talking to me? (*pause*)

BAYLEN. Yes. (*pause*)

ROMA. My name is Richard Roma. (*Baylen goes back into the inner room.*)

AARONOW. I, you know, they should be insured.

ROMA. What do *you* care . . . ?

AARONOW. Then, you know, they wouldn't be so ups . . .

ROMA. Yeah. That's swell. Yes. You're right. (*pause*) How are you?

AARONOW. I'm fine. You mean the *board*? You mean the *board* . . . ?

ROMA. I don't . . . yes. Okay, the board.

AARONOW. I'm, I'm, I'm, I'm fucked on the board. *You.* You see how . . . I . . . (*pause*) I can't . . . my mind must be in other places. 'Cause I can't do any . . .

ROMA. *What?* You can't do any *what?* (*pause*)

AARONOW. I can't close 'em.

ROMA. Well, they're old. I saw the shit that they were giving you.

AARONOW. Yes.

ROMA. Huh?

AARONOW. Yes. They are old.

ROMA. They're ancient.

AARONOW. Clear . . .

ROMA. Clear Meadows. That shit's dead. (*pause*)

AARONOW. It *is* dead.

ROMA. It's a waste of time.

AARONOW. Yes. (*long pause*) I'm no fucking good.

ROMA. That's . . .

AARONOW. Everything I . . . *you* know . . .

ROMA. That's not . . . Fuck that shit, George. You're a, *hey,* you had a bad month. You're a good man, George.

AARONOW. I am?

ROMA. You hit a bad streak. We've all . . . look at this: fifteen units Mountain View, the fucking things get stole.

AARONOW. He said he filed . . .

ROMA. He filed half of them, he file the *big* one. All the little ones, I have, I have to go back and . . . ah, *fuck,* I got to go out like a fucking schmuck hat in my and reclose the . . . (*pause*) I mean, talk about a bad streak. That would sap *anyone's* self confi . . . I got to go out and reclose all my . . . Where's the phones?

AARONOW. They stole . . .

ROMA. They stole the . . .

AARONOW. What. What kind of outfit are were running where . . . where anyone . . .

ROMA (*to himself*). They stole the phones.

AARONOW. Where criminals can come in here . . . they take the . . .

ROMA. They stole the phones. They stole the leads. They're . . . *Christ.* (*pause*) What am I going to do this month? Oh, shit . . . (*starts for the door*)

AARONOW. You think they're going to catch . . . where are you going?

ROMA. Down the street.

WILLIAMSON (*sticking his head out of the door*). Where are you going?

ROMA. To the restaura . . . what do you fucking . . . ?

WILLIAMSON. Aren't you going out today?

ROMA. With what? (*pause*) With what, John, they took the leads . . .

WILLIAMSON. I have the stuff from last year's . . .

ROMA. Oh. Oh. Oh, your "nostalgia" file, that's fine. No. Swell. 'Cause I don't have to . . .

WILLIAMSON. . . . you want to go out today . . . ?

ROMA. 'Cause I don't have to *eat* this month. No. Okay. Give 'em to me . . . (*to himself*) Fucking Mitch and Murray going to shit a br . . . what am I going to *do* all . . . (*Williamson starts back into the office. He is accosted by Aaronow.*)

AARONOW. Were the leads . . .

ROMA. . . . what am I going to *do* all month . . . ?

AARONOW. Were the leads insured?

WILLIAMSON. I don't know, George, why?

AARONOW. 'Cause, you know, 'cause they weren't, I know that Mitch and Murray uh . . . (*pause*)

WILLIAMSON. What?

AARONOW. That they're going to be upset.

WILLIAMSON. That's right. (*Going back into his office, pause; to Roma:*) You want to go out today . . . ? (*Pause, Williamson returns to his office.*)

AARONOW. He said we're all going to have to go talk to the guy.

ROMA. What?

AARONOW. He said we . . .

ROMA. To the cop?

AARONOW. Yeah.

ROMA. Yeah. That's swell. *Another* waste of time.

AARONOW. A waste of time? Why?

ROMA. *Why?* 'Cause they aren't going to find the guy.

AARONOW. The cops?

ROMA. Yes. The cops. No.

AARONOW. They aren't?

ROMA. No.

AARONOW. Why don't you think so?

ROMA. Why? Because they're *stupid*. "Where were you last night . . .

AARONOW. Where were you?

ROMA. Where was *I*?

AARONOW. Yes.

ROMA. I was at home, where were *you*?

AARONOW. At home.

ROMA. *See . . . ?* Were you the guy who broke in?

AARONOW. Was I?

ROMA. Yes.

AARONOW. No.

ROMA. Then don't sweat it, George, you know why?

AARONOW. No.

ROMA. You have nothing to hide.

AARONOW (*pause*). When I talk to the police, I get nervous.

ROMA. Yeah. You know who doesn't?

AARONOW. No, who?

ROMA. Thieves.

AARONOW. Why?

ROMA. They're inured to it.

AARONOW. You think so?

ROMA. Yes. (*pause*)

AARONOW. But what should I *tell* them?

ROMA. The truth, George. Always tell the truth. It's the easiest thing to remember. (*Williamson comes out of the office with leads. Roma takes one, reads it.*)

ROMA. *Patel*? Ravidam *Patel*? How am I going to make a living on these deadbeat *wogs*? Where did you get this, from the *morgue*?

WILLIAMSON. If you don't want it, give it back.

ROMA. I don't "want" it, if you catch my drift.

WILLIAMSON. I'm giving you *three* leads. You . . .

ROMA. What's the fucking point in *any* case . . . ? What's the *point*. I got to argue with *you*, I got to knock heads with the *cops*, I'm busting my *balls*, sell your *dirt* to fucking *deadbeats* money in the *mattress*, I come back you can't even manage to keep the contracts safe, I have to go back and close them *again*. . . . What the fuck am I wasting my time, fuck this shit. I'm going out and reclose last week's . . .

WILLIAMSON. The word from Murray is: leave them alone. If we need a new signature he'll go out himself, he'll be the *president*, just come *in*, from out of *town* . . .

ROMA. Okay, okay, okay, gimme this shit. Fine. (*takes the leads*)

WILLIAMSON. Now, I'm giving you three . . .

ROMA. Three? I count *two*.

WILLIAMSON. Three.

ROMA. Patel? Fuck *you*. Fuckin' *Shiva* handed him a million dollars, told him "sign the deal," he wouldn't sign. And Vishnu, too. Into the bargain. Fuck *that*, John. You know your business, I know mine. Your business is being an *asshole*, and I find out whose fucking *cousin* you are, I'm go-

ing to go to him and figure out a way to have your *ass* . . . fuck you—I'll wait for the new leads.

(*Shelly Levene enters.*)

LEVENE. Get the *chalk*. Get the *chalk* . . . get the chalk! I closed 'em! I *closed* the cocksucker. Get the chalk and put me on the *board*. I'm going to Hawaii! Put me on the Cadillac board, Williamson! Pick up the fuckin' chalk. Eight units. Mountain View . . .

ROMA. You sold eight Mountain View?

LEVENE. You bet your ass. Who wants to go to lunch? Who wants to go to lunch? I'm buying. (*slaps contract down on Williamson's desk*) Eighty-two fucking grand. And twelve grand in commission. John. (*pause*) On fucking deadbeat magazine subscription leads.

WILLIAMSON. Who?

LEVENE (*pointing to contract*). *Read* it. Bruce and Harriett Nyborg. (*looking around*) What happened here?

AARONOW. Fuck. I had them on River Glen. (*Levene looks around*)

LEVENE. What happened?

WILLIAMSON. Somebody broke in.

ROMA. Eight units?

LEVENE. That's right.

ROMA. *Shelly . . . !*

LEVENE. Hey, big fucking deal. Broke a bad streak . . .

AARONOW. Shelly, the Machine, Levene.

LEVENE. You . . .

AARONOW. That's great.

LEVENE. Thank you, George.

(*Baylen sticks his head out of the room; calls in, "Aaronow."*)

LEVENE. Williamson, get on the phone, call Mitch . . .

ROMA. They took the phones . . .

LEVENE. They . . .

BAYLEN. *Aaronow* . . .

ROMA. They took the typewriters, they took the leads, they took the *cash*, they took the *contracts* . . .

LEVENE. Wh . . . wh . . . Wha . . . ?

AARONOW. We had a robbery. (*goes into the inner room*)

LEVENE (*pause*). When?

ROMA. Last night, this morning. (*pause*)

LEVENE. They took the leads?

ROMA. Mmm.

(*Moss comes out of the interrogation.*)

MOSS. Fuckin' asshole.

ROMA. What, they beat you with a rubber bat?

MOSS. Cop couldn't find his dick two hands and a map. Anyone talks to this guy's an *asshole* . . .

ROMA. You going to turn State's?

MOSS. Fuck you, Ricky. I ain't going out today. I'm going home. I'm going home because nothing's *accomplished* here. . . . Anyone *talks* to this guy is . . .

ROMA. Guess what the Machine did?

MOSS. Fuck the Machine.

ROMA. Mountain View. Eight units.

MOSS. Fuckin' cop's got no right talk to me that way. I didn't rob the place . . .

ROMA. You hear what I said?

MOSS. Yeah. He closed a deal.

ROMA. Eight units. Mountain View.

MOSS (*to Levene*). You did that?

LEVENE. Yeah. (*pause*)

MOSS. Fuck you.

ROMA. Guess who?

MOSS. When . . .

LEVENE. Just now.

ROMA. Guess who?

MOSS. You just this morning . . .

ROMA. Harriet and blah blah Nyborg.

MOSS. You did that?

LEVENE. Eighty-two thousand dollars. (*pause*)

MOSS. Those fuckin' *deadbeats* . . .

LEVENE. My ass, I told 'em (*to Roma*) Listen to this: I said . . .

MOSS. Hey, I don't want to hear your fucking war stories . . .

ROMA. Fuck *you*, Dave . . .

LEVENE. "You have to believe in your*self* . . . you"—look—"alright . . . ?"

MOSS (*to Williamson*). Give me some leads. I'm going out . . . I'm getting out of . . .

LEVENE. ". . . you have to believe in your*self* . . . "

MOSS. Na, fuck the leads, I'm going home.

LEVENE. "Bruce, Harriet . . . Fuck *me*, believe in your*self* . . . "

ROMA. We haven't got a lead . . .

MOSS. Why not?

ROMA. They took 'em . . .

MOSS. Hey, they're fuckin' garbage any case. . . . This whole goddamn . . .

LEVENE. ". . . You look around, you say, 'This one has so-and-so, and I have nothing . . . '"

MOSS. *Shit.*

LEVENE. "*Why*? Why don't I get the opportunities . . . ?"

MOSS. And did they steal the contracts . . . ?

ROMA. Fuck *you* are . . . ?

LEVENE. "I want to tell you something, Harriett . . . "

MOSS. . . . the fuck is *that* supposed to mean . . . ?

LEVENE. Will you shut up, I'm telling you this . . . (*Aaronow sticks his head out.*)

AARONOW. Can we get some coffee . . . ?

MOSS. How ya doing? (*pause*)

AARONOW. Fine.

MOSS. Uh-huh.

AARONOW. If anyone's going, I could use some coffee.

LEVENE. "You *do* get the . . . " (*to Roma*) Huh? Huh?

MOSS. *Fuck* is that supposed to mean?

LEVENE. "You *do* get the opportunity. . . . You *get* them. As *I* do, as *anyone* does . . . "

MOSS. Ricky? . . . That I don't care they stole the contracts? (*pause*)

LEVENE. I got 'em in the kitchen. I'm eating her crumb cake.

MOSS. What does that mean?

ROMA. It *means*, Dave, you haven't closed a good one in a month, none of my business, you want to push me to answer you. (*pause*) And so you haven't got a contract to get stolen or so forth.

MOSS. You have a mean streak in you, Ricky, you know that . . . ?

LEVENE. Rick. Let me tell you. Wait, we're in the . . .

MOSS. Shut the fuck up. (*pause*) Ricky. You have a mean streak in you. . . . (*to Levene*) And what the fuck are *you* babbling about . . . ? (*to Roma*) Bring that shit up. Of my volume. You were on a bad one and I brought it up to *you* you'd harbor it. (*pause*) You'd harbor it a long long while. And you'd be right.

ROMA. Who said "Fuck the Machine"?

MOSS. "*Fuck the Machine*"? "*Fuck the Machine*"? What is this. *Courtesy* class . . . ? You're *fucked*, Rick—are you fucking *nuts*? You're hot, so you think you're the *ruler* of this place . . . ?! You want to . . .

LEVENE. Dave . . .

MOSS. Shut up. Decide who should be dealt with how? Is that the thing? I come into the fuckin' office today, I get humiliated by some jagoff cop. I get accused of . . . I get this *shit* thrown in my face by you, you genuine shit, because you're the top name on the board . . .

ROMA. Is that what I did? Dave? I humiliated you? My *God* . . . I'm *sorry* . . .

MOSS. Sittin' on top of the *world*, sittin' on top of the *world*, everything's fucking *peach*fuzz . . .

ROMA. Oh, and I don't get a moment to spare for a bust-out *humanitarian* down on his luck lately. Fuck *you*, Dave, you know you got a big *mouth*. And *you* make a close the whole *place* stinks with your *farts* for a week. "How much you just ingested," what a big *man* you are, "Hey, let me buy you a pack of gum. I'll show you how to *chew* it." Your *pal* closes, all that comes out of your mouth is *bile*, how fucked *up* you are . . .

MOSS. *Who's* my pal . . . ? And what are you, Ricky, huh, what are you, Bishop *Sheean*? Who the fuck are *you*, Mr. Slick . . . ? What are you, friend to the *workingman*? Big deal. Fuck *you*, you got the memory a fuckin' fly. I never liked you.

ROMA. What is this, your farewell speech?

MOSS. I'm going home.

ROMA. Your farewell to the troops?

MOSS. I'm not going home. I'm going to Wisconsin.

ROMA. Have a good trip.

MOSS (*simultaneously with "trip"*). And fuck *you*. Fuck the *lot* of you. Fuck you *all*. (*Moss exits. Pause.*)

ROMA (*to Levene*). You were saying? (*pause*) Come on. Come on, you got them in the kitchen, you got the stats spread out, you're in your shirtsleeves, you can *smell* it. Huh? Snap out of it, you're eating her *crumb* cake. (*pause*)

LEVENE. I'm eating her *crumb* cake . . .

ROMA. How was it . . . ?

LEVENE. From the store.

ROMA. Fuck *her* . . .

LEVENE. "What we have to do is *admit* to ourself that we see that opportunity . . . and *take* it. (*pause*) And that's it." And we *sit* there. (*pause*) I got the pen out . . .

ROMA. "Always be closing . . . "

LEVENE. That's what I'm *saying*. The *old* ways. The *old* ways . . . convert the motherfucker . . . *sell* him . . . *sell* him . . . *make him sign the check*. (*pause*) The . . . Bruce, Harriett . . . the kitchen, blah: they got their money in *government* bonds. . . . I say *fuck* it, we're going to go the whole route. I plat it out eight units. Eighty-two grand. I tell them. "This is now. This is that *thing* that you've been dreaming of, you're going to find that suitcase on the train, the guy comes in the door, the bag that's full of money. This is it, *Harriett* . . . "

ROMA (*reflectively*). Harriet . . .

LEVENE. *Bruce* . . . "I don't want to fuck *around* with you. I don't want to go *round* this, and pussyfoot *around* the thing, you have to look back on this. I do, too. I came here to do good for you and me. For *both* of us. Why take an interim position? *The only arrangement I'll accept* is full investment. Period. The whole eight units. I know that you're saying 'be safe,' I know what you're saying. I know if I left you to yourselves, you'd say 'come back tomorrow,' and when I walked out that door, you'd make a cup of *coffee* . . . you'd sit *down* . . . and you'd think 'let's be safe. . .' and not to disappoint me you'd go *one* unit or maybe two, because you'd become scared because you'd met possi*bility*. But this won't do, and that's not the subject. . . ." Listen to this, I actually said this. "That's not the subject of our *evening* together." Now I handed them the pen. I held it in my hand. I turned the contract, eight units—eighty-two grand. "Now I want you to sign." (*pause*) I sat there. Five minutes. Then, I sat there, Ricky, *twenty-two minutes* by the kitchen *clock*. (*pause*) Twenty-two minutes by the kitchen clock. Not a *word*, not a mo*tion*. What am I thinking? "My arm's getting tired?" *No.* I *did* it. I *did* it. Like in the *old* days, Ricky. Like I was taught . . . Like, like, like, I *used* to do . . . I did it.

ROMA. Like you taught me . . .

LEVENE. Bullshit, you're . . . No. That's . . . that's . . . well, if I *did*, then I'm *glad* I did. I, *well*. I locked on them. All of them, nothing on me. All my thoughts are on them. I'm holding the last thought that I spoke: "Now is the time." (*pause*) They signed, Ricky. It was *great*. It was fucking great. It was like they wilted all at once. No *gesture* . . . nothing. Like together. They, I swear to God, they both kind of *imperceptibly slumped*. And he reaches and takes the pen and signs, he passes it to her, she signs. It was so fucking solemn. I just let it sit. I nod like this. I nod again. I grasp his hands. I shake his hands. I grasp *her* hands. I nod at her like this. "Bruce . . . Harriett . . ." I'm beaming at them. I'm nodding like this. I point back in

the living room, back to the sideboard. (*pause*) *I didn't fucking know there was a sideboard there!!* He goes back, he brings us a drink. Little shot glasses. A pattern in 'em. And we toast. In silence. (*pause*)

ROMA. That was a great sale, Shelly. (*pause*)

LEVENE. Ah, fuck. Leads! Leads! Williamson! (*Williamson sticks his head out of the office.*) Send me *out*! Send me *out*!

WILLIAMSON. The leads are coming.

LEVENE. *Get* 'em to me!

WILLIAMSON. I talked to Murray and Mitch an hour ago. They're coming in, you understand they're a bit *upset* over this morning's . . .

LEVENE. Did you tell 'em my sale?

WILLIAMSON. How could I tell 'em your sale? Eh? I don't have a tel . . . I'll tell 'em your sale when they bring in the leads. Alright? Shelly. Alright? We had a little . . . You closed a deal. You made a good sale. Fine.

LEVENE. It's better than a good sale. It's a . . .

WILLIAMSON. Look: I have a lot of things on my mind, they're coming in, alright, they're very upset, I'm trying to make some *sense* . . .

LEVENE. All that I'm *telling* you: that one thing you can tell them it's a remarkable sale.

WILLIAMSON. The only thing remarkable is who you made it to.

LEVENE. What does *that* fucking mean?

WILLIAMSON. That if the sale sticks, it will be a miracle.

LEVENE. Why should the sale not stick? Hey, *fuck* you. That's what I'm saying. You have no idea of your job. A man's his job and you're *fucked* at yours. You hear what I'm saying to you? Your "end of the month board . . ." You can't run an office. I don't care. You don't know what it *is*, you don't have the *sense*, you don't have the *balls*. You ever been on a sit. *Ever*? Has this cocksucker ever been . . . you ever sit down with a cust . . .

WILLIAMSON. I were you, I'd calm down, Shelly.

LEVENE. *Would* you? *Would* you . . . ? Or you're gonna *what*, fire me?

WILLIAMSON. It's not impossible.

LEVENE. On an eighty-thousand dollar *day*? And it ain't even *noon*.

ROMA. You closed 'em today?

LEVENE. Yes. I did. This *morning*. (*to Williamson*) What I'm *saying* to you: things can *change*. You *see*? This is where you fuck *up*, because this is something you don't *know*. You can't look down the *road*. And see what's *coming*. Might be someone *else*, John. It might be someone *new*, eh? Someone *new*. And you can't look *back*. 'Cause you don't know *history*. You ask them. When we were at Rio Rancho, who was top man? A month . . . ? Two months . . . ? Eight months in twelve for three years in a row. You know what that means? You know what that means? Is that *luck*? Is that some, some, some purloined leads? That's *skill*. That's *talent*, that's, that's . . .

ROMA. . . . . *yes* . . .

LEVENE. . . . and you don't *remember*. 'Cause you weren't *around*. That's cold *calling*. Walk up to the door. I don't even know their *name*. I'm selling something they don't even *want*. You talk about soft sell . . . before we had a name for it . . . before we called it anything, we did it.

ROMA. That's right, Shel.

LEVENE. And, and, and, I *did* it. And I put a kid through *school*. My *daughter* . . . She . . . and . . . Cold *calling*, fella. Door to door. But you don't know. You don't know. You never heard of a *streak*. You never heard of "marshaling your sales force. . . ." What are you, you're a *secretary*, John. Fuck *you*. That's my message to you. Fuck you and kiss my ass. You don't like it, I'll go talk to Jerry Graff. Period. Fuck you. Put me on the board. And I want three worthwhile leads today and I don't want any bullshit about them and I want 'em close together 'cause I'm going to hit them all today. That's all I have to say to you.

ROMA. He's right, Williamson. (*Williamson goes into a side office. Pause*)

LEVENE. It's not right. I'm sorry, and I'll tell you who's to blame is Mitch and Murray. (*Roma sees something outside the window.*)

ROMA (*sotto*). Oh, Christ.

LEVENE. The hell with him. We'll go to lunch, the leads won't be up for . . .

ROMA. You're a client. I just sold you five waterfront Glengarry Farms. I rub my head, throw me the cue "Kenilworth."

LEVEN. What is it?

ROMA. Kenilw . . . (*Lingk enters the office.*)

ROMA (*to Levene*). I own the property, my *mother* owns the property, I put her *into* it. I'm going to show you on the plats. You look when you get home A-3 through A-14 and 26 through 30. You take your time and if you still feel.

LEVENE. No, Mr. Roma. I don't need the time, I've made a lot of *investments* in the last . . .

LINGK. I've got to talk to you.

ROMA (*looking up*). Jim! What are you doing here? Jim Lingk, D. Ray Morton . . .

LEVENE. Glad to meet you.

ROMA. I just put Jim into Black Creek . . . are you acquainted with . . .

LEVENE. No . . . Black *Creek*. Yes. In *Florida*?

ROMA. Yes.

LEVENE. I wanted to *speak* with you about . . .

ROMA. Well, we'll do that this weekend.

LEVENE. My *wife* told me to look into . . .

ROMA. *Beautiful.* Beautiful rolling land. I was telling Jim and Jinny, Ray, I want to tell you something. (*to Levene*) You, Ray, you eat in a lot of restaurants. I know you do. . . . (*to Lingk*) Mr. Morton's with American Express . . . he's . . . (*to Levene*) I can tell Jim what you do . . . ?

LEVENE. Sure.

ROMA. Ray is director of all European sales and services for American Ex . . . (*to Levene*) But I'm saying you haven't had a *meal* until you've tasted . . . I was at the Lingk's last . . . as a matter of fact, what was that service feature you were talking about . . . ?

LEVENE. Which . . .

ROMA. "Home Cooking" . . . what did you call it, you said . . . it was a tag phrase that you had . . .

LEVENE. Uh . . .

ROMA. Home . . .

LEVENE. Home cooking . . .

ROMA. The monthly interview . . . ?

LEVENE. Oh! For the *magazine* . . .

ROMA. Yes. Is this something that I can talk ab . . .

LEVENE. Well, it isn't coming *out* until the February iss . . . sure. Sure, go ahead, Rick.

ROMA. You're sure?

LEVENE (*nods*). Go ahead.

ROMA. Well, Ray was eating at one of his company's men's home in France . . . the man's French, isn't he?

LEVENE. No, his *wife* is.

ROMA. Ah. Ah, his wife is. Ray: what *time* do you have . . . ?

LEVENE. Twelve-fifteen.

ROMA. Oh! My God . . . I've got to get you on the *plane!*

LEVENE. Didn't I say I was taking the two o' . . .

ROMA. No. You said the one. That 's why you said we couldn't talk till Kenilworth.

LEVENE. Oh, my God, you're right! I'm on the one. . . . (*getting up*) Well, let's scoot . . .

LINGK. I've got to talk to you . . .

ROMA. I've got to get Ray to O'Hare . . . (*to Levene*) Come on, let's hustle. . . . (*over his shoulder*) John! Call American Express in *Pittsburgh* for Mr. Morton, will you, tell them he's on the one o'clock. (*to Lingk*) I'll see you. . . . Christ, I'm sorry you came all the way in. . . . I'm running Ray over to O'Hare. . . . You wait here, I'll . . . no. (*to Levene*) I'm meeting your man at the back. . . . (*to Lingk*) I wish you'd phoned. . . . I'll tell you, wait: are you and Jinny going to be home tonight? (*rubs forehead*)

LINGK. I . . .

LEVENE. Rick.

ROMA. What?

LEVENE. *Kenilworth* . . . ?

ROMA. I'm sorry . . . ?

LEVENE. *Kenilworth.*

ROMA. Oh, God . . . Oh, God . . . (*Roma takes Lingk aside, sotto*) Jim, excuse me. . . . Ray, I told you, who he is is *the* senior vice-president American Express. His family owns 32 per. . . . Over the past years I've sold him . . . I can't tell you the dollar amount, but *quite* a lot of land. I promised five *weeks* ago that I'd go to the wife's birthday party in Kenilworth tonight. (*sighs*) I *have* to go. You understand. They treat me like a member of the family, so I have to go. It's funny, you know, you get a picture of the

Corporation-Type Company Man, all business . . . this man, *no*. We'll go out to his home sometime. Let's see. (*He checks his datebook.*) Tomorrow. No. Tomorrow, I'm in L.A. . . . *Monday* . . . I'll take you to lunch, where would you like to go?

LINGK. My wife . . . (*Roma rubs his head.*)

LEVENE (*standing in the door*). Rick . . . ?

ROMA. I'm sorry, Jim. I can't talk now. I'll call you tonight . . . I'm sorry. I'm coming, Ray. (*starts for the door*)

LINGK. My wife said I have to cancel the deal.

ROMA. It's a common reaction, Jim. I'll tell you what it is, and I know that that's why you married her. One of the reasons is *prudence*. It's a sizable investment. One *thinks* twice . . . it's also something *women* have. It's just a reaction to the size of the investment. *Monday*, if you'd invite me for dinner again . . . (*to Levene*) This woman can *cook* . . .

LEVENE (*simultaneously*). I'm sure she can . . .

ROMA (*to Lingk*). We're going to talk. I'm going to *tell* you something. Because (*sotto*) there's something about your acreage I want you to know. I can't talk about it now. I really shouldn't. And, in fact, by *law*, I . . . (*shrugs, resigned*) The man next to you, he bought his lot at forty-*two*, he phoned to say that he'd *already* had an offer . . . (*Roma rubs his head.*)

LEVENE. Rick . . . ?

ROMA. I'm coming, Ray . . . what a day! I'll call you this evening, Jim. I'm sorry you had to come in . . . Monday, lunch.

LINGK. My wife . . .

LEVENE. Rick, we really have to go.

LINGK. My wife . . .

ROMA. Monday.

LINGK. She called the consumer . . . the attorney, I don't know. The attorney gen . . . they said we have three days . . .

ROMA. *Who* did she call?

LINGK. I don't know, the attorney gen . . . the . . . some consumer office.

ROMA. Why did she do *that*, Jim?

LINGK. I don't know (*pause*) They said we have three days. (*pause*) They said we have three days.

ROMA. Three days.

LINGK. To . . . you know. (*pause*)

ROMA. No, I don't know. *Tell* me.

LINGK. To change our minds.

ROMA. Of *course* you have three days. (*pause*)

LINGK. So we can't talk Monday. (*pause*)

ROMA. Jim, Jim, you saw my book . . . I *can't*, *you* saw my book . . .

LINGK. But we have to *before* Monday. To get our money ba . . .

ROMA. Three *business* days. They mean three *business* days.

LINGK. Wednesday, Thursday, Friday.

ROMA. I don't understand.

LINGK. That's what they are. Three business . . . if I wait till Monday, my time limit runs out.

ROMA. You don't count Saturday.

LINGK. I'm not.

ROMA. No, I'm saying you don't include Saturday . . . in your three days. It's not a *business* day.

LINGK. But I'm not *counting* it. (*pause*) Wednesday. Thursday. Friday. So it would have elapsed.

ROMA. What would have elapsed?

LINGK. If we wait till Mon . . .

ROMA. When did you write the check?

LINGK. Yest . . .

ROMA. What was yesterday?

LINGK. Tuesday.

ROMA. And when was that check cashed?

LINGK. I don't know.

ROMA. What was the *earliest* it could have been cashed? (*pause*)

LINGK. I don't know.

ROMA. *Today*: (*pause*) *Today*. Which, in any case, it was not, as there were a couple of points on the agreement I wanted to go over with you in any case.

LINGK. The check wasn't cashed?

ROMA. I just called downtown, and it's on their desk.

LEVENE. Rick . . .

ROMA. One moment, I'll be right with you. (*to Lingk*) In fact, a . . . *one* point, which I spoke to you of which (*looks around*) I can't talk to you about here.

(*Detective puts his head out of the doorway.*)

BAYLEN. Levene!!!

LINGK. I, I . . .

ROMA. Listen to me, the *statute*, it's for your protection. I have no complaints with that, in fact, I was a member of the board when we *drafted* it, so quite the *opposite*. It *says* that you can change your mind three working days from the time the deal is closed.

BAYLEN. Levene!

ROMA. Which, wait a second, which is not until the check is cashed.

BEYLEN. Levene!!

(*Aaronow comes out of the Detective's office.*)

AARONOW. I'm *through*, with *this* fucking meshugaas. No one should talk to a man that way. How are you *talking* to me that . . . ?

BAYLEN. Levene! (*Williamson puts his head out of the office.*)

AARONOW. . . . how can you *talk* to me that . . . that . . .

LEVENE (*to Roma*). Rick, I'm going to flag a cab.

AARONOW. *I* didn't rob . . . (*Williamson sees Levene.*)

WILLIAMSON. Shelly: Get in the office.

AARONOW. *I* didn't . . . why should *I* . . . "Where were you last . . ." Is anybody listening to me . . . ? Where's Moss . . . ? Where . . . ?

BAYLEN. Levene? (*to Williamson*) Is this Lev . . . (*Baylen accosts Lingk.*)

LEVENE (*taking Baylen into the office*). Ah. Ah. Perhaps I can advise you on that. . . . (*to Roma and Lingk, as he exits*) Excuse us, will you . . . ?

AARONOW (*simultaneous with Levene's speech above*) . . . Come in here . . . I work here, I don't come in here to be *mistreated* . . .

WILLIAMSON. Go to *lunch*, will you . . .

AARONOW. I want to *work* today, that's why I came . . .

WILLIAMSON. The leads come in, I'll let . . .

AARONOW. . . . that's why I came in. I thought I . . .

WILLIAMSON. Just go to lunch.

AARONOW. I don't *want* to go to lunch.

WILLIAMSON. Go to lunch, George.

AARONOW. Where does he get off to talk that way to a working man? It's not . . .

WILLIAMSON (*buttonholes him*). Will you take it outside, we have people trying to do *business* here . . .

AARONOW. That's what, that's what, that's what *I* was trying to do. (*pause*) That's why I came *in* . . . I meet *gestapo* tac . . .

WILLIAMSON (*going back into his office*). Excuse me . . .

AARONOW. I meet *gestapo* tactics . . . I meet *gestapo* tactics. . . . That's not right. . . . No man has the right to . . . "Call an attorney," that means you're guilt . . . you're under sus . . . "Co . . ." he says, "cooperate" or we'll go downtown. *That's* not . . . as long as I've . . .

WILLIAMSON (*bursting out of his office*). Will you get out of here. Will you get *out* of here. Will you. I'm trying to run an *office* here. Will you go to lunch? Go to lunch. Will you go to lunch? (*retreats into office*)

ROMA (*to Aaronow*). Will you excuse . . .

AARONOW. Where did Moss . . .? I . . .

ROMA. Will you excuse me please?

AARONOW. Uh, uh, did he go to the restaurant? (*pause*) I . . . I . . . (*exits*)

ROMA. I'm *very* sorry, Jimmy. I apologize to you.

LINGK. It's not me, it's my wife.

ROMA (*pause*). What is?

LINGK. I told you.

ROMA. Tell me again.

LINGK. What's going on here?

ROMA. Tell me again. Your wife.

LINGK. I told you.

ROMA. You tell me again.

LINGK. She wants her money back.

ROMA. We're going to speak to her.

LINGK. No. She told me "right now."

ROMA. We'll speak to her, Jim . . .

LINGK. She won't listen.

(*Detective sticks his head out.*)

BAYLEN. *Roma.*

LINGK. She told me if not, I have to call the State's attorney.

ROMA. No, no. That's just something she "said." We don't have to do that.

LINGK. She told me I *have* to.

ROMA. No, Jim.

LINGK. I *do*. If I don't get my *money* back . . .

BAYLEN. Roma! (*to Roma*) I'm talking to you . . .

ROMA. I've . . . look. (*generally*) Will someone get this guy off my back.

BAYLEN. You have a problem?

ROMA. Yes, I have a problem. Yes, I *do*, my fr . . . It's not me that ripped the joint off, I'm doing *business*. I'll be with you in a *while*. You got it . . . ? (*Detective goes back into inner office. Looks back, Lingk is heading for the door.*) Where are you going?

LINGK. I'm . . .

ROMA. Where are you going . . . ? This is *me*. . . . This is Ricky, Jim. Jim, anything you *want*, you *want* it, you *have* it. You understand? This is *me*. Something *upset* you. Sit down, now sit down. You tell me what it is. (*pause*) Am I going to help you fix it? You're goddamned right I am. Sit down. Tell you something . . . ? *Sometimes* we need someone from *outside*. It's . . . no, sit down. . . . Now *talk* to me.

LINGK. I can't negotiate.

ROMA. What does that mean?

LINGK. That . . .

ROMA. . . . what, what, *say* it. Say it to me . . .

LINGK. I . . .

ROMA. What . . . ?

LINGK. I . . .

ROMA. What . . . ? Say the words.

LINGK. I don't have the *power*. (*pause*) I said it.

ROMA. What power?

LINGK. The power to negotiate.

ROMA. To negotiate what? (*pause*) To negotiate what?

LINGK. *This.*

ROMA. What, "this"? (*pause*)

LINGK. The deal.

ROMA. The "deal," *forget* the deal. *Forget* the deal, you've got something on your mind, Jim, what is it?

LINGK (*rising*). I can't talk to you, *you* met my wife, I . . . (*pause*)

ROMA. What? (*pause*) What? (*pause*) What, Jim: I tell you what, let's get out of here . . . let's go get a drink.

LINGK. She told me not to talk to you.

ROMA. Let's . . . no one's going to know, let's go around the *corner* and we'll get a drink.

LINGK. She told me I had to get back the check or call the State's att . . .

ROMA. *Forget* the deal, Jimmy. (*pause*) *Forget* the deal . . . you know me. The deal's *dead*. Am I talking about the *deal*? That's *over*. Please. Let's talk about *you*. Come on. (*Pause, Roma rises and starts walking toward the front door.*) Come on. (*pause*) Come on, Jim. (*pause*) I want to tell you something. Your life is your own. You have a contract with your wife. You have certain things you do *jointly*, you have a *bond* there . . . and there are *other* things. Those things are yours. You needn't feel *ashamed*, you needn't feel that you're being *untrue* . . . or that she would abandon you if she knew. This is *your* life. (*pause*) *Yes*. Now I want to *talk* to you because you're obviously upset and that *concerns* me. Now let's go. Right now. (*Lingk gets up and they start for the door.*)

BAYLEN (*sticks his head out of the door*). Roma . . .

LINGK. . . . and . . . and . . . (*pause*)

ROMA. What?

LINGK. And the check is . . .

ROMA. What did I *tell* you? (*pause*) What did I say about the three days . . . ?

BAYLEN. Roma, would you, I'd like to get some lunch . . .

ROMA. I'm talking with Mr. Lingk. If you please, I'll be back in. (*checks watch*) I'll be back in a while. . . . I told you, check with Mr. Williamson.

BAYLEN. The people downtown said . . .

ROMA. You call them again. Mr. Williamson . . . !

WILLIAMSON (*coming out of his office*). Yes.

ROMA. Mr. Lingk and I are going to . . .

WILLIAMSON. Yes. Please. Please. (*to Lingk*) The police (*shrugs*) can be . . .

LINGK. What are the police doing?

ROMA. It's nothing.

LINGK. What are the *police* doing here . . . ?

WILLIAMSON. We had a slight burglary last night.

ROMA. It was nothing . . . I was assuring Mr. Lingk . . .

WILLIAMSON. Mr. Lingk. James Lingk. Your contract went out. Nothing to . . .

ROMA. John . . .

WILLIAMSON. Your contract went out to the bank.

LINGK. You cashed the check?

WILLIAMSON. We . . .

ROMA. . . . Mr. Williamson . . .

WILLIAMSON. Your check was cashed yesterday afternoon. And we're completely insured, as you know, in *any* case. (*pause*)

LINGK (*to Roma*). You cashed the check?

ROMA. Not to my knowledge, no . . .

WILLIAMSON. I'm sure we can . . .

LINGK. Oh, Christ . . . (*starts out the door*) Don't follow me. . . . Oh, Christ. (*pause, to Roma*) I know I've let you down. I'm sorry. For . . . Forgive . . . for . . . I don't know anymore. (*pause*) Forgive me. (*Lingk exits. Pause.*)

ROMA (*to Williamson*). You stupid fucking cunt. *You*, Williamson . . . I'm talking to *you*, shithead. . . . You just cost me *six thousand dollars*. (*pause*) Six thousand dollars. And one Cadillac. That's right. What are you going to do about it. What are you going to do about it, asshole. You fucking *shit*. Where did you learn your *trade*? You stupid fucking *cunt*. You *idiot*. Whoever told you you could work with *men*?

BAYLEN. Could I . . .

ROMA. I'm going to have your *job*, shithead. I'm going *downtown* and talk to Mitch and Murray, and I'm going to

Lemkin. I don't care *whose* nephew you are, who you know, whose dick you're sucking on. You're going *out*, I swear to you, you're going . . .

BAYLEN. Hey, fella, let's get this done . . .

ROMA. Anyone in this office lives on their *wits*. . . . (*to Baylen*) I'm going to be with you in a second. (*to Williamson*) What you're hired for is to *help* us—does that seem clear to you? To *help* us. *Not* to fuck us up . . . to help *men* who are going *out* there to try to earn a *living*. You *fairy*. You company man . . . I'll tell you something else. I hope you knocked the joint off, I can tell our friend here something might help him catch you. (*starts into the room*) You want to learn the first rule you'd know if you ever spent a day in your life . . . you never open your mouth till you know what the shot is. (*pause*) You fucking *child* . . . (*Roma goes to the inner room, followed by Baylen.*)

LEVENE. You *are* a shithead, Williamson . . . (*pause*)

WILLIAMSON. Mmm.

LEVENE. You can't think on your feet you should keep your mouth closed. (*pause*) You hear me? I'm *talking* to you. Do you hear me . . . ?

WILLIAMSON. Yes. (*pause*) I hear you.

LEVENE. You can't learn that in an office. Eh? He's right. You have to learn it on the street. You can't *buy* that. You have to *live* it.

WILLIAMSON. Mmm.

LEVENE. *Yes*. "Mmm." *Yes. Precisely. Precisely.* 'Cause your partner *depends* on it. (*pause*) I'm *talking* to you, I'm trying to tell you something.

WILLIAMSON. You are?

LEVENE. Yes, I am.

WILLIAMSON. What are you trying to tell me?

LEVENE. What Roma's trying to tell you. What I told you yesterday. Why you don't belong in this busienss.

WILLIAMSON. Why I don't . . .

LEVENE. You listen to me, someday you might say, "Hey . . ." No, fuck that, you just listen what I'm going to say: your partner *depends* on you. Your partner . . . a man who's your "partner" *depends* on you . . . you have to go *with* him and *for* him . . . or you're shit, you're *shit*, you can't exist alone . . .

WILLIAMSON (*brushing past him*). Excuse me . . .

LEVENE. . . . excuse you, *nothing*, you be as cold as you want, but you just fucked a good man out of six thousand dollars and his goddamn bonus 'cause you didn't know the *shot*, if you can do that and you aren't man enough that it gets you, then I don't know what, if you can't take *some thing* from that . . . (*blocking his way*) you're *scum*, you're fucking white-bread. You be as cold as you want. A *child* would know it, he's right. (*pause*) You're going to make something up, be sure it will *help* or keep your mouth closed. (*pause*)

WILLIAMSON. Mmm. (*Levene lifts up his arm.*)

LEVENE. Now I'm done with you. (*pause*)

WILLIAMSON. How do you know I made it up?

LEVENE (*pause*). What?

WILLIAMSON. How do you know I made it up?

LEVENE. What are you talking about?

WILLIAMSON. You said, "You don't make something up unless it's sure to help." (*pause*) How did you know that I made it up?

LEVENE. What are you talking about?

WILLIAMSON. I told the customer that his contract had gone to the bank.

LEVENE. Well, hadn't it?

WILLIAMSON. No. (*pause*) It hadn't.

LEVENE. Don't *fuck* with me, John, don't *fuck* with me . . . what are you saying?

WILLIAMSON. Well, I'm saying this, Shel: usually I take the contracts to the bank. Last night I didn't. How did you know that? One night in a year I left a contract on my desk. Nobody knew that but *you*. Now how did you know that? (*pause*) You want to talk to me, you want to talk to someone *else* . . . because this is *my* job. This is my job on the line, and you are going to *talk* to me. Now how did you know that contract was on my desk?

LEVENE. You're so full of shit.

WILLIAMSON. You robbed the office.

LEVENE (*laughs*). Sure! I robbed the office. Sure.

WILLIAMSON. What'd you do with the leads? (*Pause. Points to the Detective's room.*) You want to go in there? I tell him what I know, he's going to dig up *something*. . . . You got an alibi last night? You better have one. What did you do with the leads? If you tell me what you did with the leads, we can talk.

LEVENE. I don't know what you are saying.

WILLIAMSON. If you tell me where the leads are, I won't turn you in. If you *don't*, I am going to tell the cop you stole them, Mitch and Murray will see that you go to jail. Believe me they will. Now, what did you do with the leads? I'm walking in that door—you have five seconds to tell me: or you are going to jail.

LEVENE. I . . .

WILLIAMSON. I don't care. You understand? *Where are the leads?* (*pause*) Alright. (*Williamson goes to open the office door.*)

LEVENE. I sold them to Jerry Graff.

WILLIAMSON. How much did you get for them? (*pause*) How much did you get for them?

LEVENE. Five thousand. I kept half.

WILLIAMSON. Who kept the other half? (*pause*)

LEVENE. Do I have to tell you? (*Pause. Williamson starts to open the door.*) Moss.

WILLIAMSON. *That* was easy, *wasn't* it? (*pause*)

LEVENE. It was his idea.

WILLIAMSON. *Was* it?

LEVENE. I . . . I'm sure he got more than the five, actually.

WILLIAMSON. Ug-huh?

LEVENE. He told me my share was twenty-five.

WILLIAMSON. Mmm.

LEVENE. Okay: I . . . look: I'm going to make it worth your while. I am. I turned this thing around. I closed the *old*

stuff, I can do it again. *I'm* the one's going to close 'em. *I* am! *I* am! 'Cause I turned this thing a . . . I can do *that*, I can do *anyth* . . . last night. I'm going to tell you, I was ready to Do the Dutch. Moss gets me, "Do this, we'll get well. . . ." Why not. Big fuckin' deal. I'm halfway hoping to get caught. To put me out of my . . . (*pause*) But it *taught* me something. What it taught me, that you've got to get *out* there. Big deal. So I wasn't cut out to be a thief. I was cut out to be a salesman. And now I'm back, and I got my *balls* back . . . and, you know, John, you have the *advantage* on me now. Whatever it takes to make it right, we'll make it right. We're going to make it right.

WILLIAMSON. I want to tell you something, Shelly. You have a big mouth. (*pause*)

LEVENE. What?

WILLIAMSON. You've got a big mouth, and now I'm going to show you an even bigger one. (*starts toward the Detective's door*)

LEVENE. Where are you going, John? . . . you can't do that, you don't want to do that . . . hold, hold on . . . hold on . . . wait . . . wait . . . wait . . . (*pulls money out of his pockets*) Wait . . . uh, look . . . (*starts splitting money*) Look, twelve, twenty, two, twen . . . twenty-five hundred, it's . . . take it. (*pause*) Take it all. . . . (*pause*) Take it!

WILLIAMSON. No, I don't think so, Shel.

LEVENE. I . . .

WILLIAMSON. No, I think I don't want your money. I think you fucked up my office. And I think you're going away.

LEVENE. I . . . what? Are you, are you, that's why . . . ? Are you nuts? I'm . . . I'm going to *close* for you, I'm going to . . . (*thrusting money at him*) Here, here, I'm going to *make* this office . . . I'm going to be back there Number One. . . . Hey, hey, hey! This is only the beginning. . . . List . . . list . . . listen. Listen. Just one moment. List . . . here's what . . . here's what we're going to do. Twenty percent. I'm going to give you twenty percent of my sales. . . . (*pause*) Twenty percent. (*pause*) For as long as I am with the firm. (*pause*) Fifty percent. (*pause*) You're going to be my partner. (*pause*) Fifty percent. Of all my sales.

WILLIAMSON. What sales?

LEVENE. What sales . . . ? I just *closed* eighty-two *grand*. . . . Are you fuckin' . . . I'm *back* . . . I'm *back*, this is only the beginning.

WILLIAMSON. Only the beginning . . .

LEVENE. Abso . . .

WILLIAMSON. Where have you been, Shelly? Bruce and Harriet Nyborg. Do you want to see the *memos* . . . ? They're nuts . . . they used to call in every week. When I was with Webb. And we were selling Arizona . . . they're nuts . . . did you see how they were *living*? How can you delude yours . . .

LEVENE. I've got the check . . .

WILLIAMSON. Forget it. Frame it. It's worthless. (*pause*)

LEVENE. The check's no good?

WILLIAMSON. You stick around I'll pull the memo for you. (*starts for the door*) I'm busy now . . .

LEVENE. Their check's no good? They're nuts . . . ?

WILLIAMSON. Call up the bank. *I* called them.

LEVENE. You did?

WILLIAMSON. I called them when we had the lead . . . four months ago. (*pause*) The people are insane. They just like talking to salesmen. (*Williamson starts for door.*)

LEVENE. Don't.

WILLIAMSON. I'm sorry.

LEVENE. *Why?*

WILLIAMSON. Because I don't like you.

LEVENE. John: John: . . . my *daughter* . . .

WILLIAMSON. Fuck you. (*Roma comes out of the Detective's door. Williamson goes in.*)

ROMA (*to Baylen*). Asshole . . . (*to Levene*) Guy couldn't find his fuckin' couch the *living room* . . . Ah, Christ . . . what a day, what a day . . . I haven't even had a cup of *coffee.* . . . Jagoff John opens his mouth he blows my Cadillac . . . . (*sighs*) I swear . . . it's not a world of men . . . it's not a world of men, Machine . . . it's a world of clock watchers, bureaucrats, office-holders . . . what it is, it's a fucked-up world . . . there's no adventure *to* it. (*pause*) dying breed. Yes it is. (*pause*) We are the members of a dying breed. That's . . . that's . . . that's why we have to stick together. Shel: I want to talk to you. I've wanted to talk to you for some time. For a long time, actually. I said, "The Machine, there's a man I would work with. There's a man. . . ." You know? I never said a thing. I should have, don't know why I didn't. And that shit you were slinging on my guy today was *so* good . . . it . . . it was, and, excuse me, 'cause it isn't even my place to say it. It was admirable . . . it was the old stuff. Hey, I've been on a hot streak, so *what?* There's things that I could learn from you. You eat today?

LEVENE. Me.

ROMA. Yeah.

LEVENE. Mm.

ROMA. Well, you want to swing by the Chinks, watch me eat, we'll talk?

LEVENE. I think I'd better stay here for a while. (*Baylen sticks his head out of the room.*)

BAYLEN. Mr. *Levene* . . . ?

ROMA. You're done, come down and let's . . .

BAYLEN. Would you come in here, please?

ROMA. And let's put this together. Okay? Shel? Say okay. (*pause*)

LEVENE (*softly to himself*). Huh.

BAYLEN. Mr. Levene, I think we have to talk.

ROMA. I'm going to the Chinks. You're done, come down, we're going to smoke a cigarette.

LEVENE. I . . .

BAYLEN (*comes over*). . . . Get in the room.

ROMA. Hey, hey, hey, *easy* friend, That's the "Machine." That is Shelly "The Machine" Lev . . .

BAYLEN. Get in the goddamn room. (*Baylen starts manhandling Shelly into the room.*)

LEVENE. Ricky, I . . .

ROMA. Okay, okay, I'll be at the resta . . .

LEVENE. Ricky . . .

BAYLEN. "Ricky" can't help you, pal.

LEVENE. . . . I only want to . . .

BAYLEN. Yeah. What do you want? You want to *what?* (*He pushes Levene into the room, closes the door behind him. Pause. Roma starts adjusting his clothes preparatory to leaving the office. Aaronow enters.*)

AARONOW. Did they find the guy who broke into the office yet?

ROMA. No. *I* don't know. (*pause*)

AARONOW. Did the leads come in yet?

ROMA. No.

AARONOW (*settling into a desk chair*). Oh, God, I hate this job.

ROMA (*simultaneous with "job," existing the office*). I'll be at the restaurant.

CURTAIN

TOPICS FOR CRITICAL THINKING AND WRITING

 ### The Play on the PAGE

1. Why is Roma so successful a salesman? Analyze his sales technique as revealed in the scene with Lingk.

2. What qualities do we discover in Shelly Levene in the first scene with Williamson? How do these qualities anticipate the ending of the play?

3. In Act 2 Roma complains that salesmen "are members of a dying breed." Do you think he's right?

4. The obvious question: How do the salesmen in this play compare to those other famous American salesmen, Willy Loman in *Death of a Salesman* and Hickey in *The Iceman Cometh?*

The Play on the STAGE

5. How realistically would you stage this play?
6. What degree of sympathy for the play's characters would you, as potential director, strive to extract from your actors?
7. Why do you think Mamet is so popular with actors, who *love* to play his characters? (Teach has

been played by Mike Kellin, Robert Duvall, Dustin Hoffman, Al Pacino, William H. Macy; Shelley Levene by Robert Prosky, Jack Lemmon, Charles Durning.)

A Context for *Glengarry Glen Ross*

MATTHEW ROUDANE
*On the American Myth: Interview with David Mamet**

Roudane: *The myth of the American Dream seems central to your artistic vision. In* American Buffalo, The Water Engine, Lakeboat, Mr. Happiness, A Life in the Theatre, *and* Glengarry Glen Ross, *a whole cultural as well as spiritual dimension of the American Dream myth is present. Could you comment on why this myth engages you so much?*

Mamet: It interests me because the national culture is founded very much on the idea of strive and succeed. Instead of rising with the masses one should rise from the masses. Your extremity is my opportunity. That's what forms the basis of our economic life, and this is what forms the rest of our lives. That American myth: the idea of something out of nothing. And this also affects the spirit of the individual. It's very divisive. One feels one can only succeed at the cost of someone else. Economic life in America is a lottery. Everyone's got an equal chance, but only one guy is going to get to the top. "The more I have the less you have." So one can only succeed at the cost of, the failure of another, which is what a lot of my plays—*American Buffalo* and *Glengarry Glen Ross*—are about. . . . In *Glengarry Glen Ross* it's the Cadillac, the steak-knives, or nothing. In this play it's obvious that these fellows are put in fear for their lives and livelihood: for them it's the same thing. They have to succeed at the cost of each other. As Thorstein Veblen in *Theory of the Leisure Class* says, sharp practice inevitably shades over into fraud. Once

someone has no vested interest in behaving in an ethical manner and the only bounds on his behavior are supposedly his innate sense of fair play, then fair play becomes an outdated concept: "But wait a second! Why should I control my sense of fair play when the other person may not control his sense of fair play? So hurray for me and to hell with you."

What are your thematic concerns in Glengarry Glen Ross?

If there are any thematic concerns, they must be blatant. The play concerns how business corrupts, . . . it becomes legitimate for those in power in the business world to act unethically. The effect on the little guy is that he turns to crime. And petty crime goes punished; major crimes go unpunished. If someone wants to destroy Manhattan for personal gain, they call him a great man. . . . In *Glengarry Glen Ross*, it's interesting to watch Aaronow. He's the one who comes closest to being the character of a *raisonneur*, for throughout the whole play he's saying, "I don't understand what's going on." "I'm no good." "I can't fit in here." "I'm incapable of either grasping those things I should or doing those things which I've grasped." Or his closing lines, "Oh, God, I hate this job." It's a kind of monody throughout the play. Aaronow has some degree of conscience, some awareness; he's troubled. Corruption troubles him. The question he's troubled by is whether his inability to succeed in the society in which he's placed is a defect—that is, is he manly or sharp enough?—or if it's in effect, a positive attribute, which is to say that his conscience prohibits him. So Aaronow is left between these two things and he's incapable of choosing. This dilemma is, I think, what many of us are facing in this country right now. As Veblen, who's had a big influence on me, says, a lot of business in this country is founded on the idea that if

*www.mindspring.com/~jason-charnick/mamet-museum.html.

you don't exploit the possible opportunity, not only are you being silly, but in many cases you're being negligent, even legally negligent.

At the close of American Buffalo, *I sensed a felt compassion, some sense of understanding between all three men, but especially between Don and Bobby. However, at the close of* Glengarry Glen Ross, *I sensed little compassion, no resolution, little sense of redemption. Could you talk about these two plays in light of this?*

Glengarry Glen Ross is structurally a very different play from *American Buffalo*. *Buffalo* is a traditionally structured drama based on tragedy, whereas *Glengarry*, although it has aspects of tragedy in it, is basically a melodrama—or, a drama. Endings in tragedies are resolved. The protagonist undergoes a reversal of the situation, a recognition of the state, and we have a certain amount of cleansing. This is what Don experiences in *American Buffalo*. But this doesn't happen in *Glengarry Glen Ross*.

What engages your aesthetic imagination in American Buffalo?

I was interested in the idea of honor among thieves; of what is an unassailable moral position and what isn't. What would cause a man to abdicate a moral position he'd espoused? That's what *American Buffalo* is about. Teach is the antagonist. The play's about Donny Dubrow. His moral position is that one must conduct himself like a man and there are no extenuating circumstances for supporting the betrayal of a friend. That's how the play starts. The rest of the play is about Donny's betrayal of the fellow, Bobby, who he's teaching these things to. The same is true to a certain extent of Levene in *Glengarry Glen Ross*. All throughout the play Levene is espousing the professional doctrine of technique. What he's saying is that I am therefore owed certain support because of what I've done, because of who I am. And at the end of the play, Levene betrays himself.

Clearly you have an ear for the sounds, sense, and rhythms of street language. Could you discuss the role of language in your plays?

It's poetic language. It's not an attempt to capture language as much as it is an attempt to create language. We see this in various periods in the evolution of American drama. And when it's good, to the most extent it's called realism. All realism means is that the language strikes a responsive chord. The language in my plays is not realistic but poetic. The words sometimes have a musical quality to them. It's language which is tailor-made for the stage. People don't always talk the way my characters do in real life, although they may use some of the same words. Think of Odets, Wilder. That stuff is not realistic; it is poetic. . . . It's not a matter, in *Lakeboat* or *Sexual Perversity in Chicago* or *Edmond* or my other plays, of my "interpretation" of how these people talk. It is an illusion. It's like when Gertrude Stein said to Picasso, "That portrait doesn't look like me." Picasso said, "It will." It's an illusion. . . . My plays don't mirror what's going on in the streets. It's something different. As Oscar Wilde said, life imitates art! We didn't have those big pea-soup fogs until somebody described them. . . .

Whereas many contemporary playwrights create antimimetic plays, you seem to re-work a more classic, Ibsenesque dramatic form: the well-made play. Could you discuss the dramatic form of your work?

I'm sure *trying* to do the well-made play. It is the hardest thing to do. I like this form because it's the structure imitating human perception. It is not just something made up out of old cloth. This is the way we perceive a play; with a clear beginning, a middle, and an end. So when one wants to best utilize the theatre, one would try to structure a play in a way that is congruent with the way the mind perceives it. Everybody wants to hear a story with a beginning, middle, and end. . . . To me, recognizing the story-telling dimension of playwriting is a beginning of a mark of maturity. That's why I embrace it. Nobody in the audience wants to hear a joke without the punch line. Nobody wants to hear how *feelingly* a guy can tell a joke. But we would like to find out what happened to the farmer's daughter. That's what Ibsen did. . . .

Could you talk about the way in which form and content coalesce to generate the creative process within your plays?

There's a curious phenomena that happens when you compose a play or movie. The creation very quickly takes on a life of its own. I have no idea why; it's just words on paper. But the art I can compare it to in my experience is carving wood. Part of the wisdom of wood carving is to realize when the wood is telling you where it wants to go. Obviously it's going to be a duck if you start out to make a duck, but the kind of duck it's going to be is largely dictated by the kind of wood.

And there is a similar phenomenon in writing drama. You start out with an idea, it becomes something else, and part of the wisdom is learning to listen to the material itself. Much of the material, of course, is in the subconscious.

What is your artistic response to what some may call a "Business as Sacrament Ethic" in America?

One has to learn something that can't be taken away: you have to learn your craft. As Sherwood Anderson said, a man who has a trade is a man who can tell the rest of the world to go to hell! If you want to become a commodity, which is what most actors and actresses tend to become, then you have to rely on the goodness of others, not only for your bread, but for your happiness. That's not very much fun.

As a writer you're confronted with a universe which is largely hostile, even absurd. Given this reality, what is your artistic response to such a world?

My response is always the same thing; it's never any different. Tolstoy said it's a mistake to think that human nature ever changes. This is the only world that I live in, so a) it would be silly for me to say something else because it isn't something else, and b) I am part of it. So the ability to perceive the problem doesn't necessarily mean that one is not part of that problem. Of course I am part of the problem. It's the same thing as people driving home from the country on Sunday night. Look at all these assholes driving, getting in my way! It's modern life. I *am* one of those assholes.

Do you see yourself, as a writer, as one who shatters illusions or as some kind of truth-teller?

No. I am just a storyteller. Keep in mind that playwrights—O'Neill or Albee or myself—know as little about what we do as anyone else. We're just storytellers, that's all. It just so happens that society rewards some of us in extraordinary ways because the society is desperately betting that one of us is going to say something that might offer some comfort. Our job, as writers, is to do our jobs. I was thinking the other day, I have trouble sometimes finishing a lot of plays. But then I always try to remind myself it took Sophocles eighteen years to write *Oedipus Rex*; that's also because he wasn't trying to write *Gigi*.

The Play in PERFORMANCE

In 1983 *Glengarry Glen Ross* premiered with enormous success at the National Theatre in London, and Mamet joined his compatriots Arthur Miller and Stephen Sondheim as American theater artists the British theater particularly esteems. The play was directed by Bill Bryden, but Mamet was intensely involved in the rehearsal process. He wanted very much to convey to his British cast the dynamism and obsessiveness of his salesmen, the addictive, near-sexual nature of their pursuit of their prey, the extraordinary, near-orgasmic sense of release they experienced when a sale was actually made. Yes, they were callous, selfish, driven, but they were not villains. Mamet actually liked the salesmen he had worked with ("They made my life interesting for a year") because of the riskiness of their high-wire acts, the bravura of their performances. All this was *so* un-British that Mamet worked hard to recreate the world for his actors: He gave them copies of that ancient self-help book, *How to Make Friends and Influence People*. He arranged to have the author of a current book, *You Can Negotiate Anything*, and salespeople from IBM and Xerox lecture the cast on motivation and sales jargon.

Indeed, so intensely did Mamet work to create the milieu of the play that, for many, the rehearsal period was a harrowing time. One of the actors, Jack Shepherd (who was playing Richard Roma) recalls,

> We all went mad. The amount of information you had to take in was staggering. Things got very, very heated and tempers were lost. A chair got thrown at one point. There is just so much to remember at any one time in Mamet's work; you begin to feel like a computer that is overloading. Mamet knows exactly what he wants . . . he is very fast, very dynamic. His speech is also very quick. The rhythms in him and in his plays are similar. In trying to pick up something of the Chicago accent from him, you cannot help but pick up his quick-fire streetwise personality as well. We tried to give the impression, during rehearsals, of rapid interaction, of sharing something over a very short

period. You have to struggle to remember so much about your part, the lines, the sensation, the character, and so on. You feel rather like a thoroughbred horse; you tend to overstrain to compensate for feelings of bewilderment and confusion. It's all very, very speedy.

The work paid off: The production opened triumphantly, winning two British drama awards. Reviews were uniformly excellent: Robert Cushman felt that it was "the best play in London. . . . Here at last, carving characters and conflicts out of language, is a play with real muscle." John Barber nominated it as "a small masterpiece."

The American premiere took place in February 1984 at the Goodman Theater in Chicago. It was directed by Gregory Mosher and had an American cast composed of actors who had worked extensively or trained with Mamet, a group that might be considered his "stock company" and which includes Joe Mantegna, Mike Nussbaum, and J.T. Walsh (several of whom have gone on to major professional careers). A month later this production (with one minor cast change) opened on Broadway where it duplicated its London success, winning for Mamet both the New York Drama Critics Circle Award and the Pulitzer Prize for 1984. In 1992 the play was filmed (to Mamet's own screenplay but directed by James Foley) with a cast of established film actors: Jack Lemmon, Al Pacino, Ed Harris, Alan Arkin, Kevin Spacey. The play's corruscating, obscene language inhibits college, community, and amateur revival, but its recent presentation (2000) at the McCarter Theater, Princeton—with Charles Durning as Shelley Levene—was judged by the *New York Times* "a searing revival . . . that speaks volumes about the American psyche."

SUSAN Yankowitz

Susan Yankowitz was born in Newark, New Jersey, and graduated from Sarah Lawrence College and Yale Drama School. Her first professional theatrical experience was as a playwright with Joseph Chaikin's Open Theater, with whom she wrote *Terminal* (1969), a collaborative piece that won her the Drama Desk Award for Most Promising Playwright and was performed throughout the United States, Europe, and the Middle East. Since that time, she has had an enduring interest in the collaborative process and has worked with many groups, including the Manhattan Project, the Omaha Magic Theatre, the Academy Theatre in Atlanta, Monstrous Regiment in London, and others on collective works. In 1996, in a similar process, she created a new version of *Terminal* with Chaikin and a company of actors. This was produced in New York City, Atlanta, Los Angeles, and abroad.

On her own, she has written many plays, including *Slaughterhouse Play, Alarms, Boxes, Under the Skin,* and *A Knife in the Heart. Night Sky,* directed by Joseph Chaikin, premiered at the Women's Project in 1991, and has been seen at the Market Theatre in Johannesburg, South Africa, 7 Stages in Atlanta, the Philadelphia Theatre Company, the Odyssey in L.A., as well as in Edinburgh, Tokyo, Avignon, and Barcelona. It has been translated into French, Catalan, Spanish, and German. *Phaedra in Delirium* was recently presented at Classic Stage Company, New York City in a co-production with The Women's Project.

In addition to her work as a playwright, she has written a novel, *Silent Witness,* published by Knopf, and several films and television plays. Currently Yankowitz has been using music as a vehicle for escaping from naturalism and creating heightened theatrical experiences in such pieces as *Slain in the Spirit: The Tragedy of Jonestown* (with composer Taj Majal). Yankowitz has received grants from the Guggenheim Foundation, the National Endowment for the Arts, Berilla Kerr and Rockefeller foundations, and is a member of New Dramatists, PEN, the Dramatists Guild, and the Women's Project.

■■■■■■■■■■■■■■■

JOSEPH Chaikin

Actor, director, and theorist Joseph Chaikin was born September 16, 1935, in Brooklyn, New York, to emigré parents. His father was a teacher and the family moved to Iowa where his father taught Hebrew. He received his education from Drake University in Des Moines, which awarded him an honorary doctorate in 1972. In 1955 he moved to New York City and co-founded The Harlequin Players, with whom he acted and directed. Chaikin joined The Living Theatre in 1959 and his portrayal of Galy Gay in Brecht's *Man Is Man* (1962) earned him the first of his six Obies. In 1963 he founded The Open Theatre, which became one of the country's premier experimental ensembles. Under his direction, the group had particular success with Megan Terry's *Viet Rock* (1966), Jean-Claude van Itallie's *The Serpent* (1968–69), and Susan Yankowitz's *Terminal* (1969).

The Open Theatre disbanded in 1973 and Chaikin went on to form other ensembles: the Working Theatre and the Other Theatre (with van Itallie) where he directed productions of van Itallie's Chekhov translations. In 1976 he founded the Winter Project, an annual twelve-week workshop with actors, musicians, and writers who explored storytelling for the theater. At the New York Shakespeare Festival he directed *Electra, The Dybbuk,* and *Antigone,* and performed in *Woyzeck, Tongues, Savage/Love* (written with Sam Shepard), and the first production of Beckett's *Texts for Nothing.*

Chaikin has acted and directed in Europe and the Middle East. He assisted Peter Brook in Royal Shakespeare productions of *US* and *The Tempest,* mounted a production of *The Dybbuk* in Israel, and has conducted workshops with Jerzy Grotowski. In 1984 Chaikin suffered a stroke that left him aphasic. Since then he has persevered as a seminal figure in American theater and has drawn on the experience of his disability in such collaborations as *Struck Dumb,* with van Itallie, and *The War in Heaven* with Sam Shepard. He has been awarded six Obies, including one for lifetime achievement in the theater, the Drama Desk award, the Brandeis University Award for Distinguished Actors, the New England Theatre Conference Award, the prestigious Edwin Booth

Award, as well as two Guggenheim fellowships and grants. In 1972 he published the book, *The Presence of the Actor.* He was the first American director to be included in the *Directors in Perspective* series of books on the century's most influential theater directors. As of this writing, he continues to direct, act, conduct workshops, and teach at American universities.

■ ■ ■ ■ ■ ■ ■ ■ ■ ■ ■ ■ ■

COMMENTARY ON *TERMINAL*

To discuss an experimental theater work like *Terminal* is necessarily to consider its textual genesis *together with* its performance in history. For it forgoes the traditional theater model in which the play, the verbal construct, precedes the act of its interpretation. In this kind of collective work, rather, play and interpretation evolve simultaneously as the product of a collaboration among actors, directors, writers (however those functions are divided). In the resulting work (as the preamble to *Terminal*'s verbal text indicates), "visual and verbal patterns are interwoven; word, sound, image reinforce and elucidate each other." *Terminal* was born in the ensemble called the Open Theatre, one of the foremost theater collectives of the 1960s and 1970s, a group whose work was spare, rigorous, and disciplined, and in which the power of words was respected. It was founded in 1963 when Joseph Chaikin, an actor in the pioneering group called the Living Theatre, called a meeting of seventeen actors and four writers to consider forming a workshop to address problems related to establishing a new non-naturalistic theater technique. Despite some ground-breaking productions—such as *The Connection* and *The Brig*—the Living Theatre, led by Julian Beck and Judith Malina, improvised its theatrical experiments without a firm theoretical base. When the living Theatre's tax difficulties led to harassment by the IRS and the closing of their theater, the Becks chose expatriation and moved their group to a more welcoming European milieu. Chaikin was one who chose not to make the journey. He decided to stay in New York and work to discover a new way of doing significant theater.

The group he assembled to enter a continuing dialogue on new approaches to theater included not only adventurous young actors but artists and intellectuals like Paul Goodman, Gorgon Rogoff, Richard Gilman, and Susan Sontag. Chaikin began workshops in which he introduced a series of new acting exercises aimed at freeing acting from Stanislavskian realism. One such

was "transformations," an improvisation in which the established realities of a scene are repeatedly changed in the course of action and replaced by others. As Richard Schechner (the founder of another contemporary experimental ensemble, the Performance Group) described it, "Each unit within a set of transformations is (or can be) as 'real' as any bit of naturalistic acting: but the quick changes from one bit to another give the over-all effect of kaleidoscope, fluidity, and scenic explosion." Experiments such as this ("circles" was another) were guided by Chaikin as master teacher and discussed by all members of the collective. These acting experiments helped shape new playwriting. (See the Commentary on *True West.*)

By the end of 1963 the group decided to include the element of audience response and began to perform publicly. Its first performances at two Greenwich Village little theaters, the Open Theatre included, alongside some of its improvisations, short plays by Brecht and new young playwrights like Megan Terry and Jean-Claude van Itallie. As their public performances proliferated in the mid–1960s, short plays by T.S. Eliot, John Arden, Maria Irene Fornes, and others were added to the repertory. The group's first major work—and the one that became the model for collectively created playwriting—was Megan Terry's *Viet Rock* (1966), an antiwar piece developed in a workshop at Yale University by Terry and the ensemble. As the political climate of the 1960s intensified, Chaikin in 1967 began a workshop on the Bible with the intention of examining the unrecorded early activities of Christ as a social anarchist. For over a year the group explored the Book of Genesis physically through acting exercises and intellectually through invited speakers like Joseph Campbell. What emerged was not what was originally intended but rather a meditation on the Garden of Eden and the origin of evil that interwove contemporary social traumas like the assassination of John F. Kennedy into its performance fabric. The text was shaped and written by Jean-Claude van Itallie, and the resulting work, *The Serpent,* is one of the signature works of its time. It toured all over Europe.

When *The Serpent* opened in the company's loft in New York City in 1969, the Open Theatre began work on a new subject: death and dying, with Roberta Sklar sharing directorial chores with Chaikin and with Susan Yankowitz given responsibility for helping provide and shape the verbal text. At first glance this choice of subject may seem unusual at a time when a turbulent decade was reaching its zenith of activism. The piece indeed reflects a very personal preoccupation with mortality by Chaikin due to his living with a damaged heart (*Endgame*—with Chaikin as Hamm—was in the group's then current repertoire). But *Terminal* never turns completely inward nor despairing. It explores the "undiscovered country" of death in social as well as psychological terms, examining our complex strategies for repressing thoughts of dying, and the taboos Americans in particular impose to avoid confronting our mortality. It fearlessly, unsentimentally examines the process of dying, and finds in ritual—in both life and art—a means of acceptance, not denial. Myth can illuminate the passage from the world of the living to the world of the dead. Even as it examines our compulsion to ignore death, *Terminal* meditates on it not morbidly but lyrically. Rather than succumbing to despair, the vignettes, incantations, and evocations that comprise its plotless structure celebrate our capacity to mourn and our ability to accept the inevitable. Indeed, insofar as the piece moves us to face what we would avoid, it is much more congruent with its era's activism than it initially seems, for before we can change *anything* we must see it clearly. *Terminal* is, after all, a work by the living for the living. It is not a plea for fatalistic inaction. On the contrary, its final judgments affirm T.S. Eliot's line from "Little Gidding" that "to make an end is to make a beginning":

> You dreamed of a new beginning but moved down the plotted path to the end. And you will wait for beginning, you will dream of it and wait for it, but nothing changes in eternity and nothing ends.
>
> You are moving toward the end from which it is possible to make a new beginning. You must change your life . . . everything will be different and everything will be the same.

In the space of two years, 1969–70, the Open Theatre presented two versions of *Terminal.* The early version, the one included in this anthology, used an ensemble of fourteen performers. This version was less abstract and distilled than the version that emerged after the acting ensemble was reduced by Chaikin from fourteen to six in late 1970. *Terminal* was the only piece carried over into the reconfigured group and became part of their late repertoire (along with *The Mutation Show* and *Nightwalk*). The early large ensemble *Terminal* had a tripartite structure ("The Dance on the Graves of the Dead," "The Pregnant Dying," "The State of the Dying"), which was essentially held but simplified and modified in the later version. The greatest difference between versions was that the early *Terminal* evoked an abstract but specific sense of place: a terminal ward in an impersonal institution inhabited by a dense gathering of the dying. In the small group version, with its concomitant increase in character transformations, the ward sometimes was evoked (particularly in the "New Arrival" sequence), but essentially the performance space became metaphysical, at once inside and outside of place and time, a magic circle where the dead are summoned by the dying—who are, of course, all of us.

Twenty-seven years after its inception, twenty-three years after its demise, *Terminal* was resummoned to performance by several of its originators. The new incarnation that was presented at P.S. 122 in 1996 was based on the later small group version and included three of the performers who had appeared in both earlier versions: Shami Chaikin, Tina Shepard, and Paul Zimet. The revised text was by the original playwright, Susan Yankowitz, and Joseph Chaikin again directed. The resummoning was extremely successful, a living demonstration of the best American work in the "poor theater" tradition—no video screens, no elaborate lighting, few props, a few modular pieces—rarely seen these days. Although Ellen Maddow again served as composer and musician, essentially the music was again produced by the actors themselves with simple instruments, particularly through the percussive clash of sticks that also served as divining rods.

The major change in the new *Terminal* derived from the pairing of the three original performers (who sustained their impressive performances, including Paul Zimet's miraculous possession by Marie Leveau) with a trio of new young performers. This created a heightened awareness of aging that did not exist in the earlier versions, in which all the performers were young. Secondly, whereas the 1970 small ensemble had been all white (there was one black member of the earlier large cast), two of the new young performers—one-third of the new ensemble—were not and contributed greatly to the piece's revitalization. The wider racial inclusion was not mere "political correctness"; its cultural awareness was absolutely appropriate for a work whose theme is the universality of death's visitation. We can see this now even if we didn't see it then.

There were other emendations and updatings: The "New Arrival" sequence was reframed with references to medical insurance; AIDS made its inevitable appearance; the then impending millennium was evoked as a historical marker; the references to soldiers and violence carried resonances beyond Vietnam. But the essence of the work remained as pure and powerful as ever. It summoned forth an era in which experimental theater really mattered.

Terminal: First Version, 1969
Ensemble work with text by Susan Yankowitz
Co-directed by Joseph Chaikin and Roberta Sklar
Original composers: Richard Peaslee and Stanley Walden

Additional writers: Mark Kaminsky, Nancy Martin, and Sam Shepard
Performers: Joyce Aaron, James Barbosa, Brenda Dixon, Ron Faber, Sharon Gans, Jayne Haynes, Ralph Lee, Peter Maloney, Puriel Miguel, Mark Samuels, Ellen Schindler, Barbara Vann, and Lee Worley. Other resource persons: Marianne de Pury, Dale Whitt, Joseph Campbell, Mossa Bildner, Kesang-tomma, R.D. Laing, and Muir Wesinger

Terminal: Second Version, 1970–71
Text, co-direction: the same. Musician: Ellen Maddow. Performers: Raymond Barry, Shami Chaikin, Tom Lillard, Jo Ann Schmidman, Tina Shepard, Paul Zimet

1969 Terminal 1996, 1996
Text: Susan Yankowitz; Direction: Joseph Chaikin; Musician: Ellen Maddow
Performers: Shami Chaikin, Tina Shepard, Paul Zimet, Scott Blumenthal, Hyun Yup Lee, Nkenge Scott

TERMINAL
Text by Susan Yankowitz

A collective work created by the Open Theater Ensemble.

Co-directed by Joseph Chaikin and Roberta Sklar

NOTE FROM THE OPEN THEATRE

In a collective work there are stages equal in significance to the performance stage. When the ensemble begins to prepare directly for the performing stage, it relies entirely on the initial investigations. We would like to acknowledge the following people for their participation in the development of Terminal: Dick Peaslee and Stanley Walden, composers; Marc Kaminski, Nancy Martin and Sam Shepard, writers; Joyce Aaron, James Barbosa, Brenda Dixon, Ron Faber, Sharon Gans, Jayne Haynes, Ralph Lee, Peter Maloney, Murial Miguel, Mark Samuels, Ellen Schindler, Barbara Vann, Lee Worley, actors; and Dale Whitt, Joseph Campbell, Mossa Bildner, Kesang-tomma, Ronald Laing and Muir Weisinger.

Terminal is the product of a collaboration among actors, directors, and writers. It evolved out of a collective investigation into human mortality and a consideration of both personal and societal responses to the fact of death. The piece was conceived from its inception as a theatrical work; the text cannot be fully understood apart from its production. Visual and verbal patterns are interwoven; word, sound, and image reinforce and elucidate each other.

This scenario documents the results of more than a year's intensive work. The process through which we arrived at these results can only be suggested in these pages. Any group that wishes to perform Terminal *will have to rediscover the material for itself; it will need to use, adapt, reject, and recreate. This text is, then, a skeleton which a new group of performers will have to flesh. It is intended as a framework and guide and, to that end, attempts to reconstruct as clearly as possible the details of the Open Theatre production.*

The following notes, as well as the notes of the directions which follow the text, are meant to clarify certain basic assumptions and to describe the specific theatrical choices which are at the root of our production.

STYLE AND STRUCTURE

The style of the piece is presentational. It is constructed of general sections within which are a series of fragments. Each fragment is a self-contained entity which relates to the others and to the whole through juxtapositions and associations. Every section and fragment is introduced by a title. A single actor, or several, may perform this function during the course of the play. Blackouts are used to define the beginning and end of major sections. These blackouts not only delineate distinct thematic areas, but provide a stylistic counterpart to the cycle of life and death, presence and absence. The movement from fragment to fragment shifts the piece back and forth through various levels of experience.

THE ACTORS AND THE SPACE

The actors are always present. When an actor is not directly engaged in the events onstage, he moves into a defined area around the periphery. This space may be considered an onstage offstage area in which the actor rests, prepares, changes costume, waits. From this periphery, an actor may spontaneously enter the acting area and join in an action. The line between the onstage and offstage area may be crossed. There is only one space in which the actors are always visible.

PROPERTIES AND LIGHTS

Like the actors, all theatrical props and materials are visible. Lights are hung in plain view of the audience. Nothing is hidden or disguised, but everything can be transformed. A pallet is a bed when placed horizontally on the floor. It is a wall when upright. A rack is a structure for hanging clothes. It is also an instrument of torture. Lights may be used as spotlights or instruments of interrogation; they may be fixed overhead or held by the actors. All objects are real objects. And what is constructed for the piece is obviously makeshift. Everything is part of the theatrical world and derives its functions from the needs of that world.

THE ROLES

All roles are multiple and interchangeable. The living are also the dying; the dying are potentially the dead. And the dead will become living matter. The Guide straddles the space between the living and the dead. His presence inspires the dying to make contact with the dead. The Dying are close to death and sensitive to spiritual forces. Their heightened awareness makes possible their possession by the dead. The Team supervise the institutions of life; they are the hospital attendants, the wardens, the embalmers. They may be portrayed by one person or by many, but they, too, are the dying.

THE MUSIC

Music is used in its broadest definition: it is pure sound and rhythm. Meaning does not accompany music, but is contained within it. Some music is simply an extension of the human voice. The actors become instruments; they find and produce sounds which communicate emotions and experiences outside the usual range of human expressions. Some music is an extension of the human body. Hands and feet become instruments for eliciting music from surfaces—floors, walls, beds. Language becomes incantation and incantation becomes music. Words dissolve into fragments and sounds. Repetition of lines, sounds, and gestures recur as a means of suggesting associations between seemingly unrelated passages and evoking resonances which enrich meaning. When conventional instruments are used, they are always simple—harmonicas, tambourines, drums, sticks. The clavis maintains a regular rhythm, measuring time.

THE COSTUMES

The piece is concerned with death and, therefore, with the body. As a part of nature, the body must be revealed by the costume. As a part of society, it must also be concealed. In our production, simple white garments are worn by the actors. Each differs from the others in cut and style, but creates an overall impression of uniformity. The costumes evoke many associations: they suggest hospital wear, uniforms, mummy clothes, bones. Strips of black tape appear on the faces of the actors during the first section. Here, an eye is covered; there, a mouth or two eyes. Each taped feature represents the loss of its function. Nothing more is worn—no jewelry, shoes, or makeup.

THE SETTING

A proscenium arch or some other well-defined frame reinforces the presentational style of the piece. Two spotlights, which will later be held by the actors, lie downstage and illuminate the acting area. Five beds—bare slabs of wood on metal legs—are lined up at the rear. They are raked at different angles and stand at varying heights. The beds will be used as pallets for the dying and embalming tables for the dead; as alternate stage levels for the actors to walk upon; as walls; and as graves. A clothing rack and ladder are visible. Stools, equal in number to the actors, stand to the right and left of the stage area in the periphery. Beneath the stools lie sticks and musical instruments which will later be used by the actors. The general effect is deliberately ambiguous. The setting is a theatrical arena, a hospital ward, a graveyard, a nameless home to which people come to die and, perhaps, to be transformed.

THE SEQUENCE

I. **THE DANCE ON THE GRAVES OF THE DEAD**
The Procession
The Calling
The Dance

II. **THE PREGNANT DYING**
The Private Case
Motion
Taking In and Eliminating
Breathing
The Last Biological Rites
Reprise: The Second Calling

III. **THE STATE OF THE DYING**
The Embalming As Required by Law
The Interview
The Dying Resist
The Runner Who Never Gets Started
The Dying Are Drugged
The Dead Come Through (A): Marie Leveau and
   the Soldier
The Renovation
The Witness
The Dead Come Through (B): The One Who Was
   Hit
The Dying Pray
The Dead Come Through (C): The Responsible One
The Initiation
The Embalming As Required by Law
The Dead Come Through (D): The Executed Man
   and the Song
The Dying Imagine Their Judgment
Presence and Absence

I. THE DANCE ON THE GRAVES OF THE DEAD

Silence. Overhead lights and two small spots illuminate the beds, the stools, the empty space. A trumpet blast. Music. A light, rhythmic melody. The procession begins. The actors move down the aisle under a makeshift red canopy. They repeat the melody on simple instruments. The actors reach the stage and face the audience. The Guide steps forward and starts the incantation. His words break through the music and charge the space with a different energy. The music stops. The canopy is placed against the rear wall where it will remain. The actors move to the stools and sit. The Guide continues his incantation.

THE GUIDE.
We come among the dying to call upon the dead.
There are graves beneath this house—we call upon the dead.
Let them take my body, let them use my tongue.
There are bones beneath this floor—we call upon the dead.
Let the dead come through
                    and let it begin with me.

Individual actors begin to join in the calling. Each carries two sticks, like divining rods. All the actors eventually participate. They call up the dead in every corner of the globe,

The small ensemble version of the Open Theater's collective meditation on death and dying. *Terminal* (1970), with (from top to bottom) Shami Chaikin, Raymond Barry, Jo Anne Schmidman (hidden), Tom Lillard, Tina Shepard, and Paul Zimet.

facing each compass point. Their voices and movements merge and overlap, filling the space with sounds and words.

THE ACTORS.
We come among the dying
There are graves beneath this house
        We come among the dying
        We call upon the dead
There are graves beneath this house
There are bones beneath this floor
        We all upon the dead
We come
    We come among the dying to call upon the dead
We come
    Let them take my body   We come
Let them take my body, let them use my tongue

Let the dead come through
Let them take my body, let them use my tongue
        We come among the dying
        There are graves beneath this house
        There are bones beneath this floor
Let the dead come through and let it begin with me
        and let it begin with me
        and let is begin with me
Let the dead come through
  Let them take my body
    Let them use my tongue
We come among the dying to all upon the dead
Let the dead come through
  Let the dead come through
        and let it begin with me

The words become increasingly fragmented. A single syllable evokes the entire incantation. The sound of the calling becomes its meaning. Cacophony. One actor grows silent. Then another. Then all. They collapse from the waist; the sticks dangle from their hands. Silence. The Guide moves among the actors. His physical presence brings them into contact with the spirits they have invoked. The actors straighten and stiffen. They raise their arms in a stylized position, as if in a trance, still holding the sticks. Drumbeat. The dance begins. Hands, feet, and sticks drum on every surface. The actors knock on the floor, walls, and beds—on the graves of the dead. They dance individually and, linking upraised arms, in pairs. From time to time, they lie on the floor to let the dead come through. Dance and knocking merge with fragments from the incantation. The drumbeat increases in volume. The dance builds in pace and pitch, reaches a peak, and ceases. Silence. Tableau.

11. THE PREGNANT DYING

When the title is announced, the actors return to the periphery. The Pregnant Dying is alone onstage, stretched out on a bed. Her swollen body is seen in profile. She breathes evenly. Her large belly rises and falls with sudden, sharp motions. She lies there, silently breathing, as the other fragments are enacted.

Note: The Pregnant Dying provides a focal image for this section of the piece. She is a tunnel in which the living and the dying come into contact for a moment and then pass each other. Each fragment in this section isolates a single bodily activity which is necessary to sustain life. The succession of images are all united in their relationship to our basic biological functions.

The Private Case: The Masses of dying people huddle together. They are crowded on beds and floor. There is a great distance between them and the Private Case. The Private Case is propped up on his own bed. He is attended by two Members of the Team who hold his hand and buff his nails. The hoarse, collective breathing of the Masses is heard.

Motion: The Private Case and the Masses remain on their beds. Four actors come forward. Three run in place. One paces in a narrow circle. All participate in some form of pure movement.

Taking In and Eliminating: Two actors stand side by side and squat. They grimace and contract their pelvic regions. They simulate defecation. At the same time, the Private Case is being fed by the Team Members. One spoons the food into his mouth. The other smooths it down his throat. The Private Case swallows regularly, with a gulping sound. The movements of the ones who are eliminating are in a rhythmic relation to the gulping sound of the one who is eating.

Breathing: Two actors step forward. They walk ahead almost imperceptively, breathing. A third breathes loudly and with much difficulty. The only audible sound is the rhythmic intake and exhalation of breath.

The Last Biological Rites: One actor faces the audience. A Team Member, impassive and matter-of-fact, stands at his side.

TEAM MEMBER.
This is your last chance to use your eyes.

The actor uses his eyes. He looks, he sees. His vision fails, He can see no more.
The Team Member hands him a piece of black tape. The blind man seals off his eyes.

TEAM MEMBER.
This is your last chance to use your voice.

The actor makes a sound which presses out into the space and recedes. His voice fades. He can speak no more.
The Team Member hands him a piece of black tape. The dumb man seals off his mouth.

TEAM MEMBER.
This is your last chance to use your legs.

The actor stumbles forward on weak legs. His legs give way. He can walk no more.
The Team Member lifts his legs into a small cart and seats him on his knees.
His chest rises and falls. The only function remaining to him is breathing.
The actors on the beds breathe audibly. All motion has ceased.
The Team Member and the dying man face the audience. Tableau.

Reprise: The Second Calling   The tableau is interrupted by the voice of one actor who begins the second calling. Others join. They raise their sticks and move in a trance-like rhythm. Fragments of the calling are repeated. Gestures and movements from the dance appear and reappear throughout The State of The Dying; they are emblematic of the incantation.

THE ACTORS.
Let the dead come through
Let the dead come through
Let the dead come through
                and let it begin with me
                            with me
    Let them take my body
        Let them use my tongue
Let the dead come through and let it begin
    with me   and let it begin with me
    Let them take my body
        and let it begin with me
            Let them use my tongue
                let it begin
Let the dead come through and let it begin
    with me   and let it begin with me   and let it
    begin

Blackout.

III. THE STATE OF THE DYING

Darkness. The actors set up the props for the new section. Movement and sound. The actors return to their stools. Silence.

Note: *Everyone, except for the dead, is in the state of the dying. For those who are not yet dead, there is always the possibility of change and transformation. When the dying allow the dead to inhabit them, they are asking to be moved, to be shifted into a different perspective. To be possessed is to make oneself available to the unknown. At the moments when the dead come through, everything is altered—ideas about life, attitudes toward death, rhythms, sounds, movements. The form of the piece itself must stretch to accommodate these unfamiliar energies. During this section, the two spotlights which have been lying downstage may be picked up by the actors and used to illuminate specific aspects of the fragments.*

The Embalming As Required by Law: *The Pregnant Dying, now inert, is rolled downstage by two Team Members. Her bed becomes an embalming table. One Team Member explains the embalming procedure. The other illustrates the process in gesture and mime.*

TEAM MEMBER.
We prepare the deceased for embalming.
The body is washed thoroughly with special attention to the orifices.
A tube is inserted to drain the blood. Through another tube, embalming fluids are injected. As the fluid fills the veins, a flush appears on the face, the eyes flutter, the chest rises and falls as if the deceased were breathing. This is only temporary, of course.
An incision is made in the central abdomen. The vital organs are removed and deposited in a bin to be burned. They are replaced by cotton batting, similar to that used in upholstery, to retain the original dimensions of the body. The skin is then repaired and sutured.

Cosmetological procedures are employed to improve the appearance of the deceased. First is the correction of lip slip.

Lip slip occurs as fluids drain from the upper lip, causing it to recede in a manner suggesting a sneer. This is unsightly for those viewing the body, so we stitch the lips together into a more attractive expression. We cut out swollen facial tissues and fill the sunken cheeks by injecting massage creams into them. We then apply conventional makeup, such as rouge and lipstick, to create a natural and lifelike glow.

The deceased is now dressed in burial garments. These are backless, as the body will be viewed only from above. The corpse is finally ready to await funeral procedures in the freezer compartment of the morgue.

The Team Members exhibit the newly embalmed body to the Dying by moving it swiftly around the center of the stage. The Dying sing a ritual farewell song. The melody is light, the pace is lively.

The body is wheeled off.

The Interview: *Music is played sporadically throughout the scene. A clothesrack, filled with clothing, is rolled forward. Some actors remain on the stools. Others move to defined areas, each of which represents a different stage in the interviewing process. Each New Arrival will be welcomed, photographed, measured, questioned, and stripped before he is given a bed. When New Arrival 3 enters, the music becomes full and continuous.*

TEAM MEMBER A. Next

The New Arrival, fully dressed, enters.

NEW ARRIVAL 1. How do you do?
TEAM MEMBER A. Please remove your hat.
NEW ARRIVAL 1. Oh. Excuse me. (*He does so.*)
TEAM MEMBER A. And your coat, please.
NEW ARRIVAL 1. My coat? Certainly. (*He does so.*)

Team Member A hangs the coat and hat on the rack. The New Arrival moves to the photographing area.

A ladder serves as a tripod and camera. Team Member C, the photographer, is mounted on a rung. The New Arrival is seated in a chair.

TEAM MEMBER B. Hello. We'll take your photograph now.
NEW ARRIVAL 1. Why?
TEAM MEMBER C. To guide us in restoring your face and body after death.
NEW ARRIVAL 1. I'd like to look as natural as possible.
TEAM MEMBER B. We know.

Team Member B adjusts the position and expression of the New Arrival as Team Member C speaks.

TEAM MEMBER C. That's why we encourage anyone who is dying to spend his last days with us. Everything has been arranged so that, immediately after death, we can move

the body from the bed to the embalming table, from the embalming table to the beauty parlor, from the beauty parlor to the coffin. All our facilities are designed to make you feel as useful and attractive in death as you were in life.

The photograph is taken. The New Arrival rises and moves to the measurement area.

Team Member D holds a rope in her hands. She measures the New Arrival as he is questioned by Team Member E.

TEAM MEMBER D. Please stand still while your measurements are being taken.
TEAM MEMBER E. Is there anything you need?
NEW ARRIVAL 1. Yes. I need to be in a bed near a window.
TEAM MEMBER E. You don't need a window. Nobody *needs* a window.
NEW ARRIVAL 1. I like fresh air. I need a window near my bed.
TEAM MEMBER E. We know what you need. That's why we're here.
NEW ARRIVAL 1. Couldn't you arrange it somehow?
TEAM MEMBER E. Of course. If you really need it.
NEW ARRIVAL 1. I do.
EAM MEMBER E. Fine. We do have a bed near a window, but it's in a separate house. The building is a little far away from everything but we'll be happy to arrange it for you.
NEW ARRIVAL 1, *after a pause:* There's no one else there?
EAM MEMBER E. No. None of our other people need a window.
NEW ARRIVAL 1. Oh. (*Pause.*) Well, then, I could do without it, too.
TEAM MEMBER E. But if you need it . . .
NEW ARRIVAL 1. I wanted to be near a window, but I don't really need it.
TEAM MEMBER E. Very good. You'll be given a bed in the main room with the others.
TEAM MEMBER D. Number 34206.

She hands him the measuring rope which he takes to the next area.

TEAM MEMBER A. Next.

NEW ARRIVAL 2. How do you do?
TEAM MEMBER A. Please remove your hat.

NEW ARRIVAL 2. Excuse me, (*He does so.*)
TEAM MEMBER A. And you coat, please.
NEW ARRIVAL 2. My coat? Certainly. (*He does so.*)

Team Member A hangs up the coat. New Arrival 2 moves to the photographing area.

TEAM MEMBER B. Hello. We'll take your photograph now.
NEW ARRIVAL 2. Why?
TEAM MEMBER C. To guide us in restoring your face and body after death.
NEW ARRIVAL 2. I'd like to look as natural as possible.
TEAM MEMBER B. We know.
TEAM MEMBER C. That's why we encourage anyone who is dying to spend his

TEAM MEMBER F. Please remove your clothing.

NEW ARRIVAL 1. My clothing?

TEAM MEMBER F. Those are the instructions. I didn't invent them, they come with the job. Now please remove your clothing.

NEW ARRIVAL 1. What for?

TEAM MEMBER G. You do want to stay here, don't you?

NEW ARRIVAL 1. Yes. (*Pause. He undresses.*)

New Arrival 1 is now dressed only in his underwear. He takes a comb from his pants.

NEW ARRIVAL 1. Can I keep my comb?

TEAM MEMBER G. We'll give you everything you need.

New Arrival 1 combs his hair, then hands it over.

last days with us. Everything has been arranged so that, immediately after death, we can move the body from the bed to the embalming table, from the embalming table to the beauty parlor, from the beauty parlor to the coffin. All our facilities are designed to make you feel as useful and attractive in death as you were in life.

The photograph is taken. New Arrival 2 moves to the measurement area.

TEAM MEMBER D. Please stand still while your measurements are being taken.

TEAM MEMBER E. Is there anything you need?

NEW ARRIVAL 2. Yes. I need to be in a bed near a window.

TEAM MEMBER F. You don't need a window. Nobody *needs* a window.

NEW ARRIVAL 2. I like fresh air. I need a window near my bed.

TEAM MEMBER E. We know what you need. That's why we're here.

NEW ARRIVAL 2. Couldn't you arrange it somehow?

TEAM MEMBER E. Of course. If you really need it.

NEW ARRIVAL 2. I do.

TEAM MEMBER E. Fine. We do have a bed near a window, but it's in a separate house. The building is a little far away from everything but we'll be happy to arrange it for you.

NEW ARRIVAL 2, *after a pause:* There's no one else there?

TEAM MEMBER E. No. None of our other people need a window.

TEAM MEMBER G. Please remove your underwear.

NEW ARRIVAL 1. I'd like to keep something of my own.

TEAM MEMBER F. We'll give you everything you need. Please. Remove your underwear and dress yourself in this garment.

Pause.
The New Arrival undresses. He stands naked for a moment, then puts on the white outfit handed him.

TEAM MEMBER F. Very good.

New Arrival 1 faces the audience.
He places a patch on one eye.
He exits.

TEAM MEMBER A. Next.

NEW ARRIVAL 3. How do you do?

TEAM MEMBER A. Please remove your hat.

NEW ARRIVAL 3. Oh. Excuse me. (*He does so.*)

TEAM MEMBER A. And your coat, please.

NEW ARRIVAL 3. My coat? Certainly. (*He does so.*)

Team Member A hangs up the coat. New Arrival 3 moves to the photographing area.

TEAM MEMBER B. Hello. We'll take your photograph now.

NEW ARRIVAL 3. Why?

TEAM MEMBER C. To guide us in restoring your face and body after death.

Blackout.

The actors return to their stools.

NEW ARRIVAL 2. Oh. (*Pause.*) Well, then, maybe I could do without it, too.

TEAM MEMBER E. But if you need it . . .

NEW ARRIVAL 2. I wanted to be near a window, but I don't really need it.

TEAM MEMBER E. Very good. You'll be given a bed in the main room with the others.

TEAM MEMBER D. Number 41702.

She hands him the measuring rope which he takes to the next area.

TEAM MEMBER D. Please remove your clothing.

NEW ARRIVAL 2. My clothing?

TEAM MEMBER D. Those are the instructions. I didn't invent them, they come with the job. Now please remove our clothing.

NEW ARRIVAL 2. What for?

TEAM MEMBER F. You do want to stay here, don't you?

NEW ARRIVAL 2. Yes. (*Pause. He undresses.*)

The Dying Resist: *Lights. A circle of actors walk at a brisk, regular pace. When individuals break out of the circle, the others maintain its original size and shape by adjusting pace and distance. Two Team Members stand outside the circle. One gives instructions. The other drones words of approval, which eventually become empty sounds.*

TEAM MEMBER 1.
  Keep moving.
  Everyone is part of the
    circle   TEAM MEMBER 2.
  Everyone must keep the
    circle moving.   Very good. Nice.
  Follow instructions.   Very good. Nice.
  Don't accelerate or slow
    down.   Very good. Nice.
  Don't stop.   Very good. Nice.
  You are each responsible
    for keeping the circle   ery ood. ice.
    moving.   ery ood. ice.
  Everyone is useful.   ery ood. ice.
  You are each keeping the
    circle alive.   ery ood. ice.

Individuals step out of the circle, or stop abruptly where they are.
First one. Then another. Then more.
Individually, and finally in unison, the Resisters punctuate the drone with the word "out."

RESISTERS.   TEAM MEMBER 2.
  Out   ery   ood.   ice.
    out out   ery   ood.   ice.
        out   ery   ood.   ice.
                  (Etc.)
  out
    out
    out
    out
    out

The actors continue their circle.
They ignore both the physical obstacles presented by the Resisters and the word of protest.
The circle and the protest exist simultaneously.

The Runner Who Never Gets Started: *The Runner crouches over an imaginary starting line on hands and toes. He holds the racing position for several moments, then jumps to his feet, panting. Behind him, a Second Runner runs frantically in place. The First Runner repeats his actions.*

The Dying Are Drugged: *Several of the Dying sit or lie on the beds. We see them in their drugged condition—vacant, tranquillized, harmless. A high-pitched hum is heard.*

Note: *This fragment should bear a rhythmic and thematic relationship to The Dying Resist.*

The Dead Come Through (A): Marie Leveau and the Soldier. *The spirit of Marie Leveau possesses one of the Dying. He breaks into a strange, rhythmic dance and speech. The entire space becomes charged with the energies of the dead world. The Soldier marches in place to Marie Leveau's rhythm, then comes through independently. The Dying support and react to the possessed ones with sound and music.*

MARIE LEVEAU. Eh ye ye Mamzell Marie
  ye ye ye li konin tou
  gris gris
  li te kouri, aver vieux kokodril
  eh oui ye, Mamzelle Marie

  Eh ye ye
  my people come to me,
  they say:

    make that man poor so I grow rich
    make that one die so I can live
    kill my sister
    kill my brother

  and no one know the other
  and no one see the other

    Marie Leveau, she sees!
    See my people smile,
    then eat each other;
    wipe blood from mouth
    with dainty cloth.

  And my ocean stink with dead fish
  and my trees are hurt and broken
  and my fruit grows sick and rots
  and my air is black with poison
  that my birds cannot breathe
    and my people eat each other
    and my people live like slaves.

  Marie Leveau, she sees!
  See my people buying,
  see them selling,
  see them spending lives
  like slaves.
  Eh ye ye, Mamzelle Marie
  ye ye ye li konin tou
    (Etc.)

The Soldier moves forward in a march, mouthing "yessir."
His hand flies to his forehead in repeated salutes.
Marie Leveau grows silent as he speaks.

THE SOLDIER. Yessir
  Yessir
  Yessir

Yessir

Said yes when I wanted to say yes
Said yes when I want to say no
Said yes
Said yes
Yessir
Said yes

  And dead because I said yes
  And dead because YOU said yes
  And dead because I said yes
  And dead because YOU said yes

And dead before 'cause you never knew why
And dead before 'cause I never asked.

  Dead before and dead again
  Because I never knew

  What the FUCK I was saying yes to!

  yes
  yes
  yes

The Soldier moves into the background, but remains visible. Periodic salutes and "yessirs" break from him as Marie Leveau comes through again.

MARIE LEVEAU. Marie Leveau, she sees!
  See my people buying, see them selling
  see them spending lives
  like slaves.

I see the thief go into business
Now he can steal and not get caught.
I see the killer become policeman
Now he can murder, that's his job.

  Eh ye ye ye
  One hand holds the whip
  And one hand bleeds.

  Marie Leveau, she sees!
  See my people smile,
  then eat each other;
  wipe blood from mouth
  with dainty cloth.

And my ocean stink with dead fish
and my trees
and my fruit
and my air
and my birds
  and my people eat each other
  and my people but and sell
  and my people live
  like slaves!

Eh ye ye, Mamzelle Marie

Ye ye ye, li konin tou

                                    (*Etc.*)

The dead depart from the bodies of the possessed. Sound and movement cease.

The Renovation: *A table, covered with cosmetics and wigs is rolled onstage. Three actors begin to beautify themselves; both men and women apply makeup and wigs. The Beautician addresses the audience. She speaks precisely with a minimum of facial or bodily movement.*

THE BEAUTICIAN. A beauty parlor and vanity room are connected with the embalming station. We make up the corpse with conventional cosmetics, restyle the hair and repair the face.

We begin by massaging moisture creams into the cheeks and neck. Since no one is born with perfect skin, we smooth on a foundation base which covers any blemishes that mar the surface. We then add a touch of rouge to the cheeks, chin, and nose, and paint the mouth with lipstick.

Like all beauticians, we compensate for those faces which are not perfectly oval. Since no one is born with ideal features, we produce an illusion of symmetry through shading and spot cosmetology. Lips that are too narrow or full are reshaped with lipstick. Small eyes are made to appear larger through the addition of eyeliner, shadow, and false eyelashes.

If the hair is in good condition, it is washed and set by our hairdresser. If it is skimpy or lifeless, wigs are supplied in every color and style.

Generally speaking, we try to avoid a severe or artificial look. Our cosmeticians are trained to produce a natural appearance. Of course, we prefer to work on faces which have already been well-preserved. Our most attractive models are people who, during their lives, controlled facial expressions and avoided wrinkles by restricting grimaces and smiles to an absolute minimum. Although such people will need less attention than those whose faces are marked with laugh lines, creases, and the signs of suffering, we can transform anyone. No one need worry. We are able to erase the lines of a lifetime in less than an hour.

The three actors, completely made up, face the audience. Spotlights, held by other actors, illuminate the transformation. Tableau.

The Witness: *Three women, different aspects of the Witness, face the audience, kneeling. The first women speaks and repeats her words as the second woman, and finally the third, interpose their experiences. All three versions rhythmically interweave and overlap.*

FIRST WOMAN. Pa, why don't you do something?

SECOND WOMAN. Pa, why don't you do something?

Oh, but I do.
I sleep and I wake up.
I go to work, and I come
    home.
I get married and I get
    divorced.

Pa, why don't you do
    something?

Oh, but I do.
I invest money and
    make more money.
I train people and they
    train people.
I have children and they
    have children.

Pa, why don't you do
    something?

Oh, but I do.
I go from the bathroom
    to the bedroom
From the bedroom to
    the living room
From the living room to
    the bathroom.

SECOND WOMAN.

Hi, ma.
I see you.
(I don't see you dying.)

Hi, ma.
I see you.

(I don't see you dying.)

Hi, ma.
I see you.

(I don't see you dying.)

Hi, ma.
I see you living.
(I don't see you dying.)

Oh, but I do.
I go from the bathroom
    to the bedroom

[*Third woman begins
her speech*]

From the bedroom to
    the living room
From the living room to
    the bathroom.
From the bathroom to
    the bedroom.
From the bedroom to
    the living room.
From the living room to
    the bathroom.

THIRD WOMAN.

I saw him on his back.
    Lying here.
        Like this.
Lying there
    Like this

Lying thre
    Like this.

    Like this.

    Like this.

All the actors become part of the Witness.
*The three women multiply; fragments of their speeches
gestures, and movements are picked up and used as emblems by the others.*
*All words and signs become incresingly concentrated and
distilled.*

**The Dead Come Through (B): The One who Was
Hit:** *The One Who Was Hit comes through the bodies of
two actors. Both are possessed and both speak, sometimes in
unison and sometimes in counterpoint.*

Up in the morning

              hit on the head
Up in the evening
              hit on the head
Got up
        and   hit
Got up
        and   hit

Men have ways of breaking those they
    wish to break
              hit on the head
Men have ways and places
              jails asylums ditches

Up in the morning
              hit!

And
I
am
lying there
        (like this)
lying there
in the earth

Got up
        and   hit

I knew who I was when
your hatred set me free.
Your hatred was your prison
but your hatred set me free.

And
I
am
lying there
        (like this)
lying there
beside you
in the earth
you wouldn't share

(but
over my head
feet
are walking)

You cannot kill
the ocean
like you
killed
me!

The Dying Pray: *Semidarkness. Spotlights pick out individuals in prayer. Sounds, gestures, fragmented words.
The total stage effect resembles a dynamic collage in which*

individual parts are independently significant and, at the same time, integrated into the total picture.

The Dead Come Through (C): The Responsible One: *The spirit of the Responsible One passes into two bodies. They begin a repetitive pacing as they speak, individually and in unison.*

I was walking down the street.
Cracks in the sidewalk.
I saw a man.
Cracks in his face.
  What have I done?

I saw a child choking on air.
  What have I done?
Oceans rising.
  What have I done?
Buildings toppled.
  What have I done?

What was given me was impossible to work with.

I saw a woman
she had no teeth
nibbling at the pavement
chewing at the pavement
mouth full of stone.
  What have I done?

I saw snow falling,
flakes of sky.
  What have I done?
Forty-one dead.
  What have I done?
I saw.
I saw.
I can't say I didn't.
What have I done?

Sitting.
Standing.
Sleeping.
Sleepwalking.

What was given me was impossible to work with.

I saw blood
  What have I done?
Fire. A man on fire.
  What have I done?
I saw—agh!
  What have I done?
I saw—kkk!
  What have I done?
Ahhhhhh!
  What have I done?
Bkhhhhhh!
  What have I done?

What was given me was impossible to work with.

The Initiation: *A dead woman lies on a bed, spread-eagled, her head hanging. Four Attendants lift the New Arrival and hold him horizontally over the corpse. The motions of copulation begin. The Attendants move the New Arrival back and forth above the body. No effective resistance is possible.*

The act is completed. The New Arrival is led to another area. Two Team Members await him. One stands on a ladder, holding a stick. Another questions him. Each time he gives an incorrect answer, the sound of the stick cutting through air is heard. An internal scream is produced by the Team Members and Attendants. Everyone is involved in the inquisition and everyone receives the punishment.

TEAM MEMBER. Did you like it?
NEW ARRIVAL. Like it?!! (*He is hit.*)
TEAM MEMBER. Did you like it?
NEW ARRIVAL. No. (*He is hit.*)
TEAM MEMBER. Did you like it?
NEW ARRIVAL. I'll say I liked it if you want. (*He is hit.*)
TEAM MEMBER. Did you like it?
NEW ARRIVAL. Yes.
TEAM MEMBER. Do you mean it?
NEW ARRIVAL. What's the difference? (*He is hit.*)
TEAM MEMBER. Do you mean it?
NEW ARRIVAL. Yes. Yes.
TEAM MEMBER. So you liked it.
NEW ARRIVAL. Yes.
TEAM MEMBER. And you mean it.
NEW ARRIVAL. Yes.
TEAM MEMBER. Why did you like it?
NEW ARRIVAL. I don't now. (*He is hit.*)
TEAM MEMBER. Why did you like it?
NEW ARRIVAL. I liked it, that's all. (*He is hit.*)
TEAM MEMBER. Why did you like it?
NEW ARRIVAL. Because it was a new experience. (*He is hit.*)
TEAM MEMBER. Why did you like it?
NEW ARRIVAL. Because I always wanted—(*He is hit.*)
TEAM MEMBER. Why did you like it?
NEW ARRIVAL. Because it was necessary to like it

Silence. Blackout.

The Embalming As Required by Law: *A living person is placed on the embalming table. The Embalmers perform their jobs as before. The victim screams and writhes. His energies gradually dissipate; when his mouth is sewn, he grows completely silent.*

TEAM MEMBER. We prepare the deceased for embalming.
  The body is washed thoroughly with special attention to the orifices.
  A tube is inserted to drain the blood. Through another tube, embalming fluids are injected. As that fluid fills the veins, a flush appears on the face, the eyes flutter,

the chest rises and falls as if the deceased were breathing. This is only temporary, of course.

An incision is made in the central abdomen. The vital organs are removed and deposited in a bin to be burned. They are replaced by cotton batting, similar to that used in upholstery, to retain the original dimensions of the body. The skin is then repaired and sutured.

Cosmetological procedures are employed to improve the appearance of the deceased. First is the correction of lip slip.

Lip slip occurs as fluids drain from the upper lip, causing it to recede in a manner suggesting a sneer. This is unsightly for those viewing the body, so we stitch the lips together into a more attractive expression.

We cut out swollen facial tissues and fill the sunken cheeks by injecting massage creams into them. We then apply conventional makeup, such as rouge and lipstick, to create a natural and lifelike glow.

The deceased is now dressed in burial garments. These are backless, as the body will be viewed only from above.

The corpse is finally ready to await funeral procedures in the freezer compartment of the morgue.

The man on the embalming table is now silent and motionless. The corpse is wheeled off.

The Dead Come Through (D): The Executed Man and the Song: *A bed is raised and stood upright. A woman stands flattened against it, gripping its sides. She rocks from left to right; the bed knocks against the floor on each side. The Executed Man comes through.*

My eyes. Wide open.
My head. Full of imagination.
Like when I was a kid.
Free in my head.

Me and my friend, Joel, we used to fish in a place called "the pit." The water there was so clear you could see the fish swimming—big, beautiful fish. Me and Joel, we'd cut off their heads and rip out their stomachs and tear the scales off 'em. Yeah, me and Joel, we had fantastic imaginations.

> I was sentenced—
> just like you!

Warden!
I know you got that noose ready for me
but it's that noose that's set me free!
A man who know's he's gonna die
doesn't have anything to be afraid of.

> My prison's made of steel;
> yours is in your head.

If someone came into "the pit," me and Joel knew how to fix him. We'd take a wire and wind it 'round his cock and we'd twist it and twist it till that fella hollered—MAAAAAAAA!

> I was sentenced—
> just like you!

But that warden, he's keeping his imagination locked up real safe so when he gets up in the morning he can look at himself in the mirror and say: What a good man I am!
Everything I imagine is part of me.
Me, I knew I'd up with my head in a noose. That's why I could say:

> Yes!
> I am a thief.
> Yes!
> I am an addict.
> Yes!
> I am a homosexual, a pimp, a rapist.
> Yes!
> I am a murderer.
> Everything I imagine is part of me.
>
> I was sentenced—
> just like you!

Go on, warden, be good, be nice, do what you're told. You've been sentenced just like me, but you're keeping that locked up, too.

> My prison's made of steel;
> yours is in your head!

The sound of the wooden bed rocking against the floor grows louder. The song fills the woman; it uses her voice to sing itself. The words of the song are repeated over and over again with various intentions. The meaning of the words is secondary to the range of human emotions which can be expressed through them.

> A-nee Ma-a-meen
> A-nee Ma-a-meen
> A-nee Ma-a-meen
>
> A-nee Ma-a-meen
> A-nee Ma-a-meen
> A-nee Ma-a-meen
> (Etc.)

The song and the rocking end abruptly.

The Dying Imagine Their Judgment: *Center-stage, a ladder with a horn and megaphone. An empty chair at the side. A rack with clothing toward the rear. The Judge climbs the ladder and sits on the highest rung. He holds a book, from which he reads the judgments. The Judge speaks in the impersonal voice of a radio broadcaster; in a hoarse, authoritarian rasp; in a tired whine. The judgments are pronounced in a continuous, repetitive loop; a* *variety of images are enacted at the same time. The Judge blows the horn and begins.*

THE JUDGMENTS. The judgment of your life is your life.

You will finally possess the thing you wanted most in life—and eternity will be that thing and that thing only.

You are in the death of crowds. There are multitudes about you and they are, each one, yourself. There is not one other besides you—and yet, there are multitudes.

There is a space between what was done and what could have been done and you are rooted in that space. The judgment of your life is your life.

You are standing in a space filled with bodies and you watch their couplings and breathe their odors, but you cannot touch them and they will not reach out to you.

You saw, you saw, you can't say you didn't. The judgment of your life is your life.

You moved from the house to the office, from the office to the house; from sleep to waking and from waking to sleep; you moved from yesterday to today, from today to tomorrow—and you will repeat that movement for eternity and the circle will not open.

Did you sit on another's head or were you sat upon? Either way, you will never be free of the one who is above or he who is below. The judgment of your life is your life.

THE IMAGES.
One actor sits at a typewriter and for the duration of the scene makes a record of the proceedings.

A dead body lies on the floor. Two voyeurs lean over him, touching, kissing, speaking.

VOYEUR 1. We wash the body thoroughly with special attention to the orifices . . . to the orifices . . .

VOYEUR 2. There is a certain temptation when you're alone with the body . . . when you're alone with the body . . . there is a certain temptation . . . a temptation when you're alone with the body.

A naked body is brought out on a bed by two persons holding a scrubbing brush and pail. They set down the bed and begin to wash the floor, the bed, and the person in it. No distinctions are made between the three.
The bed and body are carried out.
One man sits on another's shoulders. The man below strains and struggles to get free, but cannot.
A clothesrack is rolled in.
Human beings hang amidst the clothing, like slabs of meat. The rack is pushed around the stage.
A woman paces alongside the empty chair. She gestures sternly.

You are standing on a bridge, but you do not know it. All around you, people come onto it and pass off of it, but you do not understand that all those who walk upon it at the same time are not strangers.

You neither faced your death nor participated in your life, but straddled the line between one place and the other, longing for both. The judgment of your life is your life.

You will finally possess the thing you wanted most in life—and eternity will be that thing and that thing only.

You are in the death of crowds. There are multitudes about you and they are, each one, yourself. There is not one other besides you—and yet, there are multitudes.

There is a space between what was done and what could have been done and you are rooted in that space. The judgment of your life is your life.

You are standing in a space filled with bodies and you watch their couplings and breathe their odors, but you cannot touch them and they will not reach out to you.

You saw, you saw, you can't say you didn't. The judgment of your life is your life.

You moved from the house to the office, from the office to the house; from sleep to waking and from waking to . . . . . .

A man is placed in the chair and bound. The woman continues her pacing.
The bound man makes sounds of protest. Others come forward, bind him more tightly and place a gag in his mouth.
The chair is raised and carried around the stage. The man gazes helplessly about him.
Someone mounts the ladder behind the Judge and, shifting from one ear to the other, whispers to him.
A chain of people crawl beneath the ladder on their bellies. They propel themselves forward by movements of their hips, arms, and legs. They seem to be swimming.
A continuous bubble of sound dribbles from their lips as they crawl. When the first person has moved as far forward as possible, he branches to the right or left. Still on his belly, he struggles to the end of the line and repeats the seemingly endless passage.
The Judge grows tired. The stream of human souls continues to pass beneath the ladder.
The voice of the Judge slurs and fades.
He is almost asleep.
The chain continues beneath him.

Blackout.

Presence and Absence: *The canopy is retrieved. The actors, with their instruments, stand beneath it, facing the audience. Drumbeat. The actors play the tune which introduced the piece. They are present through the music. The drumbeat ceases. The music ceases. The actors stand silently. They are directly present in their bodies, in the space, and in their relationship to the audience. The drumbeat begins again. The music is present. The drumbeat ceases. The music ceases. The actors are present. This sequence is repeated. This sequence is repeated. Blackout.*

Several scenes and speeches by dead ones were omitted from our final performances; we felt that the piece, as it then stood, was both concise and full enough. However, some of the extra material was used in performances in Europe and in New York and it is here included for those who, in performing the piece, would make different choices from ours.

The Dead Come Through: The Hooker:
So yes, I said
yes
when they wanted me
yes
with my body
living in it
living for it
living off of it
living off men living off me
yes, I said

you scratch my back
I'll scratch yours
so yes, I said
buying and selling
feeding off men feeding off me
yes, I said
yes
living for it
living off of it
yes, I said

you scratch my back
I'll scratch yours
and I paid for living with my life.

The Dead Come Through: The Stutterer: My voice. Bridging the distance. My voice. Shaping words. Here, in this . . . (*Gesture.*) A corridor without walls. Here, a . . . (*Gesture.*) I am squeezing myself into words. To speak at all is to speak within boundaries. Caught between the half-living and the half-dead, moving between the sound and the silence . . . we are not what we were.

What They Will Say of Him:
Yes, he was a good man
Yes, he was a man

Yes, he was
Yes Yes

Yes, he earned some money and he spent it
Yes, he travelled far and he returned (Yes, he went to other countries . . .)
Yes, he was married and yes, he was divorced
Yes, he was a man
Yes Yes

Yes, it's over now
Yes, he had possibility
Now he has none
Yes, my brother
Yes Yes

The Dying Imagine Their Judgment:
JUDGMENTS. You will be given the thing you wanted most in life, and eternity will be that thing and that thing only.

From this day on, you have whatever you wanted most in life, and eternity will be that thing and that thing only.

You are locked in a space filled with money and whether you are sitting or standing you are surrounded by it; and eternity is the sight of money and the smell of money and the touch of money and nothing else.

You will see your life stretch out around you and you will stand rooted in the space between what was done and what could have been done.

You are rooted in the space between what was done and what could have been done. The judgment of your life is your life.

There is a space between what was done and what could have been done and you are rooted there, looking at both.

You will judge yourself as harshly as you judged others and you will be forever judging and judged.

Everywhere you turn you will meet yourself and pass judgments; and there will be no distance between the judge and the accused and no relief.

You are standing in a courtroom and you are the judge and you are the accused, and you will pass sentence and there will be no relief from judging and being judged.

You will stand in a space filled with bodies and you will watch their couplings and breathe their odors, but you will not touch them and they will not reach out to you.

You are standing in the death of flesh. Bodies surround you and you watch their couplings, but you cannot touch them and they do not reach out to you.

You lived in the body and did not recognize the mind. Now you will stand in a space filled with bodies and though you will watch their couplings, you will not touch them and they will not reach out to you.

Do you live in the body or live in the mind?

You will dream of a new beginning and you will wait for it, but nothing changes in eternity and nothing ends.

You dreamed of a new beginning but moved down the plotted path to the end. And you will wait for beginning, you will dream of it and wait for it, but nothing changes in eternity and nothing ends.

You are moving toward the end from which it is possible to make a new beginning. You must change your life.

You will suffer repeatedly the agonies you have imposed on others. If you were unloving, you shall suffer the torments of the unloved; if you were an exploiter, you shall suffer the deprivations of the exploited; if you were male, you shall be female; if you were strong, you shall be weak; if you were rich, you shall be poor—and you will become wholly your opposite and suffer at your own hands.

Everything will become its opposite and each person will suffer repeatedly the agonies he imposed on others. The unloving will be unloved; the oppressor will be oppressed; the rich will be poor and the strong will be weak; the murderer will be the victim and the judge will be the accused. Everything will be different and everything will be the same.

TOPICS FOR CRITICAL THINKING AND WRITING

The Play on the STAGE and the PAGE

1. The final scene contains this statement: "The judgment of your life is your life." What do you think this means?
2. Are you bothered by the fact that this play has no plot and no fixed characters?
3. Can you think of alternative ways of staging this work than the ways suggested in the text?

4. What about costumes? How specifically should they evoke the subject matter of the scenes?
5. Certain moments seem clearly to derive from exercises. Where? And do they play a significant role in defining the piece?

A Context for *Terminal*

Writing for a Collective: Interview between Susan Yankowitz and Arthur Sainer (1972)*

Sainer: Did you supply any of the visual images that appear in Terminal, *or any that the actors used as beginning points?*

Yankowitz: To me, the question itself reveals a misunderstanding about the nature of the collective experience. In work of this sort, roles are very fluid; each individual, regardless of his or her particular function,

contributes material which can further any aspect of the work. Ultimately, the writer is responsible for the words used in the play, the actors for their performances, and the director for the integration of words, visual images, movement, and style; but during the actual process, these roles overlap. An actor may suggest dialogue; the writer may try to find a visual image rather than a verbal one; the director may ask that a new character be added. This occurs, I think, because in a collective work, there is no preset frame of reference: no characters, no words, no established acting mode, no structure. We have to find all that and it therefore becomes necessary, right from the start, to relate to the piece as a whole rather than specialized aspects of it. The "text" and the production are inextricably linked from the inception. As to whether or not I personally supplied some of the visual elements in the production, I'm sure that I did. But in a work which has

*Arthur Sainer, The Radical Theatre Notebook (New York: Avon, 1975), 147–53.

taken a very long period to evolve, it is nearly impossible to sort out where impulses began, or who generated them. And to try to do so is to miss the point.

In what ways did the ensemble experience help fulfill you as a writer, and in what ways do you feel it limited you?

Whether you are writing in collaboration with an ensemble or by yourself, the activity of writing—sitting down at the typewriter with a blank sheet of paper—is a solitary and fearful one. There are areas of experience which you are hesitant to explore because they are too painful or close to you. It's essential for a writer to find some way to push past her own limits and touch what is raw in herself. Working with a group helped me to do this. Because the fears were shared, it was easier to move through them. The attempt to break through societal and personal taboos about death helped me to open up parts of myself that I had previously kept locked. I learned a great deal about language: what it can and can't communicate; when a phrase is literary rather than theatrical, i.e., the words look beautiful on the page but sound self-conscious on an actor's tongue. I tended to overwrite; I didn't trust the actors to convey my intentions. But as the work progressed, I learned to leave space for the actor to supply meanings through his own instruments: pitch, inflection, gesture, body. My writing has become more economical, more precise as a result. . . .

Of course, a situation in which your work is subjected to the scrutiny of a large company is as much a frustration as a challenge. If Joe [Chaikin] or the actor who was to perform a speech wasn't satisfied with it, the speech had to be rewritten. I could argue or defend my work, but ultimately artistic control was not in my hands. And my ego suffered. Ultimately, *Terminal* is not my work in the way that *Slaughterhouse Play* or *Boxes* is. I am not responsible for all its successful moments nor all of its failures. . . .

You've indicated that you weren't the first writer to work on the text for Terminal. *At what stage was the work when you arrived? Were you instrumental in discarding written material that you didn't feel comfortable with?*

When I began writing for *Terminal*, the company had already been working for about four months with writers Marc Kaminsky and Nancy Fales. During that period, the idea that spirits from the dead would possess the dying and speak through them was developed; this was a central structural contribution to the piece. Additional work had been done on the "ward," which later became "The State of the Dying."

At that point, the concept for the section was essentially linear; the biology of death was virtually unexplored although the embalming ritual had been investigated and more or less set as an integral segment of the piece; there had been some character development of hospital authorities and patients, but the elitist and conformist pressures of hospital life itself were unexamined. Nancy and Marc, as well as Sam Shepard, had written some material, but as emphasis, structure, and intention changed, most of it was discarded. All these early investigations, however, were seminal to the version of *Terminal* which is now being performed. . . . Contrary to much opinion, the writer in a collective work is not a secretary or a reporter; his style and imagination are essential to determining the direction of a piece. Had Nancy or Marc remained as the writer for *Terminal*, the work undoubtedly would have been very different.

How did Joe and Roberta [Sklar, co-director] and the ensemble specifically help you in the writing?

My primary contact at all stages of the work was Joe. After workshops, we'd talk about the improvisational material and try to clarify a direction. Sometimes he'd suggest that I work on an idea which had been explored improvisationally or which had arisen out of our discussion; at other times, a scene would suggest itself and I'd go home and write it. Material grew out of improvisations, discussions, and solitary thinking. After a speech or scene was written, Joe would read it. Sometimes he'd mark the lines or ideas which particularly appealed to him; or suggest cuts; or hand the text over to an actor to work on. There were few violent disagreements; in retrospect, the process appears remarkably peaceful and rational, at least for me and Joe. But my memory is not very good. Everyone contributed to the writing. I saw my function in this way: not to "write" every word but to be responsible for every word which was used. That is, to remain open to phrases and expressions that were not my own; to take from the actors, to use their imaginations; and, at the same time, to assume absolute responsibility for all decisions pertaining to language. If an actor wanted to use a phrase which seemed inappropriate to me, I felt that it was my prerogative to insist it be deleted. This occasioned some arguments but was generally respected.

Could you conceive of your initiating an idea for the Open Theatre or another ensemble? Do you think you would then feel more "in control" of the work, if this isn't begging the question?

To have more control in the theatre, it would be necessary for me to write, direct, design and act all the roles in my play. It seems to me that the essence of the medium is collaborative. Even when I write a play in a conventional manner, I am finally dependent on others; the play goes out of my hands and into those of a producer, director, et cetera. If I wanted to have absolute control, I would choose a medium in which only language was necessary; I would write fiction. Which I am doing.

* * *

After the initial run of Terminal, *the size of the ensemble was cut to six, I believe, and the script was changed somewhat. What were the nature of the changes, and were you consulted about them? Is it possible that the piece may change further, and would you expect to be consulted about further*

changes? Would you want to be? I suppose what I'm getting at is, To what degree do you feel proprietary toward the work, proprietary in the best sense?

I still feel very attached to *Terminal.* I suppose that I am a part of it to the extent that it's a part of me. When material needed to be deleted or altered or added to accommodate a smaller company, I revised. When the piece was recently performed at the Tombs, the house of detention in Lower Manhattan, I rewrote some of the text with an aim to making it speak more directly to a prison audience. I don't imagine that the piece will change very much more. In a way, I guess it's history for all of us who created it.*

*Not true: The piece was revised 27 years after its opening and presented as 1969 Terminal 1996 *at P. S. 122, New York City. See Commentary.*

ASIAN AMERICAN THEATER

Although actors and musicians of Asian ancestry have performed in the United States for well over a century, prejudice and exclusionary practices impeded the development of a large body of stage plays. Of course, "mainstream" American plays in the twentieth century have included several with Asian themes—for instance, post–World War II Broadway hits such as *Teahouse of the August Moon, The King and I,* and *South Pacific*—but these were not written by Asian Americans and they did not succeed in removing stereotypical casting from the American stage.

In 1965, dissatisfied with the lack of roles and scripts, a group of Asian American actors and directors established the East-West Players in Los Angeles, which became a vital force on the West Coast. The players' artistic director, Mako, encouraged a number of Asian American writers, including Wakako Yamauchi, Momoko Iko, Frank Chin, Genny Lim, and Velina Hasu Houston. In 1982 an interviewer, James F. Dean, asked Mako about those early years.

Dean: Why was East-West Payers formed? Because there were actors with unfulfilled needs? Or were there Asian American plays waiting to be produced?

Mako: I think to answer the question we have to go back to the very beginning. We have to back to 1965 when our company was formed, founded. Since all of us who were founders at that time were actors, I would have to classify our theater as "actors" theater, as opposed to "directors' theater or "writers" theaters.... What is Asian American art? We do recognize Japanese art or Chinese art or Korean art, but what is this Asian American stuff?... At the same time, the whole thinking began to evolve much more: Why are we here? What do we have to do? What do we want to do?... We needed to educate our own people as well as reaching out to non-Asian audiences. And we had to educate our actors. In order to do that we had to develop writers.

Playwriting contests and grants from the Ford Foundation, the Rockefeller Foundation, and the National Endowment for the Arts all helped encourage Asian American playwrights. Several other West Coast groups sprang up, among them the Asian American Theater Company in San Francisco, the Asian Exclusion Act (now called the Northwest Asia American Theatre Company), and the Asian American Actors Ensemble in San Diego. Chicago has engendered two Asian American companies, Angel's Island Theatre Company and Mina-sama-no. In New York City, Tisa Chang established the Pan Asian Repertory Theatre in 1977, which has performed plays by Shakespeare, Ibsen, and Chekhov, as well as many scripts written by Asian American playwrights.

Perhaps today's best-known Asian American playwright is David Henry Hwang, whose early works debuted at New York's Public Theater and whose *M. Butterfly* (1988) won a Tony on Broadway. For one of Hwang's plays, see *The Dance and the Railroad,* page 1297. Other playwrights include the Chinese American Elizabeth Wong, whose "Letter to a Student Revolutionary" examined the explosive events of Tiananmen Square through letters between a Chinese American student and a Chinese student. A director who must also be mentioned is Shozo Sato, who has produced several works that synthesize traditional performance techniques of Japan with classic Western plays such as his "Kabuki Medea."

Nearly thirty companies in the country now perform Asian American material. Broadly speaking these can be divided into two groups whose purposes are widely diverse. The first consists of theater companies that focus on their local community and mount plays written by both canonical writers as well as Asian American writers. Notable examples, all founded in the 1990s, include National Asian American Theater Company in New York City, which usually produces European American canonized works such as Shakespeare and Ibsen with all Asian American actors; Ma-Yi Theater, also in New York, which focuses on Filipino American plays; Asian American Repertory Theater in San Diego, which does revivals of older Asian American plays; Theater Mu in Minneapolis, which produces intercultural Asian American works; and Lodestone Theater in Los Angeles, which does not call itself "Asian American" but which has mounted some of the most original, cutting edge works by younger Asian American playwrights. The second kind of company, also founded in the last decade, consists of performance groups that write their own materials and tour around the country, often appearing at colleges and universities. These include Slant Performance Group from New York City, consisting of three

Asian American men who incorporate rock music, dance, movement into their performances; 18 Mighty Mountain Warriors in San Francisco, a cutting-edge comic group that models itself after the Hispanic group called Culture Clash; Here and Now from Los Angeles whose material focuses on college-age Asian Americans; and Peeling the Banana, in New York, which uses autobiography in performance. Cold Tofu, founded in the early 1980s, is the only Asian American improvisational group.

DAVID Henry Hwang

David Henry Hwang (1957–) was born and raised in the middle-class Los Angeles suburb of San Gabriel, the son of Henry Hwang, an accountant turned bank president born in Shanghai, and Dorothy Hwang, a pianist and teacher born in Amoy, China, but reared in the Philippines. From his mother David received a heritage uncommon to Chinese Americans, a tradition of Protestant fundamentalism. In China, Dorothy's grandparents had been converted by Christian missionaries, her grandmother even becoming an exorcist. The family migrated to the Philippines where they became successful merchants before coming to the United States in the early 1950s, and soon after, at a dance for foreign students at the University of Southern California, Dorothy met Henry Hwang. The couple could not marry, however, until Henry converted to Christianity. In what the Chinese call "the Land of the Gold Mountain," the couple raised a family (two sisters besides David) and pursued the American dream. Henry, in particular, never looked back, identifying completely with his adopted culture.

It is a not unfamiliar immigrant tale: The parents reject the old country with its old values, but their American-born children, disturbed by this rejection, are determined to retrieve their lost inheritance. What makes Hwang's variation on this story different is the intense disparity between Protestantism and Confucianism, the latter being, as he has observed, "more a code of ethics than a religion." Hwang expresses a passionate need to escape what he clearly sees as the destructive confluence of Christian hypocrisy and prudery with the most venal aspects of American materialism. It is a debilitating legacy he feels compelled to exorcize. And yet in his plays he cannot escape the consequences of his Christian upbringing.

In 1979, as a Stanford University senior enacting a time-honored rite of passage, he directed a production of his first play in the lounge of his college dormitory. Within a year, the play, *FOB* (Fresh Off the Boat—an ironic acronym for recent immigrants) made a rapid journey from Stanford to the O'Neill Theater Center in Connecticut to Joseph Papp's Public Theater in New York (where it won an Obie award), and the fledgling Chinese American playwright received national recognition as a vigorous new voice in the American theater. A year after the impact-making debut of *FOB* at the Public Theater in 1980, Hwang confirmed his originality there with *The Dance and the Railroad.* Through the ensuing decades, Hwang has slowly increased his oeuvre, but no new effort has matched his remarkable 1988 Broadway debut with *M.Butterfly*, a play that rapidly achieved a dreamed-about level of critical appreciation and commercial success both here and abroad. Although the triumph of *M.Butterfly* has not been replicated, Hwang's later work has been diverse: family plays such as *Family Devotions,* 1981; *Rich Relations,* 1986; and *Golden Child,* 1996; adaptations from the Japanese (*The House of the Sleeping Beauties* and *The Sound of a Voice,* 1983); and collaborations with Philip Glass (*1000 Airplanes on the Roof,* 1989), and Elton John (*Aïda,* 2000).

■ ■ ■ ■ ■ ■ ■ ■ ■ ■ ■ ■ ■ ■ ■ ■

COMMENTARY ON *THE DANCE AND THE RAILROAD*

Although it is a play about young people, FOB—David Hwang's first play—is far from the familiar reenacting of adolescent coming of age. It is a chamber play about ethnic consciousness centered on three cousins, all in their early twenties, all with American first names, who represent different groups of Chinese in America: Dale is an ABC—American-born Chinese—who is completely committed to effacing his Chinese roots; his dream is to be totally assimilated into mainstream white culture. His opposite is Steve, a fresh-off-the-boat immigrant from Hong Kong on whom Dale projects all the greenhorn characteristics that he hates. The most enigmatic of the trio, Steve enters the play identifying himself with Gwan Gung, the warrior god brought to America by Chinese immigrants as a source of inspiration in a hostile and repressive land. The central action of the play focuses on the competition of the two young men for Grace, Taiwanese-born but American reared. As the competition intensifies, it is, significantly, *her* journey toward identity that powers the play.

It is no surprise that Grace rejects Dale's assimilationism, choosing the tradition embodied by Steve. But Hwang refuses to polemicize her decision by oversimplifying the theme of ethnic choice. The play's originality derives from a more complex dramatic strategy. However attracted to the theme of racial consciousness, so dominant as he was writing in emerging black and Hispanic art, Hwang is aesthetically attracted to another contemporary dramatic force: the free-associative, quasi-surreal, mythic dramaturgy of the white experimental tradition, particularly as displayed in the plays of Sam Shepard. While at Stanford, Hwang attended San Francisco's Magic Theatre where Shepard was playwright in residence, and also visited the Padua Hills Playwright's Festival in Claremont, California, where Shepard, Maria Irene Fornes, and other contemporary experimentalists worked with fledgling writers.

But whereas Shepard had to construct a personal mythology out of the heterogeneous myths of America's past and present, Hwang sensed his cultural advantage. He had available in his own ethnic tradition a powerful storehouse of legend and ritual. His dramatic inspiration was to confront the imperative theme of identity neither in naturalistic nor white experimental modes, but to move beyond realism *and* surrealism into the realm of Chinese myth. On one level, *FOB* indeed places socially and psychologically coherent characters in a concrete environment: the back room of a small Chinese restaurant in Torrance, California. But it soon explodes beyond realism by boldly moving into the realm of the legendary. The inspiration for this move was provided by two Californian, Chinese American writers to whom the young playwright is acknowledgedly indebted: Maxine Hong Kingston and Frank Chin. Hong Kingston in *The Woman Warrior* (1976) evoked the figure of Fa Mu Lan, the eponymous Woman Warrior, who takes her father's place in battle, as a symbol of the need of a people and a gender to transcend passivity. Frank Chin, the first Chinese American playwright to have major plays produced in New York (*The Chickencoop Chinaman*, 1972; *The Year of the Dragon*, 1974), identified with the rise of African American theater and challenged American racism. To combat white society's relegation of Asian Americans—particularly Chinese Americans—to states of "self-contempt, self-rejection, and disintegration," Chin evokes in many of his works the aforementioned legendary figure of Gwan Gung, the revered Chinese folk hero who fought battles for the Han dynasty. Be-

cause of his skill in battle, Gwan was deified as the God of War, and his moral virtues made him the god of writers and scholars whom in legend he protected. A century ago, he traveled to America in the novels and operas brought by the Cantonese immigrants who came to work on the railroad. For Chin, Gwan Gung represents the active, individualistic masculine ideal to which his important characters aspire.

Drawing on the mythical materials used by Hong Kingston and Chin, David Hwang evokes the figure of Gwan Gung in *The Dance and the Railroad* (1981), a play that spins variations on the themes and techniques of *FOB*. Set not in contemporary California, but in 1867 somewhere in the West where the transcontinental railroad is being completed, this is a chamber play for two actors that again confronts the theme of Chinese American identity in a theatrical style ranging from the realistic to the ritualistic. The protagonists are two immigrant Chinese men—Lone and Ma—working under repressive conditions to fulfill the white man's dream to span the continent. As they while away the time during a strike, they enter into a complex master-apprentice relationship that forces each to reexamine himself. Lone is the old hand; he has been working on the railroad for two years. Ma is the FOB, only in America for four weeks, captivated by the dream of the Gold Mountain of America where even the snow is warm. Lone is appropriately named, indeed the loner—the rebel artist who calls his compatriots "dead" because they lack spiritual goals. A would-be actor in the old country until forced abroad, he obsessively, solitarily practices his demanding craft on a secluded mountaintop.

Lone's solitude is breached by the young, ebullient Ma, who persists until Lone reluctantly accepts him as an acting disciple. Though newly arrived, Ma completely identifies with his fellow Chinese who have just embarked on a strike against their shameful working conditions. Nonetheless, he sees in the reclusive, disdainful Lone a master who can lead him to a higher plane of achievement. As Lone puts him through his paces, Ma endures difficult trials such as having to spend an entire night enacting a locust. Finally, Ma earns the right to play a major role, the heroic figure of the immigrant's favorite god, Gwan Gung. But once he has earned that cherished right, he rejects it. He does not have to play Gwan Gung; he is Gwan Gung, because he is a Chinese man who despite the odds has won his strike. As Lone pulls out a gong, master and disciple, like the characters in *FOB*, perform a climactic Chinese opera that this time ends with the triumph of the striking Chinese.

Hwang then moves his play in an ambiguous direction: At the moment of celebration, Lone informs Ma that the men did not get their full demands. Ma is appalled by "a strike that has gotten us nothing," and declares his independence from his compatriots whom he, too, now sees as dead men. If Ma is now Gwan Gung it is not because his identity is subsumed by his group, but because he has come to realize that every journey to identity must be individual. "I've got to change myself. Count my change. Learn to gamble. Learn to win. Learn to stare. Learn to deny." He will no longer blindly accept the values of the group, nor will he any longer study to be an actor. Lone, meanwhile, recognizing that the apprenticeship is over, comes to his own realization: One does not have to dance to proudly prove one's superiority over others: "Today I am dancing for no reason at all." As Ma departs for good, Lone resumes his dance.

Is Hwang endorsing his characters' final decisions? At a time when Hwang was aggressively affirming his racial militancy ("I write about Asian-Americans," he reported to the *New York Times*, "to claim our legitimate, but often neglected place in the American experience"), he appears at the end of this play to withdraw from group solidarity. Is it, perhaps, less a case of con-

tradition than of painful self-scrutiny? The young playwright indeed makes common cause with his marginalized group's right to find its authentic voice. He proudly sees his plays as part of a burgeoning Asian American theater movement comparable to the rise of African American and Latino theater, a movement that has produced artists such as Winston Tong and Frank Chin and theater groups such as the East-West Players of Los Angeles, San Francisco's Asian-American Theatre Company, and New York's Pan-Asian Repertory. He acknowledges that his plays would not exist without the energy of his new theater and, indeed, in *The Dance and the Railroad*, pays homage to the contributions of Asian American artists by giving his characters the actual names of their performers, John Lone and Tzi Ma. But as much as he cherishes his Chinese inheritance, Hwang also affirms the American part of his intense search for individuality. It is this personal dimension that he scrutinizes in several later plays such as *Family Devotions* and *Golden Child*. That he refuses to be ghettoized as a "minority" writer can be seen by his commitment to mainstream subjects and projects and experimental collaborations. Acknowledging the disparate elements in his cultural inheritance, Hwang remains an adventurous and unpredictable writer.

THE DANCE AND THE RAILROAD
David Henry Hwang

CHARACTERS

LONE, *Twenty years old, ChinaMan railroad worker.*
MA, *Eighteen years old, ChinaMan railroad worker.*

PLACE

A mountaintop near the transcontinental railroad.

TIME

June, 1867.

SYNOPSIS OF SCENES

SCENE 1, *Afternoon.*
SCENE 2, *Afternoon, a day later.*
SCENE 3, *Late afternoon, four days later.*
SCENE 4, *Late that night.*
SCENE 5, *Just before the following dawn.*

SCENE 1

A mountaintop. Lone is practicing opera steps. He swings his pigtail around like a fan. Ma enters, cautiously, watches from a hidden spot. Ma approaches Lone.

LONE. So, there are insects hiding in the bushes.
MA. Hey, listen, we haven't met, but—
LONE. I don't spend time with insects. (*Lone whips his hair into Ma's face; Ma backs off; Lone pursues him, swiping at Ma with his hair.*)
MA. What the—? Cut it out! (*Ma pushes Lone away.*)
LONE. Don't push me.
MA. What was that for?
LONE. Don't ever push me again.
MA. You mess like that, you're gonna get pushed.
LONE. Don't push me.
MA. You started it. I just wanted to watch.
LONE. You "just wanted to watch." Did you ask my permission?
MA. What?
LONE. Did you?
MA. C'mon.
LONE. You can't expect to get in for free.
MA. Listen. I got stuff you'll wanna hear.
LONE. You think so?
MA. Yeah. Some advice.
LONE. Advice? How old are you, anyway?
MA. Eighteen.
LONE. A child.
MA. Yeah. Right, a child. But listen—
LONE. A child who tries to advise a grown man—
MA. Listen, you got this kind of attitude.
LONE. —is a child who will never grow up.

MA. You know, the ChinaMen down at camp, they can't stand it.
LONE. Oh?
MA. Yeah. You gotta watch yourself. You know what they say? They call you "Prince of the Mountain." Like you're too good to spend time with them.
LONE. Perceptive of them.
MA. After all, you never sing songs, never tell stories. They say you act like your spit is too clean for them, and they got ways to fix that.
LONE. Is that so?
MA. Like they're gonna bury you in the shit buckets, so you'll have more to clean than your nails.
LONE. But I don't shit.
MA. Or they're gonna cut out your tongue, since you never speak to them.
LONE. There's no one here worth talking to.
MA. Cut it out, Lone. Look, I'm trying to help you, all right? I got a solution.
LONE. So young yet so clever.
MA. That stuff you're doing—it's beautiful. Why don't you do it for the guys at camp? Help us celebrate?
LONE. What will "this stuff" help celebrate?
MA. C'mon. The strike, of course. Guys on a railroad gang, we gotta stick together, you know.
LONE. This is something to celebrate?
MA. Yeah. Yesterday, the weak-kneed ChinaMen, they were running around like chickens without a head: "The white devils are sending their soldiers! Shoot us all!" But now, look—day four, see? Still in one piece. Those soldiers—we've never seen a gun or a bullet.
LONE. So you're all warrior-spirits, huh?
MA. They're scared of us, Lone—that's what it means.

LONE. I appreciate your advice. Tell you what—you go down—

MA. Yeah?

LONE. Down to the camp—

MA. Okay.

LONE. To where the men are—

MA. Yeah?

LONE. Sit there—

MA. Yeah.

LONE. And wait for me.

MA. Okay. (*Pause.*) That's it? What do you think I am?

LONE. I think you're an insect interrupting my practice. So fly away. Go home.

MA. Look, I didn't come here to get laughed at.

LONE. No, I suppose you didn't.

MA. So just stay up here. By yourself. You deserve it.

LONE. I do.

MA. And don't expect any more help from me.

LONE. I haven't gotten any yet.

MA. If one day, you wake up and your head is buried in the shit can—

LONE. Yes?

MA. You can't find your body, your tongue is cut out—

LONE. Yes.

MA. Don't worry, 'cuz I'll be there.

LONE. Oh.

MA. To make sure your mother's head is sitting right next to yours. (*Ma exits.*)

LONE. His head is too big for this mountain. (*Returns to practicing.*)

SCENE 2

Mountaintop. Next day. Lone is practicing. Ma enters.

MA. Hey.

LONE. You? Again?

MA. I forgive you.

LONE. You . . . what?

MA. For making fun of me yesterday. I forgive you.

LONE. You can't—

MA. No. Don't thank me.

LONE. You can't forgive me.

MA. No. Don't mention it.

LONE. You—! I never asked for your forgiveness.

MA. I know. That's just the kinda guy I am.

LONE. This is ridiculous. Why don't you leave? Go down to your friends and play soldiers, sing songs, tell stories.

MA. Ah! See? That's just it. I got other ways I wanna spend my time. Will you teach me the opera?

LONE. What?

MA. I wanna learn it. I dreamt about it all last night.

LONE. No.

MA. The dance, the opera—I can do it.

LONE. You think so?

MA. Yeah. When I get outa here, I wanna go back to China and perform.

LONE. You want to become an actor?

MA. Well, I wanna perform.

LONE. Don't you remember the story about the three sons whose parents send them away to learn a trade? After three years, they return. The first one says, "I have become a coppersmith." The parents say, "Good. Second son, what have you become?" "I've become a silversmith." "Good—and youngest son, what about you?" "I have become an actor." When the parents hear that their son has become an actor, they are very sad. The mother beats her head against the ground until the ground, out of pity, opens up and swallows her. The father is so angry he can't even speak, and the anger builds up inside him until it blows his body to pieces—little bits of his skin are found hanging from trees days later. You don't know how you endanger your relatives by becoming an actor.

MA. Well, I don't wanna become an "actor." That sounds terrible. I just wanna perform. Look, I'll be rich by the time I get out of here, right?

LONE. Oh?

MA. Sure. By the time I go back to China, I'll ride in gold sedan chairs, with twenty wives fanning me all around.

LONE. Twenty wives? This boy is ambitious.

MA. I'll give out pigs on New Year's and keep a stable of small birds to give to any woman who pleases me. And in my spare time, I'll perform.

LONE. Between your twenty wives and your birds, where will you find a free moment?

MA. I'll play Gwan Gung* and tell stories of what life was like on the Gold Mountain.

LONE. Ma, just how long have you been in "America"?

MA. Huh? About four weeks.

LONE. You are a big dreamer.

MA. Well, all us ChinaMen here are—right? Men with little dreams—have little brains to match. They walk with their eyes down, trying to find extra grains of rice on the ground.

LONE. So, you know all about "America"? Tell me, what kind of stories will you tell?

MA. I'll say, "We had laid tracks like soldiers. Mountains? We hung from cliffs in baskets and the winds blew us like birds. Snow? We lived underground like moles for days at a time. Deserts? We—"

LONE. Wait. Wait. How do you know these things after only four weeks?

MA. They told me—the other ChinaMen on the gang. We've been telling stories ever since the strike began.

LONE. They make it sound like it's very enjoyable.

MA. They said it is.

LONE. Oh? And you believe them?

---

*The warrior god brought to America by Chinese immigrants as primary inspiration in a hostile land.

MA. They're my friends. Living underground in winter—sounds exciting, huh?

LONE. Did they say anything about the cold?

MA. Oh, I already know about that. They told me about the mild winters and the warm snow.

LONE. Warm snow?

MA. When I go home, I'll bring some back to show my brothers.

LONE. Bring some—? On the boat?

MA. They'll be shocked—they never seen American snow before.

LONE. You can't. By the time you get snow to the boat, it'll have melted, evaporated, and returned as rain already.

MA. No.

LONE. No?

MA. Stupid.

LONE. Me?

MA. You been here awhile, haven't you?

LONE. Yes. Two years.

MA. Then how come you're so stupid? This is the Gold Mountain. The snow here doesn't melt. It's not wet.

LONE. That's what they told you?

MA. Yeah. It's true.

LONE. Did anyone show you any of this snow?

MA. No. It's not winter.

LONE. So where does it go?

MA. Huh?

LONE. Where does it go, if it doesn't melt? What happens to it?

MA. The snow? I dunno. I guess it just stays around.

LONE. So where is it? Do you see any?

MA. Here? Well, no but . . . (*Pause.*) This is probably one of those places where it doesn't snow—even in winter.

LONE. Oh.

MA. Anyway, what's the use of me telling you what you already know? Hey, c'mon—teach me some of that stuff. Look—I've been practicing the walk—how's this? (*Demonstrates.*)

LONE. You look like a duck in heat.

MA. Hey—it's a start, isn't it?

LONE. Tell you what—you want to play some *die siu?*

MA. *Die su?* Sure.

LONE. You know, I'm pretty good.

MA. Hey, I play with the guys at camp. You can't be any better than Lee—he's really got it down. (*Lone pulls out a case with two dice.*)

LONE. I used to play till morning.

MA. Hey, us too. We see the sun start to rise, and say, "Hey, if we go to sleep now, we'll never get up for work." So we just keep playing.

LONE. (*Holding out dice.*) Die or Siu?

MA. *Siu.*

LONE. You sure?

MA. Yeah!

LONE. All right. (*He rolls.*) Die!

MA. *Siu!* (*They see the result.*)

MA. Not bad. (*They continue taking turns rolling through the following section; Ma always loses.*)

LONE. I haven't touched these in two years.

MA. I gotta practice more.

LONE. Have you lost much money?

MA. Huh? So what?

LONE. Oh, you have gold hidden in your shirt linings, huh?

MA. Here in "America"—losing is no problem. You know—End of the Year Bonus?

LONE. Oh, right.

MA. After I get that, I'll laugh at what I lost.

LONE. Lee told you there was a bonus, right?

MA. How'd you know?

LONE. When I arrived here, Lee told me there was a bonus, too.

MA. Lee teach you how to play?

LONE. Him? He talked to me a lot.

MA. Look, why don't you come down and start playing with the guys again?

LONE. "The guys."

MA. Before we start playing, Lee uses a stick to write "Kill!" in the dirt.

LONE. You seem to live for your nights with "the guys."

MA. What's life without friends, huh?

LONE. Well, why do *you* think I stopped playing?

MA. Hey, maybe you were the one getting killed, huh?

LONE. What?

MA. Hey, just kidding.

LONE. Who's getting killed here?

MA. Just a joke.

LONE. That's not a joke, it's blasphemy.

MA. Look, obviously you stopped playing 'cause you wanted to practice the opera.

LONE. Do you understand that discipline?

MA. But, I mean, you don't have to overdo it either. You don't have to treat 'em like dirt. I mean, who are you trying to impress? (*Pause. Lone throws dice into the bushes.*)

LONE. Oooops. Better go see who won.

MA. Hey! C'mon! Help me look!

LONE. If you find them, they are yours.

MA. You serious?

LONE. Yes.

MA. Here. (*Finds the dice.*)

LONE. Who won?

MA. I didn't check.

LONE. Well, no matter. Keep the dice. Take them and go play with your friends.

MA. Here. (*He offers them to Lone.*) A present.

LONE. A present? This isn't a present!

MA. They're mine, aren't they? You gave them to me, right?

LONE. Well, yes, but—

MA. So now I'm giving the to you.

LONE. You can't give me a present. I don't want them.

MA. You wanted them enough to keep them two years.

LONE. I'd forgotten I had them.

MA. See, I know, Lone. You wanna get rid of me. But you can't. I'm paying for lessons.

LONE. With my dice.

MA. Mine now. (*He offers them again.*) Here. (*Pause. Lone runs Ma's head across his forehead.*)

LONE. Feel this.

MA. Hey!

LONE. Pretty wet, huh?

MA. Big deal.

LONE. Pretty wet, huh?

MA. Big deal.

LONE. Well, its not from playing *die siu.*

MA. I know how to sweat. I wouldn't be here if I didn't.

LONE. Yes, but are you willing to sweat after you've finished sweating? Are you willing to come up after you've spent the whole day chipping half an inch off a rock, and punish your body some more?

MA. Yeah. Even after work, I still—

LONE. No, you don't. You want to gamble, and tell dirty stories, and dress up like women to do shows.

MA. Hey, I never did that.

LONE. You've only been here a month. (*Pause.*) And what about "the guys"? They're not going to treat you so well once you stop playing with them. Are you willing to work all day listening to them whisper, "That one—let's put spiders in his soup"?

MA. They won't do that to me. With you, it's different.

LONE. Is it?

MA. You don't have to act that way.

LONE. What way?

MA. Like you're so much better than them.

LONE. No. You haven't even begun to understand. To practice every day, you must have a fear to force you up here.

MA. A fear? No—it's 'cause what you're doing is beautiful.

LONE. No.

MA. I've seen it.

LONE. It's ugly to practice when the mountain has turned your muscles to ice. When my body hurts too much to come here, I look at the other ChinaMen and think, "They are dead. Their muscles work only because the white man forces them. I live because I can still force my muscles to work for me." Say it. "They are dead."

MA. No. They're my friends.

LONE. Well, then, take your dice down to your friends.

MA. But I want to learn—

LONE. This is your first lesson.

MA. Look, it shouldn't matter—

LONE. It does,

MA. It shouldn't matter what I think.

LONE. Attitude is everything.

MA. But as long as I come up, do the exercises—

LONE. I'm not going to waste time on a quitter.

MA. I'm not!

LONE. Then say it.—"They are dead men."

MA. I can't.

LONE. Then you will never have the dedication.

MA. That doesn't prove anything.

LONE. I will not teach a dead man.

MA. What?

LONE. If you can't see it, then you're dead too.

MA. Don't start pinning—

LONE. Say it!

MA. All right.

LONE. What?

MA. All right. I'm one of them. I'm a dead man too. (*Pause.*)

LONE. I thought as much. So, go. You have your friends.

MA. But I don't have a teacher.

LONE. I don't think you need both.

MA. Are you sure?

LONE. I'm being questioned by a child. (*Lone returns to practicing. Silence.*)

MA. Look, Lone, I'll come up here every night—after work—I'll spend my time practicing, okay? (*Pause.*) But I'm not gonna say that they're dead. Look at them. They're on strike; dead men don't go on strike, Lone. The white devils—they try and stick us with a ten-hour day. We want a return to eight hours and also a fourteen-dollar-a-month raise. I learned the demon English—listen: "Eight hour a day good for white man, alla same good for ChinaMan." These are the demands of live ChinaMen, Lone. Dead men don't complain.

LONE. All right, this is something new. But no one can judge the ChinaMen till after the strike.

MA. They say we'll hold out for months if we have to. The smart men will live on what we've hoarded.

LONE. A ChinaMan's mouth can swallow the earth. (*He takes the dice.*) While the strike is on, I'll teach you.

MA. And afterwards?

LONE. Afterwards—we'll decide then whether these are dead or live men.

MA. When can we start?

LONE. We've already begun. Give me your hand.

SCENE 3

Lone and Ma are doing physical exercises.

MA. How long will it be before I can play Gwan Gung?

LONE. How long before a dog can play the violin?

MA. Old Ah Hong—have you heard him play the violin?

LONE. Yes. Now, he should take his violin and give it to a dog.

MA. I think he sounds okay.

LONE. I think he caused the avalanche last winter.

MA. He used to play for weddings back home.

LONE. Ah Hong?

MA. That's what he said.

LONE. You probably heard wrong.

MA. No.

LONE. He probably said he played for funerals.

MA. He's been playing for the guys down at camp.

LONE. He should play for the white devils—that will end this stupid strike.

MA. Yang told me for sure—it'll be over by tomorrow.

LONE. Eight days already. And Yang doesn't know anything.

MA. He said they're already down to an eight-hour and five dollar raise at the bargaining sessions.

LONE. Yang eats too much opium.

MA. That doesn't mean he's wrong about this.

LONE. You can't trust him. One time—last year—he went around camp looking in everybody's eyes and saying, "Your nails are too long. They're hurting my eyes." This went on for a week. Finally, all the men clipped their nails, made a big pile, which they wrapped in leaves and gave to him. Yang used the nails to season his food—he put it in his soup, sprinkled it on his rice, and never said a word about it again. Now tell me—are you going to trust a man who eats other men's fingernails?

MA. Well, all I know is we won't go back to work until they meet all our demands. Listen, teach me some Gwan Gung steps.

LONE. I should have expected this. A boy who wants to have twenty wives is the type who demands more than he can handle.

MA. Just a few.

LONE. It takes years before an actor can play Gwan Gung.

MA. I can do it. I spend a lot of time watching the opera when it comes around. Every time I see Gwan Gung, I say, "Yeah. That's me. The god of fighters. The god of adventurers. We have the same kind of spirit."

LONE. I tell you, if you work very hard, when you return to China, you can perhaps be the Second Clown.

MA. Second Clown?

LONE. If you work hard.

MA. What's the Second Clown?

LONE. You can play the *p'ip'a*, and dance and jump all over.

MA. I'll buy them.

LONE. Excuse me?

MA. I'm going to be rich, remember? I'll buy a troupe and force them to let me play Gwan Gung.

LONE. I hope you have enough money, then, to pay audiences to sit through your show.

MA. You mean, I'm going to have to practice here every night—and in return, all I can play is the Second Clown?

LONE. If you work hard.

MA. Am I that bad? Maybe I shouldn't even try to do this. Maybe I should just go down.

LONE. It's not you. Everyone must earn the right to play Gwan Gung. I entered opera school when I was ten years old. My parents decided to sell me for ten years to this opera company. I lived with eighty other boys and we slept in bunks four beds high and hid our candy and rice cakes from each other. After eight years, I was studying to play Gwan Gung.

MA. Eight years?

LONE. I was one of the best in my class. One day, I was summoned by my master, who told me I was to go home for two days, because my mother had fallen very ill and was dying. When I arrived home, Mother was standing at the door waiting, not sick at all. Her first words to me, the son away for eight years, were, "You've been playing while your village has starved. You must go to the Gold Mountain and work."

MA. And you never returned to school?

LONE. I went from a room with eighty boys to a ship with three hundred men. So, you see, it does not come easily to play Gwan Gung?

MA. Did you want to play Gwan Gung?

LONE. What a foolish question!

MA. Well, you're better off this way.

LONE. What?

MA. Actors—they don't make much money. Here, you make a bundle, then go back and be an actor again. Best of both worlds.

LONE. "Best of both worlds."

MA. Yeah! (*Lone drops to the ground, begins imitating a duck, waddling and quacking.*)

MA. Lone? What are you doing? (*Lone quacks.*) You're a duck? (*Lone quacks.*) I can see that. (*Lone quacks.*) Is this an exercise? Am I supposed to do this? (*Lone quacks.*) This is dumb. I never seen Gwan Gung waddle. (*Lone quacks.*) Okay. All right. I'll do it. (*Ma and Lone quack and waddle*). You know, I never realized before how uncomfortable a duck's life is. And you have to listen to yourself quacking all day. Go crazy! (*Lone stands up straight.*) Now, what was that all about?

LONE. No, no. Stay down there, duck.

MA. What's the—

LONE. (*Prompting.*) Quack, quack, quack.

MA. I don't—

LONE. Act your species!

MA. I'm not a duck!

LONE. Nothing worse than a duck that doesn't know his place.

MA. All right. (*Mechanically.*) Quack, quack.

LONE. More.

MA. Quack.

LONE. More!

MA. Quack, quack, quack! (*Ma now continues quacking, as Lone gives commands.*)

LONE. Louder! It's your mating call! Think of your twenty duck wives! Good! Louder! Project! More! Don't slow down! Put your tail feathers into it! They can't hear you! (*Ma is now quacking up a storm. Lone exits, unnoticed by Ma*).

MA. Quack! Quack! Quack! Quack. Quack . . . quack. (*He looks around.*) Quack . . . quack . . . Lone? . . . Lone? (*He waddles around the stage looking.*) Lone, where are you? Where'd you go? (*He stops, scratches his left leg with his right foot.*) C'mon—stop playing around. What is this? (*Lone enters as a tiger, unseen by Ma.*) Look, let's call it a day, okay? I'm getting hungry. (*Ma turns around, notices Lone right before Lone is to bite him.*) Aaash! Quack, quack, quack! (*They face off, in character as animals. Duck-Ma is terrified.*)

LONE. Grrrr!

MA (*As a cry for help*). Quack, quack, quack! (*Lone pounces on Ma. They struggle, in character. Ma is quacking madly, eyes tightly closed. Lone stands up straight. Ma continues to quack.*)

LONE. Stand up.

MA (*Eyes still closed*). Quack, quack, quack!

LONE (*Louder*). Stand up!

MA (*Opening his eyes.*) Oh.

LONE. What are you?

MA. Huh?

LONE. A ChinaMan or a duck?

MA. Huh? Gimme a second to remember.

LONE. You like being a duck?

MA. My feet fell asleep.

LONE. You change forms so easily.

MA. You said to.

LONE. What else could you turn into?

MA. Well, you scared me—sneaking up like that.

LONE. Perhaps a rock. That would be useful. When the men need to rest, they can sit on you.

MA. I got carried away.

LONE. Let's try . . . a locust. Can you become a locust?

MA. No. Let's cut this, okay?

LONE. Here. It's easy. You just have to know how to hop.

MA. You're not gonna get me—

LONE. Like this. (*He demonstrates.*)

MA. Forget it, Lone.

LONE. I'm a locust. (*He begins jumping toward Ma.*)

MA. Hey! Get away!

LONE. I devour whole fields.

MA. Stop it.

LONE. I starve babies before they are born.

MA. Hey, look, stop it!

LONE. I cause famines and destroy villages.

MA. I'm warning you! Get away!

LONE. What are you going to do? You can't kill a locust.

MA. You're not a locust.

LONE. You kill one, and another sits on your hand.

MA. Stop following me.

LONE. Locusts always trouble people. If not, we'd feel useless. Now, if you became a locust, too . . .

MA. I'm not going to become a locust.

LONE. Just stick your teeth out!

MA. I"m not gonna be a bug! It's stupid!

LONE. No man who's just been a duck has the right to call anything stupid.

MA. I thought you were trying teach me something.

LONE. I am. Go ahead.

MA. All right. There. That look right?

LONE. Your legs should be a little lower. Lower! There. That's adequate. So, how does it feel to be a locust? (*Lone gets up.*)

MA. I dunno. How long do I have to do this?

LONE. Could you do it for three years?

MA. Three years? Don't be—

LONE. You couldn't, could you? Could you be a duck for that long?

MA. Look, I wasn't born to be either of those.

LONE. Exactly. Well, I wasn't born to work on a railroad, either. "Best of both worlds." How can you be such an insect! (*Pause.*)

MA. Lone . . .

LONE. Stay down there! Don't move! I've never told anyone my story—the story of my parents' kidnapping me from school. All the time we were crossing the ocean, the last two years here—I've kept my mouth shut. To you, I finally tell it. And all you can say is, "Best of both worlds." You're a bug to me, a locust. You think you understand the dedication one must have to be in the opera? You think it's the same as working on a railroad.

MA. Lone, all I was saying is that you'll go back too, and—

LONE. You're no longer a student of mine.

MA. What?

LONE. You have no dedication.

MA. Lone, I'm sorry.

LONE. Get up.

MA. I'm honored that you told me that.

LONE. Get up.

MA. No.

LONE. No?

MA. I don't want to. I want to talk.

LONE. Well, I've learned from the past. You're stubborn. You don't go. All right. Stay there. If you want to prove to me that you're dedicated, be a locust till morning. I'll go.

MA. Lone, I'm really honored that you told me.

LONE. I'll return in the morning. (*Exits.*)

MA. Lone? Lone, that's ridiculous. You think I'm gonna stay like this? If you do, you're crazy. Lone? Come back here.

SCENE 4

Night. Ma, alone, as a locust.

MA. Locusts travel in huge swarms, so large that when they cross the sky, they block out the sun, like a storm. Second Uncle—back home—when he was a young man, his whole crop got wiped out by locusts one year. In the famine that followed, Second Uncle lost his eldest son and his second wife—the one he married for love. Even to this day, we look around before saying the word "locust," to make sure Second Uncle is out of hearing range. About eight years ago, my brother and I discovered Second Uncle's cave in back of the stream near our house. We saw him come out of it one day around noon. Later, just before the sun went down, we sneaked in. We only looked once. Inside, there must have been hundreds—maybe five hundred or more—grasshoppers in huge bamboo cages—and around them—stacks of grasshopper legs, grasshoppers with one leg, still trying to hop but toppling like trees coughing, grasshoppers wrapped around sharp branches rolling from side to side, grasshopper legs cut off grasshopper bodies, then tied around grasshoppers and tightened till grasshoppers died. Every conceivable stage of life and death, subjects to every conceivable grasshopper torture. We ran out quickly, my brother and I—we knew an evil place by the thickness of the air. Now, I think of Second Uncle. How sad that the locusts forced him to take out his agony on innocent grasshoppers. What if Second Uncle could see me now? Would he cut off my legs? He might as well. I can barely feel them. But then again, Second Uncle never tortured actual locusts, just weak grasshoppers.

SCENE 5

Night. Ma still as a locust.

LONE (*Off, singing.*)
> Hit your hardest
> Pound out your tears
> The more you try
> The more you'll cry
> At how little I've moved
> And how large I loom
> By the time the sun goes down

MA. You look rested.
LONE. Me?
MA. Well, you sound rested.
LONE. No, not at all.
MA. Maybe I'm just comparing you to me.
LONE. I didn't every close my eyes all last night.
MA. Aw, Lone, you didn't have to stay up for me. You coulda just came up here and—
LONE. For you?
MA. —apologized and everything woulda been—
LONE. I didn't stay up for you.
MA. Huh? You didn't?
LONE. No.
MA. Oh. You sure?
LONE. Positive. I was thinking, that's all.
MA. About me?
LONE. Well . . .
MA. Even a little?
LONE. I was thinking about the ChinaMen—and you. Get up, Ma.
MA. Aw, do I have to? I've gotten to know these grasshoppers real well.
LONE. Get up. I have a lot to tell you.
MA. What'll they think? They take me in, even though I'm a little large, then they find out I'm a human being. I stepped on their kids. No trust. Gimme a hand, will you? (*Lone helps Ma up, but Ma's legs can't support him.*) Aw, shit. My legs are coming off. (*He lies down and tries to straighten them out.*)
LONE. I have many surprises. First, you will play Gwan Gung.
MA. My legs will be sent home without me. What'll my family think? Come to port to meet me and all they get is two legs.

LONE. Did you hear me?
MA. Hold on. I can't be in agony and listen to Chinese at the same time.
LONE. Did you hear my first surprise?
MA. No. I'm too busy screaming.
LONE. I said, you'll play Gwan Gung.
MA. Gwan Gung?
LONE. Yes.
MA. Me?
LONE. Yes.
MA. Without legs?
LONE. What?
MA. That might be good.
LONE. Stop that!
MA. I'll become a legend. Like the blind man who defended Amoy.
LONE. Did you hear?
MA. "The legless man who played Gwan Gung."
LONE. Isn't this what you want? To play Gwan Gung?
MA. No, I just wanna sleep.
LONE. No, you don't. Look. Here. I brought you something.
MA. Food?
LONE. Here. Some rice.
MA. Thanks, Lone. And duck?
LONE. Just a little.
MA. Where'd you get the duck?
LONE. Just bones and skin.
MA. We don't have duck. And the white devils have been blockading the food.
LONE. Sing—he had some left over.
MA. Sing? That thief?
LONE. And something to go with it.
MA. What? Lone, where did you find the whiskey?
LONE. You know, Sing—he has almost anything.
MA. Yeah. For a price.
LONE. Once, even some thousand-day-old eggs.
MA. He's a thief. That's what they told me.
LONE. Not if you're his friend.
MA. Sing don't have any real friends. Everyone talks about him bein' tied in to the head of the klan in San Francisco. Lone, you didn't have to do this. Here. Have some.
LONE. I had plenty.
MA. Don't gimme that. This cost you plenty, Lone.
LONE. Well, I thought if we were going to celebrate, we should do it as well as we would at home.
MA. Celebrate? What for? Wait.
LONE. Ma, the strike is over.
MA. Shit, I knew it. And we won, right?
LONE. Yes, the ChinaMen have won. They can do more than just talk.
MA. I told you. Didn't I tell you?
LONE. Yes. Yes, you did.
MA. Yang told me it was gonna be done. He said—
LONE. Yes, I remember.
MA. Didn't I tell you? Huh?
LONE. Ma, eat your duck.

MA. Nine days. In nine days, we civilized the white devils. I knew it. I knew we'd hold out till their ears started twitching. So that's where you got the duck, right? At the celebration?

LONE. No, there wasn't a celebration.

MA. Huh? You sure? ChinaMen—they look for any excuse to party.

LONE. But I thought *we* should celebrate.

MA. Well, that's for sure.

LONE. So you will play Gwan Gung.

MA. God, nine days. Shit, it's finally done. Well, we'll show them how to party. Make noise. Jump off rocks. Make the mountain shake.

LONE. We'll wash your body, to prepare you for the role.

MA. What role?

LONE. Gwan Gung. I've been telling you.

MA. I don't wanna play Gwan Gung.

LONE. You've shown the dedication required to become my student, so—

MA. Lone, you think I stayed up last night 'cause I wanted to play Gwan Gung?

LONE. You said you were like him.

MA. I am. Gwan Gung stayed up all night once to prove his loyalty. Well, now I have too. Lone, I'm honored that you told me your story.

LONE. Yes . . . That is like Gwan Gung.

MA. Good. So let's do an opera about *me.*

LONE. What?

MA. You wanna party or what?

LONE. About you?

MA. You said I was like Gwan Gung, didn't you?

LONE. Yes, but—

MA. Well, look at the operas he's got. I ain't even got one.

LONE. Still, you can't—

MA. You tell me, is that fair?

LONE. You can't do an opera about yourself.

MA. I just won a victory, didn't I. I deserve an opera in my honor.

LONE. But it's not traditional.

MA. Traditional? Lone, you gotta figure any way I could do Gwan Gung wasn't gonna be traditional anyway. I may be as good a guy as him, but he's a better dancer. (*Sings.*)

Old Gwan Gung, just sits about
Till the dime-store fighters have had it out
Then he pitches his peach pit
Combs his beard
Draws his sword
And they scatter in fear

LONE. What are you talking about?

MA. I just won a great victory. I get—whatcha call it?—poetic license. C'mon. Hit the gongs. I'll immortalize my story.

LONE. I refuse. This goes against all my training. I try and give you your wish and—

MA. Do it. Gimme my wish. Hit the gongs.

LONE. I never—I can't.

MA. Can't what? Don't think I'm worth an opera? No, I guess not. I forgot—you think I'm just one of those dead men. (*Silence. Lone pulls out a gong. Ma gets into position. Lone hits the gong. They do the following in a mock-Chinese-opera style.*) I am Me. Yesterday, I was kicked out of my house by my three elder brothers, calling me the lazy dreamer of the family. I am sitting here in front of the temple trying to decide how I will avenge this indignity. Here comes the poorest beggar in this village. (*He cues Lone.*) He is called Fleaman because his body is the most popular meeting place for fleas from around the province.

LONE (*Singing*).
Fleas in love,
Find your happiness
In the gray scraps of my suit

MA. Hello, Flea—

LONE (*Continuing,*).
Fleas in need,
Shield your families
In the gray hairs of my beard

MA. Hello, Flea— (*Lone cuts Ma off, continues an extended improvised aria.*) Hello, Fleaman.

LONE. Hello, Ma. Are you interested in providing a home for these fleas?

MA. No!

LONE. This couple here—seeking to start a new home. Housing today is so hard to find. How about your left arm?

MA. I may have plenty of my own fleas in time. I have been thrown out by my elder brothers.

LONE. Are you seeking revenge? A flea epidemic on your house? (*To a flea.*) Get back there. You should be asleep. Your mother will worry.

MA. Nothing would make my brothers angrier than seeing me rich.

LONE. Rich? After the bad crops of the last three years, even the fleas are thinking of moving north.

MA. I heard a white devil talk yesterday.

LONE. Oh—with hair the color of a sick chicken and eyes round as eggs? The fleas and I call him Chicken-Laying-an-Egg.

MA. He said we can make our fortunes on the Gold Mountain, where work is play and the sun scares off snow.

LONE. Don't listen to chicken-brains.

MA. Why not? He said gold grows like weeds.

LONE. I have heard that it is slavery.

MA. Slavery? What do you know, Fleaman? Who told you? The fleas? Yes, I will go to Gold Mountain. (*Gongs. Ma strikes a submissive pose to Lone.*)

LONE. "The one hundred twenty-five dollars passage money is to be paid to the said head of said Hong, who will make arrangements with the coolies, that their wages shall be deducted until the debt is absorbed." (*Ma bows to Lone. Gongs. They pick up fighting sticks and do a water-crossing dance. Dance ends. They stoop next to each other and rock.*)

MA. I have been in the bottom of this boat for thirty-six days now. Tang, how many have died?

LONE. Not me. I'll live through this ride.

MA. I didn't ask how you are.

LONE. But why's the Gold Mountain so far?

MA. We left with three hundred and three.

LONE. My family's depending on me.

MA. So tell me, how many have died?

LONE. I'll be the last one alive.

MA. That's not what I wanted to know.

LONE. I'll find some fresh air in this hole.

MA. I asked, how many have died.

LONE. Is that a crack in the side?

MA. Are you listening to me?

LONE. If I had some air—

MA. I asked, don't you see—?

LONE. The crack—over there—

MA. Will you answer me, please?

LONE. I need to get out.

MA. The rest here agree—

LONE. I can't stand the smell.

MA. That a hundred eighty—

LONE. I can't see the air—

MA. Of us will not see—

LONE. And I can't die.

MA. Our Gold Mountain dream. (*Lone/Tang dies; Ma throws his body overboard. The boat docks. Ma exits, walks through the streets. He picks up one of the fighting sticks, while Lone becomes the mountain.*) I have been given my pickax. Now I will attack the mountain. (*Ma does a dance of labor. Lone sings.*)

LONE.

> Hit your hardest
> Pound out your tears
> The more you try
> The more you'll cry
> At how little I've moved
> And how large I loom
> By the time the sun goes down

(*Dance stops.*)

MA. This mountain is clever. But why shouldn't it be? It's fighting for its life, like we fight for ours. (*The mountain picks up a stick. Ma and the mountain do a battle dance. Dance ends.*) This mountain not only defends itself—it also attacks. It turns our strength against us. (*Lone does Ma's labor dance, while Ma plants explosives in midair. Dance ends.*) This mountain has survived for millions of years. Its wisdom is immense. (*Lone and Ma begin a second battle dance. This one ends with them working the battle sticks together. Lone breaks away, does a warrior strut.*)

LONE. I am a white devil! Listen to my stupid language: "What che doo doo blah blah." Look at my wide eyes—like I have drunk seventy-two pots of tea. Look at my funny hair—twisting, turning, like a snake telling lies. (*To Ma.*) Bla bla doo doo tee tee.

MA. We don't understand English.

LONE (*Angry*). Bla bla doo doo tee tee!

MA (*With Chinese accent*). Please you-ah speak-ah Chinese?

LONE. Oh. Work—uh—one—two—more—work—two—

MA. Two hours more? Stupid demons. As confused as your hair. We will strike! (*Gongs. Ma is on strike.*)

MA (*In broken English*). Eight hours day good for white man, alla same food for ChinaMan.

LONE. The strike is over! We've won!

MA. I knew we would.

LONE. We forced the white devil to act civilized.

MA. Tamed the barbarians!

LONE. Did you think—

MA. Who woulda thought?

LONE. —it could be done?

MA. Who?

LONE. But who?

MA. Who could tame them?

MA. and LONE. Only a ChinaMan! (*They laugh.*)

LONE. Well, c'mon.

MA. Let's celebrate!

LONE. We have.

MA. Oh.

LONE. Back to work.

MA. But we've won the strike.

LONE. I know. Congratulations! And now—

MA. —back to work?

LONE. Right.

MA. No.

LONE. But the strike is over. (*Lone tosses Ma a stick. They resume their stick battle as before, but Ma is heard over Lone's singing.*)

LONE.	MA.
Hit your hardest	Wait.
Pound out your tears	I'm tired of this!
The more you try	How do we end it?
The more you'll cry	Let's stop now, all right?
At how little I've moved	Look, I said enough!
And how large I loom	
By the time the sun goes down	

(*Ma tosses his stick away, but Lone is already aiming a blow toward it, so that Lone hits Ma instead and knocks him down.*)

MA. Oh! Shit . . .

LONE. I'm sorry! Are you all right?

MA. Yeah. I guess.

LONE. Why'd you let go? You can't just do that.

MA. I'm bleeding.

LONE. That was stupid—where?

MA. Here.

LONE. No.

MA. Ow!

LONE. There will probably be a bump.

MA. I dunno.

LONE. What?

MA. I dunno why I let go.

LONE. It was stupid.

MA. But how were we going to end the opera?

LONE. Here. (*He applies whiskey to Ma's bruise*) I don't know.

MA. Why didn't we just end it with the celebration? Ow! Careful.

LONE. Sorry. But Ma, the celebration's not the end. We're returning to work. Today. At dawn.

MA. What?

LONE. We've already lost nine days of work. But we got eight hours.

MA. Today? That's terrible.

LONE. What do you think we're here for? But they listened to our demands. We're getting a raise.

MA. Fourteen dollars.

LONE. No. Eight.

MA. What?

LONE. We had to compromise. We got an eight-dollar raise.

MA. But we wanted fourteen. Why didn't we get fourteen?

LONE. It was the best deal they could get. Congratulations.

MA. Congratulations? Look, Lone, I'm sick of you making fun of the ChinaMen.

LONE. Ma, I'm not. For the first time. I was wrong. We got eight dollars.

MA. We wanted fourteen.

LONE. But we got eight hours.

MA. We'll go back on strike.

LONE. Why?

MA. We could hold out for months.

LONE. And lose all that work?

MA. But we gave in.

LONE. You're being ridiculous. We got eight hours. Besides, it's already been decided.

MA. I didn't decide. I wasn't there. You made me stay up here.

LONE. The heads of the gangs decide.

MA. And that's it?

LONE. It's done.

MA. Back to work? That's what they decided? Lone, I don't want to go back to work.

LONE. Who does.

MA. I forgot what it's like.

LONE. You'll pick up the technique again soon enough.

MA. I mean, what's it's like to have them telling you what to do all the time. Using up your strength.

LONE. I thought you said even after work, you still feel good.

MA. Some days. But others . . . (*Pause.*) I get so frustrated sometimes. At the rock. The rock doesn't give in. It's not human. I wanna claw it with my fingers, but that would just rip them up. I wanna throw myself head first onto it, but it'd just knock my skull open. The rock would knock my skull open, then just sit there, still like nothing had happened, like a faceless Buddha. (*Pause.*) Lone, when do I get out of here?

LONE. Well, the railroad may get finished—

MA. It'll never get finished.

LONE. —or you may get rich.

MA. Rich. Right. This is the Gold Mountain. (*Pause.*) Lone, has anyone gone home rich from here?

LONE. Yes. Some.

MA. But most?

LONE. Most . . . do go home.

MA. Do you still have the fear?

LONE. The fear?

MA. That you'll become like them—dead men?

LONE. Maybe I was wrong about them.

MA. Well, I do. You wanted me to say it before. I can say it now: "They are dead men." Their greatest accomplishment was to win a strike that's gotten us nothing.

LONE. They're sending money home.

MA. No.

LONE. It's not much, I know, but it's something.

MA. Lone, I'm not even doing that. If I don't get rich here, I might as well die here. Let my brothers laugh in peace.

LONE. Ma, you're too soft to get rich here, naive—you believed the snow was warm.

MA. I've got to change myself. Toughen up. Take no shit. Count my change. Learn to gamble. Learn to win. Learn to share. Learn to deny. Learn to look at me with opaque eyes.

LONE. You want to do that?

MA. I will. 'Cause I've got the fear. You've given it to me. (*Pause.*)

LONE. Will I see you here tonight?

MA. Tonight?

LONE. I just thought I'd ask.

MA. I'm sorry, Lone. I haven't got time to be the Second Clown.

LONE. I thought you might not.

MA. Sorry.

LONE. You could have been a . . . fair actor.

MA. You coming down? I gotta get ready for work. This is gonna be a terrible day. My legs are sore and my arms are outa practice.

LONE. You go first. I'm going to practice some before work. There's still time.

MA. Practice? But you said you lost your fear. And you said that's what brings you up here.

LONE. I guess I was wrong about that, too. Today I am dancing for no reason at all.

MA. Do whatever you want. See you down at camp.

LONE. Could you do me a favor?

MA. A favor?

LONE. Could you take this down so I don't have to take it all? (*Lone points to a pile of props.*)

MA. Well, okay. (*Pause.*) But this is the last time.

LONE. Of course, Ma. (*Ma exits.*) See you soon. The last time. I suppose so. (*Lone resumes practicing. He twirls his hair around as in the beginning of the play. The sun begins to rise. It continues rising until Lone is moving and seen only in shadow.*)

CURTAIN

TOPICS FOR CRITICAL THINKING AND WRITING

The Play on the PAGE

1. What do you make of the play's ending? Is Hwang reneging on his militant ethnic stance?

2. Contrast the characters of the play's protagonists.

The Play on the STAGE

3. Research the Chinese classical theater. Discuss the radically different ways its conventions differ from the conventions of realism.

4. Research the 1867 strike of the Chinese railroad workers.

5. How could you bring the information you've discovered to bear on a possible production of the play?

6. Is there only one plausible way to stage the play or can you think of alternatives?

The Play in PERFORMANCE

From the outset of his writing career, David Hwang has been aware that his Chinese cultural inheritance provides him not only with mythic material, but with aesthetic precedents. In *FOB*, the physical conjuring of Fa Mu Lan and Gwan Gung permits the play to move beyond the realistic style with which it begins. Hwang has in mind a classical model: Beijing opera—a form that combines musical, dance, narrative elements into an acrobatic, cacaphonous theatrical spectacle, the very antithesis of realism. The call for the customary onstage presence of musician/stage managers in staging the play (one invariably observed in production) affirms this traditional indebtedness. The conventions of Chinese opera permit the play's theme—the search for ethnic identity—to shift audaciously beyond realistic comic banter and confessional monologue. The play's climax is a group improvisation by the three young people in operatic style. As the stage directions state, "By this time, the lights have dimmed, throwing shadows on the stage. Grace will strike two pots together to indicate each speaker change and the ritual will gradually take on elements of Chinese opera."

In *The Dance and the Railroad*, Hwang's classical indebtedness continues: One of his two protagonists is an actor, or would-be actor, working to build the transcontinental railroad during the 1860s. Viewed as standoffish by his compatriots, he is obsessed with his craft; the play opens with him practicing opera steps. The character is called Lone, which is the real name of the actor who played him (similarly, Lone's protegé, Ma, is named after the real actor Tzi Ma). Classically trained in Beijing opera, John Lone, an important early collaborator with Hwang, choreographed the operatic elements in *FOB*, played Steve in the Public Theater production of the play, and directed as well as starred in *The Dance and the Railroad*. An actor of striking physical grace, his performances remain vivid to all who saw them. The thematic core of the play rests, then, on a metaphor of performance: Several scenes open with the apprenticed Ma huddled alone in traditional locus position. The end of the play, like absurdist plays, is cyclical: "Lone resumes practicing. He twirls his hair around as in the beginning of the play. The sun begins to rise. It continues rising until Lone is moving and seen only in shadow." The theater, like the Chinese men themselves, will endure.

We may observe here that in his best-known play, *M.Butterfly*, Hwang again attempted (most would say with considerable success) to achieve the spectacular visual/aural ambience of Chinese classical theater in all its quintessential theatricality: its stylization, symbolism, acrobatic and conventionalized movement, beautiful costumes, emblematic makeup, and percussive music. The total visual impact of the Broadway production drew power from a startling contrast between the bright gorgeous costumes of the actors and the bare stage on which a few pieces of furniture evoked a world from Paris to Beijing. Indeed, the conceit that is at the heart of the play—the historical fact that a French diplomat unknowingly married a female impersonator—rests on the willingness of the Chinese classical theater since the era of Sun Yat-sen to accept actresses in female roles previously played by men (which they still are not permitted to do in Japanese Noh and Kabuki). Which is why the play's protagonist (a China expert, after all) is not a complete dunderhead in believing his "wife" to be a woman.

ERIC PACE
An Interview with David Henry Hwang: "I Write Plays to Claim a Place for Asian-Americans"*

The Dance and the Railroad is about ethnic Chinese in this country, set in 1867, and its two characters are immigrants who have been laboring on the transcontinental railroad and who talk, do gymnastics and even improvise their own Chinese opera as they pass time during a strike. . . .

"I wanted to try writing a historical play," says David Hwang, "even though obviously the core of that experience, particularly being a working-class experience, is rather removed from my own. For some time I had wanted to write a play about the work of Chinese-Americans on the transcontinental railroad, and I wanted to center it around a particular historical incident, the strike of 1867. Most Americans are aware that Chinese-Americans worked there, but we tend to have this impression that they were really servile and weak—little coolies who were always being knocked down by big white men on horses.

"Granted there was a lot of knocking around, but the spirit of the Chinese-American railroad workers, as far as we can tell, was much different than this picture would suggest. These were strong and hardy and rebellious men who considered themselves warriors, adventurers or soldiers, and I think their resistance in this strike best typifies that attitude.

*Excerpts from an article by Eric Pace based on an interview with David Henry Hwang, *New York Times* 12 July 1981, Arts & Leisure section: 4.

"At the same time, though, it was important to me that this be a very personal play, that the Chinese-Americans not be presented as polemics but as people, and so I decided to focus on the relationship of two workers, and how they spend their time during the strike. And while the strike affects both of them, in the play it's a background, if omnipresent, event. I suppose it was to make that experience more accessible to me that I focused on the interpersonal aspects and also on the character named Lone, whose ambition is to be a dancer, but whose career has been cut short by the need to come to America to work. I could empathize easily with that type of frustration."

Much of the material in *The Dance and the Railroad*, he says, he has taken from the lives of the Chinese-American actors who play the parts, John Lone and Tzi Ma—which is why their own real names appear in the play. They were in the cast of the Public's production of *FOB*, and in the first production of *Dance*, and they will appear also in the Public Theater production. . . .

"One very important thing for me is to give Asian-American actors a chance to work and increase our visibility," the playwright added. "I know to some degree there's the feeling that Asian-Americans have made it economically in this country, but I think the acting profession is sort of a tell-tale sign that we aren't as fully accepted as we'd like to believe. Sometimes even the few roles that are written for Asian characters end up being played by Caucasians in yellow-face. I'd like to see Asian-Americans in plays which don't deal only with ethnic issues—because we don't spend all our time thinking about being Asian: if you cut us we bleed; obviously we're as human as anyone else."

AUGUST Wilson

August Wilson, the son of a black woman and a white man, was born in Pittsburgh in 1945. After dropping out of school at the age of fifteen, Wilson took various odd jobs, such as stock clerk and short-order cook, in his spare time, while educating himself in the public library, chiefly by reading works by such black writers as Richard Wright, Ralph Ellison, Langston Hughes, and Imamu Amiri Baraka (LeRoi Jones). In 1978 the director of a black theater in St. Paul, Minnesota, who had known Wilson in Pittsburgh, invited him to write a play for the theater. Six months later Wilson moved permanently to St. Paul.

The winner of the Pulitzer Prize for drama in 1987, Wilson's *Fences* was first presented as a staged reading in 1983 and was later performed in Chicago, Seattle, Rochester (New York), and New Haven (Connecticut) before reaching New York City in 1987. An earlier play, *Ma Rainey's Black Bottom,* was voted Best Play of the Year 1984–1985 by the New York Drama Critics' Circle. In 1981 when *Ma Rainey* was first read at the O'Neill Center in Waterford, Connecticut, Wilson met Lloyd Richards, a black director with whom he has continued to work closely.

■■■■■■■■■■■■■

COMMENTARY ON *FENCES*

In 1926 W.E.B. DuBois, a black leader, organized a black theater in Harlem and enunciated his vision of a new black drama:

> The plays of a real Negro theatre must be: 1. About us. That is, they must have plots that reveal Negro life as it is. 2. By us; they must be written by Negro authors who understand from birth and continued association just what it means to be a Negro today. 3. For us; that is, the Negro theatre must cater primarily to Negro audiences and be supported by their entertainment and approval. 4. Near us. The theatre must be in a neighborhood near the mass of Negro people.

However, when it came to putting ink on paper, not every black writer was quite sure how to proceed. In 1928, in an article titled "The Dilemma of the Negro Artist," James Weldon Johnson wrote:

> The moment a Negro writer picks up his pen and sits down to his typewriter he is immediately called upon to solve, consciously or unconsciously, this problem of the double audience. To whom shall he address himself, to his own black group or to white America?

Johnson in fact went on to assert that the black writer's audience "is always both white America and black America," but, as we shall see in a moment, in the 1960s—the period when "black" displaced "Negro"—not all black writers agreed.

The plays written by blacks from, say, 1920 to the early 1960s fit rather comfortably into the mainstream of American drama. Two plays by and about blacks, Langston Hughes's *Mulatto* (1935) and Lorraine Hansberry's *A Raisin in the Sun* (1959), enjoyed long runs on Broadway, which is to say that much of their support came from whites. These plays are not fundamentally different from, say, Philip Yordan's *Anna Lucasta,* which is by a white playwright and originally dealt with a working-class Polish family in Philadelphia but was altered for a black cast and then became a Broadway hit. With the growth of the Civil Rights movement in the 1960s, however, black theater changed decisively, helping to form the black power movement.

The most talented black dramatists, including Imamu Amiri Baraka (LeRoi Jones) and Ed Bullins, largely turned their backs on white audiences and, in effect, wrote plays aimed at showing blacks that *they*— not their white oppressors—must change, must cease to accept the myths that whites had created. Today, however, strongly revolutionary plays by and about blacks have difficulty getting a hearing. Instead, the newest black writers seem to be concerned less with raising the consciousness of blacks than with depicting black life and with letting both blacks and whites respond aesthetically rather than politically. Baraka has attributed the change to a desire by many blacks to become assimilated in today's society, and surely there is much to his view. One might also say, however, that black dramatists may for other reasons have come to assume that the business of drama is not to preach but to show, and that a profound, honest depiction—in a traditional, realistic dramatic form—of things as they are, or in Wilson's play, things as they were in the 1950s—will touch audiences whatever their color. "Part of the reason I wrote *Fences*," Wilson has said, "was to illuminate that generation, which shielded its children from all of the indignities they went through."

This is not to say, of course, that *Fences* is a play about people who just happen to be black. The Polish family of *Anna Lucasta* could easily be converted to a black family (though perhaps blacks may feel that there is something unconvincing about this family), but Troy Maxson's family cannot be whitewashed. The play is very much about persons who are what they are because they are blacks living in an unjust society run by whites. We are not allowed to forget this. Troy is a baseball player who was too old to join a white team when the major leagues began to hire blacks. For Troy's friend, Bono, "Troy just came along too early," to which Troy pungently replies, "There ought not never have been no time called too early." Blacks of Troy's day were expected to subscribe to American ideals—for instance, to serve in the army in time of war—but they were also expected to sit in the back of the bus and to accept the fact that they were barred from decent jobs. Wilson shows us the scars that such treatment left. Troy is no paragon. Although he has a deep sense of responsibility to his family, his behavior toward them is deeply flawed: he oppresses his son Cory; he is unfaithful to his wife, Rose; and he exploits his brother Gabriel.

Wilson, as we have seen, calls attention to racism in baseball, and he indicates that Troy turned to crime because he could not earn money. However, Wilson does not allow *Fences* to become a prolonged protest against white oppression—though one can never quite forget that Troy insists on a high personal ideal in a world that has cheated him. The interest in the play is in Troy as a human being, or, rather, in all of the characters as human beings rather than as representatives of white victimization. As Troy sees it, by preventing Cory from engaging in athletics (the career that frustrated Troy), he is helping rather than oppressing Cory: "I don't want him to be like me. I want him to move as far from me as he can." Wilson also makes it clear, however, that Troy has other (very human) motives, of which Troy perhaps is unaware.

FENCES
August Wilson

for Lloyd Richards,
who adds to whatever he touches
When the sins of our fathers visit us
We do not have to play host.
We can banish them with forgiveness
As God, in His Largeness and Laws.
  —*August Wilson*

LIST OF CHARACTERS

TROY MAXSON

JIM BONO, *Troy's friend*

ROSE, *Troy's wife*

LYONS, *Troy's oldest son by previous marriage*

GABRIEL, *Troy's brother*

CORY, *Troy and Rose's son*

RAYNELL, *Troy's daughter*

SETTING

The setting is the yard which fronts the only entrance to the Maxson household, an ancient two-story brick house set back off a small alley in a big-city neighborhood. The entrance to the house is gained by two or three steps leading to a wooden porch badly in need of paint.

A relatively recent addition to the house and running its full width, the porch lacks congruence. It is a sturdy porch with a flat roof. One or two chairs of dubious value sit at one end where the kitchen window opens onto the porch. An old-fashioned icebox stands silent guard at the opposite end.

The yard is a small dirt yard, partially fenced, except for the last scene, with a wooden saw horse, a pile of lumber, and other fence-building equipment set off to the side. Opposite is a tree from which hangs a ball made of rags. A baseball bat leans against the tree. Two oil drums serve as garbage receptacles and sit near the house at right to complete the setting.

THE PLAY

Near the turn of the century, the destitute of Europe sprang on the city with tenacious claws and an honest and solid dream. The city devoured them. They swelled its belly until it burst into a thousand furnaces and sewing machines, a thousand butcher shops and bakers' ovens, a thousand churches and hospitals and funeral parlors and money-lenders. The city grew. It nourished itself and offered each man a partnership limited only by his talent, his guile, and his willingness and capacity for hard work. For the immigrants of Europe, a dream dared and won true.

The descendants of African slaves were offered no such welcome or participation. They came from places called the Carolinas and the Virginias, Georgia, Alabama, Mississippi, and Tennessee. They came strong, eager, searching. The city rejected them and they fled and settled along the riverbanks and under bridges in shallow, ramshackle houses made of sticks and tarpaper. They collected rags and wood. They sold the use of their muscles and their bodies. They cleaned houses and washed clothes, they shined shoes, and in quiet desperation and vengeful pride, they stole, and lived in pursuit of their own dream. That they could breathe free, finally, and stand to meet life with the force of dignity and whatever eloquence the heart could call upon.

By 1957, the hard-won victories of the European immigrants had solidified the industrial might of America. War had been confronted and won with new energies that used loyalty and patriotism as its fuel. Life was rich, full, and flourishing. The Milwaukee Braves won the World Series, and the hot winds of change that would make the sixties a turbulent, racing, dangerous, and provocative decade had not yet begun to blow full.

ACT 1

SCENE 1

It is 1957. Troy and Bono enter the yard, engaged in conversation. Troy is fifty-three years old, a large man with thick, heavy hands; it is this largeness that he strives to fill out and make an accommodation with. Together with his blackness, his largeness informs his sensibilities and the choices he has made in his life.

Of the two men, Bono is obviously the follower. His commitment to their friendship of thirty-odd years is rooted in his admiration of Troy's honesty, capacity for hard work, and his strength, which Bono seeks to emulate.

It is Friday night, payday, and the one night of the week the two men engage in a ritual of talk and drink.

Troy is usually the most talkative and at times he can be crude and almost vulgar, though he is capable of rising to profound heights of expression. The men carry lunch buckets and wear or carry burlap aprons and are dressed in clothes suitable to their jobs as garbage collectors.

BONO. Troy, you ought to stop that lying!

TROY. I ain't lying! The nigger had a watermelon this big. (*He indicates with his hands.*) Talking about . . . "What watermelon, Mr. Rand?" I liked to fell out! "What watermelon, Mr. Rand?" . . . And it sitting there big as life.

BONO. What did Mr. Rand say?

TROY. Ain't said nothing. Figure if the nigger too dumb to know he carrying a watermelon, he wasn't gonna get much sense out of him. Trying to hide that great big old watermelon under his coat. Afraid to let the white man see him carry it home.

BONO. I'm like you . . . I ain't got no time for them kind of people.

TROY. Now what he look like getting mad cause he see the man from the union talking to Mr. Rand?

BONO. He come to me talking about . . . "Maxson gonna get us fired." I told him to get away from me with that. He walked away from me calling you a troublemaker. What Mr. Rand say?

TROY. Ain't said nothing. He told me to go down the Commissioner's office next Friday. They called me down there to see them.

BONO. Well, as long as you got your complaint filed, they can't fire you. That's what one of them white fellows tell me.

TROY. I ain't worried about them firing me. They gonna fire me cause I asked a question? That's all I did. I went to Mr. Rand and asked him, "Why? Why you got the white mens driving and the colored lifting?" Told him, "what's the matter, don't I count? You think only white fellows got sense enough to drive a truck. That ain't no paper job! Hell, anybody can drive a truck. How come you got all whites driving and the colored lifting?" He told me "take it to the union." Well, hell, that's what I done! Now they wanna come up with this pack of lies.

BONO. I told Brownie if the man come and ask him any questions . . . just tell the truth! It ain't nothing but something they done trumped up on you cause you filed a complaint on them.

TROY. Brownie don't understand nothing. All I want them to do is change the job description. Give everybody a chance to drive the truck. Brownie can't see that. He ain't got that much sense.

BONO. How you figure he be making out with that gal be up at Taylor's all the time . . . that Alberta gal?

TROY. Same as you and me. Getting just as much as we is. Which is to say nothing.

BONO. It is, huh? I figure you doing a little better than me . . . and I ain't saying what I'm doing.

TROY. Aw, nigger, look here . . . I know you. If you had got anywhere near that gal, twenty minutes later you be looking to tell somebody. And the first one you gonna tell . . . that you gonna want to brag to . . . is me.

BONO. I ain't saying that. I see where you be eyeing her.

TROY. I eye all the women. I don't miss nothing. Don't never let nobody tell you Troy Maxson don't eye the women.

BONO. You been doing more than eyeing her. You done bought her a drink or two.

TROY. Hell yeah, I bought her a drink! What that mean? I bought you one, too. What that mean cause I buy her a drink? I'm just being polite.

BONO. It's all right to buy her one drink. That's what you call being polite. But when you wanna be buying two or three . . . that's what you call eyeing her.

TROY. Look here, as long as you known me . . . you ever known me to chase after women?

BONO. Hell yeah! Long as I done known you. You forgetting I knew you when.

TROY. Naw, I'm talking about since I been married to Rose?

BONO. Oh, not since you been married to Rose. Now, that's the truth, there. I can say that.

TROY. All right then! Case closed.

BONO. I see you be walking up around Alberta's house. You supposed to be at Taylors' and you be walking up around there.

TROY. What you watching where I'm walking for? I ain't watching after you.

BONO. I seen you walking around there more than once.

TROY. Hell, you liable to see me walking anywhere! That don't mean nothing cause you see me walking around there.

BONO. Where she come from anyway? She just kinda showed up one day.

TROY. Tallahassee. You can look at her and tell she one of them Florida gals. They got some big healthy women down there. Grow them right up out the ground. Got a little bit of Indian in her. Most of them niggers down in Florida got some Indian in them.

BONO. I don't know about that Indian part. But she damn sure big and healthy. Woman wear some big stockings. Got them great big old legs and hips as wide as the Mississippi River.

TROY. Legs don't mean nothing. You don't do nothing but push them out of the way. But them hips cushion the ride!

BONO. Troy, you ain't got no sense.

TROY. It's the truth! Like you riding on Goodyears!

(*Rose enters from the house. She is ten years younger than Troy, her devotion to him stems from her recognition of the possibilities of her life without him: a succession of abusive men and their babies, a life of partying and running the streets, the Church, or aloneness with its attendant pain and frustration. She recognizes Troy's spirit as a fine and illuminating one and she either ignores or forgives his faults, only some of which she recognizes. Though she doesn't drink, her presence is an integral part of the Friday night rituals. She alternates between the porch and the kitchen, where supper preparations are under way.*)

ROSE. What you all out here getting into?

TROY. What you worried about what we getting into for? This is men talk, woman.

ROSE. What I care what you all talking about? Bono, you gonna stay for supper?

BONO. No, I thank you, Rose. But Lucille say she cooking up a pot of pigfeet.

TROY. Pigfeet! Hell, I'm going home with you! Might even stay the night if you got some pigfeet. You got something in there to top them pigfeet, Rose?

ROSE. I'm cooking up some chicken. I got some chicken and collard greens.

TROY. Well, go on back in the house and let me and Bono finish what we was talking about. This is men talk. I got some talk for you later. You know what kind of talk I mean. You go on and powder it up.

ROSE. Troy Maxson, don't you start that now!

TROY (*puts his arm around her*). Aw, woman . . . come here. Look here, Bono . . . when I met this woman . . . I got out that place, say, "Hitch up my pony, saddle up my mare . . . there's a woman out there for me somewhere. I looked here. Looked there. Saw Rose and latched on to her." I latched on to her and told her—I'm gonna tell you the truth—I told her, "Baby, I don't wanna marry, I just wanna be your man." Rose told me . . . tell him what you told me, Rose.

ROSE. I told him if he wasn't the marrying kind, then move out the way so the marrying kind could find me.

TROY. That's what she told me. "Nigger, you in my way. You blocking the view! Move out the way so I can find me a husband." I thought it over two or three days. Come back—

ROSE. Ain't no two or three days nothing. You was back the same night.

TROY. Come back, told her . . . "Okay, baby . . . but I'm gonna buy me a banty rooster and put him out there in the backyard . . . and when he see a stranger come, he'll flap his wings and crow. . . . " Look here, Bono, I could watch the front door by myself . . . it was that back door I was worried about.

ROSE. Troy, you ought not talk like that. Troy ain't doing nothing but telling a lie.

TROY. Only thing is . . . when we first got married . . . forget the rooster . . . we ain't had no yard!

BONO. I hear you tell it. Me and Lucille was staying down there on Logan Street. Had two rooms with the outhouse in the back. I ain't mind the outhouse none. But when that goddamn wind blow through there in the winter . . . that's what I'm talking about! To this day I wonder why in the hell I ever stayed down there for six long years. But see, I didn't know I could do no better. I thought only white folks had inside toilets and things.

ROSE. There's a lot of people don't know they can do no better than they doing now. That's just something you got to learn. A lot of folks still shop at Bella's.

TROY. Ain't nothing wrong with shopping at Bella's. She got fresh food.

ROSE. I ain't said nothing about if she got fresh food. I'm talking about what she charge. She charge ten cents more than the A&P.

TROY. The A&P ain't never done nothing for me. I spends my money where I'm treated right. I go down to Bella, say, "I need a loaf of bread, I'll pay you Friday." She give it to me. What sense that make when I got money to go and spend it somewhere else and ignore the person who done right by me? That ain't in the Bible.

ROSE. We ain't talking about what's in the Bible. What sense it make to shop there when she overcharge?

TROY. You shop where you want to. I'll do my shopping where the people been good to me.

ROSE. Well, I don't think it's right for her to overcharge. That's all I was saying.

BONO. Look here . . . I got to get on. Lucille going be raising all kind of hell.

TROY. Where you going, nigger? We ain't finished this pint. Come here, finish this pint.

BONO. Well, hell, I am . . . if you ever turn the bottle loose.

TROY (*hands him the bottle*). The only thing I say about the A&P is I'm glad Cory got that job down there. Help him take care of his school clothes and things. Gabe done moved out and things getting tight around here. He got that job. . . . He can start to look out for himself.

ROSE. Cory done went and got recruited by a college football team.

TROY. I told that boy about that football stuff. The white man ain't gonna let him get nowhere with that football. I told him when he first come to me with it. Now you come telling me he done went and got more tied up in it. He ought to go and get recruited in how to fix cars or something where he can make a living.

ROSE. He ain't talking about making no living playing football. It's just something the boys in school do. They gonna send a recruiter by to talk to you. He'll tell you he ain't talking about making no living playing football. It's a honor to be recruited.

TROY. It ain't gonna get him nowhere. Bono'll tell you that.

BONO. If he be like you in the sports . . . he's gonna be all right. Ain't but two men ever played baseball as good as you. That's Babe Ruth and Josh Gibson.[1] Them's the only two men ever hit more home runs than you.

TROY. What it ever get me? Ain't got a pot to piss in or a window to throw it out of.

---

[1] African-American ballplayer (1911–47), known as the Babe Ruth of the Negro leagues.

ROSE. Times have changed since you was playing baseball, Troy. That was before the war. Times have changed a lot since then.

TROY. How in hell they done changed?

ROSE. They got lots of colored boys playing ball now. Baseball and football.

BONO. You right about that, Rose. Times have changed, Troy. You just come along too early.

TROY. There ought not never have been no time called too early! Now you take that fellow . . . what's that fellow they had playing right field for the Yankees back then? You know who I'm talking about, Bono. Used to play right field for the Yankees.

ROSE. Selkirk?

TROY. Selkirk! That's it! Man batting .269, understand? .269. What kind of sense that make? I was hitting .432 with thirty-seven home runs! Man batting .269 and playing right field for the Yankees! I saw Josh Gibson's daughter yesterday. She walking around with raggedy shoes on her feet. Now I bet you Selkirk's daughter ain't walking around with raggedy shoes on the feet! I bet you that!

ROSE. They got a lot of colored baseball players now. Jackie Robinson[2] was the first. Folks had to wait for Jackie Robinson.

TROY. I done seen a hundred niggers play baseball better than Jackie Robinson. Hell, I know some teams Jackie Robinson couldn't even make! What you talking about Jackie Robinson. Jackie Robinson wasn't nobody. I'm talking about if you could play ball then they ought to have let you play. Don't care what color you were. Come telling me I come along too early. If you could play . . . then they ought to have let you play.

(*Troy takes a long drink from the bottle.*)

ROSE. You gonna drink yourself to death. You don't need to be drinking like that.

TROY. Death ain't nothing. I done seen him. Done wrassled with him. You can't tell me nothing about death. Death ain't nothing but a fastball on the outside corner. And you know what I'll do to that! Lookee here, Bono . . . am I lying? You get one of them fastballs, about waist high, over the outside corner of the plate where you can get the meat of the bat on it . . . and good god! You can kiss it goodbye. Now, am I lying?

BONO. Naw, you telling the truth there. I seen you do it.

TROY. If I'm lying . . . that 450 feet worth of lying! (*Pause.*) That's all death is to me. A fastball on the outside corner.

ROSE. I don't know why you want to get on talking about death.

TROY. Ain't nothing wrong with talking about death. That's part of life. Everybody gonna die. You gonna die, I'm gonna die. Bono's gonna die. Hell, we all gonna die.

[2] In 1947 Robinson (1919–72) became the first African-American to play baseball in the major leagues.

ROSE. But you ain't got to talk about it. I don't like to talk about it.

TROY. You the one brought it up. Me and Bono was talking about baseball . . . you tell me I'm gonna drink myself to death. Ain't that right, Bono? You know I don't drink this but one night out of the week. That's Friday night. I'm gonna drink just enough to where I can handle it. Then I cuts it loose. I leave it alone. So don't you worry about me drinking myself to death. 'Cause I ain't worried about Death. I done seen him. I done wrestled with him.

Look here, Bono . . . I looked up one day and Death was marching straight at me. Like Soldiers on Parade! The Army of Death was marching straight at me. The middle of July, 1941. It got real cold just like it be winter. It seem like Death himself reached out and touched me on the shoulder. He touch me just like I touch you. I got cold as ice and Death standing there grinning at me.

ROSE. Troy, why don't you hush that talk.

TROY. I say . . . what you want, Mr. Death? You be wanting me? You done brought your army to be getting me? I looked him dead in the eye. I wasn't fearing nothing. I was ready to tangle. Just like I'm ready to tangle now. The Bible say be ever vigilant. That's why I don't get but so drunk. I got to keep watch.

ROSE. Troy was right down there in Mercy Hospital. You remember he had pneumonia? Laying there with a fever talking plumb out of his head.

TROY. Death standing there staring at me . . . carrying that sickle in his hand. Finally he say, "You want bound over for another year?" See, just like that . . . "You want bound over for another year?" I told him, "Bound over hell! Let's settle this now!"

It seem like he kinda fell back when I said that, and all the cold went out of me. I reached down and grabbed that sickle and threw it just as far as I could throw it . . . and me and him commenced to wrestling.

We wrestled for three days and three nights. I can't say where I found the strength from. Everytime it seemed like he was gonna get the best of me, I'd reach way down deep inside myself and find the strength to do him one better.

ROSE. Everytime Troy tell that story he find different ways to tell it. Different things to make up about it.

TROY. I ain't making up nothing. I'm telling you the facts of what happened. I wrestled with Death for three days and three nights and I'm standing here to tell you about it. (*Pause.*) All right. At the end of the third night we done weakened each other to where we can't hardly move. Death stood up, throwed on his robe . . . had him a white robe with a hood on it. He throwed on that robe and went off to look for his sickle. Say, "I'll be back." Just like that. "I'll be back." I told him, say, "Yeah, but . . . you gonna have to find me!" I wasn't no fool. I wasn't going looking for him. Death ain't nothing to play with. And I know he's gonna get me. I know I got to join his army . . . his camp followers. But as long as I keep my strength and see him coming . . . as long as I keep up my vigilance . . . he's gonna have to fight to get me. I ain't going easy.

BONO. Well, look here, since you got to keep up your vigilance . . . let me have the bottle.

TROY. Aw hell, I shouldn't have told you that part. I should have left out that part.

ROSE. Troy be talking that stuff and half the time don't even know what he be talking about.

TROY. Bono know me better than that.

BONO. That's right. I know you. I know you got some Uncle Remus[3] in your blood. You got more stories than the devil got sinners.

TROY. Aw hell, I done seen him too! Done talked with the devil.

ROSE. Troy, don't nobody wanna be hearing all that stuff.

(*Lyons enters the yard from the street. Thirty-four years old, Troy's son by a previous marriage, he sports a neatly trimmed goatee, sport coat, white shirt, tieless and buttoned at the collar. Though he fancies himself a musician, he is more caught up in the rituals and "idea" of being a musician than in the actual practice of the music. He has come to borrow money from Troy, and while he knows he will be successful, he is uncertain as to what extent his lifestyle will be held up to scrutiny and ridicule.*)

LYONS. Hey, Pop.

TROY. What you come "Hey, Popping" me for?

LYONS. How you doing, Rose? (*He kisses her.*) Mr. Bono. How you doing?

BONO. Hey, Lyons . . . how you been?

TROY. He must have been doing all right. I ain't seen him around here last week.

ROSE. Troy, leave your boy alone. He come by to see you and you wanna start all that nonsense.

TROY. I ain't bothering Lyons. (*Offers him the bottle.*) Here . . . get you a drink. We got an understanding. I know why he come by to see me and he know I know.

LYONS. Come on, Pop . . . I just stopped by to say hi . . . see how you was doing.

TROY. You ain't stopped by yesterday.

ROSE. You gonna stay for supper, Lyons? I got some chicken cooking in the oven.

LYONS. No, Rose . . . thanks. I was just in the neighborhood and thought I'd stop by for a minute.

TROY. You was in the neighborhood all right, nigger. You telling the truth there. You was in the neighborhood cause it's my payday.

LYONS. Well, hell, since you mentioned it . . . let me have ten dollars.

TROY. I'll be damned! I'll die and go to hell and play blackjack with the devil before I give you ten dollars.

[3]Narrator of traditional black tales in a book by Joel Chandler Harris.

BONO. That's what I wanna know about . . . that devil you done seen.

LYONS. What . . . Pop done seen the devil? You too much, Pops.

TROY. Yeah, I done seen him. Talked to him too!

ROSE. You ain't seen no devil. I done told you that man ain't had nothing to do with the devil. Anything you can't understand, you want to call it the devil.

TROY. Look here, Bono . . . I went down to see Hertzberger about some furniture. Got three rooms for two-ninety-eight. That what it say on the radio. "Three rooms . . . two-ninety-eight." Even made up a little song about it. Go down there . . . man tell me I can't get no credit. I'm working every day and can't get no credit. What to do? I got an empty house with some raggedy furniture in it. Cory ain't got no bed. He's sleeping on a pile of rags on the floor. Working every day and can't get no credit. Come back here—Rose'll tell you—madder than hell. Sit down . . . try to figure what I'm gonna do. Come a knock on the door. Ain't been living here but three days. Who know I'm here? Open the door . . . devil standing there bigger than life. White fellow . . . white fellow . . . got on good clothes and everything. Standing there with a clipboard in his hand. I ain't had to say nothing. First words come out of his mouth was . . . "I understand you need some furniture and can't get no credit." I liked to fell over. He say, "I'll give you all the credit you want, but you got to pay the interest on it." I told him, "Give me three rooms worth and charge whatever you want." Next day a truck pulled up here and two men unloaded them three rooms. Man what drove the truck give me a book. Say send ten dollars, first of every month to the address in the book and every thing will be all right. Say if I miss a payment the devil was coming back and it'll be hell to pay. That was fifteen years ago. To this day . . . the first of the month I send my ten dollars, Rose'll tell you.

ROSE. Troy lying.

TROY. I ain't never seen that man since. Now you tell me who else that could have been but the devil? I ain't sold my soul or nothing like that, you understand. Naw, I wouldn't have truck with the devil about nothing like that. I got my furniture and pays my ten dollars the first of the month just like clockwork.

BONO. How long you say you been paying this ten dollars a month?

TROY. Fifteen years!

BONO. Hell, ain't you finished paying for it yet? How much the man done charged you?

TROY. Ah hell, I done paid for it. I done paid for it ten times over! The fact is I'm scared to stop paying it.

ROSE. Troy lying. We got that furniture from Mr. Glickman. He ain't paying no ten dollars a month to nobody.

TROY. Aw hell, woman. Bono know I ain't that big a fool.

LYONS. I was just getting ready to say . . . I know where there's a bridge for sale.

TROY. Look here, I'll tell you this . . . it don't matter to me if he was the devil. It don't matter if the devil give credit. Somebody has got to give it.

ROSE. It ought to matter. You going around talking about having truck with the devil . . . God's the one you gonna have to answer to. He's the one gonna be at the Judgment.

LYONS. Yeah, well, look here, Pop . . . Let me have that ten dollars. I'll give it back to you. Bonnie got a job working at the hospital.

TROY. What I tell you, Bono? The only time I see this nigger is when he wants something. That's the only time I see him.

LYONS. Come on, Pop, Mr. Bono don't want to hear all that. Let me have the ten dollars. I told you Bonnie working.

TROY. What that mean to me? "Bonnie working." I don't care if she working. Go ask her for the ten dollars if she working. Talking about "Bonnie working." Why ain't you working?

LYONS. Aw, Pop, you know I can't find no decent job. Where am I gonna get a job at? You know I can't get no job.

TROY. I told you I know some people down there. I can get you on the rubbish if you want to work. I told you that the last time you came by here asking me for something.

LYONS. Naw, Pop . . . thanks. That ain't for me. I don't wanna be carrying nobody's rubbish. I don't wanna be punching nobody's time clock.

TROY. What's the matter, you too good to carry people's rubbish? Where you think that ten dollars you talking about come from? I'm just supposed to haul people's rubbish and give my money to you cause you too lazy to work. You too lazy to work and wanna know why you ain't got what I got.

ROSE. What hospital Bonnie working at? Mercy?

LYONS. She's down at Passavant working in the laundry.

TROY. I ain't got nothing as it is. I give you that ten dollars and I got to eat beans the rest of the week. Naw . . . you ain't getting no ten dollars here.

LYONS. You ain't got to be eating no beans. I don't know why you wanna say that.

TROY. I ain't got no extra money. Gabe done moved over to Miss Pearl's paying her the rent and things done got tight around here. I can't afford to be giving you every payday.

LYONS. I ain't asked you to give me nothing. I asked you to loan me ten dollars. I know you got ten dollars.

TROY. Yeah, I got it. You know why I got it? Cause I don't throw my money away out there in the streets. You living the fast life . . . wanna be a musician . . . running around in them clubs and things . . . then, you learn to take care of yourself. You ain't gonna find me going and asking nobody for nothing. I done spent too many years without.

LYONS. You and me is two different people, Pop.

TROY. I done learned my mistake and learned to do what's right by it. You still trying to get something for nothing. Life don't owe you nothing. You owe it to yourself. Ask Bono. He'll tell you I'm right.

LYONS. You got your way of dealing with the world . . . I got mine. The only thing that matters to me is the music.

TROY. Yeah, I can see that! It don't matter how you gonna eat . . . where your next dollar is coming from. You telling the truth there.

LYONS. I know I got to eat. But I got to live too. I need something that gonna help me to get out of the bed in the morning. Make me feel like I belong in the world. I don't bother nobody. I just stay with the music cause that's the only way I can find to live in the world. Otherwise there ain't no telling what I might do. Now I don't come criticizing you and how you live. I just come by to ask you for ten dollars. I don't wanna hear all that about how I live.

TROY. Boy, your mamma did a hell of a job raising you.

LYONS. You can't change me, Pop. I'm thirty-four years old. If you wanted to change me, you should have been there when I was growing up. I come by to see you . . . ask for ten dollars and you want to talk about how I was raised. You don't know nothing about how I was raised.

ROSE. Let the boy have ten dollars, Troy.

TROY (to Lyons). What the hell you looking at me for? I ain't got no ten dollars. You know what I do with my money. (To Rose.) Give him ten dollars if you want him to have it.

ROSE. I will. Just as soon as you turn it loose.

TROY (handing Rose the money). There it is. Seventy-six dollars and forty-two cents. You see this, Bono? Now, I ain't gonna get but six of that back.

ROSE. You ought to stop telling that lie. Here, Lyons. (She hands him the money.)

LYONS. Thanks, Rose. Look . . . I got to run . . . I'll see you later.

TROY. Wait a minute. You gonna say, "thanks, Rose" and ain't gonna look to see where she got that ten dollars from? See how they do me, Bono?

LYONS. I know she got it from you, Pop. Thanks. I'll give it back to you.

TROY. There he go telling another lie. Time I see that ten dollars . . . he'll be owing me thirty more.

LYONS. See you, Mr. Bono.

BONO. Take care, Lyons!

LYONS. Thanks, Pop. I'll see you again.

(Lyons exits the yard.)

TROY. I don't know why he don't go and get him a decent job and take care of that woman he got.

BONO. He'll be all right, Troy. The boy is still young.

TROY. The *boy* is thirty-four years old.

ROSE. Let's not get off into all that.

BONO. Look here . . . I got to be going. I got to be getting on. Lucille gonna be waiting.

TROY (puts his arm around Rose). See this woman, Bono? I love this woman. I love this woman so much it hurts. I love her so much . . . I done run out of ways of loving her. So I got to go back to basics. Don't you come by my

house Monday morning talking about time to go to work
. . . 'cause I'm still gonna be stroking!

ROSE. Troy! Stop it now!

BONO. I ain't paying him no mind, Rose. That ain't nothing
but gin-talk. Go on, Troy. I'll see you Monday.

TROY. Don't you come by my house, nigger! I done told you
what I'm gonna be doing.

(*The lights go down to black.*)

SCENE 2

(*The lights come up on Rose hanging up clothes. She hums
and sings softly to herself. It is the following morning.*)

ROSE (*sings*).

> Jesus, be a fence all around me every day
> Jesus, I want you to protect me as I travel on my way.
> Jesus, be a fence all around me every day.

(*Troy enters from the house.*)

> Jesus, I want you to protect me
> As I travel on my way.
> (*To Troy.*) 'Morning. You ready for breakfast? I can fix
> it soon as I finish hanging up these clothes?

TROY. I got the coffee on. That'll be all right. I'll just drink
some of that this morning.

ROSE. That 651 hit yesterday. That's the second time this
month. Miss Pearl hit for a dollar . . . seem like those that
need the least always get lucky. Poor folks can't get nothing.

TROY. Them numbers don't know nobody. I don't know why
you fool with them. You and Lyons both.

ROSE. It's something to do.

TROY. You ain't doing nothing but throwing your money
away.

ROSE. Troy, you know I don't play foolishly. I just play a
nickel here and a nickel there.

TROY. That's two nickels you done thrown away.

ROSE. Now I hit sometimes . . . that makes up for it. It always
comes in handy when I do hit. I don't hear you complaining then.

TROY. I ain't complaining now. I just say it's foolish. Trying
to guess out of six hundred ways which way the number
gonna come. If I had all the money niggers, these Negroes, throw away on numbers for one week—just one
week—I'd be a rich man.

ROSE. Well, you wishing and calling it foolish ain't gonna
stop folks from playing numbers. That's one thing for
sure. Besides . . . some good things come from playing
numbers. Look where Pope done bought him that restaurant off of numbers.

TROY. I can't stand niggers like that. Man ain't had two
dimes to rub together. He walking around with his shoes
all run over bumming money for cigarettes. All right.
Got lucky there and hit the numbers . . .

ROSE. Troy, I know all about it.

TROY. Had good sense, I'll say that for him. He ain't throwed
his money away. I seen niggers hit the numbers and go
through two thousand dollars in four days. Man bought
him that restaurant down there . . . fixed it up real nice . . .
and then didn't want nobody to come in it! A Negro go
in there and can't get no kind of service. I seen a white
fellow come in there and order a bowl of stew. Pope
picked all the meat out of the pot for him. Man ain't had
nothing but a bowl of meat! Negro come behind him and
ain't got nothing but the potatoes and carrots. Talking
about what numbers do for people, you picked a wrong
example. Ain't done nothing but make a worser fool out
of him than he was before.

ROSE. Troy, you ought to stop worrying about what happened
at work yesterday.

TROY. I ain't worried. Just told me to be down there at the
Commissioner's office on Friday. Everybody think they
gonna fire me. I ain't worried about them firing me. You
ain't got to worry about that. (*Pause.*) Where's Cory?
Cory in the house? (*Calls.*) Cory?

ROSE. He gone out.

TROY. Out, huh? He gone out 'cause he know I want him to
help me with this fence. I know how he is. That boy
scared of work.

(*Gabriel enters. He comes halfway down the alley and,
hearing Troy's voice, stops.*)

TROY (*continues*). He ain't done a lick of work in his life.

ROSE. He had to go to football practice. Coach wanted them
to get in a little extra practice before the season start.

TROY. I got his practice . . . running out of here before he get
his chores done.

ROSE. Troy, what is wrong with you this morning? Don't
nothing set right with you. Go on back in there and go to
bed . . . get up on the other side.

TROY. Why something got to be wrong with me? I ain't said
nothing wrong with me.

ROSE. You got something to say about everything. First it's
the numbers . . . then it's the way the man runs his
restaurant . . . then you done got on Cory. What's it
gonna be next? Take a look up there and see if the
weather suits you . . . or is it gonna be how you gonna put
up the fence with the clothes hanging in the yard.

TROY. You hit the nail on the head then.

ROSE. I know you like I know the back of my hand. Go on in
there and get you some coffee . . . see if that straighten
you up. 'Cause you ain't right this morning.

(*Troy starts into the house and sees Gabriel. Gabriel starts
singing. Troy's brother, he is seven years younger than
Troy. Injured in World War II, he has a metal plate in his
head. He carries an old trumpet tied around his waist and
believes with every fiber of his being that he is the
Archangel Gabriel. He carries a chipped basket with an*

assortment of discarded fruits and vegetables he has picked up in the strip district and which he attempts to sell.)

GABRIEL (*singing*).
>   Yes, ma'am I got plums
>   You ask me how I sell them
>   Oh ten cents apiece
>   Three for a quarter
>   Come and buy now
>   'Cause I'm here today
>   And tomorrow I'll be gone

(*Gabriel enters.*)
Hey, Rose!

ROSE. How you doing Gabe?

GABRIEL. There's Troy . . . Hey, Troy!

TROY. Hey, Gabe.

(*Exit into kitchen.*)

ROSE (*to Gabriel*). What you got there?

GABRIEL. You know what I got, Rose. I got fruits and vegetables.

ROSE (*looking in basket*). Where's all these plums you talking about?

GABRIEL. I ain't got no plums today, Rose. I was just singing that. Have some tomorrow. Put me in a big order for plums. Have enough plums tomorrow for St. Peter and everybody.

(*Troy reenters from kitchen, crosses to steps.*)

(*To Rose.*) Troy's mad at me.

TROY. I ain't mad at you. What I got to be mad at you about? You ain't done nothing to me.

GABRIEL. I just moved over to Miss Pearl's to keep out from in your way. I ain't mean no harm by it.

TROY. Who said anything about that? I ain't said anything about that.

GABRIEL. You ain't mad at me, is you?

TROY. Naw . . . I ain't mad at you, Gabe. If I was mad at you I'd tell you about it.

GABRIEL. Got me two rooms. In the basement. Got my own door too. Wanna see my key? (*He holds up a key.*) That's my own key! My two rooms!

TROY. Well, that's good, Gabe. You got your own key . . . that's good.

ROSE. You hungry, Gabe? I was just fixing to cook Troy his breakfast.

GABRIEL. I'll take some biscuits. You got some biscuits? Did you know when I was in heaven . . . every morning me and St. Peter would sit down by the gate and eat some big fat biscuits? Oh, yeah! We had us a good time. We'd sit there and eat us them biscuits and then St. Peter would go off to sleep and tell me to wake him up when it's time to open the gates for the judgment.

ROSE. Well, come on . . . I'll make up a batch of biscuits.

(*Rose exits into the house.*)

GABRIEL. Troy . . . St. Peter got your name in the book. I seen it. It say . . . Troy Maxson. I say . . . I know him! He got the same name like what I got. That's my brother!

TROY. How many times you gonna tell me that, Gabe?

GABRIEL. Ain't got my name in the book. Don't have to have my name. I done died and went to heaven. He got your name though. One morning St. Peter was looking at his book . . . marking it up for the judgment . . . and he let me see your name. Got it in there under M. Got Rose's name . . . I ain't seen it like I seen yours . . . but I know it's in there. He got a great big book. Got everybody's name what was ever been born. That's what he told me. But I seen your name. Seen it with my own eyes.

TROY. Go on in the house there. Rose going to fix you something to eat.

GABRIEL. Oh, I ain't hungry. I done had breakfast with Aunt Jemimah. She come by and cooked me up a whole mess of flapjacks. Remember how we used to eat them flapjacks?

TROY. Go on in the house and get you something to eat now.

GABRIEL. I got to sell my plums. I done sold some tomatoes. Got me two quarters. Wanna see? (*He shows Troy his quarters.*) I'm gonna save them and buy me a new horn so St. Peter can hear me when it's time to open the gates. (*Gabriel stops suddenly. Listens.*) Hear that? That's the hellhounds. I got to chase them out of here. Go on get out of here! Get out!

(*Gabriel exits singing.*)

>   Better get ready for the judgment
>   Better get ready for the judgment
>   My Lord is coming down

(*Rose enters from the house.*)

TROY. He's gone off somewhere.

GABRIEL (*offstage*).
>   Better get ready for the judgment
>   Better get ready for the judgment morning
>   Better get ready for the judgment
>   My God is coming down

ROSE. He ain't eating right. Miss Pearl say she can't get him to eat nothing.

TROY. What you want me to do about it, Rose? I done did everything I can for the man. I can't make him get well. Man got half his head blown away . . . what you expect?

ROSE. Seem like something ought to be done to help him.

TROY. Man don't bother nobody. He just mixed up from that metal plate he got in his head. Ain't no sense for him to go back into the hospital.

ROSE. Least he be eating right. They can help him take care of himself.

TROY. Don't nobody wanna be locked up, Rose. What you wanna lock him up for? Man go over there and fight the war . . . messin' around with them Japs, get half his head blow off . . . and they give him a lousy three thousand dollars. And I had to swoop down on that.

ROSE. Is you fixing to go into that again?

TROY. That's the only way I got a roof over my head . . . cause of that metal plate.

ROSE. Ain't no sense you blaming yourself for nothing. Gabe wasn't in no condition to manage that money. You done what was right by him. Can't nobody say you ain't done what was right by him. Look how long you took care of him . . . till he wanted to have his own place and moved over there with Miss Pearl.

TROY. That ain't what I'm saying, woman! I'm just stating the facts. If my brother didn't have that metal plate in his head . . . I wouldn't have a pot to piss in or a window to throw it out of. And I'm fifty-three years old. Now see if you can understand that!

(*Troy gets up from the porch and starts to exit the yard.*)

ROSE. Where you going off to? You been running out of here every Saturday for weeks. I thought you was gonna work on this fence?

TROY. I'm gonna walk down to Taylor's. Listen to the ball game. I'll be back in a bit. I'll work on it when I get back.

(*He exits the yard. The lights go to black.*)

SCENE 3

The lights come up on the yard. It is four hours later. Rose is taking down the clothes from the line. Cory enters carrying his football equipment.

ROSE. Your daddy like to had a fit with you running out of here this morning without doing your chores.

CORY. I told you I had to go to practice.

ROSE. He say you were supposed to help him with this fence.

CORY. He been saying that the last four or five Saturdays, and then he don't never do nothing, but go down to Taylors'. Did you tell him about the recruiter?

ROSE. Yeah, I told him.

CORY. What he say?

ROSE. He ain't said nothing too much. You get in there and get started on your chores before he gets back. Go on and scrub down them steps before he gets back here hollering and carrying on.

CORY. I'm hungry. What you got to eat, Mama?

ROSE. Go on and get started on your chores. I got some meat loaf in there. Go on and make you a sandwich . . . and don't leave no mess in there.

(*Cory exits into the house. Rose continues to take down the clothes. Troy enters the yard and sneaks up and grabs her from behind.*)

Troy! Go on, now. You liked to scared me to death. What was the score of the game? Lucille had me on the phone and I couldn't keep up with it.

TROY. What I care about the game? Come here, woman. (*He tries to kiss her.*)

ROSE. I thought you went down Taylors' to listen to the game. Go on, Troy! You supposed to be putting up this fence.

TROY (*attempting to kiss her again*). I'll put it up when I finish with what is at hand.

ROSE. Go on, Troy. I ain't studying you.

TROY (*chasing after her*). I'm studying you . . . fixing to do my homework!

ROSE. Troy, you better leave me alone.

TROY. Where's Cory? That boy brought his butt home yet?

ROSE. He's in the house doing his chores.

TROY (*calling*). Cory! Get your butt out here, boy!

(*Rose exits into the house with the laundry. Troy goes over to the pile of wood, picks up a board, and starts sawing. Cory enters from the house.*)

TROY. You just now coming in here from leaving this morning?

CORY. Yeah, I had to go to football practice.

TROY. Yeah, what?

CORY. Yessir.

TROY. I ain't but two seconds off you noway. The garbage sitting in there overflowing . . . you ain't done none of your chores . . . and you come in here talking about "Yeah."

CORY. I was just getting ready to do my chores now, Pop . . .

TROY. Your first chore is to help me with this fence on Saturday. Everything else come after that. Now get that saw and cut them boards.

(*Cory takes the saw and begins cutting the boards. Troy continues working. There is a long pause.*)

CORY. Hey, Pop . . . why don't you buy a TV?

TROY. What I want with a TV? What I want one of them for?

CORY. Everybody got one. Earl, Ba Bra . . . Jesse!

TROY. I ain't asked you who had one. I say what I want with one?

CORY. So you can watch it. They got lots of things on TV. Baseball games and everything. We could watch the World Series.

TROY. Yeah . . . and how much this TV cost?

CORY. I don't know. They got them on sale for around two hundred dollars.

TROY. Two hundred dollars, huh?

CORY. That ain't that much, Pop.

TROY. Naw, it's just two hundred dollars. See that roof you got over your head at night? Let me tell you something about that roof. It's been over ten years since that roof was last tarred. See now . . . the snow come this winter and sit up there on that roof like it is . . . and it's gonna seep inside. It's just gonna be a little bit . . . ain't gonna hardly notice it. Then the next thing you know, it's gonna be leaking all over the house. Then the wood rot from all that water and you gonna need a whole new roof. Now, how much you think it cost to get that roof tarred?

CORY. I don't know.

TROY. Two hundred and sixty-four dollars . . . cash money. While you thinking about a TV, I got to be thinking about the roof . . . and whatever else go wrong here. Now if you had two hundred dollars, what would you do . . . fix the roof or buy a TV?

CORY. I'd buy a TV. Then when the roof started to leak . . . when it needed fixing . . . I'd fix it.

TROY. Where you gonna get the money from? You done spent it for a TV. You gonna sit up and watch the water run all over your brand new TV.

CORY. Aw, Pop. You got money. I know you do.

TROY. Where I got it at, huh?

CORY. You got it in the bank.

TROY. You wanna see my bankbook? You wanna see that seventy-three dollars and twenty-two cents I got sitting up in there?

CORY. You ain't got to pay for it all at one time. You can put a down payment on it and carry it on home with you.

TROY. Not me. I ain't gonna owe nobody nothing if I can help it. Miss a payment and they come and snatch it right out of your house. Then what you got? Now, soon as I get two hundred dollars clear, then I'll buy a TV. Right now, as soon as I get two hundred and sixty-four dollars, I'm gonna have this roof tarred.

CORY. Aw . . . Pop!

TROY. You go on and get you two hundred dollars and buy one if ya want it. I got better things to do with my money.

CORY. I can't get no two hundred dollars. I ain't never seen two hundred dollars.

TROY. I'll tell you what . . . you get you a hundred dollars and I'll put the other hundred with it.

CORY. All right, I'm gonna show you.

TROY. You gonna show me how you can cut them boards right now.

(*Cory begins to cut the boards. There is a long pause.*)

CORY. The Pirates won today. That makes five in a row.

TROY. I ain't thinking about the Pirates. Got an all-white team. Got that boy . . . that Puerto Rican boy . . . Clemente. Don't even half-play him. That boy could be something if they give him a chance. Play him one day and sit him on the bench the next.

CORY. He gets a lot of chances to play.

TROY. I'm talking about playing regular. Playing every day so you can get your timing. That's what I'm talking about.

CORY. They got some white guys on the team that don't play every day. You can't play everybody at the same time.

TROY. If they got a white fellow sitting on the bench . . . you can bet your last dollar he can't play! The colored guy got to be twice as good before he get on the team. That's why I don't want you to get all tied up in them sports. Man on the team and what it get him? They got colored on the team and don't use them. Same as not having them. All them teams the same.

CORY. The Braves got Hank Aaron and Wes Covington. Hank Aaron hit two home runs today. That makes forty-three.

TROY. Hank Aaron ain't nobody. That what you supposed to do. That's how you supposed to play the game. Ain't nothing to it. It's just a matter of timing . . . getting the right follow-through. Hell, I can hit forty-three home runs right now!

CORY. Not off no major-league pitching, you couldn't.

TROY. We had better pitching in the Negro leagues. I hit seven home runs off of Satchel Paige.[4] You can't get no better than that!

CORY. Sandy Koufax. He's leading the league in strikeouts.

TROY. I ain't thinking of no Sandy Koufax.

CORY. You got Warren Spahn and Lew Burdette. I bet you couldn't hit no home runs off of Warren Spahn.

TROY. I'm through with it now. You go on and cut them boards. (*Pause.*) Your mama tell me you done got recruited by a college football team? Is that right?

CORY. Yeah. Coach Zellman say the recruiter gonna be coming by to talk to you. Get you to sign the permission papers.

TROY. I thought you supposed to be working down there at the A&P. Ain't you suppose to be working down there after school?

CORY. Mr. Stawicki say he gonna hold my job for me until after the football season. Say starting next week I can work weekends.

TROY. I thought we had an understanding about this football stuff? You suppose to keep up with your chores and hold that job down at the A&P. Ain't been around here all day on a Saturday. Ain't none of your chores done . . . and now you telling me you done quit your job.

CORY. I'm going to be working weekends.

TROY. You damn right you are! And ain't no need for nobody coming around here to talk to me about signing nothing.

CORY. Hey, Pop . . . you can't do that. He's coming all the way from North Carolina.

TROY. I don't care where he coming from. The white man ain't gonna let you get nowhere with that football noway. You go on and get your book-learning so you can work yourself up in that A&P or learn how to fix cars or build houses or something, get you a trade. That way you have something can't nobody take away from you. You go on and learn how to put your hands to some good use. Besides hauling people's garbage.

CORY. I get good grades, Pop. That's why the recruiter wants to talk with you. You got to keep up your grades to get recruited. This way I'll be going to college. I'll get a chance . . .

TROY. First you gonna get your butt down there to the A&P and get your job back.

CORY. Mr. Stawicki done already hired somebody else 'cause I told him I was playing football.

---

[4]Paige (1906–82) was a pitcher in the Negro leagues.

TROY. You a bigger fool than I thought . . . to let somebody take away your job so you can play some football. Where you gonna get your money to take out your girlfriend and whatnot? What kind of foolishness is that to let somebody take away your job?

CORY. I'm still gonna be working weekends.

TROY. Naw . . . naw. You getting your butt out of here and finding you another job.

CORY. Come on, Pop! I got to practice. I can't work after school and play football too. The team needs me. That's what Coach Zellman say . . .

TROY. I don't care what nobody else say. I'm the boss . . . you understand? I'm the boss around here. I do the only saying what counts.

CORY. Come on, Pop!

TROY. I asked you . . . did you understand?

CORY. Yeah . . .

TROY. What?!

CORY. Yessir.

TROY. You go on down there to that A&P and see if you can get your job back. If you can't do both . . . then you quit the football team. You've got to take the crookeds with the straights.

CORY. Yessir. (*Pause.*) Can I ask you a question?

TROY. What the hell you wanna ask me? Mr. Stawicki the one you got the questions for.

CORY. How come you ain't never liked me?

TROY. Liked you? Who the hell say I got to like you? What law is there say I got to like you? Wanna stand up in my face and ask a damn foolass question like that. Talking about liking somebody. Come here, boy, when I talk to you.

(*Cory comes over to where Troy is working. He stands slouched over and Troy shoves him on his shoulder.*)

Straighten up, goddammit! I asked you a question . . . what law is there say I got to like you?

CORY. None.

TROY. Well, all right then! Don't you eat every day? (*Pause.*) Answer me when I talk to you! Don't you eat every day?

CORY. Yeah.

TROY. Nigger, as long as you in my house, you put that sir on the end of it when you talk to me.

CORY. Yes . . . sir.

TROY. You eat every day.

CORY. Yessir!

TROY. Got a roof over your head.

CORY. Yessir!

TROY. Got clothes on your back.

CORY. Yessir.

TROY. Why you think that is?

CORY. Cause of you.

TROY. Ah, hell I know it's cause of me . . . but why do you think that is?

CORY (*hesitant*). Cause you like me.

TROY. Like you? I go out of here every morning . . . bust my butt . . . putting up with them crackers every day . . . cause I like you? You are the biggest fool I ever saw. (*Pause.*) It's my job. It's my responsibility! You understand that? A man got to take care of his family. You live in my house . . . sleep you behind on my bedclothes . . . fill you belly up with my food . . . cause you my son. You my flesh and blood. Not cause I like you! Cause it's my duty to take care of you. I owe a responsibility to you! Let's get this straight right here . . . before it go along any further . . . I ain't got to like you. Mr. Rand don't give me my money come payday cause he likes me. He gives me cause he owe me. I done give you everything I had to give you. I gave you your life! Me and your mama worked that out between us. And liking your black ass wasn't part of the bargain. Don't you try and go through life worrying about if somebody like you or not. You best be making sure they doing right by you. You understand what I'm saying boy?

CORY. Yessir.

TROY. Then get the hell out of my face, and get on down to that A&P.

(*Rose has been standing behind the screen door for much of the scene. She enters as Cory exits.*)

ROSE. Why don't you let the boy go ahead and play football, Troy? Ain't no harm in that. He's just trying to be like you with the sports.

TROY. I don't want him to be like me! I want him to move as far away from my life as he can get. You the only decent thing that ever happened to me. I wish him that. But I don't wish him a thing else from my life. I decided seventeen years ago that boy wasn't getting involved in no sports. Not after what they did to me in the sports.

ROSE. Troy, why don't you admit you was too old to play in the major leagues? For once . . . why don't you admit that?

TROY. What do you mean too old? Don't come telling me I was too old. I just wasn't the right color. Hell, I'm fifty-three years old and can do better than Selkirk's .269 right now!

ROSE. How's was you gonna play ball when you were over forty? Sometimes I can't get no sense out of you.

TROY. I got good sense, woman. I got sense enough not to let my boy get hurt over playing no sports. You been mothering that boy too much. Worried about if people like him.

ROSE. Everything that boy do . . . he do for you. He wants you to say "Good job, son." That's all.

TROY. Rose, I ain't got time for that. He's alive. He's healthy. He's got to make his own way. I made mine. Ain't nobody gonna hold his hand when he get out there in that world.

ROSE. Times have changed from when you was young, Troy. People change. The world's changing around you and you can't even see it.

TROY (*slow, methodical*). Woman . . . I do the best I can do. I come in here every Friday. I carry a sack of potatoes and a bucket of lard. You all line up at the door with your hands out. I give you the lint from my pockets. I give you my sweat and my blood. I ain't got no tears. I done spent them. We go upstairs in that room at night . . . and I fall down on you and try to blast a hole into forever. I get up Monday morning . . . find my lunch on the table. I go out. Make my way. Find my strength to carry me through to the next Friday. (*Pause.*) That's all I got, Rose. That's all I got to give. I can't give nothing else.

(*Troy exits into the house. The lights go down to black.*)

SCENE 4

It is Friday. Two weeks later. Cory starts out of the house with his football equipment. The phone rings.

CORY (*calling*). I got it! (*He answers the phone and stands in the screen door talking.*) Hello? Hey, Jesse. Naw . . . I was just getting ready to leave now.

ROSE (*calling*). Cory!

CORY. I told you, man, them spikes is all tore up. You can use them if you want, but they ain't no good. Earl got some spikes.

ROSE (*calling*). Cory!

CORY (*calling to Rose*). Mam? I'm talking to Jesse. (*Into phone.*) When she say that? (*Pause.*) Aw, you lying, man. I'm gonna tell her you said that.

ROSE (*calling*). Cory, don't you go nowhere!

CORY. I got to go to the game, Ma! (*Into the phone.*) Yeah, hey, look, I'll talk to you later. Yeah, I'll meet you over Earl's house. Later. Bye, Ma.

(*Cory exits the house and starts out the yard.*)

ROSE. Cory, where you going off to? You got that stuff all pulled out and thrown all over your room.

CORY (*in the yard*). I was looking for my spikes. Jesse wanted to borrow my spikes.

ROSE. Get up there and get that cleaned up before your daddy get back in here.

CORY. I got to go to the game! I'll clean it up *when I get back.*

(*Cory exits.*)

ROSE. That's all he need to do is see that room all messed up.

(*Rose exits into the house. Troy and Bono enter the yard. Troy is dressed in clothes other than his work clothes.*)

BONO. He told him the same thing he told you. Take it to the union.

TROY. Brownie ain't got that much sense. Man wasn't thinking about nothing. He wait until I confront them on it . . . then he wanna come crying seniority. (*Calls.*) Hey, Rose!

BONO. I wish I could have seen Mr. Rand's face when he told you.

TROY. He couldn't get it out of his mouth! Liked to bit his tongue! When they called me down there to the Commissioner's office . . . he thought they was gonna fire me. Like everybody else.

BONO. I didn't think they was gonna fire you. I thought they was gonna put you on the warning paper.

TROY. Hey, Rose! (*To Bono.*) Yeah, Mr. Rand like to bit his tongue.

(*Troy breaks the seal on the bottle, takes a drink, and hands it to Bono.*)

BONO. I see you run right down to Taylors' and told that Alberta gal.

TROY (*calling*). Hey Rose! (*To Bono.*) I told everybody. Hey, Rose! I went down there to cash my check.

ROSE (*entering from the house*). Hush all that hollering, man! I know you out here. What they say down there at the Commissioner's office?

TROY. You supposed to come when I call you, woman. Bono'll tell you that. (*To Bono.*) Don't Lucille come when you call her?

ROSE. Man, hush your mouth. I ain't no dog . . . talk about "come when you call me."

TROY (*puts his arm around Rose*). You hear this, Bono? I had me an old dog used to get uppity like that. You say, "C'mere, Blue!" . . . and he just lay there and look at you. End up getting a stick and chasing him away trying to make him come.

ROSE. I ain't studying you and your dog. I remember you used to sing that old song.

TROY (*he sings*).
     Hear it ring! Hear it ring! I had a dog his name was Blue.

ROSE. Don't nobody wanna hear you sing that old song.

TROY (*sings*).
     You know Blue was mighty true.

ROSE. Used to have Cory running around here singing that song.

BONO. Hell, I remember that song myself.

TROY (*sings*).
     You know Blue was a good old dog.
     Blue treed a possum in a hollow log.
That was my daddy's song. My daddy made up that song.

ROSE. I don't care who made it up. Don't nobody wanna hear you sing it.

TROY (*makes a song like calling a dog*). Come here, woman.

ROSE. You come in here carrying on, I reckon they ain't fired you. What they say down there at the Commissioner's office?

TROY. Look here, Rose . . . Mr. Rand called me into his office today when I got back from talking to them people down there . . . it come from up top . . . he called me in and told me they was making me a driver.

ROSE. Troy, you kidding!

TROY. No I ain't. Ask Bono.

ROSE. Well, that's great, Troy. Now you don't have to hassle them people no more.

(*Lyons enters from the street.*)

TROY. Aw hell, I wasn't looking to see you today. I thought you was in jail. Got it all over the front page of the *Courier* about them raiding Sefus's place . . . where you be hanging out with all them thugs.

LYONS. Hey, Pop . . . that ain't got nothing to do with me. I don't go down there gambling. I go down there to sit in with the band. I ain't got nothing to do with the gambling part. They got some good music down there.

TROY. They got some rogues . . . is what they got.

LYONS. How you been, Mr. Bono? Hi, Rose.

BONO. I see where you playing down at the Crawford Grill tonight.

ROSE. How come you ain't brought Bonnie like I told you? You should have brought Bonnie with you, she ain't been over in a month of Sundays.

LYONS. I was just in the neighborhood . . . thought I'd stop by.

TROY. Here he come . . .

BONO. Your daddy got a promotion on the rubbish. He's gonna be the first colored driver. Ain't got to do nothing but sit up there and read the paper like them white fellows.

LYONS. Hey, Pop . . . if you knew how to read you'd be all right.

BONO. Naw . . . naw . . . you mean if the nigger knew how to drive he'd be all right. Been fighting with them people about driving and ain't even got a license. Mr. Rand know you ain't got no driver's license?

TROY. Driving ain't nothing. All you do is point the truck where you want it to go. Driving ain't nothing.

BONO. Do Mr. Rand know you ain't got no driver's license? That's what I'm talking about. I ain't asked if driving was easy. I asked if Mr. Rand know you ain't got no driver's license.

TROY. He ain't got to know. The man ain't got to know my business. Time he find out, I have two or three driver's licenses.

LYONS (*going into his pocket*). Say, look here, Pop . . .

TROY. I knew it was coming. Didn't I tell you, Bono? I know what kind of "Look here, Pop" that was. The nigger fixing to ask me for some money. It's Friday night. It's my payday. All them rogues down there on the avenue . . . the ones that ain't in jail . . . and Lyons is hopping in his shoes to get down there with them.

LYONS. See, Pop . . . if you give somebody else a chance to talk sometimes, you'd see that I was fixing to pay you back your ten dollars like I told you. Here . . . I told you I'd pay you when Bonnie got paid.

TROY. Naw . . . you go ahead and keep that ten dollars. Put it in the bank. The next time you feel like you wanna come by here and ask me for something . . . you go on down there and get that.

LYONS. Here's your ten dollars, Pop. I told you I don't want you to give me nothing. I just wanted to borrow ten dollars.

TROY. Naw . . . you go on and keep that for the next time you want to ask me.

LYONS. Come on, Pop . . . here go your ten dollars.

ROSE. Why don't you go on and let the boy pay you back, Troy?

LYONS. Here you go, Rose. If you don't take it I'm gonna have to hear about it for the next six months. (*He hands her the money.*)

ROSE. You can hand yours over here too, Troy.

TROY. You see this, Bono. You see how they do me.

BONO. Yeah, Lucille do me the same way.

(*Gabriel is heard singing off stage. He enters.*)

GABRIEL. Better get ready for the Judgment! Better get ready for . . . Hey! . . . Hey! . . . There's Troy's boy!

LYONS. How are you doing, Uncle Gabe?

GABRIEL. Lyons . . . The King of the Jungle! Rose . . . hey, Rose. Got a flower for you. (*He takes a rose from his pocket.*) Picked it myself. That's the same rose like you is!

ROSE. That's right nice of you, Gabe.

LYONS. What you been doing, Uncle Gabe?

GABRIEL. Oh, I been chasing hellhounds and waiting on the time to tell St. Peter to open the gates.

LYONS. You been chasing hellhounds, huh? Well . . . you doing the right thing, Uncle Gabe. Somebody got to chase them.

GABRIEL. Oh, yeah . . . I know it. The devil's strong. The devil ain't no pushover. Hellhounds snipping at everybody's heels. But I got my trumpet waiting on the judgment time.

LYONS. Waiting on the Battle of Armageddon, huh?

GABRIEL. Ain't gonna be too much of a battle when God get to waving that Judgment sword. But the people's gonna have a hell of a time trying to get into heaven if them gates ain't open.

LYONS (*putting his arm around Gabriel*). You hear this, Pop. Uncle Gabe, you all right!

GABRIEL (*laughing with Lyons*). Lyons! King of the Jungle.

ROSE. You gonna stay for supper, Gabe? Want me to fix you a plate?

GABRIEL. I'll take a sandwich, Rose. Don't want no plate. Just wanna eat with my hands. I'll take a sandwich.

ROSE. How about you, Lyons? You staying? Got some short ribs cooking.

LYONS. Naw, I won't eat nothing till after we finished playing. (*Pause.*) You ought to come down and listen to me play, Pop.

TROY. I don't like that Chinese music. All that noise.

ROSE. Go on in the house and wash up, Gabe . . . I'll fix you a sandwich.

GABRIEL (*to Lyons, as he exits*). Troy's mad at me.

LYONS. What you mad at Uncle Gabe for, Pop?

ROSE. He thinks Troy's mad at him cause he moved over to Miss Pearl's.

TROY. I ain't mad at the man. He can live where he want to live at.

LYONS. What he move over there for? Miss Pearl don't like nobody.

ROSE. She don't mind him none. She treats him real nice. She just don't allow all that singing.

TROY. She don't mind that rent he be paying . . . that's what she don't mind.

ROSE. Troy, I ain't going through that with you no more. He's over there cause he want to have his own place. He can come and go as he please.

TROY. Hell, he could come and go as he please here. I wasn't stopping him. I ain't put no rules on him.

ROSE. It ain't the same thing, Troy. And you know it.

(*Gabriel comes to the door.*)

Now, that's the last I wanna hear about that. I don't wanna hear nothing else about Gabe and Miss Pearl. And next week . . .

GABRIEL. I'm ready for my sandwich, Rose.

ROSE. And next week . . . when that recruiter come from that school . . . I want you to sign that paper and go on and let Cory play football. Then that'll be the last I have to hear about that.

TROY (*to Rose as she exits into the house*). I ain't thinking about Cory nothing.

LYONS. What . . . Cory got recruited? What school he going to?

TROY. That boy walking around here smelling his piss . . . thinking he's grown. Thinking he's gonna do what he want, irrespective of what I say. Look here, Bono . . . I left the Commissioner's office and went down to the A&P . . . that boy ain't working down there. He lying to me. Telling me he got his job back . . . telling me he working weekends . . . telling me he working after school . . . Mr. Stawicki tell me he ain't working down there at all!

LYONS. Cory just growing up. He's just busting at the seams trying to fill out your shoes.

TROY. I don't care what he's doing. When he get to the point where he wanna disobey me . . . then it's time for him to move on. Bono'll tell you that. I bet he ain't never disobeyed his daddy without paying the consequences.

BONO. I ain't never had a chance. My daddy came on through . . . but I ain't never knew him to see him . . . or what he had on his mind or where he went. Just moving on through. Searching out the New Land. That's what the old folks used to call it. See a fellow moving around from place to place . . . woman to woman . . . called it searching out the New Land. I can't say if he ever found it. I come

along, didn't want no kids. Didn't know if I was gonna be in one place long enough to fix on them right as their daddy. I figured I was going searching too. As it turned out I been hooked up with Lucille near about as long as your daddy been with Rose. Going on sixteen years.

TROY. Sometimes I wish I hadn't known my daddy. He ain't cared nothing about no kids. A kid to him wasn't nothing. All he wanted was for you to learn how to walk so he could start you to working. When it come time for eating . . . he ate first. If there was anything left over, that's what you got. Man would sit down and eat two chickens and give you the wing.

LYONS. You ought to stop that, Pop. Everybody feed their kids. No matter how hard times is . . . everybody care about their kids. Make sure they have something to eat.

TROY. The only thing my daddy cared about was getting them bales of cotton in to Mr. Lubin. That's the only thing that mattered to him. Sometimes I used to wonder why he was living. Wonder why the devil hadn't come and got him. "Get them bales of cotton in to Mr. Lubin" and find out he owe him money . . .

LYONS. He should have just went on and left when he saw he couldn't get nowhere. That's what I would have done.

TROY. How he gonna leave with eleven kids? And where he gonna go? He ain't knew how to do nothing but farm. No, he was trapped and I think he knew it. But I'll say this for him . . . he felt a responsibility toward us. Maybe he ain't treated us the way I felt he should have . . . but without that responsibility he could have walked off and left us . . . made his own way.

BONO. A lot of them did. Back in those days what you talking about . . . they walk out their front door and just take on down one road or another and keep on walking.

LYONS. There you go! That's what I'm talking about.

BONO. Just keep on walking till you come to something else. Ain't you never heard of nobody having the walking blues? Well, that's what you call it when you just take off like that.

TROY. My daddy ain't had them walking blues! What you talking about? He stayed right there with his family. But he was just as evil as he could be. My mama couldn't stand him. Couldn't stand that evilness. She run off when I was about eight. She sneaked off one night after he had gone to sleep. Told me she was coming back for me. I ain't never seen her no more. All his women run off and left him. He wasn't good for nobody.

When my turn come to head out, I was fourteen and got to sniffing around Joe Canewell's daughter. Had us an old mule we called Greyboy. My daddy sent me out to do some plowing and I tied up Greyboy and went to fooling around with Joe Canewell's daughter. We done found us a nice little spot, got real cozy with each other. She about thirteen and we done figured we was grown anyway . . . so we down there enjoying ourselves . . . ain't thinking about nothing. We didn't know Greyboy had got loose and wandered back to the house and my daddy was looking for me. We down there by the creek enjoying ourselves when my daddy come up on us. Surprised us. He had them leather straps off the mule and commenced to whupping me like there was no tomorrow. I jumped up, mad and embarrassed. I was scared of my daddy. When he commenced to whupping on me . . . quite naturally I run to get out of the way. (*Pause.*) Now I thought he was mad cause I ain't done my work. But I see where he was chasing me off so he could have the gal for himself. When I see what the matter of it was, I lost all fear of my daddy. Right there is where I become a man . . . at fourteen years of age. (*Pause.*) Now it was my turn to run him off. I picked up them same reins that he had used on me. I picked up them reins and commenced to whupping on him. The gal jumped up and run off . . . and when my daddy turned to face me, I could see why the devil had never come to get him . . . cause he was the devil himself. I don't know what happened. When I woke up, I was laying right there by the creek, and Blue . . . this old dog we had . . . was licking my face. I thought I was blind. I couldn't see nothing. Both my eyes were swollen shut. I laid there and cried. I didn't know what I was gonna do. The only thing I knew was the time had come for me to leave my daddy's house. And right there the world suddenly got big. And it was a long time before I could cut it down to where I could handle it.

Part of that cutting down was when I got to the place where I could feel him kicking in my blood and knew that the only thing that separated us was the matter of a few years.

(*Gabriel enters from the house with a sandwich.*)

LYONS. What you got there, Uncle Gabe?

GABRIEL. Got me a ham sandwich. Rose gave me a ham sandwich.

TROY. I don't know what happened to him. I done lost touch with everybody except Gabriel. But I hope he's dead. I hope he found some peace.

LYONS. That's a heavy story, Pop. I didn't know you left home when you was fourteen.

TROY. And didn't know nothing. The only part of the world I knew was the forty-two acres of Mr. Lubin's land. That's all I knew about life.

LYONS. Fourteen's kinda young to be out on your own. (*Phone rings.*) I don't even think I was ready to be out on my own at fourteen. I don't know what I would have done.

TROY. I got up from the creek and walked on down to Mobile. I was through with farming. Figured I could do better in the city. So I walked the two hundred miles to Mobile.

LYONS. Wait a minute . . . you ain't walked no two hundred miles, Pop. Ain't nobody gonna walk no two hundred miles. You talking about some walking there.

BONO. That's the only way you got anywhere back in them days.

LYONS. Shhh. Damn if I wouldn't have hitched a ride with somebody!

TROY. Who you gonna hitch it with? They ain't had no cars and things like they got now. We talking about 1918.

ROSE (*entering*). What you all out here getting into?

TROY (*to Rose*). I'm telling Lyons how good he got it. He don't know nothing about this I'm talking.

ROSE. Lyons, that was Bonnie on the phone. She say you supposed to pick her up.

LYONS. Yeah, okay, Rose.

TROY. I walked on down to Mobile and hitched up with some of them fellows that was heading this way. Got up here and found out . . . not only couldn't you get a job . . . you couldn't find no place to live. I thought I was in freedom. Shhh. Colored folks living down there on the riverbanks in whatever kind of shelter they could find for themselves. Right down there under the Brady Street Bridge. Living in shacks made of sticks and tarpaper. Messed around there and went from bad to worse. Started stealing. First it was food. Then I figured, hell, if I steal money I can buy me some food. Buy me some shoes too! One thing led to another. Met your mama. I was young and anxious to be a man. Met your mama and had you. What I do that for? Now I got to worry about feeding you and her. Got to steal three times as much. Went out one day looking for somebody to rob . . . that's what I was, a robber. I'll tell you the truth. I'm ashamed of it today. But it's the truth. Went to rob this fellow . . . pulled out my knife . . . and he pulled out a gun. Shot me in the chest. I felt just like somebody had taken a hot branding iron and laid it on me. When he shot me I jumped at him with my knife. They told me I killed him and they put me in the penitentiary and locked me up for fifteen years. That's where I met Bono. That's where I learned how to play baseball. Got out that place and your mama had taken you and went on to make life without me. Fifteen years was a long time for her to wait. But that fifteen years cured me of that robbing stuff. Rose'll tell you. She asked me when I met her if I had gotten all that foolishness out of my system. And I told her, "Baby, it's you and baseball all what count with me." You hear me, Bono? I meant it too. She say, "Which one comes first?" I told her, "Baby, ain't no doubt it's baseball . . . but you stick and get old with me and we'll both outlive this baseball." Am I right, Rose? And it's true.

ROSE. Man, hush your mouth. You ain't said no such thing. Talking about, "Baby you know you'll always be number one with me." That's what you was talking.

TROY. You hear that, Bono. That's why I love her.

BONO. Rose'll keep you straight. You get off the track, she'll straighten you up.

ROSE. Lyons, you better get on up and get Bonnie. She waiting on you.

LYONS (*gets up to go*). Hey, Pop, why don't you come on down to the Grill and hear me play?

TROY. I ain't going down there. I'm too old to be sitting around in them clubs.

BONO. You got to be good to play down at the Grill.

LYONS. Come on, Pop . . .

TROY. I got to get up in the morning.

LYONS. You ain't got to stay long.

TROY. Naw, I'm gonna get my supper and go on to bed.

LYONS. Well, I got to go. I'll see you again.

TROY. Don't you come around my house on my payday.

ROSE. Pick up the phone and let somebody know you coming. And bring Bonnie with you. You know I'm always glad to see her.

LYONS. Yeah, I'll do that, Rose. You take care now. See you, Pop. See you, Mr. Bono. See you, Uncle Gabe.

GABRIEL. Lyons! King of the Jungle!

(*Lyons exits.*)

TROY. Is supper ready, woman? Me and you got some business to take care of. I'm gonna tear it up too.

ROSE. Troy, I done told you now!

TROY (*puts his arm around Bono*). Aw hell, woman . . . this is Bono. Bono like family. I done known this nigger since . . . how long I done know you?

BONO. It's been a long time.

TROY. I done know this nigger since Skippy was a pup. Me and him done been through some times.

BONO. You sure right about that.

TROY. Hell, I done know him longer than I known you. And we still standing shoulder to shoulder. Hey, look here, Bono . . . a man can't ask for no more than that. (*Drinks to him.*) I love you, nigger.

BONO. Hell, I love you too . . . I got to get home see my woman. You got yours in hand. I got to get mine.

(*Bono starts to exit as Cory enters the yard, dressed in his football uniform. He gives Troy a hard, uncompromising look.*)

CORY. What you do that for, Pop?

(*He throws his helmet down in the direction of Troy.*)

ROSE. What's the matter? Cory . . . what's the matter?

CORY. Papa done went up to the school and told Coach Zellman I can't play football no more. Wouldn't even let me play the game. Told him to tell the recruiter not to come.

ROSE. Troy . . .

TROY. What you Troying me for. Yeah, I did it. And the boy know why I did it.

CORY. Why you wanna do that to me? That was the one chance I had.

ROSE. Ain't nothing wrong with Cory playing football, Troy.

TROY. The boy lied to me. I told the nigger if he wanna play football . . . to keep up his chores and hold down that job at the A&P. That was the conditions. Stopped down there to see Mr. Stawicki . . .

CORY. I can't work after school during the football season, Pop! I tried to tell you that Mr. Stawicki's holding my job for me. You don't never want to listen to nobody. And then you wanna go and do this to me!

TROY. I ain't done nothing to you. You done it to yourself.

CORY. Just cause you didn't have a chance! You just scared I'm gonna be better than you, that's all.

TROY. Come here.

ROSE. Troy . . .

(*Cory reluctantly crosses over to Troy.*)

TROY. All right! See. You done made a mistake.

CORY. I didn't even do nothing!

TROY. I'm gonna tell you what your mistake was. See . . . you swung at the ball and didn't hit it. That's strike one. See, you in the batter's box now. You swung and you missed. That's strike one. Don't you strike out!

(*Lights fade to black.*)

ACT 2

SCENE 1

The following morning. Cory is at the tree hitting the ball with the bat. He tries to mimic Troy, but his swing is awkward, less sure. Rose enters from the house.

ROSE. Cory, I want you to help me with this cupboard.

CORY. I ain't quitting the team. I don't care what Poppa say.

ROSE. I'll talk to him when he gets back. He had to go see about your Uncle Gabe. The police done arrested him. Say he was disturbing the peace. He'll be back directly. Come on in here and help me clean out the top of this cupboard.

(*Cory exits into the house. Rose sees Troy and Bono coming down the alley.*)

Troy . . . what they say down there?

TROY. Ain't said nothing. I give them fifty dollars and they let him go. I'll talk to you about it. Where's Cory?

ROSE. He's in there helping me clean out these cupboards.

TROY. Tell him to get his butt out here.

(*Troy and Bono go over to the pile of wood. Bono picks up the saw and begins sawing.*)

TROY (*to Bono*). All they want is the money. That makes six or seven times I done went down there and got him. See me coming they stick out their hands.

BONO. Yeah. I know what you mean. That's all they care about . . . that money. They don't care about what's right. (*Pause.*) Nigger, why you got to go and get some hard wood? You ain't doing nothing but building a little old fence. Get you some soft pine wood. That's all you need.

TROY. I know what I'm doing. This is outside wood. You put pine wood inside the house. Pine wood is inside wood.

This here is outside wood. Now you tell me where the fence is gonna be?

BONO. You don't need this wood. You can put it up with pine wood and it'll stand as long as you gonna be here looking at it.

TROY. How you know how long I'm gonna be here, nigger? Hell, I might just live forever. Live longer than old man Horsely.

BONO. That's what Magee used to say.

TROY. Magee's damn fool. Now you tell me who you ever heard of gonna pull their own teeth with a pair of rusty pliers.

BONO. The old folks . . . my granddaddy used to pull his teeth with pliers. They ain't had no dentists for the colored folks back then.

TROY. Get clean pliers! You understand? Clean pliers! Sterilize them! Besides we ain't living back then. All Magee had to do was walk over to Doc Goldblum's.

BONO. I see where you and that Tallahassee gal . . . that Alberta . . . I see where you all done got tight.

TROY. What you mean "got tight"?

BONO. I see where you be laughing and joking with her all the time.

TROY. I laughs and jokes with all of them, Bono. You know me.

BONO. That ain't the kind of laughing and joking I'm talking about.

(Cory enters from the house.)

CORY. How you doing. Mr. Bono?

TROY. Cory? Get that saw from Bono and cut some wood. He talking about the wood's too hard to cut. Stand back there, Jim, and let that young boy show you how it's done.

BONO. He's sure welcome to it.

(Cory takes the saw and begins to cut the wood.)

Whew-e-e! Look at that. Big old strong boy. Look like Joe Louis. Hell, must be getting old the way I'm watching that boy whip through that wood.

CORY. I don't see why Mama want a fence around the yard noways.

TROY. Damn if I know either. What the hell she keeping out with it? She ain't got nothing nobody want.

BONO. Some people build fences to keep people out . . . and other people build fences to keep people in. Rose wants to hold on to you all. She loves you.

TROY. Hell, nigger, I don't need nobody to tell me my wife loves me. Cory . . . go on in the house and see if you can find that other saw.

CORY. Where's it at?

TROY. I said find it! Look for it till you find it!

(Cory exits into the house.)

What's that supposed to mean? Wanna keep us in?

BONO. Troy . . . I done known you seem like damn near my whole life. You and Rose both. I done know both of you

all for a long time. I remember when you met Rose. When you was hitting them baseball out the park. A lot of them old gals was after you then. You had the pick of the litter. When you picked Rose, I was happy for you. That was the first time I knew you had any sense. I said . . . My man Troy knows what he's doing . . . I'm gonna follow this nigger . . . he might take me somewhere. I been following you too. I done learned a whole heap of things about life watching you. I done learned how to tell where the shit lies. How to tell it from the alfalfa. You done learned me a lot of things. You showed me how to not make the same mistakes . . . to take life as it comes along and keep putting one foot in front of the other. (Pause.) Rose a good woman, Troy.

TROY. Hell, nigger, I know she a good woman. I been married to her for eighteen years. What you got on your mind, Bono?

BONO. I just say she a good woman. Just like I say anything. I ain't got to have nothing on my mind.

TROY. You just gonna say she a good woman and leave it hanging out there like that? Why you telling me she a good woman?

BONO. She loves you, Troy. Rose loves you.

TROY. You saying I don't measure up. That's what you trying to say. I don't measure up cause I'm seeing this other gal. I know what you trying to say.

BONO. I know what Rose means to you, Troy. I'm just trying to say I don't want to see you mess up.

TROY. Yeah, I appreciate that, Bono. If you was messing around on Lucille I'd be telling you the same thing.

BONO. Well, that's all I got to say. I just say that because I love you both.

TROY. Hell, you know me . . . I wasn't out there looking for nothing. You can't find a better woman than Rose. I know that. But seems like this woman just stuck onto me where I can't shake her loose. I done wrestled with it, tried to throw her off me . . . but she just stuck on tighter. Now she's stuck on for good.

BONO. You's in control . . . that's what you tell me all the time. You responsible for what you do.

TROY. I ain't ducking the responsibility of it. As long as it sets right in my heart . . . then I'm okay. Cause that's all I listen to. It'll tell me right from wrong every time. And I ain't talking about doing Rose no bad turn. I love Rose. She done carried me a long ways and I love and respect her for that.

BONO. I know you do. That's why I don't want to see you hurt her. But what you gonna do when she find out? What you got then? If you try and juggle both of them . . . sooner or later you gonna drop one of them. That's common sense.

TROY. Yeah, I hear what you saying, Bono. I been trying to figure a way to work it out.

BONO. Work it out right, Troy. I don't want to be getting all up between you and Rose's business . . . but work it so it come out right.

TROY. Ah hell, I get all up between you and Lucille's business. When you gonna get that woman that refrigerator she been wanting? Don't tell me you ain't got no money now. I know who your banker is. Mellon don't need that money bad as Lucille want that refrigerator. I'll tell you that.

BONO. Tell you what I'll do . . . when you finish building this fence for Rose . . . I'll buy Lucille that refrigerator.

TROY. You done stuck your foot in your mouth now!

(*Troy grabs up a board and begins to saw. Bono starts to walk out the yard.*)

Hey, nigger . . . where you going?

BONO. I'm going home. I know you don't expect me to help you now. I'm protecting my money. I wanna see you put that fence up by yourself. That's what I want to see. You'll be here another six months without me.

TROY. Nigger, you ain't right.

BONO. When it comes to my money . . . I'm right as fireworks on the Fourth of July.

TROY. All right, we gonna see now. You better get out your bankbook.

(*Bono exits, and Troy continues to work. Rose enters from the house.*)

ROSE. What they say down there? What's happening with Gabe?

TROY. I went down there and got him out. Cost me fifty dollars. Say he was disturbing the peace. Judge set up a hearing for him in three weeks. Say to show cause why he shouldn't be recommitted.

ROSE. What was he doing that cause them to arrest him?

TROY. Some kids was teasing him and he run them off home. Say he was howling and carrying on. Some folks seen him and called the police. That's all it was.

ROSE. Well, what's you say? What'd you tell the judge?

TROY. Told him I'd look after him. It didn't make no sense to recommit the man. He stuck out his big greasy palm and told me to give him fifty dollars and take him on home.

ROSE. Where's he at now? Where'd he go off to?

TROY. He's gone about his business. He don't need nobody to hold his hand.

ROSE. Well, I don't know. Seem like that would be the best place for him if they did put him into the hospital. I know what you're gonna say. But that's what I think would be best.

TROY. The man done had his life ruined fighting for what? And they wanna take and lock him up. Let him be free. He don't bother nobody.

ROSE. Well, everybody got their own way of looking at it I guess. Come on and get your lunch. I got a bowl of lima beans and some cornbread in the oven. Come and get something to eat. Ain't no sense you fretting over Gabe.

(*Rose turns to go into the house.*)

TROY. Rose . . . got something to tell you.

ROSE. Well, come on . . . wait till I get this food on the table.

TROY. Rose!

(*She stops and turns around.*)

I don't know how to say this. (*Pause.*) I can't explain it none. It just sort of grows on you till it gets out of hand. It starts out like a little bush . . . and the next thing you know it's a whole forest.

ROSE. Troy . . . what is you talking about?

TROY. I'm talking, woman, let me talk. I'm trying to find a way to tell you . . . I'm gonna be a daddy. I'm gonna be somebody's daddy.

ROSE. Troy . . . you're not telling me this? You're gonna be . . . what?

TROY. Rose . . . now . . . see . . .

ROSE. You telling me you gonna be somebody's daddy? You telling your *wife* this?

(*Gabriel enters from the street. He carries a rose in his hand.*)

GABRIEL. Hey, Troy! Hey, Rose!

ROSE. I have to wait eighteen years to hear something like this.

GABRIEL. Hey, Rose . . . I got a flower for you. (*He hands it to her.*) That's a rose. Same rose like you is.

ROSE. Thanks, Gabe.

GABRIEL. Troy, you ain't mad at me is you? Them bad mens come and put me away. You ain't mad at me is you?

TROY. Naw, Gabe, I ain't mad at you.

ROSE. Eighteen years and you wanna come with this.

GABRIEL (*takes a quarter out of his pocket*). See what I got? Got a brand new quarter.

TROY. Rose . . . it's just . . .

ROSE. Ain't nothing you can say, Troy. Ain't no way of explaining that.

GABRIEL. Fellow that give me this quarter had a whole mess of them. I'm gonna keep this quarter till it stop shining.

ROSE. Gabe, go on in the house there. I got some watermelon in the Frigidaire. Go on and get you a piece.

GABRIEL. Say, Rose . . . you know I was chasing hellhounds and them bad mens come and get me and take me away. Troy helped me. He come down there and told them they better let me go before he beat them up. Yeah, he did!

ROSE. You go on and get you a piece of watermelon, Gabe. Them bad mens is gone now.

GABRIEL. Okay, Rose . . . gonna get me some watermelon. The kind with the stripes on it.

(*Gabriel exits into the house.*)

ROSE. Why, Troy? Why? After all these years to come dragging this in to me now. It don't make no sense at your age. I could have expected this ten or fifteen years ago, but not now.

TROY. Age ain't got nothing to do with it, Rose.

ROSE. I done tried to be everything a wife should be. Everything a wife could be. Been married eighteen years and I got to live to see the day you tell me you been seeing another woman and done fathered a child by her. And you know I ain't never wanted no half nothing in my family. My whole family is half. Everybody got different fathers and mothers . . . my two sisters and my brother. Can't hardly tell who's who. Can't never sit down and talk about Papa and Mama. It's your papa and your mama and my papa and my mama . . .

TROY. Rose . . . stop it now.

ROSE. I ain't never wanted that for none of my children. And now you wanna drag your behind in here and tell me something like this.

TROY. You ought to know. It's time for you to know.

ROSE. Well, I don't want to know, goddamn it!

TROY. I can't just make it go away. It's done now. I can't wish the circumstance of the thing away.

ROSE. And you don't want to either. Maybe you want to wish me and my boy away. Maybe that's what you want? Well, you can't wish us away. I've got eighteen years of my life invested in you. You ought to have stayed upstairs in my bed where you belong.

TROY. Rose . . . now listen to me . . . we can get a handle on this thing. We can talk this out . . . come to an understanding.

ROSE. All of a sudden it's "we." Where was "we" at when you was down there rolling around with some godforsaken woman? "We" should have come to an understanding before you started making a damn fool of yourself. You're a day late and a dollar short when it comes to an understanding with me.

TROY. It's just . . . She gives me a different idea . . . a different understanding about myself. I can step out of this house and get away from the pressures and problems . . . be a different man. I ain't got to wonder how I'm gonna pay the bills or get the roof fixed. I can just be a part of myself that I ain't never been.

ROSE. What I want to know . . . is do you plan to continue seeing her. That's all you can say to me.

TROY. I can sit up in her house and laugh. Do you understand what I'm saying. I can laugh out loud . . . and it feels good. It reaches all the way down to the bottom of my shoes. (*Pause.*) Rose, I can't give that up.

ROSE. Maybe you ought to go on and stay down there with her . . . if she's a better woman than me.

TROY. It ain't about nobody being a better woman or nothing. Rose, you ain't the blame. A man couldn't ask for no woman to be a better wife than you've been. I'm responsible for it. I done locked myself into a pattern trying to take care of you all that I forgot about myself.

ROSE. What the hell was I there for? That was my job, not somebody else's.

TROY. Rose, I done tried all my life to live decent . . . to live a clean . . . hard . . . useful life. I tried to be a good husband to you. In every way I knew how. Maybe I come into the world backwards, I don't know. But . . . you born with two strikes on you before you come to the plate. You got to guard it closely . . . always looking for the curve ball on the inside corner. You can't afford to let none get past you. You can't afford a call strike. If you going down . . . you going down swinging. Everything lined up against you. What you gonna do. I fooled them, Rose. I bunted. When I found you and Cory and a halfway decent job . . . I was safe. Couldn't nothing touch me. I wasn't gonna strike out no more. I wasn't going back to the penitentiary. I wasn't gonna lay in the streets with a bottle of wine. I was safe. I had me a family. A job. I wasn't gonna get that last strike. I was on first looking for one of them boys to knock me in. To get me home.

ROSE. You should have stayed in my bed, Troy.

TROY. Then when I saw that gal . . . she firmed up my backbone. And I got to thinking that if I tried . . . I just might be able to steal second. Do you understand after eighteen years I wanted to steal second.

ROSE. You should have held me tight. You should have grabbed me and held on.

TROY. I stood on first base for eighteen years and I thought . . . well, goddamn it . . . go on for it!

ROSE. We're not talking about baseball! We're talking about you going off to lay in bed with another woman . . . and then bring it home to me. That's what we're talking about. We ain't talking about no baseball.

TROY. Rose, you're not listening to me. I'm trying the best I can to explain it to you. It's not easy for me to admit that I been standing in the same place for eighteen years.

ROSE. I been standing with you! I been right here with you, Troy. I got a life too. I gave eighteen years of my life to stand in the same spot with you. Don't you think I ever wanted other things? Don't you think I had dreams and hopes? What about my life? What about me. Don't you think it ever crossed my mind to want to know other men? That I wanted to lay up somewhere and forget about my responsibilities? That I wanted someone to make me laugh so I could feel good? You not the only one who's got wants and needs. But I held on to you, Troy. I took all my feelings, my wants and needs, my dreams . . . and I buried them inside you. I planted a seed and watched and prayed over it. I planted myself inside you and waited to bloom. And it didn't take me no eighteen years to find out the soil was hard and rocky and it wasn't never gonna bloom.

But I held on to you, Troy. I held you tighter. You was my husband. I owed you everything I had. Every part of me I could find to give you. And upstairs in that room . . .

with the darkness falling in on me . . . I gave everything I had to try and erase the doubt that you wasn't the finest man in the world. And wherever you was going . . . I wanted to be there with you. Cause you was my husband. Cause that's the only way I was gonna survive as your wife. You always talking about what you give . . . and what you don't have to give. But you take too. You take . . . and don't even know nobody's giving!

(*Rose turns to exit into the house; Troy grabs her arm.*)

TROY. You say I take and don't give!

ROSE. Troy! You're hurting me!

TROY. You say I take and don't give!

ROSE. Troy . . . you're hurting my arm! Let go!

TROY. I done give you everything I got. Don't you tell that lie on me.

ROSE. Troy!

TROY. Don't you tell that lie on me!

(*Cory enters from the house.*)

CORY. Mama!

ROSE. Troy. You're hurting me.

TROY. Don't you tell me about no taking and giving.

(*Cory comes up behind Troy and grabs him. Troy, surprised, is thrown off balance just as Cory throws a glancing blow that catches him on the chest and knocks him down. Troy is stunned, as is Cory.*)

ROSE. Troy. Troy. No!

(*Troy gets to his feet and starts at Cory.*)

Troy . . . no. Please! Troy!

(*Rose pulls on Troy to hold him back. Troy stops himself.*)

TROY (*to Cory*). All right. That's strike two. You stay away from around me, boy. Don't you strike out. You living with a full count. Don't you strike out.

(*Troy exits out the yard as the lights go down.*)

SCENE 2

It is six months later, early afternoon. Troy enters from the house and starts to exit the yard. Rose enters from the house.

ROSE. Troy, I want to talk to you.

TROY. All of a sudden, after all this time, you want to talk to me, huh? You ain't wanted to talk to me for months. You ain't wanted to talk to me last night. You ain't wanted no part of me then. What you wanna talk to me about now?

ROSE. Tomorrow's Friday.

TROY. I know what day tomorrow is. You think I don't know tomorrow's Friday? My whole life I ain't done nothing but look to see Friday coming and you got to tell me it's Friday.

ROSE. I want to know if you're coming home.

TROY. I always come home, Rose. You know that. There ain't never been a night I ain't come home.

ROSE. That ain't what I mean . . . and you know it. I want to know if you're coming straight home after work.

TROY. I figure I'd cash my check . . . hang out at Taylors' with the boys . . . maybe play a game of checkers . . .

ROSE. Troy, I can't live like this. I won't live like this. You livin' on borrowed time with me. It's been going on six months now you ain't been coming home.

TROY. I be here every night. Every night of the year. That's 365 days.

ROSE. I want you to come home tomorrow after work.

TROY. Rose . . . I don't mess up my pay. You know that now. I take my pay and I give it to you. I don't have no money but what you give me back. I just want to have a little time to myself . . . a little time to enjoy life.

ROSE. What about me? When's my time to enjoy life?

TROY. I don't know what to tell you, Rose. I'm doing the best I can.

ROSE. You ain't been home from work but time enough to change your clothes and run out . . . and you wanna call that the best you can do?

TROY. I'm going over to the hospital to see Alberta. She went into the hospital this afternoon. Look like she might have the baby early. I won't be gone long.

ROSE. Well, you ought to know. They went over to Miss Pearl's and got Gabe today. She said you told them to go ahead and lock him up.

TROY. I ain't said no such thing. Whoever told you that is telling a lie. Pearl ain't doing nothing but telling a big fat lie.

ROSE. She ain't had to tell me. I read it on the papers.

TROY. I ain't told them nothing of the kind.

ROSE. I saw it right there on the papers.

TROY. What it say, huh?

ROSE. It said you told them to take him.

TROY. Then they screwed that up, just the way they screw up everything. I ain't worried about what they got on the paper.

ROSE. Say the government send part of his check to the hospital and the other part to you.

TROY. I ain't got nothing to do with that if that's the way it works. I ain't made up the rules about how it work.

ROSE. You did Gabe just like you did Cory. You wouldn't sign the paper for Cory . . . but you signed for Gabe. You signed that paper.

(*The telephone is heard ringing inside the house.*)

TROY. I told you I ain't signed nothing, woman! The only thing I signed was the release form. Hell, I can't read, I don't know what they had on that paper! I ain't signed nothing about sending Gabe away.

ROSE. I said send him to the hospital . . . you said let him be free . . . now you done went down there and signed him to the hospital for half his money. You went back on yourself, Troy. You gonna have to answer for that.

TROY. See now . . . you been over there talking to Miss Pearl. She done got mad cause she ain't getting Gabe's rent money. That's all it is. She's liable to say anything.

ROSE. Troy, I seen where you signed the paper.

TROY. You ain't seen nothing I signed. What she doing got papers on my brother anyway? Miss Pearl telling a big fat lie. And I'm gonna tell her about it too! You ain't seen nothing I signed. Say . . . you ain't seen nothing I signed.

(*Rose exits into the house to answer the telephone. Presently she returns.*)

ROSE. Troy . . . that was the hospital. Alberta had the baby.

TROY. What she have? What is it?

ROSE. It's a girl.

TROY. I better get on down to the hospital to see her.

ROSE. Troy . . .

TROY. Rose . . . I got to go see her now. That's only right . . . what's the matter . . . the baby's all right, ain't it?

ROSE. Alberta died having the baby.

TROY. Died . . . you say she's dead? Alberta's dead?

ROSE. They said they done all they could. They couldn't do nothing for her.

TROY. The baby? How's the baby?

ROSE. They say it's healthy. I wonder who's gonna bury her.

TROY. She had family, Rose. She wasn't living in the world by herself.

ROSE. I know she wasn't living in the world by herself.

TROY. Next thing you gonna want to know if she had any insurance.

ROSE. Troy, you ain't got to talk like that.

TROY. That's the first thing that jumped out your mouth. "Who's gonna bury her?" Like I'm fixing to take on that task for myself.

ROSE. I am your wife. Don't push me away.

TROY. I ain't pushing nobody away. Just give me some space. That's all. Just give me some room to breathe.

(*Rose exists into the house. Troy walks about the yard.*)

TROY (*with a quiet rage that threatens to consume him*). All right . . . Mr. Death. See now . . . I'm gonna tell you what I'm gonna do. I'm gonna take and build me a fence around this yard. See? I'm gonna build me a fence around what belongs to me. And then I want you to stay on the other side. See? You stay over there until you're ready for me. Then you come on. Bring your army. Bring your sickle. Bring your wrestling clothes. I ain't gonna fall down on my vigilance this time. You ain't gonna sneak up on me no more. When you ready for me . . . when the top of your list say Troy Maxson . . . that's when you come around here. You come up and knock on the front door. Ain't nobody else got nothing to do with this. This is between you and me. Man to man. You stay on the other side of that fence until you ready for me. Then you

come up and knock on the front door. Anytime you want. I'll be ready for you.

(*The lights go down to black.*)

SCENE 3

The lights come up on the porch. It is late evening three days later. Rose sits listening to the ball game waiting for Troy. The final out of the game is made and Rose switches off the radio. Troy enters the yard carrying an infant wrapped in blankets. He stands back from the house and calls.

Rose enters and stands on the porch. There is a long, awkward silence, the weight of which grows heavier with each passing second.

TROY. Rose . . . I'm standing here with my daughter in my arms. She ain't but a wee bittie little old thing. She don't know nothing about grownups' business. She innocent . . . and she ain't got no mama.

ROSE. What you telling me for, Troy?

(*She turns and exits into the house.*)

TROY. Well . . . I guess we'll just sit out here on the porch.

(*He sits down on the porch. There is an awkward indelicateness about the way he handles the baby. His largeness engulfs and seems to swallow it. He speaks loud enough for Rose to hear.*)

A man's got to do what's right for him. I ain't sorry for nothing I done. It felt right in my heart. (*To the baby.*) What you smiling at? Your daddy's a big man. Got these great big old hands. But sometimes he's scared. And right now your daddy's scared cause we sitting out here and ain't got no home. Oh, I been homeless before. I ain't had no little baby with me. But I been homeless. You just be out on the road by your lonesome and you see one of them trains coming and you just kinda go like this . . .

(*He sings as a lullaby.*)

    Please, Mr. Engineer let a man ride the line
    Please, Mr. Engineer let a man ride the line
    I ain't got no ticket please let me ride the blinds.

(*Rose enters from the house. Troy, hearing her steps behind him, stands and faces her.*)

She's my daughter, Rose. My own flesh and blood. I can't deny her no more than I can deny them boys. (*Pause.*) You and them boys is my family. You and them and this child is all I got in the world. So I guess what I'm saying is . . . I'd appreciate it if you'd help me take care of her.

ROSE. Okay, Troy . . . you're right. I'll take care of your baby for you . . . cause . . . like you say . . . she's innocent . . .

and you can't visit the sins of the father upon the child. A motherless child has got a hard time. (*She takes the baby from him.*) From right now . . . this child got a mother. But you a womanless man.

(*Rose turns and exits into the house with the baby. Lights go down to black.*)

SCENE 4

It is two months later. Lyons enters the street. He knocks on the door and calls.

LYONS. Hey, Rose! (*Pause.*) Rose!

ROSE (*from inside the house*). Stop that yelling. You gonna wake up Raynell. I just got her to sleep.

LYONS. I just stopped by to pay Papa this twenty dollars I owe him. Where's Papa at?

ROSE. He should be here in a minute. I'm getting ready to go down to the church. Sit down and wait on him.

LYONS. I got to go pick up Bonnie over her mother's house.

ROSE. Well, sit it down there on the table. He'll get it.

LYONS (*enters the house and sets the money on the table*). Tell Papa I said thanks. I'll see you again.

ROSE. All right, Lyons. We'll see you.

(*Lyons starts to exit as Cory enters.*)

CORY. Hey, Lyons.

LYONS. What's happening, Cory? Say man, I'm sorry I missed your graduation. You know I had a gig and couldn't get away. Otherwise, I would have been there, man. So what you doing?

CORY. I'm trying to find a job.

LYONS. Yeah I know how that go, man. It's rough out here. Jobs are scarce.

CORY. Yeah, I know.

LYONS. Look here, I got to run. Talk to Papa . . . he know some people. He'll be able to help get you a job. Talk to him . . . see what he say.

CORY. Yeah . . . all right, Lyons.

LYONS. You take care. I'll talk to you soon. We'll find some time to talk.

(*Lyons exits the yard. Cory wanders over to the tree, picks up the bat, and assumes a batting stance. He studies an imaginary pitcher and swings. Dissatisfied with the result, he tries again. Troy enters. They eye each other for a beat. Cory puts the bat down and exits the yard. Troy starts into the house as Rose exits with Raynell. She is carrying a cake.*)

TROY. I'm coming in and everybody's going out.

ROSE. I'm taking this cake down to the church for the bake sale. Lyons was by to see you. He stopped by to pay you your twenty dollars. It's laying in there on the table.

TROY (*going into his pocket*). Well . . . here go this money.

ROSE. Put it in there on the table, Troy. I'll get it.

TROY. What time you coming back?

ROSE. Ain't no use in you studying me. It don't matter what time I come back.

TROY. I just asked you a question, woman. What's the matter . . . can't I ask you a question?

ROSE. Troy, I don't want to go into it. Your dinner's in there on the stove. All you got to do is heat it up. And don't you be eating the rest of them cakes in there. I'm coming back for them. We having a bake sale at the church tomorrow.

(*Rose exits the yard. Troy sits down on the steps, takes a pint bottle from his pocket, opens it, and drinks. He begins to sing.*)

TROY.

Hear it ring! Hear it ring!
Had an old dog his name was Blue
You know Blue was mighty true
You know Blue as a good old dog
Blue trees a possum in a hollow log
You know from that he was a good old dog.

(*Bono enters the yard.*)

BONO. Hey, Troy.

TROY. Hey, what's happening, Bono?

BONO. I just thought I'd stop by to see you.

TROY. What you stop by and see me for? You ain't stopped by in a month of Sundays. Hell, I must owe you money or something.

BONO. Since you got your promotion I can't keep up with you. Used to see you every day. Now I don't even know what route you working.

TROY. They keep switching me around. Got me out in Greentree now . . . hauling white folks' garbage.

BONO. Greentree, huh? You lucky, at least you ain't got to be lifting them barrels. Damn if they ain't getting heavier. I'm gonna put in my two years and call it quits.

TROY. I'm thinking about retiring myself.

BONO. You got it easy. You can drive for another five years.

TROY. It ain't the same, Bono. It ain't like working the back of the truck. Ain't got nobody to talk to . . . feel like you working by yourself. Naw, I'm thinking about retiring. How's Lucille?

BONO. She all right. Her arthritis get to acting up on her sometime. Saw Rose on my way in. She going down to the church, huh?

TROY. Yeah, she took up going down there. All them preachers looking for somebody to fatten their pockets. (*Pause.*) Got some gin here.

BONO. Naw, thanks. I just stopped by to say hello.

TROY. Hell, nigger . . . you can take a drink. I ain't never known you to say no to a drink. You ain't got to work tomorrow.

BONO. I just stopped by. I'm fixing to go over to Skinner's. We got us a domino game going over his house every Friday.

TROY. Nigger, you can't play no dominoes. I used to whup you four games out of five.

BONO. Well, that learned me. I'm getting better.

TROY. Yeah? Well, that's all right.

BONO. Look here . . . I got to be getting on. Stop by sometime, huh?

TROY. Yeah, I'll do that, Bono. Lucille told Rose you bought her a new refrigerator.

BONO. Yeah, Rose told Lucille you had finally built your fence . . . so I figured we'd call it even.

TROY. I knew you would.

BONO. Yeah . . . okay. I'll be talking to you.

TROY. Yeah, take care, Bono. Good to see you. I'm gonna stop over.

BONO. Yeah. Okay, Troy.

(*Bono exits. Troy drinks from the bottle.*)

TROY.

>Old Blue died and I dig his grave
>Let him down with a golden chain
>Every night when I hear old Blue bark
>I know Blue treed a possum in Noah's Ark.
>Hear it ring! Hear it ring!

(*Cory enters the yard. They eye each other for a beat. Troy is sitting in the middle of the steps. Cory walks over.*)

CORY. I got to get by.

TROY. Say what? What's you say?

CORY. You in my way. I got to get by.

TROY. You got to get by where? This is my house. Bought and paid for. In full. Took me fifteen years. And if you wanna go in my house and I'm sitting on the steps . . . you say excuse me. Like your mama taught you.

CORY. Come on, Pop . . . I got to get by.

(*Cory starts to maneuver his way past Troy. Troy grabs his leg and shoves him back.*)

TROY. You just gonna walk over top of me?

CORY. I live here too!

TROY (*advancing toward him*). You just gonna walk over top of me in my own house?

CORY. I ain't scared of you.

TROY. I ain't asked if you was scared of me. I asked you if you was fixing to walk over top of me in my own house? That's the question. You ain't gonna say excuse me? You just gonna walk over top of me?

CORY. If you wanna put it like that.

TROY. How else am I gonna put it?

CORY. I was walking by you to go into the house cause you sitting on the steps drunk, singing to yourself. You can put it like that.

TROY. Without saying excuse me???

(*Cory doesn't respond.*)

I asked you a question. Without saying excuse me???

CORY. I ain't got to say excuse me to you. You don't count around here no more.

TROY. Oh, I see . . . I don't count around here no more. You ain't got to say excuse me to your daddy. All of a sudden you done got so grown that your daddy don't count around here no more . . . Around here in his own house and yard that he done paid for with the sweat of his brow. You done got so grown to where you gonna take over. You gonna take over my house. Is that right? You gonna wear my pants. You gonna go in there and stretch out on my bed. You ain't got to say excuse me cause I don't count around here no more. Is that right?

CORY. That's right. You always talking this dumb stuff. Now, why don't you just get out my way?

TROY. I guess you got someplace to sleep and something to put in your belly. You got that, huh? You got that? That's what you need. You got that, huh?

CORY. You don't know what I got. You ain't got to worry about what I got.

TROY. You right! You one hundred percent right! I done spent the last seventeen years worrying about what you got. Now it's your turn, see? I'll tell you what to do. You grown . . . we done established that. You a man. Now, let's see you act like one. Turn your behind around and walk out this yard. And when you get out there in the alley . . . you can forget about this house. See? Cause this is my house. You go on and be a man and get your own house. You can forget about this. Cause this is mine. You go on and get yours cause I'm through with doing for you.

CORY. You talking about what you did for me . . . what'd you ever give me?

TROY. Them feet and bones! That pumping heart, nigger! I give you more than anybody else is ever gonna give you.

CORY. You ain't never gave me nothing! You ain't never done nothing but hold me back. Afraid I was gonna be better than you. All you ever did was try and make me scared of you. I used to tremble every time you called my name. Every time I heard your footsteps in the house. Wondering all the time . . . what's Papa gonna say if I do this? . . . What's he gonna say if I do that? . . . What's Papa gonna say if I turn on the radio? And Mama, too . . . she tries . . . but she's scared of you.

TROY. You leave your mama out of this. She ain't got nothing to do with this.

CORY. I don't know how she stand you . . . after what you did to her.

TROY. I told you to leave your mama out of this!

(*He advances toward Cory.*)

CORY. What you gonna do . . . give me a whupping? You can't whup me no more. You're too old. You just an old man.

TROY (*shoves him on his shoulder*). Nigger! That's what you are. You just another nigger on the street to me!

CORY. You crazy! You know that?

TROY. Go on now! You got the devil in you. Get on away from me!

CORY. You just a crazy old man . . . talking about I got the devil in me.

TROY. Yeah, I'm crazy! If you don't get on the other side of that yard . . . I'm gonna show you how crazy I am! Go on . . . get the hell out of my yard.

CORY. It ain't your yard. You took Uncle Gabe's money he got from the army to buy this house and then you put him out.

TROY (*advances on Cory*). Get your black ass out of my yard!

(*Troy's advance backs Cory up against the tree. Cory grabs up the bat.*)

CORY. I ain't going nowhere! Come on . . . put me out! I ain't scared of you.

TROY. That's my bat!

CORY. Come on!

TROY. Put my bat down!

CORY. Come on, put me out.

(*Cory swings at Troy, who backs across the yard.*)

What's the matter? You so bad . . . put me out!

(*Troy advances toward Cory.*)

CORY (*backing up*). Come on! Come on!

TROY. You're gonna have to use it! You wanna draw that bat back on me . . . you're gonna have to use it.

CORY. Come on! . . . Come on!

(*Cory swings the bat at Troy a second time. He misses. Troy continues to advance toward him.*)

TROY. You're gonna have to kill me! You wanna draw that bat back on me. You're gonna have to kill me.

(*Cory, backed up against the tree, can go no farther. Troy taunts him. He sticks out his head and offers him a target.*)

Come on! Come on!

(*Cory is unable to swing the bat. Troy grabs it.*)

TROY. Then I'll show you.

(*Cory and Troy struggle over the bat. The struggle is fierce and fully engaged. Troy ultimately is the stronger and takes the bat from Cory and stands over him ready to swing. He stops himself.*)

Go on and get away from around my house.

(*Cory, stung by his defeat, picks himself up, walks slowly out of the yard and up the alley.*)

CORY. Tell Mama I'll be back for my things.

TROY. They'll be on the other side of that fence.

(*Cory exits.*)

TROY. I can't taste nothing. Helluljah! I can't taste nothing no more. (*Troy assumes a batting posture and begins to taunt Death, the fastball on the outside corner.*) Come on! It's between you and me now! Come on! Anytime you want! Come on! I be ready for you . . . but I ain't gonna be easy.

(*The lights go down on the scene.*)

SCENE 5

The time is 1965. The lights come up in the yard. It is the morning of Troy's funeral. A funeral plaque with a light hangs beside the door. There is a small garden plot off to the side. There is noise and activity in the house as Rose, Lyons, and Bono have gathered. The door opens and Raynell, seven years old, enters dressed in a flannel night-gown. She crosses to the garden and pokes around with a stick. Rose calls from the house.

ROSE. Raynell!

RAYNELL. Mam?

ROSE. What you doing out there?

RAYNELL. Nothing.

(*Rose comes to the door.*)

ROSE. Girl, get in here and get dressed. What you doing?

RAYNELL. Seeing if my garden growed.

ROSE. I told you it ain't gonna grow overnight. You got to wait.

RAYNELL. It don't look like it never gonna grow. Dag!

ROSE. I told you a watched pot never boils. Get in here and get dressed.

RAYNELL. This ain't even no pot, Mama.

ROSE. You just have to give it a chance. It'll grow. Now you come on and do what I told you. We got to be getting ready. This ain't no morning to be playing around. You hear me?

RAYNELL. Yes, mam.

(*Rose exits into the house. Raynell continues to poke at her garden with a stick. Cory enters. He is dressed in a Marine corporal's uniform, and carries a duffelbag. His posture is that of a military man, and his speech has a clipped sternness.*)

CORY (*to Raynell*). Hi. (*Pause.*) I bet your name is Raynell.

RAYNELL. Uh huh.

CORY. Is your mama home?

(*Raynell runs up on the porch and calls through the screen door.*)

RAYNELL. Mama . . . there's some man out here. Mama?

(*Rose comes to the door.*)

ROSE. Cory? Lord have mercy! Look here, you all!

(*Rose and Cory embrace in a tearful reunion as Bono and Lyons enter from the house dressed in funeral clothes.*)

BONO. Aw, looka here . . .

ROSE. Done got all grown up!

CORY. Don't cry, Mama. What you crying about?

ROSE. I'm just so glad you made it.

CORY. Hey Lyons. How you doing, Mr. Bono.

(*Lyons goes to embrace Cory.*)

LYONS. Look at you, man. Look at you. Don't he look good, Rose. Got them Corporal stripes.

ROSE. What took you so long?

CORY. You know how the Marines are, Mama. They got to get all their paperwork straight before they let you do anything.

ROSE. Well, I'm sure glad you made it. They let Lyons come. Your Uncle Gabe's still in the hospital. They don't know if they gonna let him out or not. I just talked to them a little while ago.

LYONS. A Corporal in the United States Marines.

BONO. Your daddy knew you had it in you. He used to tell me all the time.

LYONS. Don't he look good, Mr. Bono?

BONO. Yeah, he remind me of Troy when I first met him. (*Pause.*) Say, Rose, Lucille's down at the church with the choir. I'm gonna go down and get the pallbearers lined up. I'll be back to get you all.

ROSE. Thanks, Jim.

CORY. See you, Mr. Bono.

LYONS (*with his arm around Raynell*). Cory . . . look at Raynell. Ain't she precious? She gonna break a whole lot of hearts.

ROSE. Raynell, come and say hello to your brother. This is your brother, Cory. You remember Cory.

RAYNELL. No, Mam.

CORY. She don't remember me, Mama.

ROSE. Well, we talk about you. She heard us talk about you. (*To Raynell.*) This is your brother, Cory. Come on and say hello.

RAYNELL. Hi.

CORY. Hi. So you're Raynell. Mama told me a lot about you.

ROSE. You all come on into the house and let me fix you some breakfast. Keep up your strength.

CORY. I ain't hungry, Mama.

LYONS. You can fix me something, Rose. I'll be in there in a minute.

ROSE. Cory, you sure you don't want nothing? I know they ain't feeding you right.

CORY. No, Mama . . . thanks. I don't feel like eating. I'll get something later.

ROSE. Raynell . . . get on upstairs and get that dress on like I told you.

(*Rose and Raynell exit into the house.*)

LYONS. So . . . I hear you thinking about getting married.

CORY. Yeah, I done found the right one, Lyons. It's about time.

LYONS. Me and Bonnie been split up about four years now. About the time Papa retired. I guess she just got tired of all them changes I was putting her through. (*Pause.*) I always knew you was gonna make something out yourself. Your head was always in the right direction. So . . . you gonna stay in . . . make it a career . . . put in your twenty years?

CORY. I don't know. I got six already, I think that's enough.

LYONS. Stick with Uncle Sam and retire early. Ain't nothing out here. I guess Rose told you what happened with me. They got me down the workhouse. I thought I was being slick cashing other people's checks.

CORY. How much time you doing?

LYONS. They give me three years. I got that beat now. I ain't got but nine more months. It ain't so bad. You learn to deal with it like anything else. You got to take the crookeds with the straights. That's what Papa used to say. He used to say that when he struck out. I seen him strike out three times in a row . . . and the next time up he hit the ball over the grandstand. Right out there in Homestead Field. He wasn't satisfied hitting in the seats . . . he want to hit it over everything! After the game he had two hundred people standing around waiting to shake his hand. You got to take the crookeds with the straights. Yeah, Papa was something else.

CORY. You still playing?

LYONS. Cory . . . you know I'm gonna do that. There's some fellows down there we got us a band . . . we gonna try and stay together when we get out . . . but yeah, I'm still playing. It still helps me to get out of bed in the morning. As long as it do that I'm gonna be right there playing and trying to make some sense out of it.

ROSE (*calling*). Lyons, I got these eggs in the pan.

LYONS. Let me go on and get these eggs, man. Get ready to go bury Papa. (*Pause.*) How you doing? You doing all right?

(*Cory nods. Lyons touches him on the shoulder and they share a moment of silent grief. Lyons exits into the house. Cory wanders about the yard. Raynell enters.*)

RAYNELL. Hi.

CORY. Hi.

RAYNELL. Did you used to sleep in my room?

CORY. Yeah . . . that used to be my room.

RAYNELL. That's what Papa call it. "Cory's room." It got your football in the closet.

(*Rose comes to the door.*)

ROSE. Raynell, get in there and get them good shoes on.

RAYNELL. Mama, can't I wear these? Them other one hurt my feet.

ROSE. Well, they just gonna have to hurt your feet for a while. You ain't said they hurt your feet when you went down to the store and got them.

RAYNELL. They didn't hurt then. My feet done got bigger.

ROSE. Don't you give me no backtalk now. You get in there and get them shoes on.

(*Raynell exits into the house.*)

Ain't too much changed. He still got that piece of rag tied to that tree. He was out here swinging that bat. I was just ready to go back in the house. He swung that bat and then he just fell over. Seem like he swung it and stood there with this grin on his face . . . and then he just fell over. They carried him on down to the hospital, but I knew there wasn't no need . . . why don't you come on in the house?

CORY. Mama . . . I got something to tell you. I don't know how to tell you this . . . but I've got to tell you . . . I'm not going to Papa's funeral.

ROSE. Boy, hush your mouth. That's your daddy you talking about. I don't want hear that kind of talk this morning. I done raised you to come to this? You standing there all healthy and grown talking about you ain't going to your daddy's funeral?

CORY. Mama . . . listen . . .

ROSE. I don't want to hear it, Cory. You just get that thought out of your head.

CORY. I can't drag Papa with me everywhere I go. I've got to say no to him. One time in my life I've got to say no.

ROSE. Don't nobody have to listen to nothing like that. I know you and your daddy ain't seen eye to eye, but I ain't got to listen to that kind of talk this morning. Whatever was between you and your daddy . . . the time has come to put it aside. Just take it and set it over there on the shelf and forget about it. Disrespecting your daddy ain't gonna make you a man, Cory. You got to find a way to come to that on your own. Not going to your daddy's funeral ain't gonna make you a man.

CORY. The whole time I was growing up . . . living in his house . . . Papa was like a shadow that followed you everywhere. It weighed on you and sunk into your flesh. It would wrap around you and lay there until you couldn't tell which one was you anymore. That shadow digging in your flesh. Trying to crawl in. Trying to live through you. Everywhere I looked, Troy Maxson was staring back at me . . . hiding under the bed . . . in the closet. I'm just saying I've got to find a way to get rid of that shadow, Mama.

ROSE. You just like him. You got him in you good.

CORY. Don't tell me that, Mama.

ROSE. You Troy Maxson all over again.

CORY. I don't want to be Troy Maxson. I want to be me.

ROSE. You can't be nobody but who you are, Cory. That shadow wasn't nothing but you growing into yourself. You either got to grow into it or cut it down to fit you. But that's all you got to make life with. That's all you got to measure yourself against that world out there. Your daddy wanted you to be everything he wasn't . . . and at the same time he tried to make you into everything he was. I don't know if he was right or wrong . . . but I do know he meant to do more good than he meant to do harm. He wasn't always right. Sometimes when he touched he bruised. And sometimes when he took me in his arms he cut.

When I first met your daddy I thought . . . Here is a man I can lay down with and make a baby. That's the first thing I thought when I seen him. I was thirty years old and had done seen my share of men. But when he walked up to me and said, "I can dance a waltz that'll make you dizzy," I thought, Rose Lee, here is a man that you can open yourself up to and be filled to bursting. Here is a man that can fill all them empty spaces you been tipping around the edges of. One of them empty spaces was being somebody's mother.

I married your daddy and settled down to cooking his supper and keeping clean sheets on the bed. When your daddy walked through the house he was so big he filled it up. That was my first mistake. Not to make him leave some room for me. For my part in the matter. But at that time I wanted that. I wanted a house that I could sing in. And that's what your daddy gave me. I didn't know to keep up his strength I had to give up little pieces of mine. I did that. I took on his life as mine and mixed up the pieces so that you couldn't hardly tell which was which anymore. It was my choice. It was my life and I didn't have to live it like that. But that's what life offered me in the way of being a woman and I took it. I grabbed hold of it with both hands.

By the time Raynell came into the house, me and your daddy had done lost touch with one another. I didn't want to make my blessing off of nobody's misfortune . . . but I took on to Raynell like she was all them babies I had wanted and never had.

(*The phone rings.*)

Like I'd been blessed to relive a part of my life. And if the Lord see fit to keep up my strength . . . I'm gonna do her just like your daddy did you . . . I'm gonna give her the best of what's in me.

RAYNELL (*entering, still with her old shoes*). Mama . . . Reverend Tollivier on the phone.

(*Rose exits into the house.*)

RAYNELL. Hi.

CORY. Hi.

RAYNELL. You in the Army or the Marines?

CORY. Marines.

RAYNELL. Papa said it was the Army. Did you know Blue?

CORY. Blue? Who's Blue?

RAYNELL. Papa's dog what he sing about all the time.

CORY (*singing*).

> Hear it ring! Hear it ring!
> I had a dog his name was Blue
> You know Blue was mighty true
> You know Blue was a good old dog
> Blue treed a possum in a hollow log
> You know from that he was a good old dog.
> Hear it ring! Hear it ring!

(*Raynell joins in singing.*)

CORY AND RAYNELL.

> Blue treed a possum out on a limb
> Blue looked at me and I looked at him
> Grabbed that possum and put him in a sack
> Blue stayed there till I came back
> Old Blue's feets was big and round
> Never allowed a possum to touch the ground.
>
> Old Blue died and I dug his grave
> I dug his grave with a silver spade
> Let him down with a golden chain
> And every night I call his name
> Go on Blue, you good dog you
> Go on Blue, you good dog you.

RAYNELL.

> Blue laid down and died like a man
> Blue laid down and died . . .

BOTH.

> Blue laid down and died like a man
> Now he's treeing possums in the Promised Land
> I'm gonna tell you this to let you know
> Blue's gone where the good dogs go
> When I hear old Blue bark
> When I hear old Blue bark
> Blue treed a possum in Noah's Ark.
> Blue treed a possum in Noah's Ark.

(*Rose comes to the screen door.*)

ROSE. Cory, we gonna be ready to go in a minute.

CORY (*to Raynell*). You go on in the house and change them shoes like Mama told you so we can go to Papa's funeral.

RAYNELL. Okay, I'll be back.

(*Raynell exits into the house. Cory gets up and crosses over to the tree. Rose stands in the screen door watching him. Gabriel enters from the alley.*)

GABRIEL (*calling*). Hey, Rose!

ROSE. Gabe?

GABRIEL. I'm here, Rose. Hey Rose, I'm here!

(*Rose enters from the house.*)

ROSE. Lord . . . Look here, Lyons!

LYONS. See, I told you, Rose . . . I told you they'd let him come.

CORY. How you doing, Uncle Gabe?

LYONS. How you doing, Uncle Gabe?

GABRIEL. Hey, Rose. It's time. It's time to tell St. Peter to open the gates. Troy, you ready? You ready, Troy. I'm gonna tell St. Peter to open the gates. You get ready now.

(*Gabriel, with great fanfare, braces himself to blow. The trumpet is without a mouthpiece. He puts the end of it into his mouth and blows with great force, like a man who has been waiting some twenty-odd years for this single moment. No sound comes out of the trumpet. He braces himself and blows again with the same result. A third time he blows. There is a weight of impossible description that falls away and leaves him bare and exposed to a frightful realization. It is a trauma that a sane and normal mind would be unable to withstand. He begins to dance. A slow, strange dance, eerie and life-giving. A dance of atavistic signature and ritual. Lyons attempts to embrace him. Gabriel pushes Lyons away. He begins to howl in what is an attempt at song, or perhaps a song turning back into itself in an attempt at speech. He finishes his dance and the gates of heaven stand open as wide as God's closet.*

That's the way that go!)

BLACKOUT

TOPICS FOR CRITICAL THINKING AND WRITING

 ## The Play on the PAGE

1. What do you think Bono means when he says, early in Act 2, "Some people build fences to keep people out . . . and some people build fences to keep people in"? Why is the play called *Fences*? What has fenced Troy in? What is Troy fencing in? (Take account of Troy's last speech in Act 2, Scene 2, but do not limit your discussion to this speech.)

2. What do you think Troy's reasons are—conscious and unconscious—for not wanting Cory to play football at college?

3. Compare and contrast Cory and Lyons. Consider, too, in what ways they resemble Troy and in what ways they differ from him.

4. In what ways is Troy like his father, and in what ways unlike him?

5. What do you make out of the prominence given to the song about Blue?

6. There is a good deal of anger in the play, but there is also humor. Which passages do you find humorous, and why?

7. Characterize Rose Maxson.

 ## The Play on the STAGE

8. How would Wilson's remarks in the 1987 interview (see below) help a director in staging *Fences*? For example, his assertion that every person (except Raynell) is institutionalized at the end of the play might suggest a certain tone or mood for a production.

9. In what ways is the role of Gabriel a challenge for an actor? What advice might you give to the other actors on stage during Gabriel's appearances?

10. Some scenes begin by specifying that "the lights come up." Others do not, presumably beginning with an illuminated stage. All scenes except the last one end with the lights going down to blackness. Explain Wilson's use of lighting.

A Context for *Fences*

AUGUST WILSON
Talking about Fences

[Following is part of an interview conducted with David Savran on March 13, 1987.]

Savran: In reading Fences, *I came to view Troy more and more critically as the play progressed, sharing Rose's point of view. We see that Troy has been crippled by his father. That's being replayed in Troy's relationship with Cory. Do you think there's a way out of that cycle?*

Wilson: Surely. First of all, we're all like our parents. The things we are taught early in life, how to respond to the world, our sense of morality—everything, we get from them. Now you can take that legacy and do with it anything you want to do. It's in your hands. Cory is Troy's son. How can he be Troy's son without sharing Troy's values? I was trying to get at why Troy made the choices he made, how they have influenced his values and how he attempts to pass those along to

his son. Each generation gives the succeeding generation what they think they need. One question in the play is, "Are the tools we are given sufficient to compete in a world that is different from the one our parents knew?" I think they are—it's just that we have to do different things with the tools. That's all Troy has to give. Troy's flaw is that he does not recognize that the world was changing. That's because he spent fifteen years in a penitentiary.

As African-Americans, we should demand to participate in society as Africans. That's the way out of the vicious cycle of poverty and neglect that exists in 1987 in America, where you have a huge percentage of blacks living in the equivalent of South African townships, in housing projects. No one is inviting these people to participate in society. Look at the poverty levels—$8,500 for a family of four, if you have $8,501 you're not counted. Those statistics would go up enormously if we had an honest assessment of the cost of living in America. I don't know how anybody can support a family of four on $8,500. What I'm saying is that 85 or 90 percent of blacks in America are living in abject poverty and, for the most part, are crowded into what amount to concentration camps. The situation for blacks in America is worse than it was forty years ago. Some sociologists will tell you about the tremendous progress we've made. They didn't put me out when I walked in the door. And you can always point to someone who works on Wall Street, or is a doctor. But they don't count in the larger scheme of things.

Do you have any idea how these political changes could take place?

I'm not sure. I know that blacks must be allowed their cultural differences. I think the process of assimilation to white American society was a big mistake. We don't want to be like you. Blacks living in housing projects are isolated from the society, for the most part—living as they choose, as Africans. Only they don't realize the value in what they're doing because they have accepted their victimization. They've marked themselves as victims. Once they recognize that, they can begin to move through society in a different manner, from a stronger position, and claim what is theirs.

A project of yours is to point up what happens when oppression is internalized.

Yes, transfer of aggression to the wrong target. I think it's interesting that the two roads open to blacks for "full participation" are entertainment and sports. *Ma Rainey* and *Fences*, and I didn't plan it that way. I don't think that they're the correct roads. I think Troy's right. Now with the benefit of historical perspective, I can say that the athletic scholarship was actually a way of exploiting. Now you've got two million kids who think they're going to play in the NBA. In the sixties the universities made a lot of money off of athletics. You had kids playing for free who, by and large, were not getting educated, were taking courses in basketweaving. Some of them could barely read.

Troy may be right about that issue, but it seems that he has passed on certain destructive traits in spite of himself. Take the hostility between father and son.

I think every generation says to the previous generation: you're in my way. I've got to get by. The father-son conflict is actually a normal generational conflict that happens all the time.

So it's a healthy and a good thing?

Oh, sure. Troy is seeing this boy walk around, smelling his piss. Two men cannot live in the same household. Troy would have been tremendously disappointed if Cory had not challenged him. Troy knows that this boy has to go out and do battle with that world: "So I had best prepare him because I know that's a harsh, cruel place out there. But that's going to be easy compared to what he's getting here. Ain't nobody gonna whip your ass like I'm gonna whip it." He has a tremendous love for the kid. But he's not going to say, "I love you," he's going to demonstrate it. He's carrying garbage for seventeen years just for the kid. The only world Troy knows is the one that he made. Cory's going to go on to find another one, he's going to arrive at the same place as Troy. I think one of the most important lines in the play is when Troy is talking about his father: "I got to the place where I could feel him kicking in my blood and knew that the only thing that separated us was the matter of a few years."

Hopefully, Cory will do things a bit differently with his son. For Troy, sports was not the way to go, the white man wouldn't let him get away with that. "Get you a job, with your hands, something that nobody can take away from you." The idea of school—he doesn't know what that is. That's for white folks. Very few blacks had paperwork jobs. But if you knew how to fix cars, you could always make some money. That's what Troy wants for Cory. There aren't many people who ever jumped up in Troy's face. So he's proud of the kid at the same time that he expresses a hurt that all men feel. You got to cut your kid loose at some point. There's that sense of loss and separation. You find out how Troy left his father's house and you see how Cory leaves his house. I suspect with Cory it will repeat with some differences and maybe, after five or six generations, they'll find a different way to do it.

Where Cory ends up is very ambiguous, as a marine in 1965.

Yes. For the average black kid on the street, that was an alternative. You went into the army because you could learn how to do something. I can remember my parents talking about the son of some friends: "He's in the navy. He *did* something"—as opposed to standing on the street corner, shooting drugs, drinking wine, and robbing stores. Lyons says to Cory, "I always knew you were going to make something out of yourself." It really wounds me. He's a corporal in the marines. For blacks, that is a sense of accomplishment. Therein lies one of the tragedies of blacks in America. Cory says, "I don't know. I put in six years. That's enough." Anyone who goes into the army and makes a career out of it is a loser. They sit there and are nurtured by the army and they don't have to confront life. Then they get out of the army and find there's nothing to do. They didn't learn any skills. And if they did, they can't find a job. Four months later, they're shooting dope. In the sixties a whole bunch of blacks went over, fought and died in the Vietnam War. The survivors came back to the same street corners and found out nothing had changed. They still couldn't get a job.

At the end of *Fences* every person, with the exception of Raynell, is institutionalized. Rose is in a church. Lyons is in a penitentiary. Gabriel's in a mental hospital and Cory's in the marines. The only free person is the girl, Troy's daughter, the hope for the future. That was conscious on my part because in '57 that's what I saw. Blacks have relied on institutions which are really foreign—except for the black church, which has been our saving grace. I have some problems with it but I recognize it as a central social organization and sometimes an economic organization for the black community. I would like to see blacks develop their own institutions that respond to their needs.

MARIA IRENE Fornes

Maria Irena Fornes, born to a moderately progressive family in 1930 in Havana, Cuba, was educated in Havana grammar schools. After the death of her father in 1945, she emigrated with her mother to the United States. She worked in a factory, and then at the age of twenty she went to Paris to study painting. While in Paris, Fornes saw the 1953–54 world premier of Beckett's *Waiting for Godot* and it changed her thinking, starting her on the path to a career in the theater. Her first play, *Tango Palace,* described as an absurdist drama, was produced in 1963 in San Francisco. One of the influential founders of the off-off-Broadway movement, Fornes has been described as one of the "mothers" of the American avant-garde. She is the author of over forty plays including *Promenade* (1965), *Fefu and her Friends* (1977), *Danube* (1981), *Mud* (1983), *Sarita* (1984), *Abingdon Square* (1987), *Terra Incognita* (1991), and *The Summer in Gossensass* (1997). In 1968, frustrated by what directors were doing to her plays, she began directing her own plays, and in 1981 she founded the now famous INTAR Hispanic Playwrights Lab in New York, where she helped nurture an impressive generation of Hispanic playwrights that include Milcha Sanchez-Scott, Migdalia Cruz, and Eduardo Machado. Maria Irene Fornes has received many honors and awards including a Rockefeller Foundations grant, a Guggenheim fellowship, National Endowment of the Arts grants, and multiple Obie Awards both as a playwright and a director, including one for *The Conduct of Life* in 1985. In 1982 she was awarded an Obie for Sustained Achievement. The Signature Theater Company of New York did a retrospective season of her plays in their 1999–2000 season.

COMMENTARY ON *THE CONDUCT OF LIFE*

By 1985, Maria Irene Fornes's style and politics were already well established in her contributions to American theater. Her theatrical experimentation is known for melding the formal traditions of American domestic realism with a theatrical form using abrupt, often discontinuous narrative and fragmented characterization. Her wide-ranging, innovative, feminist vision informs her work in various ways. In *The Conduct of Life* (1985) she addresses political issues specific to the Latin community in the Americas: the personal and political costs of dictatorship, class division in marginalized communities, and conflicting attitudes toward sexuality and sexual violence.

The Conduct of Life parallels the vocation of Orlando, a government-sanctioned torturer in an unnamed Latin American dictatorship, with the treatment of his wife, Leticia, and of Nena, a young girl Orlando has abducted and raped time and time again. At the same time, Fornes creates a triad of women in Leticia, Nena, and Olimpia, the housekeeper, divided by class difference and conflicting attitudes toward sexuality, servitude, and domination.

Stage settings and stage directions have always had an important place in Fornes's work. In *Mud* the set is a wooden room perched on a five-foot-high promontory of soft red earth. In *Fefu and Her Friends* the play takes place in various rooms of a country house in New England. The play requires four of the scenes, each in a different room of the house, to play simultaneously. Such requirements have led to some inventive stagings, several of which have taken place in site-specific spaces, such as an actual house or space with multiple rooms. In these instances the audience is mobile, moving from space to space to see each of the different scenes.

Fornes begins *The Conduct of Life* with this stage description: "The floor is divided in four horizontal planes." The details that follow describe a stage that is multileveled, with steps, raised surfaces, and several practical doors. Many critics have argued that the geography of the stage world Fornes describes is fundamental to the playing of the drama. Each level offers a visual clue to the separation and isolation experienced by the characters. At the same time, the stage space is the domestic environment of the characters, the levels appear connected yet contained, a wholly interior world from which there seems to be no possibility of escape.

The play is episodic, its many short scenes appearing almost as brief snapshots, or distilled single moments of time. The dialogue, or lack of dialogue, adds to the episodic style. The characters, each with their own monologues, often tell us what they feel, what they are thinking. Sometimes these words are directed at other characters, but the other characters rarely respond or do nothing with it. As one writer says of Fornes's writing style in *The Conduct of Life* "What is being said often appears to be spoken for the speaker's ears only, and for the audience. Characters listen to each other, they may even comment from time to time on what is being said to them, but they do not *hear*. They do not hear because what is being said to them is often too painful, which is why there is nothing they can do with it" (in Delgado 67).

THE CONDUCT OF LIFE
Maria Irene Fornes

CHARACTERS

ORLANDO, *An army lieutenant at the start of the play. A lieutenant commander soon after.*

LETICIA, *His wife, ten years his elder.*

ALEJO, *A lieutenant commander. Their friend.*

NENA, *A destitute girl of twelve.*

OLIMPIA, *A servant.*

A Latin American country. The present.

The floor is divided into four horizontal planes. Downstage is the livingroom, which is about ten feet deep. Center stage, eighteen inches high, is the diningroom, which is about ten feet deep. Further upstage, eighteen inches high is a hallway which is about four feet deep. At each end of the hallway there is a door. The one to the right leads to the servants' quarters, the one to the left to the basement. Upstage, three feet lower than the hallway (same level as the livingroom), is the cellar, which is about sixteen feet deep. Most of the cellar is occupied by two platforms which are eight feet wide, eight feet deep, and three feet high. Upstage of the cellar are steps that lead up. Approximately ten feet above the cellar is another level, extending from the extreme left to the extreme right, which represents a warehouse. There is a door on the left of the warehouse. On the left and the right of the livingroom there are archways that lead to hallways or antechambers, the floors of these hallways are the same level as the diningroom. On the left and the right of the diningroom there is a second set of archways that lead to hallways or antechambers, the floors of which are the same level as the hallways. All along the edge of each level there is a step that leads to the next level. All floors and steps are black marble. In the livingroom there are two chairs. One is to the left, next to a table with a telephone. The other is to the right. In the diningroom there are a large green marble table and three chairs. On the cellar floor there is a mattress to the right and a chair to the left. In the warehouse there is a table and a chair to the left, and a chair and some boxes and crates to the right.*

SCENE 1

Orlando is doing jumping-jacks in the upper left corner of the diningroom in the dark. A light, slowly, comes up on him. He wears military breeches held by suspenders, and riding boots. He does jumping-jacks as long as it can be endured. He stops, the center area starts to become visible. There is a chair upstage of the table. There is a linen towel on the left side of the table. Orlando dries his face with the towel and sits as he puts the towel around his neck.

ORLANDO. Thirty three and I'm still a lieutenant. In two years I'll receive a promotion or I'll leave the military. I promise I will not spend time feeling sorry for myself.— Instead I will study the situation and draw an effective plan of action. I must eliminate all obstacles.—I will make the acquaintance of people in high power. If I cannot achieve this on my own merit, I will marry a woman in high circles. Leticia must not be an obstacle.—Man must have an ideal, mine is to achieve maximum power. That is my destiny.—No other interest will deter me from this.—My sexual drive is detrimental to my ideals. I must no longer be overwhelmed by sexual passion or I will be degraded beyond hope of recovery. (*Lights fade to black.*)

SCENE 2

Alejo sits to the right of the diningroom table. Orlando stands to Alejo's left. He is now a lieutenant commander. He wears an army tunic, breeches, and boots. Leticia stands to the left. She wears a dress that suggests 1940s fashion.

LETICIA. What! Me go hunting? Do you think I'm going to shoot a deer, the most beautiful animal in the world? Do you think I'm going to destroy a deer? On the contrary, I would run in the field and scream and wave my arms like a mad woman and try to scare them away so the hunters could not reach them. I'd run in front of the bullets and let the mad hunters kill me—stand in the way of the bullets and let the mad hunters kill me—stand in the way of the bullets—stop the bullets with my body. I don't see how anyone can shoot a deer.

ORLANDO (*To Alejo*). Do you understand that? You, who are her friend, can you understand that? You don't think that is madness? She's mad. Tell her that—she'll think it's you who's mad. (*To Leticia.*) Hunting is a sport! A skill! Don't talk about something you know nothing about. Must you have an opinion about every damn thing! Can't you keep your mouth shut when you don't know what you're talking about? (*Orlando exits right.*)

LETICIA. He told me that he didn't love me, and that his sole relationship to me was simply a marital one. What he means is that I am to keep this house, and he is to provide for it. That's what he said. That explains why he treats me the way he treats me. I never understood why he did, but now it's clear. He doesn't love me. I thought he loved me and that he stayed with me because he loved me and that's why I didn't understand his behavior. But now I know, because he told me that he sees me as a person who runs the house. I never understood that because I would have never—if he had said, "Would you marry me to run my house even if I don't love you." I would have never—I would have never believed what I was hearing. I would have never believed that these words were coming out of his mouth. Because I loved him. (*Orlando has entered, Leticia sees him and exits left. Orlando enters and sits center.*)

ORLANDO. I didn't say any of that. I told her that she's not my heir. That's what I said. I told her that she's not in my will, and she will not receive a penny of my money if I die. That's what I said. I didn't say anything about running the house. I said she will not inherit a penny from me because I didn't want to be humiliated. She is capable of foolishness beyond anyone's imagination. Ask her what she would do if she were rich and could do anything she wants with her money. (*Leticia enters.*)

LETICIA. I would distribute it among the poor.

ORLANDO. She has no respect for money.

LETICIA. That is not true. If I had money I would give it to those who need it. I know what money is, what money can do. It can feed people, it can put a roof over their heads. Money can do that. It can clothe them. What do you know about money? What does it mean to you? What do you do with money? Buy rifles? To shoot deer?

ORLANDO. You're foolish!—You're foolish! You're a foolish woman! (*Orlando exits, He speaks from offstage.*) Foolish. . . . Foolish. . . .

LETICIA. He has no respect for me. He is insensitive. He doesn't listen. You cannot reach him. He is deaf. He is an animal. Nothing touches him except sensuality. He responds to food, to the flesh. To music sometimes, if it is romantic. To the moon. He is romantic but he is not aware of what you are feeling. I can't change him.—I'll tell you why I asked you to come. Because I want something from you.—I want you to educate me. I want to study. I want to study so I am not an ignorant person. I want to go to the university. I want to be knowledgeable. I'm tired of being ignored. I want to study political sci-

ence. Is political science what diplomats study? Is that what it is? You have to teach me elemental things because I never finished grammar school. I would have to study a great deal. A great deal so I could enter the university. I would have to go through all the subjects. I would like to be a woman who speaks in a group and have others listen.

ALEJO. Why do you want to worry about any of that? What's the use? Do you think you can change anything? Do you think anyone can change anything?

LETICIA. Why not? (*Pause.*) Do you think I'm crazy?—He can't help it.—Do you think I'm crazy?—Because I love him? (*He looks away from her. Lights fade to black.*)

SCENE 3

Orlando enters the warehouse holding Nena close to him. She wears a gray over-large uniform. She is barefoot. She resists him. She is tearful and frightened. She pulls away and runs to the right wall. He follows her.

ORLANDO (*Softly*). You called me a snake.

NENA. No, I didn't. (*He tries to reach her. She pushes his hands away from her.*) I was kidding.—I swear I was kidding.

(*He graves her and pushes her against the wall. He pushes his pelvis against her. He moves to the chair dragging her with him. She crawls to the left, pushes the table aside and stands behind it. He walks around the table. She goes under it. He grabs her foot and pulls her out toward the downstage side. He opens his fly and pushes his pelvis against her. Lights fade to black.*)

SCENE 4

Olimpia is wiping crumbs off the diningroom table. She wears a plain gray uniform. Leticia sits to the left of the table facing front. She wears a dressing gown. She writes in a notebook. There is some silverware on the table. Olimpia has a speech defect.

LETICIA. Let's do this.

OLIMPIA. O.K. (*She continues wiping the table.*)

LETICIA (*Still writing*). What are you doing?

OLIMPIA. I'm doing what I always do.

LETICIA. Let's do this.

OLIMPIA. Let's do this.

OLIMPIA (*In a mumble.*). As soon as I finish doing this. You can't just ask me to do what you want me to do, and interrupt what I'm doing. I don't stop from the time I wake up in the morning to the time I go to sleep. You can't interrupt me whenever you want, not if you want me to get to the end of my work. I wake up at 5:30. I wash. I put on my clothes and make my bed. I go to the kitchen. I get the milk and the bread from outside and I put them on the counter. I open the icebox. I put one bottle in and take the butter out. I leave the other bottle on the counter. I shut the refrigerator door. I take the pan that I use for water and put water in it. I know how much. I put the pan on the stove, light the stove, cover it. I take the top off the milk and pour it in the milk pan except for a little. (*Indicating with her finger.*) Like this. For the cat. I put the pan on the stove, light the stove. I put coffee in the thing. I know how much. I light the oven and put bread in it. I come here, get the tablecloth and I lay it on the table. I shout "Breakfast." I get the napkins. I take the cups, the saucers, and the silver out and set the table. I go to the kitchen. I put the tray on the counter, put the butter on the tray. The water and the milk are getting hot. I pick up the cat's dish. I wash it. I pour the milk I left in the bottle in the milk dish. I put it on the floor for the cat. I shout "Breakfast." The water boils. I pour it in the thing. When the milk boils I turn off the gas and cover the milk. I get the bread from the oven. I slice it down the middle and butter it. Then I cut it in pieces (*indicating*) this big. I set a piece aside for me. I put the rest of the bread in the bread dish and shout "Breakfast." I pour the coffee in the coffee pot and the milk in the milk pitcher, except I leave (*indicating*) this much for me. I put them on the tray and bring them here. If you're not in the diningroom I call again. "Breakfast." I go to the kitchen, I fill the milk pan with water and let it soak. I pour my coffee, sit at the counter and eat my breakfast. I go upstairs to make your bed and clean your bathroom. I come down here to meet you and figure out what you want for lunch and dinner. And try to get you to think quickly so I can run to the market and get it bought before all the fresh stuff is bought up. Then, I start the day.

LETICIA. So?

OLIMPIA. So I need a steam pot.

LETICIA. What is a steam pot?

OLIMPIA. A pressure cooker.

LETICIA. And you want a steam pot? Don't you have enough pots?

OLIMPIA. No.

LETICIA. Why do you want a steam pot?

OLIMPIA. It cooks faster.

LETICIA. How much is it?

OLIMPIA. Expensive.

LETICIA. How much?

OLIMPIA. Twenty.

LETICIA. Too expensive. (*Olimpia throws the silver on the floor. Leticia turns her eyes up to the ceiling.*) Why do you want one more pot?

OLIMPIA. I don't have a steam pot.

LETICIA. A pressure cooker.

OLIMPIA. A pressure cooker.

LETICIA. You have too many pots. (*Olimpia goes to the kitchen and returns with an aluminum pan. She shows it to Leticia.*)

OLIMPIA. Look at this. (*Leticia looks at it.*)

LETICIA. What? (*Olimpia hits the pan against the back of a chair, breaking off a piece of the bottom.*)

OLIMPIA. It's no good.

LETICIA. All right! (*She takes money from her pocket and gives it to Olimpia.*) Here. Buy it!—What are we having for lunch?

OLIMPIA. Fish.

LETICIA. I don't like fish.—What else?

OLIMPIA. Boiled plantains.

LETICIA. Make something I like.

OLIMPIA. Avocados. (*Leticia gives a look of resentment to Olimpia.*)

LETICIA. Why can't you make something I like?

OLIMPIA. Avocados.

LETICIA. Something that needs cooking.

OLIMPIA. Bread pudding.

LETICIA. And for dinner?

OLIMPIA. Pot roast.

LETICIA. What else?

OLIMPA. Rice.

LETICIA. What else?

OLIMPIA. Salad.

LETICIA. What kind?

OLIMPIA. Avocado.

LETICIA. Again. (*Olimpia looks at Leticia.*)

OLIMPA. You like avocados.

LETICIA. Not again.—Tomatoes. (*Olimpia mumbles.*) What's wrong with tomatoes besides that you don't like them? (*Olimpia mumbles.*) Get some. (*Olimpia mumbles.*) What does that mean? (*Olimpia doesn't answer.*) Buy tomatoes.—What else?

OLIMPIA. That's all.

LETICIA. We need a green.

OLIMPIA. Watercress.

LETICIA. What else?

OLIMPIA. Nothing.

LETICIA. For dessert.

OLIMPIA. Bread pudding.

LETICIA. Again.

OLIMPIA. Why not.?

LETICIA. Make a flan.

OLIMPIA. No flan.

LETICIA. Why not?

OLIMPIA. No good.

LETICIA. Why no good!—Buy some fruit then.

OLIMPIA. What kind?

LETICIA. Pineapple. (*Olimpia shakes her head.*) Why not? (*Olimpia shakes her head.*) Mango.

OLIMPIA. No mango.

LETICIA. Buy some fruit! That's all. Don't forget bread. (*Leticia hands Olimpia some bills. Olimpia holds it and waits for more. Leticia hands her one more bill. Lights fade to black.*)

SCENE 5

The warehouse table is propped against the door. The chair on the left faces right. The door is pushed and the table falls to the floor. Orlando enters. He wears an undershirt with short sleeves, breeches with suspenders and boots. He looks around the room for Nena. Believing she has escaped, he becomes still and downcast. He turns to the door and stands there for a moment. He takes a few steps to the right and stands there staring fixedly. He hears a sound from behind the boxes, walks to them and takes a box off. Nena is there. Her head is covered with a blanket. He pulls the blanket off. Nena is motionless and staring into space. He looks at her for a while, then walks to the chair and sits facing right staring into space. A few moments pass. Lights fade to black.

SCENE 6

Leticia speaks on the telephone to Mona.

LETICIA. Since they moved him to the new department he's different. (*Brief pause.*) He's distracted. I don't know where he goes in his mind. He doesn't listen to me. He worries. When I talk to him he doesn't listen. He's thinking about the job. He says he worries. What is there to worry about? Do you think there is anything to worry about? (*Brief pause.*) What meeting? (*Brief pause.*) Oh, sure. When is it? (*Brief pause.*) At what time? What do you mean I knew? No one told me.—I don't remember. Would you pick me up? (*Brief pause.*) At one? Isn't one early? (*Brief pause.*) Orlando may still be home at one. Sometimes he's here a little longer than usual. After lunch he sits and smokes. Don't you think one thirty will give us enough time? (*Brief pause.*) No. I can't leave while he's smoking . . . I'd rather not. I'd rather wait till he leaves. (*Brief pause.*) . . . One thirty, then. Thank you, Mona. (*Brief pause.*) See you then. Bye. (*Leticia puts down the receiver and walks to stage right area. Orlando's voice is heard offstage left. He and Alejo enter halfway through the following speech.*)

ORLANDO. He made loud sounds not high-pitched like a horse. He sounded like a whale, like a wounded whale. He was pouring liquid from everywhere, his mouth, his nose, his eyes. He was not a horse but a sexual organ.— Helpless. A viscera.—Screaming. Making strange sounds. He collapsed on top of her. She wanted him off but he collapsed on top of her and stayed there on top of her. Like gum. He looked more like a whale than a horse. A seal. His muscles were soft. What does it feel like to be without shape like that. Without pride. She was indifferent. He stayed there for a while and then lifted himself off her and to the ground. (*Pause.*) He looked like a horse again.

LETICIA. Alejo, how are you? (*Alejo kisses Leticia's hand.*)

ORLANDO (*As he walks to the livingroom. He sits left facing front*). Alejo is staying for dinner.

LETICIA. Would you like some coffee?

ALEJO. Yes, thank you.

LETICIA. Would you like some coffee, Orlando?

ORLANDO. Yes, thank you.

LETICIA. (*In a loud voice towards the kitchen*) Olimpia . . .

OLIMPIA. What?

LETICIA. Coffee . . . (*Leticia sits to the right of the table. Alejo sits center.*)

ALEJO. Have you heard?

LETICIA. Yes, he's dead and I'm glad he's dead. An evil man. I knew he'd be killed. Who killed him?

ALEJO. Someone who knew him.

LETICIA. What is there to gain? So he's murdered. Someone else will do the job. Nothing will change. To destroy them all is to say we destroy us all.

ALEJO. Do you think we're all rotten?

LETICIA. Yes.

ORLANDO. A bad germ?

LETICIA. Yes.

ORLANDO. In our hearts?

LETICIA. Yes.—In our eyes.

ORLANDO. You're silly.

LETICIA. We're blind. We can't see beyond an arm's reach. We don't believe our life will last beyond the day. We only know what we have in our hand to put in our mouth, to put in our stomach, and to put in our pocket. We take care of our pocket, but not of our country. We take care of our stomachs but not of our hungry. We are primitive. We don't believe in the future Each night when the sun goes down we think that's the end of life— so we have one last fling. We don't think we have a future. We don't think we have a country. Ask anybody, "Do you have a country?" They'll say, "Yes." Ask them, "What is your country?" They'll say, "My bed, my dinner plate." But, things can change. They can. I have changed. You have changed. He has changed.

ALEJO. Look at me. I used to be an idealist. Now I don't have any feeling for anything. I used to be strong, healthy. I looked at the future with hope.

LETICIA. Now you don't?

ALEJO. Now I don't. I know what viciousness is.

ORLANDO. What is viciousness?

ALEJO. You.

ORLANDO. Me?

ALEJO. The way you tortured Felo.

ORLANDO. I never tortured Felo.

ALEJO. You did.

ORLANDO. Boys play that way. You did too.

ALEJO. I didn't.

ORLANDO. He was repulsive to us.

ALEJO. I never hurt him.

ORLANDO. Well, you never stopped me.

ALEJO. I didn't know how to stop you. I didn't know anyone could behave the way you did. It frightened me. It changed me. I became hopeless. (*Orlando walks to the diningroom.*)

ORLANDO. You were always hopeless. (*He exits. Olimpia enters carrying three demitasse coffees on a tray. She places them on the table and exits.*)

ALEJO. I am sexually impotent. I have no feelings. Things pass through me which resemble feelings but I know they are not. I'm impotent.

LETICIA. Nonsense.

ALEJO. It's not nonsense. How can you say it's nonsense?— How can one live in a world that festers the way ours does and take any pleasure in life? (*Lights fade to black.*)

SCENE 7

Nena and Orlando stand against the wall in the warehouse. She is fully dressed. He is barebreasted. He pushes his pelvis against her gently. His lips touch her face as he speaks. The words are inaudible to the audience. On the table there is a tin plate with food and a tin cup with milk.

ORLANDO. Look this way. I'm going to do something to you. (*She makes a move away from him.*) Don't do that. Don't move away. (*As he slides his hand along her side.*) I just want to put my hand here like this. (*He puts his lips on hers softly and speaks at the same time.*) Don't hold your lips so tight. Make them soft. Let them loose. So I can do this. (*She whimpers.*) Don't cry. I won't hurt you. This is all I'm going to do to you. Just hold your lips soft. Be nice. Be a nice girl. (*He pushes against her and reaches an orgasm. He remains motionless for a moment, then steps away from her still leaning his hand on the wall.*) Go eat. I brought you food. (*She goes to the table. He sits on the floor and watches her eat. She eats voraciously. She looks at the milk.*) Drink it. It's milk. It's good for you. (*She drinks the milk, then continues eating. Lights fade to black.*)

SCENE 8

Leticia stands left of the diningroom table. She speaks words she has memorized. Olimpia sits to the left of the table. She holds a book close to her eyes. Her head moves from left to right along the written words as she mumbles the sound of imaginary words. She continues doing this through the rest of the scene.

LETICIA. The impact of war is felt particularly in the economic realm. The destruction of property, private as well as public may paralyze the country. Foreign investment is virtually . . . (*To Olimpia.*) Is that right? (*Pause.*) Is that right!

OLIMPIA. Wait a moment. (*She continues mumbling and moving her head.*)

LETICIA. What for? (*Pause.*) You can't read. (*Pause.*) You can't read!

OLIMPIA. Wait a moment. (*She continues mumbling and moving her head.*)

LETICIA (*Slapping the book off Olimpia's hand.*). Why are you pretending you can read? (*Olimpia slaps Leticia's hands. They slap each other's hands. Lights fade to black.*)

SCENE 9

Orlando sits in the livingroom. He smokes. He faces front and is thoughtful. Leticia and Olimpia are in the diningroom. Leticia wears a hat and jacket. She tries to put a leather strap through the loops of a suitcase. There is a smaller piece of luggage on the floor.

LETICIA. This strap is too wide. It doesn't fit through the loop. (*Orlando doesn't reaply.*) Is this the right strap? Is this the strap that came with this suitcase? Did the strap that came with the suitcase break? If so, where is it? And when did it break? Why doesn't this strap fit the suitcase and how did it get here. Did you buy this strap, Orlando?

ORLANDO. I may have.

LETICIA. It doesn't fit.

ORLANDO. Hm.

LETICIA. It doesn't fit through the loops.

ORLANDO. Just strap it outside the loops. (*Leticia stands. Olimpia tries to put the strap through the loop.*)

LETICIA. No. You're supposed to put it through the loops. That's what the loops are for. What happened to the other strap?

ORLANDO. It broke.

LETICIA. How?

ORLANDO. I used it for something.

LETICIA. What! (*He looks at her.*) You should have gotten me one that fit. What did you use it for?—Look at that.

ORLANDO. Strap it outside the loops.

LETICIA. That wouldn't look right.

ORLANDO (*Going to look at the suitcase.*). Why do you need the straps?

LETICIA. Because they come with it.

ORLANDO. You don't need them.

LETICIA. And travel like this?

ORLANDO. Use another suitcase.

LETICIA. What other suitcase. I don't have another. (*Orlando looks at his watch.*)

ORLANDO. You're going to miss your plane.

LETICIA. I'm not going. I'm not travelling like this.

ORLANDO. Go without it. I'll send it to you.

LETICIA. You'll get new luggage, repack it and send it to me?—All right. (*She starts to exit left.*) It's nice to travel light. (*Off stage.*) Do I have everything?—Come, Olimpia.

(*Olimpia follows with the suitcases. Orlando takes the larger suitcase from Olimpia. She exits. Orlando goes up the hallway and exists through the left door. A moment later he enters holding Nena close to him. She is pale, dishevelled and has black circles around her eyes. She has a high fever and is almost unconscious. Her dress is torn and soiled. She is barefoot. He carries a new cotton dress on his arm. He takes her to the chair in the livingroom. He takes off the soiled dress and puts the new dress on her over a soiled slip.)*

ORLANDO. That's nice. You look nice. (*Leticia's voice is heard. He hurriedly takes Nena out the door, closes it, and leans on it.*)

LETICIA (*Off stage*). It would take but a second. You run to the garage and get the little suitcase and I'll take out the things I need. (*Leticia and Olimpia enter left. Olimpia exits right.*) Hurry. Hurry. It would take but a second. (*Seeing Orlando.*) Orlando, I came back because I couldn't leave without anything at all. I came to get a few things because I have a smaller suitcase where I can take a few things. (*She puts the suitcase on the table, opens it and takes out the things she mentions.*) A pair of shoes . . . (*Olimpia enters right with a small suitcase.*)

OLIMPIA. Here.

LETICIA.	OLIMPIA.
A nightgown,	A robe
a robe,	a dress,
underwear,	a nightgown,
a dress,	underwear
a sweater.	a sweater,
	a pair of shoes.

(*Leticia closes the large suitcase. Olimpia closes the smaller suitcase.*)

LETICIA. (*Starting to exit.*) Goodbye.
OLIMPIA. (*Following Leticia*). Goodbye.
ORLANDO. Goodbye. (*Lights fade to black.*)

SCENE 10

Nena is curled on the extreme right of the mattress. Orlando sits on the mattress using Nena as a back support. Alejo sits on the chair. He holds a green paper on his hand. Olimpia sweeps the floor.

ORLANDO. Tell them to check him. See if there's a scratch on him. There's not a scratch on that body. Why the fuss! Who was he and who's making a fuss? Why is he so important?

ALEJO. He was in deep. He knew names.

ORLANDO. I was never told that. But it wouldn't have mattered if they had because he died before I touched him.

ALEJO. You have to go to headquarters. They want you there.

ORLANDO. He came in screaming and he wouldn't stop. I had to wait for him to stop screaming before I could even pose a question to him. He wouldn't stop. I had put the poker to his neck to see if he would stop. Just to see if he would shut up. He just opened his eyes wide and started shaking and screamed even louder and fell over dead.

Maybe he took something. I didn't do anything to him. If I didn't get anything from him it's because he died before I could get to him. He died of fear, not from anything I did to him. Tell them to do an autopsy. I'm telling you the truth. That's the truth. Why the fuss.

ALEJO (*Starting to put the paper in his pocket*). I'll tell them what you said.

ORLANDO. Let me see that. (*Alejo takes it to him. Orlando looks at it and puts it back in Alejo's hands.*) O.K. so it's a trap. So what side are you on? (*Pause. Alejo says nothing.*) So what do they want? (*Pause.*) Who's going to question me? That's funny. That's very funny. They want to question me. They want to punch my eyes out? I knew something was wrong because they were getting nervous. Antonio was getting nervous. I went to him and I asked him if something was wrong. He said, no, nothing was wrong. But I could tell something was wrong. He looked at Velez and Velez looked back at him. They are stupid. They want to conceal something from me and they look at each other right in front of me, as if I'm blind, as if I can't tell that they are worried about something. As if there's something happening right in front of my nose but I'm blind and I can't see it. (*He grabs the paper from Alejo's hand.*) You understand? (*He goes up the steps.*)

OLIMPIA. Like an alligator, big mouth and no brains. Lots of teeth but no brains. All tongue. (*Orlando enters through the left hallway door, and sits at the diningroom table. Alejo enters a few moments later. He stands to the right.*)

ORLANDO. What kind of way is this to treat me?—After what I've done for them?—Is this a way to treat me?—I'll come up . . . as soon as I can—I haven't been well.—O.K. I'll come up. I get depressed because things are bad and they are not going to improve. There's something malignant in the world. Destructiveness, aggressiveness.—Greed. People take what is not theirs. There is greed. I am depressed, disillusioned . . . with life . . . with work . . . family. I don't see hope. (*He sits. He speaks more to himself than to Alejo.*) Some people get a cut in a finger and die. Because their veins are right next to their skin. There are people who, if you punch them in the stomach the skin around the stomach bursts and the bowels fall out. Other people, you cut them open and you don't see any veins. You can't find their intestines. There are people who don't even bleed. There are people who bleed like pigs. There are people who have the nerves right on their skins. You touch them and they scream. They have their vital organs close to the surface. You hit them and they burst an organ. I didn't even touch this one and he died. He died of fear. (*Lights fade to black.*)

SCENE 11

Nena, Alejo and Olimpia sit cross-legged on the mattress in the basement. Nena sits right, Alejo center, Olimpia left. Nena and Olimpia play pattycake. Orlando enters. He goes close to them.

ORLANDO. What are you doing?

OLIMPIA. I'm playing with her.

ORLANDO (*To Alejo.*). What are you doing here? (*Alejo looks at Orlando as a reply. Orlando speaks sarcastically*). They're playing pattycake. (*He goes near Nena.*) So? (*Short pause. Nena giggles.*) Stop laughing! (*Nena is frightened. Olimpia holds her.*)

OLIMPIA. Why do you have to spoil everything.
We were having a good time.

ORLANDO. Shut up! (*Nena whimpers.*) Stop whimpering. I can't stand your whimpering. I can't stand it. (*Timidly, she tries to speak words as she whimpers.*) Speak up. I can't hear you! She's crazy! Take her to the crazy house!

OLIMPIA. She's not crazy! She's a baby!

ORLANDO. She's not a baby! She's crazy! You think she's a baby? She's older than you think! How old do you think she is—Don't tell me that.

OLIMPIA. She's sick. Don't you see she's sick? Let her cry! (*To Nena.*) Cry!

ORLANDO. You drive me crazy too with your . . . (*He imitates her speech defect. She punches him repeatedly.*)

OLIMPIA. You drive me crazy! (*He pushes her off.*) You drive me crazy! You are a bastard! One day I'm going to kill you when you're asleep! I'm going to open you up and cut your entrails and feed them to the snakes. (*She tries to strangle him.*) I'm going to tear your heart out and feed it to the dogs! I'm going to cut your head open and have the cats eat your brain! (*Reaching for his fly.*) I'm going to cut your peepee and hang it on a tree and feed it to the birds!

ORLANDO. Get off me! I'm getting rid of you too! (*He starts to exit.*) I can't stand you!

OLIMPIA. Oh, yeah! I'm getting rid of you.

ORLANDO. I can't stand you.

OLIMPA. I can't stand you!

ORLANDO. Meddler! (*to Alejo.*) I can't stand you either.

OLIMPIA (*Going to the stairs.*). Tell the boss! Tell her! She won't get rid of me! She'll get rid of you! What good are you! Tell her! (*She goes to Nena.*) Don't pay any attention to him. He's a coward.—You're pretty. (*Orlando enters through the hallway left door. He sits center at the diningroom table and leans his head on it. Leticia enters. He turns to look at her.*)

LETICIA. You didn't send it. (*Lights fade to black.*)

SCENE 12

Leticia sits next to the phone. She speaks to Mona in her mind.

LETICIA. I walk through the house and I know where's he's made love to her I think I hear his voice making love to her. Saying the same things he says to me, the same words.—(*There is a pause.*) There is someone here. He keeps someone here in the house. (*Pause.*) I don't dare

look. (*Pause.*) No, there's nothing I can do. I can't do anything. (*She walks to the hallway. She hears footsteps. She moves rapidly to left and hides behind a pillar. Olimpia enters from right. She takes a few steps down the hallway. She carries a plate of food. She sees Leticia and stops. She takes a few steps in various directions, then stops.*)

OLIMPIA. Here kitty, kitty. (*Leticia walks to Olimpia, looks closely at the plate, then up at Olimpia.*)

LETICIA. What is it?

OLIMPIA. Food.

LETICIA. Who is it for? (*Olimpia turns her eyes away and doesn't answer. Leticia decides to go to the cellar door. She stops halfway there.*) Who is it?

OLIMPIA. A cat. (*Leticia opens the cellar door.*)

LETICIA. It's not a cat. I'm going down. (*She opens the door to the cellar and starts to go down.*) I want to see who is there.

ORLANDO (*Offstage from the cellar*). What is it you want? (*Lights fade to black.*)

SCENE 13

Orlando leans back on the chair in the basement. His legs are outstretched. His eyes are bloodshot and leery. His tunic is open. Nena is curled on the floor. Orlando speaks quietly. He is deeply absorbed.

ORLANDO. What I do to you is out of love. Out of want. It's not what you think. I wish you didn't have to be hurt. I don't do it out of hatred. It is not out of rage. It is love. It is a quiet feeling. It's a pleasure. It is quiet and it pierces my insides in the most internal way. It is my most private self. And this I give to you.—Don't be afraid.—It is a desire to destroy and to see things destroyed and to see the inside of them.—It's my nature. I must hide this from others. But I don't feel remorse. I was born this way and I must have this.—I need love. I wish you did not feel hurt and recoil from me. (*Lights fade to black.*)

SCENE 14

Orlando sits to the right and Leticia sits to the left of the table.

LETICIA. Don't make her scream. (*There is a pause.*)

ORLANDO. You're crazy.

LETICIA. Don't I give you enough?

ORLANDO (*He's calm.*). Don't start.

LETICIA. How long is she going to be here?

ORLANDO. Not long.

LETICIA. Don't make her cry. (*He looks at her.*) I can't stand it. (*Pause.*) Why do you make her scream?

ORLANDO. I don't make her scream.

LETICIA. She screams.

ORLANDO. I can't help it. (*Pause.*)

LETICIA. I tell you I can't stand it. I'm going to ask Mona to
come and stay with me.

ORLANDO. No.

LETICIA. I want someone here with me.

ORLANDO. I don't want her here.

LETICIA. Why not?

ORLANDO. I don't.

LETICIA. I need someone here with me.

ORLANDO. Not now.

LETICIA. When?

ORLANDO. Soon enough.—She's going to stay here for a
while. She's going to work for us. She'll be a servant here.

LETICIA. . . . No.

ORLANDO. She's going to be a servant here. (*Lights fade to
black.*)

SCENE 15

*Olimpia and Nena are sitting at the diningroom table. They
are separating stones and other matter from dry beans.*

NENA. I used to clean beans when I was in the home. And
also string beans. I also pressed clothes. The days were
long. Some girls did hand sewing. They spent the day doing that. I didn't like it. When I did that, the day was even
longer and there were times when I couldn't move even if
I tried. And they said I couldn't go there anymore, that I
had to stay in the yard. I didn't mind sitting in the yard
looking at the birds. I went to the laundryroom and
watched the women work. They let me go in and sit there.
And they showed me how to press. I like to press because
my mind wanders and I find satisfaction. I can iron all day.
I like the way the wrinkles come out and things look nice.
It's a miracle isn't it? I could earn a living pressing clothes.
And I could find my grandpa and take care of him.

OLIMPIA. Where is your grandpa?

NENA. I don't know. (*They work a little in silence.*) He sleeps
in the streets. Because he's too old to remember where he
lives. He needs a person to take care of him. And I can
take care of him. But I don't know where he is.—He
doesn't know where I am.—He doesn't know who he is.
He's too old. He doesn't know anything about himself.
He only knows how to beg. And he knows that, only because he's hungry. He walks around and begs for food. He
forgets to go home. He lives in the camp for the homeless
and he has his own box. It's not an ugly box like the others. It's is a real box. I used to live there with him. He
took me with him when my mother died till they took
me to the home. It is a big box. It's big enough for two. I
could sleep in the front where it's cold. And he cold sleep
in the back where it's warmer. And he could lean on me.
The floor is hard for him because he's skinny and it's hard
on his poor bones. He could sleep on top of me if that
would make him feel comfortable. I wouldn't mind. Except that he may pee on me because he pees in his pants.

He doesn't know not to. He is incontinent. He can't hold
it. His box was a little smelly. But that doesn't matter because I could clean it. All I would need is some soap. I
could get plenty of water from the public faucet. And I
could borrow a brush. You know how clean I could get it?
As clean as new. You know what I would do? I would
make holes in the floor so the pee would go down to the
ground. And you know what else I would do?

OLIMPIA. What?

NENA. I would get straw and put it on the floor for him and
for me and it would make it comfortable and clean and
warm. How do you like that? Just as I did for my goat.

OLIMPIA. You have a goat?

NENA. . . . I did.

OLIMPIA. What happened to him?

NENA. He died. They killed him and ate him. Just like they
did Christ.

OLIMPIA. Nobody ate Christ.

NENA. . . . I thought they did. My goat was eaten though.—
In the home we had clean sheets. But that doesn't help.
You can't sleep on clean sheets, not if there isn't someone
watching over you while you sleep. And since my ma
died there just wasn't anyone watching over me. Except
you.—Aren't you? In the home they said guardian angles
watch you sleep, but I didn't see any there. There weren't
any. One day I heard my grandpa calling me and I went
to look for him. And I didn't find him. I got tired and I
slept in the street, and I was hungry and I was crying.
And then he came to me and he spoke to me very softly
so as not to scare me and he said he would give me something to eat and he said he would help me look for my
grandpa. And he put me in the back of his van . . . And
he took me to a place. And he hurt me. I fought with him
but I stopped fighting—because I couldn't fight anymore
and he did things to me. And he locked me in. And
sometimes he brought me food and sometimes he didn't.
And he did things to me. And he beat me. And he hung
me on the wall. And I got sick. And sometimes he
brought me medicine. And then he said he had to take
me somewhere. And he brought me here. And I am glad
to be here because you are here. I only wish my grandpa
were here too. He doesn't beat me so much anymore.

OLIMPIA. Why does he beat you? I hear him at night. He goes
down the steps and I hear you cry. Why does he beat you?

NENA. Because I'm dirty.

OLIMPIA. You are not dirty.

NENA. I am. That's why he beats me. The dirt won't go away
from inside me.—He comes downstairs when I'm sleeping and I hear him coming and it frightens me. And he
takes the covers off me and I don't move because I'm
frightened and because I feel cold and I think I'm going
to die. And he puts his hand on me and he recites poetry.
And he is almost naked. He wears a robe but the leaves it
open and he feels himself as he recites. He touches himself and he touches his stomach and his breasts and his

behind. He puts his fingers in my parts and he keeps reciting. Then he turns me on my stomach and puts himself inside me. And he says I belong to him. (*There is a pause.*) I want to conduct each day of my life in the best possible way. I should value the things I have. And I should value all those who are near me. And I should value the kindness that others bestow upon me. And if someone should treat me unkindly, I should not blind myself with rage, but I should see them and receive them, since maybe they are in worse pain than me. (*Lights fade to black.*)

SCENE 16

Leticia speaks on the telephone with Mona. She speaks rapidly.

LETICIA. He is violent. He has become more so. I sense it. I feel it in him.—I understand his thoughts. I know what he thinks.—I raised him. I practically did. He was a boy when I met him. I saw him grow. I was the first woman he loved. That's how young he was. I have to look after him, make sure he doesn't get into trouble. He's not wise. He's trusting. They are changing him.—He tortures people. I know he does. He tells me he doesn't but I know he does. I know it. How could I not. Sometimes he comes from headquarters and his hands are shaking. Why should he shake? What do they do there?—He should transfer. Why do that? He says he doesn't do it himself. That the officers don't do it. He says that people are not being tortured. That that is questionable.—Everybody knows it. How could he not know it when everybody knows it. Sometimes you see blood in the streets. Haven't you seen it? Why do they leave the bodies in the streets,—how evil, to frighten people? They tear their fingernails off and their poor hands are bloody and destroyed. And they mangle their genitals and expose them and they tear their eyes out and you can see the empty eyesockets in the skull. How awful, Mona. He mustn't do it. I don't care if I don't have anything! What's money! I don't need a house as big as this! He's doing it for money! What other reason could he have! What other reason could he have!! He shouldn't do it. I cannot look at him without thinking of it. He's doing it. I know he's doing it.— Shhhh! I hear steps. I'll call you later. Bye, Mona. I'll take to you. (*She hangs up the receiver. Lights fade to black.*)

SCENE 17

The livingroom. Olimpia sits to the right, Nena to the left.

OLIMPIA. I don't wear high heels because they hurt my feet. I used to have a pair but they hurt my feet and also (*Pointing to her calf.*) here in my legs. So I don't wear them anymore even if they were pretty. Did you ever wear high

heels? (*Nena shakes her head.*) Do you have ingrown nails? (*Nena looks at her questioningly.*) Nails that grow twisted into the flesh. (*Nena shakes her head.*) I don't either. Do you have sugar in the blood? (*Nena shakes her head.*) My mother had sugar in the blood and that's what she died of but she lived to be eighty six which is very old even if she many things wrong with her. She had glaucoma and high blood pressure. (*Leticia enters and sits center at the table. Nena starts to get up. Olimpia signals her to be still. Leticia is not concerned with them.*)

LETICIA. So, what are you talking about?

OLIMPIA. Ingrown nails. (*Nena turns to Leticia to make sure she may remain seated there. Leticia is involved with her own thoughts. Nena turns front. Lights fade to black.*)

SCENE 18

Orlando is sleeping on the diningroom table. The telephone rings. He speaks as someone having a nightmare.

ORLANDO. Ah! Ah! Ah! Get off me! Get off! I said get off! (*Leticia enters.*)

LETICIA (*Going to him*). Orlando! What's the matter! What are you doing here!

ORLANDO. Get off me! Ah! Ah! Ah! Get off me!

LETICIA. Why are you sleeping here! On the table. (*Holding him close to her.*) Wake up.

ORLANDO. Let go of me. (*He slaps her hands as she tries to reach him.*) Get away from me. (*He goes to the floor on his knees and staggers to the telephone.*) Yes. Yes, it's me.—You did?—So?—It's true then.—What's the name?—Yes, sure.—Thanks.—Sure. (*He hangs up the receiver. He turns to look at Leticia. Lights fade to black.*)

SCENE 19

Two chairs are placed side by side facing front in the center of the living room. Leticia sits on the right. Orlando stands on the down left corner. Nena sits to the left of the dining room table facing front. She covers her face. Olimpia stands behind her, holding Nena and leaning her head on her.

ORLANDO. Talk.

LETICIA. I can't talk like this.

ORLANDO. Why not?

LETICIA. In front of everyone.

ORLANDO. Why not?

LETICIA. It is personal. I don't need the whole world to know.

ORLANDO. Why not?

LETICIA. Because it's private. My life is private.

ORLANDO. Are you ashamed?

LETICIA. Yes, I am ashamed!

ORLANDO. What of . . . ? What of . . . ?—I want you to tell us—about your lover.

LETICIA. I don't have a lover. (*He grabs her by the hair. Olimpia holds on to Nena and hides her face. Nena covers her face.*)

ORLANDO. You have a lover.

LETICIA. That's a lie.

ORLANDO (*Moving closer to her.*). It's not a lie. (*To Leticia.*) Come on tell us. (*He pulls harder.*) What's his name? (*She emits a sound of pain. He pulls harder, leans toward her and speaks in a low tone.*) What's his name?

LETICIA. Albertico. (*He takes a moment to release her.*)

ORLANDO. Tell us about it. (*There is silence. He pulls her hair.*)

LETICIA. All right. (*He releases her.*)

ORLANDO. What's his name?

LETICIA. Albertico.

ORLANDO. Go on. (*Pause.*) Sit up! (*She does.*) Albertico what?

LETICIA. Estevez. (*Orlando sits next to her.*)

ORLANDO. Go on. (*Silence.*) Where did you first meet him?

LETICIA. At . . . I . . .

ORLANDO (*He grabs her by the hair*). In my office.

LETICIA. Yes.

ORLANDO. Don't lie.—When?

LETICIA. You know when.

ORLANDO. When! (*Silence.*) How did you meet him?

LETICIA. You introduced him to me. (*He lets her go.*)

ORLANDO. What else? (*Silence.*) Who is he!

LETICIA. He's a lieutenant.

ORLANDO (*He stands*). When did you meet with him?

LETICIA. Last week.

ORLANDO. When!

LETICIA. Last week.

ORLANDO. When!

LETICIA. Last week. I said last week.

ORLANDO. Where did you meet him?

LETICIA. . . . In a house of rendezvous . . .

ORLANDO. How did you arrange it?

LETICIA. . . . I wrote to him . . . !

ORLANDO. Did he approach you?

LETICIA. No.

ORLANDO. Did he!

LETICIA. No.

ORLANDO (*He grabs her hair again*). He did! How!

LETICIA. I approached him.

ORLANDO. How!

LETICIA (*Aggresively*). I looked at him! I looked at him! I looked at him! (*He lets her go.*)

ORLANDO. When did you look at him?

LETICIA. Please stop . . . !

ORLANDO. Where! When!

LETICIA. In your office!

ORLANDO. When?

LETICIA. I asked him to meet me!

ORLANDO. What did he say?

LETICIA (*Aggresively*). He walked away. He walked away! He walked away! I asked him to meet me.

ORLANDO. What was he like?

LETICIA. . . . Oh . . .

ORLANDO. Was he tender? Was he tender to you!

(*She doesn't answer. He puts his hand inside her blouse. She lets out an excrutiating scream. He lets her go and walks to the right of the diningroom. She goes to the telephone table, opens the drawer, takes a gun and shoots Orlando. Orlando falls dead. Nena runs to downstage of the table. Leticia is disconcerted, then puts the revolver in Nena's hand and steps away form her.*)

LETICIA. Please.

(*Nena is in a state of terror and numb acceptance. She looks at the gun. Then, up. The lights fade.*)

END

TOPICS FOR CRITICAL THINKING AND WRITING

 ### The Play on the PAGE

1. Is rape the central metaphor of the play? What does Fornes want the audience to understand about sexual aggression, power, and social institutions? About men and women?

2. Does Leticia love Orlando, as she says in Scene 2? Why does she allow the abuse of Nena to go on under her own roof?

3. In the final moment of the play, when Leticia gives Nena the gun, is she attempting to make Nena take responsibility for the Murder? Or is she expressing solidarity with the other woman, who would have gladly seen Orlando dead? What other conclusions can you draw from the play's ambiguous ending?

4. Reviews of recent performances of *The Conduct of Life* have suggested that the central images and themes of the play have become clichéd. Is this true? Or can the play speak to audiences today as forcefully as it did in 1985 when it was first produced?

5. Maria Irene Fornes is a Latina playwright and *The Conduct of Life* is set in "a Latin American country." How is the play about an ethnic and national culture? On the other hand, is it only about this?

 ## The Play on the STAGE

6. Scene 1 begins with Orlando doing jumping jacks "as long as it can be endured." What is the significance of this physical movement? How will this activity affect the way in which the actor playing Orlando will deliver his first monologue? If you were directing this scene, how would you stage this?

7. There are many disturbing moments in the play, particularly scenes of sexual assault. How might the response of an audience change if the scenes were played realistically? Symbolically? Expressionistically? How would these different styles change the meaning of the play?

8. Critics have noted the moments of comic relief in the role of the housekeeper, Olimpia. Why might a play like *The Conduct of Life* need comic relief? How does your reaction in such scenes affect the social messages of the play?

9. *The Conduct of Life* is composed of many short scenes. How does the playwright indicate how this is supposed to function on stage? How might you do it differently if you directed the play? How might the play work if it were a film?

The Play in PERFORMANCE

The Conduct of Life premiered in 1985 at the Theater for the New City in New York under Fornes's direction. Since then it has had over fifteen productions throughout the United States in cities including Los Angeles, Chicago, Williamstown, Providence, and Iowa City. It was produced by the Gate Theater in London in 1988.

In *Interviews with Contemporary Women Playwrights* (edited by Kathleen Betsko and Rachel Koenig), Fornes describes the importance of understanding the technical side of theater in her writing:

You have to find out what lights are all about or you may destroy scenes. But you see, I was a painter before. The stage for me is a very beautiful place, nice to look at. And space is very important. I'm very picky with actors. I will keep on positioning them—a little to the left, no, three inches more . . . —because for me, it's as important as focusing a camera. You reach a point, pass it, go back a little and ZING! it's in focus (161).

HERBERT MITGANG
The Conduct of Life

The following review of *The Conduct of Life** is of its premiere production, in 1985.

*Review of *The Conduct of Life*, New York Times 20 Mar. 1985: C 16.

Although the harrowing central characters in *The Conduct of Life* seems to speak their lines in heavy capital letters, it would be hard to fault any of the sentiments behind the portentous one-act drama that Maria Irene Fornes has written and directed at the Theater for the New City.

The play by Miss Fornes, a five-time Obie winner whose works include *Mud* and *Sarita*, is against corrupt military government in the unidentified Latin American land where the story takes place; against the victimization of the poor and homeless; against the use of power and ambition to brutalize women in marriage and in backstairs rooms. Dictatorship in the bedroom and in the country are linked together in an endless metaphor of sadism that rules the conduct of these hapless lives.

Called upon to emote the playwright's sentiments are the burdened wife Letitia (played by Sheila Dabney in an old-fashioned melodramatic style that comes across as one long Edvard Munch scream) and her cruel husband (Pedro Garrido, speaking in some unfathomable street accent that weakens his role as a bestial army interrogator in jackboots). Some snatches of dialogue include: "Man is propelled by power," "If I had money I would distribute it to the poor," "I want to conduct each day of my life in the best possible way."

Two of the other characters—Crystal Field, as a humorous housekeeper, and Alba Oms, as a young woman locked up and raped—do succeed, respectively, in offering comedy relief and a measure of subtlety in their performances. And a second military officer (Hermann Lademann) is an interesting though not fully realized personality.

The drama is presented in a dozen or so vignettes, some lasting only a moment or two, that are punctuated by lighting that fades slowly and repetitively over T. Owen Baumgartner's two-level set. These theatrical punctuation marks are the equivalent of the ellipses that some poets and novelists use, and abuse, to tell the reader: At this point it's time to think about the wisdom of what is being said. While the onstage proceedings in *The Conduct of Life* are numbing, what Miss Fornes finally has to say does have a certain cumulative power as a feminist statement.

ANNA Deavere Smith

As an undergraduate at Beaver College in suburban Philadelphia, Anna Deavere Smith (1950–   ), who was raised in Baltimore, was inspired by her teacher of Shakespeare to consider speech as thought in order to discover character. Later, when she herself began to teach, she began collecting and transcribing interviews as the basis for acting exercises aimed to help her students deal with characters and situations beyond themselves. Dissatisfied with the quality of professional interviews, Smith began to conduct them herself, working to create an atmosphere in which the interviewee dropped his or her guard and "experience[d] his/her own authorship." At first she had her students at Carnegie-Mellon University—where she was then teaching (she is now Ann O'Day Maples Professor of the Arts at Stanford)—reenact these encounters; but she soon developed an interest in performing them herself as a model for them. The process logically moved beyond the classroom, and she decided to create an ongoing project she named "On the Road: A Search for American Character" where she would work out her theories with herself as performer. She began to create and perform pieces in different venues and contexts: a piece for the Eureka Theater, San Francisco (*From the Outside Looking In*, 1990), and for conferences at the Rockefeller Conference Center, Bellagio, Italy, on intercultural performance, at Princeton on gender, at Crossroads Theater, New Brunswick, titled "Black Identity and Black Theater."

Her breakthrough work, *Fires in the Mirror*, was created in 1991 for producer/director George Wolfe's Festival of New Voices at the Joseph Papp Public Theater in New York City. It was a piece based on a traumatic clash earlier that year between African Americans and Hasidic Jews in the poor Brooklyn area known as Crown Heights following the death of a seven-year-old black boy. Alone onstage in white shirt and black pants, Smith inhabited almost thirty different characters from rabbi to rapper—black, white, male, female. The enthusiastic critical reaction of Frank Rich in the *New York Times* was typical, calling the play "quite simply the most compelling and sophisticated view of urban and class conflict . . . that one could hope to encounter . . ." A year later Smith repeated her triumph with a piece about a similar racial trauma on our other coast: *Twilight: Los Angeles, 1992*, which examined the civic unrest following the Rodney King verdict. Acclaimed both in L.A. and New York where it played on Broadway (and as far away as Australia when it toured), *Twilight* earned Smith many awards including two Tony nominations, an Obie, and an NAACP Theater Award. In 1996 she was awarded a prestigious MacArthur Foundation fellowship. Her most recent piece, *House Arrest* (1997–99), on the American presidency past and present, however, has had a problematic journey: It was first presented *without* Smith, in traditional fashion with individual actors in individual roles. When this proved unsatisfactory, Smith returned it to a one-person piece with herself as solo performer. The general critical reaction was still that the material was too unwieldy to be as powerful and dramatically cohesive as her major works.

▪▪▪▪▪▪▪▪▪▪▪▪▪▪

COMMENTARY ON *FIRES IN THE MIRROR*

The critical success of *Twilight: Los Angeles, 1992* led the Pulitzer Prize committee to consider it for its drama award in 1994. After deliberation, the chair of the committee struck it from consideration on two grounds: Although the piece was indeed "a creative act," it was not fiction; and, moreover, Smith was not the author of its words, which came from others. Smith and others objected to the decision, pointing out that the model of what constitutes a play has broadened: Performance art and group collaborations

(such as *My Brazil* and *Terminal* in the present collection) have blurred the traditional distinction between creator and interpreter. Much new theater experiment assumes that the relationship between text/score and performance (as in jazz or dance) is often a two-way street: The performer may create text through improvisation or bring in new text from other sources, material the playwright and director—whether distinct from the performer(s) or not—can then codify. This codification, set down in words and immobilized as written text, is clearly a *play*, a verbal score whose theatrical survival depends on successive interpretations.

Every new interpretation—even when it strives for fidelity—invariably alters the interpretation of the past. The initial impact of *Fires in the Mirror* rested on two circumstances that no longer obtain: The social wounds it described were fresh, and Smith as a solo performer was hypnotic. Now we have a verbal text without Smith's presence, and the specific events recounted have fallen back into history. Can *Fires in the Mirror* survive without these dual pillars of strength? The dramatic evidence suggests that it can and does.

What makes *Fires in the Mirror* remarkable as a play is its ability to express political passion without affirming one specific political position. Most political drama—particularly drama based on contemporary conflict—takes sides against the forces it perceives to be oppressive. In the lexicon of the 1930s, drama is a weapon in an ideological struggle in which one side is right and one side is wrong. Note the example of a dramatic form that briefly flourished in the 1930s, a form very similar to Deavere Smith's work: The Living Newspaper was created by the Federal Theater Project (1935–39), one of four divisions of the arts subsidized by the government to combat the crisis of unemployment in the arts. The happy idea arose to simultaneously combat unemployment among theater *and* newspaper workers by creating within the theater project a unit that would create and stage plays based on contemporary social problems. The reporters would compose documentary works in which historical figures would (for the most part) speak only in direct quotation. In essence, the Living Newspaper saw its function as editorial, dealing with and taking sides on current issues like the farm crisis (*Triple-A Ploughed Under*), housing (*One-Third of a Nation*), labor (*Injunction Granted*), and foreign aggression (*Ethiopia*). It was not reticent in choosing sides, often ending with a direct appeal for political action, such as this from *One-Third of a Nation*: "You know what we're going to do? We're going to holler. And we're going to keep on hollering. . . . Give me a decent place to live in! Give me a home! A home!"

Political drama then and now invariably asks, in the words of the old union song, "Which side are you on?" Smith radically departs from this model. Not only will she *not* take sides in the conflict she describes, she very consciously balances opposing "truths" as perceived by the antagonists she portrays. Note the title of this piece: The fires this time are reflected in a mirror, but it is a mirror that yields different images to different perceivers. Early in the piece she interviews an

MIT physicist who notes that mirrors are not as simple to understand as they first seem. They do not always present an undistorted image. He observes that when astronomers scrutinize the heavens they do so by constructing as big a reflecting mirror, a telescope, as they can. The large telescope magnifies light and focuses it to a narrow point. In order for this point of focus, called by physicists, "the circle of confusion," to be as undistorted as possible it must gather in as much light as it can. "If you're counting stars . . . and two look like one, you've blown it." Without drawing the parallel, Smith recognizes that to minimize social distortion in the theater mirror she is constructing, it must encompass a large, diverse cast of participants and include all points of view.

Right after the learned physicist, she pursues the theme of reflection in the comments on an anonymous black girl who struggles to verbalize what her reflected image means to her: "When I look in the mirror . . . / I don't know. / How did I find out I was Black. . . . / When I grew up and I look in the mirror and saw I was Black." (We must note here that Smith, to emphasize the lyrical nature of the language she has transcribed, consciously has it printed in poetic form.) These incomplete phrases affirm another salient theme—perhaps *the* salient theme—in *Fires in the Mirror*, a theme articulated in the play's subtitle *Crown Heights, Brooklyn and Other Identities*. Long before Smith gets to her recounting of the incidents surrounding the riots, she explores, in almost the entire first half of the piece, those genetic, social, and cultural markers that combine to create each individual's sense of his or her individual and group identity. For Smith realizes that to understand the disturbances that erupted we must try to understand how individuals and groups took the reflected images of events and filtered them through the prisms of their images of themselves. But she notes that group identity is not immutably fixed. As she writes in the play's introduction, "In America, identity is always being negotiated." The terms of these negotiations, however, vary widely.

"Identity" is the first word spoken at the beginning of the play through the persona of the poet/playwright Ntozake Shange, who defines it as "a psychic sense of place . . . a way of knowing that no matter where I put myself / that I am not necessarily / what's around me." The first section of the play pursues this theme through characters well known and unknown: Director/playwright George Wolfe reveals as much confusion in his attempt to define his postsuburban black self as the anonymous black girl. Activist Al Sharpton defends his politically incorrect hairstyle as a conscious homage to his surrogate father, music icon James Brown, who made the young Sharpton promise to always wear his hair that way. And this leads Smith to contrast Sharpton's sense of hair with that of a Lubavitcher woman who describes Chasidic rituals that necessitate the shaving of women's hair and the wearing of wigs. Smith next moves beyond physical detail into the realm of ideas. Such figures as radical professors Angela Davis and Leonard Jeffries articulate how their individual identities merge with that of the group to which they belong. Race becomes the foundation on which to construct a philosophical, revolutionary political vision of the world. The dramatic climax of what could be called the play's first act presents powerful contrasting litanies of atrocities against blacks and Jews by black Muslim minister Conrad X and author/feminist Letty Pogrebin: Conrad X recounts the horrific toll in torture and death taken by the slave trade over three centuries, and Pogrebin tells the terrible story of how during the Holocaust her uncle had to send his own wife and children to their extermination.

So when Smith then initiates the latter part of her drama—the events surrounding the death of a young black boy in a car accident, the subsequent revenge murder of a Chasidic scholar, the explosion of rioting in the neighborhood of Crown Heights, the political

reactions of the different communities within the community, the actions and inactions of the mayor, the police and other authorities, and the wider reverberations citywide, nationally, even internationally— she has given us a visceral sense of where all this is coming from. But understanding does not necessitate dispassion. Without the rhetoric of direct appeal, *Fires in the Mirror* is a passionate call for social action. But the aim of this action is not ideological victory; it aims at creating a world of common humanity in which *no* group is defeated. But the piece never negates the legitimacy of the emotions it has transcribed and presented. It genuinely feels the pain of all involved, from the horror of Jews confronting renewed cries of "Heil Hitler," to the rage of black youth crying, "ain't no justice / ain't never been no justice, / ain't never gonna be no justice." The final word, however, is given to the father of the seven-year-old boy, Gavin Cato, whose death under the wheels of a Lubavitch-driven car precipitated the disturbances. Carmel Cato's description of the accident is not sentimental, or enraged, although it works itself up finally to anger. The quality we are left with is loss: "the children laying on the ground." To lift them up we must first really see them, and ask some hard questions about how they got there. And to make us do so, Anna Deavere Smith chooses the theater to "hold its crazy mirror up to nature, and provide a momentary glance at something that at the very least raises questions, if not truths."

FIRES IN THE MIRROR
Anna Deavere Smith

THE CHARACTERS

NTOZAKE SHANGE, *Playwright, poet, novelist*

ANONYMOUS LUBAVITCHER WOMAN, *Preschool teacher*

GEORGE C. WOLFE, *Playwright, director, producing director of the New York Shakespeare Festival*

AARON M. BERNSTEIN, *Physicist at Massachusetts Institute of Technology*

ANONYMOUS GIRL, *Junior high school black girl of Haitian descent. Lives in Brooklyn near Crown Heights*

THE REVEREND AL SHARPTON, *Well-known New York activist, minister*

RIVKAH SIEGAL, *Lubavitcher woman, graphic designer*

ANGELA DAVIS, *Author, orator, activist, scholar, Professor in the History of Consciousness Department at the University of California, Santa Cruz*

MONIQUE "BIG MO" MATTHEWS, *Los Angeles rapper*

LEONARD JEFFRIES, *Professor of African American Studies at City University of New York, former head of the department*

LETTY COTTIN POGREBIN, *Author of* Deborah, Golda, and Me. *One of the founding editors of* Ms. *magazine*

MINISTER CONRAD MOHAMMED, *New York minister for the Honorable Louis Farrakhan*

ROBERT SHERMAN, *Director, Mayor of the City of New York's Increase the Peace Corps*

RABBI JOSEPH SPIELMAN, *Spokesperson in the Lubavitch community*

THE REVEREND CANON DOCTOR HERON SAM, *Pastor, St. Mark's, Crown Heights Church*

ANONYMOUS YOUNG MAN #1, *Crown Heights resident*

MICHAEL S. MILLER, *Executive Director at the Jewish Community Relations Council*

HENRY RICE, *Crown Heights resident*

NORMAN ROSENBAUM, *Brother of Yankel Rosenbaum. A barrister from Australia*

ANONYMOUS YOUNG MAN #2, *African American young man, late teens, early twenties. Resident of Crown Heights*

SONNY CARSON, *Activist*

RABBI SHEA HECHT, *Lubavitcher rabbi, spokesperson*

RICHARD GREEN, *Director, Crown Heights Youth Collective. Codirector Project CURE, a Black-Hasidic basketball team that developed after the riots*

ROSLYN MALAMUD, *Lubavitcher resident of Crown Heights*

REUVEN OSTROV, *Lubavitcher youth, member, project CURE; at the time of the riot, was seventeen years old. Worked as assistant chaplain at Kings County Hospital*

CARMEL CATO, *Father of Gavin Cato. Crown Heights resident, originally from Guyana*

CROWN HEIGHTS: A CHRONOLOGY*

August 19, 1991

8:20 P.M. A station wagon from a police-escorted entourage bearing Lubavitcher Grand Rebbe Menachem Schneerson careens into two Guyanese American children at the intersection of Utica Avenue and President Street. Seven-year-old Gavin Cato is killed, and his cousin Angela suffers a broken leg. As an angry crowd gathers, the twenty-two-year-old Hasidic driver, Yosef Lifsh, and his two Hasidic passengers are taken from the scene by a private Jewish ambulance.

11:30 P.M. Three hours later and five blocks from the car accident, Yankel Rosenbaum, a visiting twenty-nine-year-old Hasidic history professor from Melbourne, Australia, is stabbed. Just after the incident, sixteen-year-old Lemrick Nelson, Jr., a Trinidadian American from Brooklyn, is arrested in connection with the stabbing.

August 20

2:00 A.M. Yankel Rosenbaum dies at Kings County Hospital.

PRE-DAWN Rioting begins on the streets as Blacks and Lubavitchers set fires, throw stones and bottles, and unleash insults at each other and at the police. The rioting continues throughout the day.

*Edited from the published edition of *Fires in the Mirror*. New York: Anchor Books, 1993, xlvii–llll.

Yosef Lifsh leaves the United States for Israel.

By the end of the day, police report sixteen arrests and twenty policemen injured.

August 21

8:15 A.M. Yankel Rosenbaum's funeral held at Lubavitch World Headquarters in Crown Heights. Afterward, Rosenbaum's body is flown back to Australia for burial.

Rioting continues and several stores are looted.

Before leading a march of nearly two hundred Blacks down Eastern Parkway, the Reverend Al Sharpton and Alton Maddox hold a news conference demanding Yosef Lifsh's arrest.

New York mayor David Dinkins and New York Police Commissioner Lee Brown visit Crown Heights to urge peace, but both are silenced by rocks and bottles and insults.

Lemrick Nelson, Jr., is charged with the second-degree murder of Yankel Rosenbaum.

August 22

Rioting continues.

Police presence in Crown Heights is increased to over fifteen hundred officers. By the end of the day, police report 107 arrests overall.

August 24

Led by the Reverend Al Sharpton and Alton Maddox, approximately fifteen hundred protesters march through Crown Heights, while nearly as many police officers patrol the immediate area.

August 26

Gavin Cato's funeral is held in Brooklyn. The Reverend Al Sharpton delivers the eulogy.

September 5

The Brooklyn grand jury does not indict Yosef Lifsh in the death of Gavin Cato.

September 17

The Reverend Al Sharpton flies to Israel to notify Yosef Lifsh of a civil suit brought against him by the Cato family. The day is the Jewish holiday of Yom Kippur.

January 26, 1992

The Cato apartment is destroyed by fire. Fire officials determine the fire resulted from children playing with matches.

April 5

Lubavitchers demonstrate outside City Hall to mourn Yankel Rosenbaum and demand more arrests in connection with his slaying.

April 13

Brooklyn district attorney Charles Hynes says that it is unlikely there will be more arrests in connection with the death of Yankel Rosenbaum.

October 29

5:20 P.M. Lemrick Nelson, Jr., is acquitted of all four counts charged against him in the killing of Yankel Rosenbaum.

8:40 P.M. More than one thousand Hasidic Jews rally outside Lubavitch headquarters in Crown Heights. Some bottle throwing and shouting matches ensue. Police report one arrest.

Mayor Dinkins offers a $10,000 reward for information leading to the conviction of Yankel Rosenbaum's murderer.

October 30

New York governor Mario Cuomo orders a state review of the case.

New York police commissioner Raymond Kelly asks his chief of detectives, Joseph R. Borrelli, to review the entire case from the scene of the accident to the announcement of the verdict.

November 15

Despite Governor Cuomo's assertion that Mayor Dinkins is being unfairly blamed for Rosenbaum's death and the unrest in Crown Heights, the Hasidic community continues to harshly criticize the mayor for his handling of the riots.

November 17

The Lubavitch community files a federal class-action lawsuit alleging that the Dinkins administration and police department refused to conduct "any meaningful investigation" into the rioting and failed to "seek out perpetrators aggressively."

November 25

In a locally televised speech, Mayor Dinkins defends his role in the Crown Heights disturbances.

December 3

Mayor Dinkins is heckled and called a "Jew Hater" at a Democratic club meeting in Queens.

July 21

New York State Director of Criminal Justice Richard Girgenti releases a six-hundred-page report on the Crown Heights disturbances. The report is critical of both Mayor Dinkins's and former Police Commissioner Lee Brown's management and leadership during the disturbances, as well as the police investigation into Yankel Rosenbaum's death and the judge's conduct of the ensuing trial of Lemrick Nelson, Jr.

IDENTITY

NTOZAKE SHANGE

The Desert

(*This interview was done on the phone at about 4:00 P.M. Philadelphia time. The only cue Ntozake gave about her physical appearance was that she took one earring off to talk on the phone. On stage we placed her upstage center in an arm chair, smoking. Then we placed her standing, downstage.*)

Hummmm.
Identity—
it, is, uh . . . in a way it's, um . . . it's sort of, it's uh . . .
it's a psychic sense of place
it's a way of knowing I'm not a rock or that tree?
I'm this other living creature over here?
And it's a way of knowing that no matter where I put
    myself
that I am not necessarily
what's around me.
I am part of my surroundings
and I become separate from them
and it's being able to make those differentiations clearly
that lets us have an identity
and what's inside our identity
is everything that's ever happened to us.
Everything that's ever happened
to us as well as our responses to it
'cause we might be alone in a trance state,
someplace like the desert
and we begin to feel as though
we are part of the desert—
which we are right at that minute—
but we are not the desert,
uh . . .
we are part of the desert,
and when we go home
we take with us that part of the desert that the desert gave us,
but we're still not the desert.
It's an important differentiation to make because you don't
    know
what you're giving if you don't know what you have and you
    don't
know what you're taking if you don't know what's yours and
    what's
somebody else's.

ANONYMOUS LUBAVITCHER WOMAN

Static

(*This interview was actually done on the phone. Based on what she told me she was doing, and on the three visits I had made to her home for other interviews, I devised this physical scene. A Lubavitcher woman, in a wig, and loose-fitting clothes. She is in her mid-thirties. She is folding clothes. There are several children around. Three boys of different ages are lying together on the couch. The oldest is reading to the younger two. A teen-age girl with long hair, a button-down-collar shirt, and skirt is sweeping the floor.*)

Well,
it was um,
getting toward the end of Shabbas,
like around five in the afternoon,
and it was summertime
and sunset isn't until about eight, nine o'clock,
so there were still quite a few hours left to go
and my baby had been playing with the knobs on the stereo
    system
then all of a sudden he pushed the button—
the on button—
and all of a sudden came blaring out,
at full volume,
sort of like a half station
of polka music.
But just like with the static,
it was blaring, blaring
and we can't turn off,
we can't turn off electrical,
you know electricity, on Shabbas.
So um,
uh . . .
there was—
we just were trying to ignore it,
but a young boy that was visiting us,
he was going nuts already, he said
it was giving him such a headache could we do something
    about it,
couldn't we get a baby
to turn it off;
we can't make the baby turn it off but if the baby,
but if a child under three
turns something on or turns something off it's not consid-
    ered against the Torah,
so we put the baby by it and tried to get the baby to turn it off,
he just probably made it worse,
so the guest was so uncomfortable that I said I would go out-
    side
and see if I can find someone who's not Jewish and see if
    they would
like to—
see if they could turn it off,
so you can have somebody who's not Jewish do a simple act
    like
turning on the light or turning off the light,
and I hope I have the law correct,
but you can't ask them to do it directly.

If they wanna do it of their own free will—
and hopefully they would get some benefit from it too,
so I went outside
and I saw
a little
boy in the neighborhood
who I didn't know and didn't know me—
not Jewish, he was black and he wasn't wearing a yarmulke
    because you can't—
so I went up to him and I said to him
that my radio is on really loud and I can't turn it off,
could he help me,
so he looked at me a little crazy like,
Well?
And I said I don't know what to do,
so he said okay,
so he followed me into the house
and he hears this music on so loud
and so unpleasant
and so
he goes over to the
stereo
and he says, "You see this little button here
that says on and off?
Push that in
and that turns it off."
And I just sort of stood there looking kind of dumb
and then he went and pushed it,
and we laughed that he probably thought:
And people say Jewish people are really smart and they don't
    know
how to turn off their radios.

GEORGE C. WOLFE

101 Dalmations

(*The Mondrian Hotel in Los Angeles. Morning, Sunny.
A very nice room. George is wearing denim jeans, a light
blue denim shirt, and white leather tennis shoes. His hair is
in a ponytail. He wears tortoise/wire spectacles. He is
drinking tea with milk. the tea is served on a tray, the cups
and teapot are delicate porcelain. George is sitting on a
sofa, with his feet up on the coffee table.*)

I mean I grew up on a black—
a one-block street—
that was black.
My grandmother lived on that street
my cousins lived around the corner.
I went to this
Black—Black—
private Black grade school
where
I was extraordinary.

Everybody there was extraordinary.
You were told you were extraordinary.
It was very clear
that I could not go to see *101 Dalmations* at the Capital The-
    atre
because it was segregated.
And at the same time
I was treated like I was the most extraordinary creature that
    had
been born.
So I'm on my street in my house,
at my school—
and I was very spoiled too—
so I was treated like I was this special special creature.
And then I would go beyond a certain point
I was treated like I was insignificant.
Nobody was
hosing me down or calling me nigger.
It was just that I was insignificant.

   (*Slight pause*)

You know what I mean so it was very clear of

   (*Teacup on saucer strike twice on "very clear"*)

where my extraordinariness lived.
You know what I mean.
That I was extraordinary as long as I was Black.
But I am—not—going—to place myself

   (*Pause*)

in relationship to your whiteness.
I will talk about your whiteness if we want to talk about that.
But I,
but what,
that which,
what I—
what am I saying?
My blackness does not resis—ex—re—
exist in relationship to your whiteness.

   (*Pause*)

You know

   (*Not really a question, more like a hum*)
   (*Slight pause*)

it does not exist in relationship to—
it *exists*
it exists.
I come—
you know what I mean—
like I said, I, I, I,
I come from—
it's a very com*plex*,

confused,
neu-rotic,
at times destructive
reality, but it is completely
and totally a reality
contained and, and,
and full unto itself.
It's complex.
It's demonic.
It's ridiculous.
It's absurd.
It's evolved.
It's all the stuff.
That's the way I grew up.

(*Slight pause*)

So that *therefore*—
and then you're White—

(*Quick beat*)

And then there's a point when,
and then these two things come into contact.

MIRRORS

AARON M. BERNSTEIN

Mirrors and Distortions

(*Evening, Cambridge, Massachusetts. Fall. He is a man in his fifties, wearing a sweater and a shirt with a pen guard. He is seated at a round wooden table with a low-hanging lamp.*)

Okay, so a mirror is something that reflects light.
It's the simplest instrument to understand,
okay?
So a simple mirror is just a flat
reflecting
substance, like,
for example,
it's a piece of glass which is silvered on the back,
okay?
Now the notion of distortion also goes back into literature,
okay?
I'm trying to remember from art—
You probably know better than I.
You know you have a pretty young woman and she looks
   in a mirror
and she's a witch

(*He laughs*)

because she's evil on the inside.

That's not a real mirror,
as everyone knows—
where
you see the inner thing.
Now that really goes back in literature.
So everyone understood that mirrors don't distort,
so that was a play
not on words
but a concept.
But physicists do
talk about distortion.
It's a big
subject, distortions.
I'll give you an example—
if you wanna see the
stars
you make a big
reflecting mirror—
that's one of the ways—
you make a big telescope
so you can gather in a lot of light
and then it focuses at a point
and then there's always something called the circle of confusion.
So if ya don't make the thing perfectly spherical or perfectly
parabolic
then,
then, uh, if there are errors in the construction
which you can see, it's easy, if it's huge,
then you're gonna have a circle of confusion,
you see?
So that's the reason for making the
telescope as large as you can,
because you want that circle
to seem smaller,
and you want to easily see errors in the construction.
So, you see, in physics it's very practical—
if you wanna look up in the heavens
and see the stars as well as you can
without distortion.
If you're counting stars, for example,
and two look like one,
you've blown it.

HAIR

ANONYMOUS GIRL

Look in the Mirror

(*Morning. Spring. A teen-age Black girl of Haitian descent. She has hair which is straightened, and is wearing a navy blue jumper and a white shirt. She is seated in a stairwell at her junior high school in Brooklyn.*)

When I look in the mirror . . .
I don't know.
How did I find out I was Black . . .

(*Tongue sound*)

When I grew up and I look in the mirror and saw I was
   Black.
When I look at my parents,
That's how I knew I was Black.
Look at my skin.
You Black?
Black is beautiful.
I don't know.
That's what I always say.
I think White is beautiful too.
But I think Black is beautiful too.
In my class nobody is White, everybody's Black,
and some of them is Hispanic.
In my class
you can't call any of them Puerto Ricans.
They despise Puerto Ricans, I don't know why.
They think that Puerto Ricans are stuck up and everything.
They say, Oh my Gosh my nail broke, look at that cute guy
   and everything.
But they act like that themselves.
They act just like White girls.
Black girls is not like that.
Please, you should be in my class.
Like they say that Puerto Ricans act like that
and they don't see that they act like that themselves.
Black girls, they do bite off the Spanish girls,
they bite off of your clothes.
You don't know what that means? biting off?
Like biting off somebody's clothes
Like cop, following,
and last year they used to have a lot of girls like that.
They come to school with a style, right?
And if they see another girl with that style?
Oh my gosh look at her.
What she think she is,
she tryin' to bite off of me in some way
no don't be bitin' off of my sneakers
or like that.
Or doin' a hairstyle
I mean Black people are into hairstyles.
So they come to school, see somebody with a certain style,
they say uh-huh I'm gonna get me one just like that uh-huh,
that's the way Black people are
Yea-ah!
They don't like people doing that to them
and they do that to other people,
so the Black girls will follow the Spanish girls.
The Spanish girls don't bite off of us.

Some of the Black girls follow them.
But they don't mind
They don't care.
They follow each other.
Like there's three girls in my class,
they from the Dominican Republic.
They all stick together like glue.
They all three best friends.
They don't follow nobody,
like there's none of them lead or anything.
They don't hang around us either.
They're
by themselves.

THE REVEREND AL SHARPTON

Me and James's Thing

(*Early afternoon. Fall. A small room that is a part of a
suite of offices in a building on West Fifty-seventh Street
and Seventh Avenue in New York. A very large man
Black man with straightened hair. Reverend Sharpton's
hair is in the style of James Brown's hair. He is wearing a
suit, colorful tie, and a gold medallion that was given to
him by Martin Luther King, Jr. Reverend Sharpton has a
pinky ring, a very resonant voice even in this small room.
There is a very built, very tall man who sits behind me
during the interview. Reverend Sharpton's face is much
younger, and more innocent than it appears to be in the
media. His humor is in his face. He is very direct. The interview only lasts fifteen minutes because he had been
called out of a meeting in progress to do the interview.*)

James Brown raised me.
Uh . . .
I never had a father.
My father left when I was ten.
James Brown took me to the beauty parlor one day
and made my hair like his.
And made me promise
to wear it like that
'til I die.
It's a personal family thing
between me and James Brown.
I always wanted a father
and he filled that void.
And the strength that he's demonstrated—
I don't know anybody that reached his heights,
and then had to go as low as he did and come back.
And I think that if anybody I met in life deserved that type of
tribute from
somebody
that he wanted a kid
to look like him

and be like his son . . .
I just came home from spending a weekend with him now,
uh, uh,
I think James deserved that.
And just like
he was the father I never had,
his kids never even visited him when he went to jail.
So I was like the kid he never had.
And if I had to choose between arguing with people about
      my
hairstyle
or giving him that one tribute
he axed,
I'd rather give him that tribute
because he filled a void for me.
And I really don't give a damn
who doesn't understand it.
Oh, I know not you, not you.
The press and everybody do
their thing on that.
It's a personal thing between me and James Brown.
And just like
in other communities
people do their cultural thing
with who they wanna look like,
uh,
there's nothing wrong with me doing
that with James.
It's, it's, *us.*
I mean in the fifties it was a slick.
It was acting like White folks.
But today
people don't wear their hair like that.
James and I the only ones out there doing that.
So it's certainlih not
a reaction to Whites.
It's me and James's thing.

RIVKAH SIEGAL

Wigs

(*Early afternoon. Spring. The kitchen of an apartment in
Crown Heights. A very pretty Lubavitcher woman, with
clear eyes and a direct gaze, wearing a wig and a knit
sweater, that looks as though it might be hand knit. A
round wooden table. Coffee mug. Sounds of children playing in the street are outside. A neighbor, a Lubavitcher
woman with light blond hair who no longer wears the wig,
observes the interview at the table.*)

Your hair—
It only has to be—
there's different,
uhm,

customs in different
Hasidic groups.
Lubavitch
the system is
it should be two inches
long.
It's—
some groups
have
the custom
to shave their
heads.
There's—
the reason is,
when you go to the mikvah [bath]
you may, maybe,
it's better if it's short
because of what you—
the preparation
that's involved
and that
you have to go under the water.
The hair has a tendency to float
and you have to be completely submerged
including your hair.
So . . .
And I got married
when I was a little older,
and I really wanted to be married
and I really wanted to, um . . .
In some ways I was eager to cover my head.
Now if I had grown up in a Lubavitch household
and then had to cut it,
I don't know what that would be like.
I really don't.
But now that I'm wearing the wig,
you see,
with my hair I can keep it very simple
and I can change it all the time.
So with a wig you have to have like five wigs if you want to
      do that.
But I, uh,
I feel somehow like it's fake,
I feel like it's not me.
I try to be as much myself as I can,
and it just
bothers me
that I'm kind of fooling the world.
I used to go to work.
People . . .
and I would wear a different wig,
and they'd say I like your new haircut
and I'd say it's not mine!
You know,

and it was very hard for me to say it
and
it became very difficult.
I mean, I've gone through a lot with wearing wigs and not
    wearing
wigs.
It's been a big issue for me.

RACE

ANGELA DAVIS

Rope

(*Morning. Spring. Oakland, California. In reality this interview was done on the phone, with myself and Thulani Davis. Thulani and I were calling from an office at the Public Theatre. We do not know exactly what Angela was doing or wearing. I believe, from things she said, that she was sitting on her deck in her home, which overlooks a beautiful panorama of trees.*)

Race, um—
of course
for many years in the history
of African Americans in this country—
was synonymous with community.
As a matter of fact
Many of our predecessors considered themselves
"race women and race men."
Billie Holiday for example
called herself a race woman
because she supported the community
and as a child growing up in the South
my assumptions were
that if anybody in the race
came under attack
then I had to be there
to support that person,
to support the race.
I was saying to my students just the other day,
I said,
if in 1970,
when I was
in jail,
someone had told me
that in 1991,
a Black man
who
said that his, um . . .
hero—

(*Increased volume, speed, and energy*)

one of his heroes
was Malcolm X—
would be nominated to the Supreme Court
I would have celebrated
and I don't think it would have been possible at that time
to convince me
that I would
be absolutely opposed,
a Black candidate—

   A new attack, more energy

or that if anyone would have told me that
a *woman would*
Finally be elected to the Supreme Court,
It would have been very difficult—
As critical as I am with respect to feminism—
To imagine opposing her.
I don't think
it would have been possible to convince me that things
    would have so absolutely
shifted that
someone could have evoked
the specter of lynching
on national television
and that specter of lynching would be used to violate our
    history.
Yet I still feel that
We have to point out the racism involved
In the staging of the sexual harrassment story
With a Black woman and a Black man as the actors.
I mean [Ted] Kennedy was sitting right there
and it had never occurred to anyone to bring him up
On charges for his past indiscretions.
Actually we,
in our various oppressed
marginalized communities,
have been able to turn
terrible acts of racism directed against us
into victory . . .
And therefore I think
Anita Hill achieved a victory by showing the courage
to expose the sexual harrassment issue on a national
    level.
and so it's very complicated,
but I have no problems aligning myself politically
against Clarence Thomas in a real passionate way.
But at the same time we have to think about racism that
    made
The Thomas-Hill hearings possible.
So I think we need to develop
New ways of looking at community.
Race in the old sense has become
an increasingly obsolete way
of constructing community

because it is based on unchangeable
immutable biological
facts
in a very pseudo-scientific way,
Now this does not mean that we ignore *racism*.
Racism is at the origins of this concept of race.
It's not the other way around;
There were not racists.
This one race,
Who suddenly came to dominate
The others.
As a matter of fact
in order for a European colonialist
to attempt
to conquer the world,
to colonize the world,
they had to construct this notion
of,
uh,
the populations of the earth being divided into certain,
uh,
firm biological, uh,
communities,
and that's what I think we have to go back and look at.
So when I use the word race now I put it in quotations.
Because if we don't transform
this . . . this intransigent
rigid
notion of race,
we will be caught up in this cycle
of genocidal
violence
that, um,
is at the origins of our history.
So I think—
and I'm
I'm convinced—
and this is what I'm working on in my political practice right
    now—
is that we have to find ways of coming together in a different
    way,
not the old notion of coalition in which we anchor ourselves
    very solidly
in our,
communities,
and simply voice
our
solidarity with other people.
I'm not suggesting that we do not anchor ourselves in our
    communities;
I feel very anchored in,
my various communities,
but I think that,
you know,

to use a metaphor, the rope
attached to that anchor should be long enough to allow us
    to move
into other communities
to understand and learn.
I've been thinking a lot about the need to make more
    intimate
these connections and associations and to really take on
    the responsibility
of learning.
So we need to find ways of working with
in order to find ways of working with
and understanding
the vastness
of our many cultural heritages
and ways of coming together without
rendering invisible all of that heterogeneity—
I don't have the answer,
What I'm interested in is communities
that are not static,
that
can change, that can respond to new historical needs.
So I think it's a very exciting moment.

RHYTHM

MONIQUE "BIG MO" MATTHEWS

Rhythm and Poetry

(*In reality this interview was done on an afternoon in
the spring of 1989, while I was in residence at the University of California, Los Angeles, as a fellow at the
Center for Afro-American Studies. Mo was a student
of mine. We were sitting in my office, which was a narrow office, with sunlight. I performed Mo in many
shows, and in the course of performing her, I changed
the setting to a performance setting, with microphone. I
was inspired by a performance that I saw of Queen Latifah in San Francisco, and by Mo's behavior in my
class, which was performance behavior, to change the
setting to one that was more theatrical, since Mo's
everyday speech was as theatrical as Latifah's performance speech. Speaking directly to the audience, pacing
the stage.*)

And she say, "This is for the fellas,"
and she took off all her clothes and she had on a leotard
that had all cuts and stuff in it,
and she started doin' it on the floor.
They were like

"Go, girl!"
People like, "That look really stink."
But that's what a lot of female rappers do—
like to try to get off,
they sell they body or pimp they body
to, um, get play.
And you have people like Latifah who doesn't, you know,
she talks intelligent.
You have Lyte who's just hard and people are are scared by
    her
hardness,
her strength of her words.
She encompasses that whole, New York–street sound.
It's like, you know, she'll like . . .
what 's a line?
What's a line
like "Paper Thin,"
"IN ONE EAR AND RIGHT OUT THE OTHUH."
It's like,
"I don't care what you have to say,
I'm gittin' done what's gotta be done.
Man can't come across me.
A female she can't stand against me.
I'm just the toughest, I'm just the hardest/You just can't
    come up
against me/if you do you get waxed!"
It's like a lot of my songs,
I don't know if I'm gonna get blacklisted for it.
The image that I want is a strong strong African strong
    Black woman
and I'm not down with what's going on, like Big Daddy
    Kane had a song
out called "Pimpin Ain't Easy," and he sat there and he
    talk for the
whole song, and I sit there I wanna slap him, I wanna slap
    him so
hard, and he talks about, it's one point he goes, yeah
um,
"Puerto Rican girls Puerto Rican girls call me Papi and
White girls say
"*even* White girls say I'm a hunk!"
I'm like,
"What you mean 'even'?
Oh! Black girls ain't good enough for you huh?"
And one of my songs has a line that's like
"PIMPIN' AIN'T EASY BUT WHORIN' AIN'T PROPER.
    RESPECT AND
CHERISH THE ORIGINAL MOTHER."
And a couple of my friends were like,
"Aww, Mo, you good but I can't listen to you 'cause you be
    Men
bashin'."
I say,
"*It ain't men bashin', it's female assertin'*."

Shit.
I'm tired of it.
I'm tired of my friends just acceptin'
that they just considered to be a ho.
You got a song,
"Everybody's a Hotty."
A "hotty" means you a freak, you a ho,
and it's like Too Short
gets up there and he goes,
"B I AYYYYYYYYYYYYE."
Like he stretches "bitch" out for as long as possible,
like you just a ho and you can't be saved,
and 2 Live Crew. . . . "we want some pussy," and the girls!
    "La le la le la le la,"
it's like my friends say,
"Mo, if you so bad how come you don't never say nothin
    about Two
Live Crew?"
When I talk about rap,
and I talk about people demeaning rap,
I don't even mention them
because they don't understand the fundamentals of rap.
Rap, rap
is basically
broken down
Rhythm
and Poetry.
And poetry is expression.
It's just like poetry; you release so much through poetry you
    get
angry, you get it?
Poetry is like
intelligence.
You just release it all and if you don't have a complex
    rhyme
it's like,
"I'm goin to the store."
What rhymes with store?
More store for more bore
"I'm going to the store I hope I don't get bored,"
it's like,
"WHAT YOU SAYIN', MAN? WHO CARES?"
You have to have something that flows.
You have to be def,
D-E-F.
I guess I have to think of something for you that ain't
    slang.
Def is dope, def is live
when you say somethin's dope
it means it is the epitome of the experience
and you have to be def by your very presence
because you have to make people happy.
And we are living in a society where people are not happy
    with their everyday lives.

SEVEN VERSES

LEONARD JEFFRIES

Roots

(3:00 P.M. Wednesday, November 20, 1991. A very large conference room in the African American Studies Department at CUNY. Drawn venetian blinds, fluorescent lighting. Dr. Jeffries wears a light, multicolored African top, and a multicolored African hat. His shoes are black functional shoes, like the shoes to a uniform. He sits facing the table, and often sits back with the chair back from the table, often touches the table, and often sits back with the chair on its back legs only. Sometimes he scratches his head by throwing his hat forward on his head with great ease and authority. There is a bodyguard, a large heavy-set African American man, present.)

People are asking who is this guy Jeffries?
When they find out my background they're gonna be
    surprised.
They are gonna find out that I was even related to Alex
    Haley.
In fact I was a major consultant for *Roots.*
In fact there might not have been a *Roots* without me.
Now when I say that,
that's my own personal in-group joke wit' Alex.
He was in Philadelphia
getting his ticket to go down to Jamaica
and
Roots was lost.
He had it in a duffle bag,
a big duffle bag like this,
the whole manuscript.
It was lost in the airport of Philadelphia.
I got on my horse and ran around the airport of
    Philadelphia
and found *Roots.*
So that's my joke.
He had this manuscript,
Alex didn't have anything else but this manuscript.
Now if he had lost that, that would have been it.
He didn't have any photocopies.
Alex did everything on a shoestring.
u h m
so for him to deny me now . . .
He never even acknowledged
Pat
Alexander
his girlfriend/secretary who he had paid with affection and
    not with
resources.

So I didn't expect him to acknowledge me.
He called me to come down.
I called my wife who was working on her Ph.D. at Yale.
I said, "Rosalind, Alex wants us to come down to
    Brunswick, Georgia,
they're filming *Roots.*"
She said yes she'd come down and we'd go, then she called
    me back.
She said, "I got too much work," so I went down to
    Brunswick, Georgia.
He introduced me to Margulies,
who was the, um, director
of *Roots,*
as the leading expert in America on Africa, and I said,
    "Wow," to
myself, "that's kind of high."
When Margulies said,
"That makes me number two," then I realized what Alex
    was doing to keep *Roots* honest.
So for two weeks I tried to change *Roots.*
Alex would say, "Wait a
minute, let's consult the experts."
After two weeks they got tired of me, sat me down
and said, "Dr. Jeffries," at lunch,
"we are very happy to have you here
but we just bought the rights to the book *Roots*
and we are under no obligation to maintain the integrity of
    the book
and we certainly don't have to deal with the truth of Black
    history."
Now,
this was a wipeout for me
I
I, there's been very few trau*ma*tic
moments

    (Longest pause in his text)

uh, just to think.
Now I wasn't even prepared for this
but Pat had called me before and said,
"Len, I'm looking at this document and I don't know what
    to make of it."
I said, "What is it, Pat, what is it?"
and I knew she was nervous, she said,
"I'm reading a contract that says
"*Roots* has been sold to David Wolper and their heirs for
    ever and
ever

    (He is thumping his hand on table)

and their heirs for ever and ever."
Alex had signed the contract for fifty thousand dollars.

(*He is thumping his hand on table*)

Fifty thousand dollars for paperback *Roots*.
Something that made how much?
Three hundred million dollars?
He was suing them for years.
The millions he made on TV *Roots* he spent a lot of it to
    sue
Doubleday to get a better deal—I don't know if he ever got
    it.
Roots was a devastation.
The tens of millions and hundreds of millions made on
    Roots
went to produce,
not to make more Black series,
like *Roots*,
but they went to produce a *series*
maybe a dozen mini-series on *Jewish* history
as opposed to Black history.
You can document what was produced in terms of Black his-
    tory
compared to what was produced of Jewish history.
It's a devastation.
But the *one* thing that came out of this for me,
was that when these people told me, you know,
"We bought your research
We bought your history
You really have no . . . "
I was thrown off
I had to get out of there.
I stayed for another couple of days.
I told Alex I had to make a pilgrimage to my grandfather's
    grave.
Never saw my grandfather.
Then I watched one more scene in the Alex Haley thing
and that finished it for me.
A cutaway of a slave ship
that was so real that they had to bring in these high school
    kids,
and once these high school kids played the enslaved Africans
    greased
down in simulated vomit
and feces
they couldn't come back,
so they had to continue to get,
go take these youngsters,
and some little White woman
who was there sleeping with one of those guys,
they told her, "You cannot take these kids without autho-
    rization."
But she would drive a bus
up to the schoolyard,
put the kids in it, and bring them to the set.
And it almost produced a riot

there.
But anyway this slave scene
was so realistic
the trainer's up on a lower deck
and Kunta Kinte's on a bottom deck
and they call down to each other,
and the trainer says,
"Kunta Kinte,
Be strong! Be strong!
We may have to fight.
Kill the White man and return to Mother Africa."
This was high drama.
All of us grown men over hiding in the shadows in *tears*.
Then
Green rushes out and said, "Break! Break!"
He said he didn't want the scene.
We said, "What?"
Even Lou Gossett and them were ready to *fight*!
You know 'cause they had—
a movie script is just
a skeleton,
you have to put your soul in a movie script,
and they put their heart and soul into what would have
    been . . .
And with the African—
because the "earth is mother" all over Africa.
So to say to go back to Mother Africa is a very meaningful
    phrase.
But this
Englishman refused
to accept it,
and they almost had a physical fight on the set.
They compromised and said,
"We—are—all—from—one—village,"

(*Hitting his hand rhythmically on the desk*)

which is not the same thing.
After that I said, "I have to go."
I said I have to go,
And I rented a—
I flew out with Lorne Greene of all people.
He saw me and we had known each other for a couple of
    weeks from
the set,
and he's sitting there drinking his little drinks
talking about "Isn't *Roots* wonderful.
It's everybody's history,"
and I'm dying.

(*Pause*)

Get to Atlanta.
Rent a car. Cut across the Georgia countryside.

came to a fork in the road,
made the right turn,
and there
on a bluff
was a clapboard church
made by my grandfather
and
four
other trustees.
Then when
I went across the cemetery
to see, uh,
the gravesite where he was—
the tallest tombstone in the graveyard was his.
Uhm,
It was an obelisk.
On it was a Masonic symbol.
He was the master of the lodge.
On it was his vital statistics:
"*Born August the tenth 1868.*"
At the birth of the Fourteenth Amendment.
I later learned that his brother Sam was born
1865 at the birth of Thirteenth Amendment!
And this is why people say,
"Who is he?
What is he?
Why is he?"
If they only know
I've had one of the best educations on the planet.
Yeah.
So . . .
When I went to Albany
in July,
I went knowing that you might not have
much time,
just like my wife said on the radio today:
"When we speak
we speak as though it is the last speech we're gonna make."
But I knew what was at stake
ever since they branded me a conspiracy theorist,
February 12, 1990,
two-column editorial in the *New York Times*.
That was,
in the concept of Jewish thinking,
the kiss of death.
I knew I had been targeted.
Arthur Schlesinger went and wrote a book
called *The Disuniting of America*.
He has everybody in the margin
except a half-page photo of myself
which said to us,
"This is the one they got to kill."
We knew that Schlesinger
and his people had sent out a thousand letters

to CEOs around the country
and foundation heads
not to have anything to do with
all of us involved in these studies
for multicultural curriculum
so, uh . . .
Knowing that I had taken this beating for two and a half years
it was my chance to strike out,
but people don't understand
that that was my way of saying,
"You bastids! . . .
for starting this process
of destroying *me*."
That was my striking out.
But people don't know the context.
They don't know that for two and a half years
I bore this burden
by myself
and I bore it well.
And now they've got a problem.
'Cause after they destroyed me,
here he is resurrected!!!!!
I spoke at Columbia, I spoke at Queens College. . . .

LETTY COTTIN POGREBIN

Near Enough to Reach

(*Evening. The day before Thanksgiving, 1991. On the phone. Direct, passionate, confident, lots of volume. She is in a study with a rolltop desk and a lot of books.*)

I think it's about rank frustration and the old story
that you pick a scapegoat
that's much more, I mean Jews and Blacks,
that's manageable,
because we're near,
we're still near enough to each other to reach!
I mean, what can you do about the people who voted for
   David Duke?
Are Blacks going to go there and deal with that?
No, it's much easier to deal with Jews who are also panicky.
We're the only ones that pay any attention

(*Her voice makes an upward inflection*)

Do you hear?
Well, Jeffries did speak about the Mafia being, um,
Mafia,
and the Jews in Hollywood.
I didn't see
this tremendous outpouring of Italian
reaction.
Only *Jews* listen,

only *Jews* take Blacks seriously,
only *Jews* view Blacks as full human beings that you
should *address*
in their rage
and, um,
people don't seem to notice that.
But Blacks, it's like a little child kicking up against Arnold
Schwarzenegger
when they,
when they have anything to say about the dominant culture
nobody listens! Nobody reacts!
To get a headline,
to get on the evening news,
you have to attack a Jew.
Otherwise you're ignored.
And it's a shame.
We all play into it.

MINISTER CONRAD MOHAMMED

Seven Verses

(*April 1992, morning. A café/restaurant. Roosevelt Island, New York, We are sitting in the back, in an area that is surrounded by glass floor-to-ceiling windows. Mr. Mohammed is impeccably dressed in a suit of an elegant fabric. He wears a blue shirt and a bow tie. He has on fine shoes, designer socks, and a large fancy watch and wedding ring. His hair is closely cropped. He drinks black coffee, and uses a few packs of sugar. He is traveling with another man, also a Muslim, in the clothing of a Muslim, impeccable, who sits at another table and watches us.*)

The condition of the Black man in America today is part
  and parcel,
through the devilishment
that permitted Caucasian people
to rob us of our humanity,
and put us in the throes of slavery . . .
The fact that our—our Black
parents
were actually taken
as cattle
and as, as
animals
and packed into
slave ships
like sardines
amid feces
and urine—
and the suffering of our people,
for months,
in the middle passage—

Our women,
raped
before our own eyes,
so that today
some look like you,
some look like me,
some look like brother . . .

(*Indicating his companion*)

This is a crime of tremendous proportion.
In fact,
no crime in the history of humanity
has before or since
equaled that crime.
The Holocaust did not equal it
Oh, absolutely not.
First of all,
that was a horrible crime
and that is something that is a disgrace in the eyes of civilized
people.
That, uh, crime also stinks
in the nostrils of God.
But it in no way compares with the slavery of our people
because we lost over a hundred
and some say two hundred and fifty,
million
in the middle passage
coming from Africa
to America.
We were so thoroughly robbed.
We didn't just lose six million.
We didn't just
endure this
for, for
five or six years
or from '38 to '45 or '39 to—
We endured this for over three hundred years—
the total subjugation of the Black man.
You can go into Bangladesh today,
Calcutta,

(*He strikes the table with a sugar packet three or four times*)

New Delhi,
Nigeria,
some really
so-called underdeveloped nation,
and I don't care how low that person's humanity is

(*He opens the sugar packet*)

whether they never

had running water,
if they'd never seen a television or anything.
They are in better condition than the Black man and woman
in America today
right now.
Even at Harvard.
They have a contextual understanding of what identity is.

(*He strikes the table with another sugar packet three or
four times and opens it*)

But the Black man has no knowledge of that;
he's an amnesia victim

(*Starts stirring his coffee*)

He has lost knowledge of himself

(*Stirring his coffee*)

and he's living a beast life.

(*Stirring his coffee*)

So this proves that it was the greatest
crime.
Because we were cut off from our past.
Not only were we killed and murdered,
not only were our women raped
in front of their own children.
Not only did the slave master stick

(*The spoon drops onto saucer*)

at times,
daggers into a pregnant woman's stomach,
slice the stomach open
push the baby out on the ground and crush the head of the
baby
to instill fear in the Massas of the plantation.

(*Stirring again*)

Not only were these things done,
not only were our thumbs

(*Spoon drops*)

put in, in devices
that would just
slowly torture the slave
and tear the thumb off from the root.
Not only were we sold on the auction block
like cattle,
not permitted to marry.
See these are the crimes
of slavery that nobody wants to talk about.
But the most significant crime—
because we could have recovered from all of that—

but the fact that they cut off all knowledge from us,
told us that we were animals,
told us that we were subhuman,
took from us our names,
gave us names like
Smith
and Jones
and today we wear those names
with dignity
and pride,
yet these were the names given to us in one of the greatest
crimes
ever committed on the face of the earth.
So this kind of thing,
Sister,
is what qualifies slavery
as the greatest
crime
ever committed.
They have stolen
our garment.
Stolen our identity.
The Honourable Louis Farrakhan
teaches us
that *we* are the chosen of God.
We are those people
that almighty God Allah
has selected as his chosen,
and they are masquerading in our garment—
the Jews.
We don't have an identity today.
Because we are the people . . .
There are seven verses
in the Bible,
seven verses,
I believe it is in Deuteronomy,
that the Jews base
their chosen people, uh, uh,
claim the theology,
the whole theological exegesis
with respect
of being the chosen
is based upon seven verses
in the Scripture that talk
about a covenant
with Abraham.

LETTY COTTIN POGREBIN

Isaac

(*Morning. Spring. On the phone. She is in her office in
her home on West 67th Street and Central Park West in
Manhattan. Her office has an old-fashioned wooden roll-*

top desk and bookcases filled with books. She says she was
wearing leggings and a loose shirt.)

Well,
it's hard for me to do that
because
I think there's a tendency to make hay
with the Holocaust,
to push
all the buttons.
And I mean this story about my uncle Isaac—makes *me* cry
and it's going to make your audience cry
and I'm beginning to worry
that
we're trotting out our Holocaust stories
too regularly and that we're going to inure each other to the
    truth of
them.
But
I think
maybe if you let me read it,
I would prefer to read it:

    (*Reading from* Deborah, Golda, and Me)

"I remember my mother's cousin
Isaac who came to New York
immediately after the war and lived with us for several
    months.
Isaac is my connection to dozens of other family members
    who
were murdered in the concentration camps.
Because he was blond and blue-eyed he had been
chosen as the designated survivor of his town.
That is the Jewish councils had instructed him to do any-
    thing
to stay alive and tell the story.
For Isaac
anything turned out to mean this.
The Germans suspected his forged Aryan papers and de-
    cided that he
would have to prove by his actions that he was not a Jew.
They put him on a transport train with the Jews of his town
and then gave him the task of herding into the gas chambers
everyone in his train load.
After he had fulfilled that assignment
with patriotic
German efficiency,
the Nazis accepted the authenticity of his identity papers
and let him go.
Among those whom Isaac packed into the gas chambers that
    day
dispassionately as if shoving a few more items into an over-
    stuffed
closet

were his wife
and
two children.
The designated survivor
arrived in America
at about age forty

    (*Breathes in*)

with prematurely white hair and a dead gaze within the sky
    blue
eyes that'd helped save his life.
As promised he told his story to dozens of Jewish agencies
and community leaders and to groups of families and friends
    which
is how I heard the account
translated from his Yiddish
by my mother.
For months he talked,
speaking the unspeakable.
Describing a horror
that American Jews had suspected but could not conceive.
A monstrous tale
that dwarfed the demonology of legend
and gave me the nightmare I still dream to this day.
And as he talked
Isaac seemed to grow older and older
until one night
a few months later
when he finished telling everything he knew
he died."

ROBERT SHERMAN

Lousy Language

(*11:00 A.M. Wednesday, November 13, 1991. A very
sunny and large, elegant living room in a large apartment
near the Brooklyn Museum. Mr. Sherman is sitting in an
armchair near an enormous bouquet of flowers for the
birth of his first child. He wears sweats, and a bright orange long-sleeved tee shirt. Smiles frequently, upbeat, impassioned. Fingers his wedding ring. Each phrase builds on
the next, pauses are all sustained intensity, never lets up.
Full. Lots of volume, clear enunciation, teeth, and tongue
very involved in his speech. Good-humored, seems to like
the act of speech.*)

Do you have demographic information on Crown Heights?
The important thing to remember is that—
and I will check these numbers when I get back to the of-
    fice—
I think the
Hasidim
comprise only ten percent
of the population

of the neighborhood.
The Crown Heights conflict has been brewing on and off for
     twenty years
since the Hasidic community
developed some serious numbers
and some strength in Crown Heights and as African Ameri-
     cans and
Caribbean Americans came to make up the dominant cul-
     ture in
Crown Heights.
Very important to remember that
those things that are expressed really as
bias,
those things
that we at the Human Rights Commission
would consider to be bias,
have the same trappings of bias,
which is complaints based on a characteristic, not on a
     knowledge of a
specific person.
There sort of is a soup
of bias—
prejudice, racism, and discrimination.
I think bias really does relate to
feelings with a valence,
feelings with a, uhm,

     (*Breathing in*)

feelings that can go in a direction positive or negative
although we usually use bias to mean a negative.
What it means usually
is negative attitudes
that can lead to negative behaviors:
biased
acts, biased incidents,
or biased crimes.
Racism is hatred based on race.
Discrimination refers to
acts against somebody . . .
so that the words
actually tangle up.
I think in part
because vocabulary
follows general awareness. . . .
I think you know
the Eskimos have seventy words for snow?
We probably have seventy different kinds of bias, prejudice,
     racism, and
discrimination,
but it's not in our mind-set to be clear about it,
so I think that we have
sort of lousy language
on the subject

and that
is a reflection
of our unwillingness
to deal with it honestly
and to sort it out.
I think we have very, very bad language.

CROWN HEIGHTS, BROOKLYN, AUGUST 1991

RABBI JOSEPH SPIELMAN

No Blood in His Feet

(*9:30 A.M. Tuesday, November 12, 1991. A large home
on President Street in Crown Heights. Only natural light,
not very much light. Dark wood. A darkish dining room
with an enormous table, could seat twenty. The rabbi sits
at the head of the table. Lots of stuff on the table. He
wears Hasidic clothing, a black fedora, black jacket, and
reading glasses. As he talks, he slightly slides around the
tape-recorder microphone, which is in front of him at the
table. The furniture in the dining room including his chair
is, for the most part, very old, solid wood. There are children playing quietly in another room, and people come in
and out frequently, but always whispering and walking
carefully not to make noise, unless they speak to him directly. The children at one point came over and stared at
me.*)

Many people were on the sidewalk,
talking, playing,
drinking,
beer or whatever—
being that type of neighborhood.
A car
driven by an individual—
a Hasidic individual—
went through the intersection,
was hit by another car,
thereby causing it to go onto the sidewalk.
The driver on seeing
himself in such a position that he felt he was going to defi-
     nitely hit
someone,
because of the amount of people on the sidewalk,
he steered at the building,
so as to get out of the way of the people.
Obviously, for the most part,
he was successful.
But regrettably,
one child was killed
and another child
was wounded.
Um,
seeing what happened,

he jumped out of the car
and, realizing
there may be a child under the car,
he tried to physically lift
the car
from the child.
Well, as he was doing this
the Afro-Americans were beating him already.
He was beaten so much he needed stitches in the scalp and
    the face,
fifteen or sixteen stitches
and also
there were three other passengers in the car
that were being beaten too.
One of the passengers was calling 911
on the cellular phone.
A Black person
pulled the phone out of his hand and ran.
Just stole the—stole the telephone.
The Jewish community
has a volunteer
ambulance corps
which is funded totally from the nations—
there is not one penny of government funds—
and manned by volunteers—
who many times at their expense—
supplied the equipment that they carry in order to save lives.
As one of the EMS ambulances were coming,
one of the Hasidic ambulances or the Jewish ambulances
    came
on the scene.
The EMS responded with three ambulances on the scene.
They were there before
the Jewish ambulance came.
Two or three police cars were already on the scene.
The police saw the potential for violence
and saw that the occupants of the car
were being beaten and were afraid for their safety.
At the same time the EMS asked
the Hasidic ambulances for certain pieces of equipment that
    they
were out of,
that they needed to take care of the Cato kid,
and,
um,
in fact, I was . . .
The Hasidic ambulance left, leaving behind one of the pas-
    sengers.
That passenger had a walkie-talkie and he requested that I
come down to pick him up.
And at that time there was a lot of screaming and shouting
and it was a mixed crowd, Hasidic and Afro-American.
The police said, "Rabbi get your people out of here."
I told them to leave and I left.

Now,
a few hours later,
two and a half hours later,
in a different part of Crown Heights,
a scholar
from Australia,
Yankel Rosenbaum,
who, urr,
I think he had a doctorate or he was working on his doctorate,
was walking on the street
on his own—
I mean he was totally oblivious—
and he was accosted by a group of young Blacks
about twenty of them strong
which was being egged on by a Black
male approximately
forty years old and balding,
telling them,
"Kill all Jews—
look what they did to the kid,
kill all Jews,"
and all the epithets that go along with it,
"Heil Hitler" and all of it.
They stabbed him,
which later on the stab wounds were fatal
and he passed away in the hospital.
The Mayor,
hearing about the Cato kid,
came to the Kings County Hospital
to give condolences to the family of the child who had re-
    grettably been killed.
At the meantime they had already wheeled in
Mr. Rosenbaum.
He was in the emergency room
and I was at the hospital at the same time,
and the Mayor, seeing me there,
expressed his concern
that a child,
uh, innocent child, had been killed.
Where I explained to him
the fact
that,
whereas the child was killed from an unfortunate accident
where there was no malicious intent,
here
there was an individual lying in the emergency room
who had been stabbed with malicious intent
and for the sole reason—
not that he did anything to anyone—
just from the fact that he happened to be Jewish.
And the mayor went with me to the emergency room
to visit Mr. Rosenbaum.
This was approximately one and half hours before he passed
    away.

I noticed at the time that his feet
were
completely white.
And I complained to the doctor
on the scene,
"He's having a problem with blood circulation
because there's no blood in his feet."
And she gave me some asinine answer.
And the mayor asked her what his condition is:
"Serious but stable."
In the meantime he was screaming and in pain
and they weren't doing anything.
Subsequently they, um,
they started giving him anaesthesia in a time that
they weren't allowed to give him anaesthesia
and while he was under anaesthesia,
he passed away.
So there was totally mismanagement in his case.
So whereas the Mayor,
had been fed . . .
his people got
whatever information he got out of the Black community was
that
the driver had run a red light
and also,
and that the ambulance,
the Hasidic ambulance,
refused to take care of the Black child that was dying and
rather took care of their own.
Nenh?
And this is what was fed amongst the Black community.
And it was false,
it was totally false
and it was done maliciously
only with the intent to get the riots,
to start up the resulting riots.

THE REVEREND CANON DOCTOR HERON SAM

Mexican Standoff

(*November 12, 1991, 4:00 P.M. The rectory office at St. Mark's Church in Crown Heights. A small, short office. Lived in but impeccably ordered. Some light from lamps, some from overhead. Plaques and awards everywhere. The reverend is wearing a yellow shirt, priest's collar, tan summer jacket. He swears spectacles. There are clocks that make noise and sound the hour in his office and outside church bells sound during the interview, loud. Throughout the talk he is trying to get the corner of a calendar to stay down, but it continues to stick up. Finally he uses a paperweight to keep it down.*)

You can't have that kind of accident
if people are observing the speed limits.
People knew it was the Grand Rebbe.

People have seen the Grand Rebbe
charging through the community.
He is worried
about a threat on his life
from the Satmars.
These Lubavitcher people
are really very,
uh, enigmatic people.
They move so easily between
simplicity and sophistication.
Because
they fear for his life,
because the Satmars
who are their sworn enemies

(*He laughs/chuckles*)

have threatened to *kill*
the Rebbe.
So whenever he comes out
he's gotta be *whisked!*
You know like a President
or even better than a President.
He says he's an intuhnational figuh
like a Pope!
I say
then, "Why don't you get the Swiss guards
to escort you
rather than using the police
and taxpayers' money?"
He's gotta be
whisked!
Quickly through the neighborhood.
Can't walk around.
He used to walk.
When I first came here.
Now he doesn't walk at all.
They drive him.
And when he walked
you could tell he was in front
because there was,
he was protected all around
and they spilled out onto the streets
and buses had to stop
because this BIG BAND
had to escort
the Rebbe from his house over there
to the synagogue.
So the Rebbe goes to the cemetery.
Every time the Rebbe goes to the cemetery,
which is once a week
to visit his wife—dead wife—
and father-in-law,
the police
lead him in escort
charging down the street

at seventy miles an hour in a metropolis—
what do you want?

(*Swift increase in volume and suddenly businesslike*)

It happened that on this occasion that as they were coming
    back,
uh,
the police car
with its siren,
had gone over a main
intersection with the light
in favor
of the police car.
The Rebbe's Cadillac had passed
when the lights had become amber
and nobody expected the bodyguard van,
uh,
station wagon
to deliberately go through the red light.
So the traffic
that had the right of way kept coming and
BANG!
came the collision and the careening
onto the sidewalk
had to damage whoever was there
and then, um, they were more concerned about licking their
    own
wounds.
Rather than pick
the car off the boy
who died as a result.
And then the ambulance that came—
the Jewish ambulance—
was concerned about the people in the van
while some boy lay dead,
a black boy lay dead on the street.
The people showed their anger,

(*Increase in volume*)

they burned and whatever else,
upturned
police cars
and looted,
and as a result,
I think in retaliation, murdered one of the Hasidics.
But that was just the match that lit the powder keg.
It's gonna happen again and again.
There's a Mexican standoff right now
But it's gonna happen again.

ANONYMOUS YOUNG MAN #1

Wa Wa Wa

(*7:00 or 8:00 P.M. Spring. A recreation room at Ebbets
Field apartments. A very handsome young Caribbean
American man with dreadlocks, in his late teens or early
twenties, wearing a bright, loose-fitting shirt. The room is
ill equipped. There are a few pieces of broken furniture. It
is poorly lit. A woman, Kym, with dreadlocks and shells in
her hair, is at the interview. It was originally scheduled to
be her interview. The Anonymous Young Man #1 and the
other Anonymous Young Man, #2, started by watching
the interview from the side of the room but soon approached me and began to join in. Anonymous Young
Man #1 was the most vocal. Anonymous Young Man #2
stood lurking in the shadows. A third young man, younger
than both of them, wearing wire spectacles and a blue
Windbreaker, who looks quite like a young Spike Lee, sat
silent with his hands and head on the table the entire time.
There is a very bad radio or tape recorder playing music in
the background.*)

What I saw was
she was pushin'
her brother on the bike like
this,
right?
She was pushin'
him
and he kept dippin' around
like he didn't know how
to ride the bike.
So she kept runnin'
and pushin' him to the side.
So she was already runnin'
when the car was comin'.
So I don't know if she was runnin' towards him
because we was watchin' the car
weavin',
and we was goin'
"Oh, yo
it's a Jew man.
He broke the stop light, they never get arrested."
At first we was laughin', man, we was like
you see they do anything
and get away with it,
and then
we saw that he was out of control,
and den
we started regrettin' laughin',
because then
we saw where he was goin'.
First he hit a car, right,
the tore a whole front fender off a car,
and then we was like
Oh
my god,
man, look at the kids,
you know,
so we was already runnin' over there

by the time the accident happened.
That's how we know he was drinkin'
cause he was like
Wa Wa Wa Wa
and I was like
"Yo, man, he's drunk.
Grab him,
grab him.
Don't let him go anywhere."
I said,
"Grab him."
I didn't want him to limp off
in some apartment somewhere
and come back in a different black jacket.
So I was like,
"Grab him,"
and then I was like, "Is the ambulance comin' for the kids?"
'Cause I been in a lot of confrontations with Jews before
and I know that when they said an ambulance
is comin'
it most likely meant for them.
And they was like,
"oh, oh."
Jews right?
"Ambulance comin', ambulance coming',
calm down, calm down,
God will help them,
God will help them if you believe."
And he was actin' like he was dyin'.
"Wa Aww,
me too,
I'm hurt, I'm hurt, I'm hurt too."
Wan nothin wrong with him,
wan nothin wrong with him.
They say that we beat up on that man
that he had to have stitches because of us.
You don't come out of an accident like that unmarked,
without a scratch.
The most he got from us was slapped
by a little kid.
And here come the ambulance
and I was like, "That's not a city ambulance,"
not like this I was upset right
and I was like,
"YO,
the man is drunk!
He ran a red light!
Y'all ain't gonna do nothin'."
Everbody started comin' around, right,
'cause I was talkin' about
these kids is dyin' man!
I'm talkin' about the skull of the baby is on the ground man!
and he's walkin'!
I was like, "Don't let him get into that ambulance!"

And the Jews,
the Jews
was like private, private ambulance
I was like, "Grab him,"
but my buddies was like,
"We can't touch them."
Nobody wanted to grab him,
nobody wanted to touch him,
An' I was breakin' fool, man,
I was goin' mad,
I couldn't believe it.
Everybody just stood
there,
and that made me cry.
I was cryin'
so I left, I went home and watched the rest of it on TV,
it was too lackadazee
so it was like me, man, instigatin' the whole thing.
I got arrested for it
long after
in Queens.
Can't tell you no more about that,
you know.
Hey, wait a minute,
they got eyes and ears everywhere.
What color is the Israeli flag?
And what color are the police cars?
The man was *drunk*,
I open up his car door,
I was like, when—
I was like, he'd been drinkin'
I know our words don't have no meanin',
as Black people in Crown Heights.
You realize, man,
ain't no justice,
ain't' never been no justice,
ain't never gonna be no justice.

MICHAEL S. MILLER

Heil Hitler

(*A large airy office in Manhattan on Lexington in the fifties. Mr. Miller sits behind a big desk in a high-backed swivel chair drinking coffee. He's wearing a yarmulke. Plays with the swizzle stick throughout. There is an intercom in the office, so that when the receptionist calls him, you can hear it, and when she calls others in other offices, you can hear it, like a page in a public place, faintly.*)

I was at Gavin Cato's funeral,
at nearly every public event
that was conducted by the Lubavitcher community and the
   Jewish

community as a whole
words of comfort
were offered to the family of Gavin Cato.
I can show you a letter that we sent
to the Cato family expressing, uh,
our sorrow over the loss,
unnecessary loss, of their son.
I am not aware of a word
that was spoken at that funeral.
I am not aware of a—
and I was taking notes—
of a word that was uttered
of comfort to the family of Yankele Rosenbaum.
Frankly this was a political rally rather than a funeral.
The individuals you mentioned—
and again,
I am not going to participate in verbal acrimony,
not only
were there cries of, "Kill the Jews"
or,
"Kill the Jew,"
there were cries of, "Heil Hitler."
There were cries of, "Hitler didn't finish the job."
There were cries of,
"Throw them back into the ovens again."
To hear in *Crown Heights*—
and Hitler was no lover of Blacks—
"Heil Hitler"?
"Hitler didn't finish the job"?
"We should heat up the ovens"?
From *Blacks*?
Is more inexplicable
or unexplainable
or any other word that I cannot fathom.
The hatred is so
deep seated
and the hatred
knows no boundaries.
There is no boundary
to anti-Judaism.
The anti-*Judaism*—
if people don't want me
to use,
hear me use the word anti-Semitism.
And I'll be damned if,
if preferential treatment is gonna
be the excuse
for every bottle,
rock,
or pellet that's uh, directed
toward a Jew
or the window of a Jewish home
or a Jewish store.
And, frankly,

I think the response of the Lubavitcher community was relatively
passive.

HENRY RICE

Knew How to Use Certain Words

(Thursday, November 21, 1991. The Jackson Hole restaurant on Lexington Avenue in the thirties in Manhattan. Lunchtime, dimly lit, a reddish haze on everything, perhaps from a neon light. Mr. Rice, very neatly dressed, is eating a large, messy hamburger and horizontally chopped pickles. Drinking a Miller Lite. Beer is in a bottle next to a red plastic glass. He's wearing a baseball cap over very closely cut hair and a bright, multicolored, expensive-looking colored nylon jacket. Heavy new Timberland boots. Struggling to eat without making a mess of the food. At some point sits up from food and has his right hand or first on his hip—a very unaffected but truly authoritative stance. Good-natured, handsome, healthy. Patsy Cline's "Crazy" is very loud on the jukebox.)

I went back home and got my bike
because I knew I would have to be
illusive.
I was there in body and in spirit
but I didn't participate in any of the violence
because basically I have a lot to lose.
But I was there
and I would have defended myself if it was necessary,
most definitely.
I weaved around trouble.
When something broke out, I moved back,
when it calmed down, I would move back in on the front line.
I was always there.
And Richard Green heard me saying something to a bunch of kids
about *voting*
about the power of *vote*
and the power of *numbers*
and he said,
uh,
I said, "Get away from me, you're an Uncle Tom,
get away from me.
Get back in your Mercedes-Benz!"
No! I said that to Clarence Norman
and to Richard Green,
both of them.
I was tearing them apart.
Richard Green was very persistent.
He said,
"Look, Mr. Rice,
I like the way you speak.
I need you.

Please help me.
I'm a community activist. . . .
ba, ba, ba, ba, ba."

(*He drops some food on his clothes, or so it seems, he looks and grins*)

It didn't get on me.
"I'm a community activist.
I need your help,
please help me,"
and so forth.
Again,
I didn't pay him no mind
but we spoke
some
the next day after that,
after the incidents that took place on that corner
of Albany Avenue.
A brother was beat up—
cops rushing into the Black crowd
didn't rush into the Jewish crowd,
cops rushed into the Black crowd
started beatin' up
Black people.
But the next day Richard came by in a yellow van,
a New York City Department of Transportation van,
with a megaphone,
yellow light flashing,

(*Music segues from Patsy Cline's "Crazy" to Public Enemy's "Can't Truss It," or Naughty by Nature's "O.P.P."*)

the whole works
and, um,
he said,
"Henry, I need you in this van.
Drive around with me.
Let's keep some of these kids off the street tonight."
I said, "Okay."
He said,
"The blood
of Black men are on your hands tonight!"
I said, "Okay."
We drive around in the van,
"Young people stay in the house!
Mothers keep your children in the house,
please."
So I began fillin'
I began feeling like
I had to do it
after he told me that,
"the blood of the Black man"
were on my hands,
you know.
Richard Green sure know how to use certain words.

(*He giggles*)

I remember reaching Albany Avenue—
kids were being chased by the police.
I jump out with a portable megaphone,
I tell them, "Stop running!
The cops won't chase you!
and they won't hit you!"
The next thing I know,
cop grabs my megaphone hits me in the head with a stick,
handcuffs me,
and takes the megaphone out of my hand.
So I'm like,
"Wait a minute
I'm doing a community service for the mayor's office."
They don't want to hear it.
Matter of fact,
they still have the megaphone 'til this day.
I'm like,
"Richard Green get me
out of this police car, please!"
So a Black captain came by,
thank God,
and he says, "What's goin' on?"
Richard Green explained it to him.
He said, "Let him go."
Get back in the van,
there's another Brother in the van,
starts saying,
"Non violence!"
to the young Brothers.
They begin throwing bottles at the, uh,
at the van.
One guy got so upset
he had a nine-millimeter
fully loaded.
He said, "Get the hell out of this neighborhood!"
I told Richard Green, "Take me on home. Shit!"
The next day
more violence:
fires,
cars being burnt,
stores being broken into,
a perception that Black youth
are going crazy in Crown Heights
like we were angry over
nothing,
understand?

NORMAN ROSENBAUM

My Brother's Blood

(*A Sunday afternoon. Spring. Crisp, clear, and windy. Across from City Hall in New York City. Crowds of peo-*

ple, *predominantly Lubavitcher, with placards. A rally
that was organized by Lubavitcher women. All of the
speakers were men, but the women stand close to the
stage. Mr. Rosenbaum, an Australian, with a beard, hat,
and wearing a pinstripe suit, speaks passionately and
loudly from the microphone on a stage with a podium. Behind him is a man in an Australian bush hat with a very
large Australian flag which blows dramatically in the wind.
It is so windy that Mr. Rosenbaum has to hold his hat to
keep it on his head.)*

Al do lay achee so achee aylay alo dalmo
My brother's blood cries out from the ground.
Let me make it clear
why I'm here.
In August of 1991,
as you all have heard before today,
my brother was killed in the streets of Crown Heights
for no other reason
than that he was a Jew!
The only miracle was
that my brother was the only victim
who paid for being a Jew with his life.
When my brother was surrounded,
each and every American was surrounded.
When my brother was stabbed four times,
each and every American was stabbed four times
and as my brother bled to death in this city,
while the medicos stood by
and let him bleed
to death, it was the gravest of indictments against this
   country.
One person out of twenty gutless individuals
who attacked my brother has been arrested.
I for one am not convinced that it is beyond the ability of
   the New York police
to arrest others.
Let me tell you, Mayor Dinkins,
let me tell you, Commissioner Brown:
I'm here,
I'm not going home,
until there is justice.

NORMAN ROSENBAUM

Sixteen Hours Difference

*(7:00 A.M. Spring. Newark Airport, Departure Gate,
Continental Airlines. Mr. Rosenbaum is moments before
his flight to LA and then back to Australia. Wearing a pinstripe suit with an Australian fit. Hat. Suitcase. He has
sparkling blue eyes with a twinkle, rosy cheeks, and a large
smile throughout the interview.)*

There's sixteen hours difference between New York and
   Melbourne
and I had just gotten back to my office
and I had a phone call from my wife,
and she said she wanted me to come home straight
   away
and I sensed the urgency in her voice.
I said, "are you all right?" She said, "Yeah."
I said, "are the children all right, you know the kids?" She
   says, "yeah."
So I'm driving home and I'm thinking, I wonder what's the
   problem now, you know?
We had some carpenters doing some work, I wonder if there
   has been a disaster,
some sort of domestic problem,
and I thought, oh my God, you know, my parents,
I didn't even ask after them,
how insensitive not to even ask after my parents,
and I've got a grandmother eighty-five years old, same sort
   of thing.
So I get home,
I walk in the door,
and a friend of mine was standing there,
close friend,
does the same sort of work as me, he's a barrister and an academic,
and he sees me and he says,
"There's got a pro—
uh,
we've got a problem.
There's a problem."
I thought he was talking about a case were working on together,
he says, "'Z come,
come and sit down."
He goes to me,
"There's been a riot in New York,
been a riot in Crown Heights,
Yankel's been stabbed and he's dead."
And
my brother was the last in the world,
I hadn't even given him a thought.
I mean the fact that my brother
could be attacked
or die,
it just hadn't even entered my mind.
At first I appeared all cool, calm and collected.
I then
started asking questions
like who told you,
how do you know,
are you sure?
I just asked the question,
you know,
are you sure?

ANONYMOUS YOUNG MAN #2

Bad Boy

(*Evening. Spring. The same recreation room as interview with Anonymous Young Man #1. Young Man #2 is wearing a black jacket over his clothes. He has a gold tooth. He has some dreadlocks, and a very odd-shaped multicolored hat. He is soft-spoken, and has a direct gaze. He seems to be very patient with his explanation.*)

That youth,
that sixteen-year-old
didn't murder that Jew.

(*Pause*)

For one thing,
he played baseball, right?
He was a atha-lete,
right?
A bad boy
does
bad things.
Only a bad boy coulda stabbed the man.
Somebody who
does those type a things,
or who sees
those types a things
A atha-lete
sees people,
is interested in athletics,
stretchin',
exercisin',
goin' to his football games,
or his baseball games.
He's not interested
in stabbin'
people.
So
it's not in his mind
to stab,
to just jump into somethin',
that he has no idea about
and
sta—
and kill a man.
A bad boy,
somebody who's groomed in badness,
or did badness
before,
stabbed the man.
Because I used to be a atha-lete
and I used to be a bad boy,
and when I was a atha-lete,
I was a atha-lete.
All I thought about was atha-lete.

I'm not gonna jeoparsize my athleticism
or my career to do anything
that bad people do.
And when I became a bad boy
I'm not a athalete no more.
I'm a bad boy,
and I'm groomin' myself in things that is bad.
You understand, so
he's a athalete,
he's not a bad boy.
It's a big difference.
Like,
mostly the Black youth in Crown Heights have two things
    to do—
either DJ or be a bad boy, right?
You either
DJ, be a MC, a rapper
or Jamaican rapper,
ragamuffin,
or you be a bad boy,
you sell drugs or you rob people.
What do you do?
I sell drugs.
What do you do?
I rap
That's how it is in Crown Heights.
I been livin' in Crown Heights mosta my life.
I know for a fact that that youth, that sixteen-year-old,
didn't kill that Jew.
That's between me and my Creator.

SONNY CARSON

Chords

(*Lunchtime. Spring. A fancy restaurant in Brooklyn. Sonny tells me it's where all the judges come for lunch. White linen tablecloths. Light wood walls, lamplight next to the table. Tile floor. He is eating crab cakes. He is dressed in a black turtleneck and a gray jacket. He has on a mud cloth hat. He has an authority stick with him, and it lays on the table. His bodyguard, wearing a black leather jacket, enters in the middle of the interview. Sonny chides him for being late.*)

It's going to be a long hot summer.
I'm connected up with the young people all over the country
and there's a thread
leading to an eruption
and Crown Heights began the whole thing.
And the Jews come second to the police
when it comes to feelings of dislike among Black folks.
The police,
the police,

believe me, the police—
I know the police and the police know me
and they turned that whole place into an occupied camp
with the Seventy-first Precinct as the overseers.
And I don't think that everything is OK within that
    precinct among those officers
either.
Don't think that,
don't think that,
You know the media has always painted me as the bad guy—
that's OK!
I'm a good guy to pick on.
Their viewers don't like me either,
they really don't like me because I *am* the bad guy,
I am the ultimate bad guy
because of my relationship to the young people in the city.
I understand their language.
I respect them as the future.
I speak their language. They don't even engage in long dia-
    logue
anymore
just short.
"Words."
It always amazes me
how the city fathers,
the power brokers,
just continue to deny what's happening.
And it is just getting intolerable for me to continue to watch
this small
arrogant
group of people continue to get this kind of preferential
    treatment.
They sit on the school board.
A board of nine
and they have
four members, and their kids don't even go to public
    school.
So that's the kind of arrogance I'm talking about.
I have no reason to be eagerly awaiting the coming
    together of our
people.
They owe me first.
I'm not givin' in just like that,
I don't want it.
You can have it.
Like my grandmother said,
"Help the bear!
If you see me and the bear in a fight,
help the bear—
don't help me,
help the bear."
I don't need any of it from them!
And I'm not gonna advocate any coming together and
    healing of
America

and all that shit.
You kiddin'?
You kiddin'?
Just 'cause I can have the fortune of walking in here
and sitting and talking
and having a drink,
it appear that I have all the same kinds of abilities
of other folks in here.
No, it's not that way.
'Cause tonight
by nighttime it could all change for me.
So I'm always aware of that, and that's what keeps me goin'
today
and each day!

    (*He eats*)

I have
this idea
about a film.
See,
these kids, they got
another kinda rhythm now,
there's a whole new kinda
step that they do.
When I first heard rap
I was sittin' in a huge open kinda stadium,
boys and girls high school field,
and I heard these kids come out and start rappin',
and I'm listening
but it's not really clickin',
but I was mesmerized though.
But it was simontaneous
all around the country
and I said, "Oh shit,"
and everybody I knew who was young was listenin' to it
and I said, "Wow."
Because I have always been involved with young people
and all of a sudden I got it,
I really heard the rhythm,
the chords,
the discord.
There's a whole new sound
that the crackers are tryin' to get, but they can't get it.
I heard it on a television commercial.
One of the most beautiful pieces of art
that I ever witnessed
was a play
called
um,
um,
um,
'bout, 'bout the Puerto Rican gang—
no, no, no, no, no—
the Puerto Rican gang,

the musical
that was on Broad—
yeah,
West Side Story—
the answer should be
a musical.

RABBI SHEA HECHT

Ovens

(*Morning. Spring. A building on Eastern Parkway. A large room with a very long conference table. There are pictures of Lubavitcher men on the walls. Rabbi Hecht is wearing a shirt, open at the neck. He has several crisp one-dollar bills in his shirt pocket. These are, apparently, dollar bills that the Rebbe has given him. It is the custom that the Rebbe gives out one-dollar bills on Sunday. Rabbi Hecht has a beard. He wears glasses, traditional Hasidic garb, including tsitses (ceremonial fringes that hang over his belt) and a red yamulke with gold trim which is ripped. His daughter comes in frequently to get money from him. He keeps telling her to wait until he is finished. She becomes more and more agitated. His brother also enters frequently to ask him questions, and to tell him he's late.*)

What is my goal?
My goal is not
to give anybody a message
that we plan on working things out
by integrating
our two
things.
By a person understanding more of their own religion
they will automatically respect another person.
The respect that my religion teaches me has nothing to do
with understanding you.
See, there's a problem.
If
the only way I'm going to respect you
is based on how much I understand you,
no matter what it is
in certain circles you're gonna run into problems.
Number one,
we are different,
and we think we should and can be different.
When the Rebbe said to the Mayor
that we were all
one people,
I think
what the Rebbe is talking about is that,
that common denominator that we're all children of God,
    and the

respect we all have to give each other under that banner.
But that does not mean that I have to invite you to my
    house for
dinner,
because I cannot go back to your home for dinner,
because you're not gonna give me kosher food.
And I said,
so, like one Black said,
I'll bring in kosher food.
I said eh-eh.
We can't use your ovens,
we can't use your dishes,
it's, it—
it's not just a question of buying certain food,
it's buying the food,
preparing it a certain way.
We can't use your dishes, we can't use your oven.
The—the higher you go
the more common denominator.
And what the Rebbe was saying,
you as the Mayor
don't get caught up in the differences,
you're—
from your position is—
you have to look at it as one city
and one
human race.
We are all New Yorkers
and therefore I will protect all New Yorkers.
You see
preferential treatment
suggests
that you're giving the person
the police car
not because they need the police car
but because
they are who they are.
You're not gonna
give them the housing
because they
need the housing—
you're giving it because of who they are.
But
just because I'm a Jew
therefore I
shouldn't get the police car.
The question is
a synagogue
that has five thousand Jews
leave
the synagogue
at the same time,
do they have a police car to stop the traffic?
The answer is every—single—synagogue,

temple,
mosque,
in
the
world
stops traffic
when five thousand people have to walk out
at the same time.

THE REVEREND AL SHARPTON

Rain

(*As before.*)

The D.A.
came back with no indictment.
Uh, so then our only course
was to ask for a special prosecutor
which is appointed by the Governor,
who's been hostile,
and to sue civilly.
When we went into civil court
we went to get an order to show cause.
The judge signed it and gave me a deadline of three days.
The driver left the country. . . .
No one even said, "Why would he run?
If he did no wrong."
If you and I were in an accident we'd have to go to civil
    court.
Why is this man
above the law?
So they said, "He's in Israel."
So I said,
"Well, I'll go to Israel to show best effits."
And the deadline
was,
I had to serve him by Tuesday,
which was Yom Kippur—
that was the judge's decision not mine.
So we went.
Alton Maddox and I
got on a plane,
left Monday night,
landed Tuesday morning,
went and served the American embassy, uh,
so that
if this man had any decency at all
he could come to the American embassy and receive service,
which he has not done to this day.
Come back,
went to court
and showed the judge the receipts,
and the judge said, "You made best effits,
therefore you are now permitted,

by default,
to go ahead
and sue the rabbi or whomever
because you cannot do the driver."
So it wasn't just a media grandstand.
We wanted to show the world
one, this man *ran*
and was *allowed* to run, and, two, we wanted to be able to
    legally go
around him,
to sue the people he was working for so that we can bring
    them into
court and establish *why* and what happened.
And it came out in the paper the other day
that the driver in the other car didn't even have a driver's
    license.
So we're dealing with a *complete* outrage here,
we're dealing with a double standard,
we're dealing with uh, uh, a, a
situation where
Blacks do not have equal protection under the law
and the media is used to castigate us
that merely asked for justice
rather than castigate those that would hit a kid
and walk away like he just stepped on a roach!
Uh,
there also is the media
contention of the young Jewish scholar
that was stabbed that night
and they've even distorted
saying *my words at the funeral*.
I *preached* the funeral.
Uh, [the newspaper said I]
helped to, to, uh, uh,
spark or, or, or, or, or *inspire* or *incite* people to kill him
    [Yankel Rosenbaum]
when he was dead the day before
I came out there.
He was killed the night
that the young man
was killed with the car accident.
I didn't even get a call
from the family
'till eighteen hours later.
So there's a whole media distortion
to protect them [the Lubavitchers].
Nobody is talking about,
"Why
is this guy
in flight?"
If I was a rabbi
(I am a ministuh)
and my driver hit a kid,
I would not let the driver *leave*

and I certainlih would give my condolences,
or anything else I could,
to the family,
I don't care what race they are.
To this minute the Rebbe has never even uttered a word of
sympathy
to the family,
not even sent 'em a *card*
a *flower* or *nothing!*
And he's supposed to be a religious leader.
So it's treating us with absolute contempt
and I don't care how controversial it makes us.
I *won't* tolerate being insulted.
If you piss in my face I'm gonna call it *piss.*
I'm not gonna call it rain.

RICHARD GREEN

Rage

(*2:00 P.M. in a big red van. Green is in the front. He has
a driver. I am in the back. Green wears a large knit hat
with reggae colors over long dreadlocks. Driving from
Crown Heights to Brooklyn College. He turns sideways to
face me in the back, and bends down, talking with his elbow on his knee.*)

Sharpton, Carson, and Reverend Herbert Daughtry
didn't have any power out there really.
The media gave them power.
But they weren't turning those youfs on and off.
Nobody knew who controlled the switch out there.
Those young people had rage like an oil-well fire
that has to burn out.
All they were doin' was sort of orchestratin' it.
Uh, they were not really the ones that were saying, "Well
stop, go, don't go, stop, turn around, go up."
It wasn't like that.
Those young people had rage out there,
that didn't matter who was in control of that—
that rage had to get out
and that rage
has been building up.
When all those guys have come and gone,
that rage is still out here.
I can show you that rage every day
right up and down this avenue.
We see, sometimes in one month, we see three bodies
in one month. That's rage,
and that's something that nobody has control of.
And I don't know who told you that it was preferential
treatment for
Blacks that the Mayor kept the cops back. . . .
If the Mayor had turned those cops on?
We would still be in a middle of a battle.

And
I pray on both sides of the fence,
and I tell the people in the Jewish community the same thing,
"This is not something that force will hold."
Those youfs were running on cops without nothing in their
hands,
seven- and eight- and nine- and ten-year-old boys were running at
those cops
with nothing,
just running at 'em.
That's rage.
Those young people out there are angry
and that anger has to be vented,
it has to be negotiated.
And they're not angry at the Lubavitcher community
they're just as angry at you and me,
if it comes to that.
They have no
role models,
no guidance
so they're just out there growin' up on their own,
their peers are their role models,
their peers is who teach them how to move
so when they see the Lubavitchers
they don't know the difference between "Heil Hitler"
and, uh, and uh, whatever else.
They don't know the difference.
When you ask 'em to say who Hitler was they wouldn't even
be able
to tell you.
Half of them don't even know.
Three quarters of them don't even know.

(*Phone rings, Richard picks it up, it's a mobile phone*)

"Richard Green, can I help?
Aw, man I tol' you I want some color
up on that wall. Give me some colors.
Look, I'm in the middle of somethin'."

(*He returns to the conversation*)

Half them don't even know three quarters of 'em.
Just as much as they don't know who Frederick Douglass was.
They know Malcolm
because Malcolm has been played up to such an extent now
that they know Malcolm.
But ask who Nat Turner was or Mary McCleod Bethune or
Booker T.
Because the system has given 'em
Malcolm is convenient and
Spike is goin' to give 'em Malcolm even more.
It's convenient.

ROSLYN MALAMUD

The Coup

(Spring. Midafternoon. The sunny kitchen of a huge, beautiful house on Eastern Parkway in Crown Heights. It's a large, very well-equipped kitchen. We are sitting at a table in a breakfast nook area, which is separated by shelves from the cooking area. There is a window to the side. There are newspapers on the chair at the far side of the table. Mrs. Malamud offers me food at the beginning of the interview. We are drinking coffee. She is wearing a sweatshirt with a large sequined cat. Her tennis shoes have matching sequined cats. She has on a black skirt and is wearing a wig. Her nails are manicured. She has beautiful eyes that sparkle and are very warm, and a very resonant voice. There is a lot of humor in her face.)

Do you know what happened in August here?
You see when you read the newspapers.
I mean my son filmed what was going on,
but when you read the newspapers . . .
Of course I was here
I couldn't leave my house.
I only would go out early during the day.
The police were barricading here.
You see,
I wish
I could just like
go on television.
I wanna scream to the whole world.
They said
that the Blacks were rioting against the Jews in Crown
     Heights
and that the Jews were fighting back.
Do you know that the Blacks who came here to riot were
     not my
neighbors?
I don't love my neighbors.
I don't know my Black neighbors.
There's one lady on President Street—
Claire—
I adore her.
She's my girl friend's next-door neighbor.
I've had a manicure
done in her house and we sit and kibbitz
and stuff
but I don't know them.
I told you we don't mingle socially
because of the difference
of food
and religion
and what have you here.
But
the people in this community

want exactly
what I want out of life.
They want to live
in nice homes.
They all go to work.
They couldn't possibly
have houses here
if they didn't
generally—They have
two,
um,
incomes
that come in.
They want to send their kids to college.
They wanna live a nice quiet life.
They wanna shop for their groceries and cook their meals
     and go to
their Sunday picnics!
They just want to have decent homes and decent lives!
The people who came to riot here
were brought here
by this famous
Reverend Al Sharpton,
which I'd like to know who ordained him?
He brought in a bunch of kids
who didn't have jobs in
the summertime.
I wish you could see the *New York Times*,
unfortunately it was on page twenty,
I mean, they interviewed
one of the Black girls on Utica Avenue.
She said,
"The guys will make you pregnant
at night
and in the morning not know who you are."

     (Almost whispering)

And if you're sitting on a front stoop and it's very, very hot
and you have no money
and you have nothing to do with your time
and someone says, "Come on, you wanna riot?"
You know how kids are.
The fault lies with the police department.
The police department did nothing to stop them.
I was sitting here in the front of the house
when bottles were being thrown
and the sergeant tells five hundred policemen
with clubs and helmets and guns
to duck.
And I said to him,
"You're telling them to duck?
What should I do?
I don't have a club and a gun."
Had they put it—

stopped it on the first night
this kid who came from Australia . . .

(*She sucks her teeth*)

You know,
his parents were Holocaust survivors, he didn't have to die.
He worked,
did a lot of research in Holocaust studies.
He didn't have to die.
What happened on Utica Avenue
was an accident.
JEWISH PEOPLE
DO NOT DRIVE VANS INTO SEVEN-YEAR-OLD
    BOYS.
YOU WANT TO KNOW SOMETHING? BLACK
    PEOPLE DO NOT DRIVE
VANS INTO SEVEN-YEAR-OLD-BOYS.
HISPANIC PEOPLE DON'T DRIVE VANS INTO
    SEVEN-YEAR-OLD BOYS.
IT'S JUST NOT DONE.
PEOPLE LIKE JEFFREY DAHMER MAYBE THEY DO IT.
BUT AVERAGE CITIZENS DO NOT GO OUT AND
    TRY TO KILL

(*Sounds like a laugh but it's just a sound*)

SEVEN-YEAR-OLD BOYS.
It was an accident!
But it was allowed to fester and to steam and all that.
When you come here do you see anything that's going on,
    riots?
No.
But Al Sharpton and the likes of him like *Dowerty*,
who by the way has been in prison
and all of a sudden he became Reverend *Dowerty*—
they once did an exposé on him—
but
these guys live off of this,
you understand?
People are not gonna give them money,
contribute to their causes
unless they're out there rabble-rousing.
My Black neighbors?
I mean I spoke to them.
They were hiding in their houses just like I was.
We were scared.
I was scared!
I was really frightened.
I had five hundred policemen standing in front of my house
every day
I had mounted police,
but I couldn't leave my block,
because when it got dark I couldn't come back in.
I couldn't meet anyone for dinner.

Thank God, I told you my children were all out of town.
My son was in Russia.
The coup
was exactly the same day as the riot
and I was very upset about it.
He was in Russia running a summer camp
and I was very concerned when I had heard about that.
I hadn't heard from him
that night the riot started.
When I did hear from him I told him to stay in Russia,
    he'd be safer
there than here.
And he was.

REUVEN OSTROV

Pogroms

(*9:00 P.M. November 1991. In a basement of a Crown Heights house. Mr. Ostrov wears a yamulke. Eating popcorn and sliced apples. Very low, gentle-sounding* nigunim *music plays in the background, it almost sounds like New Age music, perhaps because traditional music is played on a modern electronic keyboard instrument. In the show, I wore a basketball jacket with project CURE's insignia, which Mr. Ostrov did not do at this interview, but previously had at a basketball game. He is clean-shaven, which is unusual for a Lubavitcher man his age. He had chosen to shave his beard. He has a very rich, deep voice.*)

I was working in a hospital.
I work as an assistant chaplain at
Down State Kings County Hospital.
I heard that Yankel Rosenbaum was stabbed and, um, they
were gonna give him an *aurtopsy*
and they asked if he had an
aurtopsy
or not because in the Jewish religion a person is not
    allowed to have
an aurtopsy
and I found out later that he did have one
a few days later.
I found a Jewish man in a room,
a Russian man.
His mother committed suicide
because she was, uhm, she was terrified.
She jumped out of the third floor of her apartment building,
committed suicide.
The mother originally came from Russia.
I was speaking to her son
in one of the rooms near the morgue
trying to get his mother not to have an aurtopsy
and he was telling me that the mother
came from Russia eleven years ago

and the mother left Russia eleven years ago
because of the hardships that they had over there,
and when they came to America
and when this thing started to happen in Crown Heights.
It became painful
and it felt like, like there was no place to go.
It's like you're trapped,
everywhere you go there's Jew haters.
And then he told me she commit suicide,
told me the next morning he woke up
he heard the doorbell ring.
He wasn't,
she wasn't there.
He noticed that the window was open,
which is never open
because she was afraid of the cold
even in the summertime.
And he saw his mother
with blood all over her
landed head first
on the concrete side of the apartment building.
After that we already knew this was getting serious,
because we had,
we had Sonny Carson come down
and we had, um,
Reverend Al Sharpton come down
start making pogroms.

CARMEL CATO

Lingering

(7:00 P.M. *The corner where the accident occurred in
Crown Heights. An altar to Gavin is against the wall
where the car crashed. Many pieces of cloth are draped.
Some writing in color is on the wall. Candle wax is everywhere. There is a rope around the area. Cato is wearing a
trench coat, pulled around him. He stands very close to
me. Dark outside. Reggae music is in the background.
Lights come from stores on each corner. Busy intersection.
Sounds from outside. Traffic. Stores open. People in and
out of shops. Sounds from inside apartments, televisions,
voices, cooking, etc. He speaks in a pronounced West Indian accent.*)

In the meanwhile
it was two.
Angela was on the ground
but she was trying to move. Gavin was still.
They was trying to pound him.
I was the father.
I was 'it, chucked, and pushed,
and a lot of
sarcastic words were passed towards me

from the police
while I was trying to explain: It was my kid!
These are my children.
The child was hit you know.
I saw everything, everything,
the guy radiator burst
all the hoses,
the steam,
all the garbage buckets goin' along the building.
And it was very loud,
everything burst.
It's like an atomic bomb,
That's why all these people
comin' round
wanna know what's happening.
Oh it was very outrageous.
Numerous numbers.
All the time the police sayin'
you can't get in,
you can't pass,
and the children laying on the ground.
He was hit at exactly eight-thirty.
Why?
I was standing over there.
There was a little child—
a friend of mine
came up with a little child—
and I lift the child up
and she look at her watch at the same time
and she say it was eight-thirty.
I gave the child back to her.
And then it happen.
Um, Um . . .
My child, these are the things I never dream about.
I take care of my children.
You know it's a funny thing,
if a child get sick and he dies
it won't hurt me so bad,
or if a child run out into the street and get hit down,
it wouldn't hurt me.
That's what's hurtin' me.
The whole week
before Gavin died
my body was changing,
I was having different feelings.
I stop eating,
I didn't et
nothin',
only drink water,
for two weeks;
and I was very touchy—
any least thing that drop
or any song I hear
it would effect me.

Every time I try to do something
I would have to stop.
I was
lingering, lingering, lingering, lingering,
all the time.
But I can do things,
I can see things,
I know that for a fact.
I was telling myself,
"Something is wrong somewhere,"
but I didn't want to see,
I didn't want to accept,
and it was inside of me,
and even when I go home I tell my friends,
"Something coming I could feel it
but I didn't want to see,"
and all the time I just deny deny deny,
and I never thought it was Gavin,
but I didn't have a clue.
I thought it was one of the other children—
the bigger boys
or the girl,
because she worry me,
she won't et—
but Gaven 'ee was 'ealtee,
and he don't cause no trouble.
That's what's devastating me now.
Sometime it make me feel like it's no justice,
like, uh,
the Jewish people,

they are very high up,
it's a very big thing,
they runnin' the whole show
from the judge right down.
And something I don't understand:
The Jewish people, they told me
there are certain people I cannot be seen with
and certain things I can not say
and certain people I can not talk to.
They made that very clear to me—the Jewish people—
they can throw the case out
unless
I go to them with pity.
I don't know what they talkin' about.
So I don't know what kind of crap is that.
And make me say things I don't wanna say
and make me do things I don't wanna do.
I am a special person.
I was born different.
I'm a man born by my foot.
I born by my foot.
Anytime a baby comin' by the foot
they either cut the mother
or the baby dies.
But I was born with my foot.
I'm one of the special.
There's no way they can overpower me.
No there's nothing to hide,
you can repeat every word I say.

TOPICS FOR CRITICAL THINKING AND WRITING

 The Play on the PAGE

1. In each of the characters presented—whether well known or not—the playwright has shaped the speaker's words to communicate the essence of his or her personality, in Stanislavskian acting theory terms, the *spine* of the character. Describe the spines of these characters: (a) Angela Davis, (b) Rivkah Siegal, (c) Leonard Jeffries, (d) "Big Mo" Matthews, and (e) Rabbi Shea Hecht.

2. The core theme of this play is identity. How do *you* define your own identity? What group(s) do you identify with?

3. Poet W.B. Yeats wrote, "The best lack all conviction, while the worst / Are full of passionate intensity." Discuss the truth of this observation with reference to the characters in this play.

The Play on the STAGE

4. Assuming you did not want to present *Fires in the Mirror* as a one-performer piece, what alternate ways of staging would you consider? Would you use two actors? Four actors? More? What balance of white and black? What balance of male and female? Would you use projections? Slides? Films? Any other ideas?

The Play in PERFORMANCE

The initial explosive impact of *Fires in the Mirror* at the New York Shakespeare Festival in 1992 (it subsequently played all over the country and abroad) derived from the combined skills of its creator. Anna Deavere Smith had, first of all, revealed herself as a probing investigative reporter who succeeded in getting her subjects to reveal core aspects of character that usually remain hidden. Secondly, as we have just discussed, she revealed herself as a playwright of note, for out of the mass of material she had constructed a play with memorable characters, vital and original themes, and effective dramatic structure and development. Moreover, she showed an ear for poetry, for as one reviewer noted, she "locates the poetry in her subjects' speech, in their minds and their hearts" and proved "that if you listen long enough, look deep enough, everyone is a poet." Lastly, and surely *not* least importantly, she revealed herself as a unique performer of unusual skills. As New York Theater Festival artistic director George C. Wolfe noted, "She has crafted this extraordinary technique—art form—of both embodying a person and illuminating their language."

As the result of her studies on Shakespeare's use of language with Juanita Rice at Beaver College, Smith came to understand the power that language contained. "I had not controlled the words. I had presented myself as an empty vessel, a repeater, and they had shown their power." She realized that if she listened carefully to people's words—particularly to their rhythms—she could use language to learn about her own time. When she became a teacher of acting, she became increasingly troubled by the Stanislavskian notion that an actor creates character through the process of discovering his or her own similarity to the character. She wanted to put her students in the shoes of *others*. And so she worked to establish an alternative acting technique that would "begin with the other and come to the self, a technique that would empower the other to find the actor rather than the other way around." To demonstrate her ideas to her students she began performing herself, a process, as we have noted, that led to her accepting the mantle of performer.

As a performer, she starts with a distinctive physical presence that permits her chameleon transformations: a handsome, tall, thin, light-skinned African American woman, slim-hipped, slightly androgynous. No character habitation—black or white, male or female—is ever rendered ludicrous by her appearance. Add a flexible voice capable of radical vocal transitions and a sensibility that projects both intelligence and commitment, and she becomes the perfect instrument for her textual creations. "The performer's possibility," she said in dialogue with Jessye Norman, "is to take a moment and whatever the moment is, to have authority over it and transform it." The aim is never mere mimicry, but always something more: to find the stance, the gesture, the demeanor to match the memory, the detail, the idea that most succinctly defines the character portrayed. George Wolfe, who witnessed the early multiperformer version of *House Arrest,* noted that the actors lacked a key element in Smith's performance style: "I saw a lot of talented actors playing the roles, and they were acting the roles in a way that you were witnessing the emotion instead of in a way that the language was swirling up and popping around you." They could find the motivations but not the poetry in the characters they portrayed. Gordon Davidson, artistic director of the Mark Taper Forum in

Los Angeles—where the multiactor *House Arrest* debuted—pointed out that the dramatic effect of Smith onstage was almost impossible for other actors to replicate: "the audience becomes Anna—they sit in for her because Anna is talking to them as if she were asking the questions. She creates a level of reality. When you have actors doing it, it removes it one more step. They were second generation and it lost something."

This connection between actor and audience is something very much on Smith's mind. Through performance, Smith wants to reclaim the audience from media manipulation:

> Early on, I saw, close up, that the techniques of acting and theater were being adopted by politicians and their handlers. We are now at a point where . . . peo-

ple are cynical about these techniques . . . I begin to wonder if, when politicians are accused of "acting," they are really being accused of being "inauthentic." . . . What I've come to realize is that acting, in its purest form, is not about being inauthentic at all; it's not even really about imitation. What it is really about is creating a fiction of a human being, of a character, in order to illuminate something not only about that character but about *all* of us.

In an age in which political issues are reduced to one-minute sound bytes, Anna Deavere Smith—in all her manifestations—talks to us honestly and directly. None of her performances end at final blackout: They continue far into the night in theaters, lobbies, cars, bars, and homes as people try to understand.

GREG TATE
*Bewitching the Other**

Tate: How do you go about disarming your subjects?

Smith: I don't think I do. I just don't say very much. I'm not aware of disarming them.

Do you think Americans have a propensity for the confessional mode?

They probably do, although I have made a piece . . . where the people were from different places. I think it's in the nature of speaking to put out words until you have this experience of yourself that is intellectually and physically satisfying; then you're silent. That's where the poem happens.

How do you separate your persona from the text?

Well, it's very technical what I'm doing. I'm trying to hit the notes and hit the rhythms that have been transcribed, trying to remember the tape. And I think about the people certainly, I think about the characters. I'll think about something that means something different to them. I've dreamt about some of them, so they have invaded my own psychic life. Invaded probably isn't the right word. They've appeared, so I've

probably combined something they have to say with my own awareness, but I know I'm not them. . . .

You're uncomfortable identifying with a character's issues or finding a connection between their lives and your own?

It's not a discomfort as much as to say that question is my whole project, but I have to admit that it does happen. Even with Rivkah Siegal, who talks about having to have five wigs and feels like the wig is fake. It shocked me to find out how personal that was. Because we've all worn something we were struggling with wearing, whether it was our hair or whatever.

Hair is such a major black issue that if it appeared in any other culture as an issue black folks would be able to leap the distance. But do you feel like you're cheating by identifying with a character's issues?

Well, the whole question is do we really have to identify with somebody to be somebody? I don't now the answer, but that's what really set me down this road. Isn't there another way? That's why Adrienne's [Kennedy] work just blew me open, because the difficulty was where to find a space between this [the head] and this [the gut]. . . . The fact that I'm doing so many characters is about trying to find the flow between those people. I must be the flow, that's where I am. People ask, "Where am I, do I get lost, do I take them with me?" I used to say, "I am where one stops and

* From an Interview with Anna Deavere Smith, *Village Voice*, 21 July 1992: 99

where the next one begins." But now, talking to you in this moment, I think that where I am is in the flow. The interpreter underneath.

How do you begin establishing the flow and the rhythm, the continuity between the characters and segments?

A lot happens during the interviews. I don't go back to the shop, so to speak, until I have most of the interviews done. In this piece, for example, I knew that I would use, "These young people have rage that's burning like an oil-well fire." So that begins to influence who else is going to be there. I knew I would use "If you piss in my face I'm going to call it piss, I'm not going to call it rain." I knew I would use "Jewish people don't drive vans into seven-year-old boys." So sometimes as people speak, I know. And obviously I'm interested in balance and fairness and all of that. When I got Lette's story about Isaac and the camps it meant I had to find something about slavery, and fortunately Conrad Muhammad was a very strong speaker about slavery. Once I have the tapes I go into a big room like a dance space and I find the material that I think will feel the best on my body. I lie on the floor with the head phones on and start repeating it and repeating it, and repeating it. And that becomes the core stone ground anchor of the piece, and then everything else spins out from that. In this process, my dramaturg and my director voted for the characters they liked the best. I refused to vote. I went away. I was afraid. I'd made a piece before with a director where I got killed by the intellect. This is not an intellectual thing. I really have to wear these words. Know if they fit, know how they feel, know if it has resonance, know if I am going to dream about it. And nobody can tell me that.

Do you feel you lost some of your larger goal of interrogating identity in narrowing the focus to Crown Heights?

No, I think this was a good focus. Ultimately I would like to make a piece that has an even more discrete propulsion. This piece still goes a little like this [indicates a straight line], and I would like to make a piece where you would look at one person and then another and say, "Well, what in the world do they have to do with one another?" but you would still say, like, "Wow," and that something happened. I'd like to make something more circular, with no traditional regard whatsoever for a line. But somehow it would be vital, and you knew you understood without understanding. Something like baby powder, a whole different kind of feeling where you didn't know where you were, you didn't care you didn't know, something happened.

Doing this piece in New York, it has built-in hooks already. People come with conflict.

And the fact that there was a story in the media. This piece could not be as effective if the media had not already created the vocabulary. They made the theme and then I get to do my little jazz on the theme.

There's a prepared text in the subconscious of certain of your subjects. George Wolfe, Ntozake Shange, Carson, Jeffries, Sharpton—they're all living out their textuality. Or performing it.

I would say that my goal is ultimately to question all of that, all of those prepared texts. But I would say the audience is grateful to have a prepared text because they're still looking for clarity about these issues because they're so anxious. But in the few post-play discussions we've had, you realize that even though they're grateful for the prepared texts, more of their upsetness, more of their what-am-I-going-to-do-ness, comes out. Like we had one lady the other night who said, "Well, I think some of these characters are caricatures." I didn't know how to answer that because . . . even if they were, so what? What is she really saying with that? . . . "Is it really OK for me to be making fun of people. If you had interviewed me, you would have made fun of me. I know you would have. And I wouldn't have liked that." That's what that question means. And we had a black lady say, "I think you sympathize more with Jewish people," and six Jewish people said it was very fair, which by now I expect to hear. And some people started counting how many of this or that I did, and I think that's very unfortunate.

* * *

Do you think people come to the show seeking catharsis?

Maybe the people who come do want catharsis because you wouldn't have to come see this after all. It's not required reading.

I don't think people find resolution. I think what they come looking for is a soul session, a spiritual experience, a connection with humanity that can take place within a television time frame.

But then what do you think theater can do right now?

Theater is the counter-spectacle, the critical spectacle, the communion that critiques itself. . . . I think any progressive artist working now has to perform a seduction saying really harsh things. But are you asking that old question about what is the purpose of the artist?

No, it's not that. The press is very interested in race right now. And we're in another moment where people are afraid and they want to know. So it's not so much about the purpose as what you think the dynamic can be if it's not to have a catharsis, right? Or what can be the productive way that this being together, this occasion can work, what can it do when in fact there's a national theater going on? So that people coming from the national theater come here and they're coming after the theater. . . . See, what I'm asking you is how as another black artist do you feel you could participate in this national theater that's going to get more dramatic?

I think you already answered that.

PHOTO ESSAY:
Representations of Gender in the Theater

In the section "Women's Theater" (page 950), we briefly discuss some of the reasons why women were not strongly represented as dramatists in earlier centuries. In the following pages we discuss other aspects of gender in the theater.

Contemporary thinking divides between two views of gender. The "essentialist" view holds that our species has a biologically fixed sex division between male and female (a matter of chromosomes, hormones, and anatomical differences) and that the masculine and feminine roles we live out are natural, or innate—part of our very essence. In this sense, they are "essential." The "constructivist" view, on the other hand, distinguishes between sex and gender. This second view holds that although there is a fixed sex division (again, a matter of biology), our patterns of gender (masculinity, femininity) are largely produced by cultural interpretation. Parents, siblings, advertisements, and so forth, teach us that males are masculine (strong, active, rational) and that females are feminine (weak, passive, emotional). According to this view, we (or at least most of us) play male or female roles in a social performance, "constructing" ourselves into what society expects of us. This is not exactly what Shakespeare meant when he said, "All the world's a stage," but the phrase is apt enough; we are all performers, playing many roles—for example, students, athletes, lovers, siblings, workers, dutiful (or perhaps rebellious) children, sober citizens, hearty friends, and so on.

Here are two statements setting forth the two positions. The first is by an essentialist.

> Every mother who has held a girl child in her arms has known that she was different from a boy child and that she would approach the reality around her in a different way.... She is a female and she will die fe-male, and though many centuries should pass, archaeologists would identify her skeleton as the remains of a female creature.

GERMAINE GREER, *THE CHANGE* (1991)

The second statement is by a constructivist, although he lived two centuries before the word was invented.

> The multitude will hardly believe the excessive force of education, and in the difference of modesty between men and women, [they] ascribe that to nature which is altogether owing to early instruction. *Miss* is scarce three years old, but she's spoke to every day to hide her leg, and rebuked in good earnest if she shows it; whilst *little Master* at the same age is bid to take up his coats and piss like a man.

BERNARD MANDEVILLE, *THE FABLE OF THE BEES* (1723)

With these competing views as background, let's now quickly survey the presence of women in drama.

In ancient Greece, plays were written only by men, and female roles in plays were performed by men who wore female costumes and masks. (See pages 45–46.) Possibly women attended the dramatic festivals, but the evidence is unclear. From the point of view of many feminist scholars, real women were in effect erased—they were mere household aids and machines for producing children—and their images were constructed by the male dramatists who wrote the roles and the male actors who performed the roles. One feminist scholar, Sue-Ellen Case, in *Feminism and Theatre* (1988) suggests that female roles or spectators may find that the female roles in Greek drama are mere male fantasies, images that have nothing to do with the experience of real women. Of course, when Greek plays are staged today, women perform these roles, but Case suggests that these "classic drag" roles (5) should perhaps today be performed by men, just as they were performed in ancient Greece. If they were performed by men, she says, we could all clearly see how "Other" they are.

> The feminist theatre-practitioner might, for instance, understand *Lysistrata* not as a good play for women, but as a male drag show, with burlesque jokes about breasts and phalluses playing well in the drag tradition. The feminist director might cast a man in the role of Medea, underscoring the patriarchal prejudice of ownership and jealousy and the ownership of children as male concerns. The feminist actor may no longer regard these roles as desirable for her career. (19)

By the way, notice that in Case's last sentence she uses the word *actor*, whereas other writers might use *actress*. Many people today find *actress* (like *hostess* and *stewardess*) demeaning and prefer to use *actor* for a woman as well as a man.

In the Elizabethan theater, too, female roles were played by males, in this case by boys whose voices had not yet changed. As with Greek plays, these roles today are played by women. We might ask ourselves whether the roles have, therefore, necessarily changed, whether, for example, Hippolyta, Helena, Hermia, and Titania in *A Midsummer Night's Dream* and Goneril, Regan, and Cordelia in *King Lear* must be different today from what they were in Shakespeare's day by virtue of the fact that today the parts are enacted by female bodies and female voices. One view is that they are different and they are better, since they now truly have a woman's imprint. A different view holds that the biology of the actor is irrelevant to the way in which the role is performed. A third view resembles Case's view of Greek drama—that is, one might argue that the parts (no matter who speaks them) remain "classic drag."

The fact that originally the roles were performed by boys dressed as girls has provoked much speculation about the spectators' responses. Were some spectators (knowing of course that the performers were boys) erotically aroused? Conversely, did the fact that the performers were boys provide a sort of "aesthetic distance," allowing the spectators (at least the straight ones) to enjoy the play as a *play*, free from any fantasized physical involvement with the female roles they watched on the stage? Perhaps no one gave the matter any thought, one way or another. Perhaps it was a convention they were so used to that they gave it no more thought than we give the fact that when we see Ibsen's *A Doll's House* acted in a box set, we are looking at the strangest imaginable room—a room that is realistic in countless details except that—crazy though this sounds—the fourth wall is missing.

Cross-dressing is a convention in the theater in other cultures, notably China and Japan, where it is still used in certain kinds of plays. (See page 1402.) Theorists sometimes argue, in fact, that a man can play a woman better than a woman can, because he *is acting* whereas she may be behaving naturally, and acting is something quite different from natural behavior. Of course, by this logic, women ought to play men's roles better than men can, but one rarely hears this assertion.

Cross-dressing affords women a chance to play male roles. (See page 1403.) Alternatively, roles can simply be changed, for example, from King Lear to Queen Lear. We can quote a comment by the director of such a production concerning Ruth Maleczech's desire to play Lear:

> It took me a while to understand that there were certain political imperatives inherent in that desire. What's one of the first things you see? That Lear's story, at least in part, is about the relationship between power and love. A man can be powerful and still be loved, but it's rare to see a woman loved for her power—women must be powerless. So as women gain power in our society, they also find love more difficult to attain.

QUOTED IN LESLEY FERRIS, ED., *CROSSING THE STAGE* (1993), 3.

Cross-dressing—a female in a male role, or a male in a female role—is used (chiefly by feminists) as a critique of society's construction of gender.

> We use cross-gender performances to challenge traditional representations, to illuminate gender-as-construction, and to provide actors (especially women) with access to a broader range of roles than they would otherwise have. Cross-gender casting expands a director's range in conceptualizing a production and can subvert conventional representation and realism. Crossing genders is also simply a way to increase the pleasure and fun of theatrical work.

RHONDA BLAIR, IN *UPSTAGING BIG DADDY*, ED. ELLEN DONKIN AND SUSAN CLEMENTS (1993), 291.

At least two other things ought to be said about cross-dressing. First, some playwrights vehemently oppose it. Samuel Beckett, for instance, refused to allow his plays to be produced with women taking male roles. Second, much cross-dressing, for instance in Brandon Thomas's venerable classic, *Charley's Aunt* (1892), and in films such as *Tootsie*, *Some Like It Hot*, and *Mrs. Doubtfire*, seems largely based on the idea that it is funny for a man to be dressed as a woman. What is offered is light entertainment, not a searching examination of gender roles. The humor perhaps is rooted in the assumption that a man dressed as a woman is in some sort of inferior and inherently demeaning position. Understandably, many women resent these images. Because women are expected (at least by most male viewers) to add beauty to the stage, an older (and implicitly therefore unattractive) woman may be played comically by a male.

Something should be said here about gay and lesbian theater. It is a significant fact that three of the four chief American dramatists of the middle of the century—Tennessee Williams, William Inge, and Edward Albee—were gay but could not directly put gay characters on the stage. In looking at some of their works, it now is evident (and indeed it was evident even then to those who were in the know) that they were writing about homosexual experience and that they voiced their concerns through various disguises. Thus, in Inge's *Bus Stop*, the professor (like Inge) is an alcoholic, but the professor's problem is a fondness for young girls, whereas Inge's was a forbidden fondness for men. These gay writers sometimes expressed their concerns through some of their female characters. In discussing *A Streetcar Named Desire*, it is a rare commentator today who does not say that Tennessee Williams was voicing a private concern when Blanche DuBois said, "I don't want realism. I want magic!" The usual interpretation is that this is the voice of a gay man crying out for freedom from current oppressive conventions.

Although male gay drama was common (if sufficiently disguised) on the stage from the 1920s through the 1950s, lesbian drama is almost invisible before the late 1960s. The absence of lesbian voices in the theater is not surprising, given the fact that until recently very few women wrote for the theater. (See section "Women's Theater," page 950.) True, the topic occasionally was introduced in a play, for instance in Lillian Hellman's *The Children's Hour* (1934), but the author was straight, and within the play the charge of being a lesbian is unfounded. Not until the 1970s do we get a significant number of plays about lesbians that presumably are addressed to a predominantly straight audience. Beginning with the 1980s there seems to be something of a shift from defensiveness to celebration, and the audience (for instance Ellen Galford's *The Fires of Bride* [1990]) seems to have changed from straights to lesbians. One final point, and it repeats one we have already made. Many feminists argue that the great body of dramatic literature, at least from

Greece through Arthur Miller, falsifies the experience of women. For instance, after talking about playwrights of the 1970s, Linda Ben-Zvi continues thus:

> The depiction of women by playwrights of the preceding generation is often no better. One need only think of Arthur Miller's handling of Linda Loman in *Death of a Salesman*. She is wife, she is mother, but she is never a person in her own right. . . . Unlike Winnie [in Beckett's *Happy Days*] she is never allowed to articulate her dreams, memories, or thoughts. She functions entirely as a cipher for the men in her life. Her signs are the laundry basket and the darned socks, just as the signs of the woman in the hotel room—another stereotyped figure at the other end of the gender spectrum—are her raucous laughter and her unclothed body. Both are images of women seen entirely from a male perspective. At the Loman family table only three places are set.
>
> WOMEN IN BECKETT (1990), XIV.

There is much to think about here, but we want to suggest three points. First, the men in the Loman family are hardly such that one would want them in one's own family. Second, Linda ultimately throws out her sons ("Get out of here, both of you, and don't come back. . . . Pick up this stuff, I'm not your maid any more. Pick it up, you bum, you!"). Third, the most memorable speech in the play is spoken not by any of the men but by Linda:

> Willy Loman never made a lot of money. His name was never in the paper. He's not the finest character that ever lived. But he's a human being, and a terrible thing is happening to him. So attention must be paid. He's not to be allowed to fall into his grave like an old dog. Attention, attention must be finally paid to such a person.

Of course the speech is *about* Willy, but we can never forget the speaker. If the Loman table is set with only three places—if, in effect, Linda is an outsider—Linda nevertheless is the most impressive figure in the play. (See page 1403.)

■ SUGGESTED REFERENCES

Most of the titles listed at the end of "Women's Theater" (page 950) are relevant here, but in addition see Vern L. Burrough, *Cross Dressing, Sex, and Gender* (1993); Marjorie Garber, *Vested Interests: Cross-Dressing and Cultural Anxiety* (1992); and Alisa Solomon, *Re-Dressing the Canon: Essays on Theater and Gender* (1997).

This marble relief sculpture shows the Greek comic dramatist Menander holding the mask of a young man. On the table are the mask of a woman and the grotesque mask of a slave. All of the roles were played by males. Given the great size of Greek theaters, subtle facial gestures of live actors would be invisible to most spectators, so masks were used to convey the essential type of the role. One of the questions that feminist scholars have raised is this: Can male playwrights and male actors adequately give voice to the experience of woman?

One strategy of many women playwrights in the twentieth century has been to take historic male or female figures and rewrite their stories from the viewpoint of a woman. The French feminist playwright Hélène Cixous's play, *Portrait of Dora*, veers between dream states and realistic moments as it explores the character Sigmund Freud and his first case study, Dora. The story is told from the point of view of Dora who disagrees with Freud's analysis and interpretation of her dreams. The play includes inventive staging possibilities as depicted here in a scene in which Freud (seated right) and Dora (standing right) observe one of her dreams.

A woman invented the Japanese Kabuki drama in the seventeenth century, and initially women performed in the plays. Soon, however, women were banned on grounds of immorality, and men performed female as well as male roles. The *onnagata* (female impersonator) shown here, Masakado, has been honored with the title of Living National Treasure. In Kabuki, the acting is highly stylized. Fight scenes, for instance, are almost balletic. Furthermore, stage hands, usually dressed in black, are conceived as invisible. Despite the high degree of stylization, devotees of Kabuki insist that the *onnagata* is more feminine than a real woman.

Sarah Bernhardt (1844–1923), widely regarded as the greatest performer in nineteenth-century France, occasionally played what are called *breeches parts,* that is, male roles designed to be played by women. She also played some male roles originally written for males, for example, Napoleon's son in Rostand's *L'Aiglon* (1900) and Hamlet. Special circumstances helped to make these roles acceptable. In the case of *L'Aiglon,* the play is something of a romantic costume piece about a fragile youth who died when he was twenty-one; in the case of *Hamlet,* the protagonist is sometimes regarded (wrongly) as unmanly.

A common explanation for nineteenth-century breeches parts is that they gave women a chance to show their legs, or, rather, they gave men a chance to admire women's legs. However, these explanations may trivialize the matter. The fact is that women, because of their sex, were in effect barred from performing many great parts. Think, for example, of Greek tragedy. *Oedipus the King* has seven speaking parts for men but only one for a woman; even *Antigone* has five speaking parts for males and only three for females. In *Hamlet,* there are more than twenty speaking parts for males and only two for females, Bernhardt may well have been more interested in playing the role of Hamlet than in displaying her body for the delight of men.

Linda Loman, in Arthur Miller's *Death of a Salesman,* has come in for severe criticism from some feminist writers, but others have held that she is the most decent and the most sensible character in the play. If the Loman family is essentially the father and two sons, her apartness from the family suggests her superiority.

Here in one of the fantasy sequences of *Angels in America, Part One,* Prior dresses as a woman and for a moment at least he finds pleasure in his cross-dressing masquerade. Harper, in her valium-induced hallucination, talks to him and they share a mutual sense of despair and comic relief at their very different, but also frighteningly similar situations. Later the actor who plays Harper dresses as Martin Heller, a side-kick of Roy Cohn. Kushner's use of cross-dressing draws attention to the various gender issues that permeate the play.

TONY Kushner

Tony Kushner was born in 1956 in New York City to Jewish parents who were both musicians. He grew up in Lake Charles, Louisiana, where his father conducted the symphony orchestra. His family life was intensely political, and dinner conversation covered music, politics, arts, and ethics. Kushner fell in love with theater when, as a young child, he saw his mother perform the role of Linda Loman in Miller's *Death of a Salesman* at the Little Theater in Lake Charles. A star on the high school debate team, Kushner continues to use his wide knowledge of politics and history in his plays. Growing up he kept his sexual identity—he is gay—a secret from his family, and he remained closeted for a few years after graduating from Columbia University with a degree in history in 1978. He went on to study directing at New York University, where he earned an MFA. His earliest plays, produced in the early 1980's, include *La Fin de la Baleine: An Opera for the Apocalypse* (1982) and *A Bright Room Called Day* (1985), as well as several plays for children. Later works include *Hydrotaphia, or the Death of Doctor Browne* (1987), *Slavs!* (1993), and *A Dybbuk or Between Two Worlds* (1995). He has adapted several plays, including Corneille's *The Illusion*. He has received numerous awards for *Angels in America, Part One: Millennium Approaches* (1990), and *Angels in America, Part Two: Perestroika* (1991), including the Pulitzer Prize, a Tony Award for Best New Play, the London Drama Critics' Circle Award for Best New Play, and Drama Desk Award for Best Play. Kushner is a dedicated political activist, particularly in relation to human rights issues. He is a member of ACT-UP (AIDS Coalition to Unleash Power) and in 1989 was arrested during an ACT-UP demonstration at St. Patrick's Cathedral in New York City. In 1998, through his impassioned essays and speeches, Kushner protested the murder of Matthew Shepherd, the gay student who was brutally beaten in Wyoming. In 1998 the Royal National Theater of Great Britain named *Angels in America* one of the ten best plays of the twentieth century.

COMMENTARY ON *ANGELS IN AMERICA, PART ONE: MILLENNIUM APPROACHES*

When Oskar Eustis, then artistic director of the Eureka Theater in San Francisco, offered Tony Kushner a commission in 1987, Kushner was interested in writing about three quite different subjects: Roy Cohn, who had just died, Mormons, and AIDS. When he began work on the project in 1988 the world seemed to be undergoing some major political changes: The Soviet Union was collapsing and the borders of Eastern Europe were transforming. AIDS had been identified as the "gay plague," and Ronald Reagan, as president of the United States, was continuing a strongly conservative stance in dealing with the deadly effects of the AIDS virus. For Kushner, a gay man, coming to terms with the AIDS virus and its effect on the gay community was an important issue. In the program note for the production at the Royal National Theater of Great Britain in London, Kushner said,

> AIDS reminds us, I think, that compassion has to do with passion, that health care is a political issue and a

human right, and that the politics of nursing, of love, are much-neglected and under-theorized. Progressive ideologies maintain their divorce from the ineffable, the mysterious, the spiritual. This is a blindness we can no longer afford.

The play that emerged from Kushner's concerns has an epic quality, embracing an impressive range of political issues, characters, and themes. The play stresses the importance of individual responsibility in this world where a single individual's actions affect the lives of numerous other people in unfathomable ways. *Angels in America* is the living embodiment of a multiplicity of voices—voices of the present, of the dead, of angels. This celebration of plurality questions the binary stranglehold of "us or them," gay or straight, white or black.

The "angel" of Kushner's title is both a physicalized presence, a winged character, and a metaphor for death. The story that enfolds before us is, in part, Prior's coming to terms with his disease. The first "angel" that appears in the play is the Karposi's sarcoma lesion that Prior shows Louis in Act 1, Scene 4: "the wine-dark kiss of the angel of death." Despite the inherently serious nature of ideas surrounding death, Kushner has infused his play with dazzling moments of comedy and fantasy, juxtaposed with intimate, insightful scenes of realism. But Prior's story is only one of several stories that are played out and entwined in the play. In order to stage these multiple narratives, one of the devices Kushner developed is the split scene, two scenes that happen simultaneously on the stage. One particularly powerful split scene occurs when Prior and his lover Louis are having an angry fight about split-

ting up while Harper and her husband Joe also argue about their deteriorating relationship and Joe leaves her. In both cases the partners who leave—Louis and Joe—have betrayed their lovers. Such a staging forces us to consider the connections to be made between the different stories, the many characters, the many voices. Kushner subtitled his play "A Gay Fantasia on National Themes," and the prominence of his work has helped challenge and change the ways we think about gay rights in a national context.

ANGELS IN AMERICA
PART ONE:
MILLENNIUM APPROACHES
Tony Kushner

THE CHARACTERS

ROY M. COHN, *a successful New York lawyer and unofficial power broker.*

JOSEPH PORTER PITT, *chief clerk for Justice Theodore Wilson of the Federal Court of Appeals, Second Circuit.*

HARPER AMATY PITT, *Joe's wife, an agoraphobic with a mild Valium addiction.*

LOUIS IRONSON, *a word processor working for the Second Circuit Court of Appeals.*

PRIOR WALTER, *Louis's boyfriend. Occasionally works as a club designer or caterer, otherwise lives very modestly but with great style off a small trust fund.*

HANNAH PORTER PITT, *Joe's mother, currently residing in Salt Lake City, living off her deceased husband's army pension.*

BELIZE, *a former drag queen and former lover of Prior's. A registered nurse. Belize's name was originally Norman Arriaga; Belize is a drag name that stuck.*

THE ANGEL, *four divine emanations, Fluor, Phosphor, Lumen and Candle; manifest in One: the Continental Principality of America. She has magnificent steel-gray wings.*

OTHER CHARACTERS IN PART ONE

RABBI ISIDOR CHEMELWITZ, *an orthodox Jewish rabbi, played by the actor playing Hannah.*

MR. LIES, *Harper's imaginary friend, a travel agent, who in style of dress and speech suggests a jazz musician; he always wears a large lapel badge emblazoned "IOTA" (The International Order of Travel Agents). He is played by the actor playing Belize.*

THE MAN IN THE PARK, *played by the actor playing Prior.*

THE VOICE, *the voice of The Angel.*

HENRY, *Roy's doctor, played by the actor playing Hannah.*

EMILY, *a nurse, played by the actor playing The Angel.*

MARTIN HELLER, *a Reagan Administration Justice Department flackman, played by the actor playing Harper.*

SISTER ELLA CHAPTER, *a Salt Lake City real-estate saleswoman, played by the actor playing The Angel.*

PRIOR 1, *the ghost of a dead Prior Walter from the 13th century, played by the actor playing Joe. He is a blunt, gloomy medieval farmer with a guttural Yorkshire accent.*

PRIOR 2, *the ghost of a dead Prior Walter from the 17th century, played by the actor playing Roy. He is a Londoner, sophisticated, with a High British accent.*

THE ESKIMO, *played by the actor playing Joe.*

THE WOMAN IN THE SOUTH BRONX, *played by the actor playing The Angel.*

ETHEL ROSENBERG, *played by the actor playing Hannah.*

PLAYWRIGHT'S NOTES

A DISCLAIMER: *Roy M. Cohn, the character, is based on the late Roy M. Cohn (1927–1986), who was all too real; for the most part the acts attributed to the character Roy, such as his illegal conferences with Judge Kaufmann during the trial of Ethel Rosenberg, are to be found in the historical record. But this Roy is a work of dramatic fiction; his words are my invention, and liberties have been taken.*

A NOTE ABOUT THE STAGING: *The play benefits from a pared-down style of presentation, with minimal scenery and scene shifts done rapidly (no blackouts!), employing the cast as well as stage-hands—which makes for an actor-driven event, as this must be. The moments of magic—the appearance and disappearance of Mr. Lies and the ghosts, the Book hallucination, and the ending—are to be fully realized, as bits of wonderful theatrical illusion—which means it's OK if the wires show, and maybe it's good that they do, but the magic should at the same time be thoroughly amazing.*

At the climax of *Angels in America, Part One: Millennium Approaches,* the Angel makes her first appearance by crashing through the ceiling in Prior's bedroom. Even though he is terrified, Prior still has enough wits about him to whisper, "*Very* Steven Spielberg." This production was directed by Woodie King, Jr., at the Ohio State University in 1999.

ACT ONE: BAD NEWS

October–November 1985

SCENE 1

The last days of October. Rabbi Isidor Chemelwitz alone onstage with a small coffin. It is a rough pine box with two wooden pegs, one at the foot and one at the head, holding the lid in place. A prayer shawl embroidered with a Star of David is draped over the lid, and by the head a yarzheit candle is burning.

RABBI ISIDOR CHEMELWITZ (*He speaks sonorously, with a heavy Eastern European accent, unapologetically consulting a sheet of notes for the family names*). Hello and good morning. I am Rabbi Isidor Chemelwitz of the Bronx Home for Aged Hebrews. We are here this morning to pay respects at the passing of Sarah Ironson, devoted wife of Benjamin Ironson, also deceased, loving and caring mother of her sons Morris, Abraham, and Samuel, and her daughters Esther and Rachel; beloved grandmother of Max, Mark, Louis, Lisa, Maria . . . uh . . . Lesley, Angela, Doris, Luke and Eric. (*Looks more closely at paper*) Eric? This is a Jewish name? (*Shrugs*) Eric. A large and loving family. We assemble that we may mourn collectively this good and righteous woman.

(*He looks at the coffin*)

This woman. I did not know this woman. I cannot accurately describe her attributes, nor do justice to her dimensions. She was. . . . Well, in the Bronx Home of Aged Hebrews are many like this, the old, and to many I speak but not to be frank with this one. She preferred silence. So I do not know her and yet I know her. She was . . .

(*He touches the coffin*)

. . . not a person but a whole kind of person, the ones who crossed the ocean, who brought with us to America the villages of Russia and Lithuania—and how we struggled, and how we fought, for the family, for the Jewish home, so that you would not grow up *here*, in this strange place, in the melting pot where nothing melted. Descendants of this immigrant woman, you do not grow up in America, you and your children and their children with the goyische names. You do not live in America. No such place exists. Your clay is the clay of some Litvak shtetl, your air the air of the steppes—because she carried the old world on her back across the ocean, in a boat, and she put it down on Grand Concourse Avenue, or in Flatbush, and she worked that earth into your bones, and you pass it to your children, this ancient, ancient culture and home.

(*Little pause*)

You can never make that crossing that she made, for such Great Voyages in this world do not any more exist. But every day of your lives the miles that voyage between that place and this one you cross. Every day. You understand me? In you that journey is.

So . . .

She was the last of the Mohicans, this one was. Pretty soon . . . all the old will be dead.

SCENE 2

Same day. Roy and Joe in Roy's office. Roy at an impressive desk, bare except for a very elaborate phone system, rows and rows of flashing buttons which bleep and beep and whistle incessantly, making chaotic music underneath Roy's conversations. Joe is sitting, waiting. Roy conducts business with great energy, impatience and sensual abandon: gesticulating, shouting, cajoling, crooning, playing the phone, receiver and hold button with virtuosity and love.

ROY (*Hitting a button*). Hold. (*To Joe*) I wish I was an octopus, a fucking octopus. Eight loving arms and all those suckers. Know what I mean?

JOE. No, I . . .

ROY (*Gesturing to a deli platter of little sandwiches on his desk*). You want lunch?

JOE. No, that's OK really I just . . .

ROY (*Hitting a button*). Ailene? Roy Cohn. Now what kind of a greeting is. . . . I thought we were friends, Ai. . . . Look Mrs. Soffer you don't have to get. . . . You're upset. You're yelling. You'll aggravate your condition, you shouldn't yell, you'll pop little blood vessels in your face if you yell. . . . No that was a joke, Mrs. Soffer, I was joking. . . . I already apologized sixteen times for that, Mrs. Soffer, you . . . (*While she's fulminating, Roy covers the mouthpiece with his hand and talks to Joe*) This'll take a minute, eat already, what is this tasty sandwich here it's—(*He takes a bite of a sandwich*) Mmmmm, liver or some. . . . Here.

(*He pitches the sandwich to Joe, who catches it and returns it to the platter.*)

ROY (*Back to Mrs. Soffer*). Uh huh, uh huh. . . . No, I already told you, it wasn't a vacation, it was business, Mrs. Soffer, I have clients in Haiti, Mrs. Soffer, I. . . . Listen, Ailene, YOU THINK I'M THE ONLY GODDAM LAWYER IN HISTORY EVER MISSED A COURT DATE? Don't make such a big fucking. . . . Hold. (*He hits the hold button*) You HAG!

JOE. If this is a bad time . . .

ROY. *Bad* time? This is a *good* time! (*Button*) Baby doll, get me. . . . Oh fuck, wait . . . (*Button, button*) Hello? Yah. Sorry to keep you holding, Judge Hollins, I. . . . Oh *Mrs.* Hollins, sorry dear deep voice you got. Enjoying your visit? (*Hand over mouthpiece again, to Joe*) She sounds like a truckdriver and he sounds like Kate Smith, very confusing. Nixon appointed him, all the geeks are Nixon appointees . . . (*To Mrs. Hollins*) Yeah yeah right good so how many tickets dear? Seven. For what, *Cats, 42nd Street,* what? No you wouldn't like *La Cage,* trust me, I know. Oh for godsake. . . . Hold. (*Button, button*) Baby doll, seven for *Cats* or something, anything hard to get, I don't give a fuck what and neither will they. (*Button; to Joe*) You see *La Cage?*

JOE. No, I . . .

ROY. Fabulous. Best thing on Broadway. Maybe ever. (*Button*) Who? Aw, Jesus H. Christ, Harry, *no,* Harry, Judge John Francis Grimes, Manhattan Family Court. Do I have to do every goddam thing myself? *Touch* the bastard, Harry, and don't call me on this line again, I told you not to . . .

JOE (*Starting to get up*). Roy, uh, should I wait outside or . . .

ROY (*To Joe*). Oh sit. (*To Harry*) You hold. I pay you to hold fuck you Harry you jerk. (*Button*) Half-wit dick-brain. (*Instantly philosophical*) I see the universe, Joe, as a kind of sandstorm in outer space with winds of mega-hurricane velocity, but instead of grains of sand it's shards and splinters of glass. You ever feel that way? Ever have one of those days?

JOE. I'm not sure I . . .

ROY. So how's life in Appeals? How's the Judge?

JOE. He sends his best.

ROY. He's a good man. Loyal. Not the brightest man on the bench, but he has manners. And a nice head of silver hair.

JOE. He gives me a lot of responsibility.

ROY. Yeah, like writing his decisions and signing his name.

JOE. Well . . .

ROY. He's a nice guy. And you cover admirably.

JOE. Well, thanks, Roy, I . . .

ROY (*Button*). Yah? Who is *this?* Well who the fuck are *you?* Hold— (*Button*) Harry? Eighty-seven grand, something like that. Fuck him. Eat me. New Jersey, chain of porno film stores in, uh, Weehawken. That's—Harry, that's the beauty of the law. (*Button*) So, baby doll, what? *Cats?* Bleah. (*Button*) *Cats!* It's about cats. Singing cats, you'll love it. Eight o'clock, the theatre's always at eight. (*Button*) Fucking tourists. (*Button, then to Joe*) Oh live a little, Joe, *eat* something for Christ sake—

JOE. Um, Roy, could you . . .

ROY. What? (*To Harry*) Hold a minute. (*Button*) Mrs. Soffer? Mrs. . . . (*Button*) God-fucking-dammit to hell, where is . . .

JOE (*Overlapping*). Roy, I'd really appreciate it if . . .

ROY (*Overlapping*). Well she was here a minute ago, baby doll, see if . . .

(*The phone starts making three different beeping sounds, all at once.*)

ROY (*Smashing buttons*). Jesus fuck this goddam thing . . .

JOE (*Overlapping*). I really wish you wouldn't . . .

ROY (*Overlapping*). Baby doll? Ring the *Post* get me Suzy see if . . .

(*The phone starts whistling loudly.*)

ROY. CHRIST!

JOE. *Roy.*

ROY (*Into receiver*). Hold. (*Button; to Joe*) *What?*

JOE. Could you please not take the Lord's name in vain? (*Pause*)
    I'm sorry. But please. At least while I'm . . .

ROY (*Laughs, then*). Right. Sorry. Fuck.
    Only in America. (*Punches a button*) Baby doll, tell 'em all to fuck off. Tell 'em I died. You handle Mrs. Soffer. Tell her it's on the way. Tell her I'm schtupping the judge.

I'll call her back. I *will* call her. I *know* how much I borrowed. She's got four hundred times that stuffed up her. . . . Yeah, tell her I said that. (*Button. The phone is silent*)

So, Joe.

JOE. I'm sorry Roy, I just . . .

ROY. No no no no, principles count, I respect principles, I'm not religious but I like God and God likes me. Baptist, Catholic?

JOE. Mormon.

ROY. Mormon. Delectable. Absolutely. Only in America. So, Joe. Whattya think?

JOE. It's . . . well . . .

ROY. Crazy life.

JOE. Chaotic.

ROY. Well but God bless chaos. Right?

JOE. Ummm . . .

ROY. Huh. Mormons. I knew Mormons, in, um, Nevada.

JOE. Utah, mostly.

ROY. No, these Mormons were in Vegas.

So. So, how'd you like to go to Washington and work for the Justice Department?

JOE. Sorry?

ROY. How'd you like to go to Washington and work for the Justice Department? All I gotta do is pick up the phone, talk to Ed, and you're in.

JOE. In . . . what, exactly?

ROY. Associate Assistant Something Big. Internal Affairs, heart of the woods, something nice with clout.

JOE. Ed . . . ?

ROY. Meese. The Attorney General.

JOE. Oh.

ROY. I just have to pick up the phone . . .

JOE. I have to think.

ROY. Of course.

(*Pause*)

It's a great time to be in Washington, Joe.

JOE. Roy, it's incredibly exciting . . .

ROY. And it would mean something to me. You understand?

(*Little pause.*)

JOE. I . . . can't say how much I appreciate this Roy, I'm sort of . . . well, stunned, I mean. . . . Thanks, Roy. But I have to give it some thought. I have to ask my wife.

ROY. Your wife. Of course.

JOE. But I really appreciate . . .

ROY. Of course. Talk to your wife.

SCENE 3

Later that day. Harper at home, alone. She is listening to the radio and talking to herself, as she often does. She speaks to the audience.

HARPER. People who are lonely, people left alone, sit talking nonsense to the air, imagining . . . beautiful systems dying, old fixed orders spiraling apart . . .

When you look at the ozone layer, from outside, from a spaceship, it looks like a pale blue halo, a gentle, shimmering aureole encircling the atmosphere encircling the earth. Thirty miles above our heads, a thin layer of three-atom oxygen molecules, product of photosynthesis, which explains the fussy vegetable preference for visible light, its rejection of darker rays and emanations. Danger from without. It's a kind of gift, from God, the crowning touch to the creation of the world: guardian angels, hands linked, make a spherical net, a blue-green nesting orb, a shell of safety for life itself. But everywhere, things are collapsing, lies surfacing, systems of defense giving way. . . . This is why, Joe, this is why I shouldn't be left alone.

(*Little pause*)

I'd like to go traveling. Leave you behind to worry. I'll send postcards with strange stamps and tantalizing messages on the back. "Later maybe." "Nevermore . . ."

(*Mr. Lies, a travel agent, appears.*)

HARPER. Oh! You startled me!

MR. LIES. Cash, check or credit card?

HARPER. I remember you. You're from Salt Lake. You sold us the plane tickets when we flew here. What are you doing in Brooklyn?

MR. LIES. You said you wanted to travel . . .

HARPER. And here you are. How thoughtful.

MR. LIES. Mr. Lies. Of the International Order of Travel Agents. We mobilize the globe, we set people adrift, we stir the populace and send nomads eddying across the planet. We are adepts of motion, acolytes of the flux. Cash, check or credit card. Name your destination.

HARPER. Antarctica, maybe. I want to see the hole in the ozone. I heard on the radio . . .

MR. LIES (*He has a computer terminal in his briefcase*). I can arrange a guided tour. Now?

HARPER. Soon. Maybe soon. I'm not safe here you see. Things aren't right with me. Weird stuff happens . . .

MR. LIES. Like?

HARPER. Well, like you, for instance. Just appearing. Or last week . . . well never mind.

People are like planets, you need a thick skin. Things get to me. Joe stays away and now. . . . Well look. My dreams are talking back to me.

MR. LIES. It's the price of rootlessness. Motion sickness. The only cure: to keep moving.

HARPER. I'm undecided. I feel . . . that something's going to give. It's 1985. Fifteen years till the third millennium. Maybe Christ will come again. Maybe seeds will be planted, maybe there'll be harvests then, maybe early figs to eat, maybe new life, maybe fresh blood, maybe companionship and love and protection, safety from what's outside, maybe the door will hold, or maybe . . . maybe the troubles will come, and the end will come, and the sky will collapse and there will be terrible rains and showers of poison light, or maybe my life is really fine, maybe Joe loves me and I'm only crazy thinking otherwise, or maybe not, maybe it's even worse than I know, maybe . . . I want to know, maybe I don't. The suspense, Mr. Lies, it's killing me.

MR. LIES. I suggest a vacation.

HARPER (*Hearing something*). That was the elevator. Oh God, I should fix myself up, I. . . . You have to go, you shouldn't be here . . . you aren't even real.

MR. LIES. Call me when you decide . . .

HARPER. Go!

(*The Travel Agent vanishes as Joe enters.*)

JOE. Buddy?
    Buddy? Sorry I'm late. I was just . . . out. Walking. Are you mad?

HARPER. I got a little anxious.

JOE. Buddy kiss.

(*They kiss.*)

JOE. Nothing to get anxious about.
    So. So how'd you like to move to Washington?

SCENE 4

Same day. Louis and Prior outside the funeral home, sitting on a bench, both dressed in funeral finery, talking. The funeral service for Sarah Ironson has just concluded and Louis is about to leave for the cemetery.

LOUIS. My grandmother actually saw Emma Goldman speak. In Yiddish. But all Grandma could remember was that she spoke well and wore a hat.
    What a weird service. That rabbi . . .

PRIOR. A definite find. Get his number when you go to the graveyard. I want him to bury me.

LOUIS. Better head out there. Everyone gets to put dirt on the coffin once it's lowered in.

PRIOR. Oooh. Cemetery fun. Don't want to miss that.

LOUIS. It's an old Jewish custom to express love. Here, Grandma, have a shovelful. Latecomers run the risk of finding the grave completely filled.
    She was pretty crazy. She was up there in that home for ten years, talking to herself. I never visited. She looked too much like my mother.

PRIOR (*Hugs him*). Poor Louis. I'm sorry your grandma is dead.

LOUIS. Tiny little coffin, huh?
    Sorry I didn't introduce you to. . . . I always get so closety at these family things.

PRIOR. Butch. You get butch. (*Imitating*) "Hi Cousin Doris, you don't remember me I'm Lou, Rachel's boy." Lou, not Louis, because if you say Louis they'll hear the sibilant S.

LOUIS. I don't have a . . .

PRIOR. I don't blame you, hiding. Bloodlines. Jewish curses are the worst. I personally would dissolve if anyone ever looked me in the eye and said "Feh." Fortunately WASPs don't say "Feh." Oh and by the way, darling, cousin Doris is a dyke.

LOUIS. No.
    Really?

PRIOR. You don't notice anything. If I hadn't spent the last four years fellating you I'd swear you were straight.

LOUIS. You're in a pissy mood. Cat still missing?

(*Little pause.*)

PRIOR. Not a furball in sight. It's your fault.

LOUIS. It is?

PRIOR. I warned you, Louis. Names are important. Call an animal "Little Sheba" and you can't expect it to stick around. Besides, it's a dog's name.

LOUIS. I wanted a dog in the first place, not a cat. He sprayed my books.

PRIOR. He was a female cat.

LOUIS. Cats are stupid, high-strung predators. Babylonians sealed them up in bricks. Dogs have brains.

PRIOR. Cats have intuition.

LOUIS. A sharp dog is as smart as a really dull two-year-old child.

PRIOR. Cats know when something's wrong.

LOUIS. Only if you stop feeding them.

PRIOR. They know. That's why Sheba left, because she knew.

LOUIS. Knew what?

(*Pause.*)

PRIOR. I did my best Shirley Booth this morning, floppy slippers, housecoat, curlers, can of Little Friskies; "Come back, Little Sheba, come back. . . ." To no avail. Le chat, elle ne reviendra jamais, jamais . . .

(*He removes his jacket, rolls up his sleeve, shows Louis a dark-purple spot on the underside of his arm near the shoulder*)

    See.

LOUIS. That's just a burst blood vessel.

PRIOR. Not according to the best medical authorities.

LOUIS. What?
    (*Pause*)
    Tell me.

PRIOR. K.S., baby. Lesion number one. Lookit. The wine-dark kiss of the angel of death.

LOUIS (*Very softly, holding Prior's arm*). Oh please . . .

PRIOR. I'm a lesionnaire. The Foreign Lesion. The American Lesion. Lesionnaire's disease.

LOUIS. Stop.

PRIOR. My troubles are lesion.

LOUIS. Will you *stop*.

PRIOR. Don't you think I'm handling this well?

I'm going to die.

LOUIS. Bullshit.

PRIOR. Let go of my arm.

LOUIS. No.

PRIOR. Let go.

LOUIS (*Grabbing Prior, embracing him ferociously*). No.

PRIOR. I can't find a way to spare you baby. No wall like the wall of hard scientific fact. K.S. Wham. Bang your head on that.

LOUIS. Fuck you. (*Letting go*) Fuck you fuck you fuck you.

PRIOR. Now that's what I like to hear. A mature reaction.

Let's go see if the cat's come home.

Louis?

LOUIS. When did you find this?

PRIOR. I couldn't tell you.

LOUIS. Why?

PRIOR. I was scared, Lou.

LOUIS. Of what?

PRIOR. That you'll leave me.

LOUIS. Oh.

(*Little pause.*)

PRIOR. Bad timing, funeral and all, but I figured as long as we're on the subject of death . . .

LOUIS. I have to go bury my grandma.

PRIOR. Lou?

(*Pause*)

Then you'll come home?

LOUIS. Then I'll come home.

SCENE 5

Same day, later on. Split scene: Joe and Harper at home; Louis at the cemetery with Rabbi Isidor Chemelwitz and the little coffin.

HARPER. Washington?

JOE. It's an incredible honor, buddy, and . . .

HARPER. I have to think.

JOE. Of course.

HARPER. Say no.

JOE. You said you were going to think about it.

HARPER. I don't want to move to Washington.

JOE. Well I do.

HARPER. It's a giant cemetery, huge white graves and mausoleums everywhere.

JOE. We could live in Maryland. Or Georgetown.

HARPER. We're happy here.

JOE. That's not really true, buddy, we . . .

HARPER. Well happy enough! Pretend-happy. That's better than nothing.

JOE. It's time to make some changes, Harper.

HARPER. No changes. Why?

JOE. I've been chief clerk for four years. I make twenty-nine thousand dollars a year. That's ridiculous. I graduated fourth in my class and I make less than anyone I know. And I'm . . . I'm tired of being a clerk, I want to go where something good is happening.

HARPER. Nothing good happens in Washington. We'll forget church teachings and buy furniture at . . . at *Conran's* and become yuppies. I have too much to do here.

JOE. Like what?

HARPER. I *do* have things . . .

JOE. What things?

HARPER. I have to finish painting the bedroom.

JOE. You've been painting in there for over a year.

HARPER. I know, I. . . . It just isn't done because I never get time to finish it.

JOE. Oh that's . . . that doesn't make sense. You have all the time in the world. You could finish it when I'm at work.

HARPER. I'm afraid to go in there alone.

JOE. Afraid of what?

HARPER. I heard someone in there. Metal scraping on the wall. A man with a knife, maybe.

JOE. There's no one in the bedroom, Harper.

HARPER. Not now.

JOE. Not this morning either.

HARPER. How do you know? You were at work this morning. There's something creepy about this place. Remember *Rosemary's Baby*?

JOE. *Rosemary's Baby*?

HARPER. Our apartment looks like that one. Wasn't that apartment in Brooklyn?

JOE. No, it was . . .

HARPER. Well, it looked like this. It did.

JOE. Then let's move.

HARPER. Georgetown's worse. *The Exorcist* was in Georgetown.

JOE. The devil, everywhere you turn, huh, buddy.

HARPER. Yeah. Everywhere.

JOE. How many pills today, buddy?

HARPER. None. One. Three. Only three.

LOUIS (*Pointing at the coffin*). Why are there just two little wooden pegs holding the lid down?

RABBI ISIDOR CHEMELWITZ. So she can get out easier if she wants to.

LOUIS. I hope she stays put.

I pretended for years that she was already dead. When they called to say she had died it was a surprise. I abandoned her.

RABBI ISIDOR CHEMELWITZ. "Sharfer vi di tson fun a shlang iz an umdankbar kind!"

LOUIS. I don't speak Yiddish.

RABBI ISIDOR CHEMELWITZ. Sharper than the serpent's tooth is the ingratitude of children. Shakespeare. *Kenig Lear*.

LOUIS. Rabbi, what does the Holy Writ say about someone who abandons someone he loves at a time of great need?

RABBI ISIDOR CHEMELWITZ. Why would a person do such a thing?

LOUIS. Because he has to.

Maybe because this person's sense of the world, that it will change for the better with struggle, maybe a person who has this neo-Hegelian positivist sense of constant historical progress towards happiness or perfection or something, who feels very powerful because he feels connected to these forces, moving uphill all the time ... maybe that person can't, um, incorporate sickness into his sense of how things are supposed to go. Maybe vomit ... and sores and disease ... really frighten him, maybe ... he isn't so good with death.

RABBI ISIDOR CHEMELWITZ. The Holy Scriptures have nothing to say about such a person.

LOUIS. Rabbi, I'm afraid of the crimes I may commit.

RABBI ISIDOR CHEMELWITZ. Please, mister. I'm a sick old rabbi facing a long drive home to the Bronx. You want to confess, better you should find a priest.

LOUIS. But I'm not a Catholic, I'm a Jew.

RABBI ISIDOR CHEMELWITZ. Worse luck for you, bubbulah. Catholics believe in forgiveness. Jews believe in Guilt. (He pats the coffin tenderly)

LOUIS. You just make sure those pegs are in good and tight.

RABBI ISIDOR CHEMELWITZ. Don't worry, mister. The life she had, she'll stay put. She's better off.

JOE. Look, I know this is scary for you. But try to understand what it means to me. Will you try?

HARPER. Yes.

JOE. Good. Really try.

I think things are starting to change in the world.

HARPER. But I don't want . . .

JOE. Wait. For the good. Change for the good. America has rediscovered itself. Its sacred position among nations. And people aren't ashamed of that like they used to be. This is a great thing. The truth restored. Law restored. That's what President Reagan's done, Harper. He says "Truth exists and can be spoken proudly." And the country responds to him. We become better. More good. I need to be a part of that, I need something big to lift me up. I mean, six years ago the world seemed in decline, horrible, hopeless, full of unsolvable problems and crime and confusion and hunger and . . .

HARPER. But it still seems that way. More now than before. They say the ozone layer is . . .

JOE. Harper . . .

HARPER. And today out the window on Atlantic Avenue there was a schizophrenic traffic cop who was making these . . .

JOE. Stop it! I'm trying to make a point.

HARPER. So am I.

JOE. You aren't even making sense, you . . .

HARPER. My point is the world seems just as . . .

JOE. It only seems that way to you because you never go out in the world, Harper, and you have emotional problems.

HARPER. I do so get out in the world.

JOE. You don't. You stay in all day, fretting about imaginary . . .

HARPER. I get out. I do. You don't know what I do.

JOE. You don't stay in all day.

HARPER. No.

JOE. Well. . . . Yes you do.

HARPER. That's what you think.

JOE. Where do you go?

HARPER. Where do *you* go? When you walk.

(Pause, then angrily) And I DO NOT have emotional problems.

JOE. I'm sorry.

HARPER. And if I do have emotional problems it's from living with you. Or . . .

JOE. I'm sorry buddy, I didn't mean to . . .

HARPER. Or if you do think I do then you should never have married me. You have all these secrets and lies.

JOE. I want to be married to you, Harper.

HARPER. You shouldn't. You never should.

(Pause)

Hey buddy. Hey buddy.

JOE. Buddy kiss . . .

(They kiss.)

HARPER. I heard on the radio how to give a blowjob.

JOE. What?

HARPER. You want to try?

JOE. You really shouldn't listen to stuff like that.

HARPER. Mormons can give blowjobs.

JOE. *Harper.*

HARPER (Imitating his tone). *Joe.*

It was a little Jewish lady with a German accent. This is a good time. For me to make a baby.

(Little pause. Joe turns away.)

HARPER. Then they went on to a program about holes in the ozone layer. Over Antarctica. Skin burns, birds go blind, icebergs melt. The world's coming to an end.

SCENE 6

First week of November. In the men's room of the offices of the Brooklyn Federal Court of Appeals; Louis is crying over the sink; Joe enters.

JOE. Oh, um. . . . Morning.

LOUIS. Good morning, counselor.

JOE (He watches Louis cry). Sorry, I . . . I don't know your name.

LOUIS. Don't bother. Word processor. The lowest of the low.

JOE (Holding out hand). Joe Pitt. I'm with Justice Wilson . . .

LOUIS. Oh, I know that. Counselor Pitt. Chief Clerk.

JOE. Were you . . . are you OK?

LOUIS. Oh, yeah, Thanks. What a nice man.

JOE. Not so nice.

LOUIS. What?

JOE. Not so nice. Nothing. You sure you're . . .

LOUIS. Life sucks shit. Life . . . just sucks shit.

JOE. What's wrong?

LOUIS. Run in my nylons.

JOE. Sorry . . . ?

LOUIS. Forget it. Look, thanks for asking.

JOE. Well . . .

LOUIS. I mean it really is nice of you.
  (*He starts crying again*)
  Sorry, sorry, sick friend . . .

JOE. Oh, I'm sorry.

LOUIS. Yeah, yeah, well, that's sweet.
  Three of your colleagues have preceded you to this baleful sight and you're the first one to ask. The others just opened the door, saw me, and fled. I hope they had to pee real bad.

JOE (*Handing him a wad of toilet paper*). They just didn't want to intrude.

LOUIS. Hah. Reaganite heartless macho asshole lawyers.

JOE. Oh, that's unfair.

LOUIS. What is? Heartless? Macho? Reaganite? Lawyer?

JOE. I voted for Reagan.

LOUIS. You did?

JOE. Twice.

LOUIS. Twice? Well, oh boy. A Gay Republican.

JOE. Excuse me?

LOUIS. Nothing.

JOE. I'm not . . .
  Forget it.

LOUIS. Republican? Not Republican? Or . . .

JOE. What?

LOUIS. What?

JOE. Not gay. I'm not gay.

LOUIS. Oh. Sorry.
  (*Blows his nose loudly*) It's just . . .

JOE. Yes?

LOUIS. Well, sometimes you can tell from the way a person sounds that . . . I mean you *sound* like a . . .

JOE. No I don't. Like what?

LOUIS. Like a Republican.

(*Little pause. Joe knows he's being teased; Louis knows he knows. Joe decides to be a little brave.*)

JOE (*Making sure no one else is around*). Do I? Sound like a . . . ?

LOUIS. What? Like a . . . ? Republican, or . . . ? Do I?

JOE. Do you what?

LOUIS. Sound like a . . . ?

JOE. Like a . . . ?
  I'm . . . confused.

LOUIS. Yes.
  My name is Louis. But all my friends call me Louise. I work in Word Processing. Thanks for the toilet paper.

(*Louis offers Joe his hand, Joe reaches, Louis feints and pecks Joe on the cheek, then exits.*)

SCENE 7

A week later. Mutual dream scene. Prior is at a fantastic makeup table, having a dream, applying the face. Harper is having a pill-induced hallucination. She has these from time to time. For some reason, Prior has appeared in this one. Or Harper has appeared in Prior's dream. It is bewildering.

PRIOR (*Alone, putting on makeup, then examining the results in the mirror; to the audience*). "I'm ready for my closeup, Mr. DeMille."
  One wants to move through life with elegance and grace, blossoming infrequently but with exquisite taste, and perfect timing, like a rare bloom, a zebra orchid. . . . One wants. . . . But one so seldom gets what one wants, does one? No. One does not. One gets fucked. Over. One . . . dies at thirty, robbed of . . . decades of majesty.
  Fuck this shit. Fuck this shit.
  (*He almost crumbles; he pulls himself together, he studies his handiwork in the mirror*)
  I look like a corpse. A corpsette. Oh my queen; you know you've hit rock-bottom when even drag is a drag.

(*Harper appears.*)

HARPER. Are you. . . . Who are you?

PRIOR. Who are you?

HARPER. What are doing in my hallucination?

PRIOR. I'm not in your hallucination. You're in my dream.

HARPER. You're wearing makeup.

PRIOR. So are you.

HARPER. But you're a man.

PRIOR (*Feigning dismay, shock, he mimes slashing his throat with his lipstick and dies, fabulously tragic. Then*). The hands and feet give it away.

HARPER. There must be some mistake here. I don't recognize you. You're not. . . . Are you my . . . some sort of imaginary friend?

PRIOR. No. Aren't you too old to have imaginary friends?

HARPER. I have emotional problems. I took too many pills. Why are you wearing makeup?

PRIOR. I was in the process of applying the face, trying to make myself feel better—I swiped the new fall colors at the Clinique counter at Macy's. (*Showing her*)

HARPER. You stole these?

PRIOR. I was out of cash; it was an emotional emergency!

HARPER. Joe will be so angry. I promised him. No more pills.

PRIOR. These pills you keep alluding to?

HARPER. Valium. I take Valium. Lots of Valium.

PRIOR. And you're dancing as fast as you can.

HARPER. I'm not *addicted*. I don't believe in addiction, and I never . . . well, I *never* drink. And I *never* take drugs.

PRIOR. Well, smell *you*, Nancy Drew.

HARPER. Except Valium.

PRIOR. Except Valium; in wee fistfuls.

HARPER. It's terrible. Mormons are not supposed to be addicted to anything. I'm a Mormon.

PRIOR. I'm a homosexual.

HARPER. Oh! In my church we don't believe in homosexuals.

PRIOR. In my church we don't believe in Mormons.

HARPER. What church do . . . oh! (*She laughs*) I get it.

I don't understand this. If I didn't ever see you before and I don't think I did then I don't think you should be here, in this hallucination, because in my experience the mind, which is where hallucinations come from, shouldn't be able to make up anything that wasn't there to start with, that didn't enter it from experience, from the real world. Imagination can't create anything new, can it? It only recycles bits and pieces from the world and reassembles them into visions. . . . Am I making sense right now?

PRIOR. Given the circumstances, yes.

HARPER. So when we think we've escaped the unbearable ordinariness and, well, untruthfulness of our lives, it's really only the same old ordinariness and falseness rearranged into the appearance of novelty and truth. Nothing unknown is knowable. Don't you think it's depressing?

PRIOR. The limitations of the imagination?

HARPER. Yes.

PRIOR. It's something you learn after your second theme party: It's All Been Done Before.

HARPER. The world. Finite. Terribly, terribly. . . . Well . . .

This is the most depressing hallucination I've ever had.

PRIOR. Apologies. I do try to be amusing.

HARPER. Oh, well, don't apologize, you. . . . I can't expect someone who's really sick to entertain me.

PRIOR. How on earth did you know . . .

HARPER. Oh that happens. This is the very threshhold of revelation sometimes. You can see things . . . how sick you are. Do you see anything about me?

PRIOR. Yes.

HARPER. What?

PRIOR. You are amazingly unhappy.

HARPER. Oh big deal. You meet a Valium addict and you figure out she's unhappy. That doesn't count. Of course I. . . . Something else. Something surprising.

PRIOR. Something surprising.

HARPER. Yes.

PRIOR. Your husband's a homo.

(*Pause.*)

HARPER. Oh, ridiculous.

(*Pause, then very quietly*)

Really?

PRIOR (*Shrugs*). Threshhold of revelation.

HARPER. Well I don't like your revelations. I don't think you intuit well at all. Joe's a very normal man, he . . .

Oh God. Oh God. He. . . . Do homos take, like, lots of long walks?

PRIOR. Yes, We do. In stretch pants with lavender coifs. I just looked at you, and there was . . .

HARPER. A sort of blue streak of recognition.

PRIOR. Yes.

HARPER. Like you knew me incredibly well.

PRIOR. Yes.

HARPER. Yes.

I have to go now, get back, something just . . . fell apart.

Oh God, I feel so sad . . .

PRIOR. I . . . I'm sorry. I usually say, "Fuck the truth," but mostly, the truth fucks you.

HARPER. I see something else about you . . .

PRIOR. Oh?

HARPER. Deep inside you, there's a part of you, the most inner part, entirely free of disease. I can see that.

PRIOR. Is that. . . . That isn't true.

HARPER. Threshhold of revelation.

Home . . .

(*She vanishes.*)

PRIOR. People come and go so quickly here . . .

(*To himself in the mirror*) I don't think there's any uninfected part of me. My heart is pumping polluted blood. I feel dirty.

(*He begins to wipe makeup off with his hands, smearing it around. A large gray feather falls from up above. Prior stops smearing the makeup and looks at the feather. He goes to it and picks it up.*)

A VOICE (*It is an incredibly beautiful voice*). Look up!

PRIOR (*Looking up, not seeing anyone*). Hello?

A VOICE. Look up!

PRIOR. Who is that?

A VOICE. Prepare the way!

PRIOR. I don't see any . . .

(*There is a dramatic change in lighting, from above.*)

A VOICE.

Look up, look up,
prepare the way
the infinite descent
A breath in air
floating down
Glory to . . .

(*Silence.*)

PRIOR. Hello? Is that it? Helloooo!
  What the fuck . . . ? (*He holds himself*)
  Poor me. Poor poor me. Why me? Why poor poor me?
Oh I don't feel good right now. I really don't.

SCENE 8

*That night. Split scene: Harper and Joe at home; Prior
and Louis in bed.*

HARPER. Where were you?
JOE. Out.
HARPER. Where?
JOE. Just out. Thinking.
HARPER. It's late.
JOE. I had a lot to think about.
HARPER. I burned dinner.
JOE. Sorry.
HARPER. Not my dinner. My dinner was fine. Your dinner. I
  put it back in the oven and turned everything up as high
  as it could go and I watched till it burned black. It's still
  hot. Very hot. Want it?
JOE. You didn't have to do that.
HARPER. I know. It just seemed like the kind of thing a men-
  tally deranged sex-starved pill-popping housewife would
  do.
JOE. Uh huh.
HARPER. So I did it. Who knows anymore what I have to do?
JOE. How many pills?
HARPER. A bunch. Don't change the subject.
JOE. I won't talk to you when you . . .
HARPER. No. No. Don't do that! I'm . . . I'm fine, pills are not
  the problem, not our problem, I WANT TO KNOW
  WHERE YOU'VE BEEN! I WANT TO KNOW
  WHAT'S GOING ON!
JOE. Going on with what? The job?
HARPER. Not the job.
JOE. I said I need more time.
HARPER. Not the job!
JOE. Mr. Cohn, I talked to him on the phone, he said I had
  to hurry . . .
HARPER. Not the . . .
JOE. But I can't get you to talk sensibly about anything
  so . . .
HARPER. SHUT UP!
JOE. Then what?
HARPER. Stick to the subject.
JOE. I don't know what that is. You have something you want
  to ask me? Ask me. Go.
HARPER. I . . . can't. I'm scared of you.
JOE. I'm tired, I'm going to bed.
HARPER. Tell me without making me ask. Please.
JOE. This is crazy, I'm not . . .

HARPER. When you come through the door at night your
  face is never exactly the way I remembered it. I get surprised by something . . . mean and hard about the way
  you look. Even the weight of you in the bed at night, the
  way you breathe in your sleep seems unfamiliar.
    You terrify me.
JOE (*Cold*). I know who you are.
HARPER. Yes. I'm the enemy. That's easy. That doesn't change.
    You think you're the only one who hates sex; I do; I
  hate it with you; I do. I dream that you batter away at me
  till all my joints come apart, like wax, and I fall into
  pieces. It's like a punishment. It was wrong of me to
  marry you. I knew you . . . (*She stops herself*) It's a sin, and
  it's killing us both.
JOE. I can always tell when you've taken pills because it
  makes you red-faced and sweaty and frankly that's very
  often why I don't want to . . .
HARPER. Because . . .
JOE. Well, you aren't pretty. Not like this.
HARPER. I have something to ask you.
JOE. Then ASK! ASK! What in hell are you . . .
HARPER. Are you a homo?
    (*Pause*)
    Are you? If you try to walk out right now I'll put your
  dinner back in the over and turn it up so high the whole
  building will fill with smoke and everyone in it will as-
  phyxiate. So help me God I will.
    Now answer the question.
JOE. What if I . . .

(*Small pause.*)

HARPER. Then tell me, please. And we'll see.
JOE. No. I'm not.
    I don't see what difference it makes.

LOUIS. Jews don't have any clear textual guide to the after-
  life; even that it exists. I don't think much about it. I see
  it as a perpetual rainy Thursday afternoon in March.
  Dead leaves.
PRIOR. Eeeugh. Very Greco-Roman.
LOUIS. Well for us it's not the verdict that counts, it's the act
  of judgment. That's why I could never be a lawyer. In
  court all that matters is the verdict.
PRIOR. You could never be a lawyer because you are over-
  sexed. You're too distracted.
LOUIS. Not distracted; *abs*tracted. I'm trying to make a point:
PRIOR. Namely:
LOUIS. It's the judge in his or her chambers, weighing, books
  open, pondering the evidence, ranging freely over cate-
  gories: good, evil, innocent, guilty; the judge in the
  chamber of circumspection, not the judge on the bench
  with the gavel. The shaping of the law, not its execution.
PRIOR. The point, dear, the point . . .
LOUIS. That it should be the questions and shape of a life, its
  total complexity gathered, arranged and considered,

which matters in the end, not some stamp of salvation or damnation which disperses all the complexity in some unsatisfying little decision—the balancing of the scales . . .

PRIOR. I like this; very zen; it's . . . reassuringly incomprehensible and useless. We who are about to die thank you.

LOUIS. You are not about to die.

PRIOR. It's not going well, really . . . two new lesions. My leg hurts. There's protein in my urine, the doctor says, but who knows what the fuck that portends. Anyway it shouldn't be there, the protein. My butt is chapped from diarrhea and yesterday I shat blood.

LOUIS. I really hate this. You don't tell me . . .

PRIOR. You get too upset, I wind up comforting you. It's easier . . .

LOUIS. Oh thanks.

PRIOR. If it's bad I'll tell you.

LOUIS. Shitting blood sounds bad to me.

PRIOR. And I'm telling you.

LOUIS. And I'm handling it.

PRIOR. Tell me some more about justice.

LOUIS. I *am* handling it.

PRIOR. Well Louis you win Trooper of the Month.

(*Louis starts to cry.*)

PRIOR. I take it back. You aren't Trooper of the Month.
    This isn't working . . .
    Tell me some more about justice.

LOUIS. You are not about to die.

PRIOR. Justice . . .

LOUIS. . . . is an immensity, a confusing vastness. Justice is God.
    Prior?

PRIOR. Hmmm?

LOUIS. You love me.

PRIOR. Yes.

LOUIS. What if I walked out on this?
    Would you hate me forever?

(*Prior kisses Louis on the forehead.*)

PRIOR. Yes.

JOE. I think we ought to pray. Ask God for help. Ask him together . . .

HARPER. God won't talk to me. I have to make up people to talk to me.

JOE. You have to keep asking.

HARPER. I forgot the question.
    Oh yeah. God, is my husband a . . .

JOE (*Scary*). Stop it. Stop it. I'm warning you.
    Does it make any difference? That I might be one thing deep within, no matter how wrong or ugly that thing is, so long as I have fought, with everything I have, to kill it. What do you want from me? What do you want from me, Harper? More than that? For God's sake, there's nothing left, I'm a shell. There's nothing left to kill.

As long as my behavior is what I know it has to be. Decent. Correct. That alone in the eyes of God.

HARPER. No, no, not that, that's Utah talk, Mormon talk, I hate it, Joe, tell me, say it . . .

JOE. All I will say is that I am a very good man who has worked very hard to become good and you want to destroy that. You want to destroy me, but I am not going to let you do that.

(*Pause.*)

HARPER. I'm going to have a baby.

JOE. Liar.

HARPER. You liar.
    A baby born addicted to pills. A baby who does not dream but who hallucinates, who stares up at us with big mirror eyes and who does not know who we are.

(*Pause.*)

JOE. Are you really . . .

HARPER. No. Yes. No. Yes. Get away from me.
    Now we both have a secret.

PRIOR. One of my ancestors was a ship's captain who made money bringing whale oil to Europe and returning with immigrants—Irish mostly, packed in tight, so many dollars per head. The last ship he captained foundered off the coast of Nova Scotia in a winter tempest and sank to the bottom. He went down with the ship—la Grande Geste—but his crew took seventy women and kids in the ship's only longboat, this big, open rowboat, and when the weather got too rough, and they thought the boat was overcrowded, the crew started lifting people up and hurling them into the sea. Until they got the ballast right. They walked up and down the longboat, eyes to the waterline, and when the boat rode low in the water they'd grab the nearest passenger and throw them into the sea. The boat was leaky, see; seventy people; they arrived in Halifax with nine people on board.

LOUIS. Jesus.

PRIOR. I think about that story a lot now. People in a boat, waiting, terrified, while implacable, unsmiling men, irresistibly strong, seize . . . maybe the person next to you, maybe you, and with no warning at all, with time only for a quick intake of air you are pitched into freezing, turbulent water and salt and darkness to drown.
    I like your cosmology, baby. While time is running out I find myself drawn to anything that's suspended, that lacks an ending—but it seems to me that it lets you off scot-free.

LOUIS. What do you mean?

PRIOR. No judgment, no guilt or responsibility.

LOUIS. For me.

PRIOR. For anyone. It was an editorial "you."

LOUIS. Please get better. Please.
    Please don't get any sicker.

SCENE 9

Third week in November. Roy and Henry, his doctor, in Henry's office.

HENRY. Nobody knows what causes it. And nobody knows how to cure it. The best theory is that we blame a retrovirus, the Human Immunodeficiency Virus. Its presence is made known to us by the useless antibodies which appear in reaction to its entrance into the bloodstream through a cut, or an orifice. The antibodies are powerless to protect the body against it. Why, we don't know. The body's immune system ceases to function. Sometimes the body even attacks itself. At any rate it's left open to a whole horror house of infections from microbes which it usually defends against.

Like Kaposi's sarcomas. These lesions. Or your throat problem. Or the glands.

We think it may also be able to slip past the blood-brain barrier into the brain. Which is of course very bad news.

And it's fatal in we don't know what percent of people with suppressed immune responses.

(Pause.)

ROY. This is very interesting, Mr. Wizard, but why the fuck are you telling me this?

(Pause.)

HENRY. Well, I have just removed one of three lesions which biopsy results will probably tell us is a Kaposi's sarcoma lesion. And you have a pronounced swelling of glands in your neck, groin, and armpits—lymphadenopathy is another sign. And you have oral candidiasis and maybe a little more fungus under the fingernails of two digits on your right hand. So that's why . . .

ROY. This disease . . .

HENRY. Syndrome.

ROY. Whatever. It afflicts mostly homosexuals and drug addicts.

HENRY. Mostly. Hemophiliacs are also at risk.

ROY. Homosexuals and drug addicts. So why are you implying that I . . .
(Pause)
What are you implying, Henry?

HENRY. I don't . . .

ROY. I'm not a drug addict.

HENRY. Oh come on Roy.

ROY. What, what, come on Roy what? Do you think I'm a junkie, Henry, do you see tracks?

HENRY. This is absurd.

ROY. Say it.

HENRY. Say what?

ROY. Say, "Roy Cohn, you are a . . ."

HENRY. Roy.

ROY. "You are a. . . ." Go on. Not "Roy Cohn you are a drug fiend." "Roy Marcus Cohn, you are a . . ."
Go on, Henry, it starts with an "H."

HENRY. Oh I'm not going to . . .

ROY. *With an "H,"* Henry, and it isn't "Hemophiliac." Come on . . .

HENRY. What are you doing, Roy?

ROY. No, say it. I mean it. Say: "Roy Cohn, you are a homosexual."
(Pause)
And I will proceed, systematically, to destroy your reputation and your practice and your career in New York State, Henry. Which you know I can do.

(Pause.)

HENRY. Roy, you have been seeing me since 1958. Apart from the facelifts I have treated you for everything from syphilis . . .

ROY. From a whore in Dallas.

HENRY. From syphilis to venereal warts. In your rectum. Which you may have gotten from a whore in Dallas, but it wasn't a female whore.

(Pause.)

ROY. So say it.

HENRY. Roy Cohn, you are . . .
You have had sex with men, many many times, Roy, and one of them, or any number of them, has made you very sick. You have AIDS.

ROY. AIDS.
Your problem, Henry, is that you are hung up on words, on labels, that you believe they mean what they seem to mean. AIDS. Homosexual. Gay. Lesbian. You think these are names that tell you who someone sleeps with, but they don't tell you that.

HENRY. No?

ROY. No. Like all labels they tell you one thing and one thing only: where does an individual so identified fit in the food chain, in the pecking order? Not ideology, or sexual taste, but something much simpler: clout. Not who I fuck or who fucks me, but who will pick up the phone when I call, who owes me favors. This is what a label refers to. Now to someone who does not understand this, homosexual is what I am because I have sex with men. But really this is wrong. Homosexuals are not men who sleep with other men. Homosexuals are men who in fifteen years of trying cannot get a pissant antidiscrimination bill through City Council. Homosexuals are men who know nobody and who nobody knows. Who have zero clout. Does this sound like me, Henry?

HENRY. No.

ROY. No. I have clout. A lot. I can pick up this phone, punch fifteen numbers, and you know who will be on the other end in under five minutes, Henry?

HENRY. The President.

ROY. Even better, Henry. His wife.

HENRY. I'm impressed.

ROY. I don't want you to be impressed. I want you to understand. This is not sophistry. And this is not hypocrisy. This is reality. I have sex with men. But unlike nearly every other man of whom this is true, I bring the guy I'm screwing to the White House and President Reagan smiles at us and shakes his hand. Because *what* I am is defined entirely by *who* I am. Roy Cohn is not a homosexual. Roy Cohn is a heterosexual man, Henry, who fucks around with guys.

HENRY. OK, Roy.

ROY. And what is my diagnosis, Henry?

HENRY. You have AIDS, Roy.

ROY. No, Henry, no. AIDS is what homosexuals have. I have liver cancer.

(Pause)

HENRY. Well, whatever the fuck you have, Roy, it's very serious and I haven't got a damn thing for you. The NIH in Bethesda has a new drug called AZT with a two-year waiting list that not even I can get you onto. So get on the phone, Roy, and dial fifteen numbers, and tell the First Lady you need in on an experimental treatment for liver cancer, because you can call it any damn thing you want, Roy, but what it boils down to is very bad news.

ACT TWO: IN VITRO

December 1985–January 1986

SCENE 1

Night, the third week in December. Prior alone on the floor of his bedroom; he is much worse.

PRIOR. Louis, Louis, please wake up, oh God.

(Louis runs in.)

PRIOR. I think something horrible is wrong with me I can't breathe . . .

LOUIS *(Starting to exit)*. I'm calling the ambulance.

PRIOR. No, wait, I . . .

LOUIS. *Wait?* Are you fucking crazy? Oh God you're on fire, your head is on fire.

PRIOR. It hurts, it hurts . . .

LOUIS. I'm calling the ambulance.

PRIOR. I don't want to go to the hospital, I don't want to go to the hospital please let me lie here, just . . .

LOUIS. No, no, God, Prior, stand up . . .

PRIOR. DON'T TOUCH MY LEG!

LOUIS. We have to . . . oh God this is so crazy.

PRIOR. I'll be OK if I just lie here Lou, really, if I can only sleep a little . . .

(Louis exits.)

PRIOR. Louis?

NO! NO! Don't call, you'll send me there and I won't come back, please, please Louis I'm begging, baby please . . .

(Screams) LOUIS!!

LOUIS *(From off; hysterical)*. WILL YOU SHUT THE FUCK UP!

PRIOR *(Trying to stand)*. Aaaah. I have . . . to go to the bathroom. Wait. Wait, just . . . oh. Oh God. *(He shits himself)*

LOUIS *(Entering)*. Prior? They'll be here in . . . Oh my God.

PRIOR. I'm sorry, I'm sorry.

LOUIS. What did . . . ? What?

PRIOR. I had an accident.

(Louis goes to him.)

LOUIS. This is blood.

PRIOR. Maybe you shouldn't touch it . . . me. . . . I . . . *(He faints)*

LOUIS *(Quietly)*. Oh help. Oh help. Oh God oh God oh God help me I can't I can't I can't.

SCENE 2

Same night. Harper is sitting at home, all alone, with no lights on. We can barely see her. Joe enters, but he doesn't turn on the lights.

JOE. Why are you sitting in the dark? Turn on the light.

HARPER. *No.* I heard the sounds in the bedroom again. I know someone was in there.

JOE. No one was.

HARPER. Maybe actually in the bed, under the covers with a knife.

Oh, boy. Joe. I, um, I'm thinking of going away. By which I mean: I think I'm going off again. You . . . you know what I mean?

JOE. Please don't. Stay. We can fix it. I pray for that. This is my fault, but I can correct it. You have to try too . . .

(He turns on the light. She turns it off again.)

HARPER. When you pray, what do you pray for?

JOE. I pray for God to crush me, break me up into little pieces and start all over again.

HARPER. Oh. Please. Don't pray for that.

JOE. I had a book of Bible stories when I was a kid. There was a picture I'd look at twenty times every day: Jacob wrestles with the angel. I don't really remember the story, or why the wrestling—just the picture. Jacob is young and very strong. The angel is . . . a beautiful man, with golden hair and wings, of course. I still dream about it. Many nights. I'm. . . . It's me. In that struggle. Fierce, and unfair. The angel is not human, and it holds nothing back, so how could anyone human win, what kind of fight is that? It's not just. Losing means your soul thrown down in the dust, your heart torn out from God's. But you can't not lose.

HARPER. In the whole entire world, you are the only person, the only person I love or have ever loved. And I love you terribly. Terribly. That's what's so awfully, irreducibly real. I can make up anything but I can't dream that away.

JOE. Are you . . . are you really going to have a baby?

HARPER. It's my time, and there's no blood. I don't really know. I suppose it wouldn't be a great thing. Maybe I'm just not bleeding because I take too many pills. Maybe I'll give birth to a pill. That would give a new meaning to pill-popping, huh?

I think you should go to Washington. Alone. Change, like you said.

JOE. I'm not going to leave you, Harper.

HARPER. Well maybe not. But I'm going to leave you.

SCENE 3

One AM, *the next morning. Louis and a nurse, Emily, are sitting in Prior's room in the hospital.*

EMILY. He'll be all right now.

LOUIS. No he won't.

EMILY. No, I guess not. I gave him something that makes him sleep.

LOUIS. Deep asleep?

EMILY. Orbiting the moons of Jupiter.

LOUIS. A good place to be.

EMILY. Anyplace better than here. You his . . . uh?

LOUIS. Yes. I'm his uh.

EMILY. This must be hell for you.

LOUIS. It is. Hell. The After Life. Which is not at all like a rainy afternoon in March, by the way, Prior. A lot more vivid than I'd expected. Dead leaves, but the crunchy kind. Sharp, dry air. The kind of long, luxurious dying feeling that breaks your heart.

EMILY. Yeah, well we all get to break our hearts on this one. He seems like a nice guy. Cute.

LOUIS. Not like this.

Yes, he is. Was. Whatever.

EMILY. Weird name. Prior Walter. Like, "The Walter before this one."

LOUIS. Lots of Walters before this one. Prior is an old old family name in an old old family. The Walters go back to the Mayflower and beyond. Back to the Norman Conquest. He says there's a Prior Walter stitched into the Bayeux tapestry.

EMILY. Is that impressive?

LOUIS. Well, it's old. Very old. Which in some circles equals impressive.

EMILY. Not in my circle. What's the name of the tapestry?

LOUIS. The Bayeux tapestry. Embroidered by La Reine Mathilde.

EMILY. I'll tell my mother. She embroiders. Drives me nuts.

LOUIS. Manual therapy for anxious hands.

EMILY. Maybe you should try it.

LOUIS. Mathilde stitched while William the Conqueror was off to war. She was capable of . . . more than loyalty. Devotion.

She waited for him, she stitched for years. And if he had come back broken and defeated from war, she would have loved him even more. And if he had returned mutilated, ugly, full of infection and horror, she would still have loved him; fed by pity, by a sharing of pain, she would love him even more, and she would never, never have prayed to God, please let him die if he can't return to me whole and healthy and able to live a normal life. . . . If he had died, she would have buried her heart with him.

So what the fuck is the matter with me?

(*Little pause*)

Will he sleep through the night?

EMILY. At least.

LOUIS. I'm going.

EMILY. It's one AM. Where do you have to go at . . .

LOUIS. I know what time it is. A walk. Night air, good for the. . . . The park.

EMILY. Be careful.

LOUIS. Yeah. Danger.

Tell him, if he wakes up and you're still on, tell him goodbye, tell him I had to go.

SCENE 4

An hour later. Split scene: Joe and Roy in a fancy (straight) bar; Louis and a Man in the Rambles in Central Park. Joe and Roy are sitting at the bar; the place is brightly lit. Joe has a plate of food in front of him but he isn't eating. Roy occasionally reaches over the table and forks small bites off Joe's plate. Roy is drinking heavily, Joe not at all. Louis and the Man are eyeing each other, each alternating interest and indifference.

JOE. The pills were something she started when she miscarried or . . . no, she took some before that. She had a really bad time at home, when she was a kid, her home was really bad. I think a lot of drinking and physical stuff. She doesn't talk about that, instead she talks about . . . the sky falling down, people with knives hiding under sofas. Monsters. Mormons. Everyone thinks Mormons don't come from homes like that, we aren't supposed to behave that way, but we do. It's not lying, or being two-faced. Everyone tries very hard to live up to God's strictures, which are very . . . um . . .

ROY. Strict.

JOE. I shouldn't be bothering you with this.

ROY. No, please. Heart to heart. Want another . . . What is that, seltzer?

JOE. The failure to measure up hits people very hard. From such a strong desire to be good they feel very far from goodness when they fail.

   What scares me is that maybe what I really love in her is the part of her that's farthest from the light, from God's love; maybe I was drawn to that in the first place. And I'm keeping it alive because I need it.

ROY. Why would you need it?

JOE. There are things. . . . I don't know how well we know ourselves. I mean, what if? I know I married her because she . . . because I loved it that she was always wrong, always doing something wrong, like one step out of step. In Salt Lake City that stands out. I never stood out, on the outside, but inside, it was hard for me. To pass.

ROY. Pass?

JOE. Yeah.

ROY. Pass as what?

JOE. Oh. Well. . . . As someone cheerful and strong. Those who love God with an open heart unclouded by secrets and struggles are cheerful; God's easy simple love for them shows in how strong and happy they are. The saints.

ROY. But you had secrets? Secret struggles . . .

JOE. I wanted to be one of the elect, one of the Blessed. You feel you ought to be, that the blemishes are yours by choice, which of course they aren't. Harper's sorrow, that really deep sorrow, she didn't choose that. But it's there.

ROY. You didn't put it there.

JOE. No.

ROY. You sound like you think you did.

JOE. I am responsible for her.

ROY. Because she's your wife.

JOE. That. And I do love her.

ROY. Whatever. She's your wife. And so there are obligations. To her. But also to yourself.

JOE. She'd fall apart in Washington.

ROY. Then let her stay here.

JOE. She'll fall apart if I leave her.

ROY. Then bring her to Washington.

JOE. I just can't, Roy. She needs me.

ROY. Listen, Joe. I'm the best divorce lawyer in the business.

   (*Little pause.*)

JOE. Can't Washington wait?

ROY. You do what you need to do, Joe. What *you* need. *You.* Let her life go where it wants to go. You'll both be better for that. *Somebody* should get what they want.

MAN. What do you want?

LOUIS. I want you to fuck me, hurt me, make me bleed.

MAN. I want to.

LOUIS. Yeah?

MAN. I want to hurt you.

LOUIS. Fuck me.

MAN. Yeah?

LOUIS. Hard.

MAN. Yeah? You been a bad boy?

   (*Pause. Louis laughs, softly.*)

LOUIS. Very bad. Very bad.

MAN. You need to be punished, boy?

LOUIS. Yes. I do.

MAN. Yes what?

   (*Little pause.*)

LOUIS. Um, I . . .

MAN. Yes *what*, boy?

LOUIS. Oh. Yes sir.

MAN. I want you to take me to your place, boy.

LOUIS. No, I can't do that.

MAN. No *what*?

LOUIS. No sir, I can't, I . . .
   I don't live alone, sir.

MAN. Your lover know you're out with a man tonight, boy?

LOUIS. No sir, he . . .
   My lover doesn't know.

MAN. Your lover know you . . .

LOUIS. Let's change the subject, OK? Can we go to your place?

MAN. I live with my parents.

LOUIS. Oh.

ROY. Everyone who makes it in this world makes it because somebody older and more powerful takes an interest. The most precious asset in life, I think, is the ability to be a good son. You have that, Joe. Somebody who can be a good son to a father who pushes them farther than they would otherwise go. I've had many fathers, I owe my life to them, powerful, powerful men. Walter Winchell, Edgar Hoover. Joe McCarthy most of all. He valued me because I am a good lawyer, but he loved me because I was and am a good son. He was a very difficult man, very guarded and cagey; I brought out something tender in him. He would have died for me. And me for him. Does this embarrass you?

JOE. I had a hard time with my father.

ROY. Well sometimes that's the way. Then you have to find other fathers, substitutes, I don't know. The father-son relationship is central to life. Women are for birth, beginning, but the father is continuance. The son offers the father his life as a vessel for carrying forth his father's dream. Your father's living?

JOE. Um, dead.

ROY. He was . . . what? A difficult man?

JOE. He was in the military. He could be very unfair. And cold.

ROY. But he loved you.

JOE. I don't know.

ROY. No, no, Joe, he did, I know this. Sometimes a father's love has to be very, very hard, unfair even, cold to make his son grow strong in a world like this. This isn't a good world.

MAN. Here, then.

LOUIS. I. . . . Do you have a rubber?

MAN. I don't use rubbers.

LOUIS. You should. (*He takes one from his coat pocket*) Here.

MAN. I don't use them.

LOUIS. Forget it, then. (*He starts to leave*)

MAN. No, wait.

Put it on me. Boy.

LOUIS. Forget it, I have to get back. Home. I must be going crazy.

MAN. Oh come on please he won't find out.

LOUIS. It's cold. Too cold.

MAN. It's never too cold, let me warm you up. Please?

(*They begin to fuck.*)

MAN. Relax.

LOUIS (*A small laugh*). Not a chance.

MAN. It . . .

LOUIS. What?

MAN. I think it broke. The rubber. You want me to keep going? (*Little pause*) Pull out? Should I . . .

LOUIS. Keep going.

Infect me.

I don't care. I don't care.

(*Pause. The Man pulls out.*)

MAN. I . . . um, look, I'm sorry, but I think I want to go.

LOUIS. Yeah.

Give my best to mom and dad.

(*The Man slaps him.*)

LOUIS. Ow!

(*They stare at each other.*)

LOUIS. It was a joke.

(*The Man leaves.*)

ROY. How long have we known each other?

JOE. Since 1980.

ROY. Right. A long time. I feel close to you, Joe. Do I advise you well?

JOE. You've been an incredible friend, Roy, I . . .

ROY. I want to be family. Familia, as my Italian friends call it. La Familia. A lovely word. It's important for me to help you, like I was helped.

JOE. I owe practically everything to you, Roy.

ROY. I'm dying, Joe. Cancer.

JOE. Oh my God.

ROY. Please. Let me finish.

Few people know this and I'm telling you this only because. . . . I'm not afraid of death. What can death bring that I haven't faced? I've lived; life is the worst. (*Gently mocking himself*) Listen to me, I'm a philosopher.

Joe. You must do this. You must must must. Love; that's a trap. Responsibility; that's a trap too. Like a father to a son I tell you this: Life is full of horror; nobody escapes, nobody; save yourself. Whatever pulls on you, whatever needs from you, threatens you. Don't be afraid; people are so afraid; don't be afraid to live in the raw wind, naked, alone. . . . Learn at least this: What you are capable of. Let nothing stand in your way.

SCENE 5

Three days later. Prior and Belize in Prior's hospital room. Prior is very sick but improving. Belize has just arrived.

PRIOR. Miss Thing.

BELIZE. Ma cherie bichette.

PRIOR. Stella.

BELIZE. Stella for star. Let me see. (*Scrutinizing Prior*) You look like shit, why yes indeed you do, comme la merde!

PRIOR. Merci.

BELIZE (*Taking little plastic bottles from his bag, handing them to Prior*). Not to despair, Belle Reeve. Lookie! Magic goop!

PRIOR (*Opening a bottle, sniffing*). Pooh! What kinda crap is that?

BELIZE. Beats me. Let's rub it on your poor blistered body and see what it does.

PRIOR. This is not Western medicine, these bottles . . .

BELIZE. Voodoo cream. From the botanica 'round the block.

PRIOR. And you a registered nurse.

BELIZE (*Sniffing it*). Beeswax and cheap perfume. Cut with Jergen's Lotion. Full of good vibes and love from some little black Cubana witch in Miami.

PRIOR. Get that trash away from me, I am immune-suppressed.

BELIZE. I *am* a health professional. I *know* what I'm doing.

PRIOR. It stinks. Any word from Louis?

(*Pause. Belize starts giving Prior a gentle massage.*)

PRIOR. Gone.

BELIZE. He'll be back. I know the type. Likes to keep a girl on edge.

PRIOR. It's been . . .

(*Pause.*)

BELIZE (*Trying to jog his memory*). How long?

PRIOR. I don't remember.

BELIZE. How long have you been here?

PRIOR (*Getting suddenly upset*). I don't remember, I don't give a fuck. I want Louis. I want my fucking boyfriend, where the fuck is he? I'm dying, I'm dying, where's Louis?

BELIZE. Shhhh, shh . . .

PRIOR. This is a very strange drug, this drug. Emotional liability, for starters.

BELIZE. Save a tab or two for me.

PRIOR. Oh no, not this drug, ce n'est pas pour la joyeux noël et la bonne année, this drug she is serious poisonous chemistry, ma pauvre bichette.

And not just disorienting. I hear things. Voices.

BELIZE. Voices.

PRIOR. A voice.

BELIZE. Saying what?

(*Pause.*)

PRIOR. I'm not supposed to tell.

BELIZE. You better tell the doctor. Or I will.

PRIOR. No no don't. Please. I want the voice; it's wonderful. It's all that's keeping me alive. I don't want to talk to some intern about it.

You know what happens? When I hear it, I get hard.

BELIZE. Oh my.

PRIOR. Comme ça. (*He uses his arm to demonstrate*) And you know I am slow to rise.

BELIZE. My jaw aches at the memory.

PRIOR. And would you deny me this little solace—betray my concupiscence to Florence Nightingale's storm troopers?

BELIZE. Perish the thought, ma bébé.

PRIOR. They'd change the drug just to spoil the fun.

BELIZE. You and your boner can depend on me.

PRIOR. Je t'adore, ma belle nègre.

BELIZE. All this girl-talk shit is politically incorrect, you know. We should have dropped it back when we gave up drag.

PRIOR. I'm sick, I get to be politically incorrect if it makes me feel better. You sound like Lou.

(*Little pause*)

Well, at least I have the satisfaction of knowing he's in anguish somewhere. I loved his anguish. Watching him stick his head up his asshole and eat his guts out over some relatively minor moral conundrum—it was the best show in town. But Mother warned me: if they get overwhelmed by the little things . . .

BELIZE. They'll be belly-up bustville when something big comes along.

PRIOR. Mother warned me.

BELIZE. And they do come along.

PRIOR. But I didn't listen.

BELIZE. No. (*Doing Hepburn*) Men are beasts.

PRIOR (*Also Hepburn*). The absolute lowest.

BELIZE. I have to go. If I want to spend my whole lonely life looking after white people I can get underpaid to do it.

PRIOR. You're just a Christian martyr.

BELIZE. Whatever happens, baby, I will be here for you.

PRIOR. Je t'aime.

BELIZE. Je t'aime. Don't go crazy on me, girlfriend, I already got enough crazy queens for one lifetime. For two. I can't be bothering with dementia.

PRIOR. I promise.

BELIZE (*Touching him; softly*). Ouch.

PRIOR. Ouch. Indeed.

BELIZE. Why'd they have to pick on you?

And eat more, girlfriend, you really do look like shit.

(*Belize leaves.*)

PRIOR (*After waiting a beat*). He's gone.

Are you still . . .

VOICE. I can't stay. I will return.

PRIOR. Are you one of those "Follow me to the other side" voices?

VOICE. No. I am no nightbird. I am a messenger . . .

PRIOR. You have a beautiful voice, it sounds . . . like a viola, like a perfectly tuned, tight string, balanced, the truth. . . . Stay with me.

VOICE. Not now. Soon I will return, I will reveal myself to you; I am glorious, glorious; my heart, my countenance and my message. You must prepare.

PRIOR. For what? I don't want to . . .

VOICE. No death, no:

A marvelous work and a wonder we undertake, an edifice awry we sink plumb and straighten, a great Lie we abolish, a great error correct, with the rule, sword and broom of Truth!

PRIOR. What are you talking about, I . . .

VOICE.

I am on my way; when I am manifest, our Work begins:
Prepare for the parting of the air,
The breath, the ascent,
Glory to . . .

SCENE 6

The second week of January. Martin, Roy and Joe in a fancy Manhattan restaurant.

MARTIN. It's a revolution in Washington, Joe. We have a new agenda and finally a real leader. They got back the Senate but we have the courts. By the nineties the Supreme Court will be block-solid Republican appointees, and the Federal bench—Republican judges like land mines, everywhere, everywhere they turn. Affirmative action? Take it to court. Boom! Land mine. And we'll get our way on just about everything: abortion, defense, Central America, family values, a live investment climate. We have the White House locked till the year 2000. And beyond. A permanent fix on the Oval Office?

It's possible. By '92 we'll get the Senate back, and in ten years the South is going to give us the House. It's really the end of Liberalism. The end of New Deal Socialism. The end of ipso facto secular humanism. The dawning of a genuinely American political personality. Modeled on Ronald Wilson Reagan.

JOE. It sounds great, Mr. Heller.

MARTIN. Martin. And Justice is the hub. Especially since Ed Meese took over. He doesn't specialize in Fine Points of the Law. He's a flatfoot, a cop. He reminds me of Teddy Roosevelt.

JOE. I can't wait to meet him.

MARTIN. Too bad, Joe, He's been dead for sixty years!

(*There's a little awkwardness. Joe doesn't respond.*)

MARTIN. Teddy Roosevelt. You said you wanted to. . . . Little joke. It reminds me of the story about the . . .

ROY (*Smiling, but nasty*). Aw shut the fuck up Martin.

(*To Joe*) You see that? Mr. Heller here is one of the mighty, Joseph, in D.C. he sitteth on the right hand of the man who sitteth on the right hand of The Man. And yet I can say "shut the fuck up" and he will take no offense. Loyalty. He . . .

Martin?

MARTIN. Yes, Roy?

ROY. Rub my back.

MARTIN. Roy . . .

ROY. No no really, a sore spot, I get them all the time now, these. . . . Rub it for me darling, would you do that for me?

(*Martin rubs Roy's back. They both look at Joe.*)

ROY (*To Joe*). How do you think a handful of Bolsheviks turned St. Petersburg into Leningrad in one afternoon? *Comrades.* Who do for each other. Marx and Engels. Lenin and Trotsky. Josef Stalin and Franklin Delano Roosevelt.

(*Martin laughs.*)

ROY. *Comrades*, right Martin?

MARTIN. This man, Joe, is a Saint of the Right.

JOE. I know, Mr. Heller, I . . .

ROY. And you see what I mean, Martin? He's special, right?

MARTIN. Don't embarrass him, Roy.

ROY. Gravity, decency, smarts! His strength is as the strength of ten because his heart is pure! *And* he's a Royboy, one hundred percent.

MARTIN. We're on the move, Joe. On the move.

JOE. Mr. Heller, I . . .

MARTIN (*Ending backrub*). We can't wait any longer for an answer.

(*Little pause.*)

JOE. Oh. Um, I . . .

ROY. Joe's a married man, Martin.

MARTIN. Aha.

ROY. With a wife. She doesn't care to go to D.C., and so Joe cannot go. And keeps us dangling. We've seen that kind of thing before, haven't we? These men and their wives.

MARTIN. Oh yes. Beware.

JOE. I really can't discuss this under . . .

MARTIN. Then *don't* discuss. Say yes, Joe.

ROY. Now.

MARTIN. Say yes I will.

ROY. Now.

Now. I'll hold my breath till you do, I'm turning blue waiting. . . . *Now*, goddammit!

MARTIN. Roy, calm down, it's not . . .

ROY. Aw, fuck it. (*He takes a letter from his jacket pocket, hands it to Joe*)

Read. Came today.

(*Joe reads the first paragraph, then looks up.*)

JOE. Roy. This is . . . Roy, this is terrible.

ROY. You're telling me.

A letter from the New York State Bar Association, Martin.

They're gonna try and disbar me.

MARTIN. Oh my.

JOE. Why?

ROY. Why, Martin?

MARTIN. Revenge.

ROY. The whole Establishment. Their little rules. Because I know no rules. Because I don't see the Law as a dead and arbitrary collection of antiquated dictums, thou shall, thou shalt not, because, because I know the Law's a pliable, breathing, sweating . . . *organ*, because, because . . .

MARTIN. Because he borrowed half a million from one of his clients.

ROY. Yeah, well, there's that.

MARTIN. *And* he forgot to *return* it.

JOE. Roy, that's. . . . You borrowed money from a client?

ROY. I'm deeply ashamed.

(*Little pause.*)

JOE (*Very sympathetic*). Roy, you know how much I admire you. Well I mean I know you have unorthodox ways, but I'm sure you only did what you thought at the time you needed to do. And I have faith that . . .

ROY. Not so damp, please. I'll deny it was a loan. She's got no paperwork. Can't prove a fucking thing.

(*Little pause. Martin studies the menu.*)

JOE (*Handing back the letter, more official in tone*). Roy I really appreciate your telling me this, and I'll do whatever I can to help.

ROY (*Holding up a hand, then, carefully*). I'll tell you what you can do.

I'm about to be tried, Joe, by a jury that is not a jury of my peers. The disbarment committee: genteel gentleman

Brahmin lawyers, country-club men. I offend them, to these men . . . I'm what, Martin, some sort of filthy little Jewish troll?

MARTIN. Oh well, I wouldn't go so far as . . .

ROY. Oh well I would.

Very fancy lawyers, these disbarment committee lawyers, fancy lawyers with fancy corporate clients and complicated cases. Antitrust suits. Deregulation. Environmental control. Complex cases like these need Justice Department cooperation like flowers need the sun. Wouldn't you say that's an accurate assessment, Martin?

MARTIN. I'm not here, Roy. I'm not hearing any of this.

ROY. No. Of course not.

Without the light of the sun, Joe, these cases, and the fancy lawyers who represent them, will wither and die.

A well-placed friend, someone in the Justice Department, say, can turn off the sun. Cast a deep shadow on my behalf. Make them shiver in the cold. If they overstep. They would fear that.

(*Pause.*)

JOE. Roy. I don't understand.

ROY. You do.

(*Pause.*)

JOE. You're not asking me to . . .

ROY. Sssshhhh. Careful.

JOE (*A beat, then*). Even if I said yes to the job, it would be illegal to interfere. With the hearings. It's unethical. No. I can't.

ROY. Un-ethical.

Would you excuse us, Martin?

MARTIN. Excuse you?

ROY. Take a walk, Martin. For real.

(*Martin leaves.*)

ROY. Un-ethical. Are you trying to embarrass me in front of my friend?

JOE. Well it is unethical, I can't . . .

ROY. Boy, you are really something. What the fuck do you think this is, Sunday School?

JOE. No, but Roy this is . . .

ROY. This is . . . this is gastric juices churning, this is enzymes and acids, this is intestinal is what this is, bowel movement and blood-red meat—this stinks, this is *politics*, Joe, the game of being alive. And you think you're. . . . What? Above that? Above alive is what? Dead! In the clouds! You're on earth, goddammit! Plant a foot, stay a while.

I'm sick. They smell I'm weak. They want blood this time. I must have eyes in Justice. In Justice you will protect me.

JOE. Why can't Mr. Heller . . .

ROY. Grow up, Joe. The administration can't get involved.

JOE. But I'd be part of the administration. The same as him.

ROY. Not the same. Martin's Ed's man. And Ed's Reagan's man. So Martin's Reagan's man.

And you're mine.

(*Little pause. He holds up the letter*)

This will never be. Understand me?

(*He tears the letter up*)

I'm gonna be a lawyer, Joe, I'm gonna be a lawyer, Joe, I'm gonna be a goddam motherfucking legally licensed member of the bar lawyer, just like my daddy was, till my last bitter day on earth, Joseph, until the day I die.

(*Martin returns.*)

ROY. Ah, Martin's back.

MARTIN. So are we agreed?

ROY. Joe?

(*Little pause.*)

JOE. I will think about it.

(*To Roy*) I will.

ROY. Huh.

MARTIN. It's the fear of what comes after the doing that makes the doing hard to do.

ROY. Amen.

MARTIN. But you can almost always live with the consequences.

SCENE 7

That afternoon. On the granite steps outside the Hall of Justice, Brooklyn. It is cold and sunny. A Sabrett wagon is selling hot dogs. Louis, in a shabby overcoat, is sitting on the steps contemplatively eating one. Joe enters with three hot dogs and a can of Coke.

JOE. Can I . . . ?

LOUIS. Oh sure. Sure. Crazy cold sun.

JOE (*Sitting*). Have to make the best of it.

How's your friend?

LOUIS. My . . . ? Oh. He's worse. My friend is worse.

JOE. I'm sorry.

LOUIS. Yeah, well. Thanks for asking. It's nice. You're nice. I can't believe you voted for Reagan.

JOE. I hope he gets better.

LOUIS. Reagan?

JOE. Your friend.

LOUIS. He won't. Neither will Reagan.

JOE. Let's not talk politics, OK?

LOUIS (*Pointing to Joe's lunch*). You're eating *three* of those?

JOE. Well . . . I'm . . . hungry.

LOUIS. They're really terrible for you. Full of rat-poo and beetle legs and wood shavings 'n' shit.

JOE. Huh.

LOUIS. And . . . um . . . irridium, I think. Something toxic.

JOE. You're eating one.

LOUIS. Yeah, well, the shape, I can't help myself, plus I'm *trying* to commit suicide, what's your excuse?

JOE. I don't have an excuse. I just have Pepto-Bismol.

(*Joe takes a bottle of Pepto-Bismol and chugs it. Louis shudders audibly.*)

JOE. Yeah I know but then I wash it down with Coke.

(*He does this. Louis mimes barfing in Joe's lap. Joe pushes Louis's head away.*)

JOE. Are you *always* like this?

LOUIS. I've been worrying a lot about his kids.

JOE. Whose?

LOUIS. Reagan's. Maureen and Mike and little orphan Patti and Miss Ron Reagan Jr., the you-should-pardon-the-expression heterosexual.

JOE. Ron Reagan Jr. is *not* . . . You shouldn't just make these assumptions about people. How do you know? About him? What he is? You don't know.

LOUIS (*Doing Tallulah*). Well darling he never sucked *my* cock but . . .

JOE. Look, if you're going to get vulgar . . .

LOUIS. No no really I mean. . . . What's it like to be the child of the Zeitgeist? To have the American Animus as your dad? It's not really a *family*, the Reagans, I read *People*, there aren't any connections there, no love, they don't ever even speak to each other except through their agents. So what's it like to be Reagan's kid? Enquiring minds want to know.

JOE. You can't believe everything you . . .

LOUIS (*Looking away*). But . . . I think we all know what that's like. Nowadays. No connections. No responsibilities. All of us . . . falling through the cracks that separate what we owe to our selves and . . . and what we owe to love.

JOE. You just. . . . Whatever you feel like saying or doing, you don't care, you just . . . do it.

LOUIS. Do what?

JOE. It. Whatever. Whatever it is you want to do.

LOUIS. Are you trying to tell me something?

(*Little pause, sexual. They stare at each other. Joe looks away.*)

JOE. No, I'm just observing that you . . .

LOUIS. Impulsive.

JOE. Yes, I mean it must be scary, you . . .

LOUIS (*Shrugs*). Land of the free. Home of the brave. Call me irresponsible.

JOE. It's kind of terrifying.

LOUIS. Yeah, well, freedom is. Heartless, too.

JOE. Oh you're not heartless.

LOUIS. You don't know.
  Finish your weenie.

(*He pats Joe on the knee, starts to leave.*)

JOE. Um . . .

(*Louis turns, looks at him. Joe searches for something to say.*)

JOE. Yesterday was Sunday but I've been a little unfocused recently and I thought it was Monday. So I came here like I was going to work. And the whole place was empty. And at first I couldn't figure out why, and I had this moment of incredible . . . fear and also. . . . It just flashed through my mind: The whole Hall of Justice, it's empty, it's deserted, it's gone out of business. Forever. The people that make it run have up and abandoned it.

LOUIS (*Looking at the building*). Creepy.

JOE. Well yes but. I felt that I was going to scream. Not because it was creepy, but because the emptiness felt so *fast*.
  And . . . well, good. A . . . happy scream.
  I just wondered what a thing it would be . . . if overnight everything you owe anything to, justice, or love, had really gone away. Free.
  It would be . . . heartless terror. Yes. Terrible, and . . . Very great. To shed your skin, every old skin, one by one and then walk away, unencumbered, into the morning.

(*Little pause. He looks at the building*)

  I can't go in there today.

LOUIS. Then don't.

JOE (*Not really hearing Louis*). I can't go in, I need . . .

(*He looks for what he needs. He takes a swig of Pepto-Bismol*)

  I can't *be* this anymore. I need . . . a change, I should just . . .

LOUIS (*Not a come-on, necessarily; he doesn't want to be alone*). Want some company? For whatever?

(*Pause. Joe looks at Louis and looks away, afraid. Louis shrugs.*)

LOUIS. Sometimes, even if it scares you to death, you have to be willing to break the law. Know what I mean?

(*Another little pause.*)

JOE. Yes.

(*Another little pause.*)

LOUIS. I moved out. I moved out on my . . .
  I haven't been sleeping well.

JOE. Me neither.

(*Louis goes up to Joe, licks his napkin and dabs at Joe's mouth.*)

LOUIS. Antacid moustache.

　　(*Points to the building*) Maybe the court won't convene. Ever again. Maybe we are free. To do whatever.

　　Children of the new morning, criminal minds. Selfish and greedy and loveless and blind. Reagan's children.

　　You're scared. So am I. Everybody is in the land of the free. God help us all.

SCENE 8

Late that night. Joe at a payphone phoning Hannah at home in Salt Lake City.

JOE. Mom?

HANNAH. Joe?

JOE. Hi.

HANNAH. You're calling from the street. It's . . . it must be four in the morning. What's happened?

JOE. Nothing, nothing, I . . .

HANNAH. It's Harper. Is Harper. . . . Joe? Joe?

JOE. Yeah, hi. No, Harper's fine. Well, no, she's . . . not fine. How are you, Mom?

HANNAH. What's happened?

JOE. I just wanted to talk to you. I, uh, wanted to try something out on you.

HANNAH. Joe, you haven't . . . have you been drinking, Joe?

JOE. Yes ma'am. I'm drunk.

HANNAH. That isn't like you.

JOE. No. I mean, who's to say?

HANNAH. Why are you out on the street at four AM? In that crazy city. It's dangerous.

JOE. Actually, Mom, I'm not on the street. I'm near the boathouse in the park.

HANNAH. What park?

JOE. Central Park.

HANNAH. CENTRAL PARK! Oh my Lord. What on earth are you doing in Central Park at this time of night? Are you . . .

　　Joe, I think you ought to go home right now. Call me from home.

　　(*Little pause*)

　　Joe?

JOE. I come here to watch, Mom. Sometimes. Just to watch.

HANNAH. Watch what? What's there to watch at four in the . . .

JOE. Mom, did Dad love me?

HANNAH. What?

JOE. Did he?

HANNAH. You ought to go home and call from there.

JOE. Answer.

HANNAH. Oh now really. This is maudlin. I don't like this conversation.

JOE. Yeah, well, it gets worse from here on.

(*Pause.*)

HANNAH. Joe?

JOE. Mom. Momma. I'm a homosexual, Momma.

　　Boy, did that come out awkward.

　　(*Pause*)

　　Hello? Hello?

　　I'm a homosexual.

　　(*Pause*)

　　Please, Momma. Say something.

HANNAH. You're old enough to understand that your father didn't love you without being ridiculous about it.

JOE. What?

HANNAH. You're ridiculous. You're being ridiculous.

JOE. I'm . . .

　　What?

HANNAH. You really ought to go home now to your wife. I need to go to bed. This phone call. . . . We will just forget this phone call.

JOE. Mom.

HANNAH. No more talk. Tonight. This . . .

　　(*Suddenly very angry*) Drinking is a sin! A sin! I raised you better than that. (*She hangs up*)

SCENE 9

The following morning, early. Split scene: Harper and Joe at home; Louis and Prior in Prior's hospital room. Joe and Louis have just entered. This should be fast and obviously furious; overlapping is fine; the proceedings may be a little confusing but not the final result.

HARPER. Oh God. Home. The moment of truth has arrived.

JOE. Harper.

LOUIS. I'm going to move out.

PRIOR. The fuck you are.

JOE. Harper. Please listen. I still love you very much. You're still my best buddy; I'm not going to leave you.

HARPER. No, I don't like the sound of this. I'm leaving.

LOUIS. I'm leaving.

　　I already have.

JOE. Please listen. Stay. this is really hard. We have to talk.

HARPER. We are talking. Aren't we. Now please shut up. OK?

PRIOR. Bastard. Sneaking off while I'm flat out here, that's low. If I could get up now I'd beat the holy shit out of you.

JOE. Did you take pills? How many?

HARPER. No pills. Bad for the . . . (*Pats stomach*)

JOE. You aren't pregnant. I called your gynecologist.

HARPER. I'm seeing a new gynecologist.

PRIOR. You have no right to do this.

LOUIS. Oh, that's ridiculous.

PRIOR. No right. It's criminal.

JOE. Forget about that. Just listen. You want the truth. This is the truth.

I knew this when I married you. I've known this I guess for as long as I've known anything, but . . . I don't know, I thought maybe that with enough effort and will I could change myself . . . but I can't . . .

PRIOR. Criminal.

LOUIS. There oughta be a law.

PRIOR. There is a law. You'll see.

JOE. I'm losing ground here, I go walking, you want to know where I walk, I . . . go to the park, or up and down 53rd Street, or places where. . . . And I keep swearing I won't go walking again, but I just can't.

LOUIS. I need some privacy.

PRIOR. That's new.

LOUIS. Everything's new, Prior.

JOE. I try to tighten my heart into a knot, a snarl, I try to learn to live dead, just numb, but then I see someone I want, and it's like a nail, like a hot spike through my chest, and I know I'm losing.

PRIOR. Apartment too small for three? Louis and Prior comfy but not Louis and Prior and Prior's disease?

LOUIS. Something like that.

I won't be judged by you. This isn't a crime, just—the inevitable consequence of people who run out of—whose limitations . . .

PRIOR. Bang bang bang. The court will come to order.

LOUIS. I mean let's talk practicalities, schedules; I'll come over if you want, spend nights with you when I can, I can . . .

PRIOR. Has the jury reached a verdict?

LOUIS. I'm doing the best I can.

PRIOR. Pathetic. Who cares?

JOE. My whole life has conspired to bring me to this place, and I can't despise my whole life. I think I believed when I met you I could save you, you at least if not myself, but . . .

I don't have any sexual feelings for you, Harper. And I don't think I ever did.

(*Little pause.*)

HARPER. I think you should go.

JOE. Where?

HARPER. Washington. Doesn't matter.

JOE. What are you talking about?

HARPER. Without me.

Without me, Joe. Isn't that what you want to hear?

(*Little pause.*)

JOE. Yes.

LOUIS. You can love someone and fail them. You can love someone and not be able to . . .

PRIOR. You *can*, theoretically, yes. A person can, maybe an editorial "you" can love, Louis, but not *you*, specifically you, I don't know, I think you are excluded from that general category.

HARPER. You were going to save me, but the whole time you were spinning a lie. I just don't understand that.

PRIOR. A person could theoretically love and maybe many do but we both know now you can't.

LOUIS. I do.

PRIOR. You can't even say it.

LOUIS. I love you, Prior.

PRIOR. I repeat. Who cares?

HARPER. This is so scary, I want this to stop, to go back . . .

PRIOR. We have reached a verdict, your honor. This man's heart is deficient. He loves, but his love is worth nothing.

JOE. Harper . . .

HARPER. Mr. Lies, I want to get away from here. Far away. Right now. Before he starts talking again. Please, please . . .

JOE. As long as I've known you Harper you've been afraid of . . . of men hiding under the bed, men hiding under the sofa, men with knives.

PRIOR (*Shattered; almost pleading; trying to reach him*). I'm dying! You stupid fuck! Do you know what that is! Love! Do you know what love means? We lived together four-and-a-half years, you animal, you idiot.

LOUIS. I have to find some way to save myself.

JOE. Who are these men? I never understood it. Now I know.

HARPER. What?

JOE. It's me.

HARPER. It is?

PRIOR. GET OUT OF MY ROOM!

JOE. I'm the man with the knives.

HARPER. You are?

PRIOR. If I could get up now I'd kill you. I would. Go away. Go away or I'll scream.

HARPER. Oh God . . .

JOE. I'm sorry . . .

HARPER. It is you.

LOUIS. Please don't scream.

PRIOR. Go.

HARPER. I recognize you now.

LOUIS. Please . . .

JOE. Oh. Wait, I. . . . Oh!

(*He covers his mouth with his hand, gags, and removes his had, red with blood*)

I'm bleeding.

(*Prior screams.*)

HARPER. Mr. Lies.

MR. LIES. (*appearing, dressed in antarctic explorer's apparel*). Right here.

HARPER. I want to go away. I can't see him anymore.

MR. LIES. Where?

HARPER. Anywhere. Far away.

MR. LIES. Absolutamento.

(*Harper and Mr. Lies vanish. Joe looks up, sees that she's gone.*)

PRIOR (*Closing his eyes*). When I open my eyes you'll be gone.

(*Louis leaves.*)

JOE. Harper?
PRIOR (*Opening his eyes*). Huh. It worked.
JOE (*Calling*). Harper?
PRIOR. I hurt all over. I wish I was dead.

SCENE 10

The same day, sunset. Hannah and Sister Ella Chapter, a real-estate saleswoman, Hannah Pitt's closest friend, in front of Hannah's house in Salt Lake City.

SISTER ELLA CHAPTER. Look at that view! A view of heaven. Like the living city of heaven, isn't it, it just fairly glimmers in the sun.
HANNAH. Glimmers.
SISTER ELLA CHAPTER. Even the stone and brick it just glimmers and glitters like heaven in the sunshine. Such a nice view you get, perched up on a canyon rim. Some kind of beautiful place.
HANNAH. It's just Salt Lake, and you're selling the house *for* me, not *to* me.
SISTER ELLA CHAPTER. I like to work up an enthusiasm for my properties.
HANNAH. Just get me a good price.
SISTER ELLA CHAPTER. Well, the market's off.
HANNAH. At least fifty.
SISTER ELLA CHAPTER. Forty'd be more like it.
HANNAH. Fifty.
SISTER ELLA CHAPTER. Wish you'd wait a bit.
HANNAH. Well I can't.
SISTER ELLA CHAPTER. Wish you would. You're about the only friend I got.
HANNAH. Oh well now.
SISTER ELLA CHAPTER. Know why I decided to like you? I decided to like you 'cause you're the only unfriendly Mormon I ever met.
HANNAH. Your wig is crooked.
SISTER ELLA CHAPTER. Fix it.

(*Hannah straightens Sister Ella's wig.*)

SISTER ELLA CHAPTER. New York City. All they got there is tiny rooms.

I always thought: People ought to stay put. That's why I got my license to sell real estate. It's a way of saying: Have a house! Stay put! It's a way of saying traveling's no good. Plus I needed the cash. (*She takes a pack of cigarettes out of her purse, lights one, offers pack to Hannah*)
HANNAH. Not out here, anyone could come by.

There's been days I've stood at this ledge and thought about stepping over.

It's a hard place, Salt Lake: baked dry. Abundant energy; not much intelligence. That's a combination that can wear a body out. No harm looking someplace else. I don't need much room.

My sister-in-law Libby thinks there's radon gas in the basement.
SISTER ELLA CHAPTER. Is there gas in the . . .
HANNAH. Of course not. Libby's a fool.
SISTER ELLA CHAPTER. 'Cause I'd have to include that in the description.
HANNAH. There's no gas, Ella. (*Little pause*) Give a puff. (*She takes a furtive drag of Ella's cigarette*) Put it away now.
SISTER ELLA CHAPTER. So I guess it's goodbye.
HANNAH. You'll be all right, Ella, I wasn't ever much of a friend.
SISTER ELLA CHAPTER. I'll say something but don't laugh, OK?

This is the home of saints, the godliest place on earth, they say, and I think they're right. That mean there's no evil here? No. Evil's everywhere. Sin's everywhere. But this . . . is the spring of sweet water in the desert, the desert flower. Every step a Believer takes away from here is a step fraught with peril. I fear for you, Hannah Pitt, because you are my friend. Stay put. This is the right home of saints.
HANNAH. Latter-day saints.
SISTER ELLA CHAPTER. Only kind left.
HANNAH. But still. Late in the day . . . for saints and everyone. That's all. That's all.

Fifty thousand dollars for the house, Sister Ella Chapter; don't undersell. It's an impressive view.

ACT THREE: NOT-YET-CONSCIOUS, FORWARD DAWNING

January 1986

SCENE 1

Late night, three days after the end of Act Two. The stage is completely dark. Prior is in bed in his apartment, having a nightmare. He wakes up, sits up and switches on a nightlight. He looks at his clock. Seated by the table near the bed is a man dressed in the clothing of a 13th-century British squire.

PRIOR (*Terrified*). Who are you?
PRIOR 1. My name is Prior Walter.

(*Pause.*)

PRIOR. My name is Prior Walter.
PRIOR 1. I know that.
PRIOR. Explain.
PRIOR 1. You're alive. I'm not. We have the same name. What do you want me to explain?

PRIOR. A ghost?

PRIOR 1. An ancestor.

PRIOR. Not *the* Prior Walter? The Bayeux tapestry Prior Walter?

PRIOR 1. His great-great grandson. The fifth of the name.

PRIOR. I'm the thirty-fourth, I think.

PRIOR 1. Actually the thirty-second.

PRIOR. Not according to Mother.

PRIOR 1. She's including the two bastards, then; I say leave them out. I say no room for bastards. The little things you swallow . . .

PRIOR. Pills.

PRIOR 1. Pills. For the pestilence. I too . . .

PRIOR. Pestilence. . . . You too what?

PRIOR 1. The pestilence in my time was much worse than now. Whole villages of empty houses. You could look outdoors and see Death walking in the morning, dew dampening the ragged hem of his black robe. Plain as I see you now.

PRIOR. You died of the plague.

PRIOR 1. The spotty monster. Like you, alone.

PRIOR. I'm not alone.

PRIOR 1. You have no wife, no children.

PRIOR. I'm gay.

PRIOR 1. So? Be gay, dance in your altogether for all I care, what's that to do with not having children?

PRIOR. Gay homosexual, not bonny, blithe and . . . never mind.

PRIOR 1. I had twelve. When I died.

(*The second ghost appears, this one dressed in the clothing of an elegant 17th-century Londoner.*)

PRIOR 1 (*Pointing to Prior 2*). And I was three years younger than him.

(*Prior sees the new ghost, screams.*)

PRIOR. Oh God another one.

PRIOR 2. Prior Walter. Prior to you by some seventeen others.

PRIOR 1. He's counting the bastards.

PRIOR. Are we having a convention?

PRIOR 2. We've been sent to declare her fabulous incipience. They love a well-paved entrance with lots of heralds, and . . .

PRIOR 1. The messenger come. Prepare the way. The infinite descent, a breath in air . . .

PRIOR 2. They chose us, I suspect, because of the mortal affinities. In a family as long-descended as the Walters there are bound to be a few carried off by plague.

PRIOR 1. The spotty monster.

PRIOR 2. Black Jack. Came from a water pump, half the city of London, can you imagine? His came from fleas. Yours, I understand, is the lamentable consequence of venery . . .

PRIOR 1. Fleas on rats, but who knew that?

PRIOR. Am I going to die?

PRIOR 2. We aren't allowed to discuss . . .

PRIOR 1. When you do, you don't get ancestors to help you through it. You may be surrounded by children but you die alone.

PRIOR. I'm afraid.

PRIOR 1. You should be. There aren't even torches, and the path's rocky, dark and steep.

PRIOR 2. Don't alarm him. There's good news before there's bad.

We two come to strew rose petal and palm leaf before the triumphal procession. Prophet. Seer. Revelator. It's a great honor for the family.

PRIOR 1. He hasn't got a family.

PRIOR 2. I meant for the Walters, for the family in the larger sense.

PRIOR (*Singing*).

All I want is a room somewhere,
Far away from the cold night air . . .

PRIOR 2 (*Putting a hand on Prior's forehead*). Calm, calm, this is no brain fever . . .

(*Prior calms down, but keeps his eyes closed. The lights begin to change. Distant Glorious Music.*)

PRIOR 1 (*Low chant*).

Adonai, Adonai,
Olam ha-yichud,
Zefirot, Zazahot,
Ha-adam, ha-gadol
Daughter of Light,
Daughter of Splendors,
Fluor! Phosphor!
Lumen! Candle!

PRIOR 2 (*Simultaneously*).

Even now,
From the mirror-bright halls of heaven,
Across the cold and lifeless infinity of space,
The Messenger comes
Trailing orbs of light,
Fabulous, incipient,
Oh Prophet,
To you . . .

PRIOR 1 and PRIOR 2.

Prepare, prepare,
The Infinite Descent,
A breath, a feather,
Glory to . . .

(*They vanish.*)

SCENE 2

The next day. Split scene: Louis and Belize in a coffee shop. Prior is at the outpatient clinic at the hospital with Emily, the nurse; she has him on a pentamidine IV drip.

LOUIS. Why has democracy succeeded in America? Of course by succeeded I mean comparatively, not literally, not in the present, but what makes for the prospect of some sort of radical democracy spreading outward and growing up? Why does the power that was once so carefully preserved at the top of the pyramid by the original framers of the Constitution seem drawn inexorably downward and outward in spite of the best effort of the Right to stop this? I mean it's the really hard thing about being Left in this country, the American Left can't help but trip over all these petrified little fetishes: freedom, that's the worst; you know, *Jeane Kirkpatrick* for God's sake will go on and on about freedom and so what does that mean, the word freedom, when she talks about it, or human rights; you have Bush talking about human rights, and so what are these people talking about, they might as well be talking about the mating habits of Venusians, these people don't begin to know what, ontologically, freedom is or human rights, like they see these bourgeois property-based Rights-of-Man-type rights but that's not enfranchisement, not democracy, not what's implicit, what's potential within the idea, not the idea with blood in it. That's just liberalism, the worst kind of liberalism, really, bourgeois tolerance, and what I think is that what AIDS shows us is the limits of tolerance, that it's not enough to be tolerated, because when the shit hits the fan you find out how much tolerance is worth. Nothing. And underneath all the tolerance is intense, passionate hatred.

BELIZE. Uh huh.

LOUIS. Well don't you think that's true?

BELIZE. Uh huh. It is.

LOUIS. *Power* is the object, not being tolerated. Fuck assimilation. But I mean in spite of all this the thing about America, I think, is that ultimately we're different from every other nation on earth, in that, with people here of every race, we can't. . . . Ultimately what defines us isn't race, but politics. Not like any European country where there's an insurmountable fact of a kind of racial, or ethnic, monopoly, or monolith, like all Dutchmen, I mean Dutch people, are well, Dutch, and the Jews of Europe were never Europeans, just a small problem. Facing the monolith. But here there are so many small problems, it's really just a collection of small problems, the monolith is missing. Oh, I mean, of course I suppose there's the monolith of White America. White Straight Male America.

BELIZE. Which is not unimpressive, even among monoliths.

LOUIS. Well, no, but when the race thing gets taken care of, and I don't mean to minimalize how major it is, I mean I know it is, this is a really, really incredibly racist country but it's like, well, the British. I mean, all these blue-eyed pink people. And it's just weird, you know, I mean I'm not all that Jewish-looking, or . . . well, maybe I am but, you know, in New York, everyone is . . . well, not everyone, but so many are but so but in England, in London I

walk into bars and I feel like Sid the Yid, you know I mean like Woody Allen in *Annie Hall*, with the payess and the gabardine coat, like never, never anywhere so much—I mean, not actively despised, not like they're Germans, who I think are still terribly anti-Semitic, and racist too, I mean black-racist, they pretend otherwise but, anyway, in London, there's just . . . and at one point I met this black gay guy from Jamaica who talked with a lilt but he said his family'd been living in London since before the Civil War—the American one—and how the English never let him forget for a minute that he wasn't blue-eyed and pink and I said yeah, me too, these people are anti-Semites and he said yeah but the British Jews have the clothing business all sewed up and blacks there can't get a foothold. And it was an incredibly awkward moment of just. . . . I mean here we were, in this bar that was gay but it was a *pub*, you know, the beams and the plaster and those horrible little, like, two-day-old fish and egg sandwiches—and just so British, so *old*, and I felt, well, there's no way out of this because both of us are, right now, too much immersed in this history, hope is dissolved in the sheer age of this place, where race is what counts and there's no real hope of change—it's the racial destiny of the Brits that matters to them, not their political destiny, whereas in America . . .

BELIZE. Here in America race doesn't count.

LOUIS. No, no, that's not. . . . I mean you *can't* be hearing that . . .

BELIZE. I . . .

LOUIS. It's—look, race, yes, but ultimately race here is a political question, right? Racists just try to use race here as a tool in a political struggle. It's not really about race. Like the spiritualists try to use that stuff, are you enlightened, are you centered, channeled, whatever, this reaching out for a spiritual past in a country where no indigenous spirits exist—only the Indians, I mean Native American spirits and we killed them off so now, there are no gods here, no ghosts and spirits in America, there are no angels in America, no spiritual past, no racial past, there's only the political, and the decoys and the ploys to maneuver around the inescapable battle of politics, the shifting downwards and outwards of political power to the people . . .

BELIZE. POWER to the People! AMEN! (*Looking at his watch*) *OH MY GOODNESS!* will you look at the time, I gotta . . .

LOUIS. Do you . . . You think this is, what, racist or naive or something?

BELIZE. Well it's certainly *something*. Look, I just remembered I have an appointment . . .

LOUIS. What? I mean I really don't want to, like, speak from some position of privilege and . . .

BELIZE. I'm sitting here, thinking, eventually he's *got* to run out of steam, so I let you rattle on and on saying about maybe seven or eight things I find really offensive.

LOUIS. What?

BELIZE. But I know you, Louis, and I know the guilt fueling this peculiar tirade is obviously already swollen bigger than your hemorrhoids.

LOUIS. I don't have hemorrhoids.

BELIZE. I hear different. May I finish?

LOUIS. Yes, but I don't have hemorrhoids.

BELIZE. So finally, when I . . .

LOUIS. Prior told you, he's an asshole, he shouldn't have . . .

BELIZE. You promised, Louis. Prior is not a subject.

LOUIS. You brought him up.

BELIZE. I brought up hemorrhoids.

LOUIS. So it's indirect. Passive-aggressive.

BELIZE. Unlike, I suppose, banging me over the head with your theory that America doesn't have a race problem.

LOUIS. Oh be fair I never said that.

BELIZE. Not exactly, but . . .

LOUIS. I said . . .

BELIZE. . . . but it was close enough, because if it'd been that blunt I'd've just walked out and . . .

LOUIS. You deliberately misinterpreted! I . . .

BELIZE. Stop interrupting! I haven't been able to . . .

LOUIS. Just let me . . .

BELIZE. NO! What, *talk*? You've been running your mouth nonstop since I got here, yaddadda yaddadda blah blah blah, up the hill, down the hill, playing with your MONOLITH . . .

LOUIS (*Overlapping*). Well, you could have joined in at any time instead of . . .

BELIZE (*Continuing over Louis*). . . . and girlfriend it is truly an *awesome* spectacle but I got better things to do with my time than sit here listening to this racist bullshit just because I feel sorry for you that . . .

LOUIS. I am not a racist!

BELIZE. Oh come on . . .

LOUIS. So maybe I am a racist but . . .

BELIZE. Oh I really hate that! It's no fun picking on you Louis; you're so guilty, it's like throwing darts at a glob of jello, there's no satisfying hits, just quivering, the darts just blop in and vanish.

LOUIS. I just think when you are discussing lines of oppression it gets very complicated and . . .

BELIZE. Oh is that a fact? You know, we black drag queens have a rather intimate knowledge of the complexity of the lines of . . .

LOUIS. *Ex*-black drag queen.

BELIZE. Actually ex-ex.

LOUIS. You're doing drag again?

BELIZE. I don't. . . . Maybe. I don't have to tell you. Maybe.

LOUIS. I think it's sexist.

BELIZE. I didn't ask you.

LOUIS. Well it is. The gay community, I think, has to adopt the same attitude towards drag as black women have to take towards black women blues singers.

BELIZE. Oh my we *are* walking dangerous tonight.

LOUIS. Well, it's all internalized oppression, right, I mean the masochism, the stereotypes, the . . .

BELIZE. Louis, are you deliberately trying to make me hate you?

LOUIS. No, I . . .

BELIZE. I mean, are you deliberately transforming yourself into an arrogant, sexual-political Stalinist-slash-racist flag-waving thug for my benefit?

(*Pause.*)

LOUIS. You know what I think?

BELIZE. What?

LOUIS. You hate me because I'm a Jew.

BELIZE. I'm leaving.

LOUIS. It's true.

BELIZE. You have no basis except your . . .

    Louis, it's good to know you haven't changed; you are still an honorary citizen of the Twilight Zone, and after your pale, pale white polemics on behalf of racial insensitivity you have a flaming *fuck* of a lot of nerve calling me an anti-Semite. Now I really gotta go.

LOUIS. You called me Lou the Jew.

BELIZE. That was a joke.

LOUIS. I didn't think it was funny. It was hostile.

BELIZE. It was three years ago.

LOUIS. So?

BELIZE. You just called yourself Sid the Yid.

LOUIS. That's not the same thing.

BELIZE. Sid the Yid is different from Lou the Jew.

LOUIS. Yes.

BELIZE. Someday you'll have to explain that to me, but right now . . .

    You hate me because you hate black people.

LOUIS. I do not. But I do think most black people are anti-Semitic.

BELIZE. "Most black people." *That's* racist, Louis, and I think most Jews . . .

LOUIS. Louis Farrakhan.

BELIZE. Ed Koch.

LOUIS. Jesse Jackson.

BELIZE. Jackson. Oh really, Louis, this is . . .

LOUIS. Hymietown! Hymietown!

BELIZE. Louis, you voted for Jesse Jackson. You send checks to the Rainbow Coalition.

LOUIS. I'm ambivalent. The checks bounced.

BELIZE. All your checks bounce, Louis; you're ambivalent about everything.

LOUIS. What's that supposed to mean?

BELIZE. You may be dumber than shit but I refuse to believe you can't figure it out. Try.

LOUIS. I was never ambivalent about Prior. I love him. I do. I really do.

BELIZE. Nobody said different.

LOUIS. Love and ambivalence are. . . . Real love isn't ambivalent.

BELIZE. "Real love isn't ambivalent." I'd swear that's a line from my favorite bestselling paperback novel, *In Love with the Night Mysterious*, except I don't think you ever read it.

(*Pause.*)

LOUIS. I never read it, no.

BELIZE. You ought to. Instead of spending the rest of your life trying to get through *Democracy in America*. It's about this white woman whose Daddy owns a plantation in the Deep South in the years before the Civil War—the American one—and her name is Margaret, and she's in love with her Daddy's number-one slave, and his name is Thaddeus, and she's married but her white slave-owner husband has AIDS: Antebellum Insufficiently Developed Sexorgans. And there's a lot of hot stuff going down when Margaret and Thaddeus can catch a spare torrid ten under the cotton-picking moon, and then of course the Yankees come, and they set the slaves free, and the slaves string up old Daddy, and so on. Historical fiction. Somewhere in there I recall Margaret and Thaddeus find the time to discuss the nature of love; her face is reflecting the flames of the burning plantation—you know, the way white people do—and his black face is dark in the night and she says to him, "Thaddeus, real love isn't ever ambivalent."

(*Little pause. Emily enters and turns off IV drip.*)

BELIZE. Thaddeus looks at her; he's contemplating her thesis; and he isn't sure he agrees.

EMILY (*Removing IV drip from Prior's arm*). Treatment number . . . (*Consulting chart*) four.

PRIOR. Pharmaceutical miracle. Lazarus breathes again.

LOUIS. Is he . . . How bad is he?

BELIZE. You want the laundry list?

EMILY. Shirt off, let's check the . . .

(*Prior takes his shirt off: She examines his lesions.*)

BELIZE. There's the weight problem and the shit problem and the morale problem.

EMILY. Only six. That's good. Pants.

(*He drops his pants. He's naked. She examines.*)

BELIZE. And. He thinks he's going crazy.

EMILY. Looking good. What else?

PRIOR. Ankles sore and swollen, but the leg's better. The nausea's mostly gone with the little orange pills. BM's pure liquid but not bloody anymore, for now, my eye doctor says everything's OK, for now, my dentist says "Yuck!" when he sees my fuzzy tongue, and now he wears little condoms on his thumb and forefinger. And a mask. So what? My dermatologist is in Hawaii and my mother . . . well leave my mother out of it. Which is usually where my mother is, out of it. My glands are like walnuts, my weight's holding steady for week two, and a friend died two days ago of bird tuberculosis; bird tuberculosis; that scared me and I didn't go to the funeral today because he was an Irish Catholic and it's probably open casket and I'm afraid of . . . something, the bird TB or seeing him or. . . . So I guess I'm dong OK. Except for of course I'm going nuts.

EMILY. We ran the toxoplasmosis series and there's no indication . . .

PRIOR. I know, I know, but I feel like something terrifying is on its way, you know, like a missile from outer space, and it's plummeting down towards the earth, and I'm ground zero, and . . . I am generally known where I am known as one cool, collected queen. And I am ruffled.

EMILY. There's really nothing to worry about. I think that shochen bamromim hamtzeh menucho nechono al kanfey haschino.

PRIOR. What?

EMILY. Everything's fine. Bemaalos k'doshim ut'horim kezohar horokeea mazhirim . . .

PRIOR. Oh I don't understand what you're . . .

EMILY. Es nishmas Prior sheholoch leolomoh, baavur shenodvoo z'dokoh b'ad hazkoras nishmosoh.

PRIOR. Why are you doing that?! Stop it! Stop it!

EMILY. Stop what?

PRIOR. You were just . . . weren't you just speaking in Hebrew or something.

EMILY. *Hebrew?* (*Laughs*) I'm basically Italian-American. No. I didn't speak in Hebrew.

PRIOR. Oh no, oh God please I really think I . . .

EMILY. Look, I'm sorry, I have a waiting room full of. . . . I think you're one of the lucky ones, you'll live for years, probably—and you're pretty healthy for someone with no immune system. Are you seeing someone? Loneliness is a danger. A therapist?

PRIOR. No, I don't need to see anyone, I just . . .

EMILY. Well think about it. You aren't going crazy. You're just under a lot of stress. No wonder . . . (*She starts to write in his chart*)

(*Suddenly there is an astonishing blaze of light, a huge chord sounded by a gigantic choir, and a great book with steel pages mounted atop a molten-red pillar pops up from the stage floor. The book opens; there is a large Aleph inscribed on its pages, which bursts into flames. Immediately the book slams shut and disappears instantly under the floor as the lights become normal again. Emily notices none of this, writing. Prior is agog.*)

EMILY (*Laughing, exiting*). Hebrew . . .

(*Prior flees.*)

LOUIS. Help me.

BELIZE. I beg your pardon?

LOUIS. You're a nurse, give me something, I . . . don't know what to do anymore, I. . . . Last week at work I screwed up the Xerox machine like permanently and so I . . . then I tripped on the subway steps and my glasses broke and I cut my forehead, here, see, and now I can't see much and my forehead . . . it's like the Mark of Cain, stupid, right, but it won't heal and every morning I see it and I think, Biblical things, Mark of Cain, Judas Iscariot and his silver and this noose, people who . . . in betraying what they love betray what's truest in themselves, I feel . . . nothing but cold for myself, just cold, and every night I miss him so much but then . . . those sores, and the smell and . . . where I thought it was going. . . . I could be . . . I could be sick too, maybe I'm sick too. I don't know.

Belize. Tell him I love him. Can you do that?

BELIZE. I've thought about it for a very long time, and I still don't understand what love is. Justice is simple. Democracy is simple. Those things are unambivalent. But love is very hard. And it goes bad for you if you violate the hard law of love.

LOUIS. I'm dying.

BELIZE. He's dying. You just wish you were.

Oh cheer up, Louis. Look at that heavy sky out there.

LOUIS. Purple.

BELIZE. *Purple?* Boy, what kind of homosexual are you, anyway? That's not purple, Mary, that color up there is (*Very grand*) mauve.

All day today it's felt like Thanksgiving. Soon, this . . . ruination will be blanketed white. You can smell it— can you smell it?

LOUIS. Smell what?

BELIZE. Softness, compliance, forgiveness, grace.

LOUIS. No . . .

BELIZE. I can't help you learn that. I can't help you, Louis. You're not my business. (*He exits*)

(*Louis puts his head in his hands, inadvertently touching his cut forehead.*)

LOUIS. Ow FUCK! (*He stands slowly, looks towards where Belize exited*) Smell what?

(*He looks both ways to be sure no one is watching, then inhales deeply, and is surprised*) Huh. Snow.

SCENE 3

Same day. Harper in a very white, cold place, with a brilliant blue sky above; a delicate snowfall. She is dressed in a beautiful snowsuit. The sound of the sea, faint.

HARPER. Snow! Ice! Mountains of ice! Where am I? I . . .

I feel better, I do, I . . . feel better. There are ice crystals in my lungs, wonderful and sharp. And the snow smells like cold, crushed peaches. And there's something

. . . some current of blood in the wind. How strange, it has that iron taste.

MR. LIES. Ozone.

HARPER. Ozone! Wow! Where am I?

MR. LIES. The Kingdom of Ice, the bottommost part of the world.

HARPER (*Looking around, then realizing*). Antarctica. This is Antarctica!

MR. LIES. Cold shelter for the shattered. No sorrow here, tears freeze.

HARPER. Antarctica, Antarctica, oh boy oh boy, LOOK at this, I. . . . Wow, I must've really snapped the tether, huh?

MR. LIES. Apparently . . .

HARPER. That's great. I want to stay here forever. Set up camp. Build things. Build a city, an enormous city made up of frontier forts, dark wood and green roofs and high gates made of pointed logs and bonfires burning on every street corner. I should build by a river. Where are the forests?

MR. LIES. No timber here. Too cold. Ice, no trees.

HARPER. Oh details! I'm sick of details! I'll plant them and grow them. I'll live off caribou fat, I'll melt it over the bonfires and drink it from long, curved goat-horn cups. It'll be great. I want to make a new world here. So that I never have to go home again.

MR. LIES. As long as it lasts. Ice has a way of melting . . .

HARPER. No. Forever. I can have anything I want here— maybe even companionship, someone who has . . . desire for me. You, maybe.

MR. LIES. It's against the by-laws of the International Order of Travel Agents to get involved with clients. Rules are rules. Anyway, I'm not the one you really want.

HARPER. There isn't anyone . . . maybe an Eskimo. Who could ice-fish for food. And help me build a nest for when the baby comes.

MR. LIES. There are no Eskimo in Antarctica. And you're not really pregnant. You made that up.

HARPER. Well all of this is made up. So if the snow feels cold I'm pregnant. Right? Here, I can be pregnant. And I can have any kind of baby I want.

MR. LIES. This is a retreat, a vacuum, its virtue is that it lacks everything; deep-freeze for feelings. You can be numb and safe here, that's what you came for. Respect the delicate ecology of your delusions.

HARPER. You mean like no Eskimo in Antarctica.

MR. LIES. Correcto. Ice and snow, no Eskimo. Even hallucinations have laws.

HARPER. Well then who's that?

(*The Eskimo appears.*)

MR. LIES. An Eskimo.

HARPER. An antarctic Eskimo. A fisher of the polar deep.

MR. LIES. There's something wrong with this picture.

(*The Eskimo beckons.*)

HARPER. I'm going to like this place. It's my own National Geographic Special! Oh! Oh! (*She holds her stomach*) I think . . . I think I felt her kicking. Maybe I'll give birth to a baby covered with thick white fur, and that way she won't be cold. My breasts will be full of hot cocoa so she doesn't get chilly. And if it gets really cold, she'll have a pouch I can crawl into. Like a marsupial. We'll mend together. That's what we'll do; we'll mend.

SCENE 4

Same day. An abandoned lot in the South Bronx. A homeless Woman is standing near an oil drum in which a fire is burning. Snowfall. Trash around. Hannah enters dragging two heavy suitcases.

HANNAH. Excuse me? I said excuse me? Can you tell me where I am? Is this Brooklyn? Do you know a Pineapple Street? Is there some sort of bus or train or . . . ?

I'm lost, I just arrived from Salt Lake. City. Utah? I took the bus that I was told to take and I got off—well it was the very last stop, so I had to get off, and I *asked* the driver was this Brooklyn, and he nodded yes but he was from one of those foreign countries where they think it's good manners to nod at everything even if you have no idea what it is you're nodding at, and in truth I think he spoke no English at all, which I think would make him ineligible for employment on public transportation. The public being English-speaking, mostly. Do you speak English?

(*The Woman nods.*)

HANNAH. I was supposed to be met at the airport by my son. He didn't show and I don't wait more than three and three-quarters hours for *anyone*. I should have been patient, I guess, I. . . . Is this . . .
WOMAN. Bronx.
HANNAH. Is that. . . . The *Bronx*? Well how in the name of Heaven did I get to the Bronx when the bus driver said . . .
WOMAN (*Talking to herself*). Slurp slurp slurp will you STOP that disgusting slurping! YOU DISGUSTING SLURPING FEEDING ANIMAL! Feeding yourself, just feeding yourself, what would it matter, to you or to ANYONE, if you just stopped. Feeding. And DIED?

(*Pause.*)

HANNAH. Can you just tell me where I . . .
WOMAN. Why was the Kosciusko Bridge named after a Polack?
HANNAH. I don't know what you're . . .
WOMAN. That was a joke.
HANNAH. Well what's the punchline?
WOMAN. I don't know.

HANNAH (*Looking around desperately*). Oh for pete's sake, is there anyone else who . . .
WOMAN (*Again, to herself*). Stand further off you fat loathsome whore, you can't have any more of this soup, slurp slurp slurp you animal, and the—I know you'll just go pee it all away and where will you do that? Behind what bush? It's FUCKING COLD out here and I . . .

Oh that's right, because it was supposed to have been a tunnel!

That's not very funny.

Have you read the prophecies of Nostradamus?
HANNAH. Who?
WOMAN. Some guy I went out with once somewhere, Nostradamus. Prophet, outcast, eyes like. . . . Scary shit, he . . .
HANNAH. Shut up. Please. Now I want you to stop jabbering for a minute and pull your wits together and tell me how to get to Brooklyn. Because you know! And you are going to tell me! Because there is no one else around to tell me and I am wet and cold and I am very angry! So I am sorry you're psychotic but just make the effort—take a deep breath—DO IT!

(*Hannah and the Woman breathe together.*)

HANNAH. That's good. Now exhale.

(*They do.*)

HANNAH. Good. Now how do I get to Brooklyn?
WOMAN. Don't know. Never been. Sorry. Want some soup?
HANNAH. Manhattan? Maybe you know . . . I don't suppose you know the location of the Mormon Visitor's . . .
WOMAN. 65th and Broadway.
HANNAH. How do you . . .
WOMAN. Go there all the time. Free movies. Boring, but you can stay there all day.
HANNAH. Well. . . . So how do I . . .
WOMAN. Take the D Train. Next block make a right.
HANNAH. Thank you.
WOMAN. Oh yeah. In the new century I think we will all be insane.

SCENE 5

Same day. Joe and Roy in the study of Roy's brownstone. Roy is wearing an elegant bathrobe. He has made a considerable effort to look well. He isn't well, and he hasn't succeeded much in looking it.

JOE. I can't. The answer's no. I'm sorry.
ROY. Oh, well, apologies . . .

I can't see that there's anyone asking for apologies.

(*Pause.*)

JOE. I'm sorry, Roy.

ROY. Oh, well, apologies.

JOE. My wife is missing, Roy. My mother's coming from Salt Lake to . . . to help look, I guess. I'm supposed to be at the airport now, picking her up but. . . . I just spent two days in a hospital, Roy, with a bleeding ulcer, I was spitting up blood.

ROY. Blood, huh? Look, I'm very busy here and . . .

JOE. It's just a job.

ROY. A job? A *job*? *Washington*! Dumb Utah Mormon hick shit!

JOE. Roy . . .

ROY. *WASHINGTON!* When Washington called me I was younger than you, you think I said "Aw fuck no I can't go I got two fingers up my asshole and a little moral nosebleed to boot!" When Washington calls you my pretty young punk friend you go or you can go fuck yourself sideways 'cause the train has pulled out of the station, and you are *out*, nowhere, out in the cold. Fuck you, Mary Jane, get outta here.

JOE. Just let me . . .

ROY. Explain? Ephemera. You broke my heart. Explain that. Explain that.

JOE. I love you. Roy.

There's so much that I want, to be . . . what you see in me, I want to be a participant in the world, in your world, Roy, I want to be capable of that, I've tried, really I have but . . . I can't do this. Not because I don't believe in you, but because I believe in you so much, in what you stand for, at heart, the order, the decency. I would give anything to protect you, but. . . . There are laws I can't break. It's too ingrained. It's not me. There's enough damage I've already done.

Maybe you were right, maybe I'm dead.

ROY. You're not dead, boy, you're a sissy.

You love me; that's moving, I'm moved. It's nice to be loved. I warned you about her, didn't I, Joe? But you don't listen to me, why, because you say Roy is smart and Roy's a friend but Roy . . . well, he isn't nice, and you wanna be nice. Right? A nice, nice man!

(*Little pause*)

You know what my greatest accomplishment was, Joe, in my life, what I am able to look back on and be proudest of? And I have helped make Presidents and unmake them and mayors and more goddam judges than anyone in NYC ever—AND several million dollars, tax-free—and what do you think means the most to me?

You ever hear of Ethel Rosenberg? Huh, Joe, huh?

JOE. Well, yeah, I guess I. . . . Yes.

ROY. Yes. Yes. You have heard of Ethel Rosenberg. Yes. Maybe you even read about her in the history books.

If it wasn't for me, Joe, Ethel Rosenberg would be alive today, writing some personal-advice column for *Ms.* magazine. She isn't. Because during the trial, Joe, I was on the phone every day, talking with the judge . . .

JOE. Roy . . .

ROY. Every day, doing what I do best, talking on the telephone, making sure that timid Yid nebbish on the bench did his duty to America, to history. That sweet unprepossessing woman, two kids, boo-hoo-hoo, reminded us all of our little Jewish mamas—she came this close to getting life; I pleaded till I wept to put her in the chair. Me. I did that. I would have fucking pulled the switch if they'd have let me. Why? Because I fucking hate traitors. Because I fucking hate communists. Was it legal? Fuck legal. Am I a nice man? Fuck nice. They say terrible things about me in the *Nation*. Fuck the *Nation*. You want to be Nice, or you want to be Effective? Make the law, or subject to it. Choose. Your wife chose. A week from today, she'll be back. SHE knows how to get what SHE wants. Maybe I ought to send *her* to Washington.

JOE. I don't believe you.

ROY. Gospel.

JOE. You can't possibly mean what you're saying.

Roy, you were the Assistant United States Attorney on the Rosenberg case, ex-parte communication with the judge during the trial would be . . . censurable, at least, probably conspiracy and . . . in a case that resulted in execution, it's . . .

ROY. What? Murder?

JOE. You're not well is all.

ROY. What do you mean, not well? Who's not well?

(*Pause.*)

JOE. You said . . .

ROY. No I didn't. I said what?

JOE. Roy, you have cancer.

ROY. No I don't.

(*Pause.*)

JOE. You told me you were dying.

ROY. What the fuck are you talking about, Joe? I never said that. I'm in perfect health. There's not a goddam thing wrong with me.

(*He smiles*)

Shake?

(*Joe hesitates. He holds out his hand to Roy. Roy pulls Joe into a close, strong clinch.*)

ROY (*More to himself than to Joe*). It's OK that you hurt me because I love you, baby Joe. That's why I'm so rough on you.

(*Roy releases Joe. Joe backs away a step or two.*)

ROY. Prodigal son. The world will wipe its dirty hands all over you.

JOE. It already has, Roy.

ROY. Now go.

(*Roy shoves Joe, hard. Joe turns to leave. Roy stops him, turns him around.*)

ROY (*Smoothing Joe's lapels, tenderly*). I'll always be here, waiting for you . . .
(*Then again, with sudden violence, he pulls Joe close, violently*)
What did you want from me, what was all this, what do you want, treacherous ungrateful little . . .

(*Joe, very close to belting Roy, grabs him by the front of his robe, and propels him across the length of the room. He holds Roy at arm's length, the other arm ready to hit.*)

ROY (*Laughing softly, almost pleading to be hit*). Transgress a little, Joseph.

(*Joe releases Roy.*)

ROY. There are so many laws; find one you can break.

(*Joe hesitates, then leaves, backing out. When Joe has gone, Roy doubles over in great pain, which he's been hiding throughout the scene with Joe.*)

ROY. Ah, Christ . . .
Andy! Andy! Get in here! Andy!

(*The door opens, but it isn't Andy. A small Jewish Woman dressed modestly in a fifties hat and coat stands in the doorway. The room darkens.*)

ROY. Who the fuck are you? The new nurse?

(*The figure in the doorway says nothing. She stares at Roy. A pause. Roy looks at her carefully, gets up, crosses to her. He crosses back to the chair, sits heavily.*)

ROY. Aw, fuck. Ethel.
ETHEL ROSENBERG (*Her manner is friendly, her voice is ice-cold*). You don't look good, Roy.
ROY. Well, Ethel. I don't feel good.
ETHEL ROSENBERG. But you lost a lot of weight. That suits you. You were heavy back then. Zaftig, mit hips.
ROY. I haven't been that heavy since 1960. We were all heavier back then, before the body thing started. Now I look like a skeleton. They stare.
ETHEL ROSENBERG. The shit's really hit the fan, huh, Roy?

(*Little pause. Roy nods.*)

ETHEL ROSENBERG. Well the fun's just started.
ROY. What is this, Ethel, Halloween? You trying to scare me?

(*Ethel says nothing.*)

ROY. Well you're wasting your time! I'm scarier than you any day of the week! So beat it, Ethel! BOOO! BETTER DEAD THAN RED! Somebody trying to shake me up?

HAH HAH! From the throne of God in heaven to the belly of hell, you can all fuck yourselves and then go jump in the lake because I'M NOT AFRAID OF YOU OR DEATH OR HELL OR ANYTHING!
ETHEL ROSENBERG. Be seeing you soon, Roy. Julius sends his regards.
ROY. Yeah, well send this to Julius!

(*He flips the bird in her direction, stands and moves towards her. Halfway across the room he slumps to the floor, breathing laboriously, in pain.*)

ETHEL ROSENBERG. You're a very sick man, Roy.
ROY. Oh God . . . ANDY!
ETHEL ROSENBERG. Hmmm. He doesn't hear you, I guess. We should call the ambulance.
(*She goes to the phone*)
Hah! Buttons! Such things they got now.
What do I dial, Roy?

(*Pause. Roy looks at her, then:*)

ROY. 911.
ETHEL ROSENBERG (*Dials the phone*). It sings!
(*Imitating dial tones*) La la la . . .
Huh.
Yes, you should please send an ambulance to the home of Mister Roy Cohn, the famous lawyer.
What's the address, Roy?
ROY (*A beat, then*). 244 East 87th.
ETHEL ROSENBERG. 244 East 87th Street. No apartment number, he's got the whole building.
My name? (*A beat*) Ethel Greenglass Rosenberg.
(*Small smile*) Me? No I'm not related to Mr. Cohn. An old friend.
(*She hangs up*)
They said a minute.
ROY. I have all the time in the world.
ETHEL ROSENBERG. You're immortal.
ROY. I'm immortal. Ethel. (*He forces himself to stand*)
I have *forced* my way into history. I ain't never gonna die.
ETHEL ROSENBERG (*A little laugh, then*). History is about to crack wide open. Millennium approaches.

SCENE 6

Late that night. Prior's bedroom. Prior 1 watching Prior in bed, who is staring back at him, terrified. Tonight Prior 1 is dressed in weird alchemical robes and hat over his historical clothing and he carries a long palm-leaf bundle.

PRIOR 1. Tonight's the night! Aren't you excited? Tonight she arrives! Right through the roof! Ha-adam, Ha-gadol . . .
PRIOR 2 (*Appearing, similarly attired*). Lumen! Phosphor! Fluor! Candle! An unending billowing of scarlet and . . .

PRIOR. Look. Garlic. A mirror. Holy water. A crucifix. FUCK OFF! Get the fuck out of my room! GO!

PRIOR 1 (*To Prior 2*). Hard as a hickory knob, I'll bet.

PRIOR 2. We all tumesce when they approach. We wax full, like moons.

PRIOR 1. Dance.

PRIOR. Dance?

PRIOR 1. Stand up, dammit, give us your hands, dance!

PRIOR 2. Listen . . .

(*A lone oboe begins to play a little dance tune.*)

PRIOR 2. Delightful sound. Care to dance?

PRIOR. Please leave me alone, please just let me sleep . . .

PRIOR 2. Ah, he wants someone familiar. A partner who knows his steps. (*To Prior*) Close your eyes. Imagine . . .

PRIOR. I don't . . .

PRIOR 2. Hush. Close your eyes.

(*Prior does.*)

PRIOR 2. Now open them.

(*Prior does. Louis appears. He looks gorgeous. The music builds gradually into a full-blooded, romantic dance tune.*)

PRIOR. Lou.

LOUIS. Dance with me.

PRIOR. I can't, my leg, it hurts at night . . .
     Are you . . . a ghost, Lou?

LOUIS. No. Just spectral. Lost to myself. Sitting all day on cold park benches. Wishing I could be with you. Dance with me, babe . . .

(*Prior stands up. The leg stops hurting. They begin to dance. The music is beautiful.*)

PRIOR 1 (*To Prior 2*). Hah. Now I see why he's not no children. He's a sodomite.

PRIOR 2. Oh be quiet, you medieval gnome, and let them dance.

PRIOR 1. I'm not interfering, I've done my bit. Hooray, hooray, the messenger's come, now I'm blowing off. I don't like it here.

(*Prior 1 vanishes.*)

PRIOR 2. The twentieth century. Oh dear, the world has gotten so terribly, terribly old.

(*Prior 2 vanishes. Louis and Prior waltz happily. Lights fade back to normal. Louis vanishes.*
     Prior dances alone.
     Then suddenly, the sound of wings fills the room.)

SCENE 7

Split scene: Prior alone in his apartment; Louis alone in the park.
     Again, a sound of beating wings.

PRIOR. Oh don't come in here don't come in . . . LOUIS!!
     No. My name is Prior Walter, I am . . . the scion of an ancient line, I am . . . abandoned I . . . no, my name is . . . is . . . Prior and I live . . . *here and now*, and . . . in the dark, in the dark, the Recording Angel opens its hundred eyes and snaps the spine of the Book of Life and . . . hush! Hush!
     I'm talking nonsense, I . . .
     No more mad scene, hush, hush . . .

(*Louis in the park on a bench. Joe approaches, stands at a distance. They stare at each other, then Louis turns away.*)

LOUIS. Do you know the story of Lazarus?

JOE. Lazarus?

LOUIS. Lazarus. I can't remember what happens, exactly.

JOE. I don't. . . . Well, he was dead, Lazarus, and Jesus breathed life into him. He brought him back from death.

LOUIS. Come here often?

JOE. No. Yes. Yes.

LOUIS. Back from the dead. You believe that really happened?

JOE. I don't know anymore what I believe.

LOUIS. This is quite a coincidence. Us meeting.

JOE. I followed you.
     From work. I . . . followed you here.

(*Pause.*)

LOUIS. You followed me.
     You probably saw me that day in the washroom and thought: there's a sweet guy, sensitive, cries for friends in trouble.

JOE. Yes.

LOUIS. You thought maybe I'll cry for you.

JOE. Yes.

LOUIS. Well I fooled you. Crocodile tears. Nothing . . . (*He touches his heart, shrugs*)

(*Joe reaches tentatively to touch Louis's face.*)

LOUIS (*Pulling back*). What are you doing? Don't do that.

JOE (*Withdrawing his hand*). Sorry. I'm sorry.

LOUIS. I'm . . . just not . . . I think, if you touch me, your hand might fall off or something. Worse things have happened to people who have touched me.

JOE. Please.
     Oh, boy . . .
     Can I . . .
     I . . . want . . . to touch you. Can I please just touch you . . . um, here?
     (*He puts his hand on one side of Louis's face. He holds it there*)
     I'm going to hell for doing this.

LOUIS. Big deal. You think it could be any worse than New York City?
     (*He puts his hand on Joe's hand. He takes Joe's hand away from his face, holds it for a moment, then*) Come on.

JOE. Where?

LOUIS. Home. With me.

JOE. This makes no sense. I mean I don't know you.

LOUIS. Likewise.

JOE. And what you do know about me you don't like.

LOUIS. The Republican stuff?

JOE. Yeah, well for starters.

LOUIS. I don't not like that. I *hate* that.

JOE. So why on earth should we . . .

(*Louis goes to Joe and kisses him.*)

LOUIS. Strange bedfellows. I don't know. I never made it with one of the dammed before.

I would really rather not have to spend tonight alone.

JOE. I'm a pretty terrible person, Louis.

LOUIS. Lou.

JOE. No, I really really am. I don't think I deserve being loved.

LOUIS. There? See? We already have a lot in common.

(*Louis stands, begins to walk away. He turns, looks back at Joe. Joe follows. They exit.*)

(*Prior listens. At first no sound, then once again, the sound of beating wings, frighteningly near.*)

PRIOR. That sound, that sound, it. . . . What is that, like birds or something, like a *really* big bird, I'm frightened, I . . . no, no fear, find the anger, find the . . . anger, my blood is clean, my brain is fine, I can handle pressure, I am a gay man and I am used to pressure, to trouble, I am tough and strong and. . . . Oh. Oh my goodness. I . . . (*He is washed over by an intense sexual feeling*) Ooohhhh. . . . I'm hot, I'm so . . . so . . . aw Jeez what is going on here I . . . must have a fever I . . .

(*The bedside lamp flickers wildly as the bed begins to roll forward and back. There is a deep bass creaking and groaning from the bedroom ceiling, like the timbers of a ship under immense stress, and from above a fine rain of plaster dust.*)

PRIOR. OH!

PLEASE, OH PLEASE! Something's coming in here, I'm scared, I don't like this at all, something's approaching and I. . . . OH!

(*There is a great blaze of triumphal music, heralding. The light turns an extraordinary harsh, cold, pale blue, then a rich, brilliant warm golden color, then a hot, bilious green, and then finally a spectacular royal purple. Then silence.*)

PRIOR (*An awestruck whisper*). God almighty . . .

Very Steven Spielberg.

(*A sound, like a plummeting meteor, tears down from very, very far above the earth, hurtling at an incredible velocity toward the bedroom; the light seems to be sucked out of the room as the projectile approaches; as the room reaches darkness we hear a terrifying CRASH as something immense strikes earth; the whole building shudders and a part of the bedroom ceiling, lots of plaster and lathe and wiring, crashes to the floor. And then in a shower of unearthly white light, spreading great opalescent gray-silver wings, the Angel descends into the room and floats above the bed.*)

ANGEL.

Greetings, Prophet;

The Great Work begins:

The Messenger has arrived.

(*Blackout.*)

END OF PART ONE

TOPICS FOR CRITICAL THINKING AND WRITING

 ### The Play on the PAGE

1. Through Kushner's decision to have actors play multiple roles, certain connections are made between characters. These connections exist not only between the characters who are played by the same actor, but also through pairing the bodies of actors who would not normally be on stage together. (For example, the actor who plays Harper is on stage with Roy Cohn when she plays Martin Heller.) Trace the connections created by multiple casting. What subtextual meanings do these connections bring to the play?

2. Compare and contrast Kushner's use of doubling with that used by Caryl Churchill in *Top Girls*.

3. Kushner employs the convention of split scenes throughout the play. Examine each of these split scenes, and analyze how the action in each half of the scene comments on the action of its companion half.

4. What additional information does the title of each act bring to the message of the play?

5. What information does each character's name tell you about that character?

The Play on the STAGE

6. The director of Kushner's play can decide whether to adhere to his scheme of multiple casting or not. What are some of the benefits that come from not using doubling? What elements of the play are lost? If you were to direct the play, how would you cast it and why?

7. Because of the length of *Angels in America*, scene changes and transitions must move smoothly and rapidly. Kushner himself specifies "no blackouts!" in his notes at the beginning of the play. How would you design a production of *Millennium Approaches* to meet the challenges of the play's requirements for fast pacing, multiple locations, and the mixture of natural and magical elements?

8. Through Kushner's casting requirement of doubling certain roles, women cross-dress as male characters. What does the presence of a female body and voice bring to these, otherwise, all-male scenes? How will this female presence be read by an audience today? Compare and contrast Prior's scene as a drag queen with one of the scenes where a woman plays a male role. What is Kushner saying by putting both aspects of cross-dressing in his play?

9. *Millennium Approaches* is a cliffhanger production that is not really completed until *Angels in America, Part Two: Perestroika*. It is also a production that requires an understanding of both 1980s politics and the early days of the AIDS epidemic in the United States. If you were producing *Millennium Approaches* today, what actions would you take to (a) present the first half of this two-part epic in such a way that the audience members feel satisfied having seen only *Part One*; (b) present the play in such a way that younger audience members do not feel alienated by events that took place during the early years of their childhood; and (c) make the play significant for a postmillennium audience?

10. In "A Note About the Staging" at the beginning of the play Kushner states, "The moments of magic—the appearance and disappearance of Mr. Lies and the ghosts, the Book hallucination, and the ending—are to be fully realized, as bits of *theatrical* illusion—which means it's OK if the wires show. . . ." Explain what he means about theatrical illusion. If you were directing this play, how would you realize those moments of magic?

The Play in PERFORMANCE

Angels in America, Part One: Millennium Approaches was commissioned by Oskar Eustis, the artistic director of the Eureka Theater Company in San Francisco. It was workshopped at the Mark Taper Forum in Los Angeles and first presented as a workshop production by the Center Theater Group/Mark Taper Forum in May 1990. This version, 250 pages long, was a continuous six acts. A year later the play was split into two parts. The first part was given its world premiere at the Eureka Theater. In January 1992 *Millennium Approaches* was given its British premiere at the Royal National Theater of Great Britain in an award-winning production. The following November both parts opened at the Mark Taper Forum.

A year later in May 1993 *Millennium Approaches* opened at the Walter Kerr Theater on Broadway with George C. Wolfe, head of the Public Theater,

directing. In November *Part Two: Perestroika* opened on Broadway and both parts played in repertory. The Broadway production had a national tour, and following that the play has had numerous productions all over the United States as well as in translation in other countries. In July 1994 it was the highlight of the Avignon International Theater Festival where it played outdoors against the walls of a medieval monastery.

The play opened on Broadway one month after a large, organized march on Washington for rights for sexual minorities took place. The march was a response to efforts to limit gay rights in Oregon and Colorado and to the heated public debates regarding the military's ban on homosexuals in the service.

Because of the frank treatment of homosexuality in the script, the play has stimulated some conservative

Christian protest. In February 1999 a production scheduled to open in Bucharest, Romania, met severe opposition with protestors destroying posters, blocking potential audience members from entering the theater, and threatening the theater's employees. Although the group responsible for the protests was never identified, the head of the Young Orthodox Christian Church, a group actively against homosexuality, supported the action. Here in this country, some of the trustees of a college attempted to halt a student production of *Angels in America* at Kilgore College in the fall of 1999. The college president stuck by the students and the production went ahead, but shortly afterward county officials cut a $50,000 grant intended for the Texas Shakespeare Festival as a "punishment" for producing the play.

STEVEN WINN
Angels *Gets Even Better**

Here we reprint a review of the first Broadway production of *Angels in America*. The reviewer, the theater critic from the *San Francisco Chronicle*, had seen the first workshop production of the play as well as the Mark Taper Forum production. Note in particular the discussion of the design elements. The twenty-six episodic scenes require a set design that can transition almost instantaneously from one location to another. The set should mirror the script's fluid interplay between fantasy and naturalism giving the designer both a technical and creative challenge.

Angels in America went to Broadway heaven last night, with the opening of director George C. Wolfe's soaring new production of Tony Kushner's Pulitzer Prize-winning play. This is the one show, instantly and above all others, that makes New York a destination for theater lovers as well as casual theater tourists this spring.

Technically the *Angels* journey is half complete, since only *Millennium Approaches*, the first half of Kushner's seven-hour epic about AIDS and the moral meltdown of Reagan-Bush America, is on view at the Walter Kerr Theatre. Part Two of the "gay fantasia on national themes," a rewritten *Perestroika*, is to open in October and run in repertory with *Millennium*.

What Wolfe has accomplished so far—with his fluid restaging, effective recasting of several roles and scrupulous underscoring of the play's themes, connections and vibrant humanity—revives confidence in this remarkable piece of theater that had been shaken a little by a monumental and somewhat cumbersome production of the two-part work last fall at the Mark Taper Forum in Los Angeles.

*Review of *Angels in America*, San Francisco Chronicle 5 May 1993: D1.

Eureka Origins

Angels is once again as startling and thrilling as it was when it first opened its wings at the Eureka Theatre two years ago this month. Now the multiple values of the script, its passion and rich play of ideas, rage and achingly empathic characters, humor and exuberant theatricality, are joined and given their due in a unified whole. *Angels* takes off and never falters.

On a new set by Broadway veteran Robin Wagner (*City of Angels, Dreamgirls*) that not only solves the dizzying demands of the text but also makes Kushner's leaps a theatrical asset, the stage space is defined and ingeniously redefined by a series of cloud-streaked blue panels that form a wedge inside a silver proscenium frame of classical columns and pediment.

As the panels open, turn and sometimes retreat into the wings, chairs, desks, a bed and other set pieces—including an iceberg—emerge as if by magical command. Sometimes the actors are already in place on the mobile furnishings; at other points they arrive first or trail a few moments behind.

Interlocking Stories

The approach accomplishes at least two important things. First it embodies the fantastical strains of the play, which combines the interlocking stories of two troubled couples with visitations by an angel and several ancestors from distant centuries, the universe-trotting fantasies of a Valium addict and various special effects that are aptly described, by Stephen Spinella's awe-struck but always ironic Prior Walter, as "Very Steven Spielberg!" Jules Fisher designed the lighting, as subtle, when called for, as it is showy.

Second, more crucially, Wolfe's staging gives the production a propulsive forward movement, further enhanced by Anthony Davis and Michael Ward's new mixed-idiom music of jazz, trance minimalism, opera and other motifs. In Los Angeles, under designer John

Conklin's looming classical façade, with it symbolic fissure, the action seemed to plod from scene to scene. Here Wolfe lets us see and sense the connections—Prior's bed sheet tellingly echoed by a Mormon's white nightgown is one of many exquisite touches—as Kushner twines his two stories together.

The extraordinary Spinella, one of three cast members (along with the multiply cast Ellen McLaughlin and Kathleen Chalfant) who have been with *Angels* from the beginning, plays the character diagnosed with AIDS. Whether Prior is launching into florid French with his "ex-ex-drag queen" friend Belize (droll but steely cast newcomer Jeffrey Wright) or staggering across a dark bedroom screaming in pain, Spinella crafts an utterly absorbing performance that has grown more grandiose under Wolfe's direction while remaining meticulously true.

Joe Mantello, whose performance has ripened to perfection since L.A., is Prior's lover Louis, a sniveling, didactic, self-critical coward who leaves Prior and takes up with a Mormon lawyer (David Marshall Grant) who is awakening to his own homosexuality. Grant and Marcia Gay Harden, as Joe Pitt's miserable, drug-addled wife Harper, are new to the production, and both, especially Harden, are distinct improvements.

Disguises Run Deep

With his dishwater blond pompadour and a habit of smiling toothily at the most inappropriate moments—"You have emotional problems," he tells his wife with a grin—Grant seems like a boy impersonating a man. His disguises, as we learn, run deeper than that. Grant makes you feel the fraudulence and suppressed fear in everything Joe does, from his lip-pecking "Buddy" kisses with Harper to his encounters with volcanic power lawyer Roy Cohn (Ron Leibman) that burlesque the father-son bond Joe never had.

Harden eschews the mannered delivery and spacey vagueness that became affectations in Cynthia Mace's L.A. performance. Her Harper is plainer, dull brown

hair hooked behind one ear and crazy-quilt pants worn as if she'd never seen them, and both her swirling visions about the damaged ozone layer and other "systems of defense breaking down" and her own lonely pain are delivered with a blunt, undecorated directness. Harden also turns up, in the show's cross-gender double casting, as Reagan flunky Martin Heller in a comb-over wig.

Wolfe, who wrote and directed the Broadway hit *Jelly's Last Jam* and recently took over as producer of the New York Shakespeare Festival/Joseph Papp Public Theater, has encouraged the cast to open out and be more physical and emphatic in many spots than they were under Oskar Eustis and Tony Taccone's direction at the Taper. For anyone who saw Leibman's Cohn on the West Coast, it's hard to believe he could crank it up another notch, but he does, swearing and scowling and wheedling with even more ferocity than ever.

The 'Octopus' Weakens

Bellow as he does in his frenzy of excoriating homosexuals even as his own homosexually contracted AIDS begins to bring him down, Leibman is somehow a bit more sympathetic, more human than he was before. Flailing away at his multi-line phone with a Manhattan skyline etched in glass behind him, Cohn laughingly wills himself to be an "octopus" in his first scene. By the end of the show, his tentacles have grown weak and desperate as he grabs for Joe's shoulder or clutches his own gut in pain.

The completed first half of Kushner's play has found paradise in Wolfe's production. The director has trusted the playwright's every instinct, from the most long-winded—Louis' Marxist/racist monologue and Belize's rapier rebuttal—to the most fanciful—an imaginary journey to the South Pole that fills the stage with icy fog—and given each scene, each moment, the most articulate voice imaginable. *Angels in America* is a Broadway dream come true, a profoundly serious, riotously entertaining work that takes wing onstage and flies.

SUZAN-LORI Parks

One of the brightest of the new generation of playwrights, Suzan-Lori Parks was born in Fort Knox, Kentucky, in 1967. She attended Mount Holyoke College in Massachusetts, graduating in English and German in 1985. While in college she took a class in creative writing with guest professor James Baldwin, who immediately recognized her talent and intelligence, lauding her as "an utterly astounding and beautiful creature who may become one of the most valuable artists of our time." In reading her work in class, Parks, unlike her classmates who would read their work sitting down, would always stand and act out all the parts. Baldwin suggested she write plays, a suggestion she at first resisted, but which she finally accepted. Her breakthrough play had the mysterious title *Imperceptible Mutabilities in the Third Kingdom*, and was produced in 1989 at a small theater in downtown Brooklyn, New York. It received excellent reviews from Yale University's *Theater* magazine ("startling stage imagery and a lyrical sense of wordplay that has been scarce in American playwriting for ages . . . ") and even the *New York Times*, which named her "the year's most promising new playwright." The play won a *Village Voice* Obie Award in 1990 for Best New American Play.

Since her memorable debut, her major plays include *The Death of the Last Black Man in the Whole Entire World*—an historical, surreal dreamscape of death and resurrection—produced by BACA Downtown (1990) and Yale Repertory Theatre (1992); *The America Play*—a powerful rumination on black identity, theater, and American history—Yale Repertory Theatre and The Joseph Papp Public Theatre (1994); and *Venus*—a true tale of racial and sexual exploitation based on the historical figure of the Hottentot Venus—again produced at the Papp Public Theatre (1996) and again winning her a Best Play Obie. In addition to her theater work, Parks has written for radio and film, most notably the screenplay for *Girl 6* directed by Spike Lee (1996).

She has been the recipient of major grants from the Rockefeller, Ford, Lila Wallace, and Whiting foundations and has twice been an NEA playwriting fellow. She has taught playwriting at Yale, and since fall 2000 has been the head of the A.S.K. Theater Projects Writing for Performance Program at California Institute of the Arts.

▪▪▪▪▪▪▪▪▪▪▪▪▪▪▪

COMMENTARY ON *IN THE BLOOD*

In the fall of 1988, as part of what was called a "fringe series" dedicated to providing "an innovative alternative to mainstream theater," a play opened in a tiny theater in downtown Brooklyn, BACA Downtown (the acronym stands for Brooklyn Arts Cultural Association). It had an evocative and ambiguous title, *Imperceptible Mutabilities in the Third Kingdom*, and its neophyte author was a twenty-one-year-old African American woman, Suzan-Lori Parks. Usually, such presentations receive (if they're lucky) minor mention in alternative newspapers, but word soon began to spread among those interested in new theater that something extraordinary was on view in Brooklyn. And, indeed, most of those who made the journey to see the play had that rare experience of hearing a genuinely original new dramatic voice. As with, say, the very early surreal plays of Sam Shepard, the playgoer wasn't sure *what* she

saw and heard, but nonetheless was bowled over by the sheer theatrical force of visual and verbal imagery.

First of all, it wasn't at all clear if one was seeing *one* play or a series of related one-acts: A program note helped only a little: "[This play] is an African-American experience in the shadow of the photographic image. An ensemble of actors move through four allegorical phases of African-American history." But allegories usually make their thematic point by assuming one narrative shape (think *Everyman*), whereas each of the four parts of *Imperceptible Mutabilities* centers on a different theatrical metaphor. For example, in the section called *Snails*, a white naturalist with bug-like lights on his eyeglasses watches three black women through a camera concealed in a giant cockroach; in *Open House*, an old black woman, who is in the hospital to have her teeth painfully extracted, is visited by the white children she has raised (played by black actors in whiteface). But if the "four phases" of black history are not clearly delineated in the four scenes, certain powerful themes insistently emerge: The old woman is not only losing her teeth, she is being extracted from history. In another scene, *Greeks*, an ex-soldier has opened his arms to white history by catching the mythological figure of the falling Icarus, and it has crippled him and his family. And in yet another, *Third Kingdom*, the black characters belong neither to the old world nor the new and seek for their identities at the bottom of the sea.

What Parks achieved in this startlingly mature, linguistically inventive play was to move beyond its disparate influences to create her very own dramatic vision. Stylistically, the play is completely non-naturalistic, with echoes of Beckett, Ionesco, early Shepard, Fornes—as well as Ntozake Shange and, preeminently, Adrienne Kennedy. But it also possesses the thematic fervor of African American and feminist protest drama. Not in a polemical sense, for Parks's work, as Erika Munk pointed out, "lends itself to connections and expansions, as images and wordplay flow along, inviting little riffs of interpretation." This distinctive style found further expression in Parks's next two full-length plays, *The Death of the Last Black Man in the Whole Entire World* (1990) and *The America Play* (1994). The former runs poetic variations on the theme of racism through the figures of its consciously stereotyped main characters: a "Black Man with Watermelon" and a "Black Woman with Fried Drumstick." The latter play, set in a theme park called the Great Hole of History, ruminates on the black presence in America, a history that is in reality an *absence*, since our national mythology has been created by whites.

This image of history as erasure and subordination has been increasingly on Parks's mind: In *Venus* (1996) she used the historical facts about the Hottentot Venus (whose voluminous behind made her a sensation in early nineteenth-century freak shows) to explore the themes of racial and sexual exploitation. And in *In the Blood* (1999) she turns to an acknowledged literary classic—Nathaniel Hawthorne's *The Scarlet Letter*—as a base from which to confront these same themes in America's past and present. In so doing she demonstrates that her unique poetic sensibilities can be expressed with traditional narrative coherence, a tendency that indeed had begun to be revealed in the aforementioned *Venus*.

The world she depicts in this—what can we call it?—contemporary improvisation on Hawthorne's classic tale of Puritan adultery and guilt, is a familiar one: *This* Hester, La Negrita, is a homeless woman, with five bastard children from different men who have abandoned her, struggling to survive in a hostile urban world. Living under bridges, denying herself sustenance to feed and maintain her brood, she gets no succor from those ostensibly dedicated to alleviating her impoverished situation: Street doctor, minister, welfare worker all fail her, using her desperation as an opportunity to use her, invariably sexually. Apart from her children, who range in age from two to thirteen, her only solace is another street person, the Amiga Gringa, who, despite her concern for Hester, is not above using her herself when the opportunity presents itself. Striving to "get a leg up," Hester is time and again pulled back down. "My life's my own fault," she admits, "but the world don't help." The accumulation of indifference leads to a violent, tragic conclusion.

This brief summary suggests the kind of realistic protest play we are familiar with, and, indeed, *some* of the dialogue would fit in such a play. But *In the Blood* is far from naturalism, despite her plot's traditional development. Parks has not abandoned her penchant for experimental form and poetic elaboration. The "realistic" sequences—written in prose—are interspersed with poetic confessions to the audience in which the various characters reveal themselves in heightened language. As in this excerpt from the confession of Reverend D., the father of Hester's most recent child:

> In the never ending blistering heat
> of the never ending gutter of the world
> my skin hot against the pavement
> but lying there I knew
> that I had never hurt anybody in my life
> (Rest)
> (Rest)

What do these "rests" mean in the printed text? They indicate another unconventional Parkian device. Rather than use the word "pause"—which she finds woefully inadequate to indicate what should be going on on stage—she uses the word "rest" to indicate a short break, a meaningful pause à la Harold Pinter. Two "rests" extend the moment. When she wants to indicate a dialogueless moment of importance, she calls it a "spell," and indicates it *not* by using that word but by repeating the name(s) of the character(s) involved. The more repetitions of names, the longer and more potent the stage moment. It's like a film closeup, REVEREND D./HESTER cuts from one to the other.

But by far the most radically nonrealistic element in the play is theatrical, not dramatic. Apart from Hester, all the other characters are played by five actors. Each actor doubles as one of the adults Hester confronts *and* one of her children. Sometimes the contrast is extreme: The actor who plays the oily Reverend D. also plays his illegitimate child, Baby, Hester's youngest. This is a conscious attempt to create what Bertolt Brecht called a *Verfremden-Effekt*, a distancing device to subvert realistic identification. Why? Because Parks at all costs wishes to avoid the kind of easy sentimentality and emotionality that characterizes so much popular writing, particularly in film and television. She wants us to *think* about what we're seeing. Indeed, Brechtian imprints are all over this play. Hester and her brood are not unlike Mother Courage and her children, struggling to survive in their own hundred-years' war. And Parks's characterizations of Hester's exploiters are *not* naturalistic portraits; they are consciously overdrawn as Parks searches for the essence of each person's character in a social context—another Brechtian technique he called the *gest*.

Where does Hawthorne fit in in all of this? *In the Blood* is far from a modern-day adaptation of *The Scarlet Letter*. The play makes no attempt to reproduce the plot of the novel. Apart from Hester, only one character consciously evokes Hawthorne: Reverend D., who shares with Hawthorne's Reverend Dimmesdale the fact of paternal responsibility but little else. The modern-day religious huckster is free of the tortured guilt that overwhelms the Puritan divine. And there is no equivalent in Parks's play of the potent catalytic figure of Hawthorne's Chillingworth. Indeed, *In the Blood* and *The Scarlet Letter* spring from opposite places in their creators' consciousness. Hawthorne writes with a deep sense of guilt for the sins of his Puritan forebears, one of whom was a judge in the Salem witch trials. He takes "shame upon myself for their sakes, and pray that any curse incurred by them . . . may be now and henceforth removed." Parks, on the other hand, writes from the vantage point of the oppressed, not the oppressors. As one of the historically dispossessed, she shares no complicity with the victimization of her heroine.

Still, she finds much in *The Scarlet Letter* with which she can identify, and takes several of its crucial themes to ruminate on: First of all, there is the theme of the "wild child." When first we see Hester Prynne at the prison door she is alone, clutching her illegitimate baby, Pearl, against her breast upon which is emblazoned the scarlet letter. Born out of social defiance, Pearl is so named because she was "purchased with all [Hester] had—her mother's only treasure!" Pearl is even more than an outcast, she is "an imp of evil, emblem and product of sin." As she grows, she shows a wild, untamed temperament appalling to Puritan respectability. But she remains Hester's "pearl." Similarly, Parks's Hester has given her disorderly brood names that mark their disparate personalities. Jabber, Beauty, Bully, Trouble. They are her pride, her pearls; she will sacrifice everything to maintain her family. The tragedy of *In the Blood* is that Hester is driven to destroy the one thing she had really created.

And then there is the scarlet letter itself. Hester Prynne does not hide her badge of shame; she has embroidered the A (for adultery) with fantastic flourishes of gold thread. But when, later in the novel, Pearl asks her mother what the A means, Hester has to decide whether or not to tell her daughter the truth. She decides she cannot yet do so and reduces the letter's value to its gold embroidery. But Pearl is perceptive enough to know that this is not the truth and persists asking the question until Hester identifies the A as the Devil's mark. Parks runs variations on this, but she reverses the situation so that the child has the knowledge and the mother asks the question. Hester La Negrita is illiterate, and Jabber, her eldest son, is teaching her to read. So far, she has just mastered the letter A. When the play opens, Hester asks Jabber what the graffito SLUT means. He pretends he can't read it. At the play's end he gives up his secret with direful consequences.

The strongest thematic parallel lies in the social context: how people perceive the carriers of shame, the adultress, the "welfare queen." The Puritan townfolk don't see Hester as a person but as a walking badge of sin. Similarly, at the end of *In the Blood* all characters as a chorus circle La Negrita and shout: "LOOK AT HER! . . . NO SKILLS / CEPT ONE / CAN'T READ CAN'T WRITE . . . / AND NOT A PENNY TO HER NAME / . . . I'LL BE DAMNED IF SHE GONNA LIVE OFF ME . . . FIRST LETTER OF THE ALPHABET / THAT'S AS FAR AS SHE GOT." What accounts for such hostility to suffering? The narrator of *The Scarlet Letter* posits "a feeling so irresistible . . . that it has the force of doom, which almost invariably compels human beings to linger around and haunt, ghostlike, the spot where some great and marked event has given color to their lifetime; and still the more irresistibly, the darker tinge that saddens it." Hester La Negrita has a vision of an eclipse that occurred when she was crossing a city street. "It was a big dark thing . . . Like the hand of fate with its 5 [sic] fingers coming down on me . . . And the trumpets started blaring . . . The trumpets was the taxi cabs. Wanting to run me over. Get out the road." The vision comes to pass. As the street doctor notes with finality, the imprisoned Hester "WON'T BE HAVING ANY-MORE [sic] CHILDREN." The scarlet letter is indeed written in the blood.

IN THE BLOOD
Suzan-Lori Parks

THE CHARACTERS

HESTER, LA NEGRITA
CHILLI / JABBER, *her oldest child*
REVEREND D. / BABY, *her youngest child*
THE WELFARE LADY / BULLY, *her oldest daughter*
THE DOCTOR / TROUBLE, *her middle son*
THE AMIGA GRINGA / BEAUTY, *her youngest daughter*

TIME

Now

PLACE

Here

NOTES

This play requires a cast of six adult actors, five of whom double as adults and children. The setting should be spare, to reflect the poverty of the world of the play.

Style:
I'm continuing the use of my slightly unconventional theatrical elements. Here's a road map.

(Rest)
Take a little time, a pause, a breather; make a transition.

A Spell
An elongated and heightened (*Rest*). Denoted by repetition of figures' names with no dialogue. Has sort of an architectural look:

REVEREND D.
HESTER
REVEREND D.
HESTER

This is a place where the figures experience their pure true simple state. While no action or stage business is necessary, directors should fill this moment as they best see fit.

[Brackets in the text indicate optional cuts for production.]

(Parentheses around dialogue indicate softly spoken passages (asides; sotto voce).)

SCENE 1

UNDER THE BRIDGE

Home under the bridge. The word "SLUT" scrawled on a wall. Hesters oldest child Jabber, 13, studies that scrawl. Hester lines up soda cans as her youngest child Baby, 2 yrs old, watches.

HESTER. Zit uh good word or a bad word?

JABBER.
JABBER.

HESTER. Aint like you to have your mouth shut, Jabber. Say it to me and we can figure out the meaning together.

JABBER. Naaaa—

HESTER. What I tell you about saying "Naa" when you mean no? You talk like that people wont think you got no brains and Jabbers got brains. All my kids got brains, now.

(Rest)

Lookie here, Baby. Mamma set the cans for you. Mamma gonna show you how to make some money. Watch.

JABBER. Im slow.

HESTER. Slow aint never stopped nothing, Jabber. You bring yr foot down on it and smash it flat. Howabout that, Baby? Put it in the pile and thats that. Now you try.

Baby jumps on the can smashing it flat, hollering as he smashes.

BABY. Ha!

HESTER. Yr a natural! Jabber, yr little baby brothers a natural. We gonna come out on top this month, I can feel it. Try another one, Baby.

JABBER. They wrote it in yr practice place.

HESTER. Yes they did.

JABBER. They wrote in yr practice place so you didnt practice today.

HESTER. I practiced. In my head. In the air. In the dirt underfoot.

JABBER. Lets see.

With great difficulty Hester makes an "A" in the dirt.

HESTER. The letter A.

JABBER. Almost.

HESTER. You gonna disparage me I ain't gonna practice.

BABY. Mommmmieee!

HESTER. Gimmieuhminute, Baby-child.

JABBER. Legs apart hands crost the chest like I showd you. Try again.

BABY. Mommieee!

HESTER. See the pretty can, Baby?

BABY. Ha!

JABBER. Try again.

BABY. Mommmieee!

HESTER. Later. Read that word out to me, huh? I like it when you read to me.

JABBER. Dont wanna read it.

HESTER. Cant or wont?

JABBER. —Cant.

HESTER. Jabber

He knows what the word says, but he wont say it.

HESTER. I was sick when I was carrying you. Damn you, slow fool. Aaah, my treasure, cmmeer. My oldest treasure. (*She gives him a quick hug*)

Hester looks at the word, its letters mysterious to her. Baby smashes can after can.

HESTER. Go scrub it off, then. I like my place clean.

Jabber dutifully scrubs the wall.

HESTER. We know who writ it up there. It was them bad boys writing on my home. And in my practice place. Do they write on they own homes? I dont think so. They come under the bridge and write things they dont write nowhere else. A mean ugly word, I'll bet. A word to hurt our feelings. And because we aint lucky we gotta live with it. 5 children I got. 5 treasures. 5 joys. But we aint got our leg up, just yet. So we gotta live with mean words and hurt feelings.

JABBER. Words dont hurt my feelings, Mamma.

HESTER. Dont disagree with me.

JABBER. Sticks and stones, Mamma.

HESTER. Yeah. I guess.

HESTER.

JABBER.

HESTER.

HESTER. Too late for yr sisters and brother to still be out. Yr little brother Babys gonna make us rich. He learns quick. Look at him go.

She lines up more cans and Baby jumps on them, smashing them all. Bully, her 12 yr old girl, runs in.

BULLY. Momieeeeeeeee! Mommie, Trouble he has really done it this time. I told him he was gonna be doing life and he laughed and then I said he was gonna get the electric chair and you know what he said?

HESTER. Help me sack the cans.

BULLY. He said a bad word!

HESTER. Sack the cans.

They sack the crushed cans.

BULLY. Trouble he said something really bad but Im not saying it cause if I do yll wash my mouth. What he said was bad but what he did, what he did was worse.

HESTER. Whatd he do?

BULLY. Stole something.

HESTER. Food?

BULLY. No.

HESTER. Toys?

BULLY. No.

HESTER. I dont like youall stealing toys and I dont like youall stealing food but it happens. I wont punish you for it. Yr just kids. Trouble thinks with his stomach. He hungry he takes, sees a toy, gotta have it.

BULLY. A policeman saw him steal and ran after him but Trouble ran faster cause the policeman was fat.

HESTER. Policeman chased him?

BULLY. He had a big stomach. Like he was pregnant. He was jiggling and running and yelling and red in the face.

HESTER. What he steal?

BULLY. —Nothing.

HESTER. You talk that much and you better keep talking, Miss.

Bully buttons her lips. Hester pops her upside the head.

BULLY. Owwwww!

HESTER. Get outa my sight. Worse than a thief is a snitch that dont snitch.

Trouble, age 10 and Beauty, age 7, run in, breathless. They see Hester eyeing them and stop running; they walk nonchalantly.

HESTER. What you got behind you?

TROUBLE. Nothing. Jabber, what you doing?

JABBER. Cleaning the wall.

BEAUTY. My hair needs a ribbon.

HESTER. Not right now it dont. You steal something?

TROUBLE. Me? Whats cookin?

HESTER. Soup of the day.

TROUBLE. We had soup the day yesterday.

HESTER. Todays a new day.

BEAUTY. Is it a new soup?

HESTER. Wait and see. You gonna end up in the penitentiary and embarrass your mother?

TROUBLE. No.

HESTER. If you do I'll kill you. Set the table.

JABBER. Thats girls work.

TROUBLE. Mommiee—

BULLY. Troubles doing girls work. Troubles doing girls work.

HESTER. Set the damn table or Ima make a girl outa you!

TROUBLE. You cant make a girl outa me.

HESTER. Dont push me!

(Rest)

Look, Baby. See the soup? Mommies stirring it. Dont come close, its hot.

BEAUTY. I want a ribbon.

HESTER. Get one I'll tie it in.

Beauty gets a ribbon. Trouble gets bowls, wipes them clean, hands them out. Hester follows behind him and, out of the back of his pants, yanks a policemans club.

HESTER. Whered you get this?

TROUBLE.

HESTER.

TROUBLE.

HESTER. I said—

TROUBLE. I found it. On the street. It was just lying there.

BULLY. You stole it.

TROUBLE. Did not!

HESTER. Dont lie to me.

TROUBLE. I found it. I did. It was just lying on the street. I was minding my own business.

HESTER. That why the cops was chasing you?

TROUBLE. Snitch!

BULLY. Jailbait!

Bully hits Trouble hard. They fight. Pandemonium.

HESTER. Suppertime!

Order is restored. Hester slips the club into the belt of her dress; it hangs there like a sword. She wears it like this for most of the play. Her children sit in a row holding their bowls. She ladles out the soup.

HESTER. Todays soup of the day, ladies and gents, is a very special blend of herbs and spices. The broth is chef Mommies worldwide famous "whathaveyou" stock. Theres carrots in there. Theres meat. Theres oranges. Theres pie.

TROUBLE. What kinda pie?

HESTER. What kind you like?

TROUBLE. Apple.

HESTER. Theres apple pie.

JABBER. Pumpkin.

BULLY. And cherry!

HESTER. Theres pumpkin and cherry too. And steak. And mash potatoes for Beauty. And milk for Baby.

BEAUTY. And diamonds.

JABBER. You cant eat diamonds.

HESTER. So when you find one in yr soup whatll you do?

BEAUTY. Put it on my finger.

They slurp down their soup quickly. As soon as she fills their bowls, theyre empty again. The kids eat. Hester doesnt.

JABBER. You aint hungry?

HESTER. I'll eat later.

JABBER. You always eating later.

HESTER. You did a good job with the wall, Jabber. Whatd that word say anyway?

JABBER. —Nothing.

The soup pot is empty.

HESTER.

JABBER/BULLY/TROUBLE/BEAUTY/BABY.

(Rest)

HESTER. Bedtime.

BULLY. Could we have a story?

(Rest)

HESTER. All right.

(Rest)

There were once these five brothers and they were all big and strong and handsome and didnt have a care in the world. One was known for his brains so they called him Smarts and one was known for his muscles, so they called him Toughguy, the third one was a rascal so they called him Wild, the fourth one was as goodlooking as all get out and they called him Looker and the fifth was the youngest and they called him Honeychild cause he was as young as he was sweet. And they was always together these five brothers. Everywhere they went they always went together. No matter what they was always together cause they was best friends and wasn't nothing could divide them. And there was this Princess. And she lived in a castle and she was lonesome. She was lonesome and looking for love but she couldn't leave her castle so she couldn't look very far so every day she would stick her head out her window and sing to the sun and every night she would stick her head and sing to the moon and the stars: "Where are you?" And one day the five brothers heard her and came calling and she looked upon them and she said: "There are five of you, and each one is wonderful and special in his own way. But the law of my country doesnt allow a princess to have more than one husband." And that was such bad news and they were all so in love that they all cried. Until the Princess had an idea. She was after all the Princess, so she changed the law of the land and married them all.

(Rest)

And with Bro Smarts she had a baby named Jabber. And with Bro Toughguy she had Bully. With Bro Wild came Trouble. With Bro Looker she had Beauty. With Bro Honeychild came Baby. And they was all happy.

JABBER. Until the bad news came.

HESTER. No bad news came.

JABBER. Theres always bad news.

HESTER. Bedtime.

BEAUTY. Where did the Daddys go?

HESTER. They went to bed.

TROUBLE. They ran off.

JABBER. The war came and the brothers went off to fight and they all died.

BEAUTY. They all died?

JABBER. And they fell into the ground and the dirt covered up they heads.

HESTER. Its bedtime. Now!

BEAUTY. Im scared.

TROUBLE. I aint scared. Jabber, you a spook.

BULLY. Yr the spook.

TROUBLE. Yr a bastard.

BULLY. Yr a bastard.

HESTER. Yr all bastards!

The children burst into tears.

HESTER. Cmmeer. Cmmeer. Mama loves you. Shes just tired is all. Lemmie hug you.

They nestle around her and she hugs them.

HESTER. My 5 treasures. My 5 joys.

HESTER.
JABBER/BULLY/TROUBLE/BEAUTY/BABY.
HESTER.

HESTER. Lets hit the sack! And leave yr shoes for polish and yr shirts and blouses for press. You dont wanna look like you dont got nobody.

They take off their shoes and tops and go inside leaving Hester outside alone.

HESTER.
HESTER.
HESTER.

(Rest)
She examines the empty soup pot, shines the kids shoes, "presses" their clothes. A wave of pain shoots through her.

HESTER. You didnt eat, Hester. And the pain in yr gut comes from having nothing in it.

(Rest)

Kids ate good though. Ate their soup all up. They wont starve.

(Rest)

None of these shoes shine. Never did no matter how hard you spit on em, Hester. You get a leg up the first thing you do is get shoes. New shoes for yr 5 treasures. You got yrself a good pair of shoes already.

From underneath a pile of junk she takes out a shoebox. Inside is a pair of white pumps. She looks them over then puts them away.

HESTER. Dont know where yll wear them but yll look good when you get there.

[*She takes out a small tape player. Pops in a tape. She takes a piece of chalk from her pocket and, on the freshly scrubbed wall, practices her letters: She writes the letter A over and over and over. The cassette tape plays as she writes.*

REVEREND D. (*On tape*). If you cant always do right then you got to admit that some times, some times my friends you are going to do wrong and you are going to have to *live* with that. Somehow work that into the fabric of your life. Because there aint a soul out there that is spot free. There aint a soul out there that has walked but hasn't stumbled. Aint a single solitary soul out there that has said "hello" and not "goodbye," has said "yes" to the lord and "yes" to the devil, too, has drunk water and drunk wine, loved and hated, experienced the good side of the tracks and the bad. That is what they call living, friends. L-I-V-I-N, friends. Life on earth is full of confusion. Life on earth is full of misunderstandings, reprimandings, and we focus on the trouble, friends, when it is the solution to those troubles we oughta be looking at. I have fallen and I cant get up! How many times have you heard that, friends? The fellow on the street with his whisky breath and his outstretched hand, the banker scraping the money off the top, the runaway child turned criminal all cry out "I have fallen, and I cant get up!" "I have fallen, and I cant get up!" "I have fallen—"

Hester hears someone coming and turns the tape off.] *She goes back to polishing her shoes. Amiga Gringa comes in.*

AMIGA GRINGA. Look at old Mother Hubbard or whatever.

HESTER. Keep quiet. Theyre sleeping.

AMIGA GRINGA. The old woman and the shoe Thats who you are.

HESTER. I get my leg up thats what Im getting. New shoes for my treasures.

AMIGA GRINGA. Thatll be some leg up.

HESTER. You got my money?

AMIGA GRINGA. Is that a way to greet a friend? "You got my money?" What world is this?

HESTER. You got my money, Amiga?

AMIGA GRINGA. I got *news* for you, Hester. News thats better than gold. But first—heads up.

The Doctor comes in. He wears a sandwich board and carries all his office paraphernalia on his back.

DOCTOR. Hester! Yr due for a checkup.

HESTER. My guts been hurting me.

DOCTOR. Im on my way home just now. Catch up with me tomorrow. We'll have a look at it then.

He goes on his way.

AMIGA GRINGA. Doc! I am in pain like you would not believe. My hips, Doc. When I move them—blinding flashes of light and then—down I go, flat on my back, like Im dead, Doc.

DOCTOR. I gave you something for that yesterday.

DOCTOR.
AMIGA GRINGA.

He slips Amiga a vial of pills. He goes on his way.

AMIGA GRINGA. He's a saint.

HESTER. Sometimes.

AMIGA GRINGA. Want some?

HESTER. I want my money.

AMIGA GRINGA. Patience, girl. All good things are on their way. Do you know what the word is?

HESTER. What word?

AMIGA GRINGA. Word is that yr first love is back in town, doing well and looking for you.

HESTER. Chilli? Jabbers daddy? Looking for me?

AMIGA GRINGA. Thats the word.

HESTER.
HESTER.

HESTER. Bullshit. Gimmie my money, Miga. I promised the kids cake and ice cream. How much you get?

AMIGA. First, an explanation of the economic environment.

HESTER. Just gimmie my money—

AMIGA. The Stock Market, The Bond Market, Wall Street, Grain Futures, Bulls and Bears and Pork Bellies. They all impact the price a woman such as myself can get for a piece of "found" jewelry.

HESTER. That werent jewelry I gived you that was a watch. A Mans watch. Name brand. And it was working.

AMIGA. Do you know what the Dow did today, Hester? The Dow was up twelve points. And that prize fighter, the one everyone is talking about, the one with the pretty wife and the heavyweight crown, he rang the opening bell. She wore a dress cut down to here. And the Dow shot up 43 points in the first minutes of trading, Hester. Up like a rocket. And men glanced up at the clocks on the walls of their offices and women around the country glanced into the faces of their children and time passed. [And someone looks at their watch because its lunchtime, Hester. And theyre having—lunch. And they wish it would last forever. Cause when they get back to their office where they—work, when they get back the Dow has plummeted. And theres a lot of racing around and time is brief and something must be done before the closing bell. Phone calls are made, marriages dissolve, promises lost in the shuffle, Hester, and all this time your Amiga Gringa is going from fence to fence trying to get the best price on this piece of "found" jewelry. Numbers racing on lightboards, Hester, telling those that are in the know, the value of who knows what. One man, broken down in tears in the middle of the avenue, oh my mutual funds he was saying.] The market was hot, and me, a suspicious looking mother, very much like yrself, with no real address and no valid forms of identification, walking the streets with a hot watch.

(Rest)

Here.

She gives Hester $.

HESTER. Wheres the rest?

AMIGA. Thats it.

HESTER. 5 bucks?

AMIGA. It wasnt a good day. Some days are good some days are bad. I kept a buck for myself.

HESTER. You stole from me.

AMIGA. Dont be silly. We're friends, Hester.

HESTER. I shoulda sold it myself.

AMIGA. But you had the baby to watch.

HESTER. And no ones gonna give money to me with me carrying Baby around. Still I coulda got more than 5.

AMIGA. Go nextime yrself then. The dangers I incur, working with you. You oughta send yr kids away. Like me. I got 3 kids. All under the age of 3. And do you see me looking all baggy eyed, up all night shining little shoes and flattening little shirts and going without food? Theres plenty of places that you can send them. Homes. Theres plenty of peoples, rich ones especially, that cant have kids. The rich spend days looking through the newspaper for ads where they can buy one. Or they go to the bastard homes and pick one out. Youd have some freedom. Youd have a chance at life. Like me.

HESTER. My kids is mine. I get rid of em what do I got? Nothing. I got nothing now, but if they go I got less than nothing.

AMIGA. Suit yrself. You wouldnt have to send them all away, just one or two or three.

HESTER. All I need is a leg up. I get my leg up I'll be ok.

Bully comes outside and stands there watching them. She wears pink, one-piece, flame-retardant pajamas.

HESTER. What.

BULLY. My hands stuck.

HESTER. Why you sleep with yr hands in fists?

AMIGA. Yr an angry girl, arentcha, Bully.

BULLY. Idunno. This ones stuck too.

HESTER. Maybe yll grow up to be a boxer, huh? We can watch you ringside, huh? *Wide World of Sports.*

AMIGA. Presenting in this corner weighing 82 pounds the challenger: Bully!

BULLY. Ima good girl.

HESTER. Course you are. There. You shouldnt sleep with yr hands balled up. The good fairies come by in the night with treats for little girls and they put them in yr hands. How you gonna get any treats if yr hands are all balled up?

BULLY. Jabber is bad and Trouble is bad and Beauty is bad and Baby is bad but I'm good. Bullys a good girl.

HESTER. Go on back to bed now.

BULLY. Miga. Smell.

AMIGA. You got bad breath.

BULLY. I forgot to brush my teeth.

HESTER. Go head.

Bully squats off in the "bathroom" and rubs her teeth with her finger.

AMIGA. Babys daddy, that Reverend, he ever give you money?

HESTER. No.

AMIGA. He's a gold mine. I seen the collection plate going around. It's a full plate.

HESTER. I aint seen him since before Baby was born.

AMIGA. Thats two years.

HESTER. He didnt want nothing to do with me. His heart went hard.

AMIGA. My second kids daddy had a hard heart at first. But time mushed him up. Remember when he comed around crying about his lineage and asking whered the baby go? And I'd already gived it up.

HESTER. Reverend D., his heart is real hard. Like a rock.

AMIGA. Worth a try all the same.

HESTER. Yeah.

(Rest)

Who told you Chilli was looking for me?

AMIGA. Word on the street, thats all.

Trouble, dressed in superhero pajamas, comes in. He holds a box of matches. He lights one.

HESTER. What the hell you doing?

TROUBLE. Sleepwalking.

HESTER. You sleepwalk yrself back over here and gimmie them matches or Ima kill you.

He gives her the matches. Bully has finished with her teeth.

BULLY. You wanna smell?

HESTER. Thats ok.

BULLY. Dont you wanna smell?

Hester leans in and Bully opens her mouth.

BULLY. I only did one side cause I only ate with one side today.

HESTER. Go on to bed.

Bully passes Trouble and hits him hard.

TROUBLE. Aaaaah!

BULLY. Yr a bad person!

She hits him again.

TROUBLE. Aaaaaaaaah!

HESTER. Who made you policewoman?

TROUBLE. Ima blow you sky high one day you bully bitch!

Bully goes to hit him again.

HESTER. Trouble I thought you said you was sleep. Go inside and lie down and shut up or you wont see tomorrow.

He goes back to sleepwalking and goes inside.

HESTER. Bully. Go over there. Close yr eyes and yr mouth and not a word, hear?

Bully goes a distance off curling up to sleep without a word.

HESTER. I used to wash Troubles mouth out with soap when he used bad words. Found out he likes the taste of soap. Sometimes you cant win. No matter what you do.

(Rest)

Im gonna talk to Welfare and get an upgrade. The worldll take care of the women and children.

AMIGA. Theyre gonna give you the test. See what skills you got. Make you write stuff.

HESTER. Like what?

AMIGA. Like yr name.

HESTER. I can write my damn name. Im not such a fool that I cant write my own goddamn name. I can write my goddamn name.

Inside, Baby starts crying.

HESTER. HUSH!

Baby hushes.

AMIGA. You should pay yrself a visit to Babys daddy. Dont take along the kid in the flesh thatll be too much. For a buck I'll get someone to take a snapshot.

Jabber comes in. He wears mismatched pajamas. He doesnt come too close but keeps his distance.

JABBER. I was in a row boat and the sea was flat like a blue plate and you was rowing me and it was fun.

HESTER. Go back to bed.

JABBER. It was a good day but then Bad News and the sea started rolling and the boat tipped and I fell out and—

HESTER. You wet the bed.

JABBER. I fell out the boat.

HESTER. You wet the bed.

JABBER. I wet the bed.

HESTER. 13 years old still peeing in the bed.

JABBER. It was uh accident.

HESTER. Whats wrong with you?

JABBER. Accidents happen.

HESTER. Yeah you should know cause yr uh damn accident. Shit. Take that off.

Jabber strips.

AMIGA. He aint bad looking, Hester. A little slow, but some women like that.

HESTER. Wear my coat. Gimmie a kiss.

He puts on her coat and kisses her on the cheek.

JABBER. Mommie?

HESTER. Bed.

JABBER. All our daddys died, right? All our daddys died in the war, right?

HESTER. Yeah, Jabber.

JABBER. They went to war and they died and you cried. They went to war and died but whered they go when they died?

HESTER. They into other things now.

JABBER. Like what?

HESTER. —. Worms. They all turned into worms, honey. They crawling around in the dirt happy as larks, eating the world up, never hungry. Go to bed.

Jabber goes in.
(*Rest*)

AMIGA. Worms?

HESTER. Whatever.

AMIGA. He's yr favorite. You like him the best.

HESTER. He's my first.

AMIGA. He's yr favorite.

HESTER. I dont got no *favorite.*

(*Rest*)

5 bucks. 3 for their treats. And one for that photo. Reverend D. aint the man I knew. He's got money now. A salvation business and all. Maybe his stone-heart is mush, though. Maybe.

AMIGA. Cant hurt to try.

SCENE 2

STREET PRACTICE

Hester walks alone down the street. She has a framed picture of Baby.

HESTER. Picture, it comed out pretty good. Got him sitting on a chair, and dont he look like he got everything one could want in life? He's 2 yrs old. Andll be growd up with a life of his own before I blink.

(*Rest*)

Picture comed out good. Thought Amiga was cheating me but it comed out good.

She meets the Doctor, coming the other way. As before he carries all of his office paraphernalia on his back. He wears a sandwich board with the words written on it hidden.

DOCTOR. Hester. Dont move a muscle, I'll be set up in a jiffy.

HESTER. I dont got more than a minute.

DOCTOR. Hows yr gut?

HESTER. Not great.

DOCTOR. Say "Aaaah!"

As she stands there with her mouth open, he sets up his roadside office: a thin curtain, his doctor's shingle, his instruments, his black bag.

DOCTOR. Good good good good good. Lets take yr temperature. Do you know what it takes to keep my roadside practice running? Do you know how much The Higher Ups would like to shut me down? Every blemish on your record is a blemish on mine. Take yr guts for instance. Yr pain could be nothing or it could be the end of the road. A cyst or a tumor. A lump or a virus or an infected sore. Or cancer, Hester. Undetected. There youd be, lying in yr coffin with all yr little ones gathered around motherlessly weeping and The Higher Ups pointing their fingers at me, saying I should of saved the day, but instead stood idly by. You and yr children live as you please and Im the one The Higher Ups hold responsible. Would you like a pill?

HESTER. No thanks. (*She doubles over in pain*) My gut hurts.

The Doctor takes a pill.

DOCTOR. In a minute. We'll get to that in a minute. How are yr children?

HESTER. Theyre all right.

DOCTOR. All 5?

HESTER. All 5.

DOCTOR. Havent had any more have you?

HESTER. No.

DOCTOR. But you could. But you might.

HESTER. —Maybe.

DOCTOR. Word from The Higher Ups is that one more kid outa the likes of you and theyre on the likes of me like white on rice. I'd like to propose something—. Yr running a temperature. Bit of a fever. Whats this?

HESTER. Its a club. For protection.

DOCTOR. Good thinking.

He examines her quickly and thoroughly.

DOCTOR. The Higher Ups are breathing down my back, Hester. They want answers! They want results! Solutions! Solutions! Solutions! Thats what they want.

He goes to take another pill, but doesnt.

DOCTOR. I only take one a day. I only allow myself one a day.

(Rest)
He goes back to examining her.

DOCTOR. Breath in deep. Lungs are clear. Yr heart sounds good. Strong as an ox.

HESTER. This falls been cold. The wind under the bridge is colder than the wind on the streets.

DOCTOR. Exercise. Thats what I suggest. When the temperature drops, I run in place. Hold yr hands out. Shaky. Experiencing any stress and tension?

HESTER. Not really.

DOCTOR. Howre yr meals?

HESTER. The kids come first.

DOCTOR. Course they do. Howre yr bowels. Regular?

HESTER. I dunno.

DOCTOR. Once a day?

HESTER. Sometimes. My gut—

doctor. In a minute. Gimmie the Spread & Squat right quick. Lets have a look under the hood.

Standing, Hester spreads her legs and squats. Like an otter, he slides between her legs on a dolly and looks up into her privates with a flashlight.

DOCTOR. Last sexual encounter?

HESTER. Thats been a while, now.

DOCTOR. Yve healed up well from yr last birth.

HESTER. Its been 2 years. His names Baby.

DOCTOR. Any pain, swelling, off-color discharge, strange smells?

HESTER. No.

DOCTOR. L.M.P.?

HESTER. About a week ago.

(Rest)

How *you* been feeling, Doc?

DOCTOR. Sometimes Im up, sometimes Im down.

HESTER. You said you was lonesome once. I came for a checkup and you said you was lonesome. You lonesome today, Doc?

DOCTOR. No.

HESTER. Oh.

DOCTOR. Yr intelligent. Attractive enough. You could of made something of yrself.

HESTER. Im doing all right.

DOCTOR. The Higher Ups say yr in a skid. I agree.

HESTER. Oh, I coulda been the Queen of Sheba, it just werent in the cards, Doc.

DOCTOR. Yr kids are 5 strikes against you.

HESTER. I dont need no lecture. Gimmie something for my gut so I can go.

DOCTOR. The Higher Ups, they say I'm not making an impact. But what do you care.

HESTER. My gut—

DOCTOR. Stand right here.

He draws a line in the dirt, positions her behind it and walks a few steps away. He reveals the writing on his sandwich board. It is an eye exam chart. The letters on the first line spell "SPAY."

DOCTOR. Read.

HESTER. —.A.

DOCTOR. Good.

He takes a step closer decreasing the distance between them.

DOCTOR. Read.

HESTER. —.—.—.

(Rest)

I need glasses for that.

DOCTOR. Uh huhn. (*He steps closer*) How about now?

HESTER. I need glasses I guess.

DOCTOR. I guess you do.

He steps even closer.

HESTER. ((somethin-somethin-A-somethin))

(Rest)

I need glasses.

DOCTOR. You cant read this?

HESTER. I gotta go.

She turns to go and he grabs her hand, holding her fast.

DOCTOR. When I say removal of your "womanly parts" do you know what parts Im talking about?

HESTER. Yr gonna take my womans parts?

DOCTOR. My hands are tied. The Higher Ups are calling the shots now.

(Rest)

You have 5 healthy children, itll be for the best, considering.

HESTER. My womans parts.

DOCTOR. Ive forwarded my recommendation to yr caseworker. Its out of my hands. Im sorry.

HESTER. I gotta go.

But she doesnt move. She stands there numbly.

DOCTOR. Yr gut. Lets have a listen. (*He puts his ear to her stomach and listens*) Growling hungry stomach. Heres a dollar. Go get yrself a sandwich.

She takes the money and goes.

DOCTOR.

DOCTOR.

DOCTOR.

First Confession: The Doctor "Times Are Tough: What Can We Do?"

DOCTOR.
   Times are tough:
   What can we do?
   When I see a woman begging on the streets
      I guess I could

Bring her in my house
sit her at my table
make her a member of my family, sure.
But there are hundreds and thousands of
    them
And my house cant hold them all.
Maybe we should all take in just one.
Except they wouldnt really fit.
They wouldnt really fit in with us.
Theres such a gulf between us. What can we
    do?
I am a man of the people from way back my
    streetside practice is a testament to that
so dont get me wrong
do not for a moment think
I am one of those people haters who does not
understand
who does not experience—compassion.

(Rest)

Shes been one of my neediest cases for several years
    now.
What can I do?
Each time she comes to me
looking more and more forlorn
and more and more in need
of affection
at first I wouldnt touch her without gloves
    on, but then

(Rest)

We did it once
in that alley there
she was
phenomenal.

(Rest)

I was
lonesome and
She gave herself to me in a way that I had never
    experienced,
even with women Ive paid,
she was, like she was giving me something that
    was not hers to give me but something that
    was mine
that I'd lent her
and she was returning it to me.
Sucked me off for what seemed like hours
but I was very insistent. And held back
and she understood that I wanted her in the
    traditional way.
And she was very giving, very motherly very
    obliging very understanding, very phenomenal.
Let me cumm inside her. Like I needed to.
What could I do?
I couldn't help it.

SCENE 3

THE REVEREND ON HIS SOAPBOX

Late at night. The Reverend D. On his soapbox preaching to no one in particular. There is a display of taped versions of his sermons for sale.

REVEREND D. You all know me. You all know this face. These arms. These legs. This body of mine is known to you. To all of you. There isnt a person on the street tonight that hasn't passed me by at some point. Maybe when I was low, many years ago, with a bottle in my hand and the cold hard unforgiving pavement for my dwelling place. Perhaps you know me from that. Or perhaps you know me from my more recent incarnation. The man on the soapbox, telling you of a better life thats available to you, not after the demise of your physical being, not in some heaven where we all gonna be robed in satin sheets and wearing gossamer wings, but right here on earth, my friends. Right here right now. Let the man on the soapbox tell you how to pick yourself up. Let the man on the soapbox tell you how all yr dreams can come true. Let the man on the soapbox tell you that you dont have to be down and dirty, you dont have to be ripped off and re-nounced, you dont have to be black and blue, your neck dont have to be red, your clothes dont have to be torn, your head dont have to be hanging, you dont have to *hate* yourself, you dont have to hate yr neighbor. You can pull yrself up.

Hester comes in with a framed picture of Baby. She stands a ways off. Reverend D. keeps on talking.

REVEREND D. And I am an example of that. I am a man who has crawled out of the quicksand of despair. I am a man who has pulled himself out of that never ending gutter— and you notice friends that every city and every towns got a gutter. Aint no place in the world that dont have some little trench for its waste. And the gutter, is endless, and deep and wide and if you think you gonna crawl out of the gutter by crawling along the gutter you gonna be in the gutter for the rest of your life. You gotta step out of it, friends and I am here to tell you that you can.

(Rest)
He sees Hester but doesnt recognize her.

REVEREND D. What can I do for you tonight, my sister.
HESTER. I been good.
REVEREND D. But yr life is weighing heavy on you tonight.
HESTER. I havent bothered you.
REVEREND D. Reverend D. likes to be bothered. Reverend D. enjoys having the tired, the deprived and the depraved come knocking on his door. Come gathering around his soapbox. Come closer. Come on.

Hester holds the picture of Baby in front of her face.

HESTER. This child here dont know his daddy.

REVEREND D. The ultimate disaster of modern times. Sweet child. Yours?

HESTER. Yes.

REVEREND D. Do you know the father?

HESTER. Yes.

REVEREND D. You must go to him and say "Mister, here is your child!"

HESTER. Mister here is your child!

REVEREND D. "You are wrong to deny what God has made!"

HESTER. You are wrong to deny what God has made!

REVEREND D. "He has nothing but love for you and reaches out his hands every day crying wheres daddy?"

HESTER. Wheres daddy?

REVEREND D. "Wont you answer those cries?"

HESTER. Wont you answer those cries?

REVEREND D. If he dont respond to that then he's a good for nothing deadbeat, and you report him to the authorities. They'll garnish his wages so at least you all wont starve. I have a motivational cassette which speaks to that very subject. I'll give it to you free of charge.

HESTER. I got all yr tapes. I send my eldest up here to get them.

REVEREND D. Wonderful. Thats wonderful. You should go to yr childs father and demand to be recognized.

HESTER. Its been years since I seen him. He didnt want me bothering him so I been good.

REVEREND D. Go to him. Plead with him. Show him this sweet face and yours. He cannot deny you.

Hester lowers the picture.

HESTER.

REVEREND D.

HESTER.

REVEREND D.

(Rest)

HESTER. You know me?

REVEREND D. No. God.

HESTER. I aint bothered you for 2 years.

REVEREND D. You should go. Home. Let me call you a taxi. *Taxi!* You shouldnt be out this time of night. Young mother like you. In a neighborhood like this. We'll get you home in a jiff. Where ya live? East? West? North I bet, am I right? *TAXI!* God.

HESTER. He's talking now. Not much but some. He's a good boy.

REVEREND D. I am going to send one of my people over to your home tomorrow. Theyre marvelous, the people who work with me. They'll put you in touch with all sorts of agencies that can help you. Get some food in that stomach of yours. Get you some sleep.

HESTER. Doctor says I got a fever. We aint doing so good. We been slipping. I been good. I dont complain. They breaking my back is all. 5 kids. My treasures, breaking my back.

REVEREND D. We'll take up a collection for you.

HESTER. You know me.

REVEREND D. You are under the impression that—. Your mind, having nothing better to fix itself on has fixed on me. Me, someone you've never even met.

HESTER. There aint no one here but you and me. Say it. You know me. You know my name. You know my—. You know me and I know you.

HESTER.

REVEREND D.

(Rest)

REVEREND D. Here is a card. My lawyer. He'll call you.

HESTER. We dont got no phone.

REVEREND D. He'll visit. Write yr address on—. Tell me yr address. I'll write it down. I'll give it to him in the morning and he'll visit you.

(Rest)

Do the authorities know the name of the father?

HESTER. I dont tell them nothing.

REVEREND D. They would garnish his wages if you did. That would provide you with a small income. If you agree not to ever notify the authorities, we could, through my institution, arrange for you to get a much larger amount of money.

HESTER. How much more?

REVEREND D. Twice as much.

HESTER. 3 times.

REVEREND D. Fine.

HESTER. Theres so many things we need. Food. New shoes. A regular dinner with meat and salad and bread.

REVEREND D. I should give you some money right now. As a promise to you that I'll keep my word. But Im short of cash.

HESTER. Oh.

REVEREND D. Come back in two days. Late. I'll have some then.

HESTER. You dont got no food or nothing do ya?

REVEREND D. Come back in two days. Not early. Late. And not a word to no one. Okay?

HESTER. —. K.

REVEREND D.

HESTER.

REVEREND D.

HESTER.

(Rest)

REVEREND D. You better go.

Hester goes.

SCENE 4

WITH THE WELFARE

Outside, Jabber, Trouble and Beauty sit in the dirt playing with toy cars.

TROUBLE. Green light. Red light. Green light. Red light.

JABBER. Look, a worm.

They all study the worm as it writhes in the dirt. Welfare enters.

WELFARE. Wheres your mommie?

BEAUTY. Inside.

JABBER. Mommie! Welfares here.

Hester enters.

WELFARE. Thank you.

HESTER. Go inside.

The kids go inside.

WELFARE. Are they clean?

HESTER. Yes, Maam.

WELFARE. Wash them again.

Hester washes her hands again. Dries them.

WELFARE. The welfare of the world.

HESTER. Maam?

WELFARE. Come on over, come on.

Hester stands behind Welfare, giving her a shoulder rub.

WELFARE. The welfare of the world weighs on these shoulders, Hester.

(Rest)

We at Welfare are at the end of our rope with you, Hester. We put you in a job and you quit. We put you in a shelter and you walk. We put you in school and you drop out. Yr children are also truant. Word is they steal. Stealing is a gateway crime, Hester. Perhaps your young daughter is pregnant. Who knows. We build bridges you burn them. We sew safety nets, harder, good strong safety nets and you slip through the weave.

HESTER. We was getting by all right, then I dunno, I been tired lately. Like something in me broke.

WELFARE. You and yr children live, who knows where.

HESTER. Here Maam, under the Main Bridge.

WELFARE. This is not the country, Hester. You cannot simply—live off the land. If yr hungry you go to the shelter and get a hot meal.

HESTER. The shelter hassles me. Always prying in my business. Stealing my shit. Touching my kids. We was making ends meet all right then—. Ends got further apart.

WELFARE. "Ends got further apart." God!

(Rest)

I care because it is my job to care. I am paid to stretch out these hands, Hester. Stretch out these hands. To you.

HESTER. I gived you the names of 4 daddys: Jabbers and Bullys and Troubles and Beautys. You was gonna find them. Garnish they wages.

WELFARE. No luck as yet but we're looking. Sometimes these searches take years.

HESTER. Its been years.

WELFARE. Lifetimes then. Sometimes they take that long. These men of yours, theyre deadbeats. They dont want to be found. Theyre probably all in Mexico wearing false mustaches. Ha ha ha.

(Rest)

What about the newest child?

HESTER. Baby.

WELFARE. What about Babys father?

HESTER. —. I dunno.

WELFARE. Dont know or dont remember?

HESTER. You think Im doing it with mens I dont know?

WELFARE. No need to raise your voice no need of that at all. You have to help me help you, Hester.

(Rest)

Run yr fingers through my hair. Go on. Feel it. Silky isnt it?

HESTER. Yes Maam.

WELFARE. Comes from a balanced diet. Three meals a day. Strict adherence to the food pyramid. Money in my pocket, clothes on my back, teeth in my mouth, womanly parts where they should be, hair on my head, husband in my bed.

Hester combs Welfare's hair.

WELFARE. Yr doctor recommends that you get a hysterectomy. Take out yr woman parts. A spay.

HESTER. Spay.

WELFARE. I hope things wont come to that. I will do what I can. But you have to help me out, Hester.

HESTER. ((Dont *make* me hurt you.))

WELFARE. What?

HESTER. I didnt mean it. Just slipped out.

WELFARE. Remember yr manners. We worked good and hard on yr manners. Remember? Remember that afternoon over at my house? That afternoon with the teacups?

HESTER. *Manners*, Maam?

WELFARE. Yes. Manners.

HESTER.

WELFARE.

WELFARE. Babys daddy. Whats his name?

HESTER. You wont find him no how.

WELFARE. We could get lucky. He could be right around the corner and I could walk out and there he would be and then we at Welfare would wrestle him to the ground and turn him upside down and let you and yr Baby grab all the money that falls from Deadbeat Daddys pockets. I speak metaphorically. We would garnish his wages.

HESTER. How much would that put in my pocket?

WELFARE. Depends how much he earns. Maybe 100. Maybe. We take our finders fee. Whats his name?

HESTER. I dunno.

WELFARE. You dont have to say it out loud. Write it down.

She gives Hester pencil and paper. Hester writes. Welfare looks at the paper.

WELFARE. "A."

(Rest)

Adam, Andrew, Archie, Arthur, Aloysius, "A" what?

HESTER. Looks good dont it?

WELFARE. You havent learned yr letters yet, have you?

HESTER. I want my leg up is all.

WELFARE. You wont get something for nothing.

HESTER. I been good.

WELFARE. 5 bastards is not good. 5 bastards is bad.

HESTER. Dont make me hurt you!

Hester raises her club to strike Welfare.

WELFARE. You hurt me and, kids or no kids, I'll have you locked up. We'll take yr kids away and yll never see them again.

HESTER. My lifes my own fault. I know that. But the world dont help, Maam.

WELFARE. The world is not here to help us, Hester. The world is simply here. We must help ourselves.

(Rest)

I know just the job for you. It doesnt pay well, but the work is very rewarding. Hard honest work. Unless yr afraid of hard honest work.

HESTER. I aint afraid of hard work.

WELFARE. Its sewing. You can do it at home. No work no pay but thats yr decision.

(Rest)

WELFARE. Heres the fabric. Make sure you dont get it dirty.

HESTER. Can I express myself?

WELFARE. Needles, thread and the pattern, in this bag. Take the cloth. Sew it. If you do a good job therell be more work. Have it sewn by tomorrow morning, yll get a bonus.

Hester takes the cloth and notions.

HESTER. I dont think the world likes women much.

WELFARE. Dont be silly.

HESTER. I was just thinking.

WELFARE. Im a woman too! And a black woman too just like you. Dont be silly.

HESTER.

WELFARE.

(Rest)

Hester puts her hand out, waiting.

HESTER. Yr shoulders. Plus I did yr hair.

WELFARE. Is a buck all right?

HESTER.

WELFARE.

WELFARE. Unless yll change a 50.

HESTER. I could go get change—

WELFARE. Take the buck, K? And the cloth. And go.

Welfare owes Hester more $, but after a beat, Hester just leaves.

Second Confession: The Welfare "I Walk The Line"

WELFARE.

> I walk the line
> between us and them
> between our kind and their kind.
> The balance of the system depends on a well
>   drawn boundary line
> And all parties respecting that boundary.
> I am
> I am a married woman.
> I—dont that is have never
> never in the past or even in the recent present
>   or even when I look
> look out into the future of my life I do not see
>   any interest
> any *sexual* interest
> in anyone
> other than my husband.

(Rest)

> My dear husband.
> The hours he keeps.
> The money he brings home.
> Our wonderful children.
> The vacations we go on.
> My dear husband he needed
> a little spice.
> And I agreed. We both needed spice.
> We both hold very demanding jobs.
> We put an ad in the paper: "Husband and Bi-
>   Curious Wife, seeking—"
> But the women we got
> Hookers. Neurotics. Gold diggers!
> "Bring one of those gals home from work,"
>   hubby said. And Hester,
> she came to tea.

(Rest)

> She came over and we had tea.

From my mothers china.
And marzipan on matching china plates.
Hubby sat opposite in the recliner.
hard as Gibralter. He told us what he wanted
    and we did it.
We were his little puppets.
She was surprised, but consented.
Her body is better than mine.
Not a single stretchmark on her
Im a looker too dont get me wrong just in a
    different way and
Hubby liked the contrast.
Just light petting at first.
Running our hands on each other
Then Hubby joined in
and while she and I kissed
Hubby did her and me alternately.
The thrill of it

(Rest)

I was so afraid I'd catch something
but I was swept away and couldn't stop
She stuck her tongue down my throat
and Hubby doing his thing on top
my skin shivered
She let me slap her across the face
And I crossed the line.

(Rest)

It was my first threesome
And it wont happen again.
And I should emphasize that
she is a low-class person.
What I mean by that is that we have absolutely
    nothing in common.
As her caseworker I realize that maintenance of the sys-
    tem depends on a well-drawn boundary line
And all parties respecting that boundary.
And I am, after all,
I am a married woman.

Welfare exits. Hester reenters to watch Welfare exit.

HESTER. Bitch.

Hester, alone on stage, examines the cloth.

HESTER. Sure is pretty cloth. Sewing cant be that hard. Thread the needle stick it in and pull it through. Pretty cloth. Lets see what we making. Oooooh. Uh evening dress. Go to a party in. Drink champagne and shit. Uh huh, "Dont mind if I do," and shit and la de *dah* and come up in a limo and everybody wants a picture. So many lights Im blinded. Wear dark glasses. Strut my stuff.

She has another painful stomach attack which knocks the wind out of her and doubles her over.

Far away, Chilli walks by with his picnic basket on his arm. He pauses, checks his pocketwatch, then continues on. Hester, recovering from her attack, sees him just before he disappears.

HESTER. Chilli!

SCENE 5

SMALL CHANGE AND SANDWICHES

Late at night. The children inside, all sleeping. Lots of As written in Hesters practice place.
    Hester, working on her sewing, tries to thread the needle.

HESTER. Damn needle eyes too damn small. Howmy supposed to get the thread through. Theres a catch to everything, Hester. No easy money nowheres. Wet the thread good. Damn.

She squeezes her eyes shut and opens them, trying to focus. Having difficulty threading the needle, she takes out an object wrapped in brown paper. Looks cautiously around. Begins to unwrap it. A sandwich.

HESTER. Put something in my stomach maybe my eyesll work.

Amiga Gringa comes in. Hester stashes the package, picks up her sewing.

AMIGA. Mother Hubbard sewing by street lamp. Very moving.
HESTER. I got me uh job. This here is work.
AMIGA. From Welfare?
HESTER. Shes getting me back in the workforce. I do good on this she'll give me more.
AMIGA. Whats the pay?
HESTER. Its by the piece.
AMIGA. How much?
HESTER. 10 bucks maybe.
AMIGA. Maybe?
HESTER. I get a bonus for working fast.
AMIGA. Very nice fabric. Very pretty. Very expensive. And oooh, look at what yr making.
HESTER. You good with needles? Thread this. My eyes aint good.

Amiga tries halfheartedly to thread the needle. Quits.

AMIGA. Sorry.

Hester continues trying to thread the needle.

AMIGA. Good yr working. Get some money in yr pocket. Make a good example for the kids. Pull yrself up by yr bootstraps. Get with the program. Taking responsibility for yr life. I envy you.

HESTER. Me?

AMIGA. Yr working, Im—looking for work.

HESTER. I bet I could get you some sewing.

AMIGA. Oh no. Thats not for me. If I work, Hester, I would want to be paid a living wage. You have agreed to work for less than a living wage. May as well be a slave. Or an animal.

HESTER. It's a start. She said if I do well—

AMIGA. If you do well shes gonna let you be her slave for *life*. Wouldnt catch me doing that. Chump work. No no no. But it's a good thing you are. Example to the kids.

HESTER. I aint no chump.

AMIGA. Course you arent. Yr just doing chump work is all.

HESTER. It's a leg up. Cant start from the top.

AMIGA. Why not? Plenty of people start from the top. Why not you? Sure is pretty fabric.

HESTER. All I gotta do is sew along the lines.

AMIGA. Bet the fabric cost a lot. I wonder how much we could get for it—on the open market.

HESTER. Aint mine to sell. Its gonna make a nice dress. Im gonna sew it up and try it on before I give it to her. Just for fun.

But Hester hasn't been able to thread the needle.

AMIGA. Bet we could get 100 bucks. For the fabric. A lot more than youd get for sewing it. And you wouldnt have to lift a finger. Id sell it tonight. Have the money for you in the morning.

HESTER. No thanks.

AMIGA. Suit yrself.

Hester continues trying to thread that damn needle.

AMIGA. Chump work.

HESTER. They make the eyes too small, thats the problem.

(*Rest*)

I seen Chilli right after I was with the Welfare. You said he was looking for me and there he was! Jabbers daddy walking right by with a big gold pocket watch. But did I tell? Did I run after Welfare and say "Theres Jabbers daddy?" I did not. Can you imagine?

AMIGA. I told ya he was looking for ya. He's gonna find you too.

HESTER. Jabbers daddy, after all these years!

AMIGA. Maybe yr lucks turning.

HESTER. You think?

AMIGA. Maybe.

AMIGA.

HESTER.

(*Rest*)

AMIGA. I missed my period.

HESTER. Dont look at *me*.

(*Rest*)

Whatcha gonna do.

AMIGA. Have it, I guess.

HESTER. You may not be knocked up.

AMIGA. Theres something in here all right. I can feel it growing inside. Just my luck.

HESTER. You shoulda been careful.

AMIGA. Whatever.

HESTER. So get rid of it if you dont want it.

AMIGA. Or birth it then sell it.

HESTER. You as crazy as they come.

AMIGA.

HESTER.

AMIGA.

Amiga leans toward Hester to kiss her. Hester pulls back a bit.

AMIGA. Whassamatter?

HESTER. I dont got no love for nobody cept the kids.

Amiga pulls back, takes up the fabric.

AMIGA. I'll get you a lot of money for this.

HESTER. No.

AMIGA. Whassis?

Shes discovered the brown paper package.

HESTER. Nothing.

AMIGA. Smells like something. Smells like food. Smells like egg salad.

HESTER. I was saving it.

AMIGA. Lets celebrate! Come on itll be fun. Kids!

HESTER. They *sleep*. Let em sleep.

AMIGA. Lets toast my new kid. Just you and me. A new life has begun. Am I showing? Not yet, right? Will be soon enough. Little Bastards in there living high on the hog, taking up space. Little Bastard, we toast you with: egg salad.

Amiga takes a big bite out of the sandwich. Hester grabs at it but Amiga keeps it from her reach. Bully comes outside.

BULLY. Mommie?

HESTER. Yes, Bully.

BULLY. My hands.

HESTER. Lemmie unlock em.

Bully comes over. Hester opens her hands.

BULLY. Egg salad?

AMIGA. Yeah. Its yr mommies sandwich.

Amiga gives the sandwich to Hester who almost takes a bite but sees Bully looking hungrily on. She gives the sandwich to Bully. Bully eats. Amiga takes up the fabric.

HESTER. Cheat me and I'll kill you.

AMIGA. Have a little faith, Hester. Amiga will sell this fabric for you. You will not be a chump. In the morning when the sun comes up yll be 100 bucks richer. Sleep tight.

Amiga takes the fabric and leaves. Bully sitting with her mother, licking her fingers.

Third Confession: Amiga Gringa "In My Head I Got It Going On"

AMIGA GRINGA.
In my head I got it going on
the triple X rated movie
Hester and Amiga get down and get dirty.
Chocolate and Vanilla get into the ugly.
We coulda done a sex show behind a curtain
Then make a movie and sell it
For 3 bucks a peek
I had me some delicious schemes
to get her out of that hole she calls home.
Im doing well for myself
working my money maker
Do you have any idea how much cash I'll get
    for the fruit of my white womb?!
Grow it.
Birth it.
Sell it.
And why shouldnt I?

(Rest)

Funny how a woman like Hester
driving her life all over the road
most often chooses to walk the straight and
    narrow.
Girl on girl action is a very lucrative business.
And someones gotta do something for her.
Im just trying to help her out.
And myself too, ok. They dont call it Capitalizm for
    nothing.

(Rest)

She liked the idea of the sex
at least she acted like it.
Her looking at me with those eyes of hers
You looking like you want it, Hester
Shoot, Miga, she says thats just the way I look
    she says.
It took a little cajoling to get her to do it with me
for an invited audience.
for a dime a look
Over at my place.
Every cent was profit and no overhead to
    speak of.
the guys in the neighborhood got their pleasure
and we was our own boss so we didnt have

to pay no joker off the top.
We slipped right into a very profitable situation
Like sliding into warm water.
Her breasts her bottom
She let me touch her however I wanted
I let her ride my knees
She made sounds like an animal.
She put her hand between my legs.
One day some of the guys took advantage.
Ah, what do you expect in a society based on
    Capitalizm.
I tell you the plight of the worker these days.
Still one day Im gonna get her to make the
    movie
Cause her and me we had the moves down
very sensual, very provocative, very scientific,
    very lucrative.
In my head I got it going on.

SCENE 6

THE REVEREND ON THE ROCK

Late at night. Down the road, Reverend D., cleaning his cornerstone, a white block of granite with the date in Roman numerals, and practicing his preaching.

[REVEREND D. "It is easier for a camel to go through the eye of a needle than for a rich man to enter the kingdom of God." And you hear that and you say, let me get a tax shelter and hide some of my riches so that when I stand up there in judgment, God wont be none the wiser! And that is the problem with the way we see God. For most of us, God is like the IRS. God garnishes yr wages if you dont pay up. God withholds. The wages of sin, they lead to death, so you say, let me give to the poor. But not any poor, just those respectable charities. I want my poor looking good. I want my poor to know that it was me who bought the such and such. I want my poor on tv. I want famous poor, not miscellaneous poor. And I dont want local poor. Local poor dont look good. Gimmie foreign poor. Poverty exotica. Gimmie brown and yellow skins against a non-western landscape, some savanna, some rain forest some rice paddy. Gimmie big sad eyes with the berri-berri belly and the outstretched hands struggling to say "Thank-You" the only english they know, right into the camera. And put me up there with them, holding them, comforting them, telling them everythings gonna be alright, we are gonna raise you up, we are gonna get you on the bandwagon of our ways, put a smile in yr heart and a hamburger in yr belly, baby.

(Rest)

And that is how we like our poor. At arms length. Like a distant relation with no complication. But folks, we gotta—]

Hester comes in and watches him. He notices her and stops talking.

HESTER. Nice rock.

REVEREND D. Thank you.

HESTER. Theres something on it.

REVEREND D. Dont come close. It's the date its just the date. The date. Well, the year.

HESTER. Like a calendar.

REVEREND D. It's a cornerstone. The first stone of my new church. My backers are building me a church and this is the first stone.

HESTER. Oh.

(*Rest*)

You told me to come back. Im back.

REVEREND D. Theyre putting up my church tomorrow. My church will be a beautiful place. Its not much of a neighborhood now but when my church gets built, oh therell be a turnaround. Lots of opportunity for everyone. I feel like one of the pilgrims. You know, they step out of their boats and on to that Plymouth rock. I step off my soapbox and on to my cornerstone.

HESTER. You said come back to get my money. Im back.

REVEREND D. Do you know what a "Backer" is?

HESTER. Uh-uhn.

REVEREND D. It's a person who backs you. A person who believes in you. A person who looks you over and figures you just might make something of yrself. And they get behind you. With kind words, connections to high places, money. But they want to make sure they havent been suckered, so they watch you real close, to make sure yr as good as they think you are. To make sure you wont screw up and shame them and waste their money.

(*Rest*)

My Backers are building me a church. It will be beautiful. And to make sure theyre not wasting their money on a man who was only recently a neerdowell, they watch me.

HESTER. They watching now?

REVEREND D. Not now. Now theyre in their nice beds. Between the cool sheets. Fast asleep. I dont sleep. I have this feeling that if I sleep I will miss someone. Someone in desperate need of what I have to say.

HESTER. Someone like me.

REVEREND D. I dont have your money yet but I will. I'll take up a collection for you on Sunday. I'll tell them yr story, that yr someone in need, and all the money will go to you. Every cent of it. We get good crowds on Sunday.

(*Rest*)

Ive got work to do.

He waits for her to go but she stays. He goes back to cleaning his cornerstone.

HESTER. Today we had uh E-clipse. You seen it?

REVEREND D. You should go.

HESTER. A shadow passed over the sky. Everything was dark. For a minute.

REVEREND D. It was a cloud. Or an airplane. Happens all the time.

HESTER. No clouds out today. It was uh E-clipse.

REVEREND D. I am taking a collection for you on Sunday. Youll have to wait until then. Good night.

HESTER. Uh E-clipse.

REVEREND D. There was no eclipse today! No eclipse!

(*Rest*)

Good night.

HESTER. I was crossing the street with the kids. We had a walk sign. White is walk and red is dont walk. I know white from red. Aint colorblind, right? And we was crossing. And a shadow fell over, everything started going dark and, shoot I had to look up. They say when theres uh E-clipse you shouldnt look up cause then you go blind and alls I need is to go blind, thank you. But I couldn't help myself. And so I stopped right there in the street and looked up. Never seen nothing like it.

(*Rest*)

I dont know what I expected to see but.

(*Rest*)

It was a big dark thing. Blocking the sun out. Like the hand of fate. The hand of fate with its 5 fingers coming down on me.

(*Rest*)
(*Rest*)

And then the trumpets started blaring.

(*Rest*)

And then there was Jabber saying "Come on Mommie, Come On!" The trumpets was the taxi cabs. Wanting to run me over. Get out the road.

REVEREND D.

HESTER.

REVEREND D.

HESTER.

Reverend D. sits on his rock, his back hiding his behavior which has become unseemly.

REVEREND D. Comeer.

Hester slowly goes to him.

REVEREND D. Suck me off.

HESTER. No.

REVEREND D. Itll only take a minute. Im half way there. Please.

*She goes down on him. Briefly. He cumms. Mildly. Into
his handkerchief. She stands there. Ashamed. Expectant.*

REVEREND D. Go home. Put yr children to bed.
HESTER. Maybe we could get something regular going—
REVEREND D. Go home. Go home.

HESTER.
REVEREND D.

(*Rest*)

REVEREND D. Heres something. Its all I have.

He offers her a crumpled bill which she takes.

REVEREND D. Next time you come by—. It would be better if
you could come around to the back. I'll have my church
up and—. If you want your money, it would be better if
you come around to the back.
HESTER. Yeah.

She goes. He sits there, watching her leave.

Fourth Confession: Reverend D. "Suffering Is An Enormous Turn-On"

REVEREND D.
Suffering is an enormous turn-on.

(*Rest*)

She had four kids and she came to me ask-
ing me what to do.
She had a look in her eye that invites liaisons
Eyes that say red spandex.
She had four children four fatherless children
four fatherless mouths to feed
fatherless mouths fatherless mouths.
Add insult to injury was what I was thinking
There was a certain animal magnetism
between us
And She threw herself at me.
Like a baseball in the minors
fast but not deadly
I coulda stepped aside but.
God made her
and her fatherless mouths.

(*Rest*)

I was lying in the never ending gutter of the
street of the world.
You can crawl along it forever and never crawl
out
praying for God to take my life
You can take it God
You can take my life back
you can have it
before I hurt myself somebody
before I do a damage that I cannot undo

before I do a crime that I can never pay for
In the never ending blistering heat
of the never ending gutter of the world
my skin hot against the pavement
but lying there I knew
that I had never hurt anybody in my life.

(*Rest*)
(*Rest*)

She was one of the multitude. She did not stand
out.

(*Rest*)

The intercourse was not memorable.
And when she told me of her *predicament*
I gave her enough money to take care of it.

(*Rest*)

In all my days in the gutter I never hurt any-
one.
I never held hate for anyone.
And now the hate I have for her
and her hunger
and the *hate* I have for her hunger.
God made me.
God pulled me up.
Now God, through her, wants to drag me
down
And sit me at the table
At the head of the table of her fatherless
house.

SCENE 7

MY SONG IN THE STREET

*Hester with the kids. They are all playing Freeze Tag. Af-
ter a bit, Hester is "it." She runs then stops, standing stock
still, looking up into the sky. Bully gets tagged.*

BULLY. 1 Mississippi, 2 Mississippi, 3 Mississippi, 4 Mississippi, 5 Mississippi.

Jabber gets tagged.

JABBER. 1 Mississippi, 2 Mississippi, 3 Mississippi, 4 Mississippi, 5 Mississippi, Yr it.

HESTER.
HESTER.

JABBER. Mommie?
HESTER. What.
BULLY. Whasswrong?
HESTER. You think I like you bothering me all day?

HESTER.

JABBER/BULLY/TROUBLE/BEAUTY.

(*Rest*)

HESTER. All yall. Leave Mommie be. She cant play right now. Shes tired.

Hester stands there looking up into the sky. The kids play apart.

BULLY. Lemmie see it.
TROUBLE. What?
BULLY. Yr pee.

TROUBLE.
BULLY.

BULLY. Dont got no hair or nothing on it yet. I got hair on mines. Look.

TROUBLE.
BULLY.

TROUBLE. Jabber. Lets see yrs.

TROUBLE.
JABBER.
BULLY.

BULLY. Its got hair. Not as much as mines though.
BEAUTY. I had hairs but they fell out.
TROUBLE. Like a bald man or something?
BEAUTY. Yeah.

TROUBLE.
TROUBLE.

BULLY. Dont be touching yrself like that, Trouble, dont be nasty.

TROUBLE.
TROUBLE.

JABBER. You keep playing with it ssgonna fall off. Yr pee be laying in the street like a dead worm.
TROUBLE. Mommieeee!
HESTER. Dont talk to Mommie just now.
BULLY. Shes having a nervous breakdown.
HESTER. Shut the fuck up, please.

(*Rest*)
(*Rest*)

JABBER. When I grow up I aint never gonna use mines.
TROUBLE. Not me. I be *using* mines.
JABBER. Im gonna keep mines in my pants.
BULLY. How you ever gonna get married?
HESTER. Im gonna get married but Im gonna keep it in my pants.
BULLY. When you get married you gonna have to get on top uh yr wife.
JABBER. I'll get on top of her all right but I'll keep it in my pants.

TROUBLE. Jabber, you uh tragedy.
BULLY. When I get married my husbands gonna get on top of me and—
HESTER. No ones getting on top of you, Bully.
BULLY. He'll put the ring on my finger and I'll have me uh white dress and he'll get on top of me—
HESTER. No ones getting on top of you, Bully, no ones getting on top of you, so shut yr mouth about it.
TROUBLE. How she gonna have babies if no one gets on top of her?
HESTER. Dont *make* me hurt you!

She raises her hand to Trouble who runs off. Bully starts crying.

HESTER. Shut the fuck up or I'll give you something to cry about!

The kids huddle together in a knot.

HESTER.
JABBER/BULLY/BEAUTY.
HESTER.
JABBER/BULLY/BEAUTY.
HESTER.

(*Rest*)

HESTER. Bedtime.
BEAUTY. Its too early for bed—
HESTER. BEDTIME!

They hurry off. Hester goes back to contemplating the sky.

HESTER.
HESTER.
HESTER.

HESTER. Big dark thing. Gods hand. Coming down on me. Blocking the light out. Five-fingered hand of fate. Coming down on me.

The Doctor comes on wearing his "SPAY" sandwich board. He watches her looking up. After a bit he looks up too.

DOCTOR. We've scheduled you in for the day after tomorrow. First thing in the morning. You can send yr kids off to school then come on in. We'll have childcare for the baby. We'll give you good meals during yr recovery. Yll go to sleep. Yll go to sleep and when you wake up, Whisk! Yll be all clean. No worries no troubles no trials no tribulations no more mistakes. Clean as a whistle. You wont feel a thing. Day after tomorrow. First thing in the morning. Free of charge. Itll be our pleasure. And yours. All for the best. In the long run, Hester. Congratulations.

He walks off. Hester is still looking up.
   Chillie walks in with his picnic basket on his arm. He pauses to check his pocketwatch. Hester lowers her head. The sight of him knocks the wind out of her.

HESTER. Oh.
CHILLI. I've been looking for you.
HESTER. Oh.
CHILLI. Ssbeen a long time.
HESTER. I—I—.
CHILLI. No need to speak.
HESTER. I—
CHILLI. Yr glad to see me.
HESTER. Yeah.
CHILLI. I been looking for you. Like I said. Lifes been good to me. Hows life been to you?
HESTER. Ok. —. Hard.

CHILLI.
HESTER.

HESTER. I was with the Welfare and I seed you. I called out yr name.
CHILLI. I didnt hear you. Darn.
HESTER. Yeah.

(Rest)

I woulda run after you but—
CHILLI. But you were weak in the knees. And you couldn't move a muscle.
HESTER. Running after you woulda gived you away. And Welfares been after me to know the names of my mens.
CHILLI. Mens? More than one?
HESTER. I seed you and I called out yr name but I didnt run after you.

(Rest)

You look good. I mean you always looked good but now you look better.

(Rest)

I didnt run after you. I didnt give you away.
CHILLI. Thats my girl.

(Rest)

Welfare has my name on file, though, doesnt she?
HESTER. From years ago. I—
CHILLI. Not to worry couldn't be helped. I changed my name. They'll never find me. Theres no trace of the old me left anywhere.
HESTER. Cept Jabber.
CHILLI. Who?
HESTER. Yr son.

HESTER.
CHILLI.

CHILLI. Guess what time it is?
HESTER. He takes after you.
CHILLI. Go on guess. Betcha cant guess. Go on.
HESTER. Noon?

CHILLI. Lets see. I love doing this. I love guessing the time and then pulling out my watch and seeing how close I am or how far off. I love it. I spend all day doing it. Doctor says it's a tick. A sure sign of some disorder. But I cant help it. And it doesnt hurt anyone. You guessed?
HESTER. Noon.
CHILLI. Lets see. Ah! 3.
HESTER. Oh.
CHILLI. Sorry.

(Rest)

Whats up there?
HESTER. Nothing.
CHILLI. I want you to look at me. I want you to take me in. Ive been searching for you for weeks now and now Ive found you. I wasn't much when you knew me. When we knew each other I was—I was a shit.

(Rest)

I was a shit, wasn't I?

HESTER.
CHILLI.

CHILLI. I was a shit, agree with me.
HESTER. We was young.
CHILLI. We was young. We had a romance. We had a love affair. We was young. We was in love. I was infatuated with narcotics. I got you knocked up then I split.
HESTER. Jabber, he's yr spitting image. Only he's a little slow, but—
CHILLI. Who?
HESTER. Jabber. Yr son.
CHILLI. Dont bring him into it just yet. I need time. Time to get to know you again. We need time alone together. Guess.
HESTER. 3:02.
CHILLI. Ah! 3:05. But better, yr getting better. Things move so fast these days. Ive seen the world Ive made some money Ive made a new name for myself and I have a loveless life. I dont have love in my life. Do you know what thats like? To be alone? Without love?
HESTER. I got my chi—I got Jabber. He's my treasure.

HESTER.
CHILLI.

(Rest)

CHILLI. Im looking for a wife.
HESTER. Oh.
CHILLI. I want you to try this on.

He takes a wedding dress out of his basket. He puts it on her, right over her old clothes. Hester rearranges the club, still held in her belt, to get the dress on more securely.

HESTER. I seed you and I called out your name, but you didnt hear me, and I wanted to run after you but I was like,

Hester, if Welfare finds out Chillis in town they gonna give him hell so I didnt run. I didnt move a muscle. I was mad at you. Years ago. Then I seed you and I was afraid I'd never see you again and now here you are.

CHILLI. What do you think?

HESTER. Its all so clean and nice.

CHILLI. It suits you.

HESTER. Jabber, come meet yr daddy! I got some special shoes. Theyd go good with this.

CHILLI. Not yet, kid!

(Rest)

Lets not bring him into this just yet, K?

He fiddles with his watch.

CHILLI. 14 years ago. Back in the old neighborhood. You and me and the moon and the stars. What was our song?

HESTER.

CHILLI.

HESTER. Huh?

CHILLI. What was our song?

(Rest)

Da dee dah, dah dah dee dee?

HESTER. Its been a long time.

CHILLI. Listen.

He plays their song, "The Looking Song," on a tinny tape recorder. He sings along as she stands there. After a bit he dances and gets her to dance with him. They sing as they dance and do a few moves from the old days.

THE LOOKING SONG
    Im looking for someone
    to lose my looks with
    looking for someone
    to lose my shape with
    looking for someone
    to-get-my-hip-replaced with
    looking for someone
    Could it be you?

    Im looking for someone
    to loose my teeth with
    looking for someone
    to go stone deaf with
    looking for someone
    to-lie-6-feet-underneath with
    looking for someone
    Could it be you?

    They say "seek and you shall find"
    So I will look until Im blind
    Through this big old universe
    For rich or poor better or worse
    Singing:

    Yuck up my tragedy
    Oh darling, marry me
    Walk down the aisle, walk on
    Down Down Down

    Yeah Im looking for someone
    to lose my looks with
    Looking for someone
    to lose my teeth with
    looking for someone
    I'll-lie-6-feet-underneath with
    Looking for someone
    Could it be you?

Theyre breathless from dancing.

CHILLI. This is real. The feelings I have for you, the feelings you are feeling for me, these are all real. Ive been fighting my feelings for years. With every dollar I made. Every hour I spent. I spent it fighting. Fighting my feelings. Maybe you did the same thing. Maybe you remembered me against yr will, maybe you carried a torch for me against yr better judgment.

HESTER. You were my first.

CHILLI. Likewise.

(Rest)

He silently guesses the time and checks his guess against his watch. Is he right or wrong?

CHILLI. "Yuck up my tragedy."

HESTER. Huh?

CHILLI. Marry me.

HESTER.

CHILLI.

HESTER. K.

CHILLI. There are some conditions some things we have to agree on. They dont have anything to do with money. I understand your situation.

HESTER. And my—

CHILLI. And your child—ok. *Our* child—ok. These things have to do with you and me. You would be mine and I would be yrs and all that. But I would still retain my rights to my manhood. You understand.

HESTER. Sure. My—

CHILLI. Yr kid. We'll get to him. I would rule the roost. I would call the shots. The whole roost and every single shot. Ive proven myself as a success. You've not done that. It only makes sense that I would be in charge.

HESTER. —K.

CHILLI. Some people pile mistake upon mistake. You have just the one kid. You've walked the line inspite of everything. And I respect you all the more for that.

HESTER. I love you.

CHILLI. Would you like me to get down on my knees?

He gets down on his knees, offering her a ring.

CHILLI. Heres an engagement ring. Its rather expensive. With an adjustable band. If I didnt find you I would have had to, well—. Try it on, try it on.

Chilli checks his watch. As Hester fiddles with the ring, Bully & Trouble rush in. Beauty & Baby follow them.

BULLY. Mommie!
HESTER. No.
TROUBLE. You look fine!
HESTER. No.
BEAUTY. Is that a diamond?
HESTER. No!

Hester recoils from her kids.

HESTER.
BULLY/TROUBLE/BEAUTY/BABY.

BULLY. Mommie?
CHILLI. Who do we have here, honey?

HESTER.
BULLY/TROUBLE/BEAUTY/BABY.

CHILLI. Who do we have here?
HESTER. The neighbors kids.

Chilli goes to look at his watch, doesnt.

HESTER. Chilli.
CHILLI. Honey?
HESTER. Wheres Jabber at?

BULLY.

CHILLI. Honey?
HESTER. Bully, Im asking you a question.
CHILLI. Honey?
TROUBLE. He's out with Miga.
CHILLI. So you all are the neighbors kids, huh?
TROUBLE. Who the fuck are you?
HESTER. Trouble—
CHILLI. Who the fuck are you?
BULLY. We the neighbors kids.

CHILLI.
CHILLI.

(*Rest*)

CHILLI. Honey?
HESTER. Huh?
CHILLI. Im—. I'm thinking this through. I'm thinking this all the way through. And I think—I think—.

(*Rest*)
(*Rest*)

I carried around this picture of you. Sad and lonely with our child on yr hip. Struggling to make do. Struggling against all odds. And triumphant. Triumphant against everything. Like—hell, like Jesus and Mary. And if they

could do it so could my Hester. My dear Hester. Or so I thought.

(*Rest*)

But I dont think so.

He takes her ring and her veil. He takes her dress. He packs up his basket.

(*Rest*)

HESTER. Please.
CHILLI. Im sorry.

He looks at his watch, flipping it open and then snapping it shut. He leaves.

Fifth Confession: Chilli "We Was Young"

CHILLI.
 We was young
 and we didnt think
 we didnt think that nothing we could do
  would hurt us
 nothing we did would come back to haunt
  us
 we was young and we knew all about gravity
  but gravity was a law
 That did not apply to those persons under the
  age of 18
 gravity was something that came later
 and we was young and we could
 float
 weightless
 I was her first
 and zoom to the moon if we wanted and
  couldn't nothing stop us
 We would go
 fast
 and we were gonna live forever
 and any mistakes we would shake off
 We were Death Defying
 we were Hot Lunatics
 careless as all get out
 and she needed to keep it and I needed to leave
  town.
 People get old that way.

(*Rest*)

 We didnt have a car and everything was
  pitched toward love in a car
 and there was this car lot down from where
  we worked and
 we were fearless
 late nights go sneak in those rusted Buicks
  that hadnt moved in years
 I would sit at the wheel and pretend to drive

and she would say she felt the wind in her face
surfing her hand out the window
Then we'd park
without even moving
In the full light of the lot
Making love
She was my first.
We was young.
Times change.

SCENE 8

THE HAND OF FATE

Night. The back entrance to the Reverend's new church.
Hester comes in with the kids in tow.

HESTER. Sunday night. He had people in there listening to
him this morning. He passed the plate in my name. Not
in my name directly. Keep me secret, cause, well, he has
his image. I understand that. Dont want to step on everything he's made for himself. And he still wants me. I can
tell. A woman can tell when a man eyes her and he eyed
me all right.

(Rest)

You built this just from talking. Must of said the right
things. Nobodyd ever give me nothing like this for running my mouth. Gonna get me something now. Get
something or do something. Fuck you up fuck you up!
Hold on, girl, it wont come to that.

(Rest)

[I'll only ask for 5 dollars. 5 dollars a week. That way he
cant say no. And hes got a church, so he got 5 dollars. I'll
say I need to buy something for the kids. No. I'll say I
need to—get my hair done. There is this style, curls piled
up on the head, I'll say. Takes hours to do. I need to fix
myself up, I'll say. Need to get my looks back. Need to get
my teeth done. Caps, bridges, what they called, fillers,
whatever. New teeth, dentures. Dentures. He dont cough
up I'll go straight to Welfare. Maybe.]

(Rest)

Jabber comes running around the building. He sees Hester
and sneaks up on her, touching her arm.

JABBER. Yr it.
HESTER. I aint playing.
JABBER. K.
HESTER. Where you been.
JABBER. Out with Miga.
HESTER. Oh.

(Rest)

JABBER. Mommie?

HESTER. What.
JABBER.
HESTER.

(Rest)

JABBER. I dont like the moon.
HESTER. I'll cover it up for you. (*She holds her hand up in the*
sky)
JABBER. Whered it go?
HESTER. Its gone to bed. You too.

She nudges him from her lap. He curls up with the others.

HESTER.
HESTER.

Reverend D. comes outside. He carries a large neon cross.

HESTER. Its Sunday.

He sees the children.

REVEREND D. Oh God.
HESTER. Its Sunday. —. Yesterday was—Saturday.
REVEREND D. Excuse me a minute?

He props the cross against a wall.

HESTER. Its Sunday.
REVEREND D. I passed the plate and it came back empty.
HESTER. Oh.
REVEREND D. But not to worry: I'll have some. Tomorrow
morning—
HESTER. I was gonna—get myself fixed up.
REVEREND D. —When the bank opens. 100 bucks. Tomorrow
morning. All for you. You have my word.
HESTER. I was thinking, you know, in my head, that there
was something I can do to stop that hand coming down.
Must be something—
REVEREND D. I'll have my lawyer deliver the money. Its better
if you dont come back. Its too dangerous. My following
are an angry bunch. They dont like the likes of you.
HESTER. But you do. You like me.
REVEREND D. Youd better go.
HESTER. Why you dont like me? Why you dont like me no
more?

He tries to go back inside. She holds onto his leg.

HESTER. Dont go.
REVEREND D. Take yr hands off me.
HESTER. Why you dont like me?

She crawls her hands up his leg. He shakes his leg vio-
lently, trying to shake her loose. With great difficulty, he
shakes her loose.

REVEREND D.
HESTER.
REVEREND D.
HESTER.

Suffering is an enormous turn-on. He sits beside her and kindly touches her hair. She sits very still, appreciative of the attention. Then, in a swift motion, she raises her club to strike him. He is much stronger than she. He brutally twists her hand, wrenching the club from her grasp. She recoils in pain, Jabber, wide awake, watches.

REVEREND D. Slut.

(*Rest*)

Dont ever come back here again! Ever! Yll never get nothing from me! Common Slut. Tell on me! Go on! Tell the world! I'll crush you underfoot. (*He drops the club right beside her. He goes inside.*)

HESTER.

HESTER.

HESTER.

JABBER. Mommie.

HESTER.

HESTER.

JABBER. The moon came out again.

JABBER.

HESTER.

JABBER.

(*Rest*)

JABBER. Them bad boys had writing. On our house. Remember the writing they had on our house and you told me to read it and I didnt wanna I said I couldn't but that wasn't really true I could I can read but I didnt wanna.

HESTER. Hush up now.

JABBER. I was reading it but I was only reading it in my head I wasn't reading it with my mouth, I was reading it with my mouth but not with my tongue, I was reading it only with my lips and I could hear the word outloud but only outloud in my head.

HESTER. Shhhh.

JABBER. I didnt wanna say the word outloud in your head.

HESTER.

HESTER.

JABBER. I didnt wanna say you the word. You wanna know why I didnt wanna say you the word? You wanna know why? Mommie?

HESTER.

HESTER.

(*Rest*)

HESTER. What.

JABBER. It was a bad word.

HESTER.

HESTER.

JABBER. Wanna know what it was? Wanna know what the word was?

HESTER. What.

JABBER.

JABBER.

HESTER. What?

JABBER. "Slut."

HESTER. Go to sleep, Jabber.

JABBER. It read "Slut." "Slut."

HESTER. Hush up.

JABBER. Whassa "Slut"?

HESTER. Go sleep.

JABBER. You said if I read it youd say what it means. Slut. Whassit mean?

HESTER. I said I dont wanna hear that word. How slow are you? Slomo.

JABBER. Slut.

HESTER. You need to close yr mouth, Jabber.

JABBER. I know what it means. Slut.

HESTER (Shut up).

JABBER. Slut.

HESTER. (I said shut up, now).

JABBER. I know what it means.

HESTER (And I said Shut up! Shut up).

(*Rest*)
(*Rest*)

JABBER. Slut. Sorry.

The word just popped out, a childs joke. He covers his mouth, sheepishly. They look at each other.

HESTER.

JABBER.

HESTER.

JABBER.

She quickly raises her club and hits him once. Brutally. He cries out and falls down dead. His cry wakes Bully, Trouble and Beauty. They look on. Hester beats Jabber's body again and again and again. Trouble and Bully back away. Beauty stands there watching. Jabber is dead and bloody. Hester looks up from her deed to see Beauty who runs off. Hester stands there alone. Wet with her sons blood. Grief stricken, she cradles his body. Her hands wet with blood, she writes an A on the ground.

HESTER. Looks good, Jabber, dont it?
    Dont it, huh?

Sixth Confession: Hester, La Negrita "1 Shoulda Had A Hundred-Thousand"

HESTER, LA NEGRITA.
Never shoulda had him.

Never shoulda had none of em.
Never was nothing but a pain to me:
5 mistakes!
No, dont say that.
—nnnnnnnn—
Kids? Where you gone?
Never shoulda haddem.
Me walking around big as a house
Knocked up and Showing
and always by myself.
Men come near me oh yeah but then
love never sticks longer than a quick minute
wanna see something last forever watch
    water boil, you know.
I never shoulda haddem!

(*Rest*)
She places her hand in the pool of Jabbers blood.

No:
I shoulda had a hundred
a hundred
I shoulda had a hundred-thousand
A hundred-thousand a whole *army* full I
    shoulda!
I shoulda.
One right after the other! Spitting em out with
    no years in between!
One after another:
Tail to head:
Spitting em out:
Bad mannered Bad mouthed Bad Bad *Bastards*!
A whole *army full* I shoulda!
I shoulda
—nnnnnnn—
I shoulda

*She sits there, crumpled, alone. The prison bars come
down.*

SCENE NINE

THE PRISON DOOR

All circle Hester as they speak.

ALL:
    LOOK AT HER!
    WHO DOES SHE THINK
    SHE IS

THE ANIMAL
NO SKILLS
CEPT ONE
CANT READ CANT WRITE
SHE MARRIED?
WHAT DO YOU THINK?
SHE OUGHTA BE MARRIED
SHE AINT MARRIED
THATS WHY THINGS ARE BAD LIKE
    THEY ARE
CAUSE OF
GIRLS LIKE THAT
THAT EVER HAPPEN TO ME YOU
    WOULDNT SEE ME DOING THAT
YOU WOULDNT SEE THAT HAPPENING TO ME
WHO THE HELL SHE THINK SHE IS
AND NOW SHES GOT TO PAY FOR IT
HAH!

They spit.

ALL:
    SHE DONT GOT NO SKILLS
    CEPT ONE
    CANT READ CANT WRITE
    SHE MARRIED?
    WHAT DO YOU THINK?
    JUST PLAIN STUPID IF YOU ASK ME
        AINT NO SMART WOMAN GOT ALL
        THEM BASTARDS
    AND NOT A PENNY TO HER NAME
    SOMETHINGS GOTTA BE DONE
    CAUSE I'LL BE DAMNED IF SHE GONNA
        LIVE OFF ME
WELFARE. IS SHE IN ANY PAIN?
DOCTOR. SHE SHOULDNT BE. SHE WONT
    BE HAVING ANYMORE CHILDREN.
WELFARE. NO MORE MISTAKES.
CHILLI. WHATS THAT?
WELFARE. AN A.
AMIGA. AN A.
DOCTOR. FIRST LETTER OF THE ALPHABET.
WELFARE. THATS AS FAR AS SHE GOT.

*Hester holds up her hands. Theyre covered with blood. She
looks up with outstretched arms.*

HESTER. Big hand coming down on me. Big hand coming
    down on me. Big hand coming down on me—

END OF PLAY

TOPICS FOR CRITICAL THINKING AND WRITING

The Play on the PAGE

1. On the evidence of the play, how responsible is Hester herself for her impoverished condition?
2. Do you think the characters of Reverend D. and the Welfare Lady are caricatured? Why do you think Parks draws them so broadly?
3. What about the ubiquitous role of sex in the play? Does this relate to a form of exploitation that is independent of social class?

4. If you can, read *The Scarlet Letter* and make your own comparisons.
5. Are you bothered by the play's radical shift in language from realistic dialogue to poetic solioquy?

The Play on the STAGE

6. What about Parks's instructions for each actor (save Hester) to play both an adult *and* a child? Can you envisage a production with actual children in the requisite roles?
7. The director and the designer of the original production sat the audience on two sides of the stage action. Why do you think this was done?

8. How realistic should stage detail be? Should *everything* be suggested or not?
9. Conceive of an alternate way of staging *In the Blood* that is faithful to your understanding of the play.

The Play in PERFORMANCE

In the Blood opened in November 1999 at The Joseph Papp Public Theater and ran for 55 performances. It played in the smallest of the Public's theater spaces, the 99-seat Shiva Theater. Director David Esbjornson's production, in critic Michael Feingold's words, "virtually invites you to open the discussion there and then, by seating the audience on the two long sides of the rectangular space, so that you can watch your fellow theatergoers react to Hester's travails." Of the many excellent reviews the play and production received, none was more eloquent than the *New York Times* review written *not* by one of the staff theater critics, but by a critic-at-large.

MARGO JEFFERSON
The Scarlet Letter, *Alive and Bitter in the Inner City**

Artists talk with one another across the centuries: they talk about their obsessions, their ancestors, the particulars of their time and place and about whatever can go beyond the particular to take on a new life.

New York Times 23 Nov. 1999: E 1.5.

Suzan-Lori Parks's extraordinary new play, *In the Blood*, which opened last night at the Public Theater, is a conversation with—a revision of, a set of improvisations on—Nathaniel Hawthorne's *Scarlet Letter*. Ms. Parks and Hawthorne share an obsession with American history and the large patterns of sin, cruelty, punishment and redemption that give it form and content. Hawthorne was the descendant of Salem, Mass., Puritans who persecuted Quakers, denounced witches and had their deeds recorded in the annals of New England history. His fiction unveiled and sought to redeem those ancestral crimes; in his introduction to *The Scar-*

let Letter he vowed: "I, the present writer, as their representative, hereby take shame upon myself for their sakes, and pray that any curse incurred by them . . . may be now and henceforth removed." Ms. Parks is the inheritor of an African-American history much of which has gone, in her words, "unrecorded, dismembered, washed out"; her task, she says in an essay called "Possession," is "to locate the ancestral burial ground, dig for bones, find bones, hear the bones sing, write it down."

This time around we are in New York, not Salem. The adulteress is Hester, La Negrita, played—no, embodied with stunning coherence—by Charlayne Woodard. She is a woman on welfare living under a bridge with her five children. Like Hester Prynne, she offers tortured assertions of her responsibility. ("My life's my own fault. I know that. But the world don't help. . . . I ain't afraid of hard work. It's a leg up. Can't start from the top.") But she, too, is being ground down by a society that wields power pitilessly and, when it sees fit, vengefully. (Hester Prynne longed to be the prophetess for a new truth that would "establish the whole relation between man and woman on a surer ground of mutual happiness." Three centuries later Hester can only say bleakly, "I don't think the world likes women much." As for the people around her, they are just a little more powerful (therefore better at being selfish) or just a little more canny (therefore better at manipulating things).

In the Blood is about the way we live now, and it is truly harrowing, (What is "in" Hester's blood, as the world sees it? Sin, sluttishness, the lower-class racial weakness that leads to sloth and reckless procreation.) We cannot turn away, and we do not want to. The play strikes us as Hawthorne claimed his first glimpse of the scarlet letter struck him: with "a sensation not altogether physical yet almost so, as of burning heat, as if the letter were not of red cloth but red-hot iron."

This Hester can't read or write. Her oldest son, Jabber (Rob Campbell), is supposed to be teaching her, but she hasn't gotten past A. She certainly can't make out the word "slut" scrawled on a nearby wall, and Jabber won't read it for her. They live on mean words and slim chances. Her son Trouble (Bruce MacVittie) steals a policeman's club, her daughter Bully (Gail Grate) sleeps with her hands in fists; her youngest, Baby (Reggie Montgomery), is learning how to smash the soda cans that earn them small change at the local supermarket.

Still, when we first see them all sitting around Hester as she ladles out a dinner of soup, there's a tenuous sweetness there, she is trying so hard to keep them together as a family. Then, when Hester makes up a bedtime story in which a princess changes the law of the land and gets to marry all five of the men who court her, we realize that those folk tales we love so would be narratives of misery and woe if poor and powerless storytellers hadn't invented supernatural forces to save the day.

Having no recourse to those forces, Hester's path leads no place but down. She is hungry all the time (the children get whatever food she has), and the world is eating her up. There is the doctor with the community street practice (Mr. MacVittie), her snappy drug-besotted white friend, The Amiga Gringa (Deirdre O'Connell), The Welfare Lady in the prim pink suit (Ms. Grate), the minister who is building his own church (Mr. Montgomery) and Chilli (Mr. Campbell), Jabber's father and her first love. Every one of them has used her for sex. And they try or pretend they will try to do better by her, especially the Rev. D. who is the father of Baby and promises child support money if she keeps quiet.

These exchanges are taut and packed. Ms. Parks's writing has grown leaner and hungrier since plays like *The Death of the Last Black Man on Earth* and *Venus*, with their layers of historical allusion and soliloquy-like dialogue. Here the dialogue alternates with beautifully timed and paced confessions from each character, delivered in a square of harsh white light. The confessions strip these people down to their bare selves with an insistence that comes as much from the anguished intimacy of Adrienne Kennedy's, plays as from Hawthorne: "Times are tough: what can we do?" asks the doctor. "There's a mama dog running loose and her puppies are crying because there's not / there's not enough food for those poor little pups / and the pups grow into dogs unhousebroken and ill-mannered with families of their own." The caseworker is a black woman, too. "I walk the line / between us and them / between our kind and their kind" she reminds us.

The Amiga Gringa regrets the money they could have made together as Chocolate and Vanilla: "We coulda done a sex show behind a curtain / Then make a movie and sell it / for 3 bucks a peek." The Rev. D. confides that suffering is an enormous turn-on, up to the moment when he realizes that through Hester, God "wants to drag me down / and sit me at the table / at the head of the table of her fatherless house." And Chilli, the long-gone lover who comes back to town looking for her, still remembers the days when they were so desperate to make love in a car, all-American-boy-and-girl style, they would go to a vacant lot and "sneak in those rusted Buicks that hadn't moved in years / and I would sit at the wheel and pretend to drive / and she would say she felt the wind in her face."

And finally there is Hester, moving toward tragedy, shadowed by "a big dark thing Blocking the sun out. Like the hand of fate."

This potent and terrible sense of being closed in with the characters is heightened by the fact that, apart from Ms. Woodard, each actor plays both a child and an adult. The director, David Esbjornson, has made them into a real ensemble, though I think he could encourage them to bring out more of the humor—stark and dissonant, but humor nevertheless—in the text. This is especially true of Reggie Montgomery's performance. When it comes to characters who like to season corruption with wit, Mr. Montgomery is a master: but at the moment his Rev. D. is in the grip of too many melodramatic flourishes.

Gail Grate is especially good as both the needy daughter and the repressive Welfare Lady, while Rob Campbell gives Jabber real sweetness and Chilli a languid, playful menace. The stage, with just the bare necessities, could easily be a street just blocks away from the theater: the lighting, clothing, sound (subways, harsh rhythmic music) intensify without showing off. (Kudos to Narelle Sissons, Elizabeth Hope, Clancy, Jane Cox, Don DiNicola.)

You will leave *In the Blood* feeling pity and terror. And because it is a work of art, you will leave thrilled, even comforted by its mastery.

BONNIE METZGAR AND SUZAN-LORI PARKS
*Alien Baby: An Interview**

Metzgar: What was your impulse for In the Blood*? How did it begin?*

Suzan-Lori Parks: I was writing a play called *Fucking A*, a futuristic version of *The Scarlet Letter*. I was having a lot of difficulty with it, and about a year ago I got into a conversation with the characters in the play. To make a long story short, I decided to change the names of all the characters. The main character had been called Hester, and I decided to change her name to something else. I began writing *Fucking A* afresh, and Hester said, "What about the play that I'm in?" I listened to what she had to say and let her lead me to a story about a woman with five kids.

For a long time I called this play my "alien baby," because its birth had that feeling like the scene in *Alien* where the alien leaps out of the scientist's chest. It felt just like that, the play burst out of my chest—boom! the writing process had such a strong and totally terrifying feeling. I wrote a draft, and something wasn't right. Then I realized what it was: The whole play is like a series of woodcuts. The texture of the first draft was wrong; it needed the feeling of a woodcut—very plain and spare—so I wrote the next draft with that feeling in mind.

You, together with a number of other contemporary writers are often called "language playwrights." How do you feel about that?

It always makes me laugh. People think I'm this writer who loves language. I do, but I love people more. The Greeks have always been my favorite plays. Shakespeare too. Where people are pressed and that sweet and painful language issues forth like wine. That's what I love. A lot of people say that a language play is just about language. Like language plays have to be language-gymnastics plays, where people are mostly just flipping words around. Language is not interesting to me unless it is rooted by the balls in some kind of reality—reality as it exists within the context of the play. Reality can be anything. I hate language that's just words floating around.

I'm just thinking about what you're saying: Language means nothing unless it is rooted by the balls.

Women have balls too. I'm not using balls completely in the gender/biological specific sense. I'm using them in a spiritual sense. (*laughter*) The language of the play should come from people's guts—what they want, what they don't want, what they're going through, what they're not going through, what they're thinking. I also like plays that have activity, where people are doing things. *In the Blood* is filled with people doing

**Public Access* [magazine/program of the Joseph Papp Public Theater], Nov. 1999: 50–58.

things. People think language plays are plays where people are just talking poetically, and there's no action, there's no activity. But that's silly. Shakespeare's plays are "language plays" but they're also filled with action.

You've re-read all of Shakespeare in the last year. Is there a direct relationship between reading and your writing, or is it harder to discern?

Shakespeare can write. That's the biggest thing I learned. He can really, really, really write. (*laughter*) It sounds silly to say that over and over, but where so many playwrights write these throwaway lines that have no guts, no balls, no oomph, he packs his lines with so much intensity and action and passion and emotion. He reminds me of how much language can do . . .

Shakespeare speaks through all of his characters.

Exactly. People always wonder which character speaks for the playwright, as if there is one character who stands for the writer, who presents his or her point of view, and the other characters sort of assist in elucidating that point. I don't think Shakespeare has a single point of view. That's why he's such a good writer. I learn from his ability to have a passion and not only one point of view. In *In the Blood*, there's Hester, she's a black woman, so people think she must be the voice of the playwright. And if not Hester it must be the Welfare Lady. Actually, the voice of the playwright is in all the characters equally. . . . The playwright stands behind the gap in the curtain but you cannot see where the gap is. Where is the playwright? Everywhere and nowhere. The characters speak for me but also beyond me. They know much more than I do. They speak from a deep well of knowledge—the intelligence of the Jungian collective unconscious. The voices of the characters are much larger than the voice of the playwright.

The thing about In the Blood *that is different from your previous work is that it appears to be something familiar—a mother of five children struggling to survive. There's something so simple about its structure, and yet I've never seen anything turn the way that it turns.*

The play came from a place that was bigger than me. I write very carefully and very intensely, but I do not spend a lot of time trying to figure out the "meaning"

of the play. So there's a lot about this play that is mysterious to me.

The play reads on the page as something really dark about the trouble in our society, but it doesn't play that way. Do you think the humor is in the text, or in the actors' performances?

There's a lot of humor in the play. It's not that I intentionally laid in humor to offset the dark bleak social commentary or anything like that. It's just that, if you write truthfully, you have to show the whole picture—the bleak stuff and the funny stuff. People are sometimes uncomfortable with the fact that there is humor within the bleakness, or bleakness within the humor. They like things in black and white, without complexity.

This is your third play to be produced at The Public, but your professional relationship with George C. Wolfe goes back to the BACA days, doesn't it?

George came to see *The Death of the Last Black Man in the Whole Entire World* at BACA and was very supportive, and he said then, "I'm going to do your plays" before he even had a theater. Then he came to a reading of *The America Play* at New Dramatists. [The play was produced at The Public in Wolfe's first season as Producer, 1993–94]. One of the first things of his I saw was his Haitian *Caucasian Chalk Circle*, which featured Charlayne Woodard and Reggie Montgomery [both cast members of *In the Blood*]. I remember Charlayne and Reggie in that play; they blew me away. I wrote an article about George Wolfe's *Caucasian Chalk Circle* for the *New York Times*. I interviewed him, and he talked a mile a minute (*laughter*). Actually, *In the Blood* feels like a BACA Downtown theater experience; maybe it's the size of the house [99 seats]. It's a good feeling. I still have a "small theater" mind. I like writing plays that don't have huge set requirements. You could do this play on a bare stage.

There's something about the economics that underscores the play's urgency—it feels like a play that needs to be heard now. This is a now play.

It makes me feel like I'm doing theater, something thats raw and necessary and alive. The play feels so bursting with life.

I want to ask you one last question about the song in the play which you've written. You're a musician—you play harmonica and studied cello, and most recently you're learning to play blues guitar. Is there anything you want to say about the song?

The song is called "The Looking Song". It's a country-western love song. It starts with the line "I'm looking for someone to lose my looks with." I'm looking for someone I can deteriorate with, which I think is what true love is all about. The whole play is all about love. All my plays are about love. And history.

WRITING ABOUT DRAMA

BASIC MATTERS

Why Write?

People write about plays because they want to clarify and to account for their responses to works that interest, excite, or frustrate them. In order to put words on paper, we have to take a second and a third look at what is in front of us and at what is within us. Writing, then, is a way of learning. The last word is never said about complex thoughts and feelings, but when we write, we hope to make at least a little progress in the difficult but rewarding job of talking about our responses. We learn, and then we hope to interest our reader because we are communicating our responses to something that for one reason or another is worth talking about.

This communication is, in effect, teaching. You may think that you are writing for the teacher, but such a belief is a misconception; when you write, *you* are the teacher. An essay on a play is an attempt to help someone see the play as you do. If this chapter had to be boiled down to a single sentence of advice, that sentence would be: Because you are teaching, your essay should embody those qualities that you value in teachers—probably intelligence, open-mindedness, effort, and certainly a desire to offer what help you can.

Analysis

Analysis is, literally, a separation into parts in order to understand. An analysis commonly considers one part and the relation of this part to the whole. For example, it may consider only the functions of the setting in *The Sandbox*, or of the music in *Death of a Salesman*.

Analysis is not a process used only in talking about literature. It is commonly applied in thinking about almost any complex matter. Steffi Graf plays a deadly game of tennis; what makes it so good? How does her backhand contribute to her game? What does her serve do to the opponent? Because a play is usually long and complicated, in a paper written for a college course you probably do not have enough space to analyze all aspects of the play, and so you will probably choose only one and relate it to the whole. Of course, all of the parts are related; a study of one character, for example, will have to take some account of other characters and of the plot and perhaps even of the setting. Nevertheless, an analysis may legitimately devote most of its space to one part, taking account of other parts only insofar as they are relevant to the topic.

Finding a Topic

If a work is fairly long and complex and if you are writing only a few pages, almost surely you will write an analysis of some part. Unless you have an enormous amount of time for reflection and revision, you cannot write a meaningful essay of five hundred or even a thousand words on *Oedipus* or *The Cherry Orchard*. You cannot even write on "Character in *Oedipus*" or "Symbolism in *The Cherry Orchard*." In any case, you probably won't want to write on such topics anyway. Probably *one* character or *one* symbol has caught your interest. Trust your feelings; you are probably onto something interesting, and it will be best to think about this smaller topic for the relatively few hours that you have.

A "smaller" topic need not be dull or trivial; treated properly, it may illuminate the entire work, or, to change the metaphor, it may serve as a mine shaft that gives entry to the work. "The Dramatic Function of the Gravedigger's Comedy" or "Does Hamlet Lapse into Fatalism?," carefully thought about, will in five hundred or a thousand words tell a reader more (and will have taught its author more) than will "*Hamlet* as a Tragedy." Similarly, "Imagery of Disease in *Hamlet*" is a better topic than "Imagery in *Hamlet*," and "The Meanings of 'Rashness' in *Hamlet*" is a better topic than "The Meaning of *Hamlet*."

Every play affords its own topics for analysis, and every essayist must set forth his or her own thesis (argument), but a few useful generalizations may be made. You can often find a thesis by asking one of two questions:

• **What is this doing?** That is, why is this scene in the play? Why are these lines verse and those lines prose? Why is a certain action reported to us rather than represented on the stage? What is the significance of the parts of the work? (Titles are often highly significant parts of the work: Ibsen's *A Doll's House* and Chekhov's *The Cherry Orchard* would be slightly different if they had other titles.)

• **Why do I have this response?** Why do I find this scene clever, moving, or puzzling? How did the author make this character funny, dignified, or pathetic? How did he or she communicate the idea that this character is a bore without boring me?

The first of these questions, "What is this doing?" requires that you identify yourself with the dramatist, wondering, for example, whether this opening scene is the best possible for this story. The second question, "Why do I have this response?" requires that you trust your feelings. If you are amused, bored, puzzled, or annoyed, assume that these responses are appropriate and follow them up, at least until a rereading of the play provides other responses.

On pages 1483–1484 we suggest many questions that you can ask yourself in order to stimulate ideas for an essay, but here we briefly suggest a few topics:

- Compare two somewhat similar characters.
- Discuss the function of a relatively minor character.
- Compare a play with a film version of the play (what has been added, what omitted, and why?).
- Write the director's notes for one scene.

From Topic to Thesis

How do you find a topic and then turn it into a thesis, that is, a point you want to make? An idea may hit you suddenly. For example, as you are reading you may find yourself jotting in the margin, "Contrast with Nora's earlier response," or "Note the change of costume," or "too heavy irony," or "ugh." Alternatively, an idea may come slowly on rereading. For example, perhaps you gradually become aware that in *Antigonê* the chorus may not be a static character but changes its views as the play progresses. At this point, then, you have a thesis—an angle—as well as a topic.

Think of it this way: A topic is a subject, and a thesis is an assertion about a subject. "Imagery in *Hamlet*" is a topic, but it can be turned into a thesis thus: "Im-

agery helps to distinguish the characters in *Hamlet*." Once you can formulate a thesis, you are well on the way to writing a good paper. Note that the more precise the formulation of the thesis, the better the paper will probably be. After all, "Imagery in *Hamlet* is interesting" is a thesis, but such a vague assertion gives you little to go on. Not until you can turn it into something such as "Imagery in *Hamlet* serves three important purposes" are you anywhere near being able to draft your essay.

Following is a short essay written by a student. The student told us privately that when she began work on the paper she was planning to write on the irrationality of the fairies in *A Midsummer Night's Dream* as a sort of mirror of the irrationality of the young lovers, but when she searched the play for supporting detail she found, to her surprise, that she had to revise her thesis.

Her earliest jottings—a sort of preliminary outline and guide to rereading the play—looked like this:

fairies--like lovers, irrational?
  Puck
    mischievous
  Titania and Oberon
    equally quarrelsome?
      quarrel disturbs human world
    Titania wants Indian boy
      isn't she right?
        if so, she's not irrational
    Oberon   ——
      jealous
      cruel to Titania?
      unfaithful?
  Other fairies
    do they do anything?
      T's different from O's?

In rereading the play and in jotting down notes, she came to see that the supernatural characters were not as malicious and irrational as she had thought, and so she changed the focus of her thesis. She wrote her notes on 3-by-5-inch index cards, but many students prefer to use a word processor. Beginning on page 1496 we offer suggestions about using a word processor.

A Sample Analysis

Fairy Mischief and Morality and

<u>A Midsummer Night's Dream</u>

Title is informative.

If we read <u>A Midsummer Night's Dream</u> casually, or come away from a delightful performance, we may have the vague impression that the fairies are wild, mischievous, willful creatures who perhaps represent the irrational qualities of mankind. But in fact the text lends only a little support to this view. The irrationality of mankind is really represented chiefly by the human beings in the play--we are told in the first scene, for example, that Demetrius used to love Helena, but now loves Hermia--and the fairies are really largely responsible for the happy ending finally achieved.

Opening paragraph leads into the subject.

It is, of course, easy to see why we may think of the fairies as wild and mischievous. Titania and Oberon have quarreled over a little Indian boy, and their quarrel has led to fogs, floods, and other disorders in nature. Moreover, Titania accuses Oberon of infidelity, and Oberon returns the charge:

> How canst thou thus for shame, Titania
>
> Glance at my credit with Hippolyta,
>
> Knowing I know thy love to Theseus?
>
> (2.1.74-76)[1]

Short quotation provides evidence.

Titania rejects this countercharge, saying "These are the forgeries of jealousy" (2.1.81), but we are not convinced of her innocence. It would be easy to give additional examples of speeches in which the king and queen of fairyland present unflattering pictures of each other, but probably one of the strongest pieces of evidence of their alleged irrationality is the fact that Oberon causes Titania to fall in love with the asinine Bottom. We should not forgot, however, that later Oberon will take pity on her: "Her dotage now I do begin to pity" (4.1.45).

Citation in parentheses reduces the number of footnotes.

In fact, it is largely through Oberon's sense of pity--this time for the quarreling young lovers in the forest--that the lovers finally are successfully paired off. And we should remember, too, before we

---

[1]All quotations from this play are from the text reprinted in Sylvan Barnet et al., <u>Types of Drama,</u> 8th ed. (New York: Longman, 2001). Further references to the play will be given parenthetically, within the text of the essay.

Footnote gives source and explains that other footnotes will not be necessary.

claim that the fairies are consistently quarrelsome and mischievous, that at the very end of the play Oberon and Titania join in a song and dance blessing the newlyweds and promising healthy offspring. The fairies, though quarrelsome, are fundamentally benevolent spirits.

The main point having been set forth, essayist now turns to an apparent exception.

But what of Robin Goodfellow, the Puck of the play? Is he not mischievous? One of the fairies says Robin is a "shrewd and knavish sprite" (2.1.33) who frightens maids and plays tricks on housewives; Robin admits the charge, saying "Thou speakest aright" (2.1.42), and two lines later he says "I jest to Oberon, and make him smile," and

Essayist concedes a point but then goes on in the rest of the paragraph to argue that the main point nevertheless still holds.

then he goes on to describe some of his practical jokes, including his fondness for neighing to tease a horse, and pulling a stool from under an old lady. But this is not quite the whole story. The fact is, despite this speech, that we do <u>not</u> see Robin engage in any mischievous pranks. After all, he does not deliberately anoint the eyes of the wrong Athenian lover. Oberon tells Robin that he will recognize the young man by his Athenian clothing, and when Puck encounters a young man in Athenian clothing he anoints the youth's eyes. The fault is really Oberon's, though of course Oberon meant well when he instructed Robin:

> A sweet Athenian lady is in love
> With a disdainful youth. Anoint his eyes;
> But do it when the next thing he espies
> May be the lady.
>
> (2.1.260–263)

So Robin's error is innocent. He is speaking honestly when he says, "Believe me, king of shadows, I mistook" (3.2.348). Of course he does enjoy the confusion he mistakenly causes, but we can hardly blame him severely for that. After all, we enjoy it, too.

Concluding paragraph summarizes, but it does not merely repeat what has come before; it offers a few brief new quotations. The paragraph ends by setting the conclusion (fairies are decent) in a fresh context (it's the mortals who are irrational).

The fairies, by their very nature, of course suggest a mysterious, irrational world, but--even though, as we have just seen, Oberon is called the "king of shadows"--they are not to be confused with "ghosts, wand'ring here and there," "damned spirits" who "willfully themselves exile from light/And must for aye consort with black-browed night" (3.2.382–388). Oberon explicitly says, after this speech, "But we are spirits of another sort," and his speech is filled with references not to darkness but to light: "morning," "eastern gate," "blessed beams." The closer we observe them in the play, then, the

```
closer their behavior is to that of normal, decent human beings. There
is plenty of irrationality in the play, but it is found for the most
```

Notice that this first-rate essay:

- Has a thesis, an argument
- Develops the thesis effectively

Notice also that:

- The title gives the reader some idea of what is coming.
- The first paragraph clearly sets forth the thesis.
- The essay next takes up the evidence that might seem to contradict the thesis—Oberon and Titania, and Robin Goodfellow—and it shows that this evidence is not decisive.
- The essay continues to move the thesis forward, substantiating it, especially with well-chosen quotations.
- The last paragraph slightly restates the thesis in light of what the essay has demonstrated.

Writing a Review

Your instructor may ask you to write a review of a local production. A review requires analytic skill, but it is not identical to an analysis. First of all, a reviewer normally assumes that the reader is unfamiliar with the production being reviewed and unfamiliar with the play if the play is not a classic. Thus, the first paragraph usually provides a helpful introduction.

Inevitably some retelling of the plot is necessary if the play is new, and a summary of a sentence or two is acceptable even for a familiar play. However, the focus of the review is on:

- Describing
- Analyzing
- Evaluating (most especially)

(By the way, don't confuse description with analysis. Description tells what something—for instance, the set or the costumes—looks like; analysis tells how it works, what it adds up to, and what it contributes to the total effect.) If the play is new, much of the evaluation may center on the play itself, but if the play is a classic, the evaluation probably will be devoted chiefly to the acting, the set, and the direction.

Here are other points to consider:

- **Save the playbill;** it will give you the names of the actors, and perhaps a brief biography of the author, a synopsis of the plot, and a photograph of the set, all of which may be helpful.
- **Draft your review as soon as possible,** while the performance is still fresh in your mind. If you can't draft it immediately after seeing the play, at least jot down some notes about the setting and the staging, the acting, and the audience's response.
- If possible, **read the play**—ideally, before the performance and again after it.
- **In your first draft, don't worry about limitations of space;** write as long a review as you can, putting down everything that comes to mind. Later you can cut it to the required length, retaining only the chief points and the necessary supporting details. In your first draft, try to produce a fairly full record of the performance and your response to it, so that a day or two later, when you are working on a revision, you won't have to trust a fading memory for details.

We include numerous reviews in this book; further, if you read reviews of plays in *Time, Newsweek,* or a newspaper, you will soon develop a sense of what reviews normally do.

The following example, an undergraduate's review of a college production of *Macbeth,* is typical except in one respect: Because *Macbeth* is so widely known, the reviewer has chosen not to risk offending her readers by telling them that *Macbeth* is a tragedy by Shakespeare. If the review were of a new play, it probably would include a few sentences summarizing the plot and classifying the play (a tragedy, a farce, a rock musical, or whatever), perhaps briefly putting it into the context of the author's other works.

A Sample Review

Title implies thesis.

An Effective <u>Macbeth</u>

Opening paragraph is
informative, letting the reading
know the reviewer's overall
attitude.

    <u>Macbeth</u> at the University Theater is a thoughtful and occasion-
ally exciting production, partly because the director, Mark Urice, has
trusted Shakespeare and has not imposed a gimmick on the play. The
characters do not wear cowboy costumes as they did in last year's production of <u>A Midsummer Night's Dream</u>.

Reviewer promptly turns to a
major issue.

    Probably the chief problem confronting a director of <u>Macbeth</u> is
how to present the witches so that they are powerful supernatural
forces and not silly things that look as though they came from a
Halloween party. Urice gives us ugly but not absurdly grotesque
witches, and he introduces them most effectively. The stage seems to
be a bombed-out battlefield littered with rocks and great chunks of
earth, but some of these begin to stir--the earth seems to come alive--
and the clods move, unfold, and become the witches, dressed in brown
and dark gray rags. The suggestion is that the witches are a part of
nature, elemental forces that can hardly be escaped. This effect is
increased by the moans and creaking noises that they make, all of
which could be comic but which in this production are impressive.

First sentence of this paragraph
provides an effective transition.

    The witches' power over Macbeth is further emphasized by their
actions. When the witches first meet Macbeth, they encircle him, touch
him, caress him, even embrace him, and he seems helpless, almost their
plaything. Moreover, in the scene in which he imagines that he sees a
dagger, the director has arranged for one of the witches to appear,
stand near Macbeth, and guide his hand toward the invisible dagger.
This is, of course, not in the text, but the interpretation is reasonable rather than intrusive. Finally, near the end of the play, just
before Macduff kills Macbeth, a witch appears and laughs at Macbeth as
Macduff explains that he was not "born of woman." There is no doubt
that throughout the tragedy Macbeth has been a puppet of the witches.

Paragraph begins with a broad assertion and then offers supporting
details.

    Stephen Beers (Macbeth) and Tina Peters (Lady Macbeth) are excel-
lent. Beers is sufficiently brawny to be convincing as a battlefield
hero, but he also speaks the lines sensitively, so the audience feels
that in addition to being a hero, he is a man of gentleness. One can
believe Lady Macbeth when she says that she fears he is "too full o'
the milk of human kindness" to murder Duncan. Lady Macbeth is especially effective in the scene in which she asks the spirits to "unsex

her." During this speech she is reclining on a bed and as she delivers the lines she becomes increasingly sexual in her bodily motions, deriving excitement from her own stimulating words. Her attachment to Macbeth is strongly sexual, and so is his attraction to her. The scene when she persuades him to kill Duncan ends with them passionately embracing. The strong attraction of each for the other, so evident in the early part of the play, disappears after the murder, when Macbeth keeps his distance from Lady Macbeth and does not allow her to touch him. The acting of the other performers is effective, except for John Berens (Duncan), who recites the lines mechanically and seems not to take much account of their meaning.

Reference is made to a particular scene.

The set consists of a barren plot at the rear of which stands a spidery framework of piping of the sort used by construction companies, supporting a catwalk. This framework fits with the costumes (lots of armor, leather, heavy boots), suggesting a sort of elemental, primitive, and somewhat sadistic world. The catwalk, though effectively used when Macbeth goes off to murder Duncan (whose room is presumably upstairs and offstage) is not much used in later scenes. For the most part it is an interesting piece of scenery but it is not otherwise helpful. For instance, there is no reason why the scene with Macduff's wife and children is staged on it. The costumes are not in any way Scottish--no plaids--but in several scenes the sound of a bagpipe is heard, adding another weird or primitive tone to the production.

Reviewer provides description and analysis.

Concrete details support evaluation.

This <u>Macbeth</u> appeals to the eye, the ear, and the mind. The director has given us a unified production that makes sense and that is faithful to the spirit of Shakespeare's play.

Summary is given.

Much of what we want to say about this review we have already said in our marginal notes, but three additional points should be made:

- The reviewer's feelings and evaluations are clearly expressed, not in such expressions as "furthermore, I feel," or "it is also my opinion," but in such expressions as "a thoughtful and occasionally exciting production," "excellent," and "appeals to the eye, the ear, and the mind."
- The evaluations are supported by details. For instance, the evaluation that the witches are effectively presented is supported by a brief description of their appearance.

- The reviewer is courteous, even when (as in the discussion of the catwalk, in the next-to-last paragraph) she is talking about aspects of the production she doesn't care for.

Writing a Comparison

Something should be said about an essay organized around a comparison or a contrast between, for example, two characters (in one play or even in two plays). Probably a student's first thought, after making some notes, is to discuss half of the comparison and then go on to the second half. Instructors and textbooks usually condemn such an organization, arguing that the essay breaks into two parts and that the second part involves a good deal of repetition of categories set up in the first part. Usually they recommend that the student organize his or her thoughts differently, somewhat along these lines:

1. First similarity
   a. First work (or character, or characteristic)
   b. Second work
2. Secondary similarity
   a. First work
   b. Second work
3. First difference
   a. First work
   b. Second work
4. Second difference
   a. First work
   b. Second work

The pattern would continue for as many additional differences as are considered relevant. For example, if one wishes to compare King Oedipus with Willy Loman, one may organize the material this way:

1. Each figure is a person of authority (first similarity)
   a. Oedipus
   b. Willy
2. Each figure is ignorant (second similarity)
   a. Oedipus is ignorant of the facts of his birth
   b. Willy is ignorant of his abilities
3. Stage at which the characters attain self-knowledge (first difference)
   a. Oedipus is ignorant until very late in the play
   b. Willy perhaps is ignorant right up to his death

Another way of organizing a comparison and contrast is to do so by presenting the information one point at a time. For example, if we use the same example that focuses on King Oedipus and Willy Loman, the organization of the material might look like this:

1. Lack of self-knowledge (first point)
   a. Similarities between Oedipus and Willy
   b. Differences between Oedipus and Willy
2. The corrupt world (second point)
   a. Similarities between the worlds in *Oedipus* and *Salesman*
   b. Differences between the worlds in *Oedipus* and *Salesman*
3. Degree of attainment of self-knowledge (third point)
   a. Similarities between Oedipus and Willy
   b. Differences between Oedipus and Willy

A Simple, Effective Organization for a Comparison

However, a comparison need not employ either of these structures. There is even the danger that an essay employing either of them may not come into focus until the essayist stands back from the seven-layer cake and announces, in the concluding paragraph, that the odd layers taste better. In your preparatory thinking, you may want to make comparisons in pairs (Faults: Oedipus and Willy; Relationship to wife: Oedipus and Willy; Comments by others: The chorus on Oedipus, Ben on Willy . . .), but you must come to some conclusions about what these add up to before writing the final version. This final version should not duplicate your thought processes; rather, it should be organized to make the point clearly and effectively. After reflection, you may believe that although there are superficial similarities between Oedipus and Willy, there are essential differences; then in the finished essay you probably will not wish to obscure the main point by jumping back and forth from play to play, working through a series of similarities and differences. It may be better to discuss Willy and then point out that, although Oedipus resembles him in A, B, and C, Oedipus in D, E, and F, does *not* resemble Willy. Some repetition in the second half of the essay (for example, "Oedipus comes very late to deep self-knowledge but Willy seems never to come to it") will serve to bind the two halves into a meaningful whole, making clear the degree of similarity or difference.

The point of the essay presumably is not to list pairs of similarities or differences but to illuminate a work, or works, by making a thoughtful comparison. Although in a long essay you cannot postpone until page 15 a discussion of the second half of the comparison, in an essay of, say, fewer than ten pages nothing is wrong with setting forth the first half of the comparison and then, in light of it, the second half. The essay will break into two unrelated parts if the second half makes no use of the first or if it fails to modify the first half, but this will not happen if the second half looks back to the first half and calls attention to differences that the new material reveals.

Communicating Judgments

Because a critical essay on a play is a judicious attempt to help a reader understand what is going on in a work or in a part of a work, the voice of the critic sounds, on first hearing, impartial. However, good criticism includes—at least implicitly—evaluation. You can say not only that the setting changes (a neutral expression) but also that "the playwright aptly shifts the setting" or "unconvincingly introduces a new character," or "effectively juxtaposes . . ." Support these evaluations with evidence. As we have already pointed out in our discussion of the review of *Macbeth*, reveal your feelings about the work under discussion not by continually saying "I feel" and "this moves me," but by calling attention to the degree of success or failure you perceive. Nothing is wrong with occasionally using "I." In fact, noticeable avoidance of it—using instead passives such as "it is felt," and devices such as "this writer," "we," and the like—suggests an offensive sham modesty, but too much talk of "I" makes a writer sound like an egomaniac.

Asking Questions to Get Answers

The next two pages are devoted to helping you to find topics to write about. We have already suggested that you can often find a thesis by asking two questions: "What is this doing?" and "Why do I have this response?" In the sections following we suggest many additional questions, but first we want to mention that the editorial apparatus throughout this book is intended to help you to read, enjoy, and discuss drama as fully as possible. When you are sitting down to write about a play, you may want to reread some parts of this apparatus for guidance on your topic, perhaps paying special attention to the Glossary entries on **character, convention, dialogue, diction, foil, irony, motivation, plot, suspense,** and **unity.** You may also want to reread some of the earlier material in the book, especially "The Language of Drama" and the questions that follow each play.

Following are additional questions that may help you to find topics and to sharpen a topic into a thesis.

Plot and conflict

- Does the exposition introduce elements that will be ironically fulfilled? During the exposition, do you perceive things differently from the way the characters do?
- Are certain happenings or situations recurrent? If so, what significance do you attach to them?
- If there is more than one plot, do the plots seem to you to be related? Is one plot clearly the main plot and another plot a sort of subplot, a minor variation on the theme?
- Do any scenes strike you as irrelevant?
- Are certain scenes so strongly foreshadowed that you anticipate them? If so, did the happenings in these scenes merely fulfill your expectations, or did they also in some way surprise you?
- What kinds of conflict are there—for example, one character against another, one group against another, one part of a personality against another part in the same person?
- How is the conflict resolved? Is it resolved by an unambiguous triumph of one side or by a triumph that is also in some degree a loss for the triumphant side? Do you find the resolution satisfying, unsettling, or what? Why?

Character

- A dramatic character is not likely to be thoroughly realistic, a copy of someone we might know. Still, we can ask whether the character is consistent and coherent. We can also ask whether the character is complex or is, on the other hand, a rather simple representative of some human type.
- How is the character defined? Consider what the character says and does and what others say about him or her and do to him or her. Also consider other characters who more or less resemble the character in question, because the similarities—and the differences— may be significant.
- How trustworthy are the characters when they characterize themselves? When they characterize others?
- Do characters change as the play goes on, or do we simply know them better at the end?
- What do you make of the minor characters? Are they merely necessary to the plot, or are they foils to other characters? Do they perhaps serve some other functions?
- If a character is tragic, does the tragedy seem to you to proceed from a moral flaw, from an intellectual error, from the malice of others, from sheer chance, or from some combination of these?
- What are the character's goals? To what degree do you sympathize with them? If a character is comic, do you laugh *with* or *at* the character?
- Do you think the characters are adequately motivated?
- Is a given character so meditative that you feel he or she is engaged less in a dialogue with others than in a dialogue with the self? If so, do you feel that this character is in large

degree a spokesperson for the author, commenting not only on the world of the play but also on the outside world?

Tragedy

- What causes the tragedy? Is it a flaw in the central character? a mistake (*not* the same thing as a flaw) made by this character? an outside force, such as another character or fate?
- Is the tragic character defined partly by other characters, for instance by characters who help us to sense what the character *might* have done, or who in some other way reveal the strengths or weaknesses of the protagonist?
- Does a viewer know more than the tragic figure knows? more than most or all of the characters know?
- Does the tragic character achieve any sort of wisdom at the end of the play?
- To what degree do you sympathize with the tragic character?
- Is the play depressing? If not, why not?

Comedy

- Do the comic complications arise chiefly out of the personalities of the characters (for instance, pretentiousness or amorousness) or out of the situations (for instances, mistaken identity)?
- What are the chief goals of the figures? Do we sympathize with these goals, or do we laugh at persons who pursue them? If we laugh, *why* do we laugh?
- What are the personalities of those who oppose the central characters? Do we laugh at them, or do we sympathize with them?
- What is funny about the play? Is the comedy high (including verbal comedy) or chiefly situational and physical?
- Is the play predominantly genial, or is there a strong satiric tone?
- Does the comedy have any potentially tragic elements in it? Might the plot be slightly rewritten so that it would become a tragedy?
- What, if anything, do the characters learn by the end of the play?

Nonverbal language

- If the playwright does not provide full stage directions, try to imagine for at least one scene what gestures, facial expressions, and

tones might accompany each speech. Consider, too, pauses that characters might make in delivering speeches.
- Consider the physical positions characters take on the stage in relationship to other characters.
- What do you make of the setting? Does it help to reveal character? Do changes of scene strike you as symbolic? If so, symbolic of what?
- Do certain costumes (dark suits, flowery shawls, stiff collars, etc.) or certain properties (book, pictures, toys, candlesticks, etc.) strike you as symbolic? If so, symbolic of what?

The Play on Film

Often we can gain a special pleasure from, or insight into, a dramatic work when we actually see it produced onstage or made into a film. This manifestation gives us an opportunity to think about the choices that the director has made, and, even more, it may prompt us to imagine and ponder how we would direct the play for the theater or make a film version of it ourselves.

- If you have seen the play in a film version, what has been added? What has been omitted? Why?
- In the case of a film, has the film medium been used to advantage—for example, in focusing attention through close-ups or reaction shots (shots showing not the speaker but a person reacting to the speaker)?
- Do certain plays seem to be especially suited—maybe *only* suited—to the stage? Would they not work effectively as films? Is the reverse true—that is, are some plays best presented and best understood when they are done as films?
- Critics have sometimes said about this or that play that it cannot really be staged successfully or presented well on film—that the best way to appreciate and understand it is as something to be *read*, like a poem or novel. Are there plays you have studied for which this observation appears to be true? Which features of the work—its characters, settings, dialogue, central themes—might make it difficult to transfer the play from the page to the movie screen or to the stage?
- Imagine that you are directing a film version. What would be the important decisions you would have to make about character, setting, and pacing of the action? Would you be inclined to omit certain scenes? Would you, al-

ternatively, add new scenes that are not in the work itself? What kinds of advice would you give to the performers about their roles?

WRITING ABOUT A FILM BASED ON A PLAY

This unit offers some comments about the nature of film, some definitions of indispensable technical terms, a few suggestions about topics, a sample essay by a student, and a list of questions to consider as you begin to think about writing on a film that is based on a play.

Film as a Medium

Perhaps your first thought is that a film (excluding cartoons, documentaries, newsreels, and so on) is rather like a play: A story is presented by means of actors. The film regularly uses techniques not possible in the playhouse, such as close-ups, and rapid changes of scene, but even these techniques can usually be approximated in the playhouse—for example, by means of lighting. It may seem, then, that one can experience a film as though it were a photographic record of a play. And, indeed, some films are nothing more than film records of productions of plays.

There are, however, crucial distinctions between film and drama. First, though drama uses such visual matters as gestures, tableaux effects, and scenery, the plays that we value most highly are *literature:* The word dominates, the visual component is subordinate. One need not be a film fanatic who believes that the invention of the sound track was an impediment to film in order to realize that a film is more a matter of pictures than of words. The camera usually roves, giving us crowded streets, empty skies, rainy nights, or close-ups of filled ashtrays and chipped coffee cups. A critic has aptly said that in Ingmar Bergman's *Smiles of a Summer Night* (1955) "The almost unbearably ornate crystal goblets, by their aspect and their positioning in the image, convey the oppressive luxuriousness of the diners' lives in purely and uniquely filmic terms." In the words of the Swiss director Eric Rohmer, "The cinema is the description of man and his surroundings." Dramatists can of course give us a sense of human beings cramped in their circumstances, but they cannot compete with the film in giving us a sense of space, especially a sense of human beings in vast natural surroundings. Filmmakers customarily "open out" plays, giving us scenes of skies, beaches, city streets, and so forth. In fact, some of the greatest sequences in cinema, such as the battle scene in Orson Welles's *Falstaff*

(1966; also titled *Chimes at Midnight*), have no dialogue; in such scenes the filmmaker relies entirely on visual effects.

In short, the speaker in a film does not usually dominate. In a play the speaker normally holds the spectator's attention, but in a film when a character speaks, the camera often gives us a **reaction shot,** focusing not on the speaker but on the face or gestures of a character who is affected by the speech, thus giving the spectator a visual interpretation of the words. In François Truffaut's *400 Blows* (1959), for example, we hear a reform school official verbally assault a boy, but we see the uncomfortable boy, not the official. Even when the camera does focus on the speaker, it is likely to offer an interpretation. An extreme example is a scene from David Lean's *Brief Encounter* (1945): A gossip is talking, and the camera gives us a close-up of her jabbering mouth, which monstrously fills the screen.

This distance between film and drama can be put in another way. A film is more like a novel than a play, the action being presented not directly by actors but by a camera, which, like a novelist's point of view, *comments on* the story while telling it. A novelist may, like a dramatist, convey information about a character through dialogue and gesture but may also simply tell us about the character's state of mind. Similarly a filmmaker may use the camera to inform us about unspoken thought. In F.W. Murnau's *The Last Laugh* (1924), when the hotel doorman reads a note firing him, the camera blurs; when he gets drunk, the camera spins so that the room seems to revolve. In Bernardo Bertolucci's *The Conformist* (1969), a shot of a chase through the woods is filmed with a hand-held camera whose shaky images convey to us the agitated emotions of the chase. At the end of Arthur Penn's *Bonnie and Clyde* (1968), when Clyde is riddled with bullets, because his collapse is shot in slow motion he seems endowed not only with unusual grace but also with almost superhuman powers and endurance.

The medium as everyone knows, is part of the message; Laurence Olivier made Shakespeare's *Henry V* (1944) in color but *Hamlet* (1948) in black and white because these media say different things. Peter Brook's film in *King Lear* (1970) is also in black and white, with an emphasis on an icy whiteness that catches the play's spirit of old age and desolation; a *Lear* in color probably would have an opulence that would work against the lovelessness and desolation of much of the play. John Houseman said that he produced *Julius Caesar* (1953) in black and white because he wanted "intensity" rather than "grandeur" and because black and white evoked newsreels of Hitler and thus helped establish the connection between Shakespeare's play and relatively recent politics.

The kind of lens used also helps determine what the viewer sees. In Mike Nichol's *The Graduate* (1967) Benjamin runs towards the camera (he is trying to reach a church before his girl marries another man), but he seems to make no progress because a telephoto lens was used and thus his size does not increase as it normally would. The lens, that is, helps communicate his desperate sense of frustration. Conversely, a wide-angle lens makes a character approach the camera with menacing rapidity; she or he quickly looms into the foreground. Film-makers, though resembling novelists in offering pervasive indirect comment, are not novelists any more than they are playwrights or directors of a play; the medium has its own techniques, and filmmakers work with them, not with the novel's or the drama's. The wife who came out of the movie theater saying to her husband, "What a disappointment; it was exactly like the book," knew what a film ought to be.

Film Techniques

At this point it may be well to suspend generalizations temporarily and to look more methodically at some techniques of filmmaking. What follows is a brief grammar and dictionary of film, naming and explaining the cinematic devices that help filmmakers embody their vision in a work of art. An essay on film will discuss some of these devices, but there is no merit in mechanically trotting them all out.

Shots. A **shot** is what is recorded between the time a camera starts and the time is stops, that is, between the director's call for "action" and the call to "cut." Perhaps the average shot is about ten seconds (very rarely a fraction of a second, and usually not more than fifteen or so seconds). The average film is about an hour and a half, with about 600 shots, but Alfred Hitchcock's *The Birds* (1963) uses 1,360 shots. Three common shots are (1) a **long shot** or **establishing shot,** showing the main object at a considerable distance from the camera and thus presenting it in relation to its general surroundings (for example, captured soldiers, seen across a prison yard, entering the yard); (2) a **medium shot,** showing the object in relation to its immediate surroundings (a couple of soldiers, from the knees up, with the yard's wall behind them); and (3) a **close-up,** showing only the main object, or, more often, only a part of it (a soldier's face or his bleeding feet).

In the outside world, and when we witness a play in the theater, we can narrow our vision to the detail that interests us by moving our head and by focusing our eyes, ignoring what is not of immediate interest. The close-up is the movie director's chief way of directing our vision and of emphasizing a detail. (Another way is to focus sharply on the significant image, leaving the rest of the image in soft focus.) The close-up, a way of getting emphasis, has been heavily used in many films, not always successfully. As Dwight Macdonald said of John Schlesinger's *Midnight Cowboy* (1969) and *Getting Straight* (1970), "a movie told in close-ups is like a comic book, or like a novel composed in punchy one-sentence paragraphs and set throughout in large caps. How refreshing is a long or middle shot, a glimpse of the real world, so lovely and so *far away*, in the midst of all those interminable processions of [a] hairy ogre face."

Two excellent film versions of Shakespeare's *Henry V* nicely show the different effects that long shots and close-ups can produce. Laurence Olivier's version (1944) uses abundant long shots and, on the whole, conveys a highly pictorial sweeping epic version of the war in which Henry was engaged. The film was made during World War II as a patriotic effort to inspire the English by showing the heroism of combat. On the other hand, Kenneth Branaugh's version, made in 1989, uses lots of close-ups of soldiers with mud-splattered faces, emphasizing the grittiness of war. Olivier brought out the splendor and romance, Branaugh the labor and pain of war.

While taking a shot, the camera can move: It can swing to the right or left while its base remains fixed (a **pan shot**), up or down while fixed on its axis (a **tilt shot**), forward or backward (a **traveling shot**), or in and out and up and down fastened to a crane (a **crane shot**). In Laurence Olivier's *Hamlet* the camera pans and travels through long empty corridors and over staircases, suggesting Hamlet's irresolute mind. The **zoom lens,** introduced in the 1950s and widespread by the middle 1960s, enables the camera to change its focus fluidly so that it can approach a detail—as a traveling shot does—while remaining fixed in place. Much will depend on the angle (high or low) from which the shots are made. If the camera is high (a **high-angle shot**), looking down on figures, it usually will dwarf them, perhaps even reduce them to crawling insects, making them vulnerable, pitiful, or contemptible. The higher the angle, the more likely it is to suggest a God's-eye view of entrapped people. In Olivier's *Hamlet*, the camera descends from a great height just before Hamlet delivers his first soliloquy. And when the

Ghost leaves at 1.5.96, the camera soars into the air, as though with the Ghost, and then, from above, it shows Hamlet fainting on the battlements. If the camera is low (a **low-angle shot**), close to the ground and looking up, thereby showing figures against the sky, it probably will give them added dignity.

In short, by its distance from the subject, its height from the ground, and its angle of elevation, the camera comments on or interprets what happens. It seems to record reality, but it offers its own version. It is only a slight exaggeration to say that the camera always lies, that is, gives a personal vision of reality.

Slow motion and **fast motion** also offer comments. In Branaugh's *Henry V*, as in Orson Welles's *Falstaff*, part of a battle is filmed in slow motion; thus, the weariness of the soldiers is emphasized. On the other hand, a fast-motion shot of factory workers or of vacationers betting in Las Vegas will—probably comically—emphasize their frantic activity.

Sequences. A group of related sequences—such as the three shots of soldiers mentioned on page 1486—is a **sequence,** though a sequence is more likely to have thirty scenes than three. A sequence corresponds roughly to a chapter in a novel, the shots being sentences and the scenes being paragraphs. Within a sequence may be an **intercut,** a switch to another action that, for example, provides an ironic comment on the main action of the sequence. If intercuts are so abundant in a sequence that, in effect, two or more sequences are going at once (for example, shots of the villain about to ravish the heroine, alternating with shots of the hero riding to her rescue), we have **parallel editing** (also called a **cross-cut**). In the example just given, probably the tempo would increase, the shots being progressively shorts as we get to the rescue.

Transitions. Within a sequence, the transitions normally are made by **straight cuts**—a strip of film is spliced next to another, and the result is an instantaneous transfer from one shot to the next. Usually, an audience is scarcely (if at all) conscious of transitions from, say, a long shot of a character to a medium shot of her or him, or from a close-up of a speaker to a close-up of her or his auditor. But sometimes the director wants the audience to be fully aware of the changes, as an author may emphasize a change by beginning to new paragraph, or, even more sharply, by beginning a new chapter. Two older, and now rather unfashionable, relatively conspicuous transitions are sometimes still used, usually between sequences rather than within a sequence. These are the **dissolve** (the shot dissolves while anew shot appears to emerge from

beneath it, there being a moment when we get a superimposition of both scenes), and the **fade** (in the **fade-out** the screen grows darker until black; in the **fade-in** the screen grows lighter until the new scene is fully visible). In effect the camera is saying "Let us now leave X and turn to Y," or "Two weeks later." Not surprisingly, Olivier's *Hamlet,* which emphasizes the prince's irresoluteness, uses lots of dreamlike dissolves.

Two older methods, even less in favor today then the dissolve and the fade but used in many excellent old films and in some modern films that seek an archaic effect, are the **wipe** (a sort of windshield wiper crosses the screen, wiping off the first scene and revealing the next), and the **iris** (in an **iris-in,** the new scene first appears in the center of the previous scene and then this circle expands until it fills the screen; an **iris-out** shows the new scene first appearing along the perimeter and then the circle closes in on the previous scene).

Editing. All of the transitions discussed a moment ago are examples of editing techniques. A film, no less than a poem or a play or a picture or a palace, is something made, and it is not made by simply exposing some film footage. Shots—often taken as widely separated times and places—must be appropriately joined. For example, we see a man look off to the right, and then we get a shot of what he is looking at and then a shot of his reaction. Until the shots are assembled, we don't have a film—we merely have the footage. The Russian director V. I. Pudovkin put it this way: "The film is not shot, but built, built up from the separate strips of celluloid that are its raw material." This building-up is the process of **editing.** In *Film Technique* Pudovkin gives some examples of editing:

1. In the simplest kind of editing, the film tells a story from the best viewpoints, that is, sometimes from long shots, sometimes from medium shots, sometimes from close-ups.
2. Simultaneous actions, occurring in different places, can be narrated by cutting back and forth from one to the other.
3. Relationships can be conveyed by contrast (shots of starvation cut in with shot of gluttony), by symbolism (in Pudovkin's *Mother* [1926], shots of an ice floe melting are cut into shots of a procession of workers, thereby suggesting that the workers' movements is a natural force coming to new life), and by leitmotiv (that is, repetition of the same shot to emphasize a recurring theme).

More than a story can be told, of course; something of the appropriate emotion can be communicated by juxtaposing, say, a medium-long shot of a group of impassively advancing soldiers against a close-up of a single terrified victim. Similarly, emotion can be communicated by the duration of the shots (quick shots suggest haste; prolonged shots suggest slowness) and by the lighting (progressively darker shots can suggest melancholy; progressively lighter shots can suggest hope or joy).

The Russian theorists of film called this process of building by quick cuts **montage.** The theory held that shots, when placed together, add up to more than the sum of the parts. Montage, for them, was what made a film a work of art and not a mere replica of reality. American writers commonly use the term merely to denote quick cutting, and French writers use it merely in the sense of cutting.[2]

All this talk about ingenious shots and their arrangement, then, assumes that the camera is a sort of pen, carefully setting forth images and thus at every point guiding the perceiver. The director (through the actors, camera technicians, cutters, and a host of others) makes an artifact, rather as a novelist makes a book or a sculptor makes a statue, and this artifact is an elaborate contraption that manipulates the spectators.

Getting Ready to Write

Mastery of terminology does not make anyone a perceptive film critic, but it helps writers communicate their perceptions to their readers. Probably an essay on a film will not be primarily about the use of establishing shots or of wipes or of any such matters; rather, it will be about the reasons why a particular film pleases or displeases, succeeds or fails, seems significant or insignificant, and in discussing these large matters it is sometimes necessary (or at least economical) to use the commonest technical terms. Large matters are often determined in part by such seemingly small matters as the distance of the camera from its subject or the way in which transitions are made, and one may as well use the conventional terms. But it is also true that a filmmaker's technique and technology alone cannot make a first-rate film. An idea, a personal vision, a

[2]You don't have to be in Hollywood or in Russia or France to write a script. You may find it challenging and entertaining to take a scene from a play and then recast it as a film script, indicating shots, camera angles, lighting, and sound track.

theme must be embodied in all that is flashed on the screen.

Writing an essay about a new film—one not yet available for study on the VCR—presents difficulties not encountered in writing about stories, plays, or poems. Because we experience film in a darkened room, we cannot easily take notes, and because the film may be shown only once, we cannot always take another look at passages that puzzle us. But some brief notes can be taken even in the dark; it is best to amplify them as soon as light is available, which you still know what the scrawls mean. If you can see the film more than once, do so, and, of course, if the script has been published, study it. Draft your paper as soon as possible after your first viewing, and then see the film again. You can sometimes check hazy memories of certain scenes and techniques with fellow viewers. But even with multiple viewings and the aid of friends, it is almost impossible to get all of the details right; it is best for the writer to be humble and for the reader to be tolerant.

A Sample Essay on Visual Symbols: "A Japanese *Macbeth*"

Printed here is an essay by a student, Thelma Washington, on a film. Because it is on a version of *Macbeth*, it is in some degree a comparison between a film and a play, but it does not keep shifting back and forth and does not make the obvious point that many differences are found. Rather, it announces that it will be concerned with one kind of difference—the use of visual symbols that the camera can render effectively—and it then examines four such symbols.

Here is the skeleton of the essay, "A Japanese *Macbeth*," paragraph by paragraph:

The Japanese film of *Macbeth* is not a film of a stage performance; it is a cinematic version.

The film sometimes changes Shakespeare's plot, but this essay will be concerned only with the changes that are visual symbols: the fog, the castle, the forest, the horses.

The fog, the castle, and the forest can be treated briefly. The fog shows nature blinding man; the castle shows man's brief attempt to impose his will on the natural landscape; the forest shows nature entrapping man.

The nervous, active horses—which could not be actually shown on the Elizabethan stage—suggest man's fierce, destructive passions.

The film, though literally false to the play, is artistically true.

This is a solid organization. The title, though not especially imaginative, at least catches our interest and gives a good idea of the general topic; the first paragraph introduces a significant point; and the second narrows it and states precisely what the essay will cover. The third paragraph studies three of the four symbols announced in the second paragraph, and the fourth paragraph studies the fourth, more complicated symbol. The concluding paragraph in a way reaffirms the opening paragraph, but it does so now in the light of concrete evidence that has been offered. Organizing the essay is only part of the job. The writer of this essay has done more than work out an acceptable organization; she has some perceptions to offer, and she has found the right details and provided neat transitions so that the reader can move through the essay with pleasure.

A Japanese <u>Macbeth</u>

A Japanese movie-version of <u>Macbeth</u> sounds like a bad idea--until one sees Akira Kurosawa's film <u>Throne of Blood</u>, in which Toshiro Mifune plays Washizu, the equivalent of Macbeth. It is a much more satisfying film than, say, Olivier's <u>Othello</u>, largely because it is not merely a filmed version of a play as it might be performed on a stage but a freely re-created version that is designed for the camera. The very fact that it is in Japanese is probably a great help to Westerners. If it were in English, we would be upset at the way some speeches are cut, but because it is in Japanese, we do not compare the words to Shakespeare's, and we concentrate on the visual aspects of the film.

Essayist's general position, and implicit thesis, is clear from the start.

There are several differences in the plots of the two works. Among the alterations of such things as these: Shakespeare's three witches are reduced to one; Lady Washizu has a miscarriage; Washizu is killed by his own troops and not by Macduff. But this paper will discuss another sort of change, the introduction of visual symbols, which the camera is adept at rendering, and which play an important part in the film. The four chief visual symbols are the fog, the castle, the forest, and the horses.

As the paragraph proceeds, it zooms in on the topic.

Essayist tell us exactly what will be covered in the rest of the essay.

The fog, the castle, and the forest, though highly effective, can be dealt with rather briefly. When the film begins we get a slow panoramic view of the ruined castle seen through the fog. The film ends with a similar panoramic view. These two scenes end with a dissolve, though almost all of the other scenes end abruptly with sharp

Transition (through repetition of part of previous sentence) and helpful forecast.

Analysis, not mere plot telling.

cuts, and so the effect is that of lingering sorrow at the transience of human creations, and awe at the permanence of the mysterious natural world, whose mist slowly drifts across what once was a mighty castle built by a great chief. The castle itself, when we come to see it in its original condition, is not a particular graceful Japanese building. Rather, it is a low, strong building, appropriate for an energetic warrior. The interior scenes show low, oppressive ceilings, with great exposed beams that almost seem to crush the people within the rooms. It represents one man's achievement in the center of the misty tangled forest of the mysteriously world, but it also suggests, despite its strength, how stifling that achievement is, in comparison with the floating mists and endless woods. The woods, rainy and misty, consist of curiously gnarled trees and vines and suggest a labyrinth that has entrapped the man, even though for a while he thinks he is secure in his castle. Early in the film we see Washizu riding through the woods, in and out of mists, and behind a maze of twisted trees that periodically hide him from our sight. Maybe it is not too fanciful to suggest that the branches through which we glimpse him blindly riding in the fog are a sort of net that entangles him. The trees and the mist are the vast unfathomable universe; this man can build his castle, can make his plans, but he cannot subdue nature for long. He cannot have his way forever; death will ultimately catch him, despite his strength. One later scene of the forest must be mentioned. Near the end of the film, when the forest moves (the soldiers are holding up leafy boughs to camouflage themselves), we get a spectacular shot; Shakespeare talks of the forest moving; but in the film we see it. Suddenly the forest seems to shudder and to be alive, crawling as though it is a vast horde of ants. Nature is seen to rise up against Washizu's crimes.

Shakespeare's stage could do very little about such an effect as the fog, though his poetry can call it to mind, and it could do even less about the forest. Kurosawa did not feel bound to the text of the play: He made a movie, and he took advantage of the camera's ability to present impressive and significant scenic effects. Similarly, he made much use of horses, which, though mentioned in Shakespeare's play, could not be shown on the Elizabethan stage. In fact, in <u>Macbeth</u> Shakespeare more-or-less apologizes for the absence of horses when one

Thoughtful interpretation.

Further interpretation.

Essayist moves chronologically.

Summary leads, at the end of the paragraph, to interpretation.

The first half of this paragraph is a well-handled comparison.

murderer explains to the other that when horsemen approach the palace it is customary for them to leave their horses and to walk the rest of the way. But the film gives us plenty of horses, not only at the start, when Washizu is galloping in the terrifying forest, but throughout the film, and they are used to suggest the terror of existence and the evil passions in Washizu's heart. Shakespeare provided a hint. After King Duncan is murdered, Shakespeare tells us that Duncan's horses "Turned wild in nature, broke their stalls," and even that they ate each other (2.4.16–18). In the film, when Washizu and his wife plot to murder their lord, we see the panic-struck horses running around the courtyard of the castle--a sort of parallel to the scene of Washizu chaotically riding in and out of the fog near the beginning of the movie. The horses in the courtyard apparently have sensed the villainous plots, or perhaps they are visual equivalents of the fierce emotions in the minds of Washizu and his wife. Later, when Washizu is planning to murder Miki (the equivalent of Banquo), we see Miki's white horse kicking at his attendants. Miki saddles the horse, preparing to ride into the hands of his assassins. Then Kurosawa cuts to a long shot of the courtyard at night, where Miki's attendants are nervously waiting for him to return. Then we hear a sound of a galloping horse, and suddenly the white horse comes running in, riderless. Yet another use of this motif is when we cut to a wild horse, after Washizu's wife has said that she is pregnant. In the film the wife has a miscarriage, and here again the horse is a visual symbol of the disorder engendered within her (the child would be the heir to the usurped throne), as the other horses were symbols for the disorder in her mind and in Macbeth's. All of these cuts to the horses are abrupt, contributing to the sense of violence that the unrestrained horses themselves embody. Moreover, almost the only close-ups in the film are some shots of horses, seen from a low angle, emphasizing their powerful, oppressive brutality.

A reminder of a point made earlier, but now developed at length.

Thoughtful generalization.

Throne of Blood is not Shakespeare's Macbeth--but even a filmed version of a staged version of the play would not be Shakespeare's Macbeth either, for the effect of a film is simply not identical with the effect of a play with live actors on the stage. But Throne of Blood is a fine translation of Macbeth into an approximate equivalent. Despite its lack of faithfulness to the literal text, it is in a higher way faithful. It is a work of art, like its original.

Conclusion is chiefly a restatement, but the last sentence gives it an interesting twist.

The Big Picture

All works of art are contrivances, but (as a Roman saying puts it) the art is to conceal art. Does the film seem a mere tour de force, or does it have the effect of inevitability, the effect of rightness, conveying a sense that a vision has been honestly expressed? Are characters or scenes clumsily dragged in? are unusual effects significant? Does the whole add up to something? Do we get scenes or characters or techniques that at first hold us by their novelty but then have nothing further to offer?

Some final advice: Early in the essay it is desirable to sketch enough of the plot to give readers an idea of what happens. (In the previous essay the student does not sketch the plot, but she says it is a version of *Macbeth* and thus gives the necessary information.) Do not try to recount everything that happens; it can't be done, and the attempt will frustrate you and bore your readers. Once you introduce the main characters and devote a few sentences to the plot, thus giving the readers a comfortable seat, get down to the job of convincing them that you have something interesting to say about the film—that the plot is trivial, or that the hero is not really cool but cruel, or that the plot and the characters are impressive achievements but the camera work is sometimes needlessly tricky, or that all is well.

Incidentally, a convenient way to give an actor's name in your essay is to put it in parentheses after the character's name or role, thus: "The detective (Humphrey Bogart) finds a clue . . . . " Then, as you go on to talk about the film, use the names of the characters or the roles, not the names of the actors, except of course when you are talking about the actors themselves, as in "Bogart is exactly right for the part."

A Sample Review of a Film Version of a Play

What follows is an undergraduate's review, published in a college newspaper, of Kenneth Branagh's film version of *Hamlet* (1996). In the margin we call attention to the reviewer's rhetorical strategies.

Will Saretta

Branagh's Film of <u>Hamlet</u>

The opening paragraph holds the reader's attention by (a) offering useful information, and (b) strongly stating an evaluation.

Kenneth Branagh's *Hamlet* opened last night at the Harmon Auditorium, and will be shown again on Wednesday and Thursday at 7:30 p.m. According to the clock the evening will be long—the film runs for four hours, and in addition there is one ten-minute intermission—but you will enjoy every minute of it.

The second paragraph begins with a neat transition (its first sentence slightly modifies the last sentence of the preceding paragraph), and supports its point (about the film's weak spots) with specific evidence.

Well, almost every minute. Curiously, the film begins and ends relatively weakly, but most of what occurs between is good and much of it is wonderful. The beginning is weak because it is too strong; Bernardo, the sentinel, offstage says "Who's there?" but before he gets a reply he crashes onto the screen and knocks Francisco down. The two soldiers grapple, swords flash in the darkness, and Francisco finally says, "Nay, answer me. Stand and unfold yourself." Presumably Branagh wanted to begin with a bang, but here, as often, more is less. A quieter, less physical opening in which Bernardo, coming on duty, hears a noise and demands that the maker of the noise identify himself, and Francisco, the sentinel on duty, rightly demands that the newcomer identify *himself*, would catch the uneasiness and the mystery that pervades the play much better than does Branagh's showy beginning.

The third paragraph uses a clear transition ("Similarly"), and makes its points in an orderly fashion, using effective repetition ("Second," "Hamlet is not a play about," "or about," "Hamlet is not about," "It is about . . .")

Similarly, at the end of the film, we get too much. For one thing, shots of Fortinbras's army invading Elsinore alternate with shots of the duel between Hamlet and King Claudius's pawn, Laertes, and they merely distract us from what really counts in this scene, the duel itself, which will result in Hamlet's death but also in Hamlet's successful completion of his mission to avenge his father. Second, at the very end we get shots of Fortinbras's men pulling down a massive statue of Hamlet Senior, probably influenced by television and newspaper shots of statues of Lenin being pulled down when the Soviet Union was dissolved a few years earlier. This is ridiculous; *Hamlet* is not a play about the fall of Communism, or about the one form of tyranny replacing another. Shakespeare's *Hamlet* is not about the triumph of Fortinbras. It is about Hamlet's brave and ultimately successful efforts to do what is right, against overwhelming odds, and to offer us the consolation that in a world where death always triumphs there nevertheless is something that be called nobility.

What, then, is good about the film? First of all, the film gives us the whole play, whereas almost all productions, whether on the stage or in the movie house, gives us drastically abbreviated versions. Although less is often more, when it comes to the text of *Hamlet*, more is better, and we should be grateful to Branagh for letting us hear all of the lines. Second, it is very well performed, with only a few exceptions. Jack Lemmon as Marcellus is pretty bad, but fortunately the part is small. Other big-name actors in small parts—Charlton Heston as the Player King, Robin Williams as Osric, and Billy Crystal as the First Gravedigger—are admirable. But of course the success or failure of any production of *Hamlet* will depend chiefly on the actor who plays Hamlet, and to a considerable degree on the actors who play Claudius, Gertrude, Polonius, Ophelia, Laertes, and Horatio. There isn't space here to comment on all of these roles, but let it be said that Branagh's Prince Hamlet is indeed princely, a man who strikes us as having the ability to become a king, not a wimpy whining figure. When at the end Fortinbras says that if Hamlet had lived to become the king, he would "have proved must royal," we believe him. And his adversary, King Claudius, though morally despicable, is a man of great charm and great ability. The two men are indeed "mighty opposites," to use Hamlet's own words.

Branagh's decision to set the play in the late nineteenth century rather than in the Elizabethan period of Shakespeare's day and rather than in our own day contributes to this sense of powerful forces at work. If the play were set in Shakspeare's day, the men would wear tights, and if it were set in our day they would wear suits or trousers and sports jackets and sweaters, but in the film all of the men wear military costumes (black for Hamlet, scarlet for Claudius, white for Laertes) and the women wear ball gowns of the Victorian period. Branagh gives us a world that is closer to our own than would Elizabethan costumes, but yet it is, visually at least, also distant enough to convey a sense of grandeur, which modern dress cannot suggest. Of course *Hamlet* can be done in modern dress, just as *Romeo and Juliet* was done, successfully, in the recent film staring Claire Danes and Leonardo DiCaprio, set in a world that seemed to be Miami Beach, but *Romeo and Juliet* is less concerned with heroism and grandeur than *Hamlet* is, so Branagh probably did well to avoid contemporary costumes.

Although Branagh is faithful to the text, in that he gives us the entire text, he knows that a good film cannot be made merely be recording on film a stage production, and so he gives us handsome shots of landscape, and of rich interiors—for instance, a great mirrored hall—that would be beyond the resources of any theatrical production. I have already said that at the end, when Fortinbras's army swarms over the countryside and then invades the castle we get material that is distracting, indeed irrelevant, but there are also a few other distractions. It is all very well to let us *see* the content of long narrative speeches (for instance, when the Player King talks of the fall of Troy and the death of King Praim and the lament of Queen Hecuba, Branagh shows us these things, with John Gielgud as Priam and Judi Dench as Hecuba performing in pantomime), but there surely is no need for us to see a naked Hamlet and a naked Ophelia in bed, when Polonius is warning Ophelia that Hamlet's talk of love cannot be trusted. Polonius's warning is not so long or so undramatic that we need to be entertained visually with an invention that finds not a word of support in the text. On the contrary, all of Ophelia's lines suggest that she would not be other than a dutiful young woman, obedient to the morals of the time and to her father's authority. Yet another of Branagh's unfortunate inventions is the prostitute who appears in Polonius's bedroom, during Polonius's interview with Reynaldo. A final example of unnecessary spectacle is Hamlet's killing of Claudius: He hurls his rapier the length of the hall, impaling Claudius and then like some 1930's movie star he swings on the chandelier and drops down on Claudius to finish him off.

Having discussed the weaknesses, the writer now turns to "what . . . is good about the film." Several points are made, in a reasonable sequence.

Although at first glance this paragraph may seem unconnected with the preceding paragraph, in fact it is firmly connected: "this sense of powerful forces" picks up the "mighty opposites" of the last sentence of the preceding paragraph.

The topic of this paragraph is Branagh's departures from the play, some of which are effective and some of which are not.

Having offered some negative comments, the reviewer reminds the reader that he thinks the film is very good.

The "postscript" is tacked on, but reviews often have a relatively informal touch.

But it is wrong to end this review by pointing out faults in Branagh's film of *Hamlet*. There is so much in this film that is exciting, so much that is moving, so much that is . . . , well, so much that is *Hamlet* (which is to say that is a great experience), that the film must be recommended without reservation. Go to see it. The four hours will fly.

A postscript. It is good to see that Branagh uses color-blind casting. Voltemand, Fortinbras's Captain, and the messenger who announces Laerte's return are all blacks—the messsenger is a black woman—although of course medieval Denmark and Elizabethan England, and, for that matter, Victorian England, would not have routinely included blacks. These performers are effective, and it is appropriate that actors of color take their place in the world's greatest play.

Topics for Critical Thinking and Writing

1. Does the writer give adequate evidence to support his favorable comments on the play?
2. Does he give evidence to support his unfavorable comments?
3. Given the writer's overall evaluation of the film, do you agree with his strategy of devoting the first and last paragraphs to praising the play?
4. Do you think the writer apportioned his space well, or should he have spent more time on the weaknesses, or more time on the strengths? Why?
5. Do you find the comments about the late-nineteenth-century setting relevant and thoughtful, or irrelevant and not very perceptive? Explain.
6. Do you find the *postscript* intrusive? Explain.
7. If you have seen the film, do you more or less agree with the reviewer? Do you think that the reviewer neglected to make certain points that you would have made in your review?

✓ A Checklist: Getting Ideas for Writing About a Film Based on a Play

Preliminaries.
✓ Is the title of the film the same as the title of the play? If not, what is implied?

Dramatic adaptations.
✓ Does the film closely follow its original and neglect the potentialities of the camera? Or does it so revel in cinematic devices that it distorts the original?

✓ Does the film do violence to the theme of the original? Is the film better than its source? Are the additions or omissions due to the medium or to a crude or faulty interpretation of the original?

Plot and character.
✓ Can film deal as effectively with inner action—mental processes—as with external, physical action? In a given film, how is the inner action conveyed? Olivier used voice-over for parts of Hamlet's soliloquies—that is, we hear Hamlet's voice but his lips do not move.

✓ Are shots and sequences adequately developed, or do they seem jerky? (A shot may be jerky by being extremely brief or at an odd angle; a sequence may be jerky by using discontinuous images or fast cuts. Sometimes, of course, jerkiness may be desirable.) if such cinematic techniques as wipes, dissolves, and slow motion are used, are they meaningful and effective?

✓ Are the characters believable?

✓ Are the actors appropriately cast?

Sound track.
✓ Does the sound track offer more than realistic dialogue? Is the music appropriate and functional? (Music may, among other things, imitate natural sounds, give a sense of locale or of ethnic group, suggest states of mind, provide ironic commentary, or—by repeated melodies—help establish connections.) Are volume, tempo, and pitch—whether of music or of such sounds as the wind blowing or cars moving—used to stimulate emotions?

Organizing an Essay

Like a play, an essay on a play should be organized, and one can hardly go wrong in saying (as Aristotle said of plays) that an essay should have a beginning, a middle and an end.

In the *beginning*, probably in the first paragraph, it's usually a good idea to state your thesis. You don't have to state it in the first sentence (you may, for example, want to open with a quotation from the play), but state it early and clearly.

In the *middle*, support your thesis with evidence, probably including some brief quotations from the play. The middle, like the essay as a whole, should be organized. For example, if you are discussing the development of a character, you will probably want to move through the play act by act.

In the *end*, or conclusion, it's helpful to recapitulate briefly, but try also (lest your conclusion strike the reader as nothing more than an unnecessary restatement of what you said a moment ago) to set your findings in a largest context, the context of the entire play.

Summary: How to Write an Effective Essay

All writers must work out their own procedures and rituals (John C. Calhoun liked to plow his farm before writing), but the following suggestions provide some help.

If you use a word processor (and we hope that you do because it makes the job of writing easier), we suggest that you read these pages even though they assume that the writer is using pen and index cards. For further suggestions, read "Suggestions for Writing with a Word Processor," page 1496.

1. **Read the play carefully.**

2. **Choose a worthwhile and manageable topic,** something that interests you and is not so big that your handling of it must be superficial. As you work, shape your topic into a thesis, moving, for example, from "The Character of King Oedipus" to "Change in King Oedipus."

3. **Reread the play, jotting down notes** of all relevant matters. As you read, reflect on your reading and record your reflections. If you have a feeling or an idea, jot it down; don't assume that you will remember it when you get around to writing your essay. The margins of this book are a good place for initial notes, but many people find that in the long run it is best to transfer these notes to 3-by–5 inch cards, writing on one side only. (Easiest of all is to use a word processor).

4. **Sort out your cards** into some kind of reasonable division, and reject cards irrelevant to your topic. If you have adequately formulated your thesis (for example, "Chance plays a large part in *Hamlet*"), you ought to be able to work out a tentative organization. As you work you may discover a better way to group your notes. If so, start reorganizing. Speaking generally, it is a good idea to organize your essay from the lesser material to the greater (to avoid anticlimax) or from the simple to the complex (to ensure intelligibility). If, for example, you are discussing the roles of three characters, it may be best to build up to the one of the three that you think is the most important. If you are comparing two characters, it may be best to move from the most obvious contrasts to the least obvious ones. (In your opening paragraph, which will probably be almost the last thing you will write, you should, of course, give the reader an idea of the scope of the paper, but at this stage you are organizing the material chiefly for yourself and so you need not yet worry about an introductory paragraph.) When you have arranged your notes into a meaningful sequence of packets, you have approximately divided your material into paragraphs.

5. **Get it down on paper.** Most essayists find it useful to jot down some sort of outline, indicating the main idea of each paragraph and, under each main idea, supporting details that give it substance. An outline—not necessarily anything highly formal with capital and lowercase letters and Roman and Arabic numerals but merely key phrases in some sort of order—will help you to overcome the paralysis called writer's block that commonly afflicts professionals as well as students. A page of paper with ideas in some sort of sequence, however rough, ought to assure you that you do have something to say. You should feel encouraged that, despite the temptation to sharpen another pencil, the best thing to do is to sit down and start writing.

If you don't feel that you can work from note cards and a rough outline, try another method: Get something down on paper, writing freely, sloppily, automatically, or whatever, but allow your ideas about what the work means to you and how it conveys its meaning—rough as they may be—to begin to take visible form. If you are like most people, you can't do much precise thinking until you have committed to paper at least a rough sketch of your initial ideas. Later you can push and polish your ideas into shape, perhaps even deleting all of them and starting over, but it's a lot easier to improve your ideas once you seen them in front of you than it is to do the job in your head. On paper (or on a computer screen) one word leads to another; in your head one word often blocks another.

Just keep going; you may realize, as you near the end of a sentence, that you no longer believe it. OK; be glad that your first idea led you to a better one, and pick up your better one and keep going with it. What you are doing is, in a sense, using trial and error to push your way not only toward clear expression but also toward sharper ideas and richer responses.

6. If there is time, **reread the play,** looking for additional material that strengthens or weakens your main point; take account of it in your outline or draft.

7. **With your outline or draft in front of you, write a more lucid version,** checking your notes for fuller details, such as supporting quotations. If, as you work, you find that some of the points in your earlier jottings are no longer relevant, eliminate them; it is important that the argument flows from one point to the next. As you write; your ideas will doubtless become clearer; some may prove to be poor ideas. (We rarely know exactly what our ideas are until we have them set down on paper. As the little girl said, replying to the suggestion that she should think before she spoke, "How do I know what I think until I say it?") Not until you have written a draft do you really have a strong sense of how good your essay may be.

8. After a suitable interval, preferably a few days, **read the draft with a view toward revising it,** not with a view towards congratulating yourself. A revision, after all, is a revision, a second (and presumably sharper) view. When you revise, you will be in the company of Picasso, who said that in painting a picture he advanced by a series of destructions. A revision—such as the addition of an example, the reorganization of the sequence of examples, or even the substitution of a precise word for an imprecise one—is not a matter of prettifying but of thinking. As you read, correct things that disturb you (for example, awkward repetitions that bore, inflated utterances that grate), add supporting detail where the argument is undeveloped (a paragraph of only one or two sentences is usually an undeveloped paragraph), and ruthlessly delete irrelevancies however well written they may be. Remember, though, that a deletion probably requires some adjustment in the preceding and subsequent material.

Make sure that the opening paragraph gives the readers some sense of where they will be going and that between the opening and the closing paragraphs the argument, aided by transition terms (such as *furthermore, on the other hand, in the next scene*), runs smoothly. The details should be relevant, the organization reasonable, and the argument clear. Check all quotations for accuracy. Quotations are evidence, usually intended to support your assertions, and you should not alter the evidence, even unintentionally. If there is time (there almost never is), put the revision aside, reread it in a day or two, and revise it again, especially with a view toward shortening it.

9. **Keyboard or write a clean copy,** following the principles concerning margins, pagination, footnotes, and so on, set forth on page 1498. If you have borrowed any ideas, be sure to give credit, usually in footnotes, to your sources. Remember that plagiarism is not limited to the unacknowledged borrowing of words; a borrowed idea, even when put into your own words, requires acknowledgement.

10. **Proofread and make corrections.**

Suggestions for Writing with a Word Processor

If possible, write your paper on a word processor. Writing a first draft on a word processor is physically easier than writing by hand or by typewriter, and revising the draft is incomparably easier. (You can almost effortlessly move material around or insert new material.) Furthermore, for many people the screen is less intimidating than a sheet of paper, and when you do put words down, they look at lot better than handwritten or typed material. In addition, if your paper includes footnotes or endnotes and a list of Works Cited, your software probably will automatically format them.

A word processor may not save you time, but it will allow you to use your time efficiently. In the past, writers had to spend a great deal of time on the tedious job of typing a clean copy. The more they revised, the more they doomed themselves to hours of retyping. With a word processor, you can spend all of your time reading, writing, and rewriting, and you can virtually leave to the printer the job of typing.

Prewriting. Your first notes probably will be in the margins of your text, but once you go beyond these, you can use a word processor to brainstorm, for instance. By means of *free association*—writing down whatever comes to mind, without fretting about spelling, punctuation, or logic—you will probably find that you can generate ideas, at least some of which will lead to something. Alternatively, you can try *listing*, jotting down key terms (for instance the names of characters in a play or technical terms such as *tragedy, pathos, hamartia, irony*) and then inserting further thoughts about each. Produce a printout, and then start *linking* or *clustering* (with circles and connecting lines) related items. Then return to your screen, and reorganize the material, moving *this* word or phrase over to connect it with *that* one.

Many students find *dialoguing* helpful. After writing a sentence or two, they imagine a somewhat skeptical critic who asks questions such as, "What examples can you give?" "What counterevidence might be offered?" and "Have you defined your terms?" in answering such questions, writers get additional ideas.

Back up your material. Don't run the risk of losing your work. Write on a hard drive (it's faster), and keep a floppy disk nearby for making backups at the close of each work session.

Taking Notes. Write into one file all of your notes for a paper. If the notes are for a paper on, for example, Caryl Churchill, you will probably name the file "Churchill." The name does not matter, so long as you remember it.

Put all bibliographic references in one place. If you are using written sources, you will want to keep a record of each source. Some programs automatically alphabetize each entry. However, even if your program does not alphabetize bibliographic entries, you can easily insert a new entry by scrolling down through the existing references to the appropriate alphabetic place where you can then insert the new reference, last name first.

When taking notes, be sure to check the accuracy of your transcription. If you quote directly, make certain that you have quoted exactly. Use three periods (ellipsis points) to indicate any omissions within a quotation, and use square brackets to enclose any addition that you make within a quotation. (See page 1499.) As we discuss below, when you are drafting your paper you may want to block some of this material and move it into the draft.

It's a good idea to print out all of your notes before you prepare a first draft. Because the screen shows very little of the material that constitutes your notes, print it all out so that you can survey it as a whole. Cut apart the various notes, and discard material that no longer seems helpful. Next, arrange the surviving material into a tentative sequence, just as you would arrange index cards with handwritten notes. (The word processor is a great help, but don't hesitate to produce hard copy at various stages and to work with the printed material. The screen is too small to give you a feel of the whole.)

Many writers find it helpful to put this selection of material, now in a sequence, back into the computer. They do this by *blocking* and moving the useful material. Do *not* delete the unused material; as you work on the essay, you may realize that you can use some of this material in the final version. It's advisable to copy this selected and arranged material into a new file, named "draft" or some such thing. If you simply add it to the end of the file containing all of the notes, you may

sometimes find yourself working with the unselected notes when you mean to work with the selected notes.

Writing a first draft. Even if you did not take notes on a computer, you can, of course, write your drafts and ultimately the final paper on a word processor. Use double-spacing to allow room for handwritten additions on a printed version of the draft, and start writing.

Some writers find it useful to start writing on the computer by setting down a rough outline—perhaps phrases in a sequence that, at least for the moment, seems reasonable. They then go back and fill in the outlines, expanding words or phrases into detailed sentences and paragraphs. Of course, as they write they may find that they want to rearrange some of the material, which they can easily do by cut-and-paste commands.

Let's assume, however, that you do have notes on the word processor and that you have arranged them in a sequence. You may want to begin by looking at the first note and writing an opening paragraph that will lead into it, and then go on to the next note. Of course, as you work you will find that some of the notes are unneeded. Don't delete them, since they may come in handy later. Just block them and move them (cut-and-paste) to the end of the file.

Because it is so easy to produce a clean final copy (with a keystroke or two you can tell the printer to print the file), don't hesitate in your draft to incorporate comments that you know you won't retain in the final version, such as "CHECK QUOTATION" or GET BETTER EXAMPLE." (Use capitals or boldface for such comments so that you will focus on them when you read the draft and so you cannot overlook them when the time comes to delete them.)

When you think you have come to the end of your draft, you will probably want to read it on the screen, from the beginning, to correct typos and to make other obvious corrections. That's fine, but remember that because the screen is small you cannot get a good sense of the entire essay. You won't be able to see, for instance, if a paragraph is much too long. Even when you scroll through the draft, you will not experience the material in the way that the reader of a printed copy will experience it. What you need to do at this stage is to print your draft.

Revising a draft. Read the printed draft, making necessary revisions in pen or pencil. Probably you will find that some of the quoted material can be abridged, or even deleted, and that in some places better transitions are needed. It is also likely that you will see the need to add details and to reorganize some of the material. Try to read the draft from the point of view of someone new to the material. Keep asking yourself, "Will my reader understand *why* I am making this point at this stage of the essay?" if you ask this question, you probably will find yourself not only adding helpful transitions, ("An apparent exception is . . .") but also occasionally reorganizing. Make these changes on the printed copy, incorporate them into the computer, and print the revised version.

Read the revised version with a critical eye; you probably will find that you can extensively revise even this version. You may get some help from a computer program. For instance, if you are using *Fifty-Third Street Writer,* which includes the *Scott, Foresman Handbook,* and you are uncertain about the use of the semicolon, you can consult the index to the *Handbook,* and then bring up the material on semicolons. Similarly, if you are writing a book review, you can find the material on reviews by consulting the index and can then bring to the screen the discussion of the qualities that make for a good review. Among other software programs that many writers find useful are *Grammatik, Word Plus, Right Writer,* and *Writer's Workbench.* Some of these will alert you to such matters as spelling errors, clichés, split infinitives, overuse of the passive voice, and certain kinds of grammatical errors. For instance, *Writer's Workbench* (and some of the others) lets you check troublesome pairs of words (for example, (*affect/effect*), flags words and phrases that are potentially sexist, detects most split infinitives and misspellings, and gives (among other things) help with transitions. You cannot rely entirely on these programs, but they do offer considerable help.

When you get a version that seems to you the best that you can do without further assistance ask a friend to read it. **Prepare a copy for peer review.** Print your text—doubled-spaced—and give it to your reader.

When the paper is returned to you, respond to the suggestions appropriately. Be sure to give credit in your paper to your reader (something such as "I want to thank Tina Lee for valuable suggestions," or "Martin Baratz suggested the comparison with Adrienne Kennedy's play"), and then print out this new version. Do not rely on reading the paper on the screen; you will need to read the hard copy, with an eye toward making further revisions.

Producing the final version. After you print out the version you have prepared in response to the comments by your reviewer, read it to see whether you can make any further improvements. (Even at this late date, you may think of a better title or you may sense

that a quotation doesn't sound quite right.) You can make small changes in ink, but if you make a substantial number of changes, print out a clean copy. Your paper will be neater, and there is little labor involved.

Basic Manuscript Form

Much of what follows regarding basic manuscript form is nothing more than common sense.

- Use $8^1/_2$-by-11-inch paper of good weight.
- If you use a word processor, be sure to use a reasonably fresh ribbon, double-space, and print on one side of the page only. If you must submit a handwritten copy, use lined paper and write on one side of the page only, in ink, on every other line. Most instructors do *not* want papers to be enclosed in any sort of binder. Most prefer papers to be stapled in the upper left corner; do not crimp or crease corners and expect them hold together.
- Leave an adequate margin—1 or $1^1/_2$ inches —at top, bottom, and sides.
- Number the pages consecutively, using Arabic numerals in the upper right-hand corner.
- Put your name and class or course number in the upper left-hand corner of the first page. It is a good idea to put your name in the upper right hand corner of each subsequent page so that your essay can be easily reassembled if a page gets separated.
- Create you own title, one that reflects your topic or thesis. For example, a paper on *The Glass Menagerie* should not be called "*The Glass Menagerie*" but might be called "Tom's Romanticization of Laura: A View of *The Glass Menagerie.*"
- Center the title of your essay below the top margin of the first page. Begin the first word of the title with a capital, and capitalize each subsequent word except articles (*the, an, an*) and prepositions (*in, on, or, with,* and so forth). For example:

```
The Truth of Dreams in

A Midsummer Night's Dream
```

- Begin the essay 1 or 2 inches below the title.
- Your extensive revisions should have been made in your drafts, but minor last-minute revisions may be made—neatly—on the fin-

ished copy. Proofreading may catch some typographical errors, and you may notice some small weaknesses. Additions should be made *above* the line, with a caret (^) *below* the line to indicate placement of the correction. Mark deletions by drawing a horizontal line through the word or words you wish to delete. Use a vertical line, to separate words that should not have been run together.

Quotations and Quotation Marks

Excerpts from the plays you are writing about are indispensable. Such quotations not only let the reader know what you are talking about, but they also present the material you are responding to, thus letting the reader share your responses.

Here are some mechanical matters regarding the presentation of quotations:

- **Identify the speaker or write of the quotation** so that the reader is not left with a sense of uncertainty. Usually this identification precedes the quoted material (for example, "Smith says . . .") in accordance with the principle of letting readers know where they are going, but occasionally it may follow the quotation, especially if it will provide something of a pleasant surprise. For instance, in a discussion of Williams's *The Glass Menagerie*, you might quote a comment that seems to belittle the play and then reveal that Williams himself was the speaker.
- **The quotation must fit grammatically into your sentence.** Suppose you want to use Hamlet's line, "The spirit that I have seen/ May be the devil." Do not say:

In 2.2, in a soliloquy, Hamlet says that the spirit he "have seen / May be the devil."

You'll have to say something like this:

In 2.2, in a soliloquy, Hamlet says that the spirit he has "seen / May be the devil."

Or you can say:

In 2.2, in a soliloquy, Hamlet says, "The spirit that I have seen / May be the devil."

- **The quotation must be exact.** Any material that you add—even one or two words—must be in square brackets as shown in this example:

When Hamlet says, "The spirit [who looked like Hamlet Senior] that I have seen / May be the devil," he is expressing a perfectly reasonable view.

If you wish to omit material from within a quotation, indicate the ellipsis by three spaced periods. If a sentence ends in an omission, add a closed-up period and then three spaced periods to indicate the omission. The following example is based on a quotation from the sentences immediately above this one:

The instructions say that "if you . . . omit material from within a quotation, [you must] indicate the ellipsis. . . . If a sentence ends in an omission, add a closed-up period and then three spaced periods. . . ."

Notice that although material preceded the first "if you," periods are not needed to indicate the omission because "if you" began a sentence in the original. Customarily, initial and terminal omissions are indicated only when they are part of the sentence you are quoting. Even such omissions need not be indicated when the quoted material is obviously incomplete—when, for instance, it is a word or phrase. Notice, too, that although quotations must be given word for word, the initial capitalization can be adapted, as here where "If" is changed to "if."

When a line or more of verse is omitted from a passage that is set off, the three spaced periods are printed on a separate line:

If we shadows have offended,
Think but this, and all is mended;

. . .

Give me your hands, if we be friends,
And Robin shall restore amends.

- **Distinguish between short and long quotations,** and treat each appropriately. Short quotations (usually defined as fewer than three lines of verse or five lines of prose) are enclosed within quotations marks and run into the text (rather than set off, without quotation marks). The following examples can be run in with text:

Near the end of <u>Oedipus Rex,</u> the Chorus reminds the audience that Oedipus "solved the famous riddle," but it does not tell us what the riddle was.

Shakespeare tells us, very early in the first scene of <u>Hamlet</u> that it is midnight ("'tis now struck twelve"), and he ends the scene, perhaps three or four minutes later, by telling us it is dawn, when Horatio says, "But, look, the morn in russet mantle clad/ Walks o'er the dew of yon high eastward hill."

Notice in the first passage that although only four words are being quoted, quotation marks are used, indicating that these are Sophocles's words, not the essayist's's. Notice that in the second example a slash (diagonal line, or virgule) is used to indicate the end of a line of verse other than the last line quoted. The slash is, of course, not used for prose, and it is not used if poetry is set off, indented and printed as verse, as shown here:

Horatio's speech is varied. In a single speech he can be cautious, reserved, given to understatement, as in the first line of the following quotation, and yet he can then immediately go on in a somewhat poetic or metaphoric vein, talking about the dawn, and then shift to a businesslike tone, all within the space of a few lines:

> So have I heard and do in part
> believe it.
> But, look, the morn in russet
> mantle clad
> Walks o'er the dew of yon high
> eastward hill.
> Break we our watch up, and by my
> advice
> Let us impart what we have seen
> tonight
> Unto young Hamlet; for upon my
> life,

> This spirit, dumb to us will
> speak to him.

Material that is set off (usually three or more lines of verse, five or more lines of prose) is *not* enclosed within quotation marks. To set it off, indent the quotation ten spaces from the left margin. **Poetry should be centered.** (Be sparing in your use of long quotations.) Use quotations as evidence, not as padding. Do not bore the reader with material that can be effectively reduced either by paraphrase or by cutting. If you cut, indicate ellipses as explained above.

- **Commas and periods go inside the quotation marks.** (An exception is if the quotation is immediately followed by material in parentheses or in square brackets. If that is the case, close the quotation, give the parenthetic or bracketed material, and then—after the closing parenthesis or bracket—put the comma or period.)

Semicolons, colons, and dashes go outside quotation marks. Question marks and exclamation points go inside if they are part of the quotation, outside if they are your own. In the following example, the first two question marks are Shakespeare's, so they go *inside* the quotation marks. The third question mark, however, is the essayist's, so it goes *outside* the quotation marks.

The first line we hear in <u>Hamlet</u> is a question, when Bernardo says, "Who's there?" Bernardo soon asks yet another question: "Say, what, is Horatio there?" Given this atmosphere of uncertainty, can we accept Horatio's easy confidence that the ghost "will not appear"?

- Use *single* quotation marks for material contained within a quotation that itself is within quotation marks. For example:

The editors of <u>Types of Drama</u> say, "With Puck we look at the antics in the forest, smile tolerantly, and say with a godlike perspective, 'Lord, what fools these mortals be!'"

- **Use quotation marks around titles of short works,** that is, for titles of chapters in books and for essays that might not be published by themselves. Unpublished works, even book-length dissertations, are also enclosed in quotation marks. **Use italics (indicated by underlining) for books, that is, for plays, periodicals, novels, and collections of essays.**

A Note on Footnotes and Endnotes

You may wish to use a footnote or endnote, telling the reader that the passage you are quoting is found in this book on such and such a page. Let us assume that you have already mentioned the author and the title of the play and have just quoted a passage. At the end of the sentence that includes the quotation, or at the end of the quotation if you are offering it as an independent sentence, following the period add the number *1*, elevating it slightly above the line. Do not put a period after the digit. Near the bottom of the paper, indent five spaces and insert the number *1*, elevated and without a period. Then write the appropriate information. For example:

> ¹Reprinted in Sylvan Barnet et al.,
> *Types of Drama*, 8th ed. (New York:
> Longman, 2001), p. 236.

Notice that the abbreviation for *page* is *p.*, not *pg.*; the abbreviation for *pages* is *pp.* (for example, pp. 236–237). For verse plays whose lines are numbered, the usual procedure is not to cite a page but to cite act, scene and line numbers in parentheses after the quotation. The old method was to give the act in capital roman numerals, the scene in small roman numerals, and the line in Arabic numerals, with periods following the act and scene (for example, V.i.7–11), but the preferred method today is to give the act, scene, and line (if numbers in the text) in Arabic numerals, with periods but no extra spaces.

> The lunatic, the lover and the poet
> Are of imagination all compact.
> One sees more devils than vast hell
>   can hold,
> That is the madman. The lover, all
>   as frantic,
> Sees Helen's beauty in a brow of
>   Egypt.
>
>   (5.1.11)¹

The corresponding footnote would read:

> ¹William Shakespeare, *A Midsummer Night's Dream*, 5.1.11, reprinted in Sylvan Barnet et al., *Types of Drama*, 8th ed. (New York: Longman, 2001).

If you have mentioned the author, but not the work, the note would follow this pattern:

> ¹*A Midsummer Night's Dream*, reprinted in Sylvan Barnet et al., *Types of Drama*, 8th ed. (New York: Longman, 2001).

In short, you need not give information in the note that is already given in the main body of the essay.

In order to eliminate writing many footnotes, each one merely citing the page of a quotation, you can write in the first footnote after giving the bibliographical information as above something such as this:

> All further references to this work will be given parenthetically, within the text of the essay.

Thus, when you quote the next passage from the play, at the end of the sentence—just before the period—you need only insert a pair of parentheses enclosing the page number of the act, scene, and line number. Here is an example:

> We quickly hear Willy Loman's irritation when he says, in his third speech, "I said nothing happened. Didn't you hear me?" (p.807).

Notice that in the sample analysis on pages 1477–79 the author used only one footnote and then cited all of the other quotations parenthetically.

A Note on Internal Citations

If you use secondary sources, your instructor may want you to cite your source (usually an authority you are quoting or summarizing) parenthetically within the body of your paper. Here is an example, citing page 29 of a book:

> In *Comic Women, Tragic Men*, Linda Bamber says that in Shakespeare's plays, "The natural order, the status quo, is for men to rule women" (29).

or

In Shakespeare's plays "the natural order," Bamber says, "is for men to rule women"
(29), but she goes on to modify this statement.

At the end of your paper on a separate page with
the heading "Works Cited," list all of your sources, alphabetically by author, with last name first, then the
title (underlined, to indicate italics), then the place of
publication, the publisher, and the date. After the
date, type a period.

Bamber, Linda. Comic Women, Tragic Men.
  Stanford. Stanford, UP, 1982.

For details on how to cite journals, books published
in more than one volume, translations, and dozens of
other troublesome works, see Joseph Gibaldi, *MLA
Handbook for Writers of Research Papers*, 5th ed. (New
York: MLA, 1999). (By the way, MLA stands for Modern Language Association.)

A SAMPLE STUDENT ESSAY, USING SOURCES

We have already discussed manuscript form. Here we
give a student's documented paper on Arthur Miller's
Death of a Salesman. (The play appears in this book on
page 806). The student had taken notes on index
cards, both from the play and from secondary sources,
and had arranged and rearranged the notes as her topic
and thesis became clearer to her. We preface the final
version of her essay with the rough outline that she
prepared before she wrote her first draft.

Linda
  realistic
  encourages Willy
  foolish? Loving? *Both? Not so foolish: Knows how to calm him down*
  prevented him from succeeding?
  doesn't understand W's needs? or
    nothing else to do?
  other women
  (quote some critics knocking Linda)
5 the Woman
4 the two women in restaurant *(Forsythe first, then Letta)*
3 Jenny
2 W's mother (compare with father?)
    check to see exactly what the play
    says about her
1 Howard's wife (and daughter?) *(discuss this first)*
6 discuss Linda last
  titles
    Linda Loman
    Women in Miller's Salesman
    Gender in . . . *Male and female in Death . .*
    Men and Women: Arthur M's View
    Willy Loman's Women

Here is the final version of the essay. In our marginal
comments we call attention to the essayist's rhetorical
strategies.

Ruth Katz

The Women in <u>Death of a Salesman</u>

The title announces the topic.

<u>Death of a Salesman</u>[1] is of course about a salesman, but it is also about the American dream of success. Somewhere between the narrowest topic, the death of a salesman, and the largest topic, the examination of American values, is Miller's picture of the American family. This paper will chiefly study one member of the family, Willy's wife, Linda Loman, but before examining Miller's depiction of her, it will look at Miller's depiction of other women in the play in order to make clear Linda's distinctive traits. We will see that although her role in society is extremely limited, she is an admirable figure, fulfilling the roles of wife, and mother with remarkable intelligence.

The opening paragraph explains why the chosen topic is worth looking at, and it also, at the end of the paragraph, announces the thesis (Linda Loman "is an admirable figure").

Linda is the only woman who is on stage much of the time, but there are several other women in the play: "the Woman" (the unnamed woman in Willy's hotel room), Miss Forsythe and her friend Letta (the two women who join the brothers in the restaurant), Jenny (Charley's secretary), the various women that the brothers talk about, and the voices of Howard's daughter and wife. We also hear a little about Willy's mother.

The second paragraph reminds the reader that there are other women in the play.

We will look first at the least important (but not utterly unimportant) of these, the voices of Howard's daughter and wife on the wire recorder. Of Howard's seven-year-old daughter we know only that she can whistle "Roll Out the Barrel" and that according to Howard she "is crazy about me." The other woman in Howard's life is equally under his thumb. Here is the dialogue that tells us about her--and her relation to her husband.

The opening sentence of this paragraph announces the topic.

> HOWARD's VOICE: "Go on, say something." (<u>Pause.</u>)
>   "Well, you gonna talk?"
> HIS WIFE: "I can't think of anything."
> HOWARD's VOICE: "Well, talk--it's turning."
> HIS WIFE (<u>shyly, beaten</u>). "Hello." (<u>Silence.</u>) "Oh, Howard, I can't
>   talk into this . . . "
> HOWARD (snapping the machine off). That was my wife. (824)

The quotation from the play provides evidence to support the essayist's thesis.

There is, in fact, a third woman in Howard's life, the maid. Howard says that if he can't be at home when the Jack Benny program comes on,

---

[1]<u>Death of a Salesman</u> appears in Sylvan Barnet, et al., <u>Types of Drama</u>, 8th ed. (New York: Longman, 2001). References to the play are to this edition.

he uses the wire recorder. He tells "the maid to turn the radio on when Jack Benny comes on, and this automatically goes on with the radio. . . ." (825). In short, the women in Howard's world exist to serve (and to worship) him.

The transition ("Another woman") helps the reader to see where the author is going.

Another woman who seems to have existed only to serve men is Willy Loman's mother. On one occasion, in speaking with Ben, Willy remembers being on her lap, and Ben, on learning that his mother is dead, utters a platitudinous description of her, "Fine specimen of a lady, Mother" (816), but that's as much as we learn of her. Willy is chiefly interested in learning about his father, who left the family and went to Alaska. Ben characterizes the father as "a very great and a very wild-hearted man" (817), but the fact that the father left his family and apparently had no further communication with his wife and children seems to mean nothing to Ben. Presumably the mother struggled along to bring up the boys, but her efforts are unmentioned.

A secondary source is cited, but is not blindly accepted.

Curiously, some writers defend the father's desertion of his family. Lois Gordon says, "The first generation (Willy's father) has been forced, in order to make a living, to break up the family" (278), but nothing in the play supports this assertion that the father was "forced" to break up the family.

Willy, like Ben, assumes that men are heroic and women are nothing except servants and sex machines. For instance, Willy says to Ben, "Please tell about Dad. I want my boys to hear. I want them to know the kind of stock they spring from" (817). As Kay Stanton, a feminist critic says, Willy's words imply "an Edenic birth myth," a world "with all the Loman men springing directly from their father's side, with no commingling with a female" (69).

Another secondary source is cited, this time with implicit approval.

Another woman who, like Howard's maid and Willy's mother, apparently exists only to serve is Jenny, Charley's secretary. She is courteous, and she is treated courteously by Charley and by Charley's son, Bernard, but she has no identity other than that of a secretary. And, as a secretary-- that is, as a nonentity in the eyes of at least some men--she can be addressed insensitively. Willy Loman makes off-color remarks to her:

The opening sentence connects this new figure, Jenny, with figures who have already been discussed ("like Howard's made and Willy's mother").

A quotation from the text brings us into close contact with the play.

WILLY. . . . Jenny, Jenny, good to see you. How're ya? Workin'? Or still honest?

JENNY. Fine. How've you been feeling?

WILLY. Not much any more, Jenny. Ha, ha! (828)

The first of these comments seems to suggest that a working woman is not honest--that is, is a prostitute or is engaged in some other sort of hanky-panky, as is the Woman who in exchange for silk stockings and sex sends Willy directly into the buyer's office. The second of Willy's jokes, with its remark about not feeling much, also refers to sex. In short, though readers or viewers of the play see Jenny as a thoroughly respectable woman, they see her not so much as an individual but as a person engaged in routine work and as a person to whom Willy can speak crudely.

The words "In short" clearly introduce a summary of the point being made.

It is a little harder to be certain about the characters of Miss Forsythe and Letta, the two women in the scene in Stanley's restaurant. For Happy, Miss Forsythe is "strudel," an object for a man to consume, and for Stanley she and her friend Letta are "chippies," that is, prostitutes. But is it clear that they are prostitutes? When Happy tells Miss Forsythe that he is in the business of selling, he makes a dirty joke, saying, "You don't happen to sell, do you?" (831). She replies, "No, I don't sell," and if we take this seriously and if we believe her, we can say that she is respectable and is rightly putting Happy in his place. Further, her friend Letta says, "I gotta get up very early tomorrow. I got jury duty" (835), which implies that she is a responsible citizen. Still, the girls do not seem especially thoughtful. When Biff introduces Willy to the girls, Letta says, "Isn't he cute? Sit down with us, Pop" (835), and when Willy breaks down in the restaurant, Miss Forsythe says, "Say, I don't like that temper of his" (835). Perhaps we can say this: It is going too far--on the basis of what we see--to agree with Stanley that the women are "chippies," or with Happy, who assumes that every woman is available for sex, but Miss Forsythe and Letta do not seem to be especially responsible or even interesting people. That is, as Miller presents them, they are of little substance, simply figures introduced into the play in order to show how badly Happy and Biff behave.

The writer frankly confesses some uncertainty in discussing the next two women. She quotes passages and cautiously draws inferences.

The long paragraph ends with a concise summary ("That is") of the writer's point.

The most important woman in the play, other than Linda, is "the Woman," who for money or stockings and perhaps for pleasure has sex with Willy, and who will use her influence as a receptionist or secretary in the office to send Willy directly on to the buyer, without his having to wait at the desk. But even though the Woman gets something out of the relationship, she knows that she is being used. When Biff appears in the hotel room, she asks him, "Are you football or base-

The first sentence of the paragraph clearly indicates the special status of "the Woman." She is "The most important woman in the play, other than Linda." Obviously the writer's structure involves moving from the least important, thereby avoiding an anticlimax.

ball?" Biff replies, "Football," and the Woman, "<u>angry, humiliated</u>," says, "That's me, too" (836). We can admire her vigorous response, but, again, like the other women whom we have discussed, she is not really an impressive figure. We can say that, at best, in a society that assumes women are to be exploited by men, she holds her own.

At this point, having discussed all of the women except Linda, the writer offers a brief summary.

So far, then--though we have not yet talked about Linda--the world of <u>Death of a Salesman</u> is not notable for its pictures of impressive women. True, most of the males in the play--Willy, Biff, Happy, Ben, and such lesser characters as Stanley and Howard--are themselves pretty sorry specimens, but Bernard and Charley are exceptionally decent and successful people, people who can well serve as role models. Can any female character in the play serve as a role model?

Turning now to Linda, the writer sketches some background by quoting one critical view.

Linda has evoked strongly contrasting reactions from the critics. Some of them judge her very severely. For instance, Lois Gordon says that Linda "encourages Willy's dream, yet she will not let him leave her for the New Continent, the only realm where the dream can be fulfilled" (280). True, Linda urges Willy not to follow Ben's advice of going to Alaska, but surely the spectator of the play cannot believe that Willy is the sort of man who can follow in Ben's footsteps and violently make a fortune. And, in fact, Ben is so vile a person (as when he trips Biff, threatens Biff's eye with the point of his umbrella, and says, "Never fight fair with a stranger, boy" [817]), that we would not want Willy to take Ben's advice.

The writer quotes a second critical view. Probably the reader senses that the writer will reject this view.

A second example of a harsh view of Linda is Brian Parker's comment on "the essential stupidity of Linda's behavior. Surely it is both stupid and immoral to encourage the man you love in self-deceit and lies" (54). Parker also says that Linda's speech at the end, when she says she cannot understand why Willy killed himself, "is not only pathetic, it is also an explanation of the loneliness of Willy Loman which threw him into other women's arms" (54). Nothing in the play suggests that Linda was anything other than a highly supportive wife. If Willy turned to other women, surely it was not because Linda did not understand him. Finally, one last example of the Linda-bashing school of commentary: Guerin Bliquez speaks of "Linda's facility for prodding Willy to his doom" (83).

The writer summarizes the case against Linda.

Very briefly, the arguments against Linda are that (1), she selfishly prevented Willy from going to Alaska, (2) she stupidly encourages him in the self-deceptions, and (3) she is materialistic, so that even at the end, in the Requiem, when she says she has made the last payment on the house, she is talking about money. But if we study the play we will see that all three of these charges are false. First, although Linda does indeed discourage Willy from taking Ben's advice and going to Alaska, she points out that there is no need for "everybody [to] conquer the world" and that Willy has "a beautiful job here" (827), a job with excellent prospects. She may be mistaken in thinking that Willy has a good job--he may have misled her--but, given what seems to be the situation, her comment is entirely reasonable. So far as the second charge goes, that she encourages him in self-deception, there are two answers. First, on some matters she does not know that Willy has lied to her, and so her encouragement is reasonable and right. Second, on other matters she does know that Willy is not telling the truth, but she rightly thinks it is best not to let him know that she knows, since such a revelation would crush what little self-respect remains in him. Consider, for example, this portion of dialogue, early in the play, when Willy, deeply agitated about his failure to drive and about Biff, has returned from what started out as a trip to Boston. Linda, trying to take his mind off his problems, urges his to go downstairs to the kitchen to try a new kind of cheese:

> LINDA. Go down, try it. And be quiet.
> WILLY (turning to Linda, guiltily). You're not worried about me, are you, sweetheart?
>
>   . . .
>
> LINDA. You've got too much on the ball to worry about.
> WILLY. You're my foundation and my support, Linda.
> LINDA. Just try and relax, dear. You make mountains out of mole-hills.
> WILLY. I wont' fight with him any more. If he wants to go back to Texas, let him go.
> LINDA. He'll find his way. (808)

Of course she does not really think he has a great deal on the ball, and she probably is not confident that Biff will "find his way," but surely she is doing the best thing possible--calming Willy, partly by using soothing words and partly by doing what she can to get Biff out of the house, since she knows that Biff and Willy can't live under the same roof.

The transitional word "but" clearly indicates that we are now going to get the opposing view.

Words such as "First" and "Second" and "for example" keep the reader posted, that is, the writer keeps the needs of her audience in mind.

The quotation is fairly long but not excessively long. Clearly the writer is not padding the essay with long, unnecessary quotations. Rather, she is providing evidence.

The third charge, that she is materialistic, is ridiculous. She <u>has</u> to count the pennies because <u>someone</u> has to see that the bills are paid, and Willy is obviously unable to do so. Here is an example of her supposed preoccupation with money:

> LINDA. Well, there's nine-sixty for the washing machine. And for
>   the vacuum cleaner there's three and a half due on the fif-
>   teenth. Then the roof, you got twenty-one dollars remaining.
> WILLY. It don't leak, does it?
> LINDA. No, they did a wonderful job. Then you owe Frank for the
>   carburetor.
> WILLY. I'm not going to pay that man! That goddam Chevrolet, they
>   ought to prohibit the manufacture of that car!
> LINDA. Well, you owe him three and a half. And odds and ends, comes
>   to around a hundred and twenty dollars by the fifteenth. (813)

It might be nice if Linda spent her time taking courses at an adult education center and thinking high thoughts, but it's obvious that <u>someone</u> in the Loman family (as in all families) has to keep track of the bills.

The worst that can be said of Linda is that she subscribes to three American ideas of the time--that the man is the breadwinner, that the relationship between a father and his sons is far more impor-tant than the relationship between a mother and her sons, and that a woman's sole job is to care for the house and to produce sons for her husband. She is the maidservant to her husband and to her sons, but in this she is like the vast majority of women of her time, and she should not be criticized for not being an innovator. Compared to her husband and her sons, Linda (though of course not perfect) is a tower of common sense, virtue, and strength. In fact, far from causing Willy's failure, she does what she can to give him strength to face the facts, for instance when she encourages him to talk to Howard about a job in New York: "Why don't you go down to the place tomorrow and tell Howard you've simply got to work in New York? You're too ac-commodating, dear" (807). Notice, too, her speech in which she agrees with Biff's decision that it is best for Biff to leave for good: she goes to Willy and says, "I think that's the best way, dear. 'Cause there's no use drawing it out, you'll just never get along" (839). Linda is not the most forceful person alive, or the brightest, but she is decent and she sees more clearly than do any of the other Lomans.

There is nothing in the play to suggest that Arthur Miller was a feminist or was ahead of his time in his view of the role of women. On the contrary, the play seems to give a prefeminist view, with women playing subordinate roles to men. The images of success of the best sort--not of Ben's ruthless sort—are Charley and Bernard, two males. Probably Miller, writing in the 1940s, could hardly conceive of a successful woman other than as a wife or mother. Notice, by the way, that Bernard--probably the most admirable man in the play--is not only an important lawyer but the father of two sons, apparently a sign of his complete success as a man. Still, Miller's picture of Linda is by no means condescending. Linda may not be a genius, but she is the brightest and the most realistic of the Lomans. Things turn out badly, but not because of Linda. The viewer leaves the theater with profound respect for her patience, her strength, her sense of decency, and, yes, her intelligence and her competence in dealing with incompetent men.

The final paragraph begins with a sort of overview of the play. With the transitional word "Still" (in the middle of the paragraph) the writer moves from Miller's limited view of women to a close-up of Linda.

Works Cited

Bliquez, Guerin. "Linda's role in Death of a Salesman." Modern Drama 10 (1968): 383-86.

Gordon, Lois. "Death of a Salesman: An Appreciation." The Forties: Fiction, Poetry, Drama. Ed. Warren French. Deland, Florida: Everett/Edwards, 1969. 273-83.

Koon, Helene Wickham, ed. Twentieth Century Interpretations of Death of a Salesman. Englewood Cliffs, New Jersey: Prentice, 1983.

Miller, Arthur. Death of a Salesman. Introduction to Literature. Ed. Sylvan Barnet et al. 12th ed. New York: Longman, 2000. 806-842.

Parker, Brian. "Point of View in Arthur Miller's Death of a Salesman." University of Toronto Quarterly 35 (1996): 144-47. Rpt. in Koon. 41-55.

Stanton, Kay. "Women and the American Dream in Death of a Salesman." Feminist Readings of American Drama. Ed. Judith Schlueter. Rutherford, New Jersey: Fairleigh Dickinson UP, 1989. 67-102.

USING ELECTRONIC SOURCES

Cautionary Words

First, some cautionary words. Because of the ease of using the Internet, with its access to electronic mail (e-mail), newsgroups, mailing lists, and, especially, sites and links on the World Wide Web, many students now make it their first—and, unfortunately too often their only—stop for research.

All of us, however, must be *critical* users of the material we find on the WWW. The WWW is up-to-date *and* out-of-date, helpful *and* disappointing. It can be a researcher's dream come true and also a source of errors and a time waster. For sources on the World Wide Web, as with print sources, you must evaluate what you have located and gauge how much or how little it will contribute to your analysis and your argument. Remember: Everything you find on the Internet is *not* of equal value.

Be sure to focus the topic of your research as precisely as you can before you embark on a web search. Lots of surfing and browsing can sometimes turn up good material, but using the web without a focus can prove distracting and unproductive. It takes you away from library research (where the results might be better) and from the actual planning and writing of the paper.

✓ A Checklist for Evaluating Sources on the World Wide Web

✓ Does this site or page look as if it can help me in my assignment?

✓ Whose site or page is this?

✓ What is the intended audience?

✓ What is the point of view? Are there signs of a specific slant or bias?

✓ What are the detail, depth, and quality of the material presented?

✓ Is the text well written?

✓ Can this Web information be corroborated or supported by print sources?

✓ When was the site or page made available? Has it been recently revised or updated? *Note:* Your browser will enable you to get this information; if you are using Netscape 4.01, for example, go to View, and choose Page Info.

✓ Can the person or institution, company, or agency responsible for this site or page receive e-mail comments, questions, and criticisms?

Theater Web Sites

- **E-resources! Theater**
  Resources by Subject: Theatre Indexes Humanities Abstracts Coverage: 1984 to present indexes for core scholarly journals in the humanities. Also includes theater, book, and film reviews.
  http://www.lafayette.edu/library/subject/theater.html

- **International Index to the Performing Arts**
  IIPA allows people to search by subject, author, keyword, or title in order to obtain full text arti-

cles from around two hundred international performing arts periodicals, indexes to performing arts and related articles and obituaries appearing in the *New York Times* and the *Washington Post.* Access to IIPA Full Text is available to authorized users at subscribing institutions only.
http://iipaft.cadwyck.com/

- **Resources in Theater and Drama**
  This valuable guide lists, in order of usefulness, selected sources that supply information about theater and drama. It covers items such as critical information on plays, biographical information on playwrights, and information on play production.
  http://www.bsu.edu/library/reference/guides/drama.html

- **Theatre Central**
  This news production-focused site maintained by Playbill Online provides a comprehensive directory of theater links such as listings of performances in major theatrical centers, listings of tours, and current news on theater celebrities.
  http://www1.playbill.com/cgibin/plb/central?cmd=start

- **Theater Databases**
  Theater Databases on BISON will primarily lead to articles in journals, electronic journals, magazines, and full-text literary databases including poetry and prose.
  http://ublib.buffalo.edu/libraries/e-resources/theater.html

- **Voice of the Shuttle Guide to WWW Theater and Drama Sites**
  This site provides an alphabetical listing of general links for drama, theater, and performance studies Web sites, and specific links for journals, theater departments, conferences, calls for papers, and performance events.
  http://vos.ucsb.edu/shuttle/english2.html#drama

- **Worldwide Arts Resources: Theater Resources Index**
  Though its focus is on art in general, this site provides access to thousands of theater-related resources such as journals and magazines, information about playwrights and shows, and resources for technical theater.
  http://wwar.com/theater/perform.html

- **Yahoo: Theater Resources**
  This site includes links for plays, theater companies, drama history. In addition to providing up-to-date theater news and a forum for chats, this site allows people to search for their specific interests in theater. It provides researchers with dozens of sub listings in more focused areas such as regional theater, *commedia dell'arte*, dramaturgy, improvisation, and stage combat.
  http://dir.yahoo.com/Arts/Performing_Arts/ Theater/

Citing a Web Source

Scholars and reference librarians have not reached a consensus about the correct form—what should be included, and in what order—for the citation of Web sources. But all agree on two principles: (1) Give as much information as you can; (2) Make certain that your readers can retrieve the source themselves—which means that you should check the URL (Uniform Resource Locator) carefully. For accuracy's sake, it is a good idea to copy the URL from the Location line of your browser and paste it into your list of works cited.

A Checklist for Citing WWW Sources

Provide the following information:

✓ Author
✓ Title
✓ Publication information
✓ Title of archive or database
✓ Date (if given) when the site was posted; sometimes termed the "revision" or "modification" date
✓ Name of institution/organization that supports or is associated with this site
✓ Date that you accessed this source
✓ URL (Uniform Resource Locator—the Web address)

Recommended Web Sites for Scholarly Citation and the Internet/WWW

Longman Web site: (http://longman.awl.com/ englishpages/). Includes a range of resources in five areas: Online Citation Guide; Composition; Literature; Basic Skills; Technical Writing.

MLA on the Web: (http://www.mla.org/). Includes a link to a site of guidelines for MLA (Modern Language Association) documentation style (e.g., Citing Sources from the World Wide Web).

A GLOSSARY OF DRAMATIC TERMS

absurd, theater of the. Drama of such writers as Eugène Ionesco and Samuel Beckett in France and Harold Pinter in England imitates the absurdity of our existence. "Everything, as I see it, is an aberration," Ionesco has said. Among the basic themes are loneliness in a world without God, inability to communicate, dehumanization at the hands of mass media, and impotence in the face of society and of death. Though the plays are serious, they may contain extravagantly comic scenes to depict a reality that is absurd, illogical, and senseless—a world of futility and meaningless clichés. In Ionesco's *The Chairs* (1951) an elderly couple rush about, filling a room with chairs for nonexistent visitors. Old age is a fact, but an absurdity, too, and old people are incomprehensible. At the end of *The Chairs*, an orator who is to deliver a solemn talk about the truths of life turns out to be deaf and dumb and merely makes unintelligible noises and gestures to the invisible crowd. Ionesco summarizes the theme of *The Chairs* (*New York Times*, June 1, 1958): "I have tried to deal . . . with emptiness, with frustration, with this world, at once fleeting and crushing. The characters I have used are not fully conscious of their spiritual rootlessness, but they feel it instinctively and emotionally." One basis of the inability to communicate, and one that the "absurd" dramatists seize upon, is the corruption of language. The absurdity of trying to communicate by means of a debased language is dramatized by Ionesco in *The Bald Soprano* (1948), in which the characters speak in clichés. Because the characters are incomprehensible and the happenings illogical and baffling, the spectators cannot simply sit back in ease but are continually challenged to grasp the play's meaning. The theater of the absurd can be said to be a descendant of expressionism. Consult M. Esslin, *The Theatre of the Absurd.*

act. A main division in drama or opera. Act divisions probably arose in Roman theory and derive ultimately from the Greek practice of separating episodes in a play by choral interludes, but Greek (and probably Roman) plays were performed without interruption, for the choral interludes were part of the plays themselves. The division of Elizabethan plays into five acts is often the work of editors rather than authors. No play of Shakespeare's was published in his lifetime with divisions into five acts. Today an act division is commonly indicated by lowering the curtain and turning up the houselights. A **scene** is a smaller unit, either (1) a division with no change of locale and no abrupt shift of time, or (2) a division consisting of an actor or a group of actors on the stage. According to the second definition, the departure or entrance of an actor changes the composition of the group and thus produces a new scene. In an entirely different sense, the scene is the locale where a work is set. The first speech in *Romeo and Juliet* informs the audience of the play's locale: "In fair Verona, where we lay our scene." Often the décor lets the spectator know where the play is set, but during the last hundred years playwrights have tended, for the convenience of readers, to write long stage directions describing the scene. Here is the beginning of the first stage direction in Shaw's *Candida*: "A fine morning in October 1894 in the north east quarter of London, a vast district miles away from the London of Mayfair and St. James's, and much less narrow, squalid, fetid and airless in its slums."

acting. The imitation by one person of another. The two extreme views of the actor's methods are, on the one hand, that acting is a craft, a matter of developing the technical skill to arouse certain feelings in an audience by means of gesture and voice, and, on the other hand, that acting is a matter of psychologically exploring the character, playing (so to speak) from the heart rather than the head. The first view is especially identified with Dennis Diderot, who in *The Paradox of Acting* (1773–88) said, "Actors impress the public not when they are impassioned but when they effectively imitate passion." The second view is especially associated with Constantin Stanislavski (1863–1938), who insisted that the actor must "sense" the "inner state" of the role. In America in the 1930s and 1940s, a school of acting called *The Method* was greatly influenced by Stanislavski.

action. (1) The physical movement of an actor, whether, for example, he is leaping into Ophelia's grave or speaking softly to himself. That talk is action is easily seen in the Bastard's remark (*King John*, 2.1.466): "Zounds! I was never so bethumped with words / Since I first called my brother's father dad." (2) An incident in the plot; an episode. Aristotle's statement that a drama is an "imitation of an action" (*praxis*) has provoked considerable controversy; recently there has been a tendency to regard this action as the motive underlying the outward deeds of the plot. Francis Fergusson says (in *The Human Image in Dramatic Literature*, p. 116), for example, that the action of *Oedipus the King* "is the quest for Laius's slayer, . . . which persists through the changing circumstances of the play."

acto. A short dramatic sketch, written in a mixture of Spanish and English, often with stereotyped characters satirizing the Anglo establishment. The form, developed by Luis Valdez in 1965 during a strike by farm workers in California, aims at stimulating Chicanos to value their culture and to unite against exploitation (see pages 937, 945–46). Consult *The Drama Review* 11:4 (1967).

aesthetic distance, or **sychical distance.** The detachment between the receptor and the work of art. The concept is chiefly associated with Edward Bullough (see the essay in his *Aesthetics,* reprinted in Melvin Rader, *A Modern Book of Aesthetics*). Bullough explains that there must be some sort of psychical "distance" (gap) between our practical self (our personal needs) and the work of art. Thus, an old man who has been treated harshly by his children may be unable to divorce his personal feelings from *King Lear*. He may be too involved with the piece as life to see it as art. However, "distance" does not mean that receptors are totally detached or objective. Rather, they are detached from their usual personal involvements, and because of this detachment they can look with a new vigorous interest—a new sort of passion born of a new personality—at the work of art as art. Persons who do not understand the need for distance between themselves and a work, Bullough explains, commonly say that they do not wish to see a tragedy because there is enough suffering in real life. However, the more sophisticated spectator at a tragedy realizes that as a picture is distanced by the frame, a play is distanced from the audience (the characters may speak verse, they perform behind footlights, and their deeds cohere to make a unified harmonious pattern); the feelings a play evokes are not the feelings evoked by an equivalent event in real life. In the theater we feel "rapturous awe" at what in life would be depressing. See also *dramatic illusion, empathy, epic drama.*

agit-prop. Propaganda theater. The term is derived from the Department of Agitation and Propaganda, formed in the former Soviet Union in 1920.

agon (Greed, "contest"). A debate in a Greek comedy. In the last few decades the term has been used (e.g., by Francis Fergusson, *The Idea of a Theater*) to designate a scene of conflict in tragedy, such as the agonizing struggle between Oedipus and Teiresias.

agroikos. See *character.*

alazon. See *character.*

alienation effect. See *epic drama.*

allegory. Often a narrative in which abstractions (e.g., virtue, fear) are made concrete (Mr. Virtue, Giant Fear), for the purpose of effectively communicating a moral. In essence, an allegory is merely a system of equivalents. Though allegory need not personify abstractions, allegoric drama almost always does. *Everyman* (c. 1500), an allegoric morality play, includes among its dramatis personae Death; Good Deeds; Beauty; and of course, Everyman. But morality plays may also include allegoric castles (standing for strength or chastity), roses (standing for love or virtue), and so on. Consult Bernard Spivack, *Shakespeare and the Allegory of Evil*. (See also *symbolism.*)

alternative theater. The theater that sees itself in opposition to the established bourgeois theater. For example, The Living Theatre, an experimental company founded in New York in 1951 and influential in the 1960s, held anarchist and pacifist goals and often sought to arouse the hostility of the audience. Another example is the Teatro Campesino of Luis Valdez, on which see page 937. See T. Shank, *American Alternative Theatre.*

anagnorisis, or **disclosure, discovery, recognition.** For Aristotle the "recognition," or "disclosure," seemed to be merely a recognition of who is who, by such tokens as birthmarks, clothes, and so on, but the term has been extended to include the tragic hero's recognition of his or her nature and/or the essence of life. Thus Othello, having murdered his faithful wife, learns he was beguiled into thinking her dishonest and finally recognizes himself as "one not easily jealous, but being wrought / Perplexed in the extreme"; and he exacts justice from himself by suicide.

antagonist. See *plot, protagonist.*

antecedent action. See *plot.*

anticlimax. A descent, the lines or happenings being markedly less important or less impressive than those that precede. In melodrama, a decrease in tension may cause disappointment and loss of interest; in comedy, a sharp descent (as when the beautiful princess opens her mouth and sounds like a burlesque queen) may get a desirable laugh. On the desirability of a gradual decrease in tension in tragedy (i.e., a "quiet ending"), consult Max Beerhohm, "Last Acts," in *Around Theatres.*

anti-hero. A central character who, reversing the conventional idea of a hero (attractive, brave, high-minded), forces the audience to examine its conception of heroism and indeed of society. An example is Samuel Beckett's tramps.

antimasque. See *masque.*

Apollonian. See *Dionysus.*

arena stage. (1) In British usage, a stage with a back wall and with an audience on three sides. (2) In American usage, a playing space surrounded by spectators, a **theater-in-the-round.** Proponents of arena staging (in the American sense) stress the intimacy afforded by having actors in the midst of the audience, but opponents suggest that at least for some plays the intimacy ought not to be very great. (See *aesthetic distance.*) It has been noted, too, that even in arena staging the audience normally feels set apart from the actors, for the audience is in the dark while the actors are in an illuminated playing area. Critics of arena staging cite the following difficulties: Soliloquies, asides, and direct addresses are hard to deliver in such a theater; directors, aware that the back of an actor's head is not very expressive, tend to have the actors gyrate disturbingly and meaninglessly; entrances and exits are cumbersome; and little use can be made of elevation and of groupings of actors.

arras. See page 218.

aside. See *convention, soliloquy.*

atmosphere. The mood created by setting, language, and happenings.

blocking. The director's organization of the movement on the stage in order to form effective stage positions and groupings.

bombast. Rant; speech that is too inflated for the occasion; from a word meaning "cotton stuffing." In Marlowe's *Tamburlaine* (c. 1587) Tamburlaine brags thus:

Our quivering lances, shaking in the air,
And bullets, like Jove's dreadful thunderbolts,
Enrolled in flames and fiery smoldering mists,
Shall threat the gods more than Cyclopian wars:
And with our sun-bright armor as we march,
Will chase the stars from Heaven and dim their eyes
That stand and muse at our admired arms.

bomolochos. See *character*.

bourgeois drama. A serious play with middle-class dramatis personae. There are a few Elizabethan tragedies of middle-class life, but bourgeois drama, with its emphasis on pathos, is more or less an eighteenth-century invention. Bourgeois dramas were written in the eighteenth and nineteenth centuries, apparently in response to the middle class's desire to see itself on the stage; the bourgeoisie by the eighteenth century regarded themselves as a suitable replacement for the nobleborn of earlier tragedy. Speaking generally, the characteristics of these plays are middle-class dramatis personae, virtue in distress, sentimentality, and an unreasonably high moral tone. Eighteenth-century critics, not sure what to do with pathetic plays on middle-class life, used the terms *drame, drame bourgeois, comédie larmoyante* (tearful comedy), *tragédie bourgeoise*, and *bürgerliches Trauerspiel* (bourgeois tragedy) interchangeably. (Note that a *comédie larmoyante* need not end happily, nor a *tragédie bourgeoise* end sadly.) In England, George Lillo's, *The London Merchant* (1731), "a tale of private woe. A London 'prentice ruined," depicted an apprentice who murdered his benefactor. Bourgeois drama in the nineteenth century became melodrama in many hands but tragedy in Ibsen's hands. Consult Fred O. Nolte, *Early Middle Class Drama*; and Eric Auerbach, *Mimesis*, Chapter 17. On Ibsen as a bourgeois dramatist, consult Eric Bentley, *The Playwright as Thinker*. See *domestic tragedy, sentimental*, and page 805.

box set. Flats connected to form three walls with movable doors and windows. The box set, developed in the mid-nineteenth century, replaced sliding wings and canvas backdrops on which windows, doors, and even pieces of furniture were painted. See *realism*.

burla. See *commedia dell' arte*.

burlesque. Any imitation that, by distortion, aims to amuse. Its subject matter is sometimes said to be faults rather than vices, and its tone is neither shrill nor savage. Thus, in distinction from satire it can be defined as a comic imitation of a mannerism or a minor fault (either in style or subject matter), contrived to arouse amusement rather than indignation. In the theater, a burlesque may be a play that amusingly criticizes another play by grotesquely imitating aspects of it, as Gay's *The Beggar's Opera* (1728) mimicked serious operas. In England, a burlesque may be a musical extravaganza in which fantasy has almost entirely ousted criticism. In America, burlesque (especially popular in the late nineteenth and first half of the twentieth century) is usually a sort of vaudeville or variety show stressing bawdy humor and sex. The sexual theme is most fully revealed in the striptease, introduced about 1920. See *comedy, satire*.

catastrophe. See *plot*.

catharsis. Aristotle and countless followers said that tragedy evokes pity and fear and that it produces in the spectator a catharsis (purgation, or, some scholars hold, purification) of these emotions; it drains or perhaps refines or modifies these emotions, and thus tragedy is socially useful. (Aristotle's *Poetics* is the subject of much controversy; one cannot with security assert that Aristotle said anything without a counterargument being offered. For various views of catharsis, consult F. L. Lucas, *Tragedy*; and Gerald F. Else's monumental *Aristotle's Poetics*.)

character. (1) One of the dramatis personae, for example, Hamlet. (2) The personality of such a figure. Characters are sometimes divided into **flat** and **round characters.** The former have only one "side," representing a single trait (e.g., the faithful wife, the genial drunkard); the latter have many traits and are seen, as it were, from all sides, in the round. The behavior of flat characters is thoroughly predictable; that of round characters is sometimes unexpected though credible. A **stock character** is a type that recurs in many works. For example, from Greek comedy to the present there have been numerous braggart soldiers, stubborn fathers, jealous husbands. Northrop Frye finds four chief types of comic figures: (1) the *alazon,* the imposter, boaster, hypocrite; (2) the *eiron* (see *irony*), the man who deprecates himself and exposes the boaster; (3) the *bomolochos,* the buffoon, or, more generally, the man who entertains by his mannerisms and talk; and (4) the *agroikos,* the straight man who is the unwitting butt of humor. Each of these types appears in many dresses. The *alazon,* for example, is most commonly the braggart soldier (in Latin *miles gloriosus*), but he is also the pedant, the crank, or anyone who is full of ideas that have no relation to reality. (See *commedia dell' arte*; consult Northrop Frye, *Anatomy of Criticism*, pp. 171–176, and R. L. Hunter, *The New Comedy of Greece and Rome*.) Stock characters are not limited to comedy. The proud tragic hero is a stock character, as are, for example, the cruel stepmother and the son who wishes to avenge his father. See also *motivation, plot*. Consult J. L. Styan, *The Elements of Drama*, Chapter 8.

chorus. In Greek drama, a group of singers and dancers (*khoros* in Greek means "dancer") who play a role, for example, Old Men of Corinth. (The chorus leader is the **koryphaios.**) In Aeschylus's *The Suppliants* (c. 490 B.C.E.), perhaps the earliest extant play, the chorus consists of the heroines, but in most Greek plays the chorus consists of subsidiary figures who comment rather helplessly on what is happening to the important people. Aeschylus reduced the chorus of fifty to twelve; Sophocles increased it to fifteen, where it remained. The Greek chorus, it is often said, is a sort of middleman between the unusual main figures and the humdrum spectators. Elizabethan dramas occasionally had a chorus of one actor who, not a participant in the story, commented on it. The Chorus (or prologue) in Shakespeare's *Henry V* urges the audience to

Think when we talk of horses that you see them
Printing their proud hoofs i' the receiving earth;
For 'tis your thoughts that now must deck our kings.
Carry them here and there, jumping o'er times,
Turning the accomplishment of many years
Into an hour-glass: for the which supply,
Admit me Chorus to this history:
Who prologue-like your humble patience pray,
Gently to hear, kindly to judge, our play.

A **chorus character,** or **raisonneur,** however, such as Enobarbus in *Antony and Cleopatra*, is a character who participates in the story yet seems to be the author's mouthpiece, intelligently commenting (often with irony) on the actions of the other characters. However, Alfred Harbage, in *As They Liked It*, skeptically and aptly calls such a figure "The Unreliable Spokesman." The use of the chorus, in one form or another, continues into our times. For example, in T. S. Eliot's *Murder in the Cathedral*, the "Chorus of Women of Canterbury," like a Greek chorus and like the audience, "are forced to bear witness"; and in Tennessee Williams's *The Glass Menagerie*, Tom Wingfield tells the audience he is "the narrator of the play, and also a character in it." See also *plot*.

climax. See *plot*.

closet drama. A play suited only for reading, not for acting. Most nineteenth-century English poetic dramas (e.g., Coleridge's, Shelley's, Tennyson's) fit into this category, although Byron's plays have recently been moving out of the closet. Consult Moody Prior, *The Language of Tragedy*.

comedy. Most broadly, anything amusing, whether a literary work or a situation. More specifically, comedy is (in Dr. Johnson's words) "such a dramatic representation of human life, as may excite mirth." Dramatic comedies generally depict a movement from unhappiness to happiness, from (for example) young lovers frustrated by their parents to young lovers happily married. The unhappy situation is so presented that it entertains rather than distresses the spectator; it is ridiculous or diverting rather than painful.

Comic drama seems related to fertility rituals; it celebrates generation, renewal, variety (laughing away any narrow-minded persons who seek to limit life's abundance), and it celebrates human triumphs over the chances of life. Irate parents and shipwrecks cannot prevent journeys from ending with lovers' meeting. For the kinds of Greek comedy (Old, Middle, and New), see pages 136–38. For the stock characters in Greek comedy see *character*. Consult C. Hoy, *The Hyacinth Room*; *Theories of Comedy*, edited by P. Lauter; and L. J. Potts, *Comedy*.

comedy of humors. A term sometimes applied to plays—notably those of Ben Jonson—in which the characters, though somewhat individualized, obviously represent types of moods (for example, the jealous husband, the witless pedant). A humor was a bodily liquid (such as blood [Latin: *sanguis*], phlegm, yellow bile, black bile) thought to control one's behavior. Allegedly, a proper mixture produced a well-adjusted person, but a preponderance of any one humor produced a distorted personality. The old sense of the word survives in the phrase, "He is in a bad humor"; *sanguine*, *phlegmatic*, and *bilious* are also modern survivals of the old psychology of humors. **Humor characters** are common in **situational comedy;** they are engineered by a clever plot into a situation that displays their absurdity. For example, the man who craves silence is confronted by a talkative woman, or the coward is confronted by the braggart.

comedy of manners, comedy of wit. See *high comedy*.

comic relief. Humorous episodes in tragedy, alleged to alleviate or lighten the tragic effect. Some comic scenes in tragedy, however, not only provide "relief" but enlarge the canvas of tragedy, showing us a fuller picture of life. The clown who brings Cleopatra the poisonous asp sets her tragedy against the daily world. Critics have increasingly noted that the comic scenes (such as the macabre comments of the gravediggers in *Hamlet*) often deepen rather than alleviate the tragic effect. See *tragicomedy*. Consult A. P. Rossiter, *Angel with Horns*, Chapter 14.

commedia dell'arte. Italian drama, more or less improvised, performed by professionals in Italy and abroad, mostly in the sixteenth century but still alive in the early eighteenth century. In contrast to the classically inspired written drama (***commedia erudita***) performed by actors who memorized their lines, *commedia dell'arte* (perhaps best translated "professional drama") employed sketches of plots (*scenario*; plural: *scenarii*) specifying entrances and exits and the gist of the dialogue. In performance these *scenarii* were fleshed out with stock bits of comic stage business (***lazzi***) or larger pieces of business (***burle***) such as practical jokes. (The singulars are ***lazzo*** and ***burla***, respectively.) Thus a *sce-*

nario may call for the *lazzo* of anger or the *burla* of chasing a fly and leave it to the actor to work out the swats and the smile when at last he munches the fly. Though these plays are said to have been improvised, the stock characters, stock situations, and stock stage business make them something more—or less—than improvised. The chief characters—most of whom wore masks—are Pantolone, an elderly Venetian merchant wearing a little cap, a red jacket, loose trousers (hence our word *pants*), and slippers; his age, amours, and avarice make him ridiculous; Dottore, a Bolognese doctor wearing a black academic gown, his age and his pedantry making him ridiculous; Capitano, a soldier, ridiculous in being a braggart and a coward; several servants called *zanne* (singular: *zanni*, from *Gianni*, "Johnny"), including Arlecchino (later Harlequin), who in the sixteenth century wore patches that in the next century were represented by triangles or diamonds; Brighella, a rather cruel and crafty rogue; Pulcinella, noted for his resourcefulness and his disguises; Pedrolino, a naïve valet who becomes the melancholy Pagliacci and Pierrot; Colombina, who later becomes Columbine and loves Harlequin. Furthermore, there are usually four lovers, children of the two Old Men. (See pages 49–66.) Consult Allardyce Nicoll, *Masks, Mimes and Miracles,* and *The World of Harliquin;* and K. M. Lea, *Italian Popular Comedy.*

complication. See *plot.*

confidant (feminine: **confidante**). A character in whom a principal character confides, revealing his or her state of mind and often furthering the exposition. Horatio is Hamlet's confidant; Oenone is Phèdre's. Although Horatio and Oenone are memorable, the confidant is sometimes absurdly vapid. Though the French defended the device as more plausible than the soliloquy, confidants may be more trouble than they are worth. In *The Critic* (1779), Sheridan ridiculed the confidante thus: "Enter Tilburina stark mad in white satin, and her confidante stark mad in white linen."

conflict. See *plot.*

convention. An unrealistic device that the public agrees to tolerate. Thus, a character in a drama may express her thoughts aloud and not be heard by other characters (the **aside**), or she may speak her thoughts aloud on the empty stage (the **soliloquy**). Italian characters (e.g., Desdemona and Iago) speak English, yet are understood to be speaking Italian. In motion pictures, one image fades out and another fades in, and through this convention the audience knows that there is a shift in time or place. More generally any character type, any theme or motif (e.g., the suspected butler), widely used in literature or drama is a convention. Similarly, **realism,** though apparently opposed to conventions, has its own conventions. For instance, a realistic set showing a room is, when one thinks about it, highly conventional, since the room lacks a fourth wall. Consult Harry Levin, *Refractions;* M. C. Bradbrook, *Themes and Conventions of Elizabethan Tragedy.*

cosmic irony. See *irony.*

cothurnus. See *sock and buskin.*

coup de théatre. A surprise, especially a striking turn of events in the plot. Consult Alan R. Thompson, *The Anatomy of Drama.*

crisis. See *plot.*

cruelty, theater of. Antonin Artaud (1896–1948) used the term in 1933 to refer to a drama that, working rather like a plague, would shock people out of the bonds of their "logical" or "civilized" conceptions and would release the suppressed primitive or prelogical powers within them, such as criminal instincts and erotic obsessions, revealing the "cruelty" or terrible mystery of existence. This drama, relying more on gestures, shapes, music, and light than on words (Artaud was immensely impressed by Balinese drama although he did not understand Indonesian), bypasses mere realism (i.e., psychology) and makes manifest the truly real supernatural, creating in the spectator a "kind of terror" or a purifying delirium. Artaud, a poet, actor, and director, published relatively little, but his metaphysics and his emphasis on an antirealistic theater in various ways have influenced Sartre, Camus, Beckett, Ionesco, Genet, and others. Language sometimes becomes gibberish, and madness and violence are presented in order to jolt spectators out of their comfortable false view of humankind and of the universe—or, in less metaphysical plays, in order to reflect on the stage the cruelty of the modern world. Consult Artaud's *The Theater and Its Double;* several articles in *Tulane Drama Review,* 8 (Winter 1963); and the "Conclusion" in Jacques Guicharnaud and June Beckelman, *Modern French Theatre.*

dénouement. See *plot.*

deus ex machina. Literally, a god out of a machine. (1) In Greek drama a god who descends by a cranelike arrangement and solves a problem in the story, thus allowing the play to end. It was much used by Euripides; Sophocles in his old age borrowed the idea and introduced Heracles at the end of *Philoctetes* to induce the title character to go to Troy. (2) Any unexpected and improbable device (e.g., an unexpected inheritance from a long-lost uncle in Australia) used to unknot a problem and thus conclude the work.

deuteragonist. See *protagonist.*

dialogue. The speech exchanged between characters or, loosely, even the speech of a single character. Dialogue is sometimes contrasted to action, but Elizabeth Bowen aptly says that dialogue is what the characters *do* to each other, and Shaw aptly says that his plays are all talk just as Beethoven's symphonies are all music. *Stichomythia* is a special form of dialogue, wherein two speakers in a verbal duel thrust and parry in alternating lines or fragments of lines. For example:

QUEEN.
    Hamlet, thou hast thy father much offended.
HAMLET.
    Mother, you have my father much offended.
QUEEN.
    Come, come, you answer with an idle tongue.
HAMLET.
    Go, go, you question with a wicked tongue.

See *action, soliloquy.* Consult J. L. Styan, *The Elements of Drama,* Chapters 1–2; and Eric Bentley, *The Life of the Drama.*

diction. (1) Choice of words, wording. Dr. Johnson objected to the "knife" ("an instrument used by butchers and cooks," he said) that Lady Macbeth says she will use to murder the king. "Words too familiar, or too remote," Johnson said, "defeat the purpose of a poet." Consult Moody Prior, *The Language of Tragedy.* (2) A performer's manner or style of speaking, including pronunciation and phrasing.

Dionysus. Greek god of wine, the phallus, the surge of growth, and (to join all these) irrational impulse. It is commonly held that Greek tragedy grew from choral celebrations in his honor. In any case, from the sixth century B.C.E. tragedies were performed in Athens at the **Great** (or **Greater,** or **City**) **Dionysia,** a festival in Dionysus's honor. (For a survey of theories of the origin of tragedy, see A. W. Pickard-Cambridge, *Dithyramb, Tragedy and Comedy,* 2nd ed., revised by T. B. L. Webster. For a brief rejection of the theory that drama originated in Dionysian festivals, see H. D. F. Kitto, in *Theatre Survey,* 1 [1960], 3–17.) Friedrich Nietzsche suggested in *The Birth of Tragedy* (1872) that Greek tragedy, usually considered calm and poised, was not the product of quiet minds. If tragedy, Nietzsche said, showed light and beauty (over which the god Apollo presided), it was nevertheless also indebted to Dionysus, who represented the frenzied, buried self-assertions of the mind. That is, Greek tragedy was the product of **Dionysian** ecstatic and violent self-assertion tamed by (or fused with) the **Apollonian** sense of reason, of moderation, and of external order. *Apollonian* is often associated with classicism, and "*Dionysian*" with romanticism.

direct address. See *soliloquy.*

disclosure, discovery. See *anagnorisis.*

disguising. See *masque.*

domestic tragedy. A serious play showing the misfortunes (especially within the family) of a private citizen rather than of a person of high rank who is involved in events that shake a realm. See *bourgeois drama.* Consult Henry H. Adams, *English Domestic or Homiletic Tragedy 1575 to 1642.*

double plot. See *plot.*

downstage. The front half of the stage, or any part of the stage considered in relationship to someone or something further from the audience.

drama (from Greek: *dran,* "to do"). (1) A play; a work that tells a story by means of impersonators. (2) The whole body of work written for the theater. (3) A serious but untragic play (see *drame*). (4) Events containing conflict, tension, surprise ("life is full of drama"; "the first act lacks drama"). See *closet drama, comedy, melodrama, tragedy.* A play is written by a **dramatist;** the art of writing plays is **dramaturgy.** A person who writes plays is also a **playwright.** (Note that the last syllable is not *-write* but *-wright,* denoting a maker, as a shipwright is a maker of ships.) Consult Kenneth T. Rowe, *Write That Play;* Walter Kerr, *How Not to Write a Play;* and Bernard Grebanier, *Playwriting.*

drama of ideas. See *pièce à thèse.*

dramatic illusion. The state between delusion (the spectators think the world on the stage is real) and full awareness (the spectators never forget they are looking at scenery and actors). In *A Midsummer Night's Dream,* Bottom fears that delusion will occur unless the audience is carefully warned: "Write me a prologue, and let the prologue seem to say we will do no harm with our swords, and that Pyramus is not killed indeed. And, for the more better assurance, tell them that I Pyramus am not Pyramus, but Bottom the Weaver. This will put them out of fear." See *aesthetic distance.*

George Henry Lewes (1817–78) introduced into English dramatic criticism the term ***optique de théâtre,*** taken from the French actor François René Molé (1734–1802). Spectators must have this "theater view," this understanding of "scenic illusion," if they are to enjoy the theater. If they lack it, they will complain that Hamlet ought to be speaking Danish (see *convention*). *Optique du théâtre* requires that we be given not reality but a symbolic representation of it. A stage miser should finger his gold differently from a real miser; a stage character must be heard, even though in real life the character might speak inaudibly.

Staging that aims at delusion or a high degree of illusion is **representational** staging. With this kind of staging, characters eat real food on stage, speak with their backs to the audience, and so on. (See *naturalism, realism.*) When David Belasco staged *The Governor's Lady* in 1912, he was representational, placing on the stage an exact duplicate of a particular (Child's) restaurant. On the other hand, **presentational** staging is antirealistic; in Thornton Wilder's *Our Town* (1938), a drugstore counter, for example, consisted of a board across the backs of two chairs. The staging in musical comedies, ballets, and puppet shows is, of course, presentational. Presentational staging is sometimes called **theatrical** staging. **Theatricalism,** by its unreality, continually reminds us that we are in the theater, not in the street. On theatricalism, see *style.* A derogatory way of saying a work is theatrical is to say it is "**stagy.**"

dramatic irony. See *irony.*

dramatist. See *drama*.

dramaturgy. See *drama*.

drame. A solemn but untragic play, especially an eighteenth-century play that, quietly glorifying the bourgeois virtues, preaches and appeals to the audience's emotions. See *bourgeois drama*. Consult Alan R. Thompson, *The Anatomy of Drama*, which classifies most naturalistic and realistic plays (e.g., Ibsen's and Chekhov's) as *drames*.

eiron. See *character*.

Elizabethan playhouse. See pages 217–19.

empathy. The projection of one's feelings into a perceived object. The Germans call it *Einfühling*—"a feeling into." Vernon Lee, one of the formulators of the idea, claimed that when we say "the mountain rises," we do so not because the mountain rises (it doesn't) but because we have often raised our eyes, head, and total muscular structure to look at mountains or other tall objects. In perceiving a mountain, we merge (unaware) its image with the previously accumulated idea of rising. We are said to empathize with characters if we flinch at a blow directed at them or if we feel bowed with their grief—if, in short, we *experience* as well as *see* their behavior. Empathy is often distinguished from **sympathy:** We empathize if we feel *with* the character; we sympathize if we feel *for* the character. See *aesthetic distance*. Consult Vernon Lee's essay in *A Modern Book of Aesthetics*, edited by Melvin Rader; and Herbert S. Langfield, *The Aesthetic Attitude*.

epic drama. Bertolt Brecht (1898–1956) labeled "Aristotelian" most drama before his own. He held that it aimed at enthralling the spectators by building up to a climax, thus arousing and then purging their emotions. In contrast, Brecht said, epic drama (he borrowed the phrase from Erwin Piscator) aims at arousing the audience's detached thought; it teaches, keeping the spectators alert by preventing any emotional involvement. The epic drama (probably so-called because it resembles the epic in its abundance of loosely connected scenes and its tendency to deal with a society rather than merely with a few individuals) achieves this estrangement, or **alienation effect** (German: ***Verfremdungseffekt***), by many means. For example, the epic play (e.g., Brecht's *The Good Woman of Setzuan* or his *Mother Courage*) commonly consists of a series of loosely connected scenes rather than a tightly organized plot with a climax; the settings are not realistic but merely suggest the locale, and they are often changed in full view of the audience, preventing any entrancing illusion (a night scene may be done on an illuminated stage, again to prevent the audience from emotionally entering into the play); the actor may address the audience directly, sometimes in song, aiming not at becoming the character but at presenting the character, or, to put it differently, making a comment on the character, as we might do when we put aside a cigarette and say, "He said to me, ' ... '"; loudspeakers,

films, and placards may be used; and the whole is something of a lecture-demonstration, aimed not at arousing and then quieting the audience's emotions but at making things somewhat strange to the audience so that the audience will look sharply and will think (see pages 1006–07). Consult Bertolt Brecht, "A Short Organum," in *Playwrights on Playwriting*, edited by Toby Cole; *Brecht on Theatre*, translated by John Willett; and R. Gray "Brecht," *The Tulane Drama Review*, 6 (Sept. 1961).

epilogue. (1) An appendix (usually a concluding address) to a play. (2) The actor who recites such an appendix (e.g., Puck, at the close of Shakespeare's *A Midsummer Night's Dream*).

exposition. See *plot*.

expressionism. An antinaturalistic movement chiefly associated with Germany just after World War I. It was foreshadowed by Strindberg, notably in his trilogy *To Damascus* (1898–1904) and in his *A Dream Play* (1902). Expressionism does not seek to "hold the mirror up to nature" (Hamlet's words) or to present reality dispassionately; rather, it seeks to show the world as we feel (rather than literally see) it. Thus, when Mr. Zero shakes his employer (in Elmer Rice's *The Adding Machine* [1923]), the office spins; when he is on trial, the walls of the courtroom veer crazily. In other words, the dramatist makes visible the symbolic, subjective experience of the characters (or of the dramatist) by distorting objective or literal reality. Speaking broadly, expressionist plays (in addition to being unrealistic) usually (1) depict types or classes (Rice's Mr. Zero; the Man, the Woman, the Nameless One in Ernst Toller's *Man and Masses* [1921]), (2) employ dream sequences, and (3) assume that society is responsible for our troubles. Though Arthur Miller's *Death of a Salesman* is in many ways "realistic," it also is indebted to expressionism, especially in the scenes involving Willy's memories. (Miller originally planned to call the play *The Inside of His Head*.) Note, too, the name of Miller's hero—Loman, that is, low man. Tennessee Wiliams's *The Glass Menagerie* similarly reveals a modified—one might say Americanized–expressionism. Consult John Willett, *Expressionism*.

falling action. See *plot*.

farce. A sort of comedy based not on clever language or subtleties of character but on broadly humorous situations (for example, a man mistakenly enters the ladies' locker room). Farce is lucidly defended by Eric Bentley in his introduction to *"Let's Get a Divorce" and Other Plays*, in which he suggests that farce, like dreams, shows "the disguised fulfillment of repressed wishes." Farce is usually filled with surprise, with swift physical action, and with assault. The characters are physically and intellectually insensitive, and characterization is subordinated to plot. See also Bentley's *The Life of the Drama*. **Slapstick,** named for an implement made of two slats that resound when slapped against a posterior, is farce that relies on physical assault. Farce and slapstick are **low comedy,** as is comedy that depends on obscenity.

feminist theater. A movement that seeks to expand the opportunities for women in the theater and to heighten the public's awareness of women, especially by concentrating on female experience. See pages 950–52 and H. Keysaar, *Feminist Theatre.*

foil. A character who sets off another, as Laertes and Fortinbras—young men who, like Hamlet, have lost a father—help to set off Hamlet, or as a braggart soldier helps to set off a courageous one.

foreshadowing. See *suspense.*

Great Dionysia. See *Dionysus.*

Greek theater. See section on Classical Greek Theater, page 44.

groundlings. See section on English Renaissance Theater, page 217.

guerilla theater. Dramatic performances, especially in the 1960s, seeking to help the populace throw off what was said to be an oppressive bourgeois government. Theater was viewed not as a means of producing beauty or of exploring ideas but as a weapon in a class war. Performances were given in such places as streets, fields, and gymnasiums rather than in conventional theaters. Thus, the traditional separation of players from audience was broken down. Moreover, the audience itself might be in some degree assaulted, by, for instance, obscenities or the spectacle of nudity, offered in an effort to shock the spectators into an awareness of new ideals. Furthermore, *performance* and *drama* were loosely interpreted. For example, Luis Valdez, founder of El Teatro Campesino (1965) in *Actos* wrote, "A demonstration with a thousand Chicanos, all carrying flags and picket signs, shouting 'Chicano Power!' is . . . theater." (See p. 937.) Consult Henry Lesnik, ed., *Guerilla Street Theatre*; and (especially for El Teatro Campesino) C. W. E. Bigsby, *A Critical Introduction to Twentieth-Century American Drama*, volume 3.

hamartia. A Greek word variously translated as "tragic flaw," "error," "shortcoming," or "weakness." In many plays it is a flaw or even a vice such as *hybris* (also *hubris*)—a word that in classical Greek meant bullying or even assault and battery, but that in discussions of tragedy means overweening pride, arrogance, excessive confidence. In other plays, however, it is merely a mistep, such as a choice that turns out badly. Indeed, the tragic hero may be undone by his virtue—his courage, for example, when others are not merely prudent but cowardly. (See pages 33–34.) On *harmartia* and *hybris* see Richmond Lattimore, *Story Patterns in Greek Tragedy.*

Hellenistic theater. Theaters of, say, the third and second centuries B.C.E. erected in towns to which Greek culture had been spread by Alexander's conquests seem to have been much like the Greek theater, though the *proskenion* was apparently more highly decorated, having pillars a few feet in front of it and being fitted with painted panels called *pinakes.* And the *skene*, now of stone rather than of wood, may have had projections at the sides (*paraskenia*) and a upper story (*episkenion*). The playing area on this upper level is the *logeion.* Consult Margarete Bieber, *The History of the Greek and Roman Theater.*

hero, heroine. The protagonist in a drama. Until the rise of middle-class drama in the late eighteenth century, heroes were usually persons of high rank (King Oedipus, King Lear) and therefore of political power. Heroines too were sometimes politically powerful (Clytemnestra, in Aeschylus's *Agamemnon*), but more often their power was moral (Desdemona, in Shakespeare's *Othello*). When heroines have exerted physical power, they have often been regarded—at least by men—as wicked. See T. H. Henn, "The Woman's Part," in Henn's *The Harvest of Tragedy.*

high comedy. Intellectual rather than physical, a type of comedy that requires the close attention of a sophisticated audience, flourishing (says George Meredith in his *Essay on Comedy* [1877]) in a "society of cultivated men and women . . . wherein ideas are current, and the perceptions quick." Etherege, Wycherley, Congreve, and other playwrights of the decades following the Restoration of Charles II to the throne of England (1660) wrote **Restoration comedy,** high comedy of a particular sort, often called **comedy of manners** or **comedy of wit.** Their plays abound in witty **repartee** (what Dr. Johnson called "gay remarks and unexpected answers") and often strike modern audiences as cynical. Restoration comedy has no precise terminal date but can be said to have ended about 1700 with the development of sentimental comedy, plays of venerable parents and middle-class dutiful sons who love pure young things. An example is Richard Steele's *The Conscious Lovers* (1722). Consult Thomas H. Fujimura, *The Restoration Comedy of Wit*; Louis Kronenberger, *The Thread of Laughter*; and Norman N. Holland, *The First Modern Comedies.*

hubris (**hybris**). See *hamartia.*

humor character. See *comedy of humors.*

imitation (Greek: *mimesis*). Not a pejorative term in much criticism, for it often implies a "making" or "re-creating" or "representing" of a form in a substance not natural to it. Thus, Michelangelo reproduced or imitated the form of Moses, in stone. For Aristotle, tragedy was the imitation (i.e., representation, re-creation) by means of words, gesture, music, and scenery, of an important action.

irony. Irony is of several sorts. **Socratic irony,** named for Socrates, who commonly feigned more ignorance than he possessed, denotes understatement. The *eiron* (see *character*) is the cunning fellow who plays the underdog. **Dramatic irony,** or **Sophoclean irony,** or **tragic irony** refers to a condition of affairs that is the tragic reverse of what the participants think. Thus, it is ironic that Macbeth kills Duncan, thinking he will achieve happiness, because he later finds he loses all that makes life worth living. Oedipus accuses the blind prophet of corruption, but by the end of the play Oedipus learns (as the audience knew at the outset) that he himself is corrupt, that he has been mentally blind (ignorant), and that the prophet has had vision (knowledge). Oedipus meant what he said, but his words have proved to be ironic. (Aristotle's word for reversal is *peripeteia*). We have dramatic irony, it can be said, when a speech or action is more fully understood by the spectators than by the characters. This sort of irony, based on misunderstanding, or partial knowledge, is common in tragedy, but comedy too has its misunderstandings; comic speeches or actions are ironic if they bring about the opposite of what is intended. More generally, the contrast implied in irony need be neither tragic nor comic. For example, it is ironic that the strong man is overthrown by the weak man and that the liar unknowingly tells the truth. **Irony of fate** (a phrase that H. W. Fowler's *Modern English Usage* aptly says is hackneyed), or **cosmic irony,** denotes the view that God, or fate, or some sort of supernatural figure is amused to manipulate human beings as a puppeteer manipulates puppets. Thus, by an irony of fate, the messenger delivers the prisoner's pardon an instant too late. Consult Garnett G. Sedgewick, *Of Irony*; and Alan R. Thompson, *The Dry Mock*.

koryphaios. See *chorus*.

kothurnus. See *sock and buskin*.

lazzo. See *commedia dell'arte*.

Lenaea. See section on Classical Greek Theater, page 44.

liturgical drama. A play that is part of the church service or liturgy. In the tenth century the churchmen put on a playlet of a few lines as part of the Easter liturgy. The text was based on Mark 16:1–7. Clerics dressed as the Three Marys approached the "tomb" of Christ (the altar) and were asked by a cleric, disguised as an angel, whom they sought. When they replied that they sought Christ, he told them that Christ had risen and showed them the empty "tomb." The performers were all male, and the Latin dialogue was chanted; probably the gestures were stylized. (See pages 2, 162–63.)

low comedy. See *farce*.

masque, mask, disguising. An entertainment (apparently derived from an ancient ritual) in the Renaissance court, wherein noblemen performed a dignified playlet, usually allegorical and mythological. The masque was lavishly produced, but its basic structure was generally simple: The masquers (costumed and masked noble performers) entered (supposedly having come from afar), danced with the ladies of the court, and then departed. Because the masquers were of the same rank as the ladies and because performers and audience joined in a dance, the masque was very close to the masked ball. Ben Jonson

(1572–1637) popularized what he called the **antimasque** (a grotesque dance of monsters or clowns), performed by professionals representing chaos, who were dispelled by the courtly performers. (*Anti*, from *antic*, meaning "a grotesque caper" or "a fool," is sometimes written *ante* because the antimasque precedes the masque.) Consult Enid Welsford, *The Court Masque*; E. K. Chambers, *The Elizabethan Stage*; Stephen Orgel, *The Jonsonian Masque*.

melodrama. Originally, in Renaissance Italy, an opera; later, a drama with occasional songs or with music (*melos* is Greek for "song") expressing a character's thoughts, much as in films today. In the early nineteenth century plays with musical accompaniment became so stereotyped that the word *melodrama* acquired a second (and now dominant) meaning: a play wherein characters clearly virtuous or vicious are pitted against each other in sensational situations filled with suspense, until justice triumphs. The situations, not the characters, are exciting. The exotic horror (castles and dungeons) dominant in early nineteenth-century melodramas was often replaced later in the century by local horror (the cruel landlord), but whether exotic or local, melodrama is improbable, and virtue—unsullied by any touch of guilt—triumphs over unlikely circumstances. Melodrama is sometimes said to be tragedy with character left out (i.e., it contains serious happenings), but by virtue of its happy ending and its one-sided characters, it can better be described as comedy with good humor left out. Some critics use *melodrama* without any pejorative connotation to describe such serious, often sensational, plays as Emlyn Williams's *Night Must Fall* (1935), Robert Ardrey's *Thunder Rock* (1939), and Arthur Miller's *All My Sons*. Consult Robert B. Heilman, *Tragedy and Melodrama*.

metatheater. A term used to describe a play that calls attention to itself as a work of theater and self-consciously examines the nature of drama. For instance, a dramatic character might step out of character and invite the audience to consider the concept of dramatic character. *Hamlet* and *A Midsummer Night's Dream*, because they include discussions of theatrical issues (e.g., the nature of dramatic illusion in *Dream* and the nature of acting in *Hamlet*) as well as plays within the plays, today are widely seen at metatheatrical.

miracle play, mystery play. Interchangeable terms for a medieval play on a biblical episode or a saint's life. The term *mystery play* derives from the French *metier* ("work," "occupation," "ministry") from the Latin *ministerium* ("attendant," "servant"). The plays were sponsored by *mysteries*, that is, trades or guilds. Consult Arnold Williams, *The Drama of Medieval England*. (See pages 164–67.)

monologue. See *soliloquy*.

morality play. A late medieval development, popular well into the sixteenth century, allegorically dramatizing some aspect of the moral life, including such characters as Everyman, Good Deeds, and Avarice. It usually showed the conflict between good and evil or the way in which the Christian faces death. Consult Arnold Williams, *The Drama of Medieval England*; Bernard Spivack, *Shakespeare and the Allegory of Evil*; and R. Potter, *The English Morality Play*. (See pages 182–83.)

motivation. Grounds based on character and situation that make behavior plausible. Such grounds are not always present, even in great drama. For example, when Othello asks why Iago "hath thus ensnared my soul," Iago replies, "Demand me nothing: what you know, you know." See *character*. Consult J. I. M. Stewart, *Character and Motive in Shakespeare*.

naturalism. Sometimes defined, like realism, as the portrayal of "a scientifically accurate, detached picture of life, including everything and selecting nothing." The spectators looking through the peephole of the proscenium, as a scientist looks through the eyepiece of a microscope, are to feel they are witnessing life rather than a symbolic representation of life. More commonly, however, naturalism alludes neither to a panoramic view nor to the detailed presentation of a narrow **slice of life** (French: *tranche de vie*) but to a particular attitude held by some writers since the middle of the nineteenth century. Though claiming to be dispassionate observers, they were influenced by evolutionary thought and regarded humans as creatures determined by their heredity and environment rather than as possessed of a soul and of free will. The movement in drama can be said to have begun with the Goncourt brothers' unsuccessful *Henriette Maréchal* (1865), but it is usual to say that the opening gun in the battle for naturalism was fired in Émile Zola's dramatization (1873) of his novel *Thérèse Raquin*. Thérèse and her lover drown her husband but are then so guilt-ridden that they poison themselves. In his preface Zola urged that the theater be brought "into closer relation with the great movement toward truth and experimental science which has since the last century been on the increase. . . . I have chosen characters who were completely dominated by their nerves and blood." In Paris, André Antoine opened his Théâtre Libre in 1887, devoting it mostly to plays showing the power of instincts and the influence of heredity and environment. These plays were staged as untheatrically as possible; for example, the actors turned their backs to the audience. In Germany, Otto Brahm opened the Freie Bühne in 1889, and in England J. T. Grein opened the Independent Theatre in 1891, both with Ibsen's *Ghosts* (1881), a play showing the destruction of a young man by inherited syphilis. Ibsen's greatness does not allow him to be pinned down by the label "naturalist," but he can be said to be naturalistic (among other things) by virtue of his serious interests in the effects of heredity and environment. Other drama-

tists who wrote naturalistic plays include August Strindberg (e.g., his *Miss Julie* [1888]) and Gerhart Hauptmann (early in his career with *The Weavers* [1892]), and Eugene O'Neill (again, the early plays such as *The Rope* [1918] and *Diff'rent* [1920]). Note, however, that the major naturalistic writers usually are more than naturalistic. Strindberg's *Miss Julie*, for example, has a preface that talks about the influence of heredity and environment. It deals with sordid aspects of reality, but it also has symbolic overtones, notably in Julie's and Jean's dreams. Consult Mordecai Gorelik, *New Theatres for Old; TDR: The Drama Review* 13 (Winter 1968); and (for Strindberg, O'Neill, and the sources of their ideas) Oscar Cargill, *Intellectual America*.

nuntius. See *Senecan tragedy*.

obligatory scene. See *scène à faire*.

optique du théâtre. See *dramatic illusion*.

orchestra. See section on Classical Greek Theater, page 44.

pathos. The quality that evokes pity. The pathetic is often distinguished from the tragic. In the former, the suffering is experienced by the passive and the innocent (especially women and children), while in the latter it is experienced by persons who act, struggle, and are in some measure responsible for their sufferings. Discussing Aeschylus's *The Suppliants*, H. D. F. Kitto says in *Greek Tragedy* (2nd ed.); "The Suppliants are not only pathetic, as the victims of outrage, but also tragic, as the victims of their own misconceptions." See *bourgeois drama*.

performance theater. A movement in the 1960s and early 1970s especially associated with Julian Beck, a cofounder of the Living Theatre. Influenced by Antonin Artaud's **theater of cruelty,** performance theater rejected the gap between performers and spectators (performers moving on stage, spectators impassively sitting in the dark); it therefore necessarily minimized the role of the playwright and gave the actors freedom to improvise. Verbal and visual assaults (for instance nudity) on the audience, as well as physical contact with it, supposedly gave actor and spectator freedom to celebrate bodily and spiritual unity and liberation. Consult Julian Beck, *The Life of the Theatre*, and for a critical and historical survey, see part 2 of the third volume of C. W. E. Bigsby, *A Critical Introduction to Twentieth-Century American Drama*.

peripeteia (anglicized to **peripety,** meaning "reversal"). The reversal occurs when an action produces the opposite of what was intended or expected, and it is, therefore, a kind of irony. An example of *peripeteia* occurs in *Julius Caesar*; Brutus kills Caesar in order to free Rome from tyranny, but the deed introduces tyranny into Rome. See *irony, plot*.

picture-frame stage. See *proscenium stage*.

pièce à thèse. A play with a thesis; a play in which the dramatist argues a point. Commonly the thesis is not about, for example, the benevolence of God, but about the merits or defects of some social institution; a play dealing with a social institution may also be called a **problem play** or a **drama of ideas.** Some critics distinguish between the terms, saying that a problem play merely poses a social problem, as Galsworthy does in *Strife* (1909), while a drama of ideas propounds a solution. Shaw says that "the material of the dramatist is always some conflict of human feeling with circumstances"; when the circumstances are "human institutions" (e.g., divorce laws, penal codes) rather than unchanging facts of life (e.g., death) and the audience is forced to meditate on the value of the institutions, we have a problem play. Shaw's essay, "The Problem Play," is reprinted in *Shaw on Theatre*, edited by E. J. West, a volume that also contains Shaw's "The Play of Ideas." Consult also Water Kerr, *How Not to Write a Play*, Chapter 5.

pièce bien faite, or **well-made play.** Of course, all good plays are "well made," but the term has come to mean a play with much suspense and with little depth of characterization that relies on a cleverly constructed plot—first developing a situation, then building the crisis to a climax, and then resolving the business. The type, which perhaps can be described as melodrama with the fisticuffs left out, is chiefly associated with Victorien Sardou (1831–1908), but Sardou was indebted to Eugene Scribe (1791–1861), who indeed coined the term *pièce bien faite* in describing his farces and melodramas. Shaw called their plays clockwork mice, and Sardoodledom, but the influence of Sardou on Shaw's hero, Ibsen, is undeniable. See *plot,* and consult Walter Kerr, *How Not to Write a Play*, Chapter 10; Eric Bentley, "Homage to Scribe," *What Is Theatre?*; C. E. Montague, *Dramatic Values*, pages 63–74; and *Camille and Other Plays*, edited by Stephen S. Stanton.

plot and **character.** The plot is sometimes the "story," that is the "narrative," but usually it is the happenings *as the author arranges them.* In *Hamlet,* for example, the story involves the poisoning of Hamlet's father, but Shakespeare omits this scene from his plot. Aristotle, in Chapter 6 of the *Poetics,* calls plot "the whole structure of the incidents," and he speaks of plot as the "soul of tragedy," thus making it more important than character. By *character* he means the personalities of the figures in the story. Menander (a Greek comic dramatist) is said to have told a friend that he had finished a comedy, though he had not yet written a line of dialogue. The anecdote implies that Menander had completed his idea of *what happens* (action) and in *what order* (plot), and he would find it easy then to write the lines of the characters necessary to his plot. The separation, however, between plot and character is misleading, for the two usually interplay. Although it is true that there may be much plot and little character (as in a thriller), in most great plays there is such a fusion between what is done and the personality of the doer that we feel the truth of Henry James's questions: "What is character but the determination of incident? What is incident but the illustration of character?" (See also *character.*)

Most plots entail a **conflict,** in which the protagonist is somehow opposed. If the protagonist is opposed chiefly by another person rather than by a force such as fate, God, or by an aspect of himself or herself, the opposing figure is the **antagonist.** The German critic Gustav Freytag, in *Technique of the Drama* (1863), held that a play dramatizes "the rushing forth of will power from the depths of man's soul toward the external world" and "the coming into being of a deed and its consequences on the human soul." The five-act play, he said, commonly arranged such an action into a **pyramidal structure,** consisting of a **rising action,** a **climax,** and **falling action.** (In Peter de Vries's witty formulation, a plot has a beginning, a muddle, and an end.) The rising action begins with the **exposition,** in which is given essential information, especially about the **antecedent action** (what has occurred before this piece of action begins). For example, the two gossiping servants who tell each other that after a year away in Paris the young master is coming home today with his new wife are giving the audience the exposition. The action rises through a **complication** (the protagonist is opposed) to a high point, or **crisis,** or **climax** (a moment at which tension is high and which is a decisive turning point). The falling action goes through a **reversal** (if a tragedy, the protagonist loses power), and then into a **catastrophe,** also called a *dénouement* (unknotting) or resolution. (Aristotle's word for the reversal is *peripeteia,* anglicized to **peripety,** and, translated as "irony of events," would in a comedy be a change from bad fortune to good, and the catastrophe would thus be happy.) The *dénouement* frequently involves what Aristotle called an *anagnorisis* (**recognition, disclosure, discovery**). This recognition may be as simple as the identification of a long-lost brother by a birthmark, or it may involve a character's recognition of his own true condition. Shakespeare sometimes used a pyramidal structure, placing his climax neatly in the middle of what seems to us to be the third of five acts. In *Julius Caesar,* for example, Brutus rises in the first half of the play, reaching his height in 3.1 with the death of Caesar; later in this scene he gives Marc Antony permission to speak at Caesar's funeral and thus sets in motion his own fall, which occupies the second half of the play. In *Macbeth,* the protagonist attains his height in 3.1 ("Thou hast it now: King"), but he soon perceives that he is going downhill:

I am in blood
Stepped in so far that, should I wade no more,
Returning were as tedious as go o'er.

Some works have a **double plot,** that is, two plots, usually with some sort of relationship. For example, the

subplot or **underplot** (the secondary narrative) might be a grotesque version of the serious main plot. In Shakespeare's *The Tempest,* the main plot and subplot both deal with usurpation. In *King Lear,* the main plot concerns Lear's relationship with his daughters, while the parallel subplot concerns Gloucester's relationship with his sons. For another aspect of the subplot, see *comic relief.* Consult William Empson, *Some Versions of Pastoral,* Chapter 2. On plotting, see *pièce bien faite* and *scène à faire.*

poetic justice. A term coined by Thomas Rymer in 1678, denoting the reward of the virtuous and the punishment of the vicious. Aristotle had said or implied that the tragic hero is undone partly by some sort of personal flaw—that is, he is at least partly responsible for the suffering he later encounters. (See *hamartia* and page 33.) Poetic justice, with its idea that all characters reap the harvest of their just deserts, is a hardening of Aristotle's suggestion. Consult M. A. Quinlan, *Poetic Justice in the Drama.*

poor theater. A term associated with the Polish director Jerzy Grotowski (1933–). Unlike the "rich" theater, which uses elaborate lighting, scenery, and costumes, the poor theater rejects technology and concentrates on the involvement of actor and audience in "a living collaboration." The actors' faces are the only "masks," and their voices are the only "sound effects." Gestures, at least in moments of strong emotion, tend to be stylized rather than naturalistic. See J. Grotowski, *Towards a Poor Theatre.*

postmodernism. The term came into prominence in the 1960s, to distinguish the contemporary experimental writing of such an author as Samuel Beckett from such early twentieth-century classics of modernism as James Joyce's *Ulysses* (1922) and T. S. Eliot's *The Waste Land* (1922). Although the classic modernists were considered revolutionary in their day, after World War II they seemed conservative, and their works seemed remote from today's society with its new interests in issues such as feminism, gay and lesbian rights, and pop culture. Postmodern literature, though widely varied and not always clearly distinct from modernist literature, usually is more politically concerned, more playful—it is given to parody and pastiche—and more closely related to the art forms of popular culture (e.g., vaudeville and film) than is modernist literature.

presentational theater. A type of theater in which there is little or no illusionism in the acting and staging (as opposed to realistic or naturalistic or representational theater). Communication is achieved by means of evident conventions, such as direct address to the audience (which acknowledges the existence of the audience), the soliloquy, and the aside. Similarly, a voyage in a boat may be indicated by pantomiming the motion of rowing. Virtually all drama before the middle of the nineteenth century was highly presentational, if only because of the in-ability to produce illusionistic lighting effects. However, a largely presentational theater, such as Shakespeare's (where, on the open-air stage, a night scene might be indicated in daylight by the presence of characters holding torches), also might aim at realism. For instance, in Shakespeare's *The Tempest* a stage direction specifies that the sailors are "wet." On the other hand, even highly illusionistic sets of the later nineteenth century also employ conventions; for instance, the audience agrees to pretend that there is a fourth wall for the living room it sees exposed on the stage. On one form of twentieth-century presentational theater, see *expressionism.*

problem play. See *pièce à thèse.*

prologue. (1) A preface or introduction. For the Greeks the *prologos* was the first scene, which gave the exposition. Elizabethan prologues commonly summarize the plot, as the Chorus does in the prologue to *Romeo and Juliet,* but in the English theater of the late seventeenth century, the prologue was almost an independent verse essay spoken before the play began. (2) The actor who speaks a piece of the sort just described.

properties, props. Objects used on the stage, other than scenery and costumes. Examples include umbrellas, books, and food.

proscenium stage, or **picture-frame stage.** A playing area framed in the front, and thus separated from the audience. This frame is the *proscenium arch* or the *proscenium;* the empty space it contains, sometimes filled with a curtain, is the *proscenium opening.* Basically a proscenium theater has two rooms, one for the audience and another (with a hole in the mutual wall) for the performers. Such a theater is at least as old as the early seventeenth century, when the Farnese Theater was built in Parma. Consult Allardyce Nicoll, *The Development of the Theatre.* (See pages 389–90.)

protagonist. The chief figure in a play. In Greek, the word means literally the "first contender," that is, the chief actor (*protos,* meaning "first"). The second role was given to the **deuteragonist,** and the third to the **tritagonist.** The protagonist is commonly opposed by the **antagonist,** played by the deuteragonist. For the relationship between the protagonist and the antagonist, see *plot.*

psychical distance. See *aesthetic distance.*

pyramidal structure. See *plot.*

raisonneur. See *chorus.*

realism. The reproduction of life, especially as it appears to the eye and ear; the illusion of nature. Usually realism deals with ordinary people in ordinary situations, moving in scenery that closely imitates reality. In England, T. W. Robertson (1829–71) insisted, for example, that doorknobs not be painted on the doors but be three dimensional. Wings and a backcloth (i.e., projecting flats at the sides and a painted cloth at the rear) were increasingly replaced by the box set (a room with the front wall missing, containing real furniture) for interior scenes. Gas lighting, introduced to the stage about 1820, soon became capable of producing effects of sunlight, moonlight, and so on. The dialogue, as well as the sets, came closer to what the senses perceive. Realistic plays (in prose, of course) avoid soliloquies, asides, and declamation. (On the other hand, realism makes use of its conventions. See the entry on *convention*.) The great playwrights of the movement are Ibsen and Chekhov. As Mary McCarthy says of American realistic drama (*On the Contrary*), "realism is a depreciation of the real," for in "its resolve to tell the whole truth" it tends to deflate, to reveal human littleness. (It doesn't believe in exceptional, heroic people; when it treats the upper classes, it usually tends toward satire.) The oppressive box set of realistic plays, McCarthy points out, "is the box or 'coffin' of average middle-class life opened at one end to reveal the corpse within." That realism shades into naturalism is clear; that in Ibsen it shades into symbolism is less obvious but is well demonstrated by John Northam, *Ibsen's Dramatic Method*. A simple example of Ibsen's symbolism occurs in *Hedda Gabler*. Hedda's hair is "not particularly ample," but Thea's is "unusually rich and wavy," suggesting Hedda's barrenness and Thea's fertility. Consult Mordecai Gorelik, *New Theatres for Old*; A. Nicholas Vardac, *Stage to Screen*, Chapters 4 and 9; and Ernest B. Watson, *Sheridan to Robertson*. In **selective realism,** some of the scenery (e.g., a window and a door) closely reproduce reality, but some (e.g., a framework *suggesting* a roof) does not.

recognition. See *anagnorisis*.

repartee. See *high comedy*.

Restoration comedy. See *high comedy*.

revenge play. See *Senecan tragedy*.

reversal. See *peripeteia*.

rising action. See *plot*.

Roman theater. A permanent theater was not built at Rome until the first century B.C.E. The plays of Plautus (254?–184 B.C.E.) and Terence (190?–159 B.C.E.) were performed on temporary stages erected in the Circus Maximus and the Forum during holidays. In the permanent Roman theater, the enormous audience (40,000 or more) sat in a semicircle around a level space that was a vestige of what had been called the *orchestra* ("dancing place") of the Greek theater. Behind this vestige was the stage, running through what would have been the diameter of the circle. The long, slightly elevated stage was backed by a façade (painted to resemble two or three houses) with several doors through which actors made some of their exits and entrances, the others being made at the ends of the stage. Behind the façade was the dressing room. The Roman theater, unlike the Greek and Hellenistic theaters, was a self-enclosed structure, built on level ground, not against a hillside. Consult Mar-

garete Bieber, *The History of the Greek and Roman Theater*.

satire. A work ridiculing aspects of human behavior and seeking to arouse in the audience contempt for its object. Satirists almost always justify their attacks by claiming that satire is therapeutic. Shaw says, in the preface to his *Complete Plays*, "If I make you laugh at yourself remember that my business as a classic writer of comedies is to 'chasten morals with ridicule'; and if I sometimes make you feel like a fool, remember that I have by the same action cured your folly." Satire, however, is sometimes distinguished from comedy on the grounds that satire aims to correct by ridiculing, while comedy aims simply to evoke amusement. Among notable satires are the plays of Aristophanes; Gay's *The Beggar's Opera* (1728); Brecht's *The Threepenny Opera* (1928); and Kaufman, Ryskind, and Gershwin's *Of Thee I Sing* (1931)—though Kaufman himself has defined satire as "that which closes on Saturday night." See *burlesque, comedy*. Consult Northrop Frye, *Anatomy of Criticism*.

satyr-play. A piece in which there is a chorus of lewd satyrs (creatures half-man and half either horse or goat). The Greek tragic playwrights of the fifth century B.C.E. presented three tragedies and a satyr-play for the dramatic festival. Apparently the satyr-play often burlesqued a hero, showing him in a ludicrous situation. Only one complete satyr-play (Euripides's *The Cyclops*) is extant; it travesties the legend of Odysseus's encounter with Polyphemus. Consult Philip W. Harsh, *A Handbook of Classical Drama*.

scenario. See *commedia dell'arte*.

scene. See *act*.

scène à faire, or (in William Archer's translation of Francisque Sarcey's term) **obligatory scene.** "An obligatory scene [Archer says] is one which the audience (more or less clearly and consciously) foresees and desires, and the absence of which it may with reason resent." For example, a familiar legend may make a scene obligatory, or a dramatist may cause the audience to expect a certain scene. In Hamlet the play within the play (3.2) has been called such a scene: Hamlet has doubted the ghost, and we must see the ghost's words verified. Most often, however, an obligatory scene is an expected critical confrontation in which information previously hidden from a character or from the audience is revealed. Consult William Archer, *Play-making*.

scenery. The carpentry and painted cloths (and projected images) used on a stage. Scenery may be used to conceal parts of the stage, to decorate, to imitate or suggest locales, to establish time, or to evoke mood. For comments on early scenery, see sections on Classical Greek Theater, page 44, and English Renaissance Theater, pages 217–19. The Elizabethan public theater did not use much scenery. In *Twelfth Night,* when Viola asks, "What country, friends, is this?" she is told, "This is Illyria, lady," and the audience knows all that carpenters and painters can tell it. But even before Shakespeare's birth, Renaissance Italians had placed buildings, probably of lath and cloth, at the right and left of the stage. Behind the buildings, which were three dimensional and embellished with moldings, projected flat pieces cut and painted to look like other buildings at a distance, and behind these flat pieces were yet other flats, still smaller.

selective realism. See *realism*.

Senecan tragedy. Any of the serious plays by the Roman author Seneca (4 B.C.E.–65 C.E.), or imitations of them. Of the ten extant Roman tragedies, nine are attributed to Seneca, and these were probably written not for the stage but for private readings. The heroes seem to us to be almost madmen, but perhaps they are to be regarded sympathetically as people overwhelmed by passion. Seneca's influence on the Elizabethan dramatists was considerable; the **revenge play,** with its ghosts and its deranged hero who seeks vengeance, doubtless would have been different had Seneca not existed. Among the signs of Seneca's influence are ghosts, revenge, deeds of horror (e.g., children stewed and served to their parents), occasional stoical speeches but a predominance of passionate speeches, use of *stichomythia* (see *dialogue*), and a *nuntius* (messenger) who recites in a heightened style an off-stage happening (e.g., the wounded soldier in *Macbeth*, 1.1). Of course, not every use of any of these characteristics is necessarily attributable to Seneca's influence, and there are differences. For example, the horrors in Seneca are narrated, but in *King Lear* Gloucester is blinded on the stage. Consult F. L. Lucas, *Seneca and Elizabethan Tragedy*; Madeleine Doran, *Endeavors of Art*; and William Farnham, *The Medieval Heritage of Elizabethan Tragedy*. Howard Baker, in *Induction to Tragedy*, minimizes Seneca's influence.

sensibility. See *sentimental*.

sentimental. Generally a pejorative word in criticism, indicating a superabundance of tender emotion, a disproportionate amount of sentiment (feeling). It is sentimental to be intensely distressed because one has stepped on a flower. A character, for example, Hamlet, may display deep emotions, but they are sentimental only if they are in excess of what the situation warrants. More specifically, "sentimental" writing refers to writing in which evil is facilely conquered, denied, overlooked, or bathed in a glow of forgiving tenderness. In the eighteenth century the ability to respond emotionally (usually tearfully) to acts of benevolence or malevolence was called **sensibility. In sentimental drama** there is at the expense of reason an emphasis on tearful situations; benevolent emotions are overestimated, for people are assumed to be innately good, and villains reform, usually in bursts of repenting tears. There is little wit, the characters are usually of the middle class, and they demonstrate their virtue by weeping at the sight of distress. In his "Comparison

between Sentimental and Laughing Comedy" (1772), Oliver Goldsmith attacked sentimental comedy, saying that in it

> the virtues of private life are exhibited, rather than the vices exposed; and the distresses rather than the faults of mankind make our interest in the piece. . . . Almost all the characters are good, . . . and though they want humor, have abundance of sentiment and feeling. If they happen to have faults or foibles, the spectator is taught, not only to pardon, but to applaud them, in consideration of the goodness of their hearts; so that folly, instead of being ridiculed, is commended, and the comedy aims at touching our passions, without the power of being truly pathetic.

See *bourgeois drama*. Consult Ernest Bernbaum, *The Drama of Sensibility*; and Arthur Sherbo, *English Sentimental Drama*.

sets. The scenery constructed for a theatrical performance, especially the three-dimensional environment (as opposed to two-dimensional wings) in which the characters move.

situational comedy. See *comedy of humors*.

slapstick. See *farce*.

slice of life. See *naturalism*.

sock and **buskin.** Performers of Latin comedy wore a light slipper or sandal called the *soccus*. The sock is either this piece of footwear or comedy itself. The high boot worn by Greek tragic actors was the *cothurnus* or *kothurnus*. In Hellenistic times it acquired a very thick sole, giving the performer the height appropriate to a great man. In English this footgear (or tragic drama in general) is called the buskin, apparently from Old French *broissequin*, from Middle Dutch *brosekin*, "a small leather boot." Consult Margarete Bieber, *The History of the Greek and Roman Theater*.

Socratic irony. See *irony*.

soliloquy. A monologue in which a character utters his or her thoughts aloud while alone. An **aside** is a speech in which a character expresses his or her thoughts in words audible to the spectators but supposedly unheard by the other stage characters present. Both were important conventions in Elizabethan drama and, later, in melodrama, but the late nineteenth century sought so vigorously to present on the stage the illusion of real life that both techniques were banished. They were, however, revived in the twentieth century, as in Eugene O'Neill's *Strange Interlude*, in which the asides represent the characters thoughts and unspoken desires. In **direct address,** a character turns from the world on the stage and speaks directly to the audience, telling it, for instance, to watch closely. Consult Una Ellis-Fermor, *The Frontiers of Drama*, Chapter 6; George E. Duckworth, *The Nature of Roman Comedy*; and Max Beerbohm, "Soliloquies in Drama," *Around Theatres*. The soliloquy, the aside, and direct address are all monologues, but more often a **monologue** is either a long speech delivered by one character, which may be heard but not interrupted by others in his presence, or a performance by a single actor.

Sophoclean irony. See *irony*.

sound effect. An imitative noise, usually produced by simple machinery. Though a sound effect may be a mere imitation of nature, it may also be a richly symbolic suggestion. Chekhov's *The Cherry Orchard* (1904) concludes, "There is a far-off sound as if out of the sky, the sound of a snapped string, dying away, sad. A stillness falls, and there is only the thud of an ax on a tree, far away in the orchard." Consult Frank Napier, *Noises Off*.

spectacle. The last of Aristotle's six elements of drama, spectacle denotes what appeals to the eye, such as costume and scenery. Greek drama was splendidly costumed and made some use of scenery. Aeschylus especially seems to have contrived moments that caught the eye, such as Agamemnon's entrance in a chariot. The Elizabethan stage, though sparse in scenery, apparently was architecturally impressive, and doubtless military scenes were embellished with waving banners. In the Restoration, spectacle sometimes got the upper hand. Alexander Pope complained:

> The play stands still; damn action and discourse,
> Back fly the scenes, and enter foot and horse;
> Pageants on pageants, in long order drawn,
> Peers, heralds, bishops, ermine, gold, and lawn.

In the nineteenth century the development of gas light and then electric light made possible elaborate sunrises and twilights, and at the end of the century (especially in Russia) there was an emphasis on ensemble acting that gave a tableau effect. Pictorial effects in late-nineteenth-century productions of Shakespeare were often achieved at the cost of Shakespeare's lines. At the very end of the century, William Poel rejected spectacle and helped establish a trend to stage Shakespeare in what was thought to be an Elizabethan manner: an uncluttered stage, allowing the action to proceed rapidly. Consult James Laver, *Drama*; and A. Nicholas Vardac, *Stage to Screen*, Chapters 3–4.

stage. A platform or space for theatrical performances. See *arena stage*, *Hellenistic theater*, *proscenium stage*, and *thrust stage*. (See also sections on Classical Greek Theater, page 44 and English Renaissance Theater, page 217.)

stage business. Minor physical action—including posture and facial expression—by a performer. Business ranges from head scratching to an addition Henry Irving made to *The Merchant of Venice*, 2.4. In Shakespeare's scene, Jessica and Lorenzo elope and the scene ends quietly; Irving added business in which Shylock entered and knocked on the door of his empty house while the curtain fell. Irving's successors amplified his business by having Shylock enter the house, cry out, reappear, and so on. Consult Arthur C. Sprague, *Shakespeare and the Actors*.

stichomythia. See *dialogue*.

stock character. See *character*.

structure. The arrangement of episodes.

style. The mode of expression. Cardinal Newman, talking of the writer's style, called it "a thinking out into language." This idea of "a thinking out" (but not into language) is applicable also to the style of the scene designer, the costume designer, and so on. Kenneth Tynan in *Curtains* defines good style as "a happy consonance of manner with matter, of means with end, of tools with job." To **stylize** a play commonly means to present it with a noticeable artful manner rather than to present it realistically, though in fact realism itself is a style. A **stylized production** usually is presentational or anti-illusionistic rather than representational (see *dramatic illusion*). Consult George R. Kernodle, "Style, Stylization, and Styles of Acting," *Educational Theatre Journal*, 12 (1960), 251–61.

subplot. See *plot*.

subtext. Constantin Stanislavski's term for a text assumed to be hidden beneath the surface. Thus, Stanislavski wanted his actors to discover and communicate the character's unspoken but felt life.

surprise. See *suspense*.

surrealism. A literary movement, especially vigorous in France in the 1920s and 1930s, that insisted that reality is grasped by the unconscious, the irrational, rather than by the conscious. The best art, it is held, is the dream. Among the forerunners were Alfred Jarry, whose *Ubu Roi* (1896) combined grotesque farce with antibourgeois satire; August Strindberg, whose *To Damascus* (three parts, 1898–1904) and *The Dream Play* (1902) had presented dreamlike worlds; and Guillaume Apollinaire, whose *Breasts of Tiresias* (1917) was called a "*drame surréaliste*" (the first use of the word) by the author. Perhaps the chief surrealist dramatist is Jean Cocteau, notably in his *Orpheus* (1926), in which a glazier is an angel and a horse dictates prophetic words. Consult Georges E. Lemaître, *From Cubism to Surrealism in French Literature*.

suspense. Uncertainty, often characterized by anxiety. Suspense is usually a curious mixture of pain and pleasure, as Gwendolen, in Oscar Wilde's *The Importance of Being Earnest*, implies: "This suspense is terrible. I hope it will last." Most great art relies more heavily on suspense than on **surprise** (the unexpected). One can rarely sit twice through a play depending on surprise; when the surprise is gone, the interest is gone. Suspense is usually achieved in part by **foreshadowing**—hints of what is to come. Dumas *fils* put it this way: "The art of the theater is the art of preparations." Coleridge, who held that Shakespeare gives us not surprise but expectation and then the satisfaction of perfect knowledge, once wrote: "As the feeling with which we startle at a shooting star, compared with that of watching the sunrise at the pre-established moment, such and so low is surprise compared with expectation." Thus, in *Hamlet*, the ghost does not pop up surprisingly but satisfies the eager expectations that have been aroused by references to "this thing," "this dreaded sight," and "this apparition." Often, in fact, Shakespeare—like the Greek dramatists—used traditional stories. For example, the audience presumably was not surprised by the deaths of Caesar and Brutus, and it enjoyed the suspense of anticipating them. Suspense is thus related to tragic irony. The tragic character moves closer and closer to his or her doom, and though the character may be surprised by it, we are not; we are held by suspense. On surprise, consult David L. Grossvogel, *The Self-Conscious Stage in Modern French Drama* (reprinted in paperback as *Twentieth-Century French Drama*).

symbolism. Derived from Greek *symballein,* "to throw together," which thus suggests the essential quality of symbolism, the drawing together of two worlds; it presents the concrete material world of roses, toads, caves, stars, and so on, and through them reveals an otherwise invisible world. Thus, the storm in *King Lear* symbolizes both the disorder in Lear's kingdom (brother against brother, etc.) and also the disorder in Lear's mind. The strangled canary in Glaspell's *Trifles* symbolizes the maltreatment that Minnie Wright experienced from her husband.

Symbolism is often distinguished from **allegory.** Where the allegorist commonly invents a world (the author of *Everyman* [c. 1500] invents a figure called Everyman, who seeks aid from figures called Goods, Kindred, etc.) in order to talk about the real world, the symbolist commonly presents the phenomena of what we usually call the real world in order to reveal a "higher," eternal world of which the symbol is a part. The allegorist is free to invent any number of imaginary worlds to talk about the real world, but the symbolist feels that there is only one way by which he or she can present the "higher" real world he or she envisions. The everyday world is often considered by symbolists as a concrete but transient version of a more important realm, and the symbolist who presents, for example, a rose, is (the symbolist might hold) speaking about a rose and also about the eternal beauty of womanhood in the only possible way.

In the second half of the nineteenth century, there arose in France the so-called **symbolist movement,** but it must be emphasized that symbolism of a sort is probably as old as literature. An author's insistence on some object may cause us to regard it as more than its apparent nature. For example, the forest or greenwood in *As You Like It* suggests a benevolent nature that restores humans to their best part. On the whole, however, Shakespeare's plays do not leave the world of sensible reality. The plays of the symbolists do. The symbolist writer presents a world that seems to be a dream world, a world that is not the usual world enriched, but a new world. In his preface to *The Dream Play* (1902), Strindberg says he "has tried to imitate the disconnected but seemingly logical form of the dream. Anything may happen. . . . The characters split, double, multiply, vanish, solidify, blur, clarify." A

play is the expression of a "soul-state" (Stéphane Mallarmé's term) rather than an imitation of an external action. See *surrealism.*

The best naturalists (Ibsen, Chekhov, Strindberg, and Hauptmann) at times wrote symbolic works, but the chief symbolic dramatists are the French (if we include the Belgian Maurice Maeterlinck) and William Butler Yeats. In Maeterlinck's *The Intruder* (1890) a blind old man sees with his soul the approach of Death. In *The Blind* (1896) a group of blind men are lost in a forest; their leader was a priest, but he has died. Maeterlinck occasionally said some of his plays were for marionettes, and though his statement is sometimes held to be a mildly self-deprecating joke, in fact there is much in the plays that belongs to the realm of impassive, otherworldly dolls, not surprisingly in the work of a writer who said he wished to study man "in the presence of eternity and mystery." Paul Claudel's *Tidings Brought to Mary* (written in 1892, revised in 1899 and 1912) was acted in 1912. Claudel, who said he had gained from Arthur Rimbaud (one of the leading symbolists) "an almost physical impression of the supernatural," in this play envelops his medieval characters in a divine world and dramatizes salvation. In Ireland, Yeats, who compared an artistic work to a magic talisman ("it entangles . . . a part of the Divine essence") wrote verse plays of Irish supernatural creatures and heroes. In *On Baile's Strand* (1903), for instance, Cuchulain, the protagonist, is said to have been sired by a hawk. The bird imagery is insisted on; Cuchulain's associates are called chicks and nestlings, and the Fool (who represents Cuchulain on another level) is delighted with feathers. Near the conclusion of the play, Cuchulain rushes out to fight the waves, literally doing what Hamlet spoke metaphorically of doing.

In Russia, Meyerhold in 1906 staged Ibsen's *Hedda Gabler* (1890) as symbolically as possible, turning what had been a naturalistic play into a vision suggestive of another world, something (in the words of a hostile critic) "halfway between metaphysics and ballet." (Consult Nikolai Gorchakov, *The Theater in Soviet Russia.*) For symbolism in the sense of richly suggestive images, consult Alan S. Downer, "The Life of Our Design: The Function of Imagery in the Poetic Drama," *The Hudson Review,* 2 (Summer 1949), 242–60. On the symbolist movement, consult William Butler Yeats, *Essays and Introductions*; Arthur Symons, *The Symbolist Movement in Literature*; *Yale French Studies,* No. 9; Eric Bentley, *The Playwright as Thinker*; and John Gassner, *Form and Idea in the Modern Theatre.*

sympathy. See *empathy.*

theater-in-the-round. See *arena stage.*

theater of the absurd. See *absurd, theater of the.*

theatrical. Literally, characteristic of the theater, but often (unfortunately) used pejoratively, to suggest artificially contrived, melodramatic, implausible.

theme. The underlying idea, such as the triumph of love or the failure of idealism. A *theme* can thus be distinguished from a *thesis,* which is a message, such as "Love ought to triumph" or "Idealism is short-sighted."

three unities. See *unity.*

thrust stage. A stage that projects into the auditorium. It encourages direct address to the spectators because even a large audience can be fairly close to the actors. On the other hand, since some members of the audience will be to the side of, or even behind, the performers, there may be acoustical problems.

total theater. The idea that the theater should not try to imitate realistically an aspect of life but should embody a synthesis of all of the expressive arts—music, movement, speech, lighting, and so on. The expression *total theater* is probably derived from Richard Wagner" *Gesamtkunstwerk,* "united" or "total artwork." Consult *Total Theater,* edited by E. T. Kirby.

tragedy. For Aristotle, tragedy was a dramatic imitation (representation) of an "action of high importance." A Greek tragedy was serious, but it did not necessarily end unhappily. Aeschylus's *Eumenides,* for example, ends on a note of solemn joy. For us a tragedy is generally a play that faces evil, depicts suffering, and ends with death or (especially in the naturalistic tragedies since the latter part of the nineteenth century) ends with the hero alive but spiritually crushed. Tragedy's essence, Alfred North Whitehead says (*Science and the Modern World,* Chapter 1), resides not in unhappiness but "in the solemnity of the remorseless working of things." H. D. F. Kitto says (*The Greeks,* Ch. 4) that Greek tragedy—and perhaps one might add the great tragedy of other countries—was in part the product of intellectualism and humanism. Intellectualism let the Greeks see that human life must be lived within a great framework of what might be called the will of the gods, or Necessity: "Actions must have their consequences; ill-judged actions must have uncomfortable results." Humanism denied the Greeks an easy view of a heavenly life and gave them an "almost fierce joy in life, the exultation in human achievement and in human personality." The tragic note, Kitto suggests, is produced by a tension between this unalterable framework and this passionate delight in life. Consult R. Sewall, *The Vision of Tragedy;* T. R. Henn, *The Harvest of Tragedy;* and H. J. Muller, *The Spirit of Tragedy.*

tragic irony. See *irony.*

tragicomedy. Renaissance critical theorists, embroidering on Aristotle's *Poetics,* assumed that tragedy dealt with noble (important) figures and ended with a death; comedy dealt with trivial (laughable) figures and ended with a celebration. A tragicomedy was some sort of mixture: high characters in a play ending happily, a mingling of deaths and feasts, or, most often (as in many American films), threats of death that are happily—and unconvincingly—evaded. John Fletcher (1579–1625), who with his collaborator

Francis Beaumont wrote graceful dramas relying heavily on passionate outbursts and surprising turns of plot, defined a tragicomedy as a play that lacks deaths (and thus is no tragedy) but "brings some near it, which is enough to make it no comedy." One of the speakers in John Dryden's *Essay of Dramatick Poesie* (1668) says: "There is no theater in the world has anything so absurd as the English tragicomedy, . . . here a course of mirth, there another of sadness and passion, and a third of honor and a duel: thus, in two hours and a half, we run through all the fits of Bedlam." Consult Eugene Waith, *The Pattern of Tragicomedy.* On what can roughly be called the bitter or ironic comedy of the nineteenth and twentieth centuries, consult K. S. Guthke, *Modern Tragicomedy;* C. Hoy, *The Hyacinth Room;* and Eric Bentley, *The Life of the Drama.*

trilogy. A unit of three works. Though Greek tragic dramatists submitted three tragedies at a time, the plays are a trilogy only if they have an internal unity. Aeschylus's *Oresteia* (458 B.C.E.) is the sole extant complete Greek trilogy; Sophocles's three plays on the Oedipus legend—*Antigonê* (c. 422 B.C.E.), *Oedipus the King* (c. 425), and *Oedipus at Colonus* (c. 406) are not properly a trilogy because they were written at widely separated times and do not cohere into a consistent, unified whole. An example of a modern trilogy is O'Neill's *Mourning Becomes Electra* (1931).

tritagonist. See *protagonist.*

underplot. See *plot.*

unity. Generally means something like "coherence" or "congruence"; in a unified piece the parts work together and jointly contribute to the whole. The subplot of a play may parallel the main plot, or one character may be a foil to another. In any case, unity suggests "completeness" or "pattern" resulting from a controlling intelligence. In the *Poetics,* Aristotle said that a tragedy should have a unified action, and he mentioned that most tragedies cover a period of twenty-four hours. Italian critics, making his comments rigid, in the late sixteenth century established the **Three Unities** of Time, Place, and Action: a play (1) must not cover more than twenty-four hours, (2) must be set in one locale only or, at worst, in various parts of a single city, and (3) must be either entirely tragic or entirely comic, rather than a mixture of (as Sir Philip Sidney said) "hornpipes and funerals." (Consult H. B. Charlton, *Castelvetro's Theory of Poetry.*) Actually, the time covered by Greek tragedies is vague, and characters come from distant places in the space of relatively few lines. For example, in *Oedipus the King,* a shepherd who lives in the "farthest" fields from Corinth is sent for in line 863 and arrives in line 1108. Nor is unity of place invariable in Greek tragedy; there are violations of it in, for example, Aeschylus's *The Eumenides* and Sophocles's *Ajax.*

upstage. The back half of the acting area, or any part of the stage considered in relation to someone or something nearer the audience.

well-made play. See *pièce bien faite.*

BIBLIOGRAPHY

This bibliography consists of three parts.

Part 1 consists of general books.

Part 2 consists of works on periods, proceeding chronologically, with works about ancient Greek theater, then medieval theater, then Renaissance theater, and so on, up through the present. Within these chronological units, works are arranged alphabetically by author.

Part 3, arranged alphabetically by subject, gives material specifically devoted to the playwrights represented in this book, from Albee, Anonymous (e.g., the authors of medieval plays), and Beckett, and on through Luis Valdez and Tennessee Williams.

PART 1: GENERAL WORKS

General

Aston, Elaine. *An Introduction to Feminism and Theatre*. New York: Routledge, 1995.

Austin, Gayle. *Feminist Theories for Dramatic Criticism*. Ann Arbor: U of Michigan P, 1990.

Banham, Martin, ed. *The Cambridge Guide to the Theatre*. Rev. ed. New York: Cambridge UP, 1995.

Bentley, Eric. *The Life of the Drama*. New York: Athenaeum, 1964.

Boal, Augusto. *The Theater of the Oppressed*. New York: Urizen, 1979.

Brandon, James R., ed. *Cambridge Guide to Asian Theatre*. New York: Cambridge UP, 1993.

Brockett, Oscar. *History of the Theatre*. 6th ed. Boston: Allyn, 1991.

Brown, John Russell, ed. *The Oxford Illustrated History of Theatre*. New York: Oxford UP, 1995.

Carlson, Marvin. *Theories of the Theatre: A Historical and Critical Survey from the Greeks to the Present*. Expanded ed. Ithaca: Cornell UP, 1993.

Case, Sue-Ellen. *Feminism and Theatre*. New York: Methuen, 1988.

Case, Sue-Ellen, and Janelle Reinelt, eds. *The Performance of Power: Theatrical Discourse and Politics*. Iowa City: U of Iowa P, 1991.

Elam, Keir. *The Semiotics of Theatre and Drama*. New York: Methuen, 1980.

Ferris, Lesley. *Acting Women: Images of Women in Theatre*. New York: New York UP, 1989.

———ed. *Crossing the Stage: Controversies on Cross-dressing*. New York: Routledge, 1993.

Hawkins-Dady, Mark, and Leanda Shrimpton, eds. *International Dictionary of Theatre*. 3 vols. Chicago: St. James, 1992–96.

International Bibliography of Theatre. New York: Theatre Research Data Center, 1982–.

Pavis, Patrice. *Dictionary of the Theatre: Terms, Concepts, and Analysis*. Trans. Christine Shantz. Toronto: U of Toronto P, 1998.

Watson, Jack, and Grant F. McKernie. *A Cultural History of Theatre*. New York: Longman, 1993.

Wilmeth, Don B., and Tice L. Miller, eds. *Cambridge Guide to American Theatre*. New York: Cambridge UP, 1993.

Wilson, Edwin, and Alvin Goldfarb. *Living Theater: A History*. 2nd ed. New York: McGraw, 1994.

PART 2: WORKS ON PERIODS

Greek and Roman Theater

Arnott, Peter. *The Ancient Greek and Roman Theatre*. New York: Random, 1971.

———. *Public and Performance in the Greek Theatre*. New York: Routledge, 1991.

Ashby, Clifford. *Classical Greek Theatre: New Views of an Old Subject*. Iowa City: U of Iowa P, 1999.

Aylen, Leo. *The Greek Theater*. Rutherford: Associated UP, 1985.

Beare, W. *The Roman Stage: A Short History of Latin Drama in the Time of the Republic*. 3rd ed. New York: Barnes, 1963.

Bieber, Margaret. *The History of the Greek and Roman Theater*. 2nd ed. Princeton: Princeton UP, 1961.

Duckworth, George E. *The Nature of Roman Comedy*. Princeton: Princeton UP, 1952.

Else, Gerald. *The Origin and Early Form of Greek Tragedy*. New York: Norton, 1972.

Harsh, Philip Whaley. *A Handbook of Classical Drama*. Stanford: Stanford UP, 1944.

Hartigan, Karelisa. *Greek Tragedy on the American Stage*. Westport: Greenwood, 1995.

Kitto, H. D. F. *Greek Tragedy*. London: Methuen, 1939.

Konstan, David. *Greek Comedy and Ideology*. New York: Oxford UP, 1995.

———. *Roman Comedy*. Ithaca: Cornell UP, 1983.

Pickard-Cambridge, A. *The Dramatic Festivals of Athens*. 2nd ed. Oxford: Oxford UP, 1968.

Sanbach, F. H. *The Comic Theatre of Greece and Rome*. New York: Norton, 1977.

Taplin, Oliver. *Greek Tragedy in Action*. Berkeley: U of California P, 1978.

Walton, J. Michael. *Greek Theatre Practice*. Westport: Greenwood, 1980.

———. *Living Greek Theatre: A Handbook of Classical Performance and Modern Production*. New York: Greenwood, 1987.

Wiles, David. *Tragedy in Athens: Performance Space and Theatrical Meaning*. New York: Cambridge UP, 1997.

Medieval English Theater

Beadle, Richard, ed. *The Cambridge Companion to Medieval English Theatre*. Cambridge: Cambridge UP, 1994.

Bevington, David. *Medieval Drama*. Boston: Houghton, 1975.

Cawley, A. C., et al. *The Revels History of Drama in English: Medieval Drama*. New York: Methuen, 1983.

Chambers, E. K. *The Medieval Stage*. 2 vols. Oxford: Clarendon P, 1903.

Denny, Neville. *Medieval Drama: Stratford-upon-Avon Studies 16*. London: Edward Arnold, 1973.

Emmerson, Richard, ed. *Approaches to Teaching Medieval Drama*. New York: Modern Language Association, 1990.

Harbison, O. B., Jr. *Christian Rite and Christian Drama in the Middle Ages*. Baltimore: Johns Hopkins UP, 1965.

Kahrl, Stanley J. *Traditions of Medieval English Drama*. London: Hutchinson, 1974.

Nelson, Alan H. *The Medieval English Stage: Corpus Christi Pageants and Plays*. Chicago: U of Chicago P, 1974.

Potter, Robert. *The English Morality Play*. London: Routledge, 1975.

Richardson, Christine, and Jackie Johnston. *Medieval Drama*. London: Macmillan, 1991.

Tydeman, William. *English Medieval Theatre 1400–1500*. New York: Routledge, 1986.

Vince, Ronald W. *A Companion to the Medieval Theatre*. Westport: Greenwood, 1989.

Wickham, Glynne. *The Medieval Theatre*. 3rd ed. New York: Cambridge UP, 1987.

Woolf, Rosemary. *The English Mystery Plays*. Berkeley: U of California P, 1972.

Medieval Japanese Theater

Arnott, Peter. *The Theatres of Japan*. New York: St. Martin's, 1969.

Bethe, Monica, and Karen Brazell. *Dance in the No Theater*. 3 vols. Ithaca: Cornell UP, 1982.

Brandon, J. R., ed. *Nô and Kyogen in the Contemporary World*. Honolulu: U of Hawaii P, 1996.

Brazell, Karen. *Traditional Japanese Theater: An Anthology of Plays*. New York: Columbia UP, 1998.

Keene, Donald. *Nō: The Classical Theatre of Japan*. Tokyo: Kodansha International, 1966.

———. *20 Plays of the Nō Theatre*. New York: Columbia UP, 1970.

Keene, Donald, and Kaneko Hiroshi. *Nō and Bunraku: Two Forms of Japanese Theatre*. New York: Columbia UP, 1990.

Kenney, Don. *On the Stage in Japan*. Tokyo: Shufunotomo, 1974.

O'Neill, P. G. *Early No Drama: Its Background, Character, and Development, 1300–1450*. Westport: Greenwood, 1974.

Ortolani, Benito. *The Japanese Theatre*. Princeton, Princeton UP, 1990.

Pound, Ezra, and Ernest Fenollosa. *The Classic Noh Theatre of Japan*. New York: Knopf, 1917.

Pronko, Leonard. *Theater East and West*. Berkeley: U of California P, 1967.

Shimizu, Yoshiaki, ed. *Japan: The Shaping of Daimyo Culture 1185–1868*. Washington, DC: National Gallery of Art, 1988. [Excellent color plates of Nō-related crafts—garments, masks, fans, etc.]

Tyler, Royall, ed. and trans. *Japanese Nō Dramas*. New York: Penguin, 1992.

Varley, H. Paul. *Japanese Culture*. Honolulu: U of Hawaii P, 1984.

Yasuda, Kenneth. *Masterworks of the Nō Theater*. Bloomington: Indiana UP, 1989.

Zeami. *On the Art of the Nô Drama*. Trans. J. Thomas Rimer and Yamazaki Masakazu. Princeton: Princeton UP, 1984.

Italian Theater (for *Commedia dell'Arte,* see also Part 3, under "Anonymous")

Andrews, Richard. *Scripts and Scenarios: The Performance of Comedy in Renaissance Italy*. New York: Cambridge UP, 1993.

Clubb, Louise George. *Italian Drama in Shakespeare's Time*. New Haven: Yale UP, 1989.

Gordon, Mel, ed. and trans. *Lazzi: The Comic Routines of the Commedia dell'Arte*. New York: Performing Arts Books, 1983.

Herrick, Marvin T. *Italian Comedy in the Renaissance*. Urbana: U of Illinois P, 1960.

Kernodle, George. *From Art to Theatre: Form and Convention in the Renaissance*. Chicago: U of Chicago P, 1944.

Oden, Dunbar H. *The Italian Baroque Stage*. Berkeley: U of California P, 1978.

Salerno, Henry F., ed. and trans. *Scenarios of the Commedia dell'Arte: Flaminio Scola's "Il Teatro delle favole rappresentative."* New York: Limelight, 1989.

Vince, Ronald W. *Renaissance Theatre: A Historiographical Handbook*. Westport: Greenwood, 1984.

Theater in Renaissance England

Barroll, J. L., et al., ed. *Revels History of Drama in English: 1576–1613*. London: Methuen, 1975.

Beckerman, Bernard. *Shakespeare at the Globe, 1599–1602*. New York: Macmillan, 1962.

Bentley, G. E. *The Profession of Dramatist in Shakespeare's Time, 1590–1642*. Princeton: Princeton UP, 1971.

———. *The Profession of Player in Shakespeare's Time, 1590–1642*, Princeton: Princeton UP, 1984.

Braunmuller, A. R., and Michael Hattaway, eds. *The Cambridge Companion to English Renaissance Drama*. New York: Cambridge UP, 1990.

Chambers, E. K. *The Elizabethan Stage*. 4 vols. Oxford: Clarendon, 1923.

Dessen, Alan C. *Elizabethan Stage Conventions and Modern Interpreters*. New York: Cambridge UP, 1984.

Gurr, Andrew. *Playgoing in Shakespeare's London*. New York: Cambridge UP, 1987.

———. *The Shakespearean Stage 1574–1642*. 3rd ed. New York: Cambridge UP, 1992.

Gurr, Andrew, and Mariko Ichikawa. *Staging in Shakespeare's Theatres*. New York: Oxford UP, 2000.

Gurr, Andrew, and John Orrell. *Rebuilding Shakespeare's Globe*. London: Weidenfeld, 1989.

Hattaway, Michael. *Elizabethan Popular Theatre: Plays in Performance*. New York: Routledge, 1982.

Hodges, C. Walter. *Enter the Whole Army: A Pictorial History of Shakespearean Staging, 1576–1616*. Cambridge: Cambridge UP, 1999.

———. *The Globe Restored: A Study of the Elizabethan Theatre*. New York: Coward McCann, 1953.

King, T. J. *Shakespearean Staging, 1599–1642*. Cambridge: Harvard UP, 1971.

Thomson, Peter. *Shakespeare's Theatre*. New York: Routledge, 1992.

Vince, Ronald W. *Renaissance Theatre: A Historiographical Handbook*. Westport: Greenwood, 1984.

Theater in the Spanish Golden Age

Allen, John J. *The Reconstruction of a Spanish Golden Age Playhouse: El Corrall del Principe, 1583–1744*. Gainesville: UP of Florida, 1983.

McKendrick, Melveena. *Theatre in Spain 1490–1700*. New York: Cambridge UP, 1989.

Shergold, N. D. *A History of the Spanish Stage from Medieval times until the End of the Seventeenth Century*. Oxford: Oxford UP, 1967.

Wilson, Margaret. *Spanish Drama in the Golden Age*. Oxford: Pergamon, 1969.

French Neoclassical Theater

Arnott, Peter. *An Introduction to the French Theatre*. Totowa, NJ: Rowman, 1977.

Lough, John. *Seventeenth Century French Drama*. Oxford: Clarendon, 1979.

Scott, Virginia. *The Commedia Dell'Arte in Paris*. Charlottesville: U of Virginia P, 1990.

Turnell, Martin. *The Classical Moment: Studies in Corneille, Molière, and Racine*. New York: New Directions, 1948.

English Theater: 1660–1900

Avery, Emmett L., et al. *The London Stage, A Critical Introduction*. Carbondale: Southern Illinois UP, 1968.

Booth, Michael. *English Melodrama*. London: Jenkins, 1965.

Holland, Peter. *The Ornament of Action: Text and Performance in Restoration Comedy*. Cambridge: Cambridge UP, 1979.

Hughes, Leo. *The Drama's Patrons: A Study of the Eighteenth-Century London Audience*. Austin: U of Texas P, 1971.

Loftis, John, et al. *The Revels History of Drama in English: 1660–1750*. London: Methuen, 1976.

Rowell, George. *The Victorian Theatre*. Oxford: Oxford UP, 1956.

Styan, J. L. *Restoration Comedy in Performance*. New York: Cambridge UP, 1986.

Vince, Ronald W. *Neoclassical Theatre: A Historiographical Handbook*. Westport: Greenwood, 1988.

Theater from 1870 to 1945

Abramson, Doris. *Negro Playwrights in the American Theatre, 1925–1959*. New York: Columbia UP, 1969.

Artaud, Antonin. *The Theatre and Its Double*. New York: Grove, 1958.

Becker, George J., ed. *Documents of Modern Literary Realism*. Princeton: Princeton UP, 1963.

Bentley, Eric. *The Playwright as Thinker*. New York: Reynal, 1946.

———. ed. *The Theory of the Modern Stage*. New York: Applause, 1998.

Brockett, Oscar, and Robert R. Findlay. *Century of Innovation*. 2nd ed. Boston: Allyn, 1991.

Brustein, Robert. *The Theatre of Revolt: An Approach to Modern Drama*. Boston: Little, 1964.

Clurman, Harold. *The Fervent Years: The Story of the Group Theatre and the Thirties*. New York: Knopf, 1945.

Foreman, Richard. *Unbalancing Acts: Foundations for a Theater*. New York: Pantheon, 1992.

Fowlie, Wallace. *Age of Surrealism*. New York: Morrow, 1950.

Garton, H. F. *Modern German Drama*. New York: Grove, 1962.

Gassner, John. *Form and Idea in the Modern Theatre*. New York: Holt, 1956.

Gilman, Richard. *The Making of Modern Drama*. New York: Da Capo, 1987.

Goldstein, Malcolm. *The Political Stage: American Drama and Theater of the Great Depression*. New York: Oxford UP, 1974.

Gorelik, Mordecai. *New Theaters for Old*. New York: S. French, 1940.

Hatch, James V., and Ted Shine. *Black Theatre, U.S.A.: An Introduction to Modern Drama*. New York: Macmillan, 1963.

Krutch, Joseph Wood. *American Drama since 1918*. New York: Braziller, 1957.

Orenstein, Gloria. *The Theater of the Marvelous: Surrealism and the Contemporary Stage*. New York UP, 1975.

Piscator, Erwin. *The Political Theatre: A History 1914–1929*. New York: Avon, 1978.

Rabkin, Gerald. *Drama and Commitment: Politics in the American Theatre of the Thirties*. Bloomington: Indiana UP, 1964.

Shattuck, Roger. *The Banquet Years: The Origins of the Avant-Garde in France 1885 to World War I*. New York: Vintage, 1968.

Shepherd-Barr, Kirsten. *Ibsen and Early Modernist Theatre, 1890–1900*. Westport: Greenwood, 1997.

Taylor, John Russell. *The Rise and Fall of the Well-Made Play*. New York: Methuen, 1967.

Willet, John. *Expressionism*. New York: McGraw-Hill, 1970.

Williams, Jay. *Stage Left*. New York: Scribner's, 1974.

Williams, Raymond. *Drama from Ibsen to Eliot*. London: Chatto, 1952.

Theater from 1945 to the Present

Abramson, Doris. *Negro Playwrights in the American Theatre, 1925–1959*. New York: Columbia UP, 1969.

Banes, Sally. *Greenwich Village 1963: Avant-garde Performance and the Effervescent Body*. Durham: Duke UP, 1993.

Beck, Julian. *The Life of the Theatre*. New York: Limelight, 1991.

Bigsby, C. W. E. *A Critical Introduction to Twentieth-Century American Drama*. 3 vols. New York: Cambridge UP, 1982–85.

———. *Modern American Drama, 1945–1990*. New York: Cambridge UP, 1992.

Bordman, Gerald. *American Musical Theatre: A Chronicle*. New York: Oxford UP, 1978.

Brook, Peter. *The Empty Space*. New York: Avon, 1968.

Canning, Charlotte. *Feminist Theaters in the U.S.A.* New York: Routledge, 1996.

Carr, C. *On Edge: Performance at the End of the Twentieth Century*. Hanover: UP of New England, 1993.

Cohn, Ruby. *Currents in Contemporary Drama*. Bloomington: Indiana UP, 1969.

———. *New American Dramatists, 1960–1980*. New York: Grove, 1982.

Colleran, Jeanne, and Jenny S. Spencer, eds. *Staging Resistance: Essays in Political Theatre*. Ann Arbor: U of Michigan P, 1998.

Donkin, Ellen, and Susan Clements, eds. *Upstaging Big Daddy: Directing Theater As If Gender and Race Matter*. Ann Arbor: U of Michigan P, 1993.

Esslin, Martin. *The Theatre of the Absurd*. Garden City, NY: Anchor, 1969.

Fowlie, Wallace. *Dionysus in Paris: A Guide to Contemporary French Theatre*. Cleveland: World, 1967.

Goldberg, Rose Lee. *Performance Art: From Futurism to the Present*. New York: Abrams, 1988.

Goodman, Lizbeth, ed., with Jane de Gay. *The Routledge Reader in Gender and Performance*. New York: Routledge, 1998.

Grotowski, Jerzy. *Towards a Poor Theatre*. New York: Simon, 1969.

Kanelos, Nicholás, ed. *Hispanic Theater in the United States*. Houston: Arte Público, 1984.

King, Bruce, ed. *Contemporary American Theatre*. New York: Macmillan, 1991.

Kirby, E. T., ed., *Total Theatre*. New York: Dutton, 1969.

Kirby, Michael. *Happenings*. New York: Dutton, 1966.

———, ed. *The New Theatre: Performance Documentation*. New York: New York UP, 1974.

Kolin, Philip, ed. *American Playwrights since 1945: A Guide to Scholarship, Criticism, and Performance*. Westport: Greenwood, 1989.

Lee, Josephine. *Performing Asian America: Race and Ethnicity on the Contemporary Stage*. Philadelphia: Temple UP, 1997.

Marranca, Bonnie, ed. *The Theatre of Images*. New York: Drama Book Specialists, 1977.

Marranca, Bonnie, and Gautam Dasgupta, eds. *Conversations on Art and Performance*. Baltimore: Johns Hopkins UP, 1999.

Murphy, Brenda, ed. *The Cambridge Companion to American Women Playwrights*. New York: Cambridge UP, 1999.

Rabkin, Gerald, ed. *Richard Foreman*. Baltimore: Johns Hopkins UP, 1999.

Sainer, Arthur. *The New Radical Theater Notebook*. New York: Applause, 1998.

Sanders, Leslie Catherine. *The Development of Black Theatre in America*. Baton Rouge: Louisiana State UP, 1988.

Savran, David. *In Their Own Words*. New York: New York Theatre Communications Group, 1988.

———. *The Wooster Group, 1975–1985: Breaking the Rules*. Ann Arbor: UMI Research, 1986.

Schechner, Richard. *Public Domain*. New York: Avon, 1969.

Shank, Theodore. *American Alternative Theatre*. New York: Grove, 1982.

Sinfield, Alan. *Out on Stage: Lesbian and Gay Theatre in the Twentieth Century*. New Haven: Yale UP, 1999.

Vinson, James, ed. *Contemporary Dramatists*. 2nd ed. New York: St. Martins, 1977.

Weales, Gerald. *American Drama since World War II*. New York: Harcourt, 1962.

PART 3: PLAYWRIGHTS (ANONYMOUS AUTHORS FIRST, FOLLOWED BY NAMED PLAYWRIGHTS IN ALPHABETICAL ORDER)

Anonymous (Author of *Commedia dell'Arte* scenario)

Andrews, Richard. *Scripts and Scenarios: The Performance of Comedy in Renaissance Italy*. New York: Cambridge UP, 1993.

Cairns, Christopher, ed. *The Commedia dell'Arte: From the Renaissance to the Dario Fo*. Lewiston: Mellen, 1989.

Clubb, Louise George. *Italian Drama in Shakespeare's Time*. New Haven: Yale UP, 1989.

Ducharte, Pierre Louis. *The Italian Comedy*. New York: Dover, 1966.

Gordon, Mel, ed. and trans. *Lazzi: The Comic Routines of the Commedia dell'Arte*. New York: Performing Arts Books, 1983.

Heck, Thomas F. *Commedia dell'Arte: A Guide to the Primary and Secondary Literature*. New York: Garland, 1988.

Nicoll, Allardyce. *The World of Harlequin: A Critical Study of the Commedia dell'Arte*. New York: Cambridge UP, 1963.

Oreglia, G. *The Commedia dell'Arte*. London: Methuen, 1968.

Pietropaolo, Domenico, ed. *The Science of Buffoonery: Theory and History of the Commedia dell'Arte*. Ottawa: Dovehouse, 1989.

Richards, Kenneth, and Laura Richards. *The Commedia dell'Arte: A Documentary History*. Cambridge, MA: Blackwell, 1990.

Salerno, Henry F., ed. and trans. *Scenarios of the Commedia dell'Arte: Flaminio Scola's "Il Teatro delle favole reppresentative."* New York: Limelight, 1989.

Anonymous (Author of *Dojoji*) *See earlier "Medieval Japanese Theater"*

Anonymous (Author of *Everyman*)

Bevington, David. *From Mankind to Marlowe: Growth of Structure in the Popular Drama of Tudor England.* Cambridge: Harvard UP, 1962.

Gilman, Donald, ed. *"Everyman" and Company.* New York: AMS, 1989.

Potter, Robert. *The English Morality Play.* Boston: Routledge, 1975.

Schreiber, Earl G. "*Everyman* in America." *Comparative Drama* 9 (1975): 99–115.

Spinrad, Phoebe S. "The Last Temptation of *Everyman*." *Philological Quarterly* 64 (1985): 185–94.

Tanner, Ron. "Humor in *Everyman* and the Middle English Morality Play." *Philological Quarterly* 70 (1991): 149–61.

Van Laan, Thomas F. "*Everyman*: A Structural Analysis." *PMLA* 78 (1963): 465–75.

White, D. Jerry. *Early English Drama: "Everyman" to 1580, A Reference Guide.* Boston: Hall, 1986.

Anonymous (Author of *The Second Shepherds' Play*)

Mack, Maynard, Jr. "*The Second Shepherds' Play*: A Reconsideration." *PMLA* 93 (1978): 78–85.

Ross, L. J. "Symbols and Structure in the *Secunda Pastorum*." *Comparative Drama* 1 (1967–68): 122–43.

Edward Albee

Amacher, Richard E. *Edward Albee.* Rev. ed. Boston: Twayne, 1982.

Bigsby, C. W. E. *A Critical Introduction to Twentieth-Century American Drama.* Vol. 2. New York: Cambridge UP, 1984.

———, comp. *Edward Albee: A Collection of Critical Essays.* Englewood Cliffs: Prentice, 1975.

Bloom, Harold, ed. *Edward Albee.* New York: Chelsea, 1987.

Giantvalley, Scott. *Edward Albee: A Reference Guide.* Boston: G. K. Hall, 1987.

Gussow, Mel. *Edward Albee: A Singular Journey.* New York: Simon, 1999.

Hyman, Ronald. *Edward Albee.* New York: Ungar, 1971.

Kolin, Philip, ed. *Conversations with Edward Albee.* Jackson: U of Mississippi P, 1988.

Kolin, Philip, and J. Madison Davis, eds. *Critical Essays on Edward Albee.* Boston: G. K. Hall, 1986.

Roudane, Matthew Charles. *Understanding Edward Albee.* Columbia: U of South Carolina P, 1987.

Aristophanes

Aristophanes. *Lysistrata.* Ed. Jeffrey Henderson. New York: Oxford UP, 1987.

Deardon, C. W. *The Stage of Aristophanes.* London: Athlone, 1976.

Dover, K. J. *Aristophanic Comedy.* Berkeley: U of California P, 1972.

Harriott, Rosemary. *Aristophanes: Poet and Dramatist.* Baltimore: Johns Hopkins UP, 1986.

Spatz, Lois. *Aristophanes.* Boston: Twayne, 1978.

Taaffe, Lauren. *Aristophanes and Women.* New York: Routledge, 1993.

Samuel Beckett

Aldonian, Cathleen. *Samuel Beckett: A Reference Guide.* Boston: G. K. Hall, 1989.

Alvarez, A. *Samuel Beckett.* New York: Viking, 1973.

Cohn, Ruby. *The Comic Gamut.* New Brunswick: Rutgers UP, 1962.

———. *Just Play: Beckett's Theater.* Princeton UP, 1980.

Cronin, Anthony. *Samuel Beckett: The Last Modernist.* London: Harper, 1996.

Esslin, Martin, ed. *Samuel Beckett: A Collection of Critical Essays.* Englewood Cliffs: Prentice, 1965.

Federman, Raymond, and John Fletcher. *Samuel Beckett: His Works and His Critics.* Berkeley: U of California P, 1970.

Friedman, Melvin J. *Samuel Beckett Now.* Chicago: U of Chicago P, 1970.

Gontarski, S. E. *The Beckett Studies Reader.* Gainesville: UP of Florida, 1993.

———. *On Beckett: Essays and Criticism.* New York: Grove, 1986.

Kalb, Jonathan. *Beckett in Performance.* New York: Cambridge UP, 1989.

Kenner, Hugh. *A Reader's Guide to Samuel Beckett.* London: Thames and Hudson, 1973.

Knowlson, James. *Damned to Fame: The Life of Samuel Beckett.* New York: Simon, 1996.

Mercier, Vivian. *Beckett / Beckett.* New York: Oxford UP, 1994.

Oppenheim, Lois. *Directing Beckett.* Ann Arbor: U of Michigan P, 1994.

Webb, Eugene. *The Plays of Samuel Beckett.* Seattle: U of Washington P, 1972.

Aphra Behn

Behn, Aphra. *The Rover.* Ed. Bill Naismith. London: Methuen, 1993.

Diamond, Elin. "Gestus and Signature in Aphra Behn's *The Rover*." *ELH* 56 (1989): 519–39.

Duffy, Maureen. *The Passionate Shepherdess: Aphra Behn, 1640–89*. London: Methuen, 1977.

Hobby, Elaine. *Virtue of Necessity: English Women's Writing*. Ann Arbor: U of Michigan P, 1988.

Bertolt Brecht

Brecht, Bertolt. *Brecht on Theatre: The Development of an Aesthetic*. Ed. and trans. John Willett. New York: Hill, 1964.

Demetz, Peter, ed. *Brecht: A Collection of Critical Essays*. Englewood Cliffs: Prentice, 1962.

Eddershaw, Margaret. *Performing Brecht: Forty Years of British Performances*. New York: Routledge, 1966.

Esslin, Martin. *Brecht: The Man and His Works*. Garden City, NY: Doubleday, 1971.

Fuegi, John. *Brecht and Company: Sex, Politics, and the Making of Modern Drama*. New York: Grove/Atlantic, 1994.

Thomson, Peter, and Glendyr Sachs, eds. *The Cambridge Companion to Brecht*. Cambridge: Cambridge UP, 1994.

Willett, John. *Brecht in Context: Contemporary Approaches*. London: Methuen, 1984.

Anton Chekhov

Barricelli, Jean-Pierre, ed. *Chekhov's Great Plays: A Critical Anthology*. New York: New York UP, 1981.

Eekman, Thomas A. *Critical Essays on Anton Chekhov*. Boston: Hall, 1989.

Magarshack, David. *Chekhov the Dramatist*. New York: Hill, 1960.

Peace, Richard. *Chekhov: A Study of the Four Major Plays*. New Haven: Yale UP, 1983.

Senelick, Laurence. *The Chekhov Theatre: A Century of the Plays in Performance*. New York: Cambridge UP, 1997.

Styan, J. L. *Chekhov in Performance*. Cambridge: Cambridge UP, 1971.

Valency, Maurice. *The Breaking String: The Plays of Anton Chekhov*. New York: Oxford UP, 1966.

Caryl Churchill

Brater, Enoch, ed. *Feminine Focus: The New Women Playwrights*. New York: Oxford UP, 1989.

Cousin, Geraldine. *Churchill: The Playwright*. London: Methuen, 1989.

Fitzsimmons, Linda. *File on Churchill*. London: Methuen, 1989.

Kritzer, Amelia Howe. *The Plays of Caryl Churchill: Theater of Empowerment*. London: Macmillan, 1991.

Randall, Phyllis R., ed. *Caryl Churchill: A Casebook*. New York: Garland, 1988.

Zeifman, Hersh, and Cynthia Zimmerman, eds. *Contemporary British Drama 1970–1990*. Toronto: U of Toronto P, 1993.

Pierre Corneille

Arnott, Peter. *An Introduction to the French Theatre*. Totowa: Rowman, 1977.

Corneille, Pierre. *Seven Plays*. Trans. and ed. Samuel Solomon. New York: Random, 1969.

Howarth, William D., et al., eds. *French Theatre in the Neo-Classical Era, 1550–1789*. New York: Cambridge UP, 1997.

Nelson, Robert J. *Corneille: His Heroes and Their Worlds*. Philadelphia: U of Pennsylvania P, 1963.

Turnell, Martin. *The Classical Moment: Studies in Corneille, Molière, Racine*. New York: New Directions, 1963.

Wiley, W. L. *The Early Public Theatre in France*. Cambridge: Harvard UP, 1960.

Euripides

Burian, Peter, ed. *Directions in Euripidean Criticism*. Durham: Duke UP, 1985.

Clauss, James J., and Sarah Isles Johnston, eds. *Medea: Essays on Medea in Myth, Literature, Philosophy, and Art*. Princeton: Princeton UP, 1997.

Halleran, Michael P. *Stagecraft in Euripides*. Totowa: Barnes, 1985.

Meagher, Robert E. *Mortal Vision: The Wisdom of Euripides*. New York: St. Martin's, 1989.

Michelini, Ann N. *Euripides and the Tragic Tradition*. Madison: U of Wisconsin P, 1987.

Whitman, Cedric Hubbell. *Euripides and the Full Circle of Myth*. Cambridge: Harvard UP, 1974.

Dario Fo

Behan, Tom. *Dario Fo: Revolutionary Theater*. London: Pluto, 2000.

Fo, Dario, and Franca Rame. *Dario Fo and Franca Rame Theatre Workshops at the Riverside Studios, London*. London: Red Notes, 1983.

Mitchell, Tony. *Dario Fo: People's Court Jester*. Expanded ed. London: Methuen, 1999.

———. *File on Fo*. London: Methuen, 1989.

Scuderi, Antonio. *Dario Fo and Popular Performance*. New York: Legas, 1998.

Maria Irene Fornes

Delgado, Maria M., and Caridad Svich, eds. *Conducting a Life: Reflections on the Theater of Maria Irene Fornes*. Lyme, NH: Smith and Kraus, 1999.

Gruber, William E. *Missing Persons: Characters and Characterization in Modern Drama*. Athens: U of Georgia P, 1994.

Kent, Assunta Bartolomucci. *Maria Irene Fornes and Her Critics*. Westport: Greenwood, 1996.

Marranca, Bonnie. *Ecologies of Theater: Essays at the Century Turning*. Baltimore: Johns Hopkins UP, 1996.

Moroff, Diane Lynn. *Fornes: Theater in the Present Tense*. Ann Arbor: U of Michigan P, 1996.

Robinson, Marc, ed. *The Theater of Maria Irene Fornes*. Baltimore: Johns Hopkins UP, 1999.

Susan Glaspell

Ben-Zvi, Linda. ed. *Susan Glaspell: Essays on Her Theater and Fiction*. Ann Arbor: U of Michigan Press, 1995.

Bigsby, C. W. E., ed. *Plays by Susan Glaspell*. New York: Cambridge UP, 1987.

Makowsky, Veronica. *Susan Glaspell's Century of American Women: A Critical Interpretation*. New York: Oxford UP, 1993.

David Henry Hwang

Bigsby, C. W. E. *Contemporary American Playwrights*. New York: Cambridge UP, 1999.

Chin, Frank, et al., eds. *Aiiieeeee! An Anthology of Asian-American Writers*. Washington, DC: Howard UP, 1974.

Gerard, Jeremy. "David Henry Hwang: Riding on the Hyphen." *New York Times Magazine* 13 Mar. 1988: 88.

Hong, Kingston, Maxine. *The Woman Warrior*. New York: Vintage, 1977.

Moy, James S. *Marginal Sights: Staging the Chinese in America*. Iowa City: U of Iowa P, 1993.

Henrik Ibsen

Durbach, Errol. *Ibsen's Myth of Transformation*. Boston: Twayne, 1991.

Egan, Michael, ed. *Ibsen: The Critical Heritage*. London: Routledge, 1972.

Fjelde, Rolf, ed. *Ibsen: A Collection of Critical Essays*. Englewood Cliffs: Prentice, 1965.

Hardwick, Elizabeth. *Seduction and Betrayal*. New York: Random, 1974.

Marker, Frederick J. *Ibsen's Lively Art: A Performance Study of the Major Plays*. New York: Cambridge UP, 1989.

Northam, John. *Ibsen: A Critical Study*. Cambridge: Cambridge UP, 1973.

———. *Ibsen's Dramatic Method*. London: Faber, 1953.

Shaw, Bernard. *The Quintessence of Ibsenism*. New York: Hill, 1957.

Templeton, Joan. "The Doll's House Backlash: Criticism, Feminism, and Ibsen." *PMLA* 104 (1989): 28–40.

———. *Ibsen's Women*. New York: Cambridge UP, 1997.

Adrienne Kennedy

Betsko, Kathleen, and Rachel Koenig, eds. *Interviews with Contemporary Women Playwrights*. New York: Beech Tree, 1987.

Bryant-Jackson, Paul K., and Lois More Overlook, eds. *Intersecting Boundaries: The Theatre of Adrienne Kennedy*. Minneapolis: U of Minneapolis P, 1992.

Hay, Samuel A. *African American Theatre: An Historical and Critical Analysis*. New York: Cambridge UP, 1994.

Kennedy, Adrienne. *People Who Led to My Plays*. New York: Theater Communications, 1987.

Tony Kushner

Bigsby, C. W. E. *Contemporary American Playwrights*. Cambridge: Cambridge UP, 1999.

Geis, Deborah R., and Steven F. Kruger, eds. *Approaching the Millennium: Essays on* Angel in America. Ann Arbor: U of Michigan P, 1997.

Kolin, Philip C., and Colby H. Kullman, eds. *Speaking on Stage: Interviews with Contemporary American Playwrights*. Tuscaloosa: U of Alabama P, 1996.

Kushner, Tony. *Thinking about Longstanding Problems of Virtue and Happiness*. New York: Theater Communications, 1995.

Lahr, John. *Light Fantastic: Adventures in Theater*. New York: Dial, 1996.

Savran, David, ed. *The Playwright's Voice: American Dramatization, Memory, Writing, and Politics of Culture*. New York: Theater Communications, 1999.

Vorlicky, Robert, ed. *Tony Kushner in Conversation*. Ann Arbor: U of Michigan P, 1998.

Arthur Laurents

Garebian, Keith. *The Making of West Side Story*. Toronto: ECW, 1995 [the precursor to *Gypsy*, involving three of its four major collaborators].

Gottfried, Martin. *Broadway Musicals*. New York: Abrams, 1979.

———. *Sondheim*. New York: Abrams, 1993.

Laurents, Arthur. *Original Story By: A Memoir of Broadway and Hollywood*. New York: Knopf, 2000.

Lee, Gypsy Rose. *Gypsy: A Memoir*. New York: Dell, 1959.

———. *Lady of Burlesque*. New York: World, 1941.

Rich, Frank. "Conversations with Sondheim." *New York Times Magazine* 12 Mar. 2000: 38–43.

Schlundt, Christina. *Dance in the Musical Theatre: Jerome Robbins and His Peers, 1934–1965: A Guide*. New York: Garland, 1989.

David Mamet

Bigsby, C. W. E. *Contemporary Writers—David Mamet*. London: Methuen, 1985.

———. *A Critical Introduction to Twentieth-Century American Drama*. New York: Cambridge UP, 1984.

Dean, Anne. *David Mamet: Language as Dramatic Action*. Rutherford: Fairleigh Dickinson UP, 1990.

Freedman, Samuel. "The Gritty Eloquence of David Mamet." *New York Times Magazine* 21 Apr. 1985: 40–62.

Kalb, Jonathan. "Casting New Light on the Most Visible of Playwrights." *New York Times* 11 Nov. 1999: 2:8.

Lahr, John. "Fortress Mamet." *New Yorker* 17 Nov. 1997: 70–82.

Lieberson, Jonathan. "The Prophet of Broadway." *New York Review of Books* 21 Jul. 1988: 3–6.

Lloyd Evans, Gareth. *The Language of Modern Drama*. Totowa: Rowman, 1977.

Richards, David. "Mamet's Women." *New York Times* 3 Jan. 1993: 2:1+.

Christopher Marlowe

Bartels, Emily C. *Spectacles of Strangeness: Imperialism, Alienation, and Marlowe*. Philadelphia: U of Pennsylvania P, 1993.

Bevington, David, and Eric Rasmussen, eds. *"Doctor Faustus": A- and B-Texts (1604, 1616)*. New York: Manchester UP, 1993.

Bloom, Harold, ed. *Christopher Marlowe*. New York: Chelsea, 1986.

Farnham, Willard, ed. *Twentieth Century Interpretations of Doctor Faustus*. Englewood Cliffs: Prentice, 1969.

Grantley, Darryll, and Peter Roberts, eds. *Christopher Marlowe and English Renaissance Culture*. Aldershot, Hants, Eng.: Scholar Press, 1996.

Hattaway, Michael. *Elizabethan Popular Theatre: Plays in Performance*. Boston: Routledge, 1982.

Levin, Harry. *The Overreacher: A Study of Christopher Marlowe*. Cambridge: Harvard UP, 1964.

Ricks, Christopher. "*Doctor Faustus* and Hell on Earth." *Essays in Criticism* 35 (1985): 101–20.

Sale, Roger. *Christopher Marlow*. New York: St. Martin's, 1991.

Shepherd, Simon. *Marlowe and the Politics of Elizabethan Theater*. Brighton, Sussex: Harvester, 1986.

Steane, J. B. *Marlowe; A Critical Study*. Cambridge: Cambridge UP, 1964.

Thomas, Vivien, and William Tydeman, eds. *Christopher Marlowe: The Plays and Their Sources*. New York: Routledge, 1994.

Tromly, Fred B. *Playing with Desire: Christopher Marlowe and the Art of Tantalization*. Toronto: U of Toronto P, 1998.

Tydeman, William. *"Doctor Faustus": Text and Performance*. Basingstoke: Macmillan, 1984.

Arthur Miller

Bigsby, Christopher. *Arthur Miller and Company: Arthur Miller Talks about His Work*. London: Methuen, 1990.

———, ed. *The Cambridge Companion to Arthur Miller*. New York: Cambridge UP, 1997.

Bloom, Harold, ed. *Arthur Miller's "Death of a Salesman."* New York: Chelsea, 1988.

———, ed. *Willy Loman*. New York: Chelsea, 1990.

Koon, Helene Wickham. *Twentieth Century Interpretations: "Death of a Salesman."* Englewood: Prentice, 1983.

Miller, Arthur. *The Theater Essays of Arthur Miller*. New York: Viking, 1978.

———, *Timebends: A Life*. New York: Viking, 1995.

Murphy, Brenda. *Miller: Death of a Salesman*. New York: Cambridge UP, 1995.

Molière (Jean Baptiste Poquelin)

Bermel, Albert. *Molière's Theatrical Bounty: A New View of the Plays*. Carbondale: Southern Illinois UP, 1990.

Gaines, James F. *Molière's Theater*. Columbus: Ohio State UP, 1984.

Gross, Nathan. *From Gesture to Idea: Esthetics and Ethics in Molière's Comedy*. New York: Columbia UP, 1982.

Hall, H. Gaston. *Molière: "Tartuffe."* London: Edward Arnold, 1960.

Howarth, W. D. *Molière: A Playwright and His Audience*. Cambridge: Cambridge UP, 1982.

Moore, Will G. *Molière: A New Criticism*. Oxford: Clarendon Press, 1949.

Clifford Odets

Brenman-Gibson, Margaret. *Clifford Odets: American Playwright*. New York: Athenaeum, 1982.

Clurman, Harold. *The Fervent Years*. New York: Hill and Wang, 1957.

Goldstein, Malcolm. *The Political Stage: American Drama and Theater of the Great Depression*. New York: Oxford UP, 1974.

Rabkin, Gerald. *Drama and Commitment: Politics in the American Theatre of the Thirties*. Bloomington: Indiana UP, 1964.

Smith, Wendy. *Real Life Drama: The Group Theatre and America, 1931–1940*. New York: Grove Weidenfeld, 1990.

Williams, Jay. *Stage Left*. New York: Scribner's, 1974.

Eugene O'Neill

Alexander, Doris. *The Tempering of Eugene O'Neill*. New York: Harcourt Brace, 1962.

Berlin, Normand. *Eugene O'Neill*. New York: Grove, 1987.

Bogard, Travis. *Contour in Time: The Plays of Eugene O'Neill*. New York: Oxford UP, 1988.

Clark, Barrett H. *Eugene O'Neill: The Man and His Plays*. New York: Dover, 1947.

Gelb, Arthur, and Barbara Gelb. *O'Neill*. New York: Harper, 1973.

———, *O'Neill: Life with Monte Cristo*. New York: Applause, 2000.

Manheim, Michael. *The Cambridge Companion to Eugene O'Neill*. New York: Cambridge UP, 1998.

Ranald, Margaret Loftus. *The Eugene O'Neill Companion*. Westport: Greenwood, 1984.

Suzan-Lori Parks

Ben-Zvi, Linda, ed. *Vital Voices: Twentieth-Century Texts for the Stage by American Women*. Ann Arbor: U of Michigan P, 2000.

Feingold, Michael. "Hesterectomy." *Village Voice* 30 Nov. 1999: 77.

Mahone, Sydne. "Seers on the Rim." *American Theatre* Mar. 1994: 22–24.

———, ed. *Moon Marked and Touched by Sun: Plays by African-American Women*. New York: Theatre Communications, 1994.

Malkin, Jeanette R. *Memory-Theater and Postmodern Drama*. Ann Arbor: U of Michigan P, 1999.

Parks, Suzan-Lori. *The American Play and Other Works*. New York: Theatre Communications, 1995.

Perkins, Kathy, and Roberta Uno. *Contemporary Plays by Women of Color*. New York: Routledge, 1996.

Peterson, Jane T., and Suzanne Bennett. *Women Playwrights of Diversity: A Bio-Bibliographical Sourcebook*. Westport: Greenwood, 1997.

Sova, Kathy. "A Better Mirror: An Interview with the Playwright." *American Theatre* Mar. 2000: 32.

Harold Pinter

Burkman, Katherine H. *The Dramatic World of Harold Pinter*. Columbus: Ohio State UP, 1971.

Diamond, Elin. *Pinter's Comic Play*. Lewisburg: Bucknell UP, 1985.

Homan, Sidney. *The Audience as Actor and Character*. Lewisburg: Bucknell UP, 1989.

Merritt, Susan Hollis. *Pinter in Play*. Durham: Duke UP, 1990.

Prentice, Penelope. *The Pinter Ethic*. New York: Garland, 1994.

Quigley, Austin E. *The Pinter Problem*. Princeton: Princeton UP, 1975.

Elizabeth Robins

Gates, Joanne E. *Elizabeth Robins 1862–1952: Actress, Novelist, Feminist*. Tuscaloosa: U of Alabama P, 1994.

John, Angela V. *Elizabeth Robins: Staging a Life, 1862–1952*. New York: Routledge, 1995.

Kelly, Katherine E., ed. *Modern Drama by Women 1880's–1930's: An International Anthology*. New York: Routledge, 1996.

Scullion, Adrienne, ed. *Female Playwrights of the Nineteenth Century*. London: Everyman, 1996.

Stowell, Sheila. *A Stage of Their Own: Feminist Playwrights of the Suffrage Era*. Ann Arbor: U of Michigan P, 1992.

Rachel Rosenthal

Champagne, Lenora, ed. *Out from Under: Texts by Women Performance Artists*. New York: Theater Communications Group, 1990.

Lampe, Elke. "Rachel Rosenthal Creating Her Selves." *TDR* 117 (Spring 1988): 170–90.

Roth, Moira, ed. *Rachel Rosenthal*. Baltimore: Johns Hopkins UP, 1997.

William Shakespeare (general works, followed by works on *Hamlet* and then works on *A Midsummer Night's Dream*)

Bamber, Linda. *Comic Women, Tragic Men: A Study of Gender and Genre in Shakespeare*. Stanford: Stanford UP, 1982.

Bate, Jonathan. *The Genesis of Shakespeare*. New York: Oxford UP, 1998.

Bate, Jonathan, and Russell Jackson, eds. *Shakespeare: An Illustrated Stage History*. New York: Oxford UP, 1996.

Bentley, G. E. *Shakespeare: A Biographical Handbook*. New Haven: Yale UP, 1961.

Bullough, Geoffrey, ed. *Narrative and Dramatic Sources of Shakespeare*. 8 vols. New York: Columbia UP, 1957–75.

Drakakis, John, ed. *Alternative Shakespeares*. New York: Methuen, 1985.

Dollimore, Jonathan, and Alan Sinfield, eds. *Political Shakespeare: New Essays in Cultural Materialism*. Ithaca: Cornell UP, 1985.

Jardine, Lisa. *Still Harping on Daughters: Women and Drama in the Age of Shakespeare*. 2nd ed. New York: Columbia UP, 1989.

Kahn, Coppélia. *Man's Estate: Masculine Identity in Shakespeare*. Berkeley: U of California P, 1981.

Kennedy, Dennis. *Looking at Shakespeare: A Visual History of Twentieth-Century Performance*. New York: Cambridge UP, 1993.

Rothwell, Kenneth S. *A History of Shakespeare on Screen: A Century of Film and Television*. New York: Cambridge UP, 1999.

Salingar, Leo. *Shakespeare and the Traditions of Comedy*. New York: Cambridge UP, 1986.

Schoenbaum, Samuel. *William Shakespeare: A Compact Documentary Life*. Rev. ed. New York: Oxford UP, 1987.

Styan, J. L. *Shakespeare's Stagecraft*. New York: Cambridge UP, 1967.

Weimann, Robert. *Shakespeare and the Popular Tradition in the Theater*. Baltimore: Johns Hopkins UP, 1978.

Wells, Stanley, ed. *The Cambridge Companion to Shakespeare Studies*. New York: Cambridge UP, 1986.

Hamlet

In addition to titles mentioned in the "The Play in Performance" (page 377), the following are especially recommended:

Bevington, David, ed. *Twentieth Century Interpretations of "Hamlet."* Englewood Cliffs: Prentice, 1968.

Bradley, A. C. *Shakespearean Tragedy*. 2nd ed. London: Macmillan, 1905.

Charney, Maurice. *Style in "Hamlet."* Princeton: Princeton UP, 1969.

Frye, Roland Mushat. *The Renaissance "Hamlet": Issues and Responses in 1600*. Princeton: Princeton UP, 1984.

Granville-Barker, Harley. *Prefaces to Shakespeare: "Hamlet."* London: Batsford, 1930.

Hattaway, Michael. *Hamlet*. Basingstoke: Macmillan, 1987.

Jones, Ernest. *Hamlet and Oedipus*. London: Gollancz, 1949.

Kastan, David Scott, ed. *Critical Essays on Shakespeare's "Hamlet."* New York: G. K. Hall, 1995.

Levin, Harry. *The Question of "Hamlet."* New York: Oxford UP, 1959.

Showalter, Elaine. "Representing Ophelia: Women, Madness and the Responsibilities of Feminist Criticism." *Shakespeare and the Question of Theory*. Ed. Patricia Parker and Geoffrey Hartman. New York: Methuen, 1985. 77–94.

A Midsummer Night's Dream

For a long essay on the stage history of the play, followed by an edition of the play in which the footnotes are devoted to reporting actors' stage business over the centuries, see Trevor R. Griffith's edition of *A Midsummer Night's Dream* (1996) in the series called Shakespeare in Production, published by Cambridge UP.

Fender, Stephen. *Shakespeare's "A Midsummer Night's Dream."* London: Edward Arnold, 1968.

Levine, Laura. "Rape, Repetition, and the Politics of Closure in *A Midsummer Night's Dream*." *Feminist Readings of Early Modern Culture*. Ed. Valerie Traub et al. New York: Cambridge UP, 1996. 210–28.

Montrose, Louis Adrian. *The Purpose of Playing: Shakespeare and the Cultural Politics of the Elizabethan Theatre*. Chicago: U of Chicago P, 1996.

Williams, Gary Jay. *Our Midnight Revels: "A Midsummer Night's Dream in the Theatre*. Iowa City: U of Iowa P, 1997.

Young, David. *Something of Great Constancy: The Art of "A Midsummer Night's Dream."* New Haven: Yale UP, 1966.

Bernard Shaw

Bentley, Eric. *Bernard Shaw*. 2nd ed. London: Methuen, 1967.

Compton, Louis. *Shaw the Dramatist*. Lincoln: U of Nebraska P, 1969.

Ganz, Arthur F. *George Bernard Shaw*. New York: Grove, 1983.

Meisel, Martin. *Shaw and the Nineteenth-Century Theater*. Princeton: Princeton UP, 1963.

Shaw, Bernard. *Shaw on Shakespeare: Bernard Shaw's Writings on the Plays and Production of Shakespeare*. Ed. Edwin Wilson. New York: Dutton, 1961.

Weintraub, Stanley. *The Unexpected Shaw: Biographical Approaches to G.B.S. and His Work*. New York: Ungar, 1982.

Sam Shepard

Bigsby, C. W. E. *Modern American Drama, 1945–1990*. New York: Cambridge UP, 1992.

Bottoms, Stephen J. *The Theatre of Sam Shepard*. New York: Cambridge UP, 1998.

Kolin, Philip C., ed. *American Playwrights Since 1945: A Guide to Scholarship, Criticism, and Performance*. Westport: Greenwood, 1989.

Marranca, Bonnie, ed. *American Dreams: The Imagination of Sam Shepard*. New York: PAJ Publications, 1981.

Mottram, Ron. *Inner Landscapes: The Theatre of Sam Shepard*. Columbia: U of Missouri P, 1984.

Anna Deavere Smith

Feingold, Michael. "Opposing Selves." *Village Voice* 19 May 1992: 103.

Fitzgerald, Sharon. "Anna of a Thousand Faces." *American Visions*. Oct-Nov. 1994: 14–15.

Hupp, Steven L. "A Review of Fires in the Mirror." *Library Journal*. 1 Feb. 1994: 125.

Johnson, Pamela. "Anna Deavere Smith: She's Bridging Our Vast Racial Divides Through Theater." *Essence*. Aug. 1994: 40–41.

Pogrebin, Robin. "Ms. Smith, Alone Again, Is Going to Washington." *New York Times* 27 Feb. 2000, Sec. 2: 11, 26.

Reinelt, Janelle. "Performing Race: Anna Deavere Smith's *Fires in the Mirror*." *Modern Drama*. Winter 1996: 609.

Reuben, Paul P. "Chapter 8: American Drama—Anna Deavere Smith." *PAL: Perspectives in American Reference Guide*. [http://www.csustan.edu/english/reuben/pal/chap8/smith.html] 4 June 2000.

Smith, Anna Deavere. *Plays in Progress*. New York: Theatre Communications, 1989.

———. *Talk to Me: Listening Between the Lines*. New York: Random, 2000.

Smith, Anna Deavere, and Jessye Norman. "A Moment of Transformation." *Public Access* [Program of the Public Theater] Mar. 2000: 8–12.

Smith, Iris. "Authors in America: Tony Kushner, Arthur Miller, and Anna Deavere Smith." *The Centennial Review* 40 (Winter 1996): 125–41.

Tobias, Tobi. "Alvin Ailey American Dance Theater." *New York* 3 Jan. 1994: 23.

Torrens, James S. "*Twilight: Los Angeles, 1992* (A Review)." *America* 4 Jun. 1994: 23.

Sophocles

Bloom, Harold, ed. *Sophocles*. New York: Chelsea, 1990.

———, ed. *Sophocles' "Oedipus Rex."* New York: Chelsea, 1988.

Bushnell, Rebecca. *Prophesying Tragedy: Sign and Void in Sophocles' Theban Plays*. Ithaca: Cornell UP, 1988.

Goheen, R. F. *The Imagery of Sophocles' "Antigone."* Princeton: Princeton UP, 1951.

Kitto, H. D. *Sophocles: Dramatist and Philosopher*. London: Oxford UP, 1956.

Knox, Bernard. *Oedipus at Thebes: Sophocles's Tragic Hero and His Time*. New York: Norton, 1971.

Lattimore, Richmond. *The Poetry of Greek Tragedy*. Baltimore: Johns Hopkins UP, 1958.

O'Brien, Michael J., ed. *Twentieth Century Interpretations of "Oedipus Rex."* Englewood Cliffs, Prentice, 1968.

Whitman, Cedric H. *Sophocles*. Cambridge: Harvard UP, 1951.

Wole Soyinka

Maduakor, Obi. *Wole Soyinka: An Introduction to His Writing*. New York: Garland, 1986.

Maja-Pearce, Adewale, ed. *Wole Soyinka: An Appraisal*. Oxford: Heinemann, 1994.

Soyinka, Wole. *Art, Dialogue, and Outrage: Essays on Literature and Culture*. New York: Pantheon, 1993.

Wright, Derek. *Wole Soyinka Revisited*. New York: Twayne, 1993.

Gertrude Stein

Bowers, Jane Palatini. "*They Watch Me as They Watch This*": *Gertrude Stein's Metadrama*. Philadelphia: U of Pennsylvania P, 1991.

Bridgman, Richard. *Gertrude Stein in Pieces*. New York: Oxford UP, 1970.

Cohen, Paul. "Gertrude Stein: American Librettist." *Centennial Review* 29 (1985): 389–99.

Gygax, Franziska. *Gender and Genre in Gertrude Stein*. Westport: Greenwood, 1998.

Hoffman, Michael. *Gertrude Stein*. Boston: Twayne, 1976.

Martin, Robert K. "*The Mother of Us All* and American History." *Gertrude Stein and the Making of Literature*. Ed. Shirley Neuman and Ira B. Nadel. Boston: Northeastern UP, 1988. 210–22.

Ryan, Betsy Alayne. *Gertrude Stein's Theatre of the Absolute*. Ann Arbor: UMI, 1984.

Winston, Elizabeth. "Making History in *The Mother of Us All*." *Mosaic: Journal for the Interdisciplinary Study of Literature* 20:4 (Fall 1987): 117–29.

Tom Stoppard

Bigsby, C. W. E., ed. Ian Scott-Kilvert. *Tom Stoppard*. Harlowe, Eng.: Longman, 1976.

Billington, Michael. *Stoppard, The Playwright*. New York: Methuen, 1987.

Bloom, Harold, ed. *Tom Stoppard*. New York: Chelsea House, 1986.

Brassell, Tim. *Tom Stoppard: An Assessment*. New York: St. Martin's, 1985.

Bratt, David. *Tom Stoppard: A Reference Guide*. Boston: G. K. Hall, 1982.

Brustein, Robert. *The Third Theatre*. New York: Knopf, 1969.

Cahn, Victor L. *Beyond Absurdity: The Plays of Tom Stoppard*. Rutherford: Fairleigh Dickinson UP, 1979.

Dean, Joan Fitzpatrick. *Tom Stoppard: Comedy as a Moral Matrix*. Columbia, U of Missouri P, 1981.

Gussow, Mel. *Conversations with Stoppard*. New York: Grove, 1996.

Harty, John, III, ed. *Tom Stoppard: A Casebook*. New York: Garland, 1988.

Hayman, Ronald. *Tom Stoppard*. Totowa: Rowman, 1977.

Hu, Stephen. *Tom Stoppard's Stagecraft*. New York: Lang, 1989.

Hunter, Jim. *Tom Stoppard's Plays*. London: Faber, 1982.

Jenkins, Anthony. *Critical Essays on Tom Stoppard*. Boston: G. K. Hall, 1990.

———, ed. *The Theatre of Tom Stoppard*. New York: Cambridge UP, 1987.

Kelly, Katherine E. *Tom Stoppard and the Craft of Comedy: Medium and Genre at Play*. Ann Arbor: U of Michigan P, 1991.

Londré, Felicia Hardison. *Tom Stoppard*. New York: Ungar, 1981.

Rusinko, Susan. *Tom Stoppard*. Boston: Twayne, 1986.

Sammells, Neil. *Tom Stoppard, The Artist as Critic*. New York: St. Martin's, 1988.

Taylor, John Russell. *The Second Wave: British Drama for the Seventies*. New York: Hill, 1971.

Whitaker, Tom. *Tom Stoppard*. New York: Grove, 1983.

August Strindberg

Carlson, Harry Gilbert. *Strindberg and the Poetry of Myth*. Berkeley: U of California Press, 1982.

Sprinchorn, Evert. *Strindberg as Dramatist*. New Haven: Yale UP, 1982.

Törnqvist, Egil. *Strindberg's "Miss Julie": A Play and Its Transpositions*. Norwich, Eng.: Norvik, 1988.

Sophie Treadwell

Barlow, Judith E., ed. *Plays by American Women: 1900–1930*. New York: Applause, 1985.

Dickey, Jerry. *Sophie Treadwell: A Research and Production Sourcebook*. Westport: Greenwood, 1997.

Murphy, Brenda. *The Cambridge Companion to American Women Playwrights*. New York: Cambridge UP, 1999.

Luis Valdez

Broyles-González, Yolanda. *El Teatro Campesino: Theater in the Chicano Movement*. Austin: U of Texas P, 1994.

Huerta., Jorge., ed. *Necessary Theater: Six Plays About the Chicano Experience*. Houston, Tex.: Arte Publico Press, 1989.

Lope (Felix) de (Carpio) Vega

Hayes, Francis C. *Lope de Vega*. New York: Twayne, 1967.

Ingber, Alix. "Lope Félix de Vega Carpio." *Spanish Dramatists of the Golden Age: A Bio-Bibliographical Sourcebook*. Ed. Mary Parker. Westport: Greenwood, 1998.

McKendrick, Melveena. *Theater in Spain 1490–1700*. Cambridge: Cambridge UP, 1989.

Derek Walcott

Baer, William, ed. *Conversations with Derek Walcott*. Jackson: U of Mississippi P, 1996.

King, Bruce. *Derek Walcott and West Indian Drama*. Oxford: Clarendon, 1995.

Taylor, Patrick. "Myth and Reality in Caribbean Narrative: Derek Walcott's *Pantomime*." *Critical Perspectives on Derek Walcott*. Ed. Robert D. Hamner. Washington, DC: Three Continents, 1993. 298–315.

Thieme, John. *Derek Walcott*. New York: Manchester UP, 1999.

Oscar Wilde

Beckson, Karl, ed. *Oscar Wilde: The Critical Heritage*. London: Routledge, 1970.

Bloom, Harold, ed. *Oscar Wilde's "The Importance of Being Earnest."* New York: Chelsea, 1988.

Donohue, Joseph, with Ruth Berggren. *Oscar Wilde's "The Importance of Being Earnest": A Reconstructive Critical Edition of the Text of the First Production*. Gerrards Cross, Bucks: Colin Smythe, 1995.

Ellmann, Richard. *Oscar Wilde*. New York: Knopf, 1988.

Powell, Kerry. *Oscar Wilde and the Theatre of the 1890s*. New York: Cambridge UP, 1990.

Raby, Peter. *"The Importance of Being Earnest": A Reader's Companion*. New York: Twayne, 1995.

Tennessee Williams

Boxill, Roger. *Tennessee Williams*. New York: St. Martin's, 1987.

Crandell, George, ed. *The Critical Response to Tennessee Williams*. Westport: Greenwood, 1996.

Devlin, Albert J., ed. *Conversations with Tennessee Williams*. Jackson: UP of Mississippi, 1986.

Falk, Signi. *Tennessee Williams*. Boston: Twayne, 1978.

Gunn, Drewey Wayne. *Tennessee Williams: A Bibliography*; 2nd ed. Metuchen: Scarecrow, 1991.

Frenz, Horst. *American Playwrights and Drama*. New York: Hill, 1965.

Johnston, Monica Carolyn. *Tennessee Williams and American Realism*. Berkeley: U of California P, 1987.

Kolin, Philip C., ed. *Tennessee Williams: A Guide to Research and Performance*. Westport: Greenwood, 1998.

Leavitt, Richard F. *The World of Tennessee Williams*. London: Allen, 1978.

Leverich, Lyle. *Tom: The Unknown Tennessee Williams*. New York: Crown, 1995.

Londré, Felicia Hardison. *Tennessee Williams*. New York: Ungar, 1979.

McCann, John S. *The Critical Reputation of Tennessee Williams: A Reference Guide*. Boston: Hall, 1983.

Nelson, Benjamin. *Tennessee Williams: The Man and His Work*. New York: Obolensky, 1961.

Phillips, Gene D. *The Films of Tennessee Williams*. Philadelphia: Art Alliance, 1980.

Spoto, Donald. *The Kindness of Strangers: The Life of Tennessee Williams*. New York: Ballantine, 1986.

Stanton, Stephen S., ed. *Tennessee Williams: A Collection of Critical Essays.* Englewood Cliffs: Prentice, 1977.

Tischler, Nancy M. *Tennessee Williams: Rebellious Puritan.* New York: Citadel, 1961.

Williams, Tennessee. *Memoirs.* Garden City, Long Island: Doubleday, 1978.

August Wilson

Henderson, Heather. "Building Fences: An Interview with Mary Alice and James Earl Jones." *Theater/Yale* 16:3 (1991): 67–70.

Nadel, Alan, ed. *May All Your Fences Have Gates: Essays on the Drama of August Wilson.* Iowa City: U of Iowa P, 1994.

Pereira, Kim. *August Wilson and the African American Odyssey.* Urbana: U of Illinois P, 1995.

Susan Yankowitz

Blumenthal, Eileen. *Joseph Chaikin.* New York: Cambridge UP, 1984.

Chaikin, Joseph. *The Presence of the Actor.* New York: Athenaeum, 1972.

Croyden, Margaret. *Lunatic, Lovers, and Poets: The Contemporary Experimental Theatre.* New York: McGraw-Hill, 1974.

Kerr, Walter. *God on the Gymnasium Floor.* New York: Simon, 1971.

Lahr, John. *Up Against the Fourth Wall.* New York: Grove, 1970.

Malpede, Karen. *Three Works by the Open Theatre.* New York: Drama Book Specialists, 1974.

Pasolli, Robert. *A Book on the Open Theatre.* New York: Bobbs-Merrill, 1970.

Sainer, Arthur. *The Radical Theatre Notebook.* New York: Avon, 1975.

Terry, Megan. *Viet Rock and Other Plays.* New York: Simon, 1967.

W. B. Yeats

Jeffares, A. Norman, and A. S. Knowland. *A Commentary on the Collected Plays of W. B. Yeats.* Stanford: Stanford UP, 1975.

Moore, John Rees. *Masks of Love and Death: Yeats as Dramatist.* Ithaca: Cornell UP, 1971.

Nathan, Leonard. *The Tragic Drama of William Butler Yeats.* New York: Columbia UP, 1965.

Taylor, Richard. *A Reader's Guide to the Plays of W. B. Yeats.* London: Macmillan, 1984.

Torchiana, Donald. *W. B. Yeats and Georgian Ireland.* Evanston: Northwestern UP, 1966.

Ure, Peter. *Yeats the Playwright.* London: Routledge, 1963.

Vendler, Helen. *Yeats's "Vision" and the Later Plays.* Cambridge: Harvard UP, 1963.

Yeats, W. B. *"Purgatory": Manuscript Materials Including the Author's Final Text.* Ed. Sandra F. Siegal. Ithaca: Cornell UP, 1986.

LIST OF VIDEO RESOURCES

The following list of audiovisual resources is intended to supplement the teaching of plays included in *Types of Drama*. Most of the sources can be located through World Cat, a search engine at your institutional or local library. Many others are available at your local video store. In some cases, you can order a copy of the video through its distributor. Please see List of Distributors at the end of this section.

General Resources

Black Theatre: The Making of a Movement
113 min. 1978.
VHS.
Documentary focusing on black theater arising from the civil rights activism in the 1950s, 1960s, and 1970s.
Distributor: California Newsreel.

A Day at the Globe
30 min. Color.
VHS.
Begins with an overview of early drama, then moves into seventeenth-century English drama with a focus on the Globe Playhouse. Covers production elements from acting, to costumes, to sound effects.
Distributor: Insight Media.

The Elizabethan Age
30 min. Color.
VHS.
A look at the seventeenth-century English Renaissance.
Distributor: Insight Media.

Modern British Drama
2 videocassettes, 400 min. Color. 1 booklet. 1993.
VHS.
A collection of lectures in the SuperStar Teachers Series.
Lecture 1: British Theatre, 1890–1990; 2. Comedy of Manners, Oscar Wilde and Noel Coward; 3. George Bernard Shaw, Socialist and Prophet; 4. John Osborne Looks Back in Anger; 5. Samuel Beckett, Drama of Alienation; 6. The Menace of Harold Pinter; 7. The Invitations of Tom Stoppard; 8. Caryl Churchill and David Hare.
Distributor: The Teaching Company: Springfield, VA.

The Origin of the Drama and the Theater
24 min., 2 parts. 1992.
VHS.

Part One uses still images to trace the evolution of drama from vulgar jests into comedy and hymns into tragedy. Part Two looks at the designs of theaters and the social role of Greek theater.
Distributor: Insight Media.

Panorama of African-American Theater
1 hour total, 4 parts. 1991.
VHS.
Traces the development of African American theater from the 1820s to the present using theatrical scenes, songs, and readings. Presents excerpts from plays such as August Wilson's *Fences* and George Wolfe's *Colored Museum*.
Distributor: Insight Media.

The Theatre in Ancient Greece
26 min. Color. 1989.
VHS, Beta, 3/4" U-matic cassette.
An exploration of ancient theater design and the incorporation of environmental elements in the theater such as Atticus, Corinth, Epidaurus, Herodus. Also looks at the origin of tragedy, and the roles of playwrights, actors, and audience members.
Distributor: Films for the Humanities and Sciences.

Anonymous, *Commedia dell'arte*

Commedia dell'arte
53 min. Color. 1997.
VHS.
Antonio Fava explains the history of *commedia dell'arte* and shows examples through his classes in this art form.
Produced by Teatro del Vicolo.
Distributor: HUSH Videos: Floreat, Australia.

Commedia dell'arte
13.5 min. Color. 198u, 196u.
VHS.
Based on *Theatre, The Search for Style* by John D. Mitchell. Presents the gallery of stock *commedia* characters focusing on the *maschere*, the mask characters. Giovanni Poli provides the authentic voice quality, characteristic movements, and gestures of *commedia dell'arte*.
Distributor: IASTA: New York, NY.

Anonymous, *Everyman*

Everyman
53 min. Color. 1991.
VHS.
A presentation of the classic fifteenth-century morality play directed by Bob Morris.
Distributor: Insight Media.

Everyman: A Modern Adaptation
57 min. Color. 1990.
VHS.

Produced and directed by Wayne J. Keeley; co-produced by Joanne Birkmann.
Distributor: Bennu Productions, Inc.: New York, NY.

Everyman
18 min. Color. 1989.
VHS.
David Boone's modern rendering of the symbolic fifteenth-century morality play expands to acknowledge that Everyman's base instincts apply equally to Everywoman.
Distributor: Vide-Sig: Irvine, CA.

Anonymous, The Wakefield Master, *The Second Shepherds' Play* and Anonymous, *Quem Quaeritis*
Early English Drama: The Second Shepherds' Play
52 min. Color. 1988.
VHS.
Presents the play as it would have been performed in the medieval period as an introduction to the English mystery play.
Distributor: Films for the Humanities.

Quem Quaeritis; Abraham and Isaac; The Second Shepherds' Play
53 min. Color. 1975.
VHS.
Presents three examples of early English drama ranging from the tenth-century *Quem Quaeritis* to the fourteenth-century *Second Shepherds' Play*.
Distributor: Films for the Humanities.

Edward Albee *The Sandbox*
The Sandbox
10 min. Black and white. 1965.
16 mm film.
An adaptation of the play by Albee. Uses abstract dialogue and setting to comment on contemporary American family relationships and attitudes toward the elderly.
Distributor: University of Southern California, Department of Cinema.

Edward Albee
52 min. Color. 1996, 1995.
VHS.
A look at the work and life of Edward Albee. Discusses Albee's influences, his work, and shows excerpts from performances of his plays.
Distributor: Films for the Humanities and Sciences.

Aristophanes *Lysistrata*
Lysistrata
97 min. Color. 1987.
VHS.
Shot at the Acropolis, this adaptation contains nudity and strong language and is recommended for mature students.
Distributor: Insight Media.

Lysistrata
75 min. Color. 1983.
VHS.
English-language performance of the play.
Distributor: SBS in Association with Video Images: Sydney, NSW.

Samuel Beckett *Krapp's Last Tape*
Krapp's Last Tape
46 min. Color. 1990.
VHS.
A performance of the San Quentin Drama Workshop.
Distributor: WGBH Educational Foundation: Boston, MA.

Beckett Directs Beckett
4 videocassettes, 279 min. Color. 1992/1990.
VHS.
Tape 3 is a 46-minute presentation of *Krapp's Last Tape*. Other Beckett plays included are *Waiting for Godot*, Act 1 (tape 1), and Act 2 (tape 2); and *Endgame* (tape 4).
Distributor: Smithsonian Institution Press Video Division: Washington, DC.

Samuel Beckett
80 min. Color. 1989.
VHS, Beta, 3/4" U-matic cassette.
An autobiographical portrayal of Beckett's life and work.
Distributor: Films for the Humanities and Sciences.

Aphra Behn *The Rover*
The Rover
180 min. Color. 1995.
VHS.
Produced, designed, and directed for the Women's Playhouse Trust by Jules Wright; produced and directed for the BBC/Open University by Tony Coe.
Distributor: Open University: Milton Keynes, England.

Bertolt Brecht *The Good Woman of Setzuan*
German Theatre, Brecht and Schiller
16 min. Black and white. 1982.
16 mm film.
Provides scenes from *The Good Woman of Setzuan* by Brecht and *Love and Intrigue* by Schiller to demonstrate their styles.
Distributor: IASTA: New York, NY.

Bertolt Brecht
55 min. Color. 1989.
VHS, Beta, 3/4" U-matic cassette.
A biographical study of Brecht and his art.
Distributor: Films for the Humanities and Sciences.

Anton Chekhov *The Cherry Orchard*
The Cherry Orchard, Part 1: Chekhov, Innovator of Modern Drama

21 min. Color and black and white. 1968.
VHS, Beta, U-matic cassette, 16 mm film.
Depicts important scenes paired with discussions led by
Norris Houghton.
Distributor: Encyclopaedia Britannica Educational
Corporation.

The Cherry Orchard, Part II: Comedy or Tragedy?
21 min. Color and black and white. 1967.
VHS.
Continuation of series. Examines Chekhov's use of subtext.
Distributor: Encyclopaedia Britannica Educational
Corporation.

The Cherry Orchard
120 min. Black and white. 1959.
VHS.
A presentation of the classic play starring Helen Hayes.
Distributor: Insight Media.

Anton Chekhov: A Writer's Life
37 min. Black and white. 1974.
VHS, Beta, 3/4" U-matic.
A biographical account of the playwright.
Distributor: Films for the Humanities and Sciences.

Caryl Churchill *Top Girls*
Top Girls
175 min. Color. 1996.
VHS.
A videocassette release of the 1991 stage production broad-
cast on television.
Distributor: Open University: London, England.

Modern British Drama
2 videocassettes, 400 min. Color. 1 booklet. 1993.
VHS.
The eighth lecture in this SuperStar Teachers Series covers
Churchill and David Hare.
Distributor: The Teaching Company: Springfield, VA.

Corneille *Le Cid*
Le Cid
2 hours, 57 min. Color. 1990.
VHS.
A video of a French 1963 production.
Distributor: Fil a Film: Paris.

Euripides *Medea*
Medea
118 min. Color. 1970.
VHS, Beta.
With Maria Callas, Guiseppi Gentile, and Laurent Tazieff.
Directed by Pier Paolo Passolini. In Italian with English
subtitles.
Distributor: Video Artists International.

Medea
107 min. Black and white. 1959.
VHS.
Adaptation of the play starring Judith Anderson.
Distributor: Insight Media.

Dario Fo
A Nobel for Two: Dario Fo and Franca Rame
56 min. Color with black and white. 1998.
VHS.
Portrays the life and career of this Italian husband and wife
team whose work was censored in Italy for more than sev-
enteen years.
Distributor: Cinema Guild.

Maria Irene Fornes
Maria Irene Fornes
1 hour. Color. 1990.
VHS.
An interview with Fornes conducted by Edwin Wilson for
the Spotlight Series.
Distributor: PBS Video.

Susan Glaspell *Trifles*
Trifles
22 min. Black and white. 1996.
VHS.
Adaptation of the play for video.
Distributor: AME Video: Oak Park, IL.

*Beginnings: The First Season of Plays Staged by the Province-
town Players*
Color. 1991.
VHS.
A film created to complement the conference "Beginnings
1915, The Culture Movement," sponsored by Provincetown
Playhouse in conjunction with the University of
Massachusetts.
Distributor: Rutgers University Press: New Brunswick, NJ.

David Henry Hwang *The Dance and the Railroad*
The Dance and the Railroad
58 min. Color. 1982.
U-matic.
A film version of the play intended for general audiences.
Distributor: Hearst/ABC Video Services: New York, NY.

Henrik Ibsen *A Doll's House*
A Doll's House
136 min. Color. 1995, 1991.
VHS.
With Juliet Stevenson, Trevor Eve, Geraldine James, and
Patrick Malahide. Includes teacher's guide.
Distributor: BBC Worldwide Americas: New York, NY.

A Doll's House
98 min. Color. 1973.
VHS, 16 mm film.
With Jane Fonda, Edward Fox, Trevor Howard, and David Warner.
Distributor: Prism Entertainment.

Gender and Performance: A Doll's House
180 min. Color. 1995.
VHS.
Presented by Lizbeth Goodman and Richard Allen. Examines two key scenes between Nora and Torvald to explore gender relations, and incorporates three different sets (1870s, 1950s, and 1980s) to discover how the different eras would alter the actors' approaches to the roles.
Distributor: Routledge in association with The Open University and the BBC: London.

A Doll's House, Part I: The Distinction of Illusion
34 min. Color. 1968.
VHS, Beta, U-matic, 16 mm film.
Norris Houghton discusses the subtextual tensions in the play.
Distributor: Encyclopedia Britannica Educational Corporation.

A Doll's House, Part II: Ibsen's Themes
29 min. Color. 1968.
VHS, Beta, U-matic, 16 mm film.
Norris Houghton examines the cast of characters and the themes in the play.
Distributor: Encyclopaedia Britannica Educational Corporation.

Arthur Laurents *Gypsy*
Gypsy
143 min. Color. 1962.
DVD, VHS.
Video release of the 1962 motion picture with Rosalind Russell, Natalie Wood, and Karl Malden.
Distributor: Warner Home Video.

Gypsy
150 min. Color. 1993.
VHS.
Release of the 1993 motion picture by RHI Entertainment with Bette Midler, Peter Riegert, and Cynthia Gibb.
Distributor: Hallmark Home Entertainment.

David Mamet *Glengarry Glen Ross*
Glengarry Glen Ross
100 min. Color. 1992.
DVD, VHS.
With Al Pacino, Jack Lemmon, Alec Baldwin, Ed Harris, Alan Arkin, Kevin Spacey, and Jonathan Price.
Distributor: Pioneer LDCA, Inc.

Mamet
29 min. Color. 1993.
VHS.
Number 5 from the Emerging Playwrights Series, this video provides an interview with Mamet conducted by Richard Barr.
Distributor: Insight Media.

Christopher Marlowe *Doctor Faustus*
Doctor Faustus
93 min. Color. 1995, 1967.
VHS.
A video release of the 1967 production with Richard Burton and Elizabeth Taylor.
Distributor: Columbia Tristar Video.

Faust: The Man and the Legend
28 min. Color. 1998.
VHS.
Viewers gain a sense of Europe before the Enlightenment and of the legendary figure immortalized by Marlowe, Lessing, and Goethe.
Distributor: Films for the Humanities and Sciences.

Marlowe's Parables of Power. Part III, Doctor Faustus
33 min. Color. 1988.
VHS.
Excerpts from the play and a discussion of humankind's lust for knowledge and power.
Distributor: IASTA: New York, NY.

Arthur Miller *Death of a Salesman*
Death of a Salesman
135 min. Color. 1985.
VHS, Beta.
Television adaptation of the play with Dustin Hoffman, John Malkovich, Charles Durning, and Stephen Lang.
Distributor: Video Learning Library.

Private Conversations on the Set of Death of a Salesman
82 min. Color. 1985.
VHS, Beta.
This PBS documentary presents heated discussions among actors, director, and playwright during the making of the production.
Distributor: Video Learning Library.

Molière *Tartuffe*
Tartuffe
140 min. Color. 1984.
VHS.
In French with English subtitles, this production features Gerard Depardieu and François Perier in a version based on the stage production directed by Jacques Lasalle.
Distributor: Insight Media.

Tartuffe
120 min. Color. 1978.
VHS.
Features John Wood, Victor Garber, and Geraldine Fitzgerald.
Distributor: Insight Media.

Molière and the Comédie Française
17 min. Color. 1982.
VHS.
In this overview of the Comédie Française, Jacques Charon directs excerpts from *The Misanthrope* and *Tartuffe* to highlight the playwright's comic style and to introduce the style of the Comédie.
Distributor: Insight Media.

Noh Drama
The Style of the Classic Japanese Noh Theater
17 min. Color. 1980.
VHS.
This video features Sadayo Kita's presentation of the techniques of Noh theater. It explains the meaning of movements and the system of Labanotation.
Distributor: Insight Media.

Clifford Odets
Sum and Substance with Clifford Odets and Herman Harvey
30 min. Black and white. 1990.
VHS.
Odets analyzes what he terms our "loss of innocence" by acculturation, and our inability to respond to experience directly and honestly.
Distributor: Citadel Video: Cupertino, CA.

Eugene O'Neill *The Emperor Jones*
The Emperor Jones and Paul Robeson, Tribute to an Artist
101 min. Black and white and color. 1933, 1979.
VHS.
A production of the 1933 film that Robeson starred in with an additional tribute to Robeson originally released in 1979.
Distributor: Home Vision.

Eugene O'Neill, 1888–1953
30 min. Color with black and white. 1996.
VHS.
Traces life and literary career of O'Neill and uses photographs and views of places associated with his life.
Distributor: Kultur Video.

Harold Pinter *The Dumb Waiter*
The Dumb Waiter
Approximately 1 hour. Color. 1970.
Four filmstrips, 35 mm and four tapes.

This production, which is part of the Great Plays of the Stage Series, includes a teacher's guide and uses photographs of a performance to illustrate the play.
Distributor: Schloat Productions.

Modern British Drama
Color. 1993.
VHS.
Lecture 6 of this SuperStar Teachers Series covers Pinter.
Distributor: The Teaching Company: Springfield, VA.

Harold Pinter with Benedict Nightingale
55 min. Color. 1989.
VHS.
Number 27 of the Writers in Conversation Series records an interview with Pinter.
Distributor: ICA Video: London.

Rachel Rosenthal
Rachel's Quest
53 min. Color. 1996.
VHS.
Examines the on- and offstage work of Rosenthal as it provides excerpts from performances, rehearsals, and interviews.
Distributor: Pacific Film Factory: Topanga, CA.

William Shakespeare *Hamlet* **and** *A Midsummer Night's Dream*
Hamlet
2 videocassettes, 266 min. Color. 1997.
VHS.
Kenneth Branagh's version of the play released as a film in 1996. Full-text version of the play set in a nineteenth-century world.
Distributor: Warner Home Video.

Hamlet
135 min. Color. 1990.
VHS.
With Mel Gibson, Glenn Close, and Helen Bonham-Carter. Directed by Franco Zeffirelli.
Distributor: Warner Home Video.

Hamlet
153 min. Black and white. 1948.
VHS and 16 mm film.
With Laurence Olivier, Basil Sydney, Felix Aylmer, and Jean Simmons.
Distributor: Paramount Home Video.

The Making of a Monologue: Robert Wilson's Hamlet
63 min. Color. 1995.
VHS.
Uses rehearsal and performance footage to depict how Wilson created his one-man *Hamlet*. Includes interviews with Wilson and collaborators.
Distributor: Cinema Guild.

Critical Guide to Hamlet
31 min. Color. 1998.
VHS.
Explores major themes, plots, and Shakespeare's comic relief to offer insights into the underlying meaning of *Hamlet*'s eloquent soliloquies.
Distributor: Films for the Humanities and Sciences.

Approaches to Hamlet
45 min. Color. 1979.
VHS.
Includes footage of four Hamlets created by John Barrymore, Laurence Olivier, John Gielgud, and Nicol Williamson.
Distributor: Films for the Humanities and Sciences.

A Midsummer Night's Dream
120 min. Color. 2000.
VHS.
A video version of the motion picture with Rupert Everett, Michelle Pfeiffer, and Calista Flockhart.
Distributor: Fox Video.

A Midsummer Night's Dream
165 min. Color. 1983.
VHS, Beta, U-matic.
An interpretation presented by Joseph Papp with William Hurt and Michelle Shay.
Distributor: Films for the Humanities and Sciences.

A Midsummer Night's Dream
111 min. Black and white. 1963.
VHS, Beta.
A live BBC-TV performance with Mendelssohn's incidental music.
Distributor: Video Yesteryear.

A Midsummer Night's Dream: Introduction to the Play
14 min. Black and white. 1954.
VHS.
Key scenes from the play, with a discussion of characters and language.
Distributor: Coronet/MTI Film & Video.

George Bernard Shaw *Major Barbara*
Major Barbara
131 min. Black and white. 1988, 1941.
VHS.
Video of the motion picture released by United Artists in 1941 and directed by Gabriel Pascal.
Distributor: Public Media: Concord, MA.

George Bernard Shaw
26 min. Black and white. 1964.
16 mm film.
A biographical study of Shaw narrated by Mike Wallace.
Distributor: CRM.

Sam Shepard *True West*
Sam Shepard's True West
110 min. Color. 1983.
VHS.
Directed by Gary Sinise with John Malkovich.
Distributor: Academy Home Entertainment.

Sam Shepard: Stalking Himself
60 min. Color. 1997.
VHS.
A biographical look at the life and work of Shepard. Includes excerpts from performances and interviews with colleagues and collaborators.
Distributor: Insight Media.

Anna Deavere Smith *Fires in the Mirror*
Fires in the Mirror
90 min. Color. 1993.
VHS.
In this PBS video Smith assumes the personalities of nearly thirty characters caught up in the racial turmoil that erupted in Brooklyn in 1991.
Distributor: Insight Media.

Sophocles *Antigonê* **and** *Oedipus Rex*
Antigone
120 min. Color. 1987.
VHS, Beta, U-matic.
With Juliet Stevenson, John Sharpnel, and John Gielgud. Staged version.
Distributor: Films for the Humanities and Sciences.

Antigone
89 min. Color. 1972.
VHS.
Based on Jean Anouilh's version of the play and performed by Genevieve Bujold, Stacy Keach, and Fritz Weaver.
Distributor: Insight Media.

Oedipus the King
120 min. Color. 1987.
VHS.
With John Gielgud, Michael Pennington, and Claire Bloom.
Distributor: Films for the Humanities and Sciences.

The Rise of Greek Tragedy; Sophocles: Oedipus the King
45 min. Color. 1998, 1975.
VHS.
Originally produced as a motion picture in 1975, this video shows a performance of the play in the setting of a fifth-century Greek theater, with the use of masks reproduced from the same era.
Distributor: Films for the Humanities.

Oedipus Rex
90 min. 1957.
VHS.
Tyrone Guthrie's version of the play using Yeats's translation. Performers wear period masks.
Distributor: Insight Media.

Oedipus Rex
Four videocassettes, each approximately 30 min. Color and black and white. 1959.
VHS, Beta, U-matic, 16 mm film.
1. *Age of Sophocles*, discusses Greek civilization and theatre; 2. *The Character of Oedipus*, debate between character flaw and fate; 3. *Man and God*, Oedipus's inability to overcome gods; 4. *Recovery of Oedipus*, the place of human beings in the chain of existence.
Distributor: Encyclopedia Britannica Educational Corporation.

Wole Soyinka
Wole Soyinka: A Voice of Africa
15 min. Color. 1990.
VHS.
This biographical portrait of Soyinka is part of a Nobel Prize series and includes a teacher's resource book and a student notebook.
Distributor: Sunburst Communications: Pleasantville, NY.

Wole Soyinka
57 min. Color. 1990.
VHS.
Soyinka discusses art in society and oppression of creative communities in Number 29 of this Writers in Conversation Series.
Distributor: ICA Video: Northbrook, IL.

Gertrude Stein
Gertrude Stein, "The Mother of Us All"
59 min. Color. 1998.
VHS.
In Part 8 of This Art: Transatlantic Modernism Series, Wanda Corn presents a collection of archival photographs, cubist paintings, and samples of Stein's writings to demonstrate her importance to the emergence of cubism in Paris and to the modernist movement in general.
Distributor: Chip Taylor Communications: Derry, NH.

Tom Stoppard
Modern British Drama
400 min. Color. 1993.
VHS.
Lecture 7 of this SuperStar Teacher Series covers the work of Stoppard.
Distributor: The Teaching Company: Springfield, VA.

August Strindberg *Miss Julie*
Miss Julie
101 min. Color. 1999.
VHS.
Video release of the 1999 motion picture directed by Mike Figgis.
Distributor: MGM Home Entertainment.

Miss Julie
60 min. Color. 1978.
VHS, Beta, U-matic.
With Patrick Stewart and Lisa Harrow. Opens with the rehearsal of a crucial scene and closes with a full-dress production of the play. Interspersed are discussions with actors regarding interpretations.
Distributor: Films, Inc. PMI.

Luis Valdez *Los Vendidos*
Los Vendidos / The Sellouts
24 min. Color. 2000.
VHS.
An introduction about the Teatro Campesino and its purpose followed by the play.
Distributor: CFI: Hollywood.

Bettina Gray Speaks with Luis Valdez
26 min. Color. 1993.
VHS.
Valdez discusses how his plays retrace the experience of Chicano families.
Distributor: Films for the Humanities and Sciences.

Lope de Vega *Fuente Ovejuna*
Fuente Ovejuna
2 videocassettes, 142 min. Color. 1993, 1980.
VHS.
A dramatization of the play produced for Spanish television and directed by Juan Guerrero Zamora.
Distributor: Films for the Humanities.

Derek Walcott *Pantomime*
Pantomime
26 min. Color. 1995, 1980.
VHS.
A video release of the production as it appeared as part of the Thames Television series, The English Programme.
Distributor: Films for the Humanities and Sciences.

Derek Walcott
29 min. Color. 1988.
VHS.
On a segment of the television program A *World of Ideas*, Bill Moyers interviews Walcott, who discusses the language of poetry, the language of politics, and the story of Robinson Crusoe as a metaphor.
Distributor: PBS Video.

Oscar Wilde *The Importance of Being Earnest*
The Importance of Being Earnest
99 min. Color. 1980.
VHS.
BBC production of the play.
Distributor: Time-Life Video.

The Importance of Being Earnest
95 min. Color. 1952.
VHS, Beta.
A staged version directed by Anthony Asquith and performed by Michael Redgrave, Edith Evans, Margaret Rutherford, Michael Dennison, and Joan Greenwood.
Distributor: Paramount Home Video.

The Importance of Being Earnest
50 min. Color with black and white. 1999, 1997.
VHS.
The video release of this television production aired in 1997. It is a biography of Wilde supported by quotations and excerpts from his works, comments from actors, and location filming.
Distributor: Films for the Humanities.

Tennessee Williams *Suddenly Last Summer*
Suddenly Last Summer
114 min. Black and white. 1996, 1959.
VHS.
Gore Vidal's adapted screenplay version of Williams's play released in 1959, starring Elizabeth Taylor, Montgomery Clift, and Katharine Hepburn.
Distributor: Columbia Tristar.

Tennessee Williams: Wounded Genius
42 min. Color with black and white. 1998.
VHS.
Biographical portrait of Williams.
Distributor: A&E Home Video.

August Wilson
August Wilson
51 min. Color with black and white. 1999, 1990.
VHS.
Interview with August Wilson and excerpts from his plays.
Distributor: Films for the Humanities and Sciences.

W.B. Yeats
William Butler Yeats: The Heart of Ireland
30 min. Color. 1997, 1977.
VHS.
Originally produced as 1977 television series, *Anyone for Tennyson.* Stories about the great Irish poet and the countryside he adored.
Distributor: Monterey Media: Thousand Oaks, CA.

Yeats and the Irish Theatre
55 min. Color. 1985.
VHS.
A discussion of Yeats as a dramatist, followed by an adaptation of a Theatre Emory production of *A Full Moon in March.*
Distributor: WPBA: Atlanta, GA.

List of Distributors
A&E Home Video
See local retailer.

Academy Home Entertainment
See local retailer.

Cabin Fever
See local retailer.

California Newsreel
149 9th St., Suite 420
San Francisco, CA 94103
(415) 621–6196

Cinema Guild
1697 Broadway
New York, NY 10019–5904
(212) 246–5522

Columbia Tristar
See local retailer.

Coronet/MTI Film & Video
4350 Equity Dr.
Columbus, OH 43228
(800) 777–8100

CRM
2215 Faraday Ave.
Carlsbad, CA 92008
(800) 421–0833

Encyclopedia Britannica Educational Corporation
310 South Michigan Ave.
Chicago, IL 60604
(800) 621–3900

Films for the Humanities/Films for the Humanities and Sciences
12 Perrine Rd.
Monmouth Junction, NJ 08852
(800) 257–5126

Films, Inc. PMI
5547 North Ravenswood Ave.
Chicago, IL 60640–1199
(312) 878–2600
(800) 323–4222

Hallmark Home Entertainment
See local retailer.

Home Vision & Public Media Video
5547 Ravenswood Ave.
Chicago, IL 60640–1199
(800) 826–3456

Insight Media
2162 Broadway
New York, NY 10024
(212) 721–6316
(800) 233–9910

Kultur Video
195 Hwy. No. 36
West Long Branch, NJ 07764
(800) 458–5887

MGM/UA Home Entertainment
See local retailer.

Paramount Home Video.
See local retailer.

PBS Video
1320 Braddock Pl.
Alexandria, VA 22314
(800) 344–3337

Prism Entertainment
1888 Century Park, E.
Suite 350
Los Angeles, CA 90067
(310) 277–3270

Time-Life Video and Television
1450 East Parham Rd.
Richmond, VA 23280
(800) 621–7026

Video Artists International
PO Box 158
Linwood Plaza
Suite 301
Fort Lee, NJ 07024
(201) 944–0099
(800) 477–7146

Video Learning Library
15838 N. 62nd St.
Suite 100
Scottsdale, AZ 85254

Video Yesteryear
Box C
Sandy Hook, CT 06482
(203) 426–2574
(800) 243–0987

Warner Home Video
See local retailer.

ACKNOWLEDGMENTS

TEXT CREDITS

Trifles by Susan Glaspell. Copyright © 1951 by Walter H. Baker Co. Reprinted by permission of Baker's Plays, PO Box 699222, Quincy, MA 02269.

My Brazil by Rachel Rosenthal from *Out from Under: Texts by Women Performance Artists*, edited by Leonora Champagne. Copyright © 1990 Rachel Rosenthal. Reprinted with permission of the author.

Oedipus Rex from *Sophocles, The Oedipus Cycle: An English Version* by Dudley Fitts and Robert Fitzgerald, reprinted by permission of the publisher. CAUTION: All rights, including professional, amateur, motion picture, recitation, lecturing, performance, public reading, radio broadcasting, and television are strictly reserved. Inquiries on all rights should be addressed to Harcourt, Inc., Permissions Department, Orlando, FL 32887-6777.

"The Poetics" by Aristotle from *On the Art of Fiction*, L. J. Potts, ed. Copyright 1953 by Cambridge University Press. Reprinted with the permission of Cambridge University Press.

"Directing *Oedipus* in Canada" by Tyrone Guthrie. From *World Theatre*, 6:4 (Winter 1957). Reprinted by permission of The Tyrone Guthrie Centre, Annaghmakerrig, Newbliss, Co., Menaghan, Ireland.

Interview with Alan MacVey on directing *Oedipus Rex*. Reprinted by permission of Alan MacVey.

Antigonê from *Sophocles, The Oedipus Cycle: An English Version* by Dudley Fitts and Robert Fitzgerald, reprinted by permission of the publisher. CAUTION: All rights, including professional, amateur, motion picture, recitation, lecturing, performance, public reading, radio broadcasting, and television are strictly reserved. Inquiries on all rights should be addressed to Harcourt, Inc., Permissions Department, Orlando, FL 32887-6777.

"*Antigonê* in Modern Dress" by Michael Billington from *The Guardian*, May 18, 1984. Reprinted by permission of Michael Billington, drama critic for *The Guardian*.

Medea by Euripides, translated by Mary-Kay Gamel. Originally appeared in *Quarterly West* (Spring–Summer 1995).

Reprinted by permission of the translator and *Quarterly West*.

Interview with L. L. West on directing *Medea*. Reprinted by permission of L. L. West.

"Amid Pain, Blood and Din, Diana Rigg Rises as a Mighty Medea" by David Richards from *New York Times*, April 8, 1994. Copyright © 1994 by The New York Times Company. Reprinted by permission.

Lysistrata: An English Version from *Aristophanes: Four Comedies* by Dudley Fitts, copyright 1954 by Harcourt, Inc. and renewed 1982 by Cornelia Fitts, Daniel H. Fitts and Deborah W. Fitts, reprinted by permission of the publisher.

"*Everyman* in Toronto" by John Astington from *Everyman*, edited by John Astington. Reprinted by permission of Poculi Ludique Societas and John H. Astington.

Dōjōji from *Twenty Plays of the Nō Theatre*, Donald Keene translation copyright © 1970 Columbia University Press. Reprinted by permission of the publisher.

On the Art of the Nō Drama, translated by J. Thomas Rimer & Yamazaki Masakazu, pp. 27–28. Copyright © 1984 by Princeton University Press. Reprinted by permission of Princeton University Press.

Theatre East & West: Perspectives Toward a Total Theater by Leonard Pronko, pp. 106–110. Copyright © 1967 The Regents of the University of California.

From *Doctor Faustus* by Christopher Marlowe, edited with an Introduction by Sylvan Barnet, copyright © 1969 by Sylvan Barnet. Used by permission of Dutton Signet, a division of Penguin Putnam Inc.

Dr. Faustus by Christopher Marlowe, edited with an introduction by Sylvan Barnet. Copyright © 1969 by Sylvan Barnet. Used by permission of Dutton Signet, a division of Penguin Books USA, Inc.

Excerpt from "The Royal Shakespeare Company Production of Dr. Faustus" by Gareth Lloyd Evans from *Shakespeare Survey*, Volume 22, 1969. Copyright © 1969 by Gareth Lloyd Evans. Reprinted by permission of Barbara Lloyd Evans.

A Midsummer Night's Dream and *Hamlet, Prince of Denmark* from *The Complete Works of Shakespeare*, Fourth Edition, by William Shakespeare, edited by David Bevington. Copyright © 1992 by HarperCollins Publishers.

Interview with Alan MacVey on directing *A Midsummer Night's Dream*. Reprinted by permission of Alan MacVey.

Excerpt from "Interview with Edward Albee" by William Flanagan from *Paris Review*. Reprinted by permission of *The Paris Review*.

Funnyhouse of a Negro by Adrienne Kennedy. Reprinted by permission of the author.

Los Vendidos by Luis Valdez is reprinted with permission from the publisher of *Luis Valdez—Early Works* (Houston: Arte Publico Press-University of Houston, 1971)

The Actos by Luis Valdez is reprinted with permission from the publisher of *Luis Valdez—Early Works: Actos, Bernabé, Pensamiento Serpentino* (Houston: Arte Público Press—University of Houston, 1971)

Interview with Jorge Huerta on directing *Los Vendidos*. Reprinted by permission of Jorge Huerta, Ph.D.—Chancellor's Associates Endowed Chair Professor of Theatre, University of California, San Diego.

Votes for Women by Elizabeth Robins from *How the Vote Was Won and Other Suffrage Plays* edited by Dale Spender and Carole Hayman. Copyright Methuen Publishing Ltd. Reprinted by permission.

Purgatory by William Yeats, Scribner, a division of Simon & Schuster, Inc.

Interview with Jeffery Jones on directing *Purgatory*. Reproduced by permission. All rights reserved.

The Good Woman of Szechuan by Bertolt Brecht, from *Parables for the Theatre: Two Plays by Bertolt Brecht*, translated and revised by Erik Bentley. Copyright 1947, 1948, © 1956, 1961. Epilogue copyright © 1965 by Eric Bentley. Reprinted by permission of the University of Minnesota Press.

The Dumb Waiter from *The Caretaker and The Dumb Waiter* by Harold Pinter. Copyright © 1968, 1988 by Harold Pinter. Used by permission of Grove/Atlantic, Inc.

Excerpt from "Interview with Harold Pinter" by Lawrence M. Bensky from *Paris Review*. Reprinted by permission of *The Paris Review*.

Krapp's Last Tape by Samuel Beckett. Copyright © 1958 by Samuel Beckett. Used by permission of Grove/Atlantic, Inc.

From *The Bacchae of Euripides: A Communion Rite* by Wole Soyinka. Copyright © 1973 by Wole Soyinka. Used by permission of W. W. Norton & Company, Inc. and Methuen Publishing, Ltd.

We Won't Pay! We Won't Pay! by Dario Fo, from *We Won't Pay! We Won't Pay! and Other Plays* by Dario Fo, translated by Ron Jenkins. Translation copyright © 2000 by Ron Jenkins. Published by Theatre Communications Group. Used by permission of Theatre Communications Group.

"Fo's Farce Works, 'Pay' Is Reward," by Ed Siegel, *Boston Globe*, September 2, 1999. Reprinted by permission of the *Boston Globe* via the Copyright Clearance Center, *www.copyrights.com*

Pantomime from *Remembrance and Patomime* by Derek Walcott. Copyright © 1980 by Derek Walcott. Reprinted by permission of Farrar, Straus and Giroux, LLC.

"Oft-staged Walcott Play Reaches Playwright's Neighborhood" by Frederick H. Guidry. This article first appeared in *The Christian Science Monitor* on June 17, 1986 and is reproduced with permission. Copyright © 1986 The Christian Science Publishing Society. All rights reserved.

Top Girls by Caryl Churchill. First published in Great Britain in 1982 by Methuen London, now Methuen Publishing Limited, 215 Vauxhall Bridge Road, London SW1V 1EJ, United Kingdom. Copyright © 1982, 1984, 1990, 1991 Caryl Churchill. The author has asserted her moral rights. All rights reserved.

"Making It" by Erika Munk, *Village Voice*, January 11, 1983. Used with permission of *The Village Voice*.

The Real Thing by Tom Stoppard. Copyright © 1984 by Tom Stoppard. Reprinted by permission of Faber and Faber, Inc., an affiliate of Farrar, Straus and Giroux, LLC.

"The Real Stops Here" by Erika Munk, *Village Voice*, January 17, 1984, p. 101. Reprinted by permission of *The Village Voice*.

"Poor Henry! He's So Clever, So Glib…So Vulnerable" by Ben Brantley, *New York Times*, April 18, 2000. Copyright © 2000 by The New York Times Company. Reprinted by permission.

True West by Sam Shepard, copyright © 1981 by Sam Shepard, from *Seven Plays* by Sam Shepard. Used by permission of Bantam Books, a division of Random House, Inc.

"An Unusual Case of Role Reversal" by Bruce Weber, *New York Times*, Arts & Leisure section, pp. 10, 37, February 27, 2000. Copyright © 2000 The New York Times Company. Reproduced by permission. All rights reserved.

Glengarry Glen Ross by David Mamet. Copyright © 1982, 1983 by David Mamet. Used by permission of Grove/Atlantic, Inc.

Excerpt from interview with David Mamet from *In Their Own Words: Contemporary Playwrights*, conducted by David Savran. Copyright © 1988 by David Savran. Used by permission of Theatre Communications Group.

Interview with David Mamet by Matthew Roudane, from *Studies in American Drama, 1945–Present*, Volume 1, pp. 73–81, 1986. Reprinted by permission of the author.

Terminal by Susan Yankowitz. Permission granted by Susan Yankowitz on behalf of Joseph Chaikin and the Open Theater.

The New Radical Theatre Notebook by Arthur Sainer, pp. 147–153, copyright © Applause Books. Reprinted by permission.

The Dance and The Railroad from *The Dance and The Railroad and Family Devotions* by David Henry Hwang. Reprinted by permission of the author.

Excerpts from "I Write Plays to Claim a Place for Asian-Americans" an interview with David Henry Hwang by Eric Pace, *New York Times*, Arts & Leisure section, p. 4, July 12, 1981. Copyright © 1981 The New York Times Company. Reproduced by permission. All rights reserved.

"Interview with David Henry Hwang," *Contemporary Authors*, Volume 132, copyright © The Gale Group. Reprinted by permission of The Gale Group.

Fences by August Wilson, copyright © 1986 by August Wilson. Used by permission of Dutton Signet, a division of Penguin Putnam Inc.

Excerpt from August Wilson interview in *In Their Own Words: Contemporary American Playwrights* by David Savran. Copyright © 1988 by David Savran. Reprinted by permission of Theatre Communications Group.

The Conduct of Life by Maria Irene Fornes in *Maria Irene Fornes: Plays*, copyright © 1982 by PAJ Publications. Reprinted by permission of PAJ Publications.

"Dispute over Actors' Studio Tapes" by Herbert Mitgang, *New York Times*, March 20, 1985. Copyright © 1985 by The New York Times Company. Reprinted by permission.

From *Fires in the Mirror* by Anna Deavere Smith, copyright © 1993 by Anna Deavere Smith. Used by permission of Doubleday, a division of Random House, Inc.

Chronology from *Fires in the Mirror* by Anna Deavere Smith, pp. xlvii–liii, copyright © 1993 by Anna Deavere Smith. Used by permission of Doubleday, a division of Random House, Inc.

Interview with Anna Deavere Smith by Greg Tate, *Village Voice*, July 21, 1992, pp. 99–100. Copyright © Village Voice Media. Reprinted by permission.

Angels in America, Part One: Millennium Approaches by Tony Kushner. Copyright © 1992, 1993 by Tony Kushner. Published by Theatre Communications Group. Used by permission of Theatre Communications Group, Inc.

"Angels' Gets Even Better" by Steven Winn, *The San Francisco Chronicle*, May 5, 1993, p. D1. Copyright © 1993 San Francisco Chronicle. Reprinted by permission.

In the Blood by Suzan Lori-Parks, reprinted by permission of the William Morris Agency. Copyright © 2000 by Suzan Lori-Parks. *In the Blood* is sole property of the author and is fully protected by copyright. All inquiries concerning the rights should be addressed to the William Morris Agency, 1325 Avenue of the Americas, New York, NY 10019.

"The Scarlet Letter" by Margo Jefferson, *New York Times*, November 23, 1999. Copyright © 1999 by The New York Times Company. Reprinted by permission.

"Alien Baby," an interview with Suzan-Lori Parks by Bonnie Metzgar, *Stagebill*, November 1999, pp. 50–58. Reprinted by permission.

PHOTO CREDITS

Page 11 (top): Corbis Bettmann; **12 (top):** British Library; **12 (center):** Alinari/Art Resource; **12 (bottom):** Auckland Art Gallery Toi o Tamaki, Mackelvie Trust collection, purchased 1961; **13 (top):** Bayersiche Staatsgemaldesammlungen, Neue Pinakothek, Munich/ Bildarchiv Foto Marburg/ Art Resource; **13 (center):** Ilse Buhs/Renaissance-Theater Berlin; **13 (bottom):** © Eileen Darby; **14 (top):** © Mike Yamashita/Woodfin Camp & Associates; **14 (center):** John Nunley, The St. Louis Art Museum; **14 (bottom):** Donald Cooper/Photostage; **15 (top):** © Michael Brosilow; **15 (center):** Archiv & Deutches Theatermuseum; **15 (bottom):** Courtesy of the Department of Theatre, The Ohio State University; **27:** Photo by Kim Kaufman, reprinted with permission from Rachel Rosenthal; **43:** © George E. Joseph; **50 (top):** Frederick Ayer/Photo Researchers, Inc.; **50 (center):** Photo by Peter Smith, Courtesy of Stratford Festival; **50 (bottom):** Photo by Donald McKague, Courtesy of Stratford Festival; **51 (top):** © Eileen Darby; **51 (center):** John Vickers Theatre Collection; **51 (bottom):** German Information

INDEX OF AUTHORS AND TITLES